Education and the American Workforce

Education and the American Workforce

2017

Edited by
Deirdre A. Gaquin and Mary Meghan Ryan

Lanham • Boulder •New York • Toronto • Plymouth, UK

Published by Bernan Press
A wholly owned subsidiary of
The Rowman & Littlefield Publishing Group, Inc.
4501 Forbes Boulevard, Suite 200
Lanham, Maryland 20706

Bernan Press
800-462-6420
www.rowman.com

ISBN-13: 978-1-59888-951-2
eISBN-13: 978-1-59888-952-9

∞™ The paper used in this publication meets the minimum requirements of
American National Standard for Information Sciences—Permanence of
Paper for Printed Library Materials, ANSI/NISO Z39.48-1992.
Manufactured in the United States of America.

Contents

Preface vii

Part A — National 1
Table A-1. Number of Employees, Wages and Salaries, and Job Requirements for
Detailed Occupations in the United States 5
Table A-2. Educational Attainment for Workers 25 Years and Older by Detailed
Occupation, 2014–2015 24
Table A-3. Fastest Growing Occupations, 2014 and Projected 2024 35
Table A-4. Fastest Declining Occupations, 2014 and Projected 2024 36

Part B — States. 37
Table B-1. Labor Force Participation of the Population Age 16 Years and Older 42
Table B-2. Employment and Unemployment, 2015 44
Table B-3. Employment Status and Class of Worker for the Population
Age 16 Years and Older. 46
Table B-4. Employment by Occupation. 48
Table B-5. Employment by Industry 64
Table B-6. Educational Attainment 68
Table B-7. Homeownership, Health Insurance, and Computer Access
by Educational Attainment. 72
Table B-8. Field of Degree for Persons with a Bachelor's Degree or Higher 76
Table B-9. Median Annual Earnings 80

Part C — Counties 95
Table C. County—Labor Force, Employment, and Educational Data, 2011–2015 99

Part D — Metropolitan Areas . . . . — 321
Table D. Metropolitan Statistical Area—Labor Force, Employment,
and Educational Data, 2015 325

Part E — Cities 365
Table E. Cities—Labor Force, Employment, and Educational Data, 2015 369

Part F — Congressional Districts. 529
Table F. Congressional Districts—Labor Force, Employment, and
Educational Data, 2015 533

Appendixes. 571
Appendix A. Geographic Concepts and Codes 573
Appendix B. Source Notes and Explanations 577

Preface

Education and the American Workforce is a compilation of data about employment and education from federal statistical agencies. The Census Bureau is the leading source of quality data about the nation's people and economy. The Bureau of Labor Statistics (BLS) is the principal federal agency responsible for measuring labor market activity, working conditions, and price changes in the economy. Together, these agencies produce a wealth of information about the American workforce. This book includes information about the jobs that people hold—the occupations that they pursue and the industries where they work—and the education levels that people have attained. The geographic location of jobs is important. People often move to locations where jobs are plentiful, moving away from areas where jobs have decreased as technology and trends have changed. The education level of a local population can have an impact on the type of jobs available, with employers establishing businesses where they expect to find employees with appropriate educational credentials.

The Bureau of Labor Statistics collects data from employers, using surveys of establishments to determine the occupations and industries where the jobs are. BLS also partners with the Census Bureau to conduct the Current Population Survey (CPS), the household survey that has measured employment levels since 1940. The Census Bureau conducts the decennial census every ten years, as mandated by the Constitution. In the 21st century, the American Community Survey (ACS) has replaced the more detailed portions of the census and is now the major source of information about the American people—their demographic characteristics, household relationships, income, employment, education, and much more.

A national overview in Part A is based on the Occupational Employment Statistics (OES) program of the Bureau of Labor Statistics to provide details about very specific occupations. The BLS Occupational Employment Statistics Program collects information from private nonfarm employer establishments. They do not include the self-employed, owners and partners in unincorporated firms, household workers, or unpaid family workers. In this program, the BLS collects information about more than 800 occupations as defined in the Standard Occupation Classification (SOC).

In Part A, several tables are from the BLS Employment Projections program which provides estimates of the occupations that are expected to grow and decline in the next ten years. They also use the ACS to show the educational attainment of workers in each of the SOC occupations (with some combining of occupations to protect respondents' privacy). For occupation projections, this book uses the BLS anticipated changes from 2014 to 2024. A new edition of the *Occupational Outlook Handbook* was released by BLS and will be available from Bernan Press in January 2018.

This book uses the American Community Survey to provide data on jobs and education in states, metropolitan areas, counties, cities, and congressional districts (Parts B, C, D, E, and F). The local area detail is necessarily less specific than the national data but the occupation categories use the same SOC categorization, grouped to protect the respondents' privacy. These sections include ACS data about the labor force, educational attainment, and field of degree, often by age, gender, race, and Hispanic origin. Also included are some personal and household characteristics that are relevant to employment and education, such as health insurance and computer access.

In a time of changing technology and cultural shifts, it is difficult to measure some aspects of the workforce. The exhaustive list of occupations in the SOC will be updated in 2018. The new list will reflect extensive changes, particularly in computer and technical fields. The growing popularity of the "gig economy" is difficult to measure with available sources. Uber drivers, independent musicians, Airbnb proprietors, and similar workers are likely included in ACS household survey counts of self-employed workers, but would not be counted in the BLS establishment data. The BLS Current Population Survey included a supplemental survey on contingent workers in May 2017, with results likely to be released in 2018. This supplement had been discontinued in 2005 and was recently reinstated. Contingent workers are people who do not expect their jobs to last or who reported that their jobs are temporary. They do not have an implicit or explicit contract for ongoing employment. Alternative employment arrangements include people employed as independent contractors, on-call workers, temporary help agency workers, and workers provided by contract firms. Another possible source of information about independent workers is the Census Bureau's Nonemployer Statistics data.

Multiple-job holders illustrate another issue with ACS employment data. Each person only reports on their principal job. Many artists and "gig" workers are especially likely to work more hours at another job and not be counted in the ACS or other measures of employment.

With changing technology, vocational and technical education is increasingly important, and that is difficult to measure with existing data sources. Non-degree certificate programs are not included in ACS educational attainment measures, nor are the fields of associate's degrees which often reflect vocational and technical specialties.

REFERENCES

Information about the ACS is available on the Census Bureau's website. The ACS main page is http://www.census.gov/acs/www. Data from the ACS is available from American Fact Finder at http://factfinder.census.gov.

Information about the CPS can be found at https://www.bls.gov/cps/ while information about the OES program can be found at https://www.bls.gov/oes/home.htm.

A vast amount of information is collected by the ACS, the CPS, and the OES. In this book, selections of these data have been assembled in various tables by subject and geographic type. Readers are encouraged to explore these websites to expand on the information contained here and to keep up with these constantly changing datasets.

SAMPLING ERROR

All data that are based on samples, such as the ACS, include a range of uncertainty. Two broad types of error can occur: sampling error and nonsampling error. Nonsampling errors can result from mistakes in how the data are reported or coded, problems in the sampling frame or survey questionnaires, or problems related to nonresponse or interviewer bias. The Census Bureau tries to minimize nonsampling errors by using trained interviewers and by carefully reviewing the survey's sampling methods, data processing techniques, and questionnaire design.

Sampling error occurs when data are based on a sample of a population rather than the full population. Sampling error is easier to measure than nonsampling error and can be used to assess the statistical reliability of survey data. For any given area, the larger the sample and the more months included in the data, the greater the confidence in the estimate. Margins of error are provided for every ACS estimate on the Census Bureau's website. This book includes 1-year (2015) data for most areas, but only 5-year (2011–2015) data area available for areas with fewer than 20,000 people. To include all counties in the United States, Table C uses 5-year data. For all tables, the margin of error is higher for the smaller groups in the table, and all users are encouraged to check the Census Bureau's website and to review their descriptions of sampling error.

ABOUT THE EDITORS

Deirdre A. Gaquin has been a data use consultant to private organizations, government agencies, and universities for over 30 years. Prior to that, she was Director of Data Access Services at Data Use & Access Laboratories, a pioneer in private sector distribution of federal statistical data. A former President of the Association of Public Data Users, Ms. Gaquin has served on numerous boards, panels, and task forces concerned with federal statistical data and has worked on five decennial censuses. She holds a Master of Urban Planning (MUP) degree from Hunter College. Ms. Gaquin is also an editor of Bernan Press's *The Who, What, and Where of America: Understanding the American Community Survey*; *Places, Towns and Townships*; *The Congressional District Atlas*, *The Almanac of American Education*, *Race and Employment in America*, and *the State and Metropolitan Area Data Book*.

Mary Meghan Ryan is the senior research editor for Bernan Press. She is also the editor for the *Handbook of U.S. Labor Statistics*, *Employment, Hours, and Earnings* and the associate editor for *Business Statistics of the United States*.

SYMBOLS USED

A "-" in a cell indicates that either there were no sample cases or the number of sample cases was too small.

PART A

NATIONAL

- With no formal educational requirement and a median salary of $22,680, 4.5 million people are employed as retail salespersons, the most of any single occupation. Cashiers and food preparation/serving workers account for another 3.5 million each.

- For nine occupations, the median annual salary is over $190,000. These are all specialized medical doctors and dentists. Only doctors and dentists are occupations where 90 percent or more have obtained doctoral or professional degrees.

- Eight occupations had median annual salaries under $20,000 (about $10 an hour)—all in the food preparation and serving and the personal service occupation groupings.

- Virtually all occupations with median salaries over $100,000 typically require a bachelor's degree or higher, with air traffic controllers being the only exception.

- While 8.7 percent of employed persons age 25 and older have not completed high school, and 4.2 percent

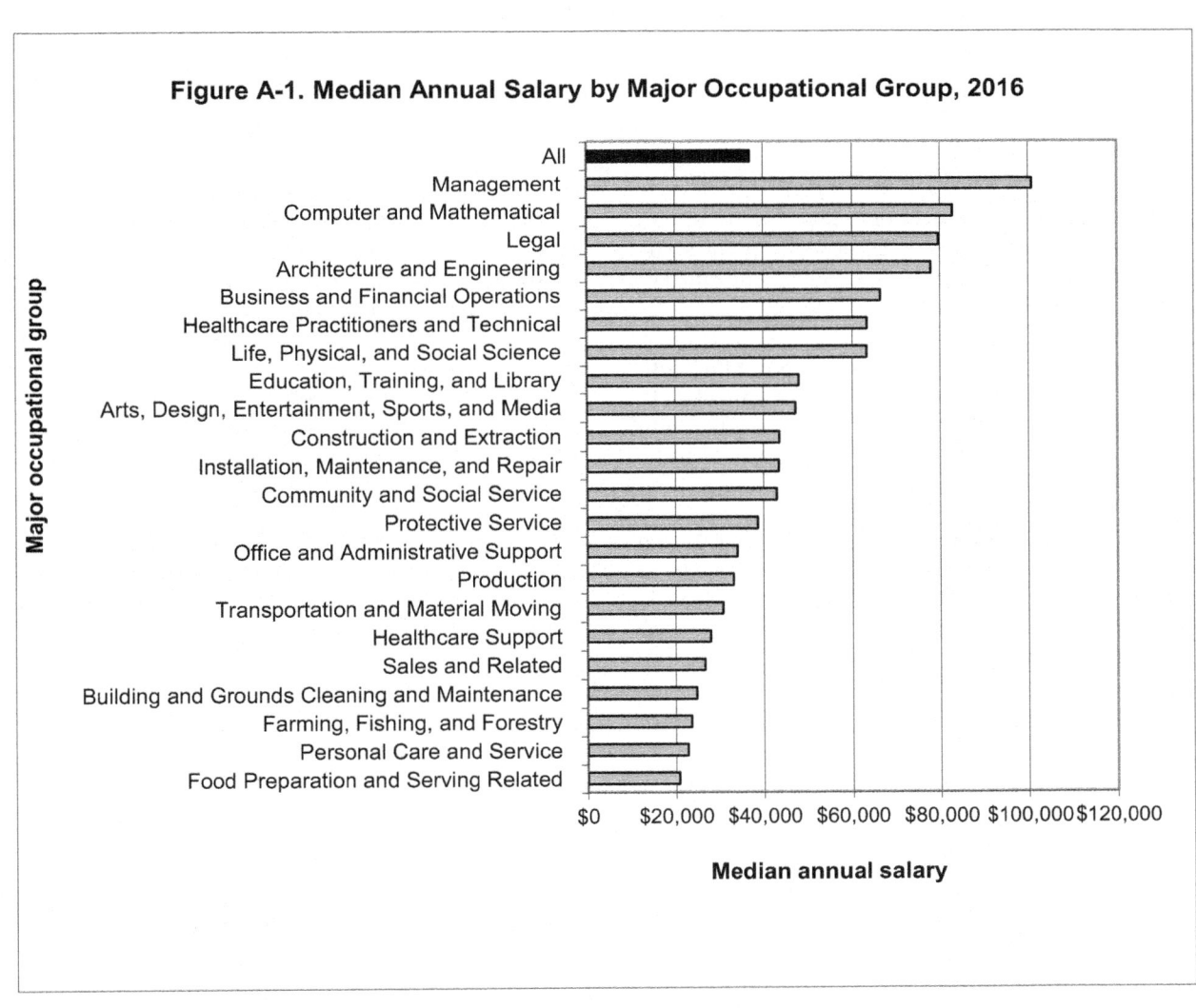

Figure A-1. Median Annual Salary by Major Occupational Group, 2016

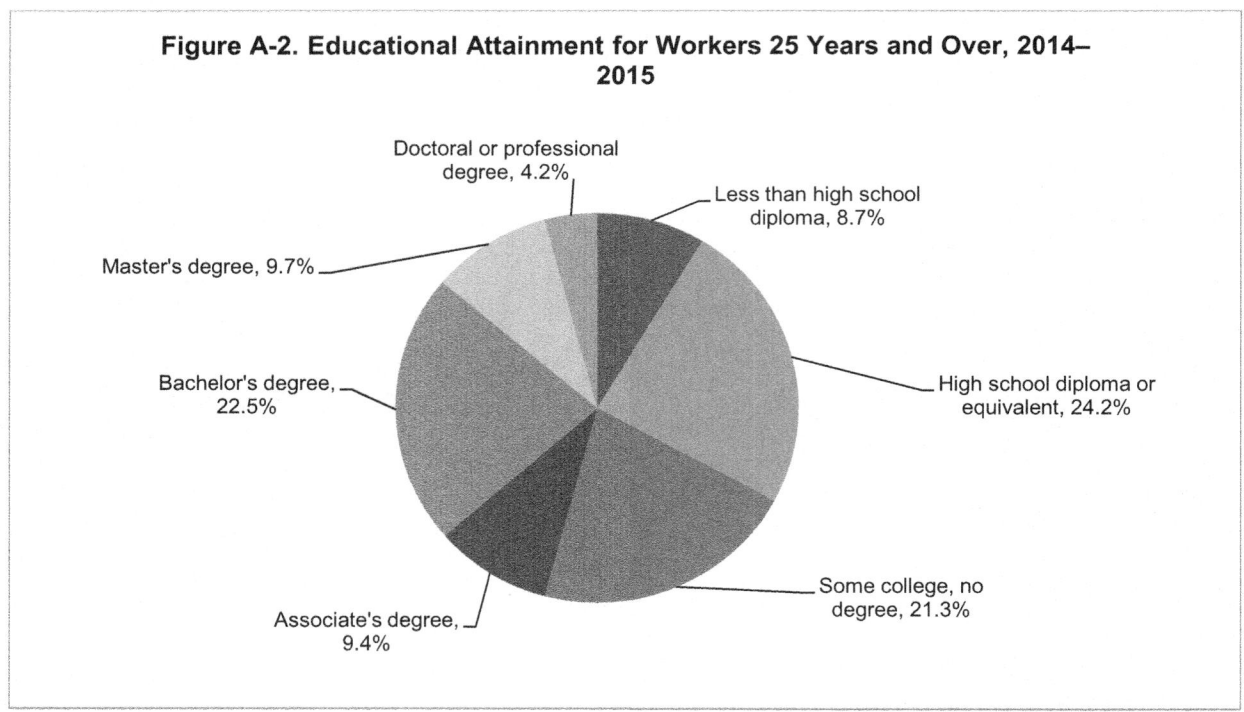

Figure A-2. Educational Attainment for Workers 25 Years and Over, 2014– 2015

- Doctoral or professional degree, 4.2%
- Less than high school diploma, 8.7%
- Master's degree, 9.7%
- High school diploma or equivalent, 24.2%
- Bachelor's degree, 22.5%
- Some college, no degree, 21.3%
- Associate's degree, 9.4%

have doctoral or professional degrees, more than half of American workers have high school diplomas, some college, or associate's degrees, and nearly one-third of workers have bachelor's or master's degrees.

- Personal care aides, home health aides, personal financial advisors, and physical therapists are expected to have the largest numeric increases, with nearly a half million additional personal care aides expected to be employed by 2024.

- The biggest numeric decline is expected for Postal Service mail carriers, dropping by about 78,000 in ten years. When combined with other Postal Service occupations—such as clerks, sorters, postmasters, and others—a decline of 140,000 jobs is expected for the Postal Service.

- Many anticipated job losses reflect changing technology: for example, the number of photographic process workers, sewing machine operators, and watch repairers is expected to decline.

- Personal care aides, home health aides, personal financial advisors, and physical therapists are expected to have the largest numeric increases, with nearly a half million additional personal care aides expected to be employed by 2024.

- Changing technology is evident in some of the occupations that are expected to increase, such as web developers, wind turbine service technicians, and solar photovoltaic installers.

Table A-1. Number of Employees, Wages and Salaries, and Job Requirements for Detailed Occupations in the United States

Occupation	Occupation code	Total employees, May 2016	Median hourly wage, 2016	Median Annual Salary, 2016	Typical education needed for entry, 2014	Work experience in a related occupation, 2014	Typical on-the-job training needed to attain competency in the occupation, 2014
All Occupations	00-0000	140,400,040	$17.81	$37,040			
Management Occupations	11-0000	7,090,790	$48.46	$100,790			
Chief Executives	11-1011	223,260	$87.12	$181,210	Bachelor's degree	5 years or more	None
General and Operations Managers	11-1021	2,188,870	$47.74	$99,310	Bachelor's degree	5 years or more	None
Legislators	11-1031	53,670		$23,470	Bachelor's degree	Less than 5 years	None
Advertising and Promotions Managers	11-2011	28,860	$48.47	$100,810	Bachelor's degree	Less than 5 years	None
Marketing Managers	11-2021	205,900	$63.07	$131,180	Bachelor's degree	5 years or more	None
Sales Managers	11-2022	365,230	$56.71	$117,960	Bachelor's degree	Less than 5 years	None
Public Relations and Fundraising Managers	11-2031	63,970	$51.59	$107,320	Bachelor's degree	5 years or more	None
Administrative Services Managers	11-3011	266,280	$43.29	$90,050	Bachelor's degree	Less than 5 years	None
Computer and Information Systems Managers	11-3021	352,510	$65.29	$135,800	Bachelor's degree	5 years or more	None
Financial Managers	11-3031	543,300	$58.54	$121,750	Bachelor's degree	5 years or more	None
Industrial Production Managers	11-3051	168,400	$46.70	$97,140	Bachelor's degree	5 years or more	None
Purchasing Managers	11-3061	71,750	$53.65	$111,590	Bachelor's degree	5 years or more	None
					High school diploma or		
Transportation, Storage, and Distribution Managers	11-3071	113,270	$42.88	$89,190	equivalent	5 years or more	None
Compensation and Benefits Managers	11-3111	15,230	$55.89	$116,240	Bachelor's degree	5 years or more	None
Human Resources Managers	11-3121	129,810	$51.40	$106,910	Bachelor's degree	5 years or more	None
Training and Development Managers	11-3131	32,880	$50.88	$105,830	Bachelor's degree	5 years or more	None
					High school diploma or		
Farmers, Ranchers, and Other Agricultural Managers	11-9013	4,560	$31.91	$66,360	equivalent	5 years or more	None
							Moderate-term on-the-job
Construction Managers	11-9021	249,650	$42.93	$89,300	Bachelor's degree	None	training
Education Administrators, Preschool and Childcare Center/Program	11-9031	48,530	$22.01	$45,790	Bachelor's degree	Less than 5 years	None
Education Administrators, Elementary and Secondary School	11-9032	242,970		$92,510	Master's degree	5 years or more	None
Education Administrators, Postsecondary	11-9033	138,430	$43.63	$90,760	Master's degree	Less than 5 years	None
Education Administrators, All Other	11-9039	34,140	$37.60	$78,210	Bachelor's degree	Less than 5 years	None
Architectural and Engineering Managers	11-9041	178,390	$64.78	$134,730	Bachelor's degree	5 years or more	None
					High school diploma or		
Food Service Managers	11-9051	201,470	$24.43	$50,820	equivalent	Less than 5 years	None
Funeral Service Managers	11-9061	8,370	$35.50	$73,830	Associate's degree	Less than 5 years	None
					High school diploma or		
Gaming Managers	11-9071	4,280	$33.26	$69,180	equivalent	Less than 5 years	None
					High school diploma or		
Lodging Managers	11-9081	35,410	$24.93	$51,840	equivalent	Less than 5 years	None
Medical and Health Services Managers	11-9111	332,150	$46.41	$96,540	Bachelor's degree	Less than 5 years	None
Natural Sciences Managers	11-9121	54,780	$57.62	$119,850	Bachelor's degree	5 years or more	None
					High school diploma or		Moderate-term on-the-job
Postmasters and Mail Superintendents	11-9131	14,720	$34.45	$71,670	equivalent	Less than 5 years	training
					High school diploma or		
Property, Real Estate, and Community Association Managers	11-9141	180,290	$27.42	$57,040	equivalent	Less than 5 years	None
Social and Community Service Managers	11-9151	126,230	$31.10	$64,680	Bachelor's degree	5 years or more	None
Emergency Management Directors	11-9161	9,570	$33.89	$70,500	Bachelor's degree	5 years or more	None
Managers, All Other	11-9199	403,670	$50.47	$104,970	Bachelor's degree	Less than 5 years	None
Business and Financial Operations Occupations	13-0000	7,281,190	$31.99	$66,530			
Agents and Business Managers of Artists, Performers, and athletes	13-1011	13,470	$29.85	$62,080	Bachelor's degree	Less than 5 years	None
							Long-term on-the-job
Buyers and Purchasing Agents, Farm Products	13-1021	11,490	$28.09	$58,430	Bachelor's degree	None	training
							Long-term on-the-job
Wholesale and Retail Buyers, Except Farm Products	13-1022	109,440	$25.65	$53,340	Bachelor's degree	None	training
							Long-term on-the-job
Purchasing Agents, Except Wholesale, Retail, and Farm products	13-1023	297,600	$30.43	$63,300	Bachelor's degree	None	training
					High school diploma or		Long-term on-the-job
Claims Adjusters, Examiners, and Investigators	13-1031	274,420	$30.62	$63,680	equivalent	None	training
					Postsecondary		Moderate-term on-the-job
Insurance Appraisers, Auto Damage	13-1032	15,130	$30.53	$63,510	nondegree award	None	training
							Moderate-term on-the-job
Compliance Officers	13-1041	273,910	$31.99	$66,540	Bachelor's degree	None	training
Cost Estimators	13-1051	214,610	$29.71	$61,790	Bachelor's degree	None	None
Human Resources Specialists	13-1071	524,800	$28.45	$59,180	Bachelor's degree	None	None
					No formal educational		Short-term on-the-job
Farm Labor Contractors	13-1074	810	$16.90	$35,160	credential	Less than 5 years	training
Labor Relations Specialists	13-1075	79,430	$29.96	$62,310	Bachelor's degree	Less than 5 years	None
Logisticians	13-1081	146,060	$35.66	$74,170	Bachelor's degree	None	None
Management Analysts	13-1111	637,690	$39.10	$81,330	Bachelor's degree	Less than 5 years	None
Meeting, Convention, and Event Planners	13-1121	95,850	$22.76	$47,350	Bachelor's degree	None	None
Fundraisers	13-1131	68,910	$26.02	$54,130	Bachelor's degree	None	None
Compensation, Benefits, and Job Analysis Specialists	13-1141	79,190	$29.85	$62,080	Bachelor's degree	Less than 5 years	None
Training and Development Specialists	13-1151	269,710	$28.37	$59,020	Bachelor's degree	Less than 5 years	None
Market Research Analysts and Marketing Specialists	13-1161	558,630	$30.08	$62,560	Bachelor's degree	None	None
Business Operations Specialists, All Other	13-1199	958,670	$33.19	$69,040	Bachelor's degree	None	None
Accountants and Auditors	13-2011	1,246,540	$32.76	$68,150	Bachelor's degree	None	None

Table A-1. Number of Employees, Wages and Salaries, and Job Requirements for Detailed Occupations in the United States—*Continued*

Occupation	Occupation code	Total employees, May 2016	Median hourly wage, 2016	Median Annual Salary, 2016	Typical education needed for entry, 2014	Work experience in a related occupation, 2014	Typical on-the-job training needed to attain competency in the occupation, 2014
Appraisers and Assessors of Real Estate	13-2021	60,770	$24.93	$51,850	Bachelor's degree	None	Long-term on-the-job training
Budget Analysts	13-2031	54,700	$35.50	$73,840	Bachelor's degree	None	None
Credit Analysts	13-2041	72,930	$33.62	$69,930	Bachelor's degree	None	None
Financial Analysts	13-2051	281,610	$39.31	$81,760	Bachelor's degree	None	None
Personal Financial Advisors	13-2052	201,850	$43.53	$90,530	Bachelor's degree	None	Long-term on-the-job training
Insurance Underwriters	13-2053	91,650	$32.54	$67,680	Bachelor's degree	None	Moderate-term on-the-job training
Financial Examiners	13-2061	49,750	$38.11	$79,280	Bachelor's degree	None	Moderate-term on-the-job training
Credit Counselors	13-2071	34,110	$21.34	$44,380	Bachelor's degree	None	Moderate-term on-the-job training
Loan Officers	13-2072	305,700	$30.60	$63,650	Bachelor's degree	None	Moderate-term on-the-job training
Tax Examiners and Collectors, and Revenue Agents	13-2081	58,450	$25.03	$52,060	Bachelor's degree	None	Moderate-term on-the-job training
Tax Preparers	13-2082	70,030	$17.57	$36,550	High school diploma or equivalent	None	Moderate-term on-the-job training
Financial Specialists, All Other	13-2099	123,270	$33.40	$69,470	Bachelor's degree	None	Moderate-term on-the-job training
Computer and Mathematical Occupations	15-0000	4,165,140	$39.82	$82,830			
Computer and Information Research Scientists	15-1111	26,580	$53.77	$111,840	Doctoral or professional degree	None	None
Computer Systems Analysts	15-1121	568,960	$41.93	$87,220	Bachelor's degree	None	None
Information Security Analysts	15-1122	96,870	$44.52	$92,600	Bachelor's degree	Less than 5 years	None
Computer Programmers	15-1131	271,200	$38.39	$79,840	Bachelor's degree	None	None
Software Developers, Applications	15-1132	794,000	$48.12	$100,080	Bachelor's degree	None	None
Software Developers, Systems Software	15-1133	409,820	$51.38	$106,860	Bachelor's degree	None	None
Web Developers	15-1134	129,540	$31.79	$66,130	Associate's degree	None	None
Database Administrators	15-1141	113,730	$40.84	$84,950	Bachelor's degree	Less than 5 years	None
Network and Computer Systems Administrators	15-1142	376,820	$38.32	$79,700	Bachelor's degree	None	None
Computer Network Architects	15-1143	157,070	$48.66	$101,210	Bachelor's degree	5 years or more	None
Computer User Support Specialists	15-1151	602,840	$23.74	$49,390	Some college, no degree	None	None
Computer Network Support Specialists	15-1152	188,740	$30.13	$62,670	Associate's degree	None	None
Computer Occupations, All Other	15-1199	261,210	$41.59	$86,510	Bachelor's degree	None	None
Actuaries	15-2011	19,940	$48.37	$100,610	Bachelor's degree	None	Long-term on-the-job training
Mathematicians	15-2021	2,730	$50.87	$105,810	Master's degree	None	None
Operations Research Analysts	15-2031	109,150	$38.08	$79,200	Bachelor's degree	None	None
Statisticians	15-2041	33,440	$38.70	$80,500	Master's degree	None	None
Mathematical Technicians	15-2091	510	$23.87	$49,660	Bachelor's degree	None	None
Mathematical Science Occupations, All Other	15-2099	2,000	$31.27	$65,050	Bachelor's degree	None	None
Architecture and Engineering Occupations	17-0000	2,499,050	$37.45	$77,900			
Architects, Except Landscape and Naval	17-1011	99,860	$36.99	$76,930	Bachelor's degree	None	Internship/residency
Landscape Architects	17-1012	19,420	$30.52	$63,480	Bachelor's degree	None	Internship/residency
Cartographers and Photogrammetrists	17-1021	12,100	$30.17	$62,750	Bachelor's degree	None	None
Surveyors	17-1022	43,340	$28.56	$59,390	Bachelor's degree	Less than 5 years	None
Aerospace Engineers	17-2011	68,510	$52.72	$109,650	Bachelor's degree	None	None
Agricultural Engineers	17-2021	1,980	$35.40	$73,640	Bachelor's degree	None	None
Biomedical Engineers	17-2031	20,590	$41.16	$85,620	Bachelor's degree	None	None
Chemical Engineers	17-2041	31,990	$47.28	$98,340	Bachelor's degree	None	None
Civil Engineers	17-2051	287,800	$40.16	$83,540	Bachelor's degree	None	None
Computer Hardware Engineers	17-2061	72,950	$55.33	$115,080	Bachelor's degree	None	None
Electrical Engineers	17-2071	183,770	$45.29	$94,210	Bachelor's degree	None	None
Electronics Engineers, Except Computer	17-2072	132,100	$47.70	$99,210	Bachelor's degree	None	None
Environmental Engineers	17-2081	52,280	$40.81	$84,890	Bachelor's degree	None	None
Health and Safety Engineers, Except Mining Safety Engineers and Inspectors	17-2111	25,410	$41.69	$86,720	Bachelor's degree	None	None
Industrial Engineers	17-2112	256,550	$40.53	$84,310	Bachelor's degree	None	None
Marine Engineers and Naval Architects	17-2121	8,120	$44.88	$93,350	Bachelor's degree	None	None
Materials Engineers	17-2131	26,800	$44.86	$93,310	Bachelor's degree	None	None
Mechanical Engineers	17-2141	285,790	$40.48	$84,190	Bachelor's degree	None	None
Mining and Geological Engineers, Including Mining Safety Engineers	17-2151	6,940	$45.06	$93,720	Bachelor's degree	None	None
Nuclear Engineers	17-2161	17,680	$49.14	$102,220	Bachelor's degree	None	None
Petroleum Engineers	17-2171	32,780	$61.65	$128,230	Bachelor's degree	None	None
Engineers, All Other	17-2199	123,390	$46.78	$97,300	Bachelor's degree	None	None
Architectural and Civil Drafters	17-3011	96,810	$24.83	$51,640	Associate's degree	None	None
Electrical and Electronics Drafters	17-3012	26,750	$28.83	$59,970	Associate's degree	None	None
Mechanical Drafters	17-3013	63,630	$26.19	$54,480	Associate's degree	None	None
Drafters, All Other	17-3019	15,530	$24.26	$50,470	Associate's degree	None	None
Aerospace Engineering and Operations Technicians	17-3021	11,970	$32.70	$68,020	Associate's degree	None	None
Civil Engineering Technicians	17-3022	72,150	$24.03	$49,980	Associate's degree	None	None
Electrical and Electronics Engineering Technicians	17-3023	134,870	$29.90	$62,190	Associate's degree	None	None
Electro-Mechanical Technicians	17-3024	13,710	$26.74	$55,610	Associate's degree	None	None

Table A-1. Number of Employees, Wages and Salaries, and Job Requirements for Detailed Occupations in the United States—*Continued*

Occupation	Occupation code	Total employees, May 2016	Median hourly wage, 2016	Median Annual Salary, 2016	Typical education needed for entry, 2014	Work experience in a related occupation, 2014	Typical on-the-job training needed to attain competency in the occupation, 2014
Environmental Engineering Technicians	17-3025	16,550	$23.64	$49,170	Associate's degree	None	None
Industrial Engineering Technicians	17-3026	63,220	$25.64	$53,330	Associate's degree	None	None
Mechanical Engineering Technicians	17-3027	45,510	$26.19	$54,480	Associate's degree	None	None
Engineering Technicians, Except Drafters, All Other	17-3029	74,290	$29.96	$62,330	Associate's degree	None	None
Surveying and Mapping Technicians	17-3031	53,920	$20.41	$42,450	High school diploma or equivalent	None	Moderate-term on-the-job training
Life, Physical, and Social Science Occupations	19-0000	1,152,840	$30.45	$63,340			
Animal Scientists	19-1011	2,470	$29.01	$60,330	Bachelor's degree	None	None
Food Scientists and Technologists	19-1012	14,200	$30.74	$63,950	Bachelor's degree	None	None
Soil and Plant Scientists	19-1013	14,690	$29.95	$62,300	Bachelor's degree	None	None
Biochemists and Biophysicists	19-1021	29,200	$39.51	$82,180	Doctoral or professional degree	None	None
Microbiologists	19-1022	21,670	$32.14	$66,850	Bachelor's degree	None	None
Zoologists and Wildlife Biologists	19-1023	17,720	$29.10	$60,520	Bachelor's degree	None	None
Biological Scientists, All Other	19-1029	35,110	$35.96	$74,790	Bachelor's degree	None	None
Conservation Scientists	19-1031	20,470	$29.72	$61,810	Bachelor's degree	None	None
Foresters	19-1032	8,420	$28.22	$58,700	Bachelor's degree	None	None
Epidemiologists	19-1041	5,690	$34.05	$70,820	Master's degree	None	None
Medical Scientists, Except Epidemiologists	19-1042	108,870	$38.72	$80,530	Doctoral or professional degree	None	None
Life Scientists, All Other	19-1099	7,890	$35.51	$73,860	Bachelor's degree	None	None
Astronomers	19-2011	1,830	$50.35	$104,740	Doctoral or professional degree	None	None
Physicists	19-2012	16,680	$55.71	$115,870	Doctoral or professional degree	None	None
Atmospheric and Space Scientists	19-2021	9,800	$44.45	$92,460	Bachelor's degree	None	None
Chemists	19-2031	86,660	$35.45	$73,740	Bachelor's degree	None	None
Materials Scientists	19-2032	7,750	$47.80	$99,430	Bachelor's degree	None	None
Environmental Scientists and Specialists, Including health	19-2041	84,250	$33.13	$68,910	Bachelor's degree	None	None
Geoscientists, Except Hydrologists and Geographers	19-2042	30,420	$43.16	$89,780	Bachelor's degree	None	None
Hydrologists	19-2043	6,300	$38.69	$80,480	Bachelor's degree	None	None
Physical Scientists, All Other	19-2099	18,960	$46.19	$96,070	Bachelor's degree	None	None
Economists	19-3011	19,380	$48.58	$101,050	Master's degree	None	None
Survey Researchers	19-3022	11,930	$26.19	$54,470	Master's degree	None	None
Clinical, Counseling, and School Psychologists	19-3031	107,980	$35.23	$73,270	Doctoral or professional degree	None	Internship/residency
Industrial-Organizational Psychologists	19-3032	1,020	$39.79	$82,760	Master's degree	None	Internship/residency
Psychologists, All Other	19-3039	13,310	$46.02	$95,710	Master's degree	None	Internship/residency
Sociologists	19-3041	2,870	$38.34	$79,750	Master's degree	None	None
Urban and Regional Planners	19-3051	34,810	$33.66	$70,020	Master's degree	None	None
Anthropologists and Archeologists	19-3091	6,470	$30.38	$63,190	Master's degree	None	None
Geographers	19-3092	1,370	$35.70	$74,260	Bachelor's degree	None	None
Historians	19-3093	2,950	$26.49	$55,110	Master's degree	None	None
Political Scientists	19-3094	6,350	$54.95	$114,290	Master's degree	None	None
Social Scientists and Related Workers, All Other	19-3099	36,380	$37.03	$77,020	Bachelor's degree	None	None
Agricultural and Food Science Technicians	19-4011	20,420	$18.05	$37,550	Associate's degree	None	Moderate-term on-the-job training
Biological Technicians	19-4021	74,720	$20.44	$42,520	Bachelor's degree	None	None
Chemical Technicians	19-4031	65,510	$22.04	$45,840	Associate's degree	None	Moderate-term on-the-job training
Geological and Petroleum Technicians	19-4041	15,100	$27.15	$56,470	Associate's degree	None	Moderate-term on-the-job training
Nuclear Technicians	19-4051	6,840	$38.05	$79,140	Associate's degree	None	Moderate-term on-the-job training
Social Science Research Assistants	19-4061	30,030	$20.76	$43,190	Bachelor's degree	None	None
Environmental Science and Protection Technicians, including Health	19-4091	32,950	$21.25	$44,190	Associate's degree	None	None
Forensic Science Technicians	19-4092	14,800	$27.29	$56,750	Bachelor's degree	None	Moderate-term on-the-job training
Forest and Conservation Technicians	19-4093	30,090	$17.10	$35,560	Associate's degree	None	None
Life, Physical, and Social Science Technicians, All Other	19-4099	68,540	$22.14	$46,040	Associate's degree	None	None
Community and Social Service Occupations	21-0000	2,019,250	$20.67	$42,990			
Substance Abuse and Behavioral Disorder Counselors	21-1011	91,040	$19.75	$41,070	Bachelor's degree	None	None
Educational, Guidance, School, and Vocational Counselors	21-1012	260,670	$26.23	$54,560	Master's degree	None	None
Marriage and Family Therapists	21-1013	36,960	$23.64	$49,170	Master's degree	None	Internship/residency
Mental Health Counselors	21-1014	139,820	$20.59	$42,840	Master's degree	None	Internship/residency
Rehabilitation Counselors	21-1015	103,030	$16.67	$34,670	Master's degree	None	None
Counselors, All Other	21-1019	28,380	$21.32	$44,350	Master's degree	None	None
Child, Family, and School Social Workers	21-1021	298,840	$20.79	$43,250	Bachelor's degree	None	None
Healthcare Social Workers	21-1022	159,310	$25.85	$53,760	Master's degree	None	None

Table A-1. Number of Employees, Wages and Salaries, and Job Requirements for Detailed Occupations in the United States—*Continued*

Occupation	Occupation code	Total employees, May 2016	Median hourly wage, 2016	Median Annual Salary, 2016	Typical education needed for entry, 2014	Work experience in a related occupation, 2014	Typical on-the-job training needed to attain competency in the occupation, 2014
Mental Health and Substance Abuse Social Workers	21-1023	114,040	$20.53	$42,700	Bachelor's degree	None	None
Social Workers, All Other	21-1029	59,540	$28.96	$60,230	Bachelor's degree	None	None
Health Educators	21-1091	57,570	$25.51	$53,070	Bachelor's degree	None	None
Probation Officers and Correctional Treatment Specialists	21-1092	87,500	$24.12	$50,160	Bachelor's degree	None	Short-term on-the-job training
Social and Human Service Assistants	21-1093	360,650	$15.29	$31,810	High school diploma or equivalent	None	Short-term on-the-job training
Community Health Workers	21-1094	51,900	$17.95	$37,330	High school diploma or equivalent	None	Short-term on-the-job training
Community and Social Service Specialists, All Other	21-1099	91,860	$20.73	$43,120	Master's degree	None	None
Clergy	21-2011	49,320	$21.99	$45,740	Bachelor's degree	None	Moderate-term on-the-job training
Directors, Religious Activities and Education	21-2021	20,590	$18.56	$38,610	Bachelor's degree	Less than 5 years	None
Religious Workers, All Other	21-2099	8,250	$13.85	$28,820	Bachelor's degree	None	None
Legal Occupations	23-0000	1,075,520	$38.30	$79,650			
Lawyers	23-1011	619,530	$56.81	$118,160	Doctoral or professional degree	None	None
Judicial Law Clerks	23-1012	13,410	$24.89	$51,760	Doctoral or professional degree	None	None
Administrative Law Judges, Adjudicators, and Hearing Officers	23-1021	14,540	$44.28	$92,110	Doctoral or professional degree	5 years or more	Short-term on-the-job training
Arbitrators, Mediators, and Conciliators	23-1022	6,300	$28.74	$59,770	Bachelor's degree	Less than 5 years	Moderate-term on-the-job training
Judges, Magistrate Judges, and Magistrates	23-1023	27,210	$60.52	$125,880	Doctoral or professional degree	5 years or more	Short-term on-the-job training
Paralegals and Legal Assistants	23-2011	277,310	$23.80	$49,500	Associate's degree	None	None
Court Reporters	23-2091	17,700	$24.68	$51,320	Postsecondary nondegree award	None	Short-term on-the-job training
Title Examiners, Abstractors, and Searchers	23-2093	54,560	$22.02	$45,800	High school diploma or equivalent	None	Short-term on-the-job training
Legal Support Workers, All Other	23-2099	44,960	$26.27	$54,650	High school diploma or equivalent	None	Short-term on-the-job training
Education, Training, and Library Occupations	25-0000	8,636,430	$23.08	$48,000			
Business Teachers, Postsecondary	25-1011	83,030		$77,490	Doctoral or professional degree	None	None
Computer Science Teachers, Postsecondary	25-1021	32,540		$77,570	Doctoral or professional degree	None	None
Mathematical Science Teachers, Postsecondary	25-1022	52,020		$69,520	Doctoral or professional degree	None	None
Architecture Teachers, Postsecondary	25-1031	7,370		$79,250	Doctoral or professional degree	None	None
Engineering Teachers, Postsecondary	25-1032	38,000		$97,530	Doctoral or professional degree	None	None
Agricultural Sciences Teachers, Postsecondary	25-1041	10,340		$91,580	Doctoral or professional degree	None	None
Biological Science Teachers, Postsecondary	25-1042	50,820		$76,650	Doctoral or professional degree	None	None
Forestry and Conservation Science Teachers, Postsecondary	25-1043	1,750		$85,880	Doctoral or professional degree	None	None
Atmospheric, Earth, Marine, and Space Sciences Teachers, Postsecondary	25-1051	10,850		$85,410	Doctoral or professional degree	None	None
Chemistry Teachers, Postsecondary	25-1052	21,250		$76,750	Doctoral or professional degree	None	None
Environmental Science Teachers, Postsecondary	25-1053	5,520		$78,340	Doctoral or professional degree	None	None
Physics Teachers, Postsecondary	25-1054	14,160		$84,570	Doctoral or professional degree	None	None
Anthropology and Archeology Teachers, Postsecondar	25-1061	5,700		$81,350	Doctoral or professional degree	None	None
Area, Ethnic, and Cultural Studies Teachers, Posts	25-1062	9,060		$73,020	Doctoral or professional degree	None	None
Economics Teachers, Postsecondary	25-1063	13,060		$95,770	Doctoral or professional degree	None	None
Geography Teachers, Postsecondary	25-1064	4,140		$76,810	Doctoral or professional degree	None	None
Political Science Teachers, Postsecondary	25-1065	16,720		$79,210	Doctoral or professional degree	None	None
Psychology Teachers, Postsecondary	25-1066	37,640		$73,140	Doctoral or professional degree	None	None
Sociology Teachers, Postsecondary	25-1067	14,580		$71,840	Doctoral or professional degree	None	None
Social Sciences Teachers, Postsecondary, All Other	25-1069	13,320		$70,740	Doctoral or professional degree	None	None
Health Specialties Teachers, Postsecondary	25-1071	186,740		$99,360	Doctoral or professional degree	Less than 5 years	None
Nursing Instructors and Teachers, Postsecondary	25-1072	56,210		$69,130	Master's degree	Less than 5 years	None
Education Teachers, Postsecondary	25-1081	58,850		$62,520	Doctoral or professional degree	Less than 5 years	None

Table A-1. Number of Employees, Wages and Salaries, and Job Requirements for Detailed Occupations in the United States—*Continued*

Occupation	Occupation code	Total employees, May 2016	Median hourly wage, 2016	Median Annual Salary, 2016	Typical education needed for entry, 2014	Work experience in a related occupation, 2014	Typical on-the-job training needed to attain competency in the occupation, 2014
Library Science Teachers, Postsecondary	25-1082	4,870		$68,410	Doctoral or professional degree	None	None
Criminal Justice and Law Enforcement Teachers, Postsecondary	25-1111	14,620		$59,590	Doctoral or professional degree	None	None
Law Teachers, Postsecondary	25-1112	16,010		$111,210	Doctoral or professional degree	None	None
Social Work Teachers, Postsecondary	25-1113	11,860		$64,030	Doctoral or professional degree	None	None
Art, Drama, and Music Teachers, Postsecondary	25-1121	99,020		$68,650	Master's degree	None	None
Communications Teachers, Postsecondary	25-1122	28,180		$65,640	Doctoral or professional degree	None	None
English Language and Literature Teachers, Postsecondary	25-1123	71,270		$63,730	Doctoral or professional degree	None	None
Foreign Language and Literature Teachers, Postsecondary	25-1124	28,720		$63,500	Doctoral or professional degree	None	None
History Teachers, Postsecondary	25-1125	21,800		$71,820	Doctoral or professional degree	None	None
Philosophy and Religion Teachers, Postsecondary	25-1126	23,180		$68,360	Doctoral or professional degree	None	None
Graduate Teaching Assistants	25-1191	135,130		$34,240	Bachelor's degree	None	None
Home Economics Teachers, Postsecondary	25-1192	2,970		$69,190	Master's degree	None	None
Recreation and Fitness Studies Teachers, Postsecondary	25-1193	17,390		$59,180	Doctoral or professional degree	None	None
Vocational Education Teachers, Postsecondary	25-1194	116,430	$24.36	$50,660	Bachelor's degree	Less than 5 years	None
Postsecondary Teachers, All Other	25-1199	194,870		$64,400	Doctoral or professional degree	None	None
Preschool Teachers, Except Special Education	25-2011	385,550	$13.84	$28,790	Associate's degree	None	None
Kindergarten Teachers, Except Special Education	25-2012	151,290		$52,620	Bachelor's degree	None	Internship/residency
Elementary School Teachers, Except Special Education	25-2021	1,392,660		$55,800	Bachelor's degree	None	Internship/residency
Middle School Teachers, Except Special and Career/Technical Education	25-2022	626,310		$56,720	Bachelor's degree	None	Internship/residency
Career/Technical Education Teachers, Middle School	25-2023	12,730		$57,560	Bachelor's degree	Less than 5 years	Internship/residency
Secondary School Teachers, Except Special and Career/Technical Education	25-2031	1,003,250		$58,030	Bachelor's degree	None	Internship/residency
Career/Technical Education Teachers, Secondary School	25-2032	80,100		$57,320	Bachelor's degree	Less than 5 years	Internship/residency
Special Education Teachers, Preschool	25-2051	28,140		$52,460	Bachelor's degree	None	Internship/residency
Special Education Teachers, Kindergarten and Elementary School	25-2052	190,530		$57,040	Bachelor's degree	None	Internship/residency
Special Education Teachers, Middle School	25-2053	90,250		$58,560	Bachelor's degree	None	Internship/residency
Special Education Teachers, Secondary School	25-2054	132,490		$59,700	Bachelor's degree	None	Internship/residency
Special Education Teachers, All Other	25-2059	40,190		$53,860	Bachelor's degree	None	Internship/residency
Adult Basic and Secondary Education and Literacy Teachers and Instructors	25-3011	58,810	$24.35	$50,650	Bachelor's degree	None	Internship/residency
Self-Enrichment Education Teachers	25-3021	229,840	$17.95	$37,330	High school diploma or equivalent	Less than 5 years	None
Teachers and Instructors, All Other, Except Substitutes	25-3097	292,950		$39,570	Bachelor's degree	None	Internship/residency
Substitute Teachers	25-3098	609,960	$13.47	$28,010	Bachelor's degree	None	Internship/residency
Archivists	25-4011	5,760	$24.28	$50,500	Master's degree	None	None
Curators	25-4012	11,170	$25.66	$53,360	Master's degree	None	None
Museum Technicians and Conservators	25-4013	10,970	$19.25	$40,040	Bachelor's degree	None	None
Librarians	25-4021	129,350	$27.73	$57,680	Master's degree	None	None
Library Technicians	25-4031	93,410	$15.81	$32,890	Postsecondary nondegree award	None	None
Audio-Visual and Multimedia Collections Specialists	25-9011	10,300	$23.00	$47,840	Bachelor's degree	Less than 5 years	None
Farm and Home Management Advisors	25-9021	8,620	$23.79	$49,490	Master's degree	None	None
Instructional Coordinators	25-9031	147,330	$30.03	$62,460	Master's degree	5 years or more	None
Teacher Assistants	25-9041	1,263,820		$25,410	Some college, no degree	None	None
Education, Training, and Library Workers, All Other	25-9099	100,640	$20.48	$42,600	Bachelor's degree	None	None
Arts, Design, Entertainment, Sports, and Media Occupations	27-0000	1,902,970	$22.69	$47,190			
Art Directors	27-1011	36,210	$43.18	$89,820	Bachelor's degree	5 years or more	None
Craft Artists	27-1012	5,070	$16.08	$33,440	No formal educational credential	None	Long-term on-the-job training
Fine Artists, Including Painters, Sculptors, and Illustators	27-1013	11,520	$24.42	$50,790	Bachelor's degree	None	Long-term on-the-job training
Multimedia Artists and Animators	27-1014	29,810	$31.40	$65,300	Bachelor's degree	None	Moderate-term on-the-job training
Artists and Related Workers, All Other	27-1019	7,010	$29.50	$61,360	No formal educational credential	None	Long-term on-the-job training
Commercial and Industrial Designers	27-1021	31,860	$32.59	$67,790	Bachelor's degree	None	None
Fashion Designers	27-1022	19,230	$31.33	$65,170	Bachelor's degree	None	None
Floral Designers	27-1023	43,990	$12.43	$25,850	High school diploma or equivalent	None	Moderate-term on-the-job training

Table A-1. Number of Employees, Wages and Salaries, and Job Requirements for Detailed Occupations in the United States—*Continued*

Occupation	Occupation code	Total employees, May 2016	Median hourly wage, 2016	Median Annual Salary, 2016	Typical education needed for entry, 2014	Work experience in a related occupation, 2014	Typical on-the-job training needed to attain competency in the occupation, 2014
Graphic Designers	27-1024	210,710	$22.90	$47,640	Bachelor's degree	None	None
Interior Designers	27-1025	53,160	$23.95	$49,810	Bachelor's degree	None	None
Merchandise Displayers and Window Trimmers	27-1026	114,690	$12.83	$26,700	High school diploma or equivalent	None	Moderate-term on-the-job training
Set and Exhibit Designers	27-1027	12,060	$24.51	$50,990	Bachelor's degree	None	None
Designers, All Other	27-1029	7,230	$25.66	$53,380	Bachelor's degree	None	None
Actors	27-2011	48,620	$18.70		Some college, no degree	None	Long-term on-the-job training
Producers and Directors	27-2012	114,510	$34.11	$70,950	Bachelor's degree	Less than 5 years	None
Athletes and Sports Competitors	27-2021	10,260		$47,710	No formal educational credential	None	Long-term on-the-job training
Coaches and Scouts	27-2022	230,930		$31,460	Bachelor's degree	None	None
Umpires, Referees, and Other Sports Officials	27-2023	18,660		$25,660	High school diploma or equivalent	None	Moderate-term on-the-job training
Dancers	27-2031	10,060	$13.74		No formal educational credential	None	Long-term on-the-job training
Choreographers	27-2032	5,160	$23.19	$48,240	High school diploma or equivalent	5 years or more	Long-term on-the-job training
Music Directors and Composers	27-2041	18,380	$24.09	$50,110	Bachelor's degree	Less than 5 years	None
Musicians and Singers	27-2042	40,110	$25.14		No formal educational credential	None	Long-term on-the-job training
Entertainers and Performers, Sports and Related Workers, All Other	27-2099	13,150	$17.34		No formal educational credential	None	Short-term on-the-job training
Radio and Television Announcers	27-3011	29,210	$15.10	$31,400	Bachelor's degree	None	Short-term on-the-job training
Public Address System and Other Announcers	27-3012	8,020	$13.91	$28,940	High school diploma or equivalent	None	Short-term on-the-job training
Broadcast News Analysts	27-3021	5,070	$27.25	$56,680	Bachelor's degree	None	None
Reporters and Correspondents	27-3022	40,090	$18.18	$37,820	Bachelor's degree	None	None
Public Relations Specialists	27-3031	226,940	$27.89	$58,020	Bachelor's degree	None	None
Editors	27-3041	97,170	$27.51	$57,210	Bachelor's degree	Less than 5 years	None
Technical Writers	27-3042	49,780	$33.58	$69,850	Bachelor's degree	Less than 5 years	Short-term on-the-job training
Writers and Authors	27-3043	44,690	$29.44	$61,240	Bachelor's degree	None	Moderate-term on-the-job training
Interpreters and Translators	27-3091	51,350	$22.17	$46,120	Bachelor's degree	None	Short-term on-the-job training
Media and Communication Workers, All Other	27-3099	23,310	$20.96	$43,600	High school diploma or equivalent	None	Short-term on-the-job training
Audio and Video Equipment Technicians	27-4011	69,670	$20.30	$42,230	Postsecondary nondegree award	None	Short-term on-the-job training
Broadcast Technicians	27-4012	30,330	$18.54	$38,550	Associate's degree	None	Short-term on-the-job training
Radio Operators	27-4013	870	$22.24	$46,250	High school diploma or equivalent	None	Short-term on-the-job training
Sound Engineering Technicians	27-4014	15,210	$25.81	$53,680	Postsecondary nondegree award	None	Short-term on-the-job training
Photographers	27-4021	48,660	$16.38	$34,070	High school diploma or equivalent	None	Long-term on-the-job training
Camera Operators, Television, Video, and Motion Picture	27-4031	21,710	$26.48	$55,080	Bachelor's degree	None	None
Film and Video Editors	27-4032	29,880	$30.18	$62,760	Bachelor's degree	None	None
Media and Communication Equipment Workers, All Other	27-4099	18,620	$36.39	$75,700	High school diploma or equivalent	None	Short-term on-the-job training
Healthcare Practitioners and Technical Occupations	29-0000	8,318,500	$30.49	$63,420			
Chiropractors	29-1011	32,960	$32.46	$67,520	Doctoral or professional degree	None	None
Dentists, General	29-1021	105,620	$73.99	$153,900	Doctoral or professional degree	None	None
Oral and Maxillofacial Surgeons	29-1022	5,380	$0.00	$208,000	Doctoral or professional degree	None	Internship/residency
Orthodontists	29-1023	5,200	$0.00	$208,000	Doctoral or professional degree	None	Internship/residency
Prosthodontists	29-1024	750	$60.60	$126,050	Doctoral or professional degree	None	Internship/residency
Dentists, All Other Specialists	29-1029	5,380	$83.17	$173,000	Doctoral or professional degree	None	Internship/residency
Dietitians and Nutritionists	29-1031	61,430	$28.33	$58,920	Bachelor's degree	None	Internship/residency
Optometrists	29-1041	36,430	$51.03	$106,140	Doctoral or professional degree	None	None
Pharmacists	29-1051	305,510	$58.77	$122,230	Doctoral or professional degree	None	None
Anesthesiologists	29-1061	30,190	$0.00	$208,000	Doctoral or professional degree	None	Internship/residency
Family and General Practitioners	29-1062	122,970	$91.58	$190,490	Doctoral or professional degree	None	Internship/residency
Internists, General	29-1063	45,290	$94.42	$196,380	Doctoral or professional degree	None	Internship/residency

Table A-1. Number of Employees, Wages and Salaries, and Job Requirements for Detailed Occupations in the United States—*Continued*

Occupation	Occupation code	Total employees, May 2016	Median hourly wage, 2016	Median Annual Salary, 2016	Typical education needed for entry, 2014	Work experience in a related occupation, 2014	Typical on-the-job training needed to attain competency in the occupation, 2014
Obstetricians and Gynecologists	29-1064	19,800	$0.00	$208,000	Doctoral or professional degree	None	Internship/residency
Pediatricians, General	29-1065	26,960	$81.24	$168,990	Doctoral or professional degree	None	Internship/residency
Psychiatrists	29-1066	24,820	$93.63	$194,740	Doctoral or professional degree	None	Internship/residency
Surgeons	29-1067	41,190	$0.00	$208,000	Doctoral or professional degree	None	Internship/residency
Physicians and Surgeons, All Other	29-1069	338,620	$99.48	$206,920	Doctoral or professional degree	None	Internship/residency
Physician Assistants	29-1071	104,050	$48.79	$101,480	Master's degree	None	None
Podiatrists	29-1081	9,800	$60.01	$124,830	Doctoral or professional degree	None	Internship/residency
Occupational Therapists	29-1122	118,070	$39.38	$81,910	Master's degree	None	None
Physical Therapists	29-1123	216,920	$41.06	$85,400	Doctoral or professional degree	None	None
Radiation Therapists	29-1124	17,450	$38.54	$80,160	Associate's degree	None	None
Recreational Therapists	29-1125	18,100	$22.31	$46,410	Bachelor's degree	None	None
Respiratory Therapists	29-1126	126,770	$28.21	$58,670	Associate's degree	None	None
Speech-Language Pathologists	29-1127	135,980	$35.90	$74,680	Master's degree	None	None
Exercise Physiologists	29-1128	6,880	$22.76	$47,340	Bachelor's degree	None	None
Therapists, All Other	29-1129	11,320	$27.26	$56,700	Bachelor's degree	None	None
Veterinarians	29-1131	67,650	$42.68	$88,770	Doctoral or professional degree	None	None
Registered Nurses	29-1141	2,857,180	$32.91	$68,450	Bachelor's degree	None	None
Nurse Anesthetists	29-1151	39,860	$77.05	$160,270	Master's degree	None	None
Nurse Midwives	29-1161	6,270	$47.97	$99,770	Master's degree	None	None
Nurse Practitioners	29-1171	150,230	$48.52	$100,910	Master's degree	None	None
Audiologists	29-1181	12,310	$36.53	$75,980	Doctoral or professional degree	None	None
Health Diagnosing and Treating Practitioners, All Other	29-1199	36,280	$35.83	$74,530	Master's degree	None	None
Medical and Clinical Laboratory Technologists	29-2011	166,730	$29.36	$61,070	Bachelor's degree	None	None
Medical and Clinical Laboratory Technicians	29-2012	160,190	$18.73	$38,950	Associate's degree	None	None
Dental Hygienists	29-2021	204,990	$35.05	$72,910	Associate's degree	None	None
Cardiovascular Technologists and Technicians	29-2031	53,760	$26.71	$55,570	Associate's degree	None	None
Diagnostic Medical Sonographers	29-2032	65,790	$33.49	$69,650	Associate's degree	None	None
Nuclear Medicine Technologists	29-2033	19,650	$35.75	$74,350	Associate's degree	None	None
Radiologic Technologists	29-2034	200,650	$27.62	$57,450	Associate's degree	None	None
Magnetic Resonance Imaging Technologists	29-2035	35,850	$32.90	$68,420	Associate's degree	Less than 5 years	None
Emergency Medical Technicians and Paramedics	29-2041	244,960	$15.71	$32,670	Postsecondary nondegree award	None	None
Dietetic Technicians	29-2051	32,240	$12.67	$26,350	Associate's degree	None	None
Pharmacy Technicians	29-2052	398,390	$14.86	$30,920	High school diploma or equivalent	None	Moderate-term on-the-job training
Psychiatric Technicians	29-2053	61,720	$14.89	$30,970	Postsecondary nondegree award	Less than 5 years	Short-term on-the-job training
Respiratory Therapy Technicians	29-2054	10,600	$23.93	$49,780	Associate's degree	None	None
Surgical Technologists	29-2055	105,720	$21.71	$45,160	Postsecondary nondegree award	None	None
Veterinary Technologists and Technicians	29-2056	99,390	$15.62	$32,490	Associate's degree	None	None
Ophthalmic Medical Technicians	29-2057	43,990	$17.08	$35,530	Postsecondary nondegree award	None	None
Licensed Practical and Licensed Vocational Nurses	29-2061	702,400	$21.20	$44,090	Postsecondary nondegree award	None	None
Medical Records and Health Information Technicians	29-2071	200,140	$18.29	$38,040	Postsecondary nondegree award	None	None
Opticians, Dispensing	29-2081	75,270	$17.08	$35,530	High school diploma or equivalent	None	Long-term on-the-job training
Orthotists and Prosthetists	29-2091	7,500	$31.55	$65,630	Master's degree	None	Internship/residency
Hearing Aid Specialists	29-2092	6,740	$24.16	$50,250	High school diploma or equivalent	None	None
Health Technologists and Technicians, All Other	29-2099	122,170	$19.75	$41,070	High school diploma or equivalent	None	None
Occupational Health and Safety Specialists	29-9011	76,630	$34.09	$70,920	Bachelor's degree	None	None
Occupational Health and Safety Technicians	29-9012	16,560	$23.47	$48,820	High school diploma or equivalent	None	Moderate-term on-the-job training
Athletic Trainers	29-9091	24,130		$45,630	Bachelor's degree	None	None
Genetic Counselors	29-9092	2,720	$35.64	$74,120	Master's degree	None	None
Healthcare Practitioners and Technical Workers, All Other	29-9099	36,000	$23.47	$48,820	Postsecondary nondegree award	None	None
Healthcare Support Occupations	31-0000	4,043,480	$13.42	$27,910			
Home Health Aides	31-1011	814,300	$10.87	$22,600	No formal educational credential	None	Short-term on-the-job training
Psychiatric Aides	31-1013	67,410	$12.85	$26,720	High school diploma or equivalent	None	Short-term on-the-job training
Nursing Assistants	31-1014	1,443,150	$12.78	$26,590	Postsecondary nondegree award	None	None
Orderlies	31-1015	52,940	$12.83	$26,690	High school diploma or equivalent	None	Short-term on-the-job training

Table A-1. Number of Employees, Wages and Salaries, and Job Requirements for Detailed Occupations in the United States—*Continued*

Occupation	Occupation code	Total employees, May 2016	Median hourly wage, 2016	Median Annual Salary, 2016	Typical education needed for entry, 2014	Work experience in a related occupation, 2014	Typical on-the-job training needed to attain competency in the occupation, 2014
Occupational Therapy Assistants	31-2011	38,170	$28.37	$59,010	Associate's degree	None	None
Occupational Therapy Aides	31-2012	7,210	$13.62	$28,330	High school diploma or equivalent	None	Short-term on-the-job training
Physical Therapist Assistants	31-2021	85,580	$27.21	$56,610	Associate's degree	None	None
Physical Therapist Aides	31-2022	50,030	$12.35	$25,680	High school diploma or equivalent	None	Short-term on-the-job training
Massage Therapists	31-9011	95,830	$19.17	$39,860	Postsecondary nondegree award	None	None
Dental Assistants	31-9091	327,290	$17.76	$36,940	Postsecondary nondegree award	None	None
Medical Assistants	31-9092	623,560	$15.17	$31,540	Postsecondary nondegree award	None	None
Medical Equipment Preparers	31-9093	52,500	$16.54	$34,400	High school diploma or equivalent	None	Moderate-term on-the-job training
Medical Transcriptionists	31-9094	54,070	$17.17	$35,720	Postsecondary nondegree award	None	None
Pharmacy Aides	31-9095	36,660	$12.14	$25,240	High school diploma or equivalent	None	Short-term on-the-job training
Veterinary Assistants and Laboratory Animal Caretakers	31-9096	79,990	$12.14	$25,250	High school diploma or equivalent	None	Short-term on-the-job training
Phlebotomists	31-9097	120,970	$15.72	$32,710	Postsecondary nondegree award	None	None
Healthcare Support Workers, All Other	31-9099	93,830	$17.46	$36,330	High school diploma or equivalent	None	None
Protective Service Occupations	33-0000	3,386,360	$18.59	$38,660			
First-Line Supervisors of Correctional Officers	33-1011	43,230	$29.12	$60,560	High school diploma or equivalent	Less than 5 years	Moderate-term on-the-job training
First-Line Supervisors of Police and Detectives	33-1012	100,200	$40.79	$84,840	High school diploma or equivalent	Less than 5 years	Moderate-term on-the-job training
First-Line Supervisors of Fire Fighting and Prevention Workers	33-1021	57,170	$35.84	$74,540	Postsecondary nondegree award	Less than 5 years	Moderate-term on-the-job training
First-Line Supervisors of Protective Service Workers, All Other	33-1099	72,880	$22.99	$47,820	High school diploma or equivalent	Less than 5 years	None
Firefighters	33-2011	315,910	$23.09	$48,030	Postsecondary nondegree award	None	Long-term on-the-job training
Fire Inspectors and Investigators	33-2021	11,910	$28.10	$58,440	Postsecondary nondegree award	5 years or more	Moderate-term on-the-job training
Forest Fire Inspectors and Prevention Specialists	33-2022	1,650	$17.42	$36,230	High school diploma or equivalent	Less than 5 years	Moderate-term on-the-job training
Bailiffs	33-3011	17,880	$20.52	$42,670	High school diploma or equivalent	None	Moderate-term on-the-job training
Correctional Officers and Jailers	33-3012	431,600	$20.59	$42,820	High school diploma or equivalent	None	Moderate-term on-the-job training
Detectives and Criminal Investigators	33-3021	104,980	$37.56	$78,120	High school diploma or equivalent	Less than 5 years	Moderate-term on-the-job training
Fish and Game Wardens	33-3031	6,610	$24.87	$51,730	Bachelor's degree	None	Moderate-term on-the-job training
Parking Enforcement Workers	33-3041	8,920	$18.25	$37,950	High school diploma or equivalent	None	Short-term on-the-job training
Police and Sheriff's Patrol Officers	33-3051	657,690	$28.69	$59,680	High school diploma or equivalent	None	Moderate-term on-the-job training
Transit and Railroad Police	33-3052	4,810	$32.03	$66,610	High school diploma or equivalent	None	Moderate-term on-the-job training
Animal Control Workers	33-9011	12,970	$16.61	$34,550	High school diploma or equivalent	None	Moderate-term on-the-job training
Private Detectives and Investigators	33-9021	28,490	$23.17	$48,190	High school diploma or equivalent	Less than 5 years	Moderate-term on-the-job training
Gaming Surveillance Officers and Gaming Investigators	33-9031	10,460	$15.69	$32,630	High school diploma or equivalent	None	Short-term on-the-job training
Security Guards	33-9032	1,103,120	$12.39	$25,770	High school diploma or equivalent	None	Short-term on-the-job training
Crossing Guards	33-9091	72,900	$12.84	$26,700	No formal educational credential	None	Short-term on-the-job training
Lifeguards, Ski Patrol, and Other Recreational Protective Service Workers	33-9092	145,100	$9.76	$20,290	No formal educational credential	None	Short-term on-the-job training
Transportation Security Screeners	33-9093	42,750	$19.08	$39,680	High school diploma or equivalent	None	Short-term on-the-job training
Protective Service Workers, All Other	33-9099	135,120	$13.81	$28,720	High school diploma or equivalent	None	Short-term on-the-job training
Food Preparation and Serving Related Occupations	35-0000	12,981,720	$10.01	$20,810			
Chefs and Head Cooks	35-1011	134,190	$20.76	$43,180	High school diploma or equivalent	5 years or more	None
First-Line Supervisors of Food Preparation and Serving workers	35-1012	908,550	$15.13	$31,480	High school diploma or equivalent	Less than 5 years	None
Cooks, Fast Food	35-2011	513,200	$9.55	$19,860	No formal educational credential	None	Short-term on-the-job training
Cooks, Institution and Cafeteria	35-2012	409,850	$11.90	$24,750	No formal educational credential	None	Short-term on-the-job training

Table A-1. Number of Employees, Wages and Salaries, and Job Requirements for Detailed Occupations in the United States—*Continued*

Occupation	Occupation code	Total employees, May 2016	Median hourly wage, 2016	Median Annual Salary, 2016	Typical education needed for entry, 2014	Work experience in a related occupation, 2014	Typical on-the-job training needed to attain competency in the occupation, 2014
Cooks, Private Household	35-2013	370	$15.42	$32,060	Postsecondary nondegree award	Less than 5 years	None
Cooks, Restaurant	35-2014	1,217,370	$11.61	$24,140	No formal educational credential	Less than 5 years	Moderate-term on-the-job training
Cooks, Short Order	35-2015	183,990	$10.52	$21,890	No formal educational credential	None	Short-term on-the-job training
Cooks, All Other	35-2019	15,490	$13.04	$27,120	No formal educational credential	None	Moderate-term on-the-job training
Food Preparation Workers	35-2021	850,670	$10.31	$21,440	No formal educational credential	None	Short-term on-the-job training
Bartenders	35-3011	603,320	$10.00	$20,800	No formal educational credential	None	Short-term on-the-job training
Combined Food Preparation and Serving Workers, Including fast food	35-3021	3,426,090	$9.35	$19,440	No formal educational credential	None	Short-term on-the-job training
Counter Attendants, Cafeteria, Food Concession, and coffee shop	35-3022	499,550	$9.60	$19,970	No formal educational credential	None	Short-term on-the-job training
Waiters and Waitresses	35-3031	2,564,610	$9.61	$19,990	No formal educational credential	None	Short-term on-the-job training
Food Servers, Nonrestaurant	35-3041	261,520	$10.21	$21,240	No formal educational credential	None	Short-term on-the-job training
Dining Room and Cafeteria Attendants and Bartender helpers	35-9011	423,080	$9.71	$20,200	No formal educational credential	None	Short-term on-the-job training
Dishwashers	35-9021	506,450	$10.00	$20,800	No formal educational credential	None	Short-term on-the-job training
Hosts and Hostesses, Restaurant, Lounge, and Coffee shop	35-9031	404,360	$9.60	$19,980	No formal educational credential	None	None
Food Preparation and Serving Related Workers, All other	35-9099	59,060	$10.14	$21,090	No formal educational credential	None	Short-term on-the-job training
Building and Grounds Cleaning and Maintenance Occupations	37-0000	4,426,090	$11.87	$24,700			
First-Line Supervisors of Housekeeping and Janitorial workers	37-1011	161,140	$18.36	$38,190	High school diploma or equivalent	Less than 5 years	None
First-Line Supervisors of Landscaping, Lawn Service, and groundskeeping workers	37-1012	103,070	$21.99	$45,740	High school diploma or equivalent	Less than 5 years	None
Janitors and Cleaners, Except Maids and Housekeeping cleaners	37-2011	2,161,740	$11.63	$24,190	No formal educational credential	None	Short-term on-the-job training
Maids and Housekeeping Cleaners	37-2012	924,640	$10.49	$21,820	No formal educational credential	None	Short-term on-the-job training
Building Cleaning Workers, All Other	37-2019	15,020	$14.28	$29,700	No formal educational credential	None	Short-term on-the-job training
Pest Control Workers	37-2021	72,830	$15.88	$33,040	High school diploma or equivalent	None	Moderate-term on-the-job training
Landscaping and Groundskeeping Workers	37-3011	906,570	$12.65	$26,320	No formal educational credential	None	Short-term on-the-job training
Pesticide Handlers, Sprayers, and Applicators, Vegetation	37-3012	25,230	$16.22	$33,740	High school diploma or equivalent	None	Moderate-term on-the-job training
Tree Trimmers and Pruners	37-3013	40,680	$16.84	$35,030	High school diploma or equivalent	None	Short-term on-the-job training
Grounds Maintenance Workers, All Other	37-3019	15,170	$13.69	$28,470	No formal educational credential	None	Short-term on-the-job training
Personal Care and Service Occupations	39-0000	4,514,960	$10.92	$22,710			
Gaming Supervisors	39-1011	22,130	$24.29	$50,520	High school diploma or equivalent	Less than 5 years	None
Slot Supervisors	39-1012	7,640	$17.35	$36,080	High school diploma or equivalent	Less than 5 years	None
First-Line Supervisors of Personal Service Workers	39-1021	190,420	$17.65	$36,700	High school diploma or equivalent	Less than 5 years	None
Animal Trainers	39-2011	13,590	$13.31	$27,690	High school diploma or equivalent	None	Moderate-term on-the-job training
Nonfarm Animal Caretakers	39-2021	187,360	$10.57	$21,990	High school diploma or equivalent	None	Short-term on-the-job training
Gaming Dealers	39-3011	94,570	$9.27	$19,290	High school diploma or equivalent	None	Short-term on-the-job training
Gaming and Sports Book Writers and Runners	39-3012	11,460	$10.87	$22,600	High school diploma or equivalent	None	Short-term on-the-job training
Gaming Service Workers, All Other	39-3019	12,140	$11.96	$24,880	High school diploma or equivalent	None	Short-term on-the-job training
Motion Picture Projectionists	39-3021	5,480	$10.62	$22,100	No formal educational credential	None	Short-term on-the-job training
Ushers, Lobby Attendants, and Ticket Takers	39-3031	117,920	$9.58	$19,920	No formal educational credential	None	Short-term on-the-job training
Amusement and Recreation Attendants	39-3091	286,740	$9.69	$20,160	No formal educational credential	None	Short-term on-the-job training
Costume Attendants	39-3092	6,640	$22.07	$45,900	High school diploma or equivalent	None	Short-term on-the-job training
Locker Room, Coatroom, and Dressing Room Attendants	39-3093	18,040	$10.44	$21,720	High school diploma or equivalent	None	Short-term on-the-job training
Entertainment Attendants and Related Workers, All other	39-3099	14,550	$11.19	$23,270	High school diploma or equivalent	None	Short-term on-the-job training
Embalmers	39-4011	3,710	$19.30	$40,150	Postsecondary nondegree award	None	Short-term on-the-job training

Table A-1. Number of Employees, Wages and Salaries, and Job Requirements for Detailed Occupations in the United States—*Continued*

Occupation	Occupation code	Total employees, May 2016	Median hourly wage, 2016	Median Annual Salary, 2016	Typical education needed for entry, 2014	Work experience in a related occupation, 2014	Typical on-the-job training needed to attain competency in the occupation, 2014
Funeral Attendants	39-4021	35,770	$11.94	$24,830	High school diploma or equivalent	None	Short-term on-the-job training
Morticians, Undertakers, and Funeral Directors	39-4031	25,850	$24.08	$50,090	Associate's degree	None	Long-term on-the-job training
Barbers	39-5011	15,900	$12.38	$25,760	Postsecondary nondegree award	None	None
Hairdressers, Hairstylists, and Cosmetologists	39-5012	352,380	$11.66	$24,260	Postsecondary nondegree award	None	None
Makeup Artists, Theatrical and Performance	39-5091	3,600	$29.31	$60,970	Postsecondary nondegree award	None	None
Manicurists and Pedicurists	39-5092	90,630	$10.65	$22,150	Postsecondary nondegree award	None	None
Shampooers	39-5093	15,240	$9.47	$19,700	No formal educational credential	None	Short-term on-the-job training
Skincare Specialists	39-5094	43,980	$14.55	$30,270	Postsecondary nondegree award	None	None
Baggage Porters and Bellhops	39-6011	44,750	$10.70	$22,260	High school diploma or equivalent	None	Short-term on-the-job training
Concierges	39-6012	32,020	$14.06	$29,250	High school diploma or equivalent	None	Moderate-term on-the-job training
Tour Guides and Escorts	39-7011	38,660	$11.98	$24,920	High school diploma or equivalent	None	Moderate-term on-the-job training
Travel Guides	39-7012	3,030	$15.44	$32,100	High school diploma or equivalent	None	Moderate-term on-the-job training
Childcare Workers	39-9011	569,370	$10.18	$21,170	High school diploma or equivalent	None	Short-term on-the-job training
Personal Care Aides	39-9021	1,492,250	$10.54	$21,920	No formal educational credential	None	Short-term on-the-job training
Fitness Trainers and Aerobics Instructors	39-9031	257,410	$18.34	$38,160	High school diploma or equivalent	None	Short-term on-the-job training
Recreation Workers	39-9032	336,880	$11.48	$23,870	High school diploma or equivalent	None	Short-term on-the-job training
Residential Advisors	39-9041	110,330	$12.29	$25,570	High school diploma or equivalent	None	Short-term on-the-job training
Personal Care and Service Workers, All Other	39-9099	54,520	$12.22	$25,420	High school diploma or equivalent	None	Short-term on-the-job training
Sales and Related Occupations	41-0000	14,536,530	$12.78	$26,590			
First-Line Supervisors of Retail Sales Workers	41-1011	1,194,220	$18.77	$39,040	High school diploma or equivalent	Less than 5 years	None
First-Line Supervisors of Non-Retail Sales Workers	41-1012	252,670	$35.17	$73,150	High school diploma or equivalent	Less than 5 years	None
Cashiers	41-2011	3,541,010	$9.70	$20,180	No formal educational credential	None	Short-term on-the-job training
Gaming Change Persons and Booth Cashiers	41-2012	23,120	$11.44	$23,780	High school diploma or equivalent	None	Short-term on-the-job training
Counter and Rental Clerks	41-2021	450,330	$12.29	$25,550	No formal educational credential	None	Short-term on-the-job training
Parts Salespersons	41-2022	248,740	$14.32	$29,780	No formal educational credential	None	Moderate-term on-the-job training
Retail Salespersons	41-2031	4,528,550	$10.90	$22,680	No formal educational credential	None	Short-term on-the-job training
Advertising Sales Agents	41-3011	141,100	$24.22	$50,380	High school diploma or equivalent	None	Moderate-term on-the-job training
Insurance Sales Agents	41-3021	385,700	$24.03	$49,990	High school diploma or equivalent	None	Moderate-term on-the-job training
Securities, Commodities, and Financial Services Sales Agents	41-3031	353,780	$32.36	$67,310	Bachelor's degree	None	Moderate-term on-the-job training
Travel Agents	41-3041	68,680	$17.53	$36,460	High school diploma or equivalent	None	Moderate-term on-the-job training
Sales Representatives, Services, All Other	41-3099	953,870	$25.23	$52,490	High school diploma or equivalent	None	Moderate-term on-the-job training
Sales Representatives, Wholesale and Manufacturing, Technical and Scientific products	41-4011	328,370	$37.97	$78,980	Bachelor's degree	None	Moderate-term on-the-job training
Sales Representatives, Wholesale and Manufacturing, except Technical and Scientific Products	41-4012	1,404,050	$27.47	$57,140	High school diploma or equivalent	None	Moderate-term on-the-job training
Demonstrators and Product Promoters	41-9011	86,500	$12.31	$25,610	High school diploma or equivalent	None	Short-term on-the-job training
Models	41-9012	4,390	$10.51	$21,870	No formal educational credential	None	None
Real Estate Brokers	41-9021	40,850	$27.30	$56,790	High school diploma or equivalent	Less than 5 years	None
Real Estate Sales Agents	41-9022	151,840	$21.20	$44,090	High school diploma or equivalent	None	Moderate-term on-the-job training
Sales Engineers	41-9031	74,330	$48.08	$100,000	Bachelor's degree	None	Moderate-term on-the-job training
Telemarketers	41-9041	215,290	$11.69	$24,300	No formal educational credential	None	Short-term on-the-job training

Table A-1. Number of Employees, Wages and Salaries, and Job Requirements for Detailed Occupations in the United States—*Continued*

Occupation	Occupation code	Total employees, May 2016	Median hourly wage, 2016	Median Annual Salary, 2016	Typical education needed for entry, 2014	Work experience in a related occupation, 2014	Typical on-the-job training needed to attain competency in the occupation, 2014
Door-to-Door Sales Workers, News and Street Vendors, and Related Workers	41-9091	8,040	$11.70	$24,330	No formal educational credential	None	Short-term on-the-job training
Sales and Related Workers, All Other	41-9099	81,080	$17.88	$37,190	High school diploma or equivalent	None	None
Office and Administrative Support Occupations	43-0000	22,026,080	$16.37	$34,050			
First-Line Supervisors of Office and Administrative Support Workers	43-1011	1,443,150	$26.12	$54,340	High school diploma or equivalent	Less than 5 years	None
Switchboard Operators, Including Answering Service	43-2011	90,910	$13.47	$28,030	High school diploma or equivalent	None	Short-term on-the-job training
Telephone Operators	43-2021	8,860	$17.79	$37,000	High school diploma or equivalent	None	Short-term on-the-job training
Communications Equipment Operators, All Other	43-2099	2,150	$19.06	$39,640	High school diploma or equivalent	None	Short-term on-the-job training
Bill and Account Collectors	43-3011	298,960	$17.00	$35,350	High school diploma or equivalent	None	Moderate-term on-the-job training
Billing and Posting Clerks	43-3021	485,220	$17.38	$36,150	High school diploma or equivalent	None	Moderate-term on-the-job training
Bookkeeping, Accounting, and Auditing Clerks	43-3031	1,566,960	$18.46	$38,390	Some college, no degree	None	Moderate-term on-the-job training
Gaming Cage Workers	43-3041	18,810	$12.49	$25,990	High school diploma or equivalent	None	Short-term on-the-job training
Payroll and Timekeeping Clerks	43-3051	159,650	$20.38	$42,390	High school diploma or equivalent	None	Moderate-term on-the-job training
Procurement Clerks	43-3061	72,120	$19.91	$41,410	High school diploma or equivalent	None	Moderate-term on-the-job training
Tellers	43-3071	496,760	$13.11	$27,260	High school diploma or equivalent	None	Short-term on-the-job training
Financial Clerks, All Other	43-3099	34,540	$19.01	$39,540	High school diploma or equivalent	None	Short-term on-the-job training
Brokerage Clerks	43-4011	59,820	$23.65	$49,200	High school diploma or equivalent	None	Moderate-term on-the-job training
Correspondence Clerks	43-4021	6,780	$17.49	$36,370	High school diploma or equivalent	None	Short-term on-the-job training
Court, Municipal, and License Clerks	43-4031	128,620	$17.63	$36,670	High school diploma or equivalent	None	Moderate-term on-the-job training
Credit Authorizers, Checkers, and Clerks	43-4041	37,680	$17.75	$36,930	High school diploma or equivalent	None	Moderate-term on-the-job training
Customer Service Representatives	43-4051	2,707,040	$15.53	$32,300	High school diploma or equivalent	None	Short-term on-the-job training
Eligibility Interviewers, Government Programs	43-4061	135,940	$20.84	$43,350	High school diploma or equivalent	None	Moderate-term on-the-job training
File Clerks	43-4071	130,950	$13.99	$29,090	High school diploma or equivalent	None	Short-term on-the-job training
Hotel, Motel, and Resort Desk Clerks	43-4081	248,440	$10.61	$22,070	High school diploma or equivalent	None	Short-term on-the-job training
Interviewers, Except Eligibility and Loan	43-4111	186,030	$15.46	$32,150	High school diploma or equivalent	None	Short-term on-the-job training
Library Assistants, Clerical	43-4121	98,560	$12.12	$25,220	High school diploma or equivalent	None	Short-term on-the-job training
Loan Interviewers and Clerks	43-4131	224,340	$18.57	$38,630	High school diploma or equivalent	None	Short-term on-the-job training
New Accounts Clerks	43-4141	41,630	$16.82	$34,990	High school diploma or equivalent	None	Moderate-term on-the-job training
Order Clerks	43-4151	176,850	$16.04	$33,370	High school diploma or equivalent	None	Short-term on-the-job training
Human Resources Assistants, Except Payroll and Timekeeping	43-4161	137,150	$18.76	$39,020	Associate's degree	None	None
Receptionists and Information Clerks	43-4171	997,770	$13.42	$27,920	High school diploma or equivalent	None	Short-term on-the-job training
Reservation and Transportation Ticket Agents and Travel Clerks	43-4181	146,350	$16.94	$35,230	High school diploma or equivalent	None	Short-term on-the-job training
Information and Record Clerks, All Other	43-4199	166,850	$18.87	$39,260	High school diploma or equivalent	None	Short-term on-the-job training
Cargo and Freight Agents	43-5011	88,920	$20.15	$41,920	High school diploma or equivalent	None	Short-term on-the-job training
Couriers and Messengers	43-5021	74,120	$13.54	$28,170	High school diploma or equivalent	None	Short-term on-the-job training
Police, Fire, and Ambulance Dispatchers	43-5031	95,170	$18.69	$38,870	High school diploma or equivalent	None	Moderate-term on-the-job training
Dispatchers, Except Police, Fire, and Ambulance	43-5032	197,910	$18.24	$37,940	High school diploma or equivalent	None	Moderate-term on-the-job training
Meter Readers, Utilities	43-5041	34,070	$18.72	$38,940	High school diploma or equivalent	None	Short-term on-the-job training
Postal Service Clerks	43-5051	82,030	$27.30	$56,790	High school diploma or equivalent	None	Short-term on-the-job training
Postal Service Mail Carriers	43-5052	328,950	$27.94	$58,110	High school diploma or equivalent	None	Short-term on-the-job training
Postal Service Mail Sorters, Processors, and Processing Machine Operators	43-5053	110,770	$27.03	$56,220	High school diploma or equivalent	None	Short-term on-the-job training

Table A-1. Number of Employees, Wages and Salaries, and Job Requirements for Detailed Occupations in the United States—*Continued*

Occupation	Occupation code	Total employees, May 2016	Median hourly wage, 2016	Median Annual Salary, 2016	Typical education needed for entry, 2014	Work experience in a related occupation, 2014	Typical on-the-job training needed to attain competency in the occupation, 2014
Production, Planning, and Expediting Clerks	43-5061	321,780	$22.48	$46,760	High school diploma or equivalent	None	Moderate-term on-the-job training
Shipping, Receiving, and Traffic Clerks	43-5071	676,990	$14.99	$31,180	High school diploma or equivalent	None	Short-term on-the-job training
Stock Clerks and Order Fillers	43-5081	2,016,340	$11.46	$23,840	No formal educational credential	None	Short-term on-the-job training
Weighers, Measurers, Checkers, and Samplers, Recordkeeping	43-5111	74,460	$13.84	$28,790	High school diploma or equivalent	None	Short-term on-the-job training
Executive Secretaries and Executive Administrative Assistants	43-6011	631,610	$26.86	$55,860	High school diploma or equivalent	Less than 5 years	None
Legal Secretaries	43-6012	191,200	$21.24	$44,180	High school diploma or equivalent	None	Moderate-term on-the-job training
Medical Secretaries	43-6013	556,820	$16.22	$33,730	High school diploma or equivalent	None	Moderate-term on-the-job training
Secretaries and Administrative Assistants, Except Legal, Medical, and Executive	43-6014	2,295,510	$16.74	$34,820	High school diploma or equivalent	None	Short-term on-the-job training
Computer Operators	43-9011	46,810	$20.32	$42,270	High school diploma or equivalent	None	Moderate-term on-the-job training
Data Entry Keyers	43-9021	194,810	$14.47	$30,100	High school diploma or equivalent	None	Moderate-term on-the-job training
Word Processors and Typists	43-9022	67,230	$18.63	$38,740	High school diploma or equivalent	None	Short-term on-the-job training
Desktop Publishers	43-9031	13,090	$19.76	$41,090	Associate's degree	None	Short-term on-the-job training
Insurance Claims and Policy Processing Clerks	43-9041	274,350	$18.48	$38,430	High school diploma or equivalent	None	Moderate-term on-the-job training
Mail Clerks and Mail Machine Operators, Except Postal Service	43-9051	91,530	$14.02	$29,160	High school diploma or equivalent	None	Short-term on-the-job training
Office Clerks, General	43-9061	2,955,550	$14.70	$30,580	High school diploma or equivalent	None	Short-term on-the-job training
Office Machine Operators, Except Computer	43-9071	58,160	$14.64	$30,460	High school diploma or equivalent	None	Short-term on-the-job training
Proofreaders and Copy Markers	43-9081	11,430	$17.77	$36,960	Bachelor's degree	None	None
Statistical Assistants	43-9111	10,900	$22.53	$46,850	Bachelor's degree	None	None
Office and Administrative Support Workers, All Other	43-9199	216,650	$16.36	$34,020	High school diploma or equivalent	None	Short-term on-the-job training
Farming, Fishing, and Forestry Occupations	45-0000	463,640	$11.30	$23,510			
First-Line Supervisors of Farming, Fishing, and Forestry Workers	45-1011	19,550	$21.79	$45,320	High school diploma or equivalent	Less than 5 years	None
Agricultural Inspectors	45-2011	14,710	$20.58	$42,800	Bachelor's degree	None	Moderate-term on-the-job training
Animal Breeders	45-2021	1,270	$17.16	$35,690	High school diploma or equivalent	None	Short-term on-the-job training
Graders and Sorters, Agricultural Products	45-2041	38,780	$10.83	$22,520	No formal educational credential	None	Short-term on-the-job training
Agricultural Equipment Operators	45-2091	28,700	$13.87	$28,850	No formal educational credential	None	Short-term on-the-job training
Farmworkers and Laborers, Crop, Nursery, and Greenhouse	45-2092	273,450	$10.58	$22,000	No formal educational credential	None	Short-term on-the-job training
Farmworkers, Farm, Ranch, and Aquacultural Animals	45-2093	35,670	$11.79	$24,520	No formal educational credential	None	Short-term on-the-job training
Agricultural Workers, All Other	45-2099	5,040	$14.98	$31,160	No formal educational credential	None	Short-term on-the-job training
Fishers and Related Fishing Workers	45-3011	520	$13.04	$27,110	No formal educational credential	None	Moderate-term on-the-job training
Forest and Conservation Workers	45-4011	7,170	$12.95	$26,940	High school diploma or equivalent	None	Moderate-term on-the-job training
Fallers	45-4021	5,370	$17.96	$37,370	High school diploma or equivalent	None	Moderate-term on-the-job training
Logging Equipment Operators	45-4022	27,250	$18.03	$37,490	High school diploma or equivalent	None	Moderate-term on-the-job training
Log Graders and Scalers	45-4023	3,020	$17.83	$37,090	High school diploma or equivalent	None	Moderate-term on-the-job training
Logging Workers, All Other	45-4029	3,010	$18.73	$38,950	High school diploma or equivalent	None	Moderate-term on-the-job training
Construction and Extraction Occupations	47-0000	5,585,420	$20.96	$43,610			
First-Line Supervisors of Construction Trades and Extraction Workers	47-1011	538,220	$30.28	$62,980	High school diploma or equivalent	5 years or more	None
Boilermakers	47-2011	16,660	$29.84	$62,060	High school diploma or equivalent	None	Apprenticeship
Brickmasons and Blockmasons	47-2021	64,370	$23.68	$49,250	High school diploma or equivalent	None	Apprenticeship
Stonemasons	47-2022	13,190	$19.13	$39,780	High school diploma or equivalent	None	Apprenticeship
Carpenters	47-2031	676,980	$20.96	$43,600	High school diploma or equivalent	None	Apprenticeship
Carpet Installers	47-2041	25,660	$18.40	$38,280	No formal educational credential	None	Short-term on-the-job training
Floor Layers, Except Carpet, Wood, and Hard Tiles	47-2042	10,340	$18.19	$37,840	No formal educational credential	None	Moderate-term on-the-job training

Table A-1. Number of Employees, Wages and Salaries, and Job Requirements for Detailed Occupations in the United States—*Continued*

Occupation	Occupation code	Total employees, May 2016	Median hourly wage, 2016	Median Annual Salary, 2016	Typical education needed for entry, 2014	Work experience in a related occupation, 2014	Typical on-the-job training needed to attain competency in the occupation, 2014
Floor Sanders and Finishers	47-2043	4,590	$17.72	$36,860	No formal educational credential	None	Moderate-term on-the-job training
Tile and Marble Setters	47-2044	36,830	$19.45	$40,460	No formal educational credential	None	Long-term on-the-job training
Cement Masons and Concrete Finishers	47-2051	173,920	$18.84	$39,180	No formal educational credential	None	Moderate-term on-the-job training
Terrazzo Workers and Finishers	47-2053	3,420	$19.68	$40,930	High school diploma or equivalent	None	Apprenticeship
Construction Laborers	47-2061	912,100	$16.07	$33,430	No formal educational credential	None	Short-term on-the-job training
Paving, Surfacing, and Tamping Equipment Operators	47-2071	51,880	$18.74	$38,970	High school diploma or equivalent	None	Moderate-term on-the-job training
Pile-Driver Operators	47-2072	3,570	$26.48	$55,070	High school diploma or equivalent	None	Moderate-term on-the-job training
Operating Engineers and Other Construction Equipment Operators	47-2073	356,750	$22.06	$45,890	High school diploma or equivalent	None	Moderate-term on-the-job training
Drywall and Ceiling Tile Installers	47-2081	93,180	$19.75	$41,090	No formal educational credential	None	Moderate-term on-the-job training
Tapers	47-2082	18,480	$23.56	$48,990	No formal educational credential	None	Moderate-term on-the-job training
Electricians	47-2111	607,120	$25.35	$52,720	High school diploma or equivalent	None	Apprenticeship
Glaziers	47-2121	47,140	$20.16	$41,920	High school diploma or equivalent	None	Apprenticeship
Insulation Workers, Floor, Ceiling, and Wall	47-2131	29,500	$17.15	$35,660	No formal educational credential	None	Short-term on-the-job training
Insulation Workers, Mechanical	47-2132	27,270	$21.84	$45,430	High school diploma or equivalent	None	Apprenticeship
Painters, Construction and Maintenance	47-2141	217,280	$18.06	$37,570	No formal educational credential	None	Moderate-term on-the-job training
Paperhangers	47-2142	3,190	$16.23	$33,770	No formal educational credential	None	Long-term on-the-job training
Pipelayers	47-2151	39,620	$18.47	$38,410	No formal educational credential	None	Short-term on-the-job training
Plumbers, Pipefitters, and Steamfitters	47-2152	411,870	$24.74	$51,450	High school diploma or equivalent	None	Apprenticeship
Plasterers and Stucco Masons	47-2161	22,810	$18.70	$38,890	No formal educational credential	None	Long-term on-the-job training
Reinforcing Iron and Rebar Workers	47-2171	20,020	$22.89	$47,600	High school diploma or equivalent	None	Apprenticeship
Roofers	47-2181	116,410	$18.15	$37,760	No formal educational credential	None	Moderate-term on-the-job training
Sheet Metal Workers	47-2211	134,450	$22.57	$46,940	High school diploma or equivalent	None	Apprenticeship
Structural Iron and Steel Workers	47-2221	69,440	$24.91	$51,800	High school diploma or equivalent	None	Apprenticeship
Solar Photovoltaic Installers	47-2231	8,870	$18.87	$39,240	High school diploma or equivalent	None	Moderate-term on-the-job training
Helpers—Brickmasons, Blockmasons, Stonemasons, and Tile and Marble Setters	47-3011	23,950	$14.70	$30,570	No formal educational credential	None	Short-term on-the-job training
Helpers—Carpenters	47-3012	35,890	$13.85	$28,810	No formal educational credential	None	Short-term on-the-job training
Helpers—Electricians	47-3013	71,890	$14.20	$29,530	High school diploma or equivalent	None	Short-term on-the-job training
Helpers—Painters, Paperhangers, Plasterers, and Stucco Masons	47-3014	10,780	$13.13	$27,310	No formal educational credential	None	Short-term on-the-job training
Helpers—Pipelayers, Plumbers, Pipefitters, and Steamfitters	47-3015	54,080	$13.96	$29,030	High school diploma or equivalent	None	Short-term on-the-job training
Helpers—Roofers	47-3016	10,190	$13.30	$27,670	No formal educational credential	None	Short-term on-the-job training
Helpers, Construction Trades, All Other	47-3019	21,820	$14.07	$29,270	No formal educational credential	None	Short-term on-the-job training
Construction and Building Inspectors	47-4011	94,960	$28.12	$58,480	High school diploma or equivalent	5 years or more	Moderate-term on-the-job training
Elevator Installers and Repairers	47-4021	22,240	$37.93	$78,890	High school diploma or equivalent	None	Apprenticeship
Fence Erectors	47-4031	21,500	$15.94	$33,150	No formal educational credential	None	Moderate-term on-the-job training
Hazardous Materials Removal Workers	47-4041	44,280	$19.54	$40,640	High school diploma or equivalent	None	Moderate-term on-the-job training
Highway Maintenance Workers	47-4051	143,320	$18.33	$38,130	High school diploma or equivalent	None	Moderate-term on-the-job training
Rail-Track Laying and Maintenance Equipment Operators	47-4061	14,250	$25.95	$53,970	High school diploma or equivalent	None	Moderate-term on-the-job training
Septic Tank Servicers and Sewer Pipe Cleaners	47-4071	26,320	$17.51	$36,430	No formal educational credential	None	Moderate-term on-the-job training
Segmental Pavers	47-4091	1,720	$16.12	$33,530	High school diploma or equivalent	None	Moderate-term on-the-job training
Construction and Related Workers, All Other	47-4099	35,340	$17.73	$36,890	High school diploma or equivalent	None	Moderate-term on-the-job training

Table A-1. Number of Employees, Wages and Salaries, and Job Requirements for Detailed Occupations in the United States—*Continued*

Occupation	Occupation code	Total employees, May 2016	Median hourly wage, 2016	Median Annual Salary, 2016	Typical education needed for entry, 2014	Work experience in a related occupation, 2014	Typical on-the-job training needed to attain competency in the occupation, 2014
Derrick Operators, Oil and Gas	47-5011	11,580	$23.14	$48,130	No formal educational credential	None	Short-term on-the-job training
Rotary Drill Operators, Oil and Gas	47-5012	17,400	$26.17	$54,430	No formal educational credential	None	Moderate-term on-the-job training
Service Unit Operators, Oil, Gas, and Mining	47-5013	42,890	$23.37	$48,610	No formal educational credential	None	Moderate-term on-the-job training
Earth Drillers, Except Oil and Gas	47-5021	18,500	$21.33	$44,360	High school diploma or equivalent	None	Moderate-term on-the-job training
Explosives Workers, Ordnance Handling Experts, and Blasters	47-5031	6,310	$25.08	$52,170	High school diploma or equivalent	Less than 5 years	Long-term on-the-job training
Continuous Mining Machine Operators	47-5041	12,030	$24.92	$51,840	No formal educational credential	None	Moderate-term on-the-job training
Mine Cutting and Channeling Machine Operators	47-5042	5,930	$24.95	$51,900	High school diploma or equivalent	None	Moderate-term on-the-job training
Mining Machine Operators, All Other	47-5049	2,160	$23.08	$48,010	High school diploma or equivalent	None	Moderate-term on-the-job training
Rock Splitters, Quarry	47-5051	3,770	$16.36	$34,020	No formal educational credential	None	Short-term on-the-job training
Roof Bolters, Mining	47-5061	3,930	$27.30	$56,780	High school diploma or equivalent	None	Moderate-term on-the-job training
Roustabouts, Oil and Gas	47-5071	51,290	$17.95	$37,340	No formal educational credential	None	Moderate-term on-the-job training
Helpers—Extraction Workers	47-5081	17,660	$17.21	$35,790	High school diploma or equivalent	None	Moderate-term on-the-job training
Extraction Workers, All Other	47-5099	4,320	$23.44	$48,750	High school diploma or equivalent	None	Moderate-term on-the-job training
Installation, Maintenance, and Repair Occupations	49-0000	5,456,640	$20.89	$43,440			
First-Line Supervisors of Mechanics, Installers, and Repairers	49-1011	453,330	$30.55	$63,540	High school diploma or equivalent	Less than 5 years	None
Computer, Automated Teller, and Office Machine Repairers	49-2011	102,170	$17.84	$37,100	Some college, no degree	None	Short-term on-the-job training
Radio, Cellular, and Tower Equipment Installers and Repairers	49-2021	14,120	$25.23	$52,480	Associate's degree	None	Moderate-term on-the-job training
Telecommunications Equipment Installers and Repairers, except Line Installers	49-2022	228,430	$25.79	$53,640	Postsecondary nondegree award	None	Moderate-term on-the-job training
Avionics Technicians	49-2091	17,330	$29.21	$60,760	Associate's degree	None	None
Electric Motor, Power Tool, and Related Repairers	49-2092	17,050	$19.99	$41,570	Postsecondary nondegree award	None	Long-term on-the-job training
Electrical and Electronics Installers and Repairer, Transportation Equipment	49-2093	13,960	$28.50	$59,280	Postsecondary nondegree award	None	Long-term on-the-job training
Electrical and Electronics Repairers, Commercial and Industrial Equipment	49-2094	67,390	$27.04	$56,250	Postsecondary nondegree award	None	Long-term on-the-job training
Electrical and Electronics Repairers, Powerhouse, Substation, and Relay	49-2095	23,060	$36.38	$75,670	Postsecondary nondegree award	None	Long-term on-the-job training
Electronic Equipment Installers and Repairers, Motor Vehicles	49-2096	11,750	$15.49	$32,220	Postsecondary nondegree award	None	Short-term on-the-job training
Electronic Home Entertainment Equipment Installers and Repairers	49-2097	25,550	$17.99	$37,410	Postsecondary nondegree award	None	Short-term on-the-job training
Security and Fire Alarm Systems Installers	49-2098	67,700	$21.31	$44,330	High school diploma or equivalent	None	Moderate-term on-the-job training
Aircraft Mechanics and Service Technicians	49-3011	128,570	$28.93	$60,170	Postsecondary nondegree award	None	None
Automotive Body and Related Repairers	49-3021	143,940	$19.97	$41,540	High school diploma or equivalent	None	Long-term on-the-job training
Automotive Glass Installers and Repairers	49-3022	18,610	$16.51	$34,340	High school diploma or equivalent	None	Moderate-term on-the-job training
Automotive Service Technicians and Mechanics	49-3023	647,380	$18.50	$38,470	Postsecondary nondegree award	None	Short-term on-the-job training
Bus and Truck Mechanics and Diesel Engine Specialists	49-3031	254,280	$21.72	$45,170	High school diploma or equivalent	None	Long-term on-the-job training
Farm Equipment Mechanics and Service Technicians	49-3041	35,110	$18.18	$37,820	High school diploma or equivalent	None	Long-term on-the-job training
Mobile Heavy Equipment Mechanics, Except Engines	49-3042	123,570	$23.73	$49,370	High school diploma or equivalent	None	Long-term on-the-job training
Rail Car Repairers	49-3043	22,090	$26.44	$55,000	High school diploma or equivalent	None	Long-term on-the-job training
Motorboat Mechanics and Service Technicians	49-3051	20,260	$18.65	$38,780	High school diploma or equivalent	None	Long-term on-the-job training
Motorcycle Mechanics	49-3052	16,000	$16.69	$34,720	Postsecondary nondegree award	None	Short-term on-the-job training
Outdoor Power Equipment and Other Small Engine Mechanics	49-3053	33,020	$16.22	$33,730	High school diploma or equivalent	None	Moderate-term on-the-job training
Bicycle Repairers	49-3091	12,560	$13.28	$27,630	High school diploma or equivalent	None	Moderate-term on-the-job training
Recreational Vehicle Service Technicians	49-3092	13,520	$17.51	$36,430	High school diploma or equivalent	None	Long-term on-the-job training
Tire Repairers and Changers	49-3093	109,350	$12.04	$25,040	High school diploma or equivalent	None	Short-term on-the-job training
Mechanical Door Repairers	49-9011	19,840	$18.50	$38,480	High school diploma or equivalent	None	Moderate-term on-the-job training

Table A-1. Number of Employees, Wages and Salaries, and Job Requirements for Detailed Occupations in the United States—*Continued*

Occupation	Occupation code	Total employees, May 2016	Median hourly wage, 2016	Median Annual Salary, 2016	Typical education needed for entry, 2014	Work experience in a related occupation, 2014	Typical on-the-job training needed to attain competency in the occupation, 2014
Control and Valve Installers and Repairers, Except Mechanical Door	49-9012	45,740	$26.21	$54,520	High school diploma or equivalent	None	Moderate-term on-the-job training
Heating, Air Conditioning, and Refrigeration Mechanics and Installers	49-9021	294,730	$22.07	$45,910	Postsecondary nondegree award	None	Long-term on-the-job training
Home Appliance Repairers	49-9031	33,480	$18.06	$37,570	High school diploma or equivalent	None	Moderate-term on-the-job training
Industrial Machinery Mechanics	49-9041	334,490	$24.06	$50,040	High school diploma or equivalent	None	Long-term on-the-job training
Maintenance Workers, Machinery	49-9043	89,630	$21.42	$44,550	High school diploma or equivalent	None	Moderate-term on-the-job training
Millwrights	49-9044	39,670	$25.21	$52,440	High school diploma or equivalent	None	Apprenticeship
Refractory Materials Repairers, Except Brickmasons	49-9045	1,540	$21.74	$45,230	High school diploma or equivalent	None	Moderate-term on-the-job training
Electrical Power-Line Installers and Repairers	49-9051	117,670	$32.70	$68,010	High school diploma or equivalent	None	Long-term on-the-job training
Telecommunications Line Installers and Repairers	49-9052	100,080	$25.28	$52,590	High school diploma or equivalent	None	Long-term on-the-job training
Camera and Photographic Equipment Repairers	49-9061	3,760	$19.74	$41,060	Associate's degree	None	Long-term on-the-job training
Medical Equipment Repairers	49-9062	43,370	$23.11	$48,070	Associate's degree	None	Moderate-term on-the-job training
Musical Instrument Repairers and Tuners	49-9063	7,980	$16.83	$35,010	High school diploma or equivalent	None	Apprenticeship
Watch Repairers	49-9064	1,620	$17.66	$36,740	High school diploma or equivalent	None	Long-term on-the-job training
Precision Instrument and Equipment Repairers, All Other	49-9069	11,640	$27.03	$56,230	High school diploma or equivalent	None	Long-term on-the-job training
Maintenance and Repair Workers, General	49-9071	1,332,480	$17.76	$36,940	High school diploma or equivalent	None	Long-term on-the-job training
Wind Turbine Service Technicians	49-9081	4,580	$25.13	$52,260	Some college, no degree	None	Long-term on-the-job training
Coin, Vending, and Amusement Machine Servicers and Repairers	49-9091	33,600	$15.90	$33,070	High school diploma or equivalent	None	Short-term on-the-job training
Commercial Divers	49-9092	3,370	$23.60	$49,090	Postsecondary nondegree award	None	Moderate-term on-the-job training
Fabric Menders, Except Garment	49-9093	550	$12.94	$26,920	No formal educational credential	None	Long-term on-the-job training
Locksmiths and Safe Repairers	49-9094	18,640	$19.43	$40,420	High school diploma or equivalent	None	Long-term on-the-job training
Manufactured Building and Mobile Home Installers	49-9095	3,200	$14.33	$29,810	High school diploma or equivalent	None	Short-term on-the-job training
Riggers	49-9096	21,020	$21.97	$45,690	High school diploma or equivalent	None	Short-term on-the-job training
Signal and Track Switch Repairers	49-9097	8,680	$31.42	$65,350	High school diploma or equivalent	None	Moderate-term on-the-job training
Helpers—Installation, Maintenance, and Repair Workers	49-9098	118,720	$13.23	$27,510	High school diploma or equivalent	None	Short-term on-the-job training
Installation, Maintenance, and Repair Workers, All Other	49-9099	146,460	$18.50	$38,480	High school diploma or equivalent	None	Moderate-term on-the-job training
Production Occupations	51-0000	9,105,650	$15.93	$33,130			
First-Line Supervisors of Production and Operating Workers	51-1011	610,480	$27.78	$57,780	High school diploma or equivalent	Less than 5 years	None
Aircraft Structure, Surfaces, Rigging, and Systems Assemblers	51-2011	42,010	$24.06	$50,050	High school diploma or equivalent	None	Moderate-term on-the-job training
Coil Winders, Tapers, and Finishers	51-2021	14,090	$16.32	$33,940	High school diploma or equivalent	None	Moderate-term on-the-job training
Electrical and Electronic Equipment Assemblers	51-2022	218,530	$15.06	$31,310	High school diploma or equivalent	None	Moderate-term on-the-job training
Electromechanical Equipment Assemblers	51-2023	45,540	$16.03	$33,350	High school diploma or equivalent	None	Moderate-term on-the-job training
Engine and Other Machine Assemblers	51-2031	38,150	$19.81	$41,210	High school diploma or equivalent	None	Moderate-term on-the-job training
Structural Metal Fabricators and Fitters	51-2041	77,270	$18.14	$37,730	High school diploma or equivalent	None	Moderate-term on-the-job training
Fiberglass Laminators and Fabricators	51-2091	19,400	$14.84	$30,870	High school diploma or equivalent	None	Moderate-term on-the-job training
Team Assemblers	51-2092	1,112,780	$14.45	$30,060	High school diploma or equivalent	None	Moderate-term on-the-job training
Timing Device Assemblers and Adjusters	51-2093	790	$17.81	$37,040	High school diploma or equivalent	None	Moderate-term on-the-job training
Assemblers and Fabricators, All Other	51-2099	230,310	$13.73	$28,550	High school diploma or equivalent	None	Moderate-term on-the-job training
Bakers	51-3011	180,450	$12.06	$25,090	No formal educational credential	None	Long-term on-the-job training
Butchers and Meat Cutters	51-3021	133,880	$14.36	$29,870	No formal educational credential	None	Long-term on-the-job training
Meat, Poultry, and Fish Cutters and Trimmers	51-3022	149,800	$11.77	$24,490	No formal educational credential	None	Short-term on-the-job training

Table A-1. Number of Employees, Wages and Salaries, and Job Requirements for Detailed Occupations in the United States—*Continued*

Occupation	Occupation code	Total employees, May 2016	Median hourly wage, 2016	Median Annual Salary, 2016	Typical education needed for entry, 2014	Work experience in a related occupation, 2014	Typical on-the-job training needed to attain competency in the occupation, 2014
Slaughterers and Meat Packers	51-3023	80,780	$12.78	$26,590	No formal educational credential	None	Short-term on-the-job training
Food and Tobacco Roasting, Baking, and Drying Machine Operators and Tenders	51-3091	20,080	$13.73	$28,570	No formal educational credential	None	Moderate-term on-the-job training
Food Batchmakers	51-3092	148,540	$13.37	$27,810	High school diploma or equivalent	None	Moderate-term on-the-job training
Food Cooking Machine Operators and Tenders	51-3093	36,520	$13.63	$28,350	High school diploma or equivalent	None	Moderate-term on-the-job training
Food Processing Workers, All Other	51-3099	43,070	$11.61	$24,160	No formal educational credential	None	Moderate-term on-the-job training
Computer-Controlled Machine Tool Operators, Metal and Plastic	51-4011	146,190	$18.21	$37,880	High school diploma or equivalent	None	Moderate-term on-the-job training
Computer Numerically Controlled Machine Tool Programmers, Metal and Plastic	51-4012	25,180	$24.32	$50,580	High school diploma or equivalent	None	Long-term on-the-job training
Extruding and Drawing Machine Setters, Operators, and Tenders, Metal and Plastic	51-4021	71,960	$16.29	$33,870	High school diploma or equivalent	None	Moderate-term on-the-job training
Forging Machine Setters, Operators, and Tenders, Metal and Plastic	51-4022	19,160	$17.76	$36,930	High school diploma or equivalent	None	Moderate-term on-the-job training
Rolling Machine Setters, Operators, and Tenders, Metal and Plastic	51-4023	29,060	$19.56	$40,680	High school diploma or equivalent	None	Moderate-term on-the-job training
Cutting, Punching, and Press Machine Setters, Operators, and Tenders, Metal and Plastic	51-4031	192,800	$15.56	$32,370	High school diploma or equivalent	None	Moderate-term on-the-job training
Drilling and Boring Machine Tool Setters, Operators and Tenders, Metal and Plastic	51-4032	12,290	$17.50	$36,410	High school diploma or equivalent	None	Moderate-term on-the-job training
Grinding, Lapping, Polishing, and Buffing Machine Tool Setters, Operators, and Tenders, Metal and Plastic	51-4033	74,600	$15.81	$32,890	High school diploma or equivalent	None	Moderate-term on-the-job training
Lathe and Turning Machine Tool Setters, Operators, and Tenders, Metal and Plastic	51-4034	33,850	$18.50	$38,480	High school diploma or equivalent	None	Moderate-term on-the-job training
Milling and Planing Machine Setters, Operators, and Tenders, Metal and Plastic	51-4035	17,560	$19.15	$39,840	High school diploma or equivalent	None	Moderate-term on-the-job training
Machinists	51-4041	391,120	$20.05	$41,700	High school diploma or equivalent	None	Long-term on-the-job training
Metal-Refining Furnace Operators and Tenders	51-4051	17,730	$19.73	$41,040	High school diploma or equivalent	None	Moderate-term on-the-job training
Pourers and Casters, Metal	51-4052	8,560	$17.39	$36,180	High school diploma or equivalent	None	Moderate-term on-the-job training
Model Makers, Metal and Plastic	51-4061	6,250	$23.34	$48,550	High school diploma or equivalent	None	Moderate-term on-the-job training
Patternmakers, Metal and Plastic	51-4062	3,420	$21.25	$44,210	High school diploma or equivalent	None	Moderate-term on-the-job training
Foundry Mold and Coremakers	51-4071	12,810	$16.73	$34,790	High school diploma or equivalent	None	Moderate-term on-the-job training
Molding, Coremaking, and Casting Machine Setters, Operators, and Tenders, Metal and Plastic	51-4072	145,560	$14.65	$30,480	High school diploma or equivalent	None	Moderate-term on-the-job training
Multiple Machine Tool Setters, Operators, and Tenders, Metal and Plastic	51-4081	117,300	$16.51	$34,340	High school diploma or equivalent	None	Moderate-term on-the-job training
Tool and Die Makers	51-4111	72,210	$24.55	$51,060	High school diploma or equivalent	None	Long-term on-the-job training
Welders, Cutters, Solderers, and Brazers	51-4121	382,730	$18.94	$39,390	High school diploma or equivalent	None	Moderate-term on-the-job training
Welding, Soldering, and Brazing Machine Setters, Operators, and Tenders	51-4122	46,920	$17.78	$36,980	High school diploma or equivalent	None	Moderate-term on-the-job training
Heat Treating Equipment Setters, Operators, and Tenders, Metal and Plastic	51-4191	19,780	$17.88	$37,180	High school diploma or equivalent	None	Moderate-term on-the-job training
Layout Workers, Metal and Plastic	51-4192	9,070	$22.03	$45,820	High school diploma or equivalent	None	Moderate-term on-the-job training
Plating and Coating Machine Setters, Operators, and Tenders, Metal and Plastic	51-4193	35,570	$15.04	$31,280	High school diploma or equivalent	None	Moderate-term on-the-job training
Tool Grinders, Filers, and Sharpeners	51-4194	9,550	$17.62	$36,650	High school diploma or equivalent	None	Moderate-term on-the-job training
Metal Workers and Plastic Workers, All Other	51-4199	22,930	$16.00	$33,280	High school diploma or equivalent	None	Moderate-term on-the-job training
Prepress Technicians and Workers	51-5111	33,340	$18.72	$38,930	Postsecondary nondegree award	None	None
Printing Press Operators	51-5112	169,910	$17.08	$35,530	High school diploma or equivalent	None	Moderate-term on-the-job training
Print Binding and Finishing Workers	51-5113	52,730	$15.10	$31,410	High school diploma or equivalent	None	Short-term on-the-job training
Laundry and Dry-Cleaning Workers	51-6011	207,710	$10.34	$21,510	No formal educational credential	None	Short-term on-the-job training
Pressers, Textile, Garment, and Related Materials	51-6021	45,150	$10.24	$21,300	No formal educational credential	None	Short-term on-the-job training
Sewing Machine Operators	51-6031	139,500	$11.38	$23,670	No formal educational credential	None	Short-term on-the-job training
Shoe and Leather Workers and Repairers	51-6041	7,780	$11.51	$23,940	High school diploma or equivalent	None	Moderate-term on-the-job training
Shoe Machine Operators and Tenders	51-6042	3,500	$12.57	$26,150	High school diploma or equivalent	None	Short-term on-the-job training

Table A-1. Number of Employees, Wages and Salaries, and Job Requirements for Detailed Occupations in the United States—*Continued*

Occupation	Occupation code	Total employees, May 2016	Median hourly wage, 2016	Median Annual Salary, 2016	Typical education needed for entry, 2014	Work experience in a related occupation, 2014	Typical on-the-job training needed to attain competency in the occupation, 2014
Sewers, Hand	51-6051	6,540	$11.79	$24,520	No formal educational credential	None	Moderate-term on-the-job training
Tailors, Dressmakers, and Custom Sewers	51-6052	21,660	$13.58	$28,240	No formal educational credential	None	Moderate-term on-the-job training
Textile Bleaching and Dyeing Machine Operators and Tenders	51-6061	10,860	$13.11	$27,270	High school diploma or equivalent	None	Short-term on-the-job training
Textile Cutting Machine Setters, Operators, and Te	51-6062	15,040	$12.55	$26,090	High school diploma or equivalent	None	Moderate-term on-the-job training
Textile Knitting and Weaving Machine Setters, Operators, and Tenders	51-6063	21,550	$13.21	$27,470	High school diploma or equivalent	None	Short-term on-the-job training
Textile Winding, Twisting, and Drawing Out Machine Setters, Operators, and Tenders	51-6064	30,340	$13.22	$27,500	High school diploma or equivalent	None	Moderate-term on-the-job training
Extruding and Forming Machine Setters, Operators, and Tenders, Synthetic and Glass Fibers	51-6091	19,340	$16.46	$34,240	High school diploma or equivalent	None	Moderate-term on-the-job training
Fabric and Apparel Patternmakers	51-6092	5,310	$19.06	$39,650	High school diploma or equivalent	None	Moderate-term on-the-job training
Upholsterers	51-6093	32,520	$15.89	$33,050	High school diploma or equivalent	None	Moderate-term on-the-job training
Textile, Apparel, and Furnishings Workers, All Other	51-6099	15,650	$12.45	$25,890	High school diploma or equivalent	None	Short-term on-the-job training
Cabinetmakers and Bench Carpenters	51-7011	97,980	$15.89	$33,050	High school diploma or equivalent	None	Moderate-term on-the-job training
Furniture Finishers	51-7021	17,370	$14.69	$30,550	High school diploma or equivalent	None	Short-term on-the-job training
Model Makers, Wood	51-7031	1,040	$19.66	$40,890	High school diploma or equivalent	None	Moderate-term on-the-job training
Patternmakers, Wood	51-7032	970	$22.36	$46,510	High school diploma or equivalent	None	Moderate-term on-the-job training
Sawing Machine Setters, Operators, and Tenders, Wood	51-7041	50,640	$13.65	$28,380	High school diploma or equivalent	None	Short-term on-the-job training
Woodworking Machine Setters, Operators, and Tenders, except Sawing	51-7042	76,130	$13.71	$28,510	High school diploma or equivalent	None	Short-term on-the-job training
Woodworkers, All Other	51-7099	6,750	$13.70	$28,500	High school diploma or equivalent	None	Moderate-term on-the-job training
Nuclear Power Reactor Operators	51-8011	7,170	$43.83	$91,170	High school diploma or equivalent	None	Long-term on-the-job training
Power Distributors and Dispatchers	51-8012	11,380	$39.37	$81,900	High school diploma or equivalent	None	Long-term on-the-job training
Power Plant Operators	51-8013	35,010	$35.91	$74,690	High school diploma or equivalent	None	Long-term on-the-job training
Stationary Engineers and Boiler Operators	51-8021	33,720	$28.56	$59,400	High school diploma or equivalent	None	Long-term on-the-job training
Water and Wastewater Treatment Plant and System Operators	51-8031	115,840	$22.00	$45,760	High school diploma or equivalent	None	Long-term on-the-job training
Chemical Plant and System Operators	51-8091	33,300	$28.81	$59,920	High school diploma or equivalent	None	Long-term on-the-job training
Gas Plant Operators	51-8092	17,350	$32.49	$67,580	High school diploma or equivalent	None	Long-term on-the-job training
Petroleum Pump System Operators, Refinery Operators, and Gaugers	51-8093	41,630	$32.40	$67,400	High school diploma or equivalent	None	Long-term on-the-job training
Plant and System Operators, All Other	51-8099	11,970	$26.41	$54,930	High school diploma or equivalent	None	Long-term on-the-job training
Chemical Equipment Operators and Tenders	51-9011	73,840	$22.97	$47,780	High school diploma or equivalent	None	Moderate-term on-the-job training
Separating, Filtering, Clarifying, Precipitating, and Still Machine Setters, Operators, and Tenders	51-9012	47,160	$18.44	$38,360	High school diploma or equivalent	None	Moderate-term on-the-job training
Crushing, Grinding, and Polishing Machine Setters, Operators, and Tenders	51-9021	29.830	$16.53	$34,390	High school diploma or equivalent	None	Moderate-term on-the-job training
Grinding and Polishing Workers, Hand	51-9022	26,670	$13.81	$28,720	No formal educational credential	None	Moderate-term on-the-job training
Mixing and Blending Machine Setters, Operators, and Tenders	51-9023	130.480	$17.16	$35,680	High school diploma or equivalent	None	Moderate-term on-the-job training
Cutters and Trimmers, Hand	51-9031	14,250	$13.27	$27,600	No formal educational credential	None	Short-term on-the-job training
Cutting and Slicing Machine Setters, Operators, and Tenders	51-9032	61,330	$15.80	$32,870	High school diploma or equivalent	None	Short-term on-the-job training
Extruding, Forming, Pressing, and Compacting Machine Setters, Operators, and Tenders	51-9041	71,260	$15.63	$32,510	High school diploma or equivalent	None	Moderate-term on-the-job training
Furnace, Kiln, Oven, Drier, and Kettle Operators and Tenders	51-9051	19,520	$17.33	$36,040	High school diploma or equivalent	None	Moderate-term on-the-job training
Inspectors, Testers, Sorters, Samplers, and Weighers	51-9061	518,950	$17.68	$36,780	High school diploma or equivalent	None	Moderate-term on-the-job training
Jewelers and Precious Stone and Metal Workers	51-9071	26,480	$18.37	$38,200	High school diploma or equivalent	None	Long-term on-the-job training
Dental Laboratory Technicians	51-9081	37,110	$18.12	$37,680	High school diploma or equivalent	None	Moderate-term on-the-job training
Medical Appliance Technicians	51-9082	14,570	$17.30	$35,980	High school diploma or equivalent	None	Long-term on-the-job training

Table A-1. Number of Employees, Wages and Salaries, and Job Requirements for Detailed Occupations in the United States—*Continued*

Occupation	Occupation code	Total employees, May 2016	Median hourly wage, 2016	Median Annual Salary, 2016	Typical education needed for entry, 2014	Work experience in a related occupation, 2014	Typical on-the-job training needed to attain competency in the occupation, 2014
Ophthalmic Laboratory Technicians	51-9083	28,570	$14.73	$30,640	High school diploma or equivalent	None	Moderate-term on-the-job training
Packaging and Filling Machine Operators and Tenders	51-9111	386,520	$13.60	$28,290	High school diploma or equivalent	None	Moderate-term on-the-job training
Coating, Painting, and Spraying Machine Setters, Operators, and Tenders	51-9121	85,760	$15.76	$32,790	High school diploma or equivalent	None	Moderate-term on-the-job training
Painters, Transportation Equipment	51-9122	54,860	$20.27	$42,150	High school diploma or equivalent	None	Moderate-term on-the-job training
Painting, Coating, and Decorating Workers	51-9123	15,450	$14.44	$30,030	No formal educational credential	None	Moderate-term on-the-job training
Semiconductor Processors	51-9141	24,430	$17.15	$35,660	Associate's degree	None	Moderate-term on-the-job training
Photographic Process Workers and Processing Machine Operators	51-9151	26,430	$12.73	$26,470	High school diploma or equivalent	None	Short-term on-the-job training
Adhesive Bonding Machine Operators and Tenders	51-9191	16,940	$15.53	$32,290	High school diploma or equivalent	None	Moderate-term on-the-job training
Cleaning, Washing, and Metal Pickling Equipment Operators, and Tenders	51-9192	17,860	$13.73	$28,550	No formal educational credential	None	Moderate-term on-the-job training
Cooling and Freezing Equipment Operators and Tenders	51-9193	8,170	$14.04	$29,190	High school diploma or equivalent	None	Moderate-term on-the-job training
Etchers and Engravers	51-9194	9,520	$14.96	$31,110	High school diploma or equivalent	None	Moderate-term on-the-job training
Molders, Shapers, and Casters, Except Metal and Plastic	51-9195	39,450	$14.72	$30,610	High school diploma or equivalent	None	Long-term on-the-job training
Paper Goods Machine Setters, Operators, and Tenders	51-9196	93,100	$17.79	$36,990	High school diploma or equivalent	None	Moderate-term on-the-job training
Tire Builders	51-9197	22,280	$20.04	$41,680	High school diploma or equivalent	None	Moderate-term on-the-job training
Helpers--Production Workers	51-9198	429,890	$11.94	$24,830	No formal educational credential	None	Short-term on-the-job training
Production Workers, All Other	51-9199	251,670	$13.83	$28,770	High school diploma or equivalent	None	Moderate-term on-the-job training
Transportation and Material Moving Occupations	53-0000	9,731,790	$14.78	$30,730			
Aircraft Cargo Handling Supervisors	53-1011	7,460	$22.77	$47,360	High school diploma or equivalent	Less than 5 years	None
First-Line Supervisors of Helpers, Laborers, and Material Movers, Hand	53-1021	183,620	$22.71	$47,230	High school diploma or equivalent	Less than 5 years	None
First-Line Supervisors of Transportation and Material-moving Machine and Vehicle Operators	53-1031	202,760	$27.54	$57,270	High school diploma or equivalent	Less than 5 years	None
Airline Pilots, Copilots, and Flight Engineers	53-2011	81,520		$127,820	Bachelor's degree	Less than 5 years	Moderate-term on-the-job training
Commercial Pilots	53-2012	38,980		$77,200	High school diploma or equivalent	None	Moderate-term on-the-job training
Air Traffic Controllers	53-2021	23,240	$58.85	$122,410	Associate's degree	None	Long-term on-the-job training
Airfield Operations Specialists	53-2022	8,760	$23.51	$48,910	High school diploma or equivalent	None	Long-term on-the-job training
Flight Attendants	53-2031	113,390		$48,500	High school diploma or equivalent	Less than 5 years	Moderate-term on-the-job training
Ambulance Drivers and Attendants, Except Emergency Medical Technicians	53-3011	17,300	$11.46	$23,850	High school diploma or equivalent	None	Moderate-term on-the-job training
Bus Drivers, Transit and Intercity	53-3021	169,680	$19.13	$39,790	High school diploma or equivalent	None	Moderate-term on-the-job training
Bus Drivers, School or Special Client	53-3022	515,020	$14.50	$30,150	High school diploma or equivalent	None	Short-term on-the-job training
Driver/Sales Workers	53-3031	426,310	$10.98	$22,830	High school diploma or equivalent	None	Short-term on-the-job training
Heavy and Tractor-Trailer Truck Drivers	53-3032	1,704,520	$19.87	$41,340	Postsecondary nondegree award	None	Short-term on-the-job training
Light Truck or Delivery Services Drivers	53-3033	858,710	$14.70	$30,580	High school diploma or equivalent	None	Short-term on-the-job training
Taxi Drivers and Chauffeurs	53-3041	188,860	$11.68	$24,300	No formal educational credential	None	Short-term on-the-job training
Motor Vehicle Operators, All Other	53-3099	53,680	$13.05	$27,150	No formal educational credential	None	Short-term on-the-job training
Locomotive Engineers	53-4011	39,900	$27.73	$57,670	High school diploma or equivalent	Less than 5 years	Moderate-term on-the-job training
Locomotive Firers	53-4012	1,210	$27.99	$58,230	High school diploma or equivalent	None	Moderate-term on-the-job training
Rail Yard Engineers, Dinkey Operators, and Hostlers	53-4013	4,530	$24.27	$50,470	High school diploma or equivalent	None	Moderate-term on-the-job training
Railroad Brake, Signal, and Switch Operators	53-4021	19,860	$27.20	$56,570	High school diploma or equivalent	None	Moderate-term on-the-job training
Railroad Conductors and Yardmasters	53-4031	42,880	$27.64	$57,480	High school diploma or equivalent	None	Moderate-term on-the-job training
Subway and Streetcar Operators	53-4041	12,350	$31.09	$64,680	High school diploma or equivalent	None	Moderate-term on-the-job training
Rail Transportation Workers, All Other	53-4099	4,470	$29.05	$60,420	High school diploma or equivalent	None	Moderate-term on-the-job training

Table A-1. Number of Employees, Wages and Salaries, and Job Requirements for Detailed Occupations in the United States—*Continued*

Occupation	Occupation code	Total employees, May 2016	Median hourly wage, 2016	Median Annual Salary, 2016	Typical education needed for entry, 2014	Work experience in a related occupation, 2014	Typical on-the-job training needed to attain competency in the occupation, 2014
Sailors and Marine Oilers	53-5011	32,530	$20.22	$42,060	No formal educational credential	None	Moderate-term on-the-job training
Captains, Mates, and Pilots of Water Vessels	53-5021	36,720	$34.94	$72,680	Postsecondary nondegree award	Less than 5 years	None
Motorboat Operators	53-5022	3,290	$19.33	$40,210	Postsecondary nondegree award	Less than 5 years	None
Ship Engineers	53-5031	9,750	$33.93	$70,570	Postsecondary nondegree award	Less than 5 years	None
Bridge and Lock Tenders	53-6011	3,510	$23.60	$49,090	High school diploma or equivalent	None	Short-term on-the-job training
Parking Lot Attendants	53-6021	146,350	$10.45	$21,730	No formal educational credential	None	Short-term on-the-job training
Automotive and Watercraft Service Attendants	53-6031	109,790	$10.78	$22,420	No formal educational credential	None	Short-term on-the-job training
Traffic Technicians	53-6041	6,410	$21.71	$45,150	High school diploma or equivalent	None	Moderate-term on-the-job training
Transportation Inspectors	53-6051	27,430	$34.72	$72,220	High school diploma or equivalent	None	Moderate-term on-the-job training
Transportation Attendants, Except Flight Attendants	53-6061	18,410	$12.53	$26,060	High school diploma or equivalent	None	Short-term on-the-job training
Transportation Workers, All Other	53-6099	37,660	$17.15	$35,660	High school diploma or equivalent	None	Short-term on-the-job training
Conveyor Operators and Tenders	53-7011	28,590	$15.10	$31,410	No formal educational credential	None	Short-term on-the-job training
Crane and Tower Operators	53-7021	45,020	$25.08	$52,170	High school diploma or equivalent	Less than 5 years	Moderate-term on-the-job training
Dredge Operators	53-7031	1,760	$20.40	$42,420	High school diploma or equivalent	None	Moderate-term on-the-job training
Excavating and Loading Machine and Dragline Operators	53-7032	48,320	$19.72	$41,030	High school diploma or equivalent	Less than 5 years	Moderate-term on-the-job training
Loading Machine Operators, Underground Mining	53-7033	2,550	$25.68	$53,420	No formal educational credential	None	Short-term on-the-job training
Hoist and Winch Operators	53-7041	2,960	$20.45	$42,530	No formal educational credential	None	Short-term on-the-job training
Industrial Truck and Tractor Operators	53-7051	542,750	$15.61	$32,460	No formal educational credential	None	Short-term on-the-job training
Cleaners of Vehicles and Equipment	53-7061	348,770	$10.68	$22,220	No formal educational credential	None	Short-term on-the-job training
Laborers and Freight, Stock, and Material Movers, Hand	53-7062	2,587,900	$12.49	$25,980	No formal educational credential	None	Short-term on-the-job training
Machine Feeders and Offbearers	53-7063	88,070	$13.66	$28,410	No formal educational credential	None	Short-term on-the-job training
Packers and Packagers, Hand	53-7064	705,660	$10.64	$22,130	No formal educational credential	None	Short-term on-the-job training
Gas Compressor and Gas Pumping Station Operators	53-7071	3,890	$29.07	$60,470	High school diploma or equivalent	None	Moderate-term on-the-job training
Pump Operators, Except Wellhead Pumpers	53-7072	12,030	$20.42	$42,470	High school diploma or equivalent	None	Moderate-term on-the-job training
Wellhead Pumpers	53-7073	11,610	$23.85	$49,610	High school diploma or equivalent	Less than 5 years	Moderate-term on-the-job training
Refuse and Recyclable Material Collectors	53-7081	114,680	$16.95	$35,270	No formal educational credential	None	Short-term on-the-job training
Mine Shuttle Car Operators	53-7111	1,590	$27.14	$56,450	No formal educational credential	None	Short-term on-the-job training
Tank Car, Truck, and Ship Loaders	53-7121	10,920	$17.20	$35,770	No formal educational credential	None	Short-term on-the-job training
Material Moving Workers, All Other	53-7199	23,880	$13.64	$28,370	No formal educational credential	None	Short-term on-the-job training

Note: An annual salary of $208,000 indicates $208,000 or more.

Table A-2. Educational Attainment for Workers 25 Years and Older by Detailed Occupation, 2014–2015

2014 National Employment Matrix title and code		Less than high school diploma	High school diploma or equivalent	Some college, no degree	Associate's degree	Bachelor's degree	Master's degree	Doctoral or professional degree
Total, All Occupations	00-0000	8.7	24.2	21.3	9.4	22.5	9.7	4.2
Chief executives[1]	11-1011	1.6	9.1	15.4	5.4	39.7	21.5	7.4
General and operations managers	11-1021	2.3	17.1	25.9	9.8	32.5	10.9	1.5
Legislators[1]	11-1031	1.6	9.1	15.4	5.4	39.7	21.5	7.4
Advertising and promotions managers	11-2011	0.6	4.4	12.4	4.2	64.2	12.1	2.0
Marketing managers[1]	11-2021	0.9	7.8	15.3	6.6	50.8	16.9	1.7
Sales managers[1]	11-2022	0.9	7.8	15.3	6.6	50.8	16.9	1.7
Public relations and fundraising managers	11-2031	0.5	2.0	9.2	2.9	58.6	23.8	2.9
Administrative services managers	11-3011	2.0	19.1	27.5	10.7	29.3	10.1	1.4
Computer and information systems managers	11-3021	0.4	4.3	14.4	8.1	45.6	24.5	2.6
Financial managers	11-3031	1.1	10.0	18.4	7.8	40.5	19.7	2.6
Industrial production managers	11-3051	4.2	20.3	21.7	7.6	32.4	12.7	1.1
Purchasing managers	11-3061	0.8	10.5	19.4	7.9	39.9	19.2	2.4
Transportation, storage, and distribution managers	11-3071	4.9	29.7	29.2	7.2	22.0	6.5	0.4
Compensation and benefits managers	11-3111	0.1	6.4	16.1	8.0	42.8	24.6	1.9
Human resources managers	11-3121	2.4	11.7	18.0	8.6	37.1	19.5	2.7
Training and development managers	11-3131	0.8	7.9	16.5	7.8	40.2	22.0	4.8
Farmers, ranchers, and other agricultural managers	11-9013	10.5	36.8	20.4	9.2	19.2	2.9	1.0
Construction managers	11-9021	6.4	25.9	25.3	8.3	27.4	5.9	0.9
Education administrators, preschool and childcare center/program[1]	11-9031	0.9	5.1	7.9	4.6	23.5	43.9	14.1
Education administrators, elementary and secondary school[1]	11-9032	0.9	5.1	7.9	4.6	23.5	43.9	14.1
Education administrators, postsecondary[1]	11-9033	0.9	5.1	7.9	4.6	23.5	43.9	14.1
Education administrators, all other[1]	11-9039	0.9	5.1	7.9	4.6	23.5	43.9	14.1
Architectural and engineering managers	11-9041	0.7	3.6	6.8	4.5	46.3	32.3	5.8
Food service managers	11-9051	8.8	28.6	27.9	9.5	21.2	3.4	0.6
Funeral service managers[1]	11-9061	2.8	14.2	18.9	7.5	35.6	17.5	3.6
Gaming managers	11-9071	3.6	24.4	32.7	11.5	21.5	5.3	0.9
Lodging managers	11-9081	3.0	18.9	25.1	10.1	32.6	8.9	1.3
Medical and health services managers	11-9111	1.2	8.3	15.6	11.3	32.2	23.4	8.1
Natural sciences managers	11-9121	0.8	1.6	3.1	2.9	36.9	31.7	22.9
Postmasters and mail superintendents[1]	11-9131	2.8	14.2	18.9	7.5	35.6	17.5	3.6
Property, real estate, and community association managers	11-9141	4.2	19.0	25.6	9.3	30.5	9.0	2.4
Social and community service managers	11-9151	0.9	7.8	14.9	5.8	37.7	27.7	5.4
Emergency management directors	11-9161	0.0	3.6	20.7	13.5	40.7	20.4	1.1
Managers, all other[1]	11-9199	2.8	14.2	18.9	7.5	35.6	17.5	3.6
Agents and business managers of artists, performers, and athletes	13-1011	2.5	12.5	20.0	7.0	43.7	10.7	3.6
Buyers and purchasing agents, farm products	13-1021	12.4	30.0	18.2	8.9	23.6	4.4	2.5
Wholesale and retail buyers, except farm products	13-1022	4.8	23.1	26.0	9.0	32.1	4.7	0.3
Purchasing agents, except wholesale, retail, and farm products	13-1023	1.8	17.0	25.3	10.9	35.0	8.8	1.3
Claims adjusters, examiners, and investigators[1]	13-1031	1.0	15.7	25.0	9.7	39.3	7.6	1.7
Insurance appraisers, auto damage[1]	13-1032	1.0	15.7	25.0	9.7	39.3	7.6	1.7
Compliance officers	13-1041	1.1	8.2	19.1	8.1	38.6	17.8	7.1
Cost estimators	13-1051	2.4	22.2	29.8	11.5	28.9	4.5	0.6
Human resources specialists[1]	13-1071	1.5	10.4	18.8	8.1	43.2	15.9	2.2
Farm labor contractors[1]	13-1074	1.5	10.4	18.8	8.1	43.2	15.9	2.2
Labor relations specialists[1]	13-1075	1.5	10.4	18.8	8.1	43.2	15.9	2.2
Logisticians	13-1081	1.3	14.5	27.7	12.7	34.2	8.7	0.8
Management analysts	13-1111	0.7	4.9	12.1	5.2	42.1	28.4	6.7
Meeting, convention, and event planners	13-1121	1.2	9.9	19.7	7.6	50.2	10.8	0.6
Fundraisers	13-1131	0.5	3.1	8.1	3.5	53.8	26.5	4.5
Compensation, benefits, and job analysis specialists	13-1141	0.4	12.8	21.7	10.3	41.7	11.5	1.6
Training and development specialists	13-1151	1.7	10.6	22.6	10.3	35.2	17.6	1.9
Market research analysts and marketing specialists	13-1161	0.9	4.2	10.0	4.5	54.1	23.4	2.9
Business operations specialists, all other	13-1199	1.6	9.7	16.8	8.1	39.5	20.0	4.3
Accountants and auditors	13-2011	0.0	4.3	8.1	9.1	55.6	20.1	2.8
Appraisers and assessors of real estate	13-2021	0.7	10.6	25.6	9.2	41.8	9.9	2.2
Budget analysts	13-2031	0.6	6.8	13.1	7.2	40.9	27.7	3.6
Credit analysts	13-2041	0.5	10.0	17.4	7.6	44.8	18.4	1.2
Financial analysts	13-2051	0.3	2.0	5.9	3.2	51.8	33.0	3.8
Personal financial advisors	13-2052	0.4	4.0	10.6	4.8	53.4	21.0	5.7
Insurance underwriters	13-2053	0.6	13.9	19.8	8.5	46.8	8.4	2.0
Financial examiners	13-2061	0.0	6.6	4.9	6.5	56.2	23.8	2.1
Credit counselors[1]	13-2071	1.0	13.8	23.3	9.8	41.0	9.8	1.3
Loan officers[1]	13-2072	1.0	13.8	23.3	9.8	41.0	9.8	1.3
Tax examiners and collectors, and revenue agents	13-2081	1.4	16.2	24.2	8.7	37.1	11.2	1.2
Tax preparers	13-2082	1.7	12.5	24.4	9.0	32.9	14.2	5.4
Financial specialists, all other	13-2099	1.1	11.2	16.5	7.7	41.4	19.6	2.6
Computer and information research scientists	15-1111	0.2	1.3	2.1	0.4	43.6	32.2	20.2
Computer systems analysts	15-1121	0.5	4.6	13.6	8.0	47.2	23.4	2.8
Information security analysts	15-1122	0.8	5.3	15.9	9.3	46.8	20.2	1.7
Computer programmers	15-1131	0.5	4.2	13.7	8.4	51.2	19.5	2.4
Software developers, applications[1]	15-1132	0.3	2.2	8.5	5.1	49.2	30.5	4.1
Software developers, systems software[1]	15-1133	0.3	2.2	8.5	5.1	49.2	30.5	4.1
Web developers	15-1134	0.6	5.1	15.8	9.8	53.6	13.7	1.4
Database administrators	15-1141	0.5	5.9	13.2	8.2	45.7	23.6	2.8
Network and computer systems administrators	15-1142	0.5	6.6	23.9	15.5	40.7	11.3	1.3
Computer network architects	15-1143	0.7	6.7	23.1	12.0	40.0	15.9	1.7
Computer user support specialists[1]	15-1151	0.8	9.5	26.7	16.4	36.2	9.4	1.0
Computer network support specialists[1]	15-1152	0.8	9.5	26.7	16.4	36.2	9.4	1.0
Computer occupations, all other	15-1199	1.1	7.2	21.1	14.7	39.0	15.5	1.3
Actuaries	15-2011	0.0	0.0	1.2	0.7	63.5	23.6	11.0

Table A-2. Educational Attainment for Workers 25 Years and Older by Detailed Occupation, 2014–2015—*Continued*

2014 National Employment Matrix title and code		Less than high school diploma	High school diploma or equivalent	Some college, no degree	Associate's degree	Bachelor's degree	Master's degree	Doctoral or professional degree
Mathematicians[1]	15-2021	0.1	0.1	3.2	3.0	32.9	39.0	21.7
Operations research analysts	15-2031	0.6	6.1	15.0	7.1	39.7	27.4	4.1
Statisticians[1]	15-2041	0.1	0.1	3.2	3.0	32.9	39.0	21.7
Mathematical technicians[1]	15-2091	0.1	0.1	3.2	3.0	32.9	39.0	21.7
Mathematical science occupations, all other[1]	15-2099	0.1	0.1	3.2	3.0	32.9	39.0	21.7
Architects, except landscape and naval[1]	17-1011	0.3	1.6	4.6	2.9	49.0	34.0	7.5
Landscape architects[1]	17-1012	0.3	1.6	4.6	2.9	49.0	34.0	7.5
Cartographers and photogrammetrists[1]	17-1021	0.4	1.8	9.4	6.7	65.8	12.6	3.2
Surveyors[1]	17-1022	0.4	1.8	9.4	6.7	65.8	12.6	3.2
Aerospace engineers	17-2011	0.4	2.1	6.7	4.7	50.0	31.3	4.7
Agricultural engineers[1]	17-2021	0.5	1.9	5.3	14.1	39.3	29.4	9.4
Biomedical engineers[1]	17-2031	0.5	1.9	5.3	14.1	39.3	29.4	9.4
Chemical engineers	17-2041	0.1	2.8	3.7	3.1	57.3	25.5	7.6
Civil engineers	17-2051	0.4	3.2	5.9	4.8	55.4	26.2	4.1
Computer hardware engineers	17-2061	0.1	3.9	10.5	8.2	47.5	25.3	4.4
Electrical engineers[1]	17-2071	0.7	3.6	8.7	8.1	48.6	24.4	5.9
Electronics engineers, except computer[1]	17-2072	0.7	3.6	8.7	8.1	48.6	24.4	5.9
Environmental engineers	17-2081	0.4	4.4	4.9	3.2	48.3	33.9	4.9
Health and safety engineers, except mining safety engineers and inspectors[1]	17-2111	0.8	6.8	12.6	9.4	50.3	17.9	2.2
Industrial engineers[1]	17-2112	0.8	6.8	12.6	9.4	50.3	17.9	2.2
Marine engineers and naval architects	17-2121	1.8	8.9	10.8	7.5	48.3	19.7	3.0
Materials engineers	17-2131	0.7	5.3	13.1	9.4	45.4	18.2	8.0
Mechanical engineers	17-2141	0.6	4.6	9.5	9.3	51.6	20.9	3.4
Mining and geological engineers, including mining safety engineers[1]	17-2151	0.7	7.8	8.0	2.7	53.7	22.6	4.4
Nuclear engineers[1]	17-2161	0.5	2.8	7.5	6.4	49.0	26.6	7.2
Petroleum engineers[1]	17-2171	0.7	7.8	8.0	2.7	53.7	22.6	4.4
Engineers, all other[1]	17-2199	0.5	2.8	7.5	6.4	49.0	26.6	7.2
Architectural and civil drafters[1]	17-3011	1.2	10.4	27.6	32.7	22.8	4.5	0.8
Electrical and electronics drafters[1]	17-3012	1.2	10.4	27.6	32.7	22.8	4.5	0.8
Mechanical drafters[1]	17-3013	1.2	10.4	27.6	32.7	22.8	4.5	0.8
Drafters, all other[1]	17-3019	1.2	10.4	27.6	32.7	22.8	4.5	0.8
Aerospace engineering and operations technicians[1]	17-3021	3.0	21.8	33.4	22.6	15.8	2.8	0.6
Civil engineering technicians[1]	17-3022	3.0	21.8	33.4	22.6	15.8	2.8	0.6
Electrical and electronics engineering technicians[1]	17-3023	3.0	21.8	33.4	22.6	15.8	2.8	0.6
Electro-mechanical technicians[1]	17-3024	3.0	21.8	33.4	22.6	15.8	2.8	0.6
Environmental engineering technicians[1]	17-3025	3.0	21.8	33.4	22.6	15.8	2.8	0.6
Industrial engineering technicians[1]	17-3026	3.0	21.8	33.4	22.6	15.8	2.8	0.6
Mechanical engineering technicians[1]	17-3027	3.0	21.8	33.4	22.6	15.8	2.8	0.6
Engineering technicians, except drafters, all other[1]	17-3029	3.0	21.8	33.4	22.6	15.8	2.8	0.6
Surveying and mapping technicians	17-3031	6.4	26.1	37.6	21.4	7.6	0.7	0.1
Animal scientists[1]	19-1011	0.0	0.0	0.0	0.0	56.4	27.6	16.0
Food scientists and technologists[1]	19-1012	0.0	0.0	0.0	0.0	56.4	27.6	16.0
Soil and plant scientists[1]	19-1013	0.0	0.0	0.0	0.0	56.4	27.6	16.0
Biochemists and biophysicists[1]	19-1021	0.0	0.0	0.0	0.0	46.4	31.9	21.7
Microbiologists[1]	19-1022	0.0	0.0	0.0	0.0	46.4	31.9	21.7
Zoologists and wildlife biologists[1]	19-1023	0.0	0.0	0.0	0.0	46.4	31.9	21.7
Biological scientists, all other[1]	19-1029	0.0	0.0	0.0	0.0	46.4	31.9	21.7
Conservation scientists[1]	19-1031	0.0	0.0	0.0	0.0	73.4	21.0	5.6
Foresters[1]	19-1032	0.0	0.0	0.0	0.0	73.4	21.0	5.6
Epidemiologists[1]	19-1041	0.4	0.6	0.5	0.9	19.3	23.8	54.5
Medical scientists, except epidemiologists[1]	19-1042	0.4	0.6	0.5	0.9	19.3	23.8	54.5
Life scientists, all other[1]	19-1099	0.4	0.6	0.5	0.9	19.3	23.8	54.5
Astronomers[1]	19-2011	0.0	0.0	0.0	0.0	17.6	28.8	53.6
Physicists[1]	19-2012	0.0	0.0	0.0	0.0	17.6	28.8	53.6
Atmospheric and space scientists	19-2021	0.0	1.2	6.5	3.8	48.6	23.7	16.2
Chemists[1]	19-2031	0.4	2.0	2.7	1.6	54.1	22.0	17.2
Materials scientists[1]	19-2032	0.4	2.0	2.7	1.6	54.1	22.0	17.2
Environmental scientists and specialists, including health[1]	19-2041	0.0	0.0	0.0	0.0	53.4	34.4	12.2
Geoscientists, except hydrologists and geographers[1]	19-2042	0.0	0.0	0.0	0.0	53.4	34.4	12.2
Hydrologists[1]	19-2043	0.0	0.0	0.0	0.0	53.4	34.4	12.2
Physical scientists, all other	19-2099	0.0	0.0	0.0	0.0	26.6	22.7	50.7
Economists	19-3011	0.0	0.0	0.0	0.0	22.8	47.7	29.5
Survey researchers[1]	19-3022	0.4	3.0	7.6	2.7	36.1	36.2	14.1
Clinical, counseling, and school psychologists[1]	19-3031	0.0	0.0	0.0	0.0	6.9	41.3	51.8
Industrial-organizational psychologists[1]	19-3032	0.0	0.0	0.0	0.0	6.9	41.3	51.8
Psychologists, all other[1]	19-3039	0.0	0.0	0.0	0.0	6.9	41.3	51.8
Sociologists[1]	19-3041	0.4	3.0	7.6	2.7	36.1	36.2	14.1
Urban and regional planners	19-3051	1.4	1.0	6.4	2.5	38.6	45.6	4.5
Anthropologists and archeologists[1]	19-3091	0.4	3.0	7.6	2.7	36.1	36.2	14.1
Geographers[1]	19-3092	0.4	3.0	7.6	2.7	36.1	36.2	14.1
Historians[1]	19-3093	0.4	3.0	7.6	2.7	36.1	36.2	14.1
Political scientists[1]	19-3094	0.4	3.0	7.6	2.7	36.1	36.2	14.1
Social scientists and related workers, all other[1]	19-3099	0.4	3.0	7.6	2.7	36.1	36.2	14.1
Agricultural and food science technicians	19-4011	8.2	20.0	30.6	12.7	22.8	3.6	2.1
Biological technicians	19-4021	4.4	17.6	23.6	16.0	28.4	5.1	4.8
Chemical technicians	19-4031	3.2	22.8	26.7	11.1	27.1	5.7	3.4
Geological and petroleum technicians[1]	19-4041	3.4	21.5	27.0	15.2	26.3	4.9	1.8
Nuclear technicians[1]	19-4051	3.4	21.5	27.0	15.2	26.3	4.9	1.8
Social science research assistants[1]	19-4061	2.8	15.7	20.3	13.2	33.5	10.8	3.7

Table A-2. Educational Attainment for Workers 25 Years and Older by Detailed Occupation, 2014–2015—*Continued*

2014 National Employment Matrix title and code		Less than high school diploma	High school diploma or equivalent	Some college, no degree	Associate's degree	Bachelor's degree	Master's degree	Doctoral or professional degree
Environmental science and protection technicians, including health[1]	19-4091	2.8	15.7	20.3	13.2	33.5	10.8	3.7
Forensic science technicians[1]	19-4092	2.8	15.7	20.3	13.2	33.5	10.8	3.7
Forest and conservation technicians[1]	19-4093	2.8	15.7	20.3	13.2	33.5	10.8	3.7
Life, physical, and social science technicians, all other[1]	19-4099	2.8	15.7	20.3	13.2	33.5	10.8	3.7
Substance abuse and behavioral disorder counselors[1]	21-1011	1.0	5.1	9.1	5.2	25.5	48.7	5.4
Educational, guidance, school, and vocational counselors[1]	21-1012	1.0	5.1	9.1	5.2	25.5	48.7	5.4
Marriage and family therapists[1]	21-1013	1.0	5.1	9.1	5.2	25.5	48.7	5.4
Mental health counselors[1]	21-1014	1.0	5.1	9.1	5.2	25.5	48.7	5.4
Rehabilitation counselors[1]	21-1015	1.0	5.1	9.1	5.2	25.5	48.7	5.4
Counselors, all other[1]	21-1019	1.0	5.1	9.1	5.2	25.5	48.7	5.4
Child, family, and school social workers[1]	21-1021	1.2	5.7	9.2	6.2	40.6	35.3	1.9
Healthcare social workers[1]	21-1022	1.2	5.7	9.2	6.2	40.6	35.3	1.9
Mental health and substance abuse social workers[1]	21-1023	1.2	5.7	9.2	6.2	40.6	35.3	1.9
Social workers, all other[1]	21-1029	1.2	5.7	9.2	6.2	40.6	35.3	1.9
Health educators[1]	21-1091	2.0	12.8	19.4	9.5	32.9	19.9	3.5
Probation officers and correctional treatment specialists	21-1092	0.7	6.0	9.4	5.5	59.0	18.2	1.0
Social and human service assistants	21-1093	2.7	14.9	24.7	10.9	33.1	11.9	1.8
Community health workers[1]	21-1094	2.0	12.8	19.4	9.5	32.9	19.9	3.5
Community and social service specialists, all other[1]	21-1099	2.0	12.8	19.4	9.5	32.9	19.9	3.5
Clergy	21-2011	2.9	6.1	11.5	4.2	24.7	35.6	15.0
Directors, religious activities and education	21-2021	1.2	10.3	16.6	6.8	36.8	23.2	5.1
Religious workers, all other	21-2099	2.4	13.3	19.3	8.3	33.0	17.6	6.1
Lawyers[1]	23-1011	0.1	0.5	0.7	0.4	5.1	4.5	88.7
Judicial law clerks	23-1012	0.1	0.7	4.3	1.8	15.6	3.7	73.8
Administrative law judges, adjudicators, and hearing officers[1]	23-1021	0.1	0.5	0.7	0.4	5.1	4.5	88.7
Arbitrators, mediators, and conciliators[1]	23-1022	0.1	0.5	0.7	0.4	5.1	4.5	88.7
Judges, magistrate judges, and magistrates[1]	23-1023	0.1	0.5	0.7	0.4	5.1	4.5	88.7
Paralegals and legal assistants	23-2011	0.9	9.6	24.6	20.3	35.2	6.2	3.1
Court reporters[1]	23-2091	1.6	17.3	25.2	14.1	30.2	7.6	4.1
Title examiners, abstractors, and searchers[1]	23-2093	1.6	17.3	25.2	14.1	30.2	7.6	4.1
Legal support workers, all other[1]	23-2099	1.6	17.3	25.2	14.1	30.2	7.6	4.1
Business teachers, postsecondary[1]	25-1011	0.5	1.3	2.4	2.1	16.5	33.6	43.7
Computer science teachers, postsecondary[1]	25-1021	0.5	1.3	2.4	2.1	16.5	33.6	43.7
Mathematical science teachers, postsecondary[1]	25-1022	0.5	1.3	2.4	2.1	16.5	33.6	43.7
Architecture teachers, postsecondary[1]	25-1031	0.5	1.3	2.4	2.1	16.5	33.6	43.7
Engineering teachers, postsecondary[1]	25-1032	0.5	1.3	2.4	2.1	16.5	33.6	43.7
Agricultural sciences teachers, postsecondary[1]	25-1041	0.5	1.3	2.4	2.1	16.5	33.6	43.7
Biological science teachers, postsecondary[1]	25-1042	0.5	1.3	2.4	2.1	16.5	33.6	43.7
Forestry and conservation science teachers, postsecondary[1]	25-1043	0.5	1.3	2.4	2.1	16.5	33.6	43.7
Atmospheric, earth, marine, and space sciences teachers, postsecondary[1]	25-1051	0.5	1.3	2.4	2.1	16.5	33.6	43.7
Chemistry teachers, postsecondary[1]	25-1052	0.5	1.3	2.4	2.1	16.5	33.6	43.7
Environmental science teachers, postsecondary[1]	25-1053	0.5	1.3	2.4	2.1	16.5	33.6	43.7
Physics teachers, postsecondary[1]	25-1054	0.5	1.3	2.4	2.1	16.5	33.6	43.7
Anthropology and archeology teachers, postsecondary[1]	25-1061	0.5	1.3	2.4	2.1	16.5	33.6	43.7
Area, ethnic, and cultural studies teachers, postsecondary[1]	25-1062	0.5	1.3	2.4	2.1	16.5	33.6	43.7
Economics teachers, postsecondary[1]	25-1063	0.5	1.3	2.4	2.1	16.5	33.6	43.7
Geography teachers, postsecondary[1]	25-1064	0.5	1.3	2.4	2.1	16.5	33.6	43.7
Political science teachers, postsecondary[1]	25-1065	0.5	1.3	2.4	2.1	16.5	33.6	43.7
Psychology teachers, postsecondary[1]	25-1066	0.5	1.3	2.4	2.1	16.5	33.6	43.7
Sociology teachers, postsecondary[1]	25-1067	0.5	1.3	2.4	2.1	16.5	33.6	43.7
Social sciences teachers, postsecondary, all other[1]	25-1069	0.5	1.3	2.4	2.1	16.5	33.6	43.7
Health specialties teachers, postsecondary[1]	25-1071	0.5	1.3	2.4	2.1	16.5	33.6	43.7
Nursing instructors and teachers, postsecondary[1]	25-1072	0.5	1.3	2.4	2.1	16.5	33.6	43.7
Education teachers, postsecondary[1]	25-1081	0.5	1.3	2.4	2.1	16.5	33.6	43.7
Library science teachers, postsecondary[1]	25-1082	0.5	1.3	2.4	2.1	16.5	33.6	43.7
Criminal justice and law enforcement teachers, postsecondary[1]	25-1111	0.5	1.3	2.4	2.1	16.5	33.6	43.7
Law teachers, postsecondary[1]	25-1112	0.5	1.3	2.4	2.1	16.5	33.6	43.7
Social work teachers, postsecondary[1]	25-1113	0.5	1.3	2.4	2.1	16.5	33.6	43.7
Art, drama, and music teachers, postsecondary[1]	25-1121	0.5	1.3	2.4	2.1	16.5	33.6	43.7
Communications teachers, postsecondary[1]	25-1122	0.5	1.3	2.4	2.1	16.5	33.6	43.7
English language and literature teachers, postsecondary[1]	25-1123	0.5	1.3	2.4	2.1	16.5	33.6	43.7
Foreign language and literature teachers, postsecondary[1]	25-1124	0.5	1.3	2.4	2.1	16.5	33.6	43.7
History teachers, postsecondary[1]	25-1125	0.5	1.3	2.4	2.1	16.5	33.6	43.7
Philosophy and religion teachers, postsecondary[1]	25-1126	0.5	1.3	2.4	2.1	16.5	33.6	43.7
Graduate teaching assistants[1]	25-1191	0.5	1.3	2.4	2.1	16.5	33.6	43.7
Home economics teachers, postsecondary[1]	25-1192	0.5	1.3	2.4	2.1	16.5	33.6	43.7
Recreation and fitness studies teachers, postsecondary[1]	25-1193	0.5	1.3	2.4	2.1	16.5	33.6	43.7
Vocational education teachers, postsecondary[1]	25-1194	0.5	1.3	2.4	2.1	16.5	33.6	43.7
Postsecondary teachers, all other[1]	25-1199	0.5	1.3	2.4	2.1	16.5	33.6	43.7
Preschool teachers, except special education[1]	25-2011	1.4	12.6	23.0	15.6	33.2	13.0	1.1
Kindergarten teachers, except special education[1]	25-2012	1.4	12.6	23.0	15.6	33.2	13.0	1.1
Elementary school teachers, except special education[1]	25-2021	0.0	0.0	3.2	2.1	43.7	46.9	4.1
Middle school teachers, except special and career/technical education[1]	25-2022	0.0	0.0	3.2	2.1	43.7	46.9	4.1
Career/technical education teachers, middle school[1]	25-2023	0.0	0.0	3.2	2.1	43.7	46.9	4.1
Secondary school teachers, except special and career/technical education[1]	25-2031	0.0	0.0	2.9	1.6	41.6	49.5	4.4
Career/technical education teachers, secondary school[1]	25-2032	0.0	0.0	2.9	1.6	41.6	49.5	4.4
Special education teachers, preschool[1]	25-2051	0.8	4.2	6.9	4.7	34.4	46.2	2.8
Special education teachers, kindergarten and elementary school[1]	25-2052	0.8	4.2	6.9	4.7	34.4	46.2	2.8

Table A-2. Educational Attainment for Workers 25 Years and Older by Detailed Occupation, 2014–2015—*Continued*

2014 National Employment Matrix title and code		Less than high school diploma	High school diploma or equivalent	Some college, no degree	Associate's degree	Bachelor's degree	Master's degree	Doctoral or professional degree
Special education teachers, middle school[1]	25-2053	0.8	4.2	6.9	4.7	34.4	46.2	2.8
Special education teachers, secondary school[1]	25-2054	0.8	4.2	6.9	4.7	34.4	46.2	2.8
Special education teachers, all other[1]	25-2059	0.8	4.2	6.9	4.7	34.4	46.2	2.8
Adult basic and secondary education and literacy teachers and instructors[1]	25-3011	1.5	10.1	19.1	8.1	35.9	20.7	4.6
Self-enrichment education teachers[1]	25-3021	1.5	10.1	19.1	8.1	35.9	20.7	4.6
Teachers and instructors, all other[1]	25-3099	1.5	10.1	19.1	8.1	35.9	20.7	4.6
Archivists[1]	25-4011	0.8	5.0	9.2	3.8	32.1	40.9	8.3
Curators[1]	25-4012	0.8	5.0	9.2	3.8	32.1	40.9	8.3
Museum technicians and conservators[1]	25-4013	0.8	5.0	9.2	3.8	32.1	40.9	8.3
Librarians	25-4021	0.4	1.9	8.2	5.0	23.8	56.1	4.8
Library technicians	25-4031	2.6	36.8	18.4	7.8	23.2	10.8	0.5
Audio-visual and multimedia collections specialists[1]	25-9011	0.5	4.5	9.0	5.1	29.7	42.5	8.7
Farm and home management advisors[1]	25-9021	0.5	4.5	9.0	5.1	29.7	42.5	8.7
Instructional coordinators[1]	25-9031	0.5	4.5	9.0	5.1	29.7	42.5	8.7
Teacher assistants	25-9041	4.2	29.7	27.2	13.8	20.3	4.2	0.6
Education, training, and library workers, all other[1]	25-9099	0.5	4.5	9.0	5.1	29.7	42.5	8.7
Art directors[1]	27-1011	2.1	10.7	19.7	8.8	45.7	11.3	1.7
Craft artists[1]	27-1012	2.1	10.7	19.7	8.8	45.7	11.3	1.7
Fine artists, including painters, sculptors, and illustrators[1]	27-1013	2.1	10.7	19.7	8.8	45.7	11.3	1.7
Multimedia artists and animators[1]	27-1014	2.1	10.7	19.7	8.8	45.7	11.3	1.7
Artists and related workers, all other[1]	27-1019	2.1	10.7	19.7	8.8	45.7	11.3	1.7
Commercial and industrial designers[1]	27-1021	2.2	10.0	16.8	12.8	48.0	8.8	1.4
Fashion designers[1]	27-1022	2.2	10.0	16.8	12.8	48.0	8.8	1.4
Floral designers[1]	27-1023	2.2	10.0	16.8	12.8	48.0	8.8	1.4
Graphic designers[1]	27-1024	2.2	10.0	16.8	12.8	48.0	8.8	1.4
Interior designers[1]	27-1025	2.2	10.0	16.8	12.8	48.0	8.8	1.4
Merchandise displayers and window trimmers[1]	27-1026	2.2	10.0	16.8	12.8	48.0	8.8	1.4
Set and exhibit designers[1]	27-1027	2.2	10.0	16.8	12.8	48.0	8.8	1.4
Designers, all other[1]	27-1029	2.2	10.0	16.8	12.8	48.0	8.8	1.4
Actors	27-2011	1.8	13.2	18.5	8.2	45.0	11.4	1.8
Producers and directors	27-2012	0.7	4.6	13.3	4.6	59.3	15.1	2.4
Athletes and sports competitors[1]	27-2021	1.6	10.9	18.9	7.4	41.6	17.6	2.0
Coaches and scouts[1]	27-2022	1.6	10.9	18.9	7.4	41.6	17.6	2.0
Umpires, referees, and other sports officials[1]	27-2023	1.6	10.9	18.9	7.4	41.6	17.6	2.0
Dancers[1]	27-2031	7.4	25.7	25.9	7.9	28.5	3.4	1.2
Choreographers[1]	27-2032	7.4	25.7	25.9	7.9	28.5	3.4	1.2
Music directors and composers[1]	27-2041	4.5	14.5	21.9	4.9	30.7	19.2	4.3
Musicians and singers[1]	27-2042	4.5	14.5	21.9	4.9	30.7	19.2	4.3
Entertainers and performers, sports and related workers, all other	27-2099	3.8	18.4	30.0	5.7	32.1	6.9	3.1
Radio and television announcers[1]	27-3011	4.7	19.0	24.4	9.1	35.6	5.7	1.4
Public address system and other announcers[1]	27-3012	4.7	19.0	24.4	9.1	35.6	5.7	1.4
Broadcast news analysts[1]	27-3021	0.6	2.5	7.7	4.1	63.7	18.7	2.6
Reporters and correspondents[1]	27-3022	0.6	2.5	7.7	4.1	63.7	18.7	2.6
Public relations specialists	27-3031	0.8	3.0	9.6	4.6	57.2	20.5	4.4
Editors	27-3041	0.5	3.1	11.0	3.3	56.2	20.0	5.9
Technical writers	27-3042	0.6	4.2	11.3	6.9	45.2	24.1	7.8
Writers and authors	27-3043	0.6	2.9	9.1	3.3	51.1	24.8	8.3
Interpreters and translators[1]	27-3091	3.6	10.9	19.5	13.7	32.3	16.1	3.9
Media and communication workers, all other[1]	27-3099	3.6	10.9	19.5	13.7	32.3	16.1	3.9
Audio and video equipment technicians[1]	27-4011	1.5	16.2	27.5	16.7	32.5	5.0	0.5
Broadcast technicians[1]	27-4012	1.5	16.2	27.5	16.7	32.5	5.0	0.5
Radio operators[1]	27-4013	1.5	16.2	27.5	16.7	32.5	5.0	0.5
Sound engineering technicians[1]	27-4014	1.5	16.2	27.5	16.7	32.5	5.0	0.5
Photographers	27-4021	1.9	10.8	24.4	11.7	41.8	8.2	1.2
Camera operators, television, video, and motion picture[1]	27-4031	1.6	8.3	17.5	11.5	51.9	8.2	1.1
Film and video editors[1]	27-4032	1.6	8.3	17.5	11.5	51.9	8.2	1.1
Media and communication equipment workers, all other[1]	27-4099	1.5	16.2	27.5	16.7	32.5	5.0	0.5
Chiropractors	29-1011	0.6	0.9	0.8	0.8	4.7	2.2	90.1
Dentists, general[1]	29-1021	0.0	0.0	0.0	0.0	0.0	1.7	98.3
Oral and maxillofacial surgeons[1]	29-1022	0.0	0.0	0.0	0.0	0.0	1.7	98.3
Orthodontists[1]	29-1023	0.0	0.0	0.0	0.0	0.0	1.7	98.3
Prosthodontists[1]	29-1024	0.0	0.0	0.0	0.0	0.0	1.7	98.3
Dentists, all other specialists[1]	29-1029	0.0	0.0	0.0	0.0	0.0	1.7	98.3
Dietitians and nutritionists	29-1031	3.0	12.0	8.7	5.1	37.2	28.0	6.0
Optometrists	29-1041	0.0	0.0	0.0	0.0	0.0	1.8	98.2
Pharmacists	29-1051	0.0	0.0	1.4	0.9	35.4	6.0	56.3
Anesthesiologists[1]	29-1061	0.1	0.1	0.0	0.0	0.9	0.3	98.6
Family and general practitioners[1]	29-1062	0.1	0.1	0.0	0.0	0.9	0.3	98.6
Internists, general[1]	29-1063	0.1	0.1	0.0	0.0	0.9	0.3	98.6
Obstetricians and gynecologists[1]	29-1064	0.1	0.1	0.0	0.0	0.9	0.3	98.6
Pediatricians, general[1]	29-1065	0.1	0.1	0.0	0.0	0.9	0.3	98.6
Psychiatrists[1]	29-1066	0.1	0.1	0.0	0.0	0.9	0.3	98.6
Surgeons[1]	29-1067	0.1	0.1	0.0	0.0	0.9	0.3	98.6
Physicians and surgeons, all other[1]	29-1069	0.1	0.1	0.0	0.0	0.9	0.3	98.6
Physician assistants	29-1071	0.2	1.0	2.6	4.6	18.0	57.7	15.9
Podiatrists	29-1081	0.0	0.0	0.0	0.0	0.0	0.9	99.1
Occupational therapists	29-1122	0.2	1.0	0.9	5.9	41.2	45.2	5.6
Physical therapists	29-1123	0.3	0.8	1.4	3.6	33.5	25.5	34.9
Radiation therapists	29-1124	0.0	0.8	9.7	36.9	43.4	6.6	2.5

Table A-2. Educational Attainment for Workers 25 Years and Older by Detailed Occupation, 2014–2015—*Continued*

2014 National Employment Matrix title and code		Less than high school diploma	High school diploma or equivalent	Some college, no degree	Associate's degree	Bachelor's degree	Master's degree	Doctoral or professional degree
Recreational therapists	29-1125	0.5	8.3	6.7	6.6	60.3	15.3	2.3
Respiratory therapists	29-1126	0.4	2.0	12.2	52.6	27.9	3.9	1.0
Speech-language pathologists	29-1127	0.1	0.9	0.6	1.1	11.7	82.6	3.0
Exercise physiologists[1]	29-1128	0.7	2.2	4.5	5.7	27.5	52.6	6.7
Therapists, all other[1]	29-1129	0.7	2.2	4.5	5.7	27.5	52.6	6.7
Veterinarians	29-1131	0.0	0.0	0.0	0.0	0.0	1.8	98.2
Registered nurses	29-1141	0.3	1.2	5.5	33.9	48.1	9.0	2.0
Nurse anesthetists	29-1151	0.0	0.0	0.0	0.0	14.4	71.9	13.7
Nurse midwives[1]	29-1161	0.0	0.0	0.0	0.0	7.1	79.0	13.9
Nurse practitioners[1]	29-1171	0.0	0.0	0.0	0.0	7.1	79.0	13.9
Audiologists	29-1181	0.0	1.6	2.3	1.7	9.4	24.9	60.1
Health diagnosing and treating practitioners, all other	29-1199	1.2	2.8	7.3	3.2	19.3	38.5	27.8
Medical and clinical laboratory technologists[1]	29-2011	1.5	10.8	19.2	19.5	39.4	6.8	2.7
Medical and clinical laboratory technicians[1]	29-2012	1.5	10.8	19.2	19.5	39.4	6.8	2.7
Dental hygienists	29-2021	0.5	2.4	7.5	52.1	31.8	3.1	2.7
Cardiovascular technologists and technicians[1]	29-2031	0.8	5.8	19.1	44.5	24.8	3.5	1.6
Diagnostic medical sonographers[1]	29-2032	0.8	5.8	19.1	44.5	24.8	3.5	1.6
Nuclear medicine technologists[1]	29-2033	0.8	5.8	19.1	44.5	24.8	3.5	1.6
Radiologic technologists[1]	29-2034	0.8	5.8	19.1	44.5	24.8	3.5	1.6
Magnetic resonance imaging technologists[1]	29-2035	0.8	5.8	19.1	44.5	24.8	3.5	1.6
Emergency medical technicians and paramedics	29-2041	0.6	12.8	44.7	22.3	16.8	2.3	0.5
Dietetic technicians[1]	29-2051	1.8	19.7	33.7	20.8	19.7	3.4	1.0
Pharmacy technicians[1]	29-2052	1.8	19.7	33.7	20.8	19.7	3.4	1.0
Psychiatric technicians[1]	29-2053	1.8	19.7	33.7	20.8	19.7	3.4	1.0
Respiratory therapy technicians[1]	29-2054	1.8	19.7	33.7	20.8	19.7	3.4	1.0
Surgical technologists[1]	29-2055	1.8	19.7	33.7	20.8	19.7	3.4	1.0
Veterinary technologists and technicians[1]	29-2056	1.8	19.7	33.7	20.8	19.7	3.4	1.0
Ophthalmic medical technicians[1]	29-2057	1.8	19.7	33.7	20.8	19.7	3.4	1.0
Licensed practical and licensed vocational nurses	29-2061	1.5	22.5	54.0	17.3	3.8	0.6	0.4
Medical records and health information technicians	29-2071	1.4	21.2	33.0	23.0	17.5	3.1	0.9
Opticians, dispensing	29-2081	2.4	26.0	33.7	17.4	17.6	1.8	1.0
Orthotists and prosthetists[1]	29-2091	1.9	17.6	30.8	17.7	22.0	6.2	3.9
Hearing aid specialists[1]	29-2092	1.9	17.6	30.8	17.7	22.0	6.2	3.9
Health technologists and technicians, all other[1]	29-2099	1.9	17.6	30.8	17.7	22.0	6.2	3.9
Occupational health and safety specialists[1]	29-9011	1.6	11.2	13.6	8.7	36.2	25.2	3.5
Occupational health and safety technicians[1]	29-9012	1.6	11.2	13.6	8.7	36.2	25.2	3.5
Athletic trainers[1]	29-9091	1.6	11.2	13.6	8.7	36.2	25.2	3.5
Genetic counselors[1]	29-9092	1.6	11.2	13.6	8.7	36.2	25.2	3.5
Healthcare practitioners and technical workers, all other[1]	29-9099	1.6	11.2	13.6	8.7	36.2	25.2	3.5
Home health aides[1]	31-1011	13.2	35.5	31.0	10.2	7.8	1.6	0.8
Psychiatric aides[1]	31-1013	13.2	35.5	31.0	10.2	7.8	1.6	0.8
Nursing assistants[1]	31-1014	13.2	35.5	31.0	10.2	7.8	1.6	0.8
Orderlies[1]	31-1015	13.2	35.5	31.0	10.2	7.8	1.6	0.8
Occupational therapy assistants[1]	31-2011	0.0	2.3	7.3	75.2	12.5	1.4	1.4
Occupational therapy aides[1]	31-2012	0.0	2.3	7.3	75.2	12.5	1.4	1.4
Physical therapist assistants[1]	31-2021	1.9	5.3	15.6	53.1	20.9	1.8	1.4
Physical therapist aides[1]	31-2022	1.9	5.3	15.6	53.1	20.9	1.8	1.4
Massage therapists	31-9011	2.9	18.6	35.2	17.1	20.0	4.0	2.2
Dental assistants	31-9091	3.2	25.3	39.5	20.5	9.0	0.8	1.6
Medical assistants	31-9092	2.2	20.9	41.3	24.0	9.1	1.8	0.7
Medical equipment preparers[1]	31-9093	8.6	35.8	30.2	11.5	10.8	2.4	0.7
Medical transcriptionists	31-9094	0.7	19.8	37.8	23.0	15.9	2.3	0.5
Pharmacy aides	31-9095	3.4	29.7	34.2	12.4	15.9	1.1	3.3
Veterinary assistants and laboratory animal caretakers	31-9096	4.6	21.6	30.3	13.5	28.0	1.3	0.7
Phlebotomists	31-9097	1.0	23.5	47.4	17.6	8.3	1.0	1.2
Healthcare support workers, all other[1]	31-9099	8.6	35.8	30.2	11.5	10.8	2.4	0.7
First-line supervisors of correctional officers	33-1011	1.0	26.2	33.5	14.1	19.8	4.9	0.7
First-line supervisors of police and detectives	33-1012	0.3	11.4	31.3	15.9	28.1	12.0	1.1
First-line supervisors of fire fighting and prevention workers	33-1021	0.4	13.7	36.4	21.6	21.8	5.3	0.7
First-line supervisors of protective service workers, all other	33-1099	1.6	23.5	29.4	11.3	22.5	10.4	1.4
Firefighters	33-2011	0.7	15.1	40.5	21.6	19.7	2.1	0.4
Fire inspectors and investigators[1]	33-2021	0.8	22.8	28.1	21.6	20.3	5.8	0.6
Forest fire inspectors and prevention specialists[1]	33-2022	0.8	22.8	28.1	21.6	20.3	5.8	0.6
Bailiffs[1]	33-3011	1.2	30.2	37.7	14.7	14.4	1.5	0.4
Correctional officers and jailers[1]	33-3012	1.2	30.2	37.7	14.7	14.4	1.5	0.4
Detectives and criminal investigators	33-3021	0.6	6.2	24.2	10.8	42.0	13.5	2.8
Fish and game wardens[1]	33-3031	3.3	23.7	27.9	11.6	29.4	3.8	0.4
Parking enforcement workers[1]	33-3041	3.3	23.7	27.9	11.6	29.4	3.8	0.4
Police and sheriff's patrol officers[1]	33-3051	0.6	12.0	33.6	16.3	31.2	5.5	0.8
Transit and railroad police[1]	33-3052	0.6	12.0	33.6	16.3	31.2	5.5	0.8
Animal control workers	33-9011	2.7	35.5	39.9	10.2	10.8	1.0	0.0
Private detectives and investigators	33-9021	0.6	8.4	22.0	8.4	43.6	13.7	3.4
Gaming surveillance officers and gaming investigators[1]	33-9031	6.4	35.3	31.7	10.7	12.8	2.6	0.5
Security guards[1]	33-9032	6.4	35.3	31.7	10.7	12.8	2.6	0.5
Crossing guards	33-9091	16.8	45.6	23.5	6.3	5.9	1.7	0.2
Lifeguards, ski patrol, and other recreational protective service workers[1]	33-9092	5.0	23.8	24.1	11.8	30.0	4.7	0.6
Transportation security screeners	33-9093	4.8	21.9	31.1	13.9	21.6	5.8	0.9
Protective service workers, all other[1]	33-9099	5.0	23.8	24.1	11.8	30.0	4.7	0.6
Chefs and head cooks	35-1011	17.4	30.1	21.6	17.6	11.4	1.5	0.3

Table A-2. Educational Attainment for Workers 25 Years and Older by Detailed Occupation, 2014–2015—*Continued*

2014 National Employment Matrix title and code		Less than high school diploma	High school diploma or equivalent	Some college, no degree	Associate's degree	Bachelor's degree	Master's degree	Doctoral or professional degree
First-line supervisors of food preparation and serving workers	35-1012	11.4	35.4	28.7	9.5	12.7	1.9	0.5
Cooks, fast food[1]	35-2011	29.7	40.7	18.5	5.6	4.7	0.7	0.2
Cooks, institution and cafeteria[1]	35-2012	29.7	40.7	18.5	5.6	4.7	0.7	0.2
Cooks, private household[1]	35-2013	29.7	40.7	18.5	5.6	4.7	0.7	0.2
Cooks, restaurant[1]	35-2014	29.7	40.7	18.5	5.6	4.7	0.7	0.2
Cooks, short order[1]	35-2015	29.7	40.7	18.5	5.6	4.7	0.7	0.2
Cooks, all other[1]	35-2019	29.7	40.7	18.5	5.6	4.7	0.7	0.2
Food preparation workers	35-2021	27.1	36.7	21.2	6.0	7.5	1.2	0.3
Bartenders	35-3011	6.5	28.3	34.2	10.2	18.5	1.8	0.5
Combined food preparation and serving workers, including fast food	35-3021	19.2	43.5	23.4	6.8	5.9	1.0	0.1
Counter attendants, cafeteria, food concession, and coffee shop	35-3022	21.3	38.2	23.3	6.5	8.6	2.1	0.0
Waiters and waitresses	35-3031	13.1	32.8	29.2	9.1	13.7	1.8	0.3
Food servers, nonrestaurant	35-3041	15.7	43.4	23.4	7.4	8.5	1.2	0.3
Dining room and cafeteria attendants and bartender helpers[1]	35-9011	26.3	44.1	17.7	5.4	5.5	0.8	0.3
Dishwashers	35-9021	44.3	38.2	10.2	2.9	3.2	0.8	0.2
Hosts and hostesses, restaurant, lounge, and coffee shop	35-9031	11.4	37.4	26.0	6.7	14.9	2.9	0.7
Food preparation and serving related workers, all other[1]	35-9099	26.3	44.1	17.7	5.4	5.5	0.8	0.3
First-line supervisors of housekeeping and janitorial workers	37-1011	15.1	38.0	24.8	8.5	10.8	2.2	0.6
First-line supervisors of landscaping, lawn service, and groundskeeping workers	37-1012	17.1	30.4	23.9	9.8	17.1	1.5	0.2
Janitors and cleaners, except maids and housekeeping cleaners[1]	37-2011	25.4	44.2	19.0	5.6	4.9	0.8	0.2
Maids and housekeeping cleaners	37-2012	38.2	39.2	13.8	3.9	4.0	0.7	0.2
Building cleaning workers, all other[1]	37-2019	25.4	44.2	19.0	5.6	4.9	0.8	0.2
Pest control workers	37-2021	7.8	42.4	29.4	8.4	10.7	1.1	0.2
Landscaping and groundskeeping workers[1]	37-3011	38.0	35.6	15.4	4.2	5.8	0.9	0.1
Pesticide handlers, sprayers, and applicators, vegetation[1]	37-3012	38.0	35.6	15.4	4.2	5.8	0.9	0.1
Tree trimmers and pruners[1]	37-3013	38.0	35.6	15.4	4.2	5.8	0.9	0.1
Grounds maintenance workers, all other[1]	37-3019	38.0	35.6	15.4	4.2	5.8	0.9	0.1
Gaming supervisors[1]	39-1011	7.0	33.3	34.4	9.8	11.9	3.2	0.4
Slot supervisors[1]	39-1012	7.0	33.3	34.4	9.8	11.9	3.2	0.4
First-line supervisors of personal service workers	39-1021	4.5	26.3	31.3	12.8	21.1	3.3	0.6
Animal trainers	39-2011	6.5	24.1	26.7	11.1	25.6	5.0	1.0
Nonfarm animal caretakers	39-2021	8.6	35.5	26.8	9.6	16.0	2.8	0.7
Gaming dealers[1]	39-3011	8.9	32.6	29.5	10.0	15.5	3.0	0.7
Gaming and sports book writers and runners[1]	39-3012	8.9	32.6	29.5	10.0	15.5	3.0	0.7
Gaming service workers, all other[1]	39-3019	8.9	32.6	29.5	10.0	15.5	3.0	0.7
Motion picture projectionists	39-3021	2.8	21.3	29.9	14.9	22.9	8.2	0.0
Ushers, lobby attendants, and ticket takers	39-3031	7.9	32.2	24.8	9.4	18.5	6.1	1.2
Amusement and recreation attendants[1]	39-3091	8.5	29.4	31.6	7.4	17.1	5.2	0.8
Costume attendants[1]	39-3092	8.5	29.4	31.6	7.4	17.1	5.2	0.8
Locker room, coatroom, and dressing room attendants[1]	39-3093	8.5	29.4	31.6	7.4	17.1	5.2	0.8
Entertainment attendants and related workers, all other[1]	39-3099	8.5	29.4	31.6	7.4	17.1	5.2	0.8
Embalmers[1]	39-4011	6.2	27.5	27.7	13.0	18.4	6.3	0.9
Funeral attendants[1]	39-4021	6.2	27.5	27.7	13.0	18.4	6.3	0.9
Morticians, undertakers, and funeral directors	39-4031	1.2	9.5	20.1	34.0	29.2	3.0	3.0
Barbers	39-5011	12.1	47.4	28.6	6.8	4.4	0.6	0.1
Hairdressers, hairstylists, and cosmetologists	39-5012	7.3	43.5	33.0	10.3	5.1	0.6	0.3
Makeup artists, theatrical and performance[1]	39-5091	22.3	37.4	21.1	7.8	9.6	1.6	0.3
Manicurists and pedicurists[1]	39-5092	22.3	37.4	21.1	7.8	9.6	1.6	0.3
Shampooers[1]	39-5093	22.3	37.4	21.1	7.8	9.6	1.6	0.3
Skincare specialists[1]	39-5094	22.3	37.4	21.1	7.8	9.6	1.6	0.3
Baggage porters and bellhops[1]	39-6011	9.4	32.0	29.8	10.7	15.6	2.0	0.5
Concierges[1]	39-6012	9.4	32.0	29.8	10.7	15.6	2.0	0.5
Tour guides and escorts[1]	39-7011	4.5	15.8	23.0	12.1	31.2	10.8	2.5
Travel guides[1]	39-7012	4.5	15.8	23.0	12.1	31.2	10.8	2.5
Childcare workers	39-9011	12.6	31.1	26.9	10.5	15.4	2.9	0.6
Personal care aides	39-9021	16.5	34.6	27.0	8.6	10.4	2.3	0.6
Fitness trainers and aerobics instructors[1]	39-9031	2.4	15.2	23.6	9.9	37.8	9.5	1.6
Recreation workers[1]	39-9032	2.4	15.2	23.6	9.9	37.8	9.5	1.6
Residential advisors	39-9041	4.6	17.8	30.5	12.0	23.6	9.2	2.2
Personal care and service workers, all other	39-9099	8.7	28.8	27.3	8.3	20.5	5.6	0.8
First-line supervisors of retail sales workers	41-1011	5.8	29.2	28.9	9.7	21.6	3.8	1.0
First-line supervisors of non-retail sales workers	41-1012	4.7	21.8	22.8	8.3	31.5	9.2	1.7
Cashiers[1]	41-2011	14.4	40.8	26.0	7.6	9.3	1.8	0.2
Gaming change persons and booth cashiers[1]	41-2012	14.4	40.8	26.0	7.6	9.3	1.8	0.2
Counter and rental clerks	41-2021	10.2	40.0	25.0	8.2	14.6	1.8	0.1
Parts salespersons	41-2022	9.4	46.8	27.5	10.4	4.9	0.6	0.4
Retail salespersons	41-2031	6.8	29.4	28.5	10.1	20.8	3.8	0.7
Advertising sales agents	41-3011	1.2	10.7	21.2	7.4	50.1	8.6	0.9
Insurance sales agents	41-3021	1.5	14.4	27.0	10.0	38.4	7.0	1.6
Securities, commodities, and financial services sales agents	41-3031	1.0	7.1	15.7	6.0	49.8	17.7	2.6
Travel agents	41-3041	1.3	17.3	33.1	14.3	27.0	6.1	0.9
Sales representatives, services, all other	41-3099	2.0	14.1	24.2	7.9	42.4	8.5	0.9
Sales representatives, wholesale and manufacturing, technical and scientific products[1]	41-4011	3.1	17.8	22.8	8.2	40.2	6.9	0.9
Sales representatives, wholesale and manufacturing, except technical and scientific products[1]	41-4012	3.1	17.8	22.8	8.2	40.2	6.9	0.9
Demonstrators and product promoters[1]	41-9011	8.1	32.0	26.7	9.4	17.7	4.8	1.2
Models[1]	41-9012	8.1	32.0	26.7	9.4	17.7	4.8	1.2

Table A-2. Educational Attainment for Workers 25 Years and Older by Detailed Occupation, 2014–2015—*Continued*

2014 National Employment Matrix title and code		Less than high school diploma	High school diploma or equivalent	Some college, no degree	Associate's degree	Bachelor's degree	Master's degree	Doctoral or professional degree
Real estate brokers[1]	41-9021	1.3	11.9	27.1	10.1	37.7	9.6	2.2
Real estate sales agents[1]	41-9022	1.3	11.9	27.1	10.1	37.7	9.6	2.2
Sales engineers	41-9031	0.6	4.1	14.2	10.5	54.6	15.3	0.6
Telemarketers	41-9041	5.8	29.8	36.2	11.3	13.2	3.5	0.2
Door-to-door sales workers, news and street vendors, and related workers	41-9091	13.2	30.8	23.6	9.6	18.2	3.8	0.8
Sales and related workers, all other	41-9099	4.0	18.8	22.3	8.7	36.1	8.8	1.3
First-line supervisors of office and administrative support workers	43-1011	2.7	22.2	28.7	11.6	25.8	7.6	1.4
Switchboard operators, including answering service	43-2011	3.7	38.9	34.7	10.7	10.1	1.1	0.7
Telephone operators	43-2021	3.4	31.5	41.3	8.9	11.9	2.1	1.0
Communications equipment operators, all other	43-2099	0.0	17.3	28.0	8.5	32.9	9.7	3.6
Bill and account collectors	43-3011	3.6	30.3	36.0	12.3	15.1	2.2	0.5
Billing and posting clerks	43-3021	2.4	29.4	33.1	15.8	15.8	2.9	0.5
Bookkeeping, accounting, and auditing clerks	43-3031	3.5	27.9	37.6	11.1	16.3	3.2	0.5
Gaming cage workers	43-3041	9.2	39.1	27.7	8.6	14.5	1.0	0.0
Payroll and timekeeping clerks	43-3051	2.0	26.1	35.9	14.0	18.9	2.7	0.4
Procurement clerks	43-3061	0.8	21.3	28.4	11.4	26.9	10.1	1.1
Tellers	43-3071	1.9	34.5	35.6	10.7	15.1	1.8	0.5
Financial clerks, all other	43-3099	1.2	16.3	24.7	9.5	33.4	13.9	1.0
Brokerage clerks	43-4011	1.0	21.0	24.0	14.9	33.3	4.5	1.3
Correspondence clerks[1]	43-4021	8.8	35.4	28.4	10.5	14.3	2.2	0.4
Court, municipal, and license clerks	43-4031	1.5	27.4	31.5	14.6	20.7	2.6	1.9
Credit authorizers, checkers, and clerks	43-4041	1.4	27.6	29.4	13.6	21.5	6.1	0.5
Customer service representatives	43-4051	3.9	26.2	32.1	11.6	21.7	4.0	0.5
Eligibility interviewers, government programs	43-4061	1.4	14.1	26.4	14.8	35.5	7.2	0.7
File clerks	43-4071	3.4	30.0	30.9	11.7	18.7	4.6	0.6
Hotel, motel, and resort desk clerks	43-4081	6.3	27.1	35.6	11.1	16.9	2.6	0.5
Interviewers, except eligibility and loan	43-4111	2.3	21.5	34.1	14.4	19.5	6.5	1.7
Library assistants, clerical	43-4121	1.6	17.9	26.8	11.6	30.5	9.7	1.8
Loan interviewers and clerks	43-4131	2.0	25.9	35.0	12.2	21.0	3.5	0.3
New accounts clerks	43-4141	1.5	20.3	35.6	11.8	27.6	2.3	0.9
Order clerks[1]	43-4151	8.8	35.4	28.4	10.5	14.3	2.2	0.4
Human resources assistants, except payroll and timekeeping	43-4161	1.7	21.8	37.6	11.5	20.3	6.8	0.3
Receptionists and information clerks	43-4171	4.0	32.8	33.9	12.3	14.0	2.6	0.3
Reservation and transportation ticket agents and travel clerks	43-4181	2.0	22.3	34.8	11.4	25.3	3.7	0.5
Information and record clerks, all other	43-4199	2.2	19.4	32.2	16.7	22.2	5.9	1.5
Cargo and freight agents	43-5011	3.5	29.9	34.7	5.6	23.5	2.2	0.7
Couriers and messengers	43-5021	8.8	36.5	31.3	9.2	11.9	2.1	0.2
Police, fire, and ambulance dispatchers[1]	43-5031	4.4	30.9	35.7	12.8	14.1	2.0	0.1
Dispatchers, except police, fire, and ambulance[1]	43-5032	4.4	30.9	35.7	12.8	14.1	2.0	0.1
Meter readers, utilities	43-5041	3.2	42.9	33.4	8.4	11.0	1.1	0.0
Postal service clerks	43-5051	3.0	30.1	38.2	11.3	15.5	1.6	0.2
Postal service mail carriers	43-5052	2.4	35.2	37.0	10.8	12.7	1.7	0.2
Postal service mail sorters, processors, and processing machine operators	43-5053	4.8	29.5	36.1	11.9	14.6	2.5	0.5
Production, planning, and expediting clerks	43-5061	2.6	22.6	29.8	12.4	24.5	7.4	0.7
Shipping, receiving, and traffic clerks	43-5071	12.6	45.8	25.4	7.7	7.3	1.0	0.2
Stock clerks and order fillers	43-5081	12.6	44.0	25.5	7.4	8.9	1.3	0.3
Weighers, measurers, checkers, and samplers, recordkeeping	43-5111	14.1	35.3	24.1	9.4	13.7	3.0	0.4
Executive secretaries and executive administrative assistants[1]	43-6011	2.1	28.1	32.8	14.7	18.4	3.4	0.5
Legal secretaries[1]	43-6012	2.1	28.1	32.8	14.7	18.4	3.4	0.5
Medical secretaries[1]	43-6013	2.1	28.1	32.8	14.7	18.4	3.4	0.5
Secretaries and administrative assistants, except legal, medical, and executive[1]	43-6014	2.1	28.1	32.8	14.7	18.4	3.4	0.5
Computer operators	43-9011	3.5	21.8	32.0	12.0	23.6	6.1	0.9
Data entry keyers	43-9021	3.0	27.2	33.7	13.1	19.0	3.7	0.4
Word processors and typists	43-9022	2.9	29.1	33.0	13.8	17.0	3.5	0.7
Desktop publishers[1]	43-9031	2.5	19.8	29.4	12.6	26.9	7.6	1.2
Insurance claims and policy processing clerks	43-9041	1.6	24.6	34.0	12.2	23.7	3.3	0.6
Mail clerks and mail machine operators, except postal service	43-9051	7.2	42.4	29.7	8.8	9.9	1.7	0.3
Office clerks, general	43-9061	3.7	30.2	31.7	12.6	17.8	3.3	0.7
Office machine operators, except computer	43-9071	6.9	32.2	31.2	13.2	14.5	1.9	0.0
Proofreaders and copy markers	43-9081	0.6	13.3	19.9	5.1	42.5	15.3	3.3
Statistical assistants	43-9111	3.1	22.9	27.6	11.5	26.3	6.8	1.8
Office and administrative support workers, all other[1]	43-9199	2.5	19.8	29.4	12.6	26.9	7.6	1.2
First-line supervisors of farming, fishing, and forestry workers	45-1011	30.7	32.2	15.6	5.9	12.7	2.3	0.4
Agricultural inspectors	45-2011	8.5	21.4	23.8	10.2	29.6	5.7	0.8
Animal breeders[1]	45-2021	56.0	25.8	9.3	3.3	4.6	0.7	0.3
Graders and sorters, agricultural products	45-2041	54.8	28.9	8.9	2.9	3.9	0.1	0.5
Agricultural equipment operators[1]	45-2091	56.0	25.8	9.3	3.3	4.6	0.7	0.3
Farmworkers and laborers, crop, nursery, and greenhouse[1]	45-2092	56.0	25.8	9.3	3.3	4.6	0.7	0.3
Farmworkers, farm, ranch, and aquacultural animals[1]	45-2093	56.0	25.8	9.3	3.3	4.6	0.7	0.3
Agricultural workers, all other[1]	45-2099	56.0	25.8	9.3	3.3	4.6	0.7	0.3
Fishers and related fishing workers[1]	45-3011	24.2	43.6	15.7	3.8	10.9	1.6	0.1
Hunters and trappers[1]	45-3021	24.2	43.6	15.7	3.8	10.9	1.6	0.1
Forest and conservation workers	45-4011	25.8	25.6	16.0	11.6	18.5	2.2	0.5
Fallers[1]	45-4021	31.7	47.2	12.4	3.3	3.8	1.5	0.2
Logging equipment operators[1]	45-4022	31.7	47.2	12.4	3.3	3.8	1.5	0.2
Log graders and scalers[1]	45-4023	31.7	47.2	12.4	3.3	3.8	1.5	0.2
Logging workers, all other[1]	45-4029	31.7	47.2	12.4	3.3	3.8	1.5	0.2
First-line supervisors of construction trades and extraction workers	47-1011	14.5	41.3	25.4	7.1	9.8	1.6	0.4

Table A-2. Educational Attainment for Workers 25 Years and Older by Detailed Occupation, 2014–2015—*Continued*

2014 National Employment Matrix title and code		Less than high school diploma	High school diploma or equivalent	Some college, no degree	Associate's degree	Bachelor's degree	Master's degree	Doctoral or professional degree
Boilermakers	47-2011	13.1	48.9	26.2	8.3	2.7	0.8	0.0
Brickmasons and blockmasons(1)	47-2021	35.5	42.8	15.2	3.5	2.5	0.3	0.1
Stonemasons(1)	47-2022	35.5	42.8	15.2	3.5	2.5	0.3	0.1
Carpenters	47-2031	26.2	42.2	19.4	5.5	5.8	0.7	0.2
Carpet installers(1)	47-2041	34.3	43.8	14.8	3.6	3.1	0.4	0.0
Floor layers, except carpet, wood, and hard tiles(1)	47-2042	34.3	43.8	14.8	3.6	3.1	0.4	0.0
Floor sanders and finishers(1)	47-2043	34.3	43.8	14.8	3.6	3.1	0.4	0.0
Tile and marble setters(1)	47-2044	34.3	43.8	14.8	3.6	3.1	0.4	0.0
Cement masons and concrete finishers(1)	47-2051	36.3	41.3	15.5	1.9	4.2	0.6	0.2
Terrazzo workers and finishers(1)	47-2053	36.3	41.3	15.5	1.9	4.2	0.6	0.2
Construction laborers	47-2061	33.2	40.7	16.5	4.2	4.6	0.6	0.1
Paving, surfacing, and tamping equipment operators	47-2071	30.6	55.5	11.2	2.1	0.6	0.0	0.0
Pile-driver operators(1)	47-2072	20.4	51.9	19.4	4.8	3.0	0.4	0.1
Operating engineers and other construction equipment operators(1)	47-2073	20.4	51.9	19.4	4.8	3.0	0.4	0.1
Drywall and ceiling tile installers(1)	47-2081	45.9	37.7	11.5	2.1	2.3	0.3	0.1
Tapers(1)	47-2082	45.9	37.7	11.5	2.1	2.3	0.3	0.1
Electricians	47-2111	7.5	37.7	31.5	15.5	6.6	0.9	0.3
Glaziers	47-2121	20.5	48.7	21.8	5.4	3.1	0.5	0.0
Insulation workers, floor, ceiling, and wall(1)	47-2131	30.1	45.4	18.2	3.7	2.0	0.1	0.5
Insulation workers, mechanical(1)	47-2132	30.1	45.4	18.2	3.7	2.0	0.1	0.5
Painters, construction and maintenance(1)	47-2141	34.9	38.7	16.2	4.2	4.9	1.0	0.2
Paperhangers(1)	47-2142	34.9	38.7	16.2	4.2	4.9	1.0	0.2
Pipelayers(1)	47-2151	17.4	46.6	24.3	6.8	4.2	0.4	0.2
Plumbers, pipefitters, and steamfitters(1)	47-2152	17.4	46.6	24.3	6.8	4.2	0.4	0.2
Plasterers and stucco masons	47-2161	49.6	36.1	9.2	1.8	3.0	0.2	0.1
Reinforcing iron and rebar workers(1)	47-2171	35.5	42.8	15.2	3.5	2.5	0.3	0.1
Roofers	47-2181	46.6	37.3	11.7	1.9	2.3	0.1	0.1
Sheet metal workers	47-2211	15.1	46.8	26.0	7.8	3.8	0.6	0.0
Structural iron and steel workers	47-2221	16.1	48.2	25.0	6.1	4.3	0.1	0.2
Solar photovoltaic installers(1)	47-2231	19.6	42.6	23.7	6.1	7.6	0.5	0.0
Helpers—brickmasons, blockmasons, stonemasons, and tile and marble setters(1)	47-3011	32.2	42.1	17.1	5.0	3.1	0.1	0.3
Helpers—carpenters(1)	47-3012	32.2	42.1	17.1	5.0	3.1	0.1	0.3
Helpers—electricians(1)	47-3013	32.2	42.1	17.1	5.0	3.1	0.1	0.3
Helpers—painters, paperhangers, plasterers, and stucco masons(1)	47-3014	32.2	42.1	17.1	5.0	3.1	0.1	0.3
Helpers—pipelayers, plumbers, pipefitters, and steamfitters(1)	47-3015	32.2	42.1	17.1	5.0	3.1	0.1	0.3
Helpers—roofers(1)	47-3016	32.2	42.1	17.1	5.0	3.1	0.1	0.3
Helpers, construction trades, all other(1)	47-3019	32.2	42.1	17.1	5.0	3.1	0.1	0.3
Construction and building inspectors	47-4011	2.0	25.6	29.8	15.5	20.9	4.8	1.3
Elevator installers and repairers	47-4021	3.4	49.7	30.2	12.0	4.5	0.2	0.0
Fence erectors	47-4031	39.0	38.2	16.0	2.8	2.4	1.2	0.4
Hazardous materials removal workers	47-4041	23.8	37.1	22.9	6.2	7.2	2.5	0.3
Highway maintenance workers	47-4051	12.6	58.1	19.0	5.8	3.6	1.0	0.0
Rail-track laying and maintenance equipment operators	47-4061	6.2	54.4	31.9	4.7	2.7	0.0	0.0
Septic tank servicers and sewer pipe cleaners(1)	47-4071	19.6	42.6	23.7	6.1	7.6	0.5	0.0
Segmental pavers(1)	47-4091	19.6	42.6	23.7	6.1	7.6	0.5	0.0
Construction and related workers, all other(1)	47-4099	19.6	42.6	23.7	6.1	7.6	0.5	0.0
Derrick operators, oil and gas(1)	47-5011	20.4	46.3	22.7	3.2	6.4	0.5	0.4
Rotary drill operators, oil and gas(1)	47-5012	20.4	46.3	22.7	3.2	6.4	0.5	0.4
Service unit operators, oil, gas, and mining(1)	47-5013	20.4	46.3	22.7	3.2	6.4	0.5	0.4
Earth drillers, except oil and gas	47-5021	17.6	51.6	20.5	6.5	3.7	0.0	0.0
Explosives workers, ordnance handling experts, and blasters	47-5031	9.4	38.7	32.7	8.0	9.6	1.2	0.4
Continuous mining machine operators(1)	47-5041	15.2	50.7	23.6	6.6	3.6	0.3	0.0
Mine cutting and channeling machine operators(1)	47-5042	15.2	50.7	23.6	6.6	3.6	0.3	0.0
Mining machine operators, all other(1)	47-5049	15.2	50.7	23.6	6.6	3.6	0.3	0.0
Rock splitters, quarry(1)	47-5051	19.2	47.4	23.9	4.6	4.0	0.4	0.3
Roof bolters, mining(1)	47-5061	19.2	47.4	23.9	4.6	4.0	0.4	0.3
Roustabouts, oil and gas(1)	47-5071	20.4	46.3	22.7	3.2	6.4	0.5	0.4
Helpers—extraction workers(1)	47-5081	19.2	47.4	23.9	4.6	4.0	0.4	0.3
Extraction workers, all other(1)	47-5099	19.2	47.4	23.9	4.6	4.0	0.4	0.3
First-line supervisors of mechanics, installers, and repairers	49-1011	6.5	35.0	30.4	13.2	12.2	2.3	0.4
Computer, automated teller, and office machine repairers	49-2011	2.3	18.2	30.8	21.3	22.5	4.1	0.8
Radio, cellular, and tower equipment installers and repairs(1)	49-2021	4.3	27.6	34.4	18.0	13.8	1.7	0.3
Telecommunications equipment installers and repairers, except line installers(1)	49-2022	4.3	27.6	34.4	18.0	13.8	1.7	0.3
Avionics technicians	49-2091	2.2	21.1	33.6	29.6	12.5	0.8	0.0
Electric motor, power tool, and related repairers	49-2092	9.4	37.9	27.1	17.8	7.7	0.0	0.1
Electrical and electronics installers and repairers, transportation equipment(1)	49-2093	4.1	31.4	36.8	14.3	13.3	0.1	0.0
Electrical and electronics repairers, commercial and industrial equipment(1)	49-2094	4.1	31.4	36.8	14.3	13.3	0.1	0.0
Electrical and electronics repairers, powerhouse, substation, and relay(1)	49-2095	4.1	31.4	36.8	14.3	13.3	0.1	0.0
Electronic equipment installers and repairers, motor vehicles	49-2096	7.1	36.7	33.9	10.1	10.4	1.5	0.3
Electronic home entertainment equipment installers and repairers	49-2097	7.2	32.0	33.7	14.0	11.2	1.7	0.2
Security and fire alarm systems installers	49-2098	7.3	42.3	29.2	10.8	9.0	0.9	0.5
Aircraft mechanics and service technicians	49-3011	2.5	24.9	39.3	21.3	10.7	0.9	0.3
Automotive body and related repairers	49-3021	24.7	47.4	18.1	6.8	2.6	0.3	0.1
Automotive glass installers and repairers	49-3022	20.8	47.6	24.0	5.1	1.8	0.7	0.0
Automotive service technicians and mechanics	49-3023	17.5	44.8	22.1	11.0	3.8	0.6	0.3

Table A-2. Educational Attainment for Workers 25 Years and Older by Detailed Occupation, 2014–2015—*Continued*

2014 National Employment Matrix title and code		Less than high school diploma	High school diploma or equivalent	Some college, no degree	Associate's degree	Bachelor's degree	Master's degree	Doctoral or professional degree
Bus and truck mechanics and diesel engine specialists	49-3031	14.0	45.7	25.2	11.8	2.6	0.4	0.2
Farm equipment mechanics and service technicians[1]	49-3041	12.1	46.4	25.1	12.3	3.4	0.6	0.1
Mobile heavy equipment mechanics, except engines[1]	49-3042	12.1	46.4	25.1	12.3	3.4	0.6	0.1
Rail car repairers[1]	49-3043	12.1	46.4	25.1	12.3	3.4	0.6	0.1
Motorboat mechanics and service technicians[1]	49-3051	13.4	46.7	24.4	11.2	3.6	0.6	0.1
Motorcycle mechanics[1]	49-3052	13.4	46.7	24.4	11.2	3.6	0.6	0.1
Outdoor power equipment and other small engine mechanics[1]	49-3053	13.4	46.7	24.4	11.2	3.6	0.6	0.1
Bicycle repairers[1]	49-3091	29.3	42.7	17.1	4.9	5.0	0.9	0.1
Recreational vehicle service technicians[1]	49-3092	29.3	42.7	17.1	4.9	5.0	0.9	0.1
Tire repairers and changers[1]	49-3093	29.3	42.7	17.1	4.9	5.0	0.9	0.1
Mechanical door repairers[1]	49-9011	6.7	48.2	31.0	9.1	4.9	0.1	0.0
Control and valve installers and repairers, except mechanical door[1]	49-9012	6.7	48.2	31.0	9.1	4.9	0.1	0.0
Heating, air conditioning, and refrigeration mechanics and installers	49-9021	10.9	40.0	29.7	14.0	4.6	0.6	0.2
Home appliance repairers	49-9031	12.0	40.0	29.4	12.3	5.0	1.0	0.2
Industrial machinery mechanics[1]	49-9041	10.5	41.0	29.5	12.9	5.3	0.7	0.1
Maintenance workers, machinery	49-9043	11.5	44.2	28.8	9.8	5.1	0.6	0.0
Millwrights	49-9044	10.1	44.3	31.5	10.5	3.1	0.4	0.1
Refractory materials repairers, except brickmasons[1]	49-9045	10.5	41.0	29.5	12.9	5.3	0.7	0.1
Electrical power-line installers and repairers	49-9051	4.4	40.7	32.1	14.6	7.1	1.1	0.0
Telecommunications line installers and repairers	49-9052	6.0	38.1	33.1	13.3	8.3	1.0	0.2
Camera and photographic equipment repairers[1]	49-9061	4.1	21.4	28.5	21.4	19.0	4.3	1.3
Medical equipment repairers[1]	49-9062	4.1	21.4	28.5	21.4	19.0	4.3	1.3
Musical instrument repairers and tuners[1]	49-9063	4.1	21.4	28.5	21.4	19.0	4.3	1.3
Watch repairers[1]	49-9064	4.1	21.4	28.5	21.4	19.0	4.3	1.3
Precision instrument and equipment repairers, all other[1]	49-9069	4.1	21.4	28.5	21.4	19.0	4.3	1.3
Maintenance and repair workers, general	49-9071	14.0	40.5	27.1	10.5	6.5	1.1	0.2
Wind turbine service technicians[1]	49-9081	13.8	39.9	26.9	9.7	7.9	1.5	0.3
Coin, vending, and amusement machine servicers and repairers	49-9091	6.6	40.8	28.7	11.2	10.6	1.5	0.6
Commercial divers[1]	49-9092	13.8	39.9	26.9	9.7	7.9	1.5	0.3
Fabric menders, except garment[1]	49-9093	13.8	39.9	26.9	9.7	7.9	1.5	0.3
Locksmiths and safe repairers	49-9094	9.5	46.0	33.0	6.0	4.5	0.9	0.2
Manufactured building and mobile home installers[1]	49-9095	13.8	39.9	26.9	9.7	7.9	1.5	0.3
Riggers	49-9096	7.3	51.6	24.5	7.0	8.8	0.8	0.0
Signal and track switch repairers[1]	49-9097	13.8	39.9	26.9	9.7	7.9	1.5	0.3
Helpers--installation, maintenance, and repair workers	49-9098	32.6	40.3	16.9	7.0	3.3	0.0	0.0
Installation, maintenance, and repair workers, all other[1]	49-9099	13.8	39.9	26.9	9.7	7.9	1.5	0.3
First-line supervisors of production and operating workers	51-1011	10.2	37.8	26.4	9.0	12.8	3.1	0.7
Aircraft structure, surfaces, rigging, and systems assemblers	51-2011	10.5	49.4	27.9	5.1	5.1	0.9	1.0
Coil winders, tapers, and finishers[1]	51-2021	18.8	44.3	21.4	8.4	6.1	0.6	0.3
Electrical and electronic equipment assemblers[1]	51-2022	18.8	44.3	21.4	8.4	6.1	0.6	0.3
Electromechanical equipment assemblers[1]	51-2023	18.8	44.3	21.4	8.4	6.1	0.6	0.3
Engine and other machine assemblers	51-2031	14.9	41.4	26.7	11.4	4.6	0.0	1.0
Structural metal fabricators and fitters	51-2041	15.2	44.7	25.8	9.2	4.6	0.4	0.1
Fiberglass laminators and fabricators[1]	51-2091	17.8	46.6	22.3	6.8	5.7	0.7	0.1
Team assemblers[1]	51-2092	17.8	46.6	22.3	6.8	5.7	0.7	0.1
Timing device assemblers and adjusters[1]	51-2093	17.8	46.6	22.3	6.8	5.7	0.7	0.1
Assemblers and fabricators, all other[1]	51-2099	17.8	46.6	22.3	6.8	5.7	0.7	0.1
Bakers	51-3011	23.4	38.3	20.9	7.3	8.7	0.9	0.5
Butchers and meat cutters[1]	51-3021	32.8	41.9	17.3	3.8	3.6	0.5	0.2
Meat, poultry, and fish cutters and trimmers[1]	51-3022	32.8	41.9	17.3	3.8	3.6	0.5	0.2
Slaughterers and meat packers[1]	51-3023	32.8	41.9	17.3	3.8	3.6	0.5	0.2
Food and tobacco roasting, baking, and drying machine operators and tenders	51-3091	22.8	38.1	25.9	3.9	7.7	1.0	0.6
Food batchmakers	51-3092	20.4	41.6	20.5	8.5	7.8	1.0	0.2
Food cooking machine operators and tenders	51-3093	27.7	37.9	24.7	4.7	5.1	0.0	0.0
Food processing workers, all other	51-3099	29.9	43.8	16.7	4.5	3.9	0.9	0.4
Computer-controlled machine tool operators, metal and plastic[1]	51-4011	6.3	40.1	33.8	12.1	6.7	0.9	0.1
Computer numerically controlled machine tool programmers, metal and plastic[1]	51-4012	6.3	40.1	33.8	12.1	6.7	0.9	0.1
Extruding and drawing machine setters, operators, and tenders, metal and plastic	51-4021	13.3	52.9	26.0	5.2	2.3	0.3	0.0
Forging machine setters, operators, and tenders, metal and plastic	51-4022	16.4	54.8	17.9	4.9	6.1	0.0	0.0
Rolling machine setters, operators, and tenders, metal and plastic	51-4023	18.8	45.5	22.6	6.1	5.6	1.4	0.0
Cutting, punching, and press machine setters, operators, and tenders, metal and plastic[1]	51-4031	21.1	50.2	19.3	4.9	3.9	0.5	0.1
Drilling and boring machine tool setters, operators, and tenders, metal and plastic[1]	51-4032	21.1	50.2	19.3	4.9	3.9	0.5	0.1
Grinding, lapping, polishing, and buffing machine tool setters, operators, and tenders, metal and plastic[1]	51-4033	21.1	50.2	19.3	4.9	3.9	0.5	0.1
Lathe and turning machine tool setters, operators, and tenders, metal and plastic[1]	51-4034	21.1	50.2	19.3	4.9	3.9	0.5	0.1
Milling and planing machine setters, operators, and tenders, metal and plastic[1]	51-4035	21.1	50.2	19.3	4.9	3.9	0.5	0.1
Machinists	51-4041	10.7	45.3	27.9	11.9	3.8	0.3	0.1
Metal-refining furnace operators and tenders[1]	51-4051	13.8	54.3	19.2	7.9	4.3	0.5	0.0
Pourers and casters, metal[1]	51-4052	13.8	54.3	19.2	7.9	4.3	0.5	0.0
Model makers, metal and plastic[1]	51-4061	16.6	47.0	21.5	7.8	7.0	0.2	0.0
Patternmakers, metal and plastic[1]	51-4062	16.6	47.0	21.5	7.8	7.0	0.2	0.0
Foundry mold and coremakers[1]	51-4071	16.6	47.0	21.5	7.8	7.0	0.2	0.0
Molding, coremaking, and casting machine setters, operators, and tenders, metal and plastic[1]	51-4072	16.6	47.0	21.5	7.8	7.0	0.2	0.0

Table A-2. Educational Attainment for Workers 25 Years and Older by Detailed Occupation, 2014–2015—*Continued*

2014 National Employment Matrix title and code		Less than high school diploma	High school diploma or equivalent	Some college, no degree	Associate's degree	Bachelor's degree	Master's degree	Doctoral or professional degree
Multiple machine tool setters, operators, and tenders, metal and plastic[1]	51-4081	19.5	47.6	22.4	6.4	3.5	0.6	0.1
Tool and die makers	51-4111	6.5	41.8	32.2	15.7	3.1	0.4	0.2
Welders, cutters, solderers, and brazers[1]	51-4121	20.4	46.8	23.0	7.1	2.3	0.3	0.1
Welding, soldering, and brazing machine setters, operators, and tenders[1]	51-4122	20.4	46.8	23.0	7.1	2.3	0.3	0.1
Heat treating equipment setters, operators, and tenders, metal and plastic[1]	51-4191	19.5	47.6	22.4	6.4	3.5	0.6	0.1
Layout workers, metal and plastic[1]	51-4192	19.5	47.6	22.4	6.4	3.5	0.6	0.1
Plating and coating machine setters, operators, and tenders, metal and plastic[1]	51-4193	19.5	47.6	22.4	6.4	3.5	0.6	0.1
Tool grinders, filers, and sharpeners[1]	51-4194	19.5	47.6	22.4	6.4	3.5	0.6	0.1
Metal workers and plastic workers, all other[1]	51-4199	19.5	47.6	22.4	6.4	3.5	0.6	0.1
Prepress technicians and workers	51-5111	8.7	32.5	28.0	15.0	13.3	2.2	0.2
Printing press operators	51-5112	12.2	45.9	25.3	7.3	8.5	0.7	0.1
Print binding and finishing workers	51-5113	10.2	54.1	21.6	5.0	7.2	1.7	0.1
Laundry and dry-cleaning workers	51-6011	32.9	41.5	16.1	3.8	4.7	0.8	0.2
Pressers, textile, garment, and related materials	51-6021	45.3	36.0	12.5	3.0	3.0	0.1	0.0
Sewing machine operators	51-6031	42.1	35.3	12.5	4.6	4.8	0.6	0.1
Shoe and leather workers and repairers[1]	51-6041	27.4	45.3	13.4	3.9	5.5	3.3	1.2
Shoe machine operators and tenders[1]	51-6042	27.4	45.3	13.4	3.9	5.5	3.3	1.2
Sewers, hand[1]	51-6051	26.1	31.3	20.0	7.1	12.2	2.8	0.5
Tailors, dressmakers, and custom sewers[1]	51-6052	26.1	31.3	20.0	7.1	12.2	2.8	0.5
Textile bleaching and dyeing machine operators and tenders[1]	51-6061	29.6	46.5	12.9	4.8	5.0	0.6	0.6
Textile cutting machine setters, operators, and tenders[1]	51-6062	29.6	46.5	12.9	4.8	5.0	0.6	0.6
Textile knitting and weaving machine setters, operators, and tenders	51-6063	25.5	39.7	20.1	1.3	8.8	3.6	0.9
Textile winding, twisting, and drawing out machine setters, operators, and tenders	51-6064	36.1	42.7	15.1	1.9	0.5	0.8	2.9
Extruding and forming machine setters, operators, and tenders, synthetic and glass fibers[1]	51-6091	31.5	37.3	14.2	6.1	9.5	1.2	0.3
Fabric and apparel patternmakers[1]	51-6092	31.5	37.3	14.2	6.1	9.5	1.2	0.3
Upholsterers	51-6093	33.2	39.1	16.6	5.4	3.7	1.8	0.3
Textile, apparel, and furnishings workers, all other[1]	51-6099	31.5	37.3	14.2	6.1	9.5	1.2	0.3
Cabinetmakers and bench carpenters	51-7011	19.1	44.0	19.4	7.3	8.7	1.3	0.1
Furniture finishers	51-7021	26.1	40.7	20.2	3.6	7.5	1.8	0.0
Model makers, wood[1]	51-7031	18.4	36.7	21.1	9.4	11.5	2.5	0.4
Patternmakers, wood[1]	51-7032	18.4	36.7	21.1	9.4	11.5	2.5	0.4
Sawing machine setters, operators, and tenders, wood	51-7041	29.7	49.6	14.1	4.3	2.1	0.0	0.0
Woodworking machine setters, operators, and tenders, except sawing	51-7042	23.6	55.4	11.1	5.1	4.0	0.8	0.0
Woodworkers, all other[1]	51-7099	18.4	36.7	21.1	9.4	11.5	2.5	0.4
Nuclear power reactor operators[1]	51-8011	1.4	30.6	32.1	18.3	14.6	2.7	0.3
Power distributors and dispatchers[1]	51-8012	1.4	30.6	32.1	18.3	14.6	2.7	0.3
Power plant operators[1]	51-8013	1.4	30.6	32.1	18.3	14.6	2.7	0.3
Stationary engineers and boiler operators	51-8021	6.1	39.2	31.7	10.6	10.1	1.7	0.6
Water and wastewater treatment plant and system operators	51-8031	3.9	38.2	33.5	12.7	9.9	1.3	0.5
Chemical plant and system operators[1]	51-8091	4.8	38.6	31.9	11.3	12.6	0.6	0.1
Gas plant operators[1]	51-8092	4.8	38.6	31.9	11.3	12.6	0.6	0.1
Petroleum pump system operators, refinery operators, and gaugers[1]	51-8093	4.8	38.6	31.9	11.3	12.6	0.6	0.1
Plant and system operators, all other[1]	51-8099	4.8	38.6	31.9	11.3	12.6	0.6	0.1
Chemical equipment operators and tenders[1]	51-9011	6.6	35.8	25.2	9.0	19.2	3.4	0.8
Separating, filtering, clarifying, precipitating, and still machine setters, operators, and tenders[1]	51-9012	6.6	35.8	25.2	9.0	19.2	3.4	0.8
Crushing, grinding, and polishing machine setters, operators, and tenders[1]	51-9021	19.4	45.1	22.4	5.5	6.6	0.6	0.4
Grinding and polishing workers, hand[1]	51-9022	19.4	45.1	22.4	5.5	6.6	0.6	0.4
Mixing and blending machine setters, operators, and tenders[1]	51-9023	19.4	45.1	22.4	5.5	6.6	0.6	0.4
Cutters and trimmers, hand[1]	51-9031	30.4	46.9	14.9	4.2	2.8	0.6	0.2
Cutting and slicing machine setters, operators, and tenders[1]	51-9032	30.4	46.9	14.9	4.2	2.8	0.6	0.2
Extruding, forming, pressing, and compacting machine setters, operators, and tenders	51-9041	18.6	51.7	20.2	4.4	3.1	1.4	0.6
Furnace, kiln, oven, drier, and kettle operators and tenders	51-9051	26.0	44.1	20.0	4.7	5.1	0.0	0.1
Inspectors, testers, sorters, samplers, and weighers	51-9061	10.7	36.3	26.4	10.0	13.1	2.8	0.6
Jewelers and precious stone and metal workers	51-9071	18.1	30.6	22.3	6.7	19.1	2.2	1.1
Dental laboratory technicians[1]	51-9081	6.0	30.3	29.7	16.3	14.8	1.8	1.1
Medical appliance technicians[1]	51-9082	6.0	30.3	29.7	16.3	14.8	1.8	1.1
Ophthalmic laboratory technicians[1]	51-9083	6.0	30.3	29.7	16.3	14.8	1.8	1.1
Packaging and filling machine operators and tenders	51-9111	34.7	42.1	14.9	3.8	3.7	0.5	0.3
Coating, painting, and spraying machine setters, operators, and tenders[1]	51-9121	22.6	47.9	19.2	5.6	4.1	0.4	0.1
Painters, transportation equipment[1]	51-9122	22.6	47.9	19.2	5.6	4.1	0.4	0.1
Painting, coating, and decorating workers[1]	51-9123	22.6	47.9	19.2	5.6	4.1	0.4	0.1
Semiconductor processors[1]	51-9141	20.1	45.5	21.4	6.3	5.6	0.9	0.2
Photographic process workers and processing machine operators	51-9151	3.2	32.1	28.7	9.1	23.6	2.6	0.8
Adhesive bonding machine operators and tenders	51-9191	17.3	55.3	21.8	2.1	3.0	0.5	0.0
Cleaning, washing, and metal pickling equipment operators and tenders[1]	51-9192	20.1	45.5	21.4	6.3	5.6	0.9	0.2
Cooling and freezing equipment operators and tenders[1]	51-9193	20.1	45.5	21.4	6.3	5.6	0.9	0.2
Etchers and engravers	51-9194	7.9	38.1	27.3	10.3	13.4	2.2	0.7
Molders, shapers, and casters, except metal and plastic	51-9195	21.9	37.2	18.6	4.3	13.1	3.7	1.3
Paper goods machine setters, operators, and tenders	51-9196	15.1	50.5	24.1	4.9	5.1	0.2	0.0
Tire builders	51-9197	2.8	55.3	30.6	6.0	4.7	0.6	0.0

Table A-2. Educational Attainment for Workers 25 Years and Older by Detailed Occupation, 2014–2015—*Continued*

2014 National Employment Matrix title and code		Less than high school diploma	High school diploma or equivalent	Some college, no degree	Associate's degree	Bachelor's degree	Master's degree	Doctoral or professional degree
Helpers—production workers	51-9198	35.9	36.1	15.0	4.3	6.7	1.4	0.5
Production workers, all other[1]	51-9199	20.1	45.5	21.4	6.3	5.6	0.9	0.2
Aircraft cargo handling supervisors[1]	53-1011	8.2	34.5	29.5	8.5	16.3	2.7	0.3
First-line supervisors of helpers, laborers, and material movers, hand[1]	53-1021	8.2	34.5	29.5	8.5	16.3	2.7	0.3
First-line supervisors of transportation and material-moving machine and vehicle operators[1]	53-1031	8.2	34.5	29.5	8.5	16.3	2.7	0.3
Airline pilots, copilots, and flight engineers[1]	53-2011	0.2	4.7	12.3	7.9	59.9	12.9	2.1
Commercial pilots[1]	53-2012	0.2	4.7	12.3	7.9	59.9	12.9	2.1
Air traffic controllers[1]	53-2021	0.6	10.2	34.2	14.2	34.4	5.2	1.2
Airfield operations specialists[1]	53-2022	0.6	10.2	34.2	14.2	34.4	5.2	1.2
Flight attendants	53-2031	1.4	12.1	33.8	13.8	32.9	4.6	1.5
Ambulance drivers and attendants, except emergency medical technicians	53-3011	5.8	36.8	35.8	7.9	10.6	2.6	0.6
Bus drivers, transit and intercity[1]	53-3021	8.4	44.0	29.6	8.5	7.2	2.0	0.4
Bus drivers, school or special client[1]	53-3022	8.4	44.0	29.6	8.5	7.2	2.0	0.4
Driver/sales workers[1]	53-3031	16.4	48.1	23.2	6.0	5.3	0.8	0.2
Heavy and tractor-trailer truck drivers[1]	53-3032	16.4	48.1	23.2	6.0	5.3	0.8	0.2
Light truck or delivery services drivers[1]	53-3033	16.4	48.1	23.2	6.0	5.3	0.8	0.2
Taxi drivers and chauffeurs	53-3041	14.5	36.4	23.7	7.7	13.4	3.5	0.7
Motor vehicle operators, all other	53-3099	11.3	43.6	23.3	9.1	10.3	1.7	0.8
Locomotive engineers[1]	53-4011	2.4	40.1	35.0	10.9	10.0	1.0	0.6
Locomotive firers[1]	53-4012	2.4	40.1	35.0	10.9	10.0	1.0	0.6
Rail yard engineers, dinkey operators, and hostlers[1]	53-4013	2.4	40.1	35.0	10.9	10.0	1.0	0.6
Railroad brake, signal, and switch operators[1]	53-4021	4.0	41.3	36.6	9.5	6.9	1.7	0.0
Railroad conductors and yardmasters	53-4031	0.9	35.6	37.3	10.9	13.7	0.9	0.7
Subway and streetcar operators[1]	53-4041	4.0	41.3	36.6	9.5	6.9	1.7	0.0
Rail transportation workers, all other[1]	53-4099	4.0	41.3	36.6	9.5	6.9	1.7	0.0
Sailors and marine oilers[1]	53-5011	9.8	38.4	30.3	4.9	11.7	4.8	0.2
Captains, mates, and pilots of water vessels[1]	53-5021	8.9	35.7	26.5	5.5	19.4	2.8	1.3
Motorboat operators[1]	53-5022	8.9	35.7	26.5	5.5	19.4	2.8	1.3
Ship engineers[1]	53-5031	9.8	38.4	30.3	4.9	11.7	4.8	0.2
Bridge and lock tenders[1]	53-6011	3.5	41.8	29.2	12.1	10.3	2.5	0.6
Parking lot attendants	53-6021	16.1	36.4	25.4	7.4	12.6	1.8	0.3
Automotive and watercraft service attendants	53-6031	17.5	46.3	23.7	4.9	6.0	1.4	0.2
Traffic technicians[1]	53-6041	3.5	41.8	29.2	12.1	10.3	2.5	0.6
Transportation inspectors	53-6051	6.1	34.1	29.1	15.5	11.5	3.2	0.5
Transportation attendants, except flight attendants	53-6061	11.6	39.2	30.6	6.3	10.4	1.5	0.4
Transportation workers, all other[1]	53-6099	3.5	41.8	29.2	12.1	10.3	2.5	0.6
Conveyor operators and tenders[1]	53-7011	20.1	53.4	12.4	7.2	6.2	0.4	0.3
Crane and tower operators	53-7021	17.5	49.1	24.7	4.5	3.5	0.7	0.1
Dredge operators[1]	53-7031	20.5	53.8	18.2	3.9	2.8	0.7	0.0
Excavating and loading machine and dragline operators[1]	53-7032	20.5	53.8	18.2	3.9	2.8	0.7	0.0
Loading machine operators, underground mining[1]	53-7033	20.5	53.8	18.2	3.9	2.8	0.7	0.0
Hoist and winch operators[1]	53-7041	20.1	53.4	12.4	7.2	6.2	0.4	0.3
Industrial truck and tractor operators	53-7051	22.0	51.1	19.7	4.1	2.7	0.3	0.0
Cleaners of vehicles and equipment	53-7061	30.9	42.0	17.1	4.7	4.3	0.8	0.2
Laborers and freight, stock, and material movers, hand	53-7062	18.9	46.8	21.8	5.9	5.6	0.7	0.2
Machine feeders and offbearers	53-7063	20.0	47.0	20.9	5.8	5.0	1.4	0.0
Packers and packagers, hand	53-7064	35.9	39.9	15.5	3.9	4.2	0.5	0.2
Gas compressor and gas pumping station operators[1]	53-7071	11.2	47.4	26.0	6.7	8.3	0.4	0.0
Pump operators, except wellhead pumpers[1]	53-7072	11.2	47.4	26.0	6.7	8.3	0.4	0.0
Wellhead pumpers[1]	53-7073	11.2	47.4	26.0	6.7	8.3	0.4	0.0
Refuse and recyclable material collectors	53-7081	27.8	47.1	16.8	4.9	2.9	0.4	0.1
Mine shuttle car operators[1]	53-7111	16.7	49.1	21.9	7.3	4.0	0.8	0.2
Tank car, truck, and ship loaders[1]	53-7121	16.7	49.1	21.9	7.3	4.0	0.8	0.2
Material moving workers, all other[1]	53-7199	16.7	49.1	21.9	7.3	4.0	0.8	0.2

[1] Data for this occupation is shared with other occupations; see http://www.bls.gov/emp/classifications-crosswalks/NEM_OccCode_ACS_Crosswalk.xlsx for details.
Data Source: 2014 and 2015 American Community Survey Public Use Microdata, U.S. Department of Commerce, U.S. Census Bureau.
Table Source: Employment Projections program, U.S. Bureau of Labor Statistics.

Table A-3. Fastest Growing Occupations, 2014 and Projected 2024 (Numbers in thousands)

2014 National Employment Matrix title and code		Employment		Change, 2014-24		Median annual wage, 2016[1]
		2014	2024	Number	Percent	
Total, All Occupations	00-0000	150,539.9	160,328.8	9,788.9	6.5	$37,040
Wind turbine service technicians	49-9081	4.4	9.2	4.8	108.0	$52,260
Occupational therapy assistants	31-2011	33.0	47.1	14.1	42.7	$59,010
Physical therapist assistants	31-2021	78.7	110.7	31.9	40.6	$56,610
Physical therapist aides	31-2022	50.0	69.5	19.5	39.0	$25,680
Home health aides	31-1011	913.5	1,261.9	348.4	38.1	$22,600
Commercial divers	49-9092	4.4	6.0	1.6	36.9	$49,090
Nurse practitioners	29-1171	126.9	171.7	44.7	35.2	$100,910
Physical therapists	29-1123	210.9	282.7	71.8	34.0	$85,400
Statisticians	15-2041	30.0	40.1	10.1	33.8	$80,500
Ambulance drivers and attendants, except emergency medical technicians	53-3011	19.6	26.1	6.5	33.0	$23,850
Occupational therapy aides	31-2012	8.8	11.6	2.7	30.6	$28,330
Physician assistants	29-1071	94.4	123.2	28.7	30.4	$101,480
Operations research analysts	15-2031	91.3	118.9	27.6	30.2	$79,200
Personal financial advisors	13-2052	249.4	323.2	73.9	29.6	$90,530
Cartographers and photogrammetrists	17-1021	12.3	15.9	3.6	29.3	$62,750
Genetic counselors	29-9092	2.4	3.1	0.7	28.8	$74,120
Interpreters and translators	27-3091	61.0	78.5	17.5	28.7	$46,120
Audiologists	29-1181	13.2	16.9	3.8	28.6	$75,980
Hearing aid specialists	29-2092	5.9	7.5	1.6	27.2	$50,250
Optometrists	29-1041	40.6	51.6	11.0	27.0	$106,140
Forensic science technicians	19-4092	14.4	18.2	3.8	26.6	$56,750
Web developers	15-1134	148.5	188.0	39.5	26.6	$66,130
Occupational therapists	29-1122	114.6	145.1	30.4	26.5	$81,910
Diagnostic medical sonographers	29-2032	60.7	76.7	16.0	26.4	$69,650
Personal care aides	39-9021	1,768.4	2,226.5	458.1	25.9	$21,920
Phlebotomists	31-9097	112.7	140.8	28.1	24.9	$32,710
Ophthalmic medical technicians	29-2057	37.0	46.1	9.1	24.7	$35,530
Nurse midwives	29-1161	5.3	6.6	1.3	24.6	$99,770
Solar photovoltaic installers	47-2231	5.9	7.4	1.4	24.3	$39,240
Emergency medical technicians and paramedics	29-2041	241.2	299.6	58.5	24.2	$32,670

[1] Data are from the Occupational Employment Statistics program, U.S. Bureau of Labor Statistics.
Source: Employment Projections program, U.S. Bureau of Labor Statistics.

Table A-4. Fastest Declining Occupations, 2014 and Projected 2024 (Numbers in thousands)

2014 National Employment Matrix title and code		Employment		Change, 2014-24		Median annual wage, 2016[1]
		2014	2024	Number	Percent	
Total, All Occupations	00-0000	150,539.9	160,328.8	9,788.9	6.5	$37,040
Locomotive firers	53-4012	1.7	0.5	-1.2	-69.9	$58,230
Electronic equipment installers and repairers, motor vehicles	49-2096	11.5	5.8	-5.8	-50.0	$32,220
Telephone operators	43-2021	13.1	7.5	-5.5	-42.4	$37,000
Postal service mail sorters, processors, and processing machine operators	43-5053	117.6	78.0	-39.7	-33.7	$56,220
Switchboard operators, including answering service	43-2011	112.4	75.4	-37.0	-32.9	$28,030
Photographic process workers and processing machine operators	51-9151	28.8	19.4	-9.5	-32.9	$26,470
Shoe machine operators and tenders	51-6042	3.5	2.5	-1.1	-30.5	$26,150
Manufactured building and mobile home installers	49-9095	4.0	2.8	-1.2	-30.0	$29,810
Foundry mold and coremakers	51-4071	12.0	8.7	-3.3	-27.7	$34,790
Sewing machine operators	51-6031	153.9	112.2	-41.7	-27.1	$23,670
Pourers and casters, metal	51-4052	9.8	7.2	-2.6	-26.6	$36,180
Postal service clerks	43-5051	69.6	51.3	-18.3	-26.2	$56,790
Postmasters and mail superintendents	11-9131	17.3	12.8	-4.6	-26.2	$71,670
Postal service mail carriers	43-5052	297.4	219.4	-78.1	-26.2	$58,110
Textile knitting and weaving machine setters, operators, and tenders	51-6063	27.9	20.6	-7.3	-26.2	$27,470
Fabric and apparel patternmakers	51-6092	5.4	4.0	-1.4	-26.0	$39,650
Textile cutting machine setters, operators, and tenders	51-6062	14.3	10.6	-3.7	-25.7	$26,090
Watch repairers	49-9064	2.7	2.0	-0.7	-25.7	$36,740
Molding, coremaking, and casting machine setters, operators, and tenders, metal and plastic	51-4072	129.5	97.2	-32.3	-25.0	$30,480
Prepress technicians and workers	51-5111	36.5	27.5	-9.0	-24.6	$38,930
Extruding and drawing machine setters, operators, and tenders, metal and plastic	51-4021	73.4	55.5	-17.9	-24.4	$33,870
Textile bleaching and dyeing machine operators and tenders	51-6061	11.7	8.9	-2.8	-23.9	$27,270
Patternmakers, metal and plastic	51-4062	3.8	2.9	-0.9	-23.4	$44,210
Grinding, lapping, polishing, and buffing machine tool setters, operators, and tenders, metal and plastic	51-4033	71.4	55.8	-15.7	-21.9	$32,890
Textile winding, twisting, and drawing out machine setters, operators, and tenders	51-6064	26.0	20.3	-5.6	-21.7	$27,500
Model makers, metal and plastic	51-4061	6.2	4.9	-1.3	-21.5	$48,550
Forging machine setters, operators, and tenders, metal and plastic	51-4022	21.6	17.0	-4.6	-21.5	$36,930
Desktop publishers	43-9031	14.8	11.7	-3.1	-21.0	$41,090
Parking enforcement workers	33-3041	9.4	7.4	-2.0	-20.8	$37,950
Milling and planing machine setters, operators, and tenders, metal and plastic	51-4035	22.4	17.8	-4.6	-20.6	$39,840

(1) Data are from the Occupational Employment Statistics program, U.S. Bureau of Labor Statistics.
Source: Employment Projections program, U.S. Bureau of Labor Statistics.

PART B
STATES

- In 2015, 62.7 percent of people age 16 and older were in the labor force—67.7 percent of men and 58 percent of women. Labor force participation shows the proportion of the population who are working or looking for work. People who are not in the labor force include those who are retired, full-time students, caring for home and family, unable to work because of disability, or other reasons.

- Minnesota, Nebraska, and the District of Columbia have the highest labor force participation, about 69 percent. At 52.8 percent, West Virginia had the lowest participation. Utah had the highest participation among men (75.9), while its labor force participation among women (59.2) was lower than 19 states and the District of Columbia. DC had the highest participation among women (66.8) and the rate for men (71.5) was even higher.

- Labor force participation varied greatly by age, with the highest (81.5) among people age 25 to 44, followed closely (79.7) by those age 45 to 54, with markedly lower levels in the youngest and oldest age groups with large numbers of students and retirees.

- The Latino population had the highest labor force participation (66.6), followed by Asians at 64.3, with the White and Black populations both at 61.6. These proportions varied widely among the states, especially in states with small populations and little racial or ethnic diversity.

- Labor force participation by educational attainment ranged from 45 percent for those with no high school diploma to 74.8 percent for those with a Bachelor's degree or more. For all education levels, the highest labor force participation was among those who speak Spanish at home, with the lowest levels among those who speak only English at home.

- In 2015, the civilian unemployment rate was 6.3 percent, with no significant difference between men and women. The highest rate was 13.5 for those in the 16- to 24-year-old age group. For those in the prime working ages of 25 to 64, the rate was 5.2 percent.

- Unemployment was highest among the African-American population, with a rate of 11.3, followed by Latinos at 7.4, with Asian and non-Hispanic White rates at 5.2 and 5.0 respectively.

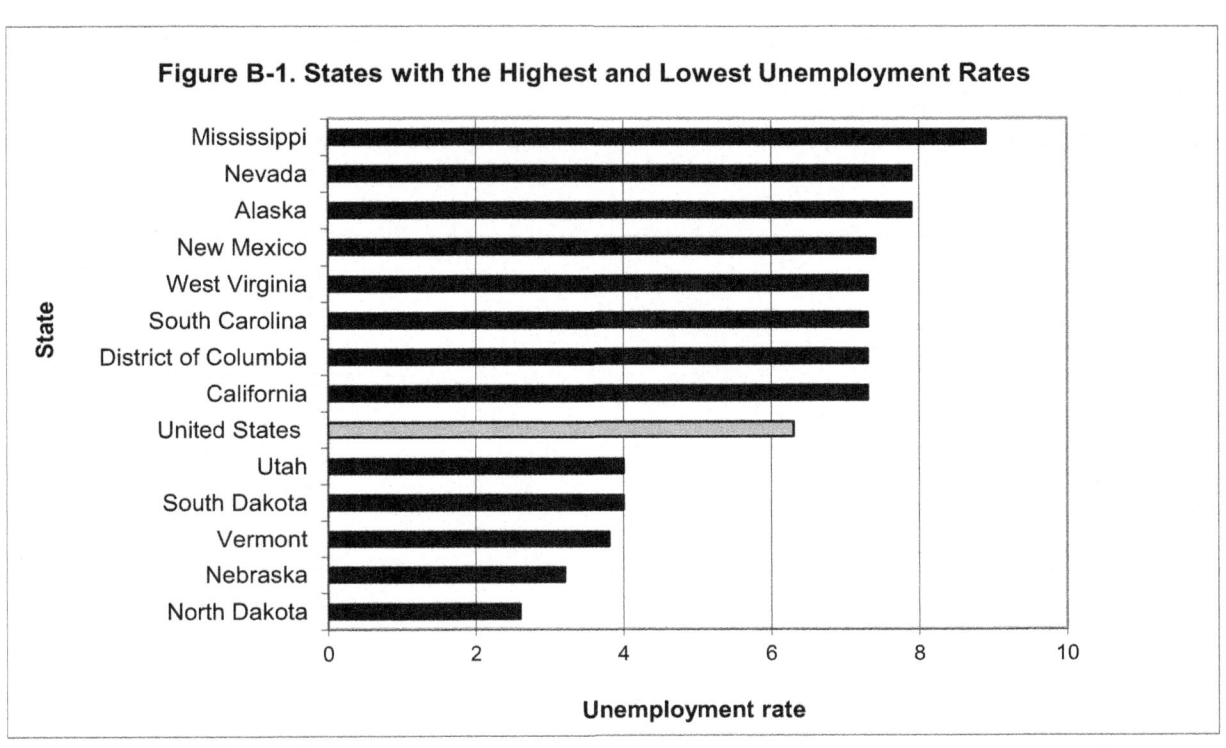

Figure B-1. States with the Highest and Lowest Unemployment Rates

- Those without high school diplomas had an unemployment rate of 9.6, while those with Bachelor's degrees or higher had a rate of 2.9.

- Mississippi had the highest unemployment rate, at 8.9, and it was higher for women (9.7) than for men (8.1). Alaska and Nevada also had high rates, both at 7.9, with higher rates for men than for women. The lowest rate was North Dakota's 2.6, followed closely by Nebraska's 3.2.

- Most workers were employed in private for-profit wage and salary jobs, accounting for 72.3 percent of all workers, with 68.8 percent of them employees and 3.5 percent employees of their own incorporated businesses.

- Self-employed individuals represented 6.1 percent of the labor force. Montana had the highest proportion of self-employed workers who had not incorporated—9.5 percent. Maine, Vermont, South Dakota, and California also had high levels of self-employed individuals.

- Government workers accounted for 13.5 percent of the labor force. At 24.5 percent, Alaska had the highest proportion of government workers, essentially the same level as the District of Columbia's 24.4 percent. New Mexico, Maryland, and Wyoming also had high levels of government workers—20 percent or more.

- At the national level, 37.1 percent of employees are in Management, business, science, and arts occupations, the largest occupation group. Sales and office occupations (23.6 percent) and Service occupations (18 percent) are also large groupings, and the lowest numbers are in Production, transportation, and material moving occupations (12.3 percent) and Natural resources, construction, and maintenance occupations (9 percent).

- In half of the states, the level of employment in the Production, transportation, and material moving occupations is above the national average of 12.3 percent, led by Indiana where 18.8 percent of employees are in this category, and other states with high levels of manufacturing industries.

- There are 30 states—especially those with mining and extraction industries—with higher than average levels of employment in Natural resources, construction, and maintenance occupations. Wyoming had the highest employment in this category (15.8 percent) followed by Montana and North Dakota, both over 13 percent.

- More than one-fifth of employees work in the Educational services and health care and social assistance group, the highest level in a single industry group. Four other industry groups each included about 10 percent of the workforce: 1/Retail trade; 2/Professional, scientific, and management, and administrative and waste management services; 3/Manufacturing, and 4/Arts, entertainment, and recreation, and accommodation and food services.

- Manufacturing provided jobs for 10.3 percent of the workforce, but the proportion was over 18 percent in Indiana, Wisconsin, and Michigan.

- In Nevada, 25.6 percent of jobs were in the Arts, entertainment, and recreation, and accommodation and food services industries, more than double the national average of 9.8 percent.

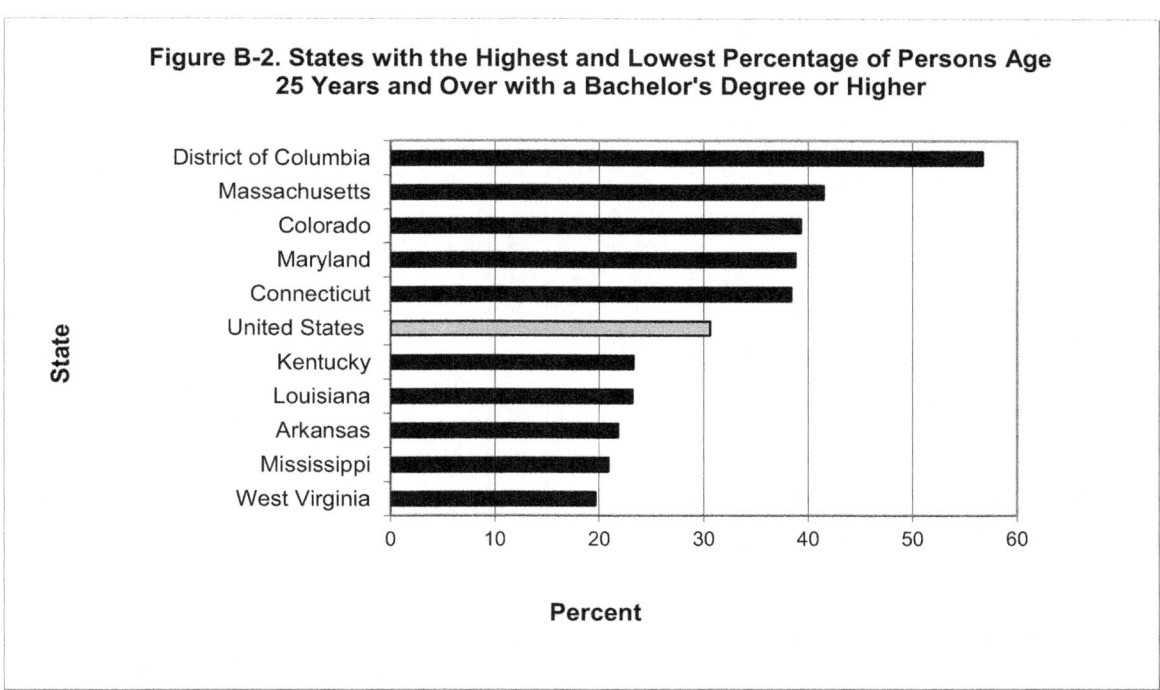

Figure B-2. States with the Highest and Lowest Percentage of Persons Age 25 Years and Over with a Bachelor's Degree or Higher

- At the national level, 30.6 percent of persons aged 25 and older have Bachelor's degrees or higher. This proportion is 56.7 percent in the District of Columbia and about 40 percent in Massachusetts and Colorado.

- For both men and women aged 25 years and older, about 30 percent have Bachelor's degrees or higher. For 18- to 24-year-olds, 12.3 percent of women have achieved this educational level, but only 8.3 percent of men. Since most college students are in this age group, it is relevant to note that women also outnumber men in the proportion who have completed some college or an Associate's degree: 49 percent of women but only 42.8 percent of men.

- More than half of Asian-Americans age 25 and older have Bachelor's degrees or higher. Among non-Hispanic Whites, 34.2 percent are college graduates. 20.2 percent of African-Americans and 14.8 percent of Latinos have Bachelor's degrees or higher.

- Persons with no education beyond high school make up 40.4 percent of the population age 25 and older. In West Virginia, 54.7 percent are in this group, as are nearly half of the populations of Louisiana, Arkansas, and Kentucky.

- 63 percent of occupied housing units are owner occupied. The level is 71.4 percent among college-graduate householders and 48.1 percent among householders who have not completed high school.

- Among 25- to 64-year-olds who have Bachelor's degrees or higher, 90 percent are covered by private health insurance policies, ranging from a low of 86 percent in New Mexico to a high of 95 percent in Nebraska and Kansas.

- Private health insurance covers only 37.4 percent of 25- to 64-year-olds who have not completed high school.

- More than 90 percent of persons with Bachelor's degrees or higher have access to the internet in their households. This access is available to only 57.4 percent of those who have not completed high school, ranging from 72 percent of Utah residents to 39 percent of Mississippi residents.

- Of the 66 million Americans who have Bachelor's degrees or higher, 44 percent earned their first Bachelor's degree in Science or Engineering or related fields. The proportion was higher—60 percent—in the Asian population.

- In 2015, the median earned income for persons age 25 and older was $36,860, with half of workers earning more and half earning less. For those with graduate or professional degrees, the median was $67,286; for those who did not complete high school, the median was $21,320.

- For persons age 16 and older in all occupations, the median earned income in 2015 was $34,656–$40,699 for men and $29,319 for women. The highest medians were about $100,000 for men in the legal and medical occupations. The lowest was about $12,000 for women in food preparation and serving occupations.

Table B-1. Labor Force Participation of the Population Age 16 Years and Older

State	Population 16 years and older	Total civilian labor force age 16 and older	Total civilian labor force participation rate	Men	Women	Age 16 to 19	Age 20 to 24	Age 25 to 44	Age 45 to 54	Age 55 to 64	Age 65 to 74	Age 75 and older	White alone, not of Hispanic origin	Black or African-American alone	Hispanic or Latino	Asian alone
United States	256,167,758	160,652,483	62.7	67.7	58.0	37.3	72.8	81.5	79.7	64.1	25.3	6.3	61.9	61.6	66.6	64.3
Alabama	3,878,471	2,197,662	56.7	61.9	51.9	32.9	70.1	77.1	72.6	53.8	21.2	5.6	56.1	56.6	68.3	60.9
Alaska	571,393	385,165	67.4	70.3	64.2	43.5	72.0	78.7	80.3	69.4	32.0	5.8	68.6	63.6	66.5	73.9
Arizona	5,393,214	3,153,950	58.5	63.2	53.9	37.7	73.3	77.8	77.4	59.2	20.4	5.0	55.5	63.0	64.2	62.1
Arkansas	2,352,507	1,349,814	57.4	62.4	52.7	36.8	72.3	77.2	72.9	55.9	22.6	6.0	56.5	57.7	65.8	67.7
California	31,068,647	19,463,807	62.6	68.7	56.8	28.6	69.4	80.3	79.0	63.8	25.9	6.2	60.2	58.9	66.1	62.7
Colorado	4,333,738	2,916,718	67.3	72.4	62.2	42.5	76.4	83.6	83.8	67.6	27.9	6.5	67.6	64.7	67.2	65.4
Connecticut	2,922,877	1,941,592	66.4	70.7	62.5	40.3	75.0	84.8	83.0	73.9	31.7	7.9	65.6	66.8	69.7	69.7
Delaware	765,250	475,209	62.1	65.9	58.7	38.9	72.9	81.8	82.7	65.4	23.8	7.1	60.1	65.3	66.2	70.9
District of Columbia	564,206	389,414	69.0	71.5	66.8	34.7	62.8	88.0	80.0	60.8	34.2	8.2	78.5	58.0	78.5	76.1
Florida	16,640,196	9,668,285	58.1	62.5	54.0	32.0	71.3	80.8	78.8	61.1	22.0	5.5	54.2	62.0	64.4	62.9
Georgia	7,998,548	4,957,832	62.0	66.5	57.8	32.4	69.0	80.0	78.4	60.2	23.1	6.7	60.4	63.0	67.6	66.2
Hawaii	1,152,884	710,239	61.6	63.9	59.2	32.3	64.8	77.8	82.5	68.6	31.2	6.5	57.3	48.6	60.9	62.6
Idaho	1,270,851	786,377	61.9	67.0	56.9	46.7	74.1	79.8	79.5	61.9	24.1	5.8	61.0	-	69.8	-
Illinois	10,240,058	6,657,355	65.0	70.3	60.1	38.8	75.1	83.5	82.2	66.4	25.8	6.4	65.0	58.7	70.4	66.0
Indiana	5,215,392	3,312,603	63.5	68.7	58.6	43.6	75.4	82.4	80.4	64.7	23.4	6.3	63.3	62.2	70.1	59.6
Iowa	2,475,140	1,669,321	67.4	71.9	63.1	53.6	80.0	87.5	86.2	70.9	28.2	7.5	67.1	69.4	72.5	67.1
Kansas	2,270,108	1,486,201	65.5	70.1	61.0	48.3	74.1	82.3	82.7	70.0	30.0	8.0	65.0	63.3	72.0	62.4
Kentucky	3,531,385	2,062,779	58.4	62.9	54.2	42.1	75.7	77.9	71.7	55.4	21.1	5.4	57.7	61.7	69.0	63.9
Louisiana	3,676,681	2,193,370	59.7	64.0	55.6	33.0	70.0	78.0	74.2	58.3	24.8	7.0	59.9	57.7	66.1	66.6
Maine	1,103,834	685,216	62.1	65.6	58.8	49.9	80.1	81.7	79.6	65.3	28.0	6.9	62.0	63.2	70.5	-
Maryland	4,814,546	3,207,268	66.6	71.0	62.6	35.6	73.0	84.2	84.5	69.4	30.2	7.4	65.1	66.8	75.4	67.7
Massachusetts	5,578,648	3,739,683	67.0	71.2	63.2	44.6	75.0	85.4	83.0	71.6	31.7	7.4	66.7	69.4	68.3	66.5
Michigan	7,982,332	4,862,037	60.9	65.5	56.5	43.2	77.4	81.8	78.7	58.8	20.6	4.8	61.0	57.9	67.0	64.3
Minnesota	4,349,038	3,039,536	69.9	73.8	66.1	53.0	85.3	88.3	87.0	72.7	27.5	6.1	69.6	69.7	76.6	70.2
Mississippi	2,345,713	1,324,308	56.5	60.4	52.8	27.2	68.6	77.3	72.5	54.0	20.9	6.3	56.1	56.9	57.4	54.5
Missouri	4,851,761	3,042,538	62.7	66.8	58.8	43.0	76.5	82.8	79.7	63.0	24.4	5.9	62.5	62.5	69.4	64.1
Montana	829,911	513,209	61.8	65.5	58.1	39.6	73.6	82.2	81.5	64.8	27.4	6.6	62.0	-	63.6	-
Nebraska	1,476,487	1,019,543	69.1	73.8	64.4	51.3	80.7	85.6	86.0	74.6	33.6	8.5	68.9	65.4	74.1	65.3
Nevada	2,292,699	1,446,814	63.1	68.0	58.2	33.9	79.0	81.4	79.6	61.0	23.9	6.0	59.8	62.3	70.6	63.4
New Hampshire	1,102,089	744,971	67.6	72.1	63.3	50.3	81.7	85.4	84.9	73.5	30.1	7.2	67.7	61.7	71.9	66.2
New Jersey	7,193,921	4,684,036	65.1	70.8	59.8	30.2	70.1	83.6	83.0	70.8	30.5	7.4	63.9	64.5	69.3	66.0
New Mexico	1,642,487	950,312	57.9	62.4	53.5	36.5	71.1	75.9	73.3	60.7	24.0	5.5	55.8	55.8	59.8	65.0
New York	16,066,508	10,128,222	63.0	67.9	58.6	30.2	67.5	82.7	80.0	66.0	26.9	6.8	63.2	61.1	64.1	62.5
North Carolina	8,011,388	4,886,759	61.0	65.7	56.6	37.8	70.7	80.3	78.1	61.4	22.6	5.8	59.9	61.0	69.8	64.9
North Dakota	603,014	415,475	68.9	73.1	64.5	48.5	77.9	87.6	85.5	71.8	29.4	8.7	68.8	-	-	-
Ohio	9,295,255	5,863,639	63.1	67.6	58.9	45.3	77.8	83.0	79.6	63.9	24.8	6.1	63.1	61.0	68.9	63.8
Oklahoma	3,053,371	1,854,533	60.7	66.2	55.5	40.2	72.9	78.8	76.2	59.9	25.9	7.8	59.9	59.7	68.9	64.0
Oregon	3,268,296	2,018,994	61.8	66.2	57.5	39.8	76.3	82.6	79.7	60.9	21.8	4.9	60.2	66.7	72.1	65.1
Pennsylvania	10,429,005	6,518,212	62.5	67.3	58.0	41.8	72.8	82.7	81.1	66.8	25.9	6.5	62.8	58.4	64.4	63.5
Rhode Island	870,136	559,733	64.3	68.2	60.8	41.2	74.6	83.9	80.6	69.3	29.1	6.0	64.1	69.4	63.9	59.4
South Carolina	3,931,185	2,336,291	59.4	63.9	55.3	36.1	70.6	80.8	77.0	58.0	22.3	5.8	58.4	59.8	69.4	64.5
South Dakota	671,301	454,996	67.8	72.4	63.2	50.3	82.3	85.1	86.3	73.0	32.6	8.9	68.9	-	69.7	-
Tennessee	5,277,935	3,198,285	60.6	65.5	56.0	41.1	74.0	79.9	75.8	59.1	23.6	6.4	59.3	64.0	71.0	64.9
Texas	21,043,248	13,437,133	63.9	70.5	57.4	34.3	71.0	79.7	79.0	64.1	27.0	7.2	62.4	64.0	65.5	65.7
Utah	2,180,281	1,472,535	67.5	75.9	59.2	51.8	81.0	80.3	80.8	66.4	27.7	6.8	66.8	71.2	72.3	66.6
Vermont	521,616	340,689	65.3	68.4	62.4	43.2	76.0	85.4	83.3	72.8	30.2	8.4	65.6	-	-	-
Virginia	6,721,590	4,317,898	64.2	68.0	60.7	36.8	69.2	81.2	81.4	67.6	28.5	6.8	62.7	63.7	73.3	68.8
Washington	5,741,873	3,613,427	62.9	68.2	57.7	37.0	73.8	80.4	80.2	64.1	24.6	4.7	61.5	68.1	69.7	65.2
West Virginia	1,508,205	796,708	52.8	57.6	48.2	34.7	66.8	74.4	69.8	51.6	18.2	4.9	52.7	53.3	-	57.4
Wisconsin	4,627,790	3,091,421	66.8	70.5	63.2	51.5	82.5	86.3	84.8	69.1	24.0	5.9	66.8	61.0	70.6	71.7
Wyoming	460,730	310,369	67.4	72.3	62.4	49.6	79.0	83.9	85.7	68.8	29.0	8.9	66.7	-	72.9	-

Table B-1. Labor Force Participation of the Population Age 16 Years and Older—*Continued*

Labor force participation rates by educational attainment and language spoken at home for persons age 25 and older

State	Less than high school graduate				High school graduate (includes equivalency)				Some college or Associate's degree				Bachelor's degree or higher			
	All persons who are less than high school graduates	Speak only English at home	Speak Spanish at home	Speak another language at home	All high school graduates (includes equivalency)	Speak only English at home	Speak Spanish at home	Speak another language at home	All persons with some college or Associate's degree:	Speak only English at home	Speak Spanish at home	Speak another language at home	All persons with Bachelor's degree or higher:	Speak only English at home	Speak Spanish at home	Speak another language at home
United States	45.0	35.7	60.1	42.1	56.8	54.8	70.2	58.7	67.7	66.7	75.8	68.8	74.8	74.5	79.9	74.4
Alabama	35.5	31.8	73.2	63.3	50.6	50.1	67.2	56.7	63.8	63.8	64.3	60.8	72.1	72.1	75.5	69.3
Alaska	49.1	49.5	74.6	42.5	66.6	65.3	85.5	70.5	72.6	72.0	74.7	77.2	78.0	77.5	90.5	77.9
Arizona	47.5	39.6	55.5	33.5	52.1	48.7	65.7	49.9	61.8	60.0	71.9	63.8	67.0	65.8	75.2	70.5
Arkansas	37.0	32.1	64.7	50.2	53.3	52.2	76.3	78.8	63.5	63.3	73.2	61.1	71.0	70.9	73.0	70.8
California	52.3	38.3	60.3	36.2	59.5	53.6	72.1	53.5	66.2	63.2	76.8	66.4	74.1	73.6	81.9	72.6
Colorado	53.1	45.8	61.1	47.1	61.6	59.9	71.8	61.7	69.7	69.4	73.1	69.6	75.5	75.7	76.0	72.4
Connecticut	43.8	35.1	55.8	43.2	60.7	58.4	73.6	62.5	71.5	70.6	81.4	68.4	76.8	76.6	81.6	76.7
Delaware	44.2	37.6	63.6	46.4	55.0	54.7	65.1	46.9	67.9	67.5	74.4	70.3	73.4	73.6	79.1	70.7
District of Columbia	44.2	28.0	82.6	55.9	54.7	53.5	67.3	56.7	66.5	64.3	88.8	72.1	84.9	85.2	84.1	83.3
Florida	42.8	37.3	49.3	46.7	53.6	49.6	65.8	59.5	63.1	60.2	73.6	69.2	67.0	64.3	76.3	70.5
Georgia	44.0	36.3	70.1	50.3	57.4	55.9	72.8	64.0	68.7	68.0	77.6	75.5	75.9	75.4	80.2	78.1
Hawaii	42.5	36.2	58.8	46.8	60.7	60.1	56.2	62.8	70.9	70.7	67.3	72.2	71.9	72.4	64.2	70.9
Idaho	48.8	39.3	71.1	30.8	57.1	55.6	78.9	62.6	63.8	63.6	72.3	60.9	70.8	70.7	76.1	70.7
Illinois	45.7	32.7	63.1	40.2	57.3	54.0	75.0	60.4	69.5	68.4	80.4	70.0	77.6	77.6	84.6	75.3
Indiana	41.8	37.1	66.1	46.9	56.8	56.2	74.9	59.1	69.7	69.7	76.5	64.6	77.4	77.8	78.2	72.0
Iowa	46.5	39.6	72.0	55.2	58.3	57.4	77.9	70.9	73.4	73.1	86.4	77.8	77.2	77.1	84.1	76.8
Kansas	49.4	37.2	76.2	49.0	58.0	56.4	76.5	69.4	69.2	68.9	73.1	75.2	76.7	76.7	80.4	74.0
Kentucky	29.6	26.8	74.2	41.3	53.0	52.6	72.3	55.1	66.0	65.8	73.4	66.8	74.5	74.3	81.9	73.8
Louisiana	37.9	36.6	61.9	34.0	55.8	55.7	70.0	47.2	68.4	68.7	70.4	60.9	75.2	75.1	80.8	74.2
Maine	30.0	30.1	76.3	26.7	54.6	54.8	78.9	49.7	67.7	68.1	66.6	60.0	71.9	72.3	74.9	63.3
Maryland	48.7	36.3	77.7	46.1	61.3	59.3	81.3	65.8	70.6	70.0	80.8	71.5	78.1	77.8	84.8	77.8
Massachusetts	41.4	34.8	53.4	41.7	59.5	56.6	72.8	67.2	70.4	69.2	77.2	74.4	78.2	78.3	82.4	76.9
Michigan	36.4	33.6	60.4	37.2	50.9	50.6	65.7	50.4	66.0	66.0	68.4	64.1	73.2	73.1	76.1	73.5
Minnesota	47.1	39.7	76.3	46.8	58.3	57.2	76.6	67.4	73.9	73.6	79.2	77.4	78.8	78.5	87.6	80.8
Mississippi	36.0	34.7	60.0	38.8	53.5	53.3	54.0	67.2	65.5	65.4	66.3	71.7	71.3	71.5	72.5	62.9
Missouri	39.7	36.6	68.9	52.5	55.0	54.5	76.6	58.3	68.2	68.0	73.8	73.7	75.9	75.9	78.2	74.7
Montana	41.1	39.8	70.4	41.9	56.6	55.9	78.6	78.3	64.0	64.2	59.3	54.9	71.8	71.8	71.1	73.9
Nebraska	53.5	44.2	70.7	50.4	59.6	58.8	75.0	50.4	73.1	73.1	82.7	63.5	79.3	79.5	80.1	74.2
Nevada	55.8	44.1	67.9	34.3	61.1	57.7	77.3	52.3	66.1	63.3	80.1	71.7	69.1	68.2	78.1	69.7
New Hampshire	41.7	39.8	68.6	39.8	60.6	61.1	70.3	47.5	71.5	71.8	70.7	65.2	75.6	75.9	68.3	73.6
New Jersey	46.1	34.2	61.1	39.2	58.8	55.6	71.1	61.0	72.1	70.2	81.3	72.0	77.1	76.9	83.2	76.0
New Mexico	42.7	41.3	45.8	30.1	55.5	55.0	55.9	57.5	62.6	62.7	61.7	64.5	66.3	65.6	68.4	70.5
New York	43.3	35.9	52.8	42.1	56.5	53.9	66.3	59.2	69.2	68.0	76.6	68.6	77.5	77.5	81.7	75.9
North Carolina	42.8	33.6	74.3	51.9	55.0	53.8	72.4	59.7	66.9	66.5	77.5	67.2	73.6	73.4	77.4	74.5
North Dakota	38.8	35.9	85.4	42.5	63.2	63.2	86.9	55.3	73.3	73.4	67.7	72.4	80.2	80.1	83.2	82.0
Ohio	35.7	33.5	55.5	45.4	55.6	55.3	68.5	57.5	69.0	69.0	73.2	67.0	76.6	76.8	83.3	73.0
Oklahoma	44.7	36.5	71.5	49.7	55.9	54.9	72.7	56.9	65.1	64.4	78.9	71.0	73.0	72.8	77.2	74.7
Oregon	52.9	41.1	75.1	53.0	53.9	51.6	80.0	60.2	62.3	61.3	77.4	68.3	70.4	70.1	75.3	71.5
Pennsylvania	36.6	32.6	50.0	46.1	55.2	54.7	65.3	57.2	70.5	70.4	74.0	68.7	76.0	76.2	76.2	73.2
Rhode Island	41.6	34.9	56.0	41.0	58.5	57.9	62.2	58.8	69.9	70.0	72.8	65.5	76.7	76.6	83.3	75.0
South Carolina	37.7	33.0	72.0	50.7	55.7	55.0	72.8	62.5	65.8	65.5	74.8	66.0	71.5	71.2	76.5	75.3
South Dakota	46.7	41.9	85.8	58.0	61.2	61.0	66.1	64.8	73.6	73.6	72.6	71.8	76.4	76.3	78.1	78.7
Tennessee	35.8	30.7	75.0	53.4	56.3	55.5	79.1	64.1	66.8	66.6	72.2	66.9	74.8	74.8	79.1	73.7
Texas	51.6	40.1	57.4	46.6	60.9	57.5	69.0	58.3	69.3	67.6	75.3	70.4	76.1	75.4	80.4	76.1
Utah	58.6	50.2	71.1	52.2	62.1	60.6	71.4	66.1	67.8	67.1	78.3	69.4	73.4	73.1	80.8	71.9
Vermont	36.8	36.0	89.5	40.1	62.5	62.7	69.6	55.6	69.2	69.5	68.7	64.9	73.4	73.5	71.8	71.5
Virginia	44.0	35.3	76.3	49.5	59.7	57.9	79.1	64.3	69.2	68.4	80.6	72.0	77.6	77.0	85.1	79.5
Washington	51.3	41.7	72.2	41.6	56.8	54.6	74.3	62.3	64.6	63.5	77.0	70.1	72.8	72.3	79.6	74.6
West Virginia	23.9	23.7	23.6	42.0	48.3	48.4	40.9	45.0	61.4	61.8	53.2	41.5	72.1	71.9	69.5	75.7
Wisconsin	43.4	37.5	70.7	40.5	58.0	57.3	73.1	62.2	71.8	71.9	72.4	69.3	76.6	76.5	84.0	75.4
Wyoming	51.2	48.3	61.3	49.8	65.4	65.2	66.7	77.0	70.8	70.6	75.1	76.8	72.3	72.2	76.2	70.3

Table B-2. Employment and Unemployment, 2015

State	Population 16 years and older	Total civilian labor force age 16 and older	Employed population 16 years and older				Unemployment		Unemployment rate by gender	
			Total	Men	Women	Percent women	Number unemployed	Unemployment rate	Men	Women
United States	256,167,758	160,652,483	150,534,773	79,120,041	71,414,732	47.4	10,117,710	6.3	6.4	6.2
Alabama	3,878,471	2,197,662	2,040,118	1,067,761	972,357	47.7	157,544	7.2	6.9	7.5
Alaska	571,393	385,165	354,766	193,392	161,374	45.5	30,399	7.9	8.9	6.7
Arizona	5,393,214	3,153,950	2,937,510	1,564,955	1,372,555	46.7	216,440	6.9	6.7	7.0
Arkansas	2,352,507	1,349,814	1,271,063	670,323	600,740	47.3	78,751	5.8	5.9	5.7
California	31,068,647	19,463,807	18,045,450	9,771,350	8,274,100	45.9	1,418,357	7.3	7.2	7.4
Colorado	4,333,738	2,916,718	2,765,115	1,485,661	1,279,454	46.3	151,603	5.2	5.3	5.0
Connecticut	2,922,877	1,941,592	1,807,098	925,935	881,163	48.8	134,494	6.9	7.1	6.8
Delaware	765,250	475,209	447,516	225,225	222,291	49.7	27,693	5.8	6.4	5.2
District of Columbia	564,206	389,414	361,179	175,876	185,303	51.3	28,235	7.3	7.2	7.3
Florida	16,640,196	9,668,285	8,990,221	4,663,492	4,326,729	48.1	678,064	7.0	7.2	6.8
Georgia	7,998,548	4,957,832	4,605,633	2,379,783	2,225,850	48.3	352,199	7.1	6.9	7.3
Hawaii	1,152,884	710,239	675,214	354,372	320,842	47.5	35,025	4.9	4.8	5.1
Idaho	1,270,851	786,377	744,228	399,344	344,884	46.3	42,149	5.4	5.3	5.4
Illinois	10,240,058	6,657,355	6,196,524	3,246,265	2,950,259	47.6	460,831	6.9	7.1	6.7
Indiana	5,215,392	3,312,603	3,119,966	1,642,149	1,477,817	47.4	192,637	5.8	5.8	5.9
Iowa	2,475,140	1,669,321	1,599,893	839,299	760,594	47.5	69,428	4.2	4.2	4.1
Kansas	2,270,108	1,486,201	1,417,069	749,555	667,514	47.1	69,132	4.7	4.7	4.6
Kentucky	3,531,385	2,062,779	1,928,967	1,006,647	922,320	47.8	133,812	6.5	6.8	6.1
Louisiana	3,676,681	2,193,370	2,037,812	1,049,048	988,764	48.5	155,558	7.1	7.6	6.6
Maine	1,103,834	685,216	648,414	327,487	320,927	49.5	36,802	5.4	6.5	4.2
Maryland	4,814,546	3,207,268	3,031,466	1,541,470	1,489,996	49.2	175,802	5.5	5.7	5.3
Massachusetts	5,578,648	3,739,683	3,522,203	1,784,929	1,737,274	49.3	217,480	5.8	6.3	5.3
Michigan	7,982,332	4,862,037	4,512,641	2,356,179	2,156,462	47.8	349,396	7.2	7.4	6.9
Minnesota	4,349,038	3,039,536	2,913,176	1,507,764	1,405,412	48.2	126,360	4.2	4.7	3.6
Mississippi	2,345,713	1,324,308	1,206,679	622,777	583,902	48.4	117,629	8.9	8.1	9.7
Missouri	4,851,761	3,042,538	2,880,309	1,484,020	1,396,289	48.5	162,229	5.3	5.7	5.0
Montana	829,911	513,209	489,875	259,333	230,542	47.1	23,334	4.5	4.9	4.1
Nebraska	1,476,487	1,019,543	986,789	519,537	467,252	47.4	32,754	3.2	3.3	3.1
Nevada	2,292,699	1,446,814	1,331,796	715,246	616,550	46.3	115,018	7.9	8.2	7.7
New Hampshire	1,102,089	744,971	713,313	371,025	342,288	48.0	31,658	4.2	4.7	3.8
New Jersey	7,193,921	4,684,036	4,374,536	2,298,798	2,075,738	47.5	309,500	6.6	6.6	6.7
New Mexico	1,642,487	950,312	879,807	463,219	416,588	47.3	70,505	7.4	8.2	6.5
New York	16,066,508	10,128,222	9,473,337	4,874,995	4,598,342	48.5	654,885	6.5	6.8	6.1
North Carolina	8,011,388	4,886,759	4,550,972	2,366,821	2,184,151	48.0	335,787	6.9	6.6	7.2
North Dakota	603,014	415,475	404,589	220,613	183,976	45.5	10,886	2.6	2.7	2.5
Ohio	9,295,255	5,863,639	5,489,742	2,839,454	2,650,288	48.3	373,897	6.4	6.6	6.2
Oklahoma	3,053,311	1,854,533	1,753,445	937,290	816,155	46.5	101,088	5.5	5.4	5.5
Oregon	3,268,296	2,018,994	1,881,255	987,483	893,772	47.5	137,739	6.8	7.1	6.5
Pennsylvania	10,429,005	6,518,212	6,109,670	3,168,719	2,940,951	48.1	408,542	6.3	6.6	5.9
Rhode Island	870,136	559,733	524,975	264,722	260,253	49.6	34,758	6.2	6.9	5.5
South Carolina	3,931,185	2,336,291	2,165,702	1,115,610	1,050,092	48.5	170,589	7.3	7.7	6.9
South Dakota	671,301	454,996	436,852	231,215	205,637	47.1	18,144	4.0	4.7	3.2
Tennessee	5,277,935	3,198,285	2,998,814	1,562,444	1,436,370	47.9	199,471	6.2	6.2	6.3
Texas	21,043,248	13,437,133	12,693,901	6,906,093	5,787,808	45.6	743,232	5.5	5.4	5.7
Utah	2,180,281	1,472,535	1,414,337	793,605	620,732	43.9	58,198	4.0	4.0	3.9
Vermont	521,616	340,689	327,841	165,927	161,914	49.4	12,848	3.8	4.5	3.1
Virginia	6,721,590	4,317,898	4,081,600	2,106,890	1,974,710	48.4	236,298	5.5	5.5	5.5
Washington	5,741,873	3,613,427	3,397,974	1,831,920	1,566,054	46.1	215,453	6.0	5.9	6.0
West Virginia	1,508,224	796,708	738,438	390,899	347,539	47.1	58,270	7.3	8.2	6.2
Wisconsin	4,627,790	3,091,421	2,959,655	1,533,690	1,425,965	48.2	131,766	4.3	4.7	3.8
Wyoming	460,730	310,369	295,328	159,435	135,893	46.0	15,041	4.8	4.7	5.1

Table B-2. Employment and Unemployment—*Continued*

| | Unemployment (Continued) | | | | | | | | | | | |
| | Unemployment rate by age group | | | | Unemployment rate by race and Hispanic origin | | | | Unemployment rate by educational attainment for persons age 25 to 64 | | | |
State	All ages	Age 16 to 24	Age 25 to 64	Age 65 and older	White alone, not of Hispanic origin	Black or African-American alone	Hispanic or Latino	Asian alone	Less than high school graduate	High school graduate (includes equivalency)	Some college or Associate's degree	Bachelor's degree or higher
United States	6.3	13.5	5.2	3.8	5.0	11.3	7.4	5.2	9.6	6.8	5.2	2.9
Alabama	7.2	15.8	5.8	4.0	5.6	11.5	5.2	2.4	12.3	7.6	5.4	2.5
Alaska	7.9	15.1	6.4	8.8	6.2	4.5	6.3	4.9	12.7	11.1	5.2	2.9
Arizona	6.9	14.4	5.5	5.0	5.6	10.5	7.7	4.8	8.9	7.0	5.5	3.2
Arkansas	5.8	13.5	4.6	2.9	4.9	10.7	5.1	4.0	8.1	5.4	4.8	2.0
California	7.3	15.8	6.0	4.6	6.2	11.9	8.2	5.7	8.5	7.9	6.4	3.8
Colorado	5.2	10.3	4.4	3.9	4.5	9.7	6.9	3.8	7.7	6.0	4.6	3.0
Connecticut	6.9	12.9	6.1	4.9	5.2	12.7	10.9	6.2	15.3	7.8	6.3	3.6
Delaware	5.8	12.2	4.9	3.8	5.5	6.8	5.2	5.0	10.4	6.8	4.4	2.7
District of Columbia	7.3	13.0	6.5	5.1	3.1	13.2	4.6	2.4	13.8	15.6	10.2	3.3
Florida	7.0	14.4	6.0	4.6	5.9	11.5	6.5	4.9	10.0	8.0	5.7	3.6
Georgia	7.1	16.3	5.7	4.1	5.2	11.1	5.6	4.5	10.5	6.9	6.2	3.1
Hawaii	4.9	10.7	4.2	2.6	5.2	10.4	6.8	3.1	7.8	5.4	4.1	3.0
Idaho	5.4	12.3	4.1	2.8	4.9	-	6.7	-	7.1	4.7	4.4	2.5
Illinois	6.9	15.5	5.6	3.7	5.0	16.4	7.8	5.5	10.7	8.2	5.7	3.0
Indiana	5.8	12.0	4.8	2.6	5.0	13.0	6.4	4.7	12.4	5.9	4.4	2.2
Iowa	4.2	9.6	3.2	2.3	3.5	13.1	7.1	7.0	6.8	4.2	3.1	1.6
Kansas	4.7	10.6	3.6	1.9	4.0	7.7	6.7	4.8	5.9	4.7	4.3	1.9
Kentucky	6.5	13.0	5.4	2.1	6.1	11.0	5.8	2.8	13.8	6.7	5.1	2.4
Louisiana	7.1	15.4	5.9	2.8	5.4	10.6	6.4	5.7	12.2	6.8	6.0	2.6
Maine	5.4	11.3	4.5	3.7	5.1	15.7	5.6	-	13.8	5.8	4.6	2.2
Maryland	5.5	12.8	4.5	3.8	4.2	7.9	5.5	4.2	9.2	6.7	4.8	2.4
Massachusetts	5.8	12.1	4.8	3.8	5.0	10.0	8.6	5.4	9.4	7.5	5.6	2.7
Michigan	7.2	14.6	5.9	3.8	5.5	16.6	9.2	6.1	14.0	8.6	5.6	2.7
Minnesota	4.2	9.0	3.3	3.2	3.4	10.1	7.4	5.6	9.1	4.6	3.2	2.0
Mississippi	8.9	19.9	7.3	2.3	5.8	14.0	6.1	5.5	15.7	9.0	6.6	2.8
Missouri	5.3	11.1	4.4	3.0	4.6	10.8	5.0	4.6	11.8	5.3	4.2	2.3
Montana	4.5	9.4	3.9	2.0	3.9	-	3.0	-	15.1	4.2	3.8	2.3
Nebraska	3.2	7.8	2.4	1.5	2.6	4.6	6.3	7.5	6.5	3.0	2.1	1.4
Nevada	7.9	12.7	7.2	6.7	7.1	11.7	8.3	6.9	9.9	9.0	6.7	4.9
New Hampshire	4.2	9.7	3.3	2.9	4.1	10.4	6.8	2.7	7.1	4.5	3.7	1.9
New Jersey	6.6	15.5	5.5	5.2	5.4	12.1	7.0	4.9	8.2	7.7	5.9	3.5
New Mexico	7.4	15.9	6.0	3.2	5.5	8.8	7.7	5.0	11.5	7.3	5.6	3.3
New York	6.5	14.9	5.4	3.9	4.9	10.9	8.5	5.6	10.1	7.0	5.3	3.4
North Carolina	6.9	15.7	5.5	4.2	5.3	11.5	7.3	4.8	10.2	7.4	5.7	2.7
North Dakota	2.6	3.7	2.4	3.0	2.2	-	-	-	7.5	4.4	2.1	0.6
Ohio	6.4	13.9	5.1	3.6	5.1	14.3	9.5	4.5	13.5	6.5	5.2	2.3
Oklahoma	5.5	11.6	4.4	2.6	4.6	9.4	5.4	4.2	7.6	6.2	4.3	1.9
Oregon	6.8	14.0	5.8	4.0	6.4	11.5	8.0	4.9	9.0	7.9	5.9	3.6
Pennsylvania	6.3	13.8	5.2	3.2	5.0	13.0	11.5	6.2	13.1	6.3	5.3	2.9
Rhode Island	6.2	13.4	5.0	4.6	5.0	11.5	10.4	7.2	9.6	7.4	4.7	2.6
South Carolina	7.3	16.6	5.9	3.5	5.6	11.8	5.9	6.2	14.4	8.1	5.0	2.5
South Dakota	4.0	7.8	3.4	1.7	2.8	-	5.1	-	10.4	5.6	2.8	0.7
Tennessee	6.2	12.1	5.3	4.0	5.2	10.9	6.2	3.6	11.8	7.1	4.5	2.5
Texas	5.5	12.1	4.5	3.2	4.5	8.1	6.1	4.2	6.5	5.6	4.6	2.7
Utah	4.0	7.6	3.1	1.9	3.7	6.4	4.2	5.5	6.7	4.1	2.7	2.0
Vermont	3.8	9.0	2.9	2.2	3.7	-	-	-	14.2	3.1	2.1	2.0
Virginia	5.5	12.5	4.5	3.1	4.3	9.2	6.0	4.4	9.9	6.2	4.4	2.7
Washington	6.0	12.9	4.9	3.9	5.4	10.4	7.5	4.7	8.9	6.5	5.4	2.9
West Virginia	7.3	16.1	6.1	3.3	7.0	11.3	-	3.9	16.5	6.9	5.9	2.7
Wisconsin	4.3	8.2	3.6	2.4	3.3	13.8	6.9	5.5	9.2	4.7	3.6	1.7
Wyoming	4.8	9.3	4.0	4.1	4.4	-	7.7	-	11.4	5.8	3.5	1.4

Table B-3. Employment Status and Class of Worker for the Population Age 16 Years and Older

State	Population 16 years and older	Total civilian labor force age 16 and older	Employed population 16 years and older			
			Total	Male	Female	Percent female
United States	256,167,758	160,652,483	150,534,773	79,120,041	71,414,732	47.4
Alabama	3,878,471	2,197,662	2,040,118	1,067,761	972,357	47.7
Alaska	571,393	385,165	354,766	193,392	161,374	45.5
Arizona	5,393,214	3,153,950	2,937,510	1,564,955	1,372,555	46.7
Arkansas	2,352,507	1,349,814	1,271,063	670,323	600,740	47.3
California	31,068,647	19,463,807	18,045,450	9,771,350	8,274,100	45.9
Colorado	4,333,738	2,916,718	2,765,115	1,485,661	1,279,454	46.3
Connecticut	2,922,877	1,941,592	1,807,098	925,935	881,163	48.8
Delaware	765,250	475,209	447,516	225,225	222,291	49.7
District of Columbia	564,206	389,414	361,179	175,876	185,303	51.3
Florida	16,640,196	9,668,285	8,990,221	4,663,492	4,326,729	48.1
Georgia	7,998,548	4,957,832	4,605,633	2,379,783	2,225,850	48.3
Hawaii	1,152,884	710,239	675,214	354,372	320,842	47.5
Idaho	1,270,851	786,377	744,228	399,344	344,884	46.3
Illinois	10,240,058	6,657,355	6,196,524	3,246,265	2,950,259	47.6
Indiana	5,215,392	3,312,603	3,119,966	1,642,149	1,477,817	47.4
Iowa	2,475,140	1,669,321	1,599,893	839,299	760,594	47.5
Kansas	2,270,108	1,486,201	1,417,069	749,555	667,514	47.1
Kentucky	3,531,385	2,062,779	1,928,967	1,006,647	922,320	47.8
Louisiana	3,676,681	2,193,370	2,037,812	1,049,048	988,764	48.5
Maine	1,103,834	685,216	648,414	327,487	320,927	49.5
Maryland	4,814,546	3,207,268	3,031,466	1,541,470	1,489,996	49.2
Massachusetts	5,578,648	3,739,683	3,522,203	1,784,929	1,737,274	49.3
Michigan	7,982,332	4,862,037	4,512,641	2,356,179	2,156,462	47.8
Minnesota	4,349,038	3,039,536	2,913,176	1,507,764	1,405,412	48.2
Mississippi	2,345,713	1,324,308	1,206,679	622,777	583,902	48.4
Missouri	4,851,761	3,042,538	2,880,309	1,484,020	1,396,289	48.5
Montana	829,911	513,209	489,875	259,333	230,542	47.1
Nebraska	1,476,487	1,019,543	986,789	519,537	467,252	47.4
Nevada	2,292,699	1,446,814	1,331,796	715,246	616,550	46.3
New Hampshire	1,102,089	744,971	713,313	371,025	342,288	48.0
New Jersey	7,193,921	4,684,036	4,374,536	2,298,798	2,075,738	47.5
New Mexico	1,642,487	950,312	879,807	463,219	416,588	47.3
New York	16,066,508	10,128,222	9,473,337	4,874,995	4,598,342	48.5
North Carolina	8,011,388	4,886,759	4,550,972	2,366,821	2,184,151	48.0
North Dakota	603,014	415,475	404,589	220,613	183,976	45.5
Ohio	9,295,255	5,863,639	5,489,742	2,839,454	2,650,288	48.3
Oklahoma	3,053,371	1,854,533	1,753,445	937,290	816,155	46.5
Oregon	3,268,296	2,018,994	1,881,255	987,483	893,772	47.5
Pennsylvania	10,429,005	6,518,212	6,109,670	3,168,719	2,940,951	48.1
Rhode Island	870,136	559,733	524,975	264,722	260,253	49.6
South Carolina	3,931,185	2,336,291	2,165,702	1,115,610	1,050,092	48.5
South Dakota	671,301	454,996	436,852	231,215	205,637	47.1
Tennessee	5,277,935	3,198,285	2,998,814	1,562,444	1,436,370	47.9
Texas	21,043,248	13,437,133	12,693,901	6,906,093	5,787,808	45.6
Utah	2,180,281	1,472,535	1,414,337	793,605	620,732	43.9
Vermont	521,616	340,689	327,841	165,927	161,914	49.4
Virginia	6,721,590	4,317,898	4,081,600	2,106,890	1,974,710	48.4
Washington	5,741,873	3,613,427	3,397,974	1,831,920	1,566,054	46.1
West Virginia	1,508,224	796,708	738,438	390,899	347,539	47.1
Wisconsin	4,627,790	3,091,421	2,959,655	1,533,690	1,425,965	48.2
Wyoming	460,730	310,369	295,328	159,435	135,893	46.0

Table B-3. Employment Status and Class of Worker for the Population Age 16 Years and Older—*Continued*

	Class of worker for civilian employed persons age 16 and older (percent)							
	Private for-profit wage and salary workers:				Government workers			
State	Total private for-profit wage and salary workers	Employee of private company workers	Self-employed in own incorporated business workers	Private not-for-profit wage and salary workers	Local government workers	State government workers	Federal government workers	Self-employed in own not incorporated business workers and unpaid family workers
United States	72.3	68.8	3.5	8.0	6.6	4.5	2.4	6.1
Alabama	73.4	70.7	2.7	6.6	6.3	5.4	3.1	5.1
Alaska	58.8	55.5	3.3	10.1	9.0	8.6	6.9	6.5
Arizona	74.1	70.6	3.5	6.1	6.4	4.7	2.7	6.0
Arkansas	70.6	67.8	2.8	7.2	5.5	8.0	2.1	6.5
California	71.8	68.5	3.3	6.5	7.5	4.0	1.8	8.3
Colorado	72.7	67.9	4.8	7.8	6.3	4.1	2.6	6.5
Connecticut	71.0	67.6	3.4	9.4	7.4	4.4	1.4	6.4
Delaware	73.4	69.7	3.7	8.2	3.2	8.8	2.1	4.2
District of Columbia	52.0	49.4	2.6	18.8	5.0	2.1	17.3	4.8
Florida	76.3	70.4	5.8	6.1	6.8	2.8	1.9	6.1
Georgia	73.6	69.7	3.9	6.1	6.9	4.8	3.0	5.6
Hawaii	65.1	61.6	3.5	7.7	3.6	9.2	7.1	7.3
Idaho	69.8	65.9	3.9	7.5	6.8	5.3	2.6	7.9
Illinois	74.9	71.4	3.5	8.7	6.5	3.6	1.6	4.7
Indiana	76.4	73.4	3.0	8.6	5.5	3.5	1.4	4.6
Iowa	71.8	68.6	3.2	8.7	6.1	5.5	1.4	6.4
Kansas	70.9	67.3	3.6	8.1	7.2	5.6	2.1	6.1
Kentucky	72.5	69.6	2.9	7.8	5.3	6.6	2.4	5.3
Louisiana	73.1	69.4	3.8	6.2	7.2	5.6	2.3	5.6
Maine	65.5	61.5	4.0	12.6	6.5	4.2	2.2	9.0
Maryland	64.1	60.6	3.5	9.7	7.5	4.1	9.8	4.8
Massachusetts	69.5	66.7	2.8	12.8	6.7	3.5	1.5	6.0
Michigan	75.3	72.0	3.3	9.5	5.0	4.0	1.4	4.9
Minnesota	71.7	67.8	3.9	11.5	6.2	3.7	1.3	5.5
Mississippi	70.9	67.7	3.2	5.9	5.6	9.2	3.2	5.2
Missouri	71.6	68.6	3.0	10.6	5.6	4.3	2.2	5.7
Montana	62.5	56.4	6.1	9.4	8.0	7.1	3.4	9.5
Nebraska	70.5	66.9	3.6	9.3	6.7	5.0	2.0	6.5
Nevada	79.9	76.8	3.0	3.5	6.2	3.0	2.2	5.2
New Hampshire	69.7	66.6	3.1	10.9	7.0	3.7	2.1	6.6
New Jersey	75.2	71.3	3.9	6.6	6.9	4.6	1.6	5.0
New Mexico	64.6	61.2	3.4	7.4	8.5	7.8	5.2	6.5
New York	68.8	65.0	3.8	10.2	9.1	4.3	1.7	6.0
North Carolina	73.0	69.5	3.5	6.9	5.3	6.7	2.3	5.9
North Dakota	66.6	63.4	3.3	10.4	6.9	5.1	2.8	8.2
Ohio	73.6	70.9	2.7	9.1	6.8	3.5	1.8	5.2
Oklahoma	70.9	67.3	3.6	6.7	5.5	6.9	3.8	6.2
Oregon	69.3	65.3	4.0	9.5	6.2	5.3	2.1	7.6
Pennsylvania	72.9	70.2	2.7	11.7	5.1	3.2	2.0	5.1
Rhode Island	72.3	69.1	3.1	10.8	6.0	3.8	2.2	4.9
South Carolina	73.6	70.6	3.0	6.2	5.4	7.1	2.2	5.5
South Dakota	65.8	61.6	4.2	11.4	6.8	4.5	2.9	8.6
Tennessee	72.1	70.1	2.1	7.6	7.0	4.1	2.4	6.8
Texas	75.0	72.2	2.7	5.5	6.3	4.5	2.1	6.6
Utah	73.4	69.2	4.2	7.6	5.6	5.5	3.1	4.8
Vermont	62.0	57.7	4.4	15.5	6.7	4.7	2.3	8.8
Virginia	67.2	63.9	3.3	7.9	7.5	4.1	8.2	5.1
Washington	70.3	66.3	4.0	7.9	6.4	6.2	3.1	6.1
West Virginia	69.2	67.2	2.0	7.8	7.0	8.0	3.5	4.6
Wisconsin	73.6	70.6	3.0	8.9	6.5	4.4	1.3	5.3
Wyoming	67.1	62.8	4.3	6.5	10.4	7.3	2.3	6.4

Table B-4. Employment by Occupation

State	Employed population 16 years and older				Employment by occupation group				
					Percent in each major occupation group				
	Total	Male	Female	Percent female	Management, business, science, and arts occupations:	Service occupations	Sales and office occupations:	Natural resources, construction, and maintenance occupations:	Production, transportation, and material moving occupations:
United States	150,534,773	79,120,041	71,414,732	47.4	37.1	18.0	23.6	9.0	12.3
Alabama	2,040,118	1,067,761	972,357	47.7	33.9	16.3	23.7	9.7	16.4
Alaska	354,766	193,392	161,374	45.5	36.4	17.7	22.6	12.1	11.1
Arizona	2,937,510	1,564,955	1,372,555	46.7	34.6	19.8	26.2	9.1	10.2
Arkansas	1,271,063	670,323	600,740	47.3	32.1	16.7	23.7	11.0	16.5
California	18,045,450	9,771,350	8,274,100	45.9	37.7	18.7	22.9	9.4	11.2
Colorado	2,765,115	1,485,661	1,279,454	46.3	41.2	16.8	23.7	9.4	8.9
Connecticut	1,807,098	925,935	881,163	48.8	42.4	17.0	23.6	7.6	9.4
Delaware	447,516	225,225	222,291	49.7	40.0	18.9	23.3	8.7	9.1
District of Columbia	361,179	175,876	185,303	51.3	61.8	15.7	17.0	2.1	3.4
Florida	8,990,221	4,663,492	4,326,729	48.1	34.5	20.1	27.0	9.2	9.3
Georgia	4,605,633	2,379,783	2,225,850	48.3	36.4	16.4	24.3	9.1	13.8
Hawaii	675,214	354,372	320,842	47.5	33.6	22.9	24.8	10.2	8.5
Idaho	744,228	399,344	344,884	46.3	33.7	19.1	23.0	11.4	12.9
Illinois	6,196,524	3,246,265	2,950,259	47.6	37.5	17.5	23.7	7.4	14.0
Indiana	3,119,966	1,642,149	1,477,817	47.4	32.9	16.5	22.8	9.0	18.8
Iowa	1,599,893	839,299	760,594	47.5	34.4	16.8	22.2	9.5	17.0
Kansas	1,417,069	749,555	667,514	47.1	37.3	17.0	22.1	9.8	13.7
Kentucky	1,928,967	1,006,647	922,320	47.8	33.2	16.7	23.8	9.2	17.1
Louisiana	2,037,812	1,049,048	988,764	48.5	33.7	19.1	23.6	11.8	11.8
Maine	648,414	327,487	320,927	49.5	36.5	17.8	23.8	10.6	11.3
Maryland	3,031,466	1,541,470	1,489,996	49.2	44.7	17.6	21.9	7.7	8.1
Massachusetts	3,522,203	1,784,929	1,737,274	49.3	44.9	17.8	21.9	6.8	8.7
Michigan	4,512,641	2,356,179	2,156,462	47.8	35.2	18.0	23.0	8.0	15.9
Minnesota	2,913,176	1,507,764	1,405,412	48.2	40.2	16.3	22.3	8.2	13.0
Mississippi	1,206,679	622,777	583,902	48.4	30.8	17.6	23.6	10.8	17.3
Missouri	2,880,309	1,484,020	1,396,289	48.5	35.4	17.6	24.4	9.0	13.6
Montana	489,875	259,333	230,542	47.1	38.1	18.7	21.3	13.7	8.2
Nebraska	986,789	519,537	467,252	47.4	36.6	16.6	23.5	10.1	13.3
Nevada	1,331,796	715,246	616,550	46.3	27.4	27.4	26.2	8.8	10.2
New Hampshire	713,313	371,025	342,288	48.0	40.1	15.9	23.7	8.5	11.7
New Jersey	4,374,536	2,298,798	2,075,738	47.5	41.3	16.6	24.2	7.3	10.6
New Mexico	879,807	463,219	416,588	47.3	34.5	21.5	24.0	11.1	8.9
New York	9,473,337	4,874,995	4,598,342	48.5	39.9	20.2	23.3	7.3	9.4
North Carolina	4,550,972	2,366,821	2,184,151	48.0	36.6	17.1	23.0	9.8	13.5
North Dakota	404,589	220,613	183,976	45.5	35.3	16.9	21.9	13.5	12.5
Ohio	5,489,742	2,839,454	2,650,288	48.3	35.7	17.3	23.3	7.5	16.1
Oklahoma	1,753,445	937,290	816,155	46.5	33.6	17.6	24.1	11.7	12.9
Oregon	1,881,255	987,483	893,772	47.5	37.7	18.7	22.7	8.9	11.9
Pennsylvania	6,109,670	3,168,719	2,940,951	48.1	37.4	17.5	23.2	8.2	13.7
Rhode Island	524,975	264,722	260,253	49.6	38.2	18.9	24.4	7.2	11.3
South Carolina	2,165,702	1,115,610	1,050,092	48.5	33.8	17.9	24.6	9.0	14.7
South Dakota	436,852	231,215	205,637	47.1	33.8	17.9	23.0	11.1	14.2
Tennessee	2,998,814	1,562,444	1,436,370	47.9	34.3	17.0	24.1	8.9	15.7
Texas	12,693,901	6,906,093	5,787,808	45.6	35.3	17.4	24.2	10.9	12.2
Utah	1,414,337	793,605	620,732	43.9	36.7	15.4	26.1	8.6	13.2
Vermont	327,841	165,927	161,914	49.4	41.1	17.1	21.3	9.4	11.0
Virginia	4,081,600	2,106,890	1,974,710	48.4	43.0	16.8	22.1	8.5	9.6
Washington	3,397,974	1,831,920	1,566,054	46.1	39.8	16.9	21.8	9.9	11.5
West Virginia	738,438	390,899	347,539	47.1	33.5	19.8	23.4	11.1	12.3
Wisconsin	2,959,655	1,533,690	1,425,965	48.2	35.2	16.9	22.4	8.6	16.9
Wyoming	295,328	159,435	135,893	46.0	31.5	17.4	22.1	15.8	13.2

Table B-4. Employment by Occupation—*Continued*

	Detailed occupation for employed persons age 16 and older								
	Number of employees in management, business, science, and arts occupations:								
		Management, business, and financial occupations:							
			Management occupations						
State	Total management, business, science, and arts occupations:	Total management, business, and financial occupations:	Total Management occupations:	Top executives	Advertising, marketing, promotions, public relations, and sales managers	Financial managers	Human resources managers	Operations specialties managers except financial managers and human resources managers	Farmers, ranchers, and other agricultural managers	Other management occupations except farmers, ranchers, and other agricultural managers
United States	55,873,365	22,657,853	15,436,375	2,079,087	1,043,601	1,178,393	388,776	1,489,764	584,812	8,671,942
Alabama	692,610	255,419	177,004	23,386	9,036	15,108	4,976	18,656	7,089	98,753
Alaska	129,291	48,442	35,108	5,603	1,330	1,826	707	3,508	712	21,422
Arizona	1,016,283	420,357	276,664	38,222	19,461	26,553	7,847	28,469	3,174	152,938
Arkansas	408,507	155,398	114,131	13,506	5,483	7,178	2,153	9,528	11,978	64,305
California	6,812,073	2,792,566	1,884,020	269,459	143,194	134,291	43,512	169,664	36,090	1,087,810
Colorado	1,138,465	490,897	335,983	47,604	24,147	23,960	7,587	29,415	10,793	192,477
Connecticut	766,642	304,441	199,235	30,927	14,951	18,116	4,250	20,313	1,603	109,075
Delaware	178,788	73,154	53,246	5,716	3,546	6,723	1,270	4,633	1,181	30,177
District of Columbia	223,262	91,807	59,429	6,607	5,836	4,083	1,076	4,774	0	37,053
Florida	3,097,672	1,323,093	923,435	147,295	68,185	68,020	18,676	75,304	14,402	531,553
Georgia	1,675,144	698,448	485,675	68,580	36,653	34,154	13,421	49,808	10,620	272,439
Hawaii	227,193	91,731	59,463	7,864	2,620	3,650	2,728	4,539	2,808	35,254
Idaho	250,456	94,904	68,653	7,884	2,966	5,288	1,703	4,848	7,704	38,260
Illinois	2,322,483	983,753	648,634	91,312	53,972	53,904	15,573	66,622	25,717	341,534
Indiana	1,025,473	414,225	289,478	36,201	18,770	19,768	7,450	32,037	17,633	157,619
Iowa	551,098	234,803	167,154	20,251	9,565	12,153	3,419	15,978	30,887	74,901
Kansas	528,954	210,187	148,545	20,600	8,768	8,227	3,701	13,370	21,617	72,262
Kentucky	641,200	250,298	171,258	22,400	10,085	13,726	4,505	15,890	12,450	92,202
Louisiana	686,168	253,417	177,868	24,587	8,964	12,135	4,767	13,536	3,572	110,307
Maine	236,807	90,654	65,425	9,593	3,504	4,355	818	5,690	3,278	38,187
Maryland	1,353,990	543,892	350,940	45,842	19,804	23,271	9,057	40,704	4,753	207,509
Massachusetts	1,581,552	610,132	405,268	57,973	31,494	37,606	9,389	42,082	3,359	223,365
Michigan	1,589,164	619,631	423,200	55,168	25,277	29,773	12,347	44,943	14,188	241,504
Minnesota	1,170,828	490,051	324,269	39,793	23,171	22,847	8,068	34,071	27,427	168,892
Mississippi	371,328	130,927	96,447	11,079	4,442	6,943	1,735	8,107	6,314	57,827
Missouri	1,018,840	410,172	278,480	34,339	17,922	20,233	7,047	31,361	22,889	144,689
Montana	186,486	82,711	61,863	6,872	2,432	3,208	1,095	3,682	12,731	31,843
Nebraska	361,038	154,383	109,832	12,204	5,531	8,698	2,310	9,265	23,456	48,368
Nevada	364,483	158,910	108,254	15,555	8,232	8,029	1,758	7,968	1,650	65,062
New Hampshire	286,270	113,383	81,110	11,975	5,055	4,885	1,503	10,244	1,466	45,982
New Jersey	1,806,345	758,093	505,355	66,351	39,065	49,419	11,685	58,153	2,903	277,779
New Mexico	303,574	108,289	78,804	10,902	3,006	5,394	2,163	6,798	3,426	47,115
New York	3,781,185	1,430,695	951,967	128,179	70,007	94,960	24,450	73,205	16,964	544,202
North Carolina	1,663,990	675,916	469,728	62,110	28,157	38,766	10,804	48,054	14,879	266,958
North Dakota	142,700	62,271	47,293	5,218	1,951	2,850	543	2,810	14,127	19,794
Ohio	1,961,686	796,974	539,859	76,012	37,015	44,370	16,202	53,450	20,487	292,323
Oklahoma	589,076	243,475	169,271	21,057	8,658	10,486	4,410	15,761	10,183	98,716
Oregon	709,914	284,101	197,898	23,864	12,991	11,460	5,130	18,375	11,603	114,475
Pennsylvania	2,284,559	899,812	601,734	78,543	44,080	45,008	17,495	61,825	17,874	336,909
Rhode Island	200,654	74,897	51,402	6,807	3,177	4,753	508	6,233	263	29,661
South Carolina	733,006	289,279	203,449	28,436	10,496	16,497	5,870	20,032	5,731	116,387
South Dakota	147,694	65,079	49,808	4,415	1,778	3,440	1,089	2,904	16,658	19,524
Tennessee	1,029,167	398,991	275,111	34,580	20,249	18,641	8,550	30,735	9,653	152,703
Texas	4,483,037	1,880,778	1,280,648	169,898	80,857	95,245	33,818	124,789	35,834	740,207
Utah	519,207	214,160	148,682	19,797	10,527	11,332	4,772	13,656	4,101	84,497
Vermont	134,584	51,059	35,836	3,729	1,766	2,015	778	2,895	3,210	21,443
Virginia	1,753,599	730,448	485,541	57,192	28,837	36,025	15,098	52,996	10,159	285,234
Washington	1,353,891	555,634	386,334	46,084	24,073	22,862	10,870	41,073	11,976	229,396
West Virginia	247,096	83,063	59,783	8,124	2,044	3,987	2,005	5,658	1,349	36,616
Wisconsin	1,042,930	425,982	289,736	36,330	19,049	20,920	7,353	30,282	27,333	148,469
Wyoming	92,923	36,671	28,065	3,062	1,422	1,252	735	1,071	4,558	15,965

Table B-4. Employment by Occupation—*Continued*

	Detailed occupation for employed persons age 16 and older										
	Number of employees in management, business, science, and arts occupations: (Continued)										
	Management, business, and financial occupations: (Continued)						Computer, engineering, and science occupations				
	Business and financial operations occupations							Computer and mathematical occupations			
				Financial Specialists					Computer occupations		
State	Total business and financial operations occupations:	Human resources workers	Other business operations specialists	Total Financial specialists	Accountants and auditors	Other financial specialists	Total Computer, engineering, and science occupations:	Total computer and mathematical occupations:	Total computer occupations:	Computer and information research scientists and analysts	Software developers and programmers
United States	7,221,478	739,945	3,158,684	3,322,849	1,930,254	1,392,595	8,276,842	4,267,389	4,051,748	574,041	1,820,187
Alabama	78,415	9,006	32,375	37,034	24,206	12,828	93,618	41,128	39,664	5,379	17,683
Alaska	13,334	1,209	6,072	6,053	4,101	1,952	19,955	5,661	5,167	901	1,005
Arizona	143,693	13,979	64,798	64,916	30,254	34,662	151,916	80,233	75,695	9,601	31,396
Arkansas	41,267	3,957	18,395	18,915	10,891	8,024	45,373	23,391	22,439	3,825	8,829
California	908,546	97,340	401,613	409,593	243,009	166,584	1,169,816	606,430	578,996	68,254	329,796
Colorado	154,914	15,696	69,384	69,834	37,881	31,953	204,258	110,996	107,488	13,018	51,886
Connecticut	105,206	8,364	42,419	54,423	27,672	26,751	109,117	53,517	49,435	6,505	22,883
Delaware	19,908	2,577	7,913	9,418	4,733	4,685	27,875	15,368	14,446	1,988	5,781
District of Columbia	32,378	2,755	20,488	9,135	3,890	5,245	39,642	22,967	15,779	2,978	6,637
Florida	399,658	38,299	178,735	182,624	106,755	75,869	361,261	194,996	187,546	23,646	75,145
Georgia	212,773	23,442	93,380	95,951	57,072	38,879	243,086	139,420	132,527	22,827	52,877
Hawaii	32,268	4,723	11,466	16,079	9,963	6,116	28,940	11,152	10,323	1,453	2,629
Idaho	26,251	3,423	12,252	10,576	6,835	3,741	36,764	15,688	15,162	1,985	5,662
Illinois	335,119	33,779	140,550	160,790	92,943	67,847	334,283	183,453	174,208	29,067	71,876
Indiana	124,747	13,542	50,750	60,455	36,588	23,867	136,080	56,182	53,256	7,299	21,300
Iowa	67,649	7,218	24,991	35,440	20,105	15,335	71,581	35,329	33,938	4,561	13,692
Kansas	61,642	6,792	24,841	30,009	16,270	13,739	73,747	37,189	35,857	4,933	14,595
Kentucky	79,040	8,244	32,156	38,640	22,245	16,395	69,118	32,458	31,255	4,295	10,578
Louisiana	75,549	6,693	29,894	38,962	25,471	13,491	79,851	28,619	27,258	3,982	9,440
Maine	25,229	1,997	13,348	9,884	5,601	4,283	27,769	12,436	11,909	1,890	3,893
Maryland	192,952	19,093	90,577	83,282	52,000	31,282	266,643	147,483	130,115	22,925	54,356
Massachusetts	204,864	20,256	91,035	93,573	52,604	40,969	281,633	141,609	135,238	20,008	73,063
Michigan	196,431	22,376	84,033	90,022	52,544	37,478	265,025	106,448	101,150	15,531	40,158
Minnesota	165,782	19,293	74,353	72,136	41,710	30,426	181,413	97,235	92,964	13,062	42,380
Mississippi	34,480	4,477	12,528	17,475	10,345	7,130	34,476	13,238	12,731	2,555	3,360
Missouri	131,692	13,317	54,662	63,713	36,041	27,672	140,025	77,600	74,070	10,546	29,751
Montana	20,848	1,182	9,714	9,952	5,825	4,127	20,374	7,089	6,733	884	2,020
Nebraska	44,551	4,449	20,120	19,982	10,953	9,029	43,382	25,442	23,926	2,988	9,996
Nevada	50,656	4,291	23,223	23,142	13,956	9,186	43,572	22,097	20,867	3,703	7,653
New Hampshire	32,273	2,495	16,532	13,246	7,453	5,793	47,874	27,069	26,442	2,497	13,829
New Jersey	252,738	22,947	107,606	122,185	73,100	49,085	272,699	167,850	160,706	23,082	75,019
New Mexico	29,485	2,770	12,139	14,576	9,371	5,205	46,455	16,200	14,839	2,460	4,375
New York	478,728	45,658	196,691	236,379	137,238	99,141	439,675	227,319	218,580	36,062	92,294
North Carolina	206,188	23,256	91,702	91,230	51,702	39,528	239,381	128,420	121,772	16,775	52,420
North Dakota	14,978	620	6,232	8,126	5,796	2,330	17,998	6,740	6,628	567	3,392
Ohio	257,115	24,711	114,191	118,213	69,226	48,987	277,681	137,420	130,708	19,148	54,573
Oklahoma	74,204	8,064	29,478	36,662	23,590	13,072	65,038	28,435	27,059	3,614	9,667
Oregon	86,203	7,031	43,224	35,948	19,488	16,460	117,200	57,378	55,691	4,919	28,093
Pennsylvania	298,078	29,636	132,581	135,861	78,242	57,619	319,419	158,018	150,615	23,089	65,055
Rhode Island	23,495	2,931	11,047	9,517	5,877	3,640	26,005	12,222	10,866	1,343	4,805
South Carolina	85,830	8,941	36,000	40,889	23,159	17,730	92,222	42,233	40,920	6,057	16,529
South Dakota	15,271	1,749	6,327	7,195	4,335	2,860	16,132	7,307	6,918	814	2,273
Tennessee	123,880	12,615	53,102	58,163	35,227	22,936	125,346	60,113	58,393	8,039	20,984
Texas	600,130	64,114	258,723	277,293	162,230	115,063	684,159	345,362	332,177	49,124	135,369
Utah	65,478	7,518	25,963	31,997	15,254	16,743	87,248	49,632	46,811	4,118	22,961
Vermont	15,223	1,415	7,665	6,143	3,282	2,861	17,843	7,692	6,973	741	2,595
Virginia	244,907	24,112	123,501	97,294	57,389	39,905	323,651	207,578	187,973	35,448	75,748
Washington	169,300	18,337	74,604	76,359	43,249	33,110	268,193	149,670	144,568	15,256	87,676
West Virginia	23,280	2,419	10,686	10,175	5,971	4,204	28,653	11,537	11,104	1,563	3,106
Wisconsin	136,246	15,787	60,944	59,515	34,278	25,237	152,808	72,067	69,707	8,614	28,752
Wyoming	8,606	1,050	3,681	3,875	2,334	1,541	10,569	2,273	2,156	122	352

Table B-4. Employment by Occupation—*Continued*

	Detailed occupation for employed persons age 16 and older											
	Number of employees in management, business, science, and arts occupations: (Continued)											
	Computer, engineering, and science occupations (Continued)											
	Computer and mathematical occupations			Architecture and engineering occupations				Life, physical, and social science occupations			
	Computer occupations										
State	Database and systems administrators and network architects	Miscellaneous computer occupations, including computer support specialists	Mathematical science occupations	Total architecture and engineering occupations:	Architects, surveyors, and cartographers	Engineers	Drafters, engineering, and mapping technicians	Total life, physical, and social science occupations:	Life and physical scientists	Social scientists and related workers	Life, physical, and social science technicians
United States	434,737	1,222,783	215,641	2,691,570	211,680	1,890,978	588,912	1,317,883	657,483	286,258	374,142
Alabama	4,758	11,844	1,464	41,727	2,618	30,881	8,228	10,763	5,195	1,577	3,991
Alaska	731	2,530	494	8,423	894	5,572	1,957	5,871	3,181	1,051	1,639
Arizona	7,748	26,950	4,538	53,745	3,532	37,667	12,546	17,938	6,383	4,984	6,571
Arkansas	2,683	7,102	952	12,761	593	8,456	3,712	9,221	3,895	1,935	3,391
California	52,092	128,854	27,434	379,146	29,309	279,785	70,052	184,240	94,584	44,871	44,785
Colorado	12,382	30,202	3,508	64,880	6,616	43,466	14,798	28,382	14,735	7,058	6,589
Connecticut	4,922	15,125	4,082	38,426	4,243	27,516	6,667	17,174	9,060	5,034	3,080
Delaware	1,810	4,867	922	6,148	265	4,250	1,633	6,359	3,249	1,001	2,109
District of Columbia	2,461	3,703	7,188	3,912	1,123	2,655	134	12,763	5,488	5,619	1,656
Florida	22,607	66,148	7,450	115,025	9,410	74,845	30,770	51,240	23,290	13,036	14,914
Georgia	14,094	42,729	6,893	69,791	5,168	47,324	17,299	33,875	17,458	5,066	11,351
Hawaii	1,734	4,507	829	11,432	1,297	7,006	3,129	6,356	2,750	1,360	2,246
Idaho	2,532	4,983	526	14,570	1,394	10,181	2,995	6,506	2,748	864	2,894
Illinois	19,206	54,059	9,245	101,067	10,116	70,663	20,288	49,763	22,953	12,324	14,486
Indiana	5,491	19,166	2,926	58,894	1,959	43,603	13,332	21,004	10,821	2,792	7,391
Iowa	3,875	11,810	1,391	22,904	857	15,448	6,599	13,348	5,939	1,679	5,730
Kansas	5,023	11,306	1,332	27,855	1,867	19,758	6,230	8,703	4,560	1,416	2,727
Kentucky	4,719	11,663	1,203	25,530	1,339	17,639	6,552	11,130	4,466	2,042	4,622
Louisiana	3,096	10,740	1,361	36,400	2,774	23,743	9,883	14,832	6,866	2,493	5,473
Maine	1,352	4,774	527	10,534	709	5,915	3,910	4,799	1,918	1,174	1,707
Maryland	14,999	37,835	17,368	65,101	6,292	48,565	10,244	54,059	34,553	10,088	9,418
Massachusetts	11,694	30,473	6,371	74,980	6,869	55,720	12,391	65,044	39,301	11,553	14,190
Michigan	12,060	33,401	5,298	126,144	3,952	101,061	21,131	32,433	15,054	6,949	10,430
Minnesota	7,838	29,684	4,271	55,255	4,452	38,133	12,670	28,923	13,864	6,837	8,222
Mississippi	1,412	5,404	507	13,285	462	8,652	4,171	7,953	4,002	741	3,210
Missouri	8,884	24,889	3,530	41,734	3,926	26,961	10,847	20,691	10,748	4,121	5,822
Montana	1,278	2,551	356	8,049	931	4,465	2,653	5,236	3,046	773	1,417
Nebraska	2,572	8,370	1,516	11,133	866	6,586	3,681	6,807	3,903	1,064	1,840
Nevada	2,997	6,514	1,230	15,309	1,052	8,735	5,522	6,166	3,780	935	1,451
New Hampshire	3,051	7,065	627	16,247	780	12,131	3,336	4,558	2,363	883	1,312
New Jersey	15,086	47,519	7,144	64,610	6,597	46,194	11,819	40,239	21,997	8,927	9,315
New Mexico	2,102	5,902	1,361	17,517	1,677	11,278	4,562	12,738	7,620	2,406	2,712
New York	22,008	68,216	8,739	128,876	20,783	80,309	27,784	83,480	33,312	30,308	19,860
North Carolina	12,233	40,344	6,648	66,946	5,560	45,655	15,731	44,015	23,046	7,492	13,477
North Dakota	511	2,158	112	7,743	556	5,240	1,947	3,515	1,412	486	1,617
Ohio	13,446	43,541	6,712	100,239	5,537	73,446	21,256	40,022	18,554	8,254	13,214
Oklahoma	2,655	11,123	1,376	24,611	1,408	15,434	7,769	11,992	5,318	1,704	4,970
Oregon	7,743	14,936	1,687	42,246	3,570	29,571	9,105	17,576	10,044	3,307	4,225
Pennsylvania	15,453	47,018	7,403	105,954	6,397	73,105	26,452	55,447	30,585	10,848	14,014
Rhode Island	1,560	3,158	1,356	8,427	667	6,160	1,600	5,356	1,980	1,564	1,812
South Carolina	4,811	13,523	1,313	37,939	2,597	25,540	9,802	12,050	5,364	2,045	4,641
South Dakota	920	2,911	389	5,163	292	2,541	2,330	3,662	2,062	630	970
Tennessee	6,923	22,447	1,720	45,155	3,575	30,008	11,572	20,078	9,641	2,894	7,543
Texas	39,167	108,517	13,185	241,881	15,740	173,470	52,671	96,916	47,111	14,239	35,566
Utah	4,769	14,963	2,821	25,424	1,720	17,813	5,891	12,192	5,598	2,264	4,330
Vermont	843	2,794	719	6,040	849	3,836	1,355	4,111	1,620	1,623	868
Virginia	23,643	53,134	19,605	77,928	7,023	55,982	14,923	38,145	17,389	13,047	7,709
Washington	11,292	30,344	5,102	84,444	7,316	62,571	14,557	34,079	17,609	6,344	10,126
West Virginia	1,288	5,147	433	10,327	396	6,235	3,696	6,789	2,943	1,358	2,488
Wisconsin	7,457	24,884	2,360	55,006	2,959	36,396	15,651	25,735	12,479	4,383	8,873
Wyoming	726	956	117	4,687	796	2,812	1,079	3,609	1,646	815	1,148

Table B-4. Employment by Occupation—*Continued*

	Detailed occupation for employed persons age 16 and older								
	Number of employees in management, business, science, and arts occupations: (Continued)								
	Education, legal, community service, arts, and media occupations:								
		Community and social service occupations:			Legal occupations				Education, training, and library occupations:	
State	Total Education, legal, community service, arts, and media occupations:	Total community and social service occupations:	Counselors, social workers, and other community and social service specialists	Religious workers	Total legal occupations:	Lawyers and judicial law clerks	Judges, magistrates, and other judicial workers	Legal support workers	Total education, training, and library occupations:	Postsecondary teachers
---	---	---	---	---	---	---	---	---	---	---
United States	16,182,850	2,575,707	2,000,412	575,295	1,684,406	1,050,575	63,949	569,882	8,957,117	1,515,921
Alabama	202,991	36,229	22,850	13,379	20,610	12,559	802	7,249	118,617	20,209
Alaska	41,149	7,624	6,345	1,279	3,758	2,045	264	1,449	23,232	2,366
Arizona	278,892	51,275	43,696	7,579	27,208	15,676	1,017	10,515	150,751	27,570
Arkansas	125,967	21,067	14,371	6,696	10,364	5,934	873	3,557	79,914	14,409
California	1,985,123	285,801	230,196	55,605	211,828	136,958	4,627	70,243	970,066	169,176
Colorado	295,561	47,967	38,285	9,682	33,589	19,023	1,495	13,071	153,989	25,500
Connecticut	237,336	37,669	34,116	3,553	24,595	15,911	578	8,106	135,189	21,948
Delaware	48,233	9,065	7,098	1,967	5,340	2,489	359	2,492	27,840	4,494
District of Columbia	81,263	9,162	8,320	842	28,065	21,541	899	5,625	22,957	6,420
Florida	873,111	127,371	97,456	29,915	118,404	62,356	3,963	52,085	457,875	72,378
Georgia	490,157	66,200	43,397	22,803	43,385	28,535	1,303	13,547	296,723	43,060
Hawaii	73,185	12,075	9,549	2,526	7,035	4,532	433	2,070	39,532	5,341
Idaho	73,362	11,252	9,313	1,939	6,222	3,456	430	2,336	45,102	8,356
Illinois	649,000	94,922	73,465	21,457	76,101	54,952	2,523	18,626	365,446	64,827
Indiana	290,902	54,155	38,650	15,505	25,095	15,417	882	8,796	169,199	34,106
Iowa	154,494	25,805	19,262	6,543	10,554	5,781	188	4,585	97,193	19,206
Kansas	154,067	22,157	15,745	6,412	13,466	8,489	679	4,298	96,227	17,707
Kentucky	191,371	40,911	30,642	10,269	17,260	11,147	1,118	4,995	109,820	19,040
Louisiana	217,332	35,596	25,425	10,171	26,551	14,855	1,140	10,556	122,502	16,729
Maine	73,847	13,446	11,379	2,067	4,888	3,497	120	1,271	43,137	6,601
Maryland	366,975	61,864	49,631	12,233	46,528	30,451	2,020	14,057	191,304	35,787
Massachusetts	457,637	74,338	66,828	7,510	46,068	34,375	1,358	10,335	260,742	59,147
Michigan	428,157	73,460	56,148	17,312	39,123	23,416	1,993	13,714	241,842	48,174
Minnesota	315,455	58,985	47,089	11,896	26,158	17,188	856	8,114	169,877	28,222
Mississippi	119,560	20,364	13,224	7,140	9,622	4,917	412	4,293	77,397	10,547
Missouri	289,361	49,099	35,136	13,963	26,278	16,422	1,061	8,795	170,009	29,907
Montana	54,692	12,800	10,790	2,010	6,236	3,009	640	2,587	27,538	5,107
Nebraska	104,341	17,594	13,317	4,277	8,021	4,456	721	2,844	65,807	14,008
Nevada	107,913	13,035	10,272	2,763	10,884	6,344	404	4,136	58,098	6,567
New Hampshire	75,568	11,334	9,786	1,548	6,449	3,974	416	2,059	47,076	5,216
New Jersey	519,762	74,699	62,798	11,901	61,690	42,072	1,594	18,024	294,262	31,712
New Mexico	99,802	15,416	11,744	3,672	9,468	5,714	217	3,537	59,965	9,452
New York	1,338,146	193,131	166,218	26,913	160,679	112,553	4,566	43,560	682,304	108,568
North Carolina	474,059	79,715	58,049	21,666	37,728	21,477	2,038	14,213	285,725	54,900
North Dakota	38,068	5,530	4,122	1,408	4,590	2,002	265	2,323	23,608	3,690
Ohio	525,427	93,640	72,496	21,144	44,328	26,691	2,898	14,739	303,757	53,176
Oklahoma	183,036	38,073	26,455	11,618	15,645	9,714	705	5,226	104,240	18,283
Oregon	200,341	36,965	29,909	7,056	18,828	10,341	475	8,012	102,753	21,592
Pennsylvania	643,934	126,455	101,563	24,892	65,425	41,817	3,198	20,410	352,586	68,999
Rhode Island	65,671	11,605	9,836	1,769	5,562	3,351	211	2,000	37,771	8,748
South Carolina	218,068	41,323	26,426	14,897	17,755	7,853	849	9,053	126,095	22,286
South Dakota	39,814	7,449	5,632	1,817	2,417	1,557	138	722	24,400	3,846
Tennessee	312,020	53,255	34,777	18,478	25,871	16,256	868	8,747	180,261	31,319
Texas	1,254,334	171,799	123,343	48,456	123,251	71,284	5,731	46,236	758,727	99,753
Utah	151,215	18,621	16,194	2,427	14,657	8,296	706	5,655	86,193	17,662
Vermont	45,020	7,946	7,314	632	3,406	1,875	352	1,179	25,035	4,798
Virginia	475,034	72,197	54,449	17,748	62,227	38,445	2,428	21,354	259,773	44,053
Washington	351,476	54,335	42,583	11,752	37,253	21,535	1,677	14,041	190,459	31,027
West Virginia	73,983	17,270	13,709	3,561	7,372	2,543	693	4,136	41,222	8,098
Wisconsin	283,949	48,477	37,098	11,379	23,653	13,649	704	9,300	162,811	29,809
Wyoming	32,689	5,184	3,916	1,268	2,916	1,845	62	1,009	20,169	2,025

Table B-4. Employment by Occupation—*Continued*

	Detailed occupation for employed persons age 16 and older									
	Number of employees in management, business, science, and arts occupations: (Continued)									
	Education, legal, community service, arts, and media occupations: (Continued)									
	Education, training, and library occupations:						Arts, design, entertainment, sports, and media occupations:			
	Primary, secondary, and special education school teachers:									
State	Total primary, secondary, and special education school teachers:	Preschool and kindergarten teachers	Elementary and middle school teachers	Secondary school teachers	Special education teachers	Librarians, curators, and archivists	Other teachers and instructors, education, training, and library occupations	Total Arts, design, entertainment, sports, and media occupations:	Art and design workers	Entertainers and performers, sports, and related workers	Media and communication equipment workers
United States	5,159,264	585,142	3,527,226	789,684	257,212	271,693	2,010,239	2,965,620	1,055,641	751,721	1,158,258
Alabama	73,013	9,663	49,082	9,951	4,317	3,049	22,346	27,535	8,756	8,247	10,532
Alaska	14,625	1,201	9,790	2,308	1,326	672	5,569	6,535	1,806	722	4,007
Arizona	80,334	8,152	53,778	14,851	3,553	4,324	38,523	49,658	18,563	12,128	18,967
Arkansas	48,010	5,202	31,713	8,598	2,497	2,205	15,290	14,622	5,464	3,464	5,694
California	523,899	56,256	352,486	87,005	28,152	29,749	247,242	517,428	180,710	145,977	190,741
Colorado	90,309	9,980	65,114	12,414	2,801	4,515	33,665	60,016	19,102	14,127	26,787
Connecticut	75,762	7,041	49,920	14,377	4,424	4,565	32,914	39,883	12,830	10,878	16,175
Delaware	17,459	2,280	11,754	2,713	712	545	5,342	5,988	2,859	1,604	1,525
District of Columbia	8,681	1,538	5,487	1,328	328	1,832	6,024	21,079	3,387	2,819	14,873
Florida	285,729	38,108	204,939	35,143	7,539	9,361	90,407	169,461	59,585	50,017	59,859
Georgia	187,853	24,420	133,727	23,199	6,507	5,550	60,260	83,849	28,280	24,694	30,875
Hawaii	20,536	1,033	14,338	3,502	1,663	2,333	11,322	14,543	3,957	3,928	6,658
Idaho	24,647	2,306	17,478	3,959	904	1,049	11,050	10,786	4,054	1,894	4,838
Illinois	208,938	22,224	130,044	44,151	12,519	15,362	76,319	112,531	42,929	24,822	44,780
Indiana	91,340	10,923	61,133	14,795	4,489	6,230	37,523	42,453	15,890	8,750	17,813
Iowa	52,948	5,421	36,346	8,656	2,525	3,241	21,798	20,942	7,965	5,473	7,504
Kansas	51,115	3,556	34,689	9,278	3,592	3,563	23,842	22,217	8,402	6,498	7,317
Kentucky	63,860	8,017	43,760	9,721	2,362	3,029	23,891	23,380	8,141	6,149	9,090
Louisiana	76,251	7,629	54,989	11,798	1,835	4,208	25,314	32,683	12,998	8,960	10,725
Maine	27,806	3,351	15,291	5,973	3,191	1,224	7,506	12,376	4,322	2,121	5,933
Maryland	105,295	11,794	73,776	14,361	5,364	7,666	42,556	67,279	18,489	14,781	34,009
Massachusetts	135,551	18,547	86,799	23,535	6,670	9,373	56,671	76,489	26,207	17,861	32,421
Michigan	130,719	12,141	93,084	18,387	7,107	6,553	56,396	73,732	31,707	17,578	24,447
Minnesota	90,689	10,411	59,372	13,927	6,979	3,359	47,607	60,435	24,655	13,329	22,451
Mississippi	48,355	6,569	31,738	8,430	1,618	2,992	15,503	12,177	3,598	4,239	4,340
Missouri	105,014	13,652	70,987	14,332	6,043	5,628	29,460	43,975	17,135	10,025	16,815
Montana	15,979	1,025	10,421	3,821	712	786	5,666	8,118	2,786	1,481	3,851
Nebraska	37,318	4,321	25,126	5,982	1,889	1,610	12,871	12,919	4,691	2,996	5,232
Nevada	37,829	3,487	27,281	5,115	1,946	1,611	12,091	25,896	8,420	8,387	9,089
New Hampshire	26,849	3,308	16,991	4,654	1,896	2,204	12,807	10,709	3,958	2,420	4,331
New Jersey	182,128	16,747	121,776	30,995	12,610	7,194	73,228	89,111	31,218	22,075	35,818
New Mexico	35,326	4,929	23,789	4,384	2,224	1,969	13,218	14,953	5,201	2,824	6,928
New York	368,185	31,098	251,450	59,541	26,096	23,641	181,910	302,032	106,366	73,997	121,669
North Carolina	166,058	25,884	113,168	21,781	5,225	7,025	57,742	70,891	22,620	20,760	27,511
North Dakota	14,044	1,462	10,098	2,070	414	450	5,424	4,340	1,459	1,011	1,870
Ohio	179,004	21,709	119,371	29,118	8,806	11,031	60,546	83,702	34,879	20,532	28,291
Oklahoma	61,507	8,794	40,201	9,294	3,218	2,348	22,102	25,078	9,082	7,243	8,753
Oregon	51,565	6,500	34,119	7,578	3,368	3,437	26,159	41,795	15,572	10,115	16,108
Pennsylvania	196,663	22,701	136,782	25,894	11,286	9,338	77,586	99,468	33,704	25,469	40,295
Rhode Island	19,275	2,118	12,837	3,113	1,207	1,167	8,581	10,733	4,950	1,923	3,860
South Carolina	74,115	7,964	50,910	12,089	3,152	4,084	25,610	32,895	11,390	9,869	11,636
South Dakota	14,728	1,420	9,973	1,952	1,383	1,340	4,486	5,548	2,766	909	1,873
Tennessee	104,356	15,156	68,732	15,202	5,266	4,329	40,257	52,633	15,748	15,707	21,178
Texas	493,748	51,390	360,949	64,997	16,412	18,420	146,806	200,557	75,439	49,683	75,435
Utah	40,757	3,539	27,471	7,925	1,822	2,737	25,037	31,744	11,635	7,594	12,515
Vermont	13,466	976	7,405	4,362	723	811	5,960	8,633	2,770	1,720	4,143
Virginia	150,050	20,332	105,685	16,625	7,408	9,595	56,075	80,837	25,752	16,252	38,833
Washington	102,617	12,260	71,894	15,338	3,125	7,359	49,456	69,429	29,263	13,608	26,558
West Virginia	25,770	2,626	17,945	3,718	1,481	584	6,770	8,119	1,945	1,620	4,554
Wisconsin	97,940	13,520	63,202	15,319	5,899	5,231	29,831	49,008	20,697	11,471	16,840
Wyoming	11,249	461	8,036	2,125	627	1,215	5,680	4,420	1,539	970	1,911

Table B-4. Employment by Occupation—*Continued*

	Detailed occupation for employed persons age 16 and older										
	Number of employees in management, business, science, and arts occupations: (Continued)									Number of employees in service occupations	
	Healthcare practitioners and technical occupations:										Healthcare support occupations
		Health diagnosing and treating practitioners and other technical occupations:									
State	Total healthcare practitioners and technical occupations:	Total Health diagnosing and treating practitioners and other technical occupations:	Physicians and surgeons	Therapists	Registered nurses	Nurses, all other	Other health diagnosing and treating practitioners and technical occupations	Health technologists and technicians	Total service occupations	Total healthcare support occupations:	Nursing, psychiatric, and home health aides
United States	8,755,820	5,894,123	889,398	781,054	3,066,554	164,123	992,994	2,861,697	27,047,705	3,588,015	2,065,790
Alabama	140,582	93,255	9,928	9,676	53,983	4,481	15,187	47,327	331,724	43,247	24,440
Alaska	19,745	13,469	1,600	1,894	5,723	373	3,879	6,276	62,930	6,412	4,089
Arizona	165,118	108,973	16,775	14,410	55,560	2,591	19,637	56,145	582,609	60,331	24,267
Arkansas	81,769	49,654	6,714	6,916	27,417	1,165	7,442	32,115	212,278	35,094	22,027
California	864,568	594,058	96,851	75,511	299,822	9,900	111,974	270,510	3,377,528	351,546	149,724
Colorado	147,749	105,292	14,051	16,939	49,477	2,493	22,332	42,457	465,588	56,065	26,461
Connecticut	115,748	80,952	12,807	9,626	41,673	2,441	14,405	34,796	308,013	46,060	29,410
Delaware	29,526	20,914	2,616	2,862	11,184	664	3,588	8,612	84,731	12,020	6,509
District of Columbia	10,550	7,504	3,145	1,301	1,731	176	1,151	3,046	56,545	5,462	3,185
Florida	540,207	356,882	52,965	45,317	191,487	10,418	56,695	183,325	1,811,206	228,053	130,790
Georgia	243,453	162,046	21,557	19,127	87,588	5,182	28,592	81,407	754,970	89,693	49,123
Hawaii	33,337	23,910	4,312	2,555	12,983	221	3,839	9,427	154,624	12,865	4,815
Idaho	45,426	29,356	3,951	5,206	15,377	768	4,054	16,070	142,118	18,077	9,745
Illinois	355,447	246,495	35,688	33,891	130,632	5,056	41,228	108,952	1,082,464	139,452	81,348
Indiana	184,266	123,022	13,981	14,698	73,486	3,075	17,782	61,244	515,832	68,222	37,323
Iowa	90,220	61,642	7,804	7,277	34,498	1,382	10,681	28,578	268,532	40,402	25,376
Kansas	90,953	62,327	8,765	7,265	34,155	2,328	9,814	28,626	240,212	36,047	23,340
Kentucky	130,413	85,952	12,046	12,196	46,406	2,270	13,034	44,461	322,198	43,071	23,523
Louisiana	135,568	81,864	10,911	9,541	44,907	2,451	14,054	53,704	389,556	48,965	31,564
Maine	44,537	31,310	4,395	5,122	16,135	1,371	4,287	13,227	115,264	19,270	11,369
Maryland	176,480	124,617	21,624	15,387	62,279	3,375	21,952	51,863	533,408	69,626	40,089
Massachusetts	232,150	168,834	31,578	22,610	84,432	5,606	24,608	63,316	625,681	91,183	56,938
Michigan	276,351	185,115	27,580	24,460	100,080	3,690	29,305	91,236	810,642	126,926	72,794
Minnesota	183,909	125,939	17,670	14,702	68,798	3,783	20,986	57,970	475,093	73,250	45,788
Mississippi	86,365	55,799	4,175	8,767	32,161	3,861	6,835	30,566	211,852	27,613	17,588
Missouri	179,282	114,503	17,180	15,414	62,839	3,833	15,237	64,779	506,401	77,188	48,231
Montana	28,709	19,806	2,385	2,633	9,540	927	4,321	8,903	91,752	10,508	6,244
Nebraska	58,932	39,648	4,774	4,957	21,546	793	7,578	19,284	163,656	25,193	15,692
Nevada	54,088	35,239	5,276	3,642	18,985	639	6,697	18,849	365,525	22,804	8,588
New Hampshire	49,445	35,093	4,532	5,684	18,783	1,003	5,091	14,352	113,207	16,908	10,279
New Jersey	255,791	178,754	30,902	26,812	89,860	3,029	28,151	77,037	725,892	102,062	58,807
New Mexico	49,028	31,225	4,698	5,192	13,981	813	6,541	17,803	188,755	23,502	12,074
New York	572,669	401,792	75,940	58,017	191,455	9,957	66,423	170,877	1,910,941	326,570	241,020
North Carolina	274,634	183,653	25,717	20,913	97,478	6,171	33,374	90,981	779,809	117,986	74,257
North Dakota	24,363	17,873	2,214	1,838	9,881	343	3,597	6,490	68,246	10,555	7,157
Ohio	361,604	237,122	35,422	29,419	131,124	7,002	34,155	124,482	949,620	151,003	97,058
Oklahoma	97,527	59,804	7,976	7,363	34,144	1,236	9,085	37,723	309,310	43,906	25,118
Oregon	108,272	73,817	12,756	9,407	33,143	3,236	15,275	34,455	352,309	44,729	17,425
Pennsylvania	421,394	281,594	44,214	43,839	141,347	8,207	43,987	139,800	1,071,792	169,029	103,405
Rhode Island	34,081	23,734	4,204	4,458	11,836	496	2,740	10,347	99,209	18,342	11,803
South Carolina	133,437	84,770	10,377	11,002	47,476	2,701	13,214	48,667	387,365	48,632	29,688
South Dakota	26,669	18,062	1,614	2,252	11,044	624	2,528	8,607	78,185	12,349	7,722
Tennessee	192,810	121,323	16,713	15,398	63,018	6,170	20,024	71,487	510,228	57,141	33,907
Texas	663,766	434,411	60,750	60,971	224,360	12,571	75,759	229,355	2,207,517	273,375	149,071
Utah	66,584	47,471	6,694	6,484	23,548	860	9,885	19,113	217,558	25,933	12,288
Vermont	20,662	14,442	3,097	2,192	6,833	336	1,984	6,220	56,149	6,282	3,776
Virginia	224,466	146,749	25,287	19,900	71,267	4,516	25,779	77,717	686,858	78,006	43,066
Washington	178,588	125,269	23,014	13,782	57,882	4,315	26,276	53,319	574,591	73,904	32,214
West Virginia	61,397	37,433	4,852	3,019	21,792	1,787	5,983	23,964	146,054	22,024	15,145
Wisconsin	180,191	121,869	14,128	17,161	67,708	3,263	19,609	58,322	499,738	76,977	47,332
Wyoming	12,994	9,486	1,193	2,049	3,710	174	2,360	3,508	51,440	4,155	2,798

Table B-4. Employment by Occupation—*Continued*

	Detailed occupation for employed persons age 16 and older									
	Number of employees in service occupations (Continued)									Food preparation and serving related occupations
	Healthcare support occupations		Protective service occupations							
State	Occupational and physical therapist assistants and aides	Other healthcare support occupations	Total protective service occupations:	First-line supervisors of law enforcement workers	First-line supervisors of fire fighting and prevention workers	First-line supervisors of protective service workers, all other	Fire fighting and prevention workers	Law enforcement workers	Other protective service workers	Total food preparation and serving related occupations:
United States	106,261	1,415,964	3,199,233	154,972	46,767	71,500	297,590	1,276,211	1,352,193	8,816,644
Alabama	1,796	17,011	42,491	2,313	1,018	933	4,478	16,818	16,931	106,011
Alaska	143	2,180	8,207	515	146	103	906	3,003	3,534	21,076
Arizona	2,990	33,074	77,490	3,924	1,376	2,716	4,911	31,452	33,111	195,798
Arkansas	1,059	12,008	24,509	1,638	271	486	2,896	12,245	6,973	67,874
California	8,174	193,648	360,032	16,503	7,048	8,073	31,253	125,014	172,141	1,039,289
Colorado	835	28,769	57,386	2,381	1,420	920	6,178	23,705	22,782	162,241
Connecticut	900	15,750	36,890	1,836	817	1,128	3,004	12,697	17,408	83,278
Delaware	369	5,142	11,490	540	40	348	419	4,741	5,402	28,125
District of Columbia	325	1,952	10,437	64	0	218	58	2,715	7,382	16,393
Florida	8,674	88,589	228,382	10,002	3,205	5,133	21,863	76,673	111,506	609,806
Georgia	2,748	37,822	100,955	3,760	953	1,934	10,511	47,914	35,883	255,288
Hawaii	268	7,782	20,836	307	175	133	1,819	6,839	11,563	52,384
Idaho	513	7,819	12,817	749	412	851	1,564	4,633	4,608	46,740
Illinois	5,183	52,921	132,795	5,815	2,014	2,914	13,549	51,886	56,617	352,707
Indiana	3,439	27,460	57,734	2,538	834	1,035	6,892	23,276	23,159	185,678
Iowa	1,108	13,918	21,461	874	182	299	1,516	9,297	9,293	90,344
Kansas	1,647	11,060	24,654	2,405	924	473	2,736	9,950	8,166	78,677
Kentucky	1,813	17,735	37,341	2,424	593	682	3,585	16,302	13,755	118,360
Louisiana	1,225	16,176	52,044	4,397	1,275	1,260	4,132	23,950	17,030	136,654
Maine	387	7,514	11,627	118	187	280	2,038	4,329	4,675	35,535
Maryland	1,914	27,623	90,491	2,689	823	3,589	7,111	36,498	39,781	153,957
Massachusetts	2,017	32,228	68,617	3,523	1,140	1,262	10,885	25,516	26,291	207,979
Michigan	4,682	49,450	79,734	4,533	919	2,072	6,670	33,451	32,089	278,132
Minnesota	2,088	25,374	38,057	2,388	558	1,188	1,905	13,698	18,320	152,670
Mississippi	1,228	8,797	26,632	1,693	271	1,004	2,532	12,156	8,976	71,930
Missouri	2,277	26,680	53,303	3,708	882	1,077	5,617	23,678	18,341	170,309
Montana	147	4,117	8,978	635	307	106	1,527	4,114	2,289	31,568
Nebraska	589	8,912	15,407	945	101	449	1,380	5,551	6,981	52,255
Nevada	472	13,744	38,289	1,373	68	1,395	2,262	8,233	24,958	140,018
New Hampshire	564	6,065	11,899	596	17	352	1,218	4,619	5,097	38,986
New Jersey	2,504	40,751	104,984	4,642	492	3,220	7,216	40,723	48,691	212,618
New Mexico	856	10,572	25,674	1,512	206	608	2,504	9,422	11,422	59,986
New York	6,511	79,039	260,191	13,983	2,168	4,207	17,397	105,868	116,568	540,035
North Carolina	2,169	41,560	87,741	4,510	1,086	1,323	11,032	40,054	29,736	257,543
North Dakota	291	3,107	5,965	176	67	368	633	2,548	2,173	21,430
Ohio	5,061	48,884	102,116	4,723	1,365	2,165	13,525	43,482	36,856	339,539
Oklahoma	1,664	17,124	35,535	1,182	746	957	4,115	13,119	15,416	107,782
Oregon	1,651	25,653	30,333	1,680	1,223	337	5,534	11,466	10,093	114,401
Pennsylvania	4,888	60,736	123,506	3,840	974	2,497	6,609	53,898	55,688	350,056
Rhode Island	582	5,957	11,741	652	186	177	2,025	4,099	4,602	31,942
South Carolina	1,464	17,480	45,487	2,891	863	1,252	5,648	17,646	17,187	131,642
South Dakota	132	4,495	5,739	313	0	196	182	3,192	1,856	26,713
Tennessee	2,356	20,878	62,331	2,870	1,256	1,740	6,032	24,646	25,787	176,924
Texas	7,401	116,903	278,483	13,162	3,560	4,836	23,302	125,058	108,565	726,158
Utah	844	12,801	25,332	1,371	461	519	2,976	9,900	10,105	74,470
Vermont	336	2,170	4,526	243	0	0	324	1,747	2,212	17,377
Virginia	3,250	31,690	101,548	5,260	2,124	2,746	9,238	43,061	39,119	222,892
Washington	2,072	39,618	58,381	2,956	712	999	8,062	19,683	25,969	186,624
West Virginia	548	6,331	17,332	639	660	267	888	8,192	6,686	44,240
Wisconsin	2,021	27,624	45,508	2,833	642	597	4,179	20,807	16,450	174,304
Wyoming	86	1,271	5,795	348	0	76	754	2,647	1,970	19,706

Table B-4. Employment by Occupation—*Continued*

	Detailed occupation for employed persons age 16 and older									
	Number of employees in service occupations (Continued)									
	Food preparation and serving related occupations					Building and grounds cleaning and maintenance occupations:				
State	First-line supervisors of food preparation and serving workers	Cooks and food preparation workers	Waiters and waitresses	Food and beverage serving workers except waiters/ waitresses	Other food preparation and serving related workers	Total building and grounds cleaning and maintenance occupations:	First-line supervisors of housekeeping and janitorial workers	First-line supervisors of landscaping, lawn service, and groundskeeping workers	Building cleaning and pest control workers	Grounds maintenance workers
United States	980,568	3,377,763	2,232,784	1,218,263	1,007,266	5,833,080	225,274	157,253	4,135,016	1,315,537
Alabama	11,272	44,459	26,274	12,336	11,670	74,729	2,602	2,121	51,629	18,377
Alaska	2,675	10,188	2,792	2,879	2,542	13,267	875	231	10,305	1,856
Arizona	23,992	74,355	44,846	28,635	23,970	135,127	6,279	3,790	83,321	41,737
Arkansas	8,296	30,616	16,108	7,162	5,692	47,678	1,370	867	34,313	11,128
California	131,059	415,301	251,588	119,393	121,948	766,769	25,372	15,227	525,517	200,653
Colorado	19,670	62,423	37,173	25,536	17,439	96,579	3,376	2,621	66,649	23,933
Connecticut	11,396	29,131	20,837	13,028	8,886	72,020	2,660	2,811	48,490	18,059
Delaware	2,510	8,794	8,986	4,431	3,404	18,808	1,029	411	13,968	3,400
District of Columbia	1,583	8,000	2,955	1,758	2,097	14,046	319	134	12,713	880
Florida	75,992	183,299	189,042	90,110	71,363	446,971	18,400	16,428	302,336	109,807
Georgia	27,814	98,465	73,765	30,902	24,342	175,456	7,115	4,687	122,404	41,250
Hawaii	5,671	18,154	14,925	6,730	6,904	42,928	1,443	692	30,371	10,422
Idaho	6,582	17,951	12,162	6,452	3,593	32,849	1,537	1,294	22,564	7,454
Illinois	38,500	137,786	84,408	53,375	38,638	218,487	6,925	4,700	161,730	45,132
Indiana	15,950	72,696	43,679	27,945	25,408	109,688	5,629	4,026	79,186	20,847
Iowa	9,615	40,144	20,819	11,886	7,880	54,099	1,922	1,382	41,082	9,713
Kansas	5,508	36,660	19,977	9,275	7,257	51,724	2,473	1,613	36,808	10,830
Kentucky	11,502	49,912	26,316	18,309	12,321	62,873	3,009	1,184	45,134	13,546
Louisiana	13,156	54,934	34,497	19,954	14,113	75,536	2,969	2,087	54,832	15,648
Maine	3,170	15,101	8,638	5,420	3,206	24,207	1,073	1,038	16,877	5,219
Maryland	19,016	57,665	41,229	16,963	19,084	115,153	5,846	4,494	79,959	24,854
Massachusetts	22,556	77,501	48,693	30,540	28,689	118,027	4,001	4,357	85,300	24,369
Michigan	27,111	105,036	71,838	43,256	30,891	161,599	6,419	6,413	113,441	35,326
Minnesota	16,450	62,082	34,655	23,902	15,581	92,402	2,492	3,392	66,589	19,929
Mississippi	6,591	32,285	16,854	7,048	9,152	46,848	1,952	958	33,613	10,325
Missouri	16,854	63,449	47,501	24,433	18,072	102,957	3,292	2,391	74,530	22,744
Montana	3,171	11,688	7,947	5,928	2,834	19,754	625	511	14,849	3,769
Nebraska	5,446	22,101	12,295	7,227	5,186	35,443	895	1,105	26,254	7,189
Nevada	13,162	42,419	32,477	27,141	24,819	84,210	2,642	1,130	67,157	13,281
New Hampshire	5,162	13,630	7,736	6,434	6,024	23,279	1,509	1,595	14,686	5,489
New Jersey	25,276	66,157	64,862	31,009	25,314	152,970	6,071	5,448	110,965	30,486
New Mexico	4,651	25,355	15,708	6,334	7,938	38,960	2,365	1,384	26,333	8,878
New York	77,041	192,958	131,435	75,113	63,488	382,000	12,455	4,770	308,734	56,041
North Carolina	28,254	100,580	67,761	31,816	29,132	178,033	8,948	5,727	116,978	46,380
North Dakota	2,302	7,406	6,272	3,142	2,308	13,563	522	210	10,775	2,056
Ohio	34,805	133,820	75,170	58,595	37,149	185,566	8,068	6,243	131,057	40,198
Oklahoma	11,891	43,384	30,730	12,699	9,078	65,502	2,439	1,713	46,225	15,125
Oregon	11,308	51,092	23,383	17,504	11,314	73,108	3,483	2,241	49,437	17,947
Pennsylvania	34,426	129,829	82,324	58,575	44,902	207,146	7,670	7,143	151,859	40,474
Rhode Island	3,997	7,939	8,522	7,666	3,818	17,239	820	466	11,570	4,383
South Carolina	15,448	52,715	37,963	13,949	11,567	93,138	4,443	3,039	62,096	23,560
South Dakota	2,603	10,353	6,225	4,053	3,479	18,164	594	139	13,208	4,223
Tennessee	16,246	72,922	45,778	23,215	18,763	109,220	3,071	3,991	77,006	25,152
Texas	68,966	291,045	198,889	80,781	86,477	505,628	19,167	8,587	357,888	119,986
Utah	7,316	31,437	18,732	9,637	7,348	50,864	2,325	1,154	34,934	12,451
Vermont	3,065	5,863	3,371	2,488	2,590	13,325	282	163	8,651	4,229
Virginia	27,410	81,979	61,044	28,169	24,290	137,281	5,995	4,710	95,898	30,678
Washington	18,665	80,925	38,558	27,452	21,024	112,855	4,132	2,731	79,678	26,314
West Virginia	4,294	21,380	10,071	5,217	3,278	33,801	1,415	1,362	25,105	5,919
Wisconsin	18,506	65,660	41,301	29,509	19,328	99,291	4,453	1,963	72,282	20,593
Wyoming	2,666	8,739	3,673	2,952	1,676	11,913	506	379	7,730	3,298

Table B-4. Employment by Occupation—*Continued*

	Detailed occupation for employed persons age 16 and older									
	Number of employees in service occupations (Continued)						Number of employees in sales and office occupations			
	Personal care and service occupations:							Sales and related occupations:		
State	Total personal care and service occupations:	First-line supervisors of personal care and service workers	Personal appearance workers	Baggage porters and concierges, and tour and travel guides	Child care workers	Other personal care and service workers except personal appearance, baggage porters, concierges, and child care workers	Total sales and office occupations:	Total sales and related occupations:	First-line supervisors of retail sales workers	First-line supervisors of non-retail sales workers
United States	5,610,733	111,700	1,282,898	146,287	1,306,329	2,763,519	35,511,295	15,966,837	3,067,480	1,213,413
Alabama	65,246	953	19,247	1,104	16,922	27,020	483,264	211,593	44,256	12,593
Alaska	13,968	193	2,320	987	3,096	7,372	80,331	30,022	6,968	1,013
Arizona	113,863	1,898	23,774	4,059	20,060	64,072	770,287	334,502	62,717	23,506
Arkansas	37,123	427	9,823	366	10,211	16,296	301,090	132,523	33,723	8,673
California	859,892	16,409	167,115	12,842	171,595	491,931	4,140,175	1,914,864	326,330	154,324
Colorado	93,317	1,346	22,567	4,570	21,902	42,932	655,674	311,360	61,037	25,330
Connecticut	69,765	1,130	12,636	887	18,569	36,543	425,896	193,436	35,225	19,976
Delaware	14,288	303	3,820	395	3,207	6,563	104,483	44,795	10,099	3,082
District of Columbia	10,207	29	2,178	874	2,200	4,926	61,396	23,297	4,399	2,087
Florida	297,994	7,663	85,697	14,990	53,129	136,515	2,423,765	1,145,924	205,401	88,610
Georgia	133,578	3,892	45,046	2,849	29,726	52,065	1,118,869	514,194	98,782	41,670
Hawaii	25,611	520	5,264	5,170	4,204	10,453	167,514	75,776	13,582	4,857
Idaho	31,635	655	8,143	742	5,710	16,385	171,150	74,448	15,168	5,018
Illinois	239,023	3,610	53,253	5,097	66,701	110,362	1,469,223	654,494	111,296	52,259
Indiana	94,510	2,056	22,870	1,679	25,589	42,316	710,805	311,494	67,379	23,737
Iowa	62,226	1,217	10,632	555	22,533	27,289	355,226	149,722	30,952	11,943
Kansas	49,110	931	10,471	306	15,639	21,763	313,690	135,026	26,742	10,579
Kentucky	60,553	770	12,702	964	15,492	30,625	458,167	197,526	44,723	14,598
Louisiana	76,357	1,190	22,092	2,308	13,987	36,780	480,891	221,546	43,212	16,269
Maine	24,625	612	3,759	524	5,038	14,692	154,108	68,866	15,724	6,536
Maryland	104,181	1,630	24,856	2,213	30,344	45,138	665,062	285,962	57,802	19,516
Massachusetts	139,875	1,793	29,768	2,922	34,494	70,898	769,643	349,800	66,940	27,581
Michigan	164,251	3,989	37,156	2,017	37,309	83,780	1,036,262	462,037	88,700	31,672
Minnesota	118,714	3,616	20,327	2,773	29,649	62,349	650,156	285,329	52,984	23,282
Mississippi	38,829	1,166	9,006	1,090	6,534	21,033	284,709	132,126	26,998	10,480
Missouri	102,644	1,707	19,827	4,012	26,294	50,804	703,392	304,045	58,316	21,982
Montana	20,944	363	3,622	798	5,229	10,932	104,236	44,774	10,956	3,398
Nebraska	35,358	933	7,893	591	12,683	13,258	231,410	101,172	22,581	9,199
Nevada	80,204	7,786	12,528	7,704	7,198	44,988	349,348	162,621	32,115	11,949
New Hampshire	22,135	369	4,551	782	4,151	12,282	169,398	81,772	17,366	6,323
New Jersey	153,258	3,584	40,352	4,063	41,516	63,743	1,060,149	481,386	88,643	46,528
New Mexico	40,633	389	7,188	460	5,378	27,218	210,762	91,073	19,161	6,608
New York	402,145	6,793	89,223	21,726	113,955	170,448	2,207,637	971,304	171,739	72,643
North Carolina	138,506	3,031	39,117	2,504	30,408	63,446	1,045,282	501,553	101,876	28,894
North Dakota	16,733	63	3,033	138	5,842	7,657	88,549	36,371	8,537	3,386
Ohio	171,396	3,021	44,255	2,190	39,163	82,767	1,280,414	550,437	110,470	40,790
Oklahoma	56,585	2,156	15,175	1,344	14,360	23,550	423,177	179,131	38,364	13,698
Oregon	89,538	1,241	14,245	1,242	16,884	55,926	426,132	182,269	36,748	13,534
Pennsylvania	222,055	2,533	49,203	4,240	49,892	116,187	1,415,523	610,272	118,394	43,871
Rhode Island	19,945	433	4,095	909	3,699	10,809	128,296	56,121	13,409	5,363
South Carolina	68,466	967	20,705	1,110	15,160	30,524	533,231	253,358	51,922	16,185
South Dakota	15,220	236	2,821	171	5,796	6,196	100,603	42,459	8,896	3,262
Tennessee	104,612	1,886	28,681	2,553	24,337	47,155	722,593	323,045	67,820	23,247
Texas	423,873	6,662	108,419	8,644	104,232	195,916	3,073,810	1,427,101	265,625	112,071
Utah	40,959	1,083	13,249	583	10,049	15,995	369,208	155,361	32,135	11,942
Vermont	14,639	209	2,201	320	3,323	8,586	69,982	30,898	7,179	2,007
Virginia	147,131	2,314	34,921	2,907	39,571	67,418	903,468	402,421	82,816	27,793
Washington	142,827	2,891	26,049	3,121	32,173	78,593	742,452	330,398	66,496	23,451
West Virginia	28,657	618	3,588	320	4,893	19,238	172,459	75,305	19,878	4,202
Wisconsin	103,658	2,340	21,501	1,062	23,073	55,682	662,702	283,654	57,200	20,041
Wyoming	9,871	94	1,934	510	3,230	4,103	65,246	27,874	7,699	1,855

Table B-4. Employment by Occupation—*Continued*

	Detailed occupation for employed persons age 16 and older									
	Number of employees in sales and office occupations (Continued)									
	Sales and related occupations: (Continued)					Office and administrative support occupations:				
State	Cashiers	Retail sales workers except cashiers	Sales representatives, services	Sales representatives, wholesale and manufacturing	Other sales and related workers	Total office and administrative support occupations:	First-line supervisors of office and administrative support workers	Communications equipment operators	Financial clerks except bookkeeping, accounting, and auditing clerks	Bookkeeping, accounting, and auditing clerks
United States	3,403,586	3,758,295	1,704,563	1,380,608	1,438,892	19,544,458	1,350,554	77,053	1,340,524	1,201,999
Alabama	49,587	55,159	18,920	16,914	14,164	271,671	20,273	2,101	19,696	16,397
Alaska	8,234	7,256	2,403	1,490	2,658	50,309	4,270	150	3,781	4,687
Arizona	69,816	71,568	41,725	24,772	40,398	435,785	28,063	2,174	31,162	27,356
Arkansas	29,579	31,091	9,068	9,591	10,798	168,567	11,158	596	12,336	9,637
California	413,189	465,217	196,616	167,310	191,878	2,225,311	150,228	7,954	129,682	140,355
Colorado	44,971	80,217	35,160	29,463	35,182	344,314	21,066	1,218	20,912	23,936
Connecticut	39,094	40,657	22,034	20,361	16,089	232,460	15,398	205	16,213	14,700
Delaware	9,133	11,896	4,281	3,329	2,975	59,688	3,724	181	5,489	3,949
District of Columbia	3,610	5,033	3,406	1,202	3,560	38,099	2,569	307	1,962	677
Florida	225,361	276,271	130,747	85,560	133,974	1,277,841	96,086	5,107	84,908	72,453
Georgia	115,025	121,788	52,098	40,913	43,918	604,675	51,302	2,555	44,962	34,174
Hawaii	15,009	23,428	6,401	4,827	7,672	91,738	7,355	457	4,821	6,574
Idaho	13,611	19,450	7,591	5,380	8,230	96,702	6,458	455	6,073	5,834
Illinois	137,049	147,989	90,063	66,180	49,658	814,729	55,850	2,845	56,873	42,806
Indiana	67,145	67,499	29,489	31,156	25,089	399,311	22,671	703	28,213	20,248
Iowa	32,969	33,512	15,992	13,648	10,706	205,504	12,162	570	15,461	13,488
Kansas	27,718	30,649	16,677	12,074	10,587	178,664	13,118	490	11,986	12,202
Kentucky	53,626	41,950	14,911	15,985	11,733	260,641	17,379	756	19,545	15,039
Louisiana	53,788	54,018	19,333	19,057	15,869	259,345	20,663	1,606	18,422	17,230
Maine	14,555	16,028	6,201	4,352	5,470	85,242	4,697	65	6,469	5,894
Maryland	64,933	67,050	30,996	20,734	24,931	379,100	36,370	1,352	24,649	23,640
Massachusetts	72,055	79,082	44,707	29,028	30,407	419,843	29,876	1,525	32,171	25,296
Michigan	106,389	110,371	43,175	45,046	36,684	574,225	33,208	1,844	41,222	30,832
Minnesota	54,474	64,691	34,800	30,338	24,760	364,827	21,945	910	26,867	24,646
Mississippi	36,536	30,956	11,686	9,038	6,432	152,583	11,210	548	10,115	9,354
Missouri	64,141	73,318	31,088	29,554	25,646	399,347	25,256	1,786	28,316	24,094
Montana	6,912	12,057	4,086	3,715	3,650	59,462	4,139	112	3,407	6,428
Nebraska	17,646	22,275	11,781	9,243	8,447	130,238	7,210	584	8,760	11,447
Nevada	38,269	37,494	15,335	8,790	18,669	186,727	14,822	1,469	11,177	9,999
New Hampshire	14,990	20,101	8,621	7,529	6,842	87,626	6,224	337	6,085	5,634
New Jersey	91,336	106,407	61,377	44,167	42,928	578,763	45,041	1,252	44,541	36,138
New Mexico	23,181	23,282	5,456	6,934	6,451	119,689	7,924	351	9,169	8,232
New York	209,346	231,669	120,784	75,452	89,671	1,236,333	86,758	4,192	90,455	77,032
North Carolina	117,690	111,396	52,417	43,442	45,838	543,729	39,072	2,851	34,464	32,308
North Dakota	7,770	8,907	3,204	2,661	1,906	52,178	3,187	478	2,593	3,155
Ohio	114,986	127,677	55,195	55,924	45,395	729,977	48,468	2,938	55,152	41,507
Oklahoma	40,447	43,097	15,147	14,702	13,676	244,046	18,917	657	19,556	16,687
Oregon	32,333	44,286	18,340	17,146	19,882	243,863	16,012	576	13,165	19,826
Pennsylvania	133,862	138,768	67,296	60,636	47,445	805,251	54,578	2,236	60,406	46,838
Rhode Island	10,751	12,547	4,253	5,514	4,284	72,175	3,784	146	3,580	4,981
South Carolina	62,176	57,156	20,098	20,811	25,010	279,873	18,266	1,587	18,468	17,850
South Dakota	8,912	9,725	4,632	3,926	3,106	58,144	3,412	405	5,811	4,922
Tennessee	74,578	75,688	30,911	26,474	24,327	399,548	25,740	1,432	31,366	23,989
Texas	308,544	341,475	157,528	121,507	120,351	1,646,709	112,372	9,089	107,295	103,558
Utah	27,591	35,324	17,312	14,167	16,890	213,847	12,549	1,537	15,463	9,458
Vermont	6,386	7,969	2,505	2,520	2,332	39,084	2,892	124	2,828	2,600
Virginia	88,497	94,185	41,520	28,265	39,345	501,047	43,740	2,444	32,743	31,827
Washington	60,224	81,558	32,064	31,830	34,775	412,054	23,818	928	27,975	30,013
West Virginia	20,730	16,342	4,894	4,951	4,308	97,154	5,869	954	5,630	6,638
Wisconsin	57,770	66,073	29,161	31,806	21,603	379,048	21,145	1,843	26,529	22,071
Wyoming	7,062	6,693	1,078	1,194	2,293	37,372	2,260	71	1,600	3,363

Table B-4. Employment by Occupation—*Continued*

	Detailed occupation for employed persons age 16 and older									
	Number of employees in sales and office occupations (Continued)					Number of employees in natural resources, construction, and maintenance occupations				
	Office and administrative support occupations: (Continued)						Farming, fishing, and forestry occupations:			
State	Information and record clerks except customer service representatives	Customer service representatives	Material recording, scheduling, dispatching, and distributing workers	Secretaries and administrative assistants	Other office and administrative support workers	Total natural resources, construction, and maintenance occupations:	Total farming, fishing, and forestry occupations:	First-line supervisors of farming, fishing, and forestry workers	Agricultural workers	Fishing and hunting, and forest, conservation, and logging workers
United States	2,565,058	2,743,369	3,733,775	3,274,608	3,257,518	13,542,970	1,102,425	61,447	931,916	109,062
Alabama	35,669	30,849	60,586	44,182	41,918	198,139	10,835	735	7,343	2,757
Alaska	7,241	3,959	10,189	7,329	8,703	42,889	3,913	277	405	3,231
Arizona	64,161	79,143	72,756	57,549	73,421	267,750	18,219	1,929	15,113	1,177
Arkansas	21,459	16,759	39,208	32,562	24,852	139,324	18,632	1,030	14,090	3,512
California	306,669	317,721	429,894	322,848	419,960	1,687,321	313,063	15,258	291,580	6,225
Colorado	51,420	63,822	60,640	52,029	49,271	259,092	15,855	955	13,932	968
Connecticut	27,033	31,312	43,473	45,567	38,559	137,403	3,434	105	2,462	867
Delaware	7,434	8,449	9,665	9,817	10,980	38,720	3,017	0	2,512	505
District of Columbia	7,725	5,703	4,274	5,903	8,979	7,533	0	0	0	0
Florida	179,667	219,785	207,974	199,723	212,138	824,719	59,550	4,694	48,923	5,933
Georgia	69,521	94,958	117,042	94,537	95,624	420,891	26,609	1,791	22,408	2,410
Hawaii	14,996	8,456	14,885	15,031	19,163	68,540	4,648	171	3,946	531
Idaho	14,081	16,714	18,042	15,999	13,046	84,577	19,887	677	17,464	1,746
Illinois	104,589	113,069	170,066	134,044	134,587	456,875	20,843	1,036	18,492	1,315
Indiana	52,717	54,830	91,828	64,738	63,363	281,205	15,289	635	12,738	1,916
Iowa	26,044	23,343	41,590	38,747	34,099	152,311	18,008	444	17,132	432
Kansas	22,732	23,001	34,097	32,273	28,765	139,368	12,011	616	11,239	156
Kentucky	31,807	33,944	60,583	40,448	41,140	177,972	13,720	334	12,155	1,231
Louisiana	34,975	21,405	51,300	50,956	42,788	240,398	12,327	1,195	6,261	4,871
Maine	11,535	10,834	16,268	16,403	13,077	68,747	10,223	684	2,235	7,304
Maryland	46,764	42,399	62,947	71,361	69,618	233,312	7,107	358	4,896	1,853
Massachusetts	47,850	56,255	72,451	79,135	75,284	238,732	9,135	375	6,463	2,297
Michigan	74,263	75,632	125,071	98,451	93,702	359,640	24,633	1,074	20,383	3,176
Minnesota	45,803	55,942	67,577	58,676	62,461	237,626	22,027	818	19,589	1,620
Mississippi	20,646	17,074	31,443	31,235	20,958	129,903	10,367	382	5,914	4,071
Missouri	56,230	54,000	75,542	65,865	68,258	259,415	19,086	875	15,913	2,298
Montana	7,929	8,068	8,891	11,607	8,881	67,153	9,092	759	7,633	700
Nebraska	17,234	15,161	24,652	23,496	21,694	99,460	13,618	359	13,010	249
Nevada	27,962	34,353	37,034	20,815	29,096	117,179	2,232	114	2,118	0
New Hampshire	11,477	10,389	19,500	16,415	11,565	60,856	2,431	473	1,464	494
New Jersey	69,790	74,462	105,572	111,997	89,970	317,343	9,248	534	7,516	1,198
New Mexico	20,504	17,373	18,773	20,773	16,590	98,089	6,816	42	6,395	379
New York	159,087	138,586	201,935	249,725	228,563	687,539	22,808	773	18,079	3,956
North Carolina	64,554	87,589	113,700	84,375	84,816	447,318	29,731	1,330	24,132	4,269
North Dakota	8,409	6,571	8,933	9,958	8,894	54,635	6,555	173	6,333	49
Ohio	90,495	105,555	151,355	120,194	114,313	413,036	16,549	1,195	13,938	1,416
Oklahoma	29,310	27,941	47,197	44,317	39,464	205,710	12,509	644	11,156	709
Oregon	33,560	38,189	47,710	38,673	36,152	168,097	36,068	2,594	27,365	6,109
Pennsylvania	96,486	97,085	152,750	157,537	137,335	498,411	29,121	1,304	24,165	3,652
Rhode Island	7,252	10,851	13,768	16,370	11,443	37,555	2,097	0	1,434	663
South Carolina	35,032	40,765	62,513	49,246	36,146	194,758	8,710	1,241	6,401	1,068
South Dakota	7,350	7,991	8,194	12,772	7,287	48,389	8,268	190	7,445	633
Tennessee	49,202	55,574	86,515	59,530	66,200	267,287	11,946	753	9,309	1,884
Texas	222,268	244,134	315,933	263,316	268,744	1,386,424	61,556	5,507	50,940	5,109
Utah	33,252	43,486	35,749	31,866	30,487	122,316	4,805	278	4,511	16
Vermont	4,585	4,990	5,968	7,539	7,558	30,920	3,204	38	2,503	663
Virginia	62,866	67,368	91,976	87,166	80,917	347,368	15,681	1,396	10,018	4,267
Washington	55,017	57,605	82,792	63,637	70,269	336,570	60,145	3,993	50,470	5,682
West Virginia	13,059	11,616	17,726	20,045	15,617	82,029	2,504	181	1,108	1,215
Wisconsin	48,689	54,566	78,871	59,337	65,997	255,344	29,883	676	27,197	2,010
Wyoming	6,658	3,743	6,377	8,494	4,806	46,782	4,410	452	3,688	270

Table B-4. Employment by Occupation—*Continued*

	Detailed occupation for employed persons age 16 and older									
	Number of employees in natural resources, construction, and maintenance (Continued)									
	Construction and extraction occupations:									
State	Total construction and extraction occupations:	First-line supervisors of construction and extraction workers	Carpenters	Construction laborers	Electricians	Painters and paperhangers	Pipelayers, plumbers, pipefitters, and steamfitters	Construction trades workers except carpenters, electricians, painters, plumbers, and construction laborers	Other construction workers and helpers	Extraction workers
United States	7,663,198	758,517	1,210,044	1,789,286	774,005	585,319	550,828	1,381,529	401,350	212,320
Alabama	105,069	10,251	15,402	21,772	11,035	8,330	7,738	21,412	5,982	3,147
Alaska	21,838	2,648	3,625	3,459	2,070	852	1,382	4,479	1,116	2,207
Arizona	147,250	14,475	19,259	36,805	11,553	11,159	8,670	33,434	8,159	3,736
Arkansas	68,438	7,929	10,207	14,024	6,492	4,543	5,913	14,378	2,642	2,310
California	876,690	80,344	121,593	273,710	74,367	81,891	62,143	132,353	40,736	9,553
Colorado	166,935	19,699	26,421	39,125	12,954	11,064	12,488	31,530	6,628	7,026
Connecticut	86,327	6,709	20,485	15,798	8,842	9,884	6,323	13,513	4,267	506
Delaware	21,756	3,014	3,381	5,339	2,551	1,285	1,330	4,011	747	98
District of Columbia	5,759	249	1,366	1,645	500	838	167	827	167	0
Florida	465,690	41,615	69,293	134,110	46,006	37,346	26,659	82,849	25,063	2,749
Georgia	231,345	23,262	39,205	51,337	22,405	24,328	14,780	43,668	10,499	1,861
Hawaii	40,729	3,959	6,070	9,050	4,648	2,727	3,323	9,047	1,728	177
Idaho	42,170	3,368	5,869	8,770	4,445	1,476	2,322	11,920	1,727	2,273
Illinois	260,137	18,384	48,572	60,316	31,634	19,083	17,933	44,625	14,937	4,653
Indiana	153,229	14,021	25,167	31,960	21,600	10,627	8,539	30,869	7,873	2,573
Iowa	80,441	7,685	10,721	19,254	10,731	4,437	6,513	14,793	5,525	782
Kansas	78,241	7,885	9,763	15,771	7,607	7,331	6,601	16,369	4,052	2,862
Kentucky	95,032	9,649	12,120	17,647	11,095	7,429	7,262	20,217	4,304	5,309
Louisiana	149,464	22,708	26,776	23,911	14,465	9,508	11,161	21,371	5,956	13,608
Maine	37,136	2,826	8,972	4,835	4,937	2,657	3,250	7,130	2,511	18
Maryland	142,497	16,013	25,831	26,893	14,813	13,588	12,379	22,457	9,440	1,083
Massachusetts	150,776	13,959	28,539	31,004	16,270	16,600	13,321	23,640	7,012	431
Michigan	185,529	18,809	31,089	38,967	22,638	11,615	14,450	35,156	9,321	3,484
Minnesota	132,285	13,836	20,950	26,126	13,185	9,599	10,668	28,003	7,518	2,400
Mississippi	72,255	8,210	10,661	14,755	7,599	3,978	6,238	12,759	3,810	4,245
Missouri	151,223	16,387	24,511	36,317	15,490	9,996	8,641	31,317	7,426	1,138
Montana	39,918	4,669	6,732	9,303	2,239	2,764	2,670	5,350	2,073	4,118
Nebraska	50,900	5,804	7,395	13,759	5,509	2,789	3,051	9,629	2,402	562
Nevada	69,103	7,129	6,430	17,910	7,885	4,105	4,187	13,335	4,105	4,017
New Hampshire	36,057	4,502	7,008	5,193	2,963	2,186	3,909	7,496	2,604	196
New Jersey	192,605	17,360	31,328	52,294	23,789	12,956	15,105	29,104	9,959	710
New Mexico	59,387	7,365	7,237	14,495	4,161	1,219	3,645	11,429	3,514	6,322
New York	432,066	35,977	72,514	118,253	44,565	36,973	31,285	61,726	28,721	2,052
North Carolina	251,458	23,410	41,809	52,960	23,901	25,343	13,461	53,533	15,664	1,377
North Dakota	31,198	5,026	3,823	4,676	2,991	525	1,626	7,890	2,046	2,595
Ohio	216,934	19,374	34,550	42,133	25,485	14,767	16,036	43,116	16,364	5,109
Oklahoma	123,561	14,521	16,961	21,816	10,591	6,967	9,521	24,533	5,471	13,180
Oregon	79,003	8,583	14,700	18,357	6,850	5,804	6,858	12,464	4,839	548
Pennsylvania	275,061	26,523	48,102	52,293	28,401	17,526	19,378	54,550	17,187	11,101
Rhode Island	22,265	1,901	4,936	5,262	1,748	1,337	3,081	2,819	1,132	49
South Carolina	106,099	13,987	16,173	21,741	12,002	8,156	7,692	18,278	6,927	1,143
South Dakota	25,933	2,917	4,354	7,435	2,458	680	2,043	3,739	1,508	799
Tennessee	145,493	12,558	23,008	30,969	17,918	11,535	10,296	32,310	5,495	1,404
Texas	867,353	88,695	128,097	204,386	73,123	62,972	71,364	150,352	34,530	53,834
Utah	73,523	7,068	8,819	16,287	7,403	4,707	4,878	16,887	3,421	4,053
Vermont	17,727	1,983	4,936	3,111	1,242	966	1,436	2,635	988	430
Virginia	203,795	23,245	32,831	44,925	23,871	14,623	14,392	36,720	10,648	2,540
Washington	165,802	15,444	30,758	31,109	20,862	14,121	9,801	32,669	9,937	1,101
West Virginia	53,442	6,753	4,741	7,356	6,372	1,389	4,101	9,781	3,203	9,746
Wisconsin	130,833	11,899	23,774	25,809	15,705	7,879	10,061	26,010	8,299	1,397
Wyoming	25,441	3,930	3,180	4,754	2,039	859	757	3,047	1,167	5,708

Table B-4. Employment by Occupation—*Continued*

	Detailed occupation for employed persons age 16 and older									
	Number of employees in natural resources, construction, and maintenance (Cont'd)				Number of employees in production, transportation, and material moving occupations:					
	Installation, maintenance, and repair occupations:					Production occupations				
State	Total installation, maintenance, and repair occupations:	First-line supervisors of mechanics, installers, and repairers	Vehicle and mobile equipment mechanics, installers, and repairers	Other installation, maintenance, and repair occupations including electrical and electronic equipment mechanics, installers, and repairers	Total production, transportation, and material moving occupations:	Total production occupations	First-line supervisors of production and operating workers	Assemblers and fabricators	Food processing workers	Metal workers and plastic workers
United States	4,777,347	268,777	1,815,483	2,693,087	18,559,438	8,970,126	885,187	1,238,458	745,518	1,807,736
Alabama	82,235	7,104	28,911	46,220	334,381	184,469	20,471	30,381	13,686	40,153
Alaska	17,138	1,221	6,744	9,173	39,325	14,811	1,693	351	2,769	1,695
Arizona	102,281	5,089	39,700	57,492	300,581	134,080	10,972	19,404	13,279	26,612
Arkansas	52,254	3,427	18,607	30,220	209,864	117,007	11,945	12,512	14,345	22,431
California	497,568	21,883	210,148	265,537	2,028,353	929,157	83,551	113,895	90,814	145,392
Colorado	76,302	4,668	32,855	38,779	246,296	104,648	9,757	11,484	12,566	16,857
Connecticut	47,642	1,399	15,623	30,620	169,144	88,502	8,733	10,835	5,443	25,599
Delaware	13,947	695	5,407	7,845	40,794	17,516	1,971	1,900	1,941	1,897
District of Columbia	1,774	0	415	1,359	12,443	2,870	352	0	293	0
Florida	299,479	17,414	106,838	175,227	832,859	309,688	25,423	32,236	35,124	48,336
Georgia	162,937	11,025	58,894	93,018	635,759	293,208	30,817	39,763	25,238	45,322
Hawaii	23,163	1,382	9,191	12,590	57,343	20,738	1,532	833	4,676	2,142
Idaho	22,520	985	8,899	12,636	95,927	43,011	4,146	3,822	4,305	8,702
Illinois	175,895	8,361	66,232	101,302	865,479	411,216	42,168	55,071	40,661	91,225
Indiana	112,687	5,389	42,718	64,580	586,651	333,452	36,638	66,498	16,460	81,290
Iowa	53,862	2,847	21,177	29,838	272,726	146,631	15,842	19,020	18,979	31,982
Kansas	49,116	3,274	20,175	25,667	194,845	103,552	9,945	14,986	10,890	21,004
Kentucky	69,220	4,158	25,945	39,117	329,430	176,284	15,295	37,632	11,338	35,973
Louisiana	78,607	7,246	25,246	46,115	240,799	115,523	13,968	6,656	7,875	27,347
Maine	21,388	1,471	9,403	10,514	73,488	36,135	3,519	2,513	3,959	8,403
Maryland	83,708	3,817	30,985	48,906	245,694	88,006	11,187	7,780	8,549	8,751
Massachusetts	78,821	2,869	30,487	45,465	306,595	147,979	11,562	23,854	15,423	28,906
Michigan	149,478	7,600	55,356	86,522	716,933	434,854	42,837	98,103	20,525	117,089
Minnesota	83,314	3,978	30,869	48,467	379,473	203,606	18,938	34,819	14,992	44,102
Mississippi	47,281	2,860	18,378	26,043	208,887	109,829	11,665	20,450	7,621	22,748
Missouri	89,106	5,200	34,496	49,410	392,261	196,616	19,770	32,604	13,677	42,185
Montana	18,143	973	8,191	8,979	40,248	16,036	1,636	1,195	1,747	3,210
Nebraska	34,942	2,000	14,320	18,622	131,225	65,312	6,394	8,333	11,295	14,184
Nevada	45,844	2,899	17,266	25,679	135,261	49,980	4,678	4,413	6,350	5,146
New Hampshire	22,368	1,311	8,405	12,652	83,582	47,113	4,802	5,910	3,094	12,027
New Jersey	115,490	5,567	42,289	67,634	464,807	171,585	18,603	14,228	16,903	21,725
New Mexico	31,886	2,088	13,694	16,104	78,627	29,097	2,057	2,775	4,209	4,440
New York	232,665	13,211	85,733	133,721	886,035	348,269	34,837	31,257	33,749	59,673
North Carolina	166,129	8,899	57,968	99,262	614,573	342,931	35,331	47,838	27,516	52,629
North Dakota	16,882	919	8,014	7,949	50,459	20,632	1,721	3,450	1,023	4,929
Ohio	179,553	11,552	63,925	104,076	884,986	471,989	48,835	81,528	27,659	120,708
Oklahoma	69,640	4,295	29,937	35,408	226,172	120,052	12,641	14,419	8,941	31,308
Oregon	53,026	2,682	19,820	30,524	224,803	112,613	9,084	12,716	10,570	20,866
Pennsylvania	194,229	11,359	78,623	104,247	839,385	398,166	38,161	47,996	33,342	84,709
Rhode Island	13,193	828	5,487	6,878	59,261	31,188	2,817	2,348	2,119	8,668
South Carolina	79,949	4,364	25,578	50,007	317,342	182,721	17,156	30,144	9,945	32,820
South Dakota	14,188	1,030	5,383	7,775	61,981	33,469	2,534	3,927	3,727	8,113
Tennessee	109,848	7,631	35,185	67,032	469,539	245,036	22,561	45,778	14,742	53,825
Texas	457,515	25,268	172,876	259,371	1,543,113	686,140	70,257	75,271	51,990	158,710
Utah	43,988	1,936	18,231	23,821	186,048	104,437	8,694	16,133	7,889	14,524
Vermont	9,989	445	4,200	5,344	36,206	20,469	1,912	2,785	1,949	3,941
Virginia	127,892	8,944	49,764	69,184	390,307	175,476	19,873	15,050	13,110	28,524
Washington	110,623	7,674	47,037	55,912	390,470	174,741	16,039	23,427	15,352	34,386
West Virginia	26,083	1,696	9,031	15,356	90,800	40,853	5,197	5,297	2,000	5,743
Wisconsin	94,628	4,949	32,165	57,514	498,941	302,220	32,378	43,547	20,145	73,069
Wyoming	16,931	895	8,662	7,374	38,937	16,213	2,292	1,291	724	3,711

Table B-4. Employment by Occupation—*Continued*

	Detailed occupation for employed persons age 16 and older										
	Number of employees in production, transportation, and material moving occupations: (Continued)										
	Production occupations (Continued)					Transportation occupations					
State	Printing workers	Textile, apparel, and furnishings workers	Woodworkers	Plant and system operators	Other production occupations	Total transportation occupations:	Supervisors of transportation and material moving workers	Air transportation workers	Rail and water transportation workers	Bus drivers	Driver/sales workers and truck drivers
United States	224,939	604,064	149,009	263,913	3,051,302	5,569,842	220,946	269,226	183,306	612,857	3,493,683
Alabama	3,038	8,872	3,628	5,459	58,781	86,712	3,054	2,534	4,788	7,459	62,674
Alaska	491	1,899	331	1,818	3,764	15,399	602	3,074	1,465	1,091	5,657
Arizona	2,303	10,624	2,120	5,467	43,299	100,764	3,409	10,611	1,917	10,300	58,334
Arkansas	1,878	4,828	2,906	3,249	42,913	52,849	2,949	1,468	1,789	4,820	37,911
California	21,338	103,997	13,240	26,613	330,317	598,674	25,288	29,044	10,520	49,858	382,452
Colorado	2,841	8,507	2,279	5,738	34,619	92,668	3,428	9,767	3,134	8,367	56,342
Connecticut	2,305	4,459	1,667	2,188	27,273	52,811	1,390	1,740	1,440	11,235	30,607
Delaware	102	1,072	238	437	7,958	12,494	361	475	565	1,878	8,390
District of Columbia	337	323	0	658	907	6,659	291	426	286	1,058	2,074
Florida	10,487	34,286	5,937	12,346	105,513	336,991	12,094	29,122	16,106	31,437	195,439
Georgia	5,181	34,154	4,747	6,642	101,344	202,005	7,673	16,245	3,240	21,848	126,634
Hawaii	891	3,504	387	1,457	5,316	24,712	1,399	3,982	969	1,890	11,513
Idaho	869	3,057	1,304	1,943	14,863	33,400	737	2,109	556	2,681	25,575
Illinois	12,940	16,570	3,669	12,028	136,884	250,140	10,508	9,323	9,793	27,365	154,240
Indiana	6,627	9,258	5,578	5,433	105,670	122,913	5,948	3,707	4,807	12,039	84,664
Iowa	2,889	5,832	2,096	3,029	46,957	64,504	1,797	682	2,032	5,613	49,311
Kansas	2,550	4,115	1,891	3,334	34,837	48,978	1,683	2,794	1,893	5,554	32,996
Kentucky	3,591	8,254	1,683	4,091	58,427	81,585	4,558	2,452	3,310	8,688	53,886
Louisiana	2,693	7,336	2,296	7,219	40,133	82,945	3,918	2,889	11,427	7,417	48,199
Maine	1,106	2,388	1,271	1,113	11,863	23,905	1,032	527	1,267	2,997	16,093
Maryland	3,174	8,850	1,975	6,162	31,578	103,208	4,362	4,260	2,490	17,255	56,241
Massachusetts	6,725	9,315	1,965	3,057	47,172	98,822	3,434	3,131	2,591	15,789	54,039
Michigan	5,015	16,527	5,669	8,470	120,619	157,807	6,045	5,216	3,349	16,219	109,175
Minnesota	8,472	7,637	4,300	5,120	65,226	100,997	3,001	6,964	3,724	12,958	63,166
Mississippi	1,146	7,910	2,366	2,321	33,602	59,917	2,563	1,552	3,535	5,931	41,405
Missouri	5,186	9,787	3,517	4,712	65,178	111,572	4,132	3,614	5,386	13,196	74,829
Montana	90	1,694	445	742	5,277	17,743	933	1,167	951	1,805	10,939
Nebraska	950	1,916	498	1,908	19,834	36,763	1,927	528	3,696	2,496	24,852
Nevada	2,978	5,682	825	4,022	15,886	49,267	1,223	4,272	406	3,142	27,371
New Hampshire	1,832	3,020	949	642	14,837	23,837	993	1,959	574	2,849	15,208
New Jersey	5,721	14,684	1,860	6,629	71,232	174,402	7,896	6,489	3,099	24,456	95,778
New Mexico	273	2,189	541	1,074	11,539	30,937	739	1,714	1,037	3,433	19,870
New York	9,854	35,805	6,117	13,371	123,606	379,217	12,839	8,839	11,354	68,801	162,796
North Carolina	6,932	39,197	7,311	6,522	119,655	159,131	5,877	8,520	2,255	15,709	114,039
North Dakota	236	899	292	1,679	6,403	18,483	212	492	1,692	1,007	13,942
Ohio	9,052	16,667	7,058	7,807	152,675	209,225	8,302	6,024	5,460	23,053	141,597
Oklahoma	3,090	5,133	885	4,834	38,801	62,163	2,665	1,598	1,617	4,106	46,495
Oregon	4,716	6,658	4,134	2,354	41,515	63,700	2,575	2,123	3,111	6,704	36,646
Pennsylvania	14,634	20,345	8,788	12,544	137,647	229,123	7,733	6,305	5,753	33,716	146,355
Rhode Island	630	2,246	249	331	11,780	18,313	432	493	733	2,241	11,859
South Carolina	3,741	14,872	1,865	4,317	67,861	73,421	4,033	2,236	1,852	6,073	50,773
South Dakota	539	1,663	959	776	11,231	17,804	896	1,150	596	1,310	12,504
Tennessee	6,439	11,869	4,450	4,445	80,927	107,732	4,594	3,791	2,128	10,120	76,173
Texas	14,917	41,909	8,891	22,938	241,257	511,027	23,310	29,418	16,600	40,244	350,678
Utah	2,742	6,713	2,763	2,924	42,055	47,006	1,675	4,110	780	3,982	32,076
Vermont	596	1,271	363	521	7,131	10,258	564	277	388	1,148	6,930
Virginia	4,210	14,727	3,138	6,294	70,550	135,301	5,949	5,648	3,739	17,424	81,094
Washington	4,183	9,552	3,417	6,661	61,724	124,321	6,032	10,952	7,200	16,613	70,081
West Virginia	1,039	2,244	1,043	2,218	16,072	31,475	866	644	1,298	4,222	22,496
Wisconsin	11,189	8,814	5,015	5,649	102,414	100,431	2,671	2,517	2,902	11,692	71,375
Wyoming	181	934	93	2,607	4,380	15,331	354	252	1,706	1,568	9,910

Table B-4. Employment by Occupation—Continued

	Detailed occupation for employed persons age 16 and older				
	Number of employees in production, transportation, and material moving occupations: (Continued)				
	Transportation occupations (Continued)		Material moving occupations:		
State	Motor vehicle operators except bus and truck drivers	Other transportation workers	Total material moving occupations:	Laborers and material movers, hand	Material moving workers except supervisors and laborers and material movers, hand
United States	493,723	296,101	4,019,470	3,139,549	879,921
Alabama	2,693	3,510	63,200	47,830	15,370
Alaska	2,030	1,480	9,115	6,910	2,205
Arizona	9,842	6,351	65,737	54,066	11,671
Arkansas	2,045	1,867	40,008	30,244	9,764
California	68,462	33,050	500,522	404,822	95,700
Colorado	7,154	4,476	48,980	40,477	8,503
Connecticut	3,428	2,971	27,831	23,328	4,503
Delaware	631	194	10,784	8,917	1,867
District of Columbia	1,514	1,010	2,914	2,220	694
Florida	33,189	19,604	186,180	156,400	29,780
Georgia	13,379	12,986	140,546	97,482	43,064
Hawaii	3,258	1,701	11,893	10,365	1,528
Idaho	919	823	19,516	15,066	4,450
Illinois	25,233	13,678	204,123	153,808	50,315
Indiana	7,221	4,527	130,286	98,415	31,871
Iowa	2,646	2,423	61,591	48,360	13,231
Kansas	2,005	2,053	42,315	32,809	9,506
Kentucky	4,634	4,057	71,561	53,762	17,799
Louisiana	5,706	3,389	42,331	28,287	14,044
Maine	1,517	472	13,448	9,964	3,484
Maryland	13,656	4,944	54,480	43,321	11,159
Massachusetts	13,218	6,620	59,794	52,596	7,198
Michigan	10,025	7,778	124,272	94,731	29,541
Minnesota	6,781	4,403	74,870	60,251	14,619
Mississippi	1,974	2,957	39,141	27,817	11,324
Missouri	5,410	5,005	84,073	67,029	17,044
Montana	575	1,373	6,469	5,099	1,370
Nebraska	1,840	1,424	29,150	22,826	6,324
Nevada	9,816	3,037	36,014	30,987	5,027
New Hampshire	1,056	1,198	12,632	10,888	1,744
New Jersey	23,428	13,256	118,820	98,988	19,832
New Mexico	2,063	2,081	18,593	13,751	4,842
New York	87,774	26,814	158,549	130,071	28,478
North Carolina	7,080	5,651	112,511	85,331	27,180
North Dakota	422	716	11,344	8,671	2,673
Ohio	14,893	9,896	203,772	162,114	41,658
Oklahoma	2,063	3,619	43,957	31,548	12,409
Oregon	4,906	7,635	48,490	37,582	10,908
Pennsylvania	18,575	10,686	212,096	168,882	43,214
Rhode Island	1,587	968	9,760	7,772	1,988
South Carolina	4,519	3,935	61,200	41,232	19,968
South Dakota	640	708	10,708	9,122	1,586
Tennessee	4,963	5,963	116,771	87,791	28,980
Texas	25,582	25,195	345,946	259,323	86,623
Utah	2,279	2,104	34,605	27,777	6,828
Vermont	547	404	5,479	4,524	955
Virginia	14,875	6,572	79,530	60,948	18,582
Washington	7,896	5,547	91,408	71,004	20,404
West Virginia	1,095	854	18,472	13,446	5,026
Wisconsin	6,022	3,252	96,290	75,563	20,727
Wyoming	657	884	7,393	5,032	2,361

Table B-5. Employment by Industry

State	Employed population 16 years and older				Employment by industry group — Percent in each major industry group							
	Total	Male	Female	Percent female	Agriculture, forestry, fishing and hunting, and mining	Construction	Manufacturing	Wholesale trade	Retail trade	Transportation and warehousing, and utilities	Information	Finance and insurance, and real estate and rental and leasing
United States	150,534,773	79,120,041	71,414,732	47.4	1.9	6.4	10.3	2.7	11.5	5.1	2.1	6.5
Alabama	2,040,118	1,067,761	972,357	47.7	1.7	6.3	14.3	2.5	11.8	5.3	1.7	5.5
Alaska	354,766	193,392	161,374	45.5	5.3	7.2	3.2	2.0	11.0	7.6	1.9	3.6
Arizona	2,937,510	1,564,955	1,372,555	46.7	1.5	6.6	7.1	2.3	12.5	5.0	1.9	8.2
Arkansas	1,271,063	670,323	600,740	47.3	3.2	6.4	13.9	2.4	13.8	5.5	1.6	4.5
California	18,045,450	9,771,350	8,274,100	45.9	2.5	6.2	9.5	2.9	10.8	5.0	2.9	6.0
Colorado	2,765,115	1,485,661	1,279,454	46.3	2.6	7.9	6.9	2.6	11.3	4.6	2.9	6.9
Connecticut	1,807,098	925,935	881,163	48.8	0.4	6.0	10.4	2.6	10.9	4.1	2.3	9.3
Delaware	447,516	225,225	222,291	49.7	1.1	6.4	8.1	1.6	12.3	4.0	1.5	9.8
District of Columbia	361,179	175,876	185,303	51.3	0.1	2.6	1.4	0.5	5.0	2.7	4.2	6.2
Florida	8,990,221	4,663,492	4,326,729	48.1	1.1	7.1	5.1	2.8	13.1	5.1	1.9	7.9
Georgia	4,605,633	2,379,783	2,225,850	48.3	1.1	6.5	10.9	2.9	12.0	6.0	2.6	6.0
Hawaii	675,214	354,372	320,842	47.5	1.4	7.9	3.0	2.6	11.5	5.7	1.7	6.8
Idaho	744,228	399,344	344,884	46.3	5.2	6.6	9.5	2.8	11.9	4.9	1.8	5.0
Illinois	6,196,524	3,246,265	2,950,259	47.6	1.1	5.3	12.3	3.1	11.0	6.1	1.9	7.3
Indiana	3,119,966	1,642,149	1,477,817	47.4	1.5	5.9	19.0	2.7	11.5	5.1	1.6	5.3
Iowa	1,599,893	839,299	760,594	47.5	3.8	6.3	15.7	2.7	11.7	4.6	1.7	7.3
Kansas	1,417,069	749,555	667,514	47.1	3.4	6.6	12.2	2.8	11.2	4.6	2.1	6.2
Kentucky	1,928,967	1,006,647	922,320	47.8	2.5	5.8	14.3	2.4	12.2	5.9	1.6	5.4
Louisiana	2,037,812	1,049,048	988,764	48.5	4.2	7.9	7.8	2.5	11.5	5.1	1.6	5.2
Maine	648,414	327,487	320,927	49.5	2.7	7.2	9.4	2.1	13.1	3.8	1.9	6.3
Maryland	3,031,466	1,541,470	1,489,996	49.2	0.5	6.8	4.6	2.0	9.9	4.6	2.2	5.9
Massachusetts	3,522,203	1,784,929	1,737,274	49.3	0.4	5.4	9.0	2.3	10.6	3.7	2.4	7.4
Michigan	4,512,641	2,356,179	2,156,462	47.8	1.2	5.1	18.1	2.5	11.4	4.3	1.5	5.4
Minnesota	2,913,176	1,507,764	1,405,412	48.2	2.2	6.1	13.4	2.9	11.0	4.6	1.7	7.3
Mississippi	1,206,679	622,777	583,902	48.4	2.9	6.9	13.6	2.7	11.9	5.8	1.2	4.7
Missouri	2,880,309	1,484,020	1,396,289	48.5	1.8	6.4	11.5	2.7	11.9	5.3	2.0	6.7
Montana	489,875	259,333	230,542	47.1	7.0	9.3	4.1	2.4	11.4	4.6	1.9	5.4
Nebraska	986,789	519,537	467,252	47.4	4.5	6.9	10.5	3.1	11.7	5.7	1.7	7.3
Nevada	1,331,796	715,246	616,550	46.3	1.6	6.2	4.5	2.0	12.1	5.2	1.4	6.1
New Hampshire	713,313	371,025	342,288	48.0	0.8	6.6	12.7	2.9	12.3	4.0	2.1	6.3
New Jersey	4,374,536	2,298,798	2,075,738	47.5	0.3	5.9	8.0	3.5	11.3	5.8	2.8	8.5
New Mexico	879,807	463,219	416,588	47.3	4.2	7.3	3.6	2.4	12.0	4.4	1.6	4.5
New York	9,473,337	4,874,995	4,598,342	48.5	0.6	5.6	6.1	2.5	10.6	5.4	3.0	7.9
North Carolina	4,550,972	2,366,821	2,184,151	48.0	1.2	7.2	12.5	2.6	11.8	4.2	1.8	6.3
North Dakota	404,589	220,613	183,976	45.5	9.5	8.0	6.8	4.0	11.6	5.8	1.2	5.1
Ohio	5,489,742	2,839,454	2,650,288	48.3	1.1	5.0	15.5	2.7	11.7	5.1	1.6	6.5
Oklahoma	1,753,445	937,290	816,155	46.5	5.0	7.3	9.5	2.6	11.8	5.2	1.7	5.6
Oregon	1,881,255	987,483	893,772	47.5	3.5	5.7	11.3	2.8	12.0	4.1	1.9	5.4
Pennsylvania	6,109,670	3,168,719	2,940,951	48.1	1.5	5.7	12.1	2.9	11.5	5.4	1.6	6.2
Rhode Island	524,975	264,722	260,253	49.6	0.4	5.2	11.4	3.1	11.7	3.7	1.6	6.5
South Carolina	2,165,702	1,115,610	1,050,092	48.5	1.0	6.4	13.9	2.7	12.2	4.6	1.9	5.9
South Dakota	436,852	231,215	205,637	47.1	6.7	7.4	10.4	2.9	10.5	4.6	1.5	7.0
Tennessee	2,998,814	1,562,444	1,436,370	47.9	1.0	6.0	13.0	2.7	12.3	6.5	1.8	5.7
Texas	12,693,901	6,906,093	5,787,808	45.6	3.4	8.1	8.7	3.0	11.7	5.7	1.8	6.6
Utah	1,414,337	793,605	620,732	43.9	2.0	6.8	11.3	2.8	12.3	4.5	2.2	6.7
Vermont	327,841	165,927	161,914	49.4	2.4	7.0	11.0	2.2	11.5	3.4	2.3	4.8
Virginia	4,081,600	2,106,890	1,974,710	48.4	1.0	6.5	7.2	2.0	10.8	4.2	2.0	6.4
Washington	3,397,974	1,831,920	1,566,054	46.1	2.7	6.5	10.3	2.9	11.7	5.4	2.2	5.4
West Virginia	738,438	390,899	347,539	47.1	4.2	6.3	7.4	2.2	12.2	5.3	1.5	4.0
Wisconsin	2,959,655	1,533,690	1,425,965	48.2	2.4	5.6	18.4	2.6	11.4	4.4	1.5	6.0
Wyoming	295,328	159,435	135,893	46.0	12.9	7.3	4.1	1.8	11.9	5.7	1.4	3.8

Table B-5. Employment by Industry—*Continued*

| | Employment by industry group (Continued) | | | | | Detailed industry for employed persons age 16 and older | | | | |
| | Percent in each major industry group (Continued) | | | | | Number of employees in agriculture, forestry, fishing and hunting, and mining industries | | | | |
State	Professional, scientific, and management, and administrative and waste management services	Educational services, and health care and social assistance	Arts, entertainment, and recreation, and accommodation and food services	Other services, except public administration	Public administration	Total in agriculture, forestry, fishing and hunting, and mining industries	Agriculture, forestry, fishing and hunting	Mining, quarrying, and oil and gas extraction	Number of employees in construction industries	Number of employees in manufacturing industries
United States	11.3	22.9	9.8	4.9	4.6	2,906,158	2,010,864	895,294	9,622,525	15,470,595
Alabama	9.6	22.5	8.4	5.2	5.2	34,383	24,462	9,921	128,389	291,477
Alaska	8.6	23.4	9.7	4.7	11.7	18,954	6,520	12,434	25,415	11,461
Arizona	12.2	21.7	11.2	4.7	5.1	43,075	27,664	15,411	193,805	207,583
Arkansas	7.2	24.4	7.7	4.7	4.6	41,301	34,955	6,346	81,587	177,030
California	13.2	20.8	10.5	5.3	4.3	446,614	412,199	34,415	1,112,236	1,715,871
Colorado	13.8	20.7	10.5	5.0	4.4	71,732	32,610	39,122	218,980	190,855
Connecticut	11.5	26.3	8.1	4.3	3.8	7,149	6,331	818	108,227	187,997
Delaware	10.1	25.0	10.1	4.5	5.3	5,106	4,963	143	28,858	36,264
District of Columbia	23.0	19.5	9.7	8.8	16.3	195	98	97	9,342	5,025
Florida	12.9	20.8	12.6	5.2	4.2	101,921	92,980	8,941	641,425	461,531
Georgia	11.8	20.9	9.2	5.1	5.0	51,889	46,946	4,943	301,380	502,776
Hawaii	9.9	19.6	15.9	4.8	9.0	9,644	9,450	194	53,542	20,047
Idaho	9.9	23.4	9.5	4.8	4.8	38,849	33,895	4,954	49,187	70,601
Illinois	11.7	22.7	9.2	4.6	3.6	69,182	56,929	12,253	330,560	761,364
Indiana	8.3	22.2	9.0	4.5	3.3	46,148	39,190	6,958	184,729	593,823
Iowa	7.1	24.3	7.7	4.0	3.0	60,661	58,083	2,578	101,009	251,893
Kansas	9.4	24.4	8.2	4.6	4.3	48,367	38,647	9,720	93,008	172,643
Kentucky	7.9	23.7	9.2	4.8	4.4	49,038	32,738	16,300	112,185	275,351
Louisiana	9.2	23.6	10.7	5.3	5.4	85,425	19,946	65,479	161,184	159,504
Maine	8.3	28.0	8.7	4.6	3.9	17,435	16,834	601	46,879	60,634
Maryland	15.5	23.2	8.9	5.3	10.7	13,956	12,326	1,630	204,648	139,239
Massachusetts	13.5	28.1	9.1	4.4	3.6	13,583	12,780	803	190,678	317,217
Michigan	9.4	23.5	9.8	4.5	3.4	52,583	44,735	7,848	232,361	816,076
Minnesota	9.8	25.0	8.4	4.5	3.1	63,248	56,808	6,440	177,870	390,950
Mississippi	6.7	24.2	9.5	4.5	5.3	34,649	21,703	12,946	82,795	164,689
Missouri	9.8	24.0	9.2	4.7	4.1	51,255	46,781	4,474	185,637	332,665
Montana	8.0	24.2	10.4	5.1	6.4	34,242	25,673	8,569	45,581	20,210
Nebraska	8.5	24.0	8.1	4.2	3.8	43,998	42,098	1,900	67,973	103,781
Nevada	11.6	15.2	25.6	4.5	4.1	20,942	5,622	15,320	82,523	59,517
New Hampshire	10.9	25.1	8.4	4.1	3.7	6,034	5,457	577	47,114	90,748
New Jersey	13.3	23.6	8.6	4.6	3.9	14,505	12,635	1,870	257,973	349,687
New Mexico	11.7	24.9	11.8	4.8	6.9	37,116	15,251	21,865	63,790	31,495
New York	11.7	27.4	9.8	5.0	4.4	52,298	45,723	6,575	535,021	577,352
North Carolina	10.7	23.0	9.5	4.7	4.3	55,694	51,199	4,495	329,035	569,884
North Dakota	6.9	23.9	8.2	4.7	4.4	38,380	23,607	14,773	32,190	27,497
Ohio	9.3	23.8	9.4	4.5	3.8	59,551	43,128	16,423	275,279	851,930
Oklahoma	8.5	22.3	9.5	5.2	5.8	87,940	25,899	62,041	127,995	167,293
Oregon	11.3	23.1	9.8	4.7	4.4	65,512	63,599	1,913	107,737	213,118
Pennsylvania	10.3	25.6	8.6	4.6	4.0	89,640	54,812	34,828	346,372	741,110
Rhode Island	9.3	27.4	11.1	4.4	4.1	2,182	2,141	41	27,396	60,010
South Carolina	9.9	21.7	10.2	5.2	4.4	22,037	19,513	2,524	138,903	301,688
South Dakota	6.5	24.3	9.5	4.4	4.4	29,093	26,767	2,326	32,182	45,422
Tennessee	9.9	22.4	9.5	5.1	4.0	28,833	24,062	4,771	178,799	390,879
Texas	11.4	21.2	9.1	5.2	4.1	434,422	113,791	320,631	1,032,811	1,102,394
Utah	11.9	20.8	9.2	4.5	5.1	27,880	11,555	16,325	95,518	160,034
Vermont	8.6	28.3	9.5	4.3	4.8	7,978	7,440	538	23,105	35,990
Virginia	14.7	21.9	9.1	5.5	8.7	41,564	31,787	9,777	264,211	292,968
Washington	12.5	21.3	9.3	4.7	5.1	90,552	87,910	2,642	220,035	350,048
West Virginia	8.0	28.6	9.4	4.2	6.7	30,840	4,538	26,302	46,635	54,976
Wisconsin	8.2	23.1	8.9	4.1	3.4	70,472	65,756	4,716	166,958	545,817
Wyoming	6.4	22.2	11.3	4.7	6.4	38,111	10,328	27,783	21,473	12,181

Table B-5. Employment by Industry—*Continued*

State	Detailed industry for employed persons age 16 and older (Continued)										
			Number of employees in transportation and warehousing, and utilities industries				Number of employees in finance and insurance, and real estate and rental and leasing industries			Number of employees in professional, scientific, and management, and administrative and waste management services industries	
	Number of employees in wholesale trade industries	Number of employees in retail trade industries	Total in transportation and warehousing, and utilities industries	Transportation and warehousing	Utilities	Number of employees in information industries	Total in finance and insurance, and real estate and rental and leasing industries	Finance and insurance	Real estate and rental and leasing	Total Professional, scientific, and management, and administrative and waste management services industries	Professional, scientific, and technical services
United States	4,092,244	17,301,650	7,682,950	6,439,323	1,243,627	3,155,281	9,822,476	6,914,315	2,908,161	17,009,744	10,342,338
Alabama	51,525	241,235	108,227	76,829	31,398	33,689	111,441	81,621	29,820	196,149	116,645
Alaska	7,250	38,999	27,012	23,492	3,520	6,916	12,651	6,795	5,856	30,351	18,100
Arizona	69,018	368,099	147,537	119,465	28,072	54,920	242,171	172,428	69,743	357,395	179,065
Arkansas	30,505	174,804	70,419	56,077	14,342	20,718	57,546	41,573	15,973	91,447	47,122
California	528,692	1,946,847	899,711	762,664	137,047	523,512	1,089,370	682,336	407,034	2,390,184	1,496,966
Colorado	71,314	312,246	126,200	102,245	23,955	81,533	190,157	125,457	64,700	380,985	257,040
Connecticut	46,464	197,043	73,296	58,904	14,392	42,062	167,826	137,075	30,751	208,216	133,349
Delaware	7,362	54,829	17,915	14,875	3,040	6,759	43,739	36,057	7,682	45,324	25,875
District of Columbia	1,932	18,086	9,754	9,134	620	14,995	22,532	11,870	10,662	83,089	67,390
Florida	251,822	1,176,106	462,347	397,285	65,062	173,543	709,646	451,747	257,899	1,164,180	600,615
Georgia	133,581	550,395	277,731	235,725	42,006	117,589	275,184	187,134	88,050	543,839	312,646
Hawaii	17,492	77,536	38,761	34,695	4,066	11,272	46,133	23,268	22,865	67,106	34,128
Idaho	20,626	88,605	36,443	29,902	6,541	13,295	37,180	25,581	11,599	73,959	40,035
Illinois	194,841	681,449	376,442	334,736	41,706	118,002	453,233	346,419	106,814	725,420	454,913
Indiana	84,131	359,998	157,851	133,194	24,657	51,180	166,396	116,528	49,868	258,117	137,015
Iowa	43,598	186,627	74,075	61,807	12,268	27,504	117,400	101,436	15,964	113,881	64,403
Kansas	40,356	158,309	65,055	52,141	12,914	29,915	87,721	67,718	20,003	132,944	81,786
Kentucky	45,617	235,867	113,365	97,130	16,235	30,394	103,324	78,605	24,719	151,808	82,233
Louisiana	51,095	233,825	103,968	83,919	20,049	32,702	105,664	68,811	36,853	186,636	111,759
Maine	13,645	84,900	24,790	20,735	4,055	12,550	40,583	29,420	11,163	54,109	33,346
Maryland	61,207	300,049	138,259	120,555	17,704	65,605	179,443	117,809	61,634	470,532	321,245
Massachusetts	80,137	374,569	129,842	107,498	22,344	84,925	259,988	195,251	64,737	475,989	339,422
Michigan	112,711	515,042	192,252	155,697	36,555	66,460	244,413	174,852	69,561	423,264	241,712
Minnesota	85,385	320,261	133,184	113,065	20,119	49,606	212,642	168,172	44,470	285,602	181,231
Mississippi	31,998	143,673	70,185	57,085	13,100	14,494	56,776	42,378	14,398	81,278	38,339
Missouri	76,466	341,614	153,838	128,432	25,406	57,136	191,685	142,346	49,339	282,024	163,128
Montana	11,549	55,990	22,500	17,508	4,992	9,067	26,248	17,910	8,338	39,136	26,249
Nebraska	30,240	115,840	56,040	45,525	10,515	16,716	71,882	58,952	12,930	83,969	47,317
Nevada	26,949	161,712	68,982	58,240	10,742	18,642	80,795	42,426	38,369	154,984	70,822
New Hampshire	20,656	87,537	28,853	22,247	6,606	15,180	45,261	32,493	12,768	77,758	52,459
New Jersey	151,810	494,289	254,649	220,174	34,475	121,905	371,069	280,867	90,202	579,806	390,633
New Mexico	21,356	105,213	38,361	26,975	11,386	13,988	39,444	24,589	14,855	102,638	66,588
New York	235,404	1,001,975	515,243	456,341	58,902	280,858	744,778	527,549	217,229	1,104,596	752,224
North Carolina	118,604	536,727	193,305	155,824	37,481	81,815	288,582	207,287	81,295	486,978	278,685
North Dakota	16,719	47,045	23,354	17,186	6,168	4,835	20,660	15,882	4,778	27,754	16,612
Ohio	149,496	644,061	277,804	233,494	44,310	90,201	357,225	271,826	85,399	511,149	295,192
Oklahoma	46,421	206,507	91,952	69,409	22,543	30,506	97,660	64,849	32,811	148,477	80,016
Oregon	53,318	225,153	77,274	62,868	14,406	34,847	101,452	64,042	37,410	212,773	132,748
Pennsylvania	174,256	701,437	330,474	273,948	56,526	99,582	381,785	300,058	81,727	630,352	386,744
Rhode Island	16,246	61,602	19,422	16,701	2,721	8,301	33,971	25,278	8,693	48,899	30,173
South Carolina	57,417	263,192	100,414	72,398	28,016	40,960	126,989	86,321	40,668	215,323	109,070
South Dakota	12,632	45,981	19,976	15,492	4,484	6,577	30,383	24,834	5,549	28,537	15,728
Tennessee	81,434	370,274	193,532	161,334	32,198	54,708	171,030	120,788	50,242	297,811	155,459
Texas	385,618	1,483,751	727,529	616,254	111,275	228,993	831,946	575,977	255,969	1,444,739	828,190
Utah	39,870	174,176	63,254	53,436	9,818	30,519	95,405	68,037	27,368	167,707	99,298
Vermont	7,070	37,554	11,140	8,721	2,419	7,587	15,579	10,728	4,851	28,190	18,506
Virginia	80,107	440,930	170,067	141,880	28,187	82,960	262,304	176,184	86,120	600,339	434,929
Washington	97,515	398,511	184,739	158,200	26,539	74,707	184,280	115,322	68,958	423,282	292,695
West Virginia	16,555	90,100	39,036	29,259	9,777	10,825	29,253	20,553	8,700	59,098	30,850
Wisconsin	77,350	336,036	129,628	106,217	23,411	45,447	178,380	142,588	35,792	242,636	139,590
Wyoming	5,422	35,044	16,963	12,406	4,557	4,279	11,271	6,288	4,983	18,985	12,053

Table B-5. Employment by Industry—*Continued*

| | Detailed industry for employed persons age 16 and older (Continued) | | | | | | | | | |
| | Number of employees in professional, scientific, and management, and administrative and waste management services industries (Continued) | | Number of employees in educational services, and health care and social assistance industries | | | Number of employees in arts, entertainment, and recreation, and accommodation and food services industries | | | | |
State	Management of companies and enterprises	Administrative and support and waste management services	Total in educational services, and health care and social assistance industries	Educational services	Health care and social assistance	Total in arts, entertainment, and recreation, and accommodation and food services industries	Arts, entertainment, and recreation	Accommodation and food services	Number of employees In other services, except public administration	Number of employees in public administration
United States	138,583	6,528,823	34,510,561	13,794,784	20,715,777	14,756,511	3,281,857	11,474,654	7,343,926	6,860,152
Alabama	889	78,615	459,777	177,730	282,047	171,239	24,634	146,605	106,030	106,557
Alaska	256	11,995	83,083	33,351	49,732	34,319	6,888	27,431	16,760	41,595
Arizona	2,763	175,567	636,623	249,541	387,082	329,444	74,308	255,136	138,387	149,453
Arkansas	1,034	43,291	309,993	123,892	186,101	97,668	14,949	82,719	59,802	58,243
California	13,148	880,070	3,750,815	1,531,478	2,219,337	1,902,121	489,975	1,412,146	954,804	784,673
Colorado	3,564	120,381	571,222	239,904	331,318	289,390	73,696	215,694	138,360	122,141
Connecticut	3,308	71,559	475,215	199,282	275,933	145,994	42,691	103,303	78,505	69,104
Delaware	247	19,202	111,772	43,886	67,886	45,372	10,646	34,726	20,336	23,880
District of Columbia	275	15,424	70,276	37,583	32,693	35,208	11,037	24,171	31,896	58,849
Florida	7,009	556,556	1,873,140	685,159	1,187,981	1,128,909	276,587	852,322	468,618	377,033
Georgia	4,268	226,925	964,170	440,316	523,854	423,122	66,166	356,956	235,504	228,473
Hawaii	339	32,639	132,463	58,740	73,723	107,685	16,937	90,748	32,454	61,079
Idaho	512	33,412	173,935	69,831	104,104	70,734	15,050	55,684	35,360	35,454
Illinois	9,111	261,396	1,404,791	571,440	833,351	568,748	121,984	446,764	286,454	226,038
Indiana	2,002	119,100	693,683	278,799	414,884	279,499	52,460	227,039	141,495	102,916
Iowa	866	48,612	388,003	156,632	231,371	122,600	27,195	95,405	64,782	47,860
Kansas	1,103	50,055	346,269	143,636	202,633	116,489	24,801	91,688	65,139	60,854
Kentucky	764	68,811	456,914	179,955	276,959	177,600	27,389	150,211	92,038	85,466
Louisiana	916	73,961	481,542	187,976	293,566	217,691	47,052	170,639	108,058	110,518
Maine	132	20,631	181,454	68,001	113,453	56,483	11,542	44,941	29,605	25,347
Maryland	2,423	146,864	702,633	295,054	407,579	268,768	64,564	204,204	162,058	325,069
Massachusetts	3,800	132,767	990,793	411,182	579,611	320,117	69,168	250,949	155,833	128,532
Michigan	3,014	178,538	1,059,969	387,646	672,323	440,253	88,889	351,364	203,191	154,066
Minnesota	4,247	100,124	726,879	257,964	468,915	246,021	60,352	185,669	129,798	91,730
Mississippi	765	42,174	292,136	116,993	175,143	115,098	27,641	87,457	54,725	64,183
Missouri	3,522	115,374	691,263	262,451	428,812	263,903	59,036	204,867	134,897	117,926
Montana	59	12,828	118,442	46,657	71,785	50,739	10,891	39,848	24,946	31,225
Nebraska	1,044	35,608	237,298	95,573	141,725	80,332	18,024	62,308	41,504	37,216
Nevada	2,984	81,178	202,212	86,103	116,109	341,021	106,213	234,808	59,490	54,027
New Hampshire	464	24,835	179,012	71,168	107,844	59,727	13,575	46,152	29,389	26,044
New Jersey	5,573	183,600	1,033,529	430,335	603,194	374,341	97,222	277,119	199,426	171,547
New Mexico	66	35,984	219,477	95,240	124,237	103,738	22,002	81,736	42,255	60,936
New York	6,474	345,898	2,599,743	1,036,475	1,563,268	933,041	239,352	693,689	473,357	419,671
North Carolina	2,343	205,950	1,046,815	410,602	636,213	434,277	84,899	349,378	215,257	193,999
North Dakota	161	10,981	96,621	35,123	61,498	33,377	7,593	25,784	19,069	17,628
Ohio	6,966	208,991	1,308,215	466,869	841,346	513,686	101,125	412,561	244,520	206,625
Oklahoma	1,540	66,921	390,813	161,114	229,699	166,058	41,914	124,144	90,762	101,061
Oregon	1,621	78,404	433,669	156,224	277,445	184,591	41,597	142,994	88,104	83,707
Pennsylvania	4,722	238,886	1,562,965	560,526	1,002,439	526,093	118,779	407,314	283,360	242,244
Rhode Island	947	17,779	143,781	56,438	87,343	58,377	15,489	42,888	23,162	21,626
South Carolina	1,344	104,909	470,753	189,873	280,880	221,811	36,899	184,912	111,964	94,251
South Dakota	40	12,769	106,014	37,020	68,994	41,711	8,988	32,723	19,241	19,103
Tennessee	3,604	138,748	672,449	255,608	416,841	286,287	54,025	232,262	153,214	119,564
Texas	16,906	599,643	2,692,663	1,174,748	1,517,915	1,158,080	188,278	969,802	654,384	516,571
Utah	629	67,780	294,547	144,682	149,865	130,400	29,437	100,963	63,294	71,733
Vermont	121	9,563	92,695	43,640	49,055	31,142	9,437	21,705	14,035	15,776
Virginia	3,263	162,147	893,646	392,273	501,373	372,891	78,807	294,084	222,770	356,843
Washington	3,787	126,800	725,258	285,829	439,429	315,472	80,427	235,045	160,199	173,376
West Virginia	114	28,134	211,493	70,823	140,670	69,272	11,964	57,308	30,674	49,681
Wisconsin	3,419	99,627	684,079	250,015	434,064	262,062	53,341	208,721	120,893	99,897
Wyoming	115	6,817	65,559	33,404	32,155	33,510	5,942	27,568	13,768	18,762

Table B-6. Educational Attainment

			Educational attainment									
		Age 18 to 24 years							Men age 18 to 24			
		Percent of all persons age 18 to 24							Percent of men age 18 to 24			
State	Population age 18 to 24 years	Less than 9th grade	9th to 12th grade, no diploma	High school graduate (includes equivalency)	Some college, no degree	Associate's degree	Bachelor's degree	Graduate or professional degree	Less than high school diploma	High school graduate (includes equivalency)	Some college or associate's degree	Bachelor's degree or higher
United States	31,341,948	1.6	11.9	30.4	40.7	5.1	9.5	0.7	15.4	33.4	42.8	8.3
Alabama	468,319	2.1	13.1	31.9	40.6	4.8	6.7	0.8	17.3	35.6	41.5	5.6
Alaska	82,518	0.7	14.3	38.1	36.9	4.1	5.4	0.4	16.2	38.3	41.2	4.3
Arizona	669,583	1.9	15.2	30.4	39.7	5.5	6.8	0.6	19.4	32.7	42.0	5.9
Arkansas	284,441	1.5	11.3	31.7	42.8	5.5	6.8	0.4	14.0	35.6	44.7	5.7
California	3,943,137	1.6	10.8	29.6	43.6	4.7	9.0	0.7	14.6	32.3	45.2	7.9
Colorado	527,949	1.8	11.6	29.9	41.0	4.6	10.6	0.5	14.4	33.0	44.4	8.2
Connecticut	352,843	1.0	9.8	27.7	42.5	4.3	13.5	1.3	13.7	30.7	43.2	12.4
Delaware	89,098	1.6	12.5	30.7	39.0	5.2	10.0	1.0	16.5	31.9	41.4	10.2
District of Columbia	81,506	0.7	5.4	23.7	44.7	1.6	21.2	2.7	9.1	24.9	48.0	18.0
Florida	1,774,002	1.7	14.7	29.7	35.8	9.3	8.1	0.7	18.9	32.7	41.7	6.8
Georgia	1,028,679	1.6	14.8	31.9	39.8	3.9	7.6	0.4	18.9	34.4	40.2	6.4
Hawaii	134,483	0.4	5.9	38.4	40.0	7.1	7.8	0.4	5.3	44.4	45.1	5.2
Idaho	156,767	0.6	13.3	34.4	41.5	4.9	4.9	0.3	15.5	38.4	41.2	4.9
Illinois	1,237,872	1.1	11.3	28.9	40.5	5.7	11.7	0.9	14.2	31.1	43.9	10.8
Indiana	676,373	2.6	13.4	31.3	40.1	3.4	8.8	0.6	18.0	34.1	39.9	8.0
Iowa	320,642	1.4	9.5	26.1	44.8	8.2	9.6	0.4	12.7	28.6	50.8	7.9
Kansas	302,928	1.5	11.0	29.7	42.8	6.1	8.4	0.5	14.1	32.1	46.5	7.3
Kentucky	425,719	1.5	12.7	34.8	39.1	4.4	6.9	0.6	16.8	38.7	37.8	6.7
Louisiana	459,284	2.5	14.2	32.8	40.5	2.6	6.6	0.9	19.0	36.2	38.4	6.4
Maine	112,229	0.9	11.0	31.1	43.7	3.7	9.0	0.5	12.3	31.4	46.9	9.3
Maryland	556,183	1.6	9.4	28.7	41.8	4.6	13.0	1.0	12.8	31.7	43.7	11.8
Massachusetts	700,584	1.3	8.9	27.5	41.4	3.7	16.1	1.3	12.6	30.8	41.3	15.4
Michigan	986,405	1.4	11.6	28.9	43.5	4.9	9.2	0.5	15.3	31.8	44.6	8.3
Minnesota	505,761	1.0	12.2	27.5	39.9	6.6	12.6	0.2	14.7	31.1	43.8	10.3
Mississippi	311,989	1.6	14.1	28.9	41.6	7.6	5.8	0.4	19.0	31.1	44.7	5.2
Missouri	593,894	1.8	12.0	30.1	41.2	5.4	8.9	0.6	15.6	33.3	43.5	7.5
Montana	100,393	2.0	14.2	35.5	38.1	4.2	5.7	0.2	17.0	36.9	42.5	3.5
Nebraska	192,977	1.0	10.7	26.2	44.1	5.5	12.1	0.4	13.7	29.1	47.3	9.8
Nevada	254,123	1.7	16.9	34.9	36.5	4.9	4.6	0.4	21.9	37.6	37.3	3.1
New Hampshire	130,063	1.5	9.6	31.8	41.3	3.6	11.1	1.1	11.9	36.7	40.9	10.5
New Jersey	792,764	1.6	10.1	27.2	40.4	5.5	14.1	1.1	13.2	29.4	44.2	13.2
New Mexico	208,145	1.3	16.8	29.9	42.5	4.9	4.3	0.4	20.9	33.2	42.3	3.5
New York	1,941,151	1.7	10.2	26.2	39.9	6.2	14.1	1.7	13.7	29.1	44.2	13.1
North Carolina	992,108	1.3	12.9	30.8	40.6	4.9	9.0	0.5	15.8	34.7	42.2	7.3
North Dakota	93,597	0.9	9.4	26.3	42.9	7.5	12.7	0.4	11.8	29.8	47.4	10.9
Ohio	1,087,145	1.7	12.0	32.7	40.0	3.8	9.1	0.7	15.2	36.3	40.4	8.1
Oklahoma	392,378	2.0	14.9	32.4	38.4	4.7	7.0	0.6	18.3	35.6	40.2	5.9
Oregon	363,364	1.4	13.8	30.2	40.1	4.9	9.1	0.6	18.6	32.4	40.9	8.1
Pennsylvania	1,214,756	1.7	10.7	32.8	39.0	4.1	11.1	0.7	14.1	35.7	40.7	9.5
Rhode Island	114,340	1.0	8.8	28.5	44.4	4.4	11.7	1.3	13.1	30.4	46.0	10.4
South Carolina	487,006	1.2	11.6	33.8	40.8	3.9	8.0	0.6	14.0	38.2	41.3	6.6
South Dakota	85,681	1.6	12.6	30.2	40.1	5.8	9.4	0.3	15.7	32.4	45.3	6.6
Tennessee	633,012	1.2	9.3	36.4	40.4	3.6	8.4	0.7	12.2	39.5	41.2	7.1
Texas	2,787,469	2.0	14.0	32.2	40.0	4.0	7.3	0.6	18.0	34.8	40.9	6.3
Utah	341,637	1.4	11.3	31.0	40.6	8.8	6.6	0.2	14.7	35.0	46.0	4.2
Vermont	67,228	0.5	7.8	26.4	47.8	3.0	13.8	0.7	9.6	27.2	50.0	13.2
Virginia	827,861	1.0	9.2	30.5	42.7	4.7	11.0	1.0	11.5	33.9	45.5	9.1
Washington	669,067	1.3	12.6	31.4	36.8	7.6	9.8	0.6	15.1	34.1	41.8	9.0
West Virginia	164,334	1.5	10.1	37.2	39.6	3.6	7.5	0.5	12.7	43.6	38.4	5.4
Wisconsin	560,301	1.3	9.8	31.4	41.5	4.9	10.7	0.5	12.4	35.3	43.3	9.0
Wyoming	57,860	1.7	13.8	34.1	36.5	9.3	3.9	0.7	16.6	39.6	40.4	3.4

Table B-6. Educational Attainment—*Continued*

	Educational attainment											
	Women age 18 to 24				Age 25 years and older							
	Percent of women age 18 to 24					Percent of all persons age 25 and older						
State	Less than high school diploma	High school graduate (includes equivalency)	Some college or associate's degree	Bachelor's degree or higher	Population age 25 years and older	Less than 9th grade	9th to 12th grade, no diploma	High school graduate (includes equivalency)	Some college, no degree	Associate's degree	Bachelor's degree	Graduate or professional degree
United States	11.5	27.3	49.0	12.3	216,447,163	5.5	7.3	27.6	20.7	8.2	19.0	11.6
Alabama	13.0	28.3	49.3	9.4	3,282,252	4.8	10.3	31.0	21.6	8.1	15.4	8.8
Alaska	13.5	37.8	40.9	7.9	469,523	2.6	4.8	27.3	27.5	8.1	18.7	11.0
Arizona	14.6	27.8	48.7	8.9	4,536,954	6.0	7.9	24.5	25.5	8.4	17.4	10.3
Arkansas	11.5	27.6	52.2	8.8	1,987,819	5.3	9.3	34.1	22.7	6.8	14.0	7.8
California	10.2	26.7	51.6	11.5	26,085,263	9.9	7.9	20.8	21.5	7.6	20.3	12.0
Colorado	12.2	26.4	47.0	14.4	3,671,853	3.7	5.1	21.7	22.0	8.2	24.8	14.5
Connecticut	7.6	24.4	50.7	17.2	2,474,718	4.2	5.6	27.4	16.9	7.6	21.7	16.7
Delaware	11.7	29.5	47.1	11.7	652,636	3.8	7.3	29.8	20.1	8.1	18.0	12.9
District of Columbia	3.7	22.6	44.7	28.9	472,884	4.3	5.9	17.4	12.7	3.0	23.8	32.9
Florida	13.8	26.5	48.8	10.9	14,394,281	5.2	7.2	29.2	20.4	9.6	18.2	10.2
Georgia	13.8	29.2	47.3	9.7	6,683,767	5.0	8.9	28.1	20.7	7.4	18.6	11.3
Hawaii	7.7	30.7	49.8	11.8	985,914	4.1	5.1	27.1	21.6	10.7	20.8	10.6
Idaho	12.3	30.3	51.8	5.6	1,065,982	3.7	6.3	27.5	27.0	9.6	17.8	8.2
Illinois	10.7	26.6	48.4	14.3	8,661,938	5.3	6.2	26.7	20.8	8.1	20.3	12.7
Indiana	13.8	28.3	47.1	10.8	4,363,573	3.8	8.0	34.3	20.6	8.3	16.0	9.0
Iowa	8.9	23.4	55.6	12.1	2,074,504	3.2	5.1	32.1	21.4	11.4	18.2	8.7
Kansas	10.6	26.9	51.7	10.7	1,888,479	3.8	5.9	26.5	23.6	8.4	20.4	11.4
Kentucky	11.4	30.8	49.5	8.3	2,988,790	6.2	8.7	33.5	20.4	7.9	13.6	9.7
Louisiana	14.3	29.1	48.1	8.5	3,095,255	5.2	10.2	34.1	21.1	6.1	15.2	8.0
Maine	11.6	30.6	48.0	9.9	961,240	2.8	5.5	32.7	19.2	9.7	19.5	10.6
Maryland	9.1	25.5	49.2	16.1	4,102,486	4.2	6.1	25.1	19.2	6.5	21.1	17.7
Massachusetts	7.8	24.2	48.8	19.2	4,706,644	4.5	5.2	25.2	15.9	7.7	23.1	18.4
Michigan	10.6	25.9	52.4	11.2	6,728,347	3.0	6.9	29.4	23.7	9.2	17.0	10.8
Minnesota	11.6	23.7	49.2	15.5	3,700,935	3.0	4.2	25.4	21.5	11.2	22.9	11.8
Mississippi	12.5	26.6	53.7	7.1	1,952,337	5.8	10.8	31.0	22.4	9.2	13.0	7.9
Missouri	12.0	26.7	49.7	11.6	4,097,212	3.6	7.5	31.0	22.4	7.7	17.3	10.6
Montana	15.2	33.9	42.2	8.8	706,329	2.0	4.4	31.5	22.8	8.6	20.4	10.2
Nebraska	9.6	23.1	52.0	15.3	1,232,583	3.9	5.1	26.9	23.8	10.1	19.8	10.4
Nevada	15.2	32.1	45.7	7.0	1,968,167	6.4	8.0	27.9	26.0	8.1	15.5	8.1
New Hampshire	10.3	26.7	49.0	14.0	937,214	1.9	4.9	28.5	19.2	9.7	21.9	13.7
New Jersey	9.9	24.9	47.8	17.4	6,166,384	5.2	5.8	28.5	16.6	6.4	23.3	14.3
New Mexico	15.1	26.3	52.7	5.9	1,377,548	6.7	8.6	26.8	23.6	7.7	14.4	12.1
New York	10.1	23.3	48.2	18.5	13,641,473	6.6	7.4	26.5	16.0	8.5	20.0	15.0
North Carolina	12.5	26.5	49.1	11.8	6,762,644	5.0	8.4	26.4	21.5	9.2	18.9	10.6
North Dakota	8.5	22.4	53.7	15.4	492,017	3.7	3.8	27.6	22.7	13.1	21.5	7.7
Ohio	12.2	28.9	47.3	11.5	7,896,470	3.0	7.3	33.7	20.6	8.6	16.8	10.0
Oklahoma	15.3	29.0	46.2	9.4	2,557,863	4.3	8.4	31.6	23.7	7.4	16.5	8.1
Oregon	11.6	28.0	49.1	11.3	2,804,461	3.7	6.3	23.4	25.8	8.8	20.2	12.0
Pennsylvania	10.6	29.7	45.5	14.1	8,895,727	3.3	7.0	35.7	16.0	8.3	18.1	11.6
Rhode Island	6.4	26.7	51.4	15.6	730,083	5.5	6.8	28.0	18.5	8.5	19.3	13.4
South Carolina	11.6	29.1	48.4	10.9	3,319,832	4.4	9.2	29.4	20.7	9.4	17.3	9.5
South Dakota	12.6	27.7	46.7	13.0	563,108	3.4	5.4	31.2	21.3	11.1	19.6	7.9
Tennessee	8.7	33.2	46.9	11.2	4,473,487	5.3	8.6	33.1	20.5	6.7	16.1	9.6
Texas	13.9	29.4	47.1	9.6	17,472,861	8.9	8.7	25.3	21.8	6.9	18.7	9.7
Utah	10.6	26.8	53.0	9.5	1,741,949	2.9	5.6	24.2	26.3	9.2	21.1	10.7
Vermont	7.0	25.5	51.6	16.0	438,654	2.8	5.5	29.0	17.1	8.6	22.3	14.6
Virginia	8.8	26.9	49.4	14.9	5,685,318	4.5	6.6	24.6	19.8	7.5	21.3	15.7
Washington	12.4	28.4	47.2	12.0	4,889,314	3.9	5.2	23.1	24.0	9.6	21.7	12.5
West Virginia	10.4	30.3	48.5	10.8	1,300,347	4.5	9.5	40.7	18.8	6.9	11.7	7.9
Wisconsin	9.7	27.5	49.5	13.3	3,918,997	3.0	5.6	31.2	21.3	10.5	18.9	9.4
Wyoming	14.2	28.1	51.7	6.0	388,747	2.0	5.8	28.8	26.3	10.9	17.3	9.0

Table B-6. Educational Attainment—*Continued*

	Educational attainment											
	Men age 25 and older				Women age 25 and older				White alone, not of Hispanic origin, age 25 and older			
	Percent of men age 25 and older				Percent of women age 25 and older				Percent of all non-Hispanic white persons age 25 and older			
State	Less than high school diploma	High school graduate (includes equivalency)	Some college or associate's degree	Bachelor's degree or higher	Less than high school diploma	High school graduate (includes equivalency)	Some college or associate's degree	Bachelor's degree or higher	Less than high school diploma	High school graduate (includes equivalency)	Some college or associate's degree	Bachelor's degree or higher
United States	13.6	28.4	27.8	30.3	12.2	26.8	30.1	30.9	7.7	27.9	30.1	34.2
Alabama	16.3	32.5	27.6	23.6	14.1	29.7	31.6	24.7	12.7	30.6	29.7	27.0
Alaska	7.2	30.2	34.9	27.8	7.6	24.1	36.5	31.8	4.1	24.0	35.3	36.6
Arizona	14.4	24.8	32.7	28.0	13.4	24.2	35.0	27.4	6.1	23.4	36.6	33.9
Arkansas	15.5	35.9	27.8	20.8	13.7	32.5	31.0	22.7	11.7	34.6	30.2	23.5
California	18.2	21.3	28.2	32.3	17.5	20.3	30.0	32.2	5.4	18.9	33.6	42.1
Colorado	9.2	22.4	29.7	38.7	8.4	21.1	30.7	39.8	3.6	19.9	30.9	45.6
Connecticut	10.4	28.6	22.8	38.1	9.2	26.4	25.9	38.5	6.0	26.8	24.3	42.9
Delaware	12.6	30.7	26.1	30.6	9.8	29.0	29.9	31.3	8.0	30.8	28.4	32.8
District of Columbia	10.8	15.6	15.0	58.6	9.6	19.0	16.2	55.1	0.4	2.1	5.9	91.6
Florida	13.2	29.2	28.7	28.8	11.6	29.1	31.2	28.0	7.3	29.0	31.8	31.9
Georgia	15.1	29.1	26.5	29.3	12.7	27.2	29.6	30.5	10.3	27.8	28.3	33.6
Hawaii	8.9	28.5	32.3	30.3	9.4	25.8	32.4	32.4	4.2	17.8	33.2	44.8
Idaho	10.6	28.1	34.2	27.0	9.4	26.8	38.9	24.9	6.9	27.5	37.8	27.7
Illinois	12.1	27.4	27.9	32.5	10.8	26.0	29.8	33.3	6.2	26.8	29.9	37.0
Indiana	12.3	35.5	27.7	24.5	11.3	33.2	30.2	25.3	10.0	35.2	29.2	25.7
Iowa	9.0	33.9	31.2	25.9	7.5	30.3	34.4	27.7	6.4	32.5	33.6	27.6
Kansas	10.5	27.8	30.5	31.3	9.0	25.4	33.5	32.1	6.3	26.6	32.9	34.3
Kentucky	16.1	35.5	26.3	22.1	13.7	31.7	30.1	24.4	14.3	33.9	28.2	23.6
Louisiana	17.5	35.4	25.4	21.7	13.5	33.0	29.0	24.6	11.6	33.9	27.5	27.1
Maine	9.5	34.3	27.6	28.7	7.2	31.3	30.1	31.4	7.9	33.2	28.8	30.1
Maryland	11.2	26.0	24.4	38.4	9.6	24.3	26.9	39.2	6.8	24.5	25.0	43.7
Massachusetts	10.3	26.6	21.8	41.4	9.3	23.9	25.2	41.6	6.4	25.0	24.1	44.5
Michigan	10.5	30.1	31.6	27.7	9.2	28.7	34.2	27.9	8.1	30.0	33.0	28.9
Minnesota	7.8	26.7	31.8	33.7	6.7	24.2	33.5	35.6	4.6	25.9	33.4	36.1
Mississippi	18.8	32.8	29.2	19.1	14.5	29.4	33.7	22.4	12.2	30.4	32.9	24.5
Missouri	12.0	32.1	29.1	26.8	10.3	29.9	31.0	28.8	9.8	31.5	29.8	28.9
Montana	6.9	32.5	30.9	29.7	6.0	30.5	32.0	31.5	5.6	30.9	31.5	32.0
Nebraska	9.6	27.9	33.2	29.3	8.4	26.0	34.6	31.1	5.4	27.0	35.5	32.1
Nevada	14.7	28.5	33.3	23.5	14.1	27.3	35.0	23.6	7.0	27.2	37.1	28.8
New Hampshire	7.9	28.9	27.6	35.6	6.0	28.1	30.2	35.7	6.3	29.0	29.2	35.5
New Jersey	11.4	28.6	22.1	37.8	10.5	28.4	23.7	37.4	6.4	28.8	23.0	41.7
New Mexico	16.3	27.8	31.0	24.9	14.4	25.9	31.6	28.0	5.4	22.0	32.8	39.8
New York	14.4	27.4	24.1	34.1	13.7	25.7	24.7	35.9	7.1	26.5	25.4	41.0
North Carolina	15.1	27.8	28.7	28.4	12.0	25.1	32.5	30.4	9.7	25.8	31.3	33.2
North Dakota	8.3	28.7	36.5	26.5	6.7	26.4	35.0	31.9	6.6	27.7	35.7	29.9
Ohio	10.7	34.9	27.8	26.7	10.0	32.7	30.5	26.9	9.1	34.6	28.6	27.7
Oklahoma	13.3	32.9	29.6	24.2	12.1	30.4	32.5	25.1	9.7	31.6	31.7	27.0
Oregon	10.5	23.9	33.8	31.9	9.5	22.8	35.3	32.4	6.6	23.8	36.0	33.6
Pennsylvania	10.8	36.3	23.3	29.6	9.9	35.1	25.2	29.8	8.3	36.5	24.1	31.1
Rhode Island	12.7	28.6	25.9	32.7	12.0	27.4	27.9	32.7	9.5	27.7	27.2	35.5
South Carolina	15.0	30.1	28.1	26.8	12.5	28.8	31.9	26.8	10.2	27.5	30.7	31.7
South Dakota	9.8	33.5	30.6	26.0	8.0	29.0	34.0	28.9	6.6	31.4	32.7	29.3
Tennessee	15.1	34.0	25.6	25.3	12.9	32.3	28.7	26.1	12.3	33.5	27.0	27.2
Texas	18.3	25.9	27.6	28.2	16.9	24.8	29.8	28.5	6.7	23.9	32.2	37.2
Utah	8.9	23.5	33.2	34.4	8.1	24.9	37.6	29.3	4.9	23.1	37.5	34.6
Vermont	10.1	31.9	23.7	34.4	6.7	26.3	27.7	39.4	7.6	29.6	25.7	37.1
Virginia	12.0	25.3	25.8	37.0	10.3	24.0	28.8	36.9	8.0	24.4	27.3	40.3
Washington	9.6	23.8	32.2	34.4	8.7	22.3	35.0	34.0	5.6	23.2	35.3	35.8
West Virginia	15.2	42.5	23.4	18.9	12.9	39.0	27.9	20.2	14.2	41.3	25.3	19.2
Wisconsin	9.3	32.4	31.2	27.1	7.8	30.1	32.5	29.6	6.3	31.6	32.2	29.9
Wyoming	7.8	31.2	34.9	26.1	7.8	26.4	39.4	26.4	5.7	28.8	37.6	27.9

Table B-6. Educational Attainment—*Continued*

| | Black or African-American alone, age 25 and older | | | | Hispanic or Latino, age 25 and older | | | | Asian alone, age 25 and older | | | |
| | Percent of all Black alone persons age 25 and older | | | | Percent of all Hispanic or Latino persons age 25 and older | | | | Percent of all Asian alone persons age 25 and older | | | |
State	Less than high school diploma	High school graduate (includes equivalency)	Some college or associate's degree	Bachelor's degree or higher	Less than high school diploma	High school graduate (includes equivalency)	Some college or associate's degree	Bachelor's degree or higher	Less than high school diploma	High school graduate (includes equivalency)	Some college or associate's degree	Bachelor's degree or higher
United States	15.3	31.5	33.0	20.2	34.0	27.6	23.6	14.8	13.5	15.5	18.7	52.3
Alabama	18.5	34.3	31.0	16.3	42.6	27.5	17.0	12.9	14.0	14.5	20.3	51.1
Alaska	4.7	26.4	49.2	19.7	11.8	23.0	46.9	18.3	18.2	26.5	30.7	24.5
Arizona	11.5	23.7	41.9	22.9	33.5	27.6	27.6	11.2	12.3	13.6	19.9	54.2
Arkansas	19.5	34.8	32.1	13.7	45.1	29.8	15.4	9.7	14.8	18.6	15.1	51.5
California	11.0	24.1	40.6	24.3	38.4	25.8	23.9	11.9	12.8	14.4	22.1	50.8
Colorado	9.9	24.3	41.5	24.3	30.0	29.4	26.3	14.2	15.1	16.7	17.6	50.6
Connecticut	13.6	34.5	29.7	22.2	29.1	31.4	23.4	16.1	9.7	13.3	14.6	62.4
Delaware	12.5	32.3	32.3	22.9	40.8	26.7	18.7	13.9	7.5	11.3	13.2	68.1
District of Columbia	15.4	33.0	25.3	26.2	28.1	14.5	13.1	44.3	6.3	4.8	11.0	77.9
Florida	18.4	33.2	30.2	18.1	22.2	28.9	26.1	22.8	12.7	19.6	19.1	48.6
Georgia	15.0	30.9	31.3	22.8	38.6	25.9	19.4	16.1	13.2	18.6	16.2	52.0
Hawaii	5.3	23.2	43.9	27.6	10.6	31.3	36.9	21.2	13.3	26.3	29.1	31.3
Idaho	11.8	18.9	36.0	33.3	39.0	28.1	24.8	8.1	10.3	16.2	28.2	45.3
Illinois	14.0	29.9	36.0	20.1	35.4	29.7	21.4	13.5	9.2	11.6	16.4	62.8
Indiana	14.6	33.4	35.1	16.9	37.2	30.3	20.6	11.9	13.7	14.1	12.1	60.1
Iowa	16.5	35.2	34.1	14.2	42.3	27.0	19.9	10.8	16.2	22.6	16.2	44.9
Kansas	13.6	30.9	36.2	19.3	37.4	26.0	23.9	12.7	15.6	21.1	17.4	45.9
Kentucky	15.9	34.5	33.4	16.3	31.7	31.2	19.3	17.8	17.1	13.0	17.7	52.2
Louisiana	21.1	36.1	27.7	15.0	26.1	32.8	23.2	17.8	26.0	19.7	18.4	35.9
Maine	16.4	22.6	34.6	26.4	7.6	18.2	30.5	43.7	17.2	16.2	24.5	42.1
Maryland	10.2	30.0	31.8	28.0	38.0	23.9	16.9	21.2	9.2	12.1	15.1	63.7
Massachusetts	15.9	29.7	31.4	22.9	31.1	30.3	20.9	17.7	15.1	14.7	12.3	57.9
Michigan	15.2	30.9	36.9	17.0	28.9	27.4	27.0	16.7	10.0	10.5	16.3	63.2
Minnesota	19.3	26.0	35.7	19.0	35.4	25.2	22.0	17.5	20.4	15.4	20.7	43.5
Mississippi	22.6	32.9	30.2	14.3	40.0	28.2	19.2	12.6	19.6	18.3	22.3	39.9
Missouri	14.7	32.7	35.5	17.1	31.0	25.4	24.9	18.6	14.2	13.0	13.3	59.5
Montana	5.0	27.3	34.9	32.7	15.9	43.3	25.5	15.3	7.4	16.8	20.9	54.9
Nebraska	12.4	29.8	35.6	22.2	43.7	27.3	18.8	10.2	21.0	14.8	13.6	50.7
Nevada	11.8	32.2	39.3	16.7	37.0	30.5	24.2	8.3	9.6	21.5	32.5	36.5
New Hampshire	10.6	24.4	44.0	20.9	20.9	25.3	27.5	26.2	10.8	11.4	10.2	67.6
New Jersey	12.2	35.9	30.1	21.8	27.5	31.6	23.1	17.8	7.8	12.1	12.5	67.6
New Mexico	9.7	21.1	37.4	31.7	25.0	31.0	29.6	14.4	15.3	22.2	18.1	44.3
New York	16.9	31.1	28.8	23.3	32.4	27.5	22.5	17.6	21.8	17.0	14.5	46.7
North Carolina	15.5	30.5	34.4	19.5	43.5	23.9	19.1	13.5	14.6	15.9	14.5	55.0
North Dakota	11.9	20.0	33.5	34.6	17.7	30.7	27.8	23.9	19.0	16.6	28.3	36.0
Ohio	15.1	32.6	35.8	16.4	23.8	32.2	27.0	17.1	13.7	14.2	11.9	60.2
Oklahoma	11.9	34.6	35.3	18.3	41.3	28.2	18.9	11.6	16.7	22.8	19.7	40.8
Oregon	12.3	21.1	37.9	28.7	38.1	22.8	23.8	15.3	13.7	15.9	21.3	49.1
Pennsylvania	15.4	37.8	29.8	17.1	30.1	31.6	23.2	15.1	16.8	15.7	13.8	53.6
Rhode Island	16.8	32.0	32.1	19.2	29.5	29.9	26.8	13.8	12.7	18.4	13.8	55.1
South Carolina	19.0	36.0	30.2	14.8	37.0	25.6	22.2	15.2	17.2	18.9	15.6	48.2
South Dakota	32.9	25.5	25.1	16.4	29.1	30.2	22.0	18.7	35.2	11.2	19.4	34.2
Tennessee	16.0	34.4	31.3	18.4	40.6	28.8	17.5	13.2	14.0	20.1	16.7	49.2
Texas	11.8	29.6	36.3	22.4	36.5	27.6	22.7	13.2	12.2	14.2	15.9	57.7
Utah	11.2	19.8	43.2	25.8	32.0	32.2	24.3	11.5	13.2	18.9	19.8	48.1
Vermont	9.6	14.5	38.3	37.6	13.2	22.2	27.8	36.8	26.7	12.8	19.5	41.1
Virginia	15.6	29.4	32.1	22.8	28.9	24.4	23.7	23.0	10.2	15.1	16.0	58.7
Washington	9.6	26.6	40.6	23.2	35.6	26.2	24.4	13.8	11.8	15.9	21.0	51.4
West Virginia	10.8	40.6	36.2	12.4	10.1	28.9	34.2	26.8	10.4	12.9	8.5	68.2
Wisconsin	18.4	32.0	36.0	13.5	35.0	29.2	24.0	11.8	15.9	19.1	20.9	44.1
Wyoming	13.5	23.4	46.3	16.8	29.2	29.8	28.2	12.8	11.2	24.0	30.6	34.2

Table B-7. Homeownership, Health Insurance, and Computer Access by Educational Attainment

	Homeownership rates by educational attainment of householder					Health insurance coverage by age and educational attainment							
	Percent of occupied housing units that are owner occupied					Persons age 25 to 64							
						With private health insurance coverage (through employer or self-purchase, including purchase through the Affordable Care Act)				With public coverage (Medicare, Medicaid, VA health care, or CHIP)			
State	All occupied housing units	Less than high school graduate	High school graduate (includes equivalency)	Some college or Associate's degree	Bachelor's degree or higher	Less than high school graduate	High school graduate (includes equivalency)	Some college or associate's degree	Bachelor's degree or higher	Less than high school graduate	High school graduate (includes equivalency)	Some college or associate's degree	Bachelor's degree or higher
United States	63.0	48.1	61.0	61.0	71.4	37.4	63.1	75.0	90.9	34.9	23.9	18.7	6.8
Alabama	67.9	56.9	66.8	65.2	77.9	38.7	64.1	77.0	93.3	34.0	21.7	17.2	6.1
Alaska	63.9	52.1	56.8	61.5	74.4	39.9	56.9	72.9	91.5	32.2	18.6	16.9	7.1
Arizona	61.9	49.1	58.0	59.4	72.4	33.3	56.3	72.4	89.4	39.6	29.6	21.7	8.6
Arkansas	65.2	58.1	65.0	61.6	74.3	38.5	60.8	70.8	89.7	40.4	28.7	24.1	8.4
California	53.6	37.9	47.6	53.4	62.9	36.5	57.1	72.0	88.9	39.3	30.6	22.8	8.7
Colorado	63.7	45.5	58.6	59.3	72.6	35.1	63.5	74.4	90.3	31.2	24.1	20.9	7.8
Connecticut	66.2	37.5	59.0	64.5	77.6	35.3	65.1	76.7	92.2	44.1	27.0	20.2	5.9
Delaware	70.8	53.4	70.9	67.5	78.3	40.6	63.3	78.1	93.3	39.9	30.9	20.6	5.7
District of Columbia	39.9	20.6	22.0	34.2	49.1	30.2	41.3	62.1	93.7	58.4	56.1	38.9	5.4
Florida	63.8	49.9	60.9	62.5	71.7	37.7	58.2	72.6	87.0	27.8	20.0	15.8	7.0
Georgia	61.8	48.3	58.8	57.8	72.8	35.9	61.6	75.0	91.5	24.1	17.2	13.8	4.8
Hawaii	56.6	47.2	51.3	53.8	64.5	60.3	74.6	82.0	92.0	33.7	22.2	16.2	8.5
Idaho	69.0	58.8	63.9	66.5	79.9	43.6	66.4	77.7	92.0	25.9	16.7	13.9	5.8
Illinois	65.3	50.1	62.9	63.9	72.4	39.9	64.7	75.8	92.1	33.8	24.7	19.7	5.9
Indiana	68.2	53.6	67.4	65.1	78.4	40.7	69.4	77.7	92.5	32.6	19.3	15.7	5.0
Iowa	70.7	56.0	70.4	67.9	78.4	48.9	74.6	82.5	94.4	34.2	21.7	16.8	6.2
Kansas	66.4	53.2	64.4	62.0	75.7	44.0	71.1	81.4	94.9	21.3	15.3	12.0	4.2
Kentucky	66.3	58.8	67.1	61.3	75.7	31.8	62.1	72.2	91.3	58.2	34.2	26.3	8.6
Louisiana	64.6	55.3	64.8	60.2	74.6	36.1	61.9	74.3	90.8	34.3	20.3	16.1	6.2
Maine	71.0	51.5	67.7	70.3	79.2	32.9	61.7	75.4	90.0	49.3	26.6	19.5	7.0
Maryland	65.9	47.4	61.1	62.6	74.2	40.7	68.1	79.4	92.9	33.9	23.8	18.9	6.5
Massachusetts	61.7	35.0	55.7	60.1	71.0	36.2	63.2	73.7	91.9	60.3	36.4	27.4	8.5
Michigan	70.4	55.8	69.4	68.7	77.6	37.0	63.6	75.0	91.7	50.9	30.4	22.0	7.4
Minnesota	70.9	47.0	68.2	69.3	78.4	41.7	69.5	79.0	93.3	44.1	25.8	20.0	6.9
Mississippi	67.4	62.0	65.5	64.7	77.6	35.9	57.0	71.3	90.4	37.8	23.6	18.0	7.1
Missouri	66.1	53.4	65.3	61.6	75.9	41.8	67.6	78.2	93.5	33.2	18.3	14.3	4.7
Montana	66.7	51.8	63.2	65.4	73.8	41.7	65.5	75.0	90.2	29.3	16.6	15.9	6.0
Nebraska	65.9	50.9	63.0	63.0	75.0	49.5	73.4	83.3	95.1	19.1	13.9	11.3	4.7
Nevada	54.0	40.7	48.9	52.8	66.4	44.2	63.9	73.4	86.2	22.8	21.2	19.6	10.2
New Hampshire	70.9	50.2	65.8	67.7	79.9	48.4	71.1	80.1	93.7	36.5	18.1	15.3	5.2
New Jersey	63.0	41.0	57.3	60.9	73.3	38.7	63.8	76.4	90.6	30.4	22.8	16.5	5.8
New Mexico	67.5	60.4	66.4	64.4	75.0	25.2	51.4	63.0	86.0	44.0	34.6	29.1	12.3
New York	53.1	30.3	52.0	54.8	59.8	32.7	59.2	72.3	87.6	49.3	31.3	23.7	9.4
North Carolina	63.9	51.3	62.3	60.5	73.2	36.3	62.4	74.7	92.7	27.7	20.6	16.6	5.3
North Dakota	61.7	51.6	60.6	58.3	69.7	48.2	76.9	83.7	94.6	29.5	14.7	12.1	4.6
Ohio	65.4	49.0	64.6	61.2	76.3	34.7	66.1	74.1	92.6	49.1	26.3	22.5	6.2
Oklahoma	65.3	54.2	63.3	62.5	75.9	38.2	60.9	73.8	90.9	24.0	18.1	15.0	5.7
Oregon	61.1	46.1	57.3	58.4	69.8	39.9	60.4	70.2	87.9	40.6	33.0	26.9	11.3
Pennsylvania	68.7	54.0	67.9	66.6	75.6	40.7	71.5	80.2	93.5	41.6	22.7	16.5	5.4
Rhode Island	59.0	37.9	53.3	55.4	73.1	39.7	63.5	73.8	91.3	49.7	30.2	23.9	8.6
South Carolina	68.1	57.2	65.5	65.8	77.8	35.4	62.3	75.0	91.1	33.8	21.9	16.9	6.4
South Dakota	68.2	50.2	65.6	66.8	77.4	47.4	69.0	81.2	93.3	24.9	14.5	11.8	5.4
Tennessee	65.8	54.9	64.2	63.5	74.9	35.9	62.7	75.1	91.6	36.7	22.8	18.0	6.1
Texas	61.1	54.1	57.4	58.2	69.9	35.8	59.4	74.5	91.1	17.3	14.9	11.9	4.4
Utah	68.9	49.6	64.5	66.3	78.2	48.4	70.3	82.1	92.6	18.4	12.6	10.0	4.5
Vermont	70.7	59.8	66.7	67.7	77.5	37.7	62.3	70.4	86.2	59.8	34.0	29.0	12.6
Virginia	65.0	53.8	61.9	61.2	72.0	45.7	68.8	80.3	94.1	24.9	16.0	13.6	4.9
Washington	62.4	46.3	58.0	60.6	69.8	42.0	65.7	76.2	90.9	33.2	26.9	22.2	8.3
West Virginia	72.3	65.9	73.5	68.6	78.9	28.4	59.3	69.7	90.4	63.6	35.9	27.8	9.1
Wisconsin	66.8	49.9	65.2	64.7	75.1	44.5	72.3	80.5	93.9	37.9	21.9	16.8	5.8
Wyoming	68.0	56.8	65.8	66.2	75.6	44.4	71.8	81.4	91.7	17.3	11.2	10.4	6.0

Table B-7. Homeownership, Health Insurance, and Computer Access by Educational Attainment—*Continued*

	Health insurance coverage by age and educational attainment (Continued)											
	Persons age 25 to 64 (Continued)				Persons age 65 and older							
	With no health insurance coverage				With private health insurance coverage (through employer or self-purchase, including purchase through the Affordable Care Act)				With public coverage (Medicare, Medicaid, VA health care, or CHIP)			
State	Less than high school graduate	High school graduate (includes equivalency)	Some college or associate's degree	Bachelor's degree or higher	Less than high school graduate	High school graduate (includes equivalency)	Some college or associate's degree	Bachelor's degree or higher	Less than high school graduate	High school graduate (includes equivalency)	Some college or associate's degree	Bachelor's degree or higher
United States	31.3	17.1	10.8	4.7	40.6	60.8	65.7	70.8	95.8	97.2	96.8	94.7
Alabama	32.9	19.3	12.0	4.0	46.3	61.7	70.1	79.4	98.1	98.4	98.2	96.3
Alaska	33.7	28.4	16.7	6.4	37.6	57.5	64.8	79.4	93.9	95.6	95.3	96.0
Arizona	30.6	18.2	10.9	5.0	35.5	53.9	60.5	64.9	94.0	96.6	97.5	95.7
Arkansas	25.6	15.9	11.0	4.8	44.2	57.4	66.7	74.3	96.8	98.2	98.6	96.0
California	26.8	15.6	9.1	4.6	25.8	48.6	59.2	63.8	94.2	96.0	95.7	93.0
Colorado	36.6	16.0	9.4	4.5	42.0	60.7	62.5	66.7	92.3	97.1	96.7	95.3
Connecticut	23.7	11.6	6.5	3.3	40.5	62.0	65.7	72.2	96.6	96.3	96.1	92.8
Delaware	23.8	11.0	5.8	3.2	45.7	65.6	73.9	76.8	96.3	95.7	96.3	96.7
District of Columbia	16.5	7.5	4.7	2.4	46.1	62.6	59.9	82.0	92.1	94.2	94.4	90.4
Florida	38.2	25.5	16.0	8.9	30.6	50.8	57.6	63.7	94.4	96.5	96.6	95.2
Georgia	43.3	25.0	15.8	6.1	40.9	57.2	65.3	71.0	96.7	96.9	97.2	95.3
Hawaii	9.7	7.3	5.8	2.9	49.0	69.6	74.7	74.3	95.4	94.0	93.0	93.9
Idaho	34.7	22.4	13.9	5.4	48.6	61.0	65.5	72.1	98.9	98.9	98.3	97.5
Illinois	28.6	14.1	8.1	3.7	44.4	63.7	67.6	71.9	95.0	97.7	96.1	93.2
Indiana	31.1	15.1	10.7	4.6	53.8	67.4	68.2	69.4	97.3	98.4	97.5	96.2
Iowa	21.9	8.6	5.3	2.2	59.8	71.7	73.2	74.2	98.5	98.7	97.5	96.6
Kansas	38.1	17.6	10.9	3.4	55.1	68.9	69.6	71.5	95.9	98.2	97.2	95.7
Kentucky	15.7	9.4	6.8	3.0	46.3	62.9	70.1	76.1	98.4	98.4	97.4	95.8
Louisiana	33.7	22.0	14.5	5.7	36.8	54.9	61.9	73.0	98.3	97.3	96.6	92.7
Maine	22.5	16.6	10.2	5.2	44.1	57.8	65.1	70.8	98.9	97.7	98.5	95.7
Maryland	29.6	12.1	6.7	3.1	50.5	68.8	75.6	79.6	93.6	96.0	95.4	92.3
Massachusetts	9.4	5.8	3.9	1.9	46.2	66.1	72.0	74.8	97.2	96.5	96.4	91.1
Michigan	17.7	11.3	8.0	3.5	62.6	74.3	76.2	80.2	98.7	98.5	97.7	96.5
Minnesota	19.1	9.1	5.4	1.9	55.6	72.2	75.2	77.1	97.7	98.6	97.8	96.2
Mississippi	31.1	23.4	15.8	5.9	35.6	54.5	64.7	74.9	98.3	98.6	97.2	97.1
Missouri	29.0	18.0	11.9	4.0	47.2	60.6	64.8	69.3	97.2	97.9	97.6	95.4
Montana	35.0	22.2	15.4	6.1	62.8	63.8	64.3	71.5	99.3	98.7	97.3	96.4
Nebraska	34.1	16.5	9.6	3.0	51.8	65.3	66.8	71.5	96.7	98.1	97.3	94.7
Nevada	35.8	18.0	12.0	7.2	32.3	49.2	57.5	62.2	88.4	94.4	96.1	94.9
New Hampshire	19.3	13.9	8.5	3.7	58.6	67.5	72.2	77.9	99.2	98.2	97.8	95.2
New Jersey	34.0	17.0	10.5	5.0	43.3	61.7	67.7	70.9	94.2	95.8	95.6	94.2
New Mexico	34.2	18.9	12.9	5.6	29.1	55.5	62.1	65.3	96.5	97.2	96.3	96.1
New York	22.8	13.8	8.4	5.0	35.1	58.8	66.2	70.7	96.1	96.2	95.6	93.9
North Carolina	40.0	21.7	14.0	4.9	45.4	61.5	66.3	73.8	97.6	98.1	98.0	96.1
North Dakota	25.8	12.5	9.1	3.2	66.0	69.0	74.1	74.5	98.9	97.6	98.1	97.8
Ohio	20.3	11.6	7.8	3.1	51.3	64.0	67.6	72.2	97.5	97.6	96.7	94.8
Oklahoma	40.9	24.7	16.2	6.6	47.0	60.4	68.3	76.7	95.6	98.2	97.5	96.2
Oregon	23.3	12.2	8.8	4.4	48.4	61.2	66.0	70.3	96.4	98.2	97.6	96.0
Pennsylvania	22.6	10.6	7.9	3.3	55.2	69.0	71.5	75.0	96.8	97.8	97.2	96.1
Rhode Island	15.9	10.5	7.1	3.5	43.9	59.3	68.0	71.6	98.5	97.8	94.5	95.9
South Carolina	35.6	20.8	13.4	6.0	40.7	59.7	68.8	74.5	98.1	98.1	97.9	97.4
South Dakota	32.0	20.6	11.9	4.3	48.9	62.2	68.2	72.1	96.6	99.1	98.2	97.9
Tennessee	31.9	19.2	11.8	5.0	43.8	58.0	65.8	69.9	98.1	98.3	96.9	95.9
Texas	48.8	28.9	17.7	6.8	29.7	55.0	62.7	69.3	92.7	96.2	96.6	93.7
Utah	36.5	20.8	11.3	5.2	46.4	62.2	68.9	68.4	90.2	95.9	96.5	95.6
Vermont	6.5	7.9	6.0	3.3	47.5	61.3	65.4	73.2	99.9	98.5	98.1	96.9
Virginia	33.0	19.0	11.2	4.1	50.2	68.5	73.8	80.9	95.7	96.8	96.1	94.2
Washington	28.9	12.4	7.4	3.5	46.0	64.1	68.2	72.5	95.2	97.0	97.2	95.1
West Virginia	13.2	9.8	8.5	3.9	50.2	66.6	72.3	79.2	99.7	98.2	97.9	96.9
Wisconsin	22.3	9.8	6.6	2.5	54.9	66.5	68.6	73.0	97.6	98.6	98.0	96.7
Wyoming	42.5	20.0	12.2	5.7	59.4	66.9	66.5	69.4	97.5	98.5	97.3	95.4

Table B-7. Homeownership, Health Insurance, and Computer Access by Educational Attainment—*Continued*

	Health insurance coverage by age and educational attainment (Continued)				Computer and internet access by educational attainment of household population 25 years and older					
	Persons age 65 and older (Continued)									
	With no health insurance coverage				Household has a computer			Household has dial-up or broadband internet subscription		
State	Less than high school graduate	High school graduate (includes equivalency)	Some college or associate's degree	Bachelor's degree or higher	Less than high school graduate or equivalency	High school graduate or equivalency, some college, or Associate's degree	Bachelor's degree or higher	Less than high school graduate or equivalency	High school graduate or equivalency, some college, or Associate's degree	Bachelor's degree or higher
United States	2.4	0.6	0.4	0.5	72.1	88.5	97.2	57.4	78.3	92.5
Alabama	0.5	0.2	0.2	0.3	60.8	83.4	95.8	45.2	70.4	90.2
Alaska	1.9	1.5	0.6	0.8	83.7	92.7	98.0	65.2	82.9	92.5
Arizona	3.8	1.2	0.4	0.4	74.7	89.1	96.5	60.4	79.6	92.0
Arkansas	2.3	0.3	0.2	0.3	63.8	84.1	95.8	42.1	66.8	86.1
California	3.3	0.9	0.5	0.7	80.0	91.5	97.7	66.4	83.2	94.0
Colorado	3.8	0.3	0.4	0.3	79.0	91.7	98.0	64.5	83.1	94.1
Connecticut	1.1	0.7	0.4	0.7	73.5	89.8	97.5	61.7	82.4	94.5
Delaware	2.0	2.7	0.0	0.4	71.9	88.4	97.2	53.3	79.0	91.8
District of Columbia	2.9	0.0	0.3	0.4	72.9	83.8	98.4	45.7	64.6	93.6
Florida	3.4	1.2	0.8	0.9	74.9	89.4	96.7	60.3	79.3	90.9
Georgia	1.8	1.0	0.4	0.5	69.0	88.3	97.5	50.6	76.1	92.1
Hawaii	0.1	1.2	0.6	0.3	79.2	90.6	96.8	68.4	84.0	92.8
Idaho	0.5	0.1	0.1	0.1	81.6	90.7	97.5	62.9	79.4	92.1
Illinois	2.9	0.4	0.6	0.4	73.3	87.1	97.1	59.2	77.7	92.6
Indiana	1.3	0.2	0.3	0.3	68.2	87.6	96.9	52.4	76.0	91.9
Iowa	0.6	0.2	0.2	0.1	69.0	86.9	96.8	55.2	77.0	91.7
Kansas	1.6	0.3	0.1	0.2	70.4	86.8	96.9	57.9	76.9	92.4
Kentucky	1.0	0.2	0.2	0.1	60.4	85.9	96.4	46.2	74.8	91.3
Louisiana	0.6	0.6	0.1	0.1	63.3	83.9	95.8	48.2	71.8	89.6
Maine	0.2	0.1	0.1	0.2	68.8	89.2	97.0	56.4	79.9	91.4
Maryland	3.1	0.8	0.6	0.8	75.4	90.4	98.0	61.0	81.3	94.2
Massachusetts	0.5	0.3	0.2	0.5	72.3	90.1	97.7	62.3	83.0	94.5
Michigan	0.6	0.3	0.2	0.3	71.6	87.8	96.9	55.7	75.9	91.4
Minnesota	1.3	0.2	0.2	0.2	74.8	89.9	97.7	60.0	80.6	93.6
Mississippi	0.5	0.4	0.3	0.1	58.9	81.6	94.8	39.0	64.1	86.4
Missouri	1.8	0.4	0.1	0.4	67.0	86.9	96.8	51.1	75.2	91.4
Montana	0.6	0.3	0.1	0.2	63.9	87.1	95.6	49.8	76.6	90.1
Nebraska	2.0	0.3	0.1	0.2	70.9	87.8	97.1	60.3	79.2	93.1
Nevada	8.9	1.8	0.7	1.4	82.6	91.8	96.7	64.9	82.4	91.8
New Hampshire	0.0	0.5	0.0	0.7	76.6	92.0	98.0	67.7	85.1	94.7
New Jersey	3.1	1.1	0.6	1.0	74.0	89.3	97.6	62.6	82.2	94.5
New Mexico	2.7	0.9	0.8	0.4	63.6	82.8	95.0	46.3	69.5	87.4
New York	1.9	0.5	0.5	0.6	74.8	88.4	96.6	62.3	79.3	91.8
North Carolina	1.4	0.3	0.3	0.3	66.1	86.8	97.1	51.5	75.5	92.1
North Dakota	0.5	0.7	0.1	0.4	60.1	87.8	95.8	49.2	79.2	89.4
Ohio	1.3	0.4	0.2	0.5	67.2	87.7	97.1	54.1	78.3	92.9
Oklahoma	2.2	0.3	0.3	0.1	68.9	86.0	95.8	52.2	72.6	88.6
Oregon	1.9	0.3	0.3	0.1	80.7	91.7	97.8	67.9	82.5	92.9
Pennsylvania	1.7	0.3	0.2	0.2	66.1	86.4	96.9	53.6	77.6	92.9
Rhode Island	0.9	0.5	0.0	0.3	71.0	89.5	97.2	59.4	81.6	93.2
South Carolina	1.1	0.4	0.2	0.2	61.9	86.2	96.7	44.3	71.6	90.1
South Dakota	0.7	0.2	0.2	0.1	62.3	86.5	96.2	51.8	77.0	90.1
Tennessee	0.8	0.3	0.3	0.5	61.2	85.2	96.3	46.4	72.6	90.3
Texas	5.1	1.3	0.7	1.0	71.0	88.7	97.5	51.8	76.3	92.5
Utah	6.7	1.4	0.5	0.4	86.8	93.9	98.4	71.9	84.8	93.2
Vermont	0.0	0.0	0.1	0.0	66.8	88.1	96.8	55.1	80.2	92.0
Virginia	2.3	0.8	0.5	0.6	68.7	89.0	97.9	55.6	78.3	94.0
Washington	2.9	0.5	0.4	0.4	80.6	92.6	97.7	69.0	85.4	94.1
West Virginia	0.0	0.2	0.0	0.2	59.5	83.8	95.6	46.7	73.5	90.7
Wisconsin	1.5	0.2	0.1	0.1	69.1	87.8	97.1	57.0	78.9	92.5
Wyoming	1.2	0.0	0.2	0.5	80.7	91.1	96.8	67.6	80.4	88.7

Table B-7. Homeownership, Health Insurance, and Computer Access by Educational Attainment—*Continued*

| | Computer and internet access by educational attainment of household population 25 years and older (Continued) | | | | | |
| | Household has a computer but no internet subscription (may have access to public internet) | | | Household has no computer | | |
State	Less than high school graduate or equivalency	High school graduate or equivalency, some college, or Associate's degree	Bachelor's degree or higher	Less than high school graduate or equivalency	High school graduate or equivalency, some college, or Associate's degree	Bachelor's degree or higher
United States	14.8	10.2	4.6	27.9	11.5	2.8
Alabama	15.6	13.0	5.6	39.2	16.6	4.2
Alaska	18.5	9.8	5.6	16.3	7.3	2.0
Arizona	14.3	9.5	4.6	25.3	10.9	3.5
Arkansas	21.6	17.4	9.7	36.2	15.9	4.2
California	13.6	8.3	3.7	20.0	8.5	2.3
Colorado	14.5	8.6	3.9	21.0	8.3	2.0
Connecticut	11.8	7.3	3.0	26.5	10.2	2.5
Delaware	18.6	9.3	5.4	28.1	11.6	2.8
District of Columbia	27.2	19.3	4.8	27.1	16.2	1.6
Florida	14.6	10.1	5.8	25.1	10.6	3.3
Georgia	18.4	12.2	5.3	31.0	11.7	2.5
Hawaii	10.8	6.7	4.0	20.8	9.4	3.2
Idaho	18.8	11.3	5.3	18.4	9.3	2.5
Illinois	14.1	9.4	4.5	26.7	12.9	2.9
Indiana	15.8	11.6	5.0	31.8	12.4	3.1
Iowa	13.8	10.0	5.2	31.0	13.1	3.2
Kansas	12.5	9.9	4.5	29.6	13.2	3.1
Kentucky	14.1	11.1	5.1	39.6	14.1	3.6
Louisiana	15.1	12.1	6.2	36.7	16.1	4.2
Maine	12.4	9.3	5.6	31.2	10.8	3.0
Maryland	14.4	9.1	3.8	24.6	9.6	2.0
Massachusetts	10.0	7.1	3.1	27.7	9.9	2.3
Michigan	15.9	11.9	5.6	28.4	12.2	3.1
Minnesota	14.8	9.3	4.2	25.2	10.1	2.3
Mississippi	19.9	17.5	8.4	41.1	18.4	5.2
Missouri	16.0	11.8	5.3	33.0	13.1	3.2
Montana	14.2	10.5	5.5	36.1	12.9	4.4
Nebraska	10.6	8.6	4.0	29.1	12.2	2.9
Nevada	17.6	9.4	4.9	17.4	8.2	3.3
New Hampshire	8.9	6.9	3.2	23.4	8.0	2.0
New Jersey	11.4	7.1	3.0	26.0	10.7	2.4
New Mexico	17.3	13.3	7.6	36.4	17.2	5.0
New York	12.4	9.2	4.8	25.2	11.6	3.4
North Carolina	14.6	11.4	5.0	33.9	13.2	2.9
North Dakota	10.9	8.6	6.4	39.9	12.2	4.2
Ohio	13.1	9.3	4.2	32.8	12.3	2.9
Oklahoma	16.7	13.5	7.1	31.1	14.0	4.2
Oregon	12.9	9.2	4.9	19.3	8.3	2.2
Pennsylvania	12.4	8.8	4.0	33.9	13.6	3.1
Rhode Island	11.6	7.8	4.0	29.0	10.5	2.8
South Carolina	17.6	14.6	6.6	38.1	13.8	3.3
South Dakota	10.5	9.5	6.1	37.7	13.5	3.8
Tennessee	14.8	12.6	5.9	38.8	14.8	3.7
Texas	19.2	12.4	4.9	29.0	11.3	2.5
Utah	14.8	9.1	5.2	13.2	6.1	1.6
Vermont	11.7	7.9	4.8	33.2	11.9	3.2
Virginia	13.0	10.8	3.9	31.3	11.0	2.1
Washington	11.6	7.2	3.6	19.4	7.4	2.3
West Virginia	12.8	10.3	4.9	40.5	16.2	4.4
Wisconsin	12.1	8.9	4.5	30.9	12.2	2.9
Wyoming	13.1	10.8	8.0	19.3	8.9	3.2

Table B-8. Field of Degree for Persons with a Bachelor's Degree or Higher

State	Total persons age 25 and older with a Bachelor's degree or higher	Detailed field of Bachelor's degree for first major for persons age 25 and older							Degrees in Science and Engineering Related Fields	Degrees in Business	Degrees in Education
		Degrees in Science and Engineering									
		Computers, Mathematics and Statistics	Biological, Agricultural, and Environmental Sciences	Physical and Related Sciences	Psychology	Social Sciences	Engineering	Multi-disciplinary Studies			
United States	66,241,553	2,994,162	4,084,323	2,072,146	3,125,659	5,102,173	5,212,950	431,426	6,180,927	13,585,532	8,417,457
Alabama	792,876	30,446	46,189	21,331	32,744	34,932	64,497	2,809	79,424	182,750	135,842
Alaska	139,416	2,381	16,425	5,333	6,853	8,015	10,361	1,219	12,854	22,495	20,385
Arizona	1,257,449	50,644	70,031	36,967	58,299	87,195	103,823	9,651	119,456	271,892	183,272
Arkansas	433,381	17,845	35,093	11,044	16,671	21,818	21,998	2,041	42,437	95,297	83,480
California	8,415,690	442,626	541,147	271,923	411,824	831,102	868,734	60,209	674,278	1,586,921	563,581
Colorado	1,440,776	71,381	102,501	56,421	72,592	122,120	118,480	10,001	121,176	286,139	147,138
Connecticut	948,044	41,513	52,105	24,939	53,956	92,777	71,925	5,420	80,873	187,022	100,734
Delaware	201,929	8,887	11,854	7,740	9,368	15,109	15,325	2,049	21,046	44,771	28,364
District of Columbia	268,345	9,869	13,210	6,503	11,922	67,875	12,458	3,330	11,869	33,555	11,676
Florida	4,092,338	151,990	197,129	112,242	197,723	285,945	318,838	19,826	414,601	995,869	589,792
Georgia	2,000,113	101,753	104,158	56,305	89,935	138,957	140,150	10,406	178,239	485,769	273,021
Hawaii	309,194	11,804	20,237	8,068	17,960	29,455	21,858	1,391	27,619	61,107	41,200
Idaho	276,912	9,331	25,036	8,296	9,837	16,721	22,438	1,127	30,241	50,346	45,560
Illinois	2,853,540	140,286	151,367	75,373	135,592	204,247	206,794	18,749	269,244	619,650	384,915
Indiana	1,088,120	40,819	59,342	32,539	40,911	50,828	76,481	4,233	134,069	226,250	185,666
Iowa	556,591	20,666	48,342	15,675	22,910	29,391	30,965	1,363	54,940	116,686	103,090
Kansas	599,063	22,914	47,044	14,920	20,577	31,209	36,722	2,203	64,756	129,649	105,871
Kentucky	696,174	21,994	48,434	21,782	30,233	40,747	36,513	3,986	78,840	137,156	119,107
Louisiana	718,058	19,933	46,969	24,754	29,307	33,563	42,372	3,369	88,487	144,280	121,677
Maine	289,553	10,408	22,415	8,023	17,907	26,284	15,772	1,923	28,277	39,879	45,189
Maryland	1,591,614	98,994	109,707	54,781	72,681	161,010	136,776	11,714	138,044	295,580	157,419
Massachusetts	1,951,689	93,417	125,856	70,768	115,907	194,343	168,797	11,748	158,139	364,241	175,035
Michigan	1,870,473	68,321	105,943	57,228	79,033	102,195	186,973	9,868	194,451	397,446	277,764
Minnesota	1,284,007	55,538	87,901	33,407	62,059	96,271	87,103	7,529	123,550	252,884	185,440
Mississippi	406,599	12,918	26,466	10,858	15,682	15,588	16,923	1,872	55,009	84,900	87,213
Missouri	1,140,860	49,080	79,600	30,234	50,997	59,279	66,277	6,554	113,391	246,469	184,485
Montana	216,174	6,397	22,591	6,446	8,174	14,935	11,846	1,167	23,757	35,787	39,252
Nebraska	372,288	12,676	31,285	11,168	14,153	16,565	15,412	2,377	40,424	84,020	71,497
Nevada	463,681	17,539	25,469	17,144	19,359	32,015	33,808	2,156	42,672	105,846	61,003
New Hampshire	334,313	16,257	22,303	9,493	18,385	24,542	30,384	2,584	31,664	63,342	42,482
New Jersey	2,318,073	141,458	121,172	83,543	116,236	184,343	197,220	10,839	195,024	527,062	259,221
New Mexico	364,462	11,374	28,064	17,163	16,031	27,618	25,763	1,314	32,978	57,214	58,421
New York	4,778,463	204,955	230,858	143,737	260,874	472,828	281,238	28,939	415,315	895,311	548,835
North Carolina	1,991,057	101,876	120,297	61,119	103,764	148,941	138,267	12,900	182,823	402,340	269,287
North Dakota	143,403	4,146	14,273	3,812	4,216	6,329	6,909	1,182	20,868	27,786	27,259
Ohio	2,115,116	77,923	122,471	64,144	86,410	128,834	160,663	10,182	233,599	448,383	342,930
Oklahoma	630,004	19,841	43,887	20,511	26,512	30,421	36,669	5,075	61,146	143,828	122,057
Oregon	901,667	35,428	74,775	35,441	47,825	77,676	67,936	8,727	79,655	131,021	100,430
Pennsylvania	2,641,023	107,542	169,950	87,778	129,119	176,846	187,430	16,021	276,665	530,252	396,210
Rhode Island	238,818	9,992	15,473	6,939	12,369	18,862	15,409	1,552	22,368	45,589	29,037
South Carolina	890,241	30,372	51,727	30,317	40,908	56,783	66,873	6,698	85,236	197,700	131,685
South Dakota	154,885	5,619	14,025	3,786	6,957	9,007	7,031	759	15,976	29,897	33,840
Tennessee	1,151,080	42,837	74,227	36,315	48,295	59,161	74,974	7,033	117,853	256,625	171,712
Texas	4,955,374	240,081	291,814	173,376	191,071	289,507	483,662	50,271	445,895	1,164,460	632,224
Utah	554,712	25,598	36,344	14,628	24,000	38,641	36,646	5,132	55,741	104,661	77,687
Vermont	162,072	5,296	13,713	6,087	10,440	13,828	9,323	1,445	12,850	18,942	22,690
Virginia	2,102,044	130,574	127,642	66,407	112,988	229,837	177,790	18,117	159,477	397,325	201,524
Washington	1,670,893	91,370	126,879	55,819	81,581	156,365	157,679	15,812	146,243	274,943	166,411
West Virginia	254,414	7,027	17,692	6,843	13,630	12,730	15,396	1,479	32,048	44,434	51,203
Wisconsin	1,112,458	40,122	80,552	28,718	44,423	72,270	69,167	4,767	125,112	225,032	182,504
Wyoming	102,034	2,104	12,339	3,958	4,510	6,313	6,102	308	10,228	14,729	21,140

Table B-8. Field of Degree for Persons with a Bachelor's Degree or Higher—*Continued*

| | Detailed field of Bachelor's degree for first major for persons age 25 and older | | | | | Field of Bachelor's degree for first major for pesons age 25 and older | | | | |
| | Degrees in Arts, Humanities, and Other | | | | | All persons with Bachelor's degree or higher | | | | |
State	Literature and Languages	Liberal Arts and History	Visual and Performing Arts	Communications	Other	Science and Engineering	Science and Engineering Related Fields	Business	Education	Arts, Humanities and Other
United States	2,851,805	3,282,681	2,687,762	2,549,845	3,662,705	34.8	9.3	20.5	12.7	22.7
Alabama	23,051	36,425	23,614	24,727	54,095	29.4	10.0	23.0	17.1	20.4
Alaska	5,134	9,458	4,035	4,803	9,665	36.3	9.2	16.1	14.6	23.7
Arizona	44,011	50,618	46,481	48,795	76,314	33.1	9.5	21.6	14.6	21.2
Arkansas	14,714	19,786	9,567	15,789	25,801	29.2	9.8	22.0	19.3	19.8
California	442,403	483,727	472,693	342,353	422,169	40.7	8.0	18.9	6.7	25.7
Colorado	59,640	67,634	59,343	66,218	79,992	38.4	8.4	19.9	10.2	23.1
Connecticut	53,748	53,668	41,080	38,244	50,001	36.1	8.5	19.7	10.6	25.0
Delaware	6,175	8,586	5,265	5,892	11,498	34.8	10.4	22.2	14.0	18.5
District of Columbia	21,808	24,290	12,577	16,815	10,588	46.6	4.4	12.5	4.4	32.1
Florida	133,919	177,220	122,006	148,969	226,269	31.4	10.1	24.3	14.4	19.8
Georgia	70,308	87,095	68,967	82,302	112,748	32.1	8.9	24.3	13.7	21.1
Hawaii	14,652	13,936	12,328	9,635	17,944	35.8	8.9	19.8	13.3	22.2
Idaho	10,152	10,864	9,855	9,609	17,499	33.5	10.9	18.2	16.5	20.9
Illinois	114,101	132,744	118,899	135,770	145,809	32.7	9.4	21.7	13.5	22.7
Indiana	31,822	64,559	33,728	40,509	66,364	28.0	12.3	20.8	17.1	21.8
Iowa	14,708	26,006	17,225	20,117	34,507	30.4	9.9	21.0	18.5	20.2
Kansas	14,548	25,386	21,126	24,949	37,189	29.3	10.8	21.6	17.7	20.6
Kentucky	27,798	36,726	18,845	29,746	44,267	29.3	11.3	19.7	17.1	22.6
Louisiana	21,052	50,820	24,949	22,139	44,387	27.9	12.3	20.1	16.9	22.7
Maine	18,193	15,910	14,041	9,231	16,101	35.5	9.8	13.8	15.6	25.4
Maryland	76,303	83,357	56,579	60,388	78,281	40.6	8.7	18.6	9.9	22.3
Massachusetts	120,817	109,870	82,991	61,419	98,341	40.0	8.1	18.7	9.0	24.3
Michigan	69,954	75,268	58,180	64,144	123,705	32.6	10.4	21.2	14.8	20.9
Minnesota	54,186	53,293	53,360	53,425	78,061	33.5	9.6	19.7	14.4	22.8
Mississippi	10,203	19,787	10,721	10,123	28,336	24.7	13.5	20.9	21.4	19.5
Missouri	37,582	53,408	41,888	50,361	71,255	30.0	9.9	21.6	16.2	22.3
Montana	7,198	10,886	8,448	6,353	12,917	33.1	11.0	16.6	18.2	21.2
Nebraska	10,750	13,663	9,145	13,437	25,716	27.8	10.9	22.6	19.2	19.5
Nevada	16,505	20,369	19,090	18,501	32,205	31.8	9.2	22.8	13.2	23.0
New Hampshire	17,880	16,053	13,636	8,933	16,375	37.1	9.5	18.9	12.7	21.8
New Jersey	96,108	105,522	90,174	89,176	100,975	36.9	8.4	22.7	11.2	20.8
New Mexico	19,006	21,968	18,093	8,052	21,403	34.9	9.0	15.7	16.0	24.3
New York	281,220	271,299	319,391	205,457	218,206	34.0	8.7	18.7	11.5	27.1
North Carolina	89,911	99,902	59,378	69,920	130,422	34.5	9.2	20.2	13.5	22.6
North Dakota	3,157	4,483	2,679	2,998	13,306	28.5	14.6	19.4	19.0	18.6
Ohio	74,813	88,717	74,933	86,797	114,317	30.8	11.0	21.2	16.2	20.8
Oklahoma	14,823	27,868	18,082	22,444	36,840	29.0	9.7	22.8	19.4	19.1
Oregon	54,871	58,838	51,324	34,193	43,527	38.6	8.8	14.5	11.1	26.9
Pennsylvania	106,586	120,257	92,951	99,426	143,990	33.1	10.5	20.1	15.0	21.3
Rhode Island	11,655	13,721	11,833	8,140	15,879	33.7	9.4	19.1	12.2	25.6
South Carolina	35,889	44,451	30,365	27,399	53,838	31.9	9.6	22.2	14.8	21.6
South Dakota	4,032	6,076	4,314	3,395	10,171	30.5	10.3	19.3	21.8	18.1
Tennessee	43,241	56,416	41,425	48,141	72,825	29.8	10.2	22.3	14.9	22.8
Texas	168,129	205,802	153,786	180,968	284,328	34.7	9.0	23.5	12.8	20.0
Utah	28,517	17,859	20,806	25,568	42,884	32.6	10.0	18.9	14.0	24.5
Vermont	13,108	11,747	9,969	5,120	7,514	37.1	7.9	11.7	14.0	29.3
Virginia	104,185	123,639	69,934	67,522	115,083	41.1	7.6	18.9	9.6	22.9
Washington	85,961	95,683	73,658	66,965	75,524	41.0	8.8	16.5	10.0	23.8
West Virginia	10,064	10,430	7,092	6,760	17,586	29.4	12.6	17.5	20.1	20.4
Wisconsin	40,191	42,915	43,970	46,020	66,695	30.6	11.2	20.2	16.4	21.6
Wyoming	3,023	3,676	2,923	1,688	8,993	34.9	10.0	14.4	20.7	19.9

Table B-8. Field of Degree for Persons with a Bachelor's Degree or Higher—*Continued*

| | Field of Bachelor's degree for first major for persons age 25 and older | | | | | | | | | |
| | White alone, not of Hispanic origin, persons with Bachelor's degree or higher | | | | | Black or African-American alone persons with a Bachelor's degree or higher | | | | |
State	Science and Engineering	Science and Engineering Related Fields	Business	Education	Arts, Humanities and Other	Science and Engineering	Science and Engineering Related Fields	Business	Education	Arts, Humanities and Other
United States	33.2	9.1	20.1	14.0	23.6	30.4	10.4	24.2	12.1	22.9
Alabama	28.9	10.1	23.1	17.6	20.3	25.6	10.4	24.0	18.5	21.4
Alaska	37.6	8.5	15.2	14.4	24.3	37.8	2.7	18.1	23.7	17.7
Arizona	32.1	9.3	21.5	15.5	21.7	31.4	8.7	24.5	11.5	23.9
Arkansas	28.4	9.8	21.9	20.1	19.8	27.0	12.6	23.1	15.6	21.7
California	39.2	6.9	17.4	7.4	29.2	34.2	9.0	21.6	8.1	27.2
Colorado	37.9	8.4	19.5	10.7	23.5	35.8	12.4	25.5	5.9	20.4
Connecticut	34.7	8.4	19.6	11.6	25.6	32.7	9.0	24.7	6.6	27.0
Delaware	33.0	10.4	21.9	14.8	19.9	28.3	9.6	28.5	15.8	17.9
District of Columbia	49.4	4.0	10.4	2.8	33.5	35.8	5.3	18.8	10.5	29.6
Florida	30.7	9.2	23.5	15.8	20.8	26.6	14.1	24.5	13.8	21.1
Georgia	30.3	8.9	24.0	15.1	21.7	29.5	9.3	26.6	13.3	21.3
Hawaii	39.0	8.6	14.3	12.7	25.4	41.5	14.3	20.4	7.7	16.1
Idaho	32.8	11.0	18.1	16.8	21.2					
Illinois	30.7	8.9	21.5	15.1	23.7	29.3	9.6	24.2	12.0	24.9
Indiana	26.5	12.4	20.9	18.4	21.9	28.3	11.2	27.3	8.8	24.3
Iowa	29.0	9.9	21.2	19.5	20.4	36.2	9.4	26.9	2.0	25.5
Kansas	28.1	10.8	21.7	18.7	20.7	25.1	14.4	23.9	10.6	25.9
Kentucky	28.5	11.3	19.6	18.0	22.5	25.0	11.6	24.5	11.5	27.4
Louisiana	28.2	12.4	20.2	16.8	22.4	22.6	12.5	20.1	20.1	24.7
Maine	35.3	9.7	13.6	16.0	25.4	43.7	8.4	15.9	4.2	27.8
Maryland	40.2	7.9	17.1	10.8	24.1	34.3	10.1	25.2	9.8	20.6
Massachusetts	38.0	8.0	18.7	9.9	25.4	35.4	10.9	22.3	7.3	24.2
Michigan	30.9	10.3	21.7	16.1	21.0	27.7	9.6	24.2	12.4	26.1
Minnesota	31.8	9.6	20.1	15.5	23.1	36.1	14.1	18.0	7.5	24.3
Mississippi	23.8	14.0	20.4	21.5	20.3	24.9	11.7	23.0	22.9	17.6
Missouri	28.9	10.0	21.5	17.1	22.5	26.6	8.8	27.2	13.9	23.5
Montana	33.0	11.1	16.3	18.7	20.9					
Nebraska	26.6	10.8	22.5	20.4	19.7	20.4	6.2	33.9	10.3	29.2
Nevada	32.2	8.3	21.1	14.2	24.2	24.7	9.2	23.9	15.8	26.4
New Hampshire	35.8	9.5	19.3	13.4	22.1	38.6	7.2	18.7	0.0	35.5
New Jersey	33.5	7.6	23.1	13.2	22.5	33.8	9.9	23.2	10.1	23.1
New Mexico	37.2	9.2	14.1	15.0	24.5	26.0	11.4	24.6	16.9	21.1
New York	32.9	7.7	17.8	13.0	28.6	31.2	12.6	21.2	10.3	24.7
North Carolina	33.2	9.5	19.9	14.1	23.3	31.7	8.5	23.7	14.3	21.9
North Dakota	27.4	14.6	20.3	19.6	18.1	55.3	14.4	11.6	2.5	16.2
Ohio	29.2	11.1	21.4	17.3	21.0	28.1	12.3	25.2	12.8	21.7
Oklahoma	28.6	9.4	22.7	20.1	19.2	26.1	10.2	27.7	15.7	20.4
Oregon	37.5	8.7	14.5	11.8	27.5	35.0	7.9	14.8	7.1	35.1
Pennsylvania	31.7	10.4	20.2	16.1	21.7	30.4	11.5	22.3	12.2	23.5
Rhode Island	32.4	9.1	18.8	13.3	26.3	42.9	10.1	24.1	3.9	19.1
South Carolina	31.7	9.4	22.1	15.2	21.6	28.1	9.7	24.6	15.2	22.4
South Dakota	30.2	10.0	19.2	22.7	18.0					
Tennessee	28.9	10.4	22.2	15.1	23.4	27.9	8.9	24.6	17.4	21.2
Texas	33.1	8.3	23.3	14.1	21.2	30.0	10.5	27.9	10.2	21.5
Utah	32.4	9.9	18.7	14.7	24.3	27.8	8.8	22.5	0.8	40.1
Vermont	36.5	7.7	11.6	14.4	29.8	36.2	11.7	13.1	5.9	33.1
Virginia	39.7	7.4	17.7	10.5	24.6	35.8	8.5	24.7	10.3	20.7
Washington	39.4	8.3	16.0	11.0	25.3	35.3	13.2	20.6	8.3	22.5
West Virginia	28.4	12.8	17.6	21.0	20.3	39.9	7.5	15.1	13.1	24.4
Wisconsin	29.8	11.4	20.2	17.2	21.5	27.9	6.8	26.7	13.8	24.8
Wyoming	34.7	10.1	14.6	21.1	19.5					

Table B-8. Field of Degree for Persons with a Bachelor's Degree or Higher—*Continued*

	Field of Bachelor's degree for first major for persons age 25 and older									
	Hispanic or Latino persons with a Bachelor's degree or higher					Asian alone persons with a Bachelor's degree or higher				
State	Science and Engineering	Science and Engineering Related Fields	Business	Education	Arts, Humanities and Other	Science and Engineering	Science and Engineering Related Fields	Business	Education	Arts, Humanities and Other
United States	34.1	8.5	23.1	11.1	23.2	50.0	11.2	19.4	4.8	14.6
Alabama	46.2	6.4	23.7	7.4	16.3	53.3	7.7	20.6	3.1	15.3
Alaska	26.9	14.9	20.0	7.6	30.5	23.3	21.2	24.3	12.4	18.8
Arizona	31.1	9.2	23.1	13.6	22.9	46.8	13.1	21.8	6.8	11.4
Arkansas	28.5	3.5	25.7	17.5	24.9	50.8	7.4	21.6	7.9	12.3
California	34.8	7.6	20.9	7.9	28.8	48.4	10.7	20.8	4.6	15.4
Colorado	37.1	7.3	22.9	9.7	23.0	52.9	8.5	19.3	4.3	14.9
Connecticut	34.8	9.0	19.8	10.0	26.4	54.6	10.5	17.6	3.8	13.5
Delaware	26.8	9.6	19.1	20.8	23.7	64.2	12.5	11.3	5.5	6.5
District of Columbia	49.9	5.1	11.1	3.3	30.6	55.1	5.1	16.1	0.6	23.1
Florida	32.4	10.2	28.1	12.1	17.2	45.1	15.1	20.8	7.0	12.0
Georgia	37.0	7.2	24.3	10.3	21.2	53.5	8.4	19.8	4.5	13.8
Hawaii	41.0	8.7	20.8	9.5	20.1	32.7	9.5	24.9	15.3	17.6
Idaho	41.2	8.0	17.5	11.1	22.2	47.8	12.8	16.8	13.7	8.9
Illinois	31.0	7.6	26.6	11.9	22.9	49.9	14.0	19.2	4.4	12.5
Indiana	33.2	10.2	22.6	11.2	22.8	55.9	14.3	9.9	5.5	14.5
Iowa	36.1	4.4	21.0	9.1	29.4	62.8	13.0	13.5	4.0	6.7
Kansas	34.2	9.9	22.8	12.8	20.3	54.7	9.9	16.4	6.2	12.9
Kentucky	37.8	6.3	17.9	15.2	22.7	52.0	14.3	14.8	3.9	15.0
Louisiana	31.6	9.6	21.6	15.0	22.2	46.3	14.3	19.2	5.4	14.7
Maine	24.2	11.8	14.4	12.3	37.4	56.5	7.0	19.4	1.9	15.2
Maryland	40.7	8.3	18.5	9.0	23.5	54.7	10.6	15.2	5.4	14.1
Massachusetts	40.1	7.6	22.6	5.0	24.7	59.9	7.8	14.9	3.6	13.8
Michigan	37.0	9.5	18.7	9.8	25.0	56.6	12.8	14.3	4.5	11.8
Minnesota	42.6	7.4	18.3	7.1	24.7	55.9	9.5	14.9	4.5	15.2
Mississippi	23.6	19.2	18.6	16.9	21.8	48.8	17.1	14.3	5.2	14.7
Missouri	33.4	9.1	19.8	11.7	25.9	56.0	9.8	16.3	3.9	14.0
Montana	34.2	17.1	12.5	9.5	26.6	40.6	2.4	25.8	2.4	28.8
Nebraska	31.0	15.8	21.5	10.8	20.9	63.8	11.6	14.2	4.8	5.5
Nevada	30.1	7.1	24.0	15.5	23.3	33.9	15.6	29.7	6.4	14.4
New Hampshire	38.5	3.9	26.9	10.1	20.6	59.5	12.5	10.3	3.6	14.1
New Jersey	33.5	7.8	26.2	12.1	20.4	52.4	11.3	19.5	3.6	13.1
New Mexico	28.3	7.6	19.2	20.4	24.4	50.3	9.1	12.5	5.1	23.0
New York	33.0	8.2	21.1	10.5	27.2	43.1	11.8	20.9	5.0	19.2
North Carolina	37.6	6.9	25.4	9.6	20.4	58.0	8.7	14.8	4.1	14.4
North Dakota	36.7	10.1	13.3	12.0	27.9	58.6	21.8	5.5	5.7	8.4
Ohio	41.6	6.6	18.2	10.1	23.5	59.0	9.9	13.5	4.2	13.4
Oklahoma	30.9	8.0	25.5	14.8	20.8	50.0	12.6	21.0	6.6	9.9
Oregon	40.3	7.6	14.2	9.8	28.1	51.9	11.6	15.2	5.0	16.3
Pennsylvania	38.4	10.2	18.7	11.2	21.5	54.2	11.5	17.6	4.1	12.6
Rhode Island	27.0	14.8	24.6	6.5	27.1	52.3	7.2	17.6	5.0	17.9
South Carolina	33.6	13.2	21.5	7.4	24.3	54.1	12.0	13.8	4.6	15.5
South Dakota	36.3	15.9	11.2	17.0	19.7					
Tennessee	32.7	10.1	23.0	9.3	24.8	52.1	10.7	17.4	5.8	14.0
Texas	32.0	8.7	24.5	15.0	19.8	52.5	12.7	19.5	4.1	11.2
Utah	28.5	11.4	23.3	8.0	28.8	45.1	10.1	20.4	7.5	16.9
Vermont	50.7	16.2	19.6	0.7	12.8	56.6	16.8	11.1	3.1	12.4
Virginia	43.3	6.6	24.1	7.1	19.0	54.2	8.4	18.9	4.0	14.5
Washington	41.4	9.1	19.4	9.0	21.1	51.7	10.6	18.1	4.0	15.6
West Virginia	18.7	7.0	22.3	19.3	32.8	54.1	13.5	13.5	2.1	16.9
Wisconsin	35.2	8.9	17.4	10.7	27.8	47.1	13.0	17.8	5.0	17.1
Wyoming	37.2	9.0	10.9	14.6	28.3					

Table B-9. Median Annual Earnings

| | Median earnings in the past 12 months for persons age 25 years and older, by educational attainment | | | | | | | | | | | |
| | All persons age 25 and older | | | | | | Men age 25 and older | | | | | |
Geography	All persons	Less than high school graduate	High school graduate (includes equivalency)	Some college or associate's degree	Bachelor's degree	Graduate or professional degree	All men	Less than high school graduate	High school graduate (includes equivalency)	Some college or associate's degree	Bachelor's degree	Graduate or professional degree
United States	$36,860	$21,320	$29,004	$34,377	$50,930	$67,286	$42,378	$25,159	$34,472	$41,582	$61,780	$85,202
Alabama	$32,468	$20,732	$27,223	$30,878	$46,740	$56,164	$40,366	$25,122	$33,864	$40,592	$60,321	$76,121
Alaska	$41,968	$21,923	$33,815	$41,036	$52,885	$70,590	$51,160	$26,389	$41,365	$50,968	$64,905	$77,073
Arizona	$35,016	$20,377	$27,947	$33,632	$49,801	$60,884	$40,163	$22,690	$31,563	$40,033	$60,684	$77,580
Arkansas	$30,983	$21,608	$26,241	$30,020	$42,828	$55,490	$35,947	$25,422	$31,159	$36,451	$52,803	$71,766
California	$37,476	$20,880	$29,108	$36,161	$57,282	$80,442	$42,110	$24,014	$32,194	$42,159	$67,274	$100,017
Colorado	$40,229	$25,304	$31,280	$35,392	$50,196	$63,270	$46,719	$30,123	$36,628	$41,441	$61,150	$82,156
Connecticut	$46,500	$22,595	$35,288	$40,982	$61,071	$77,568	$53,355	$28,932	$41,902	$48,484	$75,348	$98,411
Delaware	$40,734	$25,297	$30,752	$36,993	$52,261	$65,967	$45,135	$28,306	$37,460	$41,490	$61,339	$77,467
District of Columbia	$57,512	$23,604	$28,467	$38,881	$64,142	$84,682	$64,754	$26,203	$30,241	$41,206	$70,920	$96,219
Florida	$31,662	$19,735	$25,474	$31,137	$42,714	$57,128	$35,830	$22,216	$29,254	$35,610	$51,349	$71,555
Georgia	$35,014	$20,592	$26,802	$31,750	$49,696	$61,443	$40,612	$23,460	$31,389	$40,010	$60,816	$77,463
Hawaii	$38,609	$25,396	$31,995	$36,558	$46,167	$65,094	$42,851	$27,409	$35,842	$42,900	$52,348	$79,582
Idaho	$31,173	$20,974	$26,002	$29,633	$42,661	$57,829	$38,315	$25,828	$32,008	$37,009	$52,109	$71,006
Illinois	$40,120	$22,052	$29,773	$35,823	$52,369	$70,580	$47,097	$26,085	$36,067	$45,093	$66,277	$87,924
Indiana	$35,368	$21,431	$30,137	$32,335	$46,884	$60,699	$41,951	$26,928	$36,486	$41,588	$60,139	$74,567
Iowa	$36,469	$24,854	$30,734	$34,482	$46,518	$61,206	$42,606	$30,066	$37,410	$42,348	$57,354	$72,075
Kansas	$36,727	$23,174	$28,715	$33,462	$46,436	$59,574	$43,792	$28,124	$35,217	$41,584	$59,825	$76,850
Kentucky	$32,495	$19,482	$27,326	$31,285	$45,058	$53,986	$39,086	$21,464	$32,679	$39,972	$52,231	$66,330
Louisiana	$35,208	$20,694	$28,713	$31,959	$46,367	$57,131	$43,660	$26,765	$38,268	$42,336	$60,238	$72,160
Maine	$33,282	$20,130	$27,259	$32,010	$41,214	$54,528	$40,312	$21,871	$32,367	$40,628	$50,731	$65,953
Maryland	$47,312	$25,074	$34,243	$41,290	$60,745	$81,087	$52,469	$28,515	$40,474	$50,219	$70,850	$98,774
Massachusetts	$46,480	$23,077	$32,480	$38,797	$57,285	$74,405	$52,364	$26,660	$40,770	$48,314	$70,358	$91,712
Michigan	$35,543	$20,106	$26,835	$31,865	$49,839	$66,580	$42,581	$23,165	$32,386	$41,495	$61,593	$82,188
Minnesota	$40,851	$22,801	$31,311	$36,845	$51,601	$67,260	$47,156	$26,844	$37,256	$43,917	$62,708	$77,837
Mississippi	$31,090	$21,833	$26,411	$30,679	$39,960	$51,111	$36,874	$26,393	$31,921	$40,003	$50,472	$65,574
Missouri	$35,129	$21,161	$27,375	$32,114	$45,607	$57,209	$41,116	$25,521	$32,237	$40,747	$56,248	$71,480
Montana	$31,848	$17,549	$26,806	$30,429	$39,292	$52,284	$40,107	$20,952	$33,515	$37,416	$49,881	$60,904
Nebraska	$36,403	$22,266	$29,307	$34,836	$46,833	$60,470	$42,172	$25,734	$35,451	$42,087	$56,216	$71,396
Nevada	$33,755	$25,316	$30,254	$33,253	$45,977	$62,155	$37,724	$27,209	$32,257	$40,010	$51,898	$75,043
New Hampshire	$42,178	$29,179	$33,726	$40,122	$51,426	$67,491	$50,676	$32,413	$40,392	$47,694	$70,110	$90,846
New Jersey	$45,704	$22,278	$31,719	$39,832	$60,935	$83,032	$52,239	$26,034	$38,303	$48,082	$75,749	$101,603
New Mexico	$31,109	$18,599	$26,477	$29,996	$42,423	$57,560	$35,901	$22,223	$30,931	$36,070	$51,553	$75,074
New York	$40,996	$20,814	$30,614	$36,736	$55,360	$71,684	$46,553	$23,981	$35,668	$43,881	$63,032	$86,817
North Carolina	$33,096	$20,359	$26,632	$31,060	$46,171	$59,243	$38,557	$22,494	$30,714	$37,339	$57,212	$80,225
North Dakota	$40,741	$30,667	$33,374	$37,644	$45,787	$65,049	$50,615	$38,773	$41,998	$50,258	$57,952	$80,867
Ohio	$36,014	$20,775	$29,284	$32,285	$50,191	$62,324	$42,400	$25,295	$35,968	$41,237	$60,902	$77,102
Oklahoma	$32,950	$22,135	$27,321	$32,197	$42,195	$55,490	$40,923	$27,294	$33,366	$41,034	$55,088	$71,406
Oregon	$33,828	$21,904	$26,567	$31,625	$44,049	$61,139	$40,467	$25,691	$31,372	$38,653	$55,165	$77,190
Pennsylvania	$37,775	$21,860	$30,304	$35,547	$50,791	$66,931	$45,448	$26,723	$36,580	$43,017	$61,234	$82,479
Rhode Island	$41,130	$23,540	$34,328	$37,783	$50,880	$70,840	$46,334	$26,376	$40,411	$43,329	$61,136	$80,406
South Carolina	$32,063	$19,637	$26,184	$31,663	$44,151	$52,733	$37,769	$22,343	$30,558	$39,884	$53,775	$66,458
South Dakota	$34,248	$24,776	$29,135	$32,264	$41,273	$51,443	$40,942	$26,760	$36,472	$40,662	$51,155	$60,150
Tennessee	$32,406	$20,461	$26,490	$31,615	$45,600	$56,896	$39,198	$22,922	$31,699	$39,931	$54,746	$72,077
Texas	$36,361	$21,362	$28,000	$35,462	$51,887	$70,031	$42,054	$25,664	$33,211	$42,435	$66,212	$90,591
Utah	$36,431	$23,626	$30,517	$32,661	$46,255	$70,017	$46,519	$27,474	$36,623	$41,844	$60,964	$83,048
Vermont	$36,529	$21,884	$30,898	$36,054	$40,348	$55,525	$41,377	$29,187	$36,005	$38,966	$50,748	$66,856
Virginia	$41,361	$22,657	$29,674	$35,656	$55,799	$78,049	$50,020	$27,318	$34,544	$43,346	$71,065	$100,317
Washington	$41,140	$24,751	$31,319	$37,293	$55,795	$71,123	$50,075	$28,505	$37,320	$46,504	$70,177	$90,717
West Virginia	$31,634	$18,618	$26,658	$30,816	$41,512	$52,317	$39,828	$23,884	$34,013	$40,341	$53,355	$63,858
Wisconsin	$37,222	$22,730	$30,884	$35,361	$47,383	$61,217	$43,118	$26,670	$37,155	$42,369	$57,485	$72,205
Wyoming	$37,811	$25,376	$32,377	$35,229	$46,092	$61,476	$50,641	$31,821	$46,539	$51,053	$54,305	$70,198

Table B-9. Median Annual Earnings—*Continued*

	Median earnings in the past 12 months for persons age 25 years and older, by educational attainment (Continued)						Median earnings in the past 12 months by gender and occupation for employed persons age 16 and older								
	Women age 25 and older						Persons in all occupations			Management, business, science, and arts occupations					
										All management, business, science, and arts occupations			Management, business, and financial occupations		
													All management, business, and financial occupations		
Geography	All women	Less than high school graduate	High school graduate (includes equivalency)	Some college or associate's degree	Bachelor's degree	Graduate or professional degree	Total:	Men	Women	Total	Men	Women	Total	Men	Women
United States	$31,072	$16,151	$22,461	$28,643	$41,952	$56,726	$34,656	$40,699	$29,319	$54,687	$67,389	$46,758	$61,918	$72,267	$52,035
Alabama	$26,849	$14,134	$20,847	$25,396	$39,543	$50,413	$31,187	$37,165	$25,708	$49,649	$62,307	$41,377	$56,553	$70,067	$47,347
Alaska	$34,713	$16,073	$25,312	$31,797	$42,423	$64,785	$40,137	$48,144	$32,088	$58,543	$69,401	$51,354	$64,517	$72,878	$52,026
Arizona	$30,484	$15,639	$23,454	$30,015	$40,862	$50,530	$31,840	$36,370	$28,519	$51,225	$62,303	$43,169	$60,028	$67,250	$49,753
Arkansas	$26,448	$16,301	$20,966	$25,367	$38,758	$50,082	$29,467	$32,446	$25,020	$45,183	$56,228	$40,103	$50,793	$61,012	$41,726
California	$31,960	$16,166	$23,233	$30,683	$50,053	$66,382	$35,376	$40,334	$30,516	$62,482	$75,859	$53,838	$69,948	$80,128	$60,541
Colorado	$32,327	$16,633	$25,450	$29,651	$40,975	$52,012	$36,813	$42,186	$31,153	$55,655	$69,587	$46,766	$61,866	$72,433	$52,672
Connecticut	$39,554	$18,348	$27,322	$35,862	$49,547	$66,887	$42,307	$50,837	$36,272	$66,712	$81,485	$56,749	$81,183	$98,005	$67,589
Delaware	$35,938	$21,795	$25,000	$31,528	$47,232	$61,040	$38,062	$41,860	$33,126	$56,364	$66,434	$50,848	$61,510	$73,102	$55,423
District of Columbia	$51,981	$20,998	$26,594	$35,878	$57,796	$76,357	$52,733	$61,276	$50,477	$75,677	$84,345	$67,046	$83,188	$91,499	$76,880
Florida	$28,564	$15,978	$21,373	$27,766	$38,424	$50,339	$30,612	$33,042	$26,939	$48,095	$57,102	$42,089	$52,485	$61,646	$47,278
Georgia	$30,052	$15,891	$21,762	$26,624	$41,262	$52,399	$31,907	$37,360	$27,381	$52,000	$66,140	$45,149	$61,124	$71,406	$51,439
Hawaii	$33,381	$23,051	$29,653	$31,266	$40,741	$54,900	$36,170	$40,565	$31,942	$51,990	$61,995	$47,421	$56,967	$67,343	$50,594
Idaho	$23,534	$14,680	$18,745	$22,364	$31,865	$50,584	$29,076	$36,053	$21,661	$44,545	$55,333	$36,039	$49,016	$57,049	$39,541
Illinois	$31,942	$17,170	$22,375	$28,612	$43,487	$60,300	$36,604	$42,895	$30,437	$57,893	$71,368	$50,132	$66,746	$77,586	$55,878
Indiana	$28,272	$15,157	$22,161	$26,644	$38,824	$51,960	$31,976	$40,229	$26,195	$49,754	$61,403	$41,231	$55,814	$66,889	$46,174
Iowa	$29,520	$18,061	$22,033	$27,131	$37,581	$52,452	$32,912	$41,026	$26,775	$49,102	$60,128	$41,221	$54,621	$62,167	$47,469
Kansas	$30,123	$16,986	$21,855	$26,775	$37,313	$50,743	$33,226	$40,761	$26,792	$49,619	$60,701	$41,426	$55,091	$62,274	$47,061
Kentucky	$27,461	$15,185	$21,511	$25,453	$38,970	$50,465	$31,111	$36,302	$26,025	$47,247	$56,530	$41,508	$52,368	$61,626	$44,929
Louisiana	$27,026	$13,918	$20,576	$25,481	$40,497	$50,711	$31,907	$41,185	$25,687	$47,221	$62,457	$41,034	$55,999	$71,063	$42,287
Maine	$28,557	$15,796	$21,708	$27,097	$35,093	$50,184	$31,683	$38,086	$26,821	$46,779	$56,765	$41,429	$52,227	$61,612	$46,494
Maryland	$41,249	$18,475	$28,176	$35,791	$51,398	$68,399	$43,865	$50,606	$38,714	$67,568	$81,462	$59,449	$76,714	$87,359	$69,586
Massachusetts	$40,032	$18,551	$26,188	$32,133	$48,867	$64,312	$41,841	$50,567	$35,804	$64,230	$78,314	$55,622	$72,464	$88,563	$62,410
Michigan	$28,008	$15,103	$20,910	$25,811	$39,268	$55,453	$32,007	$40,590	$26,794	$52,252	$66,443	$44,654	$60,332	$71,630	$49,935
Minnesota	$34,598	$18,061	$24,020	$31,099	$42,703	$60,319	$37,290	$43,736	$31,429	$55,023	$66,117	$47,368	$61,986	$71,117	$54,334
Mississippi	$26,048	$14,547	$20,436	$25,007	$35,298	$45,720	$30,057	$35,102	$24,869	$42,279	$51,937	$37,981	$49,711	$57,602	$40,456
Missouri	$29,619	$16,200	$21,728	$26,626	$38,258	$50,944	$31,801	$38,452	$26,794	$48,791	$60,588	$41,208	$54,520	$64,683	$46,868
Montana	$26,231	$15,454	$20,361	$24,479	$32,546	$50,192	$30,865	$37,493	$25,111	$43,755	$52,306	$39,313	$46,888	$51,822	$40,942
Nebraska	$30,440	$16,870	$21,880	$27,610	$40,251	$52,149	$32,943	$40,200	$27,378	$49,812	$60,387	$41,583	$55,318	$61,834	$47,176
Nevada	$30,713	$20,945	$26,105	$30,389	$40,217	$55,266	$31,999	$36,193	$29,639	$51,769	$60,841	$46,799	$56,006	$63,656	$47,442
New Hampshire	$36,037	$23,518	$27,088	$33,577	$41,958	$57,362	$40,124	$46,794	$32,392	$58,032	$77,167	$47,743	$67,354	$84,011	$55,222
New Jersey	$37,223	$17,401	$25,850	$32,117	$51,054	$68,086	$41,982	$50,863	$35,479	$69,559	$86,063	$56,949	$81,711	$96,542	$66,210
New Mexico	$26,499	$13,009	$21,260	$25,060	$38,863	$50,875	$29,074	$32,121	$24,548	$48,947	$57,171	$42,380	$53,747	$60,763	$49,589
New York	$35,922	$16,203	$23,940	$31,321	$49,180	$62,172	$38,611	$43,203	$33,270	$61,112	$71,714	$52,555	$70,560	$80,033	$61,291
North Carolina	$29,576	$15,674	$21,446	$26,164	$39,364	$50,162	$31,308	$35,810	$27,235	$48,553	$61,173	$41,494	$56,231	$65,830	$47,793
North Dakota	$31,353	$17,462	$23,957	$28,483	$39,956	$51,937	$36,890	$46,884	$29,918	$48,746	$62,542	$41,183	$55,434	$66,576	$45,904
Ohio	$29,777	$15,388	$22,097	$27,034	$41,029	$54,680	$32,755	$40,869	$27,069	$51,565	$63,027	$44,242	$58,684	$69,796	$49,045
Oklahoma	$27,040	$15,608	$21,381	$26,801	$35,839	$45,524	$31,222	$37,902	$25,444	$45,499	$57,323	$37,252	$52,600	$61,887	$44,300
Oregon	$28,457	$18,147	$22,149	$26,505	$35,954	$50,988	$31,808	$38,123	$26,785	$51,806	$62,752	$44,639	$56,004	$63,159	$48,109
Pennsylvania	$31,231	$16,420	$23,178	$29,630	$41,647	$57,016	$35,786	$42,132	$29,544	$54,236	$66,455	$46,567	$61,184	$71,510	$51,053
Rhode Island	$36,076	$20,680	$27,162	$31,875	$42,157	$63,536	$37,458	$42,198	$31,997	$57,411	$67,457	$51,402	$62,091	$75,501	$55,045
South Carolina	$27,565	$14,149	$21,501	$26,308	$36,398	$49,430	$30,951	$36,011	$26,316	$46,765	$58,029	$40,659	$51,357	$62,266	$42,759
South Dakota	$28,439	$15,959	$21,713	$27,162	$35,457	$47,466	$31,640	$38,133	$26,675	$43,201	$51,173	$39,159	$50,302	$53,534	$41,392
Tennessee	$27,653	$15,653	$21,326	$26,578	$38,506	$48,477	$30,974	$36,210	$26,134	$47,373	$60,045	$40,832	$56,496	$66,803	$46,540
Texas	$30,242	$14,998	$21,930	$28,877	$45,857	$56,166	$33,001	$40,118	$27,400	$53,193	$70,123	$46,699	$61,717	$75,652	$50,935
Utah	$26,674	$17,217	$22,757	$25,276	$32,143	$51,666	$31,446	$40,424	$23,400	$50,294	$63,813	$36,760	$57,477	$69,375	$43,035
Vermont	$31,876	$13,401	$24,739	$33,670	$32,958	$47,024	$34,502	$38,744	$30,510	$48,137	$57,233	$41,515	$51,903	$58,594	$47,139
Virginia	$34,491	$16,937	$23,852	$30,483	$45,784	$60,921	$38,638	$45,820	$31,904	$61,836	$80,066	$50,988	$73,782	$85,926	$61,620
Washington	$32,776	$19,638	$24,674	$30,737	$44,389	$58,794	$38,930	$47,088	$31,387	$61,620	$76,593	$50,837	$66,860	$78,877	$57,028
West Virginia	$26,183	$13,926	$20,838	$25,615	$35,903	$48,198	$30,748	$37,275	$25,498	$42,931	$52,914	$37,917	$51,267	$61,834	$42,184
Wisconsin	$31,199	$17,163	$23,994	$29,090	$41,171	$55,515	$34,688	$41,072	$28,701	$50,539	$60,895	$42,645	$55,403	$66,018	$47,032
Wyoming	$27,361	$12,772	$21,213	$25,453	$40,543	$57,720	$35,451	$47,323	$25,714	$47,237	$60,113	$42,949	$47,189	$56,399	$43,345

Table B-9. Median Annual Earnings—*Continued*

	Median earnings in the past 12 months by gender and occupation for employed persons age 16 and older																
	Management, business, science, and arts occupations (Continued)																
	Management, business, and financial occupations (Continued)						Computer, engineering, and science occupations									
	Management occupations			Business and financial operations occupations			All computer, engineering, and science occupations			Computer and mathematical occupations			Architecture and engineering occupations		
Geography	Total	Men	Women	Total	Men	Women	Total	Men	Women	Total	Men	Women	Total	Men	Women
United States	$66,332	$76,061	$55,273	$55,903	$66,240	$50,486	$71,791	$76,289	$61,274	$75,089	$77,761	$66,396	$75,574	$77,184	$62,487
Alabama	$59,330	$71,470	$46,841	$52,357	$64,400	$47,836	$70,335	$72,236	$57,330	$68,417	$71,911	$55,172	$80,062	$80,199	$78,027
Alaska	$65,537	$75,500	$51,424	$61,436	$67,150	$54,890	$67,300	$71,289	$56,411	$67,693	$62,163	$72,317	$74,912	$77,007	$50,384
Arizona	$62,925	$71,490	$52,444	$50,807	$60,920	$45,126	$69,922	$72,004	$57,646	$67,066	$71,172	$57,288	$76,623	$77,282	$67,418
Arkansas	$51,268	$61,125	$40,979	$49,804	$60,578	$42,577	$60,206	$61,627	$52,482	$61,863	$62,179	$61,232	$56,848	$61,599	$41,157
California	$75,053	$82,197	$62,410	$60,983	$70,328	$55,775	$84,403	$90,548	$71,664	$90,092	$92,489	$80,087	$87,107	$90,963	$74,508
Colorado	$65,999	$76,100	$55,115	$56,635	$66,193	$51,796	$75,442	$80,227	$62,116	$80,452	$83,768	$70,192	$75,149	$76,835	$70,014
Connecticut	$86,568	$101,087	$71,884	$70,934	$83,967	$62,258	$77,047	$81,415	$65,258	$76,027	$81,016	$65,203	$81,409	$82,204	$73,072
Delaware	$64,786	$75,510	$59,688	$56,461	$67,485	$51,260	$71,929	$74,677	$70,764	$76,623	$77,382	$71,955	$70,179	$61,758	$71,680
District of Columbia	$89,094	$100,277	$79,652	$75,556	$80,181	$71,737	$77,968	$82,682	$67,084	$74,462	$76,934	$67,310	$90,311	$91,038	$80,696
Florida	$57,165	$65,377	$50,681	$47,353	$53,171	$43,075	$61,050	$65,117	$48,832	$61,576	$64,090	$51,967	$65,442	$67,563	$53,428
Georgia	$64,033	$75,363	$51,841	$55,733	$62,118	$50,978	$70,393	$72,157	$60,290	$71,188	$73,564	$65,211	$71,460	$73,750	$52,372
Hawaii	$61,887	$75,194	$51,959	$50,689	$52,778	$46,671	$62,449	$67,730	$58,975	$61,787	$69,886	$55,097	$71,889	$73,375	$70,385
Idaho	$47,580	$55,670	$39,321	$50,712	$58,678	$39,776	$58,209	$64,541	$32,180	$60,196	$61,671	$43,190	$70,258	$72,052	$39,742
Illinois	$71,380	$81,533	$59,012	$60,555	$70,972	$52,024	$71,513	$76,111	$60,495	$62,230	$81,076	$65,603	$71,598	$73,105	$60,858
Indiana	$60,146	$70,152	$47,608	$50,456	$60,684	$42,452	$63,145	$65,936	$57,387	$62,230	$63,630	$60,633	$68,500	$70,468	$60,143
Iowa	$57,709	$64,101	$48,076	$50,999	$57,471	$47,191	$60,626	$62,034	$49,743	$64,085	$67,672	$54,446	$61,493	$62,119	$50,062
Kansas	$57,776	$62,294	$48,198	$51,237	$62,214	$46,265	$62,151	$67,193	$50,010	$65,235	$71,175	$49,882	$66,384	$67,328	$51,672
Kentucky	$58,599	$65,177	$49,817	$45,642	$53,843	$41,636	$60,352	$61,315	$51,198	$60,881	$61,566	$55,118	$64,990	$65,678	$58,412
Louisiana	$60,492	$72,417	$45,309	$47,834	$62,946	$41,334	$63,691	$70,925	$47,164	$50,931	$51,798	$41,761	$80,553	$82,096	$53,272
Maine	$54,585	$65,521	$45,711	$50,723	$55,574	$47,246	$59,573	$60,963	$51,045	$60,026	$57,234	$61,321	$60,860	$62,500	$50,250
Maryland	$81,786	$91,106	$72,417	$69,089	$77,772	$62,716	$85,338	$89,836	$77,729	$86,360	$90,197	$80,586	$86,877	$89,055	$80,879
Massachusetts	$80,582	$94,817	$64,820	$65,923	$75,633	$61,258	$80,029	$83,229	$68,033	$85,799	$89,549	$78,641	$80,550	$81,302	$70,631
Michigan	$63,025	$75,538	$50,647	$52,159	$62,833	$47,700	$69,752	$71,915	$58,811	$63,399	$65,808	$60,904	$77,311	$79,027	$65,978
Minnesota	$67,174	$72,521	$57,124	$56,275	$64,729	$51,640	$69,906	$72,094	$61,164	$74,898	$76,655	$67,825	$70,376	$71,757	$57,189
Mississippi	$50,954	$59,283	$41,213	$43,459	$55,775	$39,973	$54,419	$56,765	$40,907	$52,103	$53,592	$50,490	$61,904	$62,165	$56,458
Missouri	$56,859	$65,081	$49,963	$50,979	$63,153	$44,978	$64,034	$68,265	$53,850	$66,859	$70,837	$60,615	$67,337	$70,634	$56,356
Montana	$46,449	$51,584	$40,156	$47,780	$53,518	$42,259	$54,252	$55,738	$51,769	$54,860	$55,799	$51,406	$60,252	$60,606	$54,009
Nebraska	$57,147	$62,435	$47,336	$51,387	$60,951	$47,050	$61,647	$65,116	$55,847	$63,044	$65,220	$61,862	$62,287	$65,690	$37,955
Nevada	$60,430	$68,333	$50,908	$51,053	$61,255	$41,982	$62,149	$65,769	$52,382	$61,255	$65,983	$50,764	$65,554	$65,062	$68,487
New Hampshire	$72,157	$87,120	$57,629	$60,664	$74,652	$51,451	$80,372	$82,842	$62,382	$82,286	$89,176	$65,069	$80,047	$80,588	$65,488
New Jersey	$90,477	$100,996	$72,060	$71,217	$83,637	$60,730	$86,658	$91,513	$72,497	$90,850	$94,029	$80,168	$84,795	$87,020	$66,619
New Mexico	$55,176	$59,628	$51,397	$51,663	$62,156	$45,597	$70,531	$73,014	$55,116	$60,810	$61,625	$53,889	$81,402	$82,297	$65,894
New York	$72,120	$80,563	$65,141	$65,260	$77,158	$55,836	$71,094	$75,748	$60,540	$72,287	$76,121	$67,205	$75,005	$76,654	$61,509
North Carolina	$60,181	$66,846	$49,261	$49,223	$62,391	$46,639	$67,747	$72,296	$56,080	$72,462	$78,777	$61,768	$66,772	$70,138	$55,280
North Dakota	$60,264	$67,122	$45,526	$49,223	$60,846	$46,207	$53,365	$60,800	$39,280	$49,600	$62,132	$36,107	$60,023	$60,013	$65,081
Ohio	$62,266	$71,685	$51,148	$51,199	$60,842	$46,493	$65,993	$68,749	$56,812	$66,546	$68,087	$61,980	$70,424	$71,386	$56,254
Oklahoma	$55,925	$62,266	$44,659	$50,611	$60,409	$43,525	$62,262	$67,867	$50,066	$70,639	$72,065	$51,653	$71,501	$75,009	$53,087
Oregon	$59,807	$65,871	$49,388	$51,608	$60,347	$46,806	$70,696	$75,290	$57,100	$70,639	$72,065	$63,493	$79,182	$82,381	$61,377
Pennsylvania	$66,111	$76,044	$53,970	$52,675	$63,059	$47,161	$67,291	$71,064	$57,299	$70,297	$71,393	$64,122	$70,056	$71,571	$53,342
Rhode Island	$67,142	$76,131	$56,450	$56,901	$66,697	$51,079	$70,674	$72,370	$57,009	$71,279	$72,064	$66,995	$71,628	$76,207	$67,824
South Carolina	$55,302	$65,469	$45,872	$46,087	$56,020	$41,250	$63,862	$68,343	$51,695	$61,743	$65,287	$57,581	$71,276	$73,569	$54,476
South Dakota	$51,568	$56,828	$41,918	$42,310	$50,265	$40,566	$51,609	$52,499	$45,533	$53,695	$53,497	$60,162	$57,212	$58,355	$40,299
Tennessee	$61,100	$70,619	$47,843	$50,775	$58,765	$45,035	$61,102	$64,082	$50,021	$60,868	$62,025	$51,530	$64,873	$67,560	$52,550
Texas	$66,255	$80,014	$51,650	$54,823	$67,106	$50,222	$75,598	$80,663	$60,817	$72,485	$77,539	$61,854	$84,528	$86,318	$72,319
Utah	$61,105	$70,487	$46,091	$50,842	$66,149	$41,112	$65,744	$69,896	$53,300	$66,246	$68,770	$57,189	$70,885	$71,644	$52,740
Vermont	$55,237	$59,398	$50,756	$48,887	$55,907	$43,512	$59,843	$65,418	$47,208	$68,119	$70,000	$61,837	$65,719	$66,024	$60,333
Virginia	$79,820	$90,386	$64,874	$65,678	$75,439	$57,144	$83,652	$88,923	$75,703	$87,393	$93,263	$80,548	$80,498	$81,724	$62,164
Washington	$71,760	$81,947	$60,668	$59,569	$66,702	$52,371	$85,338	$90,621	$71,276	$90,844	$92,493	$80,308	$87,192	$91,045	$74,030
West Virginia	$54,402	$60,860	$46,544	$45,707	$51,766	$37,384	$60,808	$62,043	$45,695	$60,796	$66,312	$53,214	$65,002	$64,967	$65,236
Wisconsin	$60,639	$70,173	$50,039	$49,070	$56,890	$45,450	$60,649	$63,031	$50,959	$62,102	$65,440	$55,708	$63,701	$66,597	$47,995
Wyoming	$46,461	$52,448	$43,371	$50,919	$67,179	$42,490	$62,141	$70,616	$50,335	$57,492	$57,103	$61,045	$70,943	$76,126	$46,356

Table B-9. Median Annual Earnings—*Continued*

	Median earnings in the past 12 months by gender and occupation for employed persons age 16 and older														
	Management, business, science, and arts occupations (Continued)														
	Computer, engineering, and science occupations (Continued)			Education, legal, community service, arts, and media occupations											
	Life, physical, and social science occupations			All education, legal, community service, arts, and media occupations			Community and social service occupations			Legal occupations			Education, training, and library occupations		
Geography	Total	Men	Women	Total	Men	Women	Total	Men	Women	Total	Men	Women	Total	Men	Women
United States	$56,061	$61,921	$50,736	$40,922	$49,243	$37,226	$38,859	$40,566	$37,941	$75,164	$102,500	$57,363	$39,589	$47,403	$36,081
Alabama	$48,418	$50,030	$47,991	$40,021	$47,999	$36,212	$36,700	$38,388	$36,348	$49,840	$96,589	$41,252	$40,164	$48,973	$36,650
Alaska	$55,630	$56,438	$52,181	$48,676	$50,925	$42,739	$49,842	$47,451	$50,348	$67,083	$75,625	$62,345	$50,301	$52,015	$41,698
Arizona	$54,323	$59,766	$50,329	$35,702	$41,465	$32,132	$35,044	$34,992	$35,063	$76,658	$102,410	$57,381	$34,607	$41,644	$31,237
Arkansas	$51,990	$56,167	$48,613	$36,857	$42,197	$35,020	$35,303	$39,188	$32,456	$52,277	$71,229	$41,823	$37,851	$46,014	$35,623
California	$62,397	$66,439	$60,758	$45,567	$52,039	$40,617	$42,208	$45,992	$41,689	$91,238	$117,464	$71,845	$40,703	$50,827	$36,056
Colorado	$52,562	$62,381	$45,868	$37,643	$44,630	$35,284	$39,371	$40,780	$38,184	$65,481	$101,164	$55,966	$34,723	$41,072	$31,457
Connecticut	$62,386	$71,852	$60,555	$48,065	$56,251	$43,410	$47,794	$51,992	$46,689	$76,733	$141,010	$63,080	$44,963	$51,267	$40,675
Delaware	$62,046	$62,229	$61,715	$42,163	$46,810	$40,647	$41,858	$46,802	$40,580	$65,525	$91,557	$60,456	$40,772	$41,364	$39,952
District of Columbia	$80,377	$86,502	$61,781	$66,946	$74,328	$59,957	$60,181	$53,760	$61,455	$100,704	$95,572	$101,612	$46,664	$68,597	$35,399
Florida	$46,526	$51,870	$41,319	$39,065	$41,904	$36,917	$37,385	$39,915	$36,642	$56,124	$75,843	$50,456	$38,444	$40,934	$37,236
Georgia	$52,271	$58,329	$46,992	$40,712	$48,182	$37,238	$36,092	$41,027	$34,888	$79,395	$109,557	$61,251	$40,344	$47,062	$37,293
Hawaii	$51,528	$51,258	$52,567	$41,668	$46,302	$40,399	$41,693	$42,049	$41,457	$71,118	$100,134	$65,298	$41,785	$49,104	$40,411
Idaho	$30,444	$40,275	$24,721	$32,099	$38,392	$30,916	$35,406	$38,538	$32,389	$58,640	$75,446	$46,586	$31,452	$34,437	$30,954
Illinois	$51,736	$60,307	$45,726	$42,179	$50,715	$40,152	$39,772	$40,288	$39,421	$86,181	$122,362	$66,171	$40,967	$48,821	$38,360
Indiana	$54,827	$54,646	$55,124	$35,928	$43,470	$32,014	$35,079	$38,100	$33,482	$64,492	$107,176	$48,110	$35,041	$46,106	$31,043
Iowa	$48,856	$51,413	$41,507	$35,880	$43,250	$32,464	$35,744	$41,153	$32,801	$54,654	$85,833	$49,287	$36,048	$46,857	$33,210
Kansas	$50,300	$55,246	$46,775	$38,396	$47,103	$34,817	$36,532	$36,148	$36,930	$75,974	$92,212	$50,605	$37,149	$46,626	$32,576
Kentucky	$45,993	$48,805	$40,455	$37,491	$42,395	$36,036	$35,316	$33,085	$35,658	$61,069	$80,601	$51,874	$40,706	$47,255	$35,589
Louisiana	$56,956	$70,367	$44,782	$40,242	$45,608	$37,344	$36,640	$37,305	$35,887	$65,566	$80,509	$56,158	$39,413	$43,266	$37,257
Maine	$52,377	$60,737	$41,112	$35,054	$42,439	$31,204	$34,836	$41,304	$32,843	$69,243	$81,400	$51,423	$34,948	$41,608	$30,681
Maryland	$77,056	$87,388	$67,285	$50,168	$59,717	$45,778	$46,355	$48,383	$45,889	$99,044	$132,076	$74,523	$46,386	$52,551	$42,421
Massachusetts	$61,755	$71,351	$55,865	$46,238	$52,687	$41,674	$41,282	$38,502	$41,782	$85,799	$110,347	$71,123	$45,194	$53,836	$40,350
Michigan	$51,332	$56,693	$45,071	$38,493	$47,292	$34,289	$40,327	$41,587	$39,492	$61,154	$85,417	$50,911	$36,454	$48,342	$31,780
Minnesota	$52,066	$54,848	$51,183	$39,582	$46,913	$35,738	$38,505	$39,717	$38,013	$67,074	$91,539	$52,056	$37,224	$46,859	$33,126
Mississippi	$41,713	$50,668	$37,085	$35,459	$44,477	$32,487	$35,137	$35,567	$33,849	$61,788	$87,256	$46,116	$34,272	$37,458	$32,323
Missouri	$47,422	$50,846	$45,237	$36,955	$45,107	$34,337	$35,079	$37,760	$33,426	$63,617	$100,155	$46,925	$36,513	$44,381	$34,437
Montana	$47,371	$47,316	$50,068	$35,437	$45,937	$31,150	$31,714	$36,751	$30,184	$53,338	$70,049	$42,718	$33,880	$47,732	$31,208
Nebraska	$52,045	$60,250	$41,133	$39,519	$48,422	$35,310	$37,067	$41,634	$35,337	$62,124	$105,376	$40,988	$40,161	$48,439	$36,484
Nevada	$60,971	$73,946	$50,226	$41,961	$47,166	$40,378	$41,772	$42,162	$40,910	$77,261	$121,620	$52,073	$41,897	$50,540	$40,633
New Hampshire	$63,203	$65,135	$57,768	$37,683	$48,224	$32,917	$41,394	$43,665	$40,052	$65,293	$91,117	$60,577	$35,187	$49,483	$30,019
New Jersey	$75,553	$85,115	$62,390	$50,431	$57,946	$46,254	$44,543	$40,676	$46,255	$90,048	$123,243	$67,363	$49,243	$58,507	$43,974
New Mexico	$67,417	$71,478	$49,345	$35,776	$41,602	$32,097	$34,230	$33,648	$35,308	$56,360	$76,925	$45,946	$33,601	$40,829	$31,643
New York	$57,190	$67,329	$50,088	$43,092	$58,446	$44,642	$41,402	$41,097	$41,528	$91,982	$120,318	$70,218	$40,895	$57,235	$41,191
North Carolina	$52,153	$57,445	$50,535	$35,825	$41,131	$33,750	$37,716	$37,478	$37,825	$61,012	$97,352	$45,147	$34,357	$41,079	$32,214
North Dakota	$48,002	$60,776	$37,533	$39,527	$50,044	$36,501	$40,063	$36,839	$40,769	$52,058	$75,787	$37,500	$38,703	$48,879	$36,846
Ohio	$52,312	$57,016	$48,665	$39,259	$46,003	$35,732	$37,518	$37,176	$37,807	$66,133	$91,375	$51,261	$38,816	$49,843	$34,243
Oklahoma	$47,001	$51,804	$41,573	$34,387	$41,962	$31,269	$34,231	$41,314	$31,122	$65,778	$86,779	$47,432	$34,214	$42,098	$31,561
Oregon	$51,532	$57,233	$46,020	$36,140	$42,675	$32,176	$35,749	$35,379	$35,873	$63,207	$101,892	$51,361	$32,227	$41,234	$30,343
Pennsylvania	$55,968	$63,623	$50,932	$41,573	$51,199	$37,260	$36,891	$38,802	$36,382	$72,266	$102,454	$53,516	$43,173	$55,428	$39,011
Rhode Island	$57,500	$71,640	$32,359	$42,457	$46,715	$41,611	$41,028	$42,128	$40,826	$75,398	$86,987	$52,252	$45,472	$46,051	$44,969
South Carolina	$48,629	$52,720	$43,781	$35,518	$42,098	$32,138	$31,839	$37,235	$30,294	$51,051	$93,500	$45,123	$36,427	$42,200	$33,914
South Dakota	$39,444	$39,814	$39,393	$34,657	$40,769	$32,246	$32,502	$32,142	$32,698	$60,381	$92,460	$51,542	$34,735	$42,102	$31,930
Tennessee	$52,418	$61,580	$46,535	$37,143	$43,440	$34,151	$36,703	$40,104	$35,592	$63,266	$104,559	$41,817	$36,959	$43,243	$35,065
Texas	$57,003	$66,423	$49,516	$42,388	$49,788	$40,592	$40,005	$42,296	$37,487	$74,205	$115,369	$56,110	$42,231	$48,081	$40,986
Utah	$52,571	$55,889	$51,003	$31,986	$46,047	$23,597	$32,560	$40,429	$30,509	$67,238	$91,684	$41,246	$27,501	$45,660	$20,654
Vermont	$41,787	$47,758	$35,181	$36,957	$46,795	$32,317	$36,366	$32,218	$37,567	$51,346	$70,641	$48,255	$39,142	$53,014	$32,485
Virginia	$70,317	$76,663	$56,761	$44,154	$52,360	$40,747	$41,100	$42,476	$40,208	$102,054	$125,773	$80,242	$41,211	$47,952	$39,072
Washington	$57,048	$59,784	$56,074	$40,893	$50,954	$35,831	$40,815	$41,769	$40,205	$80,907	$115,691	$65,118	$35,159	$47,498	$30,467
West Virginia	$41,572	$45,864	$38,710	$36,499	$41,393	$35,015	$31,952	$35,535	$30,823	$45,428	$89,177	$39,205	$38,936	$42,807	$36,772
Wisconsin	$45,696	$46,859	$43,292	$39,222	$45,993	$36,416	$38,657	$37,571	$38,747	$57,351	$90,795	$44,235	$38,450	$46,529	$35,331
Wyoming	$56,811	$65,775	$51,127	$40,462	$50,665	$33,739	$35,053	$19,477	$39,899	$61,224	$79,681	$51,128	$36,815	$56,466	$28,787

Table B-9. Median Annual Earnings—*Continued*

	Median earnings in the past 12 months by gender and occupation for employed persons age 16 and older														
	Management, business, science, and arts occupations (Continued)												Service occupations		
	Education, legal, community service, arts, and media occupations			Healthcare practitioners and technical occupations											
	Arts, design, entertainment, sports, and media occupations			All healthcare practitioners and technical occupations			Health diagnosing and treating practitioners and other technical occupations			Health technologists and technicians			All service occupations		
Geography	Total	Men	Women	Total	Men	Women	Total	Men	Women	Total	Men	Women	Total	Men	Women
United States	$36,794	$42,086	$30,868	$52,376	$71,643	$50,500	$64,805	$99,063	$60,359	$35,726	$40,729	$34,557	$18,227	$21,927	$16,013
Alabama	$34,363	$41,711	$27,085	$45,014	$61,099	$41,519	$52,464	$91,433	$50,073	$31,255	$37,041	$30,328	$15,951	$19,981	$14,191
Alaska	$30,567	$35,969	$26,226	$60,890	$81,599	$56,120	$76,188	$89,389	$70,584	$41,064	$51,847	$37,434	$23,007	$26,405	$21,053
Arizona	$29,648	$36,202	$25,670	$56,540	$71,329	$51,986	$68,389	$100,670	$62,347	$35,720	$35,519	$35,773	$17,792	$20,151	$16,170
Arkansas	$26,697	$29,585	$25,563	$45,256	$70,227	$41,544	$60,175	$91,481	$51,843	$30,963	$38,599	$30,003	$15,762	$20,136	$13,822
California	$41,634	$47,592	$35,689	$67,113	$80,219	$62,270	$82,025	$101,964	$78,090	$40,303	$45,457	$37,275	$19,324	$22,389	$16,450
Colorado	$34,814	$40,957	$28,010	$54,684	$76,220	$51,002	$62,170	$97,917	$59,265	$36,569	$42,786	$36,137	$20,275	$22,950	$17,262
Connecticut	$44,222	$52,102	$34,070	$64,791	$85,475	$61,100	$75,533	$116,752	$70,105	$46,410	$47,987	$45,722	$21,819	$26,696	$18,705
Delaware	$36,747	$40,554	$31,378	$57,990	$80,217	$55,520	$66,317	$97,800	$63,736	$38,769	$39,978	$37,876	$19,499	$21,928	$17,146
District of Columbia	$62,431	$70,620	$54,220	$61,301	$62,623	$58,071	$68,198	$64,136	$70,563	$40,934	$51,237	$40,328	$23,957	$26,155	$22,193
Florida	$30,966	$37,232	$24,235	$50,060	$61,264	$46,639	$60,378	$84,598	$55,096	$32,431	$35,754	$31,975	$19,261	$21,671	$16,980
Georgia	$36,093	$41,747	$27,396	$50,180	$73,776	$46,495	$60,597	$100,803	$55,374	$33,659	$40,782	$32,163	$17,430	$21,139	$15,597
Hawaii	$32,168	$36,948	$25,961	$64,782	$90,616	$56,121	$77,206	$105,850	$70,669	$37,426	$46,662	$36,826	$24,734	$26,852	$22,370
Idaho	$25,998	$37,441	$21,824	$50,425	$77,116	$42,998	$60,778	$100,260	$52,991	$31,258	$50,286	$29,378	$13,691	$16,607	$12,125
Illinois	$38,915	$42,036	$35,262	$52,453	$72,152	$51,112	$62,184	$102,312	$59,560	$34,272	$35,534	$33,791	$18,625	$22,160	$16,361
Indiana	$29,528	$36,879	$20,999	$48,388	$79,083	$45,893	$57,009	$108,792	$52,021	$32,480	$35,696	$32,319	$16,054	$20,142	$14,096
Iowa	$30,145	$35,028	$26,087	$46,977	$76,619	$42,426	$52,411	$102,246	$49,159	$34,342	$42,496	$32,314	$16,294	$19,887	$15,230
Kansas	$36,141	$49,221	$27,140	$47,519	$74,741	$42,963	$55,367	$96,865	$50,921	$31,939	$38,415	$31,497	$16,238	$20,553	$14,429
Kentucky	$31,134	$34,816	$25,559	$49,025	$61,965	$46,051	$56,372	$100,355	$52,478	$31,639	$35,488	$31,304	$16,708	$20,073	$15,535
Louisiana	$30,542	$37,799	$24,211	$47,305	$70,435	$42,174	$60,699	$81,241	$53,980	$34,811	$47,027	$32,061	$16,077	$20,298	$14,269
Maine	$30,437	$37,116	$24,013	$51,014	$63,769	$48,054	$61,130	$91,423	$56,274	$31,699	$26,526	$35,077	$17,306	$22,724	$15,436
Maryland	$44,975	$50,941	$40,979	$61,421	$86,395	$57,614	$72,484	$112,113	$66,935	$40,649	$42,348	$40,040	$22,730	$28,691	$20,453
Massachusetts	$41,053	$49,350	$32,341	$61,944	$80,167	$60,531	$70,908	$102,010	$66,562	$41,847	$50,120	$41,109	$20,630	$25,722	$16,768
Michigan	$31,836	$41,459	$25,119	$51,072	$66,785	$47,910	$60,708	$91,042	$56,280	$32,305	$40,321	$31,475	$15,388	$18,013	$13,962
Minnesota	$36,242	$43,826	$30,644	$53,250	$75,447	$50,566	$65,097	$101,186	$60,692	$36,076	$41,447	$35,199	$18,054	$21,271	$16,541
Mississippi	$29,513	$40,356	$25,455	$46,909	$61,236	$44,302	$55,678	$76,571	$52,172	$32,456	$40,311	$31,919	$16,246	$20,002	$15,077
Missouri	$31,938	$41,033	$27,176	$46,837	$60,957	$43,404	$55,220	$86,678	$51,462	$32,598	$41,223	$31,419	$16,062	$18,872	$14,670
Montana	$30,031	$40,670	$19,518	$50,285	$78,700	$43,349	$60,788	$91,416	$51,688	$30,891	$40,882	$29,631	$15,203	$20,123	$13,578
Nebraska	$30,883	$40,229	$23,341	$45,555	$62,992	$42,358	$51,999	$90,612	$50,510	$33,577	$41,000	$32,437	$15,430	$20,564	$12,781
Nevada	$31,960	$37,441	$26,756	$61,389	$70,198	$60,690	$75,334	$101,335	$69,609	$39,298	$37,858	$40,902	$25,839	$28,828	$22,206
New Hampshire	$33,718	$41,217	$28,339	$56,268	$96,099	$51,932	$65,974	$105,873	$62,091	$38,504	$54,566	$36,704	$20,327	$23,453	$18,159
New Jersey	$42,015	$47,000	$40,009	$66,179	$87,574	$61,412	$79,996	$109,925	$71,888	$40,986	$40,287	$41,140	$20,949	$26,317	$17,000
New Mexico	$30,945	$35,725	$24,197	$51,621	$58,182	$50,645	$62,456	$82,440	$60,130	$33,071	$40,101	$32,044	$16,427	$19,730	$14,315
New York	$48,241	$50,865	$45,632	$61,395	$75,831	$59,280	$71,883	$97,658	$67,399	$40,710	$42,249	$40,173	$21,052	$26,191	$17,533
North Carolina	$31,096	$35,597	$26,155	$49,747	$63,537	$46,374	$57,870	$93,768	$54,605	$35,257	$38,399	$33,510	$16,800	$20,629	$15,079
North Dakota	$26,435	$42,308	$22,521	$49,929	$99,839	$45,902	$54,581	$126,946	$50,257	$35,489	$58,155	$34,083	$18,954	$25,504	$16,411
Ohio	$31,267	$38,645	$24,973	$50,235	$63,961	$46,653	$57,262	$82,370	$54,296	$33,616	$38,297	$32,263	$16,267	$20,131	$14,775
Oklahoma	$26,766	$30,969	$20,912	$47,052	$62,252	$42,836	$56,896	$86,027	$52,103	$33,072	$41,456	$31,917	$16,872	$21,015	$14,963
Oregon	$31,329	$36,916	$25,669	$60,771	$89,392	$52,166	$72,610	$103,075	$66,417	$36,812	$47,452	$34,327	$17,103	$20,405	$15,414
Pennsylvania	$33,410	$43,321	$25,611	$52,100	$74,430	$50,100	$62,689	$92,407	$58,829	$35,841	$40,096	$35,188	$18,035	$22,100	$15,845
Rhode Island	$37,236	$42,099	$32,317	$62,167	$78,819	$60,410	$71,891	$85,006	$67,497	$47,214	$51,373	$44,514	$19,778	$23,049	$16,263
South Carolina	$27,709	$36,977	$21,791	$49,158	$57,883	$46,814	$58,526	$80,655	$54,935	$35,856	$40,543	$34,729	$16,790	$20,462	$15,157
South Dakota	$30,189	$31,834	$24,276	$45,030	$52,038	$44,036	$48,943	$75,082	$47,046	$34,680	$32,171	$35,012	$16,456	$19,088	$15,472
Tennessee	$31,272	$38,772	$21,730	$47,134	$60,813	$43,745	$58,812	$99,115	$53,320	$34,471	$40,651	$32,166	$16,459	$20,210	$14,580
Texas	$36,214	$41,892	$30,223	$52,436	$70,115	$50,847	$65,614	$89,834	$60,989	$34,809	$39,260	$32,484	$17,047	$21,110	$15,162
Utah	$30,754	$37,221	$17,914	$50,351	$80,152	$42,033	$61,465	$109,280	$52,351	$26,890	$30,878	$25,716	$14,121	$17,143	$12,212
Vermont	$27,533	$35,018	$21,324	$51,368	$70,906	$50,039	$59,104	$91,851	$51,668	$40,080	$40,345	$38,864	$17,330	$23,839	$15,291
Virginia	$41,532	$45,953	$37,470	$51,763	$74,417	$48,985	$64,005	$102,444	$58,266	$34,267	$42,672	$32,894	$19,332	$22,503	$16,970
Washington	$37,684	$48,036	$31,262	$61,068	$82,384	$55,208	$71,124	$106,988	$63,738	$40,523	$49,712	$36,626	$20,689	$24,008	$18,553
West Virginia	$24,903	$32,331	$18,015	$43,293	$59,306	$40,497	$55,328	$92,358	$50,792	$31,245	$36,395	$30,672	$16,204	$18,494	$14,897
Wisconsin	$32,292	$39,971	$26,337	$50,776	$74,697	$46,998	$60,251	$99,809	$55,304	$34,863	$38,092	$34,203	$16,957	$21,069	$15,432
Wyoming	$36,535	$41,236	$20,911	$57,129	$71,175	$52,046	$69,167	$80,455	$61,887	$36,415	$31,855	$37,193	$15,585	$20,819	$12,704

Table B-9. Median Annual Earnings—*Continued*

Median earnings in the past 12 months by gender and occupation for employed persons age 16 and older

Service occupations (Continued)

Geography	Healthcare support occupations			All protective service occupations			Protective service occupations						Food preparation and serving related occupations		
							Fire fighting and prevention, and other protective service workers including supervisors			Law enforcement workers including supervisors					
	Total	Men	Women	Total	Men	Women	Total	Men	Women	Total	Men	Women	Total	Men	Women
United States	$22,417	$25,079	$22,194	$41,448	$45,671	$31,135	$29,114	$31,635	$21,110	$56,221	$60,079	$45,830	$13,759	$15,887	$12,240
Alabama	$20,687	$26,633	$20,183	$35,956	$37,699	$27,545	$26,546	$32,273	$14,592	$41,603	$42,019	$40,944	$11,135	$11,129	$11,138
Alaska	$31,034	$22,008	$31,489	$50,557	$52,285	$43,029	$40,866	$42,038	$36,067	$70,342	$75,305	$50,452	$17,737	$17,850	$17,648
Arizona	$24,050	$25,729	$23,735	$40,400	$45,657	$31,568	$27,316	$28,562	$21,917	$56,451	$61,299	$40,520	$13,242	$13,364	$13,153
Arkansas	$17,922	$16,270	$18,262	$32,438	$34,649	$27,767	$31,765	$34,568	$19,029	$32,676	$34,679	$29,622	$11,269	$12,072	$10,787
California	$25,036	$25,616	$24,893	$50,305	$52,295	$37,181	$27,523	$29,306	$22,871	$82,211	$86,000	$71,555	$16,280	$18,507	$14,202
Colorado	$24,427	$24,461	$24,420	$44,752	$47,415	$39,512	$30,443	$31,575	$20,823	$57,010	$60,535	$52,533	$14,809	$17,110	$12,825
Connecticut	$27,410	$35,979	$26,739	$47,396	$50,410	$31,852	$30,813	$34,861	$17,594	$71,469	$71,828	$70,238	$15,647	$18,690	$14,000
Delaware	$25,602	$25,634	$25,589	$40,484	$39,015	$47,088	$24,844	$25,039	$19,503	$56,433	$56,579	$56,206	$13,742	$12,452	$14,728
District of Columbia	$24,238	$22,494	$24,262	$35,133	$55,897	$25,966	$27,129	$40,139	$22,092	$79,449	$79,960	$76,620	$19,320	$19,633	$19,117
Florida	$22,133	$23,969	$21,971	$36,000	$37,969	$30,156	$26,371	$27,350	$21,976	$47,932	$50,412	$43,270	$16,060	$17,665	$14,790
Georgia	$22,408	$20,949	$22,565	$34,417	$36,934	$25,369	$28,693	$31,447	$20,653	$39,300	$41,285	$31,167	$12,084	$12,664	$11,796
Hawaii	$26,270	$25,839	$26,354	$41,186	$46,406	$30,116	$31,582	$35,453	$28,883	$61,402	$62,184	$52,226	$20,513	$21,491	$19,089
Idaho	$20,281	$22,162	$19,948	$37,987	$41,596	$7,315	$31,487	$37,776	$5,625	$45,158	$47,019	$31,549	$11,165	$11,763	$10,944
Illinois	$21,555	$20,778	$21,669	$50,554	$59,526	$25,816	$26,881	$32,262	$17,466	$71,050	$72,086	$64,891	$15,310	$17,144	$13,058
Indiana	$22,223	$21,927	$22,248	$36,573	$41,180	$25,422	$24,739	$31,036	$17,086	$45,753	$47,057	$39,142	$10,972	$11,966	$10,461
Iowa	$22,374	$27,149	$21,988	$42,735	$47,916	$25,485	$25,068	$29,699	$9,855	$55,969	$58,295	$43,889	$11,328	$12,062	$11,011
Kansas	$21,040	$23,290	$20,898	$40,155	$43,390	$26,353	$28,797	$37,035	$6,996	$46,385	$47,959	$42,071	$11,206	$11,265	$11,181
Kentucky	$22,565	$26,723	$22,097	$35,340	$36,804	$24,889	$24,585	$26,129	$17,711	$41,914	$45,181	$36,305	$11,631	$11,605	$11,648
Louisiana	$18,536	$18,697	$18,513	$37,086	$41,334	$24,506	$30,916	$40,089	$22,371	$40,468	$42,012	$29,931	$12,049	$12,840	$11,786
Maine	$24,071	$26,463	$23,091	$41,657	$42,376	$22,027	$27,089	$35,265	$18,065	$52,352	$52,387	$52,133	$12,430	$15,298	$11,759
Maryland	$26,719	$27,717	$26,607	$55,255	$60,024	$46,015	$43,889	$45,602	$35,398	$62,529	$66,048	$51,567	$15,617	$17,174	$14,228
Massachusetts	$25,370	$30,598	$23,860	$59,376	$62,248	$28,860	$35,044	$46,524	$9,984	$72,298	$75,448	$66,712	$15,436	$20,066	$11,738
Michigan	$21,493	$22,196	$21,391	$45,170	$50,079	$26,864	$26,370	$32,114	$14,881	$55,640	$56,623	$51,950	$11,154	$11,481	$10,949
Minnesota	$22,203	$26,081	$21,768	$41,419	$42,109	$37,393	$26,647	$26,245	$30,360	$61,141	$62,287	$51,950	$12,515	$14,005	$12,028
Mississippi	$20,039	$25,779	$19,557	$29,666	$30,789	$26,146	$26,113	$25,955	$26,754	$34,819	$36,945	$25,803	$11,848	$11,843	$11,852
Missouri	$20,618	$19,360	$20,698	$35,539	$36,314	$31,545	$30,712	$32,107	$20,362	$39,248	$39,550	$38,880	$11,306	$11,201	$11,363
Montana	$19,094	$26,626	$18,669	$47,621	$49,898	$32,190	$35,973	$40,349	$11,051	$51,958	$55,496	$34,923	$11,767	$12,238	$11,395
Nebraska	$21,233	$26,646	$20,619	$38,834	$45,487	$17,172	$26,823	$33,023	$9,391	$50,489	$52,355	$36,567	$11,192	$12,465	$10,461
Nevada	$27,178	$30,898	$26,479	$45,170	$36,903	$22,190	$26,963	$30,139	$15,673	$72,710	$72,411	$80,693	$23,953	$26,654	$20,002
New Hampshire	$25,814	$21,777	$26,260	$50,313	$56,134	$40,522	$35,077	$43,540	$21,090	$61,911	$64,040	$51,435	$12,014	$14,076	$11,019
New Jersey	$25,527	$30,733	$25,140	$50,159	$60,196	$27,389	$26,259	$30,525	$20,386	$85,543	$90,212	$68,762	$15,879	$19,710	$12,457
New Mexico	$19,827	$21,083	$19,319	$36,779	$40,515	$25,837	$27,873	$31,248	$24,080	$46,496	$46,834	$42,203	$12,375	$12,801	$12,190
New York	$23,893	$30,764	$23,005	$51,936	$56,540	$37,605	$31,192	$35,307	$21,853	$71,812	$75,093	$66,204	$16,811	$19,642	$13,664
North Carolina	$20,830	$25,051	$20,346	$36,728	$38,474	$30,447	$29,918	$31,480	$21,558	$41,073	$41,591	$37,151	$12,340	$13,882	$11,742
North Dakota	$25,366	$28,761	$25,142	$42,459	$46,721	$22,385	$41,567	$46,003	$20,388	$47,874	$49,141	$40,805	$12,606	$13,630	$12,334
Ohio	$21,162	$26,268	$20,859	$44,900	$49,746	$30,019	$29,018	$32,425	$20,684	$52,287	$55,145	$45,002	$11,491	$12,025	$11,144
Oklahoma	$21,332	$21,516	$21,280	$33,533	$36,747	$25,726	$28,842	$30,645	$21,934	$40,441	$41,710	$30,743	$12,187	$13,869	$11,610
Oregon	$24,655	$24,959	$24,634	$50,590	$56,001	$29,045	$32,381	$41,279	$21,474	$65,746	$66,943	$57,031	$14,326	$15,986	$12,349
Pennsylvania	$23,526	$26,385	$23,131	$45,140	$50,942	$27,763	$26,641	$30,816	$11,825	$62,343	$65,987	$47,069	$11,810	$14,432	$10,957
Rhode Island	$22,412	$23,750	$22,385	$57,153	$65,598	$23,618	$50,181	$51,317	$20,763	$75,036	$76,389	$24,648	$12,024	$16,321	$10,155
South Carolina	$20,790	$24,097	$20,448	$32,063	$33,457	$28,268	$26,311	$26,985	$21,509	$37,325	$37,326	$37,320	$12,831	$14,645	$11,919
South Dakota	$21,248	$21,303	$21,244	$35,717	$38,092	$30,684	$20,248	$23,483	$6,890	$40,160	$39,745	$40,869	$10,636	$10,286	$10,873
Tennessee	$21,935	$23,006	$21,825	$34,152	$38,051	$25,118	$28,311	$31,334	$21,298	$39,828	$41,572	$29,196	$11,530	$12,619	$10,747
Texas	$21,359	$23,839	$21,106	$39,926	$41,901	$33,257	$30,215	$32,120	$22,917	$47,653	$51,733	$38,934	$13,951	$15,827	$12,548
Utah	$19,286	$18,485	$19,403	$38,802	$41,212	$25,943	$25,215	$30,967	$5,611	$42,120	$43,465	$40,216	$10,544	$10,795	$10,311
Vermont	$24,602	$30,117	$23,338	$44,107	$51,697	$15,703	$31,495	$36,561	$7,284	$60,531	$61,373	$45,601	$13,957	$16,470	$12,483
Virginia	$22,145	$20,819	$22,199	$46,342	$50,425	$37,281	$36,908	$40,926	$33,380	$52,282	$57,161	$41,212	$12,573	$14,369	$12,180
Washington	$25,959	$25,711	$26,007	$50,514	$53,760	$32,219	$33,266	$39,280	$22,837	$70,298	$72,116	$51,792	$16,540	$16,964	$16,221
West Virginia	$19,007	$25,897	$17,770	$34,787	$36,265	$28,618	$21,070	$21,277	$17,738	$42,423	$43,912	$37,039	$11,590	$11,312	$11,840
Wisconsin	$23,195	$25,577	$23,064	$47,945	$51,537	$30,996	$26,346	$36,100	$11,282	$57,047	$58,377	$52,293	$11,323	$11,776	$11,161
Wyoming	$19,269	$12,220	$19,349	$37,101	$37,352	$36,696	$17,486	$26,367	$6,488	$55,809	$48,794	$58,407	$11,991	$14,732	$11,428

Table B-9. Median Annual Earnings—Continued

	Median earnings in the past 12 months by gender and occupation for employed persons age 16 and older														
	Service occupations (Continued)						Sales and office occupations								
	Building and grounds cleaning and maintenance occupations			Personal care and service occupations			All sales and office occupations			Sales and related occupations			Office and administrative support occupations		
Geography	Total	Men	Women	Total	Men	Women	Total	Men	Women	Total	Men	Women	Total	Men	Women
United States	$18,955	$22,066	$15,235	$15,821	$19,335	$15,163	$28,665	$35,322	$25,841	$26,901	$40,342	$18,395	$29,669	$30,602	$29,162
Alabama	$17,106	$21,334	$14,362	$14,763	$16,908	$13,847	$25,494	$32,113	$23,093	$23,778	$38,525	$16,678	$26,338	$27,202	$26,121
Alaska	$19,929	$25,836	$13,417	$22,436	$24,831	$22,172	$31,038	$35,344	$30,015	$26,782	$36,807	$19,121	$32,944	$33,995	$32,894
Arizona	$17,196	$19,532	$15,079	$16,023	$18,361	$15,300	$29,194	$32,269	$26,861	$29,724	$39,248	$21,453	$28,998	$29,126	$28,963
Arkansas	$15,769	$20,904	$11,182	$15,436	$15,947	$15,362	$25,028	$30,205	$23,075	$23,329	$36,173	$16,203	$25,685	$24,935	$25,901
California	$20,109	$22,929	$15,779	$15,486	$18,344	$14,801	$30,314	$33,568	$27,165	$27,460	$38,036	$20,309	$30,940	$30,592	$31,090
Colorado	$20,071	$24,699	$15,524	$18,802	$20,500	$18,441	$30,666	$36,497	$26,855	$30,712	$41,028	$21,112	$30,640	$31,733	$30,290
Connecticut	$23,097	$27,123	$17,866	$16,005	$18,387	$15,454	$35,466	$42,005	$32,011	$35,079	$50,161	$22,478	$35,668	$35,536	$35,716
Delaware	$20,497	$26,372	$15,401	$17,949	$21,780	$16,319	$31,135	$38,158	$27,967	$30,363	$41,339	$19,314	$31,322	$32,177	$30,994
District of Columbia	$23,239	$24,263	$22,737	$26,525	$28,114	$24,388	$37,343	$40,177	$35,391	$32,842	$51,424	$25,511	$38,050	$36,827	$38,941
Florida	$18,458	$21,218	$15,507	$16,503	$18,665	$15,712	$26,312	$30,778	$24,752	$25,844	$35,477	$19,481	$26,535	$26,019	$26,684
Georgia	$17,526	$21,129	$15,023	$15,882	$19,382	$15,011	$27,083	$35,487	$24,319	$26,424	$40,831	$16,903	$27,371	$30,021	$26,934
Hawaii	$28,047	$27,534	$28,964	$20,224	$23,672	$16,084	$31,397	$36,575	$30,417	$29,594	$40,317	$22,986	$32,398	$35,071	$32,199
Idaho	$13,444	$15,685	$10,836	$13,254	$15,840	$12,668	$23,813	$33,028	$20,587	$25,035	$41,062	$16,969	$23,223	$26,097	$22,345
Illinois	$20,611	$22,435	$17,259	$15,334	$16,151	$15,153	$29,494	$38,944	$26,374	$30,181	$46,561	$18,833	$30,605	$31,442	$30,338
Indiana	$18,585	$22,404	$13,498	$14,700	$19,046	$13,817	$26,523	$35,037	$23,576	$25,890	$41,277	$16,360	$26,882	$27,641	$26,715
Iowa	$17,582	$22,137	$15,359	$15,141	$16,214	$14,905	$27,989	$36,630	$25,787	$26,631	$41,437	$16,965	$28,727	$30,568	$28,191
Kansas	$18,326	$21,639	$14,163	$14,677	$17,161	$14,081	$27,768	$36,608	$25,336	$27,184	$42,148	$18,225	$28,128	$30,698	$27,351
Kentucky	$18,061	$21,350	$14,625	$16,034	$21,116	$15,282	$25,272	$30,904	$22,419	$22,968	$35,747	$15,784	$25,850	$26,861	$25,448
Louisiana	$15,190	$17,631	$13,591	$14,711	$18,847	$13,951	$25,846	$32,003	$23,128	$22,602	$40,762	$15,525	$26,929	$29,295	$27,127
Maine	$20,024	$26,002	$13,966	$12,356	$17,447	$11,677	$26,801	$34,790	$24,413	$24,987	$36,272	$16,812	$27,478	$32,413	$26,610
Maryland	$22,138	$25,916	$18,834	$20,289	$24,481	$18,190	$33,737	$38,673	$31,642	$28,858	$40,066	$20,868	$36,184	$37,043	$35,942
Massachusetts	$21,773	$25,829	$17,099	$17,294	$21,471	$16,472	$33,713	$41,994	$30,461	$32,145	$50,597	$17,871	$34,555	$35,343	$34,124
Michigan	$16,541	$19,275	$13,362	$13,398	$15,774	$12,877	$26,095	$32,670	$23,318	$23,485	$38,320	$15,909	$27,126	$28,371	$26,899
Minnesota	$18,362	$23,222	$12,304	$17,856	$20,201	$17,465	$31,384	$39,228	$28,799	$30,737	$42,226	$20,193	$31,473	$34,026	$31,277
Mississippi	$15,669	$19,060	$13,461	$14,419	$20,653	$12,975	$24,710	$31,371	$22,076	$22,395	$35,823	$16,275	$25,520	$26,485	$25,269
Missouri	$18,736	$21,518	$14,600	$12,288	$12,760	$12,231	$26,762	$33,534	$24,879	$25,458	$37,649	$17,265	$27,278	$30,447	$26,896
Montana	$13,751	$15,466	$11,872	$14,133	$21,108	$13,486	$24,676	$28,699	$23,322	$24,106	$35,889	$19,863	$24,940	$23,279	$25,182
Nebraska	$16,379	$20,826	$11,957	$13,935	$18,532	$12,827	$28,843	$36,235	$25,653	$29,715	$42,359	$18,630	$28,443	$30,116	$28,147
Nevada	$25,118	$25,586	$24,230	$27,012	$32,057	$22,942	$27,262	$31,442	$25,685	$26,421	$35,171	$20,803	$27,812	$28,578	$27,496
New Hampshire	$21,864	$27,354	$16,979	$16,426	$12,497	$16,636	$32,495	$41,523	$29,937	$35,052	$50,548	$20,845	$32,185	$32,573	$32,123
New Jersey	$22,303	$27,913	$17,052	$15,941	$20,684	$15,089	$33,748	$41,736	$30,425	$32,389	$47,853	$21,149	$34,265	$36,367	$33,122
New Mexico	$16,493	$18,930	$12,988	$14,847	$20,786	$13,673	$23,504	$26,653	$21,968	$21,934	$27,616	$17,068	$24,602	$25,637	$24,305
New York	$21,275	$26,585	$15,572	$16,724	$21,771	$15,666	$31,475	$36,284	$29,792	$29,214	$40,728	$18,807	$32,251	$31,887	$32,388
North Carolina	$17,137	$20,750	$13,827	$14,537	$16,157	$13,960	$26,797	$32,404	$24,355	$24,649	$37,318	$15,931	$27,976	$27,921	$27,993
North Dakota	$18,058	$25,245	$13,683	$17,396	$21,941	$15,161	$30,729	$37,952	$26,718	$35,006	$44,310	$22,169	$29,336	$31,105	$28,584
Ohio	$17,787	$21,656	$13,671	$14,433	$17,015	$13,515	$27,353	$35,497	$25,077	$25,400	$40,316	$16,655	$28,772	$31,074	$27,788
Oklahoma	$17,559	$20,796	$14,037	$16,009	$22,197	$15,013	$25,996	$32,672	$23,412	$24,844	$38,608	$17,157	$26,482	$29,397	$26,056
Oregon	$17,408	$21,496	$13,534	$14,453	$16,876	$13,385	$28,011	$32,561	$25,998	$27,332	$40,056	$21,178	$28,337	$28,883	$28,137
Pennsylvania	$20,158	$23,609	$15,366	$16,421	$20,343	$15,748	$29,685	$37,026	$26,335	$27,015	$41,535	$16,840	$30,299	$32,097	$29,735
Rhode Island	$18,768	$21,064	$14,820	$20,300	$22,726	$17,497	$31,761	$37,138	$29,865	$29,862	$40,873	$16,109	$33,123	$31,847	$33,667
South Carolina	$17,698	$21,140	$14,181	$14,444	$13,292	$14,684	$25,737	$34,529	$22,934	$23,839	$39,028	$16,481	$26,440	$27,870	$26,141
South Dakota	$17,224	$24,057	$11,799	$18,054	$21,512	$17,516	$28,692	$38,706	$25,883	$28,996	$44,733	$17,671	$28,608	$34,680	$27,294
Tennessee	$16,892	$19,835	$13,435	$15,628	$19,579	$14,943	$26,281	$32,344	$23,662	$24,581	$36,996	$16,625	$26,949	$28,545	$26,644
Texas	$16,634	$20,298	$13,830	$14,658	$17,554	$13,888	$25,819	$34,685	$24,882	$26,446	$39,336	$18,344	$24,851	$30,796	$27,439
Utah	$14,822	$18,987	$10,915	$13,001	$14,248	$12,782	$25,819	$31,622	$22,455	$28,511	$38,344	$17,123	$24,851	$25,869	$24,435
Vermont	$18,601	$25,899	$13,127	$15,888	$18,498	$15,604	$30,613	$33,337	$29,702	$27,756	$38,730	$18,725	$31,539	$27,158	$32,019
Virginia	$20,005	$22,123	$16,745	$17,242	$17,363	$17,216	$30,179	$35,287	$27,314	$26,920	$37,064	$19,562	$30,900	$31,997	$30,580
Washington	$20,898	$25,320	$17,034	$17,327	$21,630	$16,777	$31,586	$39,090	$28,826	$31,595	$45,227	$22,501	$31,581	$34,372	$31,014
West Virginia	$19,599	$21,364	$15,694	$15,374	$18,374	$14,559	$24,754	$30,073	$22,777	$20,820	$31,719	$13,707	$26,365	$28,514	$25,936
Wisconsin	$20,263	$24,652	$13,053	$15,426	$17,021	$15,270	$29,117	$36,025	$26,131	$27,912	$41,362	$19,053	$29,561	$30,844	$28,890
Wyoming	$18,216	$22,165	$15,385	$14,399	$16,493	$12,709	$28,176	$40,371	$25,151	$25,144	$40,543	$20,501	$30,376	$40,242	$29,321

Table B-9. Median Annual Earnings—*Continued*

	Median earnings in the past 12 months by gender and occupation for employed persons age 16 and older												Production, transportation, and material moving occupations		
	Natural resources, construction, and maintenance occupations														
	All natural resources, construction, and maintenance occupations:			Farming, fishing, and forestry occupations			Construction and extraction occupations			Installation, maintenance, and repair occupations			All production, transportation, and material moving occupations		
Geography	Total	Men	Women	Total	Men	Women	Total	Men	Women	Total	Men	Women	Total	Men	Women
United States	$35,496	$35,982	$21,700	$20,316	$21,818	$14,362	$33,752	$34,179	$27,252	$41,286	$41,399	$34,923	$30,606	$32,527	$22,061
Alabama	$31,868	$31,968	$27,970	$21,145	$22,172	$10,310	$27,109	$27,040	$31,627	$40,615	$40,823	$32,834	$30,465	$32,612	$21,619
Alaska	$51,520	$51,563	$39,705	$31,451	$31,623	$17,276	$52,342	$52,337	$55,073	$51,712	$51,506	$83,345	$31,856	$39,516	$21,736
Arizona	$32,242	$32,413	$27,018	$20,242	$21,268	$11,699	$31,170	$31,195	$30,144	$40,432	$40,419	$41,435	$28,164	$30,764	$22,048
Arkansas	$30,798	$30,930	$27,182	$22,069	$22,522	$17,038	$29,526	$29,910	$27,316	$37,257	$37,447	$31,170	$27,730	$30,981	$21,359
California	$30,879	$31,717	$15,741	$17,915	$20,271	$12,748	$32,202	$32,203	$32,141	$40,566	$40,481	$46,120	$27,208	$30,571	$21,012
Colorado	$36,579	$36,985	$25,434	$22,588	$23,583	$16,662	$34,742	$35,114	$22,210	$43,664	$44,300	$30,090	$31,085	$33,482	$22,529
Connecticut	$44,092	$45,067	$29,240	$16,300	$21,134	$11,821	$41,730	$41,875	$28,476	$50,762	$50,956	$46,624	$32,475	$40,045	$22,135
Delaware	$39,744	$40,153	$25,021	$26,973	$27,298	$22,015	$36,632	$36,953	$25,575	$44,839	$44,992	$19,764	$30,927	$34,053	$22,679
District of Columbia	$31,379	$31,217	-	-	-	-	$30,697	$30,451	-	$45,279	$45,279	-	$35,421	$36,944	$29,005
Florida	$28,824	$29,512	$20,235	$17,377	$18,588	$14,560	$27,038	$27,096	$22,747	$35,571	$35,700	$27,231	$26,129	$28,010	$20,338
Georgia	$31,290	$31,385	$27,488	$18,851	$19,720	$16,455	$28,737	$28,960	$25,737	$39,906	$39,486	$41,337	$27,997	$30,870	$21,584
Hawaii	$45,100	$45,853	$27,784	$20,665	$21,011	$20,200	$46,479	$46,492	$46,371	$47,458	$47,368	$48,284	$32,370	$34,188	$28,805
Idaho	$31,042	$32,009	$15,928	$21,050	$23,097	$11,593	$33,733	$34,952	$19,096	$37,391	$40,045	$17,123	$30,815	$33,949	$17,347
Illinois	$41,539	$41,877	$29,716	$24,299	$24,023	$25,345	$41,413	$41,655	$32,051	$44,969	$45,206	$30,899	$31,041	$34,678	$22,231
Indiana	$37,462	$38,891	$23,040	$21,463	$27,084	$9,197	$35,398	$35,750	$25,158	$42,258	$42,656	$31,732	$32,195	$36,531	$24,449
Iowa	$40,255	$40,611	$25,226	$27,294	$29,950	$20,524	$40,849	$41,020	$24,760	$41,676	$41,834	$34,432	$32,071	$36,244	$24,726
Kansas	$36,206	$36,605	$24,541	$25,340	$27,263	$10,968	$32,889	$33,113	$27,554	$42,173	$42,447	$25,510	$31,048	$34,010	$22,067
Kentucky	$34,455	$34,934	$27,133	$22,726	$22,462	$25,672	$32,364	$32,415	$29,169	$40,587	$40,792	$26,641	$30,848	$33,946	$22,984
Louisiana	$39,878	$40,078	$32,101	$22,344	$24,081	$20,745	$38,190	$38,599	$31,255	$42,209	$42,895	$40,963	$36,097	$41,146	$19,395
Maine	$36,399	$36,929	$27,368	$28,226	$30,330	$11,912	$35,930	$36,532	$30,133	$41,074	$41,205	$27,338	$30,762	$32,124	$22,166
Maryland	$40,845	$41,046	$29,909	$28,165	$29,169	$18,047	$36,464	$36,606	$26,280	$50,752	$50,913	$40,576	$31,915	$35,187	$25,171
Massachusetts	$41,983	$42,313	$21,946	$14,675	$16,583	$12,337	$41,389	$41,475	$31,034	$47,590	$48,026	$36,580	$31,747	$35,735	$23,678
Michigan	$36,784	$37,459	$20,307	$20,864	$23,967	$14,299	$35,718	$35,946	$22,498	$41,817	$42,204	$26,915	$31,449	$35,129	$23,970
Minnesota	$41,534	$42,053	$25,613	$23,884	$25,740	$18,937	$42,324	$43,638	$30,297	$43,924	$45,134	$31,178	$32,298	$35,884	$25,283
Mississippi	$34,562	$35,602	$20,969	$21,868	$24,807	$17,623	$33,921	$32,165	$15,007	$39,805	$40,289	$25,890	$29,334	$31,418	$21,157
Missouri	$37,036	$37,330	$27,045	$21,520	$22,110	$19,339	$36,649	$36,799	$31,180	$40,794	$40,977	$30,706	$30,840	$32,476	$23,244
Montana	$37,154	$38,336	$15,671	$22,751	$25,114	$10,209	$39,069	$40,109	$30,265	$41,570	$41,619	$40,075	$32,106	$35,973	$19,613
Nebraska	$36,051	$36,335	$25,374	$27,280	$28,324	$20,733	$33,343	$33,798	$26,544	$41,894	$42,035	$35,556	$31,427	$34,221	$24,626
Nevada	$37,086	$37,346	$30,354	$31,538	$31,489	$31,620	$36,461	$36,448	$36,614	$40,110	$40,916	$21,498	$29,482	$30,995	$21,988
New Hampshire	$41,319	$41,855	$20,107	$13,456	$21,730	$9,536	$41,507	$41,794	$12,061	$42,785	$43,431	$22,376	$33,235	$36,956	$27,342
New Jersey	$42,017	$42,106	$35,657	$21,127	$24,024	$16,067	$39,906	$39,863	$42,697	$47,543	$47,837	$43,790	$29,358	$32,279	$20,889
New Mexico	$30,859	$30,975	$24,925	$14,367	$14,442	$12,117	$30,486	$30,546	$25,793	$37,521	$37,063	$43,497	$28,444	$31,361	$19,069
New York	$40,576	$40,646	$35,351	$24,383	$27,281	$11,585	$38,011	$38,029	$37,050	$45,550	$45,406	$50,754	$31,050	$32,291	$22,783
North Carolina	$30,022	$30,334	$22,426	$17,709	$17,754	$17,282	$26,767	$27,089	$21,525	$36,393	$36,569	$27,384	$27,179	$30,547	$21,597
North Dakota	$48,200	$50,170	$30,549	$31,152	$33,327	$9,548	$50,473	$50,898	$32,048	$51,338	$51,374	$28,965	$31,299	$41,236	$25,685
Ohio	$40,058	$40,462	$21,945	$21,662	$24,089	$12,651	$37,458	$38,613	$26,405	$41,915	$42,198	$28,965	$31,299	$35,074	$22,907
Oklahoma	$35,234	$35,510	$27,399	$20,909	$21,269	$18,581	$32,662	$33,130	$26,739	$41,037	$41,095	$40,367	$31,813	$35,115	$22,051
Oregon	$32,256	$34,369	$17,606	$20,955	$22,291	$13,626	$36,231	$36,745	$25,987	$40,386	$40,333	$41,701	$29,922	$31,851	$21,966
Pennsylvania	$40,886	$41,170	$24,799	$20,982	$21,758	$16,792	$40,877	$40,933	$34,501	$43,632	$43,918	$36,049	$31,689	$35,781	$22,019
Rhode Island	$41,237	$41,367	$36,980	$35,127	$23,808	$36,490	$40,836	$40,870	$40,344	$42,458	$42,592	-	$31,361	$36,160	$20,305
South Carolina	$31,628	$31,699	$27,014	$21,538	$22,102	$16,734	$28,939	$29,176	$26,704	$40,106	$40,128	$39,189	$30,787	$32,126	$25,192
South Dakota	$36,512	$36,812	$20,172	$26,595	$27,924	$16,841	$37,109	$37,277	$12,425	$41,074	$41,321	$37,083	$28,309	$31,644	$23,721
Tennessee	$31,842	$32,002	$27,468	$18,741	$18,688	$20,140	$29,868	$29,924	$27,404	$40,167	$40,559	$31,041	$28,309	$31,493	$22,028
Texas	$31,733	$31,894	$23,612	$22,076	$23,625	$13,582	$30,662	$30,689	$27,325	$38,368	$39,035	$26,257	$30,956	$34,556	$20,679
Utah	$36,608	$37,006	$18,487	$18,789	$19,615	$11,928	$35,582	$35,712	$7,294	$44,391	$41,952	$20,394	$29,736	$32,065	$21,656
Vermont	$36,387	$36,830	$29,507	$21,774	$24,448	$13,759	$34,697	$34,186	$35,852	$42,676	$42,441	$65,610	$31,000	$32,481	$22,800
Virginia	$35,886	$36,170	$30,089	$20,795	$22,032	$10,892	$33,041	$32,927	$35,494	$41,948	$42,037	$37,023	$30,546	$33,082	$21,943
Washington	$38,362	$40,519	$20,174	$21,016	$25,381	$16,553	$41,554	$41,749	$35,239	$47,174	$47,055	$49,667	$34,940	$37,493	$24,571
West Virginia	$42,350	$42,832	$29,205	$26,913	$27,055	-	$44,408	$45,255	$26,329	$41,991	$41,934	$66,056	$31,873	$35,740	$21,922
Wisconsin	$40,785	$41,281	$21,742	$23,344	$25,180	$18,386	$41,754	$42,037	$16,143	$44,017	$44,059	$43,165	$32,203	$36,266	$25,325
Wyoming	$51,144	$51,627	$26,784	$26,185	$26,619	$25,878	$51,548	$51,456	$60,875	$56,644	$60,339	$26,881	$45,103	$50,287	$18,278

Table B-9. Median Annual Earnings—*Continued*

	Median earnings in the past 12 months by gender and occupation for employed persons age 16 and older												Median earnings in the past 12 months by gender and industry for employed persons age 16 and older		
	Production, transportation, and material moving occupations													Agriculture, forestry, fishing and hunting, and mining	
	Production occupations			Transportation occupations			Material moving occupations			Persons in all industries			All agriculture, forestry, fishing and hunting, and mining:		
Geography	Total	Men	Women	Total	Men	Women	Total	Men	Women	Total:	Men	Women	Total:	Men	Women
United States	$31,759	$36,526	$23,331	$34,060	$36,357	$22,337	$22,412	$24,267	$18,029	$34,656	$40,699	$29,319	$32,630	$36,955	$21,406
Alabama	$31,087	$35,449	$22,044	$35,115	$36,621	$18,200	$25,000	$25,804	$18,509	$31,187	$37,165	$25,708	$35,456	$40,063	$20,293
Alaska	$29,445	$39,704	$22,355	$41,250	$41,963	$30,910	$23,651	$26,736	$7,530	$40,137	$48,144	$32,088	$72,020	$78,750	$52,490
Arizona	$29,735	$31,973	$21,940	$32,485	$35,156	$26,439	$20,410	$21,108	$17,186	$31,840	$36,370	$28,519	$32,026	$33,483	$26,579
Arkansas	$28,113	$31,717	$21,834	$31,781	$33,470	$19,000	$24,104	$25,551	$20,155	$29,467	$32,446	$25,020	$28,276	$30,388	$17,718
California	$28,162	$31,875	$21,525	$34,344	$35,629	$26,426	$20,744	$21,733	$17,416	$35,376	$40,334	$30,516	$21,218	$23,205	$15,728
Colorado	$31,525	$36,014	$22,109	$37,065	$38,813	$28,533	$23,455	$25,086	$20,543	$36,813	$42,186	$31,153	$52,314	$56,305	$45,549
Connecticut	$36,507	$42,124	$23,382	$35,190	$40,886	$22,480	$22,095	$25,996	$16,474	$42,307	$50,837	$36,272	$21,041	$22,045	$14,336
Delaware	$41,342	$47,180	$29,737	$32,315	$37,431	$16,858	$19,893	$20,084	$19,508	$38,062	$41,860	$33,126	$31,292	$32,132	$21,426
District of Columbia	$41,965	$62,043	$33,425	$35,512	$36,462	$31,416	$31,184	$31,715	$20,096	$52,733	$61,276	$50,477	$130,651	-	-
Florida	$26,732	$30,770	$20,797	$30,238	$31,046	$22,457	$20,038	$21,062	$16,278	$30,612	$33,042	$26,939	$21,400	$23,585	$18,194
Georgia	$28,689	$32,108	$22,023	$31,809	$35,359	$21,691	$22,542	$23,486	$16,918	$31,907	$37,360	$27,381	$27,068	$28,524	$22,404
Hawaii	$35,166	$37,448	$25,171	$35,611	$33,153	$39,052	$22,297	$22,278	$22,429	$36,170	$40,565	$31,942	$22,340	$24,078	$20,468
Idaho	$30,954	$35,373	$19,313	$36,503	$37,389	$16,929	$20,248	$20,503	$16,613	$29,076	$36,053	$21,661	$28,681	$31,045	$12,745
Illinois	$32,115	$37,853	$24,142	$35,832	$38,425	$22,294	$23,350	$25,449	$17,194	$36,604	$42,895	$30,437	$37,516	$41,029	$27,621
Indiana	$35,362	$40,023	$26,492	$36,364	$40,054	$20,272	$25,270	$26,867	$20,909	$31,976	$40,229	$26,195	$36,007	$41,338	$18,158
Iowa	$34,949	$38,780	$26,860	$35,770	$37,406	$16,716	$26,038	$29,163	$18,103	$32,912	$41,026	$26,775	$35,936	$40,259	$20,529
Kansas	$33,776	$36,991	$24,121	$33,277	$36,437	$15,257	$21,805	$23,784	$16,957	$33,226	$40,761	$26,792	$34,662	$40,684	$18,786
Kentucky	$32,388	$36,493	$25,448	$35,060	$37,238	$16,936	$22,459	$23,676	$18,469	$31,111	$36,302	$26,025	$35,131	$35,565	$30,231
Louisiana	$41,408	$47,258	$19,217	$36,121	$38,998	$21,105	$24,257	$26,793	$16,316	$31,907	$41,185	$25,687	$55,890	$60,835	$35,529
Maine	$32,015	$36,337	$26,339	$32,060	$32,901	$19,739	$21,127	$25,040	$11,530	$31,683	$38,086	$26,821	$29,783	$31,587	$19,023
Maryland	$36,200	$41,156	$25,768	$35,293	$36,971	$26,974	$23,718	$25,331	$20,019	$43,865	$50,606	$38,714	$31,039	$31,919	$22,144
Massachusetts	$35,853	$40,973	$25,771	$32,467	$36,143	$22,934	$20,997	$23,341	$15,923	$41,841	$50,567	$35,804	$20,855	$21,931	$13,833
Michigan	$33,355	$37,421	$25,880	$31,464	$34,512	$17,620	$23,728	$25,566	$18,884	$32,007	$40,590	$25,986	$27,141	$31,743	$14,456
Minnesota	$35,049	$37,984	$26,434	$36,656	$39,379	$25,918	$24,959	$26,642	$18,795	$37,290	$43,736	$31,429	$36,049	$39,474	$21,952
Mississippi	$30,010	$33,879	$21,959	$32,159	$35,205	$20,613	$21,308	$21,828	$15,007	$30,057	$35,102	$24,869	$41,265	$45,036	$17,731
Missouri	$32,000	$36,395	$25,027	$32,436	$35,738	$21,208	$22,747	$23,721	$19,676	$31,801	$38,452	$26,794	$31,321	$31,935	$22,378
Montana	$30,815	$35,558	$20,568	$36,632	$38,300	$20,143	$26,644	$28,468	$12,758	$30,865	$37,493	$25,111	$38,040	$41,446	$20,463
Nebraska	$31,931	$35,861	$26,405	$36,693	$39,395	$22,037	$25,610	$26,950	$16,643	$32,943	$40,200	$27,378	$37,937	$40,664	$22,097
Nevada	$28,004	$31,103	$23,872	$34,395	$35,865	$25,958	$21,583	$22,977	$18,596	$31,999	$36,193	$29,639	$52,745	$56,525	$46,740
New Hampshire	$36,558	$40,909	$30,218	$34,007	$36,782	$21,376	$21,376	$21,942	$17,242	$40,124	$46,794	$32,392	$25,755	$35,380	$12,062
New Jersey	$32,058	$37,433	$22,916	$32,224	$35,423	$22,106	$21,874	$25,027	$16,886	$41,982	$50,863	$35,479	$25,122	$26,992	$16,806
New Mexico	$29,551	$33,477	$18,378	$31,838	$34,470	$20,839	$21,157	$21,746	$17,658	$29,074	$32,121	$24,548	$42,177	$45,046	$29,771
New York	$32,154	$36,822	$22,196	$31,847	$32,493	$26,737	$23,957	$25,617	$17,969	$38,611	$43,203	$33,270	$27,584	$31,529	$15,709
North Carolina	$27,828	$31,516	$22,085	$31,577	$33,935	$21,193	$21,718	$22,309	$20,243	$31,308	$35,810	$27,235	$23,132	$24,063	$19,424
North Dakota	$39,351	$45,752	$26,221	$46,462	$48,228	$18,654	$24,538	$24,588	$24,213	$36,890	$46,884	$29,918	$56,129	$61,216	$30,194
Ohio	$33,445	$37,656	$25,499	$32,598	$36,731	$20,716	$24,666	$26,599	$19,780	$32,755	$40,869	$27,069	$35,195	$40,063	$16,897
Oklahoma	$35,011	$38,332	$23,553	$33,610	$36,366	$20,527	$25,269	$26,130	$17,263	$31,222	$37,902	$25,444	$51,065	$52,264	$36,704
Oregon	$32,087	$36,371	$23,236	$28,641	$31,139	$19,974	$22,257	$23,408	$18,606	$31,808	$38,123	$26,785	$26,925	$29,829	$18,787
Pennsylvania	$35,596	$40,362	$23,591	$33,076	$36,915	$17,593	$25,536	$26,978	$20,762	$35,786	$42,132	$29,544	$36,338	$40,736	$22,412
Rhode Island	$31,178	$36,269	$21,117	$36,707	$38,750	$25,805	$19,217	$22,210	$15,615	$37,458	$42,198	$31,997	$35,197	$24,433	$35,875
South Carolina	$31,997	$35,983	$26,629	$34,620	$36,766	$20,583	$21,082	$21,667	$18,565	$30,951	$36,011	$26,316	$26,992	$28,657	$17,148
South Dakota	$31,875	$36,318	$25,206	$37,409	$40,194	$27,943	$22,938	$25,785	$16,050	$31,640	$38,133	$26,675	$40,179	$40,823	$22,114
Tennessee	$30,356	$32,968	$23,991	$35,405	$39,360	$19,180	$21,622	$22,703	$19,457	$30,974	$36,210	$26,134	$26,766	$27,496	$22,323
Texas	$31,784	$37,168	$20,393	$36,802	$39,626	$23,974	$22,390	$23,759	$17,370	$33,001	$40,118	$27,400	$60,573	$61,230	$51,274
Utah	$30,228	$34,820	$21,881	$36,434	$38,225	$25,640	$20,256	$21,301	$16,366	$31,446	$40,424	$23,400	$51,022	$57,255	$25,975
Vermont	$31,899	$35,560	$22,298	$32,079	$33,939	$26,182	$22,815	$22,460	$30,315	$34,502	$38,744	$30,510	$28,048	$31,049	$15,162
Virginia	$34,703	$40,187	$26,025	$31,165	$35,016	$19,100	$22,371	$24,425	$16,056	$38,638	$45,820	$31,904	$30,452	$31,975	$16,949
Washington	$37,057	$41,243	$26,118	$39,809	$41,846	$27,122	$25,111	$26,921	$18,547	$38,930	$47,088	$31,387	$24,802	$28,261	$18,225
West Virginia	$36,932	$41,980	$21,716	$33,991	$35,600	$25,946	$22,962	$24,338	$11,098	$30,748	$37,275	$25,498	$60,691	$61,200	$42,190
Wisconsin	$34,780	$38,746	$26,491	$36,182	$38,185	$20,214	$26,062	$27,138	$22,297	$34,688	$41,072	$28,701	$27,934	$30,345	$16,908
Wyoming	$59,127	$61,957	$18,592	$40,572	$46,629	$17,793	$35,270	$37,517	$24,135	$35,451	$47,323	$25,714	$70,538	$76,164	$40,157

Table B-9. Median Annual Earnings—*Continued*

	Median earnings in the past 12 months by gender and industry for employed persons age 16 and older														
	Agriculture, forestry, fishing and hunting, and mining						Construction			Manufacturing			Wholesale Trade		
	Agriculture, forestry, fishing and hunting			Mining, quarrying, and oil and gas extraction											
Geography	Total:	Men	Women	Total:	Men	Women	Total:	Men	Women	Total:	Men	Women	Total:	Men	Women
United States	$24,977	$27,137	$16,967	$66,641	$69,785	$55,566	$36,272	$36,427	$34,642	$42,223	$47,186	$33,867	$42,365	$46,632	$36,279
Alabama	$28,425	$31,135	$15,852	$65,021	$65,619	$36,026	$30,991	$30,464	$38,338	$36,988	$41,000	$29,192	$40,148	$45,365	$30,857
Alaska	$30,033	$30,295	$28,569	$100,064	$100,800	$70,828	$51,062	$51,756	$31,985	$29,704	$41,574	$20,307	$50,912	$52,352	$25,775
Arizona	$21,570	$24,995	$16,113	$61,113	$62,019	$54,963	$33,737	$33,429	$35,180	$43,888	$46,997	$35,492	$41,342	$43,143	$36,176
Arkansas	$25,789	$26,722	$15,285	$69,141	$71,121	$43,750	$30,231	$30,388	$27,267	$33,943	$37,116	$26,998	$39,586	$42,410	$31,005
California	$20,456	$22,076	$15,110	$65,847	$65,726	$67,674	$36,533	$36,222	$41,153	$44,100	$50,327	$35,289	$40,847	$42,677	$35,361
Colorado	$30,687	$31,485	$25,359	$76,825	$80,199	$67,419	$37,154	$37,192	$36,672	$47,331	$51,850	$37,160	$49,029	$52,388	$40,770
Connecticut	$17,552	$20,837	$13,889	$70,417	$66,736	$201,630	$45,007	$45,635	$36,036	$57,587	$61,989	$44,690	$52,384	$55,707	$47,486
Delaware	$30,937	$31,777	$21,426	-	-	-	$40,008	$40,229	$35,931	$51,623	$55,369	$46,135	$48,258	$47,116	$48,866
District of Columbia	-	-	-	$101,067	-	-	$37,564	$34,626	$54,519	$62,802	$85,636	$46,770	$55,519	$56,380	$47,684
Florida	$20,191	$21,576	$17,896	$56,590	$56,050	$100,544	$30,392	$30,359	$30,739	$38,694	$41,555	$30,753	$38,411	$41,379	$31,755
Georgia	$25,706	$26,490	$21,206	$48,463	$50,674	$35,523	$31,027	$30,887	$32,345	$36,774	$41,155	$29,097	$42,167	$46,207	$37,561
Hawaii	$21,992	$23,415	$20,468	$59,367	$59,367	-	$50,325	$50,330	$50,103	$39,078	$42,943	$27,336	$39,045	$42,990	$31,861
Idaho	$26,205	$28,153	$12,360	$58,086	$59,739	$50,744	$35,297	$35,639	$22,990	$38,953	$41,590	$26,930	$36,647	$40,768	$29,019
Illinois	$35,849	$38,000	$25,592	$51,358	$52,065	$40,924	$41,995	$42,760	$35,629	$43,246	$48,492	$35,917	$46,756	$50,513	$40,566
Indiana	$31,633	$36,812	$17,560	$55,456	$60,916	$31,591	$37,259	$37,516	$32,979	$42,089	$47,204	$34,539	$41,436	$46,274	$32,437
Iowa	$35,386	$39,164	$20,099	$51,569	$53,020	$37,697	$41,069	$41,538	$31,312	$40,827	$43,914	$31,929	$41,153	$44,257	$31,896
Kansas	$32,246	$37,540	$15,699	$46,288	$46,766	$39,740	$35,725	$36,105	$32,115	$41,900	$46,849	$31,626	$45,174	$50,481	$36,464
Kentucky	$25,822	$25,981	$21,602	$58,158	$60,077	$40,716	$32,423	$32,820	$30,313	$40,418	$43,946	$32,025	$38,709	$42,163	$32,290
Louisiana	$27,454	$27,575	$26,613	$67,149	$72,371	$40,470	$36,347	$36,644	$32,152	$50,981	$56,527	$33,339	$49,183	$51,890	$33,768
Maine	$27,354	$30,770	$19,023	$67,261	$67,261	-	$35,309	$36,451	$20,725	$43,238	$47,489	$30,864	$41,231	$45,349	$35,923
Maryland	$30,208	$31,624	$21,344	$38,713	$36,128	$76,258	$41,274	$41,476	$39,911	$52,411	$56,864	$46,609	$49,366	$51,486	$39,373
Massachusetts	$20,191	$21,141	$12,402	$51,332	$51,708	$49,036	$45,351	$45,710	$39,878	$55,487	$60,428	$45,484	$50,258	$51,690	$44,809
Michigan	$23,116	$28,623	$13,518	$56,846	$57,544	$40,268	$36,701	$37,223	$30,964	$46,629	$50,978	$35,884	$41,395	$47,079	$33,419
Minnesota	$31,838	$35,823	$20,770	$67,328	$69,555	$65,437	$45,301	$46,438	$31,749	$46,372	$49,822	$39,954	$47,155	$50,696	$40,567
Mississippi	$27,699	$30,660	$12,350	$68,511	$70,877	$30,958	$32,218	$32,687	$27,003	$33,917	$40,303	$25,752	$35,859	$41,600	$24,977
Missouri	$30,523	$31,161	$21,565	$50,918	$51,015	$46,838	$37,763	$38,703	$33,436	$40,552	$42,830	$31,971	$41,046	$45,256	$31,383
Montana	$30,437	$32,209	$15,301	$66,146	$71,779	$53,045	$36,436	$37,334	$30,335	$36,659	$39,225	$26,527	$41,418	$46,687	$27,070
Nebraska	$37,170	$40,092	$22,263	$51,250	$57,292	$8,979	$36,057	$36,175	$35,202	$37,046	$40,213	$31,566	$45,138	$46,693	$34,546
Nevada	$36,947	$40,422	$26,639	$66,050	$69,955	$51,887	$36,826	$37,093	$33,235	$36,081	$40,953	$30,291	$45,018	$46,898	$35,659
New Hampshire	$21,130	$30,257	$11,597	$110,062	$111,139	-	$43,858	$44,744	$39,866	$50,656	$56,481	$37,401	$52,150	$57,835	$39,521
New Jersey	$20,301	$25,038	$16,012	$77,219	$76,938	$170,309	$45,258	$46,274	$37,412	$51,927	$56,810	$47,704	$50,669	$52,006	$46,521
New Mexico	$21,790	$22,360	$20,899	$56,324	$58,549	$37,486	$30,744	$30,601	$31,625	$40,487	$47,226	$26,482	$40,820	$46,653	$30,903
New York	$26,200	$30,607	$14,697	$39,984	$41,327	$32,341	$40,502	$40,513	$40,406	$44,061	$48,616	$35,646	$46,042	$47,127	$42,134
North Carolina	$21,514	$22,280	$17,614	$51,944	$51,834	$61,283	$30,073	$30,085	$29,880	$40,859	$40,771	$29,783	$40,296	$41,825	$34,174
North Dakota	$40,896	$45,115	$13,601	$76,986	$81,384	$42,026	$45,246	$46,998	$32,023	$42,784	$47,836	$33,148	$47,439	$53,089	$35,558
Ohio	$27,477	$31,058	$13,908	$53,249	$54,124	$46,456	$38,521	$40,370	$30,505	$42,227	$46,984	$32,984	$41,898	$45,838	$34,793
Oklahoma	$27,192	$30,083	$19,488	$61,912	$66,259	$50,359	$32,303	$32,470	$31,216	$40,859	$42,041	$31,976	$41,381	$47,099	$30,359
Oregon	$26,323	$28,828	$18,532	$50,581	$51,029	$41,490	$39,655	$40,525	$32,812	$42,431	$46,754	$35,685	$41,185	$44,482	$36,149
Pennsylvania	$24,506	$26,918	$19,198	$56,703	$60,027	$45,619	$41,472	$41,732	$36,898	$45,160	$49,317	$36,079	$42,505	$46,840	$36,498
Rhode Island	$35,029	$24,250	$35,875	-	-	-	$42,132	$42,445	$40,774	$41,386	$45,910	$36,169	$42,103	$45,578	$35,491
South Carolina	$24,816	$25,912	$17,148	$60,027	$60,027	-	$31,177	$31,075	$31,988	$40,126	$42,171	$32,254	$41,570	$47,037	$31,513
South Dakota	$37,370	$40,225	$22,240	$50,250	$50,971	-	$37,203	$38,723	$25,597	$35,568	$39,464	$30,249	$42,086	$47,220	$28,049
Tennessee	$21,477	$21,453	$21,654	$56,161	$60,604	$33,500	$31,189	$31,137	$31,818	$36,910	$41,378	$30,320	$37,453	$40,010	$35,213
Texas	$25,419	$27,343	$20,007	$73,267	$75,856	$65,891	$31,514	$31,408	$33,179	$46,151	$50,714	$35,261	$43,498	$47,082	$35,710
Utah	$28,935	$31,491	$16,819	$71,012	$75,436	$36,736	$37,085	$38,090	$26,224	$36,673	$41,962	$26,790	$41,717	$51,005	$30,947
Vermont	$25,301	$30,376	$15,162	$34,676	$34,676	-	$38,183	$39,082	$36,348	$40,404	$41,807	$35,763	$44,980	$50,342	$30,528
Virginia	$25,464	$29,425	$16,091	$50,951	$51,228	$38,693	$36,366	$36,201	$37,486	$45,201	$49,099	$35,646	$43,306	$46,846	$36,129
Washington	$24,256	$27,495	$18,222	$66,204	$66,515	$32,602	$45,833	$46,403	$40,986	$55,601	$60,059	$45,388	$45,780	$48,495	$38,152
West Virginia	$26,027	$25,959	$26,750	$65,113	$65,675	$46,372	$36,955	$38,785	$30,853	$42,340	$46,545	$31,250	$41,337	$42,945	$30,755
Wisconsin	$26,748	$29,040	$16,389	$46,000	$46,042	$41,691	$42,110	$42,699	$35,803	$41,710	$45,942	$33,102	$44,855	$47,497	$38,941
Wyoming	$27,495	$29,657	$23,068	$82,123	$85,854	$57,231	$40,144	$41,488	$26,651	$49,403	$61,754	$23,977	$45,911	$51,797	$35,646

Table B-9. Median Annual Earnings—*Continued*

Median earnings in the past 12 months by gender and industry for employed persons age 16 and older

Geography	Retail trade Total:	Men	Women	All transportation and warehousing, and utilities Total:	Men	Women	Transportation and warehousing Total:	Men	Women	Utilities Total:	Men	Women	Information Total:	Men	Women
United States	$21,734	$26,473	$17,945	$42,308	$46,371	$34,996	$40,246	$41,866	$31,652	$66,027	$70,387	$52,656	$50,587	$58,416	$40,581
Alabama	$21,093	$24,687	$18,120	$46,889	$50,353	$36,549	$41,209	$42,287	$29,642	$63,914	$70,479	$48,457	$41,589	$51,495	$31,732
Alaska	$26,051	$29,801	$21,122	$45,400	$49,935	$31,570	$41,806	$47,544	$31,336	$62,588	$76,205	$46,839	$44,388	$56,802	$40,115
Arizona	$22,715	$26,486	$20,230	$41,842	$42,571	$37,744	$40,014	$40,762	$35,339	$61,462	$65,099	$50,276	$40,915	$45,631	$31,808
Arkansas	$22,558	$26,533	$18,775	$43,399	$46,942	$32,814	$41,889	$46,045	$32,090	$51,101	$52,417	$41,110	$40,915	$45,631	$29,624
California	$22,979	$26,800	$20,054	$41,186	$42,034	$36,246	$36,630	$38,265	$31,775	$80,394	$85,056	$70,264	$61,973	$67,298	$55,338
Colorado	$23,151	$28,024	$20,002	$47,055	$49,062	$41,329	$41,848	$43,729	$37,040	$67,161	$70,665	$60,564	$55,285	$63,271	$43,602
Connecticut	$23,260	$29,017	$19,193	$49,246	$56,317	$31,856	$41,319	$48,634	$29,761	$90,117	$92,174	$64,340	$57,131	$70,002	$42,333
Delaware	$24,603	$32,157	$20,106	$51,219	$52,468	$41,563	$48,395	$50,732	$41,276	$66,839	$67,448	$59,796	$50,101	$53,843	$40,148
District of Columbia	$18,392	$25,922	$13,971	$39,247	$41,815	$38,125	$37,730	$39,304	$31,908	$112,039	$111,842	$162,683	$70,213	$75,844	$65,110
Florida	$21,320	$24,986	$18,119	$39,023	$40,654	$35,053	$36,364	$37,793	$31,547	$52,225	$55,637	$49,829	$41,990	$46,449	$36,538
Georgia	$21,373	$26,783	$17,101	$40,940	$43,341	$32,328	$38,240	$41,386	$31,031	$56,034	$60,512	$46,384	$56,499	$68,947	$42,122
Hawaii	$25,703	$29,347	$22,603	$43,116	$44,782	$40,994	$40,916	$41,974	$38,546	$68,840	$80,247	$61,965	$52,002	$60,361	$47,378
Idaho	$21,286	$27,442	$17,462	$40,813	$44,324	$24,651	$40,051	$42,241	$22,152	$46,193	$52,132	$31,702	$30,805	$36,011	$23,327
Illinois	$21,714	$26,899	$17,935	$43,370	$46,910	$35,784	$40,922	$42,193	$32,758	$76,616	$80,989	$60,593	$47,752	$60,172	$36,919
Indiana	$20,557	$25,974	$16,313	$41,555	$46,260	$30,127	$40,040	$42,163	$27,105	$60,839	$67,405	$40,207	$35,579	$41,487	$29,881
Iowa	$20,672	$26,033	$16,365	$47,436	$50,795	$32,261	$45,263	$48,388	$30,543	$60,348	$61,846	$48,964	$37,085	$47,138	$30,469
Kansas	$20,785	$26,085	$16,833	$46,213	$49,578	$35,632	$41,745	$46,252	$31,728	$60,428	$61,425	$50,867	$48,691	$64,893	$35,475
Kentucky	$20,163	$25,562	$16,285	$38,755	$42,206	$28,951	$36,505	$40,804	$27,141	$56,778	$61,509	$38,547	$36,057	$40,343	$27,389
Louisiana	$20,318	$26,342	$16,743	$46,509	$50,401	$35,623	$44,172	$48,049	$32,394	$55,712	$57,220	$42,484	$37,487	$45,713	$31,062
Maine	$20,677	$27,806	$15,954	$41,679	$45,956	$31,529	$37,200	$41,433	$29,358	$60,098	$61,758	$50,038	$36,220	$37,395	$32,297
Maryland	$22,306	$27,065	$19,935	$46,134	$47,646	$40,683	$41,774	$43,410	$36,452	$70,261	$70,817	$64,493	$62,031	$70,232	$51,237
Massachusetts	$23,749	$31,203	$17,069	$46,167	$50,133	$36,871	$40,647	$42,581	$31,437	$77,031	$80,821	$70,909	$61,194	$72,158	$50,138
Michigan	$19,210	$24,251	$15,639	$43,371	$46,713	$35,411	$39,957	$41,412	$31,249	$72,728	$80,265	$60,024	$40,947	$50,067	$30,656
Minnesota	$22,415	$28,530	$18,854	$46,921	$49,690	$39,918	$42,292	$45,535	$36,807	$71,769	$73,832	$62,060	$45,150	$50,688	$37,702
Mississippi	$20,611	$25,670	$17,496	$41,557	$45,529	$34,414	$40,368	$41,548	$34,674	$52,319	$61,841	$32,350	$30,486	$40,836	$22,267
Missouri	$20,900	$24,705	$16,874	$42,380	$46,581	$32,264	$40,886	$42,954	$30,823	$62,212	$65,833	$50,595	$45,282	$51,712	$36,776
Montana	$21,724	$24,754	$18,481	$47,346	$51,832	$31,002	$45,105	$50,772	$29,369	$66,489	$75,681	$46,728	$35,369	$40,359	$34,506
Nebraska	$21,377	$25,459	$18,183	$52,463	$55,812	$45,350	$51,226	$52,411	$37,027	$62,114	$66,451	$52,362	$42,292	$51,298	$27,229
Nevada	$22,037	$25,784	$19,713	$39,659	$41,477	$32,502	$34,500	$37,645	$30,496	$77,113	$78,261	$66,857	$45,009	$47,965	$36,582
New Hampshire	$24,321	$30,696	$18,344	$50,754	$55,298	$39,089	$46,207	$50,298	$31,535	$71,113	$71,653	$56,318	$50,118	$75,925	$37,284
New Jersey	$24,149	$29,881	$20,205	$45,735	$50,140	$36,371	$41,120	$45,189	$31,300	$75,627	$81,270	$66,067	$71,397	$84,401	$56,207
New Mexico	$20,688	$22,094	$18,559	$40,137	$43,520	$31,128	$36,121	$37,449	$30,958	$49,399	$56,958	$35,853	$40,632	$48,879	$24,406
New York	$22,090	$26,720	$17,648	$41,679	$43,150	$36,562	$38,666	$40,481	$33,341	$76,236	$80,762	$62,437	$58,640	$65,406	$51,480
North Carolina	$20,634	$25,211	$16,596	$41,870	$45,290	$34,154	$40,259	$41,431	$31,232	$57,445	$65,167	$46,094	$46,849	$55,001	$40,309
North Dakota	$25,915	$30,586	$21,946	$54,800	$62,239	$38,142	$49,022	$56,206	$33,257	$65,351	$76,487	$43,103	$41,615	$53,873	$25,779
Ohio	$20,969	$26,324	$17,011	$41,837	$45,333	$33,295	$39,085	$41,219	$31,150	$67,405	$70,696	$52,478	$42,441	$51,326	$35,365
Oklahoma	$20,820	$25,877	$17,078	$48,756	$50,909	$37,225	$46,155	$50,050	$35,662	$54,641	$56,863	$47,686	$35,857	$42,293	$28,147
Oregon	$22,848	$25,382	$20,662	$45,425	$46,666	$41,107	$41,171	$42,943	$36,011	$64,847	$67,331	$56,363	$41,583	$53,834	$29,870
Pennsylvania	$20,969	$25,963	$16,705	$42,208	$46,969	$30,069	$38,812	$42,213	$26,600	$66,470	$71,309	$52,062	$47,455	$55,589	$36,924
Rhode Island	$23,664	$31,886	$16,792	$48,471	$50,246	$36,849	$41,810	$42,165	$36,429	$76,347	$80,610	$65,897	$51,366	$52,914	$47,470
South Carolina	$20,092	$24,485	$16,648	$42,246	$48,628	$31,065	$37,004	$41,623	$28,918	$60,578	$66,641	$40,962	$40,111	$45,848	$33,851
South Dakota	$22,290	$26,449	$18,281	$49,486	$52,101	$35,390	$47,012	$50,087	$31,961	$65,643	$71,415	$36,863	$35,572	$45,293	$30,259
Tennessee	$20,799	$26,130	$16,763	$40,335	$44,237	$30,022	$36,776	$41,382	$26,801	$56,366	$62,206	$41,644	$42,697	$51,147	$32,326
Texas	$21,460	$26,061	$17,812	$42,291	$46,729	$33,781	$41,367	$45,201	$32,084	$55,936	$61,518	$41,084	$49,212	$57,350	$36,718
Utah	$21,543	$26,274	$17,230	$44,152	$50,642	$30,291	$40,813	$47,270	$29,478	$65,120	$70,583	$37,679	$36,062	$44,864	$17,280
Vermont	$21,348	$26,611	$17,324	$41,823	$45,278	$39,563	$38,253	$40,481	$35,141	$60,226	$62,130	$56,034	$43,410	$51,436	$32,407
Virginia	$21,810	$25,485	$18,466	$42,225	$45,902	$36,314	$37,930	$40,881	$32,539	$69,812	$70,749	$65,199	$59,446	$70,666	$45,737
Washington	$27,235	$32,346	$21,927	$50,146	$52,312	$38,591	$44,879	$49,994	$36,397	$75,388	$80,487	$63,843	$59,259	$72,210	$39,381
West Virginia	$20,459	$25,690	$15,725	$49,236	$51,765	$31,306	$42,086	$47,867	$30,829	$62,477	$68,460	$41,250	$32,172	$38,532	$22,504
Wisconsin	$21,739	$26,921	$17,319	$43,533	$47,384	$33,020	$40,478	$42,117	$30,982	$70,083	$71,826	$60,212	$40,800	$48,115	$31,807
Wyoming	$22,125	$28,432	$20,842	$57,342	$63,673	$31,884	$52,316	$61,174	$23,729	$66,173	$71,515	$56,338	$31,959	$41,451	$20,997

Table B-9. Median Annual Earnings—*Continued*

	Median earnings in the past 12 months by gender and industry for employed persons age 16 and older														
	Finance and insurance, and real estate and rental and leasing									Professional, scientific, and management, and administrative and waste management services					
	All finance and insurance, and real estate and rental and leasing			Finance and insurance			Real estate and rental and leasing			All professional, scientific, and management, and administrative and waste management services			Professional, scientific, and technical services		
Geography	Total:	Men	Women	Total:	Men	Women	Total:	Men	Women	Total:	Men	Women	Total:	Men	Women
United States	$47,740	$61,033	$41,069	$51,681	$75,486	$42,177	$38,070	$41,296	$35,420	$41,900	$50,763	$35,124	$60,983	$75,852	$45,830
Alabama	$39,959	$51,263	$34,031	$41,966	$69,532	$35,040	$31,653	$32,772	$30,918	$36,634	$45,304	$30,193	$51,997	$72,372	$37,337
Alaska	$42,470	$51,433	$37,496	$46,177	$72,778	$41,563	$35,538	$46,887	$26,647	$49,604	$57,132	$41,212	$61,412	$70,917	$44,423
Arizona	$42,923	$50,900	$40,790	$45,774	$54,325	$41,678	$38,782	$41,985	$36,306	$32,355	$36,969	$28,604	$52,334	$66,615	$39,471
Arkansas	$36,215	$48,852	$31,924	$37,481	$55,913	$33,424	$29,603	$35,224	$26,177	$30,539	$33,017	$26,650	$45,644	$55,151	$33,839
California	$51,531	$61,252	$46,117	$60,048	$77,073	$50,098	$41,369	$43,677	$39,382	$46,092	$51,352	$39,599	$68,790	$82,200	$52,078
Colorado	$50,211	$60,341	$43,459	$51,693	$66,421	$45,435	$45,054	$50,261	$40,081	$50,709	$60,904	$40,146	$64,811	$77,411	$49,145
Connecticut	$71,948	$99,227	$56,082	$81,241	$111,918	$60,867	$44,861	$50,478	$41,601	$50,028	$56,689	$40,789	$66,755	$81,899	$50,155
Delaware	$51,405	$61,910	$43,844	$53,786	$70,727	$45,031	$45,383	$46,221	$43,583	$45,879	$51,324	$41,490	$62,207	$73,761	$51,073
District of Columbia	$71,352	$80,641	$57,398	$91,301	$101,690	$81,065	$45,882	$52,134	$41,945	$66,889	$76,677	$57,377	$80,353	$87,389	$67,344
Florida	$41,240	$46,993	$37,970	$45,453	$60,642	$40,246	$34,069	$33,617	$34,306	$32,481	$36,981	$29,593	$48,932	$61,652	$37,018
Georgia	$46,191	$56,493	$40,222	$50,523	$69,974	$41,430	$36,322	$40,510	$33,564	$40,890	$50,048	$32,239	$61,479	$75,469	$46,542
Hawaii	$41,328	$42,378	$40,756	$47,903	$61,810	$42,018	$36,557	$37,006	$35,755	$36,807	$40,807	$33,326	$51,145	$70,955	$41,788
Idaho	$32,453	$50,352	$29,284	$36,190	$53,884	$30,856	$28,504	$32,480	$23,501	$32,046	$46,165	$23,444	$52,393	$67,729	$32,656
Illinois	$52,882	$72,970	$44,006	$58,732	$85,822	$46,045	$41,628	$46,993	$37,115	$46,524	$55,634	$37,489	$62,427	$77,543	$49,366
Indiana	$40,174	$51,947	$35,495	$42,041	$65,211	$36,633	$31,519	$32,440	$30,373	$35,419	$41,663	$29,829	$49,765	$61,872	$37,466
Iowa	$44,719	$57,968	$38,977	$46,378	$62,159	$40,109	$29,764	$32,345	$26,333	$32,455	$43,332	$27,032	$47,277	$60,068	$35,519
Kansas	$41,926	$60,237	$36,299	$43,673	$66,493	$36,588	$36,829	$40,000	$32,475	$40,892	$52,356	$31,066	$55,479	$75,455	$38,943
Kentucky	$41,198	$51,009	$37,189	$42,746	$60,872	$38,629	$33,772	$37,541	$31,567	$32,049	$37,259	$27,358	$46,937	$60,376	$36,346
Louisiana	$37,790	$51,496	$33,709	$39,975	$66,486	$35,258	$35,779	$42,343	$30,159	$37,418	$46,796	$30,415	$50,308	$62,209	$36,743
Maine	$45,028	$52,277	$40,277	$49,537	$60,432	$42,115	$33,903	$41,141	$31,353	$37,468	$45,969	$32,220	$50,639	$62,291	$39,263
Maryland	$53,905	$66,104	$50,085	$56,787	$77,461	$50,041	$50,673	$50,956	$50,244	$60,015	$67,334	$50,026	$75,499	$90,268	$60,449
Massachusetts	$61,963	$80,653	$51,824	$70,332	$95,617	$55,100	$47,114	$50,245	$45,474	$60,395	$70,393	$49,519	$72,099	$86,235	$56,551
Michigan	$41,028	$51,283	$36,109	$45,828	$65,166	$39,905	$31,027	$33,679	$27,077	$36,586	$43,366	$30,505	$50,842	$62,131	$38,008
Minnesota	$52,243	$66,421	$46,823	$57,111	$77,409	$49,085	$39,179	$40,868	$36,704	$45,759	$51,859	$38,561	$58,773	$70,601	$45,969
Mississippi	$34,685	$42,344	$31,216	$35,821	$50,544	$31,787	$31,384	$36,277	$27,153	$29,337	$32,467	$25,177	$42,511	$56,003	$28,260
Missouri	$42,398	$57,197	$37,000	$46,687	$69,530	$38,314	$34,294	$36,558	$31,863	$38,832	$47,209	$31,353	$52,347	$70,466	$39,136
Montana	$37,651	$44,161	$35,482	$40,267	$60,553	$37,154	$28,218	$36,532	$21,077	$36,633	$47,478	$29,919	$49,588	$66,366	$38,443
Nebraska	$43,441	$58,812	$37,994	$46,147	$61,893	$39,675	$35,941	$39,113	$35,537	$36,257	$46,441	$29,263	$51,128	$66,267	$36,193
Nevada	$38,396	$42,321	$35,964	$39,686	$55,703	$35,881	$37,048	$40,041	$36,135	$32,679	$40,127	$28,973	$50,400	$65,358	$35,328
New Hampshire	$51,558	$67,401	$44,992	$60,446	$91,572	$48,314	$36,374	$37,676	$36,126	$51,290	$63,354	$38,366	$65,736	$83,011	$46,960
New Jersey	$71,667	$95,928	$52,044	$82,497	$110,036	$57,368	$46,247	$52,189	$37,298	$56,197	$69,119	$45,153	$72,984	$90,378	$54,513
New Mexico	$36,497	$40,984	$34,516	$37,340	$50,615	$34,657	$29,917	$28,962	$33,413	$41,185	$50,005	$32,058	$61,219	$76,865	$42,006
New York	$61,548	$76,134	$51,313	$73,505	$101,189	$55,279	$42,842	$45,728	$41,058	$50,579	$56,615	$42,171	$64,444	$77,359	$52,027
North Carolina	$47,685	$63,489	$40,922	$53,423	$80,664	$42,389	$35,869	$38,223	$31,824	$36,949	$42,279	$30,972	$57,523	$74,385	$42,398
North Dakota	$42,369	$59,433	$39,226	$41,843	$61,537	$39,226	$46,447	$51,236	$45,994	$37,002	$47,105	$31,965	$47,569	$66,003	$35,359
Ohio	$45,753	$56,417	$38,990	$50,007	$67,007	$41,060	$33,379	$37,009	$30,224	$37,391	$45,616	$31,317	$52,825	$66,599	$40,883
Oklahoma	$35,349	$45,513	$31,539	$36,389	$51,574	$31,984	$32,204	$36,513	$29,881	$32,171	$38,524	$29,334	$46,366	$61,681	$32,967
Oregon	$42,491	$51,010	$40,203	$49,436	$65,239	$41,749	$33,915	$36,069	$31,199	$38,542	$45,247	$30,765	$53,516	$69,119	$39,971
Pennsylvania	$48,548	$61,329	$41,176	$51,272	$71,606	$42,284	$36,866	$41,793	$32,200	$42,372	$51,434	$35,137	$60,013	$72,363	$42,883
Rhode Island	$49,846	$65,828	$42,673	$54,174	$76,412	$45,560	$39,077	$43,409	$32,953	$42,499	$51,420	$40,821	$55,328	$80,954	$44,479
South Carolina	$38,762	$47,631	$35,127	$41,205	$56,034	$36,735	$32,770	$36,791	$30,756	$32,466	$40,293	$26,884	$46,972	$62,359	$36,364
South Dakota	$40,406	$55,469	$35,077	$40,945	$60,291	$35,616	$31,684	$36,717	$25,888	$32,255	$40,690	$27,477	$42,321	$51,961	$34,040
Tennessee	$39,265	$51,283	$34,324	$41,349	$61,665	$35,078	$32,764	$33,781	$32,047	$34,823	$41,147	$28,422	$50,247	$66,109	$36,185
Texas	$44,228	$55,233	$39,463	$47,013	$68,900	$40,418	$38,088	$41,135	$35,018	$40,068	$47,394	$31,606	$60,130	$75,597	$42,917
Utah	$41,611	$61,067	$33,025	$44,981	$65,562	$36,545	$34,832	$50,290	$28,277	$37,188	$48,289	$25,878	$51,759	$64,336	$36,495
Vermont	$40,035	$47,040	$37,983	$46,885	$60,967	$40,295	$31,878	$31,709	$32,131	$39,253	$47,157	$35,155	$50,912	$65,593	$39,542
Virginia	$50,772	$69,413	$42,811	$52,342	$81,758	$45,543	$44,234	$50,407	$40,081	$62,083	$76,142	$46,083	$80,580	$95,004	$61,249
Washington	$49,246	$60,658	$44,084	$54,238	$78,685	$45,961	$40,532	$40,949	$40,052	$54,938	$66,843	$41,370	$72,191	$90,614	$52,148
West Virginia	$35,531	$50,639	$30,159	$36,409	$60,766	$31,344	$30,506	$37,457	$26,076	$30,976	$33,885	$28,049	$40,120	$52,226	$30,614
Wisconsin	$42,455	$59,258	$39,206	$46,262	$66,480	$40,429	$35,265	$37,370	$32,821	$37,571	$44,948	$31,059	$50,887	$62,467	$39,939
Wyoming	$36,438	$61,123	$32,744	$37,360	$92,003	$35,184	$32,268	$38,676	$31,625	$41,253	$47,114	$33,396	$51,110	$63,589	$37,600

Table B-9. Median Annual Earnings—*Continued*

| | Professional, scientific, and management, and administrative and waste management services | | | | | | Educational services, and health care and social assistance | | | | | | | | |
| | Management of companies and enterprises | | | Administrative and support and waste management services | | | All educational services, and health care and social assistance | | | Educational services | | | Health care and social assistance | | |
Geography	Total:	Men	Women	Total:	Men	Women	Total:	Men	Women	Total:	Men	Women	Total:	Men	Women
United States	$59,817	$80,428	$50,223	$24,551	$26,456	$21,556	$35,506	$44,404	$32,195	$37,766	$42,417	$35,755	$33,393	$46,057	$31,443
Alabama	$39,989	$7,214	$48,974	$21,617	$24,008	$20,156	$31,736	$42,255	$30,220	$36,724	$40,851	$35,679	$30,314	$46,579	$27,207
Alaska	$56,511	$56,142	$87,770	$33,875	$35,509	$32,361	$41,089	$50,006	$37,590	$45,992	$48,235	$41,490	$39,825	$50,693	$36,649
Arizona	$45,179	$75,788	$38,674	$22,475	$23,523	$21,327	$33,031	$40,304	$31,580	$34,326	$39,928	$31,899	$32,398	$40,762	$31,431
Arkansas	$69,462	$85,689	$31,954	$20,459	$22,371	$15,368	$30,084	$39,774	$28,245	$33,677	$40,483	$32,176	$27,444	$38,179	$26,488
California	$66,760	$89,115	$51,379	$23,995	$25,575	$21,319	$37,952	$47,063	$35,275	$40,556	$46,790	$36,711	$36,715	$47,425	$34,332
Colorado	$71,205	$90,077	$51,640	$28,067	$30,792	$24,506	$35,674	$44,441	$32,470	$35,127	$40,102	$31,993	$36,156	$51,281	$33,072
Connecticut	$66,150	$52,333	$66,700	$27,218	$29,213	$24,191	$42,268	$50,467	$40,354	$46,320	$49,676	$44,506	$40,756	$51,671	$38,298
Delaware	$68,556	-	-	$27,516	$28,898	$24,312	$40,430	$42,040	$39,490	$42,820	$42,223	$43,534	$37,556	$41,663	$36,859
District of Columbia	$76,076	-	$76,087	$30,581	$36,159	$25,906	$41,806	$51,041	$38,167	$41,999	$55,379	$37,108	$41,663	$50,637	$40,151
Florida	$46,917	$70,538	$45,173	$23,175	$25,232	$21,491	$35,104	$41,215	$32,109	$37,375	$39,706	$36,680	$32,438	$44,281	$31,002
Georgia	$67,491	$78,114	$61,461	$22,399	$24,551	$20,797	$35,187	$43,877	$31,994	$37,648	$42,150	$35,594	$32,384	$47,206	$31,119
Hawaii	$45,118	-	$19,661	$29,555	$30,740	$27,205	$38,512	$48,565	$35,633	$38,796	$46,880	$35,303	$38,333	$52,793	$35,801
Idaho	$51,948	$56,910	$50,552	$20,639	$22,615	$17,856	$29,641	$36,201	$26,616	$29,573	$30,849	$27,485	$29,673	$46,024	$26,445
Illinois	$82,132	$100,374	$68,576	$24,771	$26,955	$21,717	$35,566	$45,664	$32,275	$40,452	$45,848	$37,395	$32,023	$45,333	$31,011
Indiana	$44,817	$67,485	$40,316	$22,337	$25,966	$21,220	$31,597	$41,158	$30,151	$31,597	$38,608	$28,684	$31,597	$42,265	$30,389
Iowa	$37,341	$53,102	$35,169	$20,231	$21,431	$18,595	$31,048	$41,455	$29,118	$34,166	$40,473	$31,541	$30,185	$42,265	$27,992
Kansas	$79,688	$104,872	$52,390	$23,454	$26,599	$21,070	$32,240	$42,984	$30,500	$35,324	$42,148	$31,462	$31,477	$45,258	$30,163
Kentucky	$43,173	$120,756	$36,835	$21,981	$24,030	$20,567	$32,016	$41,221	$30,779	$34,181	$38,064	$31,851	$31,585	$45,025	$30,402
Louisiana	$45,476	$60,959	$30,330	$24,173	$26,369	$22,113	$32,046	$43,253	$30,603	$36,734	$39,707	$35,977	$30,744	$50,421	$28,204
Maine	$37,639	-	$37,639	$25,653	$28,345	$21,445	$31,964	$38,452	$30,913	$33,188	$38,889	$30,854	$31,546	$37,324	$30,938
Maryland	$59,945	$84,059	$58,439	$29,608	$32,006	$24,921	$41,952	$51,327	$40,384	$46,483	$50,830	$44,672	$40,377	$52,042	$37,373
Massachusetts	$80,423	$106,915	$51,712	$31,033	$33,975	$26,115	$41,417	$49,706	$39,868	$45,684	$50,361	$42,423	$40,181	$47,945	$37,443
Michigan	$65,471	$71,250	$53,298	$23,286	$25,656	$21,166	$35,113	$43,915	$30,305	$35,348	$42,574	$31,389	$35,200	$45,200	$29,971
Minnesota	$76,020	$92,482	$62,340	$27,007	$28,207	$26,017	$35,681	$42,363	$32,431	$37,051	$42,035	$34,888	$35,027	$42,978	$32,141
Mississippi	$64,528	$74,598	$24,527	$20,971	$23,327	$16,337	$31,623	$37,423	$30,582	$32,429	$35,501	$31,759	$30,902	$42,401	$29,217
Missouri	$52,072	$60,765	$45,366	$24,386	$26,884	$21,522	$31,646	$40,632	$30,392	$35,671	$40,063	$34,329	$30,296	$41,483	$27,980
Montana	-	-	-	$20,568	$21,562	$18,000	$30,140	$39,967	$27,150	$30,812	$33,236	$29,402	$29,381	$48,087	$26,487
Nebraska	$55,360	$42,391	$55,462	$22,076	$26,579	$19,346	$32,221	$41,460	$30,930	$37,490	$44,351	$35,206	$30,732	$40,316	$29,855
Nevada	$40,908	$41,499	$36,799	$26,024	$27,367	$23,281	$37,116	$44,026	$35,743	$40,280	$42,491	$37,643	$35,921	$45,513	$33,746
New Hampshire	$83,125	$85,077	$43,274	$29,163	$31,774	$23,903	$38,316	$45,854	$36,249	$37,203	$43,295	$35,035	$39,468	$49,501	$36,910
New Jersey	$53,338	$84,633	$45,707	$30,123	$31,564	$25,105	$42,121	$53,159	$40,039	$50,385	$54,202	$48,099	$38,319	$51,986	$35,900
New Mexico	-	-	-	$21,505	$22,476	$16,792	$29,677	$32,197	$27,395	$31,110	$32,606	$30,475	$27,695	$31,913	$26,488
New York	$62,434	$69,188	$60,644	$27,411	$30,871	$23,614	$39,009	$48,151	$36,154	$45,289	$51,016	$41,774	$36,183	$46,056	$33,428
North Carolina	$43,894	$70,310	$40,850	$21,629	$23,938	$18,606	$33,575	$40,292	$31,948	$34,695	$37,292	$33,188	$32,489	$42,037	$31,384
North Dakota	-	-	-	$26,753	$28,639	$24,459	$33,885	$47,100	$31,634	$37,059	$46,891	$34,287	$32,201	$47,296	$30,827
Ohio	$51,342	$100,735	$41,181	$23,943	$25,782	$21,712	$33,011	$42,786	$31,134	$36,761	$42,923	$32,625	$31,859	$42,629	$30,680
Oklahoma	$47,948	$50,728	$42,325	$23,161	$25,558	$20,705	$30,816	$39,332	$28,609	$31,319	$36,392	$29,775	$30,483	$42,465	$28,248
Oregon	$52,576	$37,325	$60,313	$22,437	$24,254	$21,460	$32,050	$40,152	$30,758	$32,791	$37,917	$30,735	$31,820	$40,810	$30,765
Pennsylvania	$53,058	$50,337	$53,988	$26,043	$28,225	$22,410	$35,468	$46,160	$32,127	$40,742	$47,776	$36,735	$32,641	$44,206	$31,353
Rhode Island	$75,923	$76,409	$53,323	$21,967	$22,031	$21,759	$40,888	$45,938	$40,034	$46,449	$46,312	$46,608	$38,001	$45,603	$36,641
South Carolina	$86,987	$112,124	$51,431	$22,706	$25,712	$20,353	$32,115	$41,077	$30,936	$35,007	$38,787	$32,460	$31,367	$45,815	$30,077
South Dakota	-	-	-	$24,155	$27,990	$20,572	$31,198	$35,996	$30,210	$32,077	$36,515	$31,414	$30,638	$35,591	$29,335
Tennessee	$64,600	$66,388	$55,340	$22,469	$24,116	$21,038	$33,331	$43,553	$31,145	$35,332	$40,376	$32,360	$32,284	$49,250	$30,603
Texas	$61,448	$75,484	$50,803	$22,727	$25,021	$20,300	$35,186	$45,057	$31,673	$38,851	$41,778	$36,834	$32,047	$49,152	$30,231
Utah	$32,924	$58,712	$31,572	$23,338	$26,506	$20,275	$28,554	$40,580	$25,654	$27,022	$36,792	$22,405	$29,565	$46,125	$26,683
Vermont	$96,681	$95,776	-	$26,060	$30,248	$17,289	$35,831	$44,116	$32,674	$36,887	$44,506	$33,522	$34,771	$42,584	$32,434
Virginia	$79,430	$81,895	$75,830	$27,736	$30,982	$24,421	$35,874	$45,816	$32,524	$39,902	$44,205	$37,253	$32,988	$49,390	$31,476
Washington	$55,019	$70,650	$49,384	$27,976	$31,357	$24,434	$36,387	$47,475	$32,715	$35,968	$44,418	$31,760	$36,565	$50,380	$33,657
West Virginia	$105,806	-	-	$22,879	$24,947	$21,995	$30,711	$38,013	$28,419	$35,313	$38,535	$31,841	$28,846	$37,547	$27,305
Wisconsin	$50,613	$102,083	$41,706	$24,032	$26,734	$21,146	$34,494	$42,437	$31,776	$37,253	$41,791	$35,591	$32,190	$44,501	$31,110
Wyoming	-	-	-	$29,254	$30,284	$20,571	$31,452	$49,266	$29,663	$29,702	$45,201	$25,880	$32,339	$56,117	$31,516

Table B-9. Median Annual Earnings—*Continued*

Median earnings in the past 12 months by gender and industry for employed persons age 16 and older

Geography	All arts, entertainment, and recreation, and accommodations and food services Total:	Men	Women	Arts, entertainment, and recreation Total:	Men	Women	Accommodation and food services Total:	Men	Women	Other services except public administration Total:	Men	Women	Public administration Total:	Men	Women
United States	$16,153	$19,058	$13,899	$21,072	$24,257	$17,329	$15,420	$17,500	$13,225	$23,410	$31,120	$18,487	$51,852	$60,564	$44,748
Alabama	$12,032	$13,458	$11,487	$17,601	$19,065	$14,069	$11,794	$12,342	$11,406	$22,354	$27,979	$17,324	$46,710	$52,369	$39,748
Alaska	$19,163	$19,408	$19,000	$18,819	$11,031	$30,405	$19,217	$20,373	$18,386	$29,319	$40,615	$27,631	$56,552	$61,315	$51,522
Arizona	$16,011	$17,587	$14,521	$21,571	$26,968	$17,074	$14,888	$15,750	$13,994	$23,101	$29,997	$18,617	$47,485	$55,451	$40,086
Arkansas	$11,656	$13,571	$10,646	$13,523	$15,529	$10,870	$11,413	$12,830	$10,620	$22,750	$27,274	$19,407	$34,656	$38,203	$31,651
California	$18,671	$21,451	$16,073	$25,200	$29,875	$20,998	$17,147	$20,003	$15,285	$22,242	$29,813	$18,074	$60,982	$72,601	$49,338
Colorado	$17,485	$20,800	$15,127	$22,242	$26,158	$18,053	$16,553	$19,655	$14,430	$25,587	$32,665	$20,561	$55,352	$61,727	$48,786
Connecticut	$17,999	$22,147	$15,767	$20,311	$24,361	$16,630	$17,393	$21,653	$15,580	$25,603	$31,444	$21,076	$62,319	$69,964	$55,349
Delaware	$15,973	$16,807	$15,541	$17,115	$20,425	$15,148	$15,697	$15,914	$15,605	$23,980	$35,615	$17,759	$48,024	$53,905	$44,520
District of Columbia	$25,373	$26,012	$24,408	$35,197	$36,182	$32,917	$22,436	$23,216	$21,938	$54,235	$65,760	$51,673	$86,756	$89,031	$85,254
Florida	$18,585	$20,864	$16,617	$22,268	$24,738	$20,528	$17,414	$20,056	$16,017	$21,119	$26,663	$16,928	$46,472	$52,073	$39,318
Georgia	$14,268	$17,286	$12,157	$19,433	$24,057	$12,303	$13,570	$16,354	$12,137	$22,310	$29,538	$17,728	$42,830	$47,622	$38,631
Hawaii	$25,271	$26,002	$24,387	$25,379	$30,093	$22,505	$25,244	$25,334	$25,165	$28,420	$31,275	$25,966	$51,470	$56,408	$45,875
Idaho	$12,068	$14,673	$10,928	$17,284	$20,549	$15,476	$11,552	$13,469	$10,735	$18,475	$31,209	$13,694	$41,121	$49,105	$32,132
Illinois	$16,299	$19,277	$13,770	$17,404	$21,236	$14,702	$16,106	$18,812	$13,631	$24,793	$31,774	$20,189	$60,612	$67,438	$49,666
Indiana	$12,013	$13,700	$11,217	$15,930	$18,361	$13,713	$11,668	$12,959	$10,939	$24,359	$33,596	$17,282	$42,076	$51,359	$35,869
Iowa	$12,907	$15,671	$11,561	$16,517	$21,995	$11,928	$12,475	$14,670	$11,496	$22,961	$32,160	$16,647	$50,309	$55,970	$44,033
Kansas	$12,337	$14,282	$11,751	$15,911	$21,068	$10,784	$12,172	$12,973	$11,860	$22,658	$30,656	$16,978	$44,203	$49,679	$40,266
Kentucky	$12,190	$14,234	$11,270	$16,668	$20,666	$12,163	$11,876	$13,158	$11,196	$22,690	$30,985	$17,499	$40,994	$46,172	$36,782
Louisiana	$13,701	$16,143	$12,315	$19,459	$20,632	$18,678	$12,307	$15,017	$11,776	$21,822	$33,452	$16,559	$41,802	$47,041	$36,093
Maine	$15,378	$18,042	$12,761	$20,948	$27,251	$9,532	$14,533	$16,347	$13,036	$25,771	$35,061	$18,508	$45,863	$50,903	$41,199
Maryland	$18,546	$21,887	$15,959	$24,833	$31,788	$20,190	$17,259	$20,747	$15,600	$31,104	$38,234	$25,628	$80,098	$86,113	$71,863
Massachusetts	$16,975	$21,193	$13,251	$17,275	$23,317	$11,965	$16,900	$21,004	$13,481	$25,755	$36,070	$21,077	$65,151	$71,493	$53,961
Michigan	$12,116	$13,401	$11,546	$16,285	$17,442	$15,271	$11,799	$12,499	$11,298	$21,531	$30,505	$15,914	$51,443	$58,752	$44,067
Minnesota	$16,216	$18,649	$14,329	$20,647	$21,444	$19,635	$15,298	$17,305	$13,203	$26,360	$35,634	$21,272	$52,904	$61,077	$48,765
Mississippi	$14,911	$17,174	$13,229	$22,864	$25,326	$21,427	$12,267	$13,083	$11,932	$24,504	$30,495	$16,080	$34,955	$40,440	$31,086
Missouri	$12,623	$13,194	$12,375	$15,969	$16,538	$15,315	$12,264	$12,406	$12,172	$22,545	$31,363	$18,261	$41,059	$46,396	$35,906
Montana	$14,066	$13,863	$14,181	$17,265	$21,417	$15,454	$13,168	$12,703	$13,551	$26,159	$32,233	$18,795	$46,327	$51,880	$37,652
Nebraska	$12,110	$15,781	$10,601	$14,598	$20,830	$10,776	$11,894	$15,292	$10,587	$26,577	$36,116	$18,949	$45,788	$54,741	$36,535
Nevada	$28,322	$30,911	$25,506	$30,954	$32,218	$28,650	$26,790	$30,316	$23,519	$23,559	$28,803	$19,065	$56,723	$64,947	$46,846
New Hampshire	$13,560	$15,632	$12,061	$10,744	$10,849	$10,538	$15,122	$17,101	$12,287	$30,488	$37,395	$22,438	$52,479	$62,267	$45,787
New Jersey	$17,392	$21,296	$14,295	$20,847	$22,768	$17,699	$16,935	$21,065	$13,517	$24,042	$35,253	$17,345	$65,591	$79,077	$53,745
New Mexico	$15,211	$15,580	$14,900	$21,522	$25,078	$20,684	$13,543	$13,712	$13,406	$21,089	$28,994	$17,087	$44,983	$49,397	$41,263
New York	$19,646	$21,803	$16,134	$22,966	$26,149	$21,147	$18,357	$21,180	$15,328	$23,815	$31,424	$18,707	$61,727	$70,482	$51,836
North Carolina	$13,418	$16,395	$11,602	$18,470	$22,279	$14,354	$12,472	$15,511	$11,377	$21,975	$29,608	$17,269	$42,025	$45,520	$40,172
North Dakota	$14,349	$19,051	$11,619	$12,345	$20,461	$7,838	$14,843	$18,828	$12,009	$30,009	$41,497	$19,211	$50,317	$55,000	$45,011
Ohio	$12,307	$14,849	$11,251	$15,607	$20,913	$11,271	$12,072	$13,807	$11,248	$22,475	$30,992	$16,592	$51,161	$57,435	$42,417
Oklahoma	$15,107	$17,818	$12,694	$21,704	$24,515	$19,877	$12,880	$15,830	$11,532	$23,902	$32,176	$17,411	$43,220	$51,125	$36,751
Oregon	$15,697	$17,360	$13,242	$16,943	$21,102	$12,460	$15,374	$16,835	$13,337	$21,012	$28,112	$16,891	$51,163	$61,930	$40,962
Pennsylvania	$14,412	$17,964	$11,751	$17,586	$21,729	$12,530	$13,517	$16,867	$11,639	$24,420	$31,715	$18,613	$51,720	$60,836	$42,354
Rhode Island	$16,562	$20,079	$13,144	$22,185	$26,777	$20,324	$15,503	$17,882	$12,246	$26,856	$35,155	$22,653	$66,218	$75,565	$51,789
South Carolina	$14,039	$16,420	$12,067	$19,871	$22,888	$12,858	$13,274	$15,361	$12,012	$22,493	$30,469	$16,638	$37,998	$42,054	$33,832
South Dakota	$13,605	$16,681	$12,003	$22,485	$30,644	$17,506	$11,980	$15,086	$11,522	$27,213	$32,878	$20,484	$40,669	$41,664	$38,961
Tennessee	$14,012	$16,715	$11,703	$22,135	$25,921	$17,873	$12,693	$15,612	$11,366	$23,742	$30,785	$17,690	$40,824	$48,047	$35,777
Texas	$15,626	$17,658	$13,441	$18,053	$20,763	$15,626	$15,387	$17,338	$13,257	$22,304	$30,096	$17,310	$46,825	$52,428	$40,219
Utah	$12,101	$13,629	$11,187	$12,309	$18,550	$9,691	$12,061	$12,826	$11,535	$23,275	$36,273	$16,008	$47,152	$54,676	$39,625
Vermont	$15,749	$19,737	$13,537	$15,787	$18,191	$15,079	$15,731	$19,849	$13,309	$25,384	$33,011	$20,738	$50,505	$61,100	$43,716
Virginia	$15,419	$17,167	$13,627	$16,542	$19,320	$14,847	$15,193	$16,949	$13,446	$27,205	$33,547	$23,341	$75,634	$82,374	$63,074
Washington	$19,027	$20,988	$17,363	$23,786	$26,522	$20,850	$17,569	$19,254	$16,806	$25,502	$35,398	$21,348	$56,092	$65,524	$49,395
West Virginia	$11,824	$12,539	$11,229	$17,481	$19,208	$16,120	$11,297	$11,951	$10,660	$26,286	$31,479	$16,508	$40,714	$45,986	$35,749
Wisconsin	$12,080	$14,478	$11,374	$13,513	$17,987	$11,598	$11,937	$13,800	$11,346	$25,257	$34,469	$18,738	$50,633	$55,486	$42,186
Wyoming	$16,292	$20,877	$12,202	$25,703	$26,982	$23,705	$15,012	$20,299	$11,294	$26,593	$36,663	$16,648	$45,587	$48,290	$40,996

PART C
COUNTIES

PART C. COUNTIES

- Between 2011 and 2015, 63.3 percent of people were in the labor force in the United States. Among the 75 largest counties in the country, Hennepin County, MN had the highest labor force participation rate at 72.2 percent, followed by Travis County, TX at 72.0. Pinellas County, FL and Pima County, AZ—which both have a higher percentage of older residents— had the lowest labor participation rates at 58.5 percent and 58.4 percent respectively.

- Nearly half the residents of Chattahoochee County, Georgia were members of the armed forces—the largest percentage in the country. Fort Benning is partially located there. Eleven other counties had at least ten percent of their populations 16 years of age and over in the armed forces.

- Corson County, South Dakota had the highest unemployment rate among all counties at 29.4 percent followed by Oglala Lakota County, South Dakota at 28.7 percent. Five out of ten counties with the highest unemployment rates were located in South Dakota.

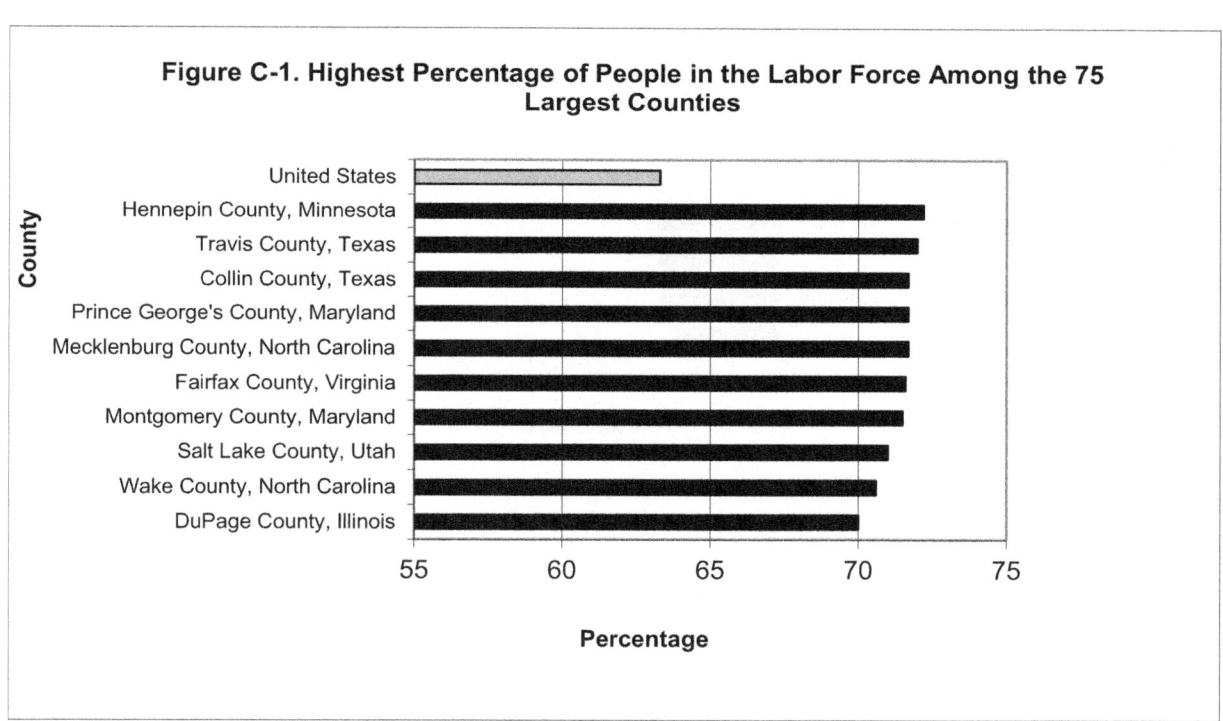

Figure C-1. Highest Percentage of People in the Labor Force Among the 75 Largest Counties

- Nationally, 68.0 percent of the employed population 16 years and over worked for private for-profit companies while another 9.4 percent were self-employed and another 8.1 percent worked for private non-profit companies. Over 14 percent of workers were employed by the government but only 0.2 percent were unpaid family members.

- Among the 75 largest counties, Bronx County, NY had the highest number of residents age 25 and over with less than a high school diploma at 29.4 percent, while Montgomery County, PA had the lowest percentage at 6.2 percent.

- Meanwhile, New York County, NY and Fairfax County, VA had the highest percentage of residents with a bachelor's degree or higher at 59.9 percent followed by Montgomery County, MD at 57.9 percent among the 75 largest counties. Nationally, between 2011 and 2015, 29.8 percent of the population had a bachelor's degree or higher.

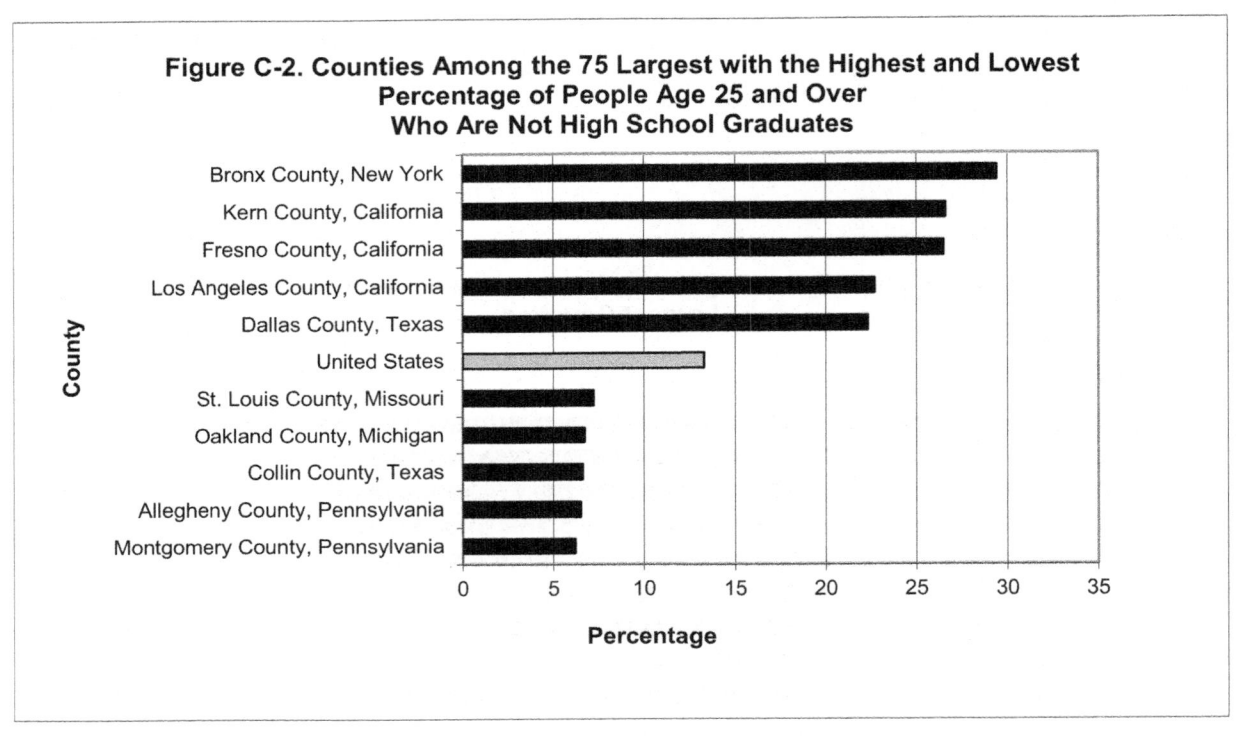

Figure C-2. Counties Among the 75 Largest with the Highest and Lowest Percentage of People Age 25 and Over Who Are Not High School Graduates

Table C. County—Labor Force, Employment, and Educational Data, 2011–2015

Fips code	State/county	Total population age 16 and older	Percent in civilian labor force	Percent in armed forces	Civilian labor force participation by gender		Civilian labor force participation by age				Civilian unemploy-ment rate	Civilian employed population age 16 and older			
					Men	Women	Age 16 to 24	Age 25 to 54	Age 55 to 64	Age 65 and older		Total	Men	Women	Percent women
00000	**United States**	251,221,309	63.3	0.4	68.3	58.5	57.1	81.1	64.2	17.0	8.3	145,747,779	76,495,493	69,252,286	47.5
01000	**Alabama**	3,846,845	58.0	0.3	63.4	53.0	54.5	76.3	55.3	14.7	9.3	2,022,325	1,059,234	963,091	47.6
01001	Autauga County, Alabama	42,801	60.7	1.0	66.6	55.2	59.1	75.9	64.8	12.6	7.6	23,986	12,732	11,254	46.9
01003	Baldwin County, Alabama	156,379	59.4	0.2	65.3	53.9	62.8	80.1	58.6	14.7	7.5	85,953	45,865	40,088	46.6
01005	Barbour County, Alabama	21,785	47.9	0.0	47.6	48.3	46.0	60.3	50.9	15.3	17.6	8,597	4,456	4,141	48.2
01007	Bibb County, Alabama	18,339	49.3	0.0	52.1	46.1	38.3	63.6	49.0	16.4	8.3	8,294	4,886	3,408	41.1
01009	Blount County, Alabama	45,839	52.4	0.1	59.3	45.8	48.9	69.3	53.2	14.4	7.7	22,189	12,242	9,947	44.8
01011	Bullock County, Alabama	8,653	54.5	0.0	56.5	52.1	61.9	65.8	58.1	13.0	18.0	3,865	2,222	1,643	42.5
01013	Butler County, Alabama	16,215	54.1	0.2	58.1	50.7	54.0	76.2	50.5	11.3	10.9	7,813	3,719	4,094	52.4
01015	Calhoun County, Alabama	93,346	57.9	0.3	64.2	52.3	59.7	77.5	52.3	12.5	12.3	47,401	24,895	22,506	47.5
01017	Chambers County, Alabama	27,492	54.7	0.1	59.2	50.6	57.8	73.5	54.9	13.0	8.9	13,689	6,958	6,731	49.2
01019	Cherokee County, Alabama	21,242	51.9	0.0	58.9	45.1	62.1	77.5	40.1	9.6	7.9	10,155	5,722	4,433	43.7
01021	Chilton County, Alabama	34,348	57.3	0.0	66.5	48.5	60.1	73.4	54.8	15.1	9.1	17,895	10,182	7,713	43.1
01023	Choctaw County, Alabama	10,900	46.8	0.0	53.4	40.9	50.4	68.6	40.4	10.4	13.6	4,405	2,420	1,985	45.1
01025	Clarke County, Alabama	20,128	50.3	0.0	57.3	44.2	54.5	69.0	42.8	13.1	19.4	8,161	4,295	3,866	47.4
01027	Clay County, Alabama	10,933	52.3	0.0	58.3	46.6	57.9	71.6	49.4	13.1	9.4	5,180	2,798	2,382	46.0
01029	Cleburne County, Alabama	11,860	55.8	0.0	65.5	46.7	57.7	74.0	57.5	13.6	8.3	6,065	3,438	2,627	43.3
01031	Coffee County, Alabama	40,161	56.0	3.4	59.9	52.3	52.4	73.7	54.9	13.9	7.1	20,912	10,984	9,928	47.5
01033	Colbert County, Alabama	44,172	53.0	0.1	60.5	46.1	50.1	74.8	50.7	11.0	9.0	21,290	11,492	9,798	46.0
01035	Conecuh County, Alabama	10,280	46.7	0.0	51.7	42.3	62.0	66.2	38.2	10.4	22.6	3,718	2,004	1,714	46.1
01037	Coosa County, Alabama	9,230	50.3	0.0	57.7	42.7	65.1	67.6	42.7	11.2	17.0	3,852	2,315	1,537	39.9
01039	Covington County, Alabama	30,519	52.4	0.1	60.0	45.6	58.1	72.6	54.3	10.5	11.2	14,202	7,814	6,388	45.0
01041	Crenshaw County, Alabama	11,111	56.0	0.3	64.0	48.7	58.6	76.1	49.9	14.9	9.7	5,620	3,097	2,523	44.9
01043	Cullman County, Alabama	64,915	53.6	0.1	61.2	46.4	50.3	73.1	54.9	11.8	7.3	32,282	18,058	14,224	44.1
01045	Dale County, Alabama	39,297	53.5	5.8	57.1	50.1	49.0	70.4	54.0	12.1	10.9	18,735	9,667	9,068	48.4
01047	Dallas County, Alabama	32,414	52.0	0.1	58.9	46.5	54.6	68.2	51.5	11.9	16.4	14,094	7,218	6,876	48.8
01049	DeKalb County, Alabama	55,469	54.3	0.0	62.3	46.6	48.3	74.5	47.0	12.7	7.7	27,778	15,453	12,325	44.4
01051	Elmore County, Alabama	64,498	56.8	0.7	58.1	55.7	54.1	70.1	58.4	16.5	8.3	33,636	16,557	17,079	50.8
01053	Escambia County, Alabama	30,527	47.7	0.0	49.8	45.5	51.1	63.2	45.3	9.1	15.6	12,294	6,588	5,706	46.4
01055	Etowah County, Alabama	83,390	54.4	0.1	59.4	49.8	55.5	73.0	51.9	13.2	9.0	41,236	21,343	19,893	48.2
01057	Fayette County, Alabama	13,666	49.8	0.1	54.1	45.7	62.2	69.5	47.6	6.2	10.0	6,122	3,211	2,911	47.5
01059	Franklin County, Alabama	24,804	54.7	0.0	65.2	44.9	58.5	71.5	52.9	12.5	9.8	12,249	7,195	5,054	41.3
01061	Geneva County, Alabama	21,558	54.4	0.5	61.1	48.1	56.0	75.4	53.8	11.6	11.2	10,419	5,710	4,709	45.2
01063	Greene County, Alabama	6,858	44.2	0.0	45.5	43.0	37.5	60.7	44.4	15.7	20.4	2,412	1,104	1,308	54.2
01065	Hale County, Alabama	12,104	50.3	0.0	52.7	48.4	45.4	71.0	41.4	17.2	13.3	5,282	2,622	2,660	50.4
01067	Henry County, Alabama	13,935	54.1	0.0	58.3	50.3	61.1	76.9	49.1	13.0	8.1	6,922	3,448	3,474	50.2
01069	Houston County, Alabama	81,625	58.9	0.2	64.9	53.6	56.6	77.4	55.9	16.3	8.3	44,067	22,734	21,333	48.4
01071	Jackson County, Alabama	42,738	54.4	0.0	61.4	47.7	55.3	72.7	56.4	13.2	10.1	20,883	11,634	9,249	44.3
01073	Jefferson County, Alabama	523,210	61.7	0.1	67.0	57.1	56.2	80.0	58.0	16.5	9.1	293,202	147,563	145,639	49.7
01075	Lamar County, Alabama	11,462	52.4	0.2	61.2	44.2	47.3	75.1	54.0	11.5	10.2	5,391	3,142	2,249	41.7
01077	Lauderdale County, Alabama	75,897	56.3	0.1	63.2	50.3	59.3	76.7	57.0	11.9	7.1	39,734	21,276	18,458	46.5
01079	Lawrence County, Alabama	27,054	52.0	0.1	61.8	42.9	55.8	69.5	47.5	9.6	9.8	12,704	7,259	5,445	42.9
01081	Lee County, Alabama	121,893	60.7	0.8	66.4	55.3	47.8	79.7	57.2	19.9	7.3	68,614	36,753	31,861	46.4
01083	Limestone County, Alabama	70,549	57.9	0.1	63.0	52.8	57.9	71.8	55.6	15.4	7.8	37,664	20,643	17,021	45.2
01085	Lowndes County, Alabama	8,487	47.1	0.5	48.6	45.8	46.7	64.4	49.3	7.0	13.2	3,471	1,654	1,817	52.3
01087	Macon County, Alabama	16,746	54.5	0.0	56.0	53.3	53.9	78.1	47.3	14.7	16.9	7,585	3,521	4,064	53.6
01089	Madison County, Alabama	277,343	64.5	0.4	70.6	58.8	56.0	82.3	63.9	17.4	8.5	163,753	87,752	76,001	46.4
01091	Marengo County, Alabama	16,162	47.9	0.1	53.6	43.1	42.7	72.7	43.6	6.5	11.4	6,860	3,587	3,273	47.7
01093	Marion County, Alabama	24,723	51.9	0.1	55.7	48.3	50.7	73.9	51.6	10.3	9.9	11,560	5,908	5,652	48.9
01095	Marshall County, Alabama	73,513	56.7	0.0	63.6	50.1	60.4	75.9	50.6	12.4	8.4	38,140	20,707	17,433	45.7
01097	Mobile County, Alabama	325,152	58.3	0.3	62.3	54.7	54.3	76.2	55.6	14.7	9.8	170,900	85,974	84,926	49.7
01099	Monroe County, Alabama	17,572	47.0	0.0	52.9	41.8	43.6	66.9	42.3	11.8	20.7	6,551	3,508	3,043	46.5
01101	Montgomery County, Alabama	179,061	60.7	1.1	64.1	57.9	53.0	76.9	61.1	18.9	8.8	99,158	48,414	50,744	51.2
01103	Morgan County, Alabama	95,186	60.0	0.0	66.8	53.7	61.5	78.4	55.0	15.2	9.9	51,472	28,126	23,346	45.4
01105	Perry County, Alabama	8,053	40.1	0.0	39.0	41.0	38.8	52.4	47.6	14.5	11.2	2,865	1,334	1,531	53.4
01107	Pickens County, Alabama	16,113	48.3	0.0	53.5	43.5	48.3	67.9	44.4	9.3	13.8	6,712	3,617	3,095	46.1
01109	Pike County, Alabama	27,455	58.6	0.1	62.9	54.9	55.4	79.9	53.9	15.5	10.2	14,462	7,508	6,954	48.1
01111	Randolph County, Alabama	18,124	53.1	0.0	58.1	48.5	55.3	78.0	44.9	10.7	10.3	8,630	4,449	4,181	48.4
01113	Russell County, Alabama	45,173	57.1	3.1	60.1	54.3	53.3	72.6	49.3	16.2	11.1	22,927	11,642	11,285	49.2
01115	St. Clair County, Alabama	68,190	59.2	0.1	63.8	54.7	60.4	77.2	51.3	14.5	8.4	36,977	19,669	17,308	46.8
01117	Shelby County, Alabama	159,063	67.4	0.1	74.5	60.8	59.4	83.8	65.1	20.4	5.5	101,343	53,731	47,612	47.0
01119	Sumter County, Alabama	10,958	48.5	0.1	50.2	47.1	49.5	67.3	49.6	8.8	16.8	4,416	2,024	2,392	54.2
01121	Talladega County, Alabama	65,264	54.4	0.0	58.7	50.4	53.7	71.7	49.3	15.7	13.8	30,618	16,103	14,515	47.4
01123	Tallapoosa County, Alabama	33,154	52.5	0.0	58.3	47.2	55.5	71.4	53.3	13.7	9.0	15,837	8,381	7,456	47.1
01125	Tuscaloosa County, Alabama	162,778	58.3	0.2	63.3	53.7	48.6	77.4	56.1	15.5	7.6	87,695	45,174	42,521	48.5
01127	Walker County, Alabama	52,945	51.2	0.0	58.0	45.0	58.5	70.0	45.4	11.5	11.4	24,043	13,222	10,821	45.0
01129	Washington County, Alabama	13,538	52.2	0.0	58.5	46.2	46.0	77.7	38.9	9.2	20.0	5,656	3,202	2,454	43.4
01131	Wilcox County, Alabama	8,851	40.5	0.3	42.5	38.7	31.7	54.7	44.7	14.9	20.8	2,838	1,294	1,544	54.4
01133	Winston County, Alabama	19,645	50.1	0.0	57.3	43.3	45.6	71.2	47.0	13.9	9.6	8,894	5,019	3,875	43.6
02000	**Alaska**	565,212	67.7	3.0	70.1	65.0	59.9	79.5	68.0	23.7	8.2	351,108	189,473	161,635	46.0
02013	Aleutians East Borough, Alaska	2,940	88.2	0.2	91.7	80.9	83.1	92.4	92.0	49.7	2.9	2,519	1,770	749	29.7
02016	Aleutians West Census Area, Alaska	4,730	81.8	1.4	88.1	70.7	60.6	90.3	79.8	65.0	2.1	3,787	2,613	1,174	31.0
02020	Anchorage Municipality, Alaska	231,795	70.4	3.6	72.8	68.0	62.5	81.8	72.1	24.1	6.7	152,355	79,665	72,690	47.7
02050	Bethel Census Area, Alaska	12,044	62.8	0.0	63.0	62.6	46.7	75.2	69.1	18.6	17.6	6,232	3,138	3,094	49.6

Table C. County—Labor Force, Employment, and Educational Data, 2011–2015—*Continued*

Fips code	State/county	Total population age 16 and older	Percent in civilian labor force	Percent in armed forces	Civilian labor force participation by gender		Civilian labor force participation by age				Civilian unemployment rate	Civilian employed population age 16 and older			
					Men	Women	Age 16 to 24	Age 25 to 54	Age 55 to 64	Age 65 and older		Total	Men	Women	Percent women
02060	Bristol Bay Borough, Alaska	766	74.7	1.3	81.7	65.0	53.8	86.7	70.8	42.0	5.4	541	340	201	37.2
02068	Denali Borough, Alaska	1,678	73.8	3.6	74.6	73.0	74.2	84.1	60.9	29.4	2.3	1,210	658	552	45.6
02070	Dillingham Census Area, Alaska	3,569	59.3	0.0	58.2	60.6	47.4	69.3	66.2	24.3	12.5	1,854	919	935	50.4
02090	Fairbanks North Star Borough, Alaska	77,480	65.4	7.8	64.8	66.2	57.4	76.4	64.6	23.3	7.9	46,661	24,821	21,840	46.8
02100	Haines Borough, Alaska	2,200	68.9	0.0	73.5	63.6	80.1	78.3	69.7	38.8	3.0	1,470	837	633	43.1
02105	Hoonah-Angoon Census Area, Alaska	1,785	70.0	0.2	70.5	69.4	67.1	86.9	71.0	22.0	13.1	1,086	610	476	43.8
02110	Juneau City and Borough, Alaska	26,087	72.1	0.5	73.9	70.3	61.5	85.1	72.6	25.2	5.2	17,836	9,311	8,525	47.8
02122	Kenai Peninsula Borough, Alaska	45,542	62.1	0.3	65.7	58.1	63.7	76.7	61.2	20.0	9.4	25,637	14,138	11,499	44.9
02130	Ketchikan Gateway Borough, Alaska	10,880	66.4	2.0	68.9	63.7	50.3	80.7	72.3	23.7	7.9	6,655	3,533	3,122	46.9
02150	Kodiak Island Borough, Alaska	10,549	71.1	6.1	71.5	70.7	65.7	78.3	77.1	34.5	6.3	7,032	3,718	3,314	47.1
02158	Kusilvak Census Area, Alaska	5,050	57.3	0.2	61.2	52.9	41.6	71.3	60.3	13.5	28.6	2,067	1,061	1,006	48.7
02164	Lake and Peninsula Borough, Alaska	1,080	67.4	0.0	66.7	68.1	52.7	80.1	69.6	20.2	9.8	657	330	327	49.8
02170	Matanuska-Susitna Borough, Alaska	72,382	62.6	0.6	68.2	56.4	57.2	74.7	58.4	20.9	9.8	40,854	23,307	17,547	43.0
02180	Nome Census Area, Alaska	6,840	64.0	0.6	64.4	63.5	52.9	76.0	61.2	27.3	16.5	3,654	1,918	1,736	47.5
02185	North Slope Borough, Alaska	7,491	81.0	0.9	83.9	75.1	66.1	88.2	83.5	42.3	9.3	5,499	3,860	1,639	29.8
02188	Northwest Arctic Borough, Alaska	5,247	63.3	0.0	66.6	59.3	52.5	76.1	64.6	17.0	21.9	2,593	1,443	1,150	44.4
02195	Petersburg Borough, Alaska	2,565	70.8	0.7	73.3	67.8	73.0	85.6	74.0	17.5	8.4	1,665	916	749	45.0
02198	Prince of Wales-Hyder Census Area, Alaska	4,993	65.6	0.1	68.2	62.3	65.7	74.7	67.6	29.2	13.9	2,819	1,599	1,220	43.3
02220	Sitka City and Borough, Alaska	7,156	69.1	1.1	71.1	67.1	57.9	85.5	66.3	27.6	3.8	4,756	2,456	2,300	48.4
02230	Skagway Municipality, Alaska	862	85.0	0.0	89.9	79.1	78.6	91.7	85.9	49.4	7.8	676	392	284	42.0
02240	Southeast Fairbanks Census Area, Alaska	5,292	63.3	3.2	66.6	59.0	50.7	75.8	64.8	31.0	9.4	3,038	1,843	1,195	39.3
02261	Valdez-Cordova Census Area, Alaska	7,444	66.4	2.0	69.8	62.5	59.3	78.4	67.4	23.8	10.7	4,415	2,393	2,022	45.8
02275	Wrangell City and Borough, Alaska	2,033	57.8	0.0	64.5	51.1	61.9	83.4	70.1	4.7	7.5	1,088	609	479	44.0
02282	Yakutat City and Borough, Alaska	509	80.0	0.0	84.0	73.6	70.4	88.8	79.2	56.5	7.9	375	237	138	36.8
02290	Yukon-Koyukuk Census Area, Alaska	4,223	60.1	0.4	59.3	61.1	54.1	74.9	62.7	21.7	18.2	2,077	1,038	1,039	50.0
04000	**Arizona**	5,207,123	59.3	0.3	64.3	54.5	56.6	78.1	59.8	14.0	8.9	2,813,406	1,499,744	1,313,662	46.7
04001	Apache County, Arizona	53,129	42.2	0.0	41.2	43.1	29.7	57.9	44.4	10.4	18.2	18,334	8,527	9,807	53.5
04003	Cochise County, Arizona	103,453	46.4	4.3	44.8	48.0	47.0	61.4	53.3	12.6	8.7	43,776	21,519	22,257	50.8
04005	Coconino County, Arizona	110,047	64.6	0.1	68.5	60.8	57.9	81.1	65.0	21.1	8.8	64,844	33,450	31,394	48.4
04007	Gila County, Arizona	43,427	47.5	0.0	50.4	44.6	59.6	71.7	49.5	12.7	12.8	17,961	9,186	8,775	48.9
04009	Graham County, Arizona	28,204	49.3	0.0	48.2	50.7	45.8	60.5	55.4	12.4	14.1	11,954	6,309	5,645	47.2
04011	Greenlee County, Arizona	6,734	55.2	0.0	68.8	40.5	49.6	70.9	55.0	7.8	10.0	3,346	2,271	1,075	32.1
04012	La Paz County, Arizona	17,244	41.7	0.0	43.5	39.8	61.6	73.0	48.7	10.3	11.2	6,386	3,397	2,989	46.8
04013	Maricopa County, Arizona	3,115,673	63.3	0.1	69.7	57.3	58.1	80.6	63.6	15.6	7.7	1,821,038	977,681	843,357	46.3
04015	Mohave County, Arizona	169,445	45.5	0.0	46.4	44.5	57.6	69.4	47.7	9.9	13.2	66,880	33,539	33,341	49.9
04017	Navajo County, Arizona	80,446	49.5	0.0	51.7	47.4	46.1	67.0	50.6	11.5	19.8	31,955	16,258	15,697	49.1
04019	Pima County, Arizona	803,330	58.4	0.6	62.8	54.3	58.6	79.0	60.1	13.6	10.0	422,371	220,749	201,622	47.7
04021	Pinal County, Arizona	302,678	49.6	0.1	51.4	47.6	50.3	67.4	47.3	10.9	10.6	134,182	73,150	61,032	45.5
04023	Santa Cruz County, Arizona	35,115	55.4	0.0	64.4	47.6	42.3	77.6	57.0	15.3	11.3	17,246	9,583	7,663	44.4
04025	Yavapai County, Arizona	182,792	49.5	0.0	53.7	45.6	61.0	76.7	54.3	12.0	10.0	81,511	42,833	38,678	47.5
04027	Yuma County, Arizona	155,406	53.0	2.1	58.8	47.0	49.5	75.4	54.0	8.7	13.1	71,622	41,292	30,330	42.3
05000	**Arkansas**	2,328,384	58.5	0.2	64.0	53.3	56.4	76.8	56.7	15.4	7.7	1,256,081	664,030	592,051	47.1
05001	Arkansas County, Arkansas	14,897	59.2	0.0	65.1	53.9	66.5	74.4	61.3	21.0	8.3	8,088	4,174	3,914	48.4
05003	Ashley County, Arkansas	16,802	52.9	0.0	58.5	47.7	51.4	73.9	50.6	11.0	11.8	7,840	4,140	3,700	47.2
05005	Baxter County, Arkansas	34,635	47.6	0.1	49.4	45.9	62.1	77.9	47.7	11.6	7.6	15,229	7,393	7,836	51.5
05007	Benton County, Arkansas	180,198	63.6	0.2	72.5	55.2	53.5	79.9	66.5	16.3	4.2	109,788	60,626	49,162	44.8
05009	Boone County, Arkansas	29,760	56.4	0.0	63.6	49.8	66.7	76.9	54.7	12.9	8.4	15,368	8,239	7,129	46.4
05011	Bradley County, Arkansas	8,797	52.4	0.0	57.5	47.8	55.5	70.5	54.8	11.7	9.4	4,180	2,275	1,905	45.6
05013	Calhoun County, Arkansas	4,362	55.4	0.0	62.0	48.6	57.0	74.7	58.4	14.9	7.2	2,243	1,266	977	43.6
05015	Carroll County, Arkansas	22,075	55.3	0.0	61.5	49.4	57.0	80.1	55.0	14.2	6.2	11,454	6,321	5,133	44.8
05017	Chicot County, Arkansas	9,013	47.2	0.0	47.1	47.3	45.9	66.3	45.3	13.9	11.5	3,769	1,831	1,938	51.4
05019	Clark County, Arkansas	18,869	56.6	0.0	59.8	53.7	50.7	81.3	53.4	18.3	8.4	9,780	4,779	5,001	51.1
05021	Clay County, Arkansas	12,513	55.5	0.0	62.0	49.2	56.4	75.3	58.9	18.1	9.5	6,283	3,441	2,842	45.2
05023	Cleburne County, Arkansas	21,306	50.7	0.0	56.5	45.0	59.9	74.1	55.8	12.9	10.2	9,699	5,376	4,323	44.6
05025	Cleveland County, Arkansas	6,810	52.9	0.0	59.4	46.7	46.3	75.3	55.0	10.6	9.7	3,256	1,775	1,481	45.5
05027	Columbia County, Arkansas	19,696	59.3	0.0	64.6	54.6	63.2	79.6	56.6	14.6	10.1	10,491	5,226	5,265	50.2
05029	Conway County, Arkansas	16,776	53.9	0.0	59.1	49.0	55.3	73.6	55.7	11.2	8.1	8,306	4,423	3,883	46.7
05031	Craighead County, Arkansas	79,002	62.3	0.0	69.5	55.7	57.8	79.9	58.3	14.7	7.5	45,526	24,414	21,112	46.4
05033	Crawford County, Arkansas	47,836	56.9	0.0	62.8	51.4	56.1	76.0	49.8	14.0	7.9	25,099	13,370	11,729	46.7

Table C. County—Labor Force, Employment, and Educational Data, 2011–2015—*Continued*

Fips code	State/county	Total population age 16 and older	Percent in civilian labor force	Percent in armed forces	Civilian labor force participation by gender		Civilian labor force participation by age				Civilian unemploy-ment rate	Civilian employed population age 16 and older			
					Men	Women	Age 16 to 24	Age 25 to 54	Age 55 to 64	Age 65 and older		Total	Men	Women	Percent women
05035	Crittenden County, Arkansas	37,225	60.6	0.0	65.3	56.6	46.8	77.5	62.9	17.4	9.9	20,336	10,320	10,016	49.3
05037	Cross County, Arkansas	13,732	56.9	0.0	64.0	50.6	47.6	76.8	57.2	17.7	8.6	7,140	3,761	3,379	47.3
05039	Dallas County, Arkansas	6,237	53.0	0.2	56.5	49.9	49.0	73.4	56.5	17.3	8.3	3,031	1,492	1,539	50.8
05041	Desha County, Arkansas	9,630	55.0	0.0	60.0	50.7	50.7	73.6	54.5	19.3	17.7	4,355	2,199	2,156	49.5
05043	Drew County, Arkansas	15,128	56.8	0.0	61.5	52.4	58.7	75.1	58.5	13.2	14.3	7,361	3,699	3,662	49.7
05045	Faulkner County, Arkansas	93,602	65.4	0.2	70.8	60.2	62.2	82.2	59.4	15.1	6.6	57,108	30,352	26,756	46.9
05047	Franklin County, Arkansas	14,118	52.5	0.1	56.2	48.9	52.1	73.5	55.4	8.2	11.0	6,592	3,329	3,263	49.5
05049	Fulton County, Arkansas	10,024	48.5	0.2	53.1	44.2	65.8	77.4	43.6	6.7	7.6	4,498	2,344	2,154	47.9
05051	Garland County, Arkansas	79,167	55.3	0.0	61.4	49.6	62.2	77.4	57.3	13.9	9.2	39,729	20,988	18,741	47.2
05053	Grant County, Arkansas	14,429	58.2	0.0	63.4	53.1	59.6	76.6	53.2	14.1	9.4	7,608	4,058	3,550	46.7
05055	Greene County, Arkansas	33,938	57.2	0.1	63.3	51.2	66.3	74.1	48.7	11.6	9.0	17,659	9,606	8,053	45.6
05057	Hempstead County, Arkansas	17,042	55.4	0.0	61.7	48.8	59.7	69.7	55.8	18.9	7.9	8,699	4,523	4,176	48.0
05059	Hot Spring County, Arkansas	26,850	53.6	0.0	57.4	49.5	63.5	69.9	49.6	13.6	7.6	13,293	7,254	6,039	45.4
05061	Howard County, Arkansas	10,334	59.2	0.0	66.5	52.4	62.1	78.4	56.9	14.7	8.5	5,596	3,032	2,564	45.8
05063	Independence County, Arkansas	29,148	56.4	0.0	64.3	49.0	64.8	73.3	55.8	11.6	6.9	15,303	8,335	6,968	45.5
05065	Izard County, Arkansas	11,280	45.4	0.0	49.0	41.6	58.4	64.8	51.0	9.7	10.0	4,607	2,500	2,107	45.7
05067	Jackson County, Arkansas	14,465	41.9	0.0	52.9	31.3	42.7	49.6	49.3	16.2	7.9	5,585	3,446	2,139	38.3
05069	Jefferson County, Arkansas	58,267	54.3	0.0	53.4	55.2	51.4	70.6	53.9	15.0	11.2	28,119	13,383	14,736	52.4
05071	Johnson County, Arkansas	20,306	54.5	0.0	61.0	48.0	48.9	76.5	47.9	10.3	6.2	10,376	5,702	4,674	45.0
05073	Lafayette County, Arkansas	5,919	48.8	0.0	52.8	45.1	49.9	64.9	52.0	19.1	12.5	2,527	1,272	1,255	49.7
05075	Lawrence County, Arkansas	13,640	51.4	0.0	57.7	45.7	58.1	69.8	47.6	15.4	6.9	6,527	3,446	3,081	47.2
05077	Lee County, Arkansas	8,278	42.5	0.0	39.2	46.9	46.3	53.5	41.6	14.3	17.3	2,910	1,499	1,411	48.5
05079	Lincoln County, Arkansas	11,756	36.3	0.0	28.9	49.2	33.7	41.3	41.7	16.1	14.2	3,666	1,809	1,857	50.7
05081	Little River County, Arkansas	10,151	51.9	0.0	55.7	48.5	54.5	72.4	42.4	16.2	8.8	4,805	2,460	2,345	48.8
05083	Logan County, Arkansas	17,655	53.7	0.1	56.0	51.5	54.0	75.7	48.9	14.4	8.1	8,718	4,514	4,204	48.2
05085	Lonoke County, Arkansas	53,710	63.2	1.9	69.0	57.8	56.5	79.5	60.3	16.4	5.9	31,944	16,694	15,250	47.7
05087	Madison County, Arkansas	12,527	58.2	0.0	63.9	52.4	50.8	78.8	61.3	14.9	7.3	6,751	3,738	3,013	44.6
05089	Marion County, Arkansas	13,977	45.6	0.0	48.9	42.4	63.6	70.9	43.5	9.7	10.9	5,679	2,910	2,769	48.8
05091	Miller County, Arkansas	34,201	59.6	0.0	64.8	54.7	53.4	78.0	55.3	18.1	9.6	18,429	9,763	8,666	47.0
05093	Mississippi County, Arkansas	34,106	57.2	0.1	62.6	52.2	56.9	71.6	55.0	17.1	12.0	17,164	9,052	8,112	47.3
05095	Monroe County, Arkansas	6,267	51.5	0.0	53.8	49.5	56.5	68.1	59.8	15.1	12.8	2,815	1,324	1,491	53.0
05097	Montgomery County, Arkansas	7,604	50.0	0.0	57.7	42.7	67.6	70.8	53.2	11.7	4.3	3,636	2,031	1,605	44.1
05099	Nevada County, Arkansas	6,879	52.4	0.3	58.3	47.1	61.5	71.3	55.9	12.1	9.5	3,265	1,761	1,504	46.1
05101	Newton County, Arkansas	6,630	51.0	0.0	55.8	46.2	59.1	74.4	47.4	15.5	4.4	3,228	1,735	1,493	46.3
05103	Ouachita County, Arkansas	19,978	56.8	0.2	63.1	51.5	60.1	76.3	54.4	17.3	8.3	10,415	5,340	5,075	48.7
05105	Perry County, Arkansas	8,252	54.4	0.2	60.3	48.5	63.0	78.7	39.0	13.7	6.8	4,184	2,371	1,813	43.3
05107	Phillips County, Arkansas	15,397	55.0	0.0	57.6	52.8	52.2	74.9	52.8	16.0	18.1	6,932	3,128	3,804	54.9
05109	Pike County, Arkansas	8,774	54.6	0.0	63.0	46.7	46.8	73.7	55.4	18.8	6.6	4,476	2,501	1,975	44.1
05111	Poinsett County, Arkansas	19,036	52.9	0.0	59.1	47.1	53.1	69.9	52.9	14.6	10.0	9,053	4,879	4,174	46.1
05113	Polk County, Arkansas	16,127	50.9	0.1	56.1	46.1	50.0	74.1	50.1	13.7	9.0	7,473	3,780	3,693	49.4
05115	Pope County, Arkansas	49,985	59.4	0.1	64.0	54.9	57.4	76.4	58.4	17.2	7.6	27,407	14,634	12,773	46.6
05117	Prairie County, Arkansas	6,897	54.3	0.3	59.2	49.6	53.7	78.1	55.9	13.2	6.2	3,513	1,877	1,636	46.6
05119	Pulaski County, Arkansas	307,550	63.4	0.7	67.9	59.4	56.9	79.3	62.5	20.0	7.5	180,430	90,983	89,447	49.6
05121	Randolph County, Arkansas	14,084	50.4	0.0	54.1	46.9	62.3	67.9	51.0	11.6	5.4	6,714	3,433	3,281	48.9
05123	St. Francis County, Arkansas	21,818	48.1	0.0	45.0	51.9	48.6	58.0	50.8	13.7	11.7	9,259	4,793	4,466	48.2
05125	Saline County, Arkansas	89,574	62.9	0.0	67.5	58.5	63.1	84.4	57.2	15.2	5.3	53,363	27,798	25,565	47.9
05127	Scott County, Arkansas	8,522	56.0	0.0	57.5	54.5	60.2	79.3	44.7	14.0	10.9	4,250	2,206	2,044	48.1
05129	Searcy County, Arkansas	6,455	46.7	0.0	50.7	42.8	51.2	67.0	48.3	13.8	5.9	2,836	1,483	1,353	47.7
05131	Sebastian County, Arkansas	99,491	58.7	0.1	65.8	52.1	55.1	75.6	57.9	14.9	6.1	54,852	29,321	25,531	46.5
05133	Sevier County, Arkansas	12,699	62.3	0.0	73.1	52.0	58.8	79.8	60.3	18.0	9.3	7,173	4,148	3,025	42.2
05135	Sharp County, Arkansas	13,942	45.3	0.0	52.2	38.8	53.4	66.4	46.8	14.1	8.8	5,764	3,219	2,545	44.2
05137	Stone County, Arkansas	10,212	45.6	0.0	51.9	39.4	47.4	69.9	43.3	14.8	7.0	4,332	2,412	1,920	44.3
05139	Union County, Arkansas	31,971	56.9	0.1	63.5	50.8	51.9	77.2	54.1	15.3	9.7	16,418	8,737	7,681	46.8
05141	Van Buren County, Arkansas	13,965	44.2	0.0	52.2	36.4	43.1	70.4	40.1	9.8	11.2	5,478	3,152	2,326	42.5
05143	Washington County, Arkansas	167,361	65.6	0.0	74.2	57.0	57.5	82.0	62.6	19.4	6.2	102,944	57,527	45,417	44.1
05145	White County, Arkansas	62,101	56.0	0.3	61.6	50.8	48.1	75.0	56.3	15.8	7.1	32,318	17,138	15,180	47.0
05147	Woodruff County, Arkansas	5,660	49.9	0.0	57.0	43.4	52.0	69.4	48.0	16.3	12.4	2,472	1,337	1,135	45.9
05149	Yell County, Arkansas	16,964	55.1	0.0	59.0	51.3	50.7	76.9	55.1	8.0	8.3	8,567	4,433	4,134	48.3
06000	**California**	30,312,429	63.1	0.4	69.2	57.2	52.1	80.1	64.1	17.2	9.9	17,246,360	9,325,675	7,920,685	45.9
06001	Alameda County, California	1,279,499	66.3	0.1	72.4	60.5	51.0	83.1	67.5	18.0	8.3	778,132	412,964	365,168	46.9
06003	Alpine County, California	932	49.0	0.0	50.2	47.5	37.5	69.1	56.1	20.1	10.7	408	227	181	44.4
06005	Amador County, California	31,994	45.7	0.1	42.7	49.3	53.8	61.7	51.0	13.9	14.0	12,573	6,352	6,221	49.5
06007	Butte County, California	182,772	55.6	0.1	59.0	52.3	57.0	75.2	55.2	13.7	12.1	89,411	45,876	43,535	48.7
06009	Calaveras County, California	37,756	48.9	0.0	52.4	45.6	57.4	70.8	54.9	12.2	12.1	16,248	8,484	7,764	47.8
06011	Colusa County, California	15,971	61.7	0.1	69.8	53.2	50.7	76.6	69.5	21.6	10.4	8,837	5,232	3,605	40.8
06013	Contra Costa County, California	865,668	64.6	0.1	71.3	58.3	53.1	82.3	67.5	18.3	8.8	509,920	271,546	238,374	46.7
06015	Del Norte County, California	22,490	43.3	0.1	39.7	47.8	39.9	52.2	48.7	15.3	11.5	8,612	4,437	4,175	48.5
06017	El Dorado County, California	148,534	60.3	0.1	65.2	55.4	57.0	80.7	60.1	17.9	11.1	79,568	41,828	37,740	47.4
06019	Fresno County, California	709,064	60.9	0.1	67.1	54.8	51.9	76.7	61.0	16.3	13.2	374,564	205,521	169,043	45.1
06021	Glenn County, California	21,373	56.3	0.0	63.5	49.2	54.0	74.2	53.2	14.9	12.6	10,523	6,019	4,504	42.8
06023	Humboldt County, California	111,660	58.5	0.1	61.7	55.3	56.3	75.3	58.5	17.7	10.5	58,449	30,526	27,923	47.8
06025	Imperial County, California	132,937	53.2	0.4	54.1	52.2	44.6	68.6	53.3	12.7	17.4	58,391	30,341	28,050	48.0
06027	Inyo County, California	15,012	59.8	0.1	61.2	58.4	61.3	85.9	62.5	13.9	6.8	8,370	4,241	4,129	49.3

Table C. County—Labor Force, Employment, and Educational Data, 2011–2015—*Continued*

					Civilian labor force participation by gender		Civilian labor force participation by age					Civilian employed population age 16 and older			
Fips code	State/county	Total population age 16 and older	Percent in civilian labor force	Percent in armed forces	Men	Women	Age 16 to 24	Age 25 to 54	Age 55 to 64	Age 65 and older	Civilian unemploy-ment rate	Total	Men	Women	Percent women
06029	Kern County, California	637,913	58.7	0.3	64.4	52.7	51.0	72.8	56.4	14.7	12.7	327,294	186,539	140,755	43.0
06031	Kings County, California	113,592	51.6	3.6	49.9	53.8	46.7	60.2	52.7	15.4	13.0	50,960	28,409	22,551	44.3
06033	Lake County, California	52,612	51.2	0.0	54.0	48.5	48.5	71.4	50.9	17.3	14.6	23,011	11,664	11,347	49.3
06035	Lassen County, California	28,228	36.1	0.2	29.0	52.0	30.6	39.0	49.4	15.5	10.9	9,082	4,966	4,116	45.3
06037	Los Angeles County, California	7,997,089	64.4	0.0	71.4	57.7	50.5	81.2	65.1	18.0	10.0	4,635,465	2,513,915	2,121,550	45.8
06039	Madera County, California	115,435	49.6	0.1	59.1	41.1	42.9	62.9	51.7	14.3	7.5	53,032	30,293	22,739	42.9
06041	Marin County, California	210,822	64.9	0.1	69.8	60.3	51.0	82.5	74.3	27.2	5.7	129,027	67,549	61,478	47.6
06043	Mariposa County, California	15,208	54.5	0.1	57.3	51.7	56.7	81.7	54.4	15.0	11.6	7,329	3,861	3,468	47.3
06045	Mendocino County, California	70,705	59.3	0.2	63.4	55.3	59.8	77.4	62.4	20.7	12.2	36,848	19,453	17,395	47.2
06047	Merced County, California	193,076	59.5	0.1	66.5	52.4	51.7	75.4	56.0	14.9	16.2	96,170	54,231	41,939	43.6
06049	Modoc County, California	7,592	48.1	0.0	43.9	52.3	50.3	68.6	47.9	16.0	8.6	3,334	1,454	1,880	56.4
06051	Mono County, California	11,556	70.6	0.5	75.3	64.9	73.4	87.0	69.1	18.3	13.4	7,061	3,732	3,329	47.1
06053	Monterey County, California	326,799	59.3	1.9	63.6	54.7	48.7	73.9	62.3	18.1	8.4	177,333	97,146	80,187	45.2
06055	Napa County, California	113,016	65.6	0.0	71.0	60.4	60.4	85.2	69.9	19.3	7.5	68,587	36,711	31,876	46.5
06057	Nevada County, California	83,161	55.3	0.3	59.5	51.3	54.4	79.3	60.0	15.2	9.8	41,473	21,685	19,788	47.7
06059	Orange County, California	2,476,835	66.0	0.1	73.6	58.6	53.5	82.8	69.3	19.6	7.6	1,508,753	824,284	684,469	45.4
06061	Placer County, California	291,432	60.9	0.3	66.3	55.8	56.2	83.1	62.0	13.2	8.3	162,616	85,088	77,528	47.7
06063	Plumas County, California	16,113	52.7	0.0	56.1	49.2	53.3	79.5	54.5	15.1	15.2	7,200	3,765	3,435	47.7
06065	Riverside County, California	1,756,103	60.2	0.2	67.1	53.4	52.6	78.0	59.3	14.2	12.9	920,603	508,256	412,347	44.8
06067	Sacramento County, California	1,145,850	62.7	0.1	67.2	58.5	56.2	80.0	59.6	14.3	11.8	633,897	325,425	308,472	48.7
06069	San Benito County, California	43,696	68.4	0.1	75.2	61.7	61.1	84.3	67.8	19.0	12.2	26,261	14,583	11,678	44.5
06071	San Bernardino County, California	1,585,031	59.9	0.7	65.6	54.2	50.1	75.2	58.1	13.9	12.6	829,145	449,149	379,996	45.8
06073	San Diego County, California	2,579,342	62.1	2.9	67.0	57.2	50.1	78.2	65.6	16.9	8.7	1,462,130	785,191	676,939	46.3
06075	San Francisco County, California	739,386	69.4	0.1	73.5	65.2	55.1	86.9	66.7	16.8	6.8	478,373	256,625	221,748	46.4
06077	San Joaquin County, California	532,449	61.0	0.1	67.5	54.8	52.9	77.5	59.4	15.4	13.7	280,460	154,010	126,450	45.1
06079	San Luis Obispo County, California	231,576	57.8	0.8	60.6	54.8	50.2	79.6	61.8	16.8	6.6	124,997	66,746	58,251	46.6
06081	San Mateo County, California	603,942	68.7	0.0	75.1	62.6	58.1	86.3	71.7	19.6	6.7	387,006	205,105	181,901	47.0
06083	Santa Barbara County, California	348,390	63.6	0.5	69.3	57.8	56.4	81.7	68.1	20.9	8.0	203,616	110,712	92,904	45.6
06085	Santa Clara County, California	1,478,517	67.1	0.0	74.5	59.6	51.9	83.7	68.5	17.7	7.7	915,619	510,751	404,868	44.2
06087	Santa Cruz County, California	221,018	64.3	0.0	69.8	59.0	52.3	82.9	67.3	23.0	7.6	131,321	70,064	61,257	46.6
06089	Shasta County, California	144,720	53.4	0.0	57.0	49.9	53.5	74.1	53.6	13.2	10.3	69,261	35,100	34,161	49.3
06091	Sierra County, California	2,618	46.1	0.0	46.3	45.8	15.8	62.2	53.6	25.0	8.0	1,110	564	546	49.2
06093	Siskiyou County, California	35,992	51.3	0.1	53.4	49.3	62.4	72.7	51.9	14.1	12.7	16,127	8,094	8,033	49.8
06095	Solano County, California	338,257	62.4	1.3	65.5	59.3	58.6	78.2	61.5	17.0	11.4	187,021	95,953	91,068	48.7
06097	Sonoma County, California	403,509	64.8	0.2	70.4	59.5	60.3	83.1	67.5	20.5	8.1	240,247	125,747	114,500	47.7
06099	Stanislaus County, California	398,487	61.7	0.0	69.4	54.3	56.5	77.9	60.4	14.2	15.2	208,428	115,796	92,632	44.4
06101	Sutter County, California	72,682	59.5	0.6	66.2	52.9	56.6	77.6	57.4	13.7	13.2	37,520	20,435	17,085	45.5
06103	Tehama County, California	49,679	53.6	0.1	58.5	48.9	54.3	71.6	54.8	14.1	13.2	23,127	12,241	10,886	47.1
06105	Trinity County, California	11,454	46.4	0.3	46.0	46.8	51.2	68.6	45.2	12.8	9.0	4,832	2,505	2,327	48.2
06107	Tulare County, California	325,404	59.6	0.1	67.5	51.9	48.2	76.1	57.8	15.8	12.0	170,780	96,349	74,431	43.6
06109	Tuolumne County, California	46,069	48.5	0.0	49.4	47.5	56.7	67.8	51.3	12.9	12.9	19,477	10,280	9,197	47.2
06111	Ventura County, California	658,777	66.1	0.5	72.8	59.7	58.0	82.7	69.4	20.4	8.6	398,116	215,769	182,347	45.8
06113	Yolo County, California	167,629	60.9	0.2	65.0	57.1	47.3	81.3	65.4	15.8	9.0	92,806	47,690	45,116	48.6
06115	Yuba County, California	55,006	54.4	3.3	60.6	48.2	45.2	69.0	53.5	14.9	14.8	25,499	14,196	11,303	44.3
08000	**Colorado**	4,168,824	67.6	0.8	72.7	62.6	61.9	83.2	67.8	19.7	6.9	2,624,436	1,405,992	1,218,444	46.4
08001	Adams County, Colorado	352,413	70.8	0.1	77.3	64.3	67.3	83.8	67.1	18.0	7.9	229,743	126,267	103,476	45.0
08003	Alamosa County, Colorado	12,586	55.7	0.0	59.8	51.8	59.9	69.4	47.8	19.2	10.4	6,283	3,392	2,891	46.0
08005	Arapahoe County, Colorado	473,975	70.8	0.3	77.0	65.0	63.7	85.5	71.5	21.9	7.2	311,498	164,237	147,261	47.3
08007	Archuleta County, Colorado	10,310	58.2	0.0	61.0	55.3	65.5	81.8	59.5	17.0	8.2	5,506	2,927	2,579	46.8
08009	Baca County, Colorado	3,008	59.3	0.0	65.9	53.2	62.3	84.7	66.2	21.7	4.5	1,702	907	795	46.7
08011	Bent County, Colorado	5,057	26.1	0.0	21.9	36.6	15.7	26.6	46.7	9.6	8.3	1,212	746	466	38.4
08013	Boulder County, Colorado	254,340	69.8	0.0	74.4	65.1	60.1	86.6	73.2	22.5	6.1	166,701	88,476	78,225	46.9
08014	Broomfield County, Colorado	47,183	71.3	0.0	78.0	65.0	62.3	87.2	73.5	15.6	5.5	31,807	17,176	14,631	46.0
08015	Chaffee County, Colorado	15,737	55.2	0.0	56.7	53.4	62.9	74.3	60.2	16.7	5.9	8,170	4,440	3,730	45.7
08017	Cheyenne County, Colorado	1,506	68.3	0.0	77.0	58.7	62.7	83.3	71.0	23.1	9.3	932	547	385	41.3
08019	Clear Creek County, Colorado	7,798	69.3	0.2	72.6	65.7	63.4	86.2	72.6	29.0	5.4	5,114	2,756	2,358	46.1
08021	Conejos County, Colorado	6,248	53.6	0.0	61.5	45.6	53.4	72.2	54.4	16.4	9.7	3,021	1,711	1,310	43.4
08023	Costilla County, Colorado	2,963	48.7	0.0	54.0	43.0	63.9	69.8	48.3	16.6	14.0	1,240	703	537	43.3
08025	Crowley County, Colorado	4,459	44.7	0.0	38.0	54.9	60.3	47.5	46.1	13.5	27.0	1,457	665	792	54.4
08027	Custer County, Colorado	3,642	44.4	0.0	54.7	33.5	39.1	69.6	58.2	11.1	14.0	1,390	864	526	37.8
08029	Delta County, Colorado	24,517	52.5	0.0	56.6	48.3	58.0	71.9	59.3	16.6	11.7	11,362	6,274	5,088	44.8
08031	Denver County, Colorado	525,109	70.8	0.1	76.2	65.4	63.8	84.9	64.8	19.5	6.3	348,382	186,839	161,543	46.4
08033	Dolores County, Colorado	1,477	56.9	0.0	59.8	53.4	77.5	78.7	58.2	11.8	4.6	801	447	354	44.2
08035	Douglas County, Colorado	227,628	73.2	0.2	81.4	65.4	62.9	85.9	74.5	22.5	4.1	159,911	87,091	72,820	45.5
08037	Eagle County, Colorado	41,579	80.0	0.1	85.6	73.5	67.8	90.2	76.1	35.7	4.4	31,793	18,290	13,503	42.5
08039	Elbert County, Colorado	19,134	69.3	0.1	75.3	63.4	58.3	85.9	69.4	27.1	6.7	12,373	6,569	5,804	46.9
08041	El Paso County, Colorado	506,562	62.6	5.5	65.9	59.3	54.0	76.6	66.1	18.1	8.4	290,448	153,209	137,239	47.3
08043	Fremont County, Colorado	39,857	38.6	0.2	32.8	47.2	55.0	42.8	48.9	14.5	9.2	13,983	6,875	7,108	50.8
08045	Garfield County, Colorado	43,734	71.4	0.1	78.6	63.9	62.6	84.3	71.9	26.2	6.9	29,078	16,487	12,591	43.3
08047	Gilpin County, Colorado	4,649	71.4	0.0	78.3	64.6	44.0	86.5	72.5	18.2	4.9	3,159	1,714	1,445	45.7

Table C. County—Labor Force, Employment, and Educational Data, 2011–2015—*Continued*

Fips code	State/county	Total population age 16 and older	Percent in civilian labor force	Percent in armed forces	Civilian labor force participation by gender — Men	Civilian labor force participation by gender — Women	Civilian labor force participation by age — Age 16 to 24	Civilian labor force participation by age — Age 25 to 54	Civilian labor force participation by age — Age 55 to 64	Civilian labor force participation by age — Age 65 and older	Civilian unemploy-ment rate	Civilian employed population age 16 and older — Total	Civilian employed population age 16 and older — Men	Civilian employed population age 16 and older — Women	Percent women
08049	Grand County, Colorado	12,008	73.1	0.0	73.9	72.1	74.5	90.7	69.7	21.6	5.7	8,274	4,615	3,659	44.2
08051	Gunnison County, Colorado	13,157	74.3	0.0	78.2	69.8	72.5	88.9	73.6	22.9	7.8	9,016	5,196	3,820	42.4
08053	Hinsdale County, Colorado	756	61.5	0.0	66.3	56.8	63.3	85.9	70.4	28.9	3.0	451	237	214	47.5
08055	Huerfano County, Colorado	5,541	46.9	0.0	50.8	43.0	57.5	71.6	49.3	16.6	15.0	2,211	1,184	1,027	46.4
08057	Jackson County, Colorado	1,139	68.1	0.0	76.6	58.8	57.9	81.1	82.7	37.7	1.5	764	452	312	40.8
08059	Jefferson County, Colorado	449,317	69.6	0.0	74.2	65.2	65.0	87.1	71.3	20.0	5.9	294,390	154,513	139,877	47.5
08061	Kiowa County, Colorado	1,150	64.2	0.2	70.3	58.9	55.4	86.0	75.1	27.5	2.0	723	374	349	48.3
08063	Kit Carson County, Colorado	6,303	57.7	0.1	56.0	59.9	71.9	62.0	74.7	29.0	5.9	3,421	1,847	1,574	46.0
08065	Lake County, Colorado	5,917	74.0	0.0	78.9	68.0	67.4	87.3	74.5	18.1	5.7	4,126	2,445	1,681	40.7
08067	La Plata County, Colorado	43,934	67.2	0.0	70.7	63.5	60.9	84.9	67.4	19.2	5.2	27,965	14,883	13,082	46.8
08069	Larimer County, Colorado	259,993	67.6	0.1	72.5	62.8	63.5	85.6	69.5	19.5	6.7	164,011	86,553	77,458	47.2
08071	Las Animas County, Colorado	11,971	54.3	0.0	58.8	49.7	56.5	71.8	59.0	20.2	9.2	5,903	3,203	2,700	45.7
08073	Lincoln County, Colorado	4,536	35.0	0.0	21.5	55.1	38.3	36.0	53.4	17.7	6.3	1,488	542	946	63.6
08075	Logan County, Colorado	18,250	62.6	0.2	67.1	57.2	69.2	77.9	61.9	19.8	9.0	10,407	6,104	4,303	41.3
08077	Mesa County, Colorado	117,560	63.3	0.0	69.0	57.8	63.2	82.9	64.7	17.2	8.7	67,956	36,282	31,674	46.6
08079	Mineral County, Colorado	679	46.2	0.0	51.4	41.4	40.0	83.3	58.0	9.7	1.6	309	168	141	45.6
08081	Moffat County, Colorado	10,088	66.8	0.0	77.1	56.1	62.4	80.0	68.4	26.4	5.9	6,343	3,745	2,598	41.0
08083	Montezuma County, Colorado	20,444	59.9	0.1	64.2	55.7	64.7	80.7	61.6	15.9	9.5	11,075	5,815	5,260	47.5
08085	Montrose County, Colorado	32,598	57.5	0.0	63.2	52.1	62.5	80.4	59.4	14.6	10.2	16,832	8,863	7,969	47.3
08087	Morgan County, Colorado	21,499	65.7	0.0	74.2	57.4	62.9	84.7	69.2	18.2	6.2	13,264	7,478	5,786	43.6
08089	Otero County, Colorado	14,730	55.6	0.0	60.9	50.6	51.9	75.8	59.3	18.4	10.7	7,314	3,865	3,449	47.2
08091	Ouray County, Colorado	4,010	60.4	0.0	66.6	54.5	55.4	89.3	65.5	21.1	6.7	2,261	1,220	1,041	46.0
08093	Park County, Colorado	13,829	67.6	0.2	69.1	65.9	59.2	88.6	63.0	24.8	5.6	8,822	4,796	4,026	45.6
08095	Phillips County, Colorado	3,430	61.1	0.0	69.8	51.4	52.4	85.0	66.1	24.7	5.3	1,984	1,197	787	39.7
08097	Pitkin County, Colorado	14,911	74.8	0.2	76.9	72.3	53.2	91.2	78.6	35.7	7.7	10,290	5,531	4,759	46.2
08099	Prowers County, Colorado	9,369	64.9	0.4	67.9	61.9	64.7	85.6	64.5	18.4	9.7	5,488	2,812	2,676	48.8
08101	Pueblo County, Colorado	127,720	57.3	0.2	60.8	54.0	61.1	77.0	53.1	13.7	10.8	65,300	33,296	32,004	49.0
08103	Rio Blanco County, Colorado	5,180	68.3	0.0	74.5	61.6	59.6	85.4	66.7	29.7	4.2	3,389	1,908	1,481	43.7
08105	Rio Grande County, Colorado	9,269	59.8	0.4	62.9	56.8	62.3	80.5	61.9	14.3	8.1	5,093	2,582	2,511	49.3
08107	Routt County, Colorado	19,508	75.1	0.0	78.7	71.2	67.9	92.4	65.4	27.2	4.0	14,060	7,715	6,345	45.1
08109	Saguache County, Colorado	4,960	54.7	0.0	61.1	48.3	59.0	70.9	49.8	26.1	9.7	2,452	1,367	1,085	44.2
08111	San Juan County, Colorado	545	71.7	0.0	85.0	55.3	80.3	82.3	54.6	57.3	13.8	337	220	117	34.7
08113	San Miguel County, Colorado	6,344	75.0	0.0	79.1	70.4	70.7	89.5	61.5	30.3	5.8	4,482	2,511	1,971	44.0
08115	Sedgwick County, Colorado	1,946	56.4	0.0	62.2	50.8	53.7	82.1	69.0	21.0	6.4	1,028	551	477	46.4
08117	Summit County, Colorado	24,440	78.0	0.0	85.0	69.5	71.9	89.2	76.3	30.0	4.7	18,171	10,926	7,245	39.9
08119	Teller County, Colorado	19,602	63.9	0.4	69.0	58.6	61.2	84.2	65.9	20.2	8.2	11,501	6,256	5,245	45.6
08121	Washington County, Colorado	3,910	59.2	0.0	61.7	56.5	49.6	74.4	77.0	24.3	5.1	2,196	1,162	1,034	47.1
08123	Weld County, Colorado	205,024	67.6	0.1	74.4	60.8	60.4	82.8	67.5	19.0	6.6	129,395	71,340	58,055	44.9
08125	Yuma County, Colorado	7,786	64.3	0.2	70.6	58.3	59.4	84.4	70.1	20.2	2.5	4,878	2,629	2,249	46.1
09000	**Connecticut**	2,906,229	67.2	0.3	72.0	62.8	59.7	84.8	73.6	20.9	8.8	1,781,417	914,469	866,948	48.7
09001	Fairfield County, Connecticut	743,451	68.5	0.0	75.7	61.9	59.4	84.5	75.5	23.7	9.0	463,610	245,703	217,907	47.0
09003	Hartford County, Connecticut	724,002	67.0	0.1	71.4	62.9	61.1	85.1	72.2	19.3	9.3	439,719	222,887	216,832	49.3
09005	Litchfield County, Connecticut	154,009	68.7	0.0	72.7	64.9	66.8	87.5	75.6	22.6	7.1	98,294	50,439	47,855	48.7
09007	Middlesex County, Connecticut	136,966	68.2	0.1	72.8	63.9	59.7	88.1	76.6	20.3	6.0	87,871	45,387	42,484	48.3
09009	New Haven County, Connecticut	701,443	66.2	0.1	70.2	62.5	57.5	84.1	72.7	20.5	9.5	419,901	209,780	210,121	50.0
09011	New London County, Connecticut	223,557	64.9	3.0	67.4	62.4	56.2	82.6	72.3	19.9	8.3	132,990	68,738	64,252	48.3
09013	Tolland County, Connecticut	127,080	67.7	0.0	69.7	65.7	62.1	85.9	75.3	20.0	6.8	80,190	41,232	38,958	48.6
09015	Windham County, Connecticut	95,721	67.7	0.2	71.8	63.8	63.6	86.0	70.1	16.9	9.3	58,842	30,303	28,539	48.5
10000	**Delaware**	744,949	63.1	0.4	67.1	59.4	56.9	82.9	64.8	17.7	7.7	433,816	219,250	214,566	49.5
10001	Kent County, Delaware	133,212	61.7	1.8	66.1	57.7	57.5	80.9	62.4	15.6	8.4	75,246	38,157	37,089	49.3
10003	New Castle County, Delaware	441,040	65.7	0.1	69.3	62.5	54.9	83.8	68.3	18.2	7.4	268,331	134,127	134,204	50.0
10005	Sussex County, Delaware	170,697	57.4	0.1	62.3	52.9	63.7	81.8	58.9	18.2	8.0	90,239	46,966	43,273	48.0
11000	District of Columbia	546,805	68.3	0.6	70.8	66.2	49.4	85.6	63.9	22.9	9.6	337,815	162,958	174,857	51.8
11001	**District of Columbia** District of Columbia	546,805	68.3	0.6	70.8	66.2	49.4	85.6	63.9	22.9	9.6	337,815	162,958	174,857	51.8
12000	**Florida**	16,077,778	58.8	0.3	63.2	54.7	54.5	80.4	61.4	14.5	9.7	8,541,291	4,428,975	4,112,316	48.1
12001	Alachua County, Florida	213,509	59.3	0.0	61.9	56.9	46.5	80.5	64.4	16.3	7.9	116,659	57,907	58,752	50.4
12003	Baker County, Florida	21,105	52.9	0.0	54.0	51.8	51.3	68.0	46.3	11.6	8.9	10,174	5,312	4,862	47.8
12005	Bay County, Florida	141,361	60.3	1.7	63.7	57.0	60.7	78.4	57.1	15.9	8.6	77,894	40,192	37,702	48.4
12007	Bradford County, Florida	22,474	46.8	0.0	43.2	51.4	42.0	63.2	42.4	13.4	12.4	9,225	4,744	4,481	48.6
12009	Brevard County, Florida	462,632	55.7	0.3	60.1	51.6	54.7	80.5	58.3	13.6	10.9	229,693	118,678	111,015	48.3
12011	Broward County, Florida	1,489,265	66.5	0.1	71.8	61.6	56.1	85.1	70.1	18.9	10.0	890,997	460,904	430,093	48.3
12013	Calhoun County, Florida	11,820	44.5	0.2	40.2	49.9	48.7	57.6	41.4	13.0	10.0	4,735	2,448	2,287	48.3
12015	Charlotte County, Florida	146,400	43.4	0.0	45.1	41.8	61.7	76.5	53.1	10.9	10.8	56,730	28,533	28,197	49.7
12017	Citrus County, Florida	121,430	41.2	0.0	43.9	38.7	56.1	73.4	47.4	8.5	13.1	43,486	21,803	21,683	49.9
12019	Clay County, Florida	155,146	62.3	1.2	67.3	57.6	59.0	79.7	60.3	15.5	10.7	86,374	45,279	41,095	47.6
12021	Collier County, Florida	285,308	53.6	0.0	59.1	48.4	60.2	82.9	61.3	14.8	7.8	141,106	75,906	65,200	46.2
12023	Columbia County, Florida	54,688	54.2	0.0	53.9	54.5	53.3	72.7	57.2	10.2	14.8	25,226	12,837	12,389	49.1
12027	DeSoto County, Florida	28,433	47.7	0.0	51.6	42.3	45.4	69.3	41.9	9.6	9.4	12,279	7,772	4,507	36.7
12029	Dixie County, Florida	13,414	39.4	0.0	38.1	41.1	36.3	52.1	48.3	12.2	7.2	4,910	2,633	2,277	46.4
12031	Duval County, Florida	707,294	64.3	1.5	68.2	60.8	55.9	80.9	62.4	17.5	10.0	409,421	206,841	202,580	49.5

Table C. County—Labor Force, Employment, and Educational Data, 2011–2015—*Continued*

Fips code	State/county	Total population age 16 and older	Percent in civilian labor force	Percent in armed forces	Civilian labor force participation by gender		Civilian labor force participation by age				Civilian unemployment rate	Civilian employed population age 16 and older			
					Men	Women	Age 16 to 24	Age 25 to 54	Age 55 to 64	Age 65 and older		Total	Men	Women	Percent women
12033	Escambia County, Florida	248,990	57.8	4.0	59.7	55.9	50.4	78.4	59.0	13.6	9.4	130,402	66,597	63,805	48.9
12035	Flagler County, Florida	84,508	48.2	0.0	52.0	44.8	56.1	76.2	52.0	11.0	9.3	36,923	18,714	18,209	49.3
12037	Franklin County, Florida	9,870	48.4	0.0	43.6	55.5	64.7	54.5	64.1	15.3	9.4	4,331	2,297	2,034	47.0
12039	Gadsden County, Florida	37,123	50.8	0.1	52.4	49.3	45.4	65.9	51.0	14.0	11.2	16,733	7,818	8,915	53.3
12041	Gilchrist County, Florida	13,982	50.0	0.0	49.9	50.1	34.0	77.0	50.3	15.7	10.4	6,260	3,245	3,015	48.2
12043	Glades County, Florida	11,111	38.2	0.0	38.2	38.3	52.9	53.0	49.3	5.5	12.9	3,701	2,080	1,621	43.8
12045	Gulf County, Florida	13,655	45.7	0.0	45.7	45.7	53.3	58.0	46.1	10.3	10.2	5,604	3,461	2,143	38.2
12047	Hamilton County, Florida	12,000	39.3	0.0	33.1	49.0	40.6	46.1	48.7	11.6	15.8	3,966	2,037	1,929	48.6
12049	Hardee County, Florida	20,987	50.9	0.0	55.4	45.6	50.5	68.1	40.7	11.0	11.0	9,517	5,636	3,881	40.8
12051	Hendry County, Florida	28,750	58.1	0.0	62.1	53.7	54.7	73.1	57.1	14.0	11.9	14,732	8,745	5,987	40.6
12053	Hernando County, Florida	145,482	46.5	0.1	50.5	42.9	53.4	75.0	48.5	8.5	13.7	58,359	29,827	28,532	48.9
12055	Highlands County, Florida	82,755	43.4	0.1	47.1	39.9	51.8	78.0	49.8	8.7	13.3	31,131	15,863	15,268	49.0
12057	Hillsborough County, Florida	1,034,849	64.6	0.5	69.5	60.1	55.3	82.3	63.5	15.8	9.0	608,977	315,388	293,589	48.2
12059	Holmes County, Florida	16,056	45.0	0.2	45.0	45.0	47.0	62.6	41.3	9.8	15.4	6,118	3,432	2,686	43.9
12061	Indian River County, Florida	120,494	50.3	0.1	55.2	45.8	56.5	79.8	60.6	12.0	12.2	53,211	27,538	25,673	48.2
12063	Jackson County, Florida	40,846	44.1	0.0	39.9	49.3	47.7	55.5	45.3	13.1	13.2	15,621	7,816	7,805	50.0
12065	Jefferson County, Florida	12,084	45.2	0.1	36.6	54.9	37.9	55.7	58.3	15.1	9.4	4,946	2,162	2,784	56.3
12067	Lafayette County, Florida	7,145	44.0	0.0	43.2	45.3	30.0	57.0	49.8	10.2	14.6	2,685	1,698	987	36.8
12069	Lake County, Florida	255,440	52.7	0.1	56.3	49.5	59.1	80.7	54.9	11.8	9.7	121,642	62,395	59,247	48.7
12071	Lee County, Florida	552,379	53.0	0.0	57.0	49.2	58.3	79.5	56.5	13.8	10.1	263,079	135,719	127,360	48.4
12073	Leon County, Florida	235,024	66.8	0.1	70.8	63.3	61.2	83.9	70.4	19.3	10.6	140,338	69,459	70,879	50.5
12075	Levy County, Florida	32,651	49.6	0.0	52.8	46.5	54.5	70.8	52.6	11.7	11.1	14,392	7,231	7,161	49.8
12077	Liberty County, Florida	6,935	44.1	0.0	40.7	50.1	45.8	52.7	47.0	7.1	10.2	2,748	1,568	1,180	42.9
12079	Madison County, Florida	15,360	45.3	0.0	45.4	45.3	48.0	59.5	45.7	11.6	11.8	6,141	3,330	2,811	45.8
12081	Manatee County, Florida	283,666	54.2	0.0	58.9	49.8	58.1	80.9	59.7	12.9	8.6	140,416	72,482	67,934	48.4
12083	Marion County, Florida	281,133	46.7	0.0	50.6	43.1	53.0	73.0	51.2	10.5	12.0	115,459	58,856	56,603	49.0
12085	Martin County, Florida	129,181	52.4	0.1	56.9	48.1	60.6	79.2	63.6	13.8	9.7	61,157	32,431	28,726	47.0
12086	Miami-Dade County, Florida	2,152,396	62.2	0.1	68.3	56.5	47.9	81.3	65.3	15.6	10.0	1,204,871	635,205	569,666	47.3
12087	Monroe County, Florida	65,807	62.3	1.5	64.6	59.7	57.1	82.2	64.1	21.6	6.0	38,504	21,039	17,465	45.4
12089	Nassau County, Florida	62,112	56.4	0.4	63.3	49.8	61.2	75.8	57.7	14.8	9.8	31,605	17,244	14,361	45.4
12091	Okaloosa County, Florida	153,946	59.2	5.4	62.3	56.1	57.0	74.9	60.6	16.5	6.9	84,899	45,030	39,869	47.0
12093	Okeechobee County, Florida	31,497	47.6	0.0	49.6	45.2	41.7	65.9	47.0	11.7	11.8	13,227	7,419	5,808	43.9
12095	Orange County, Florida	979,897	67.8	0.1	72.2	63.5	55.5	83.8	68.1	16.9	9.1	603,683	313,980	289,703	48.0
12097	Osceola County, Florida	233,772	62.4	0.0	67.8	57.2	53.3	79.5	57.8	17.2	9.8	131,450	68,999	62,451	47.5
12099	Palm Beach County, Florida	1,138,307	60.0	0.0	66.0	54.4	60.3	83.8	67.0	16.2	9.5	617,902	325,009	292,893	47.4
12101	Pasco County, Florida	392,316	52.7	0.1	56.9	48.9	54.4	77.3	53.0	10.6	9.4	187,556	95,874	91,682	48.9
12103	Pinellas County, Florida	790,366	58.5	0.1	62.5	54.9	58.3	82.3	63.9	14.9	8.4	423,351	212,795	210,556	49.7
12105	Polk County, Florida	499,586	55.1	0.0	59.8	50.6	51.5	77.3	57.3	13.1	10.6	245,853	128,238	117,615	47.8
12107	Putnam County, Florida	58,608	47.3	0.1	50.9	43.7	46.4	70.1	44.2	11.5	12.6	24,209	12,717	11,492	47.5
12109	St. Johns County, Florida	169,803	60.9	0.4	67.9	54.3	54.0	82.2	62.8	16.9	6.7	96,436	52,042	44,394	46.0
12111	St. Lucie County, Florida	234,119	54.7	0.0	57.9	51.8	56.7	78.8	56.8	13.1	12.4	112,310	57,130	55,180	49.1
12113	Santa Rosa County, Florida	128,550	57.0	2.8	61.0	52.8	55.5	70.5	60.0	14.6	7.9	67,510	36,834	30,676	45.4
12115	Sarasota County, Florida	339,991	49.6	0.0	53.7	46.0	60.4	83.1	58.0	12.8	8.2	155,023	78,349	76,674	49.5
12117	Seminole County, Florida	354,090	65.6	0.1	71.0	60.7	55.2	82.7	69.2	18.9	9.4	210,450	108,632	101,818	48.4
12119	Sumter County, Florida	101,007	24.2	0.0	23.4	25.2	48.8	53.5	31.2	7.9	9.0	22,298	11,084	11,214	50.3
12121	Suwannee County, Florida	35,245	50.0	0.0	56.5	43.5	56.7	70.0	44.2	13.8	11.1	15,676	8,870	6,806	43.4
12123	Taylor County, Florida	18,948	41.5	0.0	37.5	46.9	54.4	50.7	38.3	14.1	9.0	7,155	3,759	3,396	47.5
12125	Union County, Florida	12,729	35.2	0.0	26.5	54.0	44.2	45.2	21.3	5.2	11.7	3,955	2,046	1,909	48.3
12127	Volusia County, Florida	423,616	51.8	0.1	55.6	48.2	49.0	76.2	55.9	12.1	9.1	199,287	102,557	96,730	48.5
12129	Wakulla County, Florida	25,489	55.8	0.1	52.0	60.8	53.3	64.7	64.0	17.2	9.3	12,899	6,961	5,938	46.0
12131	Walton County, Florida	48,588	56.7	0.3	58.5	54.9	64.7	74.4	55.5	15.7	7.9	25,377	13,130	12,247	48.3
12133	Washington County, Florida	20,258	46.3	0.0	44.0	49.3	53.5	59.0	45.4	10.9	11.5	8,307	4,418	3,889	46.8
13000	**Georgia**	7,792,052	62.3	0.6	67.1	57.9	52.5	79.2	60.6	16.1	9.7	4,388,274	2,282,476	2,105,798	48.0
13001	Appling County, Georgia	14,292	53.7	0.2	60.8	46.7	47.0	73.7	48.6	12.2	7.9	7,071	4,018	3,053	43.2
13003	Atkinson County, Georgia	6,177	59.2	0.0	67.1	51.3	40.2	78.7	51.0	14.1	7.3	3,389	1,962	1,427	42.1
13005	Bacon County, Georgia	8,793	54.7	0.0	56.0	53.3	59.9	70.1	53.1	9.3	4.4	4,598	2,388	2,210	48.1
13007	Baker County, Georgia	2,720	50.7	0.0	48.4	53.0	28.6	71.1	56.8	16.5	7.1	1,282	601	681	53.1
13009	Baldwin County, Georgia	37,786	47.4	0.2	47.1	47.6	38.6	67.9	45.1	9.9	8.4	16,387	7,936	8,451	51.6
13011	Banks County, Georgia	14,513	58.7	0.1	66.3	51.2	55.3	76.9	60.2	14.2	8.5	7,801	4,233	3,568	45.7
13013	Barrow County, Georgia	54,463	65.6	0.1	74.3	57.4	60.0	80.2	59.8	19.3	10.1	32,137	17,559	14,578	45.4
13015	Bartow County, Georgia	78,337	62.4	0.0	69.4	55.8	58.5	79.0	60.5	11.9	8.8	44,594	23,860	20,734	46.5
13017	Ben Hill County, Georgia	13,433	49.6	0.1	54.6	45.2	41.1	68.6	45.0	13.5	9.7	6,019	3,070	2,949	49.0
13019	Berrien County, Georgia	15,024	49.8	0.9	56.9	43.1	43.9	67.3	47.8	13.0	13.8	6,457	3,614	2,843	44.0
13021	Bibb County, Georgia	119,863	57.3	0.1	61.0	54.1	50.0	76.7	51.5	14.8	12.4	60,115	29,021	31,094	51.7
13023	Bleckley County, Georgia	10,186	45.0	0.1	46.8	43.5	27.1	70.3	46.0	11.2	4.8	4,365	2,112	2,253	51.6
13025	Brantley County, Georgia	14,124	53.2	0.0	56.6	50.0	50.0	70.5	47.7	14.1	10.9	6,702	3,390	3,312	49.4
13027	Brooks County, Georgia	12,560	54.7	0.1	59.6	50.2	52.3	77.8	49.9	13.1	17.0	5,703	3,118	2,585	45.3
13029	Bryan County, Georgia	24,576	63.6	3.5	67.9	59.4	56.3	75.8	63.5	17.2	9.0	14,224	7,595	6,629	46.6
13031	Bulloch County, Georgia	59,288	57.8	0.1	61.5	54.2	43.8	80.3	62.1	17.6	9.1	31,144	16,190	14,954	48.0
13033	Burke County, Georgia	17,507	54.0	0.1	57.9	50.4	43.7	74.7	47.6	12.4	8.2	8,676	4,387	4,289	49.4
13035	Butts County, Georgia	18,991	51.1	0.0	50.0	52.4	45.5	63.0	53.0	18.1	10.3	8,700	4,649	4,051	46.6
13037	Calhoun County, Georgia	5,485	40.2	0.0	29.4	57.0	62.6	39.9	48.0	6.6	7.7	2,036	914	1,122	55.1
13039	Camden County, Georgia	39,730	56.9	8.2	58.2	55.5	46.5	72.1	61.2	10.6	8.5	20,674	11,114	9,560	46.2

Table C. County—Labor Force, Employment, and Educational Data, 2011–2015—*Continued*

Fips code	State/county	Total population age 16 and older	Percent in civilian labor force	Percent in armed forces	Civilian labor force participation by gender		Civilian labor force participation by age				Civilian unemploy-ment rate	Civilian employed population age 16 and older			
					Men	Women	Age 16 to 24	Age 25 to 54	Age 55 to 64	Age 65 and older		Total	Men	Women	Percent women
13043	Candler County, Georgia	8,444	53.7	0.0	58.5	49.3	60.0	70.6	48.3	15.6	8.1	4,168	2,174	1,994	47.8
13045	Carroll County, Georgia	88,168	61.1	0.1	68.6	54.2	58.2	77.6	60.3	13.0	12.1	47,372	25,923	21,449	45.3
13047	Catoosa County, Georgia	51,547	63.5	0.1	68.5	58.8	64.4	80.4	62.4	19.5	8.1	30,069	15,363	14,706	48.9
13049	Charlton County, Georgia	10,886	50.2	0.0	46.6	54.3	57.2	60.8	47.8	6.1	13.8	4,705	2,369	2,336	49.6
13051	Chatham County, Georgia	223,398	61.8	1.6	65.7	58.3	53.5	79.6	61.6	16.7	9.7	124,627	62,945	61,682	49.5
13053	Chattahoochee County, Georgia	9,185	28.7	49.6	26.1	35.2	17.3	37.8	60.8	6.6	16.5	2,204	1,455	749	34.0
13055	Chattooga County, Georgia	20,311	49.1	0.0	49.6	48.6	38.7	66.9	52.2	9.0	10.0	8,976	4,681	4,295	47.8
13057	Cherokee County, Georgia	172,590	68.1	0.0	75.4	61.2	59.4	83.6	67.1	18.6	6.3	110,111	59,409	50,702	46.0
13059	Clarke County, Georgia	101,854	58.3	0.2	63.3	53.8	46.7	78.0	59.2	19.3	9.2	53,922	27,288	26,634	49.4
13061	Clay County, Georgia	2,383	44.0	0.0	50.4	37.9	62.9	59.8	48.6	5.4	19.2	848	480	368	43.4
13063	Clayton County, Georgia	199,379	66.7	0.1	69.9	63.9	53.6	81.5	59.1	17.8	14.1	114,144	55,864	58,280	51.1
13065	Clinch County, Georgia	5,096	50.8	0.4	52.5	49.1	52.4	66.7	40.6	16.7	10.7	2,309	1,185	1,124	48.7
13067	Cobb County, Georgia	560,255	71.2	0.1	77.5	65.4	59.0	85.9	70.7	21.5	8.0	366,793	192,102	174,691	47.6
13069	Coffee County, Georgia	33,467	50.1	0.1	51.3	48.8	47.7	62.2	45.7	16.1	8.3	15,358	8,025	7,333	47.7
13071	Colquitt County, Georgia	34,802	57.5	0.1	62.9	52.2	49.9	73.0	58.8	18.3	8.3	18,354	9,876	8,478	46.2
13073	Columbia County, Georgia	104,789	62.6	2.5	68.6	57.1	54.4	77.2	62.5	17.0	7.1	60,928	32,070	28,858	47.4
13075	Cook County, Georgia	13,008	58.0	0.1	63.0	53.4	51.2	74.7	53.1	21.4	6.6	7,043	3,658	3,385	48.1
13077	Coweta County, Georgia	102,565	65.3	0.1	73.3	57.8	57.9	80.8	65.1	17.9	7.0	62,298	33,939	28,359	45.5
13079	Crawford County, Georgia	10,099	53.9	0.1	59.3	48.4	44.2	74.0	47.9	15.7	11.0	4,843	2,658	2,185	45.1
13081	Crisp County, Georgia	18,117	56.4	0.0	59.6	53.7	53.7	77.6	48.0	13.5	15.5	8,633	4,197	4,436	51.4
13083	Dade County, Georgia	13,796	60.6	0.1	66.3	55.2	55.6	80.3	60.3	20.4	6.1	7,848	4,083	3,765	48.0
13085	Dawson County, Georgia	18,377	58.2	0.1	65.1	51.5	65.3	75.1	57.4	16.6	8.5	9,787	5,482	4,305	44.0
13087	Decatur County, Georgia	21,471	49.3	0.5	53.6	45.3	41.9	65.0	50.2	15.2	6.5	9,892	5,145	4,747	48.0
13089	DeKalb County, Georgia	562,904	69.1	0.1	73.3	65.4	56.0	84.1	66.0	19.0	11.3	344,876	171,850	173,026	50.2
13091	Dodge County, Georgia	17,161	50.8	0.0	50.1	51.6	44.7	67.9	47.8	11.1	9.8	7,871	4,145	3,726	47.3
13093	Dooly County, Georgia	11,709	47.4	0.0	45.2	50.1	36.8	61.4	52.0	14.1	11.7	4,895	2,676	2,219	45.3
13095	Dougherty County, Georgia	72,526	57.4	0.4	59.7	55.4	56.8	75.2	50.4	13.4	18.0	34,097	16,120	17,977	52.7
13097	Douglas County, Georgia	103,719	66.6	0.0	73.3	60.7	55.9	82.3	63.4	15.5	10.5	61,844	32,018	29,826	48.2
13099	Early County, Georgia	8,245	50.1	0.0	55.5	45.6	40.9	69.3	54.5	14.5	9.4	3,742	1,843	1,899	50.7
13101	Echols County, Georgia	3,120	59.7	0.0	73.1	47.1	53.9	76.0	62.2	11.3	10.1	1,675	1,028	647	38.6
13103	Effingham County, Georgia	41,477	65.0	0.8	72.4	57.9	53.7	81.5	60.9	15.0	6.0	25,352	13,816	11,536	45.5
13105	Elbert County, Georgia	15,668	51.6	0.0	55.7	47.9	48.5	72.7	45.3	15.5	10.8	7,210	3,566	3,644	50.5
13107	Emanuel County, Georgia	17,671	54.1	0.0	58.7	49.8	46.7	74.0	51.2	13.6	13.2	8,300	4,235	4,065	49.0
13109	Evans County, Georgia	8,194	54.1	0.4	63.2	46.1	49.4	68.1	60.3	16.6	10.3	3,979	2,169	1,810	45.5
13111	Fannin County, Georgia	20,001	49.2	0.0	53.7	45.0	58.5	74.1	48.3	12.7	12.0	8,669	4,572	4,097	47.3
13113	Fayette County, Georgia	86,168	62.6	0.3	69.3	56.4	50.8	82.3	67.9	19.1	7.6	49,795	26,445	23,350	46.9
13115	Floyd County, Georgia	75,952	58.6	0.1	63.0	54.6	61.0	76.0	56.3	14.5	10.9	39,669	20,217	19,452	49.0
13117	Forsyth County, Georgia	145,162	68.0	0.1	76.8	59.5	53.9	83.4	69.4	16.6	6.2	92,504	51,267	41,237	44.6
13119	Franklin County, Georgia	17,861	49.1	0.0	55.3	43.3	38.2	73.2	45.3	11.3	8.4	8,038	4,442	3,596	44.7
13121	Fulton County, Georgia	778,889	67.3	0.1	72.4	62.5	52.8	83.3	62.7	18.1	9.9	471,816	245,412	226,404	48.0
13123	Gilmer County, Georgia	23,423	51.9	0.2	56.5	47.2	59.0	74.6	46.2	13.5	10.0	10,938	5,982	4,956	45.3
13125	Glascock County, Georgia	2,393	60.5	0.0	67.6	54.3	63.0	82.6	51.4	16.3	7.1	1,344	697	647	48.1
13127	Glynn County, Georgia	64,700	62.0	0.1	67.0	57.6	60.8	82.3	60.9	18.2	9.3	36,375	18,431	17,944	49.3
13129	Gordon County, Georgia	43,344	59.4	0.0	66.3	52.6	51.0	77.4	55.0	14.3	8.3	23,587	13,088	10,499	44.5
13131	Grady County, Georgia	19,488	53.3	0.1	60.0	47.0	51.1	71.2	48.5	15.6	10.5	9,291	5,080	4,211	45.3
13133	Greene County, Georgia	13,370	47.8	0.2	53.8	42.2	57.7	73.8	46.3	11.4	6.8	5,952	3,229	2,723	45.7
13135	Gwinnett County, Georgia	645,209	69.4	0.1	76.4	62.8	51.0	83.1	71.5	19.9	8.3	410,562	219,173	191,389	46.6
13137	Habersham County, Georgia	34,570	53.2	0.0	63.6	44.1	53.7	69.4	58.4	12.6	7.7	16,970	9,373	7,597	44.8
13139	Hall County, Georgia	143,076	63.6	0.0	71.0	56.3	58.0	80.6	64.7	15.7	7.5	84,198	46,705	37,493	44.5
13141	Hancock County, Georgia	7,554	33.5	0.0	27.8	40.6	23.5	40.7	46.1	14.1	14.6	2,159	977	1,182	54.7
13143	Haralson County, Georgia	22,434	56.6	0.1	65.2	48.6	57.2	75.4	48.0	14.8	12.3	11,136	6,247	4,889	43.9
13145	Harris County, Georgia	26,482	61.8	0.3	67.2	56.8	52.7	82.9	57.6	20.1	8.0	15,071	8,038	7,033	46.7
13147	Hart County, Georgia	20,642	49.9	0.0	54.6	45.4	52.7	70.8	47.5	12.5	6.2	9,660	5,109	4,551	47.1
13149	Heard County, Georgia	9,162	56.5	0.0	60.1	53.0	53.6	75.2	56.6	9.6	12.1	4,547	2,377	2,170	47.7
13151	Henry County, Georgia	161,180	64.4	0.3	68.8	60.4	48.1	81.7	62.2	13.7	10.3	92,993	46,772	46,221	49.7
13153	Houston County, Georgia	113,163	62.6	2.0	67.0	58.7	57.8	78.8	57.8	13.1	9.7	64,013	32,973	31,040	48.5
13155	Irwin County, Georgia	7,457	45.4	0.0	47.3	43.5	43.6	60.9	43.6	10.6	6.8	3,158	1,679	1,479	46.8
13157	Jackson County, Georgia	47,220	61.3	0.1	67.6	55.3	48.6	79.4	62.3	13.2	7.9	26,679	14,331	12,348	46.3
13159	Jasper County, Georgia	10,685	59.1	0.0	63.8	54.7	50.5	79.0	53.6	17.6	12.7	5,520	2,929	2,591	46.9
13161	Jeff Davis County, Georgia	11,117	54.0	0.2	63.2	45.2	48.5	72.3	51.3	8.6	6.6	5,606	3,276	2,330	41.6
13163	Jefferson County, Georgia	12,776	48.1	0.0	53.5	43.3	36.2	66.6	53.3	10.1	17.0	5,097	2,677	2,420	47.5
13165	Jenkins County, Georgia	6,909	49.0	0.0	58.0	40.4	40.7	73.1	47.3	9.7	10.3	3,035	1,727	1,308	43.1
13167	Johnson County, Georgia	8,087	53.1	0.0	57.2	47.8	44.8	74.9	44.6	10.5	9.0	3,909	2,365	1,544	39.5
13169	Jones County, Georgia	22,506	59.8	0.2	64.2	55.7	50.1	80.5	55.4	16.4	9.5	12,176	6,193	5,983	49.1
13171	Lamar County, Georgia	14,766	55.1	0.2	61.0	49.4	42.7	79.0	63.2	7.6	15.6	6,860	3,496	3,364	49.0
13173	Lanier County, Georgia	7,905	51.5	3.1	53.6	49.4	56.3	61.5	47.9	13.8	14.6	3,476	1,726	1,750	50.3
13175	Laurens County, Georgia	37,204	48.7	0.1	52.4	45.4	39.4	65.8	50.0	13.4	6.6	16,926	8,522	8,404	49.7
13177	Lee County, Georgia	21,970	63.7	0.5	65.5	61.9	50.7	77.9	65.7	15.4	7.2	12,990	6,582	6,408	49.3
13179	Liberty County, Georgia	47,200	56.2	12.3	55.9	56.5	45.0	68.1	56.3	16.3	12.9	23,102	11,853	11,249	48.7
13181	Lincoln County, Georgia	6,381	53.9	0.3	54.1	53.8	46.4	79.3	49.4	15.9	9.3	3,121	1,530	1,591	51.0
13183	Long County, Georgia	12,279	55.3	6.6	60.7	49.9	57.0	65.1	46.6	10.4	15.6	5,728	3,226	2,502	43.7
13185	Lowndes County, Georgia	88,014	59.5	2.8	61.7	57.4	56.4	74.7	55.3	16.2	13.0	45,595	23,336	22,259	48.8
13187	Lumpkin County, Georgia	25,777	59.9	0.7	63.7	56.3	54.4	79.1	65.9	14.9	8.2	14,185	7,313	6,872	48.4

Table C. County—Labor Force, Employment, and Educational Data, 2011–2015—*Continued*

Fips code	State/county	Total population age 16 and older	Percent in civilian labor force	Percent in armed forces	Civilian labor force participation by gender		Civilian labor force participation by age				Civilian unemploy- ment rate	Civilian employed population age 16 and older			
					Men	Women	Age 16 to 24	Age 25 to 54	Age 55 to 64	Age 65 and older		Total	Men	Women	Percent women
13189	McDuffie County, Georgia	16,628	55.2	0.0	61.0	50.3	41.7	75.6	51.3	18.5	9.5	8,314	4,337	3,977	47.8
13191	McIntosh County, Georgia	11,643	50.9	0.2	54.1	48.0	45.3	71.7	57.0	10.6	8.8	5,410	2,747	2,663	49.2
13193	Macon County, Georgia	11,644	47.1	0.0	46.2	48.4	38.4	62.1	44.9	14.6	18.7	4,461	2,457	2,004	44.9
13195	Madison County, Georgia	22,425	55.6	0.1	58.9	52.5	46.8	72.0	57.4	18.3	8.7	11,393	5,910	5,483	48.1
13197	Marion County, Georgia	7,009	53.6	0.2	62.6	43.8	33.9	73.9	56.7	17.5	14.3	3,219	1,907	1,312	40.8
13199	Meriwether County, Georgia	17,161	51.7	0.0	60.7	43.5	43.4	73.4	50.1	13.0	12.8	7,730	4,274	3,456	44.7
13201	Miller County, Georgia	4,688	54.1	0.0	59.6	49.1	53.9	73.9	54.2	18.4	6.5	2,373	1,249	1,124	47.4
13205	Mitchell County, Georgia	18,171	50.6	0.0	48.8	52.7	42.0	65.4	47.1	19.6	13.5	7,956	4,078	3,878	48.7
13207	Monroe County, Georgia	21,919	55.7	0.0	57.2	54.2	43.8	77.2	54.5	13.3	10.5	10,914	5,562	5,352	49.0
13209	Montgomery County, Georgia	7,229	50.3	0.0	53.7	46.8	43.3	67.2	45.4	18.2	6.7	3,394	1,789	1,605	47.3
13211	Morgan County, Georgia	14,167	57.8	0.2	63.9	52.2	46.0	78.5	62.4	18.9	6.9	7,624	3,946	3,678	48.2
13213	Murray County, Georgia	30,404	59.5	0.0	66.9	52.3	55.7	76.0	52.8	14.6	11.1	16,079	8,894	7,185	44.7
13215	Muscogee County, Georgia	156,445	56.4	6.2	56.0	56.8	45.2	72.4	56.6	14.1	11.0	78,531	38,026	40,505	51.6
13217	Newton County, Georgia	77,995	63.4	0.1	66.9	60.4	55.3	80.7	59.2	14.8	11.8	43,639	21,689	21,950	50.3
13219	Oconee County, Georgia	26,381	64.7	0.0	71.4	58.4	48.2	83.5	71.5	16.7	5.0	16,227	8,669	7,558	46.6
13221	Oglethorpe County, Georgia	11,784	57.0	0.1	59.8	54.3	39.7	75.5	63.4	15.7	5.3	6,355	3,169	3,186	50.1
13223	Paulding County, Georgia	110,464	69.4	0.0	75.8	63.5	60.8	83.8	64.8	14.2	8.7	70,001	36,801	33,200	47.4
13225	Peach County, Georgia	21,799	59.4	0.5	65.7	53.6	43.3	82.0	61.3	16.1	11.3	11,481	6,195	5,286	46.0
13227	Pickens County, Georgia	24,260	57.0	0.2	65.4	48.5	65.7	79.0	49.6	16.1	8.3	12,678	7,278	5,400	42.6
13229	Pierce County, Georgia	14,761	54.0	0.0	63.2	45.3	44.7	73.0	50.9	15.8	8.9	7,262	4,127	3,135	43.2
13231	Pike County, Georgia	13,988	58.5	0.1	62.6	54.6	48.9	79.3	54.8	10.3	10.4	7,323	3,908	3,415	46.6
13233	Polk County, Georgia	31,505	57.2	0.0	65.2	49.7	51.0	77.3	52.5	12.7	10.2	16,190	9,095	7,095	43.8
13235	Pulaski County, Georgia	9,679	44.0	0.2	54.4	36.8	36.1	53.6	45.7	22.1	7.4	3,949	2,100	1,849	46.8
13237	Putnam County, Georgia	17,600	57.3	0.0	59.5	55.0	57.4	81.7	58.1	12.6	6.3	9,448	4,888	4,560	48.3
13239	Quitman County, Georgia	1,937	43.8	0.0	44.0	43.5	28.3	76.0	37.8	15.7	11.2	753	366	387	51.4
13241	Rabun County, Georgia	13,798	48.7	0.2	57.0	41.0	47.1	75.8	49.7	11.1	7.3	6,236	3,495	2,741	44.0
13243	Randolph County, Georgia	5,703	49.0	0.0	53.5	44.8	47.0	64.3	59.2	10.2	10.4	2,503	1,298	1,205	48.1
13245	Richmond County, Georgia	158,038	55.2	3.5	55.5	54.9	47.7	71.1	55.2	12.7	12.0	76,807	36,191	40,616	52.9
13247	Rockdale County, Georgia	66,857	62.9	0.0	69.1	57.6	49.0	81.9	63.8	14.0	11.2	37,374	18,986	18,388	49.2
13249	Schley County, Georgia	3,848	58.3	0.0	63.2	53.4	51.8	79.5	49.4	16.9	12.4	1,964	1,085	879	44.8
13251	Screven County, Georgia	11,365	53.5	0.2	54.9	52.2	39.1	76.1	54.1	16.0	9.8	5,482	2,659	2,823	51.5
13253	Seminole County, Georgia	7,060	46.9	0.0	55.4	39.7	36.2	73.8	40.0	12.9	9.4	2,999	1,651	1,348	44.9
13255	Spalding County, Georgia	49,756	53.8	0.0	57.5	50.6	55.8	72.4	47.0	11.0	12.4	23,471	11,654	11,817	50.3
13257	Stephens County, Georgia	20,477	55.9	0.0	60.1	52.1	55.1	72.9	57.7	21.0	10.6	10,224	5,270	4,954	48.5
13259	Stewart County, Georgia	5,068	34.3	0.1	26.2	47.5	31.5	38.0	49.2	13.9	14.5	1,485	642	843	56.8
13261	Sumter County, Georgia	24,486	54.4	0.0	58.0	51.2	49.2	73.3	52.7	13.6	14.4	11,392	5,670	5,722	50.2
13263	Talbot County, Georgia	5,422	51.8	0.0	51.8	51.8	57.2	74.1	50.3	7.9	10.6	2,513	1,172	1,341	53.4
13265	Taliaferro County, Georgia	1,511	43.2	0.0	46.4	40.1	58.4	64.0	37.3	9.7	12.1	574	298	276	48.1
13267	Tattnall County, Georgia	20,576	38.6	0.1	32.0	48.3	33.9	45.0	43.2	14.6	7.9	7,310	3,593	3,717	50.8
13269	Taylor County, Georgia	6,826	52.9	0.0	55.2	50.9	47.6	73.8	51.3	14.9	20.6	2,869	1,352	1,517	52.9
13271	Telfair County, Georgia	13,790	33.9	0.0	28.9	12.6	29.4	41.5	35.8	11.2	4.4	4,472	2,323	2,149	48.1
13273	Terrell County, Georgia	7,221	51.5	0.1	52.7	50.5	54.4	67.4	52.0	15.4	14.4	3,181	1,544	1,637	51.5
13275	Thomas County, Georgia	35,097	55.3	0.1	58.9	52.1	52.3	73.1	53.8	16.5	10.5	17,359	8,555	8,804	50.7
13277	Tift County, Georgia	31,634	53.8	0.0	59.3	48.9	47.4	71.0	52.4	14.4	5.8	16,038	8,342	7,696	48.0
13279	Toombs County, Georgia	20,519	57.2	0.4	65.0	50.5	51.4	75.6	57.6	13.9	9.6	10,615	5,613	5,002	47.1
13281	Towns County, Georgia	9,448	43.8	0.1	43.2	44.2	49.8	72.1	58.1	10.5	10.0	3,722	1,694	2,028	54.5
13283	Treutlen County, Georgia	5,519	51.6	0.0	50.7	52.5	48.7	73.5	44.6	13.1	5.4	2,692	1,286	1,406	52.2
13285	Troup County, Georgia	53,426	60.9	0.1	65.1	57.1	55.2	79.5	60.1	11.9	11.9	28,677	14,672	14,005	48.8
13287	Turner County, Georgia	6,465	51.2	0.0	53.4	49.0	42.0	68.3	58.9	16.8	12.5	2,900	1,465	1,435	49.5
13289	Twiggs County, Georgia	7,019	39.4	0.0	43.3	35.8	35.1	61.1	32.5	7.3	6.7	2,581	1,390	1,191	46.1
13291	Union County, Georgia	18,481	45.3	0.0	46.9	43.8	58.5	74.4	48.0	11.3	13.0	7,291	3,688	3,603	49.4
13293	Upson County, Georgia	21,151	52.7	0.0	56.3	49.5	50.3	72.6	53.0	11.3	11.1	9,904	5,086	4,818	48.6
13295	Walker County, Georgia	54,508	56.4	0.1	61.2	51.8	57.5	73.7	55.6	13.9	8.4	28,164	14,965	13,199	46.9
13297	Walton County, Georgia	66,218	61.6	0.1	68.5	55.2	53.0	79.9	61.1	14.3	7.9	37,547	19,987	17,560	46.8
13299	Ware County, Georgia	28,312	49.6	0.0	53.5	45.7	45.4	67.2	48.2	11.2	7.2	13,022	6,905	6,117	47.0
13301	Warren County, Georgia	4,536	52.7	0.0	61.2	45.6	45.2	73.5	61.3	15.8	16.4	1,998	996	1,002	50.2
13303	Washington County, Georgia	16,556	50.7	0.0	48.4	53.0	41.3	66.5	53.3	14.6	12.2	7,370	3,522	3,848	52.2
13305	Wayne County, Georgia	23,368	50.6	0.3	52.0	49.2	48.4	67.5	45.9	7.9	11.3	10,495	5,615	4,880	46.5
13307	Webster County, Georgia	2,165	55.8	0.0	59.4	52.3	39.9	79.3	59.1	14.9	5.8	1,139	613	526	46.2
13309	Wheeler County, Georgia	6,862	21.7	0.0	12.9	41.9	10.5	26.2	24.4	10.6	10.0	1,339	593	746	55.7
13311	White County, Georgia	22,571	52.4	0.2	58.9	46.4	59.4	74.3	49.6	11.2	6.8	11,029	5,867	5,162	46.8
13313	Whitfield County, Georgia	78,210	64.6	0.0	72.7	56.8	64.7	79.9	62.0	17.6	10.3	45,345	25,021	20,324	44.8
13315	Wilcox County, Georgia	7,440	35.2	0.0	31.4	41.1	28.2	44.6	41.6	8.5	6.7	2,446	1,311	1,135	46.4
13317	Wilkes County, Georgia	8,132	51.2	0.2	56.9	46.2	44.7	77.8	46.4	13.2	8.9	3,798	1,981	1,817	47.8
13319	Wilkinson County, Georgia	7,455	47.6	0.0	53.9	41.9	42.2	68.0	43.1	11.5	7.3	3,287	1,735	1,552	47.2
13321	Worth County, Georgia	16,767	55.3	0.0	60.1	50.8	52.5	72.7	56.2	16.0	9.8	8,359	4,295	4,064	48.6
15000	**Hawaii**	1,130,491	61.5	3.7	64.2	58.8	52.0	78.6	68.3	19.4	6.1	653,284	341,056	312,228	47.8
15001	Hawaii County, Hawaii	153,443	58.3	0.1	61.0	55.5	50.6	77.9	61.2	17.3	8.1	82,124	42,364	39,760	48.4
15003	Honolulu County, Hawaii	792,760	60.9	5.1	63.5	58.2	50.5	77.2	70.3	19.6	5.6	455,481	238,839	216,642	47.6
15005	Kalawao County, Hawaii	84	76.2	6.0	78.6	73.8	33.3	92.1	89.5	47.6	0.0	64	33	31	48.4
15007	Kauai County, Hawaii	55,747	64.4	0.4	67.5	61.4	59.3	83.8	67.3	20.3	5.4	33,996	17,559	16,437	48.3
15009	Maui County, Hawaii	128,457	68.2	0.2	71.3	65.2	63.2	85.8	68.4	22.2	6.9	81,619	42,261	39,358	48.2

Table C. County—Labor Force, Employment, and Educational Data, 2011–2015—*Continued*

Fips code	State/county	Total population age 16 and older	Percent in civilian labor force	Percent in armed forces	Civilian labor force participation by gender		Civilian labor force participation by age				Civilian unemploy-ment rate	Civilian employed population age 16 and older			Percent women
					Men	Women	Age 16 to 24	Age 25 to 54	Age 55 to 64	Age 65 and older		Total	Men	Women	
16000	**Idaho**	1,232,564	62.6	0.3	68.3	56.8	60.8	80.0	63.4	15.5	7.2	715,861	388,809	327,052	45.7
16001	Ada County, Idaho	322,908	66.3	0.2	71.3	61.3	61.1	81.9	67.2	15.7	6.6	199,955	107,136	92,819	46.4
16003	Adams County, Idaho	3,246	51.2	0.0	53.0	49.2	59.8	74.1	54.3	16.5	11.3	1,474	778	696	47.2
16005	Bannock County, Idaho	63,406	63.2	0.1	67.6	58.9	60.5	79.9	64.6	12.6	7.2	37,206	19,593	17,613	47.3
16007	Bear Lake County, Idaho	4,543	59.1	0.0	66.7	51.5	58.9	82.7	63.0	16.4	3.3	2,598	1,480	1,118	43.0
16009	Benewah County, Idaho	7,296	54.9	0.0	57.9	51.8	71.4	74.3	58.8	11.8	10.1	3,600	1,853	1,747	48.5
16011	Bingham County, Idaho	32,154	64.0	0.1	71.8	56.4	64.4	79.7	67.6	15.5	7.1	19,121	10,581	8,540	44.7
16013	Blaine County, Idaho	16,870	73.8	0.0	78.2	69.2	77.3	88.0	76.8	30.9	4.1	11,941	6,427	5,514	46.2
16015	Boise County, Idaho	5,755	53.7	0.0	59.4	47.6	62.7	79.1	50.6	13.5	10.5	2,768	1,582	1,186	42.8
16017	Bonner County, Idaho	33,507	52.2	0.0	55.8	48.6	50.8	75.1	52.9	13.0	6.2	16,399	8,699	7,700	47.0
16019	Bonneville County, Idaho	77,588	64.4	0.1	72.0	57.1	64.2	78.7	66.5	16.4	5.6	47,191	25,815	21,376	45.3
16021	Boundary County, Idaho	8,700	46.9	0.0	54.1	39.3	40.2	68.7	48.4	11.4	4.7	3,888	2,286	1,602	41.2
16023	Butte County, Idaho	2,047	50.3	0.0	58.6	41.1	36.1	72.4	62.0	12.4	6.8	960	593	367	38.2
16025	Camas County, Idaho	821	64.7	0.0	68.2	60.5	45.3	89.0	69.1	19.1	5.8	500	289	211	42.2
16027	Canyon County, Idaho	144,666	62.2	0.2	68.9	55.6	58.2	78.8	61.1	15.2	9.4	81,460	44,163	37,297	45.8
16029	Caribou County, Idaho	5,019	63.1	0.0	74.6	51.5	72.4	80.5	66.8	18.9	1.5	3,121	1,856	1,265	40.5
16031	Cassia County, Idaho	16,479	62.9	0.0	74.5	50.9	62.8	78.8	66.9	17.6	5.7	9,771	5,904	3,867	39.6
16033	Clark County, Idaho	670	68.7	0.0	82.8	53.8	70.2	87.1	83.0	4.2	3.9	442	266	176	39.8
16035	Clearwater County, Idaho	7,428	41.8	0.1	41.0	42.9	48.4	57.0	47.9	12.5	7.3	2,877	1,564	1,313	45.6
16037	Custer County, Idaho	3,581	51.5	0.0	57.5	45.5	39.8	80.5	47.1	15.4	3.3	1,784	1,009	775	43.4
16039	Elmore County, Idaho	19,749	55.2	10.0	57.1	53.1	49.5	69.3	62.5	10.2	8.4	9,981	5,378	4,603	46.1
16041	Franklin County, Idaho	8,934	63.7	0.0	74.9	52.5	64.8	79.8	71.6	15.8	5.0	5,401	3,229	2,172	40.2
16043	Fremont County, Idaho	9,716	58.1	0.1	63.3	52.4	52.2	75.7	59.3	21.9	6.0	5,305	3,034	2,271	42.8
16045	Gem County, Idaho	13,386	50.4	0.0	56.8	44.3	46.5	75.3	44.0	15.0	14.2	5,789	3,065	2,724	47.1
16047	Gooding County, Idaho	11,427	62.2	0.0	70.6	53.3	64.2	81.0	66.6	18.0	3.8	6,844	3,974	2,870	41.9
16049	Idaho County, Idaho	13,448	51.8	0.0	52.4	51.2	52.5	77.8	56.1	13.0	6.4	6,526	3,432	3,094	47.4
16051	Jefferson County, Idaho	18,308	64.9	0.0	76.1	53.5	58.0	79.0	68.4	19.7	6.1	11,157	6,514	4,643	41.6
16053	Jerome County, Idaho	16,101	64.1	0.0	74.0	53.7	64.2	79.7	57.6	22.0	6.6	9,641	5,693	3,948	41.0
16055	Kootenai County, Idaho	114,358	61.9	0.2	67.8	56.3	68.3	81.6	60.3	13.2	7.9	65,216	34,757	30,459	46.7
16057	Latah County, Idaho	32,131	63.4	0.0	65.2	61.6	55.9	81.7	72.7	18.8	7.6	18,842	9,787	9,055	48.1
16059	Lemhi County, Idaho	6,579	51.2	0.0	54.1	48.2	55.8	77.9	49.6	18.0	6.1	3,165	1,705	1,460	46.1
16061	Lewis County, Idaho	3,053	54.2	0.0	57.7	50.9	58.2	77.9	62.3	15.2	6.5	1,547	802	745	48.2
16063	Lincoln County, Idaho	3,775	62.3	0.0	73.5	50.9	53.8	77.0	71.5	18.3	6.0	2,212	1,320	892	40.3
16065	Madison County, Idaho	28,507	63.1	0.0	73.0	53.4	60.7	73.8	71.0	17.7	10.2	16,153	9,412	6,741	41.7
16067	Minidoka County, Idaho	15,091	63.6	0.2	73.2	53.7	63.3	81.1	69.6	18.1	4.8	9,136	5,387	3,749	41.0
16069	Nez Perce County, Idaho	32,145	61.8	0.0	64.8	59.0	68.8	84.0	60.4	15.0	6.1	18,668	9,437	9,231	49.4
16071	Oneida County, Idaho	3,207	58.4	0.0	65.3	51.2	62.1	82.7	61.7	14.7	6.7	1,749	1,012	737	42.1
16073	Owyhee County, Idaho	8,659	56.3	0.2	63.9	48.1	54.7	76.9	58.0	10.5	11.7	4,304	2,468	1,836	42.7
16075	Payette County, Idaho	17,258	60.5	0.0	67.0	54.0	62.0	79.9	61.7	16.7	10.1	9,393	5,207	4,186	44.6
16077	Power County, Idaho	5,551	63.3	0.0	72.4	53.6	54.6	79.5	76.7	16.6	9.4	3,184	1,988	1,196	37.6
16079	Shoshone County, Idaho	10,437	54.3	0.1	58.0	50.5	55.8	78.0	55.7	12.9	11.8	4,992	2,581	2,411	48.3
16081	Teton County, Idaho	7,626	76.5	0.0	80.6	72.0	65.6	85.6	81.2	30.1	8.5	5,342	2,930	2,412	45.2
16083	Twin Falls County, Idaho	60,353	63.9	0.0	70.5	57.6	63.7	81.5	66.1	17.5	5.9	36,316	19,617	16,699	46.0
16085	Valley County, Idaho	8,083	56.3	0.0	52.7	60.2	69.0	83.1	47.2	15.2	5.7	4,292	2,073	2,219	51.7
16087	Washington County, Idaho	7,998	50.5	0.2	56.8	44.1	44.4	76.9	60.7	8.5	9.7	3,650	2,133	1,517	41.6
17000	**Illinois**	10,201,787	65.6	0.2	70.8	60.7	58.8	83.3	66.8	17.2	9.1	6,086,226	3,178,535	2,907,691	47.8
17001	Adams County, Illinois	53,491	65.0	0.1	69.8	60.6	68.8	85.4	68.0	18.8	6.8	32,400	16,576	15,824	48.8
17003	Alexander County, Illinois	5,786	48.2	0.0	49.1	47.3	47.7	65.9	53.9	10.9	13.9	2,400	1,154	1,246	51.9
17005	Bond County, Illinois	14,315	56.4	0.0	54.5	58.4	61.8	69.9	56.7	19.3	6.4	7,563	3,667	3,896	51.5
17007	Boone County, Illinois	41,209	66.4	0.0	74.1	58.8	61.1	84.5	68.0	15.8	9.7	24,714	13,787	10,927	44.2
17009	Brown County, Illinois	5,957	49.2	0.1	42.8	61.7	51.8	57.2	55.2	11.8	5.4	2,772	1,577	1,195	43.1
17011	Bureau County, Illinois	27,417	64.0	0.1	68.6	59.6	67.8	85.1	73.1	15.5	7.6	16,206	8,357	7,849	48.4
17013	Calhoun County, Illinois	4,095	57.6	0.0	63.6	51.5	60.2	82.7	58.5	15.9	5.4	2,231	1,239	992	44.5
17015	Carroll County, Illinois	12,320	60.7	0.0	64.8	56.6	65.0	84.7	69.6	15.8	8.1	6,866	3,663	3,203	46.7
17017	Cass County, Illinois	10,397	65.0	0.0	71.0	59.0	63.7	85.2	70.4	12.9	8.5	6,183	3,351	2,832	45.8
17019	Champaign County, Illinois	170,764	63.7	0.1	66.2	61.2	51.0	84.7	67.8	19.7	6.5	101,720	52,154	49,566	48.7
17021	Christian County, Illinois	27,747	57.8	0.0	58.3	57.1	60.0	76.7	60.4	14.7	5.4	15,151	7,745	7,406	48.9
17023	Clark County, Illinois	12,878	63.0	0.0	69.8	56.8	73.3	86.4	59.4	12.9	8.5	7,425	3,954	3,471	46.7
17025	Clay County, Illinois	10,867	61.8	0.0	67.1	56.8	71.6	84.7	62.4	11.4	6.7	6,270	3,267	3,003	47.9
17027	Clinton County, Illinois	30,717	65.9	0.1	65.3	66.5	68.3	83.2	67.4	17.2	4.9	19,250	9,861	9,389	48.8
17029	Coles County, Illinois	44,597	61.9	0.0	65.5	58.7	63.0	83.2	60.9	11.5	9.7	24,939	12,546	12,393	49.7
17031	Cook County, Illinois	4,173,224	66.1	0.0	71.8	61.0	56.2	83.3	65.9	17.3	10.7	2,463,655	1,278,254	1,185,401	48.1
17033	Crawford County, Illinois	16,058	55.9	0.0	57.0	54.7	64.6	74.0	54.1	12.7	6.8	8,369	4,364	4,005	47.9
17035	Cumberland County, Illinois	8,706	61.2	0.0	66.8	55.6	68.4	83.9	59.6	10.0	7.4	4,932	2,665	2,267	46.0
17037	DeKalb County, Illinois	83,697	68.8	0.0	72.5	65.3	66.6	85.6	68.6	16.2	10.4	51,637	26,871	24,766	48.0
17039	De Witt County, Illinois	13,228	66.0	0.0	72.0	60.1	73.5	86.0	66.8	17.2	7.7	8,066	4,316	3,750	46.5
17041	Douglas County, Illinois	15,320	65.4	0.0	73.1	58.3	67.6	84.7	66.9	18.1	6.1	9,415	5,080	4,335	46.0
17043	DuPage County, Illinois	736,804	70.0	0.0	77.1	63.4	60.5	86.4	74.7	21.8	7.0	479,592	255,752	223,840	46.7
17045	Edgar County, Illinois	14,550	59.4	0.0	66.8	52.3	59.1	83.1	58.6	15.8	9.6	7,807	4,227	3,580	45.9
17047	Edwards County, Illinois	5,301	61.0	0.0	67.8	54.4	60.9	85.1	65.5	12.1	8.3	2,968	1,579	1,389	46.8
17049	Effingham County, Illinois	27,116	67.8	0.0	72.8	62.9	75.4	87.9	68.1	15.4	5.4	17,382	9,079	8,303	47.8
17051	Fayette County, Illinois	17,794	56.1	0.0	56.8	55.2	59.0	71.6	60.7	13.7	10.4	8,943	4,779	4,164	46.6
17053	Ford County, Illinois	11,055	61.2	0.0	66.5	56.1	63.2	83.5	67.4	13.8	8.6	6,179	3,259	2,920	47.3

Table C. County—Labor Force, Employment, and Educational Data, 2011–2015—*Continued*

Fips code	State/county	Total population age 16 and older	Percent in civilian labor force	Percent in armed forces	Men	Women	Age 16 to 24	Age 25 to 54	Age 55 to 64	Age 65 and older	Civilian unemploy-ment rate	Total	Men	Women	Percent women
17055	Franklin County, Illinois	31,953	54.0	0.0	59.1	49.2	56.1	75.7	53.7	10.7	10.0	15,510	8,127	7,383	47.6
17057	Fulton County, Illinois	29,759	56.8	0.1	57.0	56.5	59.8	76.1	58.8	12.8	7.9	15,565	8,095	7,470	48.0
17059	Gallatin County, Illinois	4,404	56.0	0.0	64.5	48.0	68.7	78.7	60.0	12.2	7.5	2,280	1,274	1,006	44.1
17061	Greene County, Illinois	10,884	60.3	0.0	62.0	58.5	67.2	80.6	58.4	15.8	9.4	5,944	3,120	2,824	47.5
17063	Grundy County, Illinois	38,559	67.2	0.0	73.1	61.5	67.3	84.1	61.9	15.8	7.8	23,887	12,664	11,223	47.0
17065	Hamilton County, Illinois	6,677	56.7	0.0	65.6	48.3	65.5	80.8	51.8	13.0	4.5	3,618	2,054	1,564	43.2
17067	Hancock County, Illinois	15,238	60.6	0.0	68.1	53.4	55.3	84.7	68.9	18.4	6.8	8,595	4,729	3,866	45.0
17069	Hardin County, Illinois	3,474	52.5	0.0	55.2	49.6	65.6	74.1	47.7	11.2	18.1	1,493	777	716	48.0
17071	Henderson County, Illinois	5,898	61.1	0.1	65.6	56.7	66.6	87.0	71.0	12.6	7.0	3,350	1,766	1,584	47.3
17073	Henry County, Illinois	39,782	62.8	0.1	68.5	57.4	61.3	85.3	67.0	15.1	5.8	23,544	12,604	10,940	46.5
17075	Iroquois County, Illinois	23,301	62.8	0.0	68.1	57.9	66.8	85.2	66.2	18.4	7.5	13,533	7,079	6,454	47.7
17077	Jackson County, Illinois	50,270	56.9	0.0	57.3	56.4	47.5	78.5	59.4	13.2	10.4	25,623	12,890	12,733	49.7
17079	Jasper County, Illinois	7,745	64.1	0.1	69.3	58.8	66.1	85.0	67.3	15.4	5.5	4,691	2,498	2,193	46.7
17081	Jefferson County, Illinois	31,012	58.7	0.0	59.4	57.9	64.0	76.2	62.0	13.7	9.2	16,528	8,619	7,909	47.9
17083	Jersey County, Illinois	18,327	62.8	0.0	64.8	60.9	63.3	86.6	63.8	8.4	8.0	10,587	5,170	5,417	51.2
17085	Jo Daviess County, Illinois	18,489	62.9	0.0	66.6	59.3	68.0	88.6	66.8	21.4	5.6	10,991	5,770	5,221	47.5
17087	Johnson County, Illinois	10,828	43.7	0.0	39.5	49.5	49.7	56.5	46.5	10.2	10.3	4,244	2,168	2,076	48.9
17089	Kane County, Illinois	397,542	69.6	0.0	77.2	62.1	63.4	84.5	71.1	20.0	7.6	255,530	140,099	115,431	45.2
17091	Kankakee County, Illinois	88,025	62.7	0.1	66.5	59.2	57.0	82.5	63.6	15.2	9.8	49,815	25,598	24,217	48.6
17093	Kendall County, Illinois	87,815	74.2	0.0	81.0	67.7	62.9	86.9	69.9	23.6	6.0	61,270	33,096	28,174	46.0
17095	Knox County, Illinois	42,851	54.1	0.1	55.3	52.9	57.6	72.3	59.4	13.8	7.4	21,475	10,861	10,614	49.4
17097	Lake County, Illinois	543,597	67.7	1.9	73.7	61.8	54.5	84.1	72.8	21.2	7.9	338,959	181,858	157,101	46.3
17099	LaSalle County, Illinois	90,414	63.1	0.0	67.3	59.0	68.6	82.2	64.2	16.1	9.8	51,452	27,072	24,380	47.4
17101	Lawrence County, Illinois	13,872	32.2	0.0	20.7	50.7	14.9	36.6	50.5	16.4	6.1	4,197	1,606	2,591	61.7
17103	Lee County, Illinois	28,716	58.5	0.0	59.1	57.8	60.6	74.6	63.4	15.2	7.5	15,539	8,264	7,275	46.8
17105	Livingston County, Illinois	30,676	55.5	0.1	60.0	51.1	59.8	67.7	63.4	17.1	6.3	15,954	8,583	7,371	46.2
17107	Logan County, Illinois	24,858	47.3	0.1	46.3	48.4	54.3	54.6	59.0	15.4	7.8	10,856	5,472	5,384	49.6
17109	McDonough County, Illinois	27,401	57.5	0.1	60.1	55.1	47.8	82.6	68.7	15.2	9.4	14,279	7,111	7,168	50.2
17111	McHenry County, Illinois	238,924	71.6	0.1	78.2	65.1	65.3	86.6	75.3	19.9	8.0	157,226	84,121	73,105	46.5
17113	McLean County, Illinois	139,114	69.1	0.1	73.5	65.0	61.8	88.4	68.8	16.1	5.5	90,810	46,214	44,596	49.1
17115	Macon County, Illinois	87,334	62.4	0.1	66.9	58.3	67.1	82.2	65.0	15.4	10.5	48,783	24,750	24,033	49.3
17117	Macoupin County, Illinois	37,896	61.6	0.2	66.0	57.5	65.5	84.4	61.5	12.9	9.6	21,098	10,884	10,214	48.4
17119	Madison County, Illinois	214,640	63.9	0.1	69.1	59.2	63.9	83.1	63.2	14.8	8.9	125,030	64,583	60,447	48.3
17121	Marion County, Illinois	30,697	61.5	0.0	64.9	58.3	67.5	84.2	59.9	12.7	9.6	17,066	8,650	8,416	49.3
17123	Marshall County, Illinois	9,979	60.6	0.0	67.2	54.2	73.5	84.0	61.9	15.2	6.5	5,651	3,077	2,574	45.5
17125	Mason County, Illinois	11,454	59.7	0.1	64.9	54.7	61.7	83.3	61.2	15.2	9.5	6,190	3,266	2,924	47.2
17127	Massac County, Illinois	12,058	52.9	0.0	58.1	48.2	56.8	74.4	49.9	12.7	8.8	5,821	3,000	2,821	48.5
17129	Menard County, Illinois	10,075	65.8	0.0	68.8	63.0	71.3	88.6	65.4	14.1	5.7	6,252	3,076	3,176	50.8
17131	Mercer County, Illinois	12,961	62.2	0.1	68.6	56.0	71.1	87.2	58.5	15.1	6.2	7,568	4,106	3,462	45.7
17133	Monroe County, Illinois	26,716	67.6	0.0	72.2	63.3	64.7	89.5	66.8	13.0	5.2	17,120	8,756	8,364	48.9
17135	Montgomery County, Illinois	24,212	41.9	0.0	32.5	52.3	39.3	52.6	53.3	12.0	5.4	9,604	3,911	5,693	59.3
17137	Morgan County, Illinois	28,827	60.8	0.0	61.4	60.3	57.4	81.3	65.9	17.3	8.3	16,089	8,089	8,000	49.7
17139	Moultrie County, Illinois	11,720	62.5	0.2	69.3	56.2	60.5	82.8	71.3	17.4	4.9	6,963	3,733	3,230	46.4
17141	Ogle County, Illinois	41,625	65.2	0.0	70.3	60.3	63.4	86.4	67.2	16.7	8.0	24,989	13,191	11,798	47.2
17143	Peoria County, Illinois	147,041	63.8	0.2	68.7	59.2	60.7	82.9	64.0	15.6	8.7	85,639	43,273	42,366	49.5
17145	Perry County, Illinois	17,956	50.3	0.1	49.8	50.9	44.2	65.6	57.7	12.3	8.0	8,312	4,483	3,829	46.1
17147	Piatt County, Illinois	13,269	68.0	0.1	73.5	62.6	60.8	90.6	70.8	21.8	6.3	8,451	4,443	4,008	47.4
17149	Pike County, Illinois	12,945	58.9	0.0	65.3	52.6	59.1	77.9	66.8	18.4	5.6	7,197	3,914	3,283	45.6
17151	Pope County, Illinois	3,716	43.9	0.0	43.1	44.9	30.6	71.9	40.0	15.2	10.0	1,469	768	701	47.7
17153	Pulaski County, Illinois	4,630	49.9	0.0	50.5	49.3	49.3	73.6	47.3	10.9	16.2	1,935	936	999	51.6
17155	Putnam County, Illinois	4,771	65.8	0.0	74.9	56.8	65.7	86.6	72.3	21.7	9.9	2,827	1,558	1,269	44.9
17157	Randolph County, Illinois	27,409	53.6	0.1	52.7	54.6	61.4	67.8	55.3	12.6	6.7	13,698	7,287	6,411	46.8
17159	Richland County, Illinois	12,867	60.1	0.0	66.9	53.7	69.2	80.2	61.8	17.0	5.4	7,317	3,995	3,322	45.4
17161	Rock Island County, Illinois	117,609	63.2	0.1	66.9	59.6	66.4	84.5	64.8	12.8	7.9	68,438	35,101	33,337	48.7
17163	St. Clair County, Illinois	209,703	61.0	1.5	64.2	58.1	53.9	77.5	62.6	16.3	8.9	116,537	58,012	58,525	50.2
17165	Saline County, Illinois	19,961	56.7	0.0	61.8	51.9	67.6	77.6	56.1	10.2	13.0	9,841	5,099	4,742	48.2
17167	Sangamon County, Illinois	158,098	66.0	0.2	70.3	62.1	62.8	86.2	63.9	17.3	7.9	96,155	47,783	48,372	50.3
17169	Schuyler County, Illinois	6,046	53.5	0.0	53.0	54.0	68.0	68.5	55.7	13.4	5.3	3,062	1,612	1,450	47.4
17171	Scott County, Illinois	4,152	63.0	0.0	68.7	57.8	60.6	86.9	65.5	14.1	9.4	2,370	1,248	1,122	47.3
17173	Shelby County, Illinois	17,953	58.7	0.1	66.3	51.4	52.7	83.8	61.5	14.5	6.2	9,895	5,452	4,443	44.9
17175	Stark County, Illinois	4,762	58.1	0.0	64.1	52.5	62.1	83.1	62.0	18.3	7.7	2,556	1,367	1,189	46.5
17177	Stephenson County, Illinois	37,617	64.5	0.0	68.3	60.9	70.7	86.8	69.1	18.7	9.9	21,853	10,869	10,984	50.3
17179	Tazewell County, Illinois	107,801	63.7	0.1	69.0	58.7	64.5	84.5	62.6	14.5	5.5	64,883	34,094	30,789	47.5
17181	Union County, Illinois	14,254	55.4	0.0	58.7	52.0	55.0	78.5	51.5	13.9	7.0	7,339	3,820	3,519	47.9
17183	Vermilion County, Illinois	63,199	57.6	0.0	60.3	55.0	55.2	78.1	59.1	13.7	10.7	32,514	16,579	15,935	49.0
17185	Wabash County, Illinois	9,395	64.2	0.0	69.1	59.5	73.9	85.3	62.8	18.5	8.7	5,501	2,867	2,634	47.9
17187	Warren County, Illinois	14,158	62.8	0.0	68.0	58.0	61.5	85.6	68.4	15.7	9.2	8,068	4,122	3,946	48.9
17189	Washington County, Illinois	11,695	65.1	0.0	70.4	59.7	66.3	88.0	67.6	13.6	5.5	7,194	3,932	3,262	45.3
17191	Wayne County, Illinois	13,155	60.4	0.0	68.0	53.0	60.8	83.7	63.7	15.6	5.3	7,523	4,192	3,331	44.3
17193	White County, Illinois	11,604	57.6	0.0	66.8	49.0	64.5	80.0	61.3	15.2	8.8	6,095	3,388	2,707	44.4
17195	Whiteside County, Illinois	45,710	62.7	0.1	67.5	58.0	68.0	84.0	67.0	14.7	8.1	26,336	13,679	12,657	48.1
17197	Will County, Illinois	521,187	69.4	0.0	75.1	63.8	61.2	85.0	68.7	18.0	7.8	333,433	176,926	156,507	46.9
17199	Williamson County, Illinois	54,076	58.1	0.1	60.3	55.9	61.2	77.0	57.7	13.4	7.0	29,214	14,801	14,413	49.3

Table C. County—Labor Force, Employment, and Educational Data, 2011–2015—*Continued*

Fips code	State/county	Total population age 16 and older	Percent in civilian labor force	Percent in armed forces	Civilian labor force participation by gender		Civilian labor force participation by age				Civilian unemploy-ment rate	Civilian employed population age 16 and older			
					Men	Women	Age 16 to 24	Age 25 to 54	Age 55 to 64	Age 65 and older		Total	Men	Women	Percent women
17201	Winnebago County, Illinois	228,451	64.9	0.0	69.7	60.4	65.6	83.4	65.3	16.3	11.5	131,172	67,391	63,781	48.6
17203	Woodford County, Illinois	30,588	65.3	0.0	71.5	59.3	69.1	83.6	70.1	15.9	5.9	18,798	9,990	8,808	46.9
18000	**Indiana**	5,160,786	63.9	0.1	69.1	59.0	59.5	81.9	64.8	16.4	7.8	3,038,762	1,597,349	1,441,413	47.4
18001	Adams County, Indiana	24,845	64.3	0.0	73.1	55.8	65.3	82.1	73.0	13.3	6.2	14,982	8,423	6,559	43.8
18003	Allen County, Indiana	277,397	66.7	0.0	72.4	61.5	63.7	83.2	67.9	17.9	8.0	170,294	89,404	80,890	47.5
18005	Bartholomew County, Indiana	62,165	65.8	0.2	73.4	58.3	65.9	84.2	64.1	16.5	5.4	38,666	21,552	17,114	44.3
18007	Benton County, Indiana	6,778	63.8	0.0	73.6	54.6	57.2	83.9	66.7	18.1	5.3	4,096	2,287	1,809	44.2
18009	Blackford County, Indiana	10,078	57.2	0.0	61.0	53.6	59.2	79.5	61.6	11.6	9.8	5,199	2,697	2,502	48.1
18011	Boone County, Indiana	46,039	68.7	0.1	75.8	62.1	57.6	84.8	74.5	19.3	3.7	30,471	16,271	14,200	46.6
18013	Brown County, Indiana	12,394	60.6	0.0	64.2	56.9	65.6	84.0	59.5	19.4	6.2	7,039	3,758	3,281	46.6
18015	Carroll County, Indiana	15,919	63.2	0.0	71.3	55.1	62.6	85.1	65.6	14.6	8.2	9,224	5,108	4,116	44.6
18017	Cass County, Indiana	30,416	62.4	0.0	68.3	56.6	58.0	82.2	64.4	16.3	8.7	17,342	9,421	7,921	45.7
18019	Clark County, Indiana	89,746	65.5	0.1	69.9	61.4	63.2	82.8	62.8	17.6	6.8	54,754	28,099	26,655	48.7
18021	Clay County, Indiana	21,189	60.2	0.1	64.9	55.9	61.7	80.4	58.2	12.6	7.8	11,766	6,132	5,634	47.9
18023	Clinton County, Indiana	25,087	64.5	0.1	69.1	60.2	58.6	84.4	70.3	15.4	7.3	15,003	7,842	7,161	47.7
18025	Crawford County, Indiana	8,487	53.9	0.0	59.7	48.0	56.0	72.1	52.3	13.1	6.6	4,273	2,411	1,862	43.6
18027	Daviess County, Indiana	23,900	63.3	0.0	73.6	53.4	70.3	79.5	60.7	19.4	5.4	14,319	8,160	6,159	43.0
18029	Dearborn County, Indiana	39,212	67.0	0.0	70.3	63.7	69.1	84.4	68.4	17.2	8.1	24,159	12,589	11,570	47.9
18031	Decatur County, Indiana	20,510	65.5	0.0	73.6	57.8	57.6	86.7	68.0	14.9	6.3	12,601	6,817	5,784	45.9
18033	DeKalb County, Indiana	32,948	64.1	0.0	69.9	58.5	69.3	82.0	60.8	14.6	7.5	19,542	10,646	8,896	45.5
18035	Delaware County, Indiana	97,701	59.0	0.0	63.0	55.3	58.7	80.4	58.2	14.1	10.1	51,781	25,968	25,813	49.9
18037	Dubois County, Indiana	33,074	68.0	0.0	74.2	61.8	64.6	88.9	70.5	16.9	3.3	21,742	11,797	9,945	45.7
18039	Elkhart County, Indiana	150,445	65.4	0.0	74.1	57.0	63.1	80.8	69.4	18.4	7.4	91,085	50,756	40,329	44.3
18041	Fayette County, Indiana	18,999	55.4	0.0	61.6	49.4	52.1	75.4	57.4	14.4	12.1	9,245	4,899	4,346	47.0
18043	Floyd County, Indiana	60,255	66.4	0.0	71.4	61.7	63.1	84.7	64.5	18.6	7.3	37,064	18,833	18,231	49.2
18045	Fountain County, Indiana	13,421	61.4	0.1	68.9	54.1	66.3	84.0	63.4	11.7	8.6	7,533	4,141	3,392	45.0
18047	Franklin County, Indiana	18,023	65.8	0.0	71.1	60.6	65.1	83.6	70.8	17.4	6.4	11,103	5,929	5,174	46.6
18049	Fulton County, Indiana	16,152	60.1	0.0	66.8	53.5	60.8	78.7	63.9	16.7	6.0	9,122	4,977	4,145	45.4
18051	Gibson County, Indiana	26,541	63.0	0.0	69.2	57.1	61.0	83.4	65.7	13.4	4.3	16,013	8,643	7,370	46.0
18053	Grant County, Indiana	56,153	56.9	0.0	61.0	53.3	57.0	78.4	57.2	13.5	8.8	29,151	14,542	14,609	50.1
18055	Greene County, Indiana	26,257	58.1	0.0	63.7	52.6	58.9	77.9	59.3	13.9	7.0	14,187	7,600	6,587	46.4
18057	Hamilton County, Indiana	219,844	73.3	0.1	80.5	66.6	63.9	86.7	74.4	22.5	4.3	154,190	81,714	72,476	47.0
18059	Hancock County, Indiana	55,931	66.9	0.0	70.3	63.7	59.3	86.6	65.9	18.1	5.5	35,339	18,085	17,254	48.8
18061	Harrison County, Indiana	31,448	63.2	0.1	68.4	58.1	62.6	81.6	64.6	15.2	7.9	18,294	9,649	8,645	47.3
18063	Hendricks County, Indiana	117,993	68.7	0.1	72.0	65.6	56.5	86.0	71.1	16.9	5.3	76,792	39,804	36,988	48.2
18065	Henry County, Indiana	40,192	54.2	0.0	56.0	52.4	52.3	72.7	56.6	12.1	10.6	19,488	10,224	9,264	47.5
18067	Howard County, Indiana	66,021	59.6	0.1	64.8	54.9	64.5	80.8	55.6	14.6	9.2	35,740	18,347	17,393	48.7
18069	Huntington County, Indiana	29,566	65.4	0.1	70.5	60.6	65.9	84.1	68.0	16.5	7.4	17,909	9,336	8,573	47.9
18071	Jackson County, Indiana	33,972	63.1	0.0	70.7	55.7	62.9	81.6	59.9	16.6	7.3	19,885	10,995	8,890	44.7
18073	Jasper County, Indiana	26,008	62.4	0.0	72.6	52.3	59.7	81.7	60.3	18.5	6.3	15,197	8,804	6,393	42.1
18075	Jay County, Indiana	16,435	62.9	0.0	69.7	56.5	65.6	82.5	65.2	15.9	8.2	9,495	5,173	4,322	45.5
18077	Jefferson County, Indiana	26,473	59.8	0.0	66.6	53.7	55.9	78.4	64.6	13.5	9.2	14,381	7,540	6,841	47.6
18079	Jennings County, Indiana	22,066	61.7	0.0	67.6	55.8	57.1	80.1	62.9	14.1	9.7	12,285	6,536	5,749	46.8
18081	Johnson County, Indiana	112,294	67.2	0.6	72.7	62.0	62.4	84.7	68.1	16.7	6.3	70,667	36,936	33,731	47.7
18083	Knox County, Indiana	30,978	61.4	0.0	66.3	56.5	55.0	79.9	69.3	21.3	6.1	17,864	9,771	8,093	45.3
18085	Kosciusko County, Indiana	60,853	65.9	0.0	72.9	59.0	69.8	82.4	69.0	16.6	6.5	37,483	20,545	16,938	45.2
18087	LaGrange County, Indiana	26,520	62.5	0.0	77.9	47.5	69.2	74.5	67.8	18.2	5.5	15,663	9,770	5,893	37.6
18089	Lake County, Indiana	384,151	61.8	0.0	67.6	56.5	56.7	80.9	60.9	14.7	10.5	212,423	110,109	102,314	48.2
18091	LaPorte County, Indiana	89,542	58.0	0.0	57.8	58.2	54.8	72.0	65.0	17.1	9.8	46,864	24,272	22,592	48.2
18093	Lawrence County, Indiana	36,693	60.1	0.1	65.8	54.7	53.3	81.8	55.5	17.7	6.3	20,669	10,823	9,846	47.6
18095	Madison County, Indiana	104,594	57.5	0.0	59.7	55.4	61.5	75.2	55.8	14.0	9.3	54,576	27,681	26,895	49.3
18097	Marion County, Indiana	718,183	67.7	0.1	71.9	63.8	63.9	82.8	64.5	17.0	10.1	436,687	218,885	217,802	49.9
18099	Marshall County, Indiana	36,265	64.5	0.0	70.5	58.8	66.9	83.0	68.3	15.5	8.3	21,470	11,618	9,852	45.9
18101	Martin County, Indiana	8,164	61.5	0.5	64.5	58.5	55.9	82.9	57.1	20.3	6.1	4,716	2,446	2,270	48.1
18103	Miami County, Indiana	29,251	55.6	0.2	57.4	53.5	49.6	71.9	59.7	13.9	9.4	14,752	8,343	6,409	43.4
18105	Monroe County, Indiana	121,950	61.5	0.0	65.0	58.1	49.1	82.5	69.0	22.1	6.9	69,887	36,445	33,442	47.9
18107	Montgomery County, Indiana	30,222	62.2	0.0	69.4	54.9	59.0	81.2	69.3	15.3	6.9	17,497	9,822	7,675	43.9
18109	Morgan County, Indiana	54,971	64.2	0.1	69.7	58.9	63.9	82.2	62.3	17.4	7.3	32,732	17,451	15,281	46.7
18111	Newton County, Indiana	11,331	59.6	0.0	68.2	51.0	53.6	81.0	61.7	14.5	8.9	6,146	3,600	2,546	41.4
18113	Noble County, Indiana	36,863	64.8	0.2	71.5	58.2	65.6	83.4	62.1	15.2	8.8	21,795	11,919	9,876	45.3
18115	Ohio County, Indiana	4,972	63.4	0.0	67.8	59.1	68.7	85.2	66.3	13.7	7.7	2,909	1,543	1,366	47.0
18117	Orange County, Indiana	15,658	57.1	0.0	61.4	52.9	58.1	77.5	57.8	11.7	6.8	8,330	4,343	3,987	47.9
18119	Owen County, Indiana	17,109	58.9	0.0	62.7	55.2	56.5	79.3	56.7	15.5	8.0	9,276	4,859	4,417	47.6
18121	Parke County, Indiana	13,844	52.8	0.0	65.6	41.7	54.6	65.8	61.8	13.4	7.8	6,730	3,846	2,884	42.9
18123	Perry County, Indiana	15,795	56.4	0.0	57.1	55.4	66.1	70.5	59.0	13.0	5.6	8,399	4,582	3,817	45.4
18125	Pike County, Indiana	10,171	61.1	0.1	66.2	56.0	63.5	83.7	62.4	12.7	5.1	5,902	3,227	2,675	45.3
18127	Porter County, Indiana	132,709	63.6	0.0	71.3	56.2	54.5	82.1	66.1	16.0	7.3	78,219	42,826	35,393	45.2
18129	Posey County, Indiana	20,495	62.3	0.1	67.5	57.2	59.4	84.1	61.4	12.9	5.3	12,101	6,518	5,583	46.1
18131	Pulaski County, Indiana	10,470	59.9	0.0	63.7	56.0	54.6	80.5	65.9	15.6	7.0	5,831	3,145	2,686	46.1
18133	Putnam County, Indiana	30,999	54.0	0.0	55.5	52.2	45.9	71.7	56.9	14.3	7.3	15,518	8,437	7,081	45.6
18135	Randolph County, Indiana	20,273	60.5	0.0	65.9	55.3	58.8	82.5	67.4	11.4	7.8	11,319	6,012	5,307	46.9
18137	Ripley County, Indiana	22,521	62.8	0.0	67.8	57.9	66.5	82.6	62.0	15.2	7.4	13,088	6,831	6,257	47.8
18139	Rush County, Indiana	13,484	62.1	0.0	69.5	54.9	61.1	83.6	63.3	15.1	6.9	7,787	4,233	3,554	45.6

Table C. County—Labor Force, Employment, and Educational Data, 2011–2015—*Continued*

Fips code	State/county	Total population age 16 and older	Percent in civilian labor force	Percent in armed forces	Civilian labor force participation by gender — Men	Women	Civilian labor force participation by age — Age 16 to 24	Age 25 to 54	Age 55 to 64	Age 65 and older	Civilian unemployment rate	Civilian employed population age 16 and older — Total	Men	Women	Percent women
18141	St. Joseph County, Indiana	209,921	64.1	0.1	69.0	59.7	56.1	83.2	68.1	17.0	8.5	123,170	62,896	60,274	48.9
18143	Scott County, Indiana	18,886	58.3	0.0	64.6	52.3	59.4	79.7	50.0	10.1	11.0	9,803	5,319	4,484	45.7
18145	Shelby County, Indiana	35,215	66.2	0.2	72.7	59.9	61.0	83.7	71.5	19.1	8.3	21,379	11,590	9,789	45.8
18147	Spencer County, Indiana	16,640	64.1	0.0	71.3	56.7	61.7	83.7	66.0	20.8	5.6	10,060	5,667	4,393	43.7
18149	Starke County, Indiana	18,411	58.8	0.0	64.5	53.4	59.0	77.9	58.9	15.3	11.5	9,583	5,184	4,399	45.9
18151	Steuben County, Indiana	27,901	63.0	0.0	67.2	58.8	60.5	84.4	67.0	15.1	6.9	16,375	8,747	7,628	46.6
18153	Sullivan County, Indiana	17,363	50.7	0.0	52.9	48.0	53.3	63.5	52.8	13.3	6.8	8,203	4,659	3,544	43.2
18155	Switzerland County, Indiana	8,178	58.4	0.0	63.2	53.4	57.3	76.2	58.7	14.8	9.6	4,314	2,404	1,910	44.3
18157	Tippecanoe County, Indiana	147,529	62.8	0.1	66.2	59.3	51.0	83.2	68.3	17.4	6.5	86,629	46,791	39,838	46.0
18159	Tipton County, Indiana	12,630	60.7	0.0	68.2	53.5	59.3	83.4	65.7	13.4	6.2	7,195	3,958	3,237	45.0
18161	Union County, Indiana	5,843	62.8	0.0	68.3	57.4	61.0	84.0	64.3	13.8	7.7	3,384	1,796	1,588	46.9
18163	Vanderburgh County, Indiana	145,391	63.1	0.0	68.3	58.4	59.8	81.5	65.4	16.1	6.2	86,077	44,038	42,039	48.8
18165	Vermillion County, Indiana	12,761	56.0	0.1	62.0	50.6	50.9	80.5	53.5	11.3	6.5	6,686	3,568	3,118	46.6
18167	Vigo County, Indiana	88,246	58.9	0.1	60.6	57.1	58.8	74.5	61.4	15.3	8.9	47,334	24,551	22,783	48.1
18169	Wabash County, Indiana	26,320	60.9	0.0	66.0	56.0	58.2	83.6	70.2	14.1	7.0	14,892	7,894	6,998	47.0
18171	Warren County, Indiana	6,755	63.2	0.0	68.5	58.0	54.6	85.4	71.1	16.3	5.5	4,031	2,156	1,875	46.5
18173	Warrick County, Indiana	47,422	66.4	0.1	72.6	60.6	60.8	86.8	68.8	16.3	5.0	29,930	15,842	14,088	47.1
18175	Washington County, Indiana	21,949	59.7	0.0	66.2	53.4	55.2	78.8	55.2	17.5	10.1	11,783	6,433	5,350	45.4
18177	Wayne County, Indiana	54,492	57.3	0.0	61.9	53.1	53.8	77.8	59.4	14.4	9.0	28,437	14,562	13,875	48.8
18179	Wells County, Indiana	21,841	64.5	0.3	71.8	57.5	63.5	86.1	68.5	15.1	4.1	13,510	7,357	6,153	45.5
18181	White County, Indiana	19,267	63.1	0.0	68.8	57.6	63.4	84.4	64.1	19.6	6.0	11,433	6,194	5,239	45.8
18183	Whitley County, Indiana	26,420	66.0	0.0	72.6	59.6	69.9	86.1	63.3	16.4	5.3	16,503	8,996	7,507	45.5
19000	**Iowa**	2,447,401	67.6	0.1	72.1	63.3	68.2	86.6	71.3	17.9	4.9	1,573,510	822,245	751,265	47.7
19001	Adair County, Iowa	6,039	64.6	0.0	70.4	59.0	70.8	89.4	74.4	17.0	3.2	3,776	2,018	1,758	46.6
19003	Adams County, Iowa	3,164	65.1	0.0	68.3	61.9	64.9	89.9	76.3	17.6	3.2	1,994	1,017	977	49.0
19005	Allamakee County, Iowa	11,245	65.3	0.0	70.7	59.8	76.8	88.2	70.4	18.3	6.0	6,904	3,705	3,199	46.3
19007	Appanoose County, Iowa	10,149	61.2	0.0	68.1	54.7	72.9	80.7	72.5	15.7	6.6	5,799	3,097	2,702	46.6
19009	Audubon County, Iowa	4,828	63.9	0.2	72.8	55.6	80.2	85.9	73.4	20.5	2.6	3,008	1,646	1,362	45.3
19011	Benton County, Iowa	20,089	68.3	0.0	72.5	64.2	69.6	88.2	70.7	19.6	4.7	13,080	6,769	6,311	48.2
19013	Black Hawk County, Iowa	106,859	67.3	0.0	71.0	63.8	72.5	86.5	65.3	15.5	6.6	67,141	34,214	32,927	49.0
19015	Boone County, Iowa	21,311	66.0	0.2	70.8	61.4	64.9	85.3	73.3	16.8	4.7	13,403	7,062	6,341	47.3
19017	Bremer County, Iowa	19,846	67.3	0.0	72.8	62.2	68.8	89.5	77.3	16.1	3.9	12,843	6,690	6,153	47.9
19019	Buchanan County, Iowa	15,992	67.5	0.0	73.4	61.8	69.6	87.7	72.0	16.4	3.9	10,375	5,595	4,780	46.1
19021	Buena Vista County, Iowa	15,861	70.2	0.0	76.7	63.4	72.6	85.8	78.4	22.5	3.7	10,725	6,014	4,711	43.9
19023	Butler County, Iowa	11,807	65.4	0.1	69.3	61.6	70.7	90.2	71.0	17.3	4.0	7,419	3,857	3,562	48.0
19025	Calhoun County, Iowa	8,105	59.3	0.1	62.1	56.4	67.6	79.2	75.2	14.9	4.0	4,614	2,463	2,151	46.6
19027	Carroll County, Iowa	16,132	68.7	0.1	74.0	63.8	79.0	91.1	75.2	16.4	3.3	10,722	5,623	5,099	47.6
19029	Cass County, Iowa	10,852	63.9	0.0	71.2	57.1	71.1	84.3	74.3	20.2	3.2	6,712	3,582	3,130	46.6
19031	Cedar County, Iowa	14,535	69.3	0.1	72.7	65.9	63.7	90.6	72.1	25.3	3.0	9,763	5,039	4,724	48.4
19033	Cerro Gordo County, Iowa	35,633	66.4	0.1	71.0	62.0	68.6	89.0	71.3	17.9	4.4	22,601	11,624	10,977	48.6
19035	Cherokee County, Iowa	9,611	65.0	0.1	70.3	59.8	72.2	89.5	77.1	16.3	3.7	6,018	3,252	2,766	46.0
19037	Chickasaw County, Iowa	9,667	66.1	0.0	71.4	60.8	78.2	87.6	74.2	14.2	3.8	6,148	3,314	2,834	46.1
19039	Clarke County, Iowa	7,249	65.4	0.0	70.2	60.8	72.1	86.7	67.8	16.7	5.0	4,504	2,372	2,132	47.3
19041	Clay County, Iowa	13,113	67.4	0.2	72.7	62.4	76.2	88.0	77.2	16.7	3.8	8,504	4,403	4,101	48.2
19043	Clayton County, Iowa	14,300	65.7	0.0	69.9	61.5	71.8	87.6	76.0	17.9	4.2	8,996	4,736	4,260	47.4
19045	Clinton County, Iowa	38,584	64.1	0.1	68.5	59.9	63.5	85.9	17.1	4.8		23,564	12,154	11,410	48.4
19047	Crawford County, Iowa	13,220	65.1	0.1	68.6	61.5	67.3	83.4	73.6	19.2	4.8	8,192	4,350	3,842	46.9
19049	Dallas County, Iowa	55,653	74.5	0.1	80.5	68.8	68.8	89.4	71.8	21.0	2.6	40,388	21,303	19,085	47.3
19051	Davis County, Iowa	6,441	61.9	0.0	71.4	52.6	68.5	77.8	66.9	23.9	4.2	3,821	2,174	1,647	43.1
19053	Decatur County, Iowa	6,706	59.0	0.0	61.0	57.0	66.9	77.4	62.3	17.6	7.5	3,660	1,873	1,787	48.8
19055	Delaware County, Iowa	13,839	70.8	0.0	75.6	66.1	67.1	91.2	79.4	24.0	3.6	9,442	5,004	4,438	47.0
19057	Des Moines County, Iowa	31,962	62.8	0.1	67.9	58.0	66.2	82.9	67.1	17.6	6.3	18,798	9,737	9,061	48.2
19059	Dickinson County, Iowa	14,077	65.7	0.1	72.4	59.1	79.1	91.8	71.9	18.7	3.8	8,899	4,808	4,091	46.0
19061	Dubuque County, Iowa	76,221	68.7	0.1	73.1	64.4	69.9	88.7	72.2	17.1	4.3	50,102	26,055	24,047	48.0
19063	Emmet County, Iowa	8,002	64.9	0.0	68.4	61.6	68.3	88.1	72.9	15.7	4.6	4,955	2,540	2,415	48.7
19065	Fayette County, Iowa	16,676	63.5	0.0	67.6	59.3	71.0	85.1	68.6	18.6	5.1	10,050	5,304	4,746	47.2
19067	Floyd County, Iowa	12,779	64.8	0.0	70.3	59.5	65.5	86.6	76.2	20.2	3.5	7,998	4,315	3,683	46.0
19069	Franklin County, Iowa	8,360	62.6	0.0	68.9	56.5	67.3	83.3	71.8	15.4	4.2	5,012	2,730	2,282	45.5
19071	Fremont County, Iowa	5,729	62.8	0.0	68.4	57.3	53.9	86.4	71.8	21.5	3.7	3,463	1,863	1,600	46.2
19073	Greene County, Iowa	7,293	64.6	0.1	72.2	57.6	63.7	88.4	69.9	23.1	5.6	4,452	2,406	2,046	46.0
19075	Grundy County, Iowa	9,768	65.6	0.1	72.2	59.4	69.9	89.5	74.5	13.2	3.9	6,164	3,302	2,862	46.4
19077	Guthrie County, Iowa	8,610	65.2	0.2	70.7	59.9	69.3	87.6	73.1	20.5	5.4	5,312	2,854	2,458	46.3
19079	Hamilton County, Iowa	12,198	63.7	0.0	70.2	57.6	59.9	87.2	70.8	15.6	3.8	7,476	4,017	3,459	46.3
19081	Hancock County, Iowa	8,853	64.7	0.0	70.0	59.4	61.7	87.0	75.2	17.8	1.5	5,640	3,047	2,593	46.0
19083	Hardin County, Iowa	14,105	61.8	0.0	67.8	56.1	59.7	86.8	72.7	14.8	4.9	8,293	4,466	3,827	46.1
19085	Harrison County, Iowa	11,628	65.6	0.1	70.6	60.8	63.8	85.4	76.5	18.8	3.6	7,352	3,846	3,506	47.7
19087	Henry County, Iowa	16,037	59.1	0.0	61.3	56.8	52.8	77.7	67.0	16.1	5.1	8,992	4,652	4,340	48.3
19089	Howard County, Iowa	7,347	65.8	0.1	72.8	58.8	75.1	86.0	75.5	18.8	3.4	4,666	2,589	2,077	44.5
19091	Humboldt County, Iowa	7,672	63.7	0.1	71.6	56.2	72.3	85.8	73.6	15.2	4.8	4,652	2,551	2,101	45.2
19093	Ida County, Iowa	5,634	66.0	0.0	72.0	60.0	74.6	89.4	75.8	18.3	3.7	3,579	1,983	1,596	44.6
19095	Iowa County, Iowa	13,043	68.9	0.0	71.8	66.0	64.8	89.9	78.7	18.8	1.8	8,818	4,539	4,279	48.5
19097	Jackson County, Iowa	15,833	64.0	0.0	69.1	59.0	61.9	86.3	73.0	17.1	4.4	9,687	5,183	4,504	46.5
19099	Jasper County, Iowa	29,582	61.6	0.0	63.1	60.1	59.1	81.2	64.9	17.5	5.4	17,247	8,805	8,442	48.9

Table C. County—Labor Force, Employment, and Educational Data, 2011–2015—*Continued*

Fips code	State/county	Total population age 16 and older	Percent in civilian labor force	Percent in armed forces	Civilian labor force participation by gender		Civilian labor force participation by age				Civilian unemploy-ment rate	Civilian employed population age 16 and older			
					Men	Women	Age 16 to 24	Age 25 to 54	Age 55 to 64	Age 65 and older		Total	Men	Women	Percent women
19101	Jefferson County, Iowa	14,564	56.8	0.0	57.2	56.4	38.6	76.4	64.6	24.0	6.4	7,751	4,163	3,588	46.3
19103	Johnson County, Iowa	114,221	71.5	0.1	73.1	70.0	62.1	87.8	76.1	23.1	3.5	78,838	39,563	39,275	49.8
19105	Jones County, Iowa	16,580	62.3	0.0	62.0	62.7	60.6	79.4	74.3	17.3	5.0	9,815	4,992	4,823	49.1
19107	Keokuk County, Iowa	8,182	63.4	0.0	68.5	58.3	66.2	84.4	66.8	22.4	5.1	4,921	2,660	2,261	45.9
19109	Kossuth County, Iowa	12,263	64.9	0.0	70.4	59.5	68.6	91.0	75.1	16.9	2.1	7,788	4,185	3,603	46.3
19111	Lee County, Iowa	28,700	62.7	0.1	67.9	57.5	71.4	82.5	65.6	14.8	8.7	16,414	8,759	7,655	46.6
19113	Linn County, Iowa	170,386	70.4	0.0	75.0	65.9	72.1	88.2	71.2	17.0	4.8	114,142	59,101	55,041	48.2
19115	Louisa County, Iowa	8,902	66.2	0.0	70.4	61.9	64.0	86.4	67.0	19.0	4.8	5,614	3,017	2,597	46.3
19117	Lucas County, Iowa	7,048	62.1	0.2	63.8	60.3	66.2	86.1	67.9	18.5	5.8	4,122	2,053	2,069	50.2
19119	Lyon County, Iowa	8,754	69.8	0.1	76.1	63.6	74.5	89.2	79.5	19.2	2.4	5,968	3,243	2,725	45.7
19121	Madison County, Iowa	11,966	68.4	0.0	73.3	63.6	59.0	88.0	78.0	16.8	5.7	7,712	4,029	3,683	47.8
19123	Mahaska County, Iowa	17,574	67.2	0.0	74.1	60.4	77.1	84.6	69.7	20.7	8.0	10,859	5,893	4,966	45.7
19125	Marion County, Iowa	26,076	68.0	0.0	71.9	64.1	71.0	88.9	69.4	17.7	4.0	17,020	9,032	7,988	46.9
19127	Marshall County, Iowa	31,845	65.1	0.0	70.9	59.2	71.5	85.4	69.3	14.1	6.3	19,409	10,504	8,905	45.9
19129	Mills County, Iowa	11,742	62.8	0.0	69.2	56.4	55.7	82.0	61.0	21.5	3.8	7,089	3,901	3,188	45.0
19131	Mitchell County, Iowa	8,459	65.0	0.0	71.3	58.9	69.6	88.8	75.6	18.9	3.2	5,319	2,833	2,486	46.7
19133	Monona County, Iowa	7,440	59.2	0.0	67.3	51.6	65.2	87.7	62.0	15.8	5.5	4,165	2,280	1,885	45.3
19135	Monroe County, Iowa	6,281	60.8	0.0	65.3	56.2	68.5	84.6	62.7	10.4	6.2	3,580	1,954	1,626	45.4
19137	Montgomery County, Iowa	8,447	61.0	0.0	64.5	57.9	65.4	82.2	70.0	16.9	9.6	4,660	2,390	2,270	48.7
19139	Muscatine County, Iowa	33,190	67.0	0.0	72.6	61.5	67.9	85.6	69.3	16.7	4.6	21,210	11,385	9,825	46.3
19141	O'Brien County, Iowa	11,209	66.4	0.0	72.5	60.5	74.8	85.6	79.1	20.8	2.8	7,237	3,886	3,351	46.3
19143	Osceola County, Iowa	4,962	68.4	0.0	74.3	62.6	80.5	90.9	74.9	17.7	3.3	3,282	1,768	1,514	46.1
19145	Page County, Iowa	12,728	58.6	0.2	61.1	56.0	56.9	78.0	63.0	21.2	5.1	7,075	3,783	3,292	46.5
19147	Palo Alto County, Iowa	7,412	64.4	0.0	70.4	58.6	70.9	89.1	76.9	12.6	2.9	4,637	2,500	2,137	46.1
19149	Plymouth County, Iowa	19,379	69.4	0.1	74.8	64.2	68.3	90.3	80.1	18.0	3.4	12,978	6,821	6,157	47.4
19151	Pocahontas County, Iowa	5,750	63.7	0.1	70.8	56.7	64.4	86.6	76.6	20.6	4.9	3,483	1,887	1,596	45.8
19153	Polk County, Iowa	349,332	72.6	0.1	77.5	68.0	71.6	87.5	70.8	19.5	5.8	238,720	123,378	115,342	48.3
19155	Pottawattamie County, Iowa	73,416	66.6	0.1	71.0	62.4	68.2	84.8	68.6	17.6	5.0	46,439	24,162	22,277	48.0
19157	Poweshiek County, Iowa	15,258	66.3	0.0	70.5	62.5	73.3	87.4	76.8	16.9	4.8	9,636	4,883	4,753	49.3
19159	Ringgold County, Iowa	3,954	56.7	0.0	62.7	51.3	59.1	86.3	67.0	12.5	4.8	2,133	1,101	1,032	48.4
19161	Sac County, Iowa	8,134	65.9	0.0	72.2	60.1	71.5	90.9	74.7	20.5	4.0	5,151	2,717	2,434	47.3
19163	Scott County, Iowa	133,403	65.9	0.2	70.4	61.6	61.9	84.2	67.1	15.5	5.4	83,140	43,053	40,087	48.2
19165	Shelby County, Iowa	9,635	65.7	0.0	70.9	60.8	76.5	90.3	74.1	17.8	2.9	6,153	3,221	2,932	47.7
19167	Sioux County, Iowa	26,117	73.5	0.1	80.2	66.7	79.4	87.9	85.1	24.0	1.8	18,867	10,380	8,487	45.0
19169	Story County, Iowa	79,053	67.6	0.0	68.6	66.5	62.3	88.1	74.7	15.7	5.5	50,519	26,347	24,172	47.8
19171	Tama County, Iowa	13,793	63.6	0.0	69.1	58.3	61.4	85.9	70.8	18.2	5.6	8,283	4,384	3,899	47.1
19173	Taylor County, Iowa	4,903	65.3	0.0	69.6	61.2	73.2	85.2	73.9	22.1	4.4	3,061	1,575	1,486	48.5
19175	Union County, Iowa	9,968	67.7	0.0	71.7	64.1	68.1	89.4	78.5	18.3	5.4	6,385	3,168	3,217	50.4
19177	Van Buren County, Iowa	5,909	59.9	0.1	66.0	53.7	51.9	81.1	68.5	21.4	6.6	3,305	1,846	1,459	44.1
19179	Wapello County, Iowa	28,224	62.1	0.0	65.6	58.8	66.3	81.2	66.0	12.6	8.0	16,128	8,256	7,872	48.8
19181	Warren County, Iowa	36,762	71.5	0.1	76.7	66.6	75.5	89.2	73.9	19.0	4.8	25,008	12,816	12,192	48.8
19183	Washington County, Iowa	17,224	68.8	0.0	75.7	62.2	70.7	87.5	78.0	23.2	4.2	11,358	6,012	5,346	47.1
19185	Wayne County, Iowa	5,032	58.2	0.0	66.7	50.0	67.1	81.2	67.7	15.1	4.3	2,800	1,565	1,235	44.1
19187	Webster County, Iowa	30,162	60.7	0.0	62.6	58.7	62.4	79.2	64.9	15.9	8.4	16,774	8,774	8,000	47.7
19189	Winnebago County, Iowa	8,580	64.8	0.0	72.4	57.5	65.6	90.4	72.9	13.9	6.2	5,214	2,844	2,370	45.5
19191	Winneshiek County, Iowa	17,408	72.4	0.0	76.4	68.5	78.1	92.3	80.5	22.5	3.0	12,230	6,323	5,907	48.3
19193	Woodbury County, Iowa	78,489	69.3	0.1	74.6	64.3	74.1	85.0	71.8	18.6	5.2	51,599	27,108	24,491	47.5
19195	Worth County, Iowa	6,142	64.9	0.0	68.9	60.9	63.3	88.9	70.1	17.1	4.7	3,800	2,011	1,789	47.1
19197	Wright County, Iowa	10,204	62.3	0.0	67.6	57.0	72.0	86.1	73.4	11.4	5.7	5,996	3,197	2,799	46.7
20000	**Kansas**	2,247,842	66.3	0.8	71.0	61.6	62.7	83.1	70.4	19.9	5.9	1,401,197	740,411	660,786	47.2
20001	Allen County, Kansas	10,349	60.9	0.1	67.6	54.4	53.5	81.5	69.7	20.7	7.0	5,863	3,090	2,773	47.3
20003	Anderson County, Kansas	6,086	62.7	0.0	71.7	53.9	77.8	81.4	67.0	21.6	5.9	3,593	2,036	1,557	43.3
20005	Atchison County, Kansas	13,124	61.8	0.0	68.6	55.8	55.2	81.2	73.3	18.7	7.3	7,519	3,805	3,714	49.4
20007	Barber County, Kansas	3,787	64.0	0.0	69.0	59.0	65.9	82.7	71.2	25.7	3.1	2,350	1,278	1,072	45.6
20009	Barton County, Kansas	21,503	65.9	0.1	71.8	60.2	63.5	86.2	74.6	19.1	6.8	13,200	7,006	6,194	46.9
20011	Bourbon County, Kansas	11,469	59.0	0.3	64.7	53.6	64.7	79.0	64.7	13.2	3.3	6,541	3,492	3,049	46.6
20013	Brown County, Kansas	7,633	63.2	0.0	67.2	59.3	61.0	84.7	71.3	18.1	4.5	4,606	2,413	2,193	47.6
20015	Butler County, Kansas	50,746	65.3	0.3	69.4	61.1	61.7	83.3	65.9	16.8	5.6	31,277	16,690	14,587	46.6
20017	Chase County, Kansas	2,194	55.7	0.0	56.0	55.5	57.2	78.4	66.0	16.4	2.9	1,187	591	596	50.2
20019	Chautauqua County, Kansas	2,864	55.6	0.4	62.4	48.4	61.1	81.5	56.8	20.0	5.1	1,510	863	647	42.8
20021	Cherokee County, Kansas	16,456	60.5	0.1	63.3	57.9	57.0	82.1	58.4	17.5	5.8	9,378	4,694	4,684	49.9
20023	Cheyenne County, Kansas	2,214	60.8	0.0	64.0	57.7	68.5	91.3	68.5	19.1	1.9	1,321	678	643	48.7
20025	Clark County, Kansas	1,684	62.6	0.0	72.0	53.2	58.9	84.0	73.1	24.0	1.4	1,040	574	466	44.8
20027	Clay County, Kansas	6,600	64.4	2.3	69.6	59.3	72.5	80.9	78.2	25.5	1.9	4,169	2,221	1,948	46.7
20029	Cloud County, Kansas	7,659	63.2	0.0	71.3	55.3	74.7	83.0	68.3	20.9	6.8	4,514	2,468	2,046	45.3
20031	Coffey County, Kansas	6,777	65.4	0.0	71.2	59.6	65.0	87.5	70.7	19.1	5.1	4,207	2,251	1,956	46.5
20033	Comanche County, Kansas	1,574	66.8	0.5	71.6	62.2	82.3	92.6	68.1	30.0	5.4	995	544	451	45.3
20035	Cowley County, Kansas	28,327	59.5	0.1	63.1	56.0	57.2	76.5	70.7	16.9	7.0	15,686	8,329	7,357	46.9
20037	Crawford County, Kansas	31,619	62.5	0.0	66.1	58.9	59.8	80.2	72.8	16.6	5.6	18,643	9,756	8,887	47.7
20039	Decatur County, Kansas	2,433	59.4	0.0	65.2	53.5	68.5	86.0	74.3	17.3	3.8	1,389	780	609	43.8
20041	Dickinson County, Kansas	15,314	62.3	1.5	67.1	57.6	65.5	79.5	69.9	19.9	6.7	8,898	4,696	4,202	47.2
20043	Doniphan County, Kansas	6,374	63.1	0.2	65.6	60.6	55.2	86.6	67.2	19.4	5.8	3,790	1,999	1,791	47.3
20045	Douglas County, Kansas	95,425	69.0	0.1	71.3	66.7	59.8	86.8	75.4	22.3	6.0	61,881	31,710	30,171	48.8
20047	Edwards County, Kansas	2,367	62.5	0.0	71.6	52.9	58.4	81.0	73.8	23.7	2.0	1,451	863	588	40.5
20049	Elk County, Kansas	2,210	53.6	0.0	60.6	46.9	56.7	79.3	64.2	16.2	5.3	1,121	606	515	45.9

Table C. County—Labor Force, Employment, and Educational Data, 2011–2015—*Continued*

Fips code	State/county	Total population age 16 and older	Percent in civilian labor force	Percent in armed forces	Civilian labor force participation by gender		Civilian labor force participation by age				Civilian unemploy-ment rate	Civilian employed population age 16 and older			
					Men	Women	Age 16 to 24	Age 25 to 54	Age 55 to 64	Age 65 and older		Total	Men	Women	Percent women
20051	Ellis County, Kansas	23,405	71.8	0.1	76.2	67.5	77.6	88.0	72.7	21.8	4.5	16,045	8,369	7,676	47.8
20053	Ellsworth County, Kansas	5,395	54.0	0.1	49.3	60.3	50.8	65.4	67.2	22.5	4.3	2,787	1,466	1,321	47.4
20055	Finney County, Kansas	26,564	73.5	0.0	81.0	65.9	67.8	85.2	78.1	27.3	4.6	18,612	10,377	8,235	44.2
20057	Ford County, Kansas	25,048	69.3	0.0	77.1	61.0	66.7	81.1	69.8	27.1	6.4	16,237	9,322	6,915	42.6
20059	Franklin County, Kansas	20,020	68.1	0.1	74.8	61.9	65.0	84.9	75.3	23.5	6.9	12,701	6,724	5,977	47.1
20061	Geary County, Kansas	26,417	53.7	18.2	52.6	54.9	42.7	61.4	67.9	27.8	9.2	12,884	6,735	6,149	47.7
20063	Gove County, Kansas	2,183	63.9	0.0	71.2	56.7	61.0	87.7	74.8	25.3	1.9	1,367	753	614	44.9
20065	Graham County, Kansas	2,152	61.0	0.0	65.4	56.9	73.2	84.4	76.8	17.3	2.4	1,282	662	620	48.4
20067	Grant County, Kansas	5,592	69.8	0.0	81.1	58.7	74.6	81.4	64.2	26.5	7.3	3,618	2,116	1,502	41.5
20069	Gray County, Kansas	4,497	72.9	0.0	84.1	62.0	76.1	84.3	77.8	35.9	2.9	3,183	1,829	1,354	42.5
20071	Greeley County, Kansas	979	61.8	0.0	69.4	54.8	55.3	88.8	75.3	11.4	2.1	592	316	276	46.6
20073	Greenwood County, Kansas	5,118	58.2	0.0	62.2	54.3	57.9	81.8	67.5	18.6	3.5	2,876	1,536	1,340	46.6
20075	Hamilton County, Kansas	1,962	69.0	0.0	84.4	52.3	71.4	82.5	75.2	25.1	2.3	1,322	848	474	35.9
20077	Harper County, Kansas	4,610	62.0	0.0	68.8	55.2	70.6	82.8	66.3	23.1	3.7	2,750	1,527	1,223	44.5
20079	Harvey County, Kansas	27,112	63.6	0.0	71.1	56.4	64.0	85.4	68.9	15.8	4.4	16,472	8,958	7,514	45.6
20081	Haskell County, Kansas	3,049	70.9	0.3	80.1	61.9	67.2	85.9	77.5	27.9	3.9	2,078	1,167	911	43.8
20083	Hodgeman County, Kansas	1,546	66.7	0.5	76.1	57.6	51.0	88.1	78.3	33.8	2.5	1,005	570	435	43.3
20085	Jackson County, Kansas	10,350	65.7	0.0	70.3	61.2	69.6	88.0	63.2	17.3	4.4	6,496	3,446	3,050	47.0
20087	Jefferson County, Kansas	14,953	66.5	0.0	70.0	63.1	62.9	86.6	72.6	18.8	6.9	9,264	4,794	4,470	48.3
20089	Jewell County, Kansas	2,520	59.8	0.0	63.0	56.5	77.3	87.3	75.8	14.5	2.5	1,468	775	693	47.2
20091	Johnson County, Kansas	437,103	72.5	0.1	78.8	66.6	65.9	87.5	75.4	22.8	4.5	302,532	158,622	143,910	47.6
20093	Kearny County, Kansas	2,912	67.5	0.0	81.1	52.9	68.1	83.9	71.8	17.9	1.8	1,930	1,193	737	38.2
20095	Kingman County, Kansas	6,206	60.0	0.0	70.0	50.2	65.4	82.9	67.1	14.3	5.7	3,509	2,002	1,507	42.9
20097	Kiowa County, Kansas	2,061	66.5	0.0	72.3	60.8	67.1	82.0	78.9	29.5	4.0	1,315	715	600	45.6
20099	Labette County, Kansas	16,534	61.2	0.0	64.0	58.4	65.1	79.6	67.2	15.3	5.3	9,572	4,896	4,676	48.9
20101	Lane County, Kansas	1,364	69.6	0.0	76.1	63.0	75.1	91.1	83.5	23.0	2.4	926	520	406	43.8
20103	Leavenworth County, Kansas	61,229	58.2	2.7	56.8	59.8	58.8	68.8	61.2	18.1	5.9	33,513	17,503	16,010	47.8
20105	Lincoln County, Kansas	2,515	63.7	0.0	67.6	59.9	64.0	86.9	70.4	20.5	6.5	1,497	807	690	46.1
20107	Linn County, Kansas	7,656	56.8	0.0	62.4	51.5	41.4	79.6	68.1	16.3	8.3	3,987	2,161	1,826	45.8
20109	Logan County, Kansas	2,220	65.6	0.0	72.7	58.8	58.3	85.2	75.5	29.0	3.9	1,399	765	634	45.3
20111	Lyon County, Kansas	26,753	67.6	0.1	73.6	62.0	66.7	83.4	78.3	18.5	7.2	16,784	8,790	7,994	47.6
20113	McPherson County, Kansas	23,357	68.1	0.1	75.3	61.3	72.3	87.9	76.4	21.9	3.1	15,406	8,280	7,126	46.3
20115	Marion County, Kansas	9,962	61.5	0.1	64.1	58.9	61.4	84.5	73.7	19.8	5.0	5,820	3,039	2,781	47.8
20117	Marshall County, Kansas	7,943	64.0	0.5	69.3	58.9	61.5	86.5	75.0	20.8	3.0	4,933	2,651	2,282	46.3
20119	Meade County, Kansas	3,353	65.6	0.0	74.6	56.2	67.4	83.7	75.6	20.9	2.8	2,137	1,230	907	42.4
20121	Miami County, Kansas	25,283	67.2	0.0	69.8	64.7	57.9	87.5	69.8	18.2	5.6	16,030	8,125	7,905	49.3
20123	Mitchell County, Kansas	5,102	62.1	0.0	70.2	53.8	60.1	89.0	76.0	15.8	2.6	3,086	1,750	1,336	43.3
20125	Montgomery County, Kansas	26,978	59.0	0.1	63.7	54.4	57.9	79.2	65.9	14.6	8.7	14,514	7,537	6,977	48.1
20127	Morris County, Kansas	4,708	61.9	0.1	67.6	56.2	56.5	83.8	74.4	23.1	3.2	2,819	1,533	1,286	45.6
20129	Morton County, Kansas	2,464	60.6	0.0	70.1	50.7	59.0	79.9	69.4	16.2	5.8	1,408	819	589	41.8
20131	Nemaha County, Kansas	7,898	68.3	0.0	73.7	63.0	74.2	91.2	78.5	19.5	1.7	5,302	2,824	2,478	46.7
20133	Neosho County, Kansas	12,828	63.9	0.0	68.6	59.5	58.6	86.1	70.9	19.1	4.7	7,816	4,133	3,683	47.1
20135	Ness County, Kansas	2,504	62.6	0.0	70.8	53.7	52.5	87.6	76.6	23.2	2.7	1,524	892	632	41.5
20137	Norton County, Kansas	4,646	58.0	0.0	52.3	66.0	53.7	66.1	82.9	26.6	1.7	2,650	1,400	1,250	47.2
20139	Osage County, Kansas	12,667	62.5	0.2	64.7	60.4	63.6	85.4	58.2	19.4	8.2	7,264	3,726	3,538	48.7
20141	Osborne County, Kansas	3,084	63.6	0.0	70.7	56.6	75.7	85.5	68.3	28.1	4.0	1,884	1,055	829	44.0
20143	Ottawa County, Kansas	4,762	66.7	0.0	71.6	61.9	54.6	85.2	83.2	22.6	5.3	3,008	1,617	1,391	46.2
20145	Pawnee County, Kansas	5,834	52.6	0.6	49.9	56.3	46.3	63.9	67.5	20.1	1.9	3,012	1,637	1,375	45.7
20147	Phillips County, Kansas	4,350	66.0	0.2	72.4	59.8	67.5	86.1	72.9	28.3	4.3	2,746	1,490	1,256	45.7
20149	Pottawatomie County, Kansas	16,668	67.2	1.5	74.6	60.1	65.8	81.6	69.7	23.6	3.7	10,795	5,899	4,896	45.4
20151	Pratt County, Kansas	7,707	63.4	0.9	69.0	58.2	62.1	81.7	71.4	23.6	5.6	4,618	2,421	2,197	47.6
20153	Rawlins County, Kansas	2,141	59.6	0.0	68.0	51.2	66.3	83.0	70.1	22.8	2.3	1,247	709	538	43.1
20155	Reno County, Kansas	50,830	61.7	0.0	64.6	58.7	66.5	78.7	68.5	18.3	5.7	29,564	15,436	14,128	47.8
20157	Republic County, Kansas	3,970	64.3	0.0	69.9	58.8	73.3	90.5	79.0	22.7	3.8	2,455	1,305	1,150	46.8
20159	Rice County, Kansas	7,928	65.5	0.0	69.6	61.3	64.2	86.0	76.9	19.6	5.5	4,905	2,645	2,260	46.1
20161	Riley County, Kansas	62,686	57.9	9.9	58.0	57.7	50.5	69.9	71.1	24.9	5.8	34,186	18,397	15,789	46.2
20163	Rooks County, Kansas	4,157	65.9	0.1	67.8	64.0	71.7	83.2	77.3	24.1	4.1	2,626	1,322	1,304	49.7
20165	Rush County, Kansas	2,642	63.2	0.0	67.8	58.6	63.0	84.8	79.3	22.4	5.6	1,577	842	735	46.6
20167	Russell County, Kansas	5,708	65.1	0.1	71.6	58.8	79.4	86.6	71.6	23.9	6.9	3,463	1,856	1,607	46.4
20169	Saline County, Kansas	43,545	68.4	0.4	73.3	63.6	68.8	86.0	74.8	20.0	5.0	28,311	14,939	13,372	47.2
20171	Scott County, Kansas	3,869	71.7	0.0	76.1	67.4	69.0	90.3	84.0	27.1	5.8	2,613	1,408	1,205	46.1
20173	Sedgwick County, Kansas	386,080	66.5	0.6	72.0	61.3	63.4	82.5	68.1	17.4	6.9	239,060	126,773	112,287	47.0
20175	Seward County, Kansas	16,663	72.7	0.0	82.4	62.7	67.6	83.7	70.6	33.6	9.0	11,031	6,538	4,493	40.7
20177	Shawnee County, Kansas	139,769	64.6	0.1	68.1	61.4	65.5	83.1	66.7	17.3	6.8	84,199	41,931	42,268	50.2
20179	Sheridan County, Kansas	1,975	65.9	0.0	75.5	56.5	83.6	87.5	73.8	23.8	1.2	1,286	730	556	43.2
20181	Sherman County, Kansas	4,656	66.9	0.0	78.3	55.6	79.6	85.4	66.2	25.1	4.0	2,992	1,732	1,260	42.1
20183	Smith County, Kansas	3,093	61.3	0.0	67.1	55.6	63.5	86.3	73.2	24.8	3.2	1,836	1,001	835	45.5
20185	Stafford County, Kansas	3,392	63.8	0.0	69.2	58.8	68.5	83.9	75.5	18.7	2.6	2,108	1,095	1,013	48.1
20187	Stanton County, Kansas	1,571	72.8	0.0	82.2	63.6	59.0	89.4	89.3	32.7	2.4	1,116	629	487	43.6
20189	Stevens County, Kansas	4,185	66.4	0.0	80.9	51.6	64.0	78.5	74.8	23.2	3.0	2,696	1,652	1,044	38.7
20191	Sumner County, Kansas	18,497	62.5	0.2	68.3	56.8	54.0	83.8	70.9	15.7	7.0	10,758	5,869	4,889	45.4
20193	Thomas County, Kansas	6,354	70.8	0.0	76.0	65.9	71.1	88.6	77.5	23.3	2.7	4,376	2,285	2,091	47.8
20195	Trego County, Kansas	2,421	70.3	0.0	76.1	64.9	76.9	88.7	85.2	30.2	1.0	1,684	871	813	48.3

Table C. County—Labor Force, Employment, and Educational Data, 2011–2015—*Continued*

Fips code	State/county	Total population age 16 and older	Percent in civilian labor force	Percent in armed forces	Civilian labor force participation by gender — Men	Women	Civilian labor force participation by age — Age 16 to 24	Age 25 to 54	Age 55 to 64	Age 65 and older	Civilian unemploy-ment rate	Civilian employed population age 16 and older — Total	Men	Women	Percent women
20197	Wabaunsee County, Kansas	5,412	64.9	0.1	68.9	60.7	70.0	86.7	63.0	17.6	6.2	3,295	1,775	1,520	46.1
20199	Wallace County, Kansas	1,229	64.9	0.0	71.4	58.3	56.5	85.8	77.2	24.5	5.4	755	414	341	45.2
20201	Washington County, Kansas	4,575	66.6	0.0	72.6	60.3	75.7	87.6	79.9	25.0	3.1	2,950	1,611	1,339	45.4
20203	Wichita County, Kansas	1,597	69.6	0.0	80.7	59.1	77.5	87.2	72.4	29.8	3.1	1,077	608	469	43.5
20205	Wilson County, Kansas	7,211	60.1	0.0	65.6	54.8	63.3	82.7	63.8	17.1	6.5	4,052	2,161	1,891	46.7
20207	Woodson County, Kansas	2,609	62.6	0.0	72.1	52.8	65.6	81.3	71.8	26.0	4.6	1,557	903	654	42.0
20209	Wyandotte County, Kansas	120,166	66.1	0.1	71.5	60.9	64.1	81.9	60.2	16.8	11.2	70,518	37,219	33,299	47.2
21000	**Kentucky**	3,493,098	59.1	0.4	63.6	54.9	60.0	76.4	55.0	14.5	8.4	1,891,381	987,066	904,315	47.8
21001	Adair County, Kentucky	15,463	53.9	0.0	58.1	50.0	49.1	74.9	53.9	11.6	7.7	7,700	4,032	3,668	47.6
21003	Allen County, Kentucky	16,104	58.6	0.0	66.4	51.3	55.5	77.4	57.7	14.6	9.2	8,576	4,765	3,811	44.4
21005	Anderson County, Kentucky	17,055	67.0	0.0	71.2	63.2	64.4	87.0	58.2	16.8	6.9	10,646	5,351	5,295	49.7
21007	Ballard County, Kentucky	6,614	56.2	0.2	61.4	51.2	58.8	75.8	57.0	16.0	6.2	3,489	1,848	1,641	47.0
21009	Barren County, Kentucky	34,044	59.4	0.1	66.3	52.9	61.6	77.4	60.6	14.6	7.6	18,672	10,026	8,646	46.3
21011	Bath County, Kentucky	9,232	51.0	0.0	55.3	46.8	53.4	72.8	30.3	14.3	14.0	4,045	2,115	1,930	47.7
21013	Bell County, Kentucky	22,620	40.1	0.1	43.3	37.2	43.4	56.7	32.0	6.0	11.6	8,018	4,165	3,853	48.1
21015	Boone County, Kentucky	93,587	70.9	0.1	76.0	66.0	70.5	84.8	66.5	20.6	5.6	62,624	33,072	29,552	47.2
21017	Bourbon County, Kentucky	15,988	62.3	0.0	66.1	58.9	64.5	82.3	54.4	20.9	9.9	8,984	4,615	4,369	48.6
21019	Boyd County, Kentucky	39,662	51.8	0.0	55.2	48.4	60.5	70.1	43.2	12.2	10.5	18,376	9,565	8,811	47.9
21021	Boyle County, Kentucky	24,019	54.8	0.1	58.1	51.6	59.4	73.6	51.8	13.8	7.1	12,218	6,261	5,957	48.8
21023	Bracken County, Kentucky	6,584	57.8	0.0	63.9	51.8	44.6	78.8	58.2	12.2	8.3	3,486	1,876	1,610	46.2
21025	Breathitt County, Kentucky	11,127	43.5	0.0	48.5	38.6	51.4	57.4	32.5	10.2	12.4	4,239	2,282	1,957	46.2
21027	Breckinridge County, Kentucky	15,930	54.5	0.1	60.6	48.5	57.3	73.1	52.7	13.4	11.5	7,683	4,294	3,389	44.1
21029	Bullitt County, Kentucky	61,038	65.7	0.1	70.1	61.5	70.1	83.5	57.2	13.5	7.6	37,079	19,281	17,798	48.0
21031	Butler County, Kentucky	10,231	52.1	0.0	57.9	46.3	51.0	72.4	46.8	10.1	6.1	5,003	2,779	2,224	44.5
21033	Caldwell County, Kentucky	10,301	57.4	0.0	60.4	54.7	68.7	80.4	51.5	9.9	8.7	5,396	2,712	2,684	49.7
21035	Calloway County, Kentucky	32,047	58.0	0.3	60.9	55.5	56.0	78.8	60.2	15.2	9.1	16,904	8,338	8,566	50.7
21037	Campbell County, Kentucky	73,523	66.9	0.0	70.4	63.7	65.3	83.7	69.0	16.1	6.8	45,872	23,197	22,675	49.4
21039	Carlisle County, Kentucky	4,048	56.3	0.2	63.7	49.2	62.4	79.6	49.6	11.8	6.8	2,122	1,161	961	45.3
21041	Carroll County, Kentucky	8,360	58.7	0.0	66.1	51.2	71.9	74.7	51.5	12.0	13.2	4,263	2,429	1,834	43.0
21043	Carter County, Kentucky	22,045	51.2	0.1	56.5	46.2	53.5	69.4	43.3	12.3	11.1	10,039	5,369	4,670	46.5
21045	Casey County, Kentucky	12,724	51.2	0.0	58.5	44.2	54.1	68.9	46.2	17.4	9.0	5,926	3,283	2,643	44.6
21047	Christian County, Kentucky	54,889	49.8	13.1	47.9	52.0	39.0	62.4	58.5	16.4	12.7	23,856	12,270	11,586	48.6
21049	Clark County, Kentucky	28,561	60.6	0.2	64.8	56.8	62.5	79.5	53.5	17.6	7.9	15,950	8,308	7,642	47.9
21051	Clay County, Kentucky	17,296	37.5	0.0	38.8	36.0	46.3	47.1	26.9	7.9	15.9	5,459	2,994	2,465	45.2
21053	Clinton County, Kentucky	8,120	48.3	0.0	54.3	42.4	46.9	73.9	28.3	10.5	9.3	3,555	1,924	1,631	45.9
21055	Crittenden County, Kentucky	7,328	53.6	0.0	59.7	47.5	63.8	74.4	47.5	13.1	7.1	3,645	2,004	1,641	45.0
21057	Cumberland County, Kentucky	5,534	49.3	0.0	50.3	48.3	39.6	74.4	47.7	11.0	10.2	2,449	1,233	1,216	49.7
21059	Daviess County, Kentucky	76,820	61.4	0.1	67.4	55.9	68.0	80.0	57.0	14.2	6.8	43,941	22,841	21,100	48.0
21061	Edmonson County, Kentucky	9,996	52.0	0.0	59.2	44.6	58.6	73.7	42.7	10.8	8.9	4,730	2,685	2,045	43.2
21063	Elliott County, Kentucky	6,447	34.5	0.0	34.2	35.0	33.7	46.2	32.6	9.1	6.2	2,088	1,164	924	44.3
21065	Estill County, Kentucky	11,566	47.6	0.0	52.9	42.4	54.2	65.3	37.7	10.3	11.8	4,855	2,548	2,307	47.5
21067	Fayette County, Kentucky	249,544	67.6	0.1	72.1	63.4	62.4	82.6	67.4	19.9	6.9	157,198	81,439	75,759	48.2
21069	Fleming County, Kentucky	11,351	57.6	0.0	67.2	48.6	63.1	75.3	50.3	17.1	9.7	5,897	3,236	2,661	45.1
21071	Floyd County, Kentucky	31,297	42.2	0.0	45.2	39.4	39.9	59.3	31.8	9.5	9.7	11,922	6,107	5,815	48.8
21073	Franklin County, Kentucky	40,571	61.0	0.3	64.6	57.8	60.1	81.5	56.6	13.4	8.7	22,601	11,212	11,389	50.4
21075	Fulton County, Kentucky	5,215	49.6	0.0	51.8	47.4	66.5	65.8	39.8	15.3	12.0	2,274	1,214	1,060	46.6
21077	Gallatin County, Kentucky	6,588	61.7	0.1	69.1	54.3	55.6	79.6	51.2	18.0	6.0	3,821	2,126	1,695	44.4
21079	Garrard County, Kentucky	13,590	59.3	0.0	64.0	54.7	63.2	80.1	51.0	12.2	11.4	7,138	3,724	3,414	47.8
21081	Grant County, Kentucky	18,461	59.4	0.0	65.8	53.0	64.6	73.4	53.3	14.6	6.8	10,215	5,686	4,529	44.3
21083	Graves County, Kentucky	29,428	58.0	0.1	63.9	52.4	63.6	75.6	59.7	13.8	7.2	15,840	8,540	7,300	46.1
21085	Grayson County, Kentucky	20,441	55.8	0.1	60.6	51.0	68.3	73.7	46.2	12.4	9.3	10,342	5,642	4,700	45.4
21087	Green County, Kentucky	9,082	54.0	0.0	59.2	49.2	58.2	74.3	53.4	14.2	9.0	4,459	2,318	2,141	48.0
21089	Greenup County, Kentucky	29,288	51.3	0.0	56.3	46.6	55.7	73.3	45.4	8.7	10.1	13,500	7,049	6,451	47.8
21091	Hancock County, Kentucky	6,714	57.7	0.2	62.4	52.9	70.8	77.7	47.2	10.1	5.9	3,647	2,001	1,646	45.1
21093	Hardin County, Kentucky	83,181	60.2	5.4	62.7	57.8	59.6	72.7	61.5	16.5	8.2	46,001	23,691	22,310	48.5
21095	Harlan County, Kentucky	22,703	40.0	0.0	46.7	33.7	45.8	55.1	28.3	10.6	9.8	8,189	4,504	3,685	45.0
21097	Harrison County, Kentucky	14,867	53.5	0.0	60.0	47.5	45.9	75.4	51.1	9.2	8.1	7,303	3,903	3,400	46.6
21099	Hart County, Kentucky	14,479	53.2	0.0	60.5	46.0	54.2	69.6	50.8	14.9	9.6	6,958	3,984	2,974	42.7
21101	Henderson County, Kentucky	36,731	60.2	0.0	65.4	55.4	60.5	78.2	56.0	17.5	8.0	20,337	10,617	9,720	47.8
21103	Henry County, Kentucky	12,189	62.4	0.0	66.7	58.4	70.4	79.1	59.8	17.9	6.6	7,099	3,705	3,394	47.8
21105	Hickman County, Kentucky	3,851	49.6	0.0	55.3	44.6	64.2	74.6	44.2	8.5	8.8	1,742	889	853	49.0
21107	Hopkins County, Kentucky	37,056	56.1	0.1	60.8	51.7	57.2	75.5	54.6	11.5	6.7	19,388	9,994	9,394	48.5
21109	Jackson County, Kentucky	10,705	42.5	0.4	50.4	35.0	37.8	60.8	36.0	3.4	12.3	3,993	2,185	1,808	45.3
21111	Jefferson County, Kentucky	602,071	65.6	0.1	70.5	61.1	64.9	83.2	63.5	16.8	8.4	361,510	184,091	177,419	49.1
21113	Jessamine County, Kentucky	39,189	64.6	0.0	72.2	57.6	62.2	80.4	62.5	21.3	8.8	23,096	12,233	10,863	47.0
21115	Johnson County, Kentucky	18,584	42.3	0.0	46.6	38.2	44.1	56.3	36.0	11.5	9.1	7,136	3,785	3,351	47.0
21117	Kenton County, Kentucky	127,102	67.7	0.1	72.5	63.2	66.6	83.9	64.7	16.4	7.7	79,447	41,519	37,928	47.7
21119	Knott County, Kentucky	13,010	42.8	0.0	47.0	38.8	42.8	58.9	33.1	10.5	14.6	4,755	2,484	2,271	47.8
21121	Knox County, Kentucky	25,065	44.9	0.0	50.0	40.2	54.8	64.0	27.8	6.4	15.7	9,477	5,172	4,305	45.4
21123	Larue County, Kentucky	11,363	56.0	0.1	65.0	47.4	63.3	73.4	54.1	13.0	9.3	5,771	3,315	2,456	42.6
21125	Laurel County, Kentucky	47,006	53.6	0.1	56.5	50.9	61.0	70.2	44.1	9.5	12.4	22,079	11,082	10,997	49.8
21127	Lawrence County, Kentucky	12,592	46.2	0.0	52.5	40.2	53.0	61.8	40.2	6.9	7.8	5,366	2,871	2,495	46.5
21129	Lee County, Kentucky	5,842	33.0	0.0	31.4	34.9	29.5	45.2	29.5	5.1	12.2	1,694	844	850	50.2
21131	Leslie County, Kentucky	8,889	38.2	0.0	43.3	33.3	45.6	51.7	29.3	6.4	17.0	2,816	1,441	1,375	48.8

Table C. County—Labor Force, Employment, and Educational Data, 2011–2015—*Continued*

Fips code	State/county	Total population age 16 and older	Percent in civilian labor force	Percent in armed forces	Civilian labor force participation by gender Men	Women	Civilian labor force participation by age Age 16 to 24	Age 25 to 54	Age 55 to 64	Age 65 and older	Civilian unemployment rate	Civilian employed population age 16 and older Total	Men	Women	Percent women
21133	Letcher County, Kentucky	19,149	43.5	0.0	45.3	41.8	50.5	56.5	42.1	8.3	12.6	7,281	3,562	3,719	51.1
21135	Lewis County, Kentucky	11,008	46.0	0.0	50.1	42.0	41.5	64.1	39.0	11.8	8.4	4,643	2,509	2,134	46.0
21137	Lincoln County, Kentucky	19,415	52.9	0.0	59.3	47.1	53.1	71.8	43.9	14.9	10.5	9,202	4,925	4,277	46.5
21139	Livingston County, Kentucky	7,710	53.4	0.0	60.5	46.3	57.7	69.3	61.6	14.2	6.7	3,840	2,134	1,706	44.4
21141	Logan County, Kentucky	21,196	53.5	0.1	62.3	45.2	55.8	72.6	49.1	12.3	7.7	10,471	5,918	4,553	43.5
21143	Lyon County, Kentucky	7,369	39.0	0.0	40.6	37.0	53.6	53.5	42.7	5.0	7.6	2,655	1,562	1,093	41.2
21145	McCracken County, Kentucky	52,633	58.8	0.1	63.9	54.1	62.9	78.8	59.0	13.1	6.1	29,043	14,877	14,166	48.8
21147	McCreary County, Kentucky	14,394	37.5	0.0	37.9	37.1	45.6	50.3	23.8	2.6	19.0	4,377	2,308	2,069	47.3
21149	McLean County, Kentucky	7,517	57.2	0.0	65.5	49.4	60.5	75.6	58.6	16.8	8.4	3,938	2,146	1,792	45.5
21151	Madison County, Kentucky	69,587	62.0	0.1	66.2	58.2	66.3	78.4	55.1	12.0	8.6	39,435	20,169	19,266	48.9
21153	Magoffin County, Kentucky	10,376	40.2	0.0	46.5	34.1	37.3	55.5	35.0	4.5	12.2	3,663	2,042	1,621	44.3
21155	Marion County, Kentucky	15,411	55.8	0.0	57.6	54.0	59.7	71.3	51.6	14.8	9.2	7,818	4,054	3,764	48.1
21157	Marshall County, Kentucky	25,689	55.1	0.0	60.3	50.1	63.3	78.5	52.4	11.1	7.7	13,051	6,935	6,116	46.9
21159	Martin County, Kentucky	10,246	30.1	0.0	31.3	28.5	41.3	34.3	29.7	5.7	20.6	2,445	1,339	1,106	45.2
21161	Mason County, Kentucky	13,604	55.9	0.1	59.4	52.6	44.7	76.1	54.4	17.3	6.2	7,127	3,566	3,561	50.0
21163	Meade County, Kentucky	22,427	57.0	3.1	61.7	52.1	55.4	70.9	52.5	12.9	11.5	11,311	6,362	4,949	43.8
21165	Menifee County, Kentucky	5,185	49.7	0.0	51.2	48.2	53.6	68.1	32.5	14.7	14.7	2,200	1,164	1,036	47.1
21167	Mercer County, Kentucky	17,158	61.4	0.1	69.4	53.9	72.5	83.4	50.9	15.3	11.5	9,331	5,155	4,176	44.8
21169	Metcalfe County, Kentucky	7,974	54.4	0.0	61.8	47.3	54.4	73.7	56.8	12.4	7.4	4,014	2,261	1,753	43.7
21171	Monroe County, Kentucky	8,529	51.1	0.3	56.6	45.5	52.2	68.4	47.7	17.1	9.5	3,943	2,178	1,765	44.8
21173	Montgomery County, Kentucky	21,437	57.0	0.1	63.8	50.6	54.6	75.7	47.0	13.7	10.4	10,948	5,938	5,010	45.8
21175	Morgan County, Kentucky	11,132	37.2	0.0	34.7	40.4	35.2	50.4	29.5	7.6	9.6	3,744	1,953	1,791	47.8
21177	Muhlenberg County, Kentucky	25,480	50.5	0.0	54.7	46.3	46.6	71.0	44.6	12.2	10.3	11,534	6,161	5,373	46.6
21179	Nelson County, Kentucky	34,672	64.7	0.0	68.4	61.3	63.3	81.4	60.7	17.8	9.8	20,232	10,211	10,021	49.5
21181	Nicholas County, Kentucky	5,645	55.2	0.2	63.1	47.8	54.5	76.5	48.2	13.4	7.7	2,877	1,611	1,266	44.0
21183	Ohio County, Kentucky	18,765	52.5	0.0	59.1	46.2	62.0	70.8	45.8	10.0	9.6	8,906	5,006	3,900	43.8
21185	Oldham County, Kentucky	48,419	63.2	0.2	63.9	62.5	57.8	75.1	66.6	18.5	4.3	29,304	15,930	13,374	45.6
21187	Owen County, Kentucky	8,434	56.5	0.0	61.2	51.9	56.8	77.5	51.5	12.8	8.6	4,351	2,281	2,070	47.6
21189	Owsley County, Kentucky	3,803	34.9	0.0	42.1	28.8	32.3	50.7	28.9	9.5	8.8	1,211	661	550	45.4
21191	Pendleton County, Kentucky	11,579	60.0	0.0	65.8	54.4	61.2	79.3	50.2	14.5	6.4	6,507	3,518	2,989	45.9
21193	Perry County, Kentucky	22,667	48.0	0.0	51.3	44.9	50.8	65.5	33.9	10.0	13.9	9,364	4,850	4,514	48.2
21195	Pike County, Kentucky	51,326	45.5	0.0	50.4	40.9	50.3	60.8	36.7	10.8	10.7	20,861	11,018	9,843	47.2
21197	Powell County, Kentucky	9,793	48.5	0.0	53.8	43.4	53.9	63.7	38.7	10.2	8.3	4,360	2,360	2,000	45.9
21199	Pulaski County, Kentucky	50,888	55.5	0.0	58.4	52.8	63.4	75.1	50.5	11.1	9.1	25,669	12,879	12,790	49.8
21201	Robertson County, Kentucky	1,826	47.3	0.0	56.1	38.7	52.4	70.3	54.0	8.6	6.7	806	473	333	41.3
21203	Rockcastle County, Kentucky	13,570	49.8	0.0	54.0	45.6	57.6	68.3	37.3	9.6	11.0	6,015	3,251	2,764	46.0
21205	Rowan County, Kentucky	19,474	55.0	0.0	58.2	52.2	48.2	76.0	61.7	8.8	6.5	10,022	4,998	5,024	50.1
21207	Russell County, Kentucky	14,087	48.4	0.0	51.8	45.2	58.3	68.4	40.3	8.5	11.8	6,014	3,091	2,923	48.6
21209	Scott County, Kentucky	38,432	70.1	0.0	75.4	65.1	66.9	86.2	61.3	17.9	6.9	25,105	13,445	11,660	46.4
21211	Shelby County, Kentucky	34,680	64.6	0.1	71.7	58.2	63.0	79.1	63.0	22.4	5.7	21,103	10,978	10,125	48.0
21213	Simpson County, Kentucky	13,801	58.6	0.1	66.4	51.4	66.9	73.6	56.6	15.0	7.0	7,524	4,019	3,505	46.6
21215	Spencer County, Kentucky	13,874	66.9	0.0	71.1	62.8	57.9	85.7	60.1	15.3	6.4	8,691	4,576	4,115	47.3
21217	Taylor County, Kentucky	20,055	57.3	0.0	62.7	52.4	59.7	75.6	61.6	14.1	9.6	10,395	5,511	4,884	47.0
21219	Todd County, Kentucky	9,499	53.5	0.5	61.0	46.2	51.6	73.2	48.8	11.5	8.5	4,648	2,621	2,027	43.6
21221	Trigg County, Kentucky	11,444	53.3	0.2	56.8	50.0	55.9	77.7	50.3	11.9	8.4	5,584	2,891	2,693	48.2
21223	Trimble County, Kentucky	6,991	60.2	0.0	68.1	52.5	62.6	83.0	48.9	11.5	14.6	3,598	2,010	1,588	44.1
21225	Union County, Kentucky	12,244	53.9	0.0	60.5	46.7	51.4	70.5	55.5	14.7	7.8	6,085	3,559	2,526	41.5
21227	Warren County, Kentucky	94,766	65.1	0.0	69.9	60.6	65.0	81.1	61.1	16.5	7.9	56,780	29,146	27,634	48.7
21229	Washington County, Kentucky	9,536	61.1	0.0	66.7	55.7	67.0	81.8	53.1	16.7	6.1	5,468	2,959	2,509	45.9
21231	Wayne County, Kentucky	16,742	45.7	0.0	49.0	42.5	57.8	60.3	36.7	14.9	12.6	6,681	3,459	3,222	48.2
21233	Webster County, Kentucky	10,606	52.7	0.0	61.1	44.5	56.3	70.1	49.5	10.9	7.2	5,186	3,016	2,170	41.8
21235	Whitley County, Kentucky	28,052	49.2	0.2	52.3	46.3	50.3	66.2	41.7	11.5	10.2	12,406	6,213	6,193	49.9
21237	Wolfe County, Kentucky	5,717	38.1	0.0	40.2	36.1	51.7	51.3	29.3	8.7	9.7	1,967	968	999	50.8
21239	Woodford County, Kentucky	20,137	66.5	0.1	75.4	58.2	62.3	84.7	69.1	20.0	4.8	12,748	6,949	5,799	45.5
22000	**Louisiana**	3,634,163	60.4	0.4	65.0	56.0	54.6	77.3	58.1	17.1	8.1	2,016,049	1,047,601	968,448	48.0
22001	Acadia Parish, Louisiana	47,365	57.8	0.0	64.5	51.7	60.7	73.8	52.8	13.5	10.1	24,619	13,132	11,487	46.7
22003	Allen Parish, Louisiana	20,455	44.4	0.0	41.2	49.0	43.3	51.3	52.6	14.9	8.9	8,269	4,421	3,848	46.5
22005	Ascension Parish, Louisiana	86,204	68.6	0.2	75.1	62.4	59.4	84.8	63.2	15.2	6.4	55,380	29,644	25,736	46.5
22007	Assumption Parish, Louisiana	18,334	57.2	0.0	61.5	53.2	51.6	77.5	56.8	10.2	10.3	9,407	4,830	4,577	48.7
22009	Avoyelles Parish, Louisiana	32,550	51.0	0.1	51.1	50.9	58.9	63.8	48.4	13.7	9.6	14,998	7,608	7,390	49.3
22011	Beauregard Parish, Louisiana	28,293	53.6	0.8	61.8	45.1	48.5	68.5	56.4	12.8	5.7	14,287	8,416	5,871	41.1
22013	Bienville Parish, Louisiana	11,150	51.7	0.0	56.4	47.4	48.5	75.3	49.6	9.6	10.1	5,177	2,732	2,445	47.2
22015	Bossier Parish, Louisiana	95,491	62.9	3.8	65.6	60.2	54.8	78.4	63.9	18.7	5.7	56,570	28,925	27,645	48.9
22017	Caddo Parish, Louisiana	199,059	58.7	0.5	62.5	55.4	50.4	76.8	58.2	17.6	7.0	108,738	53,832	54,906	50.5
22019	Calcasieu Parish, Louisiana	152,663	62.0	0.1	68.3	56.1	59.4	79.1	59.7	16.7	8.3	86,840	46,158	40,682	46.8
22021	Caldwell Parish, Louisiana	7,950	55.4	0.0	59.9	50.5	65.4	69.9	56.4	12.8	10.2	3,955	2,179	1,776	44.9
22023	Cameron Parish, Louisiana	5,323	61.7	0.2	69.0	54.7	40.8	85.2	64.4	17.5	6.3	3,077	1,709	1,368	44.5
22025	Catahoula Parish, Louisiana	8,198	49.9	0.0	50.9	48.6	39.4	65.7	53.3	15.1	8.3	3,749	2,094	1,655	44.1
22027	Claiborne Parish, Louisiana	13,814	46.0	0.0	44.0	48.8	39.6	61.8	49.2	11.1	13.5	5,494	2,971	2,523	45.9
22029	Concordia Parish, Louisiana	15,927	50.3	0.0	51.0	49.6	50.9	60.5	58.0	17.8	11.7	7,078	3,647	3,431	48.5
22031	De Soto Parish, Louisiana	21,194	54.8	0.0	57.8	52.0	52.4	75.1	49.0	11.8	9.3	10,521	5,328	5,193	49.4
22033	East Baton Rouge Parish, Louisiana	354,109	65.8	0.1	71.0	61.2	59.8	84.3	61.2	19.7	7.6	215,513	109,926	105,587	49.0
22035	East Carroll Parish, Louisiana	5,890	39.5	0.0	33.6	47.4	33.5	48.2	41.1	15.7	19.2	1,882	962	920	48.9
22037	East Feliciana Parish, Louisiana	16,444	46.6	0.0	43.7	50.1	41.0	58.2	48.3	18.3	6.5	7,165	3,602	3,563	49.7
22039	Evangeline Parish, Louisiana	25,876	47.4	0.3	49.6	45.1	43.6	64.4	36.9	13.2	10.4	10,978	5,743	5,235	47.7

Table C. County—Labor Force, Employment, and Educational Data, 2011–2015—*Continued*

Fips code	State/county	Total population age 16 and older	Percent in civilian labor force	Percent in armed forces	Civilian labor force participation by gender		Civilian labor force participation by age				Civilian unemploy-ment rate	Civilian employed population age 16 and older			
					Men	Women	Age 16 to 24	Age 25 to 54	Age 55 to 64	Age 65 and older		Total	Men	Women	Percent women
22041	Franklin Parish, Louisiana	15,798	50.5	0.0	53.0	48.2	51.7	66.5	52.6	13.6	11.5	7,062	3,400	3,662	51.9
22043	Grant Parish, Louisiana	17,979	43.3	0.0	38.4	49.8	46.0	52.8	45.0	7.7	9.2	7,068	3,468	3,600	50.9
22045	Iberia Parish, Louisiana	56,759	62.1	0.0	68.8	55.9	61.3	78.2	58.6	18.9	10.6	31,517	17,063	14,454	45.9
22047	Iberville Parish, Louisiana	26,873	52.7	0.2	54.9	50.5	47.1	65.9	53.4	15.4	7.9	13,049	6,641	6,408	49.1
22049	Jackson Parish, Louisiana	12,885	46.1	0.0	45.8	46.5	40.3	59.2	51.3	17.3	6.9	5,536	2,829	2,707	48.9
22051	Jefferson Parish, Louisiana	350,277	64.3	0.2	70.3	58.8	55.7	82.3	65.1	19.8	6.7	210,346	110,313	100,033	47.6
22053	Jefferson Davis Parish, Louisiana	24,185	57.6	0.2	64.3	51.4	55.4	76.6	54.8	13.8	9.2	12,657	6,856	5,801	45.8
22055	Lafayette Parish, Louisiana	182,261	68.2	0.1	74.5	62.4	61.6	83.3	64.4	22.4	6.3	116,522	61,787	54,735	47.0
22057	Lafourche Parish, Louisiana	76,632	61.1	0.0	70.0	52.7	60.5	77.2	56.5	16.7	7.0	43,542	24,383	19,159	44.0
22059	LaSalle Parish, Louisiana	11,762	48.6	0.0	52.9	43.8	41.9	64.2	52.4	10.1	6.3	5,354	3,002	2,352	43.9
22061	Lincoln Parish, Louisiana	38,570	60.4	0.1	62.3	58.7	58.4	78.4	61.7	15.9	11.9	20,541	9,985	10,556	51.4
22063	Livingston Parish, Louisiana	102,033	64.9	0.1	71.8	58.4	58.3	81.2	59.5	15.8	7.0	61,631	33,167	28,464	46.2
22065	Madison Parish, Louisiana	9,300	51.3	0.0	52.1	50.5	44.1	63.1	51.4	19.7	16.9	3,967	1,926	2,041	51.4
22067	Morehouse Parish, Louisiana	21,060	51.0	0.1	53.5	48.9	49.3	67.9	52.9	13.1	8.0	9,888	4,687	5,201	52.6
22069	Natchitoches Parish, Louisiana	30,910	53.3	0.1	55.9	50.9	50.7	72.7	51.0	14.9	12.2	14,446	7,155	7,291	50.5
22071	Orleans Parish, Louisiana	307,039	61.9	0.2	64.8	59.3	48.8	78.5	57.5	18.8	10.3	170,454	84,056	86,398	50.7
22073	Ouachita Parish, Louisiana	119,961	58.5	0.0	59.7	57.5	48.4	75.0	60.2	18.3	8.0	64,578	30,948	33,630	52.1
22075	Plaquemines Parish, Louisiana	18,025	56.9	3.5	64.4	49.6	34.7	73.6	65.2	14.6	4.7	9,777	5,463	4,314	44.1
22077	Pointe Coupee Parish, Louisiana	17,701	56.1	0.0	62.9	49.8	54.0	77.2	55.2	14.1	8.3	9,105	4,780	4,325	47.5
22079	Rapides Parish, Louisiana	102,913	55.9	0.3	60.0	52.3	47.3	75.2	52.3	15.6	8.6	52,620	26,316	26,304	50.0
22081	Red River Parish, Louisiana	6,892	51.8	0.1	60.6	43.7	40.5	72.0	53.2	13.9	9.2	3,241	1,846	1,395	43.0
22083	Richland Parish, Louisiana	16,189	54.9	0.1	59.5	50.8	46.2	72.5	52.9	19.3	9.6	8,038	4,000	4,038	50.2
22085	Sabine Parish, Louisiana	19,039	51.7	0.0	60.9	43.0	47.6	75.8	44.9	12.1	10.6	8,803	5,079	3,724	42.3
22087	St. Bernard Parish, Louisiana	32,620	61.1	0.1	67.9	54.5	49.4	77.6	50.5	14.4	12.2	17,494	9,690	7,804	44.6
22089	St. Charles Parish, Louisiana	40,727	66.0	0.2	71.5	60.8	58.0	82.8	62.4	16.0	7.7	24,804	12,855	11,949	48.2
22091	St. Helena Parish, Louisiana	8,616	49.1	0.0	51.1	47.2	47.8	64.5	55.0	11.8	14.4	3,619	1,827	1,792	49.5
22093	St. James Parish, Louisiana	17,058	59.5	0.0	67.0	52.7	53.6	81.0	56.0	10.6	11.0	9,035	4,699	4,336	48.0
22095	St. John the Baptist Parish, Louisiana	34,272	63.2	0.0	66.3	60.3	53.2	82.8	57.6	14.1	9.2	19,661	9,932	9,729	49.5
22097	St. Landry Parish, Louisiana	63,354	52.4	0.0	57.3	48.0	45.1	69.8	52.0	15.4	6.1	31,154	15,858	15,296	49.1
22099	St. Martin Parish, Louisiana	41,304	62.4	0.0	66.3	58.7	62.4	79.1	56.9	15.3	7.2	23,921	12,324	11,597	48.5
22101	St. Mary Parish, Louisiana	41,769	57.7	0.2	66.3	49.4	59.5	72.9	55.3	15.9	12.2	21,161	11,747	9,414	44.5
22103	St. Tammany Parish, Louisiana	189,633	63.3	0.2	70.2	56.9	58.5	80.8	63.3	18.8	7.6	110,923	58,812	52,111	47.0
22105	Tangipahoa Parish, Louisiana	97,716	61.5	0.0	67.2	56.3	60.0	78.5	54.6	16.9	10.7	53,685	27,844	25,841	48.1
22107	Tensas Parish, Louisiana	3,846	50.4	0.0	57.6	44.0	40.9	69.1	54.3	20.3	15.6	1,636	852	784	47.9
22109	Terrebonne Parish, Louisiana	87,208	58.8	0.1	67.6	50.4	56.6	73.5	56.1	14.9	5.5	48,450	27,342	21,108	43.6
22111	Union Parish, Louisiana	17,982	48.8	0.0	55.9	41.9	43.1	66.7	53.7	12.6	7.7	8,096	4,492	3,604	44.5
22113	Vermilion Parish, Louisiana	45,202	60.5	0.0	67.5	54.2	61.6	76.7	56.9	16.0	8.5	25,011	13,389	11,622	46.5
22115	Vernon Parish, Louisiana	39,554	48.4	13.5	49.9	46.7	40.7	59.3	52.1	14.1	7.5	17,705	9,669	8,036	45.4
22117	Washington Parish, Louisiana	36,543	49.4	0.0	51.6	47.3	51.6	67.3	41.7	11.3	15.0	15,327	7,661	7,666	50.0
22119	Webster Parish, Louisiana	32,197	51.5	0.2	57.0	46.5	48.3	69.5	51.3	15.3	7.6	15,313	8,162	7,151	46.7
22121	West Baton Rouge Parish, Louisiana	19,282	65.2	0.2	68.4	62.2	59.1	79.3	65.4	21.5	6.5	11,757	5,992	5,765	49.0
22123	West Carroll Parish, Louisiana	9,064	49.1	0.0	50.4	47.8	42.4	68.6	44.8	15.3	11.9	3,917	1,933	1,984	50.7
22125	West Feliciana Parish, Louisiana	13,044	42.1	0.0	38.8	49.1	38.1	49.4	41.5	20.9	8.5	5,021	2,982	2,039	40.6
22127	Winn Parish, Louisiana	11,912	44.1	0.1	42.3	46.2	41.0	56.6	42.7	15.4	6.3	4,920	2,530	2,390	48.6
23000	**Maine**	1,098,075	63.4	0.2	67.1	59.9	65.2	82.1	66.9	18.2	6.8	648,687	329,117	319,570	49.3
23001	Androscoggin County, Maine	86,100	66.3	0.1	70.0	62.8	67.0	84.5	68.4	16.7	7.2	52,961	26,784	26,177	49.4
23003	Aroostook County, Maine	58,480	56.6	0.1	60.9	52.5	63.2	76.9	60.5	14.7	7.5	30,612	15,859	14,753	48.2
23005	Cumberland County, Maine	236,013	68.1	0.2	72.1	64.5	66.9	85.2	73.3	20.3	5.4	152,196	76,807	75,389	49.5
23007	Franklin County, Maine	25,383	61.4	0.1	65.2	57.8	68.3	82.5	61.7	16.3	7.7	14,386	7,305	7,081	49.2
23009	Hancock County, Maine	46,214	62.5	0.1	65.8	59.5	61.2	83.9	67.1	20.9	7.7	26,665	13,405	13,260	49.7
23011	Kennebec County, Maine	99,631	62.8	0.1	65.7	60.2	66.2	81.1	64.9	17.0	7.7	57,787	28,842	28,945	50.1
23013	Knox County, Maine	33,131	61.7	0.2	64.0	59.5	67.3	78.8	68.5	24.9	5.7	19,270	9,545	9,725	50.5
23015	Lincoln County, Maine	28,883	59.6	0.1	63.0	56.4	66.0	82.4	65.7	20.6	4.2	16,480	8,336	8,144	49.4
23017	Oxford County, Maine	47,397	58.2	0.0	62.7	53.9	60.7	76.2	65.4	14.0	9.2	25,041	13,039	12,002	47.9
23019	Penobscot County, Maine	128,079	60.8	0.2	63.8	58.1	61.1	79.3	61.7	15.1	7.8	71,852	36,441	35,411	49.3
23021	Piscataquis County, Maine	14,491	51.1	0.0	54.4	47.9	47.4	70.1	60.2	16.0	10.5	6,632	3,431	3,201	48.3
23023	Sagadahoc County, Maine	28,834	65.1	0.2	70.6	60.1	70.2	84.0	68.1	20.5	5.7	17,689	9,146	8,543	48.3
23025	Somerset County, Maine	42,349	58.1	0.2	61.5	54.9	66.5	75.5	61.0	14.3	9.5	22,275	11,301	10,974	49.3
23027	Waldo County, Maine	32,155	61.8	0.3	65.0	58.7	62.8	81.4	66.8	17.7	7.5	18,381	9,236	9,145	49.8
23029	Washington County, Maine	26,814	53.6	0.1	57.5	49.7	54.8	75.3	54.0	16.7	9.8	12,954	6,711	6,243	48.2
23031	York County, Maine	164,121	67.0	0.2	71.5	62.8	69.2	85.6	70.6	20.2	5.9	103,506	52,929	50,577	48.9
24000	**Maryland**	4,737,405	67.9	0.6	71.9	64.1	57.6	85.0	70.3	21.2	7.4	2,976,504	1,503,021	1,473,483	49.5
24001	Allegany County, Maryland	62,134	53.3	0.0	53.6	52.9	57.3	71.4	56.4	11.2	10.0	29,810	15,312	14,498	48.6
24003	Anne Arundel County, Maryland	442,656	68.2	2.7	71.5	65.0	59.1	83.9	70.8	22.2	5.9	284,092	145,730	138,362	48.7
24005	Baltimore County, Maryland	665,725	66.5	0.1	71.3	62.3	57.2	86.0	70.7	19.6	6.9	412,199	204,681	207,518	50.3
24009	Calvert County, Maryland	70,850	69.2	1.1	72.5	65.9	69.1	85.2	67.7	18.2	7.6	45,249	23,256	21,993	48.6
24011	Caroline County, Maryland	25,679	65.3	0.0	71.4	59.7	63.3	82.3	66.9	20.5	8.8	15,306	7,970	7,336	47.9

Table C. County—Labor Force, Employment, and Educational Data, 2011–2015—*Continued*

Fips code	State/county	Total population age 16 and older	Percent in civilian labor force	Percent in armed forces	Civilian labor force participation by gender		Civilian labor force participation by age				Civilian unemploy-ment rate	Civilian employed population age 16 and older			
					Men	Women	Age 16 to 24	Age 25 to 54	Age 55 to 64	Age 65 and older		Total	Men	Women	Percent women
24013	Carroll County, Maryland	134,464	68.8	0.1	74.5	63.3	63.6	87.3	71.8	20.5	4.6	88,196	46,596	41,600	47.2
24015	Cecil County, Maryland	80,442	65.6	0.1	71.3	60.2	64.7	82.2	64.2	17.4	7.5	48,849	25,563	23,286	47.7
24017	Charles County, Maryland	119,276	68.5	1.0	71.4	65.9	55.3	85.5	66.1	17.8	6.3	76,622	37,753	38,869	50.7
24019	Dorchester County, Maryland	26,391	64.9	0.1	67.7	62.5	67.0	85.7	68.7	20.2	10.4	15,354	7,308	8,046	52.4
24021	Frederick County, Maryland	189,847	71.0	0.4	77.4	65.1	63.5	87.1	73.6	21.2	5.8	127,105	67,530	59,575	46.9
24023	Garrett County, Maryland	24,670	60.3	0.0	65.0	55.7	69.6	80.7	62.3	14.7	7.0	13,830	7,347	6,483	46.9
24025	Harford County, Maryland	198,344	68.6	0.7	73.8	63.6	64.7	86.0	69.8	19.8	6.4	127,274	65,881	61,393	48.2
24027	Howard County, Maryland	238,290	72.1	0.5	77.9	66.6	54.1	87.5	78.9	25.0	4.9	163,278	85,200	78,078	47.8
24029	Kent County, Maryland	16,900	57.3	0.1	64.0	51.3	54.9	83.3	68.6	17.2	7.2	8,984	4,651	4,333	48.2
24031	Montgomery County, Maryland	804,704	71.5	0.4	77.3	66.2	55.6	87.8	77.4	25.9	6.1	540,333	277,601	262,732	48.6
24033	Prince George's County, Maryland	711,108	71.7	0.3	74.9	68.8	56.8	88.4	71.1	23.7	8.7	465,639	228,906	236,733	50.8
24035	Queen Anne's County, Maryland	38,955	68.6	0.5	72.6	64.7	62.6	85.6	76.5	26.4	5.3	25,305	13,035	12,270	48.5
24037	St. Mary's County, Maryland	85,124	66.6	2.1	72.1	61.1	58.3	80.6	69.4	20.8	4.8	53,945	28,954	24,991	46.3
24039	Somerset County, Maryland	22,216	39.7	0.1	35.5	45.0	29.3	49.0	54.4	18.4	8.2	8,103	3,940	4,163	51.4
24041	Talbot County, Maryland	31,557	59.8	0.1	63.3	56.8	70.4	82.8	72.6	18.6	6.7	17,620	8,716	8,904	50.5
24043	Washington County, Maryland	119,637	61.7	0.2	62.7	60.7	61.6	78.2	63.4	16.1	8.5	67,555	34,765	32,790	48.5
24045	Wicomico County, Maryland	81,313	64.6	0.1	66.8	62.7	56.8	84.3	64.1	20.6	8.8	47,947	23,188	24,759	51.6
24047	Worcester County, Maryland	43,285	58.9	0.1	63.5	54.6	63.7	83.9	66.4	17.8	9.9	22,979	11,879	11,100	48.3
24510	Baltimore city, Maryland	503,838	61.9	0.1	63.3	60.6	53.2	78.0	57.8	17.4	13.1	270,930	127,259	143,671	53.0
25000	**Massachusetts**	5,479,502	67.5	0.1	71.9	63.4	61.3	84.8	71.7	20.5	7.6	3,415,975	1,731,102	1,684,873	49.3
25001	Barnstable County, Massachusetts	184,579	60.0	0.3	64.8	55.7	65.7	85.9	70.6	20.3	7.0	102,995	51,839	51,156	49.7
25003	Berkshire County, Massachusetts	108,982	63.1	0.0	66.4	60.0	60.1	86.0	69.4	19.0	8.9	62,596	30,896	31,700	50.6
25005	Bristol County, Massachusetts	449,436	65.8	0.0	69.9	62.1	66.5	83.6	67.2	17.1	9.0	269,391	134,862	134,529	49.9
25007	Dukes County, Massachusetts	14,221	65.6	0.0	69.2	62.2	50.0	85.9	67.0	30.1	5.2	8,849	4,676	4,173	47.2
25009	Essex County, Massachusetts	614,462	67.7	0.1	72.7	63.2	64.4	85.1	72.1	20.7	7.7	383,882	193,876	190,006	49.5
25011	Franklin County, Massachusetts	59,456	67.1	0.0	70.6	63.8	64.7	85.0	72.0	23.7	6.7	37,218	18,659	18,559	49.9
25013	Hampden County, Massachusetts	374,641	63.1	0.1	67.0	59.5	61.6	80.8	65.8	16.5	10.0	212,742	106,465	106,277	50.0
25015	Hampshire County, Massachusetts	139,014	65.4	0.0	67.1	63.9	57.6	84.7	76.1	23.2	7.2	84,303	39,394	44,909	53.3
25017	Middlesex County, Massachusetts	1,272,238	69.7	0.1	74.9	64.8	59.1	85.9	75.0	23.2	6.1	832,753	431,384	401,369	48.2
25019	Nantucket County, Massachusetts	8,506	74.6	0.2	80.0	68.5	50.3	91.6	80.2	27.4	3.0	6,157	3,482	2,675	43.4
25021	Norfolk County, Massachusetts	555,861	69.2	0.0	74.0	65.0	60.8	86.5	76.3	23.1	6.9	358,283	180,420	177,863	49.6
25023	Plymouth County, Massachusetts	403,555	67.8	0.1	71.6	64.2	67.2	85.3	71.8	20.9	7.9	252,016	126,670	125,346	49.7
25025	Suffolk County, Massachusetts	641,526	68.5	0.1	72.0	65.3	58.8	84.3	65.9	17.8	8.7	401,271	201,229	200,042	49.9
25027	Worcester County, Massachusetts	653,025	67.0	0.1	71.2	63.0	59.9	84.0	71.3	19.0	7.8	403,519	207,250	196,269	48.6
26000	**Michigan**	7,925,988	61.2	0.0	65.5	57.1	61.0	80.7	58.6	13.4	9.8	4,373,518	2,259,928	2,113,590	48.3
26001	Alcona County, Michigan	9,326	40.2	0.0	42.6	37.7	54.9	73.6	42.8	8.1	12.2	3,288	1,762	1,526	46.4
26003	Alger County, Michigan	8,184	43.4	0.0	40.4	47.1	35.6	66.1	46.2	7.7	10.8	3,166	1,570	1,596	50.4
26005	Allegan County, Michigan	87,958	61.9	0.0	67.2	56.6	57.8	80.9	63.5	13.0	6.1	51,081	27,256	23,825	46.6
26007	Alpena County, Michigan	24,085	56.0	0.2	59.6	52.6	66.0	79.7	55.8	11.3	9.3	12,233	6,224	6,009	49.1
26009	Antrim County, Michigan	19,321	54.6	0.0	58.0	51.2	68.1	79.9	61.4	11.5	9.7	9,528	4,945	4,583	48.1
26011	Arenac County, Michigan	12,939	48.9	0.0	50.4	47.4	57.9	73.1	44.9	9.3	12.0	5,569	2,761	2,808	50.4
26013	Baraga County, Michigan	7,466	34.4	0.0	24.5	50.7	29.3	43.6	41.4	9.9	8.1	2,358	1,035	1,323	56.1
26015	Barry County, Michigan	47,084	62.0	0.0	67.4	56.7	60.9	84.1	61.1	12.8	7.9	26,899	14,662	12,237	45.5
26017	Bay County, Michigan	86,622	58.7	0.0	62.4	55.1	66.0	82.1	51.7	9.9	9.7	45,913	23,262	22,651	49.3
26019	Benzie County, Michigan	14,487	57.1	0.2	59.9	54.5	59.6	84.4	59.4	14.0	8.4	7,579	3,878	3,701	48.8
26021	Berrien County, Michigan	124,476	60.7	0.0	66.4	55.3	60.9	79.8	65.0	15.9	9.4	68,463	35,919	32,544	47.5
26023	Branch County, Michigan	34,414	57.3	0.0	59.6	54.8	58.4	76.2	57.4	12.5	7.0	18,328	9,894	8,434	46.0
26025	Calhoun County, Michigan	107,105	58.8	0.2	61.8	56.1	60.7	79.3	55.2	11.9	10.0	56,687	28,409	28,278	49.9
26027	Cass County, Michigan	42,122	59.3	0.0	65.1	53.6	58.8	80.2	65.0	14.0	9.7	22,556	12,348	10,208	45.3
26029	Charlevoix County, Michigan	21,421	59.7	0.3	64.7	55.0	65.7	84.0	60.2	15.6	7.8	11,793	6,202	5,591	47.4
26031	Cheboygan County, Michigan	21,649	53.8	0.3	57.1	50.6	60.2	80.7	54.7	12.6	13.9	10,029	5,257	4,772	47.6
26033	Chippewa County, Michigan	31,819	52.4	0.6	48.7	57.1	58.5	66.7	51.8	12.1	11.7	14,733	7,499	7,234	49.1
26035	Clare County, Michigan	25,279	48.8	0.0	52.6	45.0	62.5	71.4	43.1	9.9	13.2	10,708	5,740	4,968	46.4
26037	Clinton County, Michigan	61,195	63.2	0.1	66.0	60.6	57.9	85.5	60.0	12.9	6.5	36,177	18,344	17,833	49.3
26039	Crawford County, Michigan	11,642	50.7	0.1	52.9	48.6	62.0	76.6	46.2	10.2	12.0	5,197	2,683	2,514	48.4
26041	Delta County, Michigan	30,058	56.8	0.1	60.9	52.9	68.2	81.9	56.8	8.8	9.2	15,510	8,152	7,358	47.4
26043	Dickinson County, Michigan	21,357	56.2	0.1	60.8	51.7	59.1	79.6	59.5	9.8	7.0	11,161	5,872	5,289	47.4
26045	Eaton County, Michigan	87,504	63.8	0.1	67.4	60.4	65.7	84.4	61.6	13.7	7.8	51,451	25,996	25,455	49.5
26047	Emmet County, Michigan	27,131	63.9	0.0	68.2	59.7	69.6	85.7	65.4	17.1	8.4	15,869	8,100	7,769	49.0
26049	Genesee County, Michigan	329,094	56.6	0.0	59.9	53.7	56.1	78.2	47.7	10.1	13.2	161,750	79,742	82,008	50.7
26051	Gladwin County, Michigan	21,174	46.3	0.1	50.2	42.5	48.4	74.1	45.2	8.7	11.0	8,730	4,659	4,071	46.6
26053	Gogebic County, Michigan	13,648	46.6	0.0	44.0	49.7	59.7	64.0	49.4	10.9	9.5	5,759	2,975	2,784	48.3
26055	Grand Traverse County, Michigan	73,141	64.1	0.2	66.9	61.4	68.0	82.2	66.0	16.0	6.6	43,804	22,163	21,641	49.4

Table C. County—Labor Force, Employment, and Educational Data, 2011–2015—*Continued*

Fips code	State/county	Total population age 16 and older	Percent in civilian labor force	Percent in armed forces	Civilian labor force participation by gender		Civilian labor force participation by age				Civilian unemploy- ment rate	Civilian employed population age 16 and older			
					Men	Women	Age 16 to 24	Age 25 to 54	Age 55 to 64	Age 65 and older		Total	Men	Women	Percent women
26057	Gratiot County, Michigan	34,339	50.9	0.0	48.9	53.2	50.6	65.8	55.2	10.7	8.5	15,980	8,193	7,787	48.7
26059	Hillsdale County, Michigan	37,046	57.3	0.0	61.1	53.5	56.3	79.0	55.9	13.5	9.0	19,316	10,197	9,119	47.2
26061	Houghton County, Michigan	30,015	55.4	0.0	57.9	52.5	52.7	78.9	58.6	11.0	7.2	15,440	8,774	6,666	43.2
26063	Huron County, Michigan	26,720	56.3	0.0	61.2	51.4	61.1	83.2	60.1	11.7	7.8	13,869	7,407	6,462	46.6
26065	Ingham County, Michigan	232,336	63.0	0.0	66.6	59.6	57.0	81.7	61.5	16.6	9.0	133,091	66,998	66,093	49.7
26067	Ionia County, Michigan	50,682	59.0	0.0	59.2	58.8	60.6	74.5	52.7	12.4	10.4	26,785	14,286	12,499	46.7
26069	Iosco County, Michigan	21,707	46.0	0.1	48.3	43.8	56.9	75.6	46.2	8.7	12.1	8,780	4,478	4,302	49.0
26071	Iron County, Michigan	9,872	48.1	0.0	50.1	46.1	57.6	77.3	50.7	11.1	9.0	4,324	2,153	2,171	50.2
26073	Isabella County, Michigan	59,815	62.9	0.1	66.3	59.8	61.1	82.6	59.3	14.0	11.3	33,411	16,781	16,630	49.8
26075	Jackson County, Michigan	128,457	56.6	0.1	58.0	55.1	57.0	73.3	58.5	11.9	10.3	65,183	33,768	31,415	48.2
26077	Kalamazoo County, Michigan	206,012	65.6	0.1	69.7	61.8	67.2	83.8	62.8	15.1	9.1	122,809	62,492	60,317	49.1
26079	Kalkaska County, Michigan	13,994	54.3	0.0	57.3	51.2	54.6	77.0	51.5	10.6	10.4	6,815	3,629	3,186	46.7
26081	Kent County, Michigan	481,956	68.7	0.0	74.2	63.4	68.2	84.7	66.2	16.6	7.7	305,508	159,768	145,740	47.7
26083	Keweenaw County, Michigan	1,880	48.1	0.0	49.0	47.2	65.4	80.5	48.2	12.0	7.0	842	432	410	48.7
26085	Lake County, Michigan	9,733	39.0	0.0	39.6	38.4	46.3	60.4	41.1	8.3	13.2	3,297	1,627	1,670	50.7
26087	Lapeer County, Michigan	71,113	59.2	0.0	64.2	54.1	62.7	79.8	53.4	10.2	10.5	37,682	20,503	17,179	45.6
26089	Leelanau County, Michigan	18,540	55.9	0.0	61.2	50.8	61.2	83.7	66.5	15.6	7.1	9,628	5,081	4,547	47.2
26091	Lenawee County, Michigan	79,755	59.1	0.0	61.2	57.0	58.3	80.3	57.3	12.2	8.6	43,095	22,260	20,835	48.3
26093	Livingston County, Michigan	146,998	66.5	0.0	72.7	60.5	63.5	85.8	64.2	16.7	5.9	92,068	49,869	42,199	45.8
26095	Luce County, Michigan	5,511	43.2	0.0	39.4	48.7	50.9	55.7	47.6	10.2	11.6	2,103	1,122	981	46.6
26097	Mackinac County, Michigan	9,386	54.4	0.6	54.9	53.9	64.0	81.7	55.5	13.4	12.5	4,470	2,217	2,253	50.4
26099	Macomb County, Michigan	689,284	63.9	0.1	69.3	59.0	64.6	83.7	62.4	11.9	9.0	401,146	207,865	193,281	48.2
26101	Manistee County, Michigan	20,666	49.3	0.1	50.6	47.9	49.4	72.5	53.9	10.7	11.5	9,010	4,768	4,242	47.1
26103	Marquette County, Michigan	56,706	56.7	0.2	58.0	55.3	58.8	78.5	53.0	9.6	8.1	29,522	14,984	14,538	49.2
26105	Mason County, Michigan	23,400	58.3	0.0	62.8	54.0	63.4	83.4	59.9	12.8	10.7	12,183	6,291	5,892	48.4
26107	Mecosta County, Michigan	36,107	55.6	0.0	58.5	52.8	54.5	78.6	57.0	11.3	12.2	17,639	9,123	8,516	48.3
26109	Menominee County, Michigan	19,666	57.5	0.0	60.5	54.6	66.8	83.1	56.5	11.3	8.5	10,346	5,423	4,923	47.6
26111	Midland County, Michigan	67,282	60.8	0.0	66.7	55.2	58.9	82.0	58.4	12.2	8.5	37,406	19,988	17,418	46.6
26113	Missaukee County, Michigan	11,895	57.6	0.0	62.5	52.6	66.4	81.0	51.5	12.8	11.0	6,096	3,369	2,727	44.7
26115	Monroe County, Michigan	120,543	61.5	0.0	66.9	56.3	62.8	82.1	57.4	11.5	8.3	68,024	36,003	32,021	47.1
26117	Montcalm County, Michigan	50,148	55.2	0.0	57.9	52.3	56.6	72.7	53.8	10.8	11.2	24,588	13,304	11,284	45.9
26119	Montmorency County, Michigan	8,130	43.0	0.0	43.8	42.2	57.1	72.8	44.5	6.9	16.0	2,937	1,435	1,502	51.1
26121	Muskegon County, Michigan	135,213	58.5	0.1	61.0	56.1	58.5	76.9	56.1	12.4	11.9	69,673	35,609	34,064	48.9
26123	Newaygo County, Michigan	38,139	54.3	0.0	57.4	51.2	55.1	75.3	51.8	11.1	10.1	18,619	9,786	8,833	47.4
26125	Oakland County, Michigan	988,161	66.4	0.0	72.6	60.7	62.7	84.7	66.0	17.9	7.5	606,484	317,289	289,195	47.7
26127	Oceana County, Michigan	20,738	54.7	0.0	60.4	48.9	54.2	77.1	55.0	12.8	8.7	10,360	5,665	4,695	45.3
26129	Ogemaw County, Michigan	17,743	49.3	0.0	52.0	46.6	63.8	73.9	46.9	10.9	12.4	7,661	3,871	3,790	49.5
26131	Ontonagon County, Michigan	5,586	42.5	0.0	46.6	38.2	52.9	74.6	40.5	8.1	13.7	2,048	1,112	936	45.7
26133	Osceola County, Michigan	18,422	53.3	0.0	58.0	48.6	56.1	74.4	52.0	11.9	10.3	8,807	4,689	4,118	46.8
26135	Oscoda County, Michigan	7,036	45.7	0.0	49.9	41.5	58.4	71.3	44.7	11.0	13.2	2,792	1,470	1,322	47.3
26137	Otsego County, Michigan	19,646	59.5	0.1	64.0	55.2	69.0	82.6	54.7	12.8	8.2	10,733	5,596	5,137	47.9
26139	Ottawa County, Michigan	212,399	68.0	0.0	75.2	61.1	66.9	85.8	70.1	16.3	6.1	135,496	73,120	62,376	46.0
26141	Presque Isle County, Michigan	11,185	46.2	0.0	49.8	42.6	59.3	78.6	46.6	7.3	13.1	4,490	2,393	2,097	46.7
26143	Roscommon County, Michigan	20,872	42.2	0.0	45.2	39.3	64.6	72.8	37.9	7.9	14.2	7,563	3,899	3,664	48.4
26145	Saginaw County, Michigan	158,042	57.8	0.0	59.9	55.8	62.4	79.5	50.4	12.5	11.1	81,106	39,277	41,829	51.6
26147	St. Clair County, Michigan	129,374	60.3	0.0	64.3	56.5	65.7	80.4	57.0	11.2	10.4	69,940	36,514	33,426	47.8
26149	St. Joseph County, Michigan	47,359	60.8	0.1	66.9	54.9	60.1	81.7	60.3	13.4	8.6	26,332	14,126	12,206	46.4
26151	Sanilac County, Michigan	33,717	56.9	0.0	62.6	51.5	59.9	80.4	54.8	12.9	10.7	17,147	9,156	7,991	46.6
26153	Schoolcraft County, Michigan	6,976	47.6	0.0	47.0	48.2	56.8	75.9	43.3	6.6	15.6	2,803	1,301	1,502	53.6
26155	Shiawassee County, Michigan	55,685	59.5	0.1	63.9	55.2	60.6	81.3	53.4	11.4	10.3	29,702	15,558	14,144	47.6
26157	Tuscola County, Michigan	44,182	57.6	0.0	62.0	53.3	65.6	78.7	52.9	12.0	9.3	23,074	12,055	11,019	47.8
26159	Van Buren County, Michigan	59,341	59.4	0.0	63.8	55.1	57.9	79.0	58.6	13.6	8.4	32,252	16,858	15,394	47.7
26161	Washtenaw County, Michigan	292,237	65.1	0.1	69.3	61.1	56.6	82.6	67.1	19.4	7.4	176,383	91,749	84,634	48.0
26163	Wayne County, Michigan	1,396,676	58.6	0.0	62.8	54.8	58.2	76.9	52.4	11.7	14.9	696,900	349,778	347,122	49.8
26165	Wexford County, Michigan	25,864	57.4	0.0	62.3	52.6	60.0	77.1	56.8	13.1	9.5	13,441	7,160	6,281	46.7
27000	**Minnesota**	4,281,141	70.0	0.0	73.8	66.2	69.0	87.7	72.1	17.4	5.6	2,827,195	1,461,693	1,365,502	48.3
27001	Aitkin County, Minnesota	13,455	51.5	0.0	52.9	50.1	66.9	84.1	55.5	11.3	7.3	6,428	3,288	3,140	48.8
27003	Anoka County, Minnesota	264,912	72.9	0.0	76.5	69.4	67.4	89.0	73.0	17.3	6.2	181,190	93,872	87,318	48.2
27005	Becker County, Minnesota	25,920	63.7	0.0	67.2	60.1	70.3	87.3	64.5	16.1	3.5	15,929	8,399	7,530	47.3
27007	Beltrami County, Minnesota	35,186	65.4	0.0	67.1	63.7	66.4	84.7	68.5	14.5	10.6	20,579	10,261	10,318	50.1
27009	Benton County, Minnesota	30,459	70.8	0.0	75.9	65.6	74.1	87.3	71.9	13.5	6.7	20,104	10,700	9,404	46.8
27011	Big Stone County, Minnesota	4,176	59.6	0.0	65.6	53.8	79.7	86.3	75.4	10.2	3.3	2,406	1,272	1,134	47.1
27013	Blue Earth County, Minnesota	53,652	71.5	0.0	72.9	70.2	72.2	90.2	75.9	15.1	4.9	36,492	18,471	18,021	49.4
27015	Brown County, Minnesota	20,531	68.4	0.0	72.8	64.1	75.9	92.9	74.2	16.2	3.2	13,583	7,094	6,489	47.8
27017	Carlton County, Minnesota	28,064	62.1	0.1	63.5	60.5	63.4	81.5	62.1	13.0	5.4	16,478	8,598	7,880	47.8
27019	Carver County, Minnesota	71,803	76.1	0.0	81.7	70.7	65.8	89.7	79.4	22.7	3.8	52,573	27,606	24,967	47.5
27021	Cass County, Minnesota	23,111	56.9	0.0	60.3	53.3	67.1	83.6	57.9	14.6	7.4	12,165	6,442	5,723	47.0
27023	Chippewa County, Minnesota	9,709	67.3	0.1	72.1	62.8	72.1	89.5	77.6	17.3	2.6	6,367	3,294	3,073	48.3
27025	Chisago County, Minnesota	42,561	68.5	0.0	69.7	67.2	68.5	85.9	66.9	15.0	5.5	27,553	14,331	13,222	48.0
27027	Clay County, Minnesota	48,110	71.9	0.1	75.6	68.4	70.7	88.5	78.1	19.0	4.3	33,104	16,818	16,286	49.2

Table C. County—Labor Force, Employment, and Educational Data, 2011–2015—*Continued*

| | | | | | Civilian labor force participation by gender | | Civilian labor force participation by age | | | | | Civilian employed population age 16 and older | | | |
| | | | | | | | | | | | | | | | |
Fips code	State/county	Total population age 16 and older	Percent in civilian labor force	Percent in armed forces	Men	Women	Age 16 to 24	Age 25 to 54	Age 55 to 64	Age 65 and older	Civilian unemploy-ment rate	Total	Men	Women	Percent women
27029	Clearwater County, Minnesota	6,836	57.4	0.0	62.5	52.2	64.9	79.4	58.9	12.2	7.4	3,634	1,960	1,674	46.1
27031	Cook County, Minnesota	4,499	64.5	0.0	66.7	62.4	83.9	90.4	62.6	21.3	4.0	2,788	1,388	1,400	50.2
27033	Cottonwood County, Minnesota	9,132	62.3	0.0	66.7	58.1	68.2	84.3	75.2	18.9	4.9	5,408	2,819	2,589	47.9
27035	Crow Wing County, Minnesota	50,572	61.4	0.3	64.3	58.5	72.5	85.0	63.4	12.4	5.7	29,263	14,985	14,278	48.8
27037	Dakota County, Minnesota	317,479	74.2	0.1	78.8	70.0	70.6	89.9	74.9	19.5	5.0	223,989	115,426	108,563	48.5
27039	Dodge County, Minnesota	15,249	74.0	0.3	77.5	70.5	68.8	91.2	82.1	18.1	3.5	10,890	5,656	5,234	48.1
27041	Douglas County, Minnesota	29,726	66.8	0.0	72.4	61.4	78.5	90.6	70.9	18.4	4.5	18,975	10,083	8,892	46.9
27043	Faribault County, Minnesota	11,579	64.2	0.0	71.1	57.3	70.5	87.6	73.9	19.6	4.2	7,117	3,897	3,220	45.2
27045	Fillmore County, Minnesota	16,418	67.5	0.0	72.2	62.8	67.7	90.9	76.1	20.1	4.3	10,595	5,563	5,032	47.5
27047	Freeborn County, Minnesota	24,917	64.7	0.0	69.0	60.4	72.7	87.3	74.7	16.0	4.9	15,322	8,037	7,285	47.5
27049	Goodhue County, Minnesota	37,001	67.5	0.0	72.5	62.6	69.3	87.1	75.6	19.0	5.3	23,662	12,450	11,212	47.4
27051	Grant County, Minnesota	4,814	63.4	0.0	67.3	59.6	69.1	87.7	73.3	18.8	3.6	2,943	1,526	1,417	48.1
27053	Hennepin County, Minnesota	957,644	72.2	0.0	76.8	67.8	67.0	87.6	73.7	20.1	6.0	650,324	336,995	313,329	48.2
27055	Houston County, Minnesota	15,215	67.7	0.0	70.8	64.6	72.8	89.9	75.9	16.6	4.9	9,795	4,990	4,805	49.1
27057	Hubbard County, Minnesota	16,736	59.6	0.0	60.8	58.4	71.3	85.1	64.1	14.5	5.0	9,475	4,747	4,728	49.9
27059	Isanti County, Minnesota	29,885	70.4	0.0	74.1	66.6	68.0	88.4	71.6	18.0	7.3	19,504	10,170	9,334	47.9
27061	Itasca County, Minnesota	36,855	58.3	0.0	60.9	55.7	68.5	82.9	59.7	10.8	7.1	19,970	10,348	9,622	48.2
27063	Jackson County, Minnesota	8,166	68.2	0.0	72.1	64.2	73.7	88.7	79.3	20.9	3.2	5,392	2,862	2,530	46.9
27065	Kanabec County, Minnesota	12,933	62.5	0.0	66.1	58.7	71.3	82.5	63.9	15.4	9.8	7,287	3,725	3,562	48.9
27067	Kandiyohi County, Minnesota	33,543	68.2	0.0	72.2	64.1	70.2	87.0	78.8	17.5	4.8	21,757	11,479	10,278	47.2
27069	Kittson County, Minnesota	3,620	62.0	0.0	68.1	55.8	74.7	86.5	72.9	15.5	2.8	2,182	1,208	974	44.6
27071	Koochiching County, Minnesota	10,804	59.0	0.0	61.7	56.3	69.6	84.0	57.8	13.6	7.8	5,877	3,040	2,837	48.3
27073	Lac qui Parle County, Minnesota	5,770	63.1	0.0	68.5	57.7	68.9	85.7	83.2	17.7	3.7	3,506	1,887	1,619	46.2
27075	Lake County, Minnesota	9,022	56.7	0.0	60.0	53.2	72.3	84.3	61.5	9.8	4.8	4,870	2,567	2,303	47.3
27077	Lake of the Woods County, Minnesota	3,296	63.0	0.0	67.4	58.1	64.4	89.3	75.3	8.6	4.8	1,975	1,098	877	44.4
27079	Le Sueur County, Minnesota	21,604	70.6	0.1	75.3	65.9	72.8	90.1	75.8	16.4	5.3	14,456	7,631	6,825	47.2
27081	Lincoln County, Minnesota	4,655	65.7	0.0	72.2	59.3	83.1	91.3	76.6	20.2	2.8	2,974	1,614	1,360	45.7
27083	Lyon County, Minnesota	19,975	72.9	0.0	80.1	65.8	70.5	91.4	78.4	20.8	5.3	13,788	7,474	6,314	45.8
27085	McLeod County, Minnesota	28,409	69.8	0.0	75.5	64.4	75.2	89.4	75.2	18.3	4.5	18,957	10,068	8,889	46.9
27087	Mahnomen County, Minnesota	3,952	61.9	0.0	63.1	60.8	63.4	81.7	64.8	20.3	9.2	2,222	1,097	1,125	50.6
27089	Marshall County, Minnesota	7,521	65.9	0.0	70.5	61.1	64.6	88.2	75.9	18.5	4.7	4,726	2,548	2,178	46.1
27091	Martin County, Minnesota	16,444	64.8	0.0	71.0	58.7	74.4	86.6	75.1	18.2	3.5	10,273	5,481	4,792	46.6
27093	Meeker County, Minnesota	18,035	66.8	0.0	72.1	61.4	69.9	87.0	73.6	17.9	4.7	11,477	6,180	5,297	46.2
27095	Mille Lacs County, Minnesota	20,129	63.2	0.0	66.2	60.3	69.0	84.5	62.4	14.1	7.7	11,752	6,037	5,715	48.6
27097	Morrison County, Minnesota	25,999	67.5	0.0	70.9	64.0	73.7	88.8	70.8	14.5	5.8	16,533	8,624	7,909	47.8
27099	Mower County, Minnesota	30,648	66.9	0.0	71.9	62.0	72.8	88.7	71.1	15.7	6.5	19,166	10,069	9,097	47.5
27101	Murray County, Minnesota	6,946	64.0	0.0	68.4	59.7	75.7	86.2	77.9	19.0	4.5	4,244	2,201	2,043	48.1
27103	Nicollet County, Minnesota	26,518	73.4	0.0	74.9	71.9	70.1	89.8	84.6	19.5	4.0	18,672	9,470	9,202	49.3
27105	Nobles County, Minnesota	16,553	67.7	0.1	74.7	60.2	63.9	84.9	79.7	19.5	6.9	10,431	5,980	4,451	42.7
27107	Norman County, Minnesota	5,364	61.0	0.0	65.3	56.7	57.4	88.4	66.3	16.3	5.1	3,105	1,637	1,468	47.3
27109	Olmsted County, Minnesota	115,694	72.3	0.0	76.0	68.7	71.5	88.9	77.3	17.2	4.1	80,162	40,276	39,886	49.8
27111	Otter Tail County, Minnesota	46,664	62.0	0.0	66.2	57.8	69.4	87.1	68.5	15.7	4.4	27,662	14,585	13,077	47.3
27113	Pennington County, Minnesota	11,144	70.6	0.0	73.6	67.7	72.6	90.1	75.7	18.6	3.0	7,636	3,928	3,708	48.6
27115	Pine County, Minnesota	23,878	57.2	0.0	56.0	58.6	65.1	75.2	56.7	13.3	7.4	12,645	6,605	6,040	47.8
27117	Pipestone County, Minnesota	7,275	65.6	0.0	72.8	59.1	68.6	86.6	77.0	20.5	4.2	4,572	2,411	2,161	47.3
27119	Polk County, Minnesota	25,024	66.9	0.1	70.7	63.1	70.9	86.5	74.1	16.5	4.6	15,978	8,399	7,579	47.4
27121	Pope County, Minnesota	8,908	63.3	0.0	68.1	58.5	76.8	90.8	63.4	16.7	4.1	5,406	2,868	2,538	46.9
27123	Ramsey County, Minnesota	417,419	68.8	0.0	71.9	65.9	66.9	85.6	69.9	15.8	7.1	266,709	132,572	134,137	50.3
27125	Red Lake County, Minnesota	3,161	68.2	0.0	71.8	64.4	74.0	89.4	72.2	20.9	3.5	2,079	1,099	980	47.1
27127	Redwood County, Minnesota	12,264	64.3	0.0	68.8	60.0	65.2	86.7	77.5	18.8	4.0	7,577	3,972	3,605	47.6
27129	Renville County, Minnesota	12,190	65.4	0.0	70.6	60.0	66.1	88.3	75.7	16.4	5.0	7,573	4,093	3,480	46.0
27131	Rice County, Minnesota	52,068	68.1	0.0	69.0	67.2	71.5	82.4	74.3	19.1	5.6	33,503	17,333	16,170	48.3
27133	Rock County, Minnesota	7,430	65.9	0.2	71.2	60.9	70.6	86.2	73.7	23.1	3.7	4,716	2,450	2,266	48.0
27135	Roseau County, Minnesota	12,226	71.0	0.0	74.6	67.1	67.5	90.7	78.2	17.3	2.7	8,447	4,563	3,884	46.0
27137	St. Louis County, Minnesota	166,387	62.4	0.1	65.5	59.3	68.5	83.5	61.7	12.7	6.9	96,700	50,231	46,469	48.1
27139	Scott County, Minnesota	101,807	76.7	0.1	80.8	72.7	68.5	90.6	74.0	19.9	4.6	74,498	38,644	35,854	48.1
27141	Sherburne County, Minnesota	68,154	73.5	0.0	76.6	70.1	65.1	88.2	73.9	15.6	5.2	47,444	25,155	22,289	47.0
27143	Sibley County, Minnesota	11,776	70.7	0.0	75.1	66.2	70.4	90.8	81.2	18.9	5.5	7,867	4,212	3,655	46.5
27145	Stearns County, Minnesota	121,430	72.4	0.0	74.7	70.1	75.9	89.8	72.8	18.0	5.0	83,520	42,861	40,659	48.7
27147	Steele County, Minnesota	28,252	68.6	0.0	73.0	64.3	74.1	87.9	70.8	15.6	4.9	18,434	9,597	8,837	47.9
27149	Stevens County, Minnesota	7,947	65.7	0.0	68.0	63.4	62.5	88.8	77.6	19.8	3.1	5,058	2,635	2,423	47.9
27151	Swift County, Minnesota	7,696	65.8	0.0	72.1	59.4	67.7	88.6	79.7	16.6	3.9	4,865	2,686	2,179	44.8
27153	Todd County, Minnesota	19,196	62.8	0.0	66.3	59.1	62.8	86.8	68.7	14.2	5.1	11,437	6,106	5,331	46.6
27155	Traverse County, Minnesota	2,826	59.1	0.0	65.8	52.7	65.3	83.2	73.6	18.3	2.9	1,623	892	731	45.0
27157	Wabasha County, Minnesota	17,119	68.0	0.1	70.8	65.2	76.4	90.6	71.4	15.9	3.6	11,221	5,862	5,359	47.8
27159	Wadena County, Minnesota	10,812	57.2	0.0	63.0	51.5	62.2	80.7	63.5	14.8	5.2	5,859	3,153	2,706	46.2
27161	Waseca County, Minnesota	15,184	66.5	0.0	74.6	59.1	70.0	80.0	78.1	19.1	4.6	9,630	5,132	4,498	46.7
27163	Washington County, Minnesota	191,383	71.4	0.1	74.9	68.1	67.5	88.2	71.7	17.9	4.8	130,036	66,206	63,830	49.1
27165	Watonwan County, Minnesota	8,581	68.1	0.0	73.0	63.4	74.2	89.1	79.4	18.1	2.9	5,676	2,981	2,695	47.5
27167	Wilkin County, Minnesota	5,126	65.9	0.0	71.3	60.7	56.0	88.6	78.8	14.1	2.0	3,312	1,778	1,534	46.3
27169	Winona County, Minnesota	42,896	70.3	0.0	73.9	66.9	71.2	89.2	76.6	20.3	6.2	28,307	14,474	13,833	48.9

Table C. County—Labor Force, Employment, and Educational Data, 2011–2015—*Continued*

| Fips code | State/county | Total population age 16 and older | Percent in civilian labor force | Percent in armed forces | Civilian labor force participation by gender | | Civilian labor force participation by age | | | | Civilian unemploy-ment rate | Civilian employed population age 16 and older | | | Percent women |
					Men	Women	Age 16 to 24	Age 25 to 54	Age 55 to 64	Age 65 and older		Total	Men	Women	
27171	Wright County, Minnesota	95,014	75.1	0.1	79.7	70.5	72.6	90.6	73.4	17.6	5.2	67,669	35,692	31,977	47.3
27173	Yellow Medicine County, Minnesota	8,098	65.8	0.0	70.2	61.3	71.0	86.8	76.2	18.3	3.4	5,147	2,779	2,368	46.0
28000	**Mississippi**	2,333,154	57.5	0.5	61.7	53.7	50.3	76.1	55.1	14.8	10.3	1,203,914	619,773	584,141	48.5
28001	Adams County, Mississippi	25,935	46.6	0.0	47.0	46.3	43.1	58.7	53.0	14.5	11.3	10,730	5,403	5,327	49.6
28003	Alcorn County, Mississippi	29,337	55.4	0.3	63.1	48.2	61.3	73.0	51.9	13.3	9.0	14,784	8,107	6,677	45.2
28005	Amite County, Mississippi	10,357	50.5	0.0	58.8	42.7	50.5	71.1	43.0	19.6	12.7	4,562	2,579	1,983	43.5
28007	Attala County, Mississippi	14,830	51.2	0.0	58.9	44.6	58.0	74.5	39.0	11.8	12.6	6,643	3,680	2,963	44.6
28009	Benton County, Mississippi	6,729	53.7	0.0	60.5	47.4	59.0	72.3	43.5	16.3	17.1	2,994	1,565	1,429	47.7
28011	Bolivar County, Mississippi	26,227	53.3	0.0	55.5	51.4	46.5	71.2	53.7	11.1	15.3	11,834	5,734	6,100	51.5
28013	Calhoun County, Mississippi	11,589	53.6	0.0	59.0	48.8	56.9	76.1	40.1	14.3	10.1	5,580	2,867	2,713	48.6
28015	Carroll County, Mississippi	8,469	49.6	0.0	54.3	44.8	30.2	72.7	55.0	16.1	11.9	3,705	2,057	1,648	44.5
28017	Chickasaw County, Mississippi	13,489	55.3	0.0	60.6	50.5	58.2	72.9	49.3	14.3	12.2	6,554	3,458	3,096	47.2
28019	Choctaw County, Mississippi	6,653	51.2	0.0	57.1	45.7	47.3	75.9	41.2	14.3	14.2	2,921	1,576	1,345	46.0
28021	Claiborne County, Mississippi	7,474	39.1	0.0	39.7	38.6	25.2	59.9	46.6	12.1	17.5	2,411	1,020	1,391	57.7
28023	Clarke County, Mississippi	13,012	55.4	0.0	59.4	51.8	50.7	79.2	50.0	13.7	11.7	6,363	3,152	3,211	50.5
28025	Clay County, Mississippi	15,778	56.9	0.2	60.9	53.5	47.7	80.1	50.6	15.4	16.2	7,524	3,800	3,724	49.5
28027	Coahoma County, Mississippi	18,843	58.0	0.0	59.4	56.8	46.3	76.6	58.8	18.3	20.3	8,706	4,099	4,607	52.9
28029	Copiah County, Mississippi	22,659	53.0	0.0	56.7	49.6	37.1	76.9	48.5	12.4	14.3	10,280	5,126	5,154	50.1
28031	Covington County, Mississippi	15,091	50.9	0.0	57.3	45.1	61.5	67.3	52.7	8.0	13.7	6,628	3,752	2,876	43.4
28033	DeSoto County, Mississippi	128,461	69.6	0.1	74.0	65.5	61.1	86.5	67.5	17.7	7.6	82,634	42,082	40,552	49.1
28035	Forrest County, Mississippi	60,322	62.3	0.3	67.2	57.9	63.3	78.8	50.9	19.0	13.1	32,647	16,774	15,873	48.6
28037	Franklin County, Mississippi	6,074	56.1	0.0	64.5	48.4	56.3	76.5	60.0	11.4	8.9	3,102	1,744	1,358	43.8
28039	George County, Mississippi	17,591	51.6	0.0	59.2	43.8	49.7	66.9	50.2	10.7	9.0	8,260	4,708	3,552	43.0
28041	Greene County, Mississippi	11,533	39.2	0.0	36.9	42.9	49.8	46.4	29.7	10.8	12.6	3,955	2,347	1,608	40.7
28043	Grenada County, Mississippi	17,148	52.6	0.0	54.4	51.1	43.8	70.0	60.8	13.0	9.4	8,169	3,848	4,321	52.9
28045	Hancock County, Mississippi	36,671	56.1	0.2	62.6	49.9	55.0	77.5	50.1	14.5	10.1	18,482	9,944	8,538	46.2
28047	Harrison County, Mississippi	153,518	59.8	4.0	63.2	56.6	53.2	76.8	58.4	14.5	9.7	82,911	42,903	40,008	48.3
28049	Hinds County, Mississippi	190,460	61.7	0.1	64.6	59.3	49.1	80.5	58.7	17.9	10.3	105,504	50,569	54,935	52.1
28051	Holmes County, Mississippi	14,154	46.4	0.0	50.9	42.5	43.0	63.1	42.1	9.9	19.2	5,301	2,658	2,643	49.9
28053	Humphreys County, Mississippi	6,790	53.9	0.0	58.7	49.9	43.7	73.1	53.3	13.0	26.8	2,678	1,370	1,308	48.8
28055	Issaquena County, Mississippi	1,128	30.6	0.0	25.5	42.3	29.7	37.5	31.0	15.2	11.6	305	180	125	41.0
28057	Itawamba County, Mississippi	18,841	55.2	0.0	61.3	49.4	43.9	80.3	48.6	13.7	9.3	9,428	5,105	4,323	45.9
28059	Jackson County, Mississippi	109,928	58.9	0.4	65.2	52.9	53.5	77.5	55.6	11.7	9.1	58,824	31,551	27,273	46.4
28061	Jasper County, Mississippi	13,155	51.6	0.5	57.3	46.3	53.9	69.9	52.7	11.8	7.9	6,257	3,458	2,799	44.7
28063	Jefferson County, Mississippi	6,013	36.8	0.0	35.6	38.0	21.2	49.7	44.0	12.5	15.9	1,861	812	1,049	56.4
28065	Jefferson Davis County, Mississippi	9,706	48.5	0.0	48.8	48.1	53.5	69.4	43.6	8.2	12.9	4,094	1,946	2,148	52.5
28067	Jones County, Mississippi	52,696	54.2	0.1	62.1	47.1	48.7	73.1	51.1	13.8	7.4	26,436	14,299	12,137	45.9
28069	Kemper County, Mississippi	8,247	47.7	0.0	43.9	51.6	38.1	68.8	50.3	7.3	10.1	3,537	1,623	1,914	54.1
28071	Lafayette County, Mississippi	42,762	57.7	0.0	63.4	52.3	40.0	83.8	60.8	16.1	8.4	22,584	12,026	10,558	46.7
28073	Lamar County, Mississippi	45,326	65.0	1.3	69.7	60.8	58.6	81.4	57.4	18.3	8.5	26,952	14,092	12,860	47.7
28075	Lauderdale County, Mississippi	62,753	57.7	1.1	61.5	54.3	49.5	76.6	57.7	15.7	9.6	32,747	17,011	15,736	48.1
28077	Lawrence County, Mississippi	9,826	52.9	0.1	58.0	48.1	48.1	73.2	48.9	12.2	10.8	4,638	2,413	2,225	48.0
28079	Leake County, Mississippi	17,475	54.6	0.0	58.3	51.1	42.9	73.5	53.6	15.4	10.5	8,537	4,452	4,085	47.9
28081	Lee County, Mississippi	65,280	62.5	0.2	68.5	57.3	58.8	81.3	57.3	15.9	7.8	37,654	19,113	18,541	49.2
28083	Leflore County, Mississippi	23,987	47.0	0.0	49.6	44.6	36.5	62.6	47.6	11.6	16.3	9,422	4,579	4,843	51.4
28085	Lincoln County, Mississippi	26,902	53.0	0.1	60.6	46.2	42.9	72.3	55.2	10.9	7.5	13,182	7,046	6,136	46.5
28087	Lowndes County, Mississippi	46,789	59.3	2.2	65.1	54.1	52.5	77.5	58.2	15.9	12.6	24,232	12,581	11,651	48.1
28089	Madison County, Mississippi	77,266	66.4	0.4	72.0	61.6	49.8	84.0	68.6	19.5	5.4	48,562	24,772	23,790	49.0
28091	Marion County, Mississippi	20,380	50.8	0.0	57.5	44.7	48.7	68.8	47.4	12.3	10.4	9,272	5,026	4,246	45.8
28093	Marshall County, Mississippi	29,078	52.8	0.1	54.8	50.9	40.6	69.5	55.0	16.8	8.4	14,066	7,389	6,677	47.5
28095	Monroe County, Mississippi	28,649	55.7	0.0	59.9	52.0	52.7	75.3	55.3	15.4	10.9	14,217	7,224	6,993	49.2
28097	Montgomery County, Mississippi	8,242	47.9	0.0	52.3	44.0	41.3	68.5	46.1	15.9	8.5	3,608	1,787	1,821	50.5
28099	Neshoba County, Mississippi	22,051	61.7	0.0	67.2	56.8	56.9	81.0	64.2	13.7	9.8	12,268	6,214	6,054	49.3
28101	Newton County, Mississippi	16,732	55.6	0.1	58.6	52.9	47.7	79.1	52.6	10.4	10.6	8,319	4,058	4,261	51.2
28103	Noxubee County, Mississippi	8,607	55.1	0.0	58.8	51.7	56.6	72.4	47.5	17.2	19.0	3,841	1,961	1,880	48.9
28105	Oktibbeha County, Mississippi	40,939	54.6	0.1	57.8	51.4	44.8	78.9	53.0	12.5	13.3	19,381	10,340	9,041	46.6
28107	Panola County, Mississippi	26,414	54.1	0.1	56.0	52.4	46.7	73.2	50.9	11.2	10.3	12,826	6,280	6,546	51.0
28109	Pearl River County, Mississippi	43,748	52.6	0.2	59.5	46.0	49.5	73.2	48.9	12.5	12.1	20,219	11,083	9,136	45.2
28111	Perry County, Mississippi	9,642	49.2	0.2	56.4	42.5	54.9	68.7	41.0	7.1	12.9	4,131	2,273	1,858	45.0
28113	Pike County, Mississippi	30,450	52.6	0.0	56.4	49.2	47.6	71.0	50.4	14.6	9.5	14,477	7,224	7,253	50.1
28115	Pontotoc County, Mississippi	23,377	61.7	0.0	64.0	59.5	59.3	82.3	55.7	12.4	6.6	13,476	6,839	6,637	49.3
28117	Prentiss County, Mississippi	20,111	53.0	0.0	56.8	49.3	49.2	73.9	49.2	11.7	10.2	9,559	4,937	4,622	48.4
28119	Quitman County, Mississippi	6,063	51.3	0.0	54.6	48.4	37.9	67.4	55.3	18.3	25.3	2,324	1,132	1,192	51.3
28121	Rankin County, Mississippi	114,743	63.8	0.2	68.6	59.4	55.0	80.6	60.4	17.7	5.4	69,233	35,353	33,880	48.9
28123	Scott County, Mississippi	21,553	58.0	0.2	62.8	53.5	54.2	76.1	52.5	12.3	13.1	10,867	5,727	5,140	47.3
28125	Sharkey County, Mississippi	3,721	57.9	0.0	57.5	58.2	58.5	78.1	46.3	18.4	22.1	1,678	675	1,003	59.8
28127	Simpson County, Mississippi	21,076	52.3	0.0	57.3	47.7	44.3	72.2	48.2	13.3	10.9	9,821	5,438	4,383	44.6
28129	Smith County, Mississippi	12,656	53.4	0.0	62.5	45.2	38.1	74.9	59.5	13.5	4.8	6,433	3,585	2,848	44.3
28131	Stone County, Mississippi	14,297	53.6	0.3	56.4	50.8	45.3	73.3	48.3	10.5	9.7	6,920	3,541	3,379	48.8
28133	Sunflower County, Mississippi	21,949	47.8	0.0	44.9	51.1	50.4	56.4	47.3	13.2	20.1	8,382	4,183	4,199	50.1

Table C. County—Labor Force, Employment, and Educational Data, 2011–2015—*Continued*

					Civilian labor force participation by gender		Civilian labor force participation by age					Civilian employed population age 16 and older			
Fips code	State/county	Total population age 16 and older	Percent in civilian labor force	Percent in armed forces	Men	Women	Age 16 to 24	Age 25 to 54	Age 55 to 64	Age 65 and older	Civilian unemployment rate	Total	Men	Women	Percent women
28135	Tallahatchie County, Mississippi	12,845	36.6	0.0	27.5	51.0	21.9	39.9	64.6	13.8	19.0	3,806	1,713	2,093	55.0
28137	Tate County, Mississippi	22,221	57.1	0.0	60.6	53.9	37.5	79.1	58.3	17.8	10.0	11,418	5,826	5,592	49.0
28139	Tippah County, Mississippi	17,103	56.2	0.0	63.8	48.8	57.9	75.5	46.3	16.2	12.2	8,428	4,684	3,744	44.4
28141	Tishomingo County, Mississippi	15,715	56.0	0.1	63.0	49.5	59.8	76.7	56.9	13.2	10.5	7,885	4,332	3,553	45.1
28143	Tunica County, Mississippi	7,689	62.2	0.0	70.8	55.0	45.3	79.1	64.2	13.9	12.4	4,191	2,277	1,914	45.7
28145	Union County, Mississippi	21,522	57.0	0.0	63.0	51.4	51.2	74.0	54.2	20.5	10.7	10,949	5,927	5,022	45.9
28147	Walthall County, Mississippi	11,702	51.7	0.0	59.7	44.6	46.5	71.3	55.3	11.9	11.1	5,382	2,946	2,436	45.3
28149	Warren County, Mississippi	37,123	57.3	0.1	62.2	52.9	42.9	76.5	57.0	17.1	8.0	19,554	9,796	9,758	49.9
28151	Washington County, Mississippi	37,747	57.6	0.0	61.9	54.1	50.6	75.4	53.5	19.2	21.7	17,034	8,064	8,970	52.7
28153	Wayne County, Mississippi	15,988	54.6	0.0	60.7	48.9	53.0	71.0	57.8	13.0	9.4	7,906	4,252	3,654	46.2
28155	Webster County, Mississippi	7,800	51.2	0.0	55.8	46.9	53.8	70.0	47.3	8.8	11.2	3,544	1,841	1,703	48.1
28157	Wilkinson County, Mississippi	7,481	43.1	0.0	39.5	47.3	46.4	56.6	37.5	9.6	9.7	2,914	1,415	1,499	51.4
28159	Winston County, Mississippi	14,726	54.5	0.2	57.5	51.8	55.0	75.4	51.4	12.9	12.3	7,034	3,681	3,353	47.7
28161	Yalobusha County, Mississippi	9,809	54.6	0.0	56.7	52.7	49.6	79.2	52.1	10.5	5.7	5,055	2,452	2,603	51.5
28163	Yazoo County, Mississippi	21,931	47.7	0.0	43.9	52.5	53.8	56.2	46.8	12.4	19.8	8,382	4,317	4,065	48.5
29000	**Missouri**	4,803,676	63.2	0.4	67.3	59.3	62.0	81.5	63.0	16.4	7.5	2,807,996	1,443,374	1,364,622	48.6
29001	Adair County, Missouri	21,421	56.2	0.0	59.3	53.5	45.5	81.0	65.6	20.6	7.9	11,096	5,473	5,623	50.7
29003	Andrew County, Missouri	13,877	65.1	0.1	68.6	61.8	65.3	86.8	65.2	16.8	5.0	8,583	4,319	4,264	49.7
29005	Atchison County, Missouri	4,504	62.4	0.1	67.3	57.7	72.8	86.6	64.8	20.9	4.3	2,691	1,422	1,269	47.2
29007	Audrain County, Missouri	20,472	56.8	0.1	65.5	50.0	58.0	71.2	64.2	16.2	8.8	10,600	5,305	5,295	50.0
29009	Barry County, Missouri	28,413	56.7	0.0	63.9	49.7	62.0	78.6	58.0	12.6	11.4	14,259	7,881	6,378	44.7
29011	Barton County, Missouri	9,545	56.8	0.0	62.7	51.3	65.0	76.4	56.7	14.7	6.5	5,075	2,744	2,331	45.9
29013	Bates County, Missouri	13,082	58.8	0.0	63.7	54.2	67.6	78.1	60.3	15.1	6.6	7,186	3,812	3,374	47.0
29015	Benton County, Missouri	15,956	45.0	0.0	48.1	41.9	61.5	71.0	47.0	9.8	10.2	6,442	3,334	3,108	48.2
29017	Bollinger County, Missouri	9,950	53.0	0.0	59.0	47.0	52.1	73.3	50.8	12.1	4.0	5,064	2,814	2,250	44.4
29019	Boone County, Missouri	139,306	68.8	0.1	72.0	65.8	60.6	85.9	69.7	22.0	5.0	90,949	45,544	45,405	49.9
29021	Buchanan County, Missouri	70,878	64.1	0.2	68.0	60.3	68.9	78.5	67.2	17.0	7.5	42,029	22,047	19,982	47.5
29023	Butler County, Missouri	34,135	56.0	0.0	57.5	54.7	60.3	75.3	50.5	15.9	9.4	17,340	8,323	9,017	52.0
29025	Caldwell County, Missouri	7,125	57.6	0.1	61.5	53.6	55.0	78.2	60.5	15.9	5.2	3,889	2,070	1,819	46.8
29027	Callaway County, Missouri	36,229	57.7	0.2	58.0	57.4	47.5	76.5	57.6	14.7	5.1	19,844	10,068	9,776	49.3
29029	Camden County, Missouri	36,663	52.2	0.0	56.5	48.0	63.7	75.1	56.3	13.9	9.1	17,403	9,206	8,197	47.1
29031	Cape Girardeau County, Missouri	62,446	64.4	0.1	67.3	61.7	64.5	84.2	64.7	16.4	6.3	37,661	18,861	18,800	49.9
29033	Carroll County, Missouri	7,287	60.4	0.0	66.4	55.1	63.4	82.5	62.4	18.7	8.9	4,010	2,113	1,897	47.3
29035	Carter County, Missouri	4,930	54.0	0.0	53.5	54.4	56.2	72.3	56.3	12.9	9.7	2,402	1,112	1,290	53.7
29037	Cass County, Missouri	78,142	66.0	0.1	73.2	59.3	66.3	85.5	63.8	16.5	6.7	48,122	25,731	22,391	46.5
29039	Cedar County, Missouri	11,032	50.9	0.0	58.2	44.1	59.0	79.0	44.2	11.7	10.5	5,029	2,766	2,263	45.0
29041	Chariton County, Missouri	6,135	56.3	0.0	62.3	50.7	63.4	78.5	67.3	12.9	3.8	3,323	1,760	1,563	47.0
29043	Christian County, Missouri	61,746	65.0	0.0	70.6	59.8	65.3	83.3	62.1	13.8	6.4	37,578	19,267	18,311	48.7
29045	Clark County, Missouri	5,468	61.5	0.0	69.1	53.8	68.9	79.7	63.2	22.3	4.5	3,210	1,785	1,425	44.4
29047	Clay County, Missouri	178,854	70.4	0.1	75.5	65.6	68.3	86.4	68.6	18.7	6.1	118,111	61,097	57,014	48.3
29049	Clinton County, Missouri	16,196	63.2	0.2	67.3	59.3	65.7	84.0	62.6	15.1	5.8	9,653	5,038	4,615	47.8
29051	Cole County, Missouri	60,833	62.2	0.2	63.0	61.3	55.2	78.8	62.2	17.2	4.9	35,978	18,280	17,698	49.2
29053	Cooper County, Missouri	14,195	59.1	0.1	56.3	62.3	50.8	76.8	65.8	18.2	5.7	7,916	3,946	3,970	50.2
29055	Crawford County, Missouri	19,481	55.2	0.0	59.9	50.7	66.1	72.1	54.0	12.9	12.7	9,393	5,101	4,292	45.7
29057	Dade County, Missouri	6,246	57.5	0.0	61.1	53.9	68.7	78.4	64.8	14.0	7.9	3,307	1,717	1,590	48.1
29059	Dallas County, Missouri	13,059	52.4	0.0	57.3	47.5	56.9	71.9	55.7	9.9	13.2	5,943	3,212	2,731	46.0
29061	Daviess County, Missouri	6,365	57.0	0.0	63.4	50.7	62.3	73.5	61.9	19.5	5.7	3,420	1,877	1,543	45.1
29063	DeKalb County, Missouri	10,923	42.1	0.1	34.8	55.6	50.6	48.2	48.5	12.1	6.8	4,285	2,294	1,991	46.5
29065	Dent County, Missouri	12,386	52.3	0.0	56.5	48.4	62.8	70.5	53.4	13.8	9.2	5,882	3,084	2,798	47.6
29067	Douglas County, Missouri	10,974	49.1	0.0	55.2	43.0	50.6	76.0	44.4	10.2	9.0	4,897	2,644	2,253	46.0
29069	Dunklin County, Missouri	24,345	52.1	0.0	56.0	48.5	56.7	69.7	48.5	14.5	8.1	11,646	5,839	5,807	49.9
29071	Franklin County, Missouri	80,153	65.0	0.0	70.5	59.6	71.7	83.9	62.1	13.4	7.2	48,336	25,394	22,942	47.5
29073	Gasconade County, Missouri	12,112	57.7	0.0	62.8	52.9	71.3	80.2	57.7	14.0	6.1	6,567	3,425	3,142	47.8
29075	Gentry County, Missouri	5,338	59.7	0.1	64.8	55.2	68.2	80.5	61.4	17.6	6.3	2,989	1,513	1,476	49.4
29077	Greene County, Missouri	229,866	63.2	0.1	68.4	58.3	66.1	81.2	61.1	15.6	6.8	135,307	69,988	65,319	48.3
29079	Grundy County, Missouri	8,070	55.4	0.0	64.3	47.3	63.0	77.1	62.3	12.9	4.5	4,272	2,356	1,916	44.9
29081	Harrison County, Missouri	6,768	58.9	0.0	64.2	53.9	71.7	82.0	61.1	14.7	5.8	3,755	2,006	1,749	46.6
29083	Henry County, Missouri	17,642	57.3	0.3	63.3	51.6	64.8	78.0	60.5	13.5	7.4	9,359	5,009	4,350	46.5
29085	Hickory County, Missouri	7,968	43.4	0.0	41.6	45.0	46.1	71.9	44.6	15.8	12.6	3,020	1,386	1,634	54.1
29087	Holt County, Missouri	3,780	62.5	0.1	68.3	56.7	67.3	85.1	69.7	19.3	5.2	2,238	1,226	1,012	45.2
29089	Howard County, Missouri	8,120	59.6	0.0	58.9	60.2	47.4	83.2	61.3	19.1	6.3	4,533	2,240	2,293	50.6
29091	Howell County, Missouri	31,400	56.3	0.1	62.0	51.1	65.9	77.3	53.2	10.9	8.3	16,205	8,449	7,756	47.9
29093	Iron County, Missouri	8,317	52.6	0.0	53.7	51.6	67.5	69.9	47.4	13.2	11.4	3,878	1,905	1,973	50.9
29095	Jackson County, Missouri	533,825	66.1	0.0	70.3	62.3	62.9	83.1	64.4	17.6	7.6	326,275	165,092	161,183	49.4
29097	Jasper County, Missouri	90,443	65.2	0.1	70.5	60.2	70.0	81.1	63.7	16.4	6.0	55,374	28,804	26,570	48.0
29099	Jefferson County, Missouri	174,003	67.1	0.1	72.1	62.1	68.0	84.0	62.9	15.2	8.3	106,972	56,178	50,794	47.5
29101	Johnson County, Missouri	43,568	59.6	6.6	61.1	58.1	54.2	75.3	64.4	17.1	8.0	23,900	12,502	11,398	47.7
29103	Knox County, Missouri	3,175	58.1	0.0	66.3	50.1	64.5	80.5	63.9	13.0	7.4	1,709	952	757	44.3
29105	Laclede County, Missouri	27,952	57.7	0.2	64.0	51.6	58.9	74.4	60.6	15.3	8.8	14,708	8,053	6,655	45.2
29107	Lafayette County, Missouri	26,180	61.6	0.1	67.4	56.0	61.3	82.1	61.5	18.3	6.9	15,021	7,976	7,045	46.9

Table C. County—Labor Force, Employment, and Educational Data, 2011–2015—*Continued*

Fips code	State/county	Total population age 16 and older	Percent in civilian labor force	Percent in armed forces	Civilian labor force participation by gender		Civilian labor force participation by age				Civilian unemploy-ment rate	Civilian employed population age 16 and older			
					Men	Women	Age 16 to 24	Age 25 to 54	Age 55 to 64	Age 65 and older		Total	Men	Women	Percent women
29109	Lawrence County, Missouri	29,529	57.5	0.2	63.8	51.5	56.3	76.7	59.2	15.8	7.0	15,804	8,567	7,237	45.8
29111	Lewis County, Missouri	8,092	64.4	0.1	65.2	63.6	62.3	85.6	71.1	18.5	5.6	4,918	2,470	2,448	49.8
29113	Lincoln County, Missouri	41,222	63.9	0.1	69.2	58.8	61.2	81.3	56.8	14.5	9.5	23,857	12,627	11,230	47.1
29115	Linn County, Missouri	9,787	54.8	0.0	60.8	49.6	52.3	79.4	55.1	12.9	4.5	5,125	2,625	2,500	48.8
29117	Livingston County, Missouri	12,253	57.1	0.1	67.3	49.1	63.1	72.7	64.0	18.1	5.1	6,641	3,417	3,224	48.5
29119	McDonald County, Missouri	17,486	59.8	0.0	63.8	55.6	57.2	75.1	65.7	12.5	8.7	9,544	5,221	4,323	45.3
29121	Macon County, Missouri	12,178	58.8	0.0	60.9	56.9	71.5	84.2	55.8	12.0	8.7	6,541	3,322	3,219	49.2
29123	Madison County, Missouri	9,740	55.5	0.0	62.1	49.4	67.0	75.1	53.1	12.8	10.2	4,854	2,622	2,232	46.0
29125	Maries County, Missouri	7,203	54.8	0.8	57.8	51.7	61.8	73.6	57.5	14.4	10.0	3,551	1,905	1,646	46.4
29127	Marion County, Missouri	22,712	60.9	0.0	63.8	58.3	63.3	81.4	55.9	17.5	7.2	12,851	6,496	6,355	49.5
29129	Mercer County, Missouri	2,909	59.7	0.0	64.9	54.5	61.6	80.8	69.5	16.8	4.6	1,657	888	769	46.4
29131	Miller County, Missouri	19,756	59.7	0.1	61.7	57.7	66.4	78.1	59.7	15.4	8.1	10,832	5,353	5,479	50.6
29133	Mississippi County, Missouri	11,274	49.9	0.0	45.5	55.2	65.5	58.6	48.7	19.2	12.2	4,945	2,389	2,556	51.7
29135	Moniteau County, Missouri	12,238	58.8	0.1	58.1	59.7	64.1	72.6	57.5	16.3	6.7	6,712	3,486	3,226	48.1
29137	Monroe County, Missouri	6,937	58.9	0.1	62.1	55.8	67.2	79.7	58.4	20.1	5.9	3,845	2,016	1,829	47.6
29139	Montgomery County, Missouri	9,434	60.0	0.1	64.7	55.4	63.1	82.2	63.9	14.5	9.4	5,126	2,774	2,352	45.9
29141	Morgan County, Missouri	16,285	47.8	0.0	52.1	43.5	68.2	69.7	42.3	12.5	11.7	6,875	3,731	3,144	45.7
29143	New Madrid County, Missouri	14,566	54.9	0.2	59.4	51.1	52.8	74.3	49.8	18.2	8.8	7,298	3,697	3,601	49.3
29145	Newton County, Missouri	46,020	60.5	0.1	66.6	54.6	63.6	80.9	58.7	15.9	6.1	26,122	14,127	11,995	45.9
29147	Nodaway County, Missouri	19,759	61.2	0.2	62.4	59.9	60.9	80.2	67.0	16.1	7.2	11,209	5,623	5,586	49.8
29149	Oregon County, Missouri	8,839	49.7	0.0	52.5	47.1	47.6	72.1	59.2	10.7	7.1	4,083	2,085	1,998	48.9
29151	Osage County, Missouri	10,891	63.9	0.0	68.3	59.1	53.6	88.5	61.6	15.3	2.9	6,752	3,750	3,002	44.5
29153	Ozark County, Missouri	7,909	45.0	0.0	47.3	42.6	53.0	68.2	46.3	12.6	12.6	3,112	1,626	1,486	47.8
29155	Pemiscot County, Missouri	13,627	53.1	0.0	59.2	47.9	48.5	71.7	49.5	15.5	11.2	6,423	3,279	3,144	48.9
29157	Perry County, Missouri	14,957	64.9	0.3	70.3	59.7	68.4	84.7	65.5	15.7	4.2	9,292	4,813	4,479	48.2
29159	Pettis County, Missouri	32,815	61.0	0.4	66.7	55.7	62.2	77.6	61.9	17.3	6.4	18,740	9,919	8,821	47.1
29161	Phelps County, Missouri	36,437	57.4	0.3	59.1	55.5	49.5	79.1	59.0	14.5	7.0	19,451	10,513	8,938	46.0
29163	Pike County, Missouri	14,920	52.3	0.1	49.5	55.9	60.6	64.6	54.9	14.0	6.5	7,300	3,867	3,433	47.0
29165	Platte County, Missouri	73,533	71.2	0.6	76.0	66.7	68.8	86.7	71.7	20.3	5.6	49,463	25,796	23,667	47.8
29167	Polk County, Missouri	24,681	58.1	0.1	61.1	55.3	64.8	76.4	59.0	13.7	9.5	12,978	6,740	6,238	48.1
29169	Pulaski County, Missouri	42,347	41.3	30.8	39.0	44.7	24.4	56.9	47.3	11.8	12.7	15,279	8,289	6,990	45.7
29171	Putnam County, Missouri	3,943	54.7	0.0	58.1	51.4	72.0	78.1	54.9	12.8	2.8	2,097	1,102	995	47.4
29173	Ralls County, Missouri	8,313	61.8	0.0	65.8	57.7	73.9	78.7	63.4	20.8	6.2	4,821	2,576	2,245	46.6
29175	Randolph County, Missouri	20,040	52.2	0.0	53.5	50.7	57.4	65.2	55.4	10.8	8.9	9,519	5,030	4,489	47.2
29177	Ray County, Missouri	18,267	60.5	0.0	65.4	55.7	56.5	80.5	59.2	17.3	8.2	10,147	5,413	4,734	46.7
29179	Reynolds County, Missouri	5,256	51.4	0.0	54.0	48.9	54.8	73.3	50.1	17.2	11.1	2,404	1,273	1,131	47.0
29181	Ripley County, Missouri	11,147	54.7	0.1	57.9	51.7	66.8	75.4	50.6	11.5	10.1	5,480	2,816	2,664	48.6
29183	St. Charles County, Missouri	292,363	71.7	0.0	77.1	66.6	69.5	88.7	71.7	18.2	5.1	198,960	104,138	94,822	47.7
29185	St. Clair County, Missouri	7,959	47.2	0.0	50.6	43.8	64.4	70.4	43.3	13.7	9.3	3,408	1,837	1,571	46.1
29186	Ste. Genevieve County, Missouri	14,399	61.0	0.0	66.0	56.2	76.3	80.1	57.8	11.9	5.4	8,313	4,461	3,852	46.3
29187	St. Francois County, Missouri	53,297	52.0	0.0	49.1	55.4	58.0	65.1	49.5	11.9	8.3	25,384	12,953	12,431	49.0
29189	St. Louis County, Missouri	802,779	66.2	0.0	71.7	61.5	61.9	86.1	70.0	18.2	7.4	492,220	245,827	246,393	50.1
29195	Saline County, Missouri	18,612	60.5	0.0	63.9	57.2	52.9	84.5	57.0	17.4	5.5	10,642	5,499	5,143	48.3
29197	Schuyler County, Missouri	3,444	59.3	0.1	65.0	54.0	58.3	82.5	64.6	15.4	7.4	1,891	988	903	47.8
29199	Scotland County, Missouri	3,639	62.8	0.0	73.7	52.6	71.3	79.0	73.3	21.7	4.0	2,193	1,233	960	43.8
29201	Scott County, Missouri	30,742	60.3	0.0	65.3	55.7	66.5	78.4	58.0	16.0	6.8	17,280	8,908	8,372	48.4
29203	Shannon County, Missouri	6,646	55.7	0.0	64.8	46.9	70.6	78.8	43.0	14.1	9.2	3,361	1,935	1,426	42.4
29205	Shelby County, Missouri	4,861	63.1	0.1	68.8	57.5	70.2	84.2	68.2	18.6	5.8	2,888	1,558	1,330	46.1
29207	Stoddard County, Missouri	24,115	56.3	0.0	63.0	50.0	63.2	75.4	56.7	13.7	9.1	12,334	6,668	5,666	45.9
29209	Stone County, Missouri	26,541	50.7	0.0	53.6	48.0	51.1	78.5	52.8	16.0	10.8	12,009	6,165	5,844	48.7
29211	Sullivan County, Missouri	5,134	57.9	0.4	61.1	54.6	62.0	73.5	66.4	17.9	6.0	2,794	1,479	1,315	47.1
29213	Taney County, Missouri	43,442	59.3	0.0	62.5	56.3	66.2	79.9	55.3	18.6	9.0	23,414	11,794	11,620	49.6
29215	Texas County, Missouri	20,462	48.6	0.7	49.8	47.3	53.8	66.8	48.8	11.1	8.1	9,142	4,751	4,391	48.0
29217	Vernon County, Missouri	16,308	61.3	0.0	64.2	58.7	58.8	82.2	69.0	19.7	5.4	9,449	4,623	4,826	51.1
29219	Warren County, Missouri	26,021	62.7	0.0	67.7	57.7	69.5	78.1	68.1	16.4	8.9	14,863	8,046	6,817	45.9
29221	Washington County, Missouri	19,877	52.3	0.0	53.2	51.3	69.0	65.9	46.8	7.9	12.2	9,124	4,724	4,400	48.2
29223	Wayne County, Missouri	10,917	47.7	0.0	48.7	46.6	65.5	67.6	46.4	8.4	9.5	4,712	2,301	2,411	51.2
29225	Webster County, Missouri	27,770	56.1	0.0	63.2	48.9	57.9	71.6	55.8	13.3	6.3	14,583	8,296	6,287	43.1
29227	Worth County, Missouri	1,687	60.3	0.1	66.9	54.0	77.2	81.7	71.6	17.6	4.3	973	522	451	46.4
29229	Wright County, Missouri	14,351	50.7	0.0	57.3	44.4	58.6	69.2	47.0	13.7	9.4	6,583	3,588	2,995	45.5
29510	St. Louis city, Missouri	259,729	64.7	0.1	67.5	62.2	56.7	80.9	58.9	15.2	12.4	147,194	72,497	74,697	50.7
30000	**Montana**	814,661	63.6	0.4	67.6	59.5	62.7	82.5	65.6	18.8	6.2	485,446	256,417	229,029	47.2
30001	Beaverhead County, Montana	7,825	63.1	0.0	66.8	59.3	60.6	83.3	75.7	21.7	6.5	4,615	2,547	2,068	44.8
30003	Big Horn County, Montana	9,095	64.0	0.1	68.8	59.6	49.3	75.8	77.3	29.5	19.9	4,663	2,348	2,315	49.6
30005	Blaine County, Montana	4,830	61.6	0.0	69.2	54.3	51.2	78.3	63.8	28.0	13.4	2,574	1,414	1,160	45.1
30007	Broadwater County, Montana	4,587	63.0	0.0	73.7	51.7	70.9	82.7	59.8	25.7	4.5	2,759	1,683	1,076	39.0
30009	Carbon County, Montana	8,601	62.0	0.2	66.3	57.8	60.3	85.7	64.6	21.9	3.9	5,126	2,761	2,365	46.1
30011	Carter County, Montana	1,020	60.8	0.0	69.6	52.0	45.5	85.7	65.0	30.8	2.3	606	349	257	42.4
30013	Cascade County, Montana	65,504	59.7	4.2	61.3	58.0	56.3	77.4	67.1	15.9	5.1	37,069	18,822	18,247	49.2
30015	Chouteau County, Montana	4,560	57.5	0.0	63.8	51.1	44.3	75.4	66.3	25.7	4.3	2,510	1,413	1,097	43.7
30017	Custer County, Montana	9,704	66.4	0.1	70.0	62.8	65.9	86.6	71.9	22.0	3.8	6,196	3,194	3,002	48.5
30019	Daniels County, Montana	1,495	62.9	0.0	70.7	55.1	66.1	86.5	83.1	20.2	2.6	916	525	391	42.7

Table C. County—Labor Force, Employment, and Educational Data, 2011–2015—*Continued*

Fips code	State/county	Total population age 16 and older	Percent in civilian labor force	Percent in armed forces	Men	Women	Age 16 to 24	Age 25 to 54	Age 55 to 64	Age 65 and older	Civilian unemployment rate	Total	Men	Women	Percent women
30021	Dawson County, Montana	7,566	63.3	0.0	70.7	55.1	71.8	80.0	63.1	21.1	2.0	4,694	2,760	1,934	41.2
30023	Deer Lodge County, Montana	7,922	50.4	0.0	50.3	50.5	61.3	67.3	49.0	14.7	3.9	3,834	2,070	1,764	46.0
30025	Fallon County, Montana	2,348	71.9	0.0	81.3	61.8	71.7	91.0	70.1	31.2	3.3	1,632	972	660	40.4
30027	Fergus County, Montana	9,354	61.5	0.0	66.5	56.5	67.8	85.1	67.2	18.8	3.1	5,579	3,005	2,574	46.1
30029	Flathead County, Montana	74,553	63.3	0.0	67.3	59.5	63.1	83.3	64.4	17.1	7.0	43,907	22,786	21,121	48.1
30031	Gallatin County, Montana	77,670	72.0	0.1	76.1	67.6	67.4	88.5	70.9	18.9	6.3	52,450	28,656	23,794	45.4
30033	Garfield County, Montana	856	65.0	0.0	76.0	55.1	75.0	82.8	73.0	31.9	0.2	555	306	249	44.9
30035	Glacier County, Montana	9,671	54.5	0.1	59.0	50.4	43.1	69.7	53.4	18.5	14.4	4,515	2,300	2,215	49.1
30037	Golden Valley County, Montana	634	58.4	0.0	64.4	52.6	18.6	80.1	72.1	22.0	3.5	357	196	161	45.1
30039	Granite County, Montana	2,706	50.4	0.0	51.9	48.8	45.2	78.6	57.1	16.7	7.2	1,265	652	613	48.5
30041	Hill County, Montana	12,504	61.3	0.0	65.1	57.4	54.3	78.2	64.7	20.4	4.0	7,364	3,935	3,429	46.6
30043	Jefferson County, Montana	9,424	60.2	0.1	64.8	55.2	54.8	82.6	62.1	15.7	6.6	5,295	2,981	2,314	43.7
30045	Judith Basin County, Montana	1,698	57.8	0.0	61.1	54.3	55.2	81.6	58.8	20.8	3.9	943	508	435	46.1
30047	Lake County, Montana	22,757	57.6	0.0	61.0	54.3	53.2	79.8	63.3	16.3	9.9	11,798	5,966	5,832	49.4
30049	Lewis and Clark County, Montana	52,496	66.3	0.3	69.4	63.4	66.3	86.4	65.9	17.1	4.9	33,126	16,692	16,434	49.6
30051	Liberty County, Montana	1,909	52.1	0.0	64.0	41.8	37.7	71.6	63.2	20.8	4.5	950	551	399	42.0
30053	Lincoln County, Montana	16,118	48.9	0.0	51.8	46.0	53.4	74.2	49.4	12.8	13.1	6,844	3,589	3,255	47.6
30055	McCone County, Montana	1,437	64.5	0.0	69.4	59.1	71.4	87.4	73.6	21.4	0.8	920	525	395	42.9
30057	Madison County, Montana	6,699	60.9	0.0	62.3	59.2	67.7	86.2	59.8	25.7	4.8	3,880	2,098	1,782	45.9
30059	Meagher County, Montana	1,598	58.0	0.0	62.2	53.9	46.4	80.8	66.2	20.4	3.9	891	470	421	47.3
30061	Mineral County, Montana	3,611	48.0	0.0	49.4	46.5	52.1	74.0	52.3	13.2	11.8	1,527	777	750	49.1
30063	Missoula County, Montana	92,198	69.8	0.1	72.5	67.2	69.8	86.0	70.1	20.4	8.2	59,103	30,205	28,898	48.9
30065	Musselshell County, Montana	3,815	54.0	0.0	61.6	46.5	45.3	77.5	54.0	21.2	4.6	1,967	1,145	822	41.8
30067	Park County, Montana	13,128	62.7	0.2	66.7	58.7	66.7	80.7	65.3	21.4	5.4	7,782	4,098	3,684	47.3
30069	Petroleum County, Montana	384	70.8	0.0	75.9	65.2	64.1	87.3	72.0	38.0	6.6	254	136	118	46.5
30071	Phillips County, Montana	3,367	56.0	0.0	62.0	50.1	55.7	79.7	59.8	13.9	6.3	1,767	938	829	46.9
30073	Pondera County, Montana	4,873	59.8	0.0	62.9	56.8	51.9	81.3	74.9	15.5	6.0	2,738	1,432	1,306	47.7
30075	Powder River County, Montana	1,473	68.6	0.0	79.9	57.5	62.6	81.3	82.1	43.3	4.5	965	558	407	42.2
30077	Powell County, Montana	6,075	44.2	0.0	41.3	49.4	45.3	51.7	54.4	17.0	2.2	2,629	1,542	1,087	41.3
30079	Prairie County, Montana	1,111	53.2	0.0	59.8	45.5	50.5	76.2	71.9	17.1	8.1	543	316	227	41.8
30081	Ravalli County, Montana	33,281	56.2	0.1	58.8	53.6	64.8	81.6	53.1	15.9	8.2	17,159	8,582	8,577	50.0
30083	Richland County, Montana	8,709	69.5	0.0	80.8	57.5	71.8	83.2	72.7	24.4	2.5	5,904	3,543	2,361	40.0
30085	Roosevelt County, Montana	7,852	48.8	0.0	51.9	45.8	27.4	63.4	62.1	16.1	6.8	3,575	1,870	1,705	47.7
30087	Rosebud County, Montana	6,970	64.2	0.0	70.8	57.8	53.2	82.5	66.0	22.6	10.6	4,002	2,195	1,807	45.2
30089	Sanders County, Montana	9,452	47.7	0.0	50.7	44.5	51.5	70.2	53.6	14.9	9.3	4,091	2,255	1,836	44.9
30091	Sheridan County, Montana	2,952	66.3	0.0	72.8	59.7	75.9	83.8	74.5	27.8	2.7	1,904	1,056	848	44.5
30093	Silver Bow County, Montana	28,222	62.9	0.1	67.2	58.4	64.6	84.3	61.8	16.1	7.0	16,497	8,847	7,650	46.4
30095	Stillwater County, Montana	7,535	61.8	0.2	69.2	54.2	59.7	81.9	66.7	21.2	3.6	4,487	2,557	1,930	43.0
30097	Sweet Grass County, Montana	2,872	56.7	0.0	65.7	48.2	38.0	84.2	72.1	11.6	0.9	1,613	910	703	43.6
30099	Teton County, Montana	4,831	59.3	0.4	64.4	54.2	47.4	81.9	76.1	19.3	5.1	2,720	1,491	1,229	45.2
30101	Toole County, Montana	4,310	55.2	0.0	54.1	56.9	52.3	63.5	71.1	18.3	3.1	2,308	1,338	970	42.0
30103	Treasure County, Montana	691	55.3	0.0	60.0	50.2	42.3	74.6	64.3	24.1	0.8	379	213	166	43.8
30105	Valley County, Montana	6,049	63.7	0.0	70.9	56.6	58.4	86.7	70.8	24.2	2.6	3,753	2,084	1,669	44.5
30107	Wheatland County, Montana	1,686	56.3	0.0	60.4	51.8	44.7	82.5	69.6	19.9	3.4	917	512	405	44.2
30109	Wibaux County, Montana	835	56.4	0.0	63.0	49.6	55.2	86.2	54.7	23.7	3.0	457	267	190	41.6
30111	Yellowstone County, Montana	121,238	67.6	0.2	73.7	61.7	66.7	84.9	69.9	20.7	4.1	78,572	41,476	37,096	47.2
31000	**Nebraska**	1,454,157	69.9	0.3	74.6	65.2	68.8	86.4	74.1	21.9	4.7	968,134	509,118	459,016	47.4
31001	Adams County, Nebraska	24,866	67.1	0.0	73.5	60.8	64.1	87.3	74.4	20.3	5.5	15,783	8,537	7,246	45.9
31003	Antelope County, Nebraska	5,189	64.4	0.3	71.8	57.0	62.5	86.5	73.7	25.2	1.6	3,288	1,819	1,469	44.7
31005	Arthur County, Nebraska	321	62.6	0.0	67.9	57.1	59.3	81.4	75.4	21.4	4.0	193	107	86	44.6
31007	Banner County, Nebraska	692	69.5	0.0	75.7	63.4	61.5	79.7	88.2	27.7	5.4	455	248	207	45.5
31009	Blaine County, Nebraska	430	67.2	0.0	77.3	55.3	47.5	86.0	70.5	32.6	0.7	287	178	109	38.0
31011	Boone County, Nebraska	4,282	65.6	0.0	74.4	57.1	70.3	88.6	75.3	21.2	1.2	2,777	1,556	1,221	44.0
31013	Box Butte County, Nebraska	8,651	67.4	0.0	75.6	59.9	68.9	88.4	69.0	19.4	3.9	5,606	3,031	2,575	45.9
31015	Boyd County, Nebraska	1,626	60.0	0.0	65.5	54.3	52.3	88.0	73.5	21.6	1.1	964	537	427	44.3
31017	Brown County, Nebraska	2,505	63.7	0.0	73.2	55.2	60.9	83.1	74.2	30.2	0.7	1,585	858	727	45.9
31019	Buffalo County, Nebraska	37,708	74.9	0.1	78.0	71.9	74.1	91.0	78.6	25.7	3.5	27,263	14,009	13,254	48.6
31021	Burt County, Nebraska	5,310	59.3	0.0	63.6	55.3	51.2	83.5	71.4	21.4	3.3	3,046	1,564	1,482	48.7
31023	Butler County, Nebraska	6,568	68.3	0.0	74.7	62.0	65.9	88.3	76.6	28.9	4.2	4,299	2,362	1,937	45.1
31025	Cass County, Nebraska	19,986	68.2	0.7	71.8	64.6	66.1	86.5	74.4	19.0	3.8	13,103	6,804	6,299	48.1
31027	Cedar County, Nebraska	6,801	69.0	0.0	73.9	64.2	71.2	90.5	83.8	24.6	2.2	4,588	2,466	2,122	46.3
31029	Chase County, Nebraska	3,074	67.9	0.0	79.1	57.4	91.0	85.8	80.0	23.0	0.7	2,073	1,180	893	43.1
31031	Cherry County, Nebraska	4,679	71.8	0.1	77.0	67.3	72.4	91.2	78.4	33.3	2.6	3,271	1,657	1,614	49.3
31033	Cheyenne County, Nebraska	7,896	73.1	0.0	79.0	67.7	70.5	92.4	78.3	22.2	1.6	5,681	2,952	2,729	48.0
31035	Clay County, Nebraska	5,022	65.0	0.1	74.3	55.6	63.7	84.2	74.2	22.3	2.8	3,171	1,809	1,362	43.0
31037	Colfax County, Nebraska	7,707	72.4	0.0	79.6	64.6	74.7	87.9	79.5	21.2	6.4	5,224	3,047	2,177	41.7
31039	Cuming County, Nebraska	7,108	66.4	0.0	75.3	57.6	63.1	86.5	86.0	24.3	3.3	4,562	2,569	1,993	43.7
31041	Custer County, Nebraska	8,631	67.5	0.0	74.0	61.2	77.0	87.4	72.6	26.1	2.3	5,694	3,094	2,600	45.7
31043	Dakota County, Nebraska	15,328	70.6	0.0	78.2	63.7	71.6	83.3	80.5	20.7	7.4	10,025	5,373	4,652	46.4
31045	Dawes County, Nebraska	7,711	61.4	0.1	66.7	56.5	53.1	82.2	77.5	24.7	2.6	4,613	2,454	2,159	46.8
31047	Dawson County, Nebraska	18,209	71.0	0.0	76.9	65.1	69.7	88.3	77.0	23.8	4.8	12,312	6,804	5,508	44.7
31049	Deuel County, Nebraska	1,567	68.2	0.0	75.2	61.3	66.1	91.7	86.9	25.4	4.3	1,023	560	463	45.3
31051	Dixon County, Nebraska	4,545	67.2	0.1	71.4	63.1	62.5	88.4	72.9	27.0	4.5	2,916	1,557	1,359	46.6
31053	Dodge County, Nebraska	28,945	67.2	0.1	73.1	61.6	76.0	86.1	70.1	22.5	5.1	18,447	9,625	8,822	47.8

Table C. County—Labor Force, Employment, and Educational Data, 2011–2015—*Continued*

Fips code	State/county	Total population age 16 and older	Percent in civilian labor force	Percent in armed forces	Civilian labor force participation by gender — Men	Civilian labor force participation by gender — Women	Age 16 to 24	Age 25 to 54	Age 55 to 64	Age 65 and older	Civilian unemployment rate	Civilian employed population age 16 and older — Total	Men	Women	Percent women
31055	Douglas County, Nebraska	412,872	71.2	0.2	76.0	66.7	68.4	85.5	71.2	20.9	5.7	277,349	143,377	133,972	48.3
31057	Dundy County, Nebraska	1,615	60.1	0.0	68.0	51.6	55.9	82.4	72.0	20.5	4.0	932	551	381	40.9
31059	Fillmore County, Nebraska	4,690	65.5	0.0	71.4	59.9	69.4	86.6	85.0	19.7	3.4	2,969	1,590	1,379	46.4
31061	Franklin County, Nebraska	2,587	63.1	0.0	66.9	59.3	73.6	86.2	74.9	21.8	3.5	1,575	842	733	46.5
31063	Frontier County, Nebraska	2,105	63.0	0.0	68.2	57.8	67.4	86.3	68.8	21.5	2.4	1,294	706	588	45.4
31065	Furnas County, Nebraska	3,910	61.5	0.0	69.9	53.5	57.6	86.2	69.5	23.5	3.4	2,323	1,305	1,018	43.8
31067	Gage County, Nebraska	17,535	66.0	0.0	70.6	61.6	69.8	87.5	74.1	20.2	4.3	11,077	5,793	5,284	47.7
31069	Garden County, Nebraska	1,548	62.6	0.0	69.5	56.4	55.3	86.0	72.4	25.8	3.1	939	495	444	47.3
31071	Garfield County, Nebraska	1,581	65.0	0.0	66.2	63.8	74.3	89.9	66.4	35.5	3.5	992	495	497	50.1
31073	Gosper County, Nebraska	1,592	72.2	0.0	77.4	67.4	83.6	91.7	84.1	23.0	5.1	1,091	553	538	49.3
31075	Grant County, Nebraska	636	68.1	0.0	72.7	63.0	64.0	89.8	85.6	27.8	3.5	418	239	179	42.8
31077	Greeley County, Nebraska	1,940	59.2	0.0	67.3	51.3	51.6	82.2	70.1	24.2	1.9	1,127	642	485	43.0
31079	Hall County, Nebraska	46,175	71.8	0.0	77.1	66.7	77.4	87.7	72.0	22.8	6.0	31,168	16,578	14,590	46.8
31081	Hamilton County, Nebraska	7,162	67.7	0.0	71.9	63.6	63.0	88.9	77.9	18.7	2.5	4,723	2,495	2,228	47.2
31083	Harlan County, Nebraska	2,828	60.7	0.0	64.0	57.2	51.3	90.2	71.5	18.2	1.7	1,687	926	761	45.1
31085	Hayes County, Nebraska	915	61.1	0.0	65.9	55.1	46.8	78.5	77.4	30.0	1.8	549	330	219	39.9
31087	Hitchcock County, Nebraska	2,331	60.1	0.0	67.5	52.7	51.2	88.0	70.4	17.0	3.0	1,358	756	602	44.3
31089	Holt County, Nebraska	8,197	68.1	0.1	74.4	62.1	73.8	87.7	80.3	24.3	0.9	5,529	2,948	2,581	46.7
31091	Hooker County, Nebraska	579	58.9	0.0	65.9	52.1	60.6	82.8	76.6	32.4	2.9	331	185	146	44.1
31093	Howard County, Nebraska	5,034	68.0	0.0	70.7	65.3	68.3	89.2	75.9	24.2	4.0	3,287	1,721	1,566	47.6
31095	Jefferson County, Nebraska	6,020	64.6	0.0	72.2	57.5	70.5	85.2	75.3	23.6	4.0	3,734	1,998	1,736	46.5
31097	Johnson County, Nebraska	4,316	49.3	0.0	42.0	60.8	44.0	56.3	65.6	23.1	3.6	2,053	1,062	991	48.3
31099	Kearney County, Nebraska	5,138	70.4	0.0	77.6	63.6	82.7	89.1	75.4	23.5	3.8	3,478	1,887	1,591	45.7
31101	Keith County, Nebraska	6,663	63.6	0.0	69.2	58.0	71.8	89.4	69.4	18.3	2.8	4,116	2,235	1,881	45.7
31103	Keya Paha County, Nebraska	599	74.3	0.0	82.6	64.7	79.3	89.5	93.0	40.8	1.1	440	265	175	39.8
31105	Kimball County, Nebraska	2,916	59.9	0.1	64.7	55.1	63.9	84.0	77.5	18.2	5.1	1,658	899	759	45.8
31107	Knox County, Nebraska	6,771	65.3	0.1	72.0	59.1	68.1	89.0	81.3	22.7	3.3	4,277	2,307	1,970	46.1
31109	Lancaster County, Nebraska	236,077	71.8	0.2	75.2	68.3	70.4	86.6	75.2	21.9	5.1	160,866	83,646	77,220	48.0
31111	Lincoln County, Nebraska	28,058	64.6	0.0	71.7	57.8	69.9	85.5	63.1	16.4	4.2	17,360	9,549	7,811	45.0
31113	Logan County, Nebraska	650	69.7	0.2	77.5	62.3	84.6	85.0	68.1	41.6	0.9	449	244	205	45.7
31115	Loup County, Nebraska	454	65.9	0.0	69.2	62.6	37.1	83.3	78.4	40.3	0.7	297	155	142	47.8
31117	McPherson County, Nebraska	352	63.6	0.0	65.7	61.5	60.0	76.3	92.1	18.4	0.9	222	117	105	47.3
31119	Madison County, Nebraska	27,382	70.6	0.1	77.1	64.3	69.3	89.1	77.7	21.3	3.1	18,727	10,103	8,624	46.1
31121	Merrick County, Nebraska	6,224	70.8	0.0	73.1	68.6	75.6	88.9	79.7	29.2	5.2	4,177	2,093	2,084	49.9
31123	Morrill County, Nebraska	3,786	67.5	0.0	73.8	61.0	67.0	86.4	76.5	23.8	4.0	2,451	1,354	1,097	44.8
31125	Nance County, Nebraska	2,928	62.9	0.0	66.8	59.3	67.2	85.3	69.3	16.8	3.2	1,784	918	866	48.5
31127	Nemaha County, Nebraska	5,892	64.2	0.2	69.7	59.0	63.3	87.5	66.7	20.2	8.0	3,481	1,808	1,673	48.1
31129	Nuckolls County, Nebraska	3,585	63.8	0.0	68.8	58.8	70.7	87.1	77.4	24.9	2.9	2,219	1,198	1,021	46.0
31131	Otoe County, Nebraska	12,587	68.5	0.1	74.2	63.0	71.4	91.2	74.0	21.2	4.6	8,225	4,277	3,948	48.0
31133	Pawnee County, Nebraska	2,210	60.0	0.1	67.1	52.7	67.9	83.6	76.4	19.7	4.6	1,265	735	530	41.9
31135	Perkins County, Nebraska	2,320	65.7	0.0	74.2	57.6	65.4	88.6	74.9	22.4	1.7	1,499	819	680	45.4
31137	Phelps County, Nebraska	7,212	65.5	0.0	71.7	59.4	67.8	88.6	73.2	16.5	1.7	4,641	2,497	2,144	46.2
31139	Pierce County, Nebraska	5,621	68.4	0.0	70.9	65.9	65.0	90.3	78.5	19.3	4.7	3,663	1,872	1,791	48.9
31141	Platte County, Nebraska	25,041	74.1	0.0	80.2	68.0	76.7	90.0	81.2	27.9	4.5	17,701	9,654	8,047	45.5
31143	Polk County, Nebraska	4,200	69.0	0.1	76.2	61.8	61.8	90.4	77.7	30.2	1.9	2,843	1,574	1,269	44.6
31145	Red Willow County, Nebraska	8,769	68.0	0.0	70.2	65.7	78.4	89.1	74.8	16.7	4.1	5,714	2,966	2,748	48.1
31147	Richardson County, Nebraska	6,651	62.3	0.0	68.9	56.0	67.8	84.6	78.2	16.8	3.4	4,000	2,126	1,874	46.9
31149	Rock County, Nebraska	1,193	65.2	0.3	73.0	57.9	60.7	90.3	78.7	24.2	1.7	765	413	352	46.0
31151	Saline County, Nebraska	11,265	65.5	0.0	69.7	61.1	60.2	84.5	74.5	19.2	3.4	7,130	3,890	3,240	45.4
31153	Sarpy County, Nebraska	126,099	72.7	2.6	76.5	69.1	68.6	85.5	75.0	19.1	4.4	87,645	45,709	41,936	47.8
31155	Saunders County, Nebraska	16,247	67.7	0.2	73.7	61.8	65.1	86.4	73.1	23.3	3.5	10,624	5,740	4,884	46.0
31157	Scotts Bluff County, Nebraska	28,410	66.9	0.0	72.7	61.6	69.0	84.6	73.9	23.7	5.5	17,970	9,298	8,672	48.3
31159	Seward County, Nebraska	13,483	65.7	0.1	70.7	60.5	55.2	88.0	75.6	20.9	3.5	8,543	4,658	3,885	45.5
31161	Sheridan County, Nebraska	4,188	62.1	0.0	64.1	60.2	59.0	80.7	83.0	25.0	1.4	2,564	1,287	1,277	49.8
31163	Sherman County, Nebraska	2,523	64.2	0.1	72.2	56.6	75.0	84.5	74.8	29.6	3.1	1,569	874	695	44.3
31165	Sioux County, Nebraska	1,037	64.7	0.0	69.3	60.2	71.7	87.7	68.0	30.9	1.3	662	351	311	47.0
31167	Stanton County, Nebraska	4,615	70.1	0.0	73.9	66.4	66.5	87.1	75.8	25.0	2.6	3,151	1,650	1,501	47.6
31169	Thayer County, Nebraska	4,250	60.8	0.0	65.0	56.9	67.2	85.7	79.6	16.6	1.7	2,542	1,319	1,223	48.1
31171	Thomas County, Nebraska	555	69.4	0.0	76.6	62.1	53.3	90.6	77.4	30.3	0.0	385	213	172	44.7
31173	Thurston County, Nebraska	4,710	61.6	0.1	65.3	58.0	53.5	77.5	69.5	21.2	14.4	2,483	1,272	1,211	48.8
31175	Valley County, Nebraska	3,384	68.0	0.0	73.4	62.7	66.0	91.1	83.4	28.8	1.4	2,268	1,207	1,061	46.8
31177	Washington County, Nebraska	15,947	69.0	0.0	75.0	63.3	59.4	88.2	74.4	24.9	1.4	10,850	5,786	5,064	46.7
31179	Wayne County, Nebraska	7,818	68.8	0.0	70.3	67.3	59.3	90.4	87.2	25.2	3.0	5,219	2,754	2,465	47.2
31181	Webster County, Nebraska	2,980	59.5	0.0	65.3	54.0	62.5	89.1	69.3	11.2	4.7	1,689	911	778	46.1
31183	Wheeler County, Nebraska	731	69.6	0.0	75.6	63.7	59.6	90.7	81.9	27.8	2.9	494	266	228	46.2
31185	York County, Nebraska	11,111	66.8	0.0	73.5	60.5	67.3	85.0	80.6	20.8	2.0	7,274	3,878	3,396	46.7
32000	**Nevada**	2,210,559	64.0	0.4	68.8	59.3	59.3	81.0	62.9	17.3	10.5	1,267,312	677,889	589,423	46.5
32001	Churchill County, Nevada	19,157	55.0	3.9	57.1	52.8	58.7	72.6	56.3	13.1	11.9	9,274	5,001	4,273	46.1
32003	Clark County, Nevada	1,599,352	64.8	0.5	69.5	60.0	58.9	81.1	62.8	17.5	10.8	923,588	491,704	431,884	46.8
32005	Douglas County, Nevada	39,572	56.3	0.3	58.7	53.8	64.9	81.8	58.7	14.2	8.5	20,371	10,653	9,718	47.7
32007	Elko County, Nevada	38,618	70.9	0.0	78.9	62.2	64.7	81.6	72.2	28.8	5.5	25,865	15,021	10,844	41.9
32009	Esmeralda County, Nevada	949	52.3	0.0	66.8	39.2	69.8	76.8	69.5	5.0	11.9	437	256	181	41.4
32011	Eureka County, Nevada	1,332	67.2	0.0	77.7	57.1	41.8	81.4	74.7	25.1	4.7	853	482	371	43.5
32013	Humboldt County, Nevada	12,865	69.9	0.1	76.2	62.8	65.5	82.7	70.4	23.6	7.8	8,295	4,854	3,441	41.5

Table C. County—Labor Force, Employment, and Educational Data, 2011–2015—*Continued*

Fips code	State/county	Total population age 16 and older	Percent in civilian labor force	Percent in armed forces	Civilian labor force participation by gender		Civilian labor force participation by age				Civilian unemployment rate	Civilian employed population age 16 and older			
					Men	Women	Age 16 to 24	Age 25 to 54	Age 55 to 64	Age 65 and older		Total	Men	Women	Percent women
32015	Lander County, Nevada	4,424	67.9	0.0	80.1	54.1	69.6	83.3	77.0	16.9	12.0	2,644	1,644	1,000	37.8
32017	Lincoln County, Nevada	4,178	46.5	0.0	45.4	47.9	48.3	66.2	47.2	6.9	11.8	1,714	946	768	44.8
32019	Lyon County, Nevada	41,080	56.2	0.2	62.0	50.4	53.5	77.4	59.6	14.2	13.6	19,958	11,059	8,899	44.6
32021	Mineral County, Nevada	3,861	56.9	0.0	58.6	54.9	67.6	73.8	64.4	20.3	15.4	1,856	965	891	48.0
32023	Nye County, Nevada	35,600	45.9	0.0	50.7	41.1	51.0	71.6	50.2	11.3	13.4	14,143	7,850	6,293	44.5
32027	Pershing County, Nevada	5,701	40.7	0.0	34.3	54.7	28.5	48.7	51.0	14.6	9.5	2,101	1,218	883	42.0
32029	Storey County, Nevada	3,527	56.2	0.3	59.6	53.0	34.7	82.6	61.9	20.8	10.3	1,777	861	916	51.5
32031	Washoe County, Nevada	347,703	65.6	0.1	70.7	60.4	61.1	83.5	65.1	18.0	9.1	207,304	110,936	96,368	46.5
32033	White Pine County, Nevada	8,054	49.0	0.0	44.0	56.2	50.9	58.8	52.5	17.5	10.6	3,529	1,928	1,601	45.4
32510	Carson City, Nevada	44,586	59.7	0.0	63.0	56.1	64.5	79.0	62.5	14.6	11.3	23,603	12,511	11,092	47.0
33000	**New Hampshire**	1,087,512	68.2	0.1	72.8	63.8	65.3	85.4	73.4	20.4	5.8	698,810	363,241	335,569	48.0
33001	Belknap County, New Hampshire	49,974	64.2	0.0	68.6	60.0	60.8	85.0	69.4	20.3	5.3	30,396	15,620	14,776	48.6
33003	Carroll County, New Hampshire	40,587	60.1	0.0	62.7	57.6	72.8	83.1	64.2	18.0	5.8	22,992	11,651	11,341	49.3
33005	Cheshire County, New Hampshire	63,840	66.2	0.1	69.7	63.0	59.2	86.1	75.5	20.3	6.1	39,695	20,070	19,625	49.4
33007	Coos County, New Hampshire	27,039	58.2	0.0	59.1	57.2	63.8	77.3	66.2	15.9	6.9	14,644	7,454	7,190	49.1
33009	Grafton County, New Hampshire	75,658	62.9	0.0	65.9	60.0	55.9	81.6	71.7	22.4	5.0	45,198	23,216	21,982	48.6
33011	Hillsborough County, New Hampshire	325,544	70.3	0.0	76.4	64.3	67.4	85.5	74.4	20.3	5.9	215,215	114,898	100,317	46.6
33013	Merrimack County, New Hampshire	121,272	66.4	0.1	70.1	62.9	61.6	83.6	72.3	20.1	5.2	76,330	38,972	37,358	48.9
33015	Rockingham County, New Hampshire	244,654	72.1	0.3	77.1	67.2	68.3	88.8	76.7	22.3	5.6	166,354	86,891	79,463	47.8
33017	Strafford County, New Hampshire	103,288	68.7	0.3	72.9	64.7	69.9	84.1	73.3	17.7	6.5	66,369	33,691	32,678	49.2
33019	Sullivan County, New Hampshire	35,656	64.4	0.0	66.9	61.9	60.0	83.7	70.9	19.7	5.8	21,617	10,778	10,839	50.1
34000	**New Jersey**	7,120,154	65.9	0.1	71.7	60.6	54.1	83.8	70.7	20.0	8.8	4,281,760	2,245,487	2,036,273	47.6
34001	Atlantic County, New Jersey	221,065	66.2	0.2	69.7	63.0	63.3	84.4	69.5	19.4	12.5	128,151	63,802	64,349	50.2
34003	Bergen County, New Jersey	748,494	65.7	0.0	73.1	58.9	47.1	83.6	75.1	23.1	6.5	459,612	244,312	215,300	46.8
34005	Burlington County, New Jersey	363,543	66.7	1.1	70.0	63.5	59.4	83.4	73.3	21.0	8.5	221,766	113,330	108,436	48.9
34007	Camden County, New Jersey	405,272	66.4	0.1	71.4	61.9	59.7	83.9	67.6	19.2	10.2	241,708	122,723	118,985	49.2
34009	Cape May County, New Jersey	80,918	58.9	0.9	64.1	54.0	57.9	83.0	65.8	19.1	10.0	42,881	22,472	20,409	47.6
34011	Cumberland County, New Jersey	123,921	57.4	0.1	56.9	58.0	60.1	69.9	58.2	15.1	11.1	63,220	32,281	30,939	48.9
34013	Essex County, New Jersey	621,013	66.3	0.0	70.6	62.4	51.2	83.1	68.7	20.2	13.0	358,229	181,158	177,071	49.4
34015	Gloucester County, New Jersey	231,169	67.5	0.0	72.9	62.5	59.0	85.7	69.2	19.4	9.2	141,635	72,191	69,444	49.0
34017	Hudson County, New Jersey	541,254	69.2	0.0	75.7	62.8	52.4	84.8	66.4	16.7	9.3	339,606	185,133	154,473	45.5
34019	Hunterdon County, New Jersey	102,925	68.1	0.1	72.2	64.1	50.7	85.6	79.7	23.6	5.9	65,918	34,493	31,425	47.7
34021	Mercer County, New Jersey	298,596	65.7	0.0	70.0	61.6	54.6	83.2	68.4	21.1	9.4	177,609	91,059	86,550	48.7
34023	Middlesex County, New Jersey	667,176	65.3	0.0	71.6	59.2	46.3	83.6	70.8	18.6	7.5	402,766	215,552	187,214	46.5
34025	Monmouth County, New Jersey	505,316	66.0	0.1	73.3	59.2	53.2	84.3	72.2	21.4	7.9	307,183	163,855	143,328	46.7
34027	Morris County, New Jersey	400,047	69.0	0.0	75.6	62.8	55.2	86.3	78.1	23.8	6.3	258,862	138,076	120,786	46.7
34029	Ocean County, New Jersey	460,437	58.7	0.1	64.3	53.7	61.4	83.1	65.0	14.9	8.8	246,680	126,567	120,113	48.7
34031	Passaic County, New Jersey	397,711	63.2	0.0	69.7	57.2	49.6	79.6	69.1	19.5	8.6	229,762	122,384	107,378	46.7
34033	Salem County, New Jersey	52,387	62.4	0.0	66.8	58.4	57.5	82.8	63.1	17.8	10.6	29,226	15,002	14,224	48.7
34035	Somerset County, New Jersey	262,004	69.1	0.0	76.8	61.9	53.4	86.4	75.2	21.7	6.0	170,172	91,073	79,099	46.5
34037	Sussex County, New Jersey	118,179	69.8	0.1	74.7	64.9	63.0	86.7	72.4	23.9	8.2	75,669	39,651	36,018	47.6
34039	Union County, New Jersey	431,756	68.7	0.0	75.3	62.7	59.4	85.3	71.6	20.2	9.8	267,803	142,104	125,699	46.9
34041	Warren County, New Jersey	86,971	67.4	0.1	73.5	61.7	63.1	86.0	69.4	19.9	9.0	53,302	28,269	25,033	47.0
35000	**New Mexico**	1,633,310	59.1	0.5	63.4	54.9	56.5	76.3	59.3	16.6	9.2	876,035	459,827	416,208	47.5
35001	Bernalillo County, New Mexico	535,086	62.8	0.4	67.6	58.2	58.7	79.4	62.0	17.3	8.4	307,756	160,645	147,111	47.8
35003	Catron County, New Mexico	3,122	35.2	0.0	36.4	33.9	34.0	65.4	36.3	13.1	4.6	1,049	578	471	44.9
35005	Chaves County, New Mexico	49,999	57.3	0.1	61.7	52.9	53.2	74.2	58.0	18.3	7.6	26,448	14,129	12,319	46.6
35006	Cibola County, New Mexico	21,423	53.0	0.0	54.9	51.1	55.4	66.0	48.3	19.4	15.3	9,625	4,961	4,664	48.5
35007	Colfax County, New Mexico	10,878	50.6	0.0	48.7	52.5	62.0	69.7	52.5	14.8	9.5	4,981	2,323	2,658	53.4
35009	Curry County, New Mexico	38,164	59.4	5.3	64.6	53.9	61.9	71.7	58.6	14.1	9.1	20,599	11,843	8,756	42.5
35011	De Baca County, New Mexico	1,676	39.0	0.0	42.6	36.2	41.6	73.7	17.6	12.9	5.2	619	291	328	53.0
35013	Doña Ana County, New Mexico	164,798	61.0	0.6	65.3	56.9	61.8	78.4	60.5	15.6	11.5	88,919	45,845	43,074	48.4
35015	Eddy County, New Mexico	42,618	63.8	0.2	73.4	54.0	59.7	81.1	66.2	17.6	5.8	25,620	14,940	10,680	41.7
35017	Grant County, New Mexico	23,464	50.0	0.0	52.1	48.0	59.4	73.6	53.8	12.1	9.7	10,585	5,301	5,284	49.9
35019	Guadalupe County, New Mexico	3,714	35.5	0.0	27.2	47.9	42.0	42.6	46.1	12.4	1.2	1,301	596	705	54.2
35021	Harding County, New Mexico	482	45.2	0.2	40.1	50.9	29.1	78.7	58.1	12.0	6.0	205	92	113	55.1
35023	Hidalgo County, New Mexico	3,737	56.9	1.6	56.1	57.7	65.4	73.4	66.0	13.5	12.2	1,867	880	987	52.9
35025	Lea County, New Mexico	49,654	62.8	0.0	73.8	51.0	61.6	74.9	64.5	18.5	5.9	29,340	17,997	11,343	38.7
35027	Lincoln County, New Mexico	16,622	52.1	0.0	57.6	47.0	58.9	79.2	50.8	16.4	7.3	8,030	4,314	3,716	46.3
35028	Los Alamos County, New Mexico	14,363	64.4	0.2	70.4	58.1	45.2	84.9	73.6	18.1	3.5	8,916	4,914	4,002	44.9
35029	Luna County, New Mexico	18,899	51.5	0.0	53.6	49.4	57.9	72.0	54.1	13.7	13.8	8,383	4,450	3,933	46.9
35031	McKinley County, New Mexico	53,919	50.2	0.0	52.6	48.1	35.4	64.9	52.5	15.5	15.5	22,865	10,799	12,066	52.8
35033	Mora County, New Mexico	3,656	33.7	0.0	33.3	34.2	2.3	59.9	42.4	6.4	5.4	1,166	528	638	54.7
35035	Otero County, New Mexico	51,082	49.6	5.0	51.3	47.7	49.3	65.2	52.5	10.9	12.7	22,092	11,696	10,396	47.1

Table C. County—Labor Force, Employment, and Educational Data, 2011–2015—*Continued*

Fips code	State/county	Total population age 16 and older	Percent in civilian labor force	Percent in armed forces	Civilian labor force participation by gender		Civilian labor force participation by age				Civilian unemploy-ment rate	Civilian employed population age 16 and older			
					Men	Women	Age 16 to 24	Age 25 to 54	Age 55 to 64	Age 65 and older		Total	Men	Women	Percent women
35037	Quay County, New Mexico	7,058	43.8	0.0	50.8	37.2	54.2	65.3	39.2	12.8	5.0	2,937	1,656	1,281	43.6
35039	Rio Arriba County, New Mexico	31,467	54.8	0.0	54.3	55.3	58.1	73.6	49.7	13.3	11.4	15,272	7,271	8,001	52.4
35041	Roosevelt County, New Mexico	15,304	58.8	1.6	62.7	55.0	63.6	74.4	53.0	12.2	9.7	8,131	4,346	3,785	46.6
35043	Sandoval County, New Mexico	106,060	60.7	0.2	64.8	56.7	54.2	78.8	61.4	15.4	9.2	58,433	29,996	28,437	48.7
35045	San Juan County, New Mexico	94,394	60.2	0.2	66.3	54.3	52.8	75.3	62.0	19.2	9.2	51,561	27,618	23,943	46.4
35047	San Miguel County, New Mexico	23,535	44.3	0.0	45.6	43.0	42.3	61.4	42.5	12.0	6.4	9,751	4,952	4,799	49.2
35049	Santa Fe County, New Mexico	121,398	63.0	0.1	67.1	59.1	60.4	81.7	67.0	22.8	7.9	70,423	36,101	34,322	48.7
35051	Sierra County, New Mexico	9,971	42.7	0.0	45.2	40.4	63.4	73.1	52.0	9.6	6.8	3,971	2,066	1,905	48.0
35053	Socorro County, New Mexico	13,624	45.2	0.0	45.5	44.9	35.6	64.3	38.8	16.9	7.3	5,706	2,901	2,805	49.2
35055	Taos County, New Mexico	27,213	59.1	0.1	63.1	55.5	64.8	78.4	62.5	21.4	10.7	14,356	7,187	7,169	49.9
35057	Torrance County, New Mexico	12,871	46.8	0.0	49.0	44.4	41.3	64.8	42.5	16.5	11.2	5,348	2,939	2,409	45.0
35059	Union County, New Mexico	3,635	47.5	0.0	45.3	50.5	53.0	60.0	62.8	8.0	2.1	1,692	900	792	46.8
35061	Valencia County, New Mexico	59,424	54.0	0.2	58.1	49.8	53.9	70.9	50.4	13.5	12.4	28,088	14,772	13,316	47.4
36000	**New York**	15,921,937	63.3	0.1	68.4	58.7	52.0	81.8	65.9	17.6	8.2	9,254,578	4,764,729	4,489,849	48.5
36001	Albany County, New York	255,718	64.8	0.1	68.4	61.5	57.6	86.0	66.1	17.2	6.4	155,200	78,272	76,928	49.6
36003	Allegany County, New York	39,423	57.0	0.0	60.4	53.5	51.2	79.3	61.5	14.2	9.2	20,410	10,634	9,776	47.9
36005	Bronx County, New York	1,102,377	59.5	0.0	64.2	55.4	47.1	76.8	57.0	13.0	14.0	563,903	279,012	284,891	50.5
36007	Broome County, New York	164,018	58.7	0.0	63.1	54.5	52.4	80.2	65.5	15.0	7.8	88,758	45,716	43,042	48.5
36009	Cattaraugus County, New York	63,058	59.2	0.0	63.2	55.4	54.7	80.3	61.5	14.4	8.2	34,265	17,848	16,417	47.9
36011	Cayuga County, New York	65,065	61.4	0.0	62.6	60.2	64.3	78.7	61.9	17.8	7.3	37,023	19,184	17,839	48.2
36013	Chautauqua County, New York	108,265	58.1	0.0	61.8	54.5	54.6	78.4	64.5	13.9	7.8	58,012	30,128	27,884	48.1
36015	Chemung County, New York	71,067	56.9	0.0	57.8	56.0	54.4	74.4	60.5	14.2	5.4	38,219	19,010	19,209	50.3
36017	Chenango County, New York	40,359	57.7	0.1	61.0	54.5	57.9	77.9	60.0	14.6	7.1	21,652	11,249	10,403	48.0
36019	Clinton County, New York	68,491	55.7	0.0	55.9	55.5	51.7	73.7	54.2	13.0	6.9	35,522	18,336	17,186	48.4
36021	Columbia County, New York	51,969	61.8	0.0	65.3	58.3	59.6	81.4	70.6	19.8	6.7	29,962	15,708	14,254	47.6
36023	Cortland County, New York	40,396	63.5	0.0	68.9	58.4	54.5	86.7	63.6	20.3	6.1	24,080	12,451	11,629	48.3
36025	Delaware County, New York	39,500	55.5	0.0	59.7	51.3	54.4	80.2	59.2	14.3	9.5	19,850	10,524	9,326	47.0
36027	Dutchess County, New York	244,232	64.5	0.1	68.6	60.5	58.1	82.6	67.6	19.8	8.7	143,829	75,122	68,707	47.8
36029	Erie County, New York	753,286	63.0	0.1	67.1	59.2	61.5	82.4	64.9	16.1	7.0	441,369	223,252	218,117	49.4
36031	Essex County, New York	33,111	58.3	0.0	57.3	59.3	57.3	77.8	61.1	19.3	7.9	17,769	8,916	8,853	49.8
36033	Franklin County, New York	41,947	52.5	0.0	50.8	54.7	48.2	65.6	56.8	14.4	8.8	20,094	10,613	9,481	47.2
36035	Fulton County, New York	44,465	59.8	0.0	63.9	55.8	57.0	79.7	61.5	15.0	9.3	24,116	12,495	11,621	48.2
36037	Genesee County, New York	48,615	65.4	0.0	69.7	61.2	67.1	84.8	69.4	16.5	6.7	29,675	15,536	14,139	47.6
36039	Greene County, New York	40,864	53.1	0.0	53.2	53.0	48.7	72.6	57.4	14.0	9.1	19,731	10,196	9,535	48.3
36041	Hamilton County, New York	4,119	50.7	0.0	57.8	43.6	66.8	72.2	50.5	19.9	9.7	1,887	1,071	816	43.2
36043	Herkimer County, New York	51,955	61.3	0.1	66.2	56.6	59.7	84.1	64.0	14.5	8.7	29,074	15,224	13,850	47.6
36045	Jefferson County, New York	92,091	54.3	11.2	52.3	56.5	44.0	68.5	59.3	14.8	10.6	44,732	22,492	22,240	49.7
36047	Kings County, New York	2,051,603	63.2	0.0	68.4	58.7	46.0	81.1	63.7	14.4	10.0	1,167,448	582,771	584,677	50.1
36049	Lewis County, New York	21,523	60.6	0.7	67.0	54.1	58.5	82.3	61.0	11.1	8.3	11,966	6,570	5,396	45.1
36051	Livingston County, New York	54,112	58.8	0.0	60.1	57.5	50.0	78.5	67.6	14.1	5.4	30,099	15,271	14,828	49.3
36053	Madison County, New York	59,567	58.4	0.1	63.5	53.6	41.8	81.6	65.5	15.0	5.1	33,023	17,268	15,755	47.7
36055	Monroe County, New York	606,638	64.6	0.0	68.9	60.8	61.2	83.6	66.5	16.5	7.7	361,948	183,238	178,710	49.4
36057	Montgomery County, New York	39,698	60.0	0.1	64.8	55.4	62.2	80.1	61.8	13.6	8.9	21,683	11,332	10,351	47.7
36059	Nassau County, New York	1,091,381	65.2	0.0	71.6	59.5	50.6	84.9	72.6	21.9	6.4	666,184	348,703	317,481	47.7
36061	New York County, New York	1,414,565	67.6	0.0	73.0	62.9	49.0	84.6	65.7	23.8	7.5	884,457	445,370	439,087	49.6
36063	Niagara County, New York	175,463	62.1	0.1	66.1	58.4	64.2	82.1	62.7	14.3	7.6	100,718	51,533	49,185	48.8
36065	Oneida County, New York	189,310	59.3	0.1	61.4	57.3	57.7	78.1	62.9	15.6	7.4	103,944	52,965	50,979	49.0
36067	Onondaga County, New York	377,171	63.1	0.1	67.4	59.2	53.9	82.8	67.1	16.8	7.2	220,774	111,896	108,878	49.3
36069	Ontario County, New York	89,008	64.1	0.1	68.1	60.3	63.8	84.6	66.4	17.7	6.4	53,394	27,416	25,978	48.7
36071	Orange County, New York	288,626	64.1	1.5	68.3	60.0	53.7	80.7	66.8	20.1	7.3	171,651	90,369	81,282	47.4
36073	Orleans County, New York	34,614	54.9	0.0	58.1	51.7	54.6	70.9	55.7	13.3	9.0	17,285	9,048	8,237	47.7
36075	Oswego County, New York	97,741	59.1	0.2	62.2	56.1	56.7	77.2	56.9	13.1	9.7	52,204	26,741	25,463	48.8
36077	Otsego County, New York	52,428	58.4	0.0	60.9	56.2	48.4	84.2	65.2	17.0	7.1	28,464	13,984	14,480	50.9
36079	Putnam County, New York	80,497	68.5	0.0	73.3	63.9	61.6	84.8	72.8	22.0	6.8	51,412	27,110	24,302	47.3
36081	Queens County, New York	1,881,607	64.2	0.0	71.6	57.4	48.5	82.2	66.4	15.5	8.6	1,104,930	590,498	514,432	46.6
36083	Rensselaer County, New York	130,796	66.3	0.1	69.8	63.0	59.9	86.4	67.1	16.9	7.6	80,144	40,966	39,178	48.9
36085	Richmond County, New York	378,913	59.2	0.1	65.7	53.3	41.9	78.5	62.0	15.4	6.9	209,113	110,051	99,062	47.4
36087	Rockland County, New York	241,889	65.6	0.1	71.7	59.8	53.8	83.4	75.4	22.4	7.9	146,049	76,609	69,440	47.5
36089	St. Lawrence County, New York	91,474	54.3	0.2	55.4	53.2	44.3	76.7	54.0	11.3	10.0	44,714	22,806	21,908	49.0
36091	Saratoga County, New York	181,406	66.8	0.9	72.0	61.8	62.1	85.5	69.3	17.3	6.0	113,884	60,152	53,732	47.2
36093	Schenectady County, New York	124,371	64.4	0.1	68.2	60.9	63.3	83.9	64.0	15.2	7.4	74,134	37,639	36,495	49.2
36095	Schoharie County, New York	26,728	59.2	0.1	62.1	56.4	59.5	82.1	55.8	15.2	10.5	14,179	7,393	6,786	47.9
36097	Schuyler County, New York	15,265	56.8	0.1	62.2	51.6	51.1	76.9	61.6	16.0	6.4	8,125	4,358	3,767	46.4
36099	Seneca County, New York	28,743	56.7	0.1	56.5	56.8	59.9	71.9	61.3	14.4	5.5	15,385	7,980	7,405	48.1
36101	Steuben County, New York	79,166	59.5	0.1	63.7	55.3	59.0	80.6	59.6	12.8	8.2	43,199	22,650	20,549	47.6
36103	Suffolk County, New York	1,204,453	65.2	0.0	71.1	59.7	54.7	83.4	70.0	19.9	6.4	735,010	388,250	346,760	47.2
36105	Sullivan County, New York	61,736	59.0	0.1	59.8	58.2	51.8	77.3	59.4	20.0	11.5	32,243	16,479	15,764	48.9
36107	Tioga County, New York	40,547	63.4	0.0	67.7	59.4	56.2	85.1	70.0	15.0	6.9	23,960	12,518	11,442	47.8
36109	Tompkins County, New York	89,862	58.3	0.0	62.3	54.6	42.1	80.6	70.9	22.4	5.9	49,291	25,366	23,925	48.5
36111	Ulster County, New York	151,678	62.2	0.1	65.0	59.5	58.3	79.3	65.7	21.8	9.3	85,617	43,761	41,856	48.9
36113	Warren County, New York	54,361	62.8	0.0	67.5	58.3	61.4	85.7	64.2	16.8	6.6	31,866	16,515	15,351	48.2
36115	Washington County, New York	51,768	61.3	0.1	66.2	60.4	62.1	78.4	62.3	18.4	9.5	28,744	14,994	13,750	47.8
36117	Wayne County, New York	74,206	62.8	0.1	67.3	58.4	61.0	84.0	61.6	13.5	7.5	43,117	22,647	20,470	47.5
36119	Westchester County, New York	770,360	65.4	0.0	72.0	59.4	50.7	83.3	73.2	22.8	7.6	465,097	242,840	222,257	47.8

Table C. County—Labor Force, Employment, and Educational Data, 2011–2015—*Continued*

Fips code	State/county	Total population age 16 and older	Percent in civilian labor force	Percent in armed forces	Civilian labor force participation by gender		Civilian labor force participation by age				Civilian unemploy-ment rate	Civilian employed population age 16 and older			
					Men	Women	Age 16 to 24	Age 25 to 54	Age 55 to 64	Age 65 and older		Total	Men	Women	Percent women
36121	Wyoming County, New York	34,174	58.4	0.0	56.4	60.9	62.7	72.0	61.8	13.7	7.4	18,495	9,754	8,741	47.3
36123	Yates County, New York	20,098	61.4	0.1	67.0	56.3	66.4	81.1	64.7	18.1	6.9	11,496	5,929	5,567	48.4
37000	**North Carolina**	7,812,594	61.8	1.1	66.2	57.7	55.6	80.0	61.6	15.8	9.4	4,372,773	2,253,704	2,119,069	48.5
37001	Alamance County, North Carolina	123,563	62.5	0.0	67.5	58.2	55.6	82.5	66.2	15.6	7.9	71,156	35,548	35,608	50.0
37003	Alexander County, North Carolina	30,308	58.7	0.0	62.7	54.5	64.8	76.8	55.6	17.2	9.0	16,182	8,934	7,248	44.8
37005	Alleghany County, North Carolina	9,149	53.3	0.0	60.8	46.2	50.7	81.0	53.3	12.1	10.5	4,365	2,459	1,906	43.7
37007	Anson County, North Carolina	21,269	56.3	0.0	58.8	53.7	62.6	71.0	54.7	15.1	17.6	9,875	5,494	4,381	44.4
37009	Ashe County, North Carolina	22,660	56.8	0.1	62.2	51.7	64.4	81.3	59.2	12.2	8.5	11,790	6,307	5,483	46.5
37011	Avery County, North Carolina	15,259	48.4	0.0	46.4	50.9	50.0	64.0	54.0	11.5	6.9	6,873	3,546	3,327	48.4
37013	Beaufort County, North Carolina	38,676	54.9	0.0	58.1	52.0	59.1	78.1	55.7	14.0	11.5	18,786	9,398	9,388	50.0
37015	Bertie County, North Carolina	17,137	48.3	0.1	49.0	47.6	47.0	63.9	59.9	9.2	13.5	7,158	3,589	3,569	49.9
37017	Bladen County, North Carolina	27,844	53.3	0.0	55.0	51.8	53.6	73.8	51.8	12.6	12.1	13,040	6,459	6,581	50.5
37019	Brunswick County, North Carolina	97,816	52.2	0.1	57.4	47.4	64.9	79.4	49.9	14.7	11.4	45,213	23,783	21,430	47.4
37021	Buncombe County, North Carolina	203,992	61.8	0.1	65.9	58.0	63.9	81.2	63.4	14.2	7.0	117,252	59,106	58,146	49.6
37023	Burke County, North Carolina	73,671	56.2	0.1	59.7	52.8	55.0	76.2	55.8	14.0	11.6	36,632	19,103	17,529	47.9
37025	Cabarrus County, North Carolina	144,343	67.1	0.1	73.3	61.4	59.1	84.7	65.0	15.6	9.2	87,960	45,860	42,100	47.9
37027	Caldwell County, North Carolina	66,484	58.0	0.0	62.4	53.8	60.5	77.8	54.0	14.5	12.2	33,837	17,775	16,062	47.5
37029	Camden County, North Carolina	8,017	60.9	2.2	63.8	58.1	57.3	79.5	56.7	17.0	9.3	4,429	2,268	2,161	48.8
37031	Carteret County, North Carolina	56,994	57.6	1.7	61.2	54.2	67.8	78.6	56.8	16.9	10.2	29,496	15,344	14,152	48.0
37033	Caswell County, North Carolina	19,243	54.1	0.0	55.8	52.4	53.4	74.1	55.2	12.7	10.9	9,276	4,832	4,444	47.9
37035	Catawba County, North Carolina	122,904	62.0	0.0	67.9	56.5	57.8	80.0	64.5	17.7	8.2	69,954	36,771	33,183	47.4
37037	Chatham County, North Carolina	55,004	59.2	0.0	65.6	53.2	60.8	83.8	65.0	16.1	9.0	29,621	15,869	13,752	46.4
37039	Cherokee County, North Carolina	22,773	44.9	0.0	49.8	40.4	49.9	68.8	45.3	13.1	8.4	9,362	4,964	4,398	47.0
37041	Chowan County, North Carolina	11,985	54.6	0.5	63.8	46.2	61.1	80.9	52.9	9.8	12.7	5,711	3,037	2,674	46.8
37043	Clay County, North Carolina	8,843	50.6	0.0	54.7	46.8	53.9	82.8	51.4	12.7	12.3	3,920	2,059	1,861	47.5
37045	Cleveland County, North Carolina	77,775	59.7	0.0	64.7	55.2	57.9	81.5	58.4	12.8	12.6	40,571	20,845	19,726	48.6
37047	Columbus County, North Carolina	45,807	49.8	0.1	51.4	48.2	46.8	67.7	49.7	12.1	9.0	20,746	10,280	10,466	50.4
37049	Craven County, North Carolina	82,895	55.2	7.4	56.4	53.9	53.2	73.9	60.6	12.6	11.4	40,530	20,851	19,679	48.6
37051	Cumberland County, North Carolina	248,496	54.7	10.4	53.8	55.5	45.8	67.6	56.6	15.3	12.6	118,750	56,043	62,707	52.8
37053	Currituck County, North Carolina	19,656	64.9	0.8	70.9	59.1	56.6	83.7	59.5	21.9	6.6	11,913	6,413	5,500	46.2
37055	Dare County, North Carolina	28,636	69.3	0.1	73.2	65.6	70.5	89.1	70.9	23.6	6.4	18,579	9,666	8,913	48.0
37057	Davidson County, North Carolina	130,657	61.6	0.0	67.3	56.1	60.5	81.5	61.1	13.6	11.0	71,620	38,085	33,535	46.8
37059	Davie County, North Carolina	33,378	59.3	0.1	64.2	54.7	55.7	82.2	64.6	9.7	7.2	18,364	9,704	8,660	47.2
37061	Duplin County, North Carolina	46,254	60.1	0.2	68.9	51.8	59.5	78.4	60.0	15.3	11.3	24,654	13,785	10,869	44.1
37063	Durham County, North Carolina	230,809	67.5	0.1	69.8	65.4	52.2	83.0	66.9	20.9	6.8	145,135	70,749	74,386	51.3
37065	Edgecombe County, North Carolina	43,739	58.0	0.0	60.8	55.7	58.6	77.3	58.4	14.0	15.4	21,446	10,133	11,313	52.8
37067	Forsyth County, North Carolina	284,965	63.1	0.1	69.4	57.7	53.4	82.1	66.0	15.6	9.5	162,790	82,679	80,111	49.2
37069	Franklin County, North Carolina	49,496	59.9	0.0	64.4	55.6	47.7	79.2	61.3	15.7	9.9	26,738	14,327	12,411	46.4
37071	Gaston County, North Carolina	166,438	62.0	0.1	67.7	56.8	60.7	80.7	58.5	14.2	11.2	91,563	47,850	43,713	47.7
37073	Gates County, North Carolina	9,475	58.5	0.4	59.7	57.3	49.2	80.4	59.6	14.2	12.2	4,865	2,326	2,539	52.2
37075	Graham County, North Carolina	7,109	46.6	0.0	54.3	39.5	44.6	68.5	43.3	15.8	11.1	2,947	1,580	1,367	46.4
37077	Granville County, North Carolina	46,957	56.1	0.0	56.4	55.8	44.5	76.4	52.3	13.2	8.3	24,163	12,288	11,875	49.1
37079	Greene County, North Carolina	17,098	53.6	0.4	52.0	55.4	60.1	61.7	59.9	17.4	11.9	8,070	4,305	3,765	46.7
37081	Guilford County, North Carolina	404,441	64.0	0.1	69.7	59.1	51.8	82.5	66.9	18.2	8.8	236,140	120,033	116,107	49.2
37083	Halifax County, North Carolina	43,044	53.3	0.1	54.9	52.0	57.0	73.9	49.1	11.9	14.1	19,726	8,908	10,818	54.8
37085	Harnett County, North Carolina	93,412	56.0	4.9	58.7	53.3	49.5	68.1	57.5	15.1	11.3	46,375	23,702	22,673	48.9
37087	Haywood County, North Carolina	49,883	53.5	0.0	60.1	47.4	59.2	78.2	53.9	11.7	7.3	24,728	13,165	11,563	46.8
37089	Henderson County, North Carolina	90,229	54.7	0.1	60.4	49.5	60.3	79.9	57.6	13.7	6.0	46,387	24,268	22,119	47.7
37091	Hertford County, North Carolina	20,032	50.2	0.0	47.6	52.7	52.1	65.4	51.3	14.8	13.7	8,679	3,886	4,793	55.2
37093	Hoke County, North Carolina	37,499	52.7	8.2	50.1	55.1	47.2	61.0	51.3	14.9	13.1	17,168	8,027	9,141	53.2
37095	Hyde County, North Carolina	4,728	56.4	0.0	50.2	63.6	42.9	68.6	64.7	26.4	12.7	2,326	1,165	1,161	49.9
37097	Iredell County, North Carolina	129,912	65.0	0.1	72.3	58.0	62.6	82.1	64.6	17.7	9.8	76,079	41,304	34,775	45.7
37099	Jackson County, North Carolina	34,371	54.5	0.2	58.2	51.0	48.1	77.7	56.2	14.3	6.2	17,567	9,197	8,370	47.6

Table C. County—Labor Force, Employment, and Educational Data, 2011-2015—*Continued*

Fips code	State/county	Total population age 16 and older	Percent in civilian labor force	Percent in armed forces	Civilian labor force participation by gender		Civilian labor force participation by age				Civilian unemploy-ment rate	Civilian employed population age 16 and older			
					Men	Women	Age 16 to 24	Age 25 to 54	Age 55 to 64	Age 65 and older		Total	Men	Women	Percent women
37101	Johnston County, North Carolina	135,761	65.2	0.1	70.3	60.5	59.9	81.8	61.4	14.6	8.9	80,656	42,105	38,551	47.8
37103	Jones County, North Carolina	8,407	54.2	0.7	61.3	47.5	49.8	78.3	52.1	15.2	11.6	4,029	2,160	1,869	46.4
37105	Lee County, North Carolina	45,832	61.8	0.7	67.8	56.2	60.1	78.9	63.7	16.2	10.3	25,418	13,257	12,161	47.8
37107	Lenoir County, North Carolina	46,870	58.8	0.2	65.1	53.3	61.2	79.2	56.3	16.8	13.1	23,972	12,469	11,503	48.0
37109	Lincoln County, North Carolina	63,846	63.9	0.0	70.5	57.4	66.0	82.1	62.1	15.2	10.2	36,605	19,856	16,749	45.8
37111	McDowell County, North Carolina	36,666	53.4	0.2	58.4	48.5	61.5	71.5	51.3	11.0	11.1	17,404	9,333	8,071	46.4
37113	Macon County, North Carolina	28,226	51.0	0.0	57.4	45.2	59.9	77.1	52.1	14.7	7.3	13,351	7,081	6,270	47.0
37115	Madison County, North Carolina	17,619	54.7	0.0	59.9	49.7	53.5	79.4	53.2	12.1	7.3	8,935	4,697	4,238	47.4
37117	Martin County, North Carolina	19,362	55.0	0.0	58.3	52.1	54.2	79.4	54.8	13.1	14.7	9,079	4,502	4,577	50.4
37119	Mecklenburg County, North Carolina	769,714	71.7	0.1	77.8	66.2	61.7	86.0	69.0	19.4	8.9	502,455	260,394	242,061	48.2
37121	Mitchell County, North Carolina	12,891	51.1	0.0	56.3	46.2	49.5	76.9	51.9	10.5	8.6	6,014	3,222	2,792	46.4
37123	Montgomery County, North Carolina	21,887	53.1	0.0	58.3	48.1	51.4	70.9	57.0	14.4	10.5	10,397	5,466	4,931	47.4
37125	Moore County, North Carolina	74,419	53.2	2.0	57.2	49.6	52.1	76.3	62.3	14.1	8.0	36,422	18,452	17,970	49.3
37127	Nash County, North Carolina	75,653	61.1	0.0	65.4	57.2	61.2	80.3	58.7	16.2	11.9	40,735	20,399	20,336	49.9
37129	New Hanover County, North Carolina	175,886	64.8	0.4	68.8	61.1	61.2	83.2	66.8	18.4	8.9	103,718	52,478	51,240	49.4
37131	Northampton County, North Carolina	17,412	49.1	0.0	50.4	48.0	47.9	71.4	51.9	13.5	15.9	7,193	3,363	3,830	53.2
37133	Onslow County, North Carolina	140,434	49.3	21.2	44.8	54.9	38.4	61.3	60.3	16.0	11.6	61,252	31,082	30,170	49.3
37135	Orange County, North Carolina	114,029	65.8	0.0	69.2	62.9	51.6	83.8	72.0	23.5	6.4	70,264	34,343	35,921	51.1
37137	Pamlico County, North Carolina	11,125	50.8	0.1	51.9	49.8	60.1	70.8	59.7	13.6	9.7	5,107	2,645	2,462	48.2
37139	Pasquotank County, North Carolina	32,145	59.1	2.0	61.5	56.8	50.6	78.8	58.4	15.0	10.1	17,073	8,666	8,407	49.2
37141	Pender County, North Carolina	44,384	58.1	0.9	62.2	53.9	59.4	75.2	59.7	15.9	9.8	23,242	12,416	10,826	46.6
37143	Perquimans County, North Carolina	11,060	50.2	0.4	55.8	45.2	46.7	77.5	48.2	13.3	12.7	4,852	2,662	2,190	45.1
37145	Person County, North Carolina	31,344	60.2	0.1	63.8	56.8	57.8	80.7	63.8	11.3	11.9	16,612	8,306	8,306	50.0
37147	Pitt County, North Carolina	139,609	65.5	0.2	68.7	62.9	60.4	83.4	63.1	17.2	12.1	80,392	38,905	41,487	51.6
37149	Polk County, North Carolina	17,232	52.6	0.1	58.4	47.5	64.5	80.8	57.9	11.8	8.8	8,270	4,223	4,047	48.9
37151	Randolph County, North Carolina	112,379	61.8	0.0	66.8	57.0	57.0	81.3	61.7	15.9	9.0	63,160	33,379	29,781	47.2
37153	Richmond County, North Carolina	36,363	53.8	0.5	55.3	52.4	49.6	75.1	45.9	11.5	13.8	16,848	8,365	8,483	50.4
37155	Robeson County, North Carolina	103,542	52.1	0.2	55.4	49.0	43.4	69.7	49.0	11.2	12.1	47,406	23,661	23,745	50.1
37157	Rockingham County, North Carolina	75,137	57.1	0.0	61.1	53.4	52.7	78.3	55.7	15.0	10.5	38,380	19,826	18,554	48.3
37159	Rowan County, North Carolina	110,281	57.9	0.1	62.5	53.4	55.4	76.2	58.3	14.6	11.5	56,519	29,839	26,680	47.2
37161	Rutherford County, North Carolina	54,399	52.4	0.0	58.1	47.2	54.1	72.0	54.6	11.2	12.2	25,033	13,428	11,605	46.4
37163	Sampson County, North Carolina	49,913	60.0	0.1	66.6	53.8	58.6	79.9	55.3	16.5	10.4	26,833	14,622	12,211	45.5
37165	Scotland County, North Carolina	28,515	46.5	0.1	47.1	45.9	41.3	62.6	48.5	10.1	15.5	11,215	5,460	5,755	51.3
37167	Stanly County, North Carolina	48,794	60.9	0.0	64.3	57.6	62.5	80.7	61.7	14.9	12.2	26,101	13,442	12,659	48.5
37169	Stokes County, North Carolina	38,251	57.6	0.0	63.6	51.9	55.2	79.0	58.7	12.4	9.3	19,972	10,561	9,411	47.1
37171	Surry County, North Carolina	58,829	55.0	0.0	60.1	50.1	56.5	75.0	54.4	13.6	6.9	30,107	15,761	14,346	47.7
37173	Swain County, North Carolina	11,229	53.5	0.1	58.1	49.3	49.4	71.5	54.8	16.7	7.7	5,543	2,865	2,678	48.3
37175	Transylvania County, North Carolina	28,082	52.8	0.0	57.2	48.8	54.2	83.6	57.5	14.5	6.9	13,794	7,053	6,741	48.9
37177	Tyrrell County, North Carolina	3,548	44.3	0.0	42.4	47.0	60.6	51.6	54.0	12.7	14.1	1,350	759	591	43.8
37179	Union County, North Carolina	159,021	68.0	0.0	76.3	60.0	59.1	83.7	66.8	19.3	7.7	99,712	54,742	44,970	45.1
37181	Vance County, North Carolina	35,180	56.6	0.0	58.3	55.1	57.0	74.8	56.5	13.7	12.2	17,461	8,205	9,256	53.0
37183	Wake County, North Carolina	756,014	70.6	0.1	76.8	64.8	55.8	85.6	70.0	19.3	6.4	499,197	262,328	236,869	47.5
37185	Warren County, North Carolina	16,864	46.2	0.2	46.5	45.8	47.7	64.9	46.1	14.5	10.7	6,958	3,468	3,490	50.2
37187	Washington County, North Carolina	10,214	51.1	0.0	59.3	43.9	51.6	72.3	60.5	9.6	15.5	4,410	2,312	2,098	47.6
37189	Watauga County, North Carolina	46,083	57.4	0.1	62.6	52.2	48.5	83.7	63.1	16.4	9.5	23,928	12,761	11,167	46.7
37191	Wayne County, North Carolina	97,462	59.5	3.0	63.2	56.1	62.3	74.8	57.9	15.9	12.4	50,821	26,460	24,361	47.9
37193	Wilkes County, North Carolina	56,068	53.8	0.1	58.6	49.2	58.4	76.5	49.0	11.3	11.7	26,631	14,285	12,346	46.4
37195	Wilson County, North Carolina	64,204	60.1	0.2	65.2	55.8	61.3	78.1	59.5	17.1	10.1	34,701	17,343	17,358	50.0
37197	Yadkin County, North Carolina	30,651	56.0	0.0	61.6	50.7	46.7	80.3	50.5	13.2	8.3	15,747	8,389	7,358	46.7
37199	Yancey County, North Carolina	14,633	53.7	0.2	60.3	47.3	65.4	75.1	56.2	13.4	11.0	6,992	3,839	3,153	45.1
38000	**North Dakota**	575,611	69.3	1.0	73.5	65.0	67.6	86.6	74.2	20.6	2.9	387,716	209,375	178,341	46.0
38001	Adams County, North Dakota	1,976	65.5	0.0	70.0	60.8	66.0	88.4	72.7	27.6	1.2	1,279	704	575	45.0
38003	Barnes County, North Dakota	9,192	65.6	0.1	71.2	60.0	60.9	89.4	73.9	19.5	2.4	5,889	3,226	2,663	45.2
38005	Benson County, North Dakota	4,705	55.7	0.1	58.1	53.2	44.2	67.7	69.3	22.2	6.1	2,461	1,292	1,169	47.5
38007	Billings County, North Dakota	817	70.0	0.0	74.5	63.9	82.0	89.1	74.9	12.3	1.4	564	343	221	39.2
38009	Bottineau County, North Dakota	5,462	63.3	0.7	71.4	54.6	68.3	81.7	73.0	24.0	2.6	3,369	1,967	1,402	41.6

Table C. County—Labor Force, Employment, and Educational Data, 2011–2015—*Continued*

Fips code	State/county	Total population age 16 and older	Percent in civilian labor force	Percent in armed forces	Civilian labor force participation by gender		Civilian labor force participation by age				Civilian unemploy-ment rate	Civilian employed population age 16 and older			
					Men	Women	Age 16 to 24	Age 25 to 54	Age 55 to 64	Age 65 and older		Total	Men	Women	Percent women
38011	Bowman County, North Dakota	2,565	68.3	0.0	77.2	60.1	75.5	91.8	72.4	22.4	1.8	1,721	950	771	44.8
38013	Burke County, North Dakota	1,701	65.3	0.1	75.9	52.3	62.7	84.7	65.4	25.1	2.3	1,084	690	394	36.3
38015	Burleigh County, North Dakota	70,116	72.1	0.4	75.1	69.2	73.6	88.5	74.4	22.2	2.3	49,375	25,253	24,122	48.9
38017	Cass County, North Dakota	130,200	75.1	0.1	78.1	72.0	73.1	89.6	75.9	21.3	3.2	94,675	49,639	45,036	47.6
38019	Cavalier County, North Dakota	3,212	61.8	0.0	71.4	51.7	65.7	86.2	76.8	21.7	0.8	1,968	1,168	800	40.7
38021	Dickey County, North Dakota	4,152	67.3	0.0	71.5	63.2	71.0	92.6	77.3	21.0	1.5	2,755	1,457	1,298	47.1
38023	Divide County, North Dakota	1,971	64.0	0.0	75.0	52.9	95.6	82.1	76.1	22.4	0.7	1,252	737	515	41.1
38025	Dunn County, North Dakota	3,365	64.5	0.0	70.7	57.3	67.4	85.1	61.4	20.5	4.3	2,078	1,216	862	41.5
38027	Eddy County, North Dakota	1,902	64.7	0.2	70.4	59.1	60.3	90.1	72.2	20.6	1.9	1,208	649	559	46.3
38029	Emmons County, North Dakota	2,845	57.7	0.0	59.3	56.1	57.6	86.2	78.8	13.9	3.6	1,583	823	760	48.0
38031	Foster County, North Dakota	2,755	65.7	0.0	73.9	57.4	63.2	91.8	74.2	19.9	1.3	1,786	1,011	775	43.4
38033	Golden Valley County, North Dakota	1,424	68.4	0.0	76.8	61.0	54.1	89.1	73.9	36.5	1.0	964	515	449	46.6
38035	Grand Forks County, North Dakota	56,369	69.5	2.3	72.5	66.3	65.2	85.6	75.1	21.5	3.6	37,754	20,134	17,620	46.7
38037	Grant County, North Dakota	2,015	61.9	0.2	68.1	55.5	56.7	87.0	75.9	25.1	3.4	1,205	678	527	43.7
38039	Griggs County, North Dakota	1,939	63.3	0.0	72.3	54.6	69.4	91.3	80.9	23.3	2.0	1,203	667	536	44.6
38041	Hettinger County, North Dakota	2,109	58.1	0.0	68.1	49.1	53.7	78.5	71.8	24.3	1.1	1,211	673	538	44.4
38043	Kidder County, North Dakota	1,996	67.6	0.0	74.3	59.9	70.4	86.6	78.0	26.1	0.9	1,337	783	554	41.4
38045	LaMoure County, North Dakota	3,357	63.0	0.0	69.4	56.2	62.6	89.2	74.9	20.9	1.9	2,073	1,180	893	43.1
38047	Logan County, North Dakota	1,610	60.4	0.0	65.5	55.3	75.2	88.2	73.6	19.4	2.2	952	520	432	45.4
38049	McHenry County, North Dakota	4,639	63.2	0.6	69.8	55.9	68.6	83.4	67.7	20.0	3.1	2,840	1,644	1,196	42.1
38051	McIntosh County, North Dakota	2,315	58.9	0.3	64.2	54.1	54.9	89.5	74.8	23.5	1.2	1,347	702	645	47.9
38053	McKenzie County, North Dakota	7,150	68.7	0.0	77.2	58.5	66.5	81.3	68.4	20.3	3.0	4,766	2,911	1,855	38.9
38055	McLean County, North Dakota	7,751	59.5	0.3	63.4	55.5	62.2	82.8	66.0	16.6	1.6	4,541	2,446	2,095	46.1
38057	Mercer County, North Dakota	6,943	65.3	0.0	70.7	59.7	63.5	86.8	69.4	13.3	3.2	4,391	2,404	1,987	45.3
38059	Morton County, North Dakota	23,195	73.1	0.1	75.6	70.5	80.1	90.8	72.4	20.0	3.2	16,411	8,587	7,824	47.7
38061	Mountrail County, North Dakota	7,094	68.1	0.5	72.5	62.7	54.9	84.4	71.3	23.1	4.7	4,607	2,684	1,923	41.7
38063	Nelson County, North Dakota	2,593	60.4	0.1	65.3	55.2	72.2	89.9	69.9	18.2	0.7	1,554	852	702	45.2
38065	Oliver County, North Dakota	1,451	61.3	0.0	69.7	52.5	71.8	84.5	68.6	14.9	3.6	857	494	363	42.4
38067	Pembina County, North Dakota	5,858	65.4	0.6	72.0	58.5	70.2	85.7	78.4	19.7	3.5	3,694	2,073	1,621	43.9
38069	Pierce County, North Dakota	3,638	60.9	0.0	66.6	55.1	70.7	84.4	65.6	20.0	0.9	2,194	1,194	1,000	45.6
38071	Ramsey County, North Dakota	9,307	64.3	2.3	67.0	61.6	68.6	84.3	73.9	15.1	1.2	5,910	3,063	2,847	48.2
38073	Ransom County, North Dakota	4,412	65.8	0.0	72.3	59.1	77.6	88.7	69.0	19.8	2.0	2,847	1,574	1,273	44.7
38075	Renville County, North Dakota	1,980	66.8	1.4	77.2	55.3	64.6	84.1	69.9	25.5	1.6	1,301	788	513	39.4
38077	Richland County, North Dakota	13,312	68.2	0.1	72.2	63.8	58.7	89.8	80.7	19.2	3.0	8,800	4,823	3,977	45.2
38079	Rolette County, North Dakota	10,036	51.3	0.0	50.8	51.8	31.4	65.5	60.3	16.8	4.8	4,907	2,303	2,604	53.1
38081	Sargent County, North Dakota	3,154	66.7	0.0	72.2	60.5	67.6	91.0	75.2	15.3	1.2	2,078	1,180	898	43.2
38083	Sheridan County, North Dakota	1,149	55.9	0.0	67.2	43.8	46.3	73.5	70.7	27.7	2.0	629	391	238	37.8
38085	Sioux County, North Dakota	2,889	56.1	0.2	53.3	58.8	44.6	63.9	64.4	29.9	20.3	1,291	575	716	55.5
38087	Slope County, North Dakota	553	60.6	0.0	72.7	45.3	77.4	79.0	74.7	11.4	0.0	335	224	111	33.1
38089	Stark County, North Dakota	22,496	73.5	0.3	80.1	66.2	74.7	88.9	76.1	22.9	2.8	16,062	9,098	6,964	43.4
38091	Steele County, North Dakota	1,653	65.2	0.0	70.4	59.1	72.4	90.4	74.2	17.8	4.0	1,035	620	415	40.1
38093	Stutsman County, North Dakota	17,239	66.3	0.1	68.2	64.4	62.0	84.3	79.3	20.0	2.5	11,144	5,788	5,356	48.1
38095	Towner County, North Dakota	1,773	61.5	0.0	71.1	52.1	69.4	82.0	79.2	20.3	2.9	1,059	610	449	42.4
38097	Traill County, North Dakota	6,480	64.8	0.0	71.2	58.5	57.2	86.6	82.7	15.7	2.7	4,085	2,227	1,858	45.5
38099	Walsh County, North Dakota	8,849	63.8	0.1	70.2	57.3	65.9	84.3	75.9	19.8	3.3	5,457	2,999	2,458	45.0
38101	Ward County, North Dakota	53,499	68.3	6.1	70.6	65.7	61.8	84.7	73.1	19.5	2.6	35,580	19,497	16,083	45.2
38103	Wells County, North Dakota	3,510	59.3	0.0	65.6	53.4	80.4	82.7	77.2	18.5	1.3	2,055	1,118	937	45.6
38105	Williams County, North Dakota	22,938	71.8	0.3	82.3	59.0	65.1	85.1	75.7	20.2	1.7	16,193	10,231	5,962	36.8
39000	**Ohio**	9,229,397	63.3	0.1	67.9	59.0	62.4	81.8	63.7	16.0	8.2	5,366,673	2,770,301	2,596,372	48.4
39001	Adams County, Ohio	22,025	53.1	0.0	57.7	48.7	54.3	71.4	48.5	13.0	13.4	10,135	5,294	4,841	47.8
39003	Allen County, Ohio	83,408	62.9	0.1	66.7	59.0	71.1	80.6	62.3	14.1	9.2	47,604	24,986	22,618	47.5
39005	Ashland County, Ohio	42,399	61.8	0.1	66.8	57.1	58.2	83.6	68.1	13.8	7.8	24,172	12,550	11,622	48.1
39007	Ashtabula County, Ohio	79,659	55.7	0.1	59.6	51.8	56.9	74.2	56.2	12.7	8.9	40,422	21,239	19,183	47.5
39009	Athens County, Ohio	56,203	53.5	0.0	54.3	52.7	47.4	71.9	55.4	14.2	10.9	26,794	13,624	13,170	49.2
39011	Auglaize County, Ohio	35,816	66.8	0.0	72.7	61.0	69.6	87.9	70.7	14.3	5.0	22,719	12,234	10,485	46.2
39013	Belmont County, Ohio	58,005	56.0	0.0	59.2	52.6	55.6	74.3	58.5	15.1	8.5	29,728	16,008	13,720	46.2
39015	Brown County, Ohio	35,040	59.2	0.0	63.5	55.2	64.1	78.8	56.0	11.3	9.9	18,693	9,652	9,041	48.4
39017	Butler County, Ohio	291,832	65.3	0.0	70.5	60.4	59.0	83.5	65.6	17.1	7.2	176,782	92,477	84,305	47.7
39019	Carroll County, Ohio	23,000	59.2	0.0	64.8	53.7	58.7	80.2	60.8	16.5	7.1	12,657	6,846	5,811	45.9
39021	Champaign County, Ohio	31,325	64.0	0.0	69.7	58.4	65.8	82.4	64.7	17.9	9.1	18,230	9,623	8,607	47.2
39023	Clark County, Ohio	109,187	60.2	0.1	64.6	56.1	64.9	80.3	59.7	15.0	10.0	59,111	30,150	28,961	49.0
39025	Clermont County, Ohio	157,027	65.5	0.0	71.9	59.5	63.3	82.1	64.6	18.5	5.5	97,207	51,842	45,365	46.7
39027	Clinton County, Ohio	32,919	61.8	0.0	67.1	56.8	55.3	82.2	62.2	14.5	9.2	18,460	9,770	8,690	47.1
39029	Columbiana County, Ohio	86,141	59.4	0.0	64.2	54.7	65.3	77.1	60.9	16.9	9.0	46,577	25,201	21,376	45.9
39031	Coshocton County, Ohio	29,066	58.1	0.1	66.6	49.9	63.4	76.5	60.8	13.2	7.8	15,576	8,744	6,832	43.9
39033	Crawford County, Ohio	34,268	57.6	0.0	62.5	53.2	60.4	81.2	60.0	14.0	8.1	18,142	9,362	8,780	48.4
39035	Cuyahoga County, Ohio	1,021,714	63.2	0.0	67.4	59.4	62.3	82.4	64.5	16.1	10.6	576,603	284,805	291,798	50.6
39037	Darke County, Ohio	41,033	62.6	0.0	69.2	56.3	66.0	83.3	66.3	16.2	7.6	23,751	12,782	10,969	46.2
39039	Defiance County, Ohio	30,605	64.5	0.1	68.7	60.4	69.0	83.5	70.4	13.6	8.4	18,092	9,295	8,797	48.6

Table C. County—Labor Force, Employment, and Educational Data, 2011–2015—Continued

Fips code	State/county	Total population age 16 and older	Percent in civilian labor force	Percent in armed forces	Civilian labor force participation by gender		Civilian labor force participation by age				Civilian unemploy- ment rate	Civilian employed population age 16 and older			Percent women
					Men	Women	Age 16 to 24	Age 25 to 54	Age 55 to 64	Age 65 and older		Total	Men	Women	
39041	Delaware County, Ohio	139,077	70.1	0.1	76.9	63.7	53.8	87.0	70.9	19.9	3.2	94,424	50,428	43,996	46.6
39043	Erie County, Ohio	61,874	62.4	0.0	65.2	59.7	69.5	84.6	64.4	13.8	7.7	35,636	17,929	17,707	49.7
39045	Fairfield County, Ohio	116,727	64.2	0.1	68.3	60.2	64.1	81.9	63.0	14.0	6.9	69,708	36,348	33,360	47.9
39047	Fayette County, Ohio	22,756	59.5	0.2	65.8	53.6	64.3	78.1	57.4	13.8	8.6	12,385	6,620	5,765	46.5
39049	Franklin County, Ohio	956,166	69.3	0.1	73.8	65.2	62.2	84.4	66.0	19.1	7.0	616,368	314,409	301,959	49.0
39051	Fulton County, Ohio	33,270	67.2	0.0	71.7	63.0	66.2	86.9	71.0	17.7	6.7	20,872	10,814	10,058	48.2
39053	Gallia County, Ohio	24,189	50.7	0.0	56.0	45.7	46.9	71.1	46.9	11.1	7.5	11,344	6,028	5,316	46.9
39055	Geauga County, Ohio	73,801	65.8	0.0	73.0	58.9	66.4	84.4	73.4	21.5	4.1	46,540	25,178	21,362	45.9
39057	Greene County, Ohio	133,798	61.6	1.9	66.8	56.6	58.4	79.8	64.4	16.5	7.6	76,109	39,849	36,260	47.6
39059	Guernsey County, Ohio	31,454	58.7	0.1	64.1	53.6	67.5	79.0	54.8	12.3	11.7	16,310	8,532	7,778	47.7
39061	Hamilton County, Ohio	637,482	66.0	0.0	71.0	61.5	63.5	83.7	65.0	18.4	8.8	383,555	194,513	189,042	49.3
39063	Hancock County, Ohio	60,319	66.9	0.1	71.7	62.4	70.2	85.0	67.0	19.0	6.9	37,580	19,414	18,166	48.3
39065	Hardin County, Ohio	25,302	60.4	0.0	64.2	56.8	60.7	80.6	57.0	15.1	9.6	13,828	7,121	6,707	48.5
39067	Harrison County, Ohio	12,747	56.0	0.0	64.3	48.0	60.9	77.0	55.9	13.7	5.6	6,740	3,832	2,908	43.1
39069	Henry County, Ohio	22,122	65.1	0.0	71.1	59.3	64.0	86.9	70.9	13.7	6.7	13,436	7,119	6,317	47.0
39071	Highland County, Ohio	33,695	56.9	0.0	64.2	50.0	63.7	74.7	54.4	13.8	11.5	16,962	9,358	7,604	44.8
39073	Hocking County, Ohio	23,163	58.2	0.0	63.0	53.4	65.3	78.0	52.6	14.3	9.5	12,199	6,600	5,599	45.9
39075	Holmes County, Ohio	30,714	65.3	0.0	78.6	52.1	76.6	76.0	66.2	21.5	4.2	19,207	11,643	7,564	39.4
39077	Huron County, Ohio	45,662	63.7	0.0	69.5	58.1	67.9	83.0	63.0	11.4	7.2	26,987	14,301	12,686	47.0
39079	Jackson County, Ohio	25,928	57.5	0.0	62.5	52.8	62.1	75.0	52.3	14.4	11.5	13,191	6,930	6,261	47.5
39081	Jefferson County, Ohio	56,309	54.3	0.0	59.6	49.4	49.2	76.7	57.0	13.6	8.8	27,871	14,363	13,508	48.5
39083	Knox County, Ohio	48,273	62.5	0.0	69.0	56.3	59.1	83.3	67.8	14.6	6.6	28,165	15,146	13,019	46.2
39085	Lake County, Ohio	186,890	66.9	0.0	71.6	62.4	65.6	87.3	72.2	17.6	6.0	117,389	59,915	57,474	49.0
39087	Lawrence County, Ohio	49,388	53.9	0.0	58.5	49.6	59.4	72.8	50.7	10.0	8.0	24,489	12,760	11,729	47.9
39089	Licking County, Ohio	133,091	65.9	0.1	70.3	61.8	65.0	85.5	64.6	15.7	7.2	81,446	41,668	39,778	48.8
39091	Logan County, Ohio	35,766	62.9	0.0	69.8	56.3	68.6	82.1	62.3	14.7	7.6	20,773	11,359	9,414	45.3
39093	Lorain County, Ohio	241,620	62.9	0.0	66.1	59.8	66.4	81.1	64.0	14.9	8.8	138,469	70,489	67,980	49.1
39095	Lucas County, Ohio	345,775	62.9	0.1	66.8	59.4	63.9	81.1	60.3	14.9	11.1	193,466	96,739	96,727	50.0
39097	Madison County, Ohio	35,316	56.0	0.0	53.7	59.0	60.4	68.3	54.9	14.0	5.9	18,617	9,907	8,710	46.8
39099	Mahoning County, Ohio	192,019	59.4	0.1	63.0	56.0	63.2	79.7	62.3	14.8	9.5	103,169	52,327	50,842	49.3
39101	Marion County, Ohio	53,605	52.9	0.0	52.0	53.9	54.5	66.2	53.7	15.6	9.6	25,608	13,438	12,170	47.5
39103	Medina County, Ohio	138,077	67.8	0.0	73.8	62.0	68.6	86.2	66.6	18.7	5.0	88,911	47,236	41,675	46.9
39105	Meigs County, Ohio	18,891	52.8	0.0	58.3	47.5	53.4	74.3	47.4	8.8	12.1	8,770	4,582	4,188	47.8
39107	Mercer County, Ohio	31,707	68.4	0.0	74.2	62.6	74.3	90.1	71.9	13.3	5.5	20,476	10,936	9,540	46.6
39109	Miami County, Ohio	82,033	64.9	0.1	71.1	59.1	66.7	84.0	68.1	17.3	7.6	49,186	26,394	22,792	46.3
39111	Monroe County, Ohio	11,802	51.0	0.0	59.9	42.1	53.0	73.6	50.5	13.2	7.4	5,571	3,221	2,350	42.2
39113	Montgomery County, Ohio	426,467	61.3	0.4	65.6	57.4	61.2	80.0	62.6	15.9	9.4	236,657	119,720	116,937	49.4
39115	Morgan County, Ohio	12,049	51.9	0.1	59.0	45.1	50.0	74.4	51.3	9.9	9.3	5,678	3,141	2,537	44.7
39117	Morrow County, Ohio	27,420	63.1	0.1	68.0	58.4	59.5	83.6	59.6	17.3	7.0	16,096	8,534	7,562	47.0
39119	Muskingum County, Ohio	68,468	59.7	0.1	63.4	56.4	60.5	80.4	58.0	13.0	8.3	37,501	18,701	18,800	50.1
39121	Noble County, Ohio	12,642	39.5	0.0	33.8	47.3	44.3	47.9	53.8	11.0	7.0	4,641	2,338	2,303	49.6
39123	Ottawa County, Ohio	34,073	60.7	0.0	65.8	55.8	63.2	84.6	65.2	16.0	5.5	19,539	10,333	9,206	47.1
39125	Paulding County, Ohio	15,130	61.2	0.1	68.5	54.0	64.0	81.6	62.3	11.1	6.6	8,638	4,813	3,825	44.3
39127	Perry County, Ohio	28,191	57.4	0.1	64.0	50.8	50.5	76.0	58.5	11.8	9.5	14,630	8,088	6,542	44.7
39129	Pickaway County, Ohio	45,333	58.7	0.1	58.9	58.5	58.3	73.5	58.9	15.3	6.9	24,777	13,286	11,491	46.4
39131	Pike County, Ohio	22,434	50.9	0.0	54.7	47.3	52.7	69.7	44.1	9.4	13.4	9,887	5,224	4,663	47.2
39133	Portage County, Ohio	134,415	66.5	0.0	71.1	62.2	66.9	84.8	66.4	18.4	8.7	81,544	41,913	39,631	48.6
39135	Preble County, Ohio	33,060	63.0	0.0	68.5	57.8	67.9	84.7	57.9	15.1	7.3	19,308	10,210	9,098	47.1
39137	Putnam County, Ohio	26,320	69.1	0.0	74.6	63.7	69.2	89.3	74.3	15.0	3.4	17,579	9,417	8,162	46.4
39139	Richland County, Ohio	98,513	56.3	0.1	58.2	54.4	58.6	74.0	59.3	14.3	8.7	50,632	26,106	24,526	48.4
39141	Ross County, Ohio	62,284	54.5	0.0	54.5	54.4	61.0	68.8	52.1	11.7	11.3	30,096	15,945	14,151	47.0
39143	Sandusky County, Ohio	47,851	63.7	0.0	68.4	59.2	65.8	84.3	66.6	13.2	7.6	28,181	14,643	13,538	48.0
39145	Scioto County, Ohio	62,699	48.7	0.1	51.3	46.2	46.1	65.9	48.5	9.8	9.6	27,592	13,920	13,672	49.6
39147	Seneca County, Ohio	44,765	61.6	0.0	65.7	57.6	58.2	83.1	63.8	12.8	8.1	25,327	13,392	11,935	47.1
39149	Shelby County, Ohio	37,801	67.0	0.0	73.7	60.6	65.5	86.1	67.0	16.1	6.7	23,649	12,814	10,835	45.8
39151	Stark County, Ohio	302,373	63.2	0.1	67.9	58.9	65.5	83.6	61.3	15.8	8.5	174,941	89,664	85,277	48.7
39153	Summit County, Ohio	437,570	64.5	0.0	69.5	59.9	63.3	83.4	66.2	16.6	8.4	258,416	132,389	126,027	48.8
39155	Trumbull County, Ohio	168,009	56.7	0.0	61.8	51.9	59.9	79.0	56.8	11.2	7.4	88,133	46,208	41,925	47.6
39157	Tuscarawas County, Ohio	73,723	62.5	0.0	68.8	56.6	66.8	83.2	63.0	15.2	7.0	42,879	22,931	19,948	46.5
39159	Union County, Ohio	41,117	64.3	0.1	75.4	54.6	58.7	77.1	66.6	15.3	4.2	25,357	13,815	11,542	45.5
39161	Van Wert County, Ohio	22,606	62.9	0.0	69.1	57.1	68.9	82.8	69.4	12.7	7.5	13,163	7,122	6,041	45.9
39163	Vinton County, Ohio	10,464	55.0	0.0	60.1	49.8	53.8	72.9	51.0	13.8	12.0	5,060	2,735	2,325	45.9
39165	Warren County, Ohio	168,617	66.6	0.1	71.3	61.9	56.2	82.0	70.4	19.5	6.1	105,433	56,305	49,128	46.6
39167	Washington County, Ohio	50,496	55.4	0.0	61.0	50.1	54.8	77.5	54.3	13.1	6.8	26,082	13,946	12,136	46.5
39169	Wayne County, Ohio	90,117	63.6	0.0	72.2	55.4	65.1	82.5	66.1	16.7	4.8	54,503	30,188	24,315	44.6
39171	Williams County, Ohio	29,792	61.9	0.0	65.6	58.2	64.7	80.7	67.0	13.8	7.1	17,119	9,046	8,073	47.2
39173	Wood County, Ohio	105,389	66.9	0.2	71.8	62.2	66.8	85.2	67.0	18.4	7.2	65,406	33,643	31,763	48.6
39175	Wyandot County, Ohio	17,729	66.6	0.0	72.7	60.7	74.0	87.1	66.0	18.1	6.6	11,017	5,841	5,176	47.0
40000	**Oklahoma**	3,003,180	61.1	0.6	66.8	55.7	58.8	77.9	60.7	17.7	6.3	1,719,541	922,579	796,962	46.3
40001	Adair County, Oklahoma	16,940	53.4	0.0	57.0	50.0	48.5	69.7	52.8	14.0	7.9	8,336	4,390	3,946	47.3
40003	Alfalfa County, Oklahoma	4,777	47.9	0.0	47.2	49.0	56.0	56.5	53.3	21.3	4.9	2,176	1,321	855	39.3
40005	Atoka County, Oklahoma	11,107	46.3	0.0	44.4	48.5	54.2	59.2	44.3	13.9	8.7	4,695	2,378	2,317	49.4
40007	Beaver County, Oklahoma	4,291	61.4	0.1	70.3	52.4	48.1	79.0	64.4	29.0	3.0	2,555	1,471	1,084	42.4
40009	Beckham County, Oklahoma	17,915	55.2	0.0	61.1	48.4	43.8	67.9	60.5	18.6	2.9	9,611	5,759	3,852	40.1

Table C. County—Labor Force, Employment, and Educational Data, 2011–2015—*Continued*

Fips code	State/county	Total population age 16 and older	Percent in civilian labor force	Percent in armed forces	Civilian labor force participation by gender		Civilian labor force participation by age				Civilian unemployment rate	Civilian employed population age 16 and older			
					Men	Women	Age 16 to 24	Age 25 to 54	Age 55 to 64	Age 65 and older		Total	Men	Women	Percent women
40011	Blaine County, Oklahoma	7,597	44.4	0.0	38.5	51.0	55.3	50.7	52.9	19.6	3.0	3,270	1,505	1,765	54.0
40013	Bryan County, Oklahoma	34,904	57.6	0.0	62.8	52.7	61.1	76.6	55.3	14.0	8.1	18,472	9,716	8,756	47.4
40015	Caddo County, Oklahoma	22,874	54.1	0.0	59.3	48.4	45.9	72.0	50.4	17.9	9.5	11,208	6,407	4,801	42.8
40017	Canadian County, Oklahoma	96,023	68.7	0.2	73.1	64.5	62.4	83.9	68.5	20.1	4.5	63,025	33,061	29,964	47.5
40019	Carter County, Oklahoma	37,413	59.2	0.0	66.1	52.9	62.6	75.8	58.0	17.4	6.1	20,820	11,219	9,601	46.1
40021	Cherokee County, Oklahoma	38,325	54.7	0.1	56.7	52.7	52.7	73.6	52.1	14.0	7.9	19,314	9,749	9,565	49.5
40023	Choctaw County, Oklahoma	11,806	49.3	0.0	52.4	46.5	55.2	71.5	41.9	11.6	8.9	5,308	2,685	2,623	49.4
40025	Cimarron County, Oklahoma	1,861	62.1	0.0	72.0	52.5	56.8	78.6	70.5	35.1	2.2	1,131	655	476	42.1
40027	Cleveland County, Oklahoma	214,233	65.7	0.6	70.3	61.2	60.3	81.3	64.5	20.7	4.9	133,949	71,182	62,767	46.9
40029	Coal County, Oklahoma	4,558	55.4	0.0	62.7	48.8	52.3	77.7	59.1	16.7	9.1	2,296	1,220	1,076	46.9
40031	Comanche County, Oklahoma	97,949	55.5	9.8	55.2	55.8	44.2	68.3	61.9	17.1	8.6	49,641	25,974	23,667	47.7
40033	Cotton County, Oklahoma	4,841	59.3	0.5	63.9	55.0	58.5	78.0	67.7	15.6	9.2	2,607	1,387	1,220	46.8
40035	Craig County, Oklahoma	11,883	52.0	0.0	53.3	50.6	49.2	71.2	52.4	13.7	6.4	5,781	3,011	2,770	47.9
40037	Creek County, Oklahoma	55,697	56.6	0.1	64.6	49.0	54.2	75.7	55.8	15.1	5.7	29,749	16,408	13,341	44.8
40039	Custer County, Oklahoma	22,745	64.2	0.0	69.9	58.5	61.2	80.8	68.3	21.1	3.7	14,072	7,709	6,363	45.2
40041	Delaware County, Oklahoma	33,543	52.5	0.0	56.0	49.2	56.6	76.2	52.6	14.8	9.2	15,991	8,459	7,532	47.1
40043	Dewey County, Oklahoma	3,754	56.4	0.1	67.4	45.4	51.4	73.2	60.2	25.8	2.7	2,061	1,229	832	40.4
40045	Ellis County, Oklahoma	3,266	58.8	0.0	65.5	52.3	46.9	82.3	59.1	25.8	5.0	1,824	1,005	819	44.9
40047	Garfield County, Oklahoma	47,989	61.9	2.1	69.0	55.0	61.8	77.7	65.7	19.4	5.6	28,056	15,546	12,510	44.6
40049	Garvin County, Oklahoma	21,421	52.1	0.0	59.8	44.9	41.8	71.8	56.3	13.5	4.4	10,668	5,951	4,717	44.2
40051	Grady County, Oklahoma	41,935	60.0	0.1	66.8	53.5	52.4	77.7	62.8	16.1	4.3	24,086	13,110	10,976	45.6
40053	Grant County, Oklahoma	3,575	60.9	0.1	72.8	49.2	46.9	84.6	66.6	23.9	3.6	2,098	1,253	845	40.3
40055	Greer County, Oklahoma	5,078	48.3	0.0	45.4	52.5	56.8	55.8	54.4	22.3	4.4	2,344	1,305	1,039	44.3
40057	Harmon County, Oklahoma	2,238	55.8	0.0	62.1	49.7	57.6	73.9	61.4	15.7	8.7	1,139	639	500	43.9
40059	Harper County, Oklahoma	2,882	62.7	0.0	75.9	49.9	44.5	87.7	59.3	21.4	1.6	1,779	1,050	729	41.0
40061	Haskell County, Oklahoma	10,120	49.6	0.0	55.6	43.9	47.9	71.2	44.1	14.3	8.7	4,585	2,475	2,110	46.0
40063	Hughes County, Oklahoma	11,202	43.7	0.0	43.2	44.2	33.8	57.4	56.3	12.9	7.1	4,546	2,441	2,105	46.3
40065	Jackson County, Oklahoma	19,744	56.9	6.1	60.9	53.1	58.1	69.4	63.5	15.0	7.6	10,388	5,567	4,821	46.4
40067	Jefferson County, Oklahoma	4,996	53.5	0.0	59.4	47.5	48.3	71.3	65.6	15.3	6.5	2,497	1,389	1,108	44.4
40069	Johnston County, Oklahoma	8,702	50.2	0.0	55.3	45.3	48.8	69.6	49.7	11.6	6.7	4,078	2,179	1,899	46.6
40071	Kay County, Oklahoma	35,427	60.0	0.0	66.7	53.5	65.8	78.6	61.9	17.9	7.8	19,588	10,548	9,040	46.2
40073	Kingfisher County, Oklahoma	11,621	65.1	0.0	74.4	55.9	59.2	84.9	68.2	16.5	3.6	7,289	4,069	3,220	44.2
40075	Kiowa County, Oklahoma	7,386	57.9	0.3	65.6	50.4	55.2	73.7	66.3	22.6	5.5	4,037	2,248	1,789	44.3
40077	Latimer County, Oklahoma	8,626	51.1	0.0	56.3	45.9	56.9	72.8	42.1	12.4	7.8	4,068	2,214	1,854	45.6
40079	Le Flore County, Oklahoma	39,258	51.5	0.0	55.4	47.5	51.9	70.2	47.9	11.4	9.4	18,311	9,762	8,549	46.7
40081	Lincoln County, Oklahoma	26,949	58.4	0.1	64.3	52.7	62.7	77.3	54.8	16.7	7.1	14,625	7,985	6,640	45.4
40083	Logan County, Oklahoma	35,275	61.2	0.1	68.7	54.1	56.1	78.6	63.9	17.8	6.0	20,281	11,167	9,114	44.9
40085	Love County, Oklahoma	7,560	56.9	0.0	63.3	50.6	49.5	77.8	56.4	20.0	4.0	4,127	2,262	1,865	45.2
40087	McClain County, Oklahoma	28,039	62.1	0.2	68.6	55.9	56.0	80.7	59.0	18.5	3.9	16,746	9,182	7,564	45.2
40089	McCurtain County, Oklahoma	25,588	52.6	0.0	57.7	47.8	50.8	70.5	52.6	14.8	8.3	12,348	6,515	5,833	47.2
40091	McIntosh County, Oklahoma	16,571	47.0	0.1	50.2	43.9	51.0	71.3	47.6	11.5	10.8	6,944	3,604	3,340	48.1
40093	Major County, Oklahoma	5,987	62.1	0.0	72.6	51.9	64.4	80.0	70.0	22.4	5.4	3,518	2,073	1,445	41.1
40095	Marshall County, Oklahoma	12,572	52.0	0.0	56.5	47.6	60.6	73.5	44.0	17.0	7.6	6,038	3,253	2,785	46.1
40097	Mayes County, Oklahoma	32,196	56.3	0.1	64.1	48.6	55.6	74.4	56.1	16.7	7.0	16,849	9,570	7,279	43.2
40099	Murray County, Oklahoma	10,929	58.0	0.3	63.6	52.7	59.7	78.8	65.1	11.3	3.6	6,115	3,257	2,858	46.7
40101	Muskogee County, Oklahoma	54,704	54.1	0.1	59.6	48.9	55.6	70.3	53.9	13.4	8.2	27,158	14,450	12,708	46.8
40103	Noble County, Oklahoma	8,985	60.8	0.1	68.5	53.6	56.6	76.9	67.1	23.8	5.9	5,141	2,811	2,330	45.3
40105	Nowata County, Oklahoma	8,379	55.3	0.0	59.4	51.5	50.2	76.1	59.6	13.9	8.4	4,248	2,254	1,994	46.9
40107	Okfuskee County, Oklahoma	9,640	45.2	0.0	45.3	45.1	50.0	57.0	48.6	12.2	9.6	3,942	2,097	1,845	46.8
40109	Oklahoma County, Oklahoma	580,833	64.7	0.7	71.5	58.3	62.5	79.7	62.4	19.4	6.0	353,043	188,378	164,665	46.6
40111	Okmulgee County, Oklahoma	30,876	54.1	0.0	58.6	49.7	56.3	74.6	51.6	10.1	10.4	14,956	7,920	7,036	47.0
40113	Osage County, Oklahoma	38,252	54.2	0.1	59.7	48.7	54.1	72.4	57.7	14.2	7.1	19,274	10,742	8,532	44.3
40115	Ottawa County, Oklahoma	25,081	56.9	0.0	61.0	53.1	57.5	77.1	56.6	16.3	9.4	12,922	6,681	6,241	48.3
40117	Pawnee County, Oklahoma	12,954	56.8	0.0	64.8	49.1	55.3	77.2	56.0	16.5	6.3	6,890	3,858	3,032	44.0
40119	Payne County, Oklahoma	65,704	59.7	0.0	64.7	54.5	53.0	78.8	61.4	17.6	6.3	36,780	20,385	16,395	44.6
40121	Pittsburg County, Oklahoma	35,962	54.7	0.0	59.0	50.2	60.9	72.9	51.1	15.0	6.2	18,459	10,163	8,296	44.9
40123	Pontotoc County, Oklahoma	29,942	62.2	0.0	66.5	58.1	62.6	80.9	60.3	18.4	6.2	17,465	8,883	8,582	49.1
40125	Pottawatomie County, Oklahoma	55,544	56.8	0.2	64.1	50.2	58.8	73.1	54.4	16.1	6.8	29,366	15,447	13,919	47.4
40127	Pushmataha County, Oklahoma	8,997	50.7	0.1	57.0	44.7	60.1	72.7	48.1	12.2	10.6	4,074	2,196	1,878	46.1
40129	Roger Mills County, Oklahoma	2,892	59.2	0.0	67.2	51.3	42.2	78.5	66.9	23.1	0.8	1,698	959	739	43.5
40131	Rogers County, Oklahoma	69,688	63.9	0.1	70.0	57.9	63.5	81.9	66.3	15.6	5.5	42,093	22,770	19,323	45.9
40133	Seminole County, Oklahoma	19,756	51.8	0.0	57.1	47.0	46.9	72.2	50.5	13.5	8.4	9,379	4,945	4,434	47.3
40135	Sequoyah County, Oklahoma	32,643	52.8	0.2	55.7	50.0	55.5	71.4	49.9	10.2	9.8	15,545	7,997	7,548	48.6
40137	Stephens County, Oklahoma	35,388	57.5	0.2	64.0	51.5	55.8	77.8	60.0	14.8	6.6	19,029	10,155	8,874	46.6
40139	Texas County, Oklahoma	16,218	71.2	0.0	78.7	62.7	64.2	86.1	64.2	30.4	3.5	11,144	6,585	4,559	40.9
40141	Tillman County, Oklahoma	6,080	54.8	0.2	59.4	49.9	58.6	72.2	56.6	15.8	7.1	3,098	1,703	1,395	45.0
40143	Tulsa County, Oklahoma	480,773	67.3	0.1	74.4	60.7	64.5	82.6	67.2	21.3	6.5	302,471	161,179	141,292	46.7
40145	Wagoner County, Oklahoma	58,292	63.0	0.1	69.1	57.3	60.7	81.0	58.1	19.9	6.0	34,531	18,461	16,070	46.5
40147	Washington County, Oklahoma	40,835	59.5	0.0	67.5	52.3	65.1	79.7	61.7	14.4	5.3	23,028	12,252	10,776	46.8
40149	Washita County, Oklahoma	8,876	59.0	0.0	71.3	47.0	52.7	77.3	66.3	16.4	3.5	5,057	3,010	2,047	40.5
40151	Woods County, Oklahoma	7,424	60.5	0.1	62.1	58.6	58.3	77.8	67.3	20.9	2.8	4,365	2,432	1,933	44.3
40153	Woodward County, Oklahoma	16,294	60.4	0.1	65.8	54.3	57.2	73.7	65.5	20.1	5.1	9,345	5,352	3,993	42.7
41000	**Oregon**	3,177,669	62.1	0.1	66.8	57.6	59.2	81.2	62.2	14.9	9.3	1,789,807	937,742	852,065	47.6
41001	Baker County, Oregon	13,290	53.4	0.0	53.6	53.1	61.8	76.4	57.6	15.6	10.1	6,376	3,244	3,132	49.1

Table C. County—Labor Force, Employment, and Educational Data, 2011–2015—*Continued*

Fips code	State/county	Total population age 16 and older	Percent in civilian labor force	Percent in armed forces	Civilian labor force participation by gender — Men	Civilian labor force participation by gender — Women	Age 16 to 24	Age 25 to 54	Age 55 to 64	Age 65 and older	Civilian unemployment rate	Civilian employed population age 16 and older — Total	Men	Women	Percent women
41003	Benton County, Oregon	73,678	59.3	0.1	61.8	56.7	49.2	80.4	69.0	16.6	8.6	39,915	20,585	19,330	48.4
41005	Clackamas County, Oregon	313,378	64.6	0.0	71.0	58.5	59.4	83.7	67.7	17.0	8.3	185,660	99,656	86,004	46.3
41007	Clatsop County, Oregon	30,912	58.9	1.7	61.4	56.5	55.2	78.5	65.7	16.4	7.6	16,843	8,541	8,302	49.3
41009	Columbia County, Oregon	39,606	57.0	0.0	61.0	53.1	58.4	76.6	55.2	12.3	9.8	20,362	10,625	9,737	47.8
41011	Coos County, Oregon	52,487	50.6	0.6	54.0	47.4	58.5	73.7	52.9	12.3	11.7	23,458	11,836	11,622	49.5
41013	Crook County, Oregon	17,278	53.7	0.0	58.9	48.7	69.1	76.9	57.1	12.0	13.5	8,014	4,263	3,751	46.8
41015	Curry County, Oregon	19,272	46.4	0.2	47.6	45.3	57.9	78.4	52.7	8.5	11.3	7,930	3,812	4,118	51.9
41017	Deschutes County, Oregon	134,369	61.3	0.0	65.6	57.2	66.3	82.0	61.2	12.3	9.4	74,599	38,590	36,009	48.3
41019	Douglas County, Oregon	88,863	50.7	0.1	54.3	47.3	55.8	76.4	50.8	10.4	12.2	39,563	20,638	18,925	47.8
41021	Gilliam County, Oregon	1,512	57.0	0.0	65.9	48.2	48.1	78.9	63.6	24.9	9.2	783	455	328	41.9
41023	Grant County, Oregon	6,104	51.8	0.4	54.3	49.5	56.4	78.6	56.8	14.7	9.0	2,878	1,422	1,456	50.6
41025	Harney County, Oregon	5,929	58.3	0.0	66.5	50.1	64.9	81.9	56.7	19.5	16.1	2,901	1,685	1,216	41.9
41027	Hood River County, Oregon	17,669	67.1	0.0	74.4	60.0	67.6	85.5	62.5	18.7	5.1	11,251	6,163	5,088	45.2
41029	Jackson County, Oregon	169,407	58.0	0.0	61.9	54.4	61.9	80.0	58.2	15.1	10.8	87,699	44,419	43,280	49.4
41031	Jefferson County, Oregon	17,295	55.2	0.0	58.9	51.3	54.2	72.0	62.2	14.0	14.4	8,167	4,501	3,666	44.9
41033	Josephine County, Oregon	69,241	47.0	0.0	51.1	43.1	52.1	71.5	48.2	10.6	12.3	28,510	14,630	13,880	48.7
41035	Klamath County, Oregon	53,209	55.2	0.4	60.3	50.3	62.3	75.3	56.2	12.0	12.4	25,753	13,880	11,873	46.1
41037	Lake County, Oregon	6,620	51.3	0.0	52.9	49.4	65.5	70.1	49.1	16.5	10.6	3,037	1,757	1,280	42.1
41039	Lane County, Oregon	296,467	59.3	0.0	62.7	56.1	57.5	79.8	60.9	15.1	9.9	158,490	79,865	78,625	49.6
41041	Lincoln County, Oregon	39,266	53.8	0.1	56.4	51.4	56.2	78.1	59.0	15.5	7.9	19,454	9,797	9,657	49.6
41043	Linn County, Oregon	94,202	58.1	0.1	63.8	52.6	57.3	78.3	60.2	11.5	10.6	48,892	26,152	22,740	46.5
41045	Malheur County, Oregon	23,730	50.3	0.0	48.8	52.2	56.0	62.0	55.6	13.5	11.2	10,595	5,790	4,805	45.4
41047	Marion County, Oregon	249,882	61.7	0.1	65.8	57.7	57.9	80.2	61.9	14.0	10.7	137,706	71,899	65,807	47.8
41049	Morrow County, Oregon	8,428	62.7	0.0	71.6	53.2	55.6	82.6	61.6	18.5	8.6	4,827	2,896	1,931	40.0
41051	Multnomah County, Oregon	630,013	68.7	0.0	72.9	64.6	61.2	84.2	64.1	16.5	8.8	394,637	204,344	190,293	48.2
41053	Polk County, Oregon	61,201	59.9	0.2	65.1	55.1	55.8	81.9	65.1	13.5	10.8	32,687	16,692	15,995	48.9
41055	Sherman County, Oregon	1,493	54.3	0.0	64.1	44.5	69.8	76.0	64.3	11.4	7.9	746	445	301	40.3
41057	Tillamook County, Oregon	21,169	49.9	0.2	53.0	46.9	51.3	72.2	54.2	12.1	7.8	9,747	5,188	4,559	46.8
41059	Umatilla County, Oregon	58,982	60.7	0.0	61.5	59.9	60.9	75.2	64.4	16.0	9.4	32,450	17,412	15,038	46.3
41061	Union County, Oregon	20,672	57.4	0.1	62.9	52.2	58.0	79.3	61.4	12.8	7.1	11,024	5,905	5,119	46.4
41063	Wallowa County, Oregon	5,720	56.0	0.0	59.6	52.5	66.7	80.8	60.2	19.9	9.5	2,898	1,449	1,449	50.0
41065	Wasco County, Oregon	20,451	58.6	0.0	62.3	55.1	60.9	80.7	61.3	15.2	9.0	10,907	5,650	5,257	48.2
41067	Washington County, Oregon	434,453	68.9	0.1	76.6	61.6	61.7	83.7	69.0	17.9	7.6	276,371	149,901	126,470	45.8
41069	Wheeler County, Oregon	1,206	51.0	0.0	57.8	44.6	42.9	79.8	68.3	19.4	8.5	563	303	260	46.2
41071	Yamhill County, Oregon	80,215	60.9	0.0	66.1	55.9	60.3	78.8	61.9	15.7	9.7	44,114	23,352	20,762	47.1
42000	**Pennsylvania**	10,384,811	62.8	0.0	67.5	58.3	58.2	82.1	66.4	16.8	7.9	6,001,889	3,104,353	2,897,536	48.3
42001	Adams County, Pennsylvania	83,225	64.4	0.1	69.4	59.5	61.1	86.1	69.1	16.7	5.7	50,517	26,881	23,636	46.8
42003	Allegheny County, Pennsylvania	1,023,076	64.4	0.0	69.5	59.7	59.9	84.3	68.6	17.6	7.1	612,259	312,749	299,510	48.9
42005	Armstrong County, Pennsylvania	56,173	58.2	0.0	64.1	52.4	62.2	81.5	59.0	11.2	8.5	29,897	16,119	13,778	46.1
42007	Beaver County, Pennsylvania	140,026	61.9	0.1	67.5	56.8	63.4	82.9	68.5	14.9	6.8	80,816	41,728	39,088	48.4
42009	Bedford County, Pennsylvania	40,160	60.4	0.0	67.1	53.9	66.8	82.2	64.9	13.6	7.3	22,499	12,295	10,204	45.4
42011	Berks County, Pennsylvania	330,102	65.8	0.0	70.7	61.2	63.2	85.0	69.8	16.8	9.0	197,703	103,070	94,633	47.9
42013	Blair County, Pennsylvania	103,124	59.3	0.0	65.2	53.9	61.0	82.2	59.8	13.3	6.4	57,253	29,780	27,473	48.0
42015	Bradford County, Pennsylvania	50,016	56.5	0.0	62.5	50.8	58.6	78.1	57.0	12.7	5.6	26,689	14,314	12,375	46.4
42017	Bucks County, Pennsylvania	507,923	68.0	0.1	73.9	62.5	63.8	86.1	73.8	21.3	7.0	321,488	168,467	153,021	47.6
42019	Butler County, Pennsylvania	151,237	64.6	0.1	70.6	58.7	61.6	85.1	67.8	15.6	5.9	91,888	49,251	42,637	46.4
42021	Cambria County, Pennsylvania	115,597	54.9	0.1	59.0	50.9	51.3	77.9	59.4	11.8	8.5	58,018	30,111	27,907	48.1
42023	Cameron County, Pennsylvania	4,158	56.8	0.0	64.1	49.6	63.3	80.5	61.5	14.5	4.5	2,254	1,242	1,012	44.9
42025	Carbon County, Pennsylvania	53,167	59.6	0.0	64.9	54.5	62.7	81.6	62.9	11.2	8.6	28,973	15,347	13,626	47.0
42027	Centre County, Pennsylvania	136,421	58.2	0.1	60.4	55.7	43.2	82.0	68.2	15.6	5.1	75,314	40,831	34,483	45.8
42029	Chester County, Pennsylvania	402,820	68.8	0.1	75.4	62.5	58.2	85.7	76.7	22.6	5.9	260,731	138,838	121,893	46.8
42031	Clarion County, Pennsylvania	32,983	56.3	0.0	61.1	51.8	48.8	80.7	60.3	11.2	8.1	17,055	8,854	8,201	48.1
42033	Clearfield County, Pennsylvania	67,859	54.5	0.0	57.5	51.3	56.5	71.5	60.6	12.1	7.8	34,110	18,559	15,551	45.6
42035	Clinton County, Pennsylvania	32,463	58.6	0.1	62.6	54.8	54.9	81.3	64.7	12.8	6.1	17,861	9,185	8,676	48.6
42037	Columbia County, Pennsylvania	56,319	56.7	0.0	61.6	52.2	42.6	82.5	63.7	13.2	5.7	30,123	15,449	14,674	48.7
42039	Crawford County, Pennsylvania	70,717	57.6	0.0	63.9	51.8	59.3	77.7	58.7	14.9	7.2	37,783	20,141	17,642	46.7
42041	Cumberland County, Pennsylvania	197,634	65.0	0.2	69.5	60.6	61.8	84.5	69.6	17.5	5.6	121,280	63,295	57,985	47.8
42043	Dauphin County, Pennsylvania	216,854	65.6	0.1	69.2	62.4	64.6	84.1	65.1	17.0	7.1	132,283	66,281	66,002	49.9
42045	Delaware County, Pennsylvania	450,577	65.1	0.0	70.0	60.7	52.3	83.9	72.4	20.5	8.2	269,220	135,229	133,991	49.8
42047	Elk County, Pennsylvania	25,991	60.7	0.0	65.4	56.1	60.4	84.3	67.4	11.5	5.2	14,947	7,933	7,014	46.9
42049	Erie County, Pennsylvania	225,303	62.0	0.0	65.5	58.7	60.6	80.7	64.7	14.8	8.0	128,541	65,852	62,689	48.8
42051	Fayette County, Pennsylvania	111,554	52.5	0.0	57.1	48.2	57.3	70.9	53.8	11.9	8.4	53,700	28,247	25,453	47.4
42053	Forest County, Pennsylvania	7,149	18.5	0.0	11.1	39.8	6.7	15.6	47.2	10.8	4.8	1,256	554	702	55.9
42055	Franklin County, Pennsylvania	121,114	63.2	0.1	70.1	56.7	63.8	85.1	64.2	15.1	6.9	71,278	38,358	32,920	46.2
42057	Fulton County, Pennsylvania	11,917	59.9	0.1	65.4	54.2	63.3	80.6	60.1	16.2	7.5	6,598	3,617	2,981	45.2
42059	Greene County, Pennsylvania	31,595	49.8	0.0	49.8	49.8	57.4	62.4	51.2	12.8	6.4	14,728	7,613	7,115	48.3
42061	Huntingdon County, Pennsylvania	38,192	52.9	0.0	51.9	54.0	54.3	69.7	55.7	13.3	8.1	18,580	9,710	8,870	47.7
42063	Indiana County, Pennsylvania	73,542	57.4	0.0	62.3	52.4	53.8	79.2	62.2	13.2	7.8	38,903	20,924	17,979	46.2
42065	Jefferson County, Pennsylvania	36,426	58.0	0.1	64.4	51.8	62.1	79.0	62.1	11.8	6.4	19,756	10,688	9,068	45.9
42067	Juniata County, Pennsylvania	19,857	59.5	0.0	67.8	51.4	65.9	79.7	66.5	12.6	5.7	11,152	6,351	4,801	43.1

Table C. County—Labor Force, Employment, and Educational Data, 2011–2015—*Continued*

Fips code	State/county	Total population age 16 and older	Percent in civilian labor force	Percent in armed forces	Civilian labor force participation by gender — Men	Civilian labor force participation by gender — Women	Civilian labor force participation by age — Age 16 to 24	Civilian labor force participation by age — Age 25 to 54	Civilian labor force participation by age — Age 55 to 64	Civilian labor force participation by age — Age 65 and older	Civilian unemployment rate	Civilian employed population age 16 and older — Total	Civilian employed population age 16 and older — Men	Civilian employed population age 16 and older — Women	Percent women
42069	Lackawanna County, Pennsylvania	175,718	59.7	0.1	65.3	54.6	57.0	81.3	62.1	15.4	6.9	97,589	50,289	47,300	48.5
42071	Lancaster County, Pennsylvania	416,312	66.4	0.0	73.5	59.8	65.6	84.0	72.7	20.8	6.1	259,601	138,360	121,241	46.7
42073	Lawrence County, Pennsylvania	73,250	57.8	0.0	63.0	52.9	56.3	79.9	60.9	15.1	7.0	39,340	20,474	18,866	48.0
42075	Lebanon County, Pennsylvania	108,070	64.7	0.2	71.5	58.4	67.3	84.5	70.7	17.4	6.9	65,090	34,520	30,570	47.0
42077	Lehigh County, Pennsylvania	284,482	65.5	0.0	70.6	60.7	63.9	84.0	69.2	16.4	8.5	170,448	88,244	82,204	48.2
42079	Luzerne County, Pennsylvania	264,631	60.4	0.1	64.6	56.3	60.3	80.8	63.3	16.0	7.8	147,243	76,351	70,892	48.1
42081	Lycoming County, Pennsylvania	95,410	61.7	0.0	67.4	56.3	59.7	82.2	64.7	15.4	7.7	54,324	28,710	25,614	47.2
42083	McKean County, Pennsylvania	35,275	57.0	0.0	58.2	55.7	56.9	75.0	62.1	14.0	9.1	18,277	9,472	8,805	48.2
42085	Mercer County, Pennsylvania	95,058	56.5	0.0	59.3	53.9	54.6	78.7	60.1	14.5	6.8	50,055	25,367	24,688	49.3
42087	Mifflin County, Pennsylvania	37,310	56.9	0.0	63.9	50.3	61.1	78.2	61.1	12.4	6.4	19,860	10,754	9,106	45.9
42089	Monroe County, Pennsylvania	137,049	63.6	0.1	68.4	59.0	60.1	82.5	63.1	17.2	12.0	76,767	40,170	36,597	47.7
42091	Montgomery County, Pennsylvania	654,259	68.3	0.0	73.9	63.2	58.6	86.6	75.2	23.0	6.4	418,411	216,237	202,174	48.3
42093	Montour County, Pennsylvania	15,134	59.4	0.0	65.9	53.5	55.1	83.1	63.2	12.0	6.6	8,391	4,365	4,026	48.0
42095	Northampton County, Pennsylvania	244,817	63.8	0.0	69.8	58.2	56.2	85.6	69.0	15.9	7.3	144,854	76,182	68,672	47.4
42097	Northumberland County, Pennsylvania	77,797	56.9	0.1	59.2	54.5	57.2	77.0	59.5	14.4	7.2	41,033	21,404	19,629	47.8
42099	Perry County, Pennsylvania	36,833	66.3	0.1	70.7	62.0	65.1	86.1	65.6	17.0	6.3	22,893	12,213	10,680	46.7
42101	Philadelphia County, Pennsylvania	1,246,606	59.7	0.0	62.5	57.3	51.0	76.8	56.3	14.2	13.9	640,661	306,026	334,635	52.2
42103	Pike County, Pennsylvania	46,874	58.7	0.0	64.0	53.4	57.3	81.8	61.8	14.0	11.6	24,320	13,056	11,264	46.3
42105	Potter County, Pennsylvania	14,059	53.2	0.0	57.5	48.9	51.0	76.7	56.9	13.1	6.9	6,956	3,731	3,225	46.4
42107	Schuylkill County, Pennsylvania	121,125	57.2	0.0	60.2	54.2	58.5	76.5	60.4	13.8	8.8	63,264	33,530	29,734	47.0
42109	Snyder County, Pennsylvania	32,356	63.1	0.0	68.9	57.6	59.8	84.4	70.3	13.1	5.0	19,403	10,344	9,059	46.7
42111	Somerset County, Pennsylvania	64,202	55.5	0.0	58.2	52.5	61.3	74.5	60.5	11.9	6.9	33,159	18,059	15,100	45.5
42113	Sullivan County, Pennsylvania	5,701	50.6	0.1	54.7	46.1	52.4	81.1	55.5	8.7	8.7	2,632	1,476	1,156	43.9
42115	Susquehanna County, Pennsylvania	34,984	59.0	0.1	64.5	53.5	61.4	80.8	60.9	14.6	7.7	19,048	10,346	8,702	45.7
42117	Tioga County, Pennsylvania	34,785	56.8	0.0	62.3	51.5	58.8	79.8	58.7	10.9	7.4	18,289	9,877	8,412	46.0
42119	Union County, Pennsylvania	37,631	49.8	0.1	47.9	52.1	48.6	61.5	60.0	13.5	6.1	17,585	9,331	8,254	46.9
42121	Venango County, Pennsylvania	44,246	57.9	0.0	63.3	52.7	63.2	80.3	57.7	13.2	8.1	23,527	12,462	11,065	47.0
42123	Warren County, Pennsylvania	33,790	58.8	0.0	63.6	54.0	62.6	81.3	63.0	12.5	6.6	18,545	9,944	8,601	46.4
42125	Washington County, Pennsylvania	172,039	62.0	0.0	68.0	56.3	63.9	82.9	64.1	16.6	6.5	99,731	52,267	47,464	47.6
42127	Wayne County, Pennsylvania	43,660	52.7	0.0	52.6	52.8	59.5	68.4	57.5	15.5	7.8	21,211	11,195	10,016	47.2
42129	Westmoreland County, Pennsylvania	301,106	61.1	0.0	66.7	55.9	62.0	83.5	66.1	15.2	5.6	173,533	91,414	82,119	47.3
42131	Wyoming County, Pennsylvania	23,014	61.2	0.0	67.3	55.1	64.8	82.4	58.7	16.3	7.6	13,003	7,075	5,928	45.6
42133	York County, Pennsylvania	351,957	66.6	0.1	71.6	61.8	65.4	85.1	68.8	17.7	7.3	217,393	113,245	104,148	47.9
44000	**Rhode Island**	865,174	65.5	0.4	69.7	61.6	60.9	84.1	69.1	18.4	8.5	518,170	263,514	254,656	49.1
44001	Bristol County, Rhode Island	40,795	65.2	0.2	68.8	61.9	55.2	89.2	73.0	19.2	6.8	24,777	12,419	12,358	49.9
44003	Kent County, Rhode Island	136,605	68.8	0.1	74.4	63.7	70.3	87.3	72.8	19.4	8.2	86,274	44,261	42,013	48.7
44005	Newport County, Rhode Island	69,161	63.7	3.0	67.0	60.4	62.7	81.7	70.3	22.3	6.9	40,977	20,945	20,032	48.9
44007	Providence County, Rhode Island	512,519	64.9	0.1	68.9	61.3	59.9	82.7	66.7	16.6	9.5	301,318	152,539	148,779	49.4
44009	Washington County, Rhode Island	106,094	65.3	0.3	69.9	61.0	59.0	87.0	71.8	21.7	6.4	64,824	33,350	31,474	48.6
45000	**South Carolina**	3,816,548	60.1	0.8	64.3	56.2	56.1	79.4	58.4	15.5	9.5	2,075,274	1,066,845	1,008,429	48.6
45001	Abbeville County, South Carolina	20,248	51.4	0.0	56.4	46.8	53.5	75.1	44.7	11.8	10.7	9,294	4,789	4,505	48.5
45003	Aiken County, South Carolina	131,421	58.6	0.2	65.0	52.8	58.7	79.9	55.5	13.5	9.9	69,420	36,572	32,848	47.3
45005	Allendale County, South Carolina	8,084	45.8	0.0	39.4	53.4	45.8	56.0	57.7	9.0	22.6	2,866	1,174	1,692	59.0
45007	Anderson County, South Carolina	151,396	59.1	0.0	64.3	54.3	59.9	79.7	55.1	13.9	9.2	81,226	42,416	38,810	47.8
45009	Bamberg County, South Carolina	12,574	49.3	0.1	52.2	46.8	28.0	76.2	55.4	16.8	10.9	5,527	2,729	2,798	50.6
45011	Barnwell County, South Carolina	17,270	54.5	0.1	54.2	54.8	47.6	75.6	53.5	13.1	14.7	8,026	3,821	4,205	52.4
45013	Beaufort County, South Carolina	140,301	54.1	4.1	57.7	50.7	55.8	78.7	56.2	17.1	7.2	70,487	36,999	33,488	47.5
45015	Berkeley County, South Carolina	150,726	62.2	3.0	65.4	59.2	52.4	79.8	57.9	15.0	9.9	84,494	44,189	40,305	47.7
45017	Calhoun County, South Carolina	12,328	57.3	0.1	60.6	54.3	42.5	83.0	60.9	14.8	8.6	6,455	3,256	3,199	49.6
45019	Charleston County, South Carolina	304,661	65.1	0.7	68.6	61.9	56.6	83.3	63.9	19.0	7.7	183,111	92,983	90,128	49.2

Table C. County—Labor Force, Employment, and Educational Data, 2011–2015—*Continued*

Fips code	State/county	Total population age 16 and older	Percent in civilian labor force	Percent in armed forces	Civilian labor force participation by gender		Civilian labor force participation by age				Civilian unemploy-ment rate	Civilian employed population age 16 and older			
					Men	Women	Age 16 to 24	Age 25 to 54	Age 55 to 64	Age 65 and older		Total	Men	Women	Percent women
45021	Cherokee County, South Carolina	43,901	53.4	0.0	59.6	47.8	53.4	70.4	48.2	13.3	10.6	20,966	11,236	9,730	46.4
45023	Chester County, South Carolina	25,966	54.9	0.2	61.5	48.9	50.0	76.7	51.3	12.8	13.8	12,296	6,404	5,892	47.9
45025	Chesterfield County, South Carolina	36,625	54.0	0.0	59.1	49.1	48.6	73.9	48.8	12.8	10.3	17,730	9,578	8,152	46.0
45027	Clarendon County, South Carolina	27,953	48.9	0.0	48.6	49.1	43.8	71.3	49.5	11.0	16.2	11,443	5,541	5,902	51.6
45029	Colleton County, South Carolina	30,155	56.2	0.2	61.6	51.4	56.3	76.3	54.0	17.3	12.4	14,841	7,649	7,192	48.5
45031	Darlington County, South Carolina	53,954	57.2	0.0	61.2	53.7	57.5	77.3	51.7	15.2	15.9	25,949	13,014	12,935	49.8
45033	Dillon County, South Carolina	24,116	51.6	0.1	57.0	46.9	45.5	70.5	48.3	10.9	13.2	10,805	5,508	5,297	49.0
45035	Dorchester County, South Carolina	112,218	64.6	1.0	68.8	60.8	57.9	79.8	62.4	16.0	8.0	66,723	34,509	32,214	48.3
45037	Edgefield County, South Carolina	21,982	50.4	0.1	50.4	50.5	41.4	64.8	50.9	17.1	8.9	10,099	5,649	4,450	44.1
45039	Fairfield County, South Carolina	18,917	52.7	0.1	59.0	47.0	52.6	70.9	52.4	12.6	12.8	8,693	4,442	4,251	48.9
45041	Florence County, South Carolina	108,444	61.2	0.1	65.6	57.4	56.9	80.3	57.6	16.6	12.1	58,296	28,647	29,649	50.9
45043	Georgetown County, South Carolina	49,832	51.4	0.3	56.4	47.0	59.7	75.7	50.2	14.1	11.2	22,756	11,526	11,230	49.3
45045	Greenville County, South Carolina	375,054	63.4	0.1	70.0	57.4	58.0	80.4	65.3	16.5	7.6	219,810	116,424	103,386	47.0
45047	Greenwood County, South Carolina	55,478	59.0	0.0	64.5	54.3	61.5	78.5	56.7	14.0	12.9	28,506	14,351	14,155	49.7
45049	Hampton County, South Carolina	16,459	53.1	0.0	52.4	53.9	54.6	69.8	49.1	12.9	11.0	7,787	3,850	3,937	50.6
45051	Horry County, South Carolina	239,962	59.0	0.1	63.7	54.6	64.3	81.9	55.4	15.1	8.7	129,161	66,657	62,504	48.4
45053	Jasper County, South Carolina	21,243	62.5	0.6	65.6	59.5	65.0	80.4	60.2	14.0	11.9	11,707	5,941	5,766	49.3
45055	Kershaw County, South Carolina	49,514	59.5	0.6	62.9	56.3	56.3	78.5	61.0	14.8	10.5	26,360	13,019	13,341	50.6
45057	Lancaster County, South Carolina	65,089	56.6	0.0	61.3	52.1	60.6	78.8	47.5	13.5	9.9	33,151	17,290	15,861	47.8
45059	Laurens County, South Carolina	53,295	57.6	0.0	62.5	53.0	56.7	76.5	58.1	14.2	10.7	27,397	14,164	13,233	48.3
45061	Lee County, South Carolina	14,860	48.6	0.0	44.7	52.8	47.9	64.8	46.9	11.2	14.9	6,146	2,857	3,289	53.5
45063	Lexington County, South Carolina	216,261	66.0	0.2	71.5	61.0	61.3	84.1	64.0	17.7	7.5	132,105	69,289	62,816	47.6
45065	McCormick County, South Carolina	8,751	39.6	0.0	36.7	43.1	52.7	58.3	42.0	12.5	14.3	2,970	1,481	1,489	50.1
45067	Marion County, South Carolina	25,296	54.5	0.2	60.3	49.8	48.7	76.9	47.9	15.1	13.9	11,875	5,732	6,143	51.7
45069	Marlboro County, South Carolina	23,006	49.4	0.1	45.0	54.5	51.8	60.2	54.5	11.9	15.5	9,600	4,771	4,829	50.3
45071	Newberry County, South Carolina	30,395	57.8	0.2	61.5	54.3	48.5	80.8	59.2	15.7	10.2	15,784	8,044	7,740	49.0
45073	Oconee County, South Carolina	61,306	52.4	0.1	57.9	47.2	51.9	75.7	55.6	10.6	10.4	28,796	15,379	13,417	46.6
45075	Orangeburg County, South Carolina	72,350	53.6	0.0	56.9	50.8	46.4	76.3	49.7	14.0	12.8	33,811	16,632	17,179	50.8
45077	Pickens County, South Carolina	99,115	56.5	0.0	60.8	52.2	46.7	78.7	59.6	14.3	9.2	50,816	26,753	24,063	47.4
45079	Richland County, South Carolina	320,115	63.6	3.7	64.5	62.8	54.6	80.0	63.9	18.9	9.4	184,364	89,475	94,889	51.5
45081	Saluda County, South Carolina	16,024	55.6	0.0	65.0	46.1	54.9	75.7	54.6	14.1	9.0	8,107	4,765	3,342	41.2
45083	Spartanburg County, South Carolina	229,652	61.3	0.0	66.8	56.3	61.6	79.5	57.8	15.3	8.9	128,253	66,595	61,658	48.1
45085	Sumter County, South Carolina	83,962	57.1	2.8	59.5	54.9	54.4	74.6	55.7	13.2	12.4	41,972	20,864	21,108	50.3
45087	Union County, South Carolina	22,711	55.7	0.2	61.7	50.3	57.5	76.5	53.1	14.0	12.3	11,086	5,737	5,349	48.3
45089	Williamsburg County, South Carolina	26,628	48.5	0.0	47.6	49.3	46.9	66.5	49.2	9.9	11.6	11,416	5,147	6,269	54.9
45091	York County, South Carolina	186,950	66.3	0.0	72.8	60.3	58.2	84.0	66.0	16.3	8.9	112,791	58,997	53,794	47.7
46000	**South Dakota**	657,804	68.6	0.4	72.6	64.6	67.5	86.1	72.9	21.7	4.5	430,853	226,674	204,179	47.4
46003	Aurora County, South Dakota	2,122	64.9	0.1	69.5	60.1	64.6	90.9	72.7	19.4	1.9	1,352	750	602	44.5
46005	Beadle County, South Dakota	13,926	68.0	0.0	76.4	59.7	67.1	86.4	74.0	20.8	2.9	9,189	5,117	4,072	44.3
46007	Bennett County, South Dakota	2,397	57.1	0.0	60.9	53.5	33.1	77.1	58.6	27.6	14.7	1,168	590	578	49.5
46009	Bon Homme County, South Dakota	5,843	48.5	0.0	41.4	58.8	45.4	57.0	67.3	21.5	0.9	2,806	1,426	1,380	49.2
46011	Brookings County, South Dakota	27,329	71.8	0.0	76.1	67.3	68.1	89.3	75.6	22.9	3.1	19,007	10,338	8,669	45.6
46013	Brown County, South Dakota	30,154	70.6	0.2	76.5	65.1	66.6	90.8	75.6	21.8	2.5	20,762	10,811	9,951	47.9
46015	Brule County, South Dakota	4,151	63.9	0.0	68.2	59.9	51.4	82.9	82.0	18.4	2.6	2,583	1,328	1,255	48.6
46017	Buffalo County, South Dakota	1,366	57.1	0.0	64.3	50.3	44.8	73.1	52.9	20.7	16.3	653	354	299	45.8
46019	Butte County, South Dakota	7,989	64.7	0.4	72.5	57.2	58.9	84.5	69.1	25.0	3.0	5,015	2,724	2,291	45.7
46021	Campbell County, South Dakota	1,241	61.7	0.0	60.6	62.7	57.8	89.8	69.0	23.5	1.4	755	347	408	54.0
46023	Charles Mix County, South Dakota	6,850	59.9	0.1	64.8	55.2	52.4	79.7	67.7	24.1	5.1	3,894	2,049	1,845	47.4
46025	Clark County, South Dakota	2,889	65.0	0.0	75.4	54.3	65.6	86.1	78.6	22.2	2.8	1,826	1,078	748	41.0

Table C. County—Labor Force, Employment, and Educational Data, 2011–2015—*Continued*

Fips code	State/county	Total population age 16 and older	Percent in civilian labor force	Percent in armed forces	Civilian labor force participation by gender		Civilian labor force participation by age				Civilian unemploy-ment rate	Civilian employed population age 16 and older			
					Men	Women	Age 16 to 24	Age 25 to 54	Age 55 to 64	Age 65 and older		Total	Men	Women	Percent women
46027	Clay County, South Dakota	11,909	67.6	0.2	68.5	66.8	68.2	81.4	67.5	25.9	6.8	7,510	3,733	3,777	50.3
46029	Codington County, South Dakota	21,691	73.9	0.0	79.5	68.4	76.6	93.2	76.9	20.6	2.9	15,575	8,261	7,314	47.0
46031	Corson County, South Dakota	2,868	61.3	0.0	67.4	54.9	53.5	73.8	64.3	27.1	29.4	1,240	698	542	43.7
46033	Custer County, South Dakota	7,135	56.5	0.1	62.5	50.6	49.2	83.6	62.2	18.3	5.2	3,823	2,087	1,736	45.4
46035	Davison County, South Dakota	15,672	68.3	0.0	73.0	63.7	78.2	89.1	74.3	12.2	3.3	10,359	5,489	4,870	47.0
46037	Day County, South Dakota	4,487	61.5	0.0	66.4	56.5	74.3	87.0	77.2	14.2	3.9	2,652	1,442	1,210	45.6
46039	Deuel County, South Dakota	3,477	68.7	0.0	72.3	65.1	64.9	90.5	69.8	32.1	3.1	2,317	1,242	1,075	46.4
46041	Dewey County, South Dakota	3,805	66.3	0.0	70.1	62.7	58.3	78.1	69.4	31.0	24.6	1,900	955	945	49.7
46043	Douglas County, South Dakota	2,356	65.5	0.0	69.2	62.0	83.2	88.8	74.7	23.6	0.4	1,538	795	743	48.3
46045	Edmunds County, South Dakota	3,208	65.7	0.0	67.1	64.5	66.4	90.1	77.5	20.4	1.8	2,070	1,024	1,046	50.5
46047	Fall River County, South Dakota	5,868	53.4	0.2	52.8	54.1	64.3	77.6	58.1	15.8	4.1	3,005	1,497	1,508	50.2
46049	Faulk County, South Dakota	1,908	61.3	0.0	64.0	58.6	67.8	85.0	69.0	22.9	0.7	1,162	612	550	47.3
46051	Grant County, South Dakota	5,914	69.7	0.1	78.6	60.1	79.9	89.6	75.9	23.1	4.1	3,953	2,347	1,606	40.6
46053	Gregory County, South Dakota	3,363	61.0	0.1	67.0	54.9	69.0	85.5	70.6	20.1	2.1	2,007	1,109	898	44.7
46055	Haakon County, South Dakota	1,647	63.4	0.0	74.7	52.6	69.9	85.0	76.6	18.7	2.5	1,018	574	444	43.6
46057	Hamlin County, South Dakota	4,329	68.1	0.0	76.8	59.1	65.7	89.8	76.0	23.9	2.5	2,874	1,642	1,232	42.9
46059	Hand County, South Dakota	2,753	65.3	0.0	70.9	59.6	86.0	88.7	75.8	24.3	1.7	1,768	966	802	45.4
46061	Hanson County, South Dakota	2,408	70.3	0.1	75.8	64.7	54.0	90.2	73.8	29.3	1.1	1,673	916	757	45.2
46063	Harding County, South Dakota	1,065	65.2	0.0	74.1	55.3	45.3	83.7	76.3	26.4	1.4	684	410	274	40.1
46065	Hughes County, South Dakota	13,849	71.7	0.1	78.9	64.9	65.8	87.2	78.0	26.4	3.1	9,620	5,106	4,514	46.9
46067	Hutchinson County, South Dakota	5,758	67.0	0.0	71.1	62.9	64.4	92.7	76.5	27.9	3.0	3,745	1,964	1,781	47.6
46069	Hyde County, South Dakota	1,151	67.4	0.0	76.3	58.3	70.0	87.3	80.2	25.7	1.8	762	431	331	43.4
46071	Jackson County, South Dakota	2,342	62.2	0.0	66.9	57.5	49.5	83.1	65.1	24.2	17.4	1,202	645	557	46.3
46073	Jerauld County, South Dakota	1,593	65.4	0.0	74.2	57.5	50.0	89.5	76.4	28.2	0.9	1,033	555	478	46.3
46075	Jones County, South Dakota	676	74.0	0.0	76.4	71.6	91.7	93.2	85.0	26.7	3.6	482	245	237	49.2
46077	Kingsbury County, South Dakota	4,087	65.7	0.0	70.8	60.6	74.9	91.3	74.2	14.8	2.0	2,631	1,424	1,207	45.9
46079	Lake County, South Dakota	9,873	68.6	0.0	73.4	63.5	68.4	89.6	75.1	26.8	4.4	6,468	3,505	2,963	45.8
46081	Lawrence County, South Dakota	20,642	65.5	0.1	69.9	61.2	69.1	87.4	66.6	17.6	3.8	13,004	6,936	6,068	46.7
46083	Lincoln County, South Dakota	36,391	77.4	0.1	82.2	72.7	70.9	90.9	78.5	22.0	1.9	27,623	14,342	13,281	48.1
46085	Lyman County, South Dakota	2,860	64.9	0.0	68.4	61.1	57.4	81.0	76.3	23.4	7.4	1,719	957	762	44.3
46087	McCook County, South Dakota	4,311	70.4	0.1	79.3	61.7	69.0	90.4	77.5	31.1	2.1	2,974	1,658	1,316	44.3
46089	McPherson County, South Dakota	1,917	56.9	0.0	60.9	52.5	66.8	78.7	78.7	19.9	6.7	1,017	539	478	47.0
46091	Marshall County, South Dakota	3,779	63.8	0.0	68.2	59.1	66.7	89.5	64.6	16.8	0.7	2,394	1,335	1,059	44.2
46093	Meade County, South Dakota	20,655	64.0	5.5	65.6	62.2	61.2	79.5	64.2	22.5	2.3	12,907	6,905	6,002	46.5
46095	Mellette County, South Dakota	1,433	58.7	0.0	64.2	52.9	47.2	75.0	59.4	29.6	12.0	740	419	321	43.4
46097	Miner County, South Dakota	1,782	68.7	0.0	73.1	64.1	60.0	90.4	88.8	25.5	4.1	1,174	617	557	47.4
46099	Minnehaha County, South Dakota	138,870	74.2	0.2	77.8	70.6	73.6	88.7	75.6	22.6	4.4	98,459	50,993	47,466	48.2
46101	Moody County, South Dakota	4,999	72.0	0.0	76.2	67.8	81.6	90.2	77.3	20.6	6.1	3,379	1,784	1,595	47.2
46102	Oglala Lakota County, South Dakota	9,614	47.1	0.0	51.6	43.0	31.7	61.9	43.3	9.2	28.7	3,226	1,526	1,700	52.7
46103	Pennington County, South Dakota	82,954	67.9	1.4	70.1	65.6	69.2	84.2	71.2	20.9	4.8	53,612	27,450	26,162	48.8
46105	Perkins County, South Dakota	2,424	64.4	0.0	69.6	59.1	46.8	87.2	77.7	27.2	4.5	1,490	797	693	46.5
46107	Potter County, South Dakota	1,902	60.4	0.0	68.4	53.0	74.5	82.9	69.8	24.5	0.5	1,142	618	524	45.9
46109	Roberts County, South Dakota	7,705	62.0	0.0	63.6	60.4	57.5	81.5	74.7	21.0	7.6	4,416	2,254	2,162	49.0
46111	Sanborn County, South Dakota	1,975	67.6	0.4	68.3	66.8	64.4	90.0	80.6	18.0	3.4	1,289	683	606	47.0
46115	Spink County, South Dakota	5,143	64.2	0.0	69.4	58.9	63.4	85.0	75.2	20.4	1.1	3,266	1,773	1,493	45.7
46117	Stanley County, South Dakota	2,311	73.5	0.0	78.5	68.2	81.8	93.1	77.6	25.0	1.4	1,674	910	764	45.6
46119	Sully County, South Dakota	1,170	68.5	0.0	78.9	55.7	56.7	90.8	80.3	24.2	1.7	788	499	289	36.7
46121	Todd County, South Dakota	6,238	62.3	0.0	63.9	60.9	58.2	69.7	61.4	36.3	25.4	2,901	1,394	1,507	51.9
46123	Tripp County, South Dakota	4,378	66.8	0.3	72.9	60.6	75.6	83.9	74.2	28.8	2.1	2,863	1,574	1,289	45.0
46125	Turner County, South Dakota	6,554	66.5	0.1	73.8	59.3	70.4	87.8	75.3	20.0	2.5	4,248	2,318	1,930	45.4
46127	Union County, South Dakota	11,600	67.3	0.1	72.1	62.4	59.8	86.2	74.9	18.5	2.9	7,576	4,057	3,519	46.4
46129	Walworth County, South Dakota	4,433	62.1	0.2	65.7	58.8	69.2	86.7	68.1	21.1	5.8	2,595	1,342	1,253	48.3
46135	Yankton County, South Dakota	18,396	64.0	0.2	64.9	63.0	74.4	76.9	73.8	18.5	3.6	11,348	5,922	5,426	47.8
46137	Ziebach County, South Dakota	1,919	68.0	0.0	71.2	64.7	52.0	82.7	68.5	20.8	27.4	948	486	462	48.7
47000	**Tennessee**	5,174,955	61.0	0.3	66.0	56.3	58.8	78.7	59.4	15.9	8.4	2,888,742	1,506,658	1,382,084	47.8
47001	Anderson County, Tennessee	61,310	56.2	0.0	61.3	51.5	60.4	75.2	56.6	14.9	7.7	31,814	16,590	15,224	47.9
47003	Bedford County, Tennessee	35,232	61.3	0.0	68.0	54.9	60.3	77.5	60.7	18.4	7.7	19,939	10,705	9,234	46.3
47005	Benton County, Tennessee	13,503	50.5	0.1	53.3	47.8	52.8	73.5	49.7	12.4	14.3	5,844	3,029	2,815	48.2
47007	Bledsoe County, Tennessee	11,365	46.1	0.1	47.4	44.3	54.3	58.3	46.4	10.4	9.6	4,739	2,747	1,992	42.0
47009	Blount County, Tennessee	101,715	60.0	0.1	65.4	55.0	61.2	80.0	60.3	15.7	7.8	56,262	29,091	27,171	48.3
47011	Bradley County, Tennessee	81,782	60.1	0.0	65.9	54.8	61.2	79.7	53.5	14.6	11.2	43,685	23,136	20,549	47.0
47013	Campbell County, Tennessee	33,014	46.7	0.1	51.5	42.3	49.3	66.6	41.1	9.8	9.9	13,897	7,102	6,795	48.9
47015	Cannon County, Tennessee	11,168	58.8	0.1	65.6	52.3	72.2	77.9	50.1	15.0	12.9	5,724	3,142	2,582	45.1
47017	Carroll County, Tennessee	22,998	52.6	0.0	57.3	48.3	50.7	72.9	57.4	12.0	11.5	10,700	5,590	5,110	47.8
47019	Carter County, Tennessee	47,128	53.6	0.1	57.5	50.0	61.1	73.4	48.9	13.1	8.1	23,210	11,951	11,259	48.5

Table C. County—Labor Force, Employment, and Educational Data, 2011–2015—*Continued*

Fips code	State/county	Total population age 16 and older	Percent in civilian labor force	Percent in armed forces	Civilian labor force participation by gender		Civilian labor force participation by age				Civilian unemploy-ment rate	Civilian employed population age 16 and older			Percent women
					Men	Women	Age 16 to 24	Age 25 to 54	Age 55 to 64	Age 65 and older		Total	Men	Women	
47021	Cheatham County, Tennessee	31,118	64.7	0.1	70.7	59.0	62.7	81.7	63.4	13.0	7.8	18,572	9,992	8,580	46.2
47023	Chester County, Tennessee	14,146	59.1	0.0	65.5	53.4	54.2	81.3	65.3	12.6	13.5	7,235	3,885	3,350	46.3
47025	Claiborne County, Tennessee	26,300	49.5	0.0	54.8	44.4	46.7	69.8	45.5	10.9	8.2	11,935	6,332	5,603	46.9
47027	Clay County, Tennessee	6,503	45.8	0.0	50.0	41.9	46.3	72.0	39.8	10.7	7.2	2,765	1,447	1,318	47.7
47029	Cocke County, Tennessee	28,841	54.9	0.0	59.5	50.6	66.3	72.7	51.5	16.2	11.1	14,071	7,352	6,719	47.8
47031	Coffee County, Tennessee	42,136	56.9	0.1	64.0	50.3	58.1	76.2	55.0	12.2	8.8	21,841	11,875	9,966	45.6
47033	Crockett County, Tennessee	11,350	54.9	0.1	62.6	47.8	50.0	75.1	55.6	12.4	7.4	5,766	3,114	2,652	46.0
47035	Cumberland County, Tennessee	48,113	46.3	0.1	50.5	42.4	60.4	74.9	45.5	10.1	9.0	20,279	10,701	9,578	47.2
47037	Davidson County, Tennessee	529,259	69.5	0.1	74.7	64.8	62.6	83.6	66.9	21.2	7.2	341,548	175,612	165,936	48.6
47039	Decatur County, Tennessee	9,506	53.5	0.0	58.5	48.7	56.0	75.6	57.7	14.8	10.1	4,569	2,403	2,166	47.4
47041	DeKalb County, Tennessee	15,336	52.3	0.0	57.0	47.6	48.5	70.4	55.5	11.5	7.6	7,409	4,003	3,406	46.0
47043	Dickson County, Tennessee	39,957	59.1	0.0	64.1	54.4	54.2	77.8	54.7	16.7	7.5	21,847	11,659	10,188	46.6
47045	Dyer County, Tennessee	29,758	57.9	0.1	63.7	52.7	53.8	78.1	59.5	11.0	6.6	16,095	8,306	7,789	48.4
47047	Fayette County, Tennessee	31,462	59.2	0.0	66.5	52.3	58.1	78.6	59.8	17.5	8.5	17,031	9,270	7,761	45.6
47049	Fentress County, Tennessee	14,417	46.4	0.5	50.4	42.7	58.7	67.2	37.9	8.2	10.4	5,998	3,118	2,880	48.0
47051	Franklin County, Tennessee	33,524	56.1	0.1	62.2	50.3	54.3	79.6	56.4	12.5	9.5	17,027	9,220	7,807	45.9
47053	Gibson County, Tennessee	38,848	57.4	0.2	64.5	51.2	57.9	77.7	56.4	13.8	9.5	20,201	10,479	9,722	48.1
47055	Giles County, Tennessee	23,495	56.1	0.1	61.6	50.9	60.0	77.5	51.7	13.1	9.9	11,881	6,226	5,655	47.6
47057	Grainger County, Tennessee	18,559	53.2	0.0	58.0	48.6	57.1	74.5	45.4	11.2	9.5	8,940	4,861	4,079	45.6
47059	Greene County, Tennessee	56,533	54.6	0.0	57.6	51.7	56.5	75.7	52.2	13.4	8.7	28,160	14,290	13,870	49.3
47061	Grundy County, Tennessee	10,889	46.3	0.0	51.4	41.5	46.2	66.2	41.3	13.4	10.2	4,529	2,431	2,098	46.3
47063	Hamblen County, Tennessee	49,980	55.8	0.2	62.9	49.2	55.4	74.8	51.0	16.1	10.1	25,095	13,836	11,259	44.9
47065	Hamilton County, Tennessee	282,160	62.7	0.1	68.2	57.8	61.3	81.6	62.2	16.0	8.0	162,818	84,482	78,336	48.1
47067	Hancock County, Tennessee	5,398	47.2	0.0	50.1	44.4	52.2	66.5	37.3	13.0	12.1	2,240	1,151	1,089	48.6
47069	Hardeman County, Tennessee	21,538	47.1	0.0	44.7	50.1	51.2	59.9	44.1	12.5	18.7	8,256	4,368	3,888	47.1
47071	Hardin County, Tennessee	21,195	51.7	0.1	59.1	44.8	57.2	72.8	47.6	15.0	13.9	9,438	5,276	4,162	44.1
47073	Hawkins County, Tennessee	45,954	52.9	0.0	58.8	47.4	62.2	73.8	46.5	9.7	10.0	21,893	11,672	10,221	46.7
47075	Haywood County, Tennessee	14,457	55.6	0.0	58.4	53.2	47.9	72.3	60.7	16.7	10.5	7,194	3,409	3,785	52.6
47077	Henderson County, Tennessee	22,158	55.4	0.0	60.5	50.7	54.3	74.0	53.4	13.1	9.4	11,115	5,898	5,217	46.9
47079	Henry County, Tennessee	26,095	53.4	0.4	59.2	48.1	61.1	72.5	56.0	15.3	9.7	12,592	6,549	6,043	48.0
47081	Hickman County, Tennessee	19,545	52.6	0.0	53.4	51.6	57.1	64.9	58.0	11.0	8.6	9,388	4,954	4,434	47.2
47083	Houston County, Tennessee	6,578	49.6	0.0	59.7	40.0	40.5	73.3	42.1	15.2	8.1	2,997	1,778	1,219	40.7
47085	Humphreys County, Tennessee	14,703	52.7	0.1	58.2	47.4	47.2	75.1	52.3	11.5	8.9	7,067	3,857	3,210	45.4
47087	Jackson County, Tennessee	9,560	47.0	0.0	52.7	41.3	44.3	70.5	43.6	8.0	14.5	3,842	2,196	1,646	42.8
47089	Jefferson County, Tennessee	42,913	59.0	0.1	62.1	56.1	63.8	78.3	57.5	17.6	9.1	23,000	11,687	11,313	49.2
47091	Johnson County, Tennessee	15,173	43.8	0.1	41.8	46.1	52.4	58.1	48.0	7.8	9.0	6,048	3,141	2,907	48.1
47093	Knox County, Tennessee	359,557	64.1	0.1	70.6	58.0	58.8	82.9	65.3	15.1	6.5	215,253	113,718	101,535	47.2
47095	Lake County, Tennessee	6,586	31.1	0.0	24.3	44.8	30.7	34.4	41.1	12.1	10.1	1,840	952	888	48.3
47097	Lauderdale County, Tennessee	21,773	48.2	0.0	46.4	50.3	39.7	60.8	45.5	19.3	13.4	9,099	4,563	4,536	49.9
47099	Lawrence County, Tennessee	32,750	56.8	0.0	63.8	50.4	60.6	77.0	56.2	11.3	10.8	16,607	8,961	7,646	46.0
47101	Lewis County, Tennessee	9,564	55.0	0.5	56.5	53.6	61.5	72.2	60.6	14.4	7.7	4,858	2,358	2,500	51.5
47103	Lincoln County, Tennessee	26,837	57.4	0.0	63.9	51.3	62.2	77.2	58.3	13.0	7.6	14,232	7,718	6,514	45.8
47105	Loudon County, Tennessee	41,392	52.8	0.0	60.6	45.5	56.8	78.7	53.6	13.7	8.9	19,909	11,033	8,876	44.6
47107	McMinn County, Tennessee	42,470	53.9	0.3	60.0	48.3	59.0	72.9	52.8	12.9	9.3	20,767	11,317	9,450	45.5
47109	McNairy County, Tennessee	20,855	50.1	0.1	57.5	43.2	65.3	66.8	46.7	13.1	14.9	8,901	4,959	3,942	44.3
47111	Macon County, Tennessee	18,045	57.8	0.0	63.2	52.7	51.5	78.7	52.5	13.6	7.4	9,657	5,247	4,410	45.7
47113	Madison County, Tennessee	77,971	60.3	0.0	64.9	56.2	54.9	78.0	61.7	17.1	8.4	43,039	21,747	21,292	49.5
47115	Marion County, Tennessee	23,017	55.4	0.4	62.9	48.4	52.1	76.4	53.5	14.0	6.7	11,895	6,455	5,440	45.7
47117	Marshall County, Tennessee	24,602	60.5	0.0	69.2	52.5	62.9	77.1	60.7	13.1	8.4	13,637	7,526	6,111	44.8
47119	Maury County, Tennessee	65,948	63.8	0.2	68.7	59.3	66.0	82.2	57.9	17.0	7.7	38,831	19,688	19,143	49.3
47121	Meigs County, Tennessee	9,543	48.1	0.0	52.7	43.6	55.0	64.6	47.1	13.2	15.0	3,907	2,219	1,688	43.2
47123	Monroe County, Tennessee	36,695	50.4	0.0	56.2	44.8	54.4	69.5	52.4	8.4	12.5	16,178	8,876	7,302	45.1
47125	Montgomery County, Tennessee	140,281	57.7	8.8	58.6	56.9	53.5	67.0	60.2	14.7	9.7	73,139	37,303	35,836	49.0
47127	Moore County, Tennessee	5,261	61.9	0.0	68.4	55.6	63.3	87.9	64.1	13.0	6.5	3,045	1,620	1,425	46.8
47129	Morgan County, Tennessee	18,031	41.8	0.0	38.0	46.7	41.9	51.7	44.3	11.6	8.5	6,893	3,527	3,366	48.8
47131	Obion County, Tennessee	24,977	56.7	0.1	61.2	52.6	66.2	75.4	53.3	15.3	11.2	12,572	6,581	5,991	47.7
47133	Overton County, Tennessee	17,745	51.8	0.1	55.2	48.6	56.2	70.0	54.0	12.0	7.7	8,479	4,326	4,153	49.0
47135	Perry County, Tennessee	6,329	49.2	0.0	52.0	46.4	52.9	72.0	45.8	9.8	9.5	2,819	1,511	1,308	46.4
47137	Pickett County, Tennessee	4,284	53.2	0.0	58.2	48.3	58.5	81.2	55.3	12.0	4.9	2,166	1,136	1,030	47.6
47139	Polk County, Tennessee	13,646	52.6	0.0	54.2	51.0	55.1	73.6	51.5	9.8	10.9	6,397	3,247	3,150	49.2
47141	Putnam County, Tennessee	60,062	55.2	0.1	58.5	52.0	50.7	74.3	57.9	14.1	8.4	30,346	15,459	14,887	49.1
47143	Rhea County, Tennessee	25,725	54.6	0.0	59.6	49.9	57.3	72.8	52.4	15.1	11.1	12,496	6,799	5,697	45.6
47145	Roane County, Tennessee	43,937	52.0	0.1	57.6	46.6	54.9	72.0	54.8	13.2	9.8	20,586	10,813	9,773	47.5
47147	Robertson County, Tennessee	52,448	65.8	0.1	72.5	59.5	65.2	82.1	64.1	16.4	8.4	31,579	16,953	14,626	46.3
47149	Rutherford County, Tennessee	218,206	69.7	0.2	75.7	63.9	65.3	83.9	66.2	16.1	6.8	141,737	75,143	66,594	47.0
47151	Scott County, Tennessee	17,271	52.5	0.0	57.2	48.0	57.7	71.0	39.1	12.1	14.1	7,780	4,034	3,746	48.1
47153	Sequatchie County, Tennessee	11,627	53.7	0.0	58.1	49.5	60.1	73.0	50.4	13.9	9.0	5,676	3,056	2,620	46.2
47155	Sevier County, Tennessee	75,739	63.9	0.1	68.1	60.0	71.7	80.1	65.6	21.1	7.4	44,811	22,549	22,262	49.7
47157	Shelby County, Tennessee	724,428	65.4	0.2	69.4	62.0	57.1	81.2	63.1	20.6	10.3	425,295	211,999	213,296	50.2
47159	Smith County, Tennessee	15,053	56.9	0.1	64.3	49.9	52.3	73.1	57.0	18.0	5.2	8,121	4,526	3,595	44.3
47161	Stewart County, Tennessee	10,701	50.1	0.8	51.5	48.7	55.6	70.5	48.1	8.2	10.1	4,818	2,391	2,427	50.4
47163	Sullivan County, Tennessee	129,233	55.9	0.0	61.5	50.8	61.2	76.8	54.7	14.6	8.2	66,313	34,645	31,668	47.8
47165	Sumner County, Tennessee	132,923	65.8	0.2	72.0	60.0	62.0	83.4	65.1	18.8	6.0	82,224	43,263	38,961	47.4

Table C. County—Labor Force, Employment, and Educational Data, 2011–2015—*Continued*

Fips code	State/county	Total population age 16 and older	Percent in civilian labor force	Percent in armed forces	Civilian labor force participation by gender — Men	Civilian labor force participation by gender — Women	Age 16 to 24	Age 25 to 54	Age 55 to 64	Age 65 and older	Civilian unemploy-ment rate	Civilian employed population age 16 and older — Total	Men	Women	Percent women
47167	Tipton County, Tennessee	47,698	63.8	0.4	69.1	58.9	58.5	79.0	66.3	17.5	10.6	27,209	14,475	12,734	46.8
47169	Trousdale County, Tennessee	6,255	60.3	0.8	66.9	54.0	68.3	75.6	52.7	22.2	10.5	3,376	1,786	1,590	47.1
47171	Unicoi County, Tennessee	15,028	49.8	0.0	54.4	45.5	45.7	74.7	50.6	6.9	13.7	6,462	3,434	3,028	46.9
47173	Union County, Tennessee	15,304	49.0	0.0	55.6	42.6	48.6	67.6	40.8	10.0	9.5	6,792	3,792	3,000	44.2
47175	Van Buren County, Tennessee	4,641	53.8	0.0	54.6	53.0	54.5	76.2	48.9	16.5	11.2	2,218	1,086	1,132	51.0
47177	Warren County, Tennessee	31,540	56.2	0.0	62.4	50.2	56.9	74.0	51.8	16.8	8.0	16,304	9,040	7,264	44.6
47179	Washington County, Tennessee	103,070	59.2	0.1	64.4	54.3	61.0	79.6	54.7	13.2	6.2	57,193	29,798	27,395	47.9
47181	Wayne County, Tennessee	14,175	45.8	0.0	44.2	47.8	52.5	58.9	48.0	9.2	12.2	5,703	2,980	2,723	47.7
47183	Weakley County, Tennessee	28,425	56.8	0.1	62.1	51.9	51.9	79.4	58.7	14.4	11.2	14,342	7,521	6,821	47.6
47185	White County, Tennessee	21,118	51.7	0.0	58.5	45.3	52.1	73.9	46.9	11.5	10.5	9,769	5,341	4,428	45.3
47187	Williamson County, Tennessee	149,350	68.4	0.0	79.1	58.6	56.5	82.9	71.1	23.6	4.2	97,869	54,394	43,475	44.4
47189	Wilson County, Tennessee	96,167	65.7	0.1	71.4	60.4	62.3	82.8	65.4	18.7	6.5	59,107	30,880	28,227	47.8
48000	**Texas**	20,241,168	64.3	0.5	71.0	57.7	55.2	79.7	63.9	18.7	7.0	12,094,262	6,588,855	5,505,407	45.5
48001	Anderson County, Texas	47,933	43.3	0.0	39.4	50.1	46.6	49.8	46.3	15.0	4.3	19,859	11,386	8,473	42.7
48003	Andrews County, Texas	12,229	67.4	0.0	78.9	55.5	64.1	80.9	68.1	18.5	3.9	7,923	4,757	3,166	40.0
48005	Angelina County, Texas	66,768	59.6	0.1	65.2	54.3	64.2	77.8	53.4	13.5	9.1	36,182	18,919	17,263	47.7
48007	Aransas County, Texas	20,255	50.1	0.0	57.0	43.4	68.1	73.3	51.3	13.8	6.8	9,464	5,368	4,096	43.3
48009	Archer County, Texas	7,102	61.6	0.2	69.0	54.1	56.0	80.8	67.0	19.6	3.0	4,239	2,347	1,892	44.6
48011	Armstrong County, Texas	1,600	60.3	0.0	68.1	52.5	63.6	85.5	59.6	18.2	1.1	954	545	409	42.9
48013	Atascosa County, Texas	35,110	60.8	0.1	69.5	52.4	61.4	79.0	52.0	17.8	6.5	19,975	11,242	8,733	43.7
48015	Austin County, Texas	22,617	63.5	0.0	70.9	56.4	67.5	82.9	66.4	18.0	6.2	13,483	7,481	6,002	44.5
48017	Bailey County, Texas	5,096	65.4	0.0	74.8	55.4	69.1	81.3	70.0	24.6	4.3	3,191	1,874	1,317	41.3
48019	Bandera County, Texas	17,527	54.0	0.0	56.6	51.4	53.5	79.0	60.9	14.9	4.8	9,010	4,704	4,306	47.8
48021	Bastrop County, Texas	59,188	60.6	0.1	65.8	55.2	55.6	74.9	60.7	21.0	9.8	32,343	17,694	14,649	45.3
48023	Baylor County, Texas	2,988	50.4	0.0	67.8	35.7	49.9	74.6	53.6	14.5	1.4	1,486	908	578	38.9
48025	Bee County, Texas	26,625	42.2	0.0	35.7	53.3	39.3	48.4	47.8	15.2	7.0	10,451	5,494	4,957	47.4
48027	Bell County, Texas	243,040	58.0	8.3	59.4	56.6	53.1	69.3	59.0	15.7	9.5	127,550	65,220	62,330	48.9
48029	Bexar County, Texas	1,396,634	63.7	1.3	69.5	58.3	56.2	79.7	60.1	16.4	7.4	824,123	437,764	386,359	46.9
48031	Blanco County, Texas	8,904	56.0	0.1	57.1	55.0	43.7	83.8	54.8	16.6	6.4	4,670	2,266	2,404	51.5
48033	Borden County, Texas	518	54.8	0.0	70.7	39.3	45.5	76.0	68.9	18.2	0.7	282	179	103	36.5
48035	Bosque County, Texas	14,473	53.7	0.0	60.1	47.7	60.6	77.3	54.2	16.5	7.9	7,165	3,917	3,248	45.3
48037	Bowie County, Texas	73,383	53.6	0.1	54.8	52.3	48.9	70.8	50.7	13.8	8.5	35,959	18,350	17,609	49.0
48039	Brazoria County, Texas	251,661	64.8	0.0	70.0	59.4	53.1	79.9	62.3	19.1	5.4	154,290	84,132	70,158	45.5
48041	Brazos County, Texas	167,379	62.8	0.1	66.1	59.4	52.7	80.6	68.0	19.6	6.4	98,294	52,391	45,903	46.7
48043	Brewster County, Texas	7,508	61.4	0.0	67.1	55.7	71.3	80.9	61.9	15.6	4.9	4,385	2,406	1,979	45.1
48045	Briscoe County, Texas	1,304	60.9	0.0	68.7	52.8	47.5	81.9	75.9	26.1	4.7	757	443	314	41.5
48047	Brooks County, Texas	5,781	52.1	0.0	60.3	43.4	47.7	65.1	66.1	20.7	19.8	2,416	1,264	1,152	47.7
48049	Brown County, Texas	30,035	52.2	0.0	56.6	48.1	42.8	71.7	60.3	15.4	4.3	15,006	7,981	7,025	46.8
48051	Burleson County, Texas	13,696	58.0	0.0	66.2	50.2	59.5	74.4	67.9	19.3	7.5	7,352	4,108	3,244	44.1
48053	Burnet County, Texas	35,645	55.2	0.0	62.3	48.3	57.9	78.6	54.9	14.7	5.1	18,673	10,348	8,325	44.6
48055	Caldwell County, Texas	31,203	56.4	0.1	61.0	51.9	41.6	76.3	57.1	14.3	5.2	16,693	9,054	7,639	45.8
48057	Calhoun County, Texas	16,670	60.9	0.1	70.1	51.5	52.4	81.4	61.8	16.8	7.2	9,416	5,508	3,908	41.5
48059	Callahan County, Texas	10,729	50.2	0.0	59.0	41.9	29.2	71.3	58.5	14.7	5.4	5,092	2,901	2,191	43.0
48061	Cameron County, Texas	298,753	55.1	0.1	62.1	48.8	43.1	73.7	55.9	12.6	10.0	148,011	78,461	69,550	47.0
48063	Camp County, Texas	9,604	57.4	0.0	63.9	51.4	53.5	78.2	61.5	14.3	8.5	5,039	2,694	2,345	46.5
48065	Carson County, Texas	4,717	62.6	0.0	71.0	54.7	51.1	80.8	71.1	22.0	1.7	2,902	1,568	1,334	46.0
48067	Cass County, Texas	24,269	54.3	0.0	60.8	48.4	54.2	76.4	56.6	15.3	9.2	11,964	6,356	5,608	46.9
48069	Castro County, Texas	5,800	60.0	0.0	74.3	45.3	46.0	73.5	75.4	25.8	4.7	3,316	2,100	1,216	36.7
48071	Chambers County, Texas	28,155	58.4	0.1	72.3	44.5	47.9	74.5	52.1	14.1	7.8	15,166	9,460	5,706	37.6
48073	Cherokee County, Texas	39,275	53.7	0.0	56.3	50.9	52.1	70.4	52.7	16.6	6.4	19,729	10,432	9,297	47.1
48075	Childress County, Texas	5,772	47.5	0.0	45.3	51.0	27.0	59.6	56.4	24.5	5.2	2,600	1,519	1,081	41.6
48077	Clay County, Texas	8,521	58.0	0.1	65.2	50.9	55.8	79.2	57.7	21.2	6.8	4,605	2,503	2,102	45.6
48079	Cochran County, Texas	2,233	57.7	0.0	67.7	47.5	52.2	78.3	56.8	12.8	8.5	1,180	734	446	37.8
48081	Coke County, Texas	2,668	58.4	0.0	61.3	55.5	58.9	88.6	64.3	16.6	3.1	1,508	776	732	48.5
48083	Coleman County, Texas	6,926	50.9	0.0	55.2	46.6	58.0	67.8	56.0	19.6	8.2	3,235	1,752	1,483	45.8
48085	Collin County, Texas	651,701	71.7	0.1	79.6	64.2	55.9	84.9	73.6	23.7	4.9	444,189	239,993	204,196	46.0
48087	Collingsworth County, Texas	2,306	61.5	0.0	74.6	48.9	66.1	82.1	63.8	23.2	5.2	1,345	835	510	37.9
48089	Colorado County, Texas	16,508	58.0	0.0	64.5	51.8	55.0	79.5	62.3	20.2	4.2	9,169	4,911	4,258	46.4
48091	Comal County, Texas	95,162	59.9	0.2	66.5	53.6	58.4	80.6	61.1	14.0	4.9	54,190	29,586	24,604	45.4
48093	Comanche County, Texas	10,743	52.0	0.0	61.3	43.1	52.9	76.1	51.1	18.0	4.5	5,338	3,137	2,201	41.2
48095	Concho County, Texas	3,451	28.7	0.0	22.6	43.2	19.1	31.5	45.6	14.5	2.8	961	532	429	44.6
48097	Cooke County, Texas	30,611	63.2	0.0	67.2	59.4	57.7	85.4	65.9	18.8	7.0	18,012	9,495	8,517	47.3
48099	Coryell County, Texas	58,204	43.1	14.2	42.5	43.6	29.9	50.2	56.2	16.7	9.5	22,684	11,150	11,534	50.8
48101	Cottle County, Texas	1,162	57.2	0.0	68.2	48.0	61.3	83.1	65.7	25.2	7.5	615	347	268	43.6
48103	Crane County, Texas	3,441	60.7	0.0	78.3	43.6	53.7	78.0	61.5	10.8	5.2	1,980	1,267	713	36.0
48105	Crockett County, Texas	2,969	63.5	0.0	78.3	49.4	51.5	89.1	64.3	10.9	1.8	1,851	1,108	743	40.1
48107	Crosby County, Texas	4,530	60.8	0.1	68.2	54.1	57.7	83.2	65.9	17.0	10.0	2,478	1,400	1,078	43.5
48109	Culberson County, Texas	1,845	59.1	0.0	64.6	53.9	71.9	70.3	59.5	20.7	6.5	1,020	540	480	47.1
48111	Dallam County, Texas	5,079	70.5	0.0	80.3	59.9	70.9	80.8	66.6	25.4	5.6	3,381	2,045	1,336	39.5
48113	Dallas County, Texas	1,881,581	68.5	0.0	76.2	61.2	58.8	81.9	67.0	21.5	7.6	1,191,958	650,511	541,447	45.4
48115	Dawson County, Texas	10,702	50.0	0.0	50.7	49.1	41.0	60.9	53.6	25.2	9.5	4,844	2,878	1,966	40.6
48117	Deaf Smith County, Texas	13,855	64.8	0.0	75.2	54.9	58.4	79.9	66.9	23.3	5.4	8,501	4,873	3,628	42.7
48119	Delta County, Texas	4,166	50.9	0.0	56.3	45.7	43.9	73.3	52.7	15.7	13.6	1,830	1,007	823	45.0

Table C. County—Labor Force, Employment, and Educational Data, 2011–2015—*Continued*

Fips code	State/county	Total population age 16 and older	Percent in civilian labor force	Percent in armed forces	Men	Women	Age 16 to 24	Age 25 to 54	Age 55 to 64	Age 65 and older	Civilian unemployment rate	Total	Men	Women	Percent women
48121	Denton County, Texas	559,855	73.5	0.1	79.8	67.5	61.8	86.0	73.5	22.5	5.7	387,884	204,965	182,919	47.2
48123	DeWitt County, Texas	16,474	51.7	0.0	51.7	51.6	59.7	66.4	58.4	13.9	6.8	7,927	4,117	3,810	48.1
48125	Dickens County, Texas	1,864	46.2	0.0	45.2	47.3	37.8	58.6	63.0	18.4	13.6	744	375	369	49.6
48127	Dimmit County, Texas	7,960	58.9	0.0	62.7	55.3	54.5	78.0	59.8	15.7	10.3	4,210	2,181	2,029	48.2
48129	Donley County, Texas	2,966	49.5	0.5	58.9	40.2	43.1	72.2	52.7	22.9	3.9	1,411	824	587	41.6
48131	Duval County, Texas	9,149	53.2	0.0	56.0	50.0	51.7	71.9	44.4	20.1	10.9	4,336	2,398	1,938	44.7
48133	Eastland County, Texas	14,737	48.3	0.0	51.6	45.4	45.8	65.4	54.8	19.2	4.4	6,803	3,442	3,361	49.4
48135	Ector County, Texas	109,480	67.6	0.0	78.7	56.6	65.6	79.8	63.8	25.0	5.2	70,130	41,027	29,103	41.5
48137	Edwards County, Texas	1,616	59.3	0.0	70.2	51.0	73.9	80.4	77.6	23.3	4.9	912	475	437	47.9
48139	Ellis County, Texas	119,055	67.1	0.1	73.7	60.8	59.3	83.3	65.9	19.7	6.5	74,703	40,208	34,495	46.2
48141	El Paso County, Texas	619,843	57.7	3.1	64.3	51.6	47.0	73.9	58.2	14.4	8.4	327,744	175,563	152,181	46.4
48143	Erath County, Texas	32,491	61.9	0.0	67.9	56.2	57.3	81.2	64.9	20.2	4.1	19,275	10,366	8,909	46.2
48145	Falls County, Texas	14,185	46.1	0.0	51.4	41.5	45.1	58.5	51.4	13.2	7.2	6,068	3,155	2,913	48.0
48147	Fannin County, Texas	27,368	51.9	0.1	52.7	51.0	44.6	69.4	57.6	16.1	6.7	13,259	7,136	6,123	46.2
48149	Fayette County, Texas	20,260	58.7	0.0	63.9	53.7	56.4	84.7	65.4	17.7	1.8	11,669	6,150	5,519	47.3
48151	Fisher County, Texas	3,138	60.7	0.0	66.9	54.5	65.2	85.4	63.1	24.8	7.2	1,767	977	790	44.7
48153	Floyd County, Texas	4,631	61.0	0.0	74.3	48.4	57.8	81.5	73.3	16.6	8.0	2,600	1,527	1,073	41.3
48155	Foard County, Texas	983	50.3	0.0	49.2	51.4	79.7	73.2	43.7	17.6	9.7	446	228	218	48.9
48157	Fort Bend County, Texas	493,742	67.2	0.0	75.1	59.7	47.8	81.8	67.5	22.6	5.1	314,534	170,095	144,439	45.9
48159	Franklin County, Texas	8,286	55.7	0.1	58.7	52.8	53.0	78.9	55.8	15.6	6.6	4,309	2,238	2,071	48.1
48161	Freestone County, Texas	15,559	53.2	0.0	55.5	50.6	57.8	70.3	54.2	14.0	4.9	7,868	4,352	3,516	44.7
48163	Frio County, Texas	14,255	49.0	0.1	47.5	51.2	51.2	57.1	49.8	19.0	5.2	6,618	3,914	2,704	40.9
48165	Gaines County, Texas	12,919	63.4	0.0	77.8	48.8	58.6	76.3	70.4	10.5	4.0	7,868	4,829	3,039	38.6
48167	Galveston County, Texas	240,082	64.7	0.3	70.8	58.8	56.3	81.1	62.9	20.5	7.5	143,681	77,630	66,051	46.0
48169	Garza County, Texas	5,463	37.7	0.0	28.6	58.0	43.7	34.2	72.8	15.6	2.0	2,018	1,049	969	48.0
48171	Gillespie County, Texas	21,127	57.0	0.0	62.9	51.8	64.8	85.6	69.7	16.5	6.8	11,230	5,835	5,395	48.0
48173	Glasscock County, Texas	879	58.2	0.0	70.2	42.7	18.3	80.2	67.2	17.2	2.5	499	346	153	30.7
48175	Goliad County, Texas	6,089	53.6	0.4	59.4	48.1	55.8	79.1	47.7	14.6	9.3	2,962	1,650	1,312	44.3
48177	Gonzales County, Texas	15,331	58.8	0.0	64.8	52.7	51.9	78.2	57.5	21.7	6.5	8,422	4,704	3,718	44.1
48179	Gray County, Texas	17,718	56.3	0.2	61.0	50.9	67.6	67.5	60.5	17.0	5.4	9,444	5,475	3,969	42.0
48181	Grayson County, Texas	96,977	61.3	0.1	68.1	55.1	59.6	81.2	63.3	16.3	7.8	54,835	29,204	25,631	46.7
48183	Gregg County, Texas	94,994	62.0	0.0	68.8	55.6	59.4	79.3	60.8	17.4	5.9	55,402	29,826	25,576	46.2
48185	Grimes County, Texas	21,573	49.2	0.1	49.9	48.2	46.7	61.6	53.1	16.5	6.2	9,951	5,690	4,261	42.8
48187	Guadalupe County, Texas	110,286	64.3	1.1	70.7	58.1	57.2	81.0	65.3	16.7	5.7	66,822	35,606	31,216	46.7
48189	Hale County, Texas	26,603	58.3	0.0	63.3	52.8	51.0	72.9	60.7	21.2	8.1	14,265	8,094	6,171	43.3
48191	Hall County, Texas	2,555	53.7	0.0	63.6	44.6	62.6	77.4	49.9	19.9	11.5	1,214	690	524	43.2
48193	Hamilton County, Texas	6,787	51.3	0.1	56.3	46.5	72.6	73.8	56.0	13.4	5.9	3,279	1,766	1,513	46.1
48195	Hansford County, Texas	4,119	65.4	0.0	81.0	50.2	68.0	80.3	56.9	32.7	2.3	2,629	1,601	1,028	39.1
48197	Hardeman County, Texas	3,242	54.8	0.0	57.7	52.1	51.4	73.5	54.6	16.6	5.9	1,671	807	864	51.7
48199	Hardin County, Texas	42,901	59.1	0.1	67.8	50.7	59.8	77.3	54.8	14.2	5.5	23,933	13,328	10,605	44.3
48201	Harris County, Texas	3,291,654	68.4	0.0	77.2	59.8	56.1	81.8	67.5	21.9	7.5	2,081,889	1,166,187	915,702	44.0
48203	Harrison County, Texas	51,514	60.3	0.0	66.7	54.3	56.1	80.2	57.2	15.9	7.7	28,650	15,263	13,387	46.7
48205	Hartley County, Texas	4,983	47.0	0.0	42.0	55.4	62.8	51.6	45.2	23.4	2.1	2,290	1,287	1,003	43.8
48207	Haskell County, Texas	4,942	48.4	0.0	48.7	48.1	28.4	62.7	60.1	23.8	6.9	2,227	1,269	958	43.0
48209	Hays County, Texas	139,719	66.9	0.2	72.6	61.3	58.8	83.2	67.5	18.0	6.7	87,233	46,599	40,634	46.6
48211	Hemphill County, Texas	2,943	63.9	0.2	75.7	52.1	57.1	81.6	65.9	21.5	3.7	1,812	1,078	734	40.5
48213	Henderson County, Texas	63,322	52.1	0.0	59.7	45.0	52.8	73.6	53.9	13.7	7.8	30,441	16,711	13,730	45.1
48215	Hidalgo County, Texas	571,313	57.9	0.0	65.7	50.7	45.9	75.4	57.8	11.4	9.9	298,030	161,088	136,942	45.9
48217	Hill County, Texas	27,512	56.9	0.0	62.9	51.3	60.7	78.3	57.4	16.7	8.9	14,271	7,669	6,602	46.3
48219	Hockley County, Texas	17,864	64.2	0.0	73.2	55.7	59.1	82.3	64.9	21.1	6.4	10,729	5,919	4,810	44.8
48221	Hood County, Texas	43,532	53.7	0.2	59.5	48.2	55.5	76.2	62.1	15.1	5.0	22,208	11,939	10,269	46.2
48223	Hopkins County, Texas	27,526	59.6	0.1	69.1	50.5	58.4	77.4	60.6	20.6	7.1	15,235	8,654	6,581	43.2
48225	Houston County, Texas	18,983	43.3	0.1	42.4	44.3	42.4	57.6	49.0	12.8	6.4	7,694	4,004	3,690	48.0
48227	Howard County, Texas	28,982	51.3	0.0	49.0	54.5	54.9	60.4	51.0	16.8	6.4	13,924	7,603	6,321	45.4
48229	Hudspeth County, Texas	2,585	46.8	0.0	53.3	40.2	43.5	55.9	50.0	25.1	5.7	1,141	683	458	40.1
48231	Hunt County, Texas	68,988	58.3	0.0	65.1	51.6	54.8	77.2	57.5	13.6	11.4	35,598	19,316	16,282	45.7
48233	Hutchinson County, Texas	16,769	58.8	0.2	69.6	48.3	59.0	77.7	55.4	13.9	5.3	9,347	5,557	3,790	40.5
48235	Irion County, Texas	1,294	65.1	0.2	76.5	53.4	56.0	83.8	68.2	22.9	4.4	805	493	312	38.8
48237	Jack County, Texas	7,416	47.8	0.0	49.3	45.7	40.0	60.5	55.7	15.5	5.6	3,348	1,984	1,364	40.7
48239	Jackson County, Texas	11,202	58.9	0.0	70.9	47.3	56.2	78.5	54.8	20.2	5.2	6,251	3,743	2,508	40.1
48241	Jasper County, Texas	27,737	50.2	0.0	54.9	45.9	51.0	71.3	44.6	11.0	11.4	12,347	6,471	5,876	47.6
48243	Jeff Davis County, Texas	1,914	60.4	0.0	67.8	53.3	40.4	78.7	76.2	31.7	7.1	1,074	577	497	46.3
48245	Jefferson County, Texas	199,717	56.7	0.1	60.3	52.9	54.1	71.1	56.3	15.2	8.8	103,203	56,260	46,943	45.5
48247	Jim Hogg County, Texas	4,015	53.3	0.0	66.2	40.3	59.7	75.6	43.0	17.3	16.5	1,786	1,042	744	41.7
48249	Jim Wells County, Texas	30,978	57.7	0.0	64.7	51.0	48.1	74.8	60.0	19.1	6.6	16,674	9,049	7,625	45.7
48251	Johnson County, Texas	118,791	62.6	0.1	70.0	55.4	54.9	78.9	65.4	16.2	7.3	68,950	38,549	30,401	44.1
48253	Jones County, Texas	16,870	31.0	0.1	19.4	52.8	22.3	30.6	55.4	19.0	4.2	5,003	2,043	2,960	59.2
48255	Karnes County, Texas	12,050	45.8	0.0	42.9	50.3	42.5	55.9	54.5	11.9	4.8	5,251	2,999	2,252	42.9
48257	Kaufman County, Texas	82,053	65.9	0.1	72.8	59.4	59.7	81.6	63.4	18.6	8.7	49,359	26,641	22,718	46.0
48259	Kendall County, Texas	29,681	58.5	0.1	65.6	52.1	52.3	81.6	58.1	18.9	4.5	16,597	8,838	7,759	46.7
48261	Kenedy County, Texas	377	49.1	0.0	60.6	33.5	20.0	64.5	59.0	13.2	0.0	185	131	54	29.2
48263	Kent County, Texas	668	60.5	0.0	71.0	50.1	36.5	84.9	83.1	28.6	1.5	398	234	164	41.2
48265	Kerr County, Texas	41,518	53.8	0.0	60.1	48.0	63.8	81.0	55.2	16.2	8.0	20,523	10,692	9,831	47.9
48267	Kimble County, Texas	3,835	60.1	0.0	65.0	55.3	77.3	84.1	72.5	20.1	7.6	2,129	1,102	1,027	48.2

Table C. County—Labor Force, Employment, and Educational Data, 2011–2015—*Continued*

Fips code	State/county	Total population age 16 and older	Percent in civilian labor force	Percent in armed forces	Civilian labor force participation by gender		Civilian labor force participation by age				Civilian unemployment rate	Civilian employed population age 16 and older			
					Men	Women	Age 16 to 24	Age 25 to 54	Age 55 to 64	Age 65 and older		Total	Men	Women	Percent women
48269	King County, Texas	242	72.3	0.0	87.6	54.9	45.5	88.1	95.0	19.6	5.1	166	104	62	37.3
48271	Kinney County, Texas	2,936	47.6	0.3	49.7	44.7	28.8	59.3	59.9	11.8	13.2	1,213	713	500	41.2
48273	Kleberg County, Texas	25,116	60.7	1.3	66.8	54.3	59.3	78.5	60.8	14.8	11.7	13,466	7,833	5,633	41.8
48275	Knox County, Texas	2,917	56.6	0.0	65.5	48.1	48.5	83.2	57.8	14.9	7.1	1,534	897	637	41.5
48277	Lamar County, Texas	39,027	58.0	0.1	63.1	53.3	59.0	78.9	58.9	14.3	7.4	20,953	10,790	10,163	48.5
48279	Lamb County, Texas	10,235	59.4	0.0	68.2	50.8	51.7	78.0	65.4	20.8	6.2	5,709	3,266	2,443	42.8
48281	Lampasas County, Texas	15,994	56.4	1.8	63.1	49.9	49.5	76.9	59.7	14.8	8.6	8,245	4,586	3,659	44.4
48283	La Salle County, Texas	5,378	46.7	0.0	48.8	43.9	40.5	61.3	44.1	11.6	8.1	2,307	1,381	926	40.1
48285	Lavaca County, Texas	15,511	60.0	0.0	67.0	53.5	66.1	84.5	66.2	15.5	4.0	8,929	4,745	4,184	46.9
48287	Lee County, Texas	13,317	61.4	0.0	64.8	57.9	56.7	82.7	64.4	15.7	5.7	7,706	4,142	3,564	46.2
48289	Leon County, Texas	13,483	53.5	0.0	60.6	46.6	48.6	74.9	62.4	18.6	7.5	6,673	3,667	3,006	45.0
48291	Liberty County, Texas	60,371	52.0	0.0	63.9	40.7	52.4	61.5	53.3	19.2	11.5	27,767	16,708	11,059	39.8
48293	Limestone County, Texas	18,670	54.8	0.0	59.1	50.1	48.9	74.2	57.8	13.2	8.2	9,384	5,086	4,298	45.8
48295	Lipscomb County, Texas	2,676	65.4	0.0	80.4	48.9	51.2	81.1	77.2	20.9	5.0	1,662	1,070	592	35.6
48297	Live Oak County, Texas	9,664	44.7	0.0	44.2	45.4	51.2	56.1	49.1	16.6	4.3	4,140	2,268	1,872	45.2
48299	Llano County, Texas	16,663	46.8	0.3	52.9	41.2	52.6	78.9	55.4	15.3	5.8	7,348	3,994	3,354	45.6
48301	Loving County, Texas	111	65.8	0.0	73.2	52.5	100.0	100.0	62.2	0.0	15.1	62	41	21	33.9
48303	Lubbock County, Texas	227,430	66.3	0.1	71.0	61.8	62.2	82.3	67.0	21.7	6.2	141,493	74,681	66,812	47.2
48305	Lynn County, Texas	4,405	61.4	0.0	70.9	51.8	52.7	79.2	64.5	23.3	10.9	2,409	1,401	1,008	41.8
48307	McCulloch County, Texas	6,598	59.0	0.0	69.5	49.4	54.7	82.2	54.3	24.9	4.3	3,727	2,047	1,680	45.1
48309	McLennan County, Texas	187,931	61.1	0.0	65.3	57.3	52.2	80.2	64.1	18.3	6.2	107,737	55,433	52,304	48.5
48311	McMullen County, Texas	614	61.4	0.0	67.9	54.1	54.3	85.9	72.4	33.8	14.1	324	175	149	46.0
48313	Madison County, Texas	11,872	37.4	0.0	28.6	53.6	31.4	43.7	50.7	16.0	5.7	4,194	1,995	2,199	52.4
48315	Marion County, Texas	8,615	49.7	0.0	53.9	45.8	39.6	75.5	48.3	14.8	8.0	3,940	2,068	1,872	47.5
48317	Martin County, Texas	3,848	63.1	0.0	74.1	52.4	53.9	77.4	63.9	28.9	3.5	2,342	1,328	1,014	43.3
48319	Mason County, Texas	3,469	62.4	0.0	74.2	49.2	63.7	84.8	70.8	30.6	6.8	2,018	1,259	759	37.6
48321	Matagorda County, Texas	28,268	60.0	0.0	68.6	51.8	60.0	79.5	56.7	15.9	6.4	15,874	8,923	6,951	43.8
48323	Maverick County, Texas	40,324	57.9	0.0	65.1	51.0	51.2	76.2	53.2	12.8	13.1	20,309	11,303	9,006	44.3
48325	Medina County, Texas	37,413	56.1	0.1	57.8	54.4	46.4	73.4	59.0	18.1	6.6	19,610	10,465	9,145	46.6
48327	Menard County, Texas	1,692	51.4	0.0	60.0	43.9	54.9	76.8	61.1	12.7	8.3	797	415	382	47.9
48329	Midland County, Texas	113,244	70.2	0.1	81.9	58.8	66.1	83.1	70.5	23.9	3.4	76,743	44,763	31,980	41.7
48331	Milam County, Texas	18,976	53.7	0.1	57.2	50.3	50.5	75.9	53.9	15.3	9.6	9,212	4,967	4,245	46.1
48333	Mills County, Texas	3,773	51.9	0.2	61.0	44.4	42.3	76.5	57.6	21.5	3.6	1,887	1,019	868	46.0
48335	Mitchell County, Texas	7,689	40.7	0.0	37.3	46.6	22.9	48.1	58.8	20.3	5.5	2,955	1,690	1,265	42.8
48337	Montague County, Texas	15,601	56.2	0.1	64.4	48.5	48.8	77.8	62.7	19.9	6.6	8,193	4,588	3,605	44.0
48339	Montgomery County, Texas	382,384	64.1	0.1	74.4	54.3	54.3	79.0	65.6	19.9	6.1	230,258	131,772	98,486	42.8
48341	Moore County, Texas	15,900	70.3	0.3	80.9	59.2	64.6	84.1	69.7	23.1	4.1	10,714	6,342	4,372	40.8
48343	Morris County, Texas	10,135	51.8	0.0	54.9	49.1	51.0	73.3	56.2	13.4	12.7	4,588	2,304	2,284	49.8
48345	Motley County, Texas	891	57.9	0.0	71.0	40.8	60.0	84.5	65.7	17.9	11.0	459	325	134	29.2
48347	Nacogdoches County, Texas	51,573	58.6	0.1	66.5	51.6	52.3	78.6	60.2	15.5	8.6	27,638	14,947	12,691	45.9
48349	Navarro County, Texas	37,037	61.1	0.1	68.3	54.4	60.5	79.2	61.1	19.0	10.9	20,159	11,074	9,085	45.1
48351	Newton County, Texas	11,585	48.2	0.2	52.3	43.9	46.3	70.1	43.4	6.8	12.1	4,911	2,740	2,171	44.2
48353	Nolan County, Texas	11,660	59.5	0.0	70.1	49.0	60.5	76.3	66.6	18.1	7.7	6,403	3,683	2,720	42.5
48355	Nueces County, Texas	272,949	63.9	0.6	70.6	57.6	57.9	80.6	63.7	18.6	6.6	162,895	87,927	74,968	46.0
48357	Ochiltree County, Texas	7,597	70.5	0.0	81.5	59.3	63.1	82.7	75.9	27.7	5.2	5,081	2,985	2,096	41.3
48359	Oldham County, Texas	1,543	54.1	0.0	53.4	55.0	29.2	79.0	71.3	23.7	7.4	773	416	357	46.2
48361	Orange County, Texas	65,090	59.7	0.0	68.3	51.4	56.9	78.7	56.4	14.8	8.4	35,616	19,815	15,801	44.4
48363	Palo Pinto County, Texas	21,984	56.0	0.1	62.0	50.3	54.2	76.5	51.6	19.1	8.3	11,291	6,131	5,160	45.7
48365	Panola County, Texas	18,580	58.0	0.0	66.3	50.1	57.2	75.7	60.6	16.9	5.7	10,154	5,743	4,411	43.4
48367	Parker County, Texas	95,207	62.9	0.1	68.9	57.0	53.7	80.1	66.6	19.2	6.1	56,235	30,800	25,435	45.2
48369	Parmer County, Texas	7,409	65.3	0.0	75.9	53.9	58.8	81.4	65.0	24.7	3.6	4,665	2,822	1,843	39.5
48371	Pecos County, Texas	12,398	54.6	0.1	54.4	55.1	56.8	60.9	67.0	19.0	4.8	6,447	3,842	2,605	40.4
48373	Polk County, Texas	37,693	48.0	0.0	47.1	49.0	51.1	63.1	54.3	13.0	10.0	16,267	8,634	7,633	46.9
48375	Potter County, Texas	91,742	61.5	0.1	64.7	58.1	64.4	73.8	58.8	16.8	5.3	53,420	29,019	24,401	45.7
48377	Presidio County, Texas	5,488	52.6	0.0	69.5	37.0	44.3	74.8	59.2	14.0	9.6	2,610	1,669	941	36.1
48379	Rains County, Texas	9,003	53.9	0.0	56.5	51.3	69.8	78.3	53.1	12.4	7.9	4,468	2,320	2,148	48.1
48381	Randall County, Texas	98,940	68.6	0.1	75.6	62.1	66.2	85.6	68.9	19.8	3.9	65,270	34,917	30,353	46.5
48383	Reagan County, Texas	2,732	66.5	0.0	82.7	48.9	47.8	82.4	65.6	30.1	2.2	1,778	1,165	613	34.5
48385	Real County, Texas	2,857	39.6	0.0	40.9	38.4	41.5	72.4	44.8	13.0	12.0	996	541	455	45.7
48387	Red River County, Texas	10,248	49.4	0.0	54.5	44.8	41.4	75.2	46.0	14.6	7.2	4,697	2,443	2,254	48.0
48389	Reeves County, Texas	11,420	44.7	0.1	38.3	53.9	50.6	50.5	49.6	16.1	6.7	4,768	2,374	2,394	50.2
48391	Refugio County, Texas	5,841	56.8	0.0	64.2	49.4	44.9	82.2	51.0	26.4	6.7	3,096	1,752	1,344	43.4
48393	Roberts County, Texas	680	63.4	0.0	68.1	59.6	48.4	87.6	66.2	19.8	1.9	423	200	223	52.7
48395	Robertson County, Texas	12,995	57.4	0.0	63.1	51.9	54.9	77.8	62.0	17.7	9.2	6,776	3,636	3,140	46.3
48397	Rockwall County, Texas	64,057	68.5	0.1	76.6	60.8	57.8	83.5	68.0	22.8	5.9	41,300	22,699	18,601	45.0
48399	Runnels County, Texas	8,254	53.8	0.0	57.5	50.2	42.7	77.0	61.6	18.8	3.4	4,292	2,242	2,050	47.8
48401	Rusk County, Texas	42,397	52.6	0.0	54.5	50.5	51.0	64.5	58.7	16.6	4.9	21,219	11,698	9,521	44.9
48403	Sabine County, Texas	8,504	38.5	0.0	46.2	31.4	33.6	64.5	45.9	9.6	12.1	2,882	1,636	1,246	43.2
48405	San Augustine County, Texas	7,165	37.3	0.0	45.8	29.4	47.4	56.9	34.5	9.4	16.3	2,237	1,317	920	41.1
48407	San Jacinto County, Texas	21,448	53.2	0.2	62.9	43.8	49.9	77.8	47.5	15.9	12.6	9,976	5,875	4,101	41.1
48409	San Patricio County, Texas	50,200	60.2	0.3	68.5	52.0	50.5	78.0	65.1	16.1	5.2	28,627	16,167	12,460	43.5
48411	San Saba County, Texas	4,835	50.7	0.0	59.5	40.0	41.2	67.2	60.5	21.6	4.9	2,329	1,487	842	36.2
48413	Schleicher County, Texas	2,357	66.3	0.0	77.9	55.0	71.1	83.3	55.0	35.4	4.1	1,499	888	611	40.8
48415	Scurry County, Texas	13,321	57.2	0.0	59.6	54.3	48.6	68.8	68.8	23.5	3.3	7,371	4,254	3,117	42.3

Table C. County—Labor Force, Employment, and Educational Data, 2011–2015—*Continued*

Fips code	State/county	Total population age 16 and older	Percent in civilian labor force	Percent in armed forces	Civilian labor force participation by gender		Civilian labor force participation by age				Civilian unemployment rate	Civilian employed population age 16 and older			
					Men	Women	Age 16 to 24	Age 25 to 54	Age 55 to 64	Age 65 and older		Total	Men	Women	Percent women
48417	Shackelford County, Texas	2,654	58.8	0.0	71.1	47.5	52.9	76.3	59.1	27.0	3.8	1,502	883	619	41.2
48419	Shelby County, Texas	19,560	56.4	0.0	63.9	49.2	53.7	73.1	64.6	14.4	7.9	10,162	5,679	4,483	44.1
48421	Sherman County, Texas	2,357	65.9	0.3	79.2	52.1	65.7	78.6	62.6	26.2	3.7	1,497	904	593	39.6
48423	Smith County, Texas	169,042	61.1	0.1	67.9	54.9	56.6	79.9	62.1	17.6	7.2	95,841	50,384	45,457	47.4
48425	Somervell County, Texas	6,860	57.7	0.0	66.3	49.8	59.8	78.2	47.6	20.9	2.1	3,878	2,167	1,711	44.1
48427	Starr County, Texas	44,161	55.2	0.0	62.0	48.9	44.3	73.6	51.9	13.0	13.8	21,006	10,967	10,039	47.8
48429	Stephens County, Texas	7,580	52.2	0.0	58.6	45.0	43.9	69.3	59.3	19.5	3.9	3,805	2,278	1,527	40.1
48431	Sterling County, Texas	990	59.1	0.0	68.0	50.3	70.2	74.3	67.5	11.4	0.3	583	335	248	42.5
48433	Stonewall County, Texas	1,053	56.4	0.0	62.3	50.7	43.9	77.0	79.0	22.4	6.9	553	298	255	46.1
48435	Sutton County, Texas	2,962	62.5	0.0	77.1	46.5	59.4	75.3	68.9	27.1	4.3	1,771	1,169	602	34.0
48437	Swisher County, Texas	5,951	50.0	0.0	55.6	43.5	56.4	62.6	54.4	17.1	6.4	2,784	1,659	1,125	40.4
48439	Tarrant County, Texas	1,447,659	68.6	0.1	76.4	61.3	60.7	82.4	67.1	20.5	6.9	924,741	498,591	426,150	46.1
48441	Taylor County, Texas	104,781	61.6	3.0	65.5	57.9	61.1	76.7	65.3	19.2	5.9	60,708	31,139	29,569	48.7
48443	Terrell County, Texas	772	55.8	0.0	70.7	41.8	48.5	81.5	69.9	10.2	3.7	415	260	155	37.3
48445	Terry County, Texas	9,595	53.2	0.0	54.5	51.6	52.1	65.7	58.1	16.8	6.5	4,767	2,606	2,161	45.3
48447	Throckmorton County, Texas	1,276	55.2	0.0	63.6	47.4	43.2	87.4	70.5	16.7	2.6	686	374	312	45.5
48449	Titus County, Texas	24,080	62.3	0.2	70.6	54.1	62.9	78.0	61.3	16.9	7.5	13,867	7,821	6,046	43.6
48451	Tom Green County, Texas	90,874	59.5	3.9	63.7	55.5	50.0	78.5	61.8	18.1	4.7	51,528	27,289	24,239	47.0
48453	Travis County, Texas	885,869	72.0	0.1	78.7	65.2	55.6	85.3	69.6	22.0	6.0	599,597	328,334	271,263	45.2
48455	Trinity County, Texas	11,839	46.2	0.0	51.1	41.6	40.3	70.7	50.5	14.0	9.9	4,922	2,618	2,304	46.8
48457	Tyler County, Texas	17,739	46.1	0.0	47.0	45.0	45.5	63.4	51.5	11.4	11.5	7,230	3,968	3,262	45.1
48459	Upshur County, Texas	31,615	57.9	0.1	66.0	50.1	54.5	76.5	59.2	18.2	7.9	16,849	9,564	7,285	43.2
48461	Upton County, Texas	2,444	56.7	0.0	67.7	46.0	45.0	69.3	69.2	21.3	4.3	1,326	769	557	42.0
48463	Uvalde County, Texas	20,276	58.0	0.0	65.3	51.0	53.1	78.4	61.0	15.8	8.1	10,801	5,990	4,811	44.5
48465	Val Verde County, Texas	36,249	55.5	3.8	61.7	49.2	45.2	73.1	58.2	16.3	9.3	18,261	10,192	8,069	44.2
48467	Van Zandt County, Texas	41,918	55.5	0.0	61.8	49.5	54.5	77.6	57.3	14.5	6.1	21,856	11,818	10,038	45.9
48469	Victoria County, Texas	69,397	64.0	0.1	71.3	57.1	60.7	82.4	63.9	17.7	6.5	41,513	22,307	19,206	46.3
48471	Walker County, Texas	59,837	39.5	0.4	30.9	52.2	41.6	43.9	41.6	16.6	4.4	22,612	10,625	11,987	53.0
48473	Waller County, Texas	36,193	60.6	0.0	71.0	50.4	54.6	78.4	62.0	21.9	8.3	20,127	11,642	8,485	42.2
48475	Ward County, Texas	8,408	58.0	0.0	69.9	46.5	56.6	75.2	54.6	17.3	4.4	4,661	2,794	1,867	40.1
48477	Washington County, Texas	27,723	54.6	0.0	60.9	48.7	45.6	76.4	54.6	15.1	5.1	14,380	7,740	6,640	46.2
48479	Webb County, Texas	182,201	57.8	0.0	67.1	49.4	45.6	72.2	55.5	16.5	6.0	98,996	54,867	44,129	44.6
48481	Wharton County, Texas	31,559	63.1	0.0	70.2	56.2	55.0	81.6	71.2	18.8	6.6	18,584	10,088	8,496	45.7
48483	Wheeler County, Texas	4,322	64.7	0.0	78.4	51.3	66.3	79.5	73.7	24.9	3.9	2,688	1,614	1,074	40.0
48485	Wichita County, Texas	105,146	55.8	5.7	55.5	56.0	49.9	70.4	58.8	19.0	6.1	55,053	28,471	26,582	48.3
48487	Wilbarger County, Texas	10,379	62.3	0.0	65.9	58.8	66.3	81.4	62.2	17.4	7.5	5,977	3,102	2,875	48.1
48489	Willacy County, Texas	16,940	35.8	0.0	35.5	36.1	28.0	47.0	37.9	8.1	11.5	5,365	2,879	2,486	46.3
48491	Williamson County, Texas	357,045	69.5	0.3	76.1	63.3	57.6	85.0	66.7	18.4	6.0	233,418	124,553	108,865	46.6
48493	Wilson County, Texas	35,516	61.3	0.3	68.6	54.1	53.2	82.1	55.9	16.0	5.8	20,521	11,504	9,017	43.9
48495	Winkler County, Texas	5,591	60.0	0.0	72.2	47.8	52.7	76.9	57.4	13.3	2.5	3,271	1,975	1,296	39.6
48497	Wise County, Texas	47,242	62.2	0.1	67.8	56.5	61.7	77.7	63.7	16.4	7.5	27,154	15,112	12,042	44.3
48499	Wood County, Texas	35,287	49.4	0.0	53.7	45.1	56.8	76.9	50.3	12.7	8.9	15,868	8,505	7,363	46.4
48501	Yoakum County, Texas	5,797	66.5	0.0	82.0	51.7	59.3	82.4	68.4	20.4	8.1	3,546	2,228	1,318	37.2
48503	Young County, Texas	14,418	60.9	0.0	70.5	51.7	54.0	78.4	70.8	25.1	5.6	8,288	4,614	3,674	44.3
48505	Zapata County, Texas	9,942	59.4	0.0	69.6	49.9	51.8	77.8	53.6	16.0	12.2	5,184	2,954	2,230	43.0
48507	Zavala County, Texas	8,798	55.3	0.0	61.9	48.9	57.1	70.2	52.5	14.5	12.2	4,276	2,375	1,901	44.5
49000	**Utah**	2,096,916	67.7	0.2	75.9	59.5	66.7	80.6	67.4	18.3	5.8	1,337,646	747,788	589,858	44.1
49001	Beaver County, Utah	4,586	65.3	0.0	73.4	56.8	66.2	83.0	66.0	18.2	3.8	2,881	1,679	1,202	41.7
49003	Box Elder County, Utah	36,016	63.8	0.0	72.7	55.0	65.8	80.2	67.6	9.6	6.3	21,534	12,279	9,255	43.0
49005	Cache County, Utah	84,540	68.3	0.1	76.8	60.1	69.3	80.2	68.9	16.0	5.5	54,566	30,565	24,001	44.0
49007	Carbon County, Utah	15,907	62.4	0.1	68.8	56.2	68.2	80.5	63.0	13.7	7.4	9,197	4,956	4,241	46.1
49009	Daggett County, Utah	618	37.5	0.0	37.2	38.0	20.6	46.7	64.2	13.4	4.3	222	131	91	41.0
49011	Davis County, Utah	225,811	68.4	1.0	77.6	59.2	65.2	80.8	67.7	19.1	4.2	147,875	83,362	64,513	43.6
49013	Duchesne County, Utah	13,753	60.4	0.0	71.5	48.8	54.0	75.2	62.6	15.6	5.2	7,875	4,746	3,129	39.7
49015	Emery County, Utah	7,747	57.3	0.0	65.5	49.2	55.0	75.9	55.8	14.4	5.7	4,188	2,318	1,870	44.7
49017	Garfield County, Utah	3,959	55.2	0.0	60.0	50.2	60.6	71.5	58.6	20.0	8.6	2,000	1,156	844	42.2
49019	Grand County, Utah	7,469	68.3	0.0	71.7	65.0	73.9	87.3	66.0	14.9	7.1	4,741	2,430	2,311	48.7
49021	Iron County, Utah	34,907	62.9	0.0	70.4	55.3	66.7	76.2	59.8	18.2	10.5	19,636	10,975	8,661	44.1
49023	Juab County, Utah	7,171	64.1	0.0	72.3	55.9	64.9	77.4	66.5	21.1	3.8	4,422	2,470	1,952	44.1
49025	Kane County, Utah	5,747	59.9	0.0	59.3	60.4	71.0	82.2	61.3	16.3	7.0	3,201	1,404	1,797	56.1
49027	Millard County, Utah	9,127	62.9	0.2	70.9	54.6	65.3	80.9	61.9	24.6	4.3	5,499	3,193	2,306	41.9
49029	Morgan County, Utah	6,997	64.4	0.4	75.3	53.2	53.7	81.1	66.7	22.1	6.0	4,234	2,561	1,673	39.5
49031	Piute County, Utah	1,500	46.7	0.0	43.3	50.5	53.9	70.6	41.7	13.3	6.8	653	301	352	53.9
49033	Rich County, Utah	1,583	49.2	0.0	65.5	34.6	52.5	60.6	52.1	24.5	6.2	731	453	278	38.0
49035	Salt Lake County, Utah	801,589	71.0	0.1	78.5	63.5	68.4	83.0	70.6	20.7	5.8	536,170	296,090	240,080	44.8
49037	San Juan County, Utah	10,773	51.0	0.0	55.4	46.7	38.6	67.0	55.6	15.4	8.4	5,026	2,697	2,329	46.3
49039	Sanpete County, Utah	21,395	51.3	0.1	51.7	50.8	50.5	64.6	54.8	13.9	8.3	10,060	5,389	4,671	46.4
49041	Sevier County, Utah	15,217	59.0	0.0	67.0	50.9	61.8	78.5	59.9	11.8	5.9	8,449	4,777	3,672	43.5
49043	Summit County, Utah	29,279	73.2	0.0	81.2	64.9	67.7	83.9	75.5	26.8	3.2	20,741	11,688	9,053	43.6
49045	Tooele County, Utah	41,923	67.6	0.3	76.0	59.1	62.9	80.0	64.1	17.3	7.1	26,337	14,909	11,428	43.4
49047	Uintah County, Utah	24,883	65.0	0.3	75.9	53.7	63.2	76.7	64.1	19.2	5.1	15,359	9,123	6,236	40.6
49049	Utah County, Utah	377,172	67.6	0.1	78.4	56.9	68.3	76.5	69.7	19.1	5.5	241,085	139,447	101,638	42.2
49051	Wasatch County, Utah	18,821	69.4	0.1	74.9	63.8	61.4	84.1	64.2	21.9	4.7	12,451	6,982	5,469	43.9
49053	Washington County, Utah	110,144	56.8	0.0	64.4	49.7	63.6	79.8	57.2	13.1	7.7	57,785	31,564	26,221	45.4

Table C. County—Labor Force, Employment, and Educational Data, 2011–2015—*Continued*

Fips code	State/county	Total population age 16 and older	Percent in civilian labor force	Percent in armed forces	Civilian labor force participation by gender		Civilian labor force participation by age				Civilian unemployment rate	Civilian employed population age 16 and older			
					Men	Women	Age 16 to 24	Age 25 to 54	Age 55 to 64	Age 65 and older		Total	Men	Women	Percent women
49055	Wayne County, Utah	2,048	62.5	0.0	65.9	59.0	74.2	84.2	60.2	18.0	2.1	1,254	684	570	45.5
49057	Weber County, Utah	176,234	66.3	0.3	72.6	60.1	65.3	81.3	63.0	15.8	6.3	109,474	59,459	50,015	45.7
50000	**Vermont**	519,139	66.6	0.1	69.8	63.6	61.4	85.2	72.5	21.7	5.5	326,732	166,152	160,580	49.1
50001	Addison County, Vermont	30,911	67.1	0.0	70.3	64.0	55.2	88.5	74.2	23.0	5.8	19,530	10,008	9,522	48.8
50003	Bennington County, Vermont	30,373	62.9	0.0	67.8	58.4	61.6	82.8	73.6	22.0	5.7	18,014	9,339	8,675	48.2
50005	Caledonia County, Vermont	25,455	62.6	0.0	65.5	59.7	59.3	81.2	67.8	20.8	7.2	14,773	7,515	7,258	49.1
50007	Chittenden County, Vermont	133,179	70.6	0.1	74.8	66.6	62.2	88.2	76.0	22.5	5.0	89,268	45,419	43,849	49.1
50009	Essex County, Vermont	5,210	56.9	0.0	59.0	54.7	62.0	79.7	60.3	15.1	9.4	2,683	1,380	1,303	48.6
50011	Franklin County, Vermont	38,377	69.7	0.4	72.7	66.7	70.6	85.8	69.0	19.6	4.9	25,416	13,005	12,411	48.8
50013	Grand Isle County, Vermont	5,848	68.3	0.0	70.4	66.2	61.2	88.4	71.6	22.7	7.4	3,697	1,852	1,845	49.9
50015	Lamoille County, Vermont	20,365	67.5	0.0	72.7	62.3	65.7	85.1	67.2	21.2	4.3	13,147	7,043	6,104	46.4
50017	Orange County, Vermont	23,890	67.1	0.0	69.1	65.2	60.2	84.8	73.3	26.1	4.5	15,314	7,675	7,639	49.9
50019	Orleans County, Vermont	22,330	57.7	0.0	59.8	55.6	54.9	79.4	62.8	15.0	5.6	12,168	6,227	5,941	48.8
50021	Rutland County, Vermont	50,759	63.5	0.2	65.5	61.6	60.7	83.5	69.9	20.3	6.6	30,125	15,019	15,106	50.1
50023	Washington County, Vermont	48,870	68.3	0.2	69.9	66.8	61.8	86.6	74.6	23.1	4.8	31,774	15,939	15,835	49.8
50025	Windham County, Vermont	36,667	65.4	0.0	68.8	62.1	56.8	84.2	74.9	23.7	6.8	22,336	11,327	11,009	49.3
50027	Windsor County, Vermont	46,905	64.0	0.0	66.8	61.3	62.8	81.7	74.3	22.3	5.1	28,487	14,404	14,083	49.4
51000	**Virginia**	6,598,956	64.7	1.7	68.7	60.8	55.0	81.3	67.6	19.1	6.5	3,990,770	2,062,344	1,928,426	48.3
51001	Accomack County, Virginia	26,938	56.9	0.5	63.2	51.3	53.6	81.3	57.8	16.1	6.8	14,296	7,438	6,858	48.0
51003	Albemarle County, Virginia	83,759	59.8	0.4	63.9	56.1	37.8	81.2	68.4	21.3	3.8	48,206	24,331	23,875	49.5
51005	Alleghany County, Virginia	13,288	51.8	0.0	58.0	46.0	55.8	77.2	55.6	9.6	5.1	6,539	3,597	2,942	45.0
51007	Amelia County, Virginia	10,311	58.0	0.0	60.7	55.5	56.2	81.3	55.0	11.5	5.0	5,686	2,921	2,765	48.6
51009	Amherst County, Virginia	26,584	59.1	0.0	62.3	56.2	49.7	82.7	61.3	16.1	6.6	14,663	7,162	7,501	51.2
51011	Appomattox County, Virginia	12,248	57.1	0.1	61.8	52.8	51.0	78.6	57.3	16.4	6.6	6,532	3,357	3,175	48.6
51013	Arlington County, Virginia	189,882	77.3	1.4	81.5	73.1	63.0	88.3	74.1	27.1	3.7	141,305	74,018	67,287	47.6
51015	Augusta County, Virginia	61,058	58.9	0.2	61.4	56.4	56.3	75.7	64.6	20.3	4.7	34,285	18,034	16,251	47.4
51017	Bath County, Virginia	3,805	64.6	0.0	66.1	63.2	58.5	89.5	69.6	21.6	6.0	2,310	1,067	1,243	53.8
51019	Bedford County, Virginia	62,219	61.0	0.1	66.4	55.8	60.0	82.7	64.2	15.8	5.8	35,756	19,005	16,751	46.8
51021	Bland County, Virginia	5,713	48.0	0.1	44.8	52.1	60.0	59.7	51.2	14.9	8.7	2,504	1,265	1,239	49.5
51023	Botetourt County, Virginia	27,156	62.7	0.0	67.5	58.1	62.3	84.6	67.7	17.1	4.6	16,257	8,535	7,722	47.5
51025	Brunswick County, Virginia	14,350	51.4	0.0	47.5	55.8	44.4	66.0	59.1	19.2	10.5	6,601	3,118	3,483	52.8
51027	Buchanan County, Virginia	19,849	40.1	0.0	43.1	37.1	49.8	55.3	34.2	7.8	10.6	7,120	3,784	3,336	46.9
51029	Buckingham County, Virginia	14,041	51.4	0.1	47.1	56.9	54.5	63.7	53.3	15.5	11.2	6,406	3,266	3,140	49.0
51031	Campbell County, Virginia	45,087	61.6	0.1	68.0	55.8	60.9	81.7	64.8	15.6	6.0	26,131	13,806	12,325	47.2
51033	Caroline County, Virginia	23,386	63.3	4.5	63.6	63.1	51.7	79.7	71.9	19.5	8.6	13,539	6,541	6,998	51.7
51035	Carroll County, Virginia	24,684	56.6	0.0	61.2	52.1	57.7	79.6	56.0	16.8	6.7	13,033	6,878	6,155	47.2
51036	Charles City County, Virginia	6,089	59.5	0.4	62.4	56.7	59.1	81.7	60.0	17.1	8.2	3,323	1,662	1,661	50.0
51037	Charlotte County, Virginia	9,984	55.5	0.0	57.2	53.8	66.8	77.1	49.1	15.6	4.9	5,266	2,661	2,605	49.5
51041	Chesterfield County, Virginia	256,916	68.8	0.5	73.7	64.4	59.4	85.7	70.3	20.3	6.8	164,842	83,646	81,196	49.3
51043	Clarke County, Virginia	11,717	62.7	0.0	67.3	58.4	54.5	81.5	76.1	19.2	6.0	6,908	3,492	3,416	49.4
51045	Craig County, Virginia	4,091	53.5	0.0	53.4	53.6	79.3	75.5	56.5	4.9	4.1	2,101	1,039	1,062	50.5
51047	Culpeper County, Virginia	37,459	63.7	0.2	66.6	60.7	54.2	80.2	67.0	18.5	7.3	22,103	11,357	10,746	48.6
51049	Cumberland County, Virginia	8,061	63.0	0.0	67.9	58.4	66.9	83.3	62.5	21.6	10.1	4,567	2,360	2,207	48.3
51051	Dickenson County, Virginia	12,623	43.4	0.2	46.9	39.8	63.1	60.1	34.7	4.7	8.4	5,017	2,740	2,277	45.4
51053	Dinwiddie County, Virginia	22,884	61.2	0.4	62.7	59.9	62.5	81.4	59.3	11.1	9.7	12,653	6,283	6,370	50.3
51057	Essex County, Virginia	9,144	62.2	0.0	64.5	60.2	66.7	84.4	70.9	13.8	8.5	5,211	2,456	2,755	52.9
51059	Fairfax County, Virginia	886,641	71.6	1.2	77.9	65.6	56.0	85.1	77.0	26.4	4.9	603,966	322,623	281,343	46.6
51061	Fauquier County, Virginia	53,262	68.2	0.3	75.9	60.9	62.7	84.9	69.7	26.3	5.0	34,515	18,857	15,658	45.4
51063	Floyd County, Virginia	12,586	63.2	0.0	69.4	57.0	64.0	84.2	69.5	17.8	5.7	7,494	4,022	3,472	46.3
51065	Fluvanna County, Virginia	21,038	60.5	0.2	67.2	55.3	58.5	79.1	64.3	16.1	5.2	12,076	5,839	6,237	51.6
51067	Franklin County, Virginia	46,580	57.6	0.0	62.3	53.1	65.1	79.5	57.2	14.0	6.2	25,149	13,210	11,939	47.5
51069	Frederick County, Virginia	64,127	67.4	0.1	72.7	62.4	61.3	83.7	73.6	20.2	5.2	40,973	21,441	19,532	47.7
51071	Giles County, Virginia	13,733	57.5	0.1	64.1	51.2	63.7	79.6	55.3	14.5	4.8	7,510	4,068	3,442	45.8
51073	Gloucester County, Virginia	30,449	60.7	1.9	66.1	55.6	62.2	79.0	65.2	11.9	4.7	17,612	9,320	8,292	47.1
51075	Goochland County, Virginia	18,029	60.3	0.1	64.4	56.4	51.3	74.0	69.6	27.3	5.0	10,325	5,323	5,002	48.4
51077	Grayson County, Virginia	13,142	52.4	0.0	55.9	49.0	53.9	75.7	52.9	13.4	9.0	6,262	3,247	3,015	48.1
51079	Greene County, Virginia	14,876	64.8	0.3	67.9	61.8	59.0	83.7	65.3	16.5	7.4	8,932	4,600	4,332	48.5
51081	Greensville County, Virginia	10,040	35.8	0.0	20.9	61.4	34.1	36.8	50.4	20.7	6.4	3,365	1,217	2,148	63.8
51083	Halifax County, Virginia	28,830	53.4	0.0	56.3	50.9	49.0	76.1	58.2	14.7	7.5	14,234	6,922	7,312	51.4
51085	Hanover County, Virginia	80,925	68.1	0.2	72.3	64.2	60.4	87.0	74.8	18.8	4.4	52,677	26,928	25,749	48.9
51087	Henrico County, Virginia	252,172	70.1	0.1	75.8	65.2	64.8	86.6	72.1	20.1	6.7	164,837	81,909	82,968	50.3
51089	Henry County, Virginia	43,019	55.4	0.1	59.9	51.4	62.4	75.9	59.2	14.3	10.0	21,466	10,901	10,565	49.2
51091	Highland County, Virginia	1,961	51.9	0.0	53.5	50.3	56.0	81.6	73.8	15.7	1.1	1,006	504	502	49.9
51093	Isle of Wight County, Virginia	29,038	64.8	0.8	71.2	58.7	64.9	83.8	69.5	15.4	8.3	17,246	9,338	7,908	45.9
51095	James City County, Virginia	57,914	57.6	1.3	62.1	53.5	53.0	80.8	65.7	17.4	5.1	31,685	16,260	15,425	48.7
51097	King and Queen County, Virginia	5,852	60.3	0.0	70.3	50.5	62.2	81.2	68.0	13.9	5.5	3,335	1,924	1,411	42.3
51099	King George County, Virginia	19,025	68.7	1.7	75.7	61.7	69.6	81.2	68.5	21.9	7.4	12,096	6,682	5,414	44.8
51101	King William County, Virginia	12,653	66.6	0.0	74.2	59.4	52.0	85.0	68.3	18.4	5.4	7,972	4,380	3,592	45.1
51103	Lancaster County, Virginia	9,656	52.7	0.1	58.1	48.2	73.3	85.8	62.6	15.9	7.9	4,690	2,290	2,400	51.2
51105	Lee County, Virginia	20,937	43.1	0.2	41.6	44.8	58.0	53.7	44.2	10.7	12.0	7,942	3,829	4,113	51.8
51107	Loudoun County, Virginia	256,779	75.7	0.5	83.4	68.2	59.2	86.9	75.8	27.1	4.0	186,474	100,988	85,486	45.8
51109	Louisa County, Virginia	27,573	63.4	0.0	66.7	60.3	61.0	84.0	61.7	18.0	8.1	16,077	8,292	7,785	48.4
51111	Lunenburg County, Virginia	10,323	47.3	0.1	44.0	51.1	52.6	54.9	60.9	18.3	7.3	4,523	2,200	2,323	51.4

Table C. County—Labor Force, Employment, and Educational Data, 2011–2015—*Continued*

Fips code	State/county	Total population age 16 and older	Percent in civilian labor force	Percent in armed forces	Civilian labor force participation by gender		Civilian labor force participation by age				Civilian unemploy-ment rate	Civilian employed population age 16 and older			
					Men	Women	Age 16 to 24	Age 25 to 54	Age 55 to 64	Age 65 and older		Total	Men	Women	Percent women
51113	Madison County, Virginia	10,679	59.8	0.0	65.0	54.9	46.5	85.8	66.9	16.3	6.6	5,965	3,183	2,782	46.6
51115	Mathews County, Virginia	7,628	52.9	0.7	54.9	51.1	59.2	83.7	58.2	13.8	3.3	3,901	1,909	1,992	51.1
51117	Mecklenburg County, Virginia	26,188	51.1	0.0	50.6	51.6	48.8	73.0	57.7	14.1	6.9	12,460	5,843	6,617	53.1
51119	Middlesex County, Virginia	9,276	50.7	0.2	50.1	51.3	52.2	80.9	58.9	11.5	6.3	4,404	2,109	2,295	52.1
51121	Montgomery County, Virginia	82,959	58.3	0.2	58.8	57.6	42.5	82.1	67.1	19.3	5.6	45,648	23,922	21,726	47.6
51125	Nelson County, Virginia	12,306	57.7	0.0	60.7	55.0	61.5	80.7	62.4	18.3	5.7	6,694	3,346	3,348	50.0
51127	New Kent County, Virginia	15,767	66.8	0.1	68.4	65.2	55.5	86.1	67.5	18.4	6.1	9,896	5,230	4,666	47.2
51131	Northampton County, Virginia	10,048	53.1	0.5	55.0	51.5	54.8	78.4	60.2	13.8	9.5	4,830	2,294	2,536	52.5
51133	Northumberland County, Virginia	10,645	51.7	0.0	57.4	46.5	60.8	82.9	68.2	14.2	8.7	5,021	2,566	2,455	48.9
51135	Nottoway County, Virginia	12,887	49.1	0.5	47.0	51.5	49.2	62.0	52.1	17.9	10.8	5,644	2,822	2,822	50.0
51137	Orange County, Virginia	27,900	58.5	0.2	65.2	52.1	52.4	81.7	62.7	12.9	7.9	15,024	7,924	7,100	47.3
51139	Page County, Virginia	19,663	58.2	0.1	62.4	54.2	65.5	77.2	62.2	13.6	9.3	10,379	5,412	4,967	47.9
51141	Patrick County, Virginia	15,492	49.1	0.0	54.9	43.5	56.4	71.6	51.2	10.8	8.3	6,971	3,854	3,117	44.7
51143	Pittsylvania County, Virginia	51,547	58.4	0.0	61.9	55.1	56.0	79.9	60.1	16.1	7.7	27,803	14,452	13,351	48.0
51145	Powhatan County, Virginia	23,480	59.6	0.0	59.1	60.2	52.1	73.6	65.4	19.9	4.9	13,301	7,081	6,220	46.8
51147	Prince Edward County, Virginia	19,753	47.7	0.0	49.9	45.6	34.0	70.9	60.5	19.1	7.0	8,771	4,549	4,222	48.1
51149	Prince George County, Virginia	30,229	53.0	4.9	51.5	54.9	56.9	61.3	54.4	15.9	10.6	14,315	7,647	6,668	46.6
51153	Prince William County, Virginia	326,846	72.5	1.8	78.3	66.8	58.6	84.3	73.4	24.0	5.4	223,939	119,586	104,353	46.6
51155	Pulaski County, Virginia	28,861	57.9	0.1	59.7	56.2	64.5	76.2	62.1	16.4	7.4	15,480	7,833	7,647	49.4
51157	Rappahannock County, Virginia	6,261	58.7	0.0	65.4	52.0	52.6	78.2	63.6	26.6	2.9	3,570	2,041	1,529	42.8
51159	Richmond County, Virginia	7,763	45.1	0.0	40.3	51.7	50.3	52.2	60.2	15.4	8.7	3,199	1,660	1,539	48.1
51161	Roanoke County, Virginia	76,558	62.4	0.1	68.1	57.4	59.2	83.5	68.4	17.5	5.1	45,358	23,092	22,266	49.1
51163	Rockbridge County, Virginia	18,862	54.1	0.0	57.5	50.9	51.5	77.8	56.1	18.4	4.1	9,789	5,135	4,654	47.5
51165	Rockingham County, Virginia	62,140	64.8	0.0	71.2	58.9	63.4	84.6	70.9	19.1	5.4	38,108	20,166	17,942	47.1
51167	Russell County, Virginia	23,372	47.5	0.0	53.9	41.4	51.9	65.9	39.5	11.9	8.0	10,211	5,592	4,619	45.2
51169	Scott County, Virginia	18,778	50.0	0.0	55.3	44.6	61.3	68.6	50.3	11.3	9.4	8,509	4,704	3,805	44.7
51171	Shenandoah County, Virginia	34,553	61.6	0.2	67.3	56.3	66.1	83.5	65.9	14.0	6.0	19,990	10,470	9,520	47.6
51173	Smyth County, Virginia	26,130	54.3	0.0	59.8	49.2	58.3	75.0	55.5	11.8	6.4	13,278	6,973	6,305	47.5
51175	Southampton County, Virginia	15,255	56.1	0.2	54.6	57.9	53.9	74.1	51.3	20.3	7.2	7,948	3,929	4,019	50.6
51177	Spotsylvania County, Virginia	98,627	67.5	0.6	74.0	61.4	57.6	83.8	68.1	17.5	6.2	62,469	32,997	29,472	47.2
51179	Stafford County, Virginia	104,567	65.4	4.3	69.5	61.3	48.8	78.9	69.0	20.0	5.5	64,619	34,333	30,286	46.9
51181	Surry County, Virginia	5,708	63.0	0.0	66.3	59.8	58.5	85.6	64.8	17.5	10.7	3,209	1,684	1,525	47.5
51183	Sussex County, Virginia	10,216	26.8	0.0	17.1	51.0	24.4	26.1	38.1	21.2	6.9	2,551	1,164	1,387	54.4
51185	Tazewell County, Virginia	36,248	50.3	0.0	55.7	44.9	57.3	68.3	48.6	10.5	8.0	16,752	9,178	7,574	45.2
51187	Warren County, Virginia	30,714	65.6	0.1	71.9	59.3	58.1	82.9	68.2	18.8	7.2	18,689	10,223	8,466	45.3
51191	Washington County, Virginia	45,642	57.5	0.1	62.3	52.9	59.1	78.7	56.8	16.5	6.9	24,442	12,887	11,555	47.3
51193	Westmoreland County, Virginia	14,545	56.5	0.6	57.8	55.4	61.1	83.8	52.0	16.9	9.7	7,423	3,629	3,794	51.1
51195	Wise County, Virginia	33,253	46.4	0.2	50.3	42.2	52.6	60.1	39.6	11.6	11.0	13,736	7,798	5,938	43.2
51197	Wythe County, Virginia	23,878	58.5	0.2	63.9	53.5	65.3	79.5	59.3	11.9	9.6	12,631	6,556	6,075	48.1
51199	York County, Virginia	52,220	61.3	5.5	65.4	57.5	47.4	77.0	71.7	19.7	5.8	30,160	15,678	14,482	48.0
51510	Alexandria city, Virginia	124,829	77.7	1.8	82.0	73.7	62.0	87.9	79.2	29.4	4.5	92,575	46,634	45,941	49.6
51520	Bristol city, Virginia	14,255	57.4	0.1	62.6	53.0	56.0	78.3	62.5	13.2	10.7	7,306	3,676	3,630	49.7
51530	Buena Vista city, Virginia	5,452	55.9	0.0	59.5	52.7	57.3	76.5	61.1	7.5	7.3	2,824	1,410	1,414	50.1
51540	Charlottesville city, Virginia	38,945	63.3	0.3	63.6	63.1	44.6	81.3	71.0	22.4	4.3	23,605	11,340	12,265	52.0
51550	Chesapeake city, Virginia	180,680	63.4	3.5	65.4	61.5	55.0	77.0	67.9	17.6	7.5	105,953	52,952	53,001	50.0
51570	Colonial Heights city, Virginia	13,985	59.8	1.3	67.4	53.6	59.2	81.9	68.1	13.7	8.3	7,672	3,905	3,767	49.1
51580	Covington city, Virginia	4,644	50.2	2.1	55.9	44.3	62.0	68.9	49.7	7.8	7.3	2,160	1,231	929	43.0
51590	Danville city, Virginia	34,149	56.0	0.1	57.8	54.4	59.9	76.9	56.7	14.8	12.7	16,682	7,528	9,154	54.9
51595	Emporia city, Virginia	4,504	56.9	0.0	65.6	49.8	66.9	75.4	54.8	17.6	19.1	2,074	1,018	1,056	50.9
51600	Fairfax city, Virginia	19,133	70.3	0.3	75.5	65.3	61.2	88.9	76.8	18.6	5.4	12,724	6,659	6,065	47.7
51610	Falls Church city, Virginia	10,210	75.1	0.9	81.2	69.6	61.3	86.2	82.6	32.1	4.2	7,347	3,769	3,578	48.7
51620	Franklin city, Virginia	6,619	60.1	0.2	59.6	60.4	57.5	82.1	66.4	10.8	13.7	3,429	1,433	1,996	58.2
51630	Fredericksburg city, Virginia	22,148	66.4	0.6	74.1	60.1	51.9	86.2	67.2	21.1	8.9	13,384	6,561	6,823	51.0
51640	Galax city, Virginia	5,599	54.2	0.0	55.7	53.0	55.1	73.7	51.8	21.5	6.4	2,842	1,338	1,504	52.9
51650	Hampton city, Virginia	110,179	61.2	4.1	64.2	58.5	51.9	77.9	64.8	17.8	9.8	60,826	30,326	30,500	50.1
51660	Harrisonburg city, Virginia	44,000	58.3	0.1	62.1	55.0	41.4	82.8	78.1	20.8	6.5	24,011	11,904	12,107	50.4
51670	Hopewell city, Virginia	17,258	60.1	0.5	63.7	56.9	61.4	80.5	51.8	14.5	12.8	9,041	4,475	4,566	50.5
51678	Lexington city, Virginia	6,455	33.1	2.4	27.8	42.7	24.0	78.4	60.2	11.8	2.7	2,082	1,133	949	45.6
51680	Lynchburg city, Virginia	64,751	57.7	0.2	61.0	54.9	49.4	80.7	65.2	15.6	8.0	34,404	16,660	17,744	51.6
51683	Manassas city, Virginia	30,857	75.5	0.1	83.3	67.8	69.5	85.6	75.3	28.9	7.5	21,549	11,887	9,662	44.8
51685	Manassas Park city, Virginia	11,756	71.1	0.7	76.7	65.2	49.1	82.9	76.7	18.7	4.4	7,991	4,497	3,494	43.7
51690	Martinsville city, Virginia	10,924	53.4	0.1	55.0	52.1	66.2	68.3	60.6	15.7	11.5	5,156	2,323	2,833	54.9
51700	Newport News city, Virginia	142,663	63.7	5.4	65.7	61.8	52.7	79.5	67.2	17.8	9.1	82,572	40,380	42,192	51.1
51710	Norfolk city, Virginia	200,147	57.1	11.6	56.1	58.1	43.0	71.6	65.9	16.7	10.9	101,764	52,500	49,264	48.4
51720	Norton city, Virginia	3,284	62.0	0.0	65.3	59.9	86.9	78.5	44.5	11.4	11.1	1,811	724	1,087	60.0
51730	Petersburg city, Virginia	26,143	56.7	1.1	56.5	56.9	67.1	69.9	57.7	13.4	13.0	12,898	5,474	7,424	57.6
51735	Poquoson city, Virginia	9,777	63.5	0.9	70.7	56.7	53.3	83.3	75.6	16.9	4.5	5,932	3,192	2,740	46.2
51740	Portsmouth city, Virginia	75,770	61.3	3.1	63.8	59.0	57.3	79.2	59.8	13.4	11.6	41,039	20,300	20,739	50.5
51750	Radford city, Virginia	15,182	49.1	0.7	49.8	48.5	39.9	73.1	57.5	20.1	8.8	6,797	3,371	3,426	50.4
51760	Richmond city, Virginia	177,809	65.3	0.2	68.0	62.9	58.7	81.0	61.3	18.6	10.0	104,547	51,100	53,447	51.1
51770	Roanoke city, Virginia	79,184	63.8	0.1	68.7	59.4	63.7	80.6	62.2	17.9	8.3	46,331	23,713	22,618	48.8
51775	Salem city, Virginia	20,948	62.7	0.2	66.9	59.1	54.5	84.6	69.0	19.3	4.8	12,506	6,166	6,340	50.7

Table C. County—Labor Force, Employment, and Educational Data, 2011–2015—*Continued*

Fips code	State/county	Total population age 16 and older	Percent in civilian labor force	Percent in armed forces	Civilian labor force participation by gender — Men	Civilian labor force participation by gender — Women	Civilian labor force participation by age — Age 16 to 24	Civilian labor force participation by age — Age 25 to 54	Civilian labor force participation by age — Age 55 to 64	Civilian labor force participation by age — Age 65 and older	Civilian unemployment rate	Civilian employed population age 16 and older — Total	Civilian employed population age 16 and older — Men	Civilian employed population age 16 and older — Women	Civilian employed population age 16 and older — Percent women
51790	Staunton city, Virginia	20,189	59.3	0.1	68.1	52.5	59.9	79.3	64.5	18.2	5.6	11,297	5,551	5,746	50.9
51800	Suffolk city, Virginia	66,759	64.4	2.5	67.8	61.4	59.8	79.9	63.7	18.5	8.0	39,589	19,827	19,762	49.9
51810	Virginia Beach city, Virginia	356,105	64.3	6.3	66.9	61.8	54.6	77.8	70.5	19.0	6.1	214,968	108,428	106,540	49.6
51820	Waynesboro city, Virginia	16,677	60.9	0.1	68.3	54.6	55.5	80.0	70.8	15.5	4.9	9,655	4,992	4,663	48.3
51830	Williamsburg city, Virginia	13,378	48.6	0.5	52.7	45.3	36.3	81.2	61.0	19.8	8.5	5,953	2,926	3,027	50.8
51840	Winchester city, Virginia	21,679	63.0	0.3	67.1	59.1	55.6	82.8	61.4	16.4	6.7	12,748	6,657	6,091	47.8
53000	**Washington**	5,568,640	63.5	0.9	68.6	58.5	57.6	80.4	65.3	16.2	7.9	3,259,877	1,742,108	1,517,769	46.6
53001	Adams County, Washington	13,105	65.0	0.2	75.5	54.4	56.8	81.6	63.6	20.1	9.6	7,698	4,537	3,161	41.1
53003	Asotin County, Washington	18,014	57.9	0.0	60.8	55.3	70.2	81.4	56.5	11.8	9.6	9,439	4,741	4,698	49.8
53005	Benton County, Washington	140,933	62.8	0.0	70.0	55.8	55.1	80.6	65.1	14.8	6.9	82,427	45,506	36,921	44.8
53007	Chelan County, Washington	58,344	61.4	0.0	67.8	55.2	60.0	82.1	64.2	15.8	7.5	33,140	17,996	15,144	45.7
53009	Clallam County, Washington	61,180	50.2	0.4	54.2	46.4	53.8	77.3	55.3	12.7	9.9	27,697	14,634	13,063	47.2
53011	Clark County, Washington	344,185	64.0	0.1	70.3	57.8	57.7	81.5	63.6	16.0	8.6	201,261	108,645	92,616	46.0
53013	Columbia County, Washington	3,373	51.5	0.0	51.6	51.4	62.2	76.1	62.8	9.5	10.4	1,557	738	819	52.6
53015	Cowlitz County, Washington	81,246	55.7	0.1	61.0	50.6	56.9	76.6	54.2	12.0	10.7	40,418	21,682	18,736	46.4
53017	Douglas County, Washington	30,222	63.8	0.0	71.9	55.9	61.7	83.5	66.8	15.4	6.5	18,034	10,018	8,016	44.4
53019	Ferry County, Washington	6,460	43.2	0.0	44.5	41.9	47.3	58.6	45.6	15.2	12.2	2,452	1,264	1,188	48.5
53021	Franklin County, Washington	60,251	64.9	0.1	70.8	58.2	56.6	76.9	65.6	15.3	7.2	36,259	20,949	15,310	42.2
53023	Garfield County, Washington	1,799	53.0	0.0	55.9	50.3	30.3	85.5	60.9	10.8	7.4	883	442	441	49.9
53025	Grant County, Washington	67,082	63.5	0.1	71.1	55.8	59.6	80.7	65.9	15.1	10.1	38,314	21,635	16,679	43.5
53027	Grays Harbor County, Washington	58,117	52.6	0.1	54.4	50.7	59.1	69.8	53.9	12.7	14.3	26,197	13,472	12,725	48.6
53029	Island County, Washington	65,479	52.9	7.0	54.4	51.4	52.6	71.0	62.7	16.2	9.0	31,525	15,783	15,742	49.9
53031	Jefferson County, Washington	26,415	48.2	0.1	48.9	47.4	53.7	74.8	54.8	16.4	9.5	11,518	5,675	5,843	50.7
53033	King County, Washington	1,662,833	69.3	0.2	75.4	63.3	58.7	84.5	70.7	18.8	6.3	1,079,601	583,562	496,039	45.9
53035	Kitsap County, Washington	207,638	56.4	5.8	58.7	54.0	50.6	72.5	62.3	15.4	8.0	107,745	56,485	51,260	47.6
53037	Kittitas County, Washington	35,450	60.6	0.1	65.0	56.2	55.9	78.7	65.4	20.5	7.8	19,811	10,516	9,295	46.9
53039	Klickitat County, Washington	16,918	49.3	0.0	53.8	45.1	45.5	71.3	52.7	11.3	7.0	7,766	4,148	3,618	46.6
53041	Lewis County, Washington	60,634	55.0	0.1	59.2	50.8	59.2	76.8	53.3	12.2	12.1	29,297	15,383	13,914	47.5
53043	Lincoln County, Washington	8,405	50.6	0.2	54.9	46.3	50.5	72.6	56.3	15.9	4.8	4,050	2,198	1,852	45.7
53045	Mason County, Washington	50,232	50.7	0.5	53.5	47.6	55.9	71.5	51.1	10.9	12.9	22,155	11,758	10,397	46.9
53047	Okanogan County, Washington	32,729	56.9	0.1	61.6	52.2	56.9	77.8	62.2	14.9	8.9	16,969	9,110	7,859	46.3
53049	Pacific County, Washington	17,464	44.9	0.3	48.0	41.8	51.5	70.5	47.6	11.8	8.9	7,141	3,790	3,351	46.9
53051	Pend Oreille County, Washington	10,663	44.1	0.0	48.5	39.5	41.5	66.7	46.5	9.8	10.3	4,217	2,331	1,886	44.7
53053	Pierce County, Washington	645,441	62.3	2.5	66.6	58.2	56.2	77.4	63.7	16.2	9.2	365,152	192,009	173,143	47.4
53055	San Juan County, Washington	13,988	58.0	0.0	61.6	54.6	63.0	84.6	65.9	20.9	5.9	7,633	3,909	3,724	48.8
53057	Skagit County, Washington	95,511	59.0	0.5	64.3	53.9	59.5	78.6	64.1	15.1	8.2	51,761	27,698	24,063	46.5
53059	Skamania County, Washington	9,205	56.2	0.0	63.9	48.6	60.7	74.7	54.3	13.7	8.3	4,742	2,671	2,071	43.7
53061	Snohomish County, Washington	592,358	67.1	0.7	72.7	61.5	60.2	81.6	69.2	17.4	7.5	367,655	198,564	169,091	46.0
53063	Spokane County, Washington	384,138	60.1	0.6	63.8	56.6	55.9	77.2	62.1	15.1	8.4	211,522	109,605	101,917	48.2
53065	Stevens County, Washington	35,151	51.1	0.1	55.2	46.9	48.4	73.6	52.5	13.1	9.4	16,259	8,714	7,545	46.4
53067	Thurston County, Washington	211,006	61.7	1.9	64.4	59.2	59.0	78.5	65.4	14.1	8.5	119,123	59,407	59,716	50.1
53069	Wahkiakum County, Washington	3,496	39.9	0.2	39.3	40.6	45.1	62.9	48.7	8.5	10.6	1,248	565	683	54.7
53071	Walla Walla County, Washington	47,929	58.2	0.0	59.4	57.1	63.6	72.5	66.7	13.9	6.4	26,112	13,645	12,467	47.7
53073	Whatcom County, Washington	170,104	62.9	0.2	68.2	57.9	63.7	80.8	65.0	15.6	8.2	98,265	52,101	46,164	47.0
53075	Whitman County, Washington	40,550	58.6	0.1	61.1	56.0	48.2	81.3	72.6	17.9	8.8	21,665	11,514	10,151	46.9
53077	Yakima County, Washington	180,592	61.6	0.1	67.4	55.8	56.8	78.1	64.2	15.3	9.0	101,169	54,708	46,461	45.9
54000	**West Virginia**	1,512,183	53.9	0.1	58.8	49.2	53.1	73.5	51.6	12.8	7.8	751,252	397,135	354,117	47.1
54001	Barbour County, West Virginia	13,634	51.2	0.0	55.3	47.3	49.2	75.2	45.6	9.4	9.0	6,345	3,198	3,147	49.6
54003	Berkeley County, West Virginia	85,021	65.1	0.2	69.8	60.6	66.4	80.6	59.6	18.6	9.7	49,941	25,989	23,952	48.0
54005	Boone County, West Virginia	19,223	43.5	0.0	50.0	37.2	45.5	61.8	35.1	6.7	9.2	7,592	4,280	3,312	43.6
54007	Braxton County, West Virginia	11,925	51.7	0.0	57.8	45.6	54.4	68.8	56.3	14.0	14.4	5,280	2,943	2,337	44.3
54009	Brooke County, West Virginia	19,950	55.5	0.1	61.2	50.2	46.4	82.8	57.5	13.4	6.4	10,360	5,427	4,933	47.6
54011	Cabell County, West Virginia	79,665	54.0	0.0	57.2	51.1	51.5	73.4	52.9	14.0	6.8	40,103	20,427	19,676	49.1
54013	Calhoun County, West Virginia	6,294	48.7	0.0	51.8	45.6	60.9	69.1	43.1	10.5	18.1	2,511	1,378	1,133	45.1
54015	Clay County, West Virginia	7,309	45.1	0.0	49.7	40.5	49.8	66.7	36.2	5.5	12.3	2,891	1,637	1,254	43.4
54017	Doddridge County, West Virginia	6,904	43.9	0.0	46.9	40.3	39.4	61.0	36.7	14.2	6.5	2,831	1,575	1,256	44.4
54019	Fayette County, West Virginia	37,187	46.9	0.0	51.4	42.4	47.8	65.9	43.6	9.6	9.2	15,837	8,639	7,198	45.5
54021	Gilmer County, West Virginia	7,516	41.0	0.0	36.8	47.4	54.3	46.3	44.0	9.8	9.4	2,791	1,459	1,332	47.7
54023	Grant County, West Virginia	9,699	55.0	0.0	59.2	50.9	36.5	81.8	59.2	13.6	6.7	4,974	2,580	2,394	48.1
54025	Greenbrier County, West Virginia	29,301	51.9	0.0	55.8	48.2	53.2	71.5	54.7	14.4	7.2	14,116	7,270	6,846	48.5
54027	Hampshire County, West Virginia	19,294	50.1	0.0	54.8	45.1	41.1	73.7	47.7	8.4	8.1	8,878	4,955	3,923	44.2
54029	Hancock County, West Virginia	24,878	57.4	0.0	63.1	52.3	55.0	76.8	63.6	16.7	7.2	13,236	6,805	6,431	48.6
54031	Hardy County, West Virginia	11,410	58.3	0.0	61.5	55.1	55.8	78.3	56.2	20.2	7.9	6,129	3,193	2,936	47.9
54033	Harrison County, West Virginia	55,825	57.3	0.0	64.7	50.4	59.7	77.5	55.1	12.3	7.4	29,587	16,060	13,527	45.7
54035	Jackson County, West Virginia	23,621	50.2	0.0	57.9	42.8	46.0	74.5	42.6	9.6	6.8	11,050	6,100	4,950	44.8
54037	Jefferson County, West Virginia	43,776	65.9	0.1	71.0	61.0	57.8	82.5	68.1	20.9	8.4	26,418	14,021	12,397	46.9
54039	Kanawha County, West Virginia	155,883	58.3	0.1	62.8	54.1	57.8	78.5	57.2	15.2	7.0	84,406	42,903	41,503	49.2

Table C. County—Labor Force, Employment, and Educational Data, 2011–2015—*Continued*

Fips code	State/county	Total population age 16 and older	Percent in civilian labor force	Percent in armed forces	Civilian labor force participation by gender		Civilian labor force participation by age				Civilian unemployment rate	Civilian employed population age 16 and older			
					Men	Women	Age 16 to 24	Age 25 to 54	Age 55 to 64	Age 65 and older		Total	Men	Women	Percent women
54041	Lewis County, West Virginia	13,282	50.8	0.0	57.0	44.9	55.5	71.7	49.1	7.0	7.2	6,259	3,465	2,794	44.6
54043	Lincoln County, West Virginia	17,177	46.9	0.0	51.2	42.8	53.0	65.0	35.7	10.7	10.1	7,245	3,751	3,494	48.2
54045	Logan County, West Virginia	29,064	45.4	0.0	52.1	39.0	48.4	64.5	34.3	9.2	10.9	11,765	6,467	5,298	45.0
54047	McDowell County, West Virginia	17,122	31.2	0.0	32.4	29.9	39.4	41.7	28.6	6.2	13.3	4,627	2,303	2,324	50.2
54049	Marion County, West Virginia	46,576	57.4	0.0	63.2	52.0	58.7	78.2	57.0	13.5	4.9	25,422	13,502	11,920	46.9
54051	Marshall County, West Virginia	26,605	54.7	0.0	61.3	48.4	57.6	76.9	50.0	13.1	7.0	13,530	7,329	6,201	45.8
54053	Mason County, West Virginia	22,107	46.0	0.0	51.9	40.6	39.6	68.2	42.5	6.8	10.3	9,116	4,812	4,304	47.2
54055	Mercer County, West Virginia	50,340	49.1	0.0	54.3	44.4	50.0	69.4	44.3	13.4	5.1	23,443	12,101	11,342	48.4
54057	Mineral County, West Virginia	22,815	51.5	0.0	56.8	46.4	50.4	74.0	52.2	8.3	8.8	10,716	5,630	5,086	47.5
54059	Mingo County, West Virginia	20,844	44.4	0.0	52.7	36.7	48.4	61.1	33.5	8.9	14.1	7,951	4,470	3,481	43.8
54061	Monongalia County, West Virginia	87,203	58.9	0.0	62.2	55.3	46.1	78.8	60.6	16.3	5.8	48,349	26,311	22,038	45.6
54063	Monroe County, West Virginia	11,138	51.8	0.1	55.6	48.0	71.6	73.7	52.0	9.2	7.3	5,348	2,850	2,498	46.7
54065	Morgan County, West Virginia	14,490	56.2	0.3	64.4	48.4	64.9	74.1	63.1	13.0	12.3	7,144	4,041	3,103	43.4
54067	Nicholas County, West Virginia	21,130	50.7	0.0	58.8	43.0	54.9	72.7	47.1	7.4	8.4	9,824	5,439	4,385	44.6
54069	Ohio County, West Virginia	36,232	59.2	0.0	64.3	54.6	59.5	80.6	62.8	16.6	5.5	20,291	10,381	9,910	48.8
54071	Pendleton County, West Virginia	6,240	47.8	1.3	51.0	44.5	40.4	67.0	63.0	12.9	4.9	2,833	1,500	1,333	47.1
54073	Pleasants County, West Virginia	6,387	49.7	0.0	50.5	48.8	49.5	66.1	51.1	12.3	8.2	2,915	1,567	1,348	46.2
54075	Pocahontas County, West Virginia	7,348	53.7	0.0	57.6	49.6	59.1	73.3	51.6	19.2	5.7	3,723	2,013	1,710	45.9
54077	Preston County, West Virginia	27,936	53.3	0.2	57.8	48.5	59.5	67.8	55.2	12.4	7.0	13,842	7,736	6,106	44.1
54079	Putnam County, West Virginia	44,968	60.0	0.2	67.5	52.9	57.3	79.0	59.8	14.2	3.7	25,964	14,039	11,925	45.9
54081	Raleigh County, West Virginia	63,727	48.7	0.1	52.1	45.4	53.1	65.3	46.5	11.4	6.6	29,014	15,161	13,853	47.7
54083	Randolph County, West Virginia	24,295	52.2	0.0	54.4	49.9	49.1	72.0	53.2	13.5	6.7	11,833	6,191	5,642	47.7
54085	Ritchie County, West Virginia	8,318	50.2	0.0	57.7	42.9	50.0	71.4	51.3	9.5	10.6	3,730	1,999	1,731	46.4
54087	Roane County, West Virginia	11,836	45.3	0.0	50.8	40.1	47.2	61.4	49.3	10.2	8.9	4,892	2,668	2,224	45.5
54089	Summers County, West Virginia	11,513	46.9	0.0	53.8	41.2	51.7	61.7	47.1	16.8	10.0	4,857	2,535	2,322	47.8
54091	Taylor County, West Virginia	13,865	54.1	0.0	59.7	48.4	55.1	74.1	53.1	9.5	9.5	6,784	3,688	3,096	45.6
54093	Tucker County, West Virginia	5,899	56.0	0.0	61.5	50.5	61.4	78.3	57.1	16.0	7.6	3,052	1,631	1,421	46.6
54095	Tyler County, West Virginia	7,478	49.5	0.0	54.3	44.8	43.7	72.7	50.0	9.6	10.9	3,296	1,758	1,538	46.7
54097	Upshur County, West Virginia	20,084	52.4	0.0	59.1	45.8	48.1	75.9	49.6	11.3	8.0	9,682	5,393	4,289	44.3
54099	Wayne County, West Virginia	33,605	48.0	0.0	52.1	44.3	53.8	67.2	41.3	8.9	9.9	14,542	7,516	7,026	48.3
54101	Webster County, West Virginia	7,331	47.1	0.0	53.2	41.4	52.2	70.4	42.5	7.3	14.8	2,945	1,564	1,381	46.9
54103	Wetzel County, West Virginia	13,309	45.4	0.0	51.4	39.7	41.9	69.2	42.7	8.4	8.1	5,548	2,983	2,565	46.2
54105	Wirt County, West Virginia	4,733	52.2	0.0	58.5	45.9	49.3	76.4	47.9	6.6	8.4	2,265	1,251	1,014	44.8
54107	Wood County, West Virginia	70,218	57.3	0.0	63.0	52.2	59.9	78.9	54.1	12.4	8.6	36,778	18,835	17,943	48.8
54109	Wyoming County, West Virginia	18,653	38.4	0.0	43.3	33.8	42.6	56.8	27.4	6.5	10.1	6,451	3,416	3,035	47.0
55000	**Wisconsin**	4,583,931	67.1	0.1	70.9	63.5	67.1	85.9	68.5	15.9	6.3	2,883,390	1,489,667	1,393,723	48.3
55001	Adams County, Wisconsin	17,679	46.9	0.0	46.8	47.0	56.7	66.8	53.0	13.5	10.1	7,457	3,949	3,508	47.0
55003	Ashland County, Wisconsin	12,839	63.2	0.0	65.3	61.2	65.1	88.8	58.8	11.7	7.9	7,475	3,829	3,646	48.8
55005	Barron County, Wisconsin	37,073	63.9	0.0	68.3	59.4	72.8	86.1	67.9	14.3	6.0	22,257	11,918	10,339	46.5
55007	Bayfield County, Wisconsin	12,670	58.3	0.2	59.6	56.9	56.1	84.7	64.4	15.7	7.2	6,859	3,533	3,326	48.5
55009	Brown County, Wisconsin	199,290	69.7	0.0	73.7	65.8	70.9	86.1	68.6	16.3	6.1	130,354	67,589	62,765	48.1
55011	Buffalo County, Wisconsin	10,845	67.2	0.0	70.6	63.5	69.2	90.4	69.8	20.1	3.7	7,013	3,767	3,246	46.3
55013	Burnett County, Wisconsin	12,846	54.4	0.2	55.5	53.2	65.1	82.6	58.3	12.4	7.5	6,464	3,273	3,191	49.4
55015	Calumet County, Wisconsin	38,426	71.6	0.0	75.4	67.8	69.0	90.2	71.3	13.8	3.1	26,679	13,991	12,688	47.6
55017	Chippewa County, Wisconsin	50,329	65.1	0.0	65.9	64.2	68.0	83.2	65.7	16.2	5.1	31,085	16,146	14,939	48.1
55019	Clark County, Wisconsin	25,468	64.2	0.0	71.4	56.9	66.3	83.1	69.1	18.1	4.8	15,579	8,676	6,903	44.3
55021	Columbia County, Wisconsin	45,389	68.9	0.2	71.6	66.1	71.8	87.0	71.1	19.3	5.8	29,483	15,421	14,062	47.7
55023	Crawford County, Wisconsin	13,461	59.5	0.0	59.6	59.5	61.5	79.8	66.5	16.6	6.5	7,491	3,834	3,657	48.8
55025	Dane County, Wisconsin	413,418	73.1	0.1	76.6	69.6	68.9	89.1	72.8	20.6	4.9	287,151	147,264	139,887	48.7
55027	Dodge County, Wisconsin	72,158	63.9	0.0	66.4	61.1	66.5	80.1	68.1	16.5	6.0	43,362	23,682	19,680	45.4
55029	Door County, Wisconsin	23,674	59.3	0.1	63.8	55.1	65.7	87.6	66.5	15.9	6.2	13,169	6,821	6,348	48.2
55031	Douglas County, Wisconsin	35,600	64.5	0.1	65.0	64.0	69.0	85.0	61.8	12.4	7.0	21,340	10,543	10,797	50.6
55033	Dunn County, Wisconsin	36,303	66.0	0.0	69.8	62.2	64.2	86.1	68.4	16.7	6.1	22,494	11,816	10,678	47.5
55035	Eau Claire County, Wisconsin	82,797	69.3	0.1	73.2	65.7	72.5	86.9	68.4	18.1	5.8	54,079	27,550	26,529	49.1
55037	Florence County, Wisconsin	3,803	55.0	0.0	55.8	54.1	75.0	75.9	58.2	14.7	7.2	1,942	993	949	48.9
55039	Fond du Lac County, Wisconsin	81,763	68.3	0.0	72.9	63.9	74.2	88.0	70.4	14.6	5.3	52,846	27,407	25,439	48.1
55041	Forest County, Wisconsin	7,481	52.9	0.0	55.3	50.6	57.5	76.3	57.8	10.6	10.1	3,559	1,842	1,717	48.2
55043	Grant County, Wisconsin	42,053	65.2	0.0	68.1	62.1	63.8	87.9	70.8	16.2	4.6	26,157	14,156	12,001	45.9
55045	Green County, Wisconsin	29,309	70.1	0.0	74.3	66.0	72.1	89.2	71.8	21.8	3.5	19,815	10,265	9,550	48.2
55047	Green Lake County, Wisconsin	15,141	63.2	0.0	67.1	59.3	66.3	86.7	67.4	18.0	5.7	9,016	4,700	4,316	47.9
55049	Iowa County, Wisconsin	18,783	69.4	0.1	72.7	66.2	68.8	89.7	72.0	19.2	4.7	12,424	6,415	6,009	48.4
55051	Iron County, Wisconsin	5,108	53.9	0.0	55.0	52.8	63.9	84.9	57.1	12.2	7.0	2,560	1,285	1,275	49.8
55053	Jackson County, Wisconsin	16,495	59.7	0.0	59.7	59.7	61.4	77.0	61.1	17.6	5.6	9,294	5,001	4,293	46.2
55055	Jefferson County, Wisconsin	67,450	69.7	0.0	73.7	65.8	80.3	88.2	73.0	17.1	5.5	44,424	23,271	21,153	47.6
55057	Juneau County, Wisconsin	21,728	57.0	0.5	57.1	57.0	61.5	75.5	59.8	14.5	7.1	11,520	6,043	5,477	47.5
55059	Kenosha County, Wisconsin	131,465	67.2	0.2	71.3	63.2	63.5	84.8	64.0	14.1	9.7	79,753	41,106	38,647	48.5

Table C. County—Labor Force, Employment, and Educational Data, 2011–2015—*Continued*

Fips code	State/county	Total population age 16 and older	Percent in civilian labor force	Percent in armed forces	Civilian labor force participation by gender		Civilian labor force participation by age				Civilian unemployment rate	Civilian employed population age 16 and older			
					Men	Women	Age 16 to 24	Age 25 to 54	Age 55 to 64	Age 65 and older		Total	Men	Women	Percent women
55061	Kewaunee County, Wisconsin	16,416	66.5	0.0	72.4	60.4	72.1	89.0	71.4	12.8	4.7	10,404	5,713	4,691	45.1
55063	La Crosse County, Wisconsin	95,759	68.7	0.0	72.2	65.6	67.4	89.0	72.1	15.9	5.4	62,292	31,137	31,155	50.0
55065	Lafayette County, Wisconsin	13,157	68.6	0.1	72.4	64.8	61.2	88.8	74.6	22.9	3.6	8,705	4,659	4,046	46.5
55067	Langlade County, Wisconsin	16,160	59.2	0.0	62.8	55.6	66.9	82.8	65.1	12.4	8.2	8,779	4,555	4,224	48.1
55069	Lincoln County, Wisconsin	23,425	63.5	0.0	65.6	61.4	68.4	88.1	66.2	10.9	6.1	13,973	7,098	6,875	49.2
55071	Manitowoc County, Wisconsin	65,610	66.0	0.1	71.3	60.7	71.5	88.3	70.9	12.3	5.7	40,799	21,597	19,202	47.1
55073	Marathon County, Wisconsin	107,089	69.2	0.0	74.0	64.3	71.7	88.0	73.4	15.9	5.7	69,834	36,894	32,940	47.2
55075	Marinette County, Wisconsin	34,313	59.7	0.0	63.8	55.7	67.0	83.8	63.5	13.0	7.5	18,969	10,000	8,969	47.3
55077	Marquette County, Wisconsin	12,512	58.9	0.1	60.9	56.8	62.2	84.6	62.9	13.1	7.6	6,809	3,551	3,258	47.8
55078	Menominee County, Wisconsin	3,204	51.4	0.0	51.8	51.1	41.9	69.7	52.6	16.7	14.8	1,403	675	728	51.9
55079	Milwaukee County, Wisconsin	745,676	65.8	0.0	69.1	62.9	60.8	82.7	63.2	15.4	9.3	445,174	220,284	224,890	50.5
55081	Monroe County, Wisconsin	34,900	64.1	1.2	68.0	60.2	63.9	82.0	67.1	17.1	6.5	20,936	11,225	9,711	46.4
55083	Oconto County, Wisconsin	30,642	65.9	0.0	69.5	62.1	68.2	88.4	67.0	14.7	5.5	19,075	10,143	8,932	46.8
55085	Oneida County, Wisconsin	30,293	58.3	0.0	60.5	56.2	64.0	85.3	61.3	13.6	6.3	16,557	8,519	8,038	48.5
55087	Outagamie County, Wisconsin	141,717	70.9	0.0	75.6	66.3	70.0	88.3	71.9	13.5	3.9	96,532	50,475	46,057	47.7
55089	Ozaukee County, Wisconsin	70,282	67.8	0.0	73.6	62.4	66.4	87.2	74.6	19.6	4.5	45,522	23,853	21,669	47.6
55091	Pepin County, Wisconsin	5,948	63.8	0.0	66.2	61.3	62.2	87.0	73.0	16.9	4.6	3,618	1,872	1,746	48.3
55093	Pierce County, Wisconsin	33,155	70.6	0.0	72.4	68.9	67.8	88.9	72.4	16.1	3.6	22,567	11,299	11,268	49.9
55095	Polk County, Wisconsin	35,098	64.5	0.0	68.5	60.5	67.9	87.5	63.1	15.2	6.8	21,085	11,208	9,877	46.8
55097	Portage County, Wisconsin	57,926	67.6	0.0	70.5	64.8	70.5	88.1	65.6	13.2	7.2	36,371	18,644	17,727	48.7
55099	Price County, Wisconsin	11,717	59.6	0.0	63.1	56.0	62.2	85.4	67.6	13.0	4.6	6,662	3,500	3,162	47.5
55101	Racine County, Wisconsin	153,366	65.3	0.0	68.8	62.0	64.3	82.8	68.4	14.7	8.4	91,796	46,651	45,145	49.2
55103	Richland County, Wisconsin	14,179	61.7	0.0	65.5	58.0	67.8	81.5	67.8	18.6	4.8	8,332	4,393	3,939	47.3
55105	Rock County, Wisconsin	126,252	65.7	0.0	69.5	62.0	68.0	84.6	64.3	14.2	8.5	75,824	38,479	37,345	49.3
55107	Rusk County, Wisconsin	11,707	58.7	0.0	63.4	53.9	64.8	85.2	61.2	12.7	5.9	6,462	3,481	2,981	46.1
55109	St. Croix County, Wisconsin	65,924	73.0	0.2	77.1	68.9	70.1	89.9	69.8	17.0	4.6	45,882	23,853	22,029	48.0
55111	Sauk County, Wisconsin	50,149	68.7	0.0	72.9	64.6	71.1	88.8	70.4	18.5	5.5	32,534	17,070	15,464	47.5
55113	Sawyer County, Wisconsin	13,578	56.8	0.0	57.2	56.3	60.4	79.9	59.7	18.8	9.8	6,957	3,460	3,497	50.3
55115	Shawano County, Wisconsin	33,514	63.9	0.0	66.6	61.3	67.8	86.9	69.3	14.7	5.4	20,281	10,389	9,892	48.8
55117	Sheboygan County, Wisconsin	91,896	68.3	0.0	72.3	64.4	70.3	87.1	73.3	16.0	5.8	59,133	31,007	28,126	47.6
55119	Taylor County, Wisconsin	16,231	65.8	0.0	70.0	61.4	63.6	87.9	72.2	15.0	5.5	10,090	5,419	4,671	46.3
55121	Trempealeau County, Wisconsin	23,017	68.4	0.0	72.2	64.5	69.5	88.5	74.1	16.8	3.6	15,166	8,043	7,123	47.0
55123	Vernon County, Wisconsin	23,269	60.2	0.0	64.1	56.4	55.9	80.5	69.3	16.6	4.0	13,450	7,049	6,401	47.6
55125	Vilas County, Wisconsin	18,236	53.6	0.0	57.9	49.2	63.2	81.8	60.5	14.9	8.0	8,986	4,759	4,227	47.0
55127	Walworth County, Wisconsin	82,805	67.8	0.0	72.8	62.8	68.1	85.9	69.9	19.8	7.2	52,048	27,579	24,469	47.0
55129	Washburn County, Wisconsin	12,996	56.7	0.0	59.6	53.8	66.7	82.3	62.3	11.4	6.6	6,880	3,549	3,331	48.4
55131	Washington County, Wisconsin	105,685	71.7	0.0	76.9	66.6	74.8	90.0	74.9	17.3	4.5	72,365	38,163	34,202	47.3
55133	Waukesha County, Wisconsin	315,919	69.2	0.0	75.3	63.5	68.5	88.6	74.4	17.3	4.2	209,461	110,243	99,218	47.4
55135	Waupaca County, Wisconsin	42,312	64.4	0.0	68.0	60.8	72.5	86.8	67.6	13.6	5.7	25,703	13,631	12,072	47.0
55137	Waushara County, Wisconsin	20,287	55.6	0.0	56.5	54.5	66.2	75.9	61.4	12.8	7.2	10,458	5,617	4,841	46.3
55139	Winnebago County, Wisconsin	137,208	65.7	0.1	68.7	62.8	70.1	82.8	67.4	12.9	4.7	85,970	44,994	40,976	47.7
55141	Wood County, Wisconsin	59,558	65.5	0.0	69.3	61.9	69.6	88.8	68.3	12.5	6.6	36,445	18,851	17,594	48.3
56000	**Wyoming**	456,640	67.7	0.5	72.5	62.7	64.0	84.3	69.6	20.7	4.9	293,949	159,635	134,314	45.7
56001	Albany County, Wyoming	31,878	67.7	0.1	68.0	67.5	58.5	84.6	77.6	23.8	4.7	20,577	10,794	9,783	47.5
56003	Big Horn County, Wyoming	9,295	59.5	0.0	66.2	52.6	49.3	81.5	67.5	21.3	4.4	5,288	2,936	2,352	44.5
56005	Campbell County, Wyoming	35,874	76.6	0.1	84.3	68.4	71.9	87.4	70.8	24.4	4.0	26,387	15,191	11,196	42.4
56007	Carbon County, Wyoming	12,370	66.3	0.0	69.1	62.9	57.7	81.6	73.9	19.7	4.3	7,851	4,509	3,342	42.6
56009	Converse County, Wyoming	10,998	70.0	0.0	75.1	64.7	67.9	86.9	69.2	24.0	5.1	7,303	3,963	3,340	45.7
56011	Crook County, Wyoming	5,776	67.8	0.0	73.0	62.3	63.0	85.3	73.2	29.9	4.1	3,754	2,078	1,676	44.6
56013	Fremont County, Wyoming	31,632	64.3	0.1	68.6	60.0	65.1	81.7	69.2	19.5	7.8	18,736	9,773	8,963	47.8
56015	Goshen County, Wyoming	11,062	59.0	0.1	63.7	53.6	59.0	78.7	62.6	21.0	6.8	6,080	3,478	2,602	42.8
56017	Hot Springs County, Wyoming	3,872	61.2	0.0	66.3	56.4	69.7	81.6	68.6	23.1	3.3	2,292	1,211	1,081	47.2
56019	Johnson County, Wyoming	6,741	66.1	0.0	71.6	60.4	74.3	88.7	70.1	21.0	3.6	4,300	2,388	1,912	44.5
56021	Laramie County, Wyoming	75,360	64.6	2.9	67.6	61.5	56.9	83.1	65.8	17.2	5.0	46,206	24,157	22,049	47.7
56023	Lincoln County, Wyoming	13,849	67.3	0.1	73.3	61.1	56.9	85.7	70.1	21.1	6.4	8,724	4,722	4,002	45.9
56025	Natrona County, Wyoming	63,054	69.2	0.0	74.7	63.6	66.8	84.1	71.3	21.5	5.1	41,415	22,460	18,955	45.8
56027	Niobrara County, Wyoming	2,109	53.7	0.5	66.3	44.1	46.2	66.5	68.8	23.9	1.6	1,114	605	509	45.7
56029	Park County, Wyoming	23,741	67.0	0.1	69.4	64.8	77.7	89.5	68.1	17.8	3.8	15,305	7,718	7,587	49.6
56031	Platte County, Wyoming	7,217	58.7	0.1	65.8	51.5	62.3	80.2	64.8	21.2	2.4	4,133	2,315	1,818	44.0
56033	Sheridan County, Wyoming	23,825	62.3	0.3	66.1	58.6	65.3	81.2	65.2	18.5	3.4	14,336	7,327	7,009	48.9
56035	Sublette County, Wyoming	7,947	73.7	0.0	81.1	65.3	59.7	88.5	72.3	34.2	5.4	5,541	3,229	2,312	41.7
56037	Sweetwater County, Wyoming	33,637	72.3	0.0	80.2	63.6	73.6	84.0	71.5	18.6	5.4	23,010	13,401	9,609	41.8
56039	Teton County, Wyoming	18,682	78.6	0.0	83.0	73.8	62.9	93.0	79.0	25.7	2.6	14,298	7,856	6,442	45.1
56041	Uinta County, Wyoming	15,297	68.8	0.0	75.8	61.9	76.3	79.8	66.9	22.4	4.4	10,064	5,455	4,609	45.8
56043	Washakie County, Wyoming	6,632	63.0	0.0	67.2	58.6	56.7	84.0	67.6	23.6	6.8	3,892	2,110	1,782	45.8
56045	Weston County, Wyoming	5,792	60.9	0.0	66.5	54.6	59.3	77.9	70.1	17.3	5.2	3,343	1,959	1,384	41.4

Table C. County—Labor Force, Employment, and Educational Data, 2011–2015

| | | Class of worker for civilian employed population age 16 and older | | | | | | | | |
| | | Private for-profit wage and salary workers | | | | Government workers | | | | |
Fips code	State/county	Total private for-profit wage and salary workers	Employees of private companies	Self-employed in own incorporated business	Private not-for-profit wage and salary workers	Local government workers	State government workers	Federal government workers	Self-employed in own not incorporated business	Unpaid family workers
00000	**United States**	71.4	68.0	3.4	8.1	7.0	4.7	2.6	6.0	0.2
01000	**Alabama**	71.7	68.8	2.8	6.6	6.9	5.8	3.5	5.2	0.2
01001	Autauga County, Alabama	66.2	63.9	2.3	7.4	6.8	9.8	4.4	5.5	0.0
01003	Baldwin County, Alabama	75.4	70.7	4.7	6.1	6.9	3.3	2.2	5.8	0.4
01005	Barbour County, Alabama	67.5	64.2	3.3	4.3	8.7	9.7	2.4	7.3	0.1
01007	Bibb County, Alabama	69.6	68.4	1.2	7.2	9.0	5.3	1.8	6.7	0.4
01009	Blount County, Alabama	75.8	72.7	3.2	6.1	6.6	5.7	1.2	4.2	0.4
01011	Bullock County, Alabama	73.4	70.7	2.6	6.2	6.5	7.8	0.9	5.4	0.0
01013	Butler County, Alabama	73.6	71.6	2.0	3.9	7.6	6.3	2.4	6.2	0.2
01015	Calhoun County, Alabama	68.7	65.6	3.0	5.4	7.8	6.1	6.8	5.0	0.1
01017	Chambers County, Alabama	80.3	77.9	2.4	4.8	5.6	4.5	1.9	2.8	0.0
01019	Cherokee County, Alabama	69.1	67.0	2.1	4.0	10.2	5.6	2.7	7.9	0.5
01021	Chilton County, Alabama	76.3	71.5	4.8	3.9	6.4	6.2	2.6	4.1	0.5
01023	Choctaw County, Alabama	73.8	72.8	1.0	3.7	8.0	6.5	2.3	5.4	0.3
01025	Clarke County, Alabama	76.7	74.6	2.1	6.4	7.5	4.6	1.5	3.3	0.0
01027	Clay County, Alabama	72.5	69.4	3.1	5.1	8.6	5.1	1.1	7.8	0.0
01029	Cleburne County, Alabama	72.3	71.4	0.9	4.0	9.2	5.1	0.9	8.4	0.0
01031	Coffee County, Alabama	65.8	62.9	2.9	4.5	8.9	4.3	10.4	5.7	0.5
01033	Colbert County, Alabama	71.9	68.6	3.3	6.7	8.9	4.5	2.8	5.2	0.0
01035	Conecuh County, Alabama	75.4	73.6	1.7	2.5	4.0	8.1	0.9	8.3	0.8
01037	Coosa County, Alabama	74.8	73.2	1.6	1.8	8.5	4.6	4.4	5.9	0.0
01039	Covington County, Alabama	73.1	70.3	2.9	3.9	8.9	5.0	1.9	6.7	0.4
01041	Crenshaw County, Alabama	70.1	68.4	1.6	4.0	6.4	7.6	3.7	7.9	0.3
01043	Cullman County, Alabama	76.0	72.1	3.9	5.6	6.1	4.2	1.9	5.8	0.4
01045	Dale County, Alabama	69.1	67.6	1.5	4.0	7.1	4.0	9.8	5.9	0.1
01047	Dallas County, Alabama	71.0	68.7	2.3	5.6	8.0	6.7	2.1	6.2	0.4
01049	DeKalb County, Alabama	74.9	71.8	3.1	3.9	7.9	3.6	1.1	8.5	0.1
01051	Elmore County, Alabama	64.3	62.0	2.3	6.1	8.0	9.5	6.6	5.5	0.0
01053	Escambia County, Alabama	71.3	69.6	1.7	3.2	9.5	7.8	1.6	6.4	0.1
01055	Etowah County, Alabama	75.2	72.5	2.7	4.6	6.9	5.6	1.9	5.6	0.2
01057	Fayette County, Alabama	74.0	72.0	2.0	7.9	6.9	6.3	0.9	3.8	0.1
01059	Franklin County, Alabama	75.1	73.9	1.2	3.4	6.9	6.0	1.7	6.9	0.0
01061	Geneva County, Alabama	70.8	66.4	4.4	4.9	7.0	4.8	3.1	8.8	0.4
01063	Greene County, Alabama	68.1	64.1	4.1	7.7	6.4	8.1	2.8	7.0	0.0
01065	Hale County, Alabama	70.2	67.6	2.6	6.1	5.3	10.8	1.5	5.8	0.3
01067	Henry County, Alabama	71.5	67.8	3.7	7.4	7.2	6.0	2.3	5.4	0.2
01069	Houston County, Alabama	74.8	71.3	3.5	6.5	6.5	3.6	2.9	5.5	0.2
01071	Jackson County, Alabama	70.9	69.6	1.4	4.2	9.1	5.4	2.6	7.7	0.0
01073	Jefferson County, Alabama	71.9	68.7	3.1	9.0	6.6	5.2	2.5	4.6	0.2
01075	Lamar County, Alabama	73.3	70.8	2.4	6.4	9.4	5.7	0.4	3.9	0.9
01077	Lauderdale County, Alabama	71.7	69.1	2.6	5.6	6.5	6.4	3.8	5.8	0.2
01079	Lawrence County, Alabama	77.6	75.5	2.0	2.7	6.2	5.3	1.9	5.9	0.4
01081	Lee County, Alabama	69.1	66.6	2.4	6.4	7.0	10.4	2.9	4.1	0.1
01083	Limestone County, Alabama	71.8	69.0	2.7	6.2	6.4	4.1	5.9	5.5	0.2
01085	Lowndes County, Alabama	67.4	65.7	1.7	6.5	7.7	9.2	3.5	4.2	1.5
01087	Macon County, Alabama	68.2	67.4	0.8	7.5	7.4	7.5	5.5	3.8	0.2
01089	Madison County, Alabama	68.2	65.7	2.5	7.5	5.5	4.2	9.8	4.7	0.2
01091	Marengo County, Alabama	66.0	63.5	2.6	6.5	9.7	7.7	1.4	7.9	0.7
01093	Marion County, Alabama	66.2	64.7	1.5	8.8	9.1	5.4	2.0	8.0	0.5
01095	Marshall County, Alabama	73.1	70.0	3.1	4.9	8.0	4.1	2.7	7.1	0.1
01097	Mobile County, Alabama	74.1	71.8	2.3	7.4	6.6	5.1	2.0	4.6	0.1
01099	Monroe County, Alabama	72.8	71.3	1.5	4.5	9.6	6.4	2.4	4.1	0.2
01101	Montgomery County, Alabama	65.3	62.8	2.6	7.3	6.9	10.3	5.5	4.6	0.1
01103	Morgan County, Alabama	76.5	74.0	2.5	5.4	5.5	3.7	2.9	5.9	0.1
01105	Perry County, Alabama	69.1	66.5	2.6	7.2	5.7	10.2	3.1	4.7	0.0
01107	Pickens County, Alabama	69.7	68.3	1.4	8.0	8.1	7.1	2.7	4.2	0.1
01109	Pike County, Alabama	69.2	68.2	1.1	6.6	7.2	9.8	1.6	5.5	0.1
01111	Randolph County, Alabama	72.7	71.1	1.6	3.7	5.4	6.6	1.9	8.9	0.9
01113	Russell County, Alabama	69.5	68.4	1.2	6.0	9.0	4.6	6.7	4.2	0.1
01115	St. Clair County, Alabama	77.6	74.5	3.1	4.1	5.5	4.8	2.0	6.0	0.1
01117	Shelby County, Alabama	75.5	71.3	4.2	7.0	6.7	4.1	1.7	4.8	0.1
01119	Sumter County, Alabama	63.9	63.0	1.0	7.2	9.3	12.7	1.7	5.1	0.0
01121	Talladega County, Alabama	72.1	70.0	2.0	5.6	7.4	6.2	3.0	5.5	0.2
01123	Tallapoosa County, Alabama	73.6	70.4	3.2	4.8	8.6	5.0	2.0	5.5	0.5
01125	Tuscaloosa County, Alabama	68.0	64.9	3.1	9.0	6.5	10.1	2.3	4.0	0.1
01127	Walker County, Alabama	72.1	69.4	2.7	6.2	8.5	5.5	1.3	6.2	0.2
01129	Washington County, Alabama	72.1	70.9	1.2	5.3	9.7	6.3	0.1	6.0	0.4
01131	Wilcox County, Alabama	62.0	58.9	3.1	6.9	12.9	11.2	1.9	5.1	0.0
01133	Winston County, Alabama	69.5	66.6	2.9	4.8	9.5	4.1	2.4	9.6	0.1
02000	**Alaska**	58.3	55.1	3.2	10.1	9.2	8.8	7.1	6.3	0.2
02013	Aleutians East Borough, Alaska	76.6	75.7	0.9	2.0	12.2	1.8	1.3	5.9	0.2
02016	Aleutians West Census Area, Alaska	74.3	73.3	0.9	3.6	12.2	2.6	4.1	3.2	0.0
02020	Anchorage Municipality, Alaska	63.2	60.1	3.1	10.1	6.0	7.2	7.7	5.7	0.1
02050	Bethel Census Area, Alaska	27.8	27.0	0.9	25.4	21.3	20.5	3.0	2.0	0.0

Table C. County—Labor Force, Employment, and Educational Data, 2011–2015—*Continued*

| | | Class of worker for civilian employed population age 16 and older | | | | | | | | |
| | | Private for-profit wage and salary workers | | | | Government workers | | | | |
Fips code	State/county	Total private for-profit wage and salary workers	Employees of private companies	Self-employed in own incorporated business	Private not-for-profit wage and salary workers	Local government workers	State government workers	Federal government workers	Self-employed in own not incorporated business	Unpaid family workers
02060	Bristol Bay Borough, Alaska	44.7	43.3	1.5	5.0	21.3	9.6	8.3	11.1	0.0
02068	Denali Borough, Alaska	56.5	54.6	1.9	9.8	9.5	6.8	8.3	7.9	1.2
02070	Dillingham Census Area, Alaska	35.1	33.3	1.8	23.5	18.4	16.0	3.4	3.7	0.0
02090	Fairbanks North Star Borough, Alaska	56.4	53.3	3.1	9.4	6.9	11.9	11.1	4.1	0.2
02100	Haines Borough, Alaska	52.6	44.1	8.5	16.4	12.4	5.0	2.3	10.3	1.0
02105	Hoonah-Angoon Census Area, Alaska	47.6	42.3	5.3	5.9	14.3	7.0	9.7	15.6	0.0
02110	Juneau City and Borough, Alaska	44.4	41.9	2.4	9.0	10.6	21.8	6.3	7.7	0.1
02122	Kenai Peninsula Borough, Alaska	61.0	55.8	5.3	11.2	8.1	6.4	2.8	9.8	0.5
02130	Ketchikan Gateway Borough, Alaska	51.1	47.2	3.9	11.6	15.1	9.9	4.4	7.3	0.6
02150	Kodiak Island Borough, Alaska	57.5	51.7	5.9	7.4	10.9	6.0	8.3	9.4	0.3
02158	Kusilvak Census Area, Alaska	28.3	28.1	0.2	17.2	30.9	20.1	2.8	0.5	0.3
02164	Lake and Peninsula Borough, Alaska	33.2	30.0	3.2	9.0	30.3	15.2	6.1	6.1	0.2
02170	Matanuska-Susitna Borough, Alaska	63.1	59.9	3.2	7.4	8.9	6.8	5.7	7.8	0.2
02180	Nome Census Area, Alaska	32.7	32.1	0.6	17.9	24.8	14.3	5.0	5.2	0.2
02185	North Slope Borough, Alaska	67.6	67.5	0.2	6.2	20.9	2.6	1.7	0.9	0.0
02188	Northwest Arctic Borough, Alaska	36.6	36.4	0.2	17.4	27.4	11.1	5.2	2.1	0.2
02195	Petersburg Borough, Alaska	47.1	43.8	3.4	7.6	15.2	7.6	10.3	11.5	0.5
02198	Prince of Wales-Hyder Census Area, Alaska	42.9	38.7	4.2	7.5	24.0	7.5	6.2	11.8	0.1
02220	Sitka City and Borough, Alaska	43.5	38.5	5.0	16.6	11.9	9.5	6.8	11.7	0.0
02230	Skagway Municipality, Alaska	66.7	62.6	4.1	1.5	9.8	3.3	9.5	7.5	1.8
02240	Southeast Fairbanks Census Area, Alaska	54.2	52.0	2.2	9.8	7.0	7.5	13.3	7.8	0.4
02261	Valdez-Cordova Census Area, Alaska	45.0	40.7	4.3	11.6	22.2	7.7	3.0	10.1	0.4
02275	Wrangell City and Borough, Alaska	44.1	39.6	4.5	9.9	22.1	3.8	6.7	13.4	0.0
02282	Yakutat City and Borough, Alaska	47.2	44.8	2.4	5.6	20.0	4.5	12.5	10.1	0.0
02290	Yukon-Koyukuk Census Area, Alaska	24.9	23.0	1.9	8.4	38.5	10.9	12.2	5.1	0.0
04000	**Arizona**	72.9	69.3	3.6	6.3	6.9	4.9	2.9	5.9	0.2
04001	Apache County, Arizona	45.8	44.1	1.7	4.4	20.6	11.5	12.9	4.7	0.1
04003	Cochise County, Arizona	57.1	54.7	2.4	6.0	9.5	5.6	15.4	6.1	0.2
04005	Coconino County, Arizona	63.9	60.3	3.6	8.3	8.5	9.5	5.3	4.4	0.1
04007	Gila County, Arizona	65.6	60.5	5.2	6.5	13.0	6.5	3.6	4.6	0.2
04009	Graham County, Arizona	64.5	62.3	2.2	6.6	8.3	13.2	3.5	3.8	0.1
04011	Greenlee County, Arizona	79.0	78.1	0.8	2.5	9.6	3.2	1.5	4.2	0.0
04012	La Paz County, Arizona	57.4	53.9	3.4	3.4	23.5	3.3	4.6	7.9	0.0
04013	Maricopa County, Arizona	76.5	72.7	3.8	6.0	5.8	4.1	1.8	5.7	0.2
04015	Mohave County, Arizona	72.5	68.4	4.1	5.8	8.7	4.5	1.7	6.4	0.3
04017	Navajo County, Arizona	54.8	49.8	5.0	6.3	18.0	7.2	6.1	7.4	0.3
04019	Pima County, Arizona	67.2	63.8	3.4	7.7	7.2	6.8	4.4	6.6	0.2
04021	Pinal County, Arizona	71.4	69.5	1.9	4.8	9.1	5.6	3.8	5.0	0.2
04023	Santa Cruz County, Arizona	63.4	58.9	4.6	4.5	11.5	5.6	3.4	11.0	0.5
04025	Yavapai County, Arizona	67.2	62.1	5.0	9.2	7.2	4.0	3.0	9.4	0.1
04027	Yuma County, Arizona	66.3	63.8	2.5	6.7	9.6	4.8	7.5	4.9	0.1
05000	Arkansas	70.1	67.0	3.1	7.1	5.8	8.4	2.2	6.3	0.2
05001	Arkansas County, Arkansas	71.8	68.0	3.8	4.6	6.7	7.6	1.1	7.7	0.6
05003	Ashley County, Arkansas	71.0	67.4	3.6	5.7	8.2	8.6	1.2	4.8	0.5
05005	Baxter County, Arkansas	70.0	66.1	3.9	9.0	5.9	6.2	0.7	8.3	0.0
05007	Benton County, Arkansas	78.8	76.3	2.5	7.1	4.3	2.8	1.0	5.9	0.1
05009	Boone County, Arkansas	72.2	68.8	3.5	5.7	5.1	6.3	1.2	8.9	0.5
05011	Bradley County, Arkansas	68.0	64.1	3.9	4.8	8.1	12.5	1.0	5.6	0.0
05013	Calhoun County, Arkansas	71.4	64.6	6.8	3.5	8.1	8.8	0.8	7.4	0.0
05015	Carroll County, Arkansas	73.3	68.8	4.5	5.1	4.9	5.4	0.8	10.2	0.2
05017	Chicot County, Arkansas	64.3	62.1	2.2	2.3	9.6	12.3	3.0	8.6	0.0
05019	Clark County, Arkansas	63.7	61.1	2.6	9.4	7.1	12.7	1.4	5.3	0.3
05021	Clay County, Arkansas	73.2	69.6	3.6	5.4	5.1	6.7	1.6	7.9	0.1
05023	Cleburne County, Arkansas	68.4	63.6	4.9	7.0	6.2	7.7	1.5	8.9	0.4
05025	Cleveland County, Arkansas	63.0	59.2	3.8	7.2	6.1	14.0	4.4	5.3	0.0
05027	Columbia County, Arkansas	70.4	68.5	1.9	5.6	7.2	11.0	1.4	4.3	0.1
05029	Conway County, Arkansas	69.7	66.5	3.2	6.7	5.8	10.4	0.8	6.4	0.2
05031	Craighead County, Arkansas	70.0	66.6	3.4	8.3	4.7	9.0	1.0	6.9	0.1
05033	Crawford County, Arkansas	73.8	69.2	4.5	6.7	7.5	5.8	1.5	4.8	0.1
05035	Crittenden County, Arkansas	73.5	71.8	1.7	4.2	7.6	7.5	1.7	5.2	0.3
05037	Cross County, Arkansas	67.7	64.7	3.0	5.3	5.3	11.0	3.7	6.3	0.8
05039	Dallas County, Arkansas	68.1	65.5	2.7	4.1	8.3	11.5	2.4	4.8	0.7
05041	Desha County, Arkansas	63.3	59.4	3.9	6.5	8.1	15.1	2.5	4.5	0.0
05043	Drew County, Arkansas	63.0	59.5	3.5	6.9	6.7	15.0	0.8	7.5	0.1
05045	Faulkner County, Arkansas	70.6	67.1	3.5	6.2	5.9	9.9	2.1	5.1	0.1

Table C. County—Labor Force, Employment, and Educational Data, 2011–2015—*Continued*

| | | Class of worker for civilian employed population age 16 and older | | | | | | | | |
| | | Private for-profit wage and salary workers | | | | Government workers | | | | |
Fips code	State/county	Total private for-profit wage and salary workers	Employees of private companies	Self-employed in own incorporated business	Private not-for-profit wage and salary workers	Local government workers	State government workers	Federal government workers	Self-employed in own not incorporated business	Unpaid family workers
05047	Franklin County, Arkansas	65.9	63.3	2.6	5.7	7.3	9.5	3.4	7.8	0.5
05049	Fulton County, Arkansas	62.4	57.5	5.0	11.1	6.0	6.9	2.0	11.0	0.6
05051	Garland County, Arkansas	68.1	64.5	3.6	9.5	6.0	5.9	2.3	8.0	0.1
05053	Grant County, Arkansas	71.7	69.1	2.5	5.4	5.4	10.9	1.9	4.8	0.0
05055	Greene County, Arkansas	73.3	70.3	3.0	5.2	5.8	7.6	1.1	6.9	0.1
05057	Hempstead County, Arkansas	67.8	66.2	1.7	5.8	7.6	12.1	0.6	6.1	0.0
05059	Hot Spring County, Arkansas	71.1	70.0	1.2	4.5	6.8	9.7	2.1	5.6	0.0
05061	Howard County, Arkansas	73.3	70.1	3.2	4.1	9.3	5.7	0.1	7.4	0.0
05063	Independence County, Arkansas	70.2	67.4	2.8	6.9	4.4	10.3	1.1	6.9	0.2
05065	Izard County, Arkansas	60.2	56.0	4.3	12.0	7.4	8.3	0.9	11.0	0.1
05067	Jackson County, Arkansas	70.6	65.9	4.7	5.0	7.7	8.0	2.1	6.1	0.4
05069	Jefferson County, Arkansas	63.6	61.3	2.3	6.0	7.3	14.3	4.8	3.9	0.1
05071	Johnson County, Arkansas	73.3	69.4	3.9	7.0	7.1	5.5	1.3	5.5	0.2
05073	Lafayette County, Arkansas	61.3	57.1	4.2	4.0	9.0	10.1	1.7	11.5	2.5
05075	Lawrence County, Arkansas	65.8	62.0	3.8	5.5	6.3	12.1	1.6	7.8	0.9
05077	Lee County, Arkansas	60.0	57.7	2.3	4.9	6.4	13.5	5.7	9.4	0.0
05079	Lincoln County, Arkansas	59.6	56.7	2.9	8.6	6.2	15.1	2.2	7.9	0.4
05081	Little River County, Arkansas	67.9	67.1	0.8	6.1	8.4	8.4	5.3	3.9	0.0
05083	Logan County, Arkansas	65.2	61.6	3.6	7.5	6.1	10.2	2.7	8.0	0.3
05085	Lonoke County, Arkansas	69.4	66.5	3.0	7.3	5.8	6.6	5.6	5.1	0.2
05087	Madison County, Arkansas	65.9	62.9	3.0	4.6	6.4	7.6	1.7	13.8	0.1
05089	Marion County, Arkansas	66.7	66.1	0.6	6.2	9.0	5.3	0.9	11.8	0.0
05091	Miller County, Arkansas	66.9	64.4	2.5	8.4	7.7	6.0	3.2	7.8	0.0
05093	Mississippi County, Arkansas	69.7	67.6	2.1	5.8	6.0	11.0	1.0	6.4	0.0
05095	Monroe County, Arkansas	65.2	62.5	2.6	4.4	6.3	11.8	2.6	9.7	0.0
05097	Montgomery County, Arkansas	63.8	60.0	3.8	4.7	8.8	6.1	3.5	13.1	0.0
05099	Nevada County, Arkansas	66.6	64.6	2.0	2.1	9.2	11.8	1.6	8.8	0.0
05101	Newton County, Arkansas	58.4	52.5	5.9	6.2	5.6	11.8	3.7	14.3	0.0
05103	Ouachita County, Arkansas	70.0	67.4	2.6	4.4	11.2	6.9	2.6	4.9	0.0
05105	Perry County, Arkansas	63.9	62.0	1.9	8.5	5.7	11.4	1.4	8.7	0.4
05107	Phillips County, Arkansas	65.4	63.1	2.4	4.0	7.1	13.6	2.9	7.0	0.0
05109	Pike County, Arkansas	68.1	65.2	2.9	3.9	5.7	9.1	1.5	11.5	0.3
05111	Poinsett County, Arkansas	72.2	69.2	3.0	6.5	4.6	6.7	2.4	7.5	0.0
05113	Polk County, Arkansas	66.5	62.6	3.9	5.8	6.3	7.7	2.6	10.9	0.1
05115	Pope County, Arkansas	73.2	69.9	3.3	6.3	4.1	8.9	1.4	6.1	0.1
05117	Prairie County, Arkansas	70.5	66.3	4.2	3.4	5.1	7.8	2.2	11.1	0.0
05119	Pulaski County, Arkansas	65.3	62.1	3.2	9.2	5.0	11.1	4.5	4.7	0.2
05121	Randolph County, Arkansas	69.5	66.8	2.7	9.7	5.0	7.8	0.8	6.7	0.5
05123	St. Francis County, Arkansas	64.0	62.0	2.0	6.7	5.3	13.3	3.6	6.9	0.3
05125	Saline County, Arkansas	66.5	63.8	2.7	9.9	5.9	9.7	2.8	5.0	0.2
05127	Scott County, Arkansas	67.4	62.7	4.8	3.5	6.9	11.3	1.8	9.0	0.0
05129	Searcy County, Arkansas	63.3	59.2	4.1	5.6	6.3	6.3	1.0	17.6	0.0
05131	Sebastian County, Arkansas	78.2	75.2	3.1	6.5	4.5	4.8	1.4	4.3	0.3
05133	Sevier County, Arkansas	74.6	72.3	2.3	3.0	7.8	4.7	2.1	7.8	0.0
05135	Sharp County, Arkansas	66.0	63.0	3.0	8.6	5.4	7.5	1.2	11.2	0.0
05137	Stone County, Arkansas	57.8	53.6	4.2	5.0	5.8	13.0	0.4	17.7	0.2
05139	Union County, Arkansas	77.5	74.2	3.3	3.9	6.2	6.7	0.8	4.9	0.0
05141	Van Buren County, Arkansas	65.6	61.7	3.9	6.0	6.7	8.9	1.4	11.3	0.0
05143	Washington County, Arkansas	71.7	68.4	3.3	7.0	5.7	7.5	1.5	6.3	0.3
05145	White County, Arkansas	72.0	69.3	2.7	7.2	5.0	8.2	1.5	5.7	0.4
05147	Woodruff County, Arkansas	70.8	67.9	2.9	6.1	4.4	11.2	1.5	6.0	0.0
05149	Yell County, Arkansas	71.7	69.2	2.5	6.1	4.8	6.9	2.0	7.4	1.1
06000	**California**	71.0	67.8	3.3	6.7	7.6	4.2	2.0	8.3	0.2
06001	Alameda County, California	69.9	67.3	2.6	8.8	7.2	4.2	2.3	7.4	0.1
06003	Alpine County, California	54.4	51.2	3.2	2.9	19.1	7.8	5.9	9.8	0.0
06005	Amador County, California	58.6	55.9	2.6	6.0	11.8	11.0	0.6	11.8	0.3
06007	Butte County, California	62.4	59.8	2.5	9.4	9.0	6.9	1.3	10.5	0.5
06009	Calaveras County, California	58.2	56.1	2.1	7.0	12.3	6.4	1.6	13.9	0.6
06011	Colusa County, California	72.7	70.5	2.2	2.9	10.2	3.9	1.3	8.8	0.1
06013	Contra Costa County, California	69.6	66.5	3.1	7.9	8.1	3.6	1.9	8.7	0.2
06015	Del Norte County, California	44.9	43.3	1.7	12.0	15.4	15.4	1.8	10.0	0.4
06017	El Dorado County, California	64.1	60.3	3.8	7.7	9.2	6.0	1.7	11.1	0.2
06019	Fresno County, California	68.5	66.2	2.3	6.9	9.4	5.6	2.8	6.7	0.2
06021	Glenn County, California	62.1	59.9	2.3	6.0	12.6	6.0	1.3	10.9	1.1
06023	Humboldt County, California	53.1	50.8	2.3	10.7	10.7	8.8	2.5	14.0	0.3
06025	Imperial County, California	61.9	60.3	1.5	4.8	14.7	8.3	4.8	5.2	0.4
06027	Inyo County, California	55.2	53.3	1.9	7.1	18.3	6.5	3.3	9.5	0.0
06029	Kern County, California	71.3	69.4	2.0	5.0	9.6	4.7	2.9	6.2	0.2
06031	Kings County, California	62.6	60.8	1.8	5.6	10.7	8.7	6.3	5.9	0.2
06033	Lake County, California	58.9	56.1	2.8	7.1	15.6	5.1	1.4	11.7	0.2
06035	Lassen County, California	36.8	34.8	2.0	5.8	13.2	24.4	12.8	6.8	0.1
06037	Los Angeles County, California	72.6	68.8	3.8	6.4	7.1	3.0	1.3	9.4	0.2
06039	Madera County, California	72.5	70.0	2.5	4.0	8.6	5.3	2.1	7.4	0.1
06041	Marin County, California	64.2	58.9	5.3	9.5	6.3	3.1	1.3	15.4	0.1
06043	Mariposa County, California	54.8	52.8	2.0	5.5	13.8	5.6	8.3	10.5	1.5

Table C. County—Labor Force, Employment, and Educational Data, 2011–2015—*Continued*

| | | Class of worker for civilian employed population age 16 and older | | | | | | | | |
| | | Private for-profit wage and salary workers | | | | Government workers | | | | |
Fips code	State/county	Total private for-profit wage and salary workers	Employees of private companies	Self-employed in own incorporated business	Private not-for-profit wage and salary workers	Local government workers	State government workers	Federal government workers	Self-employed in own not incorporated business	Unpaid family workers
06045	Mendocino County, California	56.0	53.3	2.7	8.9	11.0	6.0	2.1	15.4	0.6
06047	Merced County, California	72.3	70.7	1.6	4.3	10.2	4.5	1.5	7.0	0.2
06049	Modoc County, California	48.3	43.5	4.8	8.2	16.6	10.6	4.1	11.6	0.6
06051	Mono County, California	58.6	54.0	4.6	3.7	14.3	4.7	7.0	10.8	0.9
06053	Monterey County, California	70.6	67.9	2.7	6.0	6.9	4.7	3.4	8.2	0.2
06055	Napa County, California	67.7	64.5	3.2	9.1	7.0	4.4	1.1	10.5	0.1
06057	Nevada County, California	60.9	56.0	4.8	7.2	8.6	4.7	1.3	16.8	0.5
06059	Orange County, California	76.8	72.5	4.3	5.0	6.1	3.0	1.2	7.8	0.2
06061	Placer County, California	67.1	63.1	4.0	8.0	8.4	6.0	1.8	8.4	0.2
06063	Plumas County, California	51.5	48.5	3.0	8.6	13.0	4.8	6.0	15.8	0.2
06065	Riverside County, California	72.2	68.9	3.3	5.0	8.8	4.1	2.0	7.8	0.2
06067	Sacramento County, California	62.8	60.7	2.1	8.0	7.8	12.0	1.9	7.3	0.2
06069	San Benito County, California	72.5	69.6	2.9	3.9	11.7	3.2	1.3	7.1	0.3
06071	San Bernardino County, California	70.3	68.0	2.2	6.2	10.2	4.3	2.3	6.7	0.2
06073	San Diego County, California	70.4	66.8	3.6	6.9	6.4	4.0	4.5	7.7	0.2
06075	San Francisco County, California	70.5	67.2	3.3	9.4	5.7	3.6	2.0	8.7	0.1
06077	San Joaquin County, California	72.4	70.2	2.1	6.4	8.4	4.2	2.0	6.4	0.2
06079	San Luis Obispo County, California	62.8	58.6	4.1	5.5	8.7	10.2	1.1	11.4	0.4
06081	San Mateo County, California	71.8	68.3	3.5	8.0	7.3	2.6	1.8	8.3	0.2
06083	Santa Barbara County, California	67.4	64.0	3.4	8.1	7.4	6.2	2.6	8.0	0.3
06085	Santa Clara County, California	77.6	74.9	2.7	6.7	6.0	2.0	1.2	6.4	0.1
06087	Santa Cruz County, California	64.6	60.9	3.6	8.5	7.7	6.5	1.1	11.4	0.2
06089	Shasta County, California	64.5	61.4	3.1	8.4	8.8	5.4	2.5	10.3	0.2
06091	Sierra County, California	43.6	41.7	1.9	1.4	28.5	9.5	4.3	9.7	3.1
06093	Siskiyou County, California	53.4	50.4	3.0	10.1	11.6	7.4	3.7	13.8	0.1
06095	Solano County, California	66.3	64.5	1.7	7.9	9.4	6.3	4.0	6.0	0.1
06097	Sonoma County, California	67.9	64.5	3.4	7.6	7.9	3.5	1.2	11.6	0.2
06099	Stanislaus County, California	72.1	69.6	2.5	6.7	9.4	3.6	1.1	6.8	0.2
06101	Sutter County, California	67.2	64.7	2.5	6.8	10.3	6.0	2.3	6.9	0.5
06103	Tehama County, California	63.3	60.6	2.8	6.8	10.8	6.9	2.5	9.6	0.2
06105	Trinity County, California	45.0	40.3	4.7	4.7	19.2	7.7	2.6	12.7	8.0
06107	Tulare County, California	71.4	68.9	2.5	5.3	9.6	5.7	1.2	6.5	0.3
06109	Tuolumne County, California	58.9	55.2	3.7	8.4	10.8	5.6	3.3	12.4	0.5
06111	Ventura County, California	72.5	68.7	3.8	5.3	8.0	2.9	2.3	8.8	0.2
06113	Yolo County, California	57.8	55.8	1.9	7.8	8.3	17.9	1.9	6.1	0.2
06115	Yuba County, California	60.8	58.2	2.7	8.2	9.5	5.7	6.2	9.3	0.2
08000	**Colorado**	71.7	66.9	4.8	7.8	6.9	4.1	2.9	6.4	0.2
08001	Adams County, Colorado	77.6	74.5	3.1	6.0	6.2	3.1	2.0	5.0	0.1
08003	Alamosa County, Colorado	56.8	55.5	1.3	10.8	8.3	16.6	2.0	5.4	0.1
08005	Arapahoe County, Colorado	75.3	70.8	4.6	7.3	5.7	3.0	2.9	5.6	0.2
08007	Archuleta County, Colorado	60.3	53.3	6.9	6.1	7.7	4.0	3.1	18.3	0.6
08009	Baca County, Colorado	44.5	39.1	5.4	7.6	15.3	11.8	2.1	17.2	1.6
08011	Bent County, Colorado	41.0	37.5	3.5	5.0	13.0	13.3	12.1	15.3	0.2
08013	Boulder County, Colorado	69.4	63.3	6.1	8.6	5.7	5.9	1.8	8.5	0.2
08014	Broomfield County, Colorado	72.4	68.2	4.2	7.5	7.0	5.2	1.7	6.0	0.2
08015	Chaffee County, Colorado	63.0	53.6	9.4	6.5	8.9	8.2	1.5	10.6	1.3
08017	Cheyenne County, Colorado	54.3	53.2	1.1	2.8	18.3	5.8	1.8	16.6	0.3
08019	Clear Creek County, Colorado	66.3	56.6	9.7	5.9	10.8	3.3	4.1	8.9	0.8
08021	Conejos County, Colorado	58.2	54.9	3.3	7.6	9.4	8.0	3.9	12.8	0.0
08023	Costilla County, Colorado	58.2	55.6	2.6	5.6	14.5	6.4	0.8	14.0	0.5
08025	Crowley County, Colorado	59.3	57.7	1.6	7.4	10.2	14.3	2.7	6.0	0.0
08027	Custer County, Colorado	34.0	29.1	4.9	15.9	19.6	3.7	0.0	26.6	0.2
08029	Delta County, Colorado	60.5	53.3	7.2	9.5	7.2	5.9	1.9	14.7	0.4
08031	Denver County, Colorado	73.8	69.6	4.2	9.4	5.3	3.7	2.1	5.6	0.1
08033	Dolores County, Colorado	68.7	65.9	2.7	0.9	17.0	2.5	2.2	8.5	0.2
08035	Douglas County, Colorado	76.7	70.7	6.1	6.2	7.4	2.3	2.2	5.1	0.1
08037	Eagle County, Colorado	78.1	69.0	9.1	6.8	6.6	1.5	0.4	6.6	0.0
08039	Elbert County, Colorado	72.6	63.6	8.9	4.7	7.1	3.5	3.2	8.6	0.4
08041	El Paso County, Colorado	67.5	63.1	4.4	9.1	7.4	2.9	7.2	5.7	0.2
08043	Fremont County, Colorado	58.9	54.8	4.1	7.3	11.0	11.3	4.8	6.7	0.1
08045	Garfield County, Colorado	68.8	62.2	6.6	8.1	8.0	4.3	1.7	8.8	0.1
08047	Gilpin County, Colorado	72.8	65.2	7.6	7.5	8.7	3.1	2.4	5.5	0.0
08049	Grand County, Colorado	71.7	65.0	6.7	9.4	8.2	4.1	2.4	4.2	0.1
08051	Gunnison County, Colorado	61.5	53.8	7.7	7.7	8.6	7.1	2.5	10.9	1.8
08053	Hinsdale County, Colorado	53.9	45.9	8.0	6.2	17.3	5.1	3.5	14.0	0.0
08055	Huerfano County, Colorado	56.2	48.1	8.1	7.0	10.6	11.8	1.7	12.2	0.5
08057	Jackson County, Colorado	63.1	56.7	6.4	3.1	9.7	9.9	4.6	8.6	0.9
08059	Jefferson County, Colorado	72.8	67.7	5.1	7.0	7.2	3.4	3.3	6.2	0.2
08061	Kiowa County, Colorado	43.8	42.3	1.5	7.1	25.3	8.0	1.9	13.8	0.0
08063	Kit Carson County, Colorado	56.6	53.2	3.3	6.3	14.5	6.4	2.0	14.0	0.2
08065	Lake County, Colorado	65.1	61.7	3.4	7.4	8.5	7.3	3.8	7.9	0.0
08067	La Plata County, Colorado	65.5	59.2	6.3	7.5	8.9	5.6	3.2	9.1	0.2
08069	Larimer County, Colorado	67.7	62.9	4.8	8.4	7.6	7.5	2.0	6.7	0.2
08071	Las Animas County, Colorado	58.7	54.5	4.3	8.6	10.9	10.5	2.2	9.0	0.1

Table C. County—Labor Force, Employment, and Educational Data, 2011–2015—*Continued*

| | | Class of worker for civilian employed population age 16 and older | | | | | | | | |
| | | Private for-profit wage and salary workers | | | | Government workers | | | | |
Fips code	State/county	Total private for-profit wage and salary workers	Employees of private companies	Self-employed in own incorporated business	Private not-for-profit wage and salary workers	Local government workers	State government workers	Federal government workers	Self-employed in own not incorporated business	Unpaid family workers
08073	Lincoln County, Colorado	45.8	42.3	3.6	8.9	13.8	12.1	1.7	16.4	1.3
08075	Logan County, Colorado	67.8	64.4	3.5	5.1	7.4	10.3	1.2	8.0	0.1
08077	Mesa County, Colorado	71.2	65.3	5.9	8.8	6.5	4.1	2.8	6.3	0.4
08079	Mineral County, Colorado	53.1	43.4	9.7	15.5	9.7	9.1	0.0	12.6	0.0
08081	Moffat County, Colorado	70.9	66.2	4.7	7.3	9.5	2.1	1.9	8.0	0.3
08083	Montezuma County, Colorado	59.6	53.9	5.7	8.4	13.6	3.6	3.2	10.9	0.7
08085	Montrose County, Colorado	63.4	58.3	5.1	9.9	11.5	2.6	1.7	10.7	0.2
08087	Morgan County, Colorado	70.0	66.6	3.3	4.9	11.8	4.4	1.3	7.3	0.3
08089	Otero County, Colorado	56.6	52.7	3.9	8.2	11.3	9.0	3.7	11.0	0.2
08091	Ouray County, Colorado	59.6	49.7	9.9	6.7	14.6	2.3	4.7	11.5	0.5
08093	Park County, Colorado	62.7	55.4	7.3	7.8	11.1	2.2	4.2	10.8	1.2
08095	Phillips County, Colorado	64.2	57.7	6.5	5.9	9.3	3.1	3.8	13.3	0.5
08097	Pitkin County, Colorado	73.0	65.5	7.5	7.5	5.8	2.8	0.8	9.8	0.2
08099	Prowers County, Colorado	63.1	58.9	4.2	4.5	13.1	9.5	1.5	8.2	0.1
08101	Pueblo County, Colorado	67.7	64.9	2.8	8.9	7.3	8.5	2.9	4.5	0.2
08103	Rio Blanco County, Colorado	65.2	61.0	4.2	9.3	9.6	6.6	3.0	6.0	0.2
08105	Rio Grande County, Colorado	60.7	57.1	3.6	9.2	11.5	6.9	2.6	8.6	0.5
08107	Routt County, Colorado	75.5	70.1	5.4	7.8	5.5	2.2	1.4	7.4	0.1
08109	Saguache County, Colorado	55.5	53.0	2.5	7.3	11.3	9.9	3.8	11.0	1.2
08111	San Juan County, Colorado	73.9	52.5	21.4	6.2	5.3	2.7	3.3	8.0	0.6
08113	San Miguel County, Colorado	71.1	59.8	11.3	4.4	8.3	2.0	1.7	12.0	0.5
08115	Sedgwick County, Colorado	56.3	51.1	5.3	9.9	13.7	4.5	3.0	12.0	0.6
08117	Summit County, Colorado	72.6	65.7	6.9	8.9	7.8	2.2	0.4	8.1	0.0
08119	Teller County, Colorado	62.1	57.5	4.6	7.7	12.3	4.5	5.6	7.4	0.3
08121	Washington County, Colorado	53.2	47.6	5.6	7.7	15.2	6.4	2.6	14.5	0.3
08123	Weld County, Colorado	73.9	69.7	4.2	6.4	7.3	4.3	1.5	6.4	0.2
08125	Yuma County, Colorado	68.8	61.7	7.1	6.7	9.9	2.2	0.8	11.4	0.2
09000	**Connecticut**	70.5	67.2	3.3	9.8	7.6	4.2	1.4	6.3	0.2
09001	Fairfield County, Connecticut	73.4	68.8	4.6	8.3	6.8	2.0	1.0	8.4	0.1
09003	Hartford County, Connecticut	71.4	68.8	2.6	9.3	7.4	5.5	1.3	4.8	0.2
09005	Litchfield County, Connecticut	67.7	63.4	4.3	9.6	8.8	3.7	0.8	9.2	0.2
09007	Middlesex County, Connecticut	70.1	66.2	3.9	9.7	7.8	4.4	0.8	7.0	0.1
09009	New Haven County, Connecticut	68.9	66.0	2.9	12.3	7.8	3.9	1.6	5.4	0.2
09011	New London County, Connecticut	69.1	66.5	2.7	9.3	9.2	3.8	3.3	5.2	0.1
09013	Tolland County, Connecticut	66.1	63.5	2.6	7.8	8.0	11.1	1.3	5.7	0.2
09015	Windham County, Connecticut	67.0	64.6	2.4	10.8	7.6	7.0	1.7	5.5	0.4
10000	**Delaware**	72.8	69.4	3.5	8.5	3.2	8.9	2.5	3.9	0.1
10001	Kent County, Delaware	67.1	63.6	3.5	6.2	3.1	14.8	4.5	3.9	0.3
10003	New Castle County, Delaware	75.1	72.3	2.9	9.4	2.8	7.2	2.2	3.1	0.1
10005	Sussex County, Delaware	70.8	65.6	5.2	8.0	4.2	8.8	1.7	6.4	0.1
11000	District of Columbia	50.8	48.1	2.7	19.2	5.3	2.1	18.1	4.4	0.1
11001	**District of Columbia** District of Columbia	50.8	48.1	2.7	19.2	5.3	2.1	18.1	4.4	0.1
12000	**Florida**	75.2	69.5	5.7	6.3	7.3	3.1	2.1	5.9	0.2
12001	Alachua County, Florida	59.2	55.0	4.2	9.8	6.6	16.9	3.0	4.3	0.1
12003	Baker County, Florida	67.5	63.0	4.5	5.7	8.0	13.3	1.0	4.4	0.1
12005	Bay County, Florida	71.1	66.3	4.7	5.3	7.0	3.5	6.5	6.4	0.3
12007	Bradford County, Florida	68.9	64.2	4.7	4.7	7.4	12.3	2.6	4.1	0.0
12009	Brevard County, Florida	73.7	68.2	5.6	6.8	7.6	2.2	4.1	5.4	0.2
12011	Broward County, Florida	76.9	69.9	7.0	5.3	7.8	1.9	1.7	6.4	0.1
12013	Calhoun County, Florida	59.3	55.9	3.3	4.4	10.2	15.1	3.0	8.0	0.0
12015	Charlotte County, Florida	74.0	66.7	7.3	5.2	8.2	3.3	1.1	7.7	0.5
12017	Citrus County, Florida	71.8	65.6	6.2	6.3	9.4	3.2	1.8	6.9	0.5
12019	Clay County, Florida	73.5	68.6	4.9	7.0	7.3	2.8	5.7	3.6	0.1
12021	Collier County, Florida	78.2	69.1	9.1	5.6	6.3	1.4	0.8	7.4	0.2
12023	Columbia County, Florida	65.5	61.8	3.7	6.0	9.9	8.7	5.5	4.4	0.1
12027	DeSoto County, Florida	76.5	73.4	3.1	4.0	8.1	5.0	1.6	4.8	0.0
12029	Dixie County, Florida	60.7	54.9	5.8	4.3	16.1	10.7	0.2	8.1	0.0
12031	Duval County, Florida	75.8	72.0	3.8	7.8	5.7	2.7	3.5	4.3	0.1
12033	Escambia County, Florida	67.9	65.1	2.7	10.3	7.1	3.4	5.2	6.0	0.1
12035	Flagler County, Florida	74.6	68.8	5.8	7.1	9.2	2.1	1.1	5.9	0.0
12037	Franklin County, Florida	53.0	48.0	5.0	5.8	14.2	10.5	1.5	14.9	0.1
12039	Gadsden County, Florida	57.0	53.5	3.5	5.2	12.2	20.3	1.6	3.5	0.1
12041	Gilchrist County, Florida	68.2	63.8	4.4	5.3	9.6	10.5	1.0	5.5	0.0
12043	Glades County, Florida	67.9	65.6	2.3	2.2	13.2	3.7	0.8	11.1	1.1
12045	Gulf County, Florida	64.9	57.3	7.6	4.7	10.6	11.2	2.3	5.9	0.3
12047	Hamilton County, Florida	61.9	57.3	4.6	4.0	14.2	8.1	2.2	8.8	0.8
12049	Hardee County, Florida	72.7	70.4	2.2	6.2	10.2	3.4	1.1	6.3	0.1
12051	Hendry County, Florida	77.3	71.6	5.6	4.0	9.3	4.8	0.4	4.0	0.2
12053	Hernando County, Florida	74.2	69.7	4.6	5.7	9.1	3.7	1.7	5.4	0.1
12055	Highlands County, Florida	69.6	65.0	4.6	8.8	8.8	5.9	1.3	5.4	0.1
12057	Hillsborough County, Florida	77.2	72.4	4.8	6.2	6.7	2.9	2.6	4.3	0.1

Table C. County—Labor Force, Employment, and Educational Data, 2011–2015—*Continued*

| | | Class of worker for civilian employed population age 16 and older | | | | | | | | |
| | | Private for-profit wage and salary workers | | | | Government workers | | | | |
Fips code	State/county	Total private for-profit wage and salary workers	Employees of private companies	Self-employed in own incorporated business	Private not-for-profit wage and salary workers	Local government workers	State government workers	Federal government workers	Self-employed in own not incorporated business	Unpaid family workers
12059	Holmes County, Florida	65.3	59.9	5.4	6.2	10.2	8.9	3.2	6.1	0.1
12061	Indian River County, Florida	74.1	67.3	6.8	6.8	8.5	2.9	1.6	6.1	0.2
12063	Jackson County, Florida	56.8	53.2	3.6	5.3	13.8	16.3	1.9	5.6	0.2
12065	Jefferson County, Florida	50.3	45.7	4.6	8.3	12.5	19.6	2.7	6.7	0.0
12067	Lafayette County, Florida	53.8	46.6	7.2	5.3	11.9	17.1	4.2	7.8	0.0
12069	Lake County, Florida	74.0	69.6	4.4	7.5	9.0	2.7	1.4	5.2	0.1
12071	Lee County, Florida	75.8	69.6	6.1	7.1	6.8	2.6	1.2	6.4	0.2
12073	Leon County, Florida	56.3	53.1	3.2	8.1	8.1	21.4	1.7	4.3	0.1
12075	Levy County, Florida	66.1	61.2	4.9	4.8	9.6	7.3	1.8	10.3	0.1
12077	Liberty County, Florida	45.9	44.3	1.6	6.3	17.1	20.1	1.4	9.2	0.0
12079	Madison County, Florida	60.5	58.6	1.9	7.0	12.8	11.1	2.7	5.7	0.1
12081	Manatee County, Florida	75.6	69.1	6.5	6.8	8.2	2.4	1.2	5.5	0.3
12083	Marion County, Florida	75.0	68.9	6.1	5.3	7.7	3.2	1.5	6.9	0.4
12085	Martin County, Florida	74.3	64.8	9.6	7.4	8.2	2.1	1.1	6.7	0.2
12086	Miami-Dade County, Florida	76.7	70.5	6.2	5.2	6.9	1.8	1.6	7.7	0.2
12087	Monroe County, Florida	70.7	61.8	8.9	6.0	7.1	2.9	4.0	9.1	0.2
12089	Nassau County, Florida	73.3	67.0	6.3	7.7	5.9	3.1	4.6	5.4	0.1
12091	Okaloosa County, Florida	68.2	63.7	4.5	5.4	6.4	2.5	11.2	6.1	0.1
12093	Okeechobee County, Florida	75.9	71.2	4.6	5.2	7.7	4.8	0.7	5.7	0.1
12095	Orange County, Florida	80.1	75.6	4.5	6.4	5.7	2.1	1.3	4.3	0.1
12097	Osceola County, Florida	80.1	76.3	3.7	4.6	7.9	1.8	1.4	4.2	0.0
12099	Palm Beach County, Florida	77.5	70.3	7.2	5.1	7.3	2.1	1.3	6.5	0.1
12101	Pasco County, Florida	74.4	69.1	5.3	6.8	8.4	2.5	2.4	5.3	0.2
12103	Pinellas County, Florida	76.2	70.4	5.8	7.5	6.9	1.9	2.1	5.2	0.2
12105	Polk County, Florida	76.2	72.4	3.8	6.3	8.4	2.5	1.1	5.3	0.1
12107	Putnam County, Florida	71.4	66.4	4.9	5.2	9.8	5.9	1.6	5.9	0.2
12109	St. Johns County, Florida	74.8	68.2	6.6	8.2	7.7	2.7	1.7	4.8	0.2
12111	St. Lucie County, Florida	74.2	68.8	5.4	6.0	9.3	3.1	1.1	6.1	0.3
12113	Santa Rosa County, Florida	67.4	63.6	3.8	7.7	8.4	3.7	5.9	6.7	0.1
12115	Sarasota County, Florida	75.0	66.8	8.2	6.5	6.7	1.9	1.1	8.5	0.2
12117	Seminole County, Florida	75.6	69.1	6.5	7.3	6.6	3.0	1.9	5.4	0.1
12119	Sumter County, Florida	71.1	66.5	4.6	8.4	9.5	2.3	1.6	7.0	0.1
12121	Suwannee County, Florida	68.2	64.5	3.7	5.6	9.5	8.5	2.6	5.5	0.1
12123	Taylor County, Florida	65.5	62.9	2.6	4.7	9.9	13.0	0.6	6.3	0.1
12125	Union County, Florida	58.5	57.6	0.9	1.8	8.6	24.7	2.2	4.0	0.2
12127	Volusia County, Florida	75.2	69.5	5.8	6.5	8.1	2.8	1.2	5.9	0.2
12129	Wakulla County, Florida	56.2	52.7	3.5	4.7	10.9	21.4	2.5	4.0	0.2
12131	Walton County, Florida	75.6	67.7	7.9	4.5	6.4	2.8	1.4	9.2	0.2
12133	Washington County, Florida	69.7	63.1	6.6	2.9	9.4	7.8	1.6	8.4	0.3
13000	**Georgia**	73.2	69.1	4.0	6.0	7.1	4.8	3.2	5.5	0.2
13001	Appling County, Georgia	75.8	71.6	4.2	4.2	7.4	5.0	1.2	6.0	0.3
13003	Atkinson County, Georgia	80.4	76.5	3.9	1.7	7.7	3.3	1.9	5.1	0.0
13005	Bacon County, Georgia	75.2	70.9	4.3	5.2	9.1	4.9	0.8	4.6	0.2
13007	Baker County, Georgia	65.4	63.9	1.5	7.8	10.8	8.4	1.6	6.1	0.0
13009	Baldwin County, Georgia	65.9	63.3	2.6	7.1	7.4	15.3	0.7	3.6	0.0
13011	Banks County, Georgia	75.1	71.2	3.9	3.1	8.8	3.8	1.1	7.2	0.8
13013	Barrow County, Georgia	76.9	74.5	2.4	5.3	9.0	3.3	1.1	4.3	0.1
13015	Bartow County, Georgia	77.2	73.7	3.5	4.5	8.5	4.6	1.2	4.0	0.1
13017	Ben Hill County, Georgia	69.0	64.7	4.2	6.7	10.2	7.3	1.4	5.3	0.1
13019	Berrien County, Georgia	67.5	66.2	1.4	5.0	6.8	9.4	4.4	6.4	0.4
13021	Bibb County, Georgia	72.2	68.8	3.4	7.0	8.0	4.8	3.6	4.3	0.2
13023	Bleckley County, Georgia	54.0	51.5	2.5	6.3	11.5	10.1	11.7	6.3	0.0
13025	Brantley County, Georgia	64.8	62.4	2.5	5.9	12.7	6.6	1.8	7.4	0.7
13027	Brooks County, Georgia	64.1	61.9	2.2	7.0	8.2	7.0	4.7	8.7	0.3
13029	Bryan County, Georgia	68.4	64.2	4.2	4.9	6.7	3.4	9.3	7.2	0.1
13031	Bulloch County, Georgia	65.9	63.2	2.7	3.6	5.8	15.0	1.7	7.6	0.3
13033	Burke County, Georgia	75.8	73.2	2.5	2.8	9.3	4.4	2.7	4.9	0.1
13035	Butts County, Georgia	72.7	67.7	5.0	3.2	10.0	6.1	2.6	4.2	1.1
13037	Calhoun County, Georgia	47.8	47.1	0.7	5.5	11.8	9.9	20.6	4.4	0.1
13039	Camden County, Georgia	62.0	58.8	3.2	5.0	7.2	4.3	16.9	4.3	0.2
13043	Candler County, Georgia	69.3	65.9	3.4	4.6	6.9	6.4	5.0	7.9	0.0
13045	Carroll County, Georgia	73.8	70.7	3.1	5.2	6.6	5.9	1.6	6.7	0.2
13047	Catoosa County, Georgia	75.7	72.9	2.8	6.4	7.6	3.3	2.1	4.8	0.0
13049	Charlton County, Georgia	66.3	62.2	4.1	5.8	7.0	11.0	6.5	3.3	0.0
13051	Chatham County, Georgia	71.5	67.7	3.8	7.3	6.7	5.2	3.9	5.3	0.2
13053	Chattahoochee County, Georgia	49.6	49.1	0.5	4.8	6.4	6.9	25.1	7.3	0.0
13055	Chattooga County, Georgia	78.4	75.4	2.9	3.0	5.0	5.5	0.5	7.0	0.7
13057	Cherokee County, Georgia	78.5	73.0	5.5	5.0	7.1	2.4	1.2	5.5	0.3
13059	Clarke County, Georgia	62.1	59.2	2.9	7.5	7.4	17.2	1.4	4.3	0.1
13061	Clay County, Georgia	67.5	62.4	5.1	2.7	11.7	2.0	7.1	7.7	1.4
13063	Clayton County, Georgia	74.0	71.7	2.3	5.5	7.5	3.5	4.4	4.9	0.1
13065	Clinch County, Georgia	70.1	65.7	4.4	2.8	13.0	8.9	0.8	4.3	0.0
13067	Cobb County, Georgia	77.6	72.8	4.8	6.2	5.4	2.9	1.9	5.9	0.1
13069	Coffee County, Georgia	73.0	69.4	3.6	5.4	6.0	6.6	1.1	7.6	0.3
13071	Colquitt County, Georgia	74.2	71.5	2.7	4.3	7.7	7.1	1.7	5.0	0.1

Table C. County—Labor Force, Employment, and Educational Data, 2011–2015—*Continued*

| | | Class of worker for civilian employed population age 16 and older | | | | | | | | |
| | | Private for-profit wage and salary workers | | | | Government workers | | | | |
Fips code	State/county	Total private for-profit wage and salary workers	Employees of private companies	Self-employed in own incorporated business	Private not-for-profit wage and salary workers	Local government workers	State government workers	Federal government workers	Self-employed in own not incorporated business	Unpaid family workers
13073	Columbia County, Georgia	69.3	65.6	3.7	5.3	6.8	5.3	8.3	5.0	0.1
13075	Cook County, Georgia	71.3	68.2	3.1	3.6	6.8	9.0	1.8	7.6	0.0
13077	Coweta County, Georgia	75.1	71.6	3.5	5.7	8.2	3.6	2.4	4.8	0.2
13079	Crawford County, Georgia	67.6	62.8	4.8	5.5	8.8	5.8	6.5	5.4	0.4
13081	Crisp County, Georgia	64.5	60.4	4.1	6.0	8.9	9.7	2.1	8.6	0.1
13083	Dade County, Georgia	64.9	61.8	3.1	12.2	5.8	2.5	2.1	12.2	0.3
13085	Dawson County, Georgia	76.1	70.8	5.3	4.5	7.5	3.0	1.2	7.4	0.3
13087	Decatur County, Georgia	68.1	64.8	3.2	3.6	9.6	10.8	0.9	7.0	0.0
13089	DeKalb County, Georgia	71.9	67.9	4.0	8.7	6.1	4.4	3.8	5.0	0.2
13091	Dodge County, Georgia	57.0	54.3	2.7	3.0	6.7	17.5	7.5	8.3	0.1
13093	Dooly County, Georgia	62.9	61.3	1.6	1.6	12.1	9.7	2.0	11.5	0.1
13095	Dougherty County, Georgia	63.3	60.6	2.8	8.8	8.1	9.8	5.9	4.1	0.1
13097	Douglas County, Georgia	73.8	70.3	3.5	6.6	7.5	3.4	2.9	5.7	0.1
13099	Early County, Georgia	67.5	64.2	3.3	4.3	7.2	11.8	2.6	6.6	0.0
13101	Echols County, Georgia	77.4	77.0	0.5	1.4	6.7	4.8	1.1	8.5	0.0
13103	Effingham County, Georgia	75.4	71.9	3.5	4.3	8.7	4.2	2.9	4.4	0.0
13105	Elbert County, Georgia	69.3	67.1	2.2	4.7	7.0	8.5	2.1	8.4	0.1
13107	Emanuel County, Georgia	69.4	65.4	4.0	2.9	6.7	10.3	2.7	7.8	0.2
13109	Evans County, Georgia	69.0	64.5	4.6	3.5	6.9	7.2	2.4	10.6	0.3
13111	Fannin County, Georgia	69.1	62.8	6.3	4.2	8.7	3.4	2.2	12.0	0.3
13113	Fayette County, Georgia	72.8	67.0	5.9	6.4	7.7	4.0	4.1	4.9	0.1
13115	Floyd County, Georgia	74.6	69.5	5.1	7.0	8.6	4.5	1.2	3.8	0.2
13117	Forsyth County, Georgia	79.5	74.1	5.4	4.6	6.9	1.8	0.9	6.2	0.1
13119	Franklin County, Georgia	71.0	66.7	4.3	7.0	9.1	4.8	0.7	7.3	0.0
13121	Fulton County, Georgia	76.0	70.7	5.2	7.2	5.0	4.2	2.3	5.2	0.1
13123	Gilmer County, Georgia	74.8	70.2	4.6	3.7	6.2	2.5	0.8	11.5	0.5
13125	Glascock County, Georgia	68.2	64.9	3.3	7.0	12.9	3.9	1.0	6.9	0.1
13127	Glynn County, Georgia	69.8	64.3	5.5	7.1	7.9	5.0	4.2	5.7	0.3
13129	Gordon County, Georgia	78.5	75.8	2.7	4.4	7.6	3.2	0.5	5.2	0.5
13131	Grady County, Georgia	69.1	66.5	2.7	4.8	7.4	7.0	1.3	9.4	1.0
13133	Greene County, Georgia	76.0	72.0	4.0	4.9	7.9	3.8	1.7	5.6	0.1
13135	Gwinnett County, Georgia	78.1	73.5	4.6	5.1	5.8	2.3	2.0	6.3	0.3
13137	Habersham County, Georgia	71.7	68.6	3.1	6.2	9.4	4.4	0.8	7.2	0.3
13139	Hall County, Georgia	78.7	74.3	4.4	5.0	7.3	2.9	1.0	5.1	0.0
13141	Hancock County, Georgia	61.0	57.8	3.2	3.8	11.8	13.4	4.3	5.7	0.0
13143	Haralson County, Georgia	71.6	67.9	3.7	3.2	11.6	6.1	0.6	6.8	0.0
13145	Harris County, Georgia	69.2	64.4	4.7	7.8	7.1	4.7	5.7	5.5	0.0
13147	Hart County, Georgia	75.1	70.6	4.4	3.7	5.2	5.1	1.4	9.1	0.4
13149	Heard County, Georgia	71.8	69.6	2.2	4.2	10.2	4.1	0.8	8.6	0.2
13151	Henry County, Georgia	72.3	68.5	3.8	5.6	9.9	4.4	4.4	3.3	0.0
13153	Houston County, Georgia	59.6	57.3	2.3	4.6	7.1	5.6	18.7	4.3	0.1
13155	Irwin County, Georgia	63.0	59.9	3.0	13.2	8.5	6.0	1.7	7.8	0.0
13157	Jackson County, Georgia	73.7	69.4	4.3	4.6	8.3	5.7	1.2	6.0	0.4
13159	Jasper County, Georgia	74.6	71.1	3.6	2.8	10.1	3.2	1.2	8.1	0.1
13161	Jeff Davis County, Georgia	70.2	67.7	2.5	2.2	11.8	8.8	2.8	4.2	0.0
13163	Jefferson County, Georgia	62.3	60.8	1.5	6.3	12.7	9.6	1.9	7.1	0.1
13165	Jenkins County, Georgia	68.5	65.8	2.7	6.1	11.1	7.7	2.1	4.4	0.0
13167	Johnson County, Georgia	69.3	63.5	5.8	1.7	5.4	12.7	2.9	7.5	0.5
13169	Jones County, Georgia	68.9	65.0	3.8	3.9	10.8	5.9	4.4	6.0	0.1
13171	Lamar County, Georgia	71.8	68.0	3.8	3.3	6.6	10.0	1.8	6.5	0.0
13173	Lanier County, Georgia	68.1	64.1	4.0	5.8	10.2	6.8	4.5	4.3	0.2
13175	Laurens County, Georgia	67.8	63.9	3.9	5.1	6.6	7.6	6.1	6.6	0.2
13177	Lee County, Georgia	60.6	55.6	5.1	8.1	11.2	6.4	8.6	5.0	0.1
13179	Liberty County, Georgia	58.8	56.5	2.3	3.0	7.8	5.4	21.5	3.4	0.1
13181	Lincoln County, Georgia	70.5	65.7	4.8	5.9	8.1	6.7	2.0	6.8	0.1
13183	Long County, Georgia	61.5	60.6	0.9	1.6	8.1	7.1	13.9	7.8	0.0
13185	Lowndes County, Georgia	70.9	67.5	3.4	5.0	7.1	7.4	4.9	4.5	0.2
13187	Lumpkin County, Georgia	65.4	61.4	4.0	7.9	8.0	7.6	1.7	9.1	0.4
13189	McDuffie County, Georgia	74.4	69.6	4.8	6.8	6.4	6.1	1.8	4.3	0.2
13191	McIntosh County, Georgia	67.9	64.8	3.1	5.2	9.6	7.5	3.8	6.0	0.0
13193	Macon County, Georgia	64.8	61.5	3.3	6.7	9.1	9.3	3.6	6.4	0.0
13195	Madison County, Georgia	65.7	61.8	3.9	8.4	7.5	8.0	1.9	8.4	0.1
13197	Marion County, Georgia	51.3	48.7	2.5	7.5	11.9	10.1	8.4	10.8	0.0
13199	Meriwether County, Georgia	71.5	69.4	2.1	4.1	8.1	6.6	1.0	8.5	0.2
13201	Miller County, Georgia	64.0	58.2	5.8	8.3	6.4	11.0	1.3	9.1	0.0
13205	Mitchell County, Georgia	66.9	61.6	5.3	5.7	8.6	6.9	2.9	7.9	1.1
13207	Monroe County, Georgia	67.1	61.0	6.1	6.5	11.0	6.5	2.7	5.8	0.4
13209	Montgomery County, Georgia	76.5	70.3	6.1	4.6	4.9	7.7	1.4	5.0	0.0
13211	Morgan County, Georgia	66.5	61.8	4.7	4.2	12.4	6.1	1.7	8.2	0.8
13213	Murray County, Georgia	79.1	76.8	2.3	4.5	6.5	3.5	0.9	4.5	0.9
13215	Muscogee County, Georgia	68.9	66.3	2.5	6.7	6.7	5.6	8.0	4.0	0.1
13217	Newton County, Georgia	72.6	69.4	3.3	5.2	11.1	4.0	2.4	4.5	0.2
13219	Oconee County, Georgia	61.0	54.6	6.3	9.0	8.7	11.9	2.2	6.9	0.2
13221	Oglethorpe County, Georgia	62.5	58.6	4.0	5.2	11.4	11.5	2.3	7.1	0.0
13223	Paulding County, Georgia	72.4	69.6	2.8	6.5	9.6	3.9	2.0	5.5	0.0

Table C. County—Labor Force, Employment, and Educational Data, 2011–2015—*Continued*

		Class of worker for civilian employed population age 16 and older								
		Private for-profit wage and salary workers				Government workers				
Fips code	State/county	Total private for-profit wage and salary workers	Employees of private companies	Self-employed in own incorporated business	Private not-for-profit wage and salary workers	Local government workers	State government workers	Federal government workers	Self-employed in own not incorporated business	Unpaid family workers
13225	Peach County, Georgia	65.7	62.8	3.0	3.2	5.8	10.9	7.8	6.6	0.0
13227	Pickens County, Georgia	73.5	68.4	5.1	5.6	9.3	2.5	2.1	7.0	0.1
13229	Pierce County, Georgia	70.3	64.5	5.7	4.1	7.7	7.4	2.2	7.9	0.6
13231	Pike County, Georgia	70.8	66.2	4.6	4.7	10.9	5.6	1.3	6.7	0.1
13233	Polk County, Georgia	74.8	72.0	2.8	4.8	8.1	5.1	0.7	6.3	0.2
13235	Pulaski County, Georgia	64.6	60.9	3.8	4.7	7.1	8.2	8.7	6.5	0.1
13237	Putnam County, Georgia	72.4	67.3	5.1	4.8	7.8	5.4	2.7	7.0	0.0
13239	Quitman County, Georgia	71.6	71.6	0.0	0.8	11.2	6.5	3.1	6.9	0.0
13241	Rabun County, Georgia	64.9	61.2	3.7	7.0	11.0	3.2	1.5	12.3	0.0
13243	Randolph County, Georgia	69.0	59.8	9.1	5.6	10.0	5.6	3.0	6.9	0.0
13245	Richmond County, Georgia	69.6	67.7	1.9	4.9	6.9	6.9	8.0	3.4	0.2
13247	Rockdale County, Georgia	70.7	66.2	4.5	5.4	10.0	4.7	4.1	5.1	0.1
13249	Schley County, Georgia	67.2	65.1	2.0	3.8	12.1	6.9	4.6	5.5	0.0
13251	Screven County, Georgia	73.7	68.5	5.2	2.0	11.8	3.9	2.1	6.1	0.4
13253	Seminole County, Georgia	71.5	69.2	2.3	5.7	6.4	7.5	1.2	7.7	0.0
13255	Spalding County, Georgia	72.8	69.1	3.7	4.5	9.8	6.2	1.8	4.6	0.3
13257	Stephens County, Georgia	70.4	66.3	4.2	5.8	9.7	6.5	1.3	6.3	0.0
13259	Stewart County, Georgia	62.2	61.3	0.8	4.0	16.2	7.2	6.4	4.0	0.0
13261	Sumter County, Georgia	60.1	56.8	3.3	8.4	8.2	14.9	2.8	4.6	1.0
13263	Talbot County, Georgia	69.8	66.4	3.4	5.7	9.2	8.6	1.5	4.8	0.5
13265	Taliaferro County, Georgia	65.5	63.1	2.4	2.4	10.5	12.9	3.5	5.2	0.0
13267	Tattnall County, Georgia	62.1	59.8	2.3	4.6	7.9	11.3	5.5	8.4	0.1
13269	Taylor County, Georgia	63.5	59.9	3.6	3.5	11.0	10.5	3.8	7.7	0.0
13271	Telfair County, Georgia	61.6	60.6	1.0	1.1	7.2	17.3	6.3	6.6	0.0
13273	Terrell County, Georgia	69.6	65.7	3.9	3.5	10.1	6.9	1.4	8.2	0.3
13275	Thomas County, Georgia	65.2	62.4	2.8	9.3	8.0	9.0	2.0	6.3	0.1
13277	Tift County, Georgia	70.0	66.6	3.4	8.4	5.3	9.0	1.2	6.0	0.1
13279	Toombs County, Georgia	72.4	68.1	4.3	3.7	7.1	8.7	1.7	6.4	0.0
13281	Towns County, Georgia	64.2	58.3	5.8	11.3	6.9	4.4	0.3	12.3	0.6
13283	Treutlen County, Georgia	69.2	68.0	1.2	5.4	6.8	9.1	3.3	6.1	0.0
13285	Troup County, Georgia	76.3	73.8	2.5	5.5	7.9	4.5	1.1	4.5	0.2
13287	Turner County, Georgia	58.9	57.2	1.7	6.0	15.4	12.6	3.2	3.9	0.0
13289	Twiggs County, Georgia	70.8	67.8	3.1	10.3	8.6	5.0	3.9	1.4	0.0
13291	Union County, Georgia	64.3	59.8	4.5	6.8	9.1	6.1	3.7	10.1	0.0
13293	Upson County, Georgia	71.8	69.1	2.7	4.5	7.8	9.0	1.5	5.4	0.1
13295	Walker County, Georgia	74.5	71.1	3.4	5.8	8.2	4.1	1.4	5.9	0.1
13297	Walton County, Georgia	75.4	69.5	5.9	3.7	11.0	3.8	0.9	4.9	0.3
13299	Ware County, Georgia	67.3	63.9	3.4	6.8	8.5	8.2	1.9	7.3	0.0
13301	Warren County, Georgia	68.6	64.2	4.4	9.4	6.9	8.1	0.3	6.9	0.0
13303	Washington County, Georgia	68.8	65.5	3.3	5.7	5.6	11.3	1.8	6.2	0.5
13305	Wayne County, Georgia	68.0	64.6	3.4	3.2	11.9	6.3	3.4	6.5	0.6
13307	Webster County, Georgia	66.2	63.6	2.6	5.0	13.4	10.5	1.8	3.0	0.0
13309	Wheeler County, Georgia	60.4	59.5	0.9	3.9	5.6	19.7	2.2	8.1	0.0
13311	White County, Georgia	73.0	68.5	4.5	4.4	9.1	4.9	1.8	6.5	0.3
13313	Whitfield County, Georgia	82.3	80.0	2.4	4.3	6.9	2.0	0.5	3.9	0.0
13315	Wilcox County, Georgia	54.0	51.6	2.4	3.1	10.2	16.6	5.2	10.7	0.2
13317	Wilkes County, Georgia	69.2	66.3	2.8	4.3	10.4	5.8	3.4	6.9	0.0
13319	Wilkinson County, Georgia	66.4	64.6	1.8	7.0	9.2	8.5	2.1	6.7	0.2
13321	Worth County, Georgia	70.9	69.2	1.7	5.0	7.0	7.2	4.3	5.7	0.0
15000	**Hawaii**	64.7	61.2	3.5	7.6	3.4	9.8	7.4	6.9	0.2
15001	Hawaii County, Hawaii	63.0	57.6	5.3	6.8	4.6	11.7	3.1	10.3	0.5
15003	Honolulu County, Hawaii	64.0	61.1	2.9	8.0	3.0	9.7	9.4	5.7	0.1
15005	Kalawao County, Hawaii	25.0	25.0	0.0	0.0	1.6	25.0	37.5	10.9	0.0
15007	Kauai County, Hawaii	67.7	64.6	3.1	5.3	3.7	9.2	3.5	10.5	0.1
15009	Maui County, Hawaii	69.0	63.9	5.1	6.7	4.0	9.1	2.0	8.8	0.4
16000	**Idaho**	69.6	65.3	4.3	6.7	7.2	5.8	2.9	7.6	0.3
16001	Ada County, Idaho	69.4	64.9	4.5	7.8	6.7	6.2	3.0	6.9	0.1
16003	Adams County, Idaho	53.2	45.7	7.5	7.3	8.9	8.8	7.5	14.2	0.1
16005	Bannock County, Idaho	68.2	65.4	2.8	4.8	7.7	10.5	2.6	6.0	0.2
16007	Bear Lake County, Idaho	65.3	59.7	5.6	6.2	9.6	5.5	2.8	10.3	0.2
16009	Benewah County, Idaho	64.7	61.3	3.4	6.6	11.8	5.3	4.7	6.7	0.2
16011	Bingham County, Idaho	67.9	64.4	3.5	4.8	8.5	6.2	4.8	7.4	0.5
16013	Blaine County, Idaho	63.0	55.1	7.9	10.2	9.5	2.6	1.9	12.6	0.2
16015	Boise County, Idaho	58.9	52.7	6.1	3.8	12.1	3.8	9.9	11.2	0.3
16017	Bonner County, Idaho	69.9	64.1	5.8	4.8	8.0	2.9	2.2	12.2	0.0
16019	Bonneville County, Idaho	72.9	68.3	4.6	5.1	6.5	4.2	4.5	6.6	0.3
16021	Boundary County, Idaho	66.3	60.6	5.8	5.3	11.5	1.7	3.6	11.1	0.4
16023	Butte County, Idaho	56.9	47.9	9.0	7.7	17.7	2.8	7.4	7.4	0.1
16025	Camas County, Idaho	52.8	51.6	1.2	13.2	11.8	6.8	3.2	11.2	1.0
16027	Canyon County, Idaho	73.7	70.7	3.0	6.1	5.7	5.5	1.5	7.2	0.3
16029	Caribou County, Idaho	65.7	60.4	5.3	6.7	9.4	7.3	1.5	8.2	1.2
16031	Cassia County, Idaho	75.2	71.6	3.6	4.5	7.7	3.1	1.6	7.7	0.1
16033	Clark County, Idaho	70.6	67.0	3.6	3.8	12.4	2.7	6.3	3.4	0.7
16035	Clearwater County, Idaho	57.8	53.0	4.8	7.7	9.8	8.6	4.9	10.2	0.9
16037	Custer County, Idaho	63.5	60.1	3.4	2.2	9.9	5.4	5.5	12.4	1.1
16039	Elmore County, Idaho	55.0	52.9	2.1	5.0	10.9	2.8	18.8	7.3	0.3

Table C. County—Labor Force, Employment, and Educational Data, 2011–2015—*Continued*

| | | Class of worker for civilian employed population age 16 and older | | | | | | | | |
| | | Private for-profit wage and salary workers | | | | Government workers | | | | |
Fips code	State/county	Total private for-profit wage and salary workers	Employees of private companies	Self-employed in own incorporated business	Private not-for-profit wage and salary workers	Local government workers	State government workers	Federal government workers	Self-employed in own not incorporated business	Unpaid family workers
16041	Franklin County, Idaho	78.9	69.8	9.1	2.4	5.2	5.6	1.2	6.4	0.3
16043	Fremont County, Idaho	64.6	56.7	7.9	6.5	9.0	7.3	2.7	9.6	0.4
16045	Gem County, Idaho	59.1	55.6	3.6	8.1	10.5	6.1	3.9	10.8	1.5
16047	Gooding County, Idaho	72.3	68.4	3.8	6.5	6.4	3.4	0.8	9.6	1.0
16049	Idaho County, Idaho	58.6	54.9	3.6	6.2	8.4	7.7	5.6	13.2	0.4
16051	Jefferson County, Idaho	71.4	66.3	5.1	5.2	6.0	5.7	4.9	6.7	0.2
16053	Jerome County, Idaho	75.7	72.1	3.6	6.9	5.9	3.2	0.9	6.9	0.5
16055	Kootenai County, Idaho	73.8	69.1	4.7	6.0	6.6	3.7	1.7	8.0	0.3
16057	Latah County, Idaho	54.3	51.7	2.7	7.8	6.4	21.4	2.6	7.2	0.2
16059	Lemhi County, Idaho	56.2	53.8	2.4	5.3	7.8	7.7	7.7	14.6	0.6
16061	Lewis County, Idaho	56.9	52.9	4.0	5.5	12.4	8.1	4.9	11.6	0.5
16063	Lincoln County, Idaho	72.7	70.2	2.5	4.1	6.8	2.8	3.6	9.8	0.2
16065	Madison County, Idaho	68.1	64.6	3.5	14.9	7.1	2.2	1.3	6.1	0.2
16067	Minidoka County, Idaho	74.5	70.7	3.9	5.3	8.6	3.5	1.6	6.3	0.1
16069	Nez Perce County, Idaho	66.9	63.4	3.5	8.1	7.5	6.9	1.9	8.5	0.3
16071	Oneida County, Idaho	63.8	59.5	4.2	4.3	13.3	3.8	5.4	8.2	1.3
16073	Owyhee County, Idaho	70.4	65.9	4.6	4.9	6.7	2.9	2.2	9.3	3.6
16075	Payette County, Idaho	69.2	63.6	5.6	6.0	8.6	5.8	1.8	8.4	0.2
16077	Power County, Idaho	74.0	69.8	4.2	1.1	12.5	6.0	0.5	5.7	0.2
16079	Shoshone County, Idaho	70.4	64.2	6.2	6.6	8.5	4.4	2.9	6.8	0.4
16081	Teton County, Idaho	72.4	68.5	3.9	4.8	9.8	1.1	2.1	9.9	0.0
16083	Twin Falls County, Idaho	72.1	67.4	4.6	8.0	6.5	4.7	0.9	7.5	0.3
16085	Valley County, Idaho	66.7	59.2	7.5	7.5	6.4	5.1	3.7	10.2	0.4
16087	Washington County, Idaho	61.1	57.4	3.7	4.4	11.3	8.1	3.6	11.4	0.1
17000	**Illinois**	73.9	70.5	3.5	8.8	6.8	3.8	1.8	4.7	0.1
17001	Adams County, Illinois	71.5	68.3	3.3	11.9	5.5	4.3	0.9	5.6	0.2
17003	Alexander County, Illinois	68.5	68.0	0.5	6.0	8.4	9.5	1.7	5.8	0.0
17005	Bond County, Illinois	72.6	69.9	2.8	9.5	5.1	4.4	2.2	6.0	0.3
17007	Boone County, Illinois	76.4	73.5	2.9	7.7	5.9	2.9	0.9	6.2	0.0
17009	Brown County, Illinois	67.2	64.0	3.2	6.6	7.0	7.3	3.1	8.8	0.0
17011	Bureau County, Illinois	72.3	70.5	1.8	7.9	7.2	3.1	1.1	8.0	0.3
17013	Calhoun County, Illinois	72.0	67.0	5.1	5.0	4.3	6.4	2.1	9.8	0.4
17015	Carroll County, Illinois	69.1	65.6	3.6	9.0	6.6	4.0	1.4	9.8	0.1
17017	Cass County, Illinois	72.1	70.5	1.7	6.4	7.6	5.8	0.9	7.2	0.0
17019	Champaign County, Illinois	56.8	54.5	2.3	9.0	6.7	20.9	1.5	5.0	0.1
17021	Christian County, Illinois	70.8	68.8	2.0	7.6	5.9	6.5	1.0	8.0	0.2
17023	Clark County, Illinois	71.5	69.5	2.0	6.9	6.2	4.5	2.0	8.7	0.2
17025	Clay County, Illinois	73.3	71.1	2.2	8.5	5.9	4.4	1.0	6.9	0.0
17027	Clinton County, Illinois	70.9	68.4	2.5	8.2	6.4	4.1	4.2	6.1	0.1
17029	Coles County, Illinois	63.4	61.3	2.1	10.1	5.9	13.0	1.1	6.4	0.1
17031	Cook County, Illinois	74.1	70.5	3.6	9.8	7.2	2.5	1.7	4.5	0.1
17033	Crawford County, Illinois	74.6	71.3	3.3	6.0	7.2	4.5	1.8	5.7	0.2
17035	Cumberland County, Illinois	70.6	67.4	3.2	9.0	4.8	6.0	0.3	8.4	0.8
17037	DeKalb County, Illinois	69.0	66.8	2.3	6.7	9.2	9.9	0.9	3.9	0.3
17039	De Witt County, Illinois	69.7	67.6	2.1	7.3	9.2	5.2	1.3	7.3	0.0
17041	Douglas County, Illinois	69.8	66.5	3.4	6.6	6.9	6.6	1.5	8.4	0.2
17043	DuPage County, Illinois	77.6	72.7	4.9	8.5	5.8	2.1	1.6	4.3	0.2
17045	Edgar County, Illinois	73.9	71.2	2.6	6.4	7.4	4.5	2.0	5.7	0.1
17047	Edwards County, Illinois	79.6	75.7	3.9	6.2	4.5	3.3	0.5	5.9	0.0
17049	Effingham County, Illinois	76.2	72.4	3.7	7.6	5.2	3.2	0.8	6.9	0.1
17051	Fayette County, Illinois	71.5	68.1	3.4	5.2	6.2	6.9	3.1	7.0	0.1
17053	Ford County, Illinois	69.9	67.5	2.5	9.1	5.9	3.4	1.3	10.2	0.1
17055	Franklin County, Illinois	69.5	67.2	2.3	7.3	6.1	7.5	2.8	6.6	0.2
17057	Fulton County, Illinois	67.5	65.0	2.5	9.8	7.4	7.1	1.8	6.4	0.1
17059	Gallatin County, Illinois	68.1	66.3	1.8	7.9	8.3	4.7	2.6	8.4	0.0
17061	Greene County, Illinois	70.3	67.0	3.3	6.0	6.0	6.0	1.0	10.2	0.5
17063	Grundy County, Illinois	76.4	74.0	2.5	7.3	7.8	3.1	1.3	4.1	0.1
17065	Hamilton County, Illinois	72.7	69.4	3.3	6.2	5.0	4.3	2.3	9.3	0.1
17067	Hancock County, Illinois	66.2	63.0	3.2	9.6	6.6	5.2	2.1	10.2	0.2
17069	Hardin County, Illinois	67.2	63.2	4.0	8.1	5.3	7.4	5.7	5.7	0.5
17071	Henderson County, Illinois	66.9	66.0	0.9	8.8	10.1	4.4	1.0	7.7	1.0
17073	Henry County, Illinois	71.6	68.7	2.8	8.0	6.6	3.9	3.2	6.6	0.1
17075	Iroquois County, Illinois	70.3	66.1	4.2	8.3	6.6	3.6	1.4	9.5	0.3
17077	Jackson County, Illinois	53.5	51.2	2.3	8.5	7.2	22.7	1.9	6.0	0.2
17079	Jasper County, Illinois	72.6	69.0	3.7	6.1	7.9	4.3	1.8	7.2	0.1
17081	Jefferson County, Illinois	72.8	70.2	2.7	8.1	6.3	4.5	1.0	7.0	0.1
17083	Jersey County, Illinois	74.7	72.5	2.2	12.0	4.2	2.2	1.0	5.8	0.1
17085	Jo Daviess County, Illinois	72.9	66.3	6.6	8.3	6.7	2.1	1.7	8.1	0.3
17087	Johnson County, Illinois	58.8	57.0	1.9	7.7	6.6	16.8	3.6	6.5	0.0
17089	Kane County, Illinois	79.4	75.9	3.4	6.5	6.8	2.1	1.3	3.7	0.2
17091	Kankakee County, Illinois	71.2	68.9	2.3	10.8	6.8	5.7	1.1	4.2	0.1
17093	Kendall County, Illinois	75.2	72.5	2.8	7.6	8.4	2.8	2.5	3.1	0.2
17095	Knox County, Illinois	70.9	68.4	2.5	10.7	6.8	4.2	1.4	5.9	0.1
17097	Lake County, Illinois	78.2	73.3	4.9	6.5	6.6	2.0	1.9	4.6	0.2
17099	LaSalle County, Illinois	76.3	73.8	2.5	8.0	6.4	4.1	0.7	4.4	0.2

Table C. County—Labor Force, Employment, and Educational Data, 2011–2015—*Continued*

| | | Class of worker for civilian employed population age 16 and older | | | | | | | | |
| | | Private for-profit wage and salary workers | | | | Government workers | | | | |
Fips code	State/county	Total private for-profit wage and salary workers	Employees of private companies	Self-employed in own incorporated business	Private not-for-profit wage and salary workers	Local government workers	State government workers	Federal government workers	Self-employed in own not incorporated business	Unpaid family workers
17101	Lawrence County, Illinois	68.6	65.8	2.9	9.9	6.7	6.0	0.5	8.3	0.0
17103	Lee County, Illinois	66.7	64.6	2.1	10.4	7.7	5.7	1.3	7.9	0.3
17105	Livingston County, Illinois	71.7	68.3	3.4	8.4	5.5	6.2	1.8	6.3	0.0
17107	Logan County, Illinois	62.6	59.8	2.8	12.4	5.4	9.5	2.1	7.9	0.2
17109	McDonough County, Illinois	55.8	54.1	1.7	10.0	8.3	19.5	0.9	5.3	0.2
17111	McHenry County, Illinois	78.4	74.0	4.4	6.3	7.2	2.3	1.0	4.7	0.1
17113	McLean County, Illinois	72.7	70.5	2.2	9.2	6.0	6.8	1.1	4.0	0.2
17115	Macon County, Illinois	72.7	70.6	2.2	9.7	6.6	4.6	1.2	4.9	0.2
17117	Macoupin County, Illinois	70.5	67.0	3.5	8.8	5.9	6.6	2.0	6.0	0.2
17119	Madison County, Illinois	74.6	72.0	2.6	8.2	6.2	4.6	2.3	4.1	0.1
17121	Marion County, Illinois	70.3	68.3	2.0	8.4	7.1	7.1	1.2	5.9	0.0
17123	Marshall County, Illinois	72.8	70.3	2.5	8.2	5.8	2.5	2.3	7.8	0.6
17125	Mason County, Illinois	66.0	63.6	2.4	8.1	9.0	6.1	1.1	9.7	0.0
17127	Massac County, Illinois	69.5	67.2	2.3	10.8	4.9	7.2	2.0	5.4	0.1
17129	Menard County, Illinois	60.3	57.9	2.4	10.7	5.5	16.1	1.6	5.6	0.1
17131	Mercer County, Illinois	73.6	70.3	3.4	6.1	6.5	2.6	2.8	8.3	0.1
17133	Monroe County, Illinois	75.5	71.6	3.9	7.7	6.1	3.8	2.2	4.6	0.1
17135	Montgomery County, Illinois	67.2	64.0	3.2	7.7	9.0	7.2	1.0	7.9	0.1
17137	Morgan County, Illinois	63.7	61.1	2.6	12.3	6.8	8.5	1.5	7.0	0.2
17139	Moultrie County, Illinois	73.1	71.7	1.3	8.6	6.8	2.6	0.7	8.0	0.1
17141	Ogle County, Illinois	71.5	68.7	2.8	8.3	9.6	3.9	1.0	5.6	0.1
17143	Peoria County, Illinois	73.8	71.8	2.0	11.9	6.0	2.5	1.9	3.7	0.1
17145	Perry County, Illinois	68.1	65.9	2.2	7.7	5.8	11.5	1.0	5.7	0.4
17147	Piatt County, Illinois	61.6	59.3	2.3	9.7	9.3	9.0	2.4	8.0	0.1
17149	Pike County, Illinois	65.0	61.6	3.4	9.2	7.6	7.9	1.5	8.3	0.6
17151	Pope County, Illinois	66.7	65.4	1.3	8.1	4.4	10.5	3.2	6.5	0.7
17153	Pulaski County, Illinois	64.2	63.4	0.8	7.1	6.1	13.4	3.0	6.0	0.1
17155	Putnam County, Illinois	73.9	70.7	3.2	5.4	5.3	6.0	2.3	7.1	0.1
17157	Randolph County, Illinois	72.0	68.3	3.7	7.1	6.4	7.7	1.3	5.4	0.2
17159	Richland County, Illinois	73.4	70.9	2.6	6.2	6.2	7.2	0.8	6.1	0.1
17161	Rock Island County, Illinois	73.6	71.3	2.3	9.2	6.1	3.0	3.8	4.1	0.2
17163	St. Clair County, Illinois	69.2	66.8	2.5	10.6	5.7	3.1	7.4	4.0	0.1
17165	Saline County, Illinois	69.9	68.5	1.3	6.9	7.2	6.5	2.2	7.0	0.3
17167	Sangamon County, Illinois	60.3	57.2	3.1	10.7	6.5	15.6	2.2	4.6	0.2
17169	Schuyler County, Illinois	64.8	61.5	3.3	4.0	10.3	9.6	1.1	10.0	0.2
17171	Scott County, Illinois	68.2	66.2	2.0	8.7	5.5	8.8	0.4	8.2	0.2
17173	Shelby County, Illinois	76.1	73.2	2.9	6.3	5.0	3.7	1.5	7.5	0.0
17175	Stark County, Illinois	70.5	66.6	4.0	6.7	7.3	3.1	2.2	9.0	1.3
17177	Stephenson County, Illinois	71.0	68.1	2.9	9.8	6.7	2.6	1.1	8.7	0.1
17179	Tazewell County, Illinois	74.4	71.6	2.7	10.2	6.1	2.8	1.8	4.7	0.1
17181	Union County, Illinois	59.3	56.9	2.4	9.7	4.8	17.3	1.7	6.5	0.8
17183	Vermilion County, Illinois	71.9	70.0	1.9	7.0	6.4	5.0	3.8	5.7	0.2
17185	Wabash County, Illinois	73.7	72.0	1.7	7.3	7.9	3.9	1.1	6.1	0.0
17187	Warren County, Illinois	64.4	61.7	2.7	15.2	7.8	3.8	0.5	8.2	0.1
17189	Washington County, Illinois	71.7	68.1	3.6	8.0	6.1	4.2	2.2	7.0	0.6
17191	Wayne County, Illinois	71.5	68.6	2.9	5.7	7.2	5.1	1.4	9.1	0.0
17193	White County, Illinois	70.0	68.0	2.0	7.5	7.1	3.9	1.2	10.1	0.2
17195	Whiteside County, Illinois	73.7	71.3	2.4	7.7	7.8	4.4	1.2	4.9	0.3
17197	Will County, Illinois	78.6	75.1	3.5	6.6	6.9	3.3	1.4	3.1	0.1
17199	Williamson County, Illinois	66.2	64.1	2.1	7.8	7.5	10.5	3.0	4.9	0.0
17201	Winnebago County, Illinois	75.9	72.8	3.0	9.1	6.2	3.2	1.0	4.5	0.2
17203	Woodford County, Illinois	72.7	69.4	3.2	10.7	5.2	4.3	1.1	6.0	0.1
18000	**Indiana**	75.2	72.3	2.9	9.1	5.8	3.7	1.5	4.6	0.1
18001	Adams County, Indiana	73.2	68.2	4.9	7.5	5.9	3.5	0.6	8.7	0.6
18003	Allen County, Indiana	76.0	72.5	3.5	10.3	5.4	2.4	1.2	4.4	0.2
18005	Bartholomew County, Indiana	79.8	77.8	2.0	8.0	5.1	1.9	0.6	4.5	0.1
18007	Benton County, Indiana	66.5	62.0	4.5	7.1	8.5	6.8	1.7	8.5	0.7
18009	Blackford County, Indiana	76.2	74.2	2.0	8.8	6.4	2.8	1.2	4.3	0.2
18011	Boone County, Indiana	74.7	69.9	4.8	9.3	5.8	2.8	1.3	6.0	0.1
18013	Brown County, Indiana	75.3	72.4	3.0	6.6	4.7	4.3	1.9	6.9	0.3
18015	Carroll County, Indiana	72.3	69.7	2.6	6.3	6.7	5.4	0.7	8.5	0.1
18017	Cass County, Indiana	74.6	72.3	2.3	7.4	6.1	6.4	0.8	4.5	0.2
18019	Clark County, Indiana	78.1	75.4	2.7	7.7	4.7	2.7	3.0	3.7	0.1
18021	Clay County, Indiana	71.3	68.4	2.9	7.1	7.5	5.7	2.2	6.1	0.1
18023	Clinton County, Indiana	79.2	76.5	2.7	8.4	4.6	2.2	0.6	4.9	0.1
18025	Crawford County, Indiana	72.4	69.6	2.8	5.4	7.2	6.5	1.6	7.0	0.0
18027	Daviess County, Indiana	72.9	69.1	3.8	6.6	5.5	3.6	4.5	6.3	0.5
18029	Dearborn County, Indiana	78.6	75.4	3.2	6.6	5.5	2.7	1.3	5.0	0.3
18031	Decatur County, Indiana	80.4	75.3	5.1	6.9	5.7	2.2	1.0	3.8	0.0
18033	DeKalb County, Indiana	79.4	76.9	2.5	7.9	5.0	2.7	0.8	3.9	0.2
18035	Delaware County, Indiana	68.4	66.4	2.0	10.8	5.9	9.1	1.0	4.6	0.1
18037	Dubois County, Indiana	78.5	75.9	2.6	8.6	4.6	2.6	1.2	4.4	0.1
18039	Elkhart County, Indiana	79.7	76.7	3.0	7.8	5.3	1.8	0.6	4.6	0.2

Table C. County—Labor Force, Employment, and Educational Data, 2011–2015—*Continued*

		Class of worker for civilian employed population age 16 and older								
		Private for-profit wage and salary workers				Government workers				
Fips code	State/county	Total private for-profit wage and salary workers	Employees of private companies	Self-employed in own incorporated business	Private not-for-profit wage and salary workers	Local government workers	State government workers	Federal government workers	Self-employed in own not incorporated business	Unpaid family workers
18041	Fayette County, Indiana	75.8	72.7	3.1	9.5	5.4	3.3	0.8	5.0	0.2
18043	Floyd County, Indiana	77.2	74.5	2.7	9.1	4.9	2.8	2.4	3.4	0.1
18045	Fountain County, Indiana	74.8	72.0	2.9	5.5	6.1	3.7	2.7	6.8	0.4
18047	Franklin County, Indiana	74.9	70.9	3.9	7.4	6.0	2.7	1.5	7.2	0.4
18049	Fulton County, Indiana	74.1	70.8	3.3	7.2	7.0	2.2	1.2	7.8	0.5
18051	Gibson County, Indiana	81.0	79.0	2.0	7.0	4.8	2.2	0.7	4.2	0.2
18053	Grant County, Indiana	70.5	68.3	2.3	12.1	6.9	2.6	3.3	4.4	0.1
18055	Greene County, Indiana	67.5	66.2	1.4	6.7	5.1	6.5	8.1	5.7	0.5
18057	Hamilton County, Indiana	75.6	70.4	5.2	9.3	6.1	2.8	1.6	4.4	0.1
18059	Hancock County, Indiana	74.9	71.4	3.5	8.5	6.9	2.5	2.9	4.2	0.0
18061	Harrison County, Indiana	76.6	74.6	2.0	7.1	6.4	3.9	2.0	4.0	0.1
18063	Hendricks County, Indiana	74.0	71.3	2.7	9.8	6.4	3.3	2.6	4.0	0.0
18065	Henry County, Indiana	73.3	70.4	2.9	8.0	6.0	4.0	1.7	6.8	0.3
18067	Howard County, Indiana	75.1	72.8	2.3	8.5	6.5	3.3	1.5	5.0	0.1
18069	Huntington County, Indiana	73.1	69.8	3.3	12.5	5.8	2.8	1.1	4.8	0.0
18071	Jackson County, Indiana	78.9	76.1	2.9	7.0	5.8	2.0	0.8	5.2	0.2
18073	Jasper County, Indiana	75.6	70.7	4.9	8.9	5.4	3.9	0.7	5.5	0.1
18075	Jay County, Indiana	75.5	72.5	3.0	5.4	7.4	2.2	0.8	8.1	0.5
18077	Jefferson County, Indiana	69.9	67.8	2.1	10.2	5.8	7.6	1.4	4.5	0.7
18079	Jennings County, Indiana	76.1	74.4	1.8	5.8	7.0	5.5	1.2	4.4	0.1
18081	Johnson County, Indiana	75.8	72.4	3.4	8.3	4.9	3.6	1.9	5.4	0.1
18083	Knox County, Indiana	72.9	69.7	3.3	9.9	6.2	5.2	1.8	3.9	0.1
18085	Kosciusko County, Indiana	80.4	77.1	3.3	7.9	4.2	2.2	0.5	4.7	0.1
18087	LaGrange County, Indiana	79.3	75.2	4.0	4.8	4.0	2.4	0.2	8.7	0.6
18089	Lake County, Indiana	76.4	73.8	2.6	8.9	6.8	2.8	1.4	3.5	0.2
18091	LaPorte County, Indiana	75.6	72.7	2.9	8.5	6.9	3.3	0.9	4.8	0.1
18093	Lawrence County, Indiana	73.8	70.8	3.0	5.9	5.9	3.9	5.1	5.4	0.1
18095	Madison County, Indiana	73.7	71.4	2.3	10.0	6.1	3.6	1.6	4.8	0.2
18097	Marion County, Indiana	76.1	73.8	2.3	9.3	5.1	3.3	2.0	4.0	0.1
18099	Marshall County, Indiana	76.1	74.1	2.1	9.1	5.9	2.2	0.9	5.6	0.2
18101	Martin County, Indiana	66.5	64.2	2.3	8.0	6.1	3.9	10.2	4.9	0.4
18103	Miami County, Indiana	72.3	70.1	2.1	6.3	7.8	4.5	3.4	5.4	0.2
18105	Monroe County, Indiana	61.7	59.1	2.6	11.5	5.7	13.2	2.3	5.5	0.1
18107	Montgomery County, Indiana	77.4	74.4	3.0	9.3	5.2	2.7	0.7	4.3	0.5
18109	Morgan County, Indiana	75.7	72.9	2.8	7.8	5.8	3.2	1.7	5.8	0.1
18111	Newton County, Indiana	76.8	75.0	1.8	5.5	7.8	1.5	1.1	7.2	0.1
18113	Noble County, Indiana	79.3	76.7	2.6	6.7	5.0	3.2	0.8	4.8	0.3
18115	Ohio County, Indiana	76.6	74.8	1.8	5.1	10.1	2.3	0.8	3.4	1.7
18117	Orange County, Indiana	79.7	78.0	1.6	5.1	4.7	3.3	0.8	6.3	0.1
18119	Owen County, Indiana	73.3	71.7	1.6	7.2	4.6	4.8	1.9	7.7	0.4
18121	Parke County, Indiana	71.5	68.2	3.3	8.1	5.0	7.1	0.9	7.1	0.2
18123	Perry County, Indiana	76.9	76.0	0.8	5.5	5.7	5.2	1.0	5.4	0.3
18125	Pike County, Indiana	81.4	79.3	2.1	5.6	6.1	2.1	1.2	3.2	0.3
18127	Porter County, Indiana	77.1	74.0	3.2	8.4	6.3	2.9	1.1	4.0	0.2
18129	Posey County, Indiana	74.3	71.5	2.8	8.9	6.7	3.5	1.0	5.6	0.0
18131	Pulaski County, Indiana	72.6	69.5	3.1	8.4	7.6	3.7	1.0	6.6	0.1
18133	Putnam County, Indiana	73.8	71.2	2.7	9.2	6.4	4.0	0.9	5.7	0.0
18135	Randolph County, Indiana	75.3	73.2	2.0	6.2	6.6	3.5	0.9	6.9	0.6
18137	Ripley County, Indiana	76.5	73.3	3.2	6.6	7.5	2.7	1.4	5.2	0.1
18139	Rush County, Indiana	75.8	74.0	1.8	4.1	7.0	3.3	1.4	8.1	0.3
18141	St. Joseph County, Indiana	72.2	69.5	2.7	13.7	6.1	2.5	0.9	4.6	0.1
18143	Scott County, Indiana	78.4	75.8	2.6	6.2	6.3	4.4	1.0	3.4	0.3
18145	Shelby County, Indiana	79.6	76.9	2.7	5.8	5.1	2.8	1.3	5.4	0.1
18147	Spencer County, Indiana	79.0	74.8	4.2	7.3	3.7	2.0	1.2	6.7	0.1
18149	Starke County, Indiana	75.6	72.1	3.5	7.8	7.7	2.6	0.8	5.3	0.1
18151	Steuben County, Indiana	75.6	72.9	2.8	8.9	6.3	2.7	1.0	5.3	0.1
18153	Sullivan County, Indiana	76.3	73.3	3.0	7.8	5.1	5.0	1.7	4.1	0.0
18155	Switzerland County, Indiana	72.2	70.9	1.3	6.8	7.9	4.4	2.5	6.2	0.0
18157	Tippecanoe County, Indiana	68.5	66.2	2.3	10.9	4.8	11.2	0.8	3.7	0.1
18159	Tipton County, Indiana	74.3	70.7	3.7	7.8	8.7	2.3	1.1	5.5	0.2
18161	Union County, Indiana	64.7	62.6	2.1	9.9	9.5	6.4	1.2	7.2	1.1
18163	Vanderburgh County, Indiana	76.3	74.2	2.1	10.8	5.4	2.8	1.0	3.7	0.1
18165	Vermillion County, Indiana	75.0	73.5	1.5	7.2	4.8	4.0	1.8	6.7	0.4
18167	Vigo County, Indiana	73.5	71.3	2.2	10.3	5.6	5.0	1.9	3.6	0.1
18169	Wabash County, Indiana	71.8	68.8	3.0	11.8	5.8	4.3	0.5	5.5	0.3
18171	Warren County, Indiana	71.1	68.9	2.2	8.1	6.7	5.4	1.0	7.7	0.0
18173	Warrick County, Indiana	77.6	73.6	4.1	8.3	6.3	1.9	1.0	4.7	0.1
18175	Washington County, Indiana	77.7	75.7	2.0	6.1	5.0	3.2	1.6	6.4	0.1
18177	Wayne County, Indiana	72.6	70.1	2.4	10.2	7.8	3.3	0.9	5.0	0.3
18179	Wells County, Indiana	78.7	75.2	3.5	6.0	5.2	2.4	1.3	6.1	0.2
18181	White County, Indiana	73.8	70.5	3.3	7.8	7.1	4.8	0.6	5.8	0.2
18183	Whitley County, Indiana	77.0	74.4	2.6	8.1	6.0	2.2	1.1	5.5	0.1
19000	**Iowa**	70.8	67.5	3.3	8.9	6.3	5.6	1.6	6.5	0.2
19001	Adair County, Iowa	68.1	65.2	2.9	5.5	9.3	4.1	2.2	10.6	0.1
19003	Adams County, Iowa	61.7	55.9	5.8	11.2	7.6	3.2	2.1	13.9	0.4

Table C. County—Labor Force, Employment, and Educational Data, 2011–2015—*Continued*

| | | Class of worker for civilian employed population age 16 and older | | | | | | | | |
| | | Private for-profit wage and salary workers | | | | Government workers | | | | |
Fips code	State/county	Total private for-profit wage and salary workers	Employees of private companies	Self-employed in own incorporated business	Private not-for-profit wage and salary workers	Local government workers	State government workers	Federal government workers	Self-employed in own not incorporated business	Unpaid family workers
19005	Allamakee County, Iowa	67.2	63.6	3.6	10.7	5.9	2.5	1.6	10.8	1.2
19007	Appanoose County, Iowa	68.5	64.7	3.8	9.9	5.9	4.6	1.4	9.1	0.6
19009	Audubon County, Iowa	64.9	59.6	5.3	7.1	8.6	3.3	1.5	14.3	0.3
19011	Benton County, Iowa	73.4	69.3	4.1	6.0	7.2	4.7	1.1	7.4	0.1
19013	Black Hawk County, Iowa	72.4	70.5	2.0	8.5	5.2	8.3	0.8	4.6	0.1
19015	Boone County, Iowa	66.5	62.0	4.5	7.8	8.8	9.0	1.9	5.8	0.2
19017	Bremer County, Iowa	70.9	67.0	3.9	11.6	6.5	3.2	0.9	6.8	0.1
19019	Buchanan County, Iowa	69.2	65.3	3.9	6.8	6.8	5.1	1.6	9.8	0.7
19021	Buena Vista County, Iowa	71.2	68.6	2.6	10.4	5.2	3.6	1.2	8.3	0.1
19023	Butler County, Iowa	69.7	67.3	2.4	6.9	6.0	4.8	0.9	11.0	0.6
19025	Calhoun County, Iowa	62.7	58.0	4.6	9.8	8.0	5.0	2.0	12.2	0.3
19027	Carroll County, Iowa	71.2	66.0	5.2	10.3	4.1	3.4	0.9	10.0	0.2
19029	Cass County, Iowa	71.2	66.1	5.1	6.5	7.4	3.3	0.7	10.6	0.4
19031	Cedar County, Iowa	66.9	62.3	4.6	6.7	6.7	7.9	1.7	9.5	0.6
19033	Cerro Gordo County, Iowa	70.0	65.9	4.1	12.5	6.2	3.9	0.8	6.3	0.2
19035	Cherokee County, Iowa	68.4	64.2	4.2	6.8	6.0	6.9	1.2	10.3	0.3
19037	Chickasaw County, Iowa	68.4	64.3	4.1	8.1	8.6	3.0	0.9	10.1	0.8
19039	Clarke County, Iowa	76.3	73.8	2.4	6.0	5.1	4.6	1.4	6.2	0.5
19041	Clay County, Iowa	72.1	68.2	3.9	9.1	6.9	2.3	0.8	8.6	0.3
19043	Clayton County, Iowa	68.5	65.2	3.3	6.8	6.4	3.4	1.3	13.2	0.4
19045	Clinton County, Iowa	76.6	72.8	3.7	8.7	6.4	2.3	0.9	5.0	0.3
19047	Crawford County, Iowa	71.7	68.2	3.6	6.1	8.0	3.4	1.4	8.4	1.0
19049	Dallas County, Iowa	76.9	73.0	3.9	6.9	5.9	3.9	1.5	4.8	0.2
19051	Davis County, Iowa	68.4	63.9	4.5	6.1	8.8	2.0	0.5	13.5	0.8
19053	Decatur County, Iowa	61.8	58.7	3.1	13.1	8.8	3.6	2.1	9.7	0.9
19055	Delaware County, Iowa	70.7	67.7	2.9	7.6	6.3	2.6	0.4	11.6	0.7
19057	Des Moines County, Iowa	72.5	69.3	3.2	9.2	6.2	4.8	1.2	6.0	0.1
19059	Dickinson County, Iowa	71.5	65.9	5.6	7.8	5.9	3.0	0.8	10.9	0.2
19061	Dubuque County, Iowa	73.0	69.8	3.3	11.7	6.3	2.9	0.7	5.2	0.2
19063	Emmet County, Iowa	73.1	69.2	3.9	7.1	7.0	3.8	0.5	8.3	0.2
19065	Fayette County, Iowa	69.1	65.5	3.5	9.9	6.5	3.5	0.5	10.2	0.2
19067	Floyd County, Iowa	71.9	67.2	4.7	8.5	8.8	1.7	0.4	8.1	0.7
19069	Franklin County, Iowa	66.1	60.6	5.5	6.9	7.5	4.2	1.0	13.9	0.5
19071	Fremont County, Iowa	64.4	58.7	5.7	9.5	8.3	7.5	1.9	8.4	0.0
19073	Greene County, Iowa	65.5	59.5	6.0	7.7	9.3	4.5	1.6	10.9	0.5
19075	Grundy County, Iowa	70.0	66.9	3.2	6.7	5.4	7.1	0.8	10.0	0.0
19077	Guthrie County, Iowa	67.2	61.1	6.1	6.6	8.1	4.7	1.8	10.9	0.7
19079	Hamilton County, Iowa	69.0	67.1	1.9	6.1	9.5	4.7	1.8	8.7	0.2
19081	Hancock County, Iowa	71.5	67.4	4.1	5.8	7.8	3.0	0.8	10.5	0.7
19083	Hardin County, Iowa	69.9	66.6	3.3	7.1	7.2	5.3	1.3	8.9	0.3
19085	Harrison County, Iowa	70.0	67.0	3.0	9.8	6.4	3.3	1.5	8.9	0.2
19087	Henry County, Iowa	66.0	62.5	3.4	9.2	7.9	8.5	1.7	6.3	0.4
19089	Howard County, Iowa	66.6	62.9	3.8	8.4	10.0	2.1	0.8	11.0	1.1
19091	Humboldt County, Iowa	71.2	67.0	4.2	7.4	7.5	2.7	1.8	9.3	0.2
19093	Ida County, Iowa	72.1	65.0	7.1	7.6	5.7	3.3	2.0	9.3	0.1
19095	Iowa County, Iowa	65.3	61.0	4.3	7.4	5.9	8.5	3.0	9.7	0.2
19097	Jackson County, Iowa	73.1	68.5	4.7	6.2	6.5	2.1	1.5	10.4	0.2
19099	Jasper County, Iowa	71.3	67.9	3.4	8.9	7.5	4.5	1.0	6.7	0.2
19101	Jefferson County, Iowa	64.7	58.4	6.3	14.9	5.1	3.2	1.1	10.5	0.5
19103	Johnson County, Iowa	57.4	54.1	3.3	9.7	5.9	20.1	2.0	4.8	0.2
19105	Jones County, Iowa	69.2	64.5	4.7	8.4	6.6	4.5	1.7	9.5	0.2
19107	Keokuk County, Iowa	62.5	58.6	3.9	7.5	8.1	6.5	1.7	13.2	0.4
19109	Kossuth County, Iowa	66.9	62.6	4.3	7.7	8.7	2.5	1.0	13.0	0.2
19111	Lee County, Iowa	73.9	71.1	2.8	7.2	6.4	5.0	1.4	5.8	0.4
19113	Linn County, Iowa	76.5	73.8	2.7	9.0	4.6	3.9	1.4	4.5	0.1
19115	Louisa County, Iowa	75.6	70.9	4.6	6.3	6.8	3.3	1.1	6.9	0.0
19117	Lucas County, Iowa	66.9	65.9	1.1	7.3	8.6	4.6	1.4	11.1	0.0
19119	Lyon County, Iowa	66.3	60.0	6.3	10.5	7.9	2.9	1.3	10.5	0.6
19121	Madison County, Iowa	73.2	69.0	4.3	6.9	7.5	3.3	2.2	6.9	0.1
19123	Mahaska County, Iowa	71.8	68.6	3.2	9.9	6.5	3.4	0.6	7.2	0.6
19125	Marion County, Iowa	69.5	66.4	3.1	13.2	5.1	4.0	2.1	5.9	0.1
19127	Marshall County, Iowa	73.4	71.4	1.9	7.1	4.7	8.0	1.3	5.1	0.3
19129	Mills County, Iowa	61.8	58.6	3.2	10.1	9.7	9.6	1.8	7.1	0.0
19131	Mitchell County, Iowa	67.2	61.5	5.7	7.8	8.7	2.9	0.9	11.7	0.8
19133	Monona County, Iowa	66.3	63.6	2.8	7.0	9.0	3.8	1.6	11.9	0.3
19135	Monroe County, Iowa	63.2	60.5	2.7	11.5	11.9	3.2	2.0	8.2	0.0
19137	Montgomery County, Iowa	67.7	64.2	3.6	9.3	7.5	3.6	0.7	10.2	1.0
19139	Muscatine County, Iowa	74.8	73.3	1.6	6.5	8.9	2.9	1.4	5.4	0.2
19141	O'Brien County, Iowa	64.1	58.1	6.0	13.7	5.6	5.8	0.6	10.2	0.0
19143	Osceola County, Iowa	66.0	61.3	4.7	10.8	4.9	4.4	1.9	11.7	0.2
19145	Page County, Iowa	67.7	65.4	2.3	8.2	6.7	7.3	1.5	8.4	0.3
19147	Palo Alto County, Iowa	64.0	60.3	3.8	9.1	10.1	6.4	1.1	9.0	0.2
19149	Plymouth County, Iowa	69.8	64.3	5.5	7.5	6.5	4.5	1.4	9.7	0.4
19151	Pocahontas County, Iowa	64.3	58.9	5.4	6.2	8.0	4.4	1.5	15.5	0.1

Table C. County—Labor Force, Employment, and Educational Data, 2011–2015—*Continued*

| | | Class of worker for civilian employed population age 16 and older | | | | | | | | |
| | | Private for-profit wage and salary workers | | | | Government workers | | | | |
Fips code	State/county	Total private for-profit wage and salary workers	Employees of private companies	Self-employed in own incorporated business	Private not-for-profit wage and salary workers	Local government workers	State government workers	Federal government workers	Self-employed in own not incorporated business	Unpaid family workers
19153	Polk County, Iowa	74.2	71.5	2.8	8.9	5.8	4.5	2.0	4.4	0.1
19155	Pottawattamie County, Iowa	74.4	71.2	3.2	8.2	5.9	4.1	2.2	5.0	0.2
19157	Poweshiek County, Iowa	68.5	63.9	4.6	15.3	4.8	3.1	1.1	7.2	0.1
19159	Ringgold County, Iowa	58.3	52.9	5.4	8.1	9.5	5.6	1.5	16.6	0.4
19161	Sac County, Iowa	70.1	64.9	5.2	6.5	8.5	3.6	1.1	9.9	0.2
19163	Scott County, Iowa	74.0	70.7	3.4	8.5	6.0	2.7	3.9	4.8	0.2
19165	Shelby County, Iowa	67.7	63.3	4.4	6.0	8.2	3.8	1.5	12.5	0.5
19167	Sioux County, Iowa	69.2	62.3	6.9	12.9	6.3	2.5	0.4	8.3	0.3
19169	Story County, Iowa	58.6	56.2	2.4	7.7	6.8	20.2	2.4	4.3	0.0
19171	Tama County, Iowa	70.1	67.3	2.8	5.5	6.5	5.8	2.1	9.6	0.4
19173	Taylor County, Iowa	64.7	62.6	2.1	6.3	7.8	6.5	1.9	12.4	0.3
19175	Union County, Iowa	68.8	66.6	2.3	8.1	8.3	3.8	0.9	9.8	0.3
19177	Van Buren County, Iowa	69.1	65.1	4.1	6.6	9.0	3.8	0.8	9.6	1.0
19179	Wapello County, Iowa	73.7	71.3	2.5	8.6	7.5	3.2	0.8	6.0	0.2
19181	Warren County, Iowa	70.7	68.0	2.7	10.1	6.4	4.3	2.7	5.8	0.1
19183	Washington County, Iowa	63.1	58.5	4.6	7.5	7.2	11.0	1.1	9.9	0.2
19185	Wayne County, Iowa	57.5	54.8	2.6	12.3	6.7	4.9	1.6	15.6	1.5
19187	Webster County, Iowa	67.5	64.0	3.5	10.5	6.3	5.1	2.0	8.4	0.2
19189	Winnebago County, Iowa	74.8	70.9	3.9	9.6	4.1	3.2	0.6	7.5	0.3
19191	Winneshiek County, Iowa	56.8	53.1	3.7	23.1	6.2	3.0	1.1	9.5	0.2
19193	Woodbury County, Iowa	75.7	73.4	2.3	9.2	5.7	3.2	1.5	4.6	0.1
19195	Worth County, Iowa	72.5	67.7	4.8	6.5	8.1	3.1	1.1	8.8	0.0
19197	Wright County, Iowa	71.2	68.2	3.0	5.7	6.6	5.3	2.7	8.5	0.0
20000	**Kansas**	69.6	66.4	3.2	8.2	7.6	5.8	2.5	6.1	0.2
20001	Allen County, Kansas	64.8	61.1	3.7	8.0	11.0	5.5	1.3	9.1	0.2
20003	Anderson County, Kansas	62.8	58.9	3.9	5.1	6.1	5.7	1.3	18.7	0.3
20005	Atchison County, Kansas	65.0	62.1	2.9	15.0	7.9	4.1	1.5	6.0	0.4
20007	Barber County, Kansas	59.5	55.2	4.3	10.8	9.8	5.3	2.2	12.0	0.5
20009	Barton County, Kansas	68.2	65.1	3.1	7.8	7.7	7.2	1.1	7.7	0.2
20011	Bourbon County, Kansas	68.5	65.4	3.1	7.3	12.0	3.8	2.5	5.8	0.1
20013	Brown County, Kansas	62.2	60.4	1.8	9.1	10.0	4.3	2.4	11.9	0.2
20015	Butler County, Kansas	70.1	67.3	2.8	7.6	10.3	5.5	1.7	4.7	0.2
20017	Chase County, Kansas	66.2	59.5	6.7	7.1	11.7	5.6	1.3	8.0	0.1
20019	Chautauqua County, Kansas	62.1	59.5	2.6	7.9	12.2	5.3	1.1	11.1	0.3
20021	Cherokee County, Kansas	64.3	63.0	1.3	9.2	9.4	7.3	1.2	8.6	0.1
20023	Cheyenne County, Kansas	53.4	45.3	8.1	6.6	15.7	6.9	1.3	15.1	1.1
20025	Clark County, Kansas	52.5	48.5	4.0	8.2	13.3	9.3	1.1	15.6	0.1
20027	Clay County, Kansas	58.8	54.5	4.3	7.6	9.9	6.0	5.9	11.3	0.4
20029	Cloud County, Kansas	65.6	61.5	4.1	9.9	8.7	5.1	1.4	9.0	0.3
20031	Coffey County, Kansas	64.7	62.4	2.3	7.3	11.9	5.3	2.1	8.6	0.0
20033	Comanche County, Kansas	58.3	53.1	5.2	4.4	12.2	6.6	1.6	16.4	0.5
20035	Cowley County, Kansas	70.4	68.4	2.0	7.3	10.1	5.0	0.9	6.0	0.2
20037	Crawford County, Kansas	68.1	66.1	2.0	7.5	6.3	10.8	1.3	5.6	0.4
20039	Decatur County, Kansas	57.1	50.0	7.1	7.8	13.5	6.6	2.2	12.2	0.6
20041	Dickinson County, Kansas	66.0	62.1	3.9	6.8	9.4	5.0	3.9	8.6	0.4
20043	Doniphan County, Kansas	64.1	59.7	4.4	9.0	10.3	6.3	1.5	7.6	1.2
20045	Douglas County, Kansas	61.4	58.2	3.3	10.4	7.4	14.0	2.0	4.7	0.1
20047	Edwards County, Kansas	65.7	58.1	7.6	3.9	12.1	6.8	1.0	10.0	0.6
20049	Elk County, Kansas	47.5	44.4	3.0	11.8	18.4	6.7	1.5	13.6	0.5
20051	Ellis County, Kansas	64.0	60.8	3.2	10.8	6.7	9.1	2.2	7.0	0.2
20053	Ellsworth County, Kansas	61.7	57.8	3.9	7.9	11.9	8.3	0.7	9.5	0.0
20055	Finney County, Kansas	71.0	68.4	2.6	7.3	9.6	4.8	1.0	6.0	0.3
20057	Ford County, Kansas	75.0	73.4	1.5	6.6	8.1	3.4	1.1	5.4	0.4
20059	Franklin County, Kansas	67.9	65.2	2.7	8.5	11.6	4.7	1.2	6.0	0.2
20061	Geary County, Kansas	55.9	53.3	2.6	4.1	12.2	3.2	19.7	4.5	0.4
20063	Gove County, Kansas	56.7	50.6	6.1	6.6	12.6	3.6	2.6	17.8	0.2
20065	Graham County, Kansas	54.1	50.0	4.1	8.1	12.1	6.4	3.9	14.9	0.5
20067	Grant County, Kansas	64.2	58.8	5.4	7.4	11.3	3.5	2.7	10.0	0.9
20069	Gray County, Kansas	59.9	52.7	7.2	11.2	8.7	3.9	1.1	14.3	0.9
20071	Greeley County, Kansas	59.1	51.9	7.3	5.1	14.4	3.9	0.8	16.6	0.2
20073	Greenwood County, Kansas	64.0	60.7	3.3	4.7	10.7	8.0	0.8	11.5	0.2
20075	Hamilton County, Kansas	61.7	53.9	7.9	3.1	8.8	6.0	1.8	17.9	0.7
20077	Harper County, Kansas	64.8	59.6	5.2	5.6	11.6	6.1	1.3	10.0	0.6
20079	Harvey County, Kansas	67.5	63.9	3.6	13.8	9.1	3.0	1.2	5.1	0.2
20081	Haskell County, Kansas	63.6	59.9	3.7	4.9	11.4	6.1	1.2	12.1	0.7
20083	Hodgeman County, Kansas	51.7	43.2	8.6	5.9	15.6	4.2	2.0	19.0	1.6
20085	Jackson County, Kansas	60.5	58.2	2.3	7.4	12.1	8.1	3.7	7.5	0.8
20087	Jefferson County, Kansas	63.5	60.5	3.0	7.9	9.5	9.7	3.2	6.2	0.0
20089	Jewell County, Kansas	50.6	45.8	4.8	10.3	11.5	5.7	1.8	19.8	0.3
20091	Johnson County, Kansas	75.5	71.3	4.2	8.4	5.4	3.3	2.2	5.2	0.1
20093	Kearny County, Kansas	59.7	54.4	5.3	5.5	14.3	8.0	2.0	10.0	0.5
20095	Kingman County, Kansas	63.2	60.3	2.9	6.5	9.8	4.1	0.7	15.6	0.1
20097	Kiowa County, Kansas	50.3	46.8	3.5	17.3	13.2	4.3	1.7	13.1	0.0
20099	Labette County, Kansas	66.1	64.2	1.9	7.8	9.0	8.8	1.2	6.9	0.2

Table C. County—Labor Force, Employment, and Educational Data, 2011–2015—*Continued*

		Class of worker for civilian employed population age 16 and older								
		Private for-profit wage and salary workers				Government workers				
Fips code	State/county	Total private for-profit wage and salary workers	Employees of private companies	Self-employed in own incorporated business	Private not-for-profit wage and salary workers	Local government workers	State government workers	Federal government workers	Self-employed in own not incorporated business	Unpaid family workers
20101	Lane County, Kansas	53.9	51.6	2.3	2.5	22.7	3.5	0.5	16.7	0.2
20103	Leavenworth County, Kansas	63.7	60.3	3.3	6.0	7.3	5.4	12.8	4.7	0.0
20105	Lincoln County, Kansas	58.7	54.0	4.6	6.2	13.9	6.6	2.5	12.2	0.0
20107	Linn County, Kansas	65.1	60.0	5.1	7.4	9.0	7.9	1.4	9.0	0.2
20109	Logan County, Kansas	55.7	50.1	5.6	4.1	13.2	7.8	2.0	16.9	0.3
20111	Lyon County, Kansas	67.2	64.8	2.3	7.8	8.5	10.3	1.0	5.2	0.1
20113	McPherson County, Kansas	67.0	63.4	3.6	10.5	8.0	2.9	1.4	9.9	0.4
20115	Marion County, Kansas	62.8	59.9	2.9	10.9	8.4	6.0	1.3	10.1	0.6
20117	Marshall County, Kansas	66.8	62.7	4.1	8.3	8.9	3.0	1.9	10.8	0.3
20119	Meade County, Kansas	55.3	50.1	5.2	5.8	17.3	10.2	0.9	10.3	0.2
20121	Miami County, Kansas	74.2	69.3	4.9	6.1	7.3	4.0	2.4	5.9	0.1
20123	Mitchell County, Kansas	64.5	59.9	4.6	8.5	10.1	3.7	1.7	11.1	0.4
20125	Montgomery County, Kansas	68.9	67.2	1.7	9.0	10.1	3.8	1.1	6.8	0.3
20127	Morris County, Kansas	60.0	57.7	2.3	6.5	9.2	5.7	4.4	13.7	0.5
20129	Morton County, Kansas	63.3	61.2	2.1	3.0	16.1	5.1	0.5	12.0	0.0
20131	Nemaha County, Kansas	66.8	63.2	3.6	10.3	7.1	4.3	1.6	9.4	0.5
20133	Neosho County, Kansas	63.6	60.0	3.6	7.3	11.4	7.2	1.9	8.4	0.2
20135	Ness County, Kansas	55.5	49.5	6.0	4.7	15.4	4.7	2.0	17.5	0.2
20137	Norton County, Kansas	56.2	54.0	2.2	9.9	11.5	8.6	1.7	12.0	0.1
20139	Osage County, Kansas	65.0	61.7	3.3	7.6	9.2	7.7	2.8	7.5	0.1
20141	Osborne County, Kansas	56.2	53.7	2.5	7.3	13.6	4.7	1.8	14.6	1.9
20143	Ottawa County, Kansas	65.0	62.5	2.5	8.1	7.8	4.0	0.7	14.0	0.3
20145	Pawnee County, Kansas	57.3	52.3	5.0	3.2	6.7	20.1	0.8	11.4	0.5
20147	Phillips County, Kansas	61.1	56.6	4.5	7.6	13.0	5.2	1.4	11.6	0.0
20149	Pottawatomie County, Kansas	62.6	59.4	3.2	6.4	9.2	11.5	2.1	7.8	0.4
20151	Pratt County, Kansas	61.1	57.5	3.6	10.8	10.5	6.2	0.5	9.6	1.3
20153	Rawlins County, Kansas	54.1	49.6	4.6	8.7	8.1	5.9	1.7	20.6	0.8
20155	Reno County, Kansas	69.3	66.0	3.2	9.4	7.9	6.0	1.4	5.8	0.3
20157	Republic County, Kansas	61.3	57.0	4.3	8.2	8.6	5.6	1.8	14.1	0.4
20159	Rice County, Kansas	64.4	61.4	3.0	10.7	10.4	5.7	1.1	7.4	0.3
20161	Riley County, Kansas	58.5	56.3	2.2	6.6	6.6	18.7	5.2	4.3	0.1
20163	Rooks County, Kansas	58.5	55.2	3.3	8.1	12.4	6.7	1.9	12.1	0.3
20165	Rush County, Kansas	53.1	49.1	3.9	6.0	10.7	10.7	1.6	17.5	0.4
20167	Russell County, Kansas	66.2	62.1	4.2	9.0	7.0	6.5	1.2	8.4	1.7
20169	Saline County, Kansas	74.5	71.8	2.7	8.4	6.1	3.3	1.1	6.3	0.3
20171	Scott County, Kansas	58.7	52.0	6.7	7.8	9.1	4.1	3.3	17.0	0.0
20173	Sedgwick County, Kansas	74.5	71.8	2.7	8.3	6.4	4.0	2.1	4.6	0.1
20175	Seward County, Kansas	73.4	71.4	2.0	5.6	7.9	5.9	1.6	5.7	0.0
20177	Shawnee County, Kansas	65.8	63.3	2.6	9.5	7.1	9.6	3.3	4.6	0.1
20179	Sheridan County, Kansas	55.1	48.8	6.3	8.0	13.1	3.0	2.0	18.6	0.2
20181	Sherman County, Kansas	66.1	59.1	7.0	4.0	12.2	7.5	2.7	7.5	0.0
20183	Smith County, Kansas	54.0	45.8	8.2	10.0	13.5	3.8	2.6	15.5	0.8
20185	Stafford County, Kansas	58.0	51.7	6.4	5.1	12.1	9.1	1.5	13.5	0.7
20187	Stanton County, Kansas	60.4	50.2	10.2	5.0	13.4	7.1	0.5	13.4	0.2
20189	Stevens County, Kansas	68.7	63.4	5.3	3.8	7.2	5.6	0.4	13.3	1.0
20191	Sumner County, Kansas	69.5	65.8	3.7	6.1	10.8	5.7	1.6	6.1	0.2
20193	Thomas County, Kansas	63.0	58.2	4.7	7.0	10.2	6.7	1.6	11.4	0.1
20195	Trego County, Kansas	57.4	51.2	6.2	9.2	14.8	4.8	1.0	12.5	0.2
20197	Wabaunsee County, Kansas	63.8	57.8	6.0	9.5	7.0	9.9	3.2	6.5	0.2
20199	Wallace County, Kansas	49.7	44.5	5.2	8.2	12.3	6.0	1.9	21.5	0.5
20201	Washington County, Kansas	64.1	60.7	3.4	8.4	9.3	6.3	1.1	10.4	0.4
20203	Wichita County, Kansas	59.9	52.6	7.3	8.1	7.7	5.4	2.7	15.9	0.4
20205	Wilson County, Kansas	64.8	62.1	2.7	5.3	12.6	4.6	1.7	10.8	0.2
20207	Woodson County, Kansas	59.3	54.1	5.3	4.4	15.1	4.6	2.8	13.4	0.4
20209	Wyandotte County, Kansas	76.1	74.8	1.3	6.8	7.0	3.4	2.4	4.0	0.2
21000	**Kentucky**	71.4	68.5	2.9	7.9	5.8	6.9	2.4	5.4	0.2
21001	Adair County, Kentucky	67.6	64.3	3.4	6.4	5.6	7.9	1.2	11.2	0.1
21003	Allen County, Kentucky	70.4	67.0	3.4	5.9	6.8	4.8	1.4	10.4	0.4
21005	Anderson County, Kentucky	62.4	60.2	2.2	4.3	7.2	16.9	2.4	6.8	0.1
21007	Ballard County, Kentucky	75.2	72.6	2.6	4.7	5.3	4.4	2.0	8.4	0.0
21009	Barren County, Kentucky	70.4	66.8	3.6	6.3	6.3	7.3	1.4	8.0	0.3
21011	Bath County, Kentucky	64.1	60.1	4.0	4.7	7.7	10.9	2.5	9.9	0.2
21013	Bell County, Kentucky	67.8	67.1	0.7	9.7	5.7	8.3	2.5	5.7	0.1
21015	Boone County, Kentucky	78.4	76.0	2.4	6.8	4.9	3.0	3.4	3.5	0.1
21017	Bourbon County, Kentucky	73.3	69.7	3.6	5.3	6.7	5.1	1.9	7.5	0.3
21019	Boyd County, Kentucky	66.0	63.4	2.6	14.3	5.9	5.4	3.2	5.0	0.3
21021	Boyle County, Kentucky	67.6	64.1	3.5	8.2	6.7	8.2	1.3	7.8	0.2
21023	Bracken County, Kentucky	71.7	70.1	1.6	6.2	4.6	7.8	2.9	6.9	0.0
21025	Breathitt County, Kentucky	61.4	59.5	1.9	7.5	7.6	14.6	2.3	6.4	0.1
21027	Breckinridge County, Kentucky	69.0	66.7	2.3	7.8	7.0	6.5	2.3	7.2	0.3
21029	Bullitt County, Kentucky	78.8	76.4	2.3	5.8	5.5	3.8	1.6	4.4	0.1
21031	Butler County, Kentucky	70.0	67.3	2.7	3.4	6.1	6.9	0.4	12.4	0.8
21033	Caldwell County, Kentucky	65.2	63.3	1.9	4.3	6.4	10.5	1.3	12.4	0.0
21035	Calloway County, Kentucky	62.9	60.7	2.3	9.0	6.4	12.7	1.8	7.0	0.1
21037	Campbell County, Kentucky	74.2	71.5	2.7	9.8	4.1	5.0	3.0	3.8	0.0
21039	Carlisle County, Kentucky	67.4	65.0	2.4	5.8	6.0	6.3	5.3	9.0	0.2

Table C. County—Labor Force, Employment, and Educational Data, 2011–2015—*Continued*

		Class of worker for civilian employed population age 16 and older								
		Private for-profit wage and salary workers				Government workers				
Fips code	State/county	Total private for-profit wage and salary workers	Employees of private companies	Self-employed in own incorporated business	Private not-for-profit wage and salary workers	Local government workers	State government workers	Federal government workers	Self-employed in own not incorporated business	Unpaid family workers
21041	Carroll County, Kentucky	80.5	76.1	4.4	2.1	7.4	5.1	0.4	4.2	0.2
21043	Carter County, Kentucky	70.6	68.6	2.0	9.5	4.9	9.4	1.2	4.3	0.1
21045	Casey County, Kentucky	71.3	68.1	3.2	3.7	6.3	8.8	1.2	8.2	0.5
21047	Christian County, Kentucky	66.8	64.7	2.1	5.9	6.3	7.5	7.0	6.2	0.2
21049	Clark County, Kentucky	73.3	69.5	3.8	6.6	7.0	4.4	2.8	5.3	0.6
21051	Clay County, Kentucky	60.4	58.6	1.8	8.6	4.9	14.7	5.2	5.7	0.5
21053	Clinton County, Kentucky	66.2	62.8	3.4	6.0	9.8	7.3	3.3	7.5	0.0
21055	Crittenden County, Kentucky	66.4	64.3	2.1	8.0	6.0	9.2	1.5	8.7	0.1
21057	Cumberland County, Kentucky	71.9	65.3	6.7	2.8	7.9	7.3	2.4	7.6	0.0
21059	Daviess County, Kentucky	73.7	70.5	3.2	9.2	5.2	5.1	1.2	5.3	0.3
21061	Edmonson County, Kentucky	66.8	64.7	2.1	5.4	6.2	11.0	3.8	6.8	0.1
21063	Elliott County, Kentucky	55.8	54.1	1.7	10.7	3.7	20.5	0.1	8.3	0.9
21065	Estill County, Kentucky	71.2	69.8	1.5	5.3	7.7	7.8	1.4	6.2	0.4
21067	Fayette County, Kentucky	69.0	65.4	3.6	9.5	5.3	9.1	2.2	4.9	0.1
21069	Fleming County, Kentucky	65.7	62.7	3.1	9.6	6.1	8.7	0.6	9.3	0.0
21071	Floyd County, Kentucky	61.9	59.3	2.7	9.3	7.2	11.4	3.6	6.4	0.0
21073	Franklin County, Kentucky	55.2	53.2	2.0	5.0	6.3	25.6	2.2	5.5	0.1
21075	Fulton County, Kentucky	67.6	66.0	1.6	7.7	8.8	6.2	2.2	6.7	0.8
21077	Gallatin County, Kentucky	79.9	78.4	1.5	2.5	5.6	5.9	1.1	4.6	0.5
21079	Garrard County, Kentucky	70.1	65.6	4.5	6.9	7.2	6.0	2.4	7.4	0.0
21081	Grant County, Kentucky	76.9	76.1	0.8	4.8	5.8	6.0	2.4	4.0	0.0
21083	Graves County, Kentucky	70.6	67.8	2.8	6.4	7.6	4.7	2.1	8.6	0.0
21085	Grayson County, Kentucky	67.5	64.9	2.5	8.0	7.2	6.8	2.6	7.6	0.3
21087	Green County, Kentucky	68.6	66.6	2.0	6.1	6.5	6.4	2.4	9.7	0.3
21089	Greenup County, Kentucky	68.1	66.4	1.7	11.8	6.8	6.2	1.9	5.0	0.1
21091	Hancock County, Kentucky	78.7	77.1	1.6	6.4	4.1	4.9	2.1	3.6	0.1
21093	Hardin County, Kentucky	66.8	64.2	2.6	6.0	6.4	5.4	10.9	4.5	0.0
21095	Harlan County, Kentucky	59.5	57.6	1.9	14.4	6.7	11.2	2.2	5.8	0.1
21097	Harrison County, Kentucky	73.9	71.2	2.8	6.2	7.3	5.5	1.5	5.6	0.0
21099	Hart County, Kentucky	67.7	66.2	1.6	3.5	4.1	8.4	2.1	13.6	0.6
21101	Henderson County, Kentucky	72.4	68.4	4.0	8.3	8.6	4.9	0.5	5.1	0.1
21103	Henry County, Kentucky	68.8	65.4	3.4	7.2	3.9	7.9	1.8	10.4	0.2
21105	Hickman County, Kentucky	67.3	60.7	6.6	8.8	7.6	7.3	0.1	9.0	0.0
21107	Hopkins County, Kentucky	68.8	67.1	1.7	8.0	7.8	7.8	1.3	6.1	0.2
21109	Jackson County, Kentucky	65.9	65.1	0.8	7.0	12.4	6.4	3.3	5.0	0.0
21111	Jefferson County, Kentucky	75.0	71.9	3.1	9.0	5.2	4.4	1.9	4.4	0.1
21113	Jessamine County, Kentucky	70.6	65.7	4.9	9.8	5.7	5.7	1.6	6.1	0.4
21115	Johnson County, Kentucky	67.5	64.4	3.1	7.6	5.2	12.2	2.5	5.0	0.0
21117	Kenton County, Kentucky	76.7	74.1	2.6	9.4	4.5	3.2	2.9	3.2	0.1
21119	Knott County, Kentucky	57.9	56.4	1.5	11.9	6.4	16.0	1.1	6.5	0.3
21121	Knox County, Kentucky	68.9	67.6	1.3	8.1	6.7	8.9	2.3	4.6	0.4
21123	Larue County, Kentucky	71.4	69.3	2.1	7.5	5.9	4.0	2.3	8.6	0.3
21125	Laurel County, Kentucky	73.8	70.6	3.2	6.2	5.2	6.8	2.9	4.9	0.1
21127	Lawrence County, Kentucky	74.5	71.1	3.4	3.6	7.3	7.3	3.1	4.3	0.0
21129	Lee County, Kentucky	60.4	59.4	1.1	3.4	13.2	12.2	4.8	5.4	0.5
21131	Leslie County, Kentucky	65.4	64.0	1.4	10.8	6.0	12.5	1.5	3.7	0.1
21133	Letcher County, Kentucky	62.6	61.0	1.6	11.3	6.6	11.2	3.0	5.1	0.2
21135	Lewis County, Kentucky	66.5	64.0	2.5	6.4	4.5	9.5	0.5	12.6	0.0
21137	Lincoln County, Kentucky	72.4	70.3	2.1	5.9	6.2	5.7	1.9	7.8	0.1
21139	Livingston County, Kentucky	73.0	71.3	1.7	7.2	6.5	4.9	2.5	5.9	0.0
21141	Logan County, Kentucky	75.1	72.9	2.2	5.3	6.2	5.0	1.6	6.5	0.2
21143	Lyon County, Kentucky	67.6	65.3	2.3	7.0	4.3	15.0	0.6	5.3	0.2
21145	McCracken County, Kentucky	69.5	66.4	3.1	9.9	5.5	5.3	2.7	7.0	0.2
21147	McCreary County, Kentucky	74.2	72.2	2.0	3.6	3.6	7.7	4.4	5.7	0.8
21149	McLean County, Kentucky	68.0	64.4	3.6	5.9	8.5	6.6	1.3	9.6	0.1
21151	Madison County, Kentucky	67.6	65.3	2.2	9.3	5.5	9.7	3.6	4.2	0.2
21153	Magoffin County, Kentucky	66.3	63.8	2.4	7.8	7.6	14.9	0.2	2.9	0.4
21155	Marion County, Kentucky	70.5	67.0	3.5	5.9	6.0	6.9	2.2	8.1	0.4
21157	Marshall County, Kentucky	68.7	66.2	2.4	9.5	6.0	7.1	1.9	6.6	0.2
21159	Martin County, Kentucky	67.3	66.0	1.3	6.9	11.9	8.0	1.2	4.8	0.0
21161	Mason County, Kentucky	70.5	68.3	2.2	7.5	7.0	8.4	0.9	5.6	0.1
21163	Meade County, Kentucky	70.7	69.2	1.5	4.5	4.7	5.5	11.4	3.3	0.0
21165	Menifee County, Kentucky	62.0	61.0	1.0	6.2	9.4	14.7	1.4	6.4	0.0
21167	Mercer County, Kentucky	67.2	63.5	3.8	8.6	5.6	9.4	1.0	7.1	1.1
21169	Metcalfe County, Kentucky	66.6	65.0	1.6	3.8	4.5	9.6	0.8	13.8	0.9
21171	Monroe County, Kentucky	65.6	61.6	4.0	6.5	5.9	8.4	1.0	11.4	1.2
21173	Montgomery County, Kentucky	73.3	70.1	3.2	4.4	6.0	8.5	2.1	5.5	0.2
21175	Morgan County, Kentucky	58.4	55.1	3.3	6.2	6.2	21.5	1.6	5.7	0.4
21177	Muhlenberg County, Kentucky	69.1	67.6	1.5	5.1	9.1	7.3	3.1	6.0	0.3
21179	Nelson County, Kentucky	75.1	71.6	3.5	6.5	5.8	5.4	1.7	5.3	0.1
21181	Nicholas County, Kentucky	70.6	68.1	2.4	7.1	6.4	6.4	1.3	8.0	0.3
21183	Ohio County, Kentucky	73.2	70.6	2.6	6.5	6.3	6.6	1.9	5.5	0.0
21185	Oldham County, Kentucky	75.2	70.1	5.1	7.6	5.2	5.1	1.6	5.2	0.2
21187	Owen County, Kentucky	63.8	61.6	2.1	5.4	9.1	12.6	0.4	8.4	0.4
21189	Owsley County, Kentucky	48.5	46.0	2.5	4.7	24.5	6.3	4.7	11.3	0.0
21191	Pendleton County, Kentucky	73.8	70.9	2.9	6.3	4.5	5.5	2.0	7.7	0.2

Table C. County—Labor Force, Employment, and Educational Data, 2011–2015—*Continued*

		Class of worker for civilian employed population age 16 and older								
		Private for-profit wage and salary workers				Government workers				
Fips code	State/county	Total private for-profit wage and salary workers	Employees of private companies	Self-employed in own incorporated business	Private not-for-profit wage and salary workers	Local government workers	State government workers	Federal government workers	Self-employed in own not incorporated business	Unpaid family workers
21193	Perry County, Kentucky	64.6	62.9	1.7	11.1	7.3	10.0	2.2	4.8	0.0
21195	Pike County, Kentucky	68.4	64.8	3.6	7.9	8.7	8.9	1.6	4.4	0.1
21197	Powell County, Kentucky	72.3	70.3	1.9	4.9	5.6	8.5	2.2	6.5	0.0
21199	Pulaski County, Kentucky	73.5	69.8	3.8	5.3	6.3	7.4	1.7	5.6	0.3
21201	Robertson County, Kentucky	76.2	69.9	6.3	2.2	6.0	12.4	0.0	3.2	0.0
21203	Rockcastle County, Kentucky	71.2	68.7	2.5	6.7	7.4	7.4	2.9	4.4	0.0
21205	Rowan County, Kentucky	61.4	58.3	3.1	8.0	8.1	15.4	1.1	5.6	0.4
21207	Russell County, Kentucky	68.3	64.1	4.2	7.1	6.4	8.6	1.7	7.8	0.0
21209	Scott County, Kentucky	73.8	71.1	2.7	6.2	7.1	6.2	1.6	5.0	0.1
21211	Shelby County, Kentucky	71.8	69.0	2.8	7.7	5.5	6.8	1.5	6.5	0.2
21213	Simpson County, Kentucky	78.5	76.8	1.8	2.4	5.0	4.7	1.0	8.2	0.2
21215	Spencer County, Kentucky	79.9	79.1	0.8	5.2	5.3	3.1	1.7	4.8	0.0
21217	Taylor County, Kentucky	71.6	67.8	3.8	7.0	6.0	7.6	0.8	7.1	0.0
21219	Todd County, Kentucky	68.9	66.8	2.1	4.8	6.0	6.3	3.1	10.3	0.6
21221	Trigg County, Kentucky	67.3	62.7	4.6	6.8	6.1	9.2	3.4	6.8	0.4
21223	Trimble County, Kentucky	78.3	76.7	1.7	4.7	2.3	7.7	1.1	5.9	0.0
21225	Union County, Kentucky	65.2	63.8	1.4	5.9	5.9	6.1	10.6	6.0	0.2
21227	Warren County, Kentucky	71.3	68.5	2.8	7.3	5.4	9.5	1.4	4.9	0.2
21229	Washington County, Kentucky	68.8	66.1	2.7	8.0	6.3	6.6	0.7	9.4	0.2
21231	Wayne County, Kentucky	71.2	69.1	2.1	4.5	7.0	10.2	1.1	5.9	0.1
21233	Webster County, Kentucky	75.0	72.6	2.5	4.7	5.4	6.1	0.8	7.5	0.4
21235	Whitley County, Kentucky	65.1	62.9	2.2	9.2	9.1	9.3	2.8	4.3	0.1
21237	Wolfe County, Kentucky	49.6	46.3	3.4	16.0	9.7	20.8	0.3	3.7	0.0
21239	Woodford County, Kentucky	68.7	65.0	3.7	8.9	5.6	7.7	1.7	7.3	0.1
22000	**Louisiana**	72.6	69.0	3.5	6.3	7.2	6.0	2.3	5.5	0.1
22001	Acadia Parish, Louisiana	76.8	72.6	4.2	5.7	5.8	3.9	0.9	7.0	0.0
22003	Allen Parish, Louisiana	66.1	64.6	1.5	3.7	11.4	7.7	7.1	3.8	0.2
22005	Ascension Parish, Louisiana	76.1	73.0	3.2	5.5	5.8	5.8	1.8	4.9	0.1
22007	Assumption Parish, Louisiana	79.0	75.9	3.1	4.3	7.2	4.7	0.7	3.6	0.6
22009	Avoyelles Parish, Louisiana	69.4	67.1	2.3	5.8	7.3	8.8	3.5	5.0	0.2
22011	Beauregard Parish, Louisiana	69.9	66.2	3.8	5.3	7.8	4.7	6.4	5.8	0.0
22013	Bienville Parish, Louisiana	63.9	59.7	4.1	3.9	10.6	11.4	1.7	7.4	1.1
22015	Bossier Parish, Louisiana	66.4	63.8	2.6	7.9	8.0	5.9	6.5	5.2	0.1
22017	Caddo Parish, Louisiana	72.2	69.5	2.7	7.8	6.7	6.4	2.4	4.4	0.1
22019	Calcasieu Parish, Louisiana	75.0	72.0	3.0	5.1	8.9	4.9	1.0	5.0	0.2
22021	Caldwell Parish, Louisiana	66.1	62.4	3.6	4.5	13.6	9.4	1.6	4.6	0.3
22023	Cameron Parish, Louisiana	67.1	64.2	2.9	3.1	14.9	6.0	1.5	7.2	0.3
22025	Catahoula Parish, Louisiana	66.7	62.5	4.2	3.1	11.3	6.1	2.9	10.0	0.0
22027	Claiborne Parish, Louisiana	64.8	60.4	4.4	6.0	10.5	11.8	1.5	5.4	0.0
22029	Concordia Parish, Louisiana	68.3	65.6	2.7	3.7	16.6	3.8	1.4	6.1	0.0
22031	De Soto Parish, Louisiana	74.9	72.6	2.2	6.1	9.4	3.6	2.1	3.8	0.2
22033	East Baton Rouge Parish, Louisiana	70.4	67.0	3.4	6.8	6.1	10.5	1.4	4.7	0.1
22035	East Carroll Parish, Louisiana	67.4	64.7	2.7	6.7	14.5	6.0	1.3	4.1	0.0
22037	East Feliciana Parish, Louisiana	61.5	58.7	2.9	6.8	9.3	14.6	2.2	5.6	0.0
22039	Evangeline Parish, Louisiana	73.9	69.2	4.7	4.6	6.3	7.4	0.8	6.9	0.0
22041	Franklin Parish, Louisiana	67.5	65.4	2.0	4.4	8.6	6.6	1.1	11.6	0.3
22043	Grant Parish, Louisiana	67.1	64.8	2.3	5.6	8.1	7.7	5.8	5.5	0.1
22045	Iberia Parish, Louisiana	77.8	74.9	2.9	3.9	6.6	4.9	0.2	6.5	0.1
22047	Iberville Parish, Louisiana	72.1	69.4	2.8	4.8	8.3	9.3	1.6	3.9	0.0
22049	Jackson Parish, Louisiana	69.9	68.0	1.9	5.0	7.8	10.5	1.5	5.1	0.3
22051	Jefferson Parish, Louisiana	75.6	71.4	4.2	6.4	6.1	3.4	2.6	5.8	0.1
22053	Jefferson Davis Parish, Louisiana	69.7	64.7	4.9	4.1	10.4	8.1	1.8	5.8	0.2
22055	Lafayette Parish, Louisiana	76.8	71.2	5.6	5.3	5.9	4.4	0.8	6.6	0.2
22057	Lafourche Parish, Louisiana	77.2	73.9	3.3	4.8	7.0	4.2	0.8	5.8	0.2
22059	LaSalle Parish, Louisiana	68.5	65.2	3.4	4.8	12.6	5.1	2.7	6.1	0.3
22061	Lincoln Parish, Louisiana	64.6	62.4	2.2	5.6	8.6	15.2	1.3	4.6	0.1
22063	Livingston Parish, Louisiana	72.5	70.1	2.5	7.6	7.7	6.8	0.9	4.4	0.1
22065	Madison Parish, Louisiana	66.9	65.7	1.1	5.6	13.9	6.0	2.8	4.6	0.1
22067	Morehouse Parish, Louisiana	80.0	77.7	2.3	4.4	6.5	4.6	1.1	3.4	0.1
22069	Natchitoches Parish, Louisiana	65.5	61.2	4.3	5.1	9.3	11.8	2.6	5.7	0.0
22071	Orleans Parish, Louisiana	68.5	64.5	4.1	11.1	5.5	5.0	3.4	6.4	0.1
22073	Ouachita Parish, Louisiana	73.8	70.6	3.2	5.9	7.1	7.3	1.3	4.4	0.1
22075	Plaquemines Parish, Louisiana	69.3	65.1	4.2	3.0	10.0	3.0	5.7	9.0	0.1
22077	Pointe Coupee Parish, Louisiana	71.7	66.6	5.1	5.7	8.7	5.2	2.5	5.7	0.4
22079	Rapides Parish, Louisiana	67.9	65.8	2.1	6.5	8.3	7.1	5.2	4.7	0.2
22081	Red River Parish, Louisiana	72.3	67.1	5.2	3.0	11.1	8.5	0.9	4.2	0.0
22083	Richland Parish, Louisiana	74.1	71.4	2.8	4.6	10.0	4.1	1.9	5.2	0.1
22085	Sabine Parish, Louisiana	69.1	66.1	3.0	10.0	8.8	4.1	2.3	5.5	0.2
22087	St. Bernard Parish, Louisiana	71.5	69.0	2.5	4.3	8.8	2.8	2.8	9.9	0.0
22089	St. Charles Parish, Louisiana	75.0	72.0	3.0	4.8	9.3	2.6	2.2	6.0	0.1
22091	St. Helena Parish, Louisiana	73.2	71.4	1.8	7.5	9.7	5.9	0.5	2.7	0.4
22093	St. James Parish, Louisiana	78.2	76.5	1.7	5.6	7.7	4.3	0.8	3.4	0.0
22095	St. John the Baptist Parish, Louisiana	79.8	77.7	2.0	4.4	6.4	3.6	1.8	3.9	0.1

Table C. County—Labor Force, Employment, and Educational Data, 2011–2015—*Continued*

		Class of worker for civilian employed population age 16 and older								
		Private for-profit wage and salary workers				Government workers				
Fips code	State/county	Total private for-profit wage and salary workers	Employees of private companies	Self-employed in own incorporated business	Private not-for-profit wage and salary workers	Local government workers	State government workers	Federal government workers	Self-employed in own not incorporated business	Unpaid family workers
22097	St. Landry Parish, Louisiana	74.0	70.4	3.6	3.7	9.9	4.9	1.4	5.9	0.1
22099	St. Martin Parish, Louisiana	76.6	72.9	3.6	5.1	8.1	4.2	1.3	4.4	0.3
22101	St. Mary Parish, Louisiana	76.0	72.2	3.8	4.4	9.7	4.1	1.0	4.7	0.0
22103	St. Tammany Parish, Louisiana	72.8	67.1	5.7	5.9	6.8	4.1	3.3	6.9	0.2
22105	Tangipahoa Parish, Louisiana	71.3	68.6	2.7	7.5	6.3	7.9	2.0	4.9	0.0
22107	Tensas Parish, Louisiana	63.8	62.4	1.4	4.9	14.9	5.7	1.7	9.0	0.0
22109	Terrebonne Parish, Louisiana	78.7	75.3	3.4	4.1	7.7	3.7	0.5	5.2	0.2
22111	Union Parish, Louisiana	79.0	76.2	2.8	5.3	5.8	3.1	1.8	4.9	0.2
22113	Vermilion Parish, Louisiana	77.3	74.1	3.2	3.0	6.6	5.1	1.2	6.8	0.0
22115	Vernon Parish, Louisiana	58.0	55.9	2.1	4.4	7.6	3.9	20.8	4.9	0.4
22117	Washington Parish, Louisiana	67.5	65.8	1.7	5.2	7.6	10.7	1.8	6.9	0.3
22119	Webster Parish, Louisiana	73.9	70.5	3.5	5.4	8.9	4.9	1.7	5.1	0.0
22121	West Baton Rouge Parish, Louisiana	71.3	67.8	3.5	5.2	6.3	10.1	1.5	5.6	0.0
22123	West Carroll Parish, Louisiana	72.4	70.1	2.3	2.5	12.3	5.1	2.1	5.2	0.4
22125	West Feliciana Parish, Louisiana	57.1	52.3	4.8	3.0	12.4	20.5	0.9	5.9	0.2
22127	Winn Parish, Louisiana	66.6	64.6	2.0	4.5	9.2	8.8	3.6	7.2	0.2
23000	**Maine**	64.3	60.5	3.9	12.7	7.4	4.2	2.4	8.7	0.1
23001	Androscoggin County, Maine	69.3	66.9	2.4	12.6	7.2	3.7	1.4	5.7	0.2
23003	Aroostook County, Maine	59.9	56.7	3.3	13.8	7.2	5.2	4.8	9.0	0.1
23005	Cumberland County, Maine	67.5	62.6	4.9	13.4	7.0	2.7	1.4	7.9	0.1
23007	Franklin County, Maine	62.4	59.7	2.7	12.3	9.4	4.2	1.3	10.3	0.1
23009	Hancock County, Maine	55.8	50.3	5.5	14.6	8.1	3.0	2.5	15.8	0.1
23011	Kennebec County, Maine	59.3	56.3	3.1	12.6	8.2	8.8	3.1	7.8	0.2
23013	Knox County, Maine	60.8	54.2	6.6	12.4	7.3	3.9	1.2	14.3	0.1
23015	Lincoln County, Maine	61.9	55.8	6.1	11.3	7.5	4.6	1.7	12.9	0.1
23017	Oxford County, Maine	66.4	63.5	3.0	10.2	8.9	2.7	1.1	10.2	0.4
23019	Penobscot County, Maine	63.5	60.6	2.9	14.4	6.3	7.1	2.4	6.2	0.1
23021	Piscataquis County, Maine	61.0	58.2	2.8	13.0	7.0	6.0	1.4	11.3	0.1
23023	Sagadahoc County, Maine	66.1	62.1	3.9	10.4	8.0	2.9	3.5	9.1	0.0
23025	Somerset County, Maine	65.5	63.0	2.5	13.1	6.9	4.4	1.4	8.6	0.1
23027	Waldo County, Maine	58.9	55.2	3.7	13.0	8.2	4.1	2.0	13.5	0.3
23029	Washington County, Maine	52.4	49.1	3.2	11.6	9.5	5.6	4.7	16.1	0.2
23031	York County, Maine	66.9	63.1	3.9	11.2	7.5	2.4	4.2	7.7	0.2
24000	**Maryland**	63.1	59.8	3.3	9.8	7.7	4.3	10.3	4.8	0.1
24001	Allegany County, Maryland	64.6	62.7	1.9	8.0	7.6	12.5	2.3	4.7	0.2
24003	Anne Arundel County, Maryland	63.9	60.3	3.6	7.7	7.6	3.7	12.7	4.3	0.2
24005	Baltimore County, Maryland	65.3	62.0	3.3	11.7	7.7	5.2	5.4	4.6	0.1
24009	Calvert County, Maryland	62.4	59.2	3.1	6.0	10.1	3.5	13.9	4.0	0.1
24011	Caroline County, Maryland	66.5	63.0	3.5	8.3	7.9	5.5	3.0	8.7	0.2
24013	Carroll County, Maryland	68.3	65.1	3.1	8.1	9.4	3.3	5.4	5.4	0.0
24015	Cecil County, Maryland	71.0	67.7	3.3	6.5	6.7	3.9	7.2	4.6	0.0
24017	Charles County, Maryland	57.2	54.5	2.6	7.2	8.5	3.9	20.2	2.9	0.2
24019	Dorchester County, Maryland	64.7	61.6	3.1	9.2	11.8	5.5	2.1	6.5	0.2
24021	Frederick County, Maryland	66.3	62.7	3.6	7.6	9.6	2.2	8.9	5.2	0.2
24023	Garrett County, Maryland	66.9	62.6	4.3	8.4	8.0	5.2	2.1	8.8	0.7
24025	Harford County, Maryland	66.2	63.0	3.2	8.2	8.9	3.2	9.1	4.2	0.2
24027	Howard County, Maryland	61.4	56.9	4.5	10.5	7.5	4.2	11.6	4.6	0.1
24029	Kent County, Maryland	66.5	61.6	4.9	9.7	5.7	4.4	3.2	10.1	0.5
24031	Montgomery County, Maryland	60.6	56.3	4.3	11.2	5.9	2.2	13.6	6.4	0.1
24033	Prince George's County, Maryland	60.3	58.3	2.0	8.8	7.6	4.4	15.1	3.6	0.1
24035	Queen Anne's County, Maryland	64.5	58.8	5.7	8.0	8.8	5.5	5.5	7.6	0.1
24037	St. Mary's County, Maryland	59.7	56.9	2.8	6.1	8.5	3.1	18.5	4.1	0.1
24039	Somerset County, Maryland	60.3	56.7	3.7	5.5	9.4	17.5	2.2	4.9	0.1
24041	Talbot County, Maryland	67.4	60.9	6.4	8.0	7.1	4.9	2.6	10.0	0.0
24043	Washington County, Maryland	69.2	66.6	2.6	7.4	8.3	4.9	4.8	5.1	0.2
24045	Wicomico County, Maryland	67.6	64.5	3.1	6.5	8.5	9.4	2.6	5.3	0.1
24047	Worcester County, Maryland	69.4	61.6	7.8	6.7	11.1	4.3	1.9	6.5	0.2
24510	Baltimore city, Maryland	62.0	59.8	2.2	14.4	8.0	6.8	5.3	3.4	0.1
25000	**Massachusetts**	68.6	65.8	2.8	12.8	7.0	3.8	1.7	6.1	0.1
25001	Barnstable County, Massachusetts	64.8	60.4	4.5	9.5	8.8	2.8	1.9	12.0	0.1
25003	Berkshire County, Massachusetts	61.4	58.3	3.1	17.0	8.5	3.8	1.1	7.9	0.2
25005	Bristol County, Massachusetts	72.6	70.2	2.4	9.2	7.5	4.0	1.7	4.9	0.1
25007	Dukes County, Massachusetts	55.3	46.1	9.2	6.0	13.6	1.6	0.7	22.6	0.2
25009	Essex County, Massachusetts	70.7	67.4	3.3	11.0	7.2	3.1	1.6	6.1	0.2
25011	Franklin County, Massachusetts	56.4	53.9	2.4	15.8	9.4	7.3	1.4	9.5	0.2
25013	Hampden County, Massachusetts	69.5	67.6	1.9	10.0	8.6	4.3	2.2	5.2	0.1
25015	Hampshire County, Massachusetts	53.3	50.4	2.9	17.8	7.1	12.5	1.8	7.4	0.1
25017	Middlesex County, Massachusetts	68.0	64.9	3.0	14.8	6.1	2.9	1.7	6.5	0.1
25019	Nantucket County, Massachusetts	63.7	54.9	8.9	6.2	9.4	2.5	0.8	17.2	0.1

Table C. County—Labor Force, Employment, and Educational Data, 2011–2015—*Continued*

		Class of worker for civilian employed population age 16 and older								
		Private for-profit wage and salary workers				Government workers				
Fips code	State/county	Total private for-profit wage and salary workers	Employees of private companies	Self-employed in own incorporated business	Private not-for-profit wage and salary workers	Local government workers	State government workers	Federal government workers	Self-employed in own not incorporated business	Unpaid family workers
25021	Norfolk County, Massachusetts	69.1	65.8	3.3	13.4	6.3	3.4	1.8	5.8	0.1
25023	Plymouth County, Massachusetts	70.4	67.2	3.2	10.5	7.5	4.1	1.7	5.7	0.1
25025	Suffolk County, Massachusetts	67.1	65.5	1.7	17.3	6.2	3.5	1.4	4.4	0.1
25027	Worcester County, Massachusetts	71.6	69.1	2.5	9.6	7.2	4.5	1.4	5.5	0.2
26000	**Michigan**	74.1	70.7	3.4	9.6	5.4	4.2	1.5	5.0	0.2
26001	Alcona County, Michigan	68.0	64.3	3.7	9.0	9.9	3.8	1.9	7.4	0.0
26003	Alger County, Michigan	65.9	62.0	3.9	8.1	6.9	9.5	3.9	5.7	0.1
26005	Allegan County, Michigan	77.2	73.4	3.8	8.0	4.5	2.7	1.0	6.4	0.2
26007	Alpena County, Michigan	70.1	66.5	3.6	9.8	7.3	3.3	1.9	7.3	0.3
26009	Antrim County, Michigan	71.5	65.7	5.8	6.7	7.3	3.3	0.9	10.0	0.3
26011	Arenac County, Michigan	69.3	65.4	3.9	11.4	4.7	5.3	1.2	7.9	0.2
26013	Baraga County, Michigan	59.8	55.6	4.2	14.2	9.5	8.2	1.6	6.4	0.2
26015	Barry County, Michigan	74.4	71.1	3.3	9.0	4.8	3.5	1.4	6.7	0.2
26017	Bay County, Michigan	74.1	71.5	2.6	9.8	6.4	3.1	1.5	5.0	0.1
26019	Benzie County, Michigan	67.2	60.8	6.4	10.8	8.8	3.8	2.4	7.0	0.1
26021	Berrien County, Michigan	73.5	69.8	3.6	11.8	5.1	2.9	0.9	5.6	0.2
26023	Branch County, Michigan	75.5	72.5	3.0	5.6	6.4	4.2	1.5	6.5	0.3
26025	Calhoun County, Michigan	74.4	72.1	2.3	9.3	5.9	2.7	3.3	4.3	0.1
26027	Cass County, Michigan	76.8	73.1	3.8	7.7	5.8	2.5	1.1	5.9	0.1
26029	Charlevoix County, Michigan	72.0	65.7	6.2	9.3	6.5	3.1	0.8	7.8	0.5
26031	Cheboygan County, Michigan	73.2	67.9	5.3	7.6	6.7	3.8	1.5	6.8	0.4
26033	Chippewa County, Michigan	52.4	49.4	3.1	11.2	13.5	11.1	4.9	6.6	0.3
26035	Clare County, Michigan	68.6	65.4	3.2	10.1	6.3	5.1	0.7	8.7	0.5
26037	Clinton County, Michigan	65.8	61.9	3.9	9.3	7.0	10.2	1.2	6.2	0.2
26039	Crawford County, Michigan	61.1	58.8	2.3	12.1	8.4	7.8	3.1	7.1	0.5
26041	Delta County, Michigan	70.7	67.5	3.2	11.3	6.5	4.0	1.3	5.9	0.3
26043	Dickinson County, Michigan	73.8	69.1	4.7	8.4	6.2	3.5	3.9	3.9	0.3
26045	Eaton County, Michigan	66.7	64.1	2.6	10.4	6.1	10.3	1.4	4.7	0.4
26047	Emmet County, Michigan	70.1	65.3	4.8	10.8	6.4	2.8	0.7	9.0	0.3
26049	Genesee County, Michigan	75.8	72.9	2.9	7.9	6.2	3.8	1.5	4.7	0.1
26051	Gladwin County, Michigan	74.2	70.4	3.9	7.3	6.4	3.5	1.2	6.6	0.8
26053	Gogebic County, Michigan	69.3	66.8	2.5	6.7	12.7	4.8	2.0	4.3	0.2
26055	Grand Traverse County, Michigan	71.3	66.4	4.9	11.7	5.5	2.7	1.3	7.3	0.2
26057	Gratiot County, Michigan	70.2	67.6	2.5	9.0	5.4	7.4	1.0	6.9	0.1
26059	Hillsdale County, Michigan	70.6	67.5	3.2	11.0	6.1	3.6	0.9	7.6	0.2
26061	Houghton County, Michigan	61.0	58.6	2.4	12.5	7.2	12.5	1.5	5.0	0.2
26063	Huron County, Michigan	73.1	68.3	4.8	6.6	7.5	2.7	0.9	8.7	0.4
26065	Ingham County, Michigan	62.3	59.8	2.5	12.8	5.8	12.9	1.2	4.9	0.1
26067	Ionia County, Michigan	70.7	68.9	1.8	7.6	5.7	7.4	1.1	7.3	0.2
26069	Iosco County, Michigan	71.9	69.0	2.8	7.9	6.7	2.8	1.3	8.8	0.6
26071	Iron County, Michigan	66.4	59.9	6.5	8.9	10.8	3.6	2.7	7.2	0.3
26073	Isabella County, Michigan	67.8	65.5	2.3	9.1	5.5	11.3	1.7	4.3	0.3
26075	Jackson County, Michigan	73.6	70.5	3.1	9.9	5.0	4.7	1.3	5.4	0.1
26077	Kalamazoo County, Michigan	70.2	67.9	2.3	12.4	4.6	5.2	1.7	5.7	0.1
26079	Kalkaska County, Michigan	72.3	69.5	2.8	7.7	5.9	4.8	0.5	8.6	0.1
26081	Kent County, Michigan	74.5	71.3	3.1	12.8	4.1	2.6	1.0	4.9	0.1
26083	Keweenaw County, Michigan	53.3	47.4	5.9	10.5	15.4	10.1	2.0	6.7	2.0
26085	Lake County, Michigan	70.5	68.3	2.2	6.5	7.9	5.4	1.9	7.4	0.5
26087	Lapeer County, Michigan	79.5	75.4	4.2	5.5	4.9	3.1	1.1	5.7	0.2
26089	Leelanau County, Michigan	66.1	58.4	7.7	11.8	7.1	2.5	1.9	9.8	0.9
26091	Lenawee County, Michigan	71.7	68.9	2.8	10.5	5.9	4.7	1.5	5.4	0.1
26093	Livingston County, Michigan	76.2	72.1	4.1	7.6	5.1	3.8	1.5	5.6	0.2
26095	Luce County, Michigan	63.3	60.4	2.9	8.3	8.6	14.4	0.8	4.3	0.3
26097	Mackinac County, Michigan	61.5	57.9	3.6	7.4	11.5	8.2	2.3	8.9	0.2
26099	Macomb County, Michigan	79.0	75.5	3.4	7.5	4.8	2.6	2.2	3.8	0.1
26101	Manistee County, Michigan	67.0	63.4	3.6	8.3	8.9	5.2	2.1	8.0	0.5
26103	Marquette County, Michigan	68.9	65.8	3.1	11.6	5.6	7.4	1.6	4.7	0.1
26105	Mason County, Michigan	72.1	68.0	4.1	7.1	7.4	4.5	1.3	6.8	0.7
26107	Mecosta County, Michigan	70.9	68.6	2.3	8.7	6.4	6.2	1.2	6.3	0.4
26109	Menominee County, Michigan	73.1	69.0	4.0	7.6	7.8	2.6	1.5	7.1	0.3
26111	Midland County, Michigan	73.9	71.3	2.6	10.6	5.3	3.2	1.2	5.7	0.2
26113	Missaukee County, Michigan	72.1	67.9	4.3	7.7	6.2	3.3	0.5	9.6	0.5
26115	Monroe County, Michigan	77.8	75.5	2.3	8.0	5.3	2.7	1.4	4.7	0.1
26117	Montcalm County, Michigan	75.5	72.2	3.3	7.0	5.0	5.0	1.6	5.6	0.3
26119	Montmorency County, Michigan	71.7	67.7	4.0	5.6	10.0	2.7	1.1	8.7	0.2
26121	Muskegon County, Michigan	75.2	72.7	2.6	9.0	6.9	3.4	0.7	4.7	0.1
26123	Newaygo County, Michigan	71.6	68.7	2.9	10.1	6.8	3.7	0.8	6.6	0.3
26125	Oakland County, Michigan	77.2	72.1	5.1	8.9	4.9	2.6	1.3	5.0	0.2
26127	Oceana County, Michigan	71.1	66.6	4.5	7.2	7.8	3.9	1.4	8.2	0.3
26129	Ogemaw County, Michigan	73.1	68.4	4.7	6.3	5.9	4.9	1.0	8.7	0.1
26131	Ontonagon County, Michigan	56.8	55.1	1.7	10.0	14.2	6.2	3.2	9.1	0.5

Table C. County—Labor Force, Employment, and Educational Data, 2011–2015—*Continued*

		Class of worker for civilian employed population age 16 and older								
		Private for-profit wage and salary workers				Government workers				
Fips code	State/county	Total private for-profit wage and salary workers	Employees of private companies	Self-employed in own incorporated business	Private not-for-profit wage and salary workers	Local government workers	State government workers	Federal government workers	Self-employed in own not incorporated business	Unpaid family workers
26133	Osceola County, Michigan	70.6	66.9	3.7	8.8	5.3	5.2	1.1	8.5	0.4
26135	Oscoda County, Michigan	66.7	60.8	5.9	6.6	8.9	4.7	2.4	10.2	0.6
26137	Otsego County, Michigan	71.7	67.2	4.5	10.5	4.2	6.2	1.8	5.3	0.3
26139	Ottawa County, Michigan	75.1	71.8	3.3	10.7	5.0	3.2	0.9	4.9	0.1
26141	Presque Isle County, Michigan	68.6	63.9	4.7	8.3	9.1	4.3	2.4	6.9	0.5
26143	Roscommon County, Michigan	71.5	67.1	4.4	8.0	6.7	6.4	0.8	6.0	0.6
26145	Saginaw County, Michigan	74.1	71.5	2.7	10.1	5.4	4.0	1.7	4.4	0.2
26147	St. Clair County, Michigan	75.5	72.2	3.3	8.0	6.2	3.2	1.8	5.1	0.1
26149	St. Joseph County, Michigan	78.2	75.1	3.1	7.1	5.9	2.7	0.5	5.4	0.2
26151	Sanilac County, Michigan	72.8	67.6	5.2	7.0	6.1	2.9	1.3	9.2	0.8
26153	Schoolcraft County, Michigan	65.6	61.3	4.4	11.1	10.0	5.3	2.8	5.1	0.1
26155	Shiawassee County, Michigan	72.1	68.7	3.4	8.3	6.1	5.2	1.2	7.0	0.2
26157	Tuscola County, Michigan	73.0	69.5	3.5	8.1	6.0	4.8	1.2	6.6	0.2
26159	Van Buren County, Michigan	72.5	69.7	2.8	8.0	7.7	3.7	1.0	6.8	0.2
26161	Washtenaw County, Michigan	62.1	58.8	3.2	14.4	5.4	11.2	2.0	4.7	0.2
26163	Wayne County, Michigan	77.0	74.3	2.7	9.1	5.3	3.0	1.8	3.8	0.1
26165	Wexford County, Michigan	73.9	70.8	3.1	8.0	5.7	3.9	1.3	6.9	0.2
27000	**Minnesota**	71.1	67.2	3.8	11.2	6.5	4.0	1.4	5.6	0.1
27001	Aitkin County, Minnesota	64.9	59.7	5.2	10.5	8.1	4.5	2.6	9.2	0.2
27003	Anoka County, Minnesota	75.8	72.3	3.6	8.9	5.9	3.8	1.3	4.2	0.1
27005	Becker County, Minnesota	65.2	60.3	4.9	9.1	9.3	4.1	3.0	9.0	0.3
27007	Beltrami County, Minnesota	59.1	55.9	3.1	7.7	15.7	8.1	3.1	6.2	0.1
27009	Benton County, Minnesota	73.1	69.5	3.6	9.8	5.7	3.9	1.6	5.7	0.2
27011	Big Stone County, Minnesota	61.1	55.9	5.2	6.8	14.0	2.7	1.7	13.5	0.2
27013	Blue Earth County, Minnesota	70.5	67.5	3.0	10.5	5.5	7.0	1.2	5.1	0.1
27015	Brown County, Minnesota	70.0	65.8	4.2	11.1	7.6	1.6	0.7	8.8	0.2
27017	Carlton County, Minnesota	61.7	59.4	2.3	11.1	10.6	7.5	2.3	6.4	0.3
27019	Carver County, Minnesota	77.2	71.4	5.8	7.5	6.5	2.0	1.1	5.5	0.2
27021	Cass County, Minnesota	62.8	56.4	6.4	8.6	11.1	4.3	2.5	10.4	0.3
27023	Chippewa County, Minnesota	68.4	64.9	3.6	8.0	11.4	2.3	1.1	8.5	0.3
27025	Chisago County, Minnesota	71.1	66.3	4.8	10.3	6.9	5.0	1.5	5.2	0.2
27027	Clay County, Minnesota	66.2	62.4	3.8	14.4	6.9	5.2	1.5	5.7	0.1
27029	Clearwater County, Minnesota	61.0	58.1	2.9	9.3	12.1	5.3	2.8	9.2	0.4
27031	Cook County, Minnesota	51.1	46.2	4.9	10.8	18.1	3.6	4.7	11.0	0.6
27033	Cottonwood County, Minnesota	61.6	59.0	2.6	13.5	9.0	2.7	1.6	11.3	0.3
27035	Crow Wing County, Minnesota	72.6	67.9	4.7	8.5	6.1	4.3	1.0	7.4	0.2
27037	Dakota County, Minnesota	74.2	70.9	3.3	9.6	5.9	3.7	2.3	4.2	0.1
27039	Dodge County, Minnesota	64.3	60.7	3.6	19.5	6.8	2.2	1.0	6.0	0.1
27041	Douglas County, Minnesota	71.1	65.3	5.8	7.9	9.1	3.4	0.6	7.7	0.2
27043	Faribault County, Minnesota	65.1	60.8	4.3	9.5	9.0	2.5	1.1	12.6	0.3
27045	Fillmore County, Minnesota	60.7	56.6	4.1	16.5	6.8	3.3	1.5	10.6	0.5
27047	Freeborn County, Minnesota	70.6	67.6	3.0	12.4	6.7	1.9	1.0	7.4	0.1
27049	Goodhue County, Minnesota	70.0	66.2	3.8	11.2	6.2	3.5	1.0	8.0	0.2
27051	Grant County, Minnesota	61.4	56.7	4.7	10.0	9.0	4.1	1.3	13.9	0.4
27053	Hennepin County, Minnesota	73.8	69.7	4.1	11.2	5.3	3.7	1.1	4.8	0.1
27055	Houston County, Minnesota	67.9	64.7	3.3	12.3	5.3	3.2	1.1	9.9	0.2
27057	Hubbard County, Minnesota	63.3	58.6	4.7	9.6	10.3	5.4	1.6	9.6	0.2
27059	Isanti County, Minnesota	71.4	66.2	5.2	11.8	6.5	4.1	0.7	5.4	0.1
27061	Itasca County, Minnesota	65.8	61.8	4.0	11.7	9.4	4.5	1.7	6.3	0.5
27063	Jackson County, Minnesota	63.7	60.7	3.0	7.6	9.6	2.3	0.9	15.3	0.5
27065	Kanabec County, Minnesota	68.4	65.4	2.9	10.2	8.8	3.7	1.1	7.8	0.1
27067	Kandiyohi County, Minnesota	69.8	66.0	3.8	8.3	8.2	5.1	1.0	7.1	0.5
27069	Kittson County, Minnesota	63.8	57.5	6.3	5.4	9.4	5.4	4.2	11.6	0.2
27071	Koochiching County, Minnesota	72.4	68.0	4.4	7.0	7.0	3.7	3.1	6.7	0.1
27073	Lac qui Parle County, Minnesota	58.5	54.4	4.1	11.9	8.9	1.6	2.3	16.5	0.3
27075	Lake County, Minnesota	64.1	61.2	3.0	10.7	8.8	7.0	1.5	7.8	0.1
27077	Lake of the Woods County, Minnesota	72.3	65.0	7.3	6.0	4.6	3.4	0.8	12.9	0.0
27079	Le Sueur County, Minnesota	71.7	67.8	3.9	7.4	8.8	4.1	1.1	6.8	0.2
27081	Lincoln County, Minnesota	61.2	57.1	4.1	11.5	7.2	3.2	1.2	15.3	0.4
27083	Lyon County, Minnesota	71.2	67.9	3.3	7.8	6.7	4.4	1.1	8.7	0.1
27085	McLeod County, Minnesota	75.6	72.5	3.1	9.9	5.6	2.1	0.8	5.9	0.1
27087	Mahnomen County, Minnesota	51.3	48.0	3.3	7.9	20.7	2.7	8.9	8.2	0.2
27089	Marshall County, Minnesota	68.5	63.9	4.6	8.4	7.0	3.8	2.1	10.0	0.3
27091	Martin County, Minnesota	68.3	64.2	4.1	11.5	6.7	1.7	0.9	10.5	0.3
27093	Meeker County, Minnesota	72.5	68.2	4.3	8.1	8.5	2.2	0.7	7.3	0.7
27095	Mille Lacs County, Minnesota	67.7	64.3	3.4	10.4	10.4	3.3	1.4	6.6	0.1
27097	Morrison County, Minnesota	66.7	62.1	4.6	11.0	6.3	3.3	2.5	9.7	0.6
27099	Mower County, Minnesota	68.7	65.1	3.6	14.7	7.2	2.1	0.9	6.3	0.1
27101	Murray County, Minnesota	59.6	54.6	5.0	11.2	10.5	2.9	1.7	13.6	0.4
27103	Nicollet County, Minnesota	66.9	62.9	4.1	11.4	6.6	7.7	1.1	6.0	0.2
27105	Nobles County, Minnesota	73.9	69.3	4.6	7.4	6.4	2.1	1.0	8.9	0.3
27107	Norman County, Minnesota	58.2	54.9	3.3	11.0	11.6	2.6	1.7	14.5	0.4
27109	Olmsted County, Minnesota	57.7	55.3	2.4	28.5	5.7	2.3	1.1	4.6	0.1
27111	Otter Tail County, Minnesota	65.4	60.9	4.5	12.1	7.6	4.3	1.1	9.2	0.3

Table C. County—Labor Force, Employment, and Educational Data, 2011–2015—*Continued*

| | | Class of worker for civilian employed population age 16 and older | | | | | | | | |
| | | Private for-profit wage and salary workers | | | | Government workers | | | | |
Fips code	State/county	Total private for-profit wage and salary workers	Employees of private companies	Self-employed in own incorporated business	Private not-for-profit wage and salary workers	Local government workers	State government workers	Federal government workers	Self-employed in own not incorporated business	Unpaid family workers
27113	Pennington County, Minnesota	74.4	70.8	3.5	8.5	4.6	3.2	1.5	7.6	0.2
27115	Pine County, Minnesota	66.6	63.2	3.4	8.9	6.8	6.6	3.4	7.3	0.3
27117	Pipestone County, Minnesota	67.0	60.8	6.2	10.4	6.8	2.3	1.5	12.0	0.2
27119	Polk County, Minnesota	61.9	57.8	4.0	13.6	8.3	6.6	1.6	7.8	0.2
27121	Pope County, Minnesota	67.1	61.5	5.6	10.6	7.7	3.8	1.7	8.5	0.5
27123	Ramsey County, Minnesota	67.7	64.8	2.9	14.1	6.2	5.9	1.6	4.4	0.1
27125	Red Lake County, Minnesota	68.9	65.3	3.6	8.3	8.0	3.4	2.1	9.0	0.3
27127	Redwood County, Minnesota	68.4	63.5	4.9	8.7	7.7	1.8	0.8	12.3	0.3
27129	Renville County, Minnesota	70.1	65.1	5.1	7.7	7.9	2.8	1.3	10.1	0.1
27131	Rice County, Minnesota	71.4	68.5	2.8	11.0	6.4	3.2	1.2	6.5	0.3
27133	Rock County, Minnesota	65.8	61.8	4.0	11.1	7.1	3.6	0.6	11.5	0.3
27135	Roseau County, Minnesota	76.1	72.0	4.1	6.7	6.3	2.3	1.9	6.5	0.2
27137	St. Louis County, Minnesota	67.5	64.4	3.1	13.0	8.0	5.0	1.7	4.7	0.1
27139	Scott County, Minnesota	79.6	74.9	4.7	7.0	5.5	2.6	1.2	4.1	0.1
27141	Sherburne County, Minnesota	75.7	70.9	4.8	8.2	7.4	2.6	1.1	4.7	0.2
27143	Sibley County, Minnesota	70.1	65.8	4.3	7.8	7.8	2.7	1.0	10.3	0.4
27145	Stearns County, Minnesota	69.8	66.0	3.8	13.4	4.9	4.2	1.9	5.6	0.2
27147	Steele County, Minnesota	76.0	73.3	2.8	7.9	6.2	3.3	0.8	5.7	0.1
27149	Stevens County, Minnesota	61.6	56.2	5.4	10.8	7.7	10.8	1.5	7.3	0.3
27151	Swift County, Minnesota	64.9	60.5	4.5	7.6	10.2	3.2	1.4	12.4	0.3
27153	Todd County, Minnesota	66.8	62.3	4.5	9.3	7.7	3.2	1.2	11.1	0.8
27155	Traverse County, Minnesota	54.8	48.9	6.0	11.5	10.4	3.6	1.5	18.0	0.2
27157	Wabasha County, Minnesota	63.9	59.6	4.3	15.6	5.6	2.6	1.2	10.9	0.2
27159	Wadena County, Minnesota	70.1	64.1	6.0	8.7	7.6	3.5	1.4	8.6	0.1
27161	Waseca County, Minnesota	70.0	65.4	4.6	9.4	6.6	3.5	1.8	8.4	0.2
27163	Washington County, Minnesota	72.1	67.8	4.3	10.3	6.9	4.6	1.7	4.3	0.1
27165	Watonwan County, Minnesota	68.7	65.0	3.7	11.0	7.8	2.7	0.7	8.5	0.7
27167	Wilkin County, Minnesota	63.3	58.7	4.6	8.4	7.1	6.9	1.9	11.7	0.8
27169	Winona County, Minnesota	69.1	66.1	2.9	13.2	4.9	5.6	0.9	6.0	0.3
27171	Wright County, Minnesota	76.4	71.8	4.6	7.3	6.7	2.5	1.0	5.9	0.1
27173	Yellow Medicine County, Minnesota	64.5	59.6	4.9	9.2	8.5	1.9	1.0	14.6	0.3
28000	**Mississippi**	70.1	67.0	3.2	5.7	6.3	9.0	3.2	5.5	0.1
28001	Adams County, Mississippi	71.9	66.4	5.5	4.7	7.5	7.2	2.1	6.4	0.2
28003	Alcorn County, Mississippi	72.3	68.0	4.3	6.1	6.9	6.9	0.9	6.8	0.2
28005	Amite County, Mississippi	67.2	65.2	2.0	6.3	4.9	8.8	2.1	9.5	1.2
28007	Attala County, Mississippi	67.7	65.5	2.2	5.7	7.7	10.7	2.1	5.8	0.3
28009	Benton County, Mississippi	79.0	73.6	5.4	5.0	5.0	4.4	1.2	5.3	0.0
28011	Bolivar County, Mississippi	61.9	57.2	4.6	3.3	8.1	18.4	2.1	6.1	0.2
28013	Calhoun County, Mississippi	75.8	73.6	2.3	2.5	3.2	7.6	1.5	9.1	0.2
28015	Carroll County, Mississippi	62.6	56.4	6.1	8.8	9.9	8.4	1.9	7.7	0.8
28017	Chickasaw County, Mississippi	76.4	72.1	4.3	3.0	6.5	6.8	1.1	6.2	0.0
28019	Choctaw County, Mississippi	66.7	62.0	4.6	4.2	9.5	10.7	1.0	7.3	0.5
28021	Claiborne County, Mississippi	63.3	62.9	0.4	2.5	6.6	20.0	2.3	5.2	0.0
28023	Clarke County, Mississippi	68.7	66.9	1.8	4.3	6.6	12.8	0.9	6.7	0.0
28025	Clay County, Mississippi	71.3	68.4	2.9	7.2	4.9	7.4	2.4	6.8	0.0
28027	Coahoma County, Mississippi	65.7	62.7	3.1	4.2	6.4	13.4	3.7	6.3	0.2
28029	Copiah County, Mississippi	76.1	72.8	3.3	3.6	4.1	9.1	1.9	5.2	0.0
28031	Covington County, Mississippi	73.9	71.9	2.0	4.5	6.8	6.8	2.1	5.9	0.1
28033	DeSoto County, Mississippi	76.1	73.7	2.5	6.2	6.6	3.3	2.7	5.0	0.0
28035	Forrest County, Mississippi	70.9	68.2	2.7	7.0	6.5	9.7	2.1	3.8	0.0
28037	Franklin County, Mississippi	66.9	64.3	2.5	3.7	6.4	13.1	2.7	7.2	0.0
28039	George County, Mississippi	75.0	72.7	2.3	6.7	7.0	3.6	2.1	5.3	0.2
28041	Greene County, Mississippi	66.6	64.9	1.7	2.2	13.7	12.1	2.0	3.4	0.0
28043	Grenada County, Mississippi	79.0	75.9	3.1	3.1	5.6	5.8	1.2	5.1	0.1
28045	Hancock County, Mississippi	71.4	69.4	2.0	5.3	5.5	4.3	4.2	8.8	0.4
28047	Harrison County, Mississippi	69.1	66.7	2.4	5.8	6.8	4.0	8.4	5.8	0.1
28049	Hinds County, Mississippi	63.5	60.5	3.0	7.4	6.3	13.4	3.5	5.8	0.1
28051	Holmes County, Mississippi	64.9	63.7	1.2	7.8	10.9	10.5	2.4	3.5	0.0
28053	Humphreys County, Mississippi	67.1	63.8	3.3	7.2	9.9	8.2	0.7	6.6	0.2
28055	Issaquena County, Mississippi	73.8	67.9	5.9	3.9	11.5	1.3	2.6	6.9	0.0
28057	Itawamba County, Mississippi	72.5	70.3	2.2	5.4	4.4	9.7	1.9	5.8	0.2
28059	Jackson County, Mississippi	72.6	69.9	2.7	5.4	8.0	4.5	4.3	5.2	0.1
28061	Jasper County, Mississippi	73.2	71.3	2.0	6.8	8.2	7.5	1.6	2.5	0.0
28063	Jefferson County, Mississippi	62.4	61.8	0.5	2.4	12.3	20.3	2.3	0.4	0.0
28065	Jefferson Davis County, Mississippi	75.7	75.0	0.7	7.2	5.4	6.2	3.2	2.3	0.0
28067	Jones County, Mississippi	69.9	66.9	3.0	6.0	7.2	10.3	1.1	5.4	0.1
28069	Kemper County, Mississippi	64.9	63.4	1.5	9.5	7.9	7.9	3.1	6.7	0.0
28071	Lafayette County, Mississippi	60.8	57.4	3.4	6.3	7.3	17.8	2.3	5.4	0.0
28073	Lamar County, Mississippi	70.0	65.4	4.6	5.4	7.1	9.8	2.1	5.6	0.1
28075	Lauderdale County, Mississippi	71.1	68.2	2.8	8.5	4.2	8.3	4.0	3.7	0.2
28077	Lawrence County, Mississippi	72.4	68.4	3.9	7.5	5.2	7.0	2.1	5.4	0.4
28079	Leake County, Mississippi	71.4	69.1	2.3	3.1	5.7	9.0	4.6	6.2	0.0
28081	Lee County, Mississippi	75.0	72.0	3.0	8.2	4.8	5.9	1.6	4.4	0.1
28083	Leflore County, Mississippi	65.3	63.6	1.7	6.8	11.7	9.1	1.1	6.0	0.1

Table C. County—Labor Force, Employment, and Educational Data, 2011–2015—*Continued*

| | | Class of worker for civilian employed population age 16 and older | | | | | | | | |
| | | Private for-profit wage and salary workers | | | | Government workers | | | | |
Fips code	State/county	Total private for-profit wage and salary workers	Employees of private companies	Self-employed in own incorporated business	Private not-for-profit wage and salary workers	Local government workers	State government workers	Federal government workers	Self-employed in own not incorporated business	Unpaid family workers
28085	Lincoln County, Mississippi	75.1	71.6	3.5	4.7	3.0	8.7	1.5	6.9	0.0
28087	Lowndes County, Mississippi	67.7	64.6	3.1	7.1	5.3	8.4	5.9	5.5	0.1
28089	Madison County, Mississippi	68.4	62.6	5.8	6.4	5.2	10.3	3.6	6.0	0.1
28091	Marion County, Mississippi	72.6	66.9	5.7	4.2	6.6	7.3	2.0	6.6	0.7
28093	Marshall County, Mississippi	75.5	71.3	4.2	4.3	5.5	4.2	2.8	7.6	0.1
28095	Monroe County, Mississippi	74.5	72.2	2.3	5.6	6.7	6.1	2.1	4.7	0.4
28097	Montgomery County, Mississippi	66.3	63.1	3.3	4.4	12.8	9.7	2.0	4.8	0.0
28099	Neshoba County, Mississippi	68.5	66.8	1.6	3.1	6.6	8.0	8.4	5.0	0.5
28101	Newton County, Mississippi	65.6	63.8	1.9	2.7	6.0	15.6	4.3	5.9	0.0
28103	Noxubee County, Mississippi	67.4	61.7	5.7	5.4	6.7	7.5	1.9	10.0	1.0
28105	Oktibbeha County, Mississippi	53.1	50.7	2.3	7.4	4.3	30.2	1.7	2.9	0.5
28107	Panola County, Mississippi	75.0	71.1	3.9	5.1	5.2	8.6	2.5	3.6	0.0
28109	Pearl River County, Mississippi	70.8	68.0	2.8	5.3	7.9	4.8	4.8	6.3	0.1
28111	Perry County, Mississippi	69.9	68.8	1.1	3.3	6.8	11.0	2.8	5.8	0.3
28113	Pike County, Mississippi	74.7	69.3	5.4	4.9	5.3	8.2	1.0	5.6	0.2
28115	Pontotoc County, Mississippi	78.5	75.9	2.6	4.5	3.5	6.9	1.4	5.3	0.1
28117	Prentiss County, Mississippi	73.1	68.6	4.5	3.6	4.7	10.3	0.3	8.0	0.0
28119	Quitman County, Mississippi	62.6	58.0	4.6	5.5	5.6	16.9	1.9	7.5	0.0
28121	Rankin County, Mississippi	70.7	66.0	4.7	5.8	4.3	12.3	2.7	4.1	0.1
28123	Scott County, Mississippi	74.9	72.4	2.5	2.6	5.7	7.4	3.0	6.3	0.1
28125	Sharkey County, Mississippi	68.1	64.2	3.9	3.6	11.9	9.3	2.3	4.7	0.1
28127	Simpson County, Mississippi	73.1	70.8	2.3	6.1	4.8	7.8	2.0	6.1	0.1
28129	Smith County, Mississippi	70.5	67.3	3.2	4.9	6.3	7.7	1.2	8.5	0.8
28131	Stone County, Mississippi	68.2	64.7	3.4	4.4	8.0	11.8	1.4	6.2	0.0
28133	Sunflower County, Mississippi	66.4	63.8	2.6	4.5	9.8	12.0	1.8	5.0	0.5
28135	Tallahatchie County, Mississippi	62.5	59.8	2.7	6.0	9.2	11.4	3.1	7.5	0.3
28137	Tate County, Mississippi	76.1	73.7	2.3	3.8	6.3	7.9	1.6	4.2	0.1
28139	Tippah County, Mississippi	76.3	73.5	2.8	3.3	4.4	8.7	0.9	6.4	0.0
28141	Tishomingo County, Mississippi	74.7	71.6	3.1	5.9	3.8	7.6	1.6	6.2	0.1
28143	Tunica County, Mississippi	77.0	73.6	3.3	5.7	7.3	7.6	0.6	1.7	0.1
28145	Union County, Mississippi	77.9	74.8	3.1	4.8	3.7	7.1	0.8	5.6	0.1
28147	Walthall County, Mississippi	68.9	61.8	7.1	3.4	7.8	9.9	2.4	6.3	1.2
28149	Warren County, Mississippi	67.3	63.9	3.5	4.5	5.8	8.6	9.9	3.7	0.2
28151	Washington County, Mississippi	65.8	61.8	4.0	4.7	8.7	11.5	3.9	5.2	0.1
28153	Wayne County, Mississippi	74.3	70.4	3.9	3.8	6.8	6.2	1.3	7.3	0.2
28155	Webster County, Mississippi	63.9	59.0	4.9	5.1	6.9	16.8	1.1	6.0	0.1
28157	Wilkinson County, Mississippi	58.1	56.0	2.1	6.1	8.6	19.4	5.1	2.7	0.0
28159	Winston County, Mississippi	68.9	65.8	3.1	4.7	6.3	11.2	2.6	6.0	0.4
28161	Yalobusha County, Mississippi	70.9	69.0	1.8	3.9	6.0	12.1	3.3	3.8	0.0
28163	Yazoo County, Mississippi	65.2	63.6	1.6	5.2	7.3	8.5	5.2	8.1	0.3
29000	**Missouri**	70.9	67.9	3.0	10.4	5.8	4.6	2.3	5.7	0.2
29001	Adair County, Missouri	63.3	60.5	2.8	8.4	5.9	14.9	1.5	5.9	0.0
29003	Andrew County, Missouri	66.3	62.1	4.3	11.1	5.4	7.8	·3.1	6.1	0.0
29005	Atchison County, Missouri	61.5	57.3	4.2	10.7	9.9	6.4	1.7	9.6	0.2
29007	Audrain County, Missouri	68.6	66.9	1.7	6.6	7.0	8.4	1.7	7.5	0.2
29009	Barry County, Missouri	70.6	67.4	3.2	7.5	6.2	4.7	0.7	10.2	0.0
29011	Barton County, Missouri	67.5	62.7	4.7	7.4	5.7	6.0	1.2	11.1	1.1
29013	Bates County, Missouri	64.7	62.3	2.4	7.5	9.3	4.2	2.0	12.0	0.3
29015	Benton County, Missouri	65.0	61.3	3.6	9.0	9.0	3.8	2.1	10.6	0.4
29017	Bollinger County, Missouri	71.2	67.6	3.6	8.2	4.7	4.9	0.9	10.0	0.1
29019	Boone County, Missouri	61.2	58.4	2.9	10.2	5.9	15.7	2.4	4.4	0.1
29021	Buchanan County, Missouri	74.2	72.3	1.9	9.9	5.1	5.2	1.1	4.3	0.1
29023	Butler County, Missouri	68.0	65.0	3.0	9.0	5.1	7.0	3.6	7.2	0.1
29025	Caldwell County, Missouri	64.0	61.3	2.6	6.8	9.6	8.2	1.2	9.7	0.5
29027	Callaway County, Missouri	64.1	62.4	1.7	6.7	7.0	15.3	1.7	4.6	0.6
29029	Camden County, Missouri	67.4	61.8	5.6	10.2	7.2	3.9	2.1	9.1	0.2
29031	Cape Girardeau County, Missouri	69.1	66.2	3.0	12.1	4.9	7.8	1.2	4.7	0.2
29033	Carroll County, Missouri	62.1	58.9	3.3	7.7	8.3	6.8	0.9	13.3	0.8
29035	Carter County, Missouri	68.9	62.1	6.8	6.5	7.3	6.0	0.7	10.5	0.0
29037	Cass County, Missouri	74.1	71.2	3.0	8.0	6.3	2.3	3.5	5.7	0.2
29039	Cedar County, Missouri	66.2	62.8	3.4	7.3	8.2	5.7	2.3	9.6	0.7
29041	Chariton County, Missouri	63.7	61.5	2.1	8.6	7.6	4.7	2.3	13.0	0.2
29043	Christian County, Missouri	69.7	66.0	3.7	11.6	6.6	3.5	2.1	6.3	0.1
29045	Clark County, Missouri	69.6	66.8	2.8	4.3	10.3	4.5	0.9	9.9	0.4
29047	Clay County, Missouri	74.6	72.0	2.6	8.6	6.4	2.9	3.0	4.4	0.1
29049	Clinton County, Missouri	71.7	67.9	3.8	7.5	8.0	4.6	2.7	4.9	0.6
29051	Cole County, Missouri	57.8	55.7	2.1	9.8	5.8	20.1	2.0	4.2	0.4
29053	Cooper County, Missouri	69.9	67.3	2.6	6.7	5.2	8.0	2.6	7.6	0.0
29055	Crawford County, Missouri	72.1	70.5	1.6	7.5	7.6	3.9	0.4	8.4	0.2
29057	Dade County, Missouri	61.2	58.1	3.1	9.6	8.0	4.8	1.5	13.8	1.1
29059	Dallas County, Missouri	71.3	66.7	4.6	6.4	3.0	6.9	1.0	10.8	0.5
29061	Daviess County, Missouri	58.2	53.6	4.6	6.6	10.1	7.2	2.3	15.4	0.3
29063	DeKalb County, Missouri	66.0	64.2	1.8	10.0	5.3	8.3	1.2	9.0	0.1
29065	Dent County, Missouri	64.3	62.1	2.2	10.9	5.3	7.6	1.6	10.0	0.2

Table C. County—Labor Force, Employment, and Educational Data, 2011–2015—*Continued*

		Class of worker for civilian employed population age 16 and older								
		Private for-profit wage and salary workers				Government workers				
Fips code	State/county	Total private for-profit wage and salary workers	Employees of private companies	Self-employed in own incorporated business	Private not-for-profit wage and salary workers	Local government workers	State government workers	Federal government workers	Self-employed in own not incorporated business	Unpaid family workers
29067	Douglas County, Missouri	74.1	71.2	3.0	6.0	4.0	6.4	1.3	7.8	0.3
29069	Dunklin County, Missouri	70.7	69.1	1.6	5.8	8.2	7.5	1.0	6.6	0.2
29071	Franklin County, Missouri	76.6	73.4	3.2	8.1	5.2	2.9	0.8	6.1	0.2
29073	Gasconade County, Missouri	71.4	68.4	3.0	7.3	5.7	3.8	1.3	10.2	0.4
29075	Gentry County, Missouri	60.2	56.7	3.4	12.5	9.2	5.9	1.3	10.2	0.7
29077	Greene County, Missouri	69.6	66.0	3.6	13.4	5.8	4.8	1.6	4.7	0.1
29079	Grundy County, Missouri	64.2	59.7	4.4	10.6	9.8	5.7	1.0	8.2	0.6
29081	Harrison County, Missouri	63.1	59.3	3.8	8.4	8.9	5.2	2.2	11.5	0.6
29083	Henry County, Missouri	69.0	66.7	2.4	8.6	6.0	4.0	3.0	8.9	0.4
29085	Hickory County, Missouri	62.5	59.5	2.9	9.9	9.8	5.5	2.0	10.4	0.0
29087	Holt County, Missouri	65.9	59.8	6.0	6.9	7.3	4.0	2.9	12.5	0.5
29089	Howard County, Missouri	61.9	59.4	2.5	8.3	8.5	9.0	2.7	9.4	0.2
29091	Howell County, Missouri	64.5	61.3	3.3	11.6	6.2	6.2	1.3	9.9	0.3
29093	Iron County, Missouri	69.9	67.3	2.7	5.3	6.3	11.5	1.3	5.5	0.1
29095	Jackson County, Missouri	71.3	68.5	2.7	11.4	5.8	3.1	3.4	4.9	0.1
29097	Jasper County, Missouri	71.9	69.6	2.3	10.0	5.7	4.6	0.9	6.8	0.2
29099	Jefferson County, Missouri	76.0	73.1	2.9	8.6	5.5	2.9	1.8	5.0	0.2
29101	Johnson County, Missouri	63.3	61.6	1.8	7.2	5.7	7.5	9.7	6.2	0.3
29103	Knox County, Missouri	62.1	61.0	1.1	7.5	5.6	3.4	2.9	17.7	0.8
29105	Laclede County, Missouri	69.9	67.3	2.6	8.6	6.5	3.8	2.5	8.5	0.2
29107	Lafayette County, Missouri	65.7	62.9	2.8	11.3	6.1	6.6	3.0	7.1	0.2
29109	Lawrence County, Missouri	68.2	66.0	2.1	9.7	5.0	5.6	1.7	9.4	0.4
29111	Lewis County, Missouri	66.7	64.0	2.6	12.5	6.5	3.3	2.3	8.4	0.3
29113	Lincoln County, Missouri	81.2	77.3	3.8	5.0	5.1	2.1	1.5	5.1	0.1
29115	Linn County, Missouri	69.4	66.8	2.5	8.5	7.3	5.1	1.2	7.9	0.6
29117	Livingston County, Missouri	62.7	59.9	2.7	10.0	6.7	8.9	1.6	9.7	0.5
29119	McDonald County, Missouri	77.1	74.8	2.3	5.8	4.7	3.9	1.6	6.6	0.2
29121	Macon County, Missouri	63.6	61.0	2.5	8.0	7.5	9.7	1.4	9.6	0.3
29123	Madison County, Missouri	66.8	64.2	2.6	9.5	8.3	7.2	3.9	4.0	0.2
29125	Maries County, Missouri	67.3	64.2	3.2	10.5	4.4	8.8	2.1	6.8	0.0
29127	Marion County, Missouri	69.1	67.2	1.9	11.8	6.0	4.0	1.3	7.7	0.1
29129	Mercer County, Missouri	63.5	59.6	3.9	3.1	6.9	8.1	3.4	14.5	0.5
29131	Miller County, Missouri	66.0	62.7	3.3	7.8	4.7	9.9	1.3	9.6	0.7
29133	Mississippi County, Missouri	65.7	63.3	2.3	7.3	7.8	7.1	2.8	9.0	0.3
29135	Moniteau County, Missouri	62.2	60.2	2.0	6.6	7.4	14.5	1.6	7.6	0.1
29137	Monroe County, Missouri	70.6	68.8	1.8	6.7	6.9	6.1	1.7	7.6	0.2
29139	Montgomery County, Missouri	68.8	66.0	2.8	6.9	8.3	4.3	1.3	10.1	0.4
29141	Morgan County, Missouri	65.5	61.9	3.6	8.9	6.7	6.0	0.6	11.9	0.4
29143	New Madrid County, Missouri	72.2	70.9	1.3	7.0	7.9	5.2	1.0	6.5	0.0
29145	Newton County, Missouri	72.4	69.7	2.7	9.9	4.7	4.2	1.9	6.7	0.3
29147	Nodaway County, Missouri	65.2	62.9	2.4	9.3	5.4	9.9	1.0	8.7	0.3
29149	Oregon County, Missouri	65.5	63.0	2.5	5.9	9.4	6.5	0.9	11.6	0.2
29151	Osage County, Missouri	64.2	61.6	2.7	6.8	5.0	14.2	2.4	5.8	1.6
29153	Ozark County, Missouri	68.0	62.6	5.4	9.1	6.1	6.7	1.0	9.1	0.0
29155	Pemiscot County, Missouri	72.3	70.9	1.3	7.8	7.7	6.6	0.6	4.9	0.1
29157	Perry County, Missouri	74.4	71.0	3.5	9.5	4.4	4.1	0.8	6.7	0.1
29159	Pettis County, Missouri	73.9	71.5	2.4	8.3	5.6	3.2	2.0	6.9	0.2
29161	Phelps County, Missouri	61.4	59.0	2.4	13.1	6.6	10.6	3.3	4.8	0.0
29163	Pike County, Missouri	71.1	68.9	2.3	6.9	7.4	6.0	0.9	7.2	0.4
29165	Platte County, Missouri	73.3	69.5	3.7	8.9	6.5	2.8	3.7	4.6	0.1
29167	Polk County, Missouri	58.7	54.8	3.9	17.0	7.6	3.9	0.9	11.1	0.9
29169	Pulaski County, Missouri	52.2	50.6	1.6	5.4	7.0	4.1	26.0	4.7	0.6
29171	Putnam County, Missouri	58.0	55.4	2.6	9.0	10.0	4.3	0.5	17.7	0.6
29173	Ralls County, Missouri	69.8	65.5	4.3	9.6	6.7	5.6	1.1	6.9	0.2
29175	Randolph County, Missouri	72.2	70.6	1.6	7.3	6.8	5.4	1.8	6.3	0.1
29177	Ray County, Missouri	71.9	69.7	2.2	9.2	8.2	2.7	2.0	5.6	0.3
29179	Reynolds County, Missouri	68.2	64.9	3.4	5.2	6.5	11.9	1.7	6.6	0.0
29181	Ripley County, Missouri	66.4	65.5	1.0	6.4	9.2	6.0	2.9	9.1	0.0
29183	St. Charles County, Missouri	77.9	74.9	3.0	9.2	5.3	2.0	1.4	4.1	0.1
29185	St. Clair County, Missouri	63.0	58.4	4.6	10.6	7.8	5.7	2.8	9.1	1.1
29186	Ste. Genevieve County, Missouri	77.2	73.5	3.7	6.6	5.6	3.8	1.1	5.2	0.4
29187	St. Francois County, Missouri	71.4	68.3	3.1	5.9	5.4	13.0	0.5	3.8	0.1
29189	St. Louis County, Missouri	73.3	69.7	3.6	12.8	4.8	2.1	2.2	4.7	0.2
29195	Saline County, Missouri	62.4	60.5	1.9	10.9	8.2	8.5	1.8	8.2	0.1
29197	Schuyler County, Missouri	62.2	60.4	1.8	5.9	11.2	5.7	0.8	13.6	0.5
29199	Scotland County, Missouri	61.4	55.1	6.3	8.3	7.5	4.7	0.9	16.5	0.7
29201	Scott County, Missouri	73.7	72.1	1.6	7.4	5.0	5.6	1.4	6.7	0.2
29203	Shannon County, Missouri	61.4	58.3	3.1	6.9	6.2	11.0	1.9	12.0	0.6
29205	Shelby County, Missouri	64.1	60.6	3.5	10.4	7.7	3.4	2.4	11.8	0.3
29207	Stoddard County, Missouri	70.6	68.1	2.5	6.7	5.6	7.0	1.3	8.8	0.0
29209	Stone County, Missouri	69.9	64.8	5.1	9.1	5.7	2.2	1.3	11.4	0.3
29211	Sullivan County, Missouri	70.0	68.9	1.1	6.2	7.2	3.1	1.9	11.0	0.7
29213	Taney County, Missouri	73.3	69.4	4.0	9.5	5.4	2.1	1.0	8.8	0.1
29215	Texas County, Missouri	60.3	55.9	4.4	10.4	5.7	10.9	4.3	7.9	0.3
29217	Vernon County, Missouri	66.8	64.3	2.6	10.2	5.9	7.0	0.9	8.4	0.7

Table C. County—Labor Force, Employment, and Educational Data, 2011–2015—*Continued*

| | | Class of worker for civilian employed population age 16 and older | | | | | | | | |
| | | Private for-profit wage and salary workers | | | | Government workers | | | | |
Fips code	State/county	Total private for-profit wage and salary workers	Employees of private companies	Self-employed in own incorporated business	Private not-for-profit wage and salary workers	Local government workers	State government workers	Federal government workers	Self-employed in own not incorporated business	Unpaid family workers
29219	Warren County, Missouri	76.8	74.3	2.5	8.3	5.8	2.6	0.7	5.5	0.3
29221	Washington County, Missouri	71.2	69.4	1.7	7.0	5.1	9.4	0.9	6.4	0.0
29223	Wayne County, Missouri	69.0	66.5	2.5	4.2	6.0	6.8	3.3	10.7	0.0
29225	Webster County, Missouri	68.8	64.7	4.0	10.8	6.2	4.0	1.7	8.4	0.1
29227	Worth County, Missouri	57.1	51.9	5.2	7.4	5.4	8.3	1.5	19.8	0.3
29229	Wright County, Missouri	58.9	56.1	2.9	14.0	4.6	8.9	0.8	12.2	0.6
29510	St. Louis city, Missouri	68.5	66.1	2.4	15.2	7.0	2.8	2.5	3.9	0.1
30000	**Montana**	62.8	57.0	5.8	9.4	7.3	6.7	4.1	9.2	0.5
30001	Beaverhead County, Montana	59.3	49.0	10.4	7.5	5.9	11.4	3.6	11.7	0.5
30003	Big Horn County, Montana	37.1	33.1	4.0	10.6	7.5	7.3	28.3	8.7	0.5
30005	Blaine County, Montana	39.9	35.1	4.8	5.7	22.2	4.5	11.3	10.2	6.0
30007	Broadwater County, Montana	58.3	48.6	9.7	7.0	5.2	10.5	5.7	12.7	0.6
30009	Carbon County, Montana	63.9	57.9	6.0	9.7	8.2	2.5	2.1	12.9	0.8
30011	Carter County, Montana	42.2	27.1	15.2	7.8	10.4	1.2	4.5	30.9	3.1
30013	Cascade County, Montana	64.7	60.9	3.8	10.7	7.2	3.8	5.5	7.7	0.3
30015	Chouteau County, Montana	52.3	40.0	12.4	6.9	19.9	2.2	2.4	15.1	1.2
30017	Custer County, Montana	63.1	57.6	5.5	9.3	6.3	7.1	3.9	10.1	0.2
30019	Daniels County, Montana	55.1	48.0	7.1	1.9	12.9	2.8	5.0	22.3	0.0
30021	Dawson County, Montana	65.5	57.6	7.9	8.4	7.7	6.2	1.3	10.5	0.5
30023	Deer Lodge County, Montana	44.7	41.8	2.9	8.3	7.5	22.4	9.4	7.7	0.1
30025	Fallon County, Montana	57.1	51.3	5.8	7.6	15.8	2.5	1.5	14.0	1.5
30027	Fergus County, Montana	56.9	51.7	5.2	10.8	7.8	9.7	2.7	11.9	0.2
30029	Flathead County, Montana	69.3	61.5	7.8	8.9	6.7	4.1	2.7	8.1	0.3
30031	Gallatin County, Montana	65.6	58.4	7.2	7.6	5.9	9.8	2.0	8.6	0.4
30033	Garfield County, Montana	37.7	35.3	2.3	2.5	16.4	1.3	3.2	36.6	2.3
30035	Glacier County, Montana	43.8	41.5	2.3	9.2	18.8	9.0	9.0	8.6	1.5
30037	Golden Valley County, Montana	58.8	50.1	8.7	4.2	16.2	3.6	3.4	12.6	1.1
30039	Granite County, Montana	59.5	45.1	14.4	4.5	9.6	7.8	5.3	12.6	0.7
30041	Hill County, Montana	58.3	53.3	5.0	9.8	15.1	7.2	3.3	4.6	1.6
30043	Jefferson County, Montana	52.7	45.1	7.6	9.4	7.0	14.8	5.9	9.6	0.6
30045	Judith Basin County, Montana	49.9	39.8	10.2	3.2	12.5	5.6	5.7	19.8	3.2
30047	Lake County, Montana	56.7	48.9	7.8	8.6	11.9	4.5	5.9	11.8	0.5
30049	Lewis and Clark County, Montana	50.5	45.9	4.6	12.3	6.6	18.2	5.9	6.4	0.2
30051	Liberty County, Montana	49.6	33.9	15.7	7.2	9.4	5.2	3.7	15.3	9.8
30053	Lincoln County, Montana	59.1	53.9	5.2	8.5	7.6	6.1	6.3	12.0	0.4
30055	McCone County, Montana	41.6	34.8	6.8	7.2	15.8	2.7	3.7	27.8	1.2
30057	Madison County, Montana	57.5	49.5	8.0	6.8	10.1	4.5	2.2	17.2	1.6
30059	Meagher County, Montana	57.5	50.1	7.4	6.4	10.0	1.0	5.5	18.0	1.7
30061	Mineral County, Montana	70.5	63.1	7.5	7.9	8.6	2.3	2.6	8.0	0.0
30063	Missoula County, Montana	64.1	59.1	5.0	11.5	5.5	8.2	3.4	7.2	0.0
30065	Musselshell County, Montana	58.1	53.1	5.0	8.3	8.5	2.8	1.7	17.9	2.7
30067	Park County, Montana	63.2	53.4	9.8	8.6	4.5	5.2	4.1	13.5	0.8
30069	Petroleum County, Montana	57.9	52.4	5.5	0.0	15.4	6.7	0.0	18.9	1.2
30071	Phillips County, Montana	54.6	44.1	10.5	4.4	13.0	3.1	8.1	15.2	1.6
30073	Pondera County, Montana	56.1	46.7	9.5	9.9	10.5	5.6	2.9	14.4	0.6
30075	Powder River County, Montana	48.9	33.9	15.0	2.3	13.7	6.9	2.9	23.2	2.1
30077	Powell County, Montana	50.8	44.0	6.7	5.6	9.4	18.4	3.5	12.4	0.0
30079	Prairie County, Montana	40.9	32.6	8.3	5.5	10.9	7.6	5.2	27.4	2.6
30081	Ravalli County, Montana	63.6	55.3	8.3	7.7	6.1	3.9	5.1	13.1	0.5
30083	Richland County, Montana	73.2	68.2	5.0	7.5	5.1	2.8	2.2	8.9	0.3
30085	Roosevelt County, Montana	40.8	38.0	2.8	4.2	31.1	6.4	5.3	11.3	0.9
30087	Rosebud County, Montana	52.6	47.7	4.8	10.9	11.2	5.9	11.7	7.0	0.8
30089	Sanders County, Montana	55.5	50.5	5.0	6.2	8.5	4.4	3.3	21.4	0.6
30091	Sheridan County, Montana	55.5	45.3	10.2	6.9	10.8	1.4	5.2	19.0	1.2
30093	Silver Bow County, Montana	65.0	60.8	4.2	11.0	5.8	7.4	3.5	6.9	0.4
30095	Stillwater County, Montana	67.8	61.7	6.1	7.1	7.1	2.9	2.2	12.2	0.8
30097	Sweet Grass County, Montana	60.9	55.1	5.8	6.7	12.3	1.9	2.4	13.6	2.0
30099	Teton County, Montana	53.8	47.9	5.9	9.4	11.1	5.1	2.9	16.5	1.2
30101	Toole County, Montana	61.8	48.7	13.1	7.4	9.7	2.7	5.5	9.8	3.2
30103	Treasure County, Montana	63.3	57.5	5.8	7.9	8.7	0.8	2.9	11.9	4.5
30105	Valley County, Montana	52.9	48.2	4.6	8.8	11.0	4.7	6.8	14.9	0.9
30107	Wheatland County, Montana	44.3	36.2	8.1	7.1	7.0	0.8	1.7	33.0	6.1
30109	Wibaux County, Montana	48.6	35.4	13.1	7.7	19.5	8.5	0.4	14.7	0.7
30111	Yellowstone County, Montana	72.4	68.5	3.9	9.9	5.3	2.6	2.7	6.9	0.2
31000	**Nebraska**	69.9	66.3	3.7	9.0	6.9	5.0	2.2	6.8	0.2
31001	Adams County, Nebraska	66.1	62.3	3.7	12.6	8.3	3.6	1.4	7.9	0.2
31003	Antelope County, Nebraska	63.7	56.4	7.3	6.0	9.1	4.3	1.2	15.4	0.4
31005	Arthur County, Nebraska	46.6	36.8	9.8	7.8	11.9	4.1	1.0	27.5	1.0
31007	Banner County, Nebraska	53.2	41.8	11.4	7.3	12.7	5.7	0.7	20.4	0.0
31009	Blaine County, Nebraska	61.0	59.2	1.7	2.8	10.8	4.5	1.7	19.2	0.0
31011	Boone County, Nebraska	63.6	58.5	5.1	9.1	8.8	1.4	1.6	15.6	0.0
31013	Box Butte County, Nebraska	68.3	64.7	3.6	6.7	8.2	4.2	1.8	10.8	0.1
31015	Boyd County, Nebraska	52.3	46.8	5.5	6.8	8.0	4.1	2.8	24.8	1.1
31017	Brown County, Nebraska	60.6	57.5	3.1	3.7	13.4	3.5	1.3	17.4	0.1
31019	Buffalo County, Nebraska	70.9	67.6	3.3	8.3	6.8	5.8	1.1	6.6	0.4

Table C. County—Labor Force, Employment, and Educational Data, 2011–2015—*Continued*

| | | Class of worker for civilian employed population age 16 and older | | | | | | | | |
| | | Private for-profit wage and salary workers | | | | Government workers | | | | |
Fips code	State/county	Total private for-profit wage and salary workers	Employees of private companies	Self-employed in own incorporated business	Private not-for-profit wage and salary workers	Local government workers	State government workers	Federal government workers	Self-employed in own not incorporated business	Unpaid family workers
31021	Burt County, Nebraska	65.8	60.5	5.3	9.7	8.6	3.3	2.3	9.6	0.8
31023	Butler County, Nebraska	70.0	66.0	4.0	5.7	8.5	2.3	2.5	11.0	0.1
31025	Cass County, Nebraska	66.6	61.0	5.6	9.5	8.7	5.3	3.5	6.1	0.2
31027	Cedar County, Nebraska	62.8	55.5	7.3	6.9	8.1	4.6	2.1	15.0	0.5
31029	Chase County, Nebraska	62.1	56.7	5.4	4.2	11.0	1.5	1.2	18.7	1.3
31031	Cherry County, Nebraska	53.2	46.3	6.9	5.3	10.7	6.6	4.2	18.6	1.3
31033	Cheyenne County, Nebraska	74.4	72.0	2.4	6.4	7.6	2.7	1.1	7.8	0.0
31035	Clay County, Nebraska	66.3	60.4	5.8	6.9	5.8	6.1	2.6	12.0	0.3
31037	Colfax County, Nebraska	78.0	72.5	5.5	5.3	5.3	2.1	0.8	8.3	0.3
31039	Cuming County, Nebraska	65.0	58.9	6.1	8.0	8.5	2.8	1.1	13.7	0.9
31041	Custer County, Nebraska	64.9	60.0	5.0	6.8	8.2	2.9	1.1	15.5	0.5
31043	Dakota County, Nebraska	80.2	78.2	1.9	7.1	4.0	1.4	1.9	5.2	0.2
31045	Dawes County, Nebraska	53.7	50.0	3.7	6.2	10.7	12.8	5.5	10.7	0.4
31047	Dawson County, Nebraska	74.9	70.2	4.7	5.5	7.3	2.8	1.4	7.9	0.1
31049	Deuel County, Nebraska	63.6	60.1	3.5	6.0	9.1	4.3	4.3	12.7	0.0
31051	Dixon County, Nebraska	64.6	60.9	3.7	7.5	9.0	6.8	2.3	9.6	0.3
31053	Dodge County, Nebraska	74.4	71.9	2.5	8.6	6.6	3.3	1.2	5.6	0.2
31055	Douglas County, Nebraska	74.6	71.3	3.3	10.2	5.6	3.2	1.9	4.2	0.1
31057	Dundy County, Nebraska	53.6	47.1	6.5	7.3	17.1	1.9	0.3	19.7	0.0
31059	Fillmore County, Nebraska	64.5	58.1	6.4	5.6	8.6	6.5	1.5	13.2	0.2
31061	Franklin County, Nebraska	59.9	53.1	6.7	8.1	13.0	1.8	3.2	13.8	0.3
31063	Frontier County, Nebraska	58.9	55.0	3.9	3.9	10.5	6.5	1.8	16.5	2.0
31065	Furnas County, Nebraska	60.1	54.8	5.2	7.5	10.4	4.0	2.2	15.1	0.6
31067	Gage County, Nebraska	63.4	59.0	4.4	10.4	6.0	8.0	1.9	10.0	0.3
31069	Garden County, Nebraska	49.7	47.6	2.1	7.2	18.6	4.9	1.0	17.9	0.6
31071	Garfield County, Nebraska	57.2	52.9	4.2	5.2	15.0	2.3	1.4	17.2	1.6
31073	Gosper County, Nebraska	56.6	50.8	5.9	9.4	10.8	5.0	1.6	15.1	1.4
31075	Grant County, Nebraska	58.6	53.3	5.3	8.6	8.1	3.3	0.7	20.6	0.0
31077	Greeley County, Nebraska	61.0	55.6	5.3	5.9	9.8	1.4	1.5	19.3	1.2
31079	Hall County, Nebraska	74.5	71.3	3.2	8.0	6.5	4.1	1.7	5.2	0.1
31081	Hamilton County, Nebraska	70.3	64.1	6.2	7.7	5.4	4.6	1.3	10.4	0.3
31083	Harlan County, Nebraska	60.7	55.7	5.0	8.6	7.5	4.9	3.3	14.5	0.7
31085	Hayes County, Nebraska	53.6	45.7	7.8	3.6	9.7	4.6	5.8	21.5	1.3
31087	Hitchcock County, Nebraska	65.0	60.2	4.9	5.0	14.1	1.8	1.6	11.2	1.3
31089	Holt County, Nebraska	59.3	54.8	4.5	8.3	9.1	4.3	0.6	18.1	0.4
31091	Hooker County, Nebraska	40.5	35.6	4.8	10.9	18.4	4.2	0.9	25.1	0.0
31093	Howard County, Nebraska	64.0	57.6	6.5	7.8	9.2	4.2	2.1	12.6	0.1
31095	Jefferson County, Nebraska	62.8	58.4	4.4	8.9	7.6	3.6	0.9	15.8	0.3
31097	Johnson County, Nebraska	53.4	48.7	4.7	7.1	10.5	12.7	1.7	14.5	0.1
31099	Kearney County, Nebraska	71.8	66.2	5.6	6.8	8.3	2.5	1.1	8.9	0.5
31101	Keith County, Nebraska	68.4	63.0	5.3	5.9	7.9	5.4	1.3	10.8	0.4
31103	Keya Paha County, Nebraska	43.6	35.5	8.2	4.3	9.3	5.7	1.6	34.3	1.1
31105	Kimball County, Nebraska	62.0	58.9	3.1	6.2	13.0	2.8	1.1	14.9	0.0
31107	Knox County, Nebraska	54.6	50.4	4.2	7.3	12.6	4.9	2.2	17.9	0.4
31109	Lancaster County, Nebraska	68.0	64.9	3.1	8.8	6.4	10.1	1.8	4.6	0.1
31111	Lincoln County, Nebraska	71.7	68.9	2.9	6.8	7.4	5.8	1.4	6.7	0.2
31113	Logan County, Nebraska	64.6	56.6	8.0	8.7	10.0	1.3	2.7	11.6	1.1
31115	Loup County, Nebraska	46.5	40.4	6.1	4.7	12.5	1.3	5.7	29.3	0.0
31117	McPherson County, Nebraska	58.1	56.8	1.4	11.3	3.2	2.7	0.0	23.9	0.9
31119	Madison County, Nebraska	71.0	67.3	3.7	9.6	6.5	4.1	1.4	7.2	0.1
31121	Merrick County, Nebraska	65.5	60.7	4.8	9.9	6.5	1.9	2.8	13.1	0.2
31123	Morrill County, Nebraska	61.9	55.9	6.0	5.3	14.2	5.8	0.9	11.8	0.2
31125	Nance County, Nebraska	62.4	57.3	5.1	4.4	12.4	3.8	0.4	14.9	1.5
31127	Nemaha County, Nebraska	51.7	48.8	3.0	10.5	8.6	17.1	1.3	10.6	0.1
31129	Nuckolls County, Nebraska	53.2	46.4	6.8	12.2	9.3	5.2	3.0	16.2	1.0
31131	Otoe County, Nebraska	67.5	63.4	4.1	8.0	8.6	5.2	2.1	8.4	0.1
31133	Pawnee County, Nebraska	46.6	43.4	3.2	5.3	15.3	5.7	1.3	25.1	0.6
31135	Perkins County, Nebraska	54.9	45.0	9.9	4.1	17.3	3.4	0.9	18.7	0.7
31137	Phelps County, Nebraska	65.8	62.1	3.7	9.3	7.5	4.1	0.5	12.3	0.5
31139	Pierce County, Nebraska	66.0	62.4	3.6	7.5	9.0	3.3	1.1	12.5	0.5
31141	Platte County, Nebraska	74.4	70.5	3.9	7.8	6.9	4.0	0.9	5.9	0.2
31143	Polk County, Nebraska	62.5	56.7	5.8	7.9	10.3	2.9	1.7	14.2	0.5
31145	Red Willow County, Nebraska	66.7	62.0	4.7	6.0	7.2	6.8	1.8	11.2	0.3
31147	Richardson County, Nebraska	58.7	52.0	6.7	11.8	7.6	8.5	2.1	11.1	0.2
31149	Rock County, Nebraska	54.2	46.3	8.0	6.3	11.1	2.6	0.7	24.1	1.0
31151	Saline County, Nebraska	69.3	68.6	0.7	8.4	7.6	4.6	0.9	8.6	0.5
31153	Sarpy County, Nebraska	70.5	67.3	3.2	9.6	6.6	3.0	6.2	4.1	0.1
31155	Saunders County, Nebraska	68.6	62.9	5.7	6.9	8.1	5.0	2.5	8.4	0.4
31157	Scotts Bluff County, Nebraska	71.4	67.6	3.8	8.3	6.8	4.4	1.6	7.2	0.2
31159	Seward County, Nebraska	67.0	62.8	4.2	9.8	7.5	5.2	1.2	9.0	0.2
31161	Sheridan County, Nebraska	54.6	50.4	4.2	9.8	10.4	5.7	4.6	14.4	0.5
31163	Sherman County, Nebraska	56.7	50.9	5.8	11.0	7.8	4.0	1.5	19.1	0.1
31165	Sioux County, Nebraska	54.5	46.2	8.3	7.6	13.9	3.8	0.0	20.2	0.0
31167	Stanton County, Nebraska	66.6	62.3	4.3	7.4	7.3	5.6	1.7	10.2	1.1
31169	Thayer County, Nebraska	61.2	56.8	4.4	10.1	8.9	2.6	1.3	15.6	0.3

Table C. County—Labor Force, Employment, and Educational Data, 2011–2015—*Continued*

| | | Class of worker for civilian employed population age 16 and older | | | | | | | | |
| | | Private for-profit wage and salary workers | | | | Government workers | | | | |
Fips code	State/county	Total private for-profit wage and salary workers	Employees of private companies	Self-employed in own incorporated business	Private not-for-profit wage and salary workers	Local government workers	State government workers	Federal government workers	Self-employed in own not incorporated business	Unpaid family workers
31171	Thomas County, Nebraska	48.8	37.1	11.7	9.1	10.6	6.8	4.9	19.2	0.5
31173	Thurston County, Nebraska	45.8	43.1	2.7	6.6	23.9	4.9	9.0	9.8	0.0
31175	Valley County, Nebraska	62.5	56.3	6.2	6.3	10.3	4.7	1.4	14.6	0.2
31177	Washington County, Nebraska	70.4	63.8	6.6	9.2	8.8	3.1	1.6	6.7	0.2
31179	Wayne County, Nebraska	59.8	58.4	1.4	9.6	5.9	14.8	0.7	9.0	0.2
31181	Webster County, Nebraska	57.6	52.9	4.7	8.9	9.8	5.5	1.5	15.7	0.8
31183	Wheeler County, Nebraska	56.1	48.0	8.1	3.0	13.6	2.6	0.6	22.7	1.4
31185	York County, Nebraska	66.7	60.5	6.1	10.1	7.3	4.9	0.9	10.0	0.1
32000	**Nevada**	78.9	75.9	3.0	3.7	6.6	3.2	2.6	5.0	0.1
32001	Churchill County, Nevada	61.0	59.4	1.6	7.2	11.6	2.9	9.6	7.5	0.1
32003	Clark County, Nevada	81.1	78.3	2.8	3.4	6.1	2.3	2.4	4.8	0.1
32005	Douglas County, Nevada	67.6	63.9	3.7	3.6	10.0	6.7	2.2	9.6	0.3
32007	Elko County, Nevada	81.2	77.6	3.5	2.4	8.4	2.9	1.7	3.2	0.2
32009	Esmeralda County, Nevada	70.9	67.5	3.4	0.0	16.5	1.8	0.0	10.8	0.0
32011	Eureka County, Nevada	56.9	50.2	6.7	1.1	31.4	2.3	0.0	8.3	0.0
32013	Humboldt County, Nevada	76.7	75.2	1.6	2.4	7.3	3.6	3.2	6.7	0.1
32015	Lander County, Nevada	80.9	79.5	1.4	1.4	7.8	1.5	4.0	4.5	0.0
32017	Lincoln County, Nevada	49.1	46.3	2.7	1.0	16.5	20.8	5.8	6.6	0.3
32019	Lyon County, Nevada	73.0	70.2	2.8	3.8	9.6	4.8	3.0	5.7	0.1
32021	Mineral County, Nevada	55.9	53.0	2.9	2.0	25.4	3.6	9.4	3.6	0.2
32023	Nye County, Nevada	71.0	66.4	4.6	3.6	11.8	4.1	4.2	5.2	0.2
32027	Pershing County, Nevada	67.3	63.7	3.5	2.0	17.3	5.6	3.8	4.0	0.0
32029	Storey County, Nevada	70.8	68.7	2.2	2.0	9.8	4.0	2.6	10.7	0.0
32031	Washoe County, Nevada	74.2	70.4	3.8	5.1	6.9	4.9	3.0	5.8	0.1
32033	White Pine County, Nevada	55.8	53.7	2.1	4.6	17.8	11.7	4.1	5.6	0.4
32510	Carson City, Nevada	65.2	62.9	2.4	5.1	7.8	15.1	1.6	4.9	0.2
33000	**New Hampshire**	68.8	65.7	3.1	10.6	7.7	3.6	2.2	6.9	0.1
33001	Belknap County, New Hampshire	63.0	59.4	3.6	11.1	10.1	4.4	1.9	9.2	0.2
33003	Carroll County, New Hampshire	60.1	56.4	3.7	11.7	10.3	2.1	1.6	14.1	0.1
33005	Cheshire County, New Hampshire	65.7	62.7	3.0	12.6	8.7	4.7	1.2	7.1	0.1
33007	Coos County, New Hampshire	58.8	55.5	3.2	13.9	10.3	5.7	2.0	9.0	0.4
33009	Grafton County, New Hampshire	58.9	55.6	3.3	16.8	8.6	4.8	2.0	8.6	0.2
33011	Hillsborough County, New Hampshire	73.7	71.1	2.6	9.1	6.8	2.0	2.4	5.8	0.1
33013	Merrimack County, New Hampshire	61.4	58.2	3.1	14.2	8.4	6.9	1.4	7.6	0.1
33015	Rockingham County, New Hampshire	72.9	68.8	4.1	8.0	7.4	2.6	2.3	6.7	0.1
33017	Strafford County, New Hampshire	69.2	66.9	2.3	9.8	6.6	5.9	3.2	5.3	0.0
33019	Sullivan County, New Hampshire	65.1	62.4	2.7	14.1	8.9	2.1	2.0	7.8	0.1
34000	**New Jersey**	74.3	70.5	3.9	6.9	7.6	4.5	1.8	4.7	0.1
34001	Atlantic County, New Jersey	74.1	71.0	3.0	5.5	8.1	5.3	2.1	4.7	0.2
34003	Bergen County, New Jersey	75.6	69.2	6.4	6.9	7.3	2.8	1.5	5.7	0.2
34005	Burlington County, New Jersey	68.7	65.8	2.8	8.8	8.1	6.2	4.0	4.2	0.1
34007	Camden County, New Jersey	72.9	69.8	3.1	9.1	6.7	4.7	2.5	4.0	0.1
34009	Cape May County, New Jersey	65.4	60.2	5.2	7.5	12.6	6.6	1.6	6.0	0.3
34011	Cumberland County, New Jersey	67.9	65.7	2.2	7.1	9.6	9.9	1.6	3.6	0.3
34013	Essex County, New Jersey	72.8	69.8	3.0	7.1	6.9	6.2	1.9	4.9	0.1
34015	Gloucester County, New Jersey	72.4	69.3	3.1	7.6	9.0	4.6	2.7	3.7	0.1
34017	Hudson County, New Jersey	79.5	77.1	2.4	5.2	6.2	3.1	1.6	4.4	0.1
34019	Hunterdon County, New Jersey	72.3	65.7	6.6	7.4	8.3	4.5	0.8	6.6	0.1
34021	Mercer County, New Jersey	67.1	64.4	2.6	11.1	7.2	8.7	1.5	4.4	0.1
34023	Middlesex County, New Jersey	77.0	73.6	3.4	6.0	7.0	4.7	1.4	3.8	0.1
34025	Monmouth County, New Jersey	74.5	69.0	5.5	6.1	8.6	3.4	1.7	5.5	0.2
34027	Morris County, New Jersey	76.2	71.5	4.6	6.6	7.5	2.8	1.6	5.3	0.1
34029	Ocean County, New Jersey	70.2	66.1	4.2	7.8	10.1	4.0	2.2	5.4	0.2
34031	Passaic County, New Jersey	78.6	75.2	3.4	5.5	7.0	3.4	1.1	4.2	0.1
34033	Salem County, New Jersey	74.0	71.5	2.5	5.7	9.4	4.6	1.6	4.6	0.1
34035	Somerset County, New Jersey	77.7	73.0	4.8	6.7	6.1	3.9	1.0	4.4	0.2
34037	Sussex County, New Jersey	72.4	68.2	4.2	6.4	9.3	3.2	1.8	6.7	0.1
34039	Union County, New Jersey	76.0	72.9	3.1	6.6	7.0	4.7	1.7	3.9	0.1
34041	Warren County, New Jersey	73.5	70.0	3.6	5.9	8.4	4.3	1.7	6.0	0.1
35000	**New Mexico**	63.4	60.4	3.1	7.5	8.4	8.0	5.8	6.7	0.2
35001	Bernalillo County, New Mexico	65.3	62.3	3.0	8.7	7.3	6.8	6.0	5.6	0.2
35003	Catron County, New Mexico	40.6	36.0	4.6	9.7	10.9	19.2	9.6	8.3	1.7
35005	Chaves County, New Mexico	68.6	65.8	2.8	4.9	8.3	8.3	2.5	7.2	0.1
35006	Cibola County, New Mexico	57.3	54.1	3.2	7.7	14.3	6.3	6.5	7.7	0.2
35007	Colfax County, New Mexico	59.0	55.2	3.8	9.6	8.5	13.9	1.8	6.7	0.4
35009	Curry County, New Mexico	64.8	62.5	2.4	8.4	5.6	5.0	11.4	4.7	0.0
35011	De Baca County, New Mexico	53.2	52.3	0.8	13.1	3.1	19.5	2.9	8.2	0.0
35013	Doña Ana County, New Mexico	63.7	61.3	2.4	4.2	8.6	10.4	5.9	7.1	0.1
35015	Eddy County, New Mexico	72.7	69.8	2.9	6.5	6.5	5.9	3.2	5.3	0.0
35017	Grant County, New Mexico	63.3	59.3	3.9	5.7	7.3	14.1	2.2	7.0	0.6

Table C. County—Labor Force, Employment, and Educational Data, 2011–2015—*Continued*

| | | Class of worker for civilian employed population age 16 and older | | | | | | | | |
| | | Private for-profit wage and salary workers | | | | Government workers | | | | |
Fips code	State/county	Total private for-profit wage and salary workers	Employees of private companies	Self-employed in own incorporated business	Private not-for-profit wage and salary workers	Local government workers	State government workers	Federal government workers	Self-employed in own not incorporated business	Unpaid family workers
35019	Guadalupe County, New Mexico	47.1	46.1	1.0	9.6	23.4	13.5	1.5	4.3	0.5
35021	Harding County, New Mexico	45.4	29.3	16.1	1.0	7.8	31.7	3.4	10.7	0.0
35023	Hidalgo County, New Mexico	66.6	62.5	4.1	2.4	9.9	9.4	6.7	4.2	0.7
35025	Lea County, New Mexico	75.9	72.9	3.0	4.9	6.8	5.4	1.4	5.5	0.1
35027	Lincoln County, New Mexico	59.9	55.7	4.2	6.3	10.9	7.9	3.7	10.3	0.9
35028	Los Alamos County, New Mexico	56.3	55.0	1.3	5.6	8.0	3.6	19.7	6.6	0.2
35029	Luna County, New Mexico	69.3	66.7	2.6	4.3	8.0	8.4	3.4	6.5	0.0
35031	McKinley County, New Mexico	51.0	49.2	1.8	7.1	16.6	8.5	8.9	7.7	0.1
35033	Mora County, New Mexico	39.5	39.5	0.0	11.2	9.3	34.1	0.5	5.2	0.2
35035	Otero County, New Mexico	54.9	52.9	2.1	7.8	10.0	6.5	15.0	5.3	0.4
35037	Quay County, New Mexico	59.9	57.9	2.0	7.1	10.7	11.3	1.9	7.4	1.8
35039	Rio Arriba County, New Mexico	48.8	46.8	2.1	6.9	13.1	11.0	12.6	7.5	0.3
35041	Roosevelt County, New Mexico	60.2	58.3	1.9	7.1	7.1	15.6	3.6	6.0	0.4
35043	Sandoval County, New Mexico	65.4	61.5	3.8	6.9	9.4	6.2	5.8	6.2	0.1
35045	San Juan County, New Mexico	68.1	65.7	2.4	8.4	9.7	5.4	4.3	3.8	0.3
35047	San Miguel County, New Mexico	48.8	47.2	1.6	8.1	11.2	22.4	3.7	5.5	0.4
35049	Santa Fe County, New Mexico	56.7	51.5	5.2	9.9	7.6	9.0	4.2	12.4	0.2
35051	Sierra County, New Mexico	54.8	52.3	2.6	4.6	16.6	9.9	3.4	10.2	0.3
35053	Socorro County, New Mexico	52.2	49.8	2.4	7.4	5.7	20.5	6.7	7.4	0.0
35055	Taos County, New Mexico	58.7	54.1	4.5	8.7	8.7	6.5	4.5	12.9	0.0
35057	Torrance County, New Mexico	58.0	52.8	5.2	8.2	7.0	8.9	4.1	13.8	0.0
35059	Union County, New Mexico	59.7	57.2	2.5	7.6	13.2	5.5	6.9	6.6	0.4
35061	Valencia County, New Mexico	64.5	61.2	3.3	6.1	7.7	10.7	4.3	6.3	0.4
36000	**New York**	68.4	64.7	3.7	10.0	9.5	4.4	1.7	5.9	0.1
36001	Albany County, New York	57.6	55.2	2.4	13.3	8.3	14.7	2.0	4.0	0.1
36003	Allegany County, New York	57.9	55.9	2.1	16.0	8.6	8.7	1.5	7.1	0.2
36005	Bronx County, New York	70.6	69.1	1.5	9.2	10.8	2.5	1.5	5.2	0.1
36007	Broome County, New York	64.0	61.7	2.4	11.0	9.3	9.5	0.8	5.4	0.1
36009	Cattaraugus County, New York	63.1	60.0	3.1	10.7	11.1	7.0	1.7	6.1	0.3
36011	Cayuga County, New York	64.7	61.6	3.2	11.4	8.3	8.1	1.2	6.1	0.3
36013	Chautauqua County, New York	63.6	61.1	2.4	10.8	10.3	6.6	0.9	7.5	0.2
36015	Chemung County, New York	64.0	62.3	1.7	14.4	8.3	7.6	0.8	4.8	0.2
36017	Chenango County, New York	61.4	59.6	1.8	8.8	11.6	8.6	1.2	8.0	0.5
36019	Clinton County, New York	60.8	58.5	2.4	9.7	9.0	12.0	2.9	5.4	0.1
36021	Columbia County, New York	58.3	53.4	4.9	12.7	10.3	8.3	1.2	8.9	0.3
36023	Cortland County, New York	62.0	59.5	2.5	10.8	10.2	9.4	1.0	6.5	0.2
36025	Delaware County, New York	56.9	52.9	4.0	8.8	13.0	8.9	1.0	11.0	0.5
36027	Dutchess County, New York	65.9	61.8	4.1	11.4	9.6	5.5	1.7	5.7	0.2
36029	Erie County, New York	68.4	65.8	2.6	10.8	8.2	6.4	2.2	4.0	0.1
36031	Essex County, New York	55.5	52.4	3.1	14.7	11.7	7.8	0.9	9.2	0.3
36033	Franklin County, New York	47.1	43.8	3.3	15.4	11.6	14.6	2.7	8.3	0.2
36035	Fulton County, New York	67.2	64.6	2.6	11.8	8.8	6.1	1.3	4.4	0.3
36037	Genesee County, New York	69.2	66.6	2.6	7.4	8.4	7.8	1.8	5.2	0.2
36039	Greene County, New York	59.5	57.3	2.2	8.6	10.9	10.3	2.1	7.8	0.8
36041	Hamilton County, New York	52.6	50.9	1.7	10.6	20.7	9.0	0.9	6.0	0.2
36043	Herkimer County, New York	63.2	60.3	2.8	13.1	9.0	6.5	1.1	6.9	0.2
36045	Jefferson County, New York	57.0	54.9	2.1	10.0	10.2	6.4	9.6	6.7	0.1
36047	Kings County, New York	69.6	66.5	3.1	9.4	10.5	2.4	1.6	6.5	0.1
36049	Lewis County, New York	56.8	54.5	2.2	7.6	14.9	7.8	3.2	9.1	0.7
36051	Livingston County, New York	64.7	62.4	2.3	9.2	8.3	10.4	0.9	5.8	0.6
36053	Madison County, New York	64.5	61.9	2.5	12.1	7.7	7.0	1.5	7.1	0.1
36055	Monroe County, New York	68.7	66.0	2.7	13.9	8.0	3.5	0.9	4.9	0.1
36057	Montgomery County, New York	65.5	63.6	1.9	10.9	8.1	7.7	1.5	6.0	0.1
36059	Nassau County, New York	69.8	63.8	6.0	8.2	11.2	3.6	1.6	5.5	0.1
36061	New York County, New York	72.3	67.6	4.7	11.3	5.5	1.5	1.5	7.8	0.1
36063	Niagara County, New York	73.3	70.7	2.6	8.6	8.2	3.9	1.8	4.0	0.1
36065	Oneida County, New York	62.1	59.4	2.7	12.5	9.8	7.6	2.4	5.3	0.2
36067	Onondaga County, New York	66.6	63.8	2.8	11.7	8.4	6.7	1.7	4.8	0.1
36069	Ontario County, New York	66.4	63.4	3.0	12.7	8.9	4.0	2.2	5.7	0.1
36071	Orange County, New York	66.1	62.4	3.7	9.7	11.9	4.8	3.1	4.3	0.1
36073	Orleans County, New York	69.6	67.2	2.4	8.2	7.9	8.0	1.1	5.1	0.1
36075	Oswego County, New York	68.5	66.7	1.8	8.0	9.3	7.1	1.4	5.6	0.2
36077	Otsego County, New York	55.2	52.6	2.6	17.1	8.5	8.0	1.2	9.5	0.6
36079	Putnam County, New York	67.3	62.9	4.5	8.7	12.6	3.8	1.2	6.1	0.3
36081	Queens County, New York	72.3	68.8	3.5	7.6	9.5	2.1	1.9	6.4	0.1
36083	Rensselaer County, New York	60.5	58.0	2.5	13.8	8.1	11.0	1.7	4.8	0.1
36085	Richmond County, New York	65.6	61.8	3.7	8.5	16.3	3.3	1.8	4.4	0.1
36087	Rockland County, New York	66.0	61.0	5.0	12.2	10.0	4.9	1.0	5.7	0.1
36089	St. Lawrence County, New York	55.3	52.8	2.5	13.4	9.6	12.4	2.3	6.8	0.1
36091	Saratoga County, New York	65.4	61.9	3.5	10.8	7.9	7.9	2.2	5.6	0.1
36093	Schenectady County, New York	64.4	62.3	2.1	11.3	7.5	9.9	2.2	4.7	0.0
36095	Schoharie County, New York	58.4	55.7	2.7	8.9	8.2	13.6	2.0	8.4	0.5
36097	Schuyler County, New York	59.0	56.5	2.5	15.7	6.7	6.7	1.8	9.9	0.1
36099	Seneca County, New York	62.5	60.5	2.0	12.0	9.2	7.4	1.8	6.9	0.2

Table C. County—Labor Force, Employment, and Educational Data, 2011–2015—*Continued*

| | | Class of worker for civilian employed population age 16 and older | | | | | | | | |
| | | Private for-profit wage and salary workers | | | | Government workers | | | | |
Fips code	State/county	Total private for-profit wage and salary workers	Employees of private companies	Self-employed in own incorporated business	Private not-for-profit wage and salary workers	Local government workers	State government workers	Federal government workers	Self-employed in own not incorporated business	Unpaid family workers
36101	Steuben County, New York	65.1	63.4	1.7	11.3	8.7	5.9	2.1	6.7	0.3
36103	Suffolk County, New York	70.0	64.4	5.6	7.1	10.0	5.9	2.2	4.7	0.1
36105	Sullivan County, New York	56.4	52.4	4.0	15.8	12.7	6.7	1.5	6.6	0.2
36107	Tioga County, New York	70.7	68.8	1.9	9.4	8.3	5.8	0.8	4.9	0.2
36109	Tompkins County, New York	50.8	48.5	2.3	27.6	6.3	6.5	0.8	7.8	0.2
36111	Ulster County, New York	62.7	58.1	4.7	11.1	10.5	6.6	1.2	7.5	0.4
36113	Warren County, New York	65.0	61.5	3.5	11.1	9.6	6.1	0.9	7.3	0.1
36115	Washington County, New York	64.5	62.5	2.1	9.4	9.1	6.2	1.6	8.9	0.2
36117	Wayne County, New York	69.6	67.1	2.6	9.0	9.5	5.7	1.0	4.9	0.2
36119	Westchester County, New York	69.0	63.6	5.3	10.4	9.6	2.7	1.5	6.6	0.1
36121	Wyoming County, New York	66.9	64.2	2.6	6.6	9.8	8.7	1.6	6.2	0.2
36123	Yates County, New York	59.0	55.6	3.4	13.0	9.3	3.6	1.1	13.2	0.9
37000	**North Carolina**	72.1	68.6	3.5	7.0	5.8	6.8	2.3	5.8	0.2
37001	Alamance County, North Carolina	75.0	72.8	2.2	6.2	5.3	6.5	1.0	5.8	0.3
37003	Alexander County, North Carolina	77.3	74.8	2.5	5.7	5.2	6.1	0.8	4.8	0.1
37005	Alleghany County, North Carolina	62.7	60.8	1.9	6.1	9.0	6.1	3.3	12.3	0.4
37007	Anson County, North Carolina	70.9	67.9	3.0	4.8	7.0	10.2	2.4	4.3	0.4
37009	Ashe County, North Carolina	64.8	62.1	2.7	7.6	6.6	7.1	1.2	12.4	0.2
37011	Avery County, North Carolina	67.6	63.4	4.3	7.6	5.1	8.9	0.9	9.5	0.3
37013	Beaufort County, North Carolina	69.2	64.6	4.6	7.5	6.9	7.5	1.6	7.2	0.1
37015	Bertie County, North Carolina	71.9	69.7	2.2	5.1	5.2	10.6	2.1	4.8	0.3
37017	Bladen County, North Carolina	68.8	66.7	2.1	3.2	9.5	12.7	1.2	4.6	0.0
37019	Brunswick County, North Carolina	72.5	68.4	4.1	5.6	6.5	5.6	1.6	8.1	0.2
37021	Buncombe County, North Carolina	68.6	63.8	4.8	10.4	4.9	5.3	2.2	8.4	0.3
37023	Burke County, North Carolina	68.8	66.6	2.2	6.5	7.6	10.5	0.6	5.7	0.3
37025	Cabarrus County, North Carolina	73.5	69.7	3.8	8.0	6.9	5.4	1.4	4.7	0.1
37027	Caldwell County, North Carolina	75.0	72.0	3.0	5.3	6.4	6.5	0.8	5.9	0.1
37029	Camden County, North Carolina	55.0	53.4	1.6	2.4	8.4	9.6	19.2	5.4	0.0
37031	Carteret County, North Carolina	62.1	56.3	5.8	4.8	7.2	7.0	8.0	10.8	0.1
37033	Caswell County, North Carolina	71.5	68.5	3.0	6.2	7.7	6.5	1.9	5.8	0.4
37035	Catawba County, North Carolina	78.1	74.7	3.4	5.7	5.2	4.9	0.8	5.2	0.1
37037	Chatham County, North Carolina	66.7	62.0	4.6	6.3	3.8	12.4	1.5	9.1	0.2
37039	Cherokee County, North Carolina	65.8	61.1	4.7	9.9	6.4	6.1	0.8	11.0	0.1
37041	Chowan County, North Carolina	65.2	62.5	2.7	4.3	10.3	13.7	1.8	4.5	0.2
37043	Clay County, North Carolina	68.8	63.8	5.0	9.1	5.5	5.6	2.4	8.2	0.4
37045	Cleveland County, North Carolina	73.6	71.7	1.9	6.8	6.7	6.1	0.9	5.7	0.2
37047	Columbus County, North Carolina	70.7	68.1	2.7	4.2	7.7	10.0	0.9	6.2	0.2
37049	Craven County, North Carolina	66.0	62.7	3.3	6.1	6.1	5.4	10.6	5.5	0.3
37051	Cumberland County, North Carolina	64.6	61.7	2.8	4.8	7.5	7.2	11.6	4.3	0.2
37053	Currituck County, North Carolina	71.8	69.2	2.7	4.6	8.7	4.6	5.2	5.0	0.1
37055	Dare County, North Carolina	69.6	62.5	7.1	5.0	8.6	4.2	1.5	10.9	0.2
37057	Davidson County, North Carolina	74.8	71.9	2.9	7.0	6.1	5.0	0.9	6.2	0.1
37059	Davie County, North Carolina	74.4	70.3	4.0	6.6	6.4	4.4	1.4	6.5	0.2
37061	Duplin County, North Carolina	72.2	69.8	2.4	4.3	5.1	8.8	1.0	8.1	0.4
37063	Durham County, North Carolina	65.0	62.4	2.6	13.2	4.3	10.0	2.5	4.9	0.1
37065	Edgecombe County, North Carolina	74.3	72.8	1.6	5.8	7.1	5.8	2.0	4.7	0.3
37067	Forsyth County, North Carolina	72.7	69.4	3.3	10.8	5.5	4.5	1.4	5.1	0.1
37069	Franklin County, North Carolina	71.2	67.0	4.2	5.8	6.4	8.5	1.6	6.4	0.1
37071	Gaston County, North Carolina	77.5	74.7	2.8	6.4	6.4	3.8	1.0	4.9	0.2
37073	Gates County, North Carolina	69.8	68.4	1.4	4.8	8.0	7.9	5.9	3.5	0.0
37075	Graham County, North Carolina	64.6	62.0	2.6	5.2	9.9	10.5	2.4	5.9	1.5
37077	Granville County, North Carolina	70.7	67.8	2.9	5.1	6.3	11.0	3.3	3.4	0.3
37079	Greene County, North Carolina	71.1	67.1	4.0	5.1	6.0	10.2	2.1	5.3	0.1
37081	Guilford County, North Carolina	74.7	71.3	3.4	7.6	5.4	5.1	1.7	5.3	0.1
37083	Halifax County, North Carolina	69.9	67.2	2.7	6.8	7.0	9.5	1.1	5.6	0.1
37085	Harnett County, North Carolina	67.8	65.0	2.9	4.4	6.2	7.4	7.9	6.1	0.2
37087	Haywood County, North Carolina	68.7	64.1	4.6	6.9	6.9	8.1	1.2	7.8	0.4
37089	Henderson County, North Carolina	71.9	67.2	4.7	7.9	5.9	4.9	1.1	8.2	0.1
37091	Hertford County, North Carolina	62.8	60.8	2.0	10.5	7.5	11.2	2.5	5.4	0.0
37093	Hoke County, North Carolina	65.7	63.2	2.5	5.4	5.0	7.0	12.1	4.7	0.0
37095	Hyde County, North Carolina	50.3	46.1	4.1	4.7	9.8	15.2	2.0	18.1	0.0
37097	Iredell County, North Carolina	77.6	73.8	3.8	6.8	5.1	4.3	1.0	5.0	0.2
37099	Jackson County, North Carolina	59.7	56.1	3.6	7.7	9.7	12.5	2.4	7.9	0.1
37101	Johnston County, North Carolina	73.1	69.4	3.7	4.4	6.6	8.8	2.0	5.0	0.1
37103	Jones County, North Carolina	64.7	61.2	3.5	6.3	6.5	9.0	4.3	8.5	0.8
37105	Lee County, North Carolina	76.3	73.0	3.3	4.7	5.7	7.9	1.5	3.7	0.3
37107	Lenoir County, North Carolina	67.1	64.1	3.0	5.8	7.1	12.0	1.1	6.7	0.3
37109	Lincoln County, North Carolina	78.0	75.0	3.0	5.0	6.5	3.5	1.1	5.8	0.1

Table C. County—Labor Force, Employment, and Educational Data, 2011–2015—*Continued*

| | | Class of worker for civilian employed population age 16 and older | | | | | | | | |
| | | Private for-profit wage and salary workers | | | | Government workers | | | | |
Fips code	State/county	Total private for-profit wage and salary workers	Employees of private companies	Self-employed in own incorporated business	Private not-for-profit wage and salary workers	Local government workers	State government workers	Federal government workers	Self-employed in own not incorporated business	Unpaid family workers
37111	McDowell County, North Carolina	70.5	68.3	2.2	7.6	6.2	9.5	1.2	5.1	0.0
37113	Macon County, North Carolina	67.0	61.9	5.2	7.3	6.5	6.5	1.2	10.6	0.8
37115	Madison County, North Carolina	62.3	58.0	4.4	13.0	6.2	6.8	1.7	9.8	0.1
37117	Martin County, North Carolina	73.2	70.6	2.5	5.2	6.1	8.8	0.9	5.7	0.2
37119	Mecklenburg County, North Carolina	78.6	74.8	3.8	7.4	4.1	3.7	1.2	4.8	0.1
37121	Mitchell County, North Carolina	67.8	62.2	5.6	5.7	7.8	10.4	1.1	7.1	0.1
37123	Montgomery County, North Carolina	71.2	67.6	3.6	5.2	6.3	10.1	0.5	6.1	0.5
37125	Moore County, North Carolina	66.5	61.9	4.7	8.3	4.9	7.7	3.5	9.0	0.1
37127	Nash County, North Carolina	73.5	70.5	3.0	5.9	6.9	6.6	1.3	5.6	0.1
37129	New Hanover County, North Carolina	73.1	67.3	5.8	6.3	5.1	6.2	1.3	7.8	0.2
37131	Northampton County, North Carolina	65.8	64.0	1.7	6.3	7.7	13.1	2.1	4.6	0.4
37133	Onslow County, North Carolina	63.1	60.5	2.6	3.2	6.2	4.2	17.3	5.9	0.1
37135	Orange County, North Carolina	55.5	52.1	3.4	12.2	4.7	18.5	2.3	6.6	0.2
37137	Pamlico County, North Carolina	69.0	64.0	5.1	4.6	6.1	7.8	4.9	6.7	0.9
37139	Pasquotank County, North Carolina	62.7	59.8	2.8	8.1	9.7	9.0	5.8	4.6	0.1
37141	Pender County, North Carolina	71.8	68.1	3.7	4.9	7.8	5.1	1.9	8.2	0.2
37143	Perquimans County, North Carolina	61.2	58.6	2.6	3.9	10.7	10.3	2.6	10.7	0.7
37145	Person County, North Carolina	74.2	71.2	3.0	4.9	7.0	5.2	2.1	6.4	0.0
37147	Pitt County, North Carolina	68.7	65.7	2.9	7.1	6.1	12.1	1.8	4.1	0.1
37149	Polk County, North Carolina	67.6	63.7	3.9	9.3	8.0	3.7	0.8	10.5	0.1
37151	Randolph County, North Carolina	75.6	73.1	2.5	5.4	6.6	4.7	0.9	6.6	0.2
37153	Richmond County, North Carolina	72.2	70.0	2.1	5.3	7.7	8.4	1.1	5.4	0.0
37155	Robeson County, North Carolina	71.0	68.8	2.2	4.8	8.0	7.8	1.9	6.3	0.3
37157	Rockingham County, North Carolina	75.4	72.8	2.6	5.2	7.0	5.2	1.2	5.9	0.2
37159	Rowan County, North Carolina	73.7	70.5	3.3	6.9	5.4	5.5	2.6	5.8	0.2
37161	Rutherford County, North Carolina	74.1	70.9	3.3	6.2	6.4	5.7	0.8	6.5	0.2
37163	Sampson County, North Carolina	73.9	70.6	3.2	4.9	6.0	6.3	1.6	7.0	0.3
37165	Scotland County, North Carolina	70.0	67.3	2.7	7.3	7.0	9.1	0.9	5.6	0.0
37167	Stanly County, North Carolina	68.8	65.9	2.9	7.7	7.0	8.3	1.1	6.9	0.2
37169	Stokes County, North Carolina	70.2	67.7	2.6	8.2	7.6	5.4	1.3	7.2	0.0
37171	Surry County, North Carolina	73.7	70.6	3.1	6.0	6.9	6.1	0.8	6.2	0.3
37173	Swain County, North Carolina	62.3	60.4	1.9	6.5	15.0	5.2	3.8	7.1	0.0
37175	Transylvania County, North Carolina	61.0	57.9	3.1	11.2	9.3	5.7	1.7	11.1	0.1
37177	Tyrrell County, North Carolina	70.4	65.9	4.6	5.1	5.2	11.2	2.9	5.2	0.0
37179	Union County, North Carolina	76.3	71.5	4.8	6.7	6.9	3.8	0.7	5.5	0.2
37181	Vance County, North Carolina	70.1	68.1	2.0	4.9	7.2	12.1	1.2	4.4	0.0
37183	Wake County, North Carolina	73.1	69.1	4.0	7.0	4.8	8.6	1.7	4.8	0.1
37185	Warren County, North Carolina	64.3	60.4	4.0	3.7	8.6	10.8	2.6	9.3	0.7
37187	Washington County, North Carolina	71.4	68.1	3.4	5.0	10.0	6.9	0.5	6.0	0.2
37189	Watauga County, North Carolina	61.5	55.4	6.1	7.8	5.3	16.6	0.9	7.3	0.5
37191	Wayne County, North Carolina	70.2	67.6	2.7	4.2	5.1	10.2	4.5	5.4	0.3
37193	Wilkes County, North Carolina	73.4	70.2	3.2	5.7	5.1	7.0	1.4	7.4	0.1
37195	Wilson County, North Carolina	75.2	72.3	2.9	6.3	7.1	6.0	0.9	4.3	0.2
37197	Yadkin County, North Carolina	74.8	71.9	2.9	6.4	5.9	4.6	1.0	7.3	0.0
37199	Yancey County, North Carolina	60.7	57.1	3.5	9.1	8.3	12.2	1.6	8.0	0.1
38000	**North Dakota**	64.7	61.5	3.3	10.5	7.4	5.9	3.2	8.1	0.3
38001	Adams County, North Dakota	53.0	48.6	4.5	12.4	9.2	2.8	2.4	19.8	0.4
38003	Barnes County, North Dakota	58.6	54.4	4.2	7.7	11.6	7.2	2.3	12.2	0.4
38005	Benson County, North Dakota	52.7	50.6	2.0	6.5	20.6	3.0	3.8	13.0	0.3
38007	Billings County, North Dakota	50.4	37.9	12.4	19.1	11.0	2.3	4.3	12.4	0.5
38009	Bottineau County, North Dakota	57.9	52.5	5.4	9.8	8.2	5.0	3.5	15.0	0.6
38011	Bowman County, North Dakota	62.9	58.1	4.8	8.7	12.6	2.6	1.5	11.4	0.3
38013	Burke County, North Dakota	63.5	57.7	5.7	7.4	8.1	2.0	4.3	14.0	0.6
38015	Burleigh County, North Dakota	64.4	61.5	2.9	12.2	6.4	8.8	2.6	5.4	0.2
38017	Cass County, North Dakota	70.6	67.8	2.8	12.3	5.4	4.8	2.4	4.5	0.1
38019	Cavalier County, North Dakota	56.3	51.7	4.6	8.3	10.1	3.5	2.4	19.0	0.5
38021	Dickey County, North Dakota	65.2	60.7	4.5	9.6	6.9	3.2	1.6	10.9	2.6
38023	Divide County, North Dakota	49.8	44.1	5.7	5.1	11.2	0.7	3.4	29.8	0.0
38025	Dunn County, North Dakota	53.2	48.0	5.2	11.8	11.2	3.0	2.6	16.3	1.9
38027	Eddy County, North Dakota	45.9	43.6	2.2	15.0	12.8	4.0	4.6	17.5	0.2
38029	Emmons County, North Dakota	53.8	45.8	8.0	4.5	10.5	4.0	3.2	22.8	1.2
38031	Foster County, North Dakota	59.4	56.4	3.0	10.2	5.7	2.9	4.3	16.3	1.1
38033	Golden Valley County, North Dakota	50.5	45.0	5.5	13.6	10.9	2.9	4.0	14.2	3.8

Table C. County—Labor Force, Employment, and Educational Data, 2011–2015—*Continued*

| | | Class of worker for civilian employed population age 16 and older | | | | | | | | |
| | | Private for-profit wage and salary workers | | | | Government workers | | | | |
Fips code	State/county	Total private for-profit wage and salary workers	Employees of private companies	Self-employed in own incorporated business	Private not-for-profit wage and salary workers	Local government workers	State government workers	Federal government workers	Self-employed in own not incorporated business	Unpaid family workers
38035	Grand Forks County, North Dakota	61.8	59.1	2.8	11.9	6.5	11.4	4.0	4.0	0.2
38037	Grant County, North Dakota	41.2	37.5	3.7	11.2	6.5	2.2	4.6	32.8	1.5
38039	Griggs County, North Dakota	62.3	56.2	6.1	8.3	7.7	2.5	0.9	17.4	0.9
38041	Hettinger County, North Dakota	54.9	51.8	3.1	6.9	9.5	5.0	1.6	20.9	1.2
38043	Kidder County, North Dakota	50.7	46.2	4.5	7.9	6.6	4.8	4.9	25.1	0.1
38045	LaMoure County, North Dakota	54.1	49.5	4.6	9.6	8.8	3.4	1.9	20.4	1.9
38047	Logan County, North Dakota	49.2	43.1	6.1	9.2	5.0	4.0	2.7	27.8	2.0
38049	McHenry County, North Dakota	58.8	54.9	4.0	7.9	7.9	2.6	3.2	19.4	0.2
38051	McIntosh County, North Dakota	49.7	43.4	6.3	13.0	12.2	2.7	1.8	19.5	1.1
38053	McKenzie County, North Dakota	68.7	64.8	3.9	7.1	6.8	3.6	2.7	10.9	0.2
38055	McLean County, North Dakota	54.9	51.9	3.0	10.9	8.8	5.3	3.8	15.4	0.9
38057	Mercer County, North Dakota	72.1	68.0	4.2	8.2	6.9	3.4	2.8	6.6	0.0
38059	Morton County, North Dakota	66.9	63.0	3.8	8.6	6.5	6.5	2.8	8.6	0.2
38061	Mountrail County, North Dakota	50.5	46.9	3.6	7.7	21.7	2.3	3.2	12.1	2.4
38063	Nelson County, North Dakota	53.6	50.3	3.3	9.8	10.7	4.9	2.4	18.5	0.1
38065	Oliver County, North Dakota	50.9	46.3	4.6	9.1	10.4	4.4	1.5	22.6	1.1
38067	Pembina County, North Dakota	61.2	58.4	2.8	10.7	8.0	3.1	5.4	11.5	0.2
38069	Pierce County, North Dakota	54.9	52.4	2.5	17.5	5.1	2.0	1.9	18.4	0.3
38071	Ramsey County, North Dakota	61.7	58.2	3.5	11.3	6.1	8.0	4.1	8.5	0.3
38073	Ransom County, North Dakota	64.1	58.8	5.3	8.5	5.8	7.1	1.8	12.2	0.6
38075	Renville County, North Dakota	60.5	56.5	4.0	3.4	9.5	2.4	6.5	17.3	0.5
38077	Richland County, North Dakota	66.9	62.8	4.1	8.0	7.4	6.3	1.6	9.7	0.1
38079	Rolette County, North Dakota	41.3	39.8	1.5	3.0	30.5	3.5	12.6	8.7	0.3
38081	Sargent County, North Dakota	68.6	63.8	4.8	5.3	7.0	3.5	2.9	11.6	1.1
38083	Sheridan County, North Dakota	52.3	49.1	3.2	7.0	7.2	3.7	2.2	27.2	0.5
38085	Sioux County, North Dakota	27.0	24.8	2.2	5.9	38.8	5.0	12.9	10.2	0.1
38087	Slope County, North Dakota	53.1	47.2	6.0	3.0	9.3	2.7	3.6	27.5	0.9
38089	Stark County, North Dakota	70.7	67.3	3.4	6.8	7.0	4.5	2.1	8.9	0.1
38091	Steele County, North Dakota	63.3	59.0	4.3	9.5	4.4	2.5	1.5	18.1	0.7
38093	Stutsman County, North Dakota	63.0	60.4	2.6	12.5	7.0	7.7	1.1	8.2	0.6
38095	Towner County, North Dakota	50.0	48.5	1.5	6.4	10.4	3.4	2.0	26.9	0.8
38097	Traill County, North Dakota	61.1	57.3	3.8	11.2	7.4	7.7	4.1	8.4	0.2
38099	Walsh County, North Dakota	63.3	57.7	5.6	10.2	7.6	5.8	1.6	11.1	0.4
38101	Ward County, North Dakota	67.2	65.3	1.9	9.6	6.4	4.1	6.2	6.4	0.1
38103	Wells County, North Dakota	57.9	50.5	7.4	9.9	9.8	2.9	2.9	16.1	0.5
38105	Williams County, North Dakota	70.2	65.1	5.1	8.1	5.9	3.4	1.9	10.3	0.2
39000	**Ohio**	73.1	70.4	2.7	9.2	7.2	3.5	1.8	5.0	0.1
39001	Adams County, Ohio	75.0	72.6	2.4	6.3	7.3	3.0	2.0	6.0	0.3
39003	Allen County, Ohio	75.0	72.8	2.2	10.2	6.7	3.3	0.5	4.1	0.2
39005	Ashland County, Ohio	73.7	71.9	1.8	10.5	6.7	3.4	0.9	4.4	0.5
39007	Ashtabula County, Ohio	76.8	74.1	2.7	7.7	7.0	2.2	1.2	5.0	0.1
39009	Athens County, Ohio	54.7	53.0	1.8	9.2	8.9	20.8	1.6	4.5	0.3
39011	Auglaize County, Ohio	77.2	75.0	2.1	7.2	7.6	2.0	1.0	4.9	0.1
39013	Belmont County, Ohio	74.6	72.8	1.7	7.6	8.0	4.7	1.2	3.8	0.1
39015	Brown County, Ohio	72.0	70.3	1.7	6.1	7.4	4.3	1.6	8.2	0.3
39017	Butler County, Ohio	77.2	74.9	2.3	7.3	6.3	3.6	1.2	4.3	0.1
39019	Carroll County, Ohio	74.6	71.0	3.6	6.7	6.5	2.2	0.9	8.8	0.3
39021	Champaign County, Ohio	71.7	69.9	1.8	9.3	8.4	3.5	1.3	5.9	0.0
39023	Clark County, Ohio	71.7	69.6	2.1	9.9	6.6	3.2	3.1	5.4	0.2
39025	Clermont County, Ohio	78.3	75.5	2.8	7.3	5.4	2.4	1.4	5.1	0.1
39027	Clinton County, Ohio	76.8	74.3	2.6	5.2	7.5	2.7	1.9	5.7	0.3
39029	Columbiana County, Ohio	76.1	74.0	2.1	6.9	7.0	2.1	1.5	6.4	0.1
39031	Coshocton County, Ohio	73.7	70.8	2.9	7.8	7.5	2.3	0.8	7.2	0.7
39033	Crawford County, Ohio	75.8	74.1	1.7	7.0	7.3	3.6	0.8	5.5	0.0
39035	Cuyahoga County, Ohio	70.4	67.4	3.1	12.7	8.4	1.8	2.4	4.2	0.1
39037	Darke County, Ohio	76.3	73.0	3.3	6.2	6.6	1.9	1.0	7.4	0.5
39039	Defiance County, Ohio	75.3	73.5	1.8	8.2	7.1	3.3	0.7	5.3	0.1
39041	Delaware County, Ohio	71.5	66.9	4.6	8.5	7.6	5.2	1.5	5.7	0.1
39043	Erie County, Ohio	73.1	70.1	2.9	8.3	7.9	3.6	1.5	5.5	0.1
39045	Fairfield County, Ohio	70.9	67.8	3.2	8.1	9.3	4.3	2.4	4.8	0.2
39047	Fayette County, Ohio	73.9	71.1	2.8	5.8	9.0	3.6	0.8	6.6	0.3
39049	Franklin County, Ohio	71.9	69.7	2.2	8.9	5.9	7.1	1.8	4.3	0.1
39051	Fulton County, Ohio	72.4	70.1	2.3	10.1	6.8	3.6	0.6	6.4	0.1
39053	Gallia County, Ohio	71.2	70.0	1.2	10.1	7.3	5.1	0.6	5.5	0.2
39055	Geauga County, Ohio	72.3	66.0	6.3	9.7	7.2	1.4	1.1	8.1	0.2
39057	Greene County, Ohio	63.7	60.9	2.8	10.0	7.3	3.7	10.2	5.0	0.2
39059	Guernsey County, Ohio	72.0	69.3	2.7	7.8	7.9	5.0	0.8	6.1	0.4
39061	Hamilton County, Ohio	73.4	70.7	2.8	11.4	6.1	2.4	2.0	4.7	0.1
39063	Hancock County, Ohio	77.9	75.4	2.4	8.4	6.5	1.9	0.6	4.7	0.1
39065	Hardin County, Ohio	74.1	72.8	1.3	7.7	8.2	2.7	0.9	6.4	0.1
39067	Harrison County, Ohio	77.3	75.6	1.7	4.6	7.3	3.6	1.5	5.0	0.7
39069	Henry County, Ohio	71.5	69.5	1.9	9.8	7.8	4.0	1.6	5.1	0.2
39071	Highland County, Ohio	72.3	69.9	2.4	5.8	7.4	4.4	0.9	8.8	0.3
39073	Hocking County, Ohio	68.4	65.4	3.0	8.2	9.2	6.2	1.2	6.2	0.6

Table C. County—Labor Force, Employment, and Educational Data, 2011–2015—*Continued*

| | | Class of worker for civilian employed population age 16 and older | | | | | | | | |
| | | Private for-profit wage and salary workers | | | | Government workers | | | | |
Fips code	State/county	Total private for-profit wage and salary workers	Employees of private companies	Self-employed in own incorporated business	Private not-for-profit wage and salary workers	Local government workers	State government workers	Federal government workers	Self-employed in own not incorporated business	Unpaid family workers
39075	Holmes County, Ohio	76.0	71.0	5.0	5.2	4.5	1.0	0.2	12.3	0.7
39077	Huron County, Ohio	77.0	74.0	3.1	7.5	6.6	2.8	0.8	5.1	0.2
39079	Jackson County, Ohio	65.6	64.3	1.3	10.8	10.8	6.0	1.4	5.0	0.3
39081	Jefferson County, Ohio	74.6	72.9	1.7	9.1	7.8	1.9	1.1	5.3	0.1
39083	Knox County, Ohio	70.9	67.9	3.0	10.1	7.6	3.1	1.1	7.1	0.2
39085	Lake County, Ohio	77.5	74.6	2.9	9.1	7.2	1.4	1.0	3.7	0.1
39087	Lawrence County, Ohio	71.1	69.8	1.3	9.5	8.8	3.5	2.8	4.4	0.0
39089	Licking County, Ohio	71.1	68.8	2.3	9.2	6.9	4.0	2.4	6.3	0.1
39091	Logan County, Ohio	75.0	73.1	1.9	7.4	6.9	2.4	0.7	7.7	0.1
39093	Lorain County, Ohio	73.5	70.8	2.7	9.8	8.6	1.9	1.9	4.1	0.1
39095	Lucas County, Ohio	72.3	70.3	2.0	10.6	6.9	4.1	1.2	4.7	0.2
39097	Madison County, Ohio	71.1	68.5	2.6	7.3	7.8	5.0	2.0	6.7	0.1
39099	Mahoning County, Ohio	73.7	71.1	2.6	8.5	7.2	3.8	1.2	5.3	0.1
39101	Marion County, Ohio	73.4	71.4	2.1	8.9	8.5	3.4	1.2	4.5	0.1
39103	Medina County, Ohio	75.8	72.1	3.6	7.7	7.5	1.8	2.0	5.1	0.1
39105	Meigs County, Ohio	65.4	64.3	1.1	6.5	11.6	7.3	1.6	7.5	0.2
39107	Mercer County, Ohio	79.9	76.7	3.2	4.7	6.8	1.7	0.7	6.1	0.1
39109	Miami County, Ohio	76.4	73.1	3.3	7.0	7.6	2.1	1.7	4.8	0.4
39111	Monroe County, Ohio	73.3	70.8	2.5	5.0	7.5	5.6	1.2	7.3	0.1
39113	Montgomery County, Ohio	70.7	68.4	2.3	10.1	7.3	2.3	4.5	5.0	0.1
39115	Morgan County, Ohio	64.3	62.8	1.5	9.1	11.7	3.8	1.3	9.2	0.5
39117	Morrow County, Ohio	70.5	68.2	2.3	7.0	11.0	3.1	0.9	6.9	0.5
39119	Muskingum County, Ohio	75.2	73.2	2.0	8.5	7.1	3.4	0.8	4.9	0.1
39121	Noble County, Ohio	69.1	65.6	3.5	9.5	7.0	5.4	2.8	6.1	0.0
39123	Ottawa County, Ohio	73.1	70.3	2.8	9.2	7.2	3.2	1.2	5.8	0.3
39125	Paulding County, Ohio	74.0	70.5	3.5	7.0	8.4	2.5	2.1	6.1	0.0
39127	Perry County, Ohio	70.9	69.3	1.6	8.4	10.4	4.3	1.3	4.8	0.2
39129	Pickaway County, Ohio	69.5	67.1	2.5	8.0	10.1	4.9	1.9	5.4	0.4
39131	Pike County, Ohio	65.9	63.3	2.6	7.9	9.3	6.7	3.2	6.6	0.4
39133	Portage County, Ohio	76.6	73.4	3.1	6.6	7.2	3.8	1.0	4.7	0.1
39135	Preble County, Ohio	75.7	73.2	2.4	6.4	6.4	3.9	1.1	6.5	0.0
39137	Putnam County, Ohio	75.7	72.3	3.4	9.0	7.2	3.0	0.9	4.1	0.1
39139	Richland County, Ohio	73.4	71.3	2.1	8.3	6.9	3.9	1.5	5.8	0.2
39141	Ross County, Ohio	68.5	66.6	1.8	9.8	7.7	6.2	3.4	4.2	0.2
39143	Sandusky County, Ohio	77.5	74.9	2.6	7.9	6.6	2.4	0.9	4.6	0.1
39145	Scioto County, Ohio	65.9	64.6	1.4	10.0	9.3	6.9	2.5	4.9	0.4
39147	Seneca County, Ohio	74.3	72.3	2.0	9.7	7.3	3.0	0.8	4.8	0.1
39149	Shelby County, Ohio	79.0	76.9	2.1	6.0	6.8	2.3	0.7	4.8	0.3
39151	Stark County, Ohio	75.2	72.5	2.8	9.1	7.2	2.0	1.0	5.3	0.1
39153	Summit County, Ohio	74.9	71.6	3.3	9.3	6.9	3.0	1.3	4.5	0.1
39155	Trumbull County, Ohio	75.4	72.9	2.5	7.5	7.3	2.8	1.5	5.4	0.2
39157	Tuscarawas County, Ohio	76.6	74.1	2.5	7.9	6.2	3.0	0.9	5.3	0.2
39159	Union County, Ohio	71.7	69.0	2.7	6.0	8.1	5.3	0.8	7.6	0.4
39161	Van Wert County, Ohio	77.4	74.4	3.0	6.3	7.4	2.1	0.5	6.1	0.3
39163	Vinton County, Ohio	67.6	66.3	1.3	8.2	8.6	7.7	2.1	5.8	0.0
39165	Warren County, Ohio	76.3	72.8	3.5	7.7	6.5	2.2	2.0	5.2	0.1
39167	Washington County, Ohio	70.4	67.7	2.7	9.6	8.5	3.6	2.8	4.8	0.1
39169	Wayne County, Ohio	72.3	69.4	2.9	8.4	6.2	3.7	1.0	8.1	0.3
39171	Williams County, Ohio	75.3	73.1	2.2	6.8	9.1	2.3	1.1	5.2	0.2
39173	Wood County, Ohio	70.6	68.5	2.0	8.7	7.6	7.5	1.0	4.5	0.1
39175	Wyandot County, Ohio	76.1	73.7	2.4	7.5	8.4	2.4	1.1	4.4	0.0
40000	**Oklahoma**	70.1	66.6	3.5	6.5	5.8	7.1	4.0	6.2	0.2
40001	Adair County, Oklahoma	65.6	63.3	2.3	4.9	8.0	9.9	4.0	7.3	0.4
40003	Alfalfa County, Oklahoma	60.9	57.9	3.1	3.0	7.8	10.2	2.1	15.6	0.4
40005	Atoka County, Oklahoma	64.7	60.7	4.0	3.6	8.1	12.1	2.7	8.3	0.4
40007	Beaver County, Oklahoma	67.5	63.1	4.4	5.8	7.6	7.5	2.2	9.3	0.2
40009	Beckham County, Oklahoma	74.8	72.5	2.3	3.2	5.7	4.0	2.7	9.2	0.4
40011	Blaine County, Oklahoma	60.5	57.2	3.3	5.1	8.5	9.7	4.3	10.8	1.1
40013	Bryan County, Oklahoma	67.9	65.1	2.8	4.4	5.4	9.5	6.5	6.1	0.1
40015	Caddo County, Oklahoma	62.7	60.4	2.2	4.5	8.4	9.5	7.2	7.7	0.1
40017	Canadian County, Oklahoma	71.4	67.4	4.0	6.3	4.7	6.2	5.4	5.9	0.1
40019	Carter County, Oklahoma	75.3	71.1	4.2	6.6	4.5	5.7	2.0	5.6	0.2
40021	Cherokee County, Oklahoma	57.8	55.1	2.7	6.7	10.5	11.5	6.9	6.5	0.2
40023	Choctaw County, Oklahoma	66.2	63.9	2.3	5.4	11.2	6.7	2.6	7.8	0.1
40025	Cimarron County, Oklahoma	57.0	51.4	5.7	6.1	13.6	7.4	2.5	13.0	0.4
40027	Cleveland County, Oklahoma	67.0	63.6	3.4	6.3	5.1	10.6	6.1	4.9	0.1
40029	Coal County, Oklahoma	60.2	59.1	1.2	4.4	6.8	16.2	2.2	9.5	0.7
40031	Comanche County, Oklahoma	60.6	58.2	2.5	5.5	6.9	7.8	13.0	5.9	0.2
40033	Cotton County, Oklahoma	63.6	60.3	3.3	4.8	10.0	6.6	4.2	10.8	0.0
40035	Craig County, Oklahoma	57.9	56.2	1.6	9.9	8.9	11.0	1.7	10.2	0.5
40037	Creek County, Oklahoma	75.9	72.2	3.7	5.8	5.3	5.7	1.3	5.7	0.2
40039	Custer County, Oklahoma	65.2	62.8	2.4	6.0	10.0	7.3	2.5	8.1	0.8
40041	Delaware County, Oklahoma	65.9	62.6	3.4	6.7	8.7	6.9	2.8	8.6	0.3
40043	Dewey County, Oklahoma	63.1	59.1	4.0	2.8	12.2	3.9	1.6	15.0	1.5

Table C. County—Labor Force, Employment, and Educational Data, 2011–2015—*Continued*

| | | Class of worker for civilian employed population age 16 and older | | | | | | | | |
| | | Private for-profit wage and salary workers | | | Private not-for-profit wage and salary workers | Government workers | | | Self-employed in own not incorporated business | Unpaid family workers |
Fips code	State/county	Total private for-profit wage and salary workers	Employees of private companies	Self-employed in own incorporated business		Local government workers	State government workers	Federal government workers		
40045	Ellis County, Oklahoma	60.9	57.2	3.6	5.6	14.4	4.2	2.3	11.5	1.2
40047	Garfield County, Oklahoma	70.6	67.4	3.2	7.0	5.3	6.1	4.1	6.7	0.2
40049	Garvin County, Oklahoma	72.7	69.1	3.6	4.5	4.8	7.3	2.5	7.8	0.4
40051	Grady County, Oklahoma	72.2	67.7	4.5	4.1	6.6	6.9	3.8	6.4	0.1
40053	Grant County, Oklahoma	60.2	56.8	3.4	4.4	8.8	7.2	1.5	17.7	0.1
40055	Greer County, Oklahoma	57.6	54.9	2.7	4.3	12.9	11.4	2.6	10.8	0.4
40057	Harmon County, Oklahoma	55.8	51.4	4.4	7.1	10.4	12.1	1.1	12.9	0.6
40059	Harper County, Oklahoma	62.7	61.0	1.7	2.0	15.9	7.8	0.8	10.2	0.6
40061	Haskell County, Oklahoma	71.8	67.9	3.9	6.5	5.3	5.1	1.7	9.4	0.2
40063	Hughes County, Oklahoma	64.2	60.8	3.4	3.6	11.6	7.3	5.3	7.4	0.6
40065	Jackson County, Oklahoma	60.7	57.3	3.4	4.4	6.2	7.0	16.1	5.7	0.1
40067	Jefferson County, Oklahoma	66.9	64.6	2.4	4.9	8.0	7.5	1.4	11.1	0.1
40069	Johnston County, Oklahoma	64.3	60.6	3.8	5.3	4.5	14.1	4.6	6.9	0.2
40071	Kay County, Oklahoma	72.6	69.8	2.8	5.5	6.3	6.9	2.6	5.9	0.2
40073	Kingfisher County, Oklahoma	73.2	67.3	5.9	4.2	5.3	6.3	1.4	9.3	0.3
40075	Kiowa County, Oklahoma	64.5	61.8	2.7	3.3	5.8	10.5	3.6	11.7	0.5
40077	Latimer County, Oklahoma	60.4	58.9	1.5	6.4	8.7	13.7	2.8	7.7	0.3
40079	Le Flore County, Oklahoma	69.7	67.0	2.7	4.6	6.6	9.6	2.4	6.8	0.2
40081	Lincoln County, Oklahoma	67.9	64.6	3.3	5.3	5.5	7.3	4.6	9.3	0.1
40083	Logan County, Oklahoma	65.9	61.8	4.1	10.0	6.3	8.4	3.2	5.8	0.2
40085	Love County, Oklahoma	74.0	68.2	5.7	4.6	5.4	3.9	3.9	8.0	0.2
40087	McClain County, Oklahoma	67.5	63.9	3.5	4.0	7.3	7.4	5.2	8.4	0.2
40089	McCurtain County, Oklahoma	70.1	67.2	2.9	5.0	5.4	8.0	3.2	8.2	0.2
40091	McIntosh County, Oklahoma	71.3	65.9	5.3	2.9	8.5	7.6	3.3	6.4	0.0
40093	Major County, Oklahoma	67.8	64.3	3.5	4.8	6.5	7.2	1.4	11.5	0.9
40095	Marshall County, Oklahoma	73.1	70.1	3.0	3.1	7.4	6.8	2.8	5.6	1.2
40097	Mayes County, Oklahoma	67.0	63.2	3.8	6.2	6.2	10.5	1.9	7.8	0.4
40099	Murray County, Oklahoma	65.2	62.3	2.9	5.6	7.6	9.6	4.8	6.2	1.0
40101	Muskogee County, Oklahoma	67.7	65.1	2.5	4.7	7.2	7.2	7.1	6.0	0.1
40103	Noble County, Oklahoma	62.3	58.1	4.2	6.0	11.6	10.7	2.9	5.9	0.7
40105	Nowata County, Oklahoma	69.0	66.4	2.6	10.2	6.5	6.8	1.8	5.5	0.3
40107	Okfuskee County, Oklahoma	64.5	58.5	6.0	3.3	8.1	12.8	3.6	7.3	0.5
40109	Oklahoma County, Oklahoma	71.5	67.6	3.9	7.2	4.3	6.2	4.6	6.1	0.2
40111	Okmulgee County, Oklahoma	66.7	64.1	2.6	7.0	9.5	7.9	2.4	6.0	0.4
40113	Osage County, Oklahoma	72.1	68.7	3.4	4.9	7.3	6.4	3.3	5.9	0.0
40115	Ottawa County, Oklahoma	66.4	64.3	2.1	7.3	8.0	10.3	2.7	5.1	0.3
40117	Pawnee County, Oklahoma	69.1	66.7	2.3	5.2	6.9	6.6	3.1	9.0	0.1
40119	Payne County, Oklahoma	59.9	57.2	2.7	7.0	6.7	18.7	2.0	5.2	0.5
40121	Pittsburg County, Oklahoma	64.5	61.4	3.1	5.0	5.8	9.2	9.8	5.8	0.0
40123	Pontotoc County, Oklahoma	58.8	55.8	3.1	6.1	6.5	17.4	5.4	5.7	0.1
40125	Pottawatomie County, Oklahoma	61.0	58.3	2.6	7.0	8.9	8.0	8.7	6.3	0.2
40127	Pushmataha County, Oklahoma	61.5	58.3	3.2	5.0	9.2	10.1	4.1	10.0	0.1
40129	Roger Mills County, Oklahoma	56.2	53.3	2.9	2.9	17.4	5.8	3.4	11.7	2.5
40131	Rogers County, Oklahoma	73.7	69.5	4.2	6.8	5.6	6.5	2.0	5.2	0.2
40133	Seminole County, Oklahoma	68.1	65.6	2.5	4.5	9.9	7.1	4.2	6.1	0.1
40135	Sequoyah County, Oklahoma	68.5	65.1	3.4	4.4	8.8	8.2	3.2	6.6	0.3
40137	Stephens County, Oklahoma	72.2	68.9	3.3	5.8	5.2	6.7	2.7	7.0	0.4
40139	Texas County, Oklahoma	75.0	71.1	3.8	3.7	6.7	7.5	1.3	5.4	0.3
40141	Tillman County, Oklahoma	62.5	58.9	3.6	3.4	9.9	10.2	4.3	9.1	0.6
40143	Tulsa County, Oklahoma	76.2	72.6	3.6	8.3	4.5	3.7	1.5	5.6	0.2
40145	Wagoner County, Oklahoma	75.4	71.7	3.7	5.8	6.1	4.5	2.5	5.5	0.2
40147	Washington County, Oklahoma	72.6	70.2	2.4	7.9	7.9	4.5	1.1	5.9	0.2
40149	Washita County, Oklahoma	66.0	60.7	5.3	5.6	10.1	5.7	1.6	10.7	0.4
40151	Woods County, Oklahoma	62.3	59.7	2.6	6.7	7.3	11.2	2.9	9.5	0.1
40153	Woodward County, Oklahoma	73.4	69.2	4.2	5.5	6.6	6.4	1.3	6.6	0.2
41000	**Oregon**	68.6	64.5	4.1	9.4	6.8	5.3	2.0	7.8	0.2
41001	Baker County, Oregon	60.7	54.4	6.3	10.5	9.9	5.0	4.2	9.5	0.3
41003	Benton County, Oregon	54.1	51.4	2.7	10.8	8.4	18.3	1.6	6.7	0.1
41005	Clackamas County, Oregon	72.9	67.4	5.5	8.1	6.1	3.5	1.5	7.8	0.2
41007	Clatsop County, Oregon	64.8	59.7	5.1	10.1	8.1	5.5	2.4	8.9	0.3
41009	Columbia County, Oregon	72.4	68.7	3.7	7.1	7.0	4.1	1.6	7.7	0.3
41011	Coos County, Oregon	64.2	59.9	4.3	7.6	8.1	7.4	2.1	9.9	0.5
41013	Crook County, Oregon	67.7	63.6	4.1	7.0	9.1	2.8	3.2	10.0	0.1
41015	Curry County, Oregon	57.8	53.4	4.4	9.9	9.6	7.6	2.3	12.9	0.0
41017	Deschutes County, Oregon	69.9	64.4	5.5	7.4	6.4	3.6	1.6	10.9	0.2
41019	Douglas County, Oregon	63.1	60.0	3.1	8.9	9.2	4.5	5.8	8.2	0.3
41021	Gilliam County, Oregon	63.7	60.5	3.2	4.0	20.1	3.2	1.1	7.5	0.4
41023	Grant County, Oregon	48.7	43.5	5.2	8.9	14.2	6.6	8.6	12.4	0.6
41025	Harney County, Oregon	48.6	43.1	5.5	4.8	12.2	6.4	10.9	16.2	1.0
41027	Hood River County, Oregon	71.4	65.9	5.5	7.6	8.4	3.4	1.5	7.7	0.0
41029	Jackson County, Oregon	66.0	61.3	4.7	9.6	6.2	4.6	3.0	10.6	0.1
41031	Jefferson County, Oregon	63.3	61.1	2.1	6.6	14.5	4.0	4.8	6.7	0.1
41033	Josephine County, Oregon	67.5	63.3	4.3	8.5	7.6	4.1	1.5	10.7	0.1
41035	Klamath County, Oregon	65.5	62.3	3.2	7.8	10.3	4.8	4.2	7.1	0.4
41037	Lake County, Oregon	54.2	48.9	5.3	5.2	10.6	8.6	8.6	11.5	1.3
41039	Lane County, Oregon	65.1	61.1	4.0	10.8	7.0	7.2	1.7	8.0	0.2

Table C. County—Labor Force, Employment, and Educational Data, 2011–2015—*Continued*

| | | Class of worker for civilian employed population age 16 and older | | | | | | | | |
| | | Private for-profit wage and salary workers | | | | Government workers | | | | |
Fips code	State/county	Total private for-profit wage and salary workers	Employees of private companies	Self-employed in own incorporated business	Private not-for-profit wage and salary workers	Local government workers	State government workers	Federal government workers	Self-employed in own not incorporated business	Unpaid family workers
41041	Lincoln County, Oregon	64.0	59.4	4.5	8.4	8.7	5.4	2.1	11.3	0.2
41043	Linn County, Oregon	69.5	65.7	3.8	8.2	7.4	6.3	1.8	6.6	0.1
41045	Malheur County, Oregon	62.5	57.7	4.8	8.1	9.9	7.7	1.6	9.8	0.5
41047	Marion County, Oregon	66.7	63.6	3.0	8.8	6.9	10.2	1.6	5.8	0.1
41049	Morrow County, Oregon	74.6	72.0	2.6	2.7	8.5	4.5	2.5	7.2	0.0
41051	Multnomah County, Oregon	68.0	63.9	4.1	12.1	6.2	3.8	1.9	7.8	0.1
41053	Polk County, Oregon	60.2	55.3	4.9	9.4	7.9	13.0	2.5	6.9	0.2
41055	Sherman County, Oregon	65.4	57.8	7.6	6.3	10.6	5.1	1.7	10.2	0.7
41057	Tillamook County, Oregon	64.0	60.0	4.0	9.6	9.2	5.5	1.8	9.8	0.1
41059	Umatilla County, Oregon	67.1	64.7	2.4	7.2	7.3	8.6	3.1	6.5	0.2
41061	Union County, Oregon	59.5	56.0	3.5	10.6	6.3	9.5	3.9	9.9	0.4
41063	Wallowa County, Oregon	58.1	46.9	11.2	7.5	9.4	6.8	4.6	13.5	0.2
41065	Wasco County, Oregon	66.0	62.7	3.3	8.9	8.8	4.9	3.1	8.3	0.1
41067	Washington County, Oregon	76.3	72.9	3.4	8.1	5.3	2.8	1.4	5.9	0.1
41069	Wheeler County, Oregon	48.0	43.3	4.6	8.2	19.0	7.6	4.1	12.8	0.4
41071	Yamhill County, Oregon	72.2	68.0	4.2	7.9	7.3	3.3	1.4	7.7	0.2
42000	**Pennsylvania**	72.4	69.6	2.8	11.5	5.5	3.4	2.0	5.1	0.1
42001	Adams County, Pennsylvania	72.0	69.5	2.6	10.9	5.6	2.8	2.6	5.9	0.2
42003	Allegheny County, Pennsylvania	70.5	67.7	2.7	15.7	5.3	2.0	2.0	4.5	0.1
42005	Armstrong County, Pennsylvania	74.8	73.0	1.8	10.2	5.6	3.1	1.3	4.9	0.1
42007	Beaver County, Pennsylvania	74.9	73.0	2.0	10.7	5.4	2.7	1.8	4.5	0.0
42009	Bedford County, Pennsylvania	73.7	71.2	2.5	7.3	4.8	4.7	1.3	7.9	0.4
42011	Berks County, Pennsylvania	76.8	74.0	2.8	9.0	5.4	2.7	1.1	5.0	0.1
42013	Blair County, Pennsylvania	72.2	69.8	2.4	10.5	5.9	4.9	2.0	4.3	0.2
42015	Bradford County, Pennsylvania	69.8	66.4	3.4	13.0	6.0	2.7	1.3	7.1	0.2
42017	Bucks County, Pennsylvania	76.8	72.5	4.3	8.7	5.2	2.3	1.5	5.3	0.2
42019	Butler County, Pennsylvania	74.2	71.2	3.0	10.7	4.2	3.2	2.4	5.2	0.1
42021	Cambria County, Pennsylvania	68.8	66.3	2.5	12.8	5.3	6.3	2.5	4.2	0.1
42023	Cameron County, Pennsylvania	74.6	70.1	4.6	6.2	7.0	5.3	0.9	5.6	0.4
42025	Carbon County, Pennsylvania	76.2	73.4	2.8	7.6	6.5	3.3	1.6	4.8	0.1
42027	Centre County, Pennsylvania	64.6	62.7	1.9	14.3	4.6	10.3	1.2	4.9	0.1
42029	Chester County, Pennsylvania	76.4	72.4	4.0	9.5	4.7	2.3	1.4	5.5	0.1
42031	Clarion County, Pennsylvania	69.2	66.8	2.4	9.6	4.8	8.1	1.3	6.7	0.4
42033	Clearfield County, Pennsylvania	70.8	68.4	2.5	9.6	5.3	6.4	1.5	6.3	0.2
42035	Clinton County, Pennsylvania	70.8	68.7	2.1	8.1	6.1	7.5	1.4	5.7	0.4
42037	Columbia County, Pennsylvania	69.3	66.9	2.4	11.2	5.6	7.1	1.4	5.2	0.1
42039	Crawford County, Pennsylvania	68.1	65.0	3.1	11.9	6.2	4.2	0.9	8.5	0.3
42041	Cumberland County, Pennsylvania	68.1	65.7	2.4	10.9	4.7	7.0	4.3	4.9	0.2
42043	Dauphin County, Pennsylvania	67.3	64.9	2.4	11.6	4.8	9.2	3.2	3.8	0.1
42045	Delaware County, Pennsylvania	72.0	68.5	3.5	13.3	5.7	2.0	2.1	4.8	0.1
42047	Elk County, Pennsylvania	77.2	74.1	3.2	9.9	3.9	3.1	0.8	4.9	0.2
42049	Erie County, Pennsylvania	72.0	69.5	2.5	13.0	5.1	3.7	1.4	4.8	0.1
42051	Fayette County, Pennsylvania	74.6	72.5	2.1	10.1	4.6	4.6	1.2	4.8	0.2
42053	Forest County, Pennsylvania	55.3	51.8	3.6	11.1	8.0	11.3	4.7	9.4	0.1
42055	Franklin County, Pennsylvania	69.9	67.8	2.2	11.1	5.3	3.1	3.8	6.4	0.3
42057	Fulton County, Pennsylvania	69.1	66.6	2.6	7.6	7.2	6.2	2.0	7.5	0.5
42059	Greene County, Pennsylvania	69.9	68.5	1.4	11.0	6.2	7.9	2.0	2.8	0.1
42061	Huntingdon County, Pennsylvania	66.8	64.5	2.3	11.0	5.0	8.3	1.8	7.0	0.2
42063	Indiana County, Pennsylvania	69.4	67.0	2.4	9.0	5.0	8.9	0.9	6.7	0.2
42065	Jefferson County, Pennsylvania	72.3	70.1	2.2	9.7	5.1	4.3	1.1	7.2	0.3
42067	Juniata County, Pennsylvania	74.9	71.9	3.1	6.7	3.2	6.5	1.3	7.2	0.2
42069	Lackawanna County, Pennsylvania	71.2	68.1	3.1	11.4	5.7	4.2	2.9	4.4	0.2
42071	Lancaster County, Pennsylvania	73.7	71.1	2.6	11.0	4.6	2.3	1.2	6.8	0.3
42073	Lawrence County, Pennsylvania	72.9	70.5	2.4	10.7	5.4	3.6	1.7	5.5	0.1
42075	Lebanon County, Pennsylvania	72.1	69.7	2.4	8.9	5.8	3.4	3.1	6.4	0.2
42077	Lehigh County, Pennsylvania	75.3	72.8	2.5	11.7	5.2	2.3	1.0	4.4	0.1
42079	Luzerne County, Pennsylvania	74.7	72.2	2.6	8.9	5.0	3.4	2.9	4.8	0.2
42081	Lycoming County, Pennsylvania	72.1	69.8	2.3	11.8	4.9	4.4	1.8	5.0	0.1
42083	McKean County, Pennsylvania	68.2	66.8	1.3	13.2	6.0	3.9	2.0	6.7	0.1
42085	Mercer County, Pennsylvania	71.1	68.7	2.4	11.7	4.8	4.6	1.5	6.0	0.2
42087	Mifflin County, Pennsylvania	72.8	70.9	1.9	10.4	4.3	3.6	1.6	7.1	0.2
42089	Monroe County, Pennsylvania	73.7	70.4	3.3	7.2	6.1	4.9	3.1	4.8	0.1
42091	Montgomery County, Pennsylvania	74.8	70.5	4.3	11.4	4.8	2.0	1.3	5.5	0.1
42093	Montour County, Pennsylvania	60.6	58.6	2.0	24.0	5.4	3.5	1.3	5.2	0.1
42095	Northampton County, Pennsylvania	73.5	71.1	2.5	11.0	6.7	2.8	1.2	4.7	0.1
42097	Northumberland County, Pennsylvania	70.1	68.1	2.0	11.8	5.4	5.4	1.9	5.1	0.3
42099	Perry County, Pennsylvania	67.6	65.6	2.0	9.0	4.8	7.9	3.9	6.4	0.4
42101	Philadelphia County, Pennsylvania	68.9	66.9	2.0	14.0	7.5	2.4	3.1	4.0	0.1

Table C. County—Labor Force, Employment, and Educational Data, 2011–2015—*Continued*

| | | Class of worker for civilian employed population age 16 and older | | | | | | | | |
| | | Private for-profit wage and salary workers | | | | Government workers | | | | |
Fips code	State/county	Total private for-profit wage and salary workers	Employees of private companies	Self-employed in own incorporated business	Private not-for-profit wage and salary workers	Local government workers	State government workers	Federal government workers	Self-employed in own not incorporated business	Unpaid family workers
42103	Pike County, Pennsylvania	68.8	66.1	2.7	9.3	7.4	3.5	2.8	8.0	0.3
42105	Potter County, Pennsylvania	69.3	66.9	2.4	9.8	6.9	4.1	0.9	8.6	0.3
42107	Schuylkill County, Pennsylvania	74.2	71.7	2.5	7.5	5.9	5.4	1.7	5.2	0.1
42109	Snyder County, Pennsylvania	71.8	69.7	2.1	9.2	3.9	5.6	1.5	7.7	0.3
42111	Somerset County, Pennsylvania	69.7	67.5	2.2	10.1	6.0	5.4	1.2	7.1	0.5
42113	Sullivan County, Pennsylvania	63.0	60.6	2.4	8.3	9.3	5.2	1.8	11.8	0.6
42115	Susquehanna County, Pennsylvania	70.3	67.2	3.1	8.0	4.4	5.4	1.4	10.2	0.3
42117	Tioga County, Pennsylvania	67.6	65.5	2.1	9.5	6.3	6.1	1.5	8.8	0.3
42119	Union County, Pennsylvania	64.0	61.2	2.8	15.0	4.1	5.2	2.1	9.2	0.4
42121	Venango County, Pennsylvania	66.5	64.3	2.2	10.9	6.2	7.7	1.8	6.6	0.2
42123	Warren County, Pennsylvania	69.5	67.9	1.7	10.4	5.5	5.3	1.7	7.3	0.3
42125	Washington County, Pennsylvania	76.1	73.1	2.9	10.2	4.4	3.2	1.2	4.9	0.1
42127	Wayne County, Pennsylvania	69.0	64.6	4.3	8.4	6.4	3.7	3.6	8.7	0.2
42129	Westmoreland County, Pennsylvania	74.5	71.5	3.0	10.9	5.0	2.9	1.4	5.2	0.1
42131	Wyoming County, Pennsylvania	77.6	75.6	2.0	7.5	4.3	2.7	1.3	6.4	0.1
42133	York County, Pennsylvania	74.5	72.0	2.5	9.7	5.3	3.4	2.4	4.7	0.1
44000	**Rhode Island**	71.0	67.8	3.2	11.4	6.2	4.1	2.4	4.9	0.1
44001	Bristol County, Rhode Island	65.4	61.0	4.5	13.6	7.1	4.0	2.5	7.0	0.4
44003	Kent County, Rhode Island	72.1	68.6	3.5	10.5	6.7	3.8	2.2	4.6	0.1
44005	Newport County, Rhode Island	64.6	59.5	5.1	12.8	5.5	2.8	6.6	7.5	0.1
44007	Providence County, Rhode Island	73.1	70.7	2.4	11.5	5.7	3.8	1.8	4.1	0.1
44009	Washington County, Rhode Island	65.7	61.1	4.6	10.3	7.6	6.5	3.1	6.7	0.1
45000	**South Carolina**	72.7	69.4	3.3	6.1	5.9	7.4	2.5	5.3	0.1
45001	Abbeville County, South Carolina	71.0	68.4	2.6	9.2	3.9	7.9	1.8	6.2	0.0
45003	Aiken County, South Carolina	71.7	69.5	2.2	5.3	6.7	5.8	5.1	5.2	0.3
45005	Allendale County, South Carolina	71.4	67.4	4.0	1.9	4.5	15.2	2.2	4.8	0.0
45007	Anderson County, South Carolina	73.9	71.3	2.6	7.3	4.6	7.4	1.0	5.5	0.2
45009	Bamberg County, South Carolina	66.5	64.2	2.3	4.4	5.7	14.0	3.4	6.0	0.0
45011	Barnwell County, South Carolina	70.3	69.2	1.0	2.4	5.9	9.3	7.1	4.9	0.1
45013	Beaufort County, South Carolina	73.2	67.2	6.0	5.7	5.7	3.9	5.0	6.2	0.2
45015	Berkeley County, South Carolina	71.9	69.5	2.4	4.6	7.7	6.6	4.8	4.3	0.1
45017	Calhoun County, South Carolina	69.3	66.9	2.4	3.9	5.9	12.0	2.7	6.3	0.0
45019	Charleston County, South Carolina	70.0	65.6	4.3	6.1	6.4	7.8	3.5	6.0	0.2
45021	Cherokee County, South Carolina	77.5	74.5	3.1	5.6	5.6	6.1	1.2	3.8	0.2
45023	Chester County, South Carolina	74.7	72.3	2.4	5.3	6.4	7.4	1.8	4.3	0.1
45025	Chesterfield County, South Carolina	73.1	70.4	2.7	5.4	6.7	7.6	1.0	6.1	0.1
45027	Clarendon County, South Carolina	69.4	66.3	3.1	6.0	8.4	7.6	1.8	6.8	0.0
45029	Colleton County, South Carolina	66.9	63.6	3.3	3.8	10.5	6.7	3.2	8.8	0.2
45031	Darlington County, South Carolina	72.2	70.1	2.2	7.5	5.2	8.1	1.2	5.5	0.3
45033	Dillon County, South Carolina	76.6	75.6	1.0	3.4	7.9	6.4	1.3	4.3	0.1
45035	Dorchester County, South Carolina	71.8	69.0	2.8	5.2	6.0	6.8	5.5	4.5	0.2
45037	Edgefield County, South Carolina	69.8	66.4	3.4	5.2	6.4	6.9	4.1	7.4	0.1
45039	Fairfield County, South Carolina	73.1	70.7	2.4	5.0	6.9	9.4	2.5	3.2	0.1
45041	Florence County, South Carolina	69.5	67.1	2.4	8.5	4.9	9.9	1.7	5.5	0.1
45043	Georgetown County, South Carolina	72.4	67.2	5.2	6.5	6.5	6.0	0.8	7.6	0.1
45045	Greenville County, South Carolina	77.4	73.8	3.6	7.5	5.0	3.7	0.9	5.3	0.1
45047	Greenwood County, South Carolina	72.2	69.0	3.2	8.9	5.1	7.8	1.0	5.0	0.1
45049	Hampton County, South Carolina	67.8	64.9	2.9	3.7	8.4	9.1	2.9	7.6	0.4
45051	Horry County, South Carolina	77.5	72.8	4.7	4.2	6.3	4.6	1.1	6.1	0.1
45053	Jasper County, South Carolina	73.0	70.7	2.3	4.6	7.9	5.3	1.5	7.7	0.1
45055	Kershaw County, South Carolina	72.5	68.9	3.7	4.6	7.1	8.1	2.4	5.2	0.2
45057	Lancaster County, South Carolina	75.7	73.4	2.3	6.8	5.7	5.3	1.4	5.2	0.2
45059	Laurens County, South Carolina	74.3	71.8	2.5	6.7	6.2	7.0	0.9	4.7	0.1
45061	Lee County, South Carolina	71.7	70.1	1.6	4.9	5.4	11.3	2.4	4.1	0.1
45063	Lexington County, South Carolina	70.6	67.0	3.6	5.5	6.1	10.6	1.7	5.3	0.2
45065	McCormick County, South Carolina	54.5	50.1	4.4	7.0	8.8	21.5	1.2	6.9	0.0
45067	Marion County, South Carolina	76.0	72.9	3.1	5.3	5.9	7.1	0.8	4.8	0.0
45069	Marlboro County, South Carolina	74.2	73.2	1.0	4.2	4.9	10.2	1.3	5.2	0.0

Table C. County—Labor Force, Employment, and Educational Data, 2011–2015—*Continued*

| | | Class of worker for civilian employed population age 16 and older | | | | | | | | |
| | | Private for-profit wage and salary workers | | | | Government workers | | | | |
Fips code	State/county	Total private for-profit wage and salary workers	Employees of private companies	Self-employed in own incorporated business	Private not-for-profit wage and salary workers	Local government workers	State government workers	Federal government workers	Self-employed in own not incorporated business	Unpaid family workers
45071	Newberry County, South Carolina	74.9	71.8	3.1	4.0	7.4	7.5	1.6	4.5	0.0
45073	Oconee County, South Carolina	69.9	66.7	3.2	6.8	6.0	10.0	0.7	6.4	0.2
45075	Orangeburg County, South Carolina	71.3	69.1	2.2	4.6	6.1	11.1	1.6	5.1	0.2
45077	Pickens County, South Carolina	69.6	67.3	2.3	6.6	6.0	11.2	1.0	5.6	0.1
45079	Richland County, South Carolina	66.9	64.1	2.8	6.7	5.0	12.4	4.7	4.3	0.1
45081	Saluda County, South Carolina	73.8	69.4	4.4	4.7	5.4	7.0	1.4	6.6	1.2
45083	Spartanburg County, South Carolina	76.3	72.9	3.4	6.7	5.7	5.4	1.0	4.7	0.1
45085	Sumter County, South Carolina	68.6	65.4	3.1	5.5	5.2	7.8	7.1	5.8	0.1
45087	Union County, South Carolina	72.6	69.5	3.2	4.4	6.9	10.0	0.9	4.9	0.3
45089	Williamsburg County, South Carolina	69.7	68.2	1.6	3.6	9.0	10.4	2.2	5.0	0.0
45091	York County, South Carolina	76.3	73.8	2.4	6.0	5.2	6.1	1.3	5.0	0.2
46000	**South Dakota**	64.8	60.7	4.1	11.2	7.3	4.6	3.6	8.2	0.3
46003	Aurora County, South Dakota	59.5	56.7	2.8	8.7	8.7	4.1	2.1	16.6	0.3
46005	Beadle County, South Dakota	67.8	64.7	3.2	10.0	6.8	4.1	3.0	8.0	0.3
46007	Bennett County, South Dakota	34.9	31.8	3.2	9.9	22.0	4.4	10.2	17.6	0.9
46009	Bon Homme County, South Dakota	51.2	46.3	4.9	9.8	8.8	10.4	1.9	17.4	0.6
46011	Brookings County, South Dakota	67.2	64.5	2.7	8.2	5.4	12.0	1.3	5.6	0.4
46013	Brown County, South Dakota	68.5	65.4	3.1	11.6	5.9	4.0	2.7	7.0	0.3
46015	Brule County, South Dakota	50.6	45.5	5.1	15.8	8.2	3.0	5.1	15.4	1.9
46017	Buffalo County, South Dakota	40.1	34.9	5.2	8.3	24.8	8.6	16.1	1.8	0.3
46019	Butte County, South Dakota	61.0	56.2	4.8	9.0	7.7	3.7	3.9	13.7	0.9
46021	Campbell County, South Dakota	48.1	41.1	7.0	11.8	8.6	3.3	3.8	24.4	0.0
46023	Charles Mix County, South Dakota	55.4	49.3	6.1	8.5	13.0	3.8	6.4	12.3	0.5
46025	Clark County, South Dakota	59.9	53.8	6.1	7.1	5.6	2.2	4.9	18.7	1.5
46027	Clay County, South Dakota	56.5	54.9	1.6	9.6	7.6	19.4	0.7	6.0	0.1
46029	Codington County, South Dakota	76.5	72.2	4.3	5.7	6.9	3.4	1.4	6.0	0.1
46031	Corson County, South Dakota	31.4	29.5	1.9	4.8	25.3	4.8	10.7	21.5	1.5
46033	Custer County, South Dakota	49.1	41.5	7.6	11.3	8.6	5.3	11.6	13.4	0.7
46035	Davison County, South Dakota	66.0	62.9	3.2	13.8	5.4	4.2	3.0	7.2	0.3
46037	Day County, South Dakota	58.8	52.6	6.2	9.7	7.3	3.4	3.8	16.5	0.7
46039	Deuel County, South Dakota	64.5	57.6	6.9	7.3	8.5	1.5	2.0	16.3	0.0
46041	Dewey County, South Dakota	31.6	29.7	1.9	3.3	29.8	4.5	14.9	14.7	1.2
46043	Douglas County, South Dakota	58.4	53.6	4.7	10.1	6.9	2.3	3.6	18.4	0.3
46045	Edmunds County, South Dakota	58.6	56.6	2.0	14.5	6.7	2.0	3.2	14.7	0.4
46047	Fall River County, South Dakota	45.2	40.2	5.0	10.9	10.8	8.7	16.0	7.8	0.6
46049	Faulk County, South Dakota	43.2	38.6	4.6	14.9	8.7	3.4	6.4	23.2	0.3
46051	Grant County, South Dakota	73.4	67.0	6.4	4.2	7.6	1.1	2.9	10.7	0.1
46053	Gregory County, South Dakota	56.1	52.4	3.7	7.0	10.5	4.8	2.3	18.6	0.7
46055	Haakon County, South Dakota	53.3	49.2	4.1	6.0	8.7	1.7	1.3	28.5	0.5
46057	Hamlin County, South Dakota	65.9	58.8	7.1	9.0	6.6	2.2	2.3	13.4	0.5
46059	Hand County, South Dakota	61.7	54.7	7.0	9.3	8.5	2.7	1.1	16.6	0.2
46061	Hanson County, South Dakota	58.0	54.3	3.8	15.4	8.6	2.6	3.8	11.4	0.2
46063	Harding County, South Dakota	52.0	44.3	7.7	1.6	12.6	1.5	4.5	24.4	3.4
46065	Hughes County, South Dakota	51.1	47.2	3.9	12.0	7.4	21.1	4.3	3.9	0.2
46067	Hutchinson County, South Dakota	55.6	53.2	2.5	13.3	6.8	3.7	2.2	18.1	0.4
46069	Hyde County, South Dakota	55.9	52.9	3.0	10.1	13.8	2.6	2.8	13.4	1.4
46071	Jackson County, South Dakota	26.4	25.2	1.2	7.7	26.0	3.4	13.6	21.5	1.2
46073	Jerauld County, South Dakota	62.1	56.8	5.3	11.0	6.2	2.3	3.4	14.9	0.0
46075	Jones County, South Dakota	57.3	52.5	4.8	5.6	8.7	2.9	3.1	20.3	2.1
46077	Kingsbury County, South Dakota	64.1	59.4	4.7	8.4	5.7	4.2	1.4	15.8	0.4
46079	Lake County, South Dakota	67.7	63.0	4.7	6.9	5.6	7.8	1.7	10.1	0.2
46081	Lawrence County, South Dakota	66.4	61.1	5.3	9.6	6.2	5.6	5.5	6.7	0.0
46083	Lincoln County, South Dakota	67.4	63.0	4.5	15.9	6.1	2.5	2.2	5.9	0.0
46085	Lyman County, South Dakota	42.9	37.2	5.7	7.6	20.1	3.7	10.4	15.0	0.3
46087	McCook County, South Dakota	59.8	53.9	5.9	15.1	5.1	2.2	2.2	15.2	0.5
46089	McPherson County, South Dakota	44.4	40.6	3.8	12.2	9.0	5.7	2.9	22.6	3.0
46091	Marshall County, South Dakota	62.1	56.2	5.8	5.6	14.0	1.7	2.3	14.2	0.2
46093	Meade County, South Dakota	64.2	59.0	5.2	9.0	6.7	3.2	8.7	8.2	0.0
46095	Mellette County, South Dakota	33.9	29.9	4.1	3.4	25.9	5.8	8.1	22.4	0.4
46097	Miner County, South Dakota	57.8	53.8	3.9	10.9	7.0	3.0	2.0	19.3	0.1
46099	Minnehaha County, South Dakota	72.0	69.2	2.8	14.2	4.8	2.2	2.3	4.6	0.1
46101	Moody County, South Dakota	54.6	49.8	4.8	11.4	10.2	2.7	5.7	14.8	0.5
46102	Oglala Lakota County, South Dakota	22.4	22.1	0.2	7.1	38.2	3.6	24.4	4.3	0.0
46103	Pennington County, South Dakota	69.0	63.4	5.6	11.0	6.3	2.9	4.7	6.1	0.1
46105	Perkins County, South Dakota	47.0	41.3	5.7	10.2	9.2	4.2	2.7	24.9	1.7

Table C. County—Labor Force, Employment, and Educational Data, 2011–2015—*Continued*

| | | Class of worker for civilian employed population age 16 and older | | | | | | | | |
| | | Private for-profit wage and salary workers | | | | Government workers | | | | |
Fips code	State/county	Total private for-profit wage and salary workers	Employees of private companies	Self-employed in own incorporated business	Private not-for-profit wage and salary workers	Local government workers	State government workers	Federal government workers	Self-employed in own not incorporated business	Unpaid family workers
46107	Potter County, South Dakota	61.5	52.5	9.0	10.9	6.8	2.9	2.8	14.9	0.2
46109	Roberts County, South Dakota	57.2	53.3	3.9	6.6	14.0	1.7	5.4	14.6	0.5
46111	Sanborn County, South Dakota	62.5	59.3	3.1	7.8	5.3	2.1	2.3	19.7	0.4
46115	Spink County, South Dakota	52.9	48.5	4.4	8.5	9.4	10.3	2.1	15.5	1.4
46117	Stanley County, South Dakota	55.3	52.7	2.6	11.2	7.8	15.0	1.2	8.7	0.8
46119	Sully County, South Dakota	62.6	57.0	5.6	5.3	6.7	6.7	1.6	16.8	0.3
46121	Todd County, South Dakota	26.4	25.7	0.7	8.0	39.2	4.0	11.8	9.8	0.8
46123	Tripp County, South Dakota	50.5	45.5	5.0	7.2	10.7	6.3	2.5	22.3	0.5
46125	Turner County, South Dakota	56.1	52.5	3.6	14.2	5.7	3.6	2.6	17.4	0.3
46127	Union County, South Dakota	68.4	63.4	5.0	10.6	7.4	4.5	1.3	7.0	0.8
46129	Walworth County, South Dakota	67.8	63.1	4.7	7.5	6.1	7.0	2.7	8.6	0.3
46135	Yankton County, South Dakota	66.5	61.0	5.5	10.7	4.6	7.7	2.5	7.9	0.1
46137	Ziebach County, South Dakota	37.7	33.9	3.8	3.3	26.8	4.0	10.9	16.6	0.8
47000	**Tennessee**	71.3	69.1	2.3	7.6	7.4	4.1	2.6	6.9	0.2
47001	Anderson County, Tennessee	67.6	65.2	2.3	8.3	9.0	3.7	5.7	5.7	0.1
47003	Bedford County, Tennessee	72.7	70.6	2.1	3.1	7.3	3.7	2.4	10.4	0.3
47005	Benton County, Tennessee	69.4	67.5	1.9	4.2	10.8	5.6	2.0	7.8	0.2
47007	Bledsoe County, Tennessee	63.7	61.6	2.1	5.5	10.6	5.6	4.2	10.3	0.2
47009	Blount County, Tennessee	72.5	69.6	2.9	7.1	8.2	3.5	1.5	7.0	0.1
47011	Bradley County, Tennessee	75.6	73.9	1.7	6.8	6.7	2.4	1.2	7.1	0.2
47013	Campbell County, Tennessee	72.9	71.2	1.7	5.1	10.0	3.9	2.0	6.1	0.0
47015	Cannon County, Tennessee	69.8	67.6	2.2	5.2	6.8	3.6	3.6	10.8	0.2
47017	Carroll County, Tennessee	70.6	69.6	1.1	5.7	8.0	6.4	1.8	7.3	0.1
47019	Carter County, Tennessee	67.2	65.2	1.9	7.5	9.1	5.3	2.8	8.0	0.0
47021	Cheatham County, Tennessee	68.2	66.1	2.1	7.8	8.0	4.3	2.3	9.2	0.3
47023	Chester County, Tennessee	67.7	65.5	2.1	9.1	8.2	7.5	1.1	6.5	0.0
47025	Claiborne County, Tennessee	71.2	69.4	1.8	6.6	9.5	2.3	1.7	8.4	0.3
47027	Clay County, Tennessee	55.8	54.4	1.4	9.5	10.5	10.5	2.2	11.6	0.0
47029	Cocke County, Tennessee	72.1	71.3	0.7	5.4	9.2	4.6	1.5	7.2	0.1
47031	Coffee County, Tennessee	73.5	71.3	2.2	4.4	8.2	3.6	2.2	7.8	0.3
47033	Crockett County, Tennessee	72.5	69.9	2.6	5.2	7.2	6.1	1.0	7.9	0.1
47035	Cumberland County, Tennessee	67.5	65.1	2.4	9.0	8.4	5.0	1.1	8.7	0.4
47037	Davidson County, Tennessee	70.9	68.6	2.3	11.2	5.2	4.0	1.8	6.8	0.1
47039	Decatur County, Tennessee	60.1	58.2	1.9	3.7	12.9	9.3	2.8	11.1	0.2
47041	DeKalb County, Tennessee	74.9	73.4	1.5	4.8	7.2	3.8	2.3	6.8	0.2
47043	Dickson County, Tennessee	72.4	69.9	2.5	6.3	7.8	4.6	2.3	6.7	0.0
47045	Dyer County, Tennessee	73.3	72.6	0.7	3.8	9.2	6.1	1.1	6.3	0.2
47047	Fayette County, Tennessee	73.1	69.3	3.7	6.7	8.4	2.8	1.8	7.1	0.1
47049	Fentress County, Tennessee	66.4	64.7	1.7	3.6	9.5	6.2	1.5	12.7	0.2
47051	Franklin County, Tennessee	68.3	66.5	1.7	7.1	9.1	4.3	3.6	7.4	0.2
47053	Gibson County, Tennessee	74.2	72.2	1.9	5.4	6.5	4.4	1.5	7.9	0.1
47055	Giles County, Tennessee	71.5	69.3	2.2	4.2	9.9	3.8	1.7	8.8	0.0
47057	Grainger County, Tennessee	71.6	69.8	1.9	4.9	7.7	2.9	2.4	10.2	0.3
47059	Greene County, Tennessee	69.1	67.7	1.5	7.3	7.8	6.7	1.3	7.5	0.2
47061	Grundy County, Tennessee	70.6	68.8	1.8	7.3	5.6	4.7	1.9	9.8	0.2
47063	Hamblen County, Tennessee	75.2	73.8	1.3	6.5	5.6	4.5	1.2	6.8	0.1
47065	Hamilton County, Tennessee	69.5	66.7	2.8	10.1	7.2	3.6	3.5	5.9	0.2
47067	Hancock County, Tennessee	61.5	59.2	2.3	2.9	12.1	8.8	1.2	13.5	0.0
47069	Hardeman County, Tennessee	64.7	62.4	2.3	6.0	12.2	8.1	1.8	7.2	0.0
47071	Hardin County, Tennessee	66.3	64.4	1.9	6.6	7.1	6.2	2.2	11.6	0.0
47073	Hawkins County, Tennessee	74.2	72.8	1.5	5.6	7.4	3.6	1.6	7.6	0.0
47075	Haywood County, Tennessee	72.9	71.3	1.6	2.8	11.3	4.4	1.8	6.2	0.6
47077	Henderson County, Tennessee	70.4	69.1	1.3	6.5	9.5	3.6	0.7	9.3	0.0
47079	Henry County, Tennessee	67.6	64.8	2.8	4.7	8.4	6.4	2.0	10.3	0.6
47081	Hickman County, Tennessee	72.6	71.1	1.5	5.0	7.8	3.7	2.5	8.3	0.0
47083	Houston County, Tennessee	62.7	61.0	1.7	4.1	8.8	5.1	5.2	13.9	0.1
47085	Humphreys County, Tennessee	67.7	66.4	1.3	5.4	9.9	6.4	2.2	7.9	0.4
47087	Jackson County, Tennessee	68.1	67.2	0.9	4.6	11.8	4.2	1.5	8.6	1.2
47089	Jefferson County, Tennessee	71.7	69.8	2.0	6.2	8.3	4.7	1.9	7.1	0.1
47091	Johnson County, Tennessee	62.9	61.8	1.1	2.7	13.1	9.8	1.9	9.4	0.2
47093	Knox County, Tennessee	71.4	69.0	2.5	8.9	5.5	5.3	2.9	5.9	0.1
47095	Lake County, Tennessee	60.8	59.5	1.3	2.3	9.2	18.8	2.0	6.4	0.5
47097	Lauderdale County, Tennessee	69.6	68.1	1.5	2.8	9.6	10.6	1.7	5.5	0.3
47099	Lawrence County, Tennessee	72.0	70.5	1.5	3.7	7.6	5.0	2.2	9.0	0.5
47101	Lewis County, Tennessee	68.6	67.0	1.6	6.2	4.9	5.2	0.1	15.0	0.0
47103	Lincoln County, Tennessee	71.9	70.5	1.4	5.9	7.2	2.3	3.4	9.0	0.2
47105	Loudon County, Tennessee	73.0	69.9	3.1	7.3	6.9	2.9	2.8	6.9	0.3
47107	McMinn County, Tennessee	79.2	77.5	1.8	3.7	6.8	3.4	1.3	5.5	0.0
47109	McNairy County, Tennessee	66.8	65.5	1.3	5.8	10.7	5.3	1.3	10.0	0.1
47111	Macon County, Tennessee	73.1	71.3	1.8	3.9	9.4	3.7	0.3	9.4	0.1
47113	Madison County, Tennessee	71.4	69.3	2.1	8.6	8.5	4.3	1.4	5.5	0.3
47115	Marion County, Tennessee	71.0	68.0	3.0	8.6	7.2	4.3	2.6	6.2	0.1
47117	Marshall County, Tennessee	76.2	74.5	1.7	4.6	8.1	3.5	1.3	6.2	0.1
47119	Maury County, Tennessee	73.8	72.3	1.5	7.5	7.1	3.3	1.1	7.0	0.2
47121	Meigs County, Tennessee	77.9	76.0	1.9	3.2	7.3	3.3	2.0	6.3	0.0

Table C. County—Labor Force, Employment, and Educational Data, 2011–2015—Continued

| | | Class of worker for civilian employed population age 16 and older | | | | | | | | |
| | | Private for-profit wage and salary workers | | | | Government workers | | | | |
Fips code	State/county	Total private for-profit wage and salary workers	Employees of private companies	Self-employed in own incorporated business	Private not-for-profit wage and salary workers	Local government workers	State government workers	Federal government workers	Self-employed in own not incorporated business	Unpaid family workers
47123	Monroe County, Tennessee	76.2	73.4	2.8	5.6	7.1	2.4	1.6	6.9	0.1
47125	Montgomery County, Tennessee	65.0	63.5	1.6	5.0	7.4	4.3	12.0	6.1	0.2
47127	Moore County, Tennessee	69.8	67.9	1.9	4.6	7.0	5.1	2.3	10.7	0.5
47129	Morgan County, Tennessee	60.8	59.7	1.1	7.8	10.1	9.6	6.9	4.7	0.1
47131	Obion County, Tennessee	71.6	68.9	2.7	5.4	7.6	4.8	1.0	9.1	0.4
47133	Overton County, Tennessee	71.0	68.9	2.2	3.4	8.2	4.8	1.9	10.7	0.1
47135	Perry County, Tennessee	65.7	63.4	2.3	5.2	10.7	7.0	2.2	9.2	0.0
47137	Pickett County, Tennessee	63.8	59.4	4.3	0.6	18.3	4.2	1.1	12.0	0.1
47139	Polk County, Tennessee	76.3	74.8	1.5	5.3	8.5	2.7	1.5	5.7	0.0
47141	Putnam County, Tennessee	70.5	68.7	1.8	5.2	8.1	5.9	1.3	8.6	0.4
47143	Rhea County, Tennessee	70.2	68.4	1.8	5.2	7.4	3.4	6.4	6.7	0.7
47145	Roane County, Tennessee	66.6	64.2	2.4	8.0	8.5	4.5	5.9	6.4	0.1
47147	Robertson County, Tennessee	71.5	69.2	2.3	5.5	8.7	4.5	1.6	8.0	0.1
47149	Rutherford County, Tennessee	74.9	72.9	2.0	5.7	6.5	4.5	2.4	5.8	0.1
47151	Scott County, Tennessee	65.8	63.8	2.0	5.1	9.2	5.4	4.1	9.9	0.4
47153	Sequatchie County, Tennessee	64.8	62.0	2.7	7.0	8.3	4.4	3.7	11.8	0.1
47155	Sevier County, Tennessee	73.8	70.9	2.8	4.8	7.6	2.6	1.4	9.4	0.5
47157	Shelby County, Tennessee	72.5	70.1	2.4	8.4	8.3	2.8	2.8	5.1	0.1
47159	Smith County, Tennessee	71.2	69.5	1.7	4.8	7.2	5.0	1.4	10.3	0.2
47161	Stewart County, Tennessee	61.9	60.0	1.9	3.7	11.0	7.8	9.6	5.7	0.2
47163	Sullivan County, Tennessee	73.1	71.1	2.0	8.1	7.1	2.8	1.9	6.9	0.1
47165	Sumner County, Tennessee	72.4	70.2	2.2	6.7	8.1	3.2	1.6	7.8	0.2
47167	Tipton County, Tennessee	70.4	68.3	2.2	8.2	8.6	3.9	4.1	4.6	0.1
47169	Trousdale County, Tennessee	72.4	70.1	2.3	3.9	9.5	4.6	1.3	8.1	0.2
47171	Unicoi County, Tennessee	70.9	67.5	3.4	6.8	10.1	4.0	2.5	5.6	0.1
47173	Union County, Tennessee	72.7	71.1	1.6	2.9	6.6	4.3	2.1	9.8	1.6
47175	Van Buren County, Tennessee	58.7	54.4	4.3	4.1	10.1	14.8	2.6	9.6	0.0
47177	Warren County, Tennessee	73.6	72.4	1.2	3.7	7.9	4.9	1.3	8.1	0.5
47179	Washington County, Tennessee	65.9	64.1	1.9	10.8	6.7	7.0	3.4	6.0	0.1
47181	Wayne County, Tennessee	62.4	61.7	0.7	7.0	11.4	8.9	2.2	8.1	0.0
47183	Weakley County, Tennessee	68.1	66.2	1.9	3.5	7.2	11.2	1.6	8.1	0.4
47185	White County, Tennessee	70.3	69.3	1.0	2.5	9.6	5.7	2.4	9.4	0.1
47187	Williamson County, Tennessee	71.4	66.8	4.5	8.9	6.6	2.7	1.2	9.0	0.2
47189	Wilson County, Tennessee	74.2	71.6	2.6	6.5	6.7	3.0	2.1	7.5	0.0
48000	**Texas**	73.7	70.9	2.8	5.7	6.7	4.8	2.3	6.6	0.2
48001	Anderson County, Texas	64.5	62.9	1.6	5.3	7.6	15.4	0.7	6.4	0.1
48003	Andrews County, Texas	79.2	76.5	2.7	3.9	6.6	2.7	0.3	6.8	0.5
48005	Angelina County, Texas	69.5	66.6	2.9	6.7	6.7	10.3	0.8	5.9	0.0
48007	Aransas County, Texas	71.0	65.7	5.2	4.5	9.3	2.3	0.8	12.2	0.1
48009	Archer County, Texas	70.2	66.5	3.7	6.4	6.7	5.4	1.7	9.5	0.2
48011	Armstrong County, Texas	60.7	57.8	2.9	4.9	10.2	9.2	5.0	9.5	0.4
48013	Atascosa County, Texas	73.8	71.5	2.3	4.3	8.8	3.6	2.0	7.5	0.1
48015	Austin County, Texas	75.1	71.8	3.3	5.3	6.9	3.4	1.6	7.7	0.1
48017	Bailey County, Texas	69.3	65.5	3.8	6.0	12.5	3.1	3.5	5.6	0.0
48019	Bandera County, Texas	62.4	59.3	3.1	6.8	9.2	6.9	2.8	11.6	0.3
48021	Bastrop County, Texas	64.9	61.9	3.0	6.4	9.2	7.1	3.8	8.3	0.3
48023	Baylor County, Texas	54.8	48.1	6.7	7.1	10.4	6.1	0.0	21.5	0.0
48025	Bee County, Texas	65.4	63.8	1.7	5.0	8.8	11.0	2.9	6.7	0.2
48027	Bell County, Texas	61.4	59.7	1.8	7.8	8.0	4.3	13.4	5.0	0.1
48029	Bexar County, Texas	73.0	70.7	2.4	6.5	5.8	4.2	4.7	5.6	0.1
48031	Blanco County, Texas	63.4	58.5	5.0	7.0	10.1	5.9	1.4	11.8	0.3
48033	Borden County, Texas	41.1	38.7	2.5	4.6	20.6	13.1	2.5	17.0	1.1
48035	Bosque County, Texas	70.1	68.1	2.0	5.5	7.1	4.0	1.8	11.2	0.4
48037	Bowie County, Texas	68.5	66.2	2.3	6.9	5.4	5.9	8.1	5.1	0.1
48039	Brazoria County, Texas	74.9	72.7	2.2	5.6	7.2	5.3	1.9	5.0	0.1
48041	Brazos County, Texas	61.8	59.7	2.1	6.6	6.3	18.1	1.2	5.8	0.2
48043	Brewster County, Texas	41.8	38.5	3.3	7.4	12.8	18.7	8.9	9.0	1.5
48045	Briscoe County, Texas	52.8	50.9	2.0	10.0	12.4	10.8	0.4	12.4	1.1
48047	Brooks County, Texas	67.6	66.0	1.6	5.3	9.4	9.7	1.8	6.3	0.0
48049	Brown County, Texas	69.2	66.7	2.4	6.1	6.0	8.9	1.5	8.2	0.1
48051	Burleson County, Texas	64.1	61.3	2.8	5.2	9.9	10.9	1.0	8.4	0.5
48053	Burnet County, Texas	68.4	64.7	3.6	5.7	9.2	3.4	1.5	11.7	0.1
48055	Caldwell County, Texas	67.5	66.1	1.4	7.2	8.1	6.2	4.2	6.7	0.1
48057	Calhoun County, Texas	76.4	72.8	3.6	4.0	10.3	2.3	0.2	6.7	0.1
48059	Callahan County, Texas	64.4	61.1	3.3	6.7	6.8	7.4	2.7	9.4	2.5
48061	Cameron County, Texas	67.9	65.4	2.5	4.7	10.1	5.5	2.6	8.9	0.2
48063	Camp County, Texas	70.1	67.9	2.1	3.6	6.3	7.6	2.2	9.9	0.4
48065	Carson County, Texas	68.6	65.2	3.4	3.9	7.4	7.8	3.1	9.2	0.0
48067	Cass County, Texas	70.0	68.0	2.0	6.0	7.6	6.1	2.2	8.1	0.0
48069	Castro County, Texas	70.0	65.7	4.3	3.5	8.8	4.6	1.1	10.8	1.2
48071	Chambers County, Texas	74.6	71.8	2.8	3.3	9.0	5.7	1.2	6.1	0.1
48073	Cherokee County, Texas	66.6	64.7	1.9	6.3	7.3	12.2	1.0	6.5	0.2
48075	Childress County, Texas	52.4	51.1	1.3	9.6	9.0	20.2	2.5	6.1	0.2
48077	Clay County, Texas	64.9	62.1	2.8	7.5	7.4	7.2	2.4	10.4	0.2
48079	Cochran County, Texas	58.9	54.8	4.1	7.7	12.2	5.4	3.3	12.0	0.4

Table C. County—Labor Force, Employment, and Educational Data, 2011–2015—*Continued*

| | | Class of worker for civilian employed population age 16 and older | | | | | | | | |
| | | Private for-profit wage and salary workers | | | | Government workers | | | | |
Fips code	State/county	Total private for-profit wage and salary workers	Employees of private companies	Self-employed in own incorporated business	Private not-for-profit wage and salary workers	Local government workers	State government workers	Federal government workers	Self-employed in own not incorporated business	Unpaid family workers
48081	Coke County, Texas	48.9	46.9	2.0	9.8	17.8	10.4	3.2	9.8	0.0
48083	Coleman County, Texas	67.4	66.0	1.4	4.0	6.8	8.0	2.6	10.9	0.2
48085	Collin County, Texas	79.4	75.5	3.9	4.7	6.0	2.8	1.2	5.8	0.2
48087	Collingsworth County, Texas	62.5	61.0	1.6	8.2	8.7	5.9	3.7	11.0	0.0
48089	Colorado County, Texas	67.4	64.4	2.9	5.2	7.9	7.7	1.7	9.0	1.1
48091	Comal County, Texas	71.0	67.0	4.0	6.3	7.3	3.2	2.8	9.1	0.4
48093	Comanche County, Texas	66.1	63.6	2.5	6.1	8.4	5.2	1.4	12.3	0.5
48095	Concho County, Texas	42.6	40.5	2.1	1.6	12.0	17.6	7.2	17.8	1.4
48097	Cooke County, Texas	72.7	70.4	2.2	4.2	6.0	7.8	1.0	8.1	0.2
48099	Coryell County, Texas	55.3	53.8	1.4	5.0	10.6	11.7	12.0	5.3	0.2
48101	Cottle County, Texas	50.6	46.2	4.4	5.9	18.4	9.9	0.7	14.0	0.7
48103	Crane County, Texas	77.4	75.4	2.1	4.7	8.4	5.0	0.5	3.9	0.0
48105	Crockett County, Texas	69.3	68.8	0.5	8.0	9.6	5.3	1.4	6.2	0.2
48107	Crosby County, Texas	66.3	65.1	1.2	6.4	10.5	5.7	1.1	9.4	0.6
48109	Culberson County, Texas	73.2	73.2	0.0	1.5	12.2	4.0	2.9	6.2	0.0
48111	Dallam County, Texas	77.5	74.4	3.1	4.6	5.6	4.5	0.9	6.7	0.1
48113	Dallas County, Texas	78.5	75.7	2.8	5.4	5.4	2.4	1.7	6.4	0.1
48115	Dawson County, Texas	61.7	59.9	1.8	6.8	9.3	11.4	1.2	9.5	0.1
48117	Deaf Smith County, Texas	71.5	67.6	3.9	6.5	7.9	4.2	1.5	7.9	0.5
48119	Delta County, Texas	70.8	68.9	1.9	2.0	4.6	10.4	1.1	11.0	0.0
48121	Denton County, Texas	77.3	74.0	3.3	4.9	6.1	4.3	1.5	5.7	0.1
48123	DeWitt County, Texas	68.6	65.4	3.2	3.8	8.3	7.6	1.8	9.6	0.3
48125	Dickens County, Texas	48.9	44.5	4.4	10.1	19.5	10.8	0.9	9.5	0.3
48127	Dimmit County, Texas	68.7	65.0	3.7	1.8	9.0	9.5	3.3	7.6	0.0
48129	Donley County, Texas	50.8	48.9	1.9	5.6	8.4	17.4	4.0	13.7	0.0
48131	Duval County, Texas	73.2	70.3	2.8	2.9	7.6	6.7	3.0	6.4	0.3
48133	Eastland County, Texas	72.1	68.2	3.8	4.3	5.4	8.9	0.8	7.8	0.7
48135	Ector County, Texas	77.9	75.2	2.7	4.0	7.6	2.9	0.8	6.7	0.1
48137	Edwards County, Texas	57.2	55.0	2.2	0.0	6.6	15.1	1.3	19.7	0.0
48139	Ellis County, Texas	71.9	68.5	3.4	6.6	7.6	4.1	2.5	7.3	0.1
48141	El Paso County, Texas	68.7	66.5	2.2	5.2	8.5	5.1	6.4	6.0	0.1
48143	Erath County, Texas	70.4	66.7	3.7	6.3	5.3	9.6	0.3	7.9	0.0
48145	Falls County, Texas	61.9	61.2	0.7	8.9	8.4	8.5	3.6	8.4	0.3
48147	Fannin County, Texas	68.0	64.9	3.1	5.1	8.1	7.6	4.1	7.1	0.1
48149	Fayette County, Texas	70.5	67.5	3.0	6.9	7.5	4.4	1.4	9.0	0.2
48151	Fisher County, Texas	62.9	59.8	3.1	9.1	7.4	8.3	2.4	9.4	0.5
48153	Floyd County, Texas	67.2	64.6	2.6	6.7	11.2	4.1	1.6	9.2	0.1
48155	Foard County, Texas	56.3	53.1	3.1	4.5	9.0	9.0	7.0	13.5	0.9
48157	Fort Bend County, Texas	76.1	72.2	3.9	5.6	6.7	4.5	1.3	5.7	0.2
48159	Franklin County, Texas	69.2	66.6	2.6	3.1	5.0	6.5	2.2	13.3	0.7
48161	Freestone County, Texas	69.3	67.5	1.8	4.3	8.7	9.6	0.6	7.3	0.2
48163	Frio County, Texas	75.3	71.0	4.4	5.8	5.9	6.0	3.4	3.4	0.1
48165	Gaines County, Texas	71.3	67.6	3.7	5.5	8.1	3.7	0.2	11.2	0.0
48167	Galveston County, Texas	70.4	67.9	2.5	5.4	7.6	7.9	2.7	5.8	0.2
48169	Garza County, Texas	65.5	63.7	1.8	5.0	9.9	6.9	0.7	12.0	0.0
48171	Gillespie County, Texas	65.9	57.9	8.0	8.9	6.0	3.2	1.3	14.3	0.5
48173	Glasscock County, Texas	68.5	49.7	18.8	0.0	13.0	2.4	1.6	14.4	0.0
48175	Goliad County, Texas	64.8	62.2	2.6	5.3	11.3	6.9	3.2	8.2	0.3
48177	Gonzales County, Texas	72.8	71.2	1.6	4.4	8.9	3.1	1.2	9.1	0.5
48179	Gray County, Texas	73.4	71.1	2.3	6.2	7.0	3.8	2.5	7.0	0.0
48181	Grayson County, Texas	73.1	70.5	2.7	5.3	7.6	4.5	1.6	7.5	0.3
48183	Gregg County, Texas	78.3	75.3	3.0	6.4	5.0	4.0	0.8	5.4	0.1
48185	Grimes County, Texas	74.6	71.2	3.5	4.6	5.9	8.5	0.6	5.7	0.1
48187	Guadalupe County, Texas	71.4	68.8	2.6	5.5	7.4	3.5	7.0	4.8	0.3
48189	Hale County, Texas	67.3	65.3	2.0	8.7	9.1	6.1	1.2	7.4	0.2
48191	Hall County, Texas	68.8	66.9	1.9	2.1	8.1	3.4	3.5	10.1	4.0
48193	Hamilton County, Texas	64.0	60.4	3.6	8.9	6.5	10.2	1.1	7.5	1.9
48195	Hansford County, Texas	61.8	56.6	5.2	9.2	8.8	7.1	2.7	10.2	0.2
48197	Hardeman County, Texas	59.8	56.3	3.5	7.4	9.5	12.8	2.9	7.5	0.0
48199	Hardin County, Texas	74.4	71.8	2.6	5.7	7.5	6.2	2.1	4.2	0.1
48201	Harris County, Texas	78.0	75.4	2.6	5.4	5.6	3.3	1.3	6.3	0.1
48203	Harrison County, Texas	73.0	69.9	3.1	7.7	6.3	5.9	1.7	5.4	0.1
48205	Hartley County, Texas	64.4	59.4	5.0	7.7	7.1	5.9	2.1	12.4	0.4
48207	Haskell County, Texas	58.6	55.2	3.3	3.8	11.7	10.2	0.5	15.0	0.2
48209	Hays County, Texas	67.6	64.6	3.1	5.8	9.2	7.9	2.3	7.0	0.2
48211	Hemphill County, Texas	66.6	62.7	3.9	4.5	7.6	7.6	1.2	12.5	0.0
48213	Henderson County, Texas	69.4	66.6	2.8	6.2	7.8	5.0	1.2	10.4	0.1
48215	Hidalgo County, Texas	67.0	64.8	2.2	3.6	8.0	7.4	1.8	11.9	0.2
48217	Hill County, Texas	71.9	66.9	5.0	5.2	9.7	3.5	1.8	7.6	0.3
48219	Hockley County, Texas	70.2	67.3	2.8	6.9	8.9	5.4	1.3	7.1	0.3
48221	Hood County, Texas	73.0	68.1	4.9	5.7	6.6	3.0	1.4	9.9	0.5
48223	Hopkins County, Texas	73.0	70.7	2.4	3.7	5.2	7.2	0.8	9.8	0.3
48225	Houston County, Texas	61.5	60.0	1.4	6.4	8.1	11.8	2.2	9.8	0.3
48227	Howard County, Texas	67.2	64.6	2.6	4.8	9.5	8.7	4.8	4.9	0.1
48229	Hudspeth County, Texas	56.0	54.4	1.6	1.6	18.6	9.1	5.3	9.3	0.1
48231	Hunt County, Texas	73.5	70.7	2.8	5.1	6.5	6.4	1.4	7.0	0.0

Table C. County—Labor Force, Employment, and Educational Data, 2011–2015—*Continued*

| | | Class of worker for civilian employed population age 16 and older | | | | | | | | |
| | | Private for-profit wage and salary workers | | | | Government workers | | | | |
Fips code	State/county	Total private for-profit wage and salary workers	Employees of private companies	Self-employed in own incorporated business	Private not-for-profit wage and salary workers	Local government workers	State government workers	Federal government workers	Self-employed in own not incorporated business	Unpaid family workers
48233	Hutchinson County, Texas	73.9	72.2	1.7	6.3	7.4	4.8	1.7	5.8	0.1
48235	Irion County, Texas	52.7	48.9	3.7	5.2	6.7	11.2	3.2	18.5	2.5
48237	Jack County, Texas	69.3	63.5	5.8	6.8	7.9	6.4	1.0	8.1	0.6
48239	Jackson County, Texas	71.3	68.4	3.0	4.7	8.7	3.7	1.2	9.3	1.0
48241	Jasper County, Texas	71.7	69.7	2.1	6.0	5.5	8.9	1.1	6.7	0.1
48243	Jeff Davis County, Texas	40.4	40.4	0.0	10.1	6.1	22.0	1.4	18.2	1.8
48245	Jefferson County, Texas	76.8	74.8	2.0	5.1	6.0	5.6	1.8	4.5	0.1
48247	Jim Hogg County, Texas	54.5	53.6	0.9	2.2	19.4	7.4	3.9	11.7	0.8
48249	Jim Wells County, Texas	74.5	71.5	3.0	5.8	6.2	4.1	2.3	7.1	0.0
48251	Johnson County, Texas	74.4	71.6	2.8	6.5	8.1	3.5	1.7	5.7	0.1
48253	Jones County, Texas	62.3	59.9	2.4	6.4	8.6	8.9	3.0	10.3	0.5
48255	Karnes County, Texas	64.1	62.0	2.1	5.6	11.8	8.2	2.1	7.8	0.5
48257	Kaufman County, Texas	72.5	70.5	2.0	4.9	10.2	4.8	1.7	5.8	0.1
48259	Kendall County, Texas	66.1	60.2	5.9	7.8	6.7	5.5	3.4	10.4	0.0
48261	Kenedy County, Texas	46.5	46.5	0.0	5.4	41.1	1.6	5.4	0.0	0.0
48263	Kent County, Texas	47.7	47.2	0.5	2.0	27.4	8.3	3.3	10.1	1.3
48265	Kerr County, Texas	62.1	57.4	4.7	10.7	8.2	5.4	3.0	10.4	0.1
48267	Kimble County, Texas	61.3	58.3	3.0	7.0	6.6	7.6	3.8	13.1	0.6
48269	King County, Texas	69.9	66.3	3.6	3.0	15.7	4.2	1.2	6.0	0.0
48271	Kinney County, Texas	43.2	37.3	5.9	5.5	20.5	12.3	5.3	13.2	0.0
48273	Kleberg County, Texas	63.4	61.7	1.8	6.1	5.8	15.2	4.8	4.4	0.2
48275	Knox County, Texas	61.1	57.2	3.8	6.1	11.1	10.0	3.9	7.0	0.8
48277	Lamar County, Texas	75.0	72.9	2.1	4.2	6.7	5.8	1.4	6.7	0.2
48279	Lamb County, Texas	68.2	64.1	4.2	5.6	11.4	3.0	1.8	9.9	0.1
48281	Lampasas County, Texas	60.1	58.3	1.8	5.4	11.5	5.8	9.2	8.0	0.0
48283	La Salle County, Texas	76.7	71.1	5.6	1.6	7.3	5.5	1.1	7.8	0.0
48285	Lavaca County, Texas	67.6	64.5	3.1	5.8	10.2	2.8	1.5	12.1	0.1
48287	Lee County, Texas	66.2	64.3	2.0	8.3	6.1	9.9	0.7	8.4	0.4
48289	Leon County, Texas	65.2	61.9	3.3	4.3	8.4	5.8	0.3	15.7	0.4
48291	Liberty County, Texas	74.8	72.1	2.7	3.6	5.5	7.1	1.0	7.8	0.2
48293	Limestone County, Texas	57.4	56.4	1.0	3.9	6.8	20.1	1.7	10.1	0.0
48295	Lipscomb County, Texas	67.8	62.9	4.9	4.9	10.3	2.8	1.5	12.2	0.4
48297	Live Oak County, Texas	71.4	67.8	3.6	2.1	9.3	3.3	1.6	12.1	0.2
48299	Llano County, Texas	66.5	60.0	6.5	5.5	8.3	2.3	0.8	16.4	0.2
48301	Loving County, Texas	71.0	71.0	0.0	0.0	27.4	0.0	0.0	1.6	0.0
48303	Lubbock County, Texas	69.8	67.3	2.5	6.7	6.2	9.2	1.4	6.5	0.2
48305	Lynn County, Texas	59.1	57.7	1.5	6.8	15.1	4.5	2.1	12.5	0.0
48307	McCulloch County, Texas	64.2	61.5	2.7	3.9	8.7	6.4	1.1	14.6	1.1
48309	McLennan County, Texas	70.7	69.0	1.7	8.8	6.4	5.5	2.8	5.7	0.1
48311	McMullen County, Texas	52.5	50.6	1.9	8.0	19.4	0.0	6.2	12.7	1.2
48313	Madison County, Texas	60.1	57.6	2.5	5.1	11.6	9.3	1.5	11.8	0.7
48315	Marion County, Texas	72.6	69.7	2.9	6.1	10.1	4.1	1.0	5.9	0.1
48317	Martin County, Texas	74.6	69.3	5.3	2.4	5.8	6.6	0.6	10.1	0.0
48319	Mason County, Texas	58.6	52.3	6.3	7.4	6.3	3.8	1.5	21.8	0.6
48321	Matagorda County, Texas	73.3	69.5	3.7	4.2	7.5	6.3	1.8	7.0	0.0
48323	Maverick County, Texas	62.6	61.0	1.6	6.2	6.9	11.9	6.2	6.1	0.1
48325	Medina County, Texas	66.9	64.4	2.5	6.7	7.7	6.5	3.1	9.0	0.1
48327	Menard County, Texas	49.6	45.4	4.1	3.4	18.6	6.0	0.0	21.0	1.5
48329	Midland County, Texas	77.1	74.0	3.1	4.1	7.5	3.1	0.8	7.1	0.3
48331	Milam County, Texas	63.0	61.5	1.5	5.5	11.5	6.8	3.0	9.8	0.4
48333	Mills County, Texas	66.3	60.2	6.1	4.9	5.2	11.6	2.7	9.0	0.2
48335	Mitchell County, Texas	61.6	59.6	2.0	5.1	9.2	15.9	0.8	7.0	0.4
48337	Montague County, Texas	71.6	68.6	3.0	4.8	7.1	5.1	1.2	9.9	0.4
48339	Montgomery County, Texas	76.1	72.6	3.5	4.4	7.0	3.5	1.2	7.8	0.1
48341	Moore County, Texas	77.2	75.4	1.8	4.8	7.2	4.0	0.5	5.9	0.4
48343	Morris County, Texas	72.0	70.2	1.8	3.3	5.3	9.6	2.7	7.1	0.0
48345	Motley County, Texas	63.0	53.8	9.2	2.6	10.0	7.2	4.4	12.9	0.0
48347	Nacogdoches County, Texas	66.8	63.6	3.2	5.2	5.4	13.4	1.2	7.9	0.1
48349	Navarro County, Texas	70.2	68.3	1.9	4.5	8.1	7.8	1.3	7.8	0.2
48351	Newton County, Texas	72.0	71.2	0.9	7.4	6.4	7.5	1.9	4.8	0.0
48353	Nolan County, Texas	70.7	68.5	2.3	5.4	8.8	7.2	1.2	6.5	0.3
48355	Nueces County, Texas	71.5	68.9	2.6	5.1	6.9	4.5	4.9	6.9	0.2
48357	Ochiltree County, Texas	76.3	74.2	2.1	3.8	7.6	1.9	1.0	9.2	0.3
48359	Oldham County, Texas	53.9	47.9	6.1	19.3	12.7	6.2	1.2	6.7	0.0
48361	Orange County, Texas	75.5	73.7	1.8	5.3	8.1	4.9	0.7	5.4	0.1
48363	Palo Pinto County, Texas	72.0	68.9	3.2	4.7	8.9	4.1	1.1	9.0	0.2
48365	Panola County, Texas	77.4	74.5	2.8	4.1	5.8	4.2	1.6	6.9	0.0
48367	Parker County, Texas	71.0	67.8	3.2	5.6	8.5	4.7	2.0	8.0	0.2
48369	Parmer County, Texas	74.0	70.3	3.6	3.7	6.8	4.0	1.7	9.3	0.5
48371	Pecos County, Texas	64.9	62.8	2.0	3.8	14.7	7.9	1.9	6.0	0.9
48373	Polk County, Texas	62.6	60.2	2.4	6.1	9.5	10.8	2.0	8.7	0.4
48375	Potter County, Texas	75.7	73.4	2.4	5.5	4.9	4.8	2.7	6.2	0.2
48377	Presidio County, Texas	45.5	44.5	1.0	9.4	20.8	4.0	8.3	11.3	0.6
48379	Rains County, Texas	73.5	72.6	0.9	1.8	9.4	5.2	1.0	9.0	0.1
48381	Randall County, Texas	67.4	64.5	2.9	8.0	7.2	6.5	3.8	7.1	0.1

Table C. County—Labor Force, Employment, and Educational Data, 2011–2015—*Continued*

		Class of worker for civilian employed population age 16 and older								
		Private for-profit wage and salary workers				Government workers				
Fips code	State/county	Total private for-profit wage and salary workers	Employees of private companies	Self-employed in own incorporated business	Private not-for-profit wage and salary workers	Local government workers	State government workers	Federal government workers	Self-employed in own not incorporated business	Unpaid family workers
48383	Reagan County, Texas	67.0	62.6	4.4	3.0	12.1	4.8	1.7	11.1	0.2
48385	Real County, Texas	46.2	43.0	3.2	15.7	8.4	9.7	2.3	17.7	0.0
48387	Red River County, Texas	65.3	63.0	2.3	3.2	7.9	5.7	3.8	13.8	0.4
48389	Reeves County, Texas	64.7	61.6	3.0	3.1	20.1	5.8	2.4	3.9	0.0
48391	Refugio County, Texas	69.5	68.2	1.2	5.7	9.1	3.8	0.9	9.8	1.2
48393	Roberts County, Texas	57.0	50.6	6.4	2.1	18.7	4.0	0.5	17.7	0.0
48395	Robertson County, Texas	64.1	60.2	3.9	5.7	11.9	8.5	2.0	7.6	0.1
48397	Rockwall County, Texas	71.2	67.0	4.2	5.7	10.0	4.8	1.4	6.7	0.2
48399	Runnels County, Texas	63.9	60.8	3.1	3.8	8.8	9.1	1.9	12.1	0.4
48401	Rusk County, Texas	75.7	73.1	2.6	3.5	5.4	6.2	1.3	7.9	0.1
48403	Sabine County, Texas	66.5	65.7	0.8	8.6	8.9	7.4	1.8	6.8	0.0
48405	San Augustine County, Texas	68.3	63.5	4.8	13.7	4.3	4.4	0.9	8.3	0.0
48407	San Jacinto County, Texas	60.8	58.5	2.4	8.3	10.1	11.0	1.9	7.6	0.2
48409	San Patricio County, Texas	74.3	72.3	1.9	3.3	12.1	3.5	2.3	4.4	0.1
48411	San Saba County, Texas	55.8	54.4	1.4	8.7	11.7	7.8	2.2	13.5	0.3
48413	Schleicher County, Texas	63.0	61.2	1.8	4.4	14.8	5.8	2.9	9.1	0.0
48415	Scurry County, Texas	71.8	69.2	2.6	5.8	6.1	9.1	1.0	6.0	0.1
48417	Shackelford County, Texas	66.0	58.7	7.3	8.1	7.9	4.3	1.3	12.3	0.3
48419	Shelby County, Texas	70.2	67.8	2.3	5.1	4.6	10.3	1.8	7.8	0.1
48421	Sherman County, Texas	65.7	63.6	2.1	9.4	9.6	3.7	0.0	11.3	0.4
48423	Smith County, Texas	72.1	69.5	2.6	8.8	5.1	6.4	1.2	6.3	0.1
48425	Somervell County, Texas	72.2	70.4	1.8	7.6	7.9	4.7	2.0	5.5	0.3
48427	Starr County, Texas	64.6	63.2	1.4	3.6	8.1	12.9	1.6	8.6	0.6
48429	Stephens County, Texas	66.1	65.2	0.9	4.6	7.4	8.1	0.8	13.0	0.0
48431	Sterling County, Texas	62.6	60.5	2.1	1.9	18.9	2.1	0.0	14.6	0.0
48433	Stonewall County, Texas	52.8	48.3	4.5	2.5	19.5	8.5	1.3	13.6	1.8
48435	Sutton County, Texas	71.4	71.2	0.2	5.0	9.8	4.2	0.7	8.6	0.3
48437	Swisher County, Texas	71.4	67.0	4.4	7.8	9.1	2.6	0.9	8.2	0.0
48439	Tarrant County, Texas	77.2	74.5	2.7	5.9	6.7	2.6	2.2	5.4	0.1
48441	Taylor County, Texas	66.8	63.5	3.3	10.7	6.9	5.9	3.7	5.7	0.2
48443	Terrell County, Texas	43.4	42.2	1.2	6.0	9.2	4.6	19.0	16.4	1.4
48445	Terry County, Texas	65.8	62.4	3.5	4.4	14.0	5.4	0.3	9.8	0.3
48447	Throckmorton County, Texas	55.4	51.7	3.6	12.1	9.9	5.8	0.4	16.3	0.0
48449	Titus County, Texas	78.1	76.0	2.1	4.4	4.3	5.2	0.5	7.4	0.1
48451	Tom Green County, Texas	69.6	66.9	2.7	7.2	6.8	5.9	3.7	6.6	0.1
48453	Travis County, Texas	69.7	66.2	3.6	6.8	6.1	8.3	1.6	7.4	0.2
48455	Trinity County, Texas	61.8	57.2	4.6	7.0	6.7	9.3	1.7	12.1	1.3
48457	Tyler County, Texas	69.8	67.1	2.8	4.7	5.6	12.5	1.7	5.3	0.3
48459	Upshur County, Texas	72.3	70.3	2.0	6.2	7.0	5.2	0.7	8.3	0.2
48461	Upton County, Texas	66.4	62.8	3.6	5.2	10.9	9.3	0.5	7.7	0.0
48463	Uvalde County, Texas	63.5	61.9	1.6	3.3	8.0	12.6	3.2	9.4	0.0
48465	Val Verde County, Texas	61.5	59.2	2.3	4.4	9.0	6.8	13.1	5.1	0.1
48467	Van Zandt County, Texas	65.7	63.5	2.2	6.0	9.8	6.0	1.1	11.1	0.4
48469	Victoria County, Texas	74.9	72.5	2.4	5.2	7.5	4.2	0.9	7.1	0.3
48471	Walker County, Texas	52.3	49.3	3.0	7.2	6.4	27.8	2.0	4.2	0.2
48473	Waller County, Texas	71.4	68.7	2.7	6.7	9.3	5.8	1.2	5.6	0.0
48475	Ward County, Texas	74.9	73.2	1.6	4.4	11.0	3.3	0.7	5.3	0.4
48477	Washington County, Texas	67.1	64.6	2.5	6.6	8.3	8.5	1.2	8.3	0.1
48479	Webb County, Texas	71.1	68.3	2.7	3.5	10.0	5.5	3.9	5.8	0.2
48481	Wharton County, Texas	73.7	71.4	2.3	5.2	6.8	5.2	0.3	8.6	0.2
48483	Wheeler County, Texas	63.3	60.1	3.2	6.0	12.3	4.5	1.6	12.1	0.2
48485	Wichita County, Texas	66.2	64.3	1.9	8.4	6.6	7.7	4.9	6.0	0.2
48487	Wilbarger County, Texas	61.3	59.4	1.9	4.8	10.9	17.8	0.9	4.4	0.1
48489	Willacy County, Texas	62.9	62.1	0.8	4.0	16.5	3.6	3.9	9.1	0.1
48491	Williamson County, Texas	72.0	69.0	2.9	7.0	7.3	6.0	1.6	6.0	0.1
48493	Wilson County, Texas	66.7	64.0	2.7	5.0	10.9	5.0	4.6	7.6	0.1
48495	Winkler County, Texas	73.8	71.3	2.4	3.8	13.1	3.1	0.6	5.5	0.1
48497	Wise County, Texas	72.4	69.4	2.9	4.5	8.1	4.8	2.1	8.1	0.1
48499	Wood County, Texas	70.2	66.9	3.3	4.7	6.4	7.9	1.4	9.0	0.4
48501	Yoakum County, Texas	69.4	68.8	0.5	4.1	13.3	3.2	0.5	9.3	0.2
48503	Young County, Texas	65.8	62.0	3.8	7.3	10.8	3.7	1.2	10.8	0.4
48505	Zapata County, Texas	69.2	67.0	2.1	4.1	7.9	8.6	1.5	8.7	0.0
48507	Zavala County, Texas	66.6	65.5	1.1	3.8	10.6	10.2	3.1	5.6	0.1
49000	**Utah**	72.7	68.6	4.1	7.3	6.2	5.9	3.2	4.6	0.2
49001	Beaver County, Utah	73.3	67.8	5.6	2.7	12.8	6.6	0.7	3.4	0.5
49003	Box Elder County, Utah	76.6	73.2	3.4	3.0	7.2	4.5	4.2	4.3	0.2
49005	Cache County, Utah	69.4	65.1	4.4	6.9	6.8	10.2	1.6	4.9	0.2
49007	Carbon County, Utah	71.4	69.2	2.1	3.1	9.9	8.7	2.3	4.2	0.4
49009	Daggett County, Utah	47.7	38.3	9.5	0.0	24.3	4.1	15.8	8.1	0.0
49011	Davis County, Utah	69.6	66.0	3.6	6.9	6.7	5.2	7.4	4.1	0.1
49013	Duchesne County, Utah	71.7	64.2	7.5	3.3	13.2	4.9	2.3	4.3	0.2
49015	Emery County, Utah	67.5	66.3	1.2	4.1	13.9	5.9	2.7	5.7	0.2
49017	Garfield County, Utah	66.1	61.4	4.7	4.8	8.9	4.8	6.5	8.9	0.3
49019	Grand County, Utah	67.7	65.0	2.7	8.5	7.5	1.6	5.7	9.0	0.0
49021	Iron County, Utah	70.6	65.6	5.0	4.0	8.4	9.8	2.7	4.5	0.0

Table C. County—Labor Force, Employment, and Educational Data, 2011–2015—*Continued*

		Class of worker for civilian employed population age 16 and older								
		Private for-profit wage and salary workers				Government workers				
Fips code	State/county	Total private for-profit wage and salary workers	Employees of private companies	Self-employed in own incorporated business	Private not-for-profit wage and salary workers	Local government workers	State government workers	Federal government workers	Self-employed in own not incorporated business	Unpaid family workers
49023	Juab County, Utah	70.8	68.1	2.7	5.6	10.5	6.8	1.9	4.4	0.0
49025	Kane County, Utah	55.3	50.5	4.8	15.3	10.5	7.1	5.8	4.1	1.9
49027	Millard County, Utah	67.4	64.8	2.6	5.7	9.3	6.4	1.7	9.2	0.2
49029	Morgan County, Utah	76.3	71.1	5.1	3.8	6.9	3.1	4.3	5.7	0.0
49031	Piute County, Utah	56.2	51.0	5.2	5.1	8.3	20.5	3.1	6.0	0.9
49033	Rich County, Utah	68.7	53.6	15.0	5.7	13.1	5.1	0.4	7.0	0.0
49035	Salt Lake County, Utah	75.1	71.3	3.8	7.0	5.1	6.1	2.1	4.5	0.1
49037	San Juan County, Utah	54.6	50.6	4.0	5.5	18.6	9.9	5.2	5.8	0.3
49039	Sanpete County, Utah	68.8	63.1	5.7	6.0	6.1	11.6	0.9	6.5	0.1
49041	Sevier County, Utah	68.2	63.5	4.7	3.7	5.9	12.3	2.8	5.6	1.5
49043	Summit County, Utah	74.4	64.4	10.0	6.2	6.6	4.3	1.7	6.6	0.1
49045	Tooele County, Utah	70.0	67.8	2.2	4.8	9.6	4.6	7.0	3.9	0.1
49047	Uintah County, Utah	74.4	70.1	4.2	4.2	8.5	4.1	3.7	4.7	0.4
49049	Utah County, Utah	72.1	68.1	4.0	11.0	6.0	5.2	1.2	4.4	0.2
49051	Wasatch County, Utah	74.4	64.7	9.7	4.7	9.4	3.8	2.1	5.4	0.2
49053	Washington County, Utah	74.4	68.4	6.0	6.5	7.2	5.1	1.3	5.3	0.2
49055	Wayne County, Utah	63.5	52.7	10.8	4.5	5.7	8.2	7.2	10.9	0.0
49057	Weber County, Utah	70.2	66.2	3.9	6.3	5.8	4.5	9.2	3.9	0.1
50000	**Vermont**	60.9	56.4	4.5	15.0	7.2	5.0	2.5	9.3	0.2
50001	Addison County, Vermont	57.6	52.8	4.8	18.5	7.4	2.9	1.1	12.2	0.2
50003	Bennington County, Vermont	63.7	58.5	5.3	13.7	5.4	3.1	1.5	12.4	0.1
50005	Caledonia County, Vermont	58.0	54.5	3.5	14.9	8.2	5.8	1.5	10.8	0.8
50007	Chittenden County, Vermont	62.1	58.0	4.2	17.3	6.0	5.8	2.6	6.0	0.1
50009	Essex County, Vermont	59.7	55.9	3.8	10.9	10.1	5.5	2.1	11.1	0.5
50011	Franklin County, Vermont	63.5	60.2	3.4	9.9	8.0	4.2	6.5	7.8	0.1
50013	Grand Isle County, Vermont	67.8	60.6	7.2	10.4	6.6	2.5	2.6	9.8	0.3
50015	Lamoille County, Vermont	66.6	59.6	7.0	10.3	5.8	5.1	1.3	10.5	0.3
50017	Orange County, Vermont	54.2	50.7	3.5	17.5	7.3	5.6	2.9	12.3	0.2
50019	Orleans County, Vermont	58.7	54.9	3.8	11.7	8.5	5.4	3.1	12.0	0.6
50021	Rutland County, Vermont	66.0	61.6	4.3	10.7	8.9	3.9	1.6	8.7	0.3
50023	Washington County, Vermont	57.0	52.4	4.7	15.1	7.4	9.4	1.6	9.1	0.3
50025	Windham County, Vermont	58.8	52.8	6.0	15.5	8.1	2.8	1.5	13.2	0.1
50027	Windsor County, Vermont	58.2	53.9	4.2	18.5	7.2	2.9	3.0	10.0	0.2
51000	**Virginia**	66.7	63.4	3.2	7.8	7.9	4.2	8.3	5.0	0.1
51001	Accomack County, Virginia	65.9	63.9	2.0	7.2	9.1	4.4	5.2	7.7	0.5
51003	Albemarle County, Virginia	56.4	52.2	4.2	10.7	7.4	14.1	3.2	8.0	0.1
51005	Alleghany County, Virginia	69.3	66.8	2.4	8.0	9.5	5.4	1.4	6.3	0.1
51007	Amelia County, Virginia	73.0	69.6	3.3	4.2	6.1	7.7	1.1	7.9	0.0
51009	Amherst County, Virginia	67.7	65.1	2.7	11.1	7.9	5.5	1.7	5.9	0.2
51011	Appomattox County, Virginia	67.1	63.8	3.2	9.3	8.3	10.4	1.7	3.2	0.2
51013	Arlington County, Virginia	58.3	55.7	2.6	11.9	5.5	1.5	18.5	4.3	0.1
51015	Augusta County, Virginia	69.1	65.8	3.3	7.3	8.6	6.8	2.1	5.8	0.2
51017	Bath County, Virginia	72.9	67.1	5.7	7.1	6.0	6.5	2.3	5.4	0.0
51019	Bedford County, Virginia	70.2	66.1	4.2	10.3	7.9	3.6	2.2	5.5	0.2
51021	Bland County, Virginia	76.0	75.1	0.8	4.8	5.2	7.9	2.0	4.3	0.0
51023	Botetourt County, Virginia	72.4	67.7	4.7	6.7	10.6	3.1	2.4	4.6	0.1
51025	Brunswick County, Virginia	63.5	59.3	4.2	5.5	8.8	11.2	2.8	8.2	0.1
51027	Buchanan County, Virginia	74.1	72.8	1.3	4.6	9.6	7.3	1.0	3.5	0.0
51029	Buckingham County, Virginia	63.8	60.3	3.5	7.8	5.3	12.8	1.3	8.9	0.2
51031	Campbell County, Virginia	71.0	67.9	3.1	11.4	6.6	4.2	1.5	5.3	0.1
51033	Caroline County, Virginia	67.0	65.0	2.0	5.2	11.7	4.1	7.2	4.7	0.1
51035	Carroll County, Virginia	68.9	66.6	2.2	5.9	7.2	6.3	2.5	9.1	0.2
51036	Charles City County, Virginia	71.4	68.4	3.0	5.8	10.7	5.3	2.7	3.9	0.1
51037	Charlotte County, Virginia	68.5	66.7	1.8	3.7	11.0	10.5	1.2	5.0	0.0
51041	Chesterfield County, Virginia	70.2	67.1	3.1	6.6	8.1	5.8	4.4	4.8	0.1
51043	Clarke County, Virginia	64.9	61.8	3.1	7.0	13.4	2.1	4.1	8.5	0.0
51045	Craig County, Virginia	64.0	62.6	1.4	8.7	5.9	12.7	2.7	6.1	0.0
51047	Culpeper County, Virginia	68.0	64.8	3.2	7.0	10.1	3.1	4.2	7.5	0.1
51049	Cumberland County, Virginia	62.8	61.3	1.6	5.2	7.8	12.4	3.1	8.6	0.0
51051	Dickenson County, Virginia	60.4	58.6	1.9	6.1	15.3	12.2	1.4	4.3	0.3
51053	Dinwiddie County, Virginia	69.9	67.8	2.1	4.3	8.8	6.3	4.4	6.0	0.4
51057	Essex County, Virginia	69.2	67.6	1.7	8.4	9.4	4.4	3.9	4.4	0.3
51059	Fairfax County, Virginia	64.0	59.9	4.1	8.9	6.1	1.8	13.7	5.4	0.1
51061	Fauquier County, Virginia	66.7	61.2	5.5	6.3	11.3	2.1	6.6	6.7	0.3
51063	Floyd County, Virginia	68.4	62.4	6.0	4.2	9.5	4.3	3.2	10.4	0.0
51065	Fluvanna County, Virginia	64.2	61.3	2.9	7.0	8.1	9.9	2.6	8.1	0.1
51067	Franklin County, Virginia	72.0	67.3	4.7	8.1	8.3	2.7	2.5	6.3	0.2
51069	Frederick County, Virginia	67.4	63.6	3.8	9.8	10.0	2.2	5.5	5.0	0.1
51071	Giles County, Virginia	66.5	62.5	3.9	7.9	10.0	7.8	1.9	6.0	0.1
51073	Gloucester County, Virginia	69.6	64.9	4.7	5.8	8.1	3.8	6.3	6.1	0.3
51075	Goochland County, Virginia	71.5	63.9	7.6	6.0	8.0	5.3	2.1	6.9	0.3
51077	Grayson County, Virginia	72.4	70.2	2.1	5.3	9.7	5.8	0.9	5.8	0.2
51079	Greene County, Virginia	64.5	61.3	3.1	6.7	7.1	8.9	5.5	7.2	0.1
51081	Greensville County, Virginia	71.9	69.4	2.5	2.8	7.8	13.3	0.4	3.9	0.0

Table C. County—Labor Force, Employment, and Educational Data, 2011–2015—*Continued*

| | | Class of worker for civilian employed population age 16 and older | | | | | | | | |
| | | Private for-profit wage and salary workers | | | | Government workers | | | | |
Fips code	State/county	Total private for-profit wage and salary workers	Employees of private companies	Self-employed in own incorporated business	Private not-for-profit wage and salary workers	Local government workers	State government workers	Federal government workers	Self-employed in own not incorporated business	Unpaid family workers
51083	Halifax County, Virginia	68.2	65.5	2.7	5.3	10.8	6.6	1.6	7.3	0.3
51085	Hanover County, Virginia	71.2	66.8	4.4	7.4	10.0	4.5	2.4	4.5	0.0
51087	Henrico County, Virginia	73.7	70.6	3.0	6.5	8.0	5.2	2.7	3.9	0.1
51089	Henry County, Virginia	76.8	73.8	3.0	4.9	8.3	4.7	0.8	4.3	0.1
51091	Highland County, Virginia	54.0	44.1	9.8	7.9	9.3	9.4	2.5	16.9	0.0
51093	Isle of Wight County, Virginia	68.1	64.4	3.8	6.3	8.7	3.9	7.3	5.5	0.2
51095	James City County, Virginia	62.7	57.7	5.0	9.3	10.2	6.2	6.4	5.0	0.2
51097	King and Queen County, Virginia	69.7	65.6	4.1	6.8	8.4	6.1	1.6	7.3	0.0
51099	King George County, Virginia	58.2	55.2	3.0	4.2	8.1	3.2	22.6	3.7	0.1
51101	King William County, Virginia	74.0	69.5	4.5	4.6	9.6	3.2	2.5	6.0	0.2
51103	Lancaster County, Virginia	64.5	60.9	3.6	9.7	9.9	3.5	2.4	9.7	0.2
51105	Lee County, Virginia	64.6	62.0	2.5	6.5	9.9	7.9	5.2	5.3	0.5
51107	Loudoun County, Virginia	71.8	67.7	4.1	6.6	7.2	1.5	8.2	4.5	0.1
51109	Louisa County, Virginia	70.5	66.7	3.8	4.7	8.2	6.2	1.9	8.1	0.3
51111	Lunenburg County, Virginia	59.6	57.7	1.9	5.1	10.3	15.7	2.6	6.4	0.3
51113	Madison County, Virginia	61.3	57.9	3.5	7.4	10.0	4.5	3.1	13.7	0.0
51115	Mathews County, Virginia	64.5	60.2	4.3	7.1	9.8	4.7	5.6	8.2	0.0
51117	Mecklenburg County, Virginia	62.3	58.5	3.8	8.0	11.3	8.2	2.0	7.9	0.2
51119	Middlesex County, Virginia	69.9	63.7	6.2	5.2	10.4	4.5	1.1	8.8	0.0
51121	Montgomery County, Virginia	58.6	56.5	2.1	6.9	7.1	21.7	1.8	3.8	0.0
51125	Nelson County, Virginia	60.5	56.6	3.9	8.6	9.1	6.4	0.6	14.2	0.6
51127	New Kent County, Virginia	67.8	63.8	4.0	6.7	9.2	6.5	2.5	6.7	0.7
51131	Northampton County, Virginia	64.4	61.2	3.3	7.9	9.4	4.9	3.0	10.2	0.1
51133	Northumberland County, Virginia	66.3	61.6	4.7	5.9	6.7	5.1	4.3	11.7	0.0
51135	Nottoway County, Virginia	56.8	55.0	1.7	6.0	12.9	13.3	6.3	4.7	0.0
51137	Orange County, Virginia	64.1	61.0	3.1	9.5	8.9	5.7	5.1	6.7	0.0
51139	Page County, Virginia	71.7	68.4	3.2	4.3	9.0	3.7	4.9	6.3	0.1
51141	Patrick County, Virginia	74.9	73.7	1.2	2.8	8.2	4.8	2.1	7.2	0.1
51143	Pittsylvania County, Virginia	74.6	71.5	3.2	5.2	8.3	4.8	1.1	5.9	0.2
51145	Powhatan County, Virginia	70.8	66.2	4.6	6.9	9.3	4.8	2.6	5.5	0.1
51147	Prince Edward County, Virginia	60.3	57.4	2.8	8.0	7.2	15.6	2.4	6.4	0.1
51149	Prince George County, Virginia	63.3	60.5	2.9	4.6	8.7	5.4	12.5	5.2	0.3
51153	Prince William County, Virginia	66.2	63.4	2.8	6.2	8.4	1.8	13.3	4.0	0.1
51155	Pulaski County, Virginia	71.5	69.7	1.8	4.8	9.5	6.9	2.5	4.7	0.0
51157	Rappahannock County, Virginia	55.9	49.5	6.4	7.6	13.4	3.8	4.3	15.0	0.0
51159	Richmond County, Virginia	60.6	59.4	1.2	5.7	13.4	5.3	2.8	11.8	0.5
51161	Roanoke County, Virginia	69.9	65.8	4.1	9.7	8.5	3.7	3.2	5.0	0.0
51163	Rockbridge County, Virginia	60.0	56.7	3.4	11.3	9.7	6.3	1.0	11.5	0.1
51165	Rockingham County, Virginia	68.9	64.9	3.9	7.4	8.7	6.0	1.1	7.4	0.5
51167	Russell County, Virginia	72.2	69.1	3.1	4.5	11.1	5.2	1.9	5.1	0.0
51169	Scott County, Virginia	70.2	68.5	1.7	8.1	9.5	5.2	1.7	5.3	0.0
51171	Shenandoah County, Virginia	72.9	69.3	3.7	6.1	9.7	3.0	2.6	5.4	0.2
51173	Smyth County, Virginia	68.6	67.2	1.4	7.0	9.4	6.8	1.4	6.6	0.2
51175	Southampton County, Virginia	65.7	63.9	1.8	4.4	10.8	10.4	2.9	5.6	0.1
51177	Spotsylvania County, Virginia	67.2	64.5	2.6	5.2	9.0	2.2	11.9	4.4	0.1
51179	Stafford County, Virginia	58.6	56.2	2.4	5.9	8.9	2.3	20.7	3.4	0.1
51181	Surry County, Virginia	70.0	66.1	4.0	7.2	12.1	4.8	1.3	4.6	0.0
51183	Sussex County, Virginia	72.0	69.1	2.9	4.8	7.4	7.3	4.3	3.7	0.4
51185	Tazewell County, Virginia	71.9	70.6	1.3	4.3	9.1	6.1	2.4	5.9	0.3
51187	Warren County, Virginia	67.1	63.9	3.1	6.9	10.4	2.9	5.6	6.8	0.3
51191	Washington County, Virginia	70.9	67.1	3.8	7.1	8.1	5.9	1.9	6.0	0.0
51193	Westmoreland County, Virginia	60.1	56.5	3.6	4.8	8.5	5.4	11.1	10.0	0.0
51195	Wise County, Virginia	69.1	66.8	2.3	5.4	10.3	9.2	3.1	2.9	0.1
51197	Wythe County, Virginia	72.8	70.7	2.1	6.3	9.1	5.5	0.9	5.2	0.2
51199	York County, Virginia	59.2	55.4	3.8	8.4	8.8	4.2	14.5	4.7	0.3
51510	Alexandria city, Virginia	56.9	54.6	2.4	13.1	5.0	1.6	18.7	4.7	0.0
51520	Bristol city, Virginia	73.6	71.8	1.8	7.5	6.5	5.0	0.7	6.5	0.3
51530	Buena Vista city, Virginia	70.6	66.0	4.7	12.0	6.0	7.3	1.7	2.3	0.0
51540	Charlottesville city, Virginia	58.3	55.1	3.2	9.8	4.5	19.0	2.3	6.0	0.0
51550	Chesapeake city, Virginia	66.8	63.8	3.0	6.3	9.6	2.9	10.1	4.2	0.1
51570	Colonial Heights city, Virginia	67.4	64.4	3.0	4.3	10.3	7.2	6.6	3.8	0.4
51580	Covington city, Virginia	73.8	72.8	1.0	9.5	10.1	5.3	0.0	1.3	0.0
51590	Danville city, Virginia	70.9	69.3	1.5	7.5	8.3	5.7	1.9	5.3	0.5
51595	Emporia city, Virginia	67.0	63.0	4.0	7.1	7.8	12.8	2.1	3.3	0.0
51600	Fairfax city, Virginia	65.1	62.1	3.0	8.3	7.8	3.2	10.9	4.5	0.2
51610	Falls Church city, Virginia	47.8	44.5	3.4	12.8	6.6	1.0	24.4	7.3	0.0
51620	Franklin city, Virginia	58.3	54.7	3.6	5.6	13.8	9.9	5.2	6.3	0.9
51630	Fredericksburg city, Virginia	66.5	63.4	3.2	8.5	6.7	4.1	10.8	3.1	0.2
51640	Galax city, Virginia	75.3	74.4	0.9	5.1	4.1	9.0	1.0	5.5	0.0
51650	Hampton city, Virginia	66.7	64.9	1.8	6.8	8.7	3.2	10.7	4.0	0.0
51660	Harrisonburg city, Virginia	67.5	64.8	2.8	9.4	5.6	11.1	2.1	4.1	0.1
51670	Hopewell city, Virginia	75.8	72.9	2.9	3.2	8.2	4.1	6.5	2.2	0.0
51678	Lexington city, Virginia	56.9	55.8	1.1	23.4	6.7	4.8	3.4	4.8	0.0
51680	Lynchburg city, Virginia	65.6	63.4	2.2	17.8	6.6	4.4	1.5	4.1	0.1
51683	Manassas city, Virginia	74.1	71.7	2.4	5.7	9.4	1.4	5.6	3.7	0.2
51685	Manassas Park city, Virginia	74.7	71.6	3.1	6.1	6.2	1.1	7.8	4.2	0.0

Table C. County—Labor Force, Employment, and Educational Data, 2011–2015—*Continued*

| | | Class of worker for civilian employed population age 16 and older | | | | | | | | |
| | | Private for-profit wage and salary workers | | | | Government workers | | | | |
Fips code	State/county	Total private for-profit wage and salary workers	Employees of private companies	Self-employed in own incorporated business	Private not-for-profit wage and salary workers	Local government workers	State government workers	Federal government workers	Self-employed in own not incorporated business	Unpaid family workers
51690	Martinsville city, Virginia	74.3	71.2	3.1	5.0	9.0	4.6	1.6	5.1	0.3
51700	Newport News city, Virginia	68.1	66.6	1.5	6.7	8.0	3.7	9.9	3.5	0.0
51710	Norfolk city, Virginia	66.5	64.4	2.1	6.8	7.6	4.4	10.7	3.9	0.1
51720	Norton city, Virginia	71.9	71.4	0.6	9.2	12.6	3.8	0.0	2.4	0.0
51730	Petersburg city, Virginia	70.1	69.1	1.0	5.5	6.0	7.9	7.8	2.6	0.0
51735	Poquoson city, Virginia	67.9	61.4	6.5	5.7	11.0	2.6	6.8	5.5	0.5
51740	Portsmouth city, Virginia	62.3	60.5	1.8	6.9	9.3	2.8	13.8	4.8	0.1
51750	Radford city, Virginia	71.2	68.5	2.7	5.2	7.4	11.2	0.4	4.2	0.3
51760	Richmond city, Virginia	69.9	67.2	2.7	9.7	6.0	7.3	3.0	4.0	0.1
51770	Roanoke city, Virginia	72.0	69.6	2.4	10.4	7.3	2.8	3.7	3.7	0.1
51775	Salem city, Virginia	71.6	68.9	2.6	8.2	10.0	3.0	4.5	2.7	0.0
51790	Staunton city, Virginia	62.3	58.9	3.4	9.5	10.8	9.7	1.7	5.9	0.2
51800	Suffolk city, Virginia	62.8	59.6	3.2	8.9	9.4	4.5	10.3	4.1	0.1
51810	Virginia Beach city, Virginia	67.3	63.5	3.8	6.7	9.2	2.3	9.8	4.5	0.1
51820	Waynesboro city, Virginia	73.0	72.2	0.8	7.6	8.0	6.3	1.6	3.5	0.0
51830	Williamsburg city, Virginia	51.6	50.6	1.0	12.1	8.3	21.1	3.7	3.1	0.1
51840	Winchester city, Virginia	70.4	66.0	4.3	10.1	7.0	2.9	3.1	6.3	0.3
53000	**Washington**	69.5	65.7	3.8	8.1	6.5	6.4	3.4	6.0	0.2
53001	Adams County, Washington	75.9	72.3	3.6	5.6	7.7	5.4	1.4	3.8	0.3
53003	Asotin County, Washington	70.3	66.5	3.8	6.6	7.6	7.1	1.9	6.5	0.0
53005	Benton County, Washington	71.6	68.3	3.3	7.1	5.7	7.1	4.1	4.3	0.1
53007	Chelan County, Washington	69.5	64.6	4.9	7.4	7.8	6.3	1.9	6.9	0.2
53009	Clallam County, Washington	62.5	57.0	5.5	7.2	11.7	6.8	3.5	8.2	0.1
53011	Clark County, Washington	72.4	68.3	4.0	7.5	6.3	4.3	2.9	6.5	0.2
53013	Columbia County, Washington	49.6	42.8	6.8	8.4	13.6	9.8	5.5	12.7	0.4
53015	Cowlitz County, Washington	69.9	66.4	3.5	9.1	7.4	5.9	1.5	5.8	0.4
53017	Douglas County, Washington	75.7	71.1	4.5	3.5	8.4	4.8	1.5	5.7	0.4
53019	Ferry County, Washington	46.4	44.9	1.4	6.1	17.9	11.5	11.3	6.4	0.5
53021	Franklin County, Washington	76.0	72.9	3.1	5.6	6.1	5.0	2.2	5.0	0.1
53023	Garfield County, Washington	45.5	43.7	1.8	2.9	19.0	9.3	4.1	19.1	0.0
53025	Grant County, Washington	71.1	68.0	3.1	4.3	8.9	8.4	2.1	5.1	0.1
53027	Grays Harbor County, Washington	63.6	60.4	3.2	7.6	10.2	9.8	1.7	7.0	0.2
53029	Island County, Washington	61.1	57.2	4.0	6.1	9.0	5.3	9.3	8.8	0.4
53031	Jefferson County, Washington	57.6	48.3	9.3	9.3	10.0	5.1	3.2	14.8	0.1
53033	King County, Washington	72.7	68.6	4.1	9.0	5.4	5.2	1.9	5.7	0.2
53035	Kitsap County, Washington	56.2	52.5	3.7	9.1	7.4	4.9	15.3	7.0	0.1
53037	Kittitas County, Washington	59.0	53.8	5.2	7.1	8.0	15.5	2.5	7.7	0.3
53039	Klickitat County, Washington	63.4	58.8	4.6	7.5	9.7	6.3	3.7	9.0	0.3
53041	Lewis County, Washington	67.6	64.6	3.0	5.9	6.8	10.4	2.0	7.1	0.2
53043	Lincoln County, Washington	59.0	49.3	9.7	5.8	12.6	10.6	3.2	8.6	0.2
53045	Mason County, Washington	57.8	54.3	3.5	6.7	8.4	12.0	5.5	9.5	0.1
53047	Okanogan County, Washington	57.6	52.8	4.8	7.5	13.3	5.8	6.0	9.5	0.3
53049	Pacific County, Washington	61.8	57.3	4.4	8.4	10.7	9.4	2.0	7.7	0.0
53051	Pend Oreille County, Washington	54.7	51.7	3.0	7.8	13.9	8.1	4.5	10.4	0.7
53053	Pierce County, Washington	67.8	64.5	3.2	8.1	7.2	5.7	5.8	5.3	0.1
53055	San Juan County, Washington	60.0	49.8	10.2	8.9	8.9	4.5	0.9	16.2	0.5
53057	Skagit County, Washington	69.3	65.2	4.1	7.1	7.8	5.2	2.6	7.8	0.1
53059	Skamania County, Washington	65.4	61.2	4.2	7.7	11.4	4.1	4.9	6.3	0.2
53061	Snohomish County, Washington	74.5	71.1	3.5	7.0	6.0	4.9	1.9	5.5	0.2
53063	Spokane County, Washington	69.0	65.3	3.7	9.4	5.9	6.7	2.9	6.0	0.2
53065	Stevens County, Washington	61.1	56.9	4.2	7.9	8.9	8.6	4.2	8.8	0.4
53067	Thurston County, Washington	55.7	52.1	3.6	7.0	6.9	17.6	6.5	6.1	0.2
53069	Wahkiakum County, Washington	61.9	56.7	5.2	1.4	14.2	11.5	1.7	9.2	0.0
53071	Walla Walla County, Washington	61.8	58.2	3.6	12.4	7.0	8.5	3.6	6.5	0.2
53073	Whatcom County, Washington	67.8	62.7	5.0	7.3	7.4	8.1	2.6	6.6	0.3
53075	Whitman County, Washington	50.4	47.3	3.1	5.7	7.1	30.3	2.0	4.4	0.1
53077	Yakima County, Washington	72.1	69.5	2.6	7.4	5.9	6.7	2.3	5.6	0.1
54000	**West Virginia**	69.1	66.9	2.2	7.4	7.3	7.8	3.9	4.4	0.1
54001	Barbour County, West Virginia	72.3	70.4	1.9	7.2	6.0	6.5	4.2	3.9	0.0
54003	Berkeley County, West Virginia	66.8	64.5	2.4	5.8	8.9	4.7	9.5	4.2	0.1
54005	Boone County, West Virginia	74.7	73.9	0.8	3.0	8.5	7.7	1.6	4.5	0.0
54007	Braxton County, West Virginia	70.9	68.5	2.4	3.9	8.7	7.1	2.8	6.1	0.5
54009	Brooke County, West Virginia	71.4	70.5	0.9	8.1	8.1	6.2	2.2	4.0	0.0
54011	Cabell County, West Virginia	70.1	67.9	2.1	9.4	6.2	7.3	3.3	3.8	0.0
54013	Calhoun County, West Virginia	70.1	66.1	3.9	7.6	5.8	10.0	1.8	3.3	1.5
54015	Clay County, West Virginia	59.3	56.7	2.6	9.8	10.5	11.1	1.2	7.0	1.0
54017	Doddridge County, West Virginia	66.9	63.3	3.6	5.8	9.3	10.3	2.1	5.7	0.0
54019	Fayette County, West Virginia	70.9	69.0	1.9	3.9	7.8	10.7	3.2	3.5	0.1
54021	Gilmer County, West Virginia	62.5	59.2	3.3	4.3	10.7	15.6	3.5	3.4	0.0
54023	Grant County, West Virginia	72.2	69.6	2.6	5.6	9.3	5.1	0.7	7.1	0.0
54025	Greenbrier County, West Virginia	69.8	68.0	1.7	6.5	7.2	6.8	2.4	7.1	0.1
54027	Hampshire County, West Virginia	68.0	66.1	1.9	6.1	7.5	7.5	2.5	8.2	0.2
54029	Hancock County, West Virginia	75.6	73.9	1.6	8.2	7.6	4.4	1.3	3.0	0.0
54031	Hardy County, West Virginia	74.9	71.5	3.4	3.9	5.7	7.8	2.3	5.1	0.3

Table C. County—Labor Force, Employment, and Educational Data, 2011–2015—*Continued*

		Class of worker for civilian employed population age 16 and older								
		Private for-profit wage and salary workers				Government workers				
Fips code	State/county	Total private for-profit wage and salary workers	Employees of private companies	Self-employed in own incorporated business	Private not-for-profit wage and salary workers	Local government workers	State government workers	Federal government workers	Self-employed in own not incorporated business	Unpaid family workers
54033	Harrison County, West Virginia	67.8	65.3	2.5	7.2	5.6	6.0	7.7	5.6	0.1
54035	Jackson County, West Virginia	68.7	66.8	1.9	6.3	7.3	9.5	2.7	5.4	0.1
54037	Jefferson County, West Virginia	66.1	63.8	2.3	5.5	9.3	4.9	9.2	4.8	0.2
54039	Kanawha County, West Virginia	65.5	63.2	2.3	10.2	7.4	10.0	2.5	4.2	0.2
54041	Lewis County, West Virginia	74.2	71.6	2.6	4.8	5.5	6.9	3.5	5.0	0.1
54043	Lincoln County, West Virginia	71.2	68.7	2.5	5.6	12.4	5.7	2.3	2.7	0.0
54045	Logan County, West Virginia	75.2	72.9	2.3	2.6	6.9	8.8	2.1	4.4	0.0
54047	McDowell County, West Virginia	60.6	59.2	1.4	5.8	11.4	14.5	4.9	2.7	0.0
54049	Marion County, West Virginia	71.4	69.9	1.5	5.8	6.2	7.1	4.4	4.8	0.2
54051	Marshall County, West Virginia	71.8	70.5	1.3	8.5	6.6	7.3	1.6	4.1	0.0
54053	Mason County, West Virginia	70.6	68.8	1.7	8.7	6.3	9.6	1.9	2.9	0.1
54055	Mercer County, West Virginia	70.2	68.5	1.7	7.1	8.0	7.8	1.9	5.0	0.1
54057	Mineral County, West Virginia	72.0	71.4	0.6	5.3	8.9	7.7	2.3	3.8	0.0
54059	Mingo County, West Virginia	68.5	66.2	2.4	5.0	9.8	9.4	2.4	4.7	0.2
54061	Monongalia County, West Virginia	64.4	62.2	2.2	9.7	4.3	14.1	3.4	4.0	0.0
54063	Monroe County, West Virginia	72.8	69.4	3.5	4.3	8.2	4.8	2.6	7.2	0.0
54065	Morgan County, West Virginia	64.4	62.1	2.3	8.1	9.7	7.7	2.6	7.6	0.0
54067	Nicholas County, West Virginia	70.1	66.6	3.4	8.5	8.5	5.8	3.0	3.5	0.6
54069	Ohio County, West Virginia	70.8	68.8	2.0	10.4	8.2	4.2	2.4	3.9	0.1
54071	Pendleton County, West Virginia	61.9	57.4	4.5	2.5	5.5	9.6	10.8	9.1	0.5
54073	Pleasants County, West Virginia	64.4	63.1	1.4	6.8	8.3	11.6	2.4	6.5	0.0
54075	Pocahontas County, West Virginia	54.2	51.2	2.9	7.1	11.2	15.4	5.4	6.7	0.1
54077	Preston County, West Virginia	70.6	68.5	2.0	5.4	6.7	8.0	3.3	5.8	0.2
54079	Putnam County, West Virginia	72.3	69.5	2.8	8.4	7.2	7.2	2.3	2.6	0.0
54081	Raleigh County, West Virginia	70.4	68.7	1.7	5.0	6.3	8.4	6.0	3.7	0.1
54083	Randolph County, West Virginia	65.3	63.3	2.0	11.9	6.1	9.7	3.2	3.9	0.0
54085	Ritchie County, West Virginia	73.4	69.5	3.9	2.9	8.4	9.0	2.8	3.5	0.0
54087	Roane County, West Virginia	67.6	63.3	4.3	8.7	8.7	5.5	2.0	7.4	0.2
54089	Summers County, West Virginia	59.7	57.6	2.1	10.1	7.2	11.0	4.2	7.7	0.1
54091	Taylor County, West Virginia	72.6	69.8	2.8	6.6	4.3	6.2	5.6	4.7	0.0
54093	Tucker County, West Virginia	57.2	54.5	2.8	6.5	9.7	18.5	3.2	4.7	0.0
54095	Tyler County, West Virginia	68.0	66.5	1.5	7.9	8.0	9.3	1.6	5.2	0.0
54097	Upshur County, West Virginia	69.6	67.5	2.2	7.3	7.2	5.0	4.9	5.7	0.3
54099	Wayne County, West Virginia	69.7	67.0	2.7	7.6	8.1	6.0	4.2	4.4	0.0
54101	Webster County, West Virginia	73.0	69.8	3.2	6.7	6.7	6.6	2.2	4.7	0.2
54103	Wetzel County, West Virginia	72.4	70.4	1.9	7.4	10.1	6.2	0.9	2.9	0.1
54105	Wirt County, West Virginia	70.2	66.1	4.1	6.8	5.9	11.2	2.0	4.0	0.0
54107	Wood County, West Virginia	74.3	72.3	2.0	7.5	5.8	4.5	4.0	3.8	0.1
54109	Wyoming County, West Virginia	73.1	72.2	1.0	4.8	9.2	7.9	3.5	1.5	0.0
55000	**Wisconsin**	73.0	70.0	3.1	9.2	6.7	4.4	1.3	5.1	0.2
55001	Adams County, Wisconsin	73.2	68.8	4.3	6.8	7.7	3.1	1.8	7.3	0.2
55003	Ashland County, Wisconsin	66.8	63.4	3.4	8.8	11.0	2.5	3.9	6.9	0.1
55005	Barron County, Wisconsin	74.0	70.4	3.6	6.8	6.8	3.2	0.9	8.1	0.2
55007	Bayfield County, Wisconsin	58.5	54.1	4.4	9.9	12.5	4.0	4.3	10.4	0.4
55009	Brown County, Wisconsin	75.5	73.0	2.5	9.0	6.9	3.0	1.1	4.3	0.1
55011	Buffalo County, Wisconsin	69.8	65.0	4.9	8.0	7.3	2.6	1.1	10.7	0.5
55013	Burnett County, Wisconsin	65.9	61.2	4.7	9.8	9.4	3.7	1.5	9.3	0.4
55015	Calumet County, Wisconsin	77.2	73.9	3.3	8.8	5.5	3.1	0.9	4.3	0.2
55017	Chippewa County, Wisconsin	73.4	70.2	3.2	7.9	6.1	3.6	1.0	7.7	0.3
55019	Clark County, Wisconsin	68.3	63.7	4.6	7.5	5.9	2.1	1.0	14.7	0.6
55021	Columbia County, Wisconsin	71.1	67.7	3.3	8.2	6.9	6.2	1.6	5.6	0.4
55023	Crawford County, Wisconsin	69.9	66.4	3.5	7.6	6.6	5.0	1.7	9.1	0.0
55025	Dane County, Wisconsin	64.6	61.6	3.0	9.7	6.2	13.4	1.5	4.5	0.1
55027	Dodge County, Wisconsin	76.0	72.8	3.2	7.5	6.1	3.5	1.4	5.2	0.4
55029	Door County, Wisconsin	70.4	65.0	5.4	8.8	7.8	3.2	0.9	8.6	0.3
55031	Douglas County, Wisconsin	68.5	66.1	2.4	12.4	7.6	5.1	1.6	4.6	0.1
55033	Dunn County, Wisconsin	69.4	66.6	2.8	8.1	6.8	7.6	0.8	7.1	0.2
55035	Eau Claire County, Wisconsin	70.9	68.7	2.3	10.7	5.6	6.6	0.9	5.2	0.1
55037	Florence County, Wisconsin	68.7	63.9	4.9	6.5	10.7	2.1	3.5	8.1	0.4
55039	Fond du Lac County, Wisconsin	75.3	71.8	3.5	8.7	6.0	3.9	0.8	5.0	0.3
55041	Forest County, Wisconsin	58.1	54.1	4.0	5.9	17.0	4.8	3.5	10.6	0.0
55043	Grant County, Wisconsin	68.1	64.5	3.5	6.7	7.2	8.5	0.9	8.0	0.7
55045	Green County, Wisconsin	70.4	65.6	4.8	8.6	6.7	4.4	1.4	8.2	0.4
55047	Green Lake County, Wisconsin	73.2	68.9	4.4	6.5	5.9	3.8	1.4	8.9	0.2
55049	Iowa County, Wisconsin	70.3	65.2	5.2	6.1	6.5	6.0	1.1	9.4	0.4
55051	Iron County, Wisconsin	66.3	62.5	3.8	8.1	12.7	3.9	2.3	6.6	0.1
55053	Jackson County, Wisconsin	66.5	63.9	2.6	6.5	8.6	6.0	3.5	8.5	0.4
55055	Jefferson County, Wisconsin	75.3	72.1	3.2	8.5	6.4	3.7	1.0	4.9	0.1
55057	Juneau County, Wisconsin	72.0	68.9	3.1	5.3	7.6	5.7	2.9	6.1	0.4
55059	Kenosha County, Wisconsin	76.8	73.7	3.1	7.6	7.5	2.4	1.9	3.6	0.1
55061	Kewaunee County, Wisconsin	77.4	74.1	3.3	4.9	6.1	1.6	1.1	8.7	0.2
55063	La Crosse County, Wisconsin	69.4	67.1	2.3	12.6	6.5	5.6	1.6	4.1	0.1
55065	Lafayette County, Wisconsin	70.0	66.1	3.9	5.2	7.4	3.4	1.4	12.1	0.6

Table C. County—Labor Force, Employment, and Educational Data, 2011–2015—*Continued*

| | | Class of worker for civilian employed population age 16 and older | | | | | | | | |
| | | Private for-profit wage and salary workers | | | | Government workers | | | | |
Fips code	State/county	Total private for-profit wage and salary workers	Employees of private companies	Self-employed in own incorporated business	Private not-for-profit wage and salary workers	Local government workers	State government workers	Federal government workers	Self-employed in own not incorporated business	Unpaid family workers
55067	Langlade County, Wisconsin	72.5	69.0	3.5	9.2	7.2	3.0	1.4	6.3	0.4
55069	Lincoln County, Wisconsin	75.0	71.5	3.4	7.6	7.3	2.5	1.2	6.1	0.2
55071	Manitowoc County, Wisconsin	77.5	74.6	2.9	8.4	6.3	1.8	0.9	4.9	0.1
55073	Marathon County, Wisconsin	75.2	72.1	3.2	9.3	6.1	2.7	0.9	5.5	0.3
55075	Marinette County, Wisconsin	74.9	72.1	2.8	7.6	6.9	2.6	0.7	6.9	0.5
55077	Marquette County, Wisconsin	72.4	69.9	2.5	6.4	7.4	4.0	2.4	7.2	0.2
55078	Menominee County, Wisconsin	28.4	28.4	0.0	8.4	51.5	3.4	4.2	3.7	0.4
55079	Milwaukee County, Wisconsin	73.2	71.1	2.0	11.6	7.3	2.8	1.6	3.4	0.1
55081	Monroe County, Wisconsin	65.0	62.4	2.6	6.9	5.6	4.4	10.6	7.2	0.3
55083	Oconto County, Wisconsin	75.4	72.1	3.3	5.6	7.2	3.2	1.6	6.6	0.3
55085	Oneida County, Wisconsin	69.8	66.6	3.2	9.1	7.7	4.2	1.2	7.7	0.2
55087	Outagamie County, Wisconsin	78.3	75.6	2.7	8.7	5.5	2.1	1.0	4.3	0.2
55089	Ozaukee County, Wisconsin	75.0	69.8	5.2	10.5	5.3	2.1	1.1	5.7	0.2
55091	Pepin County, Wisconsin	67.7	63.2	4.5	7.3	7.8	3.7	1.3	11.9	0.2
55093	Pierce County, Wisconsin	70.5	67.5	3.0	7.7	6.9	7.0	1.1	6.4	0.4
55095	Polk County, Wisconsin	70.7	66.6	4.1	8.5	7.4	3.7	1.1	8.2	0.5
55097	Portage County, Wisconsin	72.4	69.6	2.7	7.8	6.6	7.1	0.9	5.1	0.2
55099	Price County, Wisconsin	70.4	66.3	4.1	6.7	9.2	2.9	1.4	9.1	0.4
55101	Racine County, Wisconsin	75.8	73.5	2.3	9.1	6.4	3.2	1.2	4.3	0.1
55103	Richland County, Wisconsin	70.4	67.2	3.3	8.0	7.6	3.4	1.2	9.1	0.2
55105	Rock County, Wisconsin	74.6	71.3	3.3	9.1	7.9	3.1	0.8	4.5	0.1
55107	Rusk County, Wisconsin	68.7	63.8	4.8	7.3	8.7	3.6	1.0	10.0	0.7
55109	St. Croix County, Wisconsin	73.2	68.7	4.5	8.6	6.4	4.7	1.2	5.7	0.1
55111	Sauk County, Wisconsin	74.1	70.5	3.7	7.5	6.9	4.0	1.2	6.0	0.3
55113	Sawyer County, Wisconsin	60.1	55.2	4.9	9.0	14.8	2.6	2.5	10.3	0.7
55115	Shawano County, Wisconsin	70.5	67.2	3.3	6.3	9.9	2.6	1.7	8.8	0.2
55117	Sheboygan County, Wisconsin	78.4	75.6	2.8	8.4	6.7	1.4	0.6	4.4	0.1
55119	Taylor County, Wisconsin	71.2	67.5	3.8	7.9	6.2	1.6	0.8	11.9	0.4
55121	Trempealeau County, Wisconsin	72.0	68.8	3.2	6.7	6.9	3.7	1.4	9.0	0.3
55123	Vernon County, Wisconsin	65.9	62.1	3.8	10.4	7.1	3.9	1.5	10.8	0.4
55125	Vilas County, Wisconsin	63.1	56.4	6.7	7.7	11.9	2.8	1.2	13.0	0.2
55127	Walworth County, Wisconsin	73.9	70.1	3.9	7.5	7.0	3.9	1.0	6.2	0.3
55129	Washburn County, Wisconsin	67.5	63.6	3.9	7.8	7.6	4.6	2.5	9.8	0.2
55131	Washington County, Wisconsin	78.9	75.4	3.4	8.8	5.6	1.8	0.8	4.1	0.1
55133	Waukesha County, Wisconsin	77.4	73.5	3.8	10.0	5.3	1.9	1.1	4.2	0.1
55135	Waupaca County, Wisconsin	75.2	71.3	3.8	7.2	6.8	4.1	0.8	5.6	0.3
55137	Waushara County, Wisconsin	70.8	67.2	3.6	6.1	7.1	5.8	1.5	8.2	0.4
55139	Winnebago County, Wisconsin	77.3	74.8	2.5	7.6	6.2	4.5	0.7	3.6	0.1
55141	Wood County, Wisconsin	70.7	67.9	2.8	12.8	7.6	2.3	1.0	5.5	0.2
56000	**Wyoming**	65.9	62.0	4.0	6.4	10.5	7.4	3.2	6.4	0.3
56001	Albany County, Wyoming	50.7	46.7	4.0	8.0	9.8	22.9	1.5	6.9	0.2
56003	Big Horn County, Wyoming	63.0	58.5	4.5	7.2	10.2	8.0	2.6	8.7	0.3
56005	Campbell County, Wyoming	76.2	73.8	2.3	4.7	11.0	2.9	0.7	4.3	0.3
56007	Carbon County, Wyoming	69.3	66.4	2.9	3.2	11.6	6.4	3.8	5.3	0.4
56009	Converse County, Wyoming	70.3	66.9	3.3	4.7	8.4	6.1	3.2	7.0	0.3
56011	Crook County, Wyoming	67.6	60.6	7.0	5.0	9.4	4.7	1.4	11.7	0.2
56013	Fremont County, Wyoming	55.7	50.4	5.3	6.0	17.1	7.9	3.3	9.4	0.5
56015	Goshen County, Wyoming	52.3	49.2	3.0	8.8	13.2	11.0	3.6	10.9	0.3
56017	Hot Springs County, Wyoming	62.3	56.3	5.9	8.2	11.3	4.9	2.8	9.9	0.7
56019	Johnson County, Wyoming	65.9	58.2	7.7	5.8	12.1	4.5	2.6	8.2	0.9
56021	Laramie County, Wyoming	61.3	58.1	3.1	6.3	9.8	10.2	7.7	4.5	0.2
56023	Lincoln County, Wyoming	68.6	63.6	5.0	5.0	11.6	5.4	2.9	6.2	0.3
56025	Natrona County, Wyoming	71.7	67.5	4.2	7.2	7.9	4.8	2.4	5.8	0.1
56027	Niobrara County, Wyoming	38.6	35.0	3.6	3.6	16.0	17.3	4.7	18.7	1.2
56029	Park County, Wyoming	67.0	63.9	3.1	8.7	7.9	6.3	2.6	7.3	0.1
56031	Platte County, Wyoming	54.5	51.8	2.8	8.9	14.9	4.6	2.3	14.8	0.0
56033	Sheridan County, Wyoming	64.4	59.2	5.2	6.4	9.8	6.5	4.7	7.7	0.5
56035	Sublette County, Wyoming	65.6	60.7	4.9	7.5	16.6	3.9	2.3	3.9	0.1
56037	Sweetwater County, Wyoming	75.0	72.2	2.8	3.6	11.5	4.5	1.6	3.7	0.0
56039	Teton County, Wyoming	72.4	66.3	6.1	8.9	6.9	1.8	2.6	7.5	0.0
56041	Uinta County, Wyoming	68.8	65.2	3.5	6.7	12.6	5.7	0.7	5.6	0.0
56043	Washakie County, Wyoming	63.2	55.0	8.2	7.3	9.5	9.9	2.1	7.6	0.5
56045	Weston County, Wyoming	66.5	62.9	3.6	3.7	12.6	6.4	1.2	8.3	1.3

Table C. County—Labor Force, Employment, and Educational Data, 2011–2015

| | | Occupation for employed population age 16 and older | | | | | Industry for employed population age 16 and older | | |
| | | Management, business, science, and arts occupations | Service occupations | Sales and office occupations: | Natural resources, construction, and maintenance occupations | Production, transportation, and material moving occupations: | Agriculture, forestry, fishing and hunting, and mining | Construction | Manufacturing |
Fips code	State/county								
00000	**United States**	36.7	18.1	24.1	8.9	12.2	2.0	6.2	10.4
01000	**Alabama**	33.3	16.8	24.1	9.9	15.9	1.7	6.4	13.9
01001	Autauga County, Alabama	33.2	17.0	24.2	8.6	17.1	1.4	5.4	14.1
01003	Baldwin County, Alabama	33.1	17.7	27.1	10.8	11.2	1.5	8.0	9.3
01005	Barbour County, Alabama	26.8	16.1	23.1	10.8	23.1	3.4	5.6	21.8
01007	Bibb County, Alabama	21.5	17.9	17.8	19.0	23.7	5.2	10.7	19.5
01009	Blount County, Alabama	28.5	14.1	23.9	13.5	19.9	3.1	8.3	16.0
01011	Bullock County, Alabama	18.8	15.0	19.7	20.1	26.4	15.2	9.0	20.1
01013	Butler County, Alabama	27.5	16.6	21.9	10.3	23.7	3.8	7.2	19.9
01015	Calhoun County, Alabama	27.3	17.7	24.2	10.5	20.4	0.7	5.7	17.3
01017	Chambers County, Alabama	23.3	14.5	26.3	11.5	24.4	1.6	5.6	25.5
01019	Cherokee County, Alabama	29.3	16.0	19.5	13.7	21.5	1.8	7.7	21.0
01021	Chilton County, Alabama	27.2	14.3	23.7	15.3	19.5	3.2	12.4	14.2
01023	Choctaw County, Alabama	24.9	15.4	19.6	18.3	21.8	7.9	10.6	18.8
01025	Clarke County, Alabama	21.1	15.0	25.5	11.6	26.9	3.7	5.3	21.9
01027	Clay County, Alabama	21.5	13.3	20.8	15.3	29.1	4.9	5.8	30.9
01029	Cleburne County, Alabama	28.9	11.7	23.1	15.6	20.7	4.8	11.8	19.8
01031	Coffee County, Alabama	32.2	18.6	22.7	12.1	14.5	2.8	5.2	11.9
01033	Colbert County, Alabama	27.3	15.5	25.7	10.7	20.7	1.3	6.5	18.5
01035	Conecuh County, Alabama	19.4	21.0	20.4	11.4	27.9	8.1	7.7	17.1
01037	Coosa County, Alabama	18.0	19.8	21.9	12.7	27.6	1.7	6.5	22.5
01039	Covington County, Alabama	26.2	15.6	23.6	15.2	19.4	5.6	7.4	16.0
01041	Crenshaw County, Alabama	27.6	11.6	23.8	12.5	24.6	5.3	6.3	21.8
01043	Cullman County, Alabama	28.5	15.6	23.9	13.9	18.1	2.8	8.3	16.3
01045	Dale County, Alabama	27.1	17.2	24.8	14.8	16.2	3.1	5.2	10.5
01047	Dallas County, Alabama	26.5	19.5	19.3	10.1	24.5	3.8	6.1	19.4
01049	DeKalb County, Alabama	24.2	15.7	21.3	12.4	26.4	3.8	7.4	27.6
01051	Elmore County, Alabama	33.3	16.0	25.2	9.6	15.9	0.8	7.4	12.0
01053	Escambia County, Alabama	25.4	21.8	23.1	11.0	18.7	2.8	6.1	14.9
01055	Etowah County, Alabama	28.7	18.5	21.3	9.8	21.7	0.8	6.2	18.9
01057	Fayette County, Alabama	27.0	14.6	21.6	12.7	24.1	6.4	5.4	23.4
01059	Franklin County, Alabama	21.4	13.6	19.4	12.8	32.8	2.4	7.8	32.1
01061	Geneva County, Alabama	23.9	17.8	22.5	19.9	16.0	6.5	8.7	12.1
01063	Greene County, Alabama	20.1	22.3	26.0	9.5	22.1	3.0	7.3	19.1
01065	Hale County, Alabama	25.5	16.7	24.4	12.2	21.3	6.2	6.4	17.4
01067	Henry County, Alabama	33.5	17.1	18.5	10.9	20.0	4.6	6.0	13.1
01069	Houston County, Alabama	31.1	18.5	26.1	10.3	14.1	1.5	6.0	9.7
01071	Jackson County, Alabama	25.3	14.1	21.1	13.0	26.6	3.2	7.0	25.4
01073	Jefferson County, Alabama	38.7	17.0	25.2	7.4	11.6	0.7	5.3	8.6
01075	Lamar County, Alabama	25.9	14.1	20.6	14.7	24.7	3.0	7.6	20.2
01077	Lauderdale County, Alabama	29.5	19.0	24.7	11.0	15.8	1.6	7.1	13.6
01079	Lawrence County, Alabama	25.1	14.8	18.3	15.3	26.5	3.8	8.2	26.3
01081	Lee County, Alabama	39.7	16.1	22.9	8.3	13.0	1.0	5.1	12.1
01083	Limestone County, Alabama	34.2	15.2	22.3	12.4	16.0	1.6	8.2	15.9
01085	Lowndes County, Alabama	23.9	16.2	19.4	9.2	31.4	4.4	4.3	23.0
01087	Macon County, Alabama	26.7	23.1	22.6	9.1	18.6	1.1	5.4	14.7
01089	Madison County, Alabama	44.6	15.6	23.2	6.7	9.9	0.7	4.7	11.6
01091	Marengo County, Alabama	28.4	18.2	20.7	12.5	20.2	3.1	5.0	18.4
01093	Marion County, Alabama	26.2	18.1	23.0	10.5	22.2	2.7	6.8	19.2
01095	Marshall County, Alabama	28.1	14.6	22.7	13.4	21.1	3.0	7.9	20.5
01097	Mobile County, Alabama	32.4	17.4	26.2	9.7	14.3	1.2	6.8	12.0
01099	Monroe County, Alabama	22.9	20.5	21.0	13.4	22.3	3.3	6.7	19.7
01101	Montgomery County, Alabama	36.0	19.1	25.1	6.0	13.8	0.5	4.4	11.0
01103	Morgan County, Alabama	29.7	15.4	24.3	11.7	18.8	0.9	9.2	20.0
01105	Perry County, Alabama	26.5	22.8	24.4	5.5	20.8	5.9	5.8	18.9
01107	Pickens County, Alabama	19.7	17.2	22.3	13.3	27.4	5.4	7.9	19.6
01109	Pike County, Alabama	29.7	15.9	25.6	9.4	19.3	2.5	5.4	16.3
01111	Randolph County, Alabama	27.6	12.9	20.3	13.1	26.1	2.8	7.4	27.5
01113	Russell County, Alabama	28.7	21.7	23.0	10.4	16.3	1.0	6.7	12.0
01115	St. Clair County, Alabama	28.8	14.9	27.6	12.4	16.3	0.8	10.0	15.1
01117	Shelby County, Alabama	42.8	14.5	27.1	7.3	8.4	0.7	6.1	8.1
01119	Sumter County, Alabama	23.8	29.9	19.7	7.1	19.6	1.7	4.5	13.9
01121	Talladega County, Alabama	28.1	14.8	22.3	11.2	23.6	1.6	6.1	22.6
01123	Tallapoosa County, Alabama	28.6	14.2	22.0	12.1	23.2	1.7	7.8	23.6
01125	Tuscaloosa County, Alabama	35.1	18.2	21.7	9.1	15.9	1.9	6.4	13.4
01127	Walker County, Alabama	25.4	17.6	25.3	14.2	17.6	6.1	6.6	10.9
01129	Washington County, Alabama	20.3	15.2	19.6	16.8	28.2	6.3	11.7	23.7
01131	Wilcox County, Alabama	28.4	17.8	19.2	8.5	26.1	4.3	6.6	16.1
01133	Winston County, Alabama	24.5	19.0	20.8	11.0	24.8	2.8	6.8	22.0
02000	**Alaska**	36.2	17.5	22.7	12.5	11.1	5.6	7.5	3.4
02013	Aleutians East Borough, Alaska	13.6	9.4	7.2	14.2	55.6	7.4	1.7	65.6
02016	Aleutians West Census Area, Alaska	16.9	10.5	17.6	14.1	40.9	1.8	6.6	38.9
02020	Anchorage Municipality, Alaska	39.7	17.7	23.9	9.4	9.3	3.7	6.7	1.9
02050	Bethel Census Area, Alaska	35.2	19.3	24.4	8.1	13.0	0.8	3.0	0.5
02060	Bristol Bay Borough, Alaska	33.1	18.7	20.5	12.9	14.8	8.5	7.8	2.0
02068	Denali Borough, Alaska	30.3	30.4	12.6	15.8	10.9	8.7	6.2	0.7

Table C. County—Labor Force, Employment, and Educational Data, 2011–2015—*Continued*

		Occupation for employed population age 16 and older					Industry for employed population age 16 and older		
Fips code	State/county	Management, business, science, and arts occupations	Service occupations	Sales and office occupations:	Natural resources, construction, and maintenance occupations	Production, transportation, and material moving occupations:	Agriculture, forestry, fishing and hunting, and mining	Construction	Manufacturing
02070	Dillingham Census Area, Alaska	38.1	15.4	22.7	11.6	12.1	5.0	3.6	3.8
02090	Fairbanks North Star Borough, Alaska	36.6	17.0	23.4	12.9	10.1	3.2	8.4	1.7
02100	Haines Borough, Alaska	34.0	20.6	20.6	10.6	14.1	8.2	9.5	1.4
02105	Hoonah-Angoon Census Area, Alaska	35.6	18.1	16.5	18.1	11.6	11.3	7.1	8.2
02110	Juneau City and Borough, Alaska	45.4	14.3	22.0	10.7	7.7	4.1	6.7	1.2
02122	Kenai Peninsula Borough, Alaska	29.9	19.0	22.2	16.9	12.0	12.6	8.0	4.3
02130	Ketchikan Gateway Borough, Alaska	30.4	16.3	26.7	12.8	13.8	3.6	9.1	4.2
02150	Kodiak Island Borough, Alaska	27.1	21.3	19.3	9.4	22.9	8.4	3.4	11.4
02158	Kusilvak Census Area, Alaska	29.9	22.8	22.4	14.6	10.3	1.7	6.0	2.9
02164	Lake and Peninsula Borough, Alaska	34.1	20.7	13.4	16.3	15.5	10.4	6.2	6.5
02170	Matanuska-Susitna Borough, Alaska	32.8	16.6	22.3	17.9	10.5	5.7	12.0	2.7
02180	Nome Census Area, Alaska	34.7	22.4	22.1	11.4	9.4	4.5	4.1	3.6
02185	North Slope Borough, Alaska	24.0	15.0	18.4	25.0	17.5	30.7	8.4	1.9
02188	Northwest Arctic Borough, Alaska	33.8	18.2	22.4	14.9	10.8	5.7	6.2	0.8
02195	Petersburg Borough, Alaska	30.7	13.9	17.6	21.0	16.8	24.1	5.7	11.8
02198	Prince of Wales-Hyder Census Area, Alaska	27.0	17.3	19.1	20.0	16.6	17.3	6.5	6.6
02220	Sitka City and Borough, Alaska	37.6	18.6	21.4	11.6	10.8	9.1	6.3	5.5
02230	Skagway Municipality, Alaska	27.5	16.9	21.0	10.2	24.4	5.0	4.6	13.3
02240	Southeast Fairbanks Census Area, Alaska	30.4	21.2	15.6	21.5	11.2	17.8	9.4	2.3
02261	Valdez-Cordova Census Area, Alaska	35.4	18.9	19.0	20.5	6.2	10.6	9.3	6.1
02275	Wrangell City and Borough, Alaska	30.2	17.1	22.7	17.8	12.1	13.5	5.9	4.6
02282	Yakutat City and Borough, Alaska	29.6	14.7	18.1	22.4	15.2	14.9	3.7	10.1
02290	Yukon-Koyukuk Census Area, Alaska	35.7	18.7	19.5	15.6	10.5	3.9	7.7	0.7
04000	**Arizona**	35.1	19.9	26.2	9.2	9.7	1.6	6.6	7.3
04001	Apache County, Arizona	28.8	25.7	20.4	13.4	11.8	3.0	8.9	1.9
04003	Cochise County, Arizona	33.7	24.9	23.4	10.3	7.6	4.0	5.1	3.8
04005	Coconino County, Arizona	34.7	22.5	23.5	8.4	10.9	1.9	5.6	6.6
04007	Gila County, Arizona	29.4	23.1	22.2	15.4	10.0	8.2	8.7	4.2
04009	Graham County, Arizona	29.8	21.3	20.9	16.1	11.9	13.4	6.0	3.7
04011	Greenlee County, Arizona	26.4	12.7	13.6	31.4	15.9	45.0	10.3	1.7
04012	La Paz County, Arizona	25.2	21.7	21.8	20.6	10.7	15.2	3.5	3.8
04013	Maricopa County, Arizona	36.6	18.4	27.2	8.4	9.5	0.7	6.6	7.8
04015	Mohave County, Arizona	25.0	25.2	27.4	10.5	12.0	1.6	7.1	5.7
04017	Navajo County, Arizona	28.5	25.6	22.7	11.6	11.6	3.8	8.2	4.0
04019	Pima County, Arizona	36.0	21.7	25.0	8.9	8.4	1.2	6.3	6.9
04021	Pinal County, Arizona	30.5	22.2	24.8	11.0	11.6	3.9	6.0	9.7
04023	Santa Cruz County, Arizona	26.8	18.6	31.6	10.1	12.9	2.8	5.2	6.2
04025	Yavapai County, Arizona	31.3	22.9	24.0	11.9	9.8	2.8	8.3	4.9
04027	Yuma County, Arizona	25.0	24.1	22.9	16.3	11.8	10.7	5.5	4.2
05000	**Arkansas**	32.0	17.1	23.9	10.7	16.4	3.3	6.5	13.6
05001	Arkansas County, Arkansas	26.8	17.0	20.8	8.7	26.7	6.7	5.4	25.9
05003	Ashley County, Arkansas	28.0	17.5	18.7	12.2	23.6	6.7	7.3	18.5
05005	Baxter County, Arkansas	29.2	19.7	23.3	8.5	19.3	1.2	5.2	17.2
05007	Benton County, Arkansas	35.2	13.5	26.5	9.3	15.5	1.9	6.4	14.2
05009	Boone County, Arkansas	30.7	18.9	25.4	10.9	14.1	4.1	6.4	10.8
05011	Bradley County, Arkansas	25.6	17.0	21.1	16.1	20.2	9.1	7.2	15.8
05013	Calhoun County, Arkansas	22.0	15.6	17.9	18.5	25.9	7.7	9.1	25.3
05015	Carroll County, Arkansas	27.5	16.7	19.1	12.7	24.0	4.3	9.0	25.3
05017	Chicot County, Arkansas	27.9	20.5	26.6	11.8	13.3	8.9	7.5	11.0
05019	Clark County, Arkansas	35.0	21.1	22.4	7.4	14.0	3.1	3.4	14.4
05021	Clay County, Arkansas	22.6	17.7	21.9	13.3	24.5	8.8	5.6	19.9
05023	Cleburne County, Arkansas	25.9	17.3	23.4	12.6	20.7	6.1	8.5	13.7
05025	Cleveland County, Arkansas	29.2	13.8	21.3	20.1	15.7	7.1	10.0	14.8
05027	Columbia County, Arkansas	27.4	16.1	26.9	11.2	18.4	7.2	3.9	20.0
05029	Conway County, Arkansas	28.8	14.2	23.3	16.7	17.0	7.4	9.2	12.9
05031	Craighead County, Arkansas	33.8	16.7	22.9	10.0	16.7	2.4	7.4	12.9
05033	Crawford County, Arkansas	28.0	17.0	24.4	11.9	18.6	2.7	7.4	16.7
05035	Crittenden County, Arkansas	29.5	18.5	25.5	8.8	17.8	2.9	3.3	11.9
05037	Cross County, Arkansas	24.3	18.4	24.7	17.5	15.2	8.1	6.8	10.6
05039	Dallas County, Arkansas	19.8	23.0	19.4	13.3	24.6	5.6	4.9	19.9
05041	Desha County, Arkansas	27.7	16.5	22.7	16.5	16.6	13.7	5.1	11.0
05043	Drew County, Arkansas	36.0	16.0	22.3	10.6	15.1	5.5	4.3	12.1
05045	Faulkner County, Arkansas	34.5	16.9	25.7	11.8	11.0	3.2	7.7	9.0
05047	Franklin County, Arkansas	26.0	18.3	22.0	12.2	21.6	6.7	8.4	18.2
05049	Fulton County, Arkansas	26.6	20.3	20.5	15.1	17.5	3.4	9.9	9.3
05051	Garland County, Arkansas	31.5	20.7	25.0	12.1	10.7	1.2	8.8	7.5
05053	Grant County, Arkansas	29.1	16.3	21.1	12.7	20.9	3.2	7.1	17.0
05055	Greene County, Arkansas	28.3	13.7	23.5	9.7	24.8	3.2	4.5	23.0
05057	Hempstead County, Arkansas	25.6	13.8	19.4	15.9	25.3	4.5	8.1	23.9
05059	Hot Spring County, Arkansas	26.5	19.4	22.9	12.9	18.3	2.5	7.4	14.0
05061	Howard County, Arkansas	25.6	14.4	19.4	13.4	27.1	12.2	5.5	25.4
05063	Independence County, Arkansas	28.2	17.0	20.8	14.6	19.4	5.5	8.6	15.5
05065	Izard County, Arkansas	33.1	16.0	20.1	9.9	20.8	4.9	9.9	13.6
05067	Jackson County, Arkansas	22.0	17.3	21.0	13.6	26.1	8.7	5.8	18.5
05069	Jefferson County, Arkansas	28.9	21.6	21.8	7.1	20.6	1.4	3.8	16.9

Table C. County—Labor Force, Employment, and Educational Data, 2011–2015—*Continued*

		Occupation for employed population age 16 and older					Industry for employed population age 16 and older		
Fips code	State/county	Management, business, science, and arts occupations	Service occupations	Sales and office occupations:	Natural resources, construction, and maintenance occupations	Production, transportation, and material moving occupations:	Agriculture, forestry, fishing and hunting, and mining	Construction	Manufacturing
05071	Johnson County, Arkansas	25.5	15.3	19.6	11.4	28.2	4.2	6.4	28.3
05073	Lafayette County, Arkansas	27.8	16.1	19.9	18.0	18.2	12.6	4.8	15.7
05075	Lawrence County, Arkansas	25.5	21.4	20.5	15.1	17.5	8.2	8.1	13.3
05077	Lee County, Arkansas	20.9	24.9	21.2	17.3	15.6	18.4	5.1	7.1
05079	Lincoln County, Arkansas	29.2	18.9	17.8	13.0	21.0	8.4	7.2	14.3
05081	Little River County, Arkansas	26.0	19.3	19.1	10.9	24.8	2.5	5.2	19.2
05083	Logan County, Arkansas	28.2	20.3	20.3	11.5	19.6	6.3	6.8	18.1
05085	Lonoke County, Arkansas	34.1	15.4	25.1	11.3	14.0	3.0	6.4	10.7
05087	Madison County, Arkansas	27.1	14.7	19.3	15.6	23.2	11.2	9.7	17.5
05089	Marion County, Arkansas	19.4	25.8	20.1	11.7	23.0	2.0	5.5	22.6
05091	Miller County, Arkansas	26.8	17.0	25.8	9.8	20.7	2.1	5.3	13.9
05093	Mississippi County, Arkansas	23.7	17.4	21.6	11.0	26.2	5.7	4.6	26.3
05095	Monroe County, Arkansas	22.4	24.7	23.6	14.3	15.1	10.2	6.8	15.0
05097	Montgomery County, Arkansas	27.6	18.9	16.6	25.1	11.8	17.3	12.2	5.6
05099	Nevada County, Arkansas	20.3	24.7	22.2	11.7	21.1	3.9	5.4	19.5
05101	Newton County, Arkansas	23.5	20.0	18.8	14.1	23.5	6.7	8.5	12.6
05103	Ouachita County, Arkansas	24.5	17.7	22.6	10.9	24.3	2.6	6.0	26.3
05105	Perry County, Arkansas	29.3	19.0	18.0	19.3	14.4	4.8	11.6	12.4
05107	Phillips County, Arkansas	26.6	24.2	24.0	9.4	15.8	8.9	2.0	8.9
05109	Pike County, Arkansas	25.2	17.9	19.3	19.0	18.6	11.5	9.2	15.5
05111	Poinsett County, Arkansas	24.2	17.4	22.8	15.3	20.3	8.5	7.2	16.5
05113	Polk County, Arkansas	28.6	14.3	24.7	14.2	18.1	6.4	10.1	14.0
05115	Pope County, Arkansas	28.8	17.6	23.4	11.1	19.1	3.0	6.5	15.9
05117	Prairie County, Arkansas	27.8	20.8	18.1	13.6	19.7	13.0	7.8	11.7
05119	Pulaski County, Arkansas	40.3	16.7	26.0	6.8	10.3	0.5	4.8	6.5
05121	Randolph County, Arkansas	30.4	16.8	19.8	14.0	19.0	7.9	5.7	15.5
05123	St. Francis County, Arkansas	23.7	21.4	24.1	10.8	20.0	3.4	6.6	12.2
05125	Saline County, Arkansas	33.9	16.1	27.7	11.0	11.2	0.5	8.6	7.4
05127	Scott County, Arkansas	24.5	17.2	16.7	13.5	28.1	8.1	4.8	29.3
05129	Searcy County, Arkansas	27.7	11.9	26.0	16.0	18.4	5.3	10.8	15.8
05131	Sebastian County, Arkansas	29.9	17.4	24.5	8.6	19.6	2.1	5.4	19.6
05133	Sevier County, Arkansas	20.4	13.5	18.8	17.9	29.4	6.3	10.4	30.6
05135	Sharp County, Arkansas	27.7	19.4	18.5	17.7	16.7	4.1	9.6	10.7
05137	Stone County, Arkansas	31.4	21.6	14.1	21.0	11.9	10.4	8.7	8.4
05139	Union County, Arkansas	30.8	15.6	23.8	12.4	17.4	3.7	7.6	16.1
05141	Van Buren County, Arkansas	25.3	16.7	22.1	19.6	16.3	9.1	14.6	5.4
05143	Washington County, Arkansas	36.5	16.9	23.3	9.2	14.1	1.4	6.3	14.3
05145	White County, Arkansas	30.5	17.3	23.6	12.3	16.2	4.5	7.6	9.7
05147	Woodruff County, Arkansas	32.9	16.3	19.2	17.8	13.8	14.2	7.2	12.6
05149	Yell County, Arkansas	24.3	16.2	18.4	16.0	25.1	8.5	7.7	23.5
06000	**California**	37.3	18.8	23.7	9.2	11.0	2.4	6.0	9.8
06001	Alameda County, California	46.6	16.2	21.5	6.5	9.3	0.4	5.1	10.4
06003	Alpine County, California	37.3	20.3	17.9	10.3	14.2	0.0	5.9	3.7
06005	Amador County, California	30.9	22.9	25.3	10.3	10.6	1.6	6.5	4.5
06007	Butte County, California	34.6	23.3	23.7	9.1	9.3	3.6	5.2	6.0
06009	Calaveras County, California	36.1	18.9	20.7	12.4	11.8	3.1	10.2	8.2
06011	Colusa County, California	24.7	17.0	18.0	26.4	13.8	27.4	4.0	10.8
06013	Contra Costa County, California	42.9	17.5	23.6	8.2	7.7	0.8	6.9	6.9
06015	Del Norte County, California	33.9	31.5	18.8	8.9	6.8	4.0	4.0	3.4
06017	El Dorado County, California	40.2	19.2	24.9	8.7	7.1	1.2	7.4	7.6
06019	Fresno County, California	28.6	19.2	23.2	15.3	13.7	10.4	5.3	7.4
06021	Glenn County, California	21.9	21.1	18.7	24.7	13.6	19.3	4.8	7.9
06023	Humboldt County, California	34.0	22.5	23.3	11.0	9.1	4.4	7.4	4.4
06025	Imperial County, California	23.5	24.1	25.1	14.7	12.5	10.0	5.1	5.0
06027	Inyo County, California	31.5	22.3	25.8	10.1	10.3	3.9	6.8	2.8
06029	Kern County, California	25.6	18.9	21.0	20.8	13.7	16.7	6.2	6.0
06031	Kings County, California	25.1	22.4	19.5	19.6	13.5	15.5	3.6	8.2
06033	Lake County, California	27.1	25.7	23.3	14.7	9.2	7.0	7.4	4.2
06035	Lassen County, California	29.1	29.1	19.4	10.1	12.3	5.8	5.3	2.2
06037	Los Angeles County, California	35.7	19.1	24.6	7.8	12.8	0.5	5.7	10.3
06039	Madera County, California	25.3	17.0	20.8	23.5	13.3	19.9	5.5	8.6
06041	Marin County, California	51.4	15.8	22.8	5.6	4.4	0.6	5.2	4.6
06043	Mariposa County, California	31.2	30.5	21.0	9.3	8.1	3.7	6.1	2.7
06045	Mendocino County, California	30.3	21.8	24.9	14.0	9.0	5.7	8.3	6.7
06047	Merced County, California	22.7	18.6	21.2	20.2	17.4	13.6	6.3	11.6
06049	Modoc County, California	40.7	14.7	18.1	18.0	8.5	19.3	6.9	2.6
06051	Mono County, California	42.1	25.1	18.8	8.4	5.5	5.6	7.1	2.2
06053	Monterey County, California	27.6	20.5	20.7	20.0	11.2	17.5	5.7	4.9
06055	Napa County, California	34.8	22.0	20.8	11.6	10.8	6.4	6.3	11.8
06057	Nevada County, California	39.1	21.6	23.0	9.3	7.0	1.4	9.0	7.1
06059	Orange County, California	40.1	17.5	25.6	6.8	10.1	0.5	5.6	13.0
06061	Placer County, California	41.9	17.3	26.8	7.2	6.8	0.6	6.9	6.4
06063	Plumas County, California	33.2	25.4	17.0	13.4	11.0	8.9	9.0	7.5
06065	Riverside County, California	29.0	21.7	25.1	11.3	13.0	1.7	8.4	9.1

Table C. County—Labor Force, Employment, and Educational Data, 2011–2015—*Continued*

		Occupation for employed population age 16 and older					Industry for employed population age 16 and older		
Fips code	State/county	Management, business, science, and arts occupations	Service occupations	Sales and office occupations:	Natural resources, construction, and maintenance occupations	Production, transportation, and material moving occupations:	Agriculture, forestry, fishing and hunting, and mining	Construction	Manufacturing
06067	Sacramento County, California	37.7	19.4	26.0	7.9	9.0	0.8	6.3	5.6
06069	San Benito County, California	27.3	18.8	23.5	16.2	14.1	7.2	9.2	12.0
06071	San Bernardino County, California	28.7	18.9	25.4	10.2	16.7	0.7	7.1	9.9
06073	San Diego County, California	40.6	19.7	23.6	7.8	8.4	1.0	5.5	9.4
06075	San Francisco County, California	53.4	17.0	20.5	3.7	5.4	0.2	3.4	5.5
06077	San Joaquin County, California	28.0	18.4	24.1	12.9	16.5	5.0	7.1	9.8
06079	San Luis Obispo County, California	37.4	20.8	23.4	10.0	8.5	3.7	6.8	6.8
06081	San Mateo County, California	45.4	18.4	22.4	6.3	7.4	0.6	5.3	7.8
06083	Santa Barbara County, California	35.2	21.3	21.2	14.0	8.3	8.6	5.5	7.4
06085	Santa Clara County, California	50.5	15.2	19.6	6.5	8.2	0.6	5.1	18.5
06087	Santa Cruz County, California	40.4	19.2	21.9	11.3	7.2	5.5	6.6	9.1
06089	Shasta County, California	31.4	21.4	27.4	10.8	8.9	2.3	7.6	5.5
06091	Sierra County, California	33.9	11.8	18.2	17.8	18.3	7.1	13.2	2.4
06093	Siskiyou County, California	33.7	21.7	21.8	12.5	10.4	9.3	6.0	6.3
06095	Solano County, California	32.5	20.1	25.3	10.1	12.0	1.6	7.2	9.1
06097	Sonoma County, California	36.3	19.8	23.4	10.6	9.8	3.4	7.6	9.8
06099	Stanislaus County, California	26.4	18.3	24.2	14.0	17.1	5.5	6.8	12.0
06101	Sutter County, California	30.5	19.6	22.6	15.7	11.6	8.8	8.3	6.7
06103	Tehama County, California	26.1	21.5	23.4	14.5	14.6	7.1	7.8	7.9
06105	Trinity County, California	29.8	30.0	22.1	11.1	7.1	3.1	8.9	2.9
06107	Tulare County, California	23.9	18.6	20.4	22.9	14.3	19.5	4.6	8.0
06109	Tuolumne County, California	33.9	26.4	20.0	11.4	8.3	2.8	8.4	5.3
06111	Ventura County, California	37.2	17.1	24.2	11.3	10.2	5.5	6.0	10.6
06113	Yolo County, California	44.5	18.5	19.2	8.2	9.5	4.1	4.4	6.3
06115	Yuba County, California	28.1	20.9	24.7	14.7	11.7	5.2	7.5	4.8
08000	**Colorado**	40.4	17.5	23.8	9.4	8.9	2.6	7.4	7.0
08001	Adams County, Colorado	29.5	18.7	24.5	13.4	13.9	1.9	10.8	8.8
08003	Alamosa County, Colorado	30.2	19.8	25.0	16.1	8.9	4.6	5.5	2.5
08005	Arapahoe County, Colorado	41.2	16.5	26.1	7.8	8.5	1.2	6.4	5.6
08007	Archuleta County, Colorado	39.7	15.6	21.4	15.4	7.9	4.6	12.9	2.6
08009	Baca County, Colorado	38.0	20.2	15.2	17.6	9.0	18.3	10.5	2.4
08011	Bent County, Colorado	35.5	26.7	12.4	18.4	7.0	21.1	6.4	1.1
08013	Boulder County, Colorado	52.3	15.7	20.3	5.1	6.5	1.1	4.5	10.1
08014	Broomfield County, Colorado	51.4	11.5	24.2	6.1	6.9	1.2	5.2	11.1
08015	Chaffee County, Colorado	36.1	18.2	25.6	13.0	7.1	2.4	11.7	4.2
08017	Cheyenne County, Colorado	38.8	12.2	18.6	18.3	12.0	26.5	7.9	2.1
08019	Clear Creek County, Colorado	36.8	17.6	24.5	11.2	9.9	5.3	9.6	4.9
08021	Conejos County, Colorado	29.6	20.0	20.0	18.2	12.2	13.5	9.1	3.2
08023	Costilla County, Colorado	23.3	23.1	21.5	21.2	10.9	11.5	4.8	7.7
08025	Crowley County, Colorado	24.4	28.8	22.7	11.5	12.6	8.1	6.7	1.1
08027	Custer County, Colorado	24.2	25.6	19.4	23.3	7.4	5.0	15.8	1.9
08029	Delta County, Colorado	32.2	19.6	19.9	19.4	8.9	16.4	10.1	6.1
08031	Denver County, Colorado	44.6	17.6	22.3	7.5	8.1	1.3	6.9	5.4
08033	Dolores County, Colorado	30.5	25.5	21.0	12.9	10.2	13.7	8.7	4.0
08035	Douglas County, Colorado	53.0	11.9	25.7	4.6	4.8	1.5	5.4	6.7
08037	Eagle County, Colorado	34.6	25.8	20.9	12.5	6.2	2.5	11.2	2.3
08039	Elbert County, Colorado	38.9	15.6	23.5	13.8	8.2	4.4	12.5	5.3
08041	El Paso County, Colorado	40.5	18.5	24.5	8.5	8.0	0.8	6.8	6.5
08043	Fremont County, Colorado	26.6	32.2	22.8	10.7	7.6	2.9	6.6	4.6
08045	Garfield County, Colorado	30.4	19.8	21.0	18.8	10.0	5.7	16.6	2.6
08047	Gilpin County, Colorado	40.5	21.9	17.9	11.1	8.6	1.2	10.1	7.4
08049	Grand County, Colorado	33.9	19.3	19.3	19.5	8.0	4.8	11.4	1.5
08051	Gunnison County, Colorado	33.3	22.5	20.4	17.0	6.9	2.8	13.1	1.7
08053	Hinsdale County, Colorado	40.6	15.5	22.2	18.6	3.1	6.7	14.6	0.0
08055	Huerfano County, Colorado	33.2	23.7	21.7	14.0	7.5	6.2	7.3	7.2
08057	Jackson County, Colorado	32.7	14.4	15.2	25.8	11.9	28.4	9.0	1.7
08059	Jefferson County, Colorado	44.0	15.2	25.1	8.0	7.7	1.6	7.2	7.6
08061	Kiowa County, Colorado	40.5	19.6	16.9	14.5	8.4	21.6	6.9	1.4
08063	Kit Carson County, Colorado	31.4	18.1	22.7	19.1	8.7	18.7	8.6	3.9
08065	Lake County, Colorado	27.2	24.6	19.5	18.0	10.7	4.1	14.8	2.9
08067	La Plata County, Colorado	39.2	20.2	21.8	11.4	7.4	4.4	8.2	3.6
08069	Larimer County, Colorado	42.6	17.3	23.4	8.2	8.4	2.6	6.7	9.6
08071	Las Animas County, Colorado	28.3	20.0	23.0	16.2	12.4	11.7	9.0	2.3
08073	Lincoln County, Colorado	34.3	26.7	23.2	8.5	7.3	12.6	5.8	1.8
08075	Logan County, Colorado	25.4	24.3	23.5	12.2	14.5	9.2	4.4	7.6
08077	Mesa County, Colorado	32.4	18.1	25.0	12.7	11.9	7.2	7.5	4.8
08079	Mineral County, Colorado	34.6	11.0	25.9	18.8	9.7	6.1	15.9	1.6
08081	Moffat County, Colorado	23.4	19.3	25.0	20.9	11.4	13.3	9.0	1.6
08083	Montezuma County, Colorado	34.1	20.1	23.7	11.4	10.6	5.4	7.8	5.7
08085	Montrose County, Colorado	30.3	19.5	21.8	17.1	11.3	7.4	11.3	8.2
08087	Morgan County, Colorado	24.0	19.7	19.9	15.6	20.8	11.0	6.0	19.5
08089	Otero County, Colorado	32.6	22.8	23.6	10.9	10.1	7.1	5.9	5.1
08091	Ouray County, Colorado	48.0	19.7	14.8	12.3	5.2	5.6	9.9	4.4
08093	Park County, Colorado	34.4	18.4	22.3	14.7	10.2	3.2	13.0	7.2
08095	Phillips County, Colorado	35.0	13.9	23.5	18.4	9.2	19.1	6.5	5.6
08097	Pitkin County, Colorado	40.4	23.6	25.0	6.9	4.0	1.4	6.0	2.2

Table C. County—Labor Force, Employment, and Educational Data, 2011–2015—*Continued*

		Occupation for employed population age 16 and older					Industry for employed population age 16 and older		
Fips code	State/county	Management, business, science, and arts occupations	Service occupations	Sales and office occupations:	Natural resources, construction, and maintenance occupations	Production, transportation, and material moving occupations:	Agriculture, forestry, fishing and hunting, and mining	Construction	Manufacturing
08099	Prowers County, Colorado	30.1	24.4	22.4	12.6	10.6	10.7	3.7	6.4
08101	Pueblo County, Colorado	30.1	22.8	25.7	9.8	11.7	1.4	7.5	7.6
08103	Rio Blanco County, Colorado	27.8	18.5	18.8	21.1	13.8	25.1	8.5	1.9
08105	Rio Grande County, Colorado	29.0	19.9	23.0	17.8	10.3	13.6	6.3	4.8
08107	Routt County, Colorado	33.0	23.1	24.2	12.1	7.6	5.9	9.9	2.4
08109	Saguache County, Colorado	30.8	12.8	17.0	25.4	13.9	18.1	9.2	8.3
08111	San Juan County, Colorado	28.8	18.1	27.9	18.7	6.5	5.3	18.1	5.9
08113	San Miguel County, Colorado	37.1	18.9	23.2	10.9	9.8	3.9	10.7	2.4
08115	Sedgwick County, Colorado	34.4	19.9	19.3	13.6	12.7	16.6	8.9	4.4
08117	Summit County, Colorado	32.0	23.3	23.1	14.5	7.1	1.1	11.9	3.4
08119	Teller County, Colorado	38.6	21.5	21.3	11.3	7.3	4.9	9.3	4.1
08121	Washington County, Colorado	35.5	14.5	18.7	15.8	15.6	18.0	8.5	6.0
08123	Weld County, Colorado	33.1	16.8	23.3	13.1	13.7	6.5	8.1	10.4
08125	Yuma County, Colorado	28.2	14.7	22.4	25.0	9.6	26.5	8.1	2.8
09000	**Connecticut**	41.7	17.8	23.5	7.4	9.6	0.4	5.6	10.7
09001	Fairfield County, Connecticut	44.1	17.6	23.8	7.5	7.0	0.2	6.6	8.3
09003	Hartford County, Connecticut	42.6	16.9	24.0	6.2	10.4	0.2	4.6	10.7
09005	Litchfield County, Connecticut	40.1	17.6	21.7	9.9	10.6	1.0	7.8	12.5
09007	Middlesex County, Connecticut	45.7	15.4	22.9	7.8	8.2	0.3	5.8	12.4
09009	New Haven County, Connecticut	40.0	17.7	24.0	7.1	11.2	0.3	5.1	11.6
09011	New London County, Connecticut	38.4	23.4	21.3	7.8	9.2	0.5	5.2	12.9
09013	Tolland County, Connecticut	41.8	15.8	23.5	9.0	9.9	0.9	6.5	11.6
09015	Windham County, Connecticut	32.1	20.6	23.6	10.2	13.5	1.8	6.0	12.6
10000	**Delaware**	38.4	18.5	24.2	8.5	10.5	1.0	6.0	9.1
10001	Kent County, Delaware	32.7	19.8	23.4	10.4	13.7	1.4	6.5	8.8
10003	New Castle County, Delaware	42.6	17.3	24.6	6.9	8.7	0.6	5.0	8.9
10005	Sussex County, Delaware	30.5	21.0	23.5	11.7	13.3	2.1	8.4	10.0
11000	District of Columbia	60.9	15.2	17.4	2.9	3.7	0.1	3.0	1.3
	District of Columbia								
11001	District of Columbia	60.9	15.2	17.4	2.9	3.7	0.1	3.0	1.3
12000	**Florida**	34.1	20.6	27.3	9.0	9.0	1.1	6.6	5.2
12001	Alachua County, Florida	46.4	19.1	23.7	5.0	5.8	0.8	3.6	3.8
12003	Baker County, Florida	29.6	20.4	24.0	11.5	14.5	0.8	9.3	6.5
12005	Bay County, Florida	32.3	22.5	25.0	10.1	10.2	0.9	6.6	6.0
12007	Bradford County, Florida	32.8	22.5	22.8	11.1	10.7	1.0	7.7	6.8
12009	Brevard County, Florida	36.6	19.8	25.9	8.3	9.3	0.4	5.9	10.1
12011	Broward County, Florida	35.4	19.9	28.4	8.1	8.1	0.2	6.1	4.8
12013	Calhoun County, Florida	25.4	28.7	20.6	15.8	9.6	9.3	8.5	5.0
12015	Charlotte County, Florida	28.1	23.4	29.5	11.6	7.6	0.7	8.6	4.2
12017	Citrus County, Florida	28.8	24.1	25.1	10.6	11.5	0.9	7.4	4.7
12019	Clay County, Florida	33.5	18.1	26.8	10.9	10.7	0.4	7.6	5.1
12021	Collier County, Florida	29.7	24.8	25.3	12.7	7.5	3.7	10.0	3.4
12023	Columbia County, Florida	30.6	21.8	24.7	12.6	10.4	1.3	7.3	4.7
12027	DeSoto County, Florida	15.7	21.9	19.5	30.6	12.3	24.2	9.1	4.7
12029	Dixie County, Florida	23.9	20.4	21.6	12.1	22.0	5.5	8.2	11.2
12031	Duval County, Florida	35.5	18.5	27.8	7.7	10.5	0.4	5.3	5.9
12033	Escambia County, Florida	32.2	21.0	28.5	8.5	9.8	1.0	5.5	4.6
12035	Flagler County, Florida	30.0	20.9	31.0	9.0	9.0	0.8	5.9	6.7
12037	Franklin County, Florida	28.7	28.1	15.4	17.4	10.3	9.1	6.2	1.6
12039	Gadsden County, Florida	28.9	23.3	25.4	12.3	10.0	3.6	9.1	3.1
12041	Gilchrist County, Florida	27.6	20.1	23.0	14.4	14.8	4.6	10.0	5.3
12043	Glades County, Florida	23.2	18.2	32.5	13.8	12.3	16.8	4.5	6.8
12045	Gulf County, Florida	26.9	23.4	24.1	13.0	12.6	2.4	12.7	4.6
12047	Hamilton County, Florida	27.4	21.6	21.9	12.5	16.6	9.9	6.3	9.8
12049	Hardee County, Florida	20.1	17.9	20.3	27.9	13.8	25.5	9.7	5.1
12051	Hendry County, Florida	22.0	13.2	17.3	33.7	13.8	27.1	8.9	8.4
12053	Hernando County, Florida	29.1	20.0	29.6	10.9	10.3	0.9	7.5	5.4
12055	Highlands County, Florida	27.7	23.9	26.8	14.5	7.2	7.3	5.7	4.0
12057	Hillsborough County, Florida	37.4	17.7	27.7	8.8	8.4	1.4	6.6	5.1
12059	Holmes County, Florida	25.7	24.4	22.5	15.0	12.3	5.6	9.9	6.7
12061	Indian River County, Florida	32.3	22.2	26.6	10.7	8.3	2.2	7.8	5.3
12063	Jackson County, Florida	28.3	28.6	22.4	9.3	11.3	3.1	5.5	5.1
12065	Jefferson County, Florida	41.1	19.0	22.9	10.2	6.9	5.2	7.6	2.4
12067	Lafayette County, Florida	29.8	26.1	17.5	9.5	17.1	10.1	3.3	10.3
12069	Lake County, Florida	31.0	21.5	27.6	10.4	9.6	1.5	7.4	5.5
12071	Lee County, Florida	30.2	22.6	28.1	11.1	8.1	1.1	9.4	3.5
12073	Leon County, Florida	44.3	17.9	27.1	5.5	5.2	0.3	3.6	2.1
12075	Levy County, Florida	25.1	22.4	23.2	17.7	11.6	7.9	9.7	3.6
12077	Liberty County, Florida	32.3	28.4	14.3	14.0	11.0	7.8	9.0	2.8
12079	Madison County, Florida	30.1	17.0	22.4	11.4	19.1	4.6	7.9	9.2
12081	Manatee County, Florida	33.2	20.9	26.7	9.7	9.4	1.5	7.2	7.7
12083	Marion County, Florida	27.4	23.9	28.3	9.7	10.7	2.2	7.4	7.1
12085	Martin County, Florida	36.7	21.0	25.7	9.7	6.9	1.2	8.9	6.1
12086	Miami-Dade County, Florida	31.5	21.0	28.2	9.1	10.2	0.8	6.8	4.8
12087	Monroe County, Florida	32.1	23.9	25.5	10.9	7.6	2.1	6.8	2.9

Table C. County—Labor Force, Employment, and Educational Data, 2011–2015—*Continued*

		Occupation for employed population age 16 and older					Industry for employed population age 16 and older		
Fips code	State/county	Management, business, science, and arts occupations	Service occupations	Sales and office occupations:	Natural resources, construction, and maintenance occupations	Production, transportation, and material moving occupations:	Agriculture, forestry, fishing and hunting, and mining	Construction	Manufacturing
12089	Nassau County, Florida	31.3	19.4	23.3	12.5	13.5	1.0	9.0	7.9
12091	Okaloosa County, Florida	34.0	22.4	25.3	9.6	8.8	0.6	7.1	4.8
12093	Okeechobee County, Florida	21.2	20.9	23.5	20.6	13.9	13.4	8.1	2.8
12095	Orange County, Florida	35.0	21.8	27.4	6.9	8.9	0.4	5.7	4.6
12097	Osceola County, Florida	24.4	25.7	29.2	8.9	11.8	0.5	6.2	3.5
12099	Palm Beach County, Florida	35.6	22.0	26.3	8.9	7.2	1.1	6.9	4.5
12101	Pasco County, Florida	35.5	18.6	28.5	8.9	8.4	0.6	6.8	5.1
12103	Pinellas County, Florida	37.4	18.9	28.0	7.2	8.6	0.4	5.3	6.9
12105	Polk County, Florida	29.5	21.0	25.6	11.0	12.9	2.6	6.8	6.1
12107	Putnam County, Florida	23.3	21.7	25.5	14.9	14.5	5.1	7.6	8.9
12109	St. Johns County, Florida	45.1	17.0	25.3	5.7	6.9	0.4	5.4	6.5
12111	St. Lucie County, Florida	28.3	23.1	28.6	11.1	9.0	1.1	7.9	3.9
12113	Santa Rosa County, Florida	37.1	15.7	26.3	11.3	9.5	1.6	8.5	5.8
12115	Sarasota County, Florida	34.2	22.8	26.9	9.0	7.1	0.5	7.5	5.3
12117	Seminole County, Florida	42.6	15.8	28.8	6.1	6.8	0.3	5.3	5.1
12119	Sumter County, Florida	29.3	21.1	29.3	9.8	10.5	1.6	7.0	5.0
12121	Suwannee County, Florida	24.0	24.7	23.1	14.4	13.8	6.0	6.9	6.4
12123	Taylor County, Florida	26.9	24.9	21.4	9.3	17.5	4.5	4.4	16.2
12125	Union County, Florida	23.7	28.6	24.7	11.5	11.4	3.3	3.6	5.5
12127	Volusia County, Florida	31.0	21.1	27.6	10.2	10.0	0.8	7.5	6.6
12129	Wakulla County, Florida	29.5	19.8	29.5	12.6	8.7	0.8	7.4	4.2
12131	Walton County, Florida	32.0	23.0	25.5	11.3	8.2	1.3	11.8	4.4
12133	Washington County, Florida	28.8	21.9	24.5	13.6	11.2	3.0	10.9	6.1
13000	**Georgia**	35.9	16.9	24.8	9.2	13.2	1.2	6.3	10.7
13001	Appling County, Georgia	25.5	13.1	19.4	22.7	19.2	7.3	11.2	14.9
13003	Atkinson County, Georgia	18.6	13.6	23.8	20.3	23.7	12.6	5.3	22.0
13005	Bacon County, Georgia	28.7	10.9	21.7	19.7	18.9	9.7	9.1	16.3
13007	Baker County, Georgia	27.8	14.4	27.0	18.0	12.9	17.9	5.0	11.8
13009	Baldwin County, Georgia	29.9	27.2	20.6	9.8	12.5	2.5	4.6	8.5
13011	Banks County, Georgia	24.5	15.5	22.4	14.5	23.0	5.4	8.0	19.5
13013	Barrow County, Georgia	27.3	14.6	29.7	12.2	16.3	1.0	8.5	11.8
13015	Bartow County, Georgia	29.0	17.1	23.3	13.0	17.5	1.0	9.8	17.2
13017	Ben Hill County, Georgia	26.9	20.6	19.4	9.6	23.5	3.3	5.2	20.7
13019	Berrien County, Georgia	26.0	20.4	22.5	16.3	14.8	5.6	7.4	12.5
13021	Bibb County, Georgia	34.6	19.1	28.7	7.5	10.1	0.8	4.5	6.6
13023	Bleckley County, Georgia	29.5	21.8	22.9	12.9	12.9	5.5	4.7	7.0
13025	Brantley County, Georgia	27.4	18.5	22.0	18.2	14.0	3.5	15.5	8.7
13027	Brooks County, Georgia	24.8	15.7	25.1	16.0	18.4	9.0	6.4	7.9
13029	Bryan County, Georgia	34.7	18.7	23.0	11.1	12.4	0.3	9.3	13.1
13031	Bulloch County, Georgia	32.3	23.0	22.9	9.2	12.5	1.8	6.0	9.1
13033	Burke County, Georgia	27.1	19.3	20.3	14.1	19.2	4.6	7.3	17.9
13035	Butts County, Georgia	25.8	21.1	20.6	16.9	15.7	1.1	8.1	14.0
13037	Calhoun County, Georgia	21.6	30.1	19.7	14.4	14.2	16.3	3.1	10.9
13039	Camden County, Georgia	33.1	19.3	25.7	10.8	11.0	0.5	6.2	10.2
13043	Candler County, Georgia	27.0	18.6	23.8	16.1	14.6	5.7	7.2	9.6
13045	Carroll County, Georgia	26.3	18.3	22.4	13.1	19.9	1.1	9.0	15.6
13047	Catoosa County, Georgia	32.3	14.7	27.5	10.4	15.2	0.5	6.4	15.7
13049	Charlton County, Georgia	28.1	22.4	13.6	16.2	19.7	3.9	5.7	8.4
13051	Chatham County, Georgia	35.1	21.2	23.5	8.8	11.4	0.4	5.7	8.4
13053	Chattahoochee County, Georgia	28.6	18.8	21.5	11.8	19.4	2.3	6.4	4.3
13055	Chattooga County, Georgia	23.8	17.0	17.3	13.8	28.1	1.8	7.6	32.3
13057	Cherokee County, Georgia	38.0	15.4	28.2	8.9	9.4	0.6	7.8	10.3
13059	Clarke County, Georgia	39.4	22.2	21.6	5.6	11.2	1.5	3.4	7.3
13061	Clay County, Georgia	23.1	20.8	16.7	24.8	14.6	10.8	11.9	18.6
13063	Clayton County, Georgia	23.5	21.8	26.5	9.7	18.5	0.3	6.5	7.6
13065	Clinch County, Georgia	30.0	12.5	19.2	15.1	23.2	8.9	5.1	21.0
13067	Cobb County, Georgia	44.3	15.2	24.9	7.4	8.2	0.2	6.7	7.8
13069	Coffee County, Georgia	31.6	16.1	21.4	8.5	22.5	4.2	4.7	18.7
13071	Colquitt County, Georgia	25.2	16.3	18.9	20.1	19.5	13.4	5.3	16.7
13073	Columbia County, Georgia	42.9	14.6	24.6	8.6	9.2	0.7	6.8	9.8
13075	Cook County, Georgia	25.4	18.8	22.3	10.2	23.4	3.8	6.9	11.8
13077	Coweta County, Georgia	34.0	16.3	24.2	10.0	15.4	0.5	5.2	14.0
13079	Crawford County, Georgia	29.2	16.6	20.8	14.5	18.9	3.7	8.7	9.6
13081	Crisp County, Georgia	29.9	19.6	25.5	12.0	13.0	3.2	6.5	9.0
13083	Dade County, Georgia	27.2	20.0	23.3	14.7	14.9	1.4	9.6	13.7
13085	Dawson County, Georgia	32.2	13.7	26.2	13.5	14.3	2.6	8.0	10.5
13087	Decatur County, Georgia	29.3	16.4	24.4	14.2	15.8	8.6	6.8	13.5
13089	DeKalb County, Georgia	42.7	16.8	24.0	5.7	10.7	0.2	4.7	6.2
13091	Dodge County, Georgia	34.4	12.7	23.1	11.0	18.7	2.5	5.4	15.2
13093	Dooly County, Georgia	21.7	17.9	20.2	11.7	28.4	7.8	6.5	18.3
13095	Dougherty County, Georgia	30.3	21.6	22.8	7.9	17.4	1.4	3.3	10.3
13097	Douglas County, Georgia	33.3	14.5	27.7	9.4	15.1	0.5	7.9	8.6
13099	Early County, Georgia	27.7	13.3	26.3	13.4	19.3	9.1	7.9	17.2
13101	Echols County, Georgia	21.7	13.2	19.2	28.9	17.1	16.2	13.4	16.2
13103	Effingham County, Georgia	30.2	13.6	23.4	13.7	19.1	0.6	9.1	16.5
13105	Elbert County, Georgia	22.6	16.5	20.4	10.2	30.4	4.0	3.8	27.8

Table C. County—Labor Force, Employment, and Educational Data, 2011–2015—*Continued*

		Occupation for employed population age 16 and older					Industry for employed population age 16 and older		
Fips code	State/county	Management, business, science, and arts occupations	Service occupations	Sales and office occupations:	Natural resources, construction, and maintenance occupations	Production, transportation, and material moving occupations:	Agriculture, forestry, fishing and hunting, and mining	Construction	Manufacturing
13107	Emanuel County, Georgia	21.8	19.7	22.3	13.5	22.7	5.1	8.4	17.4
13109	Evans County, Georgia	31.5	11.6	18.4	18.8	19.7	5.2	10.5	16.6
13111	Fannin County, Georgia	25.4	17.0	27.3	14.4	15.7	1.5	12.0	10.4
13113	Fayette County, Georgia	43.3	13.2	25.0	6.8	11.7	0.2	3.8	9.5
13115	Floyd County, Georgia	28.3	20.7	22.3	10.9	17.8	0.7	6.9	16.6
13117	Forsyth County, Georgia	48.4	11.9	26.4	5.9	7.4	0.5	5.9	9.4
13119	Franklin County, Georgia	28.9	15.0	21.2	13.2	21.8	3.0	9.0	20.6
13121	Fulton County, Georgia	49.4	15.0	24.1	4.0	7.5	0.4	3.4	6.1
13123	Gilmer County, Georgia	27.0	18.6	26.4	14.1	13.9	2.9	10.4	16.9
13125	Glascock County, Georgia	29.0	13.0	19.3	15.0	23.7	8.5	8.2	12.2
13127	Glynn County, Georgia	31.9	23.5	24.6	8.8	11.2	0.9	5.8	7.1
13129	Gordon County, Georgia	23.4	12.5	24.4	12.8	26.9	2.1	9.1	31.6
13131	Grady County, Georgia	28.7	12.8	26.2	14.3	18.1	8.7	8.1	13.6
13133	Greene County, Georgia	24.1	25.1	24.0	10.4	16.3	5.2	6.5	11.5
13135	Gwinnett County, Georgia	37.6	16.0	26.6	10.1	9.7	0.2	8.9	8.5
13137	Habersham County, Georgia	24.6	18.9	23.8	12.3	20.4	4.0	6.4	21.1
13139	Hall County, Georgia	28.3	15.1	24.3	11.1	21.2	1.6	8.3	20.5
13141	Hancock County, Georgia	25.1	27.7	20.1	7.7	19.4	3.9	4.1	9.6
13143	Haralson County, Georgia	28.2	19.7	18.8	14.4	18.9	0.4	11.6	15.4
13145	Harris County, Georgia	36.6	13.3	25.9	10.0	14.2	1.5	7.2	12.4
13147	Hart County, Georgia	27.5	13.5	24.3	13.3	21.4	4.9	6.3	26.0
13149	Heard County, Georgia	25.2	15.0	19.0	18.1	22.7	1.8	11.4	19.2
13151	Henry County, Georgia	32.9	16.3	27.7	9.1	14.0	0.2	4.8	7.5
13153	Houston County, Georgia	35.3	17.6	23.0	11.9	12.2	0.6	4.5	9.8
13155	Irwin County, Georgia	30.9	15.0	21.7	7.0	25.3	3.9	3.5	20.6
13157	Jackson County, Georgia	31.5	15.7	26.3	10.3	16.2	1.1	7.4	14.2
13159	Jasper County, Georgia	23.3	15.0	22.6	19.0	20.1	2.2	10.8	19.6
13161	Jeff Davis County, Georgia	23.7	16.2	28.0	16.4	15.7	4.9	9.8	13.5
13163	Jefferson County, Georgia	24.4	21.8	14.9	14.5	24.4	7.6	7.3	17.3
13165	Jenkins County, Georgia	27.1	19.9	14.6	13.2	25.3	3.8	11.3	13.1
13167	Johnson County, Georgia	23.6	18.6	19.6	12.8	25.4	4.6	7.2	12.7
13169	Jones County, Georgia	31.9	14.2	28.0	13.2	12.8	1.3	8.5	7.1
13171	Lamar County, Georgia	30.8	17.5	23.8	9.3	18.6	0.7	6.0	14.8
13173	Lanier County, Georgia	28.4	15.4	31.8	10.0	14.3	5.0	4.8	6.3
13175	Laurens County, Georgia	30.7	19.3	24.6	10.2	15.3	2.2	6.6	11.3
13177	Lee County, Georgia	39.6	12.9	27.9	9.2	10.4	2.9	4.7	10.6
13179	Liberty County, Georgia	28.6	21.5	25.3	10.1	14.4	0.4	4.9	6.6
13181	Lincoln County, Georgia	19.6	18.7	25.1	19.2	17.4	5.2	13.9	12.7
13183	Long County, Georgia	27.1	18.0	27.2	13.4	14.3	5.5	11.6	7.7
13185	Lowndes County, Georgia	29.2	21.4	27.9	8.8	12.7	0.9	5.1	8.0
13187	Lumpkin County, Georgia	31.5	18.7	26.5	9.6	13.6	0.7	6.6	11.0
13189	McDuffie County, Georgia	25.7	19.6	20.5	15.2	19.0	2.9	10.6	18.2
13191	McIntosh County, Georgia	22.8	18.7	28.5	9.5	20.5	1.8	5.8	10.3
13193	Macon County, Georgia	20.5	20.4	19.5	11.8	27.8	9.6	6.0	18.7
13195	Madison County, Georgia	30.6	15.1	23.0	12.4	18.8	2.2	8.9	17.1
13197	Marion County, Georgia	26.0	11.7	20.3	20.1	22.0	3.3	11.6	13.9
13199	Meriwether County, Georgia	19.9	18.6	17.1	17.3	27.1	3.1	8.7	20.4
13201	Miller County, Georgia	27.4	18.3	24.1	17.9	12.3	14.5	4.6	11.4
13205	Mitchell County, Georgia	28.4	15.2	23.2	12.3	21.0	8.2	5.0	16.1
13207	Monroe County, Georgia	35.2	18.9	22.9	10.8	12.2	1.9	7.0	5.6
13209	Montgomery County, Georgia	25.2	19.3	21.6	10.7	23.2	4.8	6.7	11.8
13211	Morgan County, Georgia	31.3	18.9	21.1	11.0	17.6	4.5	6.7	12.1
13213	Murray County, Georgia	19.5	15.3	23.1	11.9	30.3	1.3	4.3	38.0
13215	Muscogee County, Georgia	32.9	20.9	26.8	6.8	12.5	0.2	4.9	9.5
13217	Newton County, Georgia	29.9	18.3	24.6	10.8	16.5	0.5	7.6	14.0
13219	Oconee County, Georgia	51.3	14.1	20.3	5.1	9.1	1.9	4.4	8.9
13221	Oglethorpe County, Georgia	31.3	13.4	19.9	14.1	21.4	5.8	7.5	15.8
13223	Paulding County, Georgia	33.6	14.7	28.0	11.5	12.1	0.4	7.5	9.7
13225	Peach County, Georgia	27.6	19.4	21.5	19.1	12.4	3.2	9.2	8.6
13227	Pickens County, Georgia	30.8	15.6	27.6	14.3	11.8	2.1	10.0	10.6
13229	Pierce County, Georgia	32.0	14.1	21.7	14.4	17.8	6.4	5.8	9.7
13231	Pike County, Georgia	33.2	15.2	22.4	11.4	17.9	2.2	9.1	12.4
13233	Polk County, Georgia	23.6	16.7	23.0	12.9	23.8	1.4	9.5	22.3
13235	Pulaski County, Georgia	32.6	22.8	17.1	13.0	14.4	5.0	5.0	13.8
13237	Putnam County, Georgia	29.3	22.0	24.6	10.0	14.1	3.2	6.1	12.3
13239	Quitman County, Georgia	14.5	20.8	27.0	9.0	28.7	1.3	6.0	20.3
13241	Rabun County, Georgia	31.4	20.9	21.3	17.4	9.1	1.9	16.2	4.8
13243	Randolph County, Georgia	26.8	19.5	20.7	9.7	23.4	9.6	6.6	11.7
13245	Richmond County, Georgia	29.8	21.6	27.0	8.4	13.1	0.5	5.2	9.5
13247	Rockdale County, Georgia	32.3	17.0	25.1	9.8	15.8	0.3	6.8	11.2
13249	Schley County, Georgia	28.4	14.3	23.4	13.8	20.1	7.6	9.0	14.4
13251	Screven County, Georgia	27.0	18.4	23.0	11.2	20.4	5.1	5.8	17.5
13253	Seminole County, Georgia	32.4	21.6	22.5	9.2	14.3	11.3	5.4	9.6
13255	Spalding County, Georgia	26.8	18.1	25.4	10.6	19.1	1.0	5.3	14.2
13257	Stephens County, Georgia	25.9	19.3	22.8	10.6	21.4	2.1	5.4	22.2

Table C. County—Labor Force, Employment, and Educational Data, 2011–2015—*Continued*

		Occupation for employed population age 16 and older					Industry for employed population age 16 and older		
Fips code	State/county	Management, business, science, and arts occupations	Service occupations	Sales and office occupations:	Natural resources, construction, and maintenance occupations	Production, transportation, and material moving occupations:	Agriculture, forestry, fishing and hunting, and mining	Construction	Manufacturing
13259	Stewart County, Georgia	30.0	20.8	20.6	9.9	18.7	3.2	2.7	18.2
13261	Sumter County, Georgia	33.0	20.0	21.0	7.8	18.2	4.8	3.4	13.3
13263	Talbot County, Georgia	19.9	24.2	20.1	9.2	26.5	1.2	4.8	19.5
13265	Taliaferro County, Georgia	16.0	29.3	14.5	22.8	17.4	10.1	4.0	18.6
13267	Tattnall County, Georgia	29.6	20.5	23.4	16.0	10.5	7.8	9.6	7.8
13269	Taylor County, Georgia	25.7	18.3	21.0	17.4	17.6	4.4	8.2	11.9
13271	Telfair County, Georgia	25.2	21.1	19.5	12.2	22.0	5.8	4.5	14.6
13273	Terrell County, Georgia	24.3	18.2	25.8	10.8	20.9	4.7	6.5	17.3
13275	Thomas County, Georgia	34.0	18.8	25.3	7.9	14.1	3.1	4.9	12.0
13277	Tift County, Georgia	29.6	18.8	24.4	13.5	13.7	5.1	6.8	7.7
13279	Toombs County, Georgia	26.7	16.4	23.5	17.1	16.2	6.3	9.4	12.8
13281	Towns County, Georgia	30.1	22.1	26.1	10.4	11.4	0.8	11.1	4.9
13283	Treutlen County, Georgia	18.5	24.0	23.0	13.6	21.0	4.6	10.5	10.0
13285	Troup County, Georgia	29.1	16.9	22.1	8.4	23.4	1.0	4.3	25.3
13287	Turner County, Georgia	32.8	14.0	25.6	15.1	12.6	8.4	9.7	5.7
13289	Twiggs County, Georgia	24.0	15.6	21.5	17.9	20.9	2.7	8.8	16.9
13291	Union County, Georgia	28.7	18.9	28.0	15.8	8.7	6.4	11.1	6.1
13293	Upson County, Georgia	24.7	19.7	21.8	9.8	23.9	1.8	6.7	16.7
13295	Walker County, Georgia	26.6	14.6	25.4	11.0	22.5	0.8	5.5	20.0
13297	Walton County, Georgia	29.8	17.7	27.5	11.6	13.4	0.6	9.4	12.5
13299	Ware County, Georgia	30.7	16.8	22.2	12.6	17.7	3.8	6.8	13.0
13301	Warren County, Georgia	20.7	16.6	25.5	12.0	25.3	7.7	4.7	26.0
13303	Washington County, Georgia	30.1	18.1	26.2	11.1	14.5	6.7	5.3	10.6
13305	Wayne County, Georgia	29.7	15.2	21.8	16.2	17.0	3.2	9.4	12.7
13307	Webster County, Georgia	30.9	15.9	23.7	11.2	18.3	6.7	4.8	19.4
13309	Wheeler County, Georgia	25.9	20.1	18.9	15.8	19.3	10.5	3.7	13.3
13311	White County, Georgia	29.5	16.5	27.3	13.1	13.7	2.2	9.2	13.0
13313	Whitfield County, Georgia	21.1	13.8	22.6	9.0	33.5	0.7	5.0	38.3
13315	Wilcox County, Georgia	28.9	22.8	17.7	12.8	17.7	8.4	8.1	9.4
13317	Wilkes County, Georgia	26.5	18.5	19.0	11.5	24.6	7.5	4.4	20.0
13319	Wilkinson County, Georgia	20.0	16.6	27.8	15.9	19.6	6.7	8.6	16.1
13321	Worth County, Georgia	24.5	17.3	23.5	15.5	19.3	4.1	9.2	12.5
15000	**Hawaii**	34.0	22.8	24.8	9.7	8.7	1.6	7.1	3.0
15001	Hawaii County, Hawaii	31.1	23.9	25.3	12.0	7.7	4.6	7.5	2.4
15003	Honolulu County, Hawaii	35.8	21.2	25.1	9.1	8.8	0.7	6.8	3.3
15005	Kalawao County, Hawaii	31.3	23.4	21.9	4.7	18.8	4.7	1.6	0.0
15007	Kauai County, Hawaii	29.3	29.0	22.8	11.3	7.6	3.7	7.4	2.1
15009	Maui County, Hawaii	29.0	27.9	23.2	10.7	9.2	2.6	8.1	2.4
16000	**Idaho**	33.5	18.0	24.1	11.9	12.5	5.6	7.1	9.9
16001	Ada County, Idaho	42.4	16.8	25.4	7.2	8.2	1.5	6.0	9.3
16003	Adams County, Idaho	27.9	23.5	20.4	17.0	11.2	11.6	9.1	7.0
16005	Bannock County, Idaho	34.4	18.5	24.7	8.6	13.9	2.1	5.6	9.1
16007	Bear Lake County, Idaho	25.3	19.3	23.8	16.1	15.6	16.8	5.0	7.5
16009	Benewah County, Idaho	25.3	20.1	16.7	16.1	21.9	10.8	4.6	13.8
16011	Bingham County, Idaho	30.9	15.9	20.3	16.5	16.4	9.9	7.6	11.4
16013	Blaine County, Idaho	31.9	26.2	22.6	13.8	5.5	3.4	10.4	2.9
16015	Boise County, Idaho	36.8	14.6	25.1	12.0	11.5	9.5	8.8	9.5
16017	Bonner County, Idaho	27.4	19.8	24.9	12.5	15.4	4.3	8.8	13.4
16019	Bonneville County, Idaho	34.7	17.4	25.1	10.1	12.6	2.9	7.7	9.5
16021	Boundary County, Idaho	28.4	18.0	21.2	15.4	17.0	12.4	3.8	14.7
16023	Butte County, Idaho	34.3	20.4	15.0	15.9	14.4	18.1	5.5	2.8
16025	Camas County, Idaho	28.4	19.8	17.6	21.2	13.0	12.2	17.8	8.6
16027	Canyon County, Idaho	25.7	19.5	24.4	14.3	16.0	5.1	8.8	12.0
16029	Caribou County, Idaho	32.8	15.8	18.5	17.9	15.0	16.7	11.4	15.3
16031	Cassia County, Idaho	24.5	13.2	24.1	19.0	19.3	19.7	4.3	15.2
16033	Clark County, Idaho	22.9	20.6	12.0	26.9	17.6	55.9	2.5	0.5
16035	Clearwater County, Idaho	30.0	18.2	17.2	17.8	16.8	15.0	6.9	11.5
16037	Custer County, Idaho	29.8	15.4	23.6	21.9	9.4	20.3	8.7	2.0
16039	Elmore County, Idaho	28.5	21.8	17.4	16.7	15.6	6.3	5.1	8.0
16041	Franklin County, Idaho	23.5	12.2	26.2	20.5	17.6	13.1	7.0	18.0
16043	Fremont County, Idaho	28.9	17.5	20.7	18.2	14.8	12.2	10.1	9.2
16045	Gem County, Idaho	30.8	19.2	25.6	14.3	10.1	7.1	9.1	7.2
16047	Gooding County, Idaho	27.5	18.9	11.4	28.4	13.9	26.6	5.3	11.4
16049	Idaho County, Idaho	25.6	18.7	22.6	17.5	15.7	11.1	9.8	10.3
16051	Jefferson County, Idaho	33.7	12.1	22.5	17.5	14.1	11.0	8.6	9.3
16053	Jerome County, Idaho	24.7	15.9	18.8	24.0	16.6	23.3	4.8	12.0
16055	Kootenai County, Idaho	31.0	18.4	27.2	11.6	11.9	2.5	9.2	7.9
16057	Latah County, Idaho	41.7	18.2	22.1	8.3	9.7	4.0	4.4	7.0
16059	Lemhi County, Idaho	31.2	17.8	24.5	14.5	12.0	14.8	7.3	9.6
16061	Lewis County, Idaho	29.5	22.9	20.4	13.6	13.5	14.3	7.1	6.9
16063	Lincoln County, Idaho	20.8	19.9	18.1	20.9	20.3	14.6	10.2	15.5
16065	Madison County, Idaho	37.4	17.0	27.5	8.5	9.6	5.3	4.9	4.3
16067	Minidoka County, Idaho	21.7	17.0	19.3	20.9	21.0	16.7	5.1	16.8
16069	Nez Perce County, Idaho	31.0	18.4	25.1	10.1	15.4	3.7	7.0	14.1
16071	Oneida County, Idaho	28.3	15.8	18.2	20.2	17.5	14.5	8.5	15.8
16073	Owyhee County, Idaho	22.7	14.9	17.1	26.3	19.0	29.2	4.8	14.3

Table C. County—Labor Force, Employment, and Educational Data, 2011–2015—*Continued*

| | | Occupation for employed population age 16 and older | | | | | Industry for employed population age 16 and older | | |
Fips code	State/county	Management, business, science, and arts occupations	Service occupations	Sales and office occupations:	Natural resources, construction, and maintenance occupations	Production, transportation, and material moving occupations:	Agriculture, forestry, fishing and hunting, and mining	Construction	Manufacturing
16075	Payette County, Idaho	26.3	20.0	26.3	11.8	15.7	6.7	4.8	13.3
16077	Power County, Idaho	19.9	13.5	22.7	20.2	23.6	18.1	8.0	18.4
16079	Shoshone County, Idaho	27.9	23.0	21.3	16.9	10.9	12.1	9.8	6.7
16081	Teton County, Idaho	32.3	23.5	17.1	20.1	7.0	4.0	19.6	5.5
16083	Twin Falls County, Idaho	28.4	19.3	23.6	13.5	15.3	8.7	5.2	9.6
16085	Valley County, Idaho	31.8	27.2	17.2	13.8	10.0	3.9	9.5	2.7
16087	Washington County, Idaho	26.1	20.6	18.1	16.5	18.7	12.7	6.8	8.2
17000	**Illinois**	36.8	17.4	24.5	7.3	13.9	1.1	5.1	12.6
17001	Adams County, Illinois	29.6	18.3	26.7	7.9	17.5	2.2	5.2	14.8
17003	Alexander County, Illinois	20.7	29.2	24.0	7.9	18.2	3.0	3.7	10.0
17005	Bond County, Illinois	26.4	21.2	26.2	9.0	17.3	3.8	5.6	13.0
17007	Boone County, Illinois	29.6	13.8	24.0	10.6	22.0	2.3	7.6	22.7
17009	Brown County, Illinois	26.8	15.8	20.8	16.4	20.2	5.9	6.6	5.4
17011	Bureau County, Illinois	27.4	18.8	22.9	10.8	20.1	6.5	6.5	15.4
17013	Calhoun County, Illinois	26.9	23.2	15.6	16.4	17.9	4.4	12.3	12.5
17015	Carroll County, Illinois	28.5	16.7	18.2	10.8	25.9	8.1	6.0	21.9
17017	Cass County, Illinois	24.7	16.4	20.0	11.9	27.0	6.5	6.6	22.1
17019	Champaign County, Illinois	44.8	18.7	21.4	5.4	9.7	1.4	3.3	7.4
17021	Christian County, Illinois	26.7	20.5	23.4	12.5	16.9	4.6	7.6	11.8
17023	Clark County, Illinois	29.4	17.3	20.3	13.6	19.4	5.9	9.3	20.2
17025	Clay County, Illinois	25.3	15.8	20.4	11.9	26.5	9.3	5.9	19.8
17027	Clinton County, Illinois	31.8	18.1	22.6	10.9	16.6	4.0	9.4	11.7
17029	Coles County, Illinois	28.9	21.2	25.4	7.9	16.6	2.2	5.3	13.9
17031	Cook County, Illinois	38.3	18.2	24.4	6.1	13.0	0.2	4.6	10.3
17033	Crawford County, Illinois	28.1	16.2	20.9	11.3	23.4	4.4	8.0	22.4
17035	Cumberland County, Illinois	28.9	16.0	20.5	12.8	21.9	7.5	7.6	20.8
17037	DeKalb County, Illinois	33.4	19.1	25.1	8.3	14.1	1.6	5.4	12.3
17039	De Witt County, Illinois	27.2	17.6	26.6	13.3	15.4	3.0	7.5	14.3
17041	Douglas County, Illinois	26.3	15.4	25.1	11.6	21.5	3.9	8.0	23.1
17043	DuPage County, Illinois	44.8	13.1	26.2	5.5	10.5	0.2	4.6	12.8
17045	Edgar County, Illinois	27.0	17.6	21.5	9.7	24.2	7.7	4.9	23.1
17047	Edwards County, Illinois	23.6	13.7	21.2	13.9	27.7	8.0	5.5	25.4
17049	Effingham County, Illinois	29.2	17.9	24.9	10.7	17.4	2.8	7.8	15.7
17051	Fayette County, Illinois	24.5	21.9	21.7	12.7	19.2	6.1	6.9	14.3
17053	Ford County, Illinois	29.9	17.4	20.2	12.8	19.6	8.8	6.6	14.5
17055	Franklin County, Illinois	26.9	20.8	21.8	12.0	18.5	6.9	4.8	12.8
17057	Fulton County, Illinois	28.7	20.3	20.3	10.4	20.2	3.0	6.1	15.8
17059	Gallatin County, Illinois	29.5	18.9	19.2	16.1	16.3	15.4	6.2	7.4
17061	Greene County, Illinois	27.5	20.9	18.9	12.3	20.4	8.1	6.8	13.5
17063	Grundy County, Illinois	28.9	17.6	24.0	12.7	16.7	1.6	9.3	10.6
17065	Hamilton County, Illinois	25.7	14.5	23.5	16.1	20.2	16.8	7.5	11.1
17067	Hancock County, Illinois	29.3	16.9	24.0	10.2	19.5	8.1	6.5	15.2
17069	Hardin County, Illinois	26.9	20.4	17.6	16.9	18.2	15.4	3.4	1.7
17071	Henderson County, Illinois	25.5	21.6	18.4	12.1	22.4	5.2	8.9	15.9
17073	Henry County, Illinois	30.9	16.8	23.2	11.0	18.1	3.3	7.0	18.4
17075	Iroquois County, Illinois	28.5	16.2	22.5	13.5	19.3	7.7	7.5	13.9
17077	Jackson County, Illinois	38.0	20.6	25.0	7.2	9.3	2.2	4.5	6.5
17079	Jasper County, Illinois	29.2	14.1	25.0	13.0	18.7	9.2	5.5	13.9
17081	Jefferson County, Illinois	26.6	19.8	23.5	9.2	20.8	2.9	5.4	14.3
17083	Jersey County, Illinois	31.5	18.3	25.9	9.7	14.7	2.3	5.6	12.6
17085	Jo Daviess County, Illinois	26.6	18.5	25.2	12.7	17.0	4.5	7.0	13.7
17087	Johnson County, Illinois	30.6	21.5	24.0	12.4	11.5	2.3	8.9	7.3
17089	Kane County, Illinois	33.7	16.5	25.2	7.7	16.8	0.6	6.1	16.8
17091	Kankakee County, Illinois	30.1	18.3	23.4	10.4	17.8	1.6	6.1	14.6
17093	Kendall County, Illinois	39.7	13.1	26.8	8.6	11.8	0.9	5.4	13.4
17095	Knox County, Illinois	30.0	19.5	23.6	8.5	18.4	3.1	4.4	11.4
17097	Lake County, Illinois	41.9	15.3	25.5	6.0	11.3	0.3	4.9	16.1
17099	LaSalle County, Illinois	26.4	20.2	23.5	10.2	19.7	3.6	5.9	14.0
17101	Lawrence County, Illinois	30.4	20.6	23.9	7.7	17.3	5.5	6.2	12.1
17103	Lee County, Illinois	29.2	20.2	22.4	8.4	19.7	2.7	5.1	18.1
17105	Livingston County, Illinois	26.4	18.1	22.7	12.5	20.4	6.3	7.1	19.0
17107	Logan County, Illinois	31.1	22.0	23.9	7.9	15.1	4.3	4.7	12.4
17109	McDonough County, Illinois	34.1	21.9	24.2	6.6	13.3	2.7	3.9	9.7
17111	McHenry County, Illinois	37.0	15.1	27.1	8.2	12.6	0.8	7.1	16.3
17113	McLean County, Illinois	42.2	17.8	25.5	5.8	8.7	1.3	3.7	6.5
17115	Macon County, Illinois	31.9	19.1	23.8	9.2	16.0	1.8	6.0	18.0
17117	Macoupin County, Illinois	31.1	15.4	24.6	11.7	17.2	4.4	6.8	11.9
17119	Madison County, Illinois	33.9	17.4	24.8	8.9	14.9	0.7	5.5	13.3
17121	Marion County, Illinois	27.1	21.9	19.9	8.6	22.5	2.9	4.3	18.0
17123	Marshall County, Illinois	28.2	19.6	19.8	11.8	20.6	5.7	5.4	22.4
17125	Mason County, Illinois	28.9	17.6	21.6	12.8	19.1	6.3	7.6	12.3
17127	Massac County, Illinois	28.8	21.4	20.9	12.0	16.9	3.8	9.2	6.6
17129	Menard County, Illinois	35.4	18.3	24.2	12.0	10.0	3.6	9.0	6.3
17131	Mercer County, Illinois	29.6	13.4	23.9	13.1	20.1	6.5	7.6	18.6
17133	Monroe County, Illinois	37.2	15.1	27.2	9.7	10.8	1.7	8.7	10.0
17135	Montgomery County, Illinois	32.4	20.3	24.0	9.4	13.8	4.3	6.1	8.8

Table C. County—Labor Force, Employment, and Educational Data, 2011–2015—*Continued*

| | | Occupation for employed population age 16 and older | | | | | Industry for employed population age 16 and older | | |
| | | Management, business, science, and arts occupations | Service occupations | Sales and office occupations: | Natural resources, construction, and maintenance occupations | Production, transportation, and material moving occupations: | Agriculture, forestry, fishing and hunting, and mining | Construction | Manufacturing |
Fips code	State/county								
17137	Morgan County, Illinois	32.0	19.0	23.0	8.9	17.2	3.2	5.5	11.3
17139	Moultrie County, Illinois	28.1	16.2	22.5	8.6	24.5	2.9	7.1	25.5
17141	Ogle County, Illinois	31.3	16.3	20.7	9.8	21.8	3.0	5.5	17.9
17143	Peoria County, Illinois	38.1	18.5	24.7	7.1	11.6	0.9	4.9	16.2
17145	Perry County, Illinois	24.7	21.0	18.9	15.1	20.4	5.9	7.2	16.9
17147	Piatt County, Illinois	35.9	15.0	24.1	11.8	13.2	5.4	6.6	13.1
17149	Pike County, Illinois	25.6	19.8	20.7	14.4	19.5	8.2	8.0	9.8
17151	Pope County, Illinois	21.7	23.6	20.1	13.5	21.1	5.8	4.9	8.4
17153	Pulaski County, Illinois	25.9	26.7	20.2	10.4	16.7	4.7	7.2	9.0
17155	Putnam County, Illinois	28.8	17.5	19.8	13.6	20.3	5.2	6.3	17.0
17157	Randolph County, Illinois	24.6	20.4	19.3	12.1	23.6	4.1	7.2	20.7
17159	Richland County, Illinois	27.7	16.8	22.9	10.4	22.2	6.7	4.6	14.4
17161	Rock Island County, Illinois	29.5	18.9	23.9	8.4	19.3	1.0	5.4	18.9
17163	St. Clair County, Illinois	34.7	19.5	24.7	8.1	13.0	0.6	5.4	8.8
17165	Saline County, Illinois	23.1	24.1	23.4	15.2	14.1	10.6	6.1	8.0
17167	Sangamon County, Illinois	41.2	18.1	25.1	7.0	8.6	1.4	4.4	4.9
17169	Schuyler County, Illinois	27.5	18.6	25.7	11.1	17.1	7.4	5.6	14.4
17171	Scott County, Illinois	27.9	15.3	23.1	11.9	21.8	5.9	6.7	12.7
17173	Shelby County, Illinois	27.6	18.1	20.3	12.2	21.7	5.4	6.4	20.1
17175	Stark County, Illinois	35.5	18.5	19.9	10.9	15.2	10.4	4.7	16.2
17177	Stephenson County, Illinois	29.1	17.6	23.1	10.1	20.1	5.2	5.7	19.0
17179	Tazewell County, Illinois	35.5	16.7	24.2	8.0	15.6	1.6	5.9	17.9
17181	Union County, Illinois	31.6	20.5	19.2	13.3	15.4	4.9	7.5	8.3
17183	Vermilion County, Illinois	25.7	20.3	21.6	9.3	23.1	2.3	5.7	16.8
17185	Wabash County, Illinois	26.5	19.9	17.5	13.2	22.9	7.0	6.5	17.1
17187	Warren County, Illinois	29.4	20.9	20.0	9.3	20.4	4.9	4.4	14.3
17189	Washington County, Illinois	31.6	15.9	18.8	12.3	21.4	9.9	6.2	16.3
17191	Wayne County, Illinois	26.6	15.1	21.4	13.4	23.5	9.4	5.3	21.9
17193	White County, Illinois	25.6	18.0	21.7	15.6	19.2	14.3	5.1	12.4
17195	Whiteside County, Illinois	26.9	18.5	23.7	9.5	21.4	2.5	5.1	19.6
17197	Will County, Illinois	36.4	15.8	25.3	8.6	13.9	0.4	6.1	11.7
17199	Williamson County, Illinois	31.1	22.1	25.1	9.9	11.7	2.1	6.2	8.7
17201	Winnebago County, Illinois	30.3	17.6	24.3	7.4	20.3	0.7	4.4	22.3
17203	Woodford County, Illinois	37.1	17.5	22.6	8.9	14.0	3.1	5.7	16.7
18000	**Indiana**	32.4	17.0	23.3	8.8	18.5	1.4	5.8	18.7
18001	Adams County, Indiana	26.5	15.1	19.5	13.1	25.7	3.0	8.3	28.8
18003	Allen County, Indiana	34.4	16.7	23.9	7.4	17.7	0.5	5.5	18.8
18005	Bartholomew County, Indiana	39.0	15.3	19.7	6.8	19.2	1.1	4.7	33.8
18007	Benton County, Indiana	26.6	14.3	21.7	15.0	22.5	8.6	8.0	19.0
18009	Blackford County, Indiana	21.0	15.8	20.8	7.9	34.5	2.6	3.0	30.9
18011	Boone County, Indiana	45.1	13.1	21.6	7.7	12.6	1.3	7.6	13.7
18013	Brown County, Indiana	33.5	22.4	17.4	11.1	15.6	1.4	10.2	16.0
18015	Carroll County, Indiana	24.9	16.0	22.8	12.0	24.3	3.6	6.1	26.2
18017	Cass County, Indiana	25.1	18.8	18.2	9.1	28.8	2.7	5.4	28.5
18019	Clark County, Indiana	29.6	16.6	26.6	8.1	19.2	0.5	4.9	16.0
18021	Clay County, Indiana	26.7	18.3	22.5	9.9	22.6	3.3	5.3	20.1
18023	Clinton County, Indiana	22.8	12.5	19.8	10.0	34.9	3.7	6.9	30.2
18025	Crawford County, Indiana	22.9	18.5	20.8	9.5	28.3	2.6	6.2	23.5
18027	Daviess County, Indiana	24.5	15.6	17.8	17.2	25.0	7.4	11.2	21.6
18029	Dearborn County, Indiana	29.6	18.3	22.7	11.3	18.1	1.1	8.3	17.1
18031	Decatur County, Indiana	27.8	14.9	18.0	10.1	29.2	3.1	5.6	32.4
18033	DeKalb County, Indiana	26.8	14.1	21.5	8.7	28.9	2.3	5.2	32.7
18035	Delaware County, Indiana	30.8	23.0	23.7	7.4	15.2	0.9	4.7	11.7
18037	Dubois County, Indiana	29.6	13.9	22.3	8.4	25.8	4.0	4.2	34.5
18039	Elkhart County, Indiana	24.2	15.2	21.8	7.6	31.2	1.0	4.3	36.4
18041	Fayette County, Indiana	24.0	19.9	24.5	7.8	23.8	0.9	5.3	22.5
18043	Floyd County, Indiana	34.5	15.6	26.3	7.2	16.4	0.3	6.2	17.2
18045	Fountain County, Indiana	26.6	15.8	17.1	12.1	28.4	3.8	6.5	30.0
18047	Franklin County, Indiana	31.7	14.7	20.4	14.8	18.4	3.5	8.5	21.3
18049	Fulton County, Indiana	24.9	14.5	16.7	10.9	33.0	4.9	5.3	34.0
18051	Gibson County, Indiana	26.0	16.1	17.9	13.7	26.3	5.6	5.5	25.9
18053	Grant County, Indiana	28.4	18.9	26.5	7.0	19.1	1.4	3.3	15.1
18055	Greene County, Indiana	27.7	18.6	21.2	12.9	19.7	5.0	7.6	12.7
18057	Hamilton County, Indiana	51.8	11.2	25.9	5.1	6.1	0.6	4.5	12.4
18059	Hancock County, Indiana	37.7	15.3	24.9	9.6	12.6	1.3	7.1	13.9
18061	Harrison County, Indiana	29.3	17.0	22.9	11.1	19.7	1.7	7.8	18.9
18063	Hendricks County, Indiana	40.0	13.7	25.8	7.9	12.6	0.6	5.7	12.6
18065	Henry County, Indiana	28.7	18.2	22.6	8.7	21.8	2.1	5.3	21.2
18067	Howard County, Indiana	29.3	19.6	21.8	7.9	21.4	0.9	4.5	23.6
18069	Huntington County, Indiana	27.8	16.6	20.3	7.9	27.4	2.2	5.1	27.0
18071	Jackson County, Indiana	27.1	14.7	22.6	9.0	26.6	3.4	5.0	31.3
18073	Jasper County, Indiana	27.1	15.5	19.3	18.7	19.4	5.5	11.8	17.8
18075	Jay County, Indiana	22.1	14.1	18.4	13.2	32.1	5.3	7.2	34.3
18077	Jefferson County, Indiana	27.3	18.4	18.7	10.5	25.1	2.1	5.0	28.8
18079	Jennings County, Indiana	23.6	16.5	21.8	10.1	27.9	1.8	7.4	30.1

Table C. County—Labor Force, Employment, and Educational Data, 2011–2015—*Continued*

		Occupation for employed population age 16 and older					Industry for employed population age 16 and older		
Fips code	State/county	Management, business, science, and arts occupations	Service occupations	Sales and office occupations:	Natural resources, construction, and maintenance occupations	Production, transportation, and material moving occupations:	Agriculture, forestry, fishing and hunting, and mining	Construction	Manufacturing
18081	Johnson County, Indiana	37.4	14.5	26.0	9.1	13.0	0.8	6.6	15.9
18083	Knox County, Indiana	27.5	21.4	19.8	11.4	19.8	7.9	4.3	14.8
18085	Kosciusko County, Indiana	27.4	13.3	21.4	8.2	29.7	2.5	4.6	39.0
18087	LaGrange County, Indiana	19.5	12.1	15.8	11.8	40.9	4.7	5.1	45.5
18089	Lake County, Indiana	29.9	19.1	24.0	9.7	17.3	0.5	6.7	15.2
18091	LaPorte County, Indiana	26.9	18.4	23.6	10.0	21.0	1.3	5.5	21.4
18093	Lawrence County, Indiana	29.5	17.4	21.7	11.7	19.8	1.6	7.5	18.0
18095	Madison County, Indiana	28.1	21.4	25.5	8.1	17.0	1.0	5.7	13.9
18097	Marion County, Indiana	33.7	18.4	25.7	7.6	14.7	0.3	5.5	10.7
18099	Marshall County, Indiana	26.9	12.7	21.9	10.3	28.2	3.7	6.0	30.5
18101	Martin County, Indiana	30.4	14.9	20.2	13.8	20.7	6.2	5.7	15.5
18103	Miami County, Indiana	24.7	18.9	19.4	10.9	26.2	2.5	6.8	24.3
18105	Monroe County, Indiana	42.8	19.5	21.7	6.0	10.0	0.5	3.9	10.0
18107	Montgomery County, Indiana	24.0	16.9	22.0	10.9	26.2	2.3	6.4	27.9
18109	Morgan County, Indiana	28.6	15.2	24.1	13.9	18.3	0.9	9.6	16.4
18111	Newton County, Indiana	18.9	15.9	22.0	19.9	23.2	6.8	9.7	20.2
18113	Noble County, Indiana	24.0	14.8	17.6	10.9	32.6	2.8	6.0	37.0
18115	Ohio County, Indiana	21.5	23.0	19.3	11.4	24.9	0.2	5.2	21.0
18117	Orange County, Indiana	24.8	21.3	19.9	12.0	21.9	4.8	9.1	19.9
18119	Owen County, Indiana	24.6	16.6	19.9	15.2	23.7	2.3	9.2	22.7
18121	Parke County, Indiana	21.4	18.2	23.3	14.4	22.7	5.8	7.3	20.3
18123	Perry County, Indiana	19.8	20.7	18.0	10.5	30.9	3.0	6.6	33.7
18125	Pike County, Indiana	23.6	12.7	22.0	12.6	29.1	6.8	9.1	23.0
18127	Porter County, Indiana	35.3	16.6	21.8	11.1	15.3	0.4	6.2	18.8
18129	Posey County, Indiana	31.0	15.9	19.9	12.1	21.2	3.2	8.0	23.8
18131	Pulaski County, Indiana	27.2	14.6	16.5	11.9	29.8	7.5	6.6	26.8
18133	Putnam County, Indiana	28.2	18.5	22.3	11.8	19.1	2.2	6.8	17.3
18135	Randolph County, Indiana	27.1	17.3	19.3	11.9	24.5	6.3	6.4	22.9
18137	Ripley County, Indiana	27.5	16.8	22.6	11.9	21.1	1.9	8.4	24.0
18139	Rush County, Indiana	28.8	14.8	20.8	10.5	25.2	5.8	5.1	24.7
18141	St. Joseph County, Indiana	34.6	17.6	24.6	7.1	16.1	0.4	4.7	17.4
18143	Scott County, Indiana	21.2	17.4	19.9	8.8	32.7	1.6	4.8	31.3
18145	Shelby County, Indiana	25.2	17.5	20.3	10.9	26.1	1.8	6.7	27.8
18147	Spencer County, Indiana	28.1	14.1	22.1	11.8	23.8	4.0	8.8	23.9
18149	Starke County, Indiana	24.8	17.9	18.9	12.3	26.1	2.7	6.4	26.2
18151	Steuben County, Indiana	26.5	15.3	24.7	8.4	25.1	2.1	4.1	27.0
18153	Sullivan County, Indiana	25.5	20.2	18.3	14.3	21.7	7.2	7.0	15.5
18155	Switzerland County, Indiana	17.4	24.9	20.1	14.0	23.7	2.5	9.0	17.0
18157	Tippecanoe County, Indiana	37.9	18.2	21.0	7.0	15.9	0.8	4.7	16.9
18159	Tipton County, Indiana	31.1	16.3	19.9	14.4	18.2	5.9	8.0	22.2
18161	Union County, Indiana	25.9	20.9	26.8	12.2	14.2	3.1	4.9	10.7
18163	Vanderburgh County, Indiana	30.8	18.5	25.4	8.3	16.9	0.7	5.5	15.9
18165	Vermillion County, Indiana	23.1	16.6	23.8	10.3	26.1	2.6	8.6	23.2
18167	Vigo County, Indiana	31.2	20.5	22.6	8.4	17.3	0.8	5.1	15.9
18169	Wabash County, Indiana	30.0	18.1	21.2	8.9	21.7	4.0	4.1	23.4
18171	Warren County, Indiana	27.4	13.0	18.8	11.9	28.9	6.2	4.9	29.5
18173	Warrick County, Indiana	36.3	15.8	24.5	9.9	13.4	1.6	6.8	15.7
18175	Washington County, Indiana	25.6	14.3	19.8	12.2	28.1	4.2	9.0	25.4
18177	Wayne County, Indiana	29.3	20.7	22.2	8.8	19.0	1.7	4.6	18.1
18179	Wells County, Indiana	25.7	16.6	23.0	11.4	23.3	3.2	4.7	25.0
18181	White County, Indiana	22.9	15.9	22.9	13.4	24.9	5.2	7.0	25.0
18183	Whitley County, Indiana	26.2	14.6	21.9	8.7	28.6	1.4	5.5	29.8
19000	**Iowa**	34.5	16.6	23.3	9.4	16.2	3.9	6.2	15.2
19001	Adair County, Iowa	27.1	15.5	21.0	17.6	18.8	13.0	9.0	14.7
19003	Adams County, Iowa	36.3	12.8	18.8	11.2	20.9	12.9	5.0	15.4
19005	Allamakee County, Iowa	29.8	15.2	19.6	15.1	20.4	10.5	8.0	15.4
19007	Appanoose County, Iowa	27.2	12.5	26.3	11.7	22.3	6.4	7.0	21.9
19009	Audubon County, Iowa	30.5	18.2	21.6	14.4	15.3	14.6	7.7	9.2
19011	Benton County, Iowa	32.5	13.8	23.8	11.1	18.8	4.2	7.7	16.9
19013	Black Hawk County, Iowa	32.0	18.4	24.2	7.4	18.0	1.6	5.2	17.9
19015	Boone County, Iowa	32.8	17.5	22.7	11.3	15.7	4.4	6.3	10.1
19017	Bremer County, Iowa	35.0	15.3	24.6	9.3	15.7	4.5	5.5	19.3
19019	Buchanan County, Iowa	29.6	15.2	20.8	13.0	21.5	6.5	7.7	21.2
19021	Buena Vista County, Iowa	25.8	16.9	18.8	9.0	29.5	6.9	4.6	30.0
19023	Butler County, Iowa	27.9	16.9	22.1	11.2	21.9	7.4	5.9	20.1
19025	Calhoun County, Iowa	32.8	19.2	20.9	14.0	13.2	10.6	7.2	8.9
19027	Carroll County, Iowa	29.4	16.9	23.3	12.2	18.2	7.5	5.0	12.3
19029	Cass County, Iowa	28.4	18.1	22.4	11.8	19.2	7.5	8.6	13.4
19031	Cedar County, Iowa	33.9	14.2	24.3	10.3	17.3	6.5	7.7	14.6
19033	Cerro Gordo County, Iowa	30.2	17.7	24.8	7.4	19.9	2.3	5.1	15.4
19035	Cherokee County, Iowa	27.8	15.0	23.9	14.0	19.3	9.3	7.5	18.1
19037	Chickasaw County, Iowa	27.9	14.2	21.3	13.0	23.6	9.5	6.0	24.7
19039	Clarke County, Iowa	27.0	18.7	19.7	12.2	22.4	7.5	6.6	17.3

Table C. County—Labor Force, Employment, and Educational Data, 2011–2015—*Continued*

		Occupation for employed population age 16 and older					Industry for employed population age 16 and older		
Fips code	State/county	Management, business, science, and arts occupations	Service occupations	Sales and office occupations:	Natural resources, construction, and maintenance occupations	Production, transportation, and material moving occupations	Agriculture, forestry, fishing and hunting, and mining	Construction	Manufacturing
19041	Clay County, Iowa	28.4	14.2	24.9	13.5	19.0	7.5	5.3	14.7
19043	Clayton County, Iowa	27.9	17.1	22.1	12.7	20.3	11.1	8.0	18.8
19045	Clinton County, Iowa	27.8	17.1	24.2	10.0	21.0	3.5	6.1	21.3
19047	Crawford County, Iowa	25.7	16.5	18.3	14.1	25.4	8.6	5.8	22.8
19049	Dallas County, Iowa	47.5	11.7	25.8	5.8	9.2	2.4	5.1	7.7
19051	Davis County, Iowa	28.3	12.1	23.2	15.2	21.2	8.1	10.1	19.3
19053	Decatur County, Iowa	32.8	22.9	17.7	11.8	14.9	8.1	6.9	9.9
19055	Delaware County, Iowa	28.7	14.3	20.8	11.5	24.7	9.0	6.9	22.1
19057	Des Moines County, Iowa	28.1	19.3	23.4	9.3	19.9	1.9	7.1	20.0
19059	Dickinson County, Iowa	34.3	15.3	21.8	11.1	17.5	4.3	9.1	18.3
19061	Dubuque County, Iowa	33.7	17.6	25.0	7.9	15.7	1.9	5.8	16.1
19063	Emmet County, Iowa	27.8	16.3	20.7	12.3	22.9	8.2	5.6	25.3
19065	Fayette County, Iowa	31.4	19.4	17.9	12.3	18.9	9.3	6.5	13.9
19067	Floyd County, Iowa	32.3	14.8	22.5	11.4	19.0	7.4	6.2	21.2
19069	Franklin County, Iowa	30.4	17.2	18.2	14.3	19.9	12.6	7.6	17.1
19071	Fremont County, Iowa	34.8	16.2	19.8	10.8	18.5	11.6	5.3	13.4
19073	Greene County, Iowa	33.8	19.0	19.4	11.1	16.6	11.3	5.7	14.6
19075	Grundy County, Iowa	34.1	12.8	23.6	12.5	16.9	9.1	8.9	15.4
19077	Guthrie County, Iowa	32.3	15.8	23.8	15.0	13.1	7.7	9.3	8.2
19079	Hamilton County, Iowa	30.0	15.3	21.7	12.3	20.7	8.0	6.1	15.9
19081	Hancock County, Iowa	30.9	13.6	19.6	9.3	26.6	10.0	3.8	26.6
19083	Hardin County, Iowa	29.4	17.9	19.1	12.8	20.8	10.5	8.6	13.4
19085	Harrison County, Iowa	29.5	16.7	23.7	11.5	18.5	6.9	7.3	11.0
19087	Henry County, Iowa	29.3	18.5	22.6	9.4	20.1	4.2	4.9	21.1
19089	Howard County, Iowa	29.0	15.7	16.5	14.0	24.8	9.7	7.4	26.4
19091	Humboldt County, Iowa	29.2	17.0	20.4	14.3	19.1	11.4	7.5	19.5
19093	Ida County, Iowa	33.7	16.5	17.6	11.4	20.8	10.0	5.5	21.2
19095	Iowa County, Iowa	30.7	16.0	23.2	10.2	19.9	8.9	5.1	19.2
19097	Jackson County, Iowa	25.9	16.6	22.8	11.5	23.1	7.4	6.9	18.7
19099	Jasper County, Iowa	30.2	15.5	24.2	11.1	19.0	4.2	6.2	17.3
19101	Jefferson County, Iowa	36.1	14.7	27.7	8.5	13.0	3.2	4.6	15.7
19103	Johnson County, Iowa	45.5	18.0	20.9	5.2	10.4	1.3	4.1	8.2
19105	Jones County, Iowa	29.9	18.1	19.6	12.1	20.3	6.8	8.3	17.2
19107	Keokuk County, Iowa	32.6	19.3	16.7	13.9	17.5	11.7	7.6	15.6
19109	Kossuth County, Iowa	34.0	15.6	20.7	11.0	18.7	12.8	6.4	17.4
19111	Lee County, Iowa	23.4	19.9	21.9	11.1	23.7	2.7	6.4	22.5
19113	Linn County, Iowa	38.2	15.0	25.2	8.3	13.3	0.9	6.2	17.0
19115	Louisa County, Iowa	25.5	15.0	18.7	11.1	29.7	8.1	4.7	33.1
19117	Lucas County, Iowa	27.2	17.2	28.0	12.2	15.3	4.5	5.4	9.2
19119	Lyon County, Iowa	36.9	15.1	20.8	12.7	14.5	11.6	6.0	16.0
19121	Madison County, Iowa	37.6	13.9	22.3	13.6	12.6	6.5	8.6	8.1
19123	Mahaska County, Iowa	32.3	15.3	21.0	11.4	20.1	4.9	6.9	24.5
19125	Marion County, Iowa	36.1	16.3	21.5	7.3	18.7	3.2	4.2	23.9
19127	Marshall County, Iowa	27.0	17.8	20.3	10.8	24.1	3.6	7.2	26.4
19129	Mills County, Iowa	33.4	18.6	21.8	11.1	15.1	5.2	6.3	9.6
19131	Mitchell County, Iowa	30.0	15.9	18.5	15.1	20.5	11.8	7.8	20.7
19133	Monona County, Iowa	28.7	20.3	22.5	14.7	13.7	8.6	9.3	10.9
19135	Monroe County, Iowa	32.0	18.9	19.7	11.4	17.9	9.4	4.2	20.2
19137	Montgomery County, Iowa	32.6	18.5	19.8	9.6	19.4	9.2	5.6	16.2
19139	Muscatine County, Iowa	27.9	17.4	19.8	8.5	26.4	3.3	5.8	29.3
19141	O'Brien County, Iowa	28.4	15.1	23.3	10.7	22.5	8.5	6.4	19.5
19143	Osceola County, Iowa	29.1	15.6	18.8	17.9	18.6	15.4	7.4	18.3
19145	Page County, Iowa	33.5	16.1	21.1	9.0	20.3	5.8	5.2	20.9
19147	Palo Alto County, Iowa	32.1	17.4	21.1	11.0	18.4	10.3	5.6	15.3
19149	Plymouth County, Iowa	31.8	15.2	23.9	11.3	17.7	7.2	5.5	18.9
19151	Pocahontas County, Iowa	31.6	13.3	21.4	13.4	20.4	15.8	4.8	16.4
19153	Polk County, Iowa	39.9	16.2	26.0	7.3	10.7	1.1	6.0	8.8
19155	Pottawattamie County, Iowa	29.4	17.8	26.6	10.9	15.2	2.3	7.3	10.4
19157	Poweshiek County, Iowa	33.2	18.2	22.4	8.4	17.8	7.1	6.0	17.0
19159	Ringgold County, Iowa	35.9	18.0	16.8	14.1	15.3	14.4	7.1	12.3
19161	Sac County, Iowa	27.3	18.3	23.8	11.1	19.4	9.4	6.4	14.8
19163	Scott County, Iowa	35.8	17.4	23.9	8.0	15.0	1.0	6.2	17.3
19165	Shelby County, Iowa	32.1	13.2	26.0	11.9	16.8	9.0	7.8	7.4
19167	Sioux County, Iowa	32.5	16.7	21.7	13.5	15.7	9.4	7.2	16.0
19169	Story County, Iowa	44.8	17.3	20.7	7.1	10.1	2.4	5.6	10.4
19171	Tama County, Iowa	29.4	16.6	20.6	12.8	20.6	7.5	7.8	17.2
19173	Taylor County, Iowa	28.2	16.3	16.7	13.0	25.9	9.6	6.1	23.2
19175	Union County, Iowa	25.2	17.3	21.3	8.4	27.8	5.7	5.1	25.4
19177	Van Buren County, Iowa	27.0	13.3	20.4	14.8	24.5	7.0	9.0	22.5
19179	Wapello County, Iowa	26.5	17.3	19.8	10.2	26.2	2.0	7.0	24.4
19181	Warren County, Iowa	37.7	15.2	26.6	9.8	10.7	1.7	8.8	5.9
19183	Washington County, Iowa	32.5	16.2	22.5	14.3	14.5	6.5	8.7	12.5
19185	Wayne County, Iowa	32.3	13.3	18.0	13.8	22.6	8.7	9.6	18.6
19187	Webster County, Iowa	30.5	19.8	23.3	12.0	14.4	5.3	6.8	12.4
19189	Winnebago County, Iowa	28.2	18.5	20.5	8.4	24.3	6.0	5.0	28.1
19191	Winneshiek County, Iowa	36.4	17.4	21.3	10.1	14.9	8.6	6.4	10.9
19193	Woodbury County, Iowa	28.3	18.5	24.0	9.3	19.9	2.1	5.6	18.6

Table C. County—Labor Force, Employment, and Educational Data, 2011–2015—*Continued*

Fips code	State/county	Occupation for employed population age 16 and older					Industry for employed population age 16 and older		
		Management, business, science, and arts occupations	Service occupations	Sales and office occupations:	Natural resources, construction, and maintenance occupations	Production, transportation, and material moving occupations:	Agriculture, forestry, fishing and hunting, and mining	Construction	Manufacturing
19195	Worth County, Iowa	24.7	18.4	23.1	14.2	19.7	8.1	8.9	18.5
19197	Wright County, Iowa	28.7	15.8	20.4	12.5	22.6	8.9	7.3	19.1
20000	**Kansas**	36.8	16.7	23.0	9.9	13.6	3.5	6.3	12.6
20001	Allen County, Kansas	29.6	17.3	19.8	9.2	24.1	5.8	5.3	21.0
20003	Anderson County, Kansas	27.6	22.2	17.1	17.6	15.5	11.6	10.8	8.6
20005	Atchison County, Kansas	32.8	17.1	21.7	10.1	18.3	3.4	4.7	20.2
20007	Barber County, Kansas	33.8	14.5	19.7	15.7	16.2	18.8	5.6	5.3
20009	Barton County, Kansas	29.9	18.1	24.3	14.4	13.3	10.0	7.4	8.9
20011	Bourbon County, Kansas	31.6	21.3	19.0	10.1	18.0	3.7	6.5	13.5
20013	Brown County, Kansas	31.7	19.0	19.9	8.3	21.1	8.0	3.7	17.6
20015	Butler County, Kansas	38.1	16.0	21.2	12.1	12.6	3.0	7.3	17.1
20017	Chase County, Kansas	32.3	14.7	21.4	16.1	15.5	7.4	8.7	15.6
20019	Chautauqua County, Kansas	29.7	17.2	15.2	20.7	17.2	20.1	8.9	7.4
20021	Cherokee County, Kansas	31.4	19.5	18.5	9.7	20.9	2.8	7.1	17.1
20023	Cheyenne County, Kansas	35.6	14.3	25.3	15.5	9.3	19.9	7.2	3.8
20025	Clark County, Kansas	40.9	17.6	17.4	14.7	9.4	19.6	5.1	8.4
20027	Clay County, Kansas	33.6	14.8	27.6	14.2	9.9	14.8	8.1	7.4
20029	Cloud County, Kansas	27.7	21.2	22.4	10.8	17.8	7.6	5.3	11.0
20031	Coffey County, Kansas	33.0	18.4	20.9	14.3	13.4	6.2	6.8	5.8
20033	Comanche County, Kansas	38.8	18.4	18.9	11.6	12.4	15.5	6.3	6.0
20035	Cowley County, Kansas	27.4	20.4	21.3	12.5	18.5	3.6	5.3	21.5
20037	Crawford County, Kansas	32.1	19.7	22.9	8.5	16.8	2.4	5.7	14.3
20039	Decatur County, Kansas	37.4	19.3	17.1	15.0	11.1	18.1	5.1	2.8
20041	Dickinson County, Kansas	31.4	16.4	23.0	12.9	16.3	6.0	6.7	13.3
20043	Doniphan County, Kansas	30.8	15.6	21.6	12.0	19.9	8.4	8.7	16.2
20045	Douglas County, Kansas	44.6	17.3	23.3	6.2	8.5	1.0	4.3	6.8
20047	Edwards County, Kansas	32.0	12.5	20.5	17.2	17.9	20.8	5.2	14.7
20049	Elk County, Kansas	38.4	18.6	15.5	14.5	13.0	12.8	10.3	6.1
20051	Ellis County, Kansas	32.1	18.6	27.2	10.8	11.3	7.0	5.2	7.7
20053	Ellsworth County, Kansas	36.0	18.9	18.5	14.4	12.2	14.4	7.0	10.0
20055	Finney County, Kansas	23.5	19.0	20.6	13.8	23.1	7.4	6.1	19.2
20057	Ford County, Kansas	21.5	16.3	17.8	15.2	29.2	7.5	4.6	25.6
20059	Franklin County, Kansas	30.0	16.4	22.3	12.5	18.8	3.7	8.0	13.2
20061	Geary County, Kansas	26.9	23.2	22.6	13.7	13.6	1.5	5.4	6.6
20063	Gove County, Kansas	37.5	15.5	19.8	13.8	13.4	20.1	6.1	8.1
20065	Graham County, Kansas	36.0	17.2	19.7	16.5	10.6	18.9	9.1	3.0
20067	Grant County, Kansas	27.5	15.4	20.2	22.4	14.5	18.1	7.8	9.4
20069	Gray County, Kansas	33.9	16.8	19.2	17.4	12.8	22.9	6.0	4.1
20071	Greeley County, Kansas	36.3	14.4	27.2	10.8	11.3	23.5	6.1	1.7
20073	Greenwood County, Kansas	29.3	20.4	17.5	14.9	17.9	13.0	6.6	10.4
20075	Hamilton County, Kansas	29.4	15.1	18.4	27.0	10.1	39.7	6.1	2.3
20077	Harper County, Kansas	33.1	15.6	23.5	11.9	15.9	10.5	7.6	14.1
20079	Harvey County, Kansas	35.3	17.6	19.0	8.8	19.3	2.5	7.1	22.9
20081	Haskell County, Kansas	30.6	17.4	19.3	17.9	14.7	26.1	5.9	3.6
20083	Hodgeman County, Kansas	44.0	13.6	16.2	14.5	11.6	26.8	4.0	4.4
20085	Jackson County, Kansas	31.5	19.8	18.7	13.8	16.2	4.7	8.3	10.9
20087	Jefferson County, Kansas	32.0	16.3	22.5	14.2	15.1	2.1	11.6	10.7
20089	Jewell County, Kansas	39.9	14.3	18.1	16.3	11.5	17.3	6.3	5.7
20091	Johnson County, Kansas	49.8	12.5	25.2	5.2	7.3	0.5	4.8	8.3
20093	Kearny County, Kansas	34.3	13.0	15.1	21.0	16.7	22.2	5.6	12.6
20095	Kingman County, Kansas	31.3	13.7	20.9	17.3	16.8	16.4	8.7	15.4
20097	Kiowa County, Kansas	41.4	16.7	16.7	17.0	8.1	14.1	11.3	2.0
20099	Labette County, Kansas	29.9	20.9	18.8	10.0	20.4	4.5	4.2	20.0
20101	Lane County, Kansas	34.9	17.5	21.9	18.8	6.9	26.1	8.2	1.5
20103	Leavenworth County, Kansas	36.6	18.6	23.1	10.2	11.6	1.3	7.6	7.2
20105	Lincoln County, Kansas	38.5	13.9	15.3	20.5	11.8	19.5	10.4	7.7
20107	Linn County, Kansas	31.7	16.9	22.0	16.0	13.5	5.1	12.9	7.4
20109	Logan County, Kansas	35.5	14.0	19.4	17.8	13.2	16.8	9.4	6.1
20111	Lyon County, Kansas	28.0	18.8	21.0	10.8	21.5	2.4	7.2	16.9
20113	McPherson County, Kansas	36.3	15.8	18.2	9.6	20.1	6.6	5.8	22.3
20115	Marion County, Kansas	31.7	17.2	21.3	12.3	17.5	9.5	5.5	15.6
20117	Marshall County, Kansas	29.7	16.3	20.6	12.2	21.1	9.0	6.7	18.2
20119	Meade County, Kansas	37.6	16.4	14.0	21.8	10.2	19.5	9.9	5.2
20121	Miami County, Kansas	34.2	13.0	25.4	14.0	13.5	2.3	10.0	9.6
20123	Mitchell County, Kansas	39.1	10.2	21.2	13.4	16.1	11.7	7.6	10.1
20125	Montgomery County, Kansas	27.8	17.5	21.2	9.8	23.7	3.0	4.9	22.4
20127	Morris County, Kansas	27.4	17.5	20.1	19.3	15.6	13.5	9.2	11.1
20129	Morton County, Kansas	26.1	19.2	19.2	25.2	10.3	23.6	4.5	3.6
20131	Nemaha County, Kansas	33.0	16.0	21.5	11.9	17.6	10.9	4.3	18.1
20133	Neosho County, Kansas	30.4	17.4	21.6	11.0	19.5	4.8	6.3	17.3
20135	Ness County, Kansas	32.3	15.3	21.1	17.7	13.6	25.5	5.6	3.7
20137	Norton County, Kansas	33.5	19.1	22.3	12.3	12.7	14.5	5.9	7.2
20139	Osage County, Kansas	30.1	18.8	21.1	14.6	15.4	2.9	9.8	8.3
20141	Osborne County, Kansas	40.0	15.0	18.6	10.8	15.6	12.5	5.7	11.3
20143	Ottawa County, Kansas	35.8	14.2	20.3	13.8	15.9	9.0	9.1	14.1

Table C. County—Labor Force, Employment, and Educational Data, 2011–2015—*Continued*

		Occupation for employed population age 16 and older					Industry for employed population age 16 and older		
Fips code	State/county	Management, business, science, and arts occupations	Service occupations	Sales and office occupations:	Natural resources, construction, and maintenance occupations	Production, transportation, and material moving occupations:	Agriculture, forestry, fishing and hunting, and mining	Construction	Manufacturing
20145	Pawnee County, Kansas	36.5	18.1	20.2	12.5	12.7	16.0	7.0	1.4
20147	Phillips County, Kansas	38.3	15.3	20.6	12.1	13.7	15.4	5.2	6.4
20149	Pottawatomie County, Kansas	38.8	14.0	21.7	13.0	12.6	3.7	10.0	10.4
20151	Pratt County, Kansas	34.3	17.5	20.4	15.7	12.1	14.1	6.3	3.4
20153	Rawlins County, Kansas	42.5	15.0	20.3	12.6	9.6	24.4	3.8	5.0
20155	Reno County, Kansas	29.7	20.0	24.3	10.6	15.4	3.8	6.6	12.8
20157	Republic County, Kansas	35.1	17.1	20.2	13.5	14.1	16.2	4.6	10.5
20159	Rice County, Kansas	30.7	18.9	19.3	14.0	17.1	10.7	7.9	12.9
20161	Riley County, Kansas	41.0	20.6	21.7	8.4	8.3	1.5	6.7	5.4
20163	Rooks County, Kansas	32.0	17.6	21.3	13.1	16.0	19.4	5.0	8.9
20165	Rush County, Kansas	39.0	16.9	18.1	15.1	11.0	14.2	7.0	7.0
20167	Russell County, Kansas	32.8	19.1	16.7	15.5	15.9	14.0	6.8	12.4
20169	Saline County, Kansas	31.3	18.0	20.9	9.7	20.1	2.1	6.7	20.0
20171	Scott County, Kansas	37.3	16.6	14.4	20.5	11.1	28.8	9.8	5.6
20173	Sedgwick County, Kansas	34.9	16.8	24.0	10.2	14.1	1.0	6.5	18.8
20175	Seward County, Kansas	20.5	12.9	17.6	17.4	31.6	12.3	7.3	26.4
20177	Shawnee County, Kansas	36.0	19.5	24.8	8.1	11.6	0.6	5.6	8.1
20179	Sheridan County, Kansas	39.1	8.4	20.5	14.5	17.5	28.8	8.2	3.1
20181	Sherman County, Kansas	32.0	18.9	22.9	13.5	12.7	10.4	6.9	2.0
20183	Smith County, Kansas	37.4	16.8	19.3	15.0	11.4	18.4	5.9	6.1
20185	Stafford County, Kansas	36.6	19.0	19.9	14.8	9.7	22.4	3.8	5.5
20187	Stanton County, Kansas	32.9	14.6	21.4	21.9	9.2	26.2	8.2	1.2
20189	Stevens County, Kansas	29.3	13.0	20.0	20.8	16.8	23.0	8.6	11.4
20191	Sumner County, Kansas	30.4	17.9	19.7	11.8	20.3	4.7	5.3	20.7
20193	Thomas County, Kansas	33.0	19.3	23.7	13.4	10.5	11.0	5.6	2.9
20195	Trego County, Kansas	34.0	12.4	27.6	12.6	13.3	13.3	5.2	5.9
20197	Wabaunsee County, Kansas	35.5	16.4	21.6	12.3	14.3	7.3	9.4	12.9
20199	Wallace County, Kansas	39.2	14.3	26.2	12.1	8.2	28.7	2.8	1.5
20201	Washington County, Kansas	29.9	16.2	18.4	17.4	18.1	16.3	8.4	11.8
20203	Wichita County, Kansas	32.5	17.9	11.0	20.0	18.7	36.7	4.0	5.5
20205	Wilson County, Kansas	32.6	19.2	15.6	12.5	20.1	10.4	8.4	17.3
20207	Woodson County, Kansas	27.6	16.5	17.6	15.9	22.4	14.8	6.0	10.1
20209	Wyandotte County, Kansas	22.5	21.5	24.0	12.6	19.5	0.8	9.7	12.0
21000	**Kentucky**	32.9	16.8	23.9	9.6	16.8	2.7	5.9	14.0
21001	Adair County, Kentucky	27.6	15.1	24.1	9.7	23.4	3.3	8.1	19.8
21003	Allen County, Kentucky	25.2	14.3	21.3	13.9	25.3	6.2	7.3	21.3
21005	Anderson County, Kentucky	29.0	15.9	25.5	10.5	19.0	1.1	6.3	20.1
21007	Ballard County, Kentucky	26.9	16.5	23.2	12.0	21.4	4.6	8.9	14.8
21009	Barren County, Kentucky	27.1	16.7	19.4	8.4	28.4	3.3	6.1	24.8
21011	Bath County, Kentucky	28.4	18.0	18.5	11.3	23.8	6.1	6.6	18.1
21013	Bell County, Kentucky	23.6	18.5	25.9	14.0	18.0	6.4	6.2	10.1
21015	Boone County, Kentucky	38.8	13.4	27.1	6.8	13.8	0.5	4.9	13.9
21017	Bourbon County, Kentucky	29.8	18.4	22.5	13.0	16.3	13.5	5.6	16.1
21019	Boyd County, Kentucky	34.7	17.7	23.9	10.4	13.4	0.8	6.2	8.3
21021	Boyle County, Kentucky	33.6	20.8	20.5	8.3	16.8	2.8	4.9	15.0
21023	Bracken County, Kentucky	29.9	14.1	21.2	14.9	20.0	4.9	7.8	15.2
21025	Breathitt County, Kentucky	28.4	23.1	23.1	12.4	12.9	4.6	6.4	4.2
21027	Breckinridge County, Kentucky	25.0	16.5	19.4	15.2	23.9	4.3	9.9	20.0
21029	Bullitt County, Kentucky	26.2	13.0	28.0	11.3	21.5	0.6	6.2	16.4
21031	Butler County, Kentucky	26.7	13.0	23.1	13.9	23.3	4.0	9.3	25.5
21033	Caldwell County, Kentucky	33.9	15.8	18.6	10.8	21.0	12.1	5.0	17.2
21035	Calloway County, Kentucky	31.7	17.6	26.4	9.1	15.2	1.7	6.5	11.8
21037	Campbell County, Kentucky	38.3	15.7	26.9	7.7	11.5	0.5	5.4	11.0
21039	Carlisle County, Kentucky	22.9	22.5	21.0	13.3	20.2	6.7	10.5	14.1
21041	Carroll County, Kentucky	20.6	15.5	22.3	14.5	27.1	5.3	6.8	26.8
21043	Carter County, Kentucky	25.4	17.1	23.5	15.6	18.3	1.8	9.2	14.1
21045	Casey County, Kentucky	28.4	13.3	23.0	11.1	24.1	4.0	7.4	18.5
21047	Christian County, Kentucky	29.2	17.9	22.6	9.7	20.7	3.9	4.3	18.5
21049	Clark County, Kentucky	33.2	14.6	25.5	10.4	16.3	2.0	5.9	16.3
21051	Clay County, Kentucky	25.2	18.0	24.1	15.0	17.7	6.0	8.4	9.8
21053	Clinton County, Kentucky	24.7	17.1	20.5	9.8	27.9	5.6	4.4	26.4
21055	Crittenden County, Kentucky	26.7	16.4	19.1	15.0	22.8	9.4	7.2	15.2
21057	Cumberland County, Kentucky	30.7	16.6	20.3	11.6	20.7	2.9	5.4	22.7
21059	Daviess County, Kentucky	29.6	18.0	24.6	9.3	18.6	2.4	6.2	15.5
21061	Edmonson County, Kentucky	24.7	19.4	22.4	16.4	17.1	1.5	11.4	15.7
21063	Elliott County, Kentucky	23.7	22.1	12.7	24.1	17.4	3.7	15.0	7.4
21065	Estill County, Kentucky	20.6	16.7	19.5	11.0	32.2	2.3	6.3	26.7
21067	Fayette County, Kentucky	42.5	18.9	23.4	6.2	8.9	2.0	4.6	8.9
21069	Fleming County, Kentucky	27.3	13.0	23.8	16.5	19.5	6.4	9.9	18.8
21071	Floyd County, Kentucky	29.4	18.7	25.8	15.5	10.6	9.0	7.9	4.3
21073	Franklin County, Kentucky	36.4	14.8	24.7	9.5	14.5	1.6	6.9	10.5
21075	Fulton County, Kentucky	29.1	22.8	17.8	6.9	23.4	5.1	4.4	17.0
21077	Gallatin County, Kentucky	21.3	16.8	23.5	13.1	25.3	3.3	9.1	24.9
21079	Garrard County, Kentucky	28.5	15.9	22.7	15.5	17.4	2.2	11.8	13.6
21081	Grant County, Kentucky	22.2	17.1	24.7	10.9	25.1	2.4	7.0	23.8
21083	Graves County, Kentucky	27.9	19.2	22.3	11.9	18.7	4.6	6.7	16.1

Table C. County—Labor Force, Employment, and Educational Data, 2011–2015—*Continued*

| | | Occupation for employed population age 16 and older | | | | | Industry for employed population age 16 and older | | |
Fips code	State/county	Management, business, science, and arts occupations	Service occupations	Sales and office occupations:	Natural resources, construction, and maintenance occupations	Production, transportation, and material moving occupations:	Agriculture, forestry, fishing and hunting, and mining	Construction	Manufacturing
21085	Grayson County, Kentucky	28.0	12.7	19.2	16.0	24.2	3.3	12.6	22.3
21087	Green County, Kentucky	21.9	19.0	21.6	9.1	28.4	2.5	5.7	23.6
21089	Greenup County, Kentucky	34.5	17.2	22.9	9.9	15.4	1.5	6.8	9.5
21091	Hancock County, Kentucky	23.4	15.1	18.5	11.0	32.0	1.9	4.7	36.8
21093	Hardin County, Kentucky	33.8	16.6	25.2	8.3	16.2	1.1	5.2	12.4
21095	Harlan County, Kentucky	28.2	20.0	22.8	15.0	14.0	12.8	4.6	5.3
21097	Harrison County, Kentucky	23.8	17.0	23.7	7.9	27.5	3.7	6.0	27.0
21099	Hart County, Kentucky	21.2	17.8	18.9	14.9	27.1	4.2	9.4	23.3
21101	Henderson County, Kentucky	28.7	17.6	24.3	9.4	20.1	3.3	5.2	15.9
21103	Henry County, Kentucky	26.4	19.8	19.9	12.8	21.0	5.0	8.2	16.8
21105	Hickman County, Kentucky	24.2	21.6	17.8	20.1	16.3	12.1	10.6	14.8
21107	Hopkins County, Kentucky	30.7	16.9	22.1	12.7	17.5	8.5	5.5	14.0
21109	Jackson County, Kentucky	29.5	9.9	23.9	10.9	25.8	1.2	8.1	21.1
21111	Jefferson County, Kentucky	37.0	16.4	24.8	6.6	15.3	0.4	4.7	11.3
21113	Jessamine County, Kentucky	34.5	18.4	22.8	11.5	12.8	2.3	8.9	9.9
21115	Johnson County, Kentucky	30.4	16.5	26.5	15.2	11.3	9.2	6.4	3.8
21117	Kenton County, Kentucky	35.8	15.5	26.6	7.5	14.6	0.5	5.5	12.3
21119	Knott County, Kentucky	31.4	18.1	23.8	15.2	11.5	11.4	7.8	1.6
21121	Knox County, Kentucky	25.8	18.6	25.4	11.1	19.2	2.4	6.5	12.0
21123	Larue County, Kentucky	22.0	15.1	19.6	15.9	27.4	1.7	7.2	22.1
21125	Laurel County, Kentucky	25.5	16.2	28.3	8.8	21.2	1.5	5.1	15.0
21127	Lawrence County, Kentucky	23.7	18.2	25.1	15.1	17.9	8.4	5.8	7.3
21129	Lee County, Kentucky	29.8	12.0	26.3	14.3	17.5	1.7	7.8	10.2
21131	Leslie County, Kentucky	28.8	20.5	17.7	18.3	14.7	21.0	5.4	3.4
21133	Letcher County, Kentucky	34.1	15.7	22.8	15.1	12.3	11.1	6.9	3.0
21135	Lewis County, Kentucky	26.2	17.9	13.9	19.4	22.6	7.3	13.1	18.1
21137	Lincoln County, Kentucky	25.5	17.2	20.7	13.0	23.6	3.0	8.1	16.1
21139	Livingston County, Kentucky	21.0	14.6	21.0	22.6	20.7	4.8	7.9	11.0
21141	Logan County, Kentucky	23.9	16.9	20.0	13.3	26.0	4.1	7.3	25.7
21143	Lyon County, Kentucky	29.1	21.3	24.6	10.0	15.1	3.5	9.0	14.7
21145	McCracken County, Kentucky	32.2	19.0	25.2	9.5	14.0	1.8	6.0	10.0
21147	McCreary County, Kentucky	20.7	19.4	26.5	11.3	22.1	2.7	6.7	14.9
21149	McLean County, Kentucky	30.5	14.1	20.8	12.7	21.9	8.7	8.3	15.7
21151	Madison County, Kentucky	36.2	20.4	23.2	7.1	13.1	1.5	5.3	13.4
21153	Magoffin County, Kentucky	28.1	19.1	16.1	20.0	16.8	6.1	12.7	8.3
21155	Marion County, Kentucky	25.3	18.5	17.8	10.2	28.2	4.7	5.9	27.4
21157	Marshall County, Kentucky	30.2	17.2	21.5	10.8	20.2	1.9	7.9	15.1
21159	Martin County, Kentucky	27.2	16.4	20.6	22.4	13.3	20.7	3.3	4.0
21161	Mason County, Kentucky	30.9	16.5	22.9	12.4	17.4	4.2	7.0	14.6
21163	Meade County, Kentucky	27.3	16.8	21.0	17.5	17.5	2.0	10.8	12.3
21165	Menifee County, Kentucky	21.5	22.1	17.5	13.0	25.9	4.6	7.4	23.0
21167	Mercer County, Kentucky	29.1	15.4	22.2	12.7	20.6	3.1	7.8	22.9
21169	Metcalfe County, Kentucky	24.5	12.8	24.7	10.2	27.8	8.0	5.8	24.7
21171	Monroe County, Kentucky	29.9	13.4	18.8	13.2	24.8	9.2	7.3	19.8
21173	Montgomery County, Kentucky	28.0	14.6	22.3	11.8	23.3	1.7	6.9	26.5
21175	Morgan County, Kentucky	28.4	19.7	17.8	17.0	17.1	4.9	10.1	11.1
21177	Muhlenberg County, Kentucky	24.5	17.0	19.3	14.0	25.2	6.6	6.1	17.3
21179	Nelson County, Kentucky	26.3	15.7	21.9	10.7	25.5	2.9	6.5	23.1
21181	Nicholas County, Kentucky	26.0	16.5	21.8	13.2	22.6	6.2	9.0	20.3
21183	Ohio County, Kentucky	26.4	15.8	19.4	14.6	23.8	7.5	6.8	24.5
21185	Oldham County, Kentucky	45.3	13.0	24.1	7.4	10.2	1.3	5.6	13.4
21187	Owen County, Kentucky	24.5	18.4	19.2	11.9	26.0	4.0	4.7	17.7
21189	Owsley County, Kentucky	33.0	25.3	18.7	15.4	7.7	4.5	3.6	4.0
21191	Pendleton County, Kentucky	24.2	13.2	20.6	16.8	25.1	1.9	12.0	18.3
21193	Perry County, Kentucky	30.7	18.1	26.2	13.6	11.4	10.1	6.2	2.4
21195	Pike County, Kentucky	29.2	17.5	24.1	15.7	13.5	11.9	5.8	5.7
21197	Powell County, Kentucky	24.9	18.0	18.3	12.0	26.7	2.5	7.0	20.5
21199	Pulaski County, Kentucky	29.7	18.9	26.4	9.8	15.1	2.6	7.1	12.5
21201	Robertson County, Kentucky	31.4	19.5	11.3	15.5	22.3	9.3	7.9	23.1
21203	Rockcastle County, Kentucky	21.8	21.1	24.7	11.8	20.7	2.9	5.4	20.3
21205	Rowan County, Kentucky	30.4	24.6	22.4	8.4	14.2	1.8	6.7	13.2
21207	Russell County, Kentucky	28.6	16.8	20.3	10.7	23.7	3.3	7.2	20.2
21209	Scott County, Kentucky	34.6	15.9	20.0	8.6	20.9	2.2	4.3	23.8
21211	Shelby County, Kentucky	34.4	17.6	23.4	10.3	14.2	3.5	6.2	14.5
21213	Simpson County, Kentucky	25.7	16.1	25.1	9.7	23.5	2.8	7.3	26.0
21215	Spencer County, Kentucky	32.0	12.3	25.1	12.3	18.2	1.4	7.6	19.7
21217	Taylor County, Kentucky	25.3	17.2	27.9	10.3	19.3	4.2	5.7	15.6
21219	Todd County, Kentucky	22.8	13.4	18.9	15.9	29.0	9.3	8.0	24.1
21221	Trigg County, Kentucky	34.1	12.8	23.8	8.2	21.1	5.7	6.3	17.1
21223	Trimble County, Kentucky	23.8	16.0	19.0	18.8	22.3	2.5	5.4	20.5
21225	Union County, Kentucky	24.3	16.9	20.1	19.5	19.3	19.3	2.6	12.8
21227	Warren County, Kentucky	32.2	18.0	24.9	7.5	17.4	1.3	5.3	16.1
21229	Washington County, Kentucky	25.1	14.9	21.5	13.3	25.2	5.5	6.7	25.3
21231	Wayne County, Kentucky	23.3	18.9	19.4	13.7	24.8	5.2	5.6	23.6
21233	Webster County, Kentucky	26.2	15.4	17.6	18.4	22.5	14.7	5.3	18.4
21235	Whitley County, Kentucky	27.6	17.8	28.8	9.2	16.6	2.5	3.7	14.8
21237	Wolfe County, Kentucky	22.0	29.5	22.1	13.1	13.3	3.3	8.1	11.2

Table C. County—Labor Force, Employment, and Educational Data, 2011–2015—*Continued*

| | | Occupation for employed population age 16 and older | | | | | Industry for employed population age 16 and older | | |
		Management, business, science, and arts occupations	Service occupations	Sales and office occupations:	Natural resources, construction, and maintenance occupations	Production, transportation, and material moving occupations:	Agriculture, forestry, fishing and hunting, and mining	Construction	Manufacturing
Fips code	State/county								
21239	Woodford County, Kentucky	38.0	15.0	22.4	12.7	11.9	10.7	4.7	13.1
22000	**Louisiana**	32.4	19.2	23.9	12.1	12.3	4.7	8.0	7.9
22001	Acadia Parish, Louisiana	28.0	17.4	24.3	14.9	15.4	14.8	6.0	8.4
22003	Allen Parish, Louisiana	27.5	25.9	17.1	18.3	11.2	5.5	9.9	8.0
22005	Ascension Parish, Louisiana	36.3	14.9	24.7	11.9	12.1	1.2	10.7	12.9
22007	Assumption Parish, Louisiana	26.5	18.4	19.9	17.6	17.6	6.1	14.1	13.0
22009	Avoyelles Parish, Louisiana	27.6	25.2	20.3	12.8	14.1	6.2	7.9	6.0
22011	Beauregard Parish, Louisiana	25.9	17.0	21.7	16.9	18.5	6.0	10.3	10.5
22013	Bienville Parish, Louisiana	30.5	15.3	18.9	12.6	22.7	11.1	5.3	13.3
22015	Bossier Parish, Louisiana	36.3	18.2	22.4	13.0	10.1	5.3	6.9	5.7
22017	Caddo Parish, Louisiana	32.4	22.2	23.8	8.9	12.7	3.8	5.4	6.3
22019	Calcasieu Parish, Louisiana	30.3	20.6	22.3	12.9	13.9	2.9	8.7	11.2
22021	Caldwell Parish, Louisiana	23.0	21.7	23.9	15.1	16.3	11.2	7.0	5.8
22023	Cameron Parish, Louisiana	26.4	13.5	23.8	19.8	16.7	13.2	9.0	8.4
22025	Catahoula Parish, Louisiana	29.7	15.8	21.9	23.3	9.3	19.4	11.2	2.9
22027	Claiborne Parish, Louisiana	24.7	24.5	17.3	12.1	21.5	8.9	5.4	13.0
22029	Concordia Parish, Louisiana	24.7	19.6	25.8	17.0	12.8	12.1	5.9	4.2
22031	De Soto Parish, Louisiana	25.6	18.6	23.5	14.9	17.4	9.4	8.8	10.4
22033	East Baton Rouge Parish, Louisiana	37.9	19.2	24.5	8.5	9.9	1.2	7.4	7.3
22035	East Carroll Parish, Louisiana	27.9	27.6	15.5	14.5	14.5	11.6	4.3	10.4
22037	East Feliciana Parish, Louisiana	26.8	24.4	21.0	13.6	14.1	1.8	12.3	10.8
22039	Evangeline Parish, Louisiana	26.4	19.0	21.5	19.5	13.6	11.3	7.3	8.7
22041	Franklin Parish, Louisiana	28.0	14.3	26.9	20.1	10.6	15.2	9.0	4.9
22043	Grant Parish, Louisiana	25.7	19.6	22.8	17.1	14.8	6.2	10.6	9.5
22045	Iberia Parish, Louisiana	25.7	17.4	25.6	15.9	15.4	15.1	6.9	9.8
22047	Iberville Parish, Louisiana	24.1	21.5	25.6	13.2	15.6	3.8	10.1	14.0
22049	Jackson Parish, Louisiana	25.4	18.4	23.7	17.1	15.3	9.0	7.0	15.4
22051	Jefferson Parish, Louisiana	31.9	18.5	25.7	13.1	10.8	1.9	10.0	6.4
22053	Jefferson Davis Parish, Louisiana	28.1	19.2	21.9	16.6	14.2	12.5	7.5	6.3
22055	Lafayette Parish, Louisiana	35.4	19.0	24.7	10.7	10.3	10.3	5.9	6.8
22057	Lafourche Parish, Louisiana	27.6	15.3	23.7	15.1	18.3	9.7	8.8	11.6
22059	LaSalle Parish, Louisiana	30.7	19.0	19.8	19.9	10.6	18.3	4.4	3.8
22061	Lincoln Parish, Louisiana	37.0	21.4	22.5	8.1	11.0	2.9	5.7	7.0
22063	Livingston Parish, Louisiana	30.8	14.8	24.5	16.5	13.3	2.1	14.0	10.5
22065	Madison Parish, Louisiana	25.0	31.0	20.0	11.6	12.4	7.1	6.4	5.6
22067	Morehouse Parish, Louisiana	24.6	20.5	23.4	13.4	18.0	4.1	6.3	12.5
22069	Natchitoches Parish, Louisiana	26.5	19.6	26.1	12.1	15.8	5.0	5.5	13.8
22071	Orleans Parish, Louisiana	41.8	23.1	19.8	7.0	8.3	1.3	5.4	4.0
22073	Ouachita Parish, Louisiana	33.8	18.9	27.5	8.9	10.9	1.9	5.8	6.6
22075	Plaquemines Parish, Louisiana	25.1	17.7	21.1	21.1	15.0	10.4	10.6	9.7
22077	Pointe Coupee Parish, Louisiana	25.3	18.5	25.3	16.4	14.6	4.8	13.8	9.8
22079	Rapides Parish, Louisiana	30.8	21.5	24.9	10.1	12.6	2.9	5.9	7.9
22081	Red River Parish, Louisiana	28.0	20.9	16.1	20.8	14.3	11.9	14.4	10.9
22083	Richland Parish, Louisiana	26.5	24.0	23.3	13.2	12.9	7.6	6.7	7.2
22085	Sabine Parish, Louisiana	29.5	15.7	17.7	20.6	16.5	15.4	5.8	9.8
22087	St. Bernard Parish, Louisiana	24.5	20.9	21.6	18.2	14.8	3.1	12.9	9.4
22089	St. Charles Parish, Louisiana	30.4	16.9	26.3	13.3	13.0	1.0	9.8	12.3
22091	St. Helena Parish, Louisiana	22.1	24.7	20.7	17.6	15.0	4.3	12.8	13.0
22093	St. James Parish, Louisiana	23.7	19.9	24.5	12.4	19.4	2.7	7.6	22.4
22095	St. John the Baptist Parish, Louisiana	29.3	20.3	21.5	12.5	16.4	1.6	8.6	13.7
22097	St. Landry Parish, Louisiana	26.0	20.9	24.8	15.3	12.9	7.5	9.1	5.2
22099	St. Martin Parish, Louisiana	24.2	20.1	24.1	15.3	16.3	10.9	8.8	9.2
22101	St. Mary Parish, Louisiana	25.3	19.2	21.5	12.3	21.7	9.6	7.0	11.8
22103	St. Tammany Parish, Louisiana	38.0	16.0	26.9	10.7	8.4	2.2	9.2	6.0
22105	Tangipahoa Parish, Louisiana	28.9	18.5	26.0	12.9	13.9	2.5	9.5	8.8
22107	Tensas Parish, Louisiana	23.2	25.9	19.6	18.2	13.0	19.6	3.3	3.7
22109	Terrebonne Parish, Louisiana	24.1	16.8	25.3	15.8	18.0	12.5	8.2	8.4
22111	Union Parish, Louisiana	25.8	14.8	23.4	20.0	15.9	8.1	12.7	12.0
22113	Vermilion Parish, Louisiana	25.4	16.3	26.0	16.9	15.4	15.6	7.1	7.2
22115	Vernon Parish, Louisiana	31.3	20.1	23.1	16.0	9.6	4.8	7.1	4.4
22117	Washington Parish, Louisiana	27.8	20.3	21.5	13.4	17.0	5.7	7.0	7.6
22119	Webster Parish, Louisiana	24.1	20.7	21.8	14.5	19.0	8.2	9.7	11.1
22121	West Baton Rouge Parish, Louisiana	30.3	17.8	24.2	11.9	15.6	1.2	8.5	15.6
22123	West Carroll Parish, Louisiana	28.4	18.1	23.7	17.4	12.3	12.4	8.5	6.5
22125	West Feliciana Parish, Louisiana	39.1	21.6	16.0	16.3	6.9	3.2	11.4	8.9
22127	Winn Parish, Louisiana	29.9	19.3	17.3	16.5	17.0	9.5	6.7	13.6
23000	**Maine**	35.4	18.5	23.9	10.7	11.4	2.5	6.9	9.3
23001	Androscoggin County, Maine	31.5	18.5	25.7	10.1	14.2	1.3	6.5	11.8
23003	Aroostook County, Maine	30.3	18.1	24.2	12.7	14.7	5.9	5.9	9.2
23005	Cumberland County, Maine	43.3	16.6	24.4	7.7	8.0	1.2	5.5	7.2
23007	Franklin County, Maine	30.2	20.3	23.8	12.0	13.7	3.8	8.7	10.8
23009	Hancock County, Maine	34.8	19.5	20.8	15.5	9.4	5.7	8.5	5.6
23011	Kennebec County, Maine	35.7	17.6	25.8	10.3	10.5	1.7	7.1	7.7
23013	Knox County, Maine	33.8	17.8	23.6	15.2	9.7	6.8	8.3	8.2
23015	Lincoln County, Maine	32.7	19.4	20.8	15.3	11.7	4.9	9.9	9.8
23017	Oxford County, Maine	27.1	19.2	21.9	15.2	16.6	2.9	10.3	12.5

Table C. County—Labor Force, Employment, and Educational Data, 2011–2015—*Continued*

Fips code	State/county	Occupation for employed population age 16 and older					Industry for employed population age 16 and older		
		Management, business, science, and arts occupations	Service occupations	Sales and office occupations:	Natural resources, construction, and maintenance occupations	Production, transportation, and material moving occupations:	Agriculture, forestry, fishing and hunting, and mining	Construction	Manufacturing
23019	Penobscot County, Maine	35.2	20.6	24.6	9.6	10.1	2.1	6.5	5.8
23021	Piscataquis County, Maine	29.4	20.3	17.2	12.9	20.2	3.3	8.0	18.2
23023	Sagadahoc County, Maine	36.7	19.4	22.9	10.4	10.6	1.8	6.2	14.0
23025	Somerset County, Maine	26.9	18.3	23.5	14.7	16.6	4.5	9.4	13.8
23027	Waldo County, Maine	33.8	20.0	22.0	12.1	12.1	2.8	8.2	9.1
23029	Washington County, Maine	28.1	21.3	18.8	18.1	13.7	11.9	5.7	8.3
23031	York County, Maine	34.1	19.0	24.4	9.9	12.6	1.1	7.0	12.6
24000	**Maryland**	44.6	17.2	22.6	7.8	7.8	0.5	6.7	4.7
24001	Allegany County, Maryland	29.5	23.8	25.2	8.3	13.2	1.1	5.8	7.2
24003	Anne Arundel County, Maryland	46.0	15.2	23.9	7.8	7.2	0.3	7.2	5.1
24005	Baltimore County, Maryland	43.3	16.2	24.8	7.2	8.4	0.3	5.8	5.7
24009	Calvert County, Maryland	39.9	15.3	24.9	12.2	7.7	0.3	10.1	4.1
24011	Caroline County, Maryland	26.0	22.3	22.0	15.2	14.4	3.0	9.6	9.1
24013	Carroll County, Maryland	43.0	16.0	22.8	10.4	7.8	1.1	8.9	7.4
24015	Cecil County, Maryland	35.8	18.1	21.7	10.8	13.6	1.3	8.2	9.8
24017	Charles County, Maryland	41.1	17.6	24.9	8.7	7.6	0.3	7.2	2.7
24019	Dorchester County, Maryland	31.4	20.7	22.2	11.3	14.5	3.6	7.5	11.6
24021	Frederick County, Maryland	46.1	15.3	22.9	8.9	6.8	1.2	8.1	6.0
24023	Garrett County, Maryland	31.3	17.9	22.3	15.1	13.4	4.9	9.9	7.5
24025	Harford County, Maryland	42.4	14.7	25.0	8.6	9.3	0.6	6.9	6.8
24027	Howard County, Maryland	60.0	11.2	19.6	4.4	4.8	0.3	4.5	5.2
24029	Kent County, Maryland	35.9	21.3	22.0	10.8	9.9	6.2	5.6	8.3
24031	Montgomery County, Maryland	56.2	15.5	18.2	5.8	4.3	0.2	5.8	3.0
24033	Prince George's County, Maryland	37.5	20.9	23.6	9.7	8.4	0.2	8.0	2.2
24035	Queen Anne's County, Maryland	40.6	15.5	25.7	9.2	9.1	3.0	8.4	6.1
24037	St. Mary's County, Maryland	44.0	17.0	20.7	10.9	7.4	0.9	7.5	4.5
24039	Somerset County, Maryland	26.9	24.3	25.2	11.0	12.7	6.0	5.7	4.9
24041	Talbot County, Maryland	37.6	22.4	22.3	10.1	7.5	2.2	7.8	5.4
24043	Washington County, Maryland	32.5	18.0	24.7	10.1	14.7	1.2	7.3	8.7
24045	Wicomico County, Maryland	33.7	20.8	24.0	9.2	12.2	1.4	6.4	9.6
24047	Worcester County, Maryland	36.0	21.9	24.7	9.5	7.9	1.7	7.6	4.7
24510	Baltimore city, Maryland	40.5	20.8	23.1	5.6	10.0	0.2	4.9	4.7
25000	**Massachusetts**	44.2	17.6	22.5	6.9	8.8	0.4	5.4	9.2
25001	Barnstable County, Massachusetts	37.0	20.4	24.4	11.2	7.0	0.9	9.4	3.7
25003	Berkshire County, Massachusetts	37.3	21.8	23.3	9.2	8.4	1.0	7.0	8.6
25005	Bristol County, Massachusetts	34.4	18.9	24.8	9.3	12.6	0.6	6.8	11.6
25007	Dukes County, Massachusetts	44.2	17.5	17.3	16.8	4.3	2.4	15.2	4.1
25009	Essex County, Massachusetts	40.8	18.3	23.6	7.1	10.3	0.4	5.6	11.0
25011	Franklin County, Massachusetts	41.1	18.5	19.7	8.3	12.4	2.0	5.9	10.4
25013	Hampden County, Massachusetts	33.5	21.1	25.1	7.6	12.7	0.6	4.6	11.4
25015	Hampshire County, Massachusetts	45.7	17.8	21.7	7.1	7.6	1.0	4.7	7.1
25017	Middlesex County, Massachusetts	53.4	14.5	19.8	5.7	6.5	0.2	4.7	9.9
25019	Nantucket County, Massachusetts	26.3	18.4	26.0	20.8	8.5	2.3	17.4	3.4
25021	Norfolk County, Massachusetts	51.6	13.8	22.6	5.9	6.1	0.2	5.0	7.0
25023	Plymouth County, Massachusetts	38.3	19.3	25.0	8.1	9.3	0.5	6.8	7.2
25025	Suffolk County, Massachusetts	44.4	21.8	21.4	4.8	7.6	0.1	3.8	4.8
25027	Worcester County, Massachusetts	40.9	17.5	23.1	7.5	11.0	0.4	5.7	12.8
26000	**Michigan**	34.9	18.2	23.7	7.8	15.4	1.3	4.8	17.8
26001	Alcona County, Michigan	22.8	22.5	22.5	13.0	19.1	2.7	6.5	15.8
26003	Alger County, Michigan	29.5	19.3	23.4	9.3	18.5	4.0	4.9	13.3
26005	Allegan County, Michigan	28.8	15.8	20.9	11.6	23.0	3.5	6.7	26.8
26007	Alpena County, Michigan	29.6	19.2	26.2	10.9	14.1	3.0	7.0	10.3
26009	Antrim County, Michigan	26.3	23.0	22.3	11.0	17.4	3.4	8.6	16.1
26011	Arenac County, Michigan	26.8	20.6	23.0	11.1	18.5	3.6	5.9	15.7
26013	Baraga County, Michigan	27.2	20.4	24.9	9.8	17.7	4.7	5.4	13.2
26015	Barry County, Michigan	31.3	14.5	21.8	11.8	20.6	2.5	7.5	23.5
26017	Bay County, Michigan	29.7	20.9	25.5	8.6	15.4	1.1	5.2	15.3
26019	Benzie County, Michigan	29.7	22.2	22.5	12.5	13.2	1.9	8.4	9.9
26021	Berrien County, Michigan	32.9	18.8	23.1	8.8	16.5	1.7	5.3	20.1
26023	Branch County, Michigan	22.8	19.3	23.6	9.6	24.7	3.6	4.8	23.9
26025	Calhoun County, Michigan	27.7	19.9	22.9	7.8	21.6	1.2	3.4	22.9
26027	Cass County, Michigan	28.2	15.4	21.9	11.9	22.5	2.3	6.1	26.5
26029	Charlevoix County, Michigan	29.5	20.2	24.4	9.7	16.1	1.7	6.7	17.5
26031	Cheboygan County, Michigan	24.8	22.4	26.5	13.7	12.6	2.5	10.2	8.6
26033	Chippewa County, Michigan	30.7	26.5	23.2	7.7	11.9	1.6	5.7	6.9
26035	Clare County, Michigan	23.8	23.6	22.9	12.3	17.4	3.7	8.6	13.5
26037	Clinton County, Michigan	39.3	16.8	23.3	8.3	12.3	2.9	5.4	11.0
26039	Crawford County, Michigan	27.2	23.2	21.8	11.2	16.6	1.9	4.8	10.6
26041	Delta County, Michigan	26.9	19.1	22.8	11.5	19.8	3.0	6.5	15.2
26043	Dickinson County, Michigan	32.4	17.2	23.8	10.7	15.8	1.9	6.8	16.1
26045	Eaton County, Michigan	33.9	17.4	26.1	8.0	14.7	0.7	5.0	14.7
26047	Emmet County, Michigan	35.3	22.3	23.9	9.6	8.9	0.9	8.5	8.4
26049	Genesee County, Michigan	30.5	19.9	24.8	8.1	16.8	0.6	5.1	15.7
26051	Gladwin County, Michigan	25.2	19.6	22.0	14.4	18.8	2.8	8.9	18.9

Table C. County—Labor Force, Employment, and Educational Data, 2011–2015—*Continued*

		Occupation for employed population age 16 and older					Industry for employed population age 16 and older		
Fips code	State/county	Management, business, science, and arts occupations	Service occupations	Sales and office occupations:	Natural resources, construction, and maintenance occupations	Production, transportation, and material moving occupations:	Agriculture, forestry, fishing and hunting, and mining	Construction	Manufacturing
26053	Gogebic County, Michigan	28.4	24.8	17.1	10.9	18.9	3.8	6.1	14.2
26055	Grand Traverse County, Michigan	34.9	19.6	25.9	7.9	11.7	2.0	5.6	10.1
26057	Gratiot County, Michigan	28.1	22.7	20.6	9.5	19.1	4.7	4.5	17.6
26059	Hillsdale County, Michigan	26.4	17.6	20.4	9.3	26.3	4.3	4.3	24.7
26061	Houghton County, Michigan	39.1	22.4	20.5	8.5	9.6	1.9	6.0	9.3
26063	Huron County, Michigan	27.3	16.4	22.0	13.3	20.9	9.3	5.9	21.5
26065	Ingham County, Michigan	39.6	19.4	23.9	5.3	11.8	0.7	3.2	9.7
26067	Ionia County, Michigan	26.3	17.6	23.1	13.0	20.0	4.7	6.3	19.4
26069	Iosco County, Michigan	22.4	20.4	25.9	12.2	19.1	2.3	6.2	16.1
26071	Iron County, Michigan	25.6	20.3	24.4	13.8	15.8	4.7	8.2	11.7
26073	Isabella County, Michigan	29.7	26.9	24.0	7.9	11.5	3.2	4.3	8.5
26075	Jackson County, Michigan	29.0	19.2	24.7	8.5	18.6	1.0	5.4	19.6
26077	Kalamazoo County, Michigan	38.4	19.5	23.2	6.4	12.4	1.1	3.9	17.0
26079	Kalkaska County, Michigan	20.6	21.2	25.0	15.4	17.8	6.8	9.0	10.8
26081	Kent County, Michigan	35.2	16.7	24.4	6.9	16.8	1.1	4.7	18.7
26083	Keweenaw County, Michigan	35.6	29.3	15.3	10.2	9.5	2.9	5.7	4.4
26085	Lake County, Michigan	21.5	25.0	22.5	10.2	20.9	2.6	6.3	15.8
26087	Lapeer County, Michigan	29.2	17.0	22.8	11.5	19.5	2.2	7.2	24.1
26089	Leelanau County, Michigan	38.3	18.5	22.5	10.9	9.7	5.0	8.7	8.3
26091	Lenawee County, Michigan	28.0	19.5	24.1	9.5	18.9	2.5	5.2	19.7
26093	Livingston County, Michigan	38.5	14.5	25.7	9.2	12.0	0.7	6.9	18.2
26095	Luce County, Michigan	24.4	25.0	24.1	10.4	16.1	6.4	4.6	11.9
26097	Mackinac County, Michigan	24.2	28.0	23.7	12.4	11.7	3.0	8.0	4.7
26099	Macomb County, Michigan	33.8	17.9	25.3	7.5	15.6	0.3	4.8	20.7
26101	Manistee County, Michigan	27.2	23.4	23.9	10.7	14.7	3.1	6.7	13.6
26103	Marquette County, Michigan	31.2	24.1	22.3	12.3	10.0	5.1	6.2	5.0
26105	Mason County, Michigan	30.1	19.0	22.3	9.5	19.1	3.4	6.3	17.3
26107	Mecosta County, Michigan	28.6	22.9	20.1	8.8	19.6	2.7	5.6	16.3
26109	Menominee County, Michigan	25.4	18.5	21.1	11.7	23.2	3.3	5.3	28.9
26111	Midland County, Michigan	39.3	16.3	23.2	8.7	12.4	0.8	7.2	21.9
26113	Missaukee County, Michigan	23.8	16.0	22.3	15.4	22.4	11.4	6.5	19.1
26115	Monroe County, Michigan	29.3	18.3	21.1	10.7	20.6	1.3	5.5	20.7
26117	Montcalm County, Michigan	25.0	16.2	23.5	13.0	22.3	3.2	7.0	22.2
26119	Montmorency County, Michigan	21.4	24.9	23.3	11.1	19.3	3.4	8.5	13.4
26121	Muskegon County, Michigan	28.3	20.4	22.6	7.3	21.4	0.9	5.0	25.4
26123	Newaygo County, Michigan	25.8	15.6	23.2	13.9	21.5	4.4	7.8	21.6
26125	Oakland County, Michigan	47.8	14.4	23.8	4.9	9.0	0.3	3.9	17.8
26127	Oceana County, Michigan	25.5	17.9	18.4	15.0	23.2	10.3	5.8	23.0
26129	Ogemaw County, Michigan	24.8	21.8	25.8	12.2	15.5	5.9	6.3	10.1
26131	Ontonagon County, Michigan	26.3	21.8	21.3	14.4	16.3	6.4	8.3	8.2
26133	Osceola County, Michigan	25.0	17.8	19.4	11.7	26.2	5.0	5.2	24.6
26135	Oscoda County, Michigan	22.3	22.2	24.2	11.2	20.1	4.2	6.2	19.8
26137	Otsego County, Michigan	29.0	18.3	27.7	10.7	14.4	3.1	5.4	9.9
26139	Ottawa County, Michigan	34.1	15.4	22.5	8.0	19.9	2.1	5.1	24.8
26141	Presque Isle County, Michigan	27.6	18.7	21.7	14.4	17.6	8.4	7.4	12.5
26143	Roscommon County, Michigan	24.7	18.3	28.5	12.9	15.5	1.4	9.8	9.6
26145	Saginaw County, Michigan	30.4	21.3	25.5	7.7	15.2	1.3	4.8	15.2
26147	St. Clair County, Michigan	27.2	19.6	23.1	10.5	19.7	0.9	6.9	22.1
26149	St. Joseph County, Michigan	24.6	14.4	19.3	9.6	32.1	3.8	4.0	36.4
26151	Sanilac County, Michigan	25.8	16.0	23.1	13.0	22.1	9.6	5.3	22.0
26153	Schoolcraft County, Michigan	25.8	25.2	22.1	14.0	12.9	5.4	7.6	8.7
26155	Shiawassee County, Michigan	28.2	17.3	23.8	11.4	19.3	2.3	7.6	17.1
26157	Tuscola County, Michigan	26.1	20.8	21.2	11.9	20.1	4.2	6.6	17.8
26159	Van Buren County, Michigan	29.1	19.7	21.1	12.7	17.5	4.7	6.6	18.3
26161	Washtenaw County, Michigan	51.3	16.2	20.0	4.4	8.1	0.5	3.0	10.9
26163	Wayne County, Michigan	31.3	20.5	24.4	6.9	16.8	0.3	4.0	16.7
26165	Wexford County, Michigan	26.5	17.5	21.6	9.1	25.3	2.5	4.1	20.7
27000	**Minnesota**	39.5	16.6	23.1	7.9	13.0	2.3	5.5	13.5
27001	Aitkin County, Minnesota	27.6	22.5	23.9	13.1	13.0	2.7	9.3	9.0
27003	Anoka County, Minnesota	36.7	15.4	25.1	8.5	14.3	0.7	6.4	16.6
27005	Becker County, Minnesota	32.7	17.5	20.2	13.7	15.9	4.9	8.7	13.4
27007	Beltrami County, Minnesota	31.4	22.9	24.4	9.5	11.7	2.6	7.3	7.6
27009	Benton County, Minnesota	29.5	17.4	21.3	11.5	20.3	2.8	8.0	14.4
27011	Big Stone County, Minnesota	34.3	17.0	20.3	15.4	12.9	12.9	9.5	8.1
27013	Blue Earth County, Minnesota	32.5	20.0	25.0	7.7	14.8	2.9	5.1	13.9
27015	Brown County, Minnesota	31.3	17.1	21.9	11.5	18.2	7.7	6.7	18.3
27017	Carlton County, Minnesota	30.9	23.3	20.1	10.2	15.5	1.7	6.6	10.0
27019	Carver County, Minnesota	45.0	14.3	24.6	6.8	9.4	1.5	5.8	16.0
27021	Cass County, Minnesota	29.4	21.0	23.7	13.3	12.7	3.8	10.9	8.7
27023	Chippewa County, Minnesota	29.8	20.9	18.2	12.8	18.3	8.2	6.8	15.9
27025	Chisago County, Minnesota	33.5	16.4	23.5	12.3	14.2	1.4	10.5	16.1
27027	Clay County, Minnesota	34.4	19.3	23.9	9.6	12.9	2.8	7.7	8.5
27029	Clearwater County, Minnesota	26.9	19.3	17.1	19.6	17.2	7.0	12.5	11.3
27031	Cook County, Minnesota	33.9	28.2	18.8	12.4	6.7	4.2	7.6	2.4

Table C. County—Labor Force, Employment, and Educational Data, 2011–2015—*Continued*

		Occupation for employed population age 16 and older					Industry for employed population age 16 and older		
Fips code	State/county	Management, business, science, and arts occupations	Service occupations	Sales and office occupations:	Natural resources, construction, and maintenance occupations	Production, transportation, and material moving occupations:	Agriculture, forestry, fishing and hunting, and mining	Construction	Manufacturing
27033	Cottonwood County, Minnesota	29.6	17.9	20.1	12.3	20.2	10.1	7.2	17.7
27035	Crow Wing County, Minnesota	31.7	20.0	26.0	10.1	12.2	1.5	8.3	9.8
27037	Dakota County, Minnesota	42.4	15.1	25.4	6.1	11.0	0.7	4.6	11.7
27039	Dodge County, Minnesota	36.7	15.8	20.0	10.7	16.9	5.6	7.0	14.8
27041	Douglas County, Minnesota	33.2	16.9	24.2	9.2	16.5	2.8	7.0	14.8
27043	Faribault County, Minnesota	32.1	17.6	19.5	14.1	16.7	10.8	7.8	15.2
27045	Fillmore County, Minnesota	34.7	18.2	18.7	13.8	14.6	9.2	8.5	10.8
27047	Freeborn County, Minnesota	27.4	18.6	22.0	11.7	20.3	5.5	6.1	19.1
27049	Goodhue County, Minnesota	34.5	17.0	20.3	10.7	17.5	5.2	6.0	16.3
27051	Grant County, Minnesota	34.7	15.1	22.7	14.4	13.1	10.8	8.8	9.6
27053	Hennepin County, Minnesota	47.7	15.6	23.2	4.3	9.2	0.5	3.4	11.9
27055	Houston County, Minnesota	33.9	16.8	20.3	13.9	15.0	6.5	9.4	13.5
27057	Hubbard County, Minnesota	30.3	19.9	22.7	12.4	14.8	2.9	9.0	9.2
27059	Isanti County, Minnesota	28.4	16.3	25.5	12.6	17.2	1.3	9.9	16.6
27061	Itasca County, Minnesota	31.2	20.1	21.8	12.7	14.2	4.9	7.5	9.6
27063	Jackson County, Minnesota	34.7	16.4	18.2	11.0	19.7	11.2	7.5	18.8
27065	Kanabec County, Minnesota	27.4	19.3	21.3	14.3	17.7	3.5	9.9	13.4
27067	Kandiyohi County, Minnesota	32.8	17.0	20.7	12.8	16.8	6.0	8.3	14.2
27069	Kittson County, Minnesota	33.9	14.3	17.5	11.5	22.8	16.3	5.2	15.3
27071	Koochiching County, Minnesota	27.5	18.6	23.2	11.9	18.8	2.9	5.1	18.2
27073	Lac qui Parle County, Minnesota	36.3	16.6	19.6	12.5	14.9	14.5	7.0	10.5
27075	Lake County, Minnesota	30.5	23.6	18.2	13.6	14.2	7.0	6.9	10.3
27077	Lake of the Woods County, Minnesota	27.7	16.2	18.6	12.2	25.4	9.1	5.2	22.8
27079	Le Sueur County, Minnesota	31.9	16.5	19.8	12.6	19.3	4.4	8.1	21.1
27081	Lincoln County, Minnesota	32.8	18.9	18.0	16.2	14.1	14.8	7.9	10.4
27083	Lyon County, Minnesota	33.2	15.2	21.9	10.8	18.8	6.6	6.4	17.1
27085	McLeod County, Minnesota	30.5	17.3	20.7	10.1	21.4	3.4	5.9	26.0
27087	Mahnomen County, Minnesota	26.8	31.5	18.7	13.1	9.9	6.9	7.1	4.7
27089	Marshall County, Minnesota	33.3	14.0	20.7	13.6	18.4	13.2	8.2	15.0
27091	Martin County, Minnesota	30.9	16.6	21.8	13.2	17.5	9.8	6.3	16.0
27093	Meeker County, Minnesota	32.2	15.2	18.8	11.6	22.3	6.1	7.9	24.6
27095	Mille Lacs County, Minnesota	28.2	19.3	21.2	13.5	17.8	2.5	9.2	15.6
27097	Morrison County, Minnesota	29.5	16.5	21.5	13.1	19.4	7.6	8.0	14.3
27099	Mower County, Minnesota	28.9	16.8	21.0	9.6	23.7	4.5	5.4	22.4
27101	Murray County, Minnesota	36.9	15.1	18.5	13.3	16.2	12.6	8.1	11.5
27103	Nicollet County, Minnesota	38.5	17.0	23.4	8.0	13.2	4.1	5.0	17.7
27105	Nobles County, Minnesota	24.6	15.3	19.3	13.1	27.7	8.6	7.2	25.9
27107	Norman County, Minnesota	33.5	17.5	20.4	14.6	14.0	14.6	6.7	6.7
27109	Olmsted County, Minnesota	48.1	16.2	20.0	6.3	9.5	1.5	4.5	9.2
27111	Otter Tail County, Minnesota	34.5	16.4	20.1	12.0	17.0	5.4	8.2	13.9
27113	Pennington County, Minnesota	28.4	13.8	29.7	9.6	18.5	3.8	5.3	15.4
27115	Pine County, Minnesota	25.0	23.8	20.6	14.1	16.5	4.2	9.1	9.6
27117	Pipestone County, Minnesota	28.7	17.3	21.7	16.2	16.1	11.9	10.1	11.0
27119	Polk County, Minnesota	34.8	16.7	22.6	11.4	14.4	7.5	7.2	10.7
27121	Pope County, Minnesota	35.2	14.9	22.7	9.1	18.1	7.2	5.9	17.2
27123	Ramsey County, Minnesota	43.1	17.2	23.0	5.2	11.5	0.4	3.8	11.8
27125	Red Lake County, Minnesota	29.0	13.6	26.2	13.9	17.4	8.1	8.0	15.7
27127	Redwood County, Minnesota	33.6	18.7	19.3	13.2	15.2	12.1	6.0	12.9
27129	Renville County, Minnesota	32.5	15.4	17.8	14.1	20.2	14.5	5.8	15.9
27131	Rice County, Minnesota	35.9	17.9	20.9	9.9	15.4	2.3	6.2	14.8
27133	Rock County, Minnesota	31.5	17.6	23.2	12.4	15.4	10.9	7.0	10.2
27135	Roseau County, Minnesota	28.7	13.0	16.9	8.3	33.1	5.4	4.0	37.7
27137	St. Louis County, Minnesota	33.6	21.2	23.7	10.2	11.3	3.6	6.1	7.2
27139	Scott County, Minnesota	41.1	14.6	23.8	8.1	12.3	1.2	6.0	16.1
27141	Sherburne County, Minnesota	34.0	16.1	23.4	10.7	15.8	1.5	8.6	15.4
27143	Sibley County, Minnesota	30.7	15.1	18.0	14.5	21.8	11.6	7.3	22.4
27145	Stearns County, Minnesota	31.9	18.6	24.4	9.3	15.8	3.4	6.5	14.1
27147	Steele County, Minnesota	31.7	15.7	25.7	8.3	18.6	3.3	5.6	24.0
27149	Stevens County, Minnesota	33.3	19.6	22.2	11.9	13.0	10.8	6.0	11.4
27151	Swift County, Minnesota	32.8	16.3	19.1	11.3	20.4	10.7	6.3	15.6
27153	Todd County, Minnesota	28.4	16.0	18.3	12.8	24.4	8.6	7.8	20.5
27155	Traverse County, Minnesota	42.0	18.4	18.9	11.6	9.1	18.3	6.7	5.7
27157	Wabasha County, Minnesota	33.2	15.9	22.0	12.1	16.9	8.1	7.1	14.6
27159	Wadena County, Minnesota	24.7	16.4	23.7	11.7	23.4	4.2	8.3	17.9
27161	Waseca County, Minnesota	31.7	16.5	20.8	9.7	21.3	5.1	6.3	22.4
27163	Washington County, Minnesota	45.2	15.1	23.4	6.5	9.7	0.9	5.1	14.8
27165	Watonwan County, Minnesota	28.1	13.5	18.3	16.1	24.0	10.0	8.1	24.8
27167	Wilkin County, Minnesota	32.6	15.1	21.9	14.6	15.9	13.8	7.1	12.9
27169	Winona County, Minnesota	32.8	18.3	22.9	7.5	18.6	4.4	3.9	20.0
27171	Wright County, Minnesota	35.1	14.3	24.3	11.4	15.0	1.8	8.7	15.9
27173	Yellow Medicine County, Minnesota	33.6	16.5	20.4	12.3	17.3	12.0	9.4	11.9
28000	**Mississippi**	31.1	17.8	23.6	11.1	16.4	3.1	6.8	13.3
28001	Adams County, Mississippi	27.4	21.0	25.1	12.1	14.4	4.7	6.5	6.3
28003	Alcorn County, Mississippi	29.2	18.1	22.3	10.6	19.8	1.8	6.5	20.6
28005	Amite County, Mississippi	22.8	20.8	17.9	18.1	20.3	10.3	8.1	11.4
28007	Attala County, Mississippi	27.1	17.7	19.4	16.5	19.2	7.1	10.3	14.9

Table C. County—Labor Force, Employment, and Educational Data, 2011–2015—*Continued*

		Occupation for employed population age 16 and older					Industry for employed population age 16 and older		
Fips code	State/county	Management, business, science, and arts occupations	Service occupations	Sales and office occupations:	Natural resources, construction, and maintenance occupations	Production, transportation, and material moving occupations:	Agriculture, forestry, fishing and hunting, and mining	Construction	Manufacturing
28009	Benton County, Mississippi	19.8	14.0	24.9	14.5	26.8	0.5	5.7	24.0
28011	Bolivar County, Mississippi	32.0	22.2	22.4	8.8	14.7	6.5	4.6	10.9
28013	Calhoun County, Mississippi	23.8	15.2	19.1	13.2	28.6	10.5	4.5	26.5
28015	Carroll County, Mississippi	34.1	12.2	21.9	15.4	16.4	6.2	7.0	11.5
28017	Chickasaw County, Mississippi	18.6	14.1	22.2	9.2	35.9	4.8	4.5	32.2
28019	Choctaw County, Mississippi	29.0	12.5	21.5	19.4	17.6	8.2	7.9	14.7
28021	Claiborne County, Mississippi	20.7	29.0	22.5	10.5	17.2	3.3	6.0	10.3
28023	Clarke County, Mississippi	28.6	13.9	22.3	21.4	13.8	10.3	7.7	9.3
28025	Clay County, Mississippi	25.7	18.8	22.2	9.7	23.5	4.0	4.6	20.6
28027	Coahoma County, Mississippi	30.2	26.3	20.0	8.8	14.6	5.7	4.4	8.7
28029	Copiah County, Mississippi	27.2	18.9	22.9	11.3	19.7	5.9	6.9	15.5
28031	Covington County, Mississippi	22.4	15.2	24.3	19.2	18.9	5.8	11.3	14.7
28033	DeSoto County, Mississippi	33.6	14.5	25.9	10.2	15.8	0.6	7.0	10.5
28035	Forrest County, Mississippi	32.2	18.3	26.5	9.3	13.8	2.0	5.6	9.3
28037	Franklin County, Mississippi	26.9	11.2	19.1	21.6	21.2	14.4	7.6	13.0
28039	George County, Mississippi	30.5	11.0	21.6	20.8	16.1	2.2	13.2	19.2
28041	Greene County, Mississippi	28.5	12.1	21.6	20.5	17.2	5.6	26.9	10.6
28043	Grenada County, Mississippi	25.4	15.6	23.9	8.9	26.3	2.5	5.4	30.0
28045	Hancock County, Mississippi	28.8	19.0	24.0	16.7	11.4	2.3	12.2	8.6
28047	Harrison County, Mississippi	27.9	23.8	25.0	12.2	11.2	1.1	8.4	6.3
28049	Hinds County, Mississippi	32.5	21.9	24.4	7.5	13.7	0.8	4.9	8.1
28051	Holmes County, Mississippi	23.2	20.4	18.1	11.9	26.3	5.4	6.8	18.0
28053	Humphreys County, Mississippi	24.7	17.6	17.3	13.6	26.9	10.2	6.8	16.2
28055	Issaquena County, Mississippi	19.0	23.9	19.0	13.1	24.9	28.5	3.0	11.5
28057	Itawamba County, Mississippi	26.8	12.2	19.3	13.2	28.5	1.7	7.5	27.0
28059	Jackson County, Mississippi	30.7	20.5	21.8	13.1	13.9	1.1	6.9	18.8
28061	Jasper County, Mississippi	24.4	17.2	18.8	13.3	26.3	6.1	6.9	26.1
28063	Jefferson County, Mississippi	23.5	20.4	20.0	13.8	22.3	4.9	3.1	13.6
28065	Jefferson Davis County, Mississippi	21.9	19.8	21.4	12.0	25.0	9.2	5.1	14.6
28067	Jones County, Mississippi	29.7	17.4	20.0	12.8	20.1	7.0	6.3	18.1
28069	Kemper County, Mississippi	20.1	22.1	16.6	18.4	22.8	4.6	10.1	16.5
28071	Lafayette County, Mississippi	38.2	21.3	21.4	7.2	11.9	1.2	5.6	9.1
28073	Lamar County, Mississippi	38.7	13.5	26.7	11.0	10.2	4.0	6.3	9.3
28075	Lauderdale County, Mississippi	31.5	17.3	28.0	10.6	12.5	2.8	7.3	9.0
28077	Lawrence County, Mississippi	27.3	15.0	19.4	20.8	17.5	11.6	9.7	15.2
28079	Leake County, Mississippi	24.5	20.1	18.7	15.7	21.1	8.5	4.3	19.6
28081	Lee County, Mississippi	30.8	16.3	24.2	8.0	20.7	1.0	4.1	21.8
28083	Leflore County, Mississippi	31.5	19.2	23.5	9.8	16.1	7.4	4.9	13.5
28085	Lincoln County, Mississippi	29.0	14.5	24.4	15.5	16.6	7.4	7.5	9.7
28087	Lowndes County, Mississippi	29.4	18.0	25.5	9.5	17.7	1.5	7.4	14.3
28089	Madison County, Mississippi	46.0	12.5	25.6	6.6	9.3	0.9	5.9	10.5
28091	Marion County, Mississippi	27.9	15.0	24.0	16.1	17.0	12.8	7.4	9.6
28093	Marshall County, Mississippi	22.9	16.5	24.3	12.3	23.9	0.9	7.2	18.7
28095	Monroe County, Mississippi	25.5	16.0	24.2	10.1	24.3	1.5	5.9	26.5
28097	Montgomery County, Mississippi	29.4	14.6	23.4	12.2	20.4	3.5	7.6	19.7
28099	Neshoba County, Mississippi	30.4	22.9	21.2	13.8	11.8	6.3	6.4	9.4
28101	Newton County, Mississippi	33.2	16.0	20.8	13.8	16.2	3.5	6.5	14.7
28103	Noxubee County, Mississippi	22.9	21.9	15.2	13.3	26.8	11.8	9.6	16.5
28105	Oktibbeha County, Mississippi	43.9	17.0	22.1	5.8	11.2	1.0	4.3	8.8
28107	Panola County, Mississippi	29.7	14.2	24.1	7.9	24.1	2.4	7.1	15.5
28109	Pearl River County, Mississippi	30.0	17.6	23.2	13.1	16.1	3.8	10.0	9.3
28111	Perry County, Mississippi	25.9	18.0	22.5	17.7	15.9	4.6	13.0	11.0
28113	Pike County, Mississippi	26.3	16.8	24.0	10.5	22.4	5.9	5.7	17.3
28115	Pontotoc County, Mississippi	22.8	10.7	25.7	7.9	32.9	1.6	5.3	28.2
28117	Prentiss County, Mississippi	23.5	15.9	25.3	11.4	23.9	3.0	7.4	22.2
28119	Quitman County, Mississippi	30.1	27.0	17.0	11.9	14.1	8.6	3.6	7.8
28121	Rankin County, Mississippi	41.0	14.0	25.5	10.6	8.8	0.9	6.7	8.4
28123	Scott County, Mississippi	23.4	17.2	19.7	15.6	24.1	6.1	10.1	27.4
28125	Sharkey County, Mississippi	36.4	27.4	21.3	11.6	3.3	14.2	2.7	2.7
28127	Simpson County, Mississippi	26.8	17.1	18.2	17.3	20.6	5.7	7.5	12.9
28129	Smith County, Mississippi	25.1	14.7	23.0	16.7	20.5	8.3	8.5	19.2
28131	Stone County, Mississippi	22.2	25.0	22.3	15.3	15.2	3.4	8.4	12.0
28133	Sunflower County, Mississippi	28.2	18.7	23.8	10.3	19.0	6.9	4.3	10.5
28135	Tallahatchie County, Mississippi	33.2	21.7	17.8	12.1	15.1	10.5	4.3	10.1
28137	Tate County, Mississippi	28.9	18.0	22.7	12.0	18.5	3.5	8.3	9.1
28139	Tippah County, Mississippi	25.2	10.8	22.1	9.4	32.5	2.1	6.9	29.1
28141	Tishomingo County, Mississippi	22.0	14.4	24.5	10.9	28.1	3.0	6.5	24.9
28143	Tunica County, Mississippi	23.9	36.6	21.5	3.5	14.5	5.5	1.0	7.2
28145	Union County, Mississippi	21.9	12.5	26.2	10.7	28.6	2.5	6.4	28.5
28147	Walthall County, Mississippi	28.5	11.1	23.6	17.7	19.1	12.2	11.0	14.6
28149	Warren County, Mississippi	36.6	21.2	20.2	9.0	13.1	2.1	8.6	12.3
28151	Washington County, Mississippi	33.1	18.2	25.3	7.6	15.9	4.3	4.1	8.7
28153	Wayne County, Mississippi	21.8	14.4	22.2	18.8	22.8	15.0	5.5	17.2
28155	Webster County, Mississippi	35.8	13.4	19.3	12.0	19.5	4.2	7.5	12.5
28157	Wilkinson County, Mississippi	25.3	28.3	15.0	14.8	16.6	4.8	7.5	9.3
28159	Winston County, Mississippi	31.8	17.8	16.9	12.8	20.7	7.3	7.4	17.4

Table C. County—Labor Force, Employment, and Educational Data, 2011–2015—*Continued*

		Occupation for employed population age 16 and older					Industry for employed population age 16 and older		
Fips code	State/county	Management, business, science, and arts occupations	Service occupations	Sales and office occupations:	Natural resources, construction, and maintenance occupations	Production, transportation, and material moving occupations:	Agriculture, forestry, fishing and hunting, and mining	Construction	Manufacturing
28161	Yalobusha County, Mississippi	21.8	15.1	22.8	9.3	31.0	2.5	6.9	27.7
28163	Yazoo County, Mississippi	26.6	20.1	22.8	11.7	18.8	5.9	6.2	14.4
29000	**Missouri**	35.2	18.0	24.7	8.8	13.3	1.8	6.0	11.4
29001	Adair County, Missouri	34.9	20.1	23.8	8.0	13.2	3.0	4.4	7.7
29003	Andrew County, Missouri	31.9	18.3	24.2	10.8	14.9	2.7	8.5	16.2
29005	Atchison County, Missouri	34.8	20.3	18.0	11.7	15.2	10.1	3.8	9.6
29007	Audrain County, Missouri	27.3	21.0	20.5	10.3	20.9	4.6	4.8	17.5
29009	Barry County, Missouri	25.6	15.4	19.6	13.2	26.2	7.0	7.6	22.3
29011	Barton County, Missouri	28.9	12.5	26.6	10.6	21.4	8.1	7.3	17.1
29013	Bates County, Missouri	28.0	19.9	20.9	15.5	15.6	6.5	10.2	9.2
29015	Benton County, Missouri	28.8	18.8	22.2	12.1	18.0	4.4	8.0	13.1
29017	Bollinger County, Missouri	22.5	16.5	20.1	19.0	22.0	6.4	13.5	19.5
29019	Boone County, Missouri	46.4	16.4	24.0	5.4	7.7	0.9	3.6	5.2
29021	Buchanan County, Missouri	26.7	20.9	24.3	8.2	19.9	0.9	5.3	19.0
29023	Butler County, Missouri	29.5	20.2	24.0	7.9	18.5	3.1	4.8	14.7
29025	Caldwell County, Missouri	30.3	18.2	20.6	17.6	13.3	5.9	10.6	10.8
29027	Callaway County, Missouri	31.0	18.9	24.5	11.7	14.0	3.3	7.6	8.0
29029	Camden County, Missouri	29.0	22.2	25.4	10.7	12.6	1.4	8.3	7.1
29031	Cape Girardeau County, Missouri	33.3	19.0	26.6	8.5	12.6	1.4	5.5	11.2
29033	Carroll County, Missouri	28.1	18.8	22.3	13.7	17.0	11.1	8.8	9.9
29035	Carter County, Missouri	31.0	22.5	18.4	10.1	18.0	4.6	5.5	15.7
29037	Cass County, Missouri	35.2	14.8	24.8	12.7	12.6	1.6	9.4	10.4
29039	Cedar County, Missouri	29.5	19.4	21.4	15.2	14.4	6.8	11.9	10.5
29041	Chariton County, Missouri	26.9	16.5	24.4	12.6	19.5	10.5	5.3	12.3
29043	Christian County, Missouri	35.4	17.9	26.4	8.9	11.4	1.2	6.5	7.9
29045	Clark County, Missouri	25.2	13.4	18.8	13.5	29.0	7.5	5.5	20.2
29047	Clay County, Missouri	36.8	17.1	25.2	7.3	13.6	0.5	5.2	11.2
29049	Clinton County, Missouri	25.7	19.8	25.2	12.8	16.6	2.8	7.4	11.3
29051	Cole County, Missouri	39.7	15.8	25.7	7.7	11.1	1.4	6.0	6.5
29053	Cooper County, Missouri	27.5	19.4	26.4	11.9	14.8	3.6	7.3	9.1
29055	Crawford County, Missouri	25.6	19.4	19.5	14.7	20.7	4.4	8.0	20.0
29057	Dade County, Missouri	33.3	15.3	21.7	13.0	16.6	9.6	6.6	12.8
29059	Dallas County, Missouri	26.8	16.1	25.9	11.0	20.2	4.2	8.7	12.4
29061	Daviess County, Missouri	27.6	18.0	22.3	15.2	16.9	9.4	11.6	11.5
29063	DeKalb County, Missouri	30.5	17.2	21.8	10.4	20.2	6.6	4.9	14.1
29065	Dent County, Missouri	25.7	21.6	21.1	13.9	17.7	6.0	8.0	11.4
29067	Douglas County, Missouri	20.4	15.3	25.1	17.0	22.3	6.9	6.8	16.8
29069	Dunklin County, Missouri	26.7	21.3	21.2	12.0	18.8	8.7	4.9	15.3
29071	Franklin County, Missouri	28.1	15.4	23.8	12.9	19.8	1.7	9.8	20.2
29073	Gasconade County, Missouri	26.3	17.9	19.8	12.3	23.6	2.9	7.3	27.0
29075	Gentry County, Missouri	33.2	19.2	18.8	14.2	14.6	9.2	5.4	10.9
29077	Greene County, Missouri	35.0	19.1	26.7	7.1	12.0	0.6	5.1	8.6
29079	Grundy County, Missouri	29.9	18.4	22.1	12.5	17.2	8.5	6.0	17.1
29081	Harrison County, Missouri	29.7	19.6	22.7	12.9	15.2	11.7	8.0	7.1
29083	Henry County, Missouri	28.4	18.1	21.9	15.3	16.3	3.2	9.5	14.9
29085	Hickory County, Missouri	29.2	16.8	22.7	14.9	16.3	2.5	7.7	6.5
29087	Holt County, Missouri	32.4	18.9	18.0	14.3	16.4	11.1	7.5	11.1
29089	Howard County, Missouri	34.0	16.5	22.3	11.9	15.2	5.8	6.4	8.5
29091	Howell County, Missouri	26.1	21.4	22.4	12.4	17.7	3.2	5.2	13.8
29093	Iron County, Missouri	22.5	25.2	20.9	12.1	19.3	7.2	7.6	13.9
29095	Jackson County, Missouri	36.1	18.5	25.9	7.4	12.1	0.4	5.9	8.7
29097	Jasper County, Missouri	29.6	17.9	25.8	9.4	17.3	1.5	5.5	16.9
29099	Jefferson County, Missouri	29.2	18.7	25.4	12.4	14.3	0.6	9.6	11.8
29101	Johnson County, Missouri	30.0	20.9	22.4	12.5	14.1	2.1	6.7	10.7
29103	Knox County, Missouri	30.8	16.6	21.5	16.9	14.3	12.6	7.9	7.5
29105	Laclede County, Missouri	25.7	17.3	23.2	9.1	24.8	3.8	4.1	24.7
29107	Lafayette County, Missouri	30.1	18.8	21.5	13.6	15.9	3.7	9.6	12.4
29109	Lawrence County, Missouri	28.5	21.6	18.2	11.9	19.8	5.4	5.3	19.7
29111	Lewis County, Missouri	23.3	22.6	18.6	13.0	22.5	5.3	5.3	16.2
29113	Lincoln County, Missouri	25.9	15.7	24.3	15.7	18.4	1.4	11.1	17.7
29115	Linn County, Missouri	27.3	17.2	23.3	13.1	19.2	4.1	8.2	15.5
29117	Livingston County, Missouri	30.4	18.9	22.9	9.0	18.7	5.7	6.2	13.2
29119	McDonald County, Missouri	21.2	14.8	25.2	15.6	23.2	4.2	10.3	22.1
29121	Macon County, Missouri	28.7	21.9	20.0	14.0	15.5	4.1	8.0	10.2
29123	Madison County, Missouri	19.3	23.1	24.7	13.9	19.0	2.3	7.7	12.2
29125	Maries County, Missouri	24.1	16.5	22.4	11.3	25.7	2.4	11.3	15.5
29127	Marion County, Missouri	30.3	19.6	19.6	11.1	19.5	2.6	6.0	16.4
29129	Mercer County, Missouri	30.2	14.6	20.4	13.8	21.1	20.1	4.5	10.6
29131	Miller County, Missouri	25.4	22.4	27.0	10.4	14.9	2.7	9.4	10.2
29133	Mississippi County, Missouri	23.6	23.1	24.5	12.2	16.6	9.3	4.7	11.9
29135	Moniteau County, Missouri	28.1	18.7	23.2	12.8	17.2	6.4	7.8	12.9
29137	Monroe County, Missouri	25.8	19.0	21.2	10.8	23.2	7.3	4.3	18.3
29139	Montgomery County, Missouri	27.8	19.0	19.9	11.1	22.2	7.6	8.3	18.7

Table C. County—Labor Force, Employment, and Educational Data, 2011–2015—Continued

| | | Occupation for employed population age 16 and older | | | | | Industry for employed population age 16 and older | | |
Fips code	State/county	Management, business, science, and arts occupations	Service occupations	Sales and office occupations:	Natural resources, construction, and maintenance occupations	Production, transportation, and material moving occupations:	Agriculture, forestry, fishing and hunting, and mining	Construction	Manufacturing
29141	Morgan County, Missouri	22.8	19.2	29.3	13.2	15.5	5.1	8.6	13.6
29143	New Madrid County, Missouri	25.3	20.8	20.6	11.6	21.7	7.7	5.5	16.3
29145	Newton County, Missouri	29.1	17.1	25.4	10.2	18.1	3.1	5.9	16.7
29147	Nodaway County, Missouri	28.3	22.8	20.1	10.3	18.5	5.0	6.4	15.9
29149	Oregon County, Missouri	23.4	20.4	20.5	12.4	23.4	7.0	4.1	13.5
29151	Osage County, Missouri	27.4	13.8	26.3	13.2	19.3	3.7	8.0	19.9
29153	Ozark County, Missouri	25.2	13.8	22.8	17.4	20.8	6.2	8.5	15.5
29155	Pemiscot County, Missouri	26.6	21.5	20.1	9.7	22.1	7.3	2.1	19.3
29157	Perry County, Missouri	28.2	13.2	22.7	14.5	21.4	4.6	8.7	23.6
29159	Pettis County, Missouri	27.0	17.9	21.8	9.6	23.7	3.0	5.3	20.1
29161	Phelps County, Missouri	37.9	19.7	22.7	7.9	11.8	1.8	5.0	8.2
29163	Pike County, Missouri	27.4	15.6	23.8	16.6	16.6	7.8	7.8	10.3
29165	Platte County, Missouri	42.4	14.8	25.9	6.1	10.8	0.9	5.1	8.8
29167	Polk County, Missouri	31.2	21.8	21.1	13.2	12.7	3.3	6.0	8.6
29169	Pulaski County, Missouri	32.8	20.9	21.9	12.3	12.0	1.2	5.4	7.2
29171	Putnam County, Missouri	32.4	14.8	17.5	17.9	17.4	15.5	7.3	15.5
29173	Ralls County, Missouri	24.9	16.7	23.8	14.5	20.1	5.5	8.3	18.3
29175	Randolph County, Missouri	26.8	16.5	28.4	10.6	17.7	2.1	5.4	9.9
29177	Ray County, Missouri	26.2	17.1	22.6	11.4	22.6	2.6	6.7	17.6
29179	Reynolds County, Missouri	24.2	23.4	12.8	16.0	23.6	14.7	5.9	16.0
29181	Ripley County, Missouri	25.5	22.3	20.9	11.4	19.9	4.1	6.3	15.4
29183	St. Charles County, Missouri	41.4	14.9	26.6	7.6	9.5	0.7	6.2	12.8
29185	St. Clair County, Missouri	26.2	20.7	23.2	13.7	16.2	5.7	9.5	6.5
29186	Ste. Genevieve County, Missouri	20.6	16.5	21.7	18.6	22.5	6.0	10.9	22.3
29187	St. Francois County, Missouri	26.9	23.0	23.0	10.5	16.6	1.8	7.3	12.0
29189	St. Louis County, Missouri	43.7	16.0	26.2	5.3	8.8	0.4	4.3	9.8
29195	Saline County, Missouri	29.7	18.7	20.8	12.1	18.8	5.2	5.8	16.8
29197	Schuyler County, Missouri	30.5	13.0	23.5	15.4	17.6	11.4	6.5	11.5
29199	Scotland County, Missouri	29.6	18.7	17.8	17.6	16.3	10.5	11.3	10.5
29201	Scott County, Missouri	26.7	20.8	21.9	11.2	19.4	3.0	6.5	14.9
29203	Shannon County, Missouri	26.3	16.1	12.1	17.9	27.7	12.9	5.9	22.0
29205	Shelby County, Missouri	27.1	16.1	20.9	16.9	18.9	11.0	9.5	14.4
29207	Stoddard County, Missouri	27.4	15.8	23.0	13.0	20.8	5.5	7.3	16.7
29209	Stone County, Missouri	26.9	21.5	25.7	15.1	10.9	2.8	12.1	6.9
29211	Sullivan County, Missouri	25.8	14.3	17.9	14.6	27.3	10.1	6.3	30.0
29213	Taney County, Missouri	24.6	28.1	30.2	8.8	8.3	1.2	6.3	4.4
29215	Texas County, Missouri	23.1	21.3	24.3	13.9	17.4	7.5	6.2	10.5
29217	Vernon County, Missouri	30.0	20.5	22.4	13.0	14.1	7.3	7.6	11.5
29219	Warren County, Missouri	24.6	17.9	23.3	17.0	17.1	1.8	12.5	16.4
29221	Washington County, Missouri	20.0	23.8	17.7	18.1	20.4	3.7	12.0	13.3
29223	Wayne County, Missouri	25.0	21.6	20.3	16.3	16.8	4.7	7.9	17.1
29225	Webster County, Missouri	26.6	17.1	22.5	14.0	19.9	3.5	9.1	13.3
29227	Worth County, Missouri	37.8	16.1	15.8	11.7	18.5	16.3	8.7	11.8
29229	Wright County, Missouri	24.8	21.9	18.3	15.8	19.2	9.6	6.9	13.6
29510	St. Louis city, Missouri	39.1	23.5	22.4	5.0	10.0	0.4	3.8	8.0
30000	**Montana**	35.9	19.1	22.7	12.8	9.5	7.3	8.1	4.5
30001	Beaverhead County, Montana	35.2	21.6	19.0	17.0	7.2	16.7	8.7	3.3
30003	Big Horn County, Montana	32.6	22.2	23.8	13.9	7.4	11.9	3.5	0.8
30005	Blaine County, Montana	38.0	16.6	18.6	19.7	7.1	19.1	9.0	0.9
30007	Broadwater County, Montana	31.7	13.0	20.3	21.9	13.0	14.3	14.5	6.0
30009	Carbon County, Montana	34.3	18.4	20.9	17.3	9.1	13.1	9.8	5.5
30011	Carter County, Montana	52.0	10.6	9.6	19.8	8.1	48.5	1.8	0.7
30013	Cascade County, Montana	33.9	21.8	23.2	11.2	9.9	3.3	7.0	3.3
30015	Chouteau County, Montana	40.5	20.3	19.6	12.1	7.5	26.8	5.7	3.7
30017	Custer County, Montana	32.6	20.3	25.8	13.1	8.2	8.1	9.7	3.0
30019	Daniels County, Montana	43.8	18.1	21.1	9.2	7.9	20.7	3.5	2.0
30021	Dawson County, Montana	36.0	17.9	16.4	14.7	14.9	15.8	6.9	2.5
30023	Deer Lodge County, Montana	28.3	26.7	17.0	13.6	14.5	6.1	9.2	4.9
30025	Fallon County, Montana	30.2	17.3	18.1	19.3	15.1	28.9	8.8	1.8
30027	Fergus County, Montana	39.6	17.0	18.8	13.0	11.7	13.1	9.6	4.5
30029	Flathead County, Montana	33.3	18.1	25.8	12.9	10.0	4.0	9.5	6.3
30031	Gallatin County, Montana	39.6	18.1	22.3	11.7	8.3	3.7	9.5	6.0
30033	Garfield County, Montana	50.5	11.9	16.0	16.9	4.7	45.2	9.5	0.7
30035	Glacier County, Montana	37.3	22.7	17.5	15.0	7.6	14.4	7.9	0.9
30037	Golden Valley County, Montana	35.3	12.0	16.5	22.7	13.4	29.1	10.4	2.8
30039	Granite County, Montana	37.7	19.0	17.5	16.3	9.6	19.3	10.4	4.7
30041	Hill County, Montana	33.9	17.3	22.6	12.6	13.7	7.1	6.3	1.6
30043	Jefferson County, Montana	43.1	16.8	17.8	14.3	8.0	6.8	8.7	3.6
30045	Judith Basin County, Montana	46.8	14.2	13.1	19.2	6.7	33.7	7.5	1.1
30047	Lake County, Montana	34.1	20.8	20.5	14.3	10.2	8.6	8.2	5.7
30049	Lewis and Clark County, Montana	44.6	16.9	23.4	9.0	6.0	2.5	6.5	2.7
30051	Liberty County, Montana	40.8	16.6	18.1	21.2	3.3	38.4	5.7	1.3
30053	Lincoln County, Montana	30.0	23.8	21.7	13.5	11.0	10.4	9.1	5.3
30055	McCone County, Montana	52.4	6.2	22.7	13.6	5.1	31.1	7.6	1.4
30057	Madison County, Montana	34.5	20.8	15.6	21.0	8.1	21.7	10.5	2.6
30059	Meagher County, Montana	35.5	18.9	20.2	14.3	11.2	26.4	5.2	2.4

Table C. County—Labor Force, Employment, and Educational Data, 2011–2015—*Continued*

		Occupation for employed population age 16 and older					Industry for employed population age 16 and older		
Fips code	State/county	Management, business, science, and arts occupations	Service occupations	Sales and office occupations:	Natural resources, construction, and maintenance occupations	Production, transportation, and material moving occupations:	Agriculture, forestry, fishing and hunting, and mining	Construction	Manufacturing
30061	Mineral County, Montana	28.0	22.3	24.6	10.0	15.1	6.4	7.6	9.7
30063	Missoula County, Montana	39.1	20.6	23.4	9.5	7.4	3.8	7.1	3.8
30065	Musselshell County, Montana	26.4	16.3	19.3	23.7	14.2	21.1	12.5	6.2
30067	Park County, Montana	37.2	16.2	23.0	15.2	8.3	10.4	7.6	4.9
30069	Petroleum County, Montana	43.7	8.3	21.7	20.1	6.3	37.8	7.9	3.9
30071	Phillips County, Montana	33.7	16.6	26.4	15.8	7.5	24.2	10.2	1.3
30073	Pondera County, Montana	37.1	19.2	19.5	15.5	8.7	18.4	7.9	3.8
30075	Powder River County, Montana	43.0	14.1	17.1	18.9	6.9	41.2	6.6	0.4
30077	Powell County, Montana	35.5	22.4	17.7	13.9	10.4	10.5	10.0	6.4
30079	Prairie County, Montana	40.0	16.4	15.1	21.7	6.8	33.1	9.2	0.9
30081	Ravalli County, Montana	33.4	17.5	23.2	15.5	10.3	6.4	10.2	9.1
30083	Richland County, Montana	28.7	12.4	23.4	21.7	13.8	22.2	8.4	5.2
30085	Roosevelt County, Montana	33.0	27.5	14.7	13.1	11.6	12.5	8.3	2.7
30087	Rosebud County, Montana	34.6	19.5	16.5	19.7	9.7	20.0	6.1	1.1
30089	Sanders County, Montana	27.0	21.1	20.0	20.5	11.5	10.2	12.3	5.9
30091	Sheridan County, Montana	36.6	19.6	24.8	12.6	6.3	19.3	5.8	1.9
30093	Silver Bow County, Montana	34.5	22.5	21.7	9.8	11.5	3.9	5.1	3.3
30095	Stillwater County, Montana	28.9	14.8	22.0	20.4	14.0	21.1	8.8	8.6
30097	Sweet Grass County, Montana	31.2	15.2	18.3	26.0	9.3	24.2	10.0	2.7
30099	Teton County, Montana	38.5	17.0	20.1	15.1	9.3	18.3	6.4	3.1
30101	Toole County, Montana	29.7	25.3	19.2	13.5	12.3	23.4	9.6	2.6
30103	Treasure County, Montana	31.1	12.7	18.5	33.5	4.2	43.0	4.7	1.3
30105	Valley County, Montana	39.5	18.4	18.2	13.0	11.0	15.6	5.7	1.2
30107	Wheatland County, Montana	40.2	15.0	18.1	21.9	4.7	39.8	10.6	2.0
30109	Wibaux County, Montana	37.9	19.9	10.9	15.8	15.5	26.5	3.7	1.5
30111	Yellowstone County, Montana	33.1	18.9	25.3	12.1	10.7	3.5	8.3	5.2
31000	**Nebraska**	35.6	16.7	24.0	10.2	13.4	4.6	6.7	10.9
31001	Adams County, Nebraska	33.7	20.1	20.1	9.9	16.2	5.3	8.0	13.3
31003	Antelope County, Nebraska	37.3	14.6	19.7	16.9	11.5	22.7	6.9	6.2
31005	Arthur County, Nebraska	54.9	10.9	4.1	19.7	10.4	41.5	6.7	4.7
31007	Banner County, Nebraska	44.6	9.7	22.9	14.7	8.1	29.2	4.6	5.3
31009	Blaine County, Nebraska	40.1	13.9	8.0	27.2	10.8	46.0	5.2	6.6
31011	Boone County, Nebraska	35.6	17.5	18.5	16.1	12.3	21.2	5.7	11.6
31013	Box Butte County, Nebraska	29.9	14.3	18.4	15.6	21.8	8.8	6.0	7.3
31015	Boyd County, Nebraska	41.2	14.1	14.8	16.5	13.4	23.5	7.3	5.1
31017	Brown County, Nebraska	41.3	22.0	15.3	13.1	8.3	17.5	7.2	3.3
31019	Buffalo County, Nebraska	31.7	18.4	26.1	8.8	15.0	4.6	5.7	13.1
31021	Burt County, Nebraska	32.1	17.0	22.7	16.1	12.1	11.3	9.3	9.8
31023	Butler County, Nebraska	29.4	13.3	19.0	16.9	21.4	14.6	6.4	18.8
31025	Cass County, Nebraska	32.6	16.3	25.2	12.7	13.2	3.2	7.8	7.5
31027	Cedar County, Nebraska	33.9	15.8	21.9	14.2	14.3	14.4	8.4	11.9
31029	Chase County, Nebraska	39.2	10.1	23.8	17.5	9.5	21.2	8.0	5.3
31031	Cherry County, Nebraska	36.3	17.7	20.6	15.0	10.4	28.1	9.0	3.9
31033	Cheyenne County, Nebraska	35.7	16.9	26.1	9.4	11.9	5.8	3.9	6.6
31035	Clay County, Nebraska	33.0	13.3	19.7	18.8	15.2	16.1	9.3	10.0
31037	Colfax County, Nebraska	20.6	11.9	18.5	14.5	34.5	8.1	6.4	34.0
31039	Cuming County, Nebraska	32.1	14.6	20.9	15.0	17.4	14.5	6.8	13.3
31041	Custer County, Nebraska	32.6	17.8	19.1	15.2	15.3	16.4	6.3	10.7
31043	Dakota County, Nebraska	21.6	17.5	20.9	12.7	27.3	2.8	7.2	28.4
31045	Dawes County, Nebraska	37.2	23.3	20.3	11.7	7.6	11.8	6.3	3.3
31047	Dawson County, Nebraska	23.1	14.8	17.9	14.3	29.9	9.1	6.8	25.8
31049	Deuel County, Nebraska	29.5	14.5	29.3	8.2	18.5	10.6	5.4	6.5
31051	Dixon County, Nebraska	29.5	17.0	18.3	17.6	17.6	12.2	8.0	18.9
31053	Dodge County, Nebraska	26.4	17.4	27.2	10.8	18.3	4.0	6.6	17.5
31055	Douglas County, Nebraska	39.5	16.5	26.2	7.6	10.2	0.8	6.7	8.6
31057	Dundy County, Nebraska	41.3	9.1	16.4	22.5	10.6	29.6	9.8	3.4
31059	Fillmore County, Nebraska	32.5	17.1	20.1	14.0	16.3	14.7	9.8	9.5
31061	Franklin County, Nebraska	32.3	15.9	19.0	17.3	15.6	17.1	7.1	5.6
31063	Frontier County, Nebraska	34.9	14.2	23.3	18.2	9.4	24.0	4.9	3.4
31065	Furnas County, Nebraska	36.5	14.4	20.4	13.3	15.4	18.7	4.4	9.6
31067	Gage County, Nebraska	33.1	17.6	20.8	9.8	18.7	6.0	6.6	14.1
31069	Garden County, Nebraska	33.4	20.6	19.6	15.0	11.4	16.1	8.7	1.1
31071	Garfield County, Nebraska	30.4	15.3	24.0	16.0	14.2	13.5	8.7	8.1
31073	Gosper County, Nebraska	27.4	16.4	25.8	13.2	17.2	10.7	5.2	10.3
31075	Grant County, Nebraska	40.2	12.4	15.6	20.6	11.2	36.6	5.0	3.3
31077	Greeley County, Nebraska	30.9	15.3	23.2	19.4	11.3	20.9	5.9	6.7
31079	Hall County, Nebraska	25.7	18.4	22.4	11.1	22.5	3.5	6.6	20.7
31081	Hamilton County, Nebraska	33.1	14.4	25.0	12.8	14.7	10.5	7.2	13.5
31083	Harlan County, Nebraska	31.2	15.8	22.5	16.1	14.4	15.4	8.8	8.0
31085	Hayes County, Nebraska	43.5	9.1	13.7	25.0	8.7	37.3	8.4	2.0
31087	Hitchcock County, Nebraska	28.9	14.1	24.2	14.9	17.9	13.5	7.4	10.8
31089	Holt County, Nebraska	33.5	17.9	21.5	14.8	12.2	18.6	4.9	4.3
31091	Hooker County, Nebraska	38.4	16.6	20.2	15.1	9.7	13.3	6.9	5.7
31093	Howard County, Nebraska	34.9	12.0	23.5	12.0	17.6	11.6	9.1	13.7
31095	Jefferson County, Nebraska	29.4	19.9	21.6	10.4	18.6	12.2	7.2	14.5
31097	Johnson County, Nebraska	31.9	22.3	18.9	12.4	14.5	9.2	6.0	10.6
31099	Kearney County, Nebraska	27.3	14.9	22.0	16.6	19.1	8.9	8.3	19.2

Table C. County—Labor Force, Employment, and Educational Data, 2011–2015—*Continued*

| | | Occupation for employed population age 16 and older | | | | | Industry for employed population age 16 and older | | |
Fips code	State/county	Management, business, science, and arts occupations	Service occupations	Sales and office occupations:	Natural resources, construction, and maintenance occupations	Production, transportation, and material moving occupations:	Agriculture, forestry, fishing and hunting, and mining	Construction	Manufacturing
31101	Keith County, Nebraska	30.3	19.3	23.8	13.3	13.3	11.5	5.9	7.6
31103	Keya Paha County, Nebraska	50.0	9.8	15.0	22.7	2.5	48.4	8.6	0.9
31105	Kimball County, Nebraska	31.7	12.8	23.2	12.3	20.0	15.0	7.3	10.2
31107	Knox County, Nebraska	34.8	16.9	21.3	14.4	12.6	16.4	6.9	7.4
31109	Lancaster County, Nebraska	38.5	17.4	24.5	8.3	11.3	1.3	6.4	9.6
31111	Lincoln County, Nebraska	27.1	18.9	22.5	13.8	17.7	4.4	4.8	3.6
31113	Logan County, Nebraska	29.0	14.0	25.4	22.7	8.9	24.7	4.0	1.1
31115	Loup County, Nebraska	42.1	11.4	20.2	14.5	11.8	36.7	4.4	8.1
31117	McPherson County, Nebraska	33.8	10.4	27.9	11.3	16.7	24.8	1.4	6.8
31119	Madison County, Nebraska	28.8	16.9	23.9	12.1	18.3	3.7	7.0	16.5
31121	Merrick County, Nebraska	30.2	19.2	22.6	12.5	15.5	10.2	7.5	13.1
31123	Morrill County, Nebraska	25.9	17.1	22.9	22.8	11.3	18.2	8.0	6.4
31125	Nance County, Nebraska	35.5	15.8	19.9	14.6	14.2	16.4	6.9	9.4
31127	Nemaha County, Nebraska	31.0	19.6	22.5	12.7	14.1	6.3	6.4	8.0
31129	Nuckolls County, Nebraska	36.0	17.8	20.3	14.6	11.4	19.4	5.7	5.4
31131	Otoe County, Nebraska	28.9	19.7	22.1	11.5	17.8	6.3	6.0	15.9
31133	Pawnee County, Nebraska	44.7	12.8	16.2	13.8	12.4	16.9	12.8	12.5
31135	Perkins County, Nebraska	41.8	11.8	18.5	19.1	8.8	20.1	11.8	2.5
31137	Phelps County, Nebraska	29.9	16.7	20.7	18.6	14.1	14.0	6.4	8.8
31139	Pierce County, Nebraska	34.5	13.3	21.6	12.5	18.0	12.3	5.4	14.2
31141	Platte County, Nebraska	27.5	15.0	20.8	13.0	23.6	6.3	8.2	26.0
31143	Polk County, Nebraska	35.7	11.5	21.7	15.1	16.1	18.0	7.2	14.0
31145	Red Willow County, Nebraska	26.0	18.4	25.8	11.8	18.0	8.1	6.0	9.3
31147	Richardson County, Nebraska	31.6	20.8	17.6	12.8	17.3	10.2	7.5	8.0
31149	Rock County, Nebraska	40.0	16.1	15.9	19.6	8.4	29.2	8.2	4.4
31151	Saline County, Nebraska	29.2	15.1	16.2	11.3	28.1	6.9	4.9	27.1
31153	Sarpy County, Nebraska	41.7	15.0	25.3	8.8	9.2	0.9	6.9	7.7
31155	Saunders County, Nebraska	36.3	15.3	25.1	11.1	12.2	6.6	7.5	9.6
31157	Scotts Bluff County, Nebraska	28.6	16.7	28.1	12.4	14.2	4.6	7.5	7.6
31159	Seward County, Nebraska	35.2	16.7	19.0	14.0	15.0	6.6	7.4	12.0
31161	Sheridan County, Nebraska	42.2	16.3	20.4	14.8	6.4	17.8	4.5	2.6
31163	Sherman County, Nebraska	37.5	16.0	14.8	12.9	18.8	19.6	7.6	8.5
31165	Sioux County, Nebraska	52.9	12.8	18.1	10.4	5.7	33.5	3.0	2.1
31167	Stanton County, Nebraska	28.9	20.3	17.1	13.1	20.4	11.0	6.1	13.7
31169	Thayer County, Nebraska	35.4	17.0	21.1	11.9	14.6	15.6	6.6	13.2
31171	Thomas County, Nebraska	42.3	10.6	17.9	18.4	10.6	25.5	4.7	6.5
31173	Thurston County, Nebraska	35.0	19.5	20.1	12.1	13.3	10.2	6.0	9.3
31175	Valley County, Nebraska	37.4	15.4	21.3	13.2	12.6	12.7	8.6	5.7
31177	Washington County, Nebraska	37.4	13.9	24.8	11.4	12.6	3.9	8.8	10.6
31179	Wayne County, Nebraska	35.9	19.1	23.7	12.3	9.0	11.3	3.7	10.6
31181	Webster County, Nebraska	34.7	16.4	17.9	16.2	14.9	17.9	5.6	8.9
31183	Wheeler County, Nebraska	37.2	16.8	14.2	22.3	9.5	37.7	4.3	2.4
31185	York County, Nebraska	36.7	17.3	21.9	10.5	13.6	10.6	4.8	11.6
32000	**Nevada**	27.7	27.8	26.0	8.7	9.8	1.7	6.0	4.2
32001	Churchill County, Nevada	29.7	20.9	20.5	14.7	14.2	8.0	6.2	7.9
32003	Clark County, Nevada	26.5	30.2	26.3	7.9	9.1	0.4	5.8	3.2
32005	Douglas County, Nevada	32.1	22.9	24.2	11.2	9.5	1.9	8.1	7.9
32007	Elko County, Nevada	25.5	20.9	21.2	21.6	10.8	26.2	6.9	1.7
32009	Esmeralda County, Nevada	25.9	22.4	7.1	30.9	13.7	30.9	5.0	0.9
32011	Eureka County, Nevada	37.5	11.4	15.9	23.8	11.4	36.8	9.0	0.0
32013	Humboldt County, Nevada	20.3	17.5	22.6	22.3	17.3	30.6	2.8	3.0
32015	Lander County, Nevada	21.4	12.1	12.8	40.3	13.4	48.5	6.2	0.0
32017	Lincoln County, Nevada	35.9	31.1	15.9	14.6	2.4	11.4	4.9	0.0
32019	Lyon County, Nevada	24.6	19.2	25.6	15.0	15.7	4.9	9.3	8.6
32021	Mineral County, Nevada	24.0	22.2	24.0	13.8	16.1	3.7	5.0	9.1
32023	Nye County, Nevada	23.9	25.3	25.8	15.4	9.6	8.6	8.9	3.7
32027	Pershing County, Nevada	32.4	17.1	16.9	27.9	5.7	28.9	7.6	4.7
32029	Storey County, Nevada	30.6	15.3	31.2	10.0	12.9	1.9	10.0	8.7
32031	Washoe County, Nevada	33.2	21.4	26.5	7.8	11.1	1.1	6.6	7.2
32033	White Pine County, Nevada	35.1	23.8	13.0	19.5	8.6	24.7	7.3	1.3
32510	Carson City, Nevada	30.2	22.0	25.5	8.1	14.2	0.7	4.4	10.8
33000	**New Hampshire**	39.8	15.8	24.2	9.0	11.2	0.9	7.0	12.7
33001	Belknap County, New Hampshire	37.9	16.1	23.7	11.1	11.2	0.8	9.7	11.8
33003	Carroll County, New Hampshire	32.2	23.4	22.5	11.9	10.0	1.0	9.8	7.6
33005	Cheshire County, New Hampshire	36.7	16.1	23.8	9.7	13.6	1.2	8.2	15.1
33007	Coos County, New Hampshire	31.1	22.4	21.8	11.5	13.2	3.3	6.8	9.0
33009	Grafton County, New Hampshire	42.7	18.8	19.6	8.6	10.3	1.8	6.9	9.8
33011	Hillsborough County, New Hampshire	40.7	14.8	25.1	8.3	11.1	0.6	6.5	14.1
33013	Merrimack County, New Hampshire	39.9	16.5	24.0	9.1	10.5	1.0	7.3	10.3
33015	Rockingham County, New Hampshire	42.4	13.5	25.1	9.1	9.9	0.6	7.1	13.0
33017	Strafford County, New Hampshire	37.3	17.6	24.1	8.5	12.4	0.7	5.6	12.2
33019	Sullivan County, New Hampshire	35.2	14.1	24.3	9.2	17.3	1.5	7.0	18.9
34000	**New Jersey**	40.9	16.7	24.7	7.2	10.4	0.3	5.6	8.4
34001	Atlantic County, New Jersey	29.9	29.8	24.0	8.0	8.2	0.4	5.9	3.9
34003	Bergen County, New Jersey	46.9	13.8	25.5	6.2	7.7	0.1	5.1	8.3

Table C. County—Labor Force, Employment, and Educational Data, 2011–2015—*Continued*

Fips code	State/county	Occupation for employed population age 16 and older					Industry for employed population age 16 and older		
		Management, business, science, and arts occupations	Service occupations	Sales and office occupations:	Natural resources, construction, and maintenance occupations	Production, transportation, and material moving occupations:	Agriculture, forestry, fishing and hunting, and mining	Construction	Manufacturing
34005	Burlington County, New Jersey	42.7	15.3	25.8	6.9	9.3	0.6	5.0	7.6
34007	Camden County, New Jersey	38.8	17.4	25.8	7.0	11.0	0.2	5.2	7.5
34009	Cape May County, New Jersey	35.1	22.1	24.4	11.0	7.4	1.3	8.0	3.2
34011	Cumberland County, New Jersey	26.3	23.6	22.2	11.1	16.9	3.1	5.7	11.7
34013	Essex County, New Jersey	37.3	20.0	23.9	7.3	11.4	0.1	5.8	6.9
34015	Gloucester County, New Jersey	41.0	14.7	25.8	8.0	10.5	0.5	6.0	8.2
34017	Hudson County, New Jersey	39.4	18.4	22.9	6.2	13.1	0.1	4.8	7.1
34019	Hunterdon County, New Jersey	50.8	13.4	23.2	6.6	5.9	1.1	5.7	12.4
34021	Mercer County, New Jersey	43.9	17.9	23.3	5.7	9.2	0.3	4.3	8.1
34023	Middlesex County, New Jersey	44.2	14.0	24.3	6.2	11.2	0.1	4.8	9.7
34025	Monmouth County, New Jersey	43.8	15.6	25.5	7.7	7.4	0.3	7.0	6.0
34027	Morris County, New Jersey	49.6	13.0	24.7	5.8	6.9	0.2	4.9	11.1
34029	Ocean County, New Jersey	34.5	18.5	27.4	10.7	8.9	0.3	8.1	5.2
34031	Passaic County, New Jersey	32.0	17.6	24.8	7.5	18.1	0.1	5.7	12.7
34033	Salem County, New Jersey	32.4	18.1	20.7	12.0	16.7	2.4	7.7	11.7
34035	Somerset County, New Jersey	51.0	12.4	23.5	5.5	7.5	0.3	4.4	12.4
34037	Sussex County, New Jersey	38.8	16.1	26.3	9.7	9.2	0.9	7.7	9.9
34039	Union County, New Jersey	36.0	17.5	24.6	7.6	14.4	0.1	5.6	9.7
34041	Warren County, New Jersey	35.2	17.3	26.1	10.3	11.2	1.4	8.0	10.5
35000	**New Mexico**	35.4	20.8	23.2	11.3	9.2	4.5	6.8	4.7
35001	Bernalillo County, New Mexico	40.3	19.9	23.5	8.6	7.8	1.0	6.4	5.3
35003	Catron County, New Mexico	34.3	14.8	22.7	25.5	2.7	20.6	6.7	1.0
35005	Chaves County, New Mexico	29.5	22.3	21.3	14.6	12.4	9.8	5.8	6.1
35006	Cibola County, New Mexico	28.4	27.8	21.8	12.9	9.1	7.6	5.3	3.5
35007	Colfax County, New Mexico	33.3	23.2	23.5	12.7	7.3	6.2	7.6	4.3
35009	Curry County, New Mexico	27.8	18.6	21.4	16.5	15.7	7.2	7.0	4.6
35011	De Baca County, New Mexico	27.5	27.9	15.3	22.0	7.3	15.8	8.6	0.8
35013	Doña Ana County, New Mexico	31.7	22.8	25.4	11.6	8.5	3.5	6.9	4.6
35015	Eddy County, New Mexico	26.7	16.3	21.6	19.1	16.3	18.6	7.5	6.6
35017	Grant County, New Mexico	33.7	21.2	22.4	15.7	7.0	13.5	8.3	1.5
35019	Guadalupe County, New Mexico	33.8	21.8	30.1	6.9	7.3	0.4	3.8	0.0
35021	Harding County, New Mexico	38.5	21.0	23.4	11.2	5.9	26.8	10.7	2.4
35023	Hidalgo County, New Mexico	24.5	26.9	20.8	18.4	9.3	16.7	7.2	0.5
35025	Lea County, New Mexico	24.2	14.7	22.2	20.8	18.0	21.1	7.8	4.5
35027	Lincoln County, New Mexico	32.5	26.0	23.0	11.4	7.2	5.3	10.0	1.4
35028	Los Alamos County, New Mexico	68.3	10.4	14.8	2.4	4.1	0.6	1.1	1.5
35029	Luna County, New Mexico	23.8	24.9	22.2	17.7	11.5	8.7	6.4	7.1
35031	McKinley County, New Mexico	28.4	26.2	21.5	9.8	14.2	3.1	5.9	6.3
35033	Mora County, New Mexico	31.1	30.4	16.5	14.9	7.0	17.8	7.5	0.1
35035	Otero County, New Mexico	25.2	25.9	26.0	15.4	7.4	2.9	9.0	2.2
35037	Quay County, New Mexico	31.8	19.5	22.6	14.2	11.8	7.3	7.4	3.7
35039	Rio Arriba County, New Mexico	35.2	27.1	19.9	10.8	7.0	2.1	8.4	1.5
35041	Roosevelt County, New Mexico	28.5	25.9	22.2	13.3	10.1	8.2	5.8	4.3
35043	Sandoval County, New Mexico	39.7	17.5	25.0	10.0	7.8	1.5	7.0	8.2
35045	San Juan County, New Mexico	27.1	20.0	25.6	15.6	11.7	11.1	7.5	4.0
35047	San Miguel County, New Mexico	31.8	25.1	24.5	10.4	8.3	2.2	6.2	1.1
35049	Santa Fe County, New Mexico	43.3	20.4	21.5	8.0	6.8	1.0	6.3	2.9
35051	Sierra County, New Mexico	28.7	25.9	22.9	10.6	11.9	8.6	7.2	1.8
35053	Socorro County, New Mexico	35.7	26.5	15.3	10.8	11.8	6.6	3.5	2.7
35055	Taos County, New Mexico	35.7	25.0	21.4	12.3	5.6	5.3	8.5	2.4
35057	Torrance County, New Mexico	34.6	21.6	22.3	11.4	10.1	9.6	7.2	2.7
35059	Union County, New Mexico	39.6	24.2	13.9	13.0	9.2	18.4	5.2	3.2
35061	Valencia County, New Mexico	26.5	23.8	24.6	14.5	10.5	3.0	10.5	5.0
36000	**New York**	39.2	20.3	23.8	7.3	9.5	0.6	5.6	6.5
36001	Albany County, New York	43.2	17.6	26.2	5.6	7.4	0.4	4.9	4.9
36003	Allegany County, New York	32.1	21.0	19.5	11.7	15.8	4.3	6.7	14.6
36005	Bronx County, New York	24.3	33.3	24.2	7.1	11.0	0.1	5.1	3.7
36007	Broome County, New York	36.2	19.4	24.9	8.3	11.2	0.8	5.6	10.3
36009	Cattaraugus County, New York	27.7	20.7	24.6	11.4	15.7	3.0	7.5	13.8
36011	Cayuga County, New York	32.7	19.9	22.4	10.3	14.7	3.4	6.2	14.6
36013	Chautauqua County, New York	28.9	19.9	22.5	9.8	18.9	2.5	5.5	18.3
36015	Chemung County, New York	34.4	20.4	23.1	8.2	13.9	1.7	5.5	15.2
36017	Chenango County, New York	31.2	18.6	22.0	10.0	18.1	3.8	7.1	17.1
36019	Clinton County, New York	31.2	22.8	22.9	8.9	14.3	2.4	5.2	11.7
36021	Columbia County, New York	37.4	20.0	21.5	11.0	10.1	4.1	8.0	5.7
36023	Cortland County, New York	33.3	20.3	23.7	9.0	13.7	2.6	5.9	12.0
36025	Delaware County, New York	30.8	20.9	21.5	11.7	15.1	4.0	8.7	13.4
36027	Dutchess County, New York	40.1	19.8	22.9	8.8	8.4	1.2	6.8	7.7
36029	Erie County, New York	38.1	18.6	25.7	6.3	11.3	0.4	4.4	10.6
36031	Essex County, New York	32.3	24.3	21.6	11.8	9.9	3.5	7.6	7.6
36033	Franklin County, New York	31.8	27.0	20.4	9.6	11.2	2.6	5.9	5.5
36035	Fulton County, New York	27.6	20.6	25.0	9.3	17.5	1.1	6.4	13.8
36037	Genesee County, New York	30.4	18.4	22.5	11.9	16.8	3.8	6.5	14.9
36039	Greene County, New York	34.0	19.0	22.4	10.7	13.9	2.0	7.5	6.6
36041	Hamilton County, New York	34.0	28.1	19.0	11.8	7.0	0.1	11.6	9.1
36043	Herkimer County, New York	32.3	19.7	24.1	10.1	13.7	2.2	6.6	12.4

Table C. County—Labor Force, Employment, and Educational Data, 2011–2015—*Continued*

| | | Occupation for employed population age 16 and older | | | | | Industry for employed population age 16 and older | | |
Fips code	State/county	Management, business, science, and arts occupations	Service occupations	Sales and office occupations:	Natural resources, construction, and maintenance occupations	Production, transportation, and material moving occupations:	Agriculture, forestry, fishing and hunting, and mining	Construction	Manufacturing
36045	Jefferson County, New York	32.3	21.5	25.1	11.2	9.8	1.7	6.5	6.2
36047	Kings County, New York	38.5	24.1	22.3	6.3	8.8	0.1	5.1	4.0
36049	Lewis County, New York	29.3	17.3	18.4	17.9	17.0	6.6	11.7	12.0
36051	Livingston County, New York	35.2	17.9	21.9	11.6	13.3	3.5	7.3	13.9
36053	Madison County, New York	36.9	17.5	22.6	10.3	12.7	2.7	6.9	11.5
36055	Monroe County, New York	41.9	17.8	24.3	5.7	10.3	0.4	4.0	11.9
36057	Montgomery County, New York	29.7	19.2	23.4	10.6	17.1	2.8	7.5	13.4
36059	Nassau County, New York	43.6	16.3	26.2	6.8	7.1	0.1	5.8	4.6
36061	New York County, New York	59.2	13.8	20.7	2.1	4.1	0.1	1.8	3.0
36063	Niagara County, New York	31.7	18.8	26.4	8.8	14.3	0.9	5.6	14.3
36065	Oneida County, New York	34.9	20.7	23.6	8.1	12.7	1.1	4.8	10.2
36067	Onondaga County, New York	40.8	17.1	25.8	6.8	9.4	0.6	5.1	7.7
36069	Ontario County, New York	38.8	17.0	23.7	8.8	11.6	1.6	5.6	14.3
36071	Orange County, New York	35.1	19.0	26.2	8.4	11.3	0.8	5.8	7.5
36073	Orleans County, New York	26.7	17.5	22.5	14.9	18.4	4.8	6.7	16.9
36075	Oswego County, New York	28.8	20.4	22.6	12.0	16.3	1.0	7.6	11.2
36077	Otsego County, New York	36.8	20.2	22.4	9.5	11.1	2.6	6.5	8.8
36079	Putnam County, New York	40.7	17.1	25.5	10.7	5.9	0.4	8.9	3.9
36081	Queens County, New York	32.3	24.8	24.0	8.2	10.7	0.2	6.6	4.2
36083	Rensselaer County, New York	38.9	16.7	25.4	8.6	10.3	0.5	7.1	7.7
36085	Richmond County, New York	39.2	19.5	24.3	9.0	8.0	0.1	7.4	2.9
36087	Rockland County, New York	44.0	18.5	23.5	7.0	7.0	0.3	5.6	6.2
36089	St. Lawrence County, New York	33.2	22.7	22.6	10.6	10.8	2.8	6.7	6.4
36091	Saratoga County, New York	44.1	15.4	24.1	7.9	8.6	0.9	6.1	9.7
36093	Schenectady County, New York	38.2	19.4	25.4	7.0	10.0	0.3	4.7	6.9
36095	Schoharie County, New York	33.5	18.1	22.9	12.5	13.1	4.5	8.7	7.0
36097	Schuyler County, New York	32.8	20.6	20.2	12.1	14.3	4.4	7.5	13.4
36099	Seneca County, New York	31.6	18.3	23.5	11.0	15.6	3.4	7.1	16.1
36101	Steuben County, New York	33.5	18.5	20.9	11.5	15.6	3.7	6.9	18.1
36103	Suffolk County, New York	37.8	17.5	25.7	9.4	9.5	0.4	7.7	7.6
36105	Sullivan County, New York	30.3	23.1	22.6	12.7	11.3	1.3	8.1	6.0
36107	Tioga County, New York	35.5	17.7	22.5	9.4	14.8	1.9	6.7	14.4
36109	Tompkins County, New York	51.8	17.7	18.0	6.1	6.5	1.8	3.2	5.8
36111	Ulster County, New York	38.9	18.0	23.7	9.4	10.0	1.1	7.0	6.6
36113	Warren County, New York	35.5	19.5	24.4	8.3	12.2	0.6	6.7	9.0
36115	Washington County, New York	27.4	19.7	22.2	12.9	17.9	4.0	9.5	15.4
36117	Wayne County, New York	33.0	16.8	21.7	11.5	17.0	3.3	7.6	17.6
36119	Westchester County, New York	46.4	18.8	22.1	6.5	6.2	0.2	6.0	4.1
36121	Wyoming County, New York	27.5	17.7	23.3	14.9	16.6	6.7	7.9	13.5
36123	Yates County, New York	31.3	20.5	21.8	12.7	13.7	8.1	8.1	11.6
37000	**North Carolina**	36.2	17.7	23.4	9.4	13.3	1.4	6.7	12.5
37001	Alamance County, North Carolina	31.7	18.0	24.2	10.0	16.1	1.0	6.6	16.2
37003	Alexander County, North Carolina	25.5	13.2	21.5	10.8	28.9	2.5	5.2	31.4
37005	Alleghany County, North Carolina	29.8	19.5	20.9	14.1	15.7	8.1	11.1	12.3
37007	Anson County, North Carolina	21.5	19.0	18.4	11.4	29.7	5.8	6.5	22.0
37009	Ashe County, North Carolina	26.3	19.8	20.9	15.6	17.4	3.8	11.5	12.8
37011	Avery County, North Carolina	26.5	24.2	24.0	13.5	11.9	2.8	11.4	7.4
37013	Beaufort County, North Carolina	29.3	18.1	23.0	14.9	14.7	6.6	7.1	14.7
37015	Bertie County, North Carolina	23.9	14.4	20.2	14.7	26.8	10.0	3.9	22.8
37017	Bladen County, North Carolina	24.9	18.5	17.8	16.4	22.4	8.4	6.2	20.9
37019	Brunswick County, North Carolina	28.8	21.6	25.9	13.4	10.3	1.1	10.3	6.6
37021	Buncombe County, North Carolina	38.8	18.9	23.5	8.8	10.1	1.0	6.4	9.8
37023	Burke County, North Carolina	28.5	20.5	19.6	9.5	21.9	1.4	5.8	21.6
37025	Cabarrus County, North Carolina	37.4	16.3	24.1	9.7	12.4	0.7	7.1	9.9
37027	Caldwell County, North Carolina	23.9	17.5	23.8	11.2	23.6	1.1	6.8	24.1
37029	Camden County, North Carolina	38.2	16.8	23.5	10.8	10.7	5.3	5.0	12.0
37031	Carteret County, North Carolina	35.5	20.3	21.6	12.8	9.8	2.1	8.3	6.0
37033	Caswell County, North Carolina	25.9	21.0	22.4	11.8	18.9	2.6	6.9	16.7
37035	Catawba County, North Carolina	31.4	15.8	23.1	7.0	22.8	0.6	4.7	27.2
37037	Chatham County, North Carolina	39.4	16.6	19.8	11.5	12.6	1.8	9.8	14.0
37039	Cherokee County, North Carolina	26.4	16.8	27.6	13.5	15.8	3.6	8.8	13.4
37041	Chowan County, North Carolina	33.2	18.1	24.1	10.2	14.5	5.6	8.4	6.0
37043	Clay County, North Carolina	28.9	28.5	22.6	9.2	10.8	2.3	7.6	7.3
37045	Cleveland County, North Carolina	28.1	19.3	23.4	9.1	20.0	1.1	5.7	18.9
37047	Columbus County, North Carolina	25.9	22.9	22.4	12.1	16.7	3.5	7.0	11.5
37049	Craven County, North Carolina	32.6	21.0	22.2	12.6	11.7	2.0	5.7	10.8
37051	Cumberland County, North Carolina	33.9	20.5	25.6	8.3	11.7	0.5	5.4	7.7
37053	Currituck County, North Carolina	25.7	19.1	26.6	17.9	10.7	0.9	13.7	8.0
37055	Dare County, North Carolina	30.2	20.3	27.8	14.0	7.7	2.9	9.4	4.2
37057	Davidson County, North Carolina	28.1	16.8	23.3	10.5	21.2	0.9	6.6	21.6
37059	Davie County, North Carolina	34.3	15.0	24.6	9.3	16.9	1.7	8.9	18.5
37061	Duplin County, North Carolina	25.1	17.8	17.1	17.2	22.8	10.4	7.9	20.1
37063	Durham County, North Carolina	49.5	17.2	18.5	7.2	7.7	0.5	5.8	7.1
37065	Edgecombe County, North Carolina	23.3	22.6	20.7	10.9	22.5	2.9	7.3	18.2
37067	Forsyth County, North Carolina	39.4	18.2	22.6	7.3	12.6	0.4	5.5	11.8
37069	Franklin County, North Carolina	31.7	16.5	24.7	13.5	13.5	2.2	8.2	13.7

Table C. County—Labor Force, Employment, and Educational Data, 2011–2015—*Continued*

Fips code	State/county	Occupation for employed population age 16 and older					Industry for employed population age 16 and older		
		Management, business, science, and arts occupations	Service occupations	Sales and office occupations:	Natural resources, construction, and maintenance occupations	Production, transportation, and material moving occupations:	Agriculture, forestry, fishing and hunting, and mining	Construction	Manufacturing
37071	Gaston County, North Carolina	28.9	18.0	24.6	9.6	18.9	0.4	6.0	18.0
37073	Gates County, North Carolina	26.5	16.9	22.7	12.4	21.6	3.8	4.3	21.1
37075	Graham County, North Carolina	24.7	22.6	21.2	15.5	16.1	4.0	13.7	12.2
37077	Granville County, North Carolina	33.2	16.4	22.0	10.6	17.9	2.2	7.0	15.9
37079	Greene County, North Carolina	24.7	19.2	20.4	17.7	18.0	10.9	8.2	15.3
37081	Guilford County, North Carolina	37.1	16.8	26.0	6.7	13.4	0.3	5.2	13.2
37083	Halifax County, North Carolina	25.6	21.6	22.1	9.1	21.5	2.0	5.5	18.8
37085	Harnett County, North Carolina	32.8	17.6	23.7	12.4	13.5	1.7	9.7	10.5
37087	Haywood County, North Carolina	32.3	20.1	21.6	12.8	13.3	1.7	8.4	12.3
37089	Henderson County, North Carolina	32.9	16.8	24.0	12.0	14.4	2.4	8.7	14.0
37091	Hertford County, North Carolina	28.5	22.6	22.7	7.0	19.3	3.6	2.6	16.2
37093	Hoke County, North Carolina	29.8	20.7	22.0	11.6	15.8	2.4	4.9	14.0
37095	Hyde County, North Carolina	31.5	21.9	20.6	13.5	12.5	14.7	1.5	6.6
37097	Iredell County, North Carolina	33.6	15.9	23.3	9.9	17.3	0.9	6.0	17.8
37099	Jackson County, North Carolina	31.6	29.7	21.2	11.4	6.2	1.4	8.7	2.8
37101	Johnston County, North Carolina	34.5	15.8	25.0	12.2	12.5	1.7	10.6	10.7
37103	Jones County, North Carolina	30.8	18.9	19.8	15.7	14.8	9.4	7.4	11.8
37105	Lee County, North Carolina	28.0	18.9	23.1	10.8	19.1	1.4	6.7	21.8
37107	Lenoir County, North Carolina	26.6	21.7	20.2	12.1	19.4	4.4	7.3	17.4
37109	Lincoln County, North Carolina	29.6	14.1	24.8	11.6	19.9	1.2	6.4	20.2
37111	McDowell County, North Carolina	25.2	19.9	22.2	8.0	24.8	0.6	4.4	26.4
37113	Macon County, North Carolina	29.6	24.5	24.2	11.8	9.9	2.3	10.6	7.0
37115	Madison County, North Carolina	31.3	20.3	20.6	14.3	13.4	2.4	10.1	10.7
37117	Martin County, North Carolina	29.8	17.2	21.9	11.5	19.6	4.9	6.2	18.5
37119	Mecklenburg County, North Carolina	42.4	16.3	25.1	6.7	9.4	0.2	6.1	7.8
37121	Mitchell County, North Carolina	28.9	19.0	21.0	14.8	16.3	5.9	7.4	15.4
37123	Montgomery County, North Carolina	26.6	17.6	17.3	14.0	24.5	4.1	8.0	26.0
37125	Moore County, North Carolina	38.6	20.4	21.2	9.6	10.2	3.2	5.6	8.5
37127	Nash County, North Carolina	29.6	16.7	25.3	9.7	18.6	2.8	6.5	16.3
37129	New Hanover County, North Carolina	38.8	19.5	25.5	8.2	8.0	0.3	7.4	6.6
37131	Northampton County, North Carolina	27.4	22.3	17.7	10.9	21.6	5.2	5.0	19.7
37133	Onslow County, North Carolina	29.6	22.4	26.4	12.0	9.6	1.1	7.8	3.1
37135	Orange County, North Carolina	55.1	16.2	18.0	5.5	5.2	0.8	4.9	5.9
37137	Pamlico County, North Carolina	29.4	17.9	22.9	17.6	12.2	7.1	7.8	9.0
37139	Pasquotank County, North Carolina	31.4	18.5	24.3	14.1	11.6	2.2	7.8	6.2
37141	Pender County, North Carolina	29.2	17.7	23.8	16.1	13.2	1.9	12.0	9.8
37143	Perquimans County, North Carolina	33.7	16.0	22.0	17.0	11.3	5.8	9.5	8.0
37145	Person County, North Carolina	27.9	17.6	23.7	14.5	16.3	1.7	9.2	13.6
37147	Pitt County, North Carolina	37.2	21.4	23.0	7.7	10.6	1.2	5.1	10.6
37149	Polk County, North Carolina	33.0	18.2	24.1	11.5	13.2	0.8	10.3	11.9
37151	Randolph County, North Carolina	26.1	14.6	24.3	10.6	24.4	1.5	6.7	25.6
37153	Richmond County, North Carolina	26.6	18.8	21.9	12.8	19.9	3.2	9.6	16.8
37155	Robeson County, North Carolina	25.1	20.4	20.8	13.7	19.9	2.4	9.1	17.3
37157	Rockingham County, North Carolina	25.0	18.7	24.2	11.2	20.9	1.1	7.0	20.3
37159	Rowan County, North Carolina	28.7	18.1	22.6	12.4	18.2	1.4	8.2	15.4
37161	Rutherford County, North Carolina	27.1	18.0	19.8	11.3	23.8	1.5	7.1	20.1
37163	Sampson County, North Carolina	24.6	16.4	20.6	18.4	20.0	11.2	9.2	14.4
37165	Scotland County, North Carolina	31.1	20.3	22.9	7.8	17.9	2.7	6.0	17.2
37167	Stanly County, North Carolina	29.1	19.9	22.4	13.0	15.5	1.4	10.2	15.9
37169	Stokes County, North Carolina	29.8	17.5	18.6	12.1	22.0	1.2	7.5	19.0
37171	Surry County, North Carolina	27.7	18.4	22.1	13.9	17.9	2.7	9.5	14.8
37173	Swain County, North Carolina	29.0	28.2	22.1	9.9	10.8	1.5	7.5	7.3
37175	Transylvania County, North Carolina	31.0	24.5	20.7	13.5	10.3	1.5	11.6	8.1
37177	Tyrrell County, North Carolina	13.5	23.7	22.3	23.4	17.1	12.6	14.2	9.3
37179	Union County, North Carolina	38.5	14.8	25.4	9.9	11.5	1.2	8.0	12.2
37181	Vance County, North Carolina	23.0	23.6	23.3	9.8	20.3	1.9	5.2	17.1
37183	Wake County, North Carolina	49.3	14.5	23.5	6.1	6.6	0.4	5.7	9.1
37185	Warren County, North Carolina	25.7	21.7	27.5	8.8	16.3	2.8	6.0	15.6
37187	Washington County, North Carolina	21.7	18.2	19.4	13.9	26.8	7.4	6.9	21.9
37189	Watauga County, North Carolina	35.4	25.5	24.6	8.4	6.1	0.9	7.0	3.7
37191	Wayne County, North Carolina	29.7	17.9	21.4	13.3	17.7	5.4	5.3	14.8
37193	Wilkes County, North Carolina	25.8	17.1	24.1	11.4	21.6	2.7	7.9	17.2
37195	Wilson County, North Carolina	29.9	18.3	23.0	11.2	17.6	2.9	6.4	18.7
37197	Yadkin County, North Carolina	26.0	16.5	22.5	12.8	22.1	2.7	10.3	18.5
37199	Yancey County, North Carolina	29.3	21.4	18.5	13.9	17.0	2.5	10.4	12.8
38000	**North Dakota**	35.0	16.9	22.5	13.2	12.4	9.5	7.5	6.8
38001	Adams County, North Dakota	44.3	11.5	16.0	19.0	9.1	22.8	7.3	1.9
38003	Barnes County, North Dakota	35.7	18.8	18.3	13.7	13.5	10.5	6.5	9.3
38005	Benson County, North Dakota	38.1	20.2	15.0	11.9	14.8	13.4	8.7	7.4
38007	Billings County, North Dakota	35.1	17.9	14.7	16.1	16.1	24.5	9.9	3.2
38009	Bottineau County, North Dakota	35.3	17.0	19.5	17.3	10.9	19.9	7.6	4.8
38011	Bowman County, North Dakota	31.8	17.1	19.2	23.1	8.8	21.8	7.8	2.6
38013	Burke County, North Dakota	32.7	16.7	17.0	20.8	12.8	31.5	5.4	2.7
38015	Burleigh County, North Dakota	38.5	15.6	24.0	12.7	9.2	4.3	8.2	4.3
38017	Cass County, North Dakota	37.9	16.3	24.5	9.2	12.1	2.4	7.2	9.1
38019	Cavalier County, North Dakota	43.5	8.4	20.4	14.6	13.0	23.1	4.6	2.4

Table C. County—Labor Force, Employment, and Educational Data, 2011–2015—*Continued*

| | | Occupation for employed population age 16 and older | | | | | Industry for employed population age 16 and older | | |
| | | Management, business, science, and arts occupations | Service occupations | Sales and office occupations: | Natural resources, construction, and maintenance occupations | Production, transportation, and material moving occupations: | Agriculture, forestry, fishing and hunting, and mining | Construction | Manufacturing |
Fips code	State/county								
38021	Dickey County, North Dakota	35.4	19.0	18.6	14.6	12.5	14.9	5.3	10.4
38023	Divide County, North Dakota	41.4	16.8	16.7	17.0	8.1	29.2	10.2	3.1
38025	Dunn County, North Dakota	31.3	18.5	16.0	18.0	16.1	27.7	8.4	5.1
38027	Eddy County, North Dakota	38.7	20.0	14.8	16.5	10.1	16.9	8.4	4.8
38029	Emmons County, North Dakota	39.2	16.2	20.3	17.4	6.9	25.9	8.3	1.2
38031	Foster County, North Dakota	31.6	15.8	21.6	13.5	17.4	12.2	5.5	15.9
38033	Golden Valley County, North Dakota	36.4	20.2	20.0	17.9	5.4	31.2	5.1	0.9
38035	Grand Forks County, North Dakota	35.2	19.4	24.9	11.0	9.5	3.6	6.9	5.0
38037	Grant County, North Dakota	47.5	14.9	14.2	11.2	12.3	33.3	4.9	4.8
38039	Griggs County, North Dakota	32.5	14.0	27.3	14.0	12.1	22.0	8.4	12.1
38041	Hettinger County, North Dakota	37.2	14.0	21.1	17.1	10.6	27.3	8.5	3.7
38043	Kidder County, North Dakota	41.3	11.4	21.5	16.6	9.2	28.2	8.4	3.1
38045	LaMoure County, North Dakota	37.0	14.0	19.7	15.3	14.0	23.7	7.1	7.3
38047	Logan County, North Dakota	38.2	18.9	15.7	18.7	8.5	21.1	12.2	2.0
38049	McHenry County, North Dakota	32.0	13.2	20.5	20.6	13.7	22.0	8.8	4.0
38051	McIntosh County, North Dakota	36.2	20.8	18.6	14.2	10.3	19.2	5.4	4.8
38053	McKenzie County, North Dakota	32.5	11.4	21.8	19.7	14.6	24.1	6.9	2.3
38055	McLean County, North Dakota	33.8	18.1	19.1	17.2	11.8	17.9	8.6	3.3
38057	Mercer County, North Dakota	28.5	16.1	20.5	19.9	15.0	18.5	7.4	6.4
38059	Morton County, North Dakota	34.7	17.2	23.3	12.0	12.8	6.6	8.3	6.3
38061	Mountrail County, North Dakota	33.4	20.5	19.0	13.3	13.7	19.8	6.6	2.7
38063	Nelson County, North Dakota	34.2	18.3	18.2	16.5	12.9	21.8	7.4	5.6
38065	Oliver County, North Dakota	38.5	13.3	18.1	20.4	9.7	25.9	11.3	4.2
38067	Pembina County, North Dakota	30.1	16.0	22.5	18.1	13.3	16.9	7.1	13.1
38069	Pierce County, North Dakota	32.2	18.9	20.1	18.4	10.3	12.4	9.3	2.1
38071	Ramsey County, North Dakota	34.9	17.3	26.3	11.7	9.9	7.5	7.4	5.4
38073	Ransom County, North Dakota	33.2	17.7	13.4	12.0	23.6	14.5	5.9	20.2
38075	Renville County, North Dakota	36.0	12.4	23.2	16.4	11.9	28.1	7.9	4.3
38077	Richland County, North Dakota	31.7	17.5	18.0	15.2	17.5	10.8	7.2	16.2
38079	Rolette County, North Dakota	37.5	20.9	20.8	12.6	8.2	6.8	8.7	3.8
38081	Sargent County, North Dakota	31.0	10.0	16.6	14.1	28.3	13.4	4.8	32.6
38083	Sheridan County, North Dakota	39.4	15.4	14.5	18.4	12.2	30.4	6.8	8.7
38085	Sioux County, North Dakota	40.8	26.7	19.3	5.6	7.6	10.2	3.4	1.9
38087	Slope County, North Dakota	46.3	7.5	14.9	19.7	11.6	41.8	6.9	3.3
38089	Stark County, North Dakota	27.7	16.1	23.2	17.5	15.5	16.2	8.4	8.6
38091	Steele County, North Dakota	33.0	13.6	18.6	18.2	16.6	24.9	11.0	9.5
38093	Stutsman County, North Dakota	31.6	22.0	20.0	11.7	14.8	8.0	6.2	11.8
38095	Towner County, North Dakota	45.0	16.5	20.6	10.9	7.0	32.3	3.0	2.5
38097	Traill County, North Dakota	33.3	15.6	21.4	15.1	14.6	12.6	5.4	8.5
38099	Walsh County, North Dakota	30.9	16.4	18.2	19.7	14.8	19.1	6.8	9.5
38101	Ward County, North Dakota	30.5	18.9	23.2	13.7	13.7	9.4	7.6	3.5
38103	Wells County, North Dakota	33.3	14.6	21.8	16.0	14.3	19.8	7.6	3.5
38105	Williams County, North Dakota	29.9	13.4	20.0	20.5	16.3	21.2	9.8	4.7
39000	**Ohio**	35.1	17.6	23.9	7.7	15.8	1.1	5.1	15.5
39001	Adams County, Ohio	27.9	19.3	17.4	14.0	21.5	3.2	8.5	16.7
39003	Allen County, Ohio	26.9	20.4	22.7	8.0	22.0	0.9	4.9	20.2
39005	Ashland County, Ohio	30.4	17.1	21.7	10.5	20.4	3.0	5.1	20.0
39007	Ashtabula County, Ohio	25.3	18.5	22.2	10.1	23.9	1.6	6.2	24.5
39009	Athens County, Ohio	36.7	24.2	22.5	8.3	8.3	1.2	4.7	5.4
39011	Auglaize County, Ohio	29.4	15.6	19.5	9.8	25.7	1.6	5.8	29.9
39013	Belmont County, Ohio	26.4	19.9	23.7	14.6	15.3	8.3	6.1	8.3
39015	Brown County, Ohio	25.7	21.0	21.0	11.5	20.7	1.6	7.7	17.8
39017	Butler County, Ohio	36.7	17.0	24.9	7.0	14.3	0.5	4.9	16.4
39019	Carroll County, Ohio	24.7	16.6	21.9	13.5	23.4	4.9	9.4	22.4
39021	Champaign County, Ohio	26.5	15.9	21.5	9.5	26.6	2.3	4.2	27.5
39023	Clark County, Ohio	29.2	18.2	24.4	8.5	19.7	1.0	4.7	17.4
39025	Clermont County, Ohio	35.5	15.7	25.9	9.2	13.7	0.4	6.3	14.7
39027	Clinton County, Ohio	28.0	15.6	27.1	9.5	19.8	2.8	6.1	15.7
39029	Columbiana County, Ohio	25.4	19.3	22.0	10.3	23.1	3.0	5.1	20.7
39031	Coshocton County, Ohio	21.8	18.6	18.4	14.9	26.3	5.8	5.8	25.8
39033	Crawford County, Ohio	26.3	18.6	20.0	10.2	24.9	2.7	5.6	24.6
39035	Cuyahoga County, Ohio	39.0	18.4	24.7	5.6	12.3	0.2	3.9	12.5
39037	Darke County, Ohio	24.9	14.9	19.9	13.2	27.0	5.0	7.8	26.9
39039	Defiance County, Ohio	26.4	15.6	24.1	9.8	24.1	1.6	4.9	27.1
39041	Delaware County, Ohio	51.9	11.6	24.3	5.2	7.0	0.5	4.4	9.3
39043	Erie County, Ohio	29.5	22.4	22.0	8.1	18.1	1.3	4.1	17.8
39045	Fairfield County, Ohio	36.2	17.9	24.7	8.3	13.0	1.0	6.2	10.4
39047	Fayette County, Ohio	24.6	18.1	25.5	9.9	21.8	4.4	5.7	19.1
39049	Franklin County, Ohio	41.6	17.0	25.3	5.2	10.8	0.2	4.1	7.6
39051	Fulton County, Ohio	28.5	15.4	21.7	11.7	22.8	2.5	8.2	24.4
39053	Gallia County, Ohio	28.4	17.3	23.9	11.0	19.4	1.3	6.6	13.4
39055	Geauga County, Ohio	40.3	14.1	23.5	10.6	11.4	1.7	8.7	16.1
39057	Greene County, Ohio	44.4	15.7	23.5	6.1	10.4	0.6	4.3	10.2
39059	Guernsey County, Ohio	26.4	18.7	21.7	10.9	22.3	4.1	6.7	17.0
39061	Hamilton County, Ohio	40.1	18.3	24.7	5.7	11.2	0.2	4.3	11.7
39063	Hancock County, Ohio	32.5	17.1	19.6	8.3	22.6	1.7	4.3	27.3

Table C. County—Labor Force, Employment, and Educational Data, 2011–2015—*Continued*

		Occupation for employed population age 16 and older					Industry for employed population age 16 and older		
Fips code	State/county	Management, business, science, and arts occupations	Service occupations	Sales and office occupations:	Natural resources, construction, and maintenance occupations	Production, transportation, and material moving occupations:	Agriculture, forestry, fishing and hunting, and mining	Construction	Manufacturing
39065	Hardin County, Ohio	26.5	20.1	20.2	7.2	26.1	3.3	4.9	22.6
39067	Harrison County, Ohio	23.1	17.0	20.4	18.0	21.6	9.7	9.2	15.1
39069	Henry County, Ohio	29.0	16.4	17.2	10.2	27.3	2.6	6.5	25.2
39071	Highland County, Ohio	26.5	15.4	19.5	13.8	24.8	4.0	7.2	19.2
39073	Hocking County, Ohio	29.8	19.6	20.8	13.0	16.7	1.7	8.5	13.7
39075	Holmes County, Ohio	20.8	13.5	19.3	14.7	31.6	6.7	10.5	29.4
39077	Huron County, Ohio	23.5	16.0	20.5	13.7	26.3	4.4	8.3	23.1
39079	Jackson County, Ohio	32.2	16.3	19.5	11.2	20.8	2.0	6.7	20.0
39081	Jefferson County, Ohio	28.5	21.0	23.7	11.1	15.7	2.5	5.9	10.8
39083	Knox County, Ohio	30.3	18.0	21.9	10.1	19.7	2.8	6.8	17.8
39085	Lake County, Ohio	35.6	16.7	25.1	7.0	15.6	0.5	4.8	20.0
39087	Lawrence County, Ohio	29.7	18.8	23.3	9.4	18.7	0.6	6.6	14.5
39089	Licking County, Ohio	35.0	16.1	25.7	9.0	14.2	0.9	7.0	11.9
39091	Logan County, Ohio	27.5	13.9	18.7	10.2	29.7	4.3	5.6	28.6
39093	Lorain County, Ohio	32.4	18.4	24.4	8.2	16.6	0.7	4.9	18.0
39095	Lucas County, Ohio	32.6	19.9	23.5	7.0	17.0	0.5	4.5	15.1
39097	Madison County, Ohio	31.7	16.1	23.1	10.8	18.3	2.8	6.0	16.8
39099	Mahoning County, Ohio	31.1	19.3	25.2	8.3	16.1	0.9	5.9	13.9
39101	Marion County, Ohio	27.7	17.9	20.2	8.3	25.9	2.0	3.5	25.3
39103	Medina County, Ohio	38.1	15.1	25.7	8.6	12.4	0.9	6.1	15.8
39105	Meigs County, Ohio	26.8	18.6	21.9	13.8	18.9	1.6	10.0	11.4
39107	Mercer County, Ohio	24.7	14.5	19.7	10.8	30.2	4.4	6.5	34.0
39109	Miami County, Ohio	30.4	15.7	22.6	9.4	21.9	0.9	6.3	27.0
39111	Monroe County, Ohio	22.6	14.7	23.4	21.9	17.4	10.5	10.0	10.2
39113	Montgomery County, Ohio	35.6	19.2	24.6	6.5	14.1	0.3	4.6	13.1
39115	Morgan County, Ohio	29.8	15.6	16.6	17.2	20.7	5.0	9.9	16.7
39117	Morrow County, Ohio	28.0	14.8	21.7	13.3	22.2	2.8	9.1	20.1
39119	Muskingum County, Ohio	26.4	20.0	24.8	10.1	18.6	2.1	5.8	12.7
39121	Noble County, Ohio	22.9	15.9	25.0	10.5	25.7	2.3	9.0	14.2
39123	Ottawa County, Ohio	30.0	18.1	22.3	10.6	19.0	1.9	7.1	16.7
39125	Paulding County, Ohio	23.5	16.8	18.3	9.7	31.6	5.1	5.3	27.4
39127	Perry County, Ohio	26.1	19.5	20.2	14.0	20.1	2.9	10.1	17.7
39129	Pickaway County, Ohio	32.8	16.6	23.2	9.8	17.5	2.4	5.8	11.0
39131	Pike County, Ohio	31.1	19.6	17.8	12.7	18.9	3.1	11.3	15.9
39133	Portage County, Ohio	31.9	18.2	24.9	7.7	17.3	0.9	5.3	18.4
39135	Preble County, Ohio	24.8	20.2	20.3	11.6	23.0	2.2	6.9	22.8
39137	Putnam County, Ohio	31.6	15.8	17.6	12.0	22.9	3.0	7.2	27.1
39139	Richland County, Ohio	26.7	19.7	24.2	7.1	22.4	0.9	4.5	20.3
39141	Ross County, Ohio	27.0	19.6	23.0	8.8	21.5	1.5	5.9	18.5
39143	Sandusky County, Ohio	24.2	15.9	20.2	10.6	29.1	2.3	6.0	28.7
39145	Scioto County, Ohio	32.7	21.6	21.6	9.4	14.7	1.0	5.7	8.9
39147	Seneca County, Ohio	25.4	17.1	19.5	9.2	28.8	1.9	5.6	28.3
39149	Shelby County, Ohio	27.8	15.1	19.4	9.0	28.6	2.0	5.9	33.0
39151	Stark County, Ohio	31.7	18.9	24.0	8.4	16.9	1.1	5.8	17.7
39153	Summit County, Ohio	37.5	16.9	25.8	6.7	13.2	0.3	5.1	15.4
39155	Trumbull County, Ohio	26.6	19.3	23.3	9.3	21.6	0.7	5.6	20.8
39157	Tuscarawas County, Ohio	25.9	18.4	22.1	9.8	23.8	3.1	5.5	24.3
39159	Union County, Ohio	37.0	15.2	21.8	7.7	18.4	2.4	4.9	17.7
39161	Van Wert County, Ohio	24.8	15.8	19.7	8.3	31.4	2.4	5.1	32.3
39163	Vinton County, Ohio	23.8	21.2	17.4	14.6	23.0	3.2	9.2	19.6
39165	Warren County, Ohio	46.2	13.7	23.5	5.9	10.7	0.4	4.4	17.2
39167	Washington County, Ohio	30.4	16.9	25.4	10.4	16.9	2.2	6.5	15.0
39169	Wayne County, Ohio	29.9	15.9	22.0	10.4	21.8	4.4	5.8	23.1
39171	Williams County, Ohio	24.1	13.4	21.2	9.6	31.6	2.1	5.3	34.9
39173	Wood County, Ohio	35.3	17.6	23.3	7.9	15.8	1.1	4.7	16.4
39175	Wyandot County, Ohio	25.0	15.9	18.3	12.5	28.3	5.4	6.8	27.7
40000	**Oklahoma**	33.3	17.7	24.2	11.7	13.2	5.2	7.1	9.9
40001	Adair County, Oklahoma	24.9	18.7	18.4	14.9	23.1	6.0	7.8	20.9
40003	Alfalfa County, Oklahoma	32.2	15.4	16.9	18.2	17.3	28.7	7.6	3.1
40005	Atoka County, Oklahoma	28.5	19.1	21.4	13.8	17.2	9.0	7.5	8.3
40007	Beaver County, Oklahoma	33.0	13.0	19.1	19.9	14.9	22.7	9.5	8.3
40009	Beckham County, Oklahoma	24.3	17.3	25.2	17.7	15.5	21.9	6.5	3.6
40011	Blaine County, Oklahoma	34.6	17.1	26.1	9.4	12.8	13.3	4.5	7.6
40013	Bryan County, Oklahoma	30.1	19.4	23.6	9.6	17.2	2.9	6.6	10.5
40015	Caddo County, Oklahoma	28.1	16.9	21.5	18.5	15.0	13.3	9.4	7.0
40017	Canadian County, Oklahoma	36.0	15.1	26.7	10.4	11.8	6.2	5.9	8.1
40019	Carter County, Oklahoma	27.7	18.4	24.4	12.0	17.5	6.5	6.2	14.0
40021	Cherokee County, Oklahoma	32.4	20.2	25.1	12.2	10.1	5.0	6.3	7.3
40023	Choctaw County, Oklahoma	27.8	23.2	19.3	13.5	16.3	6.7	9.2	8.1
40025	Cimarron County, Oklahoma	38.5	11.8	17.9	17.9	13.9	31.7	6.1	6.1
40027	Cleveland County, Oklahoma	39.5	17.0	25.4	9.4	8.7	2.6	5.9	6.5
40029	Coal County, Oklahoma	31.5	14.4	22.0	19.5	12.6	10.6	11.7	5.4
40031	Comanche County, Oklahoma	32.3	21.1	23.2	10.7	12.7	1.7	6.4	8.9
40033	Cotton County, Oklahoma	31.8	17.7	22.6	11.9	16.0	6.9	7.8	10.2
40035	Craig County, Oklahoma	27.3	22.2	21.2	11.6	17.8	7.4	5.9	8.6
40037	Creek County, Oklahoma	28.1	16.7	23.2	12.1	20.0	3.6	7.4	16.1

Table C. County—Labor Force, Employment, and Educational Data, 2011–2015—*Continued*

		Occupation for employed population age 16 and older					Industry for employed population age 16 and older		
Fips code	State/county	Management, business, science, and arts occupations	Service occupations	Sales and office occupations:	Natural resources, construction, and maintenance occupations	Production, transportation, and material moving occupations:	Agriculture, forestry, fishing and hunting, and mining	Construction	Manufacturing
40039	Custer County, Oklahoma	27.4	19.8	22.4	16.5	13.9	13.2	6.6	5.6
40041	Delaware County, Oklahoma	27.7	20.2	22.6	12.8	16.8	4.7	7.9	13.7
40043	Dewey County, Oklahoma	31.7	13.9	16.6	23.3	14.4	26.6	8.1	4.9
40045	Ellis County, Oklahoma	35.9	8.9	21.9	19.0	14.3	26.0	8.6	3.3
40047	Garfield County, Oklahoma	26.5	17.7	23.3	14.6	17.9	9.0	7.2	8.0
40049	Garvin County, Oklahoma	28.3	14.9	23.7	14.0	19.0	12.4	6.4	11.9
40051	Grady County, Oklahoma	29.2	17.3	23.3	14.0	16.2	9.1	7.5	9.5
40053	Grant County, Oklahoma	36.8	11.2	19.6	20.1	12.3	25.3	8.7	5.7
40055	Greer County, Oklahoma	31.8	22.7	20.5	14.0	11.0	12.3	7.7	3.5
40057	Harmon County, Oklahoma	34.9	15.4	23.6	16.1	10.1	18.2	8.2	4.7
40059	Harper County, Oklahoma	32.9	15.3	19.3	20.6	11.9	25.9	9.5	3.8
40061	Haskell County, Oklahoma	27.0	17.9	19.1	22.0	14.0	14.9	11.2	6.9
40063	Hughes County, Oklahoma	28.1	20.4	18.6	19.5	13.4	14.8	8.1	4.6
40065	Jackson County, Oklahoma	25.8	21.8	21.5	15.5	15.4	6.3	6.8	8.9
40067	Jefferson County, Oklahoma	24.3	20.8	18.4	17.1	19.3	18.5	8.9	6.0
40069	Johnston County, Oklahoma	33.3	15.2	17.6	13.6	20.4	12.2	6.7	13.1
40071	Kay County, Oklahoma	28.5	18.8	23.6	12.6	16.5	6.2	6.1	14.0
40073	Kingfisher County, Oklahoma	31.3	13.0	22.7	20.4	12.6	20.4	6.8	9.7
40075	Kiowa County, Oklahoma	30.2	19.2	19.3	13.6	17.6	12.9	4.9	8.7
40077	Latimer County, Oklahoma	32.1	16.2	19.2	17.3	15.2	11.1	7.5	6.8
40079	Le Flore County, Oklahoma	25.8	19.5	21.3	15.8	17.6	8.6	8.0	12.1
40081	Lincoln County, Oklahoma	27.7	17.4	22.6	16.3	16.0	7.0	10.3	9.8
40083	Logan County, Oklahoma	35.5	17.4	24.1	11.7	11.3	7.0	8.0	6.7
40085	Love County, Oklahoma	25.0	19.0	22.5	14.4	19.1	8.0	8.8	13.0
40087	McClain County, Oklahoma	33.8	18.2	23.5	13.9	10.7	7.7	8.6	7.5
40089	McCurtain County, Oklahoma	23.2	19.1	19.7	15.2	22.9	6.3	7.8	18.4
40091	McIntosh County, Oklahoma	28.6	18.5	21.8	13.5	17.7	5.3	10.4	9.2
40093	Major County, Oklahoma	29.4	12.6	23.6	17.5	16.9	19.3	6.7	10.8
40095	Marshall County, Oklahoma	22.0	19.8	21.9	10.8	25.4	4.8	7.0	20.4
40097	Mayes County, Oklahoma	28.3	17.8	22.1	14.4	17.5	3.6	9.0	19.2
40099	Murray County, Oklahoma	28.2	24.0	22.9	11.3	13.6	8.8	6.9	8.3
40101	Muskogee County, Oklahoma	28.2	20.5	22.9	11.3	17.2	1.6	7.3	13.6
40103	Noble County, Oklahoma	35.6	15.4	20.1	10.5	18.4	6.4	6.4	20.1
40105	Nowata County, Oklahoma	26.2	16.1	24.5	14.1	19.2	5.8	6.2	16.6
40107	Okfuskee County, Oklahoma	29.2	18.3	18.2	17.7	16.6	7.9	8.5	9.2
40109	Oklahoma County, Oklahoma	35.7	17.9	25.2	10.8	10.3	3.5	8.1	6.9
40111	Okmulgee County, Oklahoma	28.5	17.9	24.0	12.0	17.6	3.5	5.7	14.2
40113	Osage County, Oklahoma	30.0	17.1	21.8	14.0	17.1	7.5	7.9	13.7
40115	Ottawa County, Oklahoma	26.5	23.7	21.0	12.1	16.7	4.5	5.9	13.2
40117	Pawnee County, Oklahoma	28.6	16.2	20.3	14.8	20.1	6.6	8.3	13.4
40119	Payne County, Oklahoma	37.3	18.9	23.5	9.8	10.4	4.5	6.6	7.0
40121	Pittsburg County, Oklahoma	28.6	19.6	22.6	13.5	15.7	8.3	6.0	9.9
40123	Pontotoc County, Oklahoma	32.6	18.1	25.7	11.9	11.8	5.2	5.6	8.1
40125	Pottawatomie County, Oklahoma	31.0	19.3	23.5	12.4	13.8	3.7	6.4	9.5
40127	Pushmataha County, Oklahoma	30.9	18.8	18.7	17.5	14.1	11.2	9.5	4.7
40129	Roger Mills County, Oklahoma	28.9	12.6	27.4	17.7	13.4	31.1	7.9	1.4
40131	Rogers County, Oklahoma	34.1	15.0	24.8	11.3	14.9	2.7	6.0	16.0
40133	Seminole County, Oklahoma	27.2	18.6	22.8	13.8	17.6	9.5	6.6	12.4
40135	Sequoyah County, Oklahoma	28.0	21.6	20.7	12.1	17.6	4.1	7.9	12.7
40137	Stephens County, Oklahoma	28.8	16.6	24.2	14.4	16.0	14.9	6.4	9.5
40139	Texas County, Oklahoma	24.5	14.6	19.0	15.1	26.8	15.0	3.9	27.0
40141	Tillman County, Oklahoma	29.4	19.5	17.7	16.1	17.3	13.2	6.8	12.1
40143	Tulsa County, Oklahoma	36.4	16.6	25.8	9.3	11.8	2.2	6.4	11.6
40145	Wagoner County, Oklahoma	32.4	14.5	26.5	12.1	14.6	2.0	8.2	14.1
40147	Washington County, Oklahoma	36.4	18.3	23.3	10.1	11.9	5.5	7.0	11.9
40149	Washita County, Oklahoma	31.2	15.6	22.1	14.8	16.3	24.6	4.7	6.1
40151	Woods County, Oklahoma	28.2	22.8	22.7	13.7	12.6	16.4	3.6	2.7
40153	Woodward County, Oklahoma	28.2	14.8	20.5	20.1	16.5	19.8	7.3	3.9
41000	**Oregon**	37.0	18.7	23.4	8.9	12.0	3.4	5.5	11.4
41001	Baker County, Oregon	36.7	14.2	22.5	13.8	12.8	9.7	7.3	9.0
41003	Benton County, Oregon	49.4	18.7	18.1	6.6	7.3	3.7	3.9	8.5
41005	Clackamas County, Oregon	37.9	15.3	26.7	8.6	11.5	1.6	7.0	12.1
41007	Clatsop County, Oregon	28.8	21.8	25.8	9.9	13.8	3.8	6.8	8.7
41009	Columbia County, Oregon	28.1	17.9	23.0	13.0	17.9	3.0	7.2	17.3
41011	Coos County, Oregon	27.0	24.3	22.1	12.0	14.7	5.3	6.4	8.3
41013	Crook County, Oregon	22.3	25.2	26.0	9.6	16.9	6.1	6.2	13.5
41015	Curry County, Oregon	32.0	21.3	25.2	13.7	7.8	7.8	5.3	5.8
41017	Deschutes County, Oregon	37.3	18.9	24.5	9.2	10.1	3.1	7.1	8.6
41019	Douglas County, Oregon	28.1	20.4	23.4	11.2	16.9	6.0	5.7	11.3
41021	Gilliam County, Oregon	28.1	10.9	23.2	18.1	19.7	11.9	9.8	5.0
41023	Grant County, Oregon	34.8	18.3	21.4	13.7	11.7	17.5	5.7	6.4
41025	Harney County, Oregon	36.1	16.8	21.5	17.9	7.7	26.9	2.1	2.5
41027	Hood River County, Oregon	35.6	16.3	18.2	15.9	14.0	14.7	5.9	9.9
41029	Jackson County, Oregon	32.1	21.8	25.0	9.2	11.9	3.0	5.7	8.8
41031	Jefferson County, Oregon	26.3	21.0	21.8	13.5	17.4	10.6	6.6	11.9
41033	Josephine County, Oregon	29.7	21.3	24.4	9.3	15.2	2.4	5.6	11.1

Table C. County—Labor Force, Employment, and Educational Data, 2011–2015—*Continued*

		Occupation for employed population age 16 and older					Industry for employed population age 16 and older		
Fips code	State/county	Management, business, science, and arts occupations	Service occupations	Sales and office occupations:	Natural resources, construction, and maintenance occupations	Production, transportation, and material moving occupations:	Agriculture, forestry, fishing and hunting, and mining	Construction	Manufacturing
41035	Klamath County, Oregon	30.2	18.7	24.5	11.9	14.7	7.2	4.3	11.6
41037	Lake County, Oregon	29.8	23.5	15.2	21.2	10.3	25.6	7.1	6.2
41039	Lane County, Oregon	34.5	20.6	24.7	8.3	11.9	2.3	5.2	9.6
41041	Lincoln County, Oregon	28.0	27.5	24.6	9.3	10.6	4.3	5.7	4.9
41043	Linn County, Oregon	28.3	19.0	22.9	12.0	17.7	4.8	7.0	14.2
41045	Malheur County, Oregon	28.6	22.9	17.6	15.4	15.5	15.8	4.7	9.9
41047	Marion County, Oregon	30.2	19.5	24.2	12.8	13.4	6.4	6.8	9.8
41049	Morrow County, Oregon	27.1	15.8	16.9	21.5	18.5	23.9	3.3	15.7
41051	Multnomah County, Oregon	43.1	18.7	21.7	5.6	10.9	0.9	4.4	9.5
41053	Polk County, Oregon	36.0	16.8	25.6	10.3	11.4	5.7	6.1	8.9
41055	Sherman County, Oregon	35.0	17.8	15.8	16.2	15.1	18.5	6.7	2.4
41057	Tillamook County, Oregon	25.5	18.7	20.4	16.0	19.4	10.4	6.5	12.4
41059	Umatilla County, Oregon	26.9	19.8	21.3	13.5	18.5	9.1	5.1	11.1
41061	Union County, Oregon	28.9	20.4	25.4	10.9	14.4	7.0	5.5	9.5
41063	Wallowa County, Oregon	34.5	19.9	21.8	13.0	10.8	18.4	9.0	4.7
41065	Wasco County, Oregon	28.0	22.7	22.2	16.4	10.7	11.4	5.9	6.2
41067	Washington County, Oregon	43.9	15.8	23.6	7.1	9.6	1.6	4.9	17.6
41069	Wheeler County, Oregon	36.9	16.0	17.2	18.8	11.0	21.0	8.5	0.9
41071	Yamhill County, Oregon	31.5	19.6	21.5	11.3	16.1	4.7	5.8	17.1
42000	**Pennsylvania**	36.7	17.6	24.0	8.3	13.5	1.5	5.7	12.2
42001	Adams County, Pennsylvania	29.1	17.1	22.6	10.9	20.4	3.1	6.8	18.6
42003	Allegheny County, Pennsylvania	43.7	17.0	24.6	6.1	8.5	0.7	4.9	7.9
42005	Armstrong County, Pennsylvania	27.4	18.3	22.1	13.8	18.5	4.2	8.0	15.8
42007	Beaver County, Pennsylvania	32.4	18.4	25.2	8.7	15.2	1.0	5.1	12.6
42009	Bedford County, Pennsylvania	25.8	17.1	22.1	13.4	21.5	5.0	8.9	15.0
42011	Berks County, Pennsylvania	31.3	16.3	24.2	9.2	18.9	1.9	5.5	19.0
42013	Blair County, Pennsylvania	30.6	19.4	25.3	8.8	15.9	1.5	5.1	11.4
42015	Bradford County, Pennsylvania	28.3	16.1	21.0	12.4	22.2	6.0	7.2	18.3
42017	Bucks County, Pennsylvania	42.1	13.8	26.1	8.1	9.9	0.5	6.7	12.1
42019	Butler County, Pennsylvania	36.6	16.0	25.2	8.8	13.4	1.3	6.3	13.8
42021	Cambria County, Pennsylvania	32.1	19.9	23.4	9.8	14.8	2.0	5.6	9.6
42023	Cameron County, Pennsylvania	23.6	15.2	18.6	11.3	31.3	5.2	4.9	39.5
42025	Carbon County, Pennsylvania	27.2	18.9	22.6	12.2	19.0	1.0	7.0	14.4
42027	Centre County, Pennsylvania	44.6	18.4	20.5	7.0	9.5	1.9	4.8	7.4
42029	Chester County, Pennsylvania	48.8	13.5	22.8	7.4	7.6	2.7	5.3	11.7
42031	Clarion County, Pennsylvania	29.8	22.0	19.7	12.5	15.9	2.9	8.1	12.6
42033	Clearfield County, Pennsylvania	26.8	19.2	22.0	11.8	20.2	3.7	6.7	10.4
42035	Clinton County, Pennsylvania	24.8	21.1	22.6	12.4	19.1	3.8	7.3	15.7
42037	Columbia County, Pennsylvania	31.3	18.4	22.5	8.7	19.2	2.0	4.9	15.2
42039	Crawford County, Pennsylvania	30.4	18.3	20.6	10.2	20.5	3.5	6.0	20.4
42041	Cumberland County, Pennsylvania	38.6	15.5	26.5	6.4	13.1	1.1	4.7	8.4
42043	Dauphin County, Pennsylvania	37.9	18.5	25.0	6.1	12.5	0.6	4.3	8.5
42045	Delaware County, Pennsylvania	41.9	17.2	25.1	6.7	9.1	0.3	5.0	7.8
42047	Elk County, Pennsylvania	23.6	15.6	18.3	8.6	34.0	1.6	4.5	39.4
42049	Erie County, Pennsylvania	33.7	19.9	23.2	7.3	15.9	1.1	4.5	17.5
42051	Fayette County, Pennsylvania	26.5	19.2	23.7	12.0	18.6	3.7	7.5	13.1
42053	Forest County, Pennsylvania	26.2	29.9	23.0	8.5	12.4	5.6	6.8	6.5
42055	Franklin County, Pennsylvania	30.7	17.2	23.0	10.5	18.6	3.0	6.3	16.1
42057	Fulton County, Pennsylvania	23.9	16.7	21.9	14.4	23.1	4.7	9.0	20.7
42059	Greene County, Pennsylvania	30.0	18.3	21.4	17.0	13.3	11.4	9.9	5.6
42061	Huntingdon County, Pennsylvania	28.7	19.5	20.8	13.2	17.8	3.3	9.6	13.9
42063	Indiana County, Pennsylvania	29.4	18.7	24.1	12.6	15.1	5.7	6.8	9.5
42065	Jefferson County, Pennsylvania	25.1	18.2	20.4	12.9	23.4	5.5	7.3	17.1
42067	Juniata County, Pennsylvania	25.9	14.7	20.3	15.2	23.9	5.4	9.5	21.3
42069	Lackawanna County, Pennsylvania	34.9	17.9	24.8	8.1	14.3	0.7	5.6	11.0
42071	Lancaster County, Pennsylvania	32.8	16.4	23.3	10.4	17.0	2.8	7.4	16.5
42073	Lawrence County, Pennsylvania	29.9	19.3	23.7	10.1	17.1	1.5	6.4	15.4
42075	Lebanon County, Pennsylvania	29.0	18.4	23.8	10.0	18.7	2.9	6.1	16.0
42077	Lehigh County, Pennsylvania	34.3	16.8	25.4	7.3	16.2	0.5	5.3	14.9
42079	Luzerne County, Pennsylvania	30.5	18.7	26.2	7.8	16.7	0.6	5.6	12.9
42081	Lycoming County, Pennsylvania	29.8	19.0	24.4	9.8	17.0	3.0	6.2	14.9
42083	McKean County, Pennsylvania	30.7	19.5	18.8	10.6	20.5	4.7	5.7	20.7
42085	Mercer County, Pennsylvania	30.4	20.4	23.5	8.4	17.4	1.8	5.3	16.0
42087	Mifflin County, Pennsylvania	24.1	19.5	19.4	13.3	23.7	3.0	7.2	22.5
42089	Monroe County, Pennsylvania	32.2	21.5	23.9	8.5	13.9	1.0	5.2	9.1
42091	Montgomery County, Pennsylvania	49.0	13.1	23.6	6.5	7.8	0.3	5.5	11.7
42093	Montour County, Pennsylvania	39.4	16.1	22.5	7.9	14.1	2.6	3.7	11.3
42095	Northampton County, Pennsylvania	35.0	17.3	24.7	8.3	14.7	0.6	5.2	14.8
42097	Northumberland County, Pennsylvania	27.8	20.5	22.2	10.4	19.1	2.8	6.0	14.3
42099	Perry County, Pennsylvania	28.7	14.8	25.0	14.7	16.7	2.8	9.1	8.0
42101	Philadelphia County, Pennsylvania	36.0	24.0	23.7	5.6	10.7	0.2	4.0	6.7
42103	Pike County, Pennsylvania	31.9	20.2	24.7	13.1	10.1	1.0	8.0	6.4
42105	Potter County, Pennsylvania	28.3	15.0	19.7	14.1	22.9	6.9	7.2	17.6
42107	Schuylkill County, Pennsylvania	27.8	16.8	22.8	10.6	21.9	2.6	6.1	18.6
42109	Snyder County, Pennsylvania	26.5	19.2	22.0	12.4	19.9	3.3	7.9	18.5
42111	Somerset County, Pennsylvania	28.2	19.1	21.6	12.7	18.3	5.3	7.1	12.1

Table C. County—Labor Force, Employment, and Educational Data, 2011–2015—*Continued*

		Occupation for employed population age 16 and older					Industry for employed population age 16 and older		
Fips code	State/county	Management, business, science, and arts occupations	Service occupations	Sales and office occupations:	Natural resources, construction, and maintenance occupations	Production, transportation, and material moving occupations:	Agriculture, forestry, fishing and hunting, and mining	Construction	Manufacturing
42113	Sullivan County, Pennsylvania	25.9	18.4	17.6	20.5	17.7	5.5	13.0	13.9
42115	Susquehanna County, Pennsylvania	27.7	16.5	21.7	14.5	19.5	6.7	9.4	13.9
42117	Tioga County, Pennsylvania	28.8	16.9	21.2	13.0	20.1	6.3	6.4	16.5
42119	Union County, Pennsylvania	32.4	20.4	20.8	10.2	16.2	3.2	7.9	12.2
42121	Venango County, Pennsylvania	28.1	19.5	22.8	9.3	20.2	2.3	6.0	19.2
42123	Warren County, Pennsylvania	30.1	15.8	22.1	11.0	21.0	4.4	4.2	20.9
42125	Washington County, Pennsylvania	34.8	16.9	24.8	10.7	12.8	3.5	7.7	11.4
42127	Wayne County, Pennsylvania	27.9	18.0	24.6	14.8	14.7	2.7	10.5	7.0
42129	Westmoreland County, Pennsylvania	34.9	17.0	23.8	9.5	14.8	1.1	6.3	14.2
42131	Wyoming County, Pennsylvania	25.8	16.5	24.1	13.7	19.9	3.3	7.6	14.8
42133	York County, Pennsylvania	32.4	16.1	24.1	9.4	18.0	0.9	6.9	16.9
44000	**Rhode Island**	36.9	20.2	24.4	7.2	11.3	0.4	5.2	10.9
44001	Bristol County, Rhode Island	47.7	16.9	22.2	5.3	7.9	0.5	4.8	10.2
44003	Kent County, Rhode Island	36.9	18.1	26.4	7.8	10.8	0.2	5.2	11.5
44005	Newport County, Rhode Island	43.1	20.5	22.1	7.5	6.8	0.7	5.8	7.9
44007	Providence County, Rhode Island	33.6	21.2	24.9	7.2	13.1	0.3	5.0	11.6
44009	Washington County, Rhode Island	44.1	19.2	21.8	7.2	7.7	1.1	5.8	9.1
45000	**South Carolina**	33.1	18.3	24.8	9.2	14.7	1.0	6.4	13.8
45001	Abbeville County, South Carolina	25.4	18.6	19.6	11.1	25.3	1.3	7.0	24.7
45003	Aiken County, South Carolina	34.7	16.2	23.4	10.9	14.8	1.7	7.7	14.4
45005	Allendale County, South Carolina	17.2	26.0	22.6	9.0	25.3	4.6	3.9	20.5
45007	Anderson County, South Carolina	30.3	16.5	25.3	9.5	18.4	0.6	5.6	21.0
45009	Bamberg County, South Carolina	29.1	23.3	16.6	9.5	21.5	2.0	4.0	22.1
45011	Barnwell County, South Carolina	26.7	18.3	21.6	13.0	20.4	3.2	6.3	21.1
45013	Beaufort County, South Carolina	33.6	24.3	24.9	9.8	7.6	1.0	8.2	4.1
45015	Berkeley County, South Carolina	32.9	16.6	24.3	12.0	14.3	0.4	8.0	12.8
45017	Calhoun County, South Carolina	28.3	15.6	22.0	12.9	21.3	2.5	8.2	15.9
45019	Charleston County, South Carolina	39.4	19.6	24.0	7.7	9.3	0.5	6.4	7.2
45021	Cherokee County, South Carolina	25.7	16.7	24.0	7.7	25.8	0.5	4.6	25.1
45023	Chester County, South Carolina	22.3	15.8	26.6	10.6	24.8	2.5	6.8	21.2
45025	Chesterfield County, South Carolina	24.4	16.2	22.1	12.1	25.2	3.6	6.3	26.1
45027	Clarendon County, South Carolina	27.7	18.2	23.7	10.4	20.0	3.3	7.1	14.8
45029	Colleton County, South Carolina	24.6	22.5	23.1	12.7	17.1	2.5	8.3	8.9
45031	Darlington County, South Carolina	28.8	17.0	25.6	8.9	19.6	0.9	5.7	16.6
45033	Dillon County, South Carolina	18.7	18.5	24.6	12.8	25.4	4.5	4.2	23.9
45035	Dorchester County, South Carolina	34.5	16.7	26.1	10.5	12.3	0.4	7.0	13.4
45037	Edgefield County, South Carolina	27.5	16.5	20.4	15.2	20.4	4.5	6.2	16.5
45039	Fairfield County, South Carolina	24.1	21.9	20.7	10.0	23.3	2.7	4.4	19.3
45041	Florence County, South Carolina	34.1	18.9	25.4	7.9	13.7	1.1	4.5	12.9
45043	Georgetown County, South Carolina	31.6	21.7	24.1	8.8	13.7	2.8	6.8	13.0
45045	Greenville County, South Carolina	37.0	17.0	24.6	7.3	14.1	0.4	5.9	17.3
45047	Greenwood County, South Carolina	31.9	17.2	21.3	7.8	21.8	1.6	5.5	22.1
45049	Hampton County, South Carolina	23.2	20.9	24.5	12.6	18.7	4.3	7.7	14.4
45051	Horry County, South Carolina	28.2	25.6	28.4	10.2	7.5	0.9	8.5	3.9
45053	Jasper County, South Carolina	19.7	23.8	25.4	20.1	11.1	2.5	16.1	5.7
45055	Kershaw County, South Carolina	31.0	17.0	22.9	12.7	16.5	1.8	8.2	13.2
45057	Lancaster County, South Carolina	29.9	16.3	28.2	10.2	15.5	1.0	6.2	16.0
45059	Laurens County, South Carolina	24.8	18.6	21.6	9.9	25.1	0.8	6.0	25.2
45061	Lee County, South Carolina	21.6	21.6	25.8	8.3	22.8	2.5	5.5	20.7
45063	Lexington County, South Carolina	36.6	15.4	26.0	10.6	11.4	0.9	7.7	9.7
45065	McCormick County, South Carolina	25.5	21.5	21.7	9.6	21.6	0.9	7.6	19.4
45067	Marion County, South Carolina	28.4	18.6	21.6	10.1	21.4	3.8	4.3	17.8
45069	Marlboro County, South Carolina	23.0	16.5	22.1	9.7	28.7	1.8	4.2	27.1
45071	Newberry County, South Carolina	25.4	15.4	23.9	12.6	22.7	3.2	6.0	21.1
45073	Oconee County, South Carolina	31.0	18.0	22.0	10.2	18.7	1.7	6.9	19.6
45075	Orangeburg County, South Carolina	28.2	18.1	23.3	9.3	21.1	2.1	5.2	18.3
45077	Pickens County, South Carolina	33.6	17.8	22.7	9.1	16.8	0.6	6.8	16.6
45079	Richland County, South Carolina	38.7	19.6	26.4	5.5	9.8	0.6	4.0	7.2
45081	Saluda County, South Carolina	21.9	14.8	21.3	19.4	22.7	8.1	7.6	18.6
45083	Spartanburg County, South Carolina	30.8	16.1	23.8	8.8	20.6	0.5	5.8	21.5
45085	Sumter County, South Carolina	28.6	18.4	23.9	9.1	20.0	1.2	6.1	18.5
45087	Union County, South Carolina	24.3	15.4	21.4	11.2	27.7	0.9	6.5	22.7
45089	Williamsburg County, South Carolina	22.4	20.7	25.1	9.7	22.0	3.4	4.4	18.1
45091	York County, South Carolina	36.2	15.4	26.9	8.0	13.5	0.6	6.0	14.4
46000	**South Dakota**	34.8	17.3	24.0	11.0	12.9	7.0	6.8	9.9
46003	Aurora County, South Dakota	36.3	20.7	13.3	15.7	14.0	20.3	5.1	7.4
46005	Beadle County, South Dakota	27.0	15.3	24.1	9.1	24.5	5.6	4.6	20.5
46007	Bennett County, South Dakota	42.2	16.4	20.6	13.0	7.8	18.1	7.9	0.9
46009	Bon Homme County, South Dakota	39.5	19.4	16.7	8.4	15.9	13.9	4.5	11.2
46011	Brookings County, South Dakota	34.9	17.4	21.5	10.9	15.3	6.4	5.3	19.0
46013	Brown County, South Dakota	33.0	16.0	24.5	10.6	15.9	5.5	5.9	13.8
46015	Brule County, South Dakota	38.9	17.5	23.7	12.4	7.5	16.6	4.8	2.7
46017	Buffalo County, South Dakota	35.2	30.2	15.0	11.9	7.7	11.8	4.6	2.3
46019	Butte County, South Dakota	29.2	16.6	20.8	16.8	16.5	18.4	8.9	6.7
46021	Campbell County, South Dakota	43.3	20.0	17.1	8.3	11.3	27.7	4.6	4.8

Table C. County—Labor Force, Employment, and Educational Data, 2011–2015—*Continued*

Fips code	State/county	Occupation for employed population age 16 and older					Industry for employed population age 16 and older		
		Management, business, science, and arts occupations	Service occupations	Sales and office occupations:	Natural resources, construction, and maintenance occupations	Production, transportation, and material moving occupations:	Agriculture, forestry, fishing and hunting, and mining	Construction	Manufacturing
46023	Charles Mix County, South Dakota	33.5	22.7	18.9	13.8	11.0	12.4	6.5	4.0
46025	Clark County, South Dakota	38.9	14.7	18.2	16.8	11.4	25.4	9.7	8.8
46027	Clay County, South Dakota	39.6	17.7	24.6	8.9	9.1	4.6	4.9	6.3
46029	Codington County, South Dakota	25.4	17.6	25.9	11.4	19.7	5.1	5.5	20.2
46031	Corson County, South Dakota	43.0	14.9	18.7	15.8	7.6	24.4	5.7	1.5
46033	Custer County, South Dakota	38.0	17.8	20.9	14.5	8.8	13.5	7.1	2.1
46035	Davison County, South Dakota	35.3	19.6	20.4	11.5	13.1	5.3	9.1	13.4
46037	Day County, South Dakota	35.7	19.4	18.1	11.6	15.2	18.3	6.6	10.3
46039	Deuel County, South Dakota	35.2	12.3	20.1	15.2	17.1	17.8	8.6	19.4
46041	Dewey County, South Dakota	42.4	20.1	17.4	13.7	6.5	15.5	6.8	1.2
46043	Douglas County, South Dakota	34.5	20.7	19.8	12.5	12.5	18.2	6.3	7.9
46045	Edmunds County, South Dakota	39.1	11.0	25.7	13.1	11.2	18.4	3.9	4.3
46047	Fall River County, South Dakota	35.2	20.6	19.7	11.6	12.8	9.9	4.7	1.9
46049	Faulk County, South Dakota	48.6	15.6	16.5	12.1	7.1	27.9	3.3	4.3
46051	Grant County, South Dakota	27.9	14.2	25.5	19.3	13.1	18.1	7.1	7.9
46053	Gregory County, South Dakota	37.1	18.1	21.4	14.3	9.0	18.2	7.9	1.4
46055	Haakon County, South Dakota	47.0	15.1	17.2	11.2	9.5	28.2	5.5	5.3
46057	Hamlin County, South Dakota	32.1	12.5	21.8	18.1	15.4	15.9	9.7	15.5
46059	Hand County, South Dakota	36.9	15.3	21.5	18.8	7.5	25.8	6.2	3.6
46061	Hanson County, South Dakota	37.8	15.5	17.7	15.6	13.3	12.8	11.7	10.0
46063	Harding County, South Dakota	41.1	10.8	14.2	23.4	10.5	45.9	7.2	1.3
46065	Hughes County, South Dakota	45.0	13.5	24.1	10.2	7.2	4.2	6.0	4.5
46067	Hutchinson County, South Dakota	38.1	18.4	18.6	12.2	12.7	16.3	5.5	9.5
46069	Hyde County, South Dakota	37.8	18.9	15.1	18.5	9.7	23.5	6.2	0.4
46071	Jackson County, South Dakota	45.8	16.7	15.7	15.0	6.8	20.7	7.8	2.1
46073	Jerauld County, South Dakota	33.3	16.7	14.0	15.1	20.8	20.4	5.2	13.4
46075	Jones County, South Dakota	38.0	13.3	25.7	17.4	5.6	26.8	8.3	1.2
46077	Kingsbury County, South Dakota	35.1	13.9	18.3	12.6	20.1	14.3	5.9	18.3
46079	Lake County, South Dakota	30.8	18.5	23.9	8.8	17.9	4.5	5.5	18.4
46081	Lawrence County, South Dakota	30.6	22.6	23.8	14.0	9.0	7.5	9.9	3.5
46083	Lincoln County, South Dakota	44.7	11.4	25.6	8.5	9.9	2.6	8.3	8.5
46085	Lyman County, South Dakota	42.2	20.1	18.6	9.1	10.0	17.6	5.3	2.3
46087	McCook County, South Dakota	35.8	15.7	20.8	14.6	13.0	12.8	5.5	11.1
46089	McPherson County, South Dakota	39.8	16.9	18.8	11.1	13.4	23.6	6.6	9.0
46091	Marshall County, South Dakota	34.8	12.3	21.6	16.5	14.8	23.9	6.4	12.4
46093	Meade County, South Dakota	33.4	18.2	22.7	14.1	11.7	6.7	9.9	6.7
46095	Mellette County, South Dakota	48.1	15.1	13.9	15.5	7.3	27.2	6.2	0.3
46097	Miner County, South Dakota	38.3	14.2	19.1	12.5	15.8	19.0	6.3	11.2
46099	Minnehaha County, South Dakota	33.2	17.4	27.2	8.6	13.6	1.5	6.0	10.7
46101	Moody County, South Dakota	41.3	13.7	17.2	10.7	17.0	17.1	5.4	12.1
46102	Oglala Lakota County, South Dakota	37.2	26.0	19.7	7.2	10.0	3.4	2.4	1.7
46103	Pennington County, South Dakota	32.0	20.0	27.3	11.0	9.8	3.1	8.0	6.1
46105	Perkins County, South Dakota	40.2	15.3	16.2	17.6	10.7	29.1	7.7	6.4
46107	Potter County, South Dakota	33.5	18.0	20.1	16.6	11.8	20.3	8.1	3.7
46109	Roberts County, South Dakota	37.0	16.8	20.1	11.5	14.5	13.9	6.1	7.6
46111	Sanborn County, South Dakota	31.9	12.6	19.9	17.8	17.8	23.5	5.8	13.0
46115	Spink County, South Dakota	34.8	18.0	20.7	16.1	10.5	21.2	5.4	5.0
46117	Stanley County, South Dakota	38.4	14.9	17.8	18.8	10.1	13.4	9.9	2.3
46119	Sully County, South Dakota	40.9	8.2	19.4	23.1	8.4	34.5	7.7	3.7
46121	Todd County, South Dakota	35.5	25.0	22.0	10.5	7.1	9.5	4.8	0.9
46123	Tripp County, South Dakota	44.8	13.9	16.0	15.0	10.2	24.8	9.1	2.3
46125	Turner County, South Dakota	36.5	18.3	17.6	13.1	14.5	12.3	7.7	8.1
46127	Union County, South Dakota	41.8	13.9	24.1	7.8	12.4	3.4	5.4	13.6
46129	Walworth County, South Dakota	32.8	20.2	22.0	15.3	9.8	7.6	7.2	5.0
46135	Yankton County, South Dakota	32.7	19.0	23.0	8.5	16.7	3.5	8.2	16.3
46137	Ziebach County, South Dakota	48.7	12.9	17.5	15.8	5.1	21.5	7.8	1.5
47000	**Tennessee**	33.8	17.0	24.9	8.9	15.5	1.0	6.2	13.1
47001	Anderson County, Tennessee	34.1	17.6	25.5	9.7	13.1	0.3	7.0	12.2
47003	Bedford County, Tennessee	24.0	14.1	23.0	13.6	25.3	3.7	8.2	24.7
47005	Benton County, Tennessee	23.1	20.6	20.9	11.7	23.7	1.4	7.1	18.1
47007	Bledsoe County, Tennessee	24.4	19.1	20.5	15.3	20.7	5.0	15.5	15.5
47009	Blount County, Tennessee	32.4	16.7	26.1	10.7	14.1	0.8	7.1	12.9
47011	Bradley County, Tennessee	29.1	17.6	24.6	9.2	19.4	1.2	5.9	17.9
47013	Campbell County, Tennessee	23.8	18.7	24.3	13.9	19.4	1.4	9.2	16.6
47015	Cannon County, Tennessee	26.6	14.2	23.5	12.4	23.4	2.0	6.4	20.0
47017	Carroll County, Tennessee	27.1	17.0	23.3	11.0	21.6	3.3	5.8	17.1
47019	Carter County, Tennessee	27.6	21.7	22.8	11.7	16.2	0.9	8.9	12.9
47021	Cheatham County, Tennessee	29.5	16.1	24.6	13.0	16.7	1.0	11.5	12.3
47023	Chester County, Tennessee	31.1	13.4	27.7	12.0	15.8	1.4	7.8	15.6
47025	Claiborne County, Tennessee	27.5	16.7	20.4	13.5	21.9	4.7	7.9	19.9
47027	Clay County, Tennessee	26.7	20.2	19.0	15.4	18.7	2.0	10.6	16.6
47029	Cocke County, Tennessee	21.4	24.0	20.9	10.9	22.7	0.8	5.8	21.2
47031	Coffee County, Tennessee	30.1	15.5	23.2	9.6	21.6	2.0	5.0	23.8
47033	Crockett County, Tennessee	28.4	14.4	22.0	13.1	22.1	4.3	5.9	21.7
47035	Cumberland County, Tennessee	27.2	19.0	24.2	11.7	17.9	2.6	7.0	14.6
47037	Davidson County, Tennessee	39.8	16.7	25.8	7.0	10.7	0.3	5.7	7.3
47039	Decatur County, Tennessee	28.4	20.9	18.5	13.0	19.2	2.3	9.0	13.2

Table C. County—Labor Force, Employment, and Educational Data, 2011–2015—*Continued*

		Occupation for employed population age 16 and older					Industry for employed population age 16 and older		
Fips code	State/county	Management, business, science, and arts occupations	Service occupations	Sales and office occupations:	Natural resources, construction, and maintenance occupations	Production, transportation, and material moving occupations:	Agriculture, forestry, fishing and hunting, and mining	Construction	Manufacturing
47041	DeKalb County, Tennessee	27.8	12.3	21.2	9.0	29.7	2.0	7.3	29.3
47043	Dickson County, Tennessee	28.3	17.5	24.5	12.6	17.0	0.6	9.6	14.8
47045	Dyer County, Tennessee	31.0	15.7	19.9	8.6	24.8	1.7	6.6	24.2
47047	Fayette County, Tennessee	32.4	14.5	25.0	12.4	15.7	2.4	9.1	13.8
47049	Fentress County, Tennessee	23.3	23.5	18.7	14.9	19.6	4.6	10.8	13.5
47051	Franklin County, Tennessee	29.9	16.4	20.9	11.5	21.2	2.4	5.5	23.5
47053	Gibson County, Tennessee	27.1	19.0	24.7	9.6	19.7	2.2	6.7	18.8
47055	Giles County, Tennessee	26.7	14.8	22.4	9.1	26.9	2.4	6.8	25.6
47057	Grainger County, Tennessee	24.0	13.9	22.2	15.9	24.0	4.3	9.8	19.8
47059	Greene County, Tennessee	27.8	17.4	21.1	9.8	23.8	1.4	6.8	21.7
47061	Grundy County, Tennessee	22.9	22.8	17.1	12.3	25.0	5.2	6.8	24.6
47063	Hamblen County, Tennessee	25.0	15.7	22.7	10.9	25.8	0.9	8.1	25.4
47065	Hamilton County, Tennessee	37.3	17.2	25.3	7.0	13.1	0.4	5.7	12.6
47067	Hancock County, Tennessee	26.6	19.4	14.7	17.3	22.1	8.1	9.4	15.7
47069	Hardeman County, Tennessee	26.0	20.3	19.8	9.2	24.7	2.2	6.2	20.8
47071	Hardin County, Tennessee	23.6	20.4	24.1	11.4	20.6	2.6	6.1	18.4
47073	Hawkins County, Tennessee	25.8	17.5	21.9	12.6	22.2	1.8	7.7	24.1
47075	Haywood County, Tennessee	25.0	17.5	19.4	9.5	28.6	4.3	3.7	29.1
47077	Henderson County, Tennessee	26.1	14.9	21.6	12.4	25.0	1.3	9.1	22.4
47079	Henry County, Tennessee	27.0	15.4	25.3	10.9	21.4	3.4	6.7	16.4
47081	Hickman County, Tennessee	24.1	21.1	21.5	14.5	18.8	2.5	11.5	14.6
47083	Houston County, Tennessee	20.7	17.8	19.6	18.1	23.9	3.6	10.5	20.6
47085	Humphreys County, Tennessee	29.5	14.4	19.3	14.6	22.2	0.8	10.7	21.2
47087	Jackson County, Tennessee	24.3	15.8	19.1	18.3	22.6	3.0	6.1	18.6
47089	Jefferson County, Tennessee	26.0	17.4	24.6	10.3	21.8	2.9	9.5	17.1
47091	Johnson County, Tennessee	26.5	19.5	21.9	12.4	19.7	1.6	5.6	19.5
47093	Knox County, Tennessee	39.7	17.1	26.1	7.3	9.8	0.3	5.6	7.4
47095	Lake County, Tennessee	25.7	29.2	18.2	12.0	15.0	10.2	2.6	9.6
47097	Lauderdale County, Tennessee	23.3	20.4	20.6	10.7	25.0	2.9	6.0	21.9
47099	Lawrence County, Tennessee	24.0	16.4	21.7	14.5	23.5	2.3	9.2	19.7
47101	Lewis County, Tennessee	26.5	13.8	26.9	13.2	19.5	4.7	6.4	14.8
47103	Lincoln County, Tennessee	26.4	14.0	22.7	10.4	26.5	1.9	7.6	25.5
47105	Loudon County, Tennessee	30.8	16.7	22.0	11.8	18.7	2.4	7.0	17.9
47107	McMinn County, Tennessee	26.1	15.8	21.8	9.9	26.5	0.9	7.3	27.5
47109	McNairy County, Tennessee	26.5	16.5	19.4	12.5	25.0	3.1	5.6	22.8
47111	Macon County, Tennessee	22.0	14.6	21.5	15.9	25.9	6.1	8.5	21.4
47113	Madison County, Tennessee	32.9	19.4	25.2	6.9	15.6	0.6	4.7	13.3
47115	Marion County, Tennessee	27.0	13.2	25.3	12.9	21.6	1.4	6.2	20.8
47117	Marshall County, Tennessee	24.7	16.7	22.6	9.7	26.3	1.0	6.4	26.9
47119	Maury County, Tennessee	31.3	18.2	26.7	9.6	14.1	0.9	6.1	12.9
47121	Meigs County, Tennessee	19.3	15.8	18.6	15.1	31.1	0.3	11.7	29.2
47123	Monroe County, Tennessee	26.2	18.3	21.0	11.3	23.2	2.3	6.1	24.4
47125	Montgomery County, Tennessee	32.2	18.7	24.9	9.3	14.9	0.8	5.6	11.3
47127	Moore County, Tennessee	24.1	12.4	25.5	9.6	28.3	3.9	5.2	29.1
47129	Morgan County, Tennessee	23.3	22.2	22.7	13.7	18.1	2.1	8.9	12.4
47131	Obion County, Tennessee	27.6	19.2	21.8	10.1	21.3	2.6	5.5	19.7
47133	Overton County, Tennessee	28.5	16.3	20.1	12.1	22.9	3.6	8.5	16.7
47135	Perry County, Tennessee	22.1	22.0	15.0	18.1	22.8	3.4	10.4	19.3
47137	Pickett County, Tennessee	32.0	21.8	19.9	10.6	15.7	5.0	7.1	13.9
47139	Polk County, Tennessee	26.3	17.0	23.2	11.4	22.2	2.4	7.6	23.1
47141	Putnam County, Tennessee	33.1	20.6	23.0	8.9	14.4	1.0	7.7	13.3
47143	Rhea County, Tennessee	25.9	16.8	19.9	10.8	26.6	1.8	6.3	25.4
47145	Roane County, Tennessee	31.1	18.3	23.8	9.7	17.1	0.5	7.6	12.2
47147	Robertson County, Tennessee	31.3	16.7	21.1	12.9	18.0	2.4	9.7	17.2
47149	Rutherford County, Tennessee	34.6	15.1	26.7	8.3	15.3	0.4	6.0	13.7
47151	Scott County, Tennessee	22.9	18.7	19.8	14.1	24.6	2.0	8.3	20.2
47153	Sequatchie County, Tennessee	26.0	18.6	23.3	16.2	15.8	2.2	9.0	16.4
47155	Sevier County, Tennessee	24.6	24.1	31.1	9.7	10.5	0.3	7.4	6.9
47157	Shelby County, Tennessee	35.1	17.4	25.5	6.7	15.3	0.3	4.7	8.9
47159	Smith County, Tennessee	24.8	15.0	22.9	12.0	25.4	4.0	7.8	25.4
47161	Stewart County, Tennessee	31.7	19.4	21.3	11.1	16.5	2.9	7.5	13.7
47163	Sullivan County, Tennessee	32.4	17.5	27.1	9.0	14.0	1.2	6.1	16.3
47165	Sumner County, Tennessee	35.1	15.0	27.5	8.1	14.4	0.6	6.2	11.3
47167	Tipton County, Tennessee	29.2	16.1	23.9	14.4	16.4	1.1	8.8	13.2
47169	Trousdale County, Tennessee	23.1	17.3	28.4	8.7	22.4	3.1	5.7	9.2
47171	Unicoi County, Tennessee	23.2	17.5	23.1	16.5	19.7	3.5	5.5	19.2
47173	Union County, Tennessee	23.7	15.2	24.7	13.8	22.6	1.3	11.5	18.3
47175	Van Buren County, Tennessee	29.4	24.4	18.2	9.1	19.0	2.4	7.8	17.4
47177	Warren County, Tennessee	24.9	14.3	22.5	12.0	26.2	3.2	6.0	26.2
47179	Washington County, Tennessee	38.5	18.2	25.0	7.8	10.6	0.7	5.4	11.6
47181	Wayne County, Tennessee	24.0	20.1	24.3	15.1	16.5	3.1	9.4	13.5
47183	Weakley County, Tennessee	31.7	16.2	23.0	9.4	19.7	3.2	4.7	18.5
47185	White County, Tennessee	23.2	19.5	21.6	12.6	23.1	2.7	7.0	21.5
47187	Williamson County, Tennessee	54.8	11.0	24.8	3.8	5.6	0.7	4.6	8.4
47189	Wilson County, Tennessee	35.3	15.1	29.8	8.9	10.9	0.9	6.5	9.5

Table C. County—Labor Force, Employment, and Educational Data, 2011–2015—*Continued*

		Occupation for employed population age 16 and older					Industry for employed population age 16 and older		
Fips code	State/county	Management, business, science, and arts occupations	Service occupations	Sales and office occupations:	Natural resources, construction, and maintenance occupations	Production, transportation, and material moving occupations:	Agriculture, forestry, fishing and hunting, and mining	Construction	Manufacturing
48000	**Texas**	35.1	17.7	24.4	10.9	11.9	3.4	7.8	9.1
48001	Anderson County, Texas	23.4	24.0	23.7	15.0	13.9	8.9	7.2	4.1
48003	Andrews County, Texas	22.2	13.8	21.9	25.0	17.2	28.4	8.0	5.9
48005	Angelina County, Texas	26.8	20.8	22.4	13.3	16.7	3.5	6.7	13.2
48007	Aransas County, Texas	28.6	19.9	22.7	18.5	10.3	5.7	16.4	3.0
48009	Archer County, Texas	33.7	13.9	21.8	15.7	14.9	12.6	6.8	7.7
48011	Armstrong County, Texas	39.2	12.1	20.1	20.9	7.8	12.8	13.2	4.8
48013	Atascosa County, Texas	23.3	20.9	21.8	19.3	14.8	10.6	11.3	7.2
48015	Austin County, Texas	30.8	17.1	21.0	13.5	17.7	5.8	9.9	15.3
48017	Bailey County, Texas	23.2	22.4	20.6	20.7	13.2	13.1	9.7	5.1
48019	Bandera County, Texas	35.8	18.5	21.2	16.4	8.1	5.8	12.3	6.4
48021	Bastrop County, Texas	31.5	15.0	25.3	16.2	12.0	3.1	13.1	9.5
48023	Baylor County, Texas	37.6	12.0	21.9	21.7	6.8	9.2	12.2	4.8
48025	Bee County, Texas	21.3	26.4	22.4	14.5	15.5	12.8	6.1	4.2
48027	Bell County, Texas	32.1	19.9	26.2	9.8	12.0	0.9	5.9	6.3
48029	Bexar County, Texas	34.6	19.6	26.4	9.6	9.8	1.3	7.3	5.8
48031	Blanco County, Texas	36.3	20.7	19.3	15.5	8.2	5.4	16.5	7.2
48033	Borden County, Texas	52.8	11.7	14.2	14.2	7.1	18.8	5.0	4.3
48035	Bosque County, Texas	28.5	18.1	21.8	15.6	16.0	8.3	9.6	11.2
48037	Bowie County, Texas	29.7	20.4	24.0	11.7	14.2	1.5	6.8	8.7
48039	Brazoria County, Texas	41.0	14.3	20.9	11.0	12.8	2.5	9.0	14.4
48041	Brazos County, Texas	40.1	17.2	24.7	9.3	8.7	3.1	6.7	5.9
48043	Brewster County, Texas	43.4	19.5	18.8	12.5	5.8	5.3	7.0	2.1
48045	Briscoe County, Texas	33.7	16.6	16.6	20.6	12.4	15.3	11.8	7.1
48047	Brooks County, Texas	19.6	32.4	25.3	11.1	11.5	10.6	6.0	2.7
48049	Brown County, Texas	32.3	19.8	22.5	10.0	15.4	5.0	5.7	14.3
48051	Burleson County, Texas	27.4	16.4	22.8	15.9	17.6	8.7	7.7	13.2
48053	Burnet County, Texas	29.3	20.5	22.8	15.3	12.1	4.1	12.6	7.5
48055	Caldwell County, Texas	24.1	22.4	23.4	14.4	15.7	4.9	10.1	8.6
48057	Calhoun County, Texas	27.6	12.2	23.0	15.8	21.3	5.3	12.1	24.9
48059	Callahan County, Texas	25.9	16.5	25.0	14.7	17.9	6.8	8.9	10.2
48061	Cameron County, Texas	27.9	25.3	25.0	10.7	11.1	2.4	6.7	5.5
48063	Camp County, Texas	22.0	19.6	21.9	13.6	23.0	4.3	8.8	17.8
48065	Carson County, Texas	34.9	10.2	24.2	17.7	13.0	10.1	11.8	11.9
48067	Cass County, Texas	21.3	19.2	24.4	14.9	20.2	5.0	6.6	16.8
48069	Castro County, Texas	23.7	15.0	21.0	21.4	18.8	24.0	6.6	8.0
48071	Chambers County, Texas	34.4	10.7	18.9	16.4	19.6	2.3	15.8	19.4
48073	Cherokee County, Texas	26.9	22.4	20.0	15.7	15.1	6.7	8.9	11.3
48075	Childress County, Texas	34.2	21.9	18.2	8.7	17.1	4.3	3.4	7.0
48077	Clay County, Texas	28.8	18.3	24.6	14.5	13.7	10.6	7.4	7.1
48079	Cochran County, Texas	24.2	14.2	12.9	33.2	15.5	36.8	7.0	4.2
48081	Coke County, Texas	46.3	13.9	15.1	12.5	12.2	12.2	4.6	1.6
48083	Coleman County, Texas	26.2	20.8	24.1	17.6	11.3	11.3	10.5	7.6
48085	Collin County, Texas	52.1	11.8	25.2	5.2	5.7	1.2	4.7	9.9
48087	Collingsworth County, Texas	25.4	15.5	18.6	27.1	13.5	21.3	15.2	3.2
48089	Colorado County, Texas	29.0	16.9	20.4	16.2	17.5	9.3	7.8	9.9
48091	Comal County, Texas	37.8	16.6	25.6	11.0	8.9	1.9	9.6	6.8
48093	Comanche County, Texas	26.9	15.7	20.7	15.6	21.2	12.6	5.0	14.8
48095	Concho County, Texas	34.1	13.5	24.5	17.0	10.9	21.7	11.3	4.1
48097	Cooke County, Texas	27.6	22.6	19.1	11.4	19.3	8.0	5.4	17.2
48099	Coryell County, Texas	30.4	24.1	25.1	11.1	9.3	1.1	6.6	4.4
48101	Cottle County, Texas	31.4	22.6	22.9	19.2	3.9	21.0	9.9	0.5
48103	Crane County, Texas	19.0	19.4	17.3	21.9	22.3	29.2	5.4	4.2
48105	Crockett County, Texas	21.6	17.5	20.7	24.4	15.9	35.3	16.4	1.7
48107	Crosby County, Texas	28.9	19.6	20.0	22.6	9.0	18.9	8.9	3.5
48109	Culberson County, Texas	20.1	32.2	24.2	15.7	7.8	16.2	4.6	0.8
48111	Dallam County, Texas	20.3	23.2	16.5	21.6	18.4	22.8	5.2	5.9
48113	Dallas County, Texas	33.3	18.2	24.5	11.2	12.9	0.8	9.0	9.1
48115	Dawson County, Texas	24.9	19.8	22.7	16.5	16.0	14.8	5.7	5.4
48117	Deaf Smith County, Texas	26.8	13.8	20.4	17.0	22.0	14.3	7.4	14.7
48119	Delta County, Texas	32.6	14.8	22.0	11.3	19.3	6.3	6.8	17.6
48121	Denton County, Texas	43.9	14.6	26.6	6.4	8.5	1.4	5.3	8.4
48123	DeWitt County, Texas	29.1	19.2	21.0	14.7	16.1	15.9	6.5	9.4
48125	Dickens County, Texas	41.5	15.6	16.9	19.0	7.0	18.8	9.4	1.9
48127	Dimmit County, Texas	19.3	23.5	31.9	17.0	8.3	22.8	2.2	1.0
48129	Donley County, Texas	32.9	24.9	16.5	14.1	11.6	12.3	7.1	3.5
48131	Duval County, Texas	18.1	24.4	21.9	22.9	12.6	22.5	5.4	6.2
48133	Eastland County, Texas	30.7	20.6	20.9	12.0	15.8	6.9	6.4	10.1
48135	Ector County, Texas	23.5	15.4	25.9	17.4	17.8	13.8	9.4	7.6
48137	Edwards County, Texas	22.7	20.9	26.9	22.0	7.5	13.9	14.6	0.5
48139	Ellis County, Texas	31.7	14.5	27.1	10.9	15.9	1.9	7.5	13.8
48141	El Paso County, Texas	29.6	21.2	26.7	9.7	12.8	1.1	6.1	7.3
48143	Erath County, Texas	29.9	19.4	21.7	13.0	16.0	9.7	6.1	14.0
48145	Falls County, Texas	26.2	20.7	22.8	14.7	15.6	7.1	10.0	11.8
48147	Fannin County, Texas	31.5	16.6	22.6	12.9	16.4	3.9	7.4	15.1

Table C. County—Labor Force, Employment, and Educational Data, 2011–2015—*Continued*

		Occupation for employed population age 16 and older					Industry for employed population age 16 and older		
Fips code	State/county	Management, business, science, and arts occupations	Service occupations	Sales and office occupations:	Natural resources, construction, and maintenance occupations	Production, transportation, and material moving occupations:	Agriculture, forestry, fishing and hunting, and mining	Construction	Manufacturing
48149	Fayette County, Texas	22.7	17.2	25.9	17.1	17.1	9.1	9.2	13.0
48151	Fisher County, Texas	28.9	19.8	22.4	17.6	11.3	16.3	6.3	9.3
48153	Floyd County, Texas	29.4	15.8	18.4	22.9	13.5	21.1	7.0	4.8
48155	Foard County, Texas	31.8	13.5	35.4	11.7	7.6	16.6	8.1	2.2
48157	Fort Bend County, Texas	49.3	12.4	23.6	6.5	8.2	5.5	5.9	9.1
48159	Franklin County, Texas	25.5	19.4	22.9	14.6	17.6	7.6	9.6	11.2
48161	Freestone County, Texas	26.1	23.6	19.8	16.4	14.2	11.9	8.2	7.3
48163	Frio County, Texas	18.5	27.3	20.2	18.7	15.3	14.9	8.5	6.0
48165	Gaines County, Texas	24.3	12.0	19.4	26.9	17.3	22.4	13.9	3.7
48167	Galveston County, Texas	39.7	17.0	22.8	10.3	10.2	2.0	8.0	10.6
48169	Garza County, Texas	24.0	21.9	22.3	15.9	15.9	14.3	8.4	8.2
48171	Gillespie County, Texas	35.4	21.1	20.3	13.4	9.9	4.4	10.7	6.0
48173	Glasscock County, Texas	44.1	5.0	19.2	27.3	4.4	45.3	18.2	0.6
48175	Goliad County, Texas	29.5	16.7	20.8	13.8	19.2	13.8	4.6	12.3
48177	Gonzales County, Texas	22.5	17.9	23.3	17.5	18.9	13.8	7.8	15.4
48179	Gray County, Texas	24.1	15.6	24.6	18.9	16.9	17.2	8.2	8.6
48181	Grayson County, Texas	31.4	18.2	24.9	11.2	14.3	2.5	8.0	12.7
48183	Gregg County, Texas	27.7	16.6	26.2	12.1	17.4	6.3	6.3	12.8
48185	Grimes County, Texas	24.7	17.9	20.8	17.3	19.3	10.9	8.6	12.6
48187	Guadalupe County, Texas	34.4	16.1	25.0	10.0	14.6	2.2	6.2	11.1
48189	Hale County, Texas	24.5	20.5	20.9	16.6	17.4	9.0	7.5	11.0
48191	Hall County, Texas	20.6	23.9	21.9	25.9	7.7	15.2	11.5	2.1
48193	Hamilton County, Texas	28.4	21.4	21.2	19.0	10.0	12.4	7.9	7.4
48195	Hansford County, Texas	28.9	13.6	18.0	20.7	18.8	23.1	5.6	4.5
48197	Hardeman County, Texas	30.6	20.2	15.1	18.7	15.4	18.7	4.0	10.0
48199	Hardin County, Texas	32.2	13.2	23.5	15.8	15.2	3.5	11.7	13.8
48201	Harris County, Texas	34.7	17.4	23.5	11.5	12.9	3.3	9.4	10.4
48203	Harrison County, Texas	32.1	15.0	22.4	14.0	16.5	7.6	7.2	13.1
48205	Hartley County, Texas	38.6	15.4	21.0	17.7	7.3	19.7	5.4	4.2
48207	Haskell County, Texas	30.8	24.3	16.2	15.4	13.3	18.0	4.7	4.0
48209	Hays County, Texas	36.9	17.6	27.6	9.4	8.4	1.0	8.3	6.8
48211	Hemphill County, Texas	28.9	16.6	25.3	19.2	10.1	25.2	5.2	3.6
48213	Henderson County, Texas	26.8	19.4	24.3	14.8	14.7	4.9	10.1	10.5
48215	Hidalgo County, Texas	25.9	23.7	26.1	13.1	11.2	3.3	8.4	4.4
48217	Hill County, Texas	26.0	18.1	24.9	15.0	16.0	5.5	10.7	11.0
48219	Hockley County, Texas	26.1	18.0	23.2	17.6	15.0	17.5	7.6	3.7
48221	Hood County, Texas	34.6	15.0	24.5	14.3	11.5	6.1	9.7	7.4
48223	Hopkins County, Texas	28.7	18.1	23.4	11.3	18.5	6.9	7.1	11.4
48225	Houston County, Texas	24.5	22.1	24.5	13.4	15.5	7.5	8.5	7.7
48227	Howard County, Texas	28.4	20.2	21.6	14.3	15.5	13.8	7.4	5.6
48229	Hudspeth County, Texas	24.0	30.4	15.6	17.7	12.3	14.5	9.2	1.7
48231	Hunt County, Texas	30.6	17.4	23.8	13.0	15.3	1.7	8.3	15.4
48233	Hutchinson County, Texas	23.5	18.5	22.2	19.4	16.3	8.7	12.3	14.2
48235	Irion County, Texas	36.8	12.3	19.9	13.8	17.3	25.1	8.1	3.1
48237	Jack County, Texas	24.2	14.6	20.0	22.5	18.7	28.1	10.4	4.5
48239	Jackson County, Texas	26.4	15.2	18.7	20.0	19.7	15.3	9.4	20.4
48241	Jasper County, Texas	24.2	18.4	24.4	17.3	15.7	6.2	13.6	10.3
48243	Jeff Davis County, Texas	33.1	21.2	17.1	22.3	6.2	19.1	8.8	0.5
48245	Jefferson County, Texas	28.0	19.4	24.2	12.8	15.6	1.7	10.3	12.9
48247	Jim Hogg County, Texas	24.7	19.7	15.3	19.2	21.1	20.3	13.9	5.0
48249	Jim Wells County, Texas	28.2	20.5	20.9	18.2	12.2	21.3	5.5	4.3
48251	Johnson County, Texas	31.0	14.5	24.1	13.0	17.5	4.2	8.1	13.2
48253	Jones County, Texas	28.3	20.4	24.5	14.7	12.1	11.6	6.6	3.5
48255	Karnes County, Texas	27.3	18.4	22.6	19.1	12.5	16.5	7.2	5.4
48257	Kaufman County, Texas	33.0	15.9	26.7	10.8	13.7	1.2	8.0	10.1
48259	Kendall County, Texas	46.7	15.7	23.2	8.7	5.6	2.3	6.0	7.2
48261	Kenedy County, Texas	24.9	34.1	20.5	20.5	0.0	40.5	0.0	4.3
48263	Kent County, Texas	39.7	16.3	16.8	17.8	9.3	20.6	7.5	0.5
48265	Kerr County, Texas	31.6	22.4	26.3	12.0	7.6	4.0	9.4	4.5
48267	Kimble County, Texas	29.5	17.1	26.5	16.3	10.7	9.8	8.4	10.2
48269	King County, Texas	34.3	10.2	13.9	39.2	2.4	50.6	7.8	2.4
48271	Kinney County, Texas	30.0	36.5	11.6	20.5	1.3	8.5	12.9	0.4
48273	Kleberg County, Texas	30.6	23.4	18.9	17.3	9.9	11.7	6.6	5.0
48275	Knox County, Texas	26.5	16.9	19.4	28.6	8.6	28.0	4.8	2.7
48277	Lamar County, Texas	27.6	18.8	25.3	11.7	16.6	3.0	7.8	15.6
48279	Lamb County, Texas	29.5	15.4	19.4	19.7	16.0	21.1	5.0	8.9
48281	Lampasas County, Texas	30.8	21.3	20.1	16.7	11.1	3.1	12.8	5.6
48283	La Salle County, Texas	25.1	13.8	19.0	24.0	18.1	17.6	5.8	5.6
48285	Lavaca County, Texas	32.4	14.7	19.2	13.9	19.8	10.0	9.4	14.6
48287	Lee County, Texas	24.7	23.7	23.4	13.2	14.9	9.7	11.0	9.8
48289	Leon County, Texas	30.3	14.4	21.2	19.5	14.6	14.3	12.4	6.8
48291	Liberty County, Texas	23.9	14.9	23.4	17.9	19.9	6.3	12.7	16.8
48293	Limestone County, Texas	29.5	21.6	18.1	14.0	16.8	9.7	7.3	9.7
48295	Lipscomb County, Texas	32.1	8.9	16.5	20.5	22.0	26.4	10.9	7.3
48297	Live Oak County, Texas	27.1	17.1	21.7	14.2	19.9	18.0	6.2	11.4
48299	Llano County, Texas	32.2	19.5	28.5	10.0	9.8	3.6	11.1	3.7

Table C. County—Labor Force, Employment, and Educational Data, 2011–2015—*Continued*

		Occupation for employed population age 16 and older					Industry for employed population age 16 and older		
Fips code	State/county	Management, business, science, and arts occupations	Service occupations	Sales and office occupations:	Natural resources, construction, and maintenance occupations	Production, transportation, and material moving occupations:	Agriculture, forestry, fishing and hunting, and mining	Construction	Manufacturing
48301	Loving County, Texas	22.6	22.6	32.3	4.8	17.7	19.4	3.2	0.0
48303	Lubbock County, Texas	34.0	20.1	25.8	10.1	10.1	2.4	7.0	5.2
48305	Lynn County, Texas	29.4	16.5	25.6	19.5	9.0	16.4	7.7	3.5
48307	McCulloch County, Texas	26.9	22.4	22.2	15.4	13.2	16.9	4.1	6.0
48309	McLennan County, Texas	32.4	18.2	25.1	10.5	13.8	1.1	7.2	11.8
48311	McMullen County, Texas	25.9	22.2	30.9	10.8	10.2	11.4	2.5	6.2
48313	Madison County, Texas	25.6	23.4	20.3	19.8	11.0	14.3	8.7	5.5
48315	Marion County, Texas	26.7	22.1	19.5	14.4	17.4	4.9	5.9	9.8
48317	Martin County, Texas	25.6	18.3	19.5	23.9	12.6	20.2	8.2	4.7
48319	Mason County, Texas	23.4	22.2	19.4	25.9	9.1	20.7	14.4	2.8
48321	Matagorda County, Texas	22.5	20.4	23.8	17.3	16.1	6.1	10.0	11.1
48323	Maverick County, Texas	22.0	26.6	22.5	13.0	15.9	10.2	6.2	4.1
48325	Medina County, Texas	31.9	19.0	24.0	13.2	11.9	7.1	8.1	4.3
48327	Menard County, Texas	28.6	23.7	17.9	20.5	9.3	13.3	13.4	3.4
48329	Midland County, Texas	32.3	13.9	25.7	16.4	11.8	19.7	7.5	5.3
48331	Milam County, Texas	30.0	16.7	23.0	17.9	12.4	9.8	9.7	7.4
48333	Mills County, Texas	31.4	14.3	28.1	15.1	11.2	9.8	6.7	3.4
48335	Mitchell County, Texas	30.5	20.3	17.3	19.1	12.9	14.9	9.8	5.2
48337	Montague County, Texas	29.4	15.7	20.7	16.4	17.8	17.1	7.7	6.3
48339	Montgomery County, Texas	38.2	15.8	24.2	10.3	11.5	5.6	8.1	10.0
48341	Moore County, Texas	20.3	16.6	17.1	18.8	27.3	9.9	5.2	28.8
48343	Morris County, Texas	27.7	19.8	20.7	6.6	25.1	4.5	3.4	21.2
48345	Motley County, Texas	38.8	14.8	16.1	24.6	5.7	24.4	10.7	0.9
48347	Nacogdoches County, Texas	33.7	17.3	22.6	11.3	15.1	5.8	8.3	11.2
48349	Navarro County, Texas	25.2	20.0	22.4	11.5	20.9	4.6	6.5	16.3
48351	Newton County, Texas	21.8	20.8	21.8	17.0	18.7	9.6	10.5	13.2
48353	Nolan County, Texas	24.9	24.5	17.6	13.7	19.3	6.8	5.7	12.3
48355	Nueces County, Texas	28.7	21.5	24.3	13.3	12.2	3.7	8.3	6.8
48357	Ochiltree County, Texas	21.3	18.9	21.3	21.6	16.9	26.2	6.8	4.3
48359	Oldham County, Texas	39.2	19.3	19.7	11.5	10.3	13.3	4.3	3.1
48361	Orange County, Texas	28.3	15.7	24.2	15.2	16.6	1.6	9.9	15.8
48363	Palo Pinto County, Texas	25.2	16.3	22.2	16.2	20.1	9.6	9.9	14.1
48365	Panola County, Texas	22.0	17.4	22.4	22.3	15.9	23.9	8.7	7.1
48367	Parker County, Texas	37.6	14.4	24.8	12.2	11.0	5.0	8.7	12.2
48369	Parmer County, Texas	23.9	14.0	18.5	17.1	26.5	17.0	5.6	20.9
48371	Pecos County, Texas	18.9	18.5	25.4	20.3	16.9	18.1	8.6	1.8
48373	Polk County, Texas	25.2	22.6	22.9	15.4	13.9	5.2	9.8	7.8
48375	Potter County, Texas	25.2	23.1	22.5	12.4	16.8	1.9	9.2	11.3
48377	Presidio County, Texas	33.9	25.7	17.7	16.6	6.1	8.6	8.0	3.0
48379	Rains County, Texas	28.6	15.9	22.9	14.6	18.0	4.2	6.6	15.4
48381	Randall County, Texas	36.8	17.5	27.5	8.5	9.8	2.7	5.5	8.6
48383	Reagan County, Texas	20.1	10.3	22.5	21.5	25.6	36.1	6.0	1.0
48385	Real County, Texas	33.7	24.2	22.0	8.7	11.3	10.8	10.3	5.1
48387	Red River County, Texas	22.5	19.2	19.6	17.9	20.8	5.7	9.8	18.7
48389	Reeves County, Texas	25.5	26.8	20.4	14.3	12.8	14.6	6.1	4.9
48391	Refugio County, Texas	23.0	24.0	21.2	16.6	15.2	17.0	7.3	5.5
48393	Roberts County, Texas	40.2	14.9	23.9	11.8	9.2	21.5	9.9	5.7
48395	Robertson County, Texas	28.6	16.8	23.1	15.4	16.1	10.3	10.5	6.7
48397	Rockwall County, Texas	45.3	12.5	25.4	8.5	8.3	1.3	9.0	9.9
48399	Runnels County, Texas	28.4	16.9	23.8	14.8	16.1	14.4	5.1	12.5
48401	Rusk County, Texas	24.2	18.0	22.1	17.1	18.6	11.4	9.4	10.2
48403	Sabine County, Texas	23.7	21.7	20.1	19.3	15.2	10.1	12.3	5.9
48405	San Augustine County, Texas	20.5	16.9	22.0	15.6	25.0	7.4	8.4	11.6
48407	San Jacinto County, Texas	24.0	21.2	18.4	19.9	16.5	7.2	14.0	8.9
48409	San Patricio County, Texas	27.8	20.9	20.1	17.5	13.7	9.0	11.5	8.9
48411	San Saba County, Texas	26.5	16.7	17.9	21.0	17.9	19.8	9.2	7.1
48413	Schleicher County, Texas	30.8	15.1	17.2	19.5	17.3	26.6	7.4	2.6
48415	Scurry County, Texas	24.4	19.6	19.4	23.9	12.7	22.0	9.0	2.6
48417	Shackelford County, Texas	31.5	18.0	25.6	13.6	11.3	25.2	6.9	4.9
48419	Shelby County, Texas	27.0	16.7	17.5	22.1	16.8	13.2	9.7	11.9
48421	Sherman County, Texas	29.9	10.0	20.3	18.6	21.2	22.8	8.2	12.7
48423	Smith County, Texas	34.3	17.8	23.5	11.4	13.1	3.3	7.3	9.4
48425	Somervell County, Texas	35.6	13.2	21.0	16.4	13.9	10.6	9.6	7.1
48427	Starr County, Texas	21.6	30.6	18.0	17.4	12.4	7.8	11.9	1.5
48429	Stephens County, Texas	28.4	16.4	22.8	17.6	14.8	20.0	9.6	4.9
48431	Sterling County, Texas	30.7	13.9	25.2	21.4	8.7	27.6	3.4	3.4
48433	Stonewall County, Texas	34.9	19.9	15.4	15.0	14.8	22.8	11.8	2.2
48435	Sutton County, Texas	25.8	14.6	14.5	26.8	18.3	35.7	8.0	1.1
48437	Swisher County, Texas	27.4	17.6	21.2	14.7	19.0	12.9	5.8	7.9
48439	Tarrant County, Texas	36.3	16.0	25.7	8.9	13.1	1.2	6.7	11.2
48441	Taylor County, Texas	30.3	21.9	25.8	11.1	10.9	2.9	6.0	4.9
48443	Terrell County, Texas	20.0	30.6	23.9	14.9	10.6	13.5	7.7	4.8
48445	Terry County, Texas	32.1	20.1	16.6	17.8	13.4	18.8	7.1	3.7
48447	Throckmorton County, Texas	30.5	17.1	23.2	15.7	13.6	28.4	8.3	2.9
48449	Titus County, Texas	22.6	15.3	21.6	11.5	29.1	3.4	6.0	24.6
48451	Tom Green County, Texas	31.1	19.5	23.7	12.9	12.8	8.7	5.7	6.0

Table C. County—Labor Force, Employment, and Educational Data, 2011–2015—*Continued*

		Occupation for employed population age 16 and older					Industry for employed population age 16 and older		
Fips code	State/county	Management, business, science, and arts occupations	Service occupations	Sales and office occupations:	Natural resources, construction, and maintenance occupations	Production, transportation, and material moving occupations:	Agriculture, forestry, fishing and hunting, and mining	Construction	Manufacturing
48453	Travis County, Texas	46.2	16.7	22.5	8.1	6.4	0.7	7.4	7.8
48455	Trinity County, Texas	23.7	27.5	24.1	11.8	12.9	7.6	8.1	7.9
48457	Tyler County, Texas	23.7	23.2	22.3	17.2	13.7	9.3	8.2	11.2
48459	Upshur County, Texas	27.1	19.0	22.2	14.6	17.0	7.5	9.1	11.9
48461	Upton County, Texas	25.8	16.2	18.2	21.0	18.9	23.8	5.4	2.5
48463	Uvalde County, Texas	27.8	22.8	20.1	18.5	10.8	11.4	8.7	4.7
48465	Val Verde County, Texas	24.6	23.0	25.2	14.3	12.9	5.1	5.2	6.8
48467	Van Zandt County, Texas	29.6	19.0	23.5	14.5	13.4	4.6	7.8	9.7
48469	Victoria County, Texas	27.9	17.4	26.9	13.7	14.2	6.7	7.9	11.4
48471	Walker County, Texas	31.5	27.4	24.9	7.2	9.0	3.2	3.5	3.8
48473	Waller County, Texas	28.0	21.1	25.6	13.8	11.6	6.1	8.4	11.0
48475	Ward County, Texas	20.3	19.2	22.0	21.7	16.8	21.9	6.6	2.7
48477	Washington County, Texas	30.0	16.5	23.4	12.4	17.7	3.9	7.5	16.7
48479	Webb County, Texas	26.2	22.5	28.3	10.4	12.6	4.0	5.6	2.1
48481	Wharton County, Texas	27.2	19.5	20.0	17.5	15.8	12.3	8.8	9.2
48483	Wheeler County, Texas	27.7	17.7	19.6	22.1	12.9	27.0	8.0	2.5
48485	Wichita County, Texas	33.0	19.9	24.5	9.2	13.4	2.9	5.2	9.5
48487	Wilbarger County, Texas	27.8	23.2	22.2	13.7	13.0	8.3	4.9	10.5
48489	Willacy County, Texas	21.9	27.0	21.2	16.6	13.3	10.5	5.7	4.2
48491	Williamson County, Texas	45.4	14.6	24.9	7.4	7.7	1.0	6.6	10.8
48493	Wilson County, Texas	32.8	16.5	23.6	15.0	12.1	5.5	10.7	7.9
48495	Winkler County, Texas	20.6	16.2	19.2	24.4	19.7	20.5	11.2	2.9
48497	Wise County, Texas	28.5	15.6	25.1	14.0	16.8	11.0	7.3	9.3
48499	Wood County, Texas	29.5	18.3	24.0	12.8	15.4	4.5	8.0	8.8
48501	Yoakum County, Texas	25.8	13.3	15.0	31.1	14.8	33.6	5.8	1.8
48503	Young County, Texas	30.4	17.2	22.0	16.6	13.9	14.8	10.3	8.5
48505	Zapata County, Texas	16.7	29.4	16.0	20.4	17.5	19.4	8.9	1.9
48507	Zavala County, Texas	28.7	26.9	12.6	18.2	13.7	12.0	6.2	3.9
49000	**Utah**	36.8	15.6	26.2	8.9	12.5	2.0	6.5	11.0
49001	Beaver County, Utah	28.7	19.8	22.3	12.6	16.6	20.4	2.9	7.9
49003	Box Elder County, Utah	30.4	13.7	21.8	10.9	23.2	3.9	6.2	24.6
49005	Cache County, Utah	37.4	15.1	23.6	7.6	16.2	2.4	4.8	19.2
49007	Carbon County, Utah	26.1	19.1	25.6	14.5	14.8	8.5	5.9	5.9
49009	Daggett County, Utah	21.6	23.4	21.6	19.4	14.0	15.3	2.7	1.4
49011	Davis County, Utah	40.9	14.0	26.4	7.2	11.4	0.8	5.2	10.4
49013	Duchesne County, Utah	29.7	13.8	18.4	21.3	16.7	26.0	6.9	2.7
49015	Emery County, Utah	26.4	19.8	16.7	21.6	15.5	11.1	11.7	4.4
49017	Garfield County, Utah	27.6	26.4	24.1	15.8	6.2	6.6	7.0	1.5
49019	Grand County, Utah	26.1	30.1	25.1	11.8	6.9	2.8	6.6	4.0
49021	Iron County, Utah	33.5	19.1	22.9	11.9	12.7	4.2	7.6	7.1
49023	Juab County, Utah	26.5	16.5	24.9	15.4	16.7	4.1	9.7	15.1
49025	Kane County, Utah	27.7	21.8	28.7	10.2	11.5	3.6	6.9	3.9
49027	Millard County, Utah	25.8	20.3	16.5	20.0	17.4	18.4	4.1	8.0
49029	Morgan County, Utah	38.6	14.2	21.4	14.2	11.6	3.3	9.6	11.4
49031	Piute County, Utah	35.4	23.4	20.8	12.9	7.5	8.7	8.6	7.5
49033	Rich County, Utah	32.7	17.4	17.5	22.8	9.6	14.9	10.0	5.1
49035	Salt Lake County, Utah	37.4	14.9	27.5	8.2	12.0	1.0	6.5	11.1
49037	San Juan County, Utah	32.7	21.6	20.0	15.7	10.1	7.5	10.2	4.4
49039	Sanpete County, Utah	33.5	18.3	19.7	15.5	13.1	9.7	10.4	8.0
49041	Sevier County, Utah	26.2	18.2	24.4	15.3	16.0	10.9	7.3	5.5
49043	Summit County, Utah	44.3	19.3	21.3	7.3	7.8	1.7	6.7	5.3
49045	Tooele County, Utah	33.3	15.3	24.9	11.1	15.4	3.0	7.2	11.9
49047	Uintah County, Utah	28.1	11.7	25.3	18.6	16.3	22.7	5.6	2.2
49049	Utah County, Utah	40.3	15.6	26.2	7.6	10.3	1.0	6.5	9.9
49051	Wasatch County, Utah	34.6	20.3	24.8	11.2	9.0	3.0	8.6	3.4
49053	Washington County, Utah	31.2	20.3	28.4	8.8	11.2	1.4	7.0	6.5
49055	Wayne County, Utah	31.1	18.5	25.3	14.2	10.9	13.2	13.2	3.2
49057	Weber County, Utah	31.6	15.8	25.3	10.2	17.1	1.2	7.1	15.6
50000	**Vermont**	40.4	17.4	21.4	10.1	10.7	2.6	7.4	10.8
50001	Addison County, Vermont	40.8	17.6	17.4	12.2	12.1	6.2	8.7	11.0
50003	Bennington County, Vermont	34.1	20.1	22.5	9.6	13.7	2.2	7.9	14.3
50005	Caledonia County, Vermont	35.2	18.6	21.0	13.0	12.2	3.5	9.0	11.4
50007	Chittenden County, Vermont	47.2	16.9	21.6	6.5	7.8	0.9	4.9	9.8
50009	Essex County, Vermont	29.8	20.8	17.3	14.2	17.9	4.1	10.5	15.1
50011	Franklin County, Vermont	36.2	15.0	21.6	12.9	14.3	3.9	8.4	14.7
50013	Grand Isle County, Vermont	38.4	14.2	26.3	11.0	10.2	2.3	9.8	14.0
50015	Lamoille County, Vermont	37.0	21.4	20.1	12.7	8.9	2.9	10.7	9.0
50017	Orange County, Vermont	39.0	16.0	21.2	13.3	10.5	3.5	9.2	9.3
50019	Orleans County, Vermont	32.6	17.6	20.9	15.2	13.7	6.9	10.4	11.1
50021	Rutland County, Vermont	34.7	18.9	22.8	10.4	13.3	2.5	7.8	10.9
50023	Washington County, Vermont	43.4	15.2	23.8	9.0	8.6	1.8	6.1	9.1
50025	Windham County, Vermont	39.9	18.1	19.6	11.5	10.9	1.9	9.3	10.1
50027	Windsor County, Vermont	39.5	17.5	20.6	10.7	11.7	3.0	7.4	10.7
51000	**Virginia**	42.7	16.9	22.5	8.4	9.5	1.0	6.4	7.3
51001	Accomack County, Virginia	33.1	16.8	20.5	14.2	15.4	4.8	6.4	15.5

Table C. County—Labor Force, Employment, and Educational Data, 2011–2015—*Continued*

		Occupation for employed population age 16 and older					Industry for employed population age 16 and older		
Fips code	State/county	Management, business, science, and arts occupations	Service occupations	Sales and office occupations:	Natural resources, construction, and maintenance occupations	Production, transportation, and material moving occupations:	Agriculture, forestry, fishing and hunting, and mining	Construction	Manufacturing
51003	Albemarle County, Virginia	54.1	15.3	18.0	6.5	6.0	1.4	5.6	4.2
51005	Alleghany County, Virginia	29.0	18.5	17.4	14.2	21.0	2.8	6.7	19.5
51007	Amelia County, Virginia	26.2	17.1	30.1	14.6	11.9	4.7	6.5	11.0
51009	Amherst County, Virginia	28.5	20.5	25.3	10.4	15.3	1.3	7.8	16.1
51011	Appomattox County, Virginia	30.9	17.4	22.8	12.1	16.8	2.7	8.8	14.1
51013	Arlington County, Virginia	68.0	10.9	14.9	3.5	2.7	0.1	4.3	1.9
51015	Augusta County, Virginia	31.1	17.2	22.4	10.0	19.3	2.6	7.8	14.6
51017	Bath County, Virginia	28.5	25.2	23.3	10.6	12.5	3.7	6.1	6.5
51019	Bedford County, Virginia	34.6	14.9	24.5	11.0	14.9	1.1	7.7	13.7
51021	Bland County, Virginia	25.6	19.4	26.5	6.9	21.6	2.1	5.9	16.7
51023	Botetourt County, Virginia	38.3	13.3	26.4	8.7	13.3	2.0	6.7	11.8
51025	Brunswick County, Virginia	26.1	23.6	21.1	14.7	14.5	1.8	8.8	7.7
51027	Buchanan County, Virginia	22.8	15.9	25.4	21.3	14.6	17.8	7.3	4.9
51029	Buckingham County, Virginia	24.2	23.1	24.2	16.9	11.7	6.9	10.3	5.3
51031	Campbell County, Virginia	32.3	15.5	23.6	10.7	17.7	1.0	7.7	15.7
51033	Caroline County, Virginia	30.4	18.8	23.6	12.2	15.0	1.1	7.7	6.7
51035	Carroll County, Virginia	26.8	18.0	20.2	14.6	20.4	2.5	9.8	17.0
51036	Charles City County, Virginia	22.1	18.6	25.8	11.5	22.1	3.6	6.3	15.8
51037	Charlotte County, Virginia	25.1	21.6	23.1	15.8	14.4	5.8	8.3	10.9
51041	Chesterfield County, Virginia	42.4	14.8	25.3	8.2	9.3	0.4	6.5	8.2
51043	Clarke County, Virginia	43.6	16.7	19.8	10.8	9.2	4.4	8.3	5.9
51045	Craig County, Virginia	24.9	12.3	24.8	17.3	20.7	2.0	11.9	20.8
51047	Culpeper County, Virginia	35.9	16.4	24.0	12.7	11.0	3.1	8.5	8.1
51049	Cumberland County, Virginia	28.7	20.0	20.7	12.2	18.5	3.9	10.9	4.9
51051	Dickenson County, Virginia	27.1	22.1	22.3	17.7	10.8	13.5	5.4	1.6
51053	Dinwiddie County, Virginia	27.2	20.3	21.5	13.7	17.3	1.7	10.6	13.0
51057	Essex County, Virginia	22.5	23.9	26.4	11.4	15.7	2.4	8.9	10.7
51059	Fairfax County, Virginia	56.1	14.9	19.2	5.5	4.4	0.2	5.4	2.8
51061	Fauquier County, Virginia	42.6	15.4	22.3	12.2	7.5	2.8	10.4	4.4
51063	Floyd County, Virginia	29.7	13.9	22.3	15.7	18.4	7.0	10.4	17.1
51065	Fluvanna County, Virginia	43.2	15.1	24.3	11.1	6.3	1.3	8.0	4.4
51067	Franklin County, Virginia	31.5	13.5	25.1	12.8	17.1	2.3	10.2	15.4
51069	Frederick County, Virginia	38.9	14.1	23.9	10.4	12.7	1.3	8.1	9.7
51071	Giles County, Virginia	24.8	17.8	19.7	12.9	24.8	2.7	8.5	23.2
51073	Gloucester County, Virginia	28.6	19.8	24.8	13.6	13.2	1.4	9.2	11.1
51075	Goochland County, Virginia	46.6	14.9	22.4	8.8	7.4	1.7	7.7	4.5
51077	Grayson County, Virginia	23.1	19.4	21.7	9.4	26.4	5.0	5.9	18.1
51079	Greene County, Virginia	37.4	20.2	24.0	11.0	7.4	1.1	9.0	6.4
51081	Greensville County, Virginia	22.8	24.5	26.4	6.1	20.1	2.2	2.7	18.5
51083	Halifax County, Virginia	26.6	20.8	22.6	10.5	19.4	2.7	6.2	16.8
51085	Hanover County, Virginia	43.1	14.1	25.8	9.6	7.4	1.0	8.1	5.6
51087	Henrico County, Virginia	43.4	16.4	26.2	5.9	8.1	0.3	4.9	6.0
51089	Henry County, Virginia	25.0	16.5	26.7	9.4	22.4	1.0	5.6	21.9
51091	Highland County, Virginia	28.7	12.5	28.7	26.0	4.0	14.9	13.6	2.6
51093	Isle of Wight County, Virginia	36.2	14.5	22.7	13.4	13.2	2.1	6.0	18.7
51095	James City County, Virginia	45.1	18.2	23.3	7.4	6.0	1.1	5.6	6.9
51097	King and Queen County, Virginia	26.7	18.6	19.3	20.6	14.7	4.9	13.9	10.3
51099	King George County, Virginia	41.5	16.3	22.9	10.9	8.4	1.4	7.6	4.5
51101	King William County, Virginia	32.4	10.7	25.0	17.2	14.8	1.2	10.9	12.6
51103	Lancaster County, Virginia	30.3	31.2	22.8	8.1	7.6	2.8	5.4	3.9
51105	Lee County, Virginia	31.5	19.8	23.4	11.4	13.9	5.1	5.9	8.5
51107	Loudoun County, Virginia	56.4	12.9	20.8	4.6	5.3	0.6	4.8	4.4
51109	Louisa County, Virginia	33.1	16.1	24.2	13.2	13.4	2.2	10.6	8.4
51111	Lunenburg County, Virginia	27.0	20.1	22.5	12.6	17.8	4.6	10.0	11.9
51113	Madison County, Virginia	30.7	22.2	20.6	15.1	11.4	2.8	9.6	8.7
51115	Mathews County, Virginia	34.8	19.2	20.3	11.7	14.0	0.2	7.4	8.8
51117	Mecklenburg County, Virginia	30.2	20.8	25.6	9.7	13.7	2.3	7.1	9.0
51119	Middlesex County, Virginia	31.1	20.9	24.7	12.4	10.9	2.6	7.3	12.6
51121	Montgomery County, Virginia	46.6	19.0	21.2	4.9	8.3	0.7	3.8	8.2
51125	Nelson County, Virginia	33.1	22.1	21.2	12.5	11.1	4.8	10.3	8.0
51127	New Kent County, Virginia	36.1	14.4	25.7	15.5	8.3	1.6	14.4	9.4
51131	Northampton County, Virginia	30.9	20.5	21.2	15.5	11.9	7.6	8.3	5.6
51133	Northumberland County, Virginia	35.3	19.6	26.0	11.4	7.7	3.0	9.8	5.6
51135	Nottoway County, Virginia	27.3	27.0	20.9	10.8	14.1	3.4	4.9	8.5
51137	Orange County, Virginia	33.2	18.5	20.8	15.3	12.3	2.6	12.6	7.7
51139	Page County, Virginia	26.0	20.3	25.0	15.0	13.6	4.9	8.8	14.2
51141	Patrick County, Virginia	25.9	16.9	17.5	13.7	26.0	2.3	6.3	24.0
51143	Pittsylvania County, Virginia	25.6	17.3	22.7	12.3	22.0	2.2	7.6	20.3
51145	Powhatan County, Virginia	38.2	18.0	22.5	13.5	7.8	1.2	10.8	5.4
51147	Prince Edward County, Virginia	30.9	25.7	21.2	10.6	11.7	3.1	8.9	5.0
51149	Prince George County, Virginia	35.8	17.5	23.7	8.6	14.3	0.9	5.5	10.4
51153	Prince William County, Virginia	43.2	17.8	22.8	9.1	7.2	0.2	8.5	3.3
51155	Pulaski County, Virginia	29.7	15.9	23.3	8.5	22.6	0.9	5.6	22.4
51157	Rappahannock County, Virginia	35.1	19.4	25.9	13.1	6.5	3.0	10.6	1.6
51159	Richmond County, Virginia	26.2	18.7	26.9	14.0	14.2	4.6	8.3	6.3
51161	Roanoke County, Virginia	40.6	14.6	27.9	6.5	10.5	0.3	4.8	9.4
51163	Rockbridge County, Virginia	33.3	17.2	22.1	10.0	17.4	2.6	8.6	14.3

Table C. County—Labor Force, Employment, and Educational Data, 2011–2015—*Continued*

| | | Occupation for employed population age 16 and older | | | | | Industry for employed population age 16 and older | | |
| | | Management, business, science, and arts occupations | Service occupations | Sales and office occupations: | Natural resources, construction, and maintenance occupations | Production, transportation, and material moving occupations: | Agriculture, forestry, fishing and hunting, and mining | Construction | Manufacturing |
Fips code	State/county								
51165	Rockingham County, Virginia	32.0	15.1	24.0	12.6	16.3	4.4	8.2	13.9
51167	Russell County, Virginia	30.8	12.8	24.8	15.8	15.7	10.7	7.6	8.0
51169	Scott County, Virginia	23.8	19.2	24.4	13.4	19.3	3.0	6.7	18.8
51171	Shenandoah County, Virginia	28.6	17.7	21.9	12.6	19.3	3.8	8.2	16.7
51173	Smyth County, Virginia	28.5	18.6	21.0	9.0	22.9	2.1	6.0	21.0
51175	Southampton County, Virginia	29.2	18.1	23.6	14.5	14.6	6.5	7.9	10.3
51177	Spotsylvania County, Virginia	39.0	18.1	23.7	9.8	9.4	0.8	7.8	4.0
51179	Stafford County, Virginia	45.9	16.7	22.6	9.1	5.8	0.2	7.6	3.2
51181	Surry County, Virginia	23.1	15.3	22.9	15.4	23.3	2.6	10.9	16.1
51183	Sussex County, Virginia	26.1	20.6	25.3	14.0	14.0	5.2	7.7	10.7
51185	Tazewell County, Virginia	28.6	17.5	24.4	14.7	14.8	9.3	3.4	9.4
51187	Warren County, Virginia	32.7	18.2	22.1	16.2	10.7	1.3	12.9	6.1
51191	Washington County, Virginia	34.4	17.1	24.8	7.3	16.4	2.8	5.3	13.5
51193	Westmoreland County, Virginia	29.4	20.0	26.0	14.5	10.1	3.7	10.1	3.9
51195	Wise County, Virginia	33.5	13.6	23.7	16.1	13.1	9.3	5.6	4.9
51197	Wythe County, Virginia	27.8	18.9	23.0	8.7	21.6	4.5	5.6	20.8
51199	York County, Virginia	48.2	14.8	20.6	8.4	8.0	0.4	4.8	9.8
51510	Alexandria city, Virginia	58.1	15.6	17.4	4.0	4.9	0.2	4.2	2.1
51520	Bristol city, Virginia	32.7	24.5	24.7	6.0	12.0	0.5	4.2	11.4
51530	Buena Vista city, Virginia	16.2	28.7	21.1	7.0	26.9	0.0	4.1	22.8
51540	Charlottesville city, Virginia	49.5	22.6	18.4	4.4	5.1	0.8	3.6	3.5
51550	Chesapeake city, Virginia	39.1	15.3	25.2	9.7	10.7	0.5	6.6	9.0
51570	Colonial Heights city, Virginia	35.6	20.0	25.4	9.2	9.9	0.1	6.7	8.7
51580	Covington city, Virginia	18.7	18.8	27.7	13.2	21.7	0.0	8.4	20.0
51590	Danville city, Virginia	31.6	21.0	23.5	5.1	18.7	0.4	4.5	15.1
51595	Emporia city, Virginia	30.5	19.3	21.9	13.7	14.6	2.1	5.8	10.5
51600	Fairfax city, Virginia	51.8	16.4	22.4	6.1	3.3	0.3	5.8	3.4
51610	Falls Church city, Virginia	74.0	9.9	12.1	2.4	1.5	0.0	2.4	3.2
51620	Franklin city, Virginia	30.1	29.9	17.3	9.6	13.1	1.3	7.0	12.4
51630	Fredericksburg city, Virginia	42.1	22.7	23.3	5.5	6.4	0.0	4.8	2.9
51640	Galax city, Virginia	21.6	19.9	24.5	5.1	28.8	1.0	2.9	21.4
51650	Hampton city, Virginia	32.5	19.1	26.1	10.1	12.3	0.4	6.0	11.8
51660	Harrisonburg city, Virginia	34.5	25.4	21.5	7.3	11.4	2.0	4.8	8.6
51670	Hopewell city, Virginia	23.0	18.5	25.9	14.6	18.0	0.1	10.7	11.8
51678	Lexington city, Virginia	46.6	27.5	21.4	1.7	2.8	0.0	2.2	5.3
51680	Lynchburg city, Virginia	38.9	22.1	23.1	5.8	10.2	0.7	4.1	9.4
51683	Manassas city, Virginia	31.5	20.7	25.2	13.4	9.2	0.2	12.0	5.9
51685	Manassas Park city, Virginia	33.6	14.7	26.0	13.7	11.9	0.0	10.1	2.6
51690	Martinsville city, Virginia	25.6	19.8	25.1	5.6	23.9	0.0	4.2	16.3
51700	Newport News city, Virginia	33.1	20.4	24.8	9.5	12.2	0.1	5.1	12.9
51710	Norfolk city, Virginia	32.4	21.4	23.4	11.6	11.1	0.2	7.2	6.8
51720	Norton city, Virginia	33.7	25.3	23.5	6.5	10.9	4.5	2.4	5.1
51730	Petersburg city, Virginia	25.4	27.8	24.9	4.9	17.0	0.2	2.9	10.6
51735	Poquoson city, Virginia	50.0	12.6	21.2	8.0	8.2	0.5	8.9	11.9
51740	Portsmouth city, Virginia	29.9	20.2	24.4	11.8	13.6	0.4	6.6	11.7
51750	Radford city, Virginia	33.5	27.5	24.6	3.5	10.9	0.0	1.5	10.5
51760	Richmond city, Virginia	40.1	21.9	23.1	6.1	8.9	0.3	4.9	5.3
51770	Roanoke city, Virginia	32.1	22.0	23.9	7.9	14.1	0.4	5.1	9.3
51775	Salem city, Virginia	38.3	17.9	26.5	5.1	12.2	0.3	4.5	8.0
51790	Staunton city, Virginia	36.3	20.6	24.0	7.5	11.6	0.6	6.0	6.2
51800	Suffolk city, Virginia	38.1	17.3	21.9	9.4	13.2	1.0	5.8	12.1
51810	Virginia Beach city, Virginia	39.6	17.5	25.8	9.1	8.0	0.4	6.3	6.4
51820	Waynesboro city, Virginia	27.3	20.3	27.6	7.6	17.2	0.0	5.8	12.4
51830	Williamsburg city, Virginia	47.3	22.5	19.0	5.3	6.0	0.0	4.6	3.5
51840	Winchester city, Virginia	34.7	20.9	23.9	8.2	12.3	1.6	6.2	8.6
53000	**Washington**	39.0	17.5	22.6	9.6	11.3	2.6	6.1	10.5
53001	Adams County, Washington	23.9	12.3	16.3	31.1	16.4	31.1	3.3	13.3
53003	Asotin County, Washington	30.3	20.2	25.7	10.6	13.2	1.8	6.7	13.6
53005	Benton County, Washington	37.7	16.4	22.0	12.2	11.8	4.6	8.7	6.9
53007	Chelan County, Washington	29.3	19.5	20.4	16.8	14.0	12.2	6.9	4.6
53009	Clallam County, Washington	29.0	23.6	23.7	11.2	12.5	3.8	6.7	7.1
53011	Clark County, Washington	34.9	17.3	24.7	9.1	14.0	0.8	7.4	12.3
53013	Columbia County, Washington	34.9	27.3	16.3	13.0	8.5	11.0	8.3	5.2
53015	Cowlitz County, Washington	27.3	19.8	22.2	12.5	18.2	3.0	7.0	14.9
53017	Douglas County, Washington	24.9	16.3	21.9	22.2	14.7	16.5	8.3	5.5
53019	Ferry County, Washington	34.6	15.3	17.7	18.4	14.0	12.1	7.4	5.9
53021	Franklin County, Washington	23.8	18.0	18.2	22.0	18.0	15.9	6.6	11.6
53023	Garfield County, Washington	35.6	18.2	24.8	12.7	8.7	16.1	5.8	1.6
53025	Grant County, Washington	27.6	15.9	16.2	25.3	15.1	23.8	4.1	12.2
53027	Grays Harbor County, Washington	25.0	24.9	23.1	11.8	15.1	4.7	6.7	10.4
53029	Island County, Washington	35.1	19.3	22.5	13.0	10.1	1.4	7.5	11.7
53031	Jefferson County, Washington	33.5	21.6	23.7	11.9	9.3	2.3	7.8	8.7
53033	King County, Washington	49.1	15.6	21.1	5.6	8.6	0.6	4.6	10.0
53035	Kitsap County, Washington	37.9	19.1	22.4	10.2	10.4	0.7	6.6	9.8
53037	Kittitas County, Washington	32.2	22.2	22.0	11.2	12.4	5.1	6.8	5.0
53039	Klickitat County, Washington	35.6	16.0	21.1	15.5	11.8	8.9	10.4	11.6

Table C. County—Labor Force, Employment, and Educational Data, 2011–2015—*Continued*

| | | Occupation for employed population age 16 and older | | | | | Industry for employed population age 16 and older | | |
Fips code	State/county	Management, business, science, and arts occupations	Service occupations	Sales and office occupations:	Natural resources, construction, and maintenance occupations	Production, transportation, and material moving occupations:	Agriculture, forestry, fishing and hunting, and mining	Construction	Manufacturing
53041	Lewis County, Washington	25.9	20.1	23.6	12.5	18.0	6.0	6.5	9.8
53043	Lincoln County, Washington	35.3	17.7	20.1	16.7	10.1	17.2	9.2	4.9
53045	Mason County, Washington	27.6	22.0	23.6	14.7	12.0	7.6	6.5	10.3
53047	Okanogan County, Washington	30.8	20.3	18.8	17.5	12.5	15.3	8.4	3.8
53049	Pacific County, Washington	26.7	22.5	18.8	14.6	17.5	7.4	5.8	13.3
53051	Pend Oreille County, Washington	33.1	19.4	19.2	14.7	13.6	4.1	9.2	8.3
53053	Pierce County, Washington	33.3	18.3	24.7	10.6	13.1	0.7	7.5	9.9
53055	San Juan County, Washington	37.7	22.0	19.1	13.7	7.5	3.6	11.9	4.5
53057	Skagit County, Washington	31.6	20.0	22.1	12.0	14.2	3.9	8.1	12.0
53059	Skamania County, Washington	34.8	16.7	19.3	13.0	16.2	3.9	9.6	12.3
53061	Snohomish County, Washington	37.2	17.4	23.3	10.5	11.6	0.8	7.1	16.8
53063	Spokane County, Washington	35.8	19.2	26.0	7.6	11.4	1.1	5.6	8.4
53065	Stevens County, Washington	29.0	17.9	23.9	15.5	13.7	5.9	9.1	9.1
53067	Thurston County, Washington	40.0	18.1	24.0	8.4	9.5	1.5	6.1	5.7
53069	Wahkiakum County, Washington	28.0	17.6	19.5	15.4	19.6	10.2	6.1	8.4
53071	Walla Walla County, Washington	35.2	21.1	22.3	11.9	9.4	7.0	5.4	6.4
53073	Whatcom County, Washington	34.0	20.2	23.9	10.3	11.6	3.9	6.1	10.8
53075	Whitman County, Washington	46.8	19.7	18.9	6.7	7.7	4.8	2.3	7.1
53077	Yakima County, Washington	24.8	16.9	21.1	21.0	16.2	15.6	5.1	8.2
54000	**West Virginia**	32.2	18.8	24.2	11.9	12.9	5.1	6.2	8.1
54001	Barbour County, West Virginia	21.3	21.1	28.8	15.2	13.6	6.2	8.7	6.8
54003	Berkeley County, West Virginia	32.6	17.1	24.2	10.0	16.1	1.2	6.6	9.6
54005	Boone County, West Virginia	26.5	19.6	21.4	20.1	12.5	23.4	3.3	2.4
54007	Braxton County, West Virginia	25.6	20.3	23.3	14.6	16.2	10.5	11.0	5.9
54009	Brooke County, West Virginia	29.8	23.1	21.3	12.3	13.6	1.7	6.4	11.7
54011	Cabell County, West Virginia	37.8	17.9	28.5	5.9	9.8	1.0	4.2	7.7
54013	Calhoun County, West Virginia	23.5	15.8	22.5	26.9	11.4	12.5	14.3	5.7
54015	Clay County, West Virginia	24.2	23.3	16.5	22.2	13.8	10.7	13.6	3.4
54017	Doddridge County, West Virginia	26.5	14.8	26.5	23.5	8.7	16.7	5.8	3.7
54019	Fayette County, West Virginia	27.0	20.8	24.6	15.3	12.3	8.3	6.6	5.9
54021	Gilmer County, West Virginia	31.3	22.0	22.2	16.3	8.2	8.5	4.4	4.8
54023	Grant County, West Virginia	20.9	17.1	20.9	15.3	25.8	5.8	15.0	16.8
54025	Greenbrier County, West Virginia	31.9	19.3	21.6	13.0	14.1	4.5	7.3	7.6
54027	Hampshire County, West Virginia	19.3	19.0	21.3	16.8	23.5	4.1	10.1	15.1
54029	Hancock County, West Virginia	27.3	20.3	23.5	9.5	19.4	1.0	5.4	15.5
54031	Hardy County, West Virginia	20.4	21.1	17.4	12.1	29.1	3.3	6.0	26.6
54033	Harrison County, West Virginia	32.8	18.3	25.0	11.9	12.1	5.6	7.8	5.5
54035	Jackson County, West Virginia	32.0	16.5	25.0	13.4	13.2	4.0	7.6	12.0
54037	Jefferson County, West Virginia	39.9	18.2	22.8	10.5	8.6	1.6	8.0	5.6
54039	Kanawha County, West Virginia	37.9	17.7	26.9	8.2	9.3	2.7	5.0	4.7
54041	Lewis County, West Virginia	24.2	18.3	25.8	17.5	14.2	9.4	8.5	6.8
54043	Lincoln County, West Virginia	23.9	21.5	24.6	15.5	14.5	7.6	6.4	7.4
54045	Logan County, West Virginia	26.3	19.7	21.1	20.3	12.5	17.2	3.7	4.0
54047	McDowell County, West Virginia	23.4	24.9	20.6	18.2	13.0	19.0	2.1	2.0
54049	Marion County, West Virginia	33.1	18.7	23.2	13.4	11.6	7.0	6.0	7.6
54051	Marshall County, West Virginia	28.1	20.0	22.3	15.6	14.0	6.8	8.3	6.1
54053	Mason County, West Virginia	25.3	17.2	22.3	11.7	23.5	2.9	5.0	17.2
54055	Mercer County, West Virginia	31.2	19.3	27.8	10.4	11.2	3.2	5.3	7.1
54057	Mineral County, West Virginia	24.8	18.7	24.6	12.9	19.0	3.1	6.8	18.3
54059	Mingo County, West Virginia	27.7	16.3	19.9	22.5	13.6	20.4	4.2	3.8
54061	Monongalia County, West Virginia	43.0	17.7	23.2	8.9	7.2	3.7	4.7	6.2
54063	Monroe County, West Virginia	27.3	17.2	20.9	12.5	22.1	6.0	6.2	21.4
54065	Morgan County, West Virginia	30.9	19.0	19.0	15.8	15.2	4.3	7.7	9.4
54067	Nicholas County, West Virginia	24.2	18.4	24.5	16.3	16.7	12.5	6.7	7.6
54069	Ohio County, West Virginia	34.0	21.2	25.0	8.3	11.5	2.5	4.5	6.1
54071	Pendleton County, West Virginia	25.9	19.2	18.3	17.8	18.8	7.0	12.2	12.4
54073	Pleasants County, West Virginia	31.2	19.9	15.6	16.8	16.5	5.0	7.7	15.1
54075	Pocahontas County, West Virginia	30.1	22.7	18.5	16.1	12.7	6.7	8.7	7.6
54077	Preston County, West Virginia	26.4	19.3	21.6	16.1	16.6	10.1	7.3	9.8
54079	Putnam County, West Virginia	37.5	15.7	27.8	8.8	10.1	1.4	6.4	10.2
54081	Raleigh County, West Virginia	31.3	20.9	24.0	14.2	9.6	9.5	5.9	3.9
54083	Randolph County, West Virginia	29.1	23.7	23.8	11.5	11.8	3.9	6.6	6.3
54085	Ritchie County, West Virginia	25.1	16.8	22.4	13.7	22.0	10.1	5.8	17.7
54087	Roane County, West Virginia	26.5	16.4	26.5	18.2	12.4	10.0	9.9	5.6
54089	Summers County, West Virginia	29.4	19.3	20.3	14.9	16.2	4.4	11.2	4.6
54091	Taylor County, West Virginia	33.7	19.4	17.6	13.7	15.7	6.9	6.4	8.6
54093	Tucker County, West Virginia	29.6	24.2	16.1	16.0	14.3	8.0	10.5	6.3
54095	Tyler County, West Virginia	25.2	22.5	21.2	11.5	19.5	7.0	4.9	14.8
54097	Upshur County, West Virginia	31.8	18.4	19.8	14.5	15.5	10.2	5.8	8.2
54099	Wayne County, West Virginia	30.1	20.7	23.6	9.6	16.2	1.9	5.2	11.4
54101	Webster County, West Virginia	18.0	27.2	17.4	20.8	16.6	15.3	4.6	10.2
54103	Wetzel County, West Virginia	23.4	21.4	18.7	19.2	17.3	7.0	11.2	8.6
54105	Wirt County, West Virginia	28.1	18.5	17.6	17.7	18.1	3.4	12.1	16.4
54107	Wood County, West Virginia	30.7	18.3	27.9	9.2	13.9	1.6	5.8	11.7
54109	Wyoming County, West Virginia	27.6	17.0	22.4	20.1	12.9	21.9	3.2	2.8

Table C. County—Labor Force, Employment, and Educational Data, 2011–2015—Continued

		Occupation for employed population age 16 and older					Industry for employed population age 16 and older		
Fips code	State/county	Management, business, science, and arts occupations	Service occupations	Sales and office occupations:	Natural resources, construction, and maintenance occupations	Production, transportation, and material moving occupations:	Agriculture, forestry, fishing and hunting, and mining	Construction	Manufacturing
55000	**Wisconsin**	34.5	17.0	23.1	8.5	16.9	2.5	5.3	18.5
55001	Adams County, Wisconsin	23.5	24.9	20.1	11.9	19.6	3.6	7.5	13.8
55003	Ashland County, Wisconsin	30.0	22.0	21.2	12.0	14.8	4.0	7.5	13.2
55005	Barron County, Wisconsin	26.6	17.1	20.6	12.2	23.5	6.1	7.3	24.6
55007	Bayfield County, Wisconsin	34.6	19.2	19.6	13.6	13.0	4.4	10.6	9.5
55009	Brown County, Wisconsin	33.4	16.9	24.6	8.0	17.1	1.8	5.3	18.3
55011	Buffalo County, Wisconsin	31.6	14.8	19.3	14.0	20.3	11.8	7.5	18.6
55013	Burnett County, Wisconsin	26.9	21.5	21.4	13.4	16.8	3.6	9.0	15.8
55015	Calumet County, Wisconsin	33.8	12.3	25.2	8.7	20.0	3.8	4.9	27.1
55017	Chippewa County, Wisconsin	29.5	16.7	21.8	10.6	21.4	4.4	6.2	20.6
55019	Clark County, Wisconsin	28.6	15.0	17.1	13.9	25.4	14.2	6.5	23.7
55021	Columbia County, Wisconsin	31.6	15.4	24.3	11.5	17.1	3.6	7.6	17.6
55023	Crawford County, Wisconsin	24.6	19.2	19.9	11.4	24.9	6.9	7.2	17.6
55025	Dane County, Wisconsin	48.8	15.5	21.7	5.5	8.5	1.4	4.0	9.0
55027	Dodge County, Wisconsin	26.6	16.6	20.4	11.5	24.8	4.5	7.1	27.6
55029	Door County, Wisconsin	31.7	20.2	23.2	10.7	14.1	2.7	7.5	17.4
55031	Douglas County, Wisconsin	29.5	21.2	24.1	9.6	15.5	1.0	6.4	7.8
55033	Dunn County, Wisconsin	31.4	17.8	22.1	9.7	19.1	5.1	5.8	16.3
55035	Eau Claire County, Wisconsin	34.7	17.8	26.4	6.4	14.7	1.5	4.1	11.6
55037	Florence County, Wisconsin	27.2	21.0	19.1	14.3	18.5	4.4	9.0	16.7
55039	Fond du Lac County, Wisconsin	29.3	16.8	21.1	10.4	22.5	4.2	6.6	23.5
55041	Forest County, Wisconsin	29.2	22.2	17.5	15.3	15.9	6.5	8.6	10.8
55043	Grant County, Wisconsin	30.0	16.6	22.1	13.0	18.3	8.8	5.6	15.6
55045	Green County, Wisconsin	31.8	15.0	23.1	11.3	18.9	5.6	7.1	19.5
55047	Green Lake County, Wisconsin	25.8	17.5	19.3	12.6	24.8	6.6	7.0	25.8
55049	Iowa County, Wisconsin	32.4	16.3	23.2	13.4	14.7	7.5	8.0	12.0
55051	Iron County, Wisconsin	27.6	20.6	22.2	14.1	15.5	3.9	7.2	16.0
55053	Jackson County, Wisconsin	26.4	21.8	19.0	13.4	19.4	9.3	6.4	16.6
55055	Jefferson County, Wisconsin	30.5	17.3	22.8	9.7	19.7	3.0	6.3	22.4
55057	Juneau County, Wisconsin	23.9	21.4	22.0	11.4	21.4	4.5	6.2	20.1
55059	Kenosha County, Wisconsin	32.9	18.0	23.9	9.3	15.8	1.4	5.6	19.8
55061	Kewaunee County, Wisconsin	29.3	13.6	20.9	15.4	20.8	9.1	7.6	25.1
55063	La Crosse County, Wisconsin	35.2	19.7	23.5	6.5	15.2	1.1	4.7	13.5
55065	Lafayette County, Wisconsin	30.5	13.3	22.1	15.6	18.5	14.1	7.2	16.4
55067	Langlade County, Wisconsin	25.8	17.2	24.1	13.8	19.1	7.9	7.3	16.1
55069	Lincoln County, Wisconsin	25.9	16.4	24.6	10.4	22.7	2.8	5.4	23.2
55071	Manitowoc County, Wisconsin	27.3	17.6	20.5	9.9	24.7	3.2	5.3	30.3
55073	Marathon County, Wisconsin	33.6	14.0	24.2	8.7	19.4	4.0	4.8	20.3
55075	Marinette County, Wisconsin	24.9	17.5	19.9	12.3	25.5	3.6	6.7	27.6
55077	Marquette County, Wisconsin	22.5	19.2	20.4	13.5	24.4	5.8	6.4	24.7
55078	Menominee County, Wisconsin	25.5	30.8	20.0	9.8	13.9	5.0	1.8	11.3
55079	Milwaukee County, Wisconsin	35.3	20.1	23.4	5.9	15.3	0.4	3.6	14.9
55081	Monroe County, Wisconsin	28.0	18.3	21.5	10.4	21.8	5.0	5.2	17.4
55083	Oconto County, Wisconsin	27.8	15.6	19.8	14.4	22.5	4.5	8.3	22.8
55085	Oneida County, Wisconsin	30.9	18.9	24.9	10.3	15.0	2.1	6.6	13.3
55087	Outagamie County, Wisconsin	33.0	14.7	24.9	8.8	18.6	1.2	6.0	23.2
55089	Ozaukee County, Wisconsin	46.5	14.0	22.5	6.8	10.1	1.6	4.0	18.8
55091	Pepin County, Wisconsin	31.8	15.1	21.1	13.8	18.2	12.1	8.7	14.5
55093	Pierce County, Wisconsin	31.8	18.4	20.4	11.5	18.0	4.7	6.6	19.2
55095	Polk County, Wisconsin	29.1	16.3	20.8	12.5	21.3	4.5	7.3	22.5
55097	Portage County, Wisconsin	31.7	17.8	25.8	8.7	16.1	3.7	5.0	13.8
55099	Price County, Wisconsin	28.4	17.6	17.1	11.1	25.8	5.5	4.2	31.2
55101	Racine County, Wisconsin	32.5	17.0	22.8	9.1	18.6	1.4	6.0	22.4
55103	Richland County, Wisconsin	26.0	17.5	20.4	12.8	23.3	8.0	7.1	23.2
55105	Rock County, Wisconsin	30.0	17.5	22.0	9.3	21.2	1.8	5.9	22.1
55107	Rusk County, Wisconsin	24.0	14.3	23.2	13.1	25.4	7.7	6.5	25.5
55109	St. Croix County, Wisconsin	36.7	14.8	24.6	9.3	14.6	2.3	6.6	18.2
55111	Sauk County, Wisconsin	28.3	19.8	24.5	10.3	17.1	3.9	6.0	16.6
55113	Sawyer County, Wisconsin	30.6	21.0	23.8	11.1	13.5	2.8	7.2	8.8
55115	Shawano County, Wisconsin	27.5	17.4	22.7	11.8	20.6	7.5	6.2	20.6
55117	Sheboygan County, Wisconsin	29.1	17.2	21.7	8.0	24.0	2.0	4.7	32.2
55119	Taylor County, Wisconsin	27.7	11.7	17.8	14.1	28.7	10.6	7.0	27.8
55121	Trempealeau County, Wisconsin	30.3	14.3	18.3	11.7	25.4	8.1	6.0	28.0
55123	Vernon County, Wisconsin	30.4	17.8	20.6	12.6	18.6	8.2	7.2	16.5
55125	Vilas County, Wisconsin	31.2	21.2	25.2	13.9	8.4	2.2	11.6	5.1
55127	Walworth County, Wisconsin	30.2	18.7	23.3	10.4	17.4	2.4	7.2	19.8
55129	Washburn County, Wisconsin	28.2	19.6	21.9	11.9	18.5	4.4	7.3	17.3
55131	Washington County, Wisconsin	35.4	14.0	25.1	8.7	16.8	1.5	5.9	23.2
55133	Waukesha County, Wisconsin	43.6	13.1	25.5	6.6	11.1	0.5	5.2	18.7
55135	Waupaca County, Wisconsin	25.3	17.9	19.3	11.5	26.0	4.9	6.5	29.0
55137	Waushara County, Wisconsin	24.8	18.6	18.1	14.4	24.0	6.8	7.7	20.3
55139	Winnebago County, Wisconsin	30.1	17.6	24.7	7.0	20.5	1.0	4.0	25.0
55141	Wood County, Wisconsin	30.4	16.5	22.7	10.0	20.4	3.2	5.8	19.2
56000	**Wyoming**	32.5	17.7	21.3	16.0	12.4	12.7	7.6	4.0
56001	Albany County, Wyoming	42.0	20.3	20.7	9.4	7.7	4.1	5.4	2.7
56003	Big Horn County, Wyoming	32.4	17.4	18.1	19.3	12.8	17.9	11.4	8.2

Table C. County—Labor Force, Employment, and Educational Data, 2011–2015—*Continued*

Fips code	State/county	Occupation for employed population age 16 and older					Industry for employed population age 16 and older		
		Management, business, science, and arts occupations	Service occupations	Sales and office occupations:	Natural resources, construction, and maintenance occupations	Production, transportation, and material moving occupations:	Agriculture, forestry, fishing and hunting, and mining	Construction	Manufacturing
56005	Campbell County, Wyoming	25.0	14.4	21.7	24.0	14.9	25.7	7.2	2.1
56007	Carbon County, Wyoming	28.6	19.5	16.4	16.5	19.0	16.6	5.3	8.7
56009	Converse County, Wyoming	26.6	19.0	19.4	21.6	13.4	22.0	7.1	1.2
56011	Crook County, Wyoming	28.3	13.2	20.6	23.1	14.8	25.5	9.0	4.4
56013	Fremont County, Wyoming	33.5	20.0	20.7	15.3	10.5	11.1	8.3	1.5
56015	Goshen County, Wyoming	33.6	20.3	18.2	13.5	14.4	11.0	6.8	7.3
56017	Hot Springs County, Wyoming	36.3	16.6	23.3	15.4	8.4	12.4	6.2	2.4
56019	Johnson County, Wyoming	32.5	19.7	17.3	22.0	8.4	23.5	11.7	0.9
56021	Laramie County, Wyoming	37.2	16.0	23.9	11.4	11.6	3.7	7.2	4.0
56023	Lincoln County, Wyoming	30.6	16.4	19.9	20.7	12.3	13.7	11.4	3.4
56025	Natrona County, Wyoming	29.8	17.1	24.9	14.6	13.5	10.3	7.9	5.5
56027	Niobrara County, Wyoming	38.8	17.0	20.9	10.9	12.5	17.5	10.1	2.0
56029	Park County, Wyoming	30.3	22.0	22.9	16.7	8.2	14.4	8.0	2.1
56031	Platte County, Wyoming	32.5	18.2	19.5	16.6	13.2	11.7	5.6	0.7
56033	Sheridan County, Wyoming	38.7	18.1	19.7	12.3	11.3	10.2	10.3	2.7
56035	Sublette County, Wyoming	37.9	12.7	12.8	18.4	18.3	35.0	5.1	2.5
56037	Sweetwater County, Wyoming	25.4	15.2	20.6	23.1	15.7	18.6	7.8	7.2
56039	Teton County, Wyoming	39.1	25.7	19.6	9.3	6.3	4.2	6.4	1.5
56041	Uinta County, Wyoming	30.1	18.3	19.1	16.7	15.8	11.5	7.1	5.8
56043	Washakie County, Wyoming	29.3	18.2	19.3	20.4	12.7	14.4	7.3	9.9
56045	Weston County, Wyoming	32.1	12.6	14.1	22.7	18.6	28.0	5.4	7.1

Table C. County—Labor Force, Employment, and Educational Data, 2011–2015

		Industry for employed population age 16 and older								
Fips code	State/county	Wholesale trade	Retail trade	Transportation and warehousing, and utilities	Information	Finance and insurance, and real estate and rental and leasing	Professional, scientific, and management, and administrative and waste management services	Educational services, and health care and social assistance	Arts, entertainment, and recreation, and accommodation and food services	Other services, except public administration
00000	**United States**	2.7	11.6	5.0	2.1	6.6	11.0	23.1	9.6	4.9
01000	**Alabama**	2.5	12.0	5.2	1.7	5.6	9.3	22.5	8.3	5.2
01001	Autauga County, Alabama	3.4	11.2	5.9	1.2	5.2	7.7	18.8	7.9	6.4
01003	Baldwin County, Alabama	2.8	15.2	4.6	1.6	6.4	9.8	19.9	11.4	4.9
01005	Barbour County, Alabama	2.8	12.7	5.7	0.5	3.4	6.0	19.6	6.7	3.7
01007	Bibb County, Alabama	2.4	9.9	5.3	0.3	3.0	5.4	22.7	5.4	6.6
01009	Blount County, Alabama	3.5	11.6	7.0	1.3	4.2	6.5	20.8	5.5	7.0
01011	Bullock County, Alabama	1.1	11.9	3.0	0.7	5.0	4.2	15.7	3.7	3.5
01013	Butler County, Alabama	1.6	14.1	5.2	1.6	3.0	5.1	21.6	6.8	4.7
01015	Calhoun County, Alabama	2.2	12.0	4.7	1.5	3.8	7.8	22.1	9.4	4.6
01017	Chambers County, Alabama	2.4	11.7	3.2	1.7	3.7	11.7	18.5	6.1	4.6
01019	Cherokee County, Alabama	2.1	11.1	6.8	0.9	2.1	4.8	23.4	6.4	5.0
01021	Chilton County, Alabama	2.3	13.4	7.3	1.1	6.1	6.7	15.8	5.3	6.3
01023	Choctaw County, Alabama	0.8	10.6	6.1	1.8	2.4	4.8	24.9	2.9	4.9
01025	Clarke County, Alabama	1.4	17.4	6.2	1.5	4.2	6.3	16.9	5.8	4.8
01027	Clay County, Alabama	0.8	10.3	4.3	2.2	3.4	5.1	16.6	3.6	4.1
01029	Cleburne County, Alabama	2.0	14.1	5.8	0.7	2.9	4.4	18.2	6.3	4.0
01031	Coffee County, Alabama	1.5	13.9	5.9	1.0	3.4	7.9	22.0	8.8	5.5
01033	Colbert County, Alabama	2.2	13.2	6.0	1.0	5.8	9.2	19.4	8.0	5.5
01035	Conecuh County, Alabama	0.8	13.5	7.4	1.2	3.3	2.9	21.4	7.5	5.1
01037	Coosa County, Alabama	1.8	9.0	10.8	0.6	2.7	8.8	15.1	7.5	5.1
01039	Covington County, Alabama	1.8	12.9	7.8	1.2	4.5	9.0	17.5	5.0	5.0
01041	Crenshaw County, Alabama	4.4	10.6	5.6	1.1	4.4	6.2	18.9	2.7	4.9
01043	Cullman County, Alabama	3.3	13.4	5.3	1.5	4.7	7.4	21.1	6.4	6.3
01045	Dale County, Alabama	2.2	14.5	10.2	1.1	4.1	7.3	19.3	8.8	5.1
01047	Dallas County, Alabama	1.5	11.4	5.0	1.0	3.4	5.0	23.7	5.1	7.7
01049	DeKalb County, Alabama	2.6	11.6	5.2	1.0	3.0	5.1	17.2	6.7	5.1
01051	Elmore County, Alabama	2.5	10.8	4.9	1.3	5.9	9.0	19.9	7.6	4.7
01053	Escambia County, Alabama	2.3	11.5	7.6	1.5	4.0	5.1	21.8	9.3	5.9
01055	Etowah County, Alabama	3.1	11.0	5.6	1.6	4.2	5.7	24.1	8.6	5.0
01057	Fayette County, Alabama	1.0	10.7	7.0	1.3	3.6	4.1	23.9	6.6	3.5
01059	Franklin County, Alabama	2.6	9.8	6.3	1.7	2.9	3.6	19.5	5.4	3.2
01061	Geneva County, Alabama	5.5	9.9	8.3	0.7	3.4	6.5	19.9	6.8	5.6
01063	Greene County, Alabama	0.0	12.9	7.0	0.2	2.3	4.4	25.2	9.4	4.1
01065	Hale County, Alabama	1.9	15.7	3.6	0.2	3.7	7.5	25.5	3.5	3.5
01067	Henry County, Alabama	3.6	8.9	9.9	0.6	4.7	5.8	24.9	9.1	5.5
01069	Houston County, Alabama	3.8	14.2	8.3	1.4	4.2	7.6	23.6	9.3	5.6
01071	Jackson County, Alabama	1.5	11.6	6.5	0.9	4.5	5.3	19.3	6.0	4.1
01073	Jefferson County, Alabama	3.1	10.7	5.4	2.2	8.8	10.5	26.2	8.8	5.7
01075	Lamar County, Alabama	2.5	9.8	7.6	2.4	4.2	6.4	18.6	7.3	6.1
01077	Lauderdale County, Alabama	3.3	14.9	7.1	1.1	4.3	7.3	21.4	9.5	5.0
01079	Lawrence County, Alabama	1.6	9.9	5.9	0.9	2.7	6.7	17.8	5.8	5.6
01081	Lee County, Alabama	1.4	12.6	3.4	1.6	5.9	8.2	29.1	10.2	4.7
01083	Limestone County, Alabama	2.4	11.6	4.5	1.4	4.3	13.7	18.9	6.6	5.1
01085	Lowndes County, Alabama	3.9	10.5	6.3	2.2	3.5	4.6	19.9	6.0	2.6
01087	Macon County, Alabama	0.9	9.8	3.3	0.7	2.8	3.6	33.6	10.6	5.6
01089	Madison County, Alabama	1.6	10.9	3.1	2.8	3.7	18.2	20.2	8.3	5.1
01091	Marengo County, Alabama	2.1	12.8	9.7	0.8	2.5	4.2	24.9	5.1	5.3
01093	Marion County, Alabama	2.6	9.6	5.9	0.5	4.3	4.0	24.6	5.4	8.4
01095	Marshall County, Alabama	2.5	12.5	4.5	1.4	4.0	7.5	19.1	6.8	5.3
01097	Mobile County, Alabama	2.9	13.0	5.3	1.7	5.2	9.7	24.1	9.0	5.5
01099	Monroe County, Alabama	2.3	13.2	6.9	1.0	3.1	4.7	17.7	9.3	4.5
01101	Montgomery County, Alabama	1.9	11.9	3.5	1.3	5.9	10.1	21.8	10.6	5.3
01103	Morgan County, Alabama	2.2	13.9	4.0	1.1	3.9	9.3	18.3	7.7	5.2
01105	Perry County, Alabama	0.2	8.4	5.0	0.5	3.8	3.7	28.4	9.2	3.7
01107	Pickens County, Alabama	3.2	11.9	6.8	0.6	5.2	3.8	22.2	4.8	4.9
01109	Pike County, Alabama	1.6	14.5	6.2	2.1	4.0	4.9	24.6	7.7	5.3
01111	Randolph County, Alabama	1.7	9.0	6.3	1.8	4.7	5.8	18.9	5.4	5.0
01113	Russell County, Alabama	1.3	10.5	4.2	1.9	8.9	7.4	22.5	8.9	5.4
01115	St. Clair County, Alabama	3.8	13.2	7.0	2.2	6.9	8.1	17.3	6.2	4.9
01117	Shelby County, Alabama	3.0	12.0	5.0	3.5	10.9	12.2	21.3	7.5	5.6
01119	Sumter County, Alabama	1.5	10.4	6.3	0.8	3.4	6.0	27.1	13.4	4.1
01121	Talladega County, Alabama	2.5	11.6	5.6	1.2	4.2	6.9	21.0	8.0	3.8
01123	Tallapoosa County, Alabama	1.8	10.3	4.3	0.9	5.1	6.0	25.1	4.9	3.5
01125	Tuscaloosa County, Alabama	2.2	10.9	3.8	1.7	4.5	6.9	30.1	9.7	4.8
01127	Walker County, Alabama	2.1	15.1	7.5	1.3	4.2	5.8	23.4	7.3	5.4
01129	Washington County, Alabama	3.0	10.0	7.7	0.5	2.4	2.8	18.8	4.6	3.0
01131	Wilcox County, Alabama	0.8	9.2	8.2	2.2	4.8	6.0	21.4	5.6	4.1
01133	Winston County, Alabama	3.5	11.6	7.0	0.5	3.8	4.5	20.2	5.1	6.9
02000	**Alaska**	1.9	11.0	7.7	2.0	4.1	8.5	23.3	9.0	4.4
02013	Aleutians East Borough, Alaska	0.1	2.3	3.2	0.4	0.5	2.1	6.6	2.2	1.2
02016	Aleutians West Census Area, Alaska	2.0	7.6	14.6	1.2	1.7	3.8	8.0	2.8	2.9
02020	Anchorage Municipality, Alaska	2.6	11.0	7.5	2.4	5.2	11.0	23.0	10.5	4.4
02050	Bethel Census Area, Alaska	0.3	11.9	11.9	1.9	3.6	2.9	35.5	3.5	3.9

Table C. County—Labor Force, Employment, and Educational Data, 2011–2015—*Continued*

Fips code	State/county	Wholesale trade	Retail trade	Transportation and warehousing, and utilities	Information	Finance and insurance, and real estate and rental and leasing	Professional, scientific, and management, and administrative and waste management services	Educational services, and health care and social assistance	Arts, entertainment, and recreation, and accommodation and food services	Other services, except public administration
02060	Bristol Bay Borough, Alaska	1.1	7.4	16.8	4.1	2.0	4.3	18.7	11.3	2.4
02068	Denali Borough, Alaska	0.0	3.9	8.8	0.6	0.9	3.9	12.1	43.5	3.6
02070	Dillingham Census Area, Alaska	0.3	10.5	8.7	1.3	2.6	5.2	36.1	2.5	4.2
02090	Fairbanks North Star Borough, Alaska	1.3	13.3	7.3	1.4	3.2	7.8	26.0	9.1	4.5
02100	Haines Borough, Alaska	1.6	14.3	7.1	0.9	3.3	7.9	23.0	12.9	4.4
02105	Hoonah-Angoon Census Area, Alaska	0.0	8.9	11.0	3.1	1.4	5.4	15.0	15.7	2.7
02110	Juneau City and Borough, Alaska	1.4	8.7	8.3	2.3	4.0	7.4	20.3	6.6	5.1
02122	Kenai Peninsula Borough, Alaska	1.6	12.1	6.4	1.2	3.3	6.6	23.0	9.4	5.1
02130	Ketchikan Gateway Borough, Alaska	1.1	14.3	11.9	2.5	5.2	4.1	20.8	6.0	4.2
02150	Kodiak Island Borough, Alaska	2.2	11.9	6.3	0.9	4.5	7.4	19.3	8.7	3.3
02158	Kusilvak Census Area, Alaska	0.2	12.7	8.6	1.6	2.9	2.0	34.7	1.5	3.1
02164	Lake and Peninsula Borough, Alaska	0.8	3.0	8.7	0.9	0.6	3.8	28.0	7.0	2.4
02170	Matanuska-Susitna Borough, Alaska	1.8	11.3	7.6	2.2	3.4	7.7	23.1	8.2	4.8
02180	Nome Census Area, Alaska	0.6	8.3	8.4	0.7	2.8	2.2	38.5	5.9	4.0
02185	North Slope Borough, Alaska	1.2	5.7	7.5	0.4	2.5	15.2	12.2	3.5	1.1
02188	Northwest Arctic Borough, Alaska	0.6	8.8	12.8	1.5	3.5	5.1	31.5	4.6	3.2
02195	Petersburg Borough, Alaska	0.5	8.8	3.3	1.9	2.8	2.2	19.5	5.1	4.7
02198	Prince of Wales-Hyder Census Area, Alaska	1.0	11.7	8.3	0.9	2.8	2.4	23.5	7.1	2.7
02220	Sitka City and Borough, Alaska	0.9	8.8	5.9	1.8	2.5	5.0	30.9	10.3	5.6
02230	Skagway Municipality, Alaska	0.3	14.2	21.9	0.9	2.2	2.7	8.6	16.4	2.1
02240	Southeast Fairbanks Census Area, Alaska	4.1	6.5	6.9	1.7	0.8	3.6	22.5	3.0	4.7
02261	Valdez-Cordova Census Area, Alaska	0.5	4.6	7.9	4.0	3.3	7.7	23.4	8.8	2.7
02275	Wrangell City and Borough, Alaska	0.7	12.0	11.7	1.5	1.7	3.0	30.4	4.4	3.6
02282	Yakutat City and Borough, Alaska	0.5	10.4	8.0	1.1	2.1	6.7	13.9	8.8	0.8
02290	Yukon-Koyukuk Census Area, Alaska	0.6	6.2	11.5	0.9	1.0	2.3	27.4	4.8	4.7
04000	**Arizona**	2.4	12.2	4.9	1.8	8.1	11.9	22.1	10.8	4.8
04001	Apache County, Arizona	0.9	10.3	6.8	0.9	3.0	3.5	37.7	8.3	3.3
04003	Cochise County, Arizona	1.3	11.6	4.2	1.4	4.2	11.3	22.0	10.8	3.9
04005	Coconino County, Arizona	1.2	12.1	4.4	1.0	3.9	6.5	27.7	19.1	3.4
04007	Gila County, Arizona	1.2	12.8	3.7	0.9	3.6	7.0	24.9	12.5	4.5
04009	Graham County, Arizona	0.9	13.4	3.2	1.1	3.6	6.0	25.0	9.6	5.7
04011	Greenlee County, Arizona	1.6	4.6	2.4	0.9	1.5	3.7	14.8	6.8	2.1
04012	La Paz County, Arizona	1.4	10.9	5.2	0.6	5.3	4.5	14.0	17.6	4.9
04013	Maricopa County, Arizona	2.7	12.4	5.1	1.9	9.7	13.0	21.0	10.0	4.8
04015	Mohave County, Arizona	1.4	14.5	6.2	1.6	4.4	6.5	20.2	19.7	4.9
04017	Navajo County, Arizona	1.1	13.2	7.2	1.4	3.4	4.5	28.1	12.6	3.7
04019	Pima County, Arizona	1.8	11.5	4.0	1.6	5.7	11.9	25.5	11.5	5.4
04021	Pinal County, Arizona	1.7	11.4	4.6	1.8	7.0	9.8	21.4	9.9	4.1
04023	Santa Cruz County, Arizona	9.6	17.5	7.4	0.9	3.9	8.7	18.8	7.0	3.8
04025	Yavapai County, Arizona	1.9	12.7	4.6	1.5	4.6	9.5	24.5	13.9	6.1
04027	Yuma County, Arizona	3.0	11.5	3.8	1.2	3.6	8.9	20.0	10.5	5.1
05000	**Arkansas**	2.4	13.5	5.5	1.7	4.8	7.2	24.2	7.9	4.8
05001	Arkansas County, Arkansas	4.7	12.5	4.6	0.7	2.9	4.7	18.0	4.8	4.1
05003	Ashley County, Arkansas	1.3	12.5	5.8	1.3	2.9	4.7	24.3	3.7	5.5
05005	Baxter County, Arkansas	1.6	13.4	3.0	1.6	5.6	7.4	27.9	8.8	4.2
05007	Benton County, Arkansas	2.7	24.1	5.0	1.1	4.6	10.2	16.9	6.8	3.9
05009	Boone County, Arkansas	1.7	11.6	12.6	1.7	4.7	5.6	19.2	12.2	6.4
05011	Bradley County, Arkansas	2.3	13.0	3.6	0.5	4.7	4.7	26.0	3.6	3.4
05013	Calhoun County, Arkansas	1.6	8.9	6.9	2.5	1.2	6.0	20.0	2.1	5.6
05015	Carroll County, Arkansas	0.7	10.2	5.5	1.2	5.0	4.6	17.2	9.9	4.9
05017	Chicot County, Arkansas	1.8	14.1	5.0	0.0	2.5	4.9	24.3	8.5	1.8
05019	Clark County, Arkansas	0.8	11.9	3.5	0.8	4.3	5.4	29.7	12.3	4.3
05021	Clay County, Arkansas	2.2	13.6	6.4	1.1	1.7	5.0	22.7	5.0	5.5
05023	Cleburne County, Arkansas	2.7	14.9	5.9	1.1	5.0	5.8	20.1	8.7	3.5
05025	Cleveland County, Arkansas	2.2	9.0	7.1	0.4	4.4	5.8	25.8	2.9	3.7
05027	Columbia County, Arkansas	1.8	13.0	3.5	0.7	2.9	4.4	26.5	8.9	3.8
05029	Conway County, Arkansas	3.2	10.4	6.0	2.2	7.3	5.5	22.1	6.0	3.3
05031	Craighead County, Arkansas	2.6	13.3	4.4	1.7	4.8	5.8	28.4	9.2	4.5
05033	Crawford County, Arkansas	2.4	11.5	5.4	0.7	5.0	6.6	25.9	6.3	5.4
05035	Crittenden County, Arkansas	4.1	12.1	10.1	1.2	4.0	6.9	25.4	9.5	4.4
05037	Cross County, Arkansas	2.5	15.1	6.8	0.4	4.5	4.4	24.3	4.9	4.7
05039	Dallas County, Arkansas	0.9	11.7	5.9	0.5	4.2	5.2	24.8	5.6	2.9
05041	Desha County, Arkansas	0.4	12.9	4.8	1.1	2.4	2.8	24.7	6.8	5.1
05043	Drew County, Arkansas	1.7	14.4	1.4	0.4	3.9	5.0	31.4	8.8	4.7
05045	Faulkner County, Arkansas	2.5	13.4	4.3	2.9	5.7	9.1	24.9	8.7	4.3
05047	Franklin County, Arkansas	2.2	10.2	6.6	0.7	3.4	4.4	23.6	5.6	3.5
05049	Fulton County, Arkansas	3.8	11.7	8.9	0.3	3.6	5.8	24.1	6.7	8.6
05051	Garland County, Arkansas	2.2	14.5	4.3	1.7	4.8	8.8	25.0	12.6	4.7
05053	Grant County, Arkansas	2.6	9.3	9.5	1.6	4.2	5.8	22.9	6.0	4.1
05055	Greene County, Arkansas	3.5	12.3	5.8	1.1	3.9	4.3	24.0	5.9	4.8
05057	Hempstead County, Arkansas	1.2	8.9	6.1	0.8	4.1	5.5	23.0	6.0	3.0
05059	Hot Spring County, Arkansas	2.1	13.0	6.2	1.0	3.7	6.9	24.7	9.4	4.3
05061	Howard County, Arkansas	1.8	11.9	3.8	1.1	2.8	1.9	19.8	6.3	4.6

Table C. County—Labor Force, Employment, and Educational Data, 2011–2015—*Continued*

		Industry for employed population age 16 and older								
Fips code	State/county	Wholesale trade	Retail trade	Transportation and warehousing, and utilities	Information	Finance and insurance, and real estate and rental and leasing	Professional, scientific, and management, and administrative and waste management services	Educational services, and health care and social assistance	Arts, entertainment, and recreation, and accommodation and food services	Other services, except public administration
05063	Independence County, Arkansas	2.3	10.5	5.6	1.9	4.3	4.1	24.6	8.4	4.8
05065	Izard County, Arkansas	3.3	11.3	3.6	1.4	5.4	3.9	26.5	4.9	6.8
05067	Jackson County, Arkansas	2.2	13.1	9.7	0.6	4.6	4.9	18.4	4.8	3.6
05069	Jefferson County, Arkansas	2.9	10.4	5.4	1.1	4.1	6.3	27.9	5.8	4.5
05071	Johnson County, Arkansas	1.1	11.9	5.7	0.5	2.9	3.2	23.4	5.2	3.4
05073	Lafayette County, Arkansas	1.9	9.1	4.8	0.8	4.1	1.6	25.0	3.9	7.7
05075	Lawrence County, Arkansas	1.9	10.7	7.0	1.3	2.6	2.9	28.0	6.9	4.0
05077	Lee County, Arkansas	1.1	12.2	2.8	1.2	3.6	8.5	22.9	4.8	3.5
05079	Lincoln County, Arkansas	0.2	8.0	5.5	0.8	2.8	6.1	28.1	5.8	4.9
05081	Little River County, Arkansas	0.9	11.7	7.2	0.5	2.6	6.5	24.1	7.0	3.3
05083	Logan County, Arkansas	2.0	11.2	4.4	1.8	3.5	4.0	27.4	4.5	4.2
05085	Lonoke County, Arkansas	3.3	12.7	6.3	1.6	5.2	7.0	24.2	6.9	5.3
05087	Madison County, Arkansas	1.6	10.2	7.4	1.7	2.7	5.5	18.8	4.3	4.4
05089	Marion County, Arkansas	1.6	11.9	3.5	1.9	2.1	8.1	21.8	8.7	5.4
05091	Miller County, Arkansas	3.3	14.6	6.0	1.7	4.5	7.1	22.1	7.2	5.7
05093	Mississippi County, Arkansas	2.3	12.4	4.8	1.7	3.2	4.3	21.2	5.8	3.9
05095	Monroe County, Arkansas	4.3	10.2	5.8	0.5	3.4	5.6	18.9	9.5	2.8
05097	Montgomery County, Arkansas	1.9	6.1	6.0	0.3	2.5	5.9	20.9	10.7	7.1
05099	Nevada County, Arkansas	4.3	14.5	7.2	0.2	2.7	1.6	25.3	4.6	5.5
05101	Newton County, Arkansas	1.4	13.0	10.9	1.4	3.8	4.1	23.7	8.4	3.5
05103	Ouachita County, Arkansas	1.6	11.4	3.9	1.1	3.0	6.7	22.5	4.9	4.6
05105	Perry County, Arkansas	3.1	10.2	6.7	2.6	4.9	8.0	17.4	6.5	8.1
05107	Phillips County, Arkansas	3.3	12.2	6.9	0.6	1.6	3.2	29.2	14.7	3.5
05109	Pike County, Arkansas	2.9	10.0	4.8	0.2	3.8	3.1	21.7	9.2	4.0
05111	Poinsett County, Arkansas	2.3	11.7	5.3	1.8	4.5	5.2	20.3	6.5	6.2
05113	Polk County, Arkansas	1.5	14.1	5.3	0.6	4.2	5.1	24.3	6.2	4.8
05115	Pope County, Arkansas	1.9	11.2	7.3	1.7	4.0	7.3	23.7	8.7	6.2
05117	Prairie County, Arkansas	3.4	13.0	8.7	0.2	4.1	7.2	18.7	4.7	4.0
05119	Pulaski County, Arkansas	2.3	12.2	5.1	3.3	7.3	9.3	27.6	8.8	5.2
05121	Randolph County, Arkansas	1.3	10.2	7.5	1.2	3.8	1.9	31.8	6.0	4.4
05123	St. Francis County, Arkansas	4.2	12.5	6.1	1.8	1.7	5.6	24.1	6.4	5.6
05125	Saline County, Arkansas	3.3	14.1	4.8	2.6	6.2	7.4	24.9	8.1	5.5
05127	Scott County, Arkansas	1.0	10.9	3.5	1.0	3.0	3.2	23.9	3.9	2.9
05129	Searcy County, Arkansas	2.5	14.8	3.9	0.4	5.9	8.0	22.5	3.6	3.8
05131	Sebastian County, Arkansas	3.1	12.5	5.6	1.8	3.9	6.2	23.9	8.1	5.1
05133	Sevier County, Arkansas	1.7	9.7	4.4	0.7	2.3	4.3	16.4	4.4	4.6
05135	Sharp County, Arkansas	1.3	11.6	8.3	1.2	4.5	4.0	25.2	8.1	7.4
05137	Stone County, Arkansas	3.8	10.2	4.3	0.2	2.5	4.4	28.2	11.6	4.2
05139	Union County, Arkansas	2.1	13.3	5.7	1.9	4.4	5.9	23.1	6.9	5.5
05141	Van Buren County, Arkansas	2.1	15.7	7.5	0.2	3.7	6.9	20.7	5.7	4.3
05143	Washington County, Arkansas	2.6	13.0	4.5	1.6	4.9	9.2	24.8	9.7	5.2
05145	White County, Arkansas	1.5	14.5	6.8	1.2	3.6	6.8	27.4	6.7	5.0
05147	Woodruff County, Arkansas	3.2	10.3	6.1	0.7	4.6	1.6	25.1	4.5	4.2
05149	Yell County, Arkansas	1.6	9.4	5.5	1.4	2.6	6.2	19.4	6.2	4.4
06000	**California**	3.1	11.1	4.7	2.9	6.2	12.9	21.0	10.2	5.4
06001	Alameda County, California	2.7	9.7	5.0	3.1	6.1	17.1	22.4	9.1	5.2
06003	Alpine County, California	0.0	12.0	9.3	1.5	1.5	17.9	15.4	13.2	5.4
06005	Amador County, California	1.3	15.0	4.2	1.5	4.2	9.2	19.4	15.3	5.2
06007	Butte County, California	1.8	13.6	2.9	1.8	5.0	9.8	29.0	11.6	5.3
06009	Calaveras County, California	2.3	11.2	5.7	1.2	4.1	10.5	22.1	8.5	5.6
06011	Colusa County, California	1.9	7.0	5.2	0.5	4.2	4.6	13.7	13.1	2.2
06013	Contra Costa County, California	2.4	10.8	4.9	2.8	9.0	15.7	21.9	8.7	5.0
06015	Del Norte County, California	0.6	10.5	1.7	0.8	3.9	7.2	29.2	12.9	4.8
06017	El Dorado County, California	1.7	12.4	4.0	2.1	7.6	11.7	19.7	12.6	4.8
06019	Fresno County, California	4.0	10.7	4.7	1.3	4.8	8.1	23.6	8.8	4.9
06021	Glenn County, California	2.1	10.0	5.5	0.8	2.6	6.6	21.5	7.8	5.4
06023	Humboldt County, California	1.9	12.9	3.7	1.6	4.2	8.4	26.7	12.7	5.0
06025	Imperial County, California	2.7	13.7	6.5	0.9	3.0	6.3	25.1	6.9	4.0
06027	Inyo County, California	1.0	13.2	6.5	1.6	2.5	5.2	22.0	18.3	5.5
06029	Kern County, California	3.0	10.8	5.2	1.1	3.7	8.0	19.5	8.6	4.4
06031	Kings County, California	2.4	8.2	3.9	0.8	2.2	5.9	22.0	9.8	4.2
06033	Lake County, California	2.6	10.5	5.9	1.0	4.2	7.4	25.0	11.0	5.8
06035	Lassen County, California	1.7	8.3	4.4	1.5	3.4	3.5	19.2	7.4	2.0
06037	Los Angeles County, California	3.5	10.7	5.3	4.4	6.3	12.5	20.6	10.8	6.2
06039	Madera County, California	2.4	9.7	4.7	1.5	3.0	6.8	19.3	8.2	4.4
06041	Marin County, California	2.4	10.3	2.5	3.7	10.2	19.9	21.8	9.0	6.2
06043	Mariposa County, California	1.5	10.1	2.1	0.7	2.5	12.3	19.2	22.9	4.3
06045	Mendocino County, California	2.0	14.6	3.0	1.7	4.1	8.3	22.4	11.0	6.2
06047	Merced County, California	3.0	11.1	5.4	1.2	3.6	6.7	22.2	7.3	4.0
06049	Modoc County, California	1.7	10.6	2.7	1.8	0.5	5.3	29.0	6.6	4.5
06051	Mono County, California	0.1	5.1	4.0	0.1	9.1	7.0	20.5	26.0	1.6
06053	Monterey County, California	3.0	10.2	3.2	1.1	3.7	8.8	19.7	12.1	4.8
06055	Napa County, California	2.6	10.1	3.2	1.3	5.4	9.2	21.6	13.5	5.2
06057	Nevada County, California	1.7	10.5	3.7	2.3	5.4	12.6	22.0	12.8	5.9
06059	Orange County, California	3.6	11.0	3.2	2.2	8.6	14.2	19.1	10.7	5.5

Table C. County—Labor Force, Employment, and Educational Data, 2011–2015—*Continued*

		Industry for employed population age 16 and older								
Fips code	State/county	Wholesale trade	Retail trade	Transportation and warehousing, and utilities	Information	Finance and insurance, and real estate and rental and leasing	Professional, scientific, and management, and administrative and waste management services	Educational services, and health care and social assistance	Arts, entertainment, and recreation, and accommodation and food services	Other services, except public administration
06061	Placer County, California	3.1	12.1	4.3	2.4	8.2	12.1	21.8	9.8	4.9
06063	Plumas County, California	1.2	9.8	4.8	0.6	5.3	6.1	22.3	11.7	6.6
06065	Riverside County, California	3.1	13.1	5.5	1.5	5.2	10.0	20.6	11.4	5.3
06067	Sacramento County, California	2.5	11.2	4.9	2.1	7.5	11.7	22.1	9.4	5.1
06069	San Benito County, California	4.0	13.2	3.9	1.3	4.4	7.9	17.6	9.3	4.9
06071	San Bernardino County, California	3.5	13.3	8.0	1.4	5.0	9.0	22.5	8.9	5.2
06073	San Diego County, California	2.5	11.1	3.7	2.3	6.3	14.5	21.3	11.7	5.3
06075	San Francisco County, California	1.8	10.0	3.7	5.5	8.6	22.2	18.7	12.1	4.8
06077	San Joaquin County, California	4.1	12.4	7.0	1.7	4.8	9.4	21.0	8.0	4.8
06079	San Luis Obispo County, California	2.2	11.9	5.1	1.6	4.7	10.6	23.9	12.0	4.9
06081	San Mateo County, California	2.3	10.0	5.4	3.6	7.3	17.9	21.1	9.7	5.3
06083	Santa Barbara County, California	2.3	10.3	3.1	2.1	5.2	11.5	22.9	11.8	5.2
06085	Santa Clara County, California	2.2	9.5	2.8	4.4	4.8	19.0	18.5	7.9	4.2
06087	Santa Cruz County, California	2.6	11.3	2.4	1.9	4.3	12.0	24.0	12.2	5.0
06089	Shasta County, California	1.8	14.1	4.0	1.6	5.3	9.7	25.5	10.0	6.2
06091	Sierra County, California	1.0	6.4	11.3	1.5	1.3	7.1	26.9	3.0	0.7
06093	Siskiyou County, California	1.9	12.0	3.4	1.6	3.7	7.1	25.1	10.4	4.7
06095	Solano County, California	2.7	12.2	5.7	1.8	5.5	9.8	22.9	9.2	4.4
06097	Sonoma County, California	3.0	11.9	3.3	1.8	6.6	11.4	21.2	10.5	5.5
06099	Stanislaus County, California	4.5	13.7	5.6	1.2	3.7	8.6	21.6	8.2	4.8
06101	Sutter County, California	2.4	13.1	5.6	0.9	4.9	7.4	22.5	8.8	4.3
06103	Tehama County, California	2.6	14.0	5.7	1.0	5.5	7.3	20.6	9.3	4.4
06105	Trinity County, California	0.9	8.4	3.1	0.8	6.3	6.4	20.2	20.1	5.4
06107	Tulare County, California	3.9	11.2	4.5	0.8	3.7	6.3	20.5	7.1	4.1
06109	Tuolumne County, California	1.2	11.6	4.9	1.6	3.3	8.8	22.2	15.5	6.3
06111	Ventura County, California	3.4	11.3	3.1	2.6	8.0	12.0	18.6	9.2	4.9
06113	Yolo County, California	2.3	10.0	4.5	1.5	4.3	10.5	30.3	9.7	4.2
06115	Yuba County, California	2.5	12.8	4.8	1.9	3.7	10.7	22.7	9.3	4.1
08000	**Colorado**	2.6	11.1	4.5	3.0	6.9	13.5	20.5	10.8	5.1
08001	Adams County, Colorado	3.6	11.7	7.3	3.0	5.2	11.2	17.1	10.1	5.2
08003	Alamosa County, Colorado	4.5	10.9	6.7	1.3	3.2	2.5	34.8	11.6	5.6
08005	Arapahoe County, Colorado	2.7	11.8	5.4	3.9	9.3	14.6	19.9	9.9	5.2
08007	Archuleta County, Colorado	0.9	11.0	4.2	2.7	6.9	12.1	17.3	13.6	7.2
08009	Baca County, Colorado	0.6	7.1	6.1	0.4	3.3	4.9	33.5	3.1	4.8
08011	Bent County, Colorado	0.4	3.7	4.0	1.9	3.1	6.9	21.8	2.5	5.4
08013	Boulder County, Colorado	2.3	9.6	2.3	3.5	4.9	19.7	23.3	10.8	5.3
08014	Broomfield County, Colorado	3.4	10.2	3.6	4.3	5.8	17.8	21.2	8.2	4.3
08015	Chaffee County, Colorado	1.9	15.0	3.1	2.6	5.9	8.4	19.4	11.7	5.7
08017	Cheyenne County, Colorado	5.0	5.0	8.5	2.0	5.2	3.0	20.1	6.3	3.4
08019	Clear Creek County, Colorado	0.9	11.2	6.2	1.8	5.3	14.1	16.2	12.7	4.4
08021	Conejos County, Colorado	1.8	10.8	5.7	0.9	5.1	5.2	25.3	7.7	4.9
08023	Costilla County, Colorado	1.8	12.7	4.4	0.7	7.6	9.8	20.4	10.8	2.6
08025	Crowley County, Colorado	4.0	24.4	1.6	0.3	1.4	5.1	25.3	6.5	1.6
08027	Custer County, Colorado	0.9	6.4	4.3	0.8	2.7	9.4	17.6	14.5	7.8
08029	Delta County, Colorado	2.2	10.2	4.7	2.3	3.3	5.9	21.3	8.1	5.0
08031	Denver County, Colorado	2.8	9.1	4.2	3.5	8.3	17.4	20.3	11.9	5.0
08033	Dolores County, Colorado	1.1	8.1	5.9	1.5	2.2	2.2	15.9	27.0	2.6
08035	Douglas County, Colorado	3.1	10.7	3.6	5.4	11.8	16.2	18.7	8.1	4.1
08037	Eagle County, Colorado	2.0	11.3	2.6	2.4	8.7	12.5	13.0	24.2	4.4
08039	Elbert County, Colorado	2.1	11.6	6.8	3.7	7.3	13.0	15.9	7.0	5.6
08041	El Paso County, Colorado	2.0	11.3	4.0	2.8	6.6	12.9	21.9	10.8	6.2
08043	Fremont County, Colorado	1.0	13.5	4.0	1.0	5.0	7.6	23.9	9.6	4.5
08045	Garfield County, Colorado	2.7	11.2	3.7	1.9	6.1	11.3	17.3	10.6	5.4
08047	Gilpin County, Colorado	2.7	9.8	6.2	1.3	2.0	7.5	11.0	29.1	3.3
08049	Grand County, Colorado	1.5	9.6	3.7	0.7	7.7	5.1	12.0	30.1	5.4
08051	Gunnison County, Colorado	0.6	13.6	5.1	1.9	4.0	10.0	17.3	21.6	5.1
08053	Hinsdale County, Colorado	0.0	7.5	2.9	3.1	6.4	9.1	13.7	21.1	6.2
08055	Huerfano County, Colorado	0.0	9.8	5.7	0.8	4.6	4.2	32.2	9.2	4.2
08057	Jackson County, Colorado	3.1	10.5	6.8	0.0	0.0	4.6	10.2	13.0	3.9
08059	Jefferson County, Colorado	3.1	11.2	4.4	3.2	7.2	14.9	19.8	9.5	5.1
08061	Kiowa County, Colorado	1.1	9.7	3.5	1.7	3.0	2.5	33.9	4.3	5.4
08063	Kit Carson County, Colorado	1.1	11.8	6.8	0.8	3.9	1.8	21.4	7.0	6.1
08065	Lake County, Colorado	0.0	14.6	3.4	1.5	3.5	9.5	20.1	14.0	2.7
08067	La Plata County, Colorado	2.3	10.3	3.9	2.0	6.4	9.7	20.7	16.8	5.0
08069	Larimer County, Colorado	2.0	11.9	3.1	2.0	5.1	12.5	25.0	10.6	5.0
08071	Las Animas County, Colorado	1.6	10.4	6.5	1.2	4.8	6.2	25.0	8.6	4.7
08073	Lincoln County, Colorado	1.9	13.7	6.0	0.3	4.0	3.0	22.9	8.1	5.8
08075	Logan County, Colorado	1.6	14.9	3.8	0.8	3.7	6.6	17.7	13.3	7.2
08077	Mesa County, Colorado	2.7	13.1	5.5	2.0	5.9	9.3	22.9	9.8	5.4
08079	Mineral County, Colorado	1.0	15.2	3.9	1.0	3.6	12.0	14.2	12.3	8.1
08081	Moffat County, Colorado	1.8	16.2	10.0	1.3	4.0	3.3	17.1	11.4	4.9
08083	Montezuma County, Colorado	2.8	12.7	5.0	1.6	4.3	6.7	21.9	11.9	6.5
08085	Montrose County, Colorado	1.8	11.4	5.7	1.2	4.3	8.2	19.4	10.4	5.4

Table C. County—Labor Force, Employment, and Educational Data, 2011–2015—*Continued*

		Industry for employed population age 16 and older								
Fips code	State/county	Wholesale trade	Retail trade	Transportation and warehousing, and utilities	Information	Finance and insurance, and real estate and rental and leasing	Professional, scientific, and management, and administrative and waste management services	Educational services, and health care and social assistance	Arts, entertainment, and recreation, and accommodation and food services	Other services, except public administration
08087	Morgan County, Colorado	2.1	8.7	5.2	1.5	3.2	5.6	19.2	7.8	4.3
08089	Otero County, Colorado	1.7	13.3	7.8	2.1	5.2	5.8	25.1	7.1	4.7
08091	Ouray County, Colorado	0.3	9.2	4.6	1.2	5.6	9.6	20.1	17.6	4.3
08093	Park County, Colorado	1.5	10.8	6.6	1.6	4.4	12.4	16.1	10.8	5.1
08095	Phillips County, Colorado	3.6	13.0	5.0	3.5	4.6	4.2	17.1	5.4	5.3
08097	Pitkin County, Colorado	1.4	8.7	2.5	1.8	11.8	11.9	15.2	27.9	5.3
08099	Prowers County, Colorado	0.5	12.9	5.8	0.7	5.1	5.8	24.4	8.7	6.1
08101	Pueblo County, Colorado	2.1	13.5	4.2	2.1	4.4	8.6	27.0	10.6	3.8
08103	Rio Blanco County, Colorado	1.2	7.5	6.5	0.3	5.5	4.1	17.4	12.0	3.8
08105	Rio Grande County, Colorado	3.2	11.5	6.5	2.8	4.6	4.2	21.1	9.2	4.5
08107	Routt County, Colorado	3.0	8.8	5.2	2.0	8.6	8.8	17.0	19.7	5.3
08109	Saguache County, Colorado	1.5	12.2	9.3	0.9	0.7	2.6	18.4	7.3	4.3
08111	San Juan County, Colorado	0.0	22.6	4.7	0.0	3.0	8.3	7.4	21.7	0.3
08113	San Miguel County, Colorado	1.8	8.5	3.9	2.4	7.8	14.1	9.3	26.8	4.1
08115	Sedgwick County, Colorado	3.0	10.5	7.5	1.2	1.7	3.3	23.2	8.0	4.5
08117	Summit County, Colorado	0.8	12.2	3.8	0.9	8.4	8.3	13.6	27.6	2.8
08119	Teller County, Colorado	1.6	9.9	4.5	1.8	4.7	10.6	20.6	13.8	4.7
08121	Washington County, Colorado	3.8	7.7	8.2	0.9	4.0	6.1	24.0	4.0	3.9
08123	Weld County, Colorado	2.9	12.1	5.1	1.8	5.4	10.8	20.1	8.2	4.7
08125	Yuma County, Colorado	2.3	10.4	4.5	0.6	4.9	5.9	18.2	7.6	4.9
09000	**Connecticut**	2.5	10.9	3.8	2.3	9.2	11.2	26.5	8.6	4.5
09001	Fairfield County, Connecticut	2.4	10.5	3.2	2.8	12.2	15.4	22.4	8.4	5.1
09003	Hartford County, Connecticut	2.6	10.7	4.0	2.3	11.4	10.7	26.5	7.4	4.2
09005	Litchfield County, Connecticut	2.0	11.1	3.5	2.1	7.0	9.7	26.9	7.7	4.8
09007	Middlesex County, Connecticut	2.6	10.5	3.5	2.6	9.1	11.3	25.8	7.7	4.5
09009	New Haven County, Connecticut	2.9	11.2	4.0	2.3	6.4	9.2	31.2	7.7	4.4
09011	New London County, Connecticut	1.6	11.3	4.1	1.6	4.5	8.6	24.6	16.8	3.4
09013	Tolland County, Connecticut	2.3	9.6	4.0	2.0	8.8	9.0	27.9	8.6	4.3
09015	Windham County, Connecticut	2.8	13.5	4.7	1.4	4.5	7.7	27.3	10.0	3.9
10000	**Delaware**	1.9	12.3	4.7	1.7	9.7	10.0	24.5	9.1	4.5
10001	Kent County, Delaware	1.8	14.9	4.5	1.1	5.2	6.9	24.2	9.5	4.3
10003	New Castle County, Delaware	1.9	10.9	4.9	1.9	12.5	11.5	25.4	8.5	4.1
10005	Sussex County, Delaware	2.0	14.2	4.5	1.3	5.1	8.2	22.4	10.4	5.7
11000	District of Columbia	0.5	4.9	3.0	4.0	5.8	22.7	19.5	9.4	9.0
11001	**District of Columbia** District of Columbia	0.5	4.9	3.0	4.0	5.8	22.7	19.5	9.4	9.0
12000	**Florida**	2.9	13.4	5.0	2.0	7.7	12.7	21.3	12.2	5.4
12001	Alachua County, Florida	1.8	10.9	2.8	1.7	5.3	9.9	38.9	11.6	4.5
12003	Baker County, Florida	3.1	12.6	8.0	0.9	5.2	8.6	25.4	5.8	4.6
12005	Bay County, Florida	2.0	13.2	4.6	1.8	5.9	12.0	20.5	14.1	4.6
12007	Bradford County, Florida	1.0	11.1	5.2	0.3	4.4	8.9	24.9	7.9	5.7
12009	Brevard County, Florida	2.0	13.7	4.1	1.7	5.0	13.4	21.8	10.8	5.1
12011	Broward County, Florida	3.7	13.8	5.3	2.4	8.1	13.8	20.8	11.0	5.7
12013	Calhoun County, Florida	3.0	9.4	3.4	1.4	3.9	4.5	22.5	9.4	4.8
12015	Charlotte County, Florida	1.7	18.1	4.1	1.6	6.2	10.9	20.8	13.1	5.6
12017	Citrus County, Florida	1.6	15.3	6.8	1.3	4.7	8.7	25.8	11.6	6.1
12019	Clay County, Florida	3.0	13.5	7.1	1.8	8.5	10.4	22.2	8.8	5.0
12021	Collier County, Florida	2.2	13.3	3.4	1.5	8.1	12.9	17.0	15.6	6.3
12023	Columbia County, Florida	1.8	14.7	5.2	1.3	3.7	9.1	25.6	9.2	5.3
12027	DeSoto County, Florida	2.0	11.1	5.8	0.8	3.4	6.1	13.4	7.6	4.5
12029	Dixie County, Florida	0.9	11.3	5.8	0.5	5.8	3.5	21.7	8.6	2.9
12031	Duval County, Florida	2.7	12.3	7.0	1.7	11.5	12.8	20.6	10.3	4.9
12033	Escambia County, Florida	2.2	15.5	4.8	1.9	8.1	10.6	22.7	11.2	5.7
12035	Flagler County, Florida	2.8	14.6	3.3	1.8	6.8	12.4	23.7	11.7	5.4
12037	Franklin County, Florida	4.8	9.1	4.5	1.3	6.1	6.5	17.6	13.0	5.0
12039	Gadsden County, Florida	2.2	11.0	4.5	1.0	3.6	9.1	27.3	6.4	4.5
12041	Gilchrist County, Florida	2.1	12.1	5.0	1.1	7.9	10.5	22.6	7.6	3.2
12043	Glades County, Florida	0.9	9.7	11.1	1.6	2.4	7.3	15.1	13.8	3.8
12045	Gulf County, Florida	2.0	9.8	5.9	2.7	6.1	12.0	14.3	10.1	3.5
12047	Hamilton County, Florida	0.9	9.5	7.7	1.1	4.0	5.2	22.8	11.0	2.6
12049	Hardee County, Florida	2.0	10.3	5.6	0.4	2.7	6.6	17.1	6.4	3.8
12051	Hendry County, Florida	2.5	9.0	4.5	0.4	3.1	6.5	15.1	6.0	3.5
12053	Hernando County, Florida	2.2	15.4	5.5	1.8	6.9	9.5	23.4	10.6	5.9
12055	Highlands County, Florida	1.8	14.7	3.4	0.9	4.6	8.3	25.3	11.9	5.6
12057	Hillsborough County, Florida	3.1	11.8	4.6	2.5	10.5	14.1	21.6	10.1	4.7
12059	Holmes County, Florida	1.3	14.6	4.9	2.3	3.3	8.0	20.8	7.7	3.6
12061	Indian River County, Florida	2.9	13.7	3.6	1.7	7.9	12.0	21.5	11.2	5.7
12063	Jackson County, Florida	2.3	14.3	4.7	1.1	3.6	5.0	29.1	8.6	4.0
12065	Jefferson County, Florida	0.1	9.3	3.3	1.3	5.9	11.0	23.8	6.9	4.9
12067	Lafayette County, Florida	2.3	7.9	8.3	0.3	2.9	6.6	17.7	5.9	5.7
12069	Lake County, Florida	2.0	13.1	4.6	2.3	5.8	10.0	21.4	16.2	5.3
12071	Lee County, Florida	2.1	15.7	3.9	1.8	7.1	12.8	21.1	12.8	5.3

Table C. County—Labor Force, Employment, and Educational Data, 2011–2015—*Continued*

Fips code	State/county	Wholesale trade	Retail trade	Transportation and warehousing, and utilities	Information	Finance and insurance, and real estate and rental and leasing	Professional, scientific, and management, and administrative and waste management services	Educational services, and health care and social assistance	Arts, entertainment, and recreation, and accommodation and food services	Other services, except public administration
12073	Leon County, Florida	1.7	12.1	2.7	1.8	5.4	13.2	26.3	11.9	5.0
12075	Levy County, Florida	1.3	13.2	6.2	0.6	5.1	8.2	23.9	8.0	5.4
12077	Liberty County, Florida	5.9	7.4	4.9	0.5	4.6	6.7	22.5	3.9	4.2
12079	Madison County, Florida	3.4	10.7	7.1	0.5	2.7	7.1	24.5	6.7	3.3
12081	Manatee County, Florida	2.8	13.9	3.7	1.4	7.0	12.3	22.1	10.7	5.6
12083	Marion County, Florida	2.5	16.5	4.6	2.1	4.9	10.3	21.9	10.9	5.1
12085	Martin County, Florida	2.4	11.7	4.5	1.8	7.1	13.4	21.6	11.6	6.0
12086	Miami-Dade County, Florida	4.2	12.7	7.2	2.1	7.3	12.8	20.1	11.2	6.3
12087	Monroe County, Florida	2.6	13.0	5.7	1.5	6.2	9.9	13.9	24.3	4.5
12089	Nassau County, Florida	2.6	12.4	8.0	2.1	6.5	9.6	18.7	11.6	5.3
12091	Okaloosa County, Florida	1.4	12.6	4.8	1.0	6.8	11.9	16.9	14.7	6.1
12093	Okeechobee County, Florida	2.9	14.6	7.3	0.6	3.2	8.9	18.0	8.7	6.1
12095	Orange County, Florida	2.7	12.9	5.1	2.4	6.8	13.9	18.6	19.4	4.7
12097	Osceola County, Florida	2.3	15.1	5.8	1.2	4.3	10.9	17.7	24.7	4.3
12099	Palm Beach County, Florida	2.8	13.3	4.1	2.0	8.2	14.8	20.7	12.2	5.9
12101	Pasco County, Florida	2.8	14.3	4.5	2.8	8.3	11.9	23.8	10.0	5.0
12103	Pinellas County, Florida	2.6	13.3	3.7	2.1	9.5	14.0	22.6	10.8	5.2
12105	Polk County, Florida	3.0	14.6	5.5	1.4	5.8	10.6	21.1	13.5	5.1
12107	Putnam County, Florida	2.2	15.0	4.9	1.2	4.5	9.8	22.1	8.2	4.5
12109	St. Johns County, Florida	3.3	12.7	4.5	1.6	12.5	12.6	20.3	12.0	3.8
12111	St. Lucie County, Florida	2.3	15.8	5.0	1.5	5.5	11.5	24.5	11.2	5.2
12113	Santa Rosa County, Florida	1.8	13.3	5.6	1.6	6.4	10.4	21.8	9.1	5.6
12115	Sarasota County, Florida	2.0	14.3	2.9	1.7	8.0	13.5	22.3	12.7	5.7
12117	Seminole County, Florida	2.8	12.7	3.7	3.2	9.9	15.5	22.0	10.4	5.3
12119	Sumter County, Florida	3.6	16.5	4.8	2.4	6.9	9.1	20.0	12.2	4.7
12121	Suwannee County, Florida	2.8	15.3	6.2	1.2	3.9	6.4	20.5	8.2	5.9
12123	Taylor County, Florida	1.2	13.2	1.1	0.0	4.6	7.5	23.3	8.5	4.3
12125	Union County, Florida	2.3	13.3	7.4	0.6	5.1	6.3	22.9	5.5	3.8
12127	Volusia County, Florida	2.0	15.0	4.5	1.8	6.7	10.9	22.4	12.1	5.1
12129	Wakulla County, Florida	2.7	10.5	6.0	1.3	7.0	11.0	18.3	5.8	4.4
12131	Walton County, Florida	1.1	15.7	3.9	1.0	7.4	13.4	14.9	14.7	5.8
12133	Washington County, Florida	3.2	11.8	5.5	0.9	5.0	9.7	19.5	10.7	3.9
13000	**Georgia**	2.9	11.9	6.0	2.5	6.3	11.6	21.0	9.3	5.0
13001	Appling County, Georgia	5.8	9.1	6.8	1.7	4.2	4.3	19.7	4.8	4.9
13003	Atkinson County, Georgia	3.0	14.9	7.1	0.0	1.6	7.0	14.3	4.2	3.7
13005	Bacon County, Georgia	1.2	12.4	7.0	2.5	3.0	5.5	24.0	2.4	3.4
13007	Baker County, Georgia	4.8	6.8	5.4	1.8	3.0	5.1	19.7	3.8	4.7
13009	Baldwin County, Georgia	0.7	11.8	4.8	0.9	4.2	5.9	31.3	11.6	5.3
13011	Banks County, Georgia	3.9	13.7	6.4	0.6	3.7	7.1	19.1	4.3	5.2
13013	Barrow County, Georgia	4.4	16.7	5.4	1.4	5.3	9.0	20.3	6.9	5.4
13015	Bartow County, Georgia	2.5	11.9	6.4	1.7	5.0	8.0	19.3	9.0	4.1
13017	Ben Hill County, Georgia	1.6	10.6	5.9	1.0	4.1	5.1	22.3	6.1	7.3
13019	Berrien County, Georgia	3.1	12.6	3.4	1.5	4.8	7.9	22.7	7.9	3.0
13021	Bibb County, Georgia	2.1	13.9	5.0	1.9	8.3	9.5	27.2	9.4	4.6
13023	Bleckley County, Georgia	1.6	14.2	2.5	0.4	4.6	5.0	25.9	6.3	3.5
13025	Brantley County, Georgia	2.1	10.3	5.7	1.5	3.1	6.8	21.2	8.0	7.3
13027	Brooks County, Georgia	2.8	16.9	6.0	0.7	4.3	5.0	21.7	2.5	7.9
13029	Bryan County, Georgia	2.0	10.5	7.4	0.5	4.2	7.3	23.0	10.5	5.9
13031	Bulloch County, Georgia	2.3	12.4	4.1	0.9	4.3	6.4	31.2	12.1	4.8
13033	Burke County, Georgia	1.5	11.8	7.3	2.0	3.2	6.6	23.2	6.6	3.3
13035	Butts County, Georgia	5.3	10.0	10.8	1.2	3.7	6.3	19.6	8.3	4.4
13037	Calhoun County, Georgia	2.5	12.2	3.7	0.6	1.9	2.6	22.3	11.4	3.6
13039	Camden County, Georgia	1.9	13.4	4.9	1.0	4.6	7.9	16.9	12.2	4.1
13043	Candler County, Georgia	2.1	16.3	6.6	1.0	3.3	7.8	16.8	13.0	5.3
13045	Carroll County, Georgia	2.8	12.0	7.6	1.7	4.0	8.9	19.8	9.7	4.2
13047	Catoosa County, Georgia	3.6	11.9	6.9	2.1	8.1	6.4	20.4	7.3	7.7
13049	Charlton County, Georgia	5.6	8.7	9.9	0.4	2.5	3.4	26.4	7.2	9.2
13051	Chatham County, Georgia	2.0	12.5	6.7	1.5	5.4	9.6	22.9	13.6	4.6
13053	Chattahoochee County, Georgia	2.9	10.2	3.8	2.0	3.9	10.6	20.5	7.3	3.4
13055	Chattooga County, Georgia	1.3	8.4	4.3	0.7	4.1	4.8	20.5	6.0	4.5
13057	Cherokee County, Georgia	3.1	14.4	4.3	3.5	8.5	13.2	17.8	8.7	4.7
13059	Clarke County, Georgia	1.9	11.6	2.5	1.5	3.7	9.0	34.2	16.4	4.1
13061	Clay County, Georgia	0.0	5.8	6.7	0.0	4.8	3.9	18.8	8.0	5.9
13063	Clayton County, Georgia	3.2	11.6	12.9	1.7	5.2	9.7	18.1	10.9	6.1
13065	Clinch County, Georgia	0.2	12.6	4.0	1.4	2.6	6.4	25.3	3.4	2.8
13067	Cobb County, Georgia	3.4	11.7	5.1	3.9	8.3	16.2	18.6	9.7	5.0
13069	Coffee County, Georgia	2.5	13.1	4.3	0.7	4.4	5.2	23.5	9.5	4.2
13071	Colquitt County, Georgia	2.4	10.9	4.4	0.8	4.8	5.0	21.4	7.2	3.8
13073	Columbia County, Georgia	2.0	11.2	5.1	2.4	4.8	11.2	26.4	7.6	4.8
13075	Cook County, Georgia	3.6	16.5	4.6	0.9	3.4	9.3	21.5	7.8	4.0
13077	Coweta County, Georgia	3.0	11.6	11.8	2.0	5.0	9.6	19.3	8.3	5.0
13079	Crawford County, Georgia	2.5	8.9	9.8	1.6	3.5	8.0	24.6	5.5	5.0
13081	Crisp County, Georgia	3.0	13.7	3.7	0.9	7.4	6.7	24.6	7.9	6.1
13083	Dade County, Georgia	1.8	8.9	6.4	1.7	5.3	8.0	21.7	10.1	7.4

Table C. County—Labor Force, Employment, and Educational Data, 2011–2015—*Continued*

		Industry for employed population age 16 and older								
Fips code	State/county	Wholesale trade	Retail trade	Transportation and warehousing, and utilities	Information	Finance and insurance, and real estate and rental and leasing	Professional, scientific, and management, and administrative and waste management services	Educational services, and health care and social assistance	Arts, entertainment, and recreation, and accommodation and food services	Other services, except public administration
13085	Dawson County, Georgia	4.2	14.1	6.8	1.2	6.8	11.9	16.7	9.3	4.4
13087	Decatur County, Georgia	3.1	11.9	2.8	1.7	6.3	5.8	22.4	5.5	5.0
13089	DeKalb County, Georgia	2.4	10.8	6.3	3.7	7.1	15.2	23.3	9.9	4.5
13091	Dodge County, Georgia	1.2	13.2	5.3	1.0	2.5	3.5	25.5	2.9	3.5
13093	Dooly County, Georgia	6.8	7.7	5.0	0.3	5.4	4.9	17.7	4.5	4.0
13095	Dougherty County, Georgia	1.7	11.9	4.2	2.0	3.8	8.3	28.5	10.2	5.7
13097	Douglas County, Georgia	4.1	13.1	9.5	2.9	5.1	10.3	18.8	9.1	5.6
13099	Early County, Georgia	1.5	11.9	4.9	0.8	4.6	4.9	21.8	4.5	4.2
13101	Echols County, Georgia	1.3	8.7	4.8	0.6	2.9	6.5	15.2	6.2	6.1
13103	Effingham County, Georgia	2.8	13.1	11.0	1.4	3.7	6.4	16.8	6.7	6.0
13105	Elbert County, Georgia	3.8	11.3	4.2	0.3	3.0	5.8	19.5	3.8	6.4
13107	Emanuel County, Georgia	2.3	13.6	5.9	0.4	2.3	4.8	22.9	5.7	4.6
13109	Evans County, Georgia	3.0	11.1	7.1	0.3	3.6	3.9	20.5	5.1	7.5
13111	Fannin County, Georgia	3.0	14.6	6.6	2.3	7.8	8.2	13.7	9.4	4.9
13113	Fayette County, Georgia	3.2	10.2	14.1	2.3	6.3	10.4	20.6	8.3	5.1
13115	Floyd County, Georgia	2.0	9.7	4.1	1.2	4.2	7.3	26.3	10.0	6.2
13117	Forsyth County, Georgia	3.6	12.2	3.6	4.9	10.0	18.6	17.0	7.3	5.0
13119	Franklin County, Georgia	2.7	12.6	4.9	1.0	3.3	5.8	22.5	6.0	5.3
13121	Fulton County, Georgia	2.9	10.0	5.9	4.2	9.0	19.5	19.6	10.9	4.6
13123	Gilmer County, Georgia	1.7	14.7	2.6	2.2	8.0	7.3	18.0	8.5	4.4
13125	Glascock County, Georgia	0.0	10.0	10.6	0.5	6.7	8.7	24.6	1.7	3.1
13127	Glynn County, Georgia	2.7	13.2	4.1	1.0	5.3	11.4	20.0	16.3	6.0
13129	Gordon County, Georgia	3.1	10.3	5.4	1.0	3.0	5.3	16.7	6.2	3.3
13131	Grady County, Georgia	3.2	13.0	4.4	2.1	5.5	6.0	22.7	3.6	4.7
13133	Greene County, Georgia	1.2	10.1	2.5	1.6	5.7	14.2	18.3	12.0	6.1
13135	Gwinnett County, Georgia	3.8	12.8	4.4	3.4	7.5	14.1	17.8	9.6	6.0
13137	Habersham County, Georgia	4.3	12.2	2.7	1.6	3.3	7.1	19.0	8.1	4.8
13139	Hall County, Georgia	3.8	12.5	4.8	1.4	4.6	9.1	18.0	7.5	4.9
13141	Hancock County, Georgia	3.1	11.8	12.0	1.0	1.5	1.5	31.4	7.5	2.3
13143	Haralson County, Georgia	3.4	10.5	5.6	1.9	1.8	6.6	23.0	7.8	6.5
13145	Harris County, Georgia	3.9	11.0	5.4	2.1	9.5	7.2	20.3	9.4	4.7
13147	Hart County, Georgia	2.9	12.5	2.4	1.2	3.7	4.9	20.9	4.8	4.8
13149	Heard County, Georgia	1.5	13.5	7.2	1.3	4.5	6.2	17.0	4.8	7.8
13151	Henry County, Georgia	3.3	11.5	12.5	2.1	5.7	10.2	21.5	8.0	5.0
13153	Houston County, Georgia	1.8	10.9	4.7	1.1	5.1	8.7	19.8	9.3	4.9
13155	Irwin County, Georgia	2.0	8.3	8.5	3.5	4.0	9.0	18.9	6.9	4.4
13157	Jackson County, Georgia	4.3	15.3	4.8	1.5	5.7	9.0	20.2	7.2	4.6
13159	Jasper County, Georgia	2.1	9.0	5.6	2.2	4.6	4.4	20.5	8.1	6.8
13161	Jeff Davis County, Georgia	4.2	12.9	8.5	1.2	3.5	5.9	20.5	3.1	2.3
13163	Jefferson County, Georgia	0.8	7.2	8.3	1.1	3.4	3.5	25.5	4.2	4.3
13165	Jenkins County, Georgia	1.3	10.9	12.0	0.5	1.1	7.8	24.5	4.4	3.8
13167	Johnson County, Georgia	1.9	13.8	11.4	0.8	2.9	5.0	22.2	2.2	5.4
13169	Jones County, Georgia	3.5	11.0	6.5	0.6	7.7	5.3	27.8	6.8	5.2
13171	Lamar County, Georgia	3.2	13.6	6.8	0.9	4.3	5.6	24.5	7.8	6.2
13173	Lanier County, Georgia	0.9	23.6	2.8	0.4	4.1	7.7	27.4	3.9	5.1
13175	Laurens County, Georgia	1.6	14.1	4.8	1.3	4.7	5.7	27.8	7.7	5.4
13177	Lee County, Georgia	4.2	12.0	4.0	1.5	4.9	9.9	23.4	4.3	5.8
13179	Liberty County, Georgia	2.2	13.3	5.7	0.8	4.0	7.4	17.9	11.6	4.4
13181	Lincoln County, Georgia	1.0	12.2	5.8	2.5	6.8	3.7	19.5	6.8	4.8
13183	Long County, Georgia	1.1	13.0	6.2	1.3	4.4	5.9	16.6	7.0	5.3
13185	Lowndes County, Georgia	1.9	15.8	4.1	1.3	4.3	8.3	24.6	13.6	5.0
13187	Lumpkin County, Georgia	1.7	17.1	3.0	2.0	4.0	7.8	22.4	10.7	7.8
13189	McDuffie County, Georgia	3.0	13.7	3.4	1.2	4.1	9.7	18.7	7.3	2.9
13191	McIntosh County, Georgia	1.1	12.5	7.8	3.3	5.5	4.9	21.9	10.5	4.1
13193	Macon County, Georgia	1.6	7.6	6.4	1.2	2.8	5.1	21.2	4.3	5.1
13195	Madison County, Georgia	2.7	11.8	4.7	0.5	3.4	8.5	25.5	5.2	5.7
13197	Marion County, Georgia	2.7	10.9	6.9	0.0	6.6	3.2	22.5	3.3	3.4
13199	Meriwether County, Georgia	3.9	10.1	8.7	0.5	3.4	6.6	20.7	7.1	3.3
13201	Miller County, Georgia	2.2	11.7	4.5	0.5	6.2	5.9	24.7	4.3	5.0
13205	Mitchell County, Georgia	4.2	9.4	6.2	0.7	5.0	6.0	21.2	3.7	7.5
13207	Monroe County, Georgia	2.7	10.4	6.7	2.3	7.8	7.4	25.1	8.5	6.5
13209	Montgomery County, Georgia	3.2	14.5	5.7	1.1	4.7	6.9	24.8	5.8	4.6
13211	Morgan County, Georgia	1.8	9.6	6.6	2.1	5.2	9.0	21.6	9.8	6.8
13213	Murray County, Georgia	1.7	11.9	6.0	1.5	3.2	4.7	14.1	6.4	3.6
13215	Muscogee County, Georgia	1.4	11.7	3.9	1.4	11.8	7.8	22.8	11.9	4.4
13217	Newton County, Georgia	2.1	11.4	8.3	2.5	3.6	10.0	23.3	6.7	3.9
13219	Oconee County, Georgia	3.1	10.4	3.7	1.2	5.4	10.0	34.2	8.2	4.3
13221	Oglethorpe County, Georgia	3.1	10.3	4.7	0.7	3.7	5.7	27.9	3.5	3.9
13223	Paulding County, Georgia	3.5	13.6	6.8	2.5	5.1	12.2	21.3	7.0	5.3
13225	Peach County, Georgia	1.9	10.4	6.2	1.7	5.5	4.4	24.9	7.8	6.6
13227	Pickens County, Georgia	2.9	17.1	5.8	2.0	6.7	10.6	16.4	7.3	4.1
13229	Pierce County, Georgia	4.0	10.8	13.1	0.7	3.9	6.2	17.6	10.0	4.9
13231	Pike County, Georgia	2.5	9.8	9.3	1.7	5.7	6.7	22.9	6.3	5.4
13233	Polk County, Georgia	3.1	11.3	4.0	2.1	3.7	7.4	18.4	6.4	6.2
13235	Pulaski County, Georgia	2.1	6.0	2.5	1.1	5.5	6.8	25.0	12.0	4.8

Table C. County—Labor Force, Employment, and Educational Data, 2011–2015—*Continued*

Fips code	State/county	Wholesale trade	Retail trade	Transportation and warehousing, and utilities	Information	Finance and insurance, and real estate and rental and leasing	Professional, scientific, and management, and administrative and waste management services	Educational services, and health care and social assistance	Arts, entertainment, and recreation, and accommodation and food services	Other services, except public administration
13237	Putnam County, Georgia	2.6	11.3	7.3	1.7	5.6	13.7	17.1	11.8	2.7
13239	Quitman County, Georgia	2.3	23.0	9.4	0.5	6.5	1.2	12.6	4.1	1.9
13241	Rabun County, Georgia	0.8	11.8	4.3	0.7	6.8	7.8	21.4	12.5	6.9
13243	Randolph County, Georgia	0.0	12.1	8.9	0.2	2.0	4.1	25.4	6.6	6.0
13245	Richmond County, Georgia	1.4	13.1	5.4	2.1	3.5	10.3	25.9	11.2	4.4
13247	Rockdale County, Georgia	2.1	11.7	7.1	3.1	4.9	10.6	21.1	8.5	5.1
13249	Schley County, Georgia	3.4	8.7	5.5	1.7	2.9	3.1	26.6	3.9	2.5
13251	Screven County, Georgia	1.0	11.7	7.6	2.0	4.1	6.9	23.4	6.0	3.5
13253	Seminole County, Georgia	4.3	11.5	2.8	0.2	5.4	7.3	22.6	7.8	6.2
13255	Spalding County, Georgia	3.1	15.1	7.3	1.6	3.7	6.9	22.3	7.7	5.4
13257	Stephens County, Georgia	4.6	9.7	3.5	1.4	2.1	4.9	27.4	7.5	4.9
13259	Stewart County, Georgia	1.2	8.1	3.8	1.7	3.7	4.0	25.1	11.3	4.4
13261	Sumter County, Georgia	3.1	9.3	3.6	1.8	4.6	6.4	30.1	6.5	4.9
13263	Talbot County, Georgia	4.7	7.5	6.2	2.2	5.8	6.7	26.9	6.1	3.0
13265	Taliaferro County, Georgia	3.3	3.0	4.4	0.5	4.0	4.9	20.2	9.4	3.8
13267	Tattnall County, Georgia	4.3	13.5	5.8	0.6	2.9	6.1	19.9	4.8	5.6
13269	Taylor County, Georgia	2.9	7.1	4.7	3.4	4.9	3.7	25.3	7.2	6.4
13271	Telfair County, Georgia	3.9	8.8	7.2	2.2	3.6	4.5	21.8	7.4	2.7
13273	Terrell County, Georgia	3.0	15.8	3.1	0.3	5.9	5.8	18.7	9.4	4.0
13275	Thomas County, Georgia	3.4	11.1	3.6	1.4	5.0	5.7	30.2	8.9	5.7
13277	Tift County, Georgia	2.6	13.3	6.0	1.4	4.3	7.9	24.9	10.3	5.8
13279	Toombs County, Georgia	3.1	12.0	8.2	0.3	2.3	4.3	23.1	4.8	6.6
13281	Towns County, Georgia	3.1	13.0	2.9	1.0	7.1	5.4	28.7	15.1	4.7
13283	Treutlen County, Georgia	2.3	18.2	5.0	0.4	2.6	6.0	19.4	8.0	5.2
13285	Troup County, Georgia	1.9	11.1	5.5	1.8	4.3	6.5	21.2	9.0	4.3
13287	Turner County, Georgia	4.2	15.7	4.6	0.2	3.1	6.5	27.7	2.8	2.1
13289	Twiggs County, Georgia	1.8	12.3	6.2	0.9	7.0	6.0	19.3	3.7	4.9
13291	Union County, Georgia	1.7	13.9	6.2	0.3	5.6	5.0	27.0	7.4	5.1
13293	Upson County, Georgia	1.2	12.2	4.8	2.4	4.8	7.4	25.0	5.7	4.9
13295	Walker County, Georgia	2.7	12.9	6.3	1.0	5.1	7.8	18.7	8.0	6.8
13297	Walton County, Georgia	3.8	15.1	4.8	1.5	5.9	8.6	19.4	8.0	5.1
13299	Ware County, Georgia	2.2	11.6	7.5	1.6	4.2	5.4	25.6	6.7	5.0
13301	Warren County, Georgia	2.4	10.2	5.4	0.5	2.0	7.2	21.3	2.4	4.5
13303	Washington County, Georgia	1.6	13.2	9.0	0.5	4.6	6.9	25.3	4.6	3.5
13305	Wayne County, Georgia	1.2	12.3	6.6	0.7	3.9	5.3	23.3	6.2	7.3
13307	Webster County, Georgia	3.4	16.3	8.7	0.5	3.2	4.4	14.6	3.3	0.4
13309	Wheeler County, Georgia	1.0	7.9	10.1	0.5	1.9	2.0	30.5	3.1	4.1
13311	White County, Georgia	1.7	17.0	3.3	2.3	4.0	5.6	19.1	11.4	6.3
13313	Whitfield County, Georgia	2.8	12.1	3.9	1.0	3.2	6.8	12.3	7.7	3.8
13315	Wilcox County, Georgia	3.5	10.9	7.6	0.3	3.0	4.0	22.1	2.5	4.9
13317	Wilkes County, Georgia	5.2	12.6	3.3	1.1	3.2	2.5	23.7	5.3	6.7
13319	Wilkinson County, Georgia	0.2	9.6	5.9	1.0	6.3	6.4	21.2	4.3	7.2
13321	Worth County, Georgia	2.9	12.7	7.2	0.7	3.6	7.5	20.3	8.0	3.9
15000	**Hawaii**	2.3	11.8	5.9	1.6	6.4	10.2	20.5	16.3	4.5
15001	Hawaii County, Hawaii	1.9	13.4	5.4	1.2	4.9	11.2	19.4	16.6	5.2
15003	Honolulu County, Hawaii	2.4	11.6	6.2	1.7	6.6	10.0	21.5	14.4	4.4
15005	Kalawao County, Hawaii	0.0	10.9	25.0	0.0	0.0	4.7	15.6	15.6	4.7
15007	Kauai County, Hawaii	1.6	11.1	5.1	1.5	6.3	10.1	15.8	24.2	4.4
15009	Maui County, Hawaii	2.1	11.2	5.3	1.3	6.2	10.7	18.0	23.0	4.2
16000	**Idaho**	2.6	12.1	4.8	1.9	5.2	9.7	22.7	8.9	4.4
16001	Ada County, Idaho	2.7	11.9	4.2	2.7	6.6	12.5	23.6	8.7	4.1
16003	Adams County, Idaho	0.8	12.9	2.0	0.5	4.0	7.6	21.8	12.6	3.3
16005	Bannock County, Idaho	1.9	11.3	6.2	1.8	6.6	9.1	28.1	9.3	3.3
16007	Bear Lake County, Idaho	2.3	11.7	6.2	1.8	3.9	5.4	20.6	9.5	5.3
16009	Benewah County, Idaho	1.0	6.1	6.9	1.0	2.7	4.2	26.4	11.1	4.1
16011	Bingham County, Idaho	3.2	9.3	5.3	0.8	3.4	8.3	23.2	5.8	5.7
16013	Blaine County, Idaho	1.4	9.9	2.8	2.8	7.5	16.5	14.9	18.1	3.3
16015	Boise County, Idaho	0.9	8.5	9.6	1.6	5.2	13.6	14.7	6.2	1.2
16017	Bonner County, Idaho	2.5	15.5	5.6	1.5	4.9	6.4	19.3	9.6	4.6
16019	Bonneville County, Idaho	3.0	12.9	4.5	1.8	3.6	14.0	22.1	8.9	4.0
16021	Boundary County, Idaho	1.1	10.0	3.8	1.4	2.8	7.6	21.3	6.8	8.1
16023	Butte County, Idaho	1.8	6.8	8.9	0.0	4.8	12.5	21.4	5.1	3.1
16025	Camas County, Idaho	0.4	7.2	2.8	2.2	3.4	3.8	19.0	10.6	8.0
16027	Canyon County, Idaho	3.0	12.0	4.8	1.8	4.8	8.3	21.7	8.2	5.0
16029	Caribou County, Idaho	2.7	10.3	2.4	0.4	2.9	4.6	20.6	4.9	3.2
16031	Cassia County, Idaho	2.7	10.4	6.9	1.4	2.4	5.4	18.9	5.6	4.5
16033	Clark County, Idaho	1.8	7.2	0.0	2.5	0.0	0.7	10.0	11.1	0.0
16035	Clearwater County, Idaho	3.0	8.5	4.0	1.3	2.6	3.8	26.7	6.8	2.7
16037	Custer County, Idaho	0.2	15.0	7.3	1.0	2.7	4.8	16.2	13.6	5.0
16039	Elmore County, Idaho	1.2	11.1	6.1	1.2	4.4	4.9	20.2	8.4	5.1
16041	Franklin County, Idaho	3.2	12.8	3.7	1.4	3.1	5.0	19.6	5.3	5.6
16043	Fremont County, Idaho	3.9	10.4	8.1	2.2	2.3	4.2	21.6	6.1	3.7
16045	Gem County, Idaho	3.0	8.5	7.8	2.0	4.0	7.3	26.4	6.1	4.7
16047	Gooding County, Idaho	0.7	5.8	6.4	0.4	3.7	6.9	18.2	6.0	6.5

Table C. County—Labor Force, Employment, and Educational Data, 2011–2015—*Continued*

Fips code	State/county	Wholesale trade	Retail trade	Transportation and warehousing, and utilities	Information	Finance and insurance, and real estate and rental and leasing	Professional, scientific, and management, and administrative and waste management services	Educational services, and health care and social assistance	Arts, entertainment, and recreation, and accommodation and food services	Other services, except public administration
							Industry for employed population age 16 and older			
16049	Idaho County, Idaho	1.8	11.5	4.9	1.7	4.4	3.1	18.8	9.8	6.5
16051	Jefferson County, Idaho	3.7	10.8	7.0	1.6	3.1	11.1	19.1	4.9	4.2
16053	Jerome County, Idaho	2.7	10.0	5.4	0.8	4.1	7.1	16.1	7.4	3.9
16055	Kootenai County, Idaho	2.7	14.2	4.1	2.1	6.7	10.2	20.5	11.0	5.0
16057	Latah County, Idaho	1.6	11.3	2.3	1.2	3.8	7.8	39.4	10.3	3.6
16059	Lemhi County, Idaho	1.4	13.1	4.5	2.7	2.9	6.9	19.0	5.2	6.1
16061	Lewis County, Idaho	1.7	10.0	5.3	0.8	3.4	4.3	22.0	9.6	4.7
16063	Lincoln County, Idaho	1.0	12.5	5.0	1.2	2.3	7.4	15.5	8.1	2.4
16065	Madison County, Idaho	2.1	14.0	4.4	1.3	4.4	9.4	34.0	10.5	2.9
16067	Minidoka County, Idaho	6.4	10.4	7.2	0.9	2.3	3.1	18.9	5.7	4.1
16069	Nez Perce County, Idaho	2.4	13.0	3.4	1.5	6.6	7.1	23.7	8.1	4.6
16071	Oneida County, Idaho	0.5	10.9	6.8	0.7	2.9	2.3	22.2	5.9	2.6
16073	Owyhee County, Idaho	2.6	10.3	6.4	0.6	1.7	4.1	12.7	4.7	4.1
16075	Payette County, Idaho	3.2	15.8	4.7	2.3	3.4	5.2	23.7	8.5	4.2
16077	Power County, Idaho	4.5	7.7	10.5	0.3	3.6	3.7	16.1	3.3	2.4
16079	Shoshone County, Idaho	1.3	15.5	2.4	0.7	2.5	6.1	21.7	12.9	4.6
16081	Teton County, Idaho	1.9	10.5	4.3	1.5	2.5	13.6	15.5	14.9	3.4
16083	Twin Falls County, Idaho	2.9	14.5	5.7	1.6	4.5	7.7	21.7	9.1	5.3
16085	Valley County, Idaho	0.3	14.6	8.5	2.0	3.4	6.2	13.5	24.9	4.3
16087	Washington County, Idaho	3.1	13.9	6.2	2.4	3.3	4.2	19.6	6.8	3.0
17000	**Illinois**	3.0	11.0	5.9	2.0	7.3	11.4	23.0	9.1	4.7
17001	Adams County, Illinois	4.0	14.8	5.3	1.7	6.6	5.2	25.3	7.4	4.4
17003	Alexander County, Illinois	2.5	13.6	8.3	0.5	5.7	4.5	22.6	11.3	5.7
17005	Bond County, Illinois	4.0	12.3	5.5	1.3	4.7	7.2	24.4	7.8	5.7
17007	Boone County, Illinois	2.8	11.8	6.5	1.4	4.9	8.2	17.9	7.1	3.7
17009	Brown County, Illinois	18.3	8.9	8.8	3.2	2.8	7.7	14.9	5.2	2.2
17011	Bureau County, Illinois	4.4	14.6	6.3	0.9	4.4	4.3	21.4	7.8	4.2
17013	Calhoun County, Illinois	4.0	6.3	3.8	0.6	8.2	5.3	20.8	11.4	6.1
17015	Carroll County, Illinois	2.7	10.6	5.4	1.0	5.0	5.8	21.1	4.7	4.8
17017	Cass County, Illinois	5.2	9.6	5.0	1.6	3.5	2.4	22.3	5.7	4.0
17019	Champaign County, Illinois	2.8	10.3	3.7	2.1	4.9	8.6	38.8	10.1	4.0
17021	Christian County, Illinois	2.3	9.8	6.1	1.1	5.8	7.6	25.6	7.4	4.4
17023	Clark County, Illinois	1.5	10.7	5.9	1.5	4.9	4.1	21.4	6.8	4.1
17025	Clay County, Illinois	2.1	12.2	6.3	2.3	2.6	4.4	21.4	5.2	5.5
17027	Clinton County, Illinois	3.6	11.0	5.8	1.3	6.3	6.6	23.2	7.1	3.6
17029	Coles County, Illinois	1.5	11.8	3.6	3.2	4.3	5.6	30.5	11.1	4.8
17031	Cook County, Illinois	2.8	10.1	6.4	2.3	8.1	13.9	22.8	9.9	5.0
17033	Crawford County, Illinois	1.8	10.7	3.8	0.9	5.4	6.9	21.6	5.7	4.4
17035	Cumberland County, Illinois	3.8	10.1	4.8	2.2	4.1	4.7	22.8	6.0	3.5
17037	DeKalb County, Illinois	3.0	12.9	4.6	1.6	4.8	7.0	27.4	12.0	3.7
17039	De Witt County, Illinois	2.4	11.0	8.1	1.0	9.2	5.2	20.8	7.5	4.9
17041	Douglas County, Illinois	2.4	12.9	5.1	1.8	4.2	4.4	19.3	7.0	4.1
17043	DuPage County, Illinois	3.9	10.4	5.6	2.6	9.0	14.3	20.8	8.6	4.7
17045	Edgar County, Illinois	2.5	9.0	5.0	0.3	5.8	4.4	21.5	6.1	4.8
17047	Edwards County, Illinois	3.9	10.8	4.6	0.7	4.2	4.9	19.4	4.1	4.6
17049	Effingham County, Illinois	4.3	14.4	4.6	1.1	4.4	5.6	22.3	10.0	4.7
17051	Fayette County, Illinois	2.4	12.5	4.9	1.4	4.0	4.4	23.6	6.4	4.6
17053	Ford County, Illinois	2.8	12.3	5.6	1.6	5.6	4.0	24.1	6.1	6.1
17055	Franklin County, Illinois	2.1	13.6	5.1	1.3	5.6	4.8	25.9	7.6	4.5
17057	Fulton County, Illinois	3.3	11.4	5.4	1.1	4.1	6.0	27.4	6.0	4.8
17059	Gallatin County, Illinois	2.5	9.8	9.4	1.4	3.1	5.7	25.2	3.1	5.2
17061	Greene County, Illinois	4.4	12.8	5.1	1.5	4.0	5.2	23.6	5.3	4.7
17063	Grundy County, Illinois	3.7	12.7	9.0	1.1	4.7	7.3	22.8	9.8	4.3
17065	Hamilton County, Illinois	2.3	11.5	8.4	1.2	3.9	4.5	18.6	5.0	4.7
17067	Hancock County, Illinois	3.9	11.2	6.5	1.2	3.7	6.8	22.2	5.2	5.2
17069	Hardin County, Illinois	2.1	8.7	12.1	0.4	3.3	4.0	31.9	5.4	5.7
17071	Henderson County, Illinois	1.9	10.4	7.5	0.9	2.4	6.4	25.0	4.8	6.1
17073	Henry County, Illinois	3.0	11.6	6.8	1.5	4.7	6.0	20.9	7.1	4.9
17075	Iroquois County, Illinois	3.7	12.2	6.5	2.3	4.8	3.9	24.1	5.6	5.1
17077	Jackson County, Illinois	1.0	12.6	3.9	1.3	3.4	5.1	41.5	9.4	3.7
17079	Jasper County, Illinois	3.1	10.8	9.6	1.3	4.4	7.0	19.9	5.5	5.8
17081	Jefferson County, Illinois	4.2	14.8	6.0	1.0	4.1	6.4	23.9	8.8	4.3
17083	Jersey County, Illinois	1.8	15.7	5.7	1.1	6.5	5.8	27.8	8.1	3.7
17085	Jo Daviess County, Illinois	2.3	12.1	8.3	1.8	6.2	5.6	18.7	10.2	6.1
17087	Johnson County, Illinois	1.6	10.0	5.5	0.6	5.6	5.0	32.5	9.5	2.9
17089	Kane County, Illinois	4.2	11.1	4.9	2.2	6.7	13.0	18.9	8.5	4.2
17091	Kankakee County, Illinois	3.3	10.8	6.4	1.0	5.5	6.0	26.7	9.5	4.7
17093	Kendall County, Illinois	3.7	11.5	7.7	1.7	8.4	9.6	22.0	6.6	4.8
17095	Knox County, Illinois	3.2	14.6	7.7	1.4	4.7	4.9	29.8	6.3	5.2
17097	Lake County, Illinois	4.4	11.7	3.5	1.9	7.9	13.7	19.2	9.2	4.2
17099	LaSalle County, Illinois	2.9	14.9	7.3	1.1	4.4	6.3	21.1	9.1	5.5
17101	Lawrence County, Illinois	2.9	8.6	4.5	0.3	9.8	3.3	30.2	6.2	6.2
17103	Lee County, Illinois	2.9	11.1	6.0	1.2	5.0	6.0	25.2	8.9	3.4
17105	Livingston County, Illinois	2.1	11.2	5.1	1.4	6.8	4.5	20.6	6.2	4.5

Table C. County—Labor Force, Employment, and Educational Data, 2011–2015—*Continued*

		Industry for employed population age 16 and older								
Fips code	State/county	Wholesale trade	Retail trade	Transportation and warehousing, and utilities	Information	Finance and insurance, and real estate and rental and leasing	Professional, scientific, and management, and administrative and waste management services	Educational services, and health care and social assistance	Arts, entertainment, and recreation, and accommodation and food services	Other services, except public administration
17107	Logan County, Illinois	3.2	10.7	5.4	1.3	6.3	4.0	26.8	8.4	4.9
17109	McDonough County, Illinois	1.9	11.6	3.7	2.5	5.1	5.5	35.8	9.1	4.4
17111	McHenry County, Illinois	3.9	12.5	4.8	2.5	7.1	10.7	18.6	8.3	4.5
17113	McLean County, Illinois	1.8	10.9	3.1	1.2	20.9	8.8	25.0	10.7	3.9
17115	Macon County, Illinois	2.0	11.5	6.7	1.5	5.0	6.5	22.5	8.9	5.2
17117	Macoupin County, Illinois	2.7	12.3	7.0	1.3	5.6	7.0	22.8	8.6	4.7
17119	Madison County, Illinois	2.2	11.8	6.3	1.9	6.3	9.7	22.8	10.3	4.8
17121	Marion County, Illinois	2.0	11.4	7.1	0.6	3.7	4.6	28.3	7.4	5.2
17123	Marshall County, Illinois	2.7	10.8	5.3	1.6	4.8	6.2	20.1	6.2	5.6
17125	Mason County, Illinois	2.1	11.3	10.3	1.1	5.0	5.1	22.2	5.4	5.3
17127	Massac County, Illinois	0.9	11.6	10.3	1.1	4.3	5.4	24.2	12.6	5.1
17129	Menard County, Illinois	2.7	11.0	4.0	1.1	6.7	6.7	28.2	4.8	4.4
17131	Mercer County, Illinois	2.6	10.8	7.0	1.8	5.0	4.8	20.0	6.9	3.9
17133	Monroe County, Illinois	4.6	11.3	5.5	2.4	8.6	10.1	23.4	6.1	4.2
17135	Montgomery County, Illinois	2.2	11.3	6.1	1.6	5.5	4.7	32.3	4.7	4.5
17137	Morgan County, Illinois	3.5	10.6	4.6	2.0	6.3	3.8	29.0	7.6	5.4
17139	Moultrie County, Illinois	3.2	12.5	5.1	2.4	3.6	4.6	20.7	6.0	3.7
17141	Ogle County, Illinois	2.8	11.2	8.9	1.2	4.2	7.6	23.5	6.5	4.1
17143	Peoria County, Illinois	2.1	10.9	4.1	1.7	5.4	10.1	26.8	8.7	5.1
17145	Perry County, Illinois	1.8	11.0	5.8	1.5	3.0	4.3	24.3	7.1	5.3
17147	Piatt County, Illinois	3.7	11.0	7.1	1.1	5.8	6.6	25.7	4.5	4.1
17149	Pike County, Illinois	4.2	11.2	8.1	0.7	3.5	4.1	24.0	6.0	3.7
17151	Pope County, Illinois	0.5	17.9	8.4	0.9	2.4	6.1	27.1	6.3	4.4
17153	Pulaski County, Illinois	0.6	10.1	11.8	0.8	4.3	5.6	27.5	4.8	4.5
17155	Putnam County, Illinois	3.1	14.2	10.4	1.4	3.8	4.6	20.2	6.8	2.9
17157	Randolph County, Illinois	1.5	9.8	6.6	1.5	3.6	5.0	23.4	5.9	4.5
17159	Richland County, Illinois	2.4	13.7	5.6	2.1	3.3	3.9	26.0	5.9	5.7
17161	Rock Island County, Illinois	2.6	11.6	6.4	2.1	3.9	8.5	21.6	8.8	4.7
17163	St. Clair County, Illinois	2.3	11.2	6.8	1.3	6.4	11.0	24.4	9.3	4.7
17165	Saline County, Illinois	2.6	12.7	5.7	1.5	3.7	5.0	25.4	7.6	5.1
17167	Sangamon County, Illinois	2.3	10.8	4.2	1.8	8.1	8.7	26.3	8.4	5.0
17169	Schuyler County, Illinois	6.2	11.8	4.0	1.2	3.8	2.9	25.7	4.2	4.6
17171	Scott County, Illinois	6.1	11.7	6.9	2.0	6.8	3.8	21.9	3.0	5.1
17173	Shelby County, Illinois	2.6	10.5	6.0	1.8	4.8	5.7	22.4	4.9	5.1
17175	Stark County, Illinois	4.0	11.2	4.3	1.3	4.4	6.4	25.7	5.8	3.2
17177	Stephenson County, Illinois	2.4	11.0	4.5	0.7	6.4	6.7	24.2	6.6	5.1
17179	Tazewell County, Illinois	2.6	12.0	4.5	1.5	6.2	7.7	24.2	8.2	4.3
17181	Union County, Illinois	1.0	11.7	7.0	1.7	4.3	5.0	31.3	5.5	3.7
17183	Vermilion County, Illinois	3.9	11.4	6.3	1.2	5.4	6.1	24.9	6.8	4.8
17185	Wabash County, Illinois	2.3	10.6	7.2	0.3	3.9	6.3	24.3	6.5	4.9
17187	Warren County, Illinois	2.5	11.2	5.7	1.1	4.4	4.9	32.6	6.8	4.2
17189	Washington County, Illinois	2.6	11.3	7.5	1.0	3.9	5.3	21.2	8.2	3.0
17191	Wayne County, Illinois	2.5	11.2	6.2	1.0	3.4	5.3	21.0	4.1	4.8
17193	White County, Illinois	3.5	9.7	7.4	1.2	4.8	4.4	21.2	6.7	5.1
17195	Whiteside County, Illinois	2.1	14.6	5.6	1.2	4.2	6.1	22.6	7.0	5.5
17197	Will County, Illinois	3.2	12.2	7.3	2.1	6.7	11.2	22.4	8.6	4.4
17199	Williamson County, Illinois	1.8	12.6	4.2	1.4	5.7	5.9	30.6	9.8	4.0
17201	Winnebago County, Illinois	2.6	11.1	5.5	1.5	4.7	7.8	22.8	8.3	5.1
17203	Woodford County, Illinois	2.8	12.1	4.5	1.7	7.0	6.0	23.5	9.1	4.6
18000	**Indiana**	2.6	11.5	5.1	1.6	5.2	8.0	23.0	8.9	4.7
18001	Adams County, Indiana	2.3	9.9	3.8	1.8	4.1	4.0	17.4	5.5	7.9
18003	Allen County, Indiana	3.0	11.8	4.5	1.9	6.1	8.0	23.3	8.9	5.2
18005	Bartholomew County, Indiana	1.5	9.7	2.6	0.6	4.3	8.0	19.6	8.3	3.4
18007	Benton County, Indiana	2.9	11.3	6.3	1.5	4.2	5.5	21.9	3.1	3.9
18009	Blackford County, Indiana	4.3	12.3	4.4	1.4	2.6	4.4	20.2	6.5	3.8
18011	Boone County, Indiana	3.9	10.4	5.5	2.2	6.7	10.5	23.7	6.6	4.2
18013	Brown County, Indiana	1.9	7.7	4.8	0.5	4.6	6.7	23.7	14.3	4.8
18015	Carroll County, Indiana	3.1	11.1	4.3	1.3	3.7	6.5	21.6	6.2	4.4
18017	Cass County, Indiana	2.2	9.5	4.1	1.3	3.3	5.3	22.1	7.4	3.4
18019	Clark County, Indiana	2.9	12.8	7.2	1.5	6.5	8.3	20.9	9.7	4.6
18021	Clay County, Indiana	1.8	11.7	4.7	0.6	3.6	5.7	22.9	8.6	5.1
18023	Clinton County, Indiana	3.6	9.9	4.9	1.7	3.1	6.1	18.3	4.8	4.9
18025	Crawford County, Indiana	1.1	10.3	6.5	1.0	4.0	5.0	19.5	9.2	4.3
18027	Daviess County, Indiana	1.4	9.0	8.0	0.3	3.3	4.6	16.4	7.4	3.2
18029	Dearborn County, Indiana	2.8	11.0	6.7	0.8	5.4	6.9	20.9	11.9	4.2
18031	Decatur County, Indiana	2.1	11.0	2.8	0.6	3.6	7.4	16.0	8.7	3.5
18033	DeKalb County, Indiana	2.6	12.4	4.2	2.1	4.0	3.8	17.8	6.6	4.3
18035	Delaware County, Indiana	2.1	12.2	3.5	0.9	4.3	7.8	32.6	11.8	4.7
18037	Dubois County, Indiana	3.3	10.2	4.2	1.0	3.0	4.9	17.8	6.5	4.2
18039	Elkhart County, Indiana	2.6	10.3	3.8	1.0	3.4	5.1	16.9	8.0	5.1
18041	Fayette County, Indiana	3.4	11.9	4.0	1.3	3.1	5.4	25.1	8.7	5.3
18043	Floyd County, Indiana	2.3	12.3	6.0	1.5	6.8	8.2	23.3	8.4	4.4
18045	Fountain County, Indiana	1.8	9.6	4.6	1.1	5.2	4.5	17.7	6.6	5.2
18047	Franklin County, Indiana	1.2	12.7	4.7	0.9	3.9	5.9	22.5	6.3	5.8

Table C. County—Labor Force, Employment, and Educational Data, 2011–2015—*Continued*

		Industry for employed population age 16 and older								
Fips code	State/county	Wholesale trade	Retail trade	Transportation and warehousing, and utilities	Information	Finance and insurance, and real estate and rental and leasing	Professional, scientific, and management, and administrative and waste management services	Educational services, and health care and social assistance	Arts, entertainment, and recreation, and accommodation and food services	Other services, except public administration
18049	Fulton County, Indiana	3.4	8.0	5.5	1.8	3.7	4.2	16.4	4.5	5.0
18051	Gibson County, Indiana	2.2	11.0	6.8	1.7	2.7	5.9	16.9	8.4	4.9
18053	Grant County, Indiana	1.9	15.0	4.5	1.6	4.3	4.5	31.8	9.2	4.7
18055	Greene County, Indiana	1.6	10.8	5.5	1.5	3.9	8.1	21.4	7.2	4.0
18057	Hamilton County, Indiana	4.1	10.7	3.1	2.3	10.2	13.6	23.6	7.6	4.2
18059	Hancock County, Indiana	3.2	12.0	3.8	1.7	6.4	10.1	23.4	6.3	4.7
18061	Harrison County, Indiana	2.6	12.0	6.1	1.3	6.0	5.0	21.4	9.8	2.9
18063	Hendricks County, Indiana	2.8	11.6	8.7	1.8	5.8	9.8	23.5	7.4	5.4
18065	Henry County, Indiana	2.4	10.8	5.1	1.5	5.2	5.7	24.2	7.4	5.0
18067	Howard County, Indiana	1.8	11.4	3.0	2.0	4.4	6.3	21.9	11.1	5.2
18069	Huntington County, Indiana	2.8	8.7	5.4	2.0	3.9	4.8	22.2	7.3	5.7
18071	Jackson County, Indiana	2.5	14.3	4.5	0.9	3.6	4.2	16.5	5.8	4.4
18073	Jasper County, Indiana	1.6	13.2	6.1	1.0	3.6	5.5	20.1	7.1	3.5
18075	Jay County, Indiana	1.5	9.7	3.9	0.8	2.3	4.1	17.8	6.6	3.6
18077	Jefferson County, Indiana	1.5	9.8	5.1	0.9	2.8	3.1	23.7	8.6	3.7
18079	Jennings County, Indiana	2.5	11.0	4.1	1.0	2.9	4.0	19.4	7.2	3.3
18081	Johnson County, Indiana	2.3	12.3	5.4	1.8	6.1	9.8	21.9	7.2	5.5
18083	Knox County, Indiana	3.0	10.7	5.3	1.5	3.6	4.6	25.0	9.1	4.6
18085	Kosciusko County, Indiana	1.6	9.2	3.2	1.5	3.4	5.0	17.2	6.6	4.9
18087	LaGrange County, Indiana	1.7	8.9	3.1	0.6	2.6	3.2	13.0	4.9	5.0
18089	Lake County, Indiana	2.2	11.9	6.7	1.4	5.0	8.4	23.5	10.4	4.7
18091	LaPorte County, Indiana	2.2	11.8	5.9	0.9	5.0	6.6	20.4	10.8	4.8
18093	Lawrence County, Indiana	2.5	12.8	4.5	1.4	4.6	7.1	22.4	7.1	4.4
18095	Madison County, Indiana	2.4	11.5	5.4	1.5	4.9	8.8	24.3	10.4	5.6
18097	Marion County, Indiana	3.3	12.8	6.4	1.9	6.5	11.6	21.9	10.3	4.6
18099	Marshall County, Indiana	2.1	10.5	4.4	0.8	4.6	4.8	19.5	6.4	4.7
18101	Martin County, Indiana	1.2	13.0	6.2	1.4	1.7	5.4	20.8	6.3	4.5
18103	Miami County, Indiana	2.1	9.7	6.8	1.1	2.4	5.3	20.1	6.8	4.8
18105	Monroe County, Indiana	1.8	10.8	2.3	2.7	3.9	7.3	34.8	12.9	5.3
18107	Montgomery County, Indiana	2.4	11.9	3.3	1.4	3.1	6.5	19.0	7.6	4.6
18109	Morgan County, Indiana	2.8	11.3	8.7	1.1	5.6	7.8	18.9	8.2	5.0
18111	Newton County, Indiana	4.2	12.4	7.4	1.6	3.9	3.0	17.1	5.0	4.9
18113	Noble County, Indiana	1.8	8.5	3.4	0.9	3.7	5.5	17.0	6.4	4.7
18115	Ohio County, Indiana	2.1	8.4	7.0	0.4	3.4	3.4	16.9	21.6	4.2
18117	Orange County, Indiana	0.6	8.1	6.0	1.0	3.8	2.8	17.8	20.2	3.2
18119	Owen County, Indiana	1.7	10.3	6.5	1.8	3.8	5.4	20.7	6.1	6.1
18121	Parke County, Indiana	4.4	9.0	3.5	1.7	3.6	6.7	16.9	8.3	5.9
18123	Perry County, Indiana	0.4	8.1	3.5	1.3	3.3	5.9	16.4	9.8	3.0
18125	Pike County, Indiana	1.9	11.6	7.7	2.0	2.7	3.4	16.4	6.4	5.9
18127	Porter County, Indiana	2.4	10.2	5.2	1.3	4.7	8.0	25.3	9.6	5.0
18129	Posey County, Indiana	2.9	7.9	5.5	1.5	4.2	6.7	21.0	7.2	5.4
18131	Pulaski County, Indiana	2.6	8.0	6.5	1.2	3.0	4.1	21.4	4.9	3.9
18133	Putnam County, Indiana	2.6	13.3	6.1	1.3	3.5	5.7	22.8	9.3	3.6
18135	Randolph County, Indiana	2.1	12.0	4.4	0.8	4.9	4.8	22.8	6.1	3.5
18137	Ripley County, Indiana	1.4	9.8	6.4	0.7	5.1	5.5	19.4	9.7	4.5
18139	Rush County, Indiana	1.9	9.1	5.9	0.8	4.5	7.5	17.6	9.9	3.4
18141	St. Joseph County, Indiana	2.8	11.2	3.8	1.8	5.2	8.3	28.0	9.0	4.5
18143	Scott County, Indiana	1.2	14.0	5.4	0.4	2.9	5.5	18.6	6.4	3.9
18145	Shelby County, Indiana	2.6	8.6	5.4	0.7	3.7	7.3	18.4	9.2	4.3
18147	Spencer County, Indiana	3.3	8.9	8.2	1.3	4.7	5.2	17.0	7.9	4.5
18149	Starke County, Indiana	2.1	10.2	6.7	1.4	3.3	4.1	22.8	7.6	3.2
18151	Steuben County, Indiana	2.8	13.3	6.6	1.4	4.0	4.8	17.7	8.1	4.7
18153	Sullivan County, Indiana	2.2	10.7	7.9	0.9	3.4	4.1	22.6	8.6	3.1
18155	Switzerland County, Indiana	2.1	5.6	9.7	0.5	4.2	3.6	15.6	17.4	5.3
18157	Tippecanoe County, Indiana	1.9	10.7	3.0	1.3	4.2	7.0	33.5	9.6	4.1
18159	Tipton County, Indiana	1.3	8.2	3.1	1.8	3.6	6.8	21.7	6.2	5.3
18161	Union County, Indiana	2.2	14.0	6.7	1.6	4.2	5.1	28.2	11.2	3.8
18163	Vanderburgh County, Indiana	2.7	13.0	4.8	2.1	5.4	8.2	23.3	10.0	5.4
18165	Vermillion County, Indiana	2.0	11.7	6.3	1.5	3.9	7.6	19.8	6.0	3.3
18167	Vigo County, Indiana	1.7	12.3	4.0	1.5	4.4	7.4	29.5	9.8	4.0
18169	Wabash County, Indiana	1.5	9.9	3.6	0.9	4.1	6.2	26.8	7.9	4.7
18171	Warren County, Indiana	2.7	8.8	5.5	0.7	3.9	1.7	22.9	6.2	4.7
18173	Warrick County, Indiana	3.0	14.0	4.1	1.9	5.9	7.1	25.4	7.6	4.6
18175	Washington County, Indiana	2.0	11.9	5.1	1.9	3.5	4.0	22.7	4.7	2.7
18177	Wayne County, Indiana	2.8	12.0	4.4	1.4	3.8	5.4	28.6	9.4	5.0
18179	Wells County, Indiana	4.4	10.9	6.9	1.7	4.5	4.0	18.0	7.0	6.8
18181	White County, Indiana	1.4	12.2	4.4	1.1	3.5	4.3	21.4	6.2	4.1
18183	Whitley County, Indiana	1.9	13.5	4.2	1.0	4.5	6.1	18.4	6.5	4.7
19000	**Iowa**	2.8	11.7	4.6	1.8	7.4	7.2	24.3	7.5	4.2
19001	Adair County, Iowa	2.5	10.8	5.3	0.7	5.5	4.6	19.9	5.5	4.5
19003	Adams County, Iowa	4.6	8.1	5.3	1.7	4.0	2.5	28.1	2.5	6.4
19005	Allamakee County, Iowa	3.2	12.9	5.2	0.5	3.0	4.3	23.5	5.2	5.0
19007	Appanoose County, Iowa	2.9	13.7	5.6	1.2	3.0	3.9	19.5	5.6	5.6
19009	Audubon County, Iowa	3.6	11.3	5.0	1.6	3.9	5.7	21.8	6.1	6.2

Table C. County—Labor Force, Employment, and Educational Data, 2011–2015—*Continued*

Fips code	State/county	Wholesale trade	Retail trade	Transportation and warehousing, and utilities	Information	Finance and insurance, and real estate and rental and leasing	Professional, scientific, and management, and administrative and waste management services	Educational services, and health care and social assistance	Arts, entertainment, and recreation, and accommodation and food services	Other services, except public administration
						Industry for employed population age 16 and older				
19011	Benton County, Iowa	4.1	11.7	6.1	2.0	7.2	6.1	21.8	4.4	4.7
19013	Black Hawk County, Iowa	2.7	12.3	4.1	1.3	5.7	7.2	26.1	9.4	4.5
19015	Boone County, Iowa	2.3	14.7	5.8	2.0	5.5	6.8	27.4	5.9	4.7
19017	Bremer County, Iowa	2.1	11.9	2.6	1.4	7.9	5.5	27.6	4.7	5.0
19019	Buchanan County, Iowa	3.5	11.2	4.9	1.3	4.9	3.9	21.5	5.3	4.3
19021	Buena Vista County, Iowa	2.4	12.3	2.9	0.7	2.3	3.6	23.3	5.9	3.3
19023	Butler County, Iowa	2.8	11.6	4.9	1.2	5.1	5.4	23.7	3.8	5.9
19025	Calhoun County, Iowa	3.4	12.3	6.8	3.0	4.0	4.1	25.9	4.8	4.0
19027	Carroll County, Iowa	7.6	13.7	5.2	1.6	6.4	4.6	24.6	5.0	4.4
19029	Cass County, Iowa	2.8	14.5	5.4	1.5	3.9	5.1	24.4	5.5	5.4
19031	Cedar County, Iowa	3.7	13.4	5.6	1.2	3.4	8.3	23.5	4.2	4.2
19033	Cerro Gordo County, Iowa	3.5	13.7	5.2	1.8	5.4	6.6	25.5	9.0	4.0
19035	Cherokee County, Iowa	4.4	14.7	3.7	1.5	3.5	3.0	22.9	3.9	4.1
19037	Chickasaw County, Iowa	3.4	10.9	4.3	0.7	3.4	3.4	20.0	5.3	4.8
19039	Clarke County, Iowa	1.7	10.7	5.4	0.3	7.5	4.3	21.9	12.6	2.2
19041	Clay County, Iowa	5.2	16.0	4.8	3.5	4.3	4.0	23.6	6.0	3.8
19043	Clayton County, Iowa	2.4	12.7	4.7	0.7	3.4	5.2	20.2	5.8	4.5
19045	Clinton County, Iowa	2.0	13.8	4.2	1.7	4.3	7.4	22.6	6.8	3.1
19047	Crawford County, Iowa	2.2	14.2	4.1	1.3	3.6	4.5	19.2	8.7	3.3
19049	Dallas County, Iowa	3.4	10.6	4.0	1.6	21.6	10.5	21.0	5.3	3.4
19051	Davis County, Iowa	2.9	15.0	4.5	1.6	4.4	3.0	20.6	5.4	3.6
19053	Decatur County, Iowa	1.9	10.7	6.7	1.1	2.5	3.4	34.6	8.7	3.1
19055	Delaware County, Iowa	3.1	13.2	4.2	1.0	4.2	5.1	21.0	4.8	3.7
19057	Des Moines County, Iowa	2.0	13.8	5.5	1.3	4.3	5.6	21.9	8.4	5.1
19059	Dickinson County, Iowa	3.0	11.8	4.3	1.3	4.4	6.9	19.5	8.8	4.8
19061	Dubuque County, Iowa	3.3	12.8	4.1	2.6	6.4	7.2	23.6	9.0	4.9
19063	Emmet County, Iowa	3.6	9.9	4.5	1.8	3.4	3.6	21.0	6.2	4.0
19065	Fayette County, Iowa	3.6	11.5	3.5	1.4	3.5	5.2	26.8	6.6	5.7
19067	Floyd County, Iowa	2.8	12.9	3.4	2.0	5.8	5.2	22.0	4.9	3.7
19069	Franklin County, Iowa	2.8	9.0	3.5	2.2	3.4	7.2	21.6	4.6	6.1
19071	Fremont County, Iowa	3.3	11.2	6.4	1.0	4.5	3.8	26.4	3.8	4.0
19073	Greene County, Iowa	3.4	11.2	4.9	1.7	4.3	4.4	25.5	4.2	4.9
19075	Grundy County, Iowa	4.1	12.4	4.1	1.4	6.3	3.8	23.2	4.2	4.9
19077	Guthrie County, Iowa	2.4	12.1	5.9	2.1	11.0	5.7	23.9	5.0	4.2
19079	Hamilton County, Iowa	4.3	12.1	4.3	2.7	3.9	5.9	23.6	5.2	4.8
19081	Hancock County, Iowa	3.5	9.5	6.3	1.6	3.2	4.4	21.7	3.0	3.5
19083	Hardin County, Iowa	4.5	11.8	5.2	1.0	4.5	4.0	23.3	5.6	4.2
19085	Harrison County, Iowa	4.1	11.1	7.7	1.7	6.4	5.8	22.8	6.9	5.3
19087	Henry County, Iowa	1.8	13.4	4.2	0.8	4.6	5.6	26.3	5.2	3.6
19089	Howard County, Iowa	1.9	11.7	2.4	0.3	2.8	3.4	23.2	4.2	4.5
19091	Humboldt County, Iowa	4.1	9.8	6.2	0.6	3.3	5.4	20.8	3.7	4.4
19093	Ida County, Iowa	2.1	9.9	5.8	0.9	5.1	3.7	23.3	4.5	5.4
19095	Iowa County, Iowa	2.1	13.7	4.3	1.0	2.3	4.6	27.0	6.5	3.3
19097	Jackson County, Iowa	2.3	15.4	6.5	1.5	5.4	3.2	19.1	6.4	4.5
19099	Jasper County, Iowa	4.3	10.1	4.3	2.1	7.5	6.8	21.7	6.1	4.9
19101	Jefferson County, Iowa	3.8	10.7	2.5	1.9	6.7	8.9	22.7	7.7	7.5
19103	Johnson County, Iowa	1.7	9.3	3.2	1.8	5.4	8.1	40.6	10.6	3.5
19105	Jones County, Iowa	2.2	11.1	5.5	1.4	5.5	6.1	21.4	5.0	5.2
19107	Keokuk County, Iowa	2.8	9.8	4.0	0.7	3.5	3.5	26.6	5.6	5.2
19109	Kossuth County, Iowa	3.4	11.2	3.5	1.6	6.4	4.3	22.9	4.5	3.4
19111	Lee County, Iowa	1.4	13.4	5.9	0.9	3.1	5.8	20.8	7.5	4.2
19113	Linn County, Iowa	2.6	12.9	5.1	2.5	7.7	9.6	22.1	7.1	4.1
19115	Louisa County, Iowa	2.1	8.0	4.9	0.8	4.4	3.9	18.3	4.4	4.2
19117	Lucas County, Iowa	5.6	22.2	4.4	1.5	6.7	3.3	22.8	3.5	7.0
19119	Lyon County, Iowa	3.8	7.6	4.2	2.1	7.8	4.4	23.6	4.9	4.6
19121	Madison County, Iowa	2.7	12.3	6.3	2.2	13.2	7.0	20.4	6.2	3.3
19123	Mahaska County, Iowa	2.0	11.7	3.5	0.9	5.2	4.4	24.6	5.0	4.9
19125	Marion County, Iowa	2.1	9.5	3.5	1.0	4.7	5.3	26.7	7.5	5.8
19127	Marshall County, Iowa	2.6	9.9	5.1	1.3	3.3	5.6	21.9	5.7	4.6
19129	Mills County, Iowa	3.2	11.6	5.9	0.9	5.8	5.3	30.5	4.7	4.9
19131	Mitchell County, Iowa	2.4	9.9	5.1	1.0	4.4	3.4	20.8	5.9	4.0
19133	Monona County, Iowa	3.2	11.0	5.1	1.3	4.0	4.4	27.0	7.8	4.8
19135	Monroe County, Iowa	1.8	8.8	4.4	3.6	3.0	3.1	28.7	4.4	3.9
19137	Montgomery County, Iowa	4.0	11.5	4.6	2.7	3.9	3.2	26.5	4.8	5.7
19139	Muscatine County, Iowa	2.4	9.3	5.3	1.6	3.1	6.8	19.8	7.8	3.4
19141	O'Brien County, Iowa	2.6	13.0	3.8	1.8	4.8	3.8	22.4	5.4	5.2
19143	Osceola County, Iowa	2.4	9.3	6.2	1.2	3.7	2.5	21.8	5.2	3.8
19145	Page County, Iowa	1.5	13.3	3.3	2.3	3.9	4.1	27.0	5.2	3.5
19147	Palo Alto County, Iowa	4.0	11.7	4.3	1.8	3.0	2.6	23.0	8.5	3.7
19149	Plymouth County, Iowa	2.7	11.0	7.2	1.4	5.0	5.1	22.6	5.8	4.0
19151	Pocahontas County, Iowa	3.0	12.6	7.1	1.6	4.8	4.3	19.3	3.4	4.2
19153	Polk County, Iowa	2.9	10.9	4.0	2.3	16.1	10.6	20.9	8.4	4.0
19155	Pottawattamie County, Iowa	3.7	12.1	7.4	1.6	7.1	8.2	23.2	8.6	4.4
19157	Poweshiek County, Iowa	2.0	11.1	3.1	2.3	7.2	3.6	27.5	8.3	3.0
19159	Ringgold County, Iowa	4.2	8.8	3.3	1.2	2.1	3.9	30.7	4.4	5.2

Table C. County—Labor Force, Employment, and Educational Data, 2011–2015—*Continued*

		Industry for employed population age 16 and older							
Fips code	State/county	Wholesale trade	Retail trade	Transportation and warehousing, and utilities	Information	Finance and insurance, and real estate and rental and leasing	Professional, scientific, and management, and administrative and waste management services	Educational services, and health care and social assistance	Arts, entertainment, and recreation, and accommodation and food services	Other services, except public administration
19161	Sac County, Iowa	3.9	10.3	7.0	1.5	5.5	4.6	23.0	5.9	3.8
19163	Scott County, Iowa	2.9	11.8	5.1	1.7	5.7	7.9	22.8	9.0	4.1
19165	Shelby County, Iowa	5.1	14.8	7.8	1.6	6.0	7.1	22.2	3.3	5.6
19167	Sioux County, Iowa	3.6	9.7	4.5	1.0	3.9	5.4	25.5	6.7	5.1
19169	Story County, Iowa	1.5	9.9	2.6	1.9	3.8	7.2	37.1	10.1	3.4
19171	Tama County, Iowa	2.4	11.1	5.6	1.3	3.5	4.5	22.0	10.2	2.8
19173	Taylor County, Iowa	1.5	8.2	4.1	0.7	4.4	3.1	25.2	3.9	5.5
19175	Union County, Iowa	2.8	11.2	5.0	1.6	3.3	3.8	23.0	7.2	3.8
19177	Van Buren County, Iowa	2.5	8.0	5.2	1.1	7.6	4.1	22.7	3.5	4.2
19179	Wapello County, Iowa	1.8	11.8	4.4	1.0	3.8	5.1	24.9	6.8	4.5
19181	Warren County, Iowa	3.1	13.2	5.5	2.0	14.8	8.4	23.7	4.8	3.3
19183	Washington County, Iowa	1.7	13.6	3.9	1.3	3.4	5.6	29.0	5.6	5.9
19185	Wayne County, Iowa	2.4	11.9	6.1	0.8	2.2	2.9	22.9	4.1	6.4
19187	Webster County, Iowa	3.3	13.5	5.9	2.1	3.9	4.7	24.1	9.2	4.9
19189	Winnebago County, Iowa	3.6	9.5	3.4	1.7	3.4	3.8	21.6	7.9	4.5
19191	Winneshiek County, Iowa	2.8	9.9	3.7	1.2	3.8	5.3	34.5	6.4	4.8
19193	Woodbury County, Iowa	3.0	12.7	4.6	1.6	4.3	7.3	21.5	10.6	4.5
19195	Worth County, Iowa	2.2	12.3	4.4	2.3	3.9	4.7	19.3	7.9	4.3
19197	Wright County, Iowa	4.7	10.2	6.1	0.9	4.1	5.2	24.2	3.5	2.4
20000	**Kansas**	2.8	11.1	4.7	2.2	6.1	8.9	24.7	7.9	4.6
20001	Allen County, Kansas	2.4	9.3	3.6	2.2	4.4	3.5	27.2	6.1	5.8
20003	Anderson County, Kansas	0.6	10.0	7.8	1.1	3.6	3.9	21.3	9.2	7.9
20005	Atchison County, Kansas	1.1	11.0	3.1	0.7	4.1	2.9	33.0	8.5	2.8
20007	Barber County, Kansas	4.7	11.6	5.5	1.4	4.5	2.6	25.5	5.7	5.6
20009	Barton County, Kansas	2.1	10.6	5.7	1.1	6.8	5.2	26.8	6.5	4.2
20011	Bourbon County, Kansas	4.1	9.6	4.0	1.0	8.1	3.9	26.3	10.8	3.7
20013	Brown County, Kansas	1.4	9.2	4.5	1.8	3.5	4.6	28.1	7.9	3.6
20015	Butler County, Kansas	2.5	10.9	4.9	1.0	4.9	5.8	26.3	5.9	5.1
20017	Chase County, Kansas	0.7	12.0	6.4	1.8	2.3	6.6	17.7	7.2	5.8
20019	Chautauqua County, Kansas	0.5	8.5	6.8	2.0	2.0	3.0	29.7	3.4	2.9
20021	Cherokee County, Kansas	1.3	9.2	7.9	1.4	2.0	4.4	28.1	8.7	5.3
20023	Cheyenne County, Kansas	3.1	12.4	5.1	0.8	3.6	2.9	23.9	4.0	7.8
20025	Clark County, Kansas	1.4	7.5	3.8	1.6	4.4	2.7	28.2	4.3	3.9
20027	Clay County, Kansas	3.0	14.9	6.2	2.6	3.3	4.0	21.3	4.1	6.8
20029	Cloud County, Kansas	3.8	13.6	5.0	1.3	3.9	4.1	26.7	7.7	5.8
20031	Coffey County, Kansas	3.4	10.7	21.2	1.4	3.7	4.8	22.9	4.0	3.0
20033	Comanche County, Kansas	4.5	8.6	7.0	2.5	4.9	1.6	26.0	9.1	4.2
20035	Cowley County, Kansas	3.1	9.2	4.7	1.3	3.7	5.1	26.4	8.7	3.4
20037	Crawford County, Kansas	2.7	12.1	4.9	1.6	3.6	4.8	31.1	7.9	5.8
20039	Decatur County, Kansas	2.2	10.0	6.6	0.7	3.3	4.3	24.6	10.7	4.5
20041	Dickinson County, Kansas	3.0	15.1	5.1	1.5	4.8	5.7	23.0	6.2	4.1
20043	Doniphan County, Kansas	2.7	7.2	5.7	0.9	4.6	3.4	28.3	4.5	4.6
20045	Douglas County, Kansas	2.0	12.0	2.9	3.0	5.6	10.3	32.1	11.7	4.2
20047	Edwards County, Kansas	4.6	8.3	6.4	1.4	2.2	0.9	20.1	4.7	4.7
20049	Elk County, Kansas	2.9	5.4	5.9	0.6	4.3	4.0	36.0	3.6	2.1
20051	Ellis County, Kansas	2.9	13.1	3.6	2.6	4.4	5.9	30.3	8.5	4.9
20053	Ellsworth County, Kansas	1.8	8.4	3.4	1.4	2.7	6.6	25.3	6.2	4.1
20055	Finney County, Kansas	3.1	11.7	6.5	1.0	3.1	5.0	19.6	7.8	4.3
20057	Ford County, Kansas	3.8	8.8	4.7	2.8	2.7	4.7	17.7	8.7	5.1
20059	Franklin County, Kansas	2.4	13.4	6.3	1.1	3.5	6.7	24.1	8.3	5.0
20061	Geary County, Kansas	1.3	11.2	4.2	0.8	5.9	7.8	21.6	11.4	4.0
20063	Gove County, Kansas	4.5	7.7	3.9	2.0	4.5	6.5	24.8	4.0	5.2
20065	Graham County, Kansas	3.2	9.0	5.1	2.0	3.4	3.6	29.2	6.9	1.6
20067	Grant County, Kansas	3.9	6.8	6.7	4.2	2.0	5.8	19.0	6.7	3.3
20069	Gray County, Kansas	4.7	9.4	10.5	1.1	2.9	5.2	19.9	3.7	5.6
20071	Greeley County, Kansas	3.7	10.5	6.4	0.8	3.7	5.1	27.0	1.2	2.4
20073	Greenwood County, Kansas	0.8	10.7	5.1	0.6	4.0	4.2	22.8	8.4	6.2
20075	Hamilton County, Kansas	3.7	11.5	3.8	1.1	2.8	2.0	15.3	3.0	3.6
20077	Harper County, Kansas	2.7	10.5	5.3	0.5	5.9	5.2	24.0	4.8	5.9
20079	Harvey County, Kansas	1.8	7.4	4.9	1.0	3.5	5.1	29.2	6.0	4.3
20081	Haskell County, Kansas	4.9	6.0	8.6	0.2	1.7	3.7	24.6	5.4	6.0
20083	Hodgeman County, Kansas	2.8	9.4	4.9	1.2	3.6	3.3	27.6	2.3	5.4
20085	Jackson County, Kansas	2.8	9.5	6.2	0.8	3.9	5.0	24.0	10.4	4.8
20087	Jefferson County, Kansas	2.0	10.5	6.3	1.7	5.1	6.5	24.6	5.3	5.2
20089	Jewell County, Kansas	5.0	10.1	5.1	2.9	5.3	3.7	25.9	2.7	4.2
20091	Johnson County, Kansas	3.8	11.0	4.1	4.1	9.9	16.1	22.5	7.6	4.2
20093	Kearny County, Kansas	1.8	6.5	4.6	0.6	4.4	4.5	21.7	11.0	1.2
20095	Kingman County, Kansas	3.5	5.8	4.7	1.0	5.3	4.7	23.9	3.0	4.0
20097	Kiowa County, Kansas	3.0	6.9	5.8	2.3	5.6	3.8	29.3	5.4	4.6
20099	Labette County, Kansas	2.1	9.3	4.1	1.3	4.0	4.1	33.5	5.0	4.3
20101	Lane County, Kansas	3.8	7.9	5.0	2.9	1.3	3.7	25.2	1.6	8.1
20103	Leavenworth County, Kansas	1.8	11.9	5.2	1.8	6.2	8.5	26.3	6.8	3.5

Table C. County—Labor Force, Employment, and Educational Data, 2011–2015—*Continued*

		Industry for employed population age 16 and older								
Fips code	State/county	Wholesale trade	Retail trade	Transportation and warehousing, and utilities	Information	Finance and insurance, and real estate and rental and leasing	Professional, scientific, and management, and administrative and waste management services	Educational services, and health care and social assistance	Arts, entertainment, and recreation, and accommodation and food services	Other services, except public administration
20105	Lincoln County, Kansas	0.9	9.9	4.1	0.8	3.7	2.6	27.8	4.9	1.2
20107	Linn County, Kansas	3.3	12.0	9.8	0.7	5.9	7.0	25.7	3.4	3.5
20109	Logan County, Kansas	3.9	14.6	4.6	1.0	2.4	3.9	20.2	5.4	3.6
20111	Lyon County, Kansas	1.7	12.1	5.3	1.1	2.7	3.9	28.9	8.7	5.6
20113	McPherson County, Kansas	1.7	8.2	4.4	1.3	6.4	4.6	25.6	6.0	4.4
20115	Marion County, Kansas	3.0	11.4	4.5	1.0	3.2	3.6	28.4	5.1	5.4
20117	Marshall County, Kansas	2.0	9.8	7.8	2.2	3.2	5.0	24.3	5.4	3.7
20119	Meade County, Kansas	2.6	5.9	5.8	1.6	1.7	5.2	29.7	4.8	2.2
20121	Miami County, Kansas	2.6	12.4	8.1	2.0	8.7	10.4	21.1	5.7	3.8
20123	Mitchell County, Kansas	2.1	16.2	4.6	2.5	5.5	3.3	25.7	3.6	3.0
20125	Montgomery County, Kansas	1.8	11.4	5.4	1.2	2.3	5.2	28.1	6.4	4.5
20127	Morris County, Kansas	2.4	8.3	7.6	2.0	3.0	5.6	21.2	5.3	5.5
20129	Morton County, Kansas	4.3	8.2	5.8	2.3	4.5	2.7	25.6	5.1	6.3
20131	Nemaha County, Kansas	2.1	8.9	5.2	0.7	4.9	3.0	26.6	5.6	5.7
20133	Neosho County, Kansas	1.9	10.8	4.0	0.8	4.7	5.2	27.5	5.9	5.3
20135	Ness County, Kansas	5.0	5.0	5.8	1.0	7.3	3.7	25.8	1.9	4.9
20137	Norton County, Kansas	2.5	4.6	7.7	3.6	8.8	6.4	25.1	2.4	3.5
20139	Osage County, Kansas	2.8	12.2	7.0	2.1	5.5	5.1	25.1	6.2	6.2
20141	Osborne County, Kansas	6.0	9.3	4.2	1.3	5.1	4.2	23.4	4.1	5.3
20143	Ottawa County, Kansas	4.8	9.5	4.7	1.4	5.6	3.4	28.0	2.9	5.1
20145	Pawnee County, Kansas	2.2	15.4	0.9	2.9	2.7	2.8	33.4	3.9	5.9
20147	Phillips County, Kansas	2.2	7.9	7.6	2.7	7.0	7.9	24.2	4.1	5.5
20149	Pottawatomie County, Kansas	1.7	11.7	3.9	1.4	6.1	6.7	29.5	5.6	4.5
20151	Pratt County, Kansas	3.9	14.1	5.8	0.7	5.1	3.0	25.8	8.2	5.3
20153	Rawlins County, Kansas	3.6	9.1	5.7	1.6	6.7	4.9	21.2	5.4	5.3
20155	Reno County, Kansas	3.0	13.5	4.8	1.6	5.5	7.1	25.0	6.8	4.4
20157	Republic County, Kansas	3.3	14.3	4.4	2.2	4.1	4.1	22.7	3.7	5.3
20159	Rice County, Kansas	2.3	9.3	6.2	2.0	3.5	5.0	28.1	4.5	3.3
20161	Riley County, Kansas	1.4	12.8	2.0	1.6	4.9	6.7	34.6	12.1	4.5
20163	Rooks County, Kansas	4.0	9.2	4.4	1.0	3.3	5.8	26.0	4.4	3.6
20165	Rush County, Kansas	2.6	8.2	6.7	3.6	2.6	6.5	26.6	6.4	4.3
20167	Russell County, Kansas	1.3	12.1	2.2	1.4	3.2	2.6	27.9	10.3	2.7
20169	Saline County, Kansas	2.2	11.5	4.1	0.9	5.0	6.3	22.7	9.7	5.7
20171	Scott County, Kansas	3.4	3.8	4.2	1.8	6.9	0.9	18.2	3.3	8.9
20173	Sedgwick County, Kansas	2.5	11.6	4.1	1.8	4.9	8.6	23.2	8.9	4.9
20175	Seward County, Kansas	3.2	9.6	4.2	1.3	1.9	2.2	17.9	6.3	3.6
20177	Shawnee County, Kansas	1.9	11.3	4.8	1.9	8.0	8.7	26.9	8.8	4.4
20179	Sheridan County, Kansas	0.9	11.4	5.6	1.6	6.3	4.4	15.7	3.7	6.2
20181	Sherman County, Kansas	4.3	14.1	5.8	5.9	4.7	3.9	21.9	7.2	8.2
20183	Smith County, Kansas	2.9	9.8	3.1	1.7	5.0	7.1	24.3	5.6	5.6
20185	Stafford County, Kansas	4.6	6.8	5.6	0.7	2.9	6.4	26.5	5.2	3.8
20187	Stanton County, Kansas	1.8	9.2	8.0	3.0	5.5	4.3	18.2	3.3	7.5
20189	Stevens County, Kansas	1.7	8.9	6.8	0.5	4.5	5.5	17.3	4.3	6.7
20191	Sumner County, Kansas	2.8	8.3	6.5	1.3	4.9	3.9	23.6	9.1	4.0
20193	Thomas County, Kansas	4.0	14.0	4.2	2.0	5.2	5.9	27.0	9.4	4.6
20195	Trego County, Kansas	4.1	14.1	5.6	1.3	3.7	4.2	26.1	6.7	6.9
20197	Wabaunsee County, Kansas	2.8	7.8	6.5	1.1	6.3	4.8	25.9	3.7	4.3
20199	Wallace County, Kansas	3.4	11.5	8.1	0.7	4.6	4.2	23.3	3.6	3.0
20201	Washington County, Kansas	2.9	9.5	3.5	1.1	4.9	2.3	27.2	3.2	4.7
20203	Wichita County, Kansas	3.2	4.5	7.3	0.4	3.0	1.9	18.6	7.1	5.4
20205	Wilson County, Kansas	1.5	8.5	5.1	1.3	2.9	2.5	27.7	7.5	4.0
20207	Woodson County, Kansas	4.1	6.4	9.2	2.4	3.7	3.5	22.5	5.1	3.9
20209	Wyandotte County, Kansas	3.8	10.7	6.9	1.5	5.4	10.9	19.3	9.5	4.8
21000	**Kentucky**	2.5	11.9	5.9	1.6	5.4	7.8	24.2	8.7	4.7
21001	Adair County, Kentucky	1.1	15.8	5.4	1.1	3.0	3.6	25.4	5.8	3.6
21003	Allen County, Kentucky	3.1	15.1	5.4	1.3	2.3	6.0	19.3	6.0	4.0
21005	Anderson County, Kentucky	1.6	10.0	3.5	2.0	4.6	5.1	19.3	6.3	5.7
21007	Ballard County, Kentucky	3.2	14.6	6.0	2.0	4.7	8.3	18.4	6.0	5.0
21009	Barren County, Kentucky	2.1	10.6	5.4	1.1	3.3	5.0	21.3	9.0	4.7
21011	Bath County, Kentucky	2.3	7.7	6.2	0.5	2.4	6.2	23.3	9.1	5.3
21013	Bell County, Kentucky	0.8	16.7	5.4	1.5	2.9	6.0	26.5	7.4	5.2
21015	Boone County, Kentucky	3.4	12.7	8.3	1.8	7.8	10.3	19.8	8.3	4.1
21017	Bourbon County, Kentucky	2.3	11.8	3.1	1.3	4.2	5.5	19.1	8.1	4.7
21019	Boyd County, Kentucky	2.2	13.4	6.4	2.6	2.4	7.8	29.2	11.1	5.2
21021	Boyle County, Kentucky	2.5	10.5	3.8	2.8	3.7	6.2	27.8	9.5	5.9
21023	Bracken County, Kentucky	2.6	12.7	7.3	1.3	5.4	7.2	21.0	6.0	5.5
21025	Breathitt County, Kentucky	1.2	12.0	5.5	1.0	3.9	7.4	31.7	6.7	4.9
21027	Breckinridge County, Kentucky	1.0	13.1	6.7	1.0	3.8	3.7	21.9	7.4	4.2
21029	Bullitt County, Kentucky	2.8	12.8	11.8	2.6	6.7	7.3	18.6	5.7	5.3
21031	Butler County, Kentucky	1.9	9.1	4.4	1.6	6.1	6.1	20.0	3.6	4.3
21033	Caldwell County, Kentucky	1.6	12.3	3.6	0.2	4.9	3.3	22.4	7.7	4.3
21035	Calloway County, Kentucky	1.8	12.0	5.3	0.9	4.4	6.4	31.7	9.6	4.8
21037	Campbell County, Kentucky	2.8	12.0	4.8	1.9	8.4	10.9	24.6	9.7	3.9
21039	Carlisle County, Kentucky	2.2	10.1	9.8	1.2	4.1	7.0	18.9	6.2	3.4

Table C. County—Labor Force, Employment, and Educational Data, 2011–2015—_Continued_

		Industry for employed population age 16 and older								
Fips code	State/county	Wholesale trade	Retail trade	Transportation and warehousing, and utilities	Information	Finance and insurance, and real estate and rental and leasing	Professional, scientific, and management, and administrative and waste management services	Educational services, and health care and social assistance	Arts, entertainment, and recreation, and accommodation and food services	Other services, except public administration
21041	Carroll County, Kentucky	3.3	7.7	9.9	0.2	1.9	3.0	17.2	11.9	2.6
21043	Carter County, Kentucky	1.6	14.8	4.8	2.9	3.6	3.8	25.2	7.8	6.0
21045	Casey County, Kentucky	2.0	15.0	5.5	1.0	2.5	3.5	24.2	6.4	4.8
21047	Christian County, Kentucky	1.7	13.5	4.2	1.3	3.8	5.1	23.0	7.8	4.9
21049	Clark County, Kentucky	2.3	14.7	5.0	1.0	6.1	8.8	20.1	7.1	5.7
21051	Clay County, Kentucky	1.7	12.5	5.0	2.9	3.1	4.4	30.6	6.0	2.2
21053	Clinton County, Kentucky	2.8	8.1	5.7	0.3	2.4	2.2	24.2	7.0	5.3
21055	Crittenden County, Kentucky	1.3	11.6	8.4	1.5	6.0	2.7	24.4	5.0	2.5
21057	Cumberland County, Kentucky	0.9	10.0	5.8	1.1	2.7	5.0	24.9	10.0	3.5
21059	Daviess County, Kentucky	2.0	12.6	5.3	1.0	7.5	6.0	23.4	8.8	5.8
21061	Edmonson County, Kentucky	2.3	10.7	3.9	1.0	4.2	5.2	27.9	9.2	5.6
21063	Elliott County, Kentucky	1.2	6.8	9.7	2.2	0.9	4.6	24.5	6.7	8.9
21065	Estill County, Kentucky	1.5	14.6	7.9	1.0	2.6	5.8	15.7	5.7	5.5
21067	Fayette County, Kentucky	2.5	11.5	3.2	1.9	5.2	11.3	29.4	11.2	4.7
21069	Fleming County, Kentucky	1.0	13.9	6.3	1.5	2.3	3.7	24.2	4.6	3.7
21071	Floyd County, Kentucky	3.4	13.4	4.2	0.8	4.0	6.2	29.4	9.7	2.7
21073	Franklin County, Kentucky	1.0	10.1	3.9	0.7	4.2	7.1	16.7	11.3	4.8
21075	Fulton County, Kentucky	2.1	12.1	6.7	0.5	3.4	4.4	25.2	9.5	4.5
21077	Gallatin County, Kentucky	3.6	8.7	9.6	1.0	2.6	6.8	15.4	6.5	4.1
21079	Garrard County, Kentucky	3.2	12.6	4.7	1.5	4.0	6.1	26.7	4.2	5.3
21081	Grant County, Kentucky	2.2	9.1	9.6	0.8	3.9	7.3	16.5	8.3	3.3
21083	Graves County, Kentucky	1.7	11.2	5.8	1.6	4.8	5.7	24.9	6.9	6.1
21085	Grayson County, Kentucky	1.8	12.0	5.9	0.6	3.2	3.7	20.1	6.7	3.1
21087	Green County, Kentucky	0.9	13.6	6.3	1.2	3.5	5.5	23.1	5.2	4.0
21089	Greenup County, Kentucky	1.9	14.0	8.1	1.3	3.4	5.7	32.5	7.3	3.5
21091	Hancock County, Kentucky	0.7	7.9	4.8	1.1	4.6	3.8	20.0	7.0	4.1
21093	Hardin County, Kentucky	2.7	13.2	4.9	2.3	4.4	8.4	22.0	9.0	5.5
21095	Harlan County, Kentucky	0.9	12.9	5.4	0.8	3.1	5.6	33.2	6.0	4.0
21097	Harrison County, Kentucky	0.9	11.4	5.8	0.8	3.8	6.4	21.5	5.1	3.9
21099	Hart County, Kentucky	2.8	8.9	6.3	1.7	3.5	5.7	17.1	8.2	4.5
21101	Henderson County, Kentucky	3.4	14.1	5.4	1.1	3.5	7.1	25.1	7.9	4.1
21103	Henry County, Kentucky	1.4	12.0	6.0	0.9	5.1	5.2	19.3	8.2	4.6
21105	Hickman County, Kentucky	2.9	10.7	6.5	0.6	2.0	5.1	23.1	3.3	5.5
21107	Hopkins County, Kentucky	2.7	12.5	3.9	0.7	4.7	4.9	25.4	6.5	5.7
21109	Jackson County, Kentucky	1.3	12.6	9.9	3.2	3.0	3.6	25.2	2.2	3.6
21111	Jefferson County, Kentucky	3.2	10.5	7.7	2.1	8.2	9.9	24.5	9.8	4.7
21113	Jessamine County, Kentucky	3.4	14.2	5.5	0.7	3.9	7.7	27.0	8.4	5.3
21115	Johnson County, Kentucky	1.3	15.7	6.3	2.4	2.9	5.9	26.1	7.6	3.9
21117	Kenton County, Kentucky	3.7	10.7	7.0	2.1	8.4	10.5	20.8	10.2	4.0
21119	Knott County, Kentucky	5.2	13.6	3.7	2.3	3.0	4.1	31.7	5.0	4.6
21121	Knox County, Kentucky	1.0	12.9	7.5	1.5	3.8	9.8	27.8	8.2	3.1
21123	Larue County, Kentucky	2.4	12.3	5.9	1.7	4.5	4.9	16.7	8.2	8.8
21125	Laurel County, Kentucky	2.9	14.5	6.6	2.4	4.7	8.7	20.7	8.6	5.2
21127	Lawrence County, Kentucky	1.8	15.4	9.9	2.0	2.9	4.8	20.4	11.3	4.1
21129	Lee County, Kentucky	1.5	7.9	7.1	3.9	5.7	4.3	30.7	4.3	4.4
21131	Leslie County, Kentucky	0.0	12.3	2.5	0.9	3.5	6.7	36.4	0.7	3.5
21133	Letcher County, Kentucky	2.5	12.9	4.2	2.2	3.1	4.6	34.3	7.1	3.6
21135	Lewis County, Kentucky	1.0	9.3	6.9	2.4	2.5	3.6	22.3	5.1	5.2
21137	Lincoln County, Kentucky	1.8	10.9	7.6	2.3	3.7	4.5	25.2	6.1	7.2
21139	Livingston County, Kentucky	1.5	14.6	11.4	0.0	4.0	4.8	22.4	6.7	8.0
21141	Logan County, Kentucky	2.9	13.7	5.2	1.1	2.1	4.0	18.9	6.3	5.1
21143	Lyon County, Kentucky	1.5	14.7	4.7	1.2	2.1	7.6	19.6	6.9	5.5
21145	McCracken County, Kentucky	2.9	13.0	6.3	0.8	4.5	8.7	25.2	10.5	6.9
21147	McCreary County, Kentucky	2.2	14.0	9.2	2.8	4.2	5.0	25.9	6.6	1.9
21149	McLean County, Kentucky	0.7	11.0	7.6	0.7	4.3	2.4	27.0	3.2	6.4
21151	Madison County, Kentucky	1.7	12.0	2.8	1.6	3.3	6.8	29.9	10.8	5.0
21153	Magoffin County, Kentucky	0.7	12.0	5.0	0.2	2.6	5.3	34.0	6.8	1.9
21155	Marion County, Kentucky	2.3	11.1	2.2	1.2	3.0	6.1	22.1	5.1	4.8
21157	Marshall County, Kentucky	2.7	12.4	8.5	1.9	4.3	5.1	23.8	7.4	5.4
21159	Martin County, Kentucky	0.5	12.9	6.8	1.2	2.2	3.1	29.9	3.2	6.3
21161	Mason County, Kentucky	1.0	11.7	8.0	1.8	4.4	4.4	26.8	9.1	3.5
21163	Meade County, Kentucky	3.2	8.9	9.3	1.7	4.2	5.8	19.8	11.2	3.4
21165	Menifee County, Kentucky	0.9	11.0	5.1	0.5	4.0	4.1	23.2	2.8	4.2
21167	Mercer County, Kentucky	1.8	9.9	4.1	1.6	5.0	5.0	21.6	6.5	5.6
21169	Metcalfe County, Kentucky	1.9	12.6	6.3	0.5	3.5	7.8	17.0	2.9	3.7
21171	Monroe County, Kentucky	3.2	13.3	2.1	1.4	2.9	3.0	23.3	5.0	4.8
21173	Montgomery County, Kentucky	2.1	12.8	4.4	1.1	4.1	3.9	19.6	8.3	3.5
21175	Morgan County, Kentucky	1.4	12.3	5.7	3.2	4.4	2.5	24.6	4.2	3.0
21177	Muhlenberg County, Kentucky	1.8	12.6	8.4	0.6	2.2	5.3	24.8	4.5	5.4
21179	Nelson County, Kentucky	1.6	13.7	6.1	1.1	5.0	6.2	19.9	5.3	4.4
21181	Nicholas County, Kentucky	0.0	9.7	6.1	0.6	4.1	8.8	19.4	6.1	4.5
21183	Ohio County, Kentucky	1.1	11.1	5.0	0.2	2.5	5.0	21.2	5.5	6.8
21185	Oldham County, Kentucky	2.9	11.4	5.4	2.1	8.6	9.1	23.1	8.9	4.5
21187	Owen County, Kentucky	1.2	9.2	10.8	1.1	3.5	5.4	23.8	7.3	3.9

Table C. County—Labor Force, Employment, and Educational Data, 2011–2015—*Continued*

		Industry for employed population age 16 and older								
Fips code	State/county	Wholesale trade	Retail trade	Transportation and warehousing, and utilities	Information	Finance and insurance, and real estate and rental and leasing	Professional, scientific, and management, and administrative and waste management services	Educational services, and health care and social assistance	Arts, entertainment, and recreation, and accommodation and food services	Other services, except public administration
21189	Owsley County, Kentucky	0.7	10.0	9.2	4.5	3.1	3.7	28.4	5.1	7.8
21191	Pendleton County, Kentucky	3.9	13.4	6.1	1.5	3.9	7.7	19.0	4.4	4.0
21193	Perry County, Kentucky	3.0	14.4	4.9	1.3	4.0	6.1	31.8	7.0	3.6
21195	Pike County, Kentucky	1.6	12.1	4.9	1.5	4.1	6.5	29.8	7.9	3.9
21197	Powell County, Kentucky	2.8	7.7	6.6	1.0	2.3	8.1	21.6	10.0	4.7
21199	Pulaski County, Kentucky	3.0	15.5	4.1	1.2	3.6	5.8	26.1	8.9	5.0
21201	Robertson County, Kentucky	0.6	8.1	3.8	0.0	1.4	3.6	30.1	4.7	0.7
21203	Rockcastle County, Kentucky	2.6	10.0	3.1	2.9	2.6	5.7	27.5	6.0	5.7
21205	Rowan County, Kentucky	1.1	14.0	2.2	0.4	3.2	3.9	31.1	11.5	4.8
21207	Russell County, Kentucky	1.1	11.8	5.7	1.8	2.6	4.6	23.1	8.8	4.2
21209	Scott County, Kentucky	2.4	9.6	4.9	0.8	3.2	8.3	21.1	9.9	4.8
21211	Shelby County, Kentucky	2.8	11.8	4.1	1.4	7.2	8.3	20.8	8.2	4.9
21213	Simpson County, Kentucky	1.6	11.8	5.5	0.9	2.5	6.5	17.7	9.1	4.4
21215	Spencer County, Kentucky	4.2	10.4	7.2	1.0	8.2	7.7	20.7	4.5	4.9
21217	Taylor County, Kentucky	2.0	16.1	4.0	1.7	3.7	6.0	24.8	8.2	3.9
21219	Todd County, Kentucky	2.1	10.4	7.1	0.0	4.2	5.0	16.1	3.5	4.8
21221	Trigg County, Kentucky	1.1	10.8	8.1	1.7	3.5	5.9	24.9	5.9	2.9
21223	Trimble County, Kentucky	3.4	7.2	12.4	2.3	3.4	3.9	25.3	6.3	4.3
21225	Union County, Kentucky	2.1	13.1	5.6	0.4	3.1	4.6	22.9	6.1	4.4
21227	Warren County, Kentucky	2.5	13.1	4.9	1.7	3.4	7.7	25.7	11.1	4.4
21229	Washington County, Kentucky	2.1	13.3	4.5	0.1	3.7	3.9	21.5	6.2	4.0
21231	Wayne County, Kentucky	1.2	9.8	4.2	1.0	5.2	2.1	27.1	5.7	4.8
21233	Webster County, Kentucky	3.8	9.6	7.3	0.6	1.9	4.6	20.4	5.1	4.9
21235	Whitley County, Kentucky	3.9	13.4	4.0	0.7	3.7	6.9	29.5	7.8	3.2
21237	Wolfe County, Kentucky	1.0	11.7	3.5	1.2	2.8	2.1	31.3	7.9	4.8
21239	Woodford County, Kentucky	1.2	11.6	3.5	1.8	3.5	9.9	20.9	7.5	5.1
22000	**Louisiana**	2.6	11.6	5.2	1.6	5.1	8.8	23.4	10.3	5.2
22001	Acadia Parish, Louisiana	2.7	13.4	5.2	1.4	3.2	7.3	21.8	7.6	4.9
22003	Allen Parish, Louisiana	1.2	9.0	4.7	0.5	2.9	5.7	21.3	15.9	4.3
22005	Ascension Parish, Louisiana	4.0	11.2	4.9	1.7	5.5	9.8	21.9	6.9	4.1
22007	Assumption Parish, Louisiana	2.3	10.2	8.0	2.1	4.3	4.6	21.7	5.4	3.2
22009	Avoyelles Parish, Louisiana	1.8	11.0	6.8	1.3	3.6	4.6	24.5	12.4	4.6
22011	Beauregard Parish, Louisiana	1.7	10.7	6.4	0.8	4.3	7.3	18.9	8.3	6.7
22013	Bienville Parish, Louisiana	2.3	10.7	6.0	2.4	3.3	4.2	24.9	5.1	5.0
22015	Bossier Parish, Louisiana	2.7	10.2	5.3	1.6	4.8	8.7	25.2	11.5	4.5
22017	Caddo Parish, Louisiana	3.1	12.1	5.8	1.9	4.7	8.4	26.9	11.5	6.0
22019	Calcasieu Parish, Louisiana	2.1	11.9	4.8	1.1	4.1	7.3	23.4	13.2	4.4
22021	Caldwell Parish, Louisiana	1.0	12.0	6.1	1.6	3.8	8.5	21.8	6.7	3.9
22023	Cameron Parish, Louisiana	3.8	9.7	8.5	3.2	2.2	9.7	16.9	4.7	3.4
22025	Catahoula Parish, Louisiana	2.5	12.3	1.7	1.4	3.1	4.3	23.2	2.8	5.0
22027	Claiborne Parish, Louisiana	1.6	10.3	6.9	1.2	2.1	6.5	24.2	4.2	6.3
22029	Concordia Parish, Louisiana	3.2	17.2	4.5	1.3	4.6	5.5	23.7	3.0	5.3
22031	De Soto Parish, Louisiana	2.5	12.3	7.4	0.9	4.4	6.1	20.7	8.0	4.5
22033	East Baton Rouge Parish, Louisiana	2.2	12.0	4.2	1.9	5.7	10.6	25.4	10.7	5.4
22035	East Carroll Parish, Louisiana	1.5	12.4	2.3	0.4	3.5	2.0	30.2	6.3	4.8
22037	East Feliciana Parish, Louisiana	3.4	7.6	5.7	0.8	3.2	6.6	26.4	5.6	5.1
22039	Evangeline Parish, Louisiana	1.3	12.1	3.7	1.6	5.3	6.2	26.9	5.9	5.7
22041	Franklin Parish, Louisiana	2.4	14.6	4.8	0.9	2.1	7.3	23.4	5.7	4.7
22043	Grant Parish, Louisiana	2.6	8.9	6.0	2.5	3.6	5.1	28.4	5.6	4.6
22045	Iberia Parish, Louisiana	3.8	11.9	4.6	1.0	6.0	5.6	18.1	7.6	6.1
22047	Iberville Parish, Louisiana	1.3	11.2	5.4	1.4	4.7	7.2	19.8	7.7	5.1
22049	Jackson Parish, Louisiana	1.2	11.6	4.4	1.1	2.7	4.3	25.3	6.5	4.0
22051	Jefferson Parish, Louisiana	3.4	11.8	5.9	1.6	6.3	10.9	19.7	11.9	5.2
22053	Jefferson Davis Parish, Louisiana	1.6	11.5	6.2	1.2	3.7	4.5	25.0	9.0	5.3
22055	Lafayette Parish, Louisiana	2.8	11.0	3.9	1.6	5.4	10.3	22.4	11.4	5.3
22057	Lafourche Parish, Louisiana	2.1	11.2	8.0	1.4	4.1	6.9	20.0	7.2	5.8
22059	LaSalle Parish, Louisiana	1.6	11.6	4.9	1.9	4.9	6.4	26.1	3.5	4.2
22061	Lincoln Parish, Louisiana	1.7	12.5	3.5	1.3	4.0	5.9	34.4	10.9	4.9
22063	Livingston Parish, Louisiana	2.6	12.5	4.0	1.7	5.9	10.1	19.4	6.1	4.7
22065	Madison Parish, Louisiana	1.1	11.0	2.9	0.8	2.8	3.7	30.3	11.3	6.5
22067	Morehouse Parish, Louisiana	2.6	11.1	4.7	0.9	6.6	5.7	27.3	7.2	6.5
22069	Natchitoches Parish, Louisiana	2.5	13.6	5.2	1.1	2.4	4.5	25.7	8.1	5.3
22071	Orleans Parish, Louisiana	1.8	9.5	4.9	2.1	4.9	12.4	26.2	17.5	4.9
22073	Ouachita Parish, Louisiana	2.5	12.3	4.2	3.5	7.9	7.6	28.1	9.3	5.3
22075	Plaquemines Parish, Louisiana	3.3	7.9	7.2	0.7	3.6	7.0	15.7	8.2	4.9
22077	Pointe Coupee Parish, Louisiana	1.0	10.0	12.3	0.8	7.0	5.5	20.3	6.7	3.1
22079	Rapides Parish, Louisiana	2.0	12.7	5.3	1.2	4.7	6.4	29.8	8.2	5.8
22081	Red River Parish, Louisiana	1.6	9.2	6.4	0.1	1.9	5.7	21.5	7.3	3.1
22083	Richland Parish, Louisiana	1.8	10.7	5.2	2.1	5.7	5.5	30.3	6.3	5.3
22085	Sabine Parish, Louisiana	1.4	10.6	5.4	0.5	4.2	5.5	22.7	6.9	6.6
22087	St. Bernard Parish, Louisiana	2.1	10.6	6.9	1.1	4.2	10.6	17.2	9.4	6.2
22089	St. Charles Parish, Louisiana	4.4	11.1	8.0	1.2	4.4	8.4	21.2	9.0	4.9
22091	St. Helena Parish, Louisiana	2.4	12.1	2.9	0.4	6.2	6.9	29.6	3.5	1.4
22093	St. James Parish, Louisiana	2.1	11.5	6.8	0.1	3.6	9.0	18.5	7.0	4.0
22095	St. John the Baptist Parish, Louisiana	2.8	12.1	6.4	1.8	4.6	8.9	22.1	10.2	3.6

Table C. County—Labor Force, Employment, and Educational Data, 2011–2015—*Continued*

		Industry for employed population age 16 and older								
Fips code	State/county	Wholesale trade	Retail trade	Transportation and warehousing, and utilities	Information	Finance and insurance, and real estate and rental and leasing	Professional, scientific, and management, and administrative and waste management services	Educational services, and health care and social assistance	Arts, entertainment, and recreation, and accommodation and food services	Other services, except public administration
22097	St. Landry Parish, Louisiana	2.6	13.1	4.2	1.5	4.4	5.9	26.8	8.0	6.5
22099	St. Martin Parish, Louisiana	3.5	11.4	5.2	1.3	4.7	6.1	19.9	7.9	5.8
22101	St. Mary Parish, Louisiana	2.8	9.9	5.3	1.1	5.2	6.7	17.7	11.8	6.3
22103	St. Tammany Parish, Louisiana	3.6	13.1	4.9	1.5	6.2	11.5	21.6	9.6	4.8
22105	Tangipahoa Parish, Louisiana	2.6	12.8	4.7	1.3	4.5	6.4	25.5	11.0	5.2
22107	Tensas Parish, Louisiana	4.6	11.2	6.5	0.0	2.1	4.1	26.2	6.1	4.0
22109	Terrebonne Parish, Louisiana	3.0	12.5	6.6	1.2	4.6	6.9	17.5	9.6	5.5
22111	Union Parish, Louisiana	1.7	10.5	6.8	1.5	5.8	6.2	20.7	4.2	5.2
22113	Vermilion Parish, Louisiana	2.4	13.6	5.0	1.8	4.7	6.8	19.9	5.9	5.0
22115	Vernon Parish, Louisiana	1.2	11.8	4.6	1.4	4.0	6.8	21.5	8.9	5.5
22117	Washington Parish, Louisiana	1.5	11.4	7.2	0.8	4.9	7.6	27.8	7.5	4.6
22119	Webster Parish, Louisiana	2.4	11.5	5.6	1.4	3.0	4.5	21.5	9.1	6.3
22121	West Baton Rouge Parish, Louisiana	1.2	10.8	6.3	1.6	4.2	8.3	22.1	7.6	4.9
22123	West Carroll Parish, Louisiana	1.1	16.2	7.7	3.1	3.9	3.9	22.3	5.1	3.1
22125	West Feliciana Parish, Louisiana	0.4	7.6	6.8	1.6	3.4	7.0	23.9	5.6	3.5
22127	Winn Parish, Louisiana	2.0	8.1	4.3	0.4	7.0	3.1	27.3	3.8	4.7
23000	**Maine**	2.3	13.4	3.8	1.8	6.2	8.6	27.5	8.9	4.4
23001	Androscoggin County, Maine	2.0	14.8	4.1	2.3	6.9	7.9	27.0	7.7	4.0
23003	Aroostook County, Maine	1.7	14.2	6.2	1.5	3.8	5.5	30.3	6.0	4.4
23005	Cumberland County, Maine	2.6	13.0	3.2	2.2	9.2	11.8	27.5	9.4	4.5
23007	Franklin County, Maine	1.6	12.8	2.8	1.6	5.2	4.5	28.6	12.4	4.1
23009	Hancock County, Maine	1.9	12.7	3.5	1.6	4.2	11.2	25.9	11.0	5.3
23011	Kennebec County, Maine	2.9	13.4	3.8	1.4	4.4	7.8	27.9	7.8	4.6
23013	Knox County, Maine	1.6	13.3	3.1	1.5	6.1	7.4	23.4	10.3	6.1
23015	Lincoln County, Maine	1.3	12.9	2.9	1.0	5.3	8.3	24.7	9.8	4.9
23017	Oxford County, Maine	2.3	13.5	4.3	0.9	4.3	6.3	25.2	9.2	4.6
23019	Penobscot County, Maine	2.2	15.1	4.5	1.5	4.3	7.0	33.5	8.9	4.3
23021	Piscataquis County, Maine	1.5	11.2	5.6	1.4	2.7	3.8	28.5	6.9	4.2
23023	Sagadahoc County, Maine	2.4	15.5	2.7	1.1	4.4	8.2	25.0	9.1	4.4
23025	Somerset County, Maine	2.5	13.4	4.1	1.8	3.0	5.4	28.8	5.7	3.5
23027	Waldo County, Maine	1.6	11.6	3.1	1.9	6.3	8.9	27.1	9.2	5.4
23029	Washington County, Maine	2.3	11.9	4.2	0.7	4.2	4.3	27.2	7.1	5.0
23031	York County, Maine	2.5	12.6	3.6	1.9	6.9	9.1	24.6	9.7	4.1
24000	**Maryland**	2.0	9.8	4.3	2.2	6.1	15.2	23.6	8.3	5.4
24001	Allegany County, Maryland	2.0	12.0	5.6	1.6	5.0	7.7	28.0	11.0	4.3
24003	Anne Arundel County, Maryland	2.7	10.4	3.8	2.2	5.9	15.4	19.9	8.1	5.0
24005	Baltimore County, Maryland	2.3	10.6	4.7	1.9	7.9	12.4	27.7	8.1	4.7
24009	Calvert County, Maryland	2.4	11.1	5.5	2.2	4.9	13.6	17.6	7.6	5.0
24011	Caroline County, Maryland	3.2	13.4	5.2	1.3	3.7	8.1	23.2	7.1	6.4
24013	Carroll County, Maryland	2.5	10.9	3.9	2.3	6.5	12.8	22.6	7.6	5.0
24015	Cecil County, Maryland	2.3	10.6	6.1	1.3	6.2	10.5	22.5	9.0	4.4
24017	Charles County, Maryland	1.6	11.0	5.4	1.8	4.2	14.7	19.2	7.0	4.9
24019	Dorchester County, Maryland	3.7	9.4	3.6	1.0	4.3	7.3	26.6	9.4	4.2
24021	Frederick County, Maryland	2.0	10.1	2.9	2.5	6.8	16.3	22.2	7.8	4.9
24023	Garrett County, Maryland	2.2	12.2	4.5	1.6	7.2	7.5	20.2	10.5	6.0
24025	Harford County, Maryland	2.9	13.0	4.5	1.6	6.2	12.1	24.0	6.8	4.8
24027	Howard County, Maryland	2.3	8.3	3.3	2.6	7.0	19.3	24.2	6.5	4.6
24029	Kent County, Maryland	1.7	10.6	3.2	1.4	4.1	11.2	24.5	12.0	4.7
24031	Montgomery County, Maryland	1.3	7.5	2.6	2.8	6.8	21.8	21.6	8.4	7.0
24033	Prince George's County, Maryland	1.3	9.1	5.7	2.2	4.8	15.2	22.3	8.5	6.0
24035	Queen Anne's County, Maryland	3.5	11.5	3.8	1.7	5.3	12.4	20.7	9.1	5.1
24037	St. Mary's County, Maryland	1.3	9.7	5.5	1.9	3.2	16.5	18.9	8.0	4.8
24039	Somerset County, Maryland	4.2	9.7	4.3	3.0	2.0	6.9	29.7	8.3	5.5
24041	Talbot County, Maryland	2.0	10.4	4.2	1.3	6.1	13.0	22.8	13.6	6.6
24043	Washington County, Maryland	2.4	13.0	7.1	2.1	7.4	9.5	21.0	7.7	4.5
24045	Wicomico County, Maryland	2.3	12.1	4.9	1.1	4.4	7.8	27.7	10.7	5.0
24047	Worcester County, Maryland	2.6	13.5	3.5	1.3	7.1	9.5	18.4	18.7	4.0
24510	Baltimore city, Maryland	1.9	9.6	5.1	1.9	5.5	12.2	31.3	8.9	4.9
25000	**Massachusetts**	2.4	10.8	3.6	2.3	7.6	13.2	27.9	8.8	4.4
25001	Barnstable County, Massachusetts	2.0	14.0	4.1	1.9	6.5	11.9	24.1	11.7	4.9
25003	Berkshire County, Massachusetts	1.5	12.2	2.9	2.0	5.1	9.5	31.2	10.2	4.9
25005	Bristol County, Massachusetts	3.6	13.7	4.0	1.6	5.7	8.8	26.0	8.8	4.3
25007	Dukes County, Massachusetts	1.6	9.8	2.2	2.0	9.1	12.2	18.6	12.8	5.2
25009	Essex County, Massachusetts	2.5	11.1	3.7	2.2	7.2	13.0	26.0	9.0	4.6
25011	Franklin County, Massachusetts	2.5	10.2	4.0	2.3	4.5	6.3	35.2	7.8	4.7
25013	Hampden County, Massachusetts	2.8	12.5	4.6	1.7	7.1	7.9	28.7	8.8	4.4
25015	Hampshire County, Massachusetts	1.9	10.4	2.8	1.8	5.1	7.5	41.0	9.1	4.2
25017	Middlesex County, Massachusetts	2.0	9.1	2.8	3.0	7.2	17.5	28.1	7.7	4.3
25019	Nantucket County, Massachusetts	1.7	14.0	4.6	2.3	7.2	10.6	16.4	10.7	5.0
25021	Norfolk County, Massachusetts	2.3	9.9	3.5	2.6	11.3	14.8	28.0	7.5	4.0
25023	Plymouth County, Massachusetts	2.8	12.4	4.6	2.0	8.8	10.9	25.3	9.5	4.4
25025	Suffolk County, Massachusetts	1.8	8.8	3.9	2.3	8.6	15.6	30.1	11.1	4.8
25027	Worcester County, Massachusetts	2.6	11.8	3.8	1.9	6.5	11.0	27.4	7.9	4.4

Table C. County—Labor Force, Employment, and Educational Data, 2011–2015—*Continued*

Fips code	State/county	Wholesale trade	Retail trade	Transportation and warehousing, and utilities	Information	Finance and insurance, and real estate and rental and leasing	Professional, scientific, and management, and administrative and waste management services	Educational services, and health care and social assistance	Arts, entertainment, and recreation, and accommodation and food services	Other services, except public administration
26000	**Michigan**	2.4	11.4	4.2	1.6	5.4	9.3	23.9	9.5	4.7
26001	Alcona County, Michigan	1.0	11.0	8.4	1.7	3.8	7.1	19.5	9.2	6.0
26003	Alger County, Michigan	2.2	9.5	3.8	3.1	4.2	4.3	20.8	17.4	3.3
26005	Allegan County, Michigan	3.3	9.4	3.7	1.1	3.7	8.0	18.8	7.1	5.5
26007	Alpena County, Michigan	2.6	14.3	5.4	1.2	5.0	5.9	27.0	9.8	4.8
26009	Antrim County, Michigan	1.6	11.9	3.4	1.7	4.4	7.4	18.5	13.3	5.5
26011	Arenac County, Michigan	1.9	14.6	5.5	0.9	3.9	5.2	24.7	10.5	3.6
26013	Baraga County, Michigan	1.6	12.8	4.3	1.0	6.1	3.2	25.1	8.1	4.8
26015	Barry County, Michigan	3.6	9.3	4.3	1.0	5.1	7.4	21.0	6.9	4.8
26017	Bay County, Michigan	2.7	14.0	4.8	1.7	4.5	7.4	25.4	9.3	5.0
26019	Benzie County, Michigan	0.8	13.6	5.1	0.7	5.1	8.2	23.2	13.2	4.3
26021	Berrien County, Michigan	2.0	10.5	6.0	1.2	4.3	7.6	23.9	10.1	4.7
26023	Branch County, Michigan	2.1	14.6	5.3	1.0	3.6	5.4	18.7	8.8	3.7
26025	Calhoun County, Michigan	1.3	12.7	4.9	1.0	3.8	6.8	21.8	10.2	4.8
26027	Cass County, Michigan	2.8	9.8	4.5	0.7	4.6	6.1	21.2	8.0	4.6
26029	Charlevoix County, Michigan	1.8	12.8	3.4	1.1	5.0	8.1	20.3	14.2	4.1
26031	Cheboygan County, Michigan	2.0	17.1	4.9	1.6	4.6	7.1	16.9	13.5	6.1
26033	Chippewa County, Michigan	1.3	11.2	3.3	2.0	3.6	5.5	27.6	16.0	5.1
26035	Clare County, Michigan	1.8	12.0	5.2	0.9	4.6	4.9	23.5	11.3	5.8
26037	Clinton County, Michigan	2.3	9.3	3.7	1.5	7.1	9.5	25.4	7.7	5.0
26039	Crawford County, Michigan	1.5	12.2	6.9	1.2	3.6	6.0	24.4	13.0	5.1
26041	Delta County, Michigan	1.3	13.7	6.3	1.7	4.9	5.4	21.1	11.1	5.8
26043	Dickinson County, Michigan	2.4	15.3	4.7	1.9	3.0	4.5	26.5	8.6	5.2
26045	Eaton County, Michigan	1.5	11.9	4.5	1.4	6.8	7.8	21.8	9.3	4.7
26047	Emmet County, Michigan	1.3	13.0	2.8	2.5	5.2	8.0	25.4	16.3	4.9
26049	Genesee County, Michigan	2.4	13.3	4.3	1.4	4.8	8.1	26.2	9.5	5.2
26051	Gladwin County, Michigan	2.2	12.7	4.3	0.9	4.5	5.9	21.2	8.9	5.0
26053	Gogebic County, Michigan	2.0	12.7	3.4	0.8	2.2	4.2	24.7	13.6	4.8
26055	Grand Traverse County, Michigan	2.6	13.7	3.0	1.6	7.0	8.1	26.3	12.6	4.2
26057	Gratiot County, Michigan	1.5	9.0	5.1	1.4	3.4	5.0	28.8	8.6	4.4
26059	Hillsdale County, Michigan	2.5	11.7	4.8	0.9	3.0	4.3	23.8	7.5	5.0
26061	Houghton County, Michigan	1.2	10.8	1.7	1.6	5.0	6.3	37.3	11.6	4.2
26063	Huron County, Michigan	1.9	11.2	4.2	1.4	3.8	4.8	21.1	6.3	4.5
26065	Ingham County, Michigan	1.6	10.6	3.6	1.8	7.2	9.3	29.3	11.3	4.9
26067	Ionia County, Michigan	2.2	12.4	4.3	1.1	5.4	5.5	18.8	8.0	5.2
26069	Iosco County, Michigan	0.9	15.4	7.3	0.8	5.3	5.8	22.3	9.7	4.5
26071	Iron County, Michigan	1.6	12.0	4.5	1.8	3.9	8.2	23.8	8.7	5.3
26073	Isabella County, Michigan	1.4	10.7	3.1	1.3	4.5	5.1	29.5	21.4	3.6
26075	Jackson County, Michigan	2.5	11.7	5.0	1.1	5.0	7.3	23.2	8.2	5.2
26077	Kalamazoo County, Michigan	2.3	11.6	2.7	1.1	6.0	8.9	27.6	10.5	4.6
26079	Kalkaska County, Michigan	2.3	13.5	3.8	0.9	4.1	7.5	18.9	12.0	5.9
26081	Kent County, Michigan	4.1	11.6	3.5	1.5	5.9	9.7	23.0	9.0	5.0
26083	Keweenaw County, Michigan	0.1	11.4	4.0	0.2	2.9	10.0	28.4	17.3	4.4
26085	Lake County, Michigan	1.1	14.9	4.7	1.1	5.1	4.5	20.0	12.2	4.9
26087	Lapeer County, Michigan	1.6	12.5	3.6	1.1	3.8	8.3	20.4	8.2	4.7
26089	Leelanau County, Michigan	1.7	11.0	2.6	1.8	4.9	9.3	23.3	12.6	5.6
26091	Lenawee County, Michigan	2.0	11.8	3.5	1.4	4.4	6.4	25.8	8.1	5.3
26093	Livingston County, Michigan	3.3	12.4	3.3	1.7	6.4	10.3	21.0	8.1	4.8
26095	Luce County, Michigan	0.5	12.3	4.8	0.3	3.4	3.9	21.0	11.7	5.0
26097	Mackinac County, Michigan	0.8	9.6	5.6	0.9	6.2	6.1	20.3	19.8	5.9
26099	Macomb County, Michigan	2.5	12.0	3.6	1.6	5.8	9.7	21.1	9.3	4.7
26101	Manistee County, Michigan	1.9	13.2	3.9	1.9	4.4	5.8	20.0	14.5	4.1
26103	Marquette County, Michigan	1.7	11.9	4.6	1.5	4.5	6.7	30.0	12.1	5.3
26105	Mason County, Michigan	3.3	12.6	4.2	1.2	5.1	4.9	21.8	11.4	4.9
26107	Mecosta County, Michigan	1.4	12.1	4.1	1.4	4.0	5.1	28.7	11.5	4.1
26109	Menominee County, Michigan	2.3	10.1	4.5	1.0	3.7	4.2	19.0	10.3	4.0
26111	Midland County, Michigan	1.5	10.7	4.0	1.4	3.7	8.2	22.8	10.0	5.2
26113	Missaukee County, Michigan	2.1	11.8	6.6	1.1	3.0	4.2	18.4	7.3	4.5
26115	Monroe County, Michigan	2.2	10.1	7.6	1.4	4.2	7.2	23.5	8.8	5.0
26117	Montcalm County, Michigan	2.9	13.2	5.0	1.5	3.1	6.0	20.9	5.6	4.8
26119	Montmorency County, Michigan	1.4	12.5	5.2	0.7	5.8	6.0	18.8	12.1	7.1
26121	Muskegon County, Michigan	2.2	11.7	3.2	1.0	3.5	7.0	23.3	8.7	4.7
26123	Newaygo County, Michigan	2.0	13.1	3.7	1.0	4.1	7.2	20.5	5.5	5.4
26125	Oakland County, Michigan	2.7	10.2	2.7	2.1	7.7	14.0	23.1	8.6	4.2
26127	Oceana County, Michigan	2.1	9.1	3.6	0.7	3.4	6.1	18.9	7.9	4.6
26129	Ogemaw County, Michigan	3.2	15.0	5.1	1.0	2.7	6.2	25.8	10.7	4.5
26131	Ontonagon County, Michigan	0.6	10.4	7.2	2.4	4.1	3.5	22.9	12.2	6.3
26133	Osceola County, Michigan	1.3	10.7	5.7	0.8	3.0	5.7	22.5	7.1	4.7
26135	Oscoda County, Michigan	0.6	11.8	3.5	1.2	3.7	7.1	17.5	12.7	5.2
26137	Otsego County, Michigan	4.1	16.7	5.6	1.8	5.0	5.2	19.4	13.5	5.6
26139	Ottawa County, Michigan	3.3	10.7	3.3	1.3	4.5	7.9	21.5	8.2	4.9
26141	Presque Isle County, Michigan	1.6	11.2	7.9	0.9	3.5	5.1	22.8	8.7	4.2
26143	Roscommon County, Michigan	2.4	18.7	5.3	1.7	5.9	4.7	19.6	11.8	3.9
26145	Saginaw County, Michigan	2.5	13.6	4.1	1.7	4.7	7.9	25.8	10.0	5.0

Table C. County—Labor Force, Employment, and Educational Data, 2011–2015—*Continued*

		Industry for employed population age 16 and older								
Fips code	State/county	Wholesale trade	Retail trade	Transportation and warehousing, and utilities	Information	Finance and insurance, and real estate and rental and leasing	Professional, scientific, and management, and administrative and waste management services	Educational services, and health care and social assistance	Arts, entertainment, and recreation, and accommodation and food services	Other services, except public administration
26147	St. Clair County, Michigan	1.5	12.4	5.0	1.2	3.9	6.6	22.1	8.7	4.5
26149	St. Joseph County, Michigan	1.8	8.7	4.0	0.6	3.2	6.0	17.0	7.3	4.3
26151	Sanilac County, Michigan	1.8	13.9	4.7	1.4	3.3	4.7	19.4	5.8	4.4
26153	Schoolcraft County, Michigan	0.5	9.7	4.8	0.5	6.4	3.0	26.6	15.4	5.4
26155	Shiawassee County, Michigan	2.6	13.9	5.0	1.5	4.1	6.8	22.6	5.7	5.6
26157	Tuscola County, Michigan	1.9	13.0	5.3	1.0	3.8	6.2	25.2	7.1	4.9
26159	Van Buren County, Michigan	2.4	11.2	4.3	1.2	4.2	8.2	21.6	8.7	4.8
26161	Washtenaw County, Michigan	1.6	9.3	3.0	2.0	4.0	11.5	37.9	9.8	4.1
26163	Wayne County, Michigan	2.4	10.9	6.0	1.8	5.5	10.6	23.3	10.4	4.9
26165	Wexford County, Michigan	1.6	13.0	5.4	1.5	3.9	7.3	21.2	9.9	5.3
27000	**Minnesota**	2.9	11.3	4.6	1.8	7.2	9.8	24.8	8.4	4.5
27001	Aitkin County, Minnesota	2.2	12.3	5.8	1.3	4.2	4.4	23.6	14.5	5.0
27003	Anoka County, Minnesota	3.0	11.3	5.2	1.7	7.9	9.9	21.5	7.3	4.9
27005	Becker County, Minnesota	2.1	13.6	4.7	1.1	3.5	4.9	25.1	9.0	4.6
27007	Beltrami County, Minnesota	1.9	12.9	4.4	1.6	3.3	5.1	31.8	11.5	5.7
27009	Benton County, Minnesota	3.5	12.4	6.5	0.9	5.0	7.2	24.4	6.5	4.2
27011	Big Stone County, Minnesota	3.1	14.3	5.1	1.0	2.7	3.2	27.9	3.7	4.7
27013	Blue Earth County, Minnesota	2.4	13.8	3.5	2.4	3.6	6.8	27.9	10.1	4.6
27015	Brown County, Minnesota	2.4	11.7	4.9	1.8	4.0	4.7	23.5	6.9	3.1
27017	Carlton County, Minnesota	1.6	10.0	6.6	1.2	5.1	5.1	29.0	11.4	4.1
27019	Carver County, Minnesota	4.2	10.8	3.3	2.0	9.0	12.5	21.0	7.5	
27021	Cass County, Minnesota	2.2	11.0	4.1	1.5	4.8	6.4	22.5	12.7	5.2
27023	Chippewa County, Minnesota	2.8	8.0	5.8	1.1	4.4	5.3	24.9	8.8	4.8
27025	Chisago County, Minnesota	2.5	10.6	5.5	0.9	4.9	7.6	24.6	6.0	4.7
27027	Clay County, Minnesota	4.2	10.9	5.3	1.4	6.9	6.6	29.7	8.0	4.9
27029	Clearwater County, Minnesota	1.8	9.5	6.8	1.3	3.4	4.1	25.8	6.6	4.8
27031	Cook County, Minnesota	1.1	8.9	2.4	1.3	5.2	5.8	19.7	29.3	5.1
27033	Cottonwood County, Minnesota	2.8	10.9	5.1	1.0	2.5	4.7	24.8	3.7	4.8
27035	Crow Wing County, Minnesota	2.0	14.6	4.1	2.1	5.3	7.5	24.1	12.3	4.7
27037	Dakota County, Minnesota	3.4	11.2	6.2	2.7	9.7	11.3	21.4	8.5	4.6
27039	Dodge County, Minnesota	3.4	9.3	5.3	0.9	2.9	4.8	32.7	5.9	4.3
27041	Douglas County, Minnesota	3.3	15.3	4.0	1.3	6.1	6.0	23.1	9.3	4.6
27043	Faribault County, Minnesota	2.1	10.9	5.6	2.3	4.7	4.3	22.5	6.6	4.1
27045	Fillmore County, Minnesota	2.7	8.3	5.4	1.8	3.6	4.8	30.9	6.7	4.5
27047	Freeborn County, Minnesota	2.5	12.9	4.4	1.3	3.9	5.3	23.2	8.7	4.7
27049	Goodhue County, Minnesota	2.6	9.5	6.5	1.5	4.8	6.8	23.4	8.4	5.5
27051	Grant County, Minnesota	2.8	12.0	4.8	1.0	4.7	5.4	24.9	5.1	6.7
27053	Hennepin County, Minnesota	3.0	11.3	3.7	2.2	9.8	15.0	23.4	9.2	4.3
27055	Houston County, Minnesota	3.0	11.5	3.1	2.9	3.2	7.3	28.0	5.6	3.5
27057	Hubbard County, Minnesota	2.0	14.0	4.3	1.3	4.8	5.4	27.1	9.7	5.6
27059	Isanti County, Minnesota	2.2	12.9	5.8	0.8	4.9	5.9	23.6	7.6	5.1
27061	Itasca County, Minnesota	2.2	11.4	5.6	0.7	4.7	6.9	26.1	11.6	4.3
27063	Jackson County, Minnesota	2.7	9.4	5.2	1.2	3.5	3.8	21.3	6.8	4.7
27065	Kanabec County, Minnesota	2.1	13.6	4.0	1.5	4.9	4.7	24.2	9.0	5.1
27067	Kandiyohi County, Minnesota	3.4	11.1	5.3	1.1	3.7	6.5	26.5	6.5	4.2
27069	Kittson County, Minnesota	3.8	12.7	5.3	0.3	3.0	3.7	20.6	3.5	3.1
27071	Koochiching County, Minnesota	0.5	16.2	8.1	1.2	6.1	4.3	18.9	8.0	5.5
27073	Lac qui Parle County, Minnesota	3.2	11.2	5.4	1.2	5.2	3.1	25.5	4.4	5.1
27075	Lake County, Minnesota	1.0	6.6	5.2	2.2	3.9	4.9	28.5	15.4	2.9
27077	Lake of the Woods County, Minnesota	2.3	10.4	2.6	0.6	3.5	1.5	14.0	22.9	2.5
27079	Le Sueur County, Minnesota	2.9	9.3	3.9	1.3	4.7	5.9	23.3	5.7	5.0
27081	Lincoln County, Minnesota	2.3	8.9	6.3	0.9	5.0	3.7	24.8	5.2	6.3
27083	Lyon County, Minnesota	4.2	12.5	4.4	0.8	8.6	4.5	20.6	7.9	3.0
27085	McLeod County, Minnesota	1.8	9.2	3.7	1.3	3.5	7.8	22.6	7.0	4.6
27087	Mahnomen County, Minnesota	1.6	8.7	4.6	0.5	3.2	2.5	24.5	24.5	3.0
27089	Marshall County, Minnesota	7.3	8.9	4.7	1.3	3.4	3.1	21.5	5.3	4.6
27091	Martin County, Minnesota	2.8	11.8	5.2	0.8	5.3	4.8	22.3	6.1	5.3
27093	Meeker County, Minnesota	2.0	9.6	4.9	0.7	3.9	4.9	22.7	5.8	4.0
27095	Mille Lacs County, Minnesota	2.2	11.2	4.3	0.9	3.7	5.8	24.9	8.6	6.2
27097	Morrison County, Minnesota	2.2	11.3	4.9	1.0	3.6	8.0	23.1	6.7	4.9
27099	Mower County, Minnesota	2.0	9.8	4.3	1.8	3.5	6.4	27.6	5.5	4.0
27101	Murray County, Minnesota	3.0	9.8	5.3	1.0	4.5	5.3	27.2	4.4	3.9
27103	Nicollet County, Minnesota	2.0	8.0	3.6	1.8	5.1	4.7	34.1	6.7	3.4
27105	Nobles County, Minnesota	3.1	11.8	4.3	0.7	3.2	4.2	18.2	5.7	4.7
27107	Norman County, Minnesota	3.3	10.9	6.2	2.0	4.7	4.0	25.5	6.9	4.9
27109	Olmsted County, Minnesota	1.6	10.3	2.9	1.9	3.3	7.4	44.4	6.6	3.9
27111	Otter Tail County, Minnesota	2.8	10.6	5.9	1.8	4.5	6.3	25.1	6.1	5.4
27113	Pennington County, Minnesota	15.3	17.5	5.0	1.0	2.3	2.9	21.5	4.7	3.7
27115	Pine County, Minnesota	1.3	11.7	5.2	0.9	3.3	4.9	20.4	17.0	4.5
27117	Pipestone County, Minnesota	3.6	12.8	5.9	1.6	3.5	4.2	22.3	6.3	4.7
27119	Polk County, Minnesota	3.3	11.7	5.7	1.4	3.3	4.5	27.9	7.8	5.4
27121	Pope County, Minnesota	4.1	12.4	4.8	1.1	4.5	5.1	23.3	6.2	4.1
27123	Ramsey County, Minnesota	2.6	10.0	4.1	2.4	7.6	11.1	28.3	8.7	4.9
27125	Red Lake County, Minnesota	10.5	13.1	6.8	1.4	2.0	2.8	18.0	5.9	4.0

Table C. County—Labor Force, Employment, and Educational Data, 2011–2015—*Continued*

		Industry for employed population age 16 and older								
Fips code	State/county	Wholesale trade	Retail trade	Transportation and warehousing, and utilities	Information	Finance and insurance, and real estate and rental and leasing	Professional, scientific, and management, and administrative and waste management services	Educational services, and health care and social assistance	Arts, entertainment, and recreation, and accommodation and food services	Other services, except public administration
27127	Redwood County, Minnesota	3.4	10.9	3.8	0.8	4.7	3.3	21.8	11.3	5.8
27129	Renville County, Minnesota	3.4	8.9	6.5	1.0	3.5	5.3	21.6	6.0	4.3
27131	Rice County, Minnesota	2.0	9.1	4.1	1.6	4.8	6.6	34.1	6.9	4.5
27133	Rock County, Minnesota	3.2	13.0	5.8	1.0	5.7	4.1	26.0	5.4	4.9
27135	Roseau County, Minnesota	1.3	8.6	3.8	0.7	2.7	2.7	19.2	7.6	3.8
27137	St. Louis County, Minnesota	2.0	12.4	5.5	1.3	5.9	6.6	29.1	11.3	4.8
27139	Scott County, Minnesota	3.8	11.3	5.1	2.1	8.4	11.2	18.5	9.9	4.2
27141	Sherburne County, Minnesota	3.1	12.9	6.5	0.7	5.5	8.9	22.3	6.7	5.0
27143	Sibley County, Minnesota	2.6	9.3	3.9	1.2	4.2	5.0	20.1	4.8	4.1
27145	Stearns County, Minnesota	2.4	13.6	4.6	1.4	5.2	7.1	26.5	8.0	4.4
27147	Steele County, Minnesota	2.3	11.6	3.2	1.1	9.7	5.2	19.9	6.7	4.3
27149	Stevens County, Minnesota	1.1	11.0	2.3	2.8	2.1	5.0	30.3	9.3	4.4
27151	Swift County, Minnesota	4.4	10.8	5.0	2.4	3.4	5.2	22.8	4.3	4.9
27153	Todd County, Minnesota	2.2	9.6	5.6	1.6	3.5	5.1	23.7	4.7	4.7
27155	Traverse County, Minnesota	3.3	12.9	3.7	1.4	3.3	2.3	29.3	4.3	5.3
27157	Wabasha County, Minnesota	2.2	10.0	5.8	1.8	3.7	4.7	27.4	6.3	5.2
27159	Wadena County, Minnesota	4.2	14.0	6.1	1.2	3.0	3.1	22.7	7.7	4.3
27161	Waseca County, Minnesota	2.4	9.0	4.6	1.9	4.4	5.8	25.0	4.3	4.8
27163	Washington County, Minnesota	2.6	10.4	4.6	1.6	9.3	10.1	23.2	8.2	4.1
27165	Watonwan County, Minnesota	3.0	8.7	5.2	1.5	3.1	4.4	21.4	3.6	3.5
27167	Wilkin County, Minnesota	3.0	11.7	4.1	1.0	4.0	5.2	23.4	6.6	4.7
27169	Winona County, Minnesota	3.8	12.3	3.3	1.9	3.9	4.6	26.4	9.1	3.7
27171	Wright County, Minnesota	3.6	12.4	5.1	1.5	7.6	9.7	20.0	5.9	5.0
27173	Yellow Medicine County, Minnesota	3.7	10.3	5.7	1.0	4.0	3.2	24.6	6.3	4.9
28000	**Mississippi**	2.6	11.7	5.7	1.3	4.9	6.6	24.4	9.5	4.8
28001	Adams County, Mississippi	2.9	15.0	6.9	0.7	5.2	6.4	23.3	10.8	5.6
28003	Alcorn County, Mississippi	2.7	11.3	3.4	1.1	5.6	5.3	22.3	8.2	6.4
28005	Amite County, Mississippi	4.2	7.7	6.0	1.9	2.9	4.4	25.8	6.7	6.2
28007	Attala County, Mississippi	1.9	10.5	5.3	0.7	3.4	5.3	23.9	5.7	6.6
28009	Benton County, Mississippi	2.2	15.6	10.4	2.0	3.5	5.6	18.4	3.3	5.2
28011	Bolivar County, Mississippi	2.8	12.2	4.8	0.7	3.3	4.1	30.4	8.8	3.9
28013	Calhoun County, Mississippi	4.1	9.5	5.4	1.7	4.0	4.4	21.2	2.7	2.5
28015	Carroll County, Mississippi	4.3	10.6	8.0	1.5	4.1	7.6	21.4	3.5	4.7
28017	Chickasaw County, Mississippi	4.1	11.3	6.4	0.4	2.0	3.8	18.4	4.5	2.3
28019	Choctaw County, Mississippi	1.8	14.8	7.8	1.6	2.8	2.6	28.0	2.2	3.9
28021	Claiborne County, Mississippi	2.2	8.4	8.3	0.4	1.7	3.8	40.0	9.4	2.4
28023	Clarke County, Mississippi	3.1	10.5	5.5	1.6	3.7	4.1	27.9	5.9	5.7
28025	Clay County, Mississippi	2.7	12.5	7.0	1.2	3.9	6.5	21.5	7.2	4.0
28027	Coahoma County, Mississippi	2.0	10.4	2.5	0.6	5.0	4.7	31.7	13.9	4.0
28029	Copiah County, Mississippi	2.4	10.7	6.2	1.3	4.3	7.3	22.4	7.6	4.7
28031	Covington County, Mississippi	3.4	16.4	5.6	0.1	2.1	4.5	18.6	8.2	6.5
28033	DeSoto County, Mississippi	5.1	10.6	12.6	1.2	5.2	7.7	20.9	9.8	5.1
28035	Forrest County, Mississippi	2.0	15.3	4.4	1.1	3.4	7.2	29.3	11.8	4.4
28037	Franklin County, Mississippi	0.4	9.7	10.4	1.5	7.2	2.1	22.7	3.2	3.9
28039	George County, Mississippi	2.3	10.9	6.3	0.9	3.1	8.3	21.7	4.2	4.4
28041	Greene County, Mississippi	0.4	9.6	4.5	1.1	4.1	3.8	19.8	0.8	1.8
28043	Grenada County, Mississippi	1.0	15.0	3.8	0.3	2.9	4.8	21.0	4.6	4.0
28045	Hancock County, Mississippi	1.3	13.0	6.4	1.1	7.3	9.5	16.2	12.7	4.1
28047	Harrison County, Mississippi	2.2	12.8	5.0	1.1	5.0	7.4	19.1	17.8	4.4
28049	Hinds County, Mississippi	2.3	11.3	4.9	2.3	4.8	8.7	28.3	10.5	5.2
28051	Holmes County, Mississippi	1.1	9.5	4.9	0.5	3.7	5.1	27.3	5.8	5.7
28053	Humphreys County, Mississippi	3.5	12.1	6.7	0.3	4.3	2.6	21.5	6.9	3.1
28055	Issaquena County, Mississippi	0.0	11.5	10.5	0.0	3.9	1.0	11.8	5.6	3.9
28057	Itawamba County, Mississippi	1.5	12.1	6.1	0.9	4.3	4.0	22.0	4.5	5.1
28059	Jackson County, Mississippi	1.6	10.6	4.2	1.3	4.2	6.1	20.2	15.4	4.6
28061	Jasper County, Mississippi	3.8	5.2	5.0	2.3	3.5	3.3	22.2	7.6	2.5
28063	Jefferson County, Mississippi	3.0	9.1	12.1	0.0	0.0	2.0	37.1	4.4	0.0
28065	Jefferson Davis County, Mississippi	2.5	15.9	5.7	0.3	4.6	4.8	27.0	2.9	3.1
28067	Jones County, Mississippi	2.3	10.5	4.0	0.7	4.1	5.0	26.8	6.8	5.5
28069	Kemper County, Mississippi	3.7	9.0	6.2	1.0	4.4	4.8	24.4	5.4	5.1
28071	Lafayette County, Mississippi	1.0	10.9	3.8	1.3	4.3	8.5	34.5	11.4	4.0
28073	Lamar County, Mississippi	2.6	12.1	4.8	0.9	7.0	6.0	30.3	8.1	5.2
28075	Lauderdale County, Mississippi	3.1	13.5	4.9	1.5	5.8	6.0	27.8	7.7	4.9
28077	Lawrence County, Mississippi	2.0	10.5	3.0	1.7	2.0	5.2	25.2	3.2	5.1
28079	Leake County, Mississippi	0.2	11.5	4.3	0.1	5.5	5.9	22.1	7.7	4.1
28081	Lee County, Mississippi	2.5	12.1	4.5	1.3	5.8	5.7	23.0	8.7	5.8
28083	Leflore County, Mississippi	4.6	11.2	2.9	1.0	3.8	4.7	30.1	6.5	2.6
28085	Lincoln County, Mississippi	2.5	13.0	6.2	1.3	4.6	4.9	27.4	5.7	6.3
28087	Lowndes County, Mississippi	2.0	14.3	7.0	1.5	5.0	6.3	21.7	8.6	4.7
28089	Madison County, Mississippi	2.7	11.5	3.7	2.1	8.4	9.2	27.3	7.2	3.9
28091	Marion County, Mississippi	2.5	14.0	5.9	0.6	2.2	5.9	21.7	6.3	6.3
28093	Marshall County, Mississippi	1.9	12.2	10.7	2.1	3.7	6.5	20.3	6.3	5.7
28095	Monroe County, Mississippi	2.7	12.4	5.3	0.6	4.2	3.5	23.3	6.2	4.2
28097	Montgomery County, Mississippi	2.6	9.9	5.1	2.2	3.3	4.6	29.0	6.7	2.6
28099	Neshoba County, Mississippi	1.5	11.1	4.6	0.7	3.1	2.5	26.6	17.5	5.3

Table C. County—Labor Force, Employment, and Educational Data, 2011–2015—*Continued*

Fips code	State/county	Wholesale trade	Retail trade	Transportation and warehousing, and utilities	Information	Finance and insurance, and real estate and rental and leasing	Professional, scientific, and management, and administrative and waste management services	Educational services, and health care and social assistance	Arts, entertainment, and recreation, and accommodation and food services	Other services, except public administration
					Industry for employed population age 16 and older					
28101	Newton County, Mississippi	2.9	9.5	3.9	2.8	4.1	6.0	28.5	7.2	2.4
28103	Noxubee County, Mississippi	3.2	8.6	5.4	0.6	2.0	4.3	22.5	6.2	3.8
28105	Oktibbeha County, Mississippi	2.3	9.5	2.0	0.7	3.6	7.1	42.9	11.0	3.5
28107	Panola County, Mississippi	4.0	12.0	7.0	1.1	4.3	3.9	26.8	9.8	3.0
28109	Pearl River County, Mississippi	2.2	13.3	6.0	1.2	4.2	8.2	21.9	9.5	4.4
28111	Perry County, Mississippi	2.0	13.0	3.8	0.4	2.5	4.7	22.9	9.9	5.9
28113	Pike County, Mississippi	2.2	13.0	5.7	1.1	4.4	5.2	21.1	9.5	4.4
28115	Pontotoc County, Mississippi	0.9	19.1	4.5	1.1	4.5	4.0	18.2	6.9	2.3
28117	Prentiss County, Mississippi	3.8	11.7	6.7	1.1	3.6	4.8	22.4	5.8	4.7
28119	Quitman County, Mississippi	2.2	9.3	4.2	0.3	4.9	4.4	29.0	15.0	4.9
28121	Rankin County, Mississippi	3.2	10.5	4.7	1.9	8.1	9.6	24.5	7.5	6.8
28123	Scott County, Mississippi	2.3	9.7	4.1	0.4	5.3	4.3	16.7	5.3	4.2
28125	Sharkey County, Mississippi	1.5	15.1	1.4	1.4	3.0	4.9	37.1	7.2	2.1
28127	Simpson County, Mississippi	2.6	10.9	7.1	0.7	5.7	3.9	24.9	7.0	6.3
28129	Smith County, Mississippi	2.5	8.1	6.3	2.1	3.9	7.9	19.3	4.9	5.4
28131	Stone County, Mississippi	2.6	9.8	6.4	2.1	4.3	5.1	27.5	7.9	4.0
28133	Sunflower County, Mississippi	4.6	15.0	4.5	0.8	3.4	2.4	27.9	7.4	4.3
28135	Tallahatchie County, Mississippi	4.3	10.7	5.1	0.3	1.3	6.2	25.9	4.7	5.5
28137	Tate County, Mississippi	4.0	10.1	9.2	0.4	8.1	5.5	25.4	8.5	4.4
28139	Tippah County, Mississippi	2.3	11.1	4.2	1.3	4.7	7.1	18.5	4.7	4.4
28141	Tishomingo County, Mississippi	1.9	13.8	7.0	1.4	2.9	5.5	18.9	4.3	5.5
28143	Tunica County, Mississippi	1.3	10.1	5.5	0.6	2.4	6.2	17.1	37.1	2.6
28145	Union County, Mississippi	1.8	14.0	6.5	0.7	3.1	4.7	20.2	4.9	5.4
28147	Walthall County, Mississippi	0.9	9.7	6.3	0.1	4.2	5.5	20.7	4.9	3.8
28149	Warren County, Mississippi	1.4	8.8	5.6	1.2	2.2	9.9	22.3	14.8	4.9
28151	Washington County, Mississippi	2.7	12.6	5.4	1.9	3.5	7.0	27.1	9.9	5.1
28153	Wayne County, Mississippi	2.6	12.7	3.4	0.7	5.6	3.1	19.0	5.7	5.0
28155	Webster County, Mississippi	0.9	12.2	8.8	0.7	2.7	3.2	34.5	3.7	4.7
28157	Wilkinson County, Mississippi	1.2	12.0	10.6	0.6	2.8	2.3	19.5	5.3	2.9
28159	Winston County, Mississippi	1.4	8.2	4.9	1.8	2.9	4.8	27.1	8.8	3.2
28161	Yalobusha County, Mississippi	1.1	10.6	8.7	0.2	4.1	3.7	25.0	2.7	1.4
28163	Yazoo County, Mississippi	4.9	9.2	4.9	0.7	6.0	5.6	24.1	6.0	3.9
29000	**Missouri**	2.7	12.0	5.0	2.0	6.8	9.4	24.4	9.3	4.8
29001	Adair County, Missouri	1.5	12.8	3.3	2.6	3.8	6.7	34.3	11.5	3.8
29003	Andrew County, Missouri	2.9	9.9	6.4	1.4	4.0	5.4	26.3	6.0	4.6
29005	Atchison County, Missouri	1.2	11.1	9.9	1.5	3.2	4.8	26.5	6.6	7.3
29007	Audrain County, Missouri	2.3	14.9	4.6	1.9	3.1	4.2	26.1	5.5	3.6
29009	Barry County, Missouri	4.2	12.1	3.8	1.1	4.0	5.8	17.1	8.0	3.9
29011	Barton County, Missouri	2.5	14.9	4.3	0.7	5.0	6.1	21.4	3.4	5.4
29013	Bates County, Missouri	1.5	14.3	5.6	1.2	3.1	8.2	24.5	5.2	6.1
29015	Benton County, Missouri	2.0	11.7	5.9	0.8	5.1	6.7	22.3	11.8	4.7
29017	Bollinger County, Missouri	2.5	9.0	4.0	0.8	1.7	5.7	24.8	5.8	4.6
29019	Boone County, Missouri	2.1	12.8	3.4	2.0	7.9	7.5	36.4	10.9	3.1
29021	Buchanan County, Missouri	2.4	11.5	4.8	2.0	5.2	7.5	23.1	9.7	4.7
29023	Butler County, Missouri	2.2	10.9	6.1	0.6	4.9	4.0	31.5	7.3	4.7
29025	Caldwell County, Missouri	3.3	10.5	6.1	0.8	6.4	3.9	23.0	4.5	5.5
29027	Callaway County, Missouri	2.2	10.7	7.1	1.4	5.2	5.9	25.3	8.1	4.7
29029	Camden County, Missouri	1.5	15.4	4.2	1.3	6.6	8.4	21.2	13.9	6.5
29031	Cape Girardeau County, Missouri	2.6	12.3	3.9	1.8	5.8	6.4	29.8	10.8	5.0
29033	Carroll County, Missouri	2.1	12.5	6.6	1.3	4.7	4.7	22.8	6.6	3.3
29035	Carter County, Missouri	0.8	12.3	3.4	0.7	3.3	5.2	28.3	9.1	6.7
29037	Cass County, Missouri	3.1	11.8	5.4	2.2	7.6	10.6	20.8	7.2	5.5
29039	Cedar County, Missouri	4.0	13.9	6.1	1.0	3.2	3.3	20.2	7.8	5.6
29041	Chariton County, Missouri	2.6	12.6	9.4	2.7	5.0	2.4	23.7	4.5	5.1
29043	Christian County, Missouri	2.9	14.0	5.5	1.6	6.8	8.2	25.6	10.5	5.6
29045	Clark County, Missouri	2.7	13.2	10.2	0.5	2.7	4.3	20.1	4.4	3.1
29047	Clay County, Missouri	3.7	11.5	6.1	2.4	7.4	11.4	21.8	9.4	4.5
29049	Clinton County, Missouri	3.7	11.7	6.4	1.9	7.2	7.1	22.3	6.4	4.9
29051	Cole County, Missouri	2.4	11.4	4.1	2.0	6.6	9.3	21.4	6.7	4.8
29053	Cooper County, Missouri	2.5	12.0	5.9	1.6	6.8	5.5	24.1	9.7	4.7
29055	Crawford County, Missouri	2.1	9.8	4.9	1.2	3.1	5.9	20.4	10.2	5.8
29057	Dade County, Missouri	4.7	11.9	5.5	0.5	4.7	5.0	26.1	4.1	5.6
29059	Dallas County, Missouri	4.8	15.7	8.9	1.4	3.0	6.6	18.3	5.8	6.0
29061	Daviess County, Missouri	1.6	11.6	7.8	1.3	4.7	2.0	22.0	6.3	3.6
29063	DeKalb County, Missouri	4.1	11.6	4.8	0.9	6.5	6.0	24.2	5.2	3.9
29065	Dent County, Missouri	1.7	14.8	3.1	0.8	2.5	3.8	31.1	7.7	4.7
29067	Douglas County, Missouri	1.7	16.2	8.8	3.9	5.0	3.4	18.7	4.3	4.9
29069	Dunklin County, Missouri	1.3	11.8	5.2	1.6	3.4	3.9	29.2	6.5	3.3
29071	Franklin County, Missouri	2.6	12.0	5.2	1.8	4.7	8.8	19.0	7.8	4.0
29073	Gasconade County, Missouri	2.1	9.6	4.3	1.9	4.1	3.5	22.7	7.9	3.3
29075	Gentry County, Missouri	1.9	9.8	5.7	1.6	4.2	5.6	31.4	5.7	4.6
29077	Greene County, Missouri	2.9	13.5	4.8	2.4	6.5	9.3	26.9	10.8	5.7
29079	Grundy County, Missouri	1.7	13.6	3.7	0.7	2.9	5.3	25.8	5.7	5.4

Table C. County—Labor Force, Employment, and Educational Data, 2011–2015—*Continued*

		Industry for employed population age 16 and older							
Fips code	State/county	Wholesale trade	Retail trade	Transportation and warehousing, and utilities	Information	Finance and insurance, and real estate and rental and leasing	Professional, scientific, and management, and administrative and waste management services	Educational services, and health care and social assistance	Arts, entertainment, and recreation, and accommodation and food services	Other services, except public administration
29081	Harrison County, Missouri	1.6	12.5	7.9	1.2	5.0	2.7	22.8	8.3	5.0
29083	Henry County, Missouri	2.3	12.1	7.0	0.6	4.2	4.6	25.9	8.6	4.4
29085	Hickory County, Missouri	1.0	16.7	7.9	1.9	4.5	5.6	24.1	9.3	5.3
29087	Holt County, Missouri	2.4	8.3	6.7	1.3	6.1	6.0	21.2	7.9	4.3
29089	Howard County, Missouri	1.3	10.8	6.2	1.2	6.0	5.1	29.1	7.8	5.8
29091	Howell County, Missouri	2.8	12.6	5.6	1.7	3.8	4.0	28.9	7.4	5.9
29093	Iron County, Missouri	1.3	11.3	4.7	1.0	2.0	6.2	29.6	5.8	4.4
29095	Jackson County, Missouri	2.6	11.4	5.4	2.6	8.0	12.3	23.6	9.8	4.9
29097	Jasper County, Missouri	2.5	13.9	5.9	2.2	4.0	6.6	22.7	9.4	6.4
29099	Jefferson County, Missouri	3.1	12.6	4.9	1.7	7.2	9.8	21.5	8.4	5.4
29101	Johnson County, Missouri	1.5	12.6	4.0	1.6	4.3	6.6	25.6	9.8	4.3
29103	Knox County, Missouri	1.6	14.5	4.0	1.5	5.8	6.9	22.4	7.3	5.3
29105	Laclede County, Missouri	2.2	12.8	4.8	1.3	4.3	6.8	16.6	9.5	5.2
29107	Lafayette County, Missouri	2.1	9.7	5.7	1.5	7.1	7.5	24.6	6.8	4.5
29109	Lawrence County, Missouri	1.3	9.1	6.0	2.5	3.3	8.7	22.4	6.7	5.7
29111	Lewis County, Missouri	2.6	10.7	8.4	0.8	4.8	5.5	27.2	6.0	4.8
29113	Lincoln County, Missouri	3.1	13.9	6.0	1.1	6.5	6.9	17.1	7.1	5.0
29115	Linn County, Missouri	1.9	12.3	3.3	8.8	4.2	3.6	20.3	8.5	3.9
29117	Livingston County, Missouri	3.7	12.4	5.7	0.9	3.0	5.3	21.2	8.5	5.5
29119	McDonald County, Missouri	1.7	16.9	5.0	1.4	4.1	6.5	13.9	6.8	4.0
29121	Macon County, Missouri	1.7	13.6	5.5	2.9	4.2	5.7	25.8	6.7	4.3
29123	Madison County, Missouri	1.8	11.8	8.6	0.9	2.5	6.4	26.3	5.0	6.6
29125	Maries County, Missouri	1.1	13.7	7.4	0.9	3.9	5.2	23.0	4.6	3.6
29127	Marion County, Missouri	1.4	10.3	5.0	2.1	4.8	6.5	26.2	10.0	4.2
29129	Mercer County, Missouri	2.7	11.9	6.1	3.6	2.5	4.8	19.9	2.2	5.7
29131	Miller County, Missouri	1.4	18.9	2.5	1.7	3.8	7.0	19.3	10.9	5.4
29133	Mississippi County, Missouri	2.0	12.6	6.5	0.4	4.7	5.0	24.0	5.9	5.0
29135	Moniteau County, Missouri	1.8	9.0	5.2	1.3	4.4	4.8	18.5	8.8	5.2
29137	Monroe County, Missouri	2.7	10.4	7.9	1.5	3.3	5.2	24.1	5.6	3.7
29139	Montgomery County, Missouri	2.2	10.9	5.6	0.5	4.9	3.2	21.9	5.4	4.5
29141	Morgan County, Missouri	1.6	19.9	4.6	1.1	3.7	5.0	18.1	7.2	6.5
29143	New Madrid County, Missouri	3.6	13.0	6.7	1.2	3.0	5.1	25.1	5.2	3.3
29145	Newton County, Missouri	2.5	11.3	6.4	2.1	2.7	9.2	23.4	8.6	4.4
29147	Nodaway County, Missouri	1.7	9.7	2.6	2.0	2.7	5.3	26.6	14.5	4.4
29149	Oregon County, Missouri	1.1	12.8	9.3	2.2	2.8	3.6	28.6	7.1	5.3
29151	Osage County, Missouri	2.7	10.1	5.6	1.4	4.5	4.2	18.5	3.7	4.7
29153	Ozark County, Missouri	4.5	12.6	4.8	0.0	2.4	4.1	26.6	5.1	7.1
29155	Pemiscot County, Missouri	1.1	12.6	4.1	0.5	3.8	4.2	25.5	9.0	4.9
29157	Perry County, Missouri	1.2	11.5	4.8	1.2	4.3	4.3	21.9	5.9	4.9
29159	Pettis County, Missouri	2.3	12.1	5.9	1.3	3.5	8.4	22.6	7.4	4.8
29161	Phelps County, Missouri	1.2	13.9	3.6	0.8	4.3	5.2	34.4	11.7	4.5
29163	Pike County, Missouri	4.2	13.2	5.7	2.7	4.1	7.5	22.5	4.3	3.6
29165	Platte County, Missouri	3.4	11.8	7.2	2.9	8.0	12.6	20.6	9.0	4.2
29167	Polk County, Missouri	4.1	10.5	6.4	0.6	4.6	6.5	32.5	7.4	5.3
29169	Pulaski County, Missouri	0.8	13.4	3.3	1.2	4.4	6.3	19.7	11.5	4.2
29171	Putnam County, Missouri	1.9	9.9	4.2	0.4	4.5	6.0	23.7	2.2	5.0
29173	Ralls County, Missouri	2.2	12.4	5.4	1.2	2.5	6.8	21.7	6.0	4.4
29175	Randolph County, Missouri	3.3	17.8	7.3	1.7	6.8	5.5	20.3	4.9	8.6
29177	Ray County, Missouri	3.5	8.9	7.9	2.2	4.5	6.8	22.5	5.5	6.4
29179	Reynolds County, Missouri	0.8	6.5	6.6	1.4	1.7	5.0	27.2	5.2	3.6
29181	Ripley County, Missouri	1.1	11.5	4.5	0.9	5.3	5.4	32.4	4.0	3.8
29183	St. Charles County, Missouri	3.5	12.4	4.5	2.4	9.5	10.0	21.5	9.2	4.2
29185	St. Clair County, Missouri	2.0	15.0	6.7	2.2	3.9	5.1	28.0	6.2	5.0
29186	Ste. Genevieve County, Missouri	1.1	8.7	6.6	1.6	3.1	5.1	22.7	6.5	2.6
29187	St. Francois County, Missouri	2.6	14.7	5.2	0.6	4.1	7.2	26.8	6.3	3.7
29189	St. Louis County, Missouri	3.0	11.3	4.5	2.4	9.1	12.5	25.6	9.4	4.8
29195	Saline County, Missouri	2.4	12.0	3.8	0.9	3.7	3.9	28.4	6.1	4.3
29197	Schuyler County, Missouri	2.7	15.4	6.0	0.7	4.5	7.4	23.8	3.6	2.9
29199	Scotland County, Missouri	2.1	10.0	8.4	1.3	3.9	3.3	24.7	2.7	6.7
29201	Scott County, Missouri	2.6	13.3	6.4	2.3	3.6	5.3	26.7	7.2	3.6
29203	Shannon County, Missouri	2.5	6.8	4.3	0.7	2.5	2.6	23.2	7.8	4.3
29205	Shelby County, Missouri	2.5	9.3	5.0	0.9	6.2	2.8	24.7	3.9	6.8
29207	Stoddard County, Missouri	2.6	13.8	6.3	0.8	4.4	5.8	24.7	5.4	3.0
29209	Stone County, Missouri	2.5	12.8	2.9	1.2	5.4	7.1	18.7	18.2	6.9
29211	Sullivan County, Missouri	1.6	8.3	5.0	0.9	3.5	4.7	20.1	3.5	3.4
29213	Taney County, Missouri	1.0	16.0	3.8	1.7	4.7	12.0	16.4	25.1	4.6
29215	Texas County, Missouri	0.4	13.6	8.0	0.6	2.9	3.9	25.9	6.8	5.8
29217	Vernon County, Missouri	1.8	11.6	4.1	1.6	8.0	4.7	28.1	6.7	3.2
29219	Warren County, Missouri	2.5	11.5	4.8	1.0	4.8	8.9	18.5	8.6	5.7
29221	Washington County, Missouri	1.3	12.1	4.3	0.6	2.2	6.3	23.1	8.7	6.1
29223	Wayne County, Missouri	2.0	11.5	5.8	0.9	4.9	6.6	19.4	9.3	3.7
29225	Webster County, Missouri	3.1	11.0	8.3	0.9	4.9	7.4	21.4	7.8	5.3
29227	Worth County, Missouri	1.3	10.9	3.8	0.5	4.5	5.2	18.9	6.9	4.9
29229	Wright County, Missouri	3.1	11.1	6.7	0.3	3.0	3.7	25.1	4.7	6.6
29510	St. Louis city, Missouri	2.5	9.1	4.2	2.5	6.7	11.5	27.5	13.5	5.0

Table C. County—Labor Force, Employment, and Educational Data, 2011–2015—*Continued*

		Industry for employed population age 16 and older								
Fips code	State/county	Wholesale trade	Retail trade	Transportation and warehousing, and utilities	Information	Finance and insurance, and real estate and rental and leasing	Professional, scientific, and management, and administrative and waste management services	Educational services, and health care and social assistance	Arts, entertainment, and recreation, and accommodation and food services	Other services, except public administration
30000	**Montana**	2.3	12.2	4.8	1.8	5.4	8.2	23.2	10.9	4.9
30001	Beaverhead County, Montana	0.9	9.5	3.6	2.1	4.2	6.7	25.4	11.3	4.7
30003	Big Horn County, Montana	0.8	9.1	3.9	0.5	2.3	1.3	27.2	12.0	4.5
30005	Blaine County, Montana	2.3	9.0	4.6	0.5	3.7	4.4	24.4	5.6	3.3
30007	Broadwater County, Montana	1.6	9.6	6.1	0.8	4.4	4.9	16.9	5.4	5.5
30009	Carbon County, Montana	2.2	10.4	7.1	1.4	6.2	6.2	18.1	11.1	4.5
30011	Carter County, Montana	0.0	4.3	8.7	1.0	1.8	5.6	15.7	3.0	4.5
30013	Cascade County, Montana	2.3	12.6	5.9	1.6	6.7	7.9	25.5	12.3	4.9
30015	Chouteau County, Montana	2.7	8.4	4.3	1.3	4.0	4.3	22.2	7.3	4.2
30017	Custer County, Montana	3.3	14.8	4.5	1.6	5.7	6.0	23.1	9.9	3.5
30019	Daniels County, Montana	3.1	8.7	2.1	14.6	2.1	0.9	18.9	6.4	6.0
30021	Dawson County, Montana	1.6	9.3	12.0	2.7	3.7	6.1	19.3	7.9	6.6
30023	Deer Lodge County, Montana	1.5	6.7	2.1	0.3	1.7	5.8	33.8	12.8	2.9
30025	Fallon County, Montana	2.0	6.3	8.3	2.6	3.2	3.2	19.7	6.2	4.2
30027	Fergus County, Montana	1.5	9.3	3.4	1.8	3.7	7.3	25.0	6.9	7.5
30029	Flathead County, Montana	2.2	13.0	4.2	1.1	7.2	9.2	22.9	11.6	5.0
30031	Gallatin County, Montana	2.3	13.4	2.9	1.3	5.0	10.8	24.9	12.5	3.7
30033	Garfield County, Montana	0.0	11.2	3.2	2.9	3.4	0.5	12.1	3.8	3.1
30035	Glacier County, Montana	1.2	6.9	3.5	1.5	3.5	3.5	30.2	12.4	6.1
30037	Golden Valley County, Montana	1.1	9.2	5.6	0.6	2.8	2.8	20.7	4.5	4.5
30039	Granite County, Montana	1.0	8.5	4.0	0.9	5.0	5.3	24.4	10.2	3.2
30041	Hill County, Montana	1.9	14.1	10.7	0.7	4.1	4.8	28.6	8.2	4.3
30043	Jefferson County, Montana	2.0	7.6	3.6	0.7	6.7	9.9	23.1	8.0	4.0
30045	Judith Basin County, Montana	1.4	8.9	4.8	0.5	6.2	2.8	17.6	7.6	1.8
30047	Lake County, Montana	1.2	12.0	3.7	0.9	5.2	7.7	23.0	9.5	5.3
30049	Lewis and Clark County, Montana	1.4	10.2	2.7	1.2	7.0	9.7	20.5	9.8	5.6
30051	Liberty County, Montana	2.4	9.4	3.9	0.0	2.7	2.6	16.8	7.1	3.5
30053	Lincoln County, Montana	0.6	11.3	5.6	2.3	4.5	8.3	23.7	9.3	5.2
30055	McCone County, Montana	1.5	12.2	6.3	3.4	4.5	4.2	16.0	3.2	3.5
30057	Madison County, Montana	0.8	9.6	4.8	1.2	3.4	6.6	17.0	14.1	3.0
30059	Meagher County, Montana	4.3	12.5	5.6	1.5	5.1	4.0	16.6	9.3	1.6
30061	Mineral County, Montana	1.4	20.4	3.5	1.4	3.1	6.4	17.1	14.5	2.7
30063	Missoula County, Montana	2.3	12.3	3.7	3.3	4.8	10.5	26.8	12.7	5.1
30065	Musselshell County, Montana	1.0	9.2	4.5	0.6	2.3	3.5	18.9	8.8	5.5
30067	Park County, Montana	0.8	14.9	2.8	3.3	5.5	8.8	18.2	13.6	5.4
30069	Petroleum County, Montana	0.0	11.0	5.5	2.0	1.6	0.4	18.5	8.3	0.0
30071	Phillips County, Montana	0.1	10.6	7.3	2.6	2.7	4.2	17.9	7.1	4.2
30073	Pondera County, Montana	1.8	10.0	5.6	0.5	4.2	4.3	22.6	7.0	5.3
30075	Powder River County, Montana	0.7	9.4	5.7	0.8	2.0	4.9	16.5	4.6	0.7
30077	Powell County, Montana	0.3	6.7	6.7	0.8	3.7	3.3	19.4	14.5	3.6
30079	Prairie County, Montana	0.7	12.2	4.6	0.9	0.7	3.3	17.1	2.8	5.7
30081	Ravalli County, Montana	2.7	15.4	4.1	1.3	4.0	8.2	20.5	8.3	5.9
30083	Richland County, Montana	3.3	10.4	10.0	0.3	4.6	5.9	14.6	7.9	4.8
30085	Roosevelt County, Montana	1.1	10.0	5.9	1.2	2.9	2.7	29.7	6.5	2.9
30087	Rosebud County, Montana	0.1	5.4	11.8	2.2	4.7	2.7	26.8	9.1	1.9
30089	Sanders County, Montana	1.8	9.6	5.6	2.2	4.1	7.3	22.7	6.8	4.8
30091	Sheridan County, Montana	3.8	12.2	6.7	1.5	6.5	3.5	19.5	8.7	5.1
30093	Silver Bow County, Montana	2.0	14.8	7.2	1.3	3.4	8.4	27.3	11.1	5.3
30095	Stillwater County, Montana	2.9	13.3	5.1	1.1	4.3	5.8	16.6	6.2	2.8
30097	Sweet Grass County, Montana	1.2	9.2	6.6	0.5	6.0	3.7	18.2	7.2	5.5
30099	Teton County, Montana	1.9	12.5	3.7	3.6	5.3	4.0	24.4	6.3	4.4
30101	Toole County, Montana	1.6	8.1	4.5	1.1	2.9	1.8	16.8	11.8	8.0
30103	Treasure County, Montana	1.6	6.6	12.1	0.8	1.8	2.4	14.8	2.6	2.6
30105	Valley County, Montana	3.4	9.4	9.4	3.9	3.2	3.4	22.4	7.7	6.2
30107	Wheatland County, Montana	1.9	6.7	5.1	1.3	5.3	1.9	11.3	6.0	6.9
30109	Wibaux County, Montana	0.4	5.7	12.0	2.4	6.6	4.6	23.0	3.9	0.0
30111	Yellowstone County, Montana	3.7	13.5	5.5	2.2	6.7	8.7	21.5	11.8	5.5
31000	**Nebraska**	2.8	11.6	5.6	1.9	7.4	8.2	23.8	7.9	4.5
31001	Adams County, Nebraska	3.3	10.7	4.8	1.1	4.7	5.7	27.1	7.4	4.6
31003	Antelope County, Nebraska	3.7	12.6	6.8	0.7	4.2	2.4	21.5	5.0	3.8
31005	Arthur County, Nebraska	0.5	4.1	3.6	1.0	0.5	3.1	23.3	7.3	2.1
31007	Banner County, Nebraska	1.8	14.9	2.0	0.0	0.4	6.8	19.1	8.4	2.0
31009	Blaine County, Nebraska	4.9	2.4	3.5	0.0	0.0	1.4	12.9	8.4	3.8
31011	Boone County, Nebraska	3.1	9.4	5.1	1.7	4.2	1.0	23.3	8.6	3.6
31013	Box Butte County, Nebraska	2.8	6.9	22.9	0.6	4.1	5.2	21.8	4.4	5.9
31015	Boyd County, Nebraska	1.5	10.5	8.8	0.6	4.4	2.4	23.0	4.0	5.7
31017	Brown County, Nebraska	3.6	13.2	4.5	0.8	6.6	6.3	18.2	11.8	3.2
31019	Buffalo County, Nebraska	3.5	15.6	4.3	1.7	3.9	4.8	26.7	9.0	4.2
31021	Burt County, Nebraska	3.4	7.8	4.8	1.5	7.0	5.9	24.2	6.0	4.3
31023	Butler County, Nebraska	2.3	11.5	6.2	0.5	3.5	3.3	19.4	5.2	5.5
31025	Cass County, Nebraska	2.5	13.7	9.2	1.5	8.3	7.5	21.8	6.7	4.7
31027	Cedar County, Nebraska	3.0	10.3	5.2	1.8	6.4	3.5	21.4	4.4	5.1
31029	Chase County, Nebraska	2.9	15.8	5.5	3.8	5.2	3.9	14.9	4.9	4.9

Table C. County—Labor Force, Employment, and Educational Data, 2011–2015—*Continued*

		Industry for employed population age 16 and older								
Fips code	State/county	Wholesale trade	Retail trade	Transportation and warehousing, and utilities	Information	Finance and insurance, and real estate and rental and leasing	Professional, scientific, and management, and administrative and waste management services	Educational services, and health care and social assistance	Arts, entertainment, and recreation, and accommodation and food services	Other services, except public administration
31031	Cherry County, Nebraska	3.1	8.7	2.8	0.6	5.6	3.2	18.7	9.0	2.0
31033	Cheyenne County, Nebraska	4.8	28.9	7.0	1.3	2.9	5.4	19.5	7.8	4.3
31035	Clay County, Nebraska	4.4	10.1	8.2	0.8	2.9	4.7	22.2	4.6	4.0
31037	Colfax County, Nebraska	3.5	10.1	4.7	0.4	3.6	3.4	14.3	5.3	4.3
31039	Cuming County, Nebraska	3.2	11.0	6.4	0.9	4.5	4.4	22.8	5.2	4.4
31041	Custer County, Nebraska	2.9	13.5	4.3	1.2	3.1	4.3	23.5	6.1	5.5
31043	Dakota County, Nebraska	1.9	10.4	4.3	0.8	5.4	6.0	14.5	10.2	5.1
31045	Dawes County, Nebraska	0.5	13.4	3.3	0.9	4.4	5.1	31.1	12.2	2.5
31047	Dawson County, Nebraska	3.2	9.9	4.6	0.7	3.1	4.5	18.6	5.5	4.9
31049	Deuel County, Nebraska	4.0	24.8	7.8	1.1	5.1	4.4	15.9	6.9	3.0
31051	Dixon County, Nebraska	3.6	9.0	5.7	1.3	4.0	2.5	19.9	5.0	6.8
31053	Dodge County, Nebraska	2.2	15.9	4.0	1.7	6.8	5.4	22.5	6.4	4.0
31055	Douglas County, Nebraska	2.6	11.3	4.9	2.5	10.6	11.7	23.9	9.2	4.2
31057	Dundy County, Nebraska	2.3	6.3	4.6	1.2	7.9	1.5	27.1	1.0	3.8
31059	Fillmore County, Nebraska	3.4	10.1	6.7	1.8	4.8	4.0	22.3	4.1	5.0
31061	Franklin County, Nebraska	5.8	10.9	5.5	1.7	6.2	3.7	23.2	4.2	4.4
31063	Frontier County, Nebraska	2.3	11.8	7.3	1.2	5.6	4.3	23.7	2.7	3.9
31065	Furnas County, Nebraska	4.2	10.9	6.7	1.8	4.6	3.0	22.6	3.7	4.5
31067	Gage County, Nebraska	3.4	11.1	5.7	1.3	4.1	4.8	28.9	4.6	4.5
31069	Garden County, Nebraska	1.4	13.7	7.5	1.7	4.2	5.1	23.0	4.9	6.5
31071	Garfield County, Nebraska	2.1	14.1	5.1	3.2	4.1	3.1	17.8	10.4	4.7
31073	Gosper County, Nebraska	3.6	10.3	6.3	0.7	7.7	3.5	24.4	3.1	8.3
31075	Grant County, Nebraska	0.5	10.8	9.1	1.7	1.0	2.4	17.9	5.3	5.3
31077	Greeley County, Nebraska	5.1	10.6	6.0	1.7	7.5	1.2	22.4	4.1	5.9
31079	Hall County, Nebraska	3.1	13.7	4.7	1.1	4.7	5.3	19.6	8.6	4.7
31081	Hamilton County, Nebraska	4.3	10.0	6.7	1.5	6.0	4.0	20.7	6.8	4.9
31083	Harlan County, Nebraska	4.2	6.3	7.6	1.2	6.2	4.7	22.2	6.5	3.6
31085	Hayes County, Nebraska	0.5	7.7	11.5	1.1	2.4	1.1	19.7	3.8	1.1
31087	Hitchcock County, Nebraska	7.6	9.8	9.2	2.0	3.6	2.1	18.7	3.2	5.4
31089	Holt County, Nebraska	3.8	10.4	5.3	1.5	4.1	5.4	26.6	5.8	5.7
31091	Hooker County, Nebraska	2.7	8.2	5.4	1.8	1.5	6.3	22.7	15.4	7.9
31093	Howard County, Nebraska	1.6	10.7	6.2	1.1	6.7	4.4	23.5	3.9	3.5
31095	Jefferson County, Nebraska	4.3	14.1	4.7	1.6	4.3	3.6	20.1	3.2	6.9
31097	Johnson County, Nebraska	1.2	7.5	6.7	0.8	5.0	2.1	26.6	4.5	4.7
31099	Kearney County, Nebraska	4.1	13.2	4.5	1.0	3.1	2.1	20.4	5.7	5.6
31101	Keith County, Nebraska	2.7	12.9	6.7	1.8	3.5	7.0	18.1	11.4	6.3
31103	Keya Paha County, Nebraska	0.2	5.0	4.3	0.7	3.0	0.9	14.3	4.8	5.2
31105	Kimball County, Nebraska	3.0	12.6	4.5	2.1	1.5	12.5	20.6	6.3	2.8
31107	Knox County, Nebraska	1.8	12.0	6.0	1.5	4.6	2.8	24.8	6.9	3.7
31109	Lancaster County, Nebraska	2.1	11.4	4.1	2.3	7.7	9.3	26.6	8.9	4.3
31111	Lincoln County, Nebraska	2.4	14.5	18.6	1.6	3.7	4.4	24.9	8.9	4.5
31113	Logan County, Nebraska	2.7	15.4	16.0	0.9	1.1	3.6	15.1	3.1	7.1
31115	Loup County, Nebraska	1.7	1.3	10.8	0.0	0.7	1.3	19.2	5.1	3.7
31117	McPherson County, Nebraska	1.8	8.6	15.8	3.6	4.1	0.0	19.8	8.1	5.4
31119	Madison County, Nebraska	5.5	11.6	4.9	1.8	4.2	5.4	23.3	6.7	5.5
31121	Merrick County, Nebraska	3.4	12.0	5.7	1.7	6.7	3.0	23.0	5.9	5.5
31123	Morrill County, Nebraska	2.1	11.4	9.3	0.8	4.3	3.4	18.7	7.8	4.2
31125	Nance County, Nebraska	4.3	7.7	5.8	0.7	4.8	3.9	27.2	6.2	3.8
31127	Nemaha County, Nebraska	1.3	10.6	14.2	2.5	4.4	2.7	27.4	6.2	6.8
31129	Nuckolls County, Nebraska	3.2	10.6	6.7	2.2	5.6	4.4	24.4	4.7	4.6
31131	Otoe County, Nebraska	1.8	10.4	6.1	0.9	5.1	6.0	23.1	8.6	4.5
31133	Pawnee County, Nebraska	1.2	6.8	2.6	0.5	2.6	3.9	25.1	3.3	4.2
31135	Perkins County, Nebraska	5.9	7.5	7.5	0.7	5.2	2.0	24.9	2.1	4.7
31137	Phelps County, Nebraska	3.6	11.8	6.4	1.1	3.9	6.7	25.9	4.0	4.4
31139	Pierce County, Nebraska	4.1	9.5	5.0	2.3	5.3	4.4	24.4	2.9	6.4
31141	Platte County, Nebraska	1.6	10.1	6.0	1.1	3.5	5.3	17.9	7.2	4.7
31143	Polk County, Nebraska	4.0	8.7	6.5	1.3	4.1	4.4	19.1	5.1	3.1
31145	Red Willow County, Nebraska	2.3	16.6	7.5	1.1	5.8	4.9	23.2	8.5	2.3
31147	Richardson County, Nebraska	2.9	8.2	12.0	1.8	3.6	5.6	24.0	6.5	3.1
31149	Rock County, Nebraska	1.3	8.9	4.2	1.3	3.3	4.3	17.6	5.8	4.4
31151	Saline County, Nebraska	1.5	9.1	6.0	0.4	3.1	4.8	24.4	4.2	4.7
31153	Sarpy County, Nebraska	3.0	11.1	6.0	2.2	9.3	11.2	23.7	7.1	4.0
31155	Saunders County, Nebraska	4.1	11.6	6.1	1.3	5.9	8.0	23.4	5.4	4.8
31157	Scotts Bluff County, Nebraska	2.9	14.1	7.7	1.6	7.4	5.4	23.7	6.7	6.3
31159	Seward County, Nebraska	4.0	9.5	7.5	0.9	5.2	5.2	25.2	5.5	5.5
31161	Sheridan County, Nebraska	4.0	14.5	3.4	1.5	6.9	4.4	24.1	6.2	4.6
31163	Sherman County, Nebraska	3.0	9.4	8.9	0.0	3.4	3.3	24.0	3.4	6.2
31165	Sioux County, Nebraska	2.0	8.2	3.3	0.8	4.5	4.5	26.0	5.3	3.0
31167	Stanton County, Nebraska	5.2	9.1	5.1	1.3	4.9	4.4	24.4	7.7	4.2
31169	Thayer County, Nebraska	3.4	8.7	3.3	0.3	5.8	3.7	26.6	4.6	4.6
31171	Thomas County, Nebraska	1.8	8.6	5.7	1.3	4.7	4.4	16.1	6.5	5.2
31173	Thurston County, Nebraska	1.7	8.6	3.7	0.8	4.5	4.1	30.4	8.3	3.3
31175	Valley County, Nebraska	1.7	12.7	7.3	2.7	4.1	4.4	22.3	5.1	8.2
31177	Washington County, Nebraska	2.5	11.0	6.9	2.7	8.6	9.4	21.1	6.5	5.3
31179	Wayne County, Nebraska	4.3	9.1	3.6	0.8	6.7	2.0	32.6	9.4	4.1

Table C. County—Labor Force, Employment, and Educational Data, 2011–2015—*Continued*

		Industry for employed population age 16 and older								
Fips code	State/county	Wholesale trade	Retail trade	Transportation and warehousing, and utilities	Information	Finance and insurance, and real estate and rental and leasing	Professional, scientific, and management, and administrative and waste management services	Educational services, and health care and social assistance	Arts, entertainment, and recreation, and accommodation and food services	Other services, except public administration
31181	Webster County, Nebraska	3.1	12.2	4.6	3.6	3.1	2.0	23.3	3.7	7.4
31183	Wheeler County, Nebraska	3.2	8.7	3.4	0.2	2.6	3.6	22.1	5.9	2.0
31185	York County, Nebraska	2.7	8.4	6.1	1.9	5.6	8.1	23.5	8.0	5.5
32000	**Nevada**	2.1	12.0	5.1	1.7	5.7	10.9	15.4	25.9	4.6
32001	Churchill County, Nevada	1.5	11.4	6.7	1.8	2.5	8.3	19.5	9.4	6.4
32003	Clark County, Nevada	1.8	12.2	5.0	1.7	6.0	11.3	14.6	29.7	4.5
32005	Douglas County, Nevada	1.8	10.7	3.8	1.1	6.1	10.2	16.7	16.7	6.3
32007	Elko County, Nevada	1.7	8.5	4.4	1.1	3.5	6.1	11.3	19.6	3.4
32009	Esmeralda County, Nevada	0.0	3.0	8.2	1.1	0.0	12.4	11.9	12.1	6.4
32011	Eureka County, Nevada	0.0	1.1	3.4	0.0	0.0	4.8	17.6	10.9	0.9
32013	Humboldt County, Nevada	1.7	12.3	6.9	1.7	0.9	5.5	11.6	14.5	3.4
32015	Lander County, Nevada	1.7	8.3	6.9	0.9	0.6	0.9	11.4	7.4	3.2
32017	Lincoln County, Nevada	0.8	11.5	2.4	4.3	4.1	4.6	21.4	10.9	1.1
32019	Lyon County, Nevada	1.8	14.4	6.4	1.9	4.2	9.3	17.0	11.1	4.1
32021	Mineral County, Nevada	0.2	8.7	0.9	0.0	4.4	8.3	19.5	19.6	2.2
32023	Nye County, Nevada	1.2	12.6	5.3	2.0	4.0	7.7	14.6	17.5	5.5
32027	Pershing County, Nevada	0.0	9.9	6.9	1.1	4.0	2.1	12.7	6.8	1.0
32029	Storey County, Nevada	2.1	12.1	11.9	1.2	4.3	8.0	13.8	15.6	3.9
32031	Washoe County, Nevada	3.4	11.7	5.4	1.8	5.8	11.3	19.4	16.4	5.0
32033	White Pine County, Nevada	1.9	8.7	3.2	1.1	2.0	4.3	16.6	11.6	1.5
32510	Carson City, Nevada	1.7	13.1	3.3	1.1	3.6	8.7	16.5	16.3	5.4
33000	**New Hampshire**	3.0	12.3	3.9	2.2	6.3	10.4	24.5	8.5	4.3
33001	Belknap County, New Hampshire	2.4	12.7	2.8	1.9	5.8	8.7	25.1	8.9	4.2
33003	Carroll County, New Hampshire	2.2	13.1	3.8	1.8	4.3	9.2	23.5	15.8	4.6
33005	Cheshire County, New Hampshire	5.5	11.9	3.8	1.4	4.7	6.1	27.4	7.5	4.1
33007	Coos County, New Hampshire	1.6	13.4	4.8	1.2	3.6	5.6	25.8	13.6	5.1
33009	Grafton County, New Hampshire	1.6	10.5	2.9	1.7	3.4	8.9	33.7	11.3	3.8
33011	Hillsborough County, New Hampshire	3.0	12.1	4.3	2.6	7.0	12.5	22.3	7.5	4.4
33013	Merrimack County, New Hampshire	3.1	11.9	3.1	1.6	6.4	9.5	27.2	7.6	4.7
33015	Rockingham County, New Hampshire	3.7	12.6	4.3	2.6	6.8	11.8	22.0	7.5	4.1
33017	Strafford County, New Hampshire	1.9	13.0	4.2	1.8	7.8	9.0	25.7	10.7	3.9
33019	Sullivan County, New Hampshire	2.2	12.5	3.1	1.8	5.0	6.1	28.2	7.0	3.9
34000	**New Jersey**	3.4	11.3	5.7	2.8	8.5	13.0	23.7	8.4	4.5
34001	Atlantic County, New Jersey	1.8	11.2	3.8	1.5	4.8	8.9	22.3	26.2	4.2
34003	Bergen County, New Jersey	4.6	11.1	4.9	3.4	9.3	13.6	24.2	7.5	4.9
34005	Burlington County, New Jersey	3.7	11.4	5.1	2.3	8.2	11.8	25.7	7.1	4.1
34007	Camden County, New Jersey	3.1	12.2	5.8	2.0	7.4	11.8	27.2	8.6	4.5
34009	Cape May County, New Jersey	2.0	13.0	3.0	1.5	6.4	8.3	25.1	16.9	3.9
34011	Cumberland County, New Jersey	3.0	12.2	5.1	0.9	4.2	7.7	27.6	7.3	4.0
34013	Essex County, New Jersey	2.6	10.5	7.0	2.9	7.9	12.8	26.2	7.9	5.3
34015	Gloucester County, New Jersey	4.0	12.5	5.9	2.1	7.1	10.8	26.5	7.2	4.6
34017	Hudson County, New Jersey	4.0	10.3	7.9	3.2	11.5	15.1	19.1	9.1	4.7
34019	Hunterdon County, New Jersey	3.8	10.7	3.0	3.7	8.6	14.3	22.1	6.3	4.2
34021	Mercer County, New Jersey	2.7	9.5	3.8	2.5	8.1	14.1	26.2	8.1	4.5
34023	Middlesex County, New Jersey	3.7	10.9	6.7	3.1	9.2	15.2	22.3	7.0	4.0
34025	Monmouth County, New Jersey	3.1	11.7	5.0	3.6	10.2	12.7	23.5	8.9	4.1
34027	Morris County, New Jersey	3.1	10.6	3.6	3.6	10.1	16.2	22.0	7.0	4.3
34029	Ocean County, New Jersey	3.0	13.8	5.7	2.4	6.6	9.9	26.3	8.2	5.0
34031	Passaic County, New Jersey	3.7	12.7	6.5	2.1	6.5	11.0	23.2	7.8	4.9
34033	Salem County, New Jersey	3.7	9.4	10.4	1.5	5.3	8.3	23.9	6.2	4.7
34035	Somerset County, New Jersey	3.6	9.9	4.1	4.2	10.6	15.9	21.9	6.4	3.8
34037	Sussex County, New Jersey	3.4	12.5	4.9	2.5	7.3	12.1	22.4	7.4	4.5
34039	Union County, New Jersey	3.7	10.6	8.5	2.5	8.9	12.8	22.0	7.1	4.8
34041	Warren County, New Jersey	2.3	13.2	5.2	2.7	6.4	11.9	21.3	8.2	4.4
35000	**New Mexico**	2.2	11.3	4.5	1.6	4.5	11.2	25.1	11.1	4.8
35001	Bernalillo County, New Mexico	2.4	11.3	3.4	1.9	5.2	14.3	25.8	11.3	5.3
35003	Catron County, New Mexico	0.0	9.8	8.2	1.6	4.3	4.3	20.4	7.2	2.7
35005	Chaves County, New Mexico	2.4	11.2	6.6	0.6	4.7	5.9	25.8	10.0	5.9
35006	Cibola County, New Mexico	1.0	12.0	3.9	1.2	1.3	6.0	27.9	15.4	4.1
35007	Colfax County, New Mexico	0.6	10.8	5.9	0.7	6.1	7.6	25.4	16.4	3.1
35009	Curry County, New Mexico	2.4	10.8	9.3	1.4	3.9	6.2	23.2	8.4	5.1
35011	De Baca County, New Mexico	1.0	5.2	2.1	1.0	1.5	6.9	31.2	14.4	3.6
35013	Doña Ana County, New Mexico	1.9	10.9	4.0	1.7	3.9	9.7	29.3	10.6	4.1
35015	Eddy County, New Mexico	3.1	9.9	7.3	1.1	3.5	5.3	18.6	7.0	5.0
35017	Grant County, New Mexico	1.2	11.5	3.2	1.3	4.1	5.9	31.5	9.2	3.7
35019	Guadalupe County, New Mexico	5.0	19.9	6.8	3.2	1.8	2.1	23.1	10.5	2.2
35021	Harding County, New Mexico	0.5	2.4	5.9	0.5	2.0	6.8	26.3	0.5	2.4
35023	Hidalgo County, New Mexico	0.9	14.8	5.0	1.8	2.0	2.8	24.1	12.6	1.8
35025	Lea County, New Mexico	5.6	9.7	8.1	0.9	3.4	6.2	16.2	7.9	4.8
35027	Lincoln County, New Mexico	0.2	11.4	5.1	2.4	6.1	6.3	18.8	22.3	3.7
35028	Los Alamos County, New Mexico	1.3	5.3	1.6	0.6	3.1	56.8	16.5	4.5	2.1
35029	Luna County, New Mexico	1.9	13.6	5.7	0.4	2.9	6.0	22.8	12.1	3.8
35031	McKinley County, New Mexico	2.1	12.2	4.0	1.4	2.6	5.0	34.0	11.5	2.9
35033	Mora County, New Mexico	0.0	12.4	4.0	0.0	0.5	4.5	36.3	4.3	0.1

Table C. County—Labor Force, Employment, and Educational Data, 2011–2015—*Continued*

		Industry for employed population age 16 and older								
Fips code	State/county	Wholesale trade	Retail trade	Transportation and warehousing, and utilities	Information	Finance and insurance, and real estate and rental and leasing	Professional, scientific, and management, and administrative and waste management services	Educational services, and health care and social assistance	Arts, entertainment, and recreation, and accommodation and food services	Other services, except public administration
35035	Otero County, New Mexico	1.1	12.4	3.8	1.1	3.3	7.8	23.0	12.7	4.1
35037	Quay County, New Mexico	1.5	14.5	6.0	1.0	3.3	3.7	27.5	8.3	7.2
35039	Rio Arriba County, New Mexico	0.9	8.6	4.0	0.7	3.9	13.8	23.5	14.1	5.0
35041	Roosevelt County, New Mexico	1.7	12.9	5.5	0.4	2.9	5.5	30.3	11.8	4.3
35043	Sandoval County, New Mexico	2.2	11.8	4.3	2.2	5.7	10.7	24.2	10.5	4.0
35045	San Juan County, New Mexico	3.2	13.0	6.7	1.0	3.7	6.6	23.5	8.9	5.6
35047	San Miguel County, New Mexico	1.0	12.6	5.2	1.4	3.9	7.8	32.7	6.5	3.2
35049	Santa Fe County, New Mexico	1.1	11.2	3.2	1.7	5.4	15.9	21.9	14.5	6.0
35051	Sierra County, New Mexico	1.2	12.8	5.9	0.6	3.7	5.6	25.8	13.3	3.0
35053	Socorro County, New Mexico	0.8	9.9	3.7	0.9	3.0	7.7	41.8	11.5	1.7
35055	Taos County, New Mexico	0.6	11.3	3.2	2.8	5.1	8.8	23.1	18.6	4.4
35057	Torrance County, New Mexico	2.9	12.3	4.9	1.0	1.7	10.4	23.7	11.0	5.1
35059	Union County, New Mexico	0.2	8.0	5.2	0.5	3.5	4.5	26.1	8.6	2.7
35061	Valencia County, New Mexico	2.2	11.9	6.2	0.9	4.9	7.6	23.7	10.2	4.4
36000	**New York**	2.5	10.8	5.1	2.9	8.0	11.4	27.5	9.5	5.0
36001	Albany County, New York	1.8	11.0	3.9	2.1	6.9	10.6	27.0	9.1	4.7
36003	Allegany County, New York	1.5	8.7	4.3	1.5	2.0	4.9	35.1	7.4	5.1
36005	Bronx County, New York	1.8	12.0	6.7	1.9	6.8	8.4	31.9	11.9	6.1
36007	Broome County, New York	2.9	12.6	4.1	1.6	4.7	8.7	29.9	8.9	5.5
36009	Cattaraugus County, New York	2.3	11.8	3.8	0.7	3.7	5.2	26.4	11.0	4.6
36011	Cayuga County, New York	2.3	11.6	4.7	1.2	3.3	6.2	27.0	8.2	4.6
36013	Chautauqua County, New York	1.8	11.5	4.1	1.2	3.3	5.2	26.9	9.5	5.8
36015	Chemung County, New York	2.5	10.9	4.0	1.3	4.3	6.1	30.4	7.5	4.4
36017	Chenango County, New York	1.8	10.8	4.1	2.2	6.1	4.3	26.2	7.2	3.8
36019	Clinton County, New York	1.6	13.1	4.6	1.7	2.8	5.4	27.8	9.9	4.2
36021	Columbia County, New York	1.8	10.9	4.0	1.7	4.4	9.8	28.0	8.0	5.0
36023	Cortland County, New York	2.0	10.8	3.6	0.6	3.1	6.9	33.0	9.8	4.9
36025	Delaware County, New York	1.7	10.8	3.8	1.3	4.0	6.7	27.4	9.2	4.3
36027	Dutchess County, New York	2.1	11.9	4.9	2.5	5.5	10.3	29.6	8.6	4.2
36029	Erie County, New York	2.8	11.5	4.6	1.6	7.8	9.9	28.2	9.8	4.1
36031	Essex County, New York	1.5	12.8	2.9	1.5	3.8	5.5	29.2	13.1	4.4
36033	Franklin County, New York	1.6	11.5	2.9	1.6	3.6	4.7	32.8	9.7	4.3
36035	Fulton County, New York	2.1	16.0	5.2	1.6	2.2	6.1	27.9	6.8	5.2
36037	Genesee County, New York	2.7	10.5	4.0	1.4	4.4	7.4	24.3	9.4	5.4
36039	Greene County, New York	1.9	11.7	6.0	2.4	5.8	6.6	24.6	10.7	4.9
36041	Hamilton County, New York	0.1	10.2	3.8	0.7	2.6	7.6	23.5	17.4	3.7
36043	Herkimer County, New York	2.1	13.0	4.1	0.9	5.4	6.4	28.3	8.5	5.0
36045	Jefferson County, New York	2.0	14.8	3.4	1.6	4.3	7.1	25.2	9.6	5.2
36047	Kings County, New York	2.3	9.8	6.2	4.0	7.6	12.5	28.8	10.3	5.4
36049	Lewis County, New York	1.7	10.7	4.0	1.2	2.3	6.2	26.4	6.0	3.8
36051	Livingston County, New York	2.1	10.6	3.5	1.8	2.7	8.4	28.0	8.8	4.9
36053	Madison County, New York	2.5	11.4	4.3	1.6	4.7	8.5	28.7	9.2	4.2
36055	Monroe County, New York	2.5	11.5	3.2	2.5	5.3	11.9	31.0	8.3	4.4
36057	Montgomery County, New York	2.3	14.0	4.2	1.3	4.2	5.4	26.2	7.5	3.6
36059	Nassau County, New York	3.4	10.4	5.2	3.1	9.9	12.7	28.3	7.3	4.6
36061	New York County, New York	2.2	7.9	2.4	6.5	16.5	19.7	22.3	10.8	4.1
36063	Niagara County, New York	2.2	12.5	5.4	1.3	6.2	8.8	24.8	9.6	4.6
36065	Oneida County, New York	1.6	11.2	3.9	1.4	7.4	7.6	28.7	9.5	5.2
36067	Onondaga County, New York	3.2	11.8	4.9	2.3	6.5	10.0	31.0	8.6	4.5
36069	Ontario County, New York	2.3	13.3	3.0	2.1	4.6	7.8	28.5	8.9	4.3
36071	Orange County, New York	3.4	13.8	6.2	2.5	5.8	9.0	25.7	8.0	4.7
36073	Orleans County, New York	2.1	11.3	4.5	1.0	5.4	5.7	23.0	8.3	5.2
36075	Oswego County, New York	2.6	13.2	6.8	1.4	4.5	6.9	25.5	10.5	4.5
36077	Otsego County, New York	1.0	13.2	2.7	1.1	5.6	5.5	34.6	11.6	3.9
36079	Putnam County, New York	2.2	12.5	3.6	3.8	8.1	12.0	27.2	7.7	3.7
36081	Queens County, New York	2.6	10.5	7.9	2.6	8.1	11.0	23.9	11.8	6.7
36083	Rensselaer County, New York	2.2	9.9	5.1	1.8	5.9	9.4	27.5	8.0	4.5
36085	Richmond County, New York	1.8	10.0	6.6	2.5	9.9	11.3	29.1	6.9	4.5
36087	Rockland County, New York	3.0	10.5	4.1	2.8	7.0	11.5	31.6	8.0	5.2
36089	St. Lawrence County, New York	1.5	12.9	3.6	1.4	3.8	5.6	34.5	8.5	4.5
36091	Saratoga County, New York	2.6	11.9	3.1	2.0	7.5	11.1	25.4	8.7	3.9
36093	Schenectady County, New York	2.0	12.8	4.7	2.4	6.6	9.9	28.4	8.2	4.6
36095	Schoharie County, New York	1.9	12.9	5.0	1.4	5.6	7.2	26.3	7.7	5.5
36097	Schuyler County, New York	1.4	10.4	3.6	1.4	2.5	5.8	28.7	9.2	6.5
36099	Seneca County, New York	2.1	12.7	4.6	0.7	3.3	4.9	27.5	6.7	4.0
36101	Steuben County, New York	1.4	11.6	3.9	1.3	3.1	7.2	25.7	8.4	4.3
36103	Suffolk County, New York	3.2	11.8	5.3	2.7	7.1	11.1	26.5	7.3	4.4
36105	Sullivan County, New York	3.5	11.8	4.9	1.8	4.4	6.8	30.7	8.3	4.9
36107	Tioga County, New York	3.1	14.2	3.4	1.2	3.9	8.4	27.0	8.1	3.7
36109	Tompkins County, New York	0.5	8.7	2.7	1.3	3.9	9.1	46.3	9.7	4.3
36111	Ulster County, New York	2.7	12.9	4.9	2.1	5.4	8.6	29.4	9.5	4.6
36113	Warren County, New York	1.9	14.2	3.5	1.4	5.6	8.3	26.2	13.1	4.4
36115	Washington County, New York	1.6	13.4	3.9	0.8	4.1	6.7	22.8	7.7	4.4
36117	Wayne County, New York	2.3	11.8	3.9	1.9	4.2	7.9	25.4	6.2	4.6

Table C. County—Labor Force, Employment, and Educational Data, 2011–2015—*Continued*

Fips code	State/county	Wholesale trade	Retail trade	Transportation and warehousing, and utilities	Information	Finance and insurance, and real estate and rental and leasing	Professional, scientific, and management, and administrative and waste management services	Educational services, and health care and social assistance	Arts, entertainment, and recreation, and accommodation and food services	Other services, except public administration
36119	Westchester County, New York	2.4	9.8	4.0	3.3	10.2	14.6	27.4	8.4	5.9
36121	Wyoming County, New York	1.8	10.9	5.1	1.2	4.3	7.6	21.5	9.0	4.0
36123	Yates County, New York	2.0	12.7	4.0	1.0	3.8	5.4	26.0	7.2	6.2
37000	**North Carolina**	2.7	11.8	4.3	1.8	6.3	10.3	23.5	9.4	4.9
37001	Alamance County, North Carolina	2.6	13.0	2.7	1.3	5.1	8.9	25.0	9.7	4.3
37003	Alexander County, North Carolina	2.7	10.9	5.6	0.3	3.0	4.9	19.1	4.9	5.5
37005	Alleghany County, North Carolina	0.6	13.4	4.2	1.3	4.0	8.5	22.0	7.5	3.0
37007	Anson County, North Carolina	3.3	10.6	8.4	0.7	2.2	5.2	19.5	6.1	3.0
37009	Ashe County, North Carolina	1.3	11.0	4.4	2.9	5.6	6.6	21.6	9.2	5.9
37011	Avery County, North Carolina	2.3	12.7	3.0	0.6	5.2	6.9	25.4	11.6	6.6
37013	Beaufort County, North Carolina	2.8	10.7	3.6	1.3	3.5	5.4	23.9	9.4	6.4
37015	Bertie County, North Carolina	2.2	9.5	3.5	0.7	3.5	4.1	26.0	3.9	3.0
37017	Bladen County, North Carolina	1.7	10.2	4.7	0.7	3.2	3.1	25.5	4.1	3.0
37019	Brunswick County, North Carolina	1.2	15.2	6.0	1.9	6.1	11.2	19.1	12.1	4.6
37021	Buncombe County, North Carolina	2.0	13.6	2.8	1.5	5.0	10.9	26.4	12.8	4.9
37023	Burke County, North Carolina	2.6	10.0	3.4	0.7	2.7	6.2	28.4	7.2	5.5
37025	Cabarrus County, North Carolina	3.2	12.2	5.9	2.0	9.2	9.0	22.0	9.8	5.4
37027	Caldwell County, North Carolina	3.9	12.4	3.9	1.4	4.2	4.8	20.0	8.1	4.7
37029	Camden County, North Carolina	1.8	11.5	3.3	0.2	5.2	7.1	25.9	5.4	2.4
37031	Carteret County, North Carolina	1.3	12.8	4.2	1.4	6.1	10.4	19.9	13.3	5.3
37033	Caswell County, North Carolina	1.6	14.4	4.4	0.7	3.4	5.3	27.1	7.9	4.9
37035	Catawba County, North Carolina	3.8	10.9	4.1	1.1	4.6	7.6	19.8	8.6	4.5
37037	Chatham County, North Carolina	2.0	8.6	3.3	1.3	4.7	11.6	25.4	7.9	6.1
37039	Cherokee County, North Carolina	1.4	17.5	2.4	2.1	5.1	9.4	18.9	8.2	5.9
37041	Chowan County, North Carolina	1.0	15.5	5.3	1.1	2.1	6.3	27.2	7.5	5.7
37043	Clay County, North Carolina	2.2	13.7	4.0	3.1	8.2	7.9	21.9	14.1	4.0
37045	Cleveland County, North Carolina	2.0	13.4	4.9	1.2	3.1	6.2	26.6	7.6	5.3
37047	Columbus County, North Carolina	2.4	13.0	4.8	0.9	3.9	5.8	28.4	6.9	4.7
37049	Craven County, North Carolina	1.7	11.8	4.7	1.3	4.1	7.6	23.6	10.8	5.3
37051	Cumberland County, North Carolina	1.4	13.7	3.9	1.8	4.2	8.0	27.6	10.8	5.0
37053	Currituck County, North Carolina	1.4	13.9	3.4	1.3	8.5	8.1	14.3	10.5	7.4
37055	Dare County, North Carolina	2.0	13.2	3.8	2.1	12.0	9.1	12.1	18.8	4.8
37057	Davidson County, North Carolina	3.0	10.5	5.7	1.9	4.6	7.9	21.4	7.3	5.3
37059	Davie County, North Carolina	3.1	12.7	5.2	1.4	5.5	8.9	20.6	7.9	2.7
37061	Duplin County, North Carolina	2.5	9.4	3.4	0.6	2.9	4.8	20.9	7.9	5.5
37063	Durham County, North Carolina	1.7	8.1	2.5	2.1	5.0	14.1	35.9	8.9	4.5
37065	Edgecombe County, North Carolina	1.7	12.2	5.7	1.2	3.8	6.0	23.8	8.5	4.5
37067	Forsyth County, North Carolina	2.5	10.1	4.4	1.6	7.0	11.3	28.1	9.1	5.2
37069	Franklin County, North Carolina	2.5	13.9	4.2	1.7	4.6	9.4	21.6	6.2	5.5
37071	Gaston County, North Carolina	3.2	12.0	6.8	1.7	5.5	8.5	19.8	9.0	5.4
37073	Gates County, North Carolina	2.8	13.0	4.0	0.1	4.4	8.2	23.5	4.6	4.3
37075	Graham County, North Carolina	1.0	10.0	2.7	0.5	2.5	4.2	18.7	17.6	4.9
37077	Granville County, North Carolina	2.8	11.1	5.5	1.1	3.8	10.7	23.2	5.6	3.6
37079	Greene County, North Carolina	2.9	9.6	3.7	0.7	3.3	3.8	24.9	5.7	4.9
37081	Guilford County, North Carolina	3.8	12.7	5.2	1.8	7.3	9.9	23.7	9.6	4.8
37083	Halifax County, North Carolina	2.5	10.3	5.6	1.4	2.6	6.0	25.8	8.1	4.5
37085	Harnett County, North Carolina	3.2	11.2	4.0	1.6	4.3	8.8	22.9	8.0	4.6
37087	Haywood County, North Carolina	1.9	12.8	2.7	1.5	5.0	8.9	24.7	10.9	4.4
37089	Henderson County, North Carolina	2.9	12.8	2.8	1.6	5.4	8.9	24.5	8.6	4.9
37091	Hertford County, North Carolina	1.6	12.1	3.9	1.3	2.9	3.8	31.5	8.4	4.8
37093	Hoke County, North Carolina	1.3	12.2	3.2	1.4	2.4	6.5	26.9	8.9	5.3
37095	Hyde County, North Carolina	4.2	16.3	5.7	0.0	3.6	1.2	19.8	9.1	6.2
37097	Iredell County, North Carolina	2.8	14.8	5.1	1.1	5.3	9.5	19.7	9.5	4.9
37099	Jackson County, North Carolina	1.3	9.6	2.9	0.3	4.1	8.0	29.4	21.4	4.5
37101	Johnston County, North Carolina	4.3	12.8	4.6	1.4	5.2	8.1	21.3	8.5	4.2
37103	Jones County, North Carolina	1.8	7.7	4.6	1.0	3.5	6.6	29.4	5.0	5.3
37105	Lee County, North Carolina	4.3	11.8	3.6	1.4	4.5	8.2	20.5	6.2	4.9
37107	Lenoir County, North Carolina	2.2	13.9	3.1	0.9	2.7	6.2	24.5	7.4	4.7
37109	Lincoln County, North Carolina	3.4	12.2	7.5	1.7	6.1	8.6	17.4	6.7	4.7
37111	McDowell County, North Carolina	2.5	11.8	2.9	0.8	3.4	6.5	21.3	9.0	4.3
37113	Macon County, North Carolina	1.1	13.8	2.8	2.3	5.3	9.4	22.6	13.8	5.7
37115	Madison County, North Carolina	2.0	11.3	4.5	1.4	2.9	11.2	27.9	6.3	5.5
37117	Martin County, North Carolina	2.0	13.3	2.4	0.6	4.9	4.1	26.6	6.9	4.1
37119	Mecklenburg County, North Carolina	3.4	10.9	5.3	2.7	12.9	13.7	19.0	10.8	4.9
37121	Mitchell County, North Carolina	1.9	13.5	3.7	0.6	2.6	5.1	22.0	8.2	5.8
37123	Montgomery County, North Carolina	1.3	8.7	3.2	0.8	3.9	5.3	21.5	6.5	5.2
37125	Moore County, North Carolina	1.8	10.6	4.2	1.8	4.4	9.2	28.7	10.0	6.5
37127	Nash County, North Carolina	4.1	12.1	5.3	1.2	5.3	6.7	21.3	8.6	4.9
37129	New Hanover County, North Carolina	2.7	12.1	3.9	2.7	5.4	11.9	24.0	14.1	5.7
37131	Northampton County, North Carolina	1.0	10.5	6.1	0.7	1.7	5.2	23.7	5.7	4.6
37133	Onslow County, North Carolina	1.5	14.4	3.7	1.5	3.7	9.7	21.3	14.1	4.6
37135	Orange County, North Carolina	1.6	9.2	1.9	2.1	5.1	12.6	39.3	9.9	3.6
37137	Pamlico County, North Carolina	3.1	10.6	4.7	0.4	7.5	6.7	20.9	10.2	4.7
37139	Pasquotank County, North Carolina	2.7	13.4	5.2	2.0	4.2	7.4	26.5	9.9	3.9

Table C. County—Labor Force, Employment, and Educational Data, 2011–2015—*Continued*

		Industry for employed population age 16 and older								
Fips code	State/county	Wholesale trade	Retail trade	Transportation and warehousing, and utilities	Information	Finance and insurance, and real estate and rental and leasing	Professional, scientific, and management, and administrative and waste management services	Educational services, and health care and social assistance	Arts, entertainment, and recreation, and accommodation and food services	Other services, except public administration
37141	Pender County, North Carolina	2.8	14.3	5.4	1.2	4.2	10.3	18.5	8.4	6.1
37143	Perquimans County, North Carolina	1.0	8.8	6.1	2.7	6.0	8.8	24.2	6.8	3.0
37145	Person County, North Carolina	1.6	12.0	6.6	1.6	5.2	9.2	25.7	5.0	4.9
37147	Pitt County, North Carolina	2.3	11.5	2.7	1.7	4.5	6.5	32.1	10.9	5.8
37149	Polk County, North Carolina	3.0	14.9	3.7	1.1	4.1	10.3	24.3	7.5	3.5
37151	Randolph County, North Carolina	3.4	11.3	5.0	1.7	4.4	6.1	19.5	6.7	4.8
37153	Richmond County, North Carolina	1.8	12.9	4.7	0.8	2.8	6.2	23.3	7.8	4.6
37155	Robeson County, North Carolina	1.4	12.3	4.5	0.8	3.1	4.5	26.9	7.6	4.0
37157	Rockingham County, North Carolina	2.6	13.3	6.2	0.9	4.4	7.8	20.8	5.6	5.4
37159	Rowan County, North Carolina	3.5	13.2	5.0	1.2	4.6	6.5	23.8	8.6	5.4
37161	Rutherford County, North Carolina	1.5	13.8	5.0	1.3	3.3	6.4	23.8	7.8	5.1
37163	Sampson County, North Carolina	2.4	11.3	4.1	1.0	2.7	6.0	21.5	7.6	5.0
37165	Scotland County, North Carolina	1.5	12.2	3.1	0.8	3.2	5.4	30.5	7.5	5.4
37167	Stanly County, North Carolina	1.5	13.5	3.7	0.9	4.0	5.9	25.9	6.3	5.4
37169	Stokes County, North Carolina	1.9	12.6	5.5	0.8	4.9	6.9	25.4	6.0	4.9
37171	Surry County, North Carolina	2.3	14.2	5.0	0.8	4.0	6.8	23.2	8.8	4.4
37173	Swain County, North Carolina	2.3	8.9	2.1	1.6	3.3	6.2	22.5	23.6	3.9
37175	Transylvania County, North Carolina	1.4	9.6	2.7	0.9	4.6	8.8	25.8	11.7	8.0
37177	Tyrrell County, North Carolina	4.3	9.4	0.7	0.0	5.8	5.2	18.4	7.8	3.7
37179	Union County, North Carolina	3.6	12.5	3.5	2.2	9.5	10.9	20.1	7.9	5.1
37181	Vance County, North Carolina	3.2	14.5	3.4	0.6	3.4	7.0	26.9	7.2	3.0
37183	Wake County, North Carolina	2.8	10.6	3.3	3.0	7.3	18.1	21.0	9.0	4.5
37185	Warren County, North Carolina	1.5	12.5	4.7	0.8	3.0	6.9	27.0	7.0	3.7
37187	Washington County, North Carolina	2.6	8.6	3.1	1.6	3.1	5.6	19.1	9.3	4.6
37189	Watauga County, North Carolina	1.1	14.6	2.0	1.3	4.8	8.5	31.2	17.6	5.2
37191	Wayne County, North Carolina	4.3	11.3	4.2	1.4	3.5	4.9	24.2	8.5	5.4
37193	Wilkes County, North Carolina	2.4	17.0	4.4	1.0	4.1	6.4	20.7	7.5	4.7
37195	Wilson County, North Carolina	2.8	12.1	3.4	1.1	5.8	6.4	24.3	7.5	4.7
37197	Yadkin County, North Carolina	3.1	11.4	5.2	1.0	4.1	7.3	22.2	7.1	4.6
37199	Yancey County, North Carolina	0.9	10.1	5.6	0.7	3.5	6.0	27.9	6.6	5.6
38000	**North Dakota**	3.4	11.7	5.7	1.5	5.7	6.6	24.6	7.8	4.3
38001	Adams County, North Dakota	2.3	7.8	3.0	1.6	6.0	4.1	28.3	4.2	7.5
38003	Barnes County, North Dakota	3.4	8.6	5.0	0.6	6.1	4.3	27.8	7.7	5.0
38005	Benson County, North Dakota	3.0	6.2	2.4	0.4	4.1	2.5	27.0	15.6	1.6
38007	Billings County, North Dakota	6.6	6.7	3.4	0.5	1.6	10.6	11.3	8.3	8.3
38009	Bottineau County, North Dakota	3.7	12.0	5.3	0.5	3.0	5.8	23.4	5.8	3.2
38011	Bowman County, North Dakota	4.0	13.4	3.7	0.9	5.5	4.1	19.9	4.9	5.2
38013	Burke County, North Dakota	2.7	13.7	7.8	0.1	3.0	5.7	12.5	5.1	2.5
38015	Burleigh County, North Dakota	2.7	11.8	5.9	1.4	5.9	8.5	27.0	7.1	4.9
38017	Cass County, North Dakota	4.2	12.3	4.4	1.6	8.5	9.0	25.9	9.1	4.0
38019	Cavalier County, North Dakota	5.8	11.8	8.9	3.8	5.1	4.6	20.7	2.4	2.7
38021	Dickey County, North Dakota	3.9	10.1	4.5	1.7	2.6	5.4	26.4	7.8	5.0
38023	Divide County, North Dakota	4.2	7.3	6.1	0.6	4.0	3.7	13.8	8.0	4.2
38025	Dunn County, North Dakota	2.5	9.7	7.6	0.7	0.5	7.2	14.0	7.7	3.3
38027	Eddy County, North Dakota	3.7	7.0	3.8	0.1	3.3	3.1	38.5	1.4	3.5
38029	Emmons County, North Dakota	3.2	7.4	4.6	0.3	4.9	9.0	22.0	5.4	2.5
38031	Foster County, North Dakota	3.1	10.1	7.9	2.1	4.4	2.1	19.0	4.6	8.1
38033	Golden Valley County, North Dakota	3.6	15.0	5.2	2.0	0.4	2.3	18.2	8.0	2.7
38035	Grand Forks County, North Dakota	2.3	14.8	4.6	1.5	4.5	6.1	32.0	9.9	3.8
38037	Grant County, North Dakota	3.7	6.1	6.5	0.5	3.7	1.5	23.5	3.1	5.0
38039	Griggs County, North Dakota	2.6	9.1	3.7	0.5	7.0	5.5	18.3	4.5	3.7
38041	Hettinger County, North Dakota	2.8	13.3	4.4	1.2	4.5	4.2	16.7	5.1	3.5
38043	Kidder County, North Dakota	2.5	9.1	5.9	3.1	6.7	2.1	17.6	5.4	4.3
38045	LaMoure County, North Dakota	6.3	10.4	5.6	0.9	4.9	2.4	19.8	4.6	3.7
38047	Logan County, North Dakota	5.3	5.6	6.3	0.5	4.9	4.9	22.8	4.7	4.5
38049	McHenry County, North Dakota	6.5	10.7	9.0	1.0	4.4	3.7	14.8	3.7	5.3
38051	McIntosh County, North Dakota	3.6	9.8	4.4	1.0	4.8	1.7	32.7	4.4	5.2
38053	McKenzie County, North Dakota	2.3	10.7	11.8	0.7	4.8	4.6	14.7	6.9	5.6
38055	McLean County, North Dakota	3.2	8.8	8.1	1.6	3.9	4.2	23.8	6.3	5.7
38057	Mercer County, North Dakota	0.8	12.4	15.4	2.1	2.9	3.3	15.4	7.8	4.9
38059	Morton County, North Dakota	1.7	12.7	7.2	2.7	4.8	6.6	24.9	6.9	4.4
38061	Mountrail County, North Dakota	3.8	7.2	5.7	2.1	3.2	2.0	19.3	9.6	6.0
38063	Nelson County, North Dakota	6.1	6.9	5.2	0.1	6.6	3.9	21.6	6.0	2.8
38065	Oliver County, North Dakota	0.4	4.3	8.9	1.3	2.9	8.4	18.6	5.0	3.0
38067	Pembina County, North Dakota	3.5	10.0	5.2	1.0	6.0	3.0	18.7	4.4	4.0
38069	Pierce County, North Dakota	2.7	14.2	8.1	0.5	2.6	6.3	26.4	4.9	9.2
38071	Ramsey County, North Dakota	2.2	13.9	4.2	2.8	5.8	4.2	23.5	12.4	5.4
38073	Ransom County, North Dakota	2.5	8.6	6.3	0.5	2.2	2.6	26.5	5.8	2.8
38075	Renville County, North Dakota	4.3	7.9	3.1	0.8	7.5	5.5	14.8	4.2	3.9
38077	Richland County, North Dakota	4.5	11.5	3.9	0.8	3.8	3.3	25.2	6.0	3.5
38079	Rolette County, North Dakota	0.3	11.2	2.4	1.1	5.2	2.2	34.3	12.5	3.1
38081	Sargent County, North Dakota	1.3	7.9	5.3	0.4	3.9	2.5	17.5	3.3	4.6
38083	Sheridan County, North Dakota	2.2	6.7	5.6	0.5	4.1	2.5	13.5	6.0	7.3
38085	Sioux County, North Dakota	0.3	3.6	3.1	0.5	2.6	1.8	32.5	19.0	2.9

Table C. County—Labor Force, Employment, and Educational Data, 2011–2015—*Continued*

		Industry for employed population age 16 and older								
Fips code	State/county	Wholesale trade	Retail trade	Transportation and warehousing, and utilities	Information	Finance and insurance, and real estate and rental and leasing	Professional, scientific, and management, and administrative and waste management services	Educational services, and health care and social assistance	Arts, entertainment, and recreation, and accommodation and food services	Other services, except public administration
38087	Slope County, North Dakota	3.3	7.5	5.1	0.6	1.2	4.5	14.3	3.6	4.8
38089	Stark County, North Dakota	3.8	11.4	7.3	1.5	4.2	5.1	17.7	7.7	4.5
38091	Steele County, North Dakota	4.1	9.2	6.3	0.7	7.5	3.4	17.7	1.4	2.7
38093	Stutsman County, North Dakota	3.6	10.4	4.9	1.6	4.5	5.0	27.9	6.2	4.7
38095	Towner County, North Dakota	5.9	6.5	6.3	0.0	9.4	1.8	15.5	7.2	3.5
38097	Traill County, North Dakota	5.7	9.2	6.7	1.4	5.8	3.9	30.2	3.0	3.8
38099	Walsh County, North Dakota	3.3	11.1	5.8	1.8	4.4	2.6	23.7	4.3	3.8
38101	Ward County, North Dakota	4.2	13.1	6.6	1.6	5.1	7.2	21.5	9.0	4.6
38103	Wells County, North Dakota	3.1	12.9	9.1	0.6	5.5	3.7	21.4	3.0	5.8
38105	Williams County, North Dakota	4.0	8.6	7.9	1.1	4.4	7.8	18.6	4.9	4.0
39000	**Ohio**	2.7	11.6	4.8	1.7	6.4	9.3	24.2	9.1	4.5
39001	Adams County, Ohio	2.1	15.0	9.2	0.7	2.8	3.5	23.5	6.5	5.0
39003	Allen County, Ohio	3.1	10.6	3.9	1.2	4.5	6.3	25.3	9.7	5.7
39005	Ashland County, Ohio	2.0	10.0	5.6	2.1	3.5	7.5	25.3	7.8	5.2
39007	Ashtabula County, Ohio	1.7	12.1	5.8	1.5	3.6	5.4	22.8	7.1	4.5
39009	Athens County, Ohio	1.2	12.0	3.2	2.1	3.4	5.0	40.6	13.7	4.3
39011	Auglaize County, Ohio	2.1	10.0	4.4	1.5	2.8	6.8	20.4	7.3	4.7
39013	Belmont County, Ohio	2.4	14.1	5.2	1.3	4.6	6.2	26.0	8.8	3.9
39015	Brown County, Ohio	2.4	10.2	5.5	1.4	6.2	8.0	22.9	7.7	4.9
39017	Butler County, Ohio	3.0	13.4	4.2	1.4	6.9	9.7	22.7	10.1	4.4
39019	Carroll County, Ohio	2.2	11.1	5.8	0.6	4.2	6.2	18.3	7.7	4.4
39021	Champaign County, Ohio	1.8	10.1	4.9	1.1	3.9	6.2	22.7	7.5	5.2
39023	Clark County, Ohio	3.3	12.0	4.1	1.3	6.0	7.6	25.2	8.1	4.5
39025	Clermont County, Ohio	3.2	12.7	4.7	2.0	8.6	11.5	19.6	8.1	5.3
39027	Clinton County, Ohio	2.7	14.0	9.4	1.5	6.1	6.8	20.1	7.0	3.3
39029	Columbiana County, Ohio	2.6	11.1	7.8	1.3	3.6	6.0	21.4	9.6	4.9
39031	Coshocton County, Ohio	1.7	10.5	5.6	1.1	2.7	5.2	22.1	6.3	4.7
39033	Crawford County, Ohio	2.5	10.5	4.1	1.6	4.0	6.1	21.2	8.5	4.6
39035	Cuyahoga County, Ohio	2.8	10.5	4.2	1.9	7.9	11.1	27.0	9.7	4.4
39037	Darke County, Ohio	2.5	10.3	5.9	1.2	3.3	4.5	19.4	7.1	4.1
39039	Defiance County, Ohio	1.8	12.3	3.9	0.9	4.4	5.7	21.5	8.3	4.0
39041	Delaware County, Ohio	3.6	11.2	3.4	2.6	13.4	13.0	22.7	7.4	3.6
39043	Erie County, Ohio	1.9	10.8	4.7	1.6	4.0	6.0	22.4	16.5	4.8
39045	Fairfield County, Ohio	3.5	12.5	6.0	1.5	7.2	7.5	23.5	9.4	4.3
39047	Fayette County, Ohio	3.1	15.8	5.8	1.1	2.9	4.5	20.9	7.4	3.9
39049	Franklin County, Ohio	3.1	12.3	5.1	2.5	10.0	12.1	24.4	9.9	4.2
39051	Fulton County, Ohio	3.1	9.7	5.0	0.7	3.9	5.5	22.6	7.5	4.1
39053	Gallia County, Ohio	2.4	13.4	10.2	1.4	4.2	4.9	30.1	5.1	3.2
39055	Geauga County, Ohio	3.2	11.1	3.3	1.3	6.3	10.8	22.2	6.9	5.5
39057	Greene County, Ohio	1.7	11.7	3.1	1.9	4.9	11.6	26.8	9.1	4.2
39059	Guernsey County, Ohio	2.5	10.2	5.0	1.0	3.3	6.6	26.7	8.8	4.1
39061	Hamilton County, Ohio	2.9	11.3	4.6	1.8	7.9	12.6	25.2	10.0	4.3
39063	Hancock County, Ohio	2.7	10.8	5.2	1.1	3.9	6.4	20.5	9.5	4.5
39065	Hardin County, Ohio	2.0	11.8	5.0	0.9	3.8	4.8	25.2	8.9	4.0
39067	Harrison County, Ohio	2.6	11.5	6.9	1.0	1.8	5.2	23.4	7.8	2.8
39069	Henry County, Ohio	2.0	8.9	6.0	0.9	3.6	5.6	23.9	5.7	4.5
39071	Highland County, Ohio	2.8	11.5	8.6	1.9	3.8	6.8	20.6	6.7	3.4
39073	Hocking County, Ohio	2.9	13.6	5.2	1.2	4.5	5.7	26.3	7.5	4.9
39075	Holmes County, Ohio	3.8	12.0	4.3	1.4	2.7	3.4	13.3	7.5	3.8
39077	Huron County, Ohio	2.3	9.4	6.5	1.3	2.8	5.8	20.6	8.0	4.7
39079	Jackson County, Ohio	1.3	10.6	4.3	0.6	4.5	3.7	32.1	7.3	2.9
39081	Jefferson County, Ohio	2.2	13.6	6.2	1.6	4.2	6.5	30.1	7.8	5.3
39083	Knox County, Ohio	2.5	9.8	4.4	1.1	5.9	5.5	26.7	7.9	5.1
39085	Lake County, Ohio	3.0	10.7	3.8	1.5	8.0	9.2	22.5	8.2	4.6
39087	Lawrence County, Ohio	2.2	12.8	5.9	3.1	3.5	5.8	29.9	8.0	4.1
39089	Licking County, Ohio	2.8	13.5	4.5	1.7	9.6	8.2	22.4	7.8	4.2
39091	Logan County, Ohio	2.8	8.2	5.5	1.0	3.3	8.2	18.7	6.8	3.8
39093	Lorain County, Ohio	2.4	11.1	4.6	1.5	6.0	8.6	24.6	9.4	4.3
39095	Lucas County, Ohio	2.7	10.9	5.7	1.5	4.2	9.3	26.7	10.7	4.8
39097	Madison County, Ohio	2.5	13.2	6.6	1.3	6.3	8.6	19.2	6.2	4.0
39099	Mahoning County, Ohio	2.6	13.5	4.5	1.7	4.8	8.2	25.5	10.1	4.7
39101	Marion County, Ohio	1.8	11.2	3.9	2.5	3.8	5.9	23.8	7.0	4.2
39103	Medina County, Ohio	3.6	12.0	5.1	1.7	7.0	9.6	21.7	8.6	4.5
39105	Meigs County, Ohio	1.2	11.9	10.3	0.6	3.8	5.3	27.3	7.9	3.2
39107	Mercer County, Ohio	2.0	9.8	4.4	0.8	3.7	4.4	16.8	6.7	4.7
39109	Miami County, Ohio	2.4	11.5	4.6	1.6	3.3	8.0	18.8	7.6	4.4
39111	Monroe County, Ohio	1.4	13.0	8.5	2.0	4.9	7.4	21.4	4.3	3.0
39113	Montgomery County, Ohio	2.2	11.6	3.9	2.2	5.3	10.5	26.0	9.8	4.9
39115	Morgan County, Ohio	1.6	10.2	6.6	1.9	3.4	3.3	24.8	6.6	5.2
39117	Morrow County, Ohio	3.0	11.7	3.9	1.7	4.9	5.8	21.3	6.4	4.7
39119	Muskingum County, Ohio	2.7	15.8	5.2	1.3	4.4	5.6	26.2	10.0	4.8
39121	Noble County, Ohio	3.0	15.1	8.4	1.2	2.7	8.7	20.3	5.4	3.7
39123	Ottawa County, Ohio	2.0	12.4	6.2	1.2	4.0	6.7	23.3	9.9	4.8
39125	Paulding County, Ohio	2.3	11.3	6.7	0.8	3.3	5.1	20.7	6.1	3.6

Table C. County—Labor Force, Employment, and Educational Data, 2011–2015—*Continued*

Fips code	State/county	Wholesale trade	Retail trade	Transportation and warehousing, and utilities	Information	Finance and insurance, and real estate and rental and leasing	Professional, scientific, and management, and administrative and waste management services	Educational services, and health care and social assistance	Arts, entertainment, and recreation, and accommodation and food services	Other services, except public administration
39127	Perry County, Ohio	1.6	12.2	5.6	0.7	4.1	6.0	25.0	5.9	4.0
39129	Pickaway County, Ohio	3.8	11.7	8.1	1.5	7.5	8.5	22.1	7.1	4.2
39131	Pike County, Ohio	0.8	10.1	5.6	0.4	4.4	7.2	24.9	6.6	2.7
39133	Portage County, Ohio	2.3	12.7	4.6	1.2	4.7	8.3	22.5	11.2	4.9
39135	Preble County, Ohio	2.4	10.9	5.2	1.4	3.4	5.7	23.7	8.5	4.2
39137	Putnam County, Ohio	2.1	9.5	4.1	1.0	3.1	4.0	26.5	6.1	3.9
39139	Richland County, Ohio	2.2	12.7	4.7	2.1	4.6	7.1	23.4	8.8	4.3
39141	Ross County, Ohio	2.0	13.0	4.8	2.1	3.5	5.2	24.6	9.2	3.3
39143	Sandusky County, Ohio	1.8	9.3	6.2	0.8	3.0	6.3	21.5	7.3	4.7
39145	Scioto County, Ohio	1.7	14.3	6.7	0.8	3.3	5.3	32.0	10.0	4.0
39147	Seneca County, Ohio	2.6	12.4	4.4	1.0	2.6	4.0	23.6	6.1	4.6
39149	Shelby County, Ohio	2.0	9.1	5.2	1.1	2.9	6.1	17.8	6.9	4.9
39151	Stark County, Ohio	2.9	11.9	4.6	1.6	5.3	8.6	24.2	8.9	4.7
39153	Summit County, Ohio	3.6	11.8	4.5	1.9	6.5	10.0	24.3	9.0	4.6
39155	Trumbull County, Ohio	2.3	12.5	5.4	1.3	4.3	7.6	22.8	8.7	4.1
39157	Tuscarawas County, Ohio	2.3	11.0	4.1	1.6	3.4	6.6	21.3	8.8	5.3
39159	Union County, Ohio	3.1	11.1	4.6	1.8	5.9	11.6	19.9	7.4	5.2
39161	Van Wert County, Ohio	2.0	9.4	4.0	0.9	4.7	4.9	20.6	6.4	4.6
39163	Vinton County, Ohio	2.2	8.8	4.1	0.7	2.9	6.2	26.5	6.8	4.5
39165	Warren County, Ohio	2.9	11.5	3.8	1.9	7.7	12.4	21.8	7.9	4.7
39167	Washington County, Ohio	2.4	12.4	5.5	2.1	4.8	6.3	24.0	8.5	4.3
39169	Wayne County, Ohio	2.5	11.5	5.0	1.0	3.9	6.2	22.7	7.3	4.5
39171	Williams County, Ohio	1.5	11.7	4.1	1.1	2.1	5.4	17.7	5.8	4.6
39173	Wood County, Ohio	2.6	11.0	5.4	1.7	4.2	7.4	26.4	11.1	4.8
39175	Wyandot County, Ohio	2.2	9.3	4.3	0.7	3.7	5.0	19.6	6.5	4.9
40000	**Oklahoma**	2.7	11.6	5.1	1.8	5.6	8.2	22.5	9.0	5.2
40001	Adair County, Oklahoma	1.9	9.9	4.1	0.7	2.3	3.4	25.1	6.6	4.5
40003	Alfalfa County, Oklahoma	3.2	7.9	8.5	1.1	4.2	3.6	13.7	4.4	4.5
40005	Atoka County, Oklahoma	1.9	11.8	5.6	0.9	4.0	5.2	21.5	9.5	5.4
40007	Beaver County, Oklahoma	1.1	11.3	7.9	0.3	3.4	3.3	18.9	4.6	4.4
40009	Beckham County, Oklahoma	3.0	13.2	4.8	1.1	5.4	5.2	15.6	10.4	4.9
40011	Blaine County, Oklahoma	3.0	11.5	5.9	1.9	4.4	5.1	24.2	7.3	5.2
40013	Bryan County, Oklahoma	2.4	11.9	5.1	1.3	5.0	6.9	23.6	12.4	4.6
40015	Caddo County, Oklahoma	2.2	10.3	6.0	1.1	3.0	3.5	20.5	10.9	4.5
40017	Canadian County, Oklahoma	3.6	12.9	5.7	1.4	6.2	8.1	21.5	7.1	5.2
40019	Carter County, Oklahoma	2.3	13.8	4.8	1.0	5.2	7.0	19.8	9.9	5.9
40021	Cherokee County, Oklahoma	3.0	11.9	3.7	0.8	3.8	6.2	29.0	8.7	3.9
40023	Choctaw County, Oklahoma	2.6	8.3	7.0	1.0	6.0	4.0	23.9	10.6	5.9
40025	Cimarron County, Oklahoma	1.6	8.2	4.2	0.3	3.9	1.3	21.0	4.3	3.8
40027	Cleveland County, Oklahoma	2.3	12.1	4.1	1.7	6.5	8.9	26.6	9.9	4.7
40029	Coal County, Oklahoma	2.5	9.7	4.2	1.0	5.2	3.6	29.2	5.9	5.5
40031	Comanche County, Oklahoma	1.3	12.4	3.9	1.6	5.4	7.5	23.6	9.8	5.3
40033	Cotton County, Oklahoma	0.8	6.6	8.8	1.8	4.3	9.1	18.0	13.0	3.8
40035	Craig County, Oklahoma	2.8	12.8	7.7	0.6	2.7	6.1	26.2	8.3	4.8
40037	Creek County, Oklahoma	3.3	10.8	6.7	1.7	5.1	8.1	20.8	7.1	5.9
40039	Custer County, Oklahoma	3.0	11.8	4.8	0.8	4.0	5.7	22.2	10.1	6.7
40041	Delaware County, Oklahoma	1.8	12.7	5.1	1.0	5.2	6.1	20.9	9.9	5.8
40043	Dewey County, Oklahoma	2.3	11.5	6.1	0.8	2.3	4.5	20.2	3.8	4.6
40045	Ellis County, Oklahoma	3.2	8.8	5.8	0.4	5.1	3.1	22.6	2.1	4.8
40047	Garfield County, Oklahoma	3.1	11.7	6.1	1.1	5.1	6.1	22.4	8.4	5.6
40049	Garvin County, Oklahoma	2.1	13.5	6.6	0.6	4.8	4.5	19.7	7.6	4.4
40051	Grady County, Oklahoma	3.1	12.6	5.9	1.4	4.4	6.8	20.8	7.1	5.3
40053	Grant County, Oklahoma	3.3	6.9	6.7	1.3	5.7	3.4	18.2	3.8	5.0
40055	Greer County, Oklahoma	0.0	7.8	6.0	1.2	5.4	8.7	23.0	8.6	5.1
40057	Harmon County, Oklahoma	3.4	10.4	3.7	1.5	8.7	3.4	23.2	3.6	2.5
40059	Harper County, Oklahoma	1.5	7.1	4.5	1.7	3.3	4.6	20.3	4.8	3.6
40061	Haskell County, Oklahoma	1.8	12.6	5.2	1.0	2.5	3.9	24.9	5.8	5.6
40063	Hughes County, Oklahoma	1.4	9.8	7.3	1.1	3.0	4.4	26.2	6.6	2.9
40065	Jackson County, Oklahoma	2.3	11.6	3.7	1.1	3.5	4.9	23.4	9.3	2.7
40067	Jefferson County, Oklahoma	2.7	10.0	5.2	0.6	4.3	4.0	20.1	7.5	6.2
40069	Johnston County, Oklahoma	1.2	12.3	3.7	0.3	2.5	2.9	27.5	7.3	3.6
40071	Kay County, Oklahoma	2.4	11.5	5.6	1.4	4.5	6.5	20.1	12.6	4.0
40073	Kingfisher County, Oklahoma	2.8	8.7	4.3	4.3	4.9	4.1	17.3	5.1	7.0
40075	Kiowa County, Oklahoma	4.5	10.9	4.4	0.4	4.3	2.5	26.1	7.3	6.2
40077	Latimer County, Oklahoma	2.2	9.7	5.7	0.4	5.0	5.0	32.3	5.1	3.8
40079	Le Flore County, Oklahoma	2.4	11.8	6.0	1.3	4.0	5.1	24.4	7.0	4.3
40081	Lincoln County, Oklahoma	2.3	10.5	6.6	1.1	5.6	4.4	21.1	8.0	5.2
40083	Logan County, Oklahoma	1.9	12.9	5.1	1.5	6.4	6.3	25.2	7.8	4.5
40085	Love County, Oklahoma	2.1	14.8	6.7	0.8	2.1	3.7	15.6	15.5	4.2
40087	McClain County, Oklahoma	2.7	12.7	5.8	1.1	5.8	6.9	22.1	6.7	4.1
40089	McCurtain County, Oklahoma	2.7	11.3	5.6	1.1	3.0	4.1	23.4	6.2	5.9
40091	McIntosh County, Oklahoma	1.0	14.4	6.5	1.7	4.3	6.3	20.8	9.6	3.8
40093	Major County, Oklahoma	3.2	9.2	6.5	0.2	6.1	5.1	18.6	4.2	4.8
40095	Marshall County, Oklahoma	1.8	12.3	5.9	0.3	3.8	6.2	20.4	9.4	3.2
40097	Mayes County, Oklahoma	1.8	11.9	5.0	1.2	3.3	5.3	22.1	7.1	6.2

Table C. County—Labor Force, Employment, and Educational Data, 2011–2015—*Continued*

		Industry for employed population age 16 and older								
Fips code	State/county	Wholesale trade	Retail trade	Transportation and warehousing, and utilities	Information	Finance and insurance, and real estate and rental and leasing	Professional, scientific, and management, and administrative and waste management services	Educational services, and health care and social assistance	Arts, entertainment, and recreation, and accommodation and food services	Other services, except public administration
40099	Murray County, Oklahoma	2.6	12.3	3.2	1.6	3.8	5.2	21.7	16.2	3.4
40101	Muskogee County, Oklahoma	3.3	11.2	5.1	1.4	4.5	4.8	25.8	9.8	5.1
40103	Noble County, Oklahoma	2.4	7.2	4.2	0.7	5.1	6.1	23.2	7.4	4.7
40105	Nowata County, Oklahoma	3.7	10.0	6.3	0.8	4.4	5.3	25.5	7.7	5.2
40107	Okfuskee County, Oklahoma	1.6	11.3	6.8	0.9	2.8	5.9	23.5	7.9	4.1
40109	Oklahoma County, Oklahoma	2.8	12.0	4.0	1.9	6.9	10.6	21.1	9.6	5.5
40111	Okmulgee County, Oklahoma	2.7	10.7	5.2	1.5	5.1	6.4	25.4	7.3	5.6
40113	Osage County, Oklahoma	1.8	9.8	7.2	1.4	4.8	7.2	19.3	7.8	5.1
40115	Ottawa County, Oklahoma	1.4	10.8	4.9	0.6	3.9	4.7	24.7	14.9	4.6
40117	Pawnee County, Oklahoma	2.1	9.3	9.6	1.4	5.6	6.2	17.7	8.2	5.3
40119	Payne County, Oklahoma	1.8	12.2	2.7	1.5	3.7	6.4	32.5	11.2	5.3
40121	Pittsburg County, Oklahoma	2.8	11.3	5.7	1.5	4.2	5.3	21.6	8.8	3.2
40123	Pontotoc County, Oklahoma	2.1	11.5	3.5	1.3	5.9	6.3	28.7	7.6	4.9
40125	Pottawatomie County, Oklahoma	2.2	11.6	4.0	1.5	3.7	6.7	23.4	10.9	4.5
40127	Pushmataha County, Oklahoma	0.6	11.6	7.6	0.9	4.4	5.3	27.2	6.1	4.1
40129	Roger Mills County, Oklahoma	1.7	11.6	4.2	2.3	2.3	3.8	18.3	4.2	4.6
40131	Rogers County, Oklahoma	3.2	11.0	8.2	1.9	5.4	7.0	21.6	7.9	5.1
40133	Seminole County, Oklahoma	2.0	12.0	4.1	1.0	2.8	5.1	23.3	8.1	4.9
40135	Sequoyah County, Oklahoma	1.4	11.6	5.5	1.0	3.2	4.9	26.2	11.8	4.4
40137	Stephens County, Oklahoma	2.0	11.5	4.9	1.0	5.2	5.9	21.3	7.0	5.9
40139	Texas County, Oklahoma	1.8	10.4	4.2	1.9	3.1	4.3	16.4	5.1	3.6
40141	Tillman County, Oklahoma	1.8	9.5	5.2	1.2	3.4	3.8	23.6	7.6	4.9
40143	Tulsa County, Oklahoma	3.2	11.0	5.6	2.8	6.6	11.3	21.5	9.4	5.7
40145	Wagoner County, Oklahoma	3.0	11.4	7.1	2.2	6.4	8.6	21.2	6.4	5.1
40147	Washington County, Oklahoma	3.5	11.6	4.9	1.9	5.1	9.3	21.6	9.7	5.2
40149	Washita County, Oklahoma	2.5	10.0	5.9	0.8	4.0	3.6	19.7	6.2	5.3
40151	Woods County, Oklahoma	3.5	11.5	5.2	3.1	5.1	5.5	21.6	9.6	4.6
40153	Woodward County, Oklahoma	2.5	13.8	7.6	1.3	5.1	2.6	17.9	6.2	7.1
41000	**Oregon**	2.9	12.1	4.1	1.8	5.7	10.6	23.1	9.9	4.9
41001	Baker County, Oregon	1.4	12.7	6.7	1.3	5.1	5.3	23.8	8.3	3.5
41003	Benton County, Oregon	1.3	9.3	2.3	1.7	3.1	10.1	38.0	9.7	4.6
41005	Clackamas County, Oregon	4.2	13.0	4.8	1.7	7.5	11.0	20.4	7.9	5.0
41007	Clatsop County, Oregon	2.3	14.4	3.7	1.6	5.8	6.9	20.4	16.1	3.9
41009	Columbia County, Oregon	2.8	11.4	7.6	0.9	4.7	9.0	19.2	7.3	4.8
41011	Coos County, Oregon	1.2	13.3	4.7	1.4	3.0	8.7	23.1	13.0	4.8
41013	Crook County, Oregon	3.3	14.0	3.0	1.6	3.0	6.6	19.3	11.5	4.5
41015	Curry County, Oregon	0.5	12.5	4.2	1.4	4.0	4.6	24.7	11.1	7.2
41017	Deschutes County, Oregon	1.8	12.9	2.7	2.9	5.8	11.5	20.7	13.5	6.0
41019	Douglas County, Oregon	2.2	12.3	5.1	1.3	4.2	7.2	22.9	10.1	6.0
41021	Gilliam County, Oregon	3.1	13.0	16.9	1.3	1.9	10.1	9.7	5.7	2.7
41023	Grant County, Oregon	1.1	11.1	7.2	1.3	1.8	5.8	17.0	9.2	4.5
41025	Harney County, Oregon	0.5	9.7	4.6	0.9	1.7	5.1	22.3	7.2	4.0
41027	Hood River County, Oregon	4.5	9.1	4.1	1.6	2.3	7.9	22.4	9.8	5.0
41029	Jackson County, Oregon	2.2	13.9	4.3	1.9	4.6	8.4	26.1	10.6	5.9
41031	Jefferson County, Oregon	2.1	12.2	5.2	0.6	3.7	5.7	18.8	10.5	4.5
41033	Josephine County, Oregon	2.4	15.1	5.1	1.2	4.9	9.8	25.1	7.4	5.5
41035	Klamath County, Oregon	2.6	12.3	6.4	1.0	3.5	8.8	22.3	8.4	4.3
41037	Lake County, Oregon	1.8	8.2	3.4	1.3	1.8	6.9	16.9	8.3	3.2
41039	Lane County, Oregon	2.7	13.3	3.6	2.1	5.1	9.9	26.9	10.8	5.1
41041	Lincoln County, Oregon	1.5	14.4	4.4	1.6	5.1	9.2	17.3	21.0	4.9
41043	Linn County, Oregon	2.6	13.9	4.6	1.4	3.4	7.3	23.8	7.7	4.4
41045	Malheur County, Oregon	4.9	10.0	4.4	0.8	3.0	4.9	18.9	10.3	4.1
41047	Marion County, Oregon	2.4	12.4	3.4	1.1	5.4	8.2	22.4	8.4	4.7
41049	Morrow County, Oregon	4.3	7.5	6.2	0.6	3.4	3.9	12.8	9.8	3.1
41051	Multnomah County, Oregon	3.3	11.0	4.3	2.3	6.2	13.4	24.9	11.2	5.4
41053	Polk County, Oregon	1.9	11.7	2.8	1.0	5.2	7.9	26.8	7.6	4.3
41055	Sherman County, Oregon	7.9	8.8	7.2	0.7	2.5	4.7	20.4	7.9	6.3
41057	Tillamook County, Oregon	1.7	10.8	6.4	0.7	5.0	5.5	19.2	11.6	3.8
41059	Umatilla County, Oregon	2.6	13.1	6.4	1.8	3.4	7.2	19.4	8.8	4.0
41061	Union County, Oregon	2.9	12.2	5.5	2.2	4.6	5.3	27.2	6.6	5.1
41063	Wallowa County, Oregon	0.7	10.8	3.7	1.0	5.7	4.9	23.7	7.6	4.2
41065	Wasco County, Oregon	2.4	13.1	4.3	1.7	4.0	6.8	25.1	10.1	5.2
41067	Washington County, Oregon	3.2	11.1	3.5	2.2	7.5	13.3	19.6	8.4	4.2
41069	Wheeler County, Oregon	2.0	10.3	6.4	0.5	2.0	2.7	18.3	9.4	5.2
41071	Yamhill County, Oregon	3.4	10.4	3.3	1.4	5.4	8.7	21.5	9.3	4.3
42000	**Pennsylvania**	2.8	11.7	5.1	1.7	6.4	9.9	25.9	8.4	4.7
42001	Adams County, Pennsylvania	3.3	11.2	4.3	0.9	4.0	6.1	22.7	8.8	4.8
42003	Allegheny County, Pennsylvania	2.8	11.1	4.7	2.0	8.7	12.0	28.2	9.3	4.6
42005	Armstrong County, Pennsylvania	2.4	11.9	6.2	1.0	3.6	7.2	26.1	5.3	5.3
42007	Beaver County, Pennsylvania	2.9	12.3	9.3	1.2	6.1	9.4	24.4	8.0	4.8
42009	Bedford County, Pennsylvania	2.2	13.3	7.4	1.2	2.9	6.3	19.0	9.5	5.2
42011	Berks County, Pennsylvania	3.3	12.1	5.0	1.2	5.8	8.7	22.8	7.8	4.5
42013	Blair County, Pennsylvania	2.8	15.0	6.5	1.8	3.8	6.6	26.5	9.5	4.9
42015	Bradford County, Pennsylvania	2.1	12.2	7.2	1.3	3.1	6.2	24.2	5.7	3.7

Table C. County—Labor Force, Employment, and Educational Data, 2011–2015—*Continued*

		Industry for employed population age 16 and older								
Fips code	State/county	Wholesale trade	Retail trade	Transportation and warehousing, and utilities	Information	Finance and insurance, and real estate and rental and leasing	Professional, scientific, and management, and administrative and waste management services	Educational services, and health care and social assistance	Arts, entertainment, and recreation, and accommodation and food services	Other services, except public administration
42017	Bucks County, Pennsylvania	3.6	12.6	3.8	2.2	7.5	12.5	23.7	7.3	4.3
42019	Butler County, Pennsylvania	3.3	13.0	5.7	1.9	5.9	10.0	22.5	8.2	4.7
42021	Cambria County, Pennsylvania	2.7	11.7	6.0	1.4	5.2	7.2	30.1	7.8	4.9
42023	Cameron County, Pennsylvania	0.9	9.6	3.7	0.6	2.6	3.1	15.6	6.7	3.9
42025	Carbon County, Pennsylvania	3.4	11.7	6.6	2.2	4.2	6.7	26.0	7.8	5.3
42027	Centre County, Pennsylvania	1.6	10.1	3.2	1.3	4.0	8.8	38.2	11.7	3.5
42029	Chester County, Pennsylvania	3.1	10.2	3.5	2.3	10.0	14.7	22.9	6.9	4.2
42031	Clarion County, Pennsylvania	2.2	11.8	5.2	0.6	2.7	5.5	29.9	9.2	5.0
42033	Clearfield County, Pennsylvania	2.1	15.1	8.4	1.1	4.0	5.5	24.4	7.3	5.3
42035	Clinton County, Pennsylvania	1.8	12.8	5.7	1.0	3.3	6.6	22.2	9.9	4.9
42037	Columbia County, Pennsylvania	2.2	13.2	6.3	1.6	3.1	5.3	27.7	9.6	4.9
42039	Crawford County, Pennsylvania	1.9	11.3	4.6	0.9	3.3	4.8	26.7	7.1	5.6
42041	Cumberland County, Pennsylvania	2.7	13.3	6.0	1.5	8.4	10.5	22.5	7.3	4.8
42043	Dauphin County, Pennsylvania	3.1	10.9	5.9	1.5	7.3	9.8	23.6	10.1	4.5
42045	Delaware County, Pennsylvania	2.5	10.4	5.2	2.1	8.0	11.9	30.3	8.3	4.8
42047	Elk County, Pennsylvania	1.3	8.6	4.0	0.8	2.3	5.8	19.0	5.6	4.5
42049	Erie County, Pennsylvania	2.2	11.3	3.5	1.5	6.0	6.5	27.3	10.8	4.8
42051	Fayette County, Pennsylvania	1.9	13.6	6.4	1.4	3.6	7.4	24.7	8.7	4.8
42053	Forest County, Pennsylvania	1.9	8.6	5.8	1.0	6.0	3.8	26.2	9.1	6.7
42055	Franklin County, Pennsylvania	2.4	12.8	4.7	1.3	5.2	7.4	22.6	7.6	5.1
42057	Fulton County, Pennsylvania	2.0	11.7	5.8	1.2	3.6	5.0	18.8	6.0	4.6
42059	Greene County, Pennsylvania	2.1	9.8	6.0	0.9	3.2	5.6	26.9	7.1	5.1
42061	Huntingdon County, Pennsylvania	2.0	10.9	5.4	1.3	3.4	5.2	27.2	6.8	3.7
42063	Indiana County, Pennsylvania	1.9	12.8	6.4	1.4	4.7	4.8	27.6	9.9	5.1
42065	Jefferson County, Pennsylvania	2.5	11.5	6.7	1.2	2.8	4.7	24.7	6.5	5.9
42067	Juniata County, Pennsylvania	1.8	11.2	6.9	1.3	4.9	5.7	17.0	6.2	3.7
42069	Lackawanna County, Pennsylvania	3.4	12.4	5.1	1.7	6.2	7.8	28.1	8.5	4.2
42071	Lancaster County, Pennsylvania	3.6	12.3	4.7	1.2	4.7	8.0	22.7	8.0	5.4
42073	Lawrence County, Pennsylvania	2.6	12.0	5.9	1.6	4.4	7.6	25.9	7.4	5.7
42075	Lebanon County, Pennsylvania	4.2	11.6	4.7	1.2	4.7	7.4	24.3	8.3	4.4
42077	Lehigh County, Pennsylvania	3.3	12.1	6.1	1.8	5.7	10.1	24.8	8.4	4.3
42079	Luzerne County, Pennsylvania	3.4	14.0	5.9	2.0	5.2	7.8	24.7	8.7	3.9
42081	Lycoming County, Pennsylvania	2.6	12.4	5.7	1.3	4.4	7.3	25.9	7.7	4.6
42083	McKean County, Pennsylvania	2.1	9.2	4.3	1.4	3.0	4.8	28.0	7.8	4.1
42085	Mercer County, Pennsylvania	2.2	13.2	4.1	1.1	3.7	6.4	28.5	8.5	5.1
42087	Mifflin County, Pennsylvania	2.0	11.6	5.1	0.6	2.8	5.2	23.9	7.9	4.6
42089	Monroe County, Pennsylvania	2.7	12.8	6.6	1.9	5.7	9.6	24.1	13.1	3.8
42091	Montgomery County, Pennsylvania	2.9	10.4	3.2	2.3	9.5	14.6	25.5	6.9	4.7
42093	Montour County, Pennsylvania	2.6	8.1	5.0	1.4	4.4	5.5	39.6	7.0	4.0
42095	Northampton County, Pennsylvania	3.0	11.7	5.3	2.1	6.4	9.1	25.8	8.1	4.6
42097	Northumberland County, Pennsylvania	2.4	13.0	5.5	0.9	3.1	4.8	29.3	7.0	4.7
42099	Perry County, Pennsylvania	3.3	13.2	9.7	1.4	7.1	7.1	19.5	5.6	4.4
42101	Philadelphia County, Pennsylvania	2.0	10.7	5.3	1.9	6.1	11.6	30.3	10.1	4.8
42103	Pike County, Pennsylvania	2.7	12.9	5.8	1.5	7.0	9.7	22.1	12.7	5.9
42105	Potter County, Pennsylvania	1.1	10.5	7.4	4.3	2.1	5.4	23.0	5.1	5.4
42107	Schuylkill County, Pennsylvania	2.9	13.6	6.1	1.1	3.9	6.1	24.7	5.1	4.0
42109	Snyder County, Pennsylvania	2.3	13.8	4.5	0.9	2.1	4.7	25.3	7.2	4.9
42111	Somerset County, Pennsylvania	2.4	12.1	7.4	0.9	3.6	6.2	24.7	8.1	5.4
42113	Sullivan County, Pennsylvania	1.9	10.4	6.8	0.9	3.5	6.3	23.0	5.8	3.4
42115	Susquehanna County, Pennsylvania	3.9	11.1	6.7	1.3	4.2	6.4	20.6	7.5	5.2
42117	Tioga County, Pennsylvania	2.2	11.7	5.6	1.3	3.7	5.9	23.7	7.9	4.7
42119	Union County, Pennsylvania	2.3	10.9	5.7	1.0	2.7	4.1	32.4	8.9	4.0
42121	Venango County, Pennsylvania	1.8	12.4	5.9	1.1	3.0	4.9	25.2	7.4	4.8
42123	Warren County, Pennsylvania	1.8	14.6	5.2	1.0	5.7	4.9	24.2	5.6	4.6
42125	Washington County, Pennsylvania	2.6	12.7	5.1	1.6	5.9	9.8	23.6	9.1	4.2
42127	Wayne County, Pennsylvania	2.2	14.8	5.6	1.3	6.0	7.0	22.7	9.6	4.9
42129	Westmoreland County, Pennsylvania	3.1	12.8	6.2	1.3	5.1	8.6	24.8	8.0	5.2
42131	Wyoming County, Pennsylvania	3.1	14.4	7.7	1.9	5.2	7.6	19.2	7.3	4.8
42133	York County, Pennsylvania	3.6	11.9	5.5	1.3	5.2	8.7	21.7	7.5	5.1
44000	**Rhode Island**	2.6	12.0	3.7	1.6	6.8	9.7	27.4	10.9	4.6
44001	Bristol County, Rhode Island	2.6	9.6	2.8	2.5	7.3	9.3	32.1	9.9	3.5
44003	Kent County, Rhode Island	2.8	12.0	4.6	2.1	8.4	8.8	24.8	10.1	4.5
44005	Newport County, Rhode Island	2.1	9.9	2.7	1.5	6.8	11.6	26.6	14.1	4.6
44007	Providence County, Rhode Island	2.7	12.7	3.7	1.6	6.4	9.6	27.7	10.2	4.7
44009	Washington County, Rhode Island	2.0	10.7	3.4	1.2	6.5	10.1	28.0	13.3	4.3
45000	**South Carolina**	2.7	12.2	4.6	1.8	5.8	9.6	21.7	10.5	5.0
45001	Abbeville County, South Carolina	2.0	8.9	5.3	1.0	3.0	7.0	23.3	8.3	4.9
45003	Aiken County, South Carolina	1.3	12.7	5.7	1.8	4.1	11.3	21.1	8.2	5.1
45005	Allendale County, South Carolina	0.6	13.9	4.8	1.3	0.5	5.2	30.8	2.8	2.6
45007	Anderson County, South Carolina	3.3	12.9	3.8	1.6	4.1	7.6	23.3	7.7	5.2
45009	Bamberg County, South Carolina	1.8	7.0	4.3	1.6	2.5	4.4	33.3	4.6	4.0
45011	Barnwell County, South Carolina	2.2	8.6	7.0	1.7	5.5	8.0	20.6	6.0	2.9
45013	Beaufort County, South Carolina	1.5	13.3	2.9	1.9	7.0	13.4	19.4	16.9	5.0

Table C. County—Labor Force, Employment, and Educational Data, 2011–2015—*Continued*

		Industry for employed population age 16 and older								
Fips code	State/county	Wholesale trade	Retail trade	Transportation and warehousing, and utilities	Information	Finance and insurance, and real estate and rental and leasing	Professional, scientific, and management, and administrative and waste management services	Educational services, and health care and social assistance	Arts, entertainment, and recreation, and accommodation and food services	Other services, except public administration
45015	Berkeley County, South Carolina	2.4	12.8	6.0	2.3	4.5	12.1	19.3	7.6	5.1
45017	Calhoun County, South Carolina	2.5	11.4	6.8	1.8	3.4	6.8	22.1	6.8	4.8
45019	Charleston County, South Carolina	2.3	10.7	4.4	2.4	6.0	13.3	23.2	14.0	4.7
45021	Cherokee County, South Carolina	2.5	14.8	7.4	1.2	2.4	5.7	18.9	8.6	4.8
45023	Chester County, South Carolina	5.1	12.1	6.6	1.6	3.1	6.3	18.0	5.9	5.2
45025	Chesterfield County, South Carolina	2.6	12.8	4.2	1.0	2.3	3.6	21.2	7.9	4.6
45027	Clarendon County, South Carolina	1.7	14.0	5.5	1.6	5.3	6.1	22.7	8.0	4.3
45029	Colleton County, South Carolina	2.3	14.1	5.9	1.5	3.0	8.8	21.4	10.6	6.0
45031	Darlington County, South Carolina	3.9	13.1	7.5	1.1	5.1	6.3	23.9	6.4	6.1
45033	Dillon County, South Carolina	1.2	14.7	3.8	1.0	4.0	4.0	20.8	8.6	4.3
45035	Dorchester County, South Carolina	2.4	12.0	4.7	2.0	4.9	11.4	20.6	9.0	5.0
45037	Edgefield County, South Carolina	2.9	11.8	6.2	2.0	3.8	10.1	20.9	4.1	6.1
45039	Fairfield County, South Carolina	1.2	9.1	9.5	0.8	4.9	6.9	20.4	7.9	4.4
45041	Florence County, South Carolina	3.3	11.1	4.7	1.6	6.8	7.6	26.5	9.5	5.6
45043	Georgetown County, South Carolina	2.2	14.1	3.2	0.9	5.8	9.1	20.3	14.9	4.0
45045	Greenville County, South Carolina	3.7	11.2	3.9	2.1	5.6	12.2	20.9	9.4	4.9
45047	Greenwood County, South Carolina	3.3	10.3	3.9	1.1	2.6	7.1	26.5	7.7	5.6
45049	Hampton County, South Carolina	1.2	13.6	4.2	0.9	3.4	7.8	21.6	8.8	4.9
45051	Horry County, South Carolina	2.0	15.8	2.8	1.7	6.7	9.1	17.8	21.8	5.5
45053	Jasper County, South Carolina	2.2	16.4	4.6	0.8	3.2	8.8	15.5	13.8	4.3
45055	Kershaw County, South Carolina	1.7	12.5	3.9	1.1	7.9	6.9	22.9	8.4	5.1
45057	Lancaster County, South Carolina	2.6	13.5	4.4	1.7	9.0	10.6	16.7	9.6	4.7
45059	Laurens County, South Carolina	2.8	11.9	3.9	1.5	3.9	5.7	22.0	7.2	5.3
45061	Lee County, South Carolina	1.8	12.2	5.7	1.9	2.5	5.2	21.9	9.3	3.3
45063	Lexington County, South Carolina	3.3	11.6	5.1	1.8	7.9	9.4	22.2	9.0	5.0
45065	McCormick County, South Carolina	1.5	8.4	2.7	2.7	3.2	4.9	28.6	6.9	6.4
45067	Marion County, South Carolina	1.6	16.1	5.8	1.4	3.5	6.0	23.2	9.4	3.8
45069	Marlboro County, South Carolina	2.5	13.5	6.8	1.2	2.0	4.8	23.2	5.4	2.1
45071	Newberry County, South Carolina	2.5	11.1	4.5	1.8	4.5	7.9	21.1	6.4	4.4
45073	Oconee County, South Carolina	1.0	10.4	5.6	1.3	4.9	6.8	24.4	9.7	4.9
45075	Orangeburg County, South Carolina	2.5	12.2	4.6	1.8	4.1	4.8	24.9	8.8	5.6
45077	Pickens County, South Carolina	2.5	10.9	5.2	1.2	4.4	7.2	27.0	9.7	4.9
45079	Richland County, South Carolina	2.2	11.8	4.0	2.1	8.6	9.8	24.7	11.6	4.8
45081	Saluda County, South Carolina	2.8	10.6	8.9	1.5	4.2	6.5	16.3	3.7	6.4
45083	Spartanburg County, South Carolina	3.4	12.2	4.4	1.9	4.3	8.4	20.7	8.9	5.6
45085	Sumter County, South Carolina	1.8	11.1	4.3	0.9	4.3	8.5	22.0	7.2	5.0
45087	Union County, South Carolina	4.7	13.5	4.4	1.3	3.0	4.4	20.9	4.6	7.3
45089	Williamsburg County, South Carolina	2.5	10.9	5.1	1.9	4.8	7.2	23.0	8.3	4.2
45091	York County, South Carolina	4.1	12.0	6.4	2.4	8.2	10.0	19.1	8.8	4.7
46000	**South Dakota**	3.0	11.2	4.2	1.7	7.2	6.0	24.1	9.4	4.5
46003	Aurora County, South Dakota	3.4	7.6	4.4	1.0	3.3	3.6	27.7	5.3	6.2
46005	Beadle County, South Dakota	3.5	13.4	7.1	0.5	4.7	4.7	19.4	6.4	4.9
46007	Bennett County, South Dakota	1.9	10.4	5.1	2.3	2.6	1.9	31.3	5.6	1.9
46009	Bon Homme County, South Dakota	2.3	9.5	4.4	0.7	5.5	3.7	26.0	3.6	5.9
46011	Brookings County, South Dakota	2.0	9.4	2.9	2.0	3.5	4.4	27.0	11.0	4.6
46013	Brown County, South Dakota	2.9	13.5	3.3	1.9	4.9	6.1	23.8	8.7	5.1
46015	Brule County, South Dakota	3.4	8.5	3.0	2.6	5.4	4.0	30.7	8.8	2.9
46017	Buffalo County, South Dakota	1.4	2.6	1.7	0.0	2.1	2.0	28.6	22.4	0.9
46019	Butte County, South Dakota	1.6	11.9	6.9	0.6	2.9	2.9	19.4	8.8	6.6
46021	Campbell County, South Dakota	4.5	5.8	4.0	1.1	3.6	3.8	25.4	3.2	6.9
46023	Charles Mix County, South Dakota	2.2	12.7	3.7	1.1	3.4	4.7	27.6	11.4	4.0
46025	Clark County, South Dakota	2.2	8.9	5.7	0.1	5.0	4.2	15.3	5.7	7.2
46027	Clay County, South Dakota	1.3	13.7	2.3	2.1	4.4	3.6	34.4	15.3	3.8
46029	Codington County, South Dakota	2.7	12.2	4.5	1.0	6.8	5.9	16.4	10.0	6.1
46031	Corson County, South Dakota	2.7	8.7	2.8	2.3	3.0	1.3	25.2	9.8	3.4
46033	Custer County, South Dakota	1.9	7.8	4.2	0.6	5.9	7.1	21.3	15.1	4.1
46035	Davison County, South Dakota	1.9	11.9	2.7	2.5	1.9	5.7	25.1	10.3	5.4
46037	Day County, South Dakota	2.5	11.5	5.1	1.7	2.8	3.8	21.5	7.7	3.5
46039	Deuel County, South Dakota	3.1	9.3	4.8	2.2	3.8	2.9	16.1	4.1	4.5
46041	Dewey County, South Dakota	0.7	6.6	3.3	1.1	5.8	2.3	33.1	5.8	2.7
46043	Douglas County, South Dakota	2.0	13.1	5.2	0.4	2.5	4.1	22.9	7.0	6.0
46045	Edmunds County, South Dakota	6.4	9.5	6.6	0.5	6.6	4.7	22.4	4.6	8.0
46047	Fall River County, South Dakota	0.3	9.0	10.0	2.0	1.1	3.0	35.1	9.6	4.6
46049	Faulk County, South Dakota	1.5	8.0	2.8	2.2	4.1	1.6	25.3	4.0	10.4
46051	Grant County, South Dakota	8.7	8.5	8.0	2.2	7.0	3.3	16.3	5.8	4.3
46053	Gregory County, South Dakota	2.3	11.3	6.9	1.2	6.4	2.9	26.2	7.6	3.6
46055	Haakon County, South Dakota	7.3	8.1	3.0	4.0	2.7	3.0	20.6	3.1	6.0
46057	Hamlin County, South Dakota	4.5	11.6	4.9	0.7	5.7	3.0	18.9	3.4	4.1
46059	Hand County, South Dakota	3.1	10.0	5.3	0.7	5.3	6.3	19.6	3.5	7.1
46061	Hanson County, South Dakota	2.1	7.8	2.9	1.5	5.4	5.9	28.6	4.3	2.6
46063	Harding County, South Dakota	1.0	11.0	4.7	2.2	3.2	1.9	12.6	2.5	2.8
46065	Hughes County, South Dakota	1.4	9.6	3.3	2.9	8.0	7.0	18.5	7.2	4.7
46067	Hutchinson County, South Dakota	3.6	10.2	5.0	1.7	4.0	3.8	26.8	6.2	4.8
46069	Hyde County, South Dakota	4.7	10.8	4.7	6.3	6.3	1.7	22.0	4.5	0.7

Table C. County—Labor Force, Employment, and Educational Data, 2011-2015—*Continued*

		Industry for employed population age 16 and older								
Fips code	State/county	Wholesale trade	Retail trade	Transportation and warehousing, and utilities	Information	Finance and insurance, and real estate and rental and leasing	Professional, scientific, and management, and administrative and waste management services	Educational services, and health care and social assistance	Arts, entertainment, and recreation, and accommodation and food services	Other services, except public administration
46071	Jackson County, South Dakota	3.1	6.5	4.2	0.6	2.9	2.6	30.9	10.0	2.7
46073	Jerauld County, South Dakota	4.4	8.6	6.7	0.3	3.4	1.5	21.7	6.5	4.7
46075	Jones County, South Dakota	0.4	14.5	8.7	0.0	5.6	1.9	13.7	13.1	1.5
46077	Kingsbury County, South Dakota	4.6	5.3	6.7	1.7	6.9	3.3	20.5	6.6	4.5
46079	Lake County, South Dakota	3.4	11.0	5.3	2.1	6.0	8.3	23.3	7.0	2.7
46081	Lawrence County, South Dakota	2.2	8.1	3.8	2.0	5.6	7.1	22.0	18.5	5.1
46083	Lincoln County, South Dakota	3.5	10.1	3.9	1.9	12.7	8.0	27.6	4.7	4.7
46085	Lyman County, South Dakota	2.6	9.4	3.3	1.1	2.9	4.3	20.8	13.1	3.4
46087	McCook County, South Dakota	5.0	10.5	5.3	1.1	7.7	3.0	21.6	4.0	8.5
46089	McPherson County, South Dakota	0.8	8.0	1.1	0.5	5.0	3.6	24.5	6.0	4.1
46091	Marshall County, South Dakota	1.4	9.7	2.0	1.1	3.5	3.7	17.6	9.1	3.0
46093	Meade County, South Dakota	3.0	10.0	4.4	1.4	5.5	5.6	21.9	11.8	3.6
46095	Mellette County, South Dakota	1.1	12.3	4.3	0.3	0.9	3.5	29.2	5.5	1.1
46097	Miner County, South Dakota	4.7	6.0	5.3	0.9	5.2	7.8	22.4	4.1	3.0
46099	Minnehaha County, South Dakota	3.6	12.3	4.3	2.1	11.5	7.2	24.6	9.2	4.0
46101	Moody County, South Dakota	1.8	8.5	6.1	0.5	5.0	4.0	21.9	9.0	5.6
46102	Oglala Lakota County, South Dakota	0.3	6.9	1.5	0.2	3.3	2.0	44.2	11.9	2.5
46103	Pennington County, South Dakota	2.6	12.8	3.6	2.0	7.2	8.1	23.4	13.2	4.9
46105	Perkins County, South Dakota	1.5	8.0	4.2	0.5	3.6	5.2	21.3	3.4	4.5
46107	Potter County, South Dakota	6.8	11.8	5.1	0.9	5.8	2.2	22.4	5.2	3.9
46109	Roberts County, South Dakota	3.0	10.1	3.7	1.0	4.3	3.4	24.0	10.7	4.3
46111	Sanborn County, South Dakota	4.1	7.8	3.8	1.9	3.0	4.2	21.2	4.6	2.9
46115	Spink County, South Dakota	3.0	9.8	5.2	0.5	4.6	2.6	25.3	5.4	4.9
46117	Stanley County, South Dakota	4.8	12.1	4.0	2.3	8.4	4.5	17.7	5.3	2.9
46119	Sully County, South Dakota	4.6	11.9	2.8	0.3	5.7	2.2	12.4	5.6	2.5
46121	Todd County, South Dakota	1.3	7.4	3.3	0.9	6.8	2.8	37.3	8.1	4.7
46123	Tripp County, South Dakota	1.4	11.6	1.9	1.7	5.0	1.3	25.5	5.0	5.5
46125	Turner County, South Dakota	4.1	10.5	6.0	1.6	4.8	4.8	26.7	4.4	4.3
46127	Union County, South Dakota	4.6	11.0	5.0	1.9	6.8	6.3	26.1	8.0	4.7
46129	Walworth County, South Dakota	3.5	11.2	6.2	2.1	4.4	4.4	25.4	10.5	6.1
46135	Yankton County, South Dakota	2.2	14.1	3.2	0.4	6.1	5.1	21.0	10.7	3.6
46137	Ziebach County, South Dakota	1.3	8.4	1.4	0.9	7.4	3.4	30.1	3.2	1.3
47000	**Tennessee**	2.7	12.2	6.3	1.9	5.7	9.4	22.8	9.3	4.9
47001	Anderson County, Tennessee	1.5	12.5	4.8	1.3	4.6	16.3	20.8	7.7	4.9
47003	Bedford County, Tennessee	2.2	13.8	6.3	1.2	4.7	6.4	15.7	4.5	4.2
47005	Benton County, Tennessee	1.9	11.7	9.8	0.6	5.3	4.3	22.5	8.1	4.0
47007	Bledsoe County, Tennessee	2.5	8.8	5.6	2.6	4.6	5.4	19.7	5.4	2.1
47009	Blount County, Tennessee	3.0	12.5	5.2	1.4	6.0	9.4	24.5	8.8	5.2
47011	Bradley County, Tennessee	2.4	11.8	6.4	1.4	4.8	6.8	22.0	10.7	6.5
47013	Campbell County, Tennessee	2.3	14.2	4.5	0.9	4.4	7.2	21.9	8.6	4.2
47015	Cannon County, Tennessee	2.7	10.2	8.3	1.2	6.6	6.8	22.9	4.0	5.2
47017	Carroll County, Tennessee	1.5	12.2	8.6	1.7	4.1	6.2	22.4	8.1	5.3
47019	Carter County, Tennessee	1.9	12.7	3.7	1.4	3.1	7.0	28.8	8.7	6.3
47021	Cheatham County, Tennessee	2.9	11.2	6.3	1.6	6.1	8.1	20.5	6.7	5.6
47023	Chester County, Tennessee	3.9	12.8	5.5	1.5	4.2	5.5	25.0	6.9	4.1
47025	Claiborne County, Tennessee	3.5	9.8	4.4	0.6	6.0	5.6	25.8	5.9	3.2
47027	Clay County, Tennessee	0.6	12.3	3.2	3.1	3.5	5.2	27.6	6.3	3.6
47029	Cocke County, Tennessee	0.9	12.9	4.2	0.7	3.4	6.4	19.2	15.1	5.0
47031	Coffee County, Tennessee	2.2	12.6	4.4	1.2	3.9	8.7	18.6	8.4	4.4
47033	Crockett County, Tennessee	2.0	8.2	7.1	1.8	4.4	10.5	20.7	5.7	4.2
47035	Cumberland County, Tennessee	2.8	13.8	5.5	1.9	3.5	6.5	21.2	10.5	5.3
47037	Davidson County, Tennessee	2.5	10.9	4.3	3.1	7.1	12.5	24.5	12.0	5.4
47039	Decatur County, Tennessee	1.9	9.8	8.8	0.8	3.3	4.1	26.3	5.3	6.5
47041	DeKalb County, Tennessee	3.7	11.0	3.5	1.3	4.6	5.2	19.7	5.0	3.9
47043	Dickson County, Tennessee	1.4	13.0	5.8	2.2	4.3	6.9	21.5	10.4	5.0
47045	Dyer County, Tennessee	1.7	10.6	5.3	0.5	4.1	3.9	23.5	7.1	5.6
47047	Fayette County, Tennessee	3.6	13.7	8.4	1.0	5.3	7.7	19.2	5.3	5.6
47049	Fentress County, Tennessee	2.7	12.4	4.7	1.3	3.0	3.8	28.1	8.2	5.1
47051	Franklin County, Tennessee	1.7	11.8	2.7	1.4	3.5	6.9	24.8	6.3	5.0
47053	Gibson County, Tennessee	2.7	13.5	4.4	1.4	4.7	6.6	23.3	6.1	5.7
47055	Giles County, Tennessee	2.3	12.5	4.4	1.1	3.9	5.5	20.6	5.7	4.3
47057	Grainger County, Tennessee	2.3	14.5	8.7	1.2	2.7	5.1	18.7	5.1	4.4
47059	Greene County, Tennessee	1.2	11.7	5.6	0.9	3.2	6.0	24.8	7.4	4.6
47061	Grundy County, Tennessee	0.6	10.0	5.2	0.4	2.9	5.1	23.5	8.6	4.6
47063	Hamblen County, Tennessee	2.8	14.1	5.0	1.4	3.6	5.7	20.7	6.7	3.4
47065	Hamilton County, Tennessee	2.5	11.9	7.2	1.6	8.0	9.4	23.1	9.6	4.8
47067	Hancock County, Tennessee	1.5	12.2	6.3	0.2	3.6	3.0	27.4	2.5	4.9
47069	Hardeman County, Tennessee	2.0	12.6	6.3	1.0	2.6	4.7	25.3	3.8	4.8
47071	Hardin County, Tennessee	0.9	13.2	7.5	0.9	4.4	5.0	17.8	9.1	8.0
47073	Hawkins County, Tennessee	1.7	12.3	6.6	1.1	4.1	5.6	21.3	7.3	3.5
47075	Haywood County, Tennessee	0.8	9.8	5.9	0.7	1.6	3.5	22.2	5.7	5.5
47077	Henderson County, Tennessee	2.3	13.1	6.8	0.7	3.6	5.8	21.7	4.6	5.1
47079	Henry County, Tennessee	4.1	14.3	7.0	0.9	3.4	5.5	22.1	6.3	5.4
47081	Hickman County, Tennessee	1.7	11.9	5.1	1.3	4.8	5.5	20.6	10.0	5.2

Table C. County—Labor Force, Employment, and Educational Data, 2011–2015—*Continued*

		Industry for employed population age 16 and older								
Fips code	State/county	Wholesale trade	Retail trade	Transportation and warehousing, and utilities	Information	Finance and insurance, and real estate and rental and leasing	Professional, scientific, and management, and administrative and waste management services	Educational services, and health care and social assistance	Arts, entertainment, and recreation, and accommodation and food services	Other services, except public administration
47083	Houston County, Tennessee	0.6	11.6	6.8	1.0	2.2	7.5	22.4	4.6	5.5
47085	Humphreys County, Tennessee	1.8	10.7	8.2	0.3	2.9	5.8	22.5	5.9	4.2
47087	Jackson County, Tennessee	2.2	10.5	9.8	2.7	2.8	5.2	22.6	3.5	4.0
47089	Jefferson County, Tennessee	2.8	12.9	6.5	1.5	4.2	6.5	19.0	10.9	5.9
47091	Johnson County, Tennessee	0.6	12.5	4.9	0.4	1.6	5.7	24.0	6.0	4.1
47093	Knox County, Tennessee	3.2	13.5	4.6	2.8	6.3	12.7	24.8	10.4	5.1
47095	Lake County, Tennessee	0.5	11.0	5.2	1.2	1.8	5.2	23.6	10.7	3.6
47097	Lauderdale County, Tennessee	4.1	10.2	5.6	0.3	3.9	4.5	19.7	5.9	4.0
47099	Lawrence County, Tennessee	3.3	11.6	6.7	1.3	3.1	5.4	23.2	5.9	4.3
47101	Lewis County, Tennessee	1.3	13.4	6.8	2.3	7.9	4.6	24.2	5.0	6.7
47103	Lincoln County, Tennessee	2.4	13.1	3.7	1.2	4.3	7.2	16.1	6.4	4.8
47105	Loudon County, Tennessee	1.8	12.2	6.7	1.0	4.6	11.3	19.5	7.4	5.0
47107	McMinn County, Tennessee	2.7	12.5	4.4	1.1	4.3	5.8	19.6	8.0	3.7
47109	McNairy County, Tennessee	2.6	10.7	6.8	0.9	2.7	6.6	22.3	7.8	4.1
47111	Macon County, Tennessee	1.0	13.1	6.1	1.7	4.3	6.0	20.9	3.4	4.5
47113	Madison County, Tennessee	2.5	14.3	4.4	1.0	4.0	7.6	28.1	9.2	5.0
47115	Marion County, Tennessee	2.8	13.6	9.2	1.9	4.7	4.9	19.1	6.2	5.6
47117	Marshall County, Tennessee	1.6	11.7	6.1	1.3	5.0	7.3	18.0	6.6	4.0
47119	Maury County, Tennessee	2.3	13.8	4.8	1.9	6.6	9.8	22.9	9.2	5.0
47121	Meigs County, Tennessee	1.0	12.3	7.4	0.4	4.1	6.1	15.1	4.5	4.2
47123	Monroe County, Tennessee	2.1	11.5	5.4	1.3	3.5	7.9	21.7	7.2	3.3
47125	Montgomery County, Tennessee	1.5	13.2	4.8	1.4	4.5	9.0	23.3	10.5	4.3
47127	Moore County, Tennessee	2.3	10.0	4.2	4.4	3.3	7.2	16.2	5.1	3.7
47129	Morgan County, Tennessee	1.5	10.4	7.7	1.5	2.0	9.8	20.8	5.8	4.7
47131	Obion County, Tennessee	2.5	12.1	4.9	1.3	5.0	8.5	20.9	7.5	5.5
47133	Overton County, Tennessee	2.1	10.2	9.0	1.2	3.5	6.1	24.2	7.3	4.2
47135	Perry County, Tennessee	1.5	7.7	10.9	2.2	3.4	3.2	23.0	4.5	3.4
47137	Pickett County, Tennessee	0.8	8.1	6.9	0.9	5.9	4.0	31.5	6.7	2.9
47139	Polk County, Tennessee	1.8	13.5	5.7	2.0	4.2	4.3	20.2	7.1	3.2
47141	Putnam County, Tennessee	2.8	11.6	4.5	1.2	4.0	6.8	25.2	13.1	4.5
47143	Rhea County, Tennessee	1.0	13.4	9.9	1.4	3.3	6.7	18.1	6.3	3.4
47145	Roane County, Tennessee	2.2	13.4	6.7	1.1	4.2	10.3	22.3	7.8	5.4
47147	Robertson County, Tennessee	2.3	10.4	5.2	1.4	5.5	8.4	19.3	8.1	4.6
47149	Rutherford County, Tennessee	3.2	12.6	5.8	3.1	6.7	9.0	21.3	9.6	4.5
47151	Scott County, Tennessee	1.3	11.9	7.5	1.3	3.0	5.3	23.1	5.6	4.7
47153	Sequatchie County, Tennessee	1.9	9.9	6.3	1.0	7.4	12.1	16.6	6.6	3.9
47155	Sevier County, Tennessee	2.0	16.6	3.7	1.7	6.9	9.3	13.5	24.4	4.1
47157	Shelby County, Tennessee	3.3	11.6	11.7	1.6	5.7	10.2	23.0	9.1	5.0
47159	Smith County, Tennessee	2.8	10.1	6.0	0.6	2.9	6.6	18.6	5.5	5.2
47161	Stewart County, Tennessee	0.9	12.3	6.4	1.2	2.9	7.6	22.0	7.6	5.8
47163	Sullivan County, Tennessee	2.6	14.2	4.2	1.9	5.0	7.6	22.7	9.1	5.6
47165	Sumner County, Tennessee	4.3	13.1	6.0	1.8	6.5	10.2	21.0	9.4	5.1
47167	Tipton County, Tennessee	3.6	10.9	7.3	0.8	5.7	7.6	21.2	7.6	6.3
47169	Trousdale County, Tennessee	6.6	14.6	10.0	0.0	4.6	6.8	26.9	3.6	4.3
47171	Unicoi County, Tennessee	1.7	8.4	7.2	1.8	2.9	10.5	23.1	7.1	3.9
47173	Union County, Tennessee	4.4	10.6	6.9	1.5	3.9	11.3	20.1	4.9	2.0
47175	Van Buren County, Tennessee	0.7	8.2	5.1	1.5	5.4	4.1	25.3	9.9	3.0
47177	Warren County, Tennessee	2.6	14.0	5.5	1.4	4.2	5.8	19.1	4.2	3.8
47179	Washington County, Tennessee	2.2	13.6	3.4	1.8	5.1	7.6	31.3	9.5	4.7
47181	Wayne County, Tennessee	1.9	13.5	5.6	0.6	5.2	2.2	26.5	5.3	4.8
47183	Weakley County, Tennessee	3.4	12.0	4.8	0.9	3.3	5.2	28.2	6.4	4.4
47185	White County, Tennessee	2.0	10.3	7.4	0.8	3.4	3.9	22.8	7.6	3.8
47187	Williamson County, Tennessee	3.6	10.3	3.0	3.4	9.9	14.0	25.4	8.2	5.3
47189	Wilson County, Tennessee	4.4	13.8	6.2	2.2	7.6	10.5	18.4	9.7	5.3
48000	**Texas**	3.0	11.6	5.5	1.8	6.6	11.1	21.6	8.9	5.3
48001	Anderson County, Texas	1.7	16.6	6.1	0.8	3.3	6.6	21.8	6.2	4.2
48003	Andrews County, Texas	2.1	6.8	9.1	0.7	4.4	6.9	16.5	4.9	4.3
48005	Angelina County, Texas	2.7	12.0	4.7	1.0	3.1	7.3	26.6	9.5	5.5
48007	Aransas County, Texas	2.7	15.6	3.4	0.7	4.0	9.8	17.8	11.8	6.6
48009	Archer County, Texas	3.8	12.6	5.8	1.3	5.2	6.3	24.1	3.9	5.4
48011	Armstrong County, Texas	4.2	9.9	5.2	1.6	4.4	5.0	23.7	5.5	3.4
48013	Atascosa County, Texas	2.3	11.4	6.8	0.9	5.2	6.5	20.4	8.6	3.9
48015	Austin County, Texas	3.4	13.2	7.2	1.3	4.8	8.0	17.7	5.7	4.1
48017	Bailey County, Texas	6.4	8.5	12.4	0.4	2.4	4.2	20.3	9.9	5.2
48019	Bandera County, Texas	1.4	10.5	1.1	1.2	5.5	8.4	24.3	7.6	8.2
48021	Bastrop County, Texas	1.7	12.0	8.0	1.4	3.7	8.7	17.9	7.0	5.0
48023	Baylor County, Texas	1.6	3.7	6.6	1.7	7.7	4.5	30.3	5.8	7.4
48025	Bee County, Texas	1.1	15.0	5.3	1.0	2.8	3.8	23.7	5.7	7.6
48027	Bell County, Texas	2.4	12.4	4.6	1.5	4.6	9.4	25.3	9.3	5.0
48029	Bexar County, Texas	2.4	12.1	4.3	1.9	9.1	11.1	23.2	11.4	5.0
48031	Blanco County, Texas	1.7	8.2	3.1	0.7	4.7	9.0	25.0	8.1	6.7
48033	Borden County, Texas	3.9	7.1	2.1	0.0	4.6	4.6	25.5	3.2	2.8
48035	Bosque County, Texas	2.5	11.2	7.9	1.0	4.6	7.2	22.1	7.1	4.1
48037	Bowie County, Texas	2.7	12.5	4.6	1.0	5.3	8.3	24.0	8.7	5.5
48039	Brazoria County, Texas	2.5	9.6	4.9	1.4	4.7	10.6	24.0	6.9	4.6

Table C. County—Labor Force, Employment, and Educational Data, 2011–2015—*Continued*

		Industry for employed population age 16 and older								
Fips code	State/county	Wholesale trade	Retail trade	Transportation and warehousing, and utilities	Information	Finance and insurance, and real estate and rental and leasing	Professional, scientific, and management, and administrative and waste management services	Educational services, and health care and social assistance	Arts, entertainment, and recreation, and accommodation and food services	Other services, except public administration
48041	Brazos County, Texas	2.3	11.6	2.6	1.4	4.9	8.9	32.7	11.9	4.4
48043	Brewster County, Texas	2.7	9.3	1.7	1.6	4.8	4.5	36.6	12.5	2.3
48045	Briscoe County, Texas	1.6	7.8	7.8	0.3	2.1	2.5	18.5	9.2	8.6
48047	Brooks County, Texas	1.1	13.1	5.7	0.5	2.4	2.3	31.8	9.2	7.7
48049	Brown County, Texas	1.5	11.5	4.6	1.1	3.3	5.1	26.9	7.3	6.3
48051	Burleson County, Texas	2.2	10.0	5.0	1.0	3.6	6.0	25.8	5.4	6.8
48053	Burnet County, Texas	2.0	13.3	4.1	2.0	4.6	9.5	16.4	13.3	5.1
48055	Caldwell County, Texas	2.4	12.6	3.8	1.1	4.6	7.2	21.9	7.9	6.6
48057	Calhoun County, Texas	2.5	10.8	3.9	1.2	4.5	6.1	18.5	5.2	2.5
48059	Callahan County, Texas	3.3	11.8	6.9	0.3	4.3	4.6	21.9	6.7	7.7
48061	Cameron County, Texas	2.4	12.9	4.9	1.6	4.5	8.2	31.8	8.6	5.2
48063	Camp County, Texas	4.5	12.5	3.7	0.2	4.2	5.3	24.2	5.8	5.4
48065	Carson County, Texas	2.0	11.4	5.8	0.5	4.5	7.7	19.8	2.8	6.7
48067	Cass County, Texas	2.1	12.6	4.8	0.4	4.1	4.2	26.1	5.5	7.3
48069	Castro County, Texas	1.9	11.9	8.4	2.1	2.6	3.4	15.5	5.5	6.3
48071	Chambers County, Texas	5.9	5.8	7.1	1.1	3.4	8.2	18.9	5.8	3.9
48073	Cherokee County, Texas	3.0	10.7	3.7	1.5	3.0	8.0	26.4	5.9	4.8
48075	Childress County, Texas	1.3	6.7	5.3	1.1	3.7	4.8	32.4	5.3	10.8
48077	Clay County, Texas	4.1	11.1	5.4	1.6	5.5	6.3	22.5	7.1	5.4
48079	Cochran County, Texas	1.1	8.1	5.3	0.2	2.4	0.6	20.5	4.0	4.3
48081	Coke County, Texas	0.1	9.2	10.0	4.4	4.6	2.8	33.6	7.0	3.1
48083	Coleman County, Texas	1.5	11.0	6.6	1.1	4.3	2.4	25.6	7.8	5.8
48085	Collin County, Texas	3.1	11.9	3.1	3.9	11.5	16.4	19.8	7.8	4.5
48087	Collingsworth County, Texas	0.7	6.3	6.8	0.4	3.8	4.1	20.5	7.0	2.8
48089	Colorado County, Texas	4.4	12.4	7.2	0.7	5.8	4.3	24.0	6.0	4.6
48091	Comal County, Texas	3.3	12.7	4.4	2.4	7.0	12.2	22.0	8.9	4.9
48093	Comanche County, Texas	1.9	11.1	7.5	0.7	3.4	4.2	24.1	4.0	6.2
48095	Concho County, Texas	0.3	3.4	1.9	3.0	4.8	2.3	21.2	4.9	4.5
48097	Cooke County, Texas	1.7	10.6	5.9	0.8	3.1	5.6	19.4	13.5	4.5
48099	Coryell County, Texas	2.0	11.3	4.1	1.8	5.0	8.0	24.7	8.6	5.1
48101	Cottle County, Texas	0.0	6.0	2.9	0.3	8.9	2.6	28.5	3.6	4.6
48103	Crane County, Texas	2.9	7.9	9.1	0.3	0.2	3.4	19.4	5.1	8.2
48105	Crockett County, Texas	0.0	4.2	5.4	0.0	1.8	1.4	17.6	7.0	2.9
48107	Crosby County, Texas	5.3	12.5	3.7	2.1	2.7	3.4	26.7	3.8	4.6
48109	Culberson County, Texas	1.0	16.5	5.0	0.5	2.5	4.1	17.4	20.2	3.7
48111	Dallam County, Texas	2.9	10.9	8.0	0.7	2.5	4.6	14.4	13.1	3.7
48113	Dallas County, Texas	3.1	11.0	5.7	2.4	8.7	14.1	18.4	9.8	5.6
48115	Dawson County, Texas	2.2	13.2	6.5	1.7	2.5	4.0	19.5	9.6	4.9
48117	Deaf Smith County, Texas	2.0	11.6	7.1	1.4	3.4	4.1	18.4	4.0	7.0
48119	Delta County, Texas	1.7	11.1	3.8	0.7	6.4	5.1	29.2	3.2	4.9
48121	Denton County, Texas	3.8	12.3	5.1	3.0	10.0	13.8	20.4	8.7	4.8
48123	DeWitt County, Texas	3.1	7.9	3.4	1.0	4.3	4.9	21.5	8.6	5.9
48125	Dickens County, Texas	0.4	6.9	7.4	4.0	2.3	3.9	29.7	4.3	3.8
48127	Dimmit County, Texas	2.3	17.9	2.6	0.0	3.9	3.3	20.3	11.5	4.5
48129	Donley County, Texas	0.7	7.8	7.2	0.1	3.5	3.0	27.9	7.9	7.3
48131	Duval County, Texas	1.3	12.5	4.7	0.2	2.9	2.7	22.1	5.7	5.0
48133	Eastland County, Texas	1.5	16.8	3.9	0.9	5.4	5.2	27.2	6.2	4.7
48135	Ector County, Texas	3.8	11.5	5.8	1.0	4.6	6.5	17.2	9.5	6.6
48137	Edwards County, Texas	1.2	3.4	6.3	4.7	9.5	6.5	26.5	5.0	6.0
48139	Ellis County, Texas	3.4	11.9	7.2	2.2	7.0	9.4	19.3	6.4	5.9
48141	El Paso County, Texas	2.9	11.9	6.6	1.7	5.2	9.9	25.2	9.9	4.6
48143	Erath County, Texas	1.8	12.1	3.2	0.5	3.4	8.1	22.7	9.7	5.5
48145	Falls County, Texas	1.9	11.1	5.4	0.6	4.8	4.7	26.9	5.2	3.4
48147	Fannin County, Texas	2.7	12.9	5.5	1.0	5.9	5.7	23.1	4.9	4.5
48149	Fayette County, Texas	4.1	12.0	7.5	0.7	4.6	5.0	17.3	8.4	5.0
48151	Fisher County, Texas	0.3	9.7	7.4	1.4	3.2	5.3	24.1	4.2	7.9
48153	Floyd County, Texas	1.4	10.0	8.6	0.4	3.9	4.5	24.9	3.2	4.0
48155	Foard County, Texas	1.8	16.4	6.3	1.1	2.9	4.0	22.9	5.4	4.0
48157	Fort Bend County, Texas	3.8	11.1	4.8	1.6	7.0	13.6	24.1	6.2	4.2
48159	Franklin County, Texas	1.3	14.3	7.8	0.1	5.1	7.0	21.4	6.8	2.9
48161	Freestone County, Texas	1.5	6.7	8.6	0.8	4.8	5.9	22.4	8.6	5.3
48163	Frio County, Texas	2.0	12.4	7.2	0.0	3.8	3.8	20.0	8.4	3.0
48165	Gaines County, Texas	2.0	7.9	9.9	0.7	1.4	4.0	19.0	5.9	7.4
48167	Galveston County, Texas	2.5	9.8	5.5	1.2	5.8	10.8	25.0	9.2	4.8
48169	Garza County, Texas	4.9	6.2	2.7	1.1	2.6	15.1	13.3	6.6	6.7
48171	Gillespie County, Texas	3.0	12.7	5.2	1.6	3.9	9.4	21.7	13.2	5.8
48173	Glasscock County, Texas	2.6	3.8	7.8	0.0	0.6	3.0	12.4	1.2	1.4
48175	Goliad County, Texas	2.0	9.5	4.6	2.6	2.1	5.2	25.0	6.2	4.7
48177	Gonzales County, Texas	4.4	11.6	4.8	1.5	3.8	5.7	18.6	4.8	4.1
48179	Gray County, Texas	2.5	11.7	6.2	1.5	4.0	4.5	16.7	8.2	6.0
48181	Grayson County, Texas	2.6	12.3	3.8	1.3	6.9	8.2	23.0	9.2	4.7
48183	Gregg County, Texas	3.3	13.7	4.4	1.1	5.5	7.4	21.5	9.0	5.9
48185	Grimes County, Texas	1.7	12.6	6.5	0.5	4.2	9.0	15.5	8.3	4.4
48187	Guadalupe County, Texas	3.0	14.5	4.4	1.8	5.9	7.5	21.0	8.5	5.9

Table C. County—Labor Force, Employment, and Educational Data, 2011–2015—*Continued*

Fips code	State/county	Wholesale trade	Retail trade	Transportation and warehousing, and utilities	Information	Finance and insurance, and real estate and rental and leasing	Professional, scientific, and management, and administrative and waste management services	Educational services, and health care and social assistance	Arts, entertainment, and recreation, and accommodation and food services	Other services, except public administration
48189	Hale County, Texas	2.4	12.5	5.6	0.7	3.8	4.8	22.9	7.6	6.4
48191	Hall County, Texas	3.6	14.9	7.5	0.6	3.5	2.9	24.7	5.3	3.5
48193	Hamilton County, Texas	3.3	11.4	4.2	0.7	3.2	4.9	27.4	7.0	5.6
48195	Hansford County, Texas	3.4	9.7	5.2	0.5	4.2	6.9	23.9	4.7	3.7
48197	Hardeman County, Texas	1.6	6.3	5.6	0.6	5.4	3.6	26.0	7.6	5.4
48199	Hardin County, Texas	3.0	12.1	6.0	1.2	4.6	5.6	21.2	6.8	5.5
48201	Harris County, Texas	3.7	10.9	6.2	1.3	5.8	13.0	18.8	8.6	5.9
48203	Harrison County, Texas	2.9	11.0	6.1	0.8	5.0	5.8	24.5	6.9	5.6
48205	Hartley County, Texas	2.8	7.9	6.7	1.1	6.2	6.2	23.1	6.8	4.9
48207	Haskell County, Texas	1.7	10.1	7.9	0.2	3.8	3.5	24.7	6.3	7.5
48209	Hays County, Texas	2.7	14.4	3.9	2.1	5.7	10.5	23.3	10.9	4.5
48211	Hemphill County, Texas	1.0	13.4	6.2	2.4	8.3	8.0	14.7	4.7	3.9
48213	Henderson County, Texas	2.2	12.3	4.1	1.6	4.6	9.5	21.4	8.7	5.8
48215	Hidalgo County, Texas	3.3	14.3	5.1	1.2	3.9	8.3	29.3	8.0	6.0
48217	Hill County, Texas	2.3	12.9	5.7	1.1	5.1	5.4	21.4	9.0	4.8
48219	Hockley County, Texas	2.7	10.5	4.6	2.2	4.3	5.0	24.7	7.6	6.7
48221	Hood County, Texas	2.4	14.6	7.2	1.8	5.2	9.8	21.0	5.8	5.1
48223	Hopkins County, Texas	5.1	13.2	6.2	1.1	5.4	6.0	22.0	7.4	4.5
48225	Houston County, Texas	1.8	13.5	6.7	0.3	5.4	3.5	24.1	5.7	5.7
48227	Howard County, Texas	2.2	10.1	5.0	1.1	4.3	4.3	26.2	7.2	6.0
48229	Hudspeth County, Texas	1.1	7.5	4.1	2.9	2.5	6.9	18.0	13.1	1.8
48231	Hunt County, Texas	2.4	12.4	6.3	1.4	4.7	8.2	22.2	7.1	6.0
48233	Hutchinson County, Texas	1.9	11.5	4.8	1.0	3.4	6.4	17.1	8.4	4.3
48235	Irion County, Texas	3.2	8.0	5.2	0.1	2.9	5.2	24.1	2.0	5.6
48237	Jack County, Texas	2.8	9.5	6.5	0.5	3.3	4.2	14.5	5.3	4.7
48239	Jackson County, Texas	0.8	7.0	6.8	0.4	4.4	4.3	18.1	6.5	3.9
48241	Jasper County, Texas	1.4	13.8	4.4	0.4	4.4	5.7	23.6	6.3	4.5
48243	Jeff Davis County, Texas	0.8	6.1	0.4	1.2	4.5	7.2	26.5	11.9	7.1
48245	Jefferson County, Texas	2.6	12.1	4.6	1.2	4.1	9.0	22.4	9.0	5.4
48247	Jim Hogg County, Texas	0.8	4.9	2.2	1.7	2.7	2.1	26.5	3.7	3.1
48249	Jim Wells County, Texas	2.7	7.7	4.9	0.4	3.7	5.8	23.4	7.7	7.7
48251	Johnson County, Texas	3.0	12.6	7.9	1.3	4.9	7.1	21.2	6.6	5.2
48253	Jones County, Texas	1.6	10.4	9.7	0.1	6.5	5.5	25.3	3.3	7.4
48255	Karnes County, Texas	1.7	12.5	6.8	0.5	3.2	3.7	21.1	3.8	5.5
48257	Kaufman County, Texas	3.8	12.0	7.0	1.4	6.6	9.4	23.3	7.3	4.7
48259	Kendall County, Texas	2.8	10.6	4.9	1.4	8.9	13.2	21.5	9.9	6.0
48261	Kenedy County, Texas	0.0	2.7	7.0	0.0	5.4	3.2	15.1	0.0	1.1
48263	Kent County, Texas	2.5	8.0	5.8	0.0	5.5	1.8	30.7	1.0	4.3
48265	Kerr County, Texas	1.8	12.1	2.8	1.6	6.0	7.8	26.4	12.5	7.2
48267	Kimble County, Texas	2.7	11.7	5.6	2.2	3.8	4.1	18.7	9.3	8.0
48269	King County, Texas	0.6	1.8	1.2	1.2	4.8	6.6	13.9	1.2	1.2
48271	Kinney County, Texas	0.0	5.0	10.8	0.9	2.5	2.2	23.0	4.6	3.5
48273	Kleberg County, Texas	0.6	10.6	3.3	0.6	3.7	4.5	30.9	11.9	5.2
48275	Knox County, Texas	0.5	13.2	4.6	0.0	4.7	1.8	25.0	1.5	4.3
48277	Lamar County, Texas	1.4	14.4	4.7	0.8	3.3	4.2	27.9	7.7	5.1
48279	Lamb County, Texas	2.5	10.1	8.7	1.3	3.7	5.7	19.7	5.7	3.2
48281	Lampasas County, Texas	3.6	12.5	2.4	1.8	3.0	7.4	24.8	6.3	6.6
48283	La Salle County, Texas	1.7	8.1	14.4	0.0	0.4	5.5	17.5	15.8	3.9
48285	Lavaca County, Texas	3.4	10.8	5.3	0.9	5.8	5.1	21.2	5.0	5.1
48287	Lee County, Texas	1.9	10.5	6.0	0.5	2.9	5.1	22.7	7.6	6.4
48289	Leon County, Texas	2.3	12.9	5.4	0.7	5.2	6.8	15.5	8.9	4.7
48291	Liberty County, Texas	2.6	11.2	6.8	0.6	3.8	5.3	17.4	5.2	6.9
48293	Limestone County, Texas	1.7	6.7	4.9	0.6	3.4	6.3	31.9	5.7	6.0
48295	Lipscomb County, Texas	2.0	7.8	10.3	1.7	3.5	2.3	15.5	3.0	6.0
48297	Live Oak County, Texas	2.0	8.8	6.8	0.5	6.2	4.9	13.5	8.9	7.4
48299	Llano County, Texas	2.7	11.6	4.3	1.3	9.4	11.6	18.3	12.3	7.0
48301	Loving County, Texas	0.0	3.2	8.1	0.0	4.8	0.0	3.2	30.6	16.1
48303	Lubbock County, Texas	3.5	12.8	4.1	2.0	5.9	7.3	29.1	11.2	5.9
48305	Lynn County, Texas	4.2	12.3	7.8	0.7	4.3	3.9	21.3	4.9	4.5
48307	McCulloch County, Texas	1.0	13.4	7.8	0.2	4.2	5.7	16.9	9.6	9.7
48309	McLennan County, Texas	2.6	12.5	4.0	1.2	6.5	7.8	26.5	8.9	5.0
48311	McMullen County, Texas	0.0	11.1	5.2	0.0	10.8	2.5	12.0	11.4	8.6
48313	Madison County, Texas	2.0	10.1	6.8	0.2	1.7	8.5	21.8	6.5	3.7
48315	Marion County, Texas	4.2	11.9	6.8	1.0	2.1	7.1	26.3	9.4	5.3
48317	Martin County, Texas	1.7	10.8	8.9	0.9	3.1	3.9	18.8	5.3	10.3
48319	Mason County, Texas	0.6	9.2	6.1	0.3	3.5	5.9	13.1	6.5	11.4
48321	Matagorda County, Texas	2.2	10.3	10.8	0.4	3.4	9.3	20.5	8.4	5.6
48323	Maverick County, Texas	1.7	11.9	6.8	0.5	4.2	3.0	29.2	9.6	3.3
48325	Medina County, Texas	2.7	11.1	6.2	1.0	6.9	10.5	24.5	7.3	5.1
48327	Menard County, Texas	0.0	11.3	6.6	0.0	2.0	7.3	27.4	6.1	2.4
48329	Midland County, Texas	3.4	11.1	5.4	1.3	4.7	8.0	17.5	7.9	5.7
48331	Milam County, Texas	1.3	10.2	8.7	0.7	5.1	5.3	24.9	6.2	4.5
48333	Mills County, Texas	1.5	20.4	4.5	2.2	6.9	3.4	27.4	2.5	7.0
48335	Mitchell County, Texas	1.6	8.5	6.4	0.0	2.6	4.8	27.1	2.6	4.7
48337	Montague County, Texas	2.2	11.8	6.5	0.9	4.7	5.1	17.9	7.8	7.1

Table C. County—Labor Force, Employment, and Educational Data, 2011–2015—*Continued*

Fips code	State/county	Wholesale trade	Retail trade	Transportation and warehousing, and utilities	Information	Finance and insurance, and real estate and rental and leasing	Professional, scientific, and management, and administrative and waste management services	Educational services, and health care and social assistance	Arts, entertainment, and recreation, and accommodation and food services	Other services, except public administration
48339	Montgomery County, Texas	4.2	11.0	7.2	1.3	5.8	11.8	18.7	8.0	5.3
48341	Moore County, Texas	3.1	8.7	3.9	0.9	1.8	4.9	15.2	9.0	4.8
48343	Morris County, Texas	4.3	10.8	8.2	0.5	4.4	3.8	22.1	2.8	7.1
48345	Motley County, Texas	0.9	8.9	10.2	2.8	2.4	1.7	17.4	7.0	7.0
48347	Nacogdoches County, Texas	2.2	10.5	2.8	0.9	3.7	6.9	30.8	9.0	4.6
48349	Navarro County, Texas	2.1	13.0	6.0	1.1	4.1	7.1	19.9	7.7	4.7
48351	Newton County, Texas	0.3	13.2	4.9	2.4	1.6	6.1	26.9	3.9	2.4
48353	Nolan County, Texas	1.0	8.7	9.9	1.0	3.7	4.3	25.5	12.9	4.0
48355	Nueces County, Texas	2.5	11.9	4.7	1.5	5.3	8.1	23.6	11.6	5.6
48357	Ochiltree County, Texas	3.9	9.6	5.8	2.9	3.7	5.3	15.8	8.5	3.9
48359	Oldham County, Texas	3.4	7.6	6.6	0.4	4.9	3.6	32.3	9.3	4.1
48361	Orange County, Texas	2.7	12.1	6.3	0.9	4.9	8.4	20.8	7.8	5.3
48363	Palo Pinto County, Texas	2.0	12.1	3.9	1.0	5.0	4.3	17.1	9.8	5.7
48365	Panola County, Texas	2.1	10.1	4.8	0.8	4.1	6.7	18.5	3.8	4.3
48367	Parker County, Texas	2.3	11.1	7.1	1.7	5.9	7.9	20.7	7.1	5.1
48369	Parmer County, Texas	3.7	8.4	4.5	0.8	3.6	3.9	17.0	7.5	4.1
48371	Pecos County, Texas	1.3	13.5	10.5	0.2	4.1	3.1	16.7	6.8	6.6
48373	Polk County, Texas	1.6	10.7	6.2	1.3	4.0	6.4	22.5	6.4	7.9
48375	Potter County, Texas	3.1	12.5	6.0	1.4	5.0	7.3	20.7	11.2	6.7
48377	Presidio County, Texas	0.6	6.4	7.3	0.0	3.6	4.0	27.8	11.0	8.3
48379	Rains County, Texas	1.2	15.2	8.0	0.6	5.9	7.3	17.8	9.4	3.6
48381	Randall County, Texas	3.9	12.3	5.3	1.7	7.4	7.1	25.1	9.4	5.9
48383	Reagan County, Texas	1.0	5.6	12.1	0.0	5.5	3.7	13.7	4.7	7.6
48385	Real County, Texas	0.0	9.6	5.4	2.7	2.4	3.5	17.1	22.6	5.7
48387	Red River County, Texas	1.5	10.0	5.2	0.8	4.6	3.3	24.9	5.2	4.6
48389	Reeves County, Texas	1.2	8.1	7.3	1.0	4.5	3.1	22.3	12.6	3.1
48391	Refugio County, Texas	3.1	10.9	4.9	0.7	6.5	6.4	16.9	7.4	7.3
48393	Roberts County, Texas	5.2	7.3	5.7	0.0	2.1	7.8	21.5	3.1	4.5
48395	Robertson County, Texas	0.6	11.6	9.4	0.4	2.0	6.9	25.0	5.0	5.2
48397	Rockwall County, Texas	2.9	11.4	5.0	2.9	7.6	11.4	23.1	5.8	5.0
48399	Runnels County, Texas	0.8	11.3	4.8	0.8	4.7	4.8	24.6	3.3	6.4
48401	Rusk County, Texas	3.1	11.1	6.3	0.9	3.3	9.4	17.1	7.5	5.4
48403	Sabine County, Texas	2.4	8.7	7.3	0.0	2.9	4.9	28.3	4.9	6.3
48405	San Augustine County, Texas	0.9	15.7	9.7	0.5	2.1	3.9	22.5	5.7	6.2
48407	San Jacinto County, Texas	0.6	9.9	8.2	1.8	4.3	6.6	15.0	5.3	7.1
48409	San Patricio County, Texas	2.0	8.6	5.5	0.5	3.7	7.3	23.0	9.3	4.5
48411	San Saba County, Texas	3.8	12.9	7.0	0.1	1.6	2.7	18.0	5.5	3.0
48413	Schleicher County, Texas	0.7	5.1	10.9	0.7	5.6	2.6	20.8	8.9	5.7
48415	Scurry County, Texas	1.6	12.9	4.7	1.1	4.9	1.3	21.1	8.6	4.7
48417	Shackelford County, Texas	2.9	8.1	4.1	0.8	5.5	3.2	15.0	9.1	8.1
48419	Shelby County, Texas	2.3	8.1	4.9	0.5	4.5	4.8	22.6	7.3	7.1
48421	Sherman County, Texas	1.1	11.1	7.1	1.4	4.0	0.9	19.7	3.1	5.7
48423	Smith County, Texas	2.7	14.0	4.3	2.0	5.2	7.5	26.6	8.5	6.0
48425	Somervell County, Texas	2.4	7.5	14.7	0.6	4.7	6.8	16.1	8.9	5.3
48427	Starr County, Texas	1.3	10.5	6.2	0.2	2.2	5.2	37.1	5.3	6.2
48429	Stephens County, Texas	1.0	12.8	5.4	1.3	5.4	5.6	20.4	4.3	4.9
48431	Sterling County, Texas	3.3	10.5	6.2	1.4	3.6	6.5	20.8	2.6	4.8
48433	Stonewall County, Texas	2.9	7.1	4.9	0.0	6.1	1.1	28.4	2.5	1.3
48435	Sutton County, Texas	2.3	4.1	5.3	1.1	1.6	6.7	15.6	9.9	5.6
48437	Swisher County, Texas	6.2	15.1	6.4	1.5	3.3	2.8	18.8	7.7	7.5
48439	Tarrant County, Texas	3.2	12.0	7.3	2.0	7.8	10.8	19.9	9.1	5.3
48441	Taylor County, Texas	2.2	12.9	5.0	1.5	6.2	6.4	27.6	11.7	5.8
48443	Terrell County, Texas	0.0	9.9	0.7	0.0	6.0	9.9	9.2	3.4	9.2
48445	Terry County, Texas	3.8	11.5	3.3	1.5	3.3	4.2	26.4	4.1	6.4
48447	Throckmorton County, Texas	3.2	8.9	6.9	0.0	6.1	2.6	22.4	1.9	4.8
48449	Titus County, Texas	2.1	14.7	7.0	0.4	4.5	5.6	16.8	8.6	4.4
48451	Tom Green County, Texas	2.5	12.8	3.3	1.7	4.8	8.4	25.3	8.6	5.5
48453	Travis County, Texas	2.1	10.0	3.2	2.9	7.3	16.2	20.4	10.6	5.3
48455	Trinity County, Texas	1.7	11.9	8.3	0.9	2.1	8.6	14.0	15.3	3.6
48457	Tyler County, Texas	1.4	10.7	5.2	2.0	5.2	5.7	23.7	4.1	4.7
48459	Upshur County, Texas	2.3	13.4	5.6	1.1	3.6	6.1	22.9	5.6	6.7
48461	Upton County, Texas	3.2	6.3	15.6	0.8	2.4	6.3	25.2	2.9	1.1
48463	Uvalde County, Texas	1.5	11.7	6.3	0.2	3.4	6.6	25.7	6.8	5.5
48465	Val Verde County, Texas	1.5	13.6	5.7	0.5	4.8	4.4	25.0	8.5	3.3
48467	Van Zandt County, Texas	2.9	14.3	5.2	2.1	4.0	6.3	22.4	7.7	7.4
48469	Victoria County, Texas	3.2	13.6	4.6	0.7	4.7	7.8	23.2	7.2	5.1
48471	Walker County, Texas	1.9	12.7	3.3	1.6	4.1	5.4	27.9	8.3	4.8
48473	Waller County, Texas	2.9	12.5	4.6	1.3	5.1	8.7	21.6	8.0	5.0
48475	Ward County, Texas	4.0	9.7	9.2	1.0	6.6	4.0	16.4	5.9	6.1
48477	Washington County, Texas	3.1	12.5	4.1	1.7	5.0	6.3	23.7	6.6	4.9
48479	Webb County, Texas	3.0	13.3	13.8	0.8	3.9	7.5	25.6	8.5	4.9
48481	Wharton County, Texas	3.9	12.2	5.2	0.6	4.0	6.4	23.8	5.3	5.3
48483	Wheeler County, Texas	0.8	8.1	7.7	0.9	4.2	4.4	19.7	6.3	6.2
48485	Wichita County, Texas	2.4	12.9	3.8	2.2	4.1	7.6	26.5	10.7	5.4

Table C. County—Labor Force, Employment, and Educational Data, 2011–2015—*Continued*

Fips code	State/county	Wholesale trade	Retail trade	Transportation and warehousing, and utilities	Information	Finance and insurance, and real estate and rental and leasing	Professional, scientific, and management, and administrative and waste management services	Educational services, and health care and social assistance	Arts, entertainment, and recreation, and accommodation and food services	Other services, except public administration
							Industry for employed population age 16 and older			
48487	Wilbarger County, Texas	1.3	11.1	4.5	1.2	4.7	5.4	32.4	7.3	4.9
48489	Willacy County, Texas	2.4	9.3	6.7	1.4	2.5	5.8	29.4	8.7	3.8
48491	Williamson County, Texas	2.8	12.1	3.0	2.4	7.2	14.3	21.1	7.8	4.8
48493	Wilson County, Texas	3.4	11.1	7.9	1.1	5.2	8.1	20.7	6.0	3.4
48495	Winkler County, Texas	6.1	8.7	12.2	0.4	3.6	3.8	17.3	4.8	3.9
48497	Wise County, Texas	2.4	11.4	9.7	1.8	4.2	6.5	20.3	6.4	5.0
48499	Wood County, Texas	2.6	14.0	6.2	2.2	6.0	6.6	22.8	5.9	6.5
48501	Yoakum County, Texas	2.7	8.0	9.5	1.7	1.6	4.7	17.9	4.9	5.0
48503	Young County, Texas	1.5	10.9	4.2	0.9	4.7	4.7	21.4	7.6	5.9
48505	Zapata County, Texas	0.0	8.4	6.8	1.7	3.7	2.7	22.6	5.0	11.1
48507	Zavala County, Texas	0.7	3.4	4.2	1.3	3.3	6.2	33.9	11.7	6.7
49000	**Utah**	2.6	12.1	4.7	2.2	6.5	11.8	21.9	9.0	4.6
49001	Beaver County, Utah	0.8	12.8	11.2	0.1	2.0	4.0	15.8	13.4	2.4
49003	Box Elder County, Utah	2.5	13.5	4.5	1.4	3.2	6.8	17.6	6.5	2.9
49005	Cache County, Utah	1.6	11.5	2.4	1.9	3.6	10.9	26.8	7.9	4.3
49007	Carbon County, Utah	2.3	11.8	9.5	2.9	2.8	7.2	23.4	9.2	5.4
49009	Daggett County, Utah	0.0	10.8	17.6	0.0	0.0	5.0	17.1	10.4	1.8
49011	Davis County, Utah	2.7	12.3	4.7	1.9	6.9	11.3	21.0	9.2	4.6
49013	Duchesne County, Utah	2.1	7.7	8.4	2.9	2.8	4.6	20.5	5.1	3.6
49015	Emery County, Utah	2.5	13.3	9.3	2.2	1.6	3.7	22.4	6.2	5.6
49017	Garfield County, Utah	0.9	11.5	5.9	2.7	3.7	2.8	15.5	35.2	3.7
49019	Grand County, Utah	4.4	10.4	4.4	2.2	5.4	7.0	14.3	29.8	1.9
49021	Iron County, Utah	1.7	11.4	4.9	1.6	4.9	7.5	27.2	12.6	4.4
49023	Juab County, Utah	1.1	8.9	7.9	0.2	2.0	8.3	24.3	8.7	4.4
49025	Kane County, Utah	1.4	16.5	6.9	0.7	4.3	5.4	17.2	14.3	10.1
49027	Millard County, Utah	1.8	9.4	13.0	0.8	1.7	6.2	18.6	9.9	4.1
49029	Morgan County, Utah	2.6	12.0	3.9	0.2	6.8	12.6	18.7	4.1	7.0
49031	Piute County, Utah	0.3	15.8	7.0	0.0	2.5	2.0	27.0	11.8	2.6
49033	Rich County, Utah	3.4	10.1	6.2	0.8	6.2	11.1	16.3	8.6	3.0
49035	Salt Lake County, Utah	2.9	11.8	5.3	2.5	8.6	13.0	20.3	8.8	4.7
49037	San Juan County, Utah	1.7	8.1	3.6	1.5	3.6	4.6	29.1	13.4	4.7
49039	Sanpete County, Utah	2.2	10.8	4.2	1.2	1.7	6.1	28.1	7.9	4.1
49041	Sevier County, Utah	2.9	17.2	9.2	0.4	2.0	4.7	20.6	8.0	3.9
49043	Summit County, Utah	1.4	9.8	5.8	1.7	8.3	14.4	17.3	19.4	5.1
49045	Tooele County, Utah	2.4	11.6	5.9	1.8	5.1	11.2	17.9	7.9	4.8
49047	Uintah County, Utah	3.0	12.9	7.7	1.4	2.9	6.9	15.0	9.3	5.1
49049	Utah County, Utah	2.6	12.6	2.7	2.7	5.1	14.1	27.2	7.7	4.6
49051	Wasatch County, Utah	1.8	13.4	7.4	1.3	5.1	11.4	18.8	16.4	4.4
49053	Washington County, Utah	2.4	16.4	4.6	2.0	5.8	9.3	23.0	13.2	4.6
49055	Wayne County, Utah	0.3	10.0	4.5	0.2	3.1	3.9	19.8	19.9	3.7
49057	Weber County, Utah	2.5	11.0	3.8	1.5	5.0	9.8	20.0	7.6	4.5
50000	**Vermont**	2.2	11.3	3.3	2.0	4.8	8.5	28.6	9.2	4.5
50001	Addison County, Vermont	1.7	9.3	3.1	1.7	3.7	7.9	31.5	7.4	4.4
50003	Bennington County, Vermont	1.5	13.4	2.7	2.1	4.4	8.1	26.1	10.1	5.0
50005	Caledonia County, Vermont	1.3	12.4	3.0	1.7	4.7	6.0	29.6	6.1	5.8
50007	Chittenden County, Vermont	1.9	11.4	3.2	2.4	5.4	10.3	31.0	9.8	4.7
50009	Essex County, Vermont	0.2	11.9	3.2	0.9	2.5	5.4	26.4	8.2	4.9
50011	Franklin County, Vermont	2.3	10.9	4.2	1.3	3.0	7.8	25.2	6.2	3.2
50013	Grand Isle County, Vermont	2.3	13.0	3.1	1.5	4.9	11.6	22.9	5.7	3.6
50015	Lamoille County, Vermont	2.2	11.1	2.1	2.1	4.6	9.7	22.8	15.9	3.5
50017	Orange County, Vermont	1.6	12.0	3.7	1.9	4.8	7.1	29.9	6.4	5.4
50019	Orleans County, Vermont	1.5	10.4	3.9	1.0	4.2	5.1	24.4	9.7	4.2
50021	Rutland County, Vermont	2.8	14.0	3.9	2.1	3.4	7.5	27.4	9.9	4.6
50023	Washington County, Vermont	3.1	10.5	2.4	2.5	7.4	8.0	26.9	8.5	5.1
50025	Windham County, Vermont	3.3	10.0	4.0	2.1	4.5	7.7	29.6	9.6	5.2
50027	Windsor County, Vermont	2.5	9.9	3.1	2.0	4.6	9.0	30.0	10.8	3.5
51000	**Virginia**	1.9	10.8	4.2	2.1	6.3	14.7	21.8	8.9	5.3
51001	Accomack County, Virginia	3.4	11.6	2.3	0.9	2.1	8.8	21.5	10.6	3.9
51003	Albemarle County, Virginia	1.5	8.6	2.7	1.8	5.7	12.1	36.9	9.5	5.2
51005	Alleghany County, Virginia	1.3	10.4	5.4	1.5	2.8	6.0	24.9	8.7	5.8
51007	Amelia County, Virginia	3.5	14.7	4.6	0.2	7.5	7.8	21.4	5.6	4.8
51009	Amherst County, Virginia	2.1	12.2	4.0	0.5	6.0	7.2	25.8	6.3	6.3
51011	Appomattox County, Virginia	2.1	11.4	5.0	1.2	6.0	6.4	25.7	4.1	5.1
51013	Arlington County, Virginia	0.9	4.3	1.8	3.1	7.6	28.3	15.6	7.8	6.7
51015	Augusta County, Virginia	2.7	12.2	6.9	1.7	3.3	6.9	26.2	6.7	4.8
51017	Bath County, Virginia	2.0	10.8	6.0	1.3	3.5	3.7	19.1	28.8	5.1
51019	Bedford County, Virginia	2.8	13.1	6.4	1.5	5.6	8.6	22.2	6.8	5.6
51021	Bland County, Virginia	5.0	13.7	6.8	0.6	5.6	6.3	20.6	7.9	2.2
51023	Botetourt County, Virginia	3.3	12.3	7.5	1.4	8.3	8.2	22.8	6.7	4.4
51025	Brunswick County, Virginia	3.0	13.1	5.5	1.1	1.8	6.3	28.8	8.1	4.2
51027	Buchanan County, Virginia	1.6	11.4	6.6	1.2	3.9	9.0	21.8	4.9	4.4
51029	Buckingham County, Virginia	2.8	10.4	5.3	0.9	4.7	5.8	25.0	6.2	7.1
51031	Campbell County, Virginia	2.6	12.1	5.4	1.5	3.5	8.5	24.3	7.3	6.4
51033	Caroline County, Virginia	4.8	14.7	6.6	1.1	6.4	8.5	21.1	4.7	6.8

Table C. County—Labor Force, Employment, and Educational Data, 2011–2015—*Continued*

		Industry for employed population age 16 and older								
Fips code	State/county	Wholesale trade	Retail trade	Transportation and warehousing, and utilities	Information	Finance and insurance, and real estate and rental and leasing	Professional, scientific, and management, and administrative and waste management services	Educational services, and health care and social assistance	Arts, entertainment, and recreation, and accommodation and food services	Other services, except public administration
51035	Carroll County, Virginia	1.7	12.8	6.5	1.3	2.5	4.1	24.2	7.2	6.2
51036	Charles City County, Virginia	2.6	10.3	6.4	0.7	5.5	7.7	22.4	8.1	4.4
51037	Charlotte County, Virginia	0.9	11.8	5.8	0.2	4.2	6.7	28.0	5.5	3.8
51041	Chesterfield County, Virginia	2.9	11.9	5.6	1.6	9.0	10.7	23.0	8.2	4.6
51043	Clarke County, Virginia	1.2	10.7	5.3	2.1	5.4	14.4	21.4	7.0	5.9
51045	Craig County, Virginia	0.7	2.9	4.9	1.7	7.8	4.6	24.3	3.5	7.8
51047	Culpeper County, Virginia	3.1	11.7	4.7	2.5	5.2	13.4	23.3	5.8	4.9
51049	Cumberland County, Virginia	1.8	13.5	5.3	2.4	6.2	4.9	23.2	7.3	2.5
51051	Dickenson County, Virginia	1.0	12.0	6.4	1.4	3.0	7.1	26.5	5.9	5.1
51053	Dinwiddie County, Virginia	2.0	11.7	7.0	0.6	3.4	5.0	25.5	7.4	4.7
51057	Essex County, Virginia	0.6	16.2	2.8	2.3	6.2	6.3	20.5	12.2	3.3
51059	Fairfax County, Virginia	1.3	8.1	2.9	3.0	6.7	24.8	17.7	8.5	6.4
51061	Fauquier County, Virginia	1.8	10.5	3.8	2.8	6.4	16.0	19.9	5.9	6.2
51063	Floyd County, Virginia	2.8	11.5	4.0	2.6	2.4	7.6	20.2	4.9	4.6
51065	Fluvanna County, Virginia	1.9	13.3	3.5	1.3	8.1	13.5	29.5	6.7	3.0
51067	Franklin County, Virginia	3.2	11.1	5.7	1.0	4.7	7.5	21.5	8.5	5.0
51069	Frederick County, Virginia	1.8	12.5	5.4	2.0	5.9	10.1	24.1	7.2	5.3
51071	Giles County, Virginia	0.4	8.6	4.4	1.3	4.4	5.9	26.2	6.1	3.9
51073	Gloucester County, Virginia	1.4	15.1	5.9	0.7	4.3	9.8	17.7	9.6	5.6
51075	Goochland County, Virginia	2.9	11.2	4.8	1.5	11.9	11.6	21.6	8.4	4.9
51077	Grayson County, Virginia	1.3	13.8	4.2	1.6	3.2	5.0	24.9	6.3	5.0
51079	Greene County, Virginia	1.7	12.1	4.8	1.2	4.2	13.9	24.7	6.3	7.6
51081	Greensville County, Virginia	3.3	12.0	5.6	0.4	1.8	4.2	26.6	7.0	4.6
51083	Halifax County, Virginia	1.0	16.2	5.6	1.0	2.2	5.4	25.1	6.5	5.1
51085	Hanover County, Virginia	4.2	10.0	5.1	2.0	10.9	11.2	22.6	8.0	4.8
51087	Henrico County, Virginia	2.4	11.7	4.8	2.0	13.4	12.0	22.5	9.1	4.7
51089	Henry County, Virginia	2.1	13.1	4.9	0.6	4.7	7.3	23.1	6.4	5.5
51091	Highland County, Virginia	0.0	10.4	5.4	4.6	5.5	3.7	14.5	8.5	7.3
51093	Isle of Wight County, Virginia	1.5	10.0	5.2	1.0	4.9	12.9	20.4	6.4	3.9
51095	James City County, Virginia	2.3	12.4	2.9	1.7	4.2	12.5	26.3	11.6	4.5
51097	King and Queen County, Virginia	2.0	10.7	4.0	1.3	5.2	11.9	18.4	7.1	3.4
51099	King George County, Virginia	1.9	12.9	3.6	0.8	3.5	13.3	15.0	8.8	4.4
51101	King William County, Virginia	4.8	9.8	7.0	1.2	6.4	9.6	20.9	4.3	6.3
51103	Lancaster County, Virginia	1.9	10.6	4.6	0.8	7.1	11.5	29.4	7.7	6.3
51105	Lee County, Virginia	2.1	14.5	5.8	1.0	4.6	6.2	27.0	6.7	4.5
51107	Loudoun County, Virginia	1.5	9.5	4.0	4.4	7.2	26.2	16.4	7.8	4.9
51109	Louisa County, Virginia	2.8	13.1	4.9	1.1	7.5	10.9	22.4	7.1	4.2
51111	Lunenburg County, Virginia	1.4	11.5	3.6	2.4	3.1	6.4	25.2	4.3	5.1
51113	Madison County, Virginia	0.8	14.0	4.1	2.1	3.1	12.4	20.5	8.5	6.7
51115	Mathews County, Virginia	0.2	11.6	9.4	1.5	2.5	5.6	32.5	9.0	3.3
51117	Mecklenburg County, Virginia	2.6	14.0	6.1	1.3	4.1	6.6	24.9	7.0	5.3
51119	Middlesex County, Virginia	3.1	13.5	3.3	0.5	5.5	6.7	21.8	10.3	6.5
51121	Montgomery County, Virginia	1.3	11.0	2.4	1.5	3.9	9.9	38.9	11.8	3.6
51125	Nelson County, Virginia	1.7	12.9	4.1	2.4	5.4	7.8	22.8	8.4	6.9
51127	New Kent County, Virginia	2.3	13.1	3.3	2.2	5.8	12.0	18.3	6.0	5.0
51131	Northampton County, Virginia	7.4	11.8	2.2	0.3	2.8	8.4	27.7	9.7	3.0
51133	Northumberland County, Virginia	2.8	11.2	8.1	0.6	8.8	10.5	21.8	5.5	6.4
51135	Nottoway County, Virginia	0.7	8.0	6.1	1.2	5.8	3.9	29.6	8.1	6.0
51137	Orange County, Virginia	2.7	9.9	4.0	1.8	5.2	9.8	23.5	6.4	5.1
51139	Page County, Virginia	1.4	13.2	4.7	1.0	5.2	7.3	17.6	11.9	3.4
51141	Patrick County, Virginia	1.5	11.0	4.9	0.5	3.1	8.9	20.1	6.6	7.9
51143	Pittsylvania County, Virginia	2.3	12.9	5.1	0.9	3.2	6.3	22.7	6.3	5.7
51145	Powhatan County, Virginia	2.4	12.3	4.3	1.2	8.4	12.6	19.7	7.2	6.1
51147	Prince Edward County, Virginia	0.5	11.5	3.7	1.5	3.0	4.4	32.4	14.5	4.7
51149	Prince George County, Virginia	2.2	12.4	6.1	1.6	3.6	11.0	21.4	6.5	6.8
51153	Prince William County, Virginia	1.6	11.0	4.8	2.1	5.3	18.8	17.9	8.4	5.3
51155	Pulaski County, Virginia	1.4	13.2	4.4	1.2	2.8	6.1	26.1	7.5	3.7
51157	Rappahannock County, Virginia	1.3	15.7	3.1	2.4	5.1	14.6	19.2	6.8	7.0
51159	Richmond County, Virginia	2.5	14.6	3.4	1.3	4.9	5.0	25.9	6.2	7.9
51161	Roanoke County, Virginia	3.2	13.5	5.5	1.7	8.7	10.2	25.7	7.1	5.0
51163	Rockbridge County, Virginia	0.4	12.8	4.3	1.5	4.0	8.4	24.6	6.9	6.0
51165	Rockingham County, Virginia	2.4	14.1	4.2	1.5	4.3	7.0	24.9	7.7	4.2
51167	Russell County, Virginia	1.2	13.7	7.3	2.3	4.4	6.8	25.8	3.2	4.6
51169	Scott County, Virginia	1.1	13.1	3.6	2.4	3.5	6.9	24.5	5.9	4.9
51171	Shenandoah County, Virginia	2.5	11.9	5.2	2.7	3.4	7.7	20.1	8.0	4.6
51173	Smyth County, Virginia	1.7	13.0	3.1	1.3	3.3	5.7	25.7	7.2	4.6
51175	Southampton County, Virginia	2.7	12.2	4.9	1.5	2.7	5.3	26.3	5.0	4.7
51177	Spotsylvania County, Virginia	2.4	12.2	5.3	2.0	6.3	12.3	20.6	9.5	4.9
51179	Stafford County, Virginia	1.3	10.2	4.1	1.6	5.5	14.8	19.1	7.6	4.3
51181	Surry County, Virginia	1.2	12.8	7.5	0.8	2.5	6.2	17.5	9.8	4.7
51183	Sussex County, Virginia	3.8	14.4	10.0	0.7	1.6	7.9	18.5	4.6	5.1
51185	Tazewell County, Virginia	2.9	14.4	4.9	2.3	5.0	6.5	23.1	6.2	5.7
51187	Warren County, Virginia	3.1	10.4	4.4	1.8	3.8	13.8	21.6	7.5	5.3
51191	Washington County, Virginia	3.4	13.7	4.1	1.3	4.4	7.9	24.6	8.9	4.8

Table C. County—Labor Force, Employment, and Educational Data, 2011–2015—*Continued*

Fips code	State/county	Wholesale trade	Retail trade	Transportation and warehousing, and utilities	Information	Finance and insurance, and real estate and rental and leasing	Professional, scientific, and management, and administrative and waste management services	Educational services, and health care and social assistance	Arts, entertainment, and recreation, and accommodation and food services	Other services, except public administration
							Industry for employed population age 16 and older			
51193	Westmoreland County, Virginia	2.2	11.0	6.9	2.0	4.7	13.5	14.9	9.7	5.1
51195	Wise County, Virginia	2.6	15.1	4.6	1.5	3.9	8.3	25.7	5.1	5.5
51197	Wythe County, Virginia	0.8	14.1	4.0	0.9	2.0	6.7	24.1	9.2	3.3
51199	York County, Virginia	2.3	9.5	3.3	1.1	4.1	12.6	22.3	10.2	5.4
51510	Alexandria city, Virginia	0.9	7.0	3.4	2.8	6.9	22.5	17.1	9.6	6.8
51520	Bristol city, Virginia	2.5	13.6	3.4	2.8	4.6	10.2	23.9	12.9	5.8
51530	Buena Vista city, Virginia	0.5	7.0	4.5	0.0	4.5	5.7	26.3	12.3	8.6
51540	Charlottesville city, Virginia	0.9	9.1	1.9	2.3	3.4	13.3	38.4	14.0	5.4
51550	Chesapeake city, Virginia	2.5	12.1	5.2	2.1	6.0	11.8	22.2	7.7	4.9
51570	Colonial Heights city, Virginia	2.3	14.6	4.7	1.6	5.3	8.0	25.0	8.1	5.7
51580	Covington city, Virginia	0.3	17.9	3.9	3.9	1.4	5.5	20.0	9.4	6.8
51590	Danville city, Virginia	1.6	12.7	3.3	1.4	4.9	7.2	29.4	10.1	4.1
51595	Emporia city, Virginia	1.2	12.7	4.7	0.0	3.5	5.5	23.8	4.4	14.1
51600	Fairfax city, Virginia	1.4	10.7	2.1	2.2	6.7	21.4	19.6	9.7	5.4
51610	Falls Church city, Virginia	0.6	6.0	0.8	2.8	7.4	27.3	13.4	4.9	9.2
51620	Franklin city, Virginia	0.4	8.3	4.3	2.0	2.0	5.7	28.6	7.3	7.2
51630	Fredericksburg city, Virginia	1.5	12.5	2.6	1.2	9.0	14.6	22.7	13.5	5.0
51640	Galax city, Virginia	1.2	16.7	5.0	0.9	2.5	8.3	19.8	11.0	5.6
51650	Hampton city, Virginia	2.0	10.5	4.3	1.9	5.7	10.4	22.8	9.3	5.1
51660	Harrisonburg city, Virginia	1.6	10.5	2.8	1.9	4.2	7.8	28.3	20.3	4.4
51670	Hopewell city, Virginia	0.9	14.4	4.3	0.9	5.6	7.7	18.6	11.6	6.8
51678	Lexington city, Virginia	0.0	5.4	0.6	7.3	3.1	3.3	39.3	24.0	5.1
51680	Lynchburg city, Virginia	1.8	11.3	2.7	2.1	4.4	9.8	33.6	11.8	5.3
51683	Manassas city, Virginia	2.0	13.9	5.8	1.5	3.5	15.0	18.1	9.1	5.8
51685	Manassas Park city, Virginia	2.3	11.8	6.0	1.3	7.9	17.4	13.0	12.8	7.0
51690	Martinsville city, Virginia	3.7	13.6	5.6	0.9	5.4	12.0	18.3	10.1	6.1
51700	Newport News city, Virginia	2.1	13.3	3.8	1.3	4.4	10.3	22.4	11.0	4.4
51710	Norfolk city, Virginia	1.6	12.5	5.1	1.6	5.4	10.7	22.8	11.7	5.1
51720	Norton city, Virginia	0.3	14.1	0.2	1.8	0.0	14.0	32.3	14.6	5.6
51730	Petersburg city, Virginia	1.4	14.1	6.4	1.2	3.2	9.2	27.3	11.1	4.3
51735	Poquoson city, Virginia	4.1	8.7	3.5	1.4	5.4	15.2	20.4	7.9	4.6
51740	Portsmouth city, Virginia	1.9	11.9	4.8	1.4	4.6	9.1	23.8	9.1	4.8
51750	Radford city, Virginia	0.8	14.4	2.6	0.5	3.6	6.7	31.3	21.7	4.3
51760	Richmond city, Virginia	1.7	10.4	4.2	1.8	8.2	13.4	26.9	12.1	5.5
51770	Roanoke city, Virginia	2.5	12.8	4.9	1.6	7.0	8.7	25.6	13.3	4.7
51775	Salem city, Virginia	3.9	11.6	5.8	1.7	7.9	7.4	29.3	9.2	4.4
51790	Staunton city, Virginia	2.9	16.9	4.1	1.5	3.7	7.6	29.4	10.8	4.2
51800	Suffolk city, Virginia	2.3	11.5	5.5	1.6	4.4	10.2	24.3	6.9	5.1
51810	Virginia Beach city, Virginia	2.0	11.8	3.7	2.2	7.6	11.9	21.9	11.0	4.9
51820	Waynesboro city, Virginia	1.3	18.7	5.1	2.1	4.7	7.9	21.6	11.1	4.3
51830	Williamsburg city, Virginia	0.9	9.4	2.4	1.1	2.7	8.3	36.5	20.9	3.3
51840	Winchester city, Virginia	4.5	12.4	2.8	3.1	3.1	9.4	26.3	12.7	4.2
53000	**Washington**	2.9	11.8	5.2	2.3	5.4	12.3	21.5	9.3	4.8
53001	Adams County, Washington	4.1	8.7	5.3	0.4	1.2	3.7	18.9	4.6	2.9
53003	Asotin County, Washington	2.2	14.2	3.2	1.2	6.1	6.0	26.2	9.5	4.9
53005	Benton County, Washington	2.1	12.4	6.2	1.1	4.3	16.3	21.2	7.9	3.9
53007	Chelan County, Washington	4.7	12.1	7.0	1.9	4.7	7.8	20.9	10.5	3.4
53009	Clallam County, Washington	2.1	14.3	4.9	1.8	4.4	6.7	23.5	11.2	5.4
53011	Clark County, Washington	3.2	11.5	7.7	1.9	6.1	10.4	20.8	8.2	5.3
53013	Columbia County, Washington	3.5	5.7	4.9	0.6	3.5	6.0	27.9	10.1	4.8
53015	Cowlitz County, Washington	2.6	13.1	6.9	1.2	3.9	7.5	21.9	7.0	6.0
53017	Douglas County, Washington	4.7	14.6	7.5	0.7	2.5	5.5	20.2	7.0	3.6
53019	Ferry County, Washington	1.0	10.7	4.0	3.7	2.7	4.2	25.6	5.6	5.3
53021	Franklin County, Washington	3.6	9.2	6.8	0.9	2.6	9.6	17.6	8.1	3.2
53023	Garfield County, Washington	4.4	15.7	8.4	1.6	2.8	2.0	27.2	2.7	3.5
53025	Grant County, Washington	2.9	9.6	6.0	0.5	3.0	5.2	17.9	5.9	3.4
53027	Grays Harbor County, Washington	2.8	11.3	5.8	1.7	4.1	5.5	21.3	11.6	4.4
53029	Island County, Washington	1.9	11.1	4.9	1.9	4.8	9.4	20.8	9.3	4.6
53031	Jefferson County, Washington	1.5	9.9	5.1	1.7	4.9	10.0	23.0	10.2	8.8
53033	King County, Washington	2.9	11.6	4.6	3.6	6.0	18.2	20.2	9.7	4.7
53035	Kitsap County, Washington	1.6	11.2	4.0	1.7	4.6	12.0	21.5	10.5	4.8
53037	Kittitas County, Washington	2.5	13.5	5.2	1.3	2.8	5.1	27.9	14.2	4.9
53039	Klickitat County, Washington	2.2	8.5	7.5	3.6	2.9	10.0	18.8	6.2	4.3
53041	Lewis County, Washington	3.0	13.9	7.1	1.1	3.9	6.7	21.6	8.8	4.3
53043	Lincoln County, Washington	3.8	7.1	6.0	2.1	3.0	5.1	22.2	8.2	4.4
53045	Mason County, Washington	2.5	9.5	5.0	0.8	4.3	8.3	20.5	9.5	4.3
53047	Okanogan County, Washington	2.9	10.1	5.1	1.5	2.9	4.8	22.9	8.3	5.0
53049	Pacific County, Washington	2.4	9.4	5.5	1.5	3.3	5.3	25.3	9.8	4.5
53051	Pend Oreille County, Washington	2.2	9.3	7.0	2.3	4.4	6.5	22.1	11.2	3.4
53053	Pierce County, Washington	3.4	12.3	6.5	1.7	5.5	8.8	23.0	8.8	4.8
53055	San Juan County, Washington	1.5	9.8	5.0	2.3	6.6	11.8	17.1	15.4	6.0
53057	Skagit County, Washington	2.9	12.2	4.6	1.0	4.6	8.7	21.3	11.1	4.9
53059	Skamania County, Washington	3.0	8.8	6.8	2.4	4.1	9.4	18.7	11.1	4.1
53061	Snohomish County, Washington	2.6	12.5	4.2	2.3	5.9	10.7	19.5	8.6	5.1

Table C. County—Labor Force, Employment, and Educational Data, 2011–2015—*Continued*

						Industry for employed population age 16 and older				
Fips code	State/county	Wholesale trade	Retail trade	Transportation and warehousing, and utilities	Information	Finance and insurance, and real estate and rental and leasing	Professional, scientific, and management, and administrative and waste management services	Educational services, and health care and social assistance	Arts, entertainment, and recreation, and accommodation and food services	Other services, except public administration
53063	Spokane County, Washington	3.6	12.7	4.9	1.7	6.8	9.5	26.1	9.8	5.0
53065	Stevens County, Washington	2.1	13.7	5.4	0.7	4.0	6.7	22.7	8.8	5.2
53067	Thurston County, Washington	1.9	11.4	4.4	1.4	5.3	9.2	21.3	9.4	5.0
53069	Wahkiakum County, Washington	3.4	7.5	7.0	1.8	0.6	7.0	23.3	8.9	5.4
53071	Walla Walla County, Washington	2.4	10.4	2.7	1.5	5.1	7.9	30.3	9.3	5.3
53073	Whatcom County, Washington	2.1	12.4	4.7	1.5	4.9	9.2	24.3	10.1	4.9
53075	Whitman County, Washington	1.4	10.1	2.8	1.3	2.7	6.2	43.3	10.7	4.3
53077	Yakima County, Washington	5.7	11.0	6.4	1.0	3.2	6.1	20.9	7.2	4.8
54000	**West Virginia**	2.2	12.6	5.4	1.7	4.1	7.8	26.7	9.2	4.3
54001	Barbour County, West Virginia	2.6	13.4	6.4	2.2	3.1	6.2	25.9	8.3	3.3
54003	Berkeley County, West Virginia	2.9	12.5	6.4	2.6	5.0	7.5	23.3	8.2	3.5
54005	Boone County, West Virginia	1.5	12.1	4.1	0.6	3.6	5.3	26.8	7.3	3.9
54007	Braxton County, West Virginia	2.1	14.3	4.8	0.8	1.3	8.8	18.9	10.4	1.9
54009	Brooke County, West Virginia	1.4	13.6	5.9	1.3	4.1	6.6	27.8	8.7	5.0
54011	Cabell County, West Virginia	2.9	15.3	3.8	2.0	3.6	8.1	33.9	10.5	3.7
54013	Calhoun County, West Virginia	0.0	10.2	6.9	0.0	4.8	4.4	24.7	3.8	6.2
54015	Clay County, West Virginia	0.4	8.5	5.7	0.3	5.1	5.6	26.2	5.9	5.4
54017	Doddridge County, West Virginia	4.1	17.7	5.3	2.0	3.4	3.3	19.1	5.6	5.0
54019	Fayette County, West Virginia	2.5	15.1	4.8	1.9	4.1	5.6	27.0	7.9	3.5
54021	Gilmer County, West Virginia	0.5	8.3	5.2	1.4	1.6	3.2	32.9	11.2	8.0
54023	Grant County, West Virginia	2.0	9.8	6.5	1.3	3.8	5.0	21.5	5.4	4.0
54025	Greenbrier County, West Virginia	2.1	13.8	4.9	1.3	3.3	6.1	24.7	14.6	5.1
54027	Hampshire County, West Virginia	2.0	14.8	3.6	0.5	2.7	4.8	26.2	3.7	5.4
54029	Hancock County, West Virginia	2.6	11.3	6.3	1.3	5.8	7.7	22.5	11.8	3.9
54031	Hardy County, West Virginia	2.3	10.5	4.2	0.6	2.9	4.5	20.2	9.9	3.9
54033	Harrison County, West Virginia	2.6	13.5	6.5	1.9	3.5	9.3	24.5	7.0	4.4
54035	Jackson County, West Virginia	2.5	9.0	6.2	1.4	4.4	8.2	25.9	6.8	4.5
54037	Jefferson County, West Virginia	1.3	10.1	4.3	2.9	4.6	13.3	21.4	13.2	3.8
54039	Kanawha County, West Virginia	2.5	11.7	5.4	2.7	6.3	10.9	25.0	9.4	4.4
54041	Lewis County, West Virginia	1.2	15.3	7.4	1.5	3.6	5.2	24.9	8.2	3.4
54043	Lincoln County, West Virginia	2.5	12.1	7.4	1.1	4.7	7.2	22.4	7.3	7.4
54045	Logan County, West Virginia	2.2	11.3	5.4	1.5	2.9	5.6	25.8	8.1	7.1
54047	McDowell County, West Virginia	0.2	14.2	9.1	0.9	4.6	5.0	29.5	1.9	3.1
54049	Marion County, West Virginia	1.6	10.2	4.7	2.1	3.7	8.4	27.2	9.4	5.1
54051	Marshall County, West Virginia	2.0	13.3	4.9	1.8	3.9	7.2	27.2	8.0	4.6
54053	Mason County, West Virginia	2.3	12.2	10.0	0.3	2.3	6.9	23.7	8.8	3.1
54055	Mercer County, West Virginia	1.8	15.6	4.9	2.0	3.5	6.9	30.4	9.4	4.8
54057	Mineral County, West Virginia	0.7	13.7	5.2	1.2	2.7	2.8	24.5	10.0	3.5
54059	Mingo County, West Virginia	2.5	12.0	7.2	1.0	2.4	4.6	26.4	5.6	3.8
54061	Monongalia County, West Virginia	1.6	11.0	3.0	1.8	2.9	9.8	36.9	10.4	3.7
54063	Monroe County, West Virginia	0.5	10.9	7.3	0.4	2.3	3.3	25.5	9.8	3.1
54065	Morgan County, West Virginia	1.9	11.6	3.2	1.6	4.8	8.1	27.3	9.1	5.1
54067	Nicholas County, West Virginia	2.9	14.8	5.2	0.6	2.4	7.1	24.2	6.2	4.5
54069	Ohio County, West Virginia	2.9	13.5	4.9	1.3	5.8	7.8	27.8	12.9	4.6
54071	Pendleton County, West Virginia	0.4	10.5	5.3	0.9	1.9	4.7	27.1	5.7	3.0
54073	Pleasants County, West Virginia	1.7	6.7	6.6	0.4	4.5	6.1	30.2	5.9	3.6
54075	Pocahontas County, West Virginia	0.8	6.2	7.5	2.8	5.1	5.1	20.9	14.9	4.3
54077	Preston County, West Virginia	1.2	12.5	5.8	1.4	3.1	7.5	25.2	6.9	4.7
54079	Putnam County, West Virginia	3.8	13.8	6.5	1.6	6.0	6.8	24.7	9.4	4.1
54081	Raleigh County, West Virginia	2.7	14.9	4.3	1.1	3.2	6.3	27.0	10.3	4.4
54083	Randolph County, West Virginia	2.1	12.8	5.0	1.7	4.1	7.8	30.5	8.5	3.1
54085	Ritchie County, West Virginia	1.7	11.2	6.5	0.7	3.6	7.3	19.1	6.9	2.2
54087	Roane County, West Virginia	1.1	16.2	6.5	1.3	5.0	5.0	24.5	6.7	4.7
54089	Summers County, West Virginia	1.7	8.4	6.7	0.7	2.9	5.9	31.6	9.8	6.4
54091	Taylor County, West Virginia	3.7	10.9	6.0	1.3	2.6	6.6	28.6	5.6	6.0
54093	Tucker County, West Virginia	0.1	6.8	5.6	1.1	4.1	5.0	24.8	14.0	4.3
54095	Tyler County, West Virginia	1.4	11.2	5.2	2.0	2.4	6.2	26.9	5.0	6.4
54097	Upshur County, West Virginia	1.4	10.7	5.9	0.5	4.0	5.4	28.1	8.5	4.9
54099	Wayne County, West Virginia	2.4	12.1	7.8	1.2	3.1	6.9	29.8	9.5	3.9
54101	Webster County, West Virginia	1.3	10.4	8.5	1.2	1.5	4.3	27.9	5.2	3.6
54103	Wetzel County, West Virginia	1.1	9.6	8.0	1.3	3.0	6.9	27.8	6.7	3.4
54105	Wirt County, West Virginia	3.0	10.4	3.2	0.3	1.0	12.0	18.8	8.2	4.9
54107	Wood County, West Virginia	1.8	14.9	5.0	1.6	5.4	8.1	23.7	10.3	4.1
54109	Wyoming County, West Virginia	1.9	13.1	4.8	1.9	2.2	4.8	27.4	7.1	2.7
55000	**Wisconsin**	2.7	11.3	4.3	1.7	6.1	8.1	23.3	8.7	4.2
55001	Adams County, Wisconsin	2.3	12.6	6.7	1.1	4.2	5.4	18.6	15.5	4.5
55003	Ashland County, Wisconsin	1.1	13.2	3.7	1.6	4.1	4.7	27.1	10.8	3.1
55005	Barron County, Wisconsin	1.5	12.3	3.7	1.2	3.5	4.6	19.5	8.0	5.0
55007	Bayfield County, Wisconsin	0.8	10.7	4.8	1.8	5.0	4.5	24.4	11.6	4.3
55009	Brown County, Wisconsin	3.2	11.7	6.1	1.6	7.0	7.6	20.9	9.1	4.1
55011	Buffalo County, Wisconsin	2.5	9.2	6.1	1.0	4.4	3.8	21.5	6.4	4.2
55013	Burnett County, Wisconsin	1.1	10.9	4.4	1.3	4.1	4.0	22.4	13.6	4.7
55015	Calumet County, Wisconsin	3.3	11.8	3.8	1.4	5.6	6.3	19.2	6.2	4.3
55017	Chippewa County, Wisconsin	1.9	13.1	5.0	1.2	5.3	6.0	22.6	5.9	4.4
55019	Clark County, Wisconsin	2.3	9.7	4.8	0.6	2.7	3.6	20.3	4.7	4.1

Table C. County—Labor Force, Employment, and Educational Data, 2011–2015—*Continued*

		Industry for employed population age 16 and older								
Fips code	State/county	Wholesale trade	Retail trade	Transportation and warehousing, and utilities	Information	Finance and insurance, and real estate and rental and leasing	Professional, scientific, and management, and administrative and waste management services	Educational services, and health care and social assistance	Arts, entertainment, and recreation, and accommodation and food services	Other services, except public administration
55021	Columbia County, Wisconsin	2.5	10.4	5.5	1.9	6.5	6.4	19.8	8.8	3.6
55023	Crawford County, Wisconsin	1.8	16.1	4.9	0.9	3.4	4.5	21.2	7.2	3.1
55025	Dane County, Wisconsin	2.3	9.9	2.7	2.9	8.4	12.9	28.5	8.9	4.2
55027	Dodge County, Wisconsin	2.1	10.8	4.2	1.6	3.2	5.3	19.0	6.3	4.2
55029	Door County, Wisconsin	1.9	11.6	3.4	1.1	4.8	7.1	17.9	14.8	5.2
55031	Douglas County, Wisconsin	2.7	12.0	8.4	0.9	6.1	5.7	28.8	11.4	4.8
55033	Dunn County, Wisconsin	2.8	13.2	4.8	0.7	4.4	5.7	25.7	8.9	4.0
55035	Eau Claire County, Wisconsin	1.8	16.6	4.2	1.4	7.3	6.8	28.6	9.1	4.2
55037	Florence County, Wisconsin	1.9	11.3	4.8	2.9	2.9	3.7	25.2	10.8	3.1
55039	Fond du Lac County, Wisconsin	2.2	10.1	4.2	1.6	5.1	5.1	20.8	7.6	4.7
55041	Forest County, Wisconsin	0.7	9.5	4.9	1.2	3.7	4.8	23.8	13.7	3.4
55043	Grant County, Wisconsin	1.6	14.2	3.7	1.4	4.2	5.7	24.1	8.2	3.6
55045	Green County, Wisconsin	2.6	12.9	4.1	2.1	5.2	6.3	21.2	6.2	4.0
55047	Green Lake County, Wisconsin	1.8	9.0	5.0	1.0	4.6	4.7	17.8	8.0	4.2
55049	Iowa County, Wisconsin	2.3	19.3	4.0	1.5	3.8	6.2	22.6	6.2	3.2
55051	Iron County, Wisconsin	1.6	9.8	3.9	1.2	3.3	5.8	23.7	12.8	4.5
55053	Jackson County, Wisconsin	1.2	10.0	4.6	0.8	3.6	3.6	21.5	10.2	3.4
55055	Jefferson County, Wisconsin	3.3	11.3	3.9	1.4	4.3	6.9	22.6	7.9	3.4
55057	Juneau County, Wisconsin	1.7	13.6	4.8	0.8	3.2	4.0	18.6	12.3	3.7
55059	Kenosha County, Wisconsin	3.6	12.1	4.2	1.5	4.4	7.6	22.7	9.0	4.4
55061	Kewaunee County, Wisconsin	1.9	9.8	7.4	1.1	3.9	5.1	17.7	5.3	3.6
55063	La Crosse County, Wisconsin	2.8	14.3	4.1	2.1	4.8	5.9	29.5	9.7	3.9
55065	Lafayette County, Wisconsin	2.6	13.8	5.4	1.1	4.1	4.7	19.0	5.3	3.8
55067	Langlade County, Wisconsin	2.4	11.2	5.8	2.1	5.1	4.6	21.0	9.1	3.9
55069	Lincoln County, Wisconsin	3.1	12.1	4.7	1.0	8.9	4.8	19.2	7.4	3.9
55071	Manitowoc County, Wisconsin	1.9	9.5	5.2	0.9	3.9	5.7	20.8	7.2	3.8
55073	Marathon County, Wisconsin	3.3	12.3	4.9	1.2	8.2	5.3	22.8	6.9	3.6
55075	Marinette County, Wisconsin	2.1	10.7	4.3	1.8	3.2	4.5	19.5	9.7	3.4
55077	Marquette County, Wisconsin	1.6	10.0	5.5	1.3	3.5	4.4	16.8	9.3	4.5
55078	Menominee County, Wisconsin	0.4	1.7	4.4	1.6	4.6	4.3	26.3	24.0	2.5
55079	Milwaukee County, Wisconsin	2.5	10.1	4.6	1.9	6.9	10.7	26.7	10.0	4.4
55081	Monroe County, Wisconsin	1.8	11.8	6.3	0.9	3.4	5.3	20.8	8.7	4.7
55083	Oconto County, Wisconsin	2.4	10.6	6.6	1.0	5.5	5.2	19.7	6.3	3.6
55085	Oneida County, Wisconsin	1.8	15.9	3.3	2.0	5.1	5.8	24.8	9.5	4.3
55087	Outagamie County, Wisconsin	2.9	10.8	4.1	1.7	7.2	8.7	19.0	8.7	3.8
55089	Ozaukee County, Wisconsin	2.8	10.1	2.4	1.5	8.3	11.4	24.8	7.9	4.3
55091	Pepin County, Wisconsin	2.9	11.2	6.7	1.2	4.0	3.2	21.4	5.6	4.0
55093	Pierce County, Wisconsin	1.6	10.5	4.4	0.9	5.4	7.3	23.2	9.1	3.6
55095	Polk County, Wisconsin	2.3	10.8	4.2	1.1	3.9	6.5	21.4	8.1	3.9
55097	Portage County, Wisconsin	2.0	13.5	5.0	1.8	10.2	5.7	22.5	10.4	3.7
55099	Price County, Wisconsin	1.6	8.5	3.6	1.2	3.8	5.0	19.2	7.0	4.1
55101	Racine County, Wisconsin	2.5	10.5	5.6	1.2	5.3	8.2	21.7	7.6	4.3
55103	Richland County, Wisconsin	2.3	12.1	3.2	1.3	3.8	3.5	21.6	7.0	3.8
55105	Rock County, Wisconsin	3.7	11.8	5.0	1.6	3.8	6.6	22.5	7.7	4.2
55107	Rusk County, Wisconsin	2.5	12.7	5.0	2.0	2.8	3.8	18.3	4.6	4.4
55109	St. Croix County, Wisconsin	3.5	11.3	5.6	1.3	6.7	8.5	21.0	6.7	4.4
55111	Sauk County, Wisconsin	3.0	13.9	3.2	1.2	4.8	5.9	18.8	14.9	4.2
55113	Sawyer County, Wisconsin	1.2	13.9	3.9	1.3	5.7	6.3	21.8	16.0	5.3
55115	Shawano County, Wisconsin	3.3	10.2	4.4	1.0	4.9	4.4	19.6	10.9	3.5
55117	Sheboygan County, Wisconsin	1.9	10.8	3.2	0.9	4.9	5.6	18.9	8.3	4.4
55119	Taylor County, Wisconsin	1.8	9.8	5.7	0.9	4.0	3.5	18.0	5.4	3.3
55121	Trempealeau County, Wisconsin	2.2	9.4	4.2	1.2	4.2	4.6	21.2	4.9	3.3
55123	Vernon County, Wisconsin	3.7	11.4	5.0	1.5	3.6	5.3	24.8	5.8	4.1
55125	Vilas County, Wisconsin	2.9	13.1	4.9	1.6	6.0	7.0	18.3	18.4	4.5
55127	Walworth County, Wisconsin	2.7	11.2	3.9	1.6	4.2	7.5	21.5	11.0	4.0
55129	Washburn County, Wisconsin	2.1	12.5	5.5	0.7	3.8	6.0	21.2	9.1	4.7
55131	Washington County, Wisconsin	3.4	12.2	4.0	1.5	7.1	8.1	20.6	6.1	4.0
55133	Waukesha County, Wisconsin	3.9	11.4	3.5	1.7	8.2	10.1	22.9	7.5	4.4
55135	Waupaca County, Wisconsin	2.1	8.8	4.2	1.5	3.6	5.0	19.8	7.4	4.2
55137	Waushara County, Wisconsin	2.0	9.5	6.1	1.2	4.0	4.9	20.0	9.0	3.6
55139	Winnebago County, Wisconsin	2.7	12.2	4.1	1.7	4.6	8.4	20.0	8.9	4.1
55141	Wood County, Wisconsin	2.0	12.0	5.3	1.4	4.4	4.4	26.9	7.7	4.6
56000	**Wyoming**	2.1	11.0	6.3	1.5	4.2	6.7	22.4	10.3	4.5
56001	Albany County, Wyoming	0.9	11.1	2.5	1.1	3.8	7.3	42.0	10.1	4.3
56003	Big Horn County, Wyoming	0.9	9.6	4.9	2.1	2.3	3.4	23.4	6.1	4.3
56005	Campbell County, Wyoming	3.8	10.0	7.7	1.6	3.4	6.0	17.0	7.3	4.4
56007	Carbon County, Wyoming	0.7	9.6	10.1	1.2	4.2	4.0	14.2	12.5	2.4
56009	Converse County, Wyoming	2.1	9.0	9.9	0.6	3.8	4.6	17.0	11.9	5.6
56011	Crook County, Wyoming	1.1	8.3	6.9	1.1	4.9	3.9	14.9	9.5	5.7
56013	Fremont County, Wyoming	1.2	11.4	4.1	1.3	2.9	5.8	26.3	13.5	5.7
56015	Goshen County, Wyoming	1.4	7.9	9.6	0.8	3.3	3.4	27.5	6.2	3.0
56017	Hot Springs County, Wyoming	0.8	6.3	4.8	1.2	5.0	7.4	27.6	14.5	5.7
56019	Johnson County, Wyoming	1.4	6.0	4.1	0.7	3.8	7.5	22.6	10.7	2.4

Table C. County—Labor Force, Employment, and Educational Data, 2011–2015—_Continued_

Fips code	State/county	Industry for employed population age 16 and older								
		Wholesale trade	Retail trade	Transportation and warehousing, and utilities	Information	Finance and insurance, and real estate and rental and leasing	Professional, scientific, and management, and administrative and waste management services	Educational services, and health care and social assistance	Arts, entertainment, and recreation, and accommodation and food services	Other services, except public administration
56021	Laramie County, Wyoming	1.6	13.5	7.0	2.4	5.2	9.1	20.3	7.5	3.8
56023	Lincoln County, Wyoming	0.7	11.9	8.1	2.3	4.7	6.0	22.5	8.3	2.3
56025	Natrona County, Wyoming	3.7	11.5	5.6	1.4	4.4	7.7	20.8	9.8	6.4
56027	Niobrara County, Wyoming	0.0	9.2	6.3	1.1	5.4	3.9	16.5	4.8	0.9
56029	Park County, Wyoming	1.5	13.5	3.8	1.1	3.9	6.1	24.2	12.4	4.9
56031	Platte County, Wyoming	1.9	14.9	15.0	1.3	3.6	3.0	19.2	12.4	4.1
56033	Sheridan County, Wyoming	0.5	9.6	5.6	1.7	5.5	8.9	27.5	9.7	3.8
56035	Sublette County, Wyoming	1.3	6.0	6.0	0.6	3.6	2.6	13.6	7.3	6.1
56037	Sweetwater County, Wyoming	3.2	11.2	8.5	1.1	2.6	4.5	17.6	8.5	5.1
56039	Teton County, Wyoming	1.0	8.2	3.8	2.0	7.8	10.0	19.1	29.9	3.2
56041	Uinta County, Wyoming	2.6	12.2	7.2	1.8	3.4	6.6	25.2	8.5	3.6
56043	Washakie County, Wyoming	3.5	8.7	4.3	1.7	2.8	4.3	24.0	6.0	6.6
56045	Weston County, Wyoming	1.5	7.9	7.9	1.0	2.5	4.3	20.9	5.6	3.6

Table C. County—Labor Force, Employment, and Educational Data, 2011–2015

| | | Industry for employed population age 16 and older | Educational attainment for the population age 25 and older | | | |
| | | | | Educational attainment | | |
Fips code	State/county	Public administration	Total population age 25 and older	Less than high school graduate	High school graduate (includes equivalency)	Some college or Associate's degree	Bachelor's degree or higher
00000	United States	4.8	211,462,522	13.3	27.8	29.1	29.8
01000	**Alabama**	5.7	3,239,351	15.7	31.0	29.7	23.5
01001	Autauga County, Alabama	11.2	36,319	12.8	33.5	30.4	23.2
01003	Baldwin County, Alabama	4.7	137,001	10.5	28.8	31.8	29.0
01005	Barbour County, Alabama	8.0	18,808	26.7	34.5	26.3	12.5
01007	Bibb County, Alabama	3.7	15,629	19.3	42.1	27.9	10.6
01009	Blount County, Alabama	5.1	39,408	21.5	33.4	32.2	12.9
01011	Bullock County, Alabama	7.0	7,438	35.1	33.3	17.7	13.9
01013	Butler County, Alabama	5.5	13,996	22.2	37.7	25.6	14.5
01015	Calhoun County, Alabama	8.2	78,700	19.1	31.8	31.5	17.6
01017	Chambers County, Alabama	3.7	23,814	21.1	38.4	29.0	11.6
01019	Cherokee County, Alabama	6.8	18,734	20.5	36.4	29.3	13.8
01021	Chilton County, Alabama	5.9	29,472	21.6	39.2	25.1	14.1
01023	Choctaw County, Alabama	3.3	9,534	23.6	36.8	27.8	11.8
01025	Clarke County, Alabama	4.6	17,128	19.5	43.9	23.7	12.9
01027	Clay County, Alabama	7.8	9,535	24.9	36.3	29.2	9.6
01029	Cleburne County, Alabama	5.2	10,420	24.9	38.3	24.8	12.1
01031	Coffee County, Alabama	10.2	34,464	15.4	29.5	31.3	23.9
01033	Colbert County, Alabama	3.4	38,008	16.1	34.5	30.7	18.6
01035	Conecuh County, Alabama	4.0	8,905	21.9	44.5	25.4	8.2
01037	Coosa County, Alabama	7.9	8,022	25.9	37.6	28.0	8.5
01039	Covington County, Alabama	6.2	26,470	20.2	33.6	31.9	14.3
01041	Crenshaw County, Alabama	7.7	9,548	22.0	38.0	25.7	14.3
01043	Cullman County, Alabama	3.2	55,773	18.2	34.7	32.6	14.6
01045	Dale County, Alabama	8.5	33,245	14.6	32.2	36.8	16.4
01047	Dallas County, Alabama	6.9	27,453	21.9	34.6	29.4	14.0
01049	DeKalb County, Alabama	3.7	47,227	27.6	35.2	26.0	11.2
01051	Elmore County, Alabama	13.2	54,452	13.4	35.4	29.8	21.4
01053	Escambia County, Alabama	7.2	26,007	20.1	42.1	25.2	12.5
01055	Etowah County, Alabama	5.1	71,591	17.5	31.9	34.5	16.0
01057	Fayette County, Alabama	3.1	11,880	22.4	38.8	24.6	14.1
01059	Franklin County, Alabama	2.9	21,075	25.4	37.5	25.7	11.4
01061	Geneva County, Alabama	6.1	18,762	21.0	37.1	29.6	12.3
01063	Greene County, Alabama	5.1	5,923	24.1	38.9	26.0	10.9
01065	Hale County, Alabama	4.7	10,271	19.3	42.9	23.9	13.9
01067	Henry County, Alabama	3.2	12,213	21.2	35.5	26.8	16.5
01069	Houston County, Alabama	5.0	70,274	15.3	33.1	31.0	20.6
01071	Jackson County, Alabama	4.7	37,190	23.1	39.8	24.6	12.4
01073	Jefferson County, Alabama	4.0	444,969	11.6	26.5	31.2	30.8
01075	Lamar County, Alabama	4.2	10,017	22.6	37.1	28.8	11.5
01077	Lauderdale County, Alabama	3.8	62,870	15.7	34.1	28.4	21.8
01079	Lawrence County, Alabama	4.8	23,292	21.1	40.6	27.1	11.1
01081	Lee County, Alabama	4.8	87,947	11.4	25.5	29.1	34.0
01083	Limestone County, Alabama	5.8	61,004	16.9	32.1	27.8	23.2
01085	Lowndes County, Alabama	8.8	7,205	25.9	35.3	24.7	14.1
01087	Macon County, Alabama	7.9	12,382	18.6	30.9	31.2	19.3
01089	Madison County, Alabama	9.1	233,276	9.3	21.3	30.0	39.4
01091	Marengo County, Alabama	6.2	13,783	15.4	42.0	27.4	15.3
01093	Marion County, Alabama	6.1	21,650	21.9	34.5	32.1	11.5
01095	Marshall County, Alabama	5.1	63,035	22.5	31.9	29.0	16.6
01097	Mobile County, Alabama	3.7	273,199	14.7	32.8	30.5	22.0
01099	Monroe County, Alabama	7.6	14,913	19.2	44.7	23.9	12.2
01101	Montgomery County, Alabama	11.7	147,536	14.6	26.0	28.2	31.1
01103	Morgan County, Alabama	4.2	81,977	17.2	31.0	30.5	21.3
01105	Perry County, Alabama	6.5	6,115	25.4	38.6	22.7	13.2
01107	Pickens County, Alabama	3.9	13,839	21.3	42.2	26.6	9.9
01109	Pike County, Alabama	5.0	19,506	20.3	33.9	22.5	23.4
01111	Randolph County, Alabama	3.8	15,549	24.3	35.6	25.1	15.1
01113	Russell County, Alabama	9.4	38,172	17.7	31.4	33.8	17.1
01115	St. Clair County, Alabama	4.4	59,246	16.8	35.5	32.0	15.6
01117	Shelby County, Alabama	4.1	137,126	8.6	21.4	29.2	40.8
01119	Sumter County, Alabama	6.8	8,128	21.7	40.5	21.5	16.3
01121	Talladega County, Alabama	4.9	56,114	20.7	36.3	29.9	13.1
01123	Tallapoosa County, Alabama	4.8	28,908	20.2	34.4	28.1	17.3
01125	Tuscaloosa County, Alabama	3.7	120,960	13.0	30.5	28.0	28.5
01127	Walker County, Alabama	4.3	45,786	21.7	36.5	31.0	10.8
01129	Washington County, Alabama	5.4	11,508	19.5	46.1	24.5	9.9
01131	Wilcox County, Alabama	10.8	7,399	22.6	41.3	23.5	12.5
01133	Winston County, Alabama	5.2	17,251	25.6	33.7	29.3	11.4
02000	**Alaska**	11.5	464,440	7.9	27.8	36.3	28.0
02013	Aleutians East Borough, Alaska	6.7	2,520	18.3	39.4	28.2	14.0
02016	Aleutians West Census Area, Alaska	8.1	3,908	16.0	37.0	32.2	14.7
02020	Anchorage Municipality, Alaska	10.3	189,300	7.0	24.1	35.6	33.2
02050	Bethel Census Area, Alaska	20.4	9,444	21.0	43.6	23.7	11.6
02060	Bristol Bay Borough, Alaska	13.7	649	8.0	30.7	41.3	20.0
02068	Denali Borough, Alaska	7.4	1,383	4.8	23.9	38.0	33.3

Table C. County—Labor Force, Employment, and Educational Data, 2011–2015—*Continued*

| | | Industry for employed population age 16 and older | Educational attainment for the population age 25 and older | | | |
| | | | | Educational attainment | | |
Fips code	State/county	Public administration	Total population age 25 and older	Less than high school graduate	High school graduate (includes equivalency)	Some college or Associate's degree	Bachelor's degree or higher
02070	Dillingham Census Area, Alaska	16.3	2,829	13.5	38.1	32.2	16.2
02090	Fairbanks North Star Borough, Alaska	13.0	60,737	5.6	23.4	39.2	31.7
02100	Haines Borough, Alaska	5.5	1,934	4.6	27.7	32.1	35.6
02105	Hoonah-Angoon Census Area, Alaska	10.0	1,615	9.6	31.3	32.4	26.6
02110	Juneau City and Borough, Alaska	23.8	22,269	5.2	21.1	35.2	38.5
02122	Kenai Peninsula Borough, Alaska	6.3	39,037	6.6	33.1	37.5	22.8
02130	Ketchikan Gateway Borough, Alaska	13.0	9,320	8.1	32.8	35.3	23.8
02150	Kodiak Island Borough, Alaska	12.5	8,536	9.6	27.3	38.4	24.7
02158	Kusilvak Census Area, Alaska	22.0	3,698	22.5	49.0	23.5	5.0
02164	Lake and Peninsula Borough, Alaska	21.6	858	12.7	42.9	31.5	12.9
02170	Matanuska-Susitna Borough, Alaska	9.5	60,694	7.7	31.6	39.9	20.7
02180	Nome Census Area, Alaska	16.4	5,391	15.4	41.3	29.2	14.1
02185	North Slope Borough, Alaska	9.5	6,283	11.3	36.8	38.0	13.9
02188	Northwest Arctic Borough, Alaska	15.8	4,025	21.3	43.6	24.5	10.6
02195	Petersburg Borough, Alaska	9.5	2,172	6.0	31.2	37.4	25.3
02198	Prince of Wales-Hyder Census Area, Alaska	9.4	4,300	9.4	40.9	34.1	15.5
02220	Sitka City and Borough, Alaska	7.5	6,173	7.2	22.1	39.5	31.2
02230	Skagway Municipality, Alaska	7.8	792	2.7	29.0	32.4	35.9
02240	Southeast Fairbanks Census Area, Alaska	16.6	4,450	7.9	33.2	41.0	17.9
02261	Valdez-Cordova Census Area, Alaska	11.2	6,324	7.5	27.2	36.6	28.7
02275	Wrangell City and Borough, Alaska	6.9	1,818	9.8	35.6	34.7	19.9
02282	Yakutat City and Borough, Alaska	18.9	438	5.5	44.7	34.5	15.3
02290	Yukon-Koyukuk Census Area, Alaska	28.3	3,543	17.8	40.1	31.0	11.2
04000	**Arizona**	5.5	4,361,304	14.0	24.4	34.1	27.5
04001	Apache County, Arizona	11.4	43,194	23.2	33.4	32.6	10.8
04003	Cochise County, Arizona	16.4	88,549	13.4	23.4	40.4	22.9
04005	Coconino County, Arizona	6.5	79,562	11.6	21.3	33.5	33.6
04007	Gila County, Arizona	7.7	38,397	16.0	30.0	37.3	16.7
04009	Graham County, Arizona	8.6	22,786	15.2	32.9	38.7	13.2
04011	Greenlee County, Arizona	4.7	5,648	14.3	37.5	37.4	10.8
04012	La Paz County, Arizona	12.9	15,508	24.1	36.6	29.4	9.9
04013	Maricopa County, Arizona	4.2	2,612,345	13.2	23.0	33.3	30.4
04015	Mohave County, Arizona	6.1	150,498	16.0	35.7	36.5	11.8
04017	Navajo County, Arizona	8.9	67,160	18.5	29.5	37.2	14.7
04019	Pima County, Arizona	6.8	658,596	12.4	22.8	34.5	30.3
04021	Pinal County, Arizona	8.6	261,865	15.0	30.1	36.9	18.0
04023	Santa Cruz County, Arizona	8.3	29,062	26.8	25.3	25.9	22.0
04025	Yavapai County, Arizona	4.9	162,724	10.3	25.6	38.4	25.6
04027	Yuma County, Arizona	11.8	125,410	28.9	25.0	31.7	14.4
05000	**Arkansas**	4.7	1,962,741	15.2	34.9	28.7	21.1
05001	Arkansas County, Arkansas	4.9	12,947	17.9	42.5	27.2	12.4
05003	Ashley County, Arkansas	5.7	14,457	15.1	41.4	30.3	13.2
05005	Baxter County, Arkansas	3.0	31,405	12.6	35.6	34.0	17.9
05007	Benton County, Arkansas	2.1	154,240	13.2	30.8	25.8	30.2
05009	Boone County, Arkansas	3.0	25,902	14.2	35.9	35.2	14.7
05011	Bradley County, Arkansas	6.1	7,649	20.5	42.1	24.5	13.0
05013	Calhoun County, Arkansas	3.0	3,736	19.3	49.3	21.0	10.4
05015	Carroll County, Arkansas	2.2	19,373	16.8	35.0	31.5	16.7
05017	Chicot County, Arkansas	9.8	7,815	21.1	44.6	23.3	11.1
05019	Clark County, Arkansas	6.2	13,182	13.2	33.6	29.4	23.9
05021	Clay County, Arkansas	2.6	10,922	21.4	43.8	23.9	11.0
05023	Cleburne County, Arkansas	3.9	18,855	15.0	39.2	29.0	16.8
05025	Cleveland County, Arkansas	6.9	5,778	13.8	44.8	26.1	15.4
05027	Columbia County, Arkansas	3.4	15,036	15.8	38.2	25.9	20.0
05029	Conway County, Arkansas	4.6	14,483	15.7	42.1	25.7	16.5
05031	Craighead County, Arkansas	2.5	64,232	12.5	32.8	29.3	25.4
05033	Crawford County, Arkansas	4.1	41,042	14.5	38.7	32.3	14.5
05035	Crittenden County, Arkansas	4.2	31,179	18.9	36.3	28.3	16.4
05037	Cross County, Arkansas	6.8	11,826	19.9	45.8	20.6	13.7
05039	Dallas County, Arkansas	8.0	5,394	16.9	50.5	19.5	13.1
05041	Desha County, Arkansas	9.0	8,183	22.5	40.4	25.1	11.9
05043	Drew County, Arkansas	6.5	11,640	17.4	35.5	26.6	20.5
05045	Faulkner County, Arkansas	4.2	71,977	9.1	30.6	31.9	28.3
05047	Franklin County, Arkansas	6.5	12,091	17.9	40.4	29.4	12.3
05049	Fulton County, Arkansas	3.8	8,973	14.5	43.0	31.9	10.6
05051	Garland County, Arkansas	3.8	69,253	11.9	32.2	34.6	21.4
05053	Grant County, Arkansas	6.6	12,395	11.1	43.1	28.7	17.1
05055	Greene County, Arkansas	3.7	28,719	16.1	43.1	25.5	15.4
05057	Hempstead County, Arkansas	5.0	14,794	21.9	38.0	27.9	12.2
05059	Hot Spring County, Arkansas	4.8	23,321	15.2	42.1	29.6	13.0
05061	Howard County, Arkansas	2.9	8,942	22.0	33.5	29.4	15.1
05063	Independence County, Arkansas	4.1	24,951	17.1	38.9	28.2	15.9

Table C. County—Labor Force, Employment, and Educational Data, 2011–2015—*Continued*

| | | Industry for employed population age 16 and older | Educational attainment for the population age 25 and older | | | | |
| | | | | Educational attainment | | | |
Fips code	State/county	Public administration	Total population age 25 and older	Less than high school graduate	High school graduate (includes equivalency)	Some college or Associate's degree	Bachelor's degree or higher
05065	Izard County, Arkansas	4.6	10,050	17.9	40.0	29.4	12.7
05067	Jackson County, Arkansas	5.2	12,592	23.0	45.3	22.8	8.8
05069	Jefferson County, Arkansas	9.5	48,746	15.2	38.7	28.6	17.5
05071	Johnson County, Arkansas	3.8	16,978	20.7	41.1	21.1	17.1
05073	Lafayette County, Arkansas	8.0	5,153	21.6	43.3	23.3	11.8
05075	Lawrence County, Arkansas	5.1	11,492	17.9	42.7	26.5	12.9
05077	Lee County, Arkansas	8.9	6,975	31.2	39.5	21.4	7.9
05079	Lincoln County, Arkansas	8.0	10,087	21.6	48.0	21.5	8.9
05081	Little River County, Arkansas	9.4	9,010	15.2	40.6	34.3	10.0
05083	Logan County, Arkansas	5.7	15,203	17.5	43.7	26.2	12.6
05085	Lonoke County, Arkansas	7.3	45,833	12.8	34.0	34.1	19.1
05087	Madison County, Arkansas	5.0	10,775	21.6	46.0	21.7	10.7
05089	Marion County, Arkansas	4.9	12,588	14.6	43.4	28.8	13.2
05091	Miller County, Arkansas	6.4	29,405	14.8	39.3	31.7	14.3
05093	Mississippi County, Arkansas	3.9	28,519	20.4	36.6	29.9	13.2
05095	Monroe County, Arkansas	7.1	5,415	23.1	41.2	26.3	9.4
05097	Montgomery County, Arkansas	3.5	6,722	19.6	37.6	30.4	12.3
05099	Nevada County, Arkansas	5.3	6,032	16.6	42.8	26.4	14.1
05101	Newton County, Arkansas	1.8	5,924	18.1	42.4	25.0	14.6
05103	Ouachita County, Arkansas	5.4	17,318	13.9	43.2	26.8	16.1
05105	Perry County, Arkansas	3.8	7,171	18.7	42.1	27.7	11.5
05107	Phillips County, Arkansas	5.0	12,913	24.6	31.7	33.0	10.8
05109	Pike County, Arkansas	4.0	7,673	18.5	35.6	31.4	14.6
05111	Poinsett County, Arkansas	4.1	16,304	23.1	42.6	26.0	8.4
05113	Polk County, Arkansas	3.5	14,125	14.9	39.0	34.1	12.0
05115	Pope County, Arkansas	2.6	39,501	17.3	33.2	28.6	20.9
05117	Prairie County, Arkansas	3.6	6,072	20.7	41.8	27.1	10.3
05119	Pulaski County, Arkansas	7.2	261,924	10.3	27.0	29.8	32.9
05121	Randolph County, Arkansas	2.8	12,271	17.5	39.3	29.8	13.4
05123	St. Francis County, Arkansas	9.7	18,682	21.5	39.7	27.4	11.4
05125	Saline County, Arkansas	6.7	78,379	11.4	33.9	31.7	23.0
05127	Scott County, Arkansas	4.6	7,265	22.7	39.6	26.1	11.6
05129	Searcy County, Arkansas	2.7	5,842	18.1	40.2	27.8	13.9
05131	Sebastian County, Arkansas	2.7	83,713	17.8	31.9	31.1	19.2
05133	Sevier County, Arkansas	4.2	10,662	30.8	34.9	26.4	7.9
05135	Sharp County, Arkansas	4.0	12,274	16.8	45.9	27.4	9.9
05137	Stone County, Arkansas	3.0	9,015	20.9	35.4	27.8	15.9
05139	Union County, Arkansas	3.6	27,648	16.6	37.7	28.2	17.5
05141	Van Buren County, Arkansas	4.3	12,440	18.1	42.7	27.0	12.3
05143	Washington County, Arkansas	2.6	129,651	16.5	27.9	25.2	30.5
05145	White County, Arkansas	4.7	50,205	16.7	37.6	26.2	19.5
05147	Woodruff County, Arkansas	5.5	4,924	26.5	44.5	18.6	10.4
05149	Yell County, Arkansas	3.5	14,578	24.2	40.6	22.6	12.6
06000	**California**	4.5	25,257,858	18.2	20.7	29.6	31.4
06001	Alameda County, California	3.6	1,092,189	13.1	18.5	25.5	43.0
06003	Alpine County, California	14.2	764	10.5	30.6	31.4	27.5
06005	Amador County, California	12.1	28,676	11.6	27.0	40.1	21.3
06007	Butte County, California	4.3	143,094	12.0	22.6	39.5	25.9
06009	Calaveras County, California	7.4	33,649	8.4	27.6	43.2	20.9
06011	Colusa County, California	5.2	13,296	31.8	21.7	31.9	14.6
06013	Contra Costa County, California	4.2	742,043	11.1	18.7	30.6	39.6
06015	Del Norte County, California	16.9	19,572	20.0	29.1	35.7	15.1
06017	El Dorado County, California	7.2	128,896	7.7	21.8	38.4	32.1
06019	Fresno County, California	6.1	571,585	26.5	22.8	31.3	19.4
06021	Glenn County, California	5.8	17,876	25.0	29.6	30.6	14.9
06023	Humboldt County, California	6.6	90,585	10.2	25.2	36.6	28.0
06025	Imperial County, California	10.9	107,251	33.7	21.9	30.4	14.1
06027	Inyo County, California	10.7	13,236	12.4	30.9	32.9	23.9
06029	Kern County, California	7.0	513,437	26.6	27.3	30.8	15.4
06031	Kings County, California	13.1	92,122	27.8	24.8	34.0	13.4
06033	Lake County, California	8.1	46,120	15.6	28.3	40.1	16.0
06035	Lassen County, California	35.4	23,860	20.1	28.8	38.9	12.3
06037	Los Angeles County, California	3.2	6,653,174	22.7	20.7	26.3	30.3
06039	Madera County, California	6.0	94,739	29.2	25.1	32.4	13.3
06041	Marin County, California	3.6	189,160	7.1	11.8	25.3	55.8
06043	Mariposa County, California	11.8	13,687	10.5	28.5	38.9	22.1
06045	Mendocino County, California	6.0	61,297	13.2	26.5	36.6	23.7
06047	Merced County, California	4.0	152,405	32.1	24.8	29.9	13.1
06049	Modoc County, California	8.5	6,734	13.2	26.1	42.7	18.0
06051	Mono County, California	11.6	9,690	15.1	16.8	35.8	32.3
06053	Monterey County, California	5.4	268,809	29.3	20.8	26.8	23.1
06055	Napa County, California	3.6	96,568	16.8	19.3	31.5	32.4
06057	Nevada County, California	5.7	73,917	6.1	20.2	40.0	33.7
06059	Orange County, California	2.8	2,077,783	15.7	17.7	28.8	37.7

Table C. County—Labor Force, Employment, and Educational Data, 2011–2015—*Continued*

| | | Industry for employed population age 16 and older | Educational attainment for the population age 25 and older | | | |
| | | | Educational attainment | | | |
Fips code	State/county	Public administration	Total population age 25 and older	Less than high school graduate	High school graduate (includes equivalency)	Some college or Associate's degree	Bachelor's degree or higher
06061	Placer County, California	7.3	252,156	5.9	19.4	38.2	36.4
06063	Plumas County, California	6.2	14,470	9.5	23.9	44.7	22.0
06065	Riverside County, California	5.0	1,441,999	19.9	25.8	33.3	20.9
06067	Sacramento County, California	10.8	962,874	13.4	22.3	35.6	28.8
06069	San Benito County, California	5.1	36,178	22.0	24.4	34.6	19.0
06071	San Bernardino County, California	5.6	1,277,155	21.4	26.2	33.4	19.0
06073	San Diego County, California	5.5	2,128,434	14.0	19.0	31.3	35.7
06075	San Francisco County, California	3.4	659,772	13.0	12.7	20.5	53.8
06077	San Joaquin County, California	4.9	435,702	22.0	26.4	33.2	18.4
06079	San Luis Obispo County, California	5.7	182,629	10.3	19.7	37.0	33.0
06081	San Mateo County, California	3.5	530,221	11.7	16.5	26.2	45.6
06083	Santa Barbara County, California	4.3	268,017	20.4	17.7	29.7	32.2
06085	Santa Clara County, California	2.4	1,268,629	13.0	15.2	23.9	47.9
06087	Santa Cruz County, California	3.3	173,902	14.4	15.5	31.9	38.2
06089	Shasta County, California	6.3	124,396	10.7	25.8	43.8	19.6
06091	Sierra County, California	18.0	2,435	7.4	34.5	39.3	18.9
06093	Siskiyou County, California	8.3	31,835	11.6	24.9	40.9	22.7
06095	Solano County, California	7.9	284,771	12.5	23.8	38.7	24.9
06097	Sonoma County, California	4.0	346,159	12.9	19.9	34.4	32.9
06099	Stanislaus County, California	3.8	327,571	22.8	28.3	32.4	16.5
06101	Sutter County, California	6.3	60,812	21.5	24.8	36.0	17.6
06103	Tehama County, California	6.8	42,760	17.7	30.5	37.4	14.4
06105	Trinity County, California	13.5	10,320	9.2	31.0	39.8	20.0
06107	Tulare County, California	5.8	260,964	31.6	25.2	29.3	13.8
06109	Tuolumne County, California	8.2	40,871	9.7	29.7	40.2	20.4
06111	Ventura County, California	4.7	550,767	16.9	19.0	32.4	31.7
06113	Yolo County, California	7.9	120,693	14.5	19.7	26.8	39.0
06115	Yuba County, California	10.1	45,152	19.2	25.0	41.5	14.3
08000	**Colorado**	4.9	3,520,177	9.3	21.8	30.8	38.1
08001	Adams County, Colorado	4.2	296,842	17.7	28.8	31.3	22.2
08003	Alamosa County, Colorado	6.2	9,250	15.2	25.9	33.5	25.5
08005	Arapahoe County, Colorado	4.0	405,311	8.0	20.4	31.5	40.1
08007	Archuleta County, Colorado	4.1	9,056	8.4	26.0	30.5	35.0
08009	Baca County, Colorado	5.1	2,674	12.8	31.6	36.6	19.0
08011	Bent County, Colorado	21.7	4,859	23.8	44.5	24.7	7.0
08013	Boulder County, Colorado	2.7	198,949	5.9	12.7	22.5	58.9
08014	Broomfield County, Colorado	3.7	40,880	4.3	14.7	29.1	51.9
08015	Chaffee County, Colorado	7.9	14,310	8.9	26.7	30.3	34.1
08017	Cheyenne County, Colorado	4.8	1,286	9.0	33.6	34.9	22.5
08019	Clear Creek County, Colorado	7.4	7,050	3.2	22.0	33.3	41.5
08021	Conejos County, Colorado	7.0	5,297	15.3	32.8	32.4	19.5
08023	Costilla County, Colorado	5.2	2,647	24.1	27.4	30.6	17.9
08025	Crowley County, Colorado	13.9	3,562	16.6	39.1	33.2	11.1
08027	Custer County, Colorado	13.0	3,371	6.5	18.7	39.3	35.5
08029	Delta County, Colorado	4.4	21,764	11.1	37.5	31.4	20.0
08031	Denver County, Colorado	4.1	455,409	13.9	17.7	23.5	45.0
08033	Dolores County, Colorado	7.0	1,339	10.8	37.8	30.5	21.0
08035	Douglas County, Colorado	4.7	197,863	2.3	12.9	28.2	56.6
08037	Eagle County, Colorado	2.9	36,139	10.9	17.9	24.5	46.7
08039	Elbert County, Colorado	4.7	16,623	4.1	27.0	38.3	30.6
08041	El Paso County, Colorado	7.5	414,724	6.2	21.0	36.9	35.9
08043	Fremont County, Colorado	15.8	35,871	13.2	39.2	32.3	15.2
08045	Garfield County, Colorado	4.9	37,456	14.1	26.1	30.1	29.7
08047	Gilpin County, Colorado	8.3	4,322	4.2	24.4	39.3	32.1
08049	Grand County, Colorado	6.5	10,462	5.5	25.5	32.5	36.4
08051	Gunnison County, Colorado	3.2	9,831	4.9	17.0	23.6	54.4
08053	Hinsdale County, Colorado	8.6	726	5.0	21.5	33.2	40.4
08055	Huerfano County, Colorado	8.8	5,136	11.6	27.0	34.3	27.1
08057	Jackson County, Colorado	8.8	1,032	12.4	41.5	28.0	18.1
08059	Jefferson County, Colorado	5.5	388,427	6.0	21.3	31.1	41.6
08061	Kiowa County, Colorado	5.1	957	9.0	34.3	36.5	20.3
08063	Kit Carson County, Colorado	8.0	5,538	16.5	38.5	31.7	13.3
08065	Lake County, Colorado	8.8	5,000	8.0	35.5	29.1	27.4
08067	La Plata County, Colorado	6.7	37,134	5.3	19.4	31.9	43.3
08069	Larimer County, Colorado	3.9	205,285	4.7	19.0	32.1	44.3
08071	Las Animas County, Colorado	8.0	10,400	15.7	28.3	39.0	17.0
08073	Lincoln County, Colorado	14.0	3,967	20.3	42.2	22.4	15.1
08075	Logan County, Colorado	9.1	14,659	13.2	31.3	39.7	15.8
08077	Mesa County, Colorado	4.0	99,217	10.1	29.1	34.5	26.3
08079	Mineral County, Colorado	5.2	659	2.1	21.4	34.1	42.3
08081	Moffat County, Colorado	5.8	8,617	10.0	40.3	34.4	15.3
08083	Montezuma County, Colorado	7.8	18,073	10.2	29.0	34.0	26.7
08085	Montrose County, Colorado	5.4	28,760	12.6	31.6	31.3	24.5
08087	Morgan County, Colorado	6.0	18,219	19.8	32.1	33.2	14.9
08089	Otero County, Colorado	9.2	12,406	15.2	28.9	40.3	15.6

Table C. County—Labor Force, Employment, and Educational Data, 2011–2015—*Continued*

Fips code	State/county	Industry for employed population age 16 and older	Educational attainment for the population age 25 and older				
				Educational attainment			
		Public administration	Total population age 25 and older	Less than high school graduate	High school graduate (includes equivalency)	Some college or Associate's degree	Bachelor's degree or higher
08091	Ouray County, Colorado	7.7	3,696	1.9	19.4	26.7	52.0
08093	Park County, Colorado	7.2	12,524	4.3	25.5	41.0	29.2
08095	Phillips County, Colorado	7.2	2,976	11.8	29.1	37.8	21.2
08097	Pitkin County, Colorado	4.0	13,284	4.9	11.5	24.6	59.1
08099	Prowers County, Colorado	9.2	7,783	18.6	27.8	40.0	13.5
08101	Pueblo County, Colorado	7.1	108,247	12.0	29.0	37.3	21.6
08103	Rio Blanco County, Colorado	6.1	4,314	8.9	33.7	35.4	22.0
08105	Rio Grande County, Colorado	7.7	7,987	16.8	29.5	31.8	22.0
08107	Routt County, Colorado	3.5	16,961	3.0	20.5	26.0	50.4
08109	Saguache County, Colorado	7.3	4,431	21.3	24.7	26.9	27.0
08111	San Juan County, Colorado	2.7	474	7.6	33.5	29.7	29.1
08113	San Miguel County, Colorado	4.2	5,751	5.5	18.0	22.7	53.9
08115	Sedgwick County, Colorado	7.4	1,702	9.3	35.1	35.1	20.6
08117	Summit County, Colorado	5.2	21,453	5.2	17.2	28.8	48.8
08119	Teller County, Colorado	9.5	17,391	7.0	24.8	36.4	31.8
08121	Washington County, Colorado	5.1	3,414	9.1	35.1	39.5	16.3
08123	Weld County, Colorado	3.9	169,668	13.3	27.0	33.7	26.1
08125	Yuma County, Colorado	3.2	6,762	11.6	31.7	35.2	21.5
09000	**Connecticut**	3.7	2,462,855	10.1	27.4	24.9	37.6
09001	Fairfield County, Connecticut	2.4	634,872	10.3	22.6	21.3	45.8
09003	Hartford County, Connecticut	4.5	618,464	11.1	27.1	25.4	36.3
09005	Litchfield County, Connecticut	3.8	135,358	8.6	29.3	28.5	33.6
09007	Middlesex County, Connecticut	3.9	118,409	6.3	26.8	26.4	40.6
09009	New Haven County, Connecticut	3.8	591,088	10.9	30.2	24.9	34.0
09011	New London County, Connecticut	5.1	188,870	8.7	31.2	27.9	32.1
09013	Tolland County, Connecticut	4.5	95,408	6.5	27.4	28.0	38.0
09015	Windham County, Connecticut	3.7	80,386	11.7	34.3	30.8	23.1
10000	**Delaware**	5.7	631,118	11.6	31.1	27.3	30.0
10001	Kent County, Delaware	10.9	110,480	13.6	33.5	30.3	22.5
10003	New Castle County, Delaware	4.2	369,089	9.8	28.6	26.5	35.0
10005	Sussex County, Delaware	5.7	151,549	14.5	35.3	27.0	23.2
11000	District of Columbia	16.7	453,952	10.7	18.0	16.8	54.6
11001	**District of Columbia** District of Columbia	16.7	453,952	10.7	18.0	16.8	54.6
12000	**Florida**	4.6	13,824,205	13.1	29.5	30.1	27.3
12001	Alachua County, Florida	4.3	151,184	7.4	21.5	29.5	41.6
12003	Baker County, Florida	9.1	17,786	18.3	43.8	26.3	11.5
12005	Bay County, Florida	7.8	121,739	12.0	30.6	35.1	22.2
12007	Bradford County, Florida	14.9	19,499	23.5	37.0	28.7	10.9
12009	Brevard County, Florida	6.0	405,195	9.3	28.8	34.6	27.3
12011	Broward County, Florida	4.3	1,286,262	11.8	27.6	29.8	30.8
12013	Calhoun County, Florida	14.9	10,326	24.8	37.5	27.3	10.5
12015	Charlotte County, Florida	4.4	134,210	10.7	34.9	33.6	20.8
12017	Citrus County, Florida	5.0	110,144	13.4	38.2	31.5	16.9
12019	Clay County, Florida	6.8	131,378	9.7	30.7	35.9	23.8
12021	Collier County, Florida	2.8	254,178	14.0	26.7	26.1	33.2
12023	Columbia County, Florida	10.8	46,593	14.3	36.1	34.4	15.1
12027	DeSoto County, Florida	7.4	23,946	29.2	40.9	20.2	9.7
12029	Dixie County, Florida	14.0	11,981	21.2	41.0	29.9	7.9
12031	Duval County, Florida	4.8	597,484	11.4	28.6	32.7	27.3
12033	Escambia County, Florida	6.2	202,078	10.4	28.9	36.2	24.5
12035	Flagler County, Florida	3.8	75,111	9.1	34.7	33.3	23.0
12037	Franklin County, Florida	15.2	8,845	21.1	35.4	27.9	15.5
12039	Gadsden County, Florida	14.6	31,887	22.0	34.6	26.5	17.0
12041	Gilchrist County, Florida	8.1	11,298	17.1	38.8	32.7	11.4
12043	Glades County, Florida	6.3	9,919	23.1	44.5	24.0	8.4
12045	Gulf County, Florida	14.0	11,884	18.0	34.7	31.4	16.0
12047	Hamilton County, Florida	9.3	9,611	26.3	37.4	26.3	9.9
12049	Hardee County, Florida	4.7	17,531	30.7	41.1	17.5	10.7
12051	Hendry County, Florida	5.1	23,915	37.0	32.2	21.0	9.8
12053	Hernando County, Florida	5.1	129,497	12.9	37.5	33.9	15.6
12055	Highlands County, Florida	6.3	74,390	17.4	36.3	29.6	16.7
12057	Hillsborough County, Florida	4.1	871,891	12.5	27.3	29.6	30.6
12059	Holmes County, Florida	11.5	13,884	24.2	36.9	27.6	11.3
12061	Indian River County, Florida	4.6	107,647	11.7	30.3	31.2	26.8
12063	Jackson County, Florida	13.6	35,317	20.7	36.5	29.1	13.7
12065	Jefferson County, Florida	18.4	10,838	20.1	31.5	29.9	18.5
12067	Lafayette County, Florida	18.7	5,946	24.5	36.7	27.1	11.6
12069	Lake County, Florida	4.9	226,558	12.6	33.5	32.4	21.5
12071	Lee County, Florida	3.5	489,379	13.0	31.6	29.4	26.0
12073	Leon County, Florida	14.0	163,429	7.7	19.0	28.3	45.0
12075	Levy County, Florida	6.9	28,861	18.5	40.9	29.7	10.9
12077	Liberty County, Florida	19.9	5,716	22.8	43.5	22.6	11.2

Table C. County—Labor Force, Employment, and Educational Data, 2011–2015—*Continued*

| | | Industry for employed population age 16 and older | Educational attainment for the population age 25 and older | | | |
| | | | | Educational attainment | | |
Fips code	State/county	Public administration	Total population age 25 and older	Less than high school graduate	High school graduate (includes equivalency)	Some college or Associate's degree	Bachelor's degree or higher
12079	Madison County, Florida	12.4	13,112	18.0	39.0	31.7	11.3
12081	Manatee County, Florida	4.1	251,699	12.1	30.7	29.5	27.7
12083	Marion County, Florida	4.6	248,893	14.0	36.6	31.6	17.8
12085	Martin County, Florida	3.9	115,814	10.2	26.1	32.1	31.6
12086	Miami-Dade County, Florida	3.6	1,838,746	19.9	28.5	24.7	26.9
12087	Monroe County, Florida	6.7	59,040	9.1	27.9	31.7	31.3
12089	Nassau County, Florida	5.4	54,293	10.4	35.5	31.0	23.0
12091	Okaloosa County, Florida	11.2	130,117	8.8	26.2	36.2	28.8
12093	Okeechobee County, Florida	5.2	26,698	29.7	37.0	22.7	10.6
12095	Orange County, Florida	2.8	802,130	12.4	26.1	30.4	31.1
12097	Osceola County, Florida	3.6	195,118	14.8	34.3	33.0	18.0
12099	Palm Beach County, Florida	3.6	996,222	12.2	25.5	28.7	33.6
12101	Pasco County, Florida	4.2	345,901	12.0	33.7	32.9	21.4
12103	Pinellas County, Florida	3.8	703,720	10.0	29.5	31.7	28.9
12105	Polk County, Florida	4.0	427,658	16.5	36.2	28.5	18.9
12107	Putnam County, Florida	6.0	51,118	21.5	38.8	27.8	11.8
12109	St. Johns County, Florida	4.4	147,127	6.1	21.2	30.5	42.1
12111	St. Lucie County, Florida	4.6	204,758	14.6	33.4	32.2	19.9
12113	Santa Rosa County, Florida	8.6	110,220	9.6	28.0	35.8	26.6
12115	Sarasota County, Florida	3.6	308,938	7.6	30.2	29.7	32.4
12117	Seminole County, Florida	3.8	300,693	7.0	24.1	33.6	35.3
12119	Sumter County, Florida	6.1	96,219	10.5	30.6	30.9	28.0
12121	Suwannee County, Florida	10.5	30,323	21.2	40.8	26.4	11.6
12123	Taylor County, Florida	11.2	16,448	23.7	39.2	28.1	9.0
12125	Union County, Florida	20.5	11,003	25.9	37.4	28.9	7.8
12127	Volusia County, Florida	4.8	367,935	11.3	33.8	33.3	21.6
12129	Wakulla County, Florida	20.7	22,141	11.1	39.4	33.4	16.1
12131	Walton County, Florida	4.7	43,287	14.8	28.1	31.2	25.9
12133	Washington County, Florida	9.8	17,497	19.7	41.3	27.9	11.1
13000	**Georgia**	5.3	6,500,205	14.6	28.4	28.2	28.8
13001	Appling County, Georgia	5.3	12,197	23.8	42.8	20.3	13.1
13003	Atkinson County, Georgia	4.3	5,244	30.5	39.2	22.5	7.8
13005	Bacon County, Georgia	3.3	7,335	22.5	40.5	24.3	12.8
13007	Baker County, Georgia	10.2	2,262	19.7	42.2	29.5	8.6
13009	Baldwin County, Georgia	8.1	27,773	17.4	39.0	25.8	17.7
13011	Banks County, Georgia	3.3	12,394	21.9	45.5	21.4	11.2
13013	Barrow County, Georgia	3.7	46,437	18.1	35.0	30.4	16.5
13015	Bartow County, Georgia	4.0	66,442	18.3	35.0	28.9	17.8
13017	Ben Hill County, Georgia	6.7	11,366	20.3	41.7	27.1	10.9
13019	Berrien County, Georgia	7.6	12,743	18.7	38.0	30.8	12.5
13021	Bibb County, Georgia	6.3	99,442	16.8	32.6	26.8	23.8
13023	Bleckley County, Georgia	18.8	7,898	15.9	44.8	22.8	16.5
13025	Brantley County, Georgia	6.3	12,057	21.0	45.6	25.0	8.4
13027	Brooks County, Georgia	8.9	10,722	22.0	38.0	28.3	11.7
13029	Bryan County, Georgia	6.1	20,937	10.4	27.6	30.9	31.1
13031	Bulloch County, Georgia	4.6	38,297	13.2	28.0	29.8	29.0
13033	Burke County, Georgia	4.7	14,667	22.4	39.9	28.1	9.6
13035	Butts County, Georgia	7.4	16,079	23.9	43.8	22.2	10.1
13037	Calhoun County, Georgia	8.9	4,536	27.2	38.6	24.3	9.9
13039	Camden County, Georgia	16.1	31,575	8.8	31.4	38.7	21.1
13043	Candler County, Georgia	5.3	7,100	26.2	34.9	23.6	15.4
13045	Carroll County, Georgia	3.6	69,642	19.7	35.8	26.6	17.9
13047	Catoosa County, Georgia	2.9	44,169	15.8	31.7	33.9	18.6
13049	Charlton County, Georgia	8.5	9,394	25.4	41.8	22.8	10.0
13051	Chatham County, Georgia	6.7	182,813	11.0	25.5	30.9	32.6
13053	Chattahoochee County, Georgia	22.5	5,205	8.2	27.0	39.1	25.7
13055	Chattooga County, Georgia	3.9	17,336	29.3	39.7	22.2	8.8
13057	Cherokee County, Georgia	3.0	148,064	10.6	24.8	30.0	34.7
13059	Clarke County, Georgia	2.9	64,822	13.7	21.8	24.3	40.2
13061	Clay County, Georgia	4.7	2,043	20.3	44.8	27.1	7.8
13063	Clayton County, Georgia	6.3	163,245	17.5	32.0	32.1	18.3
13065	Clinch County, Georgia	6.3	4,483	26.8	35.4	24.3	13.5
13067	Cobb County, Georgia	3.2	473,749	9.0	19.5	27.4	44.1
13069	Coffee County, Georgia	4.9	27,341	22.6	39.1	24.7	13.7
13071	Colquitt County, Georgia	3.9	29,476	27.2	36.7	23.0	13.1
13073	Columbia County, Georgia	7.3	88,824	8.2	23.8	32.7	35.3
13075	Cook County, Georgia	5.9	11,159	24.8	39.5	22.9	12.9
13077	Coweta County, Georgia	4.8	87,515	11.6	31.6	29.2	27.6
13079	Crawford County, Georgia	8.6	8,765	21.7	35.6	29.9	12.8
13081	Crisp County, Georgia	7.3	15,358	21.8	35.7	27.9	14.6
13083	Dade County, Georgia	3.9	11,182	19.7	35.5	30.7	14.1
13085	Dawson County, Georgia	3.4	15,974	14.2	29.0	29.2	27.6

Table C. County—Labor Force, Employment, and Educational Data, 2011–2015—*Continued*

| | | Industry for employed population age 16 and older | Educational attainment for the population age 25 and older | | | |
| | | | | Educational attainment | | |
Fips code	State/county	Public administration	Total population age 25 and older	Less than high school graduate	High school graduate (includes equivalency)	Some college or Associate's degree	Bachelor's degree or higher
13087	Decatur County, Georgia	6.3	17,999	20.2	34.9	29.1	15.8
13089	DeKalb County, Georgia	5.5	479,320	11.7	21.0	26.2	41.1
13091	Dodge County, Georgia	18.3	14,509	19.0	42.1	24.2	14.7
13093	Dooly County, Georgia	11.1	9,955	25.1	43.4	22.3	9.2
13095	Dougherty County, Georgia	8.5	58,304	19.1	29.3	32.8	18.9
13097	Douglas County, Georgia	4.6	87,156	12.2	31.2	30.6	26.0
13099	Early County, Georgia	6.7	7,058	20.9	38.1	25.8	15.2
13101	Echols County, Georgia	2.0	2,565	28.5	36.2	27.0	8.3
13103	Effingham County, Georgia	5.9	34,974	14.0	38.2	30.8	16.9
13105	Elbert County, Georgia	6.3	13,539	23.2	45.7	20.5	10.6
13107	Emanuel County, Georgia	6.6	14,801	23.5	40.2	25.5	10.8
13109	Evans County, Georgia	5.5	6,971	25.7	37.9	21.1	15.4
13111	Fannin County, Georgia	5.4	18,036	19.1	38.8	26.0	16.2
13113	Fayette County, Georgia	6.0	72,846	6.1	21.5	28.6	43.8
13115	Floyd County, Georgia	4.7	63,344	21.0	31.0	29.4	18.6
13117	Forsyth County, Georgia	2.0	125,848	8.0	19.3	27.1	45.6
13119	Franklin County, Georgia	3.4	15,104	25.4	38.3	23.7	12.6
13121	Fulton County, Georgia	3.7	650,445	9.1	18.0	23.6	49.3
13123	Gilmer County, Georgia	2.3	20,596	21.9	35.5	25.9	16.7
13125	Glascock County, Georgia	5.2	2,077	20.7	44.6	26.6	8.1
13127	Glynn County, Georgia	6.2	55,802	12.7	28.2	31.8	27.3
13129	Gordon County, Georgia	2.9	36,477	24.0	35.7	26.6	13.7
13131	Grady County, Georgia	4.4	16,745	24.4	36.8	25.6	13.3
13133	Greene County, Georgia	5.2	12,038	18.1	35.6	21.6	24.7
13135	Gwinnett County, Georgia	3.0	540,173	12.8	23.4	29.2	34.7
13137	Habersham County, Georgia	5.4	29,403	21.8	34.0	26.7	17.5
13139	Hall County, Georgia	3.1	119,969	22.0	28.1	27.2	22.7
13141	Hancock County, Georgia	10.2	6,471	27.4	40.6	21.7	10.3
13143	Haralson County, Georgia	5.3	19,040	21.6	37.7	26.6	14.1
13145	Harris County, Georgia	5.7	22,842	10.4	27.4	35.5	26.6
13147	Hart County, Georgia	4.6	17,817	19.5	37.9	29.0	13.6
13149	Heard County, Georgia	3.8	7,792	23.5	43.2	23.2	10.1
13151	Henry County, Georgia	7.8	133,759	10.4	30.5	32.1	27.0
13153	Houston County, Georgia	18.9	94,781	10.4	30.0	36.1	23.5
13155	Irwin County, Georgia	6.3	6,446	14.9	44.2	30.2	10.6
13157	Jackson County, Georgia	4.5	40,623	17.3	34.3	29.2	19.2
13159	Jasper County, Georgia	4.1	9,171	21.3	40.2	26.6	11.9
13161	Jeff Davis County, Georgia	9.6	9,631	21.3	40.2	28.9	9.7
13163	Jefferson County, Georgia	9.4	10,893	27.2	41.2	21.6	10.1
13165	Jenkins County, Georgia	5.4	5,944	28.8	36.8	22.2	12.2
13167	Johnson County, Georgia	9.8	6,724	24.3	39.3	27.4	8.9
13169	Jones County, Georgia	8.7	19,232	13.3	37.3	29.7	19.7
13171	Lamar County, Georgia	5.7	11,645	15.3	37.9	29.7	17.1
13173	Lanier County, Georgia	8.0	6,970	23.6	30.5	33.2	12.7
13175	Laurens County, Georgia	6.9	31,873	18.9	43.6	22.4	15.1
13177	Lee County, Georgia	11.7	18,801	13.2	28.6	34.9	23.2
13179	Liberty County, Georgia	20.7	35,998	10.0	31.5	39.8	18.7
13181	Lincoln County, Georgia	5.3	5,625	18.7	42.2	26.9	12.1
13183	Long County, Georgia	14.4	9,879	14.8	36.9	33.2	15.0
13185	Lowndes County, Georgia	7.3	64,465	16.2	28.3	32.0	23.5
13187	Lumpkin County, Georgia	5.2	19,966	15.0	28.6	28.3	28.1
13189	McDuffie County, Georgia	4.5	14,240	23.1	38.6	24.1	14.2
13191	McIntosh County, Georgia	10.5	10,378	18.6	35.8	32.5	13.1
13193	Macon County, Georgia	10.4	9,718	28.3	37.8	26.0	7.9
13195	Madison County, Georgia	3.7	19,272	18.4	39.9	26.1	15.6
13197	Marion County, Georgia	11.6	6,059	24.4	37.5	25.9	12.2
13199	Meriwether County, Georgia	3.4	14,714	26.4	39.0	25.3	9.3
13201	Miller County, Georgia	4.6	4,028	20.4	40.3	26.4	12.8
13205	Mitchell County, Georgia	6.9	15,371	25.9	39.8	23.0	11.4
13207	Monroe County, Georgia	8.3	18,753	18.3	35.4	25.0	21.3
13209	Montgomery County, Georgia	5.5	5,937	19.5	42.3	23.6	14.6
13211	Morgan County, Georgia	4.2	12,106	17.6	34.8	25.5	22.1
13213	Murray County, Georgia	3.4	25,666	30.0	36.8	22.9	10.3
13215	Muscogee County, Georgia	8.2	127,557	13.6	27.7	34.6	24.1
13217	Newton County, Georgia	6.0	64,747	15.7	32.0	32.1	20.2
13219	Oconee County, Georgia	4.3	22,334	6.8	21.3	27.0	44.9
13221	Oglethorpe County, Georgia	7.4	10,523	20.8	36.1	25.9	17.2
13223	Paulding County, Georgia	5.0	92,676	10.4	35.6	30.2	23.8
13225	Peach County, Georgia	9.8	16,643	14.9	30.1	34.1	20.9
13227	Pickens County, Georgia	4.2	21,577	16.6	30.8	27.5	25.1
13229	Pierce County, Georgia	6.9	12,456	20.1	39.3	26.3	14.2
13231	Pike County, Georgia	6.2	11,886	13.1	39.2	31.7	16.0
13233	Polk County, Georgia	4.3	26,815	24.8	38.1	24.1	13.1
13235	Pulaski County, Georgia	10.4	8,459	19.1	43.6	25.2	12.1
13237	Putnam County, Georgia	4.7	15,700	15.5	39.0	28.0	17.5

Table C. County—Labor Force, Employment, and Educational Data, 2011–2015—*Continued*

| | | Industry for employed population age 16 and older | Educational attainment for the population age 25 and older | | | |
| | | | | Educational attainment | | |
Fips code	State/county	Public administration	Total population age 25 and older	Less than high school graduate	High school graduate (includes equivalency)	Some college or Associate's degree	Bachelor's degree or higher
13239	Quitman County, Georgia	10.9	1,704	26.9	40.7	25.7	6.7
13241	Rabun County, Georgia	4.3	12,051	13.9	34.0	26.2	25.9
13243	Randolph County, Georgia	7.0	4,927	27.1	35.3	22.9	14.7
13245	Richmond County, Georgia	7.5	128,857	16.7	31.1	31.7	20.4
13247	Rockdale County, Georgia	7.5	56,170	13.9	31.2	29.4	25.5
13249	Schley County, Georgia	10.7	3,198	22.8	34.4	28.1	14.7
13251	Screven County, Georgia	5.3	9,401	19.0	42.2	25.5	13.3
13253	Seminole County, Georgia	5.5	6,092	17.4	40.3	27.2	15.1
13255	Spalding County, Georgia	6.4	42,434	21.1	36.5	26.6	15.9
13257	Stephens County, Georgia	4.3	17,162	20.0	38.3	25.6	16.2
13259	Stewart County, Georgia	12.5	4,247	39.0	35.6	14.7	10.8
13261	Sumter County, Georgia	8.3	19,621	23.5	31.4	26.1	19.0
13263	Talbot County, Georgia	5.3	4,716	22.0	43.3	21.1	13.7
13265	Taliaferro County, Georgia	13.8	1,309	31.0	43.9	15.1	9.9
13267	Tattnall County, Georgia	11.5	17,465	26.4	38.0	24.7	11.0
13269	Taylor County, Georgia	9.8	5,717	24.5	36.5	27.9	11.1
13271	Telfair County, Georgia	12.9	12,291	26.4	49.3	14.9	9.3
13273	Terrell County, Georgia	5.6	6,130	30.0	31.5	27.3	11.2
13275	Thomas County, Georgia	5.1	30,269	18.9	32.7	29.2	19.2
13277	Tift County, Georgia	3.9	25,552	20.4	33.6	29.3	16.8
13279	Toombs County, Georgia	6.5	17,427	20.8	39.2	24.4	15.7
13281	Towns County, Georgia	2.2	7,897	11.5	34.9	31.3	22.4
13283	Treutlen County, Georgia	7.7	4,770	22.9	41.6	20.8	14.8
13285	Troup County, Georgia	3.8	44,007	16.0	35.8	29.5	18.7
13287	Turner County, Georgia	9.2	5,501	25.9	35.9	26.5	11.7
13289	Twiggs County, Georgia	9.6	6,043	31.6	38.7	19.9	9.7
13291	Union County, Georgia	4.1	16,789	12.2	33.4	32.5	21.9
13293	Upson County, Georgia	6.6	18,037	23.4	35.4	29.1	12.1
13295	Walker County, Georgia	4.3	47,214	20.0	37.2	28.1	14.7
13297	Walton County, Georgia	5.2	56,685	14.7	35.6	31.8	17.9
13299	Ware County, Georgia	6.6	23,849	18.7	40.8	27.7	12.9
13301	Warren County, Georgia	5.8	3,831	28.9	42.3	16.3	12.5
13303	Washington County, Georgia	8.2	14,154	22.0	41.5	23.6	12.9
13305	Wayne County, Georgia	7.9	20,136	17.9	42.1	26.9	13.1
13307	Webster County, Georgia	14.1	1,857	24.3	46.3	21.8	7.6
13309	Wheeler County, Georgia	11.3	5,931	23.1	54.8	16.4	5.6
13311	White County, Georgia	4.8	19,365	14.7	31.2	33.4	20.7
13313	Whitfield County, Georgia	2.5	65,109	31.4	28.9	25.6	14.0
13315	Wilcox County, Georgia	15.3	6,418	22.3	50.0	19.3	8.5
13317	Wilkes County, Georgia	4.6	7,041	20.3	43.4	20.6	15.7
13319	Wilkinson County, Georgia	6.5	6,406	18.7	51.2	22.6	7.4
13321	Worth County, Georgia	7.4	14,306	25.4	41.1	24.2	9.4
15000	**Hawaii**	8.9	962,052	9.0	27.9	32.3	30.8
15001	Hawaii County, Hawaii	6.3	133,135	8.7	31.9	32.6	26.8
15003	Honolulu County, Hawaii	10.3	667,370	9.1	26.4	31.8	32.7
15005	Kalawao County, Hawaii	17.2	78	11.5	29.5	24.4	34.6
15007	Kauai County, Hawaii	6.8	48,963	8.4	30.0	33.6	28.0
15009	Maui County, Hawaii	4.9	112,506	8.5	31.2	34.2	26.1
16000	**Idaho**	5.2	1,030,748	10.5	27.5	36.1	25.9
16001	Ada County, Idaho	6.2	274,388	5.8	21.4	35.8	37.1
16003	Adams County, Idaho	6.7	2,890	11.5	35.4	31.6	21.5
16005	Bannock County, Idaho	5.5	51,764	8.4	26.6	38.6	26.4
16007	Bear Lake County, Idaho	4.0	3,915	6.8	39.0	35.1	19.1
16009	Benewah County, Idaho	7.4	6,382	14.0	40.8	31.9	13.3
16011	Bingham County, Idaho	6.0	27,044	14.8	29.4	38.3	17.5
16013	Blaine County, Idaho	6.1	14,992	9.7	18.0	29.4	42.9
16015	Boise County, Idaho	10.7	5,205	5.9	27.8	41.3	25.1
16017	Bonner County, Idaho	3.6	30,068	8.8	31.4	38.9	20.9
16019	Bonneville County, Idaho	5.0	65,086	8.9	27.5	36.4	27.2
16021	Boundary County, Idaho	6.2	7,648	11.5	36.8	35.7	16.0
16023	Butte County, Idaho	9.3	1,753	10.3	36.5	37.6	15.6
16025	Camas County, Idaho	4.0	726	12.9	27.8	40.9	18.3
16027	Canyon County, Idaho	4.5	119,771	16.8	32.0	33.4	17.7
16029	Caribou County, Idaho	4.6	4,407	8.6	35.5	36.6	19.3
16031	Cassia County, Idaho	2.8	13,650	20.1	26.9	35.2	17.8
16033	Clark County, Idaho	7.9	539	27.1	34.1	23.7	15.0
16035	Clearwater County, Idaho	7.2	6,667	13.6	34.0	35.5	16.9
16037	Custer County, Idaho	3.3	3,292	9.2	34.8	28.9	27.1
16039	Elmore County, Idaho	18.1	15,650	14.4	27.9	41.2	16.6
16041	Franklin County, Idaho	2.3	7,447	9.8	33.4	38.4	18.4
16043	Fremont County, Idaho	6.0	8,184	10.8	34.2	34.5	20.5
16045	Gem County, Idaho	6.8	11,804	13.1	37.7	33.2	16.0
16047	Gooding County, Idaho	1.9	9,564	24.2	33.1	28.4	14.3
16049	Idaho County, Idaho	6.3	11,919	10.6	37.3	32.7	19.3

Table C. County—Labor Force, Employment, and Educational Data, 2011–2015—*Continued*

| | | Industry for employed population age 16 and older | Educational attainment for the population age 25 and older | | | |
| | | | | Educational attainment | | |
Fips code	State/county	Public administration	Total population age 25 and older	Less than high school graduate	High school graduate (includes equivalency)	Some college or Associate's degree	Bachelor's degree or higher
16051	Jefferson County, Idaho	5.4	15,227	12.1	30.8	36.9	20.2
16053	Jerome County, Idaho	2.5	13,470	27.7	28.2	30.1	14.0
16055	Kootenai County, Idaho	3.8	98,196	7.8	28.4	40.5	23.3
16057	Latah County, Idaho	3.3	21,379	4.5	19.8	30.1	45.6
16059	Lemhi County, Idaho	6.4	5,955	8.6	33.7	36.2	21.5
16061	Lewis County, Idaho	9.8	2,730	11.4	34.3	39.1	15.2
16063	Lincoln County, Idaho	4.5	3,150	21.4	38.3	28.7	11.6
16065	Madison County, Idaho	2.6	15,633	4.6	15.8	44.8	34.8
16067	Minidoka County, Idaho	2.4	12,691	23.3	29.2	34.6	12.9
16069	Nez Perce County, Idaho	5.1	27,509	8.7	30.7	37.3	23.4
16071	Oneida County, Idaho	6.3	2,679	6.4	38.4	41.1	14.1
16073	Owyhee County, Idaho	4.6	7,305	25.4	36.9	28.9	8.9
16075	Payette County, Idaho	4.2	14,774	13.8	33.1	37.4	15.7
16077	Power County, Idaho	3.5	4,686	21.9	39.8	25.4	13.0
16079	Shoshone County, Idaho	3.8	9,187	13.8	36.2	36.0	14.1
16081	Teton County, Idaho	2.6	6,644	9.8	20.1	30.3	39.8
16083	Twin Falls County, Idaho	3.6	50,530	14.5	28.9	38.9	17.7
16085	Valley County, Idaho	6.1	7,268	6.5	28.6	35.0	29.8
16087	Washington County, Idaho	9.9	6,980	17.2	34.4	34.5	13.9
17000	**Illinois**	3.8	8,600,178	12.1	26.8	28.8	32.3
17001	Adams County, Illinois	3.1	46,090	8.7	36.1	34.0	21.2
17003	Alexander County, Illinois	8.6	4,951	22.3	35.8	33.8	8.0
17005	Bond County, Illinois	4.8	11,964	13.1	39.8	29.6	17.6
17007	Boone County, Illinois	3.0	34,670	13.3	36.0	30.6	20.2
17009	Brown County, Illinois	10.0	5,059	14.2	41.9	29.9	14.0
17011	Bureau County, Illinois	3.3	23,976	10.0	39.4	32.7	17.9
17013	Calhoun County, Illinois	4.3	3,605	8.6	43.5	32.3	15.6
17015	Carroll County, Illinois	3.0	10,925	9.5	43.3	31.0	16.2
17017	Cass County, Illinois	5.6	8,913	14.5	46.5	25.2	13.9
17019	Champaign County, Illinois	2.5	117,746	5.7	22.8	28.1	43.4
17021	Christian County, Illinois	5.7	24,019	11.8	44.1	29.8	14.2
17023	Clark County, Illinois	3.6	11,221	9.8	38.2	33.9	18.1
17025	Clay County, Illinois	3.1	9,366	12.0	38.6	34.6	14.8
17027	Clinton County, Illinois	6.4	26,599	10.4	32.7	36.0	20.8
17029	Coles County, Illinois	2.2	32,350	9.7	32.2	34.0	24.1
17031	Cook County, Illinois	3.6	3,537,179	14.7	24.0	25.6	35.8
17033	Crawford County, Illinois	3.9	13,928	11.0	33.6	36.6	18.8
17035	Cumberland County, Illinois	2.1	7,587	11.8	37.2	37.4	13.6
17037	DeKalb County, Illinois	3.9	60,466	7.8	26.3	35.9	30.0
17039	De Witt County, Illinois	5.1	11,618	7.6	38.6	34.5	19.2
17041	Douglas County, Illinois	3.7	13,182	16.1	36.2	29.9	17.8
17043	DuPage County, Illinois	2.4	627,482	7.6	19.0	26.6	46.7
17045	Edgar County, Illinois	4.8	12,791	12.5	39.2	30.1	18.1
17047	Edwards County, Illinois	3.7	4,631	11.6	36.8	40.5	11.0
17049	Effingham County, Illinois	2.4	23,140	8.8	36.4	33.8	20.9
17051	Fayette County, Illinois	8.4	15,284	17.3	40.0	29.5	13.2
17053	Ford County, Illinois	2.0	9,665	10.9	38.8	33.7	16.6
17055	Franklin County, Illinois	4.9	27,687	12.4	34.4	38.4	14.8
17057	Fulton County, Illinois	5.6	26,041	12.3	35.9	35.8	16.0
17059	Gallatin County, Illinois	5.6	3,893	14.0	41.4	35.1	9.5
17061	Greene County, Illinois	4.9	9,490	14.3	40.9	32.8	11.9
17063	Grundy County, Illinois	3.0	33,005	7.5	37.6	34.0	20.8
17065	Hamilton County, Illinois	4.4	5,842	12.3	35.3	38.4	14.0
17067	Hancock County, Illinois	4.5	13,470	8.1	37.5	34.0	20.3
17069	Hardin County, Illinois	5.8	3,055	16.6	34.3	37.3	11.8
17071	Henderson County, Illinois	4.7	5,206	12.0	44.0	30.1	13.9
17073	Henry County, Illinois	4.8	34,483	10.3	35.2	33.8	20.6
17075	Iroquois County, Illinois	2.6	20,316	11.3	41.1	32.3	15.3
17077	Jackson County, Illinois	4.9	35,056	8.3	25.0	31.4	35.3
17079	Jasper County, Illinois	4.0	6,768	10.4	39.1	32.9	17.6
17081	Jefferson County, Illinois	3.8	26,773	14.0	32.8	36.9	16.3
17083	Jersey County, Illinois	3.2	15,521	9.1	37.7	35.8	17.4
17085	Jo Daviess County, Illinois	3.4	16,422	7.7	38.2	30.4	23.6
17087	Johnson County, Illinois	8.2	9,346	15.9	31.4	36.0	16.7
17089	Kane County, Illinois	2.7	334,407	17.3	23.5	27.6	31.6
17091	Kankakee County, Illinois	3.7	73,073	12.3	34.1	34.8	18.8
17093	Kendall County, Illinois	4.2	75,012	6.3	24.6	34.2	34.8
17095	Knox County, Illinois	3.4	36,351	12.8	36.6	32.9	17.7
17097	Lake County, Illinois	2.9	451,898	10.6	21.3	24.9	43.2
17099	LaSalle County, Illinois	3.7	78,046	11.8	37.5	34.5	16.2
17101	Lawrence County, Illinois	4.2	12,313	22.9	34.3	33.5	9.4
17103	Lee County, Illinois	4.4	24,945	12.0	37.7	33.0	17.3

Table C. County—Labor Force, Employment, and Educational Data, 2011–2015—*Continued*

		Industry for employed population age 16 and older	Educational attainment for the population age 25 and older			
				Educational attainment		
Fips code	State/county	Public administration	Total population age 25 and older	Less than high school graduate	High school graduate (includes equivalency)	Some college or Associate's degree	Bachelor's degree or higher
17105	Livingston County, Illinois	5.2	26,556	12.5	40.5	31.9	15.2
17107	Logan County, Illinois	7.7	20,846	13.9	33.3	35.6	17.2
17109	McDonough County, Illinois	4.2	18,342	7.7	29.2	29.0	34.1
17111	McHenry County, Illinois	3.0	202,962	7.6	26.5	33.4	32.5
17113	McLean County, Illinois	2.3	103,933	5.0	25.7	25.3	44.0
17115	Macon County, Illinois	4.3	74,408	11.0	34.6	31.5	22.9
17117	Macoupin County, Illinois	4.9	32,811	10.2	37.3	34.4	18.1
17119	Madison County, Illinois	4.4	182,966	8.0	32.3	34.4	25.3
17121	Marion County, Illinois	4.5	26,574	12.4	35.4	37.8	14.5
17123	Marshall County, Illinois	3.2	8,713	8.4	40.3	34.6	16.8
17125	Mason County, Illinois	6.0	10,047	12.7	41.3	31.9	14.1
17127	Massac County, Illinois	4.8	10,598	17.9	31.7	35.8	14.7
17129	Menard County, Illinois	11.4	8,817	7.6	37.2	32.0	23.1
17131	Mercer County, Illinois	4.3	11,377	8.3	41.9	34.1	15.7
17133	Monroe County, Illinois	3.3	23,364	6.0	33.7	32.8	27.5
17135	Montgomery County, Illinois	8.0	20,886	14.5	41.7	30.9	13.0
17137	Morgan County, Illinois	7.1	24,088	9.4	41.4	26.8	22.3
17139	Moultrie County, Illinois	2.7	10,186	15.6	36.9	31.8	15.7
17141	Ogle County, Illinois	3.7	35,909	11.7	33.7	34.7	19.8
17143	Peoria County, Illinois	3.2	124,036	9.8	28.6	32.4	29.2
17145	Perry County, Illinois	6.0	15,317	14.1	38.3	34.1	13.4
17147	Piatt County, Illinois	5.3	11,567	5.5	34.7	32.2	27.6
17149	Pike County, Illinois	8.4	11,247	12.5	43.0	29.3	15.2
17151	Pope County, Illinois	7.1	3,148	14.3	32.3	38.3	15.1
17153	Pulaski County, Illinois	9.0	4,054	19.5	35.5	33.3	11.6
17155	Putnam County, Illinois	4.0	4,200	9.8	42.7	35.1	12.5
17157	Randolph County, Illinois	6.1	24,041	15.3	42.4	30.3	12.0
17159	Richland County, Illinois	5.9	11,243	11.6	33.3	34.1	20.9
17161	Rock Island County, Illinois	4.5	100,858	11.9	31.8	34.3	22.0
17163	St. Clair County, Illinois	7.8	177,595	9.7	28.1	36.2	26.0
17165	Saline County, Illinois	5.9	17,210	14.2	33.1	38.7	14.0
17167	Sangamon County, Illinois	14.0	135,955	7.9	28.1	30.6	33.4
17169	Schuyler County, Illinois	8.1	5,409	12.4	39.0	32.7	15.9
17171	Scott County, Illinois	7.5	3,637	9.2	49.4	29.5	11.9
17173	Shelby County, Illinois	4.3	15,670	8.3	45.5	31.3	14.9
17175	Stark County, Illinois	2.3	4,177	11.5	38.8	32.1	17.6
17177	Stephenson County, Illinois	2.4	32,774	9.5	35.3	37.1	18.1
17179	Tazewell County, Illinois	3.5	94,102	7.3	33.1	34.6	25.0
17181	Union County, Illinois	8.1	12,480	15.3	31.0	32.1	21.6
17183	Vermilion County, Illinois	4.3	54,239	13.2	40.6	32.4	13.8
17185	Wabash County, Illinois	3.2	8,113	10.7	32.2	41.5	15.6
17187	Warren County, Illinois	3.1	11,603	12.2	35.0	31.9	20.9
17189	Washington County, Illinois	3.6	10,266	8.7	35.0	35.4	20.9
17191	Wayne County, Illinois	4.0	11,549	13.4	34.4	38.4	13.8
17193	White County, Illinois	4.0	10,318	12.3	35.1	39.0	13.6
17195	Whiteside County, Illinois	3.8	39,785	11.9	35.0	36.2	16.9
17197	Will County, Illinois	3.7	437,079	9.5	27.0	30.4	33.0
17199	Williamson County, Illinois	6.9	47,041	10.3	30.4	38.3	21.0
17201	Winnebago County, Illinois	3.0	195,388	12.8	33.3	32.1	21.9
17203	Woodford County, Illinois	3.4	25,868	6.3	32.7	32.7	28.4
18000	**Indiana**	3.5	4,316,273	12.2	34.6	29.1	24.1
18001	Adams County, Indiana	3.0	20,912	14.8	44.1	26.1	15.0
18003	Allen County, Indiana	2.7	233,222	10.7	29.4	32.9	27.0
18005	Bartholomew County, Indiana	2.5	53,618	9.7	34.3	26.6	29.4
18007	Benton County, Indiana	3.9	5,892	11.0	45.2	26.8	16.9
18009	Blackford County, Indiana	3.6	8,739	14.5	49.5	25.9	10.1
18011	Boone County, Indiana	3.6	39,913	6.7	26.7	23.9	42.7
18013	Brown County, Indiana	3.4	11,036	10.2	37.9	29.6	22.3
18015	Carroll County, Indiana	1.9	13,748	12.0	41.3	29.6	17.0
18017	Cass County, Indiana	4.8	25,838	17.2	40.8	27.9	14.2
18019	Clark County, Indiana	4.1	77,603	12.8	34.0	33.1	20.1
18021	Clay County, Indiana	6.7	18,235	12.7	44.9	27.3	15.1
18023	Clinton County, Indiana	2.0	21,499	13.7	45.6	25.6	15.1
18025	Crawford County, Indiana	6.8	7,389	17.6	49.7	23.0	9.7
18027	Daviess County, Indiana	6.3	20,092	25.2	37.2	23.9	13.7
18029	Dearborn County, Indiana	3.0	33,990	9.6	39.6	31.3	19.5
18031	Decatur County, Indiana	3.2	17,634	11.4	45.3	27.0	16.2
18033	DeKalb County, Indiana	2.0	28,125	11.9	40.6	30.5	17.0
18035	Delaware County, Indiana	3.0	71,099	11.3	35.5	29.9	23.2
18037	Dubois County, Indiana	2.3	28,503	12.1	41.9	27.3	18.7
18039	Elkhart County, Indiana	2.0	126,571	19.2	36.9	25.8	18.1
18041	Fayette County, Indiana	3.0	16,551	19.6	42.8	27.8	9.8
18043	Floyd County, Indiana	3.0	51,455	10.8	32.1	31.2	25.8

Table C. County—Labor Force, Employment, and Educational Data, 2011–2015—*Continued*

| | | Industry for employed population age 16 and older | Educational attainment for the population age 25 and older | | | |
| | | | | Educational attainment | | |
Fips code	State/county	Public administration	Total population age 25 and older	Less than high school graduate	High school graduate (includes equivalency)	Some college or Associate's degree	Bachelor's degree or higher
18045	Fountain County, Indiana	3.5	11,656	12.3	44.2	29.9	13.6
18047	Franklin County, Indiana	2.6	15,561	13.1	42.6	25.1	19.3
18049	Fulton County, Indiana	3.2	13,991	14.7	43.6	28.4	13.2
18051	Gibson County, Indiana	2.3	22,878	10.2	40.3	34.4	15.1
18053	Grant County, Indiana	2.7	45,070	13.7	41.5	27.6	17.3
18055	Greene County, Indiana	10.9	22,774	14.4	41.1	30.7	13.7
18057	Hamilton County, Indiana	3.1	190,788	3.9	15.9	24.3	55.9
18059	Hancock County, Indiana	6.1	48,118	6.0	33.3	32.4	28.3
18061	Harrison County, Indiana	4.4	27,167	12.2	41.9	29.9	16.0
18063	Hendricks County, Indiana	4.2	100,853	6.2	28.9	31.4	33.4
18065	Henry County, Indiana	4.2	34,723	13.5	43.5	27.5	15.6
18067	Howard County, Indiana	3.7	57,030	11.9	36.4	32.8	18.9
18069	Huntington County, Indiana	2.9	24,821	10.3	43.4	28.3	18.0
18071	Jackson County, Indiana	3.7	29,371	12.5	48.1	24.4	15.0
18073	Jasper County, Indiana	3.1	22,029	12.1	42.8	29.8	15.3
18075	Jay County, Indiana	2.9	13,920	15.9	48.6	25.4	10.1
18077	Jefferson County, Indiana	4.9	21,976	13.3	39.5	29.6	17.6
18079	Jennings County, Indiana	5.4	18,691	16.1	47.4	26.0	10.4
18081	Johnson County, Indiana	4.4	96,050	8.0	33.8	29.7	28.5
18083	Knox County, Indiana	5.7	24,882	12.0	37.8	34.9	15.2
18085	Kosciusko County, Indiana	1.3	51,316	14.6	37.7	27.0	20.7
18087	LaGrange County, Indiana	1.8	21,662	37.0	33.1	20.1	9.8
18089	Lake County, Indiana	3.4	325,777	12.8	35.4	31.4	20.4
18091	LaPorte County, Indiana	3.4	77,149	13.4	39.2	30.2	17.2
18093	Lawrence County, Indiana	6.1	32,002	12.7	42.9	30.6	13.8
18095	Madison County, Indiana	4.7	89,672	12.7	39.1	30.6	17.5
18097	Marion County, Indiana	4.2	603,299	15.0	28.5	28.3	28.3
18099	Marshall County, Indiana	2.0	30,883	15.5	40.5	25.8	18.3
18101	Martin County, Indiana	12.1	7,131	17.0	43.1	27.8	12.1
18103	Miami County, Indiana	7.2	24,915	15.3	42.7	30.1	11.9
18105	Monroe County, Indiana	3.9	79,416	7.6	22.3	25.1	45.0
18107	Montgomery County, Indiana	3.4	25,465	11.6	44.2	28.2	16.0
18109	Morgan County, Indiana	3.7	47,126	11.7	41.6	31.0	15.7
18111	Newton County, Indiana	3.8	9,843	14.0	49.5	26.8	9.7
18113	Noble County, Indiana	2.3	31,266	15.7	41.1	28.9	14.3
18115	Ohio County, Indiana	6.2	4,397	12.6	49.4	25.0	12.9
18117	Orange County, Indiana	2.7	13,437	17.0	46.5	25.1	11.4
18119	Owen County, Indiana	3.2	14,932	16.7	43.7	29.1	10.5
18121	Parke County, Indiana	6.6	12,066	14.6	40.5	31.4	13.5
18123	Perry County, Indiana	5.0	13,657	14.3	51.2	23.1	11.5
18125	Pike County, Indiana	3.1	8,977	13.7	46.7	28.0	11.6
18127	Porter County, Indiana	2.8	112,289	8.1	35.2	30.4	26.4
18129	Posey County, Indiana	2.7	17,633	6.6	39.5	33.3	20.6
18131	Pulaski County, Indiana	3.4	9,031	13.9	46.2	28.6	11.4
18133	Putnam County, Indiana	5.5	24,705	12.1	42.8	29.9	15.2
18135	Randolph County, Indiana	3.0	17,583	14.5	44.0	29.1	12.3
18137	Ripley County, Indiana	3.2	19,321	12.8	44.9	25.9	16.4
18139	Rush County, Indiana	3.8	11,670	14.2	47.4	23.5	14.9
18141	St. Joseph County, Indiana	2.8	172,854	12.0	31.2	28.9	27.9
18143	Scott County, Indiana	4.1	16,254	17.0	42.6	28.2	12.2
18145	Shelby County, Indiana	3.3	30,456	12.8	44.1	28.3	14.8
18147	Spencer County, Indiana	2.3	14,471	11.0	43.6	30.4	15.0
18149	Starke County, Indiana	3.2	15,800	17.7	42.3	28.3	11.6
18151	Steuben County, Indiana	3.3	23,141	10.4	38.1	31.5	20.0
18153	Sullivan County, Indiana	6.9	15,024	14.3	42.1	30.4	13.2
18155	Switzerland County, Indiana	7.4	7,055	15.7	46.6	28.7	9.1
18157	Tippecanoe County, Indiana	2.3	99,327	9.7	26.6	28.5	35.2
18159	Tipton County, Indiana	6.1	10,981	11.6	40.5	28.5	19.4
18161	Union County, Indiana	4.2	4,963	12.0	42.6	26.8	18.6
18163	Vanderburgh County, Indiana	2.8	121,733	10.1	34.5	31.3	24.2
18165	Vermillion County, Indiana	3.3	11,097	11.1	43.9	31.5	13.5
18167	Vigo County, Indiana	3.6	69,381	12.6	33.6	31.3	22.5
18169	Wabash County, Indiana	3.0	22,061	11.9	42.5	26.9	18.8
18171	Warren County, Indiana	2.3	5,933	11.2	43.8	26.3	18.6
18173	Warrick County, Indiana	2.4	41,492	6.8	33.8	32.3	27.0
18175	Washington County, Indiana	3.0	18,908	15.9	45.9	25.8	12.4
18177	Wayne County, Indiana	2.9	46,353	16.0	38.6	28.0	17.4
18179	Wells County, Indiana	2.8	18,746	9.3	41.8	31.3	17.6
18181	White County, Indiana	4.3	16,792	10.5	44.3	29.7	15.5
18183	Whitley County, Indiana	2.5	22,818	9.2	42.3	30.1	18.4
19000	**Iowa**	3.2	2,049,344	8.5	32.2	32.6	26.7
19001	Adair County, Iowa	4.1	5,337	7.5	44.7	32.5	15.3

Table C. County—Labor Force, Employment, and Educational Data, 2011–2015—*Continued*

		Industry for employed population age 16 and older	Educational attainment for the population age 25 and older				
				Educational attainment			
Fips code	State/county	Public administration	Total population age 25 and older	Less than high school graduate	High school graduate (includes equivalency)	Some college or Associate's degree	Bachelor's degree or higher
19003	Adams County, Iowa	3.6	2,808	7.4	39.1	38.5	15.1
19005	Allamakee County, Iowa	3.3	9,928	11.6	42.1	30.1	16.3
19007	Appanoose County, Iowa	3.6	9,004	11.4	36.3	34.7	17.6
19009	Audubon County, Iowa	3.4	4,251	10.0	42.3	33.4	14.3
19011	Benton County, Iowa	3.2	17,470	7.3	36.4	34.7	21.6
19013	Black Hawk County, Iowa	1.9	83,037	9.5	32.7	30.7	27.0
19015	Boone County, Iowa	4.0	18,317	6.1	34.8	35.9	23.2
19017	Bremer County, Iowa	1.9	16,111	5.3	33.4	32.7	28.6
19019	Buchanan County, Iowa	3.9	13,944	7.7	42.9	32.6	16.8
19021	Buena Vista County, Iowa	1.7	12,946	21.1	31.0	29.0	18.9
19023	Butler County, Iowa	2.1	10,460	7.8	40.8	36.3	15.2
19025	Calhoun County, Iowa	4.9	7,100	7.6	37.0	37.0	18.4
19027	Carroll County, Iowa	2.0	14,105	7.7	40.6	31.7	20.1
19029	Cass County, Iowa	2.0	9,602	8.2	44.3	27.7	19.9
19031	Cedar County, Iowa	3.7	12,837	7.4	37.0	34.1	21.5
19033	Cerro Gordo County, Iowa	2.5	30,861	6.4	31.8	39.7	22.2
19035	Cherokee County, Iowa	3.4	8,494	9.4	35.6	36.2	18.8
19037	Chickasaw County, Iowa	3.8	8,414	10.3	43.2	31.5	15.0
19039	Clarke County, Iowa	2.0	6,172	11.4	44.6	30.2	13.9
19041	Clay County, Iowa	1.5	11,541	6.7	36.9	37.1	19.3
19043	Clayton County, Iowa	2.5	12,560	8.1	44.5	30.5	16.8
19045	Clinton County, Iowa	3.0	33,322	8.5	36.3	35.6	19.6
19047	Crawford County, Iowa	1.6	11,236	22.5	35.8	28.2	13.5
19049	Dallas County, Iowa	3.5	48,854	5.1	21.1	29.6	44.2
19051	Davis County, Iowa	1.5	5,548	14.2	37.4	31.6	16.8
19053	Decatur County, Iowa	2.4	5,043	12.9	38.6	28.7	19.8
19055	Delaware County, Iowa	1.7	11,950	10.1	44.1	31.0	14.8
19057	Des Moines County, Iowa	3.1	27,964	8.6	35.6	35.8	20.0
19059	Dickinson County, Iowa	3.4	12,647	5.2	29.6	37.8	27.4
19061	Dubuque County, Iowa	2.4	63,714	7.9	35.4	28.0	28.7
19063	Emmet County, Iowa	2.9	6,690	10.6	34.6	38.5	16.2
19065	Fayette County, Iowa	2.5	14,015	10.5	39.5	31.5	18.5
19067	Floyd County, Iowa	2.6	11,118	12.0	35.5	34.3	18.2
19069	Franklin County, Iowa	2.1	7,337	11.9	38.1	33.4	16.7
19071	Fremont County, Iowa	5.3	5,059	7.7	36.4	34.3	21.5
19073	Greene County, Iowa	4.0	6,412	8.4	35.7	37.3	18.6
19075	Grundy County, Iowa	2.3	8,577	5.2	35.3	36.8	22.7
19077	Guthrie County, Iowa	2.6	7,650	8.0	39.3	33.5	19.2
19079	Hamilton County, Iowa	3.2	10,717	9.0	33.2	37.9	19.9
19081	Hancock County, Iowa	2.7	7,853	7.9	36.4	37.6	18.1
19083	Hardin County, Iowa	3.5	12,240	9.2	34.9	37.6	18.2
19085	Harrison County, Iowa	2.9	10,082	9.2	38.1	35.4	17.4
19087	Henry County, Iowa	4.4	13,736	8.2	37.3	35.7	18.8
19089	Howard County, Iowa	2.3	6,449	11.5	44.0	31.7	12.8
19091	Humboldt County, Iowa	3.3	6,753	8.0	37.1	37.2	17.6
19093	Ida County, Iowa	2.5	4,989	8.3	40.1	32.2	19.3
19095	Iowa County, Iowa	2.0	11,368	7.2	38.4	33.7	20.7
19097	Jackson County, Iowa	2.6	13,757	9.3	44.8	30.6	15.3
19099	Jasper County, Iowa	4.4	25,768	7.7	39.7	34.5	18.2
19101	Jefferson County, Iowa	4.1	12,167	5.7	30.4	32.0	31.9
19103	Johnson County, Iowa	2.3	81,699	5.2	17.1	26.4	51.3
19105	Jones County, Iowa	4.2	14,574	7.9	39.6	35.9	16.6
19107	Keokuk County, Iowa	3.3	7,188	9.5	42.8	32.2	15.5
19109	Kossuth County, Iowa	2.2	10,829	6.1	38.0	36.8	19.1
19111	Lee County, Iowa	5.3	24,860	8.5	41.7	34.3	15.5
19113	Linn County, Iowa	2.4	143,440	5.6	27.2	35.8	31.5
19115	Louisa County, Iowa	2.9	7,667	17.6	37.3	31.9	13.2
19117	Lucas County, Iowa	3.8	6,105	9.2	44.9	30.9	14.9
19119	Lyon County, Iowa	3.3	7,611	9.6	37.1	32.6	20.8
19121	Madison County, Iowa	3.1	10,580	6.0	38.9	33.4	21.7
19123	Mahaska County, Iowa	1.6	14,974	8.5	37.6	31.1	22.7
19125	Marion County, Iowa	2.5	21,599	8.0	35.7	31.5	24.8
19127	Marshall County, Iowa	2.9	27,259	16.5	32.9	31.0	19.7
19129	Mills County, Iowa	6.1	10,187	6.9	35.9	33.3	23.8
19131	Mitchell County, Iowa	2.7	7,331	9.1	44.2	31.8	14.9
19133	Monona County, Iowa	2.8	6,632	8.5	43.3	33.8	14.5
19135	Monroe County, Iowa	4.4	5,387	11.0	44.8	27.0	17.2
19137	Montgomery County, Iowa	2.0	7,388	11.6	37.6	35.8	14.9
19139	Muscatine County, Iowa	1.9	28,364	13.8	35.0	32.4	18.8
19141	O'Brien County, Iowa	2.9	9,823	7.9	37.7	35.6	18.8
19143	Osceola County, Iowa	2.7	4,378	14.2	37.6	30.8	17.4
19145	Page County, Iowa	3.9	11,109	11.7	34.7	33.5	20.0
19147	Palo Alto County, Iowa	6.0	6,349	7.2	30.9	41.9	20.0
19149	Plymouth County, Iowa	3.5	16,883	7.9	35.6	36.0	20.5
19151	Pocahontas County, Iowa	2.7	5,051	7.3	38.9	36.3	17.4

Table C. County—Labor Force, Employment, and Educational Data, 2011–2015—*Continued*

| | | Industry for employed population age 16 and older | Educational attainment for the population age 25 and older | | | | |
| | | | | Educational attainment | | | |
Fips code	State/county	Public administration	Total population age 25 and older	Less than high school graduate	High school graduate (includes equivalency)	Some college or Associate's degree	Bachelor's degree or higher
19153	Polk County, Iowa	4.0	297,135	8.2	25.3	30.7	35.8
19155	Pottawattamie County, Iowa	3.5	62,552	10.8	34.9	34.1	20.2
19157	Poweshiek County, Iowa	1.9	12,124	7.1	36.8	31.5	24.6
19159	Ringgold County, Iowa	2.5	3,538	10.2	35.5	33.6	20.8
19161	Sac County, Iowa	4.0	7,171	8.1	39.3	32.9	19.7
19163	Scott County, Iowa	4.4	114,193	7.4	28.3	32.2	32.1
19165	Shelby County, Iowa	2.4	8,481	8.3	36.8	33.6	21.3
19167	Sioux County, Iowa	2.1	20,488	10.8	31.9	31.8	25.5
19169	Story County, Iowa	4.2	48,099	4.1	18.8	28.8	48.3
19171	Tama County, Iowa	4.0	11,965	9.1	41.0	34.2	15.7
19173	Taylor County, Iowa	4.6	4,385	8.7	42.0	34.8	14.5
19175	Union County, Iowa	2.2	8,503	7.3	40.0	38.0	14.7
19177	Van Buren County, Iowa	2.5	5,210	11.0	43.5	32.8	12.7
19179	Wapello County, Iowa	2.5	24,039	13.8	36.7	32.8	16.8
19181	Warren County, Iowa	4.8	30,916	4.5	32.6	34.8	28.2
19183	Washington County, Iowa	2.4	15,007	9.7	35.8	33.6	20.9
19185	Wayne County, Iowa	3.4	4,388	10.4	43.5	32.1	13.9
19187	Webster County, Iowa	4.0	25,141	9.8	32.5	39.0	18.8
19189	Winnebago County, Iowa	1.5	7,390	7.8	35.1	36.5	20.6
19191	Winneshiek County, Iowa	1.6	13,571	5.9	35.1	31.3	27.7
19193	Woodbury County, Iowa	3.6	65,099	14.4	34.2	30.2	21.1
19195	Worth County, Iowa	3.3	5,358	7.4	36.6	40.5	15.4
19197	Wright County, Iowa	3.5	9,010	10.1	37.5	35.4	17.0
20000	**Kansas**	4.6	1,869,698	9.8	27.0	32.1	31.0
20001	Allen County, Kansas	3.5	8,825	9.4	33.4	39.0	18.2
20003	Anderson County, Kansas	3.6	5,364	9.4	39.1	35.1	16.5
20005	Atchison County, Kansas	4.5	10,150	7.2	41.0	31.9	19.9
20007	Barber County, Kansas	3.2	3,362	8.4	36.6	34.8	20.2
20009	Barton County, Kansas	4.7	18,207	13.9	33.9	35.3	16.9
20011	Bourbon County, Kansas	4.6	9,569	10.6	31.2	36.1	22.1
20013	Brown County, Kansas	5.9	6,694	7.3	39.8	33.1	19.8
20015	Butler County, Kansas	5.4	42,787	7.1	26.8	38.2	28.0
20017	Chase County, Kansas	7.8	1,930	9.8	33.5	32.3	24.3
20019	Chautauqua County, Kansas	4.8	2,548	13.9	36.1	32.4	17.5
20021	Cherokee County, Kansas	4.6	14,336	13.0	34.6	35.0	17.4
20023	Cheyenne County, Kansas	5.5	1,947	7.1	31.5	39.0	22.3
20025	Clark County, Kansas	8.9	1,492	8.1	26.1	36.1	29.7
20027	Clay County, Kansas	3.6	5,854	3.7	33.7	38.9	23.7
20029	Cloud County, Kansas	4.4	6,354	8.9	34.2	39.4	17.5
20031	Coffey County, Kansas	6.2	5,948	7.2	36.8	35.0	21.0
20033	Comanche County, Kansas	3.5	1,393	8.3	28.4	39.3	24.0
20035	Cowley County, Kansas	3.9	23,444	9.8	30.5	40.5	19.2
20037	Crawford County, Kansas	3.1	23,597	10.0	28.2	33.2	28.6
20039	Decatur County, Kansas	7.0	2,195	9.5	37.6	26.3	26.6
20041	Dickinson County, Kansas	5.5	13,394	10.5	36.0	33.4	20.0
20043	Doniphan County, Kansas	4.7	5,133	9.9	38.7	34.9	16.5
20045	Douglas County, Kansas	4.1	64,749	5.1	20.0	25.8	49.1
20047	Edwards County, Kansas	5.9	2,100	17.7	30.7	32.9	18.7
20049	Elk County, Kansas	6.1	2,016	11.0	35.3	36.3	17.4
20051	Ellis County, Kansas	4.0	17,534	6.6	27.7	33.3	32.3
20053	Ellsworth County, Kansas	8.7	4,683	10.4	32.2	36.2	21.2
20055	Finney County, Kansas	5.0	21,536	28.1	23.1	30.3	18.6
20057	Ford County, Kansas	3.2	20,386	30.6	23.0	28.4	17.9
20059	Franklin County, Kansas	4.4	16,992	7.5	36.1	35.2	21.2
20061	Geary County, Kansas	18.2	19,707	7.6	29.8	42.3	20.4
20063	Gove County, Kansas	2.7	1,978	6.9	37.7	33.9	21.4
20065	Graham County, Kansas	5.1	1,917	6.7	32.7	34.1	26.5
20067	Grant County, Kansas	6.3	4,755	28.4	28.9	24.5	18.2
20069	Gray County, Kansas	3.9	3,778	23.8	25.6	31.5	19.1
20071	Greeley County, Kansas	7.9	894	11.9	30.3	32.3	25.5
20073	Greenwood County, Kansas	7.0	4,596	10.1	40.1	33.2	16.5
20075	Hamilton County, Kansas	5.1	1,710	20.2	34.8	31.6	13.3
20077	Harper County, Kansas	2.9	4,087	11.4	36.6	32.2	19.7
20079	Harvey County, Kansas	4.3	22,957	10.1	29.6	33.8	26.5
20081	Haskell County, Kansas	3.3	2,527	29.3	20.9	32.1	17.7
20083	Hodgeman County, Kansas	4.6	1,391	7.4	25.9	43.1	23.7
20085	Jackson County, Kansas	8.6	8,993	6.0	40.6	34.7	18.7
20087	Jefferson County, Kansas	8.4	13,141	7.2	40.7	32.6	19.5
20089	Jewell County, Kansas	5.7	2,282	6.7	39.4	38.6	15.4
20091	Johnson County, Kansas	3.2	378,407	4.2	15.2	27.8	52.8
20093	Kearny County, Kansas	3.4	2,508	22.4	23.4	37.0	17.2
20095	Kingman County, Kansas	3.7	5,480	9.6	34.8	35.1	20.5
20097	Kiowa County, Kansas	5.9	1,690	8.6	26.9	37.2	27.3
20099	Labette County, Kansas	3.7	14,201	11.3	33.1	36.1	19.5

Table C. County—Labor Force, Employment, and Educational Data, 2011–2015—*Continued*

Fips code	State/county	Industry for employed population age 16 and older Public administration	Total population age 25 and older	Educational attainment for the population age 25 and older Less than high school graduate	High school graduate (includes equivalency)	Some college or Associate's degree	Bachelor's degree or higher
20101	Lane County, Kansas	4.8	1,159	7.2	29.7	41.7	21.4
20103	Leavenworth County, Kansas	11.8	52,345	8.7	30.9	31.5	29.0
20105	Lincoln County, Kansas	6.5	2,251	5.9	32.3	41.5	20.3
20107	Linn County, Kansas	3.3	6,661	11.8	37.2	36.0	15.0
20109	Logan County, Kansas	8.1	1,944	7.7	35.5	38.6	18.2
20111	Lyon County, Kansas	3.3	19,821	12.1	33.4	28.9	25.6
20113	McPherson County, Kansas	2.8	19,905	9.1	29.1	34.4	27.4
20115	Marion County, Kansas	3.6	8,468	11.3	36.4	29.7	22.6
20117	Marshall County, Kansas	2.7	7,055	5.8	44.8	32.7	16.6
20119	Meade County, Kansas	5.7	2,865	14.3	31.1	32.4	22.2
20121	Miami County, Kansas	3.1	21,758	5.5	32.5	38.7	23.3
20123	Mitchell County, Kansas	4.0	4,323	5.0	34.0	35.3	25.7
20125	Montgomery County, Kansas	3.2	22,784	11.3	32.1	39.6	17.1
20127	Morris County, Kansas	5.4	4,186	11.3	35.7	35.5	17.6
20129	Morton County, Kansas	3.4	2,005	14.4	32.5	39.2	13.9
20131	Nemaha County, Kansas	3.8	6,792	9.4	41.9	26.0	22.6
20133	Neosho County, Kansas	5.4	10,886	8.3	33.6	39.5	18.6
20135	Ness County, Kansas	4.8	2,285	9.0	35.9	35.3	19.8
20137	Norton County, Kansas	7.8	4,097	13.7	34.6	34.3	17.4
20139	Osage County, Kansas	6.8	11,069	9.2	40.5	30.8	19.5
20141	Osborne County, Kansas	7.5	2,743	9.8	36.3	33.4	20.6
20143	Ottawa County, Kansas	2.4	4,158	6.9	32.9	38.8	21.4
20145	Pawnee County, Kansas	5.5	4,981	10.9	28.0	39.3	21.7
20147	Phillips County, Kansas	4.0	3,812	7.8	35.3	35.3	21.6
20149	Pottawatomie County, Kansas	4.8	14,178	4.3	31.2	32.3	32.2
20151	Pratt County, Kansas	4.2	6,383	10.3	26.5	37.3	25.9
20153	Rawlins County, Kansas	3.4	1,913	7.9	30.8	36.2	25.0
20155	Reno County, Kansas	5.3	43,341	11.9	28.6	39.3	20.2
20157	Republic County, Kansas	4.8	3,607	7.2	35.1	37.7	20.0
20159	Rice County, Kansas	4.4	6,401	12.0	30.5	36.3	21.2
20161	Riley County, Kansas	5.9	36,876	4.9	17.4	32.7	44.9
20163	Rooks County, Kansas	5.0	3,651	8.1	36.8	33.1	22.0
20165	Rush County, Kansas	4.2	2,350	9.6	33.0	35.7	21.7
20167	Russell County, Kansas	3.0	4,989	10.3	32.8	32.9	24.0
20169	Saline County, Kansas	3.1	36,610	10.2	33.5	32.9	23.4
20171	Scott County, Kansas	4.5	3,440	15.1	33.4	31.0	20.5
20173	Sedgwick County, Kansas	3.2	323,131	11.0	26.8	32.7	29.4
20175	Seward County, Kansas	4.1	13,258	36.0	24.8	27.3	11.8
20177	Shawnee County, Kansas	9.0	119,669	9.2	31.1	30.8	29.0
20179	Sheridan County, Kansas	4.2	1,804	8.4	33.8	36.1	21.6
20181	Sherman County, Kansas	4.7	4,113	10.7	33.3	41.9	14.1
20183	Smith County, Kansas	4.5	2,745	9.3	35.3	37.3	18.1
20185	Stafford County, Kansas	5.8	3,005	12.5	28.7	36.9	21.8
20187	Stanton County, Kansas	3.7	1,332	17.3	27.4	33.1	22.2
20189	Stevens County, Kansas	0.8	3,616	17.2	35.6	31.8	15.4
20191	Sumner County, Kansas	5.0	15,769	8.0	35.9	36.2	19.9
20193	Thomas County, Kansas	4.3	5,001	6.9	28.9	36.0	28.3
20195	Trego County, Kansas	2.8	2,122	6.0	33.2	35.8	25.0
20197	Wabaunsee County, Kansas	7.3	4,795	5.0	38.9	33.2	23.0
20199	Wallace County, Kansas	4.5	1,075	8.5	32.9	33.4	25.2
20201	Washington County, Kansas	4.3	4,032	9.9	38.0	35.1	17.0
20203	Wichita County, Kansas	2.7	1,397	22.2	29.6	32.1	16.1
20205	Wilson County, Kansas	3.0	6,271	14.4	36.8	34.2	14.7
20207	Woodson County, Kansas	8.2	2,347	9.8	38.8	35.4	16.0
20209	Wyandotte County, Kansas	4.8	100,606	21.4	32.9	29.8	15.9
21000	**Kentucky**	4.5	2,955,216	15.8	33.6	28.2	22.3
21001	Adair County, Kentucky	4.0	12,634	25.0	36.3	22.8	15.9
21003	Allen County, Kentucky	2.8	13,724	22.5	36.0	28.0	13.6
21005	Anderson County, Kentucky	14.5	14,725	11.9	38.8	30.4	18.9
21007	Ballard County, Kentucky	3.4	5,804	15.0	39.4	32.0	13.6
21009	Barren County, Kentucky	3.4	29,283	18.8	41.5	24.1	15.6
21011	Bath County, Kentucky	6.1	8,037	24.4	39.2	24.3	12.2
21013	Bell County, Kentucky	5.0	19,492	33.8	35.6	20.8	9.8
21015	Boone County, Kentucky	4.3	80,765	8.0	28.1	33.1	30.8
21017	Bourbon County, Kentucky	4.7	13,852	17.1	36.7	30.2	16.0
21019	Boyd County, Kentucky	4.3	34,832	11.5	35.9	34.9	17.7
21021	Boyle County, Kentucky	4.5	19,713	14.3	35.0	28.0	22.7
21023	Bracken County, Kentucky	3.0	5,674	17.0	43.4	25.5	14.0
21025	Breathitt County, Kentucky	10.5	9,452	31.1	34.3	23.3	11.2
21027	Breckinridge County, Kentucky	2.9	13,832	21.8	44.0	24.6	9.5
21029	Bullitt County, Kentucky	3.2	52,336	13.7	40.8	31.2	14.3
21031	Butler County, Kentucky	4.0	8,952	24.9	43.3	23.1	8.7
21033	Caldwell County, Kentucky	5.3	9,003	13.2	44.9	25.6	16.4
21035	Calloway County, Kentucky	3.2	23,019	12.6	31.6	28.3	27.5
21037	Campbell County, Kentucky	4.0	61,352	10.7	31.0	29.2	29.1

Table C. County—Labor Force, Employment, and Educational Data, 2011–2015—*Continued*

		Industry for employed population age 16 and older	Educational attainment for the population age 25 and older				
				Educational attainment			
Fips code	State/county	Public administration	Total population age 25 and older	Less than high school graduate	High school graduate (includes equivalency)	Some college or Associate's degree	Bachelor's degree or higher
21039	Carlisle County, Kentucky	5.9	3,535	17.9	38.2	30.6	13.3
21041	Carroll County, Kentucky	3.4	7,087	21.9	44.0	22.9	11.2
21043	Carter County, Kentucky	4.3	18,393	20.2	41.4	25.6	12.8
21045	Casey County, Kentucky	5.2	11,050	27.3	37.4	24.0	11.2
21047	Christian County, Kentucky	7.9	42,158	14.7	32.7	36.0	16.6
21049	Clark County, Kentucky	5.0	24,835	16.0	35.2	28.1	20.7
21051	Clay County, Kentucky	7.5	14,919	36.3	36.9	17.2	9.6
21053	Clinton County, Kentucky	5.6	6,967	30.4	36.2	23.8	9.6
21055	Crittenden County, Kentucky	4.9	6,476	20.1	37.9	30.7	11.4
21057	Cumberland County, Kentucky	5.1	4,782	22.9	39.1	24.6	13.4
21059	Daviess County, Kentucky	3.5	66,181	12.1	37.8	29.9	20.3
21061	Edmonson County, Kentucky	1.4	8,526	21.2	42.1	23.4	13.3
21063	Elliott County, Kentucky	8.4	5,655	25.2	42.0	25.3	7.5
21065	Estill County, Kentucky	4.4	10,210	25.7	48.6	17.9	7.8
21067	Fayette County, Kentucky	3.6	199,042	10.2	20.6	28.0	41.2
21069	Fleming County, Kentucky	3.7	9,818	21.6	38.9	26.6	12.8
21071	Floyd County, Kentucky	5.2	26,910	24.9	34.7	27.6	12.8
21073	Franklin County, Kentucky	21.2	34,510	13.2	31.8	28.0	27.0
21075	Fulton County, Kentucky	4.9	4,498	24.6	34.8	27.5	13.1
21077	Gallatin County, Kentucky	4.4	5,613	17.9	44.2	27.8	10.1
21079	Garrard County, Kentucky	4.2	11,950	20.4	38.8	25.7	15.1
21081	Grant County, Kentucky	5.7	15,714	17.4	44.8	25.3	12.4
21083	Graves County, Kentucky	3.8	25,384	17.5	36.7	28.5	17.3
21085	Grayson County, Kentucky	4.7	17,540	22.9	42.2	25.8	9.1
21087	Green County, Kentucky	5.0	7,915	21.6	46.0	22.2	10.2
21089	Greenup County, Kentucky	4.4	25,779	14.2	37.4	31.5	16.9
21091	Hancock County, Kentucky	2.6	5,795	11.8	46.8	30.2	11.2
21093	Hardin County, Kentucky	9.1	69,451	10.9	32.1	33.8	23.2
21095	Harlan County, Kentucky	5.5	19,523	28.3	35.6	24.4	11.7
21097	Harrison County, Kentucky	3.7	12,810	18.6	42.5	24.9	14.0
21099	Hart County, Kentucky	4.3	12,444	27.2	41.3	21.1	10.3
21101	Henderson County, Kentucky	4.0	32,024	14.0	36.6	32.6	16.8
21103	Henry County, Kentucky	7.2	10,549	18.8	44.6	25.5	11.2
21105	Hickman County, Kentucky	2.9	3,399	19.2	41.2	30.4	9.2
21107	Hopkins County, Kentucky	5.1	32,279	15.5	39.5	29.7	15.3
21109	Jackson County, Kentucky	5.0	9,241	27.9	43.4	19.0	9.7
21111	Jefferson County, Kentucky	3.2	515,934	11.1	27.5	29.9	31.5
21113	Jessamine County, Kentucky	2.8	32,484	14.9	28.9	27.3	29.0
21115	Johnson County, Kentucky	8.5	16,189	22.9	37.3	29.0	10.8
21117	Kenton County, Kentucky	4.4	109,078	10.8	29.4	30.9	28.9
21119	Knott County, Kentucky	6.1	10,934	29.5	35.1	23.2	12.3
21121	Knox County, Kentucky	3.5	21,295	29.7	40.7	18.6	11.0
21123	Larue County, Kentucky	3.6	9,816	17.1	43.1	29.6	10.3
21125	Laurel County, Kentucky	4.3	40,652	23.9	37.9	26.0	12.3
21127	Lawrence County, Kentucky	5.9	10,897	22.6	41.5	24.1	11.9
21129	Lee County, Kentucky	10.6	5,136	28.6	42.5	21.0	7.9
21131	Leslie County, Kentucky	3.8	7,724	34.9	33.8	22.7	8.6
21133	Letcher County, Kentucky	4.5	16,744	26.5	36.1	25.6	11.8
21135	Lewis County, Kentucky	3.3	9,505	26.4	42.2	20.6	10.9
21137	Lincoln County, Kentucky	3.7	16,790	22.0	44.5	22.9	10.6
21139	Livingston County, Kentucky	3.0	6,813	17.0	46.9	25.7	10.4
21141	Logan County, Kentucky	3.5	18,250	21.7	40.3	24.8	13.2
21143	Lyon County, Kentucky	8.9	6,629	12.4	39.0	30.8	17.8
21145	McCracken County, Kentucky	3.5	46,038	12.1	31.3	33.6	23.0
21147	McCreary County, Kentucky	3.9	12,275	27.6	40.5	24.9	7.0
21149	McLean County, Kentucky	3.9	6,575	18.3	39.9	30.8	10.9
21151	Madison County, Kentucky	6.0	52,635	14.1	29.5	27.8	28.6
21153	Magoffin County, Kentucky	4.3	8,912	31.0	37.8	22.6	8.5
21155	Marion County, Kentucky	4.2	13,406	18.4	44.8	23.4	13.4
21157	Marshall County, Kentucky	3.4	22,617	13.9	41.0	29.3	15.8
21159	Martin County, Kentucky	5.9	8,765	28.1	39.5	25.8	6.5
21161	Mason County, Kentucky	3.5	11,688	16.8	38.3	28.9	16.0
21163	Meade County, Kentucky	7.5	19,206	13.5	39.8	31.8	14.8
21165	Menifee County, Kentucky	9.3	4,504	26.1	39.1	24.1	10.7
21167	Mercer County, Kentucky	5.2	14,954	15.4	38.8	27.0	18.8
21169	Metcalfe County, Kentucky	5.2	6,954	24.2	40.9	23.3	11.6
21171	Monroe County, Kentucky	4.5	7,487	25.2	41.8	18.8	14.1
21173	Montgomery County, Kentucky	5.1	18,436	17.6	39.1	26.2	17.1
21175	Morgan County, Kentucky	12.7	9,810	27.3	36.2	24.6	11.8
21177	Muhlenberg County, Kentucky	4.3	21,777	22.4	42.1	25.1	10.4
21179	Nelson County, Kentucky	4.1	29,502	12.8	42.0	29.0	16.2
21181	Nicholas County, Kentucky	5.1	4,886	20.8	40.7	27.4	11.2
21183	Ohio County, Kentucky	3.0	16,270	21.7	42.8	25.8	9.7

Table C. County—Labor Force, Employment, and Educational Data, 2011–2015—*Continued*

Fips code	State/county	Industry for employed population age 16 and older	Educational attainment for the population age 25 and older				
				Educational attainment			
		Public administration	Total population age 25 and older	Less than high school graduate	High school graduate (includes equivalency)	Some college or Associate's degree	Bachelor's degree or higher
21185	Oldham County, Kentucky	3.6	41,887	7.8	23.0	29.8	39.4
21187	Owen County, Kentucky	7.2	7,338	16.1	47.0	24.7	12.2
21189	Owsley County, Kentucky	15.5	3,268	32.0	34.6	16.8	16.6
21191	Pendleton County, Kentucky	3.9	9,872	16.1	47.9	25.2	10.8
21193	Perry County, Kentucky	5.1	19,537	26.9	32.2	26.9	14.0
21195	Pike County, Kentucky	4.3	44,383	26.5	36.4	23.8	13.3
21197	Powell County, Kentucky	5.2	8,390	25.9	40.7	20.4	13.0
21199	Pulaski County, Kentucky	4.6	44,353	19.0	41.2	25.3	14.4
21201	Robertson County, Kentucky	6.6	1,572	25.4	36.1	22.5	16.0
21203	Rockcastle County, Kentucky	5.5	11,820	24.1	43.2	22.9	9.8
21205	Rowan County, Kentucky	6.0	13,617	18.0	31.0	24.1	26.9
21207	Russell County, Kentucky	5.5	12,374	25.2	36.6	25.8	12.4
21209	Scott County, Kentucky	4.6	32,276	10.9	30.7	30.6	27.8
21211	Shelby County, Kentucky	6.1	29,906	13.8	31.8	30.6	23.8
21213	Simpson County, Kentucky	4.0	12,019	15.5	42.6	26.8	15.1
21215	Spencer County, Kentucky	2.5	12,021	12.2	35.6	33.8	18.5
21217	Taylor County, Kentucky	4.1	16,378	17.5	40.6	26.2	15.8
21219	Todd County, Kentucky	5.4	8,120	22.6	41.9	24.7	10.8
21221	Trigg County, Kentucky	6.1	10,205	17.3	30.1	34.9	17.6
21223	Trimble County, Kentucky	3.0	6,021	15.9	47.2	26.6	10.3
21225	Union County, Kentucky	2.9	9,581	16.8	40.2	31.7	11.3
21227	Warren County, Kentucky	2.7	72,191	12.7	30.9	28.4	28.1
21229	Washington County, Kentucky	3.2	7,971	19.8	41.6	24.0	14.5
21231	Wayne County, Kentucky	4.5	14,539	28.9	37.0	24.1	10.0
21233	Webster County, Kentucky	3.5	9,150	21.4	42.3	27.2	9.2
21235	Whitley County, Kentucky	5.8	22,954	24.2	37.1	22.8	15.9
21237	Wolfe County, Kentucky	11.2	5,032	32.6	38.5	17.0	11.9
21239	Woodford County, Kentucky	6.5	17,431	10.9	28.9	27.3	32.9
22000	**Louisiana**	5.5	3,040,041	16.6	33.9	26.9	22.5
22001	Acadia Parish, Louisiana	3.4	39,781	26.2	39.2	24.1	10.5
22003	Allen Parish, Louisiana	11.1	17,767	20.6	44.0	23.7	11.6
22005	Ascension Parish, Louisiana	5.2	73,240	11.9	34.6	27.5	26.0
22007	Assumption Parish, Louisiana	5.0	15,450	27.3	39.5	22.5	10.7
22009	Avoyelles Parish, Louisiana	9.3	27,932	27.6	41.3	21.7	9.5
22011	Beauregard Parish, Louisiana	8.0	23,897	16.1	42.7	26.1	15.1
22013	Bienville Parish, Louisiana	6.4	9,598	18.0	42.7	28.1	11.2
22015	Bossier Parish, Louisiana	7.6	80,195	11.7	29.4	33.3	25.7
22017	Caddo Parish, Louisiana	4.2	168,163	14.1	32.9	29.2	23.8
22019	Calcasieu Parish, Louisiana	4.9	127,638	14.2	35.8	29.3	20.7
22021	Caldwell Parish, Louisiana	10.6	6,796	25.3	42.8	21.8	10.2
22023	Cameron Parish, Louisiana	7.1	4,527	17.1	38.5	28.5	15.8
22025	Catahoula Parish, Louisiana	10.1	6,971	25.1	42.2	20.3	12.3
22027	Claiborne Parish, Louisiana	9.2	11,794	23.8	40.7	22.7	12.8
22029	Concordia Parish, Louisiana	9.6	13,648	23.6	41.3	23.6	11.6
22031	De Soto Parish, Louisiana	4.6	18,149	19.5	41.2	27.3	12.1
22033	East Baton Rouge Parish, Louisiana	6.0	277,497	10.6	26.7	28.6	34.1
22035	East Carroll Parish, Louisiana	10.4	4,958	31.2	38.5	21.5	8.8
22037	East Feliciana Parish, Louisiana	10.6	14,215	18.1	43.5	26.1	12.3
22039	Evangeline Parish, Louisiana	4.1	21,642	30.6	34.6	22.2	12.6
22041	Franklin Parish, Louisiana	4.9	13,552	26.7	40.3	22.1	10.8
22043	Grant Parish, Louisiana	6.4	15,614	21.5	42.3	27.6	8.6
22045	Iberia Parish, Louisiana	3.4	47,432	22.5	42.1	22.4	13.0
22047	Iberville Parish, Louisiana	8.4	22,845	23.7	38.3	24.9	13.1
22049	Jackson Parish, Louisiana	7.6	11,186	21.0	41.9	24.1	13.0
22051	Jefferson Parish, Louisiana	5.0	301,812	15.5	31.1	28.8	24.6
22053	Jefferson Davis Parish, Louisiana	5.8	20,661	21.2	41.1	23.7	14.0
22055	Lafayette Parish, Louisiana	3.1	150,461	13.7	28.7	27.6	29.9
22057	Lafourche Parish, Louisiana	3.3	64,634	25.5	39.1	19.9	15.4
22059	LaSalle Parish, Louisiana	8.3	10,162	21.9	43.6	22.8	11.7
22061	Lincoln Parish, Louisiana	5.1	25,458	13.3	27.7	23.4	35.6
22063	Livingston Parish, Louisiana	6.3	86,802	15.8	40.2	25.7	18.3
22065	Madison Parish, Louisiana	10.5	7,834	24.3	39.6	24.7	11.4
22067	Morehouse Parish, Louisiana	4.7	18,048	20.9	43.5	22.9	12.7
22069	Natchitoches Parish, Louisiana	7.5	23,438	17.3	33.7	28.6	20.4
22071	Orleans Parish, Louisiana	5.1	258,654	14.8	23.2	26.7	35.3
22073	Ouachita Parish, Louisiana	5.0	98,946	15.6	32.9	27.5	24.0
22075	Plaquemines Parish, Louisiana	10.7	15,130	19.9	39.3	26.6	14.2
22077	Pointe Coupee Parish, Louisiana	4.9	15,472	19.6	41.7	25.4	13.4
22079	Rapides Parish, Louisiana	7.2	86,541	16.5	37.0	28.1	18.4
22081	Red River Parish, Louisiana	6.0	5,787	22.8	44.3	21.0	12.0
22083	Richland Parish, Louisiana	5.6	13,765	21.2	41.0	23.3	14.5
22085	Sabine Parish, Louisiana	5.0	16,352	17.6	42.0	26.3	14.1
22087	St. Bernard Parish, Louisiana	6.5	27,281	18.5	40.9	28.1	12.5
22089	St. Charles Parish, Louisiana	4.3	34,456	12.7	36.7	30.4	20.3
22091	St. Helena Parish, Louisiana	4.3	7,245	20.2	45.7	24.1	10.0

Table C. County—Labor Force, Employment, and Educational Data, 2011–2015—*Continued*

| | | Industry for employed population age 16 and older | Educational attainment for the population age 25 and older | | | | |
| | | | | | Educational attainment | | |
Fips code	State/county	Public administration	Total population age 25 and older	Less than high school graduate	High school graduate (includes equivalency)	Some college or Associate's degree	Bachelor's degree or higher
22093	St. James Parish, Louisiana	4.7	14,472	15.8	44.8	25.2	14.2
22095	St. John the Baptist Parish, Louisiana	3.4	28,691	17.3	37.5	28.6	16.5
22097	St. Landry Parish, Louisiana	5.2	53,773	23.9	44.5	18.9	12.8
22099	St. Martin Parish, Louisiana	5.3	34,994	21.6	42.1	23.0	13.2
22101	St. Mary Parish, Louisiana	5.0	35,290	24.8	43.4	20.7	11.1
22103	St. Tammany Parish, Louisiana	5.7	163,931	11.5	27.0	30.9	30.6
22105	Tangipahoa Parish, Louisiana	5.3	79,747	18.3	35.6	26.8	19.3
22107	Tensas Parish, Louisiana	8.6	3,335	20.6	45.6	23.5	10.3
22109	Terrebonne Parish, Louisiana	3.6	72,821	22.9	40.0	23.5	13.7
22111	Union Parish, Louisiana	4.6	15,479	16.4	44.9	27.0	11.7
22113	Vermilion Parish, Louisiana	5.0	38,457	23.8	41.0	22.9	12.4
22115	Vernon Parish, Louisiana	18.0	31,158	12.5	35.8	32.5	19.2
22117	Washington Parish, Louisiana	6.5	31,352	23.1	40.5	24.0	12.3
22119	Webster Parish, Louisiana	5.7	27,732	19.8	40.5	25.7	14.0
22121	West Baton Rouge Parish, Louisiana	7.6	16,332	15.1	39.2	26.0	19.7
22123	West Carroll Parish, Louisiana	6.3	7,758	25.0	44.0	19.9	11.1
22125	West Feliciana Parish, Louisiana	16.7	11,012	21.4	33.7	23.2	21.6
22127	Winn Parish, Louisiana	9.5	10,281	21.6	42.0	23.9	12.5
23000	**Maine**	4.4	952,777	8.4	33.2	29.4	29.0
23001	Androscoggin County, Maine	3.7	74,022	11.4	37.2	31.1	20.3
23003	Aroostook County, Maine	5.5	51,150	13.4	39.0	30.4	17.2
23005	Cumberland County, Maine	2.7	203,465	5.6	24.1	27.4	43.0
23007	Franklin County, Maine	3.2	21,445	7.8	36.9	29.7	25.6
23009	Hancock County, Maine	3.0	40,814	6.3	33.1	27.9	32.7
23011	Kennebec County, Maine	9.3	86,458	8.5	35.6	30.8	25.0
23013	Knox County, Maine	3.9	29,762	7.0	34.8	27.0	31.2
23015	Lincoln County, Maine	4.5	25,951	7.3	32.1	29.4	31.2
23017	Oxford County, Maine	3.8	41,817	8.9	45.6	27.4	18.1
23019	Penobscot County, Maine	4.2	106,040	9.2	34.9	31.4	24.5
23021	Piscataquis County, Maine	4.5	13,068	11.4	40.5	30.7	17.4
23023	Sagadahoc County, Maine	5.2	25,706	6.4	31.6	29.8	32.2
23025	Somerset County, Maine	4.1	37,463	12.1	41.3	31.2	15.4
23027	Waldo County, Maine	4.8	28,240	7.8	34.0	27.8	30.3
23029	Washington County, Maine	7.2	23,579	12.3	38.3	29.3	20.1
23031	York County, Maine	4.3	143,797	7.7	31.6	30.1	30.5
24000	**Maryland**	11.1	4,018,459	10.6	25.5	25.9	37.9
24001	Allegany County, Maryland	8.8	51,103	11.7	42.0	29.0	17.4
24003	Anne Arundel County, Maryland	13.9	378,655	8.4	25.0	28.3	38.3
24005	Baltimore County, Maryland	8.0	564,976	9.4	27.2	26.8	36.6
24009	Calvert County, Maryland	15.6	60,190	6.7	31.5	32.6	29.1
24011	Caroline County, Maryland	6.6	21,961	17.2	40.7	26.6	15.5
24013	Carroll County, Maryland	8.5	113,973	7.9	30.6	28.4	33.1
24015	Cecil County, Maryland	7.7	68,433	12.1	37.8	28.1	22.0
24017	Charles County, Maryland	20.1	100,163	7.7	32.2	32.7	27.4
24019	Dorchester County, Maryland	7.9	23,096	15.0	38.3	26.4	20.2
24021	Frederick County, Maryland	9.2	161,783	7.6	25.2	28.2	39.1
24023	Garrett County, Maryland	5.7	21,284	11.6	42.2	27.1	19.0
24025	Harford County, Maryland	9.9	169,738	7.1	28.1	30.9	33.8
24027	Howard County, Maryland	11.9	204,318	4.8	14.2	20.3	60.6
24029	Kent County, Maryland	6.4	13,870	13.0	33.2	23.9	30.0
24031	Montgomery County, Maryland	11.2	698,595	8.8	14.0	19.3	57.9
24033	Prince George's County, Maryland	14.4	590,874	14.4	26.1	28.5	31.1
24035	Queen Anne's County, Maryland	9.4	33,916	8.6	29.9	26.5	34.9
24037	St. Mary's County, Maryland	17.4	71,445	9.4	30.6	29.5	30.6
24039	Somerset County, Maryland	9.9	16,907	19.5	43.2	22.5	14.8
24041	Talbot County, Maryland	4.5	28,173	11.5	27.9	26.7	33.9
24043	Washington County, Maryland	8.1	103,305	13.3	38.1	28.7	19.9
24045	Wicomico County, Maryland	6.6	63,138	12.1	31.9	27.5	28.5
24047	Worcester County, Maryland	7.3	38,407	10.8	31.6	27.4	30.2
24510	Baltimore city, Maryland	8.8	420,156	17.5	29.8	24.1	28.7
25000	**Massachusetts**	4.0	4,610,510	10.2	25.4	23.9	40.5
25001	Barnstable County, Massachusetts	4.8	164,458	4.9	24.9	30.1	40.1
25003	Berkshire County, Massachusetts	3.8	93,114	9.3	31.7	27.4	31.6
25005	Bristol County, Massachusetts	4.4	380,990	17.2	30.2	26.7	25.9
25007	Dukes County, Massachusetts	4.8	12,774	6.8	23.1	29.8	40.3
25009	Essex County, Massachusetts	3.7	523,024	10.7	26.2	25.6	37.5
25011	Franklin County, Massachusetts	4.2	52,268	7.8	27.1	29.8	35.2
25013	Hampden County, Massachusetts	4.8	310,367	15.2	30.8	28.3	25.8
25015	Hampshire County, Massachusetts	3.7	98,119	6.1	24.2	25.5	44.2
25017	Middlesex County, Massachusetts	3.5	1,083,024	7.6	21.1	19.3	52.0
25019	Nantucket County, Massachusetts	4.3	7,617	5.2	25.4	25.7	43.7
25021	Norfolk County, Massachusetts	3.8	478,767	6.1	21.0	22.2	50.6
25023	Plymouth County, Massachusetts	4.7	345,295	7.7	29.0	28.9	34.4

Table C. County—Labor Force, Employment, and Educational Data, 2011–2015—*Continued*

Fips code	State/county	Industry for employed population age 16 and older — Public administration	Total population age 25 and older	Less than high school graduate	High school graduate (includes equivalency)	Some college or Associate's degree	Bachelor's degree or higher
25025	Suffolk County, Massachusetts	4.2	511,404	15.7	23.6	19.0	41.7
25027	Worcester County, Massachusetts	3.8	549,289	10.2	28.9	26.5	34.4
26000	**Michigan**	3.6	6,652,665	10.4	29.9	32.8	26.9
26001	Alcona County, Michigan	7.3	8,594	11.5	39.9	34.4	14.3
26003	Alger County, Michigan	9.3	7,330	11.2	43.2	27.1	18.4
26005	Allegan County, Michigan	2.4	75,605	10.1	38.3	30.0	21.5
26007	Alpena County, Michigan	3.8	21,197	10.3	33.4	39.8	16.5
26009	Antrim County, Michigan	4.4	17,297	9.9	33.7	31.1	25.3
26011	Arenac County, Michigan	4.0	11,417	14.9	42.8	30.6	11.7
26013	Baraga County, Michigan	9.7	6,593	17.6	44.1	25.2	13.1
26015	Barry County, Michigan	3.1	40,874	8.7	36.6	35.5	19.2
26017	Bay County, Michigan	3.6	75,039	10.7	35.6	35.4	18.3
26019	Benzie County, Michigan	5.6	12,931	8.6	34.2	33.0	24.2
26021	Berrien County, Michigan	2.7	106,841	11.3	30.6	32.0	26.1
26023	Branch County, Michigan	4.5	29,832	12.0	40.8	33.7	13.5
26025	Calhoun County, Michigan	5.0	90,820	10.0	35.7	34.3	20.1
26027	Cass County, Michigan	2.8	36,366	11.9	36.2	35.0	16.9
26029	Charlevoix County, Michigan	3.2	18,916	7.8	31.8	32.5	27.9
26031	Cheboygan County, Michigan	5.1	19,200	10.9	39.4	31.6	18.1
26033	Chippewa County, Michigan	10.2	26,283	11.0	37.8	32.1	19.1
26035	Clare County, Michigan	4.2	22,184	15.8	39.3	33.2	11.6
26037	Clinton County, Michigan	9.2	51,430	6.8	27.9	35.6	29.7
26039	Crawford County, Michigan	8.9	10,349	12.5	35.4	34.9	17.2
26041	Delta County, Michigan	3.9	26,538	7.9	35.3	37.9	18.9
26043	Dickinson County, Michigan	3.1	18,835	6.9	39.9	30.9	22.4
26045	Eaton County, Michigan	9.8	74,682	6.3	29.7	39.2	24.7
26047	Emmet County, Michigan	2.7	23,485	6.3	26.2	34.2	33.2
26049	Genesee County, Michigan	3.4	278,937	10.7	32.8	37.1	19.3
26051	Gladwin County, Michigan	3.6	18,818	15.0	40.2	32.5	12.3
26053	Gogebic County, Michigan	7.4	12,033	7.6	38.4	35.7	18.3
26055	Grand Traverse County, Michigan	3.0	63,727	6.3	26.9	35.4	31.5
26057	Gratiot County, Michigan	6.2	28,340	11.1	41.1	33.8	14.1
26059	Hillsdale County, Michigan	3.4	31,182	13.2	40.2	31.0	15.5
26061	Houghton County, Michigan	3.3	21,481	7.9	33.8	27.2	31.1
26063	Huron County, Michigan	4.1	23,671	12.1	44.3	29.4	14.1
26065	Ingham County, Michigan	6.8	169,257	8.2	21.6	32.9	37.2
26067	Ionia County, Michigan	6.8	43,017	11.8	38.1	35.2	14.9
26069	Iosco County, Michigan	3.4	19,516	11.9	40.0	32.0	16.1
26071	Iron County, Michigan	5.6	8,980	8.8	45.0	27.0	19.3
26073	Isabella County, Michigan	3.4	36,821	8.9	31.8	32.0	27.3
26075	Jackson County, Michigan	4.9	109,316	10.2	34.8	35.0	20.0
26077	Kalamazoo County, Michigan	2.9	158,739	6.7	23.1	35.0	35.1
26079	Kalkaska County, Michigan	4.7	12,324	13.4	42.4	31.5	12.7
26081	Kent County, Michigan	2.2	401,985	10.5	25.5	30.8	33.3
26083	Keweenaw County, Michigan	8.3	1,724	7.6	32.6	37.0	22.8
26085	Lake County, Michigan	6.9	8,798	18.1	41.5	31.0	9.4
26087	Lapeer County, Michigan	2.3	61,029	9.2	37.1	36.2	17.5
26089	Leelanau County, Michigan	5.1	16,572	5.0	22.4	32.7	40.0
26091	Lenawee County, Michigan	3.7	67,319	10.2	36.7	33.8	19.2
26093	Livingston County, Michigan	2.9	126,354	4.9	25.6	35.9	33.6
26095	Luce County, Michigan	14.2	4,866	11.7	45.0	31.0	12.4
26097	Mackinac County, Michigan	9.2	8,412	11.6	36.5	33.5	18.3
26099	Macomb County, Michigan	3.9	592,575	11.1	30.6	35.0	23.3
26101	Manistee County, Michigan	6.9	18,127	10.4	37.3	32.7	19.7
26103	Marquette County, Michigan	5.4	44,640	5.5	33.1	32.6	28.8
26105	Mason County, Michigan	3.6	20,531	8.3	34.4	37.1	20.2
26107	Mecosta County, Michigan	2.9	26,471	10.6	34.4	32.2	22.7
26109	Menominee County, Michigan	3.5	17,343	9.8	42.2	32.9	15.1
26111	Midland County, Michigan	2.7	57,296	6.5	29.6	31.4	32.5
26113	Missaukee County, Michigan	4.0	10,373	13.4	42.8	30.7	13.1
26115	Monroe County, Michigan	2.7	103,337	9.8	36.2	35.4	18.6
26117	Montcalm County, Michigan	4.5	43,161	12.7	39.0	35.2	13.1
26119	Montmorency County, Michigan	5.1	7,465	14.5	41.9	32.9	10.7
26121	Muskegon County, Michigan	3.7	114,891	11.2	34.8	35.8	18.2
26123	Newaygo County, Michigan	3.7	32,890	14.0	41.1	31.0	13.9
26125	Oakland County, Michigan	2.8	854,509	6.7	20.1	28.8	44.4
26127	Oceana County, Michigan	4.4	17,791	14.7	34.7	33.8	16.8
26129	Ogemaw County, Michigan	3.3	15,701	15.0	40.9	32.5	11.7
26131	Ontonagon County, Michigan	7.5	5,140	8.6	40.6	35.7	15.1
26133	Osceola County, Michigan	3.7	15,947	12.0	44.7	30.1	13.2
26135	Oscoda County, Michigan	6.3	6,277	16.3	40.6	33.4	9.7
26137	Otsego County, Michigan	4.8	16,985	8.1	36.6	34.8	20.5
26139	Ottawa County, Michigan	2.4	167,263	8.6	28.9	31.3	31.1
26141	Presque Isle County, Michigan	5.5	10,127	11.9	40.6	30.5	16.9

Table C. County—Labor Force, Employment, and Educational Data, 2011–2015—*Continued*

| | | Industry for employed population age 16 and older | Educational attainment for the population age 25 and older | | | |
| | | | | Educational attainment | | |
Fips code	State/county	Public administration	Total population age 25 and older	Less than high school graduate	High school graduate (includes equivalency)	Some college or Associate's degree	Bachelor's degree or higher
26143	Roscommon County, Michigan	5.3	18,994	11.8	38.9	34.8	14.4
26145	Saginaw County, Michigan	3.6	132,135	12.0	34.2	33.6	20.2
26147	St. Clair County, Michigan	4.3	111,510	10.4	35.3	36.9	17.4
26149	St. Joseph County, Michigan	2.9	40,598	14.8	38.9	31.6	14.7
26151	Sanilac County, Michigan	3.6	29,344	12.2	45.1	30.5	12.3
26153	Schoolcraft County, Michigan	6.0	6,184	12.6	46.8	27.3	13.2
26155	Shiawassee County, Michigan	5.2	47,399	9.0	36.6	38.6	15.7
26157	Tuscola County, Michigan	3.1	38,134	11.3	42.0	32.9	13.9
26159	Van Buren County, Michigan	3.8	50,855	13.7	34.0	32.8	19.5
26161	Washtenaw County, Michigan	2.4	219,618	5.5	15.7	26.1	52.6
26163	Wayne County, Michigan	3.4	1,170,589	15.3	30.3	32.4	22.0
26165	Wexford County, Michigan	3.6	22,609	11.2	38.8	33.2	16.8
27000	**Minnesota**	3.4	3,632,992	7.6	26.1	32.7	33.7
27001	Aitkin County, Minnesota	5.9	12,246	9.4	39.9	35.2	15.5
27003	Anoka County, Minnesota	3.6	227,438	6.7	28.4	37.1	27.8
27005	Becker County, Minnesota	4.3	22,674	8.4	33.5	35.8	22.4
27007	Beltrami County, Minnesota	5.6	27,380	9.5	26.1	37.9	26.6
27009	Benton County, Minnesota	2.8	26,171	8.5	32.1	37.9	21.5
27011	Big Stone County, Minnesota	4.3	3,743	10.0	42.4	30.2	17.4
27013	Blue Earth County, Minnesota	2.8	37,634	5.7	28.1	34.9	31.3
27015	Brown County, Minnesota	2.8	17,447	9.4	37.6	31.7	21.3
27017	Carlton County, Minnesota	8.5	24,452	5.8	36.4	35.0	22.8
27019	Carver County, Minnesota	2.4	61,321	4.8	21.2	28.7	45.2
27021	Cass County, Minnesota	6.2	20,621	8.7	35.4	35.7	20.2
27023	Chippewa County, Minnesota	3.1	8,449	10.4	36.0	37.7	15.9
27025	Chisago County, Minnesota	4.7	36,698	6.1	34.6	37.3	22.0
27027	Clay County, Minnesota	3.1	36,548	6.1	27.3	34.9	31.7
27029	Clearwater County, Minnesota	5.0	5,968	13.4	38.1	33.6	14.9
27031	Cook County, Minnesota	7.1	4,089	4.4	25.1	31.6	39.0
27033	Cottonwood County, Minnesota	4.7	7,958	10.6	36.2	34.8	18.5
27035	Crow Wing County, Minnesota	3.7	44,314	6.9	31.4	38.5	23.2
27037	Dakota County, Minnesota	4.0	272,845	5.3	21.6	32.9	40.3
27039	Dodge County, Minnesota	3.1	13,115	6.0	33.5	36.8	23.7
27041	Douglas County, Minnesota	2.4	25,980	6.0	29.9	39.4	24.7
27043	Faribault County, Minnesota	3.1	10,245	9.8	39.9	33.4	16.9
27045	Fillmore County, Minnesota	2.8	14,437	9.1	35.7	35.7	19.5
27047	Freeborn County, Minnesota	2.4	21,941	11.1	36.7	36.2	16.1
27049	Goodhue County, Minnesota	3.4	32,356	7.1	33.0	36.5	23.4
27051	Grant County, Minnesota	3.4	4,274	7.3	33.4	40.5	18.9
27053	Hennepin County, Minnesota	2.3	821,362	7.4	17.8	27.8	47.0
27055	Houston County, Minnesota	2.5	13,358	7.2	34.3	37.2	21.4
27057	Hubbard County, Minnesota	4.9	14,968	7.3	31.8	35.9	25.0
27059	Isanti County, Minnesota	3.4	25,881	9.3	37.8	35.2	17.7
27061	Itasca County, Minnesota	4.4	32,514	7.2	31.8	39.1	21.9
27063	Jackson County, Minnesota	3.8	7,165	8.7	34.8	37.7	18.8
27065	Kanabec County, Minnesota	4.0	11,283	11.9	39.7	35.0	13.5
27067	Kandiyohi County, Minnesota	3.2	28,582	11.2	27.9	38.6	22.2
27069	Kittson County, Minnesota	7.2	3,205	9.7	35.0	34.4	20.9
27071	Koochiching County, Minnesota	5.0	9,595	10.6	36.5	34.5	18.4
27073	Lac qui Parle County, Minnesota	3.7	5,143	7.9	38.3	36.2	17.7
27075	Lake County, Minnesota	5.2	8,142	5.1	36.2	34.3	24.4
27077	Lake of the Woods County, Minnesota	2.7	2,959	8.6	44.8	31.1	15.5
27079	Le Sueur County, Minnesota	4.5	18,866	9.4	35.5	33.9	21.2
27081	Lincoln County, Minnesota	3.6	4,151	8.1	40.5	32.2	19.2
27083	Lyon County, Minnesota	3.5	16,375	7.9	35.1	31.2	25.8
27085	McLeod County, Minnesota	3.1	24,642	8.1	38.0	35.9	18.0
27087	Mahnomen County, Minnesota	8.1	3,378	14.3	37.1	35.7	12.9
27089	Marshall County, Minnesota	3.6	6,615	11.2	37.4	32.7	18.7
27091	Martin County, Minnesota	3.5	14,533	11.0	38.6	31.5	18.9
27093	Meeker County, Minnesota	2.9	15,765	8.4	38.3	34.3	18.9
27095	Mille Lacs County, Minnesota	4.9	17,655	10.4	38.3	36.6	14.7
27097	Morrison County, Minnesota	4.4	22,702	10.5	38.6	33.9	17.0
27099	Mower County, Minnesota	2.9	25,970	12.0	32.6	36.4	19.0
27101	Murray County, Minnesota	3.4	6,161	10.9	36.5	34.5	18.1
27103	Nicollet County, Minnesota	3.8	21,339	5.9	27.0	34.6	32.5
27105	Nobles County, Minnesota	2.3	13,940	20.9	34.3	31.0	13.8
27107	Norman County, Minnesota	3.7	4,699	11.3	38.5	35.1	15.1
27109	Olmsted County, Minnesota	2.4	100,329	5.9	20.9	31.9	41.3
27111	Otter Tail County, Minnesota	3.9	41,151	8.7	30.5	36.3	24.5
27113	Pennington County, Minnesota	1.5	9,559	8.9	36.0	39.0	16.1
27115	Pine County, Minnesota	7.9	21,105	10.9	42.6	33.2	13.2
27117	Pipestone County, Minnesota	2.2	6,357	13.5	36.0	31.5	19.0
27119	Polk County, Minnesota	3.8	21,001	9.2	31.1	36.5	23.2
27121	Pope County, Minnesota	3.9	7,944	5.6	34.1	38.1	22.2

Table C. County—Labor Force, Employment, and Educational Data, 2011–2015—*Continued*

Fips code	State/county	Industry for employed population age 16 and older — Public administration	Educational attainment for the population age 25 and older — Total population age 25 and older	Educational attainment — Less than high school graduate	High school graduate (includes equivalency)	Some college or Associate's degree	Bachelor's degree or higher
27123	Ramsey County, Minnesota	4.3	346,106	10.0	21.9	27.7	40.4
27125	Red Lake County, Minnesota	3.7	2,803	8.2	40.9	35.5	15.4
27127	Redwood County, Minnesota	3.4	10,694	11.7	37.9	33.4	17.0
27129	Renville County, Minnesota	3.1	10,697	10.5	37.5	36.3	15.7
27131	Rice County, Minnesota	3.0	40,740	9.6	31.8	31.0	27.6
27133	Rock County, Minnesota	2.7	6,501	10.2	38.5	30.9	20.4
27135	Roseau County, Minnesota	2.7	10,520	8.1	37.3	35.6	19.0
27137	St. Louis County, Minnesota	4.2	136,107	6.8	29.5	36.7	27.0
27139	Scott County, Minnesota	2.3	87,575	5.3	23.4	33.1	38.2
27141	Sherburne County, Minnesota	3.1	57,754	6.3	26.6	40.6	26.5
27143	Sibley County, Minnesota	3.6	10,262	10.6	40.8	32.3	16.3
27145	Stearns County, Minnesota	2.6	93,806	8.2	30.2	35.6	25.9
27147	Steele County, Minnesota	3.2	24,227	8.2	35.5	31.0	25.4
27149	Stevens County, Minnesota	3.6	5,732	8.7	27.2	35.8	28.3
27151	Swift County, Minnesota	4.2	6,748	11.4	38.6	33.8	16.2
27153	Todd County, Minnesota	2.5	16,646	12.2	37.1	35.5	15.2
27155	Traverse County, Minnesota	3.6	2,509	9.8	34.8	37.3	18.0
27157	Wabasha County, Minnesota	3.2	15,064	6.8	39.1	33.0	21.2
27159	Wadena County, Minnesota	3.2	9,436	11.1	39.3	36.9	12.7
27161	Waseca County, Minnesota	3.9	13,357	7.9	35.2	36.5	20.4
27163	Washington County, Minnesota	4.9	164,696	4.0	22.0	32.4	41.6
27165	Watonwan County, Minnesota	2.7	7,491	14.7	40.0	29.5	15.8
27167	Wilkin County, Minnesota	2.5	4,537	8.5	30.5	43.4	17.5
27169	Winona County, Minnesota	2.6	30,978	8.4	29.6	33.8	28.2
27171	Wright County, Minnesota	3.0	82,238	6.0	28.9	37.8	27.3
27173	Yellow Medicine County, Minnesota	3.2	7,030	9.5	36.8	37.5	16.1
28000	**Mississippi**	5.5	1,940,365	17.7	30.3	31.4	20.7
28001	Adams County, Mississippi	5.8	22,512	19.3	35.9	27.0	17.8
28003	Alcorn County, Mississippi	4.7	25,278	19.2	36.3	28.4	16.2
28005	Amite County, Mississippi	4.4	9,276	25.4	36.6	26.0	12.1
28007	Attala County, Mississippi	4.3	12,751	23.2	31.4	30.6	14.9
28009	Benton County, Mississippi	3.4	5,700	23.2	38.1	28.2	10.6
28011	Bolivar County, Mississippi	6.9	21,311	26.5	25.0	27.4	21.1
28013	Calhoun County, Mississippi	3.2	9,927	27.1	34.2	27.6	11.2
28015	Carroll County, Mississippi	9.7	7,322	21.1	37.3	28.0	13.6
28017	Chickasaw County, Mississippi	5.2	11,330	27.8	37.3	24.2	10.7
28019	Choctaw County, Mississippi	3.7	5,701	21.1	33.4	32.1	13.5
28021	Claiborne County, Mississippi	3.9	5,334	21.9	29.8	32.7	15.6
28023	Clarke County, Mississippi	5.0	11,165	20.2	34.4	31.4	13.9
28025	Clay County, Mississippi	4.2	13,385	21.4	32.9	27.9	17.8
28027	Coahoma County, Mississippi	6.4	15,296	22.9	27.6	31.9	17.6
28029	Copiah County, Mississippi	4.8	18,791	20.5	31.5	33.8	14.1
28031	Covington County, Mississippi	2.8	12,808	21.4	36.8	26.5	15.3
28033	DeSoto County, Mississippi	3.7	108,640	11.3	29.9	36.4	22.4
28035	Forrest County, Mississippi	4.0	46,287	15.2	28.2	29.9	26.7
28037	Franklin County, Mississippi	3.9	5,308	17.7	37.3	27.1	17.9
28039	George County, Mississippi	3.4	14,940	20.0	40.7	27.2	12.0
28041	Greene County, Mississippi	10.9	10,022	25.7	36.7	29.4	8.2
28043	Grenada County, Mississippi	4.7	14,325	23.1	30.2	31.2	15.6
28045	Hancock County, Mississippi	5.1	31,667	15.7	29.2	34.0	21.0
28047	Harrison County, Mississippi	9.4	127,792	14.5	28.8	35.3	21.3
28049	Hinds County, Mississippi	7.9	153,972	14.2	24.9	33.3	27.7
28051	Holmes County, Mississippi	6.4	11,302	28.1	36.9	22.7	12.3
28053	Humphreys County, Mississippi	5.7	5,663	36.5	27.8	23.6	12.1
28055	Issaquena County, Mississippi	8.9	1,017	39.5	34.9	18.4	7.2
28057	Itawamba County, Mississippi	3.2	15,561	20.2	31.8	34.8	13.2
28059	Jackson County, Mississippi	4.9	93,759	12.5	31.4	36.0	20.1
28061	Jasper County, Mississippi	5.7	11,274	21.1	36.4	29.2	13.4
28063	Jefferson County, Mississippi	10.6	4,916	23.4	36.4	23.7	16.5
28065	Jefferson Davis County, Mississippi	4.3	8,288	20.1	39.1	26.6	14.2
28067	Jones County, Mississippi	3.1	44,503	20.6	28.2	32.9	18.4
28069	Kemper County, Mississippi	4.8	6,745	23.2	31.1	34.2	11.5
28071	Lafayette County, Mississippi	4.4	28,578	10.8	20.9	29.9	38.3
28073	Lamar County, Mississippi	3.5	37,756	8.8	23.9	31.3	35.9
28075	Lauderdale County, Mississippi	5.5	52,568	14.3	30.9	36.1	18.7
28077	Lawrence County, Mississippi	5.4	8,408	20.7	35.4	31.8	12.1
28079	Leake County, Mississippi	6.2	14,503	24.6	35.1	28.5	11.8
28081	Lee County, Mississippi	3.5	55,648	16.1	27.5	34.5	21.8
28083	Leflore County, Mississippi	6.9	19,319	23.7	33.8	25.0	17.5
28085	Lincoln County, Mississippi	3.4	22,782	15.7	35.7	33.4	15.2
28087	Lowndes County, Mississippi	5.7	38,939	17.0	29.0	32.2	21.8
28089	Madison County, Mississippi	6.8	65,786	10.2	16.0	27.8	46.0
28091	Marion County, Mississippi	4.8	17,537	23.3	36.5	27.2	13.0
28093	Marshall County, Mississippi	3.7	24,462	22.5	37.7	26.4	13.4
28095	Monroe County, Mississippi	3.7	24,633	22.9	33.8	28.7	14.6

Table C. County—Labor Force, Employment, and Educational Data, 2011–2015—*Continued*

Fips code	State/county	Industry for employed population age 16 and older — Public administration	Educational attainment for the population age 25 and older — Total population age 25 and older	Educational attainment — Less than high school graduate	High school graduate (includes equivalency)	Some college or Associate's degree	Bachelor's degree or higher
28097	Montgomery County, Mississippi	3.2	6,924	26.8	32.1	25.3	15.8
28099	Neshoba County, Mississippi	5.0	18,618	22.3	32.7	31.6	13.5
28101	Newton County, Mississippi	7.8	13,888	17.5	30.1	36.6	15.8
28103	Noxubee County, Mississippi	5.6	7,275	34.7	30.5	22.9	11.9
28105	Oktibbeha County, Mississippi	3.2	24,496	13.8	19.3	24.0	43.0
28107	Panola County, Mississippi	3.0	22,175	19.5	36.7	28.9	14.9
28109	Pearl River County, Mississippi	5.9	36,741	18.0	31.4	36.6	13.9
28111	Perry County, Mississippi	6.3	8,266	18.0	41.3	32.3	8.3
28113	Pike County, Mississippi	4.6	25,575	19.5	34.5	29.7	16.3
28115	Pontotoc County, Mississippi	3.4	19,630	22.6	34.7	29.8	13.0
28117	Prentiss County, Mississippi	2.8	16,700	23.8	33.9	30.3	11.9
28119	Quitman County, Mississippi	5.8	5,103	32.6	29.1	25.4	12.9
28121	Rankin County, Mississippi	7.2	99,098	10.3	26.9	33.8	29.0
28123	Scott County, Mississippi	4.2	18,311	29.0	34.4	25.3	11.2
28125	Sharkey County, Mississippi	6.7	3,118	22.5	30.6	26.8	20.0
28127	Simpson County, Mississippi	4.9	17,945	20.4	38.9	28.0	12.7
28129	Smith County, Mississippi	3.6	10,737	18.5	42.2	26.3	13.0
28131	Stone County, Mississippi	6.4	11,684	16.4	34.4	35.7	13.4
28133	Sunflower County, Mississippi	8.1	18,049	28.6	28.3	28.8	14.4
28135	Tallahatchie County, Mississippi	11.1	10,936	35.9	32.1	23.4	8.5
28137	Tate County, Mississippi	3.5	18,204	20.2	29.6	33.5	16.7
28139	Tippah County, Mississippi	3.6	14,468	24.9	32.0	30.2	12.9
28141	Tishomingo County, Mississippi	4.4	13,616	22.9	38.3	27.5	11.2
28143	Tunica County, Mississippi	3.4	6,429	23.8	30.6	28.3	17.3
28145	Union County, Mississippi	1.1	18,405	23.8	33.3	29.1	13.8
28147	Walthall County, Mississippi	6.0	9,909	21.8	41.0	26.3	11.0
28149	Warren County, Mississippi	5.9	31,806	14.0	30.1	31.6	24.4
28151	Washington County, Mississippi	7.8	31,395	23.2	30.1	27.8	18.8
28153	Wayne County, Mississippi	4.5	13,388	23.4	36.4	26.6	13.6
28155	Webster County, Mississippi	4.3	6,748	17.3	34.5	31.0	17.2
28157	Wilkinson County, Mississippi	21.2	6,395	29.1	36.1	20.2	14.5
28159	Winston County, Mississippi	5.0	12,620	22.4	31.5	29.7	16.5
28161	Yalobusha County, Mississippi	5.3	8,457	21.7	38.5	27.5	12.4
28163	Yazoo County, Mississippi	8.2	18,469	24.5	36.2	26.0	13.3
29000	**Missouri**	4.4	4,052,300	11.6	31.3	30.0	27.1
29001	Adair County, Missouri	4.4	13,588	11.4	33.9	24.6	30.0
29003	Andrew County, Missouri	5.6	12,011	9.5	40.5	26.7	23.3
29005	Atchison County, Missouri	4.4	3,964	10.1	42.1	25.1	22.7
29007	Audrain County, Missouri	6.9	17,535	16.0	46.9	25.5	11.5
29009	Barry County, Missouri	3.2	24,684	18.4	41.3	26.2	14.0
29011	Barton County, Missouri	3.8	8,212	13.1	39.5	30.7	16.7
29013	Bates County, Missouri	4.3	11,420	15.0	43.3	28.6	13.1
29015	Benton County, Missouri	3.4	14,469	15.2	44.8	28.7	11.3
29017	Bollinger County, Missouri	1.7	8,594	20.9	45.4	23.7	10.0
29019	Boone County, Missouri	4.2	99,851	6.6	20.2	25.9	47.3
29021	Buchanan County, Missouri	3.9	59,643	12.7	36.8	31.0	19.5
29023	Butler County, Missouri	5.2	29,357	18.8	36.7	30.0	14.6
29025	Caldwell County, Missouri	8.6	6,253	11.4	44.0	27.1	17.4
29027	Callaway County, Missouri	10.5	29,750	14.3	38.3	27.0	20.4
29029	Camden County, Missouri	4.3	32,867	12.3	36.0	30.7	21.0
29031	Cape Girardeau County, Missouri	3.6	49,602	10.9	32.0	28.4	28.7
29033	Carroll County, Missouri	5.6	6,255	11.4	49.6	22.3	16.7
29035	Carter County, Missouri	4.4	4,252	21.7	31.3	35.7	11.4
29037	Cass County, Missouri	4.3	67,217	7.7	34.8	32.8	24.7
29039	Cedar County, Missouri	5.8	9,733	16.4	42.4	27.0	14.3
29041	Chariton County, Missouri	3.8	5,422	14.5	49.2	21.3	15.0
29043	Christian County, Missouri	3.7	53,381	8.7	31.6	33.7	26.0
29045	Clark County, Missouri	5.5	4,805	13.0	43.3	30.9	12.8
29047	Clay County, Missouri	4.7	153,656	8.0	28.9	32.2	31.0
29049	Clinton County, Missouri	6.8	14,011	8.0	38.7	35.7	17.6
29051	Cole County, Missouri	17.4	52,014	8.5	31.1	28.7	31.6
29053	Cooper County, Missouri	7.1	11,957	11.9	41.4	27.2	19.5
29055	Crawford County, Missouri	4.1	16,908	23.0	38.4	26.4	12.2
29057	Dade County, Missouri	2.9	5,492	14.2	41.3	29.1	15.3
29059	Dallas County, Missouri	4.3	11,419	18.2	41.9	25.2	14.7
29061	Daviess County, Missouri	6.6	5,477	17.0	40.5	26.7	15.8
29063	DeKalb County, Missouri	7.1	9,506	14.5	48.9	25.1	11.5
29065	Dent County, Missouri	4.4	10,900	22.3	39.2	25.5	13.0
29067	Douglas County, Missouri	2.6	9,696	20.8	42.4	27.6	9.2
29069	Dunklin County, Missouri	4.8	20,723	27.0	38.6	22.6	11.8
29071	Franklin County, Missouri	2.5	69,207	13.4	34.3	33.7	18.6
29073	Gasconade County, Missouri	3.4	10,639	15.4	43.2	26.3	15.0
29075	Gentry County, Missouri	3.9	4,608	11.1	43.5	26.8	18.6
29077	Greene County, Missouri	3.0	183,911	9.5	27.9	33.1	29.5

Table C. County—Labor Force, Employment, and Educational Data, 2011–2015—*Continued*

Fips code	State/county	Industry for employed population age 16 and older	Educational attainment for the population age 25 and older				
				Educational attainment			
		Public administration	Total population age 25 and older	Less than high school graduate	High school graduate (includes equivalency)	Some college or Associate's degree	Bachelor's degree or higher
29079	Grundy County, Missouri	3.4	6,886	13.4	39.3	30.1	17.2
29081	Harrison County, Missouri	6.2	5,991	16.5	48.6	22.6	12.3
29083	Henry County, Missouri	2.7	15,610	12.2	41.3	31.0	15.4
29085	Hickory County, Missouri	7.1	7,211	16.9	42.7	30.2	10.3
29087	Holt County, Missouri	6.1	3,398	9.8	44.4	26.7	19.2
29089	Howard County, Missouri	5.8	6,583	12.6	36.2	26.9	24.2
29091	Howell County, Missouri	5.0	27,172	15.7	39.0	30.3	14.9
29093	Iron County, Missouri	5.1	7,249	19.4	40.4	28.2	12.0
29095	Jackson County, Missouri	4.6	455,938	11.0	29.1	31.2	28.8
29097	Jasper County, Missouri	2.5	75,697	13.6	35.6	28.8	22.0
29099	Jefferson County, Missouri	3.6	149,808	12.4	33.6	35.8	18.2
29101	Johnson County, Missouri	10.2	30,949	9.0	30.7	33.8	26.5
29103	Knox County, Missouri	2.9	2,744	16.3	41.9	26.7	15.2
29105	Laclede County, Missouri	3.8	24,031	18.6	38.9	28.6	13.9
29107	Lafayette County, Missouri	4.8	22,467	10.9	42.4	28.4	18.3
29109	Lawrence County, Missouri	3.8	25,497	16.1	38.7	28.4	16.8
29111	Lewis County, Missouri	2.5	6,648	12.4	47.7	26.4	13.5
29113	Lincoln County, Missouri	3.1	35,000	13.6	43.4	28.2	14.8
29115	Linn County, Missouri	5.5	8,507	12.2	49.5	24.0	14.2
29117	Livingston County, Missouri	8.7	10,674	13.7	42.6	23.7	20.0
29119	McDonald County, Missouri	3.1	14,806	22.4	34.2	31.0	12.4
29121	Macon County, Missouri	7.2	10,650	12.4	43.8	28.3	15.5
29123	Madison County, Missouri	7.8	8,472	23.6	36.4	28.8	11.2
29125	Maries County, Missouri	7.5	6,378	16.8	42.8	25.4	15.0
29127	Marion County, Missouri	4.4	19,278	15.7	38.5	26.5	19.4
29129	Mercer County, Missouri	5.5	2,552	11.8	50.1	24.2	13.9
29131	Miller County, Missouri	6.7	17,126	13.8	42.5	27.3	16.4
29133	Mississippi County, Missouri	8.0	9,876	26.9	40.7	21.6	10.8
29135	Moniteau County, Missouri	13.8	10,565	17.0	43.4	21.5	18.1
29137	Monroe County, Missouri	5.6	6,102	9.5	48.7	27.7	14.1
29139	Montgomery County, Missouri	6.2	8,322	17.6	42.3	27.7	12.5
29141	Morgan County, Missouri	5.0	14,426	20.8	41.3	24.4	13.4
29143	New Madrid County, Missouri	4.3	12,587	23.7	41.3	23.3	11.6
29145	Newton County, Missouri	3.6	39,008	14.2	33.1	33.9	18.8
29147	Nodaway County, Missouri	3.3	12,495	8.6	41.2	26.3	23.9
29149	Oregon County, Missouri	2.6	7,706	18.4	39.6	30.9	11.0
29151	Osage County, Missouri	12.8	9,200	10.8	46.6	25.1	17.5
29153	Ozark County, Missouri	2.6	7,119	16.5	44.2	26.4	12.9
29155	Pemiscot County, Missouri	5.6	11,430	26.3	37.8	24.2	11.7
29157	Perry County, Missouri	3.1	12,868	13.7	44.4	26.0	15.9
29159	Pettis County, Missouri	3.6	27,798	17.0	32.2	33.2	17.5
29161	Phelps County, Missouri	5.6	27,786	12.8	33.2	26.2	27.8
29163	Pike County, Missouri	6.2	12,768	20.9	43.8	22.6	12.7
29165	Platte County, Missouri	5.4	63,284	4.7	22.4	32.4	40.4
29167	Polk County, Missouri	4.2	19,729	13.0	38.8	29.4	18.8
29169	Pulaski County, Missouri	21.5	28,558	10.2	31.3	34.4	24.1
29171	Putnam County, Missouri	3.6	3,472	12.5	41.7	27.8	18.1
29173	Ralls County, Missouri	5.3	7,308	12.6	48.5	26.6	12.3
29175	Randolph County, Missouri	6.3	17,090	14.3	38.9	33.1	13.7
29177	Ray County, Missouri	4.9	15,758	11.3	47.3	27.6	13.8
29179	Reynolds County, Missouri	5.3	4,745	23.5	44.0	24.4	8.1
29181	Ripley County, Missouri	5.2	9,657	22.7	39.1	27.1	11.1
29183	St. Charles County, Missouri	3.1	249,690	5.9	26.1	32.5	35.5
29185	St. Clair County, Missouri	4.1	7,082	18.6	45.7	24.9	10.8
29186	Ste. Genevieve County, Missouri	2.8	12,417	13.3	42.0	31.4	13.3
29187	St. Francois County, Missouri	7.6	45,948	18.9	34.2	32.8	14.1
29189	St. Louis County, Missouri	2.8	686,619	7.2	22.0	29.2	41.6
29195	Saline County, Missouri	6.7	15,202	14.6	39.4	27.2	18.8
29197	Schuyler County, Missouri	3.6	2,921	14.1	45.9	27.6	12.4
29199	Scotland County, Missouri	4.6	3,106	20.0	40.7	24.5	14.8
29201	Scott County, Missouri	4.5	26,390	18.5	42.0	26.3	13.2
29203	Shannon County, Missouri	4.5	5,793	18.6	37.9	28.4	15.1
29205	Shelby County, Missouri	3.0	4,274	9.6	46.4	31.0	13.1
29207	Stoddard County, Missouri	3.7	20,774	19.6	39.9	26.8	13.7
29209	Stone County, Missouri	2.5	23,856	13.9	40.1	29.7	16.3
29211	Sullivan County, Missouri	2.6	4,468	16.0	47.3	23.8	12.9
29213	Taney County, Missouri	2.9	36,777	13.1	35.5	33.0	18.3
29215	Texas County, Missouri	7.8	17,682	17.4	43.8	25.9	13.0
29217	Vernon County, Missouri	3.8	13,912	12.4	41.0	30.3	16.3
29219	Warren County, Missouri	3.1	22,700	15.5	37.0	31.7	15.8
29221	Washington County, Missouri	6.0	17,222	24.7	42.0	26.1	7.1
29223	Wayne County, Missouri	6.0	9,625	25.1	36.6	27.6	10.7
29225	Webster County, Missouri	3.9	23,843	14.3	40.5	29.5	15.8
29227	Worth County, Missouri	6.1	1,481	11.9	42.3	28.4	17.5

Table C. County—Labor Force, Employment, and Educational Data, 2011–2015—*Continued*

| | | Industry for employed population age 16 and older | Educational attainment for the population age 25 and older | | | |
| | | | | Educational attainment | | |
Fips code	State/county	Public administration	Total population age 25 and older	Less than high school graduate	High school graduate (includes equivalency)	Some college or Associate's degree	Bachelor's degree or higher
29229	Wright County, Missouri	5.4	12,442	22.3	40.8	24.5	12.4
29510	St. Louis city, Missouri	5.5	218,108	15.9	23.6	28.6	31.9
30000	**Montana**	6.4	690,448	7.2	30.1	33.2	29.5
30001	Beaverhead County, Montana	3.0	6,209	6.6	30.1	33.0	30.3
30003	Big Horn County, Montana	22.2	7,464	14.2	34.9	35.3	15.6
30005	Blaine County, Montana	13.3	4,027	10.9	28.1	40.7	20.3
30007	Broadwater County, Montana	9.9	4,106	7.2	39.1	29.8	23.9
30009	Carbon County, Montana	4.3	7,764	7.0	28.4	35.5	29.2
30011	Carter County, Montana	4.5	910	6.7	38.6	39.1	15.6
30013	Cascade County, Montana	6.7	55,320	8.7	31.8	34.1	25.5
30015	Chouteau County, Montana	5.1	3,865	7.6	34.5	34.6	23.3
30017	Custer County, Montana	6.9	8,277	8.6	29.3	42.1	20.0
30019	Daniels County, Montana	11.0	1,327	6.2	31.2	40.4	22.2
30021	Dawson County, Montana	5.7	6,504	8.0	35.6	37.6	18.8
30023	Deer Lodge County, Montana	12.3	6,719	9.1	38.7	35.3	16.8
30025	Fallon County, Montana	4.9	2,101	5.7	37.6	40.6	16.1
30027	Fergus County, Montana	6.5	8,467	6.1	35.6	30.1	28.2
30029	Flathead County, Montana	3.7	65,114	5.7	29.9	35.3	29.1
30031	Gallatin County, Montana	4.0	60,120	3.3	20.0	28.7	48.0
30033	Garfield County, Montana	4.3	756	7.8	44.4	32.9	14.8
30035	Glacier County, Montana	8.0	7,939	11.4	37.8	33.0	17.7
30037	Golden Valley County, Montana	5.9	575	7.1	42.8	29.7	20.3
30039	Granite County, Montana	3.1	2,485	11.1	36.0	27.0	25.8
30041	Hill County, Montana	7.5	10,303	9.5	28.3	39.0	23.2
30043	Jefferson County, Montana	15.3	8,337	5.3	28.6	33.5	32.6
30045	Judith Basin County, Montana	6.2	1,526	5.8	37.7	26.6	29.9
30047	Lake County, Montana	9.1	19,702	9.2	31.4	35.0	24.4
30049	Lewis and Clark County, Montana	20.2	45,364	5.4	23.7	32.8	38.0
30051	Liberty County, Montana	6.2	1,673	21.0	22.1	35.2	21.6
30053	Lincoln County, Montana	4.3	14,529	10.9	33.6	36.1	19.4
30055	McCone County, Montana	5.2	1,304	6.7	45.9	30.0	17.5
30057	Madison County, Montana	4.7	6,028	5.8	35.9	31.8	26.4
30059	Meagher County, Montana	5.7	1,406	7.0	39.7	30.0	23.3
30061	Mineral County, Montana	5.9	3,122	10.6	41.8	34.5	13.1
30063	Missoula County, Montana	3.8	73,249	4.7	22.7	31.9	40.7
30065	Musselshell County, Montana	5.9	3,422	9.1	40.2	34.0	16.8
30067	Park County, Montana	3.8	11,768	4.2	33.1	27.6	35.0
30069	Petroleum County, Montana	3.1	345	3.2	52.5	23.8	20.6
30071	Phillips County, Montana	7.4	2,970	8.7	37.3	34.7	19.3
30073	Pondera County, Montana	8.3	4,208	10.7	33.0	34.2	22.1
30075	Powder River County, Montana	6.4	1,318	6.1	29.4	40.0	24.4
30077	Powell County, Montana	13.9	5,369	11.1	37.0	32.6	19.3
30079	Prairie County, Montana	8.7	1,010	9.6	46.4	28.2	15.7
30081	Ravalli County, Montana	4.0	29,736	8.1	33.9	33.6	24.4
30083	Richland County, Montana	2.4	7,442	7.6	38.5	37.4	16.5
30085	Roosevelt County, Montana	13.8	6,278	16.7	38.8	31.1	13.5
30087	Rosebud County, Montana	8.0	5,879	12.5	32.7	34.9	19.8
30089	Sanders County, Montana	6.6	8,533	11.6	41.9	30.0	16.4
30091	Sheridan County, Montana	5.5	2,645	8.6	30.4	39.7	21.3
30093	Silver Bow County, Montana	6.9	23,336	9.1	34.9	31.4	24.6
30095	Stillwater County, Montana	3.4	6,703	6.0	37.2	33.1	23.7
30097	Sweet Grass County, Montana	5.0	2,567	7.6	38.1	29.2	25.2
30099	Teton County, Montana	6.2	4,209	7.5	34.3	34.9	23.3
30101	Toole County, Montana	7.8	3,696	15.4	36.6	34.6	13.4
30103	Treasure County, Montana	5.5	587	10.2	35.1	35.8	18.9
30105	Valley County, Montana	8.6	5,368	7.2	37.8	35.7	19.4
30107	Wheatland County, Montana	1.3	1,496	22.8	36.4	22.8	18.0
30109	Wibaux County, Montana	9.6	719	14.6	37.4	28.0	20.0
30111	Yellowstone County, Montana	3.9	104,252	7.4	31.2	32.9	28.5
31000	**Nebraska**	4.2	1,215,400	9.3	27.5	33.9	29.3
31001	Adams County, Nebraska	3.8	20,321	9.3	32.0	35.7	23.0
31003	Antelope County, Nebraska	3.3	4,571	9.1	33.1	40.1	17.7
31005	Arthur County, Nebraska	1.6	294	3.4	24.1	39.8	32.7
31007	Banner County, Nebraska	5.5	627	5.4	29.3	47.8	17.4
31009	Blaine County, Nebraska	4.9	371	1.9	39.6	40.2	18.3
31011	Boone County, Nebraska	1.6	3,726	6.7	42.3	34.5	16.6
31013	Box Butte County, Nebraska	3.2	7,522	9.4	33.8	40.9	15.9
31015	Boyd County, Nebraska	3.2	1,473	6.4	41.5	34.1	18.1
31017	Brown County, Nebraska	3.8	2,308	11.4	41.2	31.1	16.3
31019	Buffalo County, Nebraska	3.0	29,027	6.5	25.6	35.2	32.7
31021	Burt County, Nebraska	4.5	4,745	9.3	39.2	34.5	17.0
31023	Butler County, Nebraska	3.0	5,753	9.3	39.9	35.5	15.2
31025	Cass County, Nebraska	5.6	17,301	5.3	32.1	37.5	25.1

Table C. County—Labor Force, Employment, and Educational Data, 2011–2015—*Continued*

		Industry for employed population age 16 and older	Educational attainment for the population age 25 and older				
					Educational attainment		
Fips code	State/county	Public administration	Total population age 25 and older	Less than high school graduate	High school graduate (includes equivalency)	Some college or Associate's degree	Bachelor's degree or higher
31027	Cedar County, Nebraska	4.2	5,909	6.9	40.6	34.8	17.7
31029	Chase County, Nebraska	3.8	2,773	11.1	33.2	37.5	18.2
31031	Cherry County, Nebraska	5.5	4,222	9.0	31.0	40.2	19.7
31033	Cheyenne County, Nebraska	2.0	6,978	6.0	27.1	43.5	23.4
31035	Clay County, Nebraska	2.9	4,388	10.8	32.6	37.6	19.0
31037	Colfax County, Nebraska	1.8	6,505	28.1	33.2	25.4	13.4
31039	Cuming County, Nebraska	2.6	6,098	12.0	38.9	30.3	18.8
31041	Custer County, Nebraska	2.1	7,551	8.1	32.8	38.1	21.0
31043	Dakota County, Nebraska	3.0	12,732	26.4	34.9	27.5	11.2
31045	Dawes County, Nebraska	5.2	5,522	5.7	29.1	31.9	33.2
31047	Dawson County, Nebraska	3.2	15,292	24.1	33.4	27.6	14.9
31049	Deuel County, Nebraska	4.4	1,384	9.4	36.3	37.1	17.3
31051	Dixon County, Nebraska	3.3	3,975	12.3	38.6	30.8	18.3
31053	Dodge County, Nebraska	3.1	24,925	12.2	36.8	32.0	18.9
31055	Douglas County, Nebraska	2.9	346,992	10.4	21.9	30.6	37.1
31057	Dundy County, Nebraska	1.5	1,420	6.7	32.5	41.2	19.6
31059	Fillmore County, Nebraska	4.0	4,112	7.2	39.1	35.3	18.5
31061	Franklin County, Nebraska	4.5	2,288	7.8	37.1	36.4	18.7
31063	Frontier County, Nebraska	4.7	1,722	5.2	34.7	41.8	18.3
31065	Furnas County, Nebraska	5.2	3,464	12.0	33.7	36.9	17.3
31067	Gage County, Nebraska	5.0	15,450	10.6	34.6	35.1	19.7
31069	Garden County, Nebraska	6.2	1,454	5.9	32.5	38.1	23.5
31071	Garfield County, Nebraska	4.9	1,402	5.9	39.5	38.4	16.2
31073	Gosper County, Nebraska	5.9	1,391	5.3	34.8	40.5	19.4
31075	Grant County, Nebraska	1.2	525	2.9	42.3	34.5	20.4
31077	Greeley County, Nebraska	2.1	1,723	7.7	39.8	38.2	14.4
31079	Hall County, Nebraska	3.7	39,038	17.2	32.5	32.0	18.3
31081	Hamilton County, Nebraska	3.8	6,178	6.2	31.8	36.8	25.2
31083	Harlan County, Nebraska	5.2	2,518	9.1	37.6	37.2	16.1
31085	Hayes County, Nebraska	3.5	806	10.9	26.7	42.7	19.7
31087	Hitchcock County, Nebraska	6.8	2,087	6.7	37.4	40.8	15.1
31089	Holt County, Nebraska	3.5	7,241	7.9	34.0	37.1	20.9
31091	Hooker County, Nebraska	2.1	546	6.6	34.1	36.3	23.1
31093	Howard County, Nebraska	4.0	4,441	8.1	41.6	31.2	19.2
31095	Jefferson County, Nebraska	3.4	5,318	10.4	42.6	33.3	13.7
31097	Johnson County, Nebraska	15.1	3,757	12.2	40.7	32.4	14.7
31099	Kearney County, Nebraska	3.8	4,544	7.0	32.5	36.4	24.1
31101	Keith County, Nebraska	4.7	5,976	8.1	34.5	36.7	20.7
31103	Keya Paha County, Nebraska	3.6	541	7.9	42.3	34.2	15.5
31105	Kimball County, Nebraska	1.7	2,614	12.2	34.0	36.3	17.4
31107	Knox County, Nebraska	5.0	5,962	9.0	37.2	34.7	19.1
31109	Lancaster County, Nebraska	5.9	184,111	6.5	22.6	34.2	36.7
31111	Lincoln County, Nebraska	3.8	24,406	8.4	31.4	40.2	20.0
31113	Logan County, Nebraska	5.1	572	8.4	28.7	40.9	22.0
31115	Loup County, Nebraska	7.1	419	4.1	41.5	35.8	18.6
31117	McPherson County, Nebraska	0.0	327	5.2	28.4	41.9	24.5
31119	Madison County, Nebraska	3.9	22,886	11.7	29.3	38.8	20.2
31121	Merrick County, Nebraska	2.1	5,430	7.8	34.5	40.9	16.8
31123	Morrill County, Nebraska	5.4	3,356	12.7	32.3	37.2	17.8
31125	Nance County, Nebraska	3.0	2,574	10.6	38.1	34.8	16.5
31127	Nemaha County, Nebraska	3.3	4,682	5.2	34.9	32.1	27.8
31129	Nuckolls County, Nebraska	3.2	3,240	6.5	42.1	34.1	17.3
31131	Otoe County, Nebraska	5.2	10,843	9.0	37.7	31.7	21.5
31133	Pawnee County, Nebraska	7.7	1,973	7.2	45.3	31.2	16.3
31135	Perkins County, Nebraska	5.1	2,057	10.1	31.1	36.8	22.0
31137	Phelps County, Nebraska	3.0	6,338	7.3	33.0	37.0	22.7
31139	Pierce County, Nebraska	3.6	4,880	6.1	36.0	37.4	20.5
31141	Platte County, Nebraska	2.1	21,248	12.0	31.0	36.9	20.1
31143	Polk County, Nebraska	4.4	3,676	6.4	32.5	41.4	19.6
31145	Red Willow County, Nebraska	4.7	7,391	6.7	36.4	39.3	17.7
31147	Richardson County, Nebraska	6.8	5,953	8.3	39.7	31.3	20.7
31149	Rock County, Nebraska	7.1	1,053	7.6	41.7	32.7	18.0
31151	Saline County, Nebraska	2.9	8,737	15.9	34.7	35.2	14.2
31153	Sarpy County, Nebraska	6.8	106,521	4.6	22.5	36.1	36.7
31155	Saunders County, Nebraska	5.7	14,171	6.6	33.0	35.9	24.6
31157	Scotts Bluff County, Nebraska	4.6	24,492	13.4	30.0	35.2	21.5
31159	Seward County, Nebraska	5.5	10,783	7.0	29.5	37.4	26.1
31161	Sheridan County, Nebraska	5.5	3,790	9.8	31.1	34.6	24.5
31163	Sherman County, Nebraska	2.7	2,263	9.5	42.3	33.5	14.7
31165	Sioux County, Nebraska	3.8	899	6.5	33.4	33.6	26.6
31167	Stanton County, Nebraska	3.0	4,018	8.1	35.0	38.6	18.3
31169	Thayer County, Nebraska	3.7	3,781	8.3	37.0	35.4	19.3
31171	Thomas County, Nebraska	9.1	480	6.0	32.1	34.4	27.5
31173	Thurston County, Nebraska	9.3	3,796	13.2	35.5	37.4	13.9
31175	Valley County, Nebraska	4.5	2,990	6.5	42.6	31.7	19.2

Table C. County—Labor Force, Employment, and Educational Data, 2011–2015—*Continued*

Fips code	State/county	Industry for employed population age 16 and older — Public administration	Educational attainment for the population age 25 and older — Total population age 25 and older	Less than high school graduate	High school graduate (includes equivalency)	Some college or Associate's degree	Bachelor's degree or higher
31177	Washington County, Nebraska	2.8	13,633	4.3	31.1	35.0	29.6
31179	Wayne County, Nebraska	1.7	5,193	5.6	20.5	36.2	37.8
31181	Webster County, Nebraska	4.7	2,604	9.3	36.1	34.9	19.8
31183	Wheeler County, Nebraska	3.8	632	5.1	42.1	34.5	18.4
31185	York County, Nebraska	3.1	9,399	6.0	32.6	35.4	26.1
32000	**Nevada**	4.7	1,884,237	14.9	28.2	33.8	23.0
32001	Churchill County, Nevada	10.6	16,254	10.4	35.0	38.7	15.9
32003	Clark County, Nevada	3.9	1,361,667	15.5	28.8	33.1	22.6
32005	Douglas County, Nevada	8.8	35,422	7.2	24.7	42.9	25.2
32007	Elko County, Nevada	5.5	32,112	16.6	26.8	38.5	18.1
32009	Esmeralda County, Nevada	8.0	843	13.0	43.2	28.1	15.7
32011	Eureka County, Nevada	15.5	1,241	8.9	35.8	33.1	22.2
32013	Humboldt County, Nevada	5.2	10,768	16.1	37.4	32.8	13.7
32015	Lander County, Nevada	4.1	3,812	19.0	37.5	35.9	7.6
32017	Lincoln County, Nevada	22.8	3,492	9.9	32.1	37.7	20.3
32019	Lyon County, Nevada	6.9	36,096	15.1	30.2	38.2	16.6
32021	Mineral County, Nevada	18.5	3,414	12.6	31.2	44.8	11.3
32023	Nye County, Nevada	8.5	31,997	15.1	35.6	36.1	13.2
32027	Pershing County, Nevada	14.4	5,013	21.7	35.4	30.5	12.4
32029	Storey County, Nevada	6.5	3,302	7.6	29.5	41.6	21.4
32031	Washoe County, Nevada	4.9	293,259	13.3	24.0	34.0	28.7
32033	White Pine County, Nevada	15.7	6,976	16.4	34.5	35.2	13.9
32510	Carson City, Nevada	14.5	38,569	13.2	28.6	37.5	20.7
33000	**New Hampshire**	3.9	925,145	7.7	28.8	28.6	34.9
33001	Belknap County, New Hampshire	5.2	44,039	8.3	31.5	30.6	29.6
33003	Carroll County, New Hampshire	3.3	36,319	6.9	31.4	29.6	32.1
33005	Cheshire County, New Hampshire	3.1	52,285	7.7	33.8	26.9	31.6
33007	Coos County, New Hampshire	6.1	24,070	12.7	39.1	30.4	17.8
33009	Grafton County, New Hampshire	3.5	61,450	7.9	28.6	25.4	38.1
33011	Hillsborough County, New Hampshire	3.2	278,907	8.8	27.2	28.2	35.9
33013	Merrimack County, New Hampshire	6.3	103,146	7.2	28.4	30.1	34.4
33015	Rockingham County, New Hampshire	3.7	212,961	5.3	26.9	29.1	38.8
33017	Strafford County, New Hampshire	3.6	80,575	8.1	28.0	29.8	34.1
33019	Sullivan County, New Hampshire	2.7	31,393	10.5	37.0	26.0	26.5
34000	**New Jersey**	4.2	6,091,495	11.4	28.6	23.2	36.8
34001	Atlantic County, New Jersey	5.1	187,414	15.4	32.9	26.6	25.1
34003	Bergen County, New Jersey	3.0	650,522	8.4	24.3	20.4	46.9
34005	Burlington County, New Jersey	7.4	311,645	7.3	29.5	27.4	35.7
34007	Camden County, New Jersey	4.6	346,315	12.1	31.3	26.4	30.2
34009	Cape May County, New Jersey	7.3	70,660	10.5	34.1	25.5	29.9
34011	Cumberland County, New Jersey	7.5	105,641	22.5	39.4	23.5	14.6
34013	Essex County, New Jersey	4.1	524,610	15.8	28.7	22.8	32.7
34015	Gloucester County, New Jersey	4.7	196,038	8.3	34.3	28.0	29.3
34017	Hudson County, New Jersey	3.2	466,297	17.1	26.1	19.3	37.5
34019	Hunterdon County, New Jersey	4.0	88,556	5.6	22.7	23.0	48.7
34021	Mercer County, New Jersey	7.8	247,262	12.6	25.6	22.2	39.6
34023	Middlesex County, New Jersey	3.3	563,333	11.2	26.3	21.4	41.0
34025	Monmouth County, New Jersey	4.1	434,934	7.3	25.6	24.6	42.5
34027	Morris County, New Jersey	3.2	345,850	6.2	22.5	20.3	51.0
34029	Ocean County, New Jersey	5.6	402,477	9.5	36.1	27.5	26.9
34031	Passaic County, New Jersey	3.0	331,616	17.7	34.8	21.4	26.0
34033	Salem County, New Jersey	4.8	45,003	13.6	38.6	27.5	20.3
34035	Somerset County, New Jersey	2.5	227,726	5.8	21.9	19.8	52.5
34037	Sussex County, New Jersey	4.7	101,656	6.1	31.0	29.1	33.8
34039	Union County, New Jersey	3.8	369,180	14.4	29.7	23.3	32.6
34041	Warren County, New Jersey	4.5	74,760	9.9	34.0	26.2	29.9
35000	**New Mexico**	7.7	1,367,822	15.8	26.4	31.4	26.3
35001	Bernalillo County, New Mexico	6.5	451,402	12.1	23.8	31.5	32.6
35003	Catron County, New Mexico	13.3	2,822	5.9	36.3	31.8	26.0
35005	Chaves County, New Mexico	5.3	41,078	21.9	27.0	33.0	18.1
35006	Cibola County, New Mexico	10.7	18,155	18.6	36.5	33.0	12.0
35007	Colfax County, New Mexico	5.3	9,474	11.4	33.9	33.3	21.5
35009	Curry County, New Mexico	10.7	30,415	17.6	25.2	36.3	20.8
35011	De Baca County, New Mexico	8.1	1,385	16.8	42.9	30.6	9.7
35013	Doña Ana County, New Mexico	9.0	127,379	21.7	22.0	28.5	27.7
35015	Eddy County, New Mexico	6.4	36,145	16.8	34.0	31.4	17.8
35017	Grant County, New Mexico	5.0	20,517	15.3	26.9	31.6	26.2
35019	Guadalupe County, New Mexico	21.1	3,290	25.1	40.2	21.2	13.5
35021	Harding County, New Mexico	12.7	427	11.5	39.1	23.9	25.5
35023	Hidalgo County, New Mexico	9.9	3,076	23.6	31.0	31.1	14.2
35025	Lea County, New Mexico	3.8	40,910	28.1	30.5	28.2	13.2
35027	Lincoln County, New Mexico	7.1	15,024	11.7	26.6	33.3	28.4
35028	Los Alamos County, New Mexico	5.1	12,713	3.0	10.8	21.9	64.2
35029	Luna County, New Mexico	8.6	15,965	31.3	31.6	25.0	12.1

Table C. County—Labor Force, Employment, and Educational Data, 2011–2015—*Continued*

| | | Industry for employed population age 16 and older | Educational attainment for the population age 25 and older | | | |
| | | | | Educational attainment | | |
Fips code	State/county	Public administration	Total population age 25 and older	Less than high school graduate	High school graduate (includes equivalency)	Some college or Associate's degree	Bachelor's degree or higher
35031	McKinley County, New Mexico	9.2	43,015	26.4	33.1	29.4	11.1
35033	Mora County, New Mexico	12.4	3,168	16.4	35.6	34.1	13.9
35035	Otero County, New Mexico	16.4	42,102	17.0	29.5	37.1	16.4
35037	Quay County, New Mexico	8.6	6,119	16.0	38.8	29.6	15.5
35039	Rio Arriba County, New Mexico	13.6	26,809	18.5	31.8	33.0	16.6
35041	Roosevelt County, New Mexico	6.3	11,176	19.9	25.3	31.8	23.1
35043	Sandoval County, New Mexico	7.6	91,188	9.5	25.9	36.1	28.5
35045	San Juan County, New Mexico	5.4	78,855	17.8	32.1	34.9	15.2
35047	San Miguel County, New Mexico	16.1	19,538	18.3	28.4	33.2	20.0
35049	Santa Fe County, New Mexico	8.9	106,755	12.3	21.4	26.1	40.1
35051	Sierra County, New Mexico	10.5	9,015	16.9	33.7	31.8	17.6
35053	Socorro County, New Mexico	6.0	11,277	23.2	33.4	25.9	17.5
35055	Taos County, New Mexico	6.0	24,358	12.6	25.4	33.4	28.6
35057	Torrance County, New Mexico	7.5	10,949	16.9	34.2	32.4	16.5
35059	Union County, New Mexico	13.9	3,116	19.9	35.3	27.7	17.1
35061	Valencia County, New Mexico	9.5	50,205	18.6	31.9	32.9	16.5
36000	**New York**	4.6	13,435,795	14.4	26.7	24.7	34.2
36001	Albany County, New York	12.6	204,024	7.2	26.5	27.7	38.6
36003	Allegany County, New York	4.1	30,568	11.4	38.7	29.8	20.0
36005	Bronx County, New York	3.6	895,181	29.4	27.3	24.3	18.9
36007	Broome County, New York	4.5	131,269	10.1	32.2	30.4	27.2
36009	Cattaraugus County, New York	6.0	53,408	12.1	40.9	29.1	17.8
36011	Cayuga County, New York	6.5	55,593	12.3	34.1	32.3	21.4
36013	Chautauqua County, New York	4.6	90,321	11.8	35.5	31.8	20.9
36015	Chemung County, New York	6.2	60,733	10.3	35.6	30.6	23.4
36017	Chenango County, New York	5.5	34,918	12.8	39.2	30.6	17.4
36019	Clinton County, New York	9.8	55,148	14.3	35.3	28.3	22.1
36021	Columbia County, New York	8.5	45,591	11.6	30.7	28.4	29.3
36023	Cortland County, New York	4.8	30,462	10.1	34.7	31.6	23.6
36025	Delaware County, New York	4.8	33,253	13.0	38.7	28.1	20.2
36027	Dutchess County, New York	4.9	202,121	10.1	27.0	29.6	33.4
36029	Erie County, New York	4.6	634,345	9.6	28.4	30.5	31.6
36031	Essex County, New York	6.6	28,949	11.2	34.5	30.2	24.2
36033	Franklin County, New York	13.4	35,748	15.1	36.2	31.0	17.7
36035	Fulton County, New York	5.3	38,780	14.0	38.5	31.3	16.2
36037	Genesee County, New York	5.1	41,496	9.2	37.2	33.5	20.0
36039	Greene County, New York	9.2	35,219	13.5	36.3	29.7	20.6
36041	Hamilton County, New York	9.5	3,546	9.3	32.3	33.9	24.5
36043	Herkimer County, New York	5.0	44,536	10.2	34.5	32.8	22.4
36045	Jefferson County, New York	12.4	73,898	10.6	33.5	35.2	20.7
36047	Kings County, New York	3.8	1,735,647	20.7	26.2	20.2	32.8
36049	Lewis County, New York	7.4	18,500	11.0	45.3	28.5	15.2
36051	Livingston County, New York	4.6	42,546	11.4	33.7	31.3	23.6
36053	Madison County, New York	3.7	47,612	9.6	33.7	30.5	26.2
36055	Monroe County, New York	3.1	504,452	9.8	25.0	29.0	36.2
36057	Montgomery County, New York	7.6	34,275	15.7	36.6	31.5	16.2
36059	Nassau County, New York	4.7	931,785	9.2	24.2	23.7	42.8
36061	New York County, New York	2.6	1,229,036	13.4	12.6	14.1	59.9
36063	Niagara County, New York	3.9	150,210	9.5	35.1	32.1	23.2
36065	Oneida County, New York	7.3	160,092	12.2	33.4	31.2	23.2
36067	Onondaga County, New York	3.9	313,724	9.8	26.2	30.0	34.1
36069	Ontario County, New York	3.8	75,472	7.7	28.3	32.2	31.7
36071	Orange County, New York	6.8	237,282	10.9	29.3	30.6	29.2
36073	Orleans County, New York	5.1	29,584	14.6	39.8	30.2	15.4
36075	Oswego County, New York	4.3	79,996	13.6	39.9	28.9	17.6
36077	Otsego County, New York	2.8	40,102	10.1	34.5	27.7	27.7
36079	Putnam County, New York	6.1	69,527	7.6	27.3	27.2	37.9
36081	Queens County, New York	4.0	1,619,173	19.6	27.3	22.7	30.4
36083	Rensselaer County, New York	10.6	109,306	9.2	29.0	33.2	28.6
36085	Richmond County, New York	7.0	322,287	11.3	32.0	25.9	30.8
36087	Rockland County, New York	4.1	201,901	12.7	23.0	24.0	40.3
36089	St. Lawrence County, New York	7.7	72,096	12.0	36.1	29.5	22.3
36091	Saratoga County, New York	7.1	156,862	5.9	25.9	29.3	39.0
36093	Schenectady County, New York	8.3	105,720	9.5	30.0	30.0	30.5
36095	Schoharie County, New York	6.3	22,149	11.8	38.5	30.2	19.6
36097	Schuyler County, New York	5.4	13,283	10.1	38.9	31.6	19.5
36099	Seneca County, New York	6.8	24,921	14.7	34.6	30.4	20.2
36101	Steuben County, New York	4.2	68,314	10.7	37.6	30.4	21.3
36103	Suffolk County, New York	4.9	1,022,970	10.1	29.3	26.6	34.0
36105	Sullivan County, New York	7.6	53,118	14.0	34.0	29.8	22.2
36107	Tioga County, New York	4.0	35,148	9.1	35.9	30.6	24.4
36109	Tompkins County, New York	2.8	59,323	5.8	19.8	23.6	50.8
36111	Ulster County, New York	5.1	128,759	10.3	30.2	29.4	30.1
36113	Warren County, New York	4.9	47,243	9.1	33.3	29.4	28.2

Table C. County—Labor Force, Employment, and Educational Data, 2011–2015—*Continued*

| | | Industry for employed population age 16 and older | Educational attainment for the population age 25 and older | | | |
| | | | | Educational attainment | | |
Fips code	State/county	Public administration	Total population age 25 and older	Less than high school graduate	High school graduate (includes equivalency)	Some college or Associate's degree	Bachelor's degree or higher
36115	Washington County, New York	5.6	44,741	11.5	41.6	27.5	19.4
36117	Wayne County, New York	3.3	64,078	10.4	37.0	31.9	20.6
36119	Westchester County, New York	3.7	659,258	12.5	20.3	20.5	46.7
36121	Wyoming County, New York	6.4	29,663	12.8	40.8	31.2	15.2
36123	Yates County, New York	3.9	16,533	14.2	34.5	27.5	23.7
37000	**North Carolina**	4.5	6,582,301	14.2	26.7	30.8	28.4
37001	Alamance County, North Carolina	3.4	103,609	16.8	28.5	33.1	21.6
37003	Alexander County, North Carolina	3.8	26,160	19.3	39.4	28.2	13.2
37005	Alleghany County, North Carolina	4.0	8,021	19.5	33.7	29.5	17.4
37007	Anson County, North Carolina	6.7	18,172	20.8	41.6	27.8	9.8
37009	Ashe County, North Carolina	3.4	20,219	17.8	31.5	32.0	18.8
37011	Avery County, North Carolina	4.2	13,061	20.5	30.5	30.2	18.9
37013	Beaufort County, North Carolina	4.6	33,649	16.5	33.2	32.9	17.3
37015	Bertie County, North Carolina	6.9	14,741	24.7	40.3	25.0	10.0
37017	Bladen County, North Carolina	8.4	24,004	20.8	33.2	32.3	13.8
37019	Brunswick County, North Carolina	4.5	88,679	13.4	27.3	33.2	26.1
37021	Buncombe County, North Carolina	3.0	177,725	10.3	24.7	29.1	35.9
37023	Burke County, North Carolina	4.4	62,854	20.9	29.8	32.2	17.2
37025	Cabarrus County, North Carolina	3.4	123,216	11.7	28.0	33.2	27.2
37027	Caldwell County, North Carolina	4.7	57,620	23.3	31.6	31.4	13.7
37029	Camden County, North Carolina	14.8	6,848	13.7	23.2	40.8	22.4
37031	Carteret County, North Carolina	8.9	50,729	10.5	27.7	36.5	25.3
37033	Caswell County, North Carolina	4.2	16,907	23.9	35.3	29.2	11.6
37035	Catawba County, North Carolina	2.7	105,756	17.4	30.3	30.6	21.7
37037	Chatham County, North Carolina	3.5	49,325	13.5	23.3	26.4	36.8
37039	Cherokee County, North Carolina	3.3	20,475	17.2	33.2	31.1	18.6
37041	Chowan County, North Carolina	8.3	10,518	17.4	33.7	28.8	20.1
37043	Clay County, North Carolina	3.8	7,938	11.8	29.3	37.8	21.2
37045	Cleveland County, North Carolina	4.1	65,976	17.6	34.6	31.8	16.0
37047	Columbus County, North Carolina	7.2	39,328	20.4	31.7	35.8	12.1
37049	Craven County, North Carolina	10.5	67,182	12.7	27.9	37.1	22.3
37051	Cumberland County, North Carolina	10.0	199,222	10.0	26.0	40.7	23.3
37053	Currituck County, North Carolina	8.6	17,243	13.6	29.3	36.6	20.5
37055	Dare County, North Carolina	5.5	25,736	7.9	24.4	38.3	29.4
37057	Davidson County, North Carolina	3.4	113,458	18.1	33.2	30.0	18.7
37059	Davie County, North Carolina	3.1	29,227	14.9	31.7	29.0	24.4
37061	Duplin County, North Carolina	3.7	39,501	28.0	30.1	31.3	10.7
37063	Durham County, North Carolina	3.7	193,842	12.5	17.4	24.3	45.8
37065	Edgecombe County, North Carolina	4.2	37,239	23.1	35.7	30.5	10.6
37067	Forsyth County, North Carolina	3.0	239,062	12.7	25.6	28.7	32.9
37069	Franklin County, North Carolina	6.1	42,360	17.1	31.3	32.2	19.4
37071	Gaston County, North Carolina	3.7	142,652	17.1	30.1	33.7	19.0
37073	Gates County, North Carolina	5.9	8,186	15.4	37.5	33.8	13.2
37075	Graham County, North Carolina	7.9	6,016	21.6	34.9	29.1	14.3
37077	Granville County, North Carolina	7.4	40,001	18.7	31.1	32.5	17.6
37079	Greene County, North Carolina	6.1	14,746	25.1	31.5	33.4	10.1
37081	Guilford County, North Carolina	2.5	334,008	11.8	24.6	29.5	34.1
37083	Halifax County, North Carolina	6.9	36,900	23.4	35.8	28.1	12.7
37085	Harnett County, North Carolina	9.5	78,061	14.4	30.8	35.2	19.6
37087	Haywood County, North Carolina	4.8	43,917	13.1	28.6	34.4	23.9
37089	Henderson County, North Carolina	2.6	80,661	11.9	26.4	33.1	28.6
37091	Hertford County, North Carolina	7.1	16,832	20.1	32.9	32.9	14.0
37093	Hoke County, North Carolina	10.7	31,669	15.1	27.5	38.1	19.3
37095	Hyde County, North Carolina	11.0	4,150	20.6	35.2	33.9	10.3
37097	Iredell County, North Carolina	2.5	111,146	12.8	28.1	33.2	25.9
37099	Jackson County, North Carolina	5.5	26,024	11.8	27.6	31.1	29.5
37101	Johnston County, North Carolina	6.6	116,344	16.0	30.4	33.4	20.3
37103	Jones County, North Carolina	6.4	7,464	18.1	31.2	37.6	13.1
37105	Lee County, North Carolina	4.7	39,106	19.3	26.4	33.8	20.5
37107	Lenoir County, North Carolina	5.2	40,272	20.5	31.8	34.9	12.7
37109	Lincoln County, North Carolina	4.0	55,475	17.1	30.4	32.3	20.2
37111	McDowell County, North Carolina	6.1	31,920	18.3	36.9	31.3	13.5
37113	Macon County, North Carolina	3.2	25,318	12.9	29.8	34.7	22.5
37115	Madison County, North Carolina	3.7	14,865	19.3	31.0	28.0	21.7
37117	Martin County, North Carolina	5.5	16,866	17.4	37.6	31.4	13.7
37119	Mecklenburg County, North Carolina	2.1	651,782	10.6	19.1	28.0	42.3
37121	Mitchell County, North Carolina	7.8	11,213	19.2	33.5	30.5	16.8
37123	Montgomery County, North Carolina	5.6	18,922	25.0	30.0	30.5	14.5
37125	Moore County, North Carolina	5.5	66,107	10.8	25.8	30.9	32.6
37127	Nash County, North Carolina	5.1	64,548	16.0	33.9	30.9	19.2
37129	New Hanover County, North Carolina	3.1	143,710	8.3	22.1	32.7	36.9
37131	Northampton County, North Carolina	10.9	15,184	23.7	35.9	29.1	11.3
37133	Onslow County, North Carolina	13.4	97,763	9.2	28.9	42.6	19.3
37135	Orange County, North Carolina	3.1	84,359	7.9	15.6	19.8	56.6

Table C. County—Labor Force, Employment, and Educational Data, 2011–2015—*Continued*

Fips code	State/county	Industry for employed population age 16 and older — Public administration	Educational attainment for the population age 25 and older — Total population age 25 and older	Less than high school graduate	High school graduate (includes equivalency)	Some college or Associate's degree	Bachelor's degree or higher
37137	Pamlico County, North Carolina	7.2	9,884	13.1	32.2	35.4	19.3
37139	Pasquotank County, North Carolina	8.5	26,679	16.2	29.9	34.5	19.4
37141	Pender County, North Carolina	5.3	38,543	14.3	31.2	33.3	21.2
37143	Perquimans County, North Carolina	9.2	9,941	16.1	35.0	32.6	16.3
37145	Person County, North Carolina	3.6	27,385	17.0	35.5	32.8	14.7
37147	Pitt County, North Carolina	5.1	102,483	11.9	25.2	33.2	29.7
37149	Polk County, North Carolina	4.6	15,436	11.9	27.2	29.7	31.3
37151	Randolph County, North Carolina	3.3	96,916	20.2	35.1	30.2	14.5
37153	Richmond County, North Carolina	5.5	30,695	19.4	36.5	31.3	12.8
37155	Robeson County, North Carolina	6.0	84,750	24.9	33.5	28.8	12.8
37157	Rockingham County, North Carolina	4.8	65,388	19.6	36.5	30.2	13.8
37159	Rowan County, North Carolina	3.4	94,015	17.5	32.8	32.1	17.6
37161	Rutherford County, North Carolina	3.4	47,325	18.9	31.8	33.1	16.2
37163	Sampson County, North Carolina	3.5	42,550	24.8	33.2	29.6	12.4
37165	Scotland County, North Carolina	4.3	23,737	21.3	34.0	28.9	15.8
37167	Stanly County, North Carolina	5.5	41,659	17.2	34.3	32.2	16.2
37169	Stokes County, North Carolina	3.6	33,550	19.2	38.1	29.1	13.6
37171	Surry County, North Carolina	3.4	50,895	23.2	31.1	30.8	14.9
37173	Swain County, North Carolina	9.4	9,839	19.4	31.2	33.4	15.9
37175	Transylvania County, North Carolina	5.2	24,546	11.5	28.4	30.3	29.7
37177	Tyrrell County, North Carolina	8.5	3,127	30.3	37.1	24.6	8.0
37179	Union County, North Carolina	3.2	133,737	11.0	25.2	30.4	33.4
37181	Vance County, North Carolina	6.6	29,658	23.2	37.6	27.8	11.4
37183	Wake County, North Carolina	5.2	637,100	8.1	16.8	26.1	49.0
37185	Warren County, North Carolina	8.4	14,743	22.2	34.8	27.6	15.4
37187	Washington County, North Carolina	6.3	8,704	20.6	38.0	31.0	10.4
37189	Watauga County, North Carolina	2.2	28,821	11.0	20.4	30.2	38.4
37191	Wayne County, North Carolina	6.8	81,354	17.3	29.7	34.6	18.4
37193	Wilkes County, North Carolina	4.0	48,785	25.0	32.2	30.1	12.8
37195	Wilson County, North Carolina	3.8	54,799	20.2	33.0	28.8	18.0
37197	Yadkin County, North Carolina	2.5	26,486	22.5	34.3	31.3	11.9
37199	Yancey County, North Carolina	7.5	12,982	17.6	33.2	30.0	19.3
38000	**North Dakota**	4.8	468,030	8.3	27.4	36.7	27.7
38001	Adams County, North Dakota	3.4	1,726	4.1	35.1	36.1	24.8
38003	Barnes County, North Dakota	5.3	7,793	8.4	31.3	34.8	25.4
38005	Benson County, North Dakota	7.8	3,857	15.0	32.5	38.0	14.6
38007	Billings County, North Dakota	5.0	717	10.3	34.0	30.4	25.2
38009	Bottineau County, North Dakota	5.0	4,670	10.2	31.3	37.6	20.9
38011	Bowman County, North Dakota	6.2	2,234	10.3	30.0	37.6	22.1
38013	Burke County, North Dakota	7.3	1,446	12.7	30.8	36.9	19.6
38015	Burleigh County, North Dakota	8.0	59,286	6.5	24.5	35.0	34.0
38017	Cass County, North Dakota	2.3	100,516	5.1	20.6	37.5	36.8
38019	Cavalier County, North Dakota	4.0	2,883	10.5	27.6	44.2	17.7
38021	Dickey County, North Dakota	1.9	3,534	13.4	28.7	31.3	26.6
38023	Divide County, North Dakota	5.5	1,836	10.7	34.3	34.4	20.6
38025	Dunn County, North Dakota	5.7	2,914	9.0	34.3	37.1	19.6
38027	Eddy County, North Dakota	5.5	1,713	11.6	28.7	37.8	22.0
38029	Emmons County, North Dakota	5.3	2,503	16.2	36.9	31.6	15.3
38031	Foster County, North Dakota	5.0	2,426	12.3	31.4	37.5	18.8
38033	Golden Valley County, North Dakota	5.4	1,206	8.3	24.0	45.0	22.7
38035	Grand Forks County, North Dakota	5.0	39,696	7.2	24.7	35.2	33.0
38037	Grant County, North Dakota	3.7	1,851	11.1	38.2	33.5	17.1
38039	Griggs County, North Dakota	2.7	1,766	11.7	37.6	32.4	18.3
38041	Hettinger County, North Dakota	4.8	1,921	11.2	37.1	36.9	14.8
38043	Kidder County, North Dakota	3.7	1,790	11.6	32.6	36.3	19.5
38045	LaMoure County, North Dakota	3.3	2,993	13.0	31.7	34.1	21.1
38047	Logan County, North Dakota	5.1	1,445	18.1	39.3	30.0	12.7
38049	McHenry County, North Dakota	6.0	4,078	10.3	37.0	34.0	18.8
38051	McIntosh County, North Dakota	3.2	2,182	20.3	31.5	29.5	18.7
38053	McKenzie County, North Dakota	4.5	5,890	8.3	28.4	40.5	22.8
38055	McLean County, North Dakota	4.8	6,884	8.8	33.8	38.4	19.0
38057	Mercer County, North Dakota	2.6	6,198	10.0	29.7	39.8	20.5
38059	Morton County, North Dakota	7.0	20,059	8.4	30.2	35.5	25.9
38061	Mountrail County, North Dakota	12.1	5,911	8.0	29.7	40.3	22.0
38063	Nelson County, North Dakota	6.0	2,348	9.2	30.8	40.8	19.2
38065	Oliver County, North Dakota	5.8	1,302	13.0	30.3	39.2	17.5
38067	Pembina County, North Dakota	7.1	5,237	10.4	38.6	32.0	19.0
38069	Pierce County, North Dakota	1.4	3,198	14.1	33.2	37.5	15.2
38071	Ramsey County, North Dakota	5.3	7,892	9.8	30.2	37.0	23.0
38073	Ransom County, North Dakota	1.6	3,844	10.1	36.4	35.4	18.1
38075	Renville County, North Dakota	7.7	1,720	6.9	30.1	47.0	15.9
38077	Richland County, North Dakota	3.4	10,461	8.7	28.5	41.1	21.8
38079	Rolette County, North Dakota	8.5	8,191	17.3	21.8	40.0	20.9
38081	Sargent County, North Dakota	2.5	2,756	8.3	32.8	39.1	19.8

Table C. County—Labor Force, Employment, and Educational Data, 2011–2015—*Continued*

Fips code	State/county	Industry for employed population age 16 and older — Public administration	Educational attainment for the population age 25 and older — Total population age 25 and older	Educational attainment — Less than high school graduate	High school graduate (includes equivalency)	Some college or Associate's degree	Bachelor's degree or higher
38083	Sheridan County, North Dakota	5.6	1,054	13.9	36.8	34.2	15.2
38085	Sioux County, North Dakota	18.2	2,281	15.9	31.8	35.1	17.3
38087	Slope County, North Dakota	3.3	522	11.9	32.4	30.1	25.7
38089	Stark County, North Dakota	3.6	18,796	10.0	30.5	35.2	24.3
38091	Steele County, North Dakota	1.7	1,468	6.8	30.9	42.6	19.7
38093	Stutsman County, North Dakota	5.2	14,526	11.0	35.5	29.9	23.6
38095	Towner County, North Dakota	6.0	1,649	8.1	33.2	41.0	17.7
38097	Traill County, North Dakota	3.7	5,465	8.1	25.2	40.3	26.4
38099	Walsh County, North Dakota	3.8	7,732	13.8	36.0	33.0	17.2
38101	Ward County, North Dakota	6.6	41,266	7.0	29.3	37.9	25.8
38103	Wells County, North Dakota	3.9	3,142	16.3	33.8	30.0	19.8
38105	Williams County, North Dakota	2.9	19,256	9.3	28.5	41.2	21.0
39000	**Ohio**	3.9	7,817,508	10.9	34.1	28.9	26.1
39001	Adams County, Ohio	3.3	19,116	22.0	43.6	23.9	10.5
39003	Allen County, Ohio	3.8	69,372	10.7	39.7	32.3	17.4
39005	Ashland County, Ohio	2.7	35,149	12.2	42.8	24.6	20.4
39007	Ashtabula County, Ohio	3.3	69,039	14.5	44.9	27.3	13.3
39009	Athens County, Ohio	3.2	35,371	10.2	32.3	28.3	29.1
39011	Auglaize County, Ohio	2.7	30,970	7.5	43.9	31.2	17.5
39013	Belmont County, Ohio	4.7	50,842	10.5	43.5	31.0	15.1
39015	Brown County, Ohio	3.9	30,342	16.2	48.1	23.6	12.1
39017	Butler County, Ohio	2.6	237,038	10.4	34.0	27.2	28.4
39019	Carroll County, Ohio	2.8	20,172	13.0	47.5	28.2	11.4
39021	Champaign County, Ohio	2.6	26,699	12.2	45.1	27.2	15.5
39023	Clark County, Ohio	4.9	93,110	13.2	36.4	32.3	18.1
39025	Clermont County, Ohio	2.8	134,899	10.5	34.0	28.4	27.1
39027	Clinton County, Ohio	4.5	27,701	12.0	40.6	31.5	15.8
39029	Columbiana County, Ohio	2.8	75,559	12.9	46.5	26.7	13.9
39031	Coshocton County, Ohio	2.6	25,224	15.0	50.3	22.6	12.1
39033	Crawford County, Ohio	4.0	29,818	12.3	44.9	30.1	12.6
39035	Cuyahoga County, Ohio	4.0	872,905	12.0	28.3	29.2	30.5
39037	Darke County, Ohio	2.0	35,565	11.8	49.9	26.0	12.3
39039	Defiance County, Ohio	3.5	25,869	10.1	44.2	29.1	16.7
39041	Delaware County, Ohio	4.9	120,295	3.4	20.6	24.2	51.8
39043	Erie County, Ohio	3.9	53,947	9.8	39.5	29.5	21.2
39045	Fairfield County, Ohio	6.9	99,454	8.3	34.4	31.3	26.0
39047	Fayette County, Ohio	5.2	19,663	14.6	46.7	24.6	14.1
39049	Franklin County, Ohio	4.6	797,167	10.0	25.1	27.3	37.6
39051	Fulton County, Ohio	2.8	28,520	9.8	40.8	32.2	17.2
39053	Gallia County, Ohio	3.9	20,732	20.2	40.5	24.2	15.1
39055	Geauga County, Ohio	2.9	63,602	9.0	27.3	26.7	37.0
39057	Greene County, Ohio	9.9	108,078	7.8	25.6	29.4	37.1
39059	Guernsey County, Ohio	4.0	27,307	14.9	43.1	28.6	13.5
39061	Hamilton County, Ohio	3.2	536,866	10.4	27.1	27.5	35.0
39063	Hancock County, Ohio	2.1	50,913	8.4	36.1	29.6	25.8
39065	Hardin County, Ohio	2.9	19,322	10.8	49.2	26.4	13.5
39067	Harrison County, Ohio	3.1	11,219	13.0	48.7	29.7	8.6
39069	Henry County, Ohio	4.5	19,041	9.8	43.9	30.3	16.1
39071	Highland County, Ohio	3.5	29,251	15.5	43.1	29.2	12.1
39073	Hocking County, Ohio	4.3	20,019	12.1	43.7	29.1	15.1
39075	Holmes County, Ohio	1.1	24,612	42.3	35.1	14.8	7.8
39077	Huron County, Ohio	2.8	39,359	12.1	48.1	26.7	13.1
39079	Jackson County, Ohio	4.0	22,211	17.3	41.8	23.7	17.2
39081	Jefferson County, Ohio	3.2	47,972	9.9	42.5	32.5	15.1
39083	Knox County, Ohio	3.5	39,473	11.0	41.2	25.9	21.8
39085	Lake County, Ohio	3.3	162,923	8.3	33.9	31.5	26.3
39087	Lawrence County, Ohio	3.1	42,829	14.0	43.1	28.2	14.7
39089	Licking County, Ohio	5.5	113,169	10.1	37.2	29.8	22.8
39091	Logan County, Ohio	3.2	30,956	11.6	49.4	23.4	15.7
39093	Lorain County, Ohio	3.8	206,754	10.9	33.4	32.9	22.8
39095	Lucas County, Ohio	3.3	289,567	11.6	31.2	32.9	24.2
39097	Madison County, Ohio	6.7	30,521	13.6	40.7	28.6	17.1
39099	Mahoning County, Ohio	3.5	165,403	10.6	38.1	29.2	22.2
39101	Marion County, Ohio	5.1	46,161	13.8	42.6	31.3	12.4
39103	Medina County, Ohio	3.3	120,032	6.5	32.4	30.3	30.8
39105	Meigs County, Ohio	5.6	16,521	15.8	43.5	27.8	12.9
39107	Mercer County, Ohio	1.9	27,110	8.4	49.1	26.7	15.7
39109	Miami County, Ohio	3.7	71,468	11.4	36.9	31.1	20.6
39111	Monroe County, Ohio	3.5	10,462	14.1	51.2	24.9	9.9
39113	Montgomery County, Ohio	5.7	362,413	10.8	28.8	34.6	25.7
39115	Morgan County, Ohio	4.9	10,448	13.4	47.5	28.0	11.1
39117	Morrow County, Ohio	4.7	23,714	12.8	46.2	27.1	13.9
39119	Muskingum County, Ohio	3.3	57,949	13.4	42.9	28.7	15.1
39121	Noble County, Ohio	5.9	11,303	17.0	52.1	21.6	9.3

Table C. County—Labor Force, Employment, and Educational Data, 2011–2015—*Continued*

Fips code	State/county	Industry for employed population age 16 and older — Public administration	Total population age 25 and older	Educational attainment for the population age 25 and older — Less than high school graduate	High school graduate (includes equivalency)	Some college or Associate's degree	Bachelor's degree or higher
39123	Ottawa County, Ohio	3.7	30,287	7.4	38.6	32.3	21.7
39125	Paulding County, Ohio	2.2	13,152	10.3	50.1	26.8	12.7
39127	Perry County, Ohio	4.1	24,118	16.6	43.9	28.5	11.0
39129	Pickaway County, Ohio	6.3	38,535	13.6	42.9	26.5	17.1
39131	Pike County, Ohio	7.0	19,168	22.2	42.0	24.0	11.8
39133	Portage County, Ohio	3.0	103,292	8.6	37.8	27.6	26.0
39135	Preble County, Ohio	2.7	28,685	11.9	46.0	30.3	11.8
39137	Putnam County, Ohio	2.3	22,610	7.3	42.8	30.5	19.4
39139	Richland County, Ohio	4.5	85,144	13.3	41.2	29.9	15.7
39141	Ross County, Ohio	6.4	54,140	15.4	42.8	27.2	14.7
39143	Sandusky County, Ohio	2.1	41,263	10.2	43.0	32.4	14.5
39145	Scioto County, Ohio	6.3	53,267	17.5	40.5	27.6	14.4
39147	Seneca County, Ohio	2.8	37,082	9.5	46.0	30.3	14.2
39149	Shelby County, Ohio	3.0	32,267	9.9	44.1	29.7	16.3
39151	Stark County, Ohio	2.6	258,395	10.0	38.3	29.8	21.9
39153	Summit County, Ohio	2.9	373,837	9.1	32.3	28.3	30.3
39155	Trumbull County, Ohio	3.9	145,804	11.5	45.2	25.9	17.3
39157	Tuscarawas County, Ohio	2.7	64,070	14.1	46.9	24.5	14.4
39159	Union County, Ohio	4.6	35,402	7.8	36.8	29.2	26.2
39161	Van Wert County, Ohio	2.6	19,530	8.4	48.7	27.2	15.7
39163	Vinton County, Ohio	5.5	9,010	18.1	45.9	26.8	9.1
39165	Warren County, Ohio	3.5	146,044	7.1	26.8	26.6	39.6
39167	Washington County, Ohio	5.9	43,327	10.4	41.5	30.6	17.5
39169	Wayne County, Ohio	2.2	75,138	15.0	41.0	22.9	21.2
39171	Williams County, Ohio	3.6	25,874	11.0	45.4	29.8	13.9
39173	Wood County, Ohio	3.4	79,133	5.9	31.3	31.6	31.1
39175	Wyandot County, Ohio	3.7	15,448	9.9	48.2	27.7	14.1
40000	**Oklahoma**	6.2	2,512,392	13.1	31.7	31.1	24.1
40001	Adair County, Oklahoma	6.9	14,280	21.0	42.6	22.6	13.8
40003	Alfalfa County, Oklahoma	9.4	4,307	11.8	40.6	27.4	20.2
40005	Atoka County, Oklahoma	9.3	9,593	18.2	40.8	27.0	14.0
40007	Beaver County, Oklahoma	4.2	3,699	17.3	37.7	24.9	20.1
40009	Beckham County, Oklahoma	4.5	15,251	16.7	40.4	25.3	17.6
40011	Blaine County, Oklahoma	6.0	6,787	14.6	39.4	29.7	16.3
40013	Bryan County, Oklahoma	6.8	29,035	15.8	33.4	29.4	21.5
40015	Caddo County, Oklahoma	8.3	19,471	15.4	41.2	27.5	15.8
40017	Canadian County, Oklahoma	8.1	82,680	8.3	29.3	36.8	25.5
40019	Carter County, Oklahoma	3.6	32,120	14.2	39.6	27.4	18.8
40021	Cherokee County, Oklahoma	10.3	29,738	14.4	31.1	30.0	24.4
40023	Choctaw County, Oklahoma	6.7	10,236	19.9	40.1	26.9	13.2
40025	Cimarron County, Oklahoma	7.4	1,655	15.6	36.3	28.9	19.1
40027	Cleveland County, Oklahoma	8.3	168,029	8.8	26.6	33.6	31.0
40029	Coal County, Oklahoma	5.4	3,898	17.2	42.8	25.2	14.8
40031	Comanche County, Oklahoma	12.4	77,824	10.7	33.2	35.3	20.8
40033	Cotton County, Oklahoma	9.1	4,190	15.3	40.7	28.6	15.4
40035	Craig County, Oklahoma	6.0	10,252	15.4	40.3	30.4	13.9
40037	Creek County, Oklahoma	3.5	47,827	14.7	40.0	30.4	15.0
40039	Custer County, Oklahoma	5.5	16,977	13.7	35.1	24.3	26.9
40041	Delaware County, Oklahoma	5.1	29,522	15.1	37.2	30.9	16.8
40043	Dewey County, Oklahoma	4.2	3,254	10.0	42.3	25.8	21.8
40045	Ellis County, Oklahoma	6.2	2,874	11.7	37.4	28.9	22.0
40047	Garfield County, Oklahoma	6.1	40,729	13.5	35.6	29.2	21.7
40049	Garvin County, Oklahoma	5.3	18,359	15.4	43.5	25.9	15.2
40051	Grady County, Oklahoma	6.6	35,814	13.2	37.7	31.5	17.6
40053	Grant County, Oklahoma	5.9	3,151	8.9	36.0	31.5	23.5
40055	Greer County, Oklahoma	10.7	4,501	15.6	37.0	34.2	13.1
40057	Harmon County, Oklahoma	8.4	1,950	20.7	26.6	29.9	22.8
40059	Harper County, Oklahoma	9.4	2,545	16.7	38.6	24.0	20.7
40061	Haskell County, Oklahoma	3.6	8,697	21.2	38.7	28.6	11.5
40063	Hughes County, Oklahoma	9.8	9,666	20.6	38.0	29.3	12.2
40065	Jackson County, Oklahoma	15.5	16,536	17.7	27.2	35.4	19.7
40067	Jefferson County, Oklahoma	6.0	4,311	15.5	44.8	28.0	11.7
40069	Johnston County, Oklahoma	7.0	7,471	18.1	35.5	30.3	16.1
40071	Kay County, Oklahoma	5.2	30,048	13.5	34.0	34.0	18.4
40073	Kingfisher County, Oklahoma	4.5	10,061	12.7	36.1	31.4	19.7
40075	Kiowa County, Oklahoma	6.9	6,480	15.4	34.7	31.2	18.8
40077	Latimer County, Oklahoma	5.3	7,191	16.5	34.4	35.1	14.0
40079	Le Flore County, Oklahoma	5.1	33,538	18.5	39.8	27.8	13.8
40081	Lincoln County, Oklahoma	8.1	23,304	15.3	39.5	31.7	13.4
40083	Logan County, Oklahoma	6.8	29,641	9.7	34.4	29.8	26.1
40085	Love County, Oklahoma	4.7	6,400	15.9	42.5	27.5	14.2
40087	McClain County, Oklahoma	8.3	24,053	12.7	34.7	30.2	22.4
40089	McCurtain County, Oklahoma	4.2	21,725	19.0	41.6	26.0	13.4
40091	McIntosh County, Oklahoma	6.7	14,684	17.3	38.0	31.0	13.8
40093	Major County, Oklahoma	5.2	5,239	12.8	41.2	29.4	16.7

Table C. County—Labor Force, Employment, and Educational Data, 2011–2015—*Continued*

		Industry for employed population age 16 and older	Educational attainment for the population age 25 and older				
					Educational attainment		
Fips code	State/county	Public administration	Total population age 25 and older	Less than high school graduate	High school graduate (includes equivalency)	Some college or Associate's degree	Bachelor's degree or higher
40095	Marshall County, Oklahoma	4.4	10,967	20.3	35.1	31.2	13.4
40097	Mayes County, Oklahoma	4.2	27,432	13.8	37.5	32.4	16.3
40099	Murray County, Oklahoma	5.9	9,345	17.7	39.2	22.9	20.2
40101	Muskogee County, Oklahoma	6.5	46,538	14.9	35.8	30.9	18.4
40103	Noble County, Oklahoma	6.0	7,843	11.3	35.4	30.6	22.7
40105	Nowata County, Oklahoma	2.5	7,228	15.0	42.1	29.2	13.8
40107	Okfuskee County, Oklahoma	9.8	8,277	20.0	37.3	30.6	12.1
40109	Oklahoma County, Oklahoma	7.1	487,987	13.8	25.3	30.3	30.6
40111	Okmulgee County, Oklahoma	6.9	25,968	13.1	37.0	34.7	15.2
40113	Osage County, Oklahoma	6.4	33,168	12.5	41.9	29.5	16.1
40115	Ottawa County, Oklahoma	5.8	20,887	16.3	36.4	33.6	13.7
40117	Pawnee County, Oklahoma	6.5	11,251	12.8	42.3	28.4	16.5
40119	Payne County, Oklahoma	4.6	42,518	8.7	27.4	27.0	36.9
40121	Pittsburg County, Oklahoma	11.5	31,369	14.8	36.4	32.6	16.2
40123	Pontotoc County, Oklahoma	9.2	24,351	12.1	33.5	27.3	27.1
40125	Pottawatomie County, Oklahoma	11.9	46,422	13.0	35.5	33.4	18.1
40127	Pushmataha County, Oklahoma	6.8	7,930	19.0	39.2	28.6	13.2
40129	Roger Mills County, Oklahoma	6.6	2,565	9.4	39.7	30.5	20.4
40131	Rogers County, Oklahoma	4.1	58,971	8.9	33.1	34.6	23.4
40133	Seminole County, Oklahoma	8.2	16,678	16.7	36.2	33.4	13.7
40135	Sequoyah County, Oklahoma	5.3	28,005	18.2	39.5	28.8	13.5
40137	Stephens County, Oklahoma	4.5	30,505	14.4	38.9	29.4	17.3
40139	Texas County, Oklahoma	3.4	13,044	30.4	28.4	22.2	19.1
40141	Tillman County, Oklahoma	6.9	5,227	23.5	35.8	24.0	16.7
40143	Tulsa County, Oklahoma	2.7	405,621	11.2	25.8	32.6	30.4
40145	Wagoner County, Oklahoma	4.3	50,211	10.4	35.3	32.5	21.8
40147	Washington County, Oklahoma	2.9	35,222	9.8	33.8	29.5	26.9
40149	Washita County, Oklahoma	6.7	7,752	13.1	40.0	26.9	20.0
40151	Woods County, Oklahoma	7.7	5,718	12.1	33.5	27.3	27.2
40153	Woodward County, Oklahoma	5.0	13,799	13.4	39.7	28.8	18.1
41000	**Oregon**	4.5	2,714,972	10.2	24.3	34.8	30.8
41001	Baker County, Oregon	5.8	11,823	10.7	31.8	37.0	20.6
41003	Benton County, Oregon	3.9	52,134	5.1	14.9	27.2	52.8
41005	Clackamas County, Oregon	3.8	270,451	6.9	23.5	36.5	33.1
41007	Clatsop County, Oregon	5.7	26,885	8.9	26.3	41.3	23.6
41009	Columbia County, Oregon	4.7	34,538	10.3	33.8	37.7	18.2
41011	Coos County, Oregon	6.8	46,383	10.9	32.6	38.1	18.3
41013	Crook County, Oregon	7.2	15,572	12.9	37.8	33.9	15.5
41015	Curry County, Oregon	10.9	17,647	9.9	27.7	38.9	23.5
41017	Deschutes County, Oregon	3.4	118,366	6.5	22.9	38.1	32.6
41019	Douglas County, Oregon	5.7	78,377	11.3	32.1	40.9	15.7
41021	Gilliam County, Oregon	8.9	1,352	8.7	39.3	35.9	16.1
41023	Grant County, Oregon	11.5	5,503	11.2	32.3	37.4	19.1
41025	Harney County, Oregon	12.6	5,157	12.4	33.9	36.7	17.0
41027	Hood River County, Oregon	2.8	15,254	18.8	25.6	23.8	31.7
41029	Jackson County, Oregon	4.7	147,024	11.2	27.4	35.8	25.6
41031	Jefferson County, Oregon	7.8	14,789	16.1	29.5	38.5	16.0
41033	Josephine County, Oregon	4.6	61,068	10.9	32.1	40.2	16.7
41035	Klamath County, Oregon	7.4	45,693	11.9	29.9	38.4	19.7
41037	Lake County, Oregon	9.3	5,866	15.6	33.4	33.3	17.7
41039	Lane County, Oregon	3.3	241,134	8.9	25.0	37.7	28.4
41041	Lincoln County, Oregon	5.8	35,290	11.2	28.1	37.0	23.7
41043	Linn County, Oregon	4.9	80,945	10.5	31.0	41.2	17.3
41045	Malheur County, Oregon	8.2	19,892	19.8	29.9	36.5	13.8
41047	Marion County, Oregon	8.6	209,106	15.7	27.2	35.1	22.0
41049	Morrow County, Oregon	5.5	7,082	24.1	35.4	30.0	10.5
41051	Multnomah County, Oregon	3.2	547,704	9.7	18.4	30.6	41.3
41053	Polk County, Oregon	10.0	49,104	8.7	26.8	35.1	29.4
41055	Sherman County, Oregon	5.9	1,314	8.1	36.7	37.9	17.3
41057	Tillamook County, Oregon	6.1	18,918	10.5	34.6	33.8	21.0
41059	Umatilla County, Oregon	8.1	49,470	16.7	29.1	38.0	16.3
41061	Union County, Oregon	6.4	17,094	7.7	33.4	35.7	23.2
41063	Wallowa County, Oregon	5.5	5,278	6.6	33.1	36.0	24.3
41065	Wasco County, Oregon	4.0	17,606	15.2	28.5	37.7	18.7
41067	Washington County, Oregon	3.0	373,592	9.3	19.0	31.0	40.7
41069	Wheeler County, Oregon	13.0	1,101	10.8	36.1	37.7	15.4
41071	Yamhill County, Oregon	4.9	66,460	12.5	29.8	34.4	23.2
42000	**Pennsylvania**	4.1	8,814,112	10.8	36.4	24.2	28.6
42001	Adams County, Pennsylvania	5.2	70,365	12.7	42.0	23.7	21.7
42003	Allegheny County, Pennsylvania	3.2	877,398	6.5	29.8	26.0	37.8
42005	Armstrong County, Pennsylvania	3.1	49,652	11.1	49.4	24.5	15.0
42007	Beaver County, Pennsylvania	3.1	122,666	8.3	39.2	29.8	22.8
42009	Bedford County, Pennsylvania	4.1	35,334	14.0	50.8	21.7	13.5
42011	Berks County, Pennsylvania	2.4	277,030	14.9	38.4	23.5	23.2

Table C. County—Labor Force, Employment, and Educational Data, 2011–2015—*Continued*

Fips code	State/county	Industry for employed population age 16 and older Public administration	Educational attainment for the population age 25 and older Total population age 25 and older	Educational attainment Less than high school graduate	High school graduate (includes equivalency)	Some college or Associate's degree	Bachelor's degree or higher
42013	Blair County, Pennsylvania	4.6	88,860	9.5	48.2	22.8	19.6
42015	Bradford County, Pennsylvania	2.8	43,825	11.5	48.0	22.8	17.6
42017	Bucks County, Pennsylvania	3.1	440,969	6.5	30.7	25.4	37.4
42019	Butler County, Pennsylvania	3.3	129,399	7.0	34.9	25.8	32.3
42021	Cambria County, Pennsylvania	5.8	99,301	10.4	46.3	24.3	19.1
42023	Cameron County, Pennsylvania	3.8	3,678	10.5	48.7	25.1	15.7
42025	Carbon County, Pennsylvania	3.7	47,170	11.3	46.2	27.0	15.5
42027	Centre County, Pennsylvania	3.5	91,495	6.8	31.6	20.2	41.4
42029	Chester County, Pennsylvania	2.4	342,356	7.3	23.2	20.4	49.1
42031	Clarion County, Pennsylvania	4.4	26,041	11.3	47.0	21.6	20.1
42033	Clearfield County, Pennsylvania	5.9	59,280	12.9	50.9	23.0	13.2
42035	Clinton County, Pennsylvania	4.9	25,059	12.9	45.6	24.6	16.9
42037	Columbia County, Pennsylvania	3.8	43,764	11.5	45.7	21.7	21.1
42039	Crawford County, Pennsylvania	4.1	59,974	12.3	45.0	22.9	19.8
42041	Cumberland County, Pennsylvania	8.7	167,431	8.5	35.0	23.7	32.7
42043	Dauphin County, Pennsylvania	10.0	186,900	11.2	34.8	25.6	28.4
42045	Delaware County, Pennsylvania	3.3	376,325	7.8	31.8	24.4	36.0
42047	Elk County, Pennsylvania	2.7	22,983	8.9	50.4	24.0	16.8
42049	Erie County, Pennsylvania	3.2	187,105	9.2	40.0	24.7	26.1
42051	Fayette County, Pennsylvania	3.3	97,832	13.2	49.9	22.7	14.2
42053	Forest County, Pennsylvania	12.0	6,255	19.5	53.6	18.4	8.5
42055	Franklin County, Pennsylvania	5.5	104,988	14.0	43.9	23.1	19.0
42057	Fulton County, Pennsylvania	6.9	10,413	14.9	51.1	20.9	13.1
42059	Greene County, Pennsylvania	6.5	26,804	13.1	47.3	21.9	17.7
42061	Huntingdon County, Pennsylvania	7.3	32,681	11.2	51.7	22.9	14.3
42063	Indiana County, Pennsylvania	3.4	56,291	11.5	43.9	22.0	22.6
42065	Jefferson County, Pennsylvania	3.8	31,603	11.4	51.2	22.8	14.6
42067	Juniata County, Pennsylvania	5.2	17,317	18.3	51.0	17.5	13.1
42069	Lackawanna County, Pennsylvania	5.4	149,695	10.1	37.7	26.3	25.9
42071	Lancaster County, Pennsylvania	2.6	351,025	15.5	38.2	21.1	25.2
42073	Lawrence County, Pennsylvania	3.7	63,496	10.8	45.0	24.5	19.7
42075	Lebanon County, Pennsylvania	4.3	93,031	14.3	43.9	22.1	19.6
42077	Lehigh County, Pennsylvania	2.7	242,376	12.6	33.1	25.8	28.5
42079	Luzerne County, Pennsylvania	5.3	226,983	11.1	39.5	28.0	21.4
42081	Lycoming County, Pennsylvania	3.9	80,594	12.0	41.1	26.5	20.4
42083	McKean County, Pennsylvania	4.3	30,199	10.3	48.2	24.8	16.7
42085	Mercer County, Pennsylvania	4.1	80,186	10.9	44.4	23.2	21.5
42087	Mifflin County, Pennsylvania	3.5	32,674	17.8	50.2	20.4	11.6
42089	Monroe County, Pennsylvania	4.4	112,801	10.3	36.6	30.0	23.0
42091	Montgomery County, Pennsylvania	2.5	568,085	6.2	24.8	22.1	46.9
42093	Montour County, Pennsylvania	4.8	13,349	10.6	39.8	20.8	28.8
42095	Northampton County, Pennsylvania	3.2	206,993	10.2	35.3	27.3	27.2
42097	Northumberland County, Pennsylvania	6.2	68,199	14.4	50.3	20.7	14.6
42099	Perry County, Pennsylvania	8.6	31,931	11.5	46.0	26.5	16.0
42101	Philadelphia County, Pennsylvania	6.3	1,024,009	18.0	33.8	22.8	25.4
42103	Pike County, Pennsylvania	4.3	40,482	9.0	35.8	31.4	23.7
42105	Potter County, Pennsylvania	3.9	12,332	12.2	48.2	23.9	15.7
42107	Schuylkill County, Pennsylvania	5.3	106,674	12.5	47.7	24.3	15.4
42109	Snyder County, Pennsylvania	4.5	26,464	17.6	46.0	20.0	16.5
42111	Somerset County, Pennsylvania	4.9	56,685	13.5	49.3	21.9	15.3
42113	Sullivan County, Pennsylvania	5.6	4,921	10.4	49.1	24.3	16.1
42115	Susquehanna County, Pennsylvania	3.2	30,720	10.9	46.7	25.3	17.1
42117	Tioga County, Pennsylvania	4.0	29,332	11.6	44.6	24.2	19.6
42119	Union County, Pennsylvania	4.6	30,478	16.1	41.2	22.3	20.5
42121	Venango County, Pennsylvania	5.9	38,780	11.0	49.7	23.6	15.8
42123	Warren County, Pennsylvania	2.9	29,821	9.5	47.2	25.3	18.1
42125	Washington County, Pennsylvania	2.8	148,204	8.7	39.3	24.6	27.4
42127	Wayne County, Pennsylvania	5.8	38,609	10.7	44.3	25.4	19.7
42129	Westmoreland County, Pennsylvania	3.2	263,887	7.3	38.9	27.4	26.4
42131	Wyoming County, Pennsylvania	3.2	19,711	8.8	48.2	24.8	18.2
42133	York County, Pennsylvania	4.9	302,842	11.7	41.0	24.6	22.8
44000	**Rhode Island**	4.3	720,641	13.8	27.3	26.9	31.9
44001	Bristol County, Rhode Island	4.8	33,968	9.3	22.4	23.3	45.1
44003	Kent County, Rhode Island	4.8	120,091	9.3	28.6	31.3	30.9
44005	Newport County, Rhode Island	5.7	59,154	7.3	23.1	24.6	45.1
44007	Providence County, Rhode Island	3.8	422,402	17.9	28.8	26.5	26.8
44009	Washington County, Rhode Island	4.8	85,026	6.5	23.3	26.1	44.1
45000	**South Carolina**	4.9	3,210,007	14.4	29.8	30.0	25.8
45001	Abbeville County, South Carolina	3.3	17,036	21.9	37.5	28.3	12.3
45003	Aiken County, South Carolina	4.8	112,845	14.7	31.0	29.1	25.3
45005	Allendale County, South Carolina	8.3	6,870	25.3	39.4	22.8	12.6
45007	Anderson County, South Carolina	3.4	130,096	17.2	31.5	31.8	19.5
45009	Bamberg County, South Carolina	8.4	9,876	23.6	25.2	33.0	18.2
45011	Barnwell County, South Carolina	6.9	14,327	20.7	37.5	29.8	11.9

Table C. County—Labor Force, Employment, and Educational Data, 2011–2015—*Continued*

| | | Industry for employed population age 16 and older | Educational attainment for the population age 25 and older | | | |
| | | | | Educational attainment | | |
Fips code	State/county	Public administration	Total population age 25 and older	Less than high school graduate	High school graduate (includes equivalency)	Some college or Associate's degree	Bachelor's degree or higher
45013	Beaufort County, South Carolina	5.5	120,118	7.9	23.4	29.9	38.8
45015	Berkeley County, South Carolina	6.7	125,957	12.2	31.1	34.5	22.3
45017	Calhoun County, South Carolina	7.1	10,714	16.0	37.2	30.0	16.8
45019	Charleston County, South Carolina	4.9	258,098	10.3	21.6	27.7	40.4
45021	Cherokee County, South Carolina	3.3	36,901	22.4	36.9	25.5	15.3
45023	Chester County, South Carolina	5.6	22,039	21.4	36.5	28.4	13.8
45025	Chesterfield County, South Carolina	3.8	31,215	23.7	39.6	24.9	11.8
45027	Clarendon County, South Carolina	5.7	23,569	20.7	36.4	28.6	14.3
45029	Colleton County, South Carolina	6.6	25,950	17.8	37.9	30.3	14.0
45031	Darlington County, South Carolina	3.3	45,799	19.3	36.5	27.4	16.9
45033	Dillon County, South Carolina	5.0	20,408	27.1	38.9	25.0	9.0
45035	Dorchester County, South Carolina	7.2	95,188	10.0	29.2	35.8	25.0
45037	Edgefield County, South Carolina	5.0	18,980	18.7	36.3	26.8	18.3
45039	Fairfield County, South Carolina	8.4	16,357	20.0	39.8	25.9	14.3
45041	Florence County, South Carolina	4.9	91,563	15.8	33.7	28.8	21.7
45043	Georgetown County, South Carolina	2.8	43,992	13.9	31.3	29.1	25.8
45045	Greenville County, South Carolina	2.6	317,863	13.3	26.3	28.4	32.1
45047	Greenwood County, South Carolina	3.0	46,245	19.2	29.7	28.0	23.0
45049	Hampton County, South Carolina	7.1	13,935	22.2	41.8	25.5	10.6
45051	Horry County, South Carolina	3.5	208,920	11.8	32.4	33.0	22.8
45053	Jasper County, South Carolina	6.1	17,514	21.2	36.9	27.0	15.0
45055	Kershaw County, South Carolina	6.5	42,739	14.8	34.8	30.1	20.3
45057	Lancaster County, South Carolina	3.9	56,827	15.6	34.0	28.5	21.9
45059	Laurens County, South Carolina	3.6	44,775	20.8	35.4	29.3	14.6
45061	Lee County, South Carolina	7.4	12,488	24.4	39.8	25.2	10.7
45063	Lexington County, South Carolina	6.3	185,655	11.3	28.0	31.5	29.2
45065	McCormick County, South Carolina	6.7	8,019	21.3	30.2	30.6	18.0
45067	Marion County, South Carolina	3.4	21,714	18.6	39.1	26.6	15.6
45069	Marlboro County, South Carolina	5.5	19,872	26.0	41.0	24.5	8.5
45071	Newberry County, South Carolina	5.3	25,444	21.5	34.9	26.9	16.6
45073	Oconee County, South Carolina	2.8	53,547	16.8	31.8	28.6	22.8
45075	Orangeburg County, South Carolina	5.2	59,478	17.7	34.8	28.2	19.3
45077	Pickens County, South Carolina	3.2	74,249	16.2	32.0	29.3	22.4
45079	Richland County, South Carolina	8.5	245,449	9.9	22.5	31.2	36.4
45081	Saluda County, South Carolina	4.7	13,778	22.7	39.2	24.1	14.0
45083	Spartanburg County, South Carolina	2.4	193,180	16.8	29.8	30.7	22.7
45085	Sumter County, South Carolina	9.2	69,237	18.3	29.2	33.3	19.2
45087	Union County, South Carolina	5.8	19,754	22.0	37.8	28.0	12.2
45089	Williamsburg County, South Carolina	6.2	22,930	21.4	40.3	27.0	11.3
45091	York County, South Carolina	3.4	158,497	11.6	27.8	31.1	29.5
46000	**South Dakota**	5.0	551,039	9.1	31.3	32.6	27.0
46003	Aurora County, South Dakota	4.8	1,837	12.0	37.1	33.0	17.9
46005	Beadle County, South Dakota	4.7	12,173	16.2	33.3	30.8	19.7
46007	Bennett County, South Dakota	10.1	1,929	20.4	28.8	33.3	17.5
46009	Bon Homme County, South Dakota	9.0	5,081	12.1	37.5	31.9	18.5
46011	Brookings County, South Dakota	2.4	17,285	5.3	26.1	27.8	40.8
46013	Brown County, South Dakota	4.5	25,239	7.5	33.3	31.0	28.3
46015	Brule County, South Dakota	6.6	3,561	14.9	30.4	30.4	24.3
46017	Buffalo County, South Dakota	19.6	1,051	18.1	43.4	29.0	9.5
46019	Butte County, South Dakota	4.6	6,985	11.7	35.1	35.4	17.7
46021	Campbell County, South Dakota	4.6	1,094	10.1	42.0	26.1	21.8
46023	Charles Mix County, South Dakota	6.4	5,742	11.4	37.9	32.5	18.3
46025	Clark County, South Dakota	1.8	2,511	10.4	37.3	31.0	21.3
46027	Clay County, South Dakota	3.3	7,047	4.3	27.8	22.9	45.0
46029	Codington County, South Dakota	3.6	18,496	8.8	39.7	31.2	20.3
46031	Corson County, South Dakota	9.3	2,328	17.9	34.4	31.7	16.1
46033	Custer County, South Dakota	9.3	6,556	7.0	30.9	36.1	26.0
46035	Davison County, South Dakota	4.8	13,052	9.0	26.9	36.9	27.2
46037	Day County, South Dakota	4.8	4,043	11.2	38.8	32.9	17.1
46039	Deuel County, South Dakota	3.5	3,058	9.9	40.8	28.9	20.3
46041	Dewey County, South Dakota	15.1	3,069	16.1	35.4	34.5	14.0
46043	Douglas County, South Dakota	4.6	2,112	14.1	41.1	25.5	19.3
46045	Edmunds County, South Dakota	3.9	2,764	11.1	33.9	31.1	24.0
46047	Fall River County, South Dakota	8.7	5,308	7.5	31.0	38.2	23.2
46049	Faulk County, South Dakota	4.6	1,597	9.2	34.3	33.2	23.2
46051	Grant County, South Dakota	2.7	5,028	8.4	44.3	30.2	17.1
46053	Gregory County, South Dakota	4.2	3,015	13.2	38.6	30.9	17.2
46055	Haakon County, South Dakota	3.1	1,464	10.0	37.6	32.3	20.1
46057	Hamlin County, South Dakota	2.2	3,667	8.6	43.3	28.0	20.1
46059	Hand County, South Dakota	3.7	2,453	11.2	33.6	32.7	22.5
46061	Hanson County, South Dakota	4.5	2,062	6.1	34.4	33.5	26.0
46063	Harding County, South Dakota	3.8	853	7.2	30.1	32.8	29.9
46065	Hughes County, South Dakota	22.8	12,097	9.5	27.2	30.4	32.9
46067	Hutchinson County, South Dakota	2.6	5,069	12.6	32.9	27.8	26.7

Table C. County—Labor Force, Employment, and Educational Data, 2011–2015—*Continued*

Fips code	State/county	Industry for employed population age 16 and older	Educational attainment for the population age 25 and older				
				Educational attainment			
		Public administration	Total population age 25 and older	Less than high school graduate	High school graduate (includes equivalency)	Some college or Associate's degree	Bachelor's degree or higher
46069	Hyde County, South Dakota	8.3	1,001	8.1	47.6	28.3	16.1
46071	Jackson County, South Dakota	5.8	1,833	11.7	32.2	36.3	19.8
46073	Jerauld County, South Dakota	3.3	1,449	11.1	40.9	32.0	16.0
46075	Jones County, South Dakota	4.4	616	7.6	38.8	37.0	16.6
46077	Kingsbury County, South Dakota	1.3	3,665	8.8	37.4	32.0	21.8
46079	Lake County, South Dakota	2.5	8,090	6.9	32.0	28.7	32.4
46081	Lawrence County, South Dakota	4.8	16,840	5.2	33.7	31.5	29.5
46083	Lincoln County, South Dakota	3.5	31,974	4.5	21.8	33.3	40.4
46085	Lyman County, South Dakota	14.0	2,421	11.5	36.5	32.8	19.2
46087	McCook County, South Dakota	3.7	3,785	9.3	33.2	33.5	23.9
46089	McPherson County, South Dakota	7.2	1,724	20.6	30.2	33.8	15.4
46091	Marshall County, South Dakota	6.1	3,227	11.5	31.8	34.4	22.3
46093	Meade County, South Dakota	9.3	17,159	7.7	32.3	37.1	23.0
46095	Mellette County, South Dakota	8.1	1,217	15.5	38.7	30.5	15.3
46097	Miner County, South Dakota	4.1	1,597	8.7	39.1	29.1	23.0
46099	Minnehaha County, South Dakota	3.0	116,899	9.0	29.3	32.3	29.4
46101	Moody County, South Dakota	3.0	4,281	9.2	33.8	31.3	25.6
46102	Oglala Lakota County, South Dakota	19.5	7,106	22.2	28.2	38.3	11.4
46103	Pennington County, South Dakota	5.0	70,952	7.4	28.1	36.3	28.2
46105	Perkins County, South Dakota	4.6	2,236	10.5	37.6	32.6	19.2
46107	Potter County, South Dakota	3.9	1,749	9.8	40.7	29.0	20.5
46109	Roberts County, South Dakota	8.0	6,528	13.4	37.5	32.4	16.7
46111	Sanborn County, South Dakota	4.3	1,705	8.6	38.8	35.1	17.5
46115	Spink County, South Dakota	7.1	4,504	9.2	36.4	32.1	22.3
46117	Stanley County, South Dakota	12.2	2,036	10.2	34.7	28.1	26.9
46119	Sully County, South Dakota	6.1	992	8.3	35.6	32.4	23.8
46121	Todd County, South Dakota	12.3	4,837	23.0	22.2	40.4	14.4
46123	Tripp County, South Dakota	5.0	3,866	13.3	34.7	29.9	22.1
46125	Turner County, South Dakota	4.7	5,837	8.0	36.3	34.7	21.0
46127	Union County, South Dakota	3.3	10,039	8.3	30.0	30.2	31.5
46129	Walworth County, South Dakota	6.2	3,916	11.4	36.9	30.1	21.7
46135	Yankton County, South Dakota	5.6	15,819	8.2	35.3	29.8	26.7
46137	Ziebach County, South Dakota	11.9	1,513	13.6	40.4	32.1	13.9
47000	**Tennessee**	4.4	4,380,036	14.5	33.0	27.5	24.9
47001	Anderson County, Tennessee	6.2	53,360	14.9	33.8	27.3	24.0
47003	Bedford County, Tennessee	4.4	29,957	20.9	41.2	24.2	13.7
47005	Benton County, Tennessee	5.3	11,893	20.7	46.1	22.4	10.8
47007	Bledsoe County, Tennessee	7.3	9,902	24.8	42.8	21.7	10.7
47009	Blount County, Tennessee	3.3	88,202	12.4	34.9	29.9	22.8
47011	Bradley County, Tennessee	2.3	68,303	17.3	32.3	30.5	19.9
47013	Campbell County, Tennessee	4.5	28,657	27.8	41.8	20.2	10.2
47015	Cannon County, Tennessee	3.8	9,767	19.0	42.2	24.8	13.9
47017	Carroll County, Tennessee	3.7	19,529	21.6	41.4	22.9	14.2
47019	Carter County, Tennessee	3.8	41,044	19.4	38.9	25.5	16.1
47021	Cheatham County, Tennessee	6.1	26,794	16.0	36.6	28.1	19.3
47023	Chester County, Tennessee	5.8	10,891	17.5	38.5	28.4	15.7
47025	Claiborne County, Tennessee	2.8	22,377	21.7	42.3	21.8	14.2
47027	Clay County, Tennessee	5.6	5,662	24.4	44.7	16.2	14.7
47029	Cocke County, Tennessee	4.3	25,273	20.8	46.6	22.5	10.1
47031	Coffee County, Tennessee	4.8	36,199	15.7	39.2	26.8	18.3
47033	Crockett County, Tennessee	3.6	9,879	23.7	40.4	22.9	13.0
47035	Cumberland County, Tennessee	4.9	43,211	16.8	38.3	26.7	18.2
47037	Davidson County, Tennessee	4.4	446,174	12.7	24.1	25.9	37.3
47039	Decatur County, Tennessee	8.6	8,432	18.7	44.6	24.0	12.7
47041	DeKalb County, Tennessee	3.7	13,168	22.1	43.2	20.9	13.8
47043	Dickson County, Tennessee	4.6	34,145	16.5	43.7	25.3	14.5
47045	Dyer County, Tennessee	5.2	25,478	15.8	40.2	24.7	19.2
47047	Fayette County, Tennessee	4.9	27,842	12.5	35.8	28.7	22.9
47049	Fentress County, Tennessee	1.8	12,633	25.3	44.2	19.6	10.9
47051	Franklin County, Tennessee	4.5	27,960	17.2	37.0	26.3	19.5
47053	Gibson County, Tennessee	3.8	33,608	16.2	38.4	29.4	16.0
47055	Giles County, Tennessee	4.9	20,254	18.1	42.3	24.7	14.8
47057	Grainger County, Tennessee	3.3	16,214	21.7	45.3	21.9	11.1
47059	Greene County, Tennessee	4.9	48,955	19.0	42.6	23.5	15.0
47061	Grundy County, Tennessee	2.5	9,466	28.7	42.0	18.4	10.8
47063	Hamblen County, Tennessee	2.3	43,447	19.2	42.1	23.3	15.5
47065	Hamilton County, Tennessee	3.2	240,006	12.6	27.3	31.4	28.7
47067	Hancock County, Tennessee	5.1	4,754	26.7	39.4	23.3	10.6
47069	Hardeman County, Tennessee	7.7	18,537	23.2	44.4	22.2	10.1
47071	Hardin County, Tennessee	6.1	18,604	21.1	43.6	22.5	12.7
47073	Hawkins County, Tennessee	3.0	40,330	19.0	44.2	24.2	12.6
47075	Haywood County, Tennessee	7.2	12,322	21.0	42.1	24.1	12.8
47077	Henderson County, Tennessee	3.4	19,091	20.2	39.8	27.2	12.8
47079	Henry County, Tennessee	4.6	23,167	16.7	45.1	22.7	15.5

Table C. County—Labor Force, Employment, and Educational Data, 2011–2015—*Continued*

		Industry for employed population age 16 and older	Educational attainment for the population age 25 and older				
				Educational attainment			
Fips code	State/county	Public administration	Total population age 25 and older	Less than high school graduate	High school graduate (includes equivalency)	Some college or Associate's degree	Bachelor's degree or higher
47081	Hickman County, Tennessee	5.3	16,883	23.8	43.3	22.4	10.6
47083	Houston County, Tennessee	3.0	5,737	20.5	46.3	22.7	10.5
47085	Humphreys County, Tennessee	5.0	12,778	16.4	42.8	27.4	13.4
47087	Jackson County, Tennessee	4.6	8,352	25.5	47.7	18.7	8.1
47089	Jefferson County, Tennessee	3.7	36,420	17.6	39.5	27.3	15.6
47091	Johnson County, Tennessee	9.5	13,450	25.2	40.9	24.7	9.2
47093	Knox County, Tennessee	3.4	294,599	9.8	26.5	29.2	34.5
47095	Lake County, Tennessee	14.7	5,711	28.3	44.6	18.3	8.9
47097	Lauderdale County, Tennessee	11.0	18,404	24.5	44.5	21.9	9.1
47099	Lawrence County, Tennessee	3.9	28,362	20.8	42.2	24.6	12.4
47101	Lewis County, Tennessee	2.0	8,396	17.7	43.2	27.0	12.1
47103	Lincoln County, Tennessee	5.8	23,331	17.6	41.9	23.9	16.7
47105	Loudon County, Tennessee	3.2	36,799	14.0	34.2	26.3	25.5
47107	McMinn County, Tennessee	2.4	36,522	17.4	42.7	24.9	15.0
47109	McNairy County, Tennessee	4.1	18,273	20.6	44.2	23.8	11.4
47111	Macon County, Tennessee	3.0	15,311	26.1	43.9	20.4	9.5
47113	Madison County, Tennessee	5.2	64,324	12.3	32.9	29.4	25.4
47115	Marion County, Tennessee	3.4	20,113	22.1	37.2	27.4	13.3
47117	Marshall County, Tennessee	4.3	21,272	18.0	42.0	26.6	13.4
47119	Maury County, Tennessee	3.9	57,355	12.5	36.6	31.7	19.2
47121	Meigs County, Tennessee	3.6	8,417	23.5	42.7	25.6	8.2
47123	Monroe County, Tennessee	3.4	31,531	21.1	42.0	24.7	12.1
47125	Montgomery County, Tennessee	9.8	112,956	8.1	30.8	36.5	24.6
47127	Moore County, Tennessee	5.2	4,616	12.8	40.2	29.4	17.6
47129	Morgan County, Tennessee	12.4	15,585	20.0	51.3	22.3	6.4
47131	Obion County, Tennessee	4.1	21,571	17.8	41.3	24.1	16.8
47133	Overton County, Tennessee	3.4	15,383	21.1	43.7	21.8	13.4
47135	Perry County, Tennessee	7.1	5,523	24.5	41.4	23.0	11.0
47137	Pickett County, Tennessee	6.4	3,853	22.7	38.4	27.6	11.4
47139	Polk County, Tennessee	4.9	11,942	21.6	43.3	25.3	9.8
47141	Putnam County, Tennessee	4.3	46,945	16.1	37.8	22.7	23.3
47143	Rhea County, Tennessee	3.2	21,881	24.4	38.1	24.7	12.9
47145	Roane County, Tennessee	6.3	38,688	15.2	36.6	29.9	18.4
47147	Robertson County, Tennessee	5.4	45,055	13.8	38.4	30.0	17.8
47149	Rutherford County, Tennessee	4.1	174,081	9.7	29.6	30.6	30.1
47151	Scott County, Tennessee	5.8	14,737	22.7	47.6	20.8	9.0
47153	Sequatchie County, Tennessee	6.6	10,167	18.0	40.2	28.9	13.0
47155	Sevier County, Tennessee	3.3	65,714	17.6	37.5	28.5	16.4
47157	Shelby County, Tennessee	4.8	600,635	13.1	27.1	29.5	30.2
47159	Smith County, Tennessee	4.5	13,073	18.3	48.0	23.6	10.2
47161	Stewart County, Tennessee	9.3	9,276	13.4	42.0	30.4	14.2
47163	Sullivan County, Tennessee	3.4	113,045	14.5	34.8	28.7	21.9
47165	Sumner County, Tennessee	4.6	114,723	10.8	32.8	31.8	24.6
47167	Tipton County, Tennessee	5.9	40,008	14.4	39.0	31.6	15.0
47169	Trousdale County, Tennessee	4.4	5,325	21.3	42.8	21.6	14.3
47171	Unicoi County, Tennessee	5.3	13,261	20.8	41.6	25.2	12.4
47173	Union County, Tennessee	3.4	13,225	25.6	44.2	21.0	9.1
47175	Van Buren County, Tennessee	9.2	4,109	20.3	50.1	17.0	12.6
47177	Warren County, Tennessee	4.1	27,268	21.9	42.5	22.1	13.5
47179	Washington County, Tennessee	2.9	85,228	11.9	30.7	26.9	30.6
47181	Wayne County, Tennessee	8.4	12,300	23.5	43.6	24.1	8.8
47183	Weakley County, Tennessee	5.1	21,647	16.1	39.8	23.6	20.4
47185	White County, Tennessee	6.8	18,380	18.9	45.3	23.8	12.1
47187	Williamson County, Tennessee	3.2	128,761	4.7	16.4	23.2	55.7
47189	Wilson County, Tennessee	4.9	83,248	10.6	32.1	29.0	28.3
48000	**Texas**	4.3	16,765,143	18.1	25.2	29.2	27.6
48001	Anderson County, Texas	12.5	41,678	20.2	36.9	31.5	11.3
48003	Andrews County, Texas	2.0	9,980	25.6	33.6	29.2	11.7
48005	Angelina County, Texas	4.2	56,564	20.8	31.6	32.3	15.2
48007	Aransas County, Texas	2.6	17,888	15.8	30.9	33.8	19.5
48009	Archer County, Texas	4.6	6,085	11.2	36.5	31.6	20.6
48011	Armstrong County, Texas	6.4	1,375	9.3	24.3	43.4	23.0
48013	Atascosa County, Texas	4.8	29,641	24.2	36.0	25.8	14.0
48015	Austin County, Texas	3.4	19,347	15.6	30.3	34.0	20.1
48017	Bailey County, Texas	2.4	4,299	31.8	32.4	28.0	7.8
48019	Bandera County, Texas	7.2	15,840	14.2	29.2	34.0	22.6
48021	Bastrop County, Texas	8.9	51,089	19.3	30.4	32.3	17.9
48023	Baylor County, Texas	4.4	2,643	11.6	31.7	30.8	25.8
48025	Bee County, Texas	10.8	22,094	27.4	33.1	29.8	9.7
48027	Bell County, Texas	12.3	194,614	10.1	28.2	38.5	23.1
48029	Bexar County, Texas	5.2	1,145,479	16.7	25.2	31.4	26.7
48031	Blanco County, Texas	3.8	7,901	11.1	30.7	29.8	28.4
48033	Borden County, Texas	18.1	474	6.3	28.9	32.9	31.9
48035	Bosque County, Texas	3.1	12,739	18.2	34.7	30.1	17.0
48037	Bowie County, Texas	10.3	62,572	12.7	36.0	33.0	18.2

Table C. County—Labor Force, Employment, and Educational Data, 2011–2015—*Continued*

Fips code	State/county	Industry for employed population age 16 and older — Public administration	Educational attainment for the population age 25 and older — Total population age 25 and older	Educational attainment — Less than high school graduate	High school graduate (includes equivalency)	Some college or Associate's degree	Bachelor's degree or higher
48039	Brazoria County, Texas	4.9	213,913	14.0	25.7	31.8	28.6
48041	Brazos County, Texas	3.4	103,564	14.6	20.4	26.1	38.9
48043	Brewster County, Texas	9.4	6,535	11.9	21.4	27.6	39.1
48045	Briscoe County, Texas	7.4	1,123	24.2	25.6	28.4	21.8
48047	Brooks County, Texas	7.1	4,494	29.4	37.6	21.3	11.7
48049	Brown County, Texas	7.5	25,560	14.6	37.9	29.6	17.9
48051	Burleson County, Texas	4.7	11,987	21.8	36.4	26.9	14.9
48053	Burnet County, Texas	5.4	30,751	14.9	31.9	30.4	22.7
48055	Caldwell County, Texas	8.2	25,019	21.0	36.0	27.6	15.4
48057	Calhoun County, Texas	2.5	14,403	20.1	31.8	31.9	16.2
48059	Callahan County, Texas	6.7	9,466	12.4	38.7	34.5	14.3
48061	Cameron County, Texas	5.4	240,350	35.2	24.0	24.4	16.4
48063	Camp County, Texas	3.2	8,118	21.6	36.5	27.5	14.3
48065	Carson County, Texas	5.0	4,071	10.2	28.4	37.0	24.4
48067	Cass County, Texas	4.4	21,270	14.4	44.0	27.9	13.6
48069	Castro County, Texas	3.7	4,773	29.9	33.1	23.7	13.2
48071	Chambers County, Texas	2.4	23,796	16.9	31.8	32.5	18.7
48073	Cherokee County, Texas	6.1	33,172	21.8	33.4	28.6	16.3
48075	Childress County, Texas	13.7	4,806	13.1	40.1	30.1	16.7
48077	Clay County, Texas	5.8	7,457	11.2	39.5	33.4	15.9
48079	Cochran County, Texas	5.4	1,821	34.2	29.7	23.9	12.2
48081	Coke County, Texas	7.0	2,427	11.8	33.5	34.0	20.6
48083	Coleman County, Texas	4.5	6,057	17.8	41.1	29.3	11.8
48085	Collin County, Texas	2.3	557,114	6.6	15.5	28.2	49.8
48087	Collingsworth County, Texas	8.0	2,052	21.3	32.7	30.9	15.2
48089	Colorado County, Texas	3.5	14,328	17.5	38.8	25.5	18.2
48091	Comal County, Texas	4.0	82,814	9.5	25.5	31.5	33.4
48093	Comanche County, Texas	4.5	9,364	21.3	37.0	24.9	16.7
48095	Concho County, Texas	16.5	3,068	36.8	30.1	21.4	11.6
48097	Cooke County, Texas	4.3	25,864	12.9	32.1	34.0	21.0
48099	Coryell County, Texas	17.1	46,703	11.8	30.3	43.1	14.8
48101	Cottle County, Texas	11.2	1,056	24.7	30.9	29.2	15.2
48103	Crane County, Texas	4.8	2,899	27.8	30.4	29.1	12.8
48105	Crockett County, Texas	6.4	2,528	28.8	27.2	30.6	13.4
48107	Crosby County, Texas	4.0	3,846	30.3	30.7	27.3	11.7
48109	Culberson County, Texas	7.6	1,443	37.9	32.9	19.3	9.9
48111	Dallam County, Texas	5.3	4,091	25.4	33.3	30.1	11.1
48113	Dallas County, Texas	2.4	1,568,849	22.3	22.9	25.7	29.1
48115	Dawson County, Texas	9.9	8,853	27.5	37.4	24.1	11.0
48117	Deaf Smith County, Texas	4.5	11,192	27.8	30.8	26.5	14.8
48119	Delta County, Texas	3.1	3,637	14.5	33.6	33.1	18.8
48121	Denton County, Texas	2.8	466,487	8.1	19.3	31.3	41.3
48123	DeWitt County, Texas	7.8	14,491	21.4	37.5	26.6	14.5
48125	Dickens County, Texas	7.3	1,634	23.7	28.3	32.6	15.5
48127	Dimmit County, Texas	7.9	6,490	31.8	29.8	26.5	11.9
48129	Donley County, Texas	11.5	2,400	16.5	33.5	34.8	15.2
48131	Duval County, Texas	8.9	7,461	31.6	33.3	27.1	8.1
48133	Eastland County, Texas	4.8	12,239	17.3	35.9	32.4	14.4
48135	Ector County, Texas	2.6	88,691	25.9	28.7	30.8	14.6
48137	Edwards County, Texas	1.8	1,367	20.8	28.8	25.2	25.1
48139	Ellis County, Texas	4.2	99,361	15.4	29.7	33.8	21.2
48141	El Paso County, Texas	7.6	495,453	24.3	24.5	29.9	21.3
48143	Erath County, Texas	3.2	22,713	15.6	27.1	30.7	26.6
48145	Falls County, Texas	7.0	11,943	23.7	37.7	26.7	11.8
48147	Fannin County, Texas	7.4	23,530	17.6	35.2	31.3	16.0
48149	Fayette County, Texas	4.1	17,857	20.3	36.9	26.8	16.0
48151	Fisher County, Texas	4.4	2,670	16.9	33.4	33.4	16.3
48153	Floyd County, Texas	6.3	3,963	26.2	29.1	28.2	16.6
48155	Foard County, Texas	8.3	904	20.2	28.1	29.0	22.7
48157	Fort Bend County, Texas	3.1	416,757	11.1	17.5	27.7	43.7
48159	Franklin County, Texas	4.8	7,259	14.8	33.5	33.6	18.1
48161	Freestone County, Texas	8.0	13,640	18.2	33.9	35.7	12.3
48163	Frio County, Texas	10.0	10,961	34.4	33.8	23.8	8.0
48165	Gaines County, Texas	1.8	10,685	39.4	27.9	20.9	11.8
48167	Galveston County, Texas	4.9	203,891	12.5	24.5	33.8	29.3
48169	Garza County, Texas	9.8	4,877	40.3	27.8	22.5	9.4
48171	Gillespie County, Texas	2.3	18,728	13.3	26.6	26.8	33.4
48173	Glasscock County, Texas	3.0	786	20.7	25.8	28.9	24.6
48175	Goliad County, Texas	7.5	5,198	11.5	39.5	35.1	13.9
48177	Gonzales County, Texas	3.8	12,918	27.9	33.7	24.6	13.8
48179	Gray County, Texas	4.6	15,366	19.5	33.0	33.9	13.6
48181	Grayson County, Texas	4.7	82,272	12.9	32.0	34.8	20.3
48183	Gregg County, Texas	2.8	78,906	15.9	28.2	35.5	20.5
48185	Grimes County, Texas	5.4	18,676	21.7	35.9	31.0	11.5

Table C. County—Labor Force, Employment, and Educational Data, 2011–2015—*Continued*

| | | Industry for employed population age 16 and older | Educational attainment for the population age 25 and older | | | | |
| | | | | Educational attainment | | | |
Fips code	State/county	Public administration	Total population age 25 and older	Less than high school graduate	High school graduate (includes equivalency)	Some college or Associate's degree	Bachelor's degree or higher
48187	Guadalupe County, Texas	8.2	92,461	12.6	29.7	31.7	26.1
48189	Hale County, Texas	5.8	21,328	27.6	32.2	25.4	14.7
48191	Hall County, Texas	4.6	2,095	26.5	27.9	32.8	12.7
48193	Hamilton County, Texas	4.6	5,979	19.3	33.2	26.2	21.3
48195	Hansford County, Texas	4.6	3,465	24.7	29.6	26.3	19.4
48197	Hardeman County, Texas	5.3	2,861	20.6	33.1	28.6	17.7
48199	Hardin County, Texas	5.0	37,025	13.7	38.2	32.7	15.4
48201	Harris County, Texas	2.6	2,734,398	20.4	23.3	26.8	29.5
48203	Harrison County, Texas	3.6	43,561	16.2	34.0	30.7	19.1
48205	Hartley County, Texas	4.8	4,529	20.2	34.3	24.2	21.3
48207	Haskell County, Texas	7.8	4,393	28.2	32.6	24.5	14.7
48209	Hays County, Texas	5.9	103,614	11.0	21.4	31.4	36.1
48211	Hemphill County, Texas	3.3	2,547	17.6	25.8	32.2	24.4
48213	Henderson County, Texas	4.5	54,979	18.1	34.3	31.2	16.5
48215	Hidalgo County, Texas	4.4	451,492	37.9	23.2	22.1	16.7
48217	Hill County, Texas	5.0	23,723	20.6	33.1	31.5	14.8
48219	Hockley County, Texas	3.1	14,184	22.2	26.2	35.9	15.7
48221	Hood County, Texas	3.9	38,287	11.6	28.4	34.5	25.5
48223	Hopkins County, Texas	3.7	23,710	17.7	37.3	28.8	16.2
48225	Houston County, Texas	9.3	16,706	17.5	37.3	30.7	14.5
48227	Howard County, Texas	6.8	24,225	22.0	31.3	33.9	12.8
48229	Hudspeth County, Texas	16.7	2,238	48.7	24.5	18.5	8.2
48231	Hunt County, Texas	3.9	57,974	16.6	34.6	31.3	17.5
48233	Hutchinson County, Texas	5.9	14,262	15.8	31.2	37.8	15.1
48235	Irion County, Texas	7.5	1,126	11.2	34.9	39.3	14.7
48237	Jack County, Texas	5.6	6,134	20.4	40.5	28.0	11.1
48239	Jackson County, Texas	2.8	9,621	19.1	33.9	29.6	17.4
48241	Jasper County, Texas	5.3	23,939	15.9	44.0	30.5	9.6
48243	Jeff Davis County, Texas	6.0	1,778	19.2	21.1	23.1	36.6
48245	Jefferson County, Texas	4.8	166,637	17.0	33.3	31.3	18.4
48247	Jim Hogg County, Texas	12.8	3,380	28.6	30.2	28.4	12.8
48249	Jim Wells County, Texas	4.9	25,677	28.9	34.1	26.0	11.0
48251	Johnson County, Texas	4.6	100,643	16.8	31.7	34.3	17.3
48253	Jones County, Texas	8.5	14,517	26.1	39.0	25.2	9.7
48255	Karnes County, Texas	12.0	10,186	26.3	36.3	24.5	13.0
48257	Kaufman County, Texas	5.1	69,926	16.4	31.4	33.2	19.0
48259	Kendall County, Texas	5.4	25,551	9.2	21.1	28.9	40.8
48261	Kenedy County, Texas	20.5	332	32.2	33.4	19.3	15.1
48263	Kent County, Texas	11.8	616	21.3	26.1	27.8	24.8
48265	Kerr County, Texas	3.9	36,128	12.4	27.8	31.7	28.1
48267	Kimble County, Texas	5.4	3,470	16.9	35.4	30.6	17.1
48269	King County, Texas	6.6	220	20.0	39.5	18.6	21.8
48271	Kinney County, Texas	25.6	2,613	33.6	27.9	26.0	12.5
48273	Kleberg County, Texas	5.4	17,767	25.4	22.1	27.1	25.4
48275	Knox County, Texas	9.0	2,552	18.8	37.0	29.0	15.2
48277	Lamar County, Texas	4.3	33,228	14.9	34.7	34.2	16.2
48279	Lamb County, Texas	4.4	8,607	26.1	30.5	27.0	16.3
48281	Lampasas County, Texas	10.0	13,768	12.3	25.8	40.8	21.0
48283	La Salle County, Texas	3.8	4,455	38.6	32.7	13.8	14.9
48285	Lavaca County, Texas	3.3	13,578	18.2	41.6	24.3	15.9
48287	Lee County, Texas	5.8	11,155	16.9	39.1	26.8	17.2
48289	Leon County, Texas	4.1	11,843	16.2	36.2	30.4	17.2
48291	Liberty County, Texas	4.4	50,708	23.8	38.0	28.6	9.6
48293	Limestone County, Texas	6.1	15,970	19.6	35.7	30.9	13.8
48295	Lipscomb County, Texas	3.3	2,221	17.4	37.2	26.8	18.6
48297	Live Oak County, Texas	5.5	8,583	19.4	36.0	31.8	12.7
48299	Llano County, Texas	3.1	15,168	12.2	27.2	33.0	27.6
48301	Loving County, Texas	11.3	106	19.8	51.9	26.4	1.9
48303	Lubbock County, Texas	3.7	169,930	15.3	25.9	31.3	27.5
48305	Lynn County, Texas	8.6	3,771	22.6	31.9	29.0	16.5
48307	McCulloch County, Texas	4.6	5,881	22.3	31.3	30.8	15.6
48309	McLennan County, Texas	4.8	145,233	16.6	27.9	33.2	22.2
48311	McMullen County, Texas	18.2	544	23.7	29.0	31.8	15.4
48313	Madison County, Texas	10.1	9,569	23.5	36.8	29.1	10.6
48315	Marion County, Texas	5.3	7,764	16.5	37.6	31.6	14.3
48317	Martin County, Texas	3.1	3,117	20.6	35.5	26.5	17.5
48319	Mason County, Texas	5.4	3,053	15.0	34.7	27.9	22.4
48321	Matagorda County, Texas	1.8	23,859	22.7	35.4	26.6	15.3
48323	Maverick County, Texas	9.4	31,775	40.9	22.4	25.9	10.7
48325	Medina County, Texas	5.3	31,240	18.3	31.9	30.9	18.9
48327	Menard County, Texas	6.8	1,550	22.8	30.3	29.5	17.4
48329	Midland County, Texas	2.5	94,044	17.0	23.6	33.8	25.6
48331	Milam County, Texas	6.1	16,292	18.6	37.5	27.3	16.7
48333	Mills County, Texas	4.4	3,347	17.1	26.8	34.0	22.1
48335	Mitchell County, Texas	11.8	6,352	26.2	33.4	29.5	11.0

Table C. County—Labor Force, Employment, and Educational Data, 2011–2015—*Continued*

Fips code	State/county	Industry for employed population age 16 and older	Educational attainment for the population age 25 and older				
				Educational attainment			
		Public administration	Total population age 25 and older	Less than high school graduate	High school graduate (includes equivalency)	Some college or Associate's degree	Bachelor's degree or higher
48337	Montague County, Texas	4.9	13,604	17.6	34.1	32.5	15.8
48339	Montgomery County, Texas	3.1	325,211	13.7	24.3	29.8	32.2
48341	Moore County, Texas	3.9	12,889	35.9	26.1	25.9	12.0
48343	Morris County, Texas	7.0	8,886	16.8	34.7	34.0	14.5
48345	Motley County, Texas	5.7	716	16.1	31.8	34.9	17.2
48347	Nacogdoches County, Texas	3.2	37,136	18.0	28.1	28.8	25.1
48349	Navarro County, Texas	6.9	31,308	22.7	30.5	31.2	15.7
48351	Newton County, Texas	5.0	9,621	12.4	50.1	31.1	6.4
48353	Nolan County, Texas	4.2	9,762	21.3	34.8	31.8	12.1
48355	Nueces County, Texas	6.4	226,272	19.2	28.2	32.4	20.2
48357	Ochiltree County, Texas	3.3	6,282	25.2	29.3	30.3	15.2
48359	Oldham County, Texas	7.0	1,166	16.4	19.6	36.2	27.8
48361	Orange County, Texas	3.5	55,379	11.2	40.0	34.2	14.6
48363	Palo Pinto County, Texas	5.7	18,819	18.4	37.0	28.8	15.8
48365	Panola County, Texas	5.2	16,015	17.0	32.5	37.6	12.8
48367	Parker County, Texas	5.3	81,156	11.0	26.9	35.6	26.5
48369	Parmer County, Texas	3.1	6,038	32.3	30.4	22.0	15.3
48371	Pecos County, Texas	8.7	10,658	30.7	35.2	24.1	10.0
48373	Polk County, Texas	10.1	32,916	20.3	37.7	29.7	12.3
48375	Potter County, Texas	3.7	76,622	23.9	27.8	33.4	14.9
48377	Presidio County, Texas	11.5	4,834	42.6	17.3	14.1	25.9
48379	Rains County, Texas	4.8	8,065	17.0	39.5	32.9	10.6
48381	Randall County, Texas	5.3	82,432	8.2	22.1	39.3	30.4
48383	Reagan County, Texas	3.0	2,366	31.3	37.1	21.2	10.5
48385	Real County, Texas	4.6	2,481	18.8	28.6	30.7	22.0
48387	Red River County, Texas	5.9	9,003	20.7	39.0	27.2	13.1
48389	Reeves County, Texas	11.2	9,511	40.2	25.8	23.2	10.8
48391	Refugio County, Texas	5.9	4,936	20.0	35.9	34.3	9.7
48393	Roberts County, Texas	5.7	616	3.4	30.2	34.6	31.8
48395	Robertson County, Texas	6.4	10,974	20.1	37.5	26.0	16.5
48397	Rockwall County, Texas	4.6	55,187	8.4	22.2	32.4	36.9
48399	Runnels County, Texas	6.3	6,994	20.5	38.8	23.2	17.5
48401	Rusk County, Texas	4.9	36,246	19.6	33.7	32.9	13.7
48403	Sabine County, Texas	5.9	7,630	14.7	44.8	28.6	12.0
48405	San Augustine County, Texas	5.2	6,347	20.1	42.9	26.2	10.8
48407	San Jacinto County, Texas	11.2	18,655	18.5	45.0	25.1	11.4
48409	San Patricio County, Texas	6.3	41,749	22.5	31.1	31.4	15.1
48411	San Saba County, Texas	9.3	4,207	22.1	30.7	32.7	14.5
48413	Schleicher County, Texas	2.4	1,903	23.8	23.6	33.0	19.5
48415	Scurry County, Texas	5.3	11,171	18.7	30.7	35.2	15.3
48417	Shackelford County, Texas	6.1	2,308	14.1	33.9	29.4	22.6
48419	Shelby County, Texas	3.2	16,397	22.9	35.7	26.6	14.8
48421	Sherman County, Texas	2.2	2,045	26.6	27.9	24.9	20.6
48423	Smith County, Texas	3.3	140,170	15.6	25.6	33.9	24.9
48425	Somervell County, Texas	5.5	5,895	18.2	26.3	32.9	22.7
48427	Starr County, Texas	4.6	34,607	53.7	22.2	15.0	9.1
48429	Stephens County, Texas	4.5	6,416	18.8	35.0	27.2	19.1
48431	Sterling County, Texas	6.0	876	21.5	32.1	24.2	22.3
48433	Stonewall County, Texas	9.0	1,012	19.7	37.5	27.3	15.6
48435	Sutton County, Texas	2.9	2,524	25.4	28.2	26.2	20.2
48437	Swisher County, Texas	4.3	4,956	21.8	35.0	27.3	15.9
48439	Tarrant County, Texas	3.5	1,210,423	14.9	23.8	31.1	30.3
48441	Taylor County, Texas	7.0	81,434	13.7	29.1	32.6	24.6
48443	Terrell County, Texas	25.8	739	19.2	36.0	27.5	17.3
48445	Terry County, Texas	6.0	8,027	30.8	29.5	27.1	12.6
48447	Throckmorton County, Texas	3.5	1,137	14.2	31.3	32.6	21.9
48449	Titus County, Texas	2.0	19,551	27.4	29.4	28.3	15.0
48451	Tom Green County, Texas	6.5	72,819	16.8	30.3	30.8	22.1
48453	Travis County, Texas	6.1	742,369	12.2	17.1	24.8	46.0
48455	Trinity County, Texas	10.0	10,594	16.7	41.9	30.4	11.1
48457	Tyler County, Texas	8.5	15,102	15.7	41.8	31.3	11.2
48459	Upshur County, Texas	4.1	26,951	17.2	32.6	35.7	14.5
48461	Upton County, Texas	4.5	2,055	23.9	39.4	26.5	10.1
48463	Uvalde County, Texas	7.3	16,518	29.5	23.2	32.0	15.3
48465	Val Verde County, Texas	15.5	29,268	34.0	26.6	22.5	17.0
48467	Van Zandt County, Texas	5.7	36,417	18.4	35.4	30.8	15.5
48469	Victoria County, Texas	3.8	58,076	17.5	31.3	33.0	18.2
48471	Walker County, Texas	19.5	44,515	18.1	35.8	27.2	18.9
48473	Waller County, Texas	4.8	24,740	21.9	31.4	27.9	18.8
48475	Ward County, Texas	5.9	7,008	24.6	35.0	29.0	11.4
48477	Washington County, Texas	3.9	22,846	17.3	31.3	29.8	21.6
48479	Webb County, Texas	7.0	142,944	34.8	24.4	23.8	17.1
48481	Wharton County, Texas	2.9	26,694	23.5	33.6	28.8	14.1
48483	Wheeler County, Texas	4.4	3,791	18.7	31.3	33.2	16.9

Table C. County—Labor Force, Employment, and Educational Data, 2011–2015—*Continued*

		Industry for employed population age 16 and older	Educational attainment for the population age 25 and older				
				Educational attainment			
Fips code	State/county	Public administration	Total population age 25 and older	Less than high school graduate	High school graduate (includes equivalency)	Some college or Associate's degree	Bachelor's degree or higher
48485	Wichita County, Texas	6.7	83,603	13.9	32.4	32.1	21.6
48487	Wilbarger County, Texas	3.6	8,662	21.1	29.9	32.5	16.5
48489	Willacy County, Texas	9.5	13,541	37.1	35.5	19.1	8.3
48491	Williamson County, Texas	6.0	306,409	7.5	20.7	32.6	39.3
48493	Wilson County, Texas	8.8	30,423	14.9	34.8	30.8	19.5
48495	Winkler County, Texas	4.6	4,584	28.7	31.2	29.1	11.1
48497	Wise County, Texas	4.7	40,786	15.8	36.8	30.8	16.5
48499	Wood County, Texas	6.0	30,901	15.4	34.7	32.8	17.0
48501	Yoakum County, Texas	2.9	4,832	29.1	29.7	26.5	14.7
48503	Young County, Texas	4.5	12,500	19.0	35.9	27.6	17.6
48505	Zapata County, Texas	7.7	7,958	46.7	26.0	18.9	8.4
48507	Zavala County, Texas	6.7	6,887	39.8	27.0	24.2	9.0
49000	**Utah**	5.1	1,674,198	8.8	23.2	36.9	31.1
49001	Beaver County, Utah	6.2	3,752	7.9	37.2	35.0	20.0
49003	Box Elder County, Utah	6.5	29,835	7.9	32.5	38.1	21.5
49005	Cache County, Utah	2.7	58,796	7.5	21.9	34.4	36.1
49007	Carbon County, Utah	5.3	13,145	12.0	26.9	46.0	15.1
49009	Daggett County, Utah	18.0	521	6.5	34.7	42.8	15.9
49011	Davis County, Utah	9.1	184,501	4.8	21.2	39.2	34.8
49013	Duchesne County, Utah	6.5	11,317	12.3	36.0	36.7	15.0
49015	Emery County, Utah	6.0	6,570	9.8	32.9	44.7	12.6
49017	Garfield County, Utah	3.2	3,334	8.7	34.5	37.1	19.7
49019	Grand County, Utah	6.9	6,543	9.9	24.1	42.3	23.7
49021	Iron County, Utah	5.1	25,604	8.4	24.7	38.3	28.6
49023	Juab County, Utah	5.2	5,742	8.8	35.0	40.3	15.8
49025	Kane County, Utah	8.7	5,140	4.7	28.8	41.6	24.8
49027	Millard County, Utah	4.0	7,609	12.0	29.1	38.9	20.0
49029	Morgan County, Utah	7.7	5,780	1.6	24.4	39.4	34.6
49031	Piute County, Utah	6.3	1,322	16.5	39.8	26.2	17.5
49033	Rich County, Utah	4.4	1,400	2.9	37.6	40.3	19.1
49035	Salt Lake County, Utah	3.8	663,851	10.4	22.8	34.6	32.1
49037	San Juan County, Utah	7.5	8,519	16.4	31.5	33.2	18.9
49039	Sanpete County, Utah	5.6	15,841	11.2	27.0	41.3	20.5
49041	Sevier County, Utah	7.5	12,724	9.6	33.7	40.4	16.4
49043	Summit County, Utah	3.2	25,303	6.6	15.5	27.1	50.8
49045	Tooele County, Utah	9.3	34,734	7.6	32.1	37.9	22.4
49047	Uintah County, Utah	5.4	20,367	13.2	34.7	36.2	15.9
49049	Utah County, Utah	3.1	267,427	6.7	16.8	39.2	37.3
49051	Wasatch County, Utah	5.0	15,737	8.4	20.7	37.4	33.5
49053	Washington County, Utah	3.7	91,894	7.4	24.6	40.9	27.1
49055	Wayne County, Utah	5.0	1,777	7.3	25.3	40.6	26.8
49057	Weber County, Utah	10.5	145,113	10.5	29.1	37.4	23.0
50000	**Vermont**	4.8	436,657	8.2	30.1	25.8	36.0
50001	Addison County, Vermont	3.5	25,159	7.9	32.0	24.6	35.5
50003	Bennington County, Vermont	2.3	26,092	9.3	30.7	26.6	33.5
50005	Caledonia County, Vermont	5.3	21,639	9.9	36.1	26.9	27.0
50007	Chittenden County, Vermont	4.2	103,786	6.2	20.6	24.5	48.7
50009	Essex County, Vermont	6.7	4,689	15.5	43.3	25.2	16.0
50011	Franklin County, Vermont	8.8	33,462	10.5	37.6	28.3	23.6
50013	Grand Isle County, Vermont	5.2	5,139	6.1	29.7	29.1	35.1
50015	Lamoille County, Vermont	3.6	17,205	7.9	28.6	27.2	36.2
50017	Orange County, Vermont	5.2	20,802	8.5	34.9	25.8	30.8
50019	Orleans County, Vermont	7.1	19,585	13.7	38.7	25.5	22.1
50021	Rutland County, Vermont	3.3	43,342	9.3	34.2	27.4	29.1
50023	Washington County, Vermont	8.6	41,992	6.1	29.2	24.8	39.9
50025	Windham County, Vermont	2.6	31,887	8.4	30.7	25.1	35.8
50027	Windsor County, Vermont	3.6	41,878	7.6	31.7	25.6	35.1
51000	**Virginia**	9.2	5,566,373	11.7	24.8	27.2	36.3
51001	Accomack County, Virginia	8.1	23,650	19.7	39.9	21.7	18.8
51003	Albemarle County, Virginia	4.7	69,085	8.7	18.2	21.5	51.7
51005	Alleghany County, Virginia	4.2	11,778	16.4	36.9	30.9	15.7
51007	Amelia County, Virginia	7.7	9,018	20.3	34.1	31.1	14.5
51009	Amherst County, Virginia	4.3	22,435	17.2	35.7	28.8	18.3
51011	Appomattox County, Virginia	7.3	10,766	16.0	36.1	30.2	17.7
51013	Arlington County, Virginia	17.4	168,459	6.5	8.3	12.3	72.9
51015	Augusta County, Virginia	3.6	53,321	14.0	40.1	23.8	22.0
51017	Bath County, Virginia	3.3	3,419	12.1	38.9	27.2	21.8
51019	Bedford County, Virginia	5.0	54,606	11.9	31.0	30.4	26.7
51021	Bland County, Virginia	6.6	5,078	14.7	39.5	31.6	14.1
51023	Botetourt County, Virginia	4.5	23,850	8.9	35.0	29.9	26.2
51025	Brunswick County, Virginia	9.8	12,080	24.1	35.7	27.1	13.1
51027	Buchanan County, Virginia	5.2	17,537	30.2	34.4	25.6	9.9

Table C. County—Labor Force, Employment, and Educational Data, 2011–2015—*Continued*

| | | Industry for employed population age 16 and older | Educational attainment for the population age 25 and older | | | |
| | | | | Educational attainment | | |
Fips code	State/county	Public administration	Total population age 25 and older	Less than high school graduate	High school graduate (includes equivalency)	Some college or Associate's degree	Bachelor's degree or higher
51029	Buckingham County, Virginia	9.1	12,311	22.8	43.5	23.3	10.4
51031	Campbell County, Virginia	4.0	38,643	15.2	36.1	29.5	19.3
51033	Caroline County, Virginia	9.7	19,905	17.8	36.7	26.4	19.2
51035	Carroll County, Virginia	4.2	21,928	20.2	34.5	30.8	14.5
51036	Charles City County, Virginia	6.2	5,419	24.4	39.3	23.3	13.0
51037	Charlotte County, Virginia	8.0	8,549	22.0	37.6	26.4	14.0
51041	Chesterfield County, Virginia	7.3	216,740	9.0	24.1	30.0	36.9
51043	Clarke County, Virginia	7.9	10,189	12.3	28.0	28.7	31.0
51045	Craig County, Virginia	7.0	3,849	10.4	48.4	26.5	14.7
51047	Culpeper County, Virginia	5.9	32,258	16.2	34.1	27.8	21.9
51049	Cumberland County, Virginia	13.1	6,800	22.5	36.5	26.4	14.5
51051	Dickenson County, Virginia	11.1	11,116	24.9	35.6	28.5	11.0
51053	Dinwiddie County, Virginia	7.3	19,558	18.2	39.7	26.8	15.3
51057	Essex County, Virginia	7.6	7,830	17.7	38.5	28.6	15.2
51059	Fairfax County, Virginia	12.3	766,502	8.0	13.0	19.1	59.9
51061	Fauquier County, Virginia	9.1	45,852	8.8	28.5	29.2	33.5
51063	Floyd County, Virginia	4.9	11,279	16.8	35.6	29.4	18.2
51065	Fluvanna County, Virginia	5.5	18,442	11.3	28.4	28.7	31.5
51067	Franklin County, Virginia	4.0	40,435	16.0	32.0	31.5	20.5
51069	Frederick County, Virginia	6.6	55,621	12.6	30.5	27.8	29.1
51071	Giles County, Virginia	4.3	12,079	16.0	40.0	28.1	15.8
51073	Gloucester County, Virginia	8.2	26,365	9.8	33.9	34.3	22.1
51075	Goochland County, Virginia	7.3	16,121	10.0	26.9	25.8	37.4
51077	Grayson County, Virginia	5.6	11,676	21.4	41.1	27.5	10.0
51079	Greene County, Virginia	7.3	13,012	15.2	34.9	26.1	23.7
51081	Greensville County, Virginia	11.0	8,807	23.8	42.3	25.3	8.6
51083	Halifax County, Virginia	6.3	25,321	20.2	36.5	27.8	15.5
51085	Hanover County, Virginia	6.6	68,702	7.8	27.6	28.8	35.7
51087	Henrico County, Virginia	6.3	217,423	9.3	22.8	27.1	40.7
51089	Henry County, Virginia	3.7	38,173	21.6	34.1	32.9	11.4
51091	Highland County, Virginia	9.0	1,802	16.3	38.6	23.4	21.6
51093	Isle of Wight County, Virginia	7.1	25,420	13.7	27.7	31.7	26.9
51095	James City County, Virginia	7.9	50,954	6.2	21.1	25.7	47.0
51097	King and Queen County, Virginia	6.7	5,209	15.2	41.1	25.6	18.1
51099	King George County, Virginia	22.2	16,141	7.3	30.3	30.0	32.3
51101	King William County, Virginia	4.9	11,169	12.3	39.4	29.9	18.4
51103	Lancaster County, Virginia	8.1	8,807	10.0	32.8	29.2	27.9
51105	Lee County, Virginia	7.9	18,499	25.5	33.6	28.8	12.0
51107	Loudoun County, Virginia	8.3	223,162	6.4	13.8	21.6	58.2
51109	Louisa County, Virginia	4.8	24,324	17.2	37.0	25.2	20.6
51111	Lunenburg County, Virginia	10.5	9,130	25.6	34.9	27.4	12.2
51113	Madison County, Virginia	6.6	9,274	16.9	36.4	23.5	23.2
51115	Mathews County, Virginia	8.0	6,805	7.9	33.3	29.7	29.2
51117	Mecklenburg County, Virginia	9.7	23,117	21.2	32.5	30.8	15.6
51119	Middlesex County, Virginia	6.3	8,276	12.3	32.5	31.0	24.2
51121	Montgomery County, Virginia	3.0	52,809	8.7	21.8	23.8	45.7
51125	Nelson County, Virginia	4.5	10,886	16.1	33.6	22.2	28.2
51127	New Kent County, Virginia	6.6	13,831	9.9	33.0	32.5	24.6
51131	Northampton County, Virginia	5.2	8,933	20.3	34.2	25.0	20.6
51133	Northumberland County, Virginia	5.8	9,671	11.9	31.1	31.7	25.4
51135	Nottoway County, Virginia	13.8	11,148	22.3	37.1	25.4	15.2
51137	Orange County, Virginia	8.8	24,371	12.1	34.7	28.1	25.1
51139	Page County, Virginia	6.4	17,138	22.9	42.9	21.4	12.8
51141	Patrick County, Virginia	2.9	13,738	21.3	36.0	30.1	12.6
51143	Pittsylvania County, Virginia	4.4	45,528	19.3	35.3	31.2	14.1
51145	Powhatan County, Virginia	8.3	20,198	10.9	28.6	32.6	27.9
51147	Prince Edward County, Virginia	6.8	12,908	18.0	34.6	23.0	24.4
51149	Prince George County, Virginia	11.5	25,481	12.3	33.4	32.9	21.3
51153	Prince William County, Virginia	12.8	275,632	10.3	21.7	29.2	38.8
51155	Pulaski County, Virginia	4.7	25,580	16.0	34.2	31.9	17.8
51157	Rappahannock County, Virginia	9.5	5,628	13.5	25.6	25.8	35.1
51159	Richmond County, Virginia	9.3	6,890	20.9	40.2	26.2	12.7
51161	Roanoke County, Virginia	4.9	66,877	8.1	26.4	31.4	34.2
51163	Rockbridge County, Virginia	5.6	16,808	14.2	36.3	24.0	25.5
51165	Rockingham County, Virginia	3.1	52,819	18.7	35.5	22.0	23.8
51167	Russell County, Virginia	4.4	20,452	23.4	36.7	27.5	12.4
51169	Scott County, Virginia	5.5	16,657	23.5	36.2	28.5	11.7
51171	Shenandoah County, Virginia	5.1	30,669	15.5	39.5	26.0	19.0
51173	Smyth County, Virginia	5.4	22,825	18.2	38.8	27.9	15.0
51175	Southampton County, Virginia	9.9	13,397	19.6	34.8	30.7	15.0
51177	Spotsylvania County, Virginia	12.0	83,464	10.5	31.7	28.6	29.3
51179	Stafford County, Virginia	20.6	85,795	6.7	23.7	32.8	36.8
51181	Surry County, Virginia	7.2	4,944	18.4	29.2	31.3	21.2
51183	Sussex County, Virginia	9.8	9,071	29.3	40.3	20.8	9.6
51185	Tazewell County, Virginia	6.8	31,619	20.8	35.8	29.9	13.5

Table C. County—Labor Force, Employment, and Educational Data, 2011–2015—*Continued*

		Industry for employed population age 16 and older	Educational attainment for the population age 25 and older				
				Educational attainment			
Fips code	State/county	Public administration	Total population age 25 and older	Less than high school graduate	High school graduate (includes equivalency)	Some college or Associate's degree	Bachelor's degree or higher
51187	Warren County, Virginia	8.0	26,368	14.5	36.6	28.2	20.7
51191	Washington County, Virginia	5.3	39,734	15.9	32.9	27.8	23.3
51193	Westmoreland County, Virginia	12.2	12,713	18.9	36.3	26.4	18.3
51195	Wise County, Virginia	7.8	28,104	26.0	32.4	27.6	14.0
51197	Wythe County, Virginia	3.9	21,175	18.8	36.4	28.8	16.0
51199	York County, Virginia	14.2	43,962	6.0	19.6	32.3	42.2
51510	Alexandria city, Virginia	16.3	113,816	8.5	12.1	18.0	61.4
51520	Bristol city, Virginia	4.4	12,375	17.6	32.8	26.3	23.3
51530	Buena Vista city, Virginia	3.6	4,106	18.1	40.5	24.9	16.4
51540	Charlottesville city, Virginia	3.4	27,803	9.8	22.2	18.2	49.8
51550	Chesapeake city, Virginia	9.5	152,122	8.9	26.5	35.0	29.6
51570	Colonial Heights city, Virginia	9.2	12,059	12.1	35.2	31.0	21.7
51580	Covington city, Virginia	2.5	3,976	16.8	43.5	30.5	9.3
51590	Danville city, Virginia	5.3	29,209	21.3	28.1	32.7	17.9
51595	Emporia city, Virginia	11.7	3,930	25.3	32.6	24.0	18.1
51600	Fairfax city, Virginia	11.2	16,493	7.6	15.2	22.4	54.9
51610	Falls Church city, Virginia	21.9	9,077	2.3	7.5	11.4	78.8
51620	Franklin city, Virginia	13.6	5,701	19.8	24.9	29.1	26.2
51630	Fredericksburg city, Virginia	9.8	16,063	9.0	26.9	26.7	37.3
51640	Galax city, Virginia	3.7	5,009	27.7	33.7	27.1	11.6
51650	Hampton city, Virginia	9.7	89,933	10.1	27.3	39.3	23.2
51660	Harrisonburg city, Virginia	2.7	24,427	15.9	26.5	21.8	35.8
51670	Hopewell city, Virginia	6.5	14,819	19.1	38.3	30.3	12.3
51678	Lexington city, Virginia	4.4	2,249	20.0	18.1	18.1	43.8
51680	Lynchburg city, Virginia	3.0	43,635	11.7	25.1	30.1	33.1
51683	Manassas city, Virginia	7.2	25,806	18.5	26.0	26.6	28.8
51685	Manassas Park city, Virginia	7.9	9,902	17.7	26.0	28.0	28.3
51690	Martinsville city, Virginia	4.0	9,513	21.9	29.7	30.6	17.8
51700	Newport News city, Virginia	8.9	114,982	11.0	28.2	36.8	24.0
51710	Norfolk city, Virginia	9.4	149,072	13.0	26.9	34.0	26.1
51720	Norton city, Virginia	5.1	2,666	18.0	19.4	43.0	19.6
51730	Petersburg city, Virginia	7.9	22,020	22.1	34.0	28.0	15.9
51735	Poquoson city, Virginia	7.4	8,417	6.4	27.0	29.5	37.1
51740	Portsmouth city, Virginia	9.8	63,396	16.4	28.9	34.0	20.8
51750	Radford city, Virginia	2.1	7,024	10.6	22.6	31.3	35.5
51760	Richmond city, Virginia	5.4	143,240	16.8	23.0	24.1	36.0
51770	Roanoke city, Virginia	4.1	68,622	15.6	30.4	30.4	23.6
51775	Salem city, Virginia	5.9	16,888	10.0	29.8	31.8	28.4
51790	Staunton city, Virginia	6.1	17,175	12.8	30.9	25.0	31.3
51800	Suffolk city, Virginia	9.4	57,071	12.5	28.3	32.9	26.4
51810	Virginia Beach city, Virginia	9.7	298,183	6.7	22.4	37.1	33.8
51820	Waynesboro city, Virginia	5.0	14,555	15.1	38.5	28.0	18.4
51830	Williamsburg city, Virginia	6.3	7,223	8.3	15.5	23.7	52.4
51840	Winchester city, Virginia	5.3	17,917	15.8	30.4	25.6	28.3
53000	**Washington**	5.3	4,721,438	9.6	23.3	34.3	32.9
53001	Adams County, Washington	2.4	10,462	33.4	25.9	27.0	13.6
53003	Asotin County, Washington	4.3	15,589	10.6	30.5	40.7	18.2
53005	Benton County, Washington	4.5	118,423	11.1	24.4	35.1	29.4
53007	Chelan County, Washington	3.2	49,530	16.5	30.1	28.8	24.5
53009	Clallam County, Washington	8.2	54,247	7.7	27.9	39.7	24.7
53011	Clark County, Washington	4.2	294,043	8.6	25.3	38.9	27.2
53013	Columbia County, Washington	8.6	2,950	9.9	27.5	39.5	23.0
53015	Cowlitz County, Washington	5.1	70,149	12.2	30.9	40.9	16.0
53017	Douglas County, Washington	3.4	25,786	19.2	27.7	35.7	17.4
53019	Ferry County, Washington	12.0	5,589	12.7	31.2	39.4	16.7
53021	Franklin County, Washington	4.2	49,013	26.4	27.3	30.5	15.9
53023	Garfield County, Washington	8.2	1,654	4.4	29.4	41.7	24.5
53025	Grant County, Washington	5.4	55,059	24.5	26.8	32.3	16.4
53027	Grays Harbor County, Washington	9.7	50,652	12.1	32.1	41.1	14.7
53029	Island County, Washington	10.6	56,695	5.5	23.3	39.5	31.7
53031	Jefferson County, Washington	6.2	24,216	5.9	23.2	33.9	37.0
53033	King County, Washington	3.3	1,435,467	7.7	16.5	28.0	47.9
53035	Kitsap County, Washington	11.0	173,927	5.5	23.2	41.0	30.3
53037	Kittitas County, Washington	5.7	25,073	9.2	26.0	31.2	33.6
53039	Klickitat County, Washington	5.1	14,966	11.4	29.0	36.2	23.5
53041	Lewis County, Washington	7.3	52,458	12.9	31.6	40.1	15.4
53043	Lincoln County, Washington	6.8	7,461	8.7	33.4	37.3	20.6
53045	Mason County, Washington	11.0	44,261	12.4	30.4	39.5	17.7
53047	Okanogan County, Washington	8.9	28,549	17.1	29.8	34.6	18.5
53049	Pacific County, Washington	6.6	15,712	12.6	31.6	39.0	16.8
53051	Pend Oreille County, Washington	10.0	9,640	9.0	32.2	41.6	17.1
53053	Pierce County, Washington	7.2	541,718	9.1	28.8	37.4	24.7
53055	San Juan County, Washington	4.3	12,824	4.6	17.2	31.6	46.6
53057	Skagit County, Washington	4.8	82,168	11.7	26.7	36.9	24.8

Table C. County—Labor Force, Employment, and Educational Data, 2011–2015—*Continued*

Fips code	State/county	Industry for employed population age 16 and older — Public administration	Total population age 25 and older	Educational attainment for the population age 25 and older — Less than high school graduate	High school graduate (includes equivalency)	Some college or Associate's degree	Bachelor's degree or higher
53059	Skamania County, Washington	5.7	8,032	9.3	29.2	39.6	22.0
53061	Snohomish County, Washington	3.9	506,719	8.4	24.3	37.4	29.9
53063	Spokane County, Washington	4.9	320,569	7.2	25.7	38.6	28.6
53065	Stevens County, Washington	6.7	30,802	9.7	34.4	39.2	16.7
53067	Thurston County, Washington	17.4	180,338	6.6	22.7	37.4	33.4
53069	Wahkiakum County, Washington	10.5	3,064	7.6	33.1	44.8	14.5
53071	Walla Walla County, Washington	6.4	38,691	11.3	22.6	38.9	27.2
53073	Whatcom County, Washington	5.0	134,413	8.8	23.0	35.7	32.5
53075	Whitman County, Washington	3.1	22,451	4.3	17.4	29.3	48.9
53077	Yakima County, Washington	4.8	148,078	28.1	27.8	28.3	15.7
54000	**West Virginia**	6.7	1,298,118	15.0	40.7	25.1	19.2
54001	Barbour County, West Virginia	6.9	11,398	18.9	47.1	22.1	11.9
54003	Berkeley County, West Virginia	10.5	73,466	12.9	38.2	29.1	19.7
54005	Boone County, West Virginia	5.6	16,804	21.5	49.4	20.2	8.8
54007	Braxton County, West Virginia	9.1	10,422	19.6	49.1	19.4	12.0
54009	Brooke County, West Virginia	5.9	16,925	9.2	43.7	28.6	18.5
54011	Cabell County, West Virginia	3.4	64,789	13.1	31.9	28.1	26.9
54013	Calhoun County, West Virginia	6.6	5,465	23.1	48.9	17.6	10.4
54015	Clay County, West Virginia	9.3	6,428	26.3	49.1	14.7	9.8
54017	Doddridge County, West Virginia	8.3	5,900	18.2	44.3	24.1	13.5
54019	Fayette County, West Virginia	6.7	32,756	19.7	44.4	23.5	12.4
54021	Gilmer County, West Virginia	9.9	6,093	21.7	36.6	25.1	16.6
54023	Grant County, West Virginia	3.1	8,593	18.1	50.2	19.3	12.3
54025	Greenbrier County, West Virginia	4.7	25,999	15.2	44.0	22.8	18.1
54027	Hampshire County, West Virginia	6.9	16,976	21.8	50.0	18.1	10.1
54029	Hancock County, West Virginia	4.8	22,189	13.1	42.8	26.3	17.8
54031	Hardy County, West Virginia	5.0	10,125	20.6	47.7	17.7	14.0
54033	Harrison County, West Virginia	8.1	48,867	12.5	39.5	27.7	20.4
54035	Jackson County, West Virginia	7.5	20,642	13.6	41.1	27.7	17.6
54037	Jefferson County, West Virginia	9.9	37,200	11.9	32.1	27.6	28.4
54039	Kanawha County, West Virginia	9.4	136,646	11.8	37.3	25.8	25.1
54041	Lewis County, West Virginia	4.7	11,822	13.3	49.7	22.9	14.1
54043	Lincoln County, West Virginia	6.4	15,114	21.6	43.4	25.5	9.5
54045	Logan County, West Virginia	5.3	25,704	23.6	41.6	26.7	8.1
54047	McDowell County, West Virginia	8.5	15,321	35.6	43.9	15.5	5.1
54049	Marion County, West Virginia	6.9	38,965	11.6	40.9	26.0	21.4
54051	Marshall County, West Virginia	5.9	23,427	10.8	45.1	27.3	16.8
54053	Mason County, West Virginia	5.6	19,497	15.9	47.5	26.3	10.4
54055	Mercer County, West Virginia	5.2	43,555	17.6	37.9	25.7	18.8
54057	Mineral County, West Virginia	7.5	19,415	12.0	50.2	24.9	12.9
54059	Mingo County, West Virginia	6.2	18,299	26.3	41.0	22.4	10.2
54061	Monongalia County, West Virginia	4.3	60,551	8.4	29.9	21.9	39.7
54063	Monroe County, West Virginia	3.4	9,907	18.1	49.4	19.2	13.3
54065	Morgan County, West Virginia	6.0	12,864	16.7	41.2	23.4	18.6
54067	Nicholas County, West Virginia	5.2	18,588	16.1	48.0	21.9	13.9
54069	Ohio County, West Virginia	5.4	30,539	9.0	34.5	26.8	29.8
54071	Pendleton County, West Virginia	8.9	5,520	19.8	46.0	18.8	15.3
54073	Pleasants County, West Virginia	6.6	5,535	11.6	50.1	25.3	13.0
54075	Pocahontas County, West Virginia	9.4	6,590	15.3	47.4	20.6	16.7
54077	Preston County, West Virginia	4.5	24,756	17.9	46.4	21.2	14.6
54079	Putnam County, West Virginia	5.5	39,710	8.7	37.8	28.0	25.4
54081	Raleigh County, West Virginia	6.5	55,878	17.4	39.5	24.8	18.3
54083	Randolph County, West Virginia	7.6	21,183	16.1	46.3	18.2	19.3
54085	Ritchie County, West Virginia	7.3	7,301	18.6	47.9	23.1	10.5
54087	Roane County, West Virginia	3.5	10,456	21.5	46.5	20.7	11.3
54089	Summers County, West Virginia	5.6	10,307	18.1	40.5	27.8	13.6
54091	Taylor County, West Virginia	6.9	12,229	14.9	43.6	25.0	16.6
54093	Tucker County, West Virginia	9.4	5,208	12.5	52.7	20.6	14.2
54095	Tyler County, West Virginia	6.6	6,537	13.7	49.2	25.9	11.3
54097	Upshur County, West Virginia	6.5	16,662	15.9	48.4	19.4	16.3
54099	Wayne County, West Virginia	4.8	29,136	21.3	40.9	25.5	12.3
54101	Webster County, West Virginia	5.9	6,497	29.1	43.0	18.7	9.3
54103	Wetzel County, West Virginia	5.4	11,644	16.1	48.7	24.8	10.4
54105	Wirt County, West Virginia	6.4	4,128	14.1	47.6	26.3	12.0
54107	Wood County, West Virginia	6.1	61,337	10.9	38.1	32.3	18.8
54109	Wyoming County, West Virginia	6.2	16,253	24.8	46.0	21.3	7.9
55000	**Wisconsin**	3.5	3,873,119	9.0	32.0	31.2	27.8
55001	Adams County, Wisconsin	4.1	16,163	12.8	43.7	30.7	12.8
55003	Ashland County, Wisconsin	5.9	10,810	7.7	35.0	34.1	23.2
55005	Barron County, Wisconsin	2.7	32,417	10.5	39.8	33.1	16.6
55007	Bayfield County, Wisconsin	7.5	11,447	6.0	30.2	34.5	29.3
55009	Brown County, Wisconsin	3.3	168,061	9.4	31.3	31.4	27.9
55011	Buffalo County, Wisconsin	2.9	9,531	8.7	42.5	30.8	18.0
55013	Burnett County, Wisconsin	5.1	11,633	8.6	40.0	33.7	17.7

Table C. County—Labor Force, Employment, and Educational Data, 2011–2015—*Continued*

| | | Industry for employed population age 16 and older | Educational attainment for the population age 25 and older | | | | |
| | | | | Educational attainment | | | |
Fips code	State/county	Public administration	Total population age 25 and older	Less than high school graduate	High school graduate (includes equivalency)	Some college or Associate's degree	Bachelor's degree or higher
55015	Calumet County, Wisconsin	2.3	33,123	7.1	33.8	30.7	28.4
55017	Chippewa County, Wisconsin	3.5	44,019	8.2	38.5	34.1	19.2
55019	Clark County, Wisconsin	2.7	21,763	18.6	43.3	26.6	11.5
55021	Columbia County, Wisconsin	5.9	39,733	7.5	34.9	35.5	22.1
55023	Crawford County, Wisconsin	5.2	11,849	10.1	42.7	32.1	15.1
55025	Dane County, Wisconsin	4.9	332,684	5.0	19.0	28.1	47.9
55027	Dodge County, Wisconsin	4.2	63,031	11.8	40.2	31.6	16.4
55029	Door County, Wisconsin	4.6	21,393	6.4	32.9	31.0	29.7
55031	Douglas County, Wisconsin	4.1	30,540	6.6	33.2	37.6	22.5
55033	Dunn County, Wisconsin	2.6	26,852	7.3	34.6	32.6	25.6
55035	Eau Claire County, Wisconsin	2.9	62,996	6.8	26.9	35.2	31.1
55037	Florence County, Wisconsin	3.3	3,479	8.8	39.2	34.8	17.1
55039	Fond du Lac County, Wisconsin	4.1	70,352	8.7	38.5	31.3	21.5
55041	Forest County, Wisconsin	8.5	6,463	13.2	40.7	32.4	13.8
55043	Grant County, Wisconsin	3.2	31,783	8.6	38.7	31.4	21.3
55045	Green County, Wisconsin	3.2	25,806	7.8	39.0	31.3	21.9
55047	Green Lake County, Wisconsin	4.6	13,425	12.0	42.3	28.8	16.9
55049	Iowa County, Wisconsin	3.5	16,597	6.9	36.3	33.9	22.9
55051	Iron County, Wisconsin	6.3	4,665	7.1	35.8	36.1	21.0
55053	Jackson County, Wisconsin	8.7	14,451	12.9	42.2	31.0	13.8
55055	Jefferson County, Wisconsin	3.3	56,642	8.8	36.5	32.1	22.6
55057	Juneau County, Wisconsin	6.5	19,170	14.6	42.2	30.9	12.3
55059	Kenosha County, Wisconsin	3.8	109,826	9.7	32.8	33.0	24.5
55061	Kewaunee County, Wisconsin	2.5	14,411	8.1	44.2	31.9	15.8
55063	La Crosse County, Wisconsin	3.7	73,880	5.6	27.7	35.8	30.9
55065	Lafayette County, Wisconsin	2.5	11,367	10.3	41.5	30.7	17.5
55067	Langlade County, Wisconsin	3.5	14,321	10.9	42.4	31.8	14.9
55069	Lincoln County, Wisconsin	3.4	20,633	10.0	40.5	34.1	15.3
55071	Manitowoc County, Wisconsin	2.4	57,142	9.7	39.9	30.7	19.7
55073	Marathon County, Wisconsin	2.3	92,401	9.0	37.1	30.2	23.7
55075	Marinette County, Wisconsin	2.9	30,072	9.0	42.6	34.0	14.4
55077	Marquette County, Wisconsin	6.1	11,218	12.1	43.8	31.3	12.8
55078	Menominee County, Wisconsin	12.0	2,527	10.2	43.8	29.9	16.1
55079	Milwaukee County, Wisconsin	3.4	620,247	13.5	28.1	29.3	29.1
55081	Monroe County, Wisconsin	8.8	30,440	10.7	39.4	32.8	17.1
55083	Oconto County, Wisconsin	3.6	27,119	9.8	43.7	31.1	15.4
55085	Oneida County, Wisconsin	5.6	27,070	7.5	34.3	33.2	25.0
55087	Outagamie County, Wisconsin	2.6	120,654	6.5	34.2	31.6	27.7
55089	Ozaukee County, Wisconsin	2.1	60,384	3.6	22.5	27.8	46.1
55091	Pepin County, Wisconsin	4.6	5,210	9.1	43.0	30.5	17.4
55093	Pierce County, Wisconsin	3.6	25,402	5.5	32.6	34.4	27.5
55095	Polk County, Wisconsin	3.5	30,863	7.8	39.0	33.7	19.5
55097	Portage County, Wisconsin	2.5	44,494	7.5	33.7	29.6	29.2
55099	Price County, Wisconsin	5.3	10,606	10.1	41.6	31.8	16.6
55101	Racine County, Wisconsin	3.3	131,699	11.8	30.7	33.8	23.7
55103	Richland County, Wisconsin	3.1	12,386	10.9	41.0	31.5	16.7
55105	Rock County, Wisconsin	3.3	108,006	11.1	36.8	31.7	20.4
55107	Rusk County, Wisconsin	4.0	10,336	11.9	43.2	29.8	15.0
55109	St. Croix County, Wisconsin	3.8	57,332	4.8	27.7	35.1	32.3
55111	Sauk County, Wisconsin	3.6	43,696	10.0	36.6	31.2	22.2
55113	Sawyer County, Wisconsin	5.7	12,117	9.0	34.5	34.0	22.6
55115	Shawano County, Wisconsin	3.5	29,449	9.7	45.3	29.5	15.5
55117	Sheboygan County, Wisconsin	2.4	79,546	9.0	36.7	30.9	23.4
55119	Taylor County, Wisconsin	2.2	14,258	12.4	46.3	28.0	13.3
55121	Trempealeau County, Wisconsin	2.8	20,161	11.5	38.8	30.6	19.2
55123	Vernon County, Wisconsin	2.8	20,339	11.6	38.1	29.7	20.5
55125	Vilas County, Wisconsin	4.6	16,520	7.5	31.4	35.1	26.0
55127	Walworth County, Wisconsin	3.1	67,210	9.8	31.8	31.5	26.8
55129	Washburn County, Wisconsin	5.4	11,713	8.6	38.8	31.9	20.7
55131	Washington County, Wisconsin	2.5	92,462	6.7	30.0	34.4	28.9
55133	Waukesha County, Wisconsin	2.2	274,624	4.3	24.3	30.2	41.2
55135	Waupaca County, Wisconsin	3.1	37,159	9.7	43.7	29.6	16.9
55137	Waushara County, Wisconsin	5.0	18,145	13.3	42.3	29.9	14.6
55139	Winnebago County, Wisconsin	3.5	112,646	8.0	34.0	31.4	26.6
55141	Wood County, Wisconsin	3.1	52,150	8.0	39.2	33.2	19.6
56000	**Wyoming**	6.6	384,272	7.7	29.4	37.2	25.7
56001	Albany County, Wyoming	4.6	20,238	3.5	17.0	30.2	49.3
56003	Big Horn County, Wyoming	5.3	7,953	11.2	31.3	37.9	19.6
56005	Campbell County, Wyoming	3.7	30,178	8.7	34.4	37.6	19.3
56007	Carbon County, Wyoming	10.4	10,686	9.2	35.6	35.7	19.5
56009	Converse County, Wyoming	5.3	9,489	8.7	38.0	35.8	17.5
56011	Crook County, Wyoming	4.7	5,063	7.0	34.7	39.5	18.8
56013	Fremont County, Wyoming	6.8	27,019	8.3	31.7	38.7	21.3
56015	Goshen County, Wyoming	11.9	9,462	9.1	29.9	38.1	22.8

Table C. County—Labor Force, Employment, and Educational Data, 2011–2015—*Continued*

		Industry for employed population age 16 and older	Educational attainment for the population age 25 and older				
					Educational attainment		
Fips code	State/county	Public administration	Total population age 25 and older	Less than high school graduate	High school graduate (includes equivalency)	Some college or Associate's degree	Bachelor's degree or higher
56017	Hot Springs County, Wyoming	5.5	3,515	9.1	30.8	39.5	20.6
56019	Johnson County, Wyoming	4.7	6,053	5.6	36.1	33.0	25.3
56021	Laramie County, Wyoming	14.6	63,353	6.9	26.3	38.9	27.8
56023	Lincoln County, Wyoming	4.6	12,108	6.6	31.5	40.4	21.5
56025	Natrona County, Wyoming	4.9	53,443	8.8	27.5	41.9	21.9
56027	Niobrara County, Wyoming	22.3	1,862	9.5	28.1	41.1	21.3
56029	Park County, Wyoming	3.9	20,362	6.8	28.5	36.3	28.4
56031	Platte County, Wyoming	6.8	6,363	7.7	30.8	39.8	21.7
56033	Sheridan County, Wyoming	3.8	20,869	5.5	27.2	38.0	29.4
56035	Sublette County, Wyoming	10.1	6,965	4.5	35.2	37.3	22.9
56037	Sweetwater County, Wyoming	4.1	28,502	9.5	35.4	35.5	19.6
56039	Teton County, Wyoming	2.8	16,823	4.1	17.9	24.1	53.9
56041	Uinta County, Wyoming	4.6	13,027	10.3	36.2	34.2	19.3
56043	Washakie County, Wyoming	6.4	5,816	12.6	29.3	37.0	21.1
56045	Weston County, Wyoming	4.2	5,123	11.9	32.2	37.7	18.1

PART D
METROPOLITAN AREAS

- New York-Newark-Jersey City, NY-NJ-PA was the largest metropolitan area in the country with more than 20 million residents while Carson City, NV was the smallest with only 54,521 residents.

- In Mankato-North Mankato, MN, 71.2 percent of women were in the labor force compared with only 37.5 percent in Homosassa Springs, FL. The civilian labor force participation for men was higher than the civilian labor force participation for women in all metro areas except for fourteen of them, including several university and military communities.

- The labor force participation rate of older workers has gradually been increasing over the past several years. In 68 metro areas, at least 20 percent of the population age 65 years and older was in the labor force. Manhattan, KS had the highest number of those 65 years and older in the labor force at 28.2 percent.

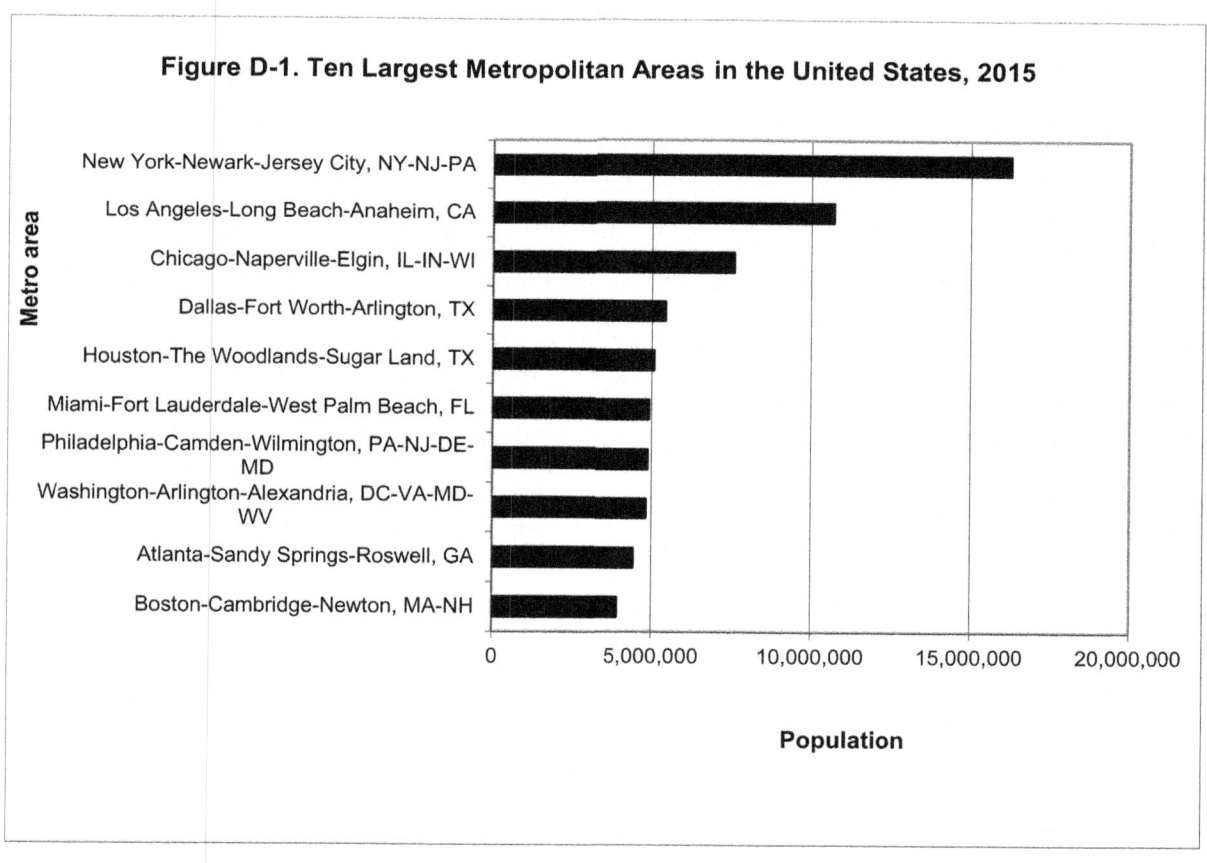

Figure D-1. Ten Largest Metropolitan Areas in the United States, 2015

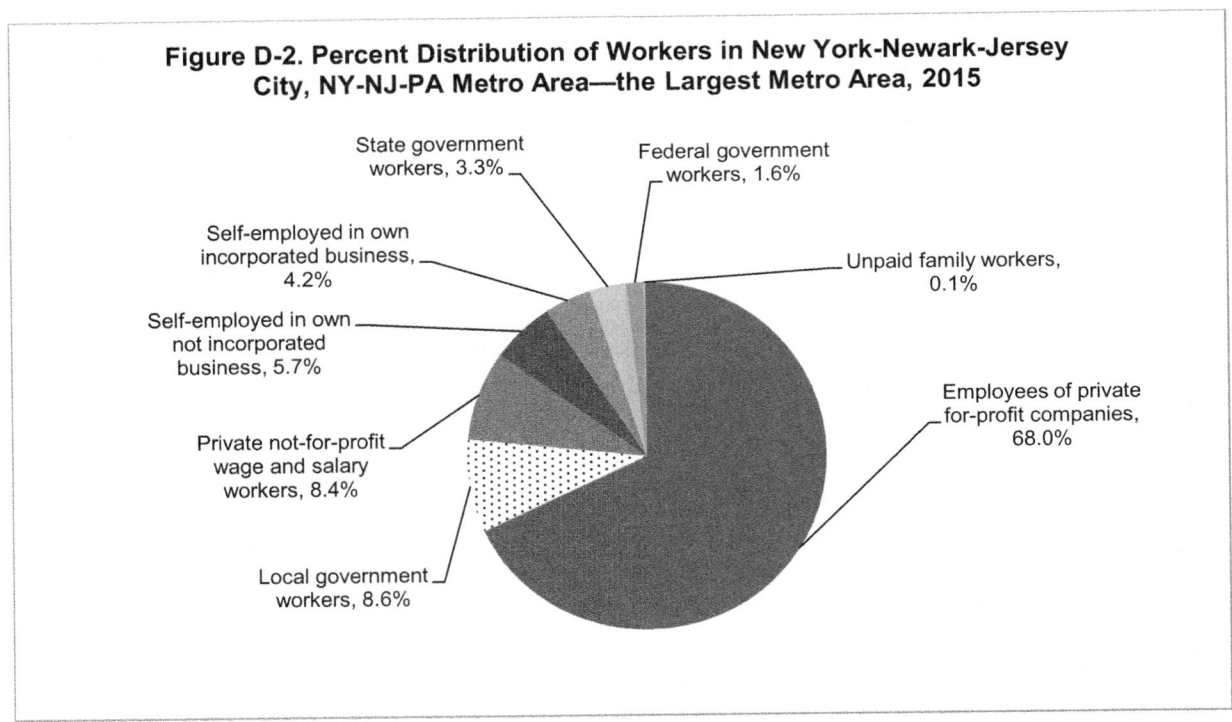

Figure D-2. Percent Distribution of Workers in New York-Newark-Jersey City, NY-NJ-PA Metro Area—the Largest Metro Area, 2015

State government workers, 3.3%

Federal government workers, 1.6%

Self-employed in own incorporated business, 4.2%

Unpaid family workers, 0.1%

Self-employed in own not incorporated business, 5.7%

Private not-for-profit wage and salary workers, 8.4%

Employees of private for-profit companies, 68.0%

Local government workers, 8.6%

- In New York-Newark-Jersey City, NY-NJ-PA—the largest metro area—68 percent of workers were employed by private for-profit companies while only 1.6 percent were federal government workers. Meanwhile, in Carson City, NV—the smallest metro area—the percentages were not much different; 67.2 percent were employed by private for-profit companies and 1.6 percent were federal government employees.

- Unemployment rates ranged from 2.3 percent in Bismarck, ND to 16.5 in El Centro, CA. Among all metro areas with a million or more residents, unemployment rates ranged from 4.3 percent in Minneapolis-St. Paul-Bloomington, MN-WI to 9.6 percent in Riverside-San Bernardino-Ontario, CA.

- Over 42 percent of employed persons age 16 years and over in Dalton, GA worked in the manufacturing industry compared with only 1.1 percent in Fairbanks, AL. In Fairbanks, AL the leading industry was educational services, and health care and social assistance with 24.8 percent of workers.

Table D. Metropolitan Statistical Area—Labor Force, Employment, and Educational Data, 2015

CBSA code/ Division code	Metropolitan area, metropolitan division	Total population age 16 and older	Percent in civilian labor force	Percent in armed forces	Civilian labor force participation by gender		Civilian labor force participation by age				Civilian unem-ployment rate	Civilian employed population age 16 and older			
					Men	Women	Age 16 to 24	Age 25 to 54	Age 55 to 64	Age 65 and older		Total	Men	Women	Percent women
10180	Abilene, TX Metro Area	134,017	56.8	3.2	58.4	55.2	53.2	71.3	61.8	19.1	4.1	73,064	37,395	35,669	48.8
10420	Akron, OH Metro Area	575,548	63.7	0.0	69.0	58.8	63.6	82.9	66.2	16.7	6.1	344,296	178,443	165,853	48.2
10500	Albany, GA Metro Area	122,083	57.0	0.3	60.8	53.7	52.6	76.0	50.3	17.0	12.6	60,786	29,689	31,097	51.2
10540	Albany, OR Metro Area	95,784	57.1	0.0	63.2	51.1	54.2	79.4	56.3	12.0	9.6	49,437	27,141	22,296	45.1
10580	Albany-Schenectady-Troy, NY Metro Area	725,304	64.7	0.3	69.1	60.4	60.0	84.5	66.5	18.2	5.2	444,595	230,899	213,696	48.1
10740	Albuquerque, NM Metro Area	722,670	60.2	0.5	64.5	56.1	57.8	77.0	61.3	16.9	6.9	405,223	210,388	194,835	48.1
10780	Alexandria, LA Metro Area	121,590	55.0	0.5	55.9	54.3	50.6	73.2	51.8	14.7	7.2	62,106	30,294	31,812	51.2
10900	Allentown-Bethlehem-Easton, PA-NJ Metro Area	675,380	64.3	0.0	70.4	58.6	62.1	84.7	68.8	15.9	5.9	408,363	215,032	193,331	47.3
11020	Altoona, PA Metro Area	103,116	57.6	0.0	64.1	51.6	59.9	80.9	57.9	12.5	5.4	56,198	29,480	26,718	47.5
11100	Amarillo, TX Metro Area	201,399	65.0	0.2	70.7	59.4	64.8	78.8	67.6	20.7	3.2	126,843	68,652	58,191	45.9
11180	Ames, IA Metro Area	81,860	64.9	0.1	62.8	67.3	57.4	87.2	76.6	14.1	4.2	50,910	25,143	25,767	50.6
11260	Anchorage, AK Metro Area	308,644	67.4	3.1	71.3	63.3	62.7	78.7	69.1	21.7	7.0	193,525	104,676	88,849	45.9
11460	Ann Arbor, MI Metro Area	297,793	64.6	0.1	69.4	59.9	57.7	82.5	65.3	20.3	5.4	181,977	96,499	85,478	47.0
11500	Anniston-Oxford-Jacksonville, AL Metro Area	93,323	56.4	0.2	61.9	51.5	66.7	73.1	53.4	11.3	10.1	47,309	24,347	22,962	48.5
11540	Appleton, WI Metro Area	183,455	71.4	0.0	75.1	67.7	74.5	89.5	71.7	14.2	3.0	127,104	66,061	61,043	48.0
11700	Asheville, NC Metro Area	371,889	56.7	0.1	62.1	51.9	61.0	78.3	58.3	14.6	5.1	200,070	103,112	96,958	48.5
12020	Athens-Clarke County, GA Metro Area	166,431	59.3	0.1	64.9	54.3	50.1	77.8	62.7	18.3	6.3	92,507	47,328	45,179	48.8
12060	Atlanta-Sandy Springs-Roswell, GA Metro Area	4,438,171	66.8	0.1	72.4	61.7	55.1	83.2	65.2	18.3	6.7	2,764,512	1,434,185	1,330,327	48.1
12100	Atlantic City-Hammonton, NJ Metro Area	220,275	65.3	0.3	68.8	62.2	64.9	82.7	71.7	19.5	10.8	128,434	64,687	63,747	49.6
12220	Auburn-Opelika, AL Metro Area	127,060	60.9	0.4	68.6	53.6	50.0	80.8	55.8	20.0	5.4	73,205	40,104	33,101	45.2
12260	Augusta-Richmond County, GA-SC Metro Area	467,608	56.5	2.3	59.6	53.7	49.3	74.2	56.6	16.1	8.4	242,071	121,846	120,225	49.7
12420	Austin-Round Rock, TX Metro Area	1,572,710	69.9	0.1	76.8	63.2	56.5	85.2	67.0	18.9	4.5	1,050,323	573,948	476,375	45.4
12540	Bakersfield, CA Metro Area	651,998	59.4	0.4	64.2	54.3	52.4	74.0	57.1	14.4	11.0	344,626	194,301	150,325	43.6
12580	Baltimore-Columbia-Towson, MD Metro Area	2,250,247	65.2	0.9	69.5	61.4	56.5	82.9	67.1	19.8	5.8	1,383,041	697,101	685,940	49.6
12620	Bangor, ME Metro Area	127,856	58.3	0.2	62.7	54.2	62.9	76.6	54.6	16.4	8.2	68,454	35,035	33,419	48.8
12700	Barnstable Town, MA Metro Area	185,313	59.7	0.3	64.9	55.1	61.0	86.6	72.8	21.4	5.2	104,949	53,887	51,062	48.7
12940	Baton Rouge, LA Metro Area	654,581	63.5	0.1	68.6	58.8	59.3	80.1	61.7	19.1	6.6	388,290	200,666	187,624	48.3
12980	Battle Creek, MI Metro Area	106,973	57.2	0.1	59.0	55.4	62.7	78.1	53.5	9.9	8.4	56,014	27,851	28,163	50.3
13020	Bay City, MI Metro Area	86,423	58.1	0.0	60.1	56.2	66.0	81.6	57.7	6.8	5.9	47,249	23,266	23,983	50.8
13140	Beaumont-Port Arthur, TX Metro Area	322,801	56.3	0.1	62.4	50.1	54.4	72.8	52.9	16.3	6.2	170,461	95,260	75,201	44.1
13220	Beckley, WV Metro Area	99,392	47.5	0.1	50.7	44.4	44.7	67.6	43.1	12.4	7.6	43,662	23,155	20,507	47.0
13380	Bellingham, WA Metro Area	175,831	61.8	0.2	65.0	58.8	64.4	80.2	60.5	17.4	6.0	102,163	52,051	50,112	49.1
13460	Bend-Redmond, OR Metro Area	142,062	61.6	0.0	65.8	57.7	68.1	85.0	59.3	14.3	6.1	82,207	42,479	39,728	48.3
13740	Billings, MT Metro Area	133,825	66.1	0.4	71.1	61.3	60.5	85.2	71.2	19.9	3.2	85,638	44,864	40,774	47.6
13780	Binghamton, NY Metro Area	203,632	59.3	0.0	62.3	56.4	53.1	81.0	67.9	15.4	7.0	112,244	56,457	55,787	49.7
13820	Birmingham-Hoover, AL Metro Area	910,443	60.8	0.1	66.1	56.0	57.7	79.4	56.4	16.9	6.9	515,386	265,464	249,922	48.5
13900	Bismarck, ND Metro Area	103,942	71.0	0.4	74.7	67.3	69.3	87.9	74.7	22.5	2.3	72,079	37,643	34,436	47.8
13980	Blacksburg-Christiansburg-Radford, VA Metro Area	153,285	57.9	0.1	61.5	54.3	44.3	81.7	64.3	19.6	5.7	83,789	44,501	39,288	46.9
14010	Bloomington, IL Metro Area	152,338	68.0	0.0	73.2	63.1	62.7	86.8	70.4	17.7	3.9	99,549	51,478	48,071	48.3
14020	Bloomington, IN Metro Area	141,099	61.4	0.1	63.6	59.2	48.3	84.1	67.4	21.1	6.2	81,252	42,415	38,837	47.8
14100	Bloomsburg-Berwick, PA Metro Area	71,830	54.9	0.0	61.7	48.7	40.0	82.0	62.7	10.9	5.4	37,317	19,737	17,580	47.1
14260	Boise City, ID Metro Area	520,982	63.8	0.4	68.7	58.9	61.3	80.6	61.9	16.9	6.2	311,753	166,753	145,000	46.5
14460	**Boston-Cambridge-Newton, MA-NH Metro Area**	3,920,656	68.7	0.1	73.4	64.4	62.4	85.7	72.9	22.2	5.3	2,553,286	1,305,356	1,247,930	48.9
14460/14454	*Boston, MA Metro Division*	1,635,248	68.5	0.1	72.9	64.5	62.3	85.4	72.2	20.7	6.2	1,050,671	530,871	519,800	49.5
14460/15764	*Cambridge-Newton-Framingham, MA Metro Division*	1,929,786	68.6	0.1	73.5	64.0	60.6	85.5	73.3	23.5	4.6	1,261,990	649,090	612,900	48.6
14460/40484	*Rockingham County-Strafford County, NH Metro Division*	355,622	70.9	0.4	75.8	66.1	71.9	88.1	74.1	21.8	4.5	240,625	125,395	115,230	47.9
14500	Boulder, CO Metro Area	263,957	68.8	0.0	72.5	65.0	59.4	86.3	70.2	25.7	5.2	172,041	89,540	82,501	48.0
14540	Bowling Green, KY Metro Area	134,415	59.6	0.0	65.3	54.2	64.2	75.2	56.8	11.9	6.4	74,982	39,732	35,250	47.0
14740	Bremerton-Silverdale, WA Metro Area	212,479	55.2	5.8	59.2	51.0	53.9	72.6	60.3	12.1	6.3	109,920	59,494	50,426	45.9
14860	Bridgeport-Stamford-Norwalk, CT Metro Area	754,903	67.8	0.0	74.6	61.5	57.9	84.1	77.3	22.8	7.7	472,541	250,305	222,236	47.0
15180	Brownsville-Harlingen, TX Metro Area	303,289	55.1	0.0	62.7	48.1	45.0	73.2	56.9	13.9	7.7	154,177	83,083	71,094	46.1
15260	Brunswick, GA Metro Area	93,346	58.0	0.1	61.2	55.0	55.6	77.1	62.4	17.3	5.0	51,415	26,236	25,179	49.0
15380	Buffalo-Cheektowaga-Niagara Falls, NY Metro Area	930,764	62.4	0.1	66.3	58.8	61.0	82.1	65.4	15.9	5.1	550,823	278,816	272,007	49.4
15500	Burlington, NC Metro Area	126,500	62.7	0.0	66.5	59.3	59.6	83.8	64.9	14.4	8.2	72,763	35,209	37,554	51.6
15540	Burlington-South Burlington, VT Metro Area	180,014	69.6	0.1	74.6	65.0	63.6	86.6	78.0	21.1	3.3	121,252	62,345	58,907	48.6
15680	California-Lexington Park, MD Metro Area	87,166	65.5	2.3	71.5	59.7	52.9	80.1	71.6	20.5	3.0	55,428	29,960	25,468	45.9
15940	Canton-Massillon, OH Metro Area	326,916	64.3	0.0	68.9	60.1	68.4	85.0	67.2	17.7	6.3	197,031	101,308	95,723	48.6

Table D. Metropolitan Statistical Area—Labor Force, Employment, and Educational Data, 2015—*Continued*

CBSA code/ Division code	Metropolitan area, metropolitan division	Total population age 16 and older	Percent in civilian labor force	Percent in armed forces	Civilian labor force participation by gender		Civilian labor force participation by age				Civilian unemployment rate	Civilian employed population age 16 and older			
					Men	Women	Age 16 to 24	Age 25 to 54	Age 55 to 64	Age 65 and older		Total	Men	Women	Percent women
15980	Cape Coral-Fort Myers, FL Metro Area	587,162	50.8	0.1	54.9	47.0	59.2	77.4	53.5	13.4	7.1	277,323	144,370	132,953	47.9
16020	Cape Girardeau, MO-IL Metro Area	77,191	60.8	0.2	62.8	58.9	59.6	81.9	61.5	15.6	2.5	45,759	22,871	22,888	50.0
16060	Carbondale-Marion, IL Metro Area	104,574	57.0	0.1	58.6	55.4	53.2	78.2	57.8	12.0	6.9	55,521	28,102	27,419	49.4
16180	Carson City, NV Metro Area	44,744	58.0	0.1							5.2	24,602			
16220	Casper, WY Metro Area	62,939	67.2	0.0	73.9	60.7	64.5	82.7	69.6	18.8	4.6	40,357	21,604	18,753	46.5
16300	Cedar Rapids, IA Metro Area	210,205	69.3	0.0	74.4	64.5	71.0	87.5	72.1	18.5	3.8	140,190	74,201	65,989	47.1
16540	Chambersburg-Waynesboro, PA Metro Area	122,313	63.7	0.0	69.9	57.8	64.3	87.2	65.8	14.3	6.4	72,851	39,039	33,812	46.4
16580	Champaign-Urbana, IL Metro Area	197,531	62.0	0.1	64.7	59.4	44.4	84.9	68.8	22.3	4.6	116,838	59,820	57,018	48.8
16620	Charleston, WV Metro Area	179,319	53.7	0.0	57.5	50.2	55.0	74.5	50.8	13.4	6.7	89,735	44,894	44,841	50.0
16700	Charleston-North Charleston, SC Metro Area	596,344	63.3	1.4	67.4	59.5	53.9	80.2	64.3	18.9	5.0	358,859	185,530	173,329	48.3
16740	Charlotte-Concord-Gastonia, NC-SC Metro Area	1,899,335	66.7	0.1	73.4	60.6	62.0	83.7	63.8	17.3	6.9	1,179,781	627,348	552,433	46.8
16820	Charlottesville, VA Metro Area	189,723	63.5	0.3	66.5	60.7	51.4	82.7	70.9	22.2	4.2	115,424	58,092	57,332	49.7
16860	Chattanooga, TN-GA Metro Area	444,120	60.1	0.1	65.9	54.8	62.8	79.7	55.8	16.1	5.9	251,262	132,147	119,115	47.4
16940	Cheyenne, WY Metro Area	77,408	63.4	2.6	67.7	59.0	59.4	82.6	60.8	17.9	6.5	45,849	25,013	20,836	45.4
16980	**Chicago-Naperville-Elgin, IL-IN-WI Metro Area**	7,568,243	66.5	0.2	72.7	60.7	58.6	83.6	67.6	18.3	7.1	4,672,798	2,468,582	2,204,216	47.2
16980/16974	*Chicago-Naperville-Arlington Heights, IL Metro Division*	5,837,383	66.7	0.0	72.9	60.9	58.1	83.8	67.2	18.4	7.3	3,607,889	1,898,553	1,709,336	47.4
16980/20994	*Elgin, IL Metro Division*	490,816	68.5	0.0	75.1	62.1	63.7	84.3	72.9	18.8	5.9	316,681	171,413	145,268	45.9
16980/23844	*Gary, IN Metro Division*	556,931	61.0	0.0	67.8	54.8	56.9	80.5	62.2	14.5	7.9	313,152	166,454	146,698	46.8
16980/29404	*Lake County-Kenosha County, IL-WI Metro Division*	683,113	67.8	1.5	73.0	62.6	59.7	84.3	72.3	20.6	6.0	435,076	232,162	202,914	46.6
17020	Chico, CA Metro Area	184,984	55.9	0.0	59.6	52.4	59.3	76.2	55.4	13.5	10.5	92,602	48,223	44,379	47.9
17140	Cincinnati, OH-KY-IN Metro Area	1,700,094	65.4	0.0	70.1	61.0	61.2	82.9	66.7	18.3	5.6	1,049,469	543,238	506,231	48.2
17300	Clarksville, TN-KY Metro Area	210,139	54.7	10.5	53.2	56.3	43.6	66.5	60.9	16.7	7.1	106,849	52,414	54,435	50.9
17420	Cleveland, TN Metro Area	97,587	58.8	0.0	64.4	53.5	64.2	74.9	55.4	19.7	7.8	52,963	28,478	24,485	46.2
17460	Cleveland-Elyria, OH Metro Area	1,665,876	63.6	0.0	67.4	60.2	65.5	83.2	65.2	17.2	7.5	980,254	493,439	486,815	49.7
17660	Coeur d'Alene, ID Metro Area	118,710	61.0	0.0	65.6	56.7	67.6	81.9	56.6	15.9	3.6	69,862	36,809	33,053	47.3
17780	College Station-Bryan, TX Metro Area	202,811	62.0	0.1	66.3	57.6	49.7	81.7	67.2	19.9	3.1	121,751	65,228	56,523	46.4
17820	Colorado Springs, CO Metro Area	546,915	62.6	4.9	65.6	59.5	57.0	77.0	66.3	17.6	6.3	320,538	170,422	150,116	46.8
17860	Columbia, MO Metro Area	142,871	66.0	0.1	66.3	65.7	47.9	87.0	71.4	21.7	4.0	90,460	43,544	46,916	51.9
17900	Columbia, SC Metro Area	651,177	63.0	1.7	66.6	59.8	54.9	81.6	63.0	18.6	7.1	381,265	191,904	189,361	49.7
17980	Columbus, GA-AL Metro Area	244,657	56.1	5.6	57.6	54.6	50.6	71.8	51.8	15.9	9.8	123,789	62,808	60,981	49.3
18020	Columbus, IN Metro Area	63,580	66.8	0.1							4.8	40,420			
18140	Columbus, OH Metro Area	1,591,691	67.3	0.1	71.3	63.4	62.5	83.6	64.9	17.7	5.6	1,011,096	521,533	489,563	48.4
18580	Corpus Christi, TX Metro Area	350,205	61.4	0.4	68.6	54.8	53.8	79.3	62.8	19.3	5.9	202,524	109,266	93,258	46.0
18700	Corvallis, OR Metro Area	74,777	59.8	0.1	62.6	56.9	44.6	84.9	73.0	16.5	6.5	41,755	21,995	19,760	47.3
18880	Crestview-Fort Walton Beach-Destin, FL Metro Area	211,614	57.9	4.2	61.7	54.0	62.3	74.5	58.7	16.0	7.8	112,924	60,801	52,123	46.2
19060	Cumberland, MD-WV Metro Area	84,585	49.7	0.1	50.9	48.3	50.7	70.1	54.7	8.2	6.7	39,185	20,352	18,833	48.1
19100	**Dallas-Fort Worth-Arlington, TX Metro Area**	5,419,936	68.2	0.1	75.6	61.1	58.7	82.4	68.6	21.0	4.9	3,513,490	1,896,646	1,616,844	46.0
19100/19124	*Dallas-Plano-Irving, TX Metro Division*	3,587,803	69.0	0.1	76.5	61.9	58.8	82.7	70.0	21.6	4.9	2,356,544	1,272,187	1,084,357	46.0
19100/23104	*Fort Worth-Arlington, TX Metro Division*	1,832,133	66.5	0.1	73.8	59.6	58.3	81.9	66.0	20.0	5.0	1,156,946	624,459	532,487	46.0
19140	Dalton, GA Metro Area	109,853	63.3	0.0	71.5	55.4	59.8	80.1	56.5	19.9	5.7	65,596	36,506	29,090	44.3
19180	Danville, IL Metro Area	62,729	55.0	0.0	58.4	51.8	47.7	74.9	64.4	12.3	7.4	31,947	16,699	15,248	47.7
19300	Daphne-Fairhope-Foley, AL Metro Area	164,125	56.4	0.0	60.2	52.8	60.2	78.5	51.0	16.0	5.1	87,864	45,290	42,574	48.5
19340	Davenport-Moline-Rock Island, IA-IL Metro Area	304,679	63.9	0.1	67.6	60.4	64.8	84.9	65.8	14.6	5.2	184,536	95,787	88,749	48.1
19380	Dayton, OH Metro Area	644,267	61.8	0.6	66.8	57.1	63.1	80.9	63.9	16.8	7.1	369,610	193,401	176,209	47.7
19460	Decatur, AL Metro Area	122,184	55.5	0.0	63.2	48.1	51.3	75.6	50.2	14.4	6.9	63,109	35,293	27,816	44.1
19500	Decatur, IL Metro Area	85,920	59.7	0.0	62.8	57.0	65.0	80.0	63.2	14.1	6.5	47,989	23,931	24,058	50.1
19660	Deltona-Daytona Beach-Ormond Beach, FL Metro Area	525,442	50.5	0.0	54.2	47.2	46.5	78.8	53.5	11.2	6.5	248,236	126,542	121,694	49.0
19740	Denver-Aurora-Lakewood, CO Metro Area	2,221,193	70.7	0.2	76.8	64.6	63.9	86.3	69.8	19.7	4.5	1,498,349	805,733	692,616	46.2
19780	Des Moines-West Des Moines, IA Metro Area	479,097	72.2	0.1	77.2	67.5	70.7	89.0	70.7	18.5	4.8	329,295	172,267	157,028	47.7
19820	**Detroit-Warren-Dearborn, MI Metro Area**	3,443,939	61.8	0.0	67.5	56.6	62.4	80.6	59.5	14.2	8.0	1,959,298	1,023,572	935,726	47.8
19820/19804	*Detroit-Dearborn-Livonia, MI Metro Division*	1,383,466	58.3	0.0	63.2	53.8	58.7	76.3	53.7	12.1	11.6	712,421	364,928	347,493	48.8

Table D. Metropolitan Statistical Area—Labor Force, Employment, and Educational Data, 2015—*Continued*

CBSA code/ Division code	Metropolitan area, metropolitan division	Total population age 16 and older	Percent in civilian labor force	Percent in armed forces	Civilian labor force participation by gender		Civilian labor force participation by age				Civilian unemployment rate	Civilian employed population age 16 and older			
					Men	Women	Age 16 to 24	Age 25 to 54	Age 55 to 64	Age 65 and older		Total	Men	Women	Percent women
19820/47664	*Warren-Troy-Farmington Hills, MI Metro Division*	2,060,473	64.2	0.1	70.3	58.5	65.1	83.6	63.3	15.5	5.8	1,246,877	658,644	588,233	47.2
20020	Dothan, AL Metro Area	117,987	56.4	0.2	61.5	51.9	57.4	76.2	52.8	15.5	8.6	60,847	30,882	29,965	49.2
20100	Dover, DE Metro Area	138,948	58.8	1.8	62.1	55.8	57.4	79.1	57.7	13.4	5.5	77,287	39,048	38,239	49.5
20220	Dubuque, IA Metro Area	77,964	67.8	0.1	70.7	65.0	64.1	91.0	71.6	16.1	4.5	50,502	25,492	25,010	49.5
20260	Duluth, MN-WI Metro Area	231,145	62.8	0.1	65.7	59.9	70.3	83.6	62.5	14.2	4.5	138,618	71,331	67,287	48.5
20500	Durham-Chapel Hill, NC Metro Area	448,623	66.4	0.1	68.7	64.4	60.0	83.8	65.5	21.9	4.9	283,410	138,342	145,068	51.2
20700	East Stroudsburg, PA Metro Area	136,679	62.3	0.1	66.1	58.6	62.9	81.6	61.1	16.1	8.0	78,375	40,416	37,959	48.4
20740	Eau Claire, WI Metro Area	133,490	66.7	0.1	69.1	64.2	69.5	85.9	66.1	17.5	2.8	86,515	44,335	42,180	48.8
20940	El Centro, CA Metro Area	134,465	53.4	0.4	51.5	55.4	50.3	69.9	45.4	13.6	16.5	59,958	29,333	30,625	51.1
21060	Elizabethtown-Fort Knox, KY Metro Area	115,972	60.2	3.1	64.1	56.5	64.0	75.5	57.2	13.9	7.7	64,449	34,167	30,282	47.0
21140	Elkhart-Goshen, IN Metro Area	152,525	63.3	0.0	72.0	55.1	65.7	77.4	66.0	20.3	4.0	92,706	51,339	41,367	44.6
21300	Elmira, NY Metro Area	70,856	57.8	0.0	59.6	56.1	54.5	75.6	61.2	17.2	4.6	39,100	19,702	19,398	49.6
21340	El Paso, TX Metro Area	629,911	58.3	3.2	64.7	52.4	48.2	74.7	57.8	16.8	6.4	343,700	185,065	158,635	46.2
21500	Erie, PA Metro Area	224,110	60.7	0.0	64.4	57.2	58.0	80.1	63.6	15.9	6.5	127,249	65,761	61,488	48.3
21660	Eugene, OR Metro Area	302,459	59.2	0.0	62.2	56.3	59.8	79.8	61.3	15.4	7.6	165,490	83,025	82,465	49.8
21780	Evansville, IN-KY Metro Area	252,606	62.4	0.0	68.0	57.2	58.7	83.0	62.7	16.0	4.0	151,363	79,413	71,950	47.5
21820	Fairbanks, AK Metro Area	78,057	66.9	7.8	65.3	68.8	58.3	80.1	65.5	20.9	7.9	48,100	25,555	22,545	46.9
22020	Fargo, ND-MN Metro Area	186,466	72.4	0.1	76.1	68.7	70.9	89.3	72.8	18.1	2.6	131,427	68,798	62,629	47.7
22140	Farmington, NM Metro Area	91,214	61.0	0.0	67.8	54.3	54.9	76.6	68.0	18.2	8.2	51,078	28,014	23,064	45.2
22180	Fayetteville, NC Metro Area	286,941	54.9	8.6	55.4	54.4	48.7	68.0	55.2	13.5	10.6	140,806	69,449	71,357	50.7
22220	Fayetteville-Springdale-Rogers, AR-MO Metro Area	396,767	63.6	0.0	71.2	56.2	55.3	80.4	65.6	17.5	4.1	242,001	133,742	108,259	44.7
22380	Flagstaff, AZ Metro Area	113,457	63.2	0.3	65.6	60.9	54.6	81.8	65.3	22.8	8.3	65,735	32,882	32,853	50.0
22420	Flint, MI Metro Area	327,202	57.3	0.0	61.3	53.7	60.9	77.8	50.5	12.7	10.0	168,901	84,846	84,055	49.8
22500	Florence, SC Metro Area	162,868	58.7	0.0	61.8	56.0	56.9	79.8	51.8	15.6	10.7	85,295	41,301	43,994	51.6
22520	Florence-Muscle Shoals, AL Metro Area	119,504	53.0	0.1	58.2	48.5	62.7	72.7	48.4	11.7	5.9	59,658	31,016	28,642	48.0
22540	Fond du Lac, WI Metro Area	82,435	67.3	0.0	70.3	64.5	71.1	87.8	70.4	16.2	3.9	53,310	27,193	26,117	49.0
22660	Fort Collins, CO Metro Area	273,136	67.4	0.1	71.9	63.0	66.9	84.9	69.8	19.1	5.2	174,576	92,224	82,352	47.2
22900	Fort Smith, AR-OK Metro Area	220,662	54.5	0.1	59.4	49.7	51.2	73.9	50.7	13.0	5.7	113,330	59,946	53,384	47.1
23060	Fort Wayne, IN Metro Area	330,064	66.3	0.1	72.7	60.2	62.7	84.4	68.9	17.3	5.6	206,340	109,857	96,483	46.8
23420	Fresno, CA Metro Area	725,355	60.8	0.0	67.1	54.6	51.1	77.0	61.6	16.9	9.9	397,209	217,759	179,450	45.2
23460	Gadsden, AL Metro Area	82,860	55.3	0.0	60.4	50.6	61.6	73.3	53.1	14.3	4.6	43,713	22,746	20,967	48.0
23540	Gainesville, FL Metro Area	230,540	58.6	0.1	59.7	57.5	43.9	81.6	65.7	15.1	5.4	127,725	61,927	65,798	51.5
23580	Gainesville, GA Metro Area	149,148	61.3	0.0	68.2	54.7	55.4	76.9	65.8	17.9	5.0	86,852	47,754	39,098	45.0
23900	Gettysburg, PA Metro Area	83,698	63.3	0.1	68.7	58.2	62.1	86.2	67.8	15.7	3.6	51,023	26,972	24,051	47.1
24020	Glens Falls, NY Metro Area	106,056	61.3	0.0	63.6	58.9	67.7	78.6	65.1	19.2	3.9	62,435	32,466	29,969	48.0
24140	Goldsboro, NC Metro Area	98,376	58.0	2.1	63.3	53.0	62.3	74.2	54.0	16.2	9.1	51,874	27,761	24,113	46.5
24220	Grand Forks, ND-MN Metro Area	82,829	69.5	1.7	73.8	65.0	73.7	85.1	72.9	18.2	2.6	56,090	30,201	25,889	46.2
24260	Grand Island, NE Metro Area	65,493	72.3	0.0	78.2	66.3	76.2	89.5	77.1	24.8	3.7	45,562	24,617	20,945	46.0
24300	Grand Junction, CO Metro Area	119,434	62.6	0.1	68.8	56.6	58.8	84.1	62.6	20.7	7.4	69,184	36,589	32,595	47.1
24340	Grand Rapids-Wyoming, MI Metro Area	811,300	67.6	0.0	73.3	62.1	69.6	85.1	65.6	16.3	5.1	520,509	277,326	243,183	46.7
24420	Grants Pass, OR Metro Area	70,644	50.0	0.1	50.4	49.7	60.5	74.3	56.8	10.7	9.8	31,876	15,480	16,396	51.4
24500	Great Falls, MT Metro Area	65,471	59.3	3.9	61.0	57.7	59.9	77.5	64.9	18.5	4.0	37,292	19,067	18,225	48.9
24540	Greeley, CO Metro Area	216,693	67.3	0.0	75.2	59.4	59.1	82.4	68.9	21.3	4.5	139,270	78,942	60,328	43.3
24580	Green Bay, WI Metro Area	250,763	68.9	0.1	73.2	64.7	71.3	87.1	70.5	16.2	3.9	166,056	87,547	78,509	47.3
24660	Greensboro-High Point, NC Metro Area	602,038	61.7	0.0	67.6	56.4	52.2	81.4	65.0	15.4	5.7	350,314	181,518	168,796	48.2
24780	Greenville, NC Metro Area	142,012	65.2	0.0	70.4	60.7	64.6	81.9	64.0	15.0	11.6	81,798	41,366	40,432	49.4
24860	Greenville-Anderson-Mauldin, SC Metro Area	700,221	60.4	0.0	66.2	55.0	54.0	79.9	62.2	15.6	6.2	396,669	208,393	188,276	47.5
25060	Gulfport-Biloxi-Pascagoula, MS Metro Area	306,505	56.3	2.5	60.0	52.8	50.5	74.8	53.4	14.3	8.7	157,634	82,791	74,843	47.5
25180	Hagerstown-Martinsburg, MD-WV Metro Area	208,378	61.4	0.2	65.5	57.4	61.3	77.1	61.7	18.7	6.6	119,497	63,326	56,171	47.0
25220	Hammond, LA Metro Area	100,145	62.6	0.0	68.5	57.0	59.7	78.5	63.2	19.0	6.8	58,396	30,626	27,770	47.6
25260	Hanford-Corcoran, CA Metro Area	113,391	51.1	3.8	49.5	53.2	42.6	61.9	48.1	17.3	8.8	52,823	28,540	24,283	46.0
25420	Harrisburg-Carlisle, PA Metro Area	457,024	64.9	0.1	68.7	61.3	64.5	84.3	68.3	17.5	5.0	281,708	144,244	137,464	48.8
25500	Harrisonburg, VA Metro Area	108,470	60.3	0.0	64.9	56.2	46.7	82.3	70.0	19.9	5.2	62,036	32,331	29,705	47.9
25540	Hartford-West Hartford-East Hartford, CT Metro Area	992,389	66.6	0.0	70.2	63.3	61.9	84.8	73.0	20.4	6.5	617,809	313,530	304,279	49.3
25620	Hattiesburg, MS Metro Area	115,431	62.7	0.5	67.9	58.1	59.4	81.6	49.4	20.7	12.1	63,584	32,948	30,636	48.2
25860	Hickory-Lenoir-Morganton, NC Metro Area	293,900	57.0	0.0	63.0	51.1	59.7	75.3	58.5	14.5	7.1	155,633	84,151	71,482	45.9
25940	Hilton Head Island-Bluffton-Beaufort, SC Metro Area	171,174	53.9	3.5	57.5	50.3	54.7	80.0	54.9	16.4	8.1	84,769	44,820	39,949	47.1
25980	Hinesville, GA Metro Area	58,506	52.4	10.7	53.7	51.0	36.4	66.1	46.1	21.1	11.7	27,064	14,460	12,604	46.6
26140	Homosassa Springs, FL Metro Area	122,740	40.1	0.0	43.0	37.5	48.0	73.7	51.4	7.9	9.7	44,459	23,082	21,377	48.1
26300	Hot Springs, AR Metro Area	80,176	54.7	0.0	59.7	50.1	65.9	74.6	57.5	15.4	6.1	41,167	21,229	19,938	48.4

Table D. Metropolitan Statistical Area—Labor Force, Employment, and Educational Data, 2015—*Continued*

CBSA code/ Division code	Metropolitan area, metropolitan division	Total population age 16 and older	Percent in civilian labor force	Percent in armed forces	Civilian labor force participation by gender		Civilian labor force participation by age				Civilian unemployment rate	Civilian employed population age 16 and older			
					Men	Women	Age 16 to 24	Age 25 to 54	Age 55 to 64	Age 65 and older		Total	Men	Women	Percent women
26380	Houma-Thibodaux, LA Metro Area	164,504	59.1	0.1	67.7	51.1	60.3	74.7	53.1	16.5	5.1	92,297	51,752	40,545	43.9
26420	Houston-The Woodlands-Sugar Land, TX Metro Area	5,065,851	66.7	0.1	75.1	58.6	55.0	80.7	67.3	21.8	5.6	3,190,721	1,772,990	1,417,731	44.4
26580	Huntington-Ashland, WV-KY-OH Metro Area	292,086	52.2	0.0	56.5	48.1	56.9	71.4	46.8	12.0	6.7	142,194	74,332	67,862	47.7
26620	Huntsville, AL Metro Area	357,481	61.3	0.3	66.9	56.0	51.9	78.8	62.5	17.3	7.6	202,518	108,266	94,252	46.5
26820	Idaho Falls, ID Metro Area	100,307	62.9	0.0	70.5	55.4	61.1	78.7	66.8	15.0	3.8	60,709	33,550	27,159	44.7
26900	Indianapolis-Carmel-Anderson, IN Metro Area	1,541,162	67.4	0.1	71.7	63.5	65.6	83.6	66.2	17.5	5.8	978,453	499,069	479,384	49.0
26980	Iowa City, IA Metro Area	135,470	72.8	0.0	76.3	69.4	69.1	88.5	76.5	23.8	4.2	94,463	47,875	46,588	49.3
27060	Ithaca, NY Metro Area	91,619	57.9	0.0	62.9	53.2	41.2	82.5	71.2	21.3	4.7	50,549	26,254	24,295	48.1
27100	Jackson, MI Metro Area	128,972	53.9	0.2	56.1	51.6	56.9	70.5	57.5	9.5	6.9	64,672	33,723	30,949	47.9
27140	Jackson, MS Metro Area	448,743	61.5	0.1	65.8	57.8	51.2	79.7	60.8	17.1	7.4	255,733	128,218	127,515	49.9
27180	Jackson, TN Metro Area	103,293	60.7	0.0	66.3	55.7	52.1	81.0	64.8	17.4	4.8	59,719	31,141	28,578	47.9
27260	Jacksonville, FL Metro Area	1,155,620	62.3	1.2	67.3	57.7	59.5	79.9	61.1	16.2	7.3	667,491	344,096	323,395	48.4
27340	Jacksonville, NC Metro Area	142,234	49.9	20.3	43.7	57.3	41.0	61.3	58.6	15.5	9.7	64,037	31,516	32,521	50.8
27500	Janesville-Beloit, WI Metro Area	127,612	66.4	0.0	70.1	62.9	70.6	84.7	69.7	14.9	7.0	78,782	39,240	39,542	50.2
27620	Jefferson City, MO Metro Area	120,923	61.1	0.2	62.4	59.7	56.5	78.6	63.4	17.0	4.4	70,678	36,462	34,216	48.4
27740	Johnson City, TN Metro Area	166,469	55.0	0.0	59.5	50.8	58.8	74.2	54.2	14.0	6.5	85,582	44,610	40,972	47.9
27780	Johnstown, PA Metro Area	113,741	55.3	0.0	59.5	51.4	50.3	79.9	61.9	12.4	7.2	58,413	30,633	27,780	47.6
27860	Jonesboro, AR Metro Area	100,723	60.7	0.1	67.1	54.9	59.7	76.7	54.5	19.7	6.2	57,367	30,374	26,993	47.1
27900	Joplin, MO Metro Area	138,334	64.0	0.1	68.9	59.5	69.1	81.4	63.8	16.9	3.9	85,148	44,470	40,678	47.8
27980	Kahului-Wailuku-Lahaina, HI Metro Area	131,431	66.2	0.4	69.2	63.3	55.1	85.8	64.2	23.9	4.4	83,258	44,067	39,191	47.1
28020	Kalamazoo-Portage, MI Metro Area	267,956	65.8	0.1	70.0	61.9	69.5	84.8	61.1	18.3	7.3	163,560	83,955	79,605	48.7
28100	Kankakee, IL Metro Area	87,001	60.4	0.0	65.1	55.9	63.6	78.3	63.2	11.3	7.6	48,556	25,623	22,933	47.2
28140	Kansas City, MO-KS Metro Area	1,628,022	67.6	0.2	72.5	62.9	65.3	84.6	67.3	19.0	4.4	1,051,623	547,459	504,164	47.9
28420	Kennewick-Richland, WA Metro Area	207,843	63.1	0.0	69.4	56.8	57.7	80.3	63.1	16.6	5.6	123,880	69,189	54,691	44.1
28660	Killeen-Temple, TX Metro Area	325,262	54.8	9.3	57.0	52.6	48.3	65.8	58.0	16.8	8.3	163,295	85,271	78,024	47.8
28700	Kingsport-Bristol-Bristol, TN-VA Metro Area	252,751	54.2	0.0	58.5	50.2	61.2	74.7	53.6	14.0	6.6	127,958	66,202	61,756	48.3
28740	Kingston, NY Metro Area	151,238	60.3	0.1	62.2	58.5	52.5	77.5	65.6	24.3	5.6	86,146	43,832	42,314	49.1
28940	Knoxville, TN Metro Area	704,977	59.8	0.0	65.5	54.4	62.0	79.6	58.3	15.9	5.9	396,624	209,170	187,454	47.3
29020	Kokomo, IN Metro Area	66,010	58.8	0.1	65.8	52.6	69.1	81.5	56.9	9.8	8.6	35,488	18,313	17,175	48.4
29100	La Crosse-Onalaska, WI-MN Metro Area	112,298	67.9	0.0	71.7	64.5	69.4	89.0	71.5	15.9	3.8	73,374	36,873	36,501	49.7
29180	Lafayette, LA Metro Area	380,454	63.4	0.0	68.3	58.8	61.6	79.6	60.4	16.7	7.0	224,114	115,581	108,533	48.4
29200	Lafayette-West Lafayette, IN Metro Area	174,303	65.3	0.1	69.1	61.3	56.7	85.7	68.2	17.7	4.5	108,749	59,289	49,460	45.5
29340	Lake Charles, LA Metro Area	160,351	61.9	0.1	66.7	57.4	61.6	79.7	59.3	15.2	6.3	93,008	47,611	45,397	48.8
29420	Lake Havasu City-Kingman, AZ Metro Area	172,689	45.1	0.0	48.8	41.4	65.8	71.2	44.2	8.8	8.2	71,494	38,926	32,568	45.6
29460	Lakeland-Winter Haven, FL Metro Area	518,961	54.5	0.1	59.6	49.7	53.5	75.9	57.0	13.5	8.5	258,761	136,094	122,667	47.4
29540	Lancaster, PA Metro Area	423,280	66.1	0.0	73.6	59.1	63.9	83.4	76.1	22.1	4.7	266,353	143,314	123,039	46.2
29620	Lansing-East Lansing, MI Metro Area	385,406	63.0	0.0	67.2	59.0	57.4	84.2	59.9	16.7	6.3	227,433	116,076	111,357	49.0
29700	Laredo, TX Metro Area	188,937	59.8	0.0	69.1	51.2	49.0	74.2	61.2	15.3	5.8	106,380	59,506	46,874	44.1
29740	Las Cruces, NM Metro Area	165,791	58.0	0.6	62.7	53.6	58.0	75.9	56.3	16.0	7.8	88,709	46,005	42,704	48.1
29820	Las Vegas-Henderson-Paradise, NV Metro Area	1,668,793	63.8	0.4	68.9	58.6	58.4	81.0	61.1	17.3	8.3	975,157	524,164	450,993	46.2
29940	Lawrence, KS Metro Area	98,265	67.8	0.2	70.1	65.6	64.4	84.1	71.1	19.4	4.1	63,871	32,290	31,581	49.4
30020	Lawton, OK Metro Area	102,095	57.6	9.7	55.0	60.3	45.8	71.4	63.2	20.0	6.7	54,848	27,502	27,346	49.9
30140	Lebanon, PA Metro Area	108,946	64.4	0.3	70.7	58.4	74.0	81.1	73.5	19.3	3.9	67,361	35,614	31,747	47.1
30300	Lewiston, ID-WA Metro Area	51,668	59.5	0.0							7.3	28,504			
30340	Lewiston-Auburn, ME Metro Area	86,334	65.5	0.1	70.1	61.4	63.7	82.8	71.9	18.7	3.4	54,658	27,625	27,033	49.5
30460	Lexington-Fayette, KY Metro Area	402,690	65.8	0.1	71.2	60.6	61.2	82.2	64.5	21.0	5.3	250,933	131,322	119,611	47.7
30620	Lima, OH Metro Area	83,188	63.3	0.1	68.0	58.7	64.8	83.4	63.2	15.9	5.3	49,872	26,829	23,043	46.2
30700	Lincoln, NE Metro Area	255,500	70.8	0.2	73.6	67.9	66.9	87.1	77.3	22.0	2.8	175,745	91,107	84,638	48.2
30780	Little Rock-North Little Rock-Conway, AR Metro Area	575,157	61.1	0.8	66.9	55.8	58.3	78.6	58.2	16.7	4.8	334,707	175,702	159,005	47.5
30860	Logan, UT-ID Metro Area	97,411	67.3	0.0	77.8	57.0	66.3	79.8	72.5	18.0	3.4	63,344	36,560	26,784	42.3
30980	Longview, TX Metro Area	169,086	57.8	0.0	62.2	53.4	57.2	75.5	54.8	16.9	5.4	92,425	49,235	43,190	46.7
31020	Longview, WA Metro Area	82,099	56.6	0.0	62.0	51.4	61.5	78.7	52.4	12.8	5.4	43,976	23,815	20,161	45.8
31080	**Los Angeles-Long Beach-Anaheim, CA Metro Area**	10,696,249	64.1	0.0	71.2	57.3	51.0	81.2	65.6	18.4	6.8	6,390,533	3,475,378	2,915,155	45.6
31080/11244	*Anaheim-Santa Ana-Irvine, CA Metro Division*	2,539,295	65.0	0.1	72.9	57.4	53.1	82.4	68.5	19.0	5.5	1,559,173	854,480	704,693	45.2
31080/31084	*Los Angeles-Long Beach-Glendale, CA Metro Division*	8,156,954	63.8	0.0	70.7	57.2	50.4	80.8	64.7	18.2	7.2	4,831,360	2,620,898	2,210,462	45.8
31140	Louisville/Jefferson County, KY-IN Metro Area	1,020,043	64.4	0.1	69.4	59.8	65.5	81.9	62.4	17.4	5.7	619,385	319,644	299,741	48.4
31180	Lubbock, TX Metro Area	243,242	63.4	0.0	68.8	58.2	53.8	81.7	68.0	20.2	4.1	147,968	78,855	69,113	46.7

Table D. Metropolitan Statistical Area—Labor Force, Employment, and Educational Data, 2015—*Continued*

CBSA code/ Division code	Metropolitan area, metropolitan division	Total population age 16 and older	Percent in civilian labor force	Percent in armed forces	Civilian labor force participation by gender		Civilian labor force participation by age				Civilian unemployment rate	Civilian employed population age 16 and older			
					Men	Women	Age 16 to 24	Age 25 to 54	Age 55 to 64	Age 65 and older		Total	Men	Women	Percent women
31340	Lynchburg, VA Metro Area	216,625	58.3	0.0	61.9	54.8	48.5	80.9	65.2	16.1	4.6	120,389	61,507	58,882	48.9
31420	Macon, GA Metro Area	182,186	55.0	0.2	58.6	51.8	43.9	76.9	49.5	14.8	8.5	91,634	45,321	46,313	50.5
31460	Madera, CA Metro Area	117,782	52.8	0.1	62.7	43.9	50.9	65.4	54.1	17.6	6.3	58,279	33,441	24,838	42.6
31540	Madison, WI Metro Area	519,875	72.6	0.0	76.8	68.4	72.2	89.3	73.2	20.8	3.8	362,860	188,086	174,774	48.2
31700	Manchester-Nashua, NH Metro Area	331,285	69.9	0.1	75.9	64.1	68.0	85.8	75.9	20.9	4.5	221,277	118,090	103,187	46.6
31740	Manhattan, KS Metro Area	80,587	59.9	8.5	62.3	57.3	57.1	70.5	60.2	28.2	7.1	44,871	24,363	20,508	45.7
31860	Mankato-North Mankato, MN Metro Area	81,664	73.0	0.0	74.8	71.2	76.8	88.6	78.1	22.6	4.0	57,219	29,251	27,968	48.9
31900	Mansfield, OH Metro Area	98,229	56.1	0.0	59.1	53.0	60.0	72.6	60.5	17.4	6.0	51,798	27,520	24,278	46.9
32580	McAllen-Edinburg-Mission, TX Metro Area	591,772	57.2	0.1	63.3	51.6	45.1	74.8	55.2	14.8	8.7	309,408	162,598	146,810	47.4
32780	Medford, OR Metro Area	174,038	56.3	0.0	59.2	53.5	57.5	79.4	54.0	17.4	7.3	90,729	46,426	44,303	48.8
32820	Memphis, TN-MS-AR Metro Area	1,044,114	64.0	0.2	68.3	60.3	55.2	80.9	63.0	20.2	8.0	614,879	308,844	306,035	49.8
32900	Merced, CA Metro Area	198,216	56.4	0.0	63.3	49.4	48.5	71.3	56.4	16.2	12.0	98,425	57,578	40,847	41.5
33100	**Miami-Fort Lauderdale-West Palm Beach, FL Metro Area**	4,919,039	62.5	0.0	68.4	57.1	52.8	82.9	66.4	17.3	7.1	2,858,008	1,501,312	1,356,696	47.5
33100/22744	*Fort Lauderdale-Pompano Beach-Deerfield Beach, FL Metro Division;*	1,535,382	66.6	0.0	72.0	61.7	56.2	86.0	69.9	19.5	7.8	942,614	489,292	453,322	48.1
33100/33124	*Miami-Miami Beach-Kendall, FL Metro Division*	2,204,515	61.3	0.0	67.7	55.4	46.9	80.6	64.3	15.9	6.6	1,261,863	670,342	591,521	46.9
33100/48424	*West Palm Beach-Boca Raton-Delray Beach, FL Metro Division*	1,179,142	59.5	0.0	65.2	54.4	60.6	83.5	65.5	17.1	6.9	653,531	341,678	311,853	47.7
33140	Michigan City-La Porte, IN Metro Area	89,265	56.7	0.1	56.6	56.8	54.0	69.6	67.9	17.1	7.8	46,640	24,571	22,069	47.3
33220	Midland, MI Metro Area	67,364	62.1	0.1	68.7	55.7	62.7	83.0	62.5	14.0	7.9	38,497	21,004	17,493	45.4
33260	Midland, TX Metro Area	124,168	71.1	0.0	82.9	59.3	67.7	82.7	73.7	24.1	4.4	84,441	50,066	34,375	40.7
33340	Milwaukee-Waukesha-West Allis, WI Metro Area	1,246,149	67.0	0.0	70.7	63.6	66.2	84.3	68.9	17.0	4.8	794,353	402,640	391,713	49.3
33460	Minneapolis-St. Paul-Bloomington, MN-WI Metro Area	2,772,146	72.0	0.0	76.2	68.1	69.6	88.4	73.6	18.7	4.3	1,911,709	985,503	926,206	48.4
33540	Missoula, MT Metro Area	93,433	67.9	0.1	67.8	68.0	68.9	86.1	62.7	19.9	4.5	60,583	30,082	30,501	50.3
33660	Mobile, AL Metro Area	326,702	57.3	0.2	61.3	53.7	52.7	76.7	53.0	13.6	6.6	174,686	87,991	86,695	49.6
33700	Modesto, CA Metro Area	408,949	59.5	0.1	67.4	52.0	54.7	75.3	61.0	13.0	11.3	215,825	122,417	93,408	43.3
33740	Monroe, LA Metro Area	138,394	56.1	0.0	60.1	52.6	44.0	76.1	53.3	14.9	7.9	71,483	35,282	36,201	50.6
33780	Monroe, MI Metro Area	121,267	60.4	0.0	66.1	55.0	61.8	80.8	57.7	14.2	5.4	69,299	36,673	32,626	47.1
33860	Montgomery, AL Metro Area	295,792	57.9	0.8	61.9	54.4	55.0	72.9	58.0	17.2	7.1	159,169	80,490	78,679	49.4
34060	Morgantown, WV Metro Area	117,974	54.2	0.0	57.5	50.5	41.0	73.3	57.8	12.4	4.9	60,782	33,598	27,184	44.7
34100	Morristown, TN Metro Area	93,706	56.3	0.0	63.4	49.5	61.8	73.3	53.6	20.0	7.2	48,912	26,298	22,614	46.2
34580	Mount Vernon-Anacortes, WA Metro Area	97,906	59.8	0.3	66.1	53.5	58.3	80.8	65.2	18.0	6.2	54,890	29,697	25,193	45.9
34620	Muncie, IN Metro Area	97,275	58.7	0.0	64.8	53.1	64.7	79.3	56.5	10.6	7.4	52,858	27,743	25,115	47.5
34740	Muskegon, MI Metro Area	136,526	57.8	0.0	60.2	55.4	62.0	76.0	53.0	13.6	7.5	72,983	37,982	35,001	48.0
34820	Myrtle Beach-Conway-North Myrtle Beach, SC-NC Metro Area	362,000	54.6	0.1	60.2	49.5	59.8	81.0	52.5	14.0	6.4	184,995	97,383	87,612	47.4
34900	Napa, CA Metro Area	115,251	64.1	0.0	70.9	57.5	59.0	84.3	68.3	20.8	4.4	70,701	38,487	32,214	45.6
34940	Naples-Immokalee-Marco Island, FL Metro Area	300,290	53.1	0.0	57.7	48.8	62.9	84.5	58.7	14.7	4.8	151,828	80,827	71,001	46.8
34980	Nashville-Davidson–Murfreesboro–Franklin, TN Metro Area	1,446,261	67.4	0.1	73.8	61.6	65.3	83.0	65.2	18.7	4.9	927,745	490,100	437,645	47.2
35100	New Bern, NC Metro Area	100,744	54.4	5.4	57.4	51.2	52.7	74.8	60.1	11.7	7.7	50,585	27,812	22,773	45.0
35300	New Haven-Milford, CT Metro Area	704,794	65.2	0.1	68.8	62.0	54.7	83.5	73.8	21.1	6.9	427,933	213,830	214,103	50.0
35380	New Orleans-Metairie, LA Metro Area	1,009,182	63.1	0.3	68.1	58.6	52.9	80.7	62.3	20.0	7.0	592,425	304,387	288,038	48.6
35620	**New York-Newark-Jersey City, NY-NJ-PA Metro Area**	16,265,767	64.4	0.1	70.3	59.0	49.8	82.7	68.3	19.5	6.5	9,795,868	5,101,015	4,694,853	47.9
35620/20524	*Dutchess County-Putnam County, NY Metro Division*	326,247	62.8	0.0	66.8	58.9	56.3	81.1	66.3	19.6	7.0	190,579	99,203	91,376	47.9
35620/35004	*Nassau County-Suffolk County, NY Metro Division*	2,316,694	64.8	0.1	70.9	59.1	52.6	84.0	72.2	21.3	4.9	1,428,225	752,681	675,544	47.3
35620/35084	*Newark, NJ-PA Metro Division*	2,005,406	67.2	0.0	72.7	62.2	55.1	84.8	72.9	21.2	7.2	1,250,744	652,933	597,811	47.8
35620/35614	*New York-Jersey City-White Plains, NY-NJ Metro Division*	11,617,420	63.9	0.1	69.9	58.5	48.0	82.1	66.6	18.8	6.7	6,926,320	3,596,198	3,330,122	48.1
35660	Niles-Benton Harbor, MI Metro Area	124,552	61.6	0.0	68.8	54.7	64.6	81.0	65.2	17.4	8.0	70,514	38,622	31,892	45.2

Table D. Metropolitan Statistical Area—Labor Force, Employment, and Educational Data, 2015—*Continued*

CBSA code/ Division code	Metropolitan area, metropolitan division	Total population age 16 and older	Percent in civilian labor force	Percent in armed forces	Civilian labor force participation by gender		Civilian labor force participation by age				Civilian unem-ployment rate	Civilian employed population age 16 and older			
					Men	Women	Age 16 to 24	Age 25 to 54	Age 55 to 64	Age 65 and older		Total	Men	Women	Percent women
35840	North Port-Sarasota-Bradenton, FL Metro Area	654,653	50.2	0.0	54.6	46.2	55.8	81.0	58.5	13.1	6.5	307,210	157,559	149,651	48.7
35980	Norwich-New London, CT Metro Area	223,781	63.8	3.1	65.8	61.9	61.1	81.5	67.5	21.1	8.1	131,346	68,702	62,644	47.7
36100	Ocala, FL Metro Area	286,389	43.9	0.0	47.5	40.6	44.4	69.5	52.9	10.6	11.6	111,085	56,128	54,957	49.5
36140	Ocean City, NJ Metro Area	80,467	56.4	1.5	64.0	49.4	46.2	81.6	66.0	19.9	8.5	41,556	22,015	19,541	47.0
36220	Odessa, TX Metro Area	116,445	68.1	0.1	78.6	57.3	62.4	80.5	65.0	27.4	5.2	75,131	44,061	31,070	41.4
36260	Ogden-Clearfield, UT Metro Area	461,810	67.5	0.4	76.5	58.5	68.0	80.5	65.6	19.5	4.2	298,430	168,328	130,102	43.6
36420	Oklahoma City, OK Metro Area	1,053,263	64.4	0.5	70.8	58.3	60.8	80.6	61.9	20.2	4.7	646,240	345,704	300,536	46.5
36500	Olympia-Tumwater, WA Metro Area	217,609	59.9	1.4	63.0	56.9	60.3	76.0	66.0	13.7	7.1	121,109	61,668	59,441	49.1
36540	Omaha-Council Bluffs, NE-IA Metro Area	703,448	69.6	0.7	74.0	65.2	68.1	84.4	71.7	21.0	3.4	472,752	246,324	226,428	47.9
36740	Orlando-Kissimmee-Sanford, FL Metro Area	1,917,585	63.9	0.1	68.5	59.6	54.6	82.1	64.7	16.8	6.4	1,147,148	596,379	550,769	48.0
36780	Oshkosh-Neenah, WI Metro Area	138,422	64.2	0.0	68.9	59.6	69.6	81.8	65.7	12.1	3.0	86,222	46,166	40,056	46.5
36980	Owensboro, KY Metro Area	92,223	61.3	0.0	65.1	57.8	71.8	79.3	60.5	16.2	6.6	52,816	26,068	26,748	50.6
37100	Oxnard-Thousand Oaks-Ventura, CA Metro Area	672,407	64.7	0.5	70.6	58.9	56.2	81.8	69.8	19.5	6.7	405,614	218,591	187,023	46.1
37340	Palm Bay-Melbourne-Titusville, FL Metro Area	476,378	54.1	0.3	57.6	50.9	52.1	79.1	60.5	12.6	6.1	241,881	122,656	119,225	49.3
37460	Panama City, FL Metro Area	158,872	58.0	2.1	59.8	56.2	59.8	76.4	52.9	15.8	5.3	87,315	44,531	42,784	49.0
37620	Parkersburg-Vienna, WV Metro Area	75,111	55.7	0.0	62.4	49.6	59.5	79.9	47.3	10.1	5.8	39,401	20,926	18,475	46.9
37860	Pensacola-Ferry Pass-Brent, FL Metro Area	388,577	57.6	3.2	59.4	55.7	54.4	76.9	59.1	11.6	6.5	209,273	109,094	100,179	47.9
37900	Peoria, IL Metro Area	297,218	63.7	0.1	68.3	59.4	67.7	82.7	65.6	16.0	6.3	177,396	90,212	87,184	49.1
37980	**Philadelphia-Camden-Wilmington, PA-NJ-DE-MD Metro Area**	4,883,842	64.9	0.1	69.4	60.9	56.2	82.8	69.0	19.8	7.1	2,945,673	1,492,690	1,452,983	49.3
37980/15804	*Camden, NJ Metro Division*	1,006,396	65.8	0.6	70.3	61.6	57.9	83.8	70.7	19.0	7.7	610,773	311,806	298,967	48.9
37980/33874	*Montgomery County-Bucks County-Chester County, PA Metro Division*	1,584,219	67.7	0.0	73.6	62.2	60.0	86.1	75.4	22.7	4.9	1,019,839	534,518	485,321	47.6
37980/37964	*Philadelphia, PA Metro Division*	1,710,953	61.8	0.0	65.2	58.8	52.3	79.2	61.0	17.5	9.5	956,497	466,004	490,493	51.3
37980/48864	*Wilmington, DE-MD-NJ Metro Division*	582,274	65.3	0.1	68.8	62.1	57.0	83.6	68.6	18.6	5.7	358,564	180,362	178,202	49.7
38060	Phoenix-Mesa-Scottsdale, AZ Metro Area	3,576,384	61.5	0.1	66.9	56.3	58.9	79.3	61.6	15.1	5.9	2,070,696	1,110,397	960,299	46.4
38220	Pine Bluff, AR Metro Area	75,954	50.1	0.0	46.0	54.5	54.1	62.1	53.2	14.6	10.1	34,239	15,764	18,475	54.0
38300	Pittsburgh, PA Metro Area	1,955,221	62.4	0.0	68.1	57.1	61.0	83.5	66.9	16.3	5.7	1,151,035	603,286	547,749	47.6
38340	Pittsfield, MA Metro Area	108,789	62.6	0.0	65.8	59.7	66.7	87.3	69.3	15.4	6.1	63,926	31,782	32,144	50.3
38540	Pocatello, ID Metro Area	63,487	59.9	0.3	63.2	56.9	56.3	79.2	56.0	11.5	8.4	34,863	17,441	17,422	50.0
38860	Portland-South Portland, ME Metro Area	437,593	66.7	0.3	70.5	63.2	70.1	84.5	71.0	22.0	4.2	279,601	141,466	138,135	49.4
38900	Portland-Vancouver-Hillsboro, OR-WA Metro Area	1,920,269	66.2	0.1	71.6	61.0	61.9	83.4	64.3	17.1	6.1	1,194,135	633,340	560,795	47.0
38940	Port St. Lucie, FL Metro Area	377,607	53.1	0.0	56.0	50.5	61.0	76.3	65.3	12.0	7.2	186,242	93,727	92,515	49.7
39140	Prescott, AZ Metro Area	188,960	47.6	0.0	51.4	44.1	59.6	76.9	52.5	10.9	6.0	84,647	44,810	39,837	47.1
39300	Providence-Warwick, RI-MA Metro Area	1,325,178	64.8	0.2	68.3	61.6	63.0	82.7	68.8	19.1	6.6	802,404	401,359	401,045	50.0
39340	Provo-Orem, UT Metro Area	404,065	67.9	0.1	79.1	56.6	69.3	77.6	67.0	20.2	3.6	264,524	155,126	109,398	41.4
39380	Pueblo, CO Metro Area	130,047	55.8	0.2	59.1	52.7	65.4	74.9	49.2	14.9	9.7	65,558	34,281	31,277	47.7
39460	Punta Gorda, FL Metro Area	153,663	43.9	0.0	46.3	41.7	55.7	77.4	61.0	11.2	8.3	61,895	31,641	30,254	48.9
39540	Racine, WI Metro Area	154,457	65.1	0.0	68.5	61.9	65.7	84.0	69.3	13.2	5.5	95,117	48,216	46,901	49.3
39580	Raleigh, NC Metro Area	992,118	68.6	0.0	74.8	62.7	56.4	84.9	67.3	18.0	5.1	645,308	340,694	304,614	47.2
39660	Rapid City, SD Metro Area	114,731	64.5	1.8	69.1	59.9	63.6	81.8	72.5	19.4	3.1	71,748	38,500	33,248	46.3
39740	Reading, PA Metro Area	331,330	65.8	0.0	70.7	61.1	68.2	84.9	68.5	16.7	7.9	200,854	105,172	95,682	47.6
39820	Redding, CA Metro Area	145,944	52.5	0.0	54.2	51.0	54.7	72.6	54.8	13.4	5.7	72,329	36,369	35,960	49.7
39900	Reno, NV Metro Area	362,309	65.6	0.1	70.5	60.6	66.4	84.2	62.7	18.4	6.7	221,541	117,946	103,595	46.8
40060	Richmond, VA Metro Area	1,025,345	66.0	0.6	68.6	63.6	60.8	82.8	68.4	19.9	5.8	637,833	315,447	322,386	50.5
40140	Riverside-San Bernardino-Ontario, CA Metro Area	3,445,866	59.6	0.4	66.0	53.4	52.3	76.3	58.5	14.4	9.6	1,858,130	1,015,647	842,483	45.3
40220	Roanoke, VA Metro Area	253,757	59.8	0.0	66.0	54.3	60.4	80.8	61.8	15.2	4.8	144,562	75,848	68,714	47.5
40340	Rochester, MN Metro Area	167,202	70.3	0.0	73.0	67.7	71.3	88.5	75.7	18.6	3.6	113,303	56,869	56,434	49.8
40380	Rochester, NY Metro Area	880,839	63.4	0.0	67.3	59.6	62.0	83.0	66.1	16.3	6.3	522,737	267,255	255,482	48.9
40420	Rockford, IL Metro Area	267,231	64.4	0.0	70.6	58.6	68.3	83.8	62.3	16.7	9.0	156,695	82,682	74,013	47.2
40580	Rocky Mount, NC Metro Area	117,828	58.4	0.0	64.2	53.5	60.6	77.7	56.3	17.9	5.7	64,856	32,273	32,583	50.2
40660	Rome, GA Metro Area	76,222	56.7	0.0	59.4	54.2	56.4	75.3	51.1	16.1	7.6	39,913	20,002	19,911	49.9
40900	Sacramento--Roseville--Arden-Arcade, CA Metro Area	1,804,752	61.1	0.1	65.6	56.9	52.6	80.7	60.5	14.7	7.9	1,015,471	525,654	489,817	48.2
40980	Saginaw, MI Metro Area	157,282	57.4	0.0	58.8	56.1	66.6	78.8	50.4	12.7	9.1	82,058	40,019	42,039	51.2
41060	St. Cloud, MN Metro Area	154,284	72.6	0.0	76.0	69.1	78.4	88.9	75.9	17.7	3.8	107,724	56,013	51,711	48.0

Table D. Metropolitan Statistical Area—Labor Force, Employment, and Educational Data, 2015—*Continued*

CBSA code/ Division code	Metropolitan area, metropolitan division	Total population age 16 and older	Percent in civilian labor force	Percent in armed forces	Civilian labor force participation by gender		Civilian labor force participation by age				Civilian unemployment rate	Civilian employed population age 16 and older			
					Men	Women	Age 16 to 24	Age 25 to 54	Age 55 to 64	Age 65 and older		Total	Men	Women	Percent women
41100	St. George, UT Metro Area	117,406	56.1	0.0	63.7	49.0	66.8	77.8	55.2	14.8	4.6	62,786	34,153	28,633	45.6
41140	St. Joseph, MO-KS Metro Area	102,589	62.6	0.1	65.9	59.1	66.3	77.2	65.8	20.2	4.9	61,067	32,738	28,329	46.4
41180	St. Louis, MO-IL Metro Area	2,250,742	65.6	0.2	70.3	61.2	64.5	84.5	66.0	16.4	6.0	1,387,444	707,548	679,896	49.0
41420	Salem, OR Metro Area	321,097	61.5	0.0	66.5	56.8	60.3	82.3	59.8	12.4	7.0	183,850	97,606	86,244	46.9
41500	Salinas, CA Metro Area	331,326	58.3	1.9	63.5	53.0	48.2	72.8	64.0	17.6	5.7	182,151	101,253	80,898	44.4
41540	Salisbury, MD-DE Metro Area	325,690	56.7	0.1	60.4	53.3	56.3	78.4	62.8	19.1	6.2	173,250	88,209	85,041	49.1
41620	Salt Lake City, UT Metro Area	871,393	70.5	0.1	77.9	63.2	69.9	82.9	69.3	20.0	3.8	591,175	324,979	266,196	45.0
41660	San Angelo, TX Metro Area	94,722	57.7	3.6	64.4	51.1	46.4	76.1	60.6	19.3	2.8	53,145	29,771	23,374	44.0
41700	San Antonio-New Braunfels, TX Metro Area	1,837,018	62.1	1.0	67.4	57.2	56.2	78.8	59.8	16.1	5.8	1,075,502	568,519	506,983	47.1
41740	San Diego-Carlsbad, CA Metro Area	2,652,326	62.9	2.5	67.7	58.1	51.4	80.0	64.3	18.1	6.9	1,552,867	839,117	713,750	46.0
41860	**San Francisco-Oakland-Hayward, CA Metro Area**	3,818,210	66.7	0.1	72.6	61.0	55.3	83.9	68.8	19.3	5.4	2,409,944	1,286,841	1,123,103	46.6
41860/36084	*Oakland-Hayward-Berkeley, CA Metro Division*	2,223,173	65.5	0.1	71.9	59.5	54.0	82.5	67.6	18.5	5.7	1,372,611	731,406	641,205	46.7
41860/41884	*San Francisco-Redwood City-South San Francisco, CA Metro Division*	1,381,434	69.2	0.0	74.3	64.0	58.0	86.5	69.7	19.4	5.1	907,232	486,892	420,340	46.3
41860/42034	*San Rafael, CA Metro Division*	213,603	63.1	0.1	69.0	57.6	53.4	81.6	74.3	24.5	3.5	130,101	68,543	61,558	47.3
41940	San Jose-Sunnyvale-Santa Clara, CA Metro Area	1,574,490	66.8	0.1	74.1	59.6	52.7	83.8	69.0	17.3	5.4	995,869	553,515	442,354	44.4
42020	San Luis Obispo-Paso Robles-Arroyo Grande, CA Metro Area	236,308	57.4	0.8	61.2	53.5	48.8	81.1	59.9	18.8	4.9	128,903	69,920	58,983	45.8
42100	Santa Cruz-Watsonville, CA Metro Area	226,071	61.6	0.0	66.3	57.0	51.6	80.5	64.2	22.3	5.1	132,081	70,144	61,937	46.9
42140	Santa Fe, NM Metro Area	123,712	60.6	0.0	63.9	57.5	52.5	81.2	68.3	23.2	4.5	71,599	36,209	35,390	49.4
42200	Santa Maria-Santa Barbara, CA Metro Area	356,206	64.1	0.6	69.2	59.0	55.6	82.4	71.7	23.3	6.2	214,133	115,709	98,424	46.0
42220	Santa Rosa, CA Metro Area	411,102	64.6	0.2	69.5	59.9	62.7	81.8	68.7	23.8	5.8	250,066	130,905	119,161	47.7
42340	Savannah, GA Metro Area	300,506	63.9	1.5	67.1	61.0	57.7	80.1	63.7	20.5	8.7	175,342	88,112	87,230	49.7
42540	Scranton--Wilkes-Barre--Hazleton, PA Metro Area	460,733	60.8	0.0	64.9	57.0	57.6	82.2	65.5	16.8	6.6	261,710	133,990	127,720	48.8
42660	**Seattle-Tacoma-Bellevue, WA Metro Area**	3,007,037	67.0	0.7	72.9	61.1	58.8	82.6	68.1	18.2	5.5	1,903,626	1,032,060	871,566	45.8
42660/42644	*Seattle-Bellevue-Everett, WA Metro Division*	2,343,162	68.6	0.2	74.7	62.5	59.4	84.2	69.8	18.8	5.1	1,524,853	829,778	695,075	45.6
42660/45104	*Tacoma-Lakewood, WA Metro Division*	663,875	61.3	2.3	66.2	56.5	56.8	76.7	62.2	16.1	6.9	378,773	202,282	176,491	46.6
42680	Sebastian-Vero Beach, FL Metro Area	124,878	46.7	0.1	53.5	40.6	56.0	78.1	50.2	12.3	10.0	52,438	27,845	24,593	46.9
42700	Sebring, FL Metro Area	84,228	41.6	0.0							8.6	32,038			
43100	Sheboygan, WI Metro Area	92,339	67.2	0.1	71.1	63.4	68.5	86.6	74.4	15.3	3.9	59,624	31,305	28,319	47.5
43300	Sherman-Denison, TX Metro Area	99,482	62.9	0.3	70.8	55.6	60.5	84.0	63.8	19.0	5.8	58,993	31,892	27,101	45.9
43340	Shreveport-Bossier City, LA Metro Area	346,648	56.7	1.6	59.8	53.9	48.3	74.8	56.2	16.3	6.2	184,336	92,000	92,336	50.1
43420	Sierra Vista-Douglas, AZ Metro Area	102,342	41.9	4.1	40.1	43.7	37.2	57.2	52.7	11.8	7.5	39,648	18,755	20,893	52.7
43580	Sioux City, IA-NE-SD Metro Area	127,825	67.4	0.0	73.2	62.0	68.6	85.8	72.6	17.8	4.4	82,382	43,313	39,069	47.4
43620	Sioux Falls, SD Metro Area	192,947	72.3	0.1	76.2	68.3	72.7	87.9	73.4	19.9	3.4	134,674	70,861	63,813	47.4
43780	South Bend-Mishawaka, IN-MI Metro Area	253,682	61.8	0.1	66.8	57.2	55.1	81.3	66.1	17.5	6.0	147,249	76,448	70,801	48.1
43900	Spartanburg, SC Metro Area	258,134	60.5	0.1	66.4	55.1	64.4	78.2	57.5	16.7	6.5	145,938	76,933	69,005	47.3
44060	Spokane-Spokane Valley, WA Metro Area	439,083	56.9	0.7	60.5	53.4	52.3	75.5	57.5	15.2	7.3	231,789	121,279	110,510	47.7
44100	Springfield, IL Metro Area	168,481	63.5	0.1	66.9	60.5	59.0	84.6	62.7	16.1	6.9	99,663	48,520	51,143	51.3
44140	Springfield, MA Metro Area	518,816	62.9	0.0	65.7	60.4	61.8	80.0	68.6	18.0	6.7	304,555	149,151	155,404	51.0
44180	Springfield, MO Metro Area	363,488	60.8	0.1	66.1	55.9	64.0	79.5	60.5	13.3	4.7	210,655	109,861	100,794	47.8
44220	Springfield, OH Metro Area	108,468	60.6	0.1	64.5	57.0	66.5	81.2	62.3	14.8	7.5	60,796	31,215	29,581	48.7
44300	State College, PA Metro Area	138,761	58.8	0.0	58.6	59.0	46.1	80.2	65.3	17.7	5.1	77,408	40,012	37,396	48.3
44420	Staunton-Waynesboro, VA Metro Area	99,298	58.6	0.0	62.5	54.9	57.2	75.4	66.1	18.9	5.1	55,230	28,666	26,564	48.1
44700	Stockton-Lodi, CA Metro Area	548,879	60.0	0.1	66.9	53.2	53.5	76.2	58.9	14.9	11.1	292,491	160,686	131,805	45.1
44940	Sumter, SC Metro Area	84,642	58.1	2.1	62.1	54.6	63.5	76.4	53.7	11.1	10.2	44,206	21,701	22,505	50.9
45060	Syracuse, NY Metro Area	535,993	61.9	0.1	65.9	58.2	52.0	82.2	68.1	16.0	6.7	309,687	156,819	152,868	49.4
45220	Tallahassee, FL Metro Area	314,083	61.7	0.0	64.5	59.1	63.0	76.8	59.1	18.5	9.3	175,785	87,724	88,061	50.1
45300	Tampa-St. Petersburg-Clearwater, FL Metro Area	2,440,504	59.2	0.3	63.6	55.2	55.9	80.9	61.7	14.4	6.5	1,350,375	690,096	660,279	48.9
45460	Terre Haute, IN Metro Area	140,222	57.1	0.0	60.5	53.5	59.2	74.3	57.8	14.5	8.9	72,906	38,748	34,158	46.9
45500	Texarkana, TX-AR Metro Area	118,450	53.9	0.1	58.1	49.7	53.3	71.2	51.2	13.4	9.2	57,963	31,069	26,894	46.4
45540	The Villages, FL Metro Area	111,323	22.9	0.0							5.2	24,153			
45780	Toledo, OH Metro Area	484,139	64.1	0.1	68.3	60.3	66.8	82.3	62.2	17.7	7.2	288,198	146,769	141,429	49.1

Table D. Metropolitan Statistical Area—Labor Force, Employment, and Educational Data, 2015—*Continued*

CBSA code/ Division code	Metropolitan area, metropolitan division	Total population age 16 and older	Percent in civilian labor force	Percent in armed forces	Civilian labor force participation by gender		Civilian labor force participation by age				Civilian unemployment rate	Civilian employed population age 16 and older			
					Men	Women	Age 16 to 24	Age 25 to 54	Age 55 to 64	Age 65 and older		Total	Men	Women	Percent women
45820	Topeka, KS Metro Area	183,614	63.3	0.2	67.0	59.8	67.8	83.8	63.8	16.6	6.0	109,226	55,526	53,700	49.2
45940	Trenton, NJ Metro Area	299,994	64.9	0.0	70.2	59.9	51.4	83.8	68.5	20.8	7.4	180,186	92,807	87,379	48.5
46060	Tucson, AZ Metro Area	817,168	57.3	0.6	61.3	53.6	59.5	78.3	59.6	13.9	8.3	429,496	224,501	204,995	47.7
46140	Tulsa, OK Metro Area	762,865	64.7	0.1	71.2	58.6	63.9	81.4	63.9	20.5	5.6	465,851	248,299	217,552	46.7
46220	Tuscaloosa, AL Metro Area	196,841	53.9	0.0	59.1	49.3	42.2	74.1	50.7	13.9	6.7	99,055	51,356	47,699	48.2
46340	Tyler, TX Metro Area	172,866	59.6	0.0	65.0	54.8	55.6	76.0	62.3	22.0	4.6	98,334	50,520	47,814	48.6
46520	Urban Honolulu, HI Metro Area	806,782	61.3	5.4	63.7	58.9	51.5	77.9	70.9	20.7	4.8	471,067	248,282	222,785	47.3
46540	Utica-Rome, NY Metro Area	238,964	57.6	0.0	60.3	54.9	58.7	76.9	59.9	15.1	6.2	129,071	65,830	63,241	49.0
46660	Valdosta, GA Metro Area	109,622	55.7	2.2	56.7	54.8	47.9	73.5	53.4	12.4	10.1	54,903	27,148	27,755	50.6
46700	Vallejo-Fairfield, CA Metro Area	348,462	60.9	1.2	63.4	58.4	56.5	78.6	57.2	17.2	8.7	193,706	97,984	95,722	49.4
47020	Victoria, TX Metro Area	76,674	62.8	0.2	68.9	57.3	58.8	84.2	58.4	18.3	7.5	44,562	22,689	21,873	49.1
47220	Vineland-Bridgeton, NJ Metro Area	123,260	57.1	0.0	56.6	57.6	56.6	70.1	58.8	16.3	5.8	66,220	34,300	31,920	48.2
47260	Virginia Beach-Norfolk-Newport News, VA-NC Metro Area	1,383,422	60.4	5.9	62.0	58.9	50.3	76.0	66.5	18.7	6.8	779,180	391,729	387,451	49.7
47300	Visalia-Porterville, CA Metro Area	330,900	56.7	0.0	65.5	48.1	43.7	74.4	53.4	13.9	9.3	170,090	97,222	72,868	42.8
47380	Waco, TX Metro Area	205,473	60.0	0.0	64.2	56.1	53.6	76.9	66.1	20.3	5.3	116,676	61,033	55,643	47.7
47460	Walla Walla, WA Metro Area	52,436	55.5	0.0	56.1	54.8	61.0	74.7	54.2	13.5	5.2	27,562	14,430	13,132	47.6
47580	Warner Robins, GA Metro Area	144,877	61.5	1.6	66.8	56.6	55.8	80.0	55.3	14.7	8.7	81,293	42,782	38,511	47.4
47900	**Washington-Arlington-Alexandria, DC-VA-MD-WV Metro Area**	4,832,622	70.9	0.9	76.0	66.1	57.7	86.3	72.5	24.2	5.1	3,250,230	1,683,519	1,566,711	48.2
47900/43524	*Silver Spring-Frederick-Rockville, MD Metro Division*	1,016,889	71.0	0.4	76.8	65.6	58.7	87.7	76.9	25.1	4.8	687,230	356,134	331,096	48.2
47900/47894	*Washington-Arlington-Alexandria, DC-VA-MD-WV Metro Division*	3,815,733	70.9	1.0	75.8	66.3	57.5	86.0	71.1	23.8	5.2	2,563,000	1,327,385	1,235,615	48.2
47940	Waterloo-Cedar Falls, IA Metro Area	137,204	66.8	0.0	70.4	63.5	73.9	87.1	66.6	15.7	2.7	89,190	45,795	43,395	48.7
48060	Watertown-Fort Drum, NY Metro Area	90,978	54.4	10.7	52.3	56.8	47.2	69.1	59.7	12.8	8.0	45,588	23,635	21,953	48.2
48140	Wausau, WI Metro Area	107,859	68.5	0.0	74.9	62.0	76.5	86.2	74.3	17.0	2.7	71,878	39,457	32,421	45.1
48260	Weirton-Steubenville, WV-OH Metro Area	100,578	58.1	0.1	63.5	53.1	62.2	77.5	59.2	18.9	7.3	54,171	28,294	25,877	47.8
48300	Wenatchee, WA Metro Area	90,189	61.3	0.1	67.6	55.0	58.1	82.1	64.5	18.5	4.6	52,750	29,641	23,109	43.8
48540	Wheeling, WV-OH Metro Area	119,803	55.0	0.0	59.4	50.6	60.8	74.4	54.8	15.1	6.0	61,910	32,911	28,999	46.8
48620	Wichita, KS Metro Area	494,351	64.9	0.5	69.6	60.4	60.6	82.3	68.4	17.8	4.6	306,300	161,549	144,751	47.3
48660	Wichita Falls, TX Metro Area	121,428	54.3	4.4	55.3	53.3	48.4	68.6	58.1	20.7	5.8	62,193	33,009	29,184	46.9
48700	Williamsport, PA Metro Area	94,792	61.9	0.0	68.1	56.2	62.9	81.6	67.8	14.8	5.1	55,739	29,134	26,605	47.7
48900	Wilmington, NC Metro Area	229,344	60.9	0.4	63.6	58.4	54.7	78.3	65.7	21.0	6.9	129,936	65,333	64,603	49.7
49020	Winchester, VA-WV Metro Area	107,297	62.0	0.1	67.3	57.1	48.9	83.7	68.2	15.1	3.7	64,068	33,176	30,892	48.2
49180	Winston-Salem, NC Metro Area	526,838	61.1	0.1	67.5	55.2	55.6	81.3	64.6	13.8	7.5	297,528	155,828	141,700	47.6
49340	Worcester, MA-CT Metro Area	758,205	66.2	0.0	69.7	62.8	60.1	83.8	70.4	18.6	6.6	468,421	239,038	229,383	49.0
49420	Yakima, WA Metro Area	181,328	62.4	0.0	69.2	55.7	63.3	77.3	64.4	18.6	7.3	104,851	57,190	47,661	45.5
49620	York-Hanover, PA Metro Area	355,190	66.0	0.1	71.3	60.9	69.5	84.7	68.3	17.3	5.1	222,498	116,099	106,399	47.8
49660	Youngstown-Warren-Boardman, OH-PA Metro Area	450,796	57.6	0.0	62.1	53.3	60.2	80.0	59.3	14.5	6.7	242,168	124,804	117,364	48.5
49700	Yuba City, CA Metro Area	130,171	56.3	1.4	62.5	50.3	51.6	72.4	58.7	13.9	11.1	65,196	35,512	29,684	45.5
49740	Yuma, AZ Metro Area	158,011	52.1	2.2	58.1	45.8	49.6	74.3	55.2	9.7	12.5	72,053	41,419	30,634	42.5

Table D. Metropolitan Statistical Area—Labor Force, Employment, and Educational Data, 2015

CBSA code/ Division code	Metropolitan area, metropolitan division	Class of worker for civilian employed population age 16 and older								
		Private for-profit wage and salary workers			Private not-for-profit wage and salary workers	Government workers			Self-employed in own not incorporated business	Unpaid family workers
		Total private for-profit wage and salary workers	Employees of private companies	Self-employed in own incorporated business		Local government workers	State government workers	Federal government workers		
10180	Abilene, TX Metro Area	65.6	62.7	2.9	12.2	6.9	5.8	3.1	6.2	0.3
10420	Akron, OH Metro Area	75.6	72.3	3.3	8.9	6.2	3.6	0.8	4.7	0.1
10500	Albany, GA Metro Area	65.4	63.6	1.8	7.3	9.4	6.6	6.6	4.6	0.1
10540	Albany, OR Metro Area	68.1	64.6	3.4	7.4	8.7	7.8	2.5	5.4	0.2
10580	Albany-Schenectady-Troy, NY Metro Area	61.4	58.7	2.8	11.6	8.6	11.1	2.4	4.7	0.1
10740	Albuquerque, NM Metro Area	66.9	63.5	3.4	8.1	7.2	6.6	5.7	5.5	0.1
10780	Alexandria, LA Metro Area	67.4	66.5	0.8	5.5	8.7	7.0	6.3	5.1	0.0
10900	Allentown-Bethlehem-Easton, PA-NJ Metro Area	74.5	72.3	2.2	11.6	5.5	2.6	1.2	4.5	0.1
11020	Altoona, PA Metro Area	73.5	71.1	2.4	9.7	5.3	6.4	1.9	3.2	0.0
11100	Amarillo, TX Metro Area	72.8	70.3	2.5	7.2	5.7	4.5	2.1	7.6	0.1
11180	Ames, IA Metro Area	57.5	54.7	2.8	7.4	6.8	22.6	2.3	3.3	0.1
11260	Anchorage, AK Metro Area	64.3	60.8	3.5	10.0	6.0	7.1	6.6	5.7	0.2
11460	Ann Arbor, MI Metro Area	63.0	59.4	3.7	14.4	4.9	10.6	2.1	4.8	0.2
11500	Anniston-Oxford-Jacksonville, AL Metro Area	72.6	70.4	2.2	5.2	5.5	5.4	5.2	6.0	0.1
11540	Appleton, WI Metro Area	77.9	75.1	2.8	7.7	5.6	3.1	0.9	4.7	0.2
11700	Asheville, NC Metro Area	69.2	64.4	4.8	8.5	4.7	5.5	2.4	9.3	0.4
12020	Athens-Clarke County, GA Metro Area	63.0	59.3	3.7	8.0	7.8	13.6	1.4	6.1	0.1
12060	Atlanta-Sandy Springs-Roswell, GA Metro Area	75.2	70.8	4.4	6.4	6.8	3.7	2.3	5.4	0.2
12100	Atlantic City-Hammonton, NJ Metro Area	74.9	71.8	3.1	6.3	7.1	4.1	2.4	5.1	0.1
12220	Auburn-Opelika, AL Metro Area	75.3	73.2	2.1	3.7	6.8	6.9	2.9	4.3	0.1
12260	Augusta-Richmond County, GA-SC Metro Area	72.9	70.0	2.9	4.6	5.9	5.8	5.4	5.2	0.2
12420	Austin-Round Rock, TX Metro Area	72.2	68.5	3.6	5.9	6.4	6.8	1.7	6.8	0.3
12540	Bakersfield, CA Metro Area	72.3	70.4	1.9	4.2	9.7	4.5	2.5	6.3	0.3
12580	Baltimore-Columbia-Towson, MD Metro Area	65.1	61.7	3.4	10.6	7.6	4.5	7.6	4.4	0.1
12620	Bangor, ME Metro Area	61.5	58.3	3.2	15.6	5.3	7.4	2.7	7.4	0.0
12700	Barnstable Town, MA Metro Area	66.9	61.9	5.0	7.1	8.4	2.3	1.6	13.8	0.0
12940	Baton Rouge, LA Metro Area	72.4	68.8	3.6	6.3	7.3	8.2	1.1	4.6	0.1
12980	Battle Creek, MI Metro Area	74.1	71.3	2.7	10.5	5.6	3.8	1.7	4.0	0.1
13020	Bay City, MI Metro Area	76.7	75.0	1.7	11.8	4.6	2.5	0.8	3.6	0.0
13140	Beaumont-Port Arthur, TX Metro Area	76.7	74.8	2.0	4.7	5.8	5.4	1.7	5.5	0.1
13220	Beckley, WV Metro Area	70.5	68.6	2.0	6.0	7.8	8.4	3.0	4.2	0.0
13380	Bellingham, WA Metro Area	68.6	63.4	5.2	7.2	7.6	7.7	2.8	5.9	0.2
13460	Bend-Redmond, OR Metro Area	70.3	62.8	7.5	6.6	5.9	3.3	1.1	12.4	0.5
13740	Billings, MT Metro Area	71.8	68.0	3.8	7.7	6.1	3.0	2.5	8.6	0.3
13780	Binghamton, NY Metro Area	68.4	65.7	2.7	10.7	7.4	8.2	0.8	4.6	0.0
13820	Birmingham-Hoover, AL Metro Area	74.2	70.9	3.3	7.6	6.2	4.9	2.2	4.7	0.2
13900	Bismarck, ND Metro Area	65.0	61.9	3.1	12.9	7.4	6.8	1.8	6.0	0.1
13980	Blacksburg-Christiansburg-Radford, VA Metro Area	64.5	61.7	2.8	5.8	8.5	14.1	2.2	4.8	0.1
14010	Bloomington, IL Metro Area	74.0	71.7	2.2	9.4	6.6	5.2	0.8	4.1	0.0
14020	Bloomington, IN Metro Area	66.1	62.5	3.5	10.5	6.5	10.2	1.8	4.8	0.2
14100	Bloomsburg-Berwick, PA Metro Area	65.2	63.8	1.4	16.8	4.3	6.9	1.5	5.0	0.3
14260	Boise City, ID Metro Area	70.8	66.6	4.2	8.6	5.5	4.7	2.0	8.2	0.1
14460	**Boston-Cambridge-Newton, MA-NH Metro Area**	70.0	67.1	2.9	13.4	6.3	3.0	1.6	5.6	0.1
14460/14454	*Boston, MA Metro Division*	69.8	67.4	2.4	14.4	6.3	3.2	1.4	4.8	0.1
14460/15764	*Cambridge-Newton-Framingham, MA Metro Division*	69.4	66.3	3.1	13.5	6.2	2.9	1.6	6.3	0.1
14460/40484	*Rockingham County-Strafford County, NH Metro Division*	73.8	70.1	3.8	8.2	6.4	3.5	2.7	5.3	0.0
14500	Boulder, CO Metro Area	72.0	66.1	5.9	7.9	5.4	5.5	1.4	7.6	0.2
14540	Bowling Green, KY Metro Area	71.0	67.7	3.3	5.8	6.1	9.8	1.7	5.4	0.1
14740	Bremerton-Silverdale, WA Metro Area	57.6	53.8	3.8	8.0	7.9	5.6	14.9	5.8	0.2
14860	Bridgeport-Stamford-Norwalk, CT Metro Area	73.5	69.0	4.5	7.8	7.4	2.0	0.9	8.1	0.3
15180	Brownsville-Harlingen, TX Metro Area	71.4	68.2	3.2	3.6	9.6	4.5	2.4	8.4	0.1
15260	Brunswick, GA Metro Area	73.0	68.8	4.1	5.8	9.0	4.5	3.6	4.2	0.0
15380	Buffalo-Cheektowaga-Niagara Falls, NY Metro Area	71.5	68.7	2.8	9.6	7.2	5.6	1.9	4.0	0.0
15500	Burlington, NC Metro Area	76.2	74.4	1.7	6.3	4.9	6.2	0.9	5.3	0.2
15540	Burlington-South Burlington, VT Metro Area	64.3	60.6	3.7	15.8	6.3	4.2	3.0	6.2	0.1
15680	California-Lexington Park, MD Metro Area	54.6	51.0	3.5	6.3	9.6	1.9	23.4	4.3	0.0
15940	Canton-Massillon, OH Metro Area	75.7	72.4	3.3	8.2	6.8	1.9	0.9	6.6	0.0

Table D. Metropolitan Statistical Area—Labor Force, Employment, and Educational Data, 2015—*Continued*

| | | Class of worker for civilian employed population age 16 and older | | | | | | | | |
| | | Private for-profit wage and salary workers | | | Private not-for-profit wage and salary workers | Government workers | | | Self-employed in own not incorporated business | Unpaid family workers |
CBSA code/ Division code	Metropolitan area, metropolitan division	Total private for-profit wage and salary workers	Employees of private companies	Self-employed in own incorporated business		Local government workers	State government workers	Federal government workers		
15980	Cape Coral-Fort Myers, FL Metro Area	76.7	69.4	7.3	6.6	6.4	1.8	1.2	7.1	0.1
16020	Cape Girardeau, MO-IL Metro Area	69.3	65.8	3.5	13.2	4.0	7.7	1.5	4.1	0.2
16060	Carbondale-Marion, IL Metro Area	62.1	60.4	1.7	7.4	6.1	15.7	2.5	6.1	0.1
16180	Carson City, NV Metro Area	69.6	67.2	2.3	5.5	3.8	15.9	1.6	3.0	0.6
16220	Casper, WY Metro Area	73.1	69.8	3.3	8.4	6.4	5.1	1.4	5.6	0.1
16300	Cedar Rapids, IA Metro Area	76.1	73.7	2.4	8.9	4.4	3.8	1.5	5.1	0.2
16540	Chambersburg-Waynesboro, PA Metro Area	71.0	69.7	1.4	9.5	7.3	2.8	3.4	5.8	0.1
16580	Champaign-Urbana, IL Metro Area	58.8	55.8	3.0	11.2	6.4	17.4	1.9	4.0	0.1
16620	Charleston, WV Metro Area	67.0	65.0	1.9	9.4	7.9	10.0	1.8	3.9	0.0
16700	Charleston-North Charleston, SC Metro Area	72.1	69.1	3.0	5.7	6.3	6.5	4.3	5.1	0.2
16740	Charlotte-Concord-Gastonia, NC-SC Metro Area	78.6	74.9	3.7	7.0	4.5	4.0	1.2	4.6	0.1
16820	Charlottesville, VA Metro Area	60.8	56.3	4.4	10.4	6.4	12.5	2.8	7.0	0.1
16860	Chattanooga, TN-GA Metro Area	72.3	69.8	2.5	8.7	5.4	3.6	3.1	6.8	0.1
16940	Cheyenne, WY Metro Area	66.0	63.7	2.3	5.9	9.9	10.1	4.3	3.6	0.2
16980	**Chicago-Naperville-Elgin, IL-IN-WI Metro Area**	76.8	73.0	3.8	8.5	6.6	2.5	1.4	4.2	0.1
16980/16974	*Chicago-Naperville-Arlington Heights, IL Metro Division*	76.1	72.3	3.9	9.0	6.6	2.4	1.4	4.3	0.1
16980/20994	*Elgin, IL Metro Division*	78.7	74.9	3.8	6.7	7.3	3.2	1.0	3.1	0.1
16980/23844	*Gary, IN Metro Division*	77.7	75.0	2.8	8.0	6.4	2.9	1.0	3.8	0.1
16980/29404	*Lake County-Kenosha County, IL-WI Metro Division; Chicago-Naperville-Elgin, IL-IN-WI Metro Area*	79.9	75.5	4.4	6.0	6.0	2.0	1.7	4.2	0.2
17020	Chico, CA Metro Area	65.7	63.9	1.8	9.1	8.1	5.9	1.5	9.4	0.3
17140	Cincinnati, OH-KY-IN Metro Area	75.2	72.6	2.6	9.6	5.7	2.7	2.0	4.7	0.1
17300	Clarksville, TN-KY Metro Area	69.3	67.7	1.6	4.8	6.6	5.4	8.9	4.6	0.3
17420	Cleveland, TN Metro Area	74.6	73.0	1.6	6.8	5.4	3.9	1.3	7.7	0.3
17460	Cleveland-Elyria, OH Metro Area	72.2	69.2	3.0	11.1	7.9	1.7	2.4	4.6	0.1
17660	Coeur d'Alene, ID Metro Area	71.4	67.3	4.0	6.0	8.5	4.8	1.7	7.4	0.2
17780	College Station-Bryan, TX Metro Area	64.2	62.2	2.0	6.4	6.3	17.0	1.2	4.8	0.1
17820	Colorado Springs, CO Metro Area	68.4	63.5	4.8	8.6	7.3	3.8	6.1	5.7	0.3
17860	Columbia, MO Metro Area	62.6	58.9	3.7	10.6	7.1	12.2	2.6	4.6	0.3
17900	Columbia, SC Metro Area	69.7	66.5	3.2	6.0	5.1	11.6	2.7	4.9	0.1
17980	Columbus, GA-AL Metro Area	68.3	66.4	1.9	7.3	6.5	5.9	7.1	4.8	0.1
18020	Columbus, IN Metro Area	82.1	79.5	2.6	5.9	3.8	1.5	0.8	5.8	0.1
18140	Columbus, OH Metro Area	72.6	70.0	2.6	8.8	6.1	5.9	1.6	4.9	0.1
18580	Corpus Christi, TX Metro Area	72.8	70.4	2.3	4.2	8.2	4.1	3.6	7.1	0.1
18700	Corvallis, OR Metro Area	55.0	52.8	2.1	13.3	7.4	15.6	2.0	6.6	0.2
18880	Crestview-Fort Walton Beach-Destin, FL Metro Area	70.3	64.6	5.6	4.3	7.1	2.3	7.9	8.0	0.0
19060	Cumberland, MD-WV Metro Area	70.9	69.0	1.9	6.4	6.8	11.5	1.2	3.1	0.1
19100	**Dallas-Fort Worth-Arlington, TX Metro Area**	78.4	75.4	3.0	5.3	6.0	2.8	1.6	5.8	0.1
19100/19124	*Dallas-Plano-Irving, TX Metro Division*	78.9	75.8	3.1	5.0	5.8	2.8	1.5	5.9	0.1
19100/23104	*Fort Worth-Arlington, TX Metro Division*	77.5	74.7	2.8	6.0	6.5	2.7	1.8	5.4	0.1
19140	Dalton, GA Metro Area	85.3	83.0	2.3	3.5	6.1	1.8	0.5	2.9	0.0
19180	Danville, IL Metro Area	73.3	69.3	4.0	8.2	3.8	4.5	3.9	6.1	0.3
19300	Daphne-Fairhope-Foley, AL Metro Area	78.0	72.8	5.2	6.9	5.7	1.9	1.7	5.6	0.1
19340	Davenport-Moline-Rock Island, IA-IL Metro Area	74.6	71.9	2.8	8.1	6.4	2.9	3.0	4.8	0.1
19380	Dayton, OH Metro Area	70.5	68.0	2.5	9.7	7.1	2.2	5.2	5.3	0.1
19460	Decatur, AL Metro Area	75.2	72.1	3.1	5.6	5.3	4.1	3.6	6.2	0.0
19500	Decatur, IL Metro Area	77.7	76.0	1.7	8.3	5.4	3.7	1.1	3.8	0.0
19660	Deltona-Daytona Beach-Ormond Beach, FL Metro Area	77.7	71.8	5.9	6.3	7.0	2.3	1.0	5.7	0.1
19740	Denver-Aurora-Lakewood, CO Metro Area	75.8	71.0	4.7	7.4	5.5	3.1	2.4	5.7	0.2
19780	Des Moines-West Des Moines, IA Metro Area	75.8	72.6	3.2	8.4	5.7	3.9	1.9	4.3	0.1
19820	**Detroit-Warren-Dearborn, MI Metro Area**	78.9	75.1	3.7	8.2	4.5	2.7	1.6	4.0	0.1
19820/19804	*Detroit-Dearborn-Livonia, MI Metro Division*	78.9	76.2	2.7	8.6	4.7	2.6	1.6	3.5	0.1
19820/47664	*Warren-Troy-Farmington Hills, MI Metro Division*	78.8	74.5	4.3	8.0	4.4	2.7	1.6	4.3	0.1
20020	Dothan, AL Metro Area	74.3	70.6	3.7	6.6	5.2	4.2	2.8	6.6	0.3

Table D. Metropolitan Statistical Area—Labor Force, Employment, and Educational Data, 2015—*Continued*

| | | Class of worker for civilian employed population age 16 and older | | | | | | | | |
| | | Private for-profit wage and salary workers | | | Private not-for-profit wage and salary workers | Government workers | | | Self-employed in own not incorporated business | Unpaid family workers |
CBSA code/ Division code	Metropolitan area, metropolitan division	Total private for-profit wage and salary workers	Employees of private companies	Self-employed in own incorporated business		Local government workers	State government workers	Federal government workers		
20100	Dover, DE Metro Area	69.3	65.9	3.5	4.9	2.7	14.7	4.3	3.9	0.1
20220	Dubuque, IA Metro Area	74.4	71.2	3.2	13.1	4.8	2.5	0.8	4.3	0.1
20260	Duluth, MN-WI Metro Area	67.4	65.0	2.4	12.7	8.7	5.3	1.3	4.4	0.1
20500	Durham-Chapel Hill, NC Metro Area	63.8	60.8	3.0	11.9	4.4	12.0	2.3	5.3	0.2
20700	East Stroudsburg, PA Metro Area	71.2	68.3	2.9	8.6	5.3	6.8	2.2	5.7	0.1
20740	Eau Claire, WI Metro Area	72.4	69.8	2.6	9.5	5.3	6.1	1.1	5.3	0.3
20940	El Centro, CA Metro Area	61.8	60.8	1.0	3.8	15.1	9.2	3.8	6.1	0.1
21060	Elizabethtown-Fort Knox, KY Metro Area	72.1	70.3	1.7	5.0	4.1	4.7	9.8	4.4	0.0
21140	Elkhart-Goshen, IN Metro Area	79.7	76.6	3.0	7.9	5.0	1.9	0.5	4.5	0.5
21300	Elmira, NY Metro Area	68.2	66.9	1.3	13.2	6.4	7.1	1.0	4.1	0.0
21340	El Paso, TX Metro Area	68.5	67.0	1.6	4.8	9.2	5.0	6.0	6.3	0.1
21500	Erie, PA Metro Area	73.8	71.1	2.7	11.8	5.1	2.8	1.6	4.8	0.1
21660	Eugene, OR Metro Area	67.9	64.1	3.8	11.1	6.1	5.5	2.1	7.1	0.2
21780	Evansville, IN-KY Metro Area	78.3	74.8	3.5	8.9	5.7	2.3	1.0	3.6	0.3
21820	Fairbanks, AK Metro Area	57.9	55.0	2.9	9.6	7.0	9.1	12.9	3.4	0.1
22020	Fargo, ND-MN Metro Area	70.7	67.9	2.8	12.8	5.4	3.8	2.1	5.2	0.0
22140	Farmington, NM Metro Area	69.3	67.1	2.2	6.7	11.0	4.2	3.7	4.9	0.2
22180	Fayetteville, NC Metro Area	65.8	63.7	2.1	5.3	6.0	7.5	11.0	4.2	0.1
22220	Fayetteville-Springdale-Rogers, AR-MO Metro Area	74.9	72.4	2.5	7.6	4.7	5.0	1.2	6.4	0.2
22380	Flagstaff, AZ Metro Area	64.0	60.9	3.1	7.3	8.7	11.5	5.0	3.4	0.0
22420	Flint, MI Metro Area	78.8	76.2	2.6	7.8	5.6	2.9	0.6	4.2	0.1
22500	Florence, SC Metro Area	70.8	69.0	1.8	8.5	5.2	8.9	1.4	5.0	0.2
22520	Florence-Muscle Shoals, AL Metro Area	75.5	72.2	3.2	5.9	6.2	5.3	2.2	4.8	0.1
22540	Fond du Lac, WI Metro Area	74.6	72.0	2.7	8.5	5.9	3.4	1.4	5.7	0.5
22660	Fort Collins, CO Metro Area	68.2	64.3	3.9	7.8	7.3	8.4	2.0	6.1	0.1
22900	Fort Smith, AR-OK Metro Area	75.4	72.6	2.8	5.6	5.7	6.7	1.5	5.1	0.1
23060	Fort Wayne, IN Metro Area	77.5	73.4	4.2	9.7	4.7	2.5	1.2	4.2	0.2
23420	Fresno, CA Metro Area	67.9	65.8	2.1	6.2	11.1	6.1	2.4	6.2	0.1
23460	Gadsden, AL Metro Area	75.4	72.7	2.7	5.8	6.7	5.0	1.4	5.2	0.4
23540	Gainesville, FL Metro Area	61.6	57.8	3.8	10.0	6.9	14.4	2.8	4.3	0.0
23580	Gainesville, GA Metro Area	78.7	74.6	4.1	4.8	5.8	3.0	1.4	6.2	0.1
23900	Gettysburg, PA Metro Area	72.7	69.4	3.3	10.2	6.4	2.5	2.8	5.2	0.3
24020	Glens Falls, NY Metro Area	68.0	64.9	3.1	10.5	7.5	5.4	1.3	7.1	0.2
24140	Goldsboro, NC Metro Area	70.6	67.7	2.9	2.7	4.2	11.8	4.4	6.0	0.3
24220	Grand Forks, ND-MN Metro Area	68.1	65.4	2.7	8.5	6.4	9.3	3.5	4.0	0.1
24260	Grand Island, NE Metro Area	72.8	70.1	2.7	8.4	5.7	3.4	2.5	7.2	0.0
24300	Grand Junction, CO Metro Area	70.0	64.6	5.4	8.9	6.9	4.1	2.5	7.2	0.2
24340	Grand Rapids-Wyoming, MI Metro Area	76.4	73.0	3.4	11.2	4.2	2.7	1.0	4.5	0.1
24420	Grants Pass, OR Metro Area	66.7	63.5	3.2	10.6	7.2	3.7	1.4	9.9	0.4
24500	Great Falls, MT Metro Area	66.6	62.0	4.6	10.3	6.2	3.2	5.3	8.0	0.4
24540	Greeley, CO Metro Area	74.1	70.7	3.4	7.5	6.8	4.4	1.4	5.5	0.2
24580	Green Bay, WI Metro Area	77.5	75.1	2.4	7.9	5.6	3.1	0.8	5.0	0.1
24660	Greensboro-High Point, NC Metro Area	74.0	70.5	3.5	7.7	5.8	5.4	1.5	5.4	0.1
24780	Greenville, NC Metro Area	70.8	67.3	3.4	7.4	3.8	11.2	2.2	4.6	0.1
24860	Greenville-Anderson-Mauldin, SC Metro Area	75.2	72.3	2.9	7.8	4.8	5.6	1.0	5.5	0.2
25060	Gulfport-Biloxi-Pascagoula, MS Metro Area	70.8	69.3	1.5	6.2	6.7	4.0	6.2	6.0	0.1
25180	Hagerstown-Martinsburg, MD-WV Metro Area	68.1	65.9	2.2	6.3	9.1	5.6	6.5	4.2	0.1
25220	Hammond, LA Metro Area	70.9	67.3	3.7	7.4	6.3	7.8	2.0	5.6	0.0
25260	Hanford-Corcoran, CA Metro Area	61.9	59.5	2.4	5.3	11.7	8.9	6.3	5.9	0.2
25420	Harrisburg-Carlisle, PA Metro Area	69.5	67.5	2.0	10.3	3.6	7.7	4.2	4.5	0.2
25500	Harrisonburg, VA Metro Area	69.3	65.1	4.2	7.7	6.9	9.0	0.9	5.9	0.2
25540	Hartford-West Hartford-East Hartford, CT Metro Area	71.3	68.3	3.0	9.0	7.1	6.2	1.1	4.9	0.3
25620	Hattiesburg, MS Metro Area	73.5	68.1	5.5	5.2	4.4	10.1	2.6	4.1	0.0
25860	Hickory-Lenoir-Morganton, NC Metro Area	75.9	73.3	2.6	4.4	5.3	7.6	0.8	5.9	0.1
25940	Hilton Head Island-Bluffton-Beaufort, SC Metro Area	74.8	68.7	6.1	5.5	5.7	3.5	3.3	7.1	0.1
25980	Hinesville, GA Metro Area	69.0	68.2	0.8	2.7	7.1	5.1	13.2	2.8	0.2
26140	Homosassa Springs, FL Metro Area	73.1	66.8	6.3	5.0	6.7	2.9	1.7	9.9	0.7
26300	Hot Springs, AR Metro Area	70.0	64.1	5.8	6.4	5.1	7.8	2.4	8.2	0.2
26380	Houma-Thibodaux, LA Metro Area	79.5	75.9	3.6	4.2	6.6	3.5	1.0	5.2	0.1
26420	Houston-The Woodlands-Sugar Land, TX Metro Area	77.8	75.2	2.6	5.3	5.6	3.5	1.2	6.4	0.1
26580	Huntington-Ashland, WV-KY-OH Metro Area	71.9	70.1	1.8	9.4	6.7	5.0	3.2	3.6	0.1
26620	Huntsville, AL Metro Area	70.4	68.8	1.6	6.9	5.5	4.2	8.0	4.5	0.4
26820	Idaho Falls, ID Metro Area	70.2	64.5	5.7	6.3	6.3	4.8	5.4	6.9	0.1

Table D. Metropolitan Statistical Area—Labor Force, Employment, and Educational Data, 2015—*Continued*

		Class of worker for civilian employed population age 16 and older								
		Private for-profit wage and salary workers			Private not-for-profit wage and salary workers	Government workers			Self-employed in own not incorporated business	Unpaid family workers
CBSA code/ Division code	Metropolitan area, metropolitan division	Total private for-profit wage and salary workers	Employees of private companies	Self-employed in own incorporated business		Local government workers	State government workers	Federal government workers		
26900	Indianapolis-Carmel-Anderson, IN Metro Area	77.0	73.6	3.4	8.5	5.4	3.3	1.6	4.0	0.1
26980	Iowa City, IA Metro Area	60.9	59.0	1.9	8.7	6.6	18.4	1.5	3.7	0.2
27060	Ithaca, NY Metro Area	53.9	51.3	2.6	27.2	5.5	6.0	0.5	6.7	0.2
27100	Jackson, MI Metro Area	74.5	71.6	2.9	10.0	4.0	5.6	1.0	4.8	0.0
27140	Jackson, MS Metro Area	68.4	64.0	4.3	7.3	4.8	11.3	3.1	5.1	0.1
27180	Jackson, TN Metro Area	72.5	70.7	1.8	10.4	6.4	5.2	1.0	4.4	0.1
27260	Jacksonville, FL Metro Area	75.6	71.3	4.3	7.6	6.3	3.2	3.1	4.1	0.1
27340	Jacksonville, NC Metro Area	69.5	66.6	2.9	1.7	5.0	3.4	13.9	6.3	0.1
27500	Janesville-Beloit, WI Metro Area	75.4	72.0	3.4	8.9	6.8	3.5	0.6	4.8	0.0
27620	Jefferson City, MO Metro Area	60.8	58.7	2.1	7.6	6.7	17.6	2.2	5.1	0.0
27740	Johnson City, TN Metro Area	68.8	66.4	2.5	9.5	5.3	6.6	3.1	6.6	0.1
27780	Johnstown, PA Metro Area	70.4	67.2	3.2	10.7	5.1	7.3	2.3	4.0	0.3
27860	Jonesboro, AR Metro Area	72.4	69.5	2.9	9.3	3.9	6.6	0.7	7.0	0.1
27900	Joplin, MO Metro Area	71.2	69.0	2.2	10.8	4.9	4.9	1.3	6.3	0.5
27980	Kahului-Wailuku-Lahaina, HI Metro Area	69.8	65.7	4.1	6.0	4.9	8.1	2.0	9.0	0.2
28020	Kalamazoo-Portage, MI Metro Area	71.3	68.9	2.4	11.5	5.6	4.3	1.5	5.6	0.2
28100	Kankakee, IL Metro Area	71.8	70.3	1.5	11.5	7.3	4.2	1.1	3.9	0.2
28140	Kansas City, MO-KS Metro Area	74.0	70.6	3.4	8.8	5.9	3.4	3.1	4.7	0.2
28420	Kennewick-Richland, WA Metro Area	73.4	69.8	3.7	6.5	6.1	6.0	3.1	4.5	0.2
28660	Killeen-Temple, TX Metro Area	61.2	59.6	1.6	7.2	7.8	6.5	12.1	5.0	0.1
28700	Kingsport-Bristol-Bristol, TN-VA Metro Area	73.3	71.0	2.2	7.7	6.9	4.2	1.4	6.3	0.2
28740	Kingston, NY Metro Area	65.2	60.2	5.0	9.4	9.1	6.9	1.0	8.2	0.2
28940	Knoxville, TN Metro Area	71.5	69.0	2.5	7.7	7.1	4.7	3.0	5.9	0.1
29020	Kokomo, IN Metro Area	78.2	76.2	1.9	5.9	6.2	4.8	0.8	4.1	0.0
29100	La Crosse-Onalaska, WI-MN Metro Area	70.4	68.0	2.4	11.2	5.8	6.4	1.6	4.6	0.1
29180	Lafayette, LA Metro Area	73.6	68.5	5.2	5.9	7.9	5.0	0.8	6.5	0.2
29200	Lafayette-West Lafayette, IN Metro Area	73.4	71.4	2.1	10.1	4.2	8.1	0.7	3.1	0.2
29340	Lake Charles, LA Metro Area	76.8	74.0	2.8	5.4	9.5	3.8	0.2	4.3	0.0
29420	Lake Havasu City-Kingman, AZ Metro Area	73.8	70.5	3.2	3.4	10.0	3.9	1.7	7.0	0.1
29460	Lakeland-Winter Haven, FL Metro Area	76.9	72.9	4.0	7.7	7.0	2.1	1.0	5.1	0.2
29540	Lancaster, PA Metro Area	72.3	69.8	2.5	10.8	4.8	2.8	1.3	7.6	0.4
29620	Lansing-East Lansing, MI Metro Area	64.0	61.5	2.4	12.3	6.4	11.5	1.0	4.7	0.2
29700	Laredo, TX Metro Area	74.0	70.6	3.5	2.9	8.9	5.8	2.8	5.3	0.1
29740	Las Cruces, NM Metro Area	63.2	59.9	3.3	5.7	9.7	8.7	6.2	6.4	0.1
29820	Las Vegas-Henderson-Paradise, NV Metro Area	81.8	79.1	2.8	3.3	5.7	2.3	2.2	4.7	0.1
29940	Lawrence, KS Metro Area	65.2	60.8	4.5	10.3	6.0	13.6	1.4	3.4	0.0
30020	Lawton, OK Metro Area	61.9	58.8	3.1	6.3	9.3	6.2	10.1	6.0	0.2
30140	Lebanon, PA Metro Area	73.6	72.0	1.7	10.2	4.7	3.0	2.2	6.4	0.0
30300	Lewiston, ID-WA Metro Area	68.6	67.0	1.7	7.0	7.3	7.7	1.5	7.8	0.1
30340	Lewiston-Auburn, ME Metro Area	68.2	65.4	2.8	12.7	5.8	4.2	1.7	7.3	0.2
30460	Lexington-Fayette, KY Metro Area	72.2	68.5	3.7	8.0	5.4	6.9	2.3	5.1	0.1
30620	Lima, OH Metro Area	75.5	73.2	2.3	9.8	6.0	3.8	0.6	4.0	0.3
30700	Lincoln, NE Metro Area	67.5	64.9	2.7	9.6	6.8	10.0	1.9	4.2	0.0
30780	Little Rock-North Little Rock-Conway, AR Metro Area	67.5	64.1	3.4	8.7	5.4	9.4	3.8	5.0	0.2
30860	Logan, UT-ID Metro Area	71.4	65.6	5.9	7.7	6.2	8.0	1.5	4.9	0.2
30980	Longview, TX Metro Area	76.2	74.2	2.0	5.4	5.4	5.5	0.8	6.6	0.1
31020	Longview, WA Metro Area	72.5	68.6	3.9	7.8	8.3	6.3	1.0	3.5	0.6
31080	**Los Angeles-Long Beach-Anaheim, CA Metro Area**	74.3	70.1	4.2	5.9	6.6	2.8	1.2	9.0	0.2
31080/11244	*Anaheim-Santa Ana-Irvine, CA Metro Division*	76.9	72.5	4.4	4.9	6.0	2.9	1.1	8.0	0.2
31080/31084	*Los Angeles-Long Beach-Glendale, CA Metro Division*	73.5	69.4	4.1	6.2	6.8	2.8	1.2	9.3	0.2
31140	Louisville/Jefferson County, KY-IN Metro Area	76.1	73.2	2.9	8.5	4.3	4.1	2.0	4.8	0.1
31180	Lubbock, TX Metro Area	73.8	71.3	2.5	5.5	5.7	7.8	0.9	5.9	0.3
31340	Lynchburg, VA Metro Area	67.2	64.3	3.0	14.5	7.7	4.8	1.3	4.4	0.1
31420	Macon, GA Metro Area	71.1	67.5	3.6	8.8	7.7	4.2	3.6	4.1	0.4
31460	Madera, CA Metro Area	73.4	71.5	1.9	3.6	8.2	5.8	1.3	7.6	0.1
31540	Madison, WI Metro Area	66.3	62.9	3.5	9.5	6.3	11.6	1.6	4.5	0.2
31700	Manchester-Nashua, NH Metro Area	73.9	71.8	2.1	9.3	6.3	2.6	1.9	5.8	0.2
31740	Manhattan, KS Metro Area	61.9	58.8	3.1	6.2	6.3	16.6	3.4	5.6	0.0
31860	Mankato-North Mankato, MN Metro Area	69.1	65.9	3.2	12.1	6.4	6.5	0.9	5.0	0.0
31900	Mansfield, OH Metro Area	75.6	73.2	2.3	7.3	6.4	4.0	1.0	5.7	0.0

Table D. Metropolitan Statistical Area—Labor Force, Employment, and Educational Data, 2015—*Continued*

		Class of worker for civilian employed population age 16 and older								
		Private for-profit wage and salary workers			Private not-for-profit wage and salary workers	Government workers			Self-employed in own not incorporated business	Unpaid family workers
CBSA code/ Division code	Metropolitan area, metropolitan division	Total private for-profit wage and salary workers	Employees of private companies	Self-employed in own incorporated business		Local government workers	State government workers	Federal government workers		
32580	McAllen-Edinburg-Mission, TX Metro Area	69.1	66.5	2.6	3.9	6.2	6.7	2.1	11.9	0.2
32780	Medford, OR Metro Area	67.1	63.5	3.6	7.8	5.2	5.4	2.7	11.6	0.1
32820	Memphis, TN-MS-AR Metro Area	74.7	72.4	2.3	7.0	7.4	3.2	2.7	4.9	0.1
32900	Merced, CA Metro Area	73.3	72.2	1.1	5.7	9.1	3.9	0.7	7.0	0.2
33100	**Miami-Fort Lauderdale-West Palm Beach, FL Metro Area**	78.1	71.2	6.9	4.8	6.8	1.8	1.4	7.0	0.1
33100/22744	*Fort Lauderdale-Pompano Beach-Deerfield Beach, FL Metro Division*	77.6	70.8	6.8	4.9	7.4	1.8	1.3	6.8	0.1
33100/33124	*Miami-Miami Beach-Kendall, FL Metro Division*	78.1	71.2	6.9	4.7	6.4	1.7	1.4	7.5	0.2
33100/48424	*West Palm Beach-Boca Raton-Delray Beach, FL Metro Division*	78.9	71.9	7.0	4.7	6.7	1.9	1.4	6.3	0.1
33140	Michigan City-La Porte, IN Metro Area	75.9	72.8	3.1	9.5	5.6	4.0	1.1	3.8	0.2
33220	Midland, MI Metro Area	76.8	74.8	2.0	9.1	4.8	2.3	1.2	5.8	0.0
33260	Midland, TX Metro Area	80.0	76.2	3.8	4.3	6.1	2.5	0.4	6.3	0.4
33340	Milwaukee-Waukesha-West Allis, WI Metro Area	75.6	72.8	2.8	10.4	6.1	2.4	1.4	4.0	0.1
33460	Minneapolis-St. Paul-Bloomington, MN-WI Metro Area	73.7	69.7	4.0	10.8	5.8	3.8	1.3	4.5	0.1
33540	Missoula, MT Metro Area	63.7	59.2	4.4	11.7	5.8	9.8	2.4	6.6	0.0
33660	Mobile, AL Metro Area	75.7	73.2	2.5	7.2	6.8	4.2	2.0	4.1	0.1
33700	Modesto, CA Metro Area	72.5	70.1	2.3	6.7	10.0	3.6	0.8	6.1	0.2
33740	Monroe, LA Metro Area	75.9	72.6	3.3	7.1	5.9	6.7	0.9	3.3	0.1
33780	Monroe, MI Metro Area	78.1	76.1	2.0	7.7	5.8	2.0	1.1	5.3	0.1
33860	Montgomery, AL Metro Area	68.1	65.9	2.2	6.6	7.4	9.2	4.7	4.0	0.0
34060	Morgantown, WV Metro Area	63.9	61.0	2.9	11.8	5.3	11.5	2.8	4.7	0.1
34100	Morristown, TN Metro Area	73.6	71.6	2.0	8.1	5.1	6.0	1.2	5.9	0.2
34580	Mount Vernon-Anacortes, WA Metro Area	72.1	67.7	4.5	6.1	6.8	4.6	2.4	7.7	0.1
34620	Muncie, IN Metro Area	71.6	69.3	2.3	10.1	4.0	9.0	1.3	4.0	0.0
34740	Muskegon, MI Metro Area	77.0	74.9	2.1	10.0	5.5	2.8	0.8	3.8	0.2
34820	Myrtle Beach-Conway-North Myrtle Beach, SC-NC Metro Area	77.1	73.1	4.1	3.6	5.5	5.2	1.0	7.3	0.2
34900	Napa, CA Metro Area	71.5	68.2	3.2	7.3	7.3	4.3	0.5	8.9	0.2
34940	Naples-Immokalee-Marco Island, FL Metro Area	79.7	70.8	8.9	4.5	5.5	0.6	1.1	8.4	0.2
34980	Nashville-Davidson--Murfreesboro--Franklin, TN Metro Area	72.2	70.0	2.2	8.8	6.2	3.9	1.5	7.2	0.1
35100	New Bern, NC Metro Area	67.5	64.6	2.9	5.9	6.1	4.8	11.2	4.2	0.3
35300	New Haven-Milford, CT Metro Area	68.7	66.0	2.7	12.5	7.1	4.1	1.7	5.8	0.1
35380	New Orleans-Metairie, LA Metro Area	73.3	68.7	4.5	7.0	6.5	4.0	2.8	6.4	0.1
35620	**New York-Newark-Jersey City, NY-NJ-PA Metro Area**	72.2	68.0	4.2	8.4	8.6	3.3	1.6	5.7	0.1
35620/20524	*Dutchess County-Putnam County, NY Metro Division*	68.0	63.7	4.3	10.5	9.2	5.4	1.5	5.2	0.3
35620/35004	*Nassau County-Suffolk County, NY Metro Division*	70.2	64.5	5.7	7.9	10.4	4.7	1.8	4.9	0.1
35620/35084	*Newark, NJ-PA Metro Division*	75.4	71.6	3.8	6.5	6.7	4.6	1.6	5.0	0.1
35620/35614	*New York-Jersey City-White Plains, NY-NJ Metro Division*	72.2	68.2	3.9	8.8	8.6	2.8	1.5	6.0	0.1
35660	Niles-Benton Harbor, MI Metro Area	74.9	71.2	3.7	11.9	3.6	2.6	0.6	6.2	0.2
35840	North Port-Sarasota-Bradenton, FL Metro Area	76.3	68.6	7.7	7.0	6.4	2.0	0.9	7.1	0.2
35980	Norwich-New London, CT Metro Area	70.3	67.6	2.7	8.4	8.4	3.7	4.0	5.2	0.1
36100	Ocala, FL Metro Area	74.2	68.5	5.7	4.6	8.3	2.9	1.3	7.8	0.9
36140	Ocean City, NJ Metro Area	64.6	57.5	7.1	4.8	14.5	6.4	1.1	8.4	0.2
36220	Odessa, TX Metro Area	77.4	74.6	2.8	3.1	8.9	3.1	0.6	6.5	0.4
36260	Ogden-Clearfield, UT Metro Area	71.7	67.6	4.1	7.1	6.0	4.3	7.1	3.6	0.1
36420	Oklahoma City, OK Metro Area	71.5	66.9	4.6	7.1	4.4	6.9	4.3	5.6	0.1
36500	Olympia-Tumwater, WA Metro Area	57.0	53.4	3.6	6.6	7.6	16.7	6.0	6.2	0.0
36540	Omaha-Council Bluffs, NE-IA Metro Area	73.6	70.2	3.4	10.2	6.0	3.2	2.3	4.5	0.2
36740	Orlando-Kissimmee-Sanford, FL Metro Area	79.0	74.3	4.7	6.5	6.0	2.2	1.4	4.8	0.2
36780	Oshkosh-Neenah, WI Metro Area	77.9	74.4	3.4	7.0	5.9	5.0	0.3	3.5	0.3

Table D. Metropolitan Statistical Area—Labor Force, Employment, and Educational Data, 2015—*Continued*

| | | Class of worker for civilian employed population age 16 and older | | | | | | | | |
| | | Private for-profit wage and salary workers | | | Private not-for-profit wage and salary workers | Government workers | | | Self-employed in own not incorporated business | Unpaid family workers |
CBSA code/ Division code	Metropolitan area, metropolitan division	Total private for-profit wage and salary workers	Employees of private companies	Self-employed in own incorporated business		Local government workers	State government workers	Federal government workers		
36980	Owensboro, KY Metro Area	71.0	68.3	2.7	10.1	5.7	5.4	1.1	6.7	0.0
37100	Oxnard-Thousand Oaks-Ventura, CA Metro Area	73.7	69.7	4.1	4.8	8.1	2.7	2.3	8.2	0.1
37340	Palm Bay-Melbourne-Titusville, FL Metro Area	76.7	70.7	5.9	6.5	6.5	1.9	3.7	4.5	0.1
37460	Panama City, FL Metro Area	70.8	66.1	4.7	5.5	6.5	3.1	6.4	7.4	0.2
37620	Parkersburg-Vienna, WV Metro Area	73.4	71.4	1.9	7.6	4.6	6.9	3.3	4.1	0.1
37860	Pensacola-Ferry Pass-Brent, FL Metro Area	68.2	65.4	2.8	10.1	6.6	3.0	5.0	6.9	0.1
37900	Peoria, IL Metro Area	73.8	71.4	2.4	10.9	4.9	3.3	2.2	4.7	0.1
37980	**Philadelphia-Camden-Wilmington, PA-NJ-DE-MD Metro Area**	73.2	70.0	3.2	11.0	5.7	3.3	2.3	4.4	0.1
37980/15804	*Camden, NJ Metro Division*	71.9	68.9	3.0	8.1	7.3	5.5	2.5	4.4	0.3
37980/33874	*Montgomery County-Bucks County-Chester County, PA Metro Division*	77.1	72.9	4.2	10.2	4.4	1.9	1.4	4.9	0.1
37980/37964	*Philadelphia, PA Metro Division*	69.2	67.1	2.2	14.6	6.6	2.3	3.1	4.2	0.1
37980/48864	*Wilmington, DE-MD-NJ Metro Division*	75.0	71.8	3.2	8.8	4.3	6.0	2.4	3.4	0.1
38060	Phoenix-Mesa-Scottsdale, AZ Metro Area	77.3	73.7	3.6	5.7	5.3	4.1	1.8	5.6	0.2
38220	Pine Bluff, AR Metro Area	64.5	61.9	2.5	7.5	6.7	14.4	2.8	3.8	0.3
38300	Pittsburgh, PA Metro Area	73.0	70.3	2.7	13.7	4.7	2.2	1.6	4.6	0.1
38340	Pittsfield, MA Metro Area	62.1	59.4	2.6	17.7	8.1	3.1	0.9	8.0	0.1
38540	Pocatello, ID Metro Area	70.1	67.9	2.2	4.9	7.0	9.9	2.3	5.5	0.3
38860	Portland-South Portland, ME Metro Area	68.9	64.2	4.7	11.9	6.6	2.5	2.0	7.9	0.1
38900	Portland-Vancouver-Hillsboro, OR-WA Metro Area	72.0	67.9	4.1	9.7	5.7	3.9	1.9	6.8	0.1
38940	Port St. Lucie, FL Metro Area	76.6	69.0	7.6	7.0	7.2	2.4	0.9	5.5	0.2
39140	Prescott, AZ Metro Area	69.6	64.3	5.4	9.3	5.9	4.5	2.7	7.8	0.2
39300	Providence-Warwick, RI-MA Metro Area	72.3	69.4	2.8	10.6	6.5	3.8	2.0	4.7	0.1
39340	Provo-Orem, UT Metro Area	72.4	68.4	4.0	10.3	6.2	5.1	1.0	4.7	0.3
39380	Pueblo, CO Metro Area	67.3	65.2	2.1	10.3	5.7	9.0	1.8	5.3	0.5
39460	Punta Gorda, FL Metro Area	79.2	70.0	9.1	4.4	4.8	4.1	1.3	6.1	0.2
39540	Racine, WI Metro Area	76.0	73.6	2.4	8.7	6.8	3.0	1.1	4.3	0.0
39580	Raleigh, NC Metro Area	73.3	69.5	3.8	6.2	5.1	8.4	1.7	5.2	0.1
39660	Rapid City, SD Metro Area	68.1	62.0	6.1	11.6	6.1	3.4	4.3	6.3	0.3
39740	Reading, PA Metro Area	77.7	75.2	2.5	8.3	5.1	3.0	1.2	4.5	0.2
39820	Redding, CA Metro Area	66.1	62.4	3.7	5.8	8.6	5.8	2.9	10.5	0.3
39900	Reno, NV Metro Area	75.9	72.1	3.8	4.6	6.4	4.5	2.0	6.5	0.2
40060	Richmond, VA Metro Area	71.6	68.3	3.3	7.3	7.8	5.2	3.5	4.4	0.2
40140	Riverside-San Bernardino-Ontario, CA Metro Area	72.2	69.6	2.6	5.6	9.1	3.8	1.8	7.3	0.2
40220	Roanoke, VA Metro Area	74.0	70.8	3.2	9.3	7.1	3.1	2.6	3.9	0.0
40340	Rochester, MN Metro Area	58.8	55.8	3.0	26.5	5.8	2.3	1.2	5.4	0.2
40380	Rochester, NY Metro Area	68.5	65.6	3.0	13.6	7.3	4.5	1.1	4.9	0.2
40420	Rockford, IL Metro Area	76.5	73.7	2.8	8.0	5.7	3.9	1.0	4.6	0.2
40580	Rocky Mount, NC Metro Area	74.8	72.3	2.5	5.4	5.9	7.0	0.6	6.2	0.1
40660	Rome, GA Metro Area	76.8	72.7	4.1	9.2	6.5	3.3	0.3	3.9	0.0
40900	Sacramento--Roseville--Arden-Arcade, CA Metro Area	64.5	62.1	2.4	7.3	8.0	10.9	1.8	7.4	0.2
40980	Saginaw, MI Metro Area	74.9	72.0	2.9	10.9	4.7	3.7	1.5	4.0	0.3
41060	St. Cloud, MN Metro Area	68.8	66.1	2.7	14.3	4.9	3.8	1.5	6.5	0.2
41100	St. George, UT Metro Area	76.6	69.8	6.8	5.3	4.7	6.0	1.0	6.1	0.3
41140	St. Joseph, MO-KS Metro Area	72.2	69.5	2.7	11.0	5.3	4.5	1.2	5.5	0.2
41180	St. Louis, MO-IL Metro Area	74.3	71.1	3.1	11.3	5.3	2.5	2.0	4.5	0.2
41420	Salem, OR Metro Area	70.8	67.0	3.7	7.6	6.0	9.3	1.6	4.6	0.1
41500	Salinas, CA Metro Area	71.9	68.7	3.1	5.6	7.3	4.4	2.7	7.8	0.3
41540	Salisbury, MD-DE Metro Area	70.1	64.9	5.2	6.1	6.2	9.4	1.6	6.4	0.1
41620	Salt Lake City, UT Metro Area	75.5	71.8	3.7	7.1	4.6	5.7	2.4	4.7	0.1
41660	San Angelo, TX Metro Area	72.3	68.8	3.5	5.6	7.7	4.6	3.4	6.4	0.0
41700	San Antonio-New Braunfels, TX Metro Area	74.1	71.7	2.5	6.1	5.4	3.9	4.8	5.5	0.1
41740	San Diego-Carlsbad, CA Metro Area	70.7	67.4	3.4	7.1	6.1	3.9	4.0	7.9	0.1
41860	**San Francisco-Oakland-Hayward, CA Metro Area**	71.2	68.0	3.2	8.3	7.0	3.4	1.7	8.3	0.2
41860/36084	*Oakland-Hayward-Berkeley, CA Metro Division*	70.8	67.9	2.9	8.1	7.5	3.6	1.9	7.9	0.2

Table D. Metropolitan Statistical Area—Labor Force, Employment, and Educational Data, 2015—*Continued*

CBSA code/ Division code	Metropolitan area, metropolitan division	Private for-profit wage and salary workers			Private not-for-profit wage and salary workers	Government workers			Self-employed in own not incorporated business	Unpaid family workers
		Total private for-profit wage and salary workers	Employees of private companies	Self-employed in own incorporated business		Local government workers	State government workers	Federal government workers		
	San Francisco-Redwood City-South									
41860/41884	*San Francisco, CA Metro Division*	72.6	69.5	3.1	8.5	6.2	3.0	1.6	7.9	0.2
41860/42034	*San Rafael, CA Metro Division*	65.5	59.1	6.4	9.3	6.9	2.5	1.2	14.4	0.2
41940	San Jose-Sunnyvale-Santa Clara, CA Metro Area	77.6	74.9	2.7	6.6	6.8	2.2	1.2	5.6	0.1
42020	San Luis Obispo-Paso Robles-Arroyo Grande, CA Metro Area	63.1	58.6	4.5	5.9	8.7	9.9	1.1	11.0	0.3
42100	Santa Cruz-Watsonville, CA Metro Area	63.0	60.0	3.0	9.8	7.1	6.3	0.7	12.7	0.4
42140	Santa Fe, NM Metro Area	57.3	51.3	6.0	9.4	6.8	10.3	3.3	12.6	0.3
42200	Santa Maria-Santa Barbara, CA Metro Area	67.4	64.0	3.4	9.7	7.0	5.8	1.4	8.5	0.1
42220	Santa Rosa, CA Metro Area	67.6	65.0	2.6	7.6	8.2	3.6	1.1	11.8	0.1
42340	Savannah, GA Metro Area	73.3	69.8	3.5	6.9	5.5	5.9	3.6	4.7	0.1
42540	Scranton--Wilkes-Barre--Hazleton, PA Metro Area	73.5	70.8	2.7	10.1	5.2	3.7	2.5	4.8	0.2
42660	**Seattle-Tacoma-Bellevue, WA Metro Area**	72.5	68.8	3.7	8.3	6.0	5.1	2.4	5.5	0.2
42660/42644	*Seattle-Bellevue-Everett, WA Metro Division*	73.4	69.6	3.8	8.5	5.6	5.0	1.7	5.7	0.2
42660/45104	*Tacoma-Lakewood, WA Metro Division*	68.9	65.8	3.1	7.4	7.6	5.7	5.5	4.7	0.2
42680	Sebastian-Vero Beach, FL Metro Area	76.4	67.4	9.0	5.6	6.5	3.2	1.0	6.9	0.5
42700	Sebring, FL Metro Area	74.7	69.7	5.0	7.7	8.5	3.2	0.6	5.2	0.0
43100	Sheboygan, WI Metro Area	78.3	75.5	2.7	8.2	6.5	1.6	0.6	4.7	0.2
43300	Sherman-Denison, TX Metro Area	72.5	69.1	3.3	5.9	7.5	4.3	1.3	8.2	0.4
43340	Shreveport-Bossier City, LA Metro Area	71.8	68.8	3.0	7.0	6.4	5.1	4.5	5.0	0.1
43420	Sierra Vista-Douglas, AZ Metro Area	54.6	51.0	3.5	6.7	9.7	7.2	17.5	4.2	0.2
43580	Sioux City, IA-NE-SD Metro Area	74.2	70.6	3.6	9.4	5.1	3.2	1.7	6.1	0.4
43620	Sioux Falls, SD Metro Area	71.5	68.7	2.9	14.7	4.2	1.8	2.1	5.6	0.1
43780	South Bend-Mishawaka, IN-MI Metro Area	73.5	71.0	2.5	13.3	5.7	1.6	1.0	4.7	0.2
43900	Spartanburg, SC Metro Area	77.8	74.8	3.0	7.0	4.0	5.2	0.9	4.9	0.2
44060	Spokane-Spokane Valley, WA Metro Area	67.2	62.3	4.8	10.3	6.0	6.7	2.6	6.9	0.2
44100	Springfield, IL Metro Area	61.6	58.4	3.2	11.9	6.0	14.7	1.8	3.8	0.2
44140	Springfield, MA Metro Area	66.4	64.4	2.0	12.0	8.1	5.7	2.1	5.6	0.1
44180	Springfield, MO Metro Area	68.8	65.7	3.1	13.7	6.2	3.8	1.8	5.7	0.1
44220	Springfield, OH Metro Area	74.2	72.0	2.2	9.6	5.8	2.8	1.8	5.5	0.3
44300	State College, PA Metro Area	68.7	65.6	3.1	14.1	4.1	8.5	0.6	3.9	0.1
44420	Staunton-Waynesboro, VA Metro Area	75.5	72.3	3.3	5.9	6.3	6.5	1.8	3.9	0.0
44700	Stockton-Lodi, CA Metro Area	75.2	72.7	2.5	5.3	7.3	4.2	2.2	5.7	0.1
44940	Sumter, SC Metro Area	69.2	67.8	1.4	6.1	4.4	8.8	4.9	6.6	0.0
45060	Syracuse, NY Metro Area	66.9	64.4	2.5	10.7	8.2	7.0	1.9	5.3	0.1
45220	Tallahassee, FL Metro Area	58.1	54.6	3.5	7.4	9.0	18.9	1.9	4.6	0.2
45300	Tampa-St. Petersburg-Clearwater, FL Metro Area	76.5	71.0	5.5	6.6	7.2	2.4	2.1	5.2	0.2
45460	Terre Haute, IN Metro Area	73.1	71.2	1.9	9.1	5.1	6.9	1.1	4.6	0.0
45500	Texarkana, TX-AR Metro Area	70.3	69.2	1.1	7.9	5.6	4.9	5.4	5.8	0.0
45540	The Villages, FL Metro Area	70.7	67.0	3.7	4.6	13.6	3.3	0.4	6.7	0.6
45780	Toledo, OH Metro Area	72.0	70.1	2.0	10.5	6.3	5.3	1.1	4.7	0.1
45820	Topeka, KS Metro Area	66.4	63.6	2.8	8.7	8.2	8.8	3.0	4.8	0.1
45940	Trenton, NJ Metro Area	70.3	67.6	2.7	9.6	5.4	9.2	1.2	4.2	0.1
46060	Tucson, AZ Metro Area	68.0	64.6	3.4	7.6	7.1	6.2	4.3	6.6	0.2
46140	Tulsa, OK Metro Area	75.3	72.0	3.3	7.5	4.9	4.5	2.0	5.6	0.2
46220	Tuscaloosa, AL Metro Area	69.0	65.4	3.7	9.2	5.6	10.7	1.4	3.9	0.2
46340	Tyler, TX Metro Area	70.0	67.6	2.4	11.3	5.5	5.4	1.1	6.6	0.2
46520	Urban Honolulu, HI Metro Area	64.5	61.2	3.2	8.6	3.1	8.9	8.8	6.0	0.2
46540	Utica-Rome, NY Metro Area	62.7	59.2	3.5	13.1	9.1	7.2	2.3	5.4	0.1
46660	Valdosta, GA Metro Area	68.2	65.2	3.1	7.3	7.9	7.2	4.4	4.6	0.3
46700	Vallejo-Fairfield, CA Metro Area	66.6	64.7	1.9	7.7	8.8	5.9	4.4	6.4	0.2
47020	Victoria, TX Metro Area	71.8	69.5	2.3	5.9	6.9	7.2	1.7	6.3	0.2
47220	Vineland-Bridgeton, NJ Metro Area	70.8	68.8	2.0	6.8	8.2	9.6	1.4	3.1	0.0
47260	Virginia Beach-Norfolk-Newport News, VA-NC Metro Area	66.6	63.5	3.1	6.8	8.5	4.0	9.8	4.2	0.1
47300	Visalia-Porterville, CA Metro Area	72.9	70.1	2.8	6.0	8.6	6.0	0.7	5.4	0.4
47380	Waco, TX Metro Area	71.1	70.1	1.0	8.6	7.4	4.9	3.1	4.9	0.1
47460	Walla Walla, WA Metro Area	61.5	58.3	3.2	9.7	6.1	11.4	4.4	6.3	0.7
47580	Warner Robins, GA Metro Area	62.3	58.2	4.2	4.1	7.9	5.9	16.5	2.8	0.4
47900	**Washington-Arlington-Alexandria, DC-VA-MD-WV Metro Area**	62.3	58.9	3.4	10.0	6.6	2.4	13.7	4.9	0.1

Table D. Metropolitan Statistical Area—Labor Force, Employment, and Educational Data, 2015—*Continued*

CBSA code/ Division code	Metropolitan area, metropolitan division	Class of worker for civilian employed population age 16 and older								
		Private for-profit wage and salary workers			Private not-for-profit wage and salary workers	Government workers			Self-employed in own not incorporated business	Unpaid family workers
		Total private for-profit wage and salary workers	Employees of private companies	Self-employed in own incorporated business		Local government workers	State government workers	Federal government workers		
47900/43524	Silver Spring-Frederick-Rockville, MD Metro Division	63.0	58.6	4.4	10.3	6.2	2.4	11.9	6.0	0.1
47900/47894	Washington-Arlington-Alexandria, DC-VA-MD-WV Metro Division	62.1	59.0	3.1	10.0	6.6	2.4	14.2	4.6	0.1
47940	Waterloo-Cedar Falls, IA Metro Area	73.3	70.6	2.7	9.6	5.1	6.8	0.4	4.8	0.1
48060	Watertown-Fort Drum, NY Metro Area	57.2	55.3	2.0	10.0	8.8	6.1	10.5	7.1	0.2
48140	Wausau, WI Metro Area	76.4	74.1	2.3	8.5	5.5	2.5	0.7	6.1	0.3
48260	Weirton-Steubenville, WV-OH Metro Area	76.4	75.3	1.1	8.5	5.6	4.1	1.3	4.1	0.0
48300	Wenatchee, WA Metro Area	70.4	65.2	5.1	6.1	7.7	4.9	2.6	7.7	0.6
48540	Wheeling, WV-OH Metro Area	72.1	70.8	1.4	8.6	7.5	5.8	1.2	4.5	0.2
48620	Wichita, KS Metro Area	76.2	73.4	2.8	7.5	6.4	3.4	1.6	4.8	0.1
48660	Wichita Falls, TX Metro Area	70.4	68.2	2.2	6.7	6.0	7.6	3.6	5.8	0.0
48700	Williamsport, PA Metro Area	72.3	70.3	2.0	14.0	4.4	3.6	1.4	4.1	0.1
48900	Wilmington, NC Metro Area	74.4	68.4	6.0	6.6	5.0	6.3	1.1	6.7	0.0
49020	Winchester, VA-WV Metro Area	67.0	62.7	4.3	7.5	10.0	3.4	3.8	7.9	0.4
49180	Winston-Salem, NC Metro Area	72.5	69.7	2.8	9.5	6.0	4.5	1.4	6.0	0.1
49340	Worcester, MA-CT Metro Area	71.7	68.8	2.9	9.6	7.1	4.8	1.1	5.4	0.3
49420	Yakima, WA Metro Area	72.4	70.3	2.1	7.2	5.1	6.2	1.9	7.1	0.0
49620	York-Hanover, PA Metro Area	75.4	72.9	2.5	9.4	4.7	3.5	2.2	4.6	0.2
49660	Youngstown-Warren-Boardman, OH-PA Metro Area	76.3	72.8	3.5	7.5	5.2	3.7	1.4	5.8	0.2
49700	Yuba City, CA Metro Area	65.4	62.7	2.7	4.3	10.2	6.6	5.1	7.5	0.8
49740	Yuma, AZ Metro Area	68.0	65.9	2.1	7.7	10.1	3.9	6.7	3.5	0.1

Table D. Metropolitan Statistical Area—Labor Force, Employment, and Educational Data, 2015

CBSA code/ Division code	Metropolitan area, metropolitan division	Occupation for employed population age 16 and older					Industry for employed population age 16 and older			
		Management, business, science, and arts occupations	Service occupations	Sales and office occupations:	Natural resources, construction, and maintenance occupations	Production, transportation, and material moving occupations:	Agriculture, forestry, fishing and hunting, and mining	Construction	Manufacturing	Wholesale trade
10180	Abilene, TX Metro Area	30.6	21.9	23.4	10.9	13.3	3.7	6.0	5.1	2.3
10420	Akron, OH Metro Area	37.4	17.2	25.4	6.2	13.9	0.4	4.5	16.3	2.7
10500	Albany, GA Metro Area	35.3	16.2	23.2	9.0	16.2	1.9	3.4	11.9	2.4
10540	Albany, OR Metro Area	30.9	18.8	19.2	12.7	18.4	5.3	6.0	15.0	2.0
10580	Albany-Schenectady-Troy, NY Metro Area	42.1	17.4	25.2	6.7	8.6	0.7	5.5	6.9	2.0
10740	Albuquerque, NM Metro Area	38.2	21.0	23.9	9.3	7.7	1.4	7.0	4.0	2.8
10780	Alexandria, LA Metro Area	30.8	24.2	21.8	11.2	12.1	2.5	5.9	7.2	1.0
10900	Allentown-Bethlehem-Easton, PA-NJ Metro Area	34.7	17.7	23.6	7.5	16.4	0.7	5.2	13.7	2.9
11020	Altoona, PA Metro Area	34.0	17.3	27.2	7.5	14.1	1.3	6.1	11.4	2.9
11100	Amarillo, TX Metro Area	32.4	18.5	24.4	12.1	12.6	2.5	8.3	7.6	4.2
11180	Ames, IA Metro Area	48.7	16.9	20.0	5.6	8.9	1.3	3.5	10.8	1.7
11260	Anchorage, AK Metro Area	38.8	17.6	23.8	10.8	8.9	3.9	7.4	2.1	2.5
11460	Ann Arbor, MI Metro Area	52.9	15.1	19.1	4.9	8.0	0.6	3.5	10.1	1.5
11500	Anniston-Oxford-Jacksonville, AL Metro Area	28.0	15.5	25.9	11.0	19.7	0.9	5.8	17.7	2.2
11540	Appleton, WI Metro Area	34.2	14.3	24.0	9.1	18.4	1.4	7.6	22.5	2.9
11700	Asheville, NC Metro Area	38.4	17.8	20.6	11.0	12.2	1.3	7.4	10.6	2.1
12020	Athens-Clarke County, GA Metro Area	40.4	20.4	20.0	7.7	11.6	1.2	6.1	8.0	2.0
12060	Atlanta-Sandy Springs-Roswell, GA Metro Area	40.0	15.5	24.8	8.1	11.7	0.4	6.6	8.7	3.2
12100	Atlantic City-Hammonton, NJ Metro Area	30.2	29.1	24.0	8.3	8.4	0.4	6.5	3.9	2.0
12220	Auburn-Opelika, AL Metro Area	38.0	17.1	22.1	8.5	14.2	0.6	4.7	14.2	1.5
12260	Augusta-Richmond County, GA-SC Metro Area	34.0	15.8	26.8	10.9	12.5	1.1	8.0	11.6	1.7
12420	Austin-Round Rock, TX Metro Area	44.5	15.7	23.4	8.8	7.6	1.1	7.7	8.1	2.5
12540	Bakersfield, CA Metro Area	25.4	18.4	20.6	22.2	13.4	17.3	6.5	5.1	3.3
12580	Baltimore-Columbia-Towson, MD Metro Area	45.3	16.1	23.5	6.6	8.5	0.3	6.0	5.3	2.6
12620	Bangor, ME Metro Area	37.3	19.4	23.8	9.1	10.4	1.8	6.1	5.9	1.2
12700	Barnstable Town, MA Metro Area	36.3	20.4	23.5	11.4	8.4	1.4	9.0	3.8	1.7
12940	Baton Rouge, LA Metro Area	37.5	17.3	23.4	10.3	11.6	1.2	8.9	10.4	2.6
12980	Battle Creek, MI Metro Area	26.6	20.5	20.1	7.4	25.4	1.2	2.9	25.2	0.8
13020	Bay City, MI Metro Area	27.6	21.4	27.6	9.7	13.7	0.9	6.5	14.3	3.0
13140	Beaumont-Port Arthur, TX Metro Area	28.7	16.6	23.7	15.2	15.9	2.4	11.4	13.4	3.1
13220	Beckley, WV Metro Area	32.2	23.1	21.6	13.5	9.7	6.7	8.1	4.5	2.1
13380	Bellingham, WA Metro Area	34.2	18.1	24.0	9.7	14.0	3.8	5.7	10.2	2.1
13460	Bend-Redmond, OR Metro Area	39.4	17.8	23.4	10.8	8.6	2.5	9.1	7.6	1.6
13740	Billings, MT Metro Area	34.9	19.7	22.5	13.4	9.5	3.9	9.6	4.9	2.9
13780	Binghamton, NY Metro Area	36.8	19.2	23.7	8.0	12.3	1.5	4.7	9.7	2.7
13820	Birmingham-Hoover, AL Metro Area	37.1	16.3	25.1	8.8	12.8	1.4	6.0	10.0	3.4
13900	Bismarck, ND Metro Area	37.8	16.9	21.4	12.8	11.2	5.0	9.3	4.9	3.0
13980	Blacksburg-Christiansburg-Radford, VA Metro Area	42.2	16.7	20.5	7.1	13.5	1.6	4.5	14.0	0.9
14010	Bloomington, IL Metro Area	42.4	18.9	25.7	4.3	8.7	1.4	3.9	6.6	2.1
14020	Bloomington, IN Metro Area	38.7	23.2	21.1	5.8	11.1	0.6	3.5	11.2	2.1
14100	Bloomsburg-Berwick, PA Metro Area	36.7	19.3	20.4	6.1	17.6	1.6	3.9	13.4	1.5
14260	Boise City, ID Metro Area	37.4	18.6	24.1	9.5	10.4	3.1	6.6	9.6	2.7
14460	**Boston-Cambridge-Newton, MA-NH Metro Area**	47.8	16.9	21.1	6.2	7.9	0.3	5.2	8.7	2.1
14460/14454	*Boston, MA Metro Division*	45.5	18.5	22.4	6.1	7.5	0.2	5.1	6.0	2.2
14460/15764	*Cambridge-Newton-Framingham, MA Metro Division*	50.7	16.1	19.6	6.1	7.5	0.2	5.2	10.0	2.0
14460/40484	*Rockingham County-Strafford County, NH Metro Division*	42.7	14.6	23.0	7.6	12.1	0.7	5.6	13.6	2.7
14500	Boulder, CO Metro Area	52.6	15.9	21.1	4.1	6.3	1.0	4.4	9.7	2.2
14540	Bowling Green, KY Metro Area	32.6	17.9	22.2	9.0	18.4	2.0	8.0	17.5	2.1
14740	Bremerton-Silverdale, WA Metro Area	37.2	18.9	21.4	11.5	11.0	0.7	7.1	10.9	1.7
14860	Bridgeport-Stamford-Norwalk, CT Metro Area	45.9	16.9	22.5	7.9	6.9	0.3	6.9	7.7	2.9
15180	Brownsville-Harlingen, TX Metro Area	27.0	26.3	24.6	11.5	10.6	2.1	7.5	5.4	2.6
15260	Brunswick, GA Metro Area	32.5	18.9	26.8	8.5	13.3	0.8	6.7	9.1	1.7
15380	Buffalo-Cheektowaga-Niagara Falls, NY Metro Area	37.0	18.7	25.7	7.0	11.6	0.3	5.4	10.7	2.9
15500	Burlington, NC Metro Area	29.7	19.4	24.5	11.1	15.3	0.8	6.8	16.5	2.3
15540	Burlington-South Burlington, VT Metro Area	45.1	15.8	21.9	7.8	9.3	1.6	6.0	10.7	2.3
15680	California-Lexington Park, MD Metro Area	49.1	15.8	19.8	8.5	6.7	1.4	6.3	3.8	1.1
15940	Canton-Massillon, OH Metro Area	31.9	18.4	22.6	9.7	17.4	2.0	6.7	16.8	3.8
15980	Cape Coral-Fort Myers, FL Metro Area	29.0	21.7	28.3	12.0	9.0	0.9	11.2	4.1	2.0

Table D. Metropolitan Statistical Area—Labor Force, Employment, and Educational Data, 2015—*Continued*

		Occupation for employed population age 16 and older					Industry for employed population age 16 and older			
CBSA code/ Division code	Metropolitan area, metropolitan division	Management, business, science, and arts occupations	Service occupations	Sales and office occupations:	Natural resources, construction, and maintenance occupations	Production, transportation, and material moving occupations:	Agriculture, forestry, fishing and hunting, and mining	Construction	Manufacturing	Wholesale trade
16020	Cape Girardeau, MO-IL Metro Area	36.0	16.8	24.8	8.6	13.8	1.1	6.4	14.0	2.6
16060	Carbondale-Marion, IL Metro Area	37.2	19.7	22.5	8.3	12.2	2.8	6.1	8.3	1.2
16180	Carson City, NV Metro Area	25.8	22.1	25.1	11.4	15.7	0.3	6.1	14.6	0.7
16220	Casper, WY Metro Area	28.0	17.8	26.3	15.9	12.1	9.9	6.9	5.6	3.2
16300	Cedar Rapids, IA Metro Area	37.2	15.9	21.4	9.4	16.0	1.5	6.4	16.3	2.6
16540	Chambersburg-Waynesboro, PA Metro Area	29.2	16.2	26.2	10.2	18.2	2.5	5.9	16.4	2.8
16580	Champaign-Urbana, IL Metro Area	44.9	17.2	19.4	6.3	12.3	1.2	4.3	10.0	2.6
16620	Charleston, WV Metro Area	36.7	19.1	25.9	8.0	10.4	3.4	4.7	4.7	1.9
16700	Charleston-North Charleston, SC Metro Area	38.0	17.8	24.2	9.3	10.8	0.4	6.6	8.8	2.6
16740	Charlotte-Concord-Gastonia, NC-SC Metro Area	38.3	15.5	24.3	8.7	13.2	0.5	6.8	12.0	3.4
16820	Charlottesville, VA Metro Area	47.9	17.2	20.6	7.5	6.8	1.4	5.7	4.8	1.4
16860	Chattanooga, TN-GA Metro Area	34.2	16.2	26.7	7.5	15.4	0.6	5.1	14.6	2.8
16940	Cheyenne, WY Metro Area	37.3	13.0	24.6	10.9	14.2	6.5	4.7	4.4	1.6
16980	**Chicago-Naperville-Elgin, IL-IN-WI Metro Area**	38.6	17.1	24.0	6.9	13.4	0.4	5.4	12.1	3.3
16980/16974	*Chicago-Naperville-Arlington Heights, IL Metro Division*	39.5	17.2	24.1	6.4	12.8	0.3	5.1	10.7	3.2
16980/20994	*Elgin, IL Metro Division*	34.1	17.1	23.4	9.3	16.0	1.1	6.6	15.6	3.8
16980/23844	*Gary, IN Metro Division*	31.4	17.3	22.9	10.0	18.4	0.8	6.9	16.9	2.1
16980/29404	*Lake County-Kenosha County, IL-WI Metro Division*	39.7	16.2	24.2	7.1	12.8	0.4	5.1	17.3	4.7
17020	Chico, CA Metro Area	37.3	22.0	23.8	8.6	8.3	4.5	5.8	6.0	1.4
17140	Cincinnati, OH-KY-IN Metro Area	39.6	16.2	24.1	7.0	13.1	0.5	5.1	13.7	3.0
17300	Clarksville, TN-KY Metro Area	32.6	15.6	24.4	10.0	17.5	1.4	5.2	14.3	1.6
17420	Cleveland, TN Metro Area	31.9	17.2	20.2	10.5	20.2	0.6	7.3	19.7	2.3
17460	Cleveland-Elyria, OH Metro Area	37.5	17.7	24.6	6.7	13.6	0.4	4.6	14.7	2.9
17660	Coeur d'Alene, ID Metro Area	33.1	19.3	25.7	9.8	12.0	1.6	8.7	8.1	3.1
17780	College Station-Bryan, TX Metro Area	39.9	14.8	26.3	10.6	8.4	3.7	7.0	6.0	2.6
17820	Colorado Springs, CO Metro Area	39.4	18.3	25.2	9.2	8.0	0.9	6.9	5.6	1.7
17860	Columbia, MO Metro Area	48.3	13.3	25.4	5.3	7.7	0.8	4.2	6.5	1.9
17900	Columbia, SC Metro Area	37.7	17.7	25.2	7.7	11.7	0.9	6.0	9.4	2.4
17980	Columbus, GA-AL Metro Area	32.6	18.4	25.2	8.4	15.4	0.7	5.1	12.5	1.5
18020	Columbus, IN Metro Area	38.5	12.5	21.7	7.9	19.4	0.7	6.0	37.4	1.8
18140	Columbus, OH Metro Area	41.5	16.2	24.2	6.0	12.1	0.5	4.6	8.9	2.9
18580	Corpus Christi, TX Metro Area	28.7	21.9	23.0	13.9	12.5	4.0	9.6	7.2	2.6
18700	Corvallis, OR Metro Area	52.6	17.2	17.0	5.5	7.6	3.4	4.5	9.0	0.9
18880	Crestview-Fort Walton Beach-Destin, FL Metro Area	36.2	23.0	23.8	8.6	8.3	0.6	7.7	4.0	2.0
19060	Cumberland, MD-WV Metro Area	27.2	21.9	26.5	9.7	14.8	1.0	5.9	10.4	2.4
19100	**Dallas-Fort Worth-Arlington, TX Metro Area**	38.1	15.4	25.1	9.4	12.0	1.3	7.6	9.4	3.2
19100/19124	*Dallas-Plano-Irving, TX Metro Division*	39.5	15.5	24.9	9.1	11.0	1.0	7.8	8.9	3.1
19100/23104	*Fort Worth-Arlington, TX Metro Division*	35.4	15.2	25.6	9.9	14.0	2.1	7.2	10.3	3.4
19140	Dalton, GA Metro Area	18.2	9.5	24.3	10.6	37.5	0.6	5.4	42.5	3.9
19180	Danville, IL Metro Area	25.8	19.4	23.0	11.3	20.5	2.1	5.7	16.0	4.2
19300	Daphne-Fairhope-Foley, AL Metro Area	32.7	21.2	28.1	8.1	9.9	0.9	7.6	8.7	2.9
19340	Davenport-Moline-Rock Island, IA-IL Metro Area	31.8	18.6	22.0	9.3	18.3	1.3	6.8	19.0	2.5
19380	Dayton, OH Metro Area	37.4	18.2	23.0	7.2	14.2	0.4	5.0	14.2	2.1
19460	Decatur, AL Metro Area	30.3	12.9	24.2	13.4	19.2	1.6	9.1	19.8	2.0
19500	Decatur, IL Metro Area	34.3	20.0	21.9	8.9	14.9	2.7	6.5	16.1	2.4
19660	Deltona-Daytona Beach-Ormond Beach, FL Metro Area	32.0	21.1	27.0	10.9	9.1	0.7	7.6	6.6	2.3
19740	Denver-Aurora-Lakewood, CO Metro Area	42.9	15.6	24.2	8.7	8.7	1.7	8.2	6.7	2.9
19780	Des Moines-West Des Moines, IA Metro Area	39.8	15.5	24.9	8.3	11.5	1.5	7.0	9.0	2.6
19820	**Detroit-Warren-Dearborn, MI Metro Area**	37.6	17.5	23.5	6.9	14.5	0.3	4.8	18.6	2.6
19820/19804	*Detroit-Dearborn-Livonia, MI Metro Division*	31.4	19.6	24.2	7.0	17.9	0.3	4.0	17.1	2.4
19820/47664	*Warren-Troy-Farmington Hills, MI Metro Division*	41.2	16.2	23.1	6.8	12.6	0.4	5.2	19.4	2.7
20020	Dothan, AL Metro Area	31.6	19.3	22.9	10.7	15.5	2.9	5.9	10.5	3.8

Table D. Metropolitan Statistical Area—Labor Force, Employment, and Educational Data, 2015—*Continued*

		Occupation for employed population age 16 and older					Industry for employed population age 16 and older			
CBSA code/ Division code	Metropolitan area, metropolitan division	Management, business, science, and arts occupations	Service occupations	Sales and office occupations:	Natural resources, construction, and maintenance occupations	Production, transportation, and material moving occupations:	Agriculture, forestry, fishing and hunting, and mining	Construction	Manufacturing	Wholesale trade
20100	Dover, DE Metro Area	32.0	23.0	21.8	10.2	12.8	0.9	6.3	8.0	2.1
20220	Dubuque, IA Metro Area	37.5	15.9	25.2	7.0	14.4	2.1	5.1	17.0	4.0
20260	Duluth, MN-WI Metro Area	34.3	21.2	22.3	8.7	13.5	2.3	5.9	7.7	2.6
20500	Durham-Chapel Hill, NC Metro Area	48.0	16.3	17.9	8.7	9.0	0.9	6.7	8.5	1.2
20700	East Stroudsburg, PA Metro Area	31.2	22.8	24.3	10.7	11.0	1.3	6.5	8.5	2.3
20740	Eau Claire, WI Metro Area	34.9	15.1	24.8	7.6	17.6	2.5	4.4	15.7	2.4
20940	El Centro, CA Metro Area	24.6	25.3	26.0	14.1	10.0	8.6	6.8	2.7	1.8
21060	Elizabethtown-Fort Knox, KY Metro Area	26.0	18.8	24.0	11.1	20.2	1.1	7.2	12.9	2.4
21140	Elkhart-Goshen, IN Metro Area	25.5	14.2	20.4	8.5	31.4	0.8	4.2	37.3	1.9
21300	Elmira, NY Metro Area	34.2	21.9	21.6	8.9	13.4	1.2	5.0	15.6	3.5
21340	El Paso, TX Metro Area	29.0	20.4	27.8	9.1	13.7	1.2	5.3	6.8	2.7
21500	Erie, PA Metro Area	34.0	19.7	23.3	6.2	16.8	1.2	3.9	18.0	2.1
21660	Eugene, OR Metro Area	35.6	19.8	23.7	8.4	12.5	2.2	5.5	10.6	2.6
21780	Evansville, IN-KY Metro Area	31.0	17.5	24.2	8.3	19.1	1.7	6.3	16.7	3.8
21820	Fairbanks, AK Metro Area	31.9	18.0	25.4	12.3	12.4	3.4	9.1	1.1	1.4
22020	Fargo, ND-MN Metro Area	36.2	17.9	23.4	10.1	12.4	2.3	7.7	9.5	4.5
22140	Farmington, NM Metro Area	27.0	20.4	24.3	17.1	11.2	11.4	9.2	3.0	3.9
22180	Fayetteville, NC Metro Area	33.0	19.8	26.9	9.1	11.2	0.8	5.4	8.1	1.4
22220	Fayetteville-Springdale-Rogers, AR-MO Metro Area	35.7	13.5	24.7	10.3	15.8	2.2	6.8	15.7	2.7
22380	Flagstaff, AZ Metro Area	37.3	24.4	21.4	6.8	10.0	1.1	3.8	7.3	0.4
22420	Flint, MI Metro Area	31.4	19.2	23.7	8.5	17.3	0.5	5.6	16.5	2.3
22500	Florence, SC Metro Area	33.3	17.8	24.9	7.1	16.9	0.6	4.1	16.0	3.8
22520	Florence-Muscle Shoals, AL Metro Area	29.6	16.3	25.8	8.9	19.4	0.9	5.4	15.2	3.8
22540	Fond du Lac, WI Metro Area	31.4	17.5	20.6	9.7	20.9	4.2	6.6	20.9	1.6
22660	Fort Collins, CO Metro Area	44.6	17.0	22.5	7.7	8.3	2.4	7.4	10.5	2.1
22900	Fort Smith, AR-OK Metro Area	29.3	19.6	22.4	11.2	17.5	3.2	5.9	15.9	3.1
23060	Fort Wayne, IN Metro Area	33.9	16.5	21.9	7.9	19.7	0.8	5.8	20.4	3.0
23420	Fresno, CA Metro Area	28.8	19.9	22.5	15.3	13.6	10.7	5.4	7.7	3.4
23460	Gadsden, AL Metro Area	30.4	16.6	20.2	9.6	23.2	1.1	7.0	20.2	2.9
23540	Gainesville, FL Metro Area	46.9	19.3	21.5	5.6	6.7	2.1	3.7	3.3	1.1
23580	Gainesville, GA Metro Area	28.8	13.6	24.2	10.4	23.0	2.0	7.6	20.8	4.8
23900	Gettysburg, PA Metro Area	29.6	18.7	20.6	9.4	21.7	2.1	6.5	19.0	2.0
24020	Glens Falls, NY Metro Area	32.2	21.7	22.5	8.5	15.1	2.2	7.3	11.0	1.4
24140	Goldsboro, NC Metro Area	30.2	15.6	26.1	11.2	16.9	1.8	6.3	17.2	3.2
24220	Grand Forks, ND-MN Metro Area	35.5	18.2	24.2	10.7	11.4	5.3	7.1	6.9	3.3
24260	Grand Island, NE Metro Area	28.5	18.4	23.4	10.7	19.1	7.3	6.1	17.3	4.1
24300	Grand Junction, CO Metro Area	35.6	18.0	24.7	10.6	11.1	6.5	7.3	4.3	2.6
24340	Grand Rapids-Wyoming, MI Metro Area	33.4	16.2	23.2	8.1	19.2	1.4	5.3	21.0	4.0
24420	Grants Pass, OR Metro Area	26.6	21.7	21.9	13.3	16.5	0.9	7.5	10.3	3.3
24500	Great Falls, MT Metro Area	36.8	21.0	21.4	10.4	10.5	4.9	7.9	4.1	1.9
24540	Greeley, CO Metro Area	33.7	15.7	23.6	13.2	13.9	7.9	8.5	10.7	3.0
24580	Green Bay, WI Metro Area	32.5	15.0	23.6	10.3	18.6	2.1	6.8	21.0	2.3
24660	Greensboro-High Point, NC Metro Area	33.9	17.6	23.7	8.7	16.1	0.7	6.5	14.9	3.4
24780	Greenville, NC Metro Area	36.0	22.6	21.9	8.9	10.6	1.3	6.4	11.1	1.7
24860	Greenville-Anderson-Mauldin, SC Metro Area	34.4	17.7	23.5	8.5	15.9	0.6	5.9	19.6	2.5
25060	Gulfport-Biloxi-Pascagoula, MS Metro Area	29.7	21.1	22.7	14.1	12.4	0.8	9.7	10.7	1.9
25180	Hagerstown-Martinsburg, MD-WV Metro Area	32.4	19.3	23.1	9.3	15.8	0.7	7.5	8.8	2.9
25220	Hammond, LA Metro Area	27.8	22.0	28.5	11.2	10.5	1.6	8.5	5.3	2.9
25260	Hanford-Corcoran, CA Metro Area	26.9	24.9	19.0	17.9	11.3	14.4	3.5	6.2	1.7
25420	Harrisburg-Carlisle, PA Metro Area	38.0	16.1	26.6	6.9	12.4	1.1	4.7	8.7	2.8
25500	Harrisonburg, VA Metro Area	35.7	19.1	21.2	11.7	12.3	3.5	6.5	9.7	3.1
25540	Hartford-West Hartford-East Hartford, CT Metro Area	43.6	16.0	23.9	6.6	9.9	0.4	5.3	11.4	2.5
25620	Hattiesburg, MS Metro Area	34.3	13.8	30.3	9.7	12.0	1.8	6.5	8.3	2.8
25860	Hickory-Lenoir-Morganton, NC Metro Area	30.0	15.5	20.7	10.0	23.8	0.8	6.4	27.3	3.6
25940	Hilton Head Island-Bluffton-Beaufort, SC Metro Area	34.1	23.1	23.6	11.1	8.1	1.1	8.5	4.4	1.6
25980	Hinesville, GA Metro Area	23.6	23.0	26.1	12.6	14.8	0.5	8.7	7.9	0.9
26140	Homosassa Springs, FL Metro Area	30.6	22.1	23.4	12.8	11.1	2.2	8.4	4.6	1.7
26300	Hot Springs, AR Metro Area	28.0	23.7	24.3	14.0	10.0	1.2	10.4	8.2	1.3
26380	Houma-Thibodaux, LA Metro Area	26.8	15.7	24.6	15.3	17.5	10.1	9.7	9.4	2.4
26420	Houston-The Woodlands-Sugar Land, TX Metro Area	37.1	16.4	23.0	10.9	12.6	4.0	9.4	9.9	3.5
26580	Huntington-Ashland, WV-KY-OH Metro Area	33.5	19.3	24.3	9.0	14.0	1.0	5.3	10.5	2.9
26620	Huntsville, AL Metro Area	45.1	15.1	22.1	7.5	10.2	0.8	4.8	11.3	2.0

Table D. Metropolitan Statistical Area—Labor Force, Employment, and Educational Data, 2015—*Continued*

CBSA code/ Division code	Metropolitan area, metropolitan division	Occupation for employed population age 16 and older					Industry for employed population age 16 and older			
		Management, business, science, and arts occupations	Service occupations	Sales and office occupations:	Natural resources, construction, and maintenance occupations	Production, transportation, and material moving occupations:	Agriculture, forestry, fishing and hunting, and mining	Construction	Manufacturing	Wholesale trade
26820	Idaho Falls, ID Metro Area	36.4	16.2	22.7	11.4	13.3	5.6	6.2	9.1	3.1
26900	Indianapolis-Carmel-Anderson, IN Metro Area	37.8	15.8	25.3	7.7	13.4	0.6	5.8	12.6	3.2
26980	Iowa City, IA Metro Area	41.2	19.1	20.3	7.1	12.3	1.8	5.0	8.4	0.9
27060	Ithaca, NY Metro Area	55.0	16.3	16.4	5.6	6.7	1.6	2.9	6.0	0.3
27100	Jackson, MI Metro Area	28.6	20.7	23.0	9.2	18.6	1.5	5.5	21.2	2.5
27140	Jackson, MS Metro Area	36.2	18.0	23.6	8.8	13.3	1.3	6.5	10.4	2.3
27180	Jackson, TN Metro Area	34.4	17.0	23.8	9.8	15.0	1.3	5.1	14.2	2.1
27260	Jacksonville, FL Metro Area	37.2	17.1	27.4	8.1	10.2	0.5	5.8	7.1	3.0
27340	Jacksonville, NC Metro Area	27.2	24.0	27.8	12.4	8.6	0.2	7.4	4.1	1.8
27500	Janesville-Beloit, WI Metro Area	33.1	17.0	20.5	9.0	20.3	1.8	6.0	22.3	2.7
27620	Jefferson City, MO Metro Area	35.7	15.2	25.6	9.8	13.6	3.0	6.6	9.8	1.8
27740	Johnson City, TN Metro Area	35.5	21.4	21.8	8.6	12.7	1.2	5.4	13.6	1.3
27780	Johnstown, PA Metro Area	31.6	19.4	22.8	9.2	16.9	2.0	5.1	8.6	3.1
27860	Jonesboro, AR Metro Area	31.0	17.4	22.3	12.3	17.0	2.8	7.1	16.1	3.8
27900	Joplin, MO Metro Area	31.0	17.8	25.6	8.8	16.7	1.4	5.3	15.3	1.4
27980	Kahului-Wailuku-Lahaina, HI Metro Area	31.3	27.3	22.9	10.0	8.4	2.3	7.7	1.8	3.0
28020	Kalamazoo-Portage, MI Metro Area	38.6	19.0	22.8	7.5	12.1	1.7	4.5	16.5	2.1
28100	Kankakee, IL Metro Area	31.8	15.6	23.7	10.4	18.6	0.7	6.0	15.4	2.0
28140	Kansas City, MO-KS Metro Area	39.1	16.5	24.3	7.9	12.2	0.8	6.3	9.6	3.3
28420	Kennewick-Richland, WA Metro Area	34.5	18.0	18.1	15.7	13.6	8.7	7.5	7.6	1.8
28660	Killeen-Temple, TX Metro Area	31.8	20.5	25.1	9.4	13.3	1.3	6.4	7.2	2.6
28700	Kingsport-Bristol-Bristol, TN-VA Metro Area	31.8	18.1	24.9	9.5	15.7	1.3	6.1	16.5	3.3
28740	Kingston, NY Metro Area	37.6	18.5	24.2	9.7	10.0	1.2	7.9	6.5	3.1
28940	Knoxville, TN Metro Area	35.9	17.0	24.9	9.1	13.1	0.7	5.5	10.4	2.5
29020	Kokomo, IN Metro Area	30.3	16.9	20.4	8.2	24.2	1.3	4.1	30.6	2.1
29100	La Crosse-Onalaska, WI-MN Metro Area	34.8	21.0	23.6	7.2	13.5	1.3	4.9	11.9	3.4
29180	Lafayette, LA Metro Area	32.7	20.4	24.0	12.2	10.8	10.6	6.3	7.0	2.8
29200	Lafayette-West Lafayette, IN Metro Area	35.4	17.5	19.6	9.5	18.1	1.6	5.3	18.9	2.2
29340	Lake Charles, LA Metro Area	30.8	18.9	21.3	13.4	15.7	2.9	8.0	12.6	1.7
29420	Lake Havasu City-Kingman, AZ Metro Area	22.3	23.9	27.8	10.0	16.0	0.7	5.9	5.3	2.2
29460	Lakeland-Winter Haven, FL Metro Area	29.0	21.1	27.6	9.8	12.4	2.2	7.0	5.4	3.6
29540	Lancaster, PA Metro Area	32.7	16.2	22.8	11.1	17.3	3.4	7.9	16.2	3.8
29620	Lansing-East Lansing, MI Metro Area	38.0	18.5	23.7	7.3	12.5	1.0	4.1	11.3	2.0
29700	Laredo, TX Metro Area	28.7	22.4	27.5	8.8	12.6	3.0	5.8	1.7	3.9
29740	Las Cruces, NM Metro Area	30.6	24.4	26.3	11.0	7.6	2.7	7.2	3.6	1.9
29820	Las Vegas-Henderson-Paradise, NV Metro Area	26.4	29.7	26.3	8.1	9.5	0.3	6.1	3.6	1.8
29940	Lawrence, KS Metro Area	44.1	16.9	23.9	6.0	9.1	1.6	4.8	5.8	2.4
30020	Lawton, OK Metro Area	35.1	19.1	21.9	11.8	12.1	2.0	6.1	7.3	0.8
30140	Lebanon, PA Metro Area	27.8	22.2	22.7	9.1	18.2	2.2	6.2	14.3	2.7
30300	Lewiston, ID-WA Metro Area	33.4	19.4	25.4	8.1	13.7	2.6	4.6	16.1	4.3
30340	Lewiston-Auburn, ME Metro Area	33.6	17.9	24.2	10.0	14.2	1.5	6.5	10.7	2.8
30460	Lexington-Fayette, KY Metro Area	38.3	19.4	23.5	7.6	11.3	3.2	5.0	11.7	2.0
30620	Lima, OH Metro Area	30.1	18.6	20.5	7.5	23.3	0.8	4.6	21.5	3.6
30700	Lincoln, NE Metro Area	39.4	17.4	23.1	9.1	11.0	1.3	7.0	9.4	2.4
30780	Little Rock-North Little Rock-Conway, AR Metro Area	37.9	15.3	26.1	8.4	12.2	1.1	5.6	8.7	2.4
30860	Logan, UT-ID Metro Area	36.7	14.7	23.5	9.2	15.9	3.8	5.6	17.4	1.5
30980	Longview, TX Metro Area	27.5	19.0	24.1	11.9	17.6	6.7	5.1	12.4	1.9
31020	Longview, WA Metro Area	27.2	17.6	22.3	13.8	19.0	2.6	8.5	14.7	2.2
31080	**Los Angeles-Long Beach-Anaheim, CA Metro Area**	37.6	18.4	24.1	7.4	12.5	0.6	5.8	10.7	3.4
31080/11244	Anaheim-Santa Ana-Irvine, CA Metro Division	40.9	17.3	24.1	6.9	10.8	0.6	6.0	13.4	3.5
31080/31084	Los Angeles-Long Beach-Glendale, CA Metro Division	36.5	18.7	24.1	7.6	13.0	0.5	5.8	9.8	3.4
31140	Louisville/Jefferson County, KY-IN Metro Area	36.2	15.3	24.3	7.9	16.3	1.1	5.4	13.9	2.9
31180	Lubbock, TX Metro Area	33.3	20.4	24.9	10.4	11.2	2.9	7.3	6.3	2.8
31340	Lynchburg, VA Metro Area	35.3	19.8	22.6	9.0	13.4	1.3	5.6	12.8	2.2
31420	Macon, GA Metro Area	37.2	15.6	25.6	7.7	14.0	0.9	4.5	9.0	2.2
31460	Madera, CA Metro Area	22.9	17.8	20.1	24.3	14.8	19.0	4.6	12.1	2.1
31540	Madison, WI Metro Area	46.5	16.1	21.2	6.8	9.5	1.7	5.0	9.9	2.4
31700	Manchester-Nashua, NH Metro Area	40.3	15.6	25.0	8.1	11.0	0.6	5.9	13.7	3.2
31740	Manhattan, KS Metro Area	38.2	21.5	23.4	9.0	7.9	2.8	8.0	6.3	1.3
31860	Mankato-North Mankato, MN Metro Area	36.5	18.7	23.1	8.3	13.4	2.4	5.3	14.3	2.4

Table D. Metropolitan Statistical Area—Labor Force, Employment, and Educational Data, 2015—*Continued*

CBSA code/ Division code	Metropolitan area, metropolitan division	Occupation for employed population age 16 and older					Industry for employed population age 16 and older			
		Management, business, science, and arts occupations	Service occupations	Sales and office occupations:	Natural resources, construction, and maintenance occupations	Production, transportation, and material moving occupations:	Agriculture, forestry, fishing and hunting, and mining	Construction	Manufacturing	Wholesale trade
31900	Mansfield, OH Metro Area	24.3	21.2	22.9	8.7	22.8	1.4	4.7	19.9	1.7
32580	McAllen-Edinburg-Mission, TX Metro Area	26.4	23.7	26.1	12.8	11.1	4.2	7.8	4.5	3.6
32780	Medford, OR Metro Area	32.5	20.9	25.2	10.0	11.4	4.1	6.2	9.5	1.4
32820	Memphis, TN-MS-AR Metro Area	33.4	16.9	25.2	7.9	16.5	0.5	5.3	9.5	3.8
32900	Merced, CA Metro Area	23.0	20.2	20.0	21.7	15.1	15.2	7.3	11.5	2.5
33100	**Miami-Fort Lauderdale-West Palm Beach, FL Metro Area**	34.0	20.7	27.1	9.1	9.1	0.7	7.4	4.4	3.5
33100/22744	*Fort Lauderdale-Pompano Beach-Deerfield Beach, FL Metro Division*	35.3	19.9	27.1	8.7	9.0	0.4	6.5	4.7	3.4
33100/33124	*Miami-Miami Beach-Kendall, FL Metro Division*	31.7	21.1	27.5	9.7	10.0	0.8	7.8	4.3	3.7
33100/48424	*West Palm Beach-Boca Raton-Delray Beach, FL Metro Division*	36.6	20.9	26.3	8.8	7.4	1.1	7.7	4.0	3.1
33140	Michigan City-La Porte, IN Metro Area	24.4	18.1	24.0	11.8	21.7	1.5	5.3	22.8	1.9
33220	Midland, MI Metro Area	40.4	16.0	21.1	10.0	12.6	0.7	8.3	24.6	1.5
33260	Midland, TX Metro Area	32.2	14.6	24.6	17.3	11.3	20.9	6.3	4.8	2.8
33340	Milwaukee-Waukesha-West Allis, WI Metro Area	39.0	17.5	23.2	6.3	14.0	0.6	4.5	17.2	3.0
33460	Minneapolis-St. Paul-Bloomington, MN-WI Metro Area	43.3	15.5	23.0	6.8	11.4	0.8	5.6	13.2	3.0
33540	Missoula, MT Metro Area	41.4	20.4	23.3	7.3	7.6	2.2	5.8	2.9	2.4
33660	Mobile, AL Metro Area	34.3	17.1	22.2	10.7	15.6	1.0	7.0	13.3	2.6
33700	Modesto, CA Metro Area	27.3	17.6	24.5	13.7	16.8	6.0	6.7	12.1	5.0
33740	Monroe, LA Metro Area	34.5	17.0	26.0	9.9	12.6	2.2	7.3	6.7	2.3
33780	Monroe, MI Metro Area	31.0	17.3	21.1	10.2	20.4	1.9	5.8	22.4	2.0
33860	Montgomery, AL Metro Area	35.8	18.5	23.5	7.4	14.7	0.8	5.2	12.7	2.2
34060	Morgantown, WV Metro Area	44.4	16.6	20.7	10.1	8.2	4.6	5.5	6.9	1.4
34100	Morristown, TN Metro Area	25.4	17.6	21.0	10.9	25.2	2.1	6.3	25.0	2.5
34580	Mount Vernon-Anacortes, WA Metro Area	31.0	19.5	21.4	14.2	13.9	4.7	8.8	12.6	4.5
34620	Muncie, IN Metro Area	30.2	24.6	20.9	8.6	15.8	0.9	4.9	11.0	2.4
34740	Muskegon, MI Metro Area	26.3	22.7	20.7	6.7	23.6	0.7	5.6	26.8	2.0
34820	Myrtle Beach-Conway-North Myrtle Beach, SC-NC Metro Area	28.5	23.1	29.2	10.9	8.3	0.8	10.2	5.8	1.7
34900	Napa, CA Metro Area	34.6	21.5	19.7	13.8	10.4	7.2	6.8	12.7	3.5
34940	Naples-Immokalee-Marco Island, FL Metro Area	31.1	23.3	23.6	12.7	9.3	3.9	10.8	4.6	2.2
34980	Nashville-Davidson--Murfreesboro--Franklin, TN Metro Area	38.8	15.9	24.5	8.1	12.8	0.6	6.0	10.4	3.0
35100	New Bern, NC Metro Area	31.2	17.7	22.8	14.0	14.4	2.4	6.5	11.0	3.2
35300	New Haven-Milford, CT Metro Area	40.1	16.8	25.1	7.3	10.6	0.2	5.8	10.7	2.8
35380	New Orleans-Metairie, LA Metro Area	36.5	19.4	23.6	10.9	9.6	1.7	8.3	6.0	2.8
35620	**New York-Newark-Jersey City, NY-NJ-PA Metro Area**	41.5	19.2	23.4	6.9	9.0	0.2	5.7	5.5	2.9
35620/20524	*Dutchess County-Putnam County, NY Metro Division*	39.3	19.6	24.5	8.6	8.0	0.6	7.7	6.9	2.1
35620/35004	*Nassau County-Suffolk County, NY Metro Division*	41.3	16.8	25.3	8.3	8.3	0.3	6.7	5.7	3.2
35620/35084	*Newark, NJ-PA Metro Division*	42.6	17.1	23.8	6.6	9.9	0.3	5.4	8.7	3.3
35620/35614	*New York-Jersey City-White Plains, NY-NJ Metro Division*	41.3	20.1	22.9	6.6	9.1	0.1	5.5	4.9	2.8
35660	Niles-Benton Harbor, MI Metro Area	33.5	17.6	24.2	9.0	15.6	1.0	5.2	20.6	2.2
35840	North Port-Sarasota-Bradenton, FL Metro Area	34.6	20.0	26.5	9.5	9.4	0.6	8.0	7.1	2.5
35980	Norwich-New London, CT Metro Area	38.5	22.5	21.5	8.2	9.1	0.5	5.2	11.4	1.6
36100	Ocala, FL Metro Area	28.3	22.6	27.1	9.7	12.4	2.6	6.8	6.7	2.6
36140	Ocean City, NJ Metro Area	37.4	20.4	23.1	11.3	7.8	0.9	9.8	3.6	2.2
36220	Odessa, TX Metro Area	24.0	15.2	26.9	16.3	17.6	14.8	9.9	5.4	4.6
36260	Ogden-Clearfield, UT Metro Area	36.6	13.2	26.0	8.1	16.0	1.2	6.5	14.6	3.0
36420	Oklahoma City, OK Metro Area	36.9	17.6	24.2	10.9	10.4	4.1	7.9	7.2	2.6
36500	Olympia-Tumwater, WA Metro Area	41.8	19.3	20.3	7.9	10.7	2.1	6.8	5.6	1.7
36540	Omaha-Council Bluffs, NE-IA Metro Area	39.2	16.2	24.8	8.5	11.2	1.6	6.9	8.5	3.2
36740	Orlando-Kissimmee-Sanford, FL Metro Area	36.0	20.4	27.3	7.1	9.3	0.4	6.2	4.7	2.7
36780	Oshkosh-Neenah, WI Metro Area	30.9	18.3	23.7	6.5	20.7	1.2	4.1	25.0	2.2

Table D. Metropolitan Statistical Area—Labor Force, Employment, and Educational Data, 2015—*Continued*

CBSA code/ Division code	Metropolitan area, metropolitan division	Occupation for employed population age 16 and older					Industry for employed population age 16 and older			
		Management, business, science, and arts occupations	Service occupations	Sales and office occupations:	Natural resources, construction, and maintenance occupations	Production, transportation, and material moving occupations:	Agriculture, forestry, fishing and hunting, and mining	Construction	Manufacturing	Wholesale trade
36980	Owensboro, KY Metro Area	28.3	17.2	25.2	9.6	19.7	2.4	6.0	16.5	1.9
37100	Oxnard-Thousand Oaks-Ventura, CA Metro Area	37.7	17.2	22.8	11.8	10.5	5.7	6.1	10.8	2.6
37340	Palm Bay-Melbourne-Titusville, FL Metro Area	37.7	19.5	26.1	7.9	8.7	0.7	6.1	9.6	2.0
37460	Panama City, FL Metro Area	32.0	22.6	25.5	9.4	10.5	1.3	7.1	6.3	1.0
37620	Parkersburg-Vienna, WV Metro Area	28.2	22.1	25.8	12.9	11.0	1.9	7.5	7.3	1.8
37860	Pensacola-Ferry Pass-Brent, FL Metro Area	32.6	20.5	27.2	9.7	10.0	1.0	6.6	4.5	1.9
37900	Peoria, IL Metro Area	36.2	17.2	25.2	8.3	13.1	1.9	5.2	16.5	2.7
37980	**Philadelphia-Camden-Wilmington, PA-NJ-DE-MD Metro Area**	42.8	17.4	23.3	6.8	9.7	0.7	5.3	8.7	2.8
37980/15804	*Camden, NJ Metro Division*	41.6	16.3	24.8	7.0	10.4	0.4	5.4	7.4	3.3
37980/33874	*Montgomery County-Bucks County-Chester County, PA Metro Division*	48.1	13.7	22.6	7.3	8.3	1.0	6.1	11.3	3.3
37980/37964	*Philadelphia, PA Metro Division*	38.2	22.1	22.9	5.7	11.1	0.3	4.1	6.9	2.3
37980/48864	*Wilmington, DE-MD-NJ Metro Division*	42.2	17.7	23.8	7.7	8.6	0.9	5.9	8.2	1.5
38060	Phoenix-Mesa-Scottsdale, AZ Metro Area	35.4	18.8	27.0	8.5	10.2	0.9	6.5	7.8	2.6
38220	Pine Bluff, AR Metro Area	29.5	19.2	17.6	8.0	25.6	1.7	3.2	20.5	2.5
38300	Pittsburgh, PA Metro Area	39.9	16.9	23.6	8.2	11.3	1.5	5.8	10.7	3.0
38340	Pittsfield, MA Metro Area	34.0	24.3	23.8	9.2	8.8	0.7	7.2	8.0	1.5
38540	Pocatello, ID Metro Area	31.4	20.5	23.4	10.1	14.6	3.0	6.4	8.3	1.3
38860	Portland-South Portland, ME Metro Area	39.9	17.5	24.2	9.1	9.4	1.4	6.9	9.8	2.5
38900	Portland-Vancouver-Hillsboro, OR-WA Metro Area	40.8	17.8	23.0	7.4	11.0	1.6	5.7	12.4	3.4
38940	Port St. Lucie, FL Metro Area	29.4	23.5	27.3	11.5	8.2	1.3	9.4	4.0	2.3
39140	Prescott, AZ Metro Area	32.1	22.7	23.9	10.4	10.9	2.3	7.4	5.4	1.7
39300	Providence-Warwick, RI-MA Metro Area	37.7	18.6	24.2	7.9	11.6	0.5	6.0	11.5	3.2
39340	Provo-Orem, UT Metro Area	40.6	15.5	24.8	7.7	11.4	0.8	7.7	9.8	3.0
39380	Pueblo, CO Metro Area	32.4	17.3	27.1	10.3	12.8	1.3	8.2	8.4	2.3
39460	Punta Gorda, FL Metro Area	26.0	20.5	30.5	14.0	9.1	0.4	9.8	4.3	2.0
39540	Racine, WI Metro Area	31.7	16.9	23.1	8.5	19.9	1.1	5.8	21.4	3.4
39580	Raleigh, NC Metro Area	46.0	14.4	23.7	8.1	7.8	0.7	7.3	8.3	2.9
39660	Rapid City, SD Metro Area	33.4	19.3	25.0	11.5	10.8	3.8	8.0	6.4	2.4
39740	Reading, PA Metro Area	32.1	15.4	23.6	8.1	20.7	1.3	5.4	19.6	3.6
39820	Redding, CA Metro Area	29.9	24.1	27.2	10.8	8.0	2.8	7.8	5.2	1.6
39900	Reno, NV Metro Area	32.5	21.5	27.1	8.0	10.8	0.9	6.3	6.7	3.5
40060	Richmond, VA Metro Area	40.5	16.3	25.6	7.9	9.8	0.7	6.3	6.7	3.1
40140	Riverside-San Bernardino-Ontario, CA Metro Area	28.3	20.7	24.6	11.2	15.1	1.2	8.2	8.9	3.1
40220	Roanoke, VA Metro Area	35.7	16.9	23.7	9.7	14.0	0.7	7.1	10.6	3.0
40340	Rochester, MN Metro Area	46.0	15.5	19.8	7.8	10.9	3.8	5.0	10.1	2.2
40380	Rochester, NY Metro Area	39.7	17.3	23.9	7.7	11.5	1.2	5.3	11.7	2.3
40420	Rockford, IL Metro Area	29.4	18.8	23.7	7.8	20.3	0.9	5.2	21.2	2.5
40580	Rocky Mount, NC Metro Area	27.2	20.0	22.1	10.1	20.6	2.7	7.6	15.4	2.3
40660	Rome, GA Metro Area	29.2	23.7	19.0	10.4	17.8	1.1	5.7	18.7	1.8
40900	Sacramento--Roseville--Arden-Arcade, CA Metro Area	39.7	18.8	24.8	7.8	9.0	1.2	6.4	5.9	2.5
40980	Saginaw, MI Metro Area	30.3	21.4	24.2	8.1	16.0	1.4	4.9	15.1	2.2
41060	St. Cloud, MN Metro Area	31.6	19.3	22.7	8.9	17.4	2.9	7.7	14.7	2.6
41100	St. George, UT Metro Area	31.3	20.3	28.6	8.8	11.1	1.9	7.3	6.3	2.0
41140	St. Joseph, MO-KS Metro Area	31.1	19.0	24.7	8.9	16.4	2.5	6.4	16.0	2.6
41180	St. Louis, MO-IL Metro Area	38.7	17.3	24.5	7.8	11.8	0.9	5.9	11.2	2.9
41420	Salem, OR Metro Area	30.1	17.9	23.8	14.6	13.6	6.8	8.0	10.4	2.4
41500	Salinas, CA Metro Area	26.8	20.9	19.1	21.5	11.7	19.4	6.2	4.5	3.5
41540	Salisbury, MD-DE Metro Area	32.7	20.6	23.2	12.0	11.5	2.4	9.0	9.2	2.2
41620	Salt Lake City, UT Metro Area	36.4	15.1	27.5	8.3	12.7	1.1	6.6	11.5	2.9
41660	San Angelo, TX Metro Area	31.0	17.0	24.6	12.2	15.3	7.8	6.9	5.2	3.2
41700	San Antonio-New Braunfels, TX Metro Area	33.8	19.5	25.8	10.5	10.5	2.0	7.5	6.4	2.8
41740	San Diego-Carlsbad, CA Metro Area	40.3	20.2	23.3	7.8	8.4	0.9	5.5	9.1	2.8
41860	**San Francisco-Oakland-Hayward, CA Metro Area**	48.1	16.4	21.2	6.4	7.8	0.6	5.3	7.5	2.3
41860/36084	*Oakland-Hayward-Berkeley, CA Metro Division*	46.0	16.5	20.9	7.5	9.0	0.6	6.2	8.5	2.6

Table D. Metropolitan Statistical Area—Labor Force, Employment, and Educational Data, 2015—*Continued*

CBSA code/ Division code	Metropolitan area, metropolitan division	Occupation for employed population age 16 and older					Industry for employed population age 16 and older			
		Management, business, science, and arts occupations	Service occupations	Sales and office occupations:	Natural resources, construction, and maintenance occupations	Production, transportation, and material moving occupations:	Agriculture, forestry, fishing and hunting, and mining	Construction	Manufacturing	Wholesale trade
41860/41884	San Francisco-Redwood City-South San Francisco, CA Metro Division	50.7	16.6	21.2	4.9	6.5	0.5	4.1	6.5	1.9
41860/42034	San Rafael, CA Metro Division	52.0	14.3	24.1	5.3	4.3	0.7	4.4	4.7	3.3
41940	San Jose-Sunnyvale-Santa Clara, CA Metro Area	51.4	16.0	18.0	6.7	7.9	0.7	5.3	17.6	1.8
42020	San Luis Obispo-Paso Robles-Arroyo Grande, CA Metro Area	41.9	21.1	20.0	9.3	7.7	3.1	7.5	6.9	1.6
42100	Santa Cruz-Watsonville, CA Metro Area	39.6	20.8	19.8	11.7	8.2	6.4	6.7	7.9	2.8
42140	Santa Fe, NM Metro Area	43.8	19.8	22.2	7.1	7.1	1.4	6.2	2.5	1.0
42200	Santa Maria-Santa Barbara, CA Metro Area	35.3	20.0	19.8	15.4	9.5	9.5	5.4	8.2	2.2
42220	Santa Rosa, CA Metro Area	36.0	19.7	21.3	12.5	10.4	3.8	9.1	9.4	3.0
42340	Savannah, GA Metro Area	34.1	20.9	22.7	8.8	13.5	0.3	6.1	9.9	2.1
42540	Scranton--Wilkes-Barre--Hazleton, PA Metro Area	32.8	17.9	25.2	7.5	16.6	0.8	5.2	12.5	3.8
42660	**Seattle-Tacoma-Bellevue, WA Metro Area**	44.8	15.6	21.6	7.9	10.1	0.6	6.2	11.0	2.9
42660/42644	Seattle-Bellevue-Everett, WA Metro Division	47.8	15.0	20.8	7.1	9.3	0.6	5.7	11.0	2.8
42660/45104	Tacoma-Lakewood, WA Metro Division	32.8	17.8	25.0	10.9	13.5	0.6	8.1	10.7	3.1
42680	Sebastian-Vero Beach, FL Metro Area	30.9	22.3	25.7	9.5	11.5	2.9	10.2	4.6	2.6
42700	Sebring, FL Metro Area	29.9	20.6	29.4	12.1	8.0	7.4	3.7	4.5	0.8
43100	Sheboygan, WI Metro Area	29.5	16.1	20.6	8.1	25.7	1.7	4.4	33.1	1.8
43300	Sherman-Denison, TX Metro Area	31.4	20.5	21.1	9.7	17.3	1.1	10.3	13.9	2.1
43340	Shreveport-Bossier City, LA Metro Area	31.8	20.3	24.6	11.3	12.0	4.5	6.9	7.2	2.7
43420	Sierra Vista-Douglas, AZ Metro Area	30.1	27.0	24.6	11.0	7.3	3.1	7.3	2.8	1.2
43580	Sioux City, IA-NE-SD Metro Area	30.2	17.6	22.0	10.3	20.0	3.3	6.4	18.6	3.1
43620	Sioux Falls, SD Metro Area	34.1	16.5	25.3	9.4	14.7	2.0	7.5	11.2	3.8
43780	South Bend-Mishawaka, IN-MI Metro Area	34.8	16.0	23.1	7.5	18.6	0.7	4.7	20.0	3.0
43900	Spartanburg, SC Metro Area	28.2	15.3	23.9	10.2	22.3	0.7	6.1	21.9	4.4
44060	Spokane-Spokane Valley, WA Metro Area	35.4	18.8	25.7	8.1	12.0	1.9	6.1	8.6	3.1
44100	Springfield, IL Metro Area	42.3	17.6	24.1	7.6	8.4	1.4	5.0	5.4	2.3
44140	Springfield, MA Metro Area	37.5	20.2	24.5	6.2	11.6	0.8	3.7	9.7	2.7
44180	Springfield, MO Metro Area	33.8	18.1	26.1	8.8	13.3	1.3	6.9	9.3	2.7
44220	Springfield, OH Metro Area	28.7	19.2	22.4	7.8	21.8	0.8	4.3	19.0	3.1
44300	State College, PA Metro Area	47.3	17.5	17.8	7.5	10.0	1.6	4.6	8.7	1.5
44420	Staunton-Waynesboro, VA Metro Area	27.9	17.0	24.8	11.4	18.8	1.5	8.1	14.4	3.2
44700	Stockton-Lodi, CA Metro Area	27.0	17.4	24.5	14.1	17.1	5.0	8.2	10.0	3.5
44940	Sumter, SC Metro Area	26.1	19.7	22.5	10.4	21.4	1.5	7.6	19.9	1.4
45060	Syracuse, NY Metro Area	38.1	17.9	25.2	8.2	10.5	0.8	5.9	8.6	3.0
45220	Tallahassee, FL Metro Area	39.5	21.6	27.2	6.3	5.5	0.8	4.0	1.8	1.9
45300	Tampa-St. Petersburg-Clearwater, FL Metro Area	37.1	18.0	27.7	8.6	8.6	1.0	6.9	5.6	2.8
45460	Terre Haute, IN Metro Area	31.0	19.1	19.2	12.2	18.4	2.6	7.3	18.0	2.4
45500	Texarkana, TX-AR Metro Area	32.0	18.8	24.3	9.8	15.1	2.0	7.4	10.2	2.7
45540	The Villages, FL Metro Area	34.6	20.6	26.8	8.7	9.4	0.9	3.7	5.0	2.9
45780	Toledo, OH Metro Area	33.7	17.8	21.9	7.5	19.0	0.5	4.8	17.8	2.6
45820	Topeka, KS Metro Area	35.5	18.5	21.9	9.7	14.3	1.1	7.2	9.2	1.7
45940	Trenton, NJ Metro Area	43.2	17.4	23.5	5.7	10.2	0.2	4.2	8.3	2.7
46060	Tucson, AZ Metro Area	35.9	21.5	25.2	8.8	8.7	1.3	7.0	5.9	1.8
46140	Tulsa, OK Metro Area	35.4	16.2	25.1	10.3	13.0	2.5	7.0	12.2	3.1
46220	Tuscaloosa, AL Metro Area	35.2	13.7	22.5	8.6	20.0	2.0	5.8	17.4	1.9
46340	Tyler, TX Metro Area	33.4	18.3	23.9	11.7	12.7	3.7	6.6	6.8	2.4
46520	Urban Honolulu, HI Metro Area	35.0	21.8	25.2	9.2	8.8	0.7	7.4	3.5	2.8
46540	Utica-Rome, NY Metro Area	32.9	19.0	26.4	8.2	13.5	1.2	5.3	11.1	1.9
46660	Valdosta, GA Metro Area	30.8	20.7	25.0	8.2	15.3	1.5	5.0	9.2	1.5
46700	Vallejo-Fairfield, CA Metro Area	30.6	21.7	24.3	10.8	12.6	2.0	8.1	8.7	2.9
47020	Victoria, TX Metro Area	34.9	17.2	24.5	11.1	12.3	4.1	8.0	9.6	2.8
47220	Vineland-Bridgeton, NJ Metro Area	28.5	18.9	20.5	13.3	18.8	4.7	6.9	13.4	2.3
47260	Virginia Beach-Norfolk-Newport News, VA-NC Metro Area	37.5	17.7	24.6	9.9	10.3	0.4	6.7	9.4	2.0
47300	Visalia-Porterville, CA Metro Area	25.1	18.4	19.1	24.3	13.0	19.5	4.3	7.7	2.8
47380	Waco, TX Metro Area	32.8	17.9	22.6	11.3	15.3	1.5	7.7	11.0	2.9
47460	Walla Walla, WA Metro Area	40.4	19.4	19.6	11.3	9.4	8.7	4.2	7.1	2.3
47580	Warner Robins, GA Metro Area	34.5	17.4	22.3	12.1	13.8	0.8	3.9	11.2	2.3
47900	**Washington-Arlington-Alexandria, DC-VA-MD-WV Metro Area**	51.1	16.9	19.3	6.8	5.9	0.3	6.3	2.8	1.3

Table D. Metropolitan Statistical Area—Labor Force, Employment, and Educational Data, 2015—*Continued*

CBSA code/ Division code	Metropolitan area, metropolitan division	Occupation for employed population age 16 and older					Industry for employed population age 16 and older			
		Management, business, science, and arts occupations	Service occupations	Sales and office occupations:	Natural resources, construction, and maintenance occupations	Production, transportation, and material moving occupations:	Agriculture, forestry, fishing and hunting, and mining	Construction	Manufacturing	Wholesale trade
47900/43524	*Silver Spring-Frederick-Rockville, MD Metro Division*	53.6	16.1	18.5	6.6	5.2	0.4	6.4	3.5	1.5
47900/47894	*Washington-Arlington-Alexandria, DC-VA-MD-WV Metro Division*	50.5	17.2	19.5	6.9	6.1	0.3	6.3	2.7	1.2
47940	Waterloo-Cedar Falls, IA Metro Area	31.9	18.4	23.8	7.5	18.3	2.7	4.6	18.8	2.6
48060	Watertown-Fort Drum, NY Metro Area	32.3	20.3	23.5	13.6	10.3	1.6	6.6	5.5	2.7
48140	Wausau, WI Metro Area	33.8	13.0	24.3	9.2	19.8	3.9	4.6	22.2	3.5
48260	Weirton-Steubenville, WV-OH Metro Area	25.7	22.5	24.8	9.3	17.8	2.4	3.7	12.0	1.9
48300	Wenatchee, WA Metro Area	28.4	21.2	21.8	17.3	11.3	12.2	6.7	4.4	5.3
48540	Wheeling, WV-OH Metro Area	33.5	17.6	24.6	12.8	11.5	6.1	6.0	7.1	2.8
48620	Wichita, KS Metro Area	34.5	18.0	22.0	10.3	15.2	1.5	6.9	18.5	2.4
48660	Wichita Falls, TX Metro Area	31.9	19.5	23.8	11.7	13.1	5.4	6.9	7.7	2.2
48700	Williamsport, PA Metro Area	28.7	20.2	23.7	9.1	18.2	2.9	6.6	15.1	2.9
48900	Wilmington, NC Metro Area	37.9	16.5	26.0	9.8	9.7	0.4	7.9	8.3	2.6
49020	Winchester, VA-WV Metro Area	35.7	15.1	21.8	12.9	14.4	3.4	7.9	10.5	2.3
49180	Winston-Salem, NC Metro Area	34.8	16.2	23.1	9.8	16.1	1.0	7.7	15.6	2.5
49340	Worcester, MA-CT Metro Area	39.9	17.9	23.4	7.9	10.8	0.7	5.6	12.5	2.5
49420	Yakima, WA Metro Area	25.3	16.6	18.7	21.4	18.0	15.9	5.5	9.3	5.5
49620	York-Hanover, PA Metro Area	32.7	15.6	23.6	9.6	18.4	0.6	7.7	16.1	3.3
49660	Youngstown-Warren-Boardman, OH-PA Metro Area	28.9	19.5	24.0	8.2	19.4	1.1	5.1	17.3	2.0
49700	Yuba City, CA Metro Area	31.5	17.3	21.6	16.7	12.9	8.1	8.8	6.4	1.9
49740	Yuma, AZ Metro Area	27.8	21.8	19.6	18.7	12.1	11.5	7.0	3.9	1.9

Table D. Metropolitan Statistical Area—Labor Force, Employment, and Educational Data, 2015

CBSA code/ Division code	Metropolitan area, metropolitan division	Retail trade	Transportation and warehousing, and utilities	Information	Finance and insurance, and real estate and rental and leasing	Professional, scientific, and management, and administrative and waste management services	Educational services, and health care and social assistance	Arts, entertainment, and recreation, and accommodation and food services	Other services, except public administration	Public administration
10180	Abilene, TX Metro Area	11.2	6.4	0.8	6.2	6.4	29.6	10.2	5.8	6.3
10420	Akron, OH Metro Area	12.7	4.2	1.9	6.3	10.1	23.3	10.2	4.7	2.7
10500	Albany, GA Metro Area	11.0	4.5	0.9	5.0	7.9	27.6	7.7	6.5	9.4
10540	Albany, OR Metro Area	13.4	4.9	0.6	3.5	7.5	26.8	5.3	3.5	6.0
10580	Albany-Schenectady-Troy, NY Metro Area	10.8	4.3	2.2	7.1	10.2	26.8	9.0	4.7	9.8
10740	Albuquerque, NM Metro Area	12.2	3.5	1.9	5.2	13.8	24.5	12.3	5.1	6.4
10780	Alexandria, LA Metro Area	13.1	6.6	1.7	4.1	6.5	30.4	10.0	4.5	6.5
10900	Allentown-Bethlehem-Easton, PA-NJ Metro Area	12.4	6.2	1.9	5.4	11.1	24.6	8.6	4.5	2.8
11020	Altoona, PA Metro Area	16.8	7.7	2.1	3.9	4.6	26.8	8.8	3.7	3.9
11100	Amarillo, TX Metro Area	13.4	5.4	1.6	5.2	6.8	24.9	9.9	6.2	4.0
11180	Ames, IA Metro Area	10.3	2.3	1.6	4.2	6.8	38.5	12.6	2.2	4.4
11260	Anchorage, AK Metro Area	11.6	7.1	2.7	4.1	10.9	22.5	10.7	5.0	9.6
11460	Ann Arbor, MI Metro Area	9.8	3.1	2.2	3.5	11.7	37.3	10.3	4.0	2.4
11500	Anniston-Oxford-Jacksonville, AL Metro Area	13.1	4.6	1.9	5.5	8.4	20.8	8.9	4.7	5.6
11540	Appleton, WI Metro Area	11.2	4.4	1.3	6.5	8.0	18.4	9.1	3.6	3.1
11700	Asheville, NC Metro Area	13.0	3.1	1.1	5.3	9.9	26.4	11.7	4.9	3.3
12020	Athens-Clarke County, GA Metro Area	10.7	3.1	1.6	3.3	8.9	30.3	15.8	5.7	3.4
12060	Atlanta-Sandy Springs-Roswell, GA Metro Area	11.6	6.5	3.4	6.9	14.5	19.6	9.3	5.1	4.2
12100	Atlantic City-Hammonton, NJ Metro Area	11.8	3.8	1.4	4.6	8.3	23.4	25.5	3.9	4.4
12220	Auburn-Opelika, AL Metro Area	13.0	4.1	2.0	6.9	9.0	25.0	10.5	4.1	4.4
12260	Augusta-Richmond County, GA-SC Metro Area	14.1	5.9	1.7	4.3	10.9	22.7	7.8	5.1	5.3
12420	Austin-Round Rock, TX Metro Area	10.4	3.6	2.8	7.2	16.3	20.5	9.8	4.7	5.4
12540	Bakersfield, CA Metro Area	10.4	5.1	1.1	3.5	8.1	19.2	8.6	5.3	6.6
12580	Baltimore-Columbia-Towson, MD Metro Area	10.5	4.5	2.2	6.4	14.2	24.8	8.5	4.9	9.7
12620	Bangor, ME Metro Area	16.6	4.8	1.5	4.6	6.4	34.8	7.8	4.5	3.8
12700	Barnstable Town, MA Metro Area	15.9	3.8	1.3	6.3	12.4	20.8	10.9	7.3	5.2
12940	Baton Rouge, LA Metro Area	11.1	4.3	1.8	5.8	10.0	24.6	8.2	5.6	5.6
12980	Battle Creek, MI Metro Area	11.0	6.0	1.1	3.9	8.5	22.3	8.4	5.2	3.7
13020	Bay City, MI Metro Area	15.3	4.5	1.7	4.5	6.8	25.2	9.7	5.3	2.2
13140	Beaumont-Port Arthur, TX Metro Area	12.1	4.4	0.8	4.5	7.9	21.9	8.1	5.2	4.8
13220	Beckley, WV Metro Area	12.0	5.3	0.5	3.5	7.8	28.5	10.5	4.7	5.6
13380	Bellingham, WA Metro Area	12.3	7.1	2.1	4.7	8.1	23.8	9.7	5.0	5.2
13460	Bend-Redmond, OR Metro Area	10.1	3.1	3.6	5.3	13.3	21.3	12.0	8.1	2.5
13740	Billings, MT Metro Area	11.6	4.7	2.9	6.7	9.8	23.0	10.3	5.4	4.2
13780	Binghamton, NY Metro Area	13.8	4.3	1.7	3.6	9.4	29.1	10.7	4.8	3.9
13820	Birmingham-Hoover, AL Metro Area	10.8	6.2	1.9	8.1	10.5	23.8	8.1	5.8	4.0
13900	Bismarck, ND Metro Area	11.0	6.9	1.3	4.9	7.5	27.1	7.1	4.9	7.0
13980	Blacksburg-Christiansburg-Radford, VA Metro Area	10.9	4.0	1.0	3.7	9.2	33.4	10.3	3.9	2.7
14010	Bloomington, IL Metro Area	12.8	3.9	1.3	19.6	8.9	22.0	11.1	3.4	3.0
14020	Bloomington, IN Metro Area	9.9	2.1	4.4	4.8	9.5	31.0	14.0	3.8	3.2
14100	Bloomsburg-Berwick, PA Metro Area	12.6	7.0	1.6	2.2	5.6	33.8	9.8	3.4	3.5
14260	Boise City, ID Metro Area	12.1	3.9	2.0	6.1	11.8	23.2	8.4	5.4	5.1
14460	**Boston-Cambridge-Newton, MA-NH Metro Area**	9.9	3.7	2.7	7.8	15.3	27.5	9.0	4.3	3.5
14460/14454	*Boston, MA Metro Division*	10.3	4.4	2.3	9.2	14.6	28.2	9.5	4.2	3.7
14460/15764	*Cambridge-Newton-Framingham, MA Metro Division*	8.9	2.9	3.0	6.9	16.5	27.7	8.6	4.6	3.3
14460/40484	*Rockingham County-Strafford County, NH Metro Division*	12.8	5.0	2.1	6.7	11.9	23.1	8.5	3.4	3.9
14500	Boulder, CO Metro Area	10.3	2.2	3.5	4.3	20.1	24.6	10.7	5.0	2.0
14540	Bowling Green, KY Metro Area	10.3	4.8	1.8	4.2	7.4	24.8	10.7	3.5	2.9
14740	Bremerton-Silverdale, WA Metro Area	10.8	4.2	1.1	4.4	11.2	20.7	12.3	4.9	9.8
14860	Bridgeport-Stamford-Norwalk, CT Metro Area	10.3	3.6	2.8	12.0	15.7	22.9	7.7	4.7	2.5
15180	Brownsville-Harlingen, TX Metro Area	13.9	5.5	1.5	4.1	7.5	32.2	7.8	5.0	5.1
15260	Brunswick, GA Metro Area	11.7	3.7	2.0	4.1	9.8	22.9	16.0	5.6	5.8
15380	Buffalo-Cheektowaga-Niagara Falls, NY Metro Area	11.5	4.6	1.5	7.6	9.8	26.7	10.2	4.5	4.3
15500	Burlington, NC Metro Area	12.4	2.6	1.0	4.7	9.1	26.1	9.4	5.3	3.1
15540	Burlington-South Burlington, VT Metro Area	10.6	3.2	2.8	5.0	9.9	29.0	9.9	4.3	4.8

Table D. Metropolitan Statistical Area—Labor Force, Employment, and Educational Data, 2015—*Continued*

CBSA code/ Division code	Metropolitan area, metropolitan division	Retail trade	Transportation and warehousing, and utilities	Information	Finance and insurance, and real estate and rental and leasing	Professional, scientific, and management, and administrative and waste management services	Educational services, and health care and social assistance	Arts, entertainment, and recreation, and accommodation and food services	Other services, except public administration	Public administration
						Industry for employed population age 16 and older				
15680	California-Lexington Park, MD Metro Area	9.1	5.5	2.8	4.3	16.0	15.8	7.9	4.8	21.2
15940	Canton-Massillon, OH Metro Area	11.4	4.5	1.8	5.0	8.3	22.3	9.9	5.2	2.4
15980	Cape Coral-Fort Myers, FL Metro Area	16.5	3.6	1.9	7.5	13.2	19.0	12.1	5.0	3.0
16020	Cape Girardeau, MO-IL Metro Area	13.1	3.9	0.6	3.6	6.5	29.7	10.5	4.1	3.8
16060	Carbondale-Marion, IL Metro Area	11.4	5.6	1.4	4.5	5.0	35.3	10.0	3.8	4.4
16180	Carson City, NV Metro Area	11.6	3.3	2.1	3.7	5.3	15.3	19.9	3.8	13.4
16220	Casper, WY Metro Area	14.0	4.2	1.8	4.1	8.2	19.6	10.7	6.5	5.1
16300	Cedar Rapids, IA Metro Area	13.0	5.8	3.1	7.3	9.3	21.8	5.8	4.7	2.6
16540	Chambersburg-Waynesboro, PA Metro Area	11.8	6.5	1.5	6.7	7.2	21.1	6.8	5.0	6.0
16580	Champaign-Urbana, IL Metro Area	10.3	4.0	1.7	5.1	8.5	37.0	8.7	3.5	3.0
16620	Charleston, WV Metro Area	11.3	3.9	2.6	5.4	9.5	29.1	9.8	4.2	9.6
16700	Charleston-North Charleston, SC Metro Area	10.7	4.7	2.2	6.3	14.0	21.3	12.2	4.9	5.4
16740	Charlotte-Concord-Gastonia, NC-SC Metro Area	12.2	5.5	2.3	10.1	11.5	19.2	9.2	5.0	2.4
16820	Charlottesville, VA Metro Area	10.6	3.2	1.7	4.9	12.0	34.6	9.9	5.9	3.8
16860	Chattanooga, TN-GA Metro Area	12.7	8.3	1.4	6.6	9.4	21.6	8.8	5.7	2.4
16940	Cheyenne, WY Metro Area	15.3	6.5	2.2	6.6	8.9	20.9	8.2	2.0	12.3
16980	**Chicago-Naperville-Elgin, IL-IN-WI Metro Area**	10.8	6.3	2.0	7.6	13.3	21.7	9.4	4.6	3.2
16980/16974	*Chicago-Naperville-Arlington Heights, IL Metro Division*	10.5	6.6	2.2	8.1	13.8	21.9	9.5	4.7	3.3
16980/20994	*Elgin, IL Metro Division*	11.1	5.4	2.1	5.8	11.6	21.2	9.2	4.2	2.3
16980/23844	*Gary, IN Metro Division*	12.3	6.5	1.0	4.5	8.9	23.4	9.0	4.3	3.2
16980/29404	*Lake County-Kenosha County, IL-WI Metro Division*	12.0	3.8	1.3	7.0	13.4	19.0	8.4	4.5	3.1
17020	Chico, CA Metro Area	13.0	2.4	2.3	5.2	9.6	27.3	15.7	3.2	3.6
17140	Cincinnati, OH-KY-IN Metro Area	12.1	5.2	1.6	7.9	11.1	22.8	9.2	4.2	3.6
17300	Clarksville, TN-KY Metro Area	13.6	5.3	1.4	3.9	9.7	22.9	9.2	4.6	6.9
17420	Cleveland, TN Metro Area	10.6	6.5	1.6	5.5	6.8	18.9	11.1	6.3	2.7
17460	Cleveland-Elyria, OH Metro Area	11.2	4.4	1.7	7.2	9.8	25.0	9.8	4.4	4.0
17660	Coeur d'Alene, ID Metro Area	11.9	3.7	1.4	6.6	9.6	24.1	12.1	4.9	4.3
17780	College Station-Bryan, TX Metro Area	14.1	3.3	1.4	3.7	9.1	30.8	10.9	4.0	3.6
17820	Colorado Springs, CO Metro Area	12.6	4.4	2.5	7.0	13.5	22.0	11.1	5.5	6.3
17860	Columbia, MO Metro Area	12.5	3.4	2.2	8.8	8.6	35.2	9.2	3.0	3.6
17900	Columbia, SC Metro Area	11.8	5.1	1.7	7.7	9.9	23.0	9.3	5.5	7.3
17980	Columbus, GA-AL Metro Area	11.7	4.4	2.3	9.9	8.6	20.8	9.6	4.9	7.9
18020	Columbus, IN Metro Area	8.3	2.0	0.6	5.5	6.6	19.0	6.8	3.7	1.6
18140	Columbus, OH Metro Area	12.7	5.7	2.0	10.0	11.6	23.2	9.5	4.0	4.4
18580	Corpus Christi, TX Metro Area	11.0	4.6	0.9	5.4	8.9	22.7	12.4	5.0	5.7
18700	Corvallis, OR Metro Area	9.6	2.4	1.2	2.3	13.2	39.3	6.7	4.8	2.7
18880	Crestview-Fort Walton Beach-Destin, FL Metro Area	14.1	4.0	0.6	6.5	13.1	16.6	15.6	6.0	9.2
19060	Cumberland, MD-WV Metro Area	13.6	6.0	1.8	5.0	7.7	25.1	9.3	3.5	8.3
19100	**Dallas-Fort Worth-Arlington, TX Metro Area**	11.8	6.3	2.5	8.3	13.1	19.2	9.1	5.3	2.9
19100/19124	*Dallas-Plano-Irving, TX Metro Division*	11.4	5.6	2.8	9.0	14.4	18.7	9.4	5.3	2.6
19100/23104	*Fort Worth-Arlington, TX Metro Division*	12.5	7.7	1.9	6.9	10.4	20.2	8.5	5.2	3.7
19140	Dalton, GA Metro Area	11.8	5.2	0.6	2.7	5.5	11.3	5.6	2.8	2.1
19180	Danville, IL Metro Area	12.2	6.0	1.8	4.9	7.1	24.5	7.6	5.3	2.6
19300	Daphne-Fairhope-Foley, AL Metro Area	16.9	4.7	2.0	5.6	10.8	18.9	12.7	4.0	4.3
19340	Davenport-Moline-Rock Island, IA-IL Metro Area	11.6	5.8	1.8	5.1	7.2	21.5	9.5	3.9	4.0
19380	Dayton, OH Metro Area	10.4	3.6	1.7	5.7	10.5	25.9	9.9	4.7	5.7
19460	Decatur, AL Metro Area	12.7	5.1	0.8	3.6	8.9	18.7	6.8	5.5	5.4
19500	Decatur, IL Metro Area	11.6	6.0	1.6	6.4	7.3	21.0	10.4	4.4	3.6
19660	Deltona-Daytona Beach-Ormond Beach, FL Metro Area	13.0	5.0	2.1	7.3	11.7	21.5	12.5	5.6	4.0
19740	Denver-Aurora-Lakewood, CO Metro Area	11.0	5.0	3.7	8.0	15.2	19.2	9.6	4.9	4.0
19780	Des Moines-West Des Moines, IA Metro Area	11.2	4.6	1.8	14.8	10.2	22.1	7.8	3.9	3.5
19820	**Detroit-Warren-Dearborn, MI Metro Area**	11.0	4.5	1.6	6.2	11.4	22.0	9.6	4.4	3.1

Table D. Metropolitan Statistical Area—Labor Force, Employment, and Educational Data, 2015—*Continued*

CBSA code/ Division code	Metropolitan area, metropolitan division	Retail trade	Transportation and warehousing, and utilities	Information	Finance and insurance, and real estate and rental and leasing	Professional, scientific, and management, and administrative and waste management services	Educational services, and health care and social assistance	Arts, entertainment, and recreation, and accommodation and food services	Other services, except public administration	Public administration
19820/19804	Detroit-Dearborn-Livonia, MI Metro Division	11.5	6.2	1.6	5.8	10.9	22.2	10.2	4.6	3.2
19820/47664	Warren-Troy-Farmington Hills, MI Metro Division	10.7	3.5	1.7	6.5	11.7	21.9	9.3	4.2	3.0
20020	Dothan, AL Metro Area	13.2	8.5	1.1	3.1	7.5	24.6	10.1	4.8	4.0
20100	Dover, DE Metro Area	14.5	3.1	1.1	5.4	8.3	22.7	12.7	4.6	10.3
20220	Dubuque, IA Metro Area	13.0	4.7	1.9	6.1	8.2	23.5	9.4	3.3	1.8
20260	Duluth, MN-WI Metro Area	12.0	6.7	0.8	6.2	5.7	29.7	12.0	4.2	4.2
20500	Durham-Chapel Hill, NC Metro Area	8.6	2.3	1.9	5.1	11.7	34.9	10.1	4.3	3.7
20700	East Stroudsburg, PA Metro Area	11.1	6.1	1.0	5.3	8.1	23.7	15.8	5.9	4.4
20740	Eau Claire, WI Metro Area	15.2	5.2	1.4	6.6	6.4	26.2	7.1	3.7	3.3
20940	El Centro, CA Metro Area	11.6	6.9	0.8	2.6	6.4	28.7	8.6	4.3	10.2
21060	Elizabethtown-Fort Knox, KY Metro Area	13.7	6.4	2.2	5.3	7.8	19.4	9.9	4.9	6.7
21140	Elkhart-Goshen, IN Metro Area	10.3	3.9	1.1	3.4	5.7	16.7	6.7	5.7	2.5
21300	Elmira, NY Metro Area	11.5	4.7	2.2	3.2	7.4	27.2	8.9	3.6	6.1
21340	El Paso, TX Metro Area	12.1	7.0	1.7	5.5	10.8	24.0	10.4	4.5	7.9
21500	Erie, PA Metro Area	10.2	3.7	1.5	6.9	6.4	25.2	12.8	5.0	3.2
21660	Eugene, OR Metro Area	13.8	3.7	1.9	5.3	9.5	26.2	11.0	4.7	3.0
21780	Evansville, IN-KY Metro Area	12.1	4.7	2.2	5.3	8.2	21.0	10.1	4.8	3.3
21820	Fairbanks, AK Metro Area	14.1	6.4	1.1	2.8	6.7	24.8	8.3	5.8	15.1
22020	Fargo, ND-MN Metro Area	11.2	4.2	1.1	8.0	9.5	24.8	10.2	4.6	2.4
22140	Farmington, NM Metro Area	9.5	8.5	0.8	3.7	7.7	21.3	9.8	6.0	5.0
22180	Fayetteville, NC Metro Area	14.2	3.4	1.8	3.6	10.2	26.1	10.9	5.5	8.7
22220	Fayetteville-Springdale-Rogers, AR-MO Metro Area	18.3	5.1	1.2	4.9	9.4	21.0	6.1	4.5	2.1
22380	Flagstaff, AZ Metro Area	11.2	5.4	0.9	4.7	6.3	29.4	18.6	3.4	7.5
22420	Flint, MI Metro Area	13.5	4.3	1.1	5.2	8.4	24.6	9.5	5.4	3.0
22500	Florence, SC Metro Area	11.7	6.8	0.7	4.8	6.3	26.9	7.2	6.3	4.8
22520	Florence-Muscle Shoals, AL Metro Area	12.2	6.9	1.2	4.6	8.7	21.3	11.1	5.1	3.7
22540	Fond du Lac, WI Metro Area	10.5	4.7	1.4	6.4	5.4	22.3	8.5	4.3	3.3
22660	Fort Collins, CO Metro Area	10.9	2.2	2.2	5.2	11.5	26.5	10.5	4.6	4.0
22900	Fort Smith, AR-OK Metro Area	12.1	5.9	1.5	3.8	6.1	25.2	9.3	4.3	3.7
23060	Fort Wayne, IN Metro Area	11.1	3.8	1.9	7.4	7.3	22.5	8.7	5.3	2.0
23420	Fresno, CA Metro Area	10.9	4.3	1.4	4.6	7.4	24.0	9.0	4.5	6.7
23460	Gadsden, AL Metro Area	9.6	4.4	1.7	6.5	5.5	22.0	9.1	5.2	4.7
23540	Gainesville, FL Metro Area	9.7	3.5	1.9	5.7	10.5	38.7	11.0	4.9	3.8
23580	Gainesville, GA Metro Area	11.7	5.7	1.2	5.1	8.2	17.5	7.1	5.0	3.4
23900	Gettysburg, PA Metro Area	12.8	4.5	1.0	2.8	6.7	23.1	8.8	5.1	5.5
24020	Glens Falls, NY Metro Area	15.0	3.7	1.4	3.6	8.5	23.8	14.6	3.1	4.4
24140	Goldsboro, NC Metro Area	15.3	4.5	0.2	2.9	3.2	25.3	10.4	3.4	6.2
24220	Grand Forks, ND-MN Metro Area	16.1	4.7	0.6	4.2	5.0	27.7	9.3	3.8	6.1
24260	Grand Island, NE Metro Area	12.8	5.1	0.7	5.0	5.0	20.6	8.6	4.0	3.5
24300	Grand Junction, CO Metro Area	14.1	4.9	1.8	5.5	9.9	24.1	9.4	5.4	4.2
24340	Grand Rapids-Wyoming, MI Metro Area	11.6	3.6	1.4	5.4	8.9	21.4	8.6	5.1	2.4
24420	Grants Pass, OR Metro Area	13.4	6.7	0.9	5.2	8.7	23.5	7.4	7.7	4.4
24500	Great Falls, MT Metro Area	10.4	5.3	1.7	5.8	6.4	25.6	13.2	6.9	5.8
24540	Greeley, CO Metro Area	11.0	5.8	1.4	5.4	9.3	19.6	8.0	5.5	3.8
24580	Green Bay, WI Metro Area	12.4	6.1	1.3	6.9	7.9	18.6	7.9	3.9	2.7
24660	Greensboro-High Point, NC Metro Area	11.6	5.3	1.3	6.7	9.8	22.0	9.0	5.6	3.2
24780	Greenville, NC Metro Area	11.7	3.1	1.9	4.5	5.8	30.0	12.5	5.0	4.9
24860	Greenville-Anderson-Mauldin, SC Metro Area	10.7	3.9	2.4	5.2	10.2	22.4	8.6	5.2	2.8
25060	Gulfport-Biloxi-Pascagoula, MS Metro Area	12.5	4.9	1.4	3.8	7.9	19.7	16.4	4.7	5.7
25180	Hagerstown-Martinsburg, MD-WV Metro Area	12.2	7.7	1.7	5.1	10.2	21.4	8.4	3.2	10.2
25220	Hammond, LA Metro Area	10.7	3.7	0.9	4.2	7.6	25.9	15.5	6.6	6.6
25260	Hanford-Corcoran, CA Metro Area	8.8	3.6	0.6	1.9	6.5	24.3	8.9	5.4	14.3
25420	Harrisburg-Carlisle, PA Metro Area	12.2	6.7	1.7	8.4	9.6	22.2	8.1	4.3	9.5
25500	Harrisonburg, VA Metro Area	12.5	3.9	2.5	4.4	9.0	25.6	13.2	3.8	2.4
25540	Hartford-West Hartford-East Hartford, CT Metro Area	10.0	4.2	2.2	10.8	10.7	26.9	7.3	4.1	4.4
25620	Hattiesburg, MS Metro Area	17.3	5.8	1.1	5.3	7.6	26.5	8.4	4.4	4.2
25860	Hickory-Lenoir-Morganton, NC Metro Area	11.1	3.5	1.0	3.7	6.4	20.7	8.6	3.0	3.9
25940	Hilton Head Island-Bluffton-Beaufort, SC Metro Area	15.4	2.9	2.9	6.9	12.5	18.5	15.6	5.2	4.3
25980	Hinesville, GA Metro Area	14.9	7.3	0.3	2.4	9.9	17.2	12.5	5.1	12.5
26140	Homosassa Springs, FL Metro Area	12.4	8.0	0.8	5.6	11.3	27.1	10.9	4.9	2.1

Table D. Metropolitan Statistical Area—Labor Force, Employment, and Educational Data, 2015—*Continued*

		Industry for employed population age 16 and older								
CBSA code/ Division code	Metropolitan area, metropolitan division	Retail trade	Transportation and warehousing, and utilities	Information	Finance and insurance, and real estate and rental and leasing	Professional, scientific, and management, and administrative and waste management services	Educational services, and health care and social assistance	Arts, entertainment, and recreation, and accommodation and food services	Other services, except public administration	Public administration
26300	Hot Springs, AR Metro Area	13.9	4.0	2.0	4.4	8.2	22.3	14.4	4.3	5.2
26380	Houma-Thibodaux, LA Metro Area	12.3	8.1	1.2	4.7	7.2	19.6	7.3	5.0	3.0
26420	Houston-The Woodlands-Sugar Land, TX Metro Area	10.8	6.4	1.4	6.1	12.6	19.7	8.5	5.1	2.7
26580	Huntington-Ashland, WV-KY-OH Metro Area	11.5	6.0	2.1	3.2	6.0	32.5	10.7	4.4	3.8
26620	Huntsville, AL Metro Area	10.8	2.7	2.1	3.9	17.7	21.7	8.8	5.5	7.8
26820	Idaho Falls, ID Metro Area	9.4	4.9	1.8	3.0	13.7	25.3	9.2	3.7	4.6
26900	Indianapolis-Carmel-Anderson, IN Metro Area	11.9	6.1	2.0	6.6	11.3	21.4	9.7	4.9	3.9
26980	Iowa City, IA Metro Area	11.6	2.8	1.4	5.8	7.3	40.5	9.1	3.3	2.0
27060	Ithaca, NY Metro Area	9.8	1.8	2.0	3.6	8.7	47.7	9.4	4.2	1.7
27100	Jackson, MI Metro Area	11.2	5.6	0.7	5.0	5.2	23.5	8.9	4.3	5.0
27140	Jackson, MS Metro Area	10.8	5.0	1.7	5.6	8.9	26.2	9.6	5.1	6.4
27180	Jackson, TN Metro Area	13.3	5.0	0.8	3.3	6.7	29.2	9.6	6.0	3.4
27260	Jacksonville, FL Metro Area	12.8	6.3	1.7	10.9	11.7	20.9	10.0	4.7	4.8
27340	Jacksonville, NC Metro Area	16.1	1.5	2.1	4.3	13.4	20.3	13.4	5.4	9.9
27500	Janesville-Beloit, WI Metro Area	12.9	3.5	1.6	4.0	6.8	23.6	8.0	4.0	2.7
27620	Jefferson City, MO Metro Area	12.6	5.6	1.5	5.6	7.3	20.6	6.1	4.2	15.3
27740	Johnson City, TN Metro Area	11.8	3.1	2.4	3.9	6.6	28.2	12.5	7.1	2.8
27780	Johnstown, PA Metro Area	11.1	6.1	1.4	4.9	6.5	30.1	9.9	5.4	5.7
27860	Jonesboro, AR Metro Area	12.0	3.7	2.1	3.8	6.1	27.8	8.4	4.0	2.3
27900	Joplin, MO Metro Area	13.9	8.5	1.5	3.3	6.6	24.7	10.1	6.0	2.1
27980	Kahului-Wailuku-Lahaina, HI Metro Area	10.7	5.5	2.2	7.1	11.1	16.7	22.5	3.6	5.7
28020	Kalamazoo-Portage, MI Metro Area	11.0	3.2	1.0	5.8	9.1	27.8	10.4	3.7	3.2
28100	Kankakee, IL Metro Area	11.4	5.8	1.0	5.4	7.3	27.7	8.3	5.0	4.0
28140	Kansas City, MO-KS Metro Area	11.1	5.5	2.6	7.8	13.1	22.3	8.4	4.7	4.5
28420	Kennewick-Richland, WA Metro Area	10.6	5.7	1.1	4.3	13.6	21.0	9.4	4.2	4.4
28660	Killeen-Temple, TX Metro Area	12.6	4.1	1.1	4.8	10.1	24.7	8.6	4.6	11.8
28700	Kingsport-Bristol-Bristol, TN-VA Metro Area	13.4	3.7	1.9	4.3	8.0	24.8	8.4	5.0	3.3
28740	Kingston, NY Metro Area	13.0	4.5	1.7	5.7	8.9	29.2	9.2	5.0	4.2
28940	Knoxville, TN Metro Area	14.2	4.9	1.9	5.7	12.9	23.2	9.0	5.0	4.1
29020	Kokomo, IN Metro Area	10.3	2.3	1.7	4.1	6.6	20.8	8.2	4.1	3.8
29100	La Crosse-Onalaska, WI-MN Metro Area	13.6	4.7	1.9	4.7	5.4	30.2	10.7	4.3	3.0
29180	Lafayette, LA Metro Area	12.5	3.6	1.0	4.1	9.1	22.3	10.9	5.6	4.1
29200	Lafayette-West Lafayette, IN Metro Area	12.1	3.1	1.5	4.5	6.2	30.7	8.7	3.5	1.8
29340	Lake Charles, LA Metro Area	12.0	4.8	1.1	4.3	5.8	25.2	12.8	4.9	4.0
29420	Lake Havasu City-Kingman, AZ Metro Area	15.8	7.1	1.5	4.9	8.0	19.0	17.1	6.5	5.9
29460	Lakeland-Winter Haven, FL Metro Area	14.7	5.7	1.4	6.2	11.5	19.7	14.1	4.9	3.6
29540	Lancaster, PA Metro Area	11.4	4.8	1.1	4.7	9.2	22.6	7.6	4.8	2.7
29620	Lansing-East Lansing, MI Metro Area	10.7	3.6	1.5	7.4	9.2	27.5	9.8	4.5	7.3
29700	Laredo, TX Metro Area	13.3	14.4	0.6	3.5	7.2	25.1	9.6	5.8	6.0
29740	Las Cruces, NM Metro Area	10.6	4.1	1.0	4.1	11.5	30.6	9.9	4.3	8.5
29820	Las Vegas-Henderson-Paradise, NV Metro Area	12.1	5.1	1.4	6.4	12.0	14.5	28.9	4.4	3.5
29940	Lawrence, KS Metro Area	12.7	2.8	1.5	6.5	11.4	28.3	13.9	3.9	4.4
30020	Lawton, OK Metro Area	12.0	4.5	2.2	7.5	9.1	22.1	9.5	7.4	9.3
30140	Lebanon, PA Metro Area	12.3	6.1	0.9	4.8	7.4	24.8	10.1	4.6	3.6
30300	Lewiston, ID-WA Metro Area	14.1	4.3	1.8	6.0	5.9	21.2	10.3	4.4	4.3
30340	Lewiston-Auburn, ME Metro Area	12.9	4.4	2.1	7.5	9.2	27.9	7.1	3.8	3.6
30460	Lexington-Fayette, KY Metro Area	12.6	3.4	1.6	3.8	10.7	26.5	10.9	4.7	3.9
30620	Lima, OH Metro Area	7.6	4.8	0.6	5.1	6.3	24.4	10.5	5.4	4.8
30700	Lincoln, NE Metro Area	11.2	4.5	1.7	7.4	9.7	26.9	8.4	4.4	5.6
30780	Little Rock-North Little Rock-Conway, AR Metro Area	13.4	5.2	2.6	6.3	8.2	26.3	8.5	5.1	6.7
30860	Logan, UT-ID Metro Area	13.1	2.6	1.3	3.3	12.9	23.9	7.5	4.4	2.5
30980	Longview, TX Metro Area	15.0	5.0	0.5	4.8	8.5	23.0	8.4	6.0	2.8
31020	Longview, WA Metro Area	14.2	5.1	1.0	4.1	7.4	23.2	7.5	5.2	4.2
31080	**Los Angeles-Long Beach-Anaheim, CA Metro Area**	10.4	5.1	3.7	6.8	13.3	20.2	11.2	5.9	3.0
31080/11244	*Anaheim-Santa Ana-Irvine, CA Metro Division*	10.0	3.4	2.1	8.5	14.2	19.1	11.1	5.5	2.7
31080/31084	*Los Angeles-Long Beach-Glendale, CA Metro Division*	10.5	5.6	4.3	6.2	13.0	20.6	11.2	6.0	3.1
31140	Louisville/Jefferson County, KY-IN Metro Area	11.8	7.1	1.7	7.4	8.5	23.0	9.5	4.7	3.2
31180	Lubbock, TX Metro Area	13.3	4.2	2.0	5.7	7.2	28.8	10.6	5.4	3.3
31340	Lynchburg, VA Metro Area	11.0	3.0	1.7	4.8	9.9	29.0	8.6	5.4	4.8

Table D. Metropolitan Statistical Area—Labor Force, Employment, and Educational Data, 2015—*Continued*

CBSA code/ Division code	Metropolitan area, metropolitan division	Retail trade	Transportation and warehousing, and utilities	Information	Finance and insurance, and real estate and rental and leasing	Professional, scientific, and management, and administrative and waste management services	Educational services, and health care and social assistance	Arts, entertainment, and recreation, and accommodation and food services	Other services, except public administration	Public administration
						Industry for employed population age 16 and older				
31420	Macon, GA Metro Area	13.0	5.7	1.3	6.6	8.8	29.8	8.2	4.5	5.4
31460	Madera, CA Metro Area	8.7	3.8	1.1	2.5	6.9	19.2	9.8	4.2	6.2
31540	Madison, WI Metro Area	10.1	3.1	2.7	7.1	12.1	26.7	9.8	4.4	4.9
31700	Manchester-Nashua, NH Metro Area	11.4	3.7	2.6	7.3	13.3	23.4	6.9	5.2	2.8
31740	Manhattan, KS Metro Area	12.2	1.7	1.7	3.9	7.8	31.7	12.5	4.9	5.4
31860	Mankato-North Mankato, MN Metro Area	12.1	3.3	1.7	4.4	6.4	31.0	9.4	4.3	2.9
31900	Mansfield, OH Metro Area	12.8	4.8	1.6	4.6	5.7	23.6	11.1	4.1	4.1
32580	McAllen-Edinburg-Mission, TX Metro Area	14.1	5.3	1.0	4.2	8.0	29.0	8.9	5.8	3.6
32780	Medford, OR Metro Area	15.5	4.5	1.3	3.8	9.0	24.3	10.3	5.7	4.4
32820	Memphis, TN-MS-AR Metro Area	11.8	11.9	1.5	5.5	9.8	21.8	8.9	5.3	4.2
32900	Merced, CA Metro Area	10.6	5.6	0.5	2.8	7.2	21.9	7.5	4.0	3.4
33100	**Miami-Fort Lauderdale-West Palm Beach, FL Metro Area**	12.8	6.1	2.2	7.8	13.5	20.2	11.9	5.9	3.6
33100/22744	*Fort Lauderdale-Pompano Beach-Deerfield Beach, FL Metro Division*	13.7	5.9	2.4	7.3	14.1	20.4	11.6	5.5	4.0
33100/33124	*Miami-Miami Beach-Kendall, FL Metro Division*	11.8	7.5	2.1	7.7	12.5	19.7	12.0	6.5	3.4
33100/48424	*West Palm Beach-Boca Raton-Delray Beach, FL Metro Division*	13.3	3.9	1.9	8.8	14.7	20.6	12.1	5.4	3.3
33140	Michigan City-La Porte, IN Metro Area	13.7	5.8	0.9	3.7	6.8	21.0	8.6	4.8	3.2
33220	Midland, MI Metro Area	11.2	3.7	0.7	5.0	5.9	18.3	11.0	6.1	3.0
33260	Midland, TX Metro Area	9.7	8.1	0.9	4.5	7.6	18.6	8.0	5.7	2.1
33340	Milwaukee-Waukesha-West Allis, WI Metro Area	10.6	3.9	1.6	7.1	10.1	25.0	9.3	4.2	2.9
33460	Minneapolis-St. Paul-Bloomington, MN-WI Metro Area	10.8	4.5	1.9	8.8	11.8	23.4	8.6	4.5	3.2
33540	Missoula, MT Metro Area	15.0	4.0	2.9	5.7	10.2	26.0	12.5	5.9	4.3
33660	Mobile, AL Metro Area	11.5	5.2	1.7	4.6	9.4	27.1	7.9	5.9	2.8
33700	Modesto, CA Metro Area	14.0	6.3	1.2	3.6	7.0	21.4	8.2	4.9	3.6
33740	Monroe, LA Metro Area	13.1	4.3	4.2	6.9	8.5	27.2	8.9	5.2	3.3
33780	Monroe, MI Metro Area	9.2	6.3	0.7	3.2	8.2	24.2	8.8	4.6	2.7
33860	Montgomery, AL Metro Area	11.3	4.0	1.5	6.0	9.8	21.1	10.2	4.4	11.0
34060	Morgantown, WV Metro Area	11.4	1.9	1.2	3.4	7.6	38.0	9.6	3.0	5.4
34100	Morristown, TN Metro Area	12.3	5.1	1.2	3.4	5.3	21.9	8.4	4.7	1.8
34580	Mount Vernon-Anacortes, WA Metro Area	10.3	4.4	1.1	2.4	10.4	20.2	11.1	5.2	4.2
34620	Muncie, IN Metro Area	11.8	3.8	0.8	3.5	8.8	30.3	14.7	4.1	2.9
34740	Muskegon, MI Metro Area	11.9	2.3	1.4	2.4	7.0	21.5	10.1	4.6	3.5
34820	Myrtle Beach-Conway-North Myrtle Beach, SC-NC Metro Area	16.0	3.3	1.9	6.5	10.4	18.4	17.2	4.4	3.3
34900	Napa, CA Metro Area	8.5	2.7	0.8	4.6	7.2	22.0	15.1	4.9	4.0
34940	Naples-Immokalee-Marco Island, FL Metro Area	13.1	4.6	1.7	7.6	12.7	14.2	16.0	6.3	2.3
34980	Nashville-Davidson--Murfreesboro--Franklin, TN Metro Area	11.4	5.4	2.4	7.3	11.6	22.4	10.4	5.2	3.9
35100	New Bern, NC Metro Area	9.7	7.6	0.3	5.1	7.5	21.1	10.2	5.8	9.7
35300	New Haven-Milford, CT Metro Area	11.7	4.1	2.2	6.5	10.1	29.7	7.5	4.8	3.9
35380	New Orleans-Metairie, LA Metro Area	10.9	5.5	1.6	6.0	11.9	21.3	13.3	5.1	5.6
35620	**New York-Newark-Jersey City, NY-NJ-PA Metro Area**	10.4	6.0	3.4	8.9	13.2	25.6	9.3	5.0	3.8
35620/20524	*Dutchess County-Putnam County, NY Metro Division*	11.4	5.1	3.1	6.4	10.4	27.9	8.9	4.2	5.1
35620/35004	*Nassau County-Suffolk County, NY Metro Division*	10.9	5.8	3.1	8.4	11.9	27.6	7.4	4.5	4.4
35620/35084	*Newark, NJ-PA Metro Division*	10.4	5.9	3.1	8.8	14.6	23.4	8.0	4.6	3.5
35620/35614	*New York-Jersey City-White Plains, NY-NJ Metro Division*	10.3	6.1	3.5	9.2	13.3	25.6	10.0	5.3	3.7
35660	Niles-Benton Harbor, MI Metro Area	11.9	5.0	1.5	4.8	7.4	23.0	11.2	4.3	2.1
35840	North Port-Sarasota-Bradenton, FL Metro Area	13.2	3.5	1.3	7.5	12.9	21.6	12.8	5.5	3.4
35980	Norwich-New London, CT Metro Area	12.8	4.6	2.0	5.3	9.4	24.4	14.2	2.7	5.8
36100	Ocala, FL Metro Area	16.8	4.4	1.4	6.2	9.5	24.3	10.4	4.4	3.8

Table D. Metropolitan Statistical Area—Labor Force, Employment, and Educational Data, 2015—*Continued*

		Industry for employed population age 16 and older								
CBSA code/ Division code	Metropolitan area, metropolitan division	Retail trade	Transportation and warehousing, and utilities	Information	Finance and insurance, and real estate and rental and leasing	Professional, scientific, and management, and administrative and waste management services	Educational services, and health care and social assistance	Arts, entertainment, and recreation, and accommodation and food services	Other services, except public administration	Public administration
36140	Ocean City, NJ Metro Area	10.8	2.6	1.4	6.9	8.2	25.5	16.8	3.5	7.8
36220	Odessa, TX Metro Area	11.4	5.8	1.1	5.7	5.7	16.3	9.4	7.6	2.4
36260	Ogden-Clearfield, UT Metro Area	11.6	4.7	1.5	6.3	11.1	19.1	7.5	4.2	8.8
36420	Oklahoma City, OK Metro Area	12.0	4.1	1.8	6.7	9.8	22.6	9.5	5.1	6.4
36500	Olympia-Tumwater, WA Metro Area	10.8	4.3	1.6	4.7	9.8	20.5	9.9	5.6	16.7
36540	Omaha-Council Bluffs, NE-IA Metro Area	11.2	5.5	2.1	9.7	11.4	23.8	8.2	4.4	3.3
36740	Orlando-Kissimmee-Sanford, FL Metro Area	12.5	4.8	2.1	7.7	13.6	19.7	18.3	4.0	3.4
36780	Oshkosh-Neenah, WI Metro Area	12.4	3.4	1.1	4.7	9.3	21.5	8.5	3.5	3.2
36980	Owensboro, KY Metro Area	11.2	5.5	1.7	7.5	5.8	23.1	7.4	7.3	3.8
37100	Oxnard-Thousand Oaks-Ventura, CA Metro Area	11.2	3.7	2.6	7.2	11.8	18.9	9.6	5.4	4.3
37340	Palm Bay-Melbourne-Titusville, FL Metro Area	13.5	4.1	1.7	4.4	13.8	22.3	11.2	5.5	5.1
37460	Panama City, FL Metro Area	14.6	4.2	2.3	5.3	10.9	20.8	13.4	3.8	9.0
37620	Parkersburg-Vienna, WV Metro Area	15.4	3.4	1.8	4.6	9.6	24.8	10.2	5.0	6.7
37860	Pensacola-Ferry Pass-Brent, FL Metro Area	14.5	5.1	1.6	8.6	11.5	19.9	11.6	6.6	6.7
37900	Peoria, IL Metro Area	11.9	4.7	1.6	5.0	8.3	23.8	9.3	5.2	4.0
37980	**Philadelphia-Camden-Wilmington, PA-NJ-DE-MD Metro Area**	10.8	5.0	2.0	8.1	12.9	26.6	8.6	4.4	4.2
37980/15804	*Camden, NJ Metro Division*	11.2	5.6	2.0	7.7	12.5	26.8	8.4	4.2	5.1
37980/33874	*Montgomery County-Bucks County-Chester County, PA Metro Division*	10.5	3.7	2.3	9.0	14.8	23.8	7.6	4.3	2.3
37980/37964	*Philadelphia, PA Metro Division*	10.6	6.0	1.9	6.2	11.9	29.9	9.5	4.9	5.6
37980/48864	*Wilmington, DE-MD-NJ Metro Division*	11.3	5.2	1.6	11.5	10.9	25.7	9.2	4.1	4.0
38060	Phoenix-Mesa-Scottsdale, AZ Metro Area	12.5	5.2	2.0	9.8	12.8	20.7	10.6	4.6	4.0
38220	Pine Bluff, AR Metro Area	8.4	4.9	0.7	3.2	7.2	29.7	5.0	3.9	9.1
38300	Pittsburgh, PA Metro Area	11.8	5.3	1.6	7.1	11.0	25.7	8.8	4.8	2.9
38340	Pittsfield, MA Metro Area	11.8	2.7	2.6	5.4	10.4	29.5	11.0	5.9	3.1
38540	Pocatello, ID Metro Area	11.1	6.3	1.7	7.0	7.9	27.3	12.4	2.9	4.3
38860	Portland-South Portland, ME Metro Area	12.2	3.1	2.4	8.0	10.0	26.4	9.8	4.6	3.0
38900	Portland-Vancouver-Hillsboro, OR-WA Metro Area	11.1	4.7	2.1	6.4	12.7	22.0	9.8	4.5	3.7
38940	Port St. Lucie, FL Metro Area	12.9	3.2	1.5	5.8	15.4	21.2	13.2	6.0	3.8
39140	Prescott, AZ Metro Area	13.9	5.3	1.6	3.8	10.8	23.4	14.7	5.0	4.9
39300	Providence-Warwick, RI-MA Metro Area	12.2	3.6	1.6	6.1	8.9	27.2	10.7	4.3	4.1
39340	Provo-Orem, UT Metro Area	12.7	3.0	3.2	5.3	12.8	25.3	8.2	4.7	3.3
39380	Pueblo, CO Metro Area	13.4	4.9	2.0	3.9	9.3	26.4	9.2	4.4	6.1
39460	Punta Gorda, FL Metro Area	21.9	5.0	2.0	6.8	11.3	20.6	9.2	4.6	2.0
39540	Racine, WI Metro Area	11.0	5.6	1.2	4.9	9.1	21.8	7.6	4.6	2.5
39580	Raleigh, NC Metro Area	11.0	3.6	3.1	6.9	17.3	20.4	9.0	4.2	5.4
39660	Rapid City, SD Metro Area	11.4	4.4	1.2	8.0	9.3	22.5	12.4	5.6	4.9
39740	Reading, PA Metro Area	12.0	5.2	1.3	5.9	9.1	22.2	7.3	4.5	2.6
39820	Redding, CA Metro Area	13.7	3.0	2.7	5.6	7.8	26.0	9.7	6.6	7.4
39900	Reno, NV Metro Area	12.5	6.2	1.4	5.9	12.1	18.6	17.0	5.0	3.9
40060	Richmond, VA Metro Area	12.2	5.1	1.8	9.4	11.2	22.7	9.5	5.3	6.1
40140	Riverside-San Bernardino-Ontario, CA Metro Area	13.3	7.2	1.3	5.0	9.9	21.3	10.2	5.4	4.9
40220	Roanoke, VA Metro Area	10.8	5.8	1.2	8.7	9.1	23.6	9.8	4.9	4.7
40340	Rochester, MN Metro Area	10.6	3.6	1.8	3.2	6.3	40.2	6.4	4.2	2.6
40380	Rochester, NY Metro Area	11.5	3.7	2.2	4.8	10.8	29.8	8.4	4.8	3.3
40420	Rockford, IL Metro Area	12.8	5.0	1.2	4.2	8.9	21.2	9.1	4.4	3.4
40580	Rocky Mount, NC Metro Area	10.4	6.9	1.1	6.0	7.1	23.7	9.5	3.5	3.8
40660	Rome, GA Metro Area	9.3	4.4	0.8	4.1	7.0	24.6	10.0	8.9	3.7
40900	Sacramento--Roseville--Arden-Arcade, CA Metro Area	11.4	5.3	1.9	6.9	12.2	22.6	9.6	4.7	9.5
40980	Saginaw, MI Metro Area	13.6	4.6	2.1	3.3	8.2	26.5	10.0	4.1	4.1
41060	St. Cloud, MN Metro Area	12.2	4.7	1.4	4.7	7.9	26.5	7.3	5.0	2.4
41100	St. George, UT Metro Area	15.9	3.8	2.4	6.1	9.6	23.3	14.4	3.8	3.3
41140	St. Joseph, MO-KS Metro Area	10.6	5.9	1.6	5.6	8.3	24.7	9.0	3.3	3.5
41180	St. Louis, MO-IL Metro Area	11.3	5.1	2.0	7.9	11.1	23.7	9.5	4.9	3.6
41420	Salem, OR Metro Area	12.8	2.9	1.0	4.6	9.4	22.1	7.6	4.6	7.4
41500	Salinas, CA Metro Area	9.0	3.1	0.7	3.2	8.8	19.5	12.4	4.2	5.4

Table D. Metropolitan Statistical Area—Labor Force, Employment, and Educational Data, 2015—*Continued*

CBSA code/ Division code	Metropolitan area, metropolitan division	Retail trade	Transportation and warehousing, and utilities	Information	Finance and insurance, and real estate and rental and leasing	Professional, scientific, and management, and administrative and waste management services	Educational services, and health care and social assistance	Arts, entertainment, and recreation, and accommodation and food services	Other services, except public administration	Public administration
						Industry for employed population age 16 and older				
41540	Salisbury, MD-DE Metro Area	13.1	4.4	1.3	4.5	7.7	23.6	11.4	5.3	6.0
41620	Salt Lake City, UT Metro Area	12.3	4.9	2.1	8.6	12.9	19.0	9.3	4.5	4.2
41660	San Angelo, TX Metro Area	14.6	3.4	1.9	3.5	8.8	25.6	8.6	4.9	5.7
41700	San Antonio-New Braunfels, TX Metro Area	12.1	4.8	1.9	8.3	11.0	22.0	11.1	4.8	5.3
41740	San Diego-Carlsbad, CA Metro Area	10.6	3.8	2.4	5.9	15.0	21.2	12.3	5.6	4.9
41860	**San Francisco-Oakland-Hayward, CA Metro Area**	9.8	5.0	4.1	7.5	19.1	20.3	9.7	5.1	3.6
41860/36084	*Oakland-Hayward-Berkeley, CA Metro Division*	9.5	5.6	3.2	7.0	17.6	21.4	8.9	5.3	3.8
41860/41884	*San Francisco-Redwood City-South San Francisco, CA Metro Division*	10.1	4.7	5.4	7.9	21.1	18.6	11.1	4.7	3.5
41860/42034	*San Rafael, CA Metro Division*	10.5	2.0	4.1	10.9	21.0	19.9	8.1	6.6	3.8
41940	San Jose-Sunnyvale-Santa Clara, CA Metro Area	8.9	2.9	4.7	4.8	19.4	18.5	8.7	3.9	2.8
42020	San Luis Obispo-Paso Robles-Arroyo Grande, CA Metro Area	11.8	4.7	1.2	4.4	9.8	25.3	13.3	4.4	5.8
42100	Santa Cruz-Watsonville, CA Metro Area	9.7	3.1	2.0	3.9	11.0	23.4	14.5	5.8	2.8
42140	Santa Fe, NM Metro Area	11.6	3.1	1.9	4.9	16.4	22.1	14.5	5.5	8.9
42200	Santa Maria-Santa Barbara, CA Metro Area	9.2	2.9	2.3	4.5	11.2	23.0	12.3	5.5	3.7
42220	Santa Rosa, CA Metro Area	11.4	3.9	2.0	6.3	10.9	21.0	11.1	4.6	3.4
42340	Savannah, GA Metro Area	13.2	8.7	1.1	5.2	8.9	22.7	11.8	5.4	4.6
42540	Scranton--Wilkes-Barre--Hazleton, PA Metro Area	12.9	5.9	1.5	5.1	8.9	25.7	8.8	4.0	4.8
42660	**Seattle-Tacoma-Bellevue, WA Metro Area**	12.0	5.1	2.8	5.9	15.1	20.6	9.2	4.5	4.1
42660/42644	*Seattle-Bellevue-Everett, WA Metro Division*	12.0	4.8	3.1	6.1	16.7	20.1	9.2	4.5	3.4
42660/45104	*Tacoma-Lakewood, WA Metro Division*	12.3	6.6	1.6	4.9	8.4	23.0	9.1	4.6	6.8
42680	Sebastian-Vero Beach, FL Metro Area	13.6	2.9	1.5	9.2	11.0	21.6	12.5	3.5	4.1
42700	Sebring, FL Metro Area	16.4	4.8	0.8	7.8	7.5	26.6	10.7	5.2	3.9
43100	Sheboygan, WI Metro Area	11.4	5.0	0.4	4.6	6.2	17.3	7.8	4.1	2.3
43300	Sherman-Denison, TX Metro Area	9.7	3.4	1.8	4.9	8.0	25.1	8.8	5.5	5.2
43340	Shreveport-Bossier City, LA Metro Area	11.8	5.4	1.7	5.1	8.3	24.6	10.9	4.8	6.0
43420	Sierra Vista-Douglas, AZ Metro Area	12.1	4.8	1.4	3.5	11.2	25.4	8.5	3.0	15.8
43580	Sioux City, IA-NE-SD Metro Area	11.5	6.1	1.0	6.1	5.6	19.8	10.8	4.4	3.3
43620	Sioux Falls, SD Metro Area	10.6	4.5	1.7	10.6	7.7	26.2	7.6	3.9	2.7
43780	South Bend-Mishawaka, IN-MI Metro Area	11.1	3.4	2.3	4.9	8.1	26.6	8.2	4.2	2.7
43900	Spartanburg, SC Metro Area	11.9	4.4	2.1	3.9	7.7	19.5	9.3	6.0	1.9
44060	Spokane-Spokane Valley, WA Metro Area	12.5	4.9	1.5	6.9	9.1	26.7	8.4	5.6	4.7
44100	Springfield, IL Metro Area	9.4	4.0	1.8	9.5	8.9	25.9	9.6	4.4	12.3
44140	Springfield, MA Metro Area	12.6	4.5	2.0	7.0	7.6	33.2	8.5	3.6	4.1
44180	Springfield, MO Metro Area	11.9	5.7	1.8	6.2	9.6	26.1	9.7	5.5	3.3
44220	Springfield, OH Metro Area	11.4	4.5	0.9	5.7	9.0	25.4	8.0	4.5	3.4
44300	State College, PA Metro Area	10.1	2.9	0.5	2.7	9.8	38.8	10.8	4.7	3.2
44420	Staunton-Waynesboro, VA Metro Area	14.4	6.3	1.1	2.9	7.4	24.5	8.7	5.3	2.1
44700	Stockton-Lodi, CA Metro Area	12.4	8.2	1.7	5.0	9.4	19.7	8.1	4.5	4.3
44940	Sumter, SC Metro Area	10.8	3.7	1.5	4.7	6.4	21.7	8.3	4.8	7.7
45060	Syracuse, NY Metro Area	11.9	5.7	2.2	5.4	9.2	29.2	10.1	4.1	3.9
45220	Tallahassee, FL Metro Area	11.9	3.5	1.6	5.7	11.6	27.5	13.1	4.3	12.3
45300	Tampa-St. Petersburg-Clearwater, FL Metro Area	12.6	4.5	2.2	9.7	14.0	21.8	10.3	4.8	3.8
45460	Terre Haute, IN Metro Area	10.7	4.7	0.8	4.8	6.8	25.2	8.9	3.6	4.2
45500	Texarkana, TX-AR Metro Area	14.3	5.5	1.0	4.2	8.6	23.6	7.6	5.6	7.3
45540	The Villages, FL Metro Area	12.2	4.0	3.0	11.2	14.1	13.7	16.0	2.6	10.9
45780	Toledo, OH Metro Area	10.9	6.3	1.1	3.3	8.8	25.9	10.5	4.6	2.9
45820	Topeka, KS Metro Area	11.5	5.5	1.8	7.5	7.4	26.2	7.9	5.5	7.5
45940	Trenton, NJ Metro Area	11.2	4.4	1.7	8.5	14.1	24.7	8.2	4.5	7.3
46060	Tucson, AZ Metro Area	12.3	3.7	1.5	5.3	13.0	24.5	12.0	5.3	6.6
46140	Tulsa, OK Metro Area	11.0	6.2	2.3	5.9	10.3	21.5	8.7	5.5	3.8
46220	Tuscaloosa, AL Metro Area	10.8	4.3	1.9	4.2	7.1	28.2	7.5	4.8	4.1
46340	Tyler, TX Metro Area	14.5	3.8	2.7	5.8	7.9	27.7	8.7	6.6	2.8
46520	Urban Honolulu, HI Metro Area	11.4	5.9	1.8	6.9	9.7	20.5	14.7	4.8	9.9
46540	Utica-Rome, NY Metro Area	12.8	4.3	0.9	5.5	7.5	31.2	7.7	4.3	6.4

Table D. Metropolitan Statistical Area—Labor Force, Employment, and Educational Data, 2015—*Continued*

CBSA code/ Division code	Metropolitan area, metropolitan division	Industry for employed population age 16 and older								
		Retail trade	Transportation and warehousing, and utilities	Information	Finance and insurance, and real estate and rental and leasing	Professional, scientific, and management, and administrative and waste management services	Educational services, and health care and social assistance	Arts, entertainment, and recreation, and accommodation and food services	Other services, except public administration	Public administration
46660	Valdosta, GA Metro Area	15.4	4.2	1.8	4.1	9.5	25.3	11.7	4.9	5.9
46700	Vallejo-Fairfield, CA Metro Area	12.1	6.2	1.6	4.7	11.4	22.3	8.0	4.6	7.3
47020	Victoria, TX Metro Area	17.0	5.4	1.0	3.4	4.9	26.8	7.8	3.9	5.2
47220	Vineland-Bridgeton, NJ Metro Area	12.2	5.8	0.7	4.1	7.3	26.1	6.8	3.1	6.6
47260	Virginia Beach-Norfolk-Newport News, VA-NC Metro Area	11.4	4.2	1.7	6.2	10.9	22.8	10.0	4.7	9.6
47300	Visalia-Porterville, CA Metro Area	11.6	4.6	0.9	3.0	7.4	20.1	8.0	4.4	5.7
47380	Waco, TX Metro Area	11.8	4.5	1.4	7.0	8.3	24.0	8.5	5.1	6.3
47460	Walla Walla, WA Metro Area	10.6	2.8	0.6	4.6	8.0	29.9	9.4	4.6	7.1
47580	Warner Robins, GA Metro Area	11.7	5.6	1.0	3.3	8.4	19.1	8.6	6.8	17.4
47900	**Washington-Arlington-Alexandria, DC-VA-MD-WV Metro Area**	8.3	3.8	2.6	6.1	20.7	19.7	9.1	6.4	12.6
47900/43524	*Silver Spring-Frederick-Rockville, MD Metro Division*	8.2	3.0	2.5	6.5	21.0	21.6	8.7	6.3	10.3
47900/47894	*Washington-Arlington-Alexandria, DC-VA-MD-WV Metro Division*	8.4	4.0	2.7	6.0	20.6	19.2	9.2	6.4	13.2
47940	Waterloo-Cedar Falls, IA Metro Area	13.2	3.7	1.4	5.8	6.6	26.6	8.5	4.2	1.4
48060	Watertown-Fort Drum, NY Metro Area	12.7	4.3	1.3	4.6	5.3	25.4	10.2	7.5	12.4
48140	Wausau, WI Metro Area	11.8	5.1	0.6	8.3	5.3	22.6	6.5	2.8	2.6
48260	Weirton-Steubenville, WV-OH Metro Area	15.2	8.8	1.0	5.2	7.2	23.8	9.0	5.3	4.5
48300	Wenatchee, WA Metro Area	13.1	8.6	0.8	4.0	9.4	19.7	8.8	3.2	3.8
48540	Wheeling, WV-OH Metro Area	14.5	5.3	0.7	4.2	6.8	28.3	8.5	4.7	5.1
48620	Wichita, KS Metro Area	12.1	4.3	1.8	4.6	8.1	23.8	8.8	4.3	2.9
48660	Wichita Falls, TX Metro Area	14.7	3.9	2.2	3.1	7.1	24.6	11.3	5.2	5.6
48700	Williamsport, PA Metro Area	11.4	5.2	1.6	3.0	7.2	28.0	9.2	3.7	3.2
48900	Wilmington, NC Metro Area	14.1	4.4	2.8	5.3	10.8	24.8	10.7	5.3	2.5
49020	Winchester, VA-WV Metro Area	12.6	5.6	3.4	4.2	7.8	25.6	7.4	4.1	5.4
49180	Winston-Salem, NC Metro Area	11.1	4.6	1.3	5.1	9.5	25.0	8.3	4.9	3.3
49340	Worcester, MA-CT Metro Area	12.4	3.6	1.8	6.2	10.1	27.9	8.9	4.3	3.5
49420	Yakima, WA Metro Area	9.9	7.7	1.1	2.4	5.8	20.7	7.2	4.6	4.3
49620	York-Hanover, PA Metro Area	11.6	6.4	1.1	5.2	8.5	21.4	7.9	5.2	5.1
49660	Youngstown-Warren-Boardman, OH-PA Metro Area	13.2	5.2	1.3	5.1	7.9	24.2	9.4	4.8	3.5
49700	Yuba City, CA Metro Area	13.5	6.5	1.5	4.8	8.0	20.7	8.4	2.9	8.5
49740	Yuma, AZ Metro Area	10.6	3.4	1.0	4.3	8.9	19.2	12.3	5.3	10.8

Table D. Metropolitan Statistical Area—Labor Force, Employment, and Educational Data, 2015

CBSA code/ Division code	Metropolitan area, metropolitan division	Total population age 25 and older	Educational attainment for the population age 25 and older			
			Educational attainment			
			Less than high school graduate	High school graduate (includes equivalency)	Some college or Associate's degree	Bachelor's degree or higher
10180	Abilene, TX Metro Area	106,507	12.3	32.7	34.4	20.7
10420	Akron, OH Metro Area	482,473	8.5	33.4	28.0	30.1
10500	Albany, GA Metro Area	101,243	17.7	31.2	30.0	21.1
10540	Albany, OR Metro Area	83,387	10.1	30.1	42.6	17.2
10580	Albany-Schenectady-Troy, NY Metro Area	605,021	7.8	27.5	29.4	35.3
10740	Albuquerque, NM Metro Area	612,939	12.8	25.1	31.9	30.2
10780	Alexandria, LA Metro Area	103,271	17.1	39.0	26.2	17.7
10900	Allentown-Bethlehem-Easton, PA-NJ Metro Area	577,040	11.2	33.3	27.3	28.2
11020	Altoona, PA Metro Area	89,411	9.6	46.7	21.8	21.9
11100	Amarillo, TX Metro Area	168,964	15.4	24.9	35.2	24.5
11180	Ames, IA Metro Area	49,115	3.0	17.0	28.5	51.6
11260	Anchorage, AK Metro Area	253,453	6.4	26.1	35.8	31.7
11460	Ann Arbor, MI Metro Area	223,966	5.4	14.8	24.6	55.2
11500	Anniston-Oxford-Jacksonville, AL Metro Area	78,387	18.0	30.1	34.6	17.3
11540	Appleton, WI Metro Area	156,226	5.9	34.1	31.0	29.0
11700	Asheville, NC Metro Area	327,553	11.6	25.6	29.9	32.8
12020	Athens-Clarke County, GA Metro Area	119,110	14.4	25.3	22.4	38.0
12060	Atlanta-Sandy Springs-Roswell, GA Metro Area	3,734,637	11.3	24.5	27.2	37.0
12100	Atlantic City-Hammonton, NJ Metro Area	187,759	14.4	32.8	25.6	27.2
12220	Auburn-Opelika, AL Metro Area	92,177	8.6	23.5	33.7	34.3
12260	Augusta-Richmond County, GA-SC Metro Area	393,190	15.1	29.5	30.8	24.6
12420	Austin-Round Rock, TX Metro Area	1,321,572	10.8	19.6	26.9	42.6
12540	Bakersfield, CA Metro Area	528,165	26.6	29.1	28.0	16.2
12580	Baltimore-Columbia-Towson, MD Metro Area	1,921,102	9.6	25.6	26.2	38.6
12620	Bangor, ME Metro Area	107,601	10.0	33.8	31.7	24.5
12700	Barnstable Town, MA Metro Area	165,588	4.2	25.0	30.7	40.1
12940	Baton Rouge, LA Metro Area	534,104	11.9	32.9	26.9	28.2
12980	Battle Creek, MI Metro Area	90,733	9.3	38.7	32.1	20.0
13020	Bay City, MI Metro Area	74,816	10.0	34.8	37.2	18.0
13140	Beaumont-Port Arthur, TX Metro Area	271,366	14.3	36.3	31.9	17.5
13220	Beckley, WV Metro Area	87,689	18.7	41.3	25.2	14.8
13380	Bellingham, WA Metro Area	138,988	7.0	24.8	35.2	33.0
13460	Bend-Redmond, OR Metro Area	125,575	4.1	20.8	38.6	36.5
13740	Billings, MT Metro Area	116,101	6.1	32.1	31.9	29.9
13780	Binghamton, NY Metro Area	165,142	8.6	32.7	31.7	27.1
13820	Birmingham-Hoover, AL Metro Area	780,402	12.0	28.4	31.0	28.6
13900	Bismarck, ND Metro Area	88,853	7.1	25.6	33.4	33.9
13980	Blacksburg-Christiansburg-Radford, VA Metro Area	109,450	10.1	27.6	27.1	35.2
14010	Bloomington, IL Metro Area	115,006	4.9	27.3	23.8	44.0
14020	Bloomington, IN Metro Area	96,446	8.3	25.4	25.9	40.4
14100	Bloomsburg-Berwick, PA Metro Area	57,347	11.0	42.3	22.7	24.0
14260	Boise City, ID Metro Area	439,125	8.5	26.1	35.3	30.1
14460	Boston-Cambridge-Newton, MA-NH Metro Area	3,313,637	8.6	23.4	22.1	46.0
14460/14454	**Boston, MA Metro Division; Boston-Cambridge-Newton, MA-NH Metro Area**	1,373,731	9.9	23.8	22.4	43.9
14460/15764	*Cambridge-Newton-Framingham, MA Metro Division*	1,640,640	8.1	22.5	20.6	48.8
14460/40484	*Rockingham County-Strafford County, NH Metro Division*	299,266	5.6	26.0	28.5	39.9
14500	Boulder, CO Metro Area	206,135	5.4	13.0	21.0	60.6
14540	Bowling Green, KY Metro Area	106,396	15.3	29.9	29.2	25.7
14740	Bremerton-Silverdale, WA Metro Area	178,483	5.2	23.2	41.1	30.5
14860	Bridgeport-Stamford-Norwalk, CT Metro Area	641,084	9.9	23.3	20.6	46.3
15180	Brownsville-Harlingen, TX Metro Area	244,947	34.5	25.1	25.2	15.2
15260	Brunswick, GA Metro Area	81,264	14.0	31.4	30.5	24.1
15380	Buffalo-Cheektowaga-Niagara Falls, NY Metro Area	792,356	9.5	29.7	30.6	30.3
15500	Burlington, NC Metro Area	106,205	16.7	27.2	33.3	22.9
15540	Burlington-South Burlington, VT Metro Area	144,307	7.0	24.4	25.2	43.4
15680	California-Lexington Park, MD Metro Area	74,038	9.9	26.4	30.4	33.3
15940	Canton-Massillon, OH Metro Area	279,545	9.6	38.6	30.7	21.2
15980	Cape Coral-Fort Myers, FL Metro Area	522,733	13.0	31.2	29.6	26.2

Table D. Metropolitan Statistical Area—Labor Force, Employment, and Educational Data, 2015—*Continued*

CBSA code/ Division code	Metropolitan area, metropolitan division	Total population age 25 and older	Educational attainment for the population age 25 and older			
			Educational attainment			
			Less than high school graduate	High school graduate (includes equivalency)	Some college or Associate's degree	Bachelor's degree or higher
16020	Cape Girardeau, MO-IL Metro Area	62,792	11.9	32.9	30.3	24.9
16060	Carbondale-Marion, IL Metro Area	82,220	7.1	30.3	35.2	27.4
16180	Carson City, NV Metro Area	38,334	15.0	25.6	37.7	21.7
16220	Casper, WY Metro Area	53,528	10.6	29.5	37.7	22.2
16300	Cedar Rapids, IA Metro Area	179,106	5.5	30.8	35.5	28.1
16540	Chambersburg-Waynesboro, PA Metro Area	106,517	12.3	44.6	23.0	20.2
16580	Champaign-Urbana, IL Metro Area	141,822	4.9	25.2	27.4	42.6
16620	Charleston, WV Metro Area	158,868	13.3	40.4	23.5	22.8
16700	Charleston-North Charleston, SC Metro Area	508,644	9.1	26.5	29.7	34.7
16740	Charlotte-Concord-Gastonia, NC-SC Metro Area	1,617,907	12.1	24.6	29.8	33.5
16820	Charlottesville, VA Metro Area	156,796	9.7	23.1	26.3	40.9
16860	Chattanooga, TN-GA Metro Area	378,791	15.2	30.6	29.1	25.1
16940	Cheyenne, WY Metro Area	64,281	7.9	25.9	38.8	27.5
16980	**Chicago-Naperville-Elgin, IL-IN-WI Metro Area**	6,407,668	12.1	24.6	27.3	36.0
16980/16974	*Chicago-Naperville-Arlington Heights, IL Metro Division*	4,969,082	12.1	23.9	26.8	37.2
16980/20994	*Elgin, IL Metro Division*	401,765	15.7	22.8	30.3	31.2
16980/23844	*Gary, IN Metro Division*	471,073	11.1	35.3	31.1	22.5
16980/29404	*Lake County-Kenosha County, IL-WI Metro Division*	565,748	9.6	23.6	26.6	40.2
17020	Chico, CA Metro Area	146,064	11.6	21.1	39.6	27.8
17140	Cincinnati, OH-KY-IN Metro Area	1,439,532	9.5	30.1	28.3	32.1
17300	Clarksville, TN-KY Metro Area	169,045	8.4	32.5	35.1	24.0
17420	Cleveland, TN Metro Area	81,001	18.1	32.1	31.2	18.5
17460	Cleveland-Elyria, OH Metro Area	1,432,123	10.3	29.9	30.4	29.4
17660	Coeur d'Alene, ID Metro Area	103,211	8.4	27.3	41.1	23.2
17780	College Station-Bryan, TX Metro Area	136,908	14.2	21.7	27.8	36.3
17820	Colorado Springs, CO Metro Area	446,709	5.5	21.8	36.2	36.5
17860	Columbia, MO Metro Area	104,102	5.9	21.3	24.4	48.5
17900	Columbia, SC Metro Area	529,053	10.8	27.1	30.7	31.4
17980	Columbus, GA-AL Metro Area	203,174	13.7	28.0	34.9	23.3
18020	Columbus, IN Metro Area	54,548	8.2	33.5	28.6	29.6
18140	Columbus, OH Metro Area	1,348,258	9.1	28.4	27.4	35.1
18580	Corpus Christi, TX Metro Area	291,482	19.6	29.3	30.6	20.5
18700	Corvallis, OR Metro Area	52,894	5.5	14.9	24.4	55.1
18880	Crestview-Fort Walton Beach-Destin, FL Metro Area	183,142	9.3	25.6	36.6	28.5
19060	Cumberland, MD-WV Metro Area	69,579	10.6	45.1	29.1	15.3
19100	**Dallas-Fort Worth-Arlington, TX Metro Area**	4,555,092	15.6	22.6	28.5	33.4
19100/19124	*Dallas-Plano-Irving, TX Metro Division*	3,016,975	16.0	21.2	27.2	35.5
19100/23104	*Fort Worth-Arlington, TX Metro Division*	1,538,117	14.6	25.2	30.9	29.3
19140	Dalton, GA Metro Area	92,059	31.3	30.0	25.3	13.4
19180	Danville, IL Metro Area	53,843	12.5	40.9	33.5	13.0
19300	Daphne-Fairhope-Foley, AL Metro Area	143,738	9.2	31.7	29.6	29.5
19340	Davenport-Moline-Rock Island, IA-IL Metro Area	263,037	9.5	31.8	32.7	26.0
19380	Dayton, OH Metro Area	544,791	9.5	29.2	32.7	28.5
19460	Decatur, AL Metro Area	106,054	18.0	31.3	30.7	19.9
19500	Decatur, IL Metro Area	73,158	10.6	34.5	31.4	23.4
19660	Deltona-Daytona Beach-Ormond Beach, FL Metro Area	460,890	9.1	33.6	34.2	23.1
19740	Denver-Aurora-Lakewood, CO Metro Area	1,919,084	9.5	20.1	28.6	41.8
19780	Des Moines-West Des Moines, IA Metro Area	409,801	8.1	25.8	30.9	35.1
19820	**Detroit-Warren-Dearborn, MI Metro Area**	2,949,395	10.7	27.0	32.8	29.5
19820/19804	*Detroit-Dearborn-Livonia, MI Metro Division*	1,170,856	14.5	30.4	32.5	22.6
19820/47664	*Warren-Troy-Farmington Hills, MI Metro Division*	1,778,539	8.2	24.8	32.9	34.1
20020	Dothan, AL Metro Area	102,233	16.6	32.2	32.2	19.0

Table D. Metropolitan Statistical Area—Labor Force, Employment, and Educational Data, 2015—*Continued*

			Educational attainment for the population age 25 and older			
			Educational attainment			
CBSA code/ Division code	Metropolitan area, metropolitan division	Total population age 25 and older	Less than high school graduate	High school graduate (includes equivalency)	Some college or Associate's degree	Bachelor's degree or higher
20100	Dover, DE Metro Area	113,970	13.5	33.8	31.4	21.3
20220	Dubuque, IA Metro Area	64,517	8.6	32.0	28.5	30.9
20260	Duluth, MN-WI Metro Area	191,463	5.9	31.1	36.6	26.5
20500	Durham-Chapel Hill, NC Metro Area	369,442	11.9	19.9	23.2	45.1
20700	East Stroudsburg, PA Metro Area	113,149	11.2	36.0	27.9	24.9
20740	Eau Claire, WI Metro Area	108,249	7.4	29.6	36.5	26.5
20940	El Centro, CA Metro Area	109,306	33.4	21.3	31.0	14.3
21060	Elizabethtown-Fort Knox, KY Metro Area	98,204	12.5	32.3	35.1	20.1
21140	Elkhart-Goshen, IN Metro Area	127,871	20.0	35.0	26.7	18.3
21300	Elmira, NY Metro Area	60,894	9.0	35.4	31.4	24.2
21340	El Paso, TX Metro Area	507,644	22.7	25.0	29.5	22.8
21500	Erie, PA Metro Area	187,773	8.3	39.0	26.3	26.4
21660	Eugene, OR Metro Area	246,605	9.2	24.0	37.6	29.1
21780	Evansville, IN-KY Metro Area	214,725	9.6	36.4	30.6	23.3
21820	Fairbanks, AK Metro Area	59,492	4.7	19.5	41.3	34.5
22020	Fargo, ND-MN Metro Area	144,696	5.6	23.1	36.8	34.5
22140	Farmington, NM Metro Area	76,791	17.4	34.3	34.2	14.1
22180	Fayetteville, NC Metro Area	234,567	9.8	25.3	39.7	25.2
22220	Fayetteville-Springdale-Rogers, AR-MO Metro Area	324,727	14.4	29.4	25.4	30.8
22380	Flagstaff, AZ Metro Area	80,427	10.5	22.2	34.2	33.1
22420	Flint, MI Metro Area	278,345	10.0	32.0	37.2	20.8
22500	Florence, SC Metro Area	139,053	16.7	35.6	28.0	19.8
22520	Florence-Muscle Shoals, AL Metro Area	101,533	15.3	36.0	27.9	20.8
22540	Fond du Lac, WI Metro Area	70,505	8.4	38.0	32.0	21.7
22660	Fort Collins, CO Metro Area	217,339	4.2	20.0	29.6	46.2
22900	Fort Smith, AR-OK Metro Area	187,828	16.9	34.9	31.1	17.1
23060	Fort Wayne, IN Metro Area	279,140	10.4	30.8	31.9	26.9
23420	Fresno, CA Metro Area	590,620	25.6	23.4	31.8	19.2
23460	Gadsden, AL Metro Area	71,551	16.2	31.4	35.1	17.3
23540	Gainesville, FL Metro Area	166,968	7.8	22.6	27.6	42.0
23580	Gainesville, GA Metro Area	125,214	20.8	27.6	29.0	22.7
23900	Gettysburg, PA Metro Area	71,589	10.6	41.5	26.8	21.0
24020	Glens Falls, NY Metro Area	92,339	9.8	35.4	30.3	24.6
24140	Goldsboro, NC Metro Area	82,719	14.7	29.4	34.0	21.9
24220	Grand Forks, ND-MN Metro Area	62,152	6.0	26.4	34.7	32.8
24260	Grand Island, NE Metro Area	54,583	13.4	34.2	32.6	19.8
24300	Grand Junction, CO Metro Area	99,999	9.2	25.9	34.6	30.3
24340	Grand Rapids-Wyoming, MI Metro Area	673,744	9.8	27.5	31.7	31.1
24420	Grants Pass, OR Metro Area	62,429	10.9	35.0	40.2	14.0
24500	Great Falls, MT Metro Area	55,591	8.6	33.9	31.9	25.6
24540	Greeley, CO Metro Area	180,362	12.9	26.6	34.6	25.9
24580	Green Bay, WI Metro Area	214,031	8.4	33.6	31.9	26.1
24660	Greensboro-High Point, NC Metro Area	508,638	14.1	26.8	31.2	28.0
24780	Greenville, NC Metro Area	105,143	10.5	25.0	32.8	31.6
24860	Greenville-Anderson-Mauldin, SC Metro Area	586,353	14.9	28.3	30.1	26.7
25060	Gulfport-Biloxi-Pascagoula, MS Metro Area	258,547	13.9	31.2	34.5	20.4
25180	Hagerstown-Martinsburg, MD-WV Metro Area	180,660	12.4	39.1	29.4	19.1
25220	Hammond, LA Metro Area	80,916	14.1	37.0	29.8	19.1
25260	Hanford-Corcoran, CA Metro Area	92,734	27.3	23.9	32.7	16.1
25420	Harrisburg-Carlisle, PA Metro Area	389,642	9.7	35.3	25.4	29.6
25500	Harrisonburg, VA Metro Area	79,147	17.3	30.7	23.0	29.0
25540	Hartford-West Hartford-East Hartford, CT Metro Area	834,317	9.6	26.9	25.3	38.3
25620	Hattiesburg, MS Metro Area	93,004	12.6	29.0	31.7	26.8
25860	Hickory-Lenoir-Morganton, NC Metro Area	251,942	18.5	30.2	32.8	18.5
25940	Hilton Head Island-Bluffton-Beaufort, SC Metro Area	146,803	10.0	23.7	29.0	37.3
25980	Hinesville, GA Metro Area	45,740	11.1	32.8	38.6	17.5
26140	Homosassa Springs, FL Metro Area	111,992	13.9	39.7	30.2	16.2
26300	Hot Springs, AR Metro Area	69,624	12.6	31.7	36.3	19.4
26380	Houma-Thibodaux, LA Metro Area	139,275	22.3	39.5	22.2	16.0
26420	Houston-The Woodlands-Sugar Land, TX Metro Area	4,241,381	17.7	23.4	27.4	31.5
26580	Huntington-Ashland, WV-KY-OH Metro Area	250,851	11.9	38.0	30.9	19.1
26620	Huntsville, AL Metro Area	303,237	10.1	24.1	27.6	38.1
26820	Idaho Falls, ID Metro Area	83,994	10.3	28.1	34.5	27.1
26900	Indianapolis-Carmel-Anderson, IN Metro Area	1,310,888	11.1	28.5	27.5	32.9

Table D. Metropolitan Statistical Area—Labor Force, Employment, and Educational Data, 2015—*Continued*

| | | | Educational attainment for the population age 25 and older | | | |
| | | | Educational attainment | | | |
CBSA code/ Division code	Metropolitan area, metropolitan division	Total population age 25 and older	Less than high school graduate	High school graduate (includes equivalency)	Some college or Associate's degree	Bachelor's degree or higher
26980	Iowa City, IA Metro Area	99,525	5.6	23.6	27.2	43.6
27060	Ithaca, NY Metro Area	59,768	3.8	20.8	20.5	54.9
27100	Jackson, MI Metro Area	109,882	10.0	34.8	33.3	21.9
27140	Jackson, MS Metro Area	377,394	12.2	25.7	33.1	29.0
27180	Jackson, TN Metro Area	85,582	10.6	36.8	29.1	23.5
27260	Jacksonville, FL Metro Area	993,223	9.9	28.2	31.9	30.0
27340	Jacksonville, NC Metro Area	101,004	8.6	32.6	38.0	20.8
27500	Janesville-Beloit, WI Metro Area	109,280	10.2	36.8	31.2	21.8
27620	Jefferson City, MO Metro Area	101,942	11.3	33.5	28.1	27.1
27740	Johnson City, TN Metro Area	141,183	14.8	34.2	27.0	23.9
27780	Johnstown, PA Metro Area	97,536	8.7	45.6	24.6	21.1
27860	Jonesboro, AR Metro Area	82,515	12.4	35.7	30.2	21.7
27900	Joplin, MO Metro Area	115,303	12.4	33.0	31.9	22.7
27980	Kahului-Wailuku-Lahaina, HI Metro Area	116,301	9.0	30.9	34.8	25.3
28020	Kalamazoo-Portage, MI Metro Area	213,504	7.3	23.9	34.2	34.7
28100	Kankakee, IL Metro Area	72,783	13.4	33.8	32.0	20.8
28140	Kansas City, MO-KS Metro Area	1,395,502	8.8	26.3	29.1	35.8
28420	Kennewick-Richland, WA Metro Area	172,291	14.5	25.6	33.5	26.4
28660	Killeen-Temple, TX Metro Area	263,003	9.8	28.2	38.9	23.2
28700	Kingsport-Bristol-Bristol, TN-VA Metro Area	221,665	15.3	35.3	28.8	20.5
28740	Kingston, NY Metro Area	128,981	10.1	31.8	26.7	31.3
28940	Knoxville, TN Metro Area	595,198	12.9	31.6	27.6	27.9
29020	Kokomo, IN Metro Area	57,645	12.7	37.0	31.6	18.8
29100	La Crosse-Onalaska, WI-MN Metro Area	88,227	5.9	27.8	36.2	30.0
29180	Lafayette, LA Metro Area	319,495	18.1	34.6	26.1	21.2
29200	Lafayette-West Lafayette, IN Metro Area	121,172	9.2	29.1	29.1	32.5
29340	Lake Charles, LA Metro Area	135,739	13.9	34.6	29.9	21.6
29420	Lake Havasu City-Kingman, AZ Metro Area	153,740	14.4	38.9	34.7	11.9
29460	Lakeland-Winter Haven, FL Metro Area	446,224	16.4	35.9	28.6	19.1
29540	Lancaster, PA Metro Area	358,036	15.5	36.5	22.2	25.8
29620	Lansing-East Lansing, MI Metro Area	299,437	6.9	24.8	34.1	34.2
29700	Laredo, TX Metro Area	147,672	33.6	27.5	21.6	17.4
29740	Las Cruces, NM Metro Area	129,813	20.4	23.4	29.8	26.4
29820	Las Vegas-Henderson-Paradise, NV Metro Area	1,429,567	14.9	28.3	33.7	23.1
29940	Lawrence, KS Metro Area	67,537	6.9	20.7	25.5	47.0
30020	Lawton, OK Metro Area	81,608	11.1	33.4	35.6	19.9
30140	Lebanon, PA Metro Area	93,143	14.6	44.1	22.6	18.6
30300	Lewiston, ID-WA Metro Area	44,900	7.8	31.8	37.6	22.9
30340	Lewiston-Auburn, ME Metro Area	74,789	11.9	35.9	31.1	21.1
30460	Lexington-Fayette, KY Metro Area	326,802	11.2	24.7	28.5	35.5
30620	Lima, OH Metro Area	70,033	8.6	38.9	33.1	19.4
30700	Lincoln, NE Metro Area	200,253	5.9	22.4	34.9	36.7
30780	Little Rock-North Little Rock-Conway, AR Metro Area	485,979	10.7	28.2	31.0	30.0
30860	Logan, UT-ID Metro Area	68,650	7.6	23.5	35.5	33.4
30980	Longview, TX Metro Area	143,653	16.7	29.6	34.6	19.1
31020	Longview, WA Metro Area	71,960	11.1	31.9	39.9	17.2
31080	**Los Angeles-Long Beach-Anaheim, CA Metro Area**	8,999,070	20.5	20.3	26.5	32.7
31080/11244	Anaheim-Santa Ana-Irvine, CA Metro Division	2,146,420	15.9	17.3	28.1	38.8
31080/31084	Los Angeles-Long Beach-Glendale, CA Metro Division	6,852,650	21.9	21.2	26.0	30.8
31140	Louisville/Jefferson County, KY-IN Metro Area	876,489	10.4	30.5	30.4	28.7
31180	Lubbock, TX Metro Area	182,861	15.2	28.5	30.4	25.8
31340	Lynchburg, VA Metro Area	175,102	13.6	30.5	29.9	26.0
31420	Macon, GA Metro Area	152,373	15.8	32.7	27.8	23.6
31460	Madera, CA Metro Area	97,105	27.2	26.3	31.1	15.4
31540	Madison, WI Metro Area	424,196	5.4	21.6	29.4	43.5
31700	Manchester-Nashua, NH Metro Area	282,826	8.2	26.6	28.3	36.9
31740	Manhattan, KS Metro Area	51,930	4.9	21.4	33.7	40.0
31860	Mankato-North Mankato, MN Metro Area	59,064	4.7	24.6	37.0	33.7
31900	Mansfield, OH Metro Area	84,510	13.7	40.7	31.3	14.4
32580	McAllen-Edinburg-Mission, TX Metro Area	467,992	38.2	22.4	22.1	17.3
32780	Medford, OR Metro Area	152,758	10.3	29.5	34.6	25.6
32820	Memphis, TN-MS-AR Metro Area	873,656	13.5	29.8	29.7	26.9
32900	Merced, CA Metro Area	155,645	31.8	24.7	29.0	14.4

Table D. Metropolitan Statistical Area—Labor Force, Employment, and Educational Data, 2015—*Continued*

CBSA code/ Division code	Metropolitan area, metropolitan division	Total population age 25 and older	Educational attainment for the population age 25 and older			
			Educational attainment			
			Less than high school graduate	High school graduate (includes equivalency)	Some college or Associate's degree	Bachelor's degree or higher
33100	**Miami-Fort Lauderdale-West Palm Beach, FL Metro Area**	4,271,132	15.2	27.1	26.8	30.9
33100/22744	*Fort Lauderdale-Pompano Beach-Deerfield Beach, FL Metro Division*	1,332,717	11.8	27.4	28.6	32.2
33100/33124	*Miami-Miami Beach-Kendall, FL Metro Division*	1,900,999	19.7	28.6	24.4	27.4
33100/48424	*West Palm Beach-Boca Raton-Delray Beach, FL Metro Division*	1,037,416	11.4	24.1	28.8	35.7
33140	Michigan City-La Porte, IN Metro Area	77,191	12.8	38.1	31.5	17.6
33220	Midland, MI Metro Area	57,912	5.4	32.4	28.3	34.0
33260	Midland, TX Metro Area	103,081	14.8	25.9	33.1	26.2
33340	Milwaukee-Waukesha-West Allis, WI Metro Area	1,060,667	9.5	26.0	30.6	33.9
33460	Minneapolis-St. Paul-Bloomington, MN-WI Metro Area	2,374,578	6.8	21.9	31.0	40.3
33540	Missoula, MT Metro Area	75,225	3.5	24.7	28.8	42.9
33660	Mobile, AL Metro Area	277,665	14.7	32.4	29.4	23.5
33700	Modesto, CA Metro Area	338,947	22.8	28.5	32.2	16.4
33740	Monroe, LA Metro Area	115,167	15.2	33.0	26.7	25.1
33780	Monroe, MI Metro Area	104,204	9.4	36.6	35.8	18.3
33860	Montgomery, AL Metro Area	248,483	14.6	29.0	28.3	28.0
34060	Morgantown, WV Metro Area	89,593	10.1	34.4	21.2	34.3
34100	Morristown, TN Metro Area	80,828	18.9	41.1	25.2	14.9
34580	Mount Vernon-Anacortes, WA Metro Area	84,596	9.1	27.7	38.8	24.4
34620	Muncie, IN Metro Area	70,810	9.9	36.7	30.3	23.1
34740	Muskegon, MI Metro Area	117,345	10.3	35.4	35.5	18.7
34820	Myrtle Beach-Conway-North Myrtle Beach, SC-NC Metro Area	319,925	11.4	30.6	33.1	24.9
34900	Napa, CA Metro Area	98,697	15.5	17.9	33.8	32.8
34940	Naples-Immokalee-Marco Island, FL Metro Area	268,250	13.2	26.1	25.5	35.2
34980	Nashville-Davidson--Murfreesboro--Franklin, TN Metro Area	1,224,179	11.0	27.9	27.5	33.6
35100	New Bern, NC Metro Area	82,938	10.4	28.6	38.0	23.0
35300	New Haven-Milford, CT Metro Area	594,403	10.5	30.4	24.9	34.3
35380	New Orleans-Metairie, LA Metro Area	870,010	13.8	28.6	29.1	28.6
35620	**New York-Newark-Jersey City, NY-NJ-PA Metro Area**	13,918,552	14.3	25.5	21.9	38.4
35620/20524	*Dutchess County-Putnam County, NY Metro Division*	273,739	8.2	28.6	29.0	34.2
35620/35004	*Nassau County-Suffolk County, NY Metro Division*	1,973,301	9.5	26.4	25.2	38.9
35620/35084	*Newark, NJ-PA Metro Division*	1,713,541	10.4	26.6	22.1	40.9
35620/35614	*New York-Jersey City-White Plains, NY-NJ Metro Division*	9,957,971	16.0	25.0	21.0	38.0
35660	Niles-Benton Harbor, MI Metro Area	106,760	9.5	28.2	33.4	28.9
35840	North Port-Sarasota-Bradenton, FL Metro Area	588,724	9.4	30.8	28.5	31.3
35980	Norwich-New London, CT Metro Area	189,272	8.6	30.9	27.1	33.4
36100	Ocala, FL Metro Area	253,157	11.2	38.4	30.6	19.7
36140	Ocean City, NJ Metro Area	70,934	9.4	32.4	27.5	30.7
36220	Odessa, TX Metro Area	93,777	23.1	29.6	31.1	16.2
36260	Ogden-Clearfield, UT Metro Area	380,160	7.0	26.5	36.6	30.0
36420	Oklahoma City, OK Metro Area	880,297	12.0	27.8	30.9	29.3
36500	Olympia-Tumwater, WA Metro Area	186,672	8.1	22.6	36.7	32.7
36540	Omaha-Council Bluffs, NE-IA Metro Area	595,342	8.6	24.2	32.5	34.7
36740	Orlando-Kissimmee-Sanford, FL Metro Area	1,618,272	10.2	27.1	32.8	29.9
36780	Oshkosh-Neenah, WI Metro Area	113,119	8.4	33.4	32.6	25.6
36980	Owensboro, KY Metro Area	79,309	12.1	37.6	30.8	19.5
37100	Oxnard-Thousand Oaks-Ventura, CA Metro Area	564,044	17.1	18.4	31.8	32.7
37340	Palm Bay-Melbourne-Titusville, FL Metro Area	418,232	8.2	29.5	33.9	28.4
37460	Panama City, FL Metro Area	138,270	11.1	31.1	35.4	22.4

Table D. Metropolitan Statistical Area—Labor Force, Employment, and Educational Data, 2015—*Continued*

CBSA code/ Division code	Metropolitan area, metropolitan division	Total population age 25 and older	Educational attainment for the population age 25 and older			
			Educational attainment			
			Less than high school graduate	High school graduate (includes equivalency)	Some college or Associate's degree	Bachelor's degree or higher
37620	Parkersburg-Vienna, WV Metro Area	65,706	11.9	36.9	31.5	19.7
37860	Pensacola-Ferry Pass-Brent, FL Metro Area	324,088	9.5	27.3	37.0	26.2
37900	Peoria, IL Metro Area	256,463	8.8	30.6	33.1	27.4
37980	**Philadelphia-Camden-Wilmington, PA-NJ-DE-MD Metro Area**	4,154,206	10.1	29.6	24.3	36.0
37980/15804	*Camden, NJ Metro Division*	861,767	8.8	30.6	27.6	33.0
37980/33874	*Montgomery County-Bucks County-Chester County, PA Metro Division*	1,367,704	6.6	25.4	22.5	45.6
37980/37964	*Philadelphia, PA Metro Division*	1,431,025	14.4	32.8	23.0	29.8
37980/48864	*Wilmington, DE-MD-NJ Metro Division*	493,710	9.5	30.6	27.3	32.6
38060	Phoenix-Mesa-Scottsdale, AZ Metro Area	3,021,157	13.5	23.6	33.5	29.4
38220	Pine Bluff, AR Metro Area	64,784	15.1	41.1	29.6	14.2
38300	Pittsburgh, PA Metro Area	1,697,737	7.0	34.0	26.0	33.0
38340	Pittsfield, MA Metro Area	92,514	10.8	29.5	27.2	32.4
38540	Pocatello, ID Metro Area	52,113	7.9	26.8	41.0	24.3
38860	Portland-South Portland, ME Metro Area	380,388	5.8	27.6	27.0	39.6
38900	Portland-Vancouver-Hillsboro, OR-WA Metro Area	1,660,565	9.2	20.1	32.8	37.9
38940	Port St. Lucie, FL Metro Area	334,007	13.1	30.9	31.0	25.0
39140	Prescott, AZ Metro Area	169,500	9.8	24.9	38.8	26.5
39300	Providence-Warwick, RI-MA Metro Area	1,116,749	13.5	28.7	27.3	30.6
39340	Provo-Orem, UT Metro Area	285,577	7.1	17.5	37.7	37.7
39380	Pueblo, CO Metro Area	110,570	12.8	28.8	36.8	21.6
39460	Punta Gorda, FL Metro Area	141,657	9.2	38.9	30.8	21.0
39540	Racine, WI Metro Area	131,952	11.0	29.7	35.3	24.0
39580	Raleigh, NC Metro Area	839,512	9.1	19.3	27.2	44.4
39660	Rapid City, SD Metro Area	98,648	5.1	28.7	36.2	30.0
39740	Reading, PA Metro Area	280,020	13.1	37.7	24.9	24.4
39820	Redding, CA Metro Area	126,950	9.7	25.3	42.9	22.0
39900	Reno, NV Metro Area	309,592	12.9	22.9	34.6	29.6
40060	Richmond, VA Metro Area	871,695	10.7	26.1	28.1	35.2
40140	Riverside-San Bernardino-Ontario, CA Metro Area	2,828,883	20.3	26.8	32.8	20.1
40220	Roanoke, VA Metro Area	220,643	11.0	30.6	32.0	26.5
40340	Rochester, MN Metro Area	145,251	5.8	24.7	32.2	37.3
40380	Rochester, NY Metro Area	740,716	10.3	27.0	29.7	33.0
40420	Rockford, IL Metro Area	228,899	13.1	32.7	32.0	22.1
40580	Rocky Mount, NC Metro Area	100,398	18.8	32.1	32.7	16.4
40660	Rome, GA Metro Area	64,448	21.0	32.7	27.8	18.5
40900	Sacramento--Roseville--Arden-Arcade, CA Metro Area	1,519,801	11.2	21.5	35.0	32.2
40980	Saginaw, MI Metro Area	132,337	11.4	34.7	34.5	19.4
41060	St. Cloud, MN Metro Area	122,610	8.4	28.5	37.5	25.6
41100	St. George, UT Metro Area	96,848	7.6	27.1	39.3	26.0
41140	St. Joseph, MO-KS Metro Area	86,652	10.8	37.8	31.2	20.2
41180	St. Louis, MO-IL Metro Area	1,929,636	8.9	27.2	31.4	32.5
41420	Salem, OR Metro Area	267,783	13.1	27.8	36.0	23.0
41500	Salinas, CA Metro Area	273,998	31.0	19.5	26.2	23.3
41540	Salisbury, MD-DE Metro Area	278,917	13.3	32.6	28.3	25.8
41620	Salt Lake City, UT Metro Area	724,009	9.8	24.6	32.9	32.7
41660	San Angelo, TX Metro Area	76,641	16.6	29.2	30.8	23.5
41700	San Antonio-New Braunfels, TX Metro Area	1,524,281	15.9	26.8	30.6	26.6
41740	San Diego-Carlsbad, CA Metro Area	2,209,465	13.4	18.9	30.6	37.2
41860	**San Francisco-Oakland-Hayward, CA Metro Area**	3,336,089	11.8	16.1	25.0	47.2
41860/36084	*Oakland-Hayward-Berkeley, CA Metro Division*	1,915,653	11.9	18.0	26.9	43.1
41860/41884	*San Francisco-Redwood City-South San Francisco, CA Metro Division*	1,229,337	12.2	13.9	22.3	51.6
41860/42034	*San Rafael, CA Metro Division*	191,099	7.6	10.8	22.6	58.9

Table D. Metropolitan Statistical Area—Labor Force, Employment, and Educational Data, 2015—*Continued*

CBSA code/ Division code	Metropolitan area, metropolitan division	Total population age 25 and older	Educational attainment for the population age 25 and older			
			Educational attainment			
			Less than high school graduate	High school graduate (includes equivalency)	Some college or Associate's degree	Bachelor's degree or higher
41940	San Jose-Sunnyvale-Santa Clara, CA Metro Area	1,352,161	12.9	15.0	23.4	48.7
42020	San Luis Obispo-Paso Robles-Arroyo Grande, CA Metro Area	187,193	9.7	20.5	35.7	34.1
42100	Santa Cruz-Watsonville, CA Metro Area	178,043	15.9	15.5	31.5	37.1
42140	Santa Fe, NM Metro Area	108,701	11.6	21.2	26.3	40.9
42200	Santa Maria-Santa Barbara, CA Metro Area	273,982	20.0	17.8	29.0	33.2
42220	Santa Rosa, CA Metro Area	356,680	13.0	19.2	35.0	32.8
42340	Savannah, GA Metro Area	247,529	11.2	26.3	33.6	28.9
42540	Scranton--Wilkes-Barre--Hazleton, PA Metro Area	396,044	10.3	39.0	27.3	23.3
42660	**Seattle-Tacoma-Bellevue, WA Metro Area**	2,587,548	7.7	20.4	30.8	41.2
42660/42644	*Seattle-Bellevue-Everett, WA Metro Division*	2,026,680	7.4	18.1	29.0	45.4
42660/45104	*Tacoma-Lakewood, WA Metro Division*	560,868	8.4	28.8	37.1	25.7
42680	Sebastian-Vero Beach, FL Metro Area	111,187	10.8	35.1	28.5	25.6
42700	Sebring, FL Metro Area	74,414	15.6	38.0	28.7	17.6
43100	Sheboygan, WI Metro Area	80,718	8.8	37.9	30.0	23.4
43300	Sherman-Denison, TX Metro Area	84,286	13.0	33.5	34.3	19.2
43340	Shreveport-Bossier City, LA Metro Area	295,998	13.6	34.0	30.4	22.0
43420	Sierra Vista-Douglas, AZ Metro Area	89,293	13.7	23.2	43.3	19.8
43580	Sioux City, IA-NE-SD Metro Area	107,694	12.5	35.6	30.3	21.6
43620	Sioux Falls, SD Metro Area	165,046	8.3	26.4	33.6	31.7
43780	South Bend-Mishawaka, IN-MI Metro Area	210,158	12.9	31.9	29.3	25.9
43900	Spartanburg, SC Metro Area	217,872	18.0	29.1	30.8	22.2
44060	Spokane-Spokane Valley, WA Metro Area	371,769	7.2	26.8	38.9	27.2
44100	Springfield, IL Metro Area	144,684	8.0	27.3	30.7	34.1
44140	Springfield, MA Metro Area	415,653	12.2	29.4	27.3	31.1
44180	Springfield, MO Metro Area	296,166	9.3	30.9	32.7	27.1
44220	Springfield, OH Metro Area	93,014	12.6	37.4	32.2	17.7
44300	State College, PA Metro Area	96,414	6.4	32.3	18.3	43.0
44420	Staunton-Waynesboro, VA Metro Area	85,521	14.2	36.9	26.0	22.9
44700	Stockton-Lodi, CA Metro Area	452,979	21.9	26.5	32.8	18.8
44940	Sumter, SC Metro Area	68,051	17.5	29.8	35.4	17.3
45060	Syracuse, NY Metro Area	444,565	9.6	29.3	30.1	31.0
45220	Tallahassee, FL Metro Area	232,124	10.2	25.0	29.5	35.3
45300	Tampa-St. Petersburg-Clearwater, FL Metro Area	2,128,909	10.7	28.7	31.7	28.9
45460	Terre Haute, IN Metro Area	113,655	13.3	35.6	30.0	21.1
45500	Texarkana, TX-AR Metro Area	101,312	13.0	38.5	34.4	14.1
45540	The Villages, FL Metro Area	105,817	7.4	30.7	28.9	33.0
45780	Toledo, OH Metro Area	400,219	9.7	31.7	33.0	25.5
45820	Topeka, KS Metro Area	157,312	8.9	32.3	31.5	27.4
45940	Trenton, NJ Metro Area	248,659	12.1	26.5	23.3	38.1
46060	Tucson, AZ Metro Area	668,691	12.7	22.9	33.3	31.1
46140	Tulsa, OK Metro Area	647,291	10.8	29.6	32.9	26.7
46220	Tuscaloosa, AL Metro Area	152,128	14.5	32.2	25.3	28.1
46340	Tyler, TX Metro Area	144,118	17.7	24.7	33.0	24.6
46520	Urban Honolulu, HI Metro Area	681,195	9.4	25.8	31.6	33.2
46540	Utica-Rome, NY Metro Area	205,291	11.8	34.0	31.0	23.1
46660	Valdosta, GA Metro Area	85,916	18.2	30.4	29.7	21.6
46700	Vallejo-Fairfield, CA Metro Area	295,732	12.4	24.5	37.3	25.7
47020	Victoria, TX Metro Area	64,711	15.6	31.3	31.3	21.8
47220	Vineland-Bridgeton, NJ Metro Area	106,002	21.4	43.8	21.3	13.5
47260	Virginia Beach-Norfolk-Newport News, VA-NC Metro Area	1,141,907	9.3	25.3	35.3	30.2
47300	Visalia-Porterville, CA Metro Area	267,457	30.9	24.3	30.6	14.2
47380	Waco, TX Metro Area	161,027	15.6	29.6	32.3	22.5
47460	Walla Walla, WA Metro Area	42,580	12.0	21.5	37.4	29.2
47580	Warner Robins, GA Metro Area	122,322	11.3	27.7	40.3	20.7
47900	**Washington-Arlington-Alexandria, DC-VA-MD-WV Metro Area**	4,132,855	9.8	18.8	22.0	49.3
47900/43524	*Silver Spring-Frederick-Rockville, MD Metro Division*	879,029	9.5	15.8	20.4	54.3
47900/47894	*Washington-Arlington-Alexandria, DC-VA-MD-WV Metro Division*	3,253,826	9.9	19.6	22.4	48.0

Table D. Metropolitan Statistical Area—Labor Force, Employment, and Educational Data, 2015—*Continued*

CBSA code/ Division code	Metropolitan area, metropolitan division	Total population age 25 and older	Educational attainment for the population age 25 and older			
			Educational attainment			
			Less than high school graduate	High school graduate (includes equivalency)	Some college or Associate's degree	Bachelor's degree or higher
47940	Waterloo-Cedar Falls, IA Metro Area	109,498	8.0	31.0	32.0	29.0
48060	Watertown-Fort Drum, NY Metro Area	73,484	9.9	30.9	36.2	23.0
48140	Wausau, WI Metro Area	94,391	9.5	36.2	30.6	23.7
48260	Weirton-Steubenville, WV-OH Metro Area	86,277	9.3	44.2	30.0	16.5
48300	Wenatchee, WA Metro Area	78,300	18.7	28.2	31.5	21.6
48540	Wheeling, WV-OH Metro Area	104,426	9.3	36.3	32.0	22.5
48620	Wichita, KS Metro Area	416,443	10.7	27.7	33.9	27.7
48660	Wichita Falls, TX Metro Area	97,188	16.0	33.4	28.9	21.8
48700	Williamsport, PA Metro Area	81,534	11.9	41.8	23.4	22.9
48900	Wilmington, NC Metro Area	190,388	7.6	24.0	34.1	34.3
49020	Winchester, VA-WV Metro Area	92,144	13.8	33.1	26.8	26.3
49180	Winston-Salem, NC Metro Area	449,699	14.1	29.4	29.6	26.9
49340	Worcester, MA-CT Metro Area	639,714	10.6	29.3	26.8	33.3
49420	Yakima, WA Metro Area	149,845	27.2	29.8	27.3	15.7
49620	York-Hanover, PA Metro Area	307,046	10.7	41.1	25.5	22.7
49660	Youngstown-Warren-Boardman, OH-PA Metro Area	388,419	10.2	42.0	26.6	21.2
49700	Yuba City, CA Metro Area	109,075	21.1	23.7	40.0	15.2
49740	Yuma, AZ Metro Area	128,566	29.3	23.7	31.5	15.4

PART E

CITIES

- Eight of the top ten cities with the highest percentage of employment in agriculture, forestry, fishing, hunting, and mining were located in California, one was in Nevada, and one was in Florida. In Arvin City, California, 58.5 percent of workers were employed in this industry compared with only 1.9 percent nationally.

- Champlin, MN had the highest labor force participation rate in the country among all cities at 82.8 percent. However, the population age 16 years and over was less than 18,000 in 2015. Among the 75 largest cities in 2015, Minneapolis, MN had the highest labor force participation rate at 75.0 percent, followed by Austin, TX and Seattle, WA at 73.4 percent, with Detroit the lowest at 53.0 percent.

- In Washington, D.C., 17.3 percent of workers were employed by the federal government. Virginia Beach, VA was the only other city among the 75 largest with more than eight percent of its workers employed by the federal government.

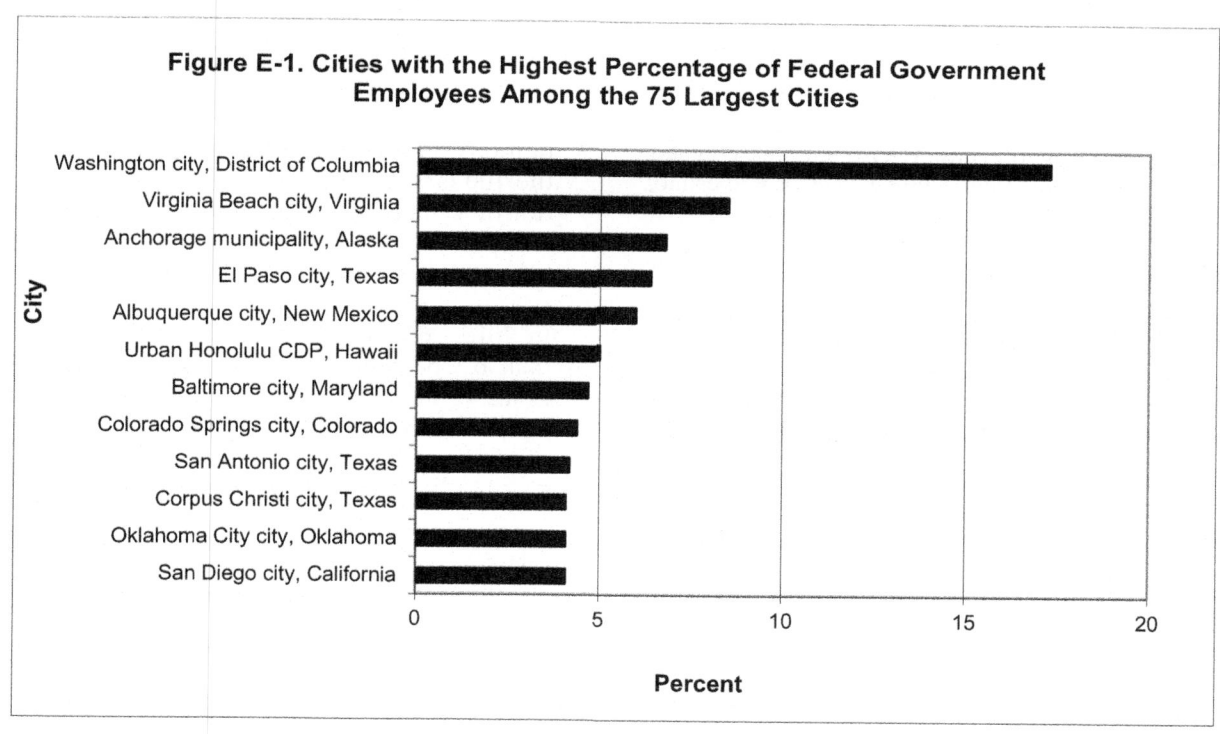

Figure E-1. Cities with the Highest Percentage of Federal Government Employees Among the 75 Largest Cities

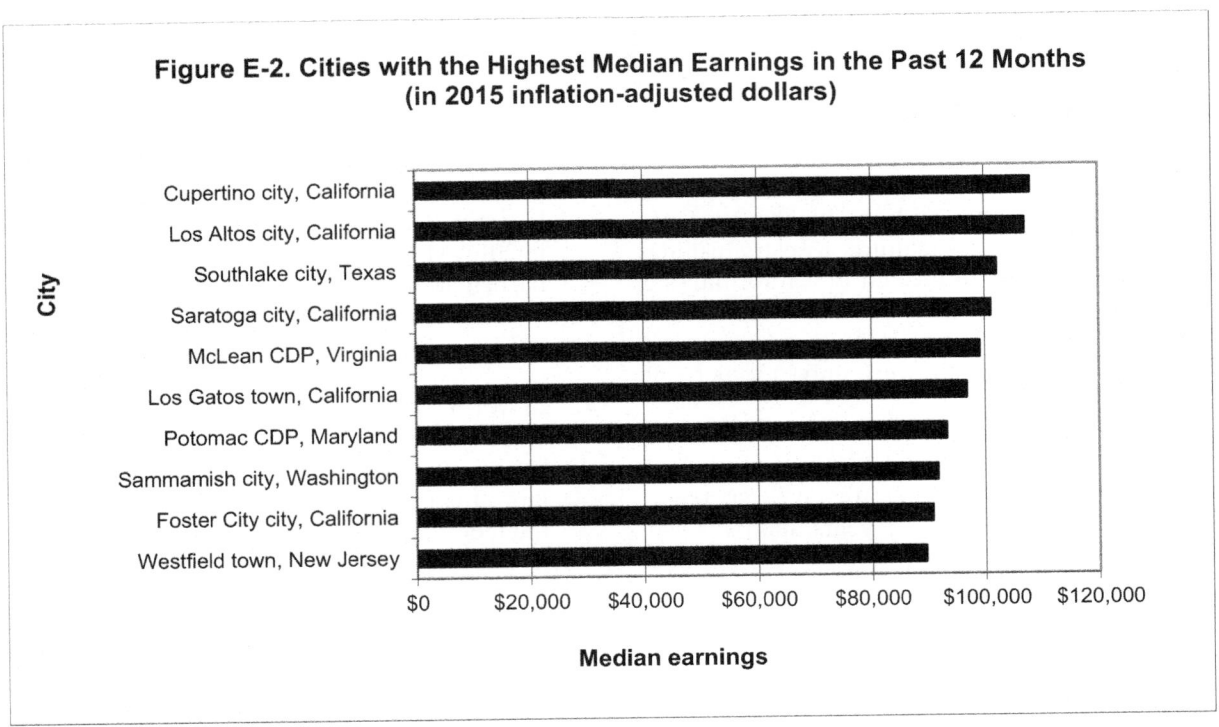

Figure E-2. Cities with the Highest Median Earnings in the Past 12 Months (in 2015 inflation-adjusted dollars)

- Median earnings in the past twelve months equaled $31,394 in the United States. Among all cities, Cupertino, CA had the highest earnings at $108,013 followed by Los Altos, CA at $107,011 and Southlake TX at $102,130. Among the top ten cities with the highest median earnings, five were located in California, and one each in Washington, Texas, Virginia, Maryland, and New Jersey.

- The median earnings of men who worked full-time year-round was approximately $10,000 higher than that of women who worked full-time year round. In the 100 largest cities, men who worked year-round full-time had higher median earnings in all cities except four: Fresno, CA; Anaheim, CA; St. Paul, MN; and Durham, NC.

- In 2015, 966 cities had unemployment rates higher than 6.3 percent—the national average. East Saint Louis, IL had the highest unemployment rate among all cities at 26.1 percent.

Table E. Cities—Labor Force, Employment, and Educational Data, 2015

FIPS state code	FIPS place code	State/city	Total population age 16 and older	Civilian labor force	Armed Forces	Unemployed	Civilian labor force participation (percent)	Percent in Armed Forces	Unemployment rate	Number of employed persons age 16 and older
00	00000	**UNITED STATES**	256,167,758	160,652,483	1,010,481	10,117,710	62.7	0.4	6.3	150,534,773
01	00000	**ALABAMA**	3,878,471	2,197,662	9,435	157,544	56.7	0.2	7.2	2,040,118
01	00820	Alabaster city, Alabama	25,758	17,631	0	682	68.4	0.0	3.9	16,949
01	00988	Albertville city, Alabama	16,782	10,160	0	89	60.5	0.0	0.9	10,071
01	01852	Anniston city, Alabama	15,419	7,651	28	1,502	49.6	0.2	19.6	6,149
01	02956	Athens city, Alabama	20,148	11,840	0	1,047	58.8	0.0	8.8	10,793
01	03076	Auburn city, Alabama	50,984	30,170	0	1,785	59.2	0.0	5.9	28,385
01	05980	Bessemer city, Alabama	21,446	11,734	0	2,526	54.7	0.0	21.5	9,208
01	07000	Birmingham city, Alabama	174,713	106,313	60	10,837	60.9	0.0	10.2	95,476
01	19648	Daphne city, Alabama	19,092	11,793	0	74	61.8	0.0	0.6	11,719
01	20104	Decatur city, Alabama	43,810	24,351	0	1,591	55.6	0.0	6.5	22,760
01	21184	Dothan city, Alabama	53,202	30,861	197	2,780	58.0	0.4	9.0	28,081
01	24184	Enterprise city, Alabama	21,409	13,221	207	836	61.8	1.0	6.3	12,385
01	26896	Florence city, Alabama	33,419	17,026	87	935	50.9	0.3	5.5	16,091
01	28696	Gadsden city, Alabama	29,426	15,936	0	725	54.2	0.0	4.5	15,211
01	35800	Homewood city, Alabama	20,460	14,322	28	500	70.0	0.1	3.5	13,822
01	35896	Hoover city, Alabama	65,649	46,317	87	1,501	70.6	0.1	3.2	44,816
01	37000	Huntsville city, Alabama	155,178	94,130	299	6,324	60.7	0.2	6.7	87,806
01	45784	Madison city, Alabama	38,670	25,316	107	1,931	65.5	0.3	7.6	23,385
01	50000	Mobile city, Alabama	157,373	90,551	401	6,572	57.5	0.3	7.3	83,979
01	51000	Montgomery city, Alabama	159,332	96,904	1,827	7,879	60.8	1.1	8.1	89,025
01	51696	Mountain Brook city, Alabama	16,268	10,039	0	370	61.7	0.0	3.7	9,669
01	55200	Northport city, Alabama	18,194	11,252	0	416	61.8	0.0	3.7	10,836
01	57048	Opelika city, Alabama	22,696	14,178	0	1,168	62.5	0.0	8.2	13,010
01	57576	Oxford city, Alabama	16,597	10,481	59	829	63.1	0.4	7.9	9,652
01	58848	Pelham city, Alabama	17,060	11,984	34	943	70.2	0.2	7.9	11,041
01	59472	Phenix City city, Alabama	29,251	17,587	391	1,038	60.1	1.3	5.9	16,549
01	62328	Prattville city, Alabama	28,095	16,012	183	907	57.0	0.7	5.7	15,105
01	62496	Prichard city, Alabama	16,037	8,032	0	1,696	50.1	0.0	21.1	6,336
01	76944	Trussville city, Alabama	14,164	9,635	0	47	68.0	0.0	0.5	9,588
01	77256	Tuscaloosa city, Alabama	84,180	42,944	0	2,818	51.0	0.0	6.6	40,126
01	78552	Vestavia Hills city, Alabama	26,442	17,514	85	420	66.2	0.3	2.4	17,094
02	00000	**ALASKA**	571,393	385,165	17,748	30,399	67.4	3.1	7.9	354,766
02	03000	Anchorage municipality, Alaska	231,969	160,783	8,981	10,258	69.3	3.9	6.4	150,525
02	05000	Badger CDP, Alaska	16,020	11,817	512	1,891	73.8	3.2	16.0	9,926
02	24230	Fairbanks city, Alaska	24,535	14,694	4,191	1,334	59.9	17.1	9.1	13,360
02	36400	Juneau city and borough, Alaska	26,251	19,557	92	870	74.5	0.4	4.4	18,687
04	00000	**ARIZONA**	5,393,214	3,153,950	17,617	216,440	58.5	0.3	6.9	2,937,510
04	02830	Apache Junction city, Arizona	32,384	14,476	0	859	44.7	0.0	5.9	13,617
04	04720	Avondale city, Arizona	57,437	38,424	255	1,923	66.9	0.4	5.0	36,501
04	07940	Buckeye town, Arizona	46,511	25,250	446	1,836	54.3	1.0	7.3	23,414
04	08220	Bullhead City city, Arizona	34,072	15,931	0	1,159	46.8	0.0	7.3	14,772
04	10530	Casa Grande city, Arizona	39,572	21,199	99	1,960	53.6	0.3	9.2	19,239
04	10670	Casas Adobes CDP, Arizona	55,313	32,551	218	1,700	58.8	0.4	5.2	30,851
04	11230	Catalina Foothills CDP, Arizona	44,078	22,368	289	1,118	50.7	0.7	5.0	21,250
04	12000	Chandler city, Arizona	200,978	141,258	301	5,687	70.3	0.1	4.0	135,571
04	20540	Drexel Heights CDP, Arizona	21,318	12,196	0	900	57.2	0.0	7.4	11,296
04	22220	El Mirage city, Arizona	22,553	15,890	0	1,290	70.5	0.0	8.1	14,600
04	23620	Flagstaff city, Arizona	58,397	39,198	0	3,091	67.1	0.0	7.9	36,107
04	23760	Florence town, Arizona	28,987	6,722	0	1,340	23.2	0.0	19.9	5,382
04	25030	Fortuna Foothills CDP, Arizona	25,271	8,498	527	878	33.6	2.1	10.3	7,620
04	25300	Fountain Hills town, Arizona	20,941	10,948	0	485	52.3	0.0	4.4	10,463
04	27400	Gilbert town, Arizona	179,208	129,052	0	5,019	72.0	0.0	3.9	124,033
04	27820	Glendale city, Arizona	185,945	114,348	1,250	7,190	61.5	0.7	6.3	107,158
04	28380	Goodyear city, Arizona	62,896	36,403	506	934	57.9	0.8	2.6	35,469
04	29710	Green Valley CDP, Arizona	21,049	3,487	0	304	16.6	0.0	8.7	3,183
04	37620	Kingman city, Arizona	23,722	11,698	0	1,127	49.3	0.0	9.6	10,571
04	39370	Lake Havasu City city, Arizona	46,630	21,850	0	925	46.9	0.0	4.2	20,925
04	44270	Marana town, Arizona	31,502	19,760	75	1,558	62.7	0.2	7.9	18,202
04	44410	Maricopa city, Arizona	35,008	21,409	32	1,107	61.2	0.1	5.2	20,302
04	46000	Mesa city, Arizona	373,724	237,452	112	13,711	63.5	0.0	5.8	223,741
04	49640	Nogales city, Arizona	16,051	8,433	0	895	52.5	0.0	10.6	7,538
04	51600	Oro Valley town, Arizona	37,810	18,160	0	1,133	48.0	0.0	6.2	17,027
04	54050	Peoria city, Arizona	129,724	83,102	54	4,528	64.1	0.0	5.4	78,574
04	55000	Phoenix city, Arizona	1,198,549	774,609	805	48,235	64.6	0.1	6.2	726,374
04	57380	Prescott city, Arizona	37,527	17,068	0	652	45.5	0.0	3.8	16,416
04	57450	Prescott Valley town, Arizona	33,876	16,971	0	1,360	50.1	0.0	8.0	15,611
04	58150	Queen Creek town, Arizona	22,738	14,387	0	168	63.3	0.0	1.2	14,219
04	62140	Sahuarita town, Arizona	19,638	11,238	381	366	57.2	1.9	3.3	10,872
04	63470	San Luis city, Arizona	23,016	12,035	0	2,705	52.3	0.0	22.5	9,330
04	64210	San Tan Valley CDP, Arizona	57,303	36,930	82	3,476	64.4	0.1	9.4	33,454
04	65000	Scottsdale city, Arizona	204,557	126,378	0	4,316	61.8	0.0	3.4	122,062
04	66820	Sierra Vista city, Arizona	33,389	15,675	4,083	1,113	46.9	12.2	7.1	14,562
04	70320	Sun City CDP, Arizona	42,475	8,741	0	1,079	20.6	0.0	12.3	7,662
04	70355	Sun City West CDP, Arizona	24,450	2,907	0	436	11.9	0.0	15.0	2,471
04	71510	Surprise city, Arizona	97,185	56,479	457	4,768	58.1	0.5	8.4	51,711
04	73000	Tempe city, Arizona	150,313	104,376	113	5,888	69.4	0.1	5.6	98,488
04	77000	Tucson city, Arizona	430,274	256,172	3,312	24,844	59.5	0.8	9.7	231,328

Table E. Cities—Labor Force, Employment, and Educational Data, 2015—*Continued*

FIPS state code	FIPS place code	State/city	Total population age 16 and older	Civilian labor force	Armed Forces	Unemployed	Civilian labor force participation (percent)	Percent in Armed Forces	Unemployment rate	Number of employed persons age 16 and older
04	85540	Yuma city, Arizona	73,504	40,788	2,793	5,154	55.5	3.8	12.6	35,634
05	00000	**ARKANSAS**	2,352,507	1,349,814	4,841	78,751	57.4	0.2	5.8	1,271,063
05	04840	Bella Vista city, Arkansas	24,209	12,378	0	536	51.1	0.0	4.3	11,842
05	05290	Benton city, Arkansas	26,510	17,087	0	612	64.5	0.0	3.6	16,475
05	05320	Bentonville city, Arkansas	32,600	21,196	0	382	65.0	0.0	1.8	20,814
05	10300	Cabot city, Arkansas	19,401	11,790	252	206	60.8	1.3	1.7	11,584
05	15190	Conway city, Arkansas	52,660	33,309	1,065	1,364	63.3	2.0	4.1	31,945
05	23290	Fayetteville city, Arkansas	68,448	43,223	0	2,208	63.1	0.0	5.1	41,015
05	24550	Fort Smith city, Arkansas	69,026	38,082	54	1,061	55.2	0.1	2.8	37,021
05	33400	Hot Springs city, Arkansas	29,915	15,986	0	1,670	53.4	0.0	10.4	14,316
05	34750	Jacksonville city, Arkansas	21,048	10,988	1,771	810	52.2	8.4	7.4	10,178
05	35710	Jonesboro city, Arkansas	58,383	36,903	77	2,402	63.2	0.1	6.5	34,501
05	41000	Little Rock city, Arkansas	157,319	102,581	236	4,950	65.2	0.2	4.8	97,631
05	50450	North Little Rock city, Arkansas	48,994	28,472	81	2,088	58.1	0.2	7.3	26,384
05	53390	Paragould city, Arkansas	21,969	13,145	0	859	59.8	0.0	6.5	12,286
05	55310	Pine Bluff city, Arkansas	34,153	18,921	0	2,887	55.4	0.0	15.3	16,034
05	60410	Rogers city, Arkansas	47,162	32,512	0	1,042	68.9	0.0	3.2	31,470
05	61670	Russellville city, Arkansas	22,891	13,029	0	939	56.9	0.0	7.2	12,090
05	63020	Searcy city, Arkansas	19,128	11,109	41	331	58.1	0.2	3.0	10,778
05	63800	Sherwood city, Arkansas	24,452	16,137	520	486	66.0	2.1	3.0	15,651
05	66080	Springdale city, Arkansas	58,828	37,857	0	1,738	64.4	0.0	4.6	36,119
05	68810	Texarkana city, Arkansas	25,157	14,394	0	1,293	57.2	0.0	9.0	13,101
05	71480	Van Buren city, Arkansas	18,282	11,048	0	1,007	60.4	0.0	9.1	10,041
05	74540	West Memphis city, Arkansas	17,792	9,839	0	682	55.3	0.0	6.9	9,157
06	00000	**CALIFORNIA**	31,068,647	19,463,807	122,879	1,418,357	62.6	0.4	7.3	18,045,450
06	00296	Adelanto city, California	21,219	10,994	0	2,004	51.8	0.0	18.2	8,990
06	00394	Agoura Hills city, California	17,404	10,449	0	457	60.0	0.0	4.4	9,992
06	00562	Alameda city, California	64,837	42,098	1,141	1,796	64.9	1.8	4.3	40,302
06	00884	Alhambra city, California	73,529	44,586	0	1,813	60.6	0.0	4.1	42,773
06	00947	Aliso Viejo city, California	39,886	29,734	0	1,496	74.5	0.0	5.0	28,238
06	01290	Altadena CDP, California	40,895	27,077	84	1,784	66.2	0.2	6.6	25,293
06	01640	American Canyon city, California	16,893	10,688	0	469	63.3	0.0	4.4	10,219
06	02000	Anaheim city, California	273,225	188,526	66	12,609	69.0	0.0	6.7	175,917
06	02210	Antelope CDP, California	36,451	23,869	54	1,052	65.5	0.1	4.4	22,817
06	02252	Antioch city, California	84,415	52,331	84	4,103	62.0	0.1	7.8	48,228
06	02364	Apple Valley town, California	54,100	28,165	0	3,242	52.1	0.0	11.5	24,923
06	02462	Arcadia city, California	47,149	27,819	0	1,864	59.0	0.0	6.7	25,955
06	02553	Arden-Arcade CDP, California	80,497	51,066	35	6,209	63.4	0.0	12.2	44,857
06	02924	Arvin city, California	16,300	10,947	0	1,133	67.2	0.0	10.3	9,814
06	02980	Ashland CDP, California	18,570	12,942	0	1,463	69.7	0.0	11.3	11,479
06	03064	Atascadero city, California	23,943	15,731	56	884	65.7	0.2	5.6	14,847
06	03162	Atwater city, California	20,351	12,092	48	1,782	59.4	0.2	14.7	10,310
06	03386	Azusa city, California	40,523	25,294	0	2,493	62.4	0.0	9.9	22,801
06	03526	Bakersfield city, California	276,600	183,321	201	19,152	66.3	0.1	10.4	164,169
06	03666	Baldwin Park city, California	59,621	35,240	0	1,599	59.1	0.0	4.5	33,641
06	03820	Banning city, California	24,010	10,634	33	1,982	44.3	0.1	18.6	8,652
06	04030	Barstow city, California	15,010	9,141	158	1,123	60.9	1.1	12.3	8,018
06	04415	Bay Point CDP, California	20,881	13,907	0	1,420	66.6	0.0	10.2	12,487
06	04758	Beaumont city, California	33,289	19,217	0	1,604	57.7	0.0	8.3	17,613
06	04870	Bell city, California	26,217	16,270	0	1,055	62.1	0.0	6.5	15,215
06	04982	Bellflower city, California	59,473	34,285	0	1,890	57.6	0.0	5.5	32,395
06	04996	Bell Gardens city, California	29,882	19,782	0	1,745	66.2	0.0	8.8	18,037
06	05108	Belmont city, California	21,797	13,829	0	774	63.4	0.0	5.6	13,055
06	05290	Benicia city, California	23,314	13,569	132	500	58.2	0.6	3.7	13,069
06	06000	Berkeley city, California	107,090	68,128	0	4,776	63.6	0.0	7.0	63,352
06	06308	Beverly Hills city, California	26,789	16,744	63	864	62.5	0.2	5.2	15,880
06	07064	Bloomington CDP, California	15,383	9,792	0	745	63.7	0.0	7.6	9,047
06	08058	Brawley city, California	20,037	10,616	0	2,079	53.0	0.0	19.6	8,537
06	08100	Brea city, California	31,998	21,329	0	1,244	66.7	0.0	5.8	20,085
06	08142	Brentwood city, California	45,686	28,630	190	2,249	62.7	0.4	7.9	26,381
06	08786	Buena Park city, California	63,979	39,199	0	3,179	61.3	0.0	8.1	36,020
06	08954	Burbank city, California	84,504	56,037	0	3,608	66.3	0.0	6.4	52,429
06	09066	Burlingame city, California	24,512	16,785	0	684	68.5	0.0	4.1	16,101
06	09598	Calabasas city, California	19,416	12,681	0	600	65.3	0.0	4.7	12,081
06	09710	Calexico city, California	29,218	16,761	0	2,815	57.4	0.0	16.8	13,946
06	10046	Camarillo city, California	53,760	31,037	379	1,621	57.7	0.7	5.2	29,416
06	10256	Cameron Park CDP, California	16,493	9,395	0	1,062	57.0	0.0	11.3	8,333
06	10345	Campbell city, California	32,585	24,626	0	429	75.6	0.0	1.7	24,197
06	11194	Carlsbad city, California	91,226	59,566	266	2,547	65.3	0.3	4.3	57,019
06	11390	Carmichael CDP, California	51,019	31,036	24	2,663	60.8	0.0	8.6	28,373
06	11530	Carson city, California	77,995	48,112	31	2,787	61.7	0.0	5.8	45,325
06	11796	Castaic CDP, California	16,445	11,211	0	808	68.2	0.0	7.2	10,403
06	11964	Castro Valley CDP, California	49,654	31,982	0	2,037	64.4	0.0	6.4	29,945
06	12048	Cathedral City city, California	41,164	23,651	0	1,732	57.5	0.0	7.3	21,919
06	12524	Ceres city, California	34,456	21,289	0	2,260	61.8	0.0	10.6	19,029

Table E. Cities—Labor Force, Employment, and Educational Data, 2015—*Continued*

FIPS state code	FIPS place code	State/city	Total population age 16 and older	Civilian labor force	Armed Forces	Unemployed	Civilian labor force participation (percent)	Percent in Armed Forces	Unemployment rate	Number of employed persons age 16 and older
06	12552	Cerritos city, California	41,971	23,523	44	1,335	56.0	0.1	5.7	22,188
06	13014	Chico city, California	75,131	47,784	0	4,920	63.6	0.0	10.3	42,864
06	13210	Chino city, California	71,209	34,730	0	3,049	48.8	0.0	8.8	31,681
06	13214	Chino Hills city, California	64,172	43,448	136	2,899	67.7	0.2	6.7	40,549
06	13392	Chula Vista city, California	204,519	128,407	2,647	8,915	62.8	1.3	6.9	119,492
06	13588	Citrus Heights city, California	70,602	42,988	0	3,687	60.9	0.0	8.6	39,301
06	13756	Claremont city, California	30,333	18,192	12	747	60.0	0.0	4.1	17,445
06	14218	Clovis city, California	81,571	51,778	0	3,175	63.5	0.0	6.1	48,603
06	14260	Coachella city, California	33,217	24,357	0	3,393	73.3	0.0	13.9	20,964
06	14890	Colton city, California	41,114	25,611	0	1,410	62.3	0.0	5.5	24,201
06	15044	Compton city, California	73,191	45,431	0	5,203	62.1	0.0	11.5	40,228
06	16000	Concord city, California	103,826	71,352	0	4,868	68.7	0.0	6.8	66,484
06	16224	Corcoran city, California	19,441	4,983	127	1,116	25.6	0.7	22.4	3,867
06	16350	Corona city, California	129,002	87,070	0	6,390	67.5	0.0	7.3	80,680
06	16378	Coronado city, California	20,157	9,006	3,520	717	44.7	17.5	8.0	8,289
06	16532	Costa Mesa city, California	93,346	68,448	252	3,809	73.3	0.3	5.6	64,639
06	16742	Covina city, California	37,228	25,612	0	1,941	68.8	0.0	7.6	23,671
06	17498	Cudahy city, California	18,135	12,114	0	1,359	66.8	0.0	11.2	10,755
06	17568	Culver City city, California	32,996	23,500	0	1,137	71.2	0.0	4.8	22,363
06	17610	Cupertino city, California	44,777	27,544	0	1,933	61.5	0.0	7.0	25,611
06	17750	Cypress city, California	40,893	25,623	0	1,366	62.7	0.0	5.3	24,257
06	17918	Daly City city, California	91,833	62,991	0	4,518	68.6	0.0	7.2	58,473
06	17946	Dana Point city, California	29,760	19,276	96	786	64.8	0.3	4.1	18,490
06	17988	Danville town, California	33,380	20,703	0	792	62.0	0.0	3.8	19,911
06	18100	Davis city, California	57,594	33,812	44	1,661	58.7	0.1	4.9	32,151
06	18394	Delano city, California	40,347	22,658	0	3,051	56.2	0.0	13.5	19,607
06	18996	Desert Hot Springs city, California	21,089	10,639	0	1,103	50.4	0.0	10.4	9,536
06	19192	Diamond Bar city, California	45,951	27,124	0	2,474	59.0	0.0	9.1	24,650
06	19318	Dinuba city, California	17,699	11,310	26	1,663	63.9	0.1	14.7	9,647
06	19766	Downey city, California	93,480	59,845	242	2,738	64.0	0.3	4.6	57,107
06	19990	Duarte city, California	18,873	12,509	0	1,185	66.3	0.0	9.5	11,324
06	20018	Dublin city, California	44,174	31,506	0	1,014	71.3	0.0	3.2	30,492
06	20802	East Los Angeles CDP, California	92,363	61,042	0	9,914	66.1	0.0	16.2	51,128
06	20956	East Palo Alto city, California	21,473	15,849	0	823	73.8	0.0	5.2	15,026
06	21230	Eastvale city, California	42,567	31,051	79	2,758	72.9	0.2	8.9	28,293
06	21712	El Cajon city, California	79,554	49,671	745	5,622	62.4	0.9	11.3	44,049
06	21782	El Centro city, California	30,777	16,603	0	2,259	53.9	0.0	13.6	14,344
06	21796	El Cerrito city, California	21,216	13,698	0	487	64.6	0.0	3.6	13,211
06	21880	El Dorado Hills CDP, California	34,772	22,030	54	1,823	63.4	0.2	8.3	20,207
06	22020	Elk Grove city, California	128,002	84,788	88	5,862	66.2	0.1	6.9	78,926
06	22230	El Monte city, California	93,817	52,433	0	2,888	55.9	0.0	5.5	49,545
06	22300	El Paso de Robles (Paso Robles) city, California	24,478	16,243	0	1,088	66.4	0.0	6.7	15,155
06	22678	Encinitas city, California	53,322	33,225	188	1,788	62.3	0.4	5.4	31,437
06	22804	Escondido city, California	119,094	78,830	792	6,364	66.2	0.7	8.1	72,466
06	23042	Eureka city, California	22,030	11,652	0	304	52.9	0.0	2.6	11,348
06	23182	Fairfield city, California	86,351	54,906	1,772	5,856	63.6	2.1	10.7	49,050
06	23294	Fair Oaks CDP, California	23,887	12,904	0	1,366	54.0	0.0	10.6	11,538
06	23462	Fallbrook CDP, California	24,987	14,803	642	693	59.2	2.6	4.7	14,110
06	24477	Florence-Graham CDP, California	48,569	30,704	0	3,339	63.2	0.0	10.9	27,365
06	24498	Florin CDP, California	36,935	22,929	0	3,263	62.1	0.0	14.2	19,666
06	24638	Folsom city, California	60,754	37,417	31	1,860	61.6	0.1	5.0	35,557
06	24680	Fontana city, California	150,800	101,007	0	9,593	67.0	0.0	9.5	91,414
06	24722	Foothill Farms CDP, California	26,808	15,231	0	1,279	56.8	0.0	8.4	13,952
06	25338	Foster City city, California	25,344	17,270	0	787	68.1	0.0	4.6	16,483
06	25380	Fountain Valley city, California	47,637	28,577	42	1,553	60.0	0.1	5.4	27,024
06	26000	Fremont city, California	186,798	121,114	0	4,592	64.8	0.0	3.8	116,522
06	26067	French Valley CDP, California	22,167	12,960	499	1,917	58.5	2.3	14.8	11,043
06	27000	Fresno city, California	382,766	236,205	102	25,694	61.7	0.0	10.9	210,511
06	28000	Fullerton city, California	114,259	75,312	0	5,558	65.9	0.0	7.4	69,754
06	28112	Galt city, California	18,598	11,919	0	684	64.1	0.0	5.7	11,235
06	28168	Gardena city, California	48,516	30,400	0	1,384	62.7	0.0	4.6	29,016
06	29000	Garden Grove city, California	141,789	90,565	0	5,509	63.9	0.0	6.1	85,056
06	29504	Gilroy city, California	40,951	28,442	0	2,050	69.5	0.0	7.2	26,392
06	30000	Glendale city, California	171,643	106,858	171	8,922	62.3	0.1	8.3	97,936
06	30014	Glendora city, California	41,172	26,293	0	3,249	63.9	0.0	12.4	23,044
06	30378	Goleta city, California	25,176	16,970	0	784	67.4	0.0	4.6	16,186
06	30693	Granite Bay CDP, California	17,253	8,968	0	713	52.0	0.0	8.0	8,255
06	31596	Hacienda Heights CDP, California	46,840	24,828	86	1,093	53.0	0.2	4.4	23,735
06	31960	Hanford city, California	41,502	24,453	388	2,356	58.9	0.9	9.6	22,097
06	32548	Hawthorne city, California	68,566	45,750	0	3,528	66.7	0.0	7.7	42,222
06	33000	Hayward city, California	125,443	82,709	0	4,625	65.9	0.0	5.6	78,084
06	33182	Hemet city, California	63,299	29,731	0	5,151	47.0	0.0	17.3	24,580
06	33308	Hercules city, California	21,471	15,428	0	530	71.9	0.0	3.4	14,898
06	33434	Hesperia city, California	67,185	39,399	0	6,338	58.6	0.0	16.1	33,061

Table E. Cities—Labor Force, Employment, and Educational Data, 2015—*Continued*

FIPS state code	FIPS place code	State/city	Total population age 16 and older	Civilian labor force	Armed Forces	Unemployed	Civilian labor force participation (percent)	Percent in Armed Forces	Unemployment rate	Number of employed persons age 16 and older
06	33588	Highland city, California	42,724	27,786	0	2,153	65.0	0.0	7.7	25,633
06	34120	Hollister city, California	28,547	20,584	126	1,491	72.1	0.4	7.2	19,093
06	36000	Huntington Beach city, California	165,642	110,698	99	5,827	66.8	0.1	5.3	104,871
06	36056	Huntington Park city, California	44,542	27,467	0	2,040	61.7	0.0	7.4	25,427
06	36294	Imperial Beach city, California	20,814	12,523	833	1,106	60.2	4.0	8.8	11,417
06	36448	Indio city, California	67,201	41,127	0	2,773	61.2	0.0	6.7	38,354
06	36546	Inglewood city, California	87,257	57,436	0	7,145	65.8	0.0	12.4	50,291
06	36770	Irvine city, California	210,577	130,318	42	6,384	61.9	0.0	4.9	123,934
06	36868	Isla Vista CDP, California	26,290	11,098	0	1,329	42.2	0.0	12.0	9,769
06	37692	Jurupa Valley city, California	78,423	48,627	0	5,641	62.0	0.0	11.6	42,986
06	39003	La Cañada Flintridge city, California	17,283	10,783	0	451	62.4	0.0	4.2	10,332
06	39114	Ladera Ranch CDP, California	18,723	14,090	0	595	75.3	0.0	4.2	13,495
06	39122	Lafayette city, California	20,780	13,415	0	696	64.6	0.0	5.2	12,719
06	39178	Laguna Beach city, California	17,968	10,835	47	566	60.3	0.3	5.2	10,269
06	39220	Laguna Hills city, California	27,163	17,319	0	796	63.8	0.0	4.6	16,523
06	39248	Laguna Niguel city, California	54,536	34,799	0	1,162	63.8	0.0	3.3	33,637
06	39290	La Habra city, California	47,567	31,838	0	3,547	66.9	0.0	11.1	28,291
06	39486	Lake Elsinore city, California	43,083	27,135	212	2,551	63.0	0.5	9.4	24,584
06	39496	Lake Forest city, California	66,507	47,552	50	2,182	71.5	0.1	4.6	45,370
06	39766	Lakeside CDP, California	19,505	12,170	132	839	62.4	0.7	6.9	11,331
06	39892	Lakewood city, California	65,974	41,660	56	2,339	63.1	0.1	5.6	39,321
06	40004	La Mesa city, California	49,538	31,402	742	2,739	63.4	1.5	8.7	28,663
06	40032	La Mirada city, California	41,668	22,653	44	1,384	54.4	0.1	6.1	21,269
06	40130	Lancaster city, California	120,525	60,702	210	4,300	50.4	0.2	7.1	56,402
06	40326	La Presa CDP, California	33,494	20,796	702	2,627	62.1	2.1	12.6	18,169
06	40340	La Puente city, California	31,822	20,625	0	1,315	64.8	0.0	6.4	19,310
06	40354	La Quinta city, California	32,633	18,344	0	1,873	56.2	0.0	10.2	16,471
06	40704	Lathrop city, California	15,604	9,904	0	799	63.5	0.0	8.1	9,105
06	40830	La Verne city, California	26,085	15,115	235	1,035	57.9	0.9	6.8	14,080
06	40886	Lawndale city, California	26,829	17,153	0	721	63.9	0.0	4.2	16,432
06	41124	Lemon Grove city, California	22,034	13,585	89	664	61.7	0.4	4.9	12,921
06	41152	Lemoore city, California	17,726	11,570	751	504	65.3	4.2	4.4	11,066
06	41180	Lennox CDP, California	14,721	10,457	0	1,064	71.0	0.0	10.2	9,393
06	41474	Lincoln city, California	36,841	17,268	201	690	46.9	0.5	4.0	16,578
06	41992	Livermore city, California	68,188	48,355	0	1,087	70.9	0.0	2.2	47,268
06	42202	Lodi city, California	48,748	30,353	140	1,985	62.3	0.3	6.5	28,368
06	42370	Loma Linda city, California	19,673	11,475	45	590	58.3	0.2	5.1	10,885
06	42468	Lomita city, California	16,410	11,275	51	664	68.7	0.3	5.9	10,611
06	42524	Lompoc city, California	35,160	21,277	356	2,479	60.5	1.0	11.7	18,798
06	43000	Long Beach city, California	376,218	239,054	206	14,370	63.5	0.1	6.0	224,684
06	43280	Los Altos city, California	23,487	14,089	0	329	60.0	0.0	2.3	13,760
06	44000	Los Angeles city, California	3,214,644	2,113,305	617	153,135	65.7	0.0	7.2	1,960,170
06	44028	Los Banos city, California	26,356	15,103	0	1,054	57.3	0.0	7.0	14,049
06	44112	Los Gatos town, California	26,085	15,227	0	362	58.4	0.0	2.4	14,865
06	44574	Lynwood city, California	53,408	33,421	0	3,193	62.6	0.0	9.6	30,228
06	45022	Madera city, California	44,699	29,179	0	1,735	65.3	0.0	5.9	27,444
06	45400	Manhattan Beach city, California	27,281	15,685	0	1,038	57.5	0.0	6.6	14,647
06	45484	Manteca city, California	57,041	34,212	0	5,050	60.0	0.0	14.8	29,162
06	45778	Marina city, California	15,246	9,347	25	329	61.3	0.2	3.5	9,018
06	46114	Martinez city, California	32,292	20,797	0	1,148	64.4	0.0	5.5	19,649
06	46492	Maywood city, California	20,426	14,230	0	1,353	69.7	0.0	9.5	12,877
06	46646	Mead Valley CDP, California	16,537	9,857	0	2,022	59.6	0.0	20.5	7,835
06	46842	Menifee city, California	66,675	35,577	518	2,688	53.4	0.8	7.6	32,889
06	46870	Menlo Park city, California	25,730	17,468	0	574	67.9	0.0	3.3	16,894
06	46898	Merced city, California	59,098	30,544	0	4,589	51.7	0.0	15.0	25,955
06	47486	Millbrae city, California	19,278	12,133	0	704	62.9	0.0	5.8	11,429
06	47766	Milpitas city, California	61,902	38,793	0	2,004	62.7	0.0	5.2	36,789
06	48256	Mission Viejo city, California	81,752	53,780	50	3,026	65.8	0.1	5.6	50,754
06	48354	Modesto city, California	163,380	96,594	0	11,482	59.1	0.0	11.9	85,112
06	48648	Monrovia city, California	30,543	21,750	0	2,043	71.2	0.0	9.4	19,707
06	48788	Montclair city, California	30,001	18,264	0	1,288	60.9	0.0	7.1	16,976
06	48816	Montebello city, California	52,634	32,360	0	2,168	61.5	0.0	6.7	30,192
06	48872	Monterey city, California	24,205	13,211	3,068	260	54.6	12.7	2.0	12,951
06	48914	Monterey Park city, California	52,330	29,581	0	1,871	56.5	0.0	6.3	27,710
06	49138	Moorpark city, California	30,677	21,624	0	1,363	70.5	0.0	6.3	20,261
06	49270	Moreno Valley city, California	154,519	98,442	302	10,037	63.7	0.2	10.2	88,405
06	49278	Morgan Hill city, California	33,018	20,996	0	843	63.6	0.0	4.0	20,153
06	49670	Mountain View city, California	64,264	49,549	0	1,602	77.1	0.0	3.2	47,947
06	50076	Murrieta city, California	84,000	51,071	243	5,832	60.8	0.3	11.4	45,239
06	50258	Napa city, California	63,073	43,527	0	1,690	69.0	0.0	3.9	41,837
06	50398	National City city, California	50,092	29,249	2,516	2,313	58.4	5.0	7.9	26,936
06	50916	Newark city, California	35,935	23,194	0	953	64.5	0.0	4.1	22,241
06	51182	Newport Beach city, California	74,168	43,944	0	1,841	59.2	0.0	4.2	42,103
06	51560	Norco city, California	21,591	11,128	0	613	51.5	0.0	5.5	10,515
06	51924	North Highlands CDP, California	40,761	23,746	0	1,597	58.3	0.0	6.7	22,149
06	52379	North Tustin CDP, California	19,590	11,740	0	376	59.9	0.0	3.2	11,364

Table E. Cities—Labor Force, Employment, and Educational Data, 2015—*Continued*

FIPS state code	FIPS place code	State/city	Total population age 16 and older	Civilian labor force	Armed Forces	Unemployed	Civilian labor force participation (percent)	Percent in Armed Forces	Unemployment rate	Number of employed persons age 16 and older
06	52526	Norwalk city, California	84,506	53,655	0	3,471	63.5	0.0	6.5	50,184
06	52582	Novato city, California	46,834	29,041	64	1,348	62.0	0.1	4.6	27,693
06	52694	Oakdale city, California	18,933	10,457	0	1,407	55.2	0.0	13.5	9,050
06	53000	Oakland city, California	342,395	234,016	0	16,435	68.3	0.0	7.0	217,581
06	53070	Oakley city, California	29,450	18,856	0	1,373	64.0	0.0	7.3	17,483
06	53322	Oceanside city, California	144,195	88,847	2,291	6,870	61.6	1.6	7.7	81,977
06	53448	Oildale CDP, California	22,670	13,003	0	1,680	57.4	0.0	12.9	11,323
06	53896	Ontario city, California	126,640	87,927	0	6,620	69.4	0.0	7.5	81,307
06	53980	Orange city, California	114,952	74,434	0	5,210	64.8	0.0	7.0	69,224
06	54092	Orangevale CDP, California	29,841	17,798	0	1,218	59.6	0.0	6.8	16,580
06	54120	Orcutt CDP, California	23,316	14,478	60	1,096	62.1	0.3	7.6	13,382
06	54652	Oxnard city, California	153,468	102,330	238	7,743	66.7	0.2	7.6	94,587
06	54806	Pacifica city, California	33,341	22,025	0	1,093	66.1	0.0	5.0	20,932
06	55156	Palmdale city, California	116,380	67,500	56	8,059	58.0	0.0	11.9	59,441
06	55184	Palm Desert city, California	45,104	22,471	0	1,361	49.8	0.0	6.1	21,110
06	55254	Palm Springs city, California	41,270	21,456	0	2,320	52.0	0.0	10.8	19,136
06	55282	Palo Alto city, California	53,183	32,315	0	853	60.8	0.0	2.6	31,462
06	55520	Paradise town, California	22,385	11,653	0	275	52.1	0.0	2.4	11,378
06	55618	Paramount city, California	41,877	27,723	0	1,142	66.2	0.0	4.1	26,581
06	56000	Pasadena city, California	116,332	79,424	0	4,673	68.3	0.0	5.9	74,751
06	56112	Patterson city, California	19,244	11,345	308	1,046	59.0	1.6	9.2	10,299
06	56700	Perris city, California	51,821	32,939	0	3,434	63.6	0.0	10.4	29,505
06	56784	Petaluma city, California	49,738	33,368	147	1,993	67.1	0.3	6.0	31,375
06	56924	Pico Rivera city, California	50,931	31,340	0	2,069	61.5	0.0	6.6	29,271
06	57456	Pittsburg city, California	54,123	35,292	125	3,583	65.2	0.2	10.2	31,709
06	57526	Placentia city, California	41,850	28,382	0	1,285	67.8	0.0	4.5	27,097
06	57764	Pleasant Hill city, California	28,274	18,384	0	1,319	65.0	0.0	7.2	17,065
06	57792	Pleasanton city, California	60,985	40,277	0	1,536	66.0	0.0	3.8	38,741
06	58072	Pomona city, California	118,860	73,483	36	6,931	61.8	0.0	9.4	66,552
06	58240	Porterville city, California	37,750	19,884	0	2,349	52.7	0.0	11.8	17,535
06	58296	Port Hueneme city, California	17,236	8,394	1,479	230	48.7	8.6	2.7	8,164
06	58520	Poway city, California	39,337	23,502	280	846	59.7	0.7	3.6	22,656
06	59346	Ramona CDP, California	17,394	11,132	70	1,156	64.0	0.4	10.4	9,976
06	59444	Rancho Cordova city, California	55,001	38,374	98	4,117	69.8	0.2	10.7	34,257
06	59451	Rancho Cucamonga city, California	135,990	90,357	146	6,068	66.4	0.1	6.7	84,289
06	59514	Rancho Palos Verdes city, California	34,946	18,430	41	729	52.7	0.1	4.0	17,701
06	59550	Rancho San Diego CDP, California	17,207	10,032	96	698	58.3	0.6	7.0	9,334
06	59587	Rancho Santa Margarita city, California	37,502	28,744	71	980	76.6	0.2	3.4	27,764
06	59920	Redding city, California	74,844	42,153	0	2,185	56.3	0.0	5.2	39,968
06	59962	Redlands city, California	56,380	32,829	0	2,489	58.2	0.0	7.6	30,340
06	60018	Redondo Beach city, California	56,565	42,127	0	2,331	74.5	0.0	5.5	39,796
06	60102	Redwood City city, California	68,194	45,997	0	1,829	67.5	0.0	4.0	44,168
06	60242	Reedley city, California	18,157	11,102	0	1,646	61.1	0.0	14.8	9,456
06	60466	Rialto city, California	79,659	49,895	0	6,117	62.6	0.0	12.3	43,778
06	60620	Richmond city, California	87,943	57,214	95	4,499	65.1	0.1	7.9	52,715
06	60704	Ridgecrest city, California	21,515	12,849	687	1,277	59.7	3.2	9.9	11,572
06	61068	Riverbank city, California	17,029	11,469	0	926	67.3	0.0	8.1	10,543
06	62000	Riverside city, California	253,708	160,318	109	12,894	63.2	0.0	8.0	147,424
06	62364	Rocklin city, California	49,293	32,480	272	2,150	65.9	0.6	6.6	30,330
06	62546	Rohnert Park city, California	34,260	23,261	59	741	67.9	0.2	3.2	22,520
06	62826	Rosamond CDP, California	14,703	8,687	283	674	59.1	1.9	7.8	8,013
06	62896	Rosemead city, California	45,318	26,734	0	1,087	59.0	0.0	4.1	25,647
06	62910	Rosemont CDP, California	18,243	10,296	0	652	56.4	0.0	6.3	9,644
06	62938	Roseville city, California	103,982	64,510	245	3,633	62.0	0.2	5.6	60,877
06	63218	Rowland Heights CDP, California	45,149	26,178	0	1,356	58.0	0.0	5.2	24,822
06	64000	Sacramento city, California	382,536	236,984	547	19,517	62.0	0.1	8.2	217,467
06	64224	Salinas city, California	112,436	71,985	193	4,669	64.0	0.2	6.5	67,316
06	65000	San Bernardino city, California	156,963	89,888	0	9,627	57.3	0.0	10.7	80,261
06	65028	San Bruno city, California	36,220	25,680	0	1,423	70.9	0.0	5.5	24,257
06	65042	San Buenaventura (Ventura) city, California	88,549	55,135	0	3,693	62.3	0.0	6.7	51,442
06	65070	San Carlos city, California	24,344	16,305	0	776	67.0	0.0	4.8	15,529
06	65084	San Clemente city, California	54,914	34,742	1,474	1,444	63.3	2.7	4.2	33,298
06	66000	San Diego city, California	1,141,329	741,945	26,489	51,492	65.0	2.3	6.9	690,453
06	66070	San Dimas city, California	29,190	16,767	0	647	57.4	0.0	3.9	16,120
06	66140	San Fernando city, California	19,721	12,373	0	629	62.7	0.0	5.1	11,744
06	67000	San Francisco city, California	760,939	533,555	274	27,235	70.1	0.0	5.1	506,320
06	67042	San Gabriel city, California	33,692	20,785	0	1,359	61.7	0.0	6.5	19,426
06	67056	Sanger city, California	18,120	11,321	0	1,135	62.5	0.0	10.0	10,186
06	67112	San Jacinto city, California	33,232	17,763	0	1,626	53.5	0.0	9.2	16,137
06	68000	San Jose city, California	815,706	548,990	254	33,630	67.3	0.0	6.1	515,360
06	68028	San Juan Capistrano city, California	28,885	16,430	0	512	56.9	0.0	3.1	15,918
06	68084	San Leandro city, California	75,506	50,524	93	2,785	66.9	0.1	5.5	47,739
06	68112	San Lorenzo CDP, California	19,722	13,613	0	608	69.0	0.0	4.5	13,005
06	68154	San Luis Obispo city, California	42,835	25,473	0	1,252	59.5	0.0	4.9	24,221

Table E. Cities—Labor Force, Employment, and Educational Data, 2015—*Continued*

FIPS state code	FIPS place code	State/city	Total population age 16 and older	Civilian labor force	Armed Forces	Unemployed	Civilian labor force participation (percent)	Percent in Armed Forces	Unemployment rate	Number of employed persons age 16 and older
06	68196	San Marcos city, California	71,298	46,064	548	1,617	64.6	0.8	3.5	44,447
06	68252	San Mateo city, California	84,032	58,925	0	2,205	70.1	0.0	3.7	56,720
06	68294	San Pablo city, California	23,465	15,648	0	1,180	66.7	0.0	7.5	14,468
06	68364	San Rafael city, California	46,304	29,738	57	788	64.2	0.1	2.6	28,950
06	68378	San Ramon city, California	55,742	36,511	72	1,385	65.5	0.1	3.8	35,126
06	69000	Santa Ana city, California	248,399	162,061	0	9,333	65.2	0.0	5.8	152,728
06	69070	Santa Barbara city, California	78,429	54,405	0	2,223	69.4	0.0	4.1	52,182
06	69084	Santa Clara city, California	104,288	72,641	71	3,008	69.7	0.1	4.1	69,633
06	69088	Santa Clarita city, California	145,539	99,115	128	6,301	68.1	0.1	6.4	92,814
06	69112	Santa Cruz city, California	57,605	33,022	0	2,363	57.3	0.0	7.2	30,659
06	69196	Santa Maria city, California	74,328	50,524	138	3,244	68.0	0.2	6.4	47,280
06	70000	Santa Monica city, California	80,790	57,878	0	3,637	71.6	0.0	6.3	54,241
06	70042	Santa Paula city, California	22,597	14,968	0	1,517	66.2	0.0	10.1	13,451
06	70098	Santa Rosa city, California	139,584	91,978	0	5,553	65.9	0.0	6.0	86,425
06	70224	Santee city, California	46,720	30,546	670	2,223	65.4	1.4	7.3	28,323
06	70280	Saratoga city, California	26,019	13,810	49	705	53.1	0.2	5.1	13,105
06	70686	Seal Beach city, California	21,585	10,075	212	394	46.7	1.0	3.9	9,681
06	70742	Seaside city, California	26,793	15,702	778	1,465	58.6	2.9	9.3	14,237
06	70882	Selma city, California	17,034	10,740	0	712	63.1	0.0	6.6	10,028
06	72016	Simi Valley city, California	102,001	70,099	0	3,816	68.7	0.0	5.4	66,283
06	72520	Soledad city, California	20,357	6,928	0	511	34.0	0.0	7.4	6,417
06	72996	South El Monte city, California	13,473	7,377	0	434	54.8	0.0	5.9	6,943
06	73080	South Gate city, California	73,179	48,413	0	5,187	66.2	0.0	10.7	43,226
06	73108	South Lake Tahoe city, California	12,425	7,874	0	995	63.4	0.0	12.6	6,879
06	73220	South Pasadena city, California	19,818	14,254	0	1,008	71.9	0.0	7.1	13,246
06	73262	South San Francisco city, California	55,039	37,722	104	2,006	68.5	0.2	5.3	35,716
06	73290	South San Jose Hills CDP, California	15,807	8,844	0	642	55.9	0.0	7.3	8,202
06	73430	South Whittier CDP, California	47,994	28,212	0	2,314	58.8	0.0	8.2	25,898
06	73696	Spring Valley CDP (San Diego County), California	23,181	16,601	101	1,773	71.6	0.4	10.7	14,828
06	73962	Stanton city, California	28,971	19,259	0	792	66.5	0.0	4.1	18,467
06	75000	Stockton city, California	230,552	132,513	59	15,583	57.5	0.0	11.8	116,930
06	75630	Suisun City city, California	23,304	15,239	768	1,281	65.4	3.3	8.4	13,958
06	77000	Sunnyvale city, California	121,269	85,537	75	4,425	70.5	0.1	5.2	81,112
06	78120	Temecula city, California	84,157	55,247	884	3,803	65.6	1.1	6.9	51,444
06	78138	Temescal Valley CDP, California	17,791	11,401	0	779	64.1	0.0	6.8	10,622
06	78148	Temple City city, California	29,004	18,077	0	769	62.3	0.0	4.3	17,308
06	78582	Thousand Oaks city, California	104,528	68,411	40	4,684	65.4	0.0	6.8	63,727
06	80000	Torrance city, California	122,542	77,630	0	4,117	63.3	0.0	5.3	73,513
06	80238	Tracy city, California	67,247	47,163	0	3,543	70.1	0.0	7.5	43,620
06	80644	Tulare city, California	45,731	25,900	0	1,361	56.6	0.0	5.3	24,539
06	80812	Turlock city, California	55,474	33,464	0	2,429	60.3	0.0	7.3	31,035
06	80854	Tustin city, California	61,967	43,764	0	2,192	70.6	0.0	5.0	41,572
06	80994	Twentynine Palms city, California	19,411	6,482	7,056	720	33.4	36.4	11.1	5,762
06	81204	Union City city, California	62,501	39,170	62	1,734	62.7	0.1	4.4	37,436
06	81344	Upland city, California	61,972	38,185	0	1,480	61.6	0.0	3.9	36,705
06	81554	Vacaville city, California	76,659	45,005	1,387	3,274	58.7	1.8	7.3	41,731
06	81638	Valinda CDP, California	20,985	14,234	0	1,744	67.8	0.0	12.3	12,490
06	81666	Vallejo city, California	99,875	60,045	100	6,121	60.1	0.1	10.2	53,924
06	82590	Victorville city, California	89,452	48,481	201	8,096	54.2	0.2	16.7	40,385
06	82852	Vineyard CDP, California	22,104	14,948	0	520	67.6	0.0	3.5	14,428
06	82954	Visalia city, California	95,618	53,872	0	3,314	56.3	0.0	6.2	50,558
06	82996	Vista city, California	74,444	51,833	611	3,185	69.6	0.8	6.1	48,648
06	83332	Walnut city, California	26,276	16,363	0	730	62.3	0.0	4.5	15,633
06	83346	Walnut Creek city, California	57,301	31,355	0	1,511	54.7	0.0	4.8	29,844
06	83542	Wasco city, California	19,166	7,643	0	1,038	39.9	0.0	13.6	6,605
06	83668	Watsonville city, California	37,550	23,954	0	1,702	63.8	0.0	7.1	22,252
06	84144	West Carson CDP, California	19,935	11,854	0	754	59.5	0.0	6.4	11,100
06	84200	West Covina city, California	89,569	57,916	0	4,117	64.7	0.0	7.1	53,799
06	84410	West Hollywood city, California	34,915	28,148	0	966	80.6	0.0	3.4	27,182
06	84550	Westminster city, California	78,214	47,412	0	2,285	60.6	0.0	4.8	45,127
06	84592	Westmont CDP, California	24,950	13,131	0	1,493	52.6	0.0	11.4	11,638
06	84774	West Puente Valley CDP, California	19,896	12,195	0	1,388	61.3	0.0	11.4	10,807
06	84780	West Rancho Dominguez CDP, California	18,090	11,755	0	809	65.0	0.0	6.9	10,946
06	84816	West Sacramento city, California	41,201	26,446	57	1,887	64.2	0.1	7.1	24,559
06	84921	West Whittier-Los Nietos CDP, California	24,140	14,470	0	781	59.9	0.0	5.4	13,689
06	85292	Whittier city, California	70,950	45,798	0	2,441	64.5	0.0	5.3	43,357
06	85446	Wildomar city, California	28,579	16,715	37	1,901	58.5	0.1	11.4	14,814
06	85922	Windsor town, California	22,833	15,326	0	908	67.1	0.0	5.9	14,418
06	85992	Winter Gardens CDP, California	16,643	11,564	82	845	69.5	0.5	7.3	10,719
06	86328	Woodland city, California	46,399	30,436	165	2,758	65.6	0.4	9.1	27,678
06	86832	Yorba Linda city, California	55,623	34,253	0	1,242	61.6	0.0	3.6	33,011
06	86972	Yuba City city, California	50,767	28,214	831	3,891	55.6	1.6	13.8	24,323
06	87042	Yucaipa city, California	42,388	23,053	0	1,748	54.4	0.0	7.6	21,305
06	87056	Yucca Valley town, California	16,381	7,475	353	484	45.6	2.2	6.5	6,991

Table E. Cities—Labor Force, Employment, and Educational Data, 2015—*Continued*

FIPS state code	FIPS place code	State/city	Total population age 16 and older	Employment status						Number of employed persons age 16 and older
				Civilian labor force	Armed Forces	Unemployed	Civilian labor force participation (percent)	Percent in Armed Forces	Unemployment rate	
08	00000	**COLORADO**	4,333,738	2,916,718	31,000	151,603	67.3	0.7	5.2	2,765,115
08	03455	Arvada city, Colorado	92,949	64,351	59	2,959	69.2	0.1	4.6	61,392
08	04000	Aurora city, Colorado	275,761	193,570	1,617	10,826	70.2	0.6	5.6	182,744
08	07850	Boulder city, Colorado	96,578	62,982	0	3,153	65.2	0.0	5.0	59,829
08	08675	Brighton city, Colorado	28,601	18,783	203	755	65.7	0.7	4.0	18,028
08	09280	Broomfield city, Colorado	51,324	37,836	0	1,397	73.7	0.0	3.7	36,439
08	12415	Castle Rock town, Colorado	41,783	33,166	393	1,207	79.4	0.9	3.6	31,959
08	12815	Centennial city, Colorado	88,155	60,750	121	2,005	68.9	0.1	3.3	58,745
08	15165	Clifton CDP, Colorado	16,005	11,110	66	1,260	69.4	0.4	11.3	9,850
08	16000	Colorado Springs city, Colorado	361,358	231,632	9,951	15,635	64.1	2.8	6.7	215,997
08	16110	Columbine CDP, Colorado	20,445	14,055	0	747	68.7	0.0	5.3	13,308
08	16495	Commerce City city, Colorado	37,010	25,719	0	1,518	69.5	0.0	5.9	24,201
08	19150	Dakota Ridge CDP, Colorado	25,533	19,247	0	1,196	75.4	0.0	6.2	18,051
08	20000	Denver city, Colorado	552,635	390,135	455	17,500	70.6	0.1	4.5	372,635
08	24785	Englewood city, Colorado	28,189	20,491	0	1,986	72.7	0.0	9.7	18,505
08	24950	Erie town, Colorado	14,543	10,771	0	315	74.1	0.0	2.9	10,456
08	25280	Evans city, Colorado	16,597	12,812	26	339	77.2	0.2	2.6	12,473
08	27425	Fort Collins city, Colorado	134,672	96,179	247	5,439	71.4	0.2	5.7	90,740
08	27865	Fountain city, Colorado	20,409	12,237	1,792	708	60.0	8.8	5.8	11,529
08	30835	Golden city, Colorado	19,438	10,919	0	299	56.2	0.0	2.7	10,620
08	31660	Grand Junction city, Colorado	48,175	28,793	109	1,958	59.8	0.2	6.8	26,835
08	32155	Greeley city, Colorado	77,802	47,670	51	2,749	61.3	0.1	5.8	44,921
08	36410	Highlands Ranch CDP, Colorado	76,506	55,477	63	1,514	72.5	0.1	2.7	53,963
08	40377	Ken Caryl CDP, Colorado	27,134	19,744	0	938	72.8	0.0	4.8	18,806
08	41835	Lafayette city, Colorado	22,019	16,433	0	441	74.6	0.0	2.7	15,992
08	43000	Lakewood city, Colorado	126,269	89,068	48	3,201	70.5	0.0	3.6	85,867
08	45255	Littleton city, Colorado	39,307	27,151	0	1,569	69.1	0.0	5.8	25,582
08	45970	Longmont city, Colorado	70,894	48,554	0	4,071	68.5	0.0	8.4	44,483
08	46355	Louisville city, Colorado	14,907	11,737	0	568	78.7	0.0	4.8	11,169
08	46465	Loveland city, Colorado	58,615	37,628	0	2,675	64.2	0.0	7.1	34,953
08	54330	Northglenn city, Colorado	30,614	22,684	0	1,995	74.1	0.0	8.8	20,689
08	57630	Parker town, Colorado	35,184	26,814	0	1,006	76.2	0.0	3.8	25,808
08	62000	Pueblo city, Colorado	87,289	47,566	69	4,637	54.5	0.1	9.7	42,929
08	62220	Pueblo West CDP, Colorado	21,762	13,870	20	832	63.7	0.1	6.0	13,038
08	68847	Security-Widefield CDP, Colorado	29,414	17,744	1,398	964	60.3	4.8	5.4	16,780
08	77290	Thornton city, Colorado	97,770	73,369	45	2,593	75.0	0.0	3.5	70,776
08	83835	Westminster city, Colorado	92,679	64,998	0	4,058	70.1	0.0	6.2	60,940
08	84440	Wheat Ridge city, Colorado	25,678	16,465	0	924	64.1	0.0	5.6	15,541
08	85485	Windsor town, Colorado	18,620	12,764	0	354	68.5	0.0	2.8	12,410
09	00000	**CONNECTICUT**	2,922,877	1,941,592	8,066	134,494	66.4	0.3	6.9	1,807,098
09	08000	Bridgeport city, Connecticut	116,892	78,654	58	10,221	67.3	0.0	13.0	68,433
09	08420	Bristol city, Connecticut	49,630	34,735	0	2,024	70.0	0.0	5.8	32,711
09	18430	Danbury city, Connecticut	70,480	49,105	0	4,685	69.7	0.0	9.5	44,420
09	18920	Darien CDP, Connecticut	15,754	9,699	0	679	61.6	0.0	7.0	9,020
09	22700	East Hartford CDP, Connecticut	40,949	26,228	57	1,960	64.1	0.1	7.5	24,268
09	22980	East Haven CDP, Connecticut	24,648	16,129	206	893	65.4	0.8	5.5	15,236
09	37000	Hartford city, Connecticut	97,874	60,468	0	9,700	61.8	0.0	16.0	50,768
09	44690	Manchester CDP, Connecticut	24,065	17,737	70	1,475	73.7	0.3	8.3	16,262
09	46450	Meriden city, Connecticut	51,053	33,883	0	2,097	66.4	0.0	6.2	31,786
09	47290	Middletown city, Connecticut	39,007	25,717	89	2,086	65.9	0.2	8.1	23,631
09	47515	Milford city (balance), Connecticut	44,267	28,954	0	1,257	65.4	0.0	4.3	27,697
09	49880	Naugatuck borough, Connecticut	24,140	15,298	0	707	63.4	0.0	4.6	14,591
09	50370	New Britain city, Connecticut	56,173	33,533	0	3,208	59.7	0.0	9.6	30,325
09	52000	New Haven city, Connecticut	104,220	65,860	71	5,887	63.2	0.1	8.9	59,973
09	52210	Newington CDP, Connecticut	26,189	19,022	0	1,143	72.6	0.0	6.0	17,879
09	52280	New London city, Connecticut	22,211	13,257	1,455	1,534	59.7	6.6	11.6	11,723
09	54940	North Haven CDP, Connecticut	18,821	12,632	0	640	67.1	0.0	5.1	11,992
09	55990	Norwalk city, Connecticut	74,219	53,213	0	4,019	71.7	0.0	7.6	49,194
09	56200	Norwich city, Connecticut	32,514	22,015	746	1,937	67.7	2.3	8.8	20,078
09	68100	Shelton city, Connecticut	34,379	22,638	0	1,887	65.8	0.0	8.3	20,751
09	73000	Stamford city, Connecticut	105,093	77,186	0	5,285	73.4	0.0	6.8	71,901
09	74260	Stratford CDP, Connecticut	43,389	29,442	0	1,717	67.9	0.0	5.8	27,725
09	76500	Torrington city, Connecticut	28,287	18,544	0	1,547	65.6	0.0	8.3	16,997
09	77270	Trumbull CDP, Connecticut	27,931	18,206	0	1,391	65.2	0.0	7.6	16,815
09	80000	Waterbury city, Connecticut	85,925	51,625	0	6,711	60.1	0.0	13.0	44,914
09	82660	West Hartford CDP, Connecticut	49,676	33,472	0	1,320	67.4	0.0	3.9	32,152
09	82800	West Haven city, Connecticut	44,816	28,347	121	3,135	63.3	0.3	11.1	25,212
09	83570	Westport CDP, Connecticut	21,236	13,199	0	973	62.2	0.0	7.4	12,226
09	84970	Wethersfield CDP, Connecticut	22,418	15,853	0	212	70.7	0.0	1.3	15,641
10	00000	**DELAWARE**	765,250	475,209	2,873	27,693	62.1	0.4	5.8	447,516
10	21200	Dover city, Delaware	29,559	17,799	861	1,098	60.2	2.9	6.2	16,701
10	50670	Newark city, Delaware	30,724	15,644	0	316	50.9	0.0	2.0	15,328
10	77580	Wilmington city, Delaware	56,503	33,894	0	1,987	60.0	0.0	5.9	31,907
11	00000	**DISTRICT OF COLUMBIA**	564,206	389,414	4,164	28,235	69.0	0.7	7.3	361,179
11	50000	Washington city, District of Columbia	564,206	389,414	4,164	28,235	69.0	0.7	7.3	361,179

Table E. Cities—Labor Force, Employment, and Educational Data, 2015—*Continued*

FIPS state code	FIPS place code	State/city	Total population age 16 and older	Employment status						Number of employed persons age 16 and older
				Civilian labor force	Armed Forces	Unemployed	Civilian labor force participation (percent)	Percent in Armed Forces	Unemployment rate	
12	00000	**FLORIDA**	16,640,196	9,668,285	53,957	678,064	58.1	0.3	7.0	8,990,221
12	00410	Alafaya CDP, Florida	66,613	46,414	0	2,441	69.7	0.0	5.3	43,973
12	00950	Altamonte Springs city, Florida	35,676	23,873	0	1,814	66.9	0.0	7.6	22,059
12	01700	Apopka city, Florida	38,064	26,229	0	2,032	68.9	0.0	7.7	24,197
12	02681	Aventura city, Florida	34,222	19,452	0	1,195	56.8	0.0	6.1	18,257
12	04162	Bayonet Point CDP, Florida	24,149	11,037	0	913	45.7	0.0	8.3	10,124
12	05462	Bellview CDP, Florida	17,144	10,792	214	666	62.9	1.2	6.2	10,126
12	06875	Bloomingdale CDP, Florida	18,954	12,452	151	371	65.7	0.8	3.0	12,081
12	07300	Boca Raton city, Florida	80,628	49,672	368	1,733	61.6	0.5	3.5	47,939
12	07525	Bonita Springs city, Florida	46,626	17,940	97	845	38.5	0.2	4.7	17,095
12	07875	Boynton Beach city, Florida	62,052	36,234	0	4,876	58.4	0.0	13.5	31,358
12	07950	Bradenton city, Florida	43,323	21,993	0	1,774	50.8	0.0	8.1	20,219
12	08150	Brandon CDP, Florida	92,871	60,135	617	4,086	64.8	0.7	6.8	56,049
12	08300	Brent CDP, Florida	20,964	12,039	0	904	57.4	0.0	7.5	11,135
12	09415	Buenaventura Lakes CDP, Florida	25,277	14,753	0	923	58.4	0.0	6.3	13,830
12	10275	Cape Coral city, Florida	147,095	81,596	384	5,659	55.5	0.3	6.9	75,937
12	10825	Carrollwood CDP, Florida	30,485	21,921	0	949	71.9	0.0	4.3	20,972
12	11050	Casselberry city, Florida	23,970	13,540	113	1,621	56.5	0.5	12.0	11,919
12	12425	Citrus Park CDP, Florida	20,444	14,982	0	332	73.3	0.0	2.2	14,650
12	12875	Clearwater city, Florida	96,892	56,963	22	3,984	58.8	0.0	7.0	52,979
12	12925	Clermont city, Florida	24,560	13,686	0	835	55.7	0.0	6.1	12,851
12	13275	Coconut Creek city, Florida	47,441	32,638	0	2,593	68.8	0.0	7.9	30,045
12	14125	Cooper City city, Florida	27,495	19,278	0	487	70.1	0.0	2.5	18,791
12	14250	Coral Gables city, Florida	43,010	25,937	55	700	60.3	0.1	2.7	25,237
12	14400	Coral Springs city, Florida	100,148	69,485	46	4,725	69.4	0.0	6.8	64,760
12	14412	Coral Terrace CDP, Florida	22,715	15,094	0	694	66.4	0.0	4.6	14,400
12	14895	Country Club CDP, Florida	39,212	27,020	0	1,057	68.9	0.0	3.9	25,963
12	15475	Crestview city, Florida	16,493	9,227	1,260	1,869	55.9	7.6	20.3	7,358
12	15968	Cutler Bay town, Florida	34,321	22,404	0	1,345	65.3	0.0	6.0	21,059
12	16335	Dania Beach city, Florida	27,059	17,904	0	1,983	66.2	0.0	11.1	15,921
12	16475	Davie town, Florida	85,696	60,903	101	2,810	71.1	0.1	4.6	58,093
12	16525	Daytona Beach city, Florida	56,410	27,476	0	1,975	48.7	0.0	7.2	25,501
12	16725	Deerfield Beach city, Florida	68,049	45,328	0	3,664	66.6	0.0	8.1	41,664
12	16875	DeLand city, Florida	24,646	10,586	0	884	43.0	0.0	8.4	9,702
12	17100	Delray Beach city, Florida	58,257	35,161	0	3,248	60.4	0.0	9.2	31,913
12	17200	Deltona city, Florida	70,604	40,283	0	2,350	57.1	0.0	5.8	37,933
12	17935	Doral city, Florida	40,542	27,530	49	1,626	67.9	0.1	5.9	25,904
12	18575	Dunedin city, Florida	32,430	18,547	0	636	57.2	0.0	3.4	17,911
12	19206	East Lake CDP, Florida	28,351	17,593	0	1,372	62.1	0.0	7.8	16,221
12	19212	East Lake-Orient Park CDP, Florida	18,705	13,248	0	1,283	70.8	0.0	9.7	11,965
12	19825	Edgewater city, Florida	18,102	10,027	0	639	55.4	0.0	6.4	9,388
12	20108	Egypt Lake-Leto CDP, Florida	32,657	22,100	0	1,649	67.7	0.0	7.5	20,451
12	20925	Ensley CDP, Florida	18,613	12,609	0	1,041	67.7	0.0	8.3	11,568
12	21150	Estero village, Florida	26,864	10,244	0	738	38.1	0.0	7.2	9,506
12	22275	Ferry Pass CDP, Florida	25,550	16,859	222	1,284	66.0	0.9	7.6	15,575
12	22660	Fleming Island CDP, Florida	20,923	13,009	755	806	62.2	3.6	6.2	12,203
12	23050	Florida Ridge CDP, Florida	16,909	9,065	0	1,750	53.6	0.0	19.3	7,315
12	24000	Fort Lauderdale city, Florida	147,592	96,724	27	8,846	65.5	0.0	9.1	87,878
12	24125	Fort Myers city, Florida	60,679	36,517	0	2,743	60.2	0.0	7.5	33,774
12	24300	Fort Pierce city, Florida	33,750	18,320	0	1,002	54.3	0.0	5.5	17,318
12	24475	Fort Walton Beach city, Florida	16,100	10,033	685	788	62.3	4.3	7.9	9,245
12	24562	Fountainebleau CDP, Florida	49,584	32,065	0	2,069	64.7	0.0	6.5	29,996
12	24581	Four Corners CDP, Florida	27,072	18,478	0	235	68.3	0.0	1.3	18,243
12	24925	Fruit Cove CDP, Florida	26,566	18,484	52	1,791	69.6	0.2	9.7	16,693
12	25175	Gainesville city, Florida	113,620	62,391	100	3,168	54.9	0.1	5.1	59,223
12	26300	Golden Gate CDP, Florida	19,839	14,259	0	519	71.9	0.0	3.6	13,740
12	26375	Golden Glades CDP, Florida	26,069	15,878	0	1,588	60.9	0.0	10.0	14,290
12	27322	Greenacres city, Florida	32,438	20,758	0	1,613	64.0	0.0	7.8	19,145
12	28400	Haines City city, Florida	19,507	10,312	0	976	52.9	0.0	9.5	9,336
12	28452	Hallandale Beach city, Florida	32,601	21,845	0	2,100	67.0	0.0	9.6	19,745
12	30000	Hialeah city, Florida	198,063	112,048	0	7,712	56.6	0.0	6.9	104,336
12	30025	Hialeah Gardens city, Florida	21,475	14,067	0	699	65.5	0.0	5.0	13,368
12	31075	Holiday CDP, Florida	17,524	8,696	0	453	49.6	0.0	5.2	8,243
12	32000	Hollywood city, Florida	121,286	81,234	80	7,461	67.0	0.1	9.2	73,773
12	32275	Homestead city, Florida	48,538	29,052	146	3,003	59.9	0.3	10.3	26,049
12	32610	Horizon West CDP, Florida	18,464	13,987	0	1,612	75.8	0.0	11.5	12,375
12	32967	Hunters Creek CDP, Florida	21,552	13,850	0	632	64.3	0.0	4.6	13,218
12	33250	Immokalee CDP, Florida	21,583	15,759	0	2,670	73.0	0.0	16.9	13,089
12	35000	Jacksonville city, Florida	684,614	440,082	11,794	31,822	64.3	1.7	7.2	408,260
12	35050	Jacksonville Beach city, Florida	20,720	12,226	109	604	59.0	0.5	4.9	11,622
12	35350	Jasmine Estates CDP, Florida	21,022	11,729	63	689	55.8	0.3	5.9	11,040
12	35875	Jupiter town, Florida	51,659	33,139	0	1,315	64.1	0.0	4.0	31,824
12	36062	Kendale Lakes CDP, Florida	50,324	32,378	0	1,564	64.3	0.0	4.8	30,814
12	36100	Kendall CDP, Florida	65,521	43,626	97	1,646	66.6	0.1	3.8	41,980
12	36121	Kendall West CDP, Florida	35,120	22,753	181	1,038	64.8	0.5	4.6	21,715
12	36462	Keystone CDP, Florida	18,295	11,808	76	548	64.5	0.4	4.6	11,260

Table E. Cities—Labor Force, Employment, and Educational Data, 2015—*Continued*

FIPS state code	FIPS place code	State/city	Total population age 16 and older	Civilian labor force	Armed Forces	Unemployed	Civilian labor force participation (percent)	Percent in Armed Forces	Unemployment rate	Number of employed persons age 16 and older
										Employment status
12	36550	Key West city, Florida	22,301	13,923	632	430	62.4	2.8	3.1	13,493
12	36950	Kissimmee city, Florida	56,372	35,592	0	2,714	63.1	0.0	7.6	32,878
12	37648	Lake Butler CDP, Florida	15,312	10,339	0	282	67.5	0.0	2.7	10,057
12	38250	Lakeland city, Florida	84,160	46,548	0	3,503	55.3	0.0	7.5	43,045
12	38350	Lake Magdalene CDP, Florida	22,264	13,655	99	857	61.3	0.4	6.3	12,798
12	38813	Lakeside CDP, Florida	25,231	15,483	121	1,562	61.4	0.5	10.1	13,921
12	39075	Lake Worth city, Florida	30,248	18,587	0	1,038	61.4	0.0	5.6	17,549
12	39200	Land O' Lakes CDP, Florida	28,245	18,653	0	642	66.0	0.0	3.4	18,011
12	39425	Largo city, Florida	67,536	40,866	130	2,326	60.5	0.2	5.7	38,540
12	39525	Lauderdale Lakes city, Florida	26,877	16,822	0	2,621	62.6	0.0	15.6	14,201
12	39550	Lauderhill city, Florida	56,295	37,086	0	3,025	65.9	0.0	8.2	34,061
12	39875	Leesburg city, Florida	17,486	8,943	0	627	51.1	0.0	7.0	8,316
12	39925	Lehigh Acres CDP, Florida	88,823	50,024	23	4,472	56.3	0.0	8.9	45,552
12	39950	Leisure City CDP, Florida	17,958	10,403	0	879	57.9	0.0	8.4	9,524
12	41775	Lutz CDP, Florida	19,019	12,949	0	464	68.1	0.0	3.6	12,485
12	41825	Lynn Haven city, Florida	16,261	10,887	76	776	67.0	0.5	7.1	10,111
12	43125	Margate city, Florida	48,540	32,861	66	4,554	67.7	0.1	13.9	28,307
12	43800	Meadow Woods CDP, Florida	24,868	17,235	0	461	69.3	0.0	2.7	16,774
12	43975	Melbourne city, Florida	67,051	38,351	76	2,126	57.2	0.1	5.5	36,225
12	44275	Merritt Island CDP, Florida	29,990	16,629	111	782	55.4	0.4	4.7	15,847
12	45000	Miami city, Florida	372,847	227,328	0	16,592	61.0	0.0	7.3	210,736
12	45025	Miami Beach city, Florida	79,969	54,612	63	1,792	68.3	0.1	3.3	52,820
12	45060	Miami Gardens city, Florida	87,724	49,317	0	5,410	56.2	0.0	11.0	43,907
12	45100	Miami Lakes town, Florida	25,690	17,811	0	284	69.3	0.0	1.6	17,527
12	45975	Miramar city, Florida	106,906	73,602	0	5,652	68.8	0.0	7.7	67,950
12	47625	Naples city, Florida	18,237	6,425	0	146	35.2	0.0	2.3	6,279
12	48050	Navarre CDP, Florida	26,042	15,262	1,380	995	58.6	5.3	6.5	14,267
12	48625	New Smyrna Beach city, Florida	21,223	9,822	10	628	46.3	0.0	6.4	9,194
12	49260	Northdale CDP, Florida	18,534	12,587	201	695	67.9	1.1	5.5	11,892
12	49350	North Fort Myers CDP, Florida	37,260	13,226	0	499	35.5	0.0	3.8	12,727
12	49425	North Lauderdale city, Florida	32,945	24,855	0	2,696	75.4	0.0	10.8	22,159
12	49450	North Miami city, Florida	50,367	32,681	0	2,821	64.9	0.0	8.6	29,860
12	49475	North Miami Beach city, Florida	35,511	20,936	0	1,032	59.0	0.0	4.9	19,904
12	49675	North Port city, Florida	47,894	22,476	0	1,108	46.9	0.0	4.9	21,368
12	50575	Oakland Park city, Florida	37,795	24,458	0	2,763	64.7	0.0	11.3	21,695
12	50630	Oakleaf Plantation CDP, Florida	18,241	13,207	419	1,139	72.4	2.3	8.6	12,068
12	50638	Oak Ridge CDP, Florida	17,659	13,840	0	412	78.4	0.0	3.0	13,428
12	50750	Ocala city, Florida	45,366	23,050	0	2,153	50.8	0.0	9.3	20,897
12	51075	Ocoee city, Florida	32,064	21,832	0	472	68.1	0.0	2.2	21,360
12	53000	Orlando city, Florida	220,510	159,484	29	11,508	72.3	0.0	7.2	147,976
12	53150	Ormond Beach city, Florida	35,220	18,590	34	1,779	52.8	0.1	9.6	16,811
12	53575	Oviedo city, Florida	30,560	20,628	146	924	67.5	0.5	4.5	19,704
12	53725	Pace CDP, Florida	18,742	11,578	155	122	61.8	0.8	1.1	11,456
12	54000	Palm Bay city, Florida	85,068	45,489	275	2,998	53.5	0.3	6.6	42,491
12	54075	Palm Beach Gardens city, Florida	46,487	26,459	0	764	56.9	0.0	2.9	25,695
12	54175	Palm City CDP, Florida	20,093	10,246	0	250	51.0	0.0	2.4	9,996
12	54200	Palm Coast city, Florida	68,329	33,568	40	2,836	49.1	0.1	8.4	30,732
12	54275	Palmetto Bay village, Florida	19,468	12,420	0	216	63.8	0.0	1.7	12,204
12	54300	Palmetto Estates CDP, Florida	18,280	12,098	0	1,191	66.2	0.0	9.8	10,907
12	54350	Palm Harbor CDP, Florida	51,977	29,418	185	1,453	56.6	0.4	4.9	27,965
12	54387	Palm River-Clair Mel CDP, Florida	16,856	10,863	158	931	64.4	0.9	8.6	9,932
12	54450	Palm Springs village, Florida	17,642	12,108	0	728	68.6	0.0	6.0	11,380
12	54525	Palm Valley CDP, Florida	17,803	10,570	39	616	59.4	0.2	5.8	9,954
12	54700	Panama City city, Florida	30,895	18,093	0	1,633	58.6	0.0	9.0	16,460
12	55125	Parkland city, Florida	21,734	14,719	0	940	67.7	0.0	6.4	13,779
12	55775	Pembroke Pines city, Florida	135,557	92,363	123	5,196	68.1	0.1	5.6	87,167
12	55925	Pensacola city, Florida	41,953	25,562	310	1,919	60.9	0.7	7.5	23,643
12	56825	Pine Hills CDP, Florida	55,703	40,562	0	3,916	72.8	0.0	9.7	36,646
12	56975	Pinellas Park city, Florida	43,564	25,674	61	1,145	58.9	0.1	4.5	24,529
12	57425	Plantation city, Florida	74,116	49,651	0	1,969	67.0	0.0	4.0	47,682
12	57550	Plant City city, Florida	27,751	17,450	0	1,069	62.9	0.0	6.1	16,381
12	57900	Poinciana CDP, Florida	58,944	30,873	0	2,343	52.4	0.0	7.6	28,530
12	58050	Pompano Beach city, Florida	88,577	52,547	40	7,273	59.3	0.0	13.8	45,274
12	58350	Port Charlotte CDP, Florida	52,643	27,286	0	3,749	51.8	0.0	13.7	23,537
12	58575	Port Orange city, Florida	50,472	24,259	0	1,143	48.1	0.0	4.7	23,116
12	58715	Port St. Lucie city, Florida	143,390	82,257	166	7,301	57.4	0.1	8.9	74,956
12	58975	Princeton CDP, Florida	19,362	12,254	81	815	63.3	0.4	6.7	11,439
12	60230	Richmond West CDP, Florida	26,564	16,726	0	1,063	63.0	0.0	6.4	15,663
12	60950	Riverview CDP, Florida	65,709	43,093	1,075	2,122	65.6	1.6	4.9	40,971
12	60975	Riviera Beach city, Florida	26,158	15,744	34	1,655	60.2	0.1	10.5	14,089
12	61500	Rockledge city, Florida	23,915	14,438	157	496	60.4	0.7	3.4	13,942
12	62100	Royal Palm Beach village, Florida	30,420	20,262	0	294	66.6	0.0	1.5	19,968
12	62275	Ruskin CDP, Florida	18,501	10,917	221	735	59.0	1.2	6.7	10,182
12	62625	St. Cloud city, Florida	33,394	21,290	0	1,805	63.8	0.0	8.5	19,485
12	63000	St. Petersburg city, Florida	214,354	133,330	388	8,461	62.2	0.2	6.3	124,869
12	63425	San Carlos Park CDP, Florida	14,806	11,145	0	1,519	75.3	0.0	13.6	9,626
12	63650	Sanford city, Florida	44,207	29,687	0	2,278	67.2	0.0	7.7	27,409

Table E. Cities—Labor Force, Employment, and Educational Data, 2015—*Continued*

					Employment status					
FIPS state code	FIPS place code	State/city	Total population age 16 and older	Civilian labor force	Armed Forces	Unemployed	Civilian labor force participation (percent)	Percent in Armed Forces	Unemployment rate	Number of employed persons age 16 and older
12	64175	Sarasota city, Florida	49,078	27,555	0	1,474	56.1	0.0	5.3	26,081
12	64825	Sebastian city, Florida	20,932	9,011	170	1,044	43.0	0.8	11.6	7,967
12	67258	South Bradenton CDP, Florida	23,910	11,673	0	617	48.8	0.0	5.3	11,056
12	67575	South Miami Heights CDP, Florida	35,364	20,760	0	1,370	58.7	0.0	6.6	19,390
12	68350	Spring Hill CDP, Florida	84,548	41,631	0	3,760	49.2	0.0	9.0	37,871
12	69250	Sun City Center CDP, Florida	22,291	4,576	0	213	20.5	0.0	4.7	4,363
12	69555	Sunny Isles Beach city, Florida	13,365	7,993	0	188	59.8	0.0	2.4	7,805
12	69700	Sunrise city, Florida	75,300	50,211	0	3,268	66.7	0.0	6.5	46,943
12	70345	Sweetwater city, Florida	15,423	9,399	0	577	60.9	0.0	6.1	8,822
12	70600	Tallahassee city, Florida	162,485	108,716	0	9,874	66.9	0.0	9.1	98,842
12	70675	Tamarac city, Florida	57,837	33,168	0	1,420	57.3	0.0	4.3	31,748
12	70700	Tamiami CDP, Florida	54,824	28,786	0	973	52.5	0.0	3.4	27,813
12	71000	Tampa city, Florida	298,188	190,556	1,872	15,815	63.9	0.6	8.3	174,741
12	71150	Tarpon Springs city, Florida	21,917	10,126	0	608	46.2	0.0	6.0	9,518
12	71400	Temple Terrace city, Florida	21,788	14,122	40	679	64.8	0.2	4.8	13,443
12	71564	The Acreage CDP, Florida	29,318	19,065	0	422	65.0	0.0	2.2	18,643
12	71567	The Crossings CDP, Florida	18,346	12,186	0	307	66.4	0.0	2.5	11,879
12	71569	The Hammocks CDP, Florida	49,574	32,853	0	1,486	66.3	0.0	4.5	31,367
12	71625	The Villages CDP, Florida	71,838	10,178	0	155	14.2	0.0	1.5	10,023
12	71741	Three Lakes CDP, Florida	15,221	11,135	0	511	73.2	0.0	4.6	10,624
12	71900	Titusville city, Florida	38,253	21,398	0	2,058	55.9	0.0	9.6	19,340
12	72145	Town 'n' Country CDP, Florida	64,771	42,664	148	3,089	65.9	0.2	7.2	39,575
12	73163	University CDP (Hillsborough County), Florida	37,921	23,987	152	3,077	63.3	0.4	12.8	20,910
12	73172	University CDP (Orange County), Florida	32,608	11,717	0	1,351	35.9	0.0	11.5	10,366
12	73287	University Park CDP, Florida	23,267	13,102	0	645	56.3	0.0	4.9	12,457
12	73700	Valrico CDP, Florida	27,122	14,788	193	858	54.5	0.7	5.8	13,930
12	73900	Venice city, Florida	22,118	8,027	0	203	36.3	0.0	2.5	7,824
12	74200	Vero Beach South CDP, Florida	19,606	11,096	0	643	56.6	0.0	5.8	10,453
12	75725	Wekiwa Springs CDP, Florida	18,660	11,675	296	552	62.6	1.6	4.7	11,123
12	75812	Wellington village, Florida	50,225	31,442	0	1,674	62.6	0.0	5.3	29,768
12	75875	Wesley Chapel CDP, Florida	40,691	27,771	138	1,965	68.2	0.3	7.1	25,806
12	76062	Westchase CDP, Florida	18,937	13,780	80	674	72.8	0.4	4.9	13,106
12	76075	Westchester CDP, Florida	24,587	15,383	0	659	62.6	0.0	4.3	14,724
12	76487	West Little River CDP, Florida	25,210	14,605	0	1,632	57.9	0.0	11.2	12,973
12	76500	West Melbourne city, Florida	20,352	11,514	0	822	56.6	0.0	7.1	10,692
12	76582	Weston city, Florida	50,490	32,447	76	1,008	64.3	0.2	3.1	31,439
12	76600	West Palm Beach city, Florida	88,834	56,164	0	5,104	63.2	0.0	9.1	51,060
12	76675	West Pensacola CDP, Florida	16,617	9,347	83	1,137	56.2	0.5	12.2	8,210
12	78250	Winter Garden city, Florida	31,383	20,448	0	267	65.2	0.0	1.3	20,181
12	78275	Winter Haven city, Florida	30,882	15,223	44	1,563	49.3	0.1	10.3	13,660
12	78300	Winter Park city, Florida	25,533	15,214	0	608	59.6	0.0	4.0	14,606
12	78325	Winter Springs city, Florida	28,480	17,678	84	1,127	62.1	0.3	6.4	16,551
12	78800	Wright CDP, Florida	20,298	12,859	1,208	458	63.4	6.0	3.6	12,401
13	00000	**GEORGIA**	7,998,548	4,957,832	47,730	352,199	62.0	0.6	7.1	4,605,633
13	00408	Acworth city, Georgia	16,616	10,943	0	1,437	65.9	0.0	13.1	9,506
13	01052	Albany city, Georgia	55,581	31,747	126	5,342	57.1	0.2	16.8	26,405
13	01696	Alpharetta city, Georgia	46,895	35,371	0	2,382	75.4	0.0	6.7	32,989
13	03440	Athens-Clarke County unified government (balance), Georgia	103,312	61,105	118	3,957	59.1	0.1	6.5	57,148
13	04000	Atlanta city, Georgia	387,266	253,208	424	18,694	65.4	0.1	7.4	234,514
13	04204	Augusta-Richmond County consolidated government (balance), Georgia	155,840	84,386	6,676	7,625	54.1	4.3	9.0	76,761
13	10944	Brookhaven city, Georgia	39,342	30,469	0	936	77.4	0.0	3.1	29,533
13	12834	Candler-McAfee CDP, Georgia	18,077	11,299	0	1,599	62.5	0.0	14.2	9,700
13	12988	Canton city, Georgia	18,540	13,402	0	643	72.3	0.0	4.8	12,759
13	13492	Carrollton city, Georgia	21,105	13,054	0	1,003	61.9	0.0	7.7	12,051
13	13688	Cartersville city, Georgia	15,749	8,767	0	211	55.7	0.0	2.4	8,556
13	15172	Chamblee city, Georgia	22,688	18,115	0	238	79.8	0.0	1.3	17,877
13	19000	Columbus city, Georgia	156,697	86,865	7,482	9,467	55.4	4.8	10.9	77,398
13	21380	Dalton city, Georgia	25,375	17,072	0	1,023	67.3	0.0	6.0	16,049
13	22052	Decatur city, Georgia	15,819	12,102	0	195	76.5	0.0	1.6	11,907
13	23900	Douglasville city, Georgia	26,842	17,996	0	2,065	67.0	0.0	11.5	15,931
13	24600	Duluth city, Georgia	23,295	17,118	0	1,361	73.5	0.0	8.0	15,757
13	24768	Dunwoody city, Georgia	36,038	25,937	0	1,351	72.0	0.0	5.2	24,586
13	25720	East Point city, Georgia	28,181	19,909	0	2,136	70.6	0.0	10.7	17,773
13	28044	Evans CDP, Georgia	29,538	17,819	357	668	60.3	1.2	3.7	17,151
13	31908	Gainesville city, Georgia	29,584	18,149	0	607	61.3	0.0	3.3	17,542
13	35324	Griffin city, Georgia	15,972	9,610	0	1,134	60.2	0.0	11.8	8,476
13	38964	Hinesville city, Georgia	25,470	14,232	2,413	1,916	55.9	9.5	13.5	12,316
13	42425	Johns Creek city, Georgia	62,986	43,910	132	4,292	69.7	0.2	9.8	39,618
13	43192	Kennesaw city, Georgia	26,948	20,610	0	598	76.5	0.0	2.9	20,012
13	44340	LaGrange city, Georgia	22,880	14,030	0	2,318	61.3	0.0	16.5	11,712
13	45488	Lawrenceville city, Georgia	24,432	14,981	0	967	61.3	0.0	6.5	14,014
13	48288	Mableton CDP, Georgia	30,249	23,321	0	1,577	77.1	0.0	6.8	21,744

Table E. Cities—Labor Force, Employment, and Educational Data, 2015—*Continued*

FIPS state code	FIPS place code	State/city	Total population age 16 and older	Civilian labor force	Armed Forces	Unemployed	Civilian labor force participation (percent)	Percent in Armed Forces	Unemployment rate	Number of employed persons age 16 and older
13	48624	McDonough city, Georgia	19,110	12,528	0	1,583	65.6	0.0	12.6	10,945
13	49008	Macon-Bibb County, Georgia	119,333	67,005	241	5,530	56.1	0.2	8.3	61,475
13	49756	Marietta city, Georgia	46,197	32,830	75	2,422	71.1	0.2	7.4	30,408
13	50036	Martinez CDP, Georgia	28,498	16,122	359	882	56.6	1.3	5.5	15,240
13	51670	Milton city, Georgia	25,587	17,693	0	613	69.1	0.0	3.5	17,080
13	55020	Newnan city, Georgia	25,779	15,483	0	796	60.1	0.0	5.1	14,687
13	56168	North Druid Hills CDP, Georgia	17,302	11,427	81	523	66.0	0.5	4.6	10,904
13	59724	Peachtree City city, Georgia	27,434	17,448	29	567	63.6	0.1	3.2	16,881
13	59735	Peachtree Corners city, Georgia	30,885	22,466	0	1,007	72.7	0.0	4.5	21,459
13	62104	Pooler city, Georgia	20,456	14,567	144	1,241	71.2	0.7	8.5	13,326
13	63952	Redan CDP, Georgia	26,174	18,514	0	2,441	70.7	0.0	13.2	16,073
13	66668	Rome city, Georgia	27,394	16,258	0	1,181	59.3	0.0	7.3	15,077
13	67284	Roswell city, Georgia	72,138	53,871	64	1,696	74.7	0.1	3.1	52,175
13	68516	Sandy Springs city, Georgia	83,950	58,932	287	2,234	70.2	0.3	3.8	56,698
13	69000	Savannah city, Georgia	117,643	72,910	1,558	7,172	62.0	1.3	9.8	65,738
13	71492	Smyrna city, Georgia	43,892	32,078	89	2,225	73.1	0.2	6.9	29,853
13	73256	Statesboro city, Georgia	26,354	14,424	0	1,302	54.7	0.0	9.0	13,122
13	73704	Stockbridge city, Georgia	21,684	14,450	0	1,149	66.6	0.0	8.0	13,301
13	74180	Sugar Hill city, Georgia	17,052	11,474	0	858	67.3	0.0	7.5	10,616
13	77652	Tucker CDP, Georgia	21,150	14,171	0	883	67.0	0.0	6.2	13,288
13	78324	Union City city, Georgia	16,860	11,313	0	998	67.1	0.0	8.8	10,315
13	78800	Valdosta city, Georgia	44,822	25,000	641	2,864	55.8	1.4	11.5	22,136
13	80508	Warner Robins city, Georgia	55,056	36,470	1,136	3,804	66.2	2.1	10.4	32,666
13	84176	Woodstock city, Georgia	21,145	14,738	0	193	69.7	0.0	1.3	14,545
15	00000	**HAWAII**	1,152,884	710,239	44,452	35,025	61.6	3.9	4.9	675,214
15	06290	East Honolulu CDP, Hawaii	38,088	23,680	135	415	62.2	0.4	1.8	23,265
15	07470	Ewa Gentry CDP, Hawaii	16,540	10,951	1,016	356	66.2	6.1	3.3	10,595
15	14650	Hilo CDP, Hawaii	36,715	20,853	237	1,595	56.8	0.6	7.6	19,258
15	22700	Kahului CDP, Hawaii	23,205	14,408	0	796	62.1	0.0	5.5	13,612
15	23150	Kailua CDP (Honolulu County), Hawaii	30,339	19,017	964	964	62.7	3.2	5.1	18,053
15	28250	Kaneohe CDP, Hawaii	27,882	18,135	1,004	684	65.0	3.6	3.8	17,451
15	30300	Kapolei CDP, Hawaii	15,220	11,493	672	1,264	75.5	4.4	11.0	10,229
15	47600	Makakilo CDP, Hawaii	19,269	13,964	414	955	72.5	2.1	6.8	13,009
15	51000	Mililani Mauka CDP, Hawaii	16,523	11,269	950	340	68.2	5.7	3.0	10,929
15	51050	Mililani Town CDP, Hawaii	22,953	14,919	458	215	65.0	2.0	1.4	14,704
15	62600	Pearl City CDP, Hawaii	36,492	19,666	2,921	413	53.9	8.0	2.1	19,253
15	69050	Schofield Barracks CDP, Hawaii	15,365	4,189	8,324	576	27.3	54.2	13.8	3,613
15	71550	Urban Honolulu CDP, Hawaii	302,566	191,802	6,025	6,905	63.4	2.0	3.6	184,897
15	79700	Waipahu CDP, Hawaii	31,688	19,993	455	1,204	63.1	1.4	6.0	18,789
16	00000	**IDAHO**	1,270,851	786,377	5,297	42,149	61.9	0.4	5.4	744,228
16	08830	Boise City city, Idaho	172,640	120,817	578	6,480	70.0	0.3	5.4	114,337
16	12250	Caldwell city, Idaho	36,079	22,133	44	2,654	61.3	0.1	12.0	19,479
16	16750	Coeur d'Alene city, Idaho	39,837	26,394	0	1,215	66.3	0.0	4.6	25,179
16	23410	Eagle city, Idaho	17,344	9,850	0	501	56.8	0.0	5.1	9,349
16	39700	Idaho Falls city, Idaho	44,575	27,235	0	1,406	61.1	0.0	5.2	25,829
16	46540	Lewiston city, Idaho	25,501	15,007	0	600	58.8	0.0	4.0	14,407
16	52120	Meridian city, Idaho	68,206	39,809	0	1,464	58.4	0.0	3.7	38,345
16	54550	Moscow city, Idaho	20,574	12,437	0	801	60.5	0.0	6.4	11,636
16	56260	Nampa city, Idaho	64,603	41,448	325	2,343	64.2	0.5	5.7	39,105
16	64090	Pocatello city, Idaho	41,866	24,916	130	2,219	59.5	0.3	8.9	22,697
16	64810	Post Falls city, Idaho	23,392	14,684	0	281	62.8	0.0	1.9	14,403
16	67420	Rexburg city, Idaho	19,784	12,312	0	713	62.2	0.0	5.8	11,599
16	82810	Twin Falls city, Idaho	35,986	24,905	0	1,105	69.2	0.0	4.4	23,800
17	00000	**ILLINOIS**	10,240,058	6,657,355	17,570	460,831	65.0	0.2	6.9	6,196,524
17	00243	Addison village, Illinois	28,058	20,837	58	780	74.3	0.2	3.7	20,057
17	00685	Algonquin village, Illinois	22,581	16,185	0	911	71.7	0.0	5.6	15,274
17	01114	Alton city, Illinois	21,445	12,802	0	1,621	59.7	0.0	12.7	11,181
17	02154	Arlington Heights village, Illinois	63,021	40,946	0	1,113	65.0	0.0	2.7	39,833
17	03012	Aurora city, Illinois	147,281	107,221	0	4,587	72.8	0.0	4.3	102,634
17	04013	Bartlett village, Illinois	31,356	23,866	0	817	76.1	0.0	3.4	23,049
17	04078	Batavia city, Illinois	21,665	15,535	0	1,468	71.7	0.0	9.4	14,067
17	04845	Belleville city, Illinois	31,736	20,604	125	1,408	64.9	0.4	6.8	19,196
17	05092	Belvidere city, Illinois	19,805	12,908	0	763	65.2	0.0	5.9	12,145
17	05573	Berwyn city, Illinois	42,784	29,258	0	1,772	68.4	0.0	6.1	27,486
17	06587	Bloomingdale village, Illinois	18,905	12,752	0	962	67.5	0.0	7.5	11,790
17	06613	Bloomington city, Illinois	63,124	43,511	0	2,393	68.9	0.0	5.5	41,118
17	06704	Blue Island city, Illinois	17,747	10,891	54	1,006	61.4	0.3	9.2	9,885
17	07133	Bolingbrook village, Illinois	54,661	40,243	0	2,281	73.6	0.0	5.7	37,962
17	09447	Buffalo Grove village, Illinois	32,893	23,604	0	1,087	71.8	0.0	4.6	22,517
17	09642	Burbank city, Illinois	24,530	14,780	0	1,498	60.3	0.0	10.1	13,282
17	10487	Calumet City city, Illinois	29,813	17,182	0	3,546	57.6	0.0	20.6	13,636
17	11163	Carbondale city, Illinois	23,034	14,079	0	1,203	61.1	0.0	8.5	12,876
17	11332	Carol Stream village, Illinois	30,441	22,027	0	1,317	72.4	0.0	6.0	20,710
17	11358	Carpentersville village, Illinois	27,345	19,084	48	903	69.8	0.2	4.7	18,181

Table E. Cities—Labor Force, Employment, and Educational Data, 2015—*Continued*

				Employment status						
FIPS state code	FIPS place code	State/city	Total population age 16 and older	Civilian labor force	Armed Forces	Unemployed	Civilian labor force participation (percent)	Percent in Armed Forces	Unemployment rate	Number of employed persons age 16 and older
17	12385	Champaign city, Illinois	74,416	47,104	94	1,974	63.3	0.1	4.2	45,130
17	12567	Charleston city, Illinois	17,083	9,742	37	728	57.0	0.2	7.5	9,014
17	14000	Chicago city, Illinois	2,200,593	1,450,688	883	137,758	65.9	0.0	9.5	1,312,930
17	14026	Chicago Heights city, Illinois	23,625	15,367	0	2,737	65.0	0.0	17.8	12,630
17	14351	Cicero town, Illinois	61,679	41,131	0	2,644	66.7	0.0	6.4	38,487
17	15599	Collinsville city, Illinois	19,889	13,432	0	836	67.5	0.0	6.2	12,596
17	17458	Crest Hill city, Illinois	15,791	7,491	0	348	47.4	0.0	4.6	7,143
17	17887	Crystal Lake city, Illinois	32,959	23,653	0	898	71.8	0.0	3.8	22,755
17	18563	Danville city, Illinois	23,615	11,940	0	1,327	50.6	0.0	11.1	10,613
17	18628	Darien city, Illinois	18,319	11,520	0	250	62.9	0.0	2.2	11,270
17	18823	Decatur city, Illinois	59,282	34,385	0	2,676	58.0	0.0	7.8	31,709
17	19161	DeKalb city, Illinois	36,133	22,709	70	2,989	62.8	0.2	13.2	19,720
17	19642	Des Plaines city, Illinois	49,159	35,581	0	2,405	72.4	0.0	6.8	33,176
17	20292	Dolton village, Illinois	18,674	12,260	0	2,444	65.7	0.0	19.9	9,816
17	20591	Downers Grove village, Illinois	39,786	27,732	0	1,234	69.7	0.0	4.4	26,498
17	22073	East Moline city, Illinois	18,654	11,839	0	620	63.5	0.0	5.2	11,219
17	22164	East Peoria city, Illinois	18,308	11,154	10	553	60.9	0.1	5.0	10,601
17	22255	East St. Louis city, Illinois	20,600	10,844	0	2,832	52.6	0.0	26.1	8,012
17	22697	Edwardsville city, Illinois	21,235	13,823	0	1,022	65.1	0.0	7.4	12,801
17	23074	Elgin city, Illinois	84,888	57,356	0	3,155	67.6	0.0	5.5	54,201
17	23256	Elk Grove Village village, Illinois	29,080	20,666	0	765	71.1	0.0	3.7	19,901
17	23620	Elmhurst city, Illinois	33,919	21,442	0	855	63.2	0.0	4.0	20,587
17	23724	Elmwood Park village, Illinois	19,076	12,747	0	964	66.8	0.0	7.6	11,783
17	24582	Evanston city, Illinois	62,725	39,540	0	1,506	63.0	0.0	3.8	38,034
17	27884	Freeport city, Illinois	17,859	11,436	0	1,187	64.0	0.0	10.4	10,249
17	28326	Galesburg city, Illinois	25,727	13,035	0	882	50.7	0.0	6.8	12,153
17	28872	Geneva city, Illinois	18,096	13,064	0	535	72.2	0.0	4.1	12,529
17	29730	Glendale Heights village, Illinois	27,411	21,335	0	1,098	77.8	0.0	5.1	20,237
17	29756	Glen Ellyn village, Illinois	21,547	13,993	0	236	64.9	0.0	1.7	13,757
17	29938	Glenview village, Illinois	36,546	21,072	0	857	57.7	0.0	4.1	20,215
17	30926	Granite City city, Illinois	24,473	15,957	0	1,838	65.2	0.0	11.5	14,119
17	31121	Grayslake village, Illinois	16,685	12,268	49	460	73.5	0.3	3.7	11,808
17	32018	Gurnee village, Illinois	24,490	17,493	158	653	71.4	0.6	3.7	16,840
17	32746	Hanover Park village, Illinois	31,566	23,783	109	1,102	75.3	0.3	4.6	22,681
17	33383	Harvey city, Illinois	16,179	8,659	0	1,439	53.5	0.0	16.6	7,220
17	34722	Highland Park city, Illinois	21,363	13,814	21	269	64.7	0.1	1.9	13,545
17	35411	Hoffman Estates village, Illinois	42,986	30,645	0	1,340	71.3	0.0	4.4	29,305
17	35835	Homer Glen village, Illinois	19,813	12,126	0	425	61.2	0.0	3.5	11,701
17	36750	Huntley village, Illinois	19,077	10,765	0	381	56.4	0.0	3.5	10,384
17	38570	Joliet city, Illinois	110,577	77,819	70	5,221	70.4	0.1	6.7	72,598
17	38934	Kankakee city, Illinois	20,172	10,139	0	1,437	50.3	0.0	14.2	8,702
17	41183	Lake in the Hills village, Illinois	22,498	17,436	0	616	77.5	0.0	3.5	16,820
17	41742	Lake Zurich village, Illinois	16,061	12,248	0	403	76.3	0.0	3.3	11,845
17	42028	Lansing village, Illinois	24,456	15,859	0	2,545	64.8	0.0	16.0	13,314
17	43250	Libertyville village, Illinois	17,208	11,086	0	662	64.4	0.0	6.0	10,424
17	43939	Lisle village, Illinois	18,409	12,891	0	920	70.0	0.0	7.1	11,971
17	44225	Lockport city, Illinois	17,772	13,307	0	502	74.9	0.0	3.8	12,805
17	44407	Lombard village, Illinois	36,460	23,607	0	1,128	64.7	0.0	4.8	22,479
17	45031	Loves Park city, Illinois	17,060	11,876	0	692	69.6	0.0	5.8	11,184
17	45694	McHenry city, Illinois	22,116	15,222	0	457	68.8	0.0	3.0	14,765
17	45726	Machesney Park village, Illinois	18,848	12,642	0	753	67.1	0.0	6.0	11,889
17	47774	Maywood village, Illinois	19,143	11,739	0	2,174	61.3	0.0	18.5	9,565
17	48242	Melrose Park village, Illinois	19,565	13,123	0	138	67.1	0.0	1.1	12,985
17	49867	Moline city, Illinois	33,727	21,366	0	1,482	63.3	0.0	6.9	19,884
17	50647	Morton Grove village, Illinois	20,294	12,144	0	215	59.8	0.0	1.8	11,929
17	51089	Mount Prospect village, Illinois	43,037	29,834	124	2,013	69.3	0.3	6.7	27,821
17	51349	Mundelein village, Illinois	22,898	16,431	64	767	71.8	0.3	4.7	15,664
17	51622	Naperville city, Illinois	113,376	78,647	153	3,565	69.4	0.1	4.5	75,082
17	52584	New Lenox village, Illinois	20,861	15,802	0	1,311	75.7	0.0	8.3	14,491
17	53000	Niles village, Illinois	25,492	14,197	0	599	55.7	0.0	4.2	13,598
17	53234	Normal town, Illinois	45,010	30,500	0	653	67.8	0.0	2.1	29,847
17	53481	Northbrook village, Illinois	26,922	13,978	0	380	51.9	0.0	2.7	13,598
17	53559	North Chicago city, Illinois	24,877	10,917	8,901	1,028	43.9	35.8	9.4	9,889
17	54638	Oak Forest city, Illinois	21,862	15,630	0	1,251	71.5	0.0	8.0	14,379
17	54820	Oak Lawn village, Illinois	43,924	26,839	156	1,697	61.1	0.4	6.3	25,142
17	54885	Oak Park village, Illinois	40,634	28,483	0	1,828	70.1	0.0	6.4	26,655
17	55249	O'Fallon city, Illinois	22,541	14,307	844	945	63.5	3.7	6.6	13,362
17	56640	Orland Park village, Illinois	48,121	29,253	0	914	60.8	0.0	3.1	28,339
17	56887	Oswego village, Illinois	25,815	20,040	0	734	77.6	0.0	3.7	19,306
17	57225	Palatine village, Illinois	55,022	40,022	0	1,447	72.7	0.0	3.6	38,575
17	57732	Park Forest village, Illinois	18,399	11,467	51	402	62.3	0.3	3.5	11,065
17	57875	Park Ridge city, Illinois	28,084	18,228	0	510	64.9	0.0	2.8	17,718
17	58447	Pekin city, Illinois	28,126	16,704	0	826	59.4	0.0	4.9	15,878
17	59000	Peoria city, Illinois	90,860	56,779	138	5,881	62.5	0.2	10.4	50,898
17	60287	Plainfield village, Illinois	30,300	22,259	76	1,197	73.5	0.3	5.4	21,062
17	62367	Quincy city, Illinois	31,813	20,109	0	1,212	63.2	0.0	6.0	18,897

Table E. Cities—Labor Force, Employment, and Educational Data, 2015—*Continued*

FIPS state code	FIPS place code	State/city	Total population age 16 and older	Civilian labor force	Armed Forces	Unemployed	Civilian labor force participation (percent)	Percent in Armed Forces	Unemployment rate	Number of employed persons age 16 and older
17	65000	Rockford city, Illinois	116,255	71,984	51	9,663	61.9	0.0	13.4	62,321
17	65078	Rock Island city, Illinois	30,422	19,490	0	1,887	64.1	0.0	9.7	17,603
17	65338	Rolling Meadows city, Illinois	16,993	12,436	0	642	73.2	0.0	5.2	11,794
17	65442	Romeoville village, Illinois	33,309	23,121	239	1,012	69.4	0.7	4.4	22,109
17	65806	Roselle village, Illinois	17,739	13,610	0	484	76.7	0.0	3.6	13,126
17	66040	Round Lake Beach village, Illinois	22,662	15,946	184	1,112	70.4	0.8	7.0	14,834
17	66703	St. Charles city, Illinois	23,214	15,953	0	428	68.7	0.0	2.7	15,525
17	68003	Schaumburg village, Illinois	59,135	43,414	41	2,545	73.4	0.1	5.9	40,869
17	70122	Skokie village, Illinois	52,699	31,053	0	1,690	58.9	0.0	5.4	29,363
17	70720	South Elgin village, Illinois	19,587	14,438	0	827	73.7	0.0	5.7	13,611
17	70850	South Holland village, Illinois	18,502	11,125	100	1,579	60.1	0.5	14.2	9,546
17	72000	Springfield city, Illinois	95,829	59,949	189	4,814	62.6	0.2	8.0	55,135
17	73157	Streamwood village, Illinois	32,251	23,612	27	1,246	73.2	0.1	5.3	22,366
17	75484	Tinley Park village, Illinois	46,519	32,332	0	1,784	69.5	0.0	5.5	30,548
17	77005	Urbana city, Illinois	36,777	19,450	0	1,435	52.9	0.0	7.4	18,015
17	77694	Vernon Hills village, Illinois	18,595	12,505	0	798	67.2	0.0	6.4	11,707
17	77993	Villa Park village, Illinois	17,623	12,748	0	969	72.3	0.0	7.6	11,779
17	79293	Waukegan city, Illinois	65,881	47,105	434	3,907	71.5	0.7	8.3	43,198
17	80060	West Chicago city, Illinois	21,415	15,251	0	428	71.2	0.0	2.8	14,823
17	80645	Westmont village, Illinois	19,780	13,538	0	903	68.4	0.0	6.7	12,635
17	81048	Wheaton city, Illinois	44,283	29,945	0	1,421	67.6	0.0	4.7	28,524
17	81087	Wheeling village, Illinois	29,128	18,714	0	486	64.2	0.0	2.6	18,228
17	82075	Wilmette village, Illinois	20,702	13,165	0	773	63.6	0.0	5.9	12,392
17	83245	Woodridge village, Illinois	26,452	18,952	0	663	71.6	0.0	3.5	18,289
17	83349	Woodstock city, Illinois	20,023	13,803	0	291	68.9	0.0	2.1	13,512
17	84220	Zion city, Illinois	18,190	12,156	0	2,086	66.8	0.0	17.2	10,070
18	00000	**INDIANA**	5,215,392	3,312,603	3,013	192,637	63.5	0.1	5.8	3,119,966
18	01468	Anderson city, Indiana	44,884	26,742	27	2,531	59.6	0.1	9.5	24,211
18	05860	Bloomington city, Indiana	75,369	42,683	0	3,232	56.6	0.0	7.6	39,451
18	08416	Brownsburg town, Indiana	20,346	16,165	0	761	79.5	0.0	4.7	15,404
18	10342	Carmel city, Indiana	67,694	48,155	0	942	71.1	0.0	2.0	47,213
18	12934	Clarksville town, Indiana	17,618	11,393	0	539	64.7	0.0	4.7	10,854
18	14734	Columbus city, Indiana	36,040	24,215	87	804	67.2	0.2	3.3	23,411
18	16138	Crown Point city, Indiana	21,706	13,185	0	762	60.7	0.0	5.8	12,423
18	19486	East Chicago city, Indiana	21,174	11,454	0	1,274	54.1	0.0	11.1	10,180
18	20728	Elkhart city, Indiana	37,548	21,626	0	1,557	57.6	0.0	7.2	20,069
18	22000	Evansville city, Indiana	96,559	58,920	0	2,355	61.0	0.0	4.0	56,565
18	23278	Fishers town, Indiana	59,272	46,708	158	911	78.8	0.3	2.0	45,797
18	25000	Fort Wayne city, Indiana	196,788	129,941	45	7,966	66.0	0.0	6.1	121,975
18	25450	Franklin city, Indiana	19,905	12,357	349	769	62.1	1.8	6.2	11,588
18	27000	Gary city, Indiana	59,768	32,884	0	5,056	55.0	0.0	15.4	27,828
18	28386	Goshen city, Indiana	27,199	17,241	0	946	63.4	0.0	5.5	16,295
18	28800	Granger CDP, Indiana	22,765	14,812	0	553	65.1	0.0	3.7	14,259
18	29520	Greenfield city, Indiana	14,925	8,828	0	453	59.1	0.0	5.1	8,375
18	29898	Greenwood city, Indiana	43,195	26,628	348	1,347	61.6	0.8	5.1	25,281
18	31000	Hammond city, Indiana	62,446	37,856	0	3,521	60.6	0.0	9.3	34,335
18	33466	Highland town, Indiana	20,311	12,992	0	510	64.0	0.0	3.9	12,482
18	34114	Hobart city, Indiana	24,821	15,633	0	1,377	63.0	0.0	8.8	14,256
18	36003	Indianapolis city (balance), Indiana	659,055	443,332	272	36,780	67.3	0.0	8.3	406,552
18	38358	Jeffersonville city, Indiana	37,492	24,510	0	1,959	65.4	0.0	8.0	22,551
18	40392	Kokomo city, Indiana	46,917	27,124	90	2,636	57.8	0.2	9.7	24,488
18	40788	Lafayette city, Indiana	56,856	40,679	0	2,509	71.5	0.0	6.2	38,170
18	42246	La Porte city, Indiana	17,782	9,918	0	862	55.8	0.0	8.7	9,056
18	42426	Lawrence city, Indiana	36,220	27,755	0	1,195	76.6	0.0	4.3	26,560
18	46908	Marion city, Indiana	24,188	13,858	0	1,483	57.3	0.0	10.7	12,375
18	48528	Merrillville town, Indiana	28,500	18,972	0	1,029	66.6	0.0	5.4	17,943
18	48798	Michigan City city, Indiana	24,799	13,351	0	1,865	53.8	0.0	14.0	11,486
18	49932	Mishawaka city, Indiana	40,932	25,163	118	1,764	61.5	0.3	7.0	23,399
18	51876	Muncie city, Indiana	58,413	34,605	0	3,217	59.2	0.0	9.3	31,388
18	51912	Munster town, Indiana	17,035	10,489	0	972	61.6	0.0	9.3	9,517
18	52326	New Albany city, Indiana	28,592	18,265	0	1,051	63.9	0.0	5.8	17,214
18	54180	Noblesville city, Indiana	45,862	33,694	92	893	73.5	0.2	2.7	32,801
18	60246	Plainfield town, Indiana	22,840	15,448	0	570	67.6	0.0	3.7	14,878
18	61092	Portage city, Indiana	28,730	17,385	0	1,148	60.5	0.0	6.6	16,237
18	64260	Richmond city, Indiana	27,699	14,245	0	1,023	51.4	0.0	7.2	13,222
18	68220	Schererville town, Indiana	23,164	14,388	0	937	62.1	0.0	6.5	13,451
18	71000	South Bend city, Indiana	76,476	48,700	0	3,171	63.7	0.0	6.5	45,529
18	75428	Terre Haute city, Indiana	51,767	28,658	0	4,483	55.4	0.0	15.6	24,175
18	78326	Valparaiso city, Indiana	28,101	17,301	0	1,352	61.6	0.0	7.8	15,949
18	82700	Westfield city, Indiana	28,429	21,265	37	812	74.8	0.1	3.8	20,453
18	82862	West Lafayette city, Indiana	36,212	17,932	34	724	49.5	0.1	4.0	17,208
18	86372	Zionsville town, Indiana	19,893	13,746	0	254	69.1	0.0	1.8	13,492
19	00000	**IOWA**	2,475,140	1,669,321	1,350	69,428	67.4	0.1	4.2	1,599,893
19	01855	Ames city, Iowa	57,719	36,138	104	1,972	62.6	0.2	5.5	34,166
19	02305	Ankeny city, Iowa	40,644	31,930	0	1,308	78.6	0.0	4.1	30,622

Table E. Cities—Labor Force, Employment, and Educational Data, 2015—*Continued*

FIPS state code	FIPS place code	State/city	Total population age 16 and older	Employment status						Number of employed persons age 16 and older
				Civilian labor force	Armed Forces	Unemployed	Civilian labor force participation (percent)	Percent in Armed Forces	Unemployment rate	
19	06355	Bettendorf city, Iowa	27,929	18,383	0	465	65.8	0.0	2.5	17,918
19	09550	Burlington city, Iowa	20,367	13,455	0	1,152	66.1	0.0	8.6	12,303
19	11755	Cedar Falls city, Iowa	33,600	23,655	0	309	70.4	0.0	1.3	23,346
19	12000	Cedar Rapids city, Iowa	104,588	75,115	0	3,521	71.8	0.0	4.7	71,594
19	14430	Clinton city, Iowa	19,889	11,976	22	878	60.2	0.1	7.3	11,098
19	16230	Coralville city, Iowa	15,782	10,660	0	408	67.5	0.0	3.8	10,252
19	16860	Council Bluffs city, Iowa	49,979	32,629	50	1,378	65.3	0.1	4.2	31,251
19	19000	Davenport city, Iowa	80,162	50,476	145	2,391	63.0	0.2	4.7	48,085
19	21000	Des Moines city, Iowa	166,628	119,077	170	8,769	71.5	0.1	7.4	110,308
19	22395	Dubuque city, Iowa	49,111	30,951	88	1,698	63.0	0.2	5.5	29,253
19	28515	Fort Dodge city, Iowa	19,691	10,798	0	767	54.8	0.0	7.1	10,031
19	38595	Iowa City city, Iowa	62,768	46,278	0	2,976	73.7	0.0	6.4	43,302
19	39765	Johnston city, Iowa	16,594	12,197	0	626	73.5	0.0	5.1	11,571
19	49485	Marion city, Iowa	28,463	19,537	0	422	68.6	0.0	2.2	19,115
19	49755	Marshalltown city, Iowa	21,768	14,305	0	1,104	65.7	0.0	7.7	13,201
19	50160	Mason City city, Iowa	21,081	13,016	0	1,181	61.7	0.0	9.1	11,835
19	55110	Muscatine city, Iowa	19,722	12,552	0	481	63.6	0.0	3.8	12,071
19	60465	Ottumwa city, Iowa	18,936	12,177	0	531	64.3	0.0	4.4	11,646
19	73335	Sioux City city, Iowa	64,505	44,017	0	2,589	68.2	0.0	5.9	41,428
19	79950	Urbandale city, Iowa	32,896	23,999	0	904	73.0	0.0	3.8	23,095
19	82425	Waterloo city, Iowa	54,208	34,948	41	1,472	64.5	0.1	4.2	33,476
19	83910	West Des Moines city, Iowa	51,490	38,793	174	1,123	75.3	0.3	2.9	37,670
20	00000	**KANSAS**	2,270,108	1,486,201	19,892	69,132	65.5	0.9	4.7	1,417,069
20	17800	Derby city, Kansas	18,036	13,002	184	323	72.1	1.0	2.5	12,679
20	18250	Dodge City city, Kansas	18,903	13,735	0	872	72.7	0.0	6.3	12,863
20	21275	Emporia city, Kansas	21,231	14,072	93	1,360	66.3	0.4	9.7	12,712
20	25325	Garden City city, Kansas	20,507	15,309	0	403	74.7	0.0	2.6	14,906
20	25425	Gardner city, Kansas	14,912	11,962	0	574	80.2	0.0	4.8	11,388
20	31100	Hays city, Kansas	16,804	12,145	0	258	72.3	0.0	2.1	11,887
20	33625	Hutchinson city, Kansas	32,281	20,526	0	1,580	63.6	0.0	7.7	18,946
20	35750	Junction City city, Kansas	18,082	8,440	3,768	688	46.7	20.8	8.2	7,752
20	36000	Kansas City city, Kansas	113,802	76,043	217	5,310	66.8	0.2	7.0	70,733
20	38900	Lawrence city, Kansas	78,699	53,156	160	2,106	67.5	0.2	4.0	51,050
20	39000	Leavenworth city, Kansas	26,797	14,664	1,341	488	54.7	5.0	3.3	14,176
20	39075	Leawood city, Kansas	25,561	16,444	0	454	64.3	0.0	2.8	15,990
20	39350	Lenexa city, Kansas	42,939	32,637	0	616	76.0	0.0	1.9	32,021
20	39825	Liberal city, Kansas	14,975	10,682	0	760	71.3	0.0	7.1	9,922
20	44250	Manhattan city, Kansas	48,758	30,292	2,215	2,077	62.1	4.5	6.9	28,215
20	52575	Olathe city, Kansas	97,718	72,376	129	2,914	74.1	0.1	4.0	69,462
20	53775	Overland Park city, Kansas	149,556	104,984	0	3,755	70.2	0.0	3.6	101,229
20	56025	Pittsburg city, Kansas	16,993	10,069	0	534	59.3	0.0	5.3	9,535
20	57575	Prairie Village city, Kansas	16,214	11,322	0	189	69.8	0.0	1.7	11,133
20	62700	Salina city, Kansas	36,042	22,901	95	1,188	63.5	0.3	5.2	21,713
20	64500	Shawnee city, Kansas	51,886	37,682	0	1,032	72.6	0.0	2.7	36,650
20	71000	Topeka city, Kansas	100,733	64,307	179	4,652	63.8	0.2	7.2	59,655
20	79000	Wichita city, Kansas	300,555	196,683	1,561	9,823	65.4	0.5	5.0	186,860
21	00000	**KENTUCKY**	3,531,385	2,062,779	12,841	133,812	58.4	0.4	6.5	1,928,967
21	02368	Ashland city, Kentucky	17,203	8,636	0	286	50.2	0.0	3.3	8,350
21	08902	Bowling Green city, Kentucky	51,256	30,282	40	2,285	59.1	0.1	7.5	27,997
21	17848	Covington city, Kentucky	32,356	20,335	0	1,827	62.8	0.0	9.0	18,508
21	24274	Elizabethtown city, Kentucky	22,946	14,408	211	1,459	62.8	0.9	10.1	12,949
21	27982	Florence city, Kentucky	24,492	17,173	0	1,720	70.1	0.0	10.0	15,453
21	28900	Frankfort city, Kentucky	19,282	12,175	0	688	63.1	0.0	5.7	11,487
21	30700	Georgetown city, Kentucky	26,161	19,126	0	923	73.1	0.0	4.8	18,203
21	35866	Henderson city, Kentucky	23,894	13,351	0	1,182	55.9	0.0	8.9	12,169
21	37918	Hopkinsville city, Kentucky	24,496	14,319	53	1,123	58.5	0.2	7.8	13,196
21	39142	Independence city, Kentucky	19,753	15,025	0	543	76.1	0.0	3.6	14,482
21	40222	Jeffersontown city, Kentucky	21,997	15,790	0	693	71.8	0.0	4.4	15,097
21	46027	Lexington-Fayette urban county, Kentucky	255,389	170,331	132	8,110	66.7	0.1	4.8	162,221
21	48006	Louisville/Jefferson County metro government (balance), Kentucky	490,481	315,379	271	20,684	64.3	0.1	6.6	294,695
21	56136	Nicholasville city, Kentucky	22,027	14,909	0	1,496	67.7	0.0	10.0	13,413
21	58620	Owensboro city, Kentucky	45,127	27,135	0	2,075	60.1	0.0	7.6	25,060
21	58836	Paducah city, Kentucky	20,964	11,893	79	1,066	56.7	0.4	9.0	10,827
21	63912	Radcliff city, Kentucky	17,081	10,133	475	1,505	59.3	2.8	14.9	8,628
21	65226	Richmond city, Kentucky	28,521	16,336	0	1,638	57.3	0.0	10.0	14,698
22	00000	**LOUISIANA**	3,676,681	2,193,370	15,033	155,558	59.7	0.4	7.1	2,037,812
22	00975	Alexandria city, Louisiana	38,739	22,004	0	2,717	56.8	0.0	12.3	19,287
22	05000	Baton Rouge city, Louisiana	185,137	119,975	0	9,765	64.8	0.0	8.1	110,210
22	05210	Bayou Cane CDP, Louisiana	17,652	10,125	147	137	57.4	0.8	1.4	9,988
22	08920	Bossier City city, Louisiana	53,363	30,802	3,634	1,402	57.7	6.8	4.6	29,400
22	13960	Central city, Louisiana	22,130	12,482	0	226	56.4	0.0	1.8	12,256
22	14135	Chalmette CDP, Louisiana	18,185	11,331	0	879	62.3	0.0	7.8	10,452
22	32755	Hammond city, Louisiana	16,987	10,222	0	806	60.2	0.0	7.9	9,416
22	33245	Harvey CDP, Louisiana	16,020	8,799	49	528	54.9	0.3	6.0	8,271

Table E. Cities—Labor Force, Employment, and Educational Data, 2015—*Continued*

FIPS state code	FIPS place code	State/city	Total population age 16 and older	Employment status						Number of employed persons age 16 and older
				Civilian labor force	Armed Forces	Unemployed	Civilian labor force participation (percent)	Percent in Armed Forces	Unemployment rate	
22	36255	Houma city, Louisiana	27,032	15,872	0	506	58.7	0.0	3.2	15,366
22	39475	Kenner city, Louisiana	53,117	33,280	55	1,337	62.7	0.1	4.0	31,943
22	40735	Lafayette city, Louisiana	101,682	69,759	24	3,188	68.6	0.0	4.6	66,571
22	41155	Lake Charles city, Louisiana	59,604	37,338	156	2,667	62.6	0.3	7.1	34,671
22	42030	Laplace CDP, Louisiana	21,627	14,522	56	598	67.1	0.3	4.1	13,924
22	48785	Marrero CDP, Louisiana	23,364	14,451	54	933	61.9	0.2	6.5	13,518
22	50115	Metairie CDP, Louisiana	122,648	81,895	541	3,947	66.8	0.4	4.8	77,948
22	51410	Monroe city, Louisiana	37,415	21,636	0	2,516	57.8	0.0	11.6	19,120
22	54035	New Iberia city, Louisiana	23,566	15,314	0	2,133	65.0	0.0	13.9	13,181
22	55000	New Orleans city, Louisiana	317,258	201,824	830	17,223	63.6	0.3	8.5	184,601
22	62385	Prairieville CDP, Louisiana	25,269	18,830	0	819	74.5	0.0	4.3	18,011
22	66655	Ruston city, Louisiana	17,009	8,947	0	592	52.6	0.0	6.6	8,355
22	70000	Shreveport city, Louisiana	153,041	86,499	708	4,658	56.5	0.5	5.4	81,841
22	70805	Slidell city, Louisiana	21,836	13,376	0	1,235	61.3	0.0	9.2	12,141
22	73640	Sulphur city, Louisiana	18,734	11,197	65	638	59.8	0.3	5.7	10,559
22	75180	Terrytown CDP, Louisiana	20,112	14,926	0	942	74.2	0.0	6.3	13,984
23	00000	**MAINE**	1,103,834	685,216	1,792	36,802	62.1	0.2	5.4	648,414
23	02060	Auburn city, Maine	18,000	11,758	0	155	65.3	0.0	1.3	11,603
23	02795	Bangor city, Maine	27,565	15,879	0	2,229	57.6	0.0	14.0	13,650
23	04860	Biddeford city, Maine	18,577	12,858	0	617	69.2	0.0	4.8	12,241
23	38740	Lewiston city, Maine	29,754	18,183	0	281	61.1	0.0	1.5	17,902
23	60545	Portland city, Maine	57,683	39,934	154	1,835	69.2	0.3	4.6	38,099
23	65725	Sanford city, Maine	17,678	11,114	0	452	62.9	0.0	4.1	10,662
23	71990	South Portland city, Maine	21,982	15,374	91	1,114	69.9	0.4	7.2	14,260
24	00000	**MARYLAND**	4,814,546	3,207,268	31,253	175,802	66.6	0.6	5.5	3,031,466
24	01600	Annapolis city, Maryland	32,832	21,521	244	1,179	65.5	0.7	5.5	20,342
24	01975	Arbutus CDP, Maryland	18,262	14,237	0	563	78.0	0.0	4.0	13,674
24	02275	Arnold CDP, Maryland	17,441	11,805	327	305	67.7	1.9	2.6	11,500
24	02825	Aspen Hill CDP, Maryland	42,061	30,770	380	1,785	73.2	0.9	5.8	28,985
24	04000	Baltimore city, Maryland	502,319	301,350	459	30,358	60.0	0.1	10.1	270,992
24	05825	Bel Air North CDP, Maryland	25,382	17,224	53	1,035	67.9	0.2	6.0	16,189
24	05950	Bel Air South CDP, Maryland	36,937	25,576	50	906	69.2	0.1	3.5	24,670
24	07125	Bethesda CDP, Maryland	47,013	32,537	519	1,294	69.2	1.1	4.0	31,243
24	08775	Bowie city, Maryland	47,219	34,194	330	2,005	72.4	0.7	5.9	32,189
24	12600	Camp Springs CDP, Maryland	21,867	15,108	0	784	69.1	0.0	5.2	14,324
24	13325	Carney CDP, Maryland	23,628	14,158	47	697	59.9	0.2	4.9	13,461
24	14125	Catonsville CDP, Maryland	34,360	19,904	68	614	57.9	0.2	3.1	19,290
24	16875	Chillum CDP, Maryland	31,389	25,099	0	1,745	80.0	0.0	7.0	23,354
24	17350	Clarksburg CDP, Maryland	15,376	11,491	44	490	74.7	0.3	4.3	11,001
24	17900	Clinton CDP, Maryland	31,169	20,972	0	1,634	67.3	0.0	7.8	19,338
24	18250	Cockeysville CDP, Maryland	18,031	13,476	0	397	74.7	0.0	2.9	13,079
24	18750	College Park city, Maryland	29,981	14,914	61	720	49.7	0.2	4.8	14,194
24	19125	Columbia CDP, Maryland	81,832	57,209	396	2,524	69.9	0.5	4.4	54,685
24	20875	Crofton CDP, Maryland	21,276	16,797	165	609	78.9	0.8	3.6	16,188
24	21325	Cumberland city, Maryland	17,112	8,660	0	664	50.6	0.0	7.7	7,996
24	23975	Dundalk CDP, Maryland	48,430	28,999	0	2,412	59.9	0.0	8.3	26,587
24	25150	Edgewood CDP, Maryland	17,549	10,919	443	458	62.2	2.5	4.2	10,461
24	25575	Eldersburg CDP, Maryland	25,986	17,106	109	678	65.8	0.4	4.0	16,428
24	26000	Ellicott City CDP, Maryland	55,059	37,128	291	1,250	67.4	0.5	3.4	35,878
24	26600	Essex CDP, Maryland	31,203	18,501	19	1,191	59.3	0.1	6.4	17,310
24	27250	Fairland CDP, Maryland	21,036	16,730	0	1,326	79.5	0.0	7.9	15,404
24	29525	Fort Washington CDP, Maryland	19,149	11,216	0	650	58.6	0.0	5.8	10,566
24	30325	Frederick city, Maryland	54,598	40,319	377	2,681	73.8	0.7	6.6	37,638
24	31175	Gaithersburg city, Maryland	53,612	39,743	233	1,072	74.1	0.4	2.7	38,671
24	32025	Germantown CDP, Maryland	63,778	46,781	427	1,550	73.3	0.7	3.3	45,231
24	32650	Glen Burnie CDP, Maryland	54,713	37,925	686	1,847	69.3	1.3	4.9	36,078
24	34775	Greenbelt city, Maryland	18,050	13,272	195	854	73.5	1.1	6.4	12,418
24	36075	Hagerstown city, Maryland	28,352	17,687	218	956	62.4	0.8	5.4	16,731
24	41475	Ilchester CDP, Maryland	20,464	15,270	384	295	74.6	1.9	1.9	14,975
24	45325	Landover CDP, Maryland	19,563	14,952	0	1,018	76.4	0.0	6.8	13,934
24	45525	Langley Park CDP, Maryland	15,582	12,114	0	485	77.7	0.0	4.0	11,629
24	45900	Laurel city, Maryland	20,086	14,890	72	755	74.1	0.4	5.1	14,135
24	47450	Lochearn CDP, Maryland	21,263	14,179	0	1,229	66.7	0.0	8.7	12,950
24	52300	Middle River CDP, Maryland	19,312	13,425	0	782	69.5	0.0	5.8	12,643
24	52562	Milford Mill CDP, Maryland	24,244	17,256	0	523	71.2	0.0	3.0	16,733
24	53325	Montgomery Village CDP, Maryland	24,275	16,691	66	760	68.8	0.3	4.6	15,931
24	56337	North Bethesda CDP, Maryland	43,736	30,584	197	1,505	69.9	0.5	4.9	29,079
24	56725	North Laurel CDP, Maryland	16,752	12,636	291	481	75.4	1.7	3.8	12,155
24	56875	North Potomac CDP, Maryland	16,483	11,634	45	291	70.6	0.3	2.5	11,343
24	58300	Odenton CDP, Maryland	30,969	21,278	1,407	477	68.7	4.5	2.2	20,801
24	58900	Olney CDP, Maryland	28,022	20,186	0	378	72.0	0.0	1.9	19,808
24	59425	Owings Mills CDP, Maryland	28,174	21,071	0	1,514	74.8	0.0	7.2	19,557
24	59500	Oxon Hill CDP, Maryland	18,378	13,809	0	1,425	75.1	0.0	10.3	12,384
24	60275	Parkville CDP, Maryland	26,819	19,129	0	1,039	71.3	0.0	5.4	18,090
24	60475	Pasadena CDP, Maryland	22,375	16,559	674	743	74.0	3.0	4.5	15,816

Table E. Cities—Labor Force, Employment, and Educational Data, 2015—*Continued*

| FIPS state code | FIPS place code | State/city | Total population age 16 and older | Employment status | | | | | | | Number of employed persons age 16 and older |
				Civilian labor force	Armed Forces	Unemployed	Civilian labor force participation (percent)	Percent in Armed Forces	Unemployment rate	
24	60975	Perry Hall CDP, Maryland	22,576	14,935	0	682	66.2	0.0	4.6	14,253
24	61400	Pikesville CDP, Maryland	26,182	16,096	275	598	61.5	1.1	3.7	15,498
24	63300	Potomac CDP, Maryland	36,463	23,046	65	1,025	63.2	0.2	4.4	22,021
24	64950	Randallstown CDP, Maryland	31,414	19,895	0	1,280	63.3	0.0	6.4	18,615
24	65600	Reisterstown CDP, Maryland	23,098	16,713	0	1,076	72.4	0.0	6.4	15,637
24	67675	Rockville city, Maryland	54,141	36,935	240	2,067	68.2	0.4	5.6	34,868
24	69925	Salisbury city, Maryland	25,869	16,750	286	1,368	64.7	1.1	8.2	15,382
24	71150	Severn CDP, Maryland	41,760	29,730	1,387	1,443	71.2	3.3	4.9	28,287
24	71200	Severna Park CDP, Maryland	30,123	19,586	226	1,377	65.0	0.8	7.0	18,209
24	72450	Silver Spring CDP, Maryland	64,661	49,819	142	3,434	77.0	0.2	6.9	46,385
24	73650	South Laurel CDP, Maryland	22,886	17,531	78	754	76.6	0.3	4.3	16,777
24	75725	Suitland CDP, Maryland	18,391	14,838	0	1,086	80.7	0.0	7.3	13,752
24	78425	Towson CDP, Maryland	48,436	29,630	0	1,429	61.2	0.0	4.8	28,201
24	81175	Waldorf CDP, Maryland	57,212	41,353	415	918	72.3	0.7	2.2	40,435
24	83775	Wheaton CDP, Maryland	37,659	28,518	179	954	75.7	0.5	3.3	27,564
24	86475	Woodlawn CDP (Baltimore County), Maryland	32,139	21,966	0	1,146	68.3	0.0	5.2	20,820
25	00000	**MASSACHUSETTS**	5,578,648	3,739,683	4,606	217,480	67.0	0.1	5.8	3,522,203
25	00840	Agawam Town city, Massachusetts	24,180	14,690	0	354	60.8	0.0	2.4	14,336
25	01640	Arlington CDP, Massachusetts	36,793	24,354	70	949	66.2	0.2	3.9	23,405
25	02690	Attleboro city, Massachusetts	34,909	24,652	0	1,694	70.6	0.0	6.9	22,958
25	03690	Barnstable Town city, Massachusetts	37,227	22,368	0	1,326	60.1	0.0	5.9	21,042
25	05105	Belmont CDP, Massachusetts	20,164	14,376	30	565	71.3	0.1	3.9	13,811
25	05595	Beverly city, Massachusetts	34,387	23,726	0	1,285	69.0	0.0	5.4	22,441
25	07000	Boston city, Massachusetts	568,577	392,593	768	26,201	69.0	0.1	6.7	366,392
25	07740	Braintree Town city, Massachusetts	29,696	20,774	0	461	70.0	0.0	2.2	20,313
25	09000	Brockton city, Massachusetts	75,269	51,549	78	5,974	68.5	0.1	11.6	45,575
25	09210	Brookline CDP, Massachusetts	48,217	32,285	44	1,090	67.0	0.1	3.4	31,195
25	09875	Burlington CDP, Massachusetts	21,373	13,806	0	845	64.6	0.0	6.1	12,961
25	11000	Cambridge city, Massachusetts	100,634	71,578	176	2,341	71.1	0.2	3.3	69,237
25	13205	Chelsea city, Massachusetts	29,159	21,424	0	1,374	73.5	0.0	6.4	20,050
25	13660	Chicopee city, Massachusetts	46,261	30,579	0	2,670	66.1	0.0	8.7	27,909
25	16285	Danvers CDP, Massachusetts	23,168	15,712	0	587	67.8	0.0	3.7	15,125
25	16530	Dedham CDP, Massachusetts	20,968	13,799	0	753	65.8	0.0	5.5	13,046
25	21990	Everett city, Massachusetts	37,146	27,406	0	1,925	73.8	0.0	7.0	25,481
25	23000	Fall River city, Massachusetts	74,121	46,123	0	5,602	62.2	0.0	12.1	40,521
25	23875	Fitchburg city, Massachusetts	31,210	20,825	61	2,762	66.7	0.2	13.3	18,063
25	24960	Framingham CDP, Massachusetts	59,346	43,229	0	1,772	72.8	0.0	4.1	41,457
25	25172	Franklin Town city, Massachusetts	24,933	17,869	0	1,249	71.7	0.0	7.0	16,620
25	25485	Gardner city, Massachusetts	17,010	9,941	0	491	58.4	0.0	4.9	9,450
25	26150	Gloucester city, Massachusetts	25,366	16,440	53	809	64.8	0.2	4.9	15,631
25	29405	Haverhill city, Massachusetts	48,946	34,966	18	2,854	71.4	0.0	8.2	32,112
25	30840	Holyoke city, Massachusetts	31,413	17,041	0	782	54.2	0.0	4.6	16,259
25	34550	Lawrence city, Massachusetts	61,482	39,223	0	3,183	63.8	0.0	8.1	36,040
25	35075	Leominster city, Massachusetts	32,632	23,533	0	2,136	72.1	0.0	9.1	21,397
25	35250	Lexington CDP, Massachusetts	26,014	17,068	42	1,125	65.6	0.2	6.6	15,943
25	37000	Lowell city, Massachusetts	88,524	56,015	0	4,402	63.3	0.0	7.9	51,613
25	37490	Lynn city, Massachusetts	71,950	50,166	29	3,081	69.7	0.0	6.1	47,085
25	37875	Malden city, Massachusetts	50,041	33,442	73	1,728	66.8	0.1	5.2	31,714
25	38435	Marblehead CDP, Massachusetts	17,028	11,507	105	798	67.6	0.6	6.9	10,709
25	38715	Marlborough city, Massachusetts	31,700	23,990	0	588	75.7	0.0	2.5	23,402
25	39835	Medford city, Massachusetts	48,193	32,354	238	952	67.1	0.5	2.9	31,402
25	40115	Melrose city, Massachusetts	22,563	15,750	70	428	69.8	0.3	2.7	15,322
25	40710	Methuen Town city, Massachusetts	40,727	29,286	166	2,042	71.9	0.4	7.0	27,244
25	41200	Milford CDP, Massachusetts	19,650	13,655	0	903	69.5	0.0	6.6	12,752
25	41725	Milton CDP, Massachusetts	22,215	15,213	0	642	68.5	0.0	4.2	14,571
25	44140	Needham CDP, Massachusetts	24,294	16,419	0	1,065	67.6	0.0	6.5	15,354
25	45000	New Bedford city, Massachusetts	77,359	47,783	0	3,946	61.8	0.0	8.3	43,837
25	45560	Newton city, Massachusetts	72,328	45,714	0	1,014	63.2	0.0	2.2	44,700
25	46330	Northampton city, Massachusetts	23,671	15,333	0	1,283	64.8	0.0	8.4	14,050
25	50285	Norwood CDP, Massachusetts	23,394	17,783	0	727	76.0	0.0	4.1	17,056
25	52490	Peabody city, Massachusetts	44,582	27,222	0	1,688	61.1	0.0	6.2	25,534
25	53960	Pittsfield city, Massachusetts	35,802	23,648	0	1,498	66.1	0.0	6.3	22,150
25	55745	Quincy city, Massachusetts	80,538	55,622	0	2,707	69.1	0.0	4.9	52,915
25	55990	Randolph CDP, Massachusetts	27,905	19,465	0	2,264	69.8	0.0	11.6	17,201
25	56165	Reading CDP, Massachusetts	19,273	13,760	0	561	71.4	0.0	4.1	13,199
25	56585	Revere city, Massachusetts	45,809	29,778	0	1,703	65.0	0.0	5.7	28,075
25	59105	Salem city, Massachusetts	36,358	26,725	0	1,254	73.5	0.0	4.7	25,471
25	60050	Saugus CDP, Massachusetts	23,301	16,257	0	1,077	69.8	0.0	6.6	15,180
25	62465	Somerset CDP, Massachusetts	15,281	9,883	0	593	64.7	0.0	6.0	9,290
25	62535	Somerville city, Massachusetts	73,778	57,376	247	2,114	77.8	0.3	3.7	55,262
25	67000	Springfield city, Massachusetts	117,828	70,968	42	6,350	60.2	0.0	8.9	64,618
25	67700	Stoneham CDP, Massachusetts	18,561	13,226	0	449	71.3	0.0	3.4	12,777
25	69170	Taunton city, Massachusetts	45,503	31,034	88	2,257	68.2	0.2	7.3	28,777
25	72250	Wakefield CDP, Massachusetts	21,965	16,058	0	441	73.1	0.0	2.7	15,617

Table E. Cities—Labor Force, Employment, and Educational Data, 2015—*Continued*

FIPS state code	FIPS place code	State/city	Total population age 16 and older	Civilian labor force	Armed Forces	Unemployed	Civilian labor force participation (percent)	Percent in Armed Forces	Unemployment rate	Number of employed persons age 16 and older
25	72600	Waltham city, Massachusetts	55,864	39,472	0	1,668	70.7	0.0	4.2	37,804
25	73440	Watertown Town city, Massachusetts	28,660	21,120	0	432	73.7	0.0	2.0	20,688
25	74210	Wellesley CDP, Massachusetts	23,013	14,105	0	728	61.3	0.0	5.2	13,377
25	76030	Westfield city, Massachusetts	35,985	24,259	0	922	67.4	0.0	3.8	23,337
25	77890	West Springfield Town city, Massachusetts	23,335	15,008	0	1,141	64.3	0.0	7.6	13,867
25	78972	Weymouth Town city, Massachusetts	47,284	32,118	94	2,373	67.9	0.2	7.4	29,745
25	80195	Wilmington CDP, Massachusetts	18,472	12,290	0	394	66.5	0.0	3.2	11,896
25	80545	Winchester CDP, Massachusetts	16,637	11,155	0	267	67.0	0.0	2.4	10,888
25	81035	Woburn city, Massachusetts	33,537	25,490	43	968	76.0	0.1	3.8	24,522
25	82000	Worcester city, Massachusetts	154,305	93,801	0	8,156	60.8	0.0	8.7	85,645
26	00000	**MICHIGAN**	7,982,332	4,862,037	4,081	349,396	60.9	0.1	7.2	4,512,641
26	00440	Adrian city, Michigan	15,584	9,796	0	865	62.9	0.0	8.8	8,931
26	01340	Allendale CDP, Michigan	16,914	10,790	0	684	63.8	0.0	6.3	10,106
26	01380	Allen Park city, Michigan	22,478	14,774	0	639	65.7	0.0	4.3	14,135
26	03000	Ann Arbor city, Michigan	104,600	62,430	31	3,496	59.7	0.0	5.6	58,934
26	04105	Auburn Hills city, Michigan	21,924	15,074	0	1,295	68.8	0.0	8.6	13,779
26	05920	Battle Creek city, Michigan	40,683	23,906	94	2,697	58.8	0.2	11.3	21,209
26	06020	Bay City city, Michigan	27,442	15,769	0	1,125	57.5	0.0	7.1	14,644
26	08640	Birmingham city, Michigan	16,401	11,231	0	284	68.5	0.0	2.5	10,947
26	12060	Burton city, Michigan	22,876	12,748	0	1,308	55.7	0.0	10.3	11,440
26	21000	Dearborn city, Michigan	70,435	39,919	0	2,605	56.7	0.0	6.5	37,314
26	21020	Dearborn Heights city, Michigan	43,456	24,384	0	1,796	56.1	0.0	7.4	22,588
26	22000	Detroit city, Michigan	524,688	277,942	116	57,235	53.0	0.0	20.6	220,707
26	24120	East Lansing city, Michigan	44,468	23,230	0	2,803	52.2	0.0	12.1	20,427
26	24290	Eastpointe city, Michigan	25,159	15,563	0	1,724	61.9	0.0	11.1	13,839
26	27440	Farmington Hills city, Michigan	65,430	41,894	0	1,811	64.0	0.0	4.3	40,083
26	27880	Ferndale city, Michigan	16,717	12,621	0	931	75.5	0.0	7.4	11,690
26	29000	Flint city, Michigan	75,799	39,113	0	7,946	51.6	0.0	20.3	31,167
26	29580	Forest Hills CDP, Michigan	20,590	13,608	0	620	66.1	0.0	4.6	12,988
26	31420	Garden City city, Michigan	22,177	13,516	0	888	60.9	0.0	6.6	12,628
26	34000	Grand Rapids city, Michigan	154,084	105,029	157	7,062	68.2	0.1	6.7	97,967
26	36280	Hamtramck city, Michigan	16,671	7,545	0	1,093	45.3	0.0	14.5	6,452
26	37100	Haslett CDP, Michigan	16,147	10,126	0	844	62.7	0.0	8.3	9,282
26	38640	Holland city, Michigan	26,331	15,537	0	564	59.0	0.0	3.6	14,973
26	38780	Holt CDP, Michigan	19,729	13,193	0	970	66.9	0.0	7.4	12,223
26	40680	Inkster city, Michigan	19,662	10,747	0	823	54.7	0.0	7.7	9,924
26	41420	Jackson city, Michigan	23,696	14,061	0	1,526	59.3	0.0	10.9	12,535
26	42160	Kalamazoo city, Michigan	62,621	42,894	0	3,836	68.5	0.0	8.9	39,058
26	42820	Kentwood city, Michigan	41,726	27,862	0	905	66.8	0.0	3.2	26,957
26	46000	Lansing city, Michigan	90,007	59,511	0	4,929	66.1	0.0	8.3	54,582
26	47800	Lincoln Park city, Michigan	28,930	16,938	0	1,336	58.5	0.0	7.9	15,602
26	49000	Livonia city, Michigan	80,166	51,692	0	2,363	64.5	0.0	4.6	49,329
26	50560	Madison Heights city, Michigan	23,828	14,758	0	643	61.9	0.0	4.4	14,115
26	51900	Marquette city, Michigan	19,227	10,554	67	935	54.9	0.3	8.9	9,619
26	53780	Midland city, Michigan	34,826	21,616	88	2,110	62.1	0.3	9.8	19,506
26	55020	Monroe city, Michigan	16,698	10,108	0	584	60.5	0.0	5.8	9,524
26	56020	Mount Pleasant city, Michigan	23,854	14,521	0	1,076	60.9	0.0	7.4	13,445
26	56320	Muskegon city, Michigan	31,030	15,688	0	1,500	50.6	0.0	9.6	14,188
26	59140	Norton Shores city, Michigan	18,104	11,814	0	538	65.3	0.0	4.6	11,276
26	59440	Novi city, Michigan	46,776	31,460	0	580	67.3	0.0	1.8	30,880
26	59920	Oak Park city, Michigan	24,016	14,308	0	949	59.6	0.0	6.6	13,359
26	60340	Okemos CDP, Michigan	18,166	11,987	0	625	66.0	0.0	5.2	11,362
26	65440	Pontiac city, Michigan	45,068	29,169	0	4,396	64.7	0.0	15.1	24,773
26	65560	Portage city, Michigan	38,537	25,756	197	1,786	66.8	0.5	6.9	23,970
26	65820	Port Huron city, Michigan	23,308	14,075	0	1,755	60.4	0.0	12.5	12,320
26	69035	Rochester Hills city, Michigan	58,726	37,491	90	1,391	63.8	0.2	3.7	36,100
26	69420	Romulus city, Michigan	16,583	9,551	0	1,256	57.6	0.0	13.2	8,295
26	69800	Roseville city, Michigan	39,615	24,653	118	2,419	62.2	0.3	9.8	22,234
26	70040	Royal Oak city, Michigan	50,793	37,093	0	1,819	73.0	0.0	4.9	35,274
26	70520	Saginaw city, Michigan	39,748	21,835	0	4,708	54.9	0.0	21.6	17,127
26	70760	St. Clair Shores city, Michigan	50,508	31,961	141	2,384	63.3	0.3	7.5	29,577
26	74900	Southfield city, Michigan	60,147	36,280	0	2,133	60.3	0.0	5.9	34,147
26	74960	Southgate city, Michigan	24,806	15,441	0	1,505	62.2	0.0	9.7	13,936
26	76460	Sterling Heights city, Michigan	108,554	67,308	43	3,001	62.0	0.0	4.5	64,307
26	79000	Taylor city, Michigan	47,027	28,278	0	2,882	60.1	0.0	10.2	25,396
26	80700	Troy city, Michigan	66,963	42,183	0	1,502	63.0	0.0	3.6	40,681
26	82960	Walker city, Michigan	20,786	14,304	0	496	68.8	0.0	3.5	13,808
26	84000	Warren city, Michigan	112,639	66,686	0	6,925	59.2	0.0	10.4	59,761
26	84800	Waverly CDP, Michigan	20,390	13,008	0	584	63.8	0.0	4.5	12,424
26	86000	Westland city, Michigan	67,026	41,639	0	2,625	62.1	0.0	6.3	39,014
26	88900	Wyandotte city, Michigan	20,282	13,137	0	1,295	64.8	0.0	9.9	11,842
26	88940	Wyoming city, Michigan	55,351	39,173	0	1,818	70.8	0.0	4.6	37,355
26	89140	Ypsilanti city, Michigan	20,006	14,058	0	1,477	70.3	0.0	10.5	12,581

Table E. Cities—Labor Force, Employment, and Educational Data, 2015—*Continued*

FIPS state code	FIPS place code	State/city	Total population age 16 and older	Civilian labor force	Armed Forces	Unemployed	Civilian labor force participation (percent)	Percent in Armed Forces	Unemployment rate	Number of employed persons age 16 and older
27	00000	**MINNESOTA**	4,349,038	3,039,536	1,576	126,360	69.9	0.0	4.2	2,913,176
27	01486	Andover city, Minnesota	23,681	17,394	0	760	73.5	0.0	4.4	16,634
27	01900	Apple Valley city, Minnesota	39,926	29,244	69	1,176	73.2	0.2	4.0	28,068
27	02908	Austin city, Minnesota	18,457	12,439	0	773	67.4	0.0	6.2	11,666
27	06382	Blaine city, Minnesota	46,885	34,979	72	1,384	74.6	0.2	4.0	33,595
27	06616	Bloomington city, Minnesota	71,398	50,305	0	1,794	70.5	0.0	3.6	48,511
27	07948	Brooklyn Center city, Minnesota	22,129	15,880	0	881	71.8	0.0	5.5	14,999
27	07966	Brooklyn Park city, Minnesota	59,360	43,094	0	2,041	72.6	0.0	4.7	41,053
27	08794	Burnsville city, Minnesota	47,468	34,762	0	1,743	73.2	0.0	5.0	33,019
27	10846	Champlin city, Minnesota	17,902	14,823	0	700	82.8	0.0	4.7	14,123
27	10918	Chanhassen city, Minnesota	19,804	14,867	0	358	75.1	0.0	2.4	14,509
27	10972	Chaska city, Minnesota	18,298	14,412	0	343	78.8	0.0	2.4	14,069
27	13114	Coon Rapids city, Minnesota	50,975	37,238	0	1,648	73.1	0.0	4.4	35,590
27	13456	Cottage Grove city, Minnesota	26,799	21,046	0	618	78.5	0.0	2.9	20,428
27	14158	Crystal city, Minnesota	17,963	13,490	0	513	75.1	0.0	3.8	12,977
27	17000	Duluth city, Minnesota	72,863	49,722	194	2,001	68.2	0.3	4.0	47,721
27	17288	Eagan city, Minnesota	53,195	41,980	0	1,437	78.9	0.0	3.4	40,543
27	18116	Eden Prairie city, Minnesota	50,737	37,452	0	1,179	73.8	0.0	3.1	36,273
27	18188	Edina city, Minnesota	40,032	25,150	62	641	62.8	0.2	2.5	24,509
27	18674	Elk River city, Minnesota	16,679	12,001	0	1,276	72.0	0.0	10.6	10,725
27	20546	Faribault city, Minnesota	17,455	10,762	0	378	61.7	0.0	3.5	10,384
27	20618	Farmington city, Minnesota	15,928	12,828	39	161	80.5	0.2	1.3	12,667
27	22814	Fridley city, Minnesota	22,083	15,137	0	339	68.5	0.0	2.2	14,798
27	24308	Golden Valley city, Minnesota	16,821	10,898	0	453	64.8	0.0	4.2	10,445
27	27530	Hastings city, Minnesota	17,326	11,970	0	296	69.1	0.0	2.5	11,674
27	31076	Inver Grove Heights city, Minnesota	27,664	18,418	119	1,178	66.6	0.4	6.4	17,240
27	35180	Lakeville city, Minnesota	46,549	36,742	0	1,602	78.9	0.0	4.4	35,140
27	37322	Lino Lakes city, Minnesota	16,004	10,992	0	217	68.7	0.0	2.0	10,775
27	39878	Mankato city, Minnesota	35,802	26,081	0	1,088	72.8	0.0	4.2	24,993
27	40166	Maple Grove city, Minnesota	52,451	38,083	0	949	72.6	0.0	2.5	37,134
27	40382	Maplewood city, Minnesota	32,365	22,018	0	920	68.0	0.0	4.2	21,098
27	43000	Minneapolis city, Minnesota	336,581	252,561	133	14,337	75.0	0.0	5.7	238,224
27	43252	Minnetonka city, Minnesota	43,533	31,218	0	1,609	71.7	0.0	5.2	29,609
27	43864	Moorhead city, Minnesota	33,082	23,012	0	1,023	69.6	0.0	4.4	21,989
27	45430	New Brighton city, Minnesota	20,957	14,987	0	771	71.5	0.0	5.1	14,216
27	45628	New Hope city, Minnesota	18,046	11,263	0	291	62.4	0.0	2.6	10,972
27	46924	Northfield city, Minnesota	17,771	12,728	0	401	71.6	0.0	3.2	12,327
27	47680	Oakdale city, Minnesota	22,492	17,121	0	1,061	76.1	0.0	6.2	16,060
27	49300	Owatonna city, Minnesota	19,364	12,888	0	459	66.6	0.0	3.6	12,429
27	51730	Plymouth city, Minnesota	59,837	42,983	0	1,332	71.8	0.0	3.1	41,651
27	52594	Prior Lake city, Minnesota	19,082	13,105	0	789	68.7	0.0	6.0	12,316
27	53026	Ramsey city, Minnesota	20,261	14,541	52	368	71.8	0.3	2.5	14,173
27	54214	Richfield city, Minnesota	27,661	20,314	0	477	73.4	0.0	2.3	19,837
27	54880	Rochester city, Minnesota	87,497	60,894	0	2,611	69.6	0.0	4.3	58,283
27	55726	Rosemount city, Minnesota	16,930	13,543	28	435	80.0	0.2	3.2	13,108
27	55852	Roseville city, Minnesota	29,822	19,226	0	1,269	64.5	0.0	6.6	17,957
27	56896	St. Cloud city, Minnesota	54,904	38,308	0	2,293	69.8	0.0	6.0	36,015
27	57220	St. Louis Park city, Minnesota	39,585	31,739	0	1,293	80.2	0.0	4.1	30,446
27	58000	St. Paul city, Minnesota	234,923	166,259	141	11,308	70.8	0.1	6.8	154,951
27	58738	Savage city, Minnesota	22,748	17,681	165	373	77.7	0.7	2.1	17,308
27	59350	Shakopee city, Minnesota	29,376	22,708	0	699	77.3	0.0	3.1	22,009
27	59998	Shoreview city, Minnesota	20,934	15,310	0	353	73.1	0.0	2.3	14,957
27	61492	South St. Paul city, Minnesota	16,055	11,065	0	118	68.9	0.0	1.1	10,947
27	69970	White Bear Lake city, Minnesota	19,045	12,857	0	561	67.5	0.0	4.4	12,296
27	71032	Winona city, Minnesota	23,317	16,497	59	1,074	70.8	0.3	6.5	15,423
27	71428	Woodbury city, Minnesota	51,541	36,759	0	730	71.3	0.0	2.0	36,029
28	00000	**MISSISSIPPI**	2,345,713	1,324,308	10,822	117,629	56.5	0.5	8.9	1,206,679
28	06220	Biloxi city, Mississippi	35,776	21,358	3,930	1,324	59.7	11.0	6.2	20,034
28	08300	Brandon city, Mississippi	18,206	12,669	154	207	69.6	0.8	1.6	12,462
28	14420	Clinton city, Mississippi	19,043	11,595	158	143	60.9	0.8	1.2	11,452
28	15380	Columbus city, Mississippi	16,064	8,124	0	1,468	50.6	0.0	18.1	6,656
28	29180	Greenville city, Mississippi	26,208	14,796	13	2,825	56.5	0.0	19.1	11,971
28	29700	Gulfport city, Mississippi	56,782	31,911	1,373	4,275	56.2	2.4	13.4	27,636
28	31020	Hattiesburg city, Mississippi	38,162	22,863	36	4,433	59.9	0.1	19.4	18,430
28	33700	Horn Lake city, Mississippi	20,714	13,850	0	2,301	66.9	0.0	16.6	11,549
28	36000	Jackson city, Mississippi	130,083	77,735	0	8,483	59.8	0.0	10.9	69,252
28	44520	Madison city, Mississippi	20,795	13,766	120	322	66.2	0.6	2.3	13,444
28	46640	Meridian city, Mississippi	31,310	17,734	80	1,962	56.6	0.3	11.1	15,772
28	54040	Olive Branch city, Mississippi	27,863	20,728	0	1,659	74.4	0.0	8.0	19,069
28	54840	Oxford city, Mississippi	15,622	7,764	0	698	49.7	0.0	9.0	7,066
28	55360	Pascagoula city, Mississippi	18,642	10,561	53	906	56.7	0.3	8.6	9,655
28	55760	Pearl city, Mississippi	20,924	13,948	0	1,391	66.7	0.0	10.0	12,557
28	62520	Ridgeland city, Mississippi	19,591	13,671	0	796	69.8	0.0	5.8	12,875
28	69280	Southaven city, Mississippi	39,434	26,191	46	1,392	66.4	0.1	5.3	24,799
28	70240	Starkville city, Mississippi	21,935	11,914	158	667	54.3	0.7	5.6	11,247
28	74840	Tupelo city, Mississippi	27,834	18,084	0	1,056	65.0	0.0	5.8	17,028

Table E. Cities—Labor Force, Employment, and Educational Data, 2015—*Continued*

FIPS state code	FIPS place code	State/city	Total population age 16 and older	Civilian labor force	Armed Forces	Unemployed	Civilian labor force participation (percent)	Percent in Armed Forces	Unemployment rate	Number of employed persons age 16 and older
28	76720	Vicksburg city, Mississippi	17,139	8,668	19	462	50.6	0.1	5.3	8,206
29	00000	**MISSOURI**	4,851,761	3,042,538	20,355	162,229	62.7	0.4	5.3	2,880,309
29	00280	Affton CDP, Missouri	16,663	12,899	0	479	77.4	0.0	3.7	12,420
29	01972	Arnold city, Missouri	17,219	10,758	0	933	62.5	0.0	8.7	9,825
29	03160	Ballwin city, Missouri	23,746	16,041	0	400	67.6	0.0	2.5	15,641
29	04384	Belton city, Missouri	16,251	11,846	0	309	72.9	0.0	2.6	11,537
29	06652	Blue Springs city, Missouri	40,470	28,699	0	1,600	70.9	0.0	5.6	27,099
29	11242	Cape Girardeau city, Missouri	32,991	20,484	83	381	62.1	0.3	1.9	20,103
29	13600	Chesterfield city, Missouri	39,776	23,968	0	1,121	60.3	0.0	4.7	22,847
29	15670	Columbia city, Missouri	99,549	65,880	164	3,175	66.2	0.2	4.8	62,705
29	16030	Concord CDP, Missouri	16,045	9,780	0	0	61.0	0.0	0.0	9,780
29	23986	Ferguson city, Missouri	13,035	9,118	0	271	70.0	0.0	3.0	8,847
29	24778	Florissant city, Missouri	40,873	28,025	0	1,888	68.6	0.0	6.7	26,137
29	25264	Fort Leonard Wood CDP, Missouri	16,695	3,261	12,375	774	19.5	74.1	23.7	2,487
29	27190	Gladstone city, Missouri	22,487	14,726	136	1,056	65.5	0.6	7.2	13,670
29	28324	Grandview city, Missouri	19,668	13,155	0	205	66.9	0.0	1.6	12,950
29	31276	Hazelwood city, Missouri	20,702	13,971	0	827	67.5	0.0	5.9	13,144
29	35000	Independence city, Missouri	93,650	57,733	40	3,902	61.6	0.0	6.8	53,831
29	37000	Jefferson City city, Missouri	35,835	20,558	75	1,033	57.4	0.2	5.0	19,525
29	37592	Joplin city, Missouri	41,208	26,813	0	1,374	65.1	0.0	5.1	25,439
29	38000	Kansas City city, Missouri	375,338	253,776	161	13,086	67.6	0.0	5.2	240,690
29	39044	Kirkwood city, Missouri	22,415	14,546	0	442	64.9	0.0	3.0	14,104
29	41348	Lee's Summit city, Missouri	71,399	49,989	0	1,494	70.0	0.0	3.0	48,495
29	42032	Liberty city, Missouri	22,975	16,882	0	764	73.5	0.0	4.5	16,118
29	46586	Maryland Heights city, Missouri	23,295	16,016	0	577	68.8	0.0	3.6	15,439
29	47180	Mehlville CDP, Missouri	25,705	17,755	0	364	69.1	0.0	2.1	17,391
29	52616	Nixa city, Missouri	17,315	9,155	0	412	52.9	0.0	4.5	8,743
29	53876	Oakville CDP, Missouri	30,976	20,262	0	499	65.4	0.0	2.5	19,763
29	54074	O'Fallon city, Missouri	64,543	48,141	0	1,618	74.6	0.0	3.4	46,523
29	60752	Raymore city, Missouri	18,234	12,365	0	124	67.8	0.0	1.0	12,241
29	60788	Raytown city, Missouri	22,790	13,823	0	460	60.7	0.0	3.3	13,363
29	62912	Rolla city, Missouri	17,200	10,646	96	1,027	61.9	0.6	9.6	9,619
29	64082	St. Charles city, Missouri	55,777	38,670	0	1,137	69.3	0.0	2.9	37,533
29	64550	St. Joseph city, Missouri	60,478	38,214	0	2,027	63.2	0.0	5.3	36,187
29	65000	St. Louis city, Missouri	258,110	168,033	367	15,983	65.1	0.1	9.5	152,050
29	65126	St. Peters city, Missouri	45,362	35,334	0	1,650	77.9	0.0	4.7	33,684
29	66440	Sedalia city, Missouri	16,791	10,370	37	1,191	61.8	0.2	11.5	9,179
29	70000	Springfield city, Missouri	142,116	85,889	157	4,598	60.4	0.1	5.4	81,291
29	75220	University City city, Missouri	28,884	21,115	0	1,308	73.1	0.0	6.2	19,807
29	78154	Webster Groves city, Missouri	19,614	12,833	0	186	65.4	0.0	1.4	12,647
29	78442	Wentzville city, Missouri	27,047	19,794	0	613	73.2	0.0	3.1	19,181
29	79820	Wildwood city, Missouri	27,668	19,273	0	570	69.7	0.0	3.0	18,703
30	00000	**MONTANA**	829,911	513,209	3,524	23,334	61.8	0.4	4.5	489,875
30	06550	Billings city, Montana	88,134	60,036	179	1,761	68.1	0.2	2.9	58,275
30	08950	Bozeman city, Montana	37,428	27,134	0	1,252	72.5	0.0	4.6	25,882
30	11397	Butte-Silver Bow (balance), Montana	27,485	15,951	0	885	58.0	0.0	5.5	15,066
30	32800	Great Falls city, Montana	46,661	27,617	675	1,044	59.2	1.4	3.8	26,573
30	35600	Helena city, Montana	25,478	15,416	74	565	60.5	0.3	3.7	14,851
30	40075	Kalispell city, Montana	18,789	11,124	0	192	59.2	0.0	1.7	10,932
30	50200	Missoula city, Montana	59,495	41,304	78	2,082	69.4	0.1	5.0	39,222
31	00000	**NEBRASKA**	1,476,487	1,019,543	5,536	32,754	69.1	0.4	3.2	986,789
31	03950	Bellevue city, Nebraska	42,861	28,480	1,092	971	66.4	2.5	3.4	27,509
31	10110	Columbus city, Nebraska	17,065	12,451	0	405	73.0	0.0	3.3	12,046
31	17670	Fremont city, Nebraska	20,222	13,248	0	420	65.5	0.0	3.2	12,828
31	19595	Grand Island city, Nebraska	38,539	28,492	0	1,275	73.9	0.0	4.5	27,217
31	21415	Hastings city, Nebraska	20,005	12,435	0	308	62.2	0.0	2.5	12,127
31	25055	Kearney city, Nebraska	27,528	20,346	0	1,105	73.9	0.0	5.4	19,241
31	28000	Lincoln city, Nebraska	219,222	155,209	529	4,835	70.8	0.2	3.1	150,374
31	34615	Norfolk city, Nebraska	19,190	13,113	0	688	68.3	0.0	5.2	12,425
31	35000	North Platte city, Nebraska	19,292	12,599	0	183	65.3	0.0	1.5	12,416
31	37000	Omaha city, Nebraska	345,585	237,996	627	9,800	68.9	0.2	4.1	228,196
31	38295	Papillion city, Nebraska	15,226	11,386	0	172	74.8	0.0	1.5	11,214
32	00000	**NEVADA**	2,292,699	1,446,814	8,491	115,018	63.1	0.4	7.9	1,331,796
32	09700	Carson City, Nevada	44,744	25,964	36	1,362	58.0	0.1	5.2	24,602
32	22500	Elko city, Nevada	16,574	11,912	0	1,141	71.9	0.0	9.6	10,771
32	23770	Enterprise CDP, Nevada	106,766	80,586	38	3,965	75.5	0.0	4.9	76,621
32	31900	Henderson city, Nevada	232,283	142,457	379	8,589	61.3	0.2	6.0	133,868
32	40000	Las Vegas city, Nevada	487,831	304,276	2,268	27,895	62.4	0.5	9.2	276,381
32	51800	North Las Vegas city, Nevada	175,553	109,213	2,310	8,273	62.2	1.3	7.6	100,940
32	53800	Pahrump CDP, Nevada	30,187	11,018	0	1,741	36.5	0.0	15.8	9,277
32	54600	Paradise CDP, Nevada	193,184	127,571	34	14,230	66.0	0.0	11.2	113,341
32	60600	Reno city, Nevada	194,472	129,034	326	8,365	66.4	0.2	6.5	120,669
32	68400	Sparks city, Nevada	74,407	49,107	42	3,992	66.0	0.1	8.1	45,115
32	68585	Spring Valley CDP, Nevada	157,486	106,803	101	6,364	67.8	0.1	6.0	100,439
32	70900	Summerlin South CDP, Nevada	21,398	12,841	0	847	60.0	0.0	6.6	11,994

Table E. Cities—Labor Force, Employment, and Educational Data, 2015—*Continued*

FIPS state code	FIPS place code	State/city	Total population age 16 and older	Employment status						Number of employed persons age 16 and older
				Civilian labor force	Armed Forces	Unemployed	Civilian labor force participation (percent)	Percent in Armed Forces	Unemployment rate	
32	71400	Sunrise Manor CDP, Nevada	146,720	94,816	519	10,360	64.6	0.4	10.9	84,456
32	71600	Sun Valley CDP, Nevada	16,068	10,659	0	827	66.3	0.0	7.8	9,832
32	83800	Whitney CDP, Nevada	34,836	23,192	0	2,091	66.6	0.0	9.0	21,101
32	84600	Winchester CDP, Nevada	25,448	18,453	0	2,625	72.5	0.0	14.2	15,828
33	00000	**NEW HAMPSHIRE**	1,102,089	744,971	1,906	31,658	67.6	0.2	4.2	713,313
33	14200	Concord city, New Hampshire	35,124	22,577	178	577	64.3	0.5	2.6	22,000
33	17860	Derry CDP, New Hampshire	18,524	14,464	0	1,339	78.1	0.0	9.3	13,125
33	18820	Dover city, New Hampshire	25,341	17,177	21	1,357	67.8	0.1	7.9	15,820
33	39300	Keene city, New Hampshire	20,059	12,641	0	543	63.0	0.0	4.3	12,098
33	45140	Manchester city, New Hampshire	90,694	62,645	46	3,326	69.1	0.1	5.3	59,319
33	50260	Nashua city, New Hampshire	71,296	49,169	128	1,934	69.0	0.2	3.9	47,235
33	62900	Portsmouth city, New Hampshire	20,836	14,429	955	548	69.3	4.6	3.8	13,881
33	65140	Rochester city, New Hampshire	24,791	15,372	75	617	62.0	0.3	4.0	14,755
34	00000	**NEW JERSEY**	7,193,921	4,684,036	9,593	309,500	65.1	0.1	6.6	4,374,536
34	02080	Atlantic City city, New Jersey	29,835	18,137	17	2,924	60.8	0.1	16.1	15,213
34	02350	Avenel CDP, New Jersey	17,272	8,293	0	328	48.0	0.0	4.0	7,965
34	03580	Bayonne city, New Jersey	52,538	33,953	29	3,224	64.6	0.1	9.5	30,729
34	05170	Bergenfield borough, New Jersey	21,527	13,926	0	469	64.7	0.0	3.4	13,457
34	07600	Bridgeton city, New Jersey	18,671	10,799	0	838	57.8	0.0	7.8	9,961
34	10000	Camden city, New Jersey	53,768	30,432	0	4,093	56.6	0.0	13.4	26,339
34	10750	Carteret borough, New Jersey	20,106	12,675	190	946	63.0	0.9	7.5	11,729
34	13570	Cliffside Park borough, New Jersey	22,181	14,796	0	335	66.7	0.0	2.3	14,461
34	13690	Clifton city, New Jersey	70,120	43,010	0	1,311	61.3	0.0	3.0	41,699
34	19390	East Orange city, New Jersey	51,858	34,513	0	5,141	66.6	0.0	14.9	29,372
34	21000	Elizabeth city, New Jersey	98,355	66,370	0	5,704	67.5	0.0	8.6	60,666
34	21300	Elmwood Park borough, New Jersey	17,893	13,154	0	543	73.5	0.0	4.1	12,611
34	21480	Englewood city, New Jersey	24,421	17,102	0	725	70.0	0.0	4.2	16,377
34	22470	Fair Lawn borough, New Jersey	28,030	18,517	0	549	66.1	0.0	3.0	17,968
34	24420	Fort Lee borough, New Jersey	31,526	19,357	0	713	61.4	0.0	3.7	18,644
34	25770	Garfield city, New Jersey	25,607	15,441	0	1,306	60.3	0.0	8.5	14,135
34	28680	Hackensack city, New Jersey	37,482	25,096	0	1,187	67.0	0.0	4.7	23,909
34	32256	Hoboken city, New Jersey	46,056	37,044	0	1,741	80.4	0.0	4.7	35,303
34	36000	Jersey City city, New Jersey	214,339	145,166	48	10,827	67.7	0.0	7.5	134,339
34	36510	Kearny town, New Jersey	33,821	21,984	0	939	65.0	0.0	4.3	21,045
34	38580	Lakewood CDP, New Jersey	27,978	16,919	0	629	60.5	0.0	3.7	16,290
34	40350	Linden city, New Jersey	34,207	24,068	0	2,165	70.4	0.0	9.0	21,903
34	41100	Lodi borough, New Jersey	19,937	13,962	0	1,100	70.0	0.0	7.9	12,862
34	41310	Long Branch city, New Jersey	25,681	18,281	0	1,636	71.2	0.0	8.9	16,645
34	46460	Millville city, New Jersey	20,251	13,077	0	914	64.6	0.0	7.0	12,163
34	51000	Newark city, New Jersey	220,398	134,542	0	20,447	61.0	0.0	15.2	114,095
34	51210	New Brunswick city, New Jersey	46,267	22,871	0	1,143	49.4	0.0	5.0	21,728
34	53280	North Plainfield borough, New Jersey	18,337	14,305	0	596	78.0	0.0	4.2	13,709
34	54690	Old Bridge CDP, New Jersey	18,985	13,284	0	831	70.0	0.0	6.3	12,453
34	55770	Palisades Park borough, New Jersey	17,465	11,821	0	442	67.7	0.0	3.7	11,379
34	55950	Paramus borough, New Jersey	24,218	15,439	0	698	63.8	0.0	4.5	14,741
34	56550	Passaic city, New Jersey	51,423	25,717	0	1,162	50.0	0.0	4.5	24,555
34	57000	Paterson city, New Jersey	112,850	62,032	0	3,657	55.0	0.0	5.9	58,375
34	58200	Perth Amboy city, New Jersey	39,225	23,593	0	920	60.1	0.0	3.9	22,673
34	59190	Plainfield city, New Jersey	39,863	27,221	0	2,413	68.3	0.0	8.9	24,808
34	59640	Pleasantville city, New Jersey	17,183	10,984	204	1,150	63.9	1.2	10.5	9,834
34	60900	Princeton, New Jersey	25,072	15,199	0	701	60.6	0.0	4.6	14,498
34	61530	Rahway city, New Jersey	25,733	17,762	93	1,148	69.0	0.4	6.5	16,614
34	63000	Ridgewood village, New Jersey	19,135	13,634	0	603	71.3	0.0	4.4	13,031
34	64620	Roselle borough, New Jersey	19,855	12,864	0	1,363	64.8	0.0	10.6	11,501
34	65790	Sayreville borough, New Jersey	35,316	24,097	0	2,082	68.2	0.0	8.6	22,015
34	68370	Somerset CDP, New Jersey	19,412	13,522	0	1,282	69.7	0.0	9.5	12,240
34	69390	South Plainfield borough, New Jersey	19,128	13,373	0	1,392	69.9	0.0	10.4	11,981
34	71430	Summit city, New Jersey	15,191	10,077	0	497	66.3	0.0	4.9	9,580
34	73110	Toms River CDP, New Jersey	69,146	44,973	65	2,955	65.0	0.1	6.6	42,018
34	74000	Trenton city, New Jersey	65,464	40,388	0	5,309	61.7	0.0	13.1	35,079
34	74630	Union City city, New Jersey	56,057	39,578	0	2,430	70.6	0.0	6.1	37,148
34	76070	Vineland city, New Jersey	47,969	28,072	0	1,477	58.5	0.0	5.3	26,595
34	79040	Westfield town, New Jersey	21,799	15,008	0	448	68.8	0.0	3.0	14,560
34	79610	West New York town, New Jersey	44,732	30,332	0	2,438	67.8	0.0	8.0	27,894
35	00000	**NEW MEXICO**	1,642,487	950,312	9,625	70,505	57.9	0.6	7.4	879,807
35	01780	Alamogordo city, New Mexico	24,356	13,519	511	665	55.5	2.1	4.9	12,854
35	02000	Albuquerque city, New Mexico	444,861	279,395	1,440	18,667	62.8	0.3	6.7	260,728
35	12150	Carlsbad city, New Mexico	20,786	13,174	0	723	63.4	0.0	5.5	12,451
35	16420	Clovis city, New Mexico	30,414	16,266	1,848	2,120	53.5	6.1	13.0	14,146
35	25800	Farmington city, New Mexico	33,024	20,920	0	922	63.3	0.0	4.4	19,998
35	28460	Gallup city, New Mexico	16,612	11,078	0	916	66.7	0.0	8.3	10,162
35	32520	Hobbs city, New Mexico	27,313	16,541	0	1,445	60.6	0.0	8.7	15,096
35	39380	Las Cruces city, New Mexico	79,096	45,967	485	3,526	58.1	0.6	7.7	42,441
35	63460	Rio Rancho city, New Mexico	73,426	46,729	182	3,574	63.6	0.2	7.6	43,155

Table E. Cities—Labor Force, Employment, and Educational Data, 2015—*Continued*

FIPS state code	FIPS place code	State/city	Total population age 16 and older	Civilian labor force	Armed Forces	Unemployed	Civilian labor force participation (percent)	Percent in Armed Forces	Unemployment rate	Number of employed persons age 16 and older
35	64930	Roswell city, New Mexico	35,737	18,651	197	836	52.2	0.6	4.5	17,815
35	70500	Santa Fe city, New Mexico	68,742	43,469	38	1,858	63.2	0.1	4.3	41,611
35	74520	South Valley CDP, New Mexico	31,856	17,746	0	1,770	55.7	0.0	10.0	15,976
36	00000	**NEW YORK**	16,066,508	10,128,222	23,097	654,885	63.0	0.1	6.5	9,473,337
36	01000	Albany city, New York	85,302	54,586	0	4,861	64.0	0.0	8.9	49,725
36	03078	Auburn city, New York	22,406	13,933	0	742	62.2	0.0	5.3	13,191
36	04143	Baldwin CDP, New York	20,891	14,315	0	503	68.5	0.0	3.5	13,812
36	04935	Bay Shore CDP, New York	24,150	15,400	0	1,074	63.8	0.0	7.0	14,326
36	06607	Binghamton city, New York	37,252	20,443	40	2,487	54.9	0.1	12.2	17,956
36	08026	Brentwood CDP, New York	49,487	33,295	0	1,115	67.3	0.0	3.3	32,180
36	08257	Brighton CDP, New York	31,034	20,014	0	930	64.5	0.0	4.6	19,084
36	11000	Buffalo city, New York	204,410	119,749	141	8,711	58.6	0.1	7.3	111,038
36	13376	Centereach CDP, New York	28,546	18,799	0	1,274	65.9	0.0	6.8	17,525
36	13552	Central Islip CDP, New York	24,205	14,277	0	730	59.0	0.0	5.1	13,547
36	15000	Cheektowaga CDP, New York	63,153	41,300	30	1,903	65.4	0.0	4.6	39,397
36	17530	Commack CDP, New York	29,864	18,832	0	436	63.1	0.0	2.3	18,396
36	18146	Copiague CDP, New York	21,611	15,062	0	1,564	69.7	0.0	10.4	13,498
36	18157	Coram CDP, New York	29,137	19,228	0	858	66.0	0.0	4.5	18,370
36	19972	Deer Park CDP, New York	21,868	13,757	0	1,166	62.9	0.0	8.5	12,591
36	20687	Dix Hills CDP, New York	20,507	12,424	0	388	60.6	0.0	3.1	12,036
36	22502	East Meadow CDP, New York	30,405	19,465	0	767	64.0	0.0	3.9	18,698
36	22612	East Northport CDP, New York	16,900	10,128	0	313	59.9	0.0	3.1	9,815
36	22733	East Patchogue CDP, New York	17,550	11,258	0	1,181	64.1	0.0	10.5	10,077
36	24229	Elmira city, New York	21,997	11,413	0	1,045	51.9	0.0	9.2	10,368
36	24273	Elmont CDP, New York	29,187	20,948	0	1,124	71.8	0.0	5.4	19,824
36	27309	Franklin Square CDP, New York	32,028	19,765	0	1,260	61.7	0.0	6.4	18,505
36	27485	Freeport village, New York	34,631	22,048	0	713	63.7	0.0	3.2	21,335
36	28178	Garden City village, New York	16,558	11,499	0	732	69.4	0.0	6.4	10,767
36	29113	Glen Cove city, New York	22,944	14,876	0	402	64.8	0.0	2.7	14,474
36	32402	Harrison village, New York	23,437	12,732	0	1,526	54.3	0.0	12.0	11,206
36	33139	Hempstead village, New York	42,531	29,985	0	1,836	70.5	0.0	6.1	28,149
36	34374	Hicksville CDP, New York	34,900	22,945	0	1,247	65.7	0.0	5.4	21,698
36	35056	Holbrook CDP, New York	20,723	15,209	47	933	73.4	0.2	6.1	14,276
36	35254	Holtsville CDP, New York	17,544	12,486	0	761	71.2	0.0	6.1	11,725
36	37044	Huntington Station CDP, New York	25,661	17,711	0	1,025	69.0	0.0	5.8	16,686
36	37737	Irondequoit CDP, New York	40,656	25,451	0	1,539	62.6	0.0	6.0	23,912
36	37869	Islip CDP, New York	18,136	11,800	0	242	65.1	0.0	2.1	11,558
36	38077	Ithaca city, New York	29,607	13,624	0	768	46.0	0.0	5.6	12,856
36	38264	Jamestown city, New York	23,803	13,598	0	1,103	57.1	0.0	8.1	12,495
36	39727	Kingston city, New York	18,417	12,393	0	963	67.3	0.0	7.8	11,430
36	39853	Kiryas Joel village, New York	9,958	4,852	0	167	48.7	0.0	3.4	4,685
36	40838	Lake Ronkonkoma CDP, New York	18,553	11,937	53	730	64.3	0.3	6.1	11,207
36	42081	Levittown CDP, New York	44,724	30,942	0	2,460	69.2	0.0	8.0	28,482
36	42554	Lindenhurst village, New York	22,071	15,247	0	801	69.1	0.0	5.3	14,446
36	43082	Lockport city, New York	16,273	9,760	0	585	60.0	0.0	6.0	9,175
36	43335	Long Beach city, New York	28,682	18,602	229	956	64.9	0.8	5.1	17,646
36	45986	Massapequa CDP, New York	17,065	11,419	0	365	66.9	0.0	3.2	11,054
36	46404	Medford CDP, New York	19,892	13,665	0	262	68.7	0.0	1.9	13,403
36	47042	Middletown city, New York	21,541	13,464	0	260	62.5	0.0	1.9	13,204
36	48010	Monsey CDP, New York	12,692	6,237	0	379	49.1	0.0	6.1	5,858
36	49121	Mount Vernon city, New York	55,917	36,340	0	4,046	65.0	0.0	11.1	32,294
36	49407	Nanuet CDP, New York	14,788	10,547	0	614	71.3	0.0	5.8	9,933
36	50034	Newburgh city, New York	17,406	11,070	0	1,117	63.6	0.0	10.1	9,953
36	50100	New City CDP, New York	28,488	18,048	0	1,402	63.4	0.0	7.8	16,646
36	50617	New Rochelle city, New York	64,143	42,204	0	2,471	65.8	0.0	5.9	39,733
36	51000	New York city, New York	6,933,836	4,421,563	1,767	329,222	63.8	0.0	7.4	4,092,341
36	51055	Niagara Falls city, New York	38,301	22,506	50	2,099	58.8	0.1	9.3	20,407
36	51396	North Amityville CDP, New York	16,001	10,909	0	556	68.2	0.0	5.1	10,353
36	53682	North Tonawanda city, New York	25,240	15,738	51	990	62.4	0.2	6.3	14,748
36	54441	Oceanside CDP, New York	25,873	17,289	0	910	66.8	0.0	5.3	16,379
36	55530	Ossining village, New York	21,968	14,703	0	1,409	66.9	0.0	9.6	13,294
36	56979	Peekskill city, New York	17,832	12,420	0	516	69.7	0.0	4.2	11,904
36	58442	Plainview CDP, New York	21,411	13,627	0	434	63.6	0.0	3.2	13,193
36	59223	Port Chester village, New York	24,533	18,122	0	1,558	73.9	0.0	8.6	16,564
36	59641	Poughkeepsie city, New York	24,437	14,757	0	2,559	60.4	0.0	17.3	12,198
36	63000	Rochester city, New York	165,183	102,538	0	14,384	62.1	0.0	14.0	88,154
36	63264	Rockville Centre village, New York	19,217	12,038	0	790	62.6	0.0	6.6	11,248
36	63418	Rome city, New York	25,796	14,043	0	834	54.4	0.0	5.9	13,209
36	63473	Ronkonkoma CDP, New York	17,251	11,737	0	772	68.0	0.0	6.6	10,965
36	63924	Rotterdam CDP, New York	15,286	9,321	0	488	61.0	0.0	5.2	8,833
36	65255	Saratoga Springs city, New York	23,461	14,485	1,062	1,561	61.7	4.5	10.8	12,924
36	65508	Schenectady city, New York	54,357	32,606	34	2,639	60.0	0.1	8.1	29,967
36	67070	Shirley CDP, New York	20,132	11,530	0	633	57.3	0.0	5.5	10,897
36	67851	Smithtown CDP, New York	23,295	15,212	0	441	65.3	0.0	2.9	14,771
36	70420	Spring Valley village, New York	23,411	16,673	0	1,694	71.2	0.0	10.2	14,979
36	72554	Syosset CDP, New York	14,451	8,675	0	43	60.0	0.0	0.5	8,632

Table E. Cities—Labor Force, Employment, and Educational Data, 2015—*Continued*

FIPS state code	FIPS place code	State/city	Total population age 16 and older	Civilian labor force	Armed Forces	Unemployed	Civilian labor force participation (percent)	Percent in Armed Forces	Unemployment rate	Number of employed persons age 16 and older
					Employment status					
36	73000	Syracuse city, New York	116,440	65,151	28	6,275	56.0	0.0	9.6	58,876
36	74183	Tonawanda CDP, New York	45,780	29,242	125	914	63.9	0.3	3.1	28,328
36	75484	Troy city, New York	42,784	26,577	0	2,238	62.1	0.0	8.4	24,339
36	76089	Uniondale CDP, New York	17,317	10,691	0	422	61.7	0.0	3.9	10,269
36	76540	Utica city, New York	46,326	26,115	24	3,657	56.4	0.1	14.0	22,458
36	76705	Valley Stream village, New York	29,431	18,881	0	1,279	64.2	0.0	6.8	17,602
36	78146	Wantagh CDP, New York	17,110	11,381	0	342	66.5	0.0	3.0	11,039
36	78608	Watertown city, New York	21,802	13,597	864	972	62.4	4.0	7.1	12,625
36	79246	West Babylon CDP, New York	34,546	23,076	0	909	66.8	0.0	3.9	22,167
36	80225	West Hempstead CDP, New York	17,618	12,665	0	594	71.9	0.0	4.7	12,071
36	80302	West Islip CDP, New York	21,824	15,146	0	666	69.4	0.0	4.4	14,480
36	80907	West Seneca CDP, New York	39,348	25,769	0	775	65.5	0.0	3.0	24,994
36	81677	White Plains city, New York	46,950	32,035	37	1,773	68.2	0.1	5.5	30,262
36	84000	Yonkers city, New York	161,871	100,583	0	6,065	62.1	0.0	6.0	94,518
37	00000	**NORTH CAROLINA**	8,011,388	4,886,759	75,039	335,787	61.0	0.9	6.9	4,550,972
37	01520	Apex town, North Carolina	33,803	25,502	25	1,460	75.4	0.1	5.7	24,042
37	02080	Asheboro city, North Carolina	19,744	13,137	0	1,201	66.5	0.0	9.1	11,936
37	02140	Asheville city, North Carolina	74,078	48,643	0	1,855	65.7	0.0	3.8	46,788
37	09060	Burlington city, North Carolina	41,836	27,037	0	2,685	64.6	0.0	9.9	24,352
37	10620	Carrboro town, North Carolina	16,069	11,792	0	484	73.4	0.0	4.1	11,308
37	10740	Cary town, North Carolina	125,190	90,668	0	3,217	72.4	0.0	3.5	87,451
37	11800	Chapel Hill town, North Carolina	51,799	33,373	0	1,002	64.4	0.0	3.0	32,371
37	12000	Charlotte city, North Carolina	650,177	463,381	274	34,016	71.3	0.0	7.3	429,365
37	14100	Concord city, North Carolina	65,935	44,787	46	2,630	67.9	0.1	5.9	42,157
37	14700	Cornelius town, North Carolina	22,435	15,660	232	570	69.8	1.0	3.6	15,090
37	19000	Durham city, North Carolina	206,441	144,813	455	7,951	70.1	0.2	5.5	136,862
37	22920	Fayetteville city, North Carolina	157,598	86,329	17,360	9,921	54.8	11.0	11.5	76,408
37	25300	Fuquay-Varina town, North Carolina	16,960	12,162	0	1,039	71.7	0.0	8.5	11,123
37	25480	Garner town, North Carolina	23,241	16,410	0	1,130	70.6	0.0	6.9	15,280
37	25580	Gastonia city, North Carolina	57,990	36,569	25	3,119	63.1	0.0	8.5	33,450
37	26880	Goldsboro city, North Carolina	28,583	15,154	1,305	1,893	53.0	4.6	12.5	13,261
37	28000	Greensboro city, North Carolina	231,341	144,312	164	7,471	62.4	0.1	5.2	136,841
37	28080	Greenville city, North Carolina	74,995	49,750	0	6,812	66.3	0.0	13.7	42,938
37	30120	Havelock city, North Carolina	13,829	6,823	4,584	329	49.3	33.1	4.8	6,494
37	31060	Hickory city, North Carolina	34,545	18,758	0	1,126	54.3	0.0	6.0	17,632
37	31400	High Point city, North Carolina	85,939	52,952	0	5,046	61.6	0.0	9.5	47,906
37	32260	Holly Springs town, North Carolina	22,101	15,732	59	598	71.2	0.3	3.8	15,134
37	33120	Huntersville town, North Carolina	36,766	28,321	0	1,290	77.0	0.0	4.6	27,031
37	33560	Indian Trail town, North Carolina	26,147	18,905	0	660	72.3	0.0	3.5	18,245
37	34200	Jacksonville city, North Carolina	54,151	24,177	17,577	2,657	44.6	32.5	11.0	21,520
37	35200	Kannapolis city, North Carolina	34,369	22,828	0	1,223	66.4	0.0	5.4	21,605
37	35600	Kernersville town, North Carolina	21,392	14,269	0	556	66.7	0.0	3.9	13,713
37	35920	Kinston city, North Carolina	16,555	8,088	0	1,384	48.9	0.0	17.1	6,704
37	39700	Lumberton city, North Carolina	17,795	8,368	0	1,244	47.0	0.0	14.9	7,124
37	41960	Matthews town, North Carolina	25,271	16,669	0	454	66.0	0.0	2.7	16,215
37	43480	Mint Hill town, North Carolina	20,239	11,778	0	753	58.2	0.0	6.4	11,025
37	43920	Monroe city, North Carolina	27,124	18,602	0	1,552	68.6	0.0	8.3	17,050
37	44220	Mooresville town, North Carolina	27,545	18,629	0	1,087	67.6	0.0	5.8	17,542
37	44520	Morrisville town, North Carolina	20,134	15,776	0	642	78.4	0.0	4.1	15,134
37	46340	New Bern city, North Carolina	24,252	13,849	456	1,171	57.1	1.9	8.5	12,678
37	55000	Raleigh city, North Carolina	361,830	250,979	183	12,311	69.4	0.1	4.9	238,668
37	57500	Rocky Mount city, North Carolina	42,083	27,528	0	1,533	65.4	0.0	5.6	25,995
37	58860	Salisbury city, North Carolina	28,971	16,855	68	1,742	58.2	0.2	10.3	15,113
37	59280	Sanford city, North Carolina	21,383	13,222	29	879	61.8	0.1	6.6	12,343
37	61200	Shelby city, North Carolina	15,194	7,660	0	1,113	50.4	0.0	14.5	6,547
37	64740	Statesville city, North Carolina	20,014	12,419	0	1,339	62.1	0.0	10.8	11,080
37	67420	Thomasville city, North Carolina	22,167	12,896	0	979	58.2	0.0	7.6	11,917
37	70540	Wake Forest town, North Carolina	27,745	18,573	75	807	66.9	0.3	4.3	17,766
37	74440	Wilmington city, North Carolina	95,965	59,746	0	5,293	62.3	0.0	8.9	54,453
37	74540	Wilson city, North Carolina	39,615	24,036	112	1,472	60.7	0.3	6.1	22,564
37	75000	Winston-Salem city, North Carolina	188,256	117,148	475	9,606	62.2	0.3	8.2	107,542
38	00000	**NORTH DAKOTA**	603,014	415,475	6,580	10,886	68.9	1.1	2.6	404,589
38	07200	Bismarck city, North Dakota	57,891	40,443	344	828	69.9	0.6	2.0	39,615
38	19620	Dickinson city, North Dakota	19,771	14,609	0	770	73.9	0.0	5.3	13,839
38	25700	Fargo city, North Dakota	97,658	70,823	88	1,813	72.5	0.1	2.6	69,010
38	32060	Grand Forks city, North Dakota	46,947	34,143	57	676	72.7	0.1	2.0	33,467
38	49900	Mandan city, North Dakota	16,003	12,129	0	121	75.8	0.0	1.0	12,008
38	53380	Minot city, North Dakota	38,439	27,014	1,523	849	70.3	4.0	3.1	26,165
38	84780	West Fargo city, North Dakota	25,720	18,913	0	213	73.5	0.0	1.1	18,700
38	86220	Williston city, North Dakota	18,732	14,833	0	592	79.2	0.0	4.0	14,241
39	00000	**OHIO**	9,295,255	5,863,639	6,859	373,897	63.1	0.1	6.4	5,489,742
39	01000	Akron city, Ohio	161,285	99,968	43	8,829	62.0	0.0	8.8	91,139
39	01420	Alliance city, Ohio	18,697	10,438	0	749	55.8	0.0	7.2	9,689
39	02568	Ashland city, Ohio	16,567	10,655	0	527	64.3	0.0	4.9	10,128
39	02736	Athens city, Ohio	23,323	11,702	0	1,447	50.2	0.0	12.4	10,255

Table E. Cities—Labor Force, Employment, and Educational Data, 2015—*Continued*

FIPS state code	FIPS place code	State/city	Total population age 16 and older	Civilian labor force	Armed Forces	Unemployed	Civilian labor force participation (percent)	Percent in Armed Forces	Unemployment rate	Number of employed persons age 16 and older
39	03184	Austintown CDP, Ohio	24,481	14,478	0	1,327	59.1	0.0	9.2	13,151
39	03352	Avon city, Ohio	15,497	10,377	0	558	67.0	0.0	5.4	9,819
39	03464	Avon Lake city, Ohio	19,065	11,631	52	76	61.0	0.3	0.7	11,555
39	03828	Barberton city, Ohio	20,503	11,405	0	871	55.6	0.0	7.6	10,534
39	04720	Beavercreek city, Ohio	36,834	23,478	268	1,168	63.7	0.7	5.0	22,310
39	07454	Boardman CDP, Ohio	28,312	19,135	0	1,350	67.6	0.0	7.1	17,785
39	07972	Bowling Green city, Ohio	28,348	18,959	0	1,466	66.9	0.0	7.7	17,493
39	09680	Brunswick city, Ohio	27,711	18,868	0	549	68.1	0.0	2.9	18,319
39	12000	Canton city, Ohio	54,974	36,811	0	4,628	67.0	0.0	12.6	32,183
39	13190	Centerville city, Ohio	18,692	10,677	0	288	57.1	0.0	2.7	10,389
39	14184	Chillicothe city, Ohio	19,209	10,566	0	352	55.0	0.0	3.3	10,214
39	15000	Cincinnati city, Ohio	241,291	154,426	27	16,199	64.0	0.0	10.5	138,227
39	16000	Cleveland city, Ohio	311,530	180,490	129	31,625	57.9	0.0	17.5	148,865
39	16014	Cleveland Heights city, Ohio	37,305	24,150	0	1,351	64.7	0.0	5.6	22,799
39	18000	Columbus city, Ohio	679,369	476,698	432	31,229	70.2	0.1	6.6	445,469
39	19778	Cuyahoga Falls city, Ohio	39,792	26,391	0	1,127	66.3	0.0	4.3	25,264
39	21000	Dayton city, Ohio	111,929	59,957	210	5,533	53.6	0.2	9.2	54,424
39	21434	Delaware city, Ohio	28,962	18,872	0	606	65.2	0.0	3.2	18,266
39	22694	Dublin city, Ohio	32,238	23,323	0	1,008	72.3	0.0	4.3	22,315
39	25256	Elyria city, Ohio	41,946	24,968	0	3,142	59.5	0.0	12.6	21,826
39	25704	Euclid city, Ohio	38,269	23,941	0	2,168	62.6	0.0	9.1	21,773
39	25914	Fairborn city, Ohio	25,219	16,119	542	1,956	63.9	2.1	12.1	14,163
39	25970	Fairfield city, Ohio	35,186	23,452	0	715	66.7	0.0	3.0	22,737
39	27048	Findlay city, Ohio	33,936	23,233	101	1,114	68.5	0.3	4.8	22,119
39	29106	Gahanna city, Ohio	27,828	18,801	0	1,059	67.6	0.0	5.6	17,742
39	29428	Garfield Heights city, Ohio	22,209	14,878	0	1,869	67.0	0.0	12.6	13,009
39	31860	Green city, Ohio	21,594	14,138	0	501	65.5	0.0	3.5	13,637
39	32592	Grove City city, Ohio	29,886	19,435	0	596	65.0	0.0	3.1	18,839
39	33012	Hamilton city, Ohio	46,460	29,008	0	2,179	62.4	0.0	7.5	26,829
39	35476	Hilliard city, Ohio	25,847	18,695	0	525	72.3	0.0	2.8	18,170
39	36610	Huber Heights city, Ohio	30,043	19,224	129	1,321	64.0	0.4	6.9	17,903
39	36651	Hudson city, Ohio	18,215	12,356	0	726	67.8	0.0	5.9	11,630
39	39872	Kent city, Ohio	25,619	14,640	0	1,060	57.1	0.0	7.2	13,580
39	40040	Kettering city, Ohio	44,054	27,811	193	1,532	63.1	0.4	5.5	26,279
39	41664	Lakewood city, Ohio	42,427	29,850	0	1,166	70.4	0.0	3.9	28,684
39	41720	Lancaster city, Ohio	30,153	18,004	38	1,345	59.7	0.1	7.5	16,659
39	42364	Lebanon city, Ohio	16,082	10,000	0	286	62.2	0.0	2.9	9,714
39	43554	Lima city, Ohio	28,960	17,594	0	1,231	60.8	0.0	7.0	16,363
39	44856	Lorain city, Ohio	47,908	29,412	0	3,328	61.4	0.0	11.3	26,084
39	47138	Mansfield city, Ohio	37,694	18,373	0	1,266	48.7	0.0	6.9	17,107
39	47306	Maple Heights city, Ohio	19,271	11,898	0	1,748	61.7	0.0	14.7	10,150
39	47754	Marion city, Ohio	30,285	13,814	0	1,648	45.6	0.0	11.9	12,166
39	48160	Marysville city, Ohio	17,771	10,292	0	337	57.9	0.0	3.3	9,955
39	48188	Mason city, Ohio	26,046	17,039	0	732	65.4	0.0	4.3	16,307
39	48244	Massillon city, Ohio	25,963	16,184	0	1,219	62.3	0.0	7.5	14,965
39	48790	Medina city, Ohio	20,026	14,181	0	484	70.8	0.0	3.4	13,697
39	49056	Mentor city, Ohio	39,496	27,330	0	1,113	69.2	0.0	4.1	26,217
39	49434	Miamisburg city, Ohio	16,862	10,190	0	522	60.4	0.0	5.1	9,668
39	49840	Middletown city, Ohio	37,182	21,877	0	2,738	58.8	0.0	12.5	19,139
39	54040	Newark city, Ohio	37,586	23,456	22	2,983	62.4	0.1	12.7	20,473
39	56882	North Olmsted city, Ohio	26,704	16,342	0	756	61.2	0.0	4.6	15,586
39	56966	North Ridgeville city, Ohio	26,415	16,950	0	109	64.2	0.0	0.6	16,841
39	57008	North Royalton city, Ohio	24,285	15,909	79	551	65.5	0.3	3.5	15,358
39	58730	Oregon city, Ohio	17,597	11,216	0	748	63.7	0.0	6.7	10,468
39	59234	Oxford city, Ohio	21,414	9,018	0	73	42.1	0.0	0.8	8,945
39	61000	Parma city, Ohio	67,531	45,800	0	3,401	67.8	0.0	7.4	42,399
39	61028	Parma Heights city, Ohio	15,626	10,123	0	948	64.8	0.0	9.4	9,175
39	62148	Perrysburg city, Ohio	18,389	12,234	204	483	66.5	1.1	3.9	11,751
39	62848	Piqua city, Ohio	15,543	9,360	0	1,749	60.2	0.0	18.7	7,611
39	64304	Portsmouth city, Ohio	15,232	7,366	63	1,159	48.4	0.4	15.7	6,207
39	66390	Reynoldsburg city, Ohio	28,932	18,107	60	856	62.6	0.2	4.7	17,251
39	67468	Riverside city, Ohio	18,559	12,199	470	896	65.7	2.5	7.3	11,303
39	68056	Rocky River city, Ohio	15,683	9,899	0	365	63.1	0.0	3.7	9,534
39	70380	Sandusky city, Ohio	19,356	12,430	0	913	64.2	0.0	7.3	11,517
39	71682	Shaker Heights city, Ohio	20,877	14,317	0	597	68.6	0.0	4.2	13,720
39	72424	Sidney city, Ohio	15,995	10,573	0	856	66.1	0.0	8.1	9,717
39	72928	Solon city, Ohio	18,479	11,617	0	319	62.9	0.0	2.7	11,298
39	73264	South Euclid city, Ohio	17,286	11,416	0	544	66.0	0.0	4.8	10,872
39	74118	Springfield city, Ohio	47,941	28,458	0	3,517	59.4	0.0	12.4	24,941
39	74944	Stow city, Ohio	28,838	19,500	0	965	67.6	0.0	4.9	18,535
39	75098	Strongsville city, Ohio	36,942	23,023	0	1,003	62.3	0.0	4.4	22,020
39	77000	Toledo city, Ohio	224,366	138,803	124	13,291	61.9	0.1	9.6	125,512
39	77504	Trotwood city, Ohio	18,677	11,076	30	1,849	59.3	0.2	16.7	9,227
39	77588	Troy city, Ohio	19,487	12,886	84	680	66.1	0.4	5.3	12,206
39	79002	Upper Arlington city, Ohio	26,405	17,831	0	697	67.5	0.0	3.9	17,134
39	80304	Wadsworth city, Ohio	17,556	11,855	0	572	67.5	0.0	4.8	11,283

Table E. Cities—Labor Force, Employment, and Educational Data, 2015—*Continued*

FIPS state code	FIPS place code	State/city	Total population age 16 and older	Employment status						Number of employed persons age 16 and older
				Civilian labor force	Armed Forces	Unemployed	Civilian labor force participation (percent)	Percent in Armed Forces	Unemployment rate	
39	80892	Warren city, Ohio	32,170	16,720	0	1,503	52.0	0.0	9.0	15,217
39	83342	Westerville city, Ohio	31,258	21,074	0	518	67.4	0.0	2.5	20,556
39	83622	Westlake city, Ohio	26,060	16,034	0	499	61.5	0.0	3.1	15,535
39	84812	White Oak CDP, Ohio	16,352	10,808	0	545	66.1	0.0	5.0	10,263
39	85484	Willoughby city, Ohio	18,393	12,386	50	239	67.3	0.3	1.9	12,147
39	86548	Wooster city, Ohio	22,044	12,989	0	673	58.9	0.0	5.2	12,316
39	86772	Xenia city, Ohio	20,235	12,877	42	1,209	63.6	0.2	9.4	11,668
39	88000	Youngstown city, Ohio	51,047	27,718	0	4,321	54.3	0.0	15.6	23,397
39	88084	Zanesville city, Ohio	19,671	10,705	42	1,136	54.4	0.2	10.6	9,569
40	00000	**OKLAHOMA**	3,053,371	1,854,533	18,633	101,088	60.7	0.6	5.5	1,753,445
40	02600	Ardmore city, Oklahoma	19,273	11,653	0	1,064	60.5	0.0	9.1	10,589
40	04450	Bartlesville city, Oklahoma	28,583	16,769	0	1,130	58.7	0.0	6.7	15,639
40	06400	Bixby city, Oklahoma	19,276	12,967	0	513	67.3	0.0	4.0	12,454
40	09050	Broken Arrow city, Oklahoma	81,538	58,848	157	3,268	72.2	0.2	5.6	55,580
40	19900	Del City city, Oklahoma	16,980	9,733	41	738	57.3	0.2	7.6	8,995
40	21900	Duncan city, Oklahoma	18,350	10,630	0	691	57.9	0.0	6.5	9,939
40	23200	Edmond city, Oklahoma	69,266	47,323	297	2,023	68.3	0.4	4.3	45,300
40	23950	Enid city, Oklahoma	38,675	23,730	1,244	1,296	61.4	3.2	5.5	22,434
40	37800	Jenks city, Oklahoma	16,145	12,252	0	289	75.9	0.0	2.4	11,963
40	41850	Lawton city, Oklahoma	75,306	42,572	9,449	2,961	56.5	12.5	7.0	39,611
40	48350	Midwest City city, Oklahoma	43,529	25,423	516	1,227	58.4	1.2	4.8	24,196
40	49200	Moore city, Oklahoma	46,552	33,034	306	1,826	71.0	0.7	5.5	31,208
40	50050	Muskogee city, Oklahoma	29,343	15,431	0	1,149	52.6	0.0	7.4	14,282
40	50100	Mustang city, Oklahoma	16,066	11,523	42	160	71.7	0.3	1.4	11,363
40	52500	Norman city, Oklahoma	99,276	64,809	360	3,011	65.3	0.4	4.6	61,798
40	55000	Oklahoma City city, Oklahoma	481,395	316,256	3,459	13,929	65.7	0.7	4.4	302,327
40	56650	Owasso city, Oklahoma	27,182	19,833	0	649	73.0	0.0	3.3	19,184
40	59850	Ponca City city, Oklahoma	20,290	12,501	0	1,309	61.6	0.0	10.5	11,192
40	65400	Sapulpa city, Oklahoma	16,307	9,661	0	412	59.2	0.0	4.3	9,249
40	66800	Shawnee city, Oklahoma	24,676	14,245	0	1,184	57.7	0.0	8.3	13,061
40	70300	Stillwater city, Oklahoma	42,366	23,501	0	1,289	55.5	0.0	5.5	22,212
40	75000	Tulsa city, Oklahoma	314,313	206,948	204	13,199	65.8	0.1	6.4	193,749
40	82950	Yukon city, Oklahoma	19,537	13,495	0	656	69.1	0.0	4.9	12,839
41	00000	**OREGON**	3,268,296	2,018,994	1,967	137,739	61.8	0.1	6.8	1,881,255
41	01000	Albany city, Oregon	42,705	26,429	0	1,890	61.9	0.0	7.2	24,539
41	01650	Aloha CDP, Oregon	43,217	30,528	0	2,914	70.6	0.0	9.5	27,614
41	03050	Ashland city, Oregon	16,022	9,489	0	662	59.2	0.0	7.0	8,827
41	05350	Beaverton city, Oregon	78,416	54,418	0	4,260	69.4	0.0	7.8	50,158
41	05800	Bend city, Oregon	69,031	46,305	0	3,248	67.1	0.0	7.0	43,057
41	05950	Bethany CDP, Oregon	15,176	10,101	0	753	66.6	0.0	7.5	9,348
41	15800	Corvallis city, Oregon	48,356	29,441	52	2,159	60.9	0.1	7.3	27,282
41	23850	Eugene city, Oregon	137,345	83,558	0	6,183	60.8	0.0	7.4	77,375
41	26200	Forest Grove city, Oregon	18,066	11,074	0	574	61.3	0.0	5.2	10,500
41	30550	Grants Pass city, Oregon	29,799	16,425	0	1,080	55.1	0.0	6.6	15,345
41	31250	Gresham city, Oregon	87,167	58,085	0	4,113	66.6	0.0	7.1	53,972
41	32850	Hayesville CDP, Oregon	16,054	10,049	0	1,254	62.6	0.0	12.5	8,795
41	34100	Hillsboro city, Oregon	79,687	53,831	0	3,663	67.6	0.0	6.8	50,168
41	38500	Keizer city, Oregon	27,685	17,294	82	1,278	62.5	0.3	7.4	16,016
41	39700	Klamath Falls city, Oregon	18,156	11,193	47	1,160	61.6	0.3	10.4	10,033
41	40550	Lake Oswego city, Oregon	32,595	20,987	0	745	64.4	0.0	3.5	20,242
41	45000	McMinnville city, Oregon	26,784	16,379	0	752	61.2	0.0	4.6	15,627
41	47000	Medford city, Oregon	63,365	37,231	0	2,933	58.8	0.0	7.9	34,298
41	48650	Milwaukie city, Oregon	16,715	10,037	0	499	60.0	0.0	5.0	9,538
41	52100	Newberg city, Oregon	17,015	10,989	0	234	64.6	0.0	2.1	10,755
41	55200	Oregon City city, Oregon	28,376	19,723	43	1,324	69.5	0.2	6.7	18,399
41	59000	Portland city, Oregon	526,781	366,610	170	23,672	69.6	0.0	6.5	342,938
41	61200	Redmond city, Oregon	21,400	12,185	0	443	56.9	0.0	3.6	11,742
41	63650	Roseburg city, Oregon	16,334	7,970	0	728	48.8	0.0	9.1	7,242
41	64900	Salem city, Oregon	129,839	80,179	0	4,716	61.8	0.0	5.9	75,463
41	69600	Springfield city, Oregon	48,224	31,950	0	2,653	66.3	0.0	8.3	29,297
41	73650	Tigard city, Oregon	41,325	28,251	0	1,883	68.4	0.0	6.7	26,368
41	74950	Tualatin city, Oregon	20,310	13,790	0	776	67.9	0.0	5.6	13,014
41	80150	West Linn city, Oregon	20,401	14,191	0	885	69.6	0.0	6.2	13,306
41	82800	Wilsonville city, Oregon	19,650	12,917	0	269	65.7	0.0	2.1	12,648
41	83750	Woodburn city, Oregon	17,748	11,070	0	301	62.4	0.0	2.7	10,769
42	00000	**PENNSYLVANIA**	10,429,005	6,518,212	3,330	408,542	62.5	0.0	6.3	6,109,670
42	02000	Allentown city, Pennsylvania	92,969	58,463	54	6,076	62.9	0.1	10.4	52,387
42	02056	Allison Park CDP, Pennsylvania	20,626	13,147	0	455	63.7	0.0	3.5	12,692
42	02184	Altoona city, Pennsylvania	37,421	21,713	0	1,326	58.0	0.0	6.1	20,387
42	06064	Bethel Park municipality, Pennsylvania	25,676	17,267	0	570	67.2	0.0	3.3	16,697
42	06088	Bethlehem city, Pennsylvania	61,586	37,444	0	1,738	60.8	0.0	4.6	35,706
42	12536	Chambersburg borough, Pennsylvania	16,901	10,574	0	714	62.6	0.0	6.8	9,860
42	13208	Chester city, Pennsylvania	27,723	14,200	0	1,690	51.2	0.0	11.9	12,510
42	19920	Drexel Hill CDP, Pennsylvania	21,968	15,354	0	930	69.9	0.0	6.1	14,424
42	21648	Easton city, Pennsylvania	21,740	12,076	0	552	55.5	0.0	4.6	11,524
42	24000	Erie city, Pennsylvania	79,084	47,728	0	3,434	60.4	0.0	7.2	44,294

Table E. Cities—Labor Force, Employment, and Educational Data, 2015—*Continued*

FIPS state code	FIPS place code	State/city	Total population age 16 and older	Civilian labor force	Armed Forces	Unemployed	Civilian labor force participation (percent)	Percent in Armed Forces	Unemployment rate	Number of employed persons age 16 and older
								Employment status		
42	32800	Harrisburg city, Pennsylvania	39,780	25,884	0	3,169	65.1	0.0	12.2	22,715
42	33408	Hazleton city, Pennsylvania	20,267	13,146	0	1,000	64.9	0.0	7.6	12,146
42	38288	Johnstown city, Pennsylvania	14,450	6,976	0	1,581	48.3	0.0	22.7	5,395
42	41216	Lancaster city, Pennsylvania	47,358	29,708	0	2,345	62.7	0.0	7.9	27,363
42	42168	Lebanon city, Pennsylvania	19,802	11,994	0	663	60.6	0.0	5.5	11,331
42	42928	Levittown CDP, Pennsylvania	38,694	27,129	0	2,219	70.1	0.0	8.2	24,910
42	50528	Monroeville municipality, Pennsylvania	23,763	14,720	0	551	61.9	0.0	3.7	14,169
42	52432	Murrysville municipality, Pennsylvania	16,009	10,364	0	373	64.7	0.0	3.6	9,991
42	53368	New Castle city, Pennsylvania	20,294	11,469	0	1,201	56.5	0.0	10.5	10,268
42	54656	Norristown borough, Pennsylvania	25,694	16,723	0	1,815	65.1	0.0	10.9	14,908
42	60000	Philadelphia city, Pennsylvania	1,256,533	759,379	126	83,008	60.4	0.0	10.9	676,371
42	61000	Pittsburgh city, Pennsylvania	263,136	161,552	0	11,330	61.4	0.0	7.0	150,222
42	61536	Plum borough, Pennsylvania	23,167	15,064	0	769	65.0	0.0	5.1	14,295
42	62416	Pottstown borough, Pennsylvania	19,563	12,877	50	1,864	65.8	0.3	14.5	11,013
42	63624	Reading city, Pennsylvania	64,458	41,748	0	8,133	64.8	0.0	19.5	33,615
42	69000	Scranton city, Pennsylvania	63,852	35,861	0	2,291	56.2	0.0	6.4	33,570
42	73808	State College borough, Pennsylvania	40,073	18,651	0	946	46.5	0.0	5.1	17,705
42	79277	Upper St. Clair CDP, Pennsylvania	14,846	8,854	0	259	59.6	0.0	2.9	8,595
42	83512	West Mifflin borough, Pennsylvania	15,304	9,596	0	660	62.7	0.0	6.9	8,936
42	85152	Wilkes-Barre city, Pennsylvania	32,079	17,867	18	2,979	55.7	0.1	16.7	14,888
42	85312	Williamsport city, Pennsylvania	24,521	16,385	0	489	66.8	0.0	3.0	15,896
42	87048	York city, Pennsylvania	33,140	20,679	93	2,433	62.4	0.3	11.8	18,246
44	00000	**RHODE ISLAND**	870,136	559,733	2,468	34,758	64.3	0.3	6.2	524,975
44	19180	Cranston city, Rhode Island	66,605	41,484	0	3,049	62.3	0.0	7.3	38,435
44	22960	East Providence city, Rhode Island	39,625	22,853	0	1,015	57.7	0.0	4.4	21,838
44	49960	Newport city, Rhode Island	21,475	13,032	1,528	373	60.7	7.1	2.9	12,659
44	54640	Pawtucket city, Rhode Island	58,745	39,085	216	2,829	66.5	0.4	7.2	36,256
44	59000	Providence city, Rhode Island	142,557	86,573	77	7,986	60.7	0.1	9.2	78,587
44	74300	Warwick city, Rhode Island	68,534	47,119	43	2,941	68.8	0.1	6.2	44,178
44	76820	Westerly CDP, Rhode Island	17,105	10,809	0	771	63.2	0.0	7.1	10,038
44	80780	Woonsocket city, Rhode Island	34,392	19,318	0	1,054	56.2	0.0	5.5	18,264
45	00000	**SOUTH CAROLINA**	3,931,185	2,336,291	28,004	170,589	59.4	0.7	7.3	2,165,702
45	00550	Aiken city, South Carolina	26,633	13,618	118	579	51.1	0.4	4.3	13,039
45	01360	Anderson city, South Carolina	21,684	11,814	69	796	54.5	0.3	6.7	11,018
45	13330	Charleston city, South Carolina	116,139	79,256	263	3,550	68.2	0.2	4.5	75,706
45	16000	Columbia city, South Carolina	113,365	65,443	8,864	6,015	57.7	7.8	9.2	59,428
45	16405	Conway city, South Carolina	14,822	8,192	0	674	55.3	0.0	8.2	7,518
45	21985	Easley city, South Carolina	16,005	9,933	0	395	62.1	0.0	4.0	9,538
45	25810	Florence city, South Carolina	30,459	19,476	0	1,499	63.9	0.0	7.7	17,977
45	29815	Goose Creek city, South Carolina	31,965	18,466	3,412	1,295	57.8	10.7	7.0	17,171
45	30850	Greenville city, South Carolina	52,373	36,510	66	2,341	69.7	0.1	6.4	34,169
45	30895	Greenwood city, South Carolina	18,353	11,235	0	1,193	61.2	0.0	10.6	10,042
45	30985	Greer city, South Carolina	24,844	17,427	0	1,135	70.1	0.0	6.5	16,292
45	32065	Hanahan city, South Carolina	18,215	12,796	33	489	70.2	0.2	3.8	12,307
45	34045	Hilton Head Island town, South Carolina	33,623	16,848	0	1,122	50.1	0.0	6.7	15,726
45	41335	Lexington town, South Carolina	16,330	9,376	81	343	57.4	0.5	3.7	9,033
45	45115	Mauldin city, South Carolina	19,187	13,719	0	753	71.5	0.0	5.5	12,966
45	48535	Mount Pleasant town, South Carolina	62,892	42,121	142	1,385	67.0	0.2	3.3	40,736
45	49075	Myrtle Beach city, South Carolina	25,368	16,106	122	1,303	63.5	0.5	8.1	14,803
45	50695	North Augusta city, South Carolina	16,973	11,149	0	1,132	65.7	0.0	10.2	10,017
45	50875	North Charleston city, South Carolina	86,280	54,403	2,949	3,638	63.1	3.4	6.7	50,765
45	61405	Rock Hill city, South Carolina	57,025	38,416	0	2,736	67.4	0.0	7.1	35,680
45	62395	St. Andrews CDP, South Carolina	20,019	14,641	37	1,452	73.1	0.2	9.9	13,189
45	66580	Simpsonville city, South Carolina	13,051	10,149	0	732	77.8	0.0	7.2	9,417
45	67390	Socastee CDP, South Carolina	19,313	11,678	0	356	60.5	0.0	3.0	11,322
45	68290	Spartanburg city, South Carolina	29,628	17,624	51	1,366	59.5	0.2	7.8	16,258
45	70270	Summerville town, South Carolina	38,437	23,455	371	507	61.0	1.0	2.2	22,948
45	70405	Sumter city, South Carolina	31,669	18,134	1,389	1,314	57.3	4.4	7.2	16,820
45	71395	Taylors CDP, South Carolina	16,046	10,327	0	236	64.4	0.0	2.3	10,091
45	73870	Wade Hampton CDP, South Carolina	19,833	10,928	0	350	55.1	0.0	3.2	10,578
46	00000	**SOUTH DAKOTA**	671,301	454,996	2,363	18,144	67.8	0.4	4.0	436,852
46	00100	Aberdeen city, South Dakota	22,285	15,521	0	669	69.6	0.0	4.3	14,852
46	07580	Brookings city, South Dakota	19,376	14,817	0	545	76.5	0.0	3.7	14,272
46	52980	Rapid City city, South Dakota	58,965	37,731	609	1,878	64.0	1.0	5.0	35,853
46	59020	Sioux Falls city, South Dakota	133,671	95,777	124	3,964	71.7	0.1	4.1	91,813
46	69300	Watertown city, South Dakota	18,823	13,253	0	417	70.4	0.0	3.1	12,836
47	00000	**TENNESSEE**	5,277,935	3,198,285	19,179	199,471	60.6	0.4	6.2	2,998,814
47	03440	Bartlett city, Tennessee	47,432	31,600	380	829	66.6	0.8	2.6	30,771
47	08280	Brentwood city, Tennessee	30,775	19,276	0	572	62.6	0.0	3.0	18,704
47	08540	Bristol city, Tennessee	21,457	12,591	0	704	58.7	0.0	5.6	11,887
47	14000	Chattanooga city, Tennessee	142,873	86,658	73	7,594	60.7	0.1	8.8	79,064
47	15160	Clarksville city, Tennessee	113,240	64,499	12,036	4,628	57.0	10.6	7.2	59,871
47	15400	Cleveland city, Tennessee	36,160	21,468	30	1,841	59.4	0.1	8.6	19,627

Table E. Cities—Labor Force, Employment, and Educational Data, 2015—*Continued*

FIPS state code	FIPS place code	State/city	Total population age 16 and older	Civilian labor force	Armed Forces	Unemployed	Civilian labor force participation (percent)	Percent in Armed Forces	Unemployment rate	Number of employed persons age 16 and older
47	16420	Collierville town, Tennessee	37,770	25,379	134	711	67.2	0.4	2.8	24,668
47	16540	Columbia city, Tennessee	28,416	16,275	0	1,118	57.3	0.0	6.9	15,157
47	16920	Cookeville city, Tennessee	26,750	13,830	0	662	51.7	0.0	4.8	13,168
47	22720	East Ridge city, Tennessee	17,988	11,657	48	504	64.8	0.3	4.3	11,153
47	25760	Farragut town, Tennessee	17,306	9,716	0	228	56.1	0.0	2.3	9,488
47	27740	Franklin city, Tennessee	55,031	39,653	0	1,840	72.1	0.0	4.6	37,813
47	28540	Gallatin city, Tennessee	28,069	16,693	53	669	59.5	0.2	4.0	16,024
47	28960	Germantown city, Tennessee	30,977	18,801	0	1,153	60.7	0.0	6.1	17,648
47	33280	Hendersonville city, Tennessee	45,059	31,437	82	1,516	69.8	0.2	4.8	29,921
47	37640	Jackson city, Tennessee	52,675	33,521	0	1,601	63.6	0.0	4.8	31,920
47	38320	Johnson City city, Tennessee	55,201	31,533	35	2,181	57.1	0.1	6.9	29,352
47	39560	Kingsport city, Tennessee	43,198	22,350	0	1,647	51.7	0.0	7.4	20,703
47	40000	Knoxville city, Tennessee	155,409	103,147	39	6,690	66.4	0.0	6.5	96,457
47	41200	La Vergne city, Tennessee	23,830	17,114	0	753	71.8	0.0	4.4	16,361
47	41520	Lebanon city, Tennessee	23,357	14,983	0	1,023	64.1	0.0	6.8	13,960
47	46380	Maryville city, Tennessee	22,019	12,751	0	599	57.9	0.0	4.7	12,152
47	48000	Memphis city, Tennessee	508,945	323,789	306	32,849	63.6	0.1	10.1	290,940
47	50280	Morristown city, Tennessee	22,784	13,312	0	957	58.4	0.0	7.2	12,355
47	50780	Mount Juliet city, Tennessee	23,465	15,950	54	1,010	68.0	0.2	6.3	14,940
47	51560	Murfreesboro city, Tennessee	101,121	71,373	0	5,116	70.6	0.0	7.2	66,257
47	52006	Nashville-Davidson metropolitan government (balance), Tennessee	526,116	370,308	627	18,239	70.4	0.1	4.9	352,069
47	55120	Oak Ridge city, Tennessee	24,637	15,281	0	1,079	62.0	0.0	7.1	14,202
47	67760	Shelbyville city, Tennessee	15,430	9,407	0	1,106	61.0	0.0	11.8	8,301
47	69420	Smyrna town, Tennessee	36,126	26,736	0	763	74.0	0.0	2.9	25,973
47	70580	Spring Hill city, Tennessee	26,189	19,457	0	873	74.3	0.0	4.5	18,584
48	00000	**TEXAS**	21,043,248	13,437,133	96,422	743,232	63.9	0.5	5.5	12,693,901
48	01000	Abilene city, Texas	99,648	57,250	4,010	2,703	57.5	4.0	4.7	54,547
48	01924	Allen city, Texas	73,187	54,288	0	2,760	74.2	0.0	5.1	51,528
48	02272	Alvin city, Texas	18,881	12,359	0	1,347	65.5	0.0	10.9	11,012
48	03000	Amarillo city, Texas	149,225	101,784	283	3,799	68.2	0.2	3.7	97,985
48	04000	Arlington city, Texas	299,334	204,173	101	8,815	68.2	0.0	4.3	195,358
48	04462	Atascocita CDP, Texas	57,672	36,979	207	1,166	64.1	0.4	3.2	35,813
48	05000	Austin city, Texas	754,228	553,250	101	23,076	73.4	0.0	4.2	530,174
48	05372	Balch Springs city, Texas	16,777	10,821	0	424	64.5	0.0	3.9	10,397
48	06128	Baytown city, Texas	58,323	39,445	0	4,016	67.6	0.0	10.2	35,429
48	07000	Beaumont city, Texas	89,764	54,481	32	2,319	60.7	0.0	4.3	52,162
48	07132	Bedford city, Texas	39,527	28,500	0	868	72.1	0.0	3.0	27,632
48	07492	Belton city, Texas	18,404	11,280	185	619	61.3	1.0	5.5	10,661
48	07552	Benbrook city, Texas	19,965	13,404	0	699	67.1	0.0	5.2	12,705
48	08236	Big Spring city, Texas	22,680	11,018	0	870	48.6	0.0	7.9	10,148
48	10768	Brownsville city, Texas	131,852	73,619	0	4,408	55.8	0.0	6.0	69,211
48	10897	Brushy Creek CDP, Texas	15,003	11,002	0	153	73.3	0.0	1.4	10,849
48	10912	Bryan city, Texas	64,829	41,565	0	1,386	64.1	0.0	3.3	40,179
48	11428	Burleson city, Texas	32,802	20,690	40	640	63.1	0.1	3.1	20,050
48	12580	Canyon Lake CDP, Texas	19,132	11,398	0	499	59.6	0.0	4.4	10,899
48	13024	Carrollton city, Texas	104,102	74,203	0	2,224	71.3	0.0	3.0	71,979
48	13492	Cedar Hill city, Texas	36,210	23,696	0	1,520	65.4	0.0	6.4	22,176
48	13552	Cedar Park city, Texas	45,142	34,088	0	1,274	75.5	0.0	3.7	32,814
48	14236	Channelview CDP, Texas	32,332	20,791	0	2,090	64.3	0.0	10.1	18,701
48	14920	Cibolo city, Texas	19,727	12,723	152	458	64.5	0.8	3.6	12,265
48	15364	Cleburne city, Texas	23,226	12,927	0	366	55.7	0.0	2.8	12,561
48	15628	Cloverleaf CDP, Texas	18,109	10,710	0	218	59.1	0.0	2.0	10,492
48	15976	College Station city, Texas	91,765	55,415	47	1,155	60.4	0.1	2.1	54,260
48	15988	Colleyville city, Texas	21,494	13,506	0	0	62.8	0.0	0.0	13,506
48	16432	Conroe city, Texas	52,574	35,785	0	2,480	68.1	0.0	6.9	33,305
48	16468	Converse city, Texas	14,016	8,525	35	278	60.8	0.2	3.3	8,247
48	16612	Coppell city, Texas	30,393	21,330	0	490	70.2	0.0	2.3	20,840
48	16624	Copperas Cove city, Texas	25,239	15,325	2,017	1,525	60.7	8.0	10.0	13,800
48	16696	Corinth city, Texas	18,369	14,888	0	296	81.0	0.0	2.0	14,592
48	17000	Corpus Christi city, Texas	253,798	161,216	1,169	9,099	63.5	0.5	5.6	152,117
48	17060	Corsicana city, Texas	17,773	11,455	0	856	64.5	0.0	7.5	10,599
48	19000	Dallas city, Texas	994,203	670,599	567	34,773	67.5	0.1	5.2	635,826
48	19624	Deer Park city, Texas	25,672	17,741	0	1,383	69.1	0.0	7.8	16,358
48	19792	Del Rio city, Texas	26,977	14,665	181	1,760	54.4	0.7	12.0	12,905
48	19900	Denison city, Texas	19,108	11,301	0	550	59.1	0.0	4.9	10,751
48	19972	Denton city, Texas	108,003	71,303	0	4,820	66.0	0.0	6.8	66,483
48	20092	DeSoto city, Texas	40,982	29,219	0	1,016	71.3	0.0	3.5	28,203
48	21628	Duncanville city, Texas	29,734	19,205	0	1,461	64.6	0.0	7.6	17,744
48	21892	Eagle Pass city, Texas	20,931	11,552	0	1,452	55.2	0.0	12.6	10,100
48	22660	Edinburg city, Texas	60,476	39,530	151	3,631	65.4	0.2	9.2	35,899
48	24000	El Paso city, Texas	518,349	307,821	13,322	19,536	59.4	2.6	6.3	288,285
48	24768	Euless city, Texas	41,418	31,123	0	994	75.1	0.0	3.2	30,129
48	25452	Farmers Branch city, Texas	26,308	20,012	0	640	76.1	0.0	3.2	19,372
48	26232	Flower Mound town, Texas	54,333	39,666	0	1,944	73.0	0.0	4.9	37,722
48	26736	Fort Hood CDP, Texas	23,180	5,547	13,637	502	23.9	58.8	9.0	5,045
48	27000	Fort Worth city, Texas	624,965	418,621	1,381	24,257	67.0	0.2	5.8	394,364

Table E. Cities—Labor Force, Employment, and Educational Data, 2015—*Continued*

FIPS state code	FIPS place code	State/city	Total population age 16 and older	Employment status						Number of employed persons age 16 and older
				Civilian labor force	Armed Forces	Unemployed	Civilian labor force participation (percent)	Percent in Armed Forces	Unemployment rate	
48	27540	Fresno CDP, Texas	14,981	10,680	0	222	71.3	0.0	2.1	10,458
48	27648	Friendswood city, Texas	29,397	19,994	61	597	68.0	0.2	3.0	19,397
48	27684	Frisco city, Texas	110,136	78,343	484	3,064	71.1	0.4	3.9	75,279
48	28068	Galveston city, Texas	42,012	24,847	146	1,864	59.1	0.3	7.5	22,983
48	29000	Garland city, Texas	178,968	126,312	0	6,455	70.6	0.0	5.1	119,857
48	29336	Georgetown city, Texas	53,570	27,777	224	1,930	51.9	0.4	6.9	25,847
48	30464	Grand Prairie city, Texas	142,048	103,252	34	6,624	72.7	0.0	6.4	96,628
48	30644	Grapevine city, Texas	40,903	30,820	0	974	75.3	0.0	3.2	29,846
48	30920	Greenville city, Texas	18,849	11,924	0	670	63.3	0.0	5.6	11,254
48	31928	Haltom City city, Texas	32,081	22,445	0	1,159	70.0	0.0	5.2	21,286
48	32312	Harker Heights city, Texas	22,050	9,838	1,748	1,368	44.6	7.9	13.9	8,470
48	32372	Harlingen city, Texas	46,288	26,421	0	1,939	57.1	0.0	7.3	24,482
48	35000	Houston city, Texas	1,771,334	1,205,150	1,170	71,115	68.0	0.1	5.9	1,134,035
48	35528	Huntsville city, Texas	36,150	16,117	0	135	44.6	0.0	0.8	15,982
48	35576	Hurst city, Texas	30,288	20,933	0	989	69.1	0.0	4.7	19,944
48	35624	Hutto city, Texas	13,787	10,720	95	808	77.8	0.7	7.5	9,912
48	37000	Irving city, Texas	178,158	131,560	65	6,301	73.8	0.0	4.8	125,259
48	38632	Keller city, Texas	33,651	21,989	0	786	65.3	0.0	3.6	21,203
48	39040	Kerrville city, Texas	19,335	9,906	0	439	51.2	0.0	4.4	9,467
48	39148	Killeen city, Texas	100,960	58,172	11,015	6,999	57.6	10.9	12.0	51,173
48	39352	Kingsville city, Texas	17,557	11,072	308	1,594	63.1	1.8	14.4	9,478
48	39952	Kyle city, Texas	25,762	19,211	99	1,096	74.6	0.4	5.7	18,115
48	40588	Lake Jackson city, Texas	21,412	15,197	0	1,025	71.0	0.0	6.7	14,172
48	41212	Lancaster city, Texas	28,559	21,003	0	1,401	73.5	0.0	6.7	19,602
48	41440	La Porte city, Texas	28,248	18,470	56	1,180	65.4	0.2	6.4	17,290
48	41464	Laredo city, Texas	180,657	108,430	0	6,090	60.0	0.0	5.6	102,340
48	41980	League City city, Texas	77,695	55,225	512	3,100	71.1	0.7	5.6	52,125
48	42016	Leander city, Texas	26,882	19,796	84	696	73.6	0.3	3.5	19,100
48	42508	Lewisville city, Texas	79,428	59,874	68	2,703	75.4	0.1	4.5	57,171
48	43012	Little Elm city, Texas	27,641	22,737	0	1,722	82.3	0.0	7.6	21,015
48	43888	Longview city, Texas	63,783	39,330	0	2,585	61.7	0.0	6.6	36,745
48	45000	Lubbock city, Texas	195,687	124,423	0	5,280	63.6	0.0	4.2	119,143
48	45072	Lufkin city, Texas	26,732	14,466	0	1,746	54.1	0.0	12.1	12,720
48	45384	McAllen city, Texas	105,042	63,522	195	6,840	60.5	0.2	10.8	56,682
48	45744	McKinney city, Texas	120,573	81,585	67	2,923	67.7	0.1	3.6	78,662
48	46452	Mansfield city, Texas	50,257	35,799	0	1,374	71.2	0.0	3.8	34,425
48	46776	Marshall city, Texas	19,046	9,979	129	588	52.4	0.7	5.9	9,391
48	47892	Mesquite city, Texas	109,765	73,375	68	5,560	66.8	0.1	7.6	67,815
48	48072	Midland city, Texas	100,572	72,019	0	3,363	71.6	0.0	4.7	68,656
48	48096	Midlothian city, Texas	16,098	11,355	0	323	70.5	0.0	2.8	11,032
48	48768	Mission city, Texas	58,640	33,406	228	2,945	57.0	0.4	8.8	30,461
48	48772	Mission Bend CDP, Texas	26,388	18,267	0	382	69.2	0.0	2.1	17,885
48	48804	Missouri City city, Texas	56,891	40,536	0	2,043	71.3	0.0	5.0	38,493
48	50100	Murphy city, Texas	18,577	12,735	0	822	68.6	0.0	6.5	11,913
48	50256	Nacogdoches city, Texas	27,943	17,292	0	2,107	61.9	0.0	12.2	15,185
48	50820	New Braunfels city, Texas	54,113	35,215	62	1,352	65.1	0.1	3.8	33,863
48	52356	North Richland Hills city, Texas	54,385	36,759	0	2,373	67.6	0.0	6.5	34,386
48	53388	Odessa city, Texas	88,459	60,412	77	2,954	68.3	0.1	4.9	57,458
48	55080	Paris city, Texas	18,819	9,679	0	545	51.4	0.0	5.6	9,134
48	56000	Pasadena city, Texas	111,303	71,376	209	5,293	64.1	0.2	7.4	66,083
48	56348	Pearland city, Texas	82,756	62,159	149	2,161	75.1	0.2	3.5	59,998
48	57176	Pflugerville city, Texas	43,074	31,000	0	1,977	72.0	0.0	6.4	29,023
48	57200	Pharr city, Texas	50,173	27,990	0	1,967	55.8	0.0	7.0	26,023
48	57980	Plainview city, Texas	15,557	9,457	0	497	60.8	0.0	5.3	8,960
48	58016	Plano city, Texas	225,838	157,582	98	5,604	69.8	0.0	3.6	151,978
48	58820	Port Arthur city, Texas	41,854	23,845	15	1,984	57.0	0.0	8.3	21,861
48	61796	Richardson city, Texas	88,211	58,986	49	2,174	66.9	0.1	3.7	56,812
48	62828	Rockwall city, Texas	32,734	22,105	0	927	67.5	0.0	4.2	21,178
48	63284	Rosenberg city, Texas	25,377	16,556	0	799	65.2	0.0	4.8	15,757
48	63500	Round Rock city, Texas	88,919	65,837	86	3,365	74.0	0.1	5.1	62,472
48	63572	Rowlett city, Texas	44,993	33,947	0	989	75.4	0.0	2.9	32,958
48	64064	Sachse city, Texas	15,765	11,064	0	609	70.2	0.0	5.5	10,455
48	64112	Saginaw city, Texas	15,847	9,868	0	766	62.3	0.0	7.8	9,102
48	64472	San Angelo city, Texas	78,897	44,745	3,452	1,234	56.7	4.4	2.8	43,511
48	65000	San Antonio city, Texas	1,138,854	713,824	7,615	43,240	62.7	0.7	6.1	670,584
48	65036	San Benito city, Texas	17,524	8,641	0	1,231	49.3	0.0	14.2	7,410
48	65516	San Juan city, Texas	24,895	14,155	0	1,165	56.9	0.0	8.2	12,990
48	65600	San Marcos city, Texas	53,664	35,418	82	2,223	66.0	0.2	6.3	33,195
48	66128	Schertz city, Texas	29,167	17,818	535	447	61.1	1.8	2.5	17,371
48	66644	Seguin city, Texas	21,648	12,818	0	268	59.2	0.0	2.1	12,550
48	67496	Sherman city, Texas	31,164	19,781	249	1,565	63.5	0.8	7.9	18,216
48	68636	Socorro city, Texas	24,874	13,785	0	659	55.4	0.0	4.8	13,126
48	69032	Southlake city, Texas	21,026	12,927	0	292	61.5	0.0	2.3	12,635
48	69596	Spring CDP, Texas	42,806	32,175	0	720	75.2	0.0	2.2	31,455
48	70208	Stephenville city, Texas	17,485	12,249	0	411	70.1	0.0	3.4	11,838
48	70808	Sugar Land city, Texas	72,007	46,896	0	1,419	65.1	0.0	3.0	45,477

Table E. Cities—Labor Force, Employment, and Educational Data, 2015—*Continued*

FIPS state code	FIPS place code	State/city	Total population age 16 and older	Civilian labor force	Armed Forces	Unemployed	Civilian labor force participation (percent)	Percent in Armed Forces	Unemployment rate	Number of employed persons age 16 and older
							Employment status			
48	72176	Temple city, Texas	54,436	34,922	436	1,677	64.2	0.8	4.8	33,245
48	72368	Texarkana city, Texas	27,087	15,927	0	1,985	58.8	0.0	12.5	13,942
48	72392	Texas City city, Texas	36,388	21,871	219	1,228	60.1	0.6	5.6	20,643
48	72530	The Colony city, Texas	33,914	27,416	0	552	80.8	0.0	2.0	26,864
48	72656	The Woodlands CDP, Texas	87,972	54,543	60	1,792	62.0	0.1	3.3	52,751
48	73057	Timberwood Park CDP, Texas	21,126	13,556	120	1,019	64.2	0.6	7.5	12,537
48	74144	Tyler city, Texas	82,549	50,055	51	2,085	60.6	0.1	4.2	47,970
48	74492	University Park city, Texas	17,861	10,802	0	79	60.5	0.0	0.7	10,723
48	75428	Victoria city, Texas	52,394	34,263	72	2,538	65.4	0.1	7.4	31,725
48	76000	Waco city, Texas	103,417	60,333	78	3,929	58.3	0.1	6.5	56,404
48	76672	Watauga city, Texas	19,728	14,621	0	715	74.1	0.0	4.9	13,906
48	76816	Waxahachie city, Texas	25,888	17,667	47	476	68.2	0.2	2.7	17,191
48	76864	Weatherford city, Texas	22,124	13,956	0	925	63.1	0.0	6.6	13,031
48	77272	Weslaco city, Texas	25,581	14,440	0	777	56.4	0.0	5.4	13,663
48	77728	West Odessa CDP, Texas	19,263	12,372	0	1,097	64.2	0.0	8.9	11,275
48	79000	Wichita Falls city, Texas	84,821	45,034	5,246	2,193	53.1	6.2	4.9	42,841
48	80356	Wylie city, Texas	35,812	25,433	0	870	71.0	0.0	3.4	24,563
49	00000	**UTAH**	2,180,281	1,472,535	2,978	58,198	67.5	0.1	4.0	1,414,337
49	01310	American Fork city, Utah	20,053	12,698	0	454	63.3	0.0	3.6	12,244
49	07690	Bountiful city, Utah	33,218	20,116	0	92	60.6	0.0	0.5	20,024
49	11320	Cedar City city, Utah	21,810	13,650	0	370	62.6	0.0	2.7	13,280
49	13850	Clearfield city, Utah	20,453	13,074	487	348	63.9	2.4	2.7	12,726
49	14290	Clinton city, Utah	13,449	10,063	68	295	74.8	0.5	2.9	9,768
49	16270	Cottonwood Heights city, Utah	27,159	19,016	95	716	70.0	0.3	3.8	18,300
49	20120	Draper city, Utah	33,024	21,400	0	1,002	64.8	0.0	4.7	20,398
49	20810	Eagle Mountain city, Utah	16,426	11,929	0	261	72.6	0.0	2.2	11,668
49	24740	Farmington city, Utah	16,944	11,697	0	422	69.0	0.0	3.6	11,275
49	34970	Herriman city, Utah	19,029	12,889	0	758	67.7	0.0	5.9	12,131
49	36070	Holladay city, Utah	22,940	15,253	0	500	66.5	0.0	3.3	14,753
49	40360	Kaysville city, Utah	19,544	13,785	0	275	70.5	0.0	2.0	13,510
49	40470	Kearns CDP, Utah	30,681	20,885	0	885	68.1	0.0	4.2	20,000
49	43660	Layton city, Utah	53,114	38,102	387	2,157	71.7	0.7	5.7	35,945
49	44320	Lehi city, Utah	33,686	23,193	163	363	68.9	0.5	1.6	22,830
49	45860	Logan city, Utah	39,198	25,992	0	687	66.3	0.0	2.6	25,305
49	47290	Magna CDP, Utah	20,578	14,990	0	539	72.8	0.0	3.6	14,451
49	49710	Midvale city, Utah	22,716	17,796	0	640	78.3	0.0	3.6	17,156
49	50150	Millcreek CDP, Utah	47,656	32,942	48	1,339	69.1	0.1	4.1	31,603
49	53230	Murray city, Utah	39,968	28,043	0	445	70.2	0.0	1.6	27,598
49	55980	Ogden city, Utah	64,802	42,444	153	2,746	65.5	0.2	6.5	39,698
49	57300	Orem city, Utah	68,793	45,873	0	1,897	66.7	0.0	4.1	43,976
49	60930	Pleasant Grove city, Utah	25,994	17,396	0	418	66.9	0.0	2.4	16,978
49	62470	Provo city, Utah	91,153	64,112	0	2,837	70.3	0.0	4.4	61,275
49	64340	Riverton city, Utah	27,401	20,273	44	243	74.0	0.2	1.2	20,030
49	65110	Roy city, Utah	26,662	17,426	169	1,430	65.4	0.6	8.2	15,996
49	65330	St. George city, Utah	63,065	35,198	0	1,531	55.8	0.0	4.3	33,667
49	67000	Salt Lake City city, Utah	157,759	111,080	78	5,157	70.4	0.0	4.6	105,923
49	67440	Sandy city, Utah	69,739	48,981	37	1,774	70.2	0.1	3.6	47,207
49	67825	Saratoga Springs city, Utah	13,067	9,396	0	250	71.9	0.0	2.7	9,146
49	70850	South Jordan city, Utah	47,336	34,061	0	414	72.0	0.0	1.2	33,647
49	71070	South Salt Lake city, Utah	19,643	13,444	0	261	68.4	0.0	1.9	13,183
49	71290	Spanish Fork city, Utah	25,538	16,973	0	406	66.5	0.0	2.4	16,567
49	72280	Springville city, Utah	20,468	13,289	0	389	64.9	0.0	2.9	12,900
49	74810	Syracuse city, Utah	18,339	12,871	86	420	70.2	0.5	3.3	12,451
49	75360	Taylorsville city, Utah	45,578	32,506	67	1,166	71.3	0.1	3.6	31,340
49	76680	Tooele city, Utah	24,427	16,769	22	1,004	68.6	0.1	6.0	15,765
49	81960	Washington city, Utah	17,151	10,622	0	0	61.9	0.0	0.0	10,622
49	82950	West Jordan city, Utah	79,865	59,810	77	2,834	74.9	0.1	4.7	56,976
49	83470	West Valley City city, Utah	100,293	71,346	0	3,249	71.1	0.0	4.6	68,097
50	00000	**VERMONT**	521,616	340,689	256	12,848	65.3	0.0	3.8	327,841
50	10675	Burlington city, Vermont	39,185	25,737	5	1,223	65.7	0.0	4.8	24,514
51	00000	**VIRGINIA**	6,721,590	4,317,898	119,242	236,298	64.2	1.8	5.5	4,081,600
51	01000	Alexandria city, Virginia	127,843	98,270	2,962	3,381	76.9	2.3	3.4	94,889
51	01912	Annandale CDP, Virginia	38,959	29,194	124	511	74.9	0.3	1.8	28,683
51	03000	Arlington CDP, Virginia	192,675	151,203	2,272	6,238	78.5	1.2	4.1	144,965
51	03320	Ashburn CDP, Virginia	39,363	30,560	19	906	77.6	0.0	3.0	29,654
51	04088	Bailey's Crossroads CDP, Virginia	19,855	14,074	37	903	70.9	0.2	6.4	13,171
51	07784	Blacksburg town, Virginia	40,936	20,594	0	1,265	50.3	0.0	6.1	19,329
51	08472	Bon Air CDP, Virginia	16,831	11,648	0	181	69.2	0.0	1.6	11,467
51	11464	Burke CDP, Virginia	29,168	18,768	916	1,011	64.3	3.1	5.4	17,757
51	13720	Cave Spring CDP, Virginia	21,293	13,239	0	395	62.2	0.0	3.0	12,844
51	14440	Centreville CDP, Virginia	57,916	45,004	482	1,839	77.7	0.8	4.1	43,165
51	14744	Chantilly CDP, Virginia	16,485	12,277	167	618	74.5	1.0	5.0	11,659
51	14968	Charlottesville city, Virginia	40,416	27,727	145	1,107	68.6	0.4	4.0	26,620
51	15176	Cherry Hill CDP, Virginia	16,572	12,669	90	357	76.4	0.5	2.8	12,312
51	16000	Chesapeake city, Virginia	185,571	114,196	8,191	6,115	61.5	4.4	5.4	108,081

Table E. Cities—Labor Force, Employment, and Educational Data, 2015—*Continued*

FIPS state code	FIPS place code	State/city	Total population age 16 and older	Civilian labor force	Armed Forces	Unemployed	Civilian labor force participation (percent)	Percent in Armed Forces	Unemployment rate	Number of employed persons age 16 and older
51	16096	Chester CDP, Virginia	19,943	12,858	0	246	64.5	0.0	1.9	12,612
51	16608	Christiansburg town, Virginia	15,090	11,753	0	731	77.9	0.0	6.2	11,022
51	21088	Dale City CDP, Virginia	53,982	38,305	760	2,891	71.0	1.4	7.5	35,414
51	21344	Danville city, Virginia	33,952	19,679	177	2,065	58.0	0.5	10.5	17,614
51	26496	Fairfax city, Virginia	20,101	15,309	0	1,145	76.2	0.0	7.5	14,164
51	26875	Fair Oaks CDP, Virginia	24,141	18,872	107	531	78.2	0.4	2.8	18,341
51	29136	Fort Hunt CDP, Virginia	14,263	9,661	488	127	67.7	3.4	1.3	9,534
51	29744	Fredericksburg city, Virginia	21,340	15,012	214	1,048	70.3	1.0	7.0	13,964
51	35000	Hampton city, Virginia	110,700	65,566	4,729	3,984	59.2	4.3	6.1	61,582
51	35624	Harrisonburg city, Virginia	44,655	25,924	47	1,768	58.1	0.1	6.8	24,156
51	36648	Herndon town, Virginia	18,187	13,751	39	1,016	75.6	0.2	7.4	12,735
51	38424	Hopewell city, Virginia	16,188	8,987	368	1,628	55.5	2.3	18.1	7,359
51	39448	Idylwood CDP, Virginia	15,787	11,482	32	186	72.7	0.2	1.6	11,296
51	43432	Lake Ridge CDP, Virginia	31,988	21,457	621	1,186	67.1	1.9	5.5	20,271
51	44280	Laurel CDP, Virginia	17,002	13,204	0	1,201	77.7	0.0	9.1	12,003
51	44984	Leesburg town, Virginia	40,271	31,822	196	748	79.0	0.5	2.4	31,074
51	45784	Lincolnia CDP, Virginia	20,191	14,341	677	1,102	71.0	3.4	7.7	13,239
51	45957	Linton Hall CDP, Virginia	28,891	22,439	97	883	77.7	0.3	3.9	21,556
51	47064	Lorton CDP, Virginia	14,453	10,562	518	464	73.1	3.6	4.4	10,098
51	47672	Lynchburg city, Virginia	66,333	36,285	0	1,719	54.7	0.0	4.7	34,566
51	48376	McLean CDP, Virginia	36,761	22,879	171	747	62.2	0.5	3.3	22,132
51	48952	Manassas city, Virginia	30,620	21,027	129	782	68.7	0.4	3.7	20,245
51	49792	Marumsco CDP, Virginia	29,447	20,811	237	1,412	70.7	0.8	6.8	19,399
51	50856	Mechanicsville CDP, Virginia	29,694	20,739	0	449	69.8	0.0	2.2	20,290
51	52658	Montclair CDP, Virginia	15,469	11,219	172	537	72.5	1.1	4.8	10,682
51	56000	Newport News city, Virginia	143,372	87,706	8,359	6,692	61.2	5.8	7.6	81,014
51	57000	Norfolk city, Virginia	201,442	111,151	25,092	10,100	55.2	12.5	9.1	101,051
51	58472	Oakton CDP, Virginia	30,493	20,989	443	1,063	68.8	1.5	5.1	19,926
51	61832	Petersburg city, Virginia	26,663	16,301	283	1,499	61.1	1.1	9.2	14,802
51	64000	Portsmouth city, Virginia	75,328	46,413	2,963	6,320	61.6	3.9	13.6	40,093
51	66672	Reston CDP, Virginia	49,750	37,154	146	1,499	74.7	0.3	4.0	35,655
51	67000	Richmond city, Virginia	184,118	120,210	682	10,362	65.3	0.4	8.6	109,848
51	68000	Roanoke city, Virginia	79,986	49,315	0	3,387	61.7	0.0	6.9	45,928
51	68880	Rose Hill CDP (Fairfax County), Virginia	17,887	13,007	307	678	72.7	1.7	5.2	12,329
51	70000	Salem city, Virginia	20,233	12,455	53	461	61.6	0.3	3.7	11,994
51	72272	Short Pump CDP, Virginia	20,023	15,964	0	394	79.7	0.0	2.5	15,570
51	74100	South Riding CDP, Virginia	20,986	15,480	89	693	73.8	0.4	4.5	14,787
51	74592	Springfield CDP, Virginia	24,580	16,791	450	1,430	68.3	1.8	8.5	15,361
51	75216	Staunton city, Virginia	21,468	12,225	0	512	56.9	0.0	4.2	11,713
51	75376	Sterling CDP, Virginia	25,211	20,486	52	1,014	81.3	0.2	4.9	19,472
51	76432	Suffolk city, Virginia	68,689	42,754	2,014	2,532	62.2	2.9	5.9	40,222
51	79560	Tuckahoe CDP, Virginia	43,193	30,924	0	1,669	71.6	0.0	5.4	29,255
51	79952	Tysons Corner CDP, Virginia	18,657	13,148	182	636	70.5	1.0	4.8	12,512
51	82000	Virginia Beach city, Virginia	362,302	230,235	25,969	12,946	63.5	7.2	5.6	217,289
51	83680	Waynesboro city, Virginia	15,983	10,969	0	255	68.6	0.0	2.3	10,714
51	84368	West Falls Church CDP, Virginia	28,257	23,322	0	2,009	82.5	0.0	8.6	21,313
51	84976	West Springfield CDP, Virginia	17,600	12,178	329	467	69.2	1.9	3.8	11,711
51	86720	Winchester city, Virginia	21,703	14,067	0	402	64.8	0.0	2.9	13,665
51	87410	Woodlawn CDP (Fairfax County), Virginia	17,653	13,649	143	1,148	77.3	0.8	8.4	12,501
53	00000	**WASHINGTON**	5,741,873	3,613,427	45,506	215,453	62.9	0.8	6.0	3,397,974
53	03180	Auburn city, Washington	61,784	40,047	44	2,296	64.8	0.1	5.7	37,751
53	03736	Bainbridge Island city, Washington	19,107	11,877	48	113	62.2	0.3	1.0	11,764
53	05210	Bellevue city, Washington	113,850	76,011	135	2,378	66.8	0.1	3.1	73,633
53	05280	Bellingham city, Washington	73,901	46,967	170	3,874	63.6	0.2	8.2	43,093
53	07380	Bothell city, Washington	36,434	25,418	0	1,380	69.8	0.0	5.4	24,038
53	07395	Bothell West CDP, Washington	15,632	10,941	0	164	70.0	0.0	1.5	10,777
53	07695	Bremerton city, Washington	33,710	16,829	4,633	1,298	49.9	13.7	7.7	15,531
53	08552	Bryn Mawr-Skyway CDP, Washington	15,897	8,874	0	184	55.8	0.0	2.1	8,690
53	08850	Burien city, Washington	38,857	26,126	40	1,564	67.2	0.1	6.0	24,562
53	09480	Camas city, Washington	16,747	11,159	0	590	66.6	0.0	5.3	10,569
53	14940	Cottage Lake CDP, Washington	16,599	10,834	0	554	65.3	0.0	5.1	10,280
53	17635	Des Moines city, Washington	25,704	17,248	0	780	67.1	0.0	4.5	16,468
53	19630	Eastmont CDP, Washington	17,423	12,192	101	399	70.0	0.6	3.3	11,793
53	20750	Edmonds city, Washington	35,919	24,306	0	1,779	67.7	0.0	7.3	22,527
53	22640	Everett city, Washington	89,099	56,984	1,440	3,180	64.0	1.6	5.6	53,804
53	23160	Fairwood CDP (King County), Washington	18,150	12,845	0	382	70.8	0.0	3.0	12,463
53	23515	Federal Way city, Washington	76,948	51,045	156	4,113	66.3	0.2	8.1	46,932
53	24188	Five Corners CDP, Washington	16,329	11,040	0	848	67.6	0.0	7.7	10,192
53	27785	Graham CDP, Washington	18,045	11,661	0	990	64.6	0.0	8.5	10,671
53	33805	Issaquah city, Washington	27,654	19,576	0	1,246	70.8	0.0	6.4	18,330
53	35170	Kenmore city, Washington	17,623	12,143	0	357	68.9	0.0	2.9	11,786
53	35275	Kennewick city, Washington	58,845	37,858	0	3,143	64.3	0.0	8.3	34,715
53	35415	Kent city, Washington	99,862	67,137	0	4,079	67.2	0.0	6.1	63,058

Table E. Cities—Labor Force, Employment, and Educational Data, 2015—*Continued*

FIPS state code	FIPS place code	State/city	Total population age 16 and older	Civilian labor force	Armed Forces	Unemployed	Civilian labor force participation (percent)	Percent in Armed Forces	Unemployment rate	Number of employed persons age 16 and older
53	35940	Kirkland city, Washington	73,033	49,902	0	1,708	68.3	0.0	3.4	48,194
53	36745	Lacey city, Washington	36,040	20,448	827	1,400	56.7	2.3	6.8	19,048
53	37900	Lake Stevens city, Washington	24,438	16,791	143	725	68.7	0.6	4.3	16,066
53	38038	Lakewood city, Washington	45,787	27,796	1,873	2,757	60.7	4.1	9.9	25,039
53	40245	Longview city, Washington	30,531	15,537	0	833	50.9	0.0	5.4	14,704
53	40840	Lynnwood city, Washington	29,754	19,681	117	612	66.1	0.4	3.1	19,069
53	43150	Maple Valley city, Washington	18,277	13,112	160	921	71.7	0.9	7.0	12,191
53	43955	Marysville city, Washington	52,094	36,133	651	2,566	69.4	1.2	7.1	33,567
53	45005	Mercer Island city, Washington	19,562	12,445	0	1,168	63.6	0.0	9.4	11,277
53	45865	Mill Creek city, Washington	16,293	10,664	56	152	65.5	0.3	1.4	10,512
53	45870	Mill Creek East CDP, Washington	14,894	10,742	0	593	72.1	0.0	5.5	10,149
53	47245	Moses Lake city, Washington	13,540	8,828	0	176	65.2	0.0	2.0	8,652
53	47490	Mountlake Terrace city, Washington	18,853	13,762	0	886	73.0	0.0	6.4	12,876
53	47560	Mount Vernon city, Washington	25,745	16,485	0	1,416	64.0	0.0	8.6	15,069
53	47735	Mukilteo city, Washington	17,689	11,293	172	1,122	63.8	1.0	9.9	10,171
53	50360	Oak Harbor city, Washington	18,224	9,612	2,072	420	52.7	11.4	4.4	9,192
53	51300	Olympia city, Washington	41,984	23,704	394	916	56.5	0.9	3.9	22,788
53	51795	Orchards CDP, Washington	17,730	12,774	46	677	72.0	0.3	5.3	12,097
53	53335	Parkland CDP, Washington	28,792	18,678	336	2,034	64.9	1.2	10.9	16,644
53	53545	Pasco city, Washington	46,999	31,968	0	2,101	68.0	0.0	6.6	29,867
53	56625	Pullman city, Washington	28,568	18,194	0	2,423	63.7	0.0	13.3	15,771
53	56695	Puyallup city, Washington	32,374	19,750	290	1,271	61.0	0.9	6.4	18,479
53	57535	Redmond city, Washington	46,572	32,891	0	1,524	70.6	0.0	4.6	31,367
53	57745	Renton city, Washington	77,648	53,351	160	2,390	68.7	0.2	4.5	50,961
53	58235	Richland city, Washington	43,151	25,932	0	708	60.1	0.0	2.7	25,224
53	61000	Salmon Creek CDP, Washington	17,190	11,557	0	845	67.2	0.0	7.3	10,712
53	61115	Sammamish city, Washington	39,020	26,318	0	804	67.4	0.0	3.1	25,514
53	62288	SeaTac city, Washington	22,720	14,495	71	917	63.8	0.3	6.3	13,578
53	63000	Seattle city, Washington	593,729	435,992	614	20,976	73.4	0.1	4.8	415,016
53	63960	Shoreline city, Washington	45,476	31,465	0	2,071	69.2	0.0	6.6	29,394
53	64380	Silver Firs CDP, Washington	15,483	11,379	0	499	73.5	0.0	4.4	10,880
53	65922	South Hill CDP, Washington	40,881	26,112	444	2,167	63.9	1.1	8.3	23,945
53	66255	Spanaway CDP, Washington	21,127	12,458	846	1,155	59.0	4.0	9.3	11,303
53	67000	Spokane city, Washington	172,362	100,731	807	8,109	58.4	0.5	8.1	92,622
53	67167	Spokane Valley city, Washington	73,538	44,586	179	2,810	60.6	0.2	6.3	41,776
53	70000	Tacoma city, Washington	171,133	102,901	2,129	6,679	60.1	1.2	6.5	96,222
53	72625	Tukwila city, Washington	14,877	10,084	0	1,011	67.8	0.0	10.0	9,073
53	73307	Union Hill-Novelty Hill CDP, Washington	15,945	9,646	0	337	60.5	0.0	3.5	9,309
53	73465	University Place city, Washington	26,176	15,462	497	863	59.1	1.9	5.6	14,599
53	74060	Vancouver city, Washington	135,831	86,977	128	4,731	64.0	0.1	5.4	82,246
53	75775	Walla Walla city, Washington	26,625	14,810	0	493	55.6	0.0	3.3	14,317
53	77105	Wenatchee city, Washington	25,886	15,000	104	275	57.9	0.4	1.8	14,725
53	80010	Yakima city, Washington	70,557	43,634	0	3,860	61.8	0.0	8.8	39,774
54	00000	**WEST VIRGINIA**	1,508,224	796,708	818	58,270	52.8	0.1	7.3	738,438
54	14600	Charleston city, West Virginia	39,572	23,749	46	1,750	60.0	0.1	7.4	21,999
54	39460	Huntington city, West Virginia	40,714	21,010	0	2,004	51.6	0.0	9.5	19,006
54	55756	Morgantown city, West Virginia	28,233	13,853	0	990	49.1	0.0	7.1	12,863
54	62140	Parkersburg city, West Virginia	25,564	14,009	0	1,362	54.8	0.0	9.7	12,647
54	86452	Wheeling city, West Virginia	21,961	12,193	0	738	55.5	0.0	6.1	11,455
55	00000	**WISCONSIN**	4,627,790	3,091,421	2,650	131,766	66.8	0.1	4.3	2,959,655
55	02375	Appleton city, Wisconsin	59,639	40,798	0	2,314	68.4	0.0	5.7	38,484
55	06500	Beloit city, Wisconsin	27,629	16,663	0	1,816	60.3	0.0	10.9	14,847
55	10025	Brookfield city, Wisconsin	30,820	19,234	0	737	62.4	0.0	3.8	18,497
55	11950	Caledonia village, Wisconsin	20,370	12,975	0	697	63.7	0.0	5.4	12,278
55	19775	De Pere city, Wisconsin	19,231	14,127	113	651	73.5	0.6	4.6	13,476
55	22300	Eau Claire city, Wisconsin	56,630	39,399	75	718	69.6	0.1	1.8	38,681
55	25950	Fitchburg city, Wisconsin	21,944	16,742	0	838	76.3	0.0	5.0	15,904
55	26275	Fond du Lac city, Wisconsin	34,100	22,453	0	1,485	65.8	0.0	6.6	20,968
55	27300	Franklin city, Wisconsin	30,374	16,984	0	77	55.9	0.0	0.5	16,907
55	31000	Green Bay city, Wisconsin	81,142	55,861	52	2,042	68.8	0.1	3.7	53,819
55	31175	Greenfield city, Wisconsin	29,239	17,623	45	652	60.3	0.2	3.7	16,971
55	37825	Janesville city, Wisconsin	51,302	35,751	0	1,810	69.7	0.0	5.1	33,941
55	39225	Kenosha city, Wisconsin	76,859	50,989	461	3,479	66.3	0.6	6.8	47,510
55	40775	La Crosse city, Wisconsin	47,440	32,243	0	1,378	68.0	0.0	4.3	30,865
55	48000	Madison city, Wisconsin	211,046	153,653	24	7,430	72.8	0.0	4.8	146,223
55	48500	Manitowoc city, Wisconsin	26,466	16,162	0	518	61.1	0.0	3.2	15,644
55	51000	Menomonee Falls village, Wisconsin	29,458	20,895	0	577	70.9	0.0	2.8	20,318
55	51150	Mequon city, Wisconsin	17,470	10,377	0	214	59.4	0.0	2.1	10,163
55	53000	Milwaukee city, Wisconsin	459,913	300,911	179	26,086	65.4	0.0	8.7	274,825
55	54875	Mount Pleasant village, Wisconsin	21,481	12,760	0	434	59.4	0.0	3.4	12,326
55	55275	Muskego city, Wisconsin	19,332	13,612	0	409	70.4	0.0	3.0	13,203
55	55750	Neenah city, Wisconsin	19,930	14,336	0	286	71.9	0.0	2.0	14,050
55	56375	New Berlin city, Wisconsin	32,560	21,260	0	224	65.3	0.0	1.1	21,036
55	58800	Oak Creek city, Wisconsin	28,417	19,754	78	616	69.5	0.3	3.1	19,138
55	60500	Oshkosh city, Wisconsin	55,861	33,769	0	1,227	60.5	0.0	3.6	32,542

Table E. Cities—Labor Force, Employment, and Educational Data, 2015—*Continued*

FIPS state code	FIPS place code	State/city	Total population age 16 and older	Employment status				Civilian labor force participation (percent)	Percent in Armed Forces	Unemployment rate	Number of employed persons age 16 and older
				Civilian labor force	Armed Forces	Unemployed					
55	63300	Pleasant Prairie village, Wisconsin	16,912	11,254	0	330	66.5	0.0	2.9	10,924
55	66000	Racine city, Wisconsin	58,384	38,594	51	3,410	66.1	0.1	8.8	35,184
55	72975	Sheboygan city, Wisconsin	38,225	25,069	75	1,664	65.6	0.2	6.6	23,405
55	75125	South Milwaukee city, Wisconsin	17,203	11,061	0	504	64.3	0.0	4.6	10,557
55	77200	Stevens Point city, Wisconsin	23,067	15,809	0	670	68.5	0.0	4.2	15,139
55	78600	Sun Prairie city, Wisconsin	26,200	18,866	0	379	72.0	0.0	2.0	18,487
55	78650	Superior city, Wisconsin	22,260	13,593	0	494	61.1	0.0	3.6	13,099
55	83975	Watertown city, Wisconsin	18,407	12,737	0	249	69.2	0.0	2.0	12,488
55	84250	Waukesha city, Wisconsin	59,000	41,954	0	1,124	71.1	0.0	2.7	40,830
55	84475	Wausau city, Wisconsin	32,341	21,732	0	870	67.2	0.0	4.0	20,862
55	84675	Wauwatosa city, Wisconsin	36,664	26,241	36	435	71.6	0.1	1.7	25,806
55	85300	West Allis city, Wisconsin	49,024	32,743	0	1,124	66.8	0.0	3.4	31,619
55	85350	West Bend city, Wisconsin	25,442	17,584	40	467	69.1	0.2	2.7	17,117
56	00000	**WYOMING**	460,730	310,369	2,172	15,041	67.4	0.5	4.8	295,328
56	13150	Casper city, Wyoming	46,121	31,967	0	1,165	69.3	0.0	3.6	30,802
56	13900	Cheyenne city, Wyoming	51,388	33,820	1,274	2,105	65.8	2.5	6.2	31,715
56	31855	Gillette city, Wyoming	25,132	18,571	0	539	73.9	0.0	2.9	18,032
56	45050	Laramie city, Wyoming	27,808	20,943	57	436	75.3	0.2	2.1	20,507
56	67235	Rock Springs city, Wyoming	17,403	12,713	65	1,215	73.1	0.4	9.6	11,498

Table E. Cities—Labor Force, Employment, and Educational Data, 2015

FIPS state code	FIPS place code	State/city	Employees of private companies	Self-employed in own incorporated business	Private not-for-profit wage and salary workers	Local	State	Federal	Self-employed in own not incorporated business	Unpaid family workers	Management, business, science, and arts occupations
00	00000	**UNITED STATES**	68.8	3.5	8.0	6.6	4.5	2.4	5.9	0.2	37.1
01	00000	**ALABAMA**	70.7	2.7	6.6	6.3	5.4	3.1	4.9	0.2	33.9
01	00820	Alabaster city, Alabama	71.7	3.9	6.9	5.4	3.0	4.3	4.6	0.3	38.7
01	00988	Albertville city, Alabama	79.8	1.8	6.4	6.1	2.8	1.3	1.7	0.0	23.0
01	01852	Anniston city, Alabama	75.2	4.4	3.7	1.9	5.2	5.4	4.1	0.0	27.3
01	02956	Athens city, Alabama	62.8	1.4	7.4	3.3	3.9	7.6	11.9	1.7	39.8
01	03076	Auburn city, Alabama	70.3	3.0	4.2	5.8	11.5	0.8	4.0	0.3	44.4
01	05980	Bessemer city, Alabama	68.2	1.8	6.3	11.8	3.8	4.6	3.4	0.0	20.2
01	07000	Birmingham city, Alabama	69.4	2.5	8.5	6.5	6.5	2.3	4.2	0.0	31.4
01	19648	Daphne city, Alabama	73.7	4.5	11.3	3.0	2.2	1.8	3.5	0.0	45.0
01	20104	Decatur city, Alabama	71.4	2.4	9.3	5.6	3.6	3.5	4.3	0.0	37.0
01	21184	Dothan city, Alabama	72.5	3.5	7.2	4.7	3.9	2.3	5.8	0.1	35.4
01	24184	Enterprise city, Alabama	59.8	1.6	9.9	5.2	6.7	12.5	4.2	0.0	38.4
01	26896	Florence city, Alabama	73.3	3.0	7.8	3.0	5.5	3.0	4.5	0.0	29.9
01	28696	Gadsden city, Alabama	75.5	3.6	5.8	5.4	4.4	2.2	3.1	0.0	24.5
01	35800	Homewood city, Alabama	66.1	4.7	12.3	3.6	9.1	1.2	3.1	0.0	53.3
01	35896	Hoover city, Alabama	67.6	5.6	10.2	3.9	3.9	3.1	5.2	0.6	53.0
01	37000	Huntsville city, Alabama	71.1	1.8	6.3	5.4	4.1	7.4	3.5	0.4	45.5
01	45784	Madison city, Alabama	67.4	0.9	7.8	4.1	4.2	11.4	4.1	0.0	61.6
01	50000	Mobile city, Alabama	71.8	2.9	7.4	6.9	5.4	2.1	3.4	0.1	36.4
01	51000	Montgomery city, Alabama	66.0	2.1	7.5	6.3	9.7	5.0	3.4	0.1	34.4
01	51696	Mountain Brook city, Alabama	55.3	9.8	15.2	3.5	6.6	3.8	5.9	0.0	71.5
01	55200	Northport city, Alabama	61.1	2.2	5.1	15.6	13.0	0.0	3.0	0.0	47.2
01	57048	Opelika city, Alabama	74.5	1.6	3.9	7.8	5.6	2.7	3.9	0.0	31.8
01	57576	Oxford city, Alabama	66.8	0.0	5.4	3.9	9.1	9.2	5.5	0.0	36.4
01	58848	Pelham city, Alabama	77.3	3.0	7.9	6.0	2.5	1.9	1.3	0.0	46.9
01	59472	Phenix City city, Alabama	69.4	2.6	4.9	7.8	1.7	6.9	6.3	0.4	35.6
01	62328	Prattville city, Alabama	59.7	2.1	7.3	8.8	9.7	6.7	5.8	0.0	39.2
01	62496	Prichard city, Alabama	72.6	0.8	9.8	9.0	2.4	4.2	1.3	0.0	24.7
01	76944	Trussville city, Alabama	78.7	4.9	5.0	7.1	1.9	0.0	2.3	0.0	46.6
01	77256	Tuscaloosa city, Alabama	58.0	4.1	12.5	6.1	13.7	1.7	3.6	0.4	37.2
01	78552	Vestavia Hills city, Alabama	61.8	4.9	12.0	6.5	5.9	2.4	5.5	0.9	61.2
02	00000	**ALASKA**	55.5	3.3	10.1	9.0	8.6	6.9	6.3	0.3	36.4
02	03000	Anchorage municipality, Alaska	61.1	3.5	10.6	5.5	7.0	6.8	5.2	0.2	41.3
02	05000	Badger CDP, Alaska	59.8	2.9	6.5	7.8	5.0	15.4	2.0	0.7	30.5
02	24230	Fairbanks city, Alaska	56.6	3.7	12.3	5.8	5.3	13.9	2.4	0.0	30.7
02	36400	Juneau city and borough, Alaska	42.3	2.7	10.9	8.3	22.1	5.3	8.4	0.0	46.9
04	00000	**ARIZONA**	70.6	3.5	6.1	6.4	4.7	2.7	5.8	0.2	34.6
04	02830	Apache Junction city, Arizona	72.1	0.7	7.5	6.3	7.3	2.6	3.4	0.0	35.5
04	04720	Avondale city, Arizona	75.6	1.1	2.5	7.2	4.9	5.4	3.0	0.3	25.2
04	07940	Buckeye town, Arizona	70.2	0.9	4.7	7.8	5.1	7.2	4.1	0.0	22.5
04	08220	Bullhead City city, Arizona	78.7	2.4	1.9	7.7	2.5	1.9	4.1	0.7	22.2
04	10530	Casa Grande city, Arizona	70.0	2.0	8.3	7.0	6.1	0.2	3.3	3.1	22.2
04	10670	Casas Adobes CDP, Arizona	66.0	4.7	9.0	7.7	4.0	1.8	6.5	0.4	40.4
04	11230	Catalina Foothills CDP, Arizona	59.0	9.4	8.9	4.7	6.5	4.4	6.4	0.7	57.5
04	12000	Chandler city, Arizona	75.0	4.4	5.3	5.9	3.7	1.4	4.1	0.2	46.4
04	20540	Drexel Heights CDP, Arizona	69.3	0.7	2.8	11.2	4.6	3.7	7.6	0.0	23.6
04	22220	El Mirage city, Arizona	72.3	1.4	13.0	6.2	1.3	1.6	3.9	0.2	24.5
04	23620	Flagstaff city, Arizona	62.2	1.6	9.9	6.1	14.1	3.7	2.4	0.0	37.4
04	23760	Florence town, Arizona	42.3	4.7	7.7	15.5	22.5	2.0	5.2	0.0	37.3
04	25030	Fortuna Foothills CDP, Arizona	52.6	2.8	7.7	7.9	2.2	20.9	5.9	0.0	36.3
04	25300	Fountain Hills town, Arizona	67.8	7.0	11.3	5.5	3.0	1.8	3.7	0.0	47.3
04	27400	Gilbert town, Arizona	73.2	3.7	6.5	5.5	4.4	1.1	5.3	0.3	43.8
04	27820	Glendale city, Arizona	75.9	2.2	5.4	6.0	3.3	1.7	5.6	0.0	28.5
04	28380	Goodyear city, Arizona	67.6	1.5	4.5	7.7	5.4	2.3	10.5	0.5	38.4
04	29710	Green Valley CDP, Arizona	56.4	2.9	8.2	2.3	8.0	6.3	16.0	0.0	43.0
04	37620	Kingman city, Arizona	60.6	2.4	7.2	17.7	4.9	2.2	4.9	0.0	27.2
04	39370	Lake Havasu City city, Arizona	71.0	6.3	0.6	5.7	2.6	1.7	12.2	0.0	22.2
04	44270	Marana town, Arizona	60.6	1.8	8.1	7.4	6.7	7.9	6.8	0.6	40.5
04	44410	Maricopa city, Arizona	76.2	0.4	6.5	5.8	5.8	2.6	2.4	0.3	33.6
04	46000	Mesa city, Arizona	74.8	3.5	5.4	6.0	3.1	1.3	5.8	0.2	32.1
04	49640	Nogales city, Arizona	61.5	1.6	11.1	15.5	3.6	0.9	5.8	0.0	27.1
04	51600	Oro Valley town, Arizona	61.7	6.4	8.4	5.1	4.9	4.8	8.7	0.0	45.3
04	54050	Peoria city, Arizona	72.7	3.1	6.9	5.1	5.2	2.0	5.0	0.1	35.4
04	55000	Phoenix city, Arizona	75.5	3.5	5.3	4.3	3.8	1.6	5.9	0.1	32.3
04	57380	Prescott city, Arizona	51.1	5.1	16.7	5.3	5.9	2.8	13.1	0.0	40.8
04	57450	Prescott Valley town, Arizona	73.1	2.4	5.4	5.5	5.0	4.3	4.2	0.0	26.6
04	58150	Queen Creek town, Arizona	69.3	7.0	3.2	7.4	5.8	1.4	6.0	0.0	49.0
04	62140	Sahuarita town, Arizona	67.0	1.9	3.7	4.3	7.4	12.7	3.1	0.0	38.1
04	63470	San Luis city, Arizona	-	-	-	-	-	-	-	-	14.5
04	64210	San Tan Valley CDP, Arizona	77.6	3.3	4.0	5.4	2.4	1.6	5.8	0.0	27.6
04	65000	Scottsdale city, Arizona	69.2	8.5	6.4	3.3	2.3	1.7	8.1	0.4	52.4
04	66820	Sierra Vista city, Arizona	52.6	0.6	4.7	6.6	2.2	31.1	2.2	0.0	36.3
04	70320	Sun City CDP, Arizona	-	-	-	-	-	-	-	-	23.8
04	70355	Sun City West CDP, Arizona	-	-	-	-	-	-	-	-	41.6

Table E. Cities—Labor Force, Employment, and Educational Data, 2015—*Continued*

FIPS state code	FIPS place code	State/city	Employees of private companies	Self-employed in own incorporated business	Private not-for-profit wage and salary workers	Government workers — Local	State	Federal	Self-employed in own not incorporated business	Unpaid family workers	Percent in each occupation group — Management, business, science, and arts occupations
04	71510	Surprise city, Arizona	73.9	1.9	6.7	4.5	5.1	2.5	5.3	0.1	33.5
04	73000	Tempe city, Arizona	74.6	2.4	4.5	5.9	6.8	0.9	4.5	0.2	43.7
04	77000	Tucson city, Arizona	65.8	2.6	7.8	7.0	6.7	3.7	6.3	0.1	33.8
04	85540	Yuma city, Arizona	66.1	2.1	8.5	10.3	3.8	6.0	3.1	0.2	32.7
05	00000	**ARKANSAS**	67.8	2.8	7.2	5.5	8.0	2.1	6.3	0.2	32.1
05	04840	Bella Vista city, Arkansas	75.0	1.8	10.4	4.4	1.4	0.5	6.5	0.0	35.1
05	05290	Benton city, Arkansas	62.8	3.1	10.1	7.7	7.3	3.2	5.6	0.2	35.3
05	05320	Bentonville city, Arkansas	78.5	3.4	6.7	3.4	2.7	0.9	4.3	0.0	46.8
05	10300	Cabot city, Arkansas	64.6	3.4	5.8	4.3	5.3	12.4	4.2	0.0	38.8
05	15190	Conway city, Arkansas	72.2	4.8	6.2	3.8	8.5	1.5	2.9	0.2	35.9
05	23290	Fayetteville city, Arkansas	62.2	2.5	11.5	5.8	12.5	0.6	4.6	0.2	47.0
05	24550	Fort Smith city, Arkansas	80.1	1.7	6.8	2.9	4.1	1.0	3.4	0.0	26.8
05	33400	Hot Springs city, Arkansas	65.6	2.7	10.3	3.3	7.6	2.3	8.1	0.0	24.1
05	34750	Jacksonville city, Arkansas	53.9	0.9	14.0	4.3	7.7	14.6	4.5	0.0	34.5
05	35710	Jonesboro city, Arkansas	68.1	3.3	11.8	3.0	7.4	0.5	5.6	0.2	34.1
05	41000	Little Rock city, Arkansas	62.3	2.5	11.1	4.9	11.2	4.2	3.8	0.0	43.4
05	50450	North Little Rock city, Arkansas	66.5	3.6	8.5	6.3	8.3	1.9	5.1	0.0	34.9
05	53390	Paragould city, Arkansas	74.2	3.6	5.8	5.5	5.9	0.5	4.0	0.6	23.3
05	55310	Pine Bluff city, Arkansas	67.7	0.9	7.7	6.4	14.1	1.4	1.8	0.0	27.3
05	60410	Rogers city, Arkansas	79.6	1.7	7.5	2.3	3.8	0.5	4.6	0.0	36.6
05	61670	Russellville city, Arkansas	74.9	0.6	4.2	4.6	11.1	1.2	3.4	0.0	22.6
05	63020	Searcy city, Arkansas	-	-	-	-	-	-	-	-	30.4
05	63800	Sherwood city, Arkansas	60.3	3.9	7.8	6.6	8.1	4.0	8.5	0.8	34.8
05	66080	Springdale city, Arkansas	78.8	1.7	5.7	3.1	2.6	2.4	5.5	0.2	27.5
05	68810	Texarkana city, Arkansas	69.6	2.5	9.5	4.8	4.9	3.3	5.3	0.0	30.0
05	71480	Van Buren city, Arkansas	74.7	5.1	4.1	9.8	2.6	1.1	2.6	0.0	45.4
05	74540	West Memphis city, Arkansas	75.8	0.4	5.0	6.8	6.2	1.6	4.3	0.0	21.1
06	00000	**CALIFORNIA**	68.5	3.3	6.5	7.5	4.0	1.8	8.2	0.2	37.7
06	00296	Adelanto city, California	-	-	-	-	-	-	-	-	9.1
06	00394	Agoura Hills city, California	-	-	-	-	-	-	-	-	57.1
06	00562	Alameda city, California	64.0	2.9	9.9	7.3	3.5	3.7	8.6	0.1	52.9
06	00884	Alhambra city, California	65.5	4.8	7.1	12.2	3.0	1.6	5.5	0.3	40.4
06	00947	Aliso Viejo city, California	74.5	5.0	5.5	3.4	2.0	2.1	7.5	0.0	51.3
06	01290	Altadena CDP, California	61.0	3.7	10.8	7.5	2.4	1.5	12.8	0.3	45.7
06	01640	American Canyon city, California	73.2	1.2	6.8	7.8	6.0	0.8	4.4	0.0	37.5
06	02000	Anaheim city, California	80.5	1.8	3.9	5.1	2.5	1.1	5.0	0.1	27.7
06	02210	Antelope CDP, California	70.3	1.7	5.0	8.2	6.4	3.5	4.8	0.0	38.9
06	02252	Antioch city, California	72.7	1.0	6.1	8.6	3.8	2.1	5.6	0.1	30.3
06	02364	Apple Valley town, California	65.3	1.9	6.2	9.7	4.4	3.1	9.1	0.3	27.9
06	02462	Arcadia city, California	67.9	10.7	5.6	8.1	3.0	0.8	3.9	0.0	54.9
06	02553	Arden-Arcade CDP, California	61.5	2.1	7.7	6.5	10.7	2.8	8.1	0.6	41.0
06	02924	Arvin city, California	84.7	0.0	4.0	2.9	0.9	1.3	6.2	0.0	1.9
06	02980	Ashland CDP, California	-	-	-	-	-	-	-	-	24.0
06	03064	Atascadero city, California	56.1	2.4	5.6	8.4	18.9	1.7	7.1	0.0	45.3
06	03162	Atwater city, California	65.5	1.1	7.1	15.4	2.0	0.8	7.4	0.7	22.6
06	03386	Azusa city, California	75.1	4.0	7.8	6.1	2.2	1.4	3.4	0.0	29.0
06	03526	Bakersfield city, California	70.8	1.9	4.6	10.5	4.7	0.7	6.3	0.6	30.0
06	03666	Baldwin Park city, California	81.1	2.8	2.5	5.8	0.6	0.8	6.1	0.1	21.0
06	03820	Banning city, California	69.8	2.5	3.2	7.2	3.3	2.1	12.1	0.0	22.5
06	04030	Barstow city, California	66.6	0.0	2.8	8.6	6.1	11.6	4.4	0.0	21.0
06	04415	Bay Point CDP, California	74.4	0.0	5.2	4.6	3.1	2.8	9.1	0.8	18.8
06	04758	Beaumont city, California	64.8	2.8	5.2	15.0	3.8	0.5	7.9	0.0	30.7
06	04870	Bell city, California	83.8	1.3	0.9	5.8	2.2	0.0	5.7	0.3	12.3
06	04982	Bellflower city, California	77.4	2.2	6.8	5.6	1.4	1.7	4.7	0.1	24.9
06	04996	Bell Gardens city, California	84.8	1.6	1.5	4.5	2.1	0.8	4.7	0.0	9.8
06	05108	Belmont city, California	73.4	2.3	9.2	5.2	2.6	1.3	6.1	0.0	64.8
06	05290	Benicia city, California	59.8	3.3	6.4	15.6	5.5	1.7	7.3	0.5	55.9
06	06000	Berkeley city, California	49.3	3.0	14.5	7.1	13.0	1.9	11.1	0.2	67.4
06	06308	Beverly Hills city, California	52.5	18.9	6.2	2.5	3.2	0.6	16.1	0.0	64.9
06	07064	Bloomington CDP, California	75.0	3.8	6.7	8.2	0.6	0.0	5.7	0.0	20.2
06	08058	Brawley city, California	59.9	2.1	3.5	13.9	14.6	0.0	5.9	0.0	27.1
06	08100	Brea city, California	67.7	4.5	5.9	8.4	3.8	3.0	6.6	0.0	51.9
06	08142	Brentwood city, California	61.8	1.9	10.4	12.9	3.8	2.2	6.6	0.3	39.8
06	08786	Buena Park city, California	75.6	5.0	4.1	5.5	3.2	0.7	5.7	0.2	31.4
06	08954	Burbank city, California	70.7	4.7	5.7	5.5	2.3	1.3	9.7	0.2	55.8
06	09066	Burlingame city, California	65.1	5.8	7.0	7.2	2.9	2.8	9.2	0.0	59.6
06	09598	Calabasas city, California	59.2	10.9	7.4	3.4	3.8	0.6	14.7	0.0	48.1
06	09710	Calexico city, California	60.1	0.4	4.8	17.0	9.2	2.8	5.7	0.0	25.0
06	10046	Camarillo city, California	67.6	5.1	4.5	8.3	2.0	4.6	7.9	0.0	43.4
06	10256	Cameron Park CDP, California	66.8	0.7	6.9	5.5	8.2	0.4	11.4	0.0	40.2
06	10345	Campbell city, California	72.2	3.0	6.0	8.4	1.8	1.9	6.8	0.0	51.9
06	11194	Carlsbad city, California	74.3	4.5	2.6	5.8	1.6	1.2	10.0	0.1	49.0
06	11390	Carmichael CDP, California	57.9	4.1	8.9	7.6	11.5	0.9	9.0	0.2	44.8
06	11530	Carson city, California	72.5	2.4	6.0	9.1	4.1	2.1	3.4	0.6	35.9

Table E. Cities—Labor Force, Employment, and Educational Data, 2015—*Continued*

			Class of worker (percent)								Percent in each occupation group
						Government workers					
FIPS state code	FIPS place code	State/city	Employees of private companies	Self-employed in own incorporated business	Private not-for-profit wage and salary workers	Local	State	Federal	Self-employed in own not incorporated business	Unpaid family workers	Management, business, science, and arts occupations
06	11796	Castaic CDP, California	65.4	4.3	6.4	15.0	4.7	1.4	2.8	0.0	34.3
06	11964	Castro Valley CDP, California	67.3	4.2	7.6	6.0	4.1	1.6	8.9	0.2	50.0
06	12048	Cathedral City city, California	76.0	1.3	6.5	5.3	1.1	0.5	8.5	0.6	14.6
06	12524	Ceres city, California	76.7	1.0	3.3	10.3	3.0	0.4	4.5	0.7	15.4
06	12552	Cerritos city, California	67.2	4.4	4.9	9.0	3.5	1.3	9.2	0.5	56.1
06	13014	Chico city, California	63.8	1.2	9.8	7.7	8.3	1.7	7.3	0.2	40.0
06	13210	Chino city, California	69.0	3.0	7.2	10.3	3.1	1.6	5.5	0.2	30.8
06	13214	Chino Hills city, California	62.0	5.8	5.7	9.4	4.0	1.9	11.1	0.2	48.8
06	13392	Chula Vista city, California	64.7	2.7	6.9	6.8	7.1	6.6	5.3	0.0	36.5
06	13588	Citrus Heights city, California	69.2	2.6	6.1	3.8	9.1	1.7	7.0	0.6	32.6
06	13756	Claremont city, California	51.4	4.9	17.7	6.3	5.4	0.2	13.1	1.0	57.7
06	14218	Clovis city, California	60.6	2.4	9.7	10.4	7.9	2.4	6.7	0.0	41.6
06	14260	Coachella city, California	80.7	0.5	3.7	6.9	2.3	2.1	3.9	0.0	7.9
06	14890	Colton city, California	71.2	1.6	7.8	8.8	2.0	0.9	7.5	0.3	21.4
06	15044	Compton city, California	75.9	2.0	4.8	8.3	2.0	1.2	5.7	0.0	16.3
06	16000	Concord city, California	70.4	2.4	7.7	5.9	2.6	1.3	9.8	0.0	39.4
06	16224	Corcoran city, California	-	-	-	-	-	-	-	-	9.4
06	16350	Corona city, California	73.2	4.9	3.9	7.5	2.9	1.8	5.6	0.2	35.6
06	16378	Coronado city, California	54.3	4.6	8.7	10.7	2.8	11.9	7.0	0.0	64.0
06	16532	Costa Mesa city, California	73.2	3.8	4.5	4.8	2.7	0.5	10.0	0.6	43.1
06	16742	Covina city, California	72.8	3.2	6.3	9.1	1.8	0.8	5.9	0.1	33.3
06	17498	Cudahy city, California	81.8	2.9	2.3	6.0	1.6	0.2	5.2	0.0	12.2
06	17568	Culver City city, California	66.1	6.7	8.9	9.6	1.9	1.0	5.9	0.0	57.7
06	17610	Cupertino city, California	80.3	2.6	4.6	4.2	2.5	0.7	5.1	0.0	80.0
06	17750	Cypress city, California	73.2	2.5	4.1	8.2	3.3	1.1	7.5	0.0	44.6
06	17918	Daly City city, California	71.5	1.8	6.6	8.5	3.9	2.4	5.1	0.2	29.8
06	17946	Dana Point city, California	61.7	4.0	7.5	6.4	2.2	0.0	18.2	0.0	40.8
06	17988	Danville town, California	72.7	5.6	6.2	4.8	0.4	1.5	8.7	0.0	56.8
06	18100	Davis city, California	46.6	2.8	9.9	7.8	25.9	2.0	4.8	0.0	61.4
06	18394	Delano city, California	82.2	0.7	1.9	8.7	4.7	0.6	1.3	0.0	11.9
06	18996	Desert Hot Springs city, California	72.3	1.8	4.5	7.2	2.8	1.6	9.1	0.6	16.8
06	19192	Diamond Bar city, California	58.8	7.0	8.0	9.3	2.8	1.8	12.2	0.2	54.4
06	19318	Dinuba city, California	78.6	0.7	2.6	9.0	3.9	1.4	3.7	0.0	23.0
06	19766	Downey city, California	66.7	4.6	4.6	11.6	1.5	1.2	9.8	0.0	32.5
06	19990	Duarte city, California	68.7	3.4	8.7	8.2	3.1	2.2	5.7	0.0	35.7
06	20018	Dublin city, California	70.4	2.4	7.3	6.9	1.9	1.5	9.0	0.5	66.8
06	20802	East Los Angeles CDP, California	85.9	0.7	2.5	4.2	1.7	1.0	3.9	0.0	14.5
06	20956	East Palo Alto city, California	74.2	0.6	10.8	4.9	2.7	1.0	5.8	0.0	21.0
06	21230	Eastvale city, California	67.7	5.3	7.8	9.4	2.5	1.8	5.5	0.0	39.8
06	21712	El Cajon city, California	71.1	2.5	6.3	8.6	2.9	3.1	5.4	0.1	22.4
06	21782	El Centro city, California	59.6	1.7	3.7	16.5	7.1	3.8	7.7	0.0	29.7
06	21796	El Cerrito city, California	48.7	6.4	15.3	7.7	7.8	1.4	12.3	0.3	65.4
06	21880	El Dorado Hills CDP, California	56.4	7.2	7.8	10.6	8.4	1.1	8.5	0.0	60.6
06	22020	Elk Grove city, California	57.3	2.2	5.7	11.3	15.6	1.8	5.9	0.1	43.9
06	22230	El Monte city, California	74.3	2.3	2.7	9.3	0.9	1.3	8.8	0.3	18.1
06	22300	El Paso de Robles (Paso Robles) city, California	66.4	3.1	3.5	10.2	7.7	2.2	6.3	0.6	31.1
06	22678	Encinitas city, California	59.4	6.8	10.9	5.1	3.5	2.8	11.4	0.1	60.6
06	22804	Escondido city, California	73.9	1.7	8.6	4.8	4.1	1.2	5.7	0.0	26.2
06	23042	Eureka city, California	51.9	1.9	13.8	7.5	7.9	1.2	15.7	0.0	28.1
06	23182	Fairfield city, California	61.1	2.8	7.2	9.2	6.3	7.5	5.9	0.1	29.0
06	23294	Fair Oaks CDP, California	49.0	7.3	10.2	9.8	11.4	1.4	10.9	0.0	59.8
06	23462	Fallbrook CDP, California	67.4	2.0	5.5	9.7	3.3	2.8	9.4	0.0	25.8
06	24477	Florence-Graham CDP, California	75.3	0.6	3.2	6.8	0.8	0.3	12.9	0.0	13.2
06	24498	Florin CDP, California	66.4	0.5	4.6	6.7	11.9	1.9	7.9	0.0	17.4
06	24638	Folsom city, California	61.2	2.4	8.3	7.6	13.9	2.0	4.7	0.0	60.1
06	24680	Fontana city, California	75.0	1.9	4.7	8.1	3.8	0.7	5.6	0.1	20.1
06	24722	Foothill Farms CDP, California	71.9	0.2	8.1	6.1	5.5	0.3	7.9	0.0	20.1
06	25338	Foster City city, California	75.0	4.2	7.7	2.4	1.7	0.4	8.3	0.4	70.8
06	25380	Fountain Valley city, California	67.0	5.2	6.6	8.3	2.7	2.3	7.6	0.4	51.0
06	26000	Fremont city, California	79.1	3.4	4.5	5.8	1.6	1.0	4.5	0.0	56.1
06	26067	French Valley CDP, California	63.8	1.0	6.1	9.8	5.6	4.6	9.1	0.0	52.6
06	27000	Fresno city, California	66.1	1.3	6.7	11.5	6.4	2.4	5.5	0.0	29.0
06	28000	Fullerton city, California	70.3	5.1	6.6	6.0	5.2	0.6	6.2	0.1	40.5
06	28112	Galt city, California	64.3	0.2	10.5	10.5	7.8	0.2	6.5	0.0	24.7
06	28168	Gardena city, California	75.0	2.4	3.2	11.2	1.7	0.9	5.6	0.0	32.5
06	29000	Garden Grove city, California	75.3	2.1	4.4	7.6	2.5	1.1	6.8	0.2	26.7
06	29504	Gilroy city, California	69.1	5.5	8.6	11.3	1.7	0.3	3.6	0.0	27.1
06	30000	Glendale city, California	64.6	3.7	7.4	8.5	3.5	0.9	10.7	0.5	42.3
06	30014	Glendora city, California	61.3	6.2	9.1	10.4	4.5	0.7	7.9	0.0	45.9
06	30378	Goleta city, California	56.2	1.9	15.4	6.0	13.2	0.8	6.6	0.0	48.3
06	30693	Granite Bay CDP, California	56.3	11.2	10.7	2.1	2.4	2.7	13.6	0.9	58.2
06	31596	Hacienda Heights CDP, California	66.4	6.0	5.9	9.8	4.1	0.5	7.1	0.2	42.4
06	31960	Hanford city, California	55.0	3.6	8.1	16.0	10.9	2.2	4.1	0.0	32.8
06	32548	Hawthorne city, California	74.0	0.8	6.4	5.5	2.7	1.8	8.8	0.0	21.8

Table E. Cities—Labor Force, Employment, and Educational Data, 2015—*Continued*

FIPS state code	FIPS place code	State/city	Employees of private companies	Self-employed in own incorporated business	Private not-for-profit wage and salary workers	Local	State	Federal	Self-employed in own not incorporated business	Unpaid family workers	Management, business, science, and arts occupations
06	33000	Hayward city, California	77.1	2.1	5.5	5.3	2.7	2.4	4.9	0.0	31.9
06	33182	Hemet city, California	71.0	2.6	3.6	9.5	5.8	0.9	6.7	0.0	24.7
06	33308	Hercules city, California	65.0	4.8	7.5	11.0	4.7	3.5	3.5	0.0	45.8
06	33434	Hesperia city, California	69.7	3.9	4.9	10.4	1.3	2.1	7.6	0.1	24.3
06	33588	Highland city, California	67.4	1.8	9.5	9.9	3.7	2.7	4.9	0.0	29.4
06	34120	Hollister city, California	73.2	1.2	4.9	11.1	2.0	1.7	5.9	0.0	20.7
06	36000	Huntington Beach city, California	70.0	3.5	4.3	7.4	3.6	1.3	9.9	0.1	45.4
06	36056	Huntington Park city, California	84.6	0.7	1.9	4.5	0.8	0.2	7.2	0.0	8.9
06	36294	Imperial Beach city, California	71.7	6.2	1.3	6.4	3.3	7.4	3.7	0.0	24.8
06	36448	Indio city, California	68.6	3.7	5.9	8.9	3.1	0.9	8.7	0.1	20.3
06	36546	Inglewood city, California	69.2	1.0	6.8	9.0	3.1	1.5	9.2	0.2	26.5
06	36770	Irvine city, California	70.8	6.9	4.7	5.0	5.0	1.5	5.9	0.2	65.8
06	36868	Isla Vista CDP, California	58.5	0.0	5.8	3.5	30.1	0.0	2.1	0.0	34.0
06	37692	Jurupa Valley city, California	73.9	1.9	5.0	7.1	3.4	0.6	8.2	0.0	17.6
06	39003	La Cañada Flintridge city, California	50.2	9.1	16.8	6.8	4.0	1.3	11.4	0.4	70.9
06	39114	Ladera Ranch CDP, California	70.2	8.4	5.5	6.9	2.0	0.0	7.1	0.0	57.7
06	39122	Lafayette city, California	63.3	4.5	6.6	7.9	4.2	2.0	11.4	0.0	72.9
06	39178	Laguna Beach city, California	60.0	7.4	5.9	4.6	2.0	0.0	19.4	0.7	58.7
06	39220	Laguna Hills city, California	66.9	9.5	4.5	6.7	3.9	0.3	7.8	0.5	49.3
06	39248	Laguna Niguel city, California	64.7	8.9	5.2	5.4	2.3	0.6	12.9	0.0	51.7
06	39290	La Habra city, California	71.7	2.8	7.0	6.0	3.3	1.9	7.3	0.0	32.6
06	39486	Lake Elsinore city, California	73.6	2.0	3.5	6.9	2.3	2.6	9.1	0.0	25.4
06	39496	Lake Forest city, California	75.3	3.7	5.6	4.9	1.9	1.4	7.2	0.0	48.3
06	39766	Lakeside CDP, California	66.4	1.6	7.8	7.4	4.9	6.6	5.3	0.0	26.9
06	39892	Lakewood city, California	71.8	1.9	8.6	9.1	2.8	0.8	4.9	0.0	41.1
06	40004	La Mesa city, California	66.3	1.9	7.5	7.5	4.8	4.8	6.9	0.3	43.5
06	40032	La Mirada city, California	69.8	0.8	9.1	10.6	3.0	1.1	5.5	0.0	38.9
06	40130	Lancaster city, California	68.1	1.7	6.2	11.7	4.9	4.3	3.1	0.0	34.5
06	40326	La Presa CDP, California	71.4	0.6	4.6	6.4	1.7	5.5	9.5	0.2	23.8
06	40340	La Puente city, California	82.4	1.1	3.6	5.3	0.4	1.2	6.0	0.0	14.4
06	40354	La Quinta city, California	68.1	7.9	2.9	11.2	3.4	0.6	5.9	0.0	35.8
06	40704	Lathrop city, California	70.9	8.5	4.1	4.0	2.7	2.3	7.5	0.0	17.8
06	40830	La Verne city, California	56.8	4.9	13.7	9.1	4.7	1.0	9.8	0.0	44.5
06	40886	Lawndale city, California	72.8	1.7	4.0	4.6	2.4	0.7	13.7	0.0	24.6
06	41124	Lemon Grove city, California	68.8	0.7	8.3	4.0	6.4	2.7	8.7	0.5	32.1
06	41152	Lemoore city, California	52.6	1.4	3.8	5.9	13.4	16.7	5.9	0.2	28.9
06	41180	Lennox CDP, California	-	-	-	-	-	-	-	-	14.5
06	41474	Lincoln city, California	62.1	2.8	10.9	8.2	4.6	3.1	8.2	0.2	39.8
06	41992	Livermore city, California	74.3	2.2	4.9	9.0	1.4	3.6	4.3	0.2	46.2
06	42202	Lodi city, California	70.7	2.2	7.8	9.4	4.0	0.6	4.9	0.3	29.0
06	42370	Loma Linda city, California	53.2	2.0	25.4	11.5	1.8	3.3	2.7	0.0	56.6
06	42468	Lomita city, California	71.7	2.7	8.2	5.8	1.5	0.7	9.4	0.0	26.7
06	42524	Lompoc city, California	72.6	0.8	6.0	6.1	3.2	5.3	5.8	0.1	25.0
06	43000	Long Beach city, California	70.2	2.5	5.4	7.6	4.2	2.1	8.0	0.1	34.8
06	43280	Los Altos city, California	68.1	7.2	8.8	4.5	2.0	0.4	9.0	0.0	84.8
06	44000	Los Angeles city, California	68.3	4.7	6.2	5.3	2.7	0.9	11.7	0.2	37.5
06	44028	Los Banos city, California	78.4	1.2	4.2	6.6	3.4	0.0	6.2	0.0	14.7
06	44112	Los Gatos town, California	70.1	4.7	8.4	2.5	0.0	0.6	13.6	0.0	72.6
06	44574	Lynwood city, California	81.2	0.6	3.1	3.9	2.3	0.8	8.1	0.0	12.2
06	45022	Madera city, California	78.3	0.7	2.2	7.7	5.4	1.1	4.6	0.0	16.8
06	45400	Manhattan Beach city, California	57.4	12.2	10.4	7.0	0.9	1.3	10.6	0.3	68.6
06	45484	Manteca city, California	72.8	2.1	3.4	10.1	2.3	2.8	6.1	0.4	23.6
06	45778	Marina city, California	56.8	2.7	7.2	7.7	6.4	6.9	11.9	0.5	29.7
06	46114	Martinez city, California	70.0	2.0	6.5	12.5	5.4	0.8	2.9	0.0	44.1
06	46492	Maywood city, California	90.8	0.5	1.8	2.8	0.7	0.0	3.4	0.0	10.1
06	46646	Mead Valley CDP, California	-	-	-	-	-	-	-	-	18.4
06	46842	Menifee city, California	60.2	3.6	5.2	10.9	4.4	4.2	10.5	1.0	36.4
06	46870	Menlo Park city, California	63.7	4.6	12.6	5.8	3.2	1.8	7.7	0.5	63.4
06	46898	Merced city, California	64.5	0.5	8.1	11.2	8.0	0.7	6.5	0.5	29.6
06	47486	Millbrae city, California	71.8	3.5	10.0	6.5	1.0	1.3	5.9	0.0	53.0
06	47766	Milpitas city, California	81.7	1.4	2.9	5.1	2.7	2.7	3.5	0.0	48.3
06	48256	Mission Viejo city, California	69.6	5.4	5.0	7.2	2.8	2.5	7.1	0.3	48.0
06	48354	Modesto city, California	67.4	2.8	8.8	11.0	2.6	1.3	6.0	0.0	31.8
06	48648	Monrovia city, California	77.6	3.1	6.2	5.0	1.3	0.5	5.7	0.6	40.0
06	48788	Montclair city, California	81.2	1.0	5.1	5.4	1.2	1.6	4.6	0.0	14.6
06	48816	Montebello city, California	73.0	1.9	5.3	8.7	2.9	1.3	7.0	0.0	25.8
06	48872	Monterey city, California	59.2	6.0	7.7	5.4	4.9	7.2	8.1	1.5	49.2
06	48914	Monterey Park city, California	69.0	6.5	3.8	8.5	4.0	1.2	7.0	0.0	44.7
06	49138	Moorpark city, California	73.7	3.8	3.5	8.9	2.0	0.9	7.2	0.0	46.5
06	49270	Moreno Valley city, California	73.1	1.0	3.8	9.4	3.6	2.1	6.7	0.4	23.7
06	49278	Morgan Hill city, California	66.4	4.5	8.4	10.2	2.7	0.7	6.6	0.5	45.4
06	49670	Mountain View city, California	76.9	1.3	8.0	5.5	1.1	1.4	5.8	0.0	67.4
06	50076	Murrieta city, California	67.9	5.2	4.5	8.6	3.9	2.4	7.4	0.0	40.1
06	50258	Napa city, California	70.5	2.1	6.5	7.4	3.9	0.5	8.6	0.4	30.9
06	50398	National City city, California	79.4	1.2	5.3	6.0	1.3	2.1	4.9	0.0	16.3

Table E. Cities—Labor Force, Employment, and Educational Data, 2015—*Continued*

FIPS state code	FIPS place code	State/city	Employees of private companies	Self-employed in own incorporated business	Private not-for-profit wage and salary workers	Local	State	Federal	Self-employed in own not incorporated business	Unpaid family workers	Management, business, science, and arts occupations
06	50916	Newark city, California	76.1	3.4	4.4	8.0	0.0	1.3	6.6	0.2	38.5
06	51182	Newport Beach city, California	65.5	11.4	3.8	3.3	3.5	0.6	11.7	0.2	58.5
06	51560	Norco city, California	66.1	3.1	2.9	12.1	3.5	2.4	9.5	0.4	24.9
06	51924	North Highlands CDP, California	81.6	1.2	1.8	3.5	5.2	0.6	6.1	0.0	16.8
06	52379	North Tustin CDP, California	52.6	13.1	7.1	10.5	1.3	2.0	12.0	1.5	57.1
06	52526	Norwalk city, California	72.7	2.1	7.3	8.1	1.7	1.0	7.0	0.0	24.4
06	52582	Novato city, California	57.1	3.5	11.2	10.2	4.5	0.6	12.8	0.2	46.7
06	52694	Oakdale city, California	67.2	4.8	3.8	16.7	2.1	0.0	5.5	0.0	30.2
06	53000	Oakland city, California	61.5	2.6	11.6	8.1	4.2	1.6	10.4	0.1	44.0
06	53070	Oakley city, California	68.3	0.0	6.5	13.6	3.5	2.5	5.5	0.0	28.1
06	53322	Oceanside city, California	68.7	2.5	5.8	6.8	2.6	5.0	8.4	0.1	35.8
06	53448	Oildale CDP, California	-	-	-	-	-	-	-	-	16.6
06	53896	Ontario city, California	76.3	0.9	5.4	7.8	3.8	0.9	5.0	0.0	22.2
06	53980	Orange city, California	71.9	3.8	5.1	6.6	2.5	0.7	9.3	0.1	41.1
06	54092	Orangevale CDP, California	62.1	2.1	4.7	7.9	13.4	1.0	8.8	0.0	40.8
06	54120	Orcutt CDP, California	59.7	3.8	12.8	9.5	3.8	1.9	8.5	0.0	34.4
06	54652	Oxnard city, California	77.4	1.4	3.0	6.5	3.2	2.7	5.8	0.0	22.9
06	54806	Pacifica city, California	67.6	3.3	9.0	7.9	3.3	2.7	6.1	0.0	45.7
06	55156	Palmdale city, California	69.8	2.1	6.0	8.9	3.3	1.5	8.0	0.4	26.4
06	55184	Palm Desert city, California	61.8	6.5	7.4	5.5	4.1	1.1	13.4	0.2	36.3
06	55254	Palm Springs city, California	63.8	4.7	6.1	7.2	3.2	2.0	13.0	0.2	38.7
06	55282	Palo Alto city, California	66.9	6.2	13.4	4.2	1.5	0.1	7.7	0.0	78.0
06	55520	Paradise town, California	69.0	3.4	8.8	4.3	5.1	0.7	8.7	0.0	34.2
06	55618	Paramount city, California	75.9	1.3	4.2	9.9	1.2	1.2	6.1	0.2	19.4
06	56000	Pasadena city, California	57.6	4.1	19.4	6.7	3.4	0.8	7.9	0.2	51.8
06	56112	Patterson city, California	-	-	-	-	-	-	-	-	12.9
06	56700	Perris city, California	80.6	0.7	3.0	4.7	1.3	1.3	8.3	0.0	12.0
06	56784	Petaluma city, California	64.0	2.1	8.8	10.1	3.1	0.7	10.9	0.2	42.5
06	56924	Pico Rivera city, California	72.6	4.5	6.3	10.0	2.2	0.6	3.9	0.0	20.3
06	57456	Pittsburg city, California	71.4	1.3	7.3	8.5	2.3	1.8	6.8	0.5	31.3
06	57526	Placentia city, California	71.6	3.0	6.6	8.7	4.4	0.4	5.1	0.3	34.7
06	57764	Pleasant Hill city, California	59.7	2.2	13.9	9.9	2.8	1.2	10.0	0.3	54.4
06	57792	Pleasanton city, California	70.5	4.4	7.1	7.3	1.8	1.9	6.7	0.3	65.5
06	58072	Pomona city, California	74.0	1.8	5.9	8.8	3.1	0.9	5.4	0.1	26.9
06	58240	Porterville city, California	65.5	3.5	8.1	10.9	6.8	0.8	4.5	0.0	24.5
06	58296	Port Hueneme city, California	76.0	1.8	2.9	2.8	2.1	7.7	6.6	0.0	28.9
06	58520	Poway city, California	71.6	6.3	4.3	4.3	3.2	2.3	8.0	0.0	48.5
06	59346	Ramona CDP, California	77.0	2.1	10.0	2.8	1.6	0.9	5.2	0.3	33.1
06	59444	Rancho Cordova city, California	69.0	2.1	7.1	4.9	8.7	2.9	5.1	0.3	35.9
06	59451	Rancho Cucamonga city, California	64.5	2.7	8.1	13.8	3.7	1.2	5.9	0.2	41.1
06	59514	Rancho Palos Verdes city, California	56.0	12.4	8.4	9.8	4.0	2.6	6.8	0.0	60.2
06	59550	Rancho San Diego CDP, California	55.5	9.3	9.2	9.8	2.3	5.6	8.3	0.0	40.9
06	59587	Rancho Santa Margarita city, California	69.9	4.7	6.7	6.6	3.4	1.5	7.0	0.2	51.7
06	59920	Redding city, California	61.1	4.3	8.3	9.1	5.4	1.9	9.4	0.5	33.9
06	59962	Redlands city, California	60.0	3.0	11.3	12.9	7.5	0.4	4.6	0.2	41.8
06	60018	Redondo Beach city, California	66.6	5.7	6.1	8.0	3.1	1.2	9.1	0.1	58.9
06	60102	Redwood City city, California	68.9	3.9	9.8	6.6	2.3	1.3	6.8	0.4	48.2
06	60242	Reedley city, California	73.3	0.0	4.3	12.6	1.5	1.1	7.2	0.0	16.3
06	60466	Rialto city, California	75.9	0.9	3.9	7.6	4.3	0.6	6.8	0.0	15.7
06	60620	Richmond city, California	65.7	2.6	9.4	6.7	4.2	2.1	9.2	0.0	25.3
06	60704	Ridgecrest city, California	47.1	0.8	4.7	6.5	4.5	22.3	14.2	0.0	38.1
06	61068	Riverbank city, California	73.5	1.4	6.9	9.2	4.0	0.4	4.7	0.0	25.1
06	62000	Riverside city, California	70.0	2.3	5.3	10.1	5.0	1.3	5.8	0.2	28.7
06	62364	Rocklin city, California	61.5	3.2	9.5	7.7	7.4	1.8	8.7	0.3	48.1
06	62546	Rohnert Park city, California	70.4	2.8	4.7	5.9	5.2	2.5	8.5	0.0	31.2
06	62826	Rosamond CDP, California	51.3	0.6	9.7	14.3	5.0	18.7	0.5	0.0	35.4
06	62896	Rosemead city, California	75.3	4.1	2.1	5.9	4.5	1.3	6.6	0.1	26.0
06	62910	Rosemont CDP, California	59.4	2.0	7.5	10.2	13.3	2.6	4.2	0.7	36.3
06	62938	Roseville city, California	69.7	2.0	6.4	7.1	6.6	2.1	5.7	0.2	45.3
06	63218	Rowland Heights CDP, California	71.4	5.7	2.2	5.7	3.5	1.8	8.7	1.0	36.5
06	64000	Sacramento city, California	62.7	1.5	7.1	7.6	13.1	1.6	6.3	0.1	37.6
06	64224	Salinas city, California	76.9	1.4	5.7	7.2	3.6	1.2	4.0	0.0	18.0
06	65000	San Bernardino city, California	72.3	1.2	5.8	10.8	3.6	0.7	5.6	0.0	18.2
06	65028	San Bruno city, California	68.2	2.7	8.4	11.1	2.1	1.7	5.6	0.0	44.7
06	65042	San Buenaventura (Ventura) city, California	65.2	3.2	6.3	10.4	3.1	3.1	8.8	0.0	37.3
06	65070	San Carlos city, California	70.3	4.1	5.0	10.3	1.4	0.3	8.6	0.0	64.7
06	65084	San Clemente city, California	60.6	7.0	6.8	8.1	1.2	1.0	15.2	0.1	50.4
06	66000	San Diego city, California	66.7	3.4	7.6	5.9	4.3	4.1	7.9	0.1	45.3
06	66070	San Dimas city, California	65.8	2.7	5.4	12.9	3.3	1.6	8.2	0.0	42.5
06	66140	San Fernando city, California	73.8	0.9	7.7	6.3	3.0	1.0	7.0	0.3	20.9
06	67000	San Francisco city, California	69.4	2.9	8.8	5.4	3.4	1.6	8.2	0.2	54.5
06	67042	San Gabriel city, California	72.3	9.9	4.5	4.6	1.7	1.4	5.5	0.0	31.5
06	67056	Sanger city, California	76.5	2.1	3.4	5.0	6.4	2.2	4.3	0.0	21.0
06	67112	San Jacinto city, California	73.1	1.7	6.7	3.9	5.8	0.8	7.9	0.0	23.0

Table E. Cities—Labor Force, Employment, and Educational Data, 2015—*Continued*

FIPS state code	FIPS place code	State/city	Employees of private companies	Self-employed in own incorporated business	Private not-for-profit wage and salary workers	Government workers			Self-employed in own not incorporated business	Unpaid family workers	Percent in each occupation group
						Local	State	Federal			Management, business, science, and arts occupations
06	68000	San Jose city, California	75.9	2.1	5.9	6.9	2.6	1.1	5.5	0.0	44.7
06	68028	San Juan Capistrano city, California	62.4	4.4	6.3	3.8	2.8	0.0	19.5	0.7	31.1
06	68084	San Leandro city, California	71.4	2.2	7.2	6.8	4.1	2.1	5.6	0.6	29.6
06	68112	San Lorenzo CDP, California	73.7	1.2	7.8	8.6	3.8	2.0	2.9	0.0	27.1
06	68154	San Luis Obispo city, California	61.4	2.3	4.7	9.7	12.1	1.4	8.5	0.0	47.6
06	68196	San Marcos city, California	71.3	2.3	7.3	4.8	2.5	2.7	9.0	0.1	36.9
06	68252	San Mateo city, California	70.7	2.7	7.1	6.3	2.9	0.9	9.3	0.1	49.0
06	68294	San Pablo city, California	72.6	0.9	6.9	6.0	2.3	0.9	10.3	0.0	14.9
06	68364	San Rafael city, California	64.0	4.2	9.0	5.6	2.2	1.3	13.8	0.0	45.5
06	68378	San Ramon city, California	74.9	3.8	5.6	7.1	1.4	1.1	5.9	0.3	62.7
06	69000	Santa Ana city, California	83.5	2.4	3.1	3.8	1.3	0.3	5.5	0.1	17.1
06	69070	Santa Barbara city, California	59.4	4.0	12.7	6.9	5.6	0.4	10.8	0.1	45.5
06	69084	Santa Clara city, California	78.1	2.1	5.8	6.5	1.8	1.5	4.3	0.0	56.0
06	69088	Santa Clarita city, California	68.2	4.4	7.4	8.8	2.6	1.6	6.9	0.2	42.5
06	69112	Santa Cruz city, California	55.6	2.7	7.9	8.3	12.5	1.0	11.7	0.3	45.3
06	69196	Santa Maria city, California	77.8	1.1	4.3	7.9	2.5	1.6	4.5	0.3	16.4
06	70000	Santa Monica city, California	63.0	6.7	7.8	5.5	3.2	1.1	12.7	0.0	65.6
06	70042	Santa Paula city, California	76.4	1.8	2.3	10.6	1.4	0.8	4.2	2.4	20.3
06	70098	Santa Rosa city, California	67.1	1.6	7.5	8.1	2.8	1.2	11.6	0.1	33.8
06	70224	Santee city, California	69.8	2.9	8.1	5.8	3.3	4.3	5.7	0.0	38.6
06	70280	Saratoga city, California	65.1	8.3	4.4	10.2	1.3	0.5	9.4	0.8	77.2
06	70686	Seal Beach city, California	69.3	2.6	4.2	9.6	0.9	1.4	11.9	0.0	46.8
06	70742	Seaside city, California	67.5	4.9	3.5	5.6	2.6	6.6	8.6	0.7	28.5
06	70882	Selma city, California	63.3	3.3	4.0	13.6	7.9	4.0	3.5	0.3	15.7
06	72016	Simi Valley city, California	69.0	3.6	7.0	8.3	1.6	1.3	9.2	0.0	43.5
06	72520	Soledad city, California	-	-	-	-	-	-	-	-	21.3
06	72996	South El Monte city, California	70.9	2.9	2.8	5.3	4.0	0.7	13.4	0.0	20.9
06	73080	South Gate city, California	81.7	1.6	4.2	5.8	2.6	0.4	3.8	0.0	17.8
06	73108	South Lake Tahoe city, California	70.6	0.7	5.1	8.5	4.6	2.1	8.4	0.0	34.2
06	73220	South Pasadena city, California	55.2	6.4	9.9	8.5	2.5	1.2	16.2	0.0	56.3
06	73262	South San Francisco city, California	73.9	1.7	5.6	10.0	2.3	1.8	4.7	0.0	31.0
06	73290	South San Jose Hills CDP, California	83.5	1.3	2.6	6.6	1.5	1.8	2.7	0.0	16.5
06	73430	South Whittier CDP, California	80.6	1.9	4.7	5.7	2.8	1.2	3.0	0.0	22.7
06	73696	Spring Valley CDP (San Diego County), California	68.7	1.4	7.9	7.0	3.1	6.1	5.0	0.7	35.3
06	73962	Stanton city, California	76.7	3.3	2.6	4.5	2.6	2.0	7.7	0.6	22.5
06	75000	Stockton city, California	71.5	1.2	6.5	7.9	5.3	1.9	5.7	0.1	24.8
06	75630	Suisun City city, California	71.9	0.0	8.3	5.1	5.0	3.4	6.4	0.0	25.4
06	77000	Sunnyvale city, California	80.1	2.9	6.3	4.2	1.0	1.2	4.3	0.0	64.9
06	78120	Temecula city, California	66.6	3.2	4.5	8.9	5.3	2.1	8.6	0.9	38.0
06	78138	Temescal Valley CDP, California	59.1	3.2	8.7	10.8	4.3	6.9	6.9	0.0	30.6
06	78148	Temple City city, California	70.3	4.3	6.6	9.3	3.3	1.1	5.2	0.0	34.9
06	78582	Thousand Oaks city, California	67.5	6.9	5.2	8.5	2.7	1.0	7.9	0.2	52.2
06	80000	Torrance city, California	66.1	5.2	7.5	7.7	2.2	1.3	9.9	0.1	49.6
06	80238	Tracy city, California	77.9	2.5	3.9	4.0	2.8	4.6	4.2	0.1	28.9
06	80644	Tulare city, California	67.2	4.2	4.8	10.9	7.1	0.7	4.5	0.5	29.5
06	80812	Turlock city, California	70.2	0.6	5.0	11.4	7.7	0.3	4.7	0.0	34.4
06	80854	Tustin city, California	71.1	3.1	6.6	6.3	1.6	1.4	9.8	0.1	38.0
06	80994	Twentynine Palms city, California	-	-	-	-	-	-	-	-	28.4
06	81204	Union City city, California	76.3	2.6	3.6	7.6	2.6	3.6	3.6	0.1	42.1
06	81344	Upland city, California	69.9	2.4	7.8	9.0	4.8	0.1	5.7	0.3	38.7
06	81554	Vacaville city, California	63.3	1.1	8.9	10.1	7.2	3.8	5.5	0.2	29.4
06	81638	Valinda CDP, California	81.0	1.6	3.0	3.9	5.0	0.2	5.3	0.0	12.1
06	81666	Vallejo city, California	68.6	1.7	7.7	6.7	5.4	2.9	6.7	0.3	28.4
06	82590	Victorville city, California	68.7	0.6	6.2	10.6	2.0	5.4	6.4	0.0	29.1
06	82852	Vineyard CDP, California	56.4	4.2	7.3	12.4	7.5	1.9	10.3	0.0	39.5
06	82954	Visalia city, California	65.2	3.1	8.3	8.2	8.4	1.0	5.2	0.7	32.0
06	82996	Vista city, California	74.1	3.0	5.0	4.1	2.2	2.0	9.4	0.3	25.6
06	83332	Walnut city, California	68.7	4.7	3.6	10.0	3.2	1.5	8.0	0.4	53.7
06	83346	Walnut Creek city, California	57.8	4.5	10.6	8.6	3.8	2.7	12.0	0.0	67.2
06	83542	Wasco city, California	-	-	-	-	-	-	-	-	11.4
06	83668	Watsonville city, California	73.8	1.9	11.3	3.0	2.7	0.2	6.3	0.8	11.4
06	84144	West Carson CDP, California	76.1	2.4	5.1	6.8	1.8	2.1	5.1	0.6	29.3
06	84200	West Covina city, California	69.7	2.8	7.8	9.3	3.1	2.0	5.2	0.1	31.9
06	84410	West Hollywood city, California	69.7	7.0	5.5	2.7	0.6	0.6	13.8	0.0	52.9
06	84550	Westminster city, California	75.2	3.0	4.6	4.9	2.0	2.6	7.4	0.3	36.6
06	84592	Westmont CDP, California	67.9	1.0	3.9	12.5	2.7	2.2	9.8	0.0	21.9
06	84774	West Puente Valley CDP, California	-	-	-	-	-	-	-	-	16.0
06	84780	West Rancho Dominguez CDP, California	81.3	0.9	3.1	8.6	0.8	1.1	4.2	0.0	26.2
06	84816	West Sacramento city, California	63.8	0.0	4.2	8.5	14.7	1.8	7.1	0.0	35.0
06	84921	West Whittier-Los Nietos CDP, California	74.6	0.3	2.7	8.5	6.2	1.7	5.9	0.0	30.1
06	85292	Whittier city, California	68.4	2.3	6.7	12.3	5.9	1.0	3.5	0.0	30.6

Table E. Cities—Labor Force, Employment, and Educational Data, 2015—*Continued*

FIPS state code	FIPS place code	State/city	Employees of private companies	Self-employed in own incorporated business	Private not-for-profit wage and salary workers	Local	State	Federal	Self-employed in own not incorporated business	Unpaid family workers	Management, business, science, and arts occupations
06	85446	Wildomar city, California	77.7	0.6	2.6	5.6	6.0	1.2	6.4	0.0	24.8
06	85922	Windsor town, California	62.6	0.6	9.4	15.7	5.1	1.7	4.9	0.0	33.9
06	85992	Winter Gardens CDP, California	69.0	0.7	10.1	3.9	6.4	4.1	6.0	0.0	34.9
06	86328	Woodland city, California	62.4	1.1	9.4	10.3	8.5	1.1	7.3	0.0	33.3
06	86832	Yorba Linda city, California	63.6	5.9	6.2	8.2	3.9	0.9	11.1	0.1	55.2
06	86972	Yuba City city, California	66.6	2.2	2.5	11.5	5.9	2.5	7.3	1.4	32.1
06	87042	Yucaipa city, California	57.5	2.7	7.2	12.1	7.3	2.3	11.0	0.0	37.5
06	87056	Yucca Valley town, California	-	-	-	-	-	-	-	-	25.5
08	00000	**COLORADO**	67.9	4.8	7.8	6.3	4.1	2.6	6.3	0.2	41.2
08	03455	Arvada city, Colorado	68.9	5.2	8.3	5.8	4.1	1.8	5.6	0.2	45.9
08	04000	Aurora city, Colorado	73.4	3.0	6.9	4.5	3.2	3.4	5.5	0.1	32.6
08	07850	Boulder city, Colorado	62.6	5.3	8.8	4.9	8.4	1.3	8.6	0.1	55.5
08	08675	Brighton city, Colorado	72.4	3.5	9.4	6.2	4.1	1.5	2.9	0.0	29.0
08	09280	Broomfield city, Colorado	71.9	3.2	7.0	4.0	5.5	1.7	6.7	0.0	55.9
08	12415	Castle Rock town, Colorado	75.1	2.3	5.5	5.7	2.8	3.9	4.7	0.0	44.1
08	12815	Centennial city, Colorado	71.3	6.5	7.5	4.9	2.4	2.4	4.8	0.2	52.9
08	15165	Clifton CDP, Colorado	82.0	2.8	4.2	5.4	0.0	1.5	4.2	0.0	15.5
08	16000	Colorado Springs city, Colorado	65.2	4.3	9.6	6.3	4.1	4.4	5.7	0.3	41.2
08	16110	Columbine CDP, Colorado	71.5	8.1	4.6	4.3	5.4	2.1	4.0	0.0	47.1
08	16495	Commerce City city, Colorado	73.5	0.7	8.1	5.6	2.9	4.5	4.7	0.0	26.7
08	19150	Dakota Ridge CDP, Colorado	68.5	5.8	6.8	8.0	1.8	3.4	5.7	0.0	40.5
08	20000	Denver city, Colorado	70.7	4.4	9.1	4.4	3.4	2.4	5.6	0.1	45.8
08	24785	Englewood city, Colorado	73.3	3.8	5.8	5.9	1.6	1.2	8.1	0.3	39.4
08	24950	Erie town, Colorado	64.2	5.6	10.5	6.8	4.8	4.4	3.7	0.0	56.1
08	25280	Evans city, Colorado	83.2	1.8	6.0	3.2	4.3	0.4	1.1	0.0	18.2
08	27425	Fort Collins city, Colorado	65.2	3.0	7.6	5.4	11.5	2.4	4.8	0.2	48.0
08	27865	Fountain city, Colorado	57.7	2.5	9.6	10.3	2.3	14.1	3.4	0.0	26.4
08	30835	Golden city, Colorado	66.9	3.5	8.6	5.5	6.2	3.9	5.4	0.0	54.8
08	31660	Grand Junction city, Colorado	63.2	5.5	7.3	7.0	5.8	2.9	8.4	0.0	38.4
08	32155	Greeley city, Colorado	74.0	1.8	7.5	6.1	4.2	2.0	4.5	0.0	29.0
08	36410	Highlands Ranch CDP, Colorado	73.1	3.9	7.2	7.2	2.1	1.6	4.7	0.3	53.7
08	40377	Ken Caryl CDP, Colorado	66.5	6.3	7.2	10.0	2.3	1.6	5.9	0.3	48.1
08	41835	Lafayette city, Colorado	69.0	4.9	6.6	7.1	3.0	1.0	8.4	0.0	43.1
08	43000	Lakewood city, Colorado	71.2	4.5	6.7	4.5	3.3	3.6	6.2	0.1	41.2
08	45255	Littleton city, Colorado	68.6	6.5	8.2	6.6	3.0	1.3	5.4	0.3	49.9
08	45970	Longmont city, Colorado	73.5	3.9	6.5	6.8	2.5	1.4	5.3	0.2	43.7
08	46355	Louisville city, Colorado	64.7	5.4	8.4	7.2	5.6	1.7	7.0	0.0	59.5
08	46465	Loveland city, Colorado	66.4	3.2	8.9	9.6	4.3	0.8	6.9	0.0	36.4
08	54330	Northglenn city, Colorado	76.0	2.1	5.2	8.5	0.9	1.2	5.7	0.4	31.4
08	57630	Parker town, Colorado	67.1	6.6	8.9	6.5	4.1	1.1	5.6	0.0	52.2
08	62000	Pueblo city, Colorado	69.3	2.0	10.3	4.3	7.4	1.5	4.6	0.6	30.2
08	62220	Pueblo West CDP, Colorado	60.9	0.5	9.3	10.1	9.9	2.9	6.4	0.0	35.3
08	68847	Security-Widefield CDP, Colorado	64.9	4.1	4.9	7.6	1.5	12.9	4.2	0.0	25.2
08	77290	Thornton city, Colorado	72.4	3.0	6.8	8.3	3.5	1.1	4.7	0.2	34.2
08	83835	Westminster city, Colorado	74.2	3.0	7.0	5.3	3.4	1.6	5.5	0.2	39.6
08	84440	Wheat Ridge city, Colorado	69.0	4.4	8.6	4.6	3.7	1.5	7.9	0.3	39.6
08	85485	Windsor town, Colorado	64.8	5.6	7.2	9.6	5.9	0.8	5.8	0.3	50.2
09	00000	CONNECTICUT	67.6	3.4	9.4	7.4	4.4	1.4	6.2	0.2	42.4
09	08000	Bridgeport city, Connecticut	73.4	2.2	8.4	6.2	1.4	1.4	6.4	0.5	27.7
09	08420	Bristol city, Connecticut	78.5	1.0	5.6	5.4	5.3	1.2	2.6	0.4	34.5
09	18430	Danbury city, Connecticut	71.9	3.9	7.4	5.7	2.0	0.2	8.4	0.4	35.6
09	18920	Darien CDP, Connecticut	63.0	12.0	10.1	5.9	1.7	0.6	6.6	0.0	65.0
09	22700	East Hartford CDP, Connecticut	72.6	3.3	6.4	6.4	5.9	1.6	3.5	0.3	28.3
09	22980	East Haven CDP, Connecticut	76.4	0.2	6.5	5.0	3.8	2.9	5.3	0.0	33.3
09	37000	Hartford city, Connecticut	72.9	1.0	11.1	5.7	5.2	0.9	2.7	0.5	28.4
09	44690	Manchester CDP, Connecticut	64.8	2.2	8.6	12.9	7.4	1.4	2.7	0.0	35.2
09	46450	Meriden city, Connecticut	66.7	1.9	7.1	7.2	6.5	1.1	8.8	0.6	34.3
09	47290	Middletown city, Connecticut	71.4	1.3	11.7	5.0	5.5	0.4	4.7	0.0	47.1
09	47515	Milford city (balance), Connecticut	70.7	2.9	7.5	6.8	1.9	2.3	8.0	0.0	44.9
09	49880	Naugatuck borough, Connecticut	71.6	0.5	8.5	8.0	3.9	1.4	6.2	0.0	40.1
09	50370	New Britain city, Connecticut	79.1	0.4	5.7	4.9	5.4	0.0	4.5	0.0	25.6
09	52000	New Haven city, Connecticut	64.3	1.4	20.8	4.7	4.2	1.7	2.8	0.0	36.5
09	52210	Newington CDP, Connecticut	67.9	3.0	11.2	6.7	4.3	2.1	4.7	0.0	44.0
09	52280	New London city, Connecticut	76.4	0.6	11.9	4.6	2.1	0.9	3.4	0.0	23.4
09	54940	North Haven CDP, Connecticut	72.2	3.9	10.4	5.0	1.7	0.6	6.3	0.0	45.1
09	55990	Norwalk city, Connecticut	68.1	4.2	9.0	7.1	1.8	1.5	8.4	0.0	39.9
09	56200	Norwich city, Connecticut	68.6	0.9	8.9	7.5	4.5	6.1	3.4	0.0	24.5
09	68100	Shelton city, Connecticut	71.7	3.9	5.6	7.8	2.3	2.4	4.9	1.3	44.6
09	73000	Stamford city, Connecticut	72.3	2.5	7.7	5.5	1.7	1.2	9.0	0.1	44.5
09	74260	Stratford CDP, Connecticut	68.9	2.3	6.8	11.7	3.2	0.8	6.0	0.3	36.8
09	76500	Torrington city, Connecticut	78.8	2.9	6.8	4.9	1.9	0.3	4.4	0.0	28.1
09	77270	Trumbull CDP, Connecticut	66.5	1.4	9.6	9.6	4.0	1.0	7.9	0.0	57.1
09	80000	Waterbury city, Connecticut	75.9	0.5	7.7	7.3	3.9	0.3	4.1	0.2	22.3
09	82660	West Hartford CDP, Connecticut	60.9	3.1	14.5	5.7	6.9	0.9	7.1	0.8	62.3
09	82800	West Haven city, Connecticut	66.0	0.7	16.3	8.2	4.5	1.2	3.2	0.0	32.6

Table E. Cities—Labor Force, Employment, and Educational Data, 2015—*Continued*

FIPS state code	FIPS place code	State/city	Employees of private companies	Self-employed in own incorporated business	Private not-for-profit wage and salary workers	Government workers Local	State	Federal	Self-employed in own not incorporated business	Unpaid family workers	Percent in each occupation group Management, business, science, and arts occupations
09	83570	Westport CDP, Connecticut	63.6	7.7	6.9	7.8	1.4	0.0	12.6	0.0	69.6
09	84970	Wethersfield CDP, Connecticut	63.1	5.1	13.5	8.9	6.8	0.0	2.6	0.0	49.3
10	00000	**DELAWARE**	69.7	3.7	8.2	3.2	8.8	2.1	4.1	0.1	40.0
10	21200	Dover city, Delaware	65.9	2.0	4.3	3.4	18.1	4.9	1.3	0.0	33.3
10	50670	Newark city, Delaware	70.6	1.3	14.6	3.2	4.6	2.2	2.9	0.6	50.0
10	77580	Wilmington city, Delaware	75.4	2.2	7.6	4.9	6.0	1.3	2.6	0.0	33.4
11	00000	**DISTRICT OF COLUMBIA**	49.4	2.6	18.8	5.0	2.1	17.3	4.7	0.1	61.8
11	50000	Washington city, District of Columbia	49.4	2.6	18.8	5.0	2.1	17.3	4.7	0.1	61.8
12	00000	**FLORIDA**	70.4	5.8	6.1	6.8	2.8	1.9	6.0	0.2	34.5
12	00410	Alafaya CDP, Florida	70.8	5.0	8.1	9.4	2.0	1.7	2.9	0.0	47.6
12	00950	Altamonte Springs city, Florida	71.8	5.3	11.6	3.9	2.5	0.9	3.9	0.0	41.0
12	01700	Apopka city, Florida	70.0	5.1	11.3	8.4	2.3	1.7	1.2	0.0	40.9
12	02681	Aventura city, Florida	65.3	18.7	2.0	0.6	1.9	0.9	9.4	1.2	46.1
12	04162	Bayonet Point CDP, Florida	70.6	2.3	4.5	15.7	1.0	0.4	5.5	0.0	15.3
12	05462	Bellview CDP, Florida	63.3	0.2	10.5	13.8	4.1	5.3	2.7	0.0	31.0
12	06875	Bloomingdale CDP, Florida	68.9	4.6	7.4	10.3	3.5	3.6	1.7	0.0	47.1
12	07300	Boca Raton city, Florida	69.1	8.7	8.0	4.3	1.9	0.3	7.4	0.3	47.6
12	07525	Bonita Springs city, Florida	72.5	11.4	5.2	4.3	1.1	1.8	3.7	0.0	29.0
12	07875	Boynton Beach city, Florida	77.8	3.4	5.1	5.4	1.1	0.4	6.8	0.0	39.2
12	07950	Bradenton city, Florida	75.6	3.4	6.8	7.9	2.3	0.2	3.9	0.0	26.3
12	08150	Brandon CDP, Florida	71.0	3.6	7.0	7.6	2.3	3.6	4.9	0.0	36.8
12	08300	Brent CDP, Florida	-	-	-	-	-	-	-	-	19.8
12	09415	Buenaventura Lakes CDP, Florida	-	-	-	-	-	-	-	-	18.3
12	10275	Cape Coral city, Florida	66.8	7.4	6.1	7.5	1.2	1.5	9.4	0.0	29.7
12	10825	Carrollwood CDP, Florida	61.7	11.2	13.5	7.4	2.7	1.2	2.2	0.0	39.7
12	11050	Casselberry city, Florida	79.8	2.4	5.1	5.7	3.7	0.7	2.6	0.0	30.5
12	12425	Citrus Park CDP, Florida	70.0	11.1	7.3	3.7	3.2	0.5	4.1	0.0	43.1
12	12875	Clearwater city, Florida	75.4	3.4	7.2	4.4	2.1	2.0	5.5	0.0	35.1
12	12925	Clermont city, Florida	58.1	0.5	7.9	14.0	3.1	8.1	8.4	0.0	53.4
12	13275	Coconut Creek city, Florida	69.8	9.1	3.9	10.1	1.7	0.2	5.1	0.0	35.1
12	14125	Cooper City, Florida	68.0	9.8	10.6	5.7	1.8	0.7	3.1	0.2	40.7
12	14250	Coral Gables city, Florida	62.0	18.2	5.8	5.5	1.8	1.4	5.0	0.2	60.7
12	14400	Coral Springs city, Florida	68.2	8.3	4.0	6.3	2.4	1.7	8.9	0.1	37.4
12	14412	Coral Terrace CDP, Florida	72.8	2.6	12.0	3.8	0.9	2.5	5.4	0.0	30.1
12	14895	Country Club CDP, Florida	75.0	7.1	3.6	5.1	1.7	0.1	7.3	0.0	29.1
12	15475	Crestview city, Florida	57.4	0.0	8.2	17.4	5.7	11.3	0.0	0.0	40.8
12	15968	Cutler Bay town, Florida	68.5	4.7	6.6	8.7	3.6	2.8	5.2	0.0	45.0
12	16335	Dania Beach city, Florida	81.2	2.4	4.8	2.9	1.3	2.2	5.0	0.2	33.4
12	16475	Davie town, Florida	67.7	7.7	6.4	9.4	1.0	1.3	6.1	0.4	37.1
12	16525	Daytona Beach city, Florida	71.6	4.8	8.3	5.1	3.1	0.6	6.4	0.0	31.9
12	16725	Deerfield Beach city, Florida	72.3	4.6	5.4	8.1	0.9	0.5	8.2	0.1	25.9
12	16875	DeLand city, Florida	76.3	6.4	4.1	6.0	1.4	1.8	3.9	0.0	33.0
12	17100	Delray Beach city, Florida	70.3	4.8	8.6	4.8	2.0	1.4	7.3	0.8	36.3
12	17200	Deltona city, Florida	78.2	3.5	4.9	4.2	2.6	1.3	5.3	0.0	29.7
12	17935	Doral city, Florida	71.1	11.5	3.7	2.2	2.3	1.1	8.1	0.0	45.0
12	18575	Dunedin city, Florida	65.5	6.0	10.5	6.5	2.3	1.8	7.0	0.4	42.4
12	19206	East Lake CDP, Florida	71.0	8.5	6.8	4.0	0.5	4.6	4.5	0.0	45.6
12	19212	East Lake-Orient Park CDP, Florida	74.7	4.2	5.7	4.9	2.9	2.3	5.3	0.0	25.9
12	19825	Edgewater city, Florida	77.1	4.0	8.5	6.1	0.9	0.9	2.5	0.0	25.2
12	20108	Egypt Lake-Leto CDP, Florida	82.5	4.4	1.2	3.0	2.3	0.7	5.5	0.4	29.0
12	20925	Ensley CDP, Florida	67.3	2.6	7.2	6.8	1.4	6.6	7.3	0.9	21.6
12	21150	Estero village, Florida	66.5	9.6	5.4	4.7	3.7	2.3	7.7	0.0	46.1
12	22275	Ferry Pass CDP, Florida	66.1	1.8	13.6	3.6	4.4	0.9	9.4	0.0	39.6
12	22660	Fleming Island CDP, Florida	70.8	5.4	1.9	9.0	2.8	4.2	5.9	0.0	46.7
12	23050	Florida Ridge CDP, Florida	-	-	-	-	-	-	-	-	22.6
12	24000	Fort Lauderdale city, Florida	70.5	8.9	4.8	7.1	1.6	1.1	5.9	0.1	37.7
12	24125	Fort Myers city, Florida	74.4	4.0	7.5	7.0	1.5	0.8	4.8	0.0	28.8
12	24300	Fort Pierce city, Florida	71.3	5.2	5.5	8.3	4.5	0.5	4.7	0.0	13.4
12	24475	Fort Walton Beach city, Florida	66.8	2.0	3.6	7.5	5.8	6.4	8.0	0.0	33.2
12	24562	Fountainebleau CDP, Florida	78.0	3.9	3.2	5.8	1.8	0.9	6.4	0.0	29.5
12	24581	Four Corners CDP, Florida	87.8	3.0	3.4	3.2	1.1	0.4	1.1	0.0	24.2
12	24925	Fruit Cove CDP, Florida	61.5	8.6	12.1	11.2	1.2	1.4	4.0	0.0	56.4
12	25175	Gainesville city, Florida	60.4	3.0	10.6	6.4	14.2	3.1	2.4	0.0	44.8
12	26300	Golden Gate CDP, Florida	81.7	3.9	3.2	1.7	0.0	0.0	9.5	0.0	12.0
12	26375	Golden Glades CDP, Florida	79.5	0.3	4.9	10.1	0.8	2.4	2.1	0.0	26.1
12	27322	Greenacres city, Florida	76.5	6.5	2.9	6.8	1.3	0.9	5.1	0.0	27.6
12	28400	Haines City city, Florida	74.4	3.7	7.5	2.6	3.1	0.3	8.4	0.0	22.7
12	28452	Hallandale Beach city, Florida	75.5	5.9	2.4	6.9	0.4	0.6	8.4	0.0	27.9
12	30000	Hialeah city, Florida	79.1	3.9	2.6	3.9	0.7	0.8	8.8	0.2	17.7
12	30025	Hialeah Gardens city, Florida	71.6	4.2	2.2	4.5	0.4	0.9	16.3	0.0	21.8
12	31075	Holiday CDP, Florida	69.2	9.8	4.1	5.5	1.6	0.0	9.7	0.0	21.0
12	32000	Hollywood city, Florida	69.8	7.4	4.7	6.9	1.4	1.0	8.5	0.2	31.9
12	32275	Homestead city, Florida	70.6	3.7	4.5	12.5	1.3	4.9	2.2	0.3	26.5

Table E. Cities—Labor Force, Employment, and Educational Data, 2015—*Continued*

			Class of worker (percent)			Government workers					Percent in each occupation group
FIPS state code	FIPS place code	State/city	Employees of private companies	Self-employed in own incorporated business	Private not-for-profit wage and salary workers	Local	State	Federal	Self-employed in own not incorporated business	Unpaid family workers	Management, business, science, and arts occupations
12	32610	Horizon West CDP, Florida	-	-	-	-	-	-	-	-	56.1
12	32967	Hunters Creek CDP, Florida	-	-	-	-	-	-	-	-	43.1
12	33250	Immokalee CDP, Florida	82.1	0.5	2.2	5.2	0.5	0.0	9.5	0.0	8.8
12	35000	Jacksonville city, Florida	73.5	3.0	7.7	5.6	3.0	3.0	4.2	0.1	36.2
12	35050	Jacksonville Beach city, Florida	70.6	10.5	6.6	2.0	2.8	1.2	6.2	0.0	42.7
12	35350	Jasmine Estates CDP, Florida	70.8	10.3	3.1	10.3	2.3	0.4	2.8	0.0	32.4
12	35875	Jupiter town, Florida	77.1	7.3	4.4	3.4	1.7	0.6	5.4	0.1	40.7
12	36062	Kendale Lakes CDP, Florida	73.3	7.2	3.8	6.7	1.6	1.4	6.0	0.0	27.6
12	36100	Kendall CDP, Florida	66.4	8.7	7.5	7.5	3.1	0.4	6.2	0.2	55.7
12	36121	Kendall West CDP, Florida	70.1	7.8	5.5	8.8	1.2	1.5	4.9	0.2	26.1
12	36462	Keystone CDP, Florida	60.0	11.3	7.7	7.6	1.0	3.1	9.2	0.0	53.1
12	36550	Key West city, Florida	63.4	4.4	6.6	7.3	3.0	10.4	4.0	0.8	35.1
12	36950	Kissimmee city, Florida	79.8	3.1	6.6	4.4	2.9	1.4	1.8	0.0	20.1
12	37648	Lake Butler CDP, Florida	-	-	-	-	-	-	-	-	65.3
12	38250	Lakeland city, Florida	74.6	4.2	6.9	7.4	2.1	0.4	4.3	0.1	32.9
12	38350	Lake Magdalene CDP, Florida	70.3	6.6	9.4	4.4	3.4	2.3	3.2	0.3	40.4
12	38813	Lakeside CDP, Florida	61.8	3.7	15.3	8.2	1.3	5.0	4.6	0.0	26.3
12	39075	Lake Worth city, Florida	75.8	6.4	5.0	5.0	0.8	0.7	6.3	0.0	25.9
12	39200	Land O' Lakes CDP, Florida	63.3	4.0	11.2	10.7	3.4	2.9	4.5	0.0	48.4
12	39425	Largo city, Florida	77.1	3.7	6.3	6.4	0.5	1.3	4.7	0.0	29.6
12	39525	Lauderdale Lakes city, Florida	76.0	4.0	2.9	5.7	1.2	0.6	9.6	0.0	8.1
12	39550	Lauderhill city, Florida	77.4	4.7	3.0	6.9	0.8	0.8	5.7	0.7	25.7
12	39875	Leesburg city, Florida	-	-	-	-	-	-	-	-	17.4
12	39925	Lehigh Acres CDP, Florida	75.2	6.1	5.3	6.5	2.0	1.2	3.8	0.1	20.4
12	39950	Leisure City CDP, Florida	-	-	-	-	-	-	-	-	4.9
12	41775	Lutz CDP, Florida	62.2	8.5	11.3	6.2	3.3	2.7	5.8	0.0	50.2
12	41825	Lynn Haven city, Florida	61.7	5.9	8.7	10.2	4.0	4.5	5.1	0.0	45.6
12	43125	Margate city, Florida	74.4	2.8	8.7	5.4	1.2	1.0	6.5	0.0	32.3
12	43800	Meadow Woods CDP, Florida	-	-	-	-	-	-	-	-	28.3
12	43975	Melbourne city, Florida	74.4	5.0	7.5	5.2	1.2	3.1	3.2	0.4	36.3
12	44275	Merritt Island CDP, Florida	65.6	10.5	6.4	7.5	0.5	1.5	7.2	0.7	37.8
12	45000	Miami city, Florida	73.9	5.4	4.8	4.1	1.6	1.5	8.6	0.0	29.3
12	45025	Miami Beach city, Florida	65.6	16.0	3.5	2.9	1.0	0.5	9.7	0.8	42.3
12	45060	Miami Gardens city, Florida	67.0	1.7	6.0	16.0	1.8	2.5	5.0	0.0	17.7
12	45100	Miami Lakes town, Florida	65.8	8.2	9.7	6.8	1.1	3.3	5.2	0.0	42.0
12	45975	Miramar city, Florida	69.3	5.0	5.0	9.1	3.1	1.7	6.8	0.0	40.7
12	47625	Naples city, Florida	56.2	17.3	7.2	5.9	0.5	0.6	12.4	0.0	43.7
12	48050	Navarre CDP, Florida	63.7	3.1	7.2	4.0	2.5	12.3	7.2	0.0	45.8
12	48625	New Smyrna Beach city, Florida	64.0	9.4	3.5	16.4	1.2	1.1	4.4	0.0	36.1
12	49260	Northdale CDP, Florida	71.8	5.0	8.9	9.2	0.7	0.7	3.7	0.0	39.6
12	49350	North Fort Myers CDP, Florida	61.6	6.1	8.3	8.2	0.7	0.3	14.8	0.0	23.9
12	49425	North Lauderdale city, Florida	76.8	3.4	2.6	7.3	1.3	0.8	7.7	0.0	17.5
12	49450	North Miami city, Florida	74.0	4.9	4.6	7.8	1.4	0.5	6.6	0.2	20.3
12	49475	North Miami Beach city, Florida	76.6	2.8	1.9	5.2	0.2	3.2	10.2	0.0	19.4
12	49675	North Port city, Florida	75.8	1.6	4.4	10.4	0.7	0.6	6.5	0.0	39.4
12	50575	Oakland Park city, Florida	73.0	2.6	6.4	6.8	0.8	1.8	8.6	0.0	31.6
12	50630	Oakleaf Plantation CDP, Florida	68.6	2.7	6.6	4.5	0.7	14.1	2.8	0.0	27.9
12	50638	Oak Ridge CDP, Florida	-	-	-	-	-	-	-	-	16.5
12	50750	Ocala city, Florida	66.8	5.0	7.2	8.4	4.3	1.6	6.8	0.0	34.5
12	51075	Ocoee city, Florida	79.9	4.0	7.0	4.6	2.0	0.0	2.5	0.1	39.9
12	53000	Orlando city, Florida	78.9	3.4	5.1	4.0	1.4	1.7	5.4	0.1	35.5
12	53150	Ormond Beach city, Florida	61.8	9.6	10.4	8.7	2.1	0.2	7.2	0.0	33.4
12	53575	Oviedo city, Florida	64.3	7.9	8.2	6.9	3.0	6.0	3.5	0.3	48.7
12	53725	Pace CDP, Florida	66.8	2.3	9.3	6.7	2.8	6.7	5.5	0.0	33.0
12	54000	Palm Bay city, Florida	73.8	5.7	7.1	6.2	1.7	3.2	2.3	0.0	32.9
12	54075	Palm Beach Gardens city, Florida	70.0	10.0	4.6	5.4	0.3	2.6	7.0	0.1	48.1
12	54175	Palm City CDP, Florida	66.1	10.9	6.7	6.6	1.7	0.4	6.6	1.0	48.5
12	54200	Palm Coast city, Florida	75.6	5.3	6.3	5.6	0.6	0.6	6.0	0.0	33.0
12	54275	Palmetto Bay village, Florida	63.6	10.1	9.9	9.8	2.0	1.3	3.1	0.0	48.1
12	54300	Palmetto Estates CDP, Florida	73.2	4.9	1.3	14.1	1.0	1.9	3.6	0.0	20.4
12	54350	Palm Harbor CDP, Florida	73.0	6.7	8.8	4.7	1.1	1.8	3.4	0.5	43.8
12	54387	Palm River-Clair Mel CDP, Florida	79.4	4.3	3.6	8.9	0.2	1.4	2.3	0.0	23.3
12	54450	Palm Springs village, Florida	80.1	2.5	3.6	6.2	0.0	0.9	6.6	0.0	15.8
12	54525	Palm Valley CDP, Florida	72.1	8.7	8.6	3.5	3.3	1.7	2.1	0.0	64.4
12	54700	Panama City city, Florida	64.4	4.0	6.1	5.8	4.3	7.2	7.7	0.4	35.3
12	55125	Parkland city, Florida	63.9	11.5	3.0	4.7	2.6	1.1	13.2	0.0	57.1
12	55775	Pembroke Pines city, Florida	67.3	4.9	5.7	9.3	2.9	3.2	6.4	0.1	43.1
12	55925	Pensacola city, Florida	69.8	1.9	12.4	5.0	3.0	2.6	5.1	0.1	37.8
12	56825	Pine Hills CDP, Florida	80.2	0.8	5.3	8.9	0.9	0.3	3.6	0.0	18.8
12	56975	Pinellas Park city, Florida	74.1	4.3	5.6	4.8	4.1	2.4	4.5	0.2	31.0
12	57425	Plantation city, Florida	68.9	11.2	5.5	5.4	2.9	1.4	4.6	0.0	43.7
12	57550	Plant City city, Florida	79.4	2.7	6.7	6.7	0.7	0.8	3.1	0.0	23.7
12	57900	Poinciana CDP, Florida	83.5	2.2	3.2	5.9	0.5	0.0	4.7	0.0	16.2
12	58050	Pompano Beach city, Florida	71.3	6.3	4.3	5.1	1.5	0.8	10.5	0.2	25.5
12	58350	Port Charlotte CDP, Florida	73.0	7.4	6.0	4.4	3.7	2.5	2.9	0.0	21.6
12	58575	Port Orange city, Florida	73.8	4.5	5.1	7.3	4.3	0.5	4.4	0.0	35.3

Table E. Cities—Labor Force, Employment, and Educational Data, 2015—*Continued*

FIPS state code	FIPS place code	State/city	Employees of private companies	Self-employed in own incorporated business	Private not-for-profit wage and salary workers	Government workers — Local	State	Federal	Self-employed in own not incorporated business	Unpaid family workers	Percent in each occupation group — Management, business, science, and arts occupations
12	58715	Port St. Lucie city, Florida	72.4	5.9	7.2	6.5	2.1	0.6	5.0	0.4	28.1
12	58975	Princeton CDP, Florida	66.3	5.8	3.1	13.8	3.2	0.7	7.2	0.0	29.4
12	60230	Richmond West CDP, Florida	62.7	8.1	6.6	9.0	3.0	1.8	8.7	0.0	33.3
12	60950	Riverview CDP, Florida	73.0	5.1	4.0	7.9	1.4	5.0	3.5	0.1	37.5
12	60975	Riviera Beach city, Florida	77.4	3.3	3.0	8.0	1.0	2.1	5.2	0.0	23.2
12	61500	Rockledge city, Florida	70.6	5.9	5.4	5.5	5.4	3.7	3.5	0.0	35.1
12	62100	Royal Palm Beach village, Florida	68.2	5.8	2.4	12.9	5.2	1.7	3.8	0.0	40.4
12	62275	Ruskin CDP, Florida	74.5	2.7	7.4	7.1	2.6	2.2	3.6	0.0	27.1
12	62625	St. Cloud city, Florida	76.3	1.8	2.7	14.5	1.2	1.7	1.9	0.0	26.4
12	63000	St. Petersburg city, Florida	67.7	5.4	7.4	8.2	2.7	1.9	6.3	0.4	40.5
12	63425	San Carlos Park CDP, Florida	76.8	4.5	6.0	5.1	4.9	0.0	2.7	0.0	21.6
12	63650	Sanford city, Florida	69.8	2.4	9.6	9.8	2.1	0.9	4.1	1.2	34.8
12	64175	Sarasota city, Florida	64.7	6.3	11.0	6.4	2.2	0.5	8.8	0.0	35.2
12	64825	Sebastian city, Florida	67.3	5.0	3.4	14.5	1.4	1.1	6.5	0.9	34.9
12	67258	South Bradenton CDP, Florida	-	-	-	-	-	-	-	-	15.5
12	67575	South Miami Heights CDP, Florida	69.0	4.8	8.1	7.7	1.2	0.6	8.7	0.0	22.8
12	68350	Spring Hill CDP, Florida	74.4	4.3	2.9	9.6	1.9	1.0	5.8	0.3	30.1
12	69250	Sun City Center CDP, Florida	-	-	-	-	-	-	-	-	48.4
12	69555	Sunny Isles Beach city, Florida	75.0	6.1	4.7	2.5	1.9	0.5	7.6	1.7	43.8
12	69700	Sunrise city, Florida	75.8	4.1	3.4	8.2	2.5	1.5	4.4	0.0	30.3
12	70345	Sweetwater city, Florida	74.0	6.3	4.6	5.7	0.2	0.0	9.2	0.0	23.8
12	70600	Tallahassee city, Florida	56.4	2.3	8.9	6.8	19.5	2.2	3.9	0.0	42.6
12	70675	Tamarac city, Florida	74.0	5.0	5.0	10.7	0.3	0.5	4.4	0.0	40.1
12	70700	Tamiami CDP, Florida	74.5	7.3	3.0	6.9	1.1	0.6	6.7	0.0	26.9
12	71000	Tampa city, Florida	71.7	4.9	7.4	6.1	3.0	2.0	4.8	0.2	40.6
12	71150	Tarpon Springs city, Florida	72.3	5.4	4.8	2.7	1.4	1.5	11.9	0.0	35.7
12	71400	Temple Terrace city, Florida	62.9	5.2	6.6	14.4	5.6	2.4	2.5	0.3	46.9
12	71564	The Acreage CDP, Florida	65.3	12.4	1.9	13.0	1.7	0.7	4.8	0.2	30.3
12	71567	The Crossings CDP, Florida	66.1	9.0	10.3	9.4	1.4	0.6	3.1	0.0	44.9
12	71569	The Hammocks CDP, Florida	76.3	6.6	6.3	5.1	2.6	0.2	2.4	0.4	34.7
12	71625	The Villages CDP, Florida	-	-	-	-	-	-	-	-	53.2
12	71741	Three Lakes CDP, Florida	73.0	7.2	5.1	6.6	0.9	3.7	3.6	0.0	35.3
12	71900	Titusville city, Florida	68.5	2.5	10.4	7.5	0.4	3.2	7.5	0.0	24.4
12	72145	Town 'n' Country CDP, Florida	75.9	3.7	6.8	7.3	0.8	1.4	4.2	0.0	33.1
12	73163	University CDP (Hillsborough County), Florida	77.4	1.4	3.2	5.0	9.0	1.0	3.0	0.0	24.4
12	73172	University CDP (Orange County), Florida	84.7	2.1	1.8	4.4	1.4	0.0	5.6	0.0	29.2
12	73287	University Park CDP, Florida	68.2	6.7	4.2	6.1	3.0	2.6	9.2	0.0	40.5
12	73700	Valrico CDP, Florida	66.5	4.6	9.1	9.4	2.7	5.9	1.9	0.0	51.9
12	73900	Venice city, Florida	68.9	3.3	4.4	7.2	1.6	0.0	14.7	0.0	28.4
12	74200	Vero Beach South CDP, Florida	61.4	7.4	7.0	8.2	3.3	1.2	10.1	1.3	26.4
12	75725	Wekiwa Springs CDP, Florida	70.8	7.3	6.3	6.3	3.5	0.8	4.8	0.4	55.6
12	75812	Wellington village, Florida	70.8	5.9	3.3	9.0	2.8	2.5	5.7	0.0	51.8
12	75875	Wesley Chapel CDP, Florida	69.2	6.1	6.3	7.8	3.5	3.3	3.7	0.0	45.9
12	76062	Westchase CDP, Florida	76.7	5.8	4.5	5.1	2.9	1.1	3.8	0.0	53.8
12	76075	Westchester CDP, Florida	73.0	8.7	3.0	3.1	2.5	1.7	8.0	0.0	29.6
12	76487	West Little River CDP, Florida	66.7	1.7	4.4	15.1	0.6	0.0	11.5	0.0	12.9
12	76500	West Melbourne city, Florida	-	-	-	-	-	-	-	-	44.7
12	76582	Weston city, Florida	69.1	10.8	6.1	5.4	3.6	1.5	3.3	0.0	52.9
12	76600	West Palm Beach city, Florida	70.9	4.1	6.3	8.9	2.8	2.0	5.0	0.0	33.6
12	76675	West Pensacola CDP, Florida	68.6	3.8	8.5	5.1	3.1	2.0	8.8	0.0	19.7
12	78250	Winter Garden city, Florida	72.7	11.4	4.9	0.9	0.8	0.0	8.9	0.4	42.4
12	78275	Winter Haven city, Florida	78.9	1.7	12.0	2.6	1.3	1.7	1.7	0.0	27.0
12	78300	Winter Park city, Florida	62.4	13.0	9.0	4.5	2.5	1.1	7.6	0.0	55.2
12	78325	Winter Springs city, Florida	64.7	10.2	8.2	5.9	3.9	1.0	6.1	0.0	51.9
12	78800	Wright CDP, Florida	74.2	2.2	6.6	5.8	0.0	7.7	3.5	0.0	30.9
13	00000	**GEORGIA**	69.7	3.9	6.1	6.9	4.8	3.0	5.4	0.2	36.4
13	00408	Acworth city, Georgia	-	-	-	-	-	-	-	-	48.0
13	01052	Albany city, Georgia	69.2	1.1	4.8	7.5	7.3	7.1	3.0	0.0	29.3
13	01696	Alpharetta city, Georgia	75.4	6.9	5.7	3.9	1.2	0.9	5.5	0.5	57.1
13	03440	Athens-Clarke County unified government (balance), Georgia	61.7	2.2	6.8	8.1	16.5	1.0	3.8	0.0	39.1
13	04000	Atlanta city, Georgia	67.0	4.8	8.8	6.5	5.5	2.4	4.9	0.1	51.2
13	04204	Augusta-Richmond County consolidated government (balance), Georgia	71.9	1.5	3.5	6.4	6.2	6.2	4.3	0.1	28.3
13	10944	Brookhaven city, Georgia	74.3	5.6	7.0	3.2	1.8	2.2	5.7	0.2	54.9
13	12834	Candler-McAfee CDP, Georgia	65.8	0.0	5.6	12.5	8.1	2.3	5.8	0.0	26.2
13	12988	Canton city, Georgia	75.5	5.4	9.0	6.9	1.4	0.0	1.8	0.0	39.3
13	13492	Carrollton city, Georgia	70.0	2.1	6.6	4.3	7.7	3.2	6.1	0.0	27.0
13	13688	Cartersville city, Georgia	75.1	2.0	8.3	5.9	7.2	1.6	0.0	0.0	24.7
13	15172	Chamblee city, Georgia	80.6	3.0	5.5	2.3	2.0	1.1	5.4	0.0	36.6
13	19000	Columbus city, Georgia	66.2	1.8	8.0	6.5	6.3	7.5	3.7	0.1	31.8
13	21380	Dalton city, Georgia	87.7	2.3	2.4	3.5	1.3	0.7	2.1	0.0	15.0

Table E. Cities—Labor Force, Employment, and Educational Data, 2015—*Continued*

| | | | Class of worker (percent) | | | | | | | | Percent in each occupation group |
| | | | | | | Government workers | | | | | |
FIPS state code	FIPS place code	State/city	Employees of private companies	Self-employed in own incorporated business	Private not-for-profit wage and salary workers	Local	State	Federal	Self-employed in own not incorporated business	Unpaid family workers	Management, business, science, and arts occupations
13	22052	Decatur city, Georgia	54.8	6.2	23.9	4.5	3.9	3.3	3.5	0.0	77.0
13	23900	Douglasville city, Georgia	65.8	3.4	10.0	10.1	6.5	2.5	1.7	0.0	41.2
13	24600	Duluth city, Georgia	76.5	2.3	7.4	4.4	2.7	1.5	5.2	0.0	42.3
13	24768	Dunwoody city, Georgia	76.1	5.0	3.9	3.7	1.2	2.4	7.5	0.1	62.6
13	25720	East Point city, Georgia	67.9	3.6	7.3	12.7	4.5	0.6	3.4	0.0	31.9
13	28044	Evans CDP, Georgia	65.1	7.6	5.4	2.6	5.4	6.9	6.9	0.0	51.3
13	31908	Gainesville city, Georgia	81.5	1.5	5.8	1.7	1.7	2.8	5.0	0.0	19.2
13	35324	Griffin city, Georgia	70.3	3.4	2.3	9.9	9.2	3.8	1.1	0.0	27.0
13	38964	Hinesville city, Georgia	66.8	0.9	4.1	6.9	6.9	10.6	3.7	0.1	24.0
13	42425	Johns Creek city, Georgia	77.3	5.6	4.6	6.3	1.4	1.5	2.8	0.4	63.4
13	43192	Kennesaw city, Georgia	76.6	2.6	6.2	5.3	4.0	2.5	2.7	0.0	34.7
13	44340	LaGrange city, Georgia	74.1	0.6	7.2	5.6	5.5	0.9	6.2	0.0	25.1
13	45488	Lawrenceville city, Georgia	77.5	0.4	5.4	9.6	1.6	2.4	2.7	0.5	34.3
13	48288	Mableton CDP, Georgia	69.1	5.3	8.3	5.7	2.5	2.0	6.7	0.4	38.2
13	48624	McDonough city, Georgia	69.3	2.5	9.0	6.5	4.4	6.5	1.7	0.0	26.7
13	49008	Macon-Bibb County, Georgia	69.2	3.7	8.5	6.8	3.7	4.2	3.7	0.3	36.3
13	49756	Marietta city, Georgia	68.9	5.9	5.6	5.6	2.1	1.4	10.5	0.0	39.5
13	50036	Martinez CDP, Georgia	65.0	5.3	7.6	6.5	4.4	4.6	6.6	0.0	44.2
13	51670	Milton city, Georgia	69.2	9.1	7.2	4.1	2.0	0.8	7.6	0.0	54.0
13	55020	Newnan city, Georgia	68.3	2.2	8.9	7.3	4.5	2.3	6.6	0.0	35.0
13	56168	North Druid Hills CDP, Georgia	54.2	4.3	15.5	7.3	7.3	4.9	5.9	0.6	69.3
13	59724	Peachtree City city, Georgia	71.9	5.6	7.8	5.7	2.8	3.1	2.9	0.2	50.2
13	59735	Peachtree Corners city, Georgia	64.1	6.3	8.4	3.3	2.5	3.3	11.0	1.1	50.6
13	62104	Pooler city, Georgia	-	-	-	-	-	-	-	-	40.2
13	63952	Redan CDP, Georgia	74.0	0.7	8.9	4.7	3.8	4.2	3.7	0.0	30.4
13	66668	Rome city, Georgia	75.8	3.4	7.6	6.8	4.1	0.3	2.0	0.0	28.8
13	67284	Roswell city, Georgia	77.5	5.2	4.5	3.0	1.8	1.0	6.9	0.0	50.4
13	68516	Sandy Springs city, Georgia	72.6	5.5	8.1	2.9	1.9	0.9	8.0	0.1	58.3
13	69000	Savannah city, Georgia	70.4	2.5	8.1	4.8	6.5	2.7	4.8	0.2	28.5
13	71492	Smyrna city, Georgia	73.9	2.7	6.1	4.5	2.5	2.6	7.7	0.0	49.2
13	73256	Statesboro city, Georgia	-	-	-	-	-	-	-	-	24.4
13	73704	Stockbridge city, Georgia	74.3	1.2	6.2	9.7	2.4	3.5	2.7	0.0	34.4
13	74180	Sugar Hill city, Georgia	72.8	7.1	0.6	5.2	2.7	3.2	7.7	0.7	49.3
13	77652	Tucker CDP, Georgia	62.6	5.0	14.1	4.6	5.8	2.8	5.1	0.0	53.6
13	78324	Union City city, Georgia	-	-	-	-	-	-	-	-	13.5
13	78800	Valdosta city, Georgia	71.2	1.4	5.9	7.9	6.4	4.4	2.9	0.0	27.6
13	80508	Warner Robins city, Georgia	59.2	2.8	3.6	8.4	5.4	16.8	2.7	1.1	29.3
13	84176	Woodstock city, Georgia	77.3	0.0	6.6	6.4	2.1	1.6	6.0	0.0	58.0
15	00000	**HAWAII**	61.6	3.5	7.7	3.6	9.2	7.1	7.2	0.2	33.6
15	06290	East Honolulu CDP, Hawaii	51.0	9.5	9.8	4.1	7.0	7.7	10.1	0.7	48.8
15	07470	Ewa Gentry CDP, Hawaii	62.7	5.1	14.1	3.0	8.1	5.1	1.8	0.0	38.7
15	14650	Hilo CDP, Hawaii	54.5	2.0	5.5	8.5	16.4	3.3	9.8	0.1	42.7
15	22700	Kahului CDP, Hawaii	62.6	1.5	6.6	3.3	13.3	5.1	6.8	0.8	26.6
15	23150	Kailua CDP (Honolulu County), Hawaii	50.3	3.1	11.5	1.8	11.1	8.2	13.2	0.8	50.3
15	28250	Kaneohe CDP, Hawaii	65.1	3.8	9.0	4.3	7.4	7.6	2.7	0.0	35.8
15	30300	Kapolei CDP, Hawaii	68.3	2.0	2.7	5.4	10.2	8.5	2.9	0.0	23.5
15	47600	Makakilo CDP, Hawaii	68.0	6.2	2.2	0.9	7.5	14.2	1.0	0.0	34.0
15	51000	Mililani Mauka CDP, Hawaii	58.6	3.1	5.3	2.7	9.6	16.5	3.6	0.6	43.5
15	51050	Mililani Town CDP, Hawaii	63.5	1.5	4.0	3.9	9.2	15.1	2.8	0.0	28.7
15	62600	Pearl City CDP, Hawaii	60.7	1.8	7.4	2.8	10.4	13.3	3.5	0.2	37.7
15	69050	Schofield Barracks CDP, Hawaii	-	-	-	-	-	-	-	-	32.6
15	71550	Urban Honolulu CDP, Hawaii	62.5	3.1	9.1	3.0	9.6	5.0	7.5	0.0	34.9
15	79700	Waipahu CDP, Hawaii	76.3	1.0	6.1	4.1	5.0	3.7	3.8	0.0	18.8
16	00000	**IDAHO**	65.9	3.9	7.5	6.8	5.3	2.6	7.8	0.2	33.7
16	08830	Boise City city, Idaho	63.7	3.5	10.6	4.6	5.2	2.4	9.7	0.2	44.0
16	12250	Caldwell city, Idaho	76.0	2.4	6.4	5.5	4.0	0.5	5.2	0.0	20.7
16	16750	Coeur d'Alene city, Idaho	68.9	2.9	6.0	10.6	6.4	1.3	3.9	0.0	33.3
16	23410	Eagle city, Idaho	56.5	10.2	11.6	6.1	3.9	3.5	8.2	0.0	60.0
16	39700	Idaho Falls city, Idaho	69.0	4.7	5.7	5.9	3.8	4.4	6.3	0.1	33.1
16	46540	Lewiston city, Idaho	66.7	1.8	9.7	6.3	7.4	1.6	6.5	0.0	36.3
16	52120	Meridian city, Idaho	71.2	4.0	6.6	7.0	4.2	1.7	5.3	0.0	37.5
16	54550	Moscow city, Idaho	54.8	1.8	7.6	6.7	22.6	2.7	3.8	0.0	50.8
16	56260	Nampa city, Idaho	69.3	4.6	9.7	5.4	4.2	1.5	5.2	0.0	29.7
16	64090	Pocatello city, Idaho	70.0	1.8	5.3	4.4	11.2	1.4	5.8	0.0	33.7
16	64810	Post Falls city, Idaho	74.2	4.0	1.9	7.5	3.5	2.1	6.7	0.0	24.4
16	67420	Rexburg city, Idaho	-	-	-	-	-	-	-	-	20.1
16	82810	Twin Falls city, Idaho	67.5	1.1	14.7	8.6	1.6	0.8	5.6	0.0	28.8
17	00000	**ILLINOIS**	71.4	3.5	8.7	6.5	3.6	1.6	4.6	0.1	37.5
17	00243	Addison village, Illinois	78.9	4.8	3.1	6.0	1.2	2.4	2.7	0.9	29.4
17	00685	Algonquin village, Illinois	77.4	3.9	6.3	5.7	1.9	1.0	3.9	0.0	46.2
17	01114	Alton city, Illinois	73.2	1.8	9.2	7.4	3.9	1.7	2.7	0.0	24.4
17	02154	Arlington Heights village, Illinois	69.0	5.0	10.7	7.4	2.3	1.0	4.4	0.2	49.9
17	03012	Aurora city, Illinois	81.5	2.7	6.1	4.1	1.8	1.1	2.6	0.0	30.0

Table E. Cities—Labor Force, Employment, and Educational Data, 2015—*Continued*

FIPS state code	FIPS place code	State/city	Employees of private companies	Self-employed in own incorporated business	Private not-for-profit wage and salary workers	Local	State	Federal	Self-employed in own not incorporated business	Unpaid family workers	Management, business, science, and arts occupations
17	04013	Bartlett village, Illinois	70.4	5.5	10.0	5.9	2.6	1.9	3.3	0.5	49.3
17	04078	Batavia city, Illinois	64.7	6.7	8.7	8.9	3.6	2.1	5.3	0.0	47.5
17	04845	Belleville city, Illinois	76.9	1.9	6.9	6.6	4.4	1.5	1.8	0.0	31.8
17	05092	Belvidere city, Illinois	-	-	-	-	-	-	-	-	15.2
17	05573	Berwyn city, Illinois	75.8	2.6	6.7	4.8	4.4	1.0	4.3	0.2	23.9
17	06587	Bloomingdale village, Illinois	73.9	5.4	8.9	5.3	2.8	2.0	1.0	0.7	37.1
17	06613	Bloomington city, Illinois	73.5	2.7	8.9	5.8	5.2	0.4	3.5	0.1	49.9
17	06704	Blue Island city, Illinois	77.7	2.2	11.8	3.0	0.9	1.7	1.8	0.8	12.5
17	07133	Bolingbrook village, Illinois	81.0	2.6	5.8	4.2	2.0	1.8	2.3	0.2	33.5
17	09447	Buffalo Grove village, Illinois	77.9	4.0	4.7	6.4	1.3	1.1	4.4	0.2	57.8
17	09642	Burbank city, Illinois	74.4	6.1	3.3	6.1	2.7	1.2	6.4	0.0	20.5
17	10487	Calumet City city, Illinois	69.9	0.5	6.8	11.1	4.8	3.3	2.3	1.3	22.8
17	11163	Carbondale city, Illinois	45.9	0.0	4.9	7.9	35.7	0.0	5.5	0.0	51.7
17	11332	Carol Stream village, Illinois	81.9	2.1	6.8	4.5	1.9	0.9	1.9	0.0	39.6
17	11358	Carpentersville village, Illinois	83.2	3.5	5.2	6.2	0.8	0.0	1.1	0.0	31.2
17	12385	Champaign city, Illinois	52.8	3.4	10.0	7.4	21.3	1.6	3.4	0.1	47.5
17	12567	Charleston city, Illinois	45.9	4.0	7.5	9.9	21.2	2.9	8.7	0.0	42.2
17	14000	Chicago city, Illinois	70.6	2.8	10.6	7.5	2.4	1.5	4.5	0.1	39.8
17	14026	Chicago Heights city, Illinois	80.5	4.0	5.3	6.3	1.2	1.1	1.7	0.0	23.3
17	14351	Cicero town, Illinois	81.4	0.3	5.3	4.6	0.5	0.5	7.3	0.0	11.9
17	15599	Collinsville city, Illinois	74.6	0.6	9.8	5.8	4.5	1.3	2.6	0.9	33.8
17	17458	Crest Hill city, Illinois	78.3	1.3	4.4	6.7	2.9	2.0	4.4	0.0	29.7
17	17887	Crystal Lake city, Illinois	79.3	3.7	5.8	5.1	0.8	1.4	3.9	0.0	44.8
17	18563	Danville city, Illinois	70.1	2.7	9.5	3.5	3.7	5.0	4.7	0.8	27.7
17	18628	Darien city, Illinois	68.2	8.0	10.2	5.6	2.4	0.9	4.7	0.0	59.6
17	18823	Decatur city, Illinois	78.4	1.4	9.1	4.5	3.9	1.0	1.8	0.0	30.6
17	19161	DeKalb city, Illinois	61.0	1.8	8.9	13.3	11.6	1.6	1.8	0.0	35.8
17	19642	Des Plaines city, Illinois	74.1	6.5	6.6	5.5	1.3	1.5	4.4	0.1	36.6
17	20292	Dolton village, Illinois	66.9	0.5	9.2	7.7	6.1	5.2	4.5	0.0	27.4
17	20591	Downers Grove village, Illinois	69.1	5.4	10.4	4.2	1.9	2.1	6.8	0.0	52.6
17	22073	East Moline city, Illinois	77.0	0.9	5.9	2.8	3.4	6.5	3.5	0.0	26.8
17	22164	East Peoria city, Illinois	75.5	1.3	9.7	6.6	2.7	0.7	3.5	0.0	38.2
17	22255	East St. Louis city, Illinois	-	-	-	-	-	-	-	-	19.6
17	22697	Edwardsville city, Illinois	59.9	5.9	12.0	8.1	7.7	1.6	4.7	0.0	49.6
17	23074	Elgin city, Illinois	78.6	2.9	4.8	5.9	2.4	1.6	3.7	0.1	25.4
17	23256	Elk Grove Village village, Illinois	75.3	4.4	7.2	6.4	1.5	0.3	4.8	0.0	37.2
17	23620	Elmhurst city, Illinois	76.0	4.9	7.3	5.4	0.9	2.4	3.0	0.0	55.1
17	23724	Elmwood Park village, Illinois	77.8	5.9	7.2	1.9	1.0	0.8	5.4	0.0	30.5
17	24582	Evanston city, Illinois	57.9	4.4	22.0	4.6	2.2	1.7	6.5	0.8	61.9
17	27884	Freeport city, Illinois	72.6	3.8	7.1	6.6	2.6	1.3	6.0	0.0	20.2
17	28326	Galesburg city, Illinois	69.6	3.8	13.8	7.9	2.2	0.0	2.6	0.0	34.2
17	28872	Geneva city, Illinois	63.4	4.3	10.1	13.3	3.6	0.0	4.8	0.6	51.2
17	29730	Glendale Heights village, Illinois	85.0	2.5	4.5	4.6	0.7	1.0	1.6	0.0	25.0
17	29756	Glen Ellyn village, Illinois	74.8	4.2	6.6	7.3	1.6	0.4	5.1	0.0	52.8
17	29938	Glenview village, Illinois	63.7	12.3	8.5	5.9	1.6	0.8	7.0	0.2	56.5
17	30926	Granite City city, Illinois	71.8	1.4	7.7	6.2	4.4	1.9	6.1	0.4	26.2
17	31121	Grayslake village, Illinois	76.7	3.3	7.0	1.9	3.0	1.2	6.3	0.7	51.9
17	32018	Gurnee village, Illinois	77.0	2.3	3.8	10.4	2.7	1.2	2.5	0.0	45.5
17	32746	Hanover Park village, Illinois	80.7	2.4	4.8	5.5	1.6	1.5	3.3	0.2	27.6
17	33383	Harvey city, Illinois	-	-	-	-	-	-	-	-	20.4
17	34722	Highland Park city, Illinois	62.5	11.2	9.2	6.6	0.4	2.1	8.0	0.0	63.4
17	35411	Hoffman Estates village, Illinois	76.7	5.9	6.1	4.7	1.7	0.7	3.5	0.7	43.0
17	35835	Homer Glen village, Illinois	74.9	5.1	5.9	8.0	2.6	1.0	2.5	0.0	41.3
17	36750	Huntley village, Illinois	-	-	-	-	-	-	-	-	39.2
17	38570	Joliet city, Illinois	80.8	2.2	2.9	7.0	2.5	1.5	3.0	0.1	25.2
17	38934	Kankakee city, Illinois	65.8	2.0	15.7	7.5	3.1	2.6	2.8	0.5	24.4
17	41183	Lake in the Hills village, Illinois	81.7	2.1	3.4	4.3	2.4	3.5	2.5	0.2	31.9
17	41742	Lake Zurich village, Illinois	74.5	3.8	7.1	5.7	3.4	0.7	4.7	0.0	46.1
17	42028	Lansing village, Illinois	74.5	3.3	10.0	6.5	2.5	0.7	2.6	0.0	35.0
17	43250	Libertyville village, Illinois	71.2	5.3	8.9	7.5	2.8	0.4	3.9	0.0	58.6
17	43939	Lisle village, Illinois	70.2	3.7	10.7	6.0	3.9	1.0	4.2	0.3	58.5
17	44225	Lockport city, Illinois	75.4	2.0	8.3	5.3	6.3	0.0	2.7	0.0	40.3
17	44407	Lombard village, Illinois	70.9	4.0	7.1	7.8	3.5	1.2	4.5	0.9	45.2
17	45031	Loves Park city, Illinois	68.7	5.3	10.4	4.7	6.4	0.8	3.7	0.0	30.9
17	45694	McHenry city, Illinois	76.8	1.3	11.1	4.9	2.0	1.0	2.9	0.0	30.4
17	45726	Machesney Park village, Illinois	73.1	2.4	12.4	4.1	4.0	1.3	2.1	0.6	26.0
17	47774	Maywood village, Illinois	76.7	0.0	4.8	7.4	6.5	1.6	3.0	0.0	25.3
17	48242	Melrose Park village, Illinois	76.2	4.4	5.3	5.6	4.1	0.8	3.4	0.4	22.0
17	49867	Moline city, Illinois	74.7	1.8	6.3	7.4	2.7	3.8	3.4	0.0	29.1
17	50647	Morton Grove village, Illinois	69.0	4.8	9.8	8.3	1.4	0.6	6.1	0.0	46.5
17	51089	Mount Prospect village, Illinois	71.7	6.0	9.0	5.8	1.7	1.7	4.1	0.0	42.9
17	51349	Mundelein village, Illinois	80.0	2.4	4.9	7.7	0.9	0.6	3.5	0.0	38.3
17	51622	Naperville city, Illinois	73.2	4.7	8.4	5.5	2.3	1.8	3.9	0.1	55.9
17	52584	New Lenox village, Illinois	69.3	1.4	8.3	11.9	3.4	0.7	5.1	0.0	43.2
17	53000	Niles village, Illinois	76.3	5.2	8.2	5.7	0.0	1.4	3.3	0.0	30.2

Table E. Cities—Labor Force, Employment, and Educational Data, 2015—*Continued*

			Class of worker (percent)								Percent in each occupation group
						Government workers					
FIPS state code	FIPS place code	State/city	Employees of private companies	Self-employed in own incorporated business	Private not-for-profit wage and salary workers	Local	State	Federal	Self-employed in own not incorporated business	Unpaid family workers	Management, business, science, and arts occupations
17	53234	Normal town, Illinois	70.8	1.7	13.0	5.6	5.9	0.3	2.7	0.0	35.7
17	53481	Northbrook village, Illinois	62.5	11.2	9.1	5.4	3.0	0.3	8.4	0.0	61.5
17	53559	North Chicago city, Illinois	67.5	2.4	6.3	6.3	1.8	11.8	3.9	0.0	21.4
17	54638	Oak Forest city, Illinois	77.4	2.0	6.1	5.5	2.4	1.0	5.6	0.0	42.8
17	54820	Oak Lawn village, Illinois	72.5	4.0	7.6	9.6	2.4	2.0	1.8	0.0	38.8
17	54885	Oak Park village, Illinois	58.8	5.1	18.0	5.1	4.3	2.9	5.8	0.0	65.2
17	55249	O'Fallon city, Illinois	67.0	2.8	11.7	4.7	2.3	9.0	2.4	0.0	45.0
17	56640	Orland Park village, Illinois	66.3	4.6	13.9	7.3	2.4	1.2	4.3	0.0	46.1
17	56887	Oswego village, Illinois	-	-	-	-	-	-	-	-	49.3
17	57225	Palatine village, Illinois	77.8	4.3	6.4	4.0	1.9	1.0	4.4	0.2	38.2
17	57732	Park Forest village, Illinois	76.9	1.6	9.3	6.1	3.1	0.8	2.1	0.0	33.4
17	57875	Park Ridge city, Illinois	64.8	7.3	10.0	7.7	1.7	2.4	6.0	0.3	52.8
17	58447	Pekin city, Illinois	73.3	2.6	11.0	3.1	3.3	4.0	2.6	0.0	26.2
17	59000	Peoria city, Illinois	71.3	1.6	12.9	4.4	3.9	2.6	3.2	0.2	41.7
17	60287	Plainfield village, Illinois	73.6	5.6	3.6	10.7	2.4	1.1	2.8	0.3	42.2
17	62367	Quincy city, Illinois	68.7	5.0	10.6	5.0	2.7	0.4	7.5	0.0	29.2
17	65000	Rockford city, Illinois	74.2	2.2	9.0	5.3	3.6	0.9	4.7	0.1	27.0
17	65078	Rock Island city, Illinois	70.2	1.5	11.1	6.2	4.9	2.7	3.0	0.4	33.6
17	65338	Rolling Meadows city, Illinois	78.3	3.6	6.4	6.7	3.3	0.7	1.1	0.0	43.4
17	65442	Romeoville village, Illinois	83.3	2.1	3.3	5.8	1.0	2.4	2.2	0.0	22.5
17	65806	Roselle village, Illinois	79.0	5.1	4.2	6.7	1.0	1.3	2.5	0.0	34.5
17	66040	Round Lake Beach village, Illinois	80.6	3.5	4.2	4.2	3.5	2.6	1.6	0.0	19.3
17	66703	St. Charles city, Illinois	75.7	2.8	9.9	5.6	1.8	0.2	3.9	0.0	47.6
17	68003	Schaumburg village, Illinois	78.6	2.8	6.7	6.1	1.1	1.3	3.5	0.0	44.1
17	70122	Skokie village, Illinois	68.3	3.9	13.8	4.8	1.5	1.1	6.3	0.2	43.4
17	70720	South Elgin village, Illinois	80.0	3.0	6.1	4.8	1.4	0.9	3.8	0.0	34.4
17	70850	South Holland village, Illinois	53.7	1.3	11.3	17.6	4.9	8.0	2.7	0.4	42.5
17	72000	Springfield city, Illinois	59.7	2.4	12.1	5.3	15.5	2.3	2.3	0.4	44.8
17	73157	Streamwood village, Illinois	78.1	3.6	7.7	6.2	2.4	0.6	1.4	0.0	39.3
17	75484	Tinley Park village, Illinois	63.9	3.8	13.4	10.4	3.1	1.7	3.8	0.0	41.7
17	77005	Urbana city, Illinois	40.4	2.4	14.0	6.4	29.7	4.0	3.1	0.0	62.6
17	77694	Vernon Hills village, Illinois	77.4	5.3	6.9	3.5	0.6	0.3	6.0	0.0	58.1
17	77993	Villa Park village, Illinois	72.4	3.0	9.2	7.3	2.6	2.7	2.5	0.4	37.6
17	79293	Waukegan city, Illinois	81.0	2.4	5.5	3.2	0.7	2.3	4.8	0.1	19.9
17	80060	West Chicago city, Illinois	84.7	2.7	5.3	2.9	1.8	1.0	1.6	0.0	26.9
17	80645	Westmont village, Illinois	80.3	4.3	5.1	2.7	0.8	0.3	6.6	0.0	43.1
17	81048	Wheaton city, Illinois	67.4	3.7	14.4	5.5	2.1	2.0	4.6	0.3	51.4
17	81087	Wheeling village, Illinois	77.1	5.0	4.4	4.4	2.0	0.6	6.3	0.2	32.5
17	82075	Wilmette village, Illinois	54.2	8.6	18.0	6.7	2.6	0.8	8.6	0.6	67.2
17	83245	Woodridge village, Illinois	72.9	4.6	8.4	4.7	0.8	2.7	4.8	1.1	45.7
17	83349	Woodstock city, Illinois	71.9	4.7	9.5	6.1	2.9	0.4	4.6	0.0	42.1
17	84220	Zion city, Illinois	79.7	1.3	5.1	5.6	2.8	2.3	3.2	0.0	26.8
18	00000	**INDIANA**	73.4	3.0	8.6	5.5	3.5	1.4	4.4	0.2	32.9
18	01468	Anderson city, Indiana	69.9	2.0	9.3	7.2	6.4	2.1	3.0	0.2	23.9
18	05860	Bloomington city, Indiana	60.8	3.1	12.0	4.8	12.9	1.1	5.1	0.2	42.3
18	08416	Brownsburg town, Indiana	-	-	-	-	-	-	-	-	37.6
18	10342	Carmel city, Indiana	66.0	10.8	13.0	3.1	2.8	1.3	3.0	0.0	58.5
18	12934	Clarksville town, Indiana	85.6	1.4	2.1	2.5	0.0	3.5	4.9	0.0	19.2
18	14734	Columbus city, Indiana	81.3	1.9	7.0	2.2	1.7	0.7	5.1	0.2	40.7
18	16138	Crown Point city, Indiana	77.3	3.5	8.2	5.2	2.3	0.8	2.8	0.0	39.7
18	19486	East Chicago city, Indiana	82.0	0.4	3.7	6.3	4.5	0.0	3.1	0.0	18.4
18	20728	Elkhart city, Indiana	80.7	2.5	5.2	3.9	2.8	0.6	3.6	0.8	19.5
18	22000	Evansville city, Indiana	77.1	2.6	10.9	3.3	1.6	1.3	3.1	0.3	26.9
18	23278	Fishers town, Indiana	69.0	7.1	7.8	5.7	3.8	2.1	4.3	0.2	60.3
18	25000	Fort Wayne city, Indiana	73.8	3.3	10.4	4.9	2.5	0.9	4.0	0.1	33.6
18	25450	Franklin city, Indiana	72.0	1.1	12.5	6.7	2.6	2.4	2.7	0.0	36.1
18	27000	Gary city, Indiana	73.2	1.0	4.8	7.5	2.7	2.9	6.9	0.9	25.1
18	28386	Goshen city, Indiana	79.0	0.3	6.4	4.2	1.8	0.9	7.4	0.0	17.6
18	28800	Granger CDP, Indiana	68.6	4.9	15.1	5.4	0.8	0.1	5.1	0.0	51.3
18	29520	Greenfield city, Indiana	-	-	-	-	-	-	-	-	33.5
18	29898	Greenwood city, Indiana	73.2	2.6	11.3	3.3	3.5	0.3	5.9	0.0	39.7
18	31000	Hammond city, Indiana	79.1	1.6	7.8	5.8	1.4	1.6	2.6	0.0	22.6
18	33466	Highland town, Indiana	70.6	1.7	12.9	7.4	0.4	1.5	5.5	0.0	32.3
18	34114	Hobart city, Indiana	74.4	2.0	8.5	7.1	5.2	0.4	2.4	0.0	35.7
18	36003	Indianapolis city (balance), Indiana	75.6	2.3	8.6	4.9	3.2	1.7	3.5	0.2	34.2
18	38358	Jeffersonville city, Indiana	74.0	2.7	8.2	5.8	1.7	2.4	5.1	0.0	30.6
18	40392	Kokomo city, Indiana	78.3	1.2	5.4	5.8	4.4	0.7	4.1	0.0	23.8
18	40788	Lafayette city, Indiana	81.8	1.7	6.4	2.9	4.7	0.3	2.1	0.0	29.0
18	42246	La Porte city, Indiana	83.5	2.3	6.3	3.3	2.3	0.0	1.8	0.4	16.7
18	42426	Lawrence city, Indiana	76.4	1.5	6.1	5.7	2.5	4.3	3.6	0.0	34.7
18	46908	Marion city, Indiana	65.8	0.4	16.2	10.6	1.6	3.0	2.3	0.1	21.8
18	48528	Merrillville town, Indiana	71.9	0.7	12.3	8.4	2.9	1.4	2.4	0.0	30.7
18	48798	Michigan City city, Indiana	71.3	0.7	10.5	8.5	3.4	2.1	3.5	0.0	15.4
18	49932	Mishawaka city, Indiana	68.7	1.9	15.3	7.2	1.5	1.9	3.1	0.3	35.1
18	51876	Muncie city, Indiana	69.8	1.6	9.9	4.1	10.7	0.9	3.0	0.0	29.2

Table E. Cities—Labor Force, Employment, and Educational Data, 2015—*Continued*

FIPS state code	FIPS place code	State/city	Employees of private companies	Self-employed in own incorporated business	Private not-for-profit wage and salary workers	Government workers Local	Government workers State	Government workers Federal	Self-employed in own not incorporated business	Unpaid family workers	Percent in each occupation group Management, business, science, and arts occupations
18	51912	Munster town, Indiana	61.0	6.5	11.2	4.3	9.0	0.0	8.1	0.0	47.1
18	52326	New Albany city, Indiana	81.7	1.5	7.7	2.7	2.8	1.0	2.6	0.0	27.8
18	54180	Noblesville city, Indiana	76.3	2.4	8.7	7.3	1.8	0.6	2.6	0.3	35.3
18	60246	Plainfield town, Indiana	65.6	1.9	11.6	2.5	4.8	3.1	10.6	0.0	32.9
18	61092	Portage city, Indiana	83.2	0.9	6.4	3.7	3.0	1.3	1.5	0.0	22.5
18	64260	Richmond city, Indiana	76.0	2.8	11.7	4.5	1.6	0.0	3.3	0.0	27.6
18	68220	Schererville town, Indiana	74.6	3.5	8.1	5.5	3.7	0.7	3.9	0.0	38.2
18	71000	South Bend city, Indiana	73.3	0.8	12.7	6.6	2.0	0.6	3.5	0.5	31.5
18	75428	Terre Haute city, Indiana	73.2	0.6	9.9	3.7	7.6	0.6	4.3	0.1	32.0
18	78326	Valparaiso city, Indiana	70.8	4.2	8.3	8.0	1.6	0.3	6.8	0.0	43.6
18	82700	Westfield city, Indiana	71.5	7.8	8.0	5.3	2.3	1.5	3.5	0.0	45.6
18	82862	West Lafayette city, Indiana	53.9	1.5	16.5	3.7	20.5	2.0	2.0	0.0	53.0
18	86372	Zionsville town, Indiana	65.5	5.6	9.1	7.4	4.6	2.9	4.9	0.0	63.3
19	00000	**IOWA**	68.6	3.2	8.7	6.1	5.5	1.4	6.2	0.2	34.4
19	01855	Ames city, Iowa	54.2	0.7	7.9	5.6	27.9	1.9	1.7	0.0	50.3
19	02305	Ankeny city, Iowa	69.6	3.6	9.0	7.5	7.1	0.8	2.5	0.0	47.5
19	06355	Bettendorf city, Iowa	69.6	5.4	10.4	7.7	2.1	1.9	3.0	0.0	50.0
19	09550	Burlington city, Iowa	70.7	2.6	10.3	4.6	6.9	0.5	4.1	0.4	26.5
19	11755	Cedar Falls city, Iowa	64.3	3.5	10.3	4.1	15.2	0.4	1.9	0.2	39.0
19	12000	Cedar Rapids city, Iowa	76.4	2.3	9.3	3.7	2.9	2.0	3.1	0.3	34.7
19	14430	Clinton city, Iowa	78.1	1.8	6.7	6.0	2.6	0.7	4.0	0.0	26.1
19	16230	Coralville city, Iowa	54.0	0.8	12.6	3.3	23.9	3.6	1.8	0.0	45.8
19	16860	Council Bluffs city, Iowa	77.5	0.7	8.7	4.4	3.5	1.3	3.9	0.0	23.5
19	19000	Davenport city, Iowa	74.8	2.6	8.5	5.9	1.1	2.1	5.1	0.0	27.9
19	21000	Des Moines city, Iowa	73.9	2.0	9.5	4.8	3.6	2.2	4.0	0.1	31.0
19	22395	Dubuque city, Iowa	71.1	2.7	15.1	3.9	2.5	1.2	3.5	0.0	37.3
19	28515	Fort Dodge city, Iowa	71.4	2.3	12.2	2.7	3.7	2.3	5.2	0.3	30.4
19	38595	Iowa City city, Iowa	58.6	1.1	9.8	6.2	19.7	1.4	3.0	0.1	44.5
19	39765	Johnston city, Iowa	76.2	0.7	13.0	3.2	3.0	1.8	2.1	0.0	56.6
19	49485	Marion city, Iowa	76.0	2.7	10.1	4.1	2.5	0.7	4.0	0.0	46.1
19	49755	Marshalltown city, Iowa	83.6	1.2	5.5	0.7	5.7	0.0	3.2	0.0	18.5
19	50160	Mason City city, Iowa	64.5	1.3	13.4	7.6	4.1	0.3	8.8	0.0	26.9
19	55110	Muscatine city, Iowa	80.6	1.9	3.3	8.2	1.7	0.0	4.2	0.0	22.8
19	60465	Ottumwa city, Iowa	70.3	1.4	9.0	10.9	1.2	0.8	6.1	0.2	23.3
19	73335	Sioux City city, Iowa	74.2	2.0	11.5	4.7	2.6	1.0	4.0	0.0	29.0
19	79950	Urbandale city, Iowa	74.8	6.1	8.1	5.2	2.1	0.4	3.4	0.0	44.3
19	82425	Waterloo city, Iowa	77.2	1.0	8.8	5.5	3.0	0.3	4.3	0.0	27.7
19	83910	West Des Moines city, Iowa	75.7	2.5	7.5	5.7	3.4	1.8	3.4	0.0	53.5
20	00000	**KANSAS**	67.3	3.6	8.1	7.2	5.6	2.1	6.0	0.2	37.3
20	17800	Derby city, Kansas	69.8	2.1	6.1	10.4	4.9	4.9	1.9	0.0	48.2
20	18250	Dodge City city, Kansas	77.1	1.3	5.5	8.8	1.8	0.7	4.5	0.2	26.3
20	21275	Emporia city, Kansas	66.8	2.2	9.6	6.5	12.2	0.9	1.7	0.2	30.8
20	25325	Garden City city, Kansas	70.6	4.7	9.2	9.0	2.1	1.6	1.8	0.9	18.5
20	25425	Gardner city, Kansas	70.7	1.9	7.8	11.3	1.9	2.1	4.3	0.0	40.2
20	31100	Hays city, Kansas	63.4	2.5	8.3	8.4	10.9	0.5	6.0	0.0	34.7
20	33625	Hutchinson city, Kansas	69.2	2.6	7.5	5.9	8.2	2.0	4.5	0.0	29.2
20	35750	Junction City city, Kansas	55.6	1.1	5.5	13.9	0.7	13.9	9.2	0.0	28.1
20	36000	Kansas City city, Kansas	75.9	0.9	6.7	6.8	2.1	1.9	5.6	0.1	21.0
20	38900	Lawrence city, Kansas	61.1	4.3	9.7	5.9	15.0	1.7	2.3	0.0	43.0
20	39000	Leavenworth city, Kansas	59.2	2.3	4.6	6.9	9.8	14.7	2.6	0.0	33.6
20	39075	Leawood city, Kansas	62.7	9.2	10.2	4.1	4.0	1.7	7.9	0.0	65.3
20	39350	Lenexa city, Kansas	75.7	4.6	7.4	5.6	2.0	1.7	3.0	0.1	49.7
20	39825	Liberal city, Kansas	74.0	1.3	6.8	6.4	2.4	2.0	7.1	0.0	21.8
20	44250	Manhattan city, Kansas	58.0	3.0	6.5	4.1	20.9	3.0	4.5	0.0	38.8
20	52575	Olathe city, Kansas	69.7	4.0	9.2	5.8	4.8	2.2	4.2	0.2	44.3
20	53775	Overland Park city, Kansas	72.5	4.5	8.8	4.1	2.8	2.1	4.9	0.1	54.8
20	56025	Pittsburg city, Kansas	61.8	1.2	6.3	5.3	20.8	1.0	3.6	0.0	48.2
20	57575	Prairie Village city, Kansas	67.5	4.6	9.3	3.0	4.0	2.4	9.2	0.0	70.7
20	62700	Salina city, Kansas	73.1	4.4	7.9	6.8	2.5	0.8	3.9	0.6	32.6
20	64500	Shawnee city, Kansas	68.4	4.2	9.0	6.4	5.4	2.1	4.6	0.0	43.0
20	71000	Topeka city, Kansas	65.2	2.6	8.8	7.7	7.7	3.5	4.3	0.1	35.8
20	79000	Wichita city, Kansas	76.7	2.5	6.9	4.8	3.2	1.3	4.6	0.1	32.0
21	00000	**KENTUCKY**	69.6	2.9	7.8	5.3	6.6	2.4	5.2	0.1	33.2
21	02368	Ashland city, Kentucky	66.9	3.1	10.1	11.4	5.4	1.2	2.0	0.0	41.4
21	08902	Bowling Green city, Kentucky	71.7	1.4	6.2	5.5	11.3	1.0	2.9	0.0	29.5
21	17848	Covington city, Kentucky	78.0	2.3	7.7	3.3	2.8	2.5	3.5	0.0	32.3
21	24274	Elizabethtown city, Kentucky	67.7	4.1	6.6	4.0	4.3	7.4	5.9	0.0	23.8
21	27982	Florence city, Kentucky	82.1	0.5	3.5	3.6	3.2	3.0	4.1	0.0	31.9
21	28900	Frankfort city, Kentucky	61.5	2.9	5.9	4.7	20.5	0.9	3.5	0.0	32.5
21	30700	Georgetown city, Kentucky	72.2	1.3	6.1	6.2	6.8	2.4	4.9	0.0	33.5
21	35866	Henderson city, Kentucky	74.4	4.5	5.9	4.8	4.2	0.6	5.6	0.0	24.8
21	37918	Hopkinsville city, Kentucky	64.8	3.3	7.5	6.2	10.2	3.6	4.4	0.0	25.3
21	39142	Independence city, Kentucky	78.5	2.5	6.9	1.1	2.5	3.8	4.7	0.0	33.4

Table E. Cities—Labor Force, Employment, and Educational Data, 2015—*Continued*

FIPS state code	FIPS place code	State/city	Employees of private companies	Self-employed in own incorporated business	Private not-for-profit wage and salary workers	Government workers Local	Government workers State	Government workers Federal	Self-employed in own not incorporated business	Unpaid family workers	Management, business, science, and arts occupations
21	40222	Jeffersontown city, Kentucky	73.2	1.8	8.9	4.1	6.5	1.5	3.2	0.8	41.2
21	46027	Lexington-Fayette urban county, Kentucky	67.0	3.8	8.9	5.2	7.7	2.3	4.9	0.1	41.2
21	48006	Louisville/Jefferson County metro government (balance), Kentucky	73.0	2.8	9.4	4.4	4.5	1.9	3.9	0.1	36.9
21	56136	Nicholasville city, Kentucky	75.1	3.3	4.7	5.9	6.8	2.2	1.9	0.0	30.4
21	58620	Owensboro city, Kentucky	69.7	2.6	12.5	4.7	5.1	0.6	4.7	0.1	27.6
21	58836	Paducah city, Kentucky	56.1	6.2	15.5	8.6	2.6	4.8	6.2	0.0	32.9
21	63912	Radcliff city, Kentucky	64.5	0.0	3.6	4.7	4.3	20.9	1.9	0.0	33.3
21	65226	Richmond city, Kentucky	67.8	2.3	8.8	4.4	11.1	3.1	2.5	0.0	29.5
22	00000	**LOUISIANA**	69.4	3.8	6.2	7.2	5.6	2.3	5.5	0.1	33.7
22	00975	Alexandria city, Louisiana	64.0	0.7	6.0	10.4	6.4	7.2	5.1	0.0	36.6
22	05000	Baton Rouge city, Louisiana	66.8	4.0	6.0	6.4	11.5	0.7	4.5	0.1	38.6
22	05210	Bayou Cane CDP, Louisiana	85.2	0.8	2.9	3.9	3.0	0.0	4.2	0.0	24.1
22	08920	Bossier City city, Louisiana	67.4	3.8	7.1	3.5	4.4	7.2	6.2	0.3	30.5
22	13960	Central city, Louisiana	70.1	4.2	6.3	8.9	9.2	0.4	0.9	0.0	43.6
22	14135	Chalmette CDP, Louisiana	72.6	2.7	4.7	8.6	3.2	1.4	6.8	0.0	24.2
22	32755	Hammond city, Louisiana	73.5	1.8	5.5	5.6	10.2	1.8	1.6	0.0	29.8
22	33245	Harvey CDP, Louisiana	77.1	0.4	9.1	7.4	1.7	1.3	3.0	0.0	21.1
22	36255	Houma city, Louisiana	73.3	4.5	5.6	12.3	1.6	0.7	2.0	0.0	24.8
22	39475	Kenner city, Louisiana	74.4	6.2	5.0	3.6	3.6	3.1	4.1	0.0	29.6
22	40735	Lafayette city, Louisiana	63.7	7.6	7.9	7.4	4.3	1.2	7.8	0.0	37.0
22	41155	Lake Charles city, Louisiana	74.4	4.8	4.3	7.6	3.9	0.4	4.6	0.0	32.4
22	42030	Laplace CDP, Louisiana	73.1	1.2	3.7	4.0	6.4	4.9	6.8	0.0	43.2
22	48785	Marrero CDP, Louisiana	77.1	1.8	3.1	10.4	4.3	0.2	3.0	0.0	24.7
22	50115	Metairie CDP, Louisiana	67.6	6.5	6.1	7.6	2.3	2.2	7.7	0.1	39.2
22	51410	Monroe city, Louisiana	67.9	2.6	9.2	6.1	7.2	0.8	6.3	0.0	35.3
22	54035	New Iberia city, Louisiana	68.1	2.7	5.8	6.8	6.0	0.3	10.1	0.2	23.6
22	55000	New Orleans city, Louisiana	64.7	4.6	10.6	5.6	4.9	2.9	6.7	0.1	42.1
22	62385	Prairieville CDP, Louisiana	68.2	2.6	8.1	4.6	7.1	0.8	8.6	0.0	44.1
22	66655	Ruston city, Louisiana	58.4	0.6	5.3	7.5	23.6	0.6	4.0	0.0	38.2
22	70000	Shreveport city, Louisiana	70.4	2.5	7.3	6.1	5.9	3.7	4.0	0.1	31.4
22	70805	Slidell city, Louisiana	77.9	2.3	3.2	2.5	5.3	4.7	4.0	0.0	35.5
22	73640	Sulphur city, Louisiana	77.2	0.3	5.8	8.3	3.6	0.0	4.4	0.4	30.4
22	75180	Terrytown CDP, Louisiana	76.0	4.3	2.4	5.7	1.4	7.5	2.7	0.0	24.5
23	00000	**MAINE**	61.5	4.0	12.6	6.5	4.2	2.2	8.9	0.1	36.5
23	02060	Auburn city, Maine	64.1	7.0	12.5	6.0	4.2	0.0	6.3	0.0	44.0
23	02795	Bangor city, Maine	55.7	3.9	13.9	5.4	6.3	3.6	11.1	0.0	44.4
23	04860	Biddeford city, Maine	69.1	2.9	16.4	4.2	1.8	1.5	4.1	0.0	27.9
23	38740	Lewiston city, Maine	65.2	0.8	15.4	5.3	1.8	2.8	8.6	0.0	28.5
23	60545	Portland city, Maine	63.5	3.7	16.0	5.7	2.4	1.0	7.7	0.0	45.1
23	65725	Sanford city, Maine	68.4	2.3	6.8	5.1	3.4	6.3	7.8	0.0	20.5
23	71990	South Portland city, Maine	69.4	3.7	12.0	4.3	2.3	0.7	7.5	0.0	41.9
24	00000	**MARYLAND**	60.6	3.5	9.7	7.5	4.1	9.8	4.7	0.1	44.7
24	01600	Annapolis city, Maryland	61.1	2.2	16.9	7.0	3.7	6.9	2.1	0.0	42.2
24	01975	Arbutus CDP, Maryland	72.5	1.3	8.9	6.3	3.7	4.3	3.0	0.0	40.4
24	02275	Arnold CDP, Maryland	48.9	6.7	5.9	12.5	4.0	8.8	13.2	0.0	59.2
24	02825	Aspen Hill CDP, Maryland	66.5	2.9	6.0	7.5	1.9	10.3	4.8	0.0	41.7
24	04000	Baltimore city, Maryland	60.2	2.2	14.6	7.7	6.3	4.7	4.1	0.1	41.7
24	05825	Bel Air North CDP, Maryland	63.6	2.9	9.9	10.0	2.6	7.3	3.7	0.0	45.4
24	05950	Bel Air South CDP, Maryland	68.0	3.1	5.7	7.6	2.4	9.4	3.8	0.0	47.1
24	07125	Bethesda CDP, Maryland	48.0	6.6	15.9	3.0	2.4	15.3	8.8	0.0	73.5
24	08775	Bowie city, Maryland	48.8	3.4	8.9	9.2	5.3	21.5	2.9	0.2	58.9
24	12600	Camp Springs CDP, Maryland	60.2	3.1	5.1	7.4	1.7	21.4	1.1	0.0	42.2
24	13325	Carney CDP, Maryland	66.3	0.3	12.4	8.4	5.4	1.7	4.7	0.8	46.3
24	14125	Catonsville CDP, Maryland	60.2	2.5	13.4	6.5	6.3	6.6	4.5	0.0	58.2
24	16875	Chillum CDP, Maryland	80.0	0.7	5.4	5.7	1.1	3.2	3.9	0.0	21.5
24	17350	Clarksburg CDP, Maryland	58.0	3.2	17.8	8.7	0.0	7.4	4.4	0.5	63.6
24	17900	Clinton CDP, Maryland	52.8	4.0	7.5	10.3	2.0	21.0	2.4	0.0	35.9
24	18250	Cockeysville CDP, Maryland	71.5	2.4	10.8	7.6	3.0	1.7	3.1	0.0	45.4
24	18750	College Park city, Maryland	50.0	3.6	9.2	4.4	23.8	6.1	2.9	0.0	53.5
24	19125	Columbia CDP, Maryland	57.8	3.5	11.9	8.4	4.1	11.6	2.8	0.0	61.6
24	20875	Crofton CDP, Maryland	49.2	3.4	9.3	10.3	3.4	24.3	0.0	0.0	59.3
24	21325	Cumberland city, Maryland	70.3	3.2	10.7	6.0	6.9	1.2	1.6	0.0	29.9
24	23975	Dundalk CDP, Maryland	72.3	3.1	7.7	7.7	4.4	3.0	1.8	0.0	25.6
24	25150	Edgewood CDP, Maryland	60.4	0.0	11.8	8.4	5.1	8.1	6.1	0.0	35.5
24	25575	Eldersburg CDP, Maryland	65.0	2.8	5.8	8.7	3.9	9.5	4.4	0.0	51.8
24	26000	Ellicott City CDP, Maryland	54.6	5.9	13.6	6.8	4.7	11.7	2.4	0.1	62.6
24	26600	Essex CDP, Maryland	66.0	3.2	11.8	7.1	2.5	4.4	4.6	0.4	25.2
24	27250	Fairland CDP, Maryland	64.9	6.1	6.4	6.5	4.0	8.2	3.1	0.8	40.0
24	29525	Fort Washington CDP, Maryland	51.1	5.9	5.0	6.7	5.1	20.0	6.2	0.0	48.3
24	30325	Frederick city, Maryland	68.5	1.6	7.4	7.7	1.9	8.8	4.2	0.0	42.1
24	31175	Gaithersburg city, Maryland	64.2	3.5	8.2	5.1	2.1	10.4	6.5	0.0	47.9
24	32025	Germantown CDP, Maryland	66.0	2.2	8.4	6.4	4.0	9.0	4.0	0.0	52.9

Table E. Cities—Labor Force, Employment, and Educational Data, 2015—*Continued*

FIPS state code	FIPS place code	State/city	Employees of private companies	Self-employed in own incorporated business	Private not-for-profit wage and salary workers	Government workers Local	Government workers State	Government workers Federal	Self-employed in own not incorporated business	Unpaid family workers	Management, business, science, and arts occupations
24	32650	Glen Burnie CDP, Maryland	69.2	2.3	8.0	7.4	4.8	6.8	1.4	0.1	34.7
24	34775	Greenbelt city, Maryland	51.0	5.6	15.1	7.0	7.8	7.8	4.5	1.2	48.8
24	36075	Hagerstown city, Maryland	71.5	2.7	7.4	7.1	3.4	2.9	4.9	0.0	28.9
24	41475	Ilchester CDP, Maryland	62.9	1.7	7.7	8.9	4.8	11.7	2.3	0.0	56.2
24	45325	Landover CDP, Maryland	67.0	1.6	6.7	7.5	2.6	11.3	3.3	0.0	22.8
24	45525	Langley Park CDP, Maryland	80.3	0.5	7.7	1.6	1.1	0.6	8.1	0.0	7.7
24	45900	Laurel city, Maryland	63.5	2.4	8.8	7.1	3.5	12.2	2.5	0.0	48.5
24	47450	Lochearn CDP, Maryland	64.7	1.2	10.7	5.5	5.7	7.6	4.6	0.0	30.7
24	52300	Middle River CDP, Maryland	70.3	3.3	12.6	3.1	2.2	2.8	5.4	0.4	29.4
24	52562	Milford Mill CDP, Maryland	59.9	2.8	10.6	4.6	6.6	12.2	3.3	0.0	29.2
24	53325	Montgomery Village CDP, Maryland	67.6	1.2	8.1	7.0	0.9	8.8	5.8	0.6	40.5
24	56337	North Bethesda CDP, Maryland	55.1	3.9	11.3	3.5	2.7	18.3	5.4	0.0	60.2
24	56725	North Laurel CDP, Maryland	57.1	2.2	7.4	5.8	5.6	13.8	5.9	2.3	50.0
24	56875	North Potomac CDP, Maryland	49.2	7.2	11.4	5.7	4.0	15.6	7.0	0.0	75.4
24	58300	Odenton CDP, Maryland	53.1	2.3	5.6	8.5	3.0	23.6	3.9	0.0	50.1
24	58900	Olney CDP, Maryland	61.4	4.1	9.7	7.1	1.8	12.2	3.7	0.0	61.5
24	59425	Owings Mills CDP, Maryland	55.8	4.1	15.0	8.6	6.1	5.8	4.6	0.0	45.8
24	59500	Oxon Hill CDP, Maryland	56.0	0.7	9.2	14.0	4.6	14.6	0.9	0.0	35.9
24	60275	Parkville CDP, Maryland	64.1	1.0	14.7	8.5	3.8	3.1	4.4	0.4	34.4
24	60475	Pasadena CDP, Maryland	62.4	2.0	7.5	12.1	2.4	9.1	4.0	0.5	40.5
24	60975	Perry Hall CDP, Maryland	64.7	4.8	10.9	10.3	3.9	4.2	1.2	0.0	45.0
24	61400	Pikesville CDP, Maryland	56.0	5.7	18.0	6.7	6.5	4.1	3.1	0.0	63.7
24	63300	Potomac CDP, Maryland	48.3	8.7	14.3	3.5	1.4	16.2	7.6	0.2	73.7
24	64950	Randallstown CDP, Maryland	55.6	2.5	12.9	6.4	3.4	11.7	7.3	0.2	40.3
24	65600	Reisterstown CDP, Maryland	64.4	3.5	10.5	3.0	5.4	5.9	6.9	0.3	38.3
24	67675	Rockville city, Maryland	46.7	3.8	12.2	7.3	2.1	22.1	5.7	0.2	64.6
24	69925	Salisbury city, Maryland	73.6	1.6	6.7	4.6	9.0	0.6	3.9	0.0	24.4
24	71150	Severn CDP, Maryland	57.0	2.3	6.8	8.0	4.2	18.5	2.8	0.3	48.2
24	71200	Severna Park CDP, Maryland	59.0	5.5	5.7	12.0	3.2	11.6	3.0	0.0	63.3
24	72450	Silver Spring CDP, Maryland	53.4	1.9	17.4	5.2	3.9	11.9	6.3	0.0	53.0
24	73650	South Laurel CDP, Maryland	58.8	2.4	9.9	12.7	2.5	9.7	4.0	0.0	42.5
24	75725	Suitland CDP, Maryland	59.1	0.6	7.6	8.0	6.8	15.2	2.7	0.0	21.5
24	78425	Towson CDP, Maryland	61.7	4.5	14.1	5.1	4.5	2.1	7.8	0.1	55.8
24	81175	Waldorf CDP, Maryland	58.4	1.1	7.0	8.4	4.0	18.1	2.4	0.6	36.3
24	83775	Wheaton CDP, Maryland	67.9	4.9	6.0	2.3	0.2	13.0	5.8	0.0	37.7
24	86475	Woodlawn CDP (Baltimore County), Maryland	59.3	1.9	12.5	8.8	5.4	8.2	3.9	0.0	41.9
25	00000	**MASSACHUSETTS**	66.7	2.8	12.8	6.7	3.5	1.5	5.9	0.1	44.9
25	00840	Agawam Town city, Massachusetts	74.3	1.2	7.4	7.9	3.6	2.3	2.6	0.7	40.5
25	01640	Arlington CDP, Massachusetts	58.9	2.9	20.6	4.4	3.2	1.2	8.8	0.0	64.3
25	02690	Attleboro city, Massachusetts	73.2	1.2	10.0	6.5	4.4	0.0	4.4	0.4	42.8
25	03690	Barnstable Town city, Massachusetts	67.2	5.0	5.9	5.5	0.5	0.6	15.3	0.0	26.4
25	05105	Belmont CDP, Massachusetts	56.8	2.8	22.1	7.4	3.0	0.8	7.0	0.0	70.4
25	05595	Beverly city, Massachusetts	64.1	3.4	10.9	8.1	3.6	1.1	8.7	0.0	47.2
25	07000	Boston city, Massachusetts	64.0	1.8	19.9	5.9	3.3	1.4	3.7	0.1	48.0
25	07740	Braintree Town city, Massachusetts	75.3	2.2	7.6	4.8	3.3	1.9	4.8	0.0	45.8
25	09000	Brockton city, Massachusetts	74.7	0.6	12.8	6.3	1.9	1.2	2.3	0.2	24.2
25	09210	Brookline CDP, Massachusetts	57.9	3.2	24.9	4.2	2.0	0.6	6.8	0.3	73.0
25	09875	Burlington CDP, Massachusetts	68.9	3.0	12.8	3.1	4.9	2.3	5.0	0.0	51.4
25	11000	Cambridge city, Massachusetts	53.1	2.3	31.5	3.4	2.2	1.7	5.9	0.0	75.1
25	13205	Chelsea city, Massachusetts	79.9	0.9	5.5	3.6	5.1	0.2	4.7	0.0	21.4
25	13660	Chicopee city, Massachusetts	74.5	0.6	8.9	6.5	3.2	3.4	2.9	0.0	29.7
25	16285	Danvers CDP, Massachusetts	67.6	3.6	7.1	10.2	0.8	1.6	9.0	0.0	41.0
25	16530	Dedham CDP, Massachusetts	61.2	0.9	19.9	7.9	5.4	1.3	3.4	0.0	45.3
25	21990	Everett city, Massachusetts	77.1	1.5	7.8	1.9	3.4	1.2	7.2	0.0	21.7
25	23000	Fall River city, Massachusetts	71.9	2.9	9.8	6.6	3.2	2.8	2.8	0.0	25.5
25	23875	Fitchburg city, Massachusetts	71.0	1.6	7.0	8.0	8.1	2.6	1.6	0.1	26.3
25	24960	Framingham CDP, Massachusetts	68.4	3.5	9.1	6.1	2.9	1.5	8.3	0.2	42.8
25	25172	Franklin Town city, Massachusetts	77.0	0.8	6.8	5.9	2.2	3.0	4.3	0.0	60.3
25	25485	Gardner city, Massachusetts	64.5	1.6	16.2	8.1	2.6	0.9	6.1	0.0	28.4
25	26150	Gloucester city, Massachusetts	67.4	2.2	9.9	9.5	2.1	0.9	8.1	0.0	37.6
25	29405	Haverhill city, Massachusetts	71.4	2.5	13.0	5.5	1.8	2.4	3.3	0.1	39.1
25	30840	Holyoke city, Massachusetts	67.3	1.7	12.9	9.1	1.9	0.7	6.3	0.0	32.9
25	34550	Lawrence city, Massachusetts	81.5	2.2	8.4	2.8	2.5	1.1	1.6	0.0	15.1
25	35075	Leominster city, Massachusetts	69.4	1.9	7.8	7.4	5.2	1.4	6.9	0.0	34.3
25	35250	Lexington CDP, Massachusetts	60.6	6.3	18.0	5.5	3.3	0.6	5.7	0.0	79.6
25	37000	Lowell city, Massachusetts	73.6	1.0	8.6	4.9	4.6	2.3	5.0	0.0	32.0
25	37490	Lynn city, Massachusetts	69.0	0.9	12.5	6.7	3.3	1.9	5.6	0.0	26.1
25	37875	Malden city, Massachusetts	70.1	2.5	14.0	4.8	3.5	0.7	4.3	0.0	41.2
25	38435	Marblehead CDP, Massachusetts	54.7	10.4	15.0	6.3	3.5	0.3	9.6	0.0	60.5
25	38715	Marlborough city, Massachusetts	72.0	2.0	9.4	4.7	2.2	0.7	9.1	0.0	43.5
25	39835	Medford city, Massachusetts	61.2	2.8	17.0	7.3	2.2	2.8	6.6	0.0	52.0
25	40115	Melrose city, Massachusetts	51.2	4.1	14.4	5.4	9.5	2.3	13.1	0.0	57.5
25	40710	Methuen Town city, Massachusetts	72.1	2.1	11.1	6.2	1.9	1.7	4.9	0.0	33.5

Table E. Cities—Labor Force, Employment, and Educational Data, 2015—*Continued*

FIPS state code	FIPS place code	State/city	Employees of private companies	Self-employed in own incorporated business	Private not-for-profit wage and salary workers	Local	State	Federal	Self-employed in own not incorporated business	Unpaid family workers	Management, business, science, and arts occupations
25	41200	Milford CDP, Massachusetts	69.5	6.9	6.2	4.6	3.4	2.9	6.0	0.5	36.8
25	41725	Milton CDP, Massachusetts	59.0	4.1	15.9	7.2	4.8	0.6	8.3	0.0	54.6
25	44140	Needham CDP, Massachusetts	56.9	3.5	21.1	5.7	2.9	0.0	9.5	0.3	67.1
25	45000	New Bedford city, Massachusetts	69.9	1.1	13.0	7.5	3.3	1.1	4.1	0.0	28.2
25	45560	Newton city, Massachusetts	53.4	5.9	22.1	4.6	2.7	1.5	9.5	0.2	70.5
25	46330	Northampton city, Massachusetts	37.1	4.4	27.7	8.4	9.6	0.8	11.6	0.6	60.2
25	50285	Norwood CDP, Massachusetts	71.4	2.8	9.5	9.5	2.9	0.3	3.3	0.3	46.8
25	52490	Peabody city, Massachusetts	69.4	5.7	9.5	7.3	3.6	2.2	2.3	0.0	41.9
25	53960	Pittsfield city, Massachusetts	63.8	2.2	15.1	9.6	2.8	1.5	5.0	0.0	26.7
25	55745	Quincy city, Massachusetts	70.5	1.3	14.0	4.6	2.8	2.8	4.0	0.0	40.7
25	55990	Randolph CDP, Massachusetts	73.5	0.0	11.7	5.0	2.2	0.9	6.8	0.0	36.7
25	56165	Reading CDP, Massachusetts	63.5	4.0	13.9	6.1	4.8	1.6	5.5	0.5	62.9
25	56585	Revere city, Massachusetts	71.7	1.4	9.4	5.3	5.1	0.6	6.3	0.1	23.2
25	59105	Salem city, Massachusetts	65.8	2.5	13.2	5.9	6.1	0.9	5.5	0.2	36.9
25	60050	Saugus CDP, Massachusetts	64.6	2.9	13.3	8.4	2.6	2.2	6.0	0.0	34.3
25	62465	Somerset CDP, Massachusetts	71.8	2.9	13.6	5.1	0.9	4.5	1.3	0.0	40.7
25	62535	Somerville city, Massachusetts	65.7	1.6	22.4	3.9	2.0	1.7	2.5	0.1	65.1
25	67000	Springfield city, Massachusetts	70.9	0.8	9.0	6.9	5.5	2.2	4.7	0.0	25.5
25	67700	Stoneham CDP, Massachusetts	67.2	3.1	12.0	7.5	5.5	3.0	1.7	0.0	44.6
25	69170	Taunton city, Massachusetts	74.9	0.7	7.2	6.9	4.7	0.9	4.6	0.1	33.5
25	72250	Wakefield CDP, Massachusetts	68.7	1.5	15.1	5.8	3.1	1.2	4.7	0.0	52.1
25	72600	Waltham city, Massachusetts	68.0	2.5	12.7	6.4	2.1	1.0	7.3	0.0	49.8
25	73440	Watertown Town city, Massachusetts	66.0	3.7	16.8	5.1	1.1	2.3	5.0	0.0	59.4
25	74210	Wellesley CDP, Massachusetts	65.0	6.6	18.5	1.9	0.7	0.3	6.1	1.0	65.2
25	76030	Westfield city, Massachusetts	67.2	2.3	11.6	7.9	3.6	2.4	4.7	0.3	37.8
25	77890	West Springfield Town city, Massachusetts	66.5	2.7	10.3	7.0	3.9	3.4	6.2	0.0	35.1
25	78972	Weymouth Town city, Massachusetts	64.1	3.4	12.7	8.7	3.1	2.9	4.8	0.3	42.1
25	80195	Wilmington CDP, Massachusetts	71.2	2.3	12.1	5.3	3.7	1.3	4.2	0.0	37.9
25	80545	Winchester CDP, Massachusetts	64.7	5.2	11.9	7.7	1.2	0.4	9.0	0.0	70.7
25	81035	Woburn city, Massachusetts	72.6	0.6	8.6	5.2	2.4	0.7	9.8	0.0	35.6
25	82000	Worcester city, Massachusetts	69.3	1.9	13.4	5.1	4.2	0.4	5.5	0.3	35.4
26	00000	**MICHIGAN**	72.0	3.3	9.5	5.0	4.0	1.4	4.7	0.2	35.2
26	00440	Adrian city, Michigan	72.2	2.2	11.0	3.8	5.4	1.2	4.2	0.0	18.7
26	01340	Allendale CDP, Michigan	72.2	0.0	12.6	7.2	7.3	0.0	0.8	0.0	28.5
26	01380	Allen Park city, Michigan	75.5	3.6	7.8	5.9	2.7	0.8	3.8	0.0	34.6
26	03000	Ann Arbor city, Michigan	50.1	2.7	18.5	3.4	18.4	1.9	4.5	0.4	65.3
26	04105	Auburn Hills city, Michigan	78.3	2.3	7.6	2.1	3.1	1.0	5.6	0.0	44.1
26	05920	Battle Creek city, Michigan	72.9	3.6	7.7	5.4	5.5	2.1	2.8	0.0	23.9
26	06020	Bay City city, Michigan	78.0	2.4	11.1	3.2	1.3	1.2	2.6	0.0	21.5
26	08640	Birmingham city, Michigan	57.8	10.8	15.8	3.6	1.9	2.2	7.8	0.0	69.2
26	12060	Burton city, Michigan	79.5	1.4	5.5	4.8	3.4	0.0	5.5	0.0	25.3
26	21000	Dearborn city, Michigan	76.8	3.2	6.2	5.1	3.8	1.1	3.7	0.2	37.6
26	21020	Dearborn Heights city, Michigan	81.1	4.5	5.4	2.1	1.2	2.0	3.6	0.0	27.9
26	22000	Detroit city, Michigan	72.9	1.8	11.0	4.8	3.9	1.8	3.7	0.1	22.4
26	24120	East Lansing city, Michigan	47.3	1.4	12.6	4.7	32.1	0.2	1.0	0.7	43.9
26	24290	Eastpointe city, Michigan	70.2	1.8	10.0	4.2	7.9	2.6	3.2	0.0	22.2
26	27440	Farmington Hills city, Michigan	74.0	5.5	9.0	2.7	4.2	1.2	3.5	0.0	54.5
26	27880	Ferndale city, Michigan	71.0	4.6	8.3	6.2	1.8	2.1	6.0	0.0	48.6
26	29000	Flint city, Michigan	78.3	1.5	8.1	5.0	2.6	0.7	3.5	0.3	21.0
26	29580	Forest Hills CDP, Michigan	67.3	7.9	13.7	2.3	2.2	0.0	6.6	0.0	56.8
26	31420	Garden City city, Michigan	-	-	-	-	-	-	-	-	21.3
26	34000	Grand Rapids city, Michigan	72.4	3.1	15.0	2.7	1.7	1.4	3.6	0.1	31.9
26	36280	Hamtramck city, Michigan	79.2	1.5	9.4	2.3	0.0	1.9	5.7	0.0	18.7
26	37100	Haslett CDP, Michigan	53.5	6.2	13.5	7.4	11.7	1.5	6.4	0.0	58.9
26	38640	Holland city, Michigan	75.0	2.8	10.9	4.8	3.2	0.3	3.1	0.0	27.8
26	38780	Holt CDP, Michigan	61.5	2.2	9.3	11.3	10.8	1.2	3.8	0.0	42.4
26	40680	Inkster city, Michigan	86.7	0.2	3.4	3.0	0.9	1.7	3.6	0.5	19.4
26	41420	Jackson city, Michigan	75.7	0.8	8.0	3.7	4.9	0.2	6.7	0.0	24.2
26	42160	Kalamazoo city, Michigan	67.0	1.5	14.1	4.8	6.2	1.3	4.8	0.3	34.9
26	42820	Kentwood city, Michigan	78.1	2.4	11.0	3.5	1.7	0.4	3.1	0.0	32.1
26	46000	Lansing city, Michigan	65.1	0.7	14.5	6.7	7.9	0.3	4.5	0.3	31.7
26	47800	Lincoln Park city, Michigan	83.8	1.3	4.7	2.9	0.6	1.9	4.8	0.0	17.8
26	49000	Livonia city, Michigan	73.8	4.0	9.7	5.4	1.7	1.8	3.6	0.1	43.7
26	50560	Madison Heights city, Michigan	77.0	2.6	9.3	1.8	5.5	2.1	1.6	0.0	31.5
26	51900	Marquette city, Michigan	67.8	2.5	10.1	6.4	9.0	0.3	2.9	1.1	34.4
26	53780	Midland city, Michigan	76.2	3.2	10.2	2.9	1.5	1.2	4.7	0.0	50.8
26	55020	Monroe city, Michigan	86.3	2.1	4.2	2.7	1.6	0.0	3.2	0.0	22.6
26	56020	Mount Pleasant city, Michigan	64.2	1.1	9.0	4.8	18.0	0.9	2.0	0.0	37.3
26	56320	Muskegon city, Michigan	80.1	0.9	8.6	6.1	1.3	0.3	2.7	0.0	29.0
26	59140	Norton Shores city, Michigan	76.5	2.3	7.1	8.2	1.0	1.0	3.9	0.0	28.5
26	59440	Novi city, Michigan	74.3	4.0	10.9	2.7	1.9	0.6	5.6	0.0	58.3
26	59920	Oak Park city, Michigan	77.2	0.9	5.2	9.3	1.3	2.5	3.6	0.0	29.7

Table E. Cities—Labor Force, Employment, and Educational Data, 2015—*Continued*

FIPS state code	FIPS place code	State/city	Employees of private companies	Self-employed in own incorporated business	Private not-for-profit wage and salary workers	Government workers Local	State	Federal	Self-employed in own not incorporated business	Unpaid family workers	Management, business, science, and arts occupations
26	60340	Okemos CDP, Michigan	52.7	5.7	14.8	5.8	13.8	0.8	6.4	0.0	62.8
26	65440	Pontiac city, Michigan	80.2	1.4	7.7	3.1	1.6	1.7	3.5	0.7	23.2
26	65560	Portage city, Michigan	72.3	2.6	10.9	5.1	3.8	2.3	3.1	0.0	43.1
26	65820	Port Huron city, Michigan	80.8	1.2	5.3	2.9	3.1	0.3	6.4	0.0	19.0
26	69035	Rochester Hills city, Michigan	72.9	6.6	7.5	4.3	2.0	1.6	4.7	0.2	55.3
26	69420	Romulus city, Michigan	73.1	3.9	7.9	6.7	0.7	1.1	5.6	1.0	20.5
26	69800	Roseville city, Michigan	77.0	2.2	10.2	3.1	2.6	1.8	3.1	0.0	21.0
26	70040	Royal Oak city, Michigan	74.3	2.3	11.5	3.4	2.2	2.1	4.1	0.1	60.0
26	70520	Saginaw city, Michigan	74.5	1.6	13.6	1.6	3.3	0.4	4.4	0.5	15.0
26	70760	St. Clair Shores city, Michigan	76.3	3.2	7.2	4.4	1.5	2.3	5.2	0.0	32.6
26	74900	Southfield city, Michigan	68.0	3.5	14.5	4.3	5.0	1.5	3.2	0.0	43.2
26	74960	Southgate city, Michigan	79.0	2.1	8.6	5.3	1.4	0.9	2.3	0.4	28.5
26	76460	Sterling Heights city, Michigan	78.9	3.0	6.9	3.2	2.1	2.1	3.8	0.0	35.6
26	79000	Taylor city, Michigan	81.1	2.8	5.7	3.9	0.9	1.3	4.2	0.0	23.6
26	80700	Troy city, Michigan	67.6	7.3	10.4	4.9	4.3	1.1	4.5	0.0	61.9
26	82960	Walker city, Michigan	69.1	7.7	14.7	1.9	1.3	1.5	3.8	0.0	28.9
26	84000	Warren city, Michigan	80.0	2.0	8.3	2.9	1.6	2.4	2.9	0.0	28.1
26	84800	Waverly CDP, Michigan	64.4	1.4	15.8	6.7	8.3	1.1	2.0	0.3	35.5
26	86000	Westland city, Michigan	85.0	2.0	5.5	2.4	1.6	1.2	2.0	0.3	28.9
26	88900	Wyandotte city, Michigan	72.9	2.4	12.0	6.7	1.5	1.5	2.4	0.6	27.5
26	88940	Wyoming city, Michigan	82.1	1.7	7.6	1.6	1.0	0.3	5.4	0.4	22.1
26	89140	Ypsilanti city, Michigan	68.3	1.4	8.6	6.8	11.1	0.6	3.1	0.0	34.4
27	00000	**MINNESOTA**	67.8	3.9	11.5	6.2	3.7	1.3	5.4	0.2	40.2
27	01486	Andover city, Minnesota	69.6	3.9	7.5	7.2	4.1	2.1	5.1	0.6	43.9
27	01900	Apple Valley city, Minnesota	69.2	2.2	11.5	4.1	6.2	2.8	3.9	0.0	43.0
27	02908	Austin city, Minnesota	73.4	3.4	10.4	8.1	0.6	0.7	3.3	0.0	30.1
27	06382	Blaine city, Minnesota	73.1	3.6	9.9	5.4	3.6	0.8	3.4	0.1	41.0
27	06616	Bloomington city, Minnesota	68.1	3.3	13.2	6.0	2.2	1.9	5.3	0.1	40.7
27	07948	Brooklyn Center city, Minnesota	74.2	3.1	10.4	6.2	1.5	1.1	3.5	0.0	32.9
27	07966	Brooklyn Park city, Minnesota	72.7	2.2	13.0	4.9	3.4	1.6	2.1	0.0	35.5
27	08794	Burnsville city, Minnesota	77.3	2.3	9.4	3.6	3.1	1.9	2.5	0.0	43.4
27	10846	Champlin city, Minnesota	75.1	3.2	9.4	4.3	2.4	1.1	4.4	0.0	46.4
27	10918	Chanhassen city, Minnesota	70.7	6.1	6.8	6.5	2.8	0.5	6.4	0.2	58.3
27	10972	Chaska city, Minnesota	80.4	3.8	4.2	3.8	2.5	0.6	4.7	0.0	40.4
27	13114	Coon Rapids city, Minnesota	72.1	2.2	9.7	5.3	3.7	1.6	5.3	0.1	34.4
27	13456	Cottage Grove city, Minnesota	69.6	4.6	4.7	8.7	7.4	2.4	2.7	0.0	34.8
27	14158	Crystal city, Minnesota	68.9	2.3	13.5	8.4	4.6	0.9	1.3	0.0	42.0
27	17000	Duluth city, Minnesota	64.5	2.2	15.1	7.8	6.0	0.6	3.8	0.0	39.9
27	17288	Eagan city, Minnesota	71.9	2.4	12.5	4.6	3.2	2.1	3.2	0.1	48.4
27	18116	Eden Prairie city, Minnesota	71.9	6.5	7.3	4.7	1.3	1.0	7.3	0.0	56.6
27	18188	Edina city, Minnesota	64.5	8.6	11.3	4.5	2.5	0.9	7.7	0.0	58.6
27	18674	Elk River city, Minnesota	64.3	8.5	12.4	6.5	4.3	0.0	2.7	1.2	44.5
27	20546	Faribault city, Minnesota	73.7	1.0	8.4	3.8	2.3	1.4	8.6	0.7	18.2
27	20618	Farmington city, Minnesota	72.1	2.0	8.7	8.5	3.6	0.9	4.2	0.0	40.4
27	22814	Fridley city, Minnesota	73.3	1.7	9.7	6.4	1.5	0.4	6.9	0.0	30.5
27	24308	Golden Valley city, Minnesota	67.6	5.3	11.3	5.2	2.7	0.5	7.5	0.0	54.9
27	27530	Hastings city, Minnesota	75.7	1.8	7.1	5.0	4.6	2.7	3.1	0.0	29.6
27	31076	Inver Grove Heights city, Minnesota	72.7	4.7	9.2	6.7	2.9	1.5	2.3	0.0	41.2
27	35180	Lakeville city, Minnesota	69.6	2.5	10.6	6.5	3.1	3.1	4.4	0.2	44.9
27	37322	Lino Lakes city, Minnesota	72.1	2.5	9.4	4.9	5.2	0.4	5.5	0.0	47.8
27	39878	Mankato city, Minnesota	67.2	2.3	14.6	5.2	7.9	0.2	2.6	0.0	32.7
27	40166	Maple Grove city, Minnesota	75.7	5.3	7.3	5.3	1.6	1.3	3.5	0.0	53.9
27	40382	Maplewood city, Minnesota	73.3	3.3	8.7	7.1	3.5	1.8	2.3	0.0	44.6
27	43000	Minneapolis city, Minnesota	65.5	3.5	14.1	5.6	5.5	1.1	4.6	0.1	49.1
27	43252	Minnetonka city, Minnesota	69.9	7.8	9.7	4.6	0.3	0.3	6.9	0.3	54.4
27	43864	Moorhead city, Minnesota	63.6	2.6	17.4	5.6	4.0	1.7	5.2	0.0	33.6
27	45430	New Brighton city, Minnesota	72.1	3.0	9.3	5.8	4.2	0.9	4.6	0.0	42.8
27	45628	New Hope city, Minnesota	76.9	2.2	9.3	4.4	1.6	1.3	4.3	0.0	45.0
27	46924	Northfield city, Minnesota	73.1	0.7	15.2	3.4	1.4	0.3	5.3	0.5	41.4
27	47680	Oakdale city, Minnesota	69.3	3.0	12.4	7.0	3.3	1.2	3.7	0.0	38.7
27	49300	Owatonna city, Minnesota	75.5	1.8	11.4	5.9	1.7	0.0	3.7	0.0	36.3
27	51730	Plymouth city, Minnesota	75.2	5.8	7.7	4.1	2.2	0.9	4.0	0.1	55.3
27	52594	Prior Lake city, Minnesota	77.6	6.0	6.1	4.2	3.1	1.4	1.3	0.3	48.3
27	53026	Ramsey city, Minnesota	72.9	5.6	7.6	8.0	1.9	0.9	3.1	0.0	38.1
27	54214	Richfield city, Minnesota	69.1	2.5	13.3	6.1	1.6	0.3	6.8	0.2	46.9
27	54880	Rochester city, Minnesota	54.4	1.4	32.5	4.9	2.3	1.2	3.2	0.0	53.5
27	55726	Rosemount city, Minnesota	67.3	2.6	7.3	13.4	2.5	2.8	4.1	0.0	40.6
27	55852	Roseville city, Minnesota	59.9	3.6	17.6	8.4	6.9	0.3	3.4	0.0	53.1
27	56896	St. Cloud city, Minnesota	64.5	1.0	16.8	6.3	4.6	1.1	5.3	0.4	27.5
27	57220	St. Louis Park city, Minnesota	68.6	2.7	12.7	7.4	4.0	0.4	3.7	0.5	59.4
27	58000	St. Paul city, Minnesota	67.8	2.2	14.6	4.7	5.5	1.1	4.0	0.0	41.0
27	58738	Savage city, Minnesota	71.9	5.3	10.2	5.9	2.7	1.8	2.2	0.0	48.6
27	59350	Shakopee city, Minnesota	78.0	2.6	6.4	5.2	2.1	1.1	4.6	0.0	35.8
27	59998	Shoreview city, Minnesota	68.4	2.1	12.5	4.2	7.7	2.3	2.8	0.0	55.6
27	61492	South St. Paul city, Minnesota	72.7	3.0	11.0	4.2	2.3	1.8	4.9	0.2	37.2

Table E. Cities—Labor Force, Employment, and Educational Data, 2015—*Continued*

			Class of worker (percent)								Percent in each occupation group
						Government workers					
FIPS state code	FIPS place code	State/city	Employees of private companies	Self-employed in own incorporated business	Private not-for-profit wage and salary workers	Local	State	Federal	Self-employed in own not incorporated business	Unpaid family workers	Management, business, science, and arts occupations
27	69970	White Bear Lake city, Minnesota	66.6	2.7	14.2	4.7	6.0	1.4	4.4	0.0	43.2
27	71032	Winona city, Minnesota	72.9	4.4	11.8	3.0	4.0	0.0	3.9	0.0	33.0
27	71428	Woodbury city, Minnesota	68.8	2.2	12.3	6.7	4.8	1.8	3.2	0.3	60.3
28	00000	**MISSISSIPPI**	67.7	3.2	5.9	5.6	9.2	3.2	5.1	0.1	30.8
28	06220	Biloxi city, Mississippi	72.7	1.3	7.0	2.4	4.4	8.8	3.5	0.0	33.0
28	08300	Brandon city, Mississippi	71.0	4.6	7.5	2.0	12.9	0.9	1.1	0.0	47.8
28	14420	Clinton city, Mississippi	61.6	3.6	14.6	2.6	10.1	1.1	6.4	0.0	41.8
28	15380	Columbus city, Mississippi	62.3	1.9	3.8	6.8	12.6	5.4	7.2	0.0	28.8
28	29180	Greenville city, Mississippi	63.5	4.6	1.8	11.7	10.4	3.9	4.2	0.0	30.4
28	29700	Gulfport city, Mississippi	72.8	1.4	3.9	6.5	3.7	8.3	3.1	0.4	25.7
28	31020	Hattiesburg city, Mississippi	69.2	4.4	5.6	3.8	11.5	3.3	2.2	0.0	32.4
28	33700	Horn Lake city, Mississippi	80.0	1.1	2.9	4.3	4.3	2.7	4.6	0.0	18.4
28	36000	Jackson city, Mississippi	57.9	3.4	6.9	6.6	15.9	3.7	5.6	0.1	32.1
28	44520	Madison city, Mississippi	66.3	6.4	7.7	2.4	7.2	1.5	8.4	0.0	49.5
28	46640	Meridian city, Mississippi	70.3	0.2	10.8	5.7	7.1	3.3	2.0	0.6	36.5
28	54040	Olive Branch city, Mississippi	73.5	3.5	4.7	5.8	3.4	3.7	5.3	0.0	34.6
28	54840	Oxford city, Mississippi	54.5	2.1	13.1	6.8	19.6	1.0	2.9	0.0	55.8
28	55360	Pascagoula city, Mississippi	76.8	1.0	5.3	8.5	3.0	0.5	4.9	0.0	25.0
28	55760	Pearl city, Mississippi	74.4	1.3	5.2	4.9	9.6	0.2	4.1	0.3	30.0
28	62520	Ridgeland city, Mississippi	62.6	6.5	6.1	4.6	10.3	5.4	4.5	0.0	43.2
28	69280	Southaven city, Mississippi	74.9	2.6	5.7	4.8	3.3	2.6	5.8	0.3	34.7
28	70240	Starkville city, Mississippi	45.0	1.6	11.7	2.3	34.8	3.1	1.6	0.0	51.5
28	74840	Tupelo city, Mississippi	75.1	3.2	8.4	5.7	4.5	1.5	1.7	0.0	26.9
28	76720	Vicksburg city, Mississippi	59.4	5.6	5.8	7.7	11.5	5.2	4.8	0.0	31.0
29	00000	**MISSOURI**	68.6	3.0	10.6	5.6	4.3	2.2	5.5	0.2	35.4
29	00280	Affton CDP, Missouri	66.6	1.4	11.3	7.6	2.3	2.7	4.9	3.3	33.3
29	01972	Arnold city, Missouri	83.9	3.9	7.0	2.3	0.6	1.2	1.2	0.0	22.6
29	03160	Ballwin city, Missouri	68.9	5.1	15.7	5.4	3.3	0.4	1.2	0.0	55.2
29	04384	Belton city, Missouri	76.1	2.9	5.7	5.3	0.5	5.2	4.3	0.0	28.0
29	06652	Blue Springs city, Missouri	73.5	3.4	10.1	6.3	2.6	1.5	2.7	0.0	38.0
29	11242	Cape Girardeau city, Missouri	61.9	5.3	14.5	4.0	11.1	1.3	1.5	0.4	42.8
29	13600	Chesterfield city, Missouri	68.5	7.5	11.5	2.9	1.8	1.8	6.0	0.0	66.8
29	15670	Columbia city, Missouri	59.8	3.4	11.3	5.3	14.4	2.5	2.8	0.5	46.9
29	16030	Concord CDP, Missouri	75.2	2.0	13.3	4.0	0.4	1.3	3.0	0.8	46.1
29	23986	Ferguson city, Missouri	77.5	2.8	6.8	5.4	2.7	3.8	0.4	0.7	29.8
29	24778	Florissant city, Missouri	70.2	1.8	16.9	3.8	1.0	2.7	3.7	0.0	32.0
29	25264	Fort Leonard Wood CDP, Missouri	-	-	-	-	-	-	-	-	-
29	27190	Gladstone city, Missouri	75.7	2.9	11.3	3.0	1.5	1.8	3.8	0.0	35.5
29	28324	Grandview city, Missouri	79.5	1.3	7.8	5.3	0.4	3.7	2.1	0.0	28.2
29	31276	Hazelwood city, Missouri	81.2	3.0	4.1	5.5	0.0	2.4	3.9	0.0	29.8
29	35000	Independence city, Missouri	77.0	2.4	6.8	6.5	2.9	1.8	2.7	0.0	24.4
29	37000	Jefferson City city, Missouri	59.6	1.7	8.8	5.8	19.2	1.9	3.1	0.0	41.7
29	37592	Joplin city, Missouri	66.7	2.9	14.9	4.2	6.1	1.2	3.9	0.1	31.6
29	38000	Kansas City city, Missouri	69.4	2.9	10.3	6.1	3.1	3.9	4.1	0.2	36.8
29	39044	Kirkwood city, Missouri	65.6	5.7	13.2	4.6	1.5	1.0	7.3	1.2	58.3
29	41348	Lee's Summit city, Missouri	66.6	3.8	10.2	6.2	4.9	4.1	4.1	0.0	51.3
29	42032	Liberty city, Missouri	72.2	2.1	8.4	7.1	1.5	4.4	3.7	0.5	34.7
29	46586	Maryland Heights city, Missouri	78.4	3.5	10.4	1.5	0.7	0.8	4.6	0.0	49.7
29	47180	Mehlville CDP, Missouri	80.1	2.0	7.8	4.4	1.5	2.1	2.1	0.0	31.1
29	52616	Nixa city, Missouri	68.6	3.0	14.4	3.4	1.2	3.8	5.7	0.0	40.1
29	53876	Oakville CDP, Missouri	77.3	2.9	8.6	4.6	0.9	3.6	2.0	0.0	39.6
29	54074	O'Fallon city, Missouri	77.1	1.3	9.7	4.8	1.4	1.8	4.0	0.0	41.5
29	60752	Raymore city, Missouri	71.2	3.2	8.5	2.4	1.6	9.1	4.0	0.0	47.9
29	60788	Raytown city, Missouri	72.1	1.5	11.1	4.5	3.5	4.4	3.0	0.0	32.7
29	62912	Rolla city, Missouri	61.4	1.4	13.0	7.6	14.5	1.3	0.8	0.0	42.1
29	64082	St. Charles city, Missouri	70.1	3.6	14.5	5.0	1.1	1.5	4.2	0.0	41.1
29	64550	St. Joseph city, Missouri	73.1	2.2	9.2	4.3	5.2	0.7	4.9	0.3	29.5
29	65000	St. Louis city, Missouri	66.5	2.1	16.4	6.4	2.2	2.4	3.8	0.2	42.0
29	65126	St. Peters city, Missouri	79.2	2.0	8.3	5.7	1.9	0.3	2.5	0.0	40.0
29	66440	Sedalia city, Missouri	73.6	0.8	9.6	4.1	2.6	2.7	6.7	0.0	22.2
29	70000	Springfield city, Missouri	68.2	2.6	14.2	5.2	4.3	1.1	4.5	0.0	32.7
29	75220	University City city, Missouri	59.1	3.7	24.4	2.9	2.5	3.4	4.0	0.0	48.0
29	78154	Webster Groves city, Missouri	65.1	3.4	18.6	5.4	1.8	1.1	4.6	0.0	55.1
29	78442	Wentzville city, Missouri	75.3	3.6	7.5	6.4	1.7	0.8	4.8	0.0	37.0
29	79820	Wildwood city, Missouri	65.5	7.4	13.7	7.2	1.0	0.7	4.6	0.0	46.7
30	00000	**MONTANA**	56.4	6.1	9.4	8.0	7.1	3.4	9.1	0.5	38.1
30	06550	Billings city, Montana	69.1	2.8	8.5	6.1	2.9	2.7	7.8	0.1	37.2
30	08950	Bozeman city, Montana	58.0	4.1	10.1	7.8	11.8	1.1	7.1	0.0	40.0
30	11397	Butte-Silver Bow (balance), Montana	58.7	1.1	12.3	12.0	10.3	1.7	3.7	0.2	43.5
30	32800	Great Falls city, Montana	65.3	3.6	10.3	6.2	3.1	3.5	7.8	0.3	35.0
30	35600	Helena city, Montana	50.6	2.6	15.0	6.1	16.9	4.5	4.3	0.0	49.9
30	40075	Kalispell city, Montana	47.9	13.6	15.6	10.6	7.7	0.0	3.7	0.9	38.3
30	50200	Missoula city, Montana	57.1	3.4	11.8	6.2	12.5	1.6	7.3	0.0	43.4

Table E. Cities—Labor Force, Employment, and Educational Data, 2015—*Continued*

FIPS state code	FIPS place code	State/city	Employees of private companies	Self-employed in own incorporated business	Private not-for-profit wage and salary workers	Local	State	Federal	Self-employed in own not incorporated business	Unpaid family workers	Management, business, science, and arts occupations
31	00000	**NEBRASKA**	66.9	3.6	9.3	6.7	5.0	2.0	6.3	0.2	36.6
31	03950	Bellevue city, Nebraska	69.4	1.4	9.3	5.2	2.8	6.7	5.2	0.0	36.7
31	10110	Columbus city, Nebraska	69.0	3.4	9.1	8.0	3.5	2.0	5.0	0.0	29.9
31	17670	Fremont city, Nebraska	73.5	1.2	8.6	6.1	5.3	0.9	4.0	0.4	26.3
31	19595	Grand Island city, Nebraska	75.3	1.0	8.4	4.6	4.6	2.9	3.3	0.0	24.5
31	21415	Hastings city, Nebraska	72.2	2.3	11.6	6.3	2.4	1.4	3.5	0.3	36.8
31	25055	Kearney city, Nebraska	73.5	1.7	8.5	5.2	7.6	0.6	2.8	0.0	27.8
31	28000	Lincoln city, Nebraska	65.1	2.0	9.3	7.0	10.6	2.0	4.0	0.0	39.4
31	34615	Norfolk city, Nebraska	68.4	4.9	8.8	7.5	4.0	1.1	5.3	0.0	30.4
31	35000	North Platte city, Nebraska	66.1	2.6	9.0	6.1	10.3	0.8	5.0	0.0	37.7
31	37000	Omaha city, Nebraska	72.1	3.4	10.4	5.4	2.9	1.7	3.9	0.1	37.8
31	38295	Papillion city, Nebraska	69.7	3.5	12.6	3.4	3.2	1.9	5.7	0.0	46.7
32	00000	**NEVADA**	76.8	3.0	3.5	6.2	3.0	2.2	5.1	0.1	27.4
32	09700	Carson City, Nevada	67.2	2.3	5.5	3.8	15.9	1.6	3.0	0.6	25.8
32	22500	Elko city, Nevada	-	-	-	-	-	-	-	-	23.4
32	23770	Enterprise CDP, Nevada	81.7	2.3	1.9	4.5	2.0	2.9	4.7	0.0	30.6
32	31900	Henderson city, Nevada	72.8	4.1	4.4	8.1	3.1	1.6	5.8	0.2	36.1
32	40000	Las Vegas city, Nevada	77.9	2.5	4.0	5.9	2.4	2.4	4.7	0.1	27.5
32	51800	North Las Vegas city, Nevada	77.9	1.8	3.9	5.8	2.5	4.0	4.1	0.0	23.4
32	53800	Pahrump CDP, Nevada	-	-	-	-	-	-	-	-	21.8
32	54600	Paradise CDP, Nevada	82.5	2.2	2.4	4.3	2.7	1.4	4.5	0.0	22.9
32	60600	Reno city, Nevada	73.3	3.6	4.0	5.6	4.9	1.7	6.6	0.2	33.9
32	68400	Sparks city, Nevada	76.9	1.7	4.9	7.7	3.5	1.8	3.4	0.1	28.8
32	68585	Spring Valley CDP, Nevada	84.2	4.0	2.7	2.8	1.0	0.7	4.3	0.2	22.1
32	70900	Summerlin South CDP, Nevada	76.6	4.4	3.9	6.7	0.5	2.1	5.8	0.0	42.2
32	71400	Sunrise Manor CDP, Nevada	82.8	1.1	2.3	6.1	2.0	2.0	3.6	0.1	13.9
32	71600	Sun Valley CDP, Nevada	79.2	0.5	6.7	2.8	2.3	1.4	7.2	0.0	11.5
32	83800	Whitney CDP, Nevada	86.1	2.5	2.1	2.0	1.5	2.4	3.4	0.0	19.4
32	84600	Winchester CDP, Nevada	83.2	3.9	2.0	4.2	1.7	1.3	3.7	0.0	20.8
33	00000	**NEW HAMPSHIRE**	66.6	3.1	10.9	7.0	3.7	2.1	6.5	0.1	40.1
33	14200	Concord city, New Hampshire	53.6	4.6	18.4	7.4	10.3	0.0	5.5	0.2	42.5
33	17860	Derry CDP, New Hampshire	82.3	2.8	4.5	4.6	2.5	0.9	2.5	0.0	25.6
33	18820	Dover city, New Hampshire	66.2	1.8	11.6	7.6	2.3	5.4	5.1	0.0	48.7
33	39300	Keene city, New Hampshire	59.9	2.2	16.1	9.7	7.0	0.0	4.6	0.5	40.3
33	45140	Manchester city, New Hampshire	74.9	1.5	10.8	4.7	2.5	2.1	3.4	0.1	33.4
33	50260	Nashua city, New Hampshire	77.7	1.5	8.7	3.8	1.7	2.0	4.6	0.0	35.7
33	62900	Portsmouth city, New Hampshire	72.1	2.4	6.8	5.7	2.9	2.6	7.4	0.0	52.7
33	65140	Rochester city, New Hampshire	75.2	0.3	7.9	5.3	2.7	4.7	4.0	0.0	31.5
34	00000	**NEW JERSEY**	71.3	3.9	6.6	6.9	4.6	1.6	4.9	0.2	41.3
34	02080	Atlantic City city, New Jersey	81.1	1.3	5.2	3.3	4.5	1.2	3.4	0.0	18.0
34	02350	Avenel CDP, New Jersey	74.3	4.7	9.2	1.6	3.7	5.5	1.0	0.0	27.2
34	03580	Bayonne city, New Jersey	71.7	2.7	5.9	13.4	2.6	0.9	2.8	0.0	37.9
34	05170	Bergenfield borough, New Jersey	70.6	3.5	11.4	6.4	3.4	1.1	3.6	0.0	48.7
34	07600	Bridgeton city, New Jersey	77.8	2.0	4.5	4.5	7.8	1.1	2.3	0.0	14.5
34	10000	Camden city, New Jersey	80.5	1.4	7.4	3.6	2.1	1.7	3.3	0.0	17.2
34	10750	Carteret borough, New Jersey	72.6	2.1	5.3	4.5	7.2	4.2	3.1	0.9	30.7
34	13570	Cliffside Park borough, New Jersey	74.6	8.2	3.5	3.0	2.8	1.5	6.4	0.0	36.3
34	13690	Clifton city, New Jersey	76.0	1.3	5.8	5.1	4.8	1.9	4.5	0.7	29.5
34	19390	East Orange city, New Jersey	68.8	1.3	6.3	10.2	7.7	2.7	2.7	0.3	27.2
34	21000	Elizabeth city, New Jersey	80.7	2.1	4.8	4.7	3.0	1.3	3.4	0.0	17.4
34	21300	Elmwood Park borough, New Jersey	79.4	4.1	4.9	4.9	3.8	1.9	1.0	0.0	33.7
34	21480	Englewood city, New Jersey	66.9	4.1	8.5	4.3	0.4	4.1	10.5	1.2	39.4
34	22470	Fair Lawn borough, New Jersey	70.9	6.1	9.0	5.1	1.1	3.7	3.7	0.4	51.2
34	24420	Fort Lee borough, New Jersey	66.1	10.3	9.6	4.3	2.6	1.4	5.7	0.0	59.5
34	25770	Garfield city, New Jersey	76.3	3.2	2.2	7.7	2.9	1.2	6.5	0.0	32.1
34	28680	Hackensack city, New Jersey	78.9	4.1	4.4	4.8	3.0	0.7	4.0	0.0	38.6
34	32250	Hoboken city, New Jersey	78.8	2.2	5.6	5.9	2.6	0.5	4.4	0.0	70.0
34	36000	Jersey City city, New Jersey	75.7	2.4	6.1	5.2	3.5	2.1	5.0	0.0	43.1
34	36510	Kearny town, New Jersey	74.0	1.6	3.8	7.3	5.2	2.9	5.2	0.0	26.5
34	38580	Lakewood CDP, New Jersey	66.0	2.9	19.9	2.0	0.4	1.2	7.6	0.0	29.5
34	40350	Linden city, New Jersey	69.2	2.6	5.1	8.3	10.4	1.2	3.2	0.0	25.9
34	41100	Lodi borough, New Jersey	79.8	4.3	1.9	8.2	2.5	0.6	2.8	0.0	37.6
34	41310	Long Branch city, New Jersey	67.1	4.4	6.0	8.2	2.0	0.8	11.5	0.0	30.8
34	46680	Millville city, New Jersey	65.0	0.9	9.7	11.7	9.5	0.0	3.3	0.0	29.8
34	51000	Newark city, New Jersey	74.4	0.8	6.2	5.3	5.9	2.4	5.0	0.0	20.8
34	51210	New Brunswick city, New Jersey	80.5	0.6	7.4	4.5	3.5	0.8	2.7	0.0	21.4
34	53280	North Plainfield borough, New Jersey	72.7	5.1	6.7	3.8	4.8	1.7	4.8	0.3	32.6
34	54690	Old Bridge CDP, New Jersey	72.4	2.6	7.4	7.1	1.5	3.3	5.6	0.0	41.1
34	55770	Palisades Park borough, New Jersey	78.2	12.1	1.2	2.9	0.0	0.3	4.2	1.0	36.4
34	55950	Paramus borough, New Jersey	63.3	9.8	8.7	7.6	2.3	0.8	7.5	0.0	46.6
34	56550	Passaic city, New Jersey	85.1	2.3	3.4	3.9	3.0	0.7	1.7	0.0	15.9
34	57000	Paterson city, New Jersey	86.1	0.8	2.5	3.9	2.3	0.8	3.6	0.0	16.5
34	58200	Perth Amboy city, New Jersey	79.8	5.0	4.3	3.6	5.8	0.2	1.2	0.1	19.1

Table E. Cities—Labor Force, Employment, and Educational Data, 2015—*Continued*

			Class of worker (percent)			Government workers					Percent in each occupation group
FIPS state code	FIPS place code	State/city	Employees of private companies	Self-employed in own incorporated business	Private not-for-profit wage and salary workers	Local	State	Federal	Self-employed in own not incorporated business	Unpaid family workers	Management, business, science, and arts occupations
34	59190	Plainfield city, New Jersey	80.9	1.1	3.6	5.1	5.4	1.3	2.6	0.0	24.1
34	59640	Pleasantville city, New Jersey	-	-	-	-	-	-	-	-	12.4
34	60900	Princeton, New Jersey	52.5	3.2	27.3	3.1	5.1	2.1	6.3	0.4	61.9
34	61530	Rahway city, New Jersey	72.2	4.1	7.2	3.8	8.2	1.9	2.6	0.0	32.0
34	63000	Ridgewood village, New Jersey	67.0	11.9	5.4	4.0	1.2	1.6	8.9	0.0	67.4
34	64620	Roselle borough, New Jersey	71.4	2.1	7.6	10.2	5.9	1.6	1.1	0.0	27.1
34	65790	Sayreville borough, New Jersey	72.5	2.8	7.2	8.0	4.0	1.6	3.8	0.2	41.0
34	68370	Somerset CDP, New Jersey	77.5	2.9	8.9	3.3	3.9	0.6	2.7	0.0	61.1
34	69390	South Plainfield borough, New Jersey	78.3	5.7	5.1	2.5	3.1	1.1	4.2	0.0	40.3
34	71430	Summit city, New Jersey	-	-	-	-	-	-	-	-	60.8
34	73110	Toms River CDP, New Jersey	65.7	5.0	8.5	8.3	4.6	2.0	4.8	1.1	33.6
34	74000	Trenton city, New Jersey	77.2	1.4	4.6	2.8	10.2	1.3	2.5	0.0	21.6
34	74630	Union City city, New Jersey	81.3	1.5	4.0	5.2	0.5	0.3	7.1	0.1	19.6
34	76070	Vineland city, New Jersey	70.0	1.5	7.2	8.2	8.7	1.5	2.9	0.0	33.1
34	79040	Westfield town, New Jersey	70.7	11.7	6.8	2.0	4.6	1.3	2.9	0.0	60.2
34	79610	West New York town, New Jersey	82.0	1.5	2.9	4.3	2.9	0.7	5.7	0.0	29.5
35	00000	**NEW MEXICO**	61.2	3.4	7.4	8.5	7.8	5.2	6.3	0.2	34.5
35	01780	Alamogordo city, New Mexico	58.4	0.6	4.0	5.0	10.8	12.2	7.5	1.3	28.2
35	02000	Albuquerque city, New Mexico	63.4	3.0	9.5	6.5	6.2	6.0	5.3	0.1	39.6
35	12150	Carlsbad city, New Mexico	71.4	0.6	6.9	6.3	10.5	1.7	2.7	0.0	22.0
35	16420	Clovis city, New Mexico	66.9	1.7	14.1	5.5	2.6	7.6	1.6	0.0	24.9
35	25800	Farmington city, New Mexico	66.8	3.7	6.7	10.8	4.0	2.3	5.8	0.0	33.1
35	28460	Gallup city, New Mexico	54.0	3.6	12.0	15.3	5.5	8.4	1.2	0.0	37.5
35	32520	Hobbs city, New Mexico	70.9	1.4	3.3	5.8	12.1	0.4	6.1	0.0	24.2
35	39380	Las Cruces city, New Mexico	62.1	3.5	5.1	9.2	7.9	7.4	4.5	0.3	30.5
35	63460	Rio Rancho city, New Mexico	67.7	3.1	6.2	6.9	4.7	5.4	6.1	0.0	35.8
35	64930	Roswell city, New Mexico	67.2	2.5	5.7	12.6	5.8	4.1	2.2	0.0	24.1
35	70500	Santa Fe city, New Mexico	53.6	5.2	10.6	5.9	9.1	2.7	12.7	0.3	41.7
35	74520	South Valley CDP, New Mexico	67.6	1.3	4.0	12.7	5.0	3.0	6.4	0.0	26.7
36	00000	**NEW YORK**	65.0	3.8	10.2	9.1	4.3	1.7	5.9	0.1	39.9
36	01000	Albany city, New York	59.0	1.5	13.2	5.1	14.2	2.7	4.2	0.0	37.3
36	03078	Auburn city, New York	63.8	0.5	16.5	4.7	8.6	0.7	5.2	0.0	38.0
36	04143	Baldwin CDP, New York	65.1	3.4	7.6	11.9	5.0	1.2	2.5	3.3	37.7
36	04935	Bay Shore CDP, New York	63.0	10.1	11.6	7.4	5.0	1.0	1.8	0.0	26.9
36	06607	Binghamton city, New York	60.4	3.0	8.9	10.4	10.4	1.3	5.5	0.0	31.1
36	08026	Brentwood CDP, New York	78.9	2.9	4.9	3.6	2.4	1.9	5.2	0.2	17.3
36	08257	Brighton CDP, New York	63.5	2.6	17.5	8.5	2.9	0.9	3.8	0.3	55.1
36	11000	Buffalo city, New York	68.3	1.2	12.2	8.8	4.8	1.4	3.2	0.1	33.0
36	13376	Centereach CDP, New York	69.1	3.4	4.8	12.3	5.5	2.6	2.2	0.0	47.4
36	13552	Central Islip CDP, New York	71.1	1.6	5.7	6.8	6.7	1.3	6.7	0.0	17.1
36	15000	Cheektowaga CDP, New York	75.7	0.5	8.5	6.3	3.9	2.5	2.4	0.0	28.3
36	17530	Commack CDP, New York	60.7	6.2	7.2	13.1	6.6	1.8	4.1	0.3	51.4
36	18146	Copiague CDP, New York	79.7	4.1	5.9	3.7	1.1	1.0	4.4	0.0	20.2
36	18157	Coram CDP, New York	62.1	3.9	9.6	7.2	11.7	2.9	2.5	0.0	35.5
36	19972	Deer Park CDP, New York	74.4	3.9	3.7	8.5	4.7	2.4	2.4	0.0	32.5
36	20687	Dix Hills CDP, New York	61.5	11.1	6.0	11.9	2.6	1.3	4.6	1.0	57.1
36	22502	East Meadow CDP, New York	69.7	4.0	7.5	11.2	2.8	0.5	4.3	0.0	46.6
36	22612	East Northport CDP, New York	68.3	5.0	8.0	5.5	5.2	3.1	4.8	0.0	41.8
36	22733	East Patchogue CDP, New York	60.6	2.1	8.7	12.9	1.5	3.8	10.3	0.0	50.7
36	24229	Elmira city, New York	70.4	1.0	13.6	6.1	5.7	0.0	3.3	0.0	24.1
36	24273	Elmont CDP, New York	67.3	3.1	6.7	15.2	3.0	0.5	4.2	0.0	29.3
36	27309	Franklin Square CDP, New York	68.2	5.4	6.1	12.0	2.4	0.9	5.1	0.0	32.2
36	27485	Freeport village, New York	76.3	0.6	7.7	8.1	1.3	1.2	4.2	0.7	33.3
36	28178	Garden City village, New York	63.9	12.8	11.3	6.2	2.7	0.9	2.1	0.0	58.5
36	29113	Glen Cove city, New York	65.3	5.7	11.0	8.2	1.6	0.7	7.6	0.0	33.0
36	32402	Harrison village, New York	70.0	5.9	9.2	6.2	0.9	0.5	7.2	0.0	47.8
36	33139	Hempstead village, New York	76.5	1.5	2.3	5.7	3.4	1.4	9.2	0.0	18.7
36	34374	Hicksville CDP, New York	72.9	2.7	6.4	8.8	1.7	2.2	5.4	0.0	32.8
36	35056	Holbrook CDP, New York	63.4	2.8	7.1	13.4	8.2	2.6	2.6	0.0	37.3
36	35254	Holtsville CDP, New York	57.4	3.6	6.0	12.4	10.3	7.7	2.6	0.0	47.1
36	37044	Huntington Station CDP, New York	65.1	6.0	5.0	14.9	4.9	1.3	2.5	0.4	35.6
36	37737	Irondequoit CDP, New York	64.0	1.8	15.3	7.7	3.9	1.9	5.4	0.0	45.1
36	37869	Islip CDP, New York	66.7	7.3	7.4	8.8	2.6	1.3	5.9	0.0	42.4
36	38077	Ithaca city, New York	49.8	1.9	29.4	7.2	7.5	0.7	3.6	0.0	60.8
36	38264	Jamestown city, New York	68.7	1.2	13.5	8.3	3.2	0.0	5.2	0.0	23.1
36	39727	Kingston city, New York	62.6	3.0	9.3	9.8	6.6	2.2	6.4	0.0	35.1
36	39853	Kiryas Joel village, New York	-	-	-	-	-	-	-	-	38.2
36	40838	Lake Ronkonkoma CDP, New York	60.2	7.5	9.2	11.4	4.8	1.6	5.3	0.0	37.6
36	42081	Levittown CDP, New York	65.1	2.1	8.9	17.1	3.1	1.7	2.1	0.0	36.4
36	42554	Lindenhurst village, New York	72.0	1.9	7.0	13.5	1.8	1.5	2.3	0.0	27.9
36	43082	Lockport city, New York	76.6	1.4	12.7	3.3	2.2	0.0	3.8	0.0	24.7
36	43335	Long Beach city, New York	57.5	6.0	11.9	10.8	6.1	0.5	7.2	0.0	41.6
36	45986	Massapequa CDP, New York	59.7	8.7	6.2	16.1	4.8	0.9	3.5	0.0	45.2
36	46404	Medford CDP, New York	70.6	6.9	7.9	4.1	5.4	3.0	1.8	0.3	32.9

Table E. Cities—Labor Force, Employment, and Educational Data, 2015—*Continued*

			Class of worker (percent)								Percent in each occupation group
						Government workers					
FIPS state code	FIPS place code	State/city	Employees of private companies	Self-employed in own incorporated business	Private not-for-profit wage and salary workers	Local	State	Federal	Self-employed in own not incorporated business	Unpaid family workers	Management, business, science, and arts occupations
36	47042	Middletown city, New York	76.7	0.0	8.3	7.7	2.8	2.2	2.3	0.0	29.7
36	48010	Monsey CDP, New York	35.5	5.6	43.4	4.8	6.0	0.0	4.8	0.0	69.5
36	49121	Mount Vernon city, New York	66.6	2.6	11.4	7.6	4.1	1.5	6.1	0.1	37.9
36	49407	Nanuet CDP, New York	60.4	8.0	7.9	16.8	2.4	0.5	4.0	0.0	40.8
36	50034	Newburgh city, New York	72.9	1.3	11.6	5.1	4.2	0.0	4.8	0.0	19.9
36	50100	New City CDP, New York	53.6	7.2	10.5	12.2	8.7	1.8	5.9	0.0	58.1
36	50617	New Rochelle city, New York	63.7	5.7	10.8	8.2	3.0	1.1	6.7	0.7	43.3
36	51000	New York city, New York	67.1	3.5	9.8	9.2	2.2	1.5	6.6	0.1	40.7
36	51055	Niagara Falls city, New York	71.7	1.2	7.7	11.6	2.4	1.2	4.2	0.0	27.4
36	51396	North Amityville CDP, New York	-	-	-	-	-	-	-	-	23.8
36	53682	North Tonawanda city, New York	74.3	2.5	7.8	6.6	3.5	2.7	2.5	0.0	27.5
36	54441	Oceanside CDP, New York	58.0	6.2	7.0	15.0	3.1	1.0	9.2	0.4	48.5
36	55530	Ossining village, New York	63.2	5.3	5.3	6.7	3.3	0.3	15.3	0.5	29.0
36	56979	Peekskill city, New York	63.9	2.8	14.1	8.2	1.7	3.5	5.8	0.0	32.0
36	58442	Plainview CDP, New York	61.0	7.0	11.5	12.4	3.3	0.6	4.2	0.0	55.9
36	59223	Port Chester village, New York	75.8	3.6	4.6	6.5	1.9	0.0	7.6	0.0	14.6
36	59641	Poughkeepsie city, New York	68.5	2.1	13.2	7.2	4.6	1.0	3.5	0.0	27.6
36	63000	Rochester city, New York	65.6	1.9	16.6	6.6	3.5	0.9	4.9	0.0	30.0
36	63264	Rockville Centre village, New York	63.6	3.3	8.2	13.3	2.2	2.1	7.2	0.0	56.8
36	63418	Rome city, New York	60.6	3.1	15.1	5.6	7.6	6.2	1.9	0.0	36.5
36	63473	Ronkonkoma CDP, New York	68.5	3.7	8.3	10.6	6.7	0.4	1.8	0.0	40.1
36	63924	Rotterdam CDP, New York	67.7	0.4	10.4	8.2	9.8	0.9	2.5	0.0	31.5
36	65255	Saratoga Springs city, New York	56.1	5.1	11.6	7.3	3.9	6.5	9.5	0.0	54.9
36	65508	Schenectady city, New York	66.2	1.1	11.0	8.1	7.0	1.2	5.4	0.0	30.8
36	67070	Shirley CDP, New York	68.2	1.7	7.8	14.2	3.1	3.6	1.4	0.0	39.3
36	67851	Smithtown CDP, New York	56.8	11.2	7.9	12.3	10.2	0.5	1.0	0.0	43.6
36	70420	Spring Valley village, New York	67.7	2.8	13.8	2.5	4.6	0.2	8.3	0.0	19.6
36	72554	Syosset CDP, New York	65.0	8.5	9.6	5.2	2.0	4.1	5.6	0.0	59.0
36	73000	Syracuse city, New York	62.9	1.7	14.1	9.6	5.5	2.7	3.6	0.0	35.2
36	74183	Tonawanda CDP, New York	67.7	1.8	15.0	4.3	5.4	2.1	3.4	0.2	36.0
36	75484	Troy city, New York	52.9	2.6	15.7	9.5	13.0	2.5	3.6	0.1	38.9
36	76089	Uniondale CDP, New York	74.6	2.4	8.4	8.6	2.6	2.1	1.3	0.0	24.2
36	76540	Utica city, New York	58.4	2.4	17.2	10.4	5.6	1.3	4.6	0.0	26.3
36	76705	Valley Stream village, New York	63.5	5.0	8.7	12.6	4.8	1.7	3.8	0.0	34.4
36	78146	Wantagh CDP, New York	56.4	3.4	8.8	22.1	3.4	0.4	5.4	0.0	50.7
36	78608	Watertown city, New York	53.7	0.5	14.3	10.7	6.3	7.6	6.9	0.0	31.9
36	79246	West Babylon CDP, New York	66.4	4.3	5.0	13.0	7.3	1.8	2.2	0.2	32.1
36	80225	West Hempstead CDP, New York	69.4	6.6	5.6	5.0	3.8	1.2	8.5	0.0	37.0
36	80302	West Islip CDP, New York	65.7	6.5	4.3	13.7	7.5	1.4	0.9	0.0	43.9
36	80907	West Seneca CDP, New York	68.8	2.1	11.0	6.3	5.5	3.2	3.3	0.0	41.8
36	81677	White Plains city, New York	61.1	4.6	14.7	7.3	3.1	1.4	7.7	0.0	50.5
36	84000	Yonkers city, New York	68.3	4.1	10.1	8.5	2.8	1.3	4.6	0.3	35.4
37	00000	**NORTH CAROLINA**	69.5	3.5	6.9	5.3	6.7	2.3	5.7	0.2	36.6
37	01520	Apex town, North Carolina	68.4	3.6	10.1	3.6	9.8	1.0	3.6	0.0	52.8
37	02080	Asheboro city, North Carolina	72.3	3.6	6.4	9.6	3.3	0.3	4.5	0.0	26.9
37	02140	Asheville city, North Carolina	63.4	5.1	10.6	4.3	4.8	1.9	9.7	0.2	42.2
37	09060	Burlington city, North Carolina	81.9	0.8	3.8	4.1	3.4	0.3	5.5	0.3	26.1
37	10620	Carrboro town, North Carolina	45.0	1.7	16.0	5.2	25.1	3.3	3.7	0.0	64.5
37	10740	Cary town, North Carolina	71.0	4.3	6.0	4.0	6.7	1.9	6.1	0.1	62.3
37	11800	Chapel Hill town, North Carolina	48.6	4.2	13.0	6.1	21.9	2.1	4.0	0.2	52.3
37	12000	Charlotte city, North Carolina	77.6	3.7	6.8	3.3	3.1	1.3	4.1	0.1	42.1
37	14100	Concord city, North Carolina	68.7	3.7	9.8	4.5	5.8	1.7	5.6	0.2	39.0
37	14700	Cornelius town, North Carolina	71.8	4.1	7.8	5.3	4.6	0.5	5.8	0.2	52.2
37	19000	Durham city, North Carolina	62.8	2.4	12.9	3.8	11.0	2.8	3.9	0.3	48.9
37	22920	Fayetteville city, North Carolina	62.3	2.3	5.7	6.5	7.9	10.4	4.7	0.1	32.5
37	25300	Fuquay-Varina town, North Carolina	74.0	0.6	3.2	8.2	4.8	3.5	5.8	0.0	41.3
37	25480	Garner town, North Carolina	65.2	4.1	7.0	5.5	9.8	5.0	3.4	0.0	38.1
37	25580	Gastonia city, North Carolina	79.8	2.3	6.2	5.3	2.4	1.2	2.8	0.0	27.7
37	26880	Goldsboro city, North Carolina	65.8	1.0	3.7	2.7	15.6	6.5	4.8	0.0	32.6
37	28000	Greensboro city, North Carolina	69.2	3.1	9.2	4.7	6.2	1.9	5.6	0.1	36.8
37	28080	Greenville city, North Carolina	68.0	2.8	7.1	3.2	13.2	2.8	3.0	0.0	32.9
37	30120	Havelock city, North Carolina	-	-	-	-	-	-	-	-	33.1
37	31060	Hickory city, North Carolina	75.4	4.1	4.7	4.9	3.5	1.6	5.8	0.0	45.1
37	31400	High Point city, North Carolina	72.8	4.5	8.4	4.3	4.6	1.5	3.7	0.1	36.3
37	32260	Holly Springs town, North Carolina	63.4	3.8	5.4	6.2	10.1	1.9	9.1	0.0	51.4
37	33120	Huntersville town, North Carolina	74.8	4.0	5.4	5.1	6.4	0.0	4.0	0.3	51.1
37	33560	Indian Trail town, North Carolina	72.0	4.6	9.4	5.3	4.1	0.4	4.1	0.0	43.9
37	34200	Jacksonville city, North Carolina	69.4	1.3	1.3	2.7	3.7	17.6	4.1	0.0	28.5
37	35200	Kannapolis city, North Carolina	73.9	1.4	10.0	6.9	3.4	2.1	2.2	0.0	30.5
37	35600	Kernersville town, North Carolina	78.5	1.4	4.0	6.8	5.3	0.4	3.2	0.4	39.8
37	35920	Kinston city, North Carolina	65.6	6.1	5.8	6.2	10.9	1.1	4.3	0.0	28.0
37	39700	Lumberton city, North Carolina	75.5	2.9	5.5	5.4	4.6	1.6	4.2	0.3	25.9
37	41960	Matthews town, North Carolina	72.7	3.2	10.1	2.1	5.8	0.6	5.6	0.0	57.1

Table E. Cities—Labor Force, Employment, and Educational Data, 2015—Continued

			Class of worker (percent)								Percent in each occupation group
						Government workers					
FIPS state code	FIPS place code	State/city	Employees of private companies	Self-employed in own incorporated business	Private not-for-profit wage and salary workers	Local	State	Federal	Self-employed in own not incorporated business	Unpaid family workers	Management, business, science, and arts occupations
37	43480	Mint Hill town, North Carolina	77.6	3.3	4.4	4.7	4.2	1.2	4.7	0.0	38.2
37	43920	Monroe city, North Carolina	78.5	1.1	6.7	8.1	3.2	0.4	2.1	0.0	26.6
37	44220	Mooresville town, North Carolina	77.2	3.9	5.2	4.7	4.5	0.7	3.9	0.0	42.8
37	44520	Morrisville town, North Carolina	77.5	1.7	6.8	2.4	3.4	1.4	6.7	0.0	65.7
37	46340	New Bern city, North Carolina	62.7	3.0	10.6	8.1	1.5	10.0	3.4	0.6	39.2
37	55000	Raleigh city, North Carolina	71.1	3.6	5.8	4.2	8.9	1.1	5.1	0.2	45.3
37	57500	Rocky Mount city, North Carolina	69.4	2.3	6.7	5.6	7.3	0.6	7.8	0.4	26.2
37	58860	Salisbury city, North Carolina	68.5	3.0	8.4	3.1	5.1	5.9	5.8	0.2	25.6
37	59280	Sanford city, North Carolina	77.3	0.7	4.7	4.1	9.7	0.2	3.2	0.0	25.7
37	61200	Shelby city, North Carolina	65.7	2.2	4.9	14.7	2.7	0.4	9.4	0.0	32.9
37	64740	Statesville city, North Carolina	76.6	2.6	5.9	3.7	5.5	2.0	3.7	0.0	24.3
37	67420	Thomasville city, North Carolina	78.4	0.5	7.1	2.4	3.2	1.8	6.7	0.0	23.0
37	70540	Wake Forest town, North Carolina	64.4	4.1	12.1	5.6	7.0	2.1	4.7	0.0	50.9
37	74440	Wilmington city, North Carolina	68.2	4.6	7.1	4.1	7.6	1.4	7.1	0.0	39.6
37	74540	Wilson city, North Carolina	70.3	2.3	8.6	6.7	7.1	0.0	5.0	0.0	36.4
37	75000	Winston-Salem city, North Carolina	67.0	3.6	13.2	4.9	4.2	1.5	5.5	0.1	38.1
38	00000	**NORTH DAKOTA**	63.4	3.3	10.4	6.9	5.1	2.8	7.9	0.2	35.3
38	07200	Bismarck city, North Dakota	62.9	2.6	14.2	7.6	7.2	1.8	3.6	0.1	38.2
38	19620	Dickinson city, North Dakota	74.6	3.3	9.6	7.0	2.7	0.6	2.1	0.0	27.6
38	25700	Fargo city, North Dakota	68.8	2.3	12.2	5.5	4.7	2.3	4.2	0.0	36.5
38	32060	Grand Forks city, North Dakota	69.1	1.6	6.7	5.2	11.2	3.6	2.5	0.0	33.3
38	49900	Mandan city, North Dakota	64.7	3.6	10.4	8.5	7.8	0.0	4.8	0.0	33.6
38	53380	Minot city, North Dakota	70.1	1.5	8.7	7.0	2.5	5.0	4.9	0.3	28.3
38	84780	West Fargo city, North Dakota	67.8	5.1	12.5	5.8	1.3	1.6	5.9	0.0	36.6
38	86220	Williston city, North Dakota	63.5	6.1	8.5	5.5	4.1	2.4	9.9	0.0	32.4
39	00000	**OHIO**	70.9	2.7	9.1	6.8	3.5	1.8	5.1	0.1	35.7
39	01000	Akron city, Ohio	75.4	2.0	8.4	5.3	3.7	0.9	4.3	0.0	27.4
39	01420	Alliance city, Ohio	81.0	1.7	8.5	5.1	0.9	0.0	2.8	0.0	18.0
39	02568	Ashland city, Ohio	69.9	2.3	13.0	9.7	1.2	0.5	3.4	0.0	40.2
39	02736	Athens city, Ohio	47.0	0.7	13.2	10.7	22.5	2.2	3.8	0.0	48.9
39	03184	Austintown CDP, Ohio	71.2	3.6	8.8	8.1	2.8	3.1	2.4	0.0	30.6
39	03352	Avon city, Ohio	73.8	7.4	6.6	7.3	3.6	0.0	1.3	0.0	37.1
39	03464	Avon Lake city, Ohio	64.0	6.4	12.9	5.6	2.8	0.9	7.3	0.0	55.8
39	03828	Barberton city, Ohio	-	-	-	-	-	-	-	-	25.2
39	04720	Beavercreek city, Ohio	64.0	2.7	11.0	7.2	2.8	10.6	1.4	0.4	48.8
39	07454	Boardman CDP, Ohio	68.8	4.0	8.8	7.3	3.1	1.6	6.4	0.0	38.5
39	07972	Bowling Green city, Ohio	68.3	0.0	4.1	9.3	14.8	1.2	2.3	0.0	31.2
39	09680	Brunswick city, Ohio	70.3	1.6	10.8	9.9	2.1	2.5	2.5	0.2	33.5
39	12000	Canton city, Ohio	74.6	2.8	9.2	6.4	2.3	0.8	3.9	0.0	22.7
39	13190	Centerville city, Ohio	61.9	1.9	12.9	6.0	4.8	7.7	4.9	0.0	51.1
39	14184	Chillicothe city, Ohio	65.9	3.3	14.0	5.3	3.8	5.3	2.3	0.0	28.9
39	15000	Cincinnati city, Ohio	69.6	2.1	13.6	5.2	2.5	1.4	5.3	0.1	40.6
39	16000	Cleveland city, Ohio	70.8	1.7	11.8	8.2	1.8	2.4	3.2	0.1	27.2
39	16014	Cleveland Heights city, Ohio	55.1	3.2	24.2	7.8	1.8	3.3	4.5	0.1	58.2
39	18000	Columbus city, Ohio	72.4	1.7	8.5	5.0	6.8	1.3	4.2	0.0	39.2
39	19778	Cuyahoga Falls city, Ohio	72.5	1.0	11.6	7.1	3.0	1.0	3.8	0.0	38.5
39	21000	Dayton city, Ohio	70.3	1.7	11.6	5.9	1.9	3.7	4.8	0.2	28.9
39	21434	Delaware city, Ohio	73.1	1.0	7.9	7.9	4.9	0.2	4.9	0.1	42.5
39	22694	Dublin city, Ohio	70.7	3.5	10.6	5.2	5.3	0.6	4.1	0.0	70.1
39	25256	Elyria city, Ohio	78.4	1.4	6.6	4.9	2.2	2.0	3.6	0.9	22.8
39	25704	Euclid city, Ohio	72.4	1.2	11.7	7.6	1.4	4.8	0.8	0.2	33.4
39	25914	Fairborn city, Ohio	64.5	1.9	8.2	10.0	2.6	8.0	4.8	0.0	37.0
39	25970	Fairfield city, Ohio	74.9	2.8	13.4	3.9	0.5	0.8	3.7	0.0	41.9
39	27048	Findlay city, Ohio	75.1	1.7	7.3	9.4	1.6	0.9	4.1	0.0	33.6
39	29106	Gahanna city, Ohio	62.0	4.6	10.3	7.8	5.4	3.8	6.2	0.0	54.2
39	29428	Garfield Heights city, Ohio	72.0	1.2	15.2	7.2	1.0	2.4	1.1	0.0	26.2
39	31860	Green city, Ohio	69.3	5.8	8.3	8.6	2.2	0.8	4.4	0.5	47.3
39	32592	Grove City city, Ohio	70.3	2.9	9.8	8.0	4.0	0.7	4.4	0.0	39.2
39	33012	Hamilton city, Ohio	80.3	2.7	3.8	8.2	1.2	0.5	3.1	0.0	24.1
39	35476	Hilliard city, Ohio	67.0	1.9	11.7	5.6	8.1	0.4	4.8	0.5	55.7
39	36610	Huber Heights city, Ohio	69.5	2.6	6.6	7.4	3.4	4.5	6.1	0.0	30.9
39	36651	Hudson city, Ohio	64.2	8.2	15.1	3.1	3.2	0.4	5.5	0.2	61.3
39	39872	Kent city, Ohio	70.0	3.1	9.4	2.9	11.9	1.3	1.4	0.0	43.0
39	40040	Kettering city, Ohio	62.1	3.3	14.6	6.2	2.5	4.5	6.5	0.3	45.9
39	41664	Lakewood city, Ohio	68.3	1.8	13.1	9.3	0.8	2.3	4.4	0.0	50.5
39	41720	Lancaster city, Ohio	69.3	3.4	11.3	6.9	4.4	1.3	3.5	0.0	36.0
39	42364	Lebanon city, Ohio	70.1	0.9	12.0	4.5	5.3	0.7	6.4	0.0	24.0
39	43554	Lima city, Ohio	76.6	1.0	9.7	4.4	2.2	0.9	5.0	0.3	24.3
39	44856	Lorain city, Ohio	75.6	2.5	6.8	7.3	1.4	1.8	4.5	0.1	22.2
39	47138	Mansfield city, Ohio	74.8	2.4	5.4	8.2	3.9	1.6	3.6	0.0	24.8
39	47306	Maple Heights city, Ohio	69.6	0.3	12.6	11.0	4.3	2.2	0.0	0.0	25.3
39	47754	Marion city, Ohio	78.6	1.2	5.6	5.5	2.6	1.1	5.4	0.0	21.2
39	48160	Marysville city, Ohio	75.9	4.9	5.2	7.2	4.3	0.0	2.6	0.0	37.6
39	48188	Mason city, Ohio	64.8	4.2	8.7	8.0	1.9	4.4	8.0	0.0	60.3
39	48244	Massillon city, Ohio	75.7	3.7	7.2	5.0	1.2	1.7	5.5	0.0	21.3

Table E. Cities—Labor Force, Employment, and Educational Data, 2015—*Continued*

FIPS state code	FIPS place code	State/city	Employees of private companies	Self-employed in own incorporated business	Private not-for-profit wage and salary workers	Government workers			Self-employed in own not incorporated business	Unpaid family workers	Percent in each occupation group — Management, business, science, and arts occupations
						Local	State	Federal			
39	48790	Medina city, Ohio	73.5	3.4	10.9	6.3	1.2	0.3	4.2	0.4	40.0
39	49056	Mentor city, Ohio	71.3	2.7	8.8	7.5	2.0	1.1	6.6	0.0	40.8
39	49434	Miamisburg city, Ohio	-	-	-	-	-	-	-	-	36.0
39	49840	Middletown city, Ohio	82.4	0.8	7.2	5.6	0.3	0.4	3.3	0.0	30.4
39	54040	Newark city, Ohio	77.0	1.3	6.3	7.4	2.8	1.4	3.6	0.2	31.5
39	56882	North Olmsted city, Ohio	74.9	1.3	8.0	7.4	1.0	2.6	4.9	0.0	31.3
39	56966	North Ridgeville city, Ohio	70.4	1.3	12.6	6.0	1.8	2.2	5.7	0.0	44.7
39	57008	North Royalton city, Ohio	68.9	3.8	13.5	5.8	1.6	1.3	4.9	0.0	45.5
39	58730	Oregon city, Ohio	69.4	3.6	10.7	11.0	3.3	0.0	2.1	0.0	28.4
39	59234	Oxford city, Ohio	56.2	1.7	10.5	9.8	20.5	1.2	0.0	0.0	36.2
39	61000	Parma city, Ohio	74.6	2.2	8.3	8.0	1.2	1.5	4.2	0.0	27.1
39	61028	Parma Heights city, Ohio	79.6	0.3	6.3	5.5	1.6	2.1	4.7	0.0	31.6
39	62148	Perrysburg city, Ohio	65.9	2.0	8.4	9.1	10.5	1.5	2.4	0.0	54.8
39	62848	Piqua city, Ohio	-	-	-	-	-	-	-	-	15.8
39	64304	Portsmouth city, Ohio	65.1	0.8	4.5	12.6	6.7	0.8	9.5	0.0	30.2
39	66390	Reynoldsburg city, Ohio	72.7	1.5	7.7	3.2	5.8	3.9	5.2	0.0	30.5
39	67468	Riverside city, Ohio	66.3	0.6	6.6	7.8	0.7	15.2	2.8	0.0	33.2
39	68056	Rocky River city, Ohio	68.4	3.5	8.3	5.2	0.8	4.1	9.8	0.0	52.1
39	70380	Sandusky city, Ohio	78.0	2.0	4.2	8.3	4.4	0.9	2.1	0.0	16.8
39	71682	Shaker Heights city, Ohio	48.8	4.6	22.8	11.5	2.3	3.2	6.7	0.0	62.2
39	72424	Sidney city, Ohio	77.8	0.0	10.4	3.5	4.0	0.0	4.3	0.0	30.5
39	72928	Solon city, Ohio	64.1	6.1	11.6	10.2	2.3	0.8	4.9	0.0	53.7
39	73264	South Euclid city, Ohio	60.0	1.2	12.4	7.2	4.1	9.3	5.9	0.0	38.3
39	74118	Springfield city, Ohio	72.4	1.4	10.7	6.5	2.1	1.0	5.3	0.6	24.5
39	74944	Stow city, Ohio	70.5	2.8	9.7	7.1	6.6	0.8	2.5	0.0	53.5
39	75098	Strongsville city, Ohio	65.6	6.2	8.8	11.6	1.7	2.7	3.4	0.0	44.0
39	77000	Toledo city, Ohio	71.3	1.1	11.2	6.2	4.0	1.4	4.6	0.0	26.7
39	77504	Trotwood city, Ohio	79.4	0.7	8.2	3.2	0.9	5.0	2.7	0.0	24.9
39	77588	Troy city, Ohio	77.7	1.3	6.5	8.4	2.5	2.1	1.4	0.0	34.8
39	79002	Upper Arlington city, Ohio	57.1	5.5	13.2	6.3	9.7	0.9	7.3	0.0	66.4
39	80304	Wadsworth city, Ohio	69.8	3.0	7.6	12.9	2.9	0.6	3.4	0.0	48.9
39	80892	Warren city, Ohio	82.6	1.3	4.9	3.5	2.3	2.4	2.5	0.4	23.1
39	83342	Westerville city, Ohio	65.0	2.5	8.9	7.4	6.4	2.6	7.3	0.0	60.2
39	83622	Westlake city, Ohio	66.2	3.3	10.0	4.6	1.2	5.8	8.4	0.4	52.8
39	84812	White Oak CDP, Ohio	71.2	3.9	9.8	4.8	0.9	6.5	2.9	0.0	34.4
39	85484	Willoughby city, Ohio	76.1	1.6	9.4	7.2	0.0	3.6	2.0	0.0	39.1
39	86548	Wooster city, Ohio	68.4	2.1	10.3	6.0	7.6	1.0	4.6	0.0	40.1
39	86772	Xenia city, Ohio	66.6	0.4	15.3	8.6	2.6	3.8	2.7	0.0	31.0
39	88000	Youngstown city, Ohio	75.1	0.6	9.6	6.3	3.6	0.7	3.8	0.1	21.2
39	88084	Zanesville city, Ohio	79.4	0.0	8.7	3.8	2.9	1.6	3.5	0.0	21.9
40	00000	**OKLAHOMA**	67.3	3.6	6.7	5.5	6.9	3.8	6.0	0.2	33.6
40	02600	Ardmore city, Oklahoma	70.4	5.3	7.1	2.4	4.6	2.7	7.4	0.0	24.2
40	04450	Bartlesville city, Oklahoma	74.9	1.3	8.1	5.6	2.9	2.5	4.7	0.0	40.8
40	06400	Bixby city, Oklahoma	74.0	3.8	6.9	4.6	1.9	2.2	6.6	0.0	39.4
40	09050	Broken Arrow city, Oklahoma	74.2	3.7	6.3	4.7	3.5	1.9	5.4	0.4	38.2
40	19900	Del City city, Oklahoma	68.9	4.1	8.4	1.0	8.1	4.4	5.1	0.0	26.4
40	21900	Duncan city, Oklahoma	73.3	1.8	2.6	4.7	6.7	6.0	4.9	0.0	27.3
40	23200	Edmond city, Oklahoma	66.1	5.6	8.3	3.9	8.0	2.3	5.9	0.0	46.3
40	23950	Enid city, Oklahoma	68.9	3.2	8.9	3.2	3.9	3.8	8.1	0.0	23.9
40	37800	Jenks city, Oklahoma	68.2	3.8	7.1	6.3	8.4	1.2	4.4	0.7	51.7
40	41850	Lawton city, Oklahoma	59.5	2.7	5.9	9.1	6.6	10.7	5.4	0.0	34.7
40	48350	Midwest City city, Oklahoma	67.9	2.6	4.5	2.2	7.2	11.4	4.2	0.0	32.0
40	49200	Moore city, Oklahoma	68.1	2.5	5.7	6.1	6.7	7.5	3.2	0.3	40.0
40	50050	Muskogee city, Oklahoma	66.1	2.8	5.8	5.2	10.1	6.1	3.9	0.0	28.1
40	50100	Mustang city, Oklahoma	66.7	5.5	9.0	2.8	4.8	9.5	1.7	0.0	35.4
40	52500	Norman city, Oklahoma	61.7	4.8	6.8	3.5	15.1	3.4	4.6	0.1	46.5
40	55000	Oklahoma City city, Oklahoma	68.7	4.6	7.9	4.1	5.1	4.1	5.4	0.1	36.4
40	56650	Owasso city, Oklahoma	74.7	1.2	10.6	3.7	3.8	2.5	3.6	0.0	41.9
40	59850	Ponca City city, Oklahoma	75.1	2.0	5.2	4.8	4.7	3.3	4.9	0.0	26.7
40	65400	Sapulpa city, Oklahoma	80.4	0.9	3.9	7.6	3.0	0.5	3.6	0.0	25.1
40	66800	Shawnee city, Oklahoma	61.6	2.8	6.9	9.8	5.1	6.7	6.6	0.6	24.2
40	70300	Stillwater city, Oklahoma	49.0	3.1	10.2	6.3	23.4	2.4	4.2	1.3	41.3
40	75000	Tulsa city, Oklahoma	72.8	3.4	8.5	3.4	3.8	1.7	6.1	0.2	36.1
40	82950	Yukon city, Oklahoma	77.9	4.7	5.7	1.0	5.6	1.1	4.0	0.0	32.7
41	00000	**OREGON**	65.3	4.0	9.5	6.2	5.3	2.1	7.4	0.2	37.7
41	01000	Albany city, Oregon	62.5	2.2	11.8	9.0	9.2	1.0	4.3	0.0	40.1
41	01650	Aloha CDP, Oregon	74.0	2.5	7.9	4.2	3.9	2.4	4.8	0.3	37.1
41	03050	Ashland city, Oregon	50.0	4.8	14.3	5.2	9.6	1.8	14.2	0.0	46.3
41	05350	Beaverton city, Oregon	74.5	3.6	8.3	5.1	2.1	1.7	4.7	0.2	46.6
41	05800	Bend city, Oregon	64.0	6.6	7.4	5.1	2.7	1.6	12.5	0.0	47.3
41	05950	Bethany CDP, Oregon	67.4	2.4	9.2	5.6	8.5	3.7	3.3	0.0	64.2
41	15800	Corvallis city, Oregon	56.3	1.7	13.8	5.1	18.9	1.0	2.9	0.3	52.1
41	23850	Eugene city, Oregon	61.1	3.6	13.2	6.3	7.0	2.3	6.3	0.2	43.0
41	26200	Forest Grove city, Oregon	76.7	1.8	8.4	5.3	2.9	2.1	2.7	0.0	26.4
41	30550	Grants Pass city, Oregon	65.5	3.4	11.9	5.5	2.6	0.4	10.2	0.5	24.3

Table E. Cities—Labor Force, Employment, and Educational Data, 2015—*Continued*

			Class of worker (percent)			Government workers					Percent in each occupation group
FIPS state code	FIPS place code	State/city	Employees of private companies	Self-employed in own incorporated business	Private not-for-profit wage and salary workers	Local	State	Federal	Self-employed in own not incorporated business	Unpaid family workers	Management, business, science, and arts occupations
41	31250	Gresham city, Oregon	71.8	2.5	8.7	6.8	3.2	2.0	5.0	0.0	27.2
41	32850	Hayesville CDP, Oregon	71.2	1.8	9.8	6.8	6.9	1.7	1.7	0.0	22.8
41	34100	Hillsboro city, Oregon	75.4	1.1	7.9	5.9	2.2	2.0	5.3	0.2	45.5
41	38500	Keizer city, Oregon	64.6	2.3	10.4	5.7	10.2	1.7	5.1	0.0	37.3
41	39700	Klamath Falls city, Oregon	64.2	6.9	7.4	5.3	4.6	3.5	7.6	0.4	30.3
41	40550	Lake Oswego city, Oregon	62.4	6.5	9.5	7.9	3.7	0.7	9.4	0.0	58.6
41	45000	McMinnville city, Oregon	69.7	0.8	11.2	8.1	3.6	1.1	5.6	0.0	27.1
41	47000	Medford city, Oregon	68.1	1.7	7.5	4.8	5.0	2.3	10.5	0.0	28.6
41	48650	Milwaukie city, Oregon	68.5	1.8	12.6	8.7	3.2	0.8	4.4	0.0	29.2
41	52100	Newberg city, Oregon	65.0	4.8	13.5	5.7	1.1	0.0	9.8	0.0	35.5
41	55200	Oregon City city, Oregon	67.7	3.2	9.3	9.9	3.8	1.5	4.5	0.0	33.1
41	59000	Portland city, Oregon	62.1	3.9	13.5	5.9	4.2	2.0	8.3	0.1	48.3
41	61200	Redmond city, Oregon	-	-	-	-	-	-	-	-	24.0
41	63650	Roseburg city, Oregon	58.1	5.6	4.5	8.6	2.4	15.7	5.0	0.0	35.1
41	64900	Salem city, Oregon	62.8	3.4	9.4	5.6	12.0	1.8	4.8	0.2	32.9
41	69600	Springfield city, Oregon	71.6	1.0	9.2	5.6	4.2	2.3	5.9	0.2	22.2
41	73650	Tigard city, Oregon	73.5	4.0	6.9	6.2	4.0	1.5	4.0	0.0	43.2
41	74950	Tualatin city, Oregon	80.4	2.0	5.6	5.2	1.9	0.4	4.6	0.0	46.6
41	80150	West Linn city, Oregon	65.5	5.5	11.2	5.3	3.7	0.8	8.0	0.0	52.2
41	82800	Wilsonville city, Oregon	68.7	8.4	6.4	4.9	3.8	0.3	7.5	0.0	47.2
41	83750	Woodburn city, Oregon	-	-	-	-	-	-	-	-	16.9
42	00000	**PENNSYLVANIA**	70.2	2.7	11.7	5.1	3.2	2.0	4.9	0.2	37.4
42	02000	Allentown city, Pennsylvania	76.1	0.7	15.0	3.1	1.3	0.9	2.7	0.1	20.9
42	02056	Allison Park CDP, Pennsylvania	72.3	3.8	15.3	1.6	1.5	2.6	3.0	0.0	46.1
42	02184	Altoona city, Pennsylvania	68.5	1.8	11.5	8.0	4.4	1.2	4.6	0.0	31.9
42	06064	Bethel Park municipality, Pennsylvania	71.3	3.8	11.3	7.3	0.7	1.3	4.4	0.0	48.8
42	06088	Bethlehem city, Pennsylvania	69.4	1.6	14.8	4.7	2.9	1.7	4.8	0.0	34.5
42	12536	Chambersburg borough, Pennsylvania	66.1	3.2	10.6	11.5	1.9	2.6	4.2	0.0	29.0
42	13208	Chester city, Pennsylvania	75.6	0.4	10.1	5.2	3.1	2.3	3.2	0.0	17.5
42	19920	Drexel Hill CDP, Pennsylvania	70.4	2.4	9.8	7.2	2.0	3.5	4.6	0.0	43.3
42	21648	Easton city, Pennsylvania	69.0	2.5	16.7	5.6	2.2	1.6	2.4	0.0	31.8
42	24000	Erie city, Pennsylvania	70.1	1.8	13.6	4.7	2.5	1.7	5.6	0.0	28.1
42	32800	Harrisburg city, Pennsylvania	69.3	2.1	7.2	1.8	12.1	3.1	4.4	0.0	29.6
42	33408	Hazleton city, Pennsylvania	80.5	1.2	8.0	3.5	2.5	0.0	4.2	0.0	17.8
42	38288	Johnstown city, Pennsylvania	76.0	0.0	7.9	4.2	6.4	1.0	4.7	0.0	19.4
42	41216	Lancaster city, Pennsylvania	78.7	1.6	9.0	5.3	1.7	0.6	3.1	0.0	23.9
42	42168	Lebanon city, Pennsylvania	76.1	0.8	8.9	5.2	4.9	2.7	1.4	0.0	19.3
42	42928	Levittown CDP, Pennsylvania	79.6	1.2	7.8	3.7	3.5	2.1	2.2	0.0	30.4
42	50528	Monroeville municipality, Pennsylvania	71.1	3.5	11.2	5.5	0.4	3.0	4.6	0.8	45.9
42	52432	Murrysville municipality, Pennsylvania	72.9	2.1	11.0	2.1	0.7	1.5	9.6	0.0	53.2
42	53368	New Castle city, Pennsylvania	74.2	1.2	7.5	3.3	5.0	2.5	6.4	0.0	20.0
42	54656	Norristown borough, Pennsylvania	76.1	2.1	11.6	4.5	1.7	1.4	2.4	0.3	31.5
42	60000	Philadelphia city, Pennsylvania	66.3	1.7	14.9	6.9	2.3	3.5	4.4	0.1	36.6
42	61000	Pittsburgh city, Pennsylvania	63.4	1.8	20.1	6.2	2.6	1.6	4.2	0.1	47.3
42	61536	Plum borough, Pennsylvania	69.4	2.3	14.1	6.1	1.8	1.8	4.5	0.0	46.2
42	62416	Pottstown borough, Pennsylvania	79.1	0.8	9.6	4.3	1.7	2.9	1.6	0.0	23.8
42	63624	Reading city, Pennsylvania	80.4	0.8	8.5	3.3	4.0	0.2	2.6	0.2	15.9
42	69000	Scranton city, Pennsylvania	68.4	2.4	14.3	6.2	1.9	2.0	4.1	0.7	28.6
42	73808	State College borough, Pennsylvania	73.8	1.0	12.2	1.5	8.9	1.1	1.5	0.0	49.7
42	79277	Upper St. Clair CDP, Pennsylvania	69.5	5.2	15.1	5.4	1.0	0.0	3.7	0.0	59.8
42	83512	West Mifflin borough, Pennsylvania	70.7	1.9	13.6	4.9	3.5	0.5	5.0	0.0	31.8
42	85152	Wilkes-Barre city, Pennsylvania	78.6	2.5	7.3	2.3	2.7	2.2	4.1	0.3	23.9
42	85312	Williamsport city, Pennsylvania	72.2	2.0	17.0	4.7	2.0	0.0	2.1	0.0	27.4
42	87048	York city, Pennsylvania	78.6	2.1	9.7	3.7	1.3	1.3	3.0	0.2	21.2
44	00000	**RHODE ISLAND**	69.1	3.1	10.8	6.0	3.8	2.2	4.8	0.1	38.2
44	19180	Cranston city, Rhode Island	72.0	2.8	8.6	6.9	4.8	1.2	3.7	0.0	41.8
44	22960	East Providence city, Rhode Island	68.7	2.8	11.4	4.1	2.8	4.5	5.7	0.0	33.3
44	49960	Newport city, Rhode Island	66.6	3.1	9.6	3.5	3.1	4.0	10.2	0.0	38.7
44	54640	Pawtucket city, Rhode Island	76.6	0.9	11.1	5.2	2.6	0.7	3.0	0.0	27.1
44	59000	Providence city, Rhode Island	71.3	3.1	15.0	3.5	2.7	0.9	3.2	0.3	36.2
44	74300	Warwick city, Rhode Island	67.9	4.2	11.0	6.8	4.4	3.1	2.7	0.0	40.8
44	76820	Westerly CDP, Rhode Island	74.1	3.8	6.5	3.6	3.4	1.5	7.2	0.0	28.3
44	80780	Woonsocket city, Rhode Island	83.8	1.5	5.1	4.8	1.3	1.1	2.4	0.0	32.3
45	00000	**SOUTH CAROLINA**	70.6	3.0	6.2	5.4	7.1	2.2	5.4	0.1	33.8
45	00550	Aiken city, South Carolina	64.3	4.2	8.0	3.5	11.4	3.1	5.5	0.0	53.6
45	01360	Anderson city, South Carolina	56.1	5.3	8.9	7.8	12.6	2.3	7.1	0.0	32.9
45	13330	Charleston city, South Carolina	67.3	3.3	7.1	5.4	7.4	3.2	6.0	0.2	47.1
45	16000	Columbia city, South Carolina	61.5	3.9	8.0	3.5	14.8	3.6	4.7	0.1	40.5
45	16405	Conway city, South Carolina	70.1	2.3	2.3	12.1	8.6	1.2	3.0	0.5	28.8
45	21985	Easley city, South Carolina	75.8	2.0	5.5	6.4	7.1	0.0	3.1	0.0	34.7

Table E. Cities—Labor Force, Employment, and Educational Data, 2015—*Continued*

FIPS state code	FIPS place code	State/city	Employees of private companies	Self-employed in own incorporated business	Private not-for-profit wage and salary workers	Local	State	Federal	Self-employed in own not incorporated business	Unpaid family workers	Management, business, science, and arts occupations
45	25810	Florence city, South Carolina	61.8	2.1	11.3	3.7	11.3	2.2	7.2	0.3	41.7
45	29815	Goose Creek city, South Carolina	67.8	3.9	3.0	3.7	4.5	12.5	4.6	0.0	34.1
45	30850	Greenville city, South Carolina	72.1	4.2	10.6	3.9	2.6	2.1	4.2	0.3	46.2
45	30895	Greenwood city, South Carolina	73.0	1.8	8.4	2.4	6.8	2.2	5.4	0.0	26.3
45	30985	Greer city, South Carolina	76.8	2.1	8.0	5.9	2.6	0.0	3.4	1.2	33.8
45	32065	Hanahan city, South Carolina	73.3	1.7	5.7	3.6	4.8	5.5	5.4	0.0	32.4
45	34045	Hilton Head Island town, South Carolina	66.0	10.3	5.6	5.6	1.8	2.4	8.4	0.0	44.8
45	41335	Lexington town, South Carolina	62.1	5.1	9.1	7.1	10.2	0.0	6.4	0.0	54.5
45	45115	Mauldin city, South Carolina	70.3	5.0	8.3	7.8	6.3	0.3	2.0	0.0	43.1
45	48535	Mount Pleasant town, South Carolina	64.7	4.5	6.2	5.6	7.2	4.5	7.2	0.1	53.0
45	49075	Myrtle Beach city, South Carolina	79.9	4.1	1.5	4.3	5.4	0.1	4.6	0.0	26.1
45	50695	North Augusta city, South Carolina	72.7	1.2	6.9	3.2	6.4	7.3	2.3	0.0	38.1
45	50875	North Charleston city, South Carolina	73.2	1.9	5.1	8.5	4.7	2.6	3.8	0.3	29.9
45	61405	Rock Hill city, South Carolina	77.5	2.1	5.4	4.3	6.4	1.1	3.1	0.0	31.7
45	62395	St. Andrews CDP, South Carolina	72.2	3.7	6.2	1.9	13.5	0.5	2.0	0.0	24.1
45	66580	Simpsonville city, South Carolina	70.6	0.0	5.8	4.9	9.8	1.1	7.7	0.0	44.6
45	67390	Socastee CDP, South Carolina	78.9	4.5	3.9	1.4	3.3	0.6	7.4	0.0	21.1
45	68290	Spartanburg city, South Carolina	75.7	3.6	7.7	3.3	3.3	1.5	4.7	0.4	25.2
45	70270	Summerville town, South Carolina	72.7	3.6	4.1	3.4	3.7	9.8	2.8	0.0	36.2
45	70405	Sumter city, South Carolina	65.8	0.6	5.6	3.8	10.2	8.2	5.8	0.0	25.7
45	71395	Taylors CDP, South Carolina	70.7	2.0	7.9	5.0	4.1	3.3	6.9	0.0	28.9
45	73870	Wade Hampton CDP, South Carolina	68.1	6.0	9.0	6.4	3.3	2.1	4.1	0.9	30.9
46	00000	**SOUTH DAKOTA**	61.6	4.2	11.4	6.8	4.5	2.9	8.3	0.3	33.8
46	00100	Aberdeen city, South Dakota	65.3	2.1	12.3	5.5	6.5	2.2	5.7	0.3	23.7
46	07580	Brookings city, South Dakota	62.2	1.5	10.9	4.4	15.1	1.1	3.6	1.2	35.0
46	52980	Rapid City city, South Dakota	62.9	5.3	12.1	6.9	3.5	3.9	5.5	0.0	33.1
46	59020	Sioux Falls city, South Dakota	70.3	2.5	15.5	3.7	1.4	1.9	4.7	0.1	33.6
46	69300	Watertown city, South Dakota	75.3	1.4	4.7	7.7	3.3	1.7	5.9	0.0	24.5
47	00000	**TENNESSEE**	70.1	2.1	7.6	7.0	4.1	2.4	6.6	0.1	34.3
47	03440	Bartlett city, Tennessee	73.7	3.0	6.5	7.7	2.7	2.1	4.2	0.0	41.7
47	08280	Brentwood city, Tennessee	62.7	6.6	9.6	3.4	2.7	0.4	14.2	0.3	61.7
47	08540	Bristol city, Tennessee	71.6	1.9	7.7	7.0	3.2	3.2	5.3	0.0	40.3
47	14000	Chattanooga city, Tennessee	70.6	2.2	9.8	5.8	2.8	2.5	6.1	0.1	35.8
47	15160	Clarksville city, Tennessee	68.2	1.1	4.5	6.8	5.3	11.5	2.6	0.0	33.3
47	15400	Cleveland city, Tennessee	74.5	2.6	7.3	5.2	3.4	0.3	6.6	0.2	34.1
47	16420	Collierville town, Tennessee	70.6	2.1	8.9	10.3	0.6	4.3	2.9	0.2	51.2
47	16540	Columbia city, Tennessee	74.0	0.6	8.2	12.0	0.9	0.0	4.2	0.0	28.4
47	16920	Cookeville city, Tennessee	71.4	0.8	8.2	7.3	5.5	0.3	6.5	0.0	33.2
47	22720	East Ridge city, Tennessee	79.7	0.0	6.9	4.9	2.6	1.6	4.3	0.0	32.4
47	25760	Farragut town, Tennessee	50.4	8.1	13.9	6.7	6.6	5.0	9.3	0.0	63.8
47	27740	Franklin city, Tennessee	69.1	3.6	9.2	6.3	3.2	1.3	7.3	0.0	52.4
47	28540	Gallatin city, Tennessee	73.1	1.6	7.4	7.2	3.0	2.0	5.7	0.0	36.2
47	28960	Germantown city, Tennessee	67.9	4.0	12.2	5.9	1.1	1.7	7.2	0.0	58.1
47	33280	Hendersonville city, Tennessee	68.9	2.5	11.4	5.4	2.2	1.5	7.3	0.9	39.4
47	37640	Jackson city, Tennessee	71.2	2.3	11.4	6.5	4.4	1.3	2.7	0.1	35.9
47	38320	Johnson City city, Tennessee	63.7	3.2	12.2	4.0	7.7	4.2	4.9	0.1	45.3
47	39560	Kingsport city, Tennessee	73.6	3.3	7.1	5.9	1.8	0.5	7.6	0.2	34.3
47	40000	Knoxville city, Tennessee	69.6	1.3	9.2	6.4	6.0	2.4	5.0	0.1	34.8
47	41200	La Vergne city, Tennessee	79.8	1.3	4.0	4.5	2.5	2.5	5.3	0.0	25.7
47	41520	Lebanon city, Tennessee	67.7	1.6	9.6	8.4	3.8	1.0	7.9	0.0	46.3
47	46380	Maryville city, Tennessee	76.2	3.8	5.8	6.4	1.9	2.9	2.7	0.2	33.3
47	48000	Memphis city, Tennessee	73.3	1.9	7.9	7.0	2.6	2.4	4.8	0.1	30.5
47	50280	Morristown city, Tennessee	73.5	0.3	4.7	3.2	9.9	2.2	6.1	0.0	19.9
47	50780	Mount Juliet city, Tennessee	69.3	2.8	6.4	6.2	2.4	2.6	10.3	0.0	47.7
47	51560	Murfreesboro city, Tennessee	72.6	0.9	5.6	7.3	7.5	1.2	4.5	0.4	38.6
47	52006	Nashville-Davidson metropolitan government (balance), Tennessee	69.4	1.7	12.3	4.8	3.8	1.6	6.3	0.1	39.5
47	55120	Oak Ridge city, Tennessee	66.7	2.2	10.8	5.9	4.7	6.3	3.4	0.0	39.5
47	67760	Shelbyville city, Tennessee	-	-	-	-	-	-	-	-	11.1
47	69420	Smyrna town, Tennessee	75.3	2.7	5.3	5.7	2.3	1.9	6.7	0.0	28.3
47	70580	Spring Hill city, Tennessee	76.9	2.6	4.7	4.0	1.1	0.0	10.7	0.0	42.1
48	00000	**TEXAS**	72.2	2.7	5.5	6.3	4.5	2.1	6.5	0.2	35.3
48	01000	Abilene city, Texas	64.3	2.7	13.3	6.3	4.9	3.3	5.1	0.1	29.8
48	01924	Allen city, Texas	71.9	2.9	6.7	5.4	4.0	2.2	7.0	0.0	53.1
48	02272	Alvin city, Texas	74.6	0.0	2.3	5.6	7.0	1.7	8.8	0.0	20.6
48	03000	Amarillo city, Texas	72.4	2.4	7.1	5.6	4.6	2.3	5.6	0.1	31.0
48	04000	Arlington city, Texas	77.0	2.9	4.7	5.9	3.2	1.8	4.6	0.0	33.8
48	04462	Atascocita CDP, Texas	71.2	2.1	4.7	9.5	5.5	4.4	2.1	0.6	41.7
48	05000	Austin city, Texas	69.2	3.7	6.2	5.0	7.5	1.6	6.7	0.2	46.5
48	05372	Balch Springs city, Texas	77.8	1.6	6.9	2.2	1.6	1.9	8.1	0.0	12.3
48	06128	Baytown city, Texas	80.3	1.3	5.6	7.0	1.2	1.5	3.3	0.0	25.1
48	07000	Beaumont city, Texas	76.4	1.4	5.3	3.9	5.7	2.3	4.9	0.0	29.7

Table E. Cities—Labor Force, Employment, and Educational Data, 2015—*Continued*

FIPS state code	FIPS place code	State/city	Employees of private companies	Self-employed in own incorporated business	Private not-for-profit wage and salary workers	Government workers Local	Government workers State	Government workers Federal	Self-employed in own not incorporated business	Unpaid family workers	Management, business, science, and arts occupations
48	07132	Bedford city, Texas	73.2	0.9	6.7	7.7	2.2	4.1	5.2	0.0	45.5
48	07492	Belton city, Texas	72.6	0.4	9.8	8.4	1.8	2.9	4.1	0.0	32.0
48	07552	Benbrook city, Texas	78.6	2.5	8.1	3.3	2.3	2.2	3.1	0.0	40.3
48	08236	Big Spring city, Texas	75.5	1.8	3.1	8.3	4.7	1.7	5.0	0.0	32.6
48	10768	Brownsville city, Texas	70.5	3.6	3.9	9.0	5.1	1.4	6.5	0.0	26.4
48	10897	Brushy Creek CDP, Texas	69.2	2.6	10.1	5.3	6.0	2.0	4.8	0.0	57.3
48	10912	Bryan city, Texas	68.1	2.4	6.6	4.3	11.7	1.5	5.4	0.0	32.8
48	11428	Burleson city, Texas	67.8	2.5	7.1	8.7	5.0	3.2	5.3	0.4	37.2
48	12580	Canyon Lake CDP, Texas	66.9	4.1	10.1	5.4	2.6	4.9	6.0	0.0	41.5
48	13024	Carrollton city, Texas	80.9	1.7	3.2	4.2	1.9	1.5	6.6	0.0	41.1
48	13492	Cedar Hill city, Texas	70.4	4.3	4.2	6.9	4.7	2.7	6.6	0.2	36.7
48	13552	Cedar Park city, Texas	72.4	1.3	6.8	6.5	7.8	0.4	4.9	0.0	58.1
48	14236	Channelview CDP, Texas	86.7	0.8	3.4	5.1	2.7	0.4	0.9	0.0	18.2
48	14920	Cibolo city, Texas	62.7	1.8	5.4	6.2	5.1	17.4	1.4	0.0	32.2
48	15364	Cleburne city, Texas	79.7	2.3	4.6	4.4	2.8	0.8	5.4	0.0	30.6
48	15628	Cloverleaf CDP, Texas	87.3	1.0	3.1	2.1	1.4	0.9	4.2	0.0	14.0
48	15976	College Station city, Texas	58.1	1.6	5.7	6.6	23.1	1.2	3.6	0.1	48.9
48	15988	Colleyville city, Texas	62.0	11.5	8.9	8.9	2.3	1.8	3.4	1.2	59.9
48	16432	Conroe city, Texas	70.3	1.8	6.4	6.9	3.4	0.5	10.6	0.2	33.3
48	16468	Converse city, Texas	77.5	0.0	5.0	2.5	3.2	8.0	3.8	0.0	42.6
48	16612	Coppell city, Texas	75.7	3.2	6.2	4.4	2.4	1.4	6.4	0.3	63.3
48	16624	Copperas Cove city, Texas	57.7	0.7	3.2	12.0	11.6	11.4	3.2	0.0	28.8
48	16696	Corinth city, Texas	67.7	4.0	2.3	9.5	7.0	0.6	8.9	0.0	46.4
48	17000	Corpus Christi city, Texas	71.1	2.0	4.1	7.0	4.6	4.1	7.0	0.1	28.1
48	17060	Corsicana city, Texas	75.0	1.6	6.3	7.4	3.4	0.3	4.7	1.2	21.7
48	19000	Dallas city, Texas	77.9	3.0	5.6	4.1	2.3	1.2	5.9	0.1	34.1
48	19624	Deer Park city, Texas	71.0	1.9	5.2	8.2	7.0	2.5	4.2	0.0	26.8
48	19792	Del Rio city, Texas	64.5	0.6	3.8	3.5	8.3	17.4	1.9	0.0	26.6
48	19900	Denison city, Texas	65.5	0.8	10.9	6.8	6.7	1.7	7.6	0.0	29.6
48	19972	Denton city, Texas	68.8	2.2	6.4	7.7	8.5	0.8	5.6	0.1	38.8
48	20092	DeSoto city, Texas	65.2	3.5	5.8	11.0	3.4	3.7	7.0	0.5	41.6
48	21628	Duncanville city, Texas	77.3	0.9	3.5	7.8	4.9	1.2	4.4	0.0	30.4
48	21892	Eagle Pass city, Texas	65.5	0.0	4.9	4.7	8.5	3.6	12.8	0.0	21.3
48	22660	Edinburg city, Texas	57.7	1.8	6.4	11.7	10.6	2.8	9.0	0.0	34.2
48	24000	El Paso city, Texas	65.7	1.5	5.1	9.5	5.1	6.4	6.5	0.1	30.6
48	24768	Euless city, Texas	75.9	1.2	7.5	4.4	4.0	1.4	5.6	0.0	38.5
48	25452	Farmers Branch city, Texas	77.8	4.5	3.1	5.4	1.5	0.7	6.8	0.2	37.0
48	26232	Flower Mound town, Texas	70.3	4.7	4.8	8.8	2.8	1.6	6.9	0.0	54.5
48	26736	Fort Hood CDP, Texas	-	-	-	-	-	-	-	-	20.3
48	27000	Fort Worth city, Texas	74.9	2.4	7.0	6.6	2.6	1.7	4.6	0.1	34.1
48	27540	Fresno CDP, Texas	72.8	0.0	7.0	4.3	7.1	2.1	6.8	0.0	34.6
48	27648	Friendswood city, Texas	73.3	2.4	8.3	3.9	5.4	1.3	5.3	0.0	53.3
48	27684	Frisco city, Texas	77.4	4.8	4.4	4.8	2.0	1.3	5.1	0.1	59.6
48	28068	Galveston city, Texas	66.6	1.9	6.4	9.1	9.8	0.8	5.4	0.1	33.7
48	29000	Garland city, Texas	75.9	2.5	5.3	5.1	2.5	1.1	7.4	0.0	26.8
48	29336	Georgetown city, Texas	62.0	3.7	11.9	7.6	6.2	0.5	8.0	0.2	40.5
48	30464	Grand Prairie city, Texas	79.9	1.0	3.2	6.4	1.9	1.9	5.4	0.2	29.2
48	30644	Grapevine city, Texas	81.2	3.8	2.3	2.7	1.9	0.4	7.4	0.2	40.1
48	30920	Greenville city, Texas	76.6	1.8	6.2	5.3	4.0	1.9	4.1	0.0	27.1
48	31928	Haltom City city, Texas	84.1	1.0	4.3	2.1	1.3	4.0	3.3	0.0	19.1
48	32312	Harker Heights city, Texas	55.2	3.1	2.7	10.6	7.5	16.3	4.6	0.0	33.6
48	32372	Harlingen city, Texas	62.3	2.0	2.8	11.7	5.2	4.1	12.0	0.0	33.9
48	35000	Houston city, Texas	76.1	2.3	6.0	4.7	3.0	1.1	6.7	0.1	33.6
48	35528	Huntsville city, Texas	-	-	-	-	-	-	-	-	35.5
48	35576	Hurst city, Texas	75.4	2.0	5.6	5.0	2.0	2.4	7.2	0.4	36.5
48	35624	Hutto city, Texas	71.0	0.0	5.0	6.1	9.8	1.4	6.6	0.0	33.0
48	37000	Irving city, Texas	81.3	2.3	3.0	4.6	1.3	1.2	6.1	0.1	36.0
48	38632	Keller city, Texas	71.1	3.5	7.5	7.7	1.4	1.5	7.1	0.2	56.7
48	39040	Kerrville city, Texas	55.8	2.5	15.4	5.6	3.8	1.4	15.4	0.0	27.1
48	39148	Killeen city, Texas	59.7	1.1	5.8	6.2	4.3	18.4	4.4	0.1	29.8
48	39352	Kingsville city, Texas	65.9	4.0	3.1	3.4	13.5	1.2	8.0	0.9	24.2
48	39952	Kyle city, Texas	71.9	0.9	5.5	7.1	8.8	1.3	4.2	0.3	30.2
48	40588	Lake Jackson city, Texas	74.0	1.8	4.6	12.3	2.8	0.7	3.7	0.2	57.1
48	41212	Lancaster city, Texas	79.0	0.0	3.9	5.6	3.1	4.3	4.2	0.0	22.2
48	41440	La Porte city, Texas	79.9	0.0	5.1	7.1	2.4	1.2	4.4	0.0	35.6
48	41464	Laredo city, Texas	70.9	3.5	3.0	9.0	5.7	2.9	4.8	0.2	29.3
48	41980	League City city, Texas	71.7	2.1	5.1	7.2	6.0	4.0	4.0	0.0	56.6
48	42016	Leander city, Texas	69.5	1.0	6.7	5.8	6.1	1.1	9.4	0.5	47.0
48	42508	Lewisville city, Texas	80.8	1.9	3.6	5.6	2.1	0.9	4.9	0.1	35.7
48	43012	Little Elm city, Texas	75.9	2.0	6.8	9.1	1.6	1.7	2.9	0.0	39.7
48	43888	Longview city, Texas	73.9	2.3	8.0	6.6	3.5	0.7	5.1	0.0	26.9
48	45000	Lubbock city, Texas	72.0	2.6	5.1	5.4	8.1	0.5	6.0	0.3	32.6
48	45072	Lufkin city, Texas	59.8	3.0	11.4	6.4	8.9	2.1	7.9	0.4	31.4
48	45384	McAllen city, Texas	67.0	3.5	4.3	6.3	6.7	3.3	8.6	0.3	38.2
48	45744	McKinney city, Texas	79.2	2.6	4.4	5.6	2.5	1.0	4.7	0.1	49.5

Table E. Cities—Labor Force, Employment, and Educational Data, 2015—*Continued*

FIPS state code	FIPS place code	State/city	Employees of private companies	Self-employed in own incorporated business	Private not-for-profit wage and salary workers	Government workers Local	State	Federal	Self-employed in own not incorporated business	Unpaid family workers	Percent in each occupation group Management, business, science, and arts occupations
48	46452	Mansfield city, Texas	67.0	4.3	7.6	9.7	4.1	2.0	5.3	0.0	48.6
48	46776	Marshall city, Texas	70.2	2.8	9.1	3.4	9.2	3.8	1.6	0.0	27.7
48	47892	Mesquite city, Texas	75.6	2.3	5.5	6.0	2.5	1.0	6.5	0.6	23.5
48	48072	Midland city, Texas	75.9	3.5	4.4	6.8	2.4	0.4	6.5	0.1	31.1
48	48096	Midlothian city, Texas	68.9	1.8	7.4	9.0	4.2	4.0	4.6	0.0	40.3
48	48768	Mission city, Texas	66.5	5.0	6.6	4.1	2.2	3.4	12.1	0.3	32.7
48	48772	Mission Bend CDP, Texas	77.7	0.8	2.0	6.8	3.0	1.1	8.7	0.0	21.5
48	48804	Missouri City city, Texas	72.6	4.8	5.8	6.3	5.3	0.7	4.6	0.0	47.8
48	50100	Murphy city, Texas	65.2	8.3	8.9	8.8	0.0	0.7	8.1	0.0	61.2
48	50256	Nacogdoches city, Texas	55.5	7.6	4.9	6.2	21.2	1.7	2.9	0.0	32.1
48	50820	New Braunfels city, Texas	66.5	4.4	4.1	9.3	3.8	3.1	8.4	0.4	35.1
48	52356	North Richland Hills city, Texas	73.2	2.6	7.2	7.0	3.4	2.0	4.4	0.3	33.7
48	53388	Odessa city, Texas	73.6	2.9	3.1	9.4	3.7	0.6	6.3	0.4	27.2
48	55080	Paris city, Texas	81.9	0.0	4.7	5.4	4.8	0.4	2.9	0.0	24.6
48	56000	Pasadena city, Texas	79.2	0.9	3.0	7.3	1.9	1.6	6.0	0.1	22.9
48	56348	Pearland city, Texas	73.4	2.1	6.6	8.1	5.2	2.3	2.4	0.0	52.1
48	57176	Pflugerville city, Texas	66.2	2.6	5.0	12.2	5.5	1.3	7.1	0.2	48.2
48	57200	Pharr city, Texas	69.1	4.0	3.2	3.8	5.0	1.4	13.6	0.0	22.2
48	57980	Plainview city, Texas	68.2	1.9	8.0	5.8	7.8	2.2	4.6	1.4	18.4
48	58016	Plano city, Texas	77.1	4.0	4.6	5.3	2.5	1.1	5.3	0.1	53.4
48	58820	Port Arthur city, Texas	83.7	0.3	2.6	4.0	3.6	1.5	4.2	0.0	16.9
48	61796	Richardson city, Texas	71.4	6.1	5.4	6.3	4.1	1.0	5.6	0.2	53.9
48	62828	Rockwall city, Texas	66.3	4.4	5.2	10.4	3.5	2.1	7.4	0.6	46.5
48	63284	Rosenberg city, Texas	76.7	2.4	2.8	8.3	3.2	0.0	6.7	0.0	31.7
48	63500	Round Rock city, Texas	71.7	2.5	5.4	8.2	4.4	2.0	5.8	0.0	42.4
48	63572	Rowlett city, Texas	76.2	2.6	5.7	6.7	2.9	2.3	3.3	0.5	43.5
48	64064	Sachse city, Texas	77.8	3.6	6.1	6.1	0.8	0.7	4.9	0.0	43.7
48	64112	Saginaw city, Texas	-	-	-	-	-	-	-	-	33.1
48	64472	San Angelo city, Texas	71.3	2.8	5.7	7.5	3.8	3.1	5.7	0.0	30.6
48	65000	San Antonio city, Texas	73.9	2.0	6.3	4.7	3.9	4.2	5.0	0.0	31.9
48	65036	San Benito city, Texas	76.0	1.7	3.7	5.9	1.8	4.2	6.7	0.0	30.3
48	65516	San Juan city, Texas	72.1	0.9	2.7	7.8	7.8	2.3	6.5	0.0	23.3
48	65600	San Marcos city, Texas	78.1	2.2	2.7	6.6	6.6	0.0	2.8	1.0	26.5
48	66128	Schertz city, Texas	66.4	1.3	6.3	3.0	1.5	19.3	2.1	0.0	43.8
48	66644	Seguin city, Texas	-	-	-	-	-	-	-	-	23.0
48	67496	Sherman city, Texas	75.1	1.5	6.7	7.3	2.4	2.0	4.5	0.3	30.8
48	68636	Socorro city, Texas	81.6	1.8	2.7	6.8	0.8	2.4	3.7	0.0	15.2
48	69032	Southlake city, Texas	77.0	7.3	3.2	2.0	0.9	0.7	9.0	0.0	66.9
48	69596	Spring CDP, Texas	69.8	1.4	5.5	7.2	4.7	1.6	9.2	0.5	30.5
48	70208	Stephenville city, Texas	75.2	0.0	4.5	4.9	9.4	0.0	5.9	0.0	23.0
48	70808	Sugar Land city, Texas	75.2	5.6	6.3	4.2	3.6	0.6	4.4	0.0	61.4
48	72176	Temple city, Texas	68.5	1.7	11.3	5.9	5.0	3.6	3.8	0.1	32.3
48	72368	Texarkana city, Texas	75.9	0.4	9.0	2.9	2.7	4.1	4.9	0.0	40.2
48	72392	Texas City city, Texas	69.6	3.3	5.8	7.1	7.5	0.6	6.0	0.0	27.1
48	72530	The Colony city, Texas	81.2	1.6	4.3	3.8	2.6	1.7	4.7	0.2	42.5
48	72656	The Woodlands CDP, Texas	74.4	4.1	5.5	4.2	2.8	2.2	6.9	0.0	62.6
48	73057	Timberwood Park CDP, Texas	59.1	5.6	8.0	7.0	6.2	7.4	6.7	0.0	51.3
48	74144	Tyler city, Texas	66.0	3.0	13.3	5.0	6.0	1.2	5.3	0.2	36.7
48	74492	University Park city, Texas	60.8	12.6	10.2	2.3	0.6	2.3	11.3	0.0	68.6
48	75428	Victoria city, Texas	69.3	2.2	6.3	7.5	6.3	2.1	6.3	0.0	35.2
48	76000	Waco city, Texas	72.6	0.8	9.8	6.8	3.8	2.7	3.4	0.1	32.9
48	76672	Watauga city, Texas	78.6	0.9	4.5	6.9	3.9	0.0	5.2	0.0	28.3
48	76816	Waxahachie city, Texas	73.3	3.5	6.8	9.2	2.3	3.3	1.6	0.0	35.6
48	76864	Weatherford city, Texas	74.9	3.6	7.0	5.9	1.5	1.4	5.7	0.0	36.2
48	77272	Weslaco city, Texas	62.6	0.0	3.9	12.8	5.8	1.4	12.4	1.0	30.5
48	77728	West Odessa CDP, Texas	76.6	2.3	2.5	9.6	2.1	0.0	6.8	0.0	16.7
48	79000	Wichita Falls city, Texas	70.2	1.5	6.6	6.0	7.7	3.8	4.3	0.0	32.4
48	80356	Wylie city, Texas	81.6	2.3	1.4	8.5	2.5	1.7	1.8	0.0	43.8
49	00000	**UTAH**	69.2	4.2	7.6	5.6	5.5	3.1	4.6	0.2	36.7
49	01310	American Fork city, Utah	72.0	6.1	6.1	6.1	6.6	0.8	2.3	0.0	44.4
49	07690	Bountiful city, Utah	64.3	4.7	8.7	6.7	5.4	3.8	6.3	0.0	47.9
49	11320	Cedar City city, Utah	64.6	4.3	7.6	4.9	12.0	2.9	3.7	0.0	40.2
49	13850	Clearfield city, Utah	75.9	0.3	2.4	1.4	4.0	11.4	4.2	0.3	24.0
49	14290	Clinton city, Utah	65.3	6.5	9.4	5.4	5.0	6.4	2.0	0.0	38.0
49	16270	Cottonwood Heights city, Utah	64.9	6.8	8.8	4.8	6.3	1.7	6.8	0.0	47.0
49	20120	Draper city, Utah	63.7	12.0	8.0	5.4	4.0	0.5	6.0	0.0	57.4
49	20810	Eagle Mountain city, Utah	71.1	6.7	4.0	5.7	3.5	1.4	4.0	3.7	44.3
49	24740	Farmington city, Utah	67.6	3.8	3.2	12.4	4.6	6.6	1.8	0.0	43.6
49	34970	Herriman city, Utah	77.9	7.1	2.5	4.6	3.1	0.7	4.0	0.0	41.4
49	36070	Holladay city, Utah	65.6	6.3	8.0	3.3	4.8	2.1	9.1	0.8	46.3
49	40360	Kaysville city, Utah	69.1	6.7	9.9	5.7	0.8	4.7	3.1	0.0	48.3
49	40470	Kearns CDP, Utah	81.1	1.6	5.5	3.6	4.8	1.8	1.4	0.2	19.9
49	43660	Layton city, Utah	70.3	4.7	5.3	5.9	3.4	8.4	2.0	0.0	37.6
49	44320	Lehi city, Utah	67.1	4.6	8.2	6.6	6.6	1.1	5.8	0.0	45.9
49	45860	Logan city, Utah	71.2	2.3	8.7	4.6	9.1	1.4	2.3	0.4	35.7

Table E. Cities—Labor Force, Employment, and Educational Data, 2015—*Continued*

FIPS state code	FIPS place code	State/city	Employees of private companies	Self-employed in own incorporated business	Private not-for-profit wage and salary workers	Local	State	Federal	Self-employed in own not incorporated business	Unpaid family workers	Management, business, science, and arts occupations
49	47290	Magna CDP, Utah	82.9	1.4	2.9	4.7	3.2	0.8	4.2	0.0	19.2
49	49710	Midvale city, Utah	74.9	2.3	10.1	2.1	4.7	2.4	3.5	0.0	32.3
49	50150	Millcreek CDP, Utah	68.2	3.4	6.6	4.8	8.7	2.2	5.7	0.4	50.2
49	53230	Murray city, Utah	75.1	2.2	6.6	4.5	4.9	2.1	4.6	0.0	32.0
49	55980	Ogden city, Utah	72.4	1.5	8.6	4.4	4.0	6.5	2.3	0.3	24.6
49	57300	Orem city, Utah	72.8	3.5	10.3	3.7	5.1	0.3	4.0	0.3	36.0
49	60930	Pleasant Grove city, Utah	61.8	3.5	8.7	9.8	8.3	1.8	6.1	0.0	42.5
49	62470	Provo city, Utah	67.0	2.0	16.9	5.5	3.6	0.6	4.2	0.1	43.8
49	64340	Riverton city, Utah	68.6	2.9	9.9	7.8	5.7	2.1	2.7	0.2	46.3
49	65110	Roy city, Utah	63.0	1.6	8.6	7.2	5.1	11.3	3.1	0.1	30.4
49	65330	St. George city, Utah	72.5	5.2	7.0	4.1	4.8	1.7	4.4	0.2	31.8
49	67000	Salt Lake City city, Utah	64.7	2.9	9.9	4.5	10.2	2.9	4.9	0.0	42.5
49	67440	Sandy city, Utah	72.5	6.4	5.6	2.7	6.6	1.2	4.9	0.1	41.7
49	67825	Saratoga Springs city, Utah	67.5	6.8	8.6	5.8	6.6	1.1	3.6	0.0	52.7
49	70850	South Jordan city, Utah	69.0	6.8	8.1	4.6	4.7	3.6	3.2	0.0	50.0
49	71070	South Salt Lake city, Utah	73.2	2.7	11.3	4.3	2.4	4.6	1.5	0.0	23.0
49	71290	Spanish Fork city, Utah	70.8	2.3	8.5	7.0	3.9	0.5	5.6	1.3	33.5
49	72280	Springville city, Utah	71.9	2.6	10.2	3.7	3.1	3.0	5.5	0.0	37.2
49	74810	Syracuse city, Utah	56.6	4.4	8.4	8.2	12.3	6.8	3.1	0.0	40.2
49	75360	Taylorsville city, Utah	77.0	2.1	5.9	3.7	5.0	1.6	4.7	0.0	30.1
49	76680	Tooele city, Utah	66.3	2.7	3.7	8.9	3.3	7.1	6.7	1.3	28.0
49	81960	Washington city, Utah	-	-	-	-	-	-	-	-	17.6
49	82950	West Jordan city, Utah	76.4	2.5	5.5	6.2	2.5	2.6	4.1	0.3	33.0
49	83470	West Valley City city, Utah	79.8	1.7	4.2	3.2	3.8	1.8	5.3	0.1	17.8
50	00000	**VERMONT**	57.7	4.4	15.5	6.7	4.7	2.3	8.6	0.2	41.1
50	10675	Burlington city, Vermont	62.5	2.8	19.2	6.1	3.9	1.9	3.5	0.1	39.4
51	00000	**VIRGINIA**	63.9	3.3	7.9	7.5	4.1	8.2	5.0	0.1	43.0
51	01000	Alexandria city, Virginia	53.1	2.7	13.1	4.4	1.6	19.8	5.4	0.0	57.5
51	01912	Annandale CDP, Virginia	63.4	2.1	7.8	5.7	2.6	10.2	8.2	0.0	39.9
51	03000	Arlington CDP, Virginia	55.2	2.8	12.2	4.5	1.7	19.5	4.0	0.1	69.8
51	03320	Ashburn CDP, Virginia	69.6	4.2	5.0	5.1	2.0	9.3	4.4	0.3	54.0
51	04088	Bailey's Crossroads CDP, Virginia	70.9	1.4	8.4	1.0	0.3	13.5	4.5	0.0	37.7
51	07784	Blacksburg town, Virginia	54.5	1.5	5.3	5.4	31.2	0.4	1.4	0.4	62.7
51	08472	Bon Air CDP, Virginia	67.0	2.1	8.6	4.6	4.1	2.1	11.5	0.0	53.3
51	11464	Burke CDP, Virginia	50.8	4.3	8.1	6.8	1.5	23.9	4.3	0.3	56.5
51	13720	Cave Spring CDP, Virginia	64.9	1.5	15.8	4.3	4.9	1.8	6.9	0.0	49.1
51	14440	Centreville CDP, Virginia	62.3	5.3	8.7	8.3	3.5	8.4	3.5	0.0	50.3
51	14744	Chantilly CDP, Virginia	72.4	3.7	4.3	7.2	1.6	4.9	5.2	0.6	49.0
51	14968	Charlottesville city, Virginia	53.7	3.8	8.9	6.9	17.5	1.9	7.2	0.0	49.4
51	15176	Cherry Hill CDP, Virginia	61.4	2.0	3.8	10.7	2.5	17.8	1.8	0.0	40.8
51	16000	Chesapeake city, Virginia	61.3	3.3	6.9	10.3	3.3	10.8	4.0	0.2	39.8
51	16096	Chester CDP, Virginia	68.3	0.4	1.6	8.5	3.4	10.1	7.7	0.0	32.0
51	16608	Christiansburg town, Virginia	56.4	2.6	7.9	14.5	8.8	5.2	4.6	0.0	47.8
51	21088	Dale City CDP, Virginia	66.4	1.9	7.1	6.1	1.5	12.2	4.7	0.1	31.5
51	21344	Danville city, Virginia	73.7	0.8	6.8	6.0	5.0	0.0	6.6	1.1	30.8
51	26496	Fairfax city, Virginia	62.1	3.1	9.3	5.3	2.9	11.5	5.2	0.5	53.7
51	26875	Fair Oaks CDP, Virginia	67.0	3.5	5.0	7.7	1.2	12.5	3.1	0.0	68.6
51	29136	Fort Hunt CDP, Virginia	45.0	5.8	7.2	5.3	2.2	28.9	5.0	0.5	64.5
51	29744	Fredericksburg city, Virginia	61.2	4.6	9.0	7.5	3.7	11.3	2.4	0.3	41.8
51	35000	Hampton city, Virginia	68.9	0.8	6.4	7.1	3.1	9.5	4.2	0.1	33.0
51	35624	Harrisonburg city, Virginia	65.9	4.7	8.7	5.1	11.6	0.4	3.5	0.0	39.6
51	36648	Herndon town, Virginia	71.4	2.2	8.0	6.6	0.3	7.3	4.2	0.0	46.4
51	38424	Hopewell city, Virginia	67.3	5.3	3.3	6.7	0.9	13.4	3.0	0.0	32.0
51	39448	Idylwood CDP, Virginia	66.0	1.4	11.6	4.9	1.1	11.6	3.4	0.0	48.2
51	43432	Lake Ridge CDP, Virginia	56.2	3.5	7.9	11.9	1.0	15.4	4.0	0.0	52.2
51	44280	Laurel CDP, Virginia	73.2	2.0	2.2	9.7	7.4	2.4	3.2	0.0	36.5
51	44984	Leesburg town, Virginia	63.4	2.6	8.2	9.8	2.3	7.4	6.2	0.0	50.8
51	45784	Lincolnia CDP, Virginia	70.8	2.7	8.1	1.2	0.9	11.5	4.7	0.0	39.4
51	45957	Linton Hall CDP, Virginia	58.3	4.5	7.4	10.9	1.9	13.9	2.4	0.7	56.4
51	47064	Lorton CDP, Virginia	58.1	1.8	4.6	7.0	2.3	17.1	8.2	0.9	49.8
51	47672	Lynchburg city, Virginia	59.9	2.3	20.7	8.7	3.8	1.6	3.1	0.0	41.5
51	48376	McLean CDP, Virginia	51.7	11.2	12.5	2.6	1.7	15.9	4.4	0.0	74.5
51	48952	Manassas city, Virginia	75.5	3.8	3.6	7.6	0.8	7.0	1.3	0.5	30.2
51	49792	Marumsco CDP, Virginia	65.0	4.6	8.1	7.2	1.0	10.8	3.3	0.0	30.7
51	50856	Mechanicsville CDP, Virginia	67.1	3.7	5.8	13.1	6.1	1.9	2.3	0.0	41.2
51	52658	Montclair CDP, Virginia	53.9	1.6	4.7	8.2	4.4	25.1	2.1	0.0	63.2
51	56000	Newport News city, Virginia	65.6	2.4	6.7	7.6	4.3	11.1	2.2	0.2	36.1
51	57000	Norfolk city, Virginia	63.8	2.7	6.2	5.7	4.4	11.8	5.3	0.2	33.1
51	58472	Oakton CDP, Virginia	56.2	4.3	12.0	6.7	2.8	13.9	4.1	0.0	64.7
51	61832	Petersburg city, Virginia	71.7	1.5	10.1	5.5	4.7	3.3	3.3	0.0	14.8
51	64000	Portsmouth city, Virginia	57.5	2.4	7.1	11.7	3.0	12.9	5.4	0.0	30.1
51	66672	Reston CDP, Virginia	66.5	2.7	8.5	5.7	1.1	9.4	5.7	0.4	61.4
51	67000	Richmond city, Virginia	65.8	2.8	9.8	7.0	7.9	3.1	3.5	0.1	41.3
51	68000	Roanoke city, Virginia	72.6	3.4	9.4	5.6	2.5	4.0	2.5	0.0	32.1
51	68880	Rose Hill CDP (Fairfax County), Virginia	58.6	3.2	11.3	4.6	1.7	14.3	6.3	0.0	49.9

Table E. Cities—Labor Force, Employment, and Educational Data, 2015—*Continued*

FIPS state code	FIPS place code	State/city	Class of worker (percent)								Percent in each occupation group
			Employees of private companies	Self-employed in own incorporated business	Private not-for-profit wage and salary workers	Government workers			Self-employed in own not incorporated business	Unpaid family workers	Management, business, science, and arts occupations
						Local	State	Federal			
51	70000	Salem city, Virginia	72.2	1.6	7.0	11.0	3.5	1.4	3.3	0.0	39.8
51	72272	Short Pump CDP, Virginia	67.9	2.8	9.1	10.3	3.6	2.9	3.4	0.0	62.5
51	74100	South Riding CDP, Virginia	69.9	4.1	7.3	3.8	0.4	8.2	5.7	0.6	65.5
51	74592	Springfield CDP, Virginia	68.5	2.3	6.1	4.4	0.3	9.8	8.7	0.0	39.9
51	75216	Staunton city, Virginia	69.5	5.3	5.6	9.1	6.1	1.3	3.2	0.0	29.6
51	75376	Sterling CDP, Virginia	71.7	1.2	8.3	2.8	0.9	6.9	8.1	0.0	32.5
51	76432	Suffolk city, Virginia	61.8	1.7	8.2	8.9	4.8	9.9	4.7	0.1	34.9
51	79560	Tuckahoe CDP, Virginia	69.9	5.0	10.0	5.6	2.4	1.3	5.8	0.0	40.2
51	79952	Tysons Corner CDP, Virginia	62.7	4.1	7.6	1.3	3.3	14.4	6.7	0.0	72.7
51	82000	Virginia Beach city, Virginia	65.2	3.5	6.7	9.1	2.9	8.5	4.0	0.1	39.3
51	83680	Waynesboro city, Virginia	77.0	0.6	7.6	4.7	7.1	0.5	2.5	0.0	18.1
51	84368	West Falls Church CDP, Virginia	66.9	2.8	7.1	3.2	1.0	10.0	9.0	0.0	36.3
51	84976	West Springfield CDP, Virginia	54.1	1.2	11.2	5.4	1.7	23.5	2.8	0.0	62.2
51	86720	Winchester city, Virginia	60.8	5.4	8.5	4.3	3.4	3.0	13.6	1.0	46.6
51	87410	Woodlawn CDP (Fairfax County), Virginia	67.6	0.3	5.1	8.3	0.0	6.7	11.9	0.0	25.4
53	00000	**WASHINGTON**	66.3	4.0	7.9	6.4	6.2	3.1	5.9	0.2	39.8
53	03180	Auburn city, Washington	72.6	2.3	7.1	6.3	4.7	2.7	4.4	0.0	28.6
53	03736	Bainbridge Island city, Washington	51.1	11.0	12.8	8.6	5.4	1.5	9.6	0.0	68.9
53	05210	Bellevue city, Washington	75.1	4.6	8.3	2.8	3.1	1.0	5.0	0.2	61.4
53	05280	Bellingham city, Washington	62.0	4.7	6.2	6.6	11.2	2.8	6.3	0.2	36.0
53	07380	Bothell city, Washington	71.1	6.7	6.1	5.4	4.4	1.2	4.9	0.3	45.9
53	07395	Bothell West CDP, Washington	80.2	2.9	5.9	4.7	1.4	0.0	4.9	0.0	54.2
53	07695	Bremerton city, Washington	61.8	1.9	6.7	3.4	4.3	19.0	2.9	0.0	30.0
53	08552	Bryn Mawr-Skyway CDP, Washington	66.3	1.3	9.7	3.9	4.7	3.2	9.9	1.0	24.8
53	08850	Burien city, Washington	74.7	2.8	7.0	7.4	1.7	2.0	4.1	0.3	28.8
53	09480	Camas city, Washington	63.0	7.8	10.3	6.2	3.2	1.6	8.0	0.0	45.4
53	14940	Cottage Lake CDP, Washington	68.4	9.0	8.9	1.7	4.2	1.6	6.2	0.0	64.7
53	17635	Des Moines city, Washington	72.3	1.8	7.2	5.4	4.1	1.9	7.3	0.0	34.0
53	19630	Eastmont CDP, Washington	76.4	4.0	1.9	3.4	7.0	1.8	5.4	0.0	37.6
53	20750	Edmonds city, Washington	69.6	3.7	8.2	4.7	3.4	1.2	8.8	0.4	44.4
53	22640	Everett city, Washington	76.2	2.2	5.6	4.2	3.8	2.6	5.4	0.0	28.3
53	23160	Fairwood CDP (King County), Washington	64.9	3.6	11.6	8.0	5.4	0.6	5.4	0.4	44.8
53	23515	Federal Way city, Washington	70.3	3.1	8.3	5.0	4.7	3.2	5.4	0.0	34.0
53	24188	Five Corners CDP, Washington	77.6	9.0	3.4	3.6	1.7	0.9	3.7	0.0	24.7
53	27785	Graham CDP, Washington	60.6	8.7	6.3	7.6	3.6	5.6	7.0	0.6	24.2
53	33805	Issaquah city, Washington	79.0	2.4	7.9	2.6	4.1	0.2	3.8	0.0	61.8
53	35170	Kenmore city, Washington	67.6	7.9	7.8	4.5	5.1	2.3	4.9	0.0	59.0
53	35275	Kennewick city, Washington	72.9	3.6	5.1	6.2	7.7	1.3	3.1	0.0	32.2
53	35415	Kent city, Washington	71.7	3.1	7.3	6.5	3.8	2.5	4.6	0.4	28.6
53	35940	Kirkland city, Washington	72.0	4.3	6.6	4.9	3.8	1.3	6.8	0.3	58.8
53	36745	Lacey city, Washington	53.1	2.3	6.5	7.8	14.7	11.6	4.0	0.0	38.2
53	37900	Lake Stevens city, Washington	69.6	1.5	9.4	7.7	7.3	1.4	3.1	0.0	33.3
53	38038	Lakewood city, Washington	64.5	1.2	4.5	4.8	11.1	9.3	4.6	0.0	29.7
53	40245	Longview city, Washington	68.2	3.8	10.2	8.7	3.8	2.3	3.0	0.0	25.7
53	40840	Lynnwood city, Washington	70.9	0.8	7.9	4.8	4.6	2.7	8.1	0.2	31.3
53	43150	Maple Valley city, Washington	75.9	6.2	3.8	6.3	3.1	2.7	2.1	0.0	47.3
53	43955	Marysville city, Washington	77.5	2.8	5.0	6.0	3.6	1.9	3.1	0.0	28.7
53	45005	Mercer Island city, Washington	61.8	8.9	8.5	5.4	7.0	1.6	6.8	0.0	81.1
53	45865	Mill Creek city, Washington	67.5	9.1	5.4	5.2	2.2	3.4	7.2	0.0	56.4
53	45870	Mill Creek East CDP, Washington	75.8	1.2	6.9	6.7	3.9	2.7	2.8	0.0	55.3
53	47245	Moses Lake city, Washington	-	-	-	-	-	-	-	-	33.9
53	47490	Mountlake Terrace city, Washington	69.0	3.3	13.1	7.6	2.3	0.3	4.3	0.0	38.7
53	47560	Mount Vernon city, Washington	70.0	3.5	8.2	6.2	3.7	2.2	6.2	0.0	29.6
53	47735	Mukilteo city, Washington	72.2	4.5	9.3	5.7	4.0	0.9	3.5	0.0	62.7
53	50360	Oak Harbor city, Washington	55.2	0.5	9.1	8.7	6.3	15.3	5.0	0.0	24.3
53	51300	Olympia city, Washington	49.3	2.0	6.9	8.5	20.5	7.2	5.4	0.1	42.4
53	51795	Orchards CDP, Washington	70.5	1.2	9.7	7.5	4.5	2.4	3.9	0.4	24.8
53	53335	Parkland CDP, Washington	67.2	1.9	12.5	5.0	4.3	6.1	2.9	0.0	22.8
53	53545	Pasco city, Washington	74.1	4.0	4.6	6.0	3.7	2.3	4.8	0.4	27.0
53	56625	Pullman city, Washington	52.3	1.6	4.9	5.9	30.1	0.9	4.3	0.0	51.4
53	56695	Puyallup city, Washington	70.3	3.4	5.9	7.2	5.7	4.6	2.9	0.0	34.1
53	57535	Redmond city, Washington	82.9	2.7	3.9	3.5	2.8	0.6	3.3	0.3	66.6
53	57745	Renton city, Washington	71.7	1.6	8.3	7.1	2.9	1.8	6.2	0.4	40.7
53	58235	Richland city, Washington	63.1	3.8	11.4	5.4	4.4	7.0	4.7	0.3	47.5
53	61000	Salmon Creek CDP, Washington	65.5	5.8	7.8	3.1	5.5	2.1	9.2	1.0	40.1
53	61115	Sammamish city, Washington	75.0	5.0	7.4	2.2	2.2	1.4	6.1	0.6	71.0
53	62288	SeaTac city, Washington	72.7	2.6	5.7	4.6	6.4	3.5	4.5	0.0	24.6
53	63000	Seattle city, Washington	63.3	4.7	12.2	4.9	7.2	1.5	6.0	0.2	59.2
53	63960	Shoreline city, Washington	65.9	2.0	10.7	6.4	5.7	1.3	7.6	0.4	46.6
53	64380	Silver Firs CDP, Washington	73.4	4.8	4.5	8.5	4.9	0.0	2.7	1.0	52.0
53	65922	South Hill CDP, Washington	64.1	2.7	8.5	10.2	3.9	5.0	5.7	0.0	33.7
53	66255	Spanaway CDP, Washington	70.2	2.3	4.2	8.6	6.2	5.8	2.7	0.0	21.1

Table E. Cities—Labor Force, Employment, and Educational Data, 2015—*Continued*

			Class of worker (percent)			Government workers					Percent in each occupation group
FIPS state code	FIPS place code	State/city	Employees of private companies	Self-employed in own incorporated business	Private not-for-profit wage and salary workers	Local	State	Federal	Self-employed in own not incorporated business	Unpaid family workers	Management, business, science, and arts occupations
53	67000	Spokane city, Washington	63.5	4.0	12.2	5.6	6.2	2.0	6.2	0.1	36.7
53	67167	Spokane Valley city, Washington	70.0	3.3	6.4	5.9	4.8	1.0	8.3	0.2	29.3
53	70000	Tacoma city, Washington	66.9	2.5	8.7	7.9	5.9	3.5	4.3	0.2	32.8
53	72625	Tukwila city, Washington	70.6	1.3	8.6	8.4	3.1	2.0	6.1	0.0	24.3
53	73307	Union Hill-Novelty Hill CDP, Washington	76.3	8.3	4.3	3.6	1.8	0.0	5.6	0.0	64.4
53	73465	University Place city, Washington	55.2	6.1	11.8	9.8	7.7	3.7	5.5	0.3	39.6
53	74060	Vancouver city, Washington	73.2	3.3	7.8	4.5	3.2	2.6	5.5	0.0	34.1
53	75775	Walla Walla city, Washington	64.0	3.2	11.6	5.6	8.7	4.5	2.0	0.4	39.5
53	77105	Wenatchee city, Washington	68.0	5.9	6.5	7.1	4.8	1.1	6.5	0.0	28.0
53	80010	Yakima city, Washington	67.6	1.4	11.7	3.8	7.4	1.9	6.1	0.1	28.2
54	00000	**WEST VIRGINIA**	67.2	2.0	7.8	7.0	8.0	3.5	4.5	0.1	33.5
54	14600	Charleston city, West Virginia	58.3	2.1	12.5	5.7	15.1	2.0	4.2	0.0	51.6
54	39460	Huntington city, West Virginia	67.4	3.0	10.6	3.2	8.8	3.2	3.7	0.0	40.8
54	55756	Morgantown city, West Virginia	52.6	4.3	16.5	1.9	17.4	3.4	4.0	0.0	56.9
54	62140	Parkersburg city, West Virginia	75.5	0.9	6.3	2.9	5.5	1.5	7.4	0.0	25.7
54	86452	Wheeling city, West Virginia	71.9	1.0	9.7	7.1	4.8	2.8	2.6	0.0	35.6
55	00000	**WISCONSIN**	70.6	3.0	8.9	6.5	4.4	1.3	5.1	0.2	35.2
55	02375	Appleton city, Wisconsin	74.1	1.3	12.2	4.8	3.7	0.6	3.3	0.1	33.8
55	06500	Beloit city, Wisconsin	73.5	2.5	9.3	8.8	3.0	1.0	1.9	0.0	25.1
55	10025	Brookfield city, Wisconsin	69.1	5.1	12.9	4.0	1.9	0.9	6.0	0.0	58.4
55	11950	Caledonia village, Wisconsin	73.5	1.9	9.1	8.6	0.8	0.8	5.3	0.0	41.8
55	19775	De Pere city, Wisconsin	74.7	2.8	9.8	6.1	2.1	0.3	4.3	0.0	40.2
55	22300	Eau Claire city, Wisconsin	68.5	1.9	12.5	5.8	6.8	1.6	2.9	0.1	38.7
55	25950	Fitchburg city, Wisconsin	61.2	4.2	6.7	7.3	12.4	1.9	5.8	0.4	53.1
55	26275	Fond du Lac city, Wisconsin	73.5	2.5	11.7	4.6	2.4	1.2	4.1	0.0	29.8
55	27300	Franklin city, Wisconsin	66.7	3.9	14.4	5.2	2.8	5.4	1.6	0.0	50.4
55	31000	Green Bay city, Wisconsin	78.9	1.0	7.7	4.5	3.1	0.9	3.8	0.0	28.4
55	31175	Greenfield city, Wisconsin	77.3	3.8	7.6	5.6	1.8	1.1	2.6	0.2	33.5
55	37825	Janesville city, Wisconsin	73.0	3.0	9.6	5.1	4.2	0.7	4.5	0.0	35.3
55	39225	Kenosha city, Wisconsin	78.2	2.4	7.4	5.2	3.6	0.9	2.3	0.0	29.1
55	40775	La Crosse city, Wisconsin	70.9	1.4	11.2	4.5	8.3	1.3	2.3	0.1	33.9
55	48000	Madison city, Wisconsin	60.0	2.0	10.8	6.0	16.7	1.5	2.9	0.0	51.3
55	48500	Manitowoc city, Wisconsin	78.4	3.8	5.1	5.0	1.6	0.7	5.4	0.0	27.9
55	51000	Menomonee Falls village, Wisconsin	79.5	1.9	11.3	2.5	2.3	0.2	2.3	0.0	51.0
55	51150	Mequon city, Wisconsin	63.1	14.1	9.3	3.4	1.9	3.1	5.1	0.0	59.5
55	53000	Milwaukee city, Wisconsin	73.7	1.2	9.5	7.4	3.1	1.3	3.6	0.1	31.7
55	54875	Mount Pleasant village, Wisconsin	71.7	5.0	10.1	7.2	3.8	1.1	1.2	0.0	34.9
55	55275	Muskego city, Wisconsin	80.8	5.0	7.8	2.6	0.3	0.6	2.9	0.0	43.4
55	55750	Neenah city, Wisconsin	78.9	2.8	6.9	4.9	2.0	1.0	3.4	0.0	33.7
55	56375	New Berlin city, Wisconsin	69.4	5.1	13.7	5.0	1.6	1.4	3.4	0.4	44.8
55	58800	Oak Creek city, Wisconsin	68.8	3.1	10.8	8.8	3.1	2.8	2.1	0.3	34.2
55	60500	Oshkosh city, Wisconsin	74.8	3.7	7.5	4.9	6.3	0.1	2.5	0.1	28.4
55	63300	Pleasant Prairie village, Wisconsin	67.9	3.9	6.3	10.5	0.5	3.3	7.6	0.0	39.1
55	66000	Racine city, Wisconsin	73.2	1.1	9.2	6.1	4.7	1.7	4.1	0.0	23.0
55	72975	Sheboygan city, Wisconsin	79.8	1.2	6.7	7.0	1.4	0.3	3.6	0.0	22.5
55	75125	South Milwaukee city, Wisconsin	69.7	0.4	14.8	1.9	1.9	2.8	8.4	0.0	23.3
55	77200	Stevens Point city, Wisconsin	67.0	2.3	8.4	7.5	9.9	1.0	3.0	1.0	33.7
55	78600	Sun Prairie city, Wisconsin	69.5	1.9	7.7	8.4	7.9	1.7	2.9	0.0	44.9
55	78650	Superior city, Wisconsin	71.5	1.4	9.7	6.7	4.7	1.7	3.8	0.6	28.8
55	83975	Watertown city, Wisconsin	80.7	1.6	6.4	5.5	2.0	0.8	3.0	0.0	26.9
55	84250	Waukesha city, Wisconsin	76.9	1.5	6.8	6.5	2.7	0.5	5.1	0.0	39.0
55	84475	Wausau city, Wisconsin	79.4	1.9	7.1	5.0	3.0	0.1	3.3	0.2	35.0
55	84675	Wauwatosa city, Wisconsin	68.0	1.8	16.7	6.8	1.6	2.0	3.1	0.0	55.2
55	85300	West Allis city, Wisconsin	75.6	1.1	12.1	5.2	1.1	2.2	2.4	0.3	31.0
55	85350	West Bend city, Wisconsin	-	-	-	-	-	-	-	-	29.8
56	00000	**WYOMING**	62.8	4.3	6.5	10.4	7.3	2.3	6.2	0.2	31.5
56	13150	Casper city, Wyoming	68.8	2.9	8.5	7.3	5.5	1.5	5.3	0.1	28.5
56	13900	Cheyenne city, Wyoming	61.1	1.9	7.2	10.5	10.3	5.1	3.8	0.2	39.8
56	31855	Gillette city, Wyoming	77.1	4.1	3.1	8.1	4.5	0.0	3.1	0.0	23.2
56	45050	Laramie city, Wyoming	41.4	5.9	9.7	9.6	24.7	2.2	6.4	0.3	39.7
56	67235	Rock Springs city, Wyoming	67.8	3.4	4.1	16.6	5.3	0.9	1.9	0.0	33.1

Table E. Cities—Labor Force, Employment, and Educational Data, 2015

FIPS state code	FIPS place code	State/city	Percent in each occupation group				Percent in each industry sector			
			Service occupations	Sales and office occupations	Natural resources, construction, and maintenance occupations	Production, transportation, and material moving occupations	Agriculture, forestry, fishing and hunting, and mining	Construction	Manufacturing	Wholesale trade
00	00000	**UNITED STATES**	18.0	23.6	9.0	12.3	1.9	6.4	10.3	2.7
01	00000	**ALABAMA**	16.3	23.7	9.7	16.4	1.7	6.3	14.3	2.5
01	00820	Alabaster city, Alabama	13.6	26.6	11.1	10.0	2.9	7.8	8.8	2.2
01	00988	Albertville city, Alabama	7.4	29.7	13.2	26.8	0.0	14.2	15.4	4.0
01	01852	Anniston city, Alabama	28.7	23.1	2.4	18.5	0.0	0.0	16.7	1.7
01	02956	Athens city, Alabama	16.0	21.3	10.8	12.0	1.3	6.4	15.4	3.1
01	03076	Auburn city, Alabama	17.6	21.8	5.9	10.3	1.0	4.9	12.9	2.6
01	05980	Bessemer city, Alabama	30.5	16.9	11.0	21.4	2.1	4.7	16.2	0.4
01	07000	Birmingham city, Alabama	25.0	24.0	5.5	14.1	0.3	3.9	9.0	3.0
01	19648	Daphne city, Alabama	14.0	35.3	1.8	3.9	0.0	2.3	7.1	3.2
01	20104	Decatur city, Alabama	14.0	23.4	9.3	16.4	0.0	9.3	20.4	1.3
01	21184	Dothan city, Alabama	20.0	23.8	7.7	13.0	2.8	4.4	9.4	3.8
01	24184	Enterprise city, Alabama	19.7	21.0	4.5	16.3	0.8	1.0	13.9	0.0
01	26896	Florence city, Alabama	21.1	26.8	6.0	16.3	0.0	5.0	12.5	5.5
01	28696	Gadsden city, Alabama	19.5	14.0	9.8	32.3	0.8	6.3	29.7	3.6
01	35800	Homewood city, Alabama	14.5	20.1	3.9	8.2	0.0	2.7	5.6	0.4
01	35896	Hoover city, Alabama	11.9	26.9	2.9	5.4	0.4	3.0	5.9	4.0
01	37000	Huntsville city, Alabama	16.9	23.2	5.5	8.9	0.5	3.8	10.0	1.7
01	45784	Madison city, Alabama	9.4	19.6	3.8	5.7	1.5	3.7	9.0	0.8
01	50000	Mobile city, Alabama	18.4	23.2	8.3	13.7	0.8	5.9	11.3	2.3
01	51000	Montgomery city, Alabama	22.4	24.9	5.2	13.0	0.3	3.9	11.0	1.8
01	51696	Mountain Brook city, Alabama	6.1	21.4	1.0	0.0	0.5	0.9	3.7	1.8
01	55200	Northport city, Alabama	11.2	23.2	4.9	13.5	0.5	4.9	16.1	0.5
01	57048	Opelika city, Alabama	18.1	23.0	9.3	17.8	0.0	3.6	16.5	1.7
01	57576	Oxford city, Alabama	14.3	15.3	18.3	15.7	2.7	6.5	20.4	0.7
01	58848	Pelham city, Alabama	15.6	29.4	2.8	5.4	0.4	3.0	9.2	1.9
01	59472	Phenix City city, Alabama	21.3	22.3	4.9	15.8	0.2	4.6	16.4	0.2
01	62328	Prattville city, Alabama	21.7	22.0	6.4	10.7	0.0	5.0	13.3	2.5
01	62496	Prichard city, Alabama	22.9	25.4	10.6	16.5	0.0	3.2	11.9	1.5
01	76944	Trussville city, Alabama	6.2	29.1	9.9	8.3	0.4	7.7	11.7	7.6
01	77256	Tuscaloosa city, Alabama	15.9	22.3	7.3	17.3	0.5	4.6	13.2	2.0
01	78552	Vestavia Hills city, Alabama	8.3	20.6	7.6	2.3	0.8	8.0	5.5	1.0
02	00000	**ALASKA**	17.7	22.6	12.1	11.1	5.3	7.2	3.2	2.0
02	03000	Anchorage municipality, Alaska	17.7	23.9	8.2	8.8	3.6	6.0	1.9	2.7
02	05000	Badger CDP, Alaska	22.7	20.9	18.0	8.0	2.5	6.8	1.6	0.7
02	24230	Fairbanks city, Alaska	20.4	27.6	7.0	14.3	1.2	3.9	1.5	1.4
02	36400	Juneau city and borough, Alaska	12.6	20.7	10.6	9.1	5.0	5.5	1.6	2.9
04	00000	**ARIZONA**	19.8	26.2	9.1	10.2	1.5	6.6	7.1	2.3
04	02830	Apache Junction city, Arizona	18.2	29.1	6.2	11.0	1.1	4.0	3.7	1.7
04	04720	Avondale city, Arizona	17.8	35.1	7.4	14.6	0.1	4.4	6.7	2.8
04	07940	Buckeye town, Arizona	24.0	30.2	10.0	13.2	2.7	5.6	4.5	1.6
04	08220	Bullhead City city, Arizona	32.7	28.4	6.4	10.3	0.5	2.4	2.6	2.4
04	10530	Casa Grande city, Arizona	23.8	25.8	9.2	19.0	2.4	5.6	17.6	1.4
04	10670	Casas Adobes CDP, Arizona	20.5	25.8	5.5	7.8	1.4	5.3	7.6	2.2
04	11230	Catalina Foothills CDP, Arizona	10.2	23.5	3.0	5.8	0.2	3.1	8.4	2.8
04	12000	Chandler city, Arizona	13.9	26.6	5.6	7.4	0.6	4.7	11.6	2.3
04	20540	Drexel Heights CDP, Arizona	19.1	33.4	10.0	13.9	1.2	9.2	6.3	2.1
04	22220	El Mirage city, Arizona	27.8	30.6	9.1	7.9	0.6	8.1	5.5	2.5
04	23620	Flagstaff city, Arizona	28.0	23.0	4.2	7.4	0.9	1.3	7.2	0.4
04	23760	Florence town, Arizona	21.1	30.7	9.8	1.1	–	–	–	–
04	25030	Fortuna Foothills CDP, Arizona	14.9	15.8	16.4	16.7	6.5	5.6	3.0	2.5
04	25300	Fountain Hills town, Arizona	19.4	26.8	2.6	3.8	0.0	1.7	1.2	5.4
04	27400	Gilbert town, Arizona	14.6	28.4	5.5	7.6	0.5	4.3	9.8	3.2
04	27820	Glendale city, Arizona	20.6	26.9	11.7	12.3	0.6	8.4	6.0	2.8
04	28380	Goodyear city, Arizona	18.9	23.3	8.5	10.8	1.5	8.0	6.8	1.6
04	29710	Green Valley CDP, Arizona	14.4	34.0	4.6	3.9	–	–	–	–
04	37620	Kingman city, Arizona	20.5	26.8	10.1	15.4	0.7	5.1	0.8	1.2
04	39370	Lake Havasu City city, Arizona	22.6	26.0	13.4	15.8	0.0	7.8	7.5	1.2
04	44270	Marana town, Arizona	21.8	23.9	6.2	7.7	1.5	2.5	7.9	2.8
04	44410	Maricopa city, Arizona	21.0	25.7	7.8	11.9	2.3	6.9	9.6	0.5
04	46000	Mesa city, Arizona	19.8	27.7	9.5	10.8	0.6	7.1	8.0	2.2
04	49640	Nogales city, Arizona	24.4	24.7	7.5	16.3	0.4	5.3	3.6	11.5
04	51600	Oro Valley town, Arizona	17.1	28.2	4.7	4.8	0.7	3.7	9.2	2.5
04	54050	Peoria city, Arizona	15.7	31.4	7.8	9.7	0.3	6.6	6.6	2.5
04	55000	Phoenix city, Arizona	20.0	26.1	10.0	11.5	0.5	7.6	7.7	2.9
04	57380	Prescott city, Arizona	18.8	28.2	6.0	6.2	0.0	4.6	3.4	2.1
04	57450	Prescott Valley town, Arizona	22.2	27.6	7.4	16.2	0.6	6.7	8.2	3.8
04	58150	Queen Creek town, Arizona	14.0	23.0	10.8	3.2	0.1	9.6	10.5	0.8
04	62140	Sahuarita town, Arizona	20.8	19.7	14.8	6.6	9.7	7.6	2.6	1.0
04	63470	San Luis city, Arizona	17.6	17.4	32.6	17.9	–	–	–	–
04	64210	San Tan Valley CDP, Arizona	28.6	24.8	7.9	11.1	0.5	4.4	9.9	3.4
04	65000	Scottsdale city, Arizona	13.7	26.3	3.0	4.6	0.4	3.5	6.0	2.2
04	66820	Sierra Vista city, Arizona	23.0	27.7	5.5	7.5	0.6	1.2	3.1	0.0
04	70320	Sun City CDP, Arizona	23.6	38.4	5.7	8.5	0.0	1.9	2.8	5.7

Table E. Cities—Labor Force, Employment, and Educational Data, 2015—*Continued*

			Percent in each occupation group				Percent in each industry sector			
FIPS state code	FIPS place code	State/city	Service occupations	Sales and office occupations	Natural resources, construction, and maintenance occupations	Production, transportation, and material moving occupations	Agriculture, forestry, fishing and hunting, and mining	Construction	Manufacturing	Wholesale trade
04	70355	Sun City West CDP, Arizona	17.1	28.2	2.9	10.2	—	—	—	—
04	71510	Surprise city, Arizona	16.1	31.0	11.1	8.3	0.3	6.5	4.8	2.0
04	73000	Tempe city, Arizona	18.9	23.3	4.4	9.8	0.8	3.8	6.8	2.6
04	77000	Tucson city, Arizona	23.6	24.8	8.7	9.0	0.5	7.3	4.9	1.5
04	85540	Yuma city, Arizona	25.2	19.2	13.7	9.2	7.2	6.3	4.0	1.2
05	00000	**ARKANSAS**	16.7	23.7	11.0	16.5	3.2	6.4	13.9	2.4
05	04840	Bella Vista city, Arkansas	15.9	31.0	9.4	8.6	0.0	5.1	6.7	1.3
05	05290	Benton city, Arkansas	17.8	25.1	10.2	11.6	0.0	8.9	6.3	0.8
05	05320	Bentonville city, Arkansas	10.8	27.6	4.7	10.1	0.3	3.0	8.8	2.6
05	10300	Cabot city, Arkansas	13.0	28.3	7.6	12.2	0.0	5.9	9.4	1.6
05	15190	Conway city, Arkansas	14.9	27.0	9.3	12.8	2.5	4.6	8.6	2.9
05	23290	Fayetteville city, Arkansas	18.8	21.8	4.9	7.5	0.6	4.3	9.1	1.3
05	24550	Fort Smith city, Arkansas	18.6	26.6	8.5	19.5	2.0	3.9	21.3	3.3
05	33400	Hot Springs city, Arkansas	27.7	23.6	12.4	12.3	1.4	10.1	9.8	1.6
05	34750	Jacksonville city, Arkansas	14.1	29.9	9.5	11.9	0.0	4.1	10.0	2.3
05	35710	Jonesboro city, Arkansas	16.2	24.7	9.6	15.4	1.0	6.4	13.8	2.4
05	41000	Little Rock city, Arkansas	15.8	24.3	4.6	11.9	0.4	4.0	7.6	2.2
05	50450	North Little Rock city, Arkansas	15.8	24.5	8.1	16.7	0.0	4.2	10.8	1.4
05	53390	Paragould city, Arkansas	15.4	25.4	7.8	28.2	1.7	3.4	21.7	1.6
05	55310	Pine Bluff city, Arkansas	22.2	16.6	4.3	29.6	1.0	0.0	27.3	2.2
05	60410	Rogers city, Arkansas	11.4	25.7	10.4	15.9	0.5	8.8	16.0	2.6
05	61670	Russellville city, Arkansas	17.7	25.4	5.6	28.8	0.4	2.6	14.7	3.8
05	63020	Searcy city, Arkansas	24.9	17.3	10.2	17.3	0.5	3.9	6.5	0.8
05	63800	Sherwood city, Arkansas	15.4	31.8	7.1	10.9	2.6	9.0	5.5	3.3
05	66080	Springdale city, Arkansas	13.9	21.2	10.8	26.7	1.6	7.9	29.1	6.2
05	68810	Texarkana city, Arkansas	15.9	27.0	9.7	17.5	1.7	7.5	10.0	2.3
05	71480	Van Buren city, Arkansas	14.3	20.9	7.7	11.7	0.3	4.8	11.5	4.5
05	74540	West Memphis city, Arkansas	24.6	30.7	8.2	15.3	1.0	2.4	12.3	6.2
06	00000	**CALIFORNIA**	18.7	22.9	9.4	11.2	2.5	6.2	9.5	2.9
06	00296	Adelanto city, California	29.6	21.5	11.6	28.1	0.0	7.3	11.8	2.5
06	00394	Agoura Hills city, California	12.6	24.9	4.0	1.4	0.0	3.3	4.1	6.6
06	00562	Alameda city, California	13.6	21.0	5.0	7.6	0.3	1.7	6.1	2.3
06	00884	Alhambra city, California	19.8	23.4	6.3	10.2	0.7	5.4	8.5	2.8
06	00947	Aliso Viejo city, California	10.6	30.3	2.4	5.5	0.0	3.7	13.2	3.2
06	01290	Altadena CDP, California	20.4	23.4	6.5	4.1	0.3	5.3	4.7	2.6
06	01640	American Canyon city, California	22.6	21.1	9.4	9.5	2.3	7.3	7.8	5.3
06	02000	Anaheim city, California	22.1	23.1	11.4	15.7	0.3	9.3	13.1	4.3
06	02210	Antelope CDP, California	15.8	22.9	10.4	11.9	0.0	7.3	4.3	1.6
06	02252	Antioch city, California	20.9	25.1	10.4	13.4	0.2	9.0	5.6	1.3
06	02364	Apple Valley town, California	20.7	23.5	9.5	18.5	0.0	6.1	11.4	0.7
06	02462	Arcadia city, California	9.8	29.7	0.9	4.7	0.0	1.8	10.2	6.4
06	02553	Arden-Arcade CDP, California	18.4	24.8	6.4	9.4	0.0	5.7	4.0	1.5
06	02924	Arvin city, California	13.0	12.3	64.1	8.7	58.5	4.8	3.4	3.5
06	02980	Ashland CDP, California	22.1	24.4	18.9	10.6	1.5	7.7	8.9	3.6
06	03064	Atascadero city, California	18.1	20.9	8.6	7.2	1.4	5.2	6.3	1.1
06	03162	Atwater city, California	15.1	23.7	19.6	18.9	17.0	4.4	11.9	0.7
06	03386	Azusa city, California	20.2	25.4	7.9	17.5	0.6	2.7	11.0	4.3
06	03526	Bakersfield city, California	19.1	22.4	14.5	14.1	10.9	7.0	5.3	4.0
06	03666	Baldwin Park city, California	22.4	23.2	11.0	22.4	1.3	6.9	19.8	3.6
06	03820	Banning city, California	19.7	28.5	13.4	15.8	0.9	10.3	7.4	4.1
06	04030	Barstow city, California	29.1	25.3	13.2	11.3	2.1	6.5	3.5	3.5
06	04415	Bay Point CDP, California	33.5	23.2	16.8	7.7	1.6	12.1	4.0	0.7
06	04758	Beaumont city, California	20.2	25.5	9.2	14.5	0.9	4.4	4.4	1.9
06	04870	Bell city, California	18.5	30.8	11.2	27.2	0.2	6.4	16.1	12.1
06	04982	Bellflower city, California	19.0	29.5	9.3	17.3	0.0	8.3	10.1	5.7
06	04996	Bell Gardens city, California	19.9	29.0	11.5	29.8	0.2	8.8	14.8	7.5
06	05108	Belmont city, California	12.3	17.5	1.9	3.5	0.8	3.0	12.2	1.1
06	05290	Benicia city, California	14.8	17.9	4.3	7.1	0.0	6.0	10.1	5.6
06	06000	Berkeley city, California	9.2	17.2	2.5	3.6	0.4	3.1	3.3	2.4
06	06308	Beverly Hills city, California	3.2	28.7	0.8	2.4	0.0	1.5	9.3	8.1
06	07064	Bloomington CDP, California	6.9	26.8	14.6	31.5	0.5	10.8	15.0	2.6
06	08058	Brawley city, California	28.1	24.4	10.0	10.3	13.0	3.3	2.7	1.7
06	08100	Brea city, California	7.7	28.3	4.6	7.5	0.8	7.4	11.9	5.8
06	08142	Brentwood city, California	21.6	19.1	10.8	8.7	0.3	9.7	5.2	2.9
06	08786	Buena Park city, California	18.6	30.0	7.1	13.0	0.2	2.4	15.9	7.1
06	08954	Burbank city, California	12.5	22.6	3.0	6.0	0.3	3.4	7.4	2.7
06	09066	Burlingame city, California	15.1	12.0	7.0	6.3	0.0	5.7	9.3	3.1
06	09598	Calabasas city, California	11.5	34.8	1.1	4.4	0.0	2.8	3.0	2.2
06	09710	Calexico city, California	27.4	22.3	14.3	11.0	4.1	8.8	4.4	2.1
06	10046	Camarillo city, California	16.7	27.6	5.3	7.1	1.5	3.8	9.9	2.2
06	10256	Cameron Park CDP, California	17.5	24.7	8.7	8.9	3.3	8.4	9.1	1.6
06	10345	Campbell city, California	15.5	20.3	7.0	5.3	0.3	6.3	21.0	1.8
06	11194	Carlsbad city, California	15.3	26.7	4.9	4.1	1.0	5.5	11.0	6.2

Table E. Cities—Labor Force, Employment, and Educational Data, 2015—*Continued*

			Percent in each occupation group				Percent in each industry sector			
FIPS state code	FIPS place code	State/city	Service occupations	Sales and office occupations	Natural resources, construction, and maintenance occupations	Production, transportation, and material moving occupations	Agriculture, forestry, fishing and hunting, and mining	Construction	Manufacturing	Wholesale trade
06	11390	Carmichael CDP, California	15.7	26.3	6.2	7.0	0.9	6.1	3.6	2.1
06	11530	Carson city, California	19.5	21.3	4.3	19.0	0.2	3.9	12.4	2.7
06	11796	Castaic CDP, California	18.2	29.9	7.3	10.2	0.6	4.3	11.1	5.4
06	11964	Castro Valley CDP, California	12.9	23.9	6.1	7.1	0.3	6.5	11.0	3.0
06	12048	Cathedral City city, California	37.2	27.6	8.8	11.9	0.7	6.9	1.6	1.4
06	12524	Ceres city, California	25.2	22.5	16.6	20.2	4.7	8.8	14.3	2.9
06	12552	Cerritos city, California	8.2	26.9	2.4	6.5	0.0	2.0	12.0	6.6
06	13014	Chico city, California	20.5	28.2	5.6	5.8	2.2	4.4	6.1	1.4
06	13210	Chino city, California	19.2	27.4	9.5	13.1	0.1	5.6	12.0	5.0
06	13214	Chino Hills city, California	14.2	25.7	6.4	4.9	0.0	4.4	9.7	7.7
06	13392	Chula Vista city, California	19.3	27.5	7.2	9.4	0.1	4.7	7.9	3.4
06	13588	Citrus Heights city, California	17.0	30.0	8.5	11.8	1.0	6.8	7.1	3.4
06	13756	Claremont city, California	15.4	19.7	2.5	4.7	0.4	3.1	4.2	2.8
06	14218	Clovis city, California	18.9	25.0	4.9	9.7	0.9	4.1	8.8	2.3
06	14260	Coachella city, California	40.8	21.9	21.0	8.4	14.0	6.7	2.2	1.1
06	14890	Colton city, California	23.1	27.7	10.5	17.3	0.4	7.4	7.3	1.6
06	15044	Compton city, California	21.4	25.0	11.8	25.5	0.8	8.0	18.1	2.4
06	16000	Concord city, California	21.2	23.1	8.4	8.0	1.7	8.1	7.0	1.8
06	16224	Corcoran city, California	27.2	16.6	35.4	11.5	–	–	–	–
06	16350	Corona city, California	14.6	28.5	9.3	12.0	0.5	7.1	14.6	4.2
06	16378	Coronado city, California	12.4	15.2	4.7	3.6	0.7	4.8	6.3	1.3
06	16532	Costa Mesa city, California	17.9	25.6	5.2	8.2	1.1	4.8	10.6	3.8
06	16742	Covina city, California	19.9	32.0	6.1	8.8	0.1	4.1	8.5	5.0
06	17498	Cudahy city, California	19.9	20.7	14.2	33.0	0.0	8.1	17.6	10.6
06	17568	Culver City city, California	8.5	27.8	2.9	3.0	0.0	1.7	4.5	4.2
06	17610	Cupertino city, California	3.8	12.6	1.7	1.9	0.4	1.0	23.6	2.4
06	17750	Cypress city, California	14.7	25.6	6.4	8.6	0.6	6.7	11.0	3.6
06	17918	Daly City city, California	24.6	27.5	6.9	11.2	0.2	4.7	5.6	2.0
06	17946	Dana Point city, California	18.6	28.5	5.5	6.5	0.0	9.1	9.5	1.4
06	17988	Danville town, California	9.2	25.4	4.7	3.9	1.0	3.8	7.4	7.6
06	18100	Davis city, California	14.2	18.0	1.9	4.5	1.3	0.8	3.9	1.8
06	18394	Delano city, California	16.8	12.7	47.9	10.7	42.3	1.2	4.4	4.4
06	18996	Desert Hot Springs city, California	39.3	21.7	14.2	7.9	0.0	14.1	2.7	1.6
06	19192	Diamond Bar city, California	8.9	29.9	2.8	4.1	0.2	1.0	7.5	7.8
06	19318	Dinuba city, California	19.7	16.7	22.3	18.3	18.6	4.8	10.7	4.6
06	19766	Downey city, California	15.8	29.3	6.8	15.6	0.1	5.3	12.5	4.4
06	19990	Duarte city, California	19.2	27.1	4.5	13.5	1.5	4.6	11.1	1.8
06	20018	Dublin city, California	9.9	14.6	2.3	6.3	0.3	2.3	12.7	2.3
06	20802	East Los Angeles CDP, California	21.0	27.3	12.8	24.5	2.3	8.7	15.2	5.8
06	20956	East Palo Alto city, California	44.9	18.1	8.0	8.1	0.0	7.9	5.5	1.4
06	21230	Eastvale city, California	14.6	27.1	5.4	13.2	0.4	6.6	12.7	5.2
06	21712	El Cajon city, California	27.0	27.6	10.2	12.9	0.0	6.8	8.5	1.1
06	21782	El Centro city, California	21.4	26.0	12.4	10.4	8.5	3.5	2.3	1.6
06	21796	El Cerrito city, California	7.3	18.9	1.7	6.7	0.3	3.8	7.3	1.5
06	21880	El Dorado Hills CDP, California	13.4	19.2	2.6	4.3	0.3	4.9	9.2	2.5
06	22020	Elk Grove city, California	17.0	22.2	5.3	11.6	1.0	4.5	6.9	2.2
06	22230	El Monte city, California	19.5	23.9	11.8	26.6	0.5	8.5	14.5	6.0
06	22300	El Paso de Robles (Paso Robles) city, California	26.1	15.7	10.6	16.5	3.5	4.8	17.6	0.5
06	22678	Encinitas city, California	11.5	20.1	3.5	4.2	0.5	3.5	11.1	2.0
06	22804	Escondido city, California	24.9	23.2	13.4	12.4	3.1	9.5	9.5	3.0
06	23042	Eureka city, California	20.5	27.2	13.6	10.6	0.0	8.4	8.1	2.1
06	23182	Fairfield city, California	22.5	25.6	9.7	13.2	2.7	6.1	10.7	1.0
06	23294	Fair Oaks CDP, California	12.1	21.6	0.8	5.7	1.1	1.8	4.7	2.7
06	23462	Fallbrook CDP, California	32.4	24.1	8.5	9.2	3.3	5.9	9.8	3.2
06	24477	Florence-Graham CDP, California	22.1	19.5	13.2	32.0	0.8	10.2	20.8	6.1
06	24498	Florin CDP, California	31.3	27.4	7.7	16.2	1.0	5.0	5.4	1.5
06	24638	Folsom city, California	12.8	20.0	4.1	2.9	0.6	4.9	13.0	1.8
06	24680	Fontana city, California	20.6	25.3	11.8	22.3	0.5	9.5	10.0	3.8
06	24722	Foothill Farms CDP, California	26.6	33.0	8.8	11.4	0.0	6.4	1.4	4.7
06	25338	Foster City city, California	6.6	16.1	2.8	3.7	0.0	1.7	11.2	2.5
06	25380	Fountain Valley city, California	12.4	23.9	3.6	9.1	0.0	2.4	15.8	3.5
06	26000	Fremont city, California	13.2	18.6	4.9	7.2	0.0	3.2	16.0	2.4
06	26067	French Valley CDP, California	13.2	23.2	5.3	5.8	1.4	9.5	8.1	2.4
06	27000	Fresno city, California	21.4	23.9	12.0	13.8	5.5	5.3	7.5	3.6
06	28000	Fullerton city, California	18.8	23.3	7.7	9.7	0.6	5.3	14.2	3.7
06	28112	Galt city, California	20.3	24.8	20.1	10.0	7.1	7.6	6.1	5.4
06	28168	Gardena city, California	19.7	25.8	6.0	16.1	0.7	4.2	8.8	3.6
06	29000	Garden Grove city, California	21.0	25.3	9.2	17.7	0.4	5.9	16.9	2.5
06	29504	Gilroy city, California	25.7	23.2	13.2	10.7	3.3	9.7	12.3	2.7
06	30000	Glendale city, California	16.5	27.4	6.2	7.5	0.4	4.6	5.3	3.0
06	30014	Glendora city, California	14.4	26.0	6.6	7.1	1.0	5.9	8.5	3.3
06	30378	Goleta city, California	18.2	23.3	5.6	4.7	0.0	3.2	9.5	1.8
06	30693	Granite Bay CDP, California	9.3	28.5	3.1	0.9	0.8	8.5	9.9	1.0
06	31596	Hacienda Heights CDP, California	15.5	25.1	5.9	11.1	0.0	3.5	9.6	5.2
06	31960	Hanford city, California	26.3	15.0	15.6	10.3	9.8	4.3	6.2	1.8

Table E. Cities—Labor Force, Employment, and Educational Data, 2015—*Continued*

FIPS state code	FIPS place code	State/city	Percent in each occupation group				Percent in each industry sector			
			Service occupations	Sales and office occupations	Natural resources, construction, and maintenance occupations	Production, transportation, and material moving occupations	Agriculture, forestry, fishing and hunting, and mining	Construction	Manufacturing	Wholesale trade
06	32548	Hawthorne city, California	27.6	26.5	7.9	16.2	0.8	5.2	7.4	2.1
06	33000	Hayward city, California	17.9	23.7	11.8	14.7	0.4	8.8	11.3	2.8
06	33182	Hemet city, California	22.6	27.0	12.3	13.4	2.2	9.0	7.0	2.5
06	33308	Hercules city, California	19.4	21.7	4.2	9.0	0.2	1.8	10.3	0.8
06	33434	Hesperia city, California	19.4	24.0	12.9	19.4	1.2	7.4	10.5	1.5
06	33588	Highland city, California	22.3	22.1	9.6	16.6	0.5	7.6	3.9	4.0
06	34120	Hollister city, California	18.9	24.5	22.6	13.2	7.8	11.6	12.9	3.5
06	36000	Huntington Beach city, California	16.2	23.2	7.6	7.6	1.3	6.9	11.4	3.0
06	36056	Huntington Park city, California	16.9	29.8	11.8	32.6	0.6	6.6	19.5	8.1
06	36294	Imperial Beach city, California	22.9	30.0	10.1	12.1	0.0	6.7	9.5	2.1
06	36448	Indio city, California	32.2	25.9	13.6	8.0	3.0	9.2	3.9	2.3
06	36546	Inglewood city, California	25.7	26.3	7.7	13.8	0.5	5.6	7.4	3.0
06	36770	Irvine city, California	8.7	20.8	0.8	3.9	0.1	2.2	13.7	4.1
06	36868	Isla Vista CDP, California	35.3	21.9	1.1	7.8	2.1	0.0	6.4	0.3
06	37692	Jurupa Valley city, California	17.1	21.8	17.7	25.7	2.0	12.9	10.7	4.8
06	39003	La Cañada Flintridge city, California	4.1	19.3	3.2	2.5	0.0	1.8	1.8	1.9
06	39114	Ladera Ranch CDP, California	11.4	20.5	1.1	9.3	0.0	3.6	9.8	8.4
06	39122	Lafayette city, California	3.9	17.6	0.4	5.2	0.0	2.1	5.1	3.4
06	39178	Laguna Beach city, California	9.5	28.8	1.3	1.6	0.0	1.9	7.7	2.9
06	39220	Laguna Hills city, California	16.4	23.0	5.5	5.8	0.2	4.4	7.3	2.3
06	39248	Laguna Niguel city, California	13.4	24.3	4.2	6.4	0.2	5.2	10.9	3.7
06	39290	La Habra city, California	19.3	26.1	9.6	12.4	1.3	6.4	14.9	5.7
06	39486	Lake Elsinore city, California	18.5	26.0	13.1	17.1	0.1	14.2	11.2	2.3
06	39496	Lake Forest city, California	14.8	24.1	5.9	6.9	0.5	6.1	14.9	2.4
06	39766	Lakeside CDP, California	18.6	32.6	12.0	9.9	0.0	10.1	9.1	1.1
06	39892	Lakewood city, California	13.7	26.5	8.0	10.7	1.0	5.0	11.1	2.9
06	40004	La Mesa city, California	15.5	24.8	9.9	6.3	0.8	5.6	6.4	1.7
06	40032	La Mirada city, California	10.5	31.9	7.2	11.5	0.0	5.1	16.9	3.5
06	40130	Lancaster city, California	18.4	22.1	11.7	13.3	0.2	6.4	8.2	1.9
06	40326	La Presa CDP, California	25.2	21.8	15.0	14.2	0.3	5.9	10.6	3.8
06	40340	La Puente city, California	23.1	24.8	12.2	25.5	1.5	8.0	21.8	4.4
06	40354	La Quinta city, California	15.2	32.6	9.8	6.6	1.3	7.8	2.5	2.9
06	40704	Lathrop city, California	13.6	21.0	15.8	31.7	4.3	10.3	10.3	1.5
06	40830	La Verne city, California	15.3	25.2	7.2	7.9	1.0	1.7	7.1	3.8
06	40886	Lawndale city, California	27.5	25.3	9.1	13.5	0.4	6.5	11.2	2.7
06	41124	Lemon Grove city, California	23.3	19.8	12.8	12.0	1.1	11.1	3.6	2.4
06	41152	Lemoore city, California	22.0	23.8	10.4	14.9	5.3	4.6	7.6	3.2
06	41180	Lennox CDP, California	32.4	27.4	13.5	12.1	1.2	13.3	3.7	1.5
06	41474	Lincoln city, California	16.6	28.6	6.2	8.7	0.0	4.8	11.3	1.6
06	41992	Livermore city, California	15.8	21.0	8.5	8.6	0.6	6.0	11.2	3.4
06	42202	Lodi city, California	18.1	24.3	14.5	14.1	7.6	9.6	10.8	3.0
06	42370	Loma Linda city, California	15.3	16.4	2.6	9.2	0.3	3.6	2.7	0.0
06	42468	Lomita city, California	9.0	39.6	10.1	14.4	0.0	7.8	13.9	1.4
06	42524	Lompoc city, California	25.4	19.4	15.5	14.7	7.3	7.1	12.6	1.2
06	43000	Long Beach city, California	19.9	23.4	8.0	13.9	0.8	5.3	10.2	3.7
06	43280	Los Altos city, California	2.8	10.0	1.2	1.3	0.0	2.1	19.1	1.5
06	44000	Los Angeles city, California	20.8	22.0	7.7	12.0	0.5	6.2	8.2	2.6
06	44028	Los Banos city, California	24.1	23.0	26.2	12.0	10.0	11.6	8.3	2.9
06	44112	Los Gatos town, California	5.0	16.7	2.8	3.0	0.3	6.4	16.9	2.4
06	44574	Lynwood city, California	27.2	22.7	8.2	29.7	0.2	6.1	13.4	3.4
06	45022	Madera city, California	16.5	19.0	31.6	16.0	28.0	2.7	11.6	1.3
06	45400	Manhattan Beach city, California	5.8	20.8	1.1	3.7	0.0	2.1	11.0	3.0
06	45484	Manteca city, California	18.7	26.0	16.2	15.5	2.5	8.5	11.9	3.9
06	45778	Marina city, California	29.1	23.4	13.8	4.0	0.5	6.7	1.9	3.5
06	46114	Martinez city, California	17.2	21.1	6.9	10.8	1.7	6.7	8.5	3.3
06	46492	Maywood city, California	17.3	24.9	12.4	35.2	1.2	8.2	17.4	6.6
06	46646	Mead Valley CDP, California	22.3	17.2	15.3	26.8	2.3	9.2	5.2	5.1
06	46842	Menifee city, California	20.4	20.6	12.6	10.0	0.5	9.6	10.5	3.5
06	46870	Menlo Park city, California	13.9	14.1	5.3	3.2	0.9	4.9	5.7	1.9
06	46898	Merced city, California	20.8	21.3	16.0	12.2	10.5	6.5	7.7	1.5
06	47486	Millbrae city, California	11.4	25.6	3.2	6.8	0.0	2.6	9.8	5.3
06	47766	Milpitas city, California	17.3	19.8	6.4	8.2	0.4	4.1	22.1	2.2
06	48256	Mission Viejo city, California	14.3	25.9	4.7	7.2	0.4	4.5	14.9	3.2
06	48354	Modesto city, California	17.3	27.8	9.1	14.0	2.4	6.0	9.7	5.3
06	48648	Monrovia city, California	19.4	23.4	6.0	11.3	0.0	5.0	10.3	2.5
06	48788	Montclair city, California	15.4	35.5	10.7	23.8	0.0	7.2	20.2	1.1
06	48816	Montebello city, California	18.7	28.6	8.3	18.6	0.1	6.6	12.3	5.9
06	48872	Monterey city, California	30.7	16.8	2.1	1.2	0.4	1.2	2.1	3.6
06	48914	Monterey Park city, California	17.7	25.8	3.7	8.1	0.0	2.7	8.3	5.3
06	49138	Moorpark city, California	14.4	26.1	5.8	7.2	2.0	4.6	16.2	4.6
06	49270	Moreno Valley city, California	21.1	23.8	12.3	19.2	0.9	9.1	8.3	3.5
06	49278	Morgan Hill city, California	17.3	25.6	5.1	6.6	0.4	5.5	11.6	2.6
06	49670	Mountain View city, California	12.8	12.8	4.2	2.7	0.4	3.4	12.1	0.7
06	50076	Murrieta city, California	19.4	24.0	6.3	10.2	1.3	7.0	8.0	2.0

Table E. Cities—Labor Force, Employment, and Educational Data, 2015—*Continued*

FIPS state code	FIPS place code	State/city	Percent in each occupation group				Percent in each industry sector			
			Service occupations	Sales and office occupations	Natural resources, construction, and maintenance occupations	Production, transportation, and material moving occupations	Agriculture, forestry, fishing and hunting, and mining	Construction	Manufacturing	Wholesale trade
06	50258	Napa city, California	20.7	20.7	16.5	11.3	8.8	6.0	12.9	3.7
06	50398	National City city, California	33.4	22.5	13.9	13.9	1.0	8.7	8.1	0.7
06	50916	Newark city, California	15.2	20.4	12.8	13.0	0.0	9.5	15.1	4.7
06	51182	Newport Beach city, California	8.6	25.6	3.4	3.9	0.2	3.4	9.8	5.2
06	51560	Norco city, California	17.6	29.0	11.7	16.7	0.7	9.2	9.5	6.4
06	51924	North Highlands CDP, California	29.2	29.3	10.3	14.5	0.0	8.2	5.2	3.5
06	52379	North Tustin CDP, California	11.5	27.2	2.3	2.0	0.0	4.7	8.1	1.7
06	52526	Norwalk city, California	17.5	29.4	9.9	18.8	0.7	6.3	10.1	4.0
06	52582	Novato city, California	14.6	28.5	6.9	3.3	0.5	5.5	3.4	2.2
06	52694	Oakdale city, California	21.9	21.7	12.0	14.2	6.4	3.0	12.9	9.8
06	53000	Oakland city, California	20.6	18.3	7.1	10.0	0.7	6.1	6.7	2.3
06	53070	Oakley city, California	15.0	29.1	20.6	7.2	1.0	17.5	3.9	2.5
06	53322	Oceanside city, California	20.6	23.5	8.5	11.6	2.3	5.7	11.9	4.6
06	53448	Oildale CDP, California	21.5	30.7	17.1	14.2	8.4	7.3	4.1	2.0
06	53896	Ontario city, California	19.6	25.2	10.5	22.5	0.6	7.8	14.2	4.8
06	53980	Orange city, California	14.6	27.4	8.6	8.3	0.2	8.0	11.2	2.4
06	54092	Orangevale CDP, California	13.5	30.0	9.5	6.3	0.9	12.2	8.5	2.1
06	54120	Orcutt CDP, California	19.2	21.8	12.2	12.4	4.7	7.3	7.9	2.9
06	54652	Oxnard city, California	18.3	21.0	21.6	16.3	14.1	6.1	12.9	2.9
06	54806	Pacifica city, California	14.1	25.2	9.8	5.2	0.7	7.3	5.4	1.2
06	55156	Palmdale city, California	23.1	24.4	13.5	12.6	1.5	8.2	11.2	2.6
06	55184	Palm Desert city, California	30.7	25.6	4.0	3.3	0.3	2.7	2.4	1.6
06	55254	Palm Springs city, California	25.3	27.6	3.2	5.3	0.3	3.2	4.5	1.5
06	55282	Palo Alto city, California	6.8	11.9	0.0	3.3	0.0	0.8	13.6	0.1
06	55520	Paradise town, California	24.2	24.2	7.1	10.3	3.6	6.1	2.9	1.5
06	55618	Paramount city, California	21.6	26.6	9.9	22.6	0.8	7.4	16.0	3.2
06	56000	Pasadena city, California	16.0	21.0	4.7	6.5	0.1	4.9	5.2	1.4
06	56112	Patterson city, California	15.6	33.4	9.6	28.6	3.1	3.8	13.8	8.5
06	56700	Perris city, California	21.8	21.6	20.4	24.2	1.5	18.8	9.0	2.6
06	56784	Petaluma city, California	17.2	23.1	9.2	8.0	2.3	8.3	6.6	2.6
06	56924	Pico Rivera city, California	16.9	31.9	10.2	20.7	0.5	7.0	13.1	10.3
06	57456	Pittsburg city, California	20.9	22.4	14.1	11.2	0.4	12.9	6.0	1.7
06	57526	Placentia city, California	17.3	24.3	11.3	12.4	0.9	8.8	17.6	2.7
06	57764	Pleasant Hill city, California	11.3	24.4	2.1	7.9	0.3	2.7	5.1	1.4
06	57792	Pleasanton city, California	10.6	17.0	2.9	4.0	0.4	2.8	11.2	3.2
06	58072	Pomona city, California	19.4	24.8	9.8	19.0	1.3	7.0	12.7	4.4
06	58240	Porterville city, California	20.3	20.1	21.1	14.0	16.5	3.5	5.8	1.5
06	58296	Port Hueneme city, California	17.7	21.0	16.3	16.1	7.1	3.4	8.1	5.5
06	58520	Poway city, California	16.3	23.3	5.6	6.2	0.0	10.0	11.6	1.8
06	59346	Ramona CDP, California	16.7	34.0	10.1	6.2	1.3	8.4	4.7	1.4
06	59444	Rancho Cordova city, California	18.6	26.8	8.8	9.9	0.3	6.8	6.9	4.8
06	59451	Rancho Cucamonga city, California	16.0	26.6	5.9	10.4	0.4	4.8	9.2	3.4
06	59514	Rancho Palos Verdes city, California	12.9	21.7	1.2	4.1	0.0	0.6	9.9	3.8
06	59550	Rancho San Diego CDP, California	16.0	35.3	3.7	4.1	0.0	2.0	8.7	4.3
06	59587	Rancho Santa Margarita city, California	12.4	25.9	3.3	6.6	0.0	2.7	12.3	2.6
06	59920	Redding city, California	22.0	29.7	8.0	6.4	1.6	6.4	3.7	1.8
06	59962	Redlands city, California	19.1	20.3	6.8	12.0	1.1	4.3	5.7	2.1
06	60018	Redondo Beach city, California	8.3	24.5	1.9	6.3	0.2	3.9	13.6	2.8
06	60102	Redwood City city, California	13.7	23.1	7.6	7.3	0.8	6.6	9.8	3.0
06	60242	Reedley city, California	14.7	18.1	30.6	20.3	29.8	3.0	6.7	7.2
06	60466	Rialto city, California	23.3	24.0	12.0	25.0	0.9	7.2	9.4	3.8
06	60620	Richmond city, California	23.4	23.2	14.1	14.0	1.0	11.2	5.0	3.0
06	60704	Ridgecrest city, California	13.5	22.5	15.6	10.3	4.8	8.6	3.8	2.0
06	61068	Riverbank city, California	18.5	22.9	15.2	18.3	14.1	5.4	14.1	1.3
06	62000	Riverside city, California	19.3	24.6	12.2	15.1	0.8	9.8	9.6	2.0
06	62364	Rocklin city, California	14.0	26.4	6.7	4.7	0.8	6.0	6.2	3.8
06	62546	Rohnert Park city, California	22.9	23.8	8.1	14.0	0.3	9.4	8.9	1.2
06	62826	Rosamond CDP, California	20.7	15.0	19.6	9.3	0.0	11.0	8.0	0.0
06	62896	Rosemead city, California	18.6	27.5	8.6	19.3	0.3	5.2	15.6	4.9
06	62910	Rosemont CDP, California	22.5	27.2	5.6	8.5	0.9	5.4	3.5	1.3
06	62938	Roseville city, California	16.3	24.5	7.0	6.9	0.8	6.4	4.4	2.8
06	63218	Rowland Heights CDP, California	20.2	25.7	5.2	12.5	0.7	5.8	8.7	5.8
06	64000	Sacramento city, California	20.0	26.0	7.5	8.9	0.7	6.6	4.8	2.7
06	64224	Salinas city, California	22.1	19.4	25.3	15.2	26.2	5.9	3.8	4.0
06	65000	San Bernardino city, California	23.1	25.5	10.3	22.9	0.4	7.8	9.3	3.6
06	65028	San Bruno city, California	16.0	26.3	6.2	6.9	0.4	3.5	6.5	2.5
06	65042	San Buenaventura (Ventura) city, California	17.0	24.3	10.6	10.8	4.7	6.0	7.3	2.3
06	65070	San Carlos city, California	8.7	20.3	3.2	3.2	0.0	2.8	11.5	2.3
06	65084	San Clemente city, California	18.0	22.4	3.6	5.6	0.0	5.0	13.6	4.0
06	66000	San Diego city, California	20.1	22.1	5.8	6.7	0.5	3.8	8.8	2.5
06	66070	San Dimas city, California	13.2	30.8	7.1	6.4	1.0	6.0	6.5	4.3
06	66140	San Fernando city, California	18.1	27.2	20.3	13.6	5.1	12.8	14.1	1.5
06	67000	San Francisco city, California	16.2	19.9	3.8	5.6	0.3	3.3	5.5	1.6

Table E. Cities—Labor Force, Employment, and Educational Data, 2015—*Continued*

FIPS state code	FIPS place code	State/city	Percent in each occupation group				Percent in each industry sector			
			Service occupations	Sales and office occupations	Natural resources, construction, and maintenance occupations	Production, transportation, and material moving occupations	Agriculture, forestry, fishing and hunting, and mining	Construction	Manufacturing	Wholesale trade
06	67042	San Gabriel city, California	20.4	25.0	9.2	13.9	0.3	6.6	10.0	3.4
06	67056	Sanger city, California	19.7	23.4	28.0	7.9	27.4	3.5	9.1	0.7
06	67112	San Jacinto city, California	20.1	27.0	17.3	12.6	3.1	9.0	7.6	4.6
06	68000	San Jose city, California	18.6	19.1	7.8	9.8	0.3	6.3	17.9	1.8
06	68028	San Juan Capistrano city, California	22.9	28.3	13.3	4.4	0.9	13.4	6.0	4.0
06	68084	San Leandro city, California	19.9	27.5	7.4	15.6	0.1	7.0	7.3	4.4
06	68112	San Lorenzo CDP, California	23.4	25.4	12.4	11.7	0.0	10.1	10.8	1.6
06	68154	San Luis Obispo city, California	21.7	16.9	3.9	10.0	0.2	5.0	5.9	2.9
06	68196	San Marcos city, California	23.4	21.2	7.8	10.6	1.8	6.9	11.1	3.6
06	68252	San Mateo city, California	14.6	23.1	5.2	8.0	0.2	4.4	9.7	1.4
06	68294	San Pablo city, California	33.5	25.7	14.4	11.4	3.1	8.5	3.7	2.2
06	68364	San Rafael city, California	21.7	19.7	6.4	6.7	1.3	3.9	5.7	2.2
06	68378	San Ramon city, California	11.4	19.5	2.2	4.3	1.4	1.5	11.3	1.4
06	69000	Santa Ana city, California	28.0	21.7	11.2	21.9	1.6	8.0	16.3	2.6
06	69070	Santa Barbara city, California	22.2	19.4	7.7	5.2	0.5	6.1	5.7	2.3
06	69084	Santa Clara city, California	12.6	18.6	4.5	8.2	0.1	2.5	21.5	2.5
06	69088	Santa Clarita city, California	16.8	25.6	6.6	8.6	0.2	6.9	8.7	2.6
06	69112	Santa Cruz city, California	25.6	19.4	4.9	4.8	1.2	5.2	4.2	1.2
06	69196	Santa Maria city, California	14.9	17.7	37.0	14.0	31.4	6.7	5.7	3.2
06	70000	Santa Monica city, California	9.7	20.3	1.1	3.2	0.3	1.6	7.5	1.5
06	70042	Santa Paula city, California	20.5	19.3	23.6	16.4	15.1	11.2	6.7	4.8
06	70098	Santa Rosa city, California	20.0	20.0	12.9	13.2	3.0	8.7	9.7	3.6
06	70224	Santee city, California	16.2	28.5	6.7	10.0	0.0	8.7	9.8	2.1
06	70280	Saratoga city, California	5.8	13.3	1.6	2.1	0.0	2.2	25.9	3.2
06	70686	Seal Beach city, California	19.2	25.3	4.6	4.2	0.0	3.2	13.0	2.9
06	70742	Seaside city, California	37.3	19.4	9.4	5.3	1.4	8.5	3.0	1.2
06	70882	Selma city, California	21.8	23.7	18.9	20.0	14.7	3.2	13.5	1.9
06	72016	Simi Valley city, California	16.6	23.5	8.9	7.5	0.8	7.1	11.1	1.8
06	72520	Soledad city, California	9.0	24.8	23.4	21.5	28.7	0.0	12.2	7.7
06	72996	South El Monte city, California	16.3	27.3	14.2	21.3	2.1	8.6	16.7	4.0
06	73080	South Gate city, California	18.0	25.8	11.6	26.7	0.1	7.6	16.6	8.5
06	73108	South Lake Tahoe city, California	29.0	20.0	3.6	13.0	1.0	4.5	7.4	0.0
06	73220	South Pasadena city, California	13.7	16.6	8.1	5.3	0.0	8.4	3.3	5.8
06	73262	South San Francisco city, California	19.9	26.2	7.2	15.6	0.3	7.3	6.1	3.3
06	73290	South San Jose Hills CDP, California	16.5	24.8	10.1	32.1	0.3	6.4	21.3	5.9
06	73430	South Whittier CDP, California	15.1	30.7	10.7	20.7	0.6	8.2	16.5	5.9
06	73696	Spring Valley CDP (San Diego County), California	17.9	20.3	10.1	16.4	0.0	9.6	10.3	1.1
06	73962	Stanton city, California	27.9	21.9	7.3	20.5	0.0	6.2	22.3	1.7
06	75000	Stockton city, California	18.5	25.5	12.4	18.8	3.2	7.2	8.6	3.1
06	75630	Suisun City city, California	18.1	27.7	12.0	16.8	0.0	6.5	13.9	3.3
06	77000	Sunnyvale city, California	13.4	14.0	3.4	4.3	0.1	2.2	18.7	1.7
06	78120	Temecula city, California	24.1	21.8	6.8	9.3	0.7	7.2	11.1	1.6
06	78138	Temescal Valley CDP, California	20.4	33.6	1.7	13.7	0.0	4.0	13.2	2.7
06	78148	Temple City city, California	22.4	31.1	6.0	5.6	0.0	4.1	6.7	2.8
06	78582	Thousand Oaks city, California	14.9	22.3	3.5	7.2	0.3	4.1	13.9	2.7
06	80000	Torrance city, California	13.8	25.5	4.0	7.1	0.0	2.9	11.8	2.5
06	80238	Tracy city, California	15.5	28.6	12.1	14.8	0.5	8.4	12.5	4.6
06	80644	Tulare city, California	19.3	20.7	18.5	12.0	12.1	5.0	6.6	2.8
06	80812	Turlock city, California	16.5	21.3	12.6	15.2	6.1	4.9	12.2	4.5
06	80854	Tustin city, California	18.5	23.8	6.4	13.3	0.4	5.6	12.1	3.7
06	80994	Twentynine Palms city, California	41.9	15.7	9.1	5.0	–	–	–	–
06	81204	Union City city, California	13.5	21.8	8.0	14.5	0.1	5.0	15.1	3.1
06	81344	Upland city, California	15.6	26.7	4.1	15.0	0.1	5.6	14.3	3.8
06	81554	Vacaville city, California	22.6	24.5	12.0	11.5	0.7	10.5	5.6	3.9
06	81638	Valinda CDP, California	21.4	26.9	17.6	22.0	0.8	9.5	17.8	2.6
06	81666	Vallejo city, California	23.8	25.4	9.7	12.7	0.9	7.3	7.0	3.6
06	82590	Victorville city, California	22.1	22.0	11.7	15.1	0.2	7.5	5.5	2.6
06	82852	Vineyard CDP, California	22.8	23.1	3.3	11.3	0.7	2.6	5.0	2.7
06	82954	Visalia city, California	20.9	22.9	12.9	11.3	4.6	4.3	9.1	2.1
06	82996	Vista city, California	24.3	21.0	13.3	15.9	2.5	6.8	11.5	3.5
06	83332	Walnut city, California	7.8	30.6	3.4	4.4	0.0	3.9	11.5	4.7
06	83346	Walnut Creek city, California	10.9	19.0	1.5	1.4	0.7	3.5	6.5	1.3
06	83542	Wasco city, California	16.1	18.0	36.7	17.8	–	–	–	–
06	83668	Watsonville city, California	20.5	18.3	30.5	19.3	25.3	5.4	10.7	5.3
06	84144	West Carson CDP, California	16.0	29.7	8.7	16.4	1.0	5.4	13.1	4.0
06	84200	West Covina city, California	17.8	30.1	7.6	12.6	0.9	4.8	10.2	4.6
06	84410	West Hollywood city, California	14.9	28.7	1.6	1.9	0.3	1.8	3.2	4.2
06	84550	Westminster city, California	19.0	20.7	6.5	17.2	1.1	3.9	17.3	2.3
06	84592	Westmont CDP, California	22.5	26.2	11.1	18.4	1.7	8.2	8.1	2.0
06	84774	West Puente Valley CDP, California	16.3	25.7	15.5	26.5	1.4	10.8	18.3	4.1
06	84780	West Rancho Dominguez CDP, California	20.9	20.9	10.0	21.9	0.0	5.4	16.3	1.0
06	84816	West Sacramento city, California	23.3	21.5	12.0	8.2	1.3	7.5	6.2	3.3
06	84921	West Whittier-Los Nietos CDP, California	15.0	28.9	12.2	13.9	0.7	4.5	20.2	4.6

Table E. Cities—Labor Force, Employment, and Educational Data, 2015—*Continued*

FIPS state code	FIPS place code	State/city	Percent in each occupation group				Percent in each industry sector			
			Service occupations	Sales and office occupations	Natural resources, construction, and maintenance occupations	Production, transportation, and material moving occupations	Agriculture, forestry, fishing and hunting, and mining	Construction	Manufacturing	Wholesale trade
06	85292	Whittier city, California	20.4	28.4	6.2	14.4	0.1	5.3	10.0	5.4
06	85446	Wildomar city, California	24.0	20.8	15.7	14.8	1.0	13.8	11.9	1.1
06	85922	Windsor town, California	22.1	23.1	11.0	10.0	2.3	9.3	12.9	2.5
06	85992	Winter Gardens CDP, California	26.4	17.3	13.9	7.5	0.0	12.3	7.8	1.1
06	86328	Woodland city, California	23.0	17.5	12.5	13.7	6.2	6.4	5.5	1.1
06	86832	Yorba Linda city, California	10.3	24.8	4.9	4.9	0.4	5.9	14.8	3.2
06	86972	Yuba City city, California	16.7	16.9	18.9	15.4	11.3	9.8	8.1	1.5
06	87042	Yucaipa city, California	21.2	23.0	9.4	8.8	0.7	5.3	4.1	1.3
06	87056	Yucca Valley town, California	18.8	30.2	21.9	3.6	–	–	–	–
08	00000	**COLORADO**	16.8	23.7	9.4	8.9	2.6	7.9	6.9	2.6
08	03455	Arvada city, Colorado	15.1	25.5	7.1	6.4	1.5	7.0	10.0	3.3
08	04000	Aurora city, Colorado	19.2	26.0	10.4	11.9	0.8	8.5	6.1	2.2
08	07850	Boulder city, Colorado	16.9	20.7	3.2	3.8	0.6	3.2	6.5	1.0
08	08675	Brighton city, Colorado	12.2	27.7	19.7	11.4	7.8	15.0	6.7	5.2
08	09280	Broomfield city, Colorado	10.5	19.1	6.9	7.5	1.8	6.3	10.5	2.6
08	12415	Castle Rock town, Colorado	16.7	26.9	5.8	6.5	0.9	8.5	5.8	2.4
08	12815	Centennial city, Colorado	11.6	23.0	6.3	6.3	2.2	5.7	5.8	3.0
08	15165	Clifton CDP, Colorado	17.7	28.6	19.8	18.4	7.2	8.5	7.4	4.2
08	16000	Colorado Springs city, Colorado	18.2	25.4	8.0	7.2	0.7	6.2	6.0	1.7
08	16110	Columbine CDP, Colorado	14.5	25.2	6.5	6.6	0.3	9.0	6.3	3.0
08	16495	Commerce City city, Colorado	14.9	28.8	14.8	14.9	0.9	11.5	8.3	5.5
08	19150	Dakota Ridge CDP, Colorado	14.7	29.5	10.2	5.1	1.9	9.0	8.3	2.5
08	20000	Denver city, Colorado	16.6	20.7	8.6	8.3	1.4	8.3	5.5	2.8
08	24785	Englewood city, Colorado	17.2	21.9	12.5	9.0	0.8	11.3	5.6	3.2
08	24950	Erie town, Colorado	11.0	21.7	4.5	6.7	6.3	3.4	10.8	2.4
08	25280	Evans city, Colorado	16.9	32.8	15.1	17.1	9.2	8.7	11.6	3.6
08	27425	Fort Collins city, Colorado	16.5	22.1	5.8	7.6	1.4	5.9	11.0	1.6
08	27865	Fountain city, Colorado	17.7	31.2	13.3	11.4	1.4	7.9	2.6	2.5
08	30835	Golden city, Colorado	15.7	24.6	2.2	2.7	2.1	4.2	9.5	2.1
08	31660	Grand Junction city, Colorado	21.3	23.7	6.0	10.6	3.6	6.2	2.3	2.2
08	32155	Greeley city, Colorado	17.5	26.4	11.7	15.3	6.3	10.0	11.2	2.1
08	36410	Highlands Ranch CDP, Colorado	10.3	28.5	3.9	3.5	1.3	4.2	6.9	2.3
08	40377	Ken Caryl CDP, Colorado	16.5	22.7	7.9	4.8	0.7	8.7	4.3	4.6
08	41835	Lafayette city, Colorado	22.7	25.1	2.4	6.7	0.7	1.8	10.8	4.5
08	43000	Lakewood city, Colorado	16.2	25.9	8.3	8.5	1.7	8.9	5.8	1.6
08	45255	Littleton city, Colorado	13.6	27.3	5.1	4.1	1.8	4.3	6.6	2.1
08	45970	Longmont city, Colorado	16.9	22.6	5.9	10.9	0.3	6.6	15.6	2.9
08	46355	Louisville city, Colorado	14.4	17.8	3.5	4.8	0.6	0.9	5.3	1.8
08	46465	Loveland city, Colorado	21.8	21.6	10.3	9.9	2.6	9.6	10.0	2.7
08	54330	Northglenn city, Colorado	13.9	22.3	16.4	15.9	0.9	12.5	5.7	4.9
08	57630	Parker town, Colorado	14.3	24.9	4.2	4.4	1.5	4.8	4.3	2.2
08	62000	Pueblo city, Colorado	17.3	30.7	9.0	12.8	0.7	8.1	7.5	2.6
08	62220	Pueblo West CDP, Colorado	22.5	21.1	9.6	11.5	1.1	4.6	10.3	2.6
08	68847	Security-Widefield CDP, Colorado	18.5	34.7	11.1	10.5	0.2	9.2	4.0	1.7
08	77290	Thornton city, Colorado	18.5	26.0	10.9	10.3	1.4	8.7	10.2	4.2
08	83835	Westminster city, Colorado	12.6	28.1	7.0	12.6	1.6	7.5	11.5	4.6
08	84440	Wheat Ridge city, Colorado	15.6	25.7	8.9	10.2	0.8	8.0	9.8	1.5
08	85485	Windsor town, Colorado	11.7	23.6	6.1	8.3	3.4	5.8	9.1	5.1
09	00000	**CONNECTICUT**	17.0	23.6	7.6	9.4	0.4	6.0	10.4	2.6
09	08000	Bridgeport city, Connecticut	26.8	23.9	9.3	12.3	0.1	7.2	9.1	1.3
09	08420	Bristol city, Connecticut	16.6	28.6	7.9	12.3	0.5	6.6	11.0	3.5
09	18430	Danbury city, Connecticut	20.1	16.3	15.0	13.0	0.5	14.7	9.7	3.1
09	18920	Darien CDP, Connecticut	5.9	26.0	1.2	1.9	0.0	2.3	3.3	4.3
09	22700	East Hartford CDP, Connecticut	17.5	27.7	8.6	17.9	0.0	5.1	13.8	3.5
09	22980	East Haven CDP, Connecticut	11.9	31.5	10.8	12.5	0.0	7.8	11.7	3.9
09	37000	Hartford city, Connecticut	29.5	21.3	6.5	14.4	0.0	4.6	6.1	0.9
09	44690	Manchester CDP, Connecticut	19.3	30.4	6.1	9.0	0.2	3.6	10.6	4.6
09	46450	Meriden city, Connecticut	18.1	27.1	8.5	12.0	0.0	4.1	10.8	3.0
09	47290	Middletown city, Connecticut	14.7	24.7	5.7	7.7	0.0	2.6	12.5	2.8
09	47515	Milford city (balance), Connecticut	11.9	27.8	5.7	9.8	0.5	5.8	10.9	4.1
09	49880	Naugatuck borough, Connecticut	16.3	21.8	10.3	11.4	0.0	7.9	17.9	4.3
09	50370	New Britain city, Connecticut	25.0	24.0	7.3	18.1	0.0	5.6	14.0	2.9
09	52000	New Haven city, Connecticut	25.8	19.2	6.7	11.8	0.2	5.7	7.0	1.6
09	52210	Newington CDP, Connecticut	12.7	26.1	4.6	12.6	0.0	3.9	14.0	3.2
09	52280	New London city, Connecticut	35.2	24.1	4.8	12.5	0.0	3.2	8.0	0.0
09	54940	North Haven CDP, Connecticut	12.8	29.0	7.6	5.5	0.0	13.6	7.7	1.3
09	55990	Norwalk city, Connecticut	18.4	25.4	9.5	6.8	0.0	8.2	4.6	4.2
09	56200	Norwich city, Connecticut	33.4	25.8	7.2	9.1	0.0	3.2	7.4	1.6
09	68100	Shelton city, Connecticut	11.7	29.7	6.1	7.9	0.0	5.9	12.9	6.1
09	73000	Stamford city, Connecticut	18.7	24.0	8.0	4.9	0.3	7.4	4.8	1.8
09	74260	Stratford CDP, Connecticut	18.8	26.4	7.7	10.3	0.1	5.4	12.6	2.3
09	76500	Torrington city, Connecticut	16.5	23.4	16.4	15.6	0.0	9.4	17.0	1.6
09	77270	Trumbull CDP, Connecticut	14.4	14.6	8.6	5.3	1.0	4.3	9.8	3.4
09	80000	Waterbury city, Connecticut	25.2	26.2	9.2	17.1	0.0	6.5	13.2	2.0

Table E. Cities—Labor Force, Employment, and Educational Data, 2015—*Continued*

FIPS state code	FIPS place code	State/city	Percent in each occupation group				Percent in each industry sector			
			Service occupations	Sales and office occupations	Natural resources, construction, and maintenance occupations	Production, transportation, and material moving occupations	Agriculture, forestry, fishing and hunting, and mining	Construction	Manufacturing	Wholesale trade
09	82660	West Hartford CDP, Connecticut	11.3	18.4	2.6	5.4	0.0	3.4	7.9	1.1
09	82800	West Haven city, Connecticut	18.3	28.3	6.2	14.6	0.0	4.6	12.2	4.0
09	83570	Westport CDP, Connecticut	6.5	17.7	3.1	3.1	0.0	2.7	2.7	2.9
09	84970	Wethersfield CDP, Connecticut	15.2	22.8	7.4	5.3	0.3	7.5	7.7	0.9
10	00000	**DELAWARE**	18.9	23.3	8.7	9.1	1.1	6.4	8.1	1.6
10	21200	Dover city, Delaware	27.7	24.2	3.4	11.4	0.9	2.9	5.6	1.3
10	50670	Newark city, Delaware	22.1	22.0	2.5	3.4	0.0	3.0	5.5	0.6
10	77580	Wilmington city, Delaware	26.8	29.4	3.1	7.3	0.3	2.1	4.4	0.5
11	00000	**DISTRICT OF COLUMBIA**	15.7	17.0	2.1	3.4	0.1	2.6	1.4	0.5
11	50000	Washington city, District of Columbia	15.7	17.0	2.1	3.4	0.1	2.6	1.4	0.5
12	00000	**FLORIDA**	20.1	27.0	9.2	9.3	1.1	7.1	5.1	2.8
12	00410	Alafaya CDP, Florida	16.6	23.6	6.6	5.6	0.0	6.5	6.6	2.2
12	00950	Altamonte Springs city, Florida	13.8	35.4	5.0	4.8	0.0	3.6	2.1	2.1
12	01700	Apopka city, Florida	11.4	28.7	6.5	12.4	2.3	6.1	2.5	4.5
12	02681	Aventura city, Florida	10.6	36.2	2.7	4.3	0.0	2.6	5.2	3.3
12	04162	Bayonet Point CDP, Florida	33.2	35.1	6.5	9.9	0.5	5.2	1.1	2.1
12	05462	Bellview CDP, Florida	16.9	43.3	3.1	5.7	0.0	1.1	3.2	1.6
12	06875	Bloomingdale CDP, Florida	14.4	29.4	1.7	7.5	0.0	2.7	5.3	6.4
12	07300	Boca Raton city, Florida	17.5	27.7	5.3	1.9	0.7	4.9	3.3	3.0
12	07525	Bonita Springs city, Florida	23.4	29.5	13.6	4.4	0.7	15.1	2.0	2.3
12	07875	Boynton Beach city, Florida	23.0	24.5	5.8	7.5	0.4	6.6	2.9	3.7
12	07950	Bradenton city, Florida	26.6	26.8	7.2	13.1	0.2	6.0	7.0	3.2
12	08150	Brandon CDP, Florida	16.0	31.9	7.8	7.6	0.6	4.3	5.8	3.1
12	08300	Brent CDP, Florida	30.4	26.3	12.6	11.0	1.9	8.0	1.6	0.0
12	09415	Buenaventura Lakes CDP, Florida	24.4	33.3	9.3	14.7	0.0	6.1	3.9	2.8
12	10275	Cape Coral city, Florida	21.3	28.5	12.0	8.5	0.5	9.8	4.1	1.4
12	10825	Carrollwood CDP, Florida	16.0	33.0	5.4	5.8	0.0	4.8	5.6	5.4
12	11050	Casselberry city, Florida	25.2	34.8	3.5	5.9	0.0	4.2	1.2	1.4
12	12425	Citrus Park CDP, Florida	17.2	28.7	8.9	2.1	0.0	8.1	5.2	3.0
12	12875	Clearwater city, Florida	18.3	28.5	9.8	8.3	0.7	6.1	7.5	2.8
12	12925	Clermont city, Florida	18.7	20.1	5.0	2.8	1.5	6.2	2.1	0.2
12	13275	Coconut Creek city, Florida	17.6	35.2	9.5	2.6	0.0	5.3	2.6	3.0
12	14125	Cooper City city, Florida	9.4	35.9	5.9	8.1	0.0	3.7	3.4	5.2
12	14250	Coral Gables city, Florida	6.0	24.8	4.1	4.4	0.0	7.8	4.2	4.8
12	14400	Coral Springs city, Florida	19.0	28.0	6.8	8.8	0.2	4.4	6.5	3.1
12	14412	Coral Terrace CDP, Florida	19.2	23.8	19.0	7.9	0.0	15.3	2.7	2.5
12	14895	Country Club CDP, Florida	13.6	29.8	10.1	17.4	0.0	6.1	6.2	4.0
12	15475	Crestview city, Florida	23.1	23.0	9.6	3.5	–	–	–	–
12	15968	Cutler Bay town, Florida	10.8	29.0	5.2	10.0	1.9	3.7	3.3	3.4
12	16335	Dania Beach city, Florida	18.2	25.6	7.9	14.9	0.0	10.6	4.7	2.0
12	16475	Davie town, Florida	17.8	27.2	10.7	7.3	3.9	5.1	3.4	3.0
12	16525	Daytona Beach city, Florida	23.6	29.9	5.9	8.7	0.0	4.9	3.5	2.0
12	16725	Deerfield Beach city, Florida	26.0	26.9	11.5	9.6	0.0	8.9	7.3	2.9
12	16875	DeLand city, Florida	31.3	18.7	9.3	7.7	1.7	6.2	5.8	1.0
12	17100	Delray Beach city, Florida	23.0	23.2	8.9	8.6	0.2	8.4	3.5	2.4
12	17200	Deltona city, Florida	16.7	29.8	12.4	11.4	0.0	8.8	7.4	2.6
12	17935	Doral city, Florida	13.5	34.5	3.8	3.3	0.0	2.8	3.4	10.9
12	18575	Dunedin city, Florida	10.8	33.4	8.7	4.6	0.0	4.7	4.4	3.0
12	19206	East Lake CDP, Florida	13.1	33.0	3.8	4.5	0.3	5.3	7.8	3.0
12	19212	East Lake-Orient Park CDP, Florida	24.0	25.2	10.5	14.4	0.3	8.9	6.7	2.2
12	19825	Edgewater city, Florida	25.9	27.7	12.2	9.0	1.6	7.0	10.1	1.0
12	20108	Egypt Lake-Leto CDP, Florida	23.6	26.2	10.1	11.1	0.1	9.9	6.1	3.3
12	20925	Ensley CDP, Florida	30.2	30.9	5.7	11.6	0.0	4.5	4.1	0.6
12	21150	Estero village, Florida	14.4	25.4	6.8	7.2	0.0	8.4	7.2	1.8
12	22275	Ferry Pass CDP, Florida	24.6	19.4	6.5	10.0	0.3	4.5	6.6	4.6
12	22660	Fleming Island CDP, Florida	14.7	28.3	5.3	5.1	0.0	6.6	1.9	6.9
12	23050	Florida Ridge CDP, Florida	30.8	24.0	17.9	4.8	–	–	–	–
12	24000	Fort Lauderdale city, Florida	22.1	22.1	8.4	9.8	0.1	5.8	4.3	3.3
12	24125	Fort Myers city, Florida	26.3	29.2	10.4	5.3	1.4	10.7	2.9	1.7
12	24300	Fort Pierce city, Florida	28.2	28.5	8.6	21.3	4.3	10.1	4.0	3.6
12	24475	Fort Walton Beach city, Florida	25.1	27.2	6.8	7.7	0.6	6.5	2.6	4.5
12	24562	Fountainebleau CDP, Florida	19.4	32.2	9.6	9.2	0.4	9.8	4.8	4.5
12	24581	Four Corners CDP, Florida	27.6	39.4	3.0	5.8	0.0	0.6	2.5	3.8
12	24925	Fruit Cove CDP, Florida	12.0	23.2	3.3	5.2	0.0	3.7	2.3	2.9
12	25175	Gainesville city, Florida	23.0	23.6	3.8	4.9	1.6	3.5	3.8	0.5
12	26300	Golden Gate CDP, Florida	31.3	15.7	20.0	21.0	1.0	18.6	3.5	1.9
12	26375	Golden Glades CDP, Florida	25.2	28.7	9.8	10.2	0.0	6.9	2.8	1.1
12	27322	Greenacres city, Florida	25.0	25.5	10.5	11.5	0.0	8.2	5.8	2.7
12	28400	Haines City city, Florida	35.1	16.1	15.1	11.0	1.3	13.2	3.2	0.7
12	28452	Hallandale Beach city, Florida	29.2	25.4	8.4	9.1	0.3	7.1	5.0	2.4
12	30000	Hialeah city, Florida	21.3	27.1	13.5	20.4	0.4	10.8	8.6	4.7
12	30025	Hialeah Gardens city, Florida	20.4	24.4	15.3	18.1	0.0	11.7	9.7	10.0
12	31075	Holiday CDP, Florida	25.0	34.6	8.8	10.6	0.3	6.6	7.2	1.2

Table E. Cities—Labor Force, Employment, and Educational Data, 2015—*Continued*

FIPS state code	FIPS place code	State/city	Percent in each occupation group				Percent in each industry sector			
			Service occupations	Sales and office occupations	Natural resources, construction, and maintenance occupations	Production, transportation, and material moving occupations	Agriculture, forestry, fishing and hunting, and mining	Construction	Manufacturing	Wholesale trade
12	32000	Hollywood city, Florida	20.9	24.3	11.3	11.5	0.5	9.8	6.5	3.0
12	32275	Homestead city, Florida	16.4	29.2	22.2	5.6	8.9	10.7	3.0	2.5
12	32610	Horizon West CDP, Florida	15.7	23.9	0.0	4.4	–	–	–	–
12	32967	Hunters Creek CDP, Florida	16.5	28.5	7.6	4.4	0.0	8.6	4.6	4.2
12	33250	Immokalee CDP, Florida	28.1	12.6	41.5	9.0	30.3	11.8	2.2	3.7
12	35000	Jacksonville city, Florida	17.2	28.1	8.0	10.6	0.6	5.3	6.7	2.7
12	35050	Jacksonville Beach city, Florida	15.7	28.1	4.5	9.0	0.0	3.8	7.4	3.5
12	35350	Jasmine Estates CDP, Florida	22.3	22.1	14.0	9.2	0.0	13.9	3.1	2.5
12	35875	Jupiter town, Florida	19.7	26.7	8.4	4.5	0.2	8.8	4.4	2.7
12	36062	Kendale Lakes CDP, Florida	19.9	36.6	8.0	7.9	0.1	6.6	4.8	3.8
12	36100	Kendall CDP, Florida	11.7	25.8	4.8	2.0	1.7	4.7	2.9	2.4
12	36121	Kendall West CDP, Florida	23.3	31.3	12.3	7.1	0.9	9.1	3.1	3.4
12	36462	Keystone CDP, Florida	9.6	27.4	4.3	5.6	0.2	4.3	3.2	3.5
12	36550	Key West city, Florida	23.4	22.7	7.2	11.6	0.0	4.2	4.6	4.0
12	36950	Kissimmee city, Florida	32.1	26.4	9.7	11.7	0.0	6.3	2.9	1.6
12	37648	Lake Butler CDP, Florida	3.7	27.9	2.2	0.9	–	–	–	–
12	38250	Lakeland city, Florida	13.8	29.7	9.2	14.4	1.7	8.5	4.5	4.8
12	38350	Lake Magdalene CDP, Florida	17.7	29.4	8.0	4.5	0.0	5.9	6.8	1.2
12	38813	Lakeside CDP, Florida	26.3	28.6	9.7	9.1	0.0	7.7	5.1	3.0
12	39075	Lake Worth city, Florida	32.8	18.6	16.2	6.5	4.8	11.4	1.9	2.7
12	39200	Land O' Lakes CDP, Florida	14.4	21.4	9.2	6.6	0.0	10.3	5.3	3.5
12	39425	Largo city, Florida	21.6	31.2	9.8	7.8	0.1	7.4	6.4	3.6
12	39525	Lauderdale Lakes city, Florida	38.7	32.4	10.6	10.2	0.3	6.9	2.1	3.4
12	39550	Lauderhill city, Florida	27.8	27.7	9.3	9.5	0.4	4.8	2.0	0.7
12	39875	Leesburg city, Florida	37.0	31.3	2.5	11.8	–	–	–	–
12	39925	Lehigh Acres CDP, Florida	21.0	27.0	16.6	15.0	0.6	14.1	4.2	2.5
12	39950	Leisure City CDP, Florida	28.8	25.2	29.0	12.1	2.7	22.2	0.9	4.0
12	41775	Lutz CDP, Florida	9.0	27.4	7.7	5.8	0.0	8.8	5.2	3.4
12	41825	Lynn Haven city, Florida	20.1	23.5	4.5	6.3	0.0	2.4	6.7	0.7
12	43125	Margate city, Florida	26.1	21.6	9.8	10.1	0.2	9.6	4.3	2.5
12	43800	Meadow Woods CDP, Florida	16.0	40.0	4.8	10.9	0.0	2.1	3.9	0.0
12	43975	Melbourne city, Florida	20.4	23.3	8.8	11.2	0.4	6.8	12.7	2.0
12	44275	Merritt Island CDP, Florida	21.8	26.4	10.1	3.9	2.0	8.7	6.5	2.1
12	45000	Miami city, Florida	25.8	21.5	12.2	11.2	0.7	10.4	3.6	3.0
12	45025	Miami Beach city, Florida	25.2	22.5	5.0	5.0	0.3	5.8	2.5	4.0
12	45060	Miami Gardens city, Florida	25.7	33.5	10.9	12.2	0.4	6.5	5.0	3.9
12	45100	Miami Lakes town, Florida	15.1	32.6	4.2	6.1	0.0	6.2	8.8	7.3
12	45975	Miramar city, Florida	17.2	24.4	8.2	9.4	0.5	5.0	4.5	3.9
12	47625	Naples city, Florida	14.8	29.4	5.7	6.4	1.2	4.3	4.4	2.2
12	48050	Navarre CDP, Florida	15.3	26.0	5.6	7.3	0.0	5.4	5.1	1.0
12	48625	New Smyrna Beach city, Florida	33.7	14.8	5.2	10.2	0.7	3.4	8.4	1.6
12	49260	Northdale CDP, Florida	13.6	28.2	10.4	8.2	0.0	8.0	0.9	4.0
12	49350	North Fort Myers CDP, Florida	23.9	34.5	9.3	8.4	0.4	9.3	4.2	1.5
12	49425	North Lauderdale city, Florida	25.7	27.6	15.1	14.2	0.2	10.6	6.3	3.8
12	49450	North Miami city, Florida	34.7	27.1	5.7	12.3	0.0	3.5	2.6	2.0
12	49475	North Miami Beach city, Florida	41.6	24.1	7.0	7.9	0.0	8.4	2.6	1.3
12	49675	North Port city, Florida	12.4	25.8	4.2	18.2	0.4	4.2	14.2	4.3
12	50575	Oakland Park city, Florida	23.2	25.7	10.3	9.2	0.0	7.5	6.1	3.6
12	50630	Oakleaf Plantation CDP, Florida	14.9	35.0	10.3	11.9	0.0	3.8	5.3	11.7
12	50638	Oak Ridge CDP, Florida	39.8	15.0	15.7	13.0	1.9	14.9	3.5	5.5
12	50750	Ocala city, Florida	24.2	26.6	7.5	7.2	2.3	3.5	7.4	2.2
12	51075	Ocoee city, Florida	12.8	28.8	11.5	6.9	0.4	10.8	6.8	2.9
12	53000	Orlando city, Florida	22.4	28.7	4.1	9.3	0.1	4.3	4.2	2.2
12	53150	Ormond Beach city, Florida	20.7	27.9	9.7	8.4	2.0	6.2	3.6	2.0
12	53575	Oviedo city, Florida	14.5	32.1	3.2	1.5	0.3	2.8	4.4	4.1
12	53725	Pace CDP, Florida	20.4	21.6	15.7	9.3	0.0	9.2	6.2	0.9
12	54000	Palm Bay city, Florida	27.7	22.1	8.3	8.9	0.6	7.7	6.0	0.3
12	54075	Palm Beach Gardens city, Florida	13.5	29.7	3.3	5.4	0.5	5.7	5.1	1.9
12	54175	Palm City CDP, Florida	18.1	26.6	1.2	5.5	0.0	8.4	6.4	2.9
12	54200	Palm Coast city, Florida	18.7	31.2	7.7	9.5	0.7	5.7	9.0	3.6
12	54275	Palmetto Bay village, Florida	21.8	24.9	3.8	1.4	0.1	4.6	2.0	3.9
12	54300	Palmetto Estates CDP, Florida	33.8	33.1	5.2	7.5	0.0	4.6	2.4	0.0
12	54350	Palm Harbor CDP, Florida	18.6	26.4	4.8	6.4	0.5	7.4	6.7	2.6
12	54387	Palm River-Clair Mel CDP, Florida	15.8	23.9	14.5	22.4	2.8	10.1	5.0	3.7
12	54450	Palm Springs village, Florida	27.7	33.6	14.3	8.7	0.0	12.7	0.4	7.2
12	54525	Palm Valley CDP, Florida	7.6	22.0	3.3	2.7	1.0	6.3	9.9	2.5
12	54700	Panama City city, Florida	28.3	21.4	7.8	7.1	0.8	3.1	4.1	0.4
12	55125	Parkland city, Florida	5.6	30.5	0.6	6.3	0.0	2.6	5.6	6.4
12	55775	Pembroke Pines city, Florida	14.5	31.1	4.3	7.0	0.1	3.4	5.3	4.3
12	55925	Pensacola city, Florida	25.3	22.2	5.8	8.8	0.7	5.9	3.3	2.9
12	56825	Pine Hills CDP, Florida	35.0	23.6	6.1	16.5	0.1	7.3	4.0	3.0
12	56975	Pinellas Park city, Florida	18.3	26.4	8.7	15.6	0.6	6.5	10.6	1.6
12	57425	Plantation city, Florida	14.8	27.9	7.8	5.8	0.2	6.1	3.5	3.8
12	57550	Plant City city, Florida	17.2	31.1	15.3	12.7	3.5	14.0	4.6	4.6
12	57900	Poinciana CDP, Florida	30.6	27.8	10.8	14.6	1.2	10.3	5.9	3.5

Table E. Cities—Labor Force, Employment, and Educational Data, 2015—*Continued*

FIPS state code	FIPS place code	State/city	Percent in each occupation group				Percent in each industry sector			
			Service occupations	Sales and office occupations	Natural resources, construction, and maintenance occupations	Production, transportation, and material moving occupations	Agriculture, forestry, fishing and hunting, and mining	Construction	Manufacturing	Wholesale trade
12	58050	Pompano Beach city, Florida	24.1	24.5	12.0	14.0	0.0	11.6	4.1	3.4
12	58350	Port Charlotte CDP, Florida	20.3	29.5	19.0	9.7	0.2	15.0	4.4	2.2
12	58575	Port Orange city, Florida	25.4	21.4	13.0	4.8	0.6	11.5	5.1	0.8
12	58715	Port St. Lucie city, Florida	23.3	30.9	11.5	6.2	0.2	7.3	3.3	1.9
12	58975	Princeton CDP, Florida	20.6	24.2	17.7	8.1	2.2	13.0	3.4	5.2
12	60230	Richmond West CDP, Florida	14.7	34.2	6.9	10.8	0.4	3.8	3.3	2.9
12	60950	Riverview CDP, Florida	16.0	30.6	7.4	8.5	1.2	5.8	6.7	2.5
12	60975	Riviera Beach city, Florida	25.4	30.2	11.8	9.4	0.0	9.2	4.0	3.0
12	61500	Rockledge city, Florida	17.1	36.8	3.3	7.8	0.7	3.4	13.5	0.8
12	62100	Royal Palm Beach village, Florida	18.9	26.6	9.1	5.0	2.0	5.7	2.2	5.1
12	62275	Ruskin CDP, Florida	15.7	26.4	18.3	12.5	8.6	10.4	6.0	3.1
12	62625	St. Cloud city, Florida	23.2	29.9	7.6	12.9	0.0	7.0	1.1	2.4
12	63000	St. Petersburg city, Florida	17.9	27.0	6.3	8.3	0.5	6.2	6.0	1.6
12	63425	San Carlos Park CDP, Florida	24.5	26.9	15.3	11.7	0.0	13.9	12.0	0.9
12	63650	Sanford city, Florida	17.7	30.1	7.2	10.3	0.4	6.3	8.0	1.0
12	64175	Sarasota city, Florida	26.4	23.8	8.6	5.9	0.4	6.4	4.0	1.6
12	64825	Sebastian city, Florida	21.7	21.3	5.2	16.9	0.8	4.1	6.3	0.0
12	67258	South Bradenton CDP, Florida	28.4	36.0	11.7	8.5	0.0	10.2	4.7	3.3
12	67575	South Miami Heights CDP, Florida	26.9	24.7	15.7	9.9	3.1	10.2	4.3	2.8
12	68350	Spring Hill CDP, Florida	24.0	26.3	8.8	10.8	0.3	5.9	3.7	2.2
12	69250	Sun City Center CDP, Florida	9.6	28.3	3.2	10.4	2.7	4.9	3.3	0.9
12	69555	Sunny Isles Beach city, Florida	22.0	22.3	4.9	7.1	0.0	5.2	3.7	2.0
12	69700	Sunrise city, Florida	22.9	31.2	6.4	9.3	0.0	4.8	2.9	2.8
12	70345	Sweetwater city, Florida	25.6	28.4	6.8	15.4	1.2	8.4	4.0	4.9
12	70600	Tallahassee city, Florida	20.6	29.8	2.8	4.3	0.3	1.8	1.1	1.9
12	70675	Tamarac city, Florida	17.0	27.8	7.0	8.1	0.3	4.9	6.9	3.2
12	70700	Tamiami CDP, Florida	20.6	31.3	12.7	8.5	0.0	5.8	5.3	4.1
12	71000	Tampa city, Florida	19.3	25.5	7.3	7.4	0.3	6.5	3.4	2.7
12	71150	Tarpon Springs city, Florida	21.4	29.4	7.0	6.5	0.0	5.1	7.5	2.4
12	71400	Temple Terrace city, Florida	11.3	33.8	5.2	2.9	0.7	5.3	0.6	3.1
12	71564	The Acreage CDP, Florida	23.0	23.5	16.1	7.0	0.8	16.4	4.9	3.0
12	71567	The Crossings CDP, Florida	16.2	24.1	5.4	9.5	0.1	4.3	7.7	3.4
12	71569	The Hammocks CDP, Florida	12.8	35.8	5.9	10.8	1.1	5.7	4.5	3.5
12	71625	The Villages CDP, Florida	13.3	25.9	1.8	5.7	1.0	0.0	6.8	0.6
12	71741	Three Lakes CDP, Florida	19.1	41.9	1.1	2.6	1.1	2.9	1.3	2.7
12	71900	Titusville city, Florida	23.3	33.3	6.7	12.2	0.0	3.8	10.1	3.2
12	72145	Town 'n' Country CDP, Florida	21.4	26.7	10.4	8.4	0.0	8.6	4.0	2.4
12	73163	University CDP (Hillsborough County), Florida	28.7	24.7	15.6	6.7	0.1	12.4	4.8	3.0
12	73172	University CDP (Orange County), Florida	17.2	35.9	8.1	9.6	0.0	7.4	1.9	5.3
12	73287	University Park CDP, Florida	24.1	17.7	4.4	13.4	0.0	3.9	3.2	0.0
12	73700	Valrico CDP, Florida	12.0	25.0	8.5	2.6	2.4	3.8	4.7	3.1
12	73900	Venice city, Florida	32.5	24.4	4.3	10.4	0.0	5.3	14.7	1.0
12	74200	Vero Beach South CDP, Florida	25.7	32.2	7.8	7.9	2.3	8.7	8.4	2.6
12	75725	Wekiwa Springs CDP, Florida	15.3	22.0	3.0	4.1	0.0	5.3	3.5	3.7
12	75812	Wellington village, Florida	17.3	24.1	4.0	2.8	2.4	5.7	4.7	2.4
12	75875	Wesley Chapel CDP, Florida	12.4	27.3	6.8	7.7	0.5	4.8	5.2	2.8
12	76062	Westchase CDP, Florida	9.8	29.1	5.0	2.3	0.0	2.0	3.8	2.3
12	76075	Westchester CDP, Florida	22.1	32.8	11.0	4.5	0.3	5.0	1.2	7.4
12	76487	West Little River CDP, Florida	23.7	27.7	10.3	25.3	0.9	9.4	5.6	0.5
12	76500	West Melbourne city, Florida	18.1	16.6	8.5	12.0	0.0	5.7	12.4	6.0
12	76582	Weston city, Florida	10.6	27.9	3.2	5.5	0.0	3.1	5.2	7.1
12	76600	West Palm Beach city, Florida	23.3	25.6	8.4	9.1	0.3	8.1	3.1	2.3
12	76675	West Pensacola CDP, Florida	30.4	32.9	7.3	9.6	0.0	4.3	1.6	2.5
12	78250	Winter Garden city, Florida	25.0	22.4	5.6	4.6	1.9	8.1	4.0	1.5
12	78275	Winter Haven city, Florida	20.0	38.5	4.7	9.9	0.2	5.6	5.8	3.4
12	78300	Winter Park city, Florida	13.9	23.2	2.2	5.5	0.3	5.5	6.2	3.6
12	78325	Winter Springs city, Florida	13.7	26.2	4.5	3.7	0.4	9.1	5.0	1.6
12	78800	Wright CDP, Florida	28.5	19.1	9.9	11.5	0.3	2.6	3.6	1.4
13	00000	**GEORGIA**	16.4	24.3	9.1	13.8	1.1	6.5	10.9	2.9
13	00408	Acworth city, Georgia	16.8	25.9	1.8	7.5	0.0	2.1	8.8	1.5
13	01052	Albany city, Georgia	19.3	24.8	9.7	17.1	1.0	3.2	10.8	0.4
13	01696	Alpharetta city, Georgia	13.7	24.2	2.3	2.6	0.0	2.7	13.3	1.8
13	03440	Athens-Clarke County unified government (balance), Georgia	23.8	20.2	6.2	10.7	1.2	4.9	4.8	1.7
13	04000	Atlanta city, Georgia	15.9	21.5	3.2	8.3	0.1	3.4	5.2	2.8
13	04204	Augusta-Richmond County consolidated government (balance), Georgia	18.0	30.6	10.4	12.5	0.7	7.2	9.6	1.2
13	10944	Brookhaven city, Georgia	18.0	16.7	5.0	5.4	0.0	6.5	6.1	2.3
13	12834	Candler-McAfee CDP, Georgia	34.2	18.9	3.0	17.7	0.5	0.8	6.6	1.5
13	12988	Canton city, Georgia	20.8	18.0	10.7	11.2	0.0	9.2	10.7	1.1
13	13492	Carrollton city, Georgia	22.7	28.8	7.1	14.4	2.4	3.6	14.6	0.7

Table E. Cities—Labor Force, Employment, and Educational Data, 2015—*Continued*

FIPS state code	FIPS place code	State/city	Percent in each occupation group				Percent in each industry sector			
			Service occupations	Sales and office occupations	Natural resources, construction, and maintenance occupations	Production, transportation, and material moving occupations	Agriculture, forestry, fishing and hunting, and mining	Construction	Manufacturing	Wholesale trade
13	13688	Cartersville city, Georgia	13.1	19.7	13.8	28.6	1.1	16.3	29.3	0.9
13	15172	Chamblee city, Georgia	22.9	14.3	17.3	8.9	0.3	16.8	2.1	3.9
13	19000	Columbus city, Georgia	19.1	25.9	8.5	14.7	0.3	6.0	11.7	1.5
13	21380	Dalton city, Georgia	8.0	25.1	5.7	46.1	0.0	4.0	39.9	5.8
13	22052	Decatur city, Georgia	6.8	14.2	0.3	1.7	0.0	4.0	6.3	2.2
13	23900	Douglasville city, Georgia	19.7	19.1	3.0	17.1	0.5	4.0	9.6	2.8
13	24600	Duluth city, Georgia	15.2	31.8	1.9	8.8	0.0	2.6	7.1	0.6
13	24768	Dunwoody city, Georgia	10.4	19.8	4.0	3.2	0.0	4.6	3.1	3.1
13	25720	East Point city, Georgia	24.9	23.6	5.6	14.0	0.0	4.1	4.2	2.1
13	28044	Evans CDP, Georgia	11.1	25.3	6.0	6.3	0.0	7.6	10.3	1.5
13	31908	Gainesville city, Georgia	19.1	20.1	14.9	26.8	1.7	12.6	24.7	5.4
13	35324	Griffin city, Georgia	25.7	25.3	9.8	12.2	0.0	2.7	8.5	0.2
13	38964	Hinesville city, Georgia	28.8	24.8	11.2	11.3	0.0	6.9	5.1	1.0
13	42425	Johns Creek city, Georgia	6.8	22.2	2.3	5.3	0.0	1.1	8.6	3.9
13	43192	Kennesaw city, Georgia	21.0	32.3	7.6	4.5	0.4	4.0	8.6	4.7
13	44340	LaGrange city, Georgia	15.1	18.9	4.9	36.1	0.0	4.6	30.8	4.9
13	45488	Lawrenceville city, Georgia	16.7	31.8	6.8	10.4	0.4	3.9	5.0	7.8
13	48288	Mableton CDP, Georgia	11.4	23.6	11.6	15.2	0.0	11.6	9.8	2.4
13	48624	McDonough city, Georgia	6.6	34.3	10.4	22.0	0.5	7.0	15.3	1.0
13	49008	Macon-Bibb County, Georgia	16.8	26.5	6.7	13.7	0.6	4.6	9.0	1.7
13	49756	Marietta city, Georgia	17.8	25.7	8.8	8.2	0.0	11.8	5.4	2.4
13	50036	Martinez CDP, Georgia	18.1	22.9	8.1	6.7	1.1	6.8	8.2	3.2
13	51670	Milton city, Georgia	9.4	28.3	1.7	6.6	0.0	2.9	8.9	2.5
13	55020	Newnan city, Georgia	12.3	31.6	4.6	16.5	0.0	3.1	11.1	5.5
13	56168	North Druid Hills CDP, Georgia	5.0	15.5	2.1	8.1	0.0	2.7	4.3	1.9
13	59724	Peachtree City city, Georgia	8.5	26.8	5.5	9.1	0.0	0.2	14.3	6.4
13	59735	Peachtree Corners city, Georgia	9.7	28.1	6.4	5.2	0.2	5.4	5.3	2.8
13	62104	Pooler city, Georgia	17.6	24.3	3.9	13.9	0.0	1.0	16.7	0.8
13	63952	Redan CDP, Georgia	22.9	28.8	3.4	14.4	0.0	3.0	2.7	0.9
13	66668	Rome city, Georgia	24.0	15.6	7.0	24.6	0.1	3.9	26.9	0.6
13	67284	Roswell city, Georgia	12.9	22.4	5.4	8.9	2.1	5.7	7.7	2.8
13	68516	Sandy Springs city, Georgia	12.7	23.4	1.4	4.2	0.1	2.3	3.3	2.4
13	69000	Savannah city, Georgia	29.7	23.0	8.0	10.8	0.4	6.2	5.7	2.2
13	71492	Smyrna city, Georgia	13.8	21.2	8.1	7.7	0.0	9.4	3.4	3.8
13	73256	Statesboro city, Georgia	30.3	29.4	5.8	10.0	0.8	3.6	7.1	1.9
13	73704	Stockbridge city, Georgia	17.6	22.7	7.1	18.2	0.0	4.3	7.5	3.7
13	74180	Sugar Hill city, Georgia	17.8	17.5	8.3	7.2	0.0	3.9	6.9	6.2
13	77652	Tucker CDP, Georgia	9.1	22.3	3.2	11.7	0.0	2.8	4.9	4.5
13	78324	Union City city, Georgia	20.1	38.2	12.3	15.8	0.0	3.9	5.3	0.6
13	78800	Valdosta city, Georgia	26.9	22.3	7.1	16.0	1.1	2.6	11.2	1.1
13	80508	Warner Robins city, Georgia	17.5	26.8	11.3	15.0	0.2	2.0	9.9	2.6
13	84176	Woodstock city, Georgia	11.5	21.9	5.1	3.5	0.0	7.2	7.0	2.5
15	00000	**HAWAII**	22.9	24.8	10.2	8.5	1.4	7.9	3.0	2.6
15	06290	East Honolulu CDP, Hawaii	16.2	23.6	5.2	6.2	0.0	5.8	2.8	3.9
15	07470	Ewa Gentry CDP, Hawaii	17.4	29.7	5.9	8.2	0.0	7.3	3.7	4.0
15	14650	Hilo CDP, Hawaii	15.8	22.8	10.3	8.4	3.8	6.1	0.8	1.0
15	22700	Kahului CDP, Hawaii	29.0	23.8	9.8	10.8	1.8	5.0	2.3	2.8
15	23150	Kailua CDP (Honolulu County), Hawaii	14.5	24.1	7.1	3.9	0.0	7.6	2.7	3.1
15	28250	Kaneohe CDP, Hawaii	19.3	24.7	13.9	6.4	0.7	10.2	3.0	2.8
15	30300	Kapolei CDP, Hawaii	20.4	30.6	8.8	16.6	0.1	5.0	2.0	4.8
15	47600	Makakilo CDP, Hawaii	18.9	32.3	8.4	6.4	3.9	9.9	2.0	0.5
15	51000	Mililani Mauka CDP, Hawaii	13.7	23.8	9.2	9.8	0.3	8.5	7.1	5.2
15	51050	Mililani Town CDP, Hawaii	22.3	28.0	13.3	7.6	0.5	6.8	4.0	2.1
15	62600	Pearl City CDP, Hawaii	15.2	28.5	11.0	7.7	0.5	6.8	4.1	1.9
15	69050	Schofield Barracks CDP, Hawaii	14.5	23.0	21.8	8.2	–	–	–	–
15	71550	Urban Honolulu CDP, Hawaii	24.8	24.8	7.4	8.0	0.3	5.8	2.7	2.4
15	79700	Waipahu CDP, Hawaii	36.6	24.1	10.1	10.4	1.1	6.2	3.3	3.6
16	00000	**IDAHO**	19.1	23.0	11.4	12.9	5.2	6.6	9.5	2.8
16	08830	Boise City city, Idaho	19.1	22.2	6.2	8.5	1.0	5.3	7.7	2.5
16	12250	Caldwell city, Idaho	20.4	27.5	15.6	15.7	2.7	4.5	17.9	2.8
16	16750	Coeur d'Alene city, Idaho	23.1	26.2	7.0	10.5	1.6	6.2	6.6	1.2
16	23410	Eagle city, Idaho	12.8	22.4	1.8	2.9	0.6	4.0	7.0	0.7
16	39700	Idaho Falls city, Idaho	22.4	21.7	8.8	14.1	3.4	6.5	10.7	2.1
16	46540	Lewiston city, Idaho	19.3	25.3	6.0	13.0	1.5	3.9	12.9	5.1
16	52120	Meridian city, Idaho	16.5	29.9	4.3	11.8	1.4	5.3	9.0	4.2
16	54550	Moscow city, Idaho	17.8	17.0	2.9	11.5	2.0	2.4	5.3	1.4
16	56260	Nampa city, Idaho	18.8	23.2	17.7	10.6	6.7	8.6	9.3	2.4
16	64090	Pocatello city, Idaho	20.9	25.0	7.1	13.3	0.2	6.1	8.5	2.0
16	64810	Post Falls city, Idaho	18.6	28.6	11.8	16.6	1.3	6.9	8.2	8.4
16	67420	Rexburg city, Idaho	28.4	29.9	10.6	11.0	8.3	7.1	1.2	0.3
16	82810	Twin Falls city, Idaho	27.0	24.8	10.8	8.6	2.1	3.2	7.4	5.2

Table E. Cities—Labor Force, Employment, and Educational Data, 2015—*Continued*

FIPS state code	FIPS place code	State/city	Percent in each occupation group				Percent in each industry sector			
			Service occupations	Sales and office occupations	Natural resources, construction, and maintenance occupations	Production, transportation, and material moving occupations	Agriculture, forestry, fishing and hunting, and mining	Construction	Manufacturing	Wholesale trade
17	00000	**ILLINOIS**	17.5	23.7	7.4	14.0	1.1	5.3	12.3	3.1
17	00243	Addison village, Illinois	18.3	19.4	9.7	23.2	0.0	7.2	17.0	3.6
17	00685	Algonquin village, Illinois	10.9	30.5	3.9	8.4	0.0	6.0	12.1	4.9
17	01114	Alton city, Illinois	21.3	26.5	9.7	18.1	0.5	5.6	10.0	2.2
17	02154	Arlington Heights village, Illinois	10.5	25.7	4.4	9.4	0.0	4.9	13.8	3.8
17	03012	Aurora city, Illinois	17.4	26.1	8.3	18.1	0.4	5.8	15.9	3.7
17	04013	Bartlett village, Illinois	10.9	23.8	7.2	8.7	0.2	7.8	10.4	3.5
17	04078	Batavia city, Illinois	13.2	25.6	6.8	6.9	0.0	5.8	15.8	3.0
17	04845	Belleville city, Illinois	23.6	21.3	9.6	13.7	2.6	2.5	12.1	1.1
17	05092	Belvidere city, Illinois	14.8	37.0	7.9	25.0	4.0	6.0	22.9	1.4
17	05573	Berwyn city, Illinois	19.4	27.0	14.4	15.3	0.0	10.3	7.1	3.8
17	06587	Bloomingdale village, Illinois	16.9	30.3	3.6	12.1	0.0	3.0	8.9	2.9
17	06613	Bloomington city, Illinois	15.4	24.4	3.2	7.1	0.0	3.5	4.8	1.8
17	06704	Blue Island city, Illinois	21.7	35.6	5.5	24.7	0.0	4.9	14.3	3.6
17	07133	Bolingbrook village, Illinois	19.3	25.3	7.0	14.9	0.0	5.1	10.1	3.8
17	09447	Buffalo Grove village, Illinois	9.7	26.1	2.7	3.7	0.7	2.0	12.9	5.0
17	09642	Burbank city, Illinois	21.0	26.5	16.2	15.8	0.3	12.6	10.6	2.8
17	10487	Calumet City city, Illinois	23.1	27.7	10.8	15.6	0.0	2.3	10.3	1.2
17	11163	Carbondale city, Illinois	20.3	17.8	0.8	9.4	0.0	0.0	5.8	0.0
17	11332	Carol Stream village, Illinois	13.7	27.0	5.1	14.6	0.0	2.9	20.2	3.1
17	11358	Carpentersville village, Illinois	21.0	21.4	7.3	19.1	0.6	8.1	17.5	2.5
17	12385	Champaign city, Illinois	16.7	20.3	4.3	11.2	0.0	4.1	8.3	2.3
17	12567	Charleston city, Illinois	15.3	28.7	3.2	10.6	0.2	4.3	8.3	0.4
17	14000	Chicago city, Illinois	19.8	22.7	5.3	12.4	0.3	4.0	8.6	2.5
17	14026	Chicago Heights city, Illinois	26.2	14.5	10.6	25.3	0.0	6.3	17.4	1.1
17	14351	Cicero town, Illinois	28.6	22.4	11.2	25.9	0.0	7.1	18.5	4.7
17	15599	Collinsville city, Illinois	24.7	21.8	7.2	12.4	0.6	3.2	11.6	5.1
17	17458	Crest Hill city, Illinois	18.9	22.2	9.0	20.2	0.0	3.7	12.2	1.6
17	17887	Crystal Lake city, Illinois	15.6	24.1	7.3	8.2	0.0	5.3	11.6	4.8
17	18563	Danville city, Illinois	21.2	16.5	8.0	26.7	0.5	4.6	17.3	2.7
17	18628	Darien city, Illinois	5.3	24.9	4.8	5.5	0.0	5.3	12.4	3.6
17	18823	Decatur city, Illinois	21.5	23.1	7.0	17.8	2.0	4.6	15.6	2.4
17	19161	DeKalb city, Illinois	20.7	25.5	6.5	11.5	0.7	2.2	10.4	1.5
17	19642	Des Plaines city, Illinois	16.6	27.0	7.9	11.9	0.1	5.2	13.8	4.9
17	20292	Dolton village, Illinois	22.3	21.9	10.3	18.0	0.0	4.5	13.8	0.0
17	20591	Downers Grove village, Illinois	9.2	24.8	3.3	10.1	0.2	4.6	10.5	3.3
17	22073	East Moline city, Illinois	14.3	18.9	7.3	32.8	1.5	4.0	29.1	1.1
17	22164	East Peoria city, Illinois	13.5	19.7	8.6	19.9	0.0	6.2	17.4	1.3
17	22255	East St. Louis city, Illinois	36.6	22.5	1.7	19.6	0.0	2.9	17.3	0.6
17	22697	Edwardsville city, Illinois	21.0	21.6	4.7	3.1	0.2	2.9	3.7	0.4
17	23074	Elgin city, Illinois	21.8	22.1	8.6	22.1	1.1	5.3	19.9	3.9
17	23256	Elk Grove Village village, Illinois	11.7	31.9	6.3	13.0	0.0	6.1	16.1	4.5
17	23620	Elmhurst city, Illinois	9.1	21.1	6.9	7.7	0.0	7.0	11.8	3.1
17	23724	Elmwood Park village, Illinois	23.4	25.7	9.0	11.4	0.0	4.6	9.0	4.3
17	24582	Evanston city, Illinois	10.7	19.5	2.5	5.5	0.5	3.0	6.2	1.8
17	27884	Freeport city, Illinois	21.6	28.6	8.3	21.3	0.4	5.3	19.3	4.0
17	28326	Galesburg city, Illinois	23.2	20.7	5.9	15.9	0.7	6.2	7.8	1.0
17	28872	Geneva city, Illinois	11.2	22.3	6.4	8.9	0.6	5.6	12.9	2.6
17	29730	Glendale Heights village, Illinois	18.2	29.1	6.2	21.5	0.0	4.6	22.3	2.8
17	29756	Glen Ellyn village, Illinois	9.7	26.0	4.7	6.8	0.0	4.0	11.1	5.8
17	29938	Glenview village, Illinois	8.0	26.4	4.4	4.6	0.4	3.9	8.2	5.7
17	30926	Granite City city, Illinois	21.9	27.3	8.2	16.4	1.1	5.6	10.3	1.7
17	31121	Grayslake village, Illinois	11.4	28.7	2.8	5.1	0.0	1.5	16.2	6.5
17	32018	Gurnee village, Illinois	15.3	23.0	5.9	10.4	0.5	3.8	19.8	5.8
17	32746	Hanover Park village, Illinois	17.9	30.1	6.6	17.8	0.3	4.3	17.0	4.3
17	33383	Harvey city, Illinois	24.2	24.0	13.7	17.7	0.0	10.6	6.9	2.2
17	34722	Highland Park city, Illinois	9.3	24.5	1.5	1.3	0.0	1.5	8.6	4.7
17	35411	Hoffman Estates village, Illinois	13.4	25.0	8.4	10.1	0.4	6.9	13.3	4.1
17	35835	Homer Glen village, Illinois	13.1	31.3	5.8	8.5	0.0	5.4	10.0	2.4
17	36750	Huntley village, Illinois	18.0	23.9	2.2	16.7	0.0	4.6	8.6	11.2
17	38570	Joliet city, Illinois	23.5	22.9	8.4	20.0	1.0	6.7	11.1	2.8
17	38934	Kankakee city, Illinois	19.9	19.3	5.8	30.5	0.4	3.5	21.8	0.9
17	41183	Lake in the Hills village, Illinois	18.3	32.8	6.2	10.8	0.0	5.2	15.2	3.6
17	41742	Lake Zurich village, Illinois	12.6	28.8	3.0	9.6	0.0	3.5	12.3	4.2
17	42028	Lansing village, Illinois	22.8	20.7	8.6	13.0	0.0	5.5	7.5	3.2
17	43250	Libertyville village, Illinois	10.8	25.0	2.2	3.3	1.1	0.5	16.7	7.9
17	43939	Lisle village, Illinois	7.9	23.1	6.1	4.3	0.0	8.1	11.2	2.5
17	44225	Lockport city, Illinois	14.7	22.4	10.3	12.4	0.0	11.5	8.2	3.2
17	44407	Lombard village, Illinois	20.4	19.0	5.8	9.7	0.3	3.6	10.1	4.3
17	45031	Loves Park city, Illinois	13.4	27.1	9.6	19.0	0.7	8.8	18.4	1.2
17	45694	McHenry city, Illinois	13.2	30.2	13.5	12.7	0.0	13.1	21.1	2.7
17	45726	Machesney Park village, Illinois	20.9	23.2	11.5	18.4	0.0	6.7	15.5	3.6
17	47774	Maywood village, Illinois	16.8	27.9	5.3	24.8	0.0	4.5	12.8	2.4
17	48242	Melrose Park village, Illinois	27.2	16.4	11.6	22.7	0.0	8.9	17.6	2.5

Table E. Cities—Labor Force, Employment, and Educational Data, 2015—*Continued*

			Percent in each occupation group				Percent in each industry sector			
FIPS state code	FIPS place code	State/city	Service occupations	Sales and office occupations	Natural resources, construction, and maintenance occupations	Production, transportation, and material moving occupations	Agriculture, forestry, fishing and hunting, and mining	Construction	Manufacturing	Wholesale trade
17	49867	Moline city, Illinois	17.7	24.1	10.9	18.1	0.1	6.3	20.5	4.3
17	50647	Morton Grove village, Illinois	13.1	17.8	8.4	14.1	0.4	5.9	10.2	5.1
17	51089	Mount Prospect village, Illinois	14.3	25.8	4.2	12.8	0.0	5.4	15.0	2.9
17	51349	Mundelein village, Illinois	18.2	23.5	5.2	14.8	0.0	3.5	15.9	7.8
17	51622	Naperville city, Illinois	12.1	23.9	3.2	4.9	0.3	3.7	12.3	3.7
17	52584	New Lenox village, Illinois	12.9	26.5	7.7	9.7	0.0	5.8	7.0	4.9
17	53000	Niles village, Illinois	23.8	27.6	5.9	12.6	0.0	4.7	9.5	2.4
17	53234	Normal town, Illinois	28.1	27.3	1.6	7.4	0.2	1.8	5.3	0.8
17	53481	Northbrook village, Illinois	7.4	26.0	1.9	3.2	0.0	3.8	5.3	4.7
17	53559	North Chicago city, Illinois	31.6	23.3	5.5	18.2	0.0	5.0	15.1	2.1
17	54638	Oak Forest city, Illinois	15.7	22.7	9.6	9.3	0.0	8.7	10.8	2.5
17	54820	Oak Lawn village, Illinois	12.4	28.8	5.6	14.4	0.0	7.0	12.0	3.0
17	54885	Oak Park village, Illinois	10.4	17.8	2.0	4.6	0.0	2.4	7.2	3.4
17	55249	O'Fallon city, Illinois	15.2	24.2	4.0	11.7	0.0	2.7	7.8	1.2
17	56640	Orland Park village, Illinois	11.7	24.7	9.8	7.8	0.2	8.8	9.2	3.4
17	56887	Oswego village, Illinois	14.6	18.5	5.7	11.9	0.0	11.3	13.6	4.9
17	57225	Palatine village, Illinois	16.1	24.9	7.7	13.2	0.0	6.2	14.3	3.2
17	57732	Park Forest village, Illinois	18.2	24.8	4.0	19.6	0.0	1.1	9.5	2.8
17	57875	Park Ridge city, Illinois	7.9	25.0	7.3	6.9	0.2	6.5	5.8	5.1
17	58447	Pekin city, Illinois	18.6	29.3	7.7	18.2	0.2	4.8	15.9	2.0
17	59000	Peoria city, Illinois	18.0	23.0	5.5	11.7	0.6	3.4	17.8	0.9
17	60287	Plainfield village, Illinois	14.7	29.5	5.0	8.6	0.4	4.4	10.4	3.5
17	62367	Quincy city, Illinois	24.2	25.9	5.1	15.5	0.3	4.2	13.8	3.8
17	65000	Rockford city, Illinois	25.5	21.8	6.3	19.4	0.4	4.2	18.9	1.6
17	65078	Rock Island city, Illinois	23.2	20.5	2.8	19.7	0.2	2.3	14.6	0.7
17	65338	Rolling Meadows city, Illinois	23.8	22.7	3.4	6.7	0.3	5.0	9.0	4.7
17	65442	Romeoville village, Illinois	17.1	23.4	8.5	28.5	0.0	5.9	19.3	4.1
17	65806	Roselle village, Illinois	13.9	24.8	8.7	18.2	0.0	8.4	10.6	3.5
17	66040	Round Lake Beach village, Illinois	25.3	26.5	13.7	15.2	0.0	7.5	18.4	1.1
17	66703	St. Charles city, Illinois	11.1	23.8	6.7	10.7	0.9	6.0	16.2	3.9
17	68003	Schaumburg village, Illinois	15.1	27.4	3.1	10.2	0.1	2.9	11.7	5.0
17	70122	Skokie village, Illinois	19.0	25.4	4.4	7.8	0.0	4.4	10.3	2.6
17	70720	South Elgin village, Illinois	16.2	27.2	6.7	15.5	0.0	6.5	15.5	4.4
17	70850	South Holland village, Illinois	17.6	22.1	7.8	10.0	0.6	1.5	6.6	1.8
17	72000	Springfield city, Illinois	19.4	23.2	5.5	7.1	0.4	4.1	4.2	1.9
17	73157	Streamwood village, Illinois	22.6	21.0	5.9	11.3	0.0	4.6	13.1	3.5
17	75484	Tinley Park village, Illinois	15.0	28.7	7.1	7.6	0.0	6.0	5.3	6.1
17	77005	Urbana city, Illinois	17.2	12.4	3.5	4.3	0.0	4.2	5.5	1.5
17	77694	Vernon Hills village, Illinois	15.4	17.1	0.8	8.6	0.0	1.2	15.9	6.0
17	77993	Villa Park village, Illinois	16.9	20.5	7.9	17.1	0.4	4.7	7.5	1.5
17	79293	Waukegan city, Illinois	23.8	20.1	9.0	27.2	0.1	7.0	26.5	4.1
17	80060	West Chicago city, Illinois	16.9	24.2	7.5	24.5	0.4	4.4	21.6	5.4
17	80645	Westmont village, Illinois	19.5	25.4	3.6	8.4	0.7	2.1	9.0	1.0
17	81048	Wheaton city, Illinois	12.5	24.5	2.3	9.2	0.1	2.1	13.7	3.7
17	81087	Wheeling village, Illinois	16.8	23.7	8.3	18.7	0.1	7.5	12.8	5.8
17	82075	Wilmette village, Illinois	4.3	23.1	1.5	3.8	0.0	0.8	8.9	2.0
17	83245	Woodridge village, Illinois	15.3	27.0	4.9	7.0	0.0	5.7	10.0	1.2
17	83349	Woodstock city, Illinois	17.9	19.4	3.5	17.1	0.0	5.3	15.1	3.2
17	84220	Zion city, Illinois	21.8	28.7	3.1	19.6	0.0	3.4	13.3	7.4
18	00000	**INDIANA**	16.5	22.8	9.0	18.8	1.5	5.9	19.0	2.7
18	01468	Anderson city, Indiana	26.3	26.9	6.9	16.0	0.6	5.0	8.1	2.7
18	05860	Bloomington city, Indiana	27.4	19.9	3.6	6.9	0.1	1.1	7.3	1.3
18	08416	Brownsburg town, Indiana	15.3	32.5	3.7	10.9	0.0	2.1	10.0	1.7
18	10342	Carmel city, Indiana	9.0	25.4	3.8	3.3	0.0	7.3	12.0	3.6
18	12934	Clarksville town, Indiana	29.7	22.8	14.5	13.8	0.0	8.5	12.7	2.4
18	14734	Columbus city, Indiana	13.4	22.3	4.7	19.0	0.6	5.0	38.5	1.3
18	16138	Crown Point city, Indiana	12.5	24.3	7.1	16.4	0.0	6.9	15.6	2.6
18	19486	East Chicago city, Indiana	27.0	24.0	9.1	21.5	0.0	12.4	16.9	2.7
18	20728	Elkhart city, Indiana	10.2	16.0	6.4	47.9	0.0	1.8	50.4	0.7
18	22000	Evansville city, Indiana	18.1	24.8	8.3	21.9	1.0	5.9	15.1	3.6
18	23278	Fishers town, Indiana	9.6	26.2	2.3	1.6	0.4	1.7	11.6	3.2
18	25000	Fort Wayne city, Indiana	17.5	23.6	7.3	17.9	0.5	5.0	18.3	3.3
18	25450	Franklin city, Indiana	21.7	19.1	5.1	17.9	0.0	3.5	17.3	2.4
18	27000	Gary city, Indiana	30.1	21.3	6.3	17.2	0.2	4.6	13.2	0.5
18	28386	Goshen city, Indiana	13.6	23.3	14.2	31.3	0.0	4.7	36.9	0.3
18	28800	Granger CDP, Indiana	7.3	26.3	6.2	8.9	0.3	4.7	20.1	2.4
18	29520	Greenfield city, Indiana	8.9	25.3	16.4	15.8	0.0	6.2	30.2	5.8
18	29898	Greenwood city, Indiana	14.4	27.7	8.3	9.9	0.0	6.9	19.2	2.2
18	31000	Hammond city, Indiana	18.8	24.5	10.7	23.4	0.0	7.1	16.2	2.5
18	33466	Highland town, Indiana	19.5	23.9	11.6	12.7	1.3	4.9	17.9	2.8
18	34114	Hobart city, Indiana	15.0	20.3	7.3	21.6	0.3	6.1	18.7	2.5
18	36003	Indianapolis city (balance), Indiana	17.7	25.9	7.1	15.2	0.2	5.4	10.5	3.5
18	38358	Jeffersonville city, Indiana	16.6	30.1	4.5	18.3	0.0	3.2	15.4	2.0
18	40392	Kokomo city, Indiana	20.2	22.3	6.8	26.8	0.6	3.3	28.8	2.4

Table E. Cities—Labor Force, Employment, and Educational Data, 2015—*Continued*

FIPS state code	FIPS place code	State/city	Percent in each occupation group				Percent in each industry sector			
			Service occupations	Sales and office occupations	Natural resources, construction, and maintenance occupations	Production, transportation, and material moving occupations	Agriculture, forestry, fishing and hunting, and mining	Construction	Manufacturing	Wholesale trade
18	40788	Lafayette city, Indiana	18.8	19.6	8.0	24.6	0.2	5.0	22.2	1.6
18	42246	La Porte city, Indiana	19.7	29.0	9.0	25.7	0.0	4.0	25.9	2.4
18	42426	Lawrence city, Indiana	16.5	25.8	15.2	7.8	0.8	10.0	7.6	1.7
18	46908	Marion city, Indiana	26.5	26.8	4.7	20.3	0.3	3.9	10.3	3.6
18	48528	Merrillville town, Indiana	20.5	25.5	9.1	14.2	0.0	2.9	16.7	0.4
18	48798	Michigan City city, Indiana	24.3	23.3	9.9	27.2	0.6	3.4	24.4	1.5
18	49932	Mishawaka city, Indiana	21.9	21.3	4.9	16.8	0.2	3.9	15.9	2.6
18	51876	Muncie city, Indiana	28.8	21.7	5.8	14.5	0.4	4.2	8.5	1.9
18	51912	Munster town, Indiana	11.1	28.6	3.7	9.5	0.0	6.8	8.0	1.5
18	52326	New Albany city, Indiana	20.2	24.5	10.4	17.1	0.0	7.5	16.1	0.8
18	54180	Noblesville city, Indiana	15.5	30.3	9.0	9.9	0.4	8.3	11.2	3.1
18	60246	Plainfield town, Indiana	15.0	26.5	7.0	18.6	0.0	4.1	10.2	4.2
18	61092	Portage city, Indiana	21.3	22.7	7.4	26.2	0.0	2.3	19.9	0.4
18	64260	Richmond city, Indiana	20.7	24.7	9.4	17.7	0.5	4.0	15.8	5.1
18	68220	Schererville town, Indiana	10.2	27.6	8.4	15.6	0.9	5.7	11.6	4.9
18	71000	South Bend city, Indiana	18.4	23.1	5.9	21.0	0.4	3.6	20.9	3.1
18	75428	Terre Haute city, Indiana	20.9	22.0	10.2	14.8	1.4	6.9	14.8	1.9
18	78326	Valparaiso city, Indiana	11.4	23.2	10.2	11.6	0.4	8.5	12.8	2.5
18	82700	Westfield city, Indiana	12.3	29.1	4.7	8.3	4.7	3.3	7.0	4.3
18	82862	West Lafayette city, Indiana	23.2	17.5	2.6	3.8	1.6	1.6	5.4	0.1
18	86372	Zionsville town, Indiana	7.4	20.1	1.4	7.8	1.4	2.6	11.4	6.2
19	00000	**IOWA**	16.8	22.2	9.5	17.0	3.8	6.3	15.7	2.7
19	01855	Ames city, Iowa	18.9	22.5	2.8	5.5	0.5	1.6	11.2	0.9
19	02305	Ankeny city, Iowa	13.5	22.9	7.6	8.5	3.3	6.8	8.3	1.7
19	06355	Bettendorf city, Iowa	12.2	19.6	8.7	9.4	0.7	6.9	15.8	4.4
19	09550	Burlington city, Iowa	20.5	22.0	11.2	19.8	0.3	9.0	21.8	3.6
19	11755	Cedar Falls city, Iowa	23.7	24.8	2.9	9.5	0.4	2.7	11.0	1.9
19	12000	Cedar Rapids city, Iowa	18.0	22.9	6.6	17.9	0.5	4.7	16.4	1.6
19	14430	Clinton city, Iowa	18.5	23.9	8.4	23.1	0.0	7.7	24.5	0.7
19	16230	Coralville city, Iowa	22.4	16.3	5.8	9.7	0.0	1.4	2.0	0.0
19	16860	Council Bluffs city, Iowa	18.8	24.8	13.2	19.7	0.5	8.7	14.0	4.3
19	19000	Davenport city, Iowa	23.7	22.9	7.8	17.6	0.0	7.2	18.2	2.0
19	21000	Des Moines city, Iowa	21.4	24.7	8.4	14.5	0.5	6.5	10.8	2.2
19	22395	Dubuque city, Iowa	17.7	24.9	5.9	14.1	1.0	3.9	15.4	2.5
19	28515	Fort Dodge city, Iowa	24.5	24.0	9.0	12.1	1.1	9.3	13.7	3.8
19	38595	Iowa City city, Iowa	20.4	18.3	4.5	12.2	0.2	4.8	6.6	0.8
19	39765	Johnston city, Iowa	16.8	21.6	3.0	1.9	2.0	3.1	10.9	0.7
19	49485	Marion city, Iowa	12.6	23.4	9.3	8.6	0.4	5.5	16.9	3.9
19	49755	Marshalltown city, Iowa	20.1	15.9	10.9	34.5	1.8	9.1	36.6	0.8
19	50160	Mason City city, Iowa	24.8	23.6	8.3	16.4	0.4	8.3	15.1	2.8
19	55110	Muscatine city, Iowa	21.1	14.3	6.1	35.7	1.9	4.2	38.5	1.9
19	60465	Ottumwa city, Iowa	16.3	20.8	7.1	32.5	1.7	4.9	25.3	0.3
19	73335	Sioux City city, Iowa	17.5	22.8	7.6	23.0	1.1	6.0	20.4	2.8
19	79950	Urbandale city, Iowa	11.1	31.0	6.0	7.6	1.8	6.5	8.3	2.4
19	82425	Waterloo city, Iowa	19.4	21.0	6.8	25.1	1.3	4.2	22.8	3.3
19	83910	West Des Moines city, Iowa	11.8	24.0	3.1	7.7	0.4	3.5	6.3	2.4
20	00000	**KANSAS**	17.0	22.1	9.8	13.7	3.4	6.6	12.2	2.8
20	17800	Derby city, Kansas	19.9	17.9	6.0	8.0	0.0	4.3	18.5	1.7
20	18250	Dodge City city, Kansas	20.3	14.5	10.6	28.3	2.7	4.8	21.1	3.9
20	21275	Emporia city, Kansas	20.3	18.3	9.7	20.9	1.2	5.9	17.0	0.6
20	25325	Garden City city, Kansas	21.4	19.4	12.3	28.3	3.8	5.0	23.5	5.3
20	25425	Gardner city, Kansas	12.7	28.5	5.8	12.7	2.0	5.5	13.2	2.8
20	31100	Hays city, Kansas	19.4	22.8	13.3	9.7	2.7	8.2	6.5	3.0
20	33625	Hutchinson city, Kansas	16.8	30.0	8.5	15.6	1.8	5.4	14.1	3.9
20	35750	Junction City city, Kansas	21.7	19.7	10.8	19.6	0.9	5.9	14.0	2.5
20	36000	Kansas City city, Kansas	23.5	23.2	13.3	19.0	0.4	10.7	12.2	3.5
20	38900	Lawrence city, Kansas	18.9	24.2	5.6	8.2	0.6	4.4	4.7	1.9
20	39000	Leavenworth city, Kansas	29.6	16.0	8.1	12.7	0.5	5.8	4.1	2.2
20	39075	Leawood city, Kansas	5.3	25.4	2.0	2.0	0.7	4.0	6.5	6.7
20	39350	Lenexa city, Kansas	12.4	25.0	4.6	8.2	0.1	3.3	12.3	4.7
20	39825	Liberal city, Kansas	13.3	19.0	16.8	29.2	6.6	13.5	22.1	1.7
20	44250	Manhattan city, Kansas	22.5	26.0	6.8	5.9	1.0	6.3	5.7	1.1
20	52575	Olathe city, Kansas	15.5	24.8	4.7	10.6	0.2	5.3	7.8	2.4
20	53775	Overland Park city, Kansas	12.0	24.9	2.7	5.5	0.3	2.5	6.7	4.7
20	56025	Pittsburg city, Kansas	15.8	15.4	6.4	14.1	4.0	1.5	14.0	2.8
20	57575	Prairie Village city, Kansas	6.3	17.6	3.1	2.3	0.0	7.4	2.6	1.7
20	62700	Salina city, Kansas	19.8	18.5	8.1	21.0	1.1	7.4	19.2	2.4
20	64500	Shawnee city, Kansas	17.2	23.3	7.0	9.5	1.5	5.4	9.6	4.2
20	71000	Topeka city, Kansas	20.3	22.0	8.6	13.2	0.4	6.0	9.0	1.2
20	79000	Wichita city, Kansas	19.7	22.8	10.3	15.3	0.9	7.0	18.6	2.6
21	00000	**KENTUCKY**	16.7	23.8	9.2	17.1	2.5	5.8	14.3	2.4
21	02368	Ashland city, Kentucky	12.2	26.8	4.0	15.6	0.0	4.7	9.0	1.9
21	08902	Bowling Green city, Kentucky	23.6	23.9	4.6	18.5	0.5	3.2	13.6	1.7

Table E. Cities—Labor Force, Employment, and Educational Data, 2015—*Continued*

FIPS state code	FIPS place code	State/city	Percent in each occupation group				Percent in each industry sector			
			Service occupations	Sales and office occupations	Natural resources, construction, and maintenance occupations	Production, transportation, and material moving occupations	Agriculture, forestry, fishing and hunting, and mining	Construction	Manufacturing	Wholesale trade
21	17848	Covington city, Kentucky	22.5	21.1	7.9	16.3	3.0	3.7	9.0	5.7
21	24274	Elizabethtown city, Kentucky	23.7	28.1	6.6	17.7	1.9	1.8	13.3	1.4
21	27982	Florence city, Kentucky	20.8	17.9	7.6	21.8	0.0	5.2	18.0	1.8
21	28900	Frankfort city, Kentucky	11.8	30.5	7.6	17.6	4.6	3.3	11.6	1.7
21	30700	Georgetown city, Kentucky	18.1	21.9	6.4	20.1	0.9	2.9	23.6	1.1
21	35866	Henderson city, Kentucky	24.0	22.1	5.7	23.3	2.0	5.5	16.5	5.1
21	37918	Hopkinsville city, Kentucky	23.4	24.2	7.9	19.2	0.9	1.9	21.4	2.6
21	39142	Independence city, Kentucky	10.0	23.0	7.9	25.7	0.6	6.4	10.0	4.1
21	40222	Jeffersontown city, Kentucky	15.7	22.8	2.9	17.3	0.0	4.4	14.1	2.3
21	46027	Lexington-Fayette urban county, Kentucky	20.3	23.8	6.2	8.4	1.7	4.9	9.2	2.0
21	48006	Louisville/Jefferson County metro government (balance), Kentucky	15.9	23.9	7.0	16.3	0.7	5.2	11.9	3.2
21	56136	Nicholasville city, Kentucky	20.2	26.9	7.5	15.1	0.2	6.4	8.7	1.4
21	58620	Owensboro city, Kentucky	18.7	29.4	5.6	18.8	1.7	2.7	14.2	1.8
21	58836	Paducah city, Kentucky	24.6	24.7	3.9	13.9	3.5	2.3	5.0	2.6
21	63912	Radcliff city, Kentucky	21.3	25.0	6.0	14.4	0.0	4.8	9.0	2.1
21	65226	Richmond city, Kentucky	24.2	29.0	5.0	12.3	0.5	3.9	11.3	0.0
22	00000	**LOUISIANA**	19.1	23.6	11.8	11.8	4.2	7.9	7.8	2.5
22	00975	Alexandria city, Louisiana	24.3	22.1	8.3	8.6	0.5	2.8	3.4	0.6
22	05000	Baton Rouge city, Louisiana	21.0	21.8	9.8	8.8	1.0	7.0	6.9	1.8
22	05210	Bayou Cane CDP, Louisiana	10.1	26.0	16.2	23.6	13.1	8.8	5.9	1.8
22	08920	Bossier City city, Louisiana	19.6	29.5	13.3	7.2	3.5	9.6	5.3	1.6
22	13960	Central city, Louisiana	10.9	24.8	11.3	9.4	0.3	8.8	13.6	1.1
22	14135	Chalmette CDP, Louisiana	23.2	26.6	17.7	8.3	0.0	15.3	4.5	1.0
22	32755	Hammond city, Louisiana	33.2	23.3	7.1	6.7	1.0	9.1	4.2	1.8
22	33245	Harvey CDP, Louisiana	18.1	27.9	19.4	13.4	1.4	16.0	4.4	3.7
22	36255	Houma city, Louisiana	20.0	25.4	10.7	19.1	7.0	8.7	14.0	1.0
22	39475	Kenner city, Louisiana	20.5	26.4	14.2	9.2	1.5	11.2	7.5	2.6
22	40735	Lafayette city, Louisiana	24.3	22.8	7.8	8.2	5.9	6.2	5.5	3.0
22	41155	Lake Charles city, Louisiana	26.7	22.0	8.1	10.8	1.2	6.5	7.5	0.3
22	42030	Laplace CDP, Louisiana	13.9	14.1	12.8	16.0	1.8	7.4	11.2	2.7
22	48785	Marrero CDP, Louisiana	29.3	21.4	14.7	9.9	3.3	5.3	8.3	1.9
22	50115	Metairie CDP, Louisiana	16.7	26.4	10.7	7.0	0.8	7.2	4.4	4.7
22	51410	Monroe city, Louisiana	24.5	26.4	4.8	9.1	0.5	2.8	3.0	0.7
22	54035	New Iberia city, Louisiana	25.6	27.8	14.9	8.0	9.4	3.3	6.8	3.8
22	55000	New Orleans city, Louisiana	23.4	19.6	7.1	7.8	0.8	5.2	4.3	1.7
22	62385	Prairieville CDP, Louisiana	10.1	29.3	7.6	8.8	0.8	4.5	10.9	5.8
22	66655	Ruston city, Louisiana	14.2	35.8	6.6	5.3	0.0	3.4	6.0	0.0
22	70000	Shreveport city, Louisiana	23.7	25.4	7.8	11.7	2.7	4.5	5.7	3.1
22	70805	Slidell city, Louisiana	17.8	28.9	6.1	11.7	0.7	6.0	5.0	4.4
22	73640	Sulphur city, Louisiana	15.4	19.9	14.9	19.5	0.0	9.4	14.6	2.8
22	75180	Terrytown CDP, Louisiana	19.8	25.4	15.6	14.7	0.8	13.0	4.7	1.0
23	00000	**MAINE**	17.8	23.8	10.6	11.3	2.7	7.2	9.4	2.1
23	02060	Auburn city, Maine	18.4	21.6	4.3	11.7	0.2	1.7	8.4	6.7
23	02795	Bangor city, Maine	22.2	23.6	3.2	6.6	0.4	2.5	1.4	1.4
23	04860	Biddeford city, Maine	27.1	27.1	3.9	14.0	1.7	7.9	12.1	2.6
23	38740	Lewiston city, Maine	23.2	26.6	9.1	12.6	0.9	7.4	10.4	2.2
23	60545	Portland city, Maine	19.3	25.0	3.8	6.7	1.3	2.5	5.7	1.9
23	65725	Sanford city, Maine	22.3	31.1	10.4	15.8	2.8	7.2	14.0	3.9
23	71990	South Portland city, Maine	18.9	27.1	4.1	8.0	1.5	2.2	8.9	1.9
24	00000	**MARYLAND**	17.6	21.9	7.7	8.1	0.5	6.8	4.6	2.0
24	01600	Annapolis city, Maryland	23.0	23.1	5.4	6.2	0.0	6.4	2.4	1.9
24	01975	Arbutus CDP, Maryland	16.1	27.2	8.3	8.0	0.0	9.5	3.0	2.8
24	02275	Arnold CDP, Maryland	11.1	17.9	6.5	5.3	0.0	7.0	2.3	2.0
24	02825	Aspen Hill CDP, Maryland	23.2	19.3	9.5	6.3	0.2	8.2	3.8	1.3
24	04000	Baltimore city, Maryland	19.1	22.7	5.2	11.3	0.1	4.4	4.9	2.0
24	05825	Bel Air North CDP, Maryland	12.8	26.2	7.2	8.3	0.4	7.8	3.7	2.3
24	05950	Bel Air South CDP, Maryland	13.0	26.3	6.9	6.6	0.2	5.7	5.0	4.0
24	07125	Bethesda CDP, Maryland	10.2	14.2	1.1	1.0	0.0	1.6	1.9	1.1
24	08775	Bowie city, Maryland	12.5	18.8	4.4	5.5	0.0	3.6	1.2	1.4
24	12600	Camp Springs CDP, Maryland	18.6	23.4	4.6	11.2	0.5	4.9	2.4	0.5
24	13325	Carney CDP, Maryland	19.1	26.9	4.5	3.3	0.3	3.0	2.9	1.6
24	14125	Catonsville CDP, Maryland	7.8	24.9	5.6	3.5	0.0	7.0	4.4	2.6
24	16875	Chillum CDP, Maryland	37.6	11.7	16.6	12.6	0.0	16.4	2.3	1.7
24	17350	Clarksburg CDP, Maryland	10.4	16.0	1.4	8.7	0.6	1.5	4.4	1.8
24	17900	Clinton CDP, Maryland	18.7	25.9	9.2	10.2	0.1	6.5	1.7	1.6
24	18250	Cockeysville CDP, Maryland	16.0	23.0	7.2	8.3	0.0	6.3	7.2	0.3
24	18750	College Park city, Maryland	18.6	17.1	3.5	7.3	0.0	4.4	0.5	0.2
24	19125	Columbia CDP, Maryland	11.5	18.9	3.5	4.6	0.1	2.5	4.6	1.0
24	20875	Crofton CDP, Maryland	8.1	23.4	6.1	3.1	0.0	6.5	1.6	3.5
24	21325	Cumberland city, Maryland	20.3	28.6	5.4	15.8	0.0	2.2	8.4	5.9
24	23975	Dundalk CDP, Maryland	19.4	28.0	11.8	15.2	0.5	7.3	8.1	4.5
24	25150	Edgewood CDP, Maryland	14.2	29.9	7.9	12.5	0.0	5.2	6.3	6.5

Table E. Cities—Labor Force, Employment, and Educational Data, 2015—*Continued*

FIPS state code	FIPS place code	State/city	Percent in each occupation group				Percent in each industry sector			
			Service occupations	Sales and office occupations	Natural resources, construction, and maintenance occupations	Production, transportation, and material moving occupations	Agriculture, forestry, fishing and hunting, and mining	Construction	Manufacturing	Wholesale trade
24	25575	Eldersburg CDP, Maryland	15.8	20.8	7.3	4.3	1.1	6.6	4.7	1.5
24	26000	Ellicott City CDP, Maryland	11.0	17.7	2.9	5.8	0.0	2.6	6.9	1.5
24	26600	Essex CDP, Maryland	22.2	30.2	12.1	10.3	0.0	10.4	8.7	2.2
24	27250	Fairland CDP, Maryland	23.4	21.8	4.6	10.2	0.0	3.7	1.6	2.5
24	29525	Fort Washington CDP, Maryland	20.2	18.3	9.1	4.1	0.0	3.4	0.8	0.4
24	30325	Frederick city, Maryland	17.3	24.1	9.1	7.4	1.4	7.4	4.5	2.0
24	31175	Gaithersburg city, Maryland	21.1	19.2	8.0	3.8	0.1	6.7	4.9	1.1
24	32025	Germantown CDP, Maryland	14.8	22.3	4.5	5.5	0.2	5.7	4.1	1.5
24	32650	Glen Burnie CDP, Maryland	18.1	24.6	11.1	11.5	0.0	8.1	7.5	2.5
24	34775	Greenbelt city, Maryland	14.4	25.2	7.5	4.2	0.0	9.6	1.7	1.7
24	36075	Hagerstown city, Maryland	17.9	28.7	9.7	14.7	0.0	8.7	7.9	1.5
24	41475	Ilchester CDP, Maryland	18.5	15.3	5.5	4.6	0.0	3.2	4.3	3.4
24	45325	Landover CDP, Maryland	40.4	18.2	10.5	8.1	0.0	6.1	0.7	2.0
24	45525	Langley Park CDP, Maryland	32.7	9.2	40.9	9.4	0.7	41.0	1.0	1.1
24	45900	Laurel city, Maryland	17.5	23.6	5.5	4.9	0.0	2.9	0.2	3.9
24	47450	Lochearn CDP, Maryland	21.8	30.4	7.3	9.7	0.0	6.8	3.5	0.9
24	52300	Middle River CDP, Maryland	19.5	29.5	6.4	15.1	0.3	6.5	9.2	2.2
24	52562	Milford Mill CDP, Maryland	20.0	36.1	4.0	10.7	0.0	4.6	2.9	1.5
24	53325	Montgomery Village CDP, Maryland	22.3	18.5	9.3	9.3	0.0	10.8	2.7	2.4
24	56337	North Bethesda CDP, Maryland	19.7	13.2	4.5	2.4	0.0	4.7	1.5	1.0
24	56725	North Laurel CDP, Maryland	12.4	21.0	9.8	6.7	0.0	6.4	2.0	1.2
24	56875	North Potomac CDP, Maryland	5.5	17.7	0.9	0.5	0.0	2.0	3.8	0.7
24	58300	Odenton CDP, Maryland	14.3	21.6	4.7	9.3	0.9	4.9	4.4	3.7
24	58900	Olney CDP, Maryland	9.4	21.8	3.6	3.7	0.0	5.1	4.0	0.9
24	59425	Owings Mills CDP, Maryland	23.7	18.0	8.5	3.9	0.2	3.8	2.9	2.0
24	59500	Oxon Hill CDP, Maryland	21.0	25.1	15.5	2.5	0.0	12.9	0.3	1.2
24	60275	Parkville CDP, Maryland	18.6	30.3	6.8	9.9	0.0	4.2	3.2	1.8
24	60475	Pasadena CDP, Maryland	18.5	24.3	6.4	10.2	0.0	5.4	4.4	2.8
24	60975	Perry Hall CDP, Maryland	13.8	32.5	3.3	5.5	0.0	4.9	6.6	4.6
24	61400	Pikesville CDP, Maryland	9.6	24.0	0.7	1.9	0.0	4.0	7.0	1.7
24	63300	Potomac CDP, Maryland	6.1	17.6	0.1	2.3	0.2	0.9	4.3	1.7
24	64950	Randallstown CDP, Maryland	14.8	30.2	4.7	10.0	0.0	3.8	3.1	0.5
24	65600	Reisterstown CDP, Maryland	21.6	27.6	7.2	5.3	0.5	8.1	5.3	2.5
24	67675	Rockville city, Maryland	9.8	17.6	5.1	2.8	0.1	5.6	1.8	1.4
24	69925	Salisbury city, Maryland	25.5	25.9	8.6	15.5	1.2	8.0	15.0	0.8
24	71150	Severn CDP, Maryland	18.3	20.1	5.3	8.1	0.0	3.7	5.7	1.5
24	71200	Severna Park CDP, Maryland	7.8	17.1	5.3	6.5	0.2	8.6	5.2	3.8
24	72450	Silver Spring CDP, Maryland	17.6	14.9	8.6	5.9	0.5	6.9	2.4	0.3
24	73650	South Laurel CDP, Maryland	18.4	19.0	12.0	8.1	0.0	8.3	1.3	3.3
24	75725	Suitland CDP, Maryland	23.5	31.9	6.5	16.5	0.0	7.4	0.9	1.3
24	78425	Towson CDP, Maryland	13.2	25.4	1.7	4.0	0.1	1.4	3.3	2.5
24	81175	Waldorf CDP, Maryland	23.8	24.5	7.6	7.8	0.3	6.6	3.4	1.4
24	83775	Wheaton CDP, Maryland	25.5	17.4	13.3	6.1	0.0	11.6	3.7	0.7
24	86475	Woodlawn CDP (Baltimore County), Maryland	16.3	24.4	6.2	11.2	0.1	3.3	4.2	1.1
25	00000	**MASSACHUSETTS**	17.8	21.9	6.8	8.7	0.4	5.4	9.0	2.3
25	00840	Agawam Town city, Massachusetts	20.8	22.8	6.8	9.2	0.3	5.1	7.7	4.6
25	01640	Arlington CDP, Massachusetts	12.3	16.1	2.7	4.7	0.0	3.1	8.4	1.2
25	02690	Attleboro city, Massachusetts	15.6	21.1	6.7	13.9	0.4	5.5	13.5	2.0
25	03690	Barnstable Town city, Massachusetts	26.8	25.2	15.7	5.8	1.0	15.3	3.8	2.5
25	05105	Belmont CDP, Massachusetts	10.1	14.2	2.3	3.0	0.0	3.3	10.2	0.3
25	05595	Beverly city, Massachusetts	22.5	17.7	6.7	5.9	0.0	5.0	9.9	0.4
25	07000	Boston city, Massachusetts	20.6	20.7	4.3	6.4	0.2	3.7	4.5	1.6
25	07740	Braintree Town city, Massachusetts	17.7	24.2	6.3	6.1	0.0	8.3	6.9	2.0
25	09000	Brockton city, Massachusetts	30.1	23.3	7.7	14.7	0.3	4.3	6.2	3.9
25	09210	Brookline CDP, Massachusetts	7.8	15.3	1.6	2.4	0.4	0.5	4.7	0.2
25	09875	Burlington CDP, Massachusetts	18.4	16.6	10.6	3.1	0.0	9.8	13.4	1.8
25	11000	Cambridge city, Massachusetts	7.8	12.3	1.4	3.4	0.1	1.6	6.5	1.2
25	13205	Chelsea city, Massachusetts	39.2	16.0	5.7	17.7	0.2	2.9	5.7	7.2
25	13660	Chicopee city, Massachusetts	18.3	28.3	6.9	16.8	0.3	3.2	15.1	1.4
25	16285	Danvers CDP, Massachusetts	12.5	29.4	6.1	11.0	0.0	10.8	9.9	2.1
25	16530	Dedham CDP, Massachusetts	13.4	27.5	6.4	7.4	0.2	5.4	4.8	3.4
25	21990	Everett city, Massachusetts	29.2	24.4	11.6	13.1	0.0	9.1	6.8	1.8
25	23000	Fall River city, Massachusetts	23.3	21.8	10.9	18.5	0.0	9.0	16.1	2.1
25	23875	Fitchburg city, Massachusetts	18.9	28.8	8.8	17.3	0.0	5.8	16.3	5.5
25	24960	Framingham CDP, Massachusetts	19.8	19.8	11.8	5.8	1.2	9.6	8.3	1.6
25	25172	Franklin Town city, Massachusetts	6.3	21.0	8.8	3.6	0.0	7.3	12.2	3.0
25	25485	Gardner city, Massachusetts	24.5	20.0	6.9	20.1	1.3	4.2	12.4	2.6
25	26150	Gloucester city, Massachusetts	20.7	21.1	7.4	13.2	0.7	5.7	13.1	3.6
25	29405	Haverhill city, Massachusetts	19.1	25.0	7.5	9.3	0.0	7.2	10.5	2.3
25	30840	Holyoke city, Massachusetts	25.3	22.8	6.5	12.6	0.0	6.4	11.2	3.5
25	34550	Lawrence city, Massachusetts	32.9	19.7	9.3	23.0	0.0	5.0	13.8	3.2
25	35075	Leominster city, Massachusetts	20.7	24.3	7.9	12.8	0.2	5.2	14.2	2.5
25	35250	Lexington CDP, Massachusetts	7.4	8.4	0.3	4.4	0.0	1.3	13.4	1.1

Table E. Cities—Labor Force, Employment, and Educational Data, 2015—*Continued*

FIPS state code	FIPS place code	State/city	Percent in each occupation group				Percent in each industry sector			
			Service occupations	Sales and office occupations	Natural resources, construction, and maintenance occupations	Production, transportation, and material moving occupations	Agriculture, forestry, fishing and hunting, and mining	Construction	Manufacturing	Wholesale trade
25	37000	Lowell city, Massachusetts	24.0	17.7	7.8	18.5	0.5	5.2	17.6	1.9
25	37490	Lynn city, Massachusetts	28.1	21.7	9.7	14.4	0.4	7.7	8.5	2.9
25	37875	Malden city, Massachusetts	22.4	21.8	5.7	8.8	0.0	4.6	5.6	1.0
25	38435	Marblehead CDP, Massachusetts	8.8	20.1	4.2	6.4	0.0	4.5	6.4	4.5
25	38715	Marlborough city, Massachusetts	19.5	18.8	9.6	8.6	0.0	9.8	12.2	1.8
25	39835	Medford city, Massachusetts	16.3	20.1	6.2	5.4	0.0	4.9	5.6	0.7
25	40115	Melrose city, Massachusetts	12.9	16.1	7.3	6.2	0.0	5.4	4.0	2.3
25	40710	Methuen Town city, Massachusetts	20.6	23.5	10.9	11.5	0.3	7.8	14.9	2.1
25	41200	Milford CDP, Massachusetts	18.8	26.3	10.1	8.0	0.0	7.8	9.5	0.5
25	41725	Milton CDP, Massachusetts	13.5	21.3	6.4	4.2	0.5	6.5	3.8	3.0
25	44140	Needham CDP, Massachusetts	10.7	15.0	6.5	0.8	0.0	7.1	3.7	0.6
25	45000	New Bedford city, Massachusetts	25.1	20.3	10.1	16.2	1.8	7.2	12.0	3.2
25	45560	Newton city, Massachusetts	9.4	15.0	2.6	2.5	0.0	2.6	5.5	1.3
25	46330	Northampton city, Massachusetts	15.3	15.3	2.5	6.6	0.0	2.4	2.2	0.0
25	50285	Norwood CDP, Massachusetts	16.1	28.6	4.5	3.9	0.0	3.8	8.5	2.6
25	52490	Peabody city, Massachusetts	20.9	24.0	3.8	9.4	0.6	4.7	7.7	2.7
25	53960	Pittsfield city, Massachusetts	30.0	22.4	8.6	12.4	0.3	3.8	10.3	2.6
25	55745	Quincy city, Massachusetts	21.1	24.3	5.7	8.2	0.2	3.9	7.3	1.0
25	55990	Randolph CDP, Massachusetts	19.9	23.3	9.3	10.9	0.0	8.4	4.5	0.9
25	56165	Reading CDP, Massachusetts	6.6	20.4	8.4	1.8	1.0	5.8	13.8	3.0
25	56585	Revere city, Massachusetts	29.8	21.3	13.2	12.6	0.6	9.8	4.0	1.9
25	59105	Salem city, Massachusetts	27.9	21.9	4.8	8.6	0.0	3.1	8.1	1.3
25	60050	Saugus CDP, Massachusetts	19.9	27.5	7.3	11.1	0.0	5.7	5.9	2.3
25	62465	Somerset CDP, Massachusetts	21.5	26.3	4.2	7.3	0.0	3.6	11.8	5.4
25	62535	Somerville city, Massachusetts	13.3	12.2	3.4	6.0	0.1	3.3	7.4	2.5
25	67000	Springfield city, Massachusetts	27.6	25.7	5.8	15.4	1.7	3.0	11.3	1.6
25	67700	Stoneham CDP, Massachusetts	13.9	27.2	10.6	3.7	0.0	6.4	7.9	1.7
25	69170	Taunton city, Massachusetts	14.9	29.3	10.1	12.4	0.0	7.3	11.5	4.7
25	72250	Wakefield CDP, Massachusetts	11.9	25.0	4.8	6.2	0.0	6.0	7.8	3.4
25	72600	Waltham city, Massachusetts	14.9	23.8	6.6	4.8	0.0	5.4	9.4	1.7
25	73440	Watertown Town city, Massachusetts	12.5	20.3	3.0	4.8	0.0	3.2	7.8	1.0
25	74210	Wellesley CDP, Massachusetts	9.5	23.6	0.6	1.1	0.0	2.4	4.5	2.9
25	76030	Westfield city, Massachusetts	16.7	23.0	6.5	16.0	0.8	2.5	8.4	6.3
25	77890	West Springfield Town city, Massachusetts	21.5	25.8	5.9	11.7	0.0	5.3	10.8	2.5
25	78972	Weymouth Town city, Massachusetts	16.4	23.2	9.0	9.2	0.6	5.7	7.9	2.0
25	80195	Wilmington CDP, Massachusetts	17.7	27.4	8.4	8.6	0.0	10.4	9.5	3.4
25	80545	Winchester CDP, Massachusetts	5.1	19.7	2.2	2.3	0.0	2.2	12.9	3.0
25	81035	Woburn city, Massachusetts	23.0	23.0	9.5	8.9	0.0	10.2	7.3	2.5
25	82000	Worcester city, Massachusetts	21.8	22.8	8.0	12.1	0.3	6.2	9.3	1.8
26	00000	**MICHIGAN**	18.0	23.0	8.0	15.9	1.2	5.1	18.1	2.5
26	00440	Adrian city, Michigan	24.8	27.2	8.0	21.2	0.0	4.7	17.9	0.0
26	01340	Allendale CDP, Michigan	19.7	30.7	7.8	13.3	2.0	3.8	11.5	1.8
26	01380	Allen Park city, Michigan	14.9	29.9	7.3	13.4	0.0	3.0	14.3	4.2
26	03000	Ann Arbor city, Michigan	12.2	16.2	1.9	4.4	0.4	1.5	6.2	0.8
26	04105	Auburn Hills city, Michigan	16.1	23.0	4.8	12.0	0.0	4.7	25.9	2.7
26	05920	Battle Creek city, Michigan	21.7	19.7	4.0	30.8	0.0	0.8	31.7	0.6
26	06020	Bay City city, Michigan	20.3	36.4	11.9	9.9	0.0	8.1	9.8	2.5
26	08640	Birmingham city, Michigan	5.1	19.7	2.5	3.5	1.2	3.7	14.5	1.9
26	12060	Burton city, Michigan	17.8	24.5	8.5	23.8	0.8	5.4	12.7	3.6
26	21000	Dearborn city, Michigan	17.5	25.3	5.7	13.8	0.1	2.8	14.4	3.4
26	21020	Dearborn Heights city, Michigan	16.6	25.1	12.2	18.2	0.3	6.9	14.1	2.9
26	22000	Detroit city, Michigan	27.4	24.1	5.8	20.3	0.4	3.1	14.0	1.7
26	24120	East Lansing city, Michigan	23.2	24.9	2.1	5.9	0.0	0.5	4.8	0.3
26	24290	Eastpointe city, Michigan	27.2	21.2	10.0	19.4	0.0	5.7	22.4	2.0
26	27440	Farmington Hills city, Michigan	12.2	22.4	3.5	7.5	0.5	2.2	15.4	3.2
26	27880	Ferndale city, Michigan	22.2	18.1	5.9	5.2	0.0	2.8	11.3	0.8
26	29000	Flint city, Michigan	26.6	24.0	10.5	17.9	0.5	6.3	14.5	1.5
26	29580	Forest Hills CDP, Michigan	10.8	23.3	2.4	6.7	0.0	1.7	15.3	2.2
26	31420	Garden City city, Michigan	18.3	17.7	17.7	25.0	0.0	9.6	23.0	5.6
26	34000	Grand Rapids city, Michigan	19.9	23.2	8.0	17.0	2.2	3.9	16.8	3.2
26	36280	Hamtramck city, Michigan	16.5	22.9	5.9	36.1	0.0	4.3	34.0	1.5
26	37100	Haslett CDP, Michigan	12.5	14.4	7.4	6.9	0.1	5.7	4.1	4.8
26	38640	Holland city, Michigan	12.7	26.6	5.2	27.6	0.0	4.3	30.0	1.0
26	38780	Holt CDP, Michigan	11.6	28.6	7.2	10.2	0.4	1.4	8.9	0.9
26	40680	Inkster city, Michigan	18.6	23.8	6.1	32.1	0.0	3.0	14.8	7.5
26	41420	Jackson city, Michigan	31.3	19.9	7.0	17.5	0.7	4.7	19.0	1.1
26	42160	Kalamazoo city, Michigan	23.3	25.2	5.8	10.8	0.8	2.0	14.0	0.4
26	42820	Kentwood city, Michigan	17.1	23.5	5.1	22.3	1.2	2.9	19.9	4.1
26	46000	Lansing city, Michigan	23.3	24.3	6.7	14.1	0.2	3.6	8.9	1.6
26	47800	Lincoln Park city, Michigan	17.6	29.4	11.1	24.2	0.2	5.7	17.8	1.1

Table E. Cities—Labor Force, Employment, and Educational Data, 2015—*Continued*

FIPS state code	FIPS place code	State/city	Percent in each occupation group				Percent in each industry sector			
			Service occupations	Sales and office occupations	Natural resources, construction, and maintenance occupations	Production, transportation, and material moving occupations	Agriculture, forestry, fishing and hunting, and mining	Construction	Manufacturing	Wholesale trade
26	49000	Livonia city, Michigan	13.9	25.7	6.5	10.3	0.4	4.8	15.5	3.8
26	50560	Madison Heights city, Michigan	17.5	20.7	8.8	21.4	0.0	7.0	20.1	1.9
26	51900	Marquette city, Michigan	28.2	22.2	10.9	4.3	0.8	10.3	2.1	1.7
26	53780	Midland city, Michigan	15.3	22.3	4.5	7.2	0.3	4.9	27.8	1.1
26	55020	Monroe city, Michigan	18.7	28.1	8.8	21.7	0.3	8.2	17.6	3.3
26	56020	Mount Pleasant city, Michigan	25.4	22.6	5.3	9.4	0.4	2.6	6.8	1.8
26	56320	Muskegon city, Michigan	27.1	14.3	6.7	23.0	0.0	6.8	21.9	1.8
26	59140	Norton Shores city, Michigan	20.2	26.1	6.8	18.5	0.0	7.2	22.1	0.9
26	59440	Novi city, Michigan	12.6	19.0	5.2	4.9	0.0	3.5	28.4	3.9
26	59920	Oak Park city, Michigan	26.4	25.3	5.1	13.4	0.0	3.9	9.8	0.0
26	60340	Okemos CDP, Michigan	12.7	18.8	3.2	2.4	1.5	3.0	6.8	3.4
26	65440	Pontiac city, Michigan	33.7	17.8	8.3	17.0	0.0	7.6	10.9	0.4
26	65560	Portage city, Michigan	20.6	24.8	3.3	8.2	0.8	1.8	16.2	1.6
26	65820	Port Huron city, Michigan	26.9	22.5	6.1	25.5	0.0	5.8	25.9	0.3
26	69035	Rochester Hills city, Michigan	10.3	25.5	3.9	5.0	0.0	3.1	21.9	4.1
26	69420	Romulus city, Michigan	18.8	20.8	4.9	34.9	0.0	1.9	16.8	0.9
26	69800	Roseville city, Michigan	22.7	26.7	9.2	20.5	0.2	6.1	20.1	1.9
26	70040	Royal Oak city, Michigan	9.6	23.5	2.8	4.1	0.0	3.4	14.0	2.9
26	70520	Saginaw city, Michigan	32.7	21.1	7.5	23.7	1.4	4.9	14.2	0.9
26	70760	St. Clair Shores city, Michigan	18.5	25.6	9.9	13.4	0.1	4.9	18.7	2.6
26	74900	Southfield city, Michigan	16.2	24.0	3.4	13.2	0.0	3.1	13.7	1.0
26	74960	Southgate city, Michigan	18.6	16.9	10.1	25.8	0.3	6.4	23.7	1.6
26	76460	Sterling Heights city, Michigan	16.1	23.7	5.4	19.2	0.1	3.2	21.6	2.7
26	79000	Taylor city, Michigan	18.0	25.6	12.1	20.8	0.4	4.1	19.2	2.1
26	80700	Troy city, Michigan	11.2	17.5	4.0	5.4	0.2	2.6	19.9	2.9
26	82960	Walker city, Michigan	19.8	26.9	8.0	16.3	0.9	6.7	17.4	2.9
26	84000	Warren city, Michigan	16.2	25.4	6.6	23.7	0.5	4.1	25.1	3.3
26	84800	Waverly CDP, Michigan	20.8	23.9	6.8	13.0	0.4	3.7	13.0	2.3
26	86000	Westland city, Michigan	17.0	28.1	6.1	20.0	0.3	4.3	20.5	4.5
26	88900	Wyandotte city, Michigan	20.0	28.5	12.3	11.6	0.2	4.6	12.8	2.3
26	88940	Wyoming city, Michigan	16.4	22.6	9.0	29.8	0.3	4.8	28.9	6.0
26	89140	Ypsilanti city, Michigan	25.5	24.5	5.3	10.3	0.3	3.4	7.9	1.6
27	00000	**MINNESOTA**	16.3	22.3	8.2	13.0	2.2	6.1	13.4	2.9
27	01486	Andover city, Minnesota	16.6	19.5	11.5	8.4	0.5	6.3	17.1	3.3
27	01900	Apple Valley city, Minnesota	14.8	26.6	6.3	9.4	0.0	4.2	11.5	4.3
27	02908	Austin city, Minnesota	19.6	15.8	9.1	25.5	3.4	7.2	25.8	1.1
27	06382	Blaine city, Minnesota	16.9	22.6	6.2	13.3	0.3	4.8	13.3	2.1
27	06616	Bloomington city, Minnesota	14.9	27.9	6.9	9.6	0.0	5.6	9.3	4.1
27	07948	Brooklyn Center city, Minnesota	21.4	22.1	6.1	17.5	0.4	4.1	13.6	3.3
27	07966	Brooklyn Park city, Minnesota	21.7	23.1	5.1	14.6	0.5	4.3	17.5	1.2
27	08794	Burnsville city, Minnesota	16.9	24.0	5.1	10.7	0.0	3.2	11.7	2.5
27	10846	Champlin city, Minnesota	12.0	25.4	8.3	8.0	1.6	6.4	15.6	1.7
27	10918	Chanhassen, Minnesota	8.4	25.7	2.4	5.2	0.4	3.5	15.7	4.7
27	10972	Chaska city, Minnesota	14.0	27.7	5.2	12.7	0.0	5.9	14.5	2.8
27	13114	Coon Rapids city, Minnesota	16.4	29.0	7.0	13.2	0.9	5.2	17.2	2.4
27	13456	Cottage Grove city, Minnesota	20.4	24.0	10.3	10.5	0.5	7.9	15.8	2.3
27	14158	Crystal city, Minnesota	14.1	27.1	4.9	11.9	0.7	5.6	12.8	2.7
27	17000	Duluth city, Minnesota	23.0	24.0	3.4	9.7	0.1	3.0	5.4	1.9
27	17288	Eagan city, Minnesota	12.8	22.9	4.8	11.1	1.4	2.0	13.0	2.9
27	18116	Eden Prairie city, Minnesota	11.2	24.4	2.7	5.0	0.3	2.8	14.9	3.8
27	18188	Edina city, Minnesota	11.5	23.2	1.1	5.5	0.5	1.2	13.4	4.6
27	18674	Elk River city, Minnesota	15.1	20.1	13.9	6.4	1.4	11.2	12.5	4.1
27	20546	Faribault city, Minnesota	21.6	17.6	11.5	31.1	2.4	8.0	25.2	1.8
27	20618	Farmington city, Minnesota	10.2	27.8	9.8	11.8	2.7	8.6	9.5	6.1
27	22814	Fridley city, Minnesota	16.4	30.1	8.0	15.0	1.3	7.1	12.5	2.5
27	24308	Golden Valley city, Minnesota	10.1	22.6	5.2	7.2	0.0	4.2	13.8	0.0
27	27530	Hastings city, Minnesota	15.2	30.7	6.9	17.6	1.2	3.9	13.3	4.1
27	31076	Inver Grove Heights city, Minnesota	17.3	20.1	8.2	13.2	0.0	7.3	10.9	3.4
27	35180	Lakeville city, Minnesota	11.3	26.3	4.8	12.7	0.2	4.0	12.0	3.0
27	37322	Lino Lakes city, Minnesota	11.2	23.2	6.1	11.6	0.0	6.6	13.7	3.0
27	39878	Mankato city, Minnesota	23.6	23.4	6.2	14.0	1.1	3.5	11.8	1.9
27	40166	Maple Grove city, Minnesota	9.4	26.5	3.7	6.5	0.6	5.5	15.9	3.9
27	40382	Maplewood city, Minnesota	13.2	20.2	7.4	14.6	0.6	6.6	12.7	3.2
27	43000	Minneapolis city, Minnesota	17.8	19.6	4.4	9.1	0.3	3.7	8.0	2.4
27	43252	Minnetonka city, Minnesota	8.7	24.9	4.0	8.0	0.3	3.5	8.9	4.2
27	43864	Moorhead city, Minnesota	20.2	27.6	8.4	10.2	1.3	7.1	7.4	3.0
27	45430	New Brighton city, Minnesota	18.8	19.7	5.1	13.7	0.0	5.9	18.8	2.5
27	45628	New Hope city, Minnesota	15.7	24.1	5.5	9.7	1.8	4.7	12.3	4.1
27	46924	Northfield city, Minnesota	19.1	23.3	6.7	9.5	0.0	5.1	7.3	3.3
27	47680	Oakdale city, Minnesota	24.7	21.6	4.1	10.9	0.8	2.1	15.0	1.7
27	49300	Owatonna city, Minnesota	14.1	24.8	6.3	18.4	1.8	3.1	22.9	3.3
27	51730	Plymouth city, Minnesota	10.6	24.1	3.0	6.9	0.0	2.7	14.1	3.7
27	52594	Prior Lake city, Minnesota	12.1	24.0	7.1	8.6	0.0	6.3	9.7	5.3

Table E. Cities—Labor Force, Employment, and Educational Data, 2015—*Continued*

FIPS state code	FIPS place code	State/city	Percent in each occupation group				Percent in each industry sector			
			Service occupations	Sales and office occupations	Natural resources, construction, and maintenance occupations	Production, transportation, and material moving occupations	Agriculture, forestry, fishing and hunting, and mining	Construction	Manufacturing	Wholesale trade
27	53026	Ramsey city, Minnesota	13.2	26.2	8.3	14.2	1.3	9.4	16.8	1.1
27	54214	Richfield city, Minnesota	18.7	18.3	6.2	10.0	0.7	6.9	7.7	2.3
27	54880	Rochester city, Minnesota	15.2	18.0	4.5	8.8	1.7	2.5	8.6	1.4
27	55726	Rosemount city, Minnesota	15.8	27.3	6.2	10.1	0.2	3.7	9.2	2.7
27	55852	Roseville city, Minnesota	14.4	19.4	2.7	10.4	0.2	2.2	8.7	3.5
27	56896	St. Cloud city, Minnesota	25.4	25.4	3.2	18.5	0.5	3.1	11.0	2.3
27	57220	St. Louis Park city, Minnesota	11.9	20.5	2.6	5.6	0.3	2.4	10.0	2.5
27	58000	St. Paul city, Minnesota	20.7	20.5	4.5	13.4	0.1	3.2	12.2	2.7
27	58738	Savage city, Minnesota	10.6	20.7	8.0	12.1	1.0	5.2	14.9	4.0
27	59350	Shakopee city, Minnesota	11.7	27.7	10.4	14.5	1.0	6.3	18.6	1.6
27	59998	Shoreview city, Minnesota	10.9	23.1	3.2	7.2	0.5	2.5	12.8	2.5
27	61492	South St. Paul city, Minnesota	18.5	23.9	6.8	13.5	0.0	6.3	13.9	3.1
27	69970	White Bear Lake city, Minnesota	14.9	23.0	9.2	9.7	0.0	8.6	6.8	4.1
27	71032	Winona city, Minnesota	23.4	23.0	6.2	14.3	0.3	5.1	15.8	5.2
27	71428	Woodbury city, Minnesota	12.3	19.1	2.7	5.6	0.2	3.3	13.5	3.3
28	00000	**MISSISSIPPI**	17.6	23.6	10.8	17.3	2.9	6.9	13.6	2.7
28	06220	Biloxi city, Mississippi	25.5	19.6	13.1	8.8	0.7	11.4	6.8	2.7
28	08300	Brandon city, Mississippi	18.8	24.0	4.6	4.8	0.2	3.1	15.3	2.5
28	14420	Clinton city, Mississippi	18.0	26.9	4.6	8.6	0.0	3.0	5.5	6.5
28	15380	Columbus city, Mississippi	16.2	28.9	1.5	24.7	0.9	4.8	14.2	5.1
28	29180	Greenville city, Mississippi	18.0	29.3	4.9	17.5	1.1	4.3	4.3	3.9
28	29700	Gulfport city, Mississippi	25.8	26.1	11.4	11.0	1.0	4.1	7.0	3.7
28	31020	Hattiesburg city, Mississippi	16.3	33.6	7.6	10.2	0.7	5.8	5.3	3.1
28	33700	Horn Lake city, Mississippi	16.1	28.3	19.1	18.0	0.9	12.3	8.6	2.3
28	36000	Jackson city, Mississippi	23.9	23.7	5.4	14.8	0.2	3.8	7.6	1.2
28	44520	Madison city, Mississippi	10.7	27.0	9.6	3.2	0.8	12.3	5.1	3.7
28	46640	Meridian city, Mississippi	19.1	25.5	5.9	12.9	0.9	0.9	10.2	3.6
28	54040	Olive Branch city, Mississippi	12.4	30.7	5.1	17.2	0.2	4.6	10.9	4.7
28	54840	Oxford city, Mississippi	13.5	23.0	5.3	2.4	0.0	5.6	1.9	0.0
28	55360	Pascagoula city, Mississippi	21.3	21.5	14.1	18.1	2.4	4.8	20.9	0.2
28	55760	Pearl city, Mississippi	26.6	20.0	10.8	12.7	2.1	4.4	10.7	2.7
28	62520	Ridgeland city, Mississippi	11.7	29.8	7.9	7.5	0.6	6.2	9.3	2.7
28	69280	Southaven city, Mississippi	15.4	26.2	7.8	15.9	1.2	5.6	7.0	6.8
28	70240	Starkville city, Mississippi	14.8	20.1	3.4	10.2	0.0	2.5	7.2	4.0
28	74840	Tupelo city, Mississippi	20.3	23.5	7.6	21.6	2.2	2.7	17.7	1.2
28	76720	Vicksburg city, Mississippi	26.7	17.7	8.9	15.7	0.7	2.9	12.9	2.7
29	00000	**MISSOURI**	17.6	24.4	9.0	13.6	1.8	6.4	11.5	2.7
29	00280	Affton CDP, Missouri	22.9	27.6	5.8	10.4	0.0	2.8	8.9	3.0
29	01972	Arnold city, Missouri	22.1	29.3	11.1	15.0	0.7	7.9	8.7	1.7
29	03160	Ballwin city, Missouri	12.4	26.1	2.6	3.6	0.3	2.6	8.1	1.3
29	04384	Belton city, Missouri	23.0	24.8	10.1	14.1	0.0	7.6	7.7	1.5
29	06652	Blue Springs city, Missouri	13.8	26.1	7.8	14.4	0.0	6.0	10.6	2.9
29	11242	Cape Girardeau city, Missouri	15.5	25.1	5.9	10.7	0.5	4.2	12.0	2.0
29	13600	Chesterfield city, Missouri	7.1	18.6	1.7	5.8	0.9	3.7	14.4	4.9
29	15670	Columbia city, Missouri	14.7	26.8	4.4	7.2	0.4	3.2	5.6	1.4
29	16030	Concord CDP, Missouri	15.8	23.4	6.9	7.9	0.0	3.7	8.9	3.4
29	23986	Ferguson city, Missouri	21.1	25.6	2.9	20.5	0.0	1.5	13.0	2.8
29	24778	Florissant city, Missouri	20.8	25.0	8.2	14.0	0.0	3.5	10.7	2.0
29	25264	Fort Leonard Wood CDP, Missouri	–	–	–	–	–	–	–	–
29	27190	Gladstone city, Missouri	17.5	24.6	5.5	16.9	2.0	5.0	10.3	2.0
29	28324	Grandview city, Missouri	18.2	30.2	8.1	15.3	0.0	7.6	11.5	4.0
29	31276	Hazelwood city, Missouri	17.3	26.3	5.5	21.1	0.0	4.9	21.4	1.2
29	35000	Independence city, Missouri	20.0	30.8	8.3	16.5	0.1	4.9	15.2	4.3
29	37000	Jefferson City city, Missouri	15.2	23.5	4.1	15.5	0.6	4.0	10.8	0.9
29	37592	Joplin city, Missouri	23.4	24.5	8.7	11.9	0.4	3.9	10.3	1.2
29	38000	Kansas City city, Missouri	18.7	24.4	7.0	13.1	0.4	5.9	8.0	3.1
29	39044	Kirkwood city, Missouri	7.0	24.8	2.8	7.0	0.4	3.3	10.1	5.8
29	41348	Lee's Summit city, Missouri	14.6	23.0	5.1	5.9	0.2	3.2	8.5	2.2
29	42032	Liberty city, Missouri	21.0	23.5	6.3	14.4	0.8	2.8	12.4	3.6
29	46586	Maryland Heights city, Missouri	12.4	21.8	7.4	8.8	0.0	6.6	13.8	0.8
29	47180	Mehlville CDP, Missouri	17.7	27.0	7.0	17.2	0.0	4.8	10.1	8.7
29	52616	Nixa city, Missouri	18.1	25.1	6.5	10.1	1.1	4.4	9.3	1.6
29	53876	Oakville CDP, Missouri	17.1	28.9	7.6	6.8	0.2	6.5	9.5	5.0
29	54074	O'Fallon city, Missouri	12.8	25.6	8.3	12.0	0.3	7.2	13.8	1.6
29	60752	Raymore city, Missouri	13.6	23.6	6.0	8.9	0.9	4.6	7.6	4.5
29	60788	Raytown city, Missouri	20.4	29.9	9.3	7.7	0.0	5.6	8.9	1.4
29	62912	Rolla city, Missouri	24.1	16.2	8.5	9.1	–	–	–	–
29	64082	St. Charles city, Missouri	18.6	23.5	7.0	9.9	0.4	5.7	11.0	3.8
29	64550	St. Joseph city, Missouri	19.9	23.4	8.6	18.7	0.6	6.5	17.8	1.3
29	65000	St. Louis city, Missouri	20.6	21.9	4.7	10.7	0.7	3.8	8.3	2.1
29	65126	St. Peters city, Missouri	19.6	24.1	7.4	8.9	0.1	3.2	12.5	2.5
29	66440	Sedalia city, Missouri	20.0	21.8	7.0	28.9	0.0	1.1	24.3	2.0
29	70000	Springfield city, Missouri	21.5	27.9	6.7	11.3	0.4	4.9	8.6	2.3
29	75220	University City city, Missouri	15.9	23.9	5.1	7.1	0.0	0.6	7.7	2.1

Table E. Cities—Labor Force, Employment, and Educational Data, 2015—Continued

FIPS state code	FIPS place code	State/city	Percent in each occupation group				Percent in each industry sector			
			Service occupations	Sales and office occupations	Natural resources, construction, and maintenance occupations	Production, transportation, and material moving occupations	Agriculture, forestry, fishing and hunting, and mining	Construction	Manufacturing	Wholesale trade
29	78154	Webster Groves city, Missouri	11.5	27.1	0.9	5.4	0.4	1.7	9.2	4.1
29	78442	Wentzville city, Missouri	22.0	24.5	7.2	9.3	0.5	8.0	7.8	2.4
29	79820	Wildwood city, Missouri	10.1	34.6	3.8	4.7	1.0	3.9	6.8	4.9
30	00000	**MONTANA**	18.7	21.3	13.7	8.2	7.0	9.3	4.1	2.4
30	06550	Billings city, Montana	20.3	21.5	13.0	8.1	2.0	9.4	4.4	2.8
30	08950	Bozeman city, Montana	18.6	25.0	9.3	7.1	2.4	9.0	3.5	1.8
30	11397	Butte-Silver Bow (balance), Montana	21.7	15.6	9.4	9.8	4.2	6.0	4.9	2.0
30	32800	Great Falls city, Montana	21.4	22.4	11.0	10.1	2.7	6.5	4.9	1.6
30	35600	Helena city, Montana	15.2	20.5	9.6	4.8	0.0	7.9	2.4	0.7
30	40075	Kalispell city, Montana	14.2	27.7	14.4	5.4	1.8	14.3	5.0	1.4
30	50200	Missoula city, Montana	22.1	21.4	6.7	6.3	2.3	5.7	1.1	2.4
31	00000	**NEBRASKA**	16.6	23.5	10.1	13.3	4.5	6.9	10.5	3.1
31	03950	Bellevue city, Nebraska	15.2	25.4	11.9	10.8	0.9	7.6	6.7	4.4
31	10110	Columbus city, Nebraska	10.7	20.7	12.5	26.2	2.4	8.8	31.3	1.4
31	17670	Fremont city, Nebraska	14.0	32.0	8.9	18.8	3.7	5.0	15.7	3.5
31	19595	Grand Island city, Nebraska	19.1	23.8	11.7	20.9	3.3	7.0	19.5	4.6
31	21415	Hastings city, Nebraska	16.5	18.9	11.1	16.7	2.1	10.5	14.7	4.7
31	25055	Kearney city, Nebraska	25.1	26.5	8.2	12.4	2.2	6.4	9.3	1.7
31	28000	Lincoln city, Nebraska	18.2	23.5	8.3	10.6	0.8	6.7	9.1	2.0
31	34615	Norfolk city, Nebraska	18.4	23.2	11.9	16.1	2.4	9.7	16.0	3.9
31	35000	North Platte city, Nebraska	18.3	22.8	8.3	12.9	2.0	5.3	2.1	1.8
31	37000	Omaha city, Nebraska	17.4	25.6	7.6	11.6	1.1	6.4	8.6	2.5
31	38295	Papillion city, Nebraska	20.8	19.0	5.9	7.6	0.3	3.6	7.2	6.7
32	00000	**NEVADA**	27.4	26.2	8.8	10.2	1.6	6.2	4.5	2.0
32	09700	Carson City, Nevada	22.1	25.1	11.4	15.7	0.3	6.1	14.6	0.7
32	22500	Elko city, Nevada	23.8	20.0	16.9	15.9	26.5	3.8	2.4	2.0
32	23770	Enterprise CDP, Nevada	30.2	25.9	5.4	7.9	0.7	2.9	4.0	2.1
32	31900	Henderson city, Nevada	22.9	26.7	6.7	7.6	0.2	6.0	5.5	1.8
32	40000	Las Vegas city, Nevada	27.4	28.4	8.6	8.1	0.2	6.8	2.8	2.0
32	51800	North Las Vegas city, Nevada	28.5	23.7	11.5	12.9	0.7	8.4	4.2	2.4
32	53800	Pahrump CDP, Nevada	19.2	31.0	13.9	14.1	0.7	5.6	2.1	3.4
32	54600	Paradise CDP, Nevada	33.8	24.8	7.3	11.2	0.1	5.9	3.7	0.9
32	60600	Reno city, Nevada	23.6	26.5	6.8	9.2	0.9	5.5	6.0	2.9
32	68400	Sparks city, Nevada	19.1	29.8	8.0	14.3	0.3	6.8	8.3	5.3
32	68585	Spring Valley CDP, Nevada	35.1	27.5	5.2	10.2	0.1	3.8	2.5	1.5
32	70900	Summerlin South CDP, Nevada	18.2	32.3	4.4	2.9	0.0	1.1	4.9	5.4
32	71400	Sunrise Manor CDP, Nevada	39.6	22.4	12.0	12.1	0.3	8.1	3.2	1.2
32	71600	Sun Valley CDP, Nevada	22.7	31.8	16.3	17.7	0.0	9.9	7.0	2.6
32	83800	Whitney CDP, Nevada	27.9	31.6	11.0	10.1	0.7	6.0	5.8	0.4
32	84600	Winchester CDP, Nevada	41.2	16.7	7.6	13.8	1.1	6.4	2.8	1.8
33	00000	**NEW HAMPSHIRE**	15.9	23.7	8.5	11.7	0.8	6.6	12.7	2.9
33	14200	Concord city, New Hampshire	19.6	23.6	5.7	8.6	0.4	3.7	7.1	1.7
33	17860	Derry CDP, New Hampshire	18.0	31.9	6.6	17.9	0.9	7.4	10.2	2.3
33	18820	Dover city, New Hampshire	16.7	19.8	4.3	10.4	0.6	2.3	13.7	0.2
33	39300	Keene city, New Hampshire	20.8	22.1	6.5	10.3	1.0	4.4	8.7	4.6
33	45140	Manchester city, New Hampshire	20.6	25.8	7.0	13.1	0.1	4.4	10.8	2.5
33	50260	Nashua city, New Hampshire	18.2	27.0	6.8	12.3	0.2	5.1	16.6	3.4
33	62900	Portsmouth city, New Hampshire	12.1	23.1	4.5	7.7	0.7	3.8	10.2	3.6
33	65140	Rochester city, New Hampshire	17.8	26.9	10.4	13.4	1.2	5.3	12.0	2.8
34	00000	**NEW JERSEY**	16.6	24.2	7.3	10.6	0.3	5.9	8.0	3.5
34	02080	Atlantic City city, New Jersey	38.0	29.8	5.3	8.9	0.0	3.1	3.1	2.0
34	02350	Avenel CDP, New Jersey	16.3	41.2	3.4	11.9	0.0	1.2	4.2	4.1
34	03580	Bayonne city, New Jersey	19.1	21.7	6.7	14.5	0.0	6.0	7.4	2.1
34	05170	Bergenfield borough, New Jersey	15.5	21.8	6.6	7.5	0.0	2.1	9.2	1.9
34	07600	Bridgeton city, New Jersey	18.7	23.2	20.9	22.7	13.9	4.1	17.5	6.3
34	10000	Camden city, New Jersey	28.8	22.9	10.2	20.9	0.6	5.2	6.0	5.9
34	10750	Carteret borough, New Jersey	12.2	31.3	5.9	19.8	0.0	2.6	4.5	6.2
34	13570	Cliffside Park borough, New Jersey	21.1	26.1	8.5	7.9	0.0	4.2	8.6	2.1
34	13690	Clifton city, New Jersey	16.2	24.7	8.0	21.6	0.0	4.1	15.3	2.9
34	19390	East Orange city, New Jersey	29.4	26.0	4.6	12.9	0.0	2.8	7.1	2.0
34	21000	Elizabeth city, New Jersey	25.7	22.1	9.5	25.3	0.1	6.7	10.8	4.3
34	21300	Elmwood Park borough, New Jersey	18.2	28.4	8.4	11.3	0.0	8.0	9.7	6.1
34	21480	Englewood city, New Jersey	23.9	25.5	5.8	5.4	0.0	3.4	3.2	1.5
34	22470	Fair Lawn borough, New Jersey	9.7	23.2	6.1	9.7	0.0	4.2	4.4	3.6
34	24420	Fort Lee borough, New Jersey	9.5	22.5	2.2	6.3	0.0	2.2	9.8	6.9
34	25770	Garfield city, New Jersey	10.0	25.3	9.6	23.0	0.5	7.7	13.3	3.8
34	28680	Hackensack city, New Jersey	20.2	19.9	7.1	14.3	0.0	5.3	8.1	2.9
34	32250	Hoboken city, New Jersey	3.1	22.6	1.0	3.2	0.0	1.7	5.3	3.5
34	36000	Jersey City city, New Jersey	16.2	22.6	5.7	12.4	0.0	3.9	6.1	3.0
34	36510	Kearny town, New Jersey	16.9	22.8	14.0	19.9	0.0	11.4	8.6	6.5
34	38580	Lakewood CDP, New Jersey	23.1	29.6	6.7	11.0	0.0	8.9	9.0	0.7
34	40350	Linden city, New Jersey	21.8	24.9	7.9	19.4	0.0	5.3	9.4	2.9

Table E. Cities—Labor Force, Employment, and Educational Data, 2015—*Continued*

FIPS state code	FIPS place code	State/city	Percent in each occupation group				Percent in each industry sector			
			Service occupations	Sales and office occupations	Natural resources, construction, and maintenance occupations	Production, transportation, and material moving occupations	Agriculture, forestry, fishing and hunting, and mining	Construction	Manufacturing	Wholesale trade
34	41100	Lodi borough, New Jersey	12.1	28.2	7.6	14.5	0.0	7.9	3.7	3.6
34	41310	Long Branch city, New Jersey	26.5	18.6	13.2	11.0	0.0	13.0	6.1	2.5
34	46680	Millville city, New Jersey	17.6	30.8	5.5	16.3	0.0	3.4	13.7	0.5
34	51000	Newark city, New Jersey	30.0	22.7	8.1	18.4	0.0	7.8	6.7	1.8
34	51210	New Brunswick city, New Jersey	26.3	15.7	9.0	27.6	0.0	5.9	19.5	4.3
34	53280	North Plainfield borough, New Jersey	19.0	20.4	12.8	15.2	0.0	10.0	12.2	1.7
34	54690	Old Bridge CDP, New Jersey	12.4	32.8	10.4	3.3	0.0	11.6	5.5	2.1
34	55770	Palisades Park borough, New Jersey	21.8	25.1	10.0	6.7	0.0	9.9	3.6	2.3
34	55950	Paramus borough, New Jersey	7.6	37.1	2.3	6.4	0.0	4.4	8.9	10.3
34	56550	Passaic city, New Jersey	15.3	16.9	16.9	34.9	0.0	13.5	22.1	1.7
34	57000	Paterson city, New Jersey	22.8	21.3	9.9	29.5	0.0	6.2	16.3	2.9
34	58200	Perth Amboy city, New Jersey	21.6	25.6	9.1	24.7	0.0	7.3	10.9	3.6
34	59190	Plainfield city, New Jersey	27.1	19.8	12.7	16.3	0.0	10.4	9.2	3.5
34	59640	Pleasantville city, New Jersey	49.5	22.1	3.4	12.6	0.0	3.8	1.6	2.0
34	60900	Princeton, New Jersey	17.6	15.6	1.4	3.5	0.0	0.2	7.4	0.7
34	61530	Rahway city, New Jersey	14.1	23.4	9.7	20.8	0.5	6.2	15.2	2.4
34	63000	Ridgewood village, New Jersey	4.9	22.0	2.5	3.3	0.0	1.4	9.7	3.3
34	64620	Roselle borough, New Jersey	23.8	25.6	2.1	21.4	0.0	2.3	9.5	1.2
34	65790	Sayreville borough, New Jersey	15.4	26.0	7.1	10.5	0.2	6.9	5.2	4.0
34	68370	Somerset CDP, New Jersey	10.6	20.5	2.5	5.3	0.5	2.2	10.7	3.1
34	69390	South Plainfield borough, New Jersey	15.7	22.4	8.5	13.2	0.0	6.2	12.3	5.1
34	71430	Summit city, New Jersey	9.9	27.6	0.4	1.3	0.0	1.2	9.3	7.3
34	73110	Toms River CDP, New Jersey	16.1	30.2	8.0	12.1	0.1	6.6	5.2	2.7
34	74000	Trenton city, New Jersey	30.6	24.1	9.4	14.3	0.1	8.3	8.0	2.5
34	74630	Union City city, New Jersey	25.9	19.8	11.9	22.8	0.1	11.2	6.4	6.4
34	76070	Vineland city, New Jersey	17.5	14.2	13.6	21.6	5.2	7.9	14.9	1.3
34	79040	Westfield town, New Jersey	7.9	25.1	3.6	3.2	0.0	1.9	11.3	3.0
34	79610	West New York town, New Jersey	23.5	21.8	8.4	16.8	0.0	6.3	7.3	3.8
35	00000	**NEW MEXICO**	21.5	24.0	11.1	8.9	4.2	7.3	3.6	2.4
35	01780	Alamogordo city, New Mexico	24.2	32.5	11.2	4.0	1.9	5.3	0.9	2.3
35	02000	Albuquerque city, New Mexico	21.3	23.8	8.3	6.9	0.7	5.8	3.6	2.4
35	12150	Carlsbad city, New Mexico	19.1	23.6	16.3	19.1	16.0	8.4	5.6	1.4
35	16420	Clovis city, New Mexico	21.4	28.8	14.6	10.3	4.9	6.2	3.4	1.4
35	25800	Farmington city, New Mexico	20.0	23.4	12.8	10.6	11.2	8.5	1.9	5.2
35	28460	Gallup city, New Mexico	19.8	26.9	10.8	4.9	3.8	5.8	1.8	0.6
35	32520	Hobbs city, New Mexico	13.0	18.5	19.0	25.3	16.9	6.6	1.5	5.7
35	39380	Las Cruces city, New Mexico	27.2	28.5	7.4	6.4	1.3	4.4	1.6	1.0
35	63460	Rio Rancho city, New Mexico	19.3	28.8	6.6	9.4	0.9	5.1	6.2	3.8
35	64930	Roswell city, New Mexico	23.9	25.4	13.5	13.0	7.7	6.0	4.3	0.1
35	70500	Santa Fe city, New Mexico	21.3	23.6	7.0	6.4	1.1	5.7	2.2	1.2
35	74520	South Valley CDP, New Mexico	26.8	21.2	18.3	6.9	2.2	17.1	1.2	4.7
36	00000	**NEW YORK**	20.2	23.3	7.3	9.4	0.6	5.6	6.1	2.5
36	01000	Albany city, New York	25.0	26.8	4.8	6.2	0.9	3.9	2.5	1.2
36	03078	Auburn city, New York	22.6	18.2	7.5	13.8	1.8	3.3	13.9	3.5
36	04143	Baldwin CDP, New York	19.2	22.6	6.3	14.1	0.0	6.7	3.0	1.8
36	04935	Bay Shore CDP, New York	25.2	23.4	11.6	12.9	0.0	4.6	17.3	0.9
36	06607	Binghamton city, New York	26.4	26.4	5.8	10.2	0.8	5.1	6.9	0.5
36	08026	Brentwood CDP, New York	25.8	24.2	11.2	21.5	0.6	7.2	14.0	4.5
36	08257	Brighton CDP, New York	11.0	19.9	5.8	8.2	0.0	5.1	7.8	2.9
36	11000	Buffalo city, New York	23.8	25.0	5.8	12.5	0.1	3.6	7.4	2.5
36	13376	Centereach CDP, New York	16.1	20.2	6.1	10.1	0.0	7.1	6.6	3.5
36	13552	Central Islip CDP, New York	26.2	22.6	14.8	19.4	0.0	7.5	13.2	1.6
36	15000	Cheektowaga CDP, New York	17.9	31.7	8.0	14.1	0.0	6.3	12.8	4.8
36	17530	Commack CDP, New York	13.2	25.1	4.3	5.9	0.0	5.5	5.5	3.9
36	18146	Copiague CDP, New York	23.1	26.8	12.3	17.6	0.0	9.7	9.5	1.1
36	18157	Coram CDP, New York	20.2	30.1	6.6	7.6	1.2	4.1	7.3	1.5
36	19972	Deer Park CDP, New York	21.0	26.9	11.4	8.2	0.0	10.9	5.0	3.7
36	20687	Dix Hills CDP, New York	6.1	22.7	0.7	13.4	0.0	3.1	9.1	1.9
36	22502	East Meadow CDP, New York	12.5	26.3	7.5	7.1	0.0	7.2	4.6	1.1
36	22612	East Northport CDP, New York	14.4	29.7	9.1	5.0	0.5	9.5	6.8	4.6
36	22733	East Patchogue CDP, New York	8.7	22.1	11.3	7.3	0.0	9.9	5.6	3.4
36	24229	Elmira city, New York	26.8	24.3	10.1	14.7	0.3	2.9	13.3	2.0
36	24273	Elmont CDP, New York	24.0	24.3	9.8	12.6	0.4	5.4	2.4	1.0
36	27309	Franklin Square CDP, New York	18.9	27.7	11.1	10.1	0.0	7.6	5.3	4.0
36	27485	Freeport village, New York	21.8	22.6	11.2	11.1	0.2	5.1	4.8	2.3
36	28178	Garden City village, New York	9.8	27.9	0.7	3.2	0.0	1.8	2.6	1.7
36	29113	Glen Cove city, New York	24.0	28.7	5.4	9.0	1.1	5.1	7.1	2.1
36	32402	Harrison village, New York	18.2	25.7	7.0	1.3	0.0	8.5	5.0	4.7
36	33139	Hempstead village, New York	32.3	26.5	10.0	12.5	0.5	6.8	4.1	4.5
36	34374	Hicksville CDP, New York	18.0	27.4	12.6	9.1	0.0	9.2	7.2	3.0
36	35056	Holbrook CDP, New York	16.0	33.2	7.8	5.7	0.0	5.7	7.4	2.7
36	35254	Holtsville CDP, New York	15.1	22.4	5.5	10.0	0.0	4.1	7.0	3.9

Table E. Cities—Labor Force, Employment, and Educational Data, 2015—*Continued*

FIPS state code	FIPS place code	State/city	Percent in each occupation group				Percent in each industry sector			
			Service occupations	Sales and office occupations	Natural resources, construction, and maintenance occupations	Production, transportation, and material moving occupations	Agriculture, forestry, fishing and hunting, and mining	Construction	Manufacturing	Wholesale trade
36	37044	Huntington Station CDP, New York	19.2	21.6	10.2	13.3	0.0	10.1	3.5	2.8
36	37737	Irondequoit CDP, New York	16.4	23.9	6.7	7.9	0.5	4.9	8.8	2.2
36	37869	Islip CDP, New York	16.8	20.2	12.5	8.2	0.0	15.3	5.9	1.1
36	38077	Ithaca city, New York	11.8	17.5	3.3	6.6	0.0	3.4	4.2	0.4
36	38264	Jamestown city, New York	21.1	30.1	3.9	21.8	1.0	4.1	20.5	1.5
36	39727	Kingston city, New York	24.6	28.0	6.1	6.2	0.6	4.5	3.3	2.2
36	39853	Kiryas Joel village, New York	14.7	36.4	0.3	10.3	0.0	1.0	14.3	4.6
36	40838	Lake Ronkonkoma CDP, New York	17.9	27.0	12.1	5.5	0.0	12.8	5.5	5.6
36	42081	Levittown CDP, New York	18.6	26.7	10.6	7.6	0.0	7.3	5.5	2.0
36	42554	Lindenhurst village, New York	15.8	33.1	13.3	9.9	0.0	9.6	7.6	3.1
36	43082	Lockport city, New York	13.4	36.3	8.9	16.6	1.4	5.4	16.9	2.7
36	43335	Long Beach city, New York	18.8	29.8	4.4	5.4	0.0	4.7	4.2	5.4
36	45986	Massapequa CDP, New York	14.4	26.0	8.8	5.7	0.0	6.5	3.7	3.5
36	46404	Medford CDP, New York	23.0	25.5	11.5	7.1	0.5	7.6	6.3	1.8
36	47042	Middletown city, New York	17.9	32.3	4.3	15.8	0.8	3.7	20.0	4.5
36	48010	Monsey CDP, New York	6.9	21.4	1.9	0.4	–	–	–	–
36	49121	Mount Vernon city, New York	27.0	22.6	5.3	7.1	0.0	4.3	4.5	1.0
36	49407	Nanuet CDP, New York	20.1	28.5	5.8	4.8	0.0	2.6	3.9	3.1
36	50034	Newburgh city, New York	29.1	20.8	5.7	24.5	0.0	5.0	14.1	2.8
36	50100	New City CDP, New York	12.9	23.1	2.0	3.8	0.0	3.6	4.0	4.3
36	50617	New Rochelle city, New York	22.0	21.7	7.0	6.0	0.0	6.7	3.1	1.8
36	51000	New York city, New York	22.8	21.9	6.2	8.5	0.1	5.0	3.4	2.2
36	51055	Niagara Falls city, New York	24.0	28.8	6.3	13.6	0.2	4.3	11.3	3.2
36	51396	North Amityville CDP, New York	32.9	20.2	11.8	11.2	0.0	5.1	10.7	1.5
36	53682	North Tonawanda city, New York	17.2	31.5	5.3	18.5	0.0	3.9	14.2	4.5
36	54441	Oceanside CDP, New York	12.4	28.7	4.2	6.2	0.0	4.4	5.5	2.4
36	55530	Ossining village, New York	20.5	26.0	15.8	8.8	0.0	14.3	2.2	3.1
36	56979	Peekskill city, New York	24.7	23.5	8.2	11.7	0.0	7.1	3.1	2.4
36	58442	Plainview CDP, New York	10.9	23.5	5.4	4.2	0.0	5.1	5.7	2.1
36	59223	Port Chester village, New York	35.7	23.3	12.5	14.0	0.0	11.5	4.6	3.1
36	59641	Poughkeepsie city, New York	31.1	24.6	4.1	12.6	0.8	5.5	6.0	0.8
36	63000	Rochester city, New York	27.1	24.2	5.3	13.3	0.1	4.2	7.6	2.0
36	63264	Rockville Centre village, New York	11.8	22.2	4.8	4.4	0.0	3.6	1.5	5.2
36	63418	Rome city, New York	15.5	28.4	5.6	13.9	0.7	2.7	12.9	0.7
36	63473	Ronkonkoma CDP, New York	15.5	26.8	7.7	9.9	0.0	7.2	6.1	5.6
36	63924	Rotterdam CDP, New York	22.0	29.2	6.9	10.3	0.0	3.1	6.1	3.0
36	65255	Saratoga Springs city, New York	12.7	22.6	6.0	3.9	0.2	7.0	14.0	3.8
36	65508	Schenectady city, New York	20.1	28.3	4.8	16.1	0.0	4.0	6.7	3.5
36	67070	Shirley CDP, New York	17.3	27.6	5.9	9.9	0.0	1.8	11.2	4.2
36	67851	Smithtown CDP, New York	17.4	26.4	6.7	5.9	0.0	8.2	7.0	5.2
36	70420	Spring Valley village, New York	33.4	26.7	7.1	13.2	0.0	7.2	5.0	4.0
36	72554	Syosset CDP, New York	4.0	28.8	5.2	3.0	0.0	5.5	3.9	5.2
36	73000	Syracuse city, New York	23.8	26.2	4.2	10.7	0.0	2.7	6.2	1.4
36	74183	Tonawanda CDP, New York	18.6	30.7	7.0	7.7	0.0	3.8	9.2	2.6
36	75484	Troy city, New York	20.1	24.7	4.8	11.5	0.1	3.4	6.5	1.4
36	76089	Uniondale CDP, New York	31.5	23.4	9.8	11.1	0.5	8.5	5.2	6.2
36	76540	Utica city, New York	26.3	26.9	5.0	15.5	0.0	4.2	11.9	1.5
36	76705	Valley Stream village, New York	22.5	24.9	10.7	7.4	0.0	4.1	7.6	1.7
36	78146	Wantagh CDP, New York	9.9	23.5	5.5	10.5	0.7	5.0	4.6	3.7
36	78608	Watertown city, New York	23.6	22.3	12.9	9.4	0.3	3.4	2.9	2.1
36	79246	West Babylon CDP, New York	14.2	33.6	12.5	7.5	0.0	7.5	5.9	3.6
36	80225	West Hempstead CDP, New York	22.3	28.2	8.7	3.8	0.0	7.3	1.2	1.7
36	80302	West Islip CDP, New York	14.4	27.7	7.4	6.6	0.0	4.0	6.7	2.4
36	80907	West Seneca CDP, New York	15.4	25.0	4.3	13.4	0.0	3.5	11.3	4.1
36	81677	White Plains city, New York	17.6	23.1	5.2	3.6	0.0	4.3	4.7	2.3
36	84000	Yonkers city, New York	21.0	25.4	8.9	9.3	0.4	7.6	3.6	2.3
37	00000	**NORTH CAROLINA**	17.1	23.0	9.8	13.5	1.2	7.2	12.5	2.6
37	01520	Apex town, North Carolina	12.7	23.4	4.1	7.1	0.3	3.1	12.7	1.7
37	02080	Asheboro city, North Carolina	21.0	16.1	6.3	29.7	0.0	9.3	28.0	1.2
37	02140	Asheville city, North Carolina	22.8	20.1	6.0	8.9	0.4	4.7	4.7	1.4
37	09060	Burlington city, North Carolina	22.7	21.8	11.7	17.6	0.4	6.8	17.6	0.8
37	10620	Carrboro town, North Carolina	11.7	16.9	2.2	4.7	0.0	1.3	6.7	0.7
37	10740	Cary town, North Carolina	10.2	18.7	3.7	5.1	0.3	3.9	10.8	2.4
37	11800	Chapel Hill town, North Carolina	18.9	21.8	3.7	3.4	0.4	3.1	3.5	2.5
37	12000	Charlotte city, North Carolina	15.6	24.4	8.0	9.9	0.2	7.1	7.6	3.2
37	14100	Concord city, North Carolina	13.1	26.1	7.2	14.6	0.3	6.9	9.6	3.5
37	14700	Cornelius town, North Carolina	14.3	26.8	4.5	2.2	1.6	6.1	10.9	4.8
37	19000	Durham city, North Carolina	17.6	16.2	7.5	9.8	0.9	5.8	8.1	1.4
37	22920	Fayetteville city, North Carolina	22.8	27.8	7.9	8.9	0.2	5.0	6.4	1.2
37	25300	Fuquay-Varina town, North Carolina	11.1	25.4	10.2	12.1	0.0	4.7	8.4	4.9
37	25480	Garner town, North Carolina	18.8	26.0	10.5	6.7	0.0	8.2	7.2	2.6
37	25580	Gastonia city, North Carolina	19.2	27.6	5.8	19.7	0.2	3.3	20.7	3.5
37	26880	Goldsboro city, North Carolina	14.6	27.5	4.8	20.4	0.0	1.5	20.1	1.9

Table E. Cities—Labor Force, Employment, and Educational Data, 2015—*Continued*

FIPS state code	FIPS place code	State/city	Percent in each occupation group				Percent in each industry sector			
			Service occupations	Sales and office occupations	Natural resources, construction, and maintenance occupations	Production, transportation, and material moving occupations	Agriculture, forestry, fishing and hunting, and mining	Construction	Manufacturing	Wholesale trade
37	28000	Greensboro city, North Carolina	19.4	24.4	7.0	12.4	0.1	5.1	10.1	3.3
37	28080	Greenville city, North Carolina	27.3	25.2	5.7	8.9	0.6	1.9	8.9	2.1
37	30120	Havelock city, North Carolina	17.5	25.3	13.2	10.8	0.0	7.1	5.9	0.0
37	31060	Hickory city, North Carolina	13.2	24.5	3.6	13.6	0.5	3.1	28.5	4.9
37	31400	High Point city, North Carolina	19.6	22.7	5.6	15.9	0.4	5.4	16.8	3.3
37	32260	Holly Springs town, North Carolina	8.3	32.9	1.5	5.9	0.3	2.1	10.3	1.2
37	33120	Huntersville town, North Carolina	10.1	29.7	4.3	4.8	0.2	3.4	9.1	5.4
37	33560	Indian Trail town, North Carolina	12.4	25.6	7.2	10.8	0.3	7.5	6.2	6.4
37	34200	Jacksonville city, North Carolina	29.6	27.9	7.2	6.7	0.1	3.8	3.6	0.6
37	35200	Kannapolis city, North Carolina	19.1	25.1	16.6	8.9	0.0	13.0	10.5	2.7
37	35600	Kernersville town, North Carolina	11.0	27.4	12.0	9.7	0.3	11.5	14.4	0.7
37	35920	Kinston city, North Carolina	20.4	15.6	8.8	27.3	0.7	9.1	25.4	7.8
37	39700	Lumberton city, North Carolina	18.1	23.4	12.0	20.6	0.4	7.9	21.2	0.5
37	41960	Matthews town, North Carolina	10.0	20.8	5.4	6.6	0.3	3.9	8.8	3.7
37	43480	Mint Hill town, North Carolina	12.1	37.4	7.3	5.0	0.0	6.9	3.8	5.0
37	43920	Monroe city, North Carolina	18.1	16.1	13.1	26.2	0.4	7.1	22.3	2.2
37	44220	Mooresville town, North Carolina	18.2	20.2	8.4	10.4	0.0	5.5	15.6	2.8
37	44520	Morrisville town, North Carolina	8.6	14.8	4.9	5.9	0.0	2.9	9.2	2.2
37	46340	New Bern city, North Carolina	21.5	19.1	5.6	14.6	0.0	1.5	15.7	3.2
37	55000	Raleigh city, North Carolina	15.4	24.9	7.2	7.2	0.2	6.9	5.8	2.7
37	57500	Rocky Mount city, North Carolina	22.9	22.4	7.7	20.8	1.1	6.2	12.7	1.2
37	58860	Salisbury city, North Carolina	28.9	19.0	9.2	17.3	0.0	6.5	15.6	0.9
37	59280	Sanford city, North Carolina	16.6	21.4	12.2	24.0	0.3	3.4	26.9	3.0
37	61200	Shelby city, North Carolina	12.2	23.8	13.3	17.8	0.6	7.8	19.9	0.0
37	64740	Statesville city, North Carolina	20.2	22.4	3.2	29.9	0.7	2.2	17.6	0.3
37	67420	Thomasville city, North Carolina	10.4	30.6	7.2	28.8	0.0	6.1	30.9	1.8
37	70540	Wake Forest town, North Carolina	11.9	27.9	4.6	4.7	0.6	5.2	8.6	3.2
37	74440	Wilmington city, North Carolina	18.7	24.2	7.6	9.9	0.0	6.1	5.7	2.2
37	74540	Wilson city, North Carolina	13.9	17.3	11.4	20.9	1.2	4.0	23.3	2.4
37	75000	Winston-Salem city, North Carolina	17.3	24.8	7.3	12.4	0.5	5.8	10.2	3.1
38	00000	**NORTH DAKOTA**	16.9	21.9	13.5	12.5	9.5	8.0	6.8	4.0
38	07200	Bismarck city, North Dakota	16.4	23.8	11.6	10.0	4.0	9.0	4.4	3.4
38	19620	Dickinson city, North Dakota	17.8	20.6	17.6	16.4	19.6	7.6	7.8	4.2
38	25700	Fargo city, North Dakota	19.0	22.7	9.2	12.5	1.0	7.4	9.7	3.0
38	32060	Grand Forks city, North Dakota	19.2	27.4	9.6	10.5	2.6	7.6	4.5	2.8
38	49900	Mandan city, North Dakota	20.7	18.5	11.7	15.5	3.4	7.6	10.5	0.0
38	53380	Minot city, North Dakota	20.4	28.1	11.6	11.6	6.1	5.8	2.7	2.5
38	84780	West Fargo city, North Dakota	14.9	22.0	10.6	15.9	3.1	7.5	12.7	9.5
38	86220	Williston city, North Dakota	13.0	21.7	20.3	12.7	17.1	9.3	4.8	3.6
39	00000	**OHIO**	17.3	23.3	7.5	16.1	1.1	5.0	15.5	2.7
39	01000	Akron city, Ohio	22.8	27.7	5.8	16.3	0.2	4.5	15.1	1.6
39	01420	Alliance city, Ohio	22.8	23.3	10.6	25.4	3.4	2.1	20.9	3.3
39	02568	Ashland city, Ohio	15.9	21.9	6.1	15.9	0.0	3.6	16.9	1.5
39	02736	Athens city, Ohio	24.9	16.5	2.0	7.8	0.8	0.9	4.4	0.4
39	03184	Austintown CDP, Ohio	20.2	20.2	9.7	19.4	0.3	5.4	15.7	2.2
39	03352	Avon city, Ohio	15.8	33.6	2.5	11.0	0.0	1.5	8.9	2.6
39	03464	Avon Lake city, Ohio	12.6	22.4	5.9	3.3	0.4	9.8	11.9	2.1
39	03828	Barberton city, Ohio	24.1	21.6	7.4	21.7	0.5	4.2	20.0	0.8
39	04720	Beavercreek city, Ohio	13.7	23.3	6.3	8.0	0.0	3.5	9.9	3.5
39	07454	Boardman CDP, Ohio	16.7	26.9	7.5	10.4	0.8	4.2	8.4	3.0
39	07972	Bowling Green city, Ohio	27.1	22.2	5.7	13.8	0.7	2.8	13.3	0.3
39	09680	Brunswick city, Ohio	16.9	28.6	6.5	14.5	0.0	1.6	13.8	2.8
39	12000	Canton city, Ohio	25.9	22.2	9.9	19.3	0.8	9.2	16.0	1.3
39	13190	Centerville city, Ohio	9.9	31.1	2.4	5.5	0.0	2.6	12.1	2.6
39	14184	Chillicothe city, Ohio	23.7	27.9	8.0	11.6	2.9	3.2	10.7	1.9
39	15000	Cincinnati city, Ohio	20.8	22.7	4.4	11.5	0.2	2.7	10.0	1.4
39	16000	Cleveland city, Ohio	26.1	23.0	5.8	17.9	0.2	4.1	13.8	2.2
39	16014	Cleveland Heights city, Ohio	14.3	15.7	4.9	7.0	0.0	4.9	7.8	1.5
39	18000	Columbus city, Ohio	17.9	25.7	4.8	12.4	0.1	3.1	7.1	2.6
39	19778	Cuyahoga Falls city, Ohio	13.2	27.9	7.8	12.7	0.4	4.7	16.8	2.8
39	21000	Dayton city, Ohio	26.2	21.4	7.4	16.2	0.0	4.8	13.8	1.2
39	21434	Delaware city, Ohio	16.9	21.1	6.3	13.2	0.9	4.8	12.0	2.5
39	22694	Dublin city, Ohio	5.0	19.4	2.3	3.2	0.0	1.1	12.1	3.9
39	25256	Elyria city, Ohio	25.0	18.5	9.7	23.9	0.3	5.7	24.1	2.4
39	25704	Euclid city, Ohio	21.1	27.9	3.6	14.0	0.2	1.1	13.6	1.3
39	25914	Fairborn city, Ohio	18.7	23.4	7.8	13.1	0.6	6.5	10.8	0.7
39	25970	Fairfield city, Ohio	11.7	24.9	7.6	13.9	0.2	5.6	12.9	6.1
39	27048	Findlay city, Ohio	19.4	15.8	10.2	21.0	0.8	3.8	24.9	2.5
39	29106	Gahanna city, Ohio	9.1	22.5	3.4	10.8	0.0	6.9	9.4	0.9
39	29428	Garfield Heights city, Ohio	15.7	32.9	6.4	18.7	0.0	4.6	17.5	1.6
39	31860	Green city, Ohio	16.0	23.6	4.0	9.0	0.8	4.0	16.7	3.0
39	32592	Grove City city, Ohio	18.5	25.6	6.2	10.5	0.5	4.5	7.9	1.6
39	33012	Hamilton city, Ohio	17.0	30.7	11.3	16.9	0.6	8.5	12.4	4.8
39	35476	Hilliard city, Ohio	14.1	24.5	2.4	3.3	0.0	2.3	6.7	3.2

Table E. Cities—Labor Force, Employment, and Educational Data, 2015—*Continued*

FIPS state code	FIPS place code	State/city	Percent in each occupation group				Percent in each industry sector			
			Service occupations	Sales and office occupations	Natural resources, construction, and maintenance occupations	Production, transportation, and material moving occupations	Agriculture, forestry, fishing and hunting, and mining	Construction	Manufacturing	Wholesale trade
39	36610	Huber Heights city, Ohio	19.1	20.7	8.1	21.2	0.0	5.5	15.8	2.5
39	36651	Hudson city, Ohio	11.4	19.2	1.8	6.2	0.0	0.8	20.8	3.7
39	39872	Kent city, Ohio	19.3	22.2	4.2	11.4	0.5	1.8	14.2	0.0
39	40040	Kettering city, Ohio	14.9	24.2	6.7	8.3	0.5	3.7	11.1	2.5
39	41664	Lakewood city, Ohio	14.6	19.8	6.1	9.1	1.0	4.8	10.6	3.1
39	41720	Lancaster city, Ohio	19.8	25.8	6.0	12.5	0.0	7.9	11.3	2.9
39	42364	Lebanon city, Ohio	22.8	24.4	14.2	14.6	0.0	12.1	12.9	2.1
39	43554	Lima city, Ohio	22.7	15.5	5.7	31.8	0.1	4.8	24.3	4.2
39	44856	Lorain city, Ohio	23.4	25.5	10.5	18.4	0.7	5.6	17.4	1.7
39	47138	Mansfield city, Ohio	28.0	24.0	6.5	16.8	0.4	3.2	16.5	2.3
39	47306	Maple Heights city, Ohio	31.4	24.0	4.4	14.8	0.0	0.0	8.1	3.2
39	47754	Marion city, Ohio	15.5	22.1	9.4	31.8	1.1	4.2	27.0	1.2
39	48160	Marysville city, Ohio	20.6	21.8	4.4	15.5	0.0	2.5	17.6	1.4
39	48188	Mason city, Ohio	10.6	22.4	2.0	4.8	0.7	1.6	13.4	5.3
39	48244	Massillon city, Ohio	16.9	24.2	9.4	28.2	0.0	5.1	19.4	2.2
39	48790	Medina city, Ohio	15.5	25.1	8.2	11.1	1.2	5.7	18.7	0.8
39	49056	Mentor city, Ohio	11.4	30.4	6.9	10.5	0.3	4.0	20.2	3.5
39	49434	Miamisburg city, Ohio	17.4	25.2	7.2	14.2	0.0	7.4	16.1	0.0
39	49840	Middletown city, Ohio	21.4	22.4	8.1	17.7	0.9	4.7	16.0	1.7
39	54040	Newark city, Ohio	20.7	22.3	9.5	16.1	1.8	5.8	14.3	1.3
39	56882	North Olmsted city, Ohio	17.5	30.8	8.0	12.3	0.5	4.3	15.5	3.0
39	56966	North Ridgeville city, Ohio	13.1	25.2	7.3	9.6	0.5	7.7	13.6	3.7
39	57008	North Royalton city, Ohio	14.5	23.8	5.9	10.2	0.9	5.1	8.1	4.0
39	58730	Oregon city, Ohio	20.7	24.7	9.0	17.3	0.0	6.5	15.6	1.3
39	59234	Oxford city, Ohio	29.6	23.1	4.6	6.5	0.6	1.2	7.4	1.0
39	61000	Parma city, Ohio	17.8	29.5	9.3	16.4	0.2	5.1	16.8	3.8
39	61028	Parma Heights city, Ohio	16.2	28.9	5.9	17.4	0.0	3.8	16.5	2.3
39	62148	Perrysburg city, Ohio	10.1	22.6	8.5	4.1	0.4	7.6	17.0	3.1
39	62848	Piqua city, Ohio	21.1	22.6	11.0	29.5	0.0	4.0	42.7	0.6
39	64304	Portsmouth city, Ohio	29.9	25.8	3.1	11.0	0.5	2.0	3.9	2.8
39	66390	Reynoldsburg city, Ohio	15.1	36.3	7.5	10.4	0.2	5.1	8.5	6.2
39	67468	Riverside city, Ohio	18.1	26.0	9.2	13.6	0.0	8.1	13.0	5.9
39	68056	Rocky River city, Ohio	8.4	22.6	3.2	13.7	0.0	4.0	14.6	2.8
39	70380	Sandusky city, Ohio	34.8	21.4	4.7	22.2	2.0	1.1	19.5	2.1
39	71682	Shaker Heights city, Ohio	10.1	19.7	2.2	5.8	0.1	1.8	7.9	2.3
39	72424	Sidney city, Ohio	12.8	28.2	6.3	22.2	0.5	6.7	23.3	1.5
39	72928	Solon city, Ohio	16.9	18.2	4.2	7.0	0.0	4.8	10.5	6.4
39	73264	South Euclid city, Ohio	16.8	30.1	5.0	9.8	0.0	1.9	12.8	2.4
39	74118	Springfield city, Ohio	23.4	22.9	6.3	22.9	0.3	4.1	17.3	4.0
39	74944	Stow city, Ohio	13.2	21.9	1.4	9.9	0.0	1.5	12.9	3.4
39	75098	Strongsville city, Ohio	14.2	26.6	4.6	10.6	0.0	3.5	13.2	3.7
39	77000	Toledo city, Ohio	21.8	22.5	6.8	22.2	0.2	4.2	17.2	2.3
39	77504	Trotwood city, Ohio	31.8	20.8	3.5	19.0	0.0	2.8	11.2	4.1
39	77588	Troy city, Ohio	21.6	26.9	6.5	10.2	0.0	1.3	25.3	1.0
39	79002	Upper Arlington city, Ohio	6.5	22.2	1.7	3.2	0.0	3.4	7.1	2.9
39	80304	Wadsworth city, Ohio	14.2	18.9	6.2	11.8	0.4	3.9	15.1	1.0
39	80892	Warren city, Ohio	25.3	25.7	5.5	20.4	0.0	2.9	19.9	0.8
39	83342	Westerville city, Ohio	12.7	19.4	3.3	4.4	0.0	5.4	7.2	1.1
39	83622	Westlake city, Ohio	14.3	24.0	2.4	6.6	0.0	1.8	6.4	3.9
39	84812	White Oak CDP, Ohio	16.3	30.8	4.5	13.9	0.0	2.7	12.1	1.5
39	85484	Willoughby city, Ohio	17.2	24.1	5.6	14.0	0.3	4.0	24.3	4.9
39	86548	Wooster city, Ohio	17.8	20.2	4.8	17.1	0.7	3.9	20.9	1.8
39	86772	Xenia city, Ohio	14.9	25.3	14.6	14.1	0.0	2.9	11.5	1.9
39	88000	Youngstown city, Ohio	28.0	23.9	5.5	21.4	0.0	3.7	15.4	2.2
39	88084	Zanesville city, Ohio	27.9	26.5	5.9	17.8	1.5	4.5	11.2	2.3
40	00000	**OKLAHOMA**	17.6	24.1	11.7	12.9	5.0	7.3	9.5	2.6
40	02600	Ardmore city, Oklahoma	18.3	26.6	11.5	19.4	1.6	7.9	16.5	4.3
40	04450	Bartlesville city, Oklahoma	19.0	26.4	6.1	7.6	5.0	4.4	11.4	2.6
40	06400	Bixby city, Oklahoma	11.0	34.5	5.8	9.3	3.0	3.9	8.2	6.6
40	09050	Broken Arrow city, Oklahoma	16.0	27.2	8.9	9.7	2.4	6.2	11.5	3.3
40	19900	Del City city, Oklahoma	20.6	32.7	9.0	11.3	6.3	3.4	7.0	2.8
40	21900	Duncan city, Oklahoma	17.9	23.6	15.4	15.9	14.0	5.3	10.6	1.1
40	23200	Edmond city, Oklahoma	16.8	23.6	6.8	6.6	5.3	5.9	5.1	2.5
40	23950	Enid city, Oklahoma	14.1	24.3	22.5	15.1	6.2	13.4	7.3	2.4
40	37800	Jenks city, Oklahoma	15.4	23.4	4.1	5.4	3.1	4.9	3.4	4.7
40	41850	Lawton city, Oklahoma	20.9	23.0	10.3	11.1	1.2	5.4	6.4	0.9
40	48350	Midwest City city, Oklahoma	16.2	26.8	13.9	11.1	2.5	6.2	7.9	2.5
40	49200	Moore city, Oklahoma	17.6	25.2	6.9	10.3	1.6	4.8	7.9	3.1
40	50050	Muskogee city, Oklahoma	22.6	26.9	9.3	13.2	0.1	5.5	13.2	4.3
40	50100	Mustang city, Oklahoma	11.4	28.8	11.1	13.3	1.8	6.6	10.3	4.6
40	52500	Norman city, Oklahoma	18.4	20.6	6.5	8.0	3.4	3.8	5.2	2.7
40	55000	Oklahoma City city, Oklahoma	17.8	23.7	11.6	10.4	3.5	9.4	6.9	2.6
40	56650	Owasso city, Oklahoma	16.4	23.6	9.0	9.1	0.9	5.8	9.4	4.6
40	59850	Ponca City city, Oklahoma	18.6	31.2	7.9	15.7	2.4	3.8	12.7	6.4
40	65400	Sapulpa city, Oklahoma	21.5	27.5	7.4	18.5	1.0	6.2	17.1	3.1

Table E. Cities—Labor Force, Employment, and Educational Data, 2015—*Continued*

FIPS state code	FIPS place code	State/city	Percent in each occupation group				Percent in each industry sector			
			Service occupations	Sales and office occupations	Natural resources, construction, and maintenance occupations	Production, transportation, and material moving occupations	Agriculture, forestry, fishing and hunting, and mining	Construction	Manufacturing	Wholesale trade
40	66800	Shawnee city, Oklahoma	26.1	24.2	8.0	17.4	3.7	4.3	10.5	1.1
40	70300	Stillwater city, Oklahoma	18.0	28.9	6.0	5.8	2.2	5.6	3.2	3.3
40	75000	Tulsa city, Oklahoma	16.3	25.1	9.7	12.8	2.0	7.0	12.1	2.7
40	82950	Yukon city, Oklahoma	10.3	28.6	14.5	13.9	2.7	10.0	11.3	2.7
41	00000	**OREGON**	18.7	22.7	8.9	11.9	3.5	5.7	11.3	2.8
41	01000	Albany city, Oregon	15.2	21.7	8.3	14.6	3.1	4.9	14.5	2.1
41	01650	Aloha CDP, Oregon	19.6	25.2	6.2	11.9	1.9	3.4	16.8	3.5
41	03050	Ashland city, Oregon	21.4	21.3	5.9	5.0	2.6	8.7	2.6	1.5
41	05350	Beaverton city, Oregon	17.3	25.2	3.5	7.4	0.2	3.9	12.8	4.3
41	05800	Bend city, Oregon	15.0	22.0	10.6	5.1	1.8	8.5	6.5	1.8
41	05950	Bethany CDP, Oregon	8.0	22.8	2.3	2.7	1.0	0.6	26.3	3.3
41	15800	Corvallis city, Oregon	19.0	17.0	4.9	7.1	2.6	2.6	7.6	1.0
41	23850	Eugene city, Oregon	19.7	22.8	4.8	9.6	1.3	3.2	7.5	2.8
41	26200	Forest Grove city, Oregon	20.6	21.4	17.4	14.3	4.2	7.7	20.4	4.2
41	30550	Grants Pass city, Oregon	26.0	24.4	11.6	13.7	0.1	5.8	11.9	0.9
41	31250	Gresham city, Oregon	25.4	21.9	9.5	16.0	4.1	3.5	10.1	4.5
41	32850	Hayesville CDP, Oregon	19.8	18.9	21.3	17.2	8.4	9.2	19.5	0.0
41	34100	Hillsboro city, Oregon	17.3	20.2	6.1	11.0	1.1	3.9	26.2	3.5
41	38500	Keizer city, Oregon	14.8	24.5	9.3	14.1	0.0	9.0	12.3	2.4
41	39700	Klamath Falls city, Oregon	20.0	25.4	9.0	15.2	3.9	3.8	9.1	2.5
41	40550	Lake Oswego city, Oregon	12.4	21.1	3.1	4.8	0.8	3.9	8.6	5.4
41	45000	McMinnville city, Oregon	22.4	19.3	12.3	19.0	7.5	5.1	18.5	3.9
41	47000	Medford city, Oregon	22.0	25.0	10.1	14.3	2.3	6.2	10.2	1.4
41	48650	Milwaukie city, Oregon	18.7	27.8	13.8	10.4	0.0	10.1	10.0	4.5
41	52100	Newberg city, Oregon	18.0	15.2	4.9	26.3	1.9	6.5	18.0	2.0
41	55200	Oregon City city, Oregon	15.4	27.3	8.7	15.5	0.0	9.2	9.6	2.8
41	59000	Portland city, Oregon	17.7	20.1	4.6	9.3	0.9	4.0	8.5	2.7
41	61200	Redmond city, Oregon	26.2	19.0	10.0	20.8	0.0	8.6	13.8	0.6
41	63650	Roseburg city, Oregon	16.3	32.4	6.2	10.1	—	—	—	—
41	64900	Salem city, Oregon	18.4	23.9	13.0	11.7	5.8	7.8	9.3	1.4
41	69600	Springfield city, Oregon	21.1	25.9	11.6	19.3	2.8	6.8	16.0	1.8
41	73650	Tigard city, Oregon	16.8	27.1	6.4	6.5	0.8	4.8	11.9	1.9
41	74950	Tualatin city, Oregon	14.6	21.9	2.9	14.0	0.3	1.9	17.4	4.0
41	80150	West Linn city, Oregon	11.9	28.7	4.0	3.2	0.7	4.5	11.8	4.7
41	82800	Wilsonville city, Oregon	15.8	23.2	7.0	6.8	2.4	5.3	7.4	6.1
41	83750	Woodburn city, Oregon	22.6	32.2	12.2	16.1	3.4	8.9	10.4	1.7
42	00000	**PENNSYLVANIA**	17.5	23.2	8.2	13.7	1.5	5.7	12.1	2.9
42	02000	Allentown city, Pennsylvania	23.2	21.7	7.9	26.4	0.4	5.5	15.2	1.8
42	02056	Allison Park CDP, Pennsylvania	20.6	24.6	1.8	6.8	0.0	3.6	4.3	3.1
42	02184	Altoona city, Pennsylvania	18.1	28.9	6.9	14.2	0.5	5.0	9.4	3.1
42	06064	Bethel Park municipality, Pennsylvania	14.7	26.3	4.6	5.6	1.7	2.0	7.7	3.5
42	06088	Bethlehem city, Pennsylvania	23.1	20.8	4.6	16.9	0.7	3.2	10.6	2.4
42	12536	Chambersburg borough, Pennsylvania	21.7	23.3	4.2	21.8	1.6	2.7	10.0	3.9
42	13208	Chester city, Pennsylvania	31.3	23.7	6.0	21.5	0.8	5.9	8.2	0.6
42	19920	Drexel Hill CDP, Pennsylvania	21.6	22.2	4.9	8.0	0.0	5.3	3.5	1.5
42	21648	Easton city, Pennsylvania	21.9	17.5	5.8	23.1	1.1	1.8	23.4	2.4
42	24000	Erie city, Pennsylvania	26.3	21.7	4.7	19.1	0.2	3.4	15.4	1.8
42	32800	Harrisburg city, Pennsylvania	25.7	24.8	5.6	14.3	0.0	3.3	8.3	3.2
42	33408	Hazleton city, Pennsylvania	14.8	28.4	4.4	34.6	0.6	2.4	16.4	2.2
42	38288	Johnstown city, Pennsylvania	26.8	35.2	6.3	12.3	0.0	4.9	3.2	2.0
42	41216	Lancaster city, Pennsylvania	23.0	21.1	4.6	27.5	0.8	2.8	20.0	3.4
42	42168	Lebanon city, Pennsylvania	28.8	19.5	3.9	28.6	0.4	2.6	20.5	1.4
42	42928	Levittown CDP, Pennsylvania	20.0	23.9	10.4	15.3	0.2	5.7	11.7	5.1
42	50528	Monroeville municipality, Pennsylvania	16.2	24.9	5.1	7.9	0.3	3.4	10.5	4.2
42	52432	Murrysville municipality, Pennsylvania	13.6	16.6	7.0	9.6	0.8	2.2	17.4	1.6
42	53368	New Castle city, Pennsylvania	24.7	25.1	6.0	24.2	0.1	2.5	15.6	2.9
42	54656	Norristown borough, Pennsylvania	27.4	16.9	12.7	11.4	0.0	9.4	7.8	0.6
42	60000	Philadelphia city, Pennsylvania	23.8	22.5	5.4	11.8	0.3	3.7	6.9	2.2
42	61000	Pittsburgh city, Pennsylvania	19.6	21.0	3.7	8.4	0.6	3.8	6.4	1.5
42	61536	Plum borough, Pennsylvania	14.6	25.8	5.2	8.2	0.0	2.8	13.4	3.3
42	62416	Pottstown borough, Pennsylvania	22.8	29.0	9.3	15.2	0.0	9.1	11.2	2.6
42	63624	Reading city, Pennsylvania	22.6	20.1	6.3	35.2	0.9	2.2	26.6	4.9
42	69000	Scranton city, Pennsylvania	21.6	24.9	6.1	18.8	0.5	4.1	10.5	5.1
42	73808	State College borough, Pennsylvania	20.8	18.0	3.1	8.4	0.0	3.8	6.8	0.0
42	79277	Upper St. Clair CDP, Pennsylvania	8.7	22.6	5.4	3.5	1.1	6.2	6.6	3.9
42	83512	West Mifflin borough, Pennsylvania	16.4	21.0	13.9	16.8	1.0	11.2	10.9	4.7
42	85152	Wilkes-Barre city, Pennsylvania	26.6	29.8	3.3	16.4	0.2	4.2	10.1	1.7
42	85312	Williamsport city, Pennsylvania	29.5	18.0	7.1	18.0	0.5	5.3	13.7	1.7
42	87048	York city, Pennsylvania	23.3	20.6	8.0	26.9	0.6	7.0	16.5	1.4
44	00000	**RHODE ISLAND**	18.9	24.4	7.2	11.3	0.4	5.2	11.4	3.1
44	19180	Cranston city, Rhode Island	15.4	28.6	5.6	8.6	0.0	3.7	12.0	3.9
44	22960	East Providence city, Rhode Island	20.0	30.2	6.5	10.0	0.0	3.8	11.1	3.7
44	49960	Newport city, Rhode Island	19.0	26.1	4.6	11.5	0.0	6.5	4.7	3.3

Table E. Cities—Labor Force, Employment, and Educational Data, 2015—*Continued*

FIPS state code	FIPS place code	State/city	Percent in each occupation group				Percent in each industry sector			
			Service occupations	Sales and office occupations	Natural resources, construction, and maintenance occupations	Production, transportation, and material moving occupations	Agriculture, forestry, fishing and hunting, and mining	Construction	Manufacturing	Wholesale trade
44	54640	Pawtucket city, Rhode Island	22.1	29.2	7.7	13.8	0.0	5.0	10.8	4.4
44	59000	Providence city, Rhode Island	19.7	22.2	5.6	16.3	0.3	2.9	15.1	3.0
44	74300	Warwick city, Rhode Island	16.7	24.9	7.3	10.3	0.1	4.9	10.5	3.9
44	76820	Westerly CDP, Rhode Island	29.0	24.0	8.3	10.4	1.1	8.3	17.1	1.9
44	80780	Woonsocket city, Rhode Island	19.4	24.6	9.7	13.9	0.0	6.6	10.9	0.9
45	00000	**SOUTH CAROLINA**	17.9	24.6	9.0	14.7	1.0	6.4	13.9	2.7
45	00550	Aiken city, South Carolina	14.2	18.4	5.2	8.6	0.4	4.5	9.2	0.0
45	01360	Anderson city, South Carolina	21.9	23.5	4.5	17.2	0.5	4.1	15.3	1.3
45	13330	Charleston city, South Carolina	17.6	22.1	6.2	7.0	0.4	5.7	4.8	2.9
45	16000	Columbia city, South Carolina	20.8	26.6	4.4	7.6	0.3	3.8	5.4	2.1
45	16405	Conway city, South Carolina	28.5	27.6	4.5	10.6	0.0	5.5	4.9	3.7
45	21985	Easley city, South Carolina	15.6	24.9	10.7	14.1	0.0	8.3	20.2	1.4
45	25810	Florence city, South Carolina	18.3	25.0	4.9	10.0	0.0	4.8	10.4	3.7
45	29815	Goose Creek city, South Carolina	17.7	21.8	10.4	16.1	0.0	7.3	15.3	2.1
45	30850	Greenville city, South Carolina	22.9	20.0	2.9	8.0	0.5	2.8	10.5	3.4
45	30895	Greenwood city, South Carolina	21.1	20.7	3.1	28.8	–	–	–	–
45	30985	Greer city, South Carolina	18.6	19.6	12.3	15.8	0.6	11.4	17.6	3.7
45	32065	Hanahan city, South Carolina	18.7	23.2	13.9	11.8	0.6	10.4	9.5	3.4
45	34045	Hilton Head Island town, South Carolina	21.9	21.0	8.6	3.7	1.0	9.1	4.0	1.0
45	41335	Lexington town, South Carolina	12.0	18.7	5.3	9.5	0.0	2.1	10.2	2.3
45	45115	Mauldin city, South Carolina	17.7	22.6	3.6	13.0	0.0	2.1	17.9	0.6
45	48535	Mount Pleasant town, South Carolina	13.3	28.3	1.3	4.1	0.3	2.9	2.3	3.4
45	49075	Myrtle Beach city, South Carolina	33.8	25.5	7.1	7.5	0.5	6.6	1.8	4.2
45	50695	North Augusta city, South Carolina	10.9	38.4	5.2	7.4	0.5	5.1	8.0	1.6
45	50875	North Charleston city, South Carolina	23.7	24.3	9.5	12.6	0.9	5.5	10.4	2.9
45	61405	Rock Hill city, South Carolina	16.4	32.3	5.0	14.6	1.1	2.0	11.6	4.6
45	62395	St. Andrews CDP, South Carolina	18.4	32.9	6.3	18.3	0.0	3.5	11.0	3.2
45	66580	Simpsonville city, South Carolina	17.8	27.6	3.0	7.1	0.0	2.3	14.2	3.9
45	67390	Socastee CDP, South Carolina	21.8	32.2	17.3	7.5	0.0	21.5	2.7	2.7
45	68290	Spartanburg city, South Carolina	21.9	26.6	2.9	23.5	0.0	1.7	24.6	8.0
45	70270	Summerville town, South Carolina	17.9	21.5	10.7	13.7	0.0	7.2	18.5	1.8
45	70405	Sumter city, South Carolina	21.9	22.0	7.4	23.0	0.9	5.9	21.0	1.0
45	71395	Taylors CDP, South Carolina	23.5	23.6	3.0	20.9	0.0	4.0	22.7	1.1
45	73870	Wade Hampton CDP, South Carolina	20.3	32.8	8.2	7.7	0.0	3.7	12.6	3.6
46	00000	**SOUTH DAKOTA**	17.9	23.0	11.1	14.2	6.7	7.4	10.4	2.9
46	00100	Aberdeen city, South Dakota	20.9	25.3	11.3	18.9	0.9	5.7	16.1	1.2
46	07580	Brookings city, South Dakota	19.7	25.6	6.0	13.7	4.5	3.2	17.5	1.3
46	52980	Rapid City city, South Dakota	19.9	27.1	8.1	11.8	1.0	6.7	5.0	2.6
46	59020	Sioux Falls city, South Dakota	16.7	25.5	8.9	15.2	0.9	8.2	11.6	3.7
46	69300	Watertown city, South Dakota	20.0	23.1	13.9	18.5	5.0	7.3	18.0	2.4
47	00000	**TENNESSEE**	17.0	24.1	8.9	15.7	1.0	6.0	13.0	2.7
47	03440	Bartlett city, Tennessee	15.9	26.6	5.0	10.8	0.0	2.6	15.7	3.5
47	08280	Brentwood city, Tennessee	10.3	24.7	1.1	2.1	0.6	2.2	8.7	3.7
47	08540	Bristol city, Tennessee	19.4	23.8	9.5	7.0	0.8	3.6	16.1	4.9
47	14000	Chattanooga city, Tennessee	18.7	25.8	5.6	14.1	0.7	4.4	11.9	2.2
47	15160	Clarksville city, Tennessee	15.0	24.9	9.7	17.1	0.5	4.8	13.4	1.7
47	15400	Cleveland city, Tennessee	25.4	18.7	6.4	15.5	0.0	6.1	14.0	1.4
47	16420	Collierville town, Tennessee	13.8	21.2	5.4	8.4	0.2	3.5	10.6	2.2
47	16540	Columbia city, Tennessee	21.1	24.4	12.2	13.8	0.0	4.8	16.0	1.3
47	16920	Cookeville city, Tennessee	27.5	18.9	6.6	13.8	1.3	2.7	10.5	0.3
47	22720	East Ridge city, Tennessee	14.2	24.3	5.3	23.8	0.0	1.9	26.2	4.3
47	25760	Farragut town, Tennessee	10.4	18.5	3.6	3.8	1.3	5.4	7.0	4.2
47	27740	Franklin city, Tennessee	14.4	25.9	2.4	5.0	0.3	2.1	9.8	2.5
47	28540	Gallatin city, Tennessee	15.9	25.0	10.7	12.1	2.6	6.5	11.2	6.1
47	28960	Germantown city, Tennessee	8.7	25.2	1.5	6.5	0.5	0.8	13.5	2.2
47	33280	Hendersonville city, Tennessee	16.2	32.8	4.3	7.2	0.2	3.5	6.9	7.7
47	37640	Jackson city, Tennessee	19.5	23.0	9.0	12.6	0.1	5.1	12.3	2.1
47	38320	Johnson City city, Tennessee	24.3	20.5	3.9	6.1	0.2	1.8	8.8	1.5
47	39560	Kingsport city, Tennessee	20.9	22.5	10.1	12.2	0.9	8.0	13.6	3.3
47	40000	Knoxville city, Tennessee	20.4	26.8	6.0	12.1	0.4	3.6	5.9	2.1
47	41200	La Vergne city, Tennessee	15.6	27.0	9.0	22.7	0.6	11.9	15.3	6.0
47	41520	Lebanon city, Tennessee	13.6	22.9	2.8	14.4	0.0	3.4	10.5	4.7
47	46380	Maryville city, Tennessee	13.1	35.1	9.8	8.8	0.3	4.9	6.9	3.0
47	48000	Memphis city, Tennessee	19.6	23.0	8.1	18.8	0.1	5.7	7.9	3.5
47	50280	Morristown city, Tennessee	20.9	14.9	16.8	27.4	1.5	10.4	27.2	1.1
47	50780	Mount Juliet city, Tennessee	17.4	26.1	3.2	5.6	0.0	4.1	7.1	2.4
47	51560	Murfreesboro city, Tennessee	17.6	26.0	5.6	12.2	0.2	3.5	12.4	2.1
47	52006	Nashville-Davidson metropolitan government (balance), Tennessee	16.9	23.7	7.9	12.0	0.1	5.6	7.6	2.4
47	55120	Oak Ridge city, Tennessee	20.2	23.2	5.3	11.9	0.3	2.2	8.2	1.8
47	67760	Shelbyville city, Tennessee	12.7	29.9	14.7	31.5	0.8	9.7	26.7	1.6
47	69420	Smyrna town, Tennessee	16.7	23.3	12.3	19.5	1.0	6.0	11.4	4.5
47	70580	Spring Hill city, Tennessee	21.2	25.1	6.3	5.3	0.1	6.6	7.5	1.2

Table E. Cities—Labor Force, Employment, and Educational Data, 2015—*Continued*

FIPS state code	FIPS place code	State/city	Percent in each occupation group				Percent in each industry sector			
			Service occupations	Sales and office occupations	Natural resources, construction, and maintenance occupations	Production, transportation, and material moving occupations	Agriculture, forestry, fishing and hunting, and mining	Construction	Manufacturing	Wholesale trade
48	00000	**TEXAS**	17.4	24.2	10.9	12.2	3.4	8.1	8.7	3.0
48	01000	Abilene city, Texas	22.8	23.8	10.4	13.2	1.7	5.3	5.7	2.0
48	01924	Allen city, Texas	10.7	25.1	4.4	6.7	0.8	6.6	8.4	3.4
48	02272	Alvin city, Texas	21.5	14.4	25.7	17.7	1.0	20.9	8.9	1.1
48	03000	Amarillo city, Texas	19.7	24.9	11.6	12.7	1.4	8.0	8.3	4.2
48	04000	Arlington city, Texas	16.5	26.3	9.4	14.1	0.4	6.7	9.3	3.7
48	04462	Atascocita CDP, Texas	15.6	24.8	5.0	12.8	4.4	5.2	8.4	5.2
48	05000	Austin city, Texas	16.9	22.0	8.0	6.6	0.7	7.5	6.7	2.0
48	05372	Balch Springs city, Texas	24.7	22.1	25.3	15.6	0.3	20.0	10.6	1.0
48	06128	Baytown city, Texas	18.9	21.5	18.4	16.2	2.0	16.0	14.0	1.5
48	07000	Beaumont city, Texas	21.3	24.3	11.4	13.3	1.0	8.0	11.5	1.2
48	07132	Bedford city, Texas	12.6	29.6	5.7	6.6	0.7	2.4	6.8	3.9
48	07492	Belton city, Texas	24.8	18.4	5.0	19.9	0.2	8.2	13.7	1.8
48	07552	Benbrook city, Texas	12.5	29.6	7.9	9.6	1.4	4.1	17.1	2.6
48	08236	Big Spring city, Texas	12.2	25.2	14.0	15.9	9.1	8.0	6.3	0.3
48	10768	Brownsville city, Texas	24.9	26.9	10.6	11.2	1.7	7.3	4.6	2.2
48	10897	Brushy Creek CDP, Texas	8.2	23.9	7.6	3.0	3.9	6.2	16.9	3.6
48	10912	Bryan city, Texas	16.2	28.5	14.0	8.5	3.4	9.3	7.2	2.8
48	11428	Burleson city, Texas	12.3	31.0	7.4	12.1	0.6	8.6	9.0	4.7
48	12580	Canyon Lake CDP, Texas	14.6	22.6	15.8	5.6	3.7	15.6	1.4	2.7
48	13024	Carrollton city, Texas	15.0	25.0	7.9	10.9	1.4	6.9	9.7	3.7
48	13492	Cedar Hill city, Texas	11.4	31.2	5.8	14.9	0.5	5.3	8.7	2.1
48	13552	Cedar Park city, Texas	10.8	21.2	6.3	3.5	1.5	4.1	10.2	1.5
48	14236	Channelview CDP, Texas	21.3	24.6	14.4	21.5	1.7	7.8	15.9	1.5
48	14920	Cibolo city, Texas	14.3	32.1	13.6	7.7	2.4	3.8	4.7	5.4
48	15364	Cleburne city, Texas	16.8	15.4	10.4	26.8	3.5	7.1	13.7	2.1
48	15628	Cloverleaf CDP, Texas	13.7	23.0	23.9	25.4	0.8	21.5	12.2	8.0
48	15976	College Station city, Texas	15.1	26.2	4.5	5.3	1.4	4.2	4.5	2.3
48	15988	Colleyville city, Texas	10.4	25.1	2.1	2.4	1.0	2.0	14.7	4.5
48	16432	Conroe city, Texas	21.2	20.9	12.1	12.6	3.5	6.8	5.8	3.9
48	16468	Converse city, Texas	9.7	30.4	3.1	14.2	2.8	1.7	7.9	3.1
48	16612	Coppell city, Texas	6.1	22.7	3.3	4.5	2.2	1.7	11.9	4.4
48	16624	Copperas Cove city, Texas	21.1	31.9	9.7	8.4	0.0	2.8	4.2	3.1
48	16696	Corinth city, Texas	11.5	24.3	7.0	10.8	0.5	8.6	8.5	2.5
48	17000	Corpus Christi city, Texas	23.8	23.2	12.5	12.4	2.7	8.9	6.6	2.6
48	17060	Corsicana city, Texas	22.8	25.2	8.0	22.2	3.4	3.1	21.0	0.8
48	19000	Dallas city, Texas	18.7	23.0	12.3	11.8	0.8	11.0	7.6	2.6
48	19624	Deer Park city, Texas	11.6	34.4	12.1	15.0	1.4	9.9	12.1	2.2
48	19792	Del Rio city, Texas	21.9	24.9	17.2	9.4	3.7	5.4	7.7	0.2
48	19900	Denison city, Texas	30.1	19.8	4.0	16.5	0.6	5.4	11.0	3.3
48	19972	Denton city, Texas	20.4	23.0	7.2	10.7	0.9	5.2	7.4	4.0
48	20092	DeSoto city, Texas	10.5	28.6	4.2	15.0	1.1	6.4	7.8	3.3
48	21628	Duncanville city, Texas	18.3	23.0	8.9	19.4	1.9	5.2	11.2	1.6
48	21892	Eagle Pass city, Texas	28.1	26.7	13.0	10.9	3.9	8.9	3.3	1.7
48	22660	Edinburg city, Texas	25.1	22.8	7.6	10.3	2.2	3.0	5.4	0.6
48	24000	El Paso city, Texas	20.4	28.4	8.0	12.6	1.1	4.0	6.8	2.7
48	24768	Euless city, Texas	13.5	27.7	6.7	13.7	0.5	6.4	7.6	4.9
48	25452	Farmers Branch city, Texas	18.9	24.7	10.4	9.0	0.8	8.3	6.0	6.5
48	26232	Flower Mound town, Texas	10.9	26.5	3.0	5.2	1.3	4.3	8.4	4.4
48	26736	Fort Hood CDP, Texas	23.9	27.8	10.4	17.6	–	–	–	–
48	27000	Fort Worth city, Texas	16.5	23.8	10.7	14.9	2.2	7.7	11.1	3.2
48	27540	Fresno CDP, Texas	16.4	29.2	5.5	14.3	5.3	2.3	4.5	2.4
48	27648	Friendswood city, Texas	8.5	23.4	6.4	8.5	5.4	6.5	10.9	2.9
48	27684	Frisco city, Texas	8.6	23.9	3.3	4.7	1.4	3.8	8.9	3.5
48	28068	Galveston city, Texas	29.8	21.5	7.0	8.1	1.6	5.9	5.2	1.6
48	29000	Garland city, Texas	20.0	27.0	11.6	14.5	1.0	8.8	10.3	2.9
48	29336	Georgetown city, Texas	20.3	27.0	5.2	7.1	0.9	5.6	7.4	2.9
48	30464	Grand Prairie city, Texas	14.1	25.5	11.0	20.3	0.7	8.4	12.2	5.0
48	30644	Grapevine city, Texas	15.1	26.8	9.2	8.8	1.0	7.4	6.2	3.4
48	30920	Greenville city, Texas	15.6	23.6	19.7	14.0	0.0	11.4	15.6	2.0
48	31928	Haltom City city, Texas	25.1	23.5	14.0	18.3	3.2	9.2	12.5	1.5
48	32312	Harker Heights city, Texas	22.6	31.6	3.4	8.8	0.0	3.0	3.2	2.6
48	32372	Harlingen city, Texas	29.1	22.0	7.6	7.3	0.7	4.5	3.9	2.8
48	35000	Houston city, Texas	19.4	22.1	12.1	12.8	3.2	11.0	8.0	3.1
48	35528	Huntsville city, Texas	31.0	25.2	4.6	3.8	–	–	–	–
48	35576	Hurst city, Texas	15.2	28.9	9.0	10.4	1.9	5.6	5.2	1.4
48	35624	Hutto city, Texas	15.2	24.0	10.5	17.3	0.8	7.4	13.0	4.4
48	37000	Irving city, Texas	15.5	22.8	11.1	14.7	0.5	8.7	7.2	3.9
48	38632	Keller city, Texas	10.2	24.7	3.1	5.4	3.3	3.0	10.0	4.3
48	39040	Kerrville city, Texas	36.0	16.0	11.8	9.1	4.6	10.2	7.7	0.8
48	39148	Killeen city, Texas	20.1	26.4	10.3	13.4	1.0	7.1	5.7	1.7
48	39352	Kingsville city, Texas	20.5	13.6	26.1	15.5	13.0	21.9	7.9	0.0
48	39952	Kyle city, Texas	17.3	31.5	8.8	12.2	0.0	7.8	5.7	8.0
48	40588	Lake Jackson city, Texas	9.1	16.0	8.9	8.8	0.0	10.2	27.0	1.1
48	41212	Lancaster city, Texas	18.4	29.5	7.1	22.8	0.0	3.2	13.9	6.8

Table E. Cities—Labor Force, Employment, and Educational Data, 2015—*Continued*

			Percent in each occupation group				Percent in each industry sector			
FIPS state code	FIPS place code	State/city	Service occupations	Sales and office occupations	Natural resources, construction, and maintenance occupations	Production, transportation, and material moving occupations	Agriculture, forestry, fishing and hunting, and mining	Construction	Manufacturing	Wholesale trade
48	41440	La Porte city, Texas	12.8	22.2	15.2	14.2	3.1	11.6	15.1	3.6
48	41464	Laredo city, Texas	22.1	27.9	8.2	12.5	2.9	5.3	1.6	3.9
48	41980	League City city, Texas	9.6	18.8	6.0	9.0	2.1	7.6	10.6	1.6
48	42016	Leander city, Texas	13.2	23.6	10.1	6.0	1.3	9.2	7.1	2.4
48	42508	Lewisville city, Texas	20.0	25.4	7.9	10.9	0.8	6.0	7.1	4.8
48	43012	Little Elm city, Texas	18.4	26.3	6.7	9.0	0.5	3.1	6.9	2.5
48	43888	Longview city, Texas	22.2	23.7	9.6	17.5	4.2	4.1	13.7	1.4
48	45000	Lubbock city, Texas	22.4	24.8	9.4	10.9	2.1	6.3	6.6	2.4
48	45072	Lufkin city, Texas	22.6	19.7	11.2	15.1	3.2	8.7	11.1	2.4
48	45384	McAllen city, Texas	18.0	28.6	6.3	8.9	2.4	4.3	6.0	3.9
48	45744	McKinney city, Texas	14.1	23.2	4.8	8.3	0.3	4.1	13.0	2.8
48	46452	Mansfield city, Texas	12.4	27.5	3.0	8.6	1.5	4.4	9.7	3.6
48	46776	Marshall city, Texas	23.7	20.7	9.7	18.2	5.5	5.9	10.1	2.7
48	47892	Mesquite city, Texas	19.3	29.7	13.5	14.1	0.8	10.1	7.7	2.6
48	48072	Midland city, Texas	14.9	25.4	16.7	12.0	20.6	6.2	3.9	2.8
48	48096	Midlothian city, Texas	14.3	31.4	7.9	6.2	0.2	10.4	2.8	1.9
48	48768	Mission city, Texas	19.4	31.8	8.4	7.7	3.1	6.9	3.4	5.8
48	48772	Mission Bend CDP, Texas	27.2	23.7	10.0	17.7	2.3	9.6	6.7	1.9
48	48804	Missouri City city, Texas	15.0	24.2	4.0	9.0	2.6	5.6	8.0	2.7
48	50100	Murphy city, Texas	10.2	22.5	4.7	1.4	–	–	–	–
48	50256	Nacogdoches city, Texas	21.5	24.1	11.9	10.4	6.2	4.6	6.7	1.2
48	50820	New Braunfels city, Texas	18.5	24.7	10.5	11.2	1.2	9.0	7.9	2.6
48	52356	North Richland Hills city, Texas	15.4	31.6	9.6	9.7	0.5	5.3	6.3	3.8
48	53388	Odessa city, Texas	15.1	26.0	15.5	16.2	14.6	9.2	4.9	5.0
48	55080	Paris city, Texas	16.4	29.7	8.7	20.6	1.5	6.4	17.6	3.0
48	56000	Pasadena city, Texas	17.8	20.6	17.7	20.9	1.8	13.5	15.3	2.4
48	56348	Pearland city, Texas	9.9	22.0	6.5	9.5	1.6	2.2	11.4	2.2
48	57176	Pflugerville city, Texas	10.7	26.1	7.4	7.6	2.2	3.4	8.4	2.0
48	57200	Pharr city, Texas	23.3	25.7	16.2	12.6	4.8	9.7	3.8	3.5
48	57980	Plainview city, Texas	16.7	35.5	11.9	17.4	7.6	7.6	4.0	2.7
48	58016	Plano city, Texas	13.7	24.0	4.5	4.3	0.8	4.2	7.5	2.8
48	58820	Port Arthur city, Texas	19.9	21.4	21.3	20.5	0.5	22.4	11.8	2.4
48	61796	Richardson city, Texas	13.7	21.9	4.8	5.7	0.9	5.6	8.8	2.2
48	62828	Rockwall city, Texas	8.1	26.6	8.9	9.9	3.4	6.6	9.7	3.0
48	63284	Rosenberg city, Texas	14.0	24.2	13.4	16.7	7.1	10.5	10.9	4.4
48	63500	Round Rock city, Texas	15.0	25.0	8.1	9.5	0.2	7.2	10.8	2.8
48	63572	Rowlett city, Texas	9.5	31.7	4.4	10.9	1.5	4.1	10.3	3.2
48	64064	Sachse city, Texas	9.4	30.6	10.1	6.3	1.9	4.5	7.3	4.7
48	64112	Saginaw city, Texas	16.1	33.8	9.0	8.0	3.6	3.7	6.4	4.7
48	64472	San Angelo city, Texas	17.1	26.6	11.2	14.5	6.7	7.1	5.4	3.5
48	65000	San Antonio city, Texas	21.0	26.0	10.6	10.5	1.2	8.0	6.0	2.7
48	65036	San Benito city, Texas	30.5	15.2	9.2	14.8	0.0	11.1	7.8	3.9
48	65516	San Juan city, Texas	27.3	23.7	14.9	10.9	2.9	11.6	1.9	5.3
48	65600	San Marcos city, Texas	16.3	32.0	15.7	9.5	2.8	10.6	3.1	1.7
48	66128	Schertz city, Texas	16.8	24.0	6.5	8.9	1.7	3.8	4.5	3.0
48	66644	Seguin city, Texas	20.6	21.8	10.5	24.0	2.7	2.8	21.9	2.0
48	67496	Sherman city, Texas	19.2	21.3	12.1	16.6	1.1	10.3	15.3	0.6
48	68636	Socorro city, Texas	25.1	23.4	15.2	21.1	0.3	10.4	6.8	1.8
48	69032	Southlake city, Texas	4.5	21.6	0.9	6.1	0.4	1.0	9.7	3.3
48	69596	Spring CDP, Texas	16.5	26.9	8.9	17.2	3.1	10.1	6.6	1.7
48	70208	Stephenville city, Texas	24.6	18.4	7.9	26.1	3.8	3.7	20.4	1.6
48	70808	Sugar Land city, Texas	7.4	23.8	3.2	4.2	4.5	4.4	10.7	3.9
48	72176	Temple city, Texas	22.9	21.3	6.8	16.7	0.7	6.0	7.4	4.0
48	72368	Texarkana city, Texas	22.2	24.2	6.6	6.8	0.0	5.1	9.5	4.0
48	72392	Texas City city, Texas	24.7	25.7	11.9	10.6	1.8	9.1	7.5	0.9
48	72530	The Colony city, Texas	14.1	32.6	5.1	5.7	0.0	3.4	5.1	3.2
48	72656	The Woodlands CDP, Texas	7.8	18.0	4.4	7.2	12.7	6.2	11.6	3.7
48	73057	Timberwood Park CDP, Texas	9.7	32.0	3.7	3.2	1.0	0.9	2.1	1.7
48	74144	Tyler city, Texas	17.7	23.8	9.9	11.9	3.4	6.7	6.7	1.5
48	74492	University Park city, Texas	5.4	24.9	0.0	1.2	2.4	1.6	5.9	1.1
48	75428	Victoria city, Texas	20.5	23.8	9.5	11.0	3.3	7.6	8.2	2.8
48	76000	Waco city, Texas	21.4	22.4	9.6	13.7	0.7	6.6	10.0	2.8
48	76672	Watauga city, Texas	17.0	28.9	7.3	18.5	0.7	6.7	9.4	4.5
48	76816	Waxahachie city, Texas	10.3	28.9	10.2	15.0	2.6	5.3	14.0	2.4
48	76864	Weatherford city, Texas	13.6	28.6	7.2	14.5	4.0	6.5	12.0	3.5
48	77272	Weslaco city, Texas	23.0	33.4	5.8	7.3	1.1	1.8	4.9	3.1
48	77728	West Odessa CDP, Texas	15.6	29.3	14.9	23.4	12.9	10.2	8.3	2.8
48	79000	Wichita Falls city, Texas	21.4	23.9	9.5	12.8	2.5	6.4	7.1	1.6
48	80356	Wylie city, Texas	12.0	32.4	7.6	4.2	1.7	2.4	14.6	2.6
49	00000	**UTAH**	15.4	26.1	8.6	13.2	2.0	6.8	11.3	2.8
49	01310	American Fork city, Utah	14.7	21.2	9.3	10.3	1.1	12.9	6.0	2.1
49	07690	Bountiful city, Utah	10.2	27.5	7.4	7.0	0.4	6.0	9.2	3.3
49	11320	Cedar City city, Utah	17.1	19.0	10.3	13.4	0.5	6.2	12.9	1.7
49	13850	Clearfield city, Utah	17.5	30.2	8.6	19.7	0.3	5.6	12.7	4.0
49	14290	Clinton city, Utah	18.0	22.5	7.4	14.2	0.0	6.8	10.6	1.8

Table E. Cities—Labor Force, Employment, and Educational Data, 2015—*Continued*

FIPS state code	FIPS place code	State/city	Percent in each occupation group				Percent in each industry sector			
			Service occupations	Sales and office occupations	Natural resources, construction, and maintenance occupations	Production, transportation, and material moving occupations	Agriculture, forestry, fishing and hunting, and mining	Construction	Manufacturing	Wholesale trade
49	16270	Cottonwood Heights city, Utah	11.4	25.8	5.5	10.2	0.0	4.4	8.5	3.8
49	20120	Draper city, Utah	11.6	22.7	2.6	5.6	1.2	3.9	6.8	5.0
49	20810	Eagle Mountain city, Utah	10.1	23.9	10.3	11.3	0.9	11.1	12.0	3.0
49	24740	Farmington city, Utah	14.5	24.0	8.2	9.7	1.1	7.9	6.1	2.0
49	34970	Herriman city, Utah	11.8	25.8	13.3	7.6	1.3	17.3	7.2	4.3
49	36070	Holladay city, Utah	15.3	30.7	3.8	3.9	0.0	2.5	5.5	3.3
49	40360	Kaysville city, Utah	11.1	25.0	8.3	7.2	0.0	6.5	10.0	3.6
49	40470	Kearns CDP, Utah	15.3	27.8	13.1	23.9	1.1	9.9	21.1	2.6
49	43660	Layton city, Utah	13.4	27.8	5.9	15.2	0.9	6.2	12.8	3.0
49	44320	Lehi city, Utah	13.3	26.0	6.8	8.0	0.3	10.1	9.4	2.2
49	45860	Logan city, Utah	17.5	23.8	8.9	14.1	1.1	4.3	15.2	0.5
49	47290	Magna CDP, Utah	18.8	24.6	15.3	22.1	2.1	12.3	19.6	2.4
49	49710	Midvale city, Utah	19.2	31.9	7.4	9.2	2.4	4.9	10.8	0.0
49	50150	Millcreek CDP, Utah	14.0	22.6	6.2	7.0	0.3	4.5	9.8	1.7
49	53230	Murray city, Utah	16.6	30.1	9.9	11.4	0.0	7.5	14.5	2.6
49	55980	Ogden city, Utah	15.6	24.1	10.2	25.5	1.5	9.0	21.3	4.0
49	57300	Orem city, Utah	18.3	26.2	7.7	11.8	0.7	7.1	9.8	2.3
49	60930	Pleasant Grove city, Utah	15.3	24.4	6.0	11.7	0.3	6.6	7.9	3.2
49	62470	Provo city, Utah	18.3	23.9	5.2	8.7	0.4	5.1	7.0	2.6
49	64340	Riverton city, Utah	11.1	27.6	5.3	9.7	0.0	6.3	6.4	5.7
49	65110	Roy city, Utah	15.4	27.5	7.2	19.5	0.0	4.3	15.9	3.7
49	65330	St. George city, Utah	23.3	26.7	8.4	9.8	0.3	5.7	6.0	1.0
49	67000	Salt Lake City city, Utah	16.1	24.4	6.3	10.6	0.7	4.6	9.6	2.0
49	67440	Sandy city, Utah	12.7	30.3	7.7	7.6	0.2	6.4	7.5	2.3
49	67825	Saratoga Springs city, Utah	10.7	26.1	4.5	6.0	0.0	10.3	8.7	5.0
49	70850	South Jordan city, Utah	11.8	25.3	4.5	8.5	2.6	3.2	12.0	4.7
49	71070	South Salt Lake city, Utah	16.5	32.0	6.3	22.3	0.6	4.7	10.6	4.1
49	71290	Spanish Fork city, Utah	14.7	24.1	12.5	15.3	0.3	10.1	16.3	3.1
49	72280	Springville city, Utah	16.8	22.8	8.7	14.5	0.0	9.2	14.4	5.1
49	74810	Syracuse city, Utah	15.0	27.1	4.3	13.4	2.4	8.1	10.4	1.0
49	75360	Taylorsville city, Utah	12.9	33.5	6.7	16.7	3.5	7.8	13.5	3.4
49	76680	Tooele city, Utah	17.2	25.9	12.9	15.9	3.9	8.5	11.4	2.6
49	81960	Washington city, Utah	20.3	42.0	11.3	8.8	8.1	8.8	5.9	2.4
49	82950	West Jordan city, Utah	15.7	27.7	9.5	14.0	1.2	7.0	13.8	2.6
49	83470	West Valley City city, Utah	19.3	29.1	12.1	21.7	0.7	8.6	15.9	3.0
50	00000	**VERMONT**	17.1	21.3	9.4	11.0	2.4	7.0	11.0	2.2
50	10675	Burlington city, Vermont	24.3	24.5	3.6	8.1	1.1	0.8	3.3	1.9
51	00000	**VIRGINIA**	16.8	22.1	8.5	9.6	1.0	6.5	7.2	2.0
51	01000	Alexandria city, Virginia	15.1	16.7	6.1	4.5	0.1	5.6	2.5	0.8
51	01912	Annandale CDP, Virginia	31.1	14.8	9.5	4.8	0.0	9.6	0.9	0.9
51	03000	Arlington CDP, Virginia	9.7	14.2	4.3	2.1	0.1	5.7	2.1	0.8
51	03320	Ashburn CDP, Virginia	10.6	25.8	3.1	6.5	1.0	3.1	2.7	1.5
51	04088	Bailey's Crossroads CDP, Virginia	29.3	15.2	10.0	7.7	0.3	9.4	1.9	0.0
51	07784	Blacksburg town, Virginia	17.7	15.8	1.8	2.0	–	–	–	–
51	08472	Bon Air CDP, Virginia	12.4	23.2	5.4	5.7	0.0	6.0	6.1	3.4
51	11464	Burke CDP, Virginia	13.5	21.3	4.6	4.0	0.0	5.1	1.7	2.3
51	13720	Cave Spring CDP, Virginia	18.0	21.1	3.0	8.8	0.0	2.9	5.9	2.4
51	14440	Centreville CDP, Virginia	16.6	22.6	4.1	6.3	0.0	4.3	3.2	1.0
51	14744	Chantilly CDP, Virginia	11.0	20.9	12.1	6.9	0.0	8.5	4.1	2.7
51	14968	Charlottesville city, Virginia	22.1	18.3	6.1	4.1	2.5	3.1	3.1	0.3
51	15176	Cherry Hill CDP, Virginia	24.7	22.3	7.0	5.2	0.0	2.6	2.4	0.7
51	16000	Chesapeake city, Virginia	16.1	24.2	9.4	10.5	0.3	6.1	8.6	1.8
51	16096	Chester CDP, Virginia	26.7	16.8	7.8	16.6	0.6	5.0	8.0	8.2
51	16608	Christiansburg town, Virginia	10.9	25.5	5.0	10.8	0.0	2.2	11.8	1.4
51	21088	Dale City CDP, Virginia	22.7	22.1	13.0	10.7	0.2	9.8	1.9	3.6
51	21344	Danville city, Virginia	24.4	23.2	4.5	17.1	0.7	4.8	11.5	0.7
51	26496	Fairfax city, Virginia	17.9	22.7	3.4	2.3	0.0	4.5	2.6	1.3
51	26875	Fair Oaks CDP, Virginia	16.2	11.9	1.6	1.7	0.5	2.3	2.0	1.3
51	29136	Fort Hunt CDP, Virginia	14.9	15.3	1.8	3.5	0.5	3.5	2.0	0.9
51	29744	Fredericksburg city, Virginia	30.3	18.1	6.7	3.0	0.0	3.5	2.3	3.2
51	35000	Hampton city, Virginia	17.2	25.6	10.8	13.3	0.3	7.2	12.3	1.2
51	35624	Harrisonburg city, Virginia	24.3	19.3	8.2	8.7	0.7	6.1	8.2	2.1
51	36648	Herndon town, Virginia	20.4	16.9	10.7	5.4	0.0	9.8	3.3	0.3
51	38424	Hopewell city, Virginia	14.9	23.4	12.2	17.5	0.7	9.4	13.0	0.7
51	39448	Idylwood CDP, Virginia	20.7	21.9	5.6	3.6	0.4	4.4	1.6	2.3
51	43432	Lake Ridge CDP, Virginia	13.4	26.4	4.5	3.5	0.5	3.8	4.1	1.4
51	44280	Laurel CDP, Virginia	20.5	30.0	4.5	8.4	2.6	5.4	5.4	1.8
51	44984	Leesburg town, Virginia	17.3	17.3	4.6	10.0	0.5	7.2	6.3	2.5
51	45784	Lincolnia CDP, Virginia	25.7	16.8	10.7	7.4	0.0	11.7	1.0	1.5
51	45957	Linton Hall CDP, Virginia	12.7	20.9	3.0	7.0	0.0	4.2	5.1	1.4
51	47064	Lorton CDP, Virginia	24.4	10.0	8.0	7.8	0.9	4.0	2.3	0.0
51	47672	Lynchburg city, Virginia	23.0	20.2	6.5	8.7	0.2	3.0	7.5	1.7
51	48376	McLean CDP, Virginia	9.1	12.6	2.2	1.6	0.4	1.7	5.2	0.3
51	48952	Manassas city, Virginia	17.9	24.6	16.4	11.0	0.8	16.9	6.4	0.9

Table E. Cities—Labor Force, Employment, and Educational Data, 2015—*Continued*

FIPS state code	FIPS place code	State/city	Percent in each occupation group				Percent in each industry sector			
			Service occupations	Sales and office occupations	Natural resources, construction, and maintenance occupations	Production, transportation, and material moving occupations	Agriculture, forestry, fishing and hunting, and mining	Construction	Manufacturing	Wholesale trade
51	49792	Marumsco CDP, Virginia	22.4	22.4	13.1	11.4	0.0	13.1	2.5	0.8
51	50856	Mechanicsville CDP, Virginia	10.7	31.1	12.0	5.0	0.5	8.8	3.8	3.1
51	52658	Montclair CDP, Virginia	17.1	13.5	2.9	3.3	0.7	3.8	1.2	1.1
51	56000	Newport News city, Virginia	16.6	26.1	8.4	12.8	0.1	3.9	17.0	1.9
51	57000	Norfolk city, Virginia	21.5	22.6	12.3	10.6	0.1	7.2	6.4	1.9
51	58472	Oakton CDP, Virginia	14.4	13.1	5.5	2.2	0.0	3.4	1.9	0.3
51	61832	Petersburg city, Virginia	26.9	28.3	3.0	27.1	0.0	1.9	10.8	1.0
51	64000	Portsmouth city, Virginia	18.7	25.0	10.9	15.4	1.1	7.4	10.2	1.1
51	66672	Reston CDP, Virginia	13.2	19.4	3.8	2.2	0.2	3.7	3.9	1.6
51	67000	Richmond city, Virginia	21.9	22.1	5.6	9.1	0.2	3.8	5.7	1.4
51	68000	Roanoke city, Virginia	21.8	22.7	8.9	14.4	0.4	7.6	9.5	2.2
51	68880	Rose Hill CDP (Fairfax County), Virginia	12.6	23.0	10.1	4.4	0.3	6.6	2.1	2.8
51	70000	Salem city, Virginia	14.6	25.7	9.2	10.7	0.9	7.6	10.1	2.8
51	72272	Short Pump CDP, Virginia	8.0	21.6	2.2	5.7	0.0	2.4	6.0	3.5
51	74100	South Riding CDP, Virginia	8.2	20.0	4.2	2.0	0.0	5.5	3.6	0.8
51	74592	Springfield CDP, Virginia	24.4	23.7	4.6	7.4	0.7	3.9	2.0	1.5
51	75216	Staunton city, Virginia	16.6	28.1	10.1	15.7	0.0	5.5	11.1	4.9
51	75376	Sterling CDP, Virginia	29.8	19.2	7.1	11.4	0.3	4.8	4.2	1.4
51	76432	Suffolk city, Virginia	21.5	24.1	8.7	10.7	0.5	6.8	11.7	1.8
51	79560	Tuckahoe CDP, Virginia	17.7	30.7	3.9	7.5	0.0	5.0	3.3	2.6
51	79952	Tysons Corner CDP, Virginia	7.2	14.4	2.5	3.3	0.0	2.4	2.6	2.1
51	82000	Virginia Beach city, Virginia	17.8	25.3	9.4	8.2	0.4	7.2	5.9	2.7
51	83680	Waynesboro city, Virginia	21.5	31.0	14.0	15.4	0.0	5.7	9.3	2.7
51	84368	West Falls Church CDP, Virginia	25.4	16.0	13.1	9.2	0.0	12.1	4.6	0.2
51	84976	West Springfield CDP, Virginia	12.5	21.4	2.1	1.8	0.0	2.1	2.0	0.3
51	86720	Winchester city, Virginia	15.1	19.1	5.1	14.1	9.4	5.6	5.1	4.3
51	87410	Woodlawn CDP (Fairfax County), Virginia	31.1	17.7	13.0	12.8	2.3	9.8	1.0	3.2
53	00000	**WASHINGTON**	16.9	21.8	9.9	11.5	2.7	6.5	10.3	2.9
53	03180	Auburn city, Washington	17.5	26.4	9.7	17.8	1.1	7.9	15.8	4.3
53	03736	Bainbridge Island city, Washington	4.4	15.6	4.0	7.1	1.9	1.3	3.9	2.3
53	05210	Bellevue city, Washington	14.2	15.1	3.2	6.1	0.7	2.3	8.9	2.7
53	05280	Bellingham city, Washington	19.8	26.4	6.8	10.9	1.8	3.7	7.7	1.9
53	07380	Bothell city, Washington	13.7	23.4	8.3	8.8	0.0	6.3	12.4	2.9
53	07395	Bothell West CDP, Washington	10.4	18.3	10.2	7.1	0.0	8.8	17.0	0.9
53	07695	Bremerton city, Washington	22.4	24.4	11.1	12.1	0.8	3.9	15.2	0.7
53	08552	Bryn Mawr-Skyway CDP, Washington	27.4	19.4	9.3	19.1	0.7	8.8	16.2	1.9
53	08850	Burien city, Washington	18.6	22.3	12.5	17.8	0.0	9.1	12.5	6.0
53	09480	Camas city, Washington	16.2	27.4	6.1	4.9	0.0	7.5	13.6	6.2
53	14940	Cottage Lake CDP, Washington	9.5	15.8	4.4	5.5	0.0	5.2	11.5	2.0
53	17635	Des Moines city, Washington	21.6	23.6	7.5	13.3	1.4	2.8	14.7	5.4
53	19630	Eastmont CDP, Washington	13.0	24.7	12.0	12.7	1.9	5.2	26.7	3.8
53	20750	Edmonds city, Washington	18.1	19.4	8.9	9.2	1.0	7.3	8.1	2.8
53	22640	Everett city, Washington	22.4	23.2	13.3	12.8	1.3	7.5	17.0	2.0
53	23160	Fairwood CDP (King County), Washington	13.9	29.7	4.8	6.8	0.0	2.0	12.0	6.0
53	23515	Federal Way city, Washington	18.2	21.8	10.8	15.2	0.2	7.7	14.1	2.3
53	24188	Five Corners CDP, Washington	18.0	26.1	10.4	20.8	0.0	12.9	14.3	3.4
53	27785	Graham CDP, Washington	13.9	28.3	16.8	16.8	1.0	13.5	9.4	2.9
53	33805	Issaquah city, Washington	10.2	21.5	1.7	4.9	0.4	1.8	7.8	3.8
53	35170	Kenmore city, Washington	9.0	20.7	4.2	7.1	0.4	5.3	10.3	2.7
53	35275	Kennewick city, Washington	21.6	19.0	14.3	12.9	5.8	9.0	6.9	1.8
53	35415	Kent city, Washington	20.6	22.0	9.6	19.1	0.7	6.8	10.0	3.2
53	35940	Kirkland city, Washington	10.9	21.5	4.8	4.0	0.3	4.7	10.6	4.1
53	36745	Lacey city, Washington	21.1	27.4	5.3	8.1	0.6	6.1	6.6	2.7
53	37900	Lake Stevens city, Washington	14.3	27.4	13.9	11.2	0.1	7.9	17.5	2.0
53	38038	Lakewood city, Washington	21.8	22.4	10.6	15.5	1.0	8.3	6.0	2.2
53	40245	Longview city, Washington	20.1	20.1	15.0	19.0	1.4	9.7	15.1	0.9
53	40840	Lynnwood city, Washington	18.0	29.5	9.4	11.9	0.0	4.9	9.8	6.1
53	43150	Maple Valley city, Washington	7.7	29.7	8.1	7.1	1.4	9.2	11.9	5.1
53	43955	Marysville city, Washington	18.6	23.1	14.9	14.7	0.7	7.4	21.8	2.8
53	45005	Mercer Island city, Washington	5.8	10.3	0.4	2.5	0.4	1.4	4.4	2.0
53	45865	Mill Creek city, Washington	11.4	23.2	7.0	1.9	0.0	4.5	14.2	1.6
53	45870	Mill Creek East CDP, Washington	7.1	22.9	3.7	11.0	0.0	3.1	16.6	0.8
53	47245	Moses Lake city, Washington	28.8	19.2	12.7	5.4	13.2	0.7	16.3	3.8
53	47490	Mountlake Terrace city, Washington	26.3	23.1	7.7	4.2	0.0	2.6	10.0	1.6
53	47560	Mount Vernon city, Washington	15.3	19.4	16.7	19.0	7.2	11.8	14.7	3.5
53	47735	Mukilteo city, Washington	9.6	17.1	3.7	6.9	0.0	1.2	31.4	1.3
53	50360	Oak Harbor city, Washington	17.9	28.3	21.2	8.3	2.1	4.3	10.9	0.3
53	51300	Olympia city, Washington	23.3	18.9	5.5	10.0	2.4	2.4	5.5	1.1
53	51795	Orchards CDP, Washington	22.6	21.6	16.8	14.1	1.2	11.8	11.2	4.4
53	53335	Parkland CDP, Washington	23.0	28.2	12.7	13.3	3.2	6.4	9.6	1.6
53	53545	Pasco city, Washington	21.0	16.5	17.6	18.0	11.1	4.0	11.6	3.5

Table E. Cities—Labor Force, Employment, and Educational Data, 2015—*Continued*

			Percent in each occupation group				Percent in each industry sector			
FIPS state code	FIPS place code	State/city	Service occupations	Sales and office occupations	Natural resources, construction, and maintenance occupations	Production, transportation, and material moving occupations	Agriculture, forestry, fishing and hunting, and mining	Construction	Manufacturing	Wholesale trade
53	56625	Pullman city, Washington	21.2	15.4	2.8	9.1	0.0	0.3	11.3	0.5
53	56695	Puyallup city, Washington	17.2	22.5	11.4	14.9	0.1	9.3	9.6	3.4
53	57535	Redmond city, Washington	9.6	18.4	2.4	3.0	0.3	1.6	8.3	2.5
53	57745	Renton city, Washington	20.2	21.6	6.3	11.2	0.0	7.7	10.7	2.7
53	58235	Richland city, Washington	15.4	19.7	7.1	10.3	0.3	8.2	5.4	0.5
53	61000	Salmon Creek CDP, Washington	12.8	24.2	11.5	11.4	0.0	12.2	11.2	2.8
53	61115	Sammamish city, Washington	5.7	19.6	2.2	1.5	0.3	3.5	8.1	1.8
53	62288	SeaTac city, Washington	19.3	22.2	8.3	25.7	0.0	8.0	8.6	1.3
53	63000	Seattle city, Washington	14.3	17.9	3.6	5.0	0.3	3.4	6.2	2.2
53	63960	Shoreline city, Washington	17.9	20.8	7.5	7.2	0.4	5.6	9.4	1.8
53	64380	Silver Firs CDP, Washington	9.2	21.4	6.5	11.0	1.9	4.7	15.7	3.8
53	65922	South Hill CDP, Washington	14.1	26.4	10.4	15.4	0.0	6.3	14.2	3.1
53	66255	Spanaway CDP, Washington	17.7	29.7	13.0	18.5	0.8	6.1	11.3	2.5
53	67000	Spokane city, Washington	21.5	23.4	6.5	11.9	0.5	4.5	7.0	4.4
53	67167	Spokane Valley city, Washington	17.2	32.1	9.4	11.9	0.5	8.1	10.5	3.7
53	70000	Tacoma city, Washington	23.4	23.6	8.4	11.8	0.5	6.2	8.7	2.9
53	72625	Tukwila city, Washington	22.8	26.5	8.3	18.2	4.4	6.9	7.8	7.9
53	73307	Union Hill-Novelty Hill CDP, Washington	9.0	14.6	6.1	5.8	1.0	5.4	5.8	1.3
53	73465	University Place city, Washington	17.4	31.2	3.6	8.2	0.3	2.8	5.8	3.4
53	74060	Vancouver city, Washington	18.5	23.9	10.5	13.0	0.6	8.1	10.8	2.9
53	75775	Walla Walla city, Washington	23.3	20.2	8.8	8.2	5.4	5.9	6.4	1.4
53	77105	Wenatchee city, Washington	25.4	29.0	8.0	9.6	5.7	5.6	3.3	5.6
53	80010	Yakima city, Washington	17.3	18.1	15.6	20.7	9.5	4.0	9.1	6.0
54	00000	**WEST VIRGINIA**	19.8	23.4	11.1	12.3	4.2	6.3	7.4	2.2
54	14600	Charleston city, West Virginia	17.1	23.6	2.7	5.0	0.9	2.7	4.2	1.7
54	39460	Huntington city, West Virginia	19.3	27.2	4.8	7.9	0.3	3.1	5.7	4.0
54	55756	Morgantown city, West Virginia	15.7	20.0	1.6	5.7	0.3	3.4	3.7	1.9
54	62140	Parkersburg city, West Virginia	26.1	27.2	11.8	9.1	3.0	7.2	6.1	1.6
54	86452	Wheeling city, West Virginia	17.1	29.4	5.3	12.6	2.5	5.4	5.2	5.4
55	00000	**WISCONSIN**	16.9	22.4	8.6	16.9	2.4	5.6	18.4	2.6
55	02375	Appleton city, Wisconsin	19.0	23.7	5.7	17.7	0.4	3.4	20.5	2.4
55	06500	Beloit city, Wisconsin	14.5	23.4	9.2	27.8	0.5	5.5	30.0	1.8
55	10025	Brookfield city, Wisconsin	9.9	20.7	5.3	5.6	0.0	4.3	13.9	1.9
55	11950	Caledonia village, Wisconsin	14.1	22.7	7.5	14.0	0.5	6.5	22.4	4.4
55	19775	De Pere city, Wisconsin	11.0	28.4	8.2	12.2	0.6	5.7	18.5	1.7
55	22300	Eau Claire city, Wisconsin	14.6	24.7	6.6	15.3	1.0	3.7	13.3	3.0
55	25950	Fitchburg city, Wisconsin	15.9	16.6	5.4	9.0	0.4	2.4	10.3	1.8
55	26275	Fond du Lac city, Wisconsin	18.9	24.7	8.3	18.4	0.4	3.5	20.6	1.4
55	27300	Franklin city, Wisconsin	10.1	27.2	4.2	8.1	0.0	2.7	11.9	3.2
55	31000	Green Bay city, Wisconsin	19.5	23.7	7.5	20.9	1.5	4.1	20.7	2.4
55	31175	Greenfield city, Wisconsin	16.2	25.4	5.3	19.5	0.3	2.6	21.9	1.7
55	37825	Janesville city, Wisconsin	16.1	20.6	7.7	20.3	0.6	5.3	20.8	3.4
55	39225	Kenosha city, Wisconsin	19.5	24.8	7.2	19.4	0.9	3.6	19.8	3.1
55	40775	La Crosse city, Wisconsin	26.2	25.0	3.7	11.1	0.6	2.6	10.3	2.2
55	48000	Madison city, Wisconsin	18.6	20.3	3.4	6.5	0.2	2.5	6.4	1.8
55	48500	Manitowoc city, Wisconsin	17.8	25.2	4.2	24.9	1.4	2.4	29.6	2.6
55	51000	Menomonee Falls village, Wisconsin	8.4	21.8	3.5	15.4	0.0	2.3	24.7	5.1
55	51150	Mequon city, Wisconsin	8.9	17.9	4.3	9.4	0.8	5.9	10.1	3.5
55	53000	Milwaukee city, Wisconsin	23.0	21.8	6.2	17.3	0.5	4.5	15.2	2.4
55	54875	Mount Pleasant village, Wisconsin	17.1	23.7	6.0	18.3	1.2	4.9	24.0	2.2
55	55275	Muskego city, Wisconsin	15.6	20.8	10.5	9.8	0.4	10.2	20.5	4.1
55	55750	Neenah city, Wisconsin	20.2	23.5	3.5	19.1	0.3	2.5	23.3	2.4
55	56375	New Berlin city, Wisconsin	13.1	28.9	3.9	9.4	0.2	2.4	15.9	5.0
55	58800	Oak Creek city, Wisconsin	16.6	22.1	5.6	21.5	0.9	2.3	20.5	3.3
55	60500	Oshkosh city, Wisconsin	21.1	27.0	4.5	19.0	0.6	2.7	22.5	1.1
55	63300	Pleasant Prairie village, Wisconsin	16.9	20.6	8.6	14.8	0.6	6.4	20.8	4.2
55	66000	Racine city, Wisconsin	22.8	23.4	7.2	23.6	0.7	4.6	19.9	2.8
55	72975	Sheboygan city, Wisconsin	17.5	18.9	6.9	34.2	1.3	2.6	37.5	1.7
55	75125	South Milwaukee city, Wisconsin	19.3	28.8	12.2	16.4	0.0	2.9	14.9	2.6
55	77200	Stevens Point city, Wisconsin	22.1	26.8	4.2	13.3	0.7	2.5	12.0	0.0
55	78600	Sun Prairie city, Wisconsin	14.9	26.6	4.2	9.5	1.5	2.5	11.2	2.6
55	78650	Superior city, Wisconsin	27.2	19.8	7.3	16.8	0.3	4.4	7.4	3.6
55	83975	Watertown city, Wisconsin	17.6	22.0	8.6	24.9	1.1	5.5	27.1	7.6
55	84250	Waukesha city, Wisconsin	16.9	25.3	5.7	13.1	0.5	4.5	18.1	2.4
55	84475	Wausau city, Wisconsin	16.5	26.8	5.1	16.6	0.4	1.8	18.6	1.8
55	84675	Wauwatosa city, Wisconsin	13.5	21.9	3.2	6.3	1.1	1.8	12.0	3.2
55	85300	West Allis city, Wisconsin	17.5	26.6	8.4	16.5	0.0	6.0	21.0	5.0
55	85350	West Bend city, Wisconsin	17.0	24.7	6.4	22.1	0.6	4.7	23.4	3.1
56	00000	**WYOMING**	17.4	22.1	15.8	13.2	12.9	7.3	4.1	1.8
56	13150	Casper city, Wyoming	19.3	25.4	14.9	11.8	8.9	5.7	5.6	2.3
56	13900	Cheyenne city, Wyoming	14.5	24.5	8.5	12.7	4.6	2.6	3.0	2.1
56	31855	Gillette city, Wyoming	19.0	20.2	17.6	20.1	22.5	5.8	3.5	3.7
56	45050	Laramie city, Wyoming	24.8	21.4	6.4	7.8	0.7	4.1	3.0	0.9
56	67235	Rock Springs city, Wyoming	11.8	20.1	24.3	10.7	16.7	13.9	4.7	2.2

Table E. Cities—Labor Force, Employment, and Educational Data, 2015

			Percent in each industry sector								
FIPS state code	FIPS place code	State/city	Retail trade	Transportation and warehousing, and utilities	Information	Finance and insurance, and real estate and rental and leasing	Professional, scientific, and management, and administrative and waste management services	Educational services, and health care and social assistance	Arts, entertainment, and recreation, and accommodation and food services	Other services, except public administration	Public administration
00	00000	**UNITED STATES**	11.5	5.1	2.1	6.5	11.3	22.9	9.8	4.9	4.6
01	00000	**ALABAMA**	11.8	5.3	1.7	5.5	9.6	22.5	8.4	5.2	5.2
01	00820	Alabaster city, Alabama	14.4	4.0	2.2	5.0	12.4	25.0	5.6	7.3	2.4
01	00988	Albertville city, Alabama	13.3	8.6	1.0	7.6	9.2	11.6	8.5	3.5	3.2
01	01852	Anniston city, Alabama	10.6	2.5	0.6	2.9	11.0	24.1	19.4	3.4	7.2
01	02956	Athens city, Alabama	8.5	4.5	0.4	3.7	12.0	23.2	9.7	6.8	4.9
01	03076	Auburn city, Alabama	10.5	2.1	2.7	5.2	7.7	30.6	13.1	4.1	2.5
01	05980	Bessemer city, Alabama	12.0	6.9	0.0	4.2	4.0	19.6	16.6	8.3	5.1
01	07000	Birmingham city, Alabama	10.1	5.0	2.4	7.2	11.0	26.3	10.7	5.5	5.6
01	19648	Daphne city, Alabama	16.7	1.8	3.1	7.2	13.3	23.6	10.6	7.4	3.5
01	20104	Decatur city, Alabama	10.9	2.7	1.1	5.6	10.0	20.9	8.1	4.4	5.4
01	21184	Dothan city, Alabama	14.5	6.5	1.5	3.3	7.3	26.2	11.2	4.9	4.3
01	24184	Enterprise city, Alabama	11.7	5.8	0.8	2.7	5.9	30.1	9.3	6.1	12.0
01	26896	Florence city, Alabama	10.0	3.5	1.0	6.6	5.2	24.3	16.3	6.4	3.9
01	28696	Gadsden city, Alabama	7.0	2.6	2.7	2.7	4.7	15.4	13.3	4.7	6.6
01	35800	Homewood city, Alabama	9.7	2.8	1.3	9.0	16.5	33.0	10.6	7.5	1.0
01	35896	Hoover city, Alabama	11.4	3.3	2.7	11.6	13.4	26.2	7.9	8.0	2.2
01	37000	Huntsville city, Alabama	12.5	1.9	2.4	3.8	16.7	25.1	10.1	4.5	7.0
01	45784	Madison city, Alabama	9.0	2.7	0.8	3.9	28.6	17.9	6.9	4.5	10.5
01	50000	Mobile city, Alabama	12.0	4.7	2.1	4.4	10.2	27.5	9.4	6.4	3.0
01	51000	Montgomery city, Alabama	12.5	2.5	1.3	6.2	10.6	21.8	11.9	5.1	11.1
01	51696	Mountain Brook city, Alabama	6.1	5.2	0.8	16.4	19.5	32.4	7.1	3.3	2.3
01	55200	Northport city, Alabama	15.4	2.3	3.2	3.3	5.8	34.1	3.1	3.9	6.8
01	57048	Opelika city, Alabama	13.5	5.0	2.1	4.4	10.6	27.5	10.3	1.6	3.1
01	57576	Oxford city, Alabama	8.7	5.4	1.8	4.2	6.3	24.1	8.1	3.6	7.5
01	58848	Pelham city, Alabama	11.7	2.7	1.7	15.6	18.6	15.2	9.5	5.0	5.5
01	59472	Phenix City city, Alabama	11.9	2.1	4.9	5.2	11.6	24.4	2.4	7.8	8.3
01	62328	Prattville city, Alabama	6.8	2.0	1.4	4.3	8.9	23.7	11.8	4.7	15.7
01	62496	Prichard city, Alabama	6.7	9.3	0.0	8.1	2.3	33.6	8.9	9.7	4.8
01	76944	Trussville city, Alabama	12.6	9.5	3.4	4.7	7.7	24.2	1.6	4.6	4.3
01	77256	Tuscaloosa city, Alabama	9.2	5.0	2.4	4.0	7.8	34.5	8.8	4.1	3.9
01	78552	Vestavia Hills city, Alabama	8.0	1.6	2.9	13.4	13.0	29.7	7.2	6.0	2.7
02	00000	**ALASKA**	11.0	7.6	1.9	3.6	8.6	23.4	9.7	4.7	11.7
02	03000	Anchorage municipality, Alaska	11.5	7.2	2.7	4.4	11.6	23.3	11.0	4.9	9.3
02	05000	Badger CDP, Alaska	12.4	10.6	1.6	0.8	6.7	24.2	8.2	9.0	14.9
02	24230	Fairbanks city, Alaska	18.8	10.3	0.0	3.5	6.9	25.6	9.9	4.6	12.4
02	36400	Juneau city and borough, Alaska	7.1	8.0	1.3	4.1	7.8	21.9	6.1	5.7	23.1
04	00000	**ARIZONA**	12.5	5.0	1.9	8.2	12.2	21.7	11.2	4.7	5.1
04	02830	Apache Junction city, Arizona	22.2	0.9	0.0	6.6	11.7	32.0	6.4	5.0	4.6
04	04720	Avondale city, Arizona	20.8	6.6	2.1	7.8	7.5	20.9	8.1	3.4	8.9
04	07940	Buckeye town, Arizona	18.7	10.0	0.3	6.3	8.0	21.9	11.7	3.0	5.6
04	08220	Bullhead City city, Arizona	17.6	6.4	2.2	5.2	5.7	16.1	29.6	6.4	2.9
04	10530	Casa Grande city, Arizona	13.3	1.9	1.3	4.9	8.2	22.4	12.2	1.9	7.0
04	10670	Casas Adobes CDP, Arizona	15.5	3.6	1.0	5.5	11.7	26.5	10.4	3.8	5.5
04	11230	Catalina Foothills CDP, Arizona	10.2	3.3	0.9	9.1	15.3	30.2	9.1	3.2	4.1
04	12000	Chandler city, Arizona	12.6	4.4	2.5	11.5	13.8	19.3	9.4	3.7	3.5
04	20540	Drexel Heights CDP, Arizona	13.7	9.8	2.0	4.7	10.4	20.2	7.5	4.4	8.5
04	22220	El Mirage city, Arizona	14.7	5.5	2.9	9.6	9.9	24.3	11.2	3.1	2.1
04	23620	Flagstaff city, Arizona	10.3	3.9	1.6	4.1	6.6	31.7	21.1	3.7	7.2
04	23760	Florence town, Arizona	–	–	–	–	–	–	–	–	–
04	25030	Fortuna Foothills CDP, Arizona	10.9	5.9	1.0	7.7	4.2	19.7	6.7	9.0	17.5
04	25300	Fountain Hills town, Arizona	6.0	6.3	0.7	11.4	11.0	23.5	25.2	5.8	1.8
04	27400	Gilbert town, Arizona	11.8	5.4	2.1	11.9	12.3	21.0	8.6	5.1	4.1
04	27820	Glendale city, Arizona	12.8	6.2	1.7	8.4	11.5	20.9	10.2	6.3	4.1
04	28380	Goodyear city, Arizona	11.3	7.4	2.0	5.9	12.2	23.4	8.4	3.9	7.5
04	29710	Green Valley CDP, Arizona									
04	37620	Kingman city, Arizona	13.7	10.7	3.5	3.7	7.5	23.9	10.5	5.5	13.2
04	39370	Lake Havasu City city, Arizona	13.7	5.7	1.7	5.4	12.4	16.7	14.6	9.9	3.4
04	44270	Marana town, Arizona	12.6	4.8	1.5	3.7	9.3	27.9	8.7	7.0	9.7
04	44410	Maricopa city, Arizona	11.0	5.1	1.7	10.5	13.4	15.7	12.1	4.0	7.1
04	46000	Mesa city, Arizona	14.1	4.9	1.7	8.7	13.2	21.1	10.5	4.7	3.2
04	49640	Nogales city, Arizona	12.0	6.6	5.1	2.6	10.9	25.3	8.2	1.6	7.0
04	51600	Oro Valley town, Arizona	14.1	2.3	3.4	10.8	9.6	22.4	6.7	7.1	7.5
04	54050	Peoria city, Arizona	16.7	5.1	1.6	10.2	9.6	23.1	7.8	4.7	5.3
04	55000	Phoenix city, Arizona	11.4	5.1	2.2	9.8	13.9	19.1	11.2	5.0	3.5
04	57380	Prescott city, Arizona	13.8	4.2	1.7	5.7	11.9	28.3	11.3	6.7	6.2
04	57450	Prescott Valley town, Arizona	16.8	7.3	1.9	4.2	4.6	23.6	15.2	2.5	4.8
04	58150	Queen Creek town, Arizona	12.0	3.1	1.4	9.1	11.4	24.8	6.3	6.1	4.7
04	62140	Sahuarita town, Arizona	10.8	4.5	1.4	9.2	10.5	21.6	4.9	0.8	15.3
04	63470	San Luis city, Arizona	–	–	–	–	–	–	–	–	–
04	64210	San Tan Valley CDP, Arizona	11.2	4.4	1.6	8.4	11.5	20.3	14.4	5.3	4.6
04	65000	Scottsdale city, Arizona	9.8	4.1	2.8	14.8	17.0	22.0	11.1	4.2	2.2

Table E. Cities—Labor Force, Employment, and Educational Data, 2015—*Continued*

			Percent in each industry sector								
FIPS state code	FIPS place code	State/city	Retail trade	Transportation and warehousing, and utilities	Information	Finance and insurance, and real estate and rental and leasing	Professional, scientific, and management, and administrative and waste management services	Educational services, and health care and social assistance	Arts, entertainment, and recreation, and accommodation and food services	Other services, except public administration	Public administration
04	66820	Sierra Vista city, Arizona	13.7	2.1	2.1	4.8	17.7	21.3	11.3	1.4	20.7
04	70320	Sun City CDP, Arizona	12.9	0.9	1.0	15.8	13.7	18.4	15.9	9.2	1.8
04	70355	Sun City West CDP, Arizona	–	–	–	–	–	–	–	–	–
04	71510	Surprise city, Arizona	15.7	6.7	1.9	10.8	8.5	26.0	7.6	4.2	5.0
04	73000	Tempe city, Arizona	11.1	4.2	2.8	8.9	14.0	25.1	14.6	3.3	2.1
04	77000	Tucson city, Arizona	12.7	3.4	1.5	4.4	13.9	24.5	14.5	5.6	5.5
04	85540	Yuma city, Arizona	9.3	2.4	1.4	4.0	10.7	20.9	17.1	5.1	10.5
05	00000	**ARKANSAS**	13.8	5.5	1.6	4.5	7.2	24.4	7.7	4.7	4.6
05	04840	Bella Vista city, Arkansas	25.6	4.1	1.0	8.7	10.7	21.3	10.4	3.1	1.9
05	05290	Benton city, Arkansas	15.7	4.4	0.6	5.4	6.9	28.8	11.0	6.5	4.6
05	05320	Bentonville city, Arkansas	34.1	3.9	1.2	5.7	11.5	13.6	8.5	5.4	1.5
05	10300	Cabot city, Arkansas	8.5	3.7	2.0	8.6	9.5	21.5	6.6	7.5	15.2
05	15190	Conway city, Arkansas	17.4	5.8	2.7	4.3	9.0	28.9	8.4	2.9	2.0
05	23290	Fayetteville city, Arkansas	11.4	4.4	1.6	4.0	10.3	35.2	9.2	5.8	2.8
05	24550	Fort Smith city, Arkansas	14.4	1.9	1.9	3.9	7.0	24.5	9.9	4.6	1.3
05	33400	Hot Springs city, Arkansas	16.0	1.7	1.3	2.0	7.0	23.0	15.6	6.6	3.7
05	34750	Jacksonville city, Arkansas	14.3	7.5	2.8	3.7	2.3	21.1	15.1	4.4	12.4
05	35710	Jonesboro city, Arkansas	13.6	3.3	2.0	5.1	6.2	32.5	8.8	3.5	1.5
05	41000	Little Rock city, Arkansas	12.3	5.1	2.7	6.6	10.4	29.4	7.6	4.5	7.1
05	50450	North Little Rock city, Arkansas	13.2	4.6	3.0	8.0	8.5	21.5	13.3	5.0	6.5
05	53390	Paragould city, Arkansas	14.4	4.7	0.2	5.8	4.4	22.0	11.9	5.3	2.8
05	55310	Pine Bluff city, Arkansas	9.6	5.2	1.2	3.0	5.2	28.9	5.9	4.3	6.2
05	60410	Rogers city, Arkansas	24.8	4.0	0.8	5.5	9.2	16.9	6.6	2.9	1.3
05	61670	Russellville city, Arkansas	17.0	6.1	0.8	6.9	6.7	28.5	8.4	2.1	2.0
05	63020	Searcy city, Arkansas	10.8	3.0	0.6	3.0	6.2	39.8	15.3	6.9	2.7
05	63800	Sherwood city, Arkansas	16.8	2.7	2.2	7.0	5.9	20.0	6.8	7.9	10.3
05	66080	Springdale city, Arkansas	9.5	3.5	1.2	4.8	8.1	15.8	6.8	3.9	1.6
05	68810	Texarkana city, Arkansas	15.6	7.1	2.5	6.3	8.1	20.2	9.2	5.0	4.6
05	71480	Van Buren city, Arkansas	10.0	7.5	0.5	2.3	12.1	31.7	8.7	4.9	1.3
05	74540	West Memphis city, Arkansas	15.3	7.9	1.3	2.9	7.2	24.0	14.7	2.0	2.8
06	00000	**CALIFORNIA**	10.8	5.0	2.9	6.0	13.2	20.8	10.5	5.3	4.3
06	00296	Adelanto city, California	13.3	15.8	0.6	3.1	7.4	15.9	15.8	4.3	2.3
06	00394	Agoura Hills city, California	10.7	3.6	4.5	15.6	26.8	12.9	7.2	1.9	3.0
06	00562	Alameda city, California	12.3	7.0	4.1	7.4	19.1	18.0	10.6	6.1	5.0
06	00884	Alhambra city, California	7.0	6.4	2.3	6.3	12.7	23.4	14.0	6.0	4.5
06	00947	Aliso Viejo city, California	9.6	3.8	4.4	17.0	15.7	18.4	5.1	3.4	2.5
06	01290	Altadena CDP, California	9.3	3.5	5.4	7.6	15.3	25.8	11.4	5.3	3.5
06	01640	American Canyon city, California	7.1	4.4	0.9	3.0	5.2	31.5	16.4	3.5	5.2
06	02000	Anaheim city, California	9.5	3.1	2.2	6.3	13.7	17.7	13.3	4.8	2.6
06	02210	Antelope CDP, California	12.1	10.2	2.5	6.5	18.6	18.2	8.5	4.4	5.7
06	02252	Antioch city, California	13.2	7.4	2.6	5.5	13.7	23.8	8.9	5.0	3.8
06	02364	Apple Valley town, California	21.1	4.4	2.2	3.9	6.1	23.0	10.8	3.7	6.5
06	02462	Arcadia city, California	8.5	5.4	1.8	14.9	14.0	19.3	9.1	3.8	4.9
06	02553	Arden-Arcade CDP, California	12.2	6.8	2.3	7.4	12.0	23.0	9.3	6.0	9.8
06	02924	Arvin city, California	6.4	3.0	0.0	1.2	3.6	9.1	3.9	1.5	1.0
06	02980	Ashland CDP, California	10.7	7.6	4.0	8.5	19.8	11.6	5.6	9.5	0.9
06	03064	Atascadero city, California	8.2	7.3	1.1	3.5	8.2	35.6	7.4	6.7	8.0
06	03162	Atwater city, California	14.8	4.7	0.7	4.9	3.7	22.7	4.5	4.3	5.6
06	03386	Azusa city, California	11.9	8.5	2.0	5.6	8.9	25.4	11.0	6.3	1.8
06	03526	Bakersfield city, California	11.2	5.5	1.3	5.2	7.2	21.7	9.9	5.7	5.0
06	03666	Baldwin Park city, California	8.7	5.6	2.2	4.2	13.8	17.7	9.6	4.9	1.7
06	03820	Banning city, California	16.7	10.0	1.4	3.7	5.4	20.9	15.7	1.3	2.4
06	04030	Barstow city, California	10.0	7.2	0.6	1.6	5.5	19.9	18.0	7.3	14.4
06	04415	Bay Point CDP, California	12.1	3.1	2.3	5.6	18.0	16.7	8.8	10.6	4.4
06	04758	Beaumont city, California	12.5	5.7	2.5	5.4	12.4	31.6	7.9	3.8	6.7
06	04870	Bell city, California	10.4	7.2	0.3	2.8	6.6	13.1	10.3	11.9	2.6
06	04982	Bellflower city, California	8.5	10.2	1.8	7.1	9.9	22.2	9.1	4.4	2.9
06	04996	Bell Gardens city, California	14.9	9.9	1.5	1.7	8.4	14.6	12.2	4.4	1.1
06	05108	Belmont city, California	12.4	1.1	3.8	8.3	25.6	22.0	5.4	1.9	2.4
06	05290	Benicia city, California	6.4	7.0	3.9	5.0	13.1	24.9	7.9	2.7	7.4
06	06000	Berkeley city, California	8.3	2.5	5.4	3.9	20.4	34.2	7.7	5.4	3.0
06	06308	Beverly Hills city, California	13.6	1.4	10.1	11.0	15.0	15.7	9.6	3.5	1.3
06	07064	Bloomington CDP, California	14.4	14.0	0.0	1.1	10.3	16.4	6.7	7.4	0.8
06	08058	Brawley city, California	19.2	1.3	0.0	2.8	2.7	30.9	9.2	2.2	11.1
06	08100	Brea city, California	10.7	5.6	1.8	12.1	6.6	22.7	8.2	3.3	3.0
06	08142	Brentwood city, California	9.4	5.1	1.8	5.5	10.2	31.7	8.9	3.7	5.5
06	08786	Buena Park city, California	15.5	4.1	1.5	4.9	11.4	17.2	10.5	5.5	3.9
06	08954	Burbank city, California	8.1	2.5	13.7	6.5	16.1	18.1	11.2	6.4	3.5
06	09066	Burlingame city, California	5.8	5.1	2.7	8.6	17.1	20.5	10.6	3.1	8.4
06	09598	Calabasas city, California	12.8	1.4	8.3	11.4	18.6	23.4	11.0	4.6	0.3
06	09710	Calexico city, California	8.8	7.8	1.1	1.7	2.5	37.0	10.9	3.8	6.9

Table E. Cities—Labor Force, Employment, and Educational Data, 2015—*Continued*

FIPS state code	FIPS place code	State/city	Retail trade	Transportation and warehousing, and utilities	Information	Finance and insurance, and real estate and rental and leasing	Professional, scientific, and management, and administrative and waste management services	Educational services, and health care and social assistance	Arts, entertainment, and recreation, and accommodation and food services	Other services, except public administration	Public administration
06	10046	Camarillo city, California	14.2	3.9	2.1	9.7	13.0	18.6	9.5	3.8	7.7
06	10256	Cameron Park CDP, California	7.5	3.9	2.4	14.7	14.1	17.6	7.6	3.1	6.7
06	10345	Campbell city, California	7.9	2.9	3.5	6.0	13.1	18.6	9.2	4.9	4.7
06	11194	Carlsbad city, California	11.3	1.6	2.0	10.2	18.6	13.2	11.3	5.2	3.0
06	11390	Carmichael CDP, California	11.8	3.1	1.8	10.9	13.1	24.1	6.5	6.6	9.4
06	11530	Carson city, California	7.2	7.4	2.1	6.6	10.3	28.3	8.5	5.8	4.4
06	11796	Castaic CDP, California	9.5	6.4	2.9	5.6	10.8	23.1	8.0	3.9	8.4
06	11964	Castro Valley CDP, California	9.0	5.1	4.1	8.9	13.9	21.9	7.4	4.5	4.4
06	12048	Cathedral City city, California	15.7	3.0	1.0	6.4	13.7	16.4	21.7	8.9	2.6
06	12524	Ceres city, California	16.7	7.9	1.0	1.0	5.0	19.7	10.3	4.4	3.4
06	12552	Cerritos city, California	10.8	5.7	1.3	8.0	10.3	26.3	7.1	4.2	5.6
06	13014	Chico city, California	16.0	1.3	2.9	6.0	11.0	26.2	16.0	3.3	3.1
06	13210	Chino city, California	13.5	8.4	0.7	4.9	9.5	21.0	8.8	6.0	4.5
06	13214	Chino Hills city, California	10.4	5.6	0.2	9.0	15.0	24.8	6.7	1.2	5.2
06	13392	Chula Vista city, California	12.5	5.0	2.1	5.4	11.4	23.3	11.5	4.3	8.5
06	13588	Citrus Heights city, California	15.2	5.6	1.8	8.9	8.7	18.3	11.3	3.8	8.0
06	13756	Claremont city, California	5.1	3.5	2.8	8.0	14.5	37.5	11.2	4.1	2.9
06	14218	Clovis city, California	11.6	3.4	2.5	5.6	7.4	30.7	10.8	4.9	7.1
06	14260	Coachella city, California	11.9	2.6	0.0	3.0	12.3	13.5	23.9	3.5	5.2
06	14890	Colton city, California	20.7	9.6	0.0	4.5	8.3	21.2	9.8	4.6	4.6
06	15044	Compton city, California	9.9	10.3	1.8	2.6	12.0	18.3	8.0	5.1	2.7
06	16000	Concord city, California	11.7	3.6	1.1	10.2	15.4	17.4	10.7	7.3	4.0
06	16224	Corcoran city, California	—	—	—	—	—	—	—	—	—
06	16350	Corona city, California	14.1	4.4	1.8	7.0	7.7	18.4	9.2	5.4	5.6
06	16378	Coronado city, California	10.3	1.2	4.1	7.0	21.6	18.3	8.5	2.3	13.7
06	16532	Costa Mesa city, California	11.6	2.3	2.3	10.2	17.4	16.7	12.9	4.8	1.4
06	16742	Covina city, California	17.1	4.2	0.5	5.7	11.8	23.6	11.7	4.8	3.0
06	17498	Cudahy city, California	16.1	8.9	1.1	1.9	4.9	16.0	7.3	6.4	1.3
06	17568	Culver City city, California	8.2	4.0	9.7	7.4	20.7	26.1	6.6	3.4	3.3
06	17610	Cupertino city, California	5.9	1.2	7.6	4.4	34.6	12.9	3.1	1.4	1.5
06	17750	Cypress city, California	10.3	7.3	2.2	7.8	12.0	19.2	11.1	4.0	4.3
06	17918	Daly City city, California	13.5	8.7	2.2	5.1	11.2	21.5	16.1	5.3	3.7
06	17946	Dana Point city, California	9.0	4.8	3.7	6.0	16.9	18.5	11.9	6.7	2.5
06	17988	Danville town, California	6.4	2.2	7.5	9.9	19.2	23.1	5.7	3.8	2.4
06	18100	Davis city, California	6.1	2.5	2.6	4.7	14.7	39.1	12.9	2.2	7.4
06	18394	Delano city, California	8.8	6.4	0.8	0.0	2.9	14.4	4.5	3.6	6.3
06	18996	Desert Hot Springs city, California	19.8	3.0	0.0	2.9	10.8	19.2	14.4	8.0	3.3
06	19192	Diamond Bar city, California	9.6	4.6	4.5	10.2	12.3	26.6	5.6	6.8	3.5
06	19318	Dinuba city, California	17.1	1.1	1.1	2.6	5.4	16.3	10.4	3.9	3.4
06	19766	Downey city, California	13.2	6.2	2.0	6.5	7.8	19.4	11.2	5.6	5.8
06	19990	Duarte city, California	12.7	4.3	2.8	6.2	12.0	25.7	11.6	4.1	1.5
06	20018	Dublin city, California	6.9	4.7	5.1	8.1	25.4	16.9	6.4	4.6	4.3
06	20802	East Los Angeles CDP, California	13.4	6.9	1.3	2.7	10.0	17.1	9.7	4.7	2.0
06	20956	East Palo Alto city, California	16.0	2.7	3.0	2.0	22.8	17.5	16.0	3.0	2.3
06	21230	Eastvale city, California	13.2	6.7	1.1	7.5	11.5	19.3	4.8	4.5	6.4
06	21712	El Cajon city, California	12.0	7.3	3.1	3.3	10.1	20.0	18.1	6.6	3.4
06	21782	El Centro city, California	13.2	5.4	0.2	3.2	11.9	30.7	7.0	3.7	8.9
06	21796	El Cerrito city, California	10.7	4.0	3.8	3.8	19.9	28.7	6.4	6.5	3.5
06	21880	El Dorado Hills CDP, California	12.8	5.5	3.2	6.5	12.7	22.1	7.8	4.0	8.4
06	22020	Elk Grove city, California	9.1	7.9	2.6	6.4	8.8	24.0	7.4	3.3	15.8
06	22230	El Monte city, California	11.1	7.6	1.2	3.6	11.1	12.6	9.0	9.9	4.3
06	22300	El Paso de Robles (Paso Robles) city, California	13.1	2.1	0.0	5.1	4.7	22.9	11.6	4.5	9.6
06	22678	Encinitas city, California	13.7	3.0	2.5	5.0	15.8	28.0	10.3	3.8	0.9
06	22804	Escondido city, California	12.0	2.4	1.2	4.0	13.8	19.9	13.2	6.0	2.4
06	23042	Eureka city, California	16.7	2.2	0.6	4.1	4.9	27.3	12.0	3.3	10.4
06	23182	Fairfield city, California	12.0	6.2	1.6	5.3	12.0	24.6	5.6	3.3	8.9
06	23294	Fair Oaks CDP, California	9.7	2.5	3.0	7.8	16.4	26.1	9.4	5.5	9.2
06	23462	Fallbrook CDP, California	10.6	2.6	1.2	5.6	15.0	20.3	11.1	5.0	6.4
06	24477	Florence-Graham CDP, California	12.0	6.9	0.4	2.4	5.7	16.0	10.3	6.9	1.5
06	24498	Florin CDP, California	13.0	7.5	1.2	3.6	11.0	25.0	10.7	5.4	9.8
06	24638	Folsom city, California	7.6	3.3	1.4	9.4	14.9	23.8	6.4	1.8	11.1
06	24680	Fontana city, California	12.7	12.3	0.9	5.0	7.2	18.1	10.3	5.2	4.4
06	24722	Foothill Farms CDP, California	17.9	7.4	1.2	6.3	9.1	17.8	16.6	6.3	4.9
06	25338	Foster City city, California	6.6	3.4	8.5	9.9	31.6	15.9	5.6	2.1	1.1
06	25380	Fountain Valley city, California	10.2	4.7	2.1	9.1	13.6	22.8	9.4	2.8	3.4
06	26000	Fremont city, California	8.1	4.6	3.8	6.8	24.4	18.3	6.5	4.0	1.9
06	26067	French Valley CDP, California	13.5	2.5	0.0	3.1	11.5	26.7	7.4	1.9	12.1
06	27000	Fresno city, California	11.7	4.4	1.3	5.0	8.1	24.7	10.8	4.7	7.4
06	28000	Fullerton city, California	9.3	2.9	3.3	7.1	11.2	23.3	13.1	3.5	2.5
06	28112	Galt city, California	10.2	4.1	3.0	7.4	5.3	19.6	5.7	7.5	10.9
06	28168	Gardena city, California	12.3	9.1	1.3	6.3	11.2	22.9	9.8	5.6	4.2
06	29000	Garden Grove city, California	11.6	3.6	1.3	5.1	10.1	18.7	12.1	8.9	2.8

Table E. Cities—Labor Force, Employment, and Educational Data, 2015—*Continued*

FIPS state code	FIPS place code	State/city	Retail trade	Transportation and warehousing, and utilities	Information	Finance and insurance, and real estate and rental and leasing	Professional, scientific, and management, and administrative and waste management services	Educational services, and health care and social assistance	Arts, entertainment, and recreation, and accommodation and food services	Other services, except public administration	Public administration
06	29504	Gilroy city, California	15.6	2.8	1.5	3.8	6.1	19.9	12.5	5.8	4.1
06	30000	Glendale city, California	10.8	4.2	5.4	6.9	14.3	26.7	8.0	5.9	4.4
06	30014	Glendora city, California	14.9	6.3	2.0	6.1	11.5	22.3	10.2	3.0	4.9
06	30378	Goleta city, California	8.4	2.9	4.7	4.0	13.5	32.6	9.0	6.8	3.7
06	30693	Granite Bay CDP, California	11.0	1.9	3.9	11.0	18.1	18.1	2.8	8.2	4.9
06	31596	Hacienda Heights CDP, California	8.9	6.5	2.0	9.2	12.1	21.1	11.8	4.1	6.1
06	31960	Hanford city, California	6.8	4.6	0.3	1.8	5.2	27.0	11.5	7.5	13.2
06	32548	Hawthorne city, California	11.0	10.3	2.8	4.7	15.4	15.7	14.6	7.4	2.7
06	33000	Hayward city, California	10.7	9.8	1.8	5.9	11.9	20.0	6.2	6.7	3.7
06	33182	Hemet city, California	14.4	4.8	2.1	3.6	7.3	18.6	14.8	8.1	5.6
06	33308	Hercules city, California	9.9	6.7	4.5	7.0	16.8	23.0	7.9	3.9	7.2
06	33434	Hesperia city, California	18.5	9.2	1.2	3.0	10.6	16.1	7.5	9.2	4.1
06	33588	Highland city, California	13.5	9.6	0.8	2.8	11.2	24.0	14.5	4.1	3.3
06	34120	Hollister city, California	15.9	3.1	1.4	3.7	4.9	15.1	11.0	5.1	3.9
06	36000	Huntington Beach city, California	10.7	3.4	2.3	8.8	12.5	19.8	11.5	5.1	3.3
06	36056	Huntington Park city, California	13.1	8.8	0.4	4.8	6.4	12.6	8.4	9.6	1.1
06	36294	Imperial Beach city, California	16.4	3.1	0.0	8.0	13.6	15.3	17.5	4.4	3.5
06	36448	Indio city, California	10.8	3.6	1.0	5.5	9.2	20.3	20.0	6.9	4.1
06	36546	Inglewood city, California	10.3	9.1	3.1	5.7	11.9	21.8	13.6	4.7	3.2
06	36770	Irvine city, California	7.8	2.6	3.3	12.5	17.6	23.0	7.6	2.7	2.7
06	36868	Isla Vista CDP, California	8.5	1.4	2.3	0.7	9.2	40.9	24.5	3.6	0.0
06	37692	Jurupa Valley city, California	13.1	11.0	1.6	2.2	11.0	15.0	7.1	5.1	3.5
06	39003	La Cañada Flintridge city, California	8.7	1.4	3.5	13.8	19.0	32.5	4.3	4.8	6.6
06	39114	Ladera Ranch CDP, California	8.4	3.6	5.1	13.2	13.8	19.5	9.8	1.9	3.0
06	39122	Lafayette city, California	9.0	4.9	3.2	15.9	23.1	21.8	5.7	2.1	3.7
06	39178	Laguna Beach city, California	12.3	0.5	3.5	18.0	20.4	16.9	5.8	6.3	3.9
06	39220	Laguna Hills city, California	12.7	3.4	0.8	9.1	14.9	23.0	14.7	2.7	4.5
06	39248	Laguna Niguel city, California	10.8	3.6	1.0	10.4	16.2	21.3	7.4	7.0	2.0
06	39290	La Habra city, California	10.0	2.9	1.7	6.4	10.5	21.5	9.3	6.7	2.5
06	39486	Lake Elsinore city, California	10.5	8.4	1.7	6.5	13.1	14.4	8.2	4.7	4.6
06	39496	Lake Forest city, California	9.1	6.3	2.7	7.7	13.9	18.4	5.8	9.1	3.0
06	39766	Lakeside CDP, California	14.8	3.7	4.4	7.6	6.4	15.2	6.9	12.1	8.6
06	39892	Lakewood city, California	14.5	5.7	2.5	6.1	8.2	26.9	8.3	5.6	2.3
06	40004	La Mesa city, California	14.0	3.0	2.0	6.6	15.2	22.2	10.7	5.3	6.5
06	40032	La Mirada city, California	14.3	5.5	2.1	6.7	6.7	22.8	7.6	4.0	5.0
06	40130	Lancaster city, California	14.4	6.0	2.2	4.5	7.8	28.2	6.8	5.8	7.5
06	40326	La Presa CDP, California	14.1	5.7	1.8	3.4	13.6	16.8	12.7	7.2	4.1
06	40340	La Puente city, California	10.0	8.1	1.3	1.9	8.7	13.4	13.7	5.3	1.9
06	40354	La Quinta city, California	18.6	1.5	1.2	9.8	8.1	18.4	19.6	5.5	2.8
06	40704	Lathrop city, California	8.6	23.0	2.3	3.6	9.2	10.8	11.4	2.7	2.2
06	40830	La Verne city, California	16.5	1.7	4.4	9.0	8.8	32.5	5.7	4.2	3.8
06	40886	Lawndale city, California	9.3	10.0	4.5	4.3	16.2	12.5	14.8	5.3	2.3
06	41124	Lemon Grove city, California	8.7	7.1	3.0	4.0	9.9	21.7	12.3	8.6	6.4
06	41152	Lemoore city, California	7.0	1.1	1.2	1.1	7.9	28.4	8.0	1.1	23.6
06	41180	Lennox CDP, California	11.5	10.1	2.2	2.1	17.3	9.8	21.5	5.7	0.0
06	41474	Lincoln city, California	16.9	4.3	1.9	7.0	13.5	20.8	8.7	2.5	6.7
06	41992	Livermore city, California	9.8	4.7	2.0	5.2	22.0	17.0	10.2	5.3	2.5
06	42202	Lodi city, California	12.2	4.9	1.2	4.9	7.1	20.0	10.0	4.6	4.1
06	42370	Loma Linda city, California	6.7	5.6	0.9	4.9	8.0	58.4	6.4	0.4	2.0
06	42468	Lomita city, California	28.8	8.4	1.0	7.1	3.7	12.3	6.5	5.9	3.1
06	42524	Lompoc city, California	10.6	2.6	0.2	3.9	10.0	20.0	14.0	4.5	6.1
06	43000	Long Beach city, California	9.5	7.4	2.0	6.0	12.7	22.2	11.7	4.9	3.7
06	43280	Los Altos city, California	5.1	2.0	7.3	7.2	28.9	19.8	3.5	1.9	1.6
06	44000	Los Angeles city, California	10.1	4.7	5.8	5.9	14.6	19.3	13.1	6.9	2.2
06	44028	Los Banos city, California	11.3	4.8	0.5	0.5	9.1	16.5	14.6	7.3	2.6
06	44112	Los Gatos town, California	5.8	2.4	6.0	6.7	28.1	15.3	5.4	2.5	1.9
06	44574	Lynwood city, California	10.4	9.8	0.9	3.5	10.9	19.5	13.3	7.5	1.2
06	45022	Madera city, California	9.9	4.2	0.8	1.9	5.4	19.4	6.4	3.2	5.4
06	45400	Manhattan Beach city, California	5.0	6.6	6.6	14.7	16.5	22.3	6.7	2.5	2.9
06	45484	Manteca city, California	13.9	8.4	2.8	4.4	8.1	19.6	7.2	3.3	5.4
06	45778	Marina city, California	8.4	3.3	1.2	5.1	16.4	23.4	17.6	5.0	7.0
06	46114	Martinez city, California	8.3	5.8	4.5	9.4	10.5	23.3	11.7	2.1	4.0
06	46492	Maywood city, California	15.1	14.4	3.0	0.7	4.0	19.2	6.2	3.5	0.3
06	46646	Mead Valley CDP, California	18.0	7.2	1.3	0.6	11.8	18.3	7.5	9.9	3.5
06	46842	Menifee city, California	12.8	3.1	0.6	4.9	9.3	23.3	9.1	5.9	6.9
06	46870	Menlo Park city, California	4.9	1.7	11.4	7.1	23.5	23.9	5.6	6.6	1.9
06	46898	Merced city, California	11.7	6.0	0.5	5.4	4.7	31.7	5.8	2.5	5.6
06	47486	Millbrae city, California	9.2	8.3	4.4	9.3	19.1	17.2	7.9	4.3	2.6
06	47766	Milpitas city, California	9.2	4.2	2.0	5.9	18.1	18.0	6.6	4.2	3.0
06	48256	Mission Viejo city, California	8.3	3.0	1.9	9.5	14.1	19.6	10.5	5.4	4.8
06	48354	Modesto city, California	15.8	6.3	1.1	4.0	8.5	23.4	9.1	4.5	3.9
06	48648	Monrovia city, California	11.1	4.5	4.4	6.4	10.0	25.2	13.4	5.6	1.6
06	48788	Montclair city, California	24.0	7.0	0.6	4.1	5.6	12.1	8.4	7.3	2.4

Table E. Cities—Labor Force, Employment, and Educational Data, 2015—*Continued*

FIPS state code	FIPS place code	State/city	Retail trade	Transportation and warehousing, and utilities	Information	Finance and insurance, and real estate and rental and leasing	Professional, scientific, and management, and administrative and waste management services	Educational services, and health care and social assistance	Arts, entertainment, and recreation, and accommodation and food services	Other services, except public administration	Public administration
								Percent in each industry sector			
06	48816	Montebello city, California	15.6	7.2	1.6	6.0	9.0	19.0	9.9	3.2	3.8
06	48872	Monterey city, California	11.9	1.9	1.8	3.9	15.9	20.3	26.1	4.2	6.6
06	48914	Monterey Park city, California	8.7	4.8	3.4	6.7	13.2	25.3	10.5	7.3	3.9
06	49138	Moorpark city, California	11.3	2.7	3.1	8.4	10.6	16.9	11.2	5.3	3.1
06	49270	Moreno Valley city, California	14.1	9.2	1.3	3.8	7.6	24.1	8.6	5.9	3.7
06	49278	Morgan Hill city, California	11.3	3.3	3.9	6.8	18.5	21.4	6.0	5.3	3.5
06	49670	Mountain View city, California	5.7	0.9	14.7	3.8	25.8	18.6	8.1	3.4	2.3
06	50076	Murrieta city, California	16.3	3.0	1.6	3.6	13.6	20.8	10.8	5.6	6.3
06	50258	Napa city, California	10.2	2.4	0.8	4.8	8.3	18.6	13.6	5.6	4.4
06	50398	National City city, California	13.1	5.8	0.7	3.4	10.4	21.3	15.1	8.1	3.6
06	50916	Newark city, California	6.9	5.6	2.4	5.2	18.0	18.0	4.6	7.5	2.6
06	51182	Newport Beach city, California	8.1	3.3	1.6	16.4	20.0	17.7	8.6	3.7	2.2
06	51560	Norco city, California	14.3	8.3	0.4	4.8	11.5	16.7	5.8	4.3	8.0
06	51924	North Highlands CDP, California	16.9	4.6	2.7	5.9	17.3	17.8	10.2	4.1	3.5
06	52379	North Tustin CDP, California	11.1	4.6	1.4	15.6	16.8	18.1	9.3	6.5	2.0
06	52526	Norwalk city, California	12.8	10.3	1.5	3.8	10.2	21.7	7.4	7.8	3.4
06	52582	Novato city, California	12.0	2.6	3.8	12.0	16.4	25.6	7.7	3.6	4.6
06	52694	Oakdale city, California	7.8	4.4	1.0	3.6	5.5	29.6	5.4	4.0	6.7
06	53000	Oakland city, California	7.5	4.9	3.5	5.4	17.7	22.6	11.9	6.8	3.9
06	53070	Oakley city, California	12.2	5.7	1.1	4.9	11.3	23.0	6.3	4.2	6.4
06	53322	Oceanside city, California	10.6	3.8	2.6	3.8	11.1	21.1	12.8	4.7	5.1
06	53448	Oildale CDP, California	15.7	5.6	0.0	0.9	15.1	21.9	9.9	4.1	5.1
06	53896	Ontario city, California	12.7	9.7	1.2	4.0	10.1	18.3	7.8	4.7	4.1
06	53980	Orange city, California	10.7	3.5	2.5	9.6	12.4	22.5	10.7	4.2	2.1
06	54092	Orangevale CDP, California	12.1	3.7	2.1	8.4	12.9	15.7	4.5	7.2	9.7
06	54120	Orcutt CDP, California	11.0	4.1	0.9	4.7	10.0	22.6	7.9	9.0	6.9
06	54652	Oxnard city, California	10.5	3.8	1.6	5.0	7.9	17.3	9.3	5.5	3.0
06	54806	Pacifica city, California	9.0	4.4	4.2	5.8	16.1	23.4	10.4	7.5	4.6
06	55156	Palmdale city, California	13.2	4.5	2.5	4.0	8.1	23.7	10.1	5.9	4.6
06	55184	Palm Desert city, California	15.1	1.7	2.3	10.9	9.8	24.3	17.8	7.5	3.7
06	55254	Palm Springs city, California	11.5	4.2	1.9	5.7	15.2	21.8	19.7	7.3	3.2
06	55282	Palo Alto city, California	5.6	1.1	7.1	9.5	29.6	24.6	4.5	2.5	1.1
06	55520	Paradise town, California	12.9	1.8	2.8	7.6	5.9	34.7	14.7	2.4	3.1
06	55618	Paramount city, California	10.0	6.9	1.6	4.5	11.0	17.9	12.8	4.6	3.5
06	56000	Pasadena city, California	8.6	3.7	4.1	7.0	17.4	27.6	11.0	5.9	3.1
06	56112	Patterson city, California	25.1	7.4	4.0	4.0	6.7	8.4	4.9	9.9	0.3
06	56700	Perris city, California	16.1	9.6	0.1	3.6	7.5	16.2	7.9	4.4	2.6
06	56784	Petaluma city, California	9.8	3.0	5.3	6.8	13.2	23.4	11.1	3.4	4.5
06	56924	Pico Rivera city, California	11.0	8.3	0.8	5.4	6.4	19.2	7.2	7.4	3.5
06	57456	Pittsburg city, California	9.6	5.8	2.0	9.5	13.9	22.2	9.9	3.6	2.5
06	57526	Placentia city, California	7.3	3.1	3.6	5.2	9.4	21.0	11.7	6.0	2.7
06	57764	Pleasant Hill city, California	16.0	6.1	1.7	12.6	16.2	22.5	7.9	3.6	3.9
06	57792	Pleasanton city, California	10.3	2.6	5.5	6.3	25.0	17.4	8.7	3.0	3.6
06	58072	Pomona city, California	11.0	6.1	1.7	4.8	10.2	20.0	11.3	5.6	4.0
06	58240	Porterville city, California	14.0	3.7	0.8	2.4	7.1	29.3	7.6	3.0	4.9
06	58296	Port Hueneme city, California	13.4	5.1	3.0	5.8	15.2	18.7	3.9	3.5	7.1
06	58520	Poway city, California	11.1	5.2	3.7	4.5	14.0	20.3	12.1	3.2	2.4
06	59346	Ramona CDP, California	10.9	4.5	3.7	6.7	15.3	21.3	10.9	9.1	1.9
06	59444	Rancho Cordova city, California	11.7	4.1	1.8	8.2	14.6	17.8	10.5	3.9	8.6
06	59451	Rancho Cucamonga city, California	10.7	7.8	2.2	6.9	9.8	26.3	8.2	3.7	6.7
06	59514	Rancho Palos Verdes city, California	10.0	5.8	1.6	13.3	11.3	29.5	2.2	6.6	5.3
06	59550	Rancho San Diego CDP, California	15.0	5.7	1.9	8.3	12.3	20.5	10.9	5.2	5.0
06	59587	Rancho Santa Margarita city, California	11.1	2.2	2.1	9.8	19.4	19.3	9.4	4.3	4.9
06	59920	Redding city, California	13.7	3.1	3.8	6.0	7.0	27.9	9.9	8.4	6.9
06	59962	Redlands city, California	12.1	5.0	1.1	5.2	10.9	33.0	6.1	6.4	7.1
06	60018	Redondo Beach city, California	10.5	5.8	6.0	8.7	15.0	20.5	7.7	2.5	2.8
06	60102	Redwood City city, California	10.9	3.7	4.6	4.6	20.5	18.9	7.9	5.4	3.2
06	60242	Reedley city, California	8.1	3.3	5.9	0.6	2.6	21.4	4.2	5.0	2.3
06	60466	Rialto city, California	15.8	12.6	1.6	2.7	8.7	17.6	8.9	6.3	4.5
06	60620	Richmond city, California	10.7	8.3	2.1	4.6	12.5	19.8	10.8	7.7	3.1
06	60704	Ridgecrest city, California	7.3	5.0	2.4	5.4	19.4	17.4	5.0	1.6	17.2
06	61068	Riverbank city, California	5.5	4.2	1.3	7.4	5.2	19.8	12.4	4.7	4.5
06	62000	Riverside city, California	13.1	5.7	1.2	5.1	9.2	23.4	9.7	5.4	5.0
06	62364	Rocklin city, California	12.4	3.8	3.3	8.0	12.0	21.9	8.4	5.9	7.4
06	62546	Rohnert Park city, California	12.5	3.5	2.7	8.2	10.0	21.4	12.8	5.4	3.8
06	62826	Rosamond CDP, California	7.0	1.7	0.7	3.7	8.0	25.5	9.1	4.5	20.8
06	62896	Rosemead city, California	11.8	5.4	3.9	7.9	8.4	19.2	8.2	5.2	4.1
06	62910	Rosemont CDP, California	9.4	6.7	1.7	4.7	10.9	22.0	10.2	5.6	17.8
06	62938	Roseville city, California	13.6	5.2	1.8	8.0	11.8	25.3	9.7	2.8	7.4
06	63218	Rowland Heights CDP, California	11.7	5.6	1.7	10.1	8.1	23.6	10.6	3.3	4.2
06	64000	Sacramento city, California	11.0	4.6	1.5	6.8	12.2	23.6	10.1	4.4	11.0
06	64224	Salinas city, California	9.5	3.1	0.6	2.0	6.4	18.7	10.4	5.3	4.0

Table E. Cities—Labor Force, Employment, and Educational Data, 2015—*Continued*

FIPS state code	FIPS place code	State/city	Retail trade	Transportation and warehousing, and utilities	Information	Finance and insurance, and real estate and rental and leasing	Professional, scientific, and management, and administrative and waste management services	Educational services, and health care and social assistance	Arts, entertainment, and recreation, and accommodation and food services	Other services, except public administration	Public administration
							Percent in each industry sector				
06	65000	San Bernardino city, California	13.1	10.0	0.6	5.0	9.7	19.7	9.2	7.0	4.6
06	65028	San Bruno city, California	12.6	6.3	3.3	5.8	18.7	17.7	14.3	3.5	4.9
06	65042	San Buenaventura (Ventura) city, California	15.3	3.9	1.6	3.7	12.4	19.1	11.5	5.7	6.5
06	65070	San Carlos city, California	8.9	1.6	4.1	6.9	28.1	21.0	5.3	1.9	5.6
06	65084	San Clemente city, California	7.3	1.9	1.0	6.0	19.6	19.8	12.5	6.3	3.0
06	66000	San Diego city, California	9.1	3.5	2.7	6.3	16.7	22.5	13.1	5.6	5.0
06	66070	San Dimas city, California	12.1	6.6	3.4	9.1	11.2	23.1	7.8	2.0	7.0
06	66140	San Fernando city, California	11.2	8.3	2.1	3.0	3.6	23.3	7.9	4.9	2.1
06	67000	San Francisco city, California	10.0	3.8	6.5	9.1	22.8	17.6	11.6	4.5	3.4
06	67042	San Gabriel city, California	10.3	4.7	0.8	7.5	10.6	16.1	18.9	7.8	2.9
06	67056	Sanger city, California	9.6	1.5	0.0	9.4	4.1	21.3	4.0	3.0	6.4
06	67112	San Jacinto city, California	19.6	11.3	1.3	2.2	8.3	23.0	3.3	3.1	3.5
06	68000	San Jose city, California	9.6	3.3	3.4	4.5	17.4	18.1	10.0	4.4	2.8
06	68028	San Juan Capistrano city, California	9.8	3.3	3.7	5.9	12.1	16.4	14.1	9.9	0.6
06	68084	San Leandro city, California	12.2	8.6	2.9	4.9	9.9	21.1	11.8	5.2	4.7
06	68112	San Lorenzo CDP, California	11.2	2.7	2.5	7.6	14.8	22.1	8.5	4.0	4.1
06	68154	San Luis Obispo city, California	9.7	2.5	1.5	2.9	8.7	28.5	22.8	5.6	3.9
06	68196	San Marcos city, California	9.9	5.2	1.0	4.8	14.6	18.3	12.0	7.9	3.0
06	68252	San Mateo city, California	6.9	6.9	5.1	7.7	20.0	19.3	11.0	5.3	2.1
06	68294	San Pablo city, California	15.1	6.5	0.4	4.4	15.7	15.4	14.1	8.7	2.2
06	68364	San Rafael city, California	11.4	2.6	2.4	7.1	19.9	17.4	12.7	9.3	4.2
06	68378	San Ramon city, California	7.4	3.8	4.2	12.3	22.3	18.4	9.0	3.0	3.9
06	69000	Santa Ana city, California	10.2	3.4	1.0	5.2	14.7	12.7	16.0	7.1	1.2
06	69070	Santa Barbara city, California	10.3	1.7	3.6	4.8	16.7	24.8	13.5	6.6	3.3
06	69084	Santa Clara city, California	8.9	2.7	5.2	2.8	21.8	18.7	7.7	2.3	3.4
06	69088	Santa Clarita city, California	11.1	2.8	4.8	8.8	11.6	20.4	11.3	5.2	5.5
06	69112	Santa Cruz city, California	8.2	2.3	3.8	1.9	11.7	29.6	20.9	6.3	3.5
06	69196	Santa Maria city, California	7.4	4.7	1.3	2.7	5.2	14.9	8.7	4.7	3.4
06	70000	Santa Monica city, California	6.0	1.6	10.1	9.6	22.8	23.5	8.4	5.0	2.2
06	70042	Santa Paula city, California	9.8	5.4	0.3	1.6	6.6	16.9	6.9	9.7	5.0
06	70098	Santa Rosa city, California	13.2	4.2	1.2	5.8	10.3	20.5	11.6	5.0	2.9
06	70224	Santee city, California	12.1	3.4	2.3	6.6	15.3	19.0	9.3	4.8	6.5
06	70280	Saratoga city, California	7.0	0.3	5.3	7.7	19.3	20.1	4.0	1.9	3.1
06	70686	Seal Beach city, California	7.2	3.2	2.7	9.5	16.7	24.6	7.6	4.0	5.4
06	70742	Seaside city, California	6.3	3.0	0.2	3.8	11.3	20.4	29.0	5.0	6.8
06	70882	Selma city, California	12.1	5.1	1.4	2.7	5.1	19.1	6.7	2.3	12.3
06	72016	Simi Valley city, California	12.0	3.5	3.6	10.9	11.1	19.7	8.5	6.6	3.4
06	72520	Soledad city, California	16.5	1.0	0.7	2.2	1.9	17.6	5.1	0.6	5.7
06	72996	South El Monte city, California	14.5	7.5	0.4	5.5	8.7	15.4	7.2	4.2	4.9
06	73080	South Gate city, California	11.6	4.4	1.0	4.2	7.2	19.0	10.9	7.1	1.8
06	73108	South Lake Tahoe city, California	10.3	3.7	1.3	6.4	12.9	17.0	31.3	1.4	2.9
06	73220	South Pasadena city, California	5.6	2.2	5.9	10.0	15.7	28.1	6.3	6.0	2.7
06	73262	South San Francisco city, California	11.6	9.3	1.5	5.6	13.1	20.8	10.6	6.2	4.4
06	73290	South San Jose Hills CDP, California	10.6	8.9	0.4	3.4	13.5	16.1	8.3	2.8	2.2
06	73430	South Whittier CDP, California	16.2	8.1	1.1	4.1	6.2	17.1	7.6	5.1	3.3
06	73696	Spring Valley CDP (San Diego County), California	11.4	7.3	0.5	4.8	14.8	25.1	7.2	2.3	5.6
06	73962	Stanton city, California	9.5	4.1	1.9	3.7	10.5	20.1	10.7	7.1	2.1
06	75000	Stockton city, California	13.3	9.4	1.4	5.4	8.6	21.6	7.7	5.1	5.3
06	75630	Suisun City city, California	16.6	4.7	0.9	4.8	9.0	22.5	11.3	3.1	3.3
06	77000	Sunnyvale city, California	6.7	1.2	8.7	4.2	27.7	14.8	8.2	3.9	1.8
06	78120	Temecula city, California	10.0	5.2	0.9	5.2	10.3	22.0	14.7	5.8	5.5
06	78138	Temescal Valley CDP, California	19.3	6.3	2.2	4.7	11.2	18.9	4.2	4.1	9.1
06	78148	Temple City city, California	9.4	5.5	1.1	10.9	12.2	21.5	18.6	5.2	2.0
06	78582	Thousand Oaks city, California	8.3	2.3	4.0	10.7	15.8	20.6	10.8	3.3	3.3
06	80000	Torrance city, California	10.3	6.3	2.6	8.7	14.3	22.3	10.4	5.0	2.9
06	80238	Tracy city, California	14.0	6.6	2.7	4.7	13.6	15.1	9.9	3.3	3.9
06	80644	Tulare city, California	13.6	7.2	1.6	2.7	7.7	21.2	7.1	3.3	9.3
06	80812	Turlock city, California	13.4	6.8	1.4	4.0	6.8	28.5	5.2	3.4	2.9
06	80854	Tustin city, California	8.5	3.4	1.4	8.8	15.0	16.9	13.4	8.4	2.5
06	80994	Twentynine Palms city, California	–	–	–	–	–	–	–	–	–
06	81204	Union City city, California	8.9	8.4	2.9	5.3	15.5	20.6	5.9	3.1	6.0
06	81344	Upland city, California	11.8	6.4	2.2	6.2	10.9	25.6	6.6	3.2	3.4
06	81554	Vacaville city, California	12.1	5.8	1.4	3.8	11.3	19.7	8.6	5.0	11.5
06	81638	Valinda CDP, California	18.5	7.1	1.0	5.1	7.6	13.1	8.6	6.3	2.1
06	81666	Vallejo city, California	13.7	7.1	1.7	5.2	11.8	21.7	8.8	6.5	4.8
06	82590	Victorville city, California	9.3	10.2	3.3	5.6	6.2	28.5	8.0	8.3	4.7
06	82852	Vineyard CDP, California	4.4	9.5	0.7	8.1	17.5	30.1	7.9	3.8	6.9
06	82954	Visalia city, California	10.0	6.6	1.2	4.4	10.9	21.8	11.4	4.3	9.2
06	82996	Vista city, California	14.1	2.5	2.3	4.1	12.9	18.0	12.2	7.2	2.5
06	83332	Walnut city, California	12.8	4.5	3.7	10.7	12.3	22.7	4.5	3.1	5.6
06	83346	Walnut Creek city, California	8.1	4.8	4.6	12.4	20.1	22.6	6.5	4.0	4.8

Table E. Cities—Labor Force, Employment, and Educational Data, 2015—*Continued*

FIPS state code	FIPS place code	State/city	Retail trade	Transportation and warehousing, and utilities	Information	Finance and insurance, and real estate and rental and leasing	Professional, scientific, and management, and administrative and waste management services	Educational services, and health care and social assistance	Arts, entertainment, and recreation, and accommodation and food services	Other services, except public administration	Public administration
							Percent in each industry sector				
06	83542	Wasco city, California	–	–	–	–	–	–	–	–	–
06	83668	Watsonville city, California	9.4	4.5	0.4	1.7	8.1	14.1	10.4	3.0	1.7
06	84144	West Carson CDP, California	12.8	7.2	4.0	6.4	9.6	18.5	7.0	7.8	3.2
06	84200	West Covina city, California	12.4	6.5	2.9	7.2	8.9	24.9	8.0	4.7	4.0
06	84410	West Hollywood city, California	10.7	0.7	13.6	7.9	19.8	7.4	20.5	7.6	2.4
06	84550	Westminster city, California	11.2	4.5	0.9	7.2	11.0	19.7	10.2	7.7	3.0
06	84592	Westmont CDP, California	14.7	13.8	1.2	3.2	14.5	20.4	4.9	4.7	2.5
06	84774	West Puente Valley CDP, California	8.3	7.6	1.8	2.3	10.4	19.7	6.1	6.7	2.5
06	84780	West Rancho Dominguez CDP, California	8.7	10.0	3.3	4.0	15.4	20.0	8.5	5.3	2.1
06	84816	West Sacramento city, California	10.9	3.5	2.4	3.7	11.8	19.9	9.0	5.5	14.9
06	84921	West Whittier-Los Nietos CDP, California	9.7	5.7	1.0	3.0	11.1	22.6	8.1	2.4	6.4
06	85292	Whittier city, California	11.8	6.4	1.5	5.1	9.9	25.9	8.9	3.7	5.9
06	85446	Wildomar city, California	10.2	4.3	0.5	6.1	11.3	17.0	12.1	6.4	4.2
06	85922	Windsor town, California	8.8	3.4	1.5	8.2	7.1	24.1	9.9	2.5	7.5
06	85992	Winter Gardens CDP, California	12.3	4.3	0.4	5.2	17.5	18.8	13.0	3.5	3.9
06	86328	Woodland city, California	14.3	6.6	0.3	2.9	8.5	23.7	10.6	7.6	6.3
06	86832	Yorba Linda city, California	9.7	1.9	1.4	12.3	14.0	23.7	5.7	3.9	3.0
06	86972	Yuba City city, California	11.7	7.2	1.1	3.8	6.0	23.0	7.9	1.8	6.7
06	87042	Yucaipa city, California	13.7	5.5	2.2	4.7	9.8	31.6	7.4	6.5	7.1
06	87056	Yucca Valley town, California	–	–	–	–	–	–	–	–	–
08	00000	**COLORADO**	11.3	4.6	2.9	6.9	13.8	20.7	10.5	5.0	4.4
08	03455	Arvada city, Colorado	10.4	3.0	3.9	7.6	14.6	19.4	8.5	6.1	4.6
08	04000	Aurora city, Colorado	12.3	7.2	3.1	8.3	12.3	19.5	10.5	4.9	4.2
08	07850	Boulder city, Colorado	9.7	1.1	3.8	2.7	22.2	28.6	14.2	4.8	1.6
08	08675	Brighton city, Colorado	13.7	3.4	2.0	3.7	8.3	19.8	5.2	3.4	6.0
08	09280	Broomfield city, Colorado	10.1	3.2	5.3	5.8	20.8	18.2	8.2	4.2	3.0
08	12415	Castle Rock town, Colorado	14.4	3.8	4.9	8.6	12.8	18.8	9.2	4.2	5.6
08	12815	Centennial city, Colorado	10.4	4.3	4.5	10.9	16.9	20.6	8.4	4.7	2.6
08	15165	Clifton CDP, Colorado	15.9	5.1	1.2	3.6	12.5	12.3	10.8	8.8	2.5
08	16000	Colorado Springs city, Colorado	12.4	4.1	2.8	7.6	14.2	23.3	11.0	5.9	4.2
08	16110	Columbine CDP, Colorado	9.2	4.8	5.5	10.2	17.0	22.3	5.0	4.9	2.6
08	16495	Commerce City city, Colorado	11.2	8.9	4.7	5.7	8.6	17.5	5.8	6.0	5.4
08	19150	Dakota Ridge CDP, Colorado	12.4	2.2	3.0	8.7	13.0	17.5	9.1	4.5	7.9
08	20000	Denver city, Colorado	9.4	4.3	3.5	7.8	17.4	19.3	11.4	5.0	3.9
08	24785	Englewood city, Colorado	11.3	3.4	3.1	9.7	16.5	19.4	7.4	6.3	2.0
08	24950	Erie town, Colorado	7.2	3.3	1.6	5.1	18.0	27.0	6.3	3.1	5.3
08	25280	Evans city, Colorado	13.6	8.1	0.3	5.6	8.4	16.1	7.3	5.5	2.0
08	27425	Fort Collins city, Colorado	9.9	2.2	1.7	5.5	11.3	29.6	12.3	4.3	3.2
08	27865	Fountain city, Colorado	16.0	6.2	2.8	4.7	6.9	20.2	8.4	3.3	17.2
08	30835	Golden city, Colorado	9.7	0.7	1.8	1.2	22.9	27.9	9.5	4.5	3.9
08	31660	Grand Junction city, Colorado	13.7	3.8	2.2	4.1	13.5	26.7	10.6	6.0	5.4
08	32155	Greeley city, Colorado	13.5	5.0	1.4	6.1	7.2	18.1	10.7	4.5	3.9
08	36410	Highlands Ranch CDP, Colorado	12.4	2.7	4.3	12.7	18.2	18.9	8.6	4.5	2.9
08	40377	Ken Caryl CDP, Colorado	10.1	3.1	4.3	6.9	18.0	22.0	10.4	4.1	2.6
08	41835	Lafayette city, Colorado	12.5	5.1	3.5	3.9	14.9	21.4	12.6	6.7	1.6
08	43000	Lakewood city, Colorado	11.7	5.0	3.4	8.3	12.9	19.7	9.6	6.6	4.8
08	45255	Littleton city, Colorado	11.4	3.6	4.7	9.2	18.2	20.5	7.9	5.7	3.9
08	45970	Longmont city, Colorado	11.0	3.1	2.1	5.0	18.0	20.7	8.1	4.0	2.7
08	46355	Louisville city, Colorado	10.2	3.6	4.7	3.2	20.8	28.1	11.8	7.4	1.8
08	46465	Loveland city, Colorado	11.0	2.5	3.1	5.2	12.2	21.5	9.0	5.8	4.8
08	54330	Northglenn city, Colorado	16.2	8.2	2.5	6.2	7.0	21.2	8.7	3.8	2.2
08	57630	Parker town, Colorado	12.0	3.2	5.2	11.3	15.0	22.3	8.4	4.5	5.4
08	62000	Pueblo city, Colorado	15.9	4.5	2.0	3.7	9.7	26.9	10.1	4.0	4.3
08	62220	Pueblo West CDP, Colorado	9.8	3.7	1.6	5.0	9.2	25.0	10.4	4.2	12.4
08	68847	Security-Widefield CDP, Colorado	20.3	7.3	1.8	4.1	7.7	17.7	10.5	3.6	11.7
08	77290	Thornton city, Colorado	11.2	6.2	2.5	6.0	11.0	20.3	9.2	4.5	4.8
08	83835	Westminster city, Colorado	11.3	5.2	4.4	7.1	12.8	16.4	10.1	3.9	3.6
08	84440	Wheat Ridge city, Colorado	13.1	4.0	2.6	6.8	16.0	17.7	9.1	6.8	3.9
08	85485	Windsor town, Colorado	9.7	5.2	0.5	8.2	11.6	23.6	7.4	4.3	6.0
09	00000	**CONNECTICUT**	10.9	4.1	2.3	9.3	11.5	26.3	8.1	4.3	3.8
09	08000	Bridgeport city, Connecticut	16.2	4.2	2.2	5.6	10.3	25.6	9.7	6.0	2.5
09	08420	Bristol city, Connecticut	12.2	3.7	7.9	12.0	9.9	15.8	9.1	2.6	5.3
09	18430	Danbury city, Connecticut	10.1	3.8	1.8	5.3	20.3	19.6	6.1	3.7	1.2
09	18920	Darien CDP, Connecticut	2.2	1.5	3.3	32.1	17.0	20.3	8.4	3.1	2.2
09	22700	East Hartford CDP, Connecticut	13.6	6.5	3.5	9.1	6.8	26.4	3.0	3.0	5.7
09	22980	East Haven CDP, Connecticut	20.6	6.0	3.1	9.2	6.4	19.6	6.9	1.3	3.5
09	37000	Hartford city, Connecticut	12.5	6.3	1.3	6.1	9.8	34.2	7.8	5.6	4.7
09	44690	Manchester CDP, Connecticut	11.1	2.9	2.0	9.7	8.0	32.2	8.5	2.5	4.0
09	46450	Meriden city, Connecticut	14.3	4.6	1.8	6.6	8.7	24.7	8.4	7.0	6.2
09	47290	Middletown city, Connecticut	7.3	3.7	5.6	9.6	10.9	30.9	6.0	5.5	2.6
09	47515	Milford city (balance), Connecticut	12.0	4.9	3.0	9.9	12.2	22.6	7.3	4.8	2.2

Table E. Cities—Labor Force, Employment, and Educational Data, 2015—*Continued*

FIPS state code	FIPS place code	State/city	Retail trade	Transportation and warehousing, and utilities	Information	Finance and insurance, and real estate and rental and leasing	Professional, scientific, and management, and administrative and waste management services	Educational services, and health care and social assistance	Arts, entertainment, and recreation, and accommodation and food services	Other services, except public administration	Public administration
							Percent in each industry sector				
09	49880	Naugatuck borough, Connecticut	9.6	2.8	1.0	6.7	9.6	23.2	7.4	5.2	4.2
09	50370	New Britain city, Connecticut	12.3	4.8	0.3	6.4	13.4	24.4	10.4	2.0	3.5
09	52000	New Haven city, Connecticut	7.7	4.3	2.1	4.1	9.8	37.6	12.1	4.0	3.8
09	52210	Newington CDP, Connecticut	12.4	4.6	1.5	12.0	8.3	25.1	7.1	3.2	4.6
09	52280	New London city, Connecticut	16.2	6.0	1.9	1.9	8.7	37.2	13.8	1.7	1.3
09	54940	North Haven CDP, Connecticut	11.1	3.6	2.5	9.9	10.5	26.5	9.9	2.1	1.3
09	55990	Norwalk city, Connecticut	11.5	4.3	2.4	10.2	15.9	21.0	10.5	4.5	2.6
09	56200	Norwich city, Connecticut	14.7	5.3	2.0	7.0	8.1	20.0	21.3	3.1	6.2
09	68100	Shelton city, Connecticut	14.7	3.1	2.1	8.7	11.0	25.0	5.1	3.2	2.1
09	73000	Stamford city, Connecticut	10.3	3.4	2.8	14.1	19.0	19.5	8.7	5.3	2.6
09	74260	Stratford CDP, Connecticut	9.6	4.4	1.7	8.2	11.1	29.4	5.4	4.7	5.1
09	76500	Torrington city, Connecticut	16.2	3.9	4.4	6.1	6.9	21.2	8.2	2.3	2.9
09	77270	Trumbull CDP, Connecticut	6.3	6.5	2.8	10.8	13.4	26.9	6.3	5.4	3.0
09	80000	Waterbury city, Connecticut	16.6	4.5	1.3	4.1	7.2	25.5	10.8	3.8	4.4
09	82660	West Hartford CDP, Connecticut	7.0	2.4	3.1	17.1	13.5	34.0	3.2	3.3	4.2
09	82800	West Haven city, Connecticut	13.5	4.4	2.5	5.6	7.0	34.2	5.6	2.6	3.7
09	83570	Westport CDP, Connecticut	4.5	4.2	2.7	24.9	23.2	24.7	5.4	1.7	0.3
09	84970	Wethersfield CDP, Connecticut	5.4	1.4	3.2	13.7	9.8	29.3	12.5	3.4	4.9
10	00000	**DELAWARE**	12.3	4.0	1.5	9.8	10.1	25.0	10.1	4.5	5.3
10	21200	Dover city, Delaware	12.3	2.3	0.0	7.7	6.4	31.4	16.9	3.7	8.7
10	50670	Newark city, Delaware	10.0	0.7	1.2	12.8	6.5	34.4	17.8	3.1	4.4
10	77580	Wilmington city, Delaware	15.3	4.7	1.4	13.2	11.3	25.1	12.8	3.8	4.9
11	00000	**DISTRICT OF COLUMBIA**	5.0	2.7	4.2	6.2	23.0	19.5	9.7	8.8	16.3
11	50000	Washington city, District of Columbia	5.0	2.7	4.2	6.2	23.0	19.5	9.7	8.8	16.3
12	00000	**FLORIDA**	13.1	5.1	1.9	7.9	12.9	20.8	12.6	5.2	4.2
12	00410	Alafaya CDP, Florida	12.4	4.7	3.8	4.3	11.3	29.0	10.5	6.2	2.4
12	00950	Altamonte Springs city, Florida	13.0	2.0	2.8	10.5	18.3	24.6	13.7	3.4	3.8
12	01700	Apopka city, Florida	11.6	4.2	2.4	8.6	11.2	30.1	7.3	4.6	4.8
12	02681	Aventura city, Florida	11.3	3.2	3.9	16.2	17.7	22.0	5.2	8.2	1.1
12	04162	Bayonet Point CDP, Florida	15.8	6.5	5.4	8.4	14.0	18.5	13.0	4.1	5.4
12	05462	Bellview CDP, Florida	26.1	3.2	0.5	7.8	10.8	21.6	10.4	3.3	10.6
12	06875	Bloomingdale CDP, Florida	9.8	5.7	0.8	12.8	16.0	23.7	5.5	2.0	9.2
12	07300	Boca Raton city, Florida	13.8	2.1	2.0	15.4	19.3	16.9	11.8	4.2	2.7
12	07525	Bonita Springs city, Florida	20.3	3.0	0.6	7.8	11.4	11.0	16.6	6.3	2.8
12	07875	Boynton Beach city, Florida	13.2	3.4	2.7	5.6	14.9	22.7	14.5	7.7	1.7
12	07950	Bradenton city, Florida	16.4	3.2	3.2	4.7	7.9	19.1	19.5	4.7	4.8
12	08150	Brandon CDP, Florida	10.6	5.3	2.4	15.7	10.9	21.0	9.7	5.7	4.8
12	08300	Brent CDP, Florida	19.1	0.6	0.8	8.1	2.7	30.1	16.4	7.8	2.7
12	09415	Buenaventura Lakes CDP, Florida	15.9	8.6	0.0	11.5	11.0	15.2	19.5	3.5	1.9
12	10275	Cape Coral city, Florida	16.2	4.0	3.1	8.0	13.3	20.5	8.6	7.0	3.6
12	10825	Carrollwood CDP, Florida	13.5	3.6	2.4	7.3	10.6	25.8	9.4	7.0	4.6
12	11050	Casselberry city, Florida	16.1	5.6	0.6	11.2	12.0	22.1	20.0	3.2	2.5
12	12425	Citrus Park CDP, Florida	7.8	4.9	2.2	11.3	19.4	18.2	15.1	2.4	2.4
12	12875	Clearwater city, Florida	14.9	2.4	1.8	9.1	16.3	17.9	11.4	6.0	3.0
12	12925	Clermont city, Florida	7.7	5.3	2.2	3.5	8.4	33.6	18.6	3.1	7.6
12	13275	Coconut Creek city, Florida	19.5	4.2	2.2	7.5	14.5	18.6	10.0	7.6	4.9
12	14125	Cooper City city, Florida	23.1	4.3	3.2	7.9	14.3	23.1	4.4	3.8	3.6
12	14250	Coral Gables city, Florida	7.4	5.4	3.9	16.9	16.0	23.9	3.3	3.1	3.4
12	14400	Coral Springs city, Florida	12.7	3.7	3.4	9.8	15.0	18.6	10.6	6.5	5.6
12	14412	Coral Terrace CDP, Florida	8.5	6.5	0.9	8.4	11.6	21.5	8.6	10.1	3.3
12	14895	Country Club CDP, Florida	14.5	12.7	1.0	5.2	11.2	22.6	6.2	6.4	3.9
12	15475	Crestview city, Florida	–	–	–	–	–	–	–	–	–
12	15968	Cutler Bay town, Florida	12.2	8.3	3.5	6.6	14.0	23.2	10.6	3.6	5.7
12	16335	Dania Beach city, Florida	10.6	11.9	1.3	4.0	8.7	13.6	20.7	9.6	2.3
12	16475	Davie town, Florida	14.4	3.0	3.7	9.2	13.6	20.2	9.1	6.0	5.5
12	16525	Daytona Beach city, Florida	16.5	3.0	2.9	9.1	10.4	21.8	15.5	7.0	3.4
12	16725	Deerfield Beach city, Florida	16.3	4.0	1.6	4.9	15.5	16.7	14.7	5.3	2.1
12	16875	DeLand city, Florida	15.0	3.9	2.1	1.6	17.4	25.6	11.9	3.4	4.3
12	17100	Delray Beach city, Florida	14.2	5.1	2.3	8.5	13.8	23.0	12.8	3.6	2.3
12	17200	Deltona city, Florida	15.1	6.5	3.1	8.0	10.9	20.6	10.9	3.2	2.8
12	17935	Doral city, Florida	8.9	8.9	4.8	10.9	17.4	14.6	11.1	2.3	4.1
12	18575	Dunedin city, Florida	17.1	5.4	3.3	14.8	11.0	19.8	11.1	3.2	2.1
12	19206	East Lake CDP, Florida	14.2	4.8	1.2	12.5	16.7	17.8	9.7	3.4	3.4
12	19212	East Lake-Orient Park CDP, Florida	13.2	7.1	0.5	7.3	13.3	16.4	15.1	6.2	2.7
12	19825	Edgewater city, Florida	20.8	7.5	0.0	2.8	9.2	18.1	11.0	7.7	3.4
12	20108	Egypt Lake-Leto CDP, Florida	12.6	7.8	3.1	7.3	18.0	20.1	4.7	4.4	2.7
12	20925	Ensley CDP, Florida	14.5	8.4	0.5	7.0	23.0	13.4	9.6	7.8	6.5
12	21150	Estero village, Florida	13.6	2.9	1.2	12.1	20.9	15.9	10.4	3.8	1.7
12	22275	Ferry Pass CDP, Florida	10.3	3.7	3.3	7.8	10.9	21.8	13.7	10.5	2.0
12	22660	Fleming Island CDP, Florida	5.4	9.3	6.1	8.0	13.4	22.0	11.0	1.6	7.7

Table E. Cities—Labor Force, Employment, and Educational Data, 2015—*Continued*

FIPS state code	FIPS place code	State/city	Retail trade	Transportation and warehousing, and utilities	Information	Finance and insurance, and real estate and rental and leasing	Professional, scientific, and management, and administrative and waste management services	Educational services, and health care and social assistance	Arts, entertainment, and recreation, and accommodation and food services	Other services, except public administration	Public administration
12	23050	Florida Ridge CDP, Florida									
12	24000	Fort Lauderdale city, Florida	12.0	5.2	2.5	7.5	16.2	17.4	17.4	4.9	3.5
12	24125	Fort Myers city, Florida	18.1	2.1	1.2	6.1	12.2	22.0	15.6	3.7	2.2
12	24300	Fort Pierce city, Florida	12.9	2.5	0.3	1.3	21.5	17.9	12.8	5.5	3.4
12	24475	Fort Walton Beach city, Florida	18.1	1.4	1.4	5.8	15.2	15.7	18.9	4.0	5.2
12	24562	Fountainebleau CDP, Florida	11.6	9.8	2.8	8.0	11.2	17.0	8.3	8.4	3.5
12	24581	Four Corners CDP, Florida	14.9	2.7	0.9	6.4	15.3	7.6	37.3	5.4	2.5
12	24925	Fruit Cove CDP, Florida	10.3	4.6	0.9	16.4	15.8	27.3	7.3	5.6	2.8
12	25175	Gainesville city, Florida	11.9	2.7	1.8	4.2	8.4	38.3	15.3	4.7	3.2
12	26300	Golden Gate CDP, Florida	13.5	4.8	0.6	2.2	15.1	13.5	12.9	11.8	0.6
12	26375	Golden Glades CDP, Florida	16.9	7.9	0.2	6.3	12.5	23.0	14.5	5.2	2.7
12	27322	Greenacres city, Florida	15.7	5.6	1.5	4.0	11.9	25.4	13.2	4.2	1.8
12	28400	Haines City city, Florida	7.8	2.1	0.8	2.0	5.0	19.5	31.1	11.1	2.1
12	28452	Hallandale Beach city, Florida	16.3	6.6	0.2	5.1	13.5	17.5	17.2	7.6	1.1
12	30000	Hialeah city, Florida	15.0	9.2	1.0	5.1	9.1	15.8	9.5	8.8	2.0
12	30025	Hialeah Gardens city, Florida	12.0	9.3	0.0	2.5	9.0	15.5	6.5	12.1	1.8
12	31075	Holiday CDP, Florida	19.8	4.6	1.5	7.7	13.7	14.9	15.3	4.5	2.8
12	32000	Hollywood city, Florida	11.5	6.1	1.5	7.0	14.0	19.1	10.8	7.0	3.0
12	32275	Homestead city, Florida	11.1	5.3	2.5	5.9	10.1	22.9	9.7	0.6	6.8
12	32610	Horizon West CDP, Florida									
12	32967	Hunters Creek CDP, Florida	17.0	4.1	4.2	6.8	16.1	14.3	16.5	2.7	0.9
12	33250	Immokalee CDP, Florida	2.7	1.0	1.0	3.8	13.6	10.6	14.4	4.6	0.5
12	35000	Jacksonville city, Florida	12.3	6.7	1.7	11.7	12.2	20.8	10.1	4.7	4.5
12	35050	Jacksonville Beach city, Florida	13.0	4.4	2.8	15.7	8.8	19.9	13.8	4.6	2.3
12	35350	Jasmine Estates CDP, Florida	18.1	2.1	0.4	1.4	11.0	30.9	12.1	4.0	0.7
12	35875	Jupiter town, Florida	11.2	3.9	2.4	9.0	18.0	19.0	13.8	4.4	2.2
12	36062	Kendale Lakes CDP, Florida	14.3	7.6	2.2	5.8	8.7	26.0	10.3	6.3	3.5
12	36100	Kendall CDP, Florida	11.0	3.2	2.8	9.8	17.4	29.5	6.8	5.4	2.4
12	36121	Kendall West CDP, Florida	14.4	6.5	0.7	7.1	8.7	19.5	15.7	7.5	3.4
12	36462	Keystone CDP, Florida	9.5	8.3	3.8	17.1	18.9	19.9	6.4	1.8	3.0
12	36550	Key West city, Florida	8.3	6.1	2.4	5.3	6.0	15.0	30.9	5.1	8.1
12	36950	Kissimmee city, Florida	17.2	3.7	0.9	1.4	11.0	17.1	31.5	3.2	3.3
12	37648	Lake Butler CDP, Florida									
12	38250	Lakeland city, Florida	18.9	3.6	1.8	7.5	10.1	22.1	8.0	5.7	2.8
12	38350	Lake Magdalene CDP, Florida	13.7	4.8	0.9	10.3	15.4	21.4	10.3	6.6	2.7
12	38813	Lakeside CDP, Florida	15.7	5.1	1.3	5.3	9.7	25.9	11.0	4.9	5.4
12	39075	Lake Worth city, Florida	9.3	1.5	2.4	5.0	15.8	13.4	22.7	7.6	1.6
12	39200	Land O' Lakes CDP, Florida	10.7	2.9	2.9	9.7	8.3	30.0	8.3	3.7	4.3
12	39425	Largo city, Florida	17.7	5.2	0.8	7.6	16.9	17.3	10.7	4.3	2.0
12	39525	Lauderdale Lakes city, Florida	24.8	6.4	1.4	3.3	8.3	24.6	12.8	5.7	0.0
12	39550	Lauderhill city, Florida	16.0	7.8	2.8	8.0	12.7	25.6	11.2	4.5	3.4
12	39875	Leesburg city, Florida									
12	39925	Lehigh Acres CDP, Florida	16.4	5.7	2.6	5.5	12.4	19.3	10.1	3.6	3.1
12	39950	Leisure City CDP, Florida	12.5	7.2	0.0	2.6	8.4	13.1	14.3	7.8	4.4
12	41775	Lutz CDP, Florida	16.5	4.4	3.6	6.6	15.3	24.7	7.3	2.9	1.3
12	41825	Lynn Haven city, Florida	11.1	3.2	2.1	9.6	8.3	32.1	12.5	1.9	9.4
12	43125	Margate city, Florida	13.6	3.1	0.9	4.6	11.0	22.3	17.7	5.6	4.6
12	43800	Meadow Woods CDP, Florida	16.7	12.9	1.3	6.5	11.0	17.0	16.9	6.7	4.9
12	43975	Melbourne city, Florida	13.1	3.6	1.7	6.5	11.0	23.9	8.4	5.8	4.2
12	44275	Merritt Island CDP, Florida	12.2	4.4	0.3	7.2	18.3	15.5	11.4	7.7	3.6
12	45000	Miami city, Florida	9.1	7.5	2.5	6.7	13.5	16.0	16.1	8.4	2.6
12	45025	Miami Beach city, Florida	7.5	4.7	3.9	12.5	15.5	13.6	24.1	4.2	1.4
12	45060	Miami Gardens city, Florida	14.4	9.9	2.7	3.9	10.1	22.0	7.1	4.4	9.8
12	45100	Miami Lakes town, Florida	11.2	6.0	0.8	7.8	7.1	25.5	6.5	8.3	4.4
12	45975	Miramar city, Florida	11.9	7.8	4.8	5.6	12.8	26.0	7.4	5.2	4.6
12	47625	Naples city, Florida	14.2	2.5	2.3	18.5	13.2	17.6	10.3	8.4	0.8
12	48050	Navarre CDP, Florida	16.3	6.7	3.3	6.4	15.2	11.3	9.9	5.4	13.9
12	48625	New Smyrna Beach city, Florida	7.7	8.0	1.8	8.9	11.3	21.4	11.0	7.6	8.3
12	49260	Northdale CDP, Florida	9.4	7.3	3.6	14.0	18.8	18.3	7.0	5.1	3.6
12	49350	North Fort Myers CDP, Florida	17.8	4.3	0.3	8.8	17.1	20.0	9.2	2.6	4.4
12	49425	North Lauderdale city, Florida	12.0	5.6	3.5	4.3	12.4	18.6	15.3	3.8	3.6
12	49450	North Miami city, Florida	15.1	8.1	0.4	4.6	8.8	21.4	23.8	6.7	3.1
12	49475	North Miami Beach city, Florida	14.7	6.4	0.2	6.6	11.3	17.5	20.6	6.0	4.3
12	49675	North Port city, Florida	7.3	6.2	2.1	9.5	11.2	24.6	8.8	2.0	5.2
12	50575	Oakland Park city, Florida	9.5	3.8	2.2	8.5	11.0	18.1	17.8	8.3	3.7
12	50630	Oakleaf Plantation CDP, Florida	11.6	13.4	0.0	10.2	4.1	19.6	4.3	6.2	9.9
12	50638	Oak Ridge CDP, Florida	12.0	4.7	0.0	1.8	14.2	12.1	20.1	5.8	3.5
12	50750	Ocala city, Florida	10.0	3.9	1.7	4.7	9.1	34.3	11.6	4.1	5.3
12	51075	Ocoee city, Florida	10.8	2.6	3.3	5.8	11.4	22.1	15.9	5.4	1.6
12	53000	Orlando city, Florida	12.1	5.8	2.4	7.6	16.3	16.7	22.4	3.6	2.3
12	53150	Ormond Beach city, Florida	11.7	3.7	2.4	6.1	12.4	22.7	13.4	9.6	4.2
12	53575	Oviedo city, Florida	14.1	6.6	5.0	9.3	11.9	22.4	7.6	4.5	7.1
12	53725	Pace CDP, Florida	9.8	5.7	1.0	11.3	10.0	20.8	11.9	8.9	4.4

Table E. Cities—Labor Force, Employment, and Educational Data, 2015—*Continued*

							Percent in each industry sector				
FIPS state code	FIPS place code	State/city	Retail trade	Transportation and warehousing, and utilities	Information	Finance and insurance, and real estate and rental and leasing	Professional, scientific, and management, and administrative and waste management services	Educational services, and health care and social assistance	Arts, entertainment, and recreation, and accommodation and food services	Other services, except public administration	Public administration
12	54000	Palm Bay city, Florida	13.5	4.1	1.4	3.8	12.6	25.5	14.6	5.7	4.1
12	54075	Palm Beach Gardens city, Florida	11.3	7.4	3.4	10.0	18.7	15.0	14.6	4.6	1.7
12	54175	Palm City CDP, Florida	12.0	1.0	0.6	12.4	16.6	17.2	14.9	4.7	3.0
12	54200	Palm Coast city, Florida	11.5	4.0	2.4	7.9	11.1	24.8	13.8	3.7	1.6
12	54275	Palmetto Bay village, Florida	11.2	5.0	1.9	8.2	14.7	22.5	17.3	4.1	4.6
12	54300	Palmetto Estates CDP, Florida	14.8	2.9	0.3	5.2	14.5	32.9	13.4	5.5	3.5
12	54350	Palm Harbor CDP, Florida	13.3	2.8	0.5	9.5	14.7	24.3	12.1	3.8	1.8
12	54387	Palm River-Clair Mel CDP, Florida	12.9	11.7	2.2	13.4	9.4	15.4	4.3	3.9	5.3
12	54450	Palm Springs village, Florida	19.6	3.1	0.3	8.7	9.8	17.6	13.1	4.3	3.2
12	54525	Palm Valley CDP, Florida	10.5	1.3	2.5	12.3	10.6	27.9	10.6	4.4	0.0
12	54700	Panama City city, Florida	19.3	2.5	3.7	4.8	12.2	21.2	14.2	4.6	9.0
12	55125	Parkland city, Florida	11.7	4.3	5.1	12.8	20.2	21.7	6.4	1.0	2.3
12	55775	Pembroke Pines city, Florida	11.8	6.6	2.5	6.5	16.3	23.5	10.5	4.4	4.9
12	55925	Pensacola city, Florida	13.2	5.6	1.0	5.3	13.7	22.7	16.9	5.4	3.5
12	56825	Pine Hills CDP, Florida	14.1	4.2	2.4	3.0	9.5	17.0	25.0	5.4	4.9
12	56975	Pinellas Park city, Florida	13.0	4.4	2.5	7.6	9.6	21.3	11.0	9.2	2.2
12	57425	Plantation city, Florida	14.8	7.2	1.6	6.9	12.9	23.4	9.5	5.2	4.9
12	57550	Plant City city, Florida	11.4	7.1	1.4	8.4	10.2	16.9	11.9	3.2	2.7
12	57900	Poinciana CDP, Florida	14.8	4.4	0.4	1.7	12.6	14.6	24.9	3.0	2.6
12	58050	Pompano Beach city, Florida	13.8	6.6	1.9	7.2	13.6	13.3	14.4	7.3	2.9
12	58350	Port Charlotte CDP, Florida	24.5	4.9	0.5	4.6	9.5	21.1	8.4	2.7	2.0
12	58575	Port Orange city, Florida	7.6	4.7	0.8	7.5	11.7	25.1	14.5	5.0	5.0
12	58715	Port St. Lucie city, Florida	16.5	2.6	2.0	5.4	14.4	25.3	13.4	4.9	2.8
12	58975	Princeton CDP, Florida	11.5	5.2	0.7	6.0	6.9	23.2	10.7	7.2	4.7
12	60230	Richmond West CDP, Florida	19.8	5.8	0.0	9.8	12.4	18.4	9.6	7.6	6.3
12	60950	Riverview CDP, Florida	12.2	7.3	0.8	13.0	14.5	21.1	5.7	1.9	7.3
12	60975	Riviera Beach city, Florida	14.1	4.0	1.2	7.7	9.4	25.6	14.5	3.7	3.5
12	61500	Rockledge city, Florida	18.3	1.6	0.3	4.8	8.6	22.9	8.4	8.8	8.0
12	62100	Royal Palm Beach village, Florida	16.4	2.9	1.6	6.9	6.9	22.1	8.9	9.8	9.4
12	62275	Ruskin CDP, Florida	10.6	10.8	0.9	5.7	10.3	15.2	10.2	2.0	6.2
12	62625	St. Cloud city, Florida	24.0	6.0	0.2	4.4	13.8	16.6	13.3	2.8	8.5
12	63000	St. Petersburg city, Florida	12.6	3.4	1.8	10.6	13.1	23.7	10.1	6.0	4.5
12	63425	San Carlos Park CDP, Florida	12.6	1.8	0.0	4.2	10.3	19.6	16.4	4.4	3.9
12	63650	Sanford city, Florida	11.8	7.1	1.9	8.9	15.1	20.5	10.2	6.2	2.7
12	64175	Sarasota city, Florida	10.9	1.9	0.9	6.4	14.0	28.8	19.2	3.6	1.9
12	64825	Sebastian city, Florida	19.1	1.4	0.9	2.4	13.7	29.8	12.6	4.5	4.5
12	67258	South Bradenton CDP, Florida	24.9	1.7	1.1	4.2	8.1	15.7	21.0	3.5	1.5
12	67575	South Miami Heights CDP, Florida	9.8	6.8	0.5	3.8	13.8	25.4	8.8	7.3	3.5
12	68350	Spring Hill CDP, Florida	16.9	4.6	1.2	8.7	9.5	21.7	13.8	6.1	5.5
12	69250	Sun City Center CDP, Florida	12.5	5.5	2.9	16.9	10.1	28.7	4.1	7.5	0.0
12	69555	Sunny Isles Beach city, Florida	8.7	4.1	0.0	18.2	13.2	17.8	15.8	11.3	0.0
12	69700	Sunrise city, Florida	16.1	7.7	2.0	8.5	10.3	23.0	11.3	5.6	5.0
12	70345	Sweetwater city, Florida	15.0	8.6	0.0	3.4	17.8	16.4	14.9	4.5	1.1
12	70600	Tallahassee city, Florida	13.6	3.1	1.3	6.0	11.8	28.7	15.6	4.3	10.4
12	70675	Tamarac city, Florida	14.1	6.5	3.0	6.2	15.6	20.1	9.1	6.2	4.1
12	70700	Tamiami CDP, Florida	11.9	10.2	3.0	8.5	10.4	17.4	9.8	9.9	3.6
12	71000	Tampa city, Florida	10.0	4.3	2.7	9.4	15.8	23.8	12.8	5.1	3.1
12	71150	Tarpon Springs city, Florida	15.2	2.7	0.7	10.2	11.7	22.2	14.7	6.4	1.1
12	71400	Temple Terrace city, Florida	14.3	1.8	2.6	9.4	18.2	29.2	9.1	0.6	5.2
12	71564	The Acreage CDP, Florida	7.8	5.0	1.9	8.2	8.8	17.4	14.2	3.2	8.3
12	71567	The Crossings CDP, Florida	8.4	6.4	1.7	9.6	15.0	26.0	9.4	5.0	3.0
12	71569	The Hammocks CDP, Florida	13.4	9.9	3.8	9.4	11.2	22.5	7.8	5.3	1.9
12	71625	The Villages CDP, Florida	15.2	1.9	1.2	15.2	20.3	11.4	13.7	3.8	8.9
12	71741	Three Lakes CDP, Florida	10.1	9.1	3.8	13.2	14.0	17.8	17.6	2.3	4.1
12	71900	Titusville city, Florida	18.5	3.4	1.0	5.0	14.0	24.2	8.6	2.2	6.1
12	72145	Town 'n' Country CDP, Florida	11.0	3.5	3.2	12.0	15.7	26.2	7.6	2.7	3.1
12	73163	University CDP (Hillsborough County), Florida	9.3	2.7	3.2	6.7	10.7	24.5	17.3	2.3	3.0
12	73172	University CDP (Orange County), Florida	18.8	3.7	1.8	10.1	4.9	19.9	20.8	4.1	1.1
12	73287	University Park CDP, Florida	9.4	8.9	2.7	10.0	16.9	22.9	10.1	9.0	3.0
12	73700	Valrico CDP, Florida	15.8	2.1	0.9	11.3	15.5	25.4	4.9	2.2	7.8
12	73900	Venice city, Florida	6.8	6.2	2.1	10.4	6.3	24.4	10.0	12.0	0.8
12	74200	Vero Beach South CDP, Florida	18.3	1.3	0.0	6.2	6.8	22.9	17.4	1.8	3.4
12	75725	Wekiwa Springs CDP, Florida	6.9	4.8	2.6	13.8	20.2	22.8	11.1	2.8	2.3
12	75812	Wellington village, Florida	11.4	3.4	2.0	6.7	15.6	26.5	9.7	3.8	5.7
12	75875	Wesley Chapel CDP, Florida	14.8	4.7	2.3	12.4	12.9	22.4	9.2	4.9	3.1
12	76062	Westchase CDP, Florida	12.6	0.5	3.7	16.1	23.9	16.2	10.7	5.0	3.2
12	76075	Westchester CDP, Florida	17.3	5.2	0.5	7.2	22.2	15.9	8.0	5.2	4.5
12	76487	West Little River CDP, Florida	15.3	11.5	1.1	1.5	10.9	23.4	10.4	6.8	2.7
12	76500	West Melbourne city, Florida	14.6	2.2	0.4	0.6	11.7	20.5	17.7	5.1	3.2
12	76582	Weston city, Florida	12.9	5.8	1.7	11.9	19.6	21.3	4.9	2.8	3.8
12	76600	West Palm Beach city, Florida	13.2	3.5	1.4	7.2	14.9	20.9	12.3	7.4	5.5

Table E. Cities—Labor Force, Employment, and Educational Data, 2015—*Continued*

FIPS state code	FIPS place code	State/city	Retail trade	Transportation and warehousing, and utilities	Information	Finance and insurance, and real estate and rental and leasing	Professional, scientific, and management, and administrative and waste management services	Educational services, and health care and social assistance	Arts, entertainment, and recreation, and accommodation and food services	Other services, except public administration	Public administration
							Percent in each industry sector				
12	76675	West Pensacola CDP, Florida	26.3	1.7	0.6	5.9	13.2	17.5	15.9	3.4	7.2
12	78250	Winter Garden city, Florida	11.8	0.4	3.6	10.8	15.7	12.4	28.4	1.3	0.0
12	78275	Winter Haven city, Florida	19.7	8.4	0.3	8.0	5.5	23.4	15.3	3.3	1.1
12	78300	Winter Park city, Florida	4.6	6.0	2.1	10.1	17.3	24.4	14.5	2.4	3.2
12	78325	Winter Springs city, Florida	9.4	3.2	3.0	14.2	18.0	19.7	9.4	4.2	2.6
12	78800	Wright CDP, Florida	17.2	4.3	0.5	6.5	13.8	19.9	16.4	9.1	4.4
13	00000	**GEORGIA**	12.0	6.0	2.6	6.0	11.8	20.9	9.2	5.1	5.0
13	00408	Acworth city, Georgia	15.4	3.9	3.8	0.7	15.3	28.3	8.9	8.7	2.6
13	01052	Albany city, Georgia	12.0	4.3	1.1	4.9	5.9	28.7	11.5	7.2	9.1
13	01696	Alpharetta city, Georgia	9.0	3.1	6.0	9.2	23.4	14.7	8.1	7.8	1.0
13	03440	Athens-Clarke County unified government (balance), Georgia	11.0	2.7	1.7	3.5	8.6	31.0	21.1	4.8	3.1
13	04000	Atlanta city, Georgia	9.3	5.8	3.9	7.6	19.4	22.0	12.0	4.1	4.3
13	04204	Augusta-Richmond County consolidated government (balance), Georgia	15.4	5.8	1.2	3.5	12.2	23.1	10.2	3.6	6.4
13	10944	Brookhaven city, Georgia	7.9	4.3	3.5	10.3	20.3	17.0	13.8	5.6	2.5
13	12834	Candler-McAfee CDP, Georgia	13.8	4.2	0.5	7.2	12.0	32.0	11.3	4.4	5.3
13	12988	Canton city, Georgia	12.6	2.5	5.3	5.5	15.3	19.6	11.7	2.2	4.2
13	13492	Carrollton city, Georgia	8.3	5.3	3.6	4.9	12.6	17.6	19.0	3.1	4.2
13	13688	Cartersville city, Georgia	9.1	6.2	1.9	0.0	9.3	15.8	2.9	2.4	4.7
13	15172	Chamblee city, Georgia	12.7	1.6	3.2	5.5	16.3	11.6	18.7	5.1	2.3
13	19000	Columbus city, Georgia	11.8	3.3	1.5	11.7	8.1	20.5	11.0	4.8	7.7
13	21380	Dalton city, Georgia	17.7	3.5	0.5	4.1	3.7	9.1	8.7	2.8	0.2
13	22052	Decatur city, Georgia	5.3	2.2	6.2	7.3	19.2	31.8	5.8	5.0	4.6
13	23900	Douglasville city, Georgia	11.5	10.2	3.3	3.4	13.2	21.5	7.9	4.9	7.1
13	24600	Duluth city, Georgia	10.9	3.7	5.9	13.5	21.0	16.9	9.9	6.6	1.5
13	24768	Dunwoody city, Georgia	5.5	3.9	6.7	9.0	36.6	11.5	7.9	4.3	3.8
13	25720	East Point city, Georgia	13.3	12.8	2.0	4.1	8.5	24.4	12.6	5.4	6.4
13	28044	Evans CDP, Georgia	18.2	6.8	3.9	5.7	7.7	26.2	4.8	3.1	4.2
13	31908	Gainesville city, Georgia	5.4	7.8	1.1	4.9	8.4	13.7	8.7	3.2	2.5
13	35324	Griffin city, Georgia	18.6	4.7	4.5	1.6	4.7	23.0	21.3	1.3	9.1
13	38964	Hinesville city, Georgia	11.3	9.2	0.2	3.5	8.2	18.0	17.2	6.9	12.6
13	42425	Johns Creek city, Georgia	9.7	5.4	5.3	9.3	25.3	19.1	7.9	1.4	3.0
13	43192	Kennesaw city, Georgia	20.7	3.0	4.2	7.2	7.5	23.0	9.3	3.6	3.8
13	44340	LaGrange city, Georgia	13.0	6.0	0.0	2.5	4.7	26.2	4.3	1.8	1.1
13	45488	Lawrenceville city, Georgia	14.2	5.0	4.4	4.8	8.2	26.8	10.0	5.0	4.5
13	48288	Mableton CDP, Georgia	12.4	7.2	3.4	6.0	9.7	22.0	7.6	5.5	2.3
13	48624	McDonough city, Georgia	11.3	6.2	4.2	5.9	13.2	22.8	4.3	1.1	7.1
13	49008	Macon-Bibb County, Georgia	11.9	5.4	1.6	8.2	9.4	29.5	9.0	4.0	5.1
13	49756	Marietta city, Georgia	14.2	5.6	4.2	6.8	16.2	12.8	13.5	4.1	2.9
13	50036	Martinez CDP, Georgia	7.8	4.5	2.3	6.9	12.0	30.4	6.1	7.5	3.1
13	51670	Milton city, Georgia	11.8	2.1	1.6	22.6	20.5	12.6	8.0	3.6	2.9
13	55020	Newnan city, Georgia	9.7	13.5	2.4	4.0	9.9	22.5	7.4	6.1	4.8
13	56168	North Druid Hills CDP, Georgia	5.6	9.1	9.5	2.1	13.6	38.6	4.8	1.8	5.9
13	59724	Peachtree City city, Georgia	8.1	11.2	6.1	9.2	10.6	18.4	6.1	6.2	3.2
13	59735	Peachtree Corners city, Georgia	13.5	4.1	4.5	11.7	18.9	17.7	6.4	7.1	2.6
13	62104	Pooler city, Georgia	16.6	10.5	0.0	11.9	14.7	10.8	4.0	2.9	10.1
13	63952	Redan CDP, Georgia	13.0	11.7	3.4	4.1	13.0	28.3	13.0	2.2	4.8
13	66668	Rome city, Georgia	8.9	3.3	1.3	4.8	4.7	23.8	11.2	7.3	3.2
13	67284	Roswell city, Georgia	11.3	3.9	2.9	13.3	18.8	12.9	12.7	4.7	1.2
13	68516	Sandy Springs city, Georgia	8.5	3.0	6.0	10.9	24.6	20.3	10.5	6.4	1.7
13	69000	Savannah city, Georgia	13.7	6.4	1.4	2.9	9.5	24.1	17.2	6.5	3.9
13	71492	Smyrna city, Georgia	12.2	3.7	5.5	8.6	17.5	20.2	8.8	4.4	2.5
13	73256	Statesboro city, Georgia	12.0	1.2	1.0	6.4	5.6	35.6	19.7	2.4	2.8
13	73704	Stockbridge city, Georgia	6.4	11.2	4.5	11.1	14.5	19.0	8.7	1.7	7.4
13	74180	Sugar Hill city, Georgia	11.7	2.0	4.4	9.6	22.1	15.3	9.1	1.4	7.5
13	77652	Tucker CDP, Georgia	13.4	4.7	3.7	3.7	10.8	28.5	10.8	5.2	7.1
13	78324	Union City city, Georgia	21.4	6.3	4.9	3.6	6.0	10.8	19.9	11.1	6.2
13	78800	Valdosta city, Georgia	13.4	1.9	3.1	2.0	12.4	28.8	15.4	2.3	4.8
13	80508	Warner Robins city, Georgia	14.6	8.7	0.8	3.6	6.9	18.5	7.4	4.9	19.8
13	84176	Woodstock city, Georgia	8.5	2.7	8.9	10.3	17.1	18.3	9.5	4.4	3.6
15	00000	HAWAII	11.5	5.7	1.7	6.8	9.9	19.6	15.9	4.8	9.0
15	06290	East Honolulu CDP, Hawaii	9.4	5.7	0.8	9.8	12.7	22.0	13.7	3.6	9.7
15	07470	Ewa Gentry CDP, Hawaii	11.9	4.6	6.3	3.9	9.6	31.8	6.5	1.9	8.2
15	14650	Hilo CDP, Hawaii	14.4	8.3	1.8	7.8	8.0	23.0	10.8	2.3	11.9
15	22700	Kahului CDP, Hawaii	14.1	7.7	0.9	6.9	7.3	20.0	17.2	4.3	9.7
15	23150	Kailua CDP (Honolulu County), Hawaii	10.5	2.8	4.1	6.8	13.8	24.5	11.6	3.2	9.3
15	28250	Kaneohe CDP, Hawaii	10.5	8.5	1.4	8.9	8.9	22.2	11.0	3.8	8.2
15	30300	Kapolei CDP, Hawaii	15.4	14.0	1.6	4.5	8.5	10.2	13.7	7.4	12.8
15	47600	Makakilo CDP, Hawaii	16.3	4.0	0.7	11.3	5.7	18.2	9.9	3.1	14.7

Table E. Cities—Labor Force, Employment, and Educational Data, 2015—*Continued*

							Percent in each industry sector				
FIPS state code	FIPS place code	State/city	Retail trade	Transportation and warehousing, and utilities	Information	Finance and insurance, and real estate and rental and leasing	Professional, scientific, and management, and administrative and waste management services	Educational services, and health care and social assistance	Arts, entertainment, and recreation, and accommodation and food services	Other services, except public administration	Public administration
15	51000	Mililani Mauka CDP, Hawaii	11.8	8.8	1.9	7.8	7.8	23.4	5.5	1.0	11.0
15	51050	Mililani Town CDP, Hawaii	15.7	6.3	0.5	6.7	6.3	19.6	15.5	3.7	12.3
15	62600	Pearl City CDP, Hawaii	14.2	6.3	2.0	7.0	10.5	17.7	9.2	5.2	14.7
15	69050	Schofield Barracks CDP, Hawaii	–	–	–	–	–	–	–	–	–
15	71550	Urban Honolulu CDP, Hawaii	11.0	5.3	1.7	7.5	10.8	20.7	18.2	6.0	7.5
15	79700	Waipahu CDP, Hawaii	15.8	6.0	0.9	5.6	9.6	16.6	22.9	2.2	6.2
16	00000	**IDAHO**	11.9	4.9	1.8	5.0	9.9	23.4	9.5	4.8	4.8
16	08830	Boise City city, Idaho	12.3	3.2	2.8	5.5	14.5	23.7	11.3	5.2	5.1
16	12250	Caldwell city, Idaho	12.7	2.8	1.6	4.3	10.4	24.2	5.3	5.3	5.5
16	16750	Coeur d'Alene city, Idaho	14.4	5.3	0.5	6.8	10.6	22.1	15.0	3.7	6.0
16	23410	Eagle city, Idaho	12.8	3.4	7.9	7.6	17.1	22.0	6.6	3.6	6.8
16	39700	Idaho Falls city, Idaho	8.7	2.5	1.4	3.3	14.7	25.8	12.8	3.6	4.3
16	46540	Lewiston city, Idaho	14.8	5.9	1.4	6.6	5.3	23.2	11.1	5.5	2.8
16	52120	Meridian city, Idaho	8.6	5.4	0.5	10.8	13.4	24.4	6.2	5.2	5.5
16	54550	Moscow city, Idaho	13.2	1.6	1.7	1.9	7.4	47.5	13.7	0.5	1.6
16	56260	Nampa city, Idaho	13.6	3.0	1.8	3.9	11.2	21.7	7.7	5.7	4.5
16	64090	Pocatello city, Idaho	12.1	4.6	2.2	7.2	8.5	30.8	12.3	3.4	2.0
16	64810	Post Falls city, Idaho	10.7	1.2	0.8	10.7	12.5	20.7	10.2	5.9	2.4
16	67420	Rexburg city, Idaho	20.1	0.9	1.3	2.6	7.0	29.1	19.8	0.6	1.6
16	82810	Twin Falls city, Idaho	20.1	1.3	2.7	3.8	5.1	24.7	14.0	5.5	5.0
17	00000	**ILLINOIS**	11.0	6.1	1.9	7.3	11.7	22.7	9.2	4.6	3.6
17	00243	Addison village, Illinois	12.2	7.5	1.0	5.2	11.4	17.8	8.8	5.0	3.3
17	00685	Algonquin village, Illinois	14.9	4.7	1.6	7.5	12.5	20.0	10.8	2.9	2.1
17	01114	Alton city, Illinois	13.1	9.0	2.6	5.4	6.2	22.3	9.7	5.5	8.0
17	02154	Arlington Heights village, Illinois	8.8	6.1	2.2	9.8	15.2	23.7	6.1	3.3	2.1
17	03012	Aurora city, Illinois	10.0	5.9	3.1	8.8	12.3	18.1	11.4	3.6	1.0
17	04013	Bartlett village, Illinois	10.4	10.2	2.8	10.1	13.9	20.8	6.1	2.4	1.3
17	04078	Batavia city, Illinois	16.9	3.8	2.6	8.0	8.7	23.2	4.8	2.9	4.5
17	04845	Belleville city, Illinois	13.3	4.1	0.3	8.7	8.3	23.4	15.5	4.8	3.3
17	05092	Belvidere city, Illinois	21.3	6.1	0.0	3.7	8.3	10.0	8.4	1.7	6.2
17	05573	Berwyn city, Illinois	8.1	8.1	3.1	7.0	8.9	20.9	12.4	8.3	2.0
17	06587	Bloomingdale village, Illinois	12.3	10.2	6.2	6.9	10.4	18.4	13.5	3.9	3.5
17	06613	Bloomington city, Illinois	12.1	1.4	1.0	26.3	12.1	23.1	8.7	3.9	1.3
17	06704	Blue Island city, Illinois	23.0	7.2	0.0	6.4	9.2	15.9	8.4	3.7	3.3
17	07133	Bolingbrook village, Illinois	14.6	6.1	2.3	5.7	12.9	22.1	10.9	2.9	3.6
17	09447	Buffalo Grove village, Illinois	12.6	1.7	1.5	11.1	19.3	22.0	6.0	3.6	1.7
17	09642	Burbank city, Illinois	13.8	10.7	0.8	3.3	8.6	18.6	11.2	5.4	1.3
17	10487	Calumet City city, Illinois	13.9	14.3	1.1	7.4	6.1	24.9	3.8	4.9	9.9
17	11163	Carbondale city, Illinois	10.2	4.6	0.5	2.6	5.2	54.2	13.2	1.9	1.7
17	11332	Carol Stream village, Illinois	12.9	5.7	3.6	8.0	11.9	18.7	7.1	4.6	1.4
17	11358	Carpentersville village, Illinois	11.2	6.3	3.3	1.7	16.7	12.5	13.8	3.7	2.1
17	12385	Champaign city, Illinois	9.6	2.3	2.0	4.7	7.6	42.0	11.7	2.8	2.7
17	12567	Charleston city, Illinois	8.4	3.2	1.7	6.0	7.9	46.3	8.9	3.2	1.1
17	14000	Chicago city, Illinois	9.3	6.3	2.3	8.4	15.8	22.7	11.0	4.7	4.1
17	14026	Chicago Heights city, Illinois	5.6	9.9	1.9	4.5	10.7	25.0	13.2	3.3	1.2
17	14351	Cicero town, Illinois	10.6	6.9	0.8	4.2	10.3	12.3	18.0	5.1	1.4
17	15599	Collinsville city, Illinois	11.3	7.4	0.5	5.4	7.4	19.6	20.2	4.7	3.1
17	17458	Crest Hill city, Illinois	12.6	11.2	0.9	6.7	7.0	21.8	17.1	0.8	4.4
17	17887	Crystal Lake city, Illinois	9.5	4.8	5.3	9.5	14.4	16.3	11.9	3.9	2.7
17	18563	Danville city, Illinois	11.5	7.0	0.5	5.8	9.8	23.0	6.4	7.6	3.3
17	18628	Darien city, Illinois	11.9	8.2	2.6	12.8	13.2	23.4	2.1	3.0	1.5
17	18823	Decatur city, Illinois	12.3	6.2	1.9	6.0	8.7	20.5	12.1	4.5	3.3
17	19161	DeKalb city, Illinois	17.7	3.6	1.9	3.1	4.5	34.3	15.0	2.3	2.6
17	19642	Des Plaines city, Illinois	13.5	6.3	1.6	7.1	11.0	20.8	7.1	6.2	2.2
17	20292	Dolton village, Illinois	7.9	9.3	3.6	6.5	8.8	27.1	6.5	4.7	7.2
17	20591	Downers Grove village, Illinois	10.2	7.3	2.5	11.6	14.5	21.1	7.2	4.9	2.3
17	22073	East Moline city, Illinois	13.1	5.4	0.6	3.5	5.8	19.3	9.2	2.4	5.0
17	22164	East Peoria city, Illinois	10.2	7.4	0.8	3.9	7.8	21.6	15.1	6.4	1.9
17	22255	East St. Louis city, Illinois	5.8	8.7	1.1	2.3	11.2	33.9	12.5	2.7	0.9
17	22697	Edwardsville city, Illinois	8.5	3.0	3.4	9.9	12.5	31.9	15.9	3.8	3.9
17	23074	Elgin city, Illinois	8.7	6.7	2.4	4.8	10.9	18.7	11.1	4.9	1.8
17	23256	Elk Grove Village village, Illinois	10.4	9.8	1.8	7.7	12.8	17.0	4.9	5.2	3.7
17	23620	Elmhurst city, Illinois	8.3	4.5	1.2	9.8	21.8	19.9	5.8	3.5	3.3
17	23724	Elmwood Park village, Illinois	15.3	7.6	0.7	7.9	12.3	21.4	6.7	8.6	1.5
17	24582	Evanston city, Illinois	7.4	2.4	2.2	8.1	18.9	34.2	7.5	6.0	1.6
17	27884	Freeport city, Illinois	8.2	4.1	0.5	4.2	11.7	26.9	5.9	5.3	4.3
17	28326	Galesburg city, Illinois	16.8	8.9	0.4	3.2	4.2	36.2	6.6	4.8	3.2
17	28872	Geneva city, Illinois	7.2	3.4	3.5	6.1	14.0	32.1	3.2	6.7	2.2
17	29730	Glendale Heights village, Illinois	10.4	7.3	0.5	5.2	12.7	17.3	11.6	2.7	2.6
17	29756	Glen Ellyn village, Illinois	6.0	2.0	3.0	11.5	15.3	20.3	16.4	3.4	1.2
17	29938	Glenview village, Illinois	10.2	5.0	3.4	9.6	15.8	26.2	7.0	3.4	1.3

Table E. Cities—Labor Force, Employment, and Educational Data, 2015—*Continued*

									Percent in each industry sector		
FIPS state code	FIPS place code	State/city	Retail trade	Transportation and warehousing, and utilities	Information	Finance and insurance, and real estate and rental and leasing	Professional, scientific, and management, and administrative and waste management services	Educational services, and health care and social assistance	Arts, entertainment, and recreation, and accommodation and food services	Other services, except public administration	Public administration
17	30926	Granite City city, Illinois	11.2	8.5	1.0	5.4	6.7	21.9	10.3	10.0	6.4
17	31121	Grayslake village, Illinois	14.9	1.6	0.6	4.7	16.7	21.0	11.7	1.2	3.3
17	32018	Gurnee village, Illinois	11.3	3.5	1.5	5.7	12.0	19.6	10.5	3.8	2.2
17	32746	Hanover Park village, Illinois	13.9	7.9	1.4	5.7	11.3	21.3	6.1	5.1	1.4
17	33383	Harvey city, Illinois	14.5	13.0	0.4	2.2	3.1	25.0	12.3	6.6	3.2
17	34722	Highland Park city, Illinois	10.8	1.8	2.5	11.7	17.8	27.2	6.7	4.5	2.1
17	35411	Hoffman Estates village, Illinois	15.6	4.3	3.0	11.1	12.2	15.3	8.3	3.8	1.6
17	35835	Homer Glen village, Illinois	8.6	10.6	2.4	9.9	13.1	23.4	5.5	5.0	3.6
17	36750	Huntley village, Illinois	12.2	7.8	0.5	5.3	14.6	21.9	9.7	2.4	1.1
17	38570	Joliet city, Illinois	13.7	7.8	1.8	5.3	10.8	19.6	11.4	4.0	4.0
17	38934	Kankakee city, Illinois	6.3	7.5	1.3	4.4	3.9	29.2	11.0	7.0	2.7
17	41183	Lake in the Hills village, Illinois	17.0	7.8	2.8	6.9	7.9	15.2	12.4	4.5	1.4
17	41742	Lake Zurich village, Illinois	14.7	3.7	0.4	7.0	18.1	19.3	8.3	5.5	3.1
17	42028	Lansing village, Illinois	11.3	10.8	0.7	8.4	6.6	24.1	12.3	4.9	4.8
17	43250	Libertyville village, Illinois	11.0	0.5	1.3	9.0	15.8	23.0	5.8	5.3	2.2
17	43939	Lisle village, Illinois	11.3	3.1	2.8	10.8	15.3	24.6	3.4	3.3	3.4
17	44225	Lockport city, Illinois	8.1	9.1	1.4	7.4	6.8	32.2	6.2	3.0	2.7
17	44407	Lombard village, Illinois	11.3	8.4	0.9	5.1	15.5	18.2	15.3	4.5	2.5
17	45031	Loves Park city, Illinois	11.0	2.7	0.8	8.9	5.6	30.0	6.5	2.4	2.8
17	45694	McHenry city, Illinois	11.9	2.4	1.3	8.9	8.9	15.7	6.9	4.6	2.4
17	45726	Machesney Park village, Illinois	13.2	2.6	1.4	4.7	7.4	24.2	10.8	7.9	2.2
17	47774	Maywood village, Illinois	11.6	12.1	0.4	6.6	12.5	20.7	7.0	2.4	7.1
17	48242	Melrose Park village, Illinois	7.6	8.4	2.5	4.6	10.8	14.2	14.0	2.8	6.1
17	49867	Moline city, Illinois	15.4	5.2	2.2	3.3	8.7	17.8	7.9	5.2	3.1
17	50647	Morton Grove village, Illinois	8.5	6.8	4.2	5.5	12.8	30.0	5.4	4.0	1.2
17	51089	Mount Prospect village, Illinois	8.2	5.1	2.4	8.6	17.1	22.2	6.9	4.1	2.0
17	51349	Mundelein village, Illinois	12.3	2.8	1.6	8.2	15.5	15.1	9.4	6.1	1.6
17	51622	Naperville city, Illinois	8.2	3.9	3.4	11.1	17.2	22.2	8.5	3.2	2.4
17	52584	New Lenox village, Illinois	13.2	8.1	3.6	6.6	10.1	27.8	5.2	4.0	3.7
17	53000	Niles village, Illinois	14.3	7.4	2.8	6.2	9.1	29.0	10.4	2.8	1.4
17	53234	Normal town, Illinois	15.4	4.9	1.3	15.6	6.0	23.6	18.4	2.8	3.9
17	53481	Northbrook village, Illinois	11.7	2.4	3.2	16.6	19.3	24.7	4.9	1.8	1.6
17	53559	North Chicago city, Illinois	13.4	4.1	0.3	2.0	9.6	22.7	11.9	5.2	8.6
17	54638	Oak Forest city, Illinois	9.5	6.7	1.5	6.1	13.0	22.2	11.6	4.5	2.9
17	54820	Oak Lawn village, Illinois	10.3	8.9	0.8	8.9	12.5	23.8	5.5	4.0	3.4
17	54885	Oak Park village, Illinois	8.1	3.8	2.5	9.0	17.2	28.0	8.7	7.3	2.4
17	55249	O'Fallon city, Illinois	9.4	8.1	0.9	7.3	10.9	29.8	5.6	4.9	11.4
17	56640	Orland Park village, Illinois	8.2	7.0	1.4	10.0	10.8	27.2	6.3	4.2	3.4
17	56887	Oswego village, Illinois	10.8	5.1	0.5	2.0	9.4	26.0	6.3	2.7	7.4
17	57225	Palatine village, Illinois	14.1	6.4	1.5	6.9	15.3	17.0	9.9	3.9	1.3
17	57732	Park Forest village, Illinois	9.8	8.6	2.7	12.0	6.6	35.4	7.3	3.4	0.8
17	57875	Park Ridge city, Illinois	9.2	4.2	2.3	14.8	15.9	20.8	5.5	6.3	3.3
17	58447	Pekin city, Illinois	15.2	4.1	1.5	4.9	4.8	24.9	9.2	5.4	7.1
17	59000	Peoria city, Illinois	9.6	4.7	1.3	4.0	10.8	28.9	9.2	4.9	3.9
17	60287	Plainfield village, Illinois	16.8	5.0	1.6	8.8	12.4	24.3	4.9	2.7	5.1
17	62367	Quincy city, Illinois	13.9	3.8	1.8	9.6	8.2	24.8	7.9	5.0	2.9
17	65000	Rockford city, Illinois	11.9	4.2	1.3	3.7	11.8	22.4	11.3	4.9	3.4
17	65078	Rock Island city, Illinois	10.1	7.1	3.7	4.2	7.0	32.5	8.8	4.8	4.2
17	65338	Rolling Meadows city, Illinois	4.6	5.1	0.6	8.1	13.7	23.2	21.0	2.1	2.6
17	65442	Romeoville village, Illinois	18.2	7.3	2.6	2.3	9.4	16.2	8.4	2.6	3.8
17	65806	Roselle village, Illinois	9.7	9.1	1.0	4.7	15.4	17.6	9.2	8.7	2.2
17	66040	Round Lake Beach village, Illinois	19.9	2.0	0.5	3.3	14.3	12.7	11.7	3.0	5.3
17	66703	St. Charles city, Illinois	14.2	1.1	0.7	11.2	11.3	24.6	6.1	2.8	1.1
17	68003	Schaumburg village, Illinois	12.8	7.5	3.1	9.0	13.8	17.6	8.7	5.3	2.5
17	70122	Skokie village, Illinois	12.4	5.9	1.3	8.9	10.6	29.6	7.8	5.0	1.2
17	70720	South Elgin village, Illinois	13.4	5.4	1.8	7.0	10.2	19.4	7.3	5.3	3.8
17	70850	South Holland village, Illinois	5.3	8.0	2.7	6.6	11.5	31.2	7.5	8.2	8.6
17	72000	Springfield city, Illinois	10.2	4.5	1.5	9.0	8.8	27.6	10.6	4.8	12.4
17	73157	Streamwood village, Illinois	11.6	5.0	3.4	3.5	14.6	19.1	12.9	6.4	2.3
17	75484	Tinley Park village, Illinois	11.9	6.5	2.7	8.5	8.1	25.6	7.9	5.4	6.0
17	77005	Urbana city, Illinois	7.8	1.7	2.0	3.0	10.0	46.4	9.4	3.9	4.6
17	77694	Vernon Hills village, Illinois	7.4	2.9	1.9	11.7	23.0	23.7	3.4	1.9	1.2
17	77993	Villa Park village, Illinois	12.6	7.6	1.8	9.1	20.5	15.5	7.9	6.2	4.7
17	79293	Waukegan city, Illinois	9.1	5.1	1.0	2.7	13.2	12.0	10.5	6.7	2.0
17	80060	West Chicago city, Illinois	8.5	7.1	1.3	3.6	14.3	14.7	10.9	6.2	1.6
17	80645	Westmont village, Illinois	9.1	3.9	5.9	15.0	13.4	22.7	12.1	4.7	0.5
17	81048	Wheaton city, Illinois	5.7	3.6	2.3	9.1	14.4	25.7	8.2	7.7	3.5
17	81087	Wheeling village, Illinois	12.6	7.0	0.7	5.0	13.3	15.0	12.3	7.0	0.9
17	82075	Wilmette village, Illinois	8.0	1.0	1.8	14.7	23.5	27.2	5.1	4.3	2.7
17	83245	Woodridge village, Illinois	10.8	4.5	3.5	8.0	12.0	26.4	10.5	4.9	2.5
17	83349	Woodstock city, Illinois	12.1	3.3	1.1	6.7	9.7	26.5	10.9	5.6	0.5
17	84220	Zion city, Illinois	16.4	6.5	1.3	6.4	9.1	22.0	8.5	2.3	3.3

Table E. Cities—Labor Force, Employment, and Educational Data, 2015—*Continued*

FIPS state code	FIPS place code	State/city	Retail trade	Transportation and warehousing, and utilities	Information	Finance and insurance, and real estate and rental and leasing	Professional, scientific, and management, and administrative and waste management services	Educational services, and health care and social assistance	Arts, entertainment, and recreation, and accommodation and food services	Other services, except public administration	Public administration
							Percent in each industry sector				
18	00000	**INDIANA**	11.5	5.1	1.6	5.3	8.3	22.2	9.0	4.5	3.3
18	01468	Anderson city, Indiana	11.7	5.0	0.7	3.5	12.0	26.5	10.5	6.0	7.6
18	05860	Bloomington city, Indiana	11.7	1.1	5.0	3.6	8.8	30.4	22.8	4.8	2.1
18	08416	Brownsburg town, Indiana	9.0	9.0	2.1	4.8	10.7	27.4	13.7	8.1	1.4
18	10342	Carmel city, Indiana	6.5	3.7	3.4	10.2	15.6	24.3	8.8	2.4	2.2
18	12934	Clarksville town, Indiana	12.4	10.0	1.7	6.4	7.4	13.5	19.4	4.5	1.0
18	14734	Columbus city, Indiana	10.5	1.4	0.7	5.6	6.2	20.3	5.9	3.0	1.1
18	16138	Crown Point city, Indiana	11.8	9.1	0.6	5.4	10.0	22.0	10.4	4.3	1.2
18	19486	East Chicago city, Indiana	9.6	2.4	0.0	5.2	9.3	15.2	20.6	2.8	2.8
18	20728	Elkhart city, Indiana	10.7	3.9	1.0	2.4	5.9	13.1	2.4	4.7	2.9
18	22000	Evansville city, Indiana	11.4	5.0	3.8	5.4	11.1	19.3	12.1	4.5	1.7
18	23278	Fishers town, Indiana	9.3	1.8	2.0	14.5	16.5	23.9	5.8	5.7	3.6
18	25000	Fort Wayne city, Indiana	11.7	3.4	2.0	7.9	8.1	22.7	10.1	5.4	1.6
18	25450	Franklin city, Indiana	10.8	6.3	0.8	2.1	7.5	25.8	10.5	5.8	7.1
18	27000	Gary city, Indiana	14.9	6.2	1.2	4.4	8.5	23.9	12.3	6.0	4.2
18	28386	Goshen city, Indiana	10.9	3.0	1.1	2.0	6.0	18.0	6.2	9.9	1.0
18	28800	Granger CDP, Indiana	12.0	3.0	1.3	7.3	8.1	33.3	2.8	3.1	1.6
18	29520	Greenfield city, Indiana	19.6	3.1	3.5	4.4	5.1	15.5	2.5	0.8	3.2
18	29898	Greenwood city, Indiana	10.1	3.8	1.2	5.0	8.5	25.3	9.1	6.7	2.1
18	31000	Hammond city, Indiana	11.6	9.6	2.0	3.6	9.3	20.8	10.7	4.4	2.3
18	33466	Highland town, Indiana	12.5	6.1	1.0	7.6	5.8	21.8	10.4	4.9	3.0
18	34114	Hobart city, Indiana	12.9	3.7	1.0	1.9	11.6	24.6	5.1	5.9	5.5
18	36003	Indianapolis city (balance), Indiana	13.2	6.8	2.1	6.1	11.9	20.5	11.2	5.0	3.5
18	38358	Jeffersonville city, Indiana	14.0	7.6	1.4	10.6	7.3	19.7	7.6	7.2	4.0
18	40392	Kokomo city, Indiana	11.0	2.6	2.1	4.5	7.6	18.8	10.1	4.3	3.7
18	40788	Lafayette city, Indiana	13.2	5.0	0.7	4.7	7.4	25.4	10.5	2.3	1.8
18	42246	La Porte city, Indiana	21.7	6.1	0.8	2.6	3.0	19.2	12.7	0.9	0.6
18	42426	Lawrence city, Indiana	13.4	3.1	3.7	7.5	9.5	19.3	10.9	7.0	5.6
18	46908	Marion city, Indiana	14.0	2.2	2.8	2.8	7.0	36.3	10.1	4.8	1.8
18	48528	Merrillville town, Indiana	8.5	8.8	2.0	3.3	10.5	25.5	11.0	4.0	6.3
18	48798	Michigan City city, Indiana	12.2	6.3	1.8	1.4	7.7	20.7	9.0	6.7	4.2
18	49932	Mishawaka city, Indiana	12.2	2.6	0.5	3.1	9.8	31.4	10.0	4.0	3.8
18	51876	Muncie city, Indiana	13.0	2.5	1.2	3.0	8.0	30.0	20.0	5.0	2.2
18	51912	Munster town, Indiana	20.6	3.2	1.3	5.2	11.9	28.3	5.9	2.5	4.7
18	52326	New Albany city, Indiana	18.8	4.1	0.6	5.4	7.9	24.2	10.6	3.3	0.8
18	54180	Noblesville city, Indiana	13.1	4.5	0.9	9.1	10.5	21.1	10.5	5.7	1.6
18	60246	Plainfield town, Indiana	11.1	19.6	2.2	3.0	5.7	19.3	10.2	8.4	2.2
18	61092	Portage city, Indiana	14.8	7.8	0.7	5.4	13.2	20.5	10.2	2.8	2.1
18	64260	Richmond city, Indiana	13.0	2.5	1.0	2.3	4.7	31.2	14.6	4.8	0.6
18	68220	Schererville town, Indiana	14.9	5.0	1.0	11.8	7.9	25.0	4.6	5.5	1.1
18	71000	South Bend city, Indiana	12.3	2.2	4.4	4.0	9.2	26.0	7.8	3.3	3.0
18	75428	Terre Haute city, Indiana	13.9	2.1	1.3	3.8	7.2	24.4	16.3	3.9	2.1
18	78326	Valparaiso city, Indiana	14.4	3.5	0.0	4.1	8.0	33.7	5.8	3.2	3.1
18	82700	Westfield city, Indiana	16.4	5.2	1.4	9.5	15.0	18.6	8.5	2.6	3.4
18	82862	West Lafayette city, Indiana	6.9	2.5	3.1	1.9	7.3	47.8	16.6	4.8	0.7
18	86372	Zionsville town, Indiana	8.6	3.7	1.8	10.5	14.2	23.8	4.1	5.6	5.9
19	00000	**IOWA**	11.7	4.6	1.7	7.3	7.1	24.3	7.7	4.0	3.0
19	01855	Ames city, Iowa	11.7	1.0	1.6	3.3	6.2	41.8	14.1	1.7	4.3
19	02305	Ankeny city, Iowa	8.5	5.4	0.9	13.0	6.5	29.2	9.3	2.2	5.1
19	06355	Bettendorf city, Iowa	9.1	3.1	2.2	9.7	9.5	23.1	6.9	4.5	4.0
19	09550	Burlington city, Iowa	10.1	3.7	0.9	4.9	7.3	18.8	10.0	6.3	3.1
19	11755	Cedar Falls city, Iowa	15.6	3.0	2.0	6.3	6.8	34.4	13.1	2.6	0.3
19	12000	Cedar Rapids city, Iowa	15.1	6.3	3.9	6.2	10.9	21.1	6.8	4.2	2.2
19	14430	Clinton city, Iowa	14.0	1.8	1.1	2.1	8.0	27.9	7.3	3.4	1.5
19	16230	Coralville city, Iowa	10.9	3.8	1.4	4.3	9.3	47.7	14.1	3.2	2.0
19	16860	Council Bluffs city, Iowa	12.9	5.8	2.1	5.9	7.2	22.4	9.0	4.5	2.7
19	19000	Davenport city, Iowa	11.9	4.8	1.5	5.8	8.1	22.0	12.5	3.3	2.6
19	21000	Des Moines city, Iowa	11.5	4.4	2.2	11.7	10.9	21.3	10.8	3.7	3.3
19	22395	Dubuque city, Iowa	13.2	4.8	2.2	6.1	9.5	24.3	12.1	3.5	1.6
19	28515	Fort Dodge city, Iowa	11.5	6.3	1.7	5.3	1.8	23.4	15.9	4.8	1.5
19	38595	Iowa City city, Iowa	9.6	1.7	1.6	4.0	8.8	45.1	11.7	4.0	1.2
19	39765	Johnston city, Iowa	6.2	0.0	6.1	19.4	12.7	29.0	4.7	2.7	2.7
19	49485	Marion city, Iowa	13.2	4.5	2.3	7.2	9.5	22.2	5.5	5.4	3.4
19	49755	Marshalltown city, Iowa	8.9	4.5	0.7	3.9	5.9	16.4	8.2	2.4	0.8
19	50160	Mason City city, Iowa	12.2	6.2	0.7	3.5	4.8	24.7	12.5	3.4	5.4
19	55110	Muscatine city, Iowa	9.4	6.4	1.7	0.5	2.8	20.8	9.0	1.2	1.8
19	60465	Ottumwa city, Iowa	10.1	6.1	4.2	7.4	3.8	21.9	4.5	5.8	4.0
19	73335	Sioux City city, Iowa	12.9	5.5	1.1	6.2	6.9	17.4	12.7	3.6	3.3
19	79950	Urbandale city, Iowa	18.8	3.3	2.5	16.3	9.4	18.3	8.1	3.3	1.2
19	82425	Waterloo city, Iowa	12.0	4.0	1.4	4.6	7.9	25.0	8.6	3.1	1.8
19	83910	West Des Moines city, Iowa	10.1	5.1	1.4	22.0	12.3	21.1	7.2	4.0	4.0

Table E. Cities—Labor Force, Employment, and Educational Data, 2015—*Continued*

FIPS state code	FIPS place code	State/city	Retail trade	Transportation and warehousing, and utilities	Information	Finance and insurance, and real estate and rental and leasing	Professional, scientific, and management, and administrative and waste management services	Educational services, and health care and social assistance	Arts, entertainment, and recreation, and accommodation and food services	Other services, except public administration	Public administration
							Percent in each industry sector				
20	00000	**KANSAS**	11.2	4.6	2.1	6.2	9.4	24.4	8.2	4.6	4.3
20	17800	Derby city, Kansas	9.5	5.6	1.3	2.7	8.2	24.0	13.6	4.9	5.7
20	18250	Dodge City city, Kansas	8.1	5.7	6.3	0.5	6.9	18.2	12.5	7.8	1.5
20	21275	Emporia city, Kansas	9.7	4.6	1.7	0.7	3.4	37.0	11.9	5.1	1.4
20	25325	Garden City city, Kansas	9.6	6.8	0.5	0.9	5.9	20.0	8.0	2.7	7.9
20	25425	Gardner city, Kansas	14.1	5.5	5.2	5.6	6.9	21.4	6.0	5.2	6.6
20	31100	Hays city, Kansas	9.0	1.4	3.2	4.3	10.4	31.5	13.0	4.6	2.1
20	33625	Hutchinson city, Kansas	16.0	4.3	0.3	6.0	7.2	30.1	4.8	1.5	4.5
20	35750	Junction City city, Kansas	9.1	5.6	0.0	4.4	12.3	27.1	8.3	0.9	9.0
20	36000	Kansas City city, Kansas	11.5	7.5	1.1	4.7	11.4	17.4	8.9	6.0	4.6
20	38900	Lawrence city, Kansas	12.5	2.6	1.5	7.3	10.9	28.7	16.4	3.9	4.5
20	39000	Leavenworth city, Kansas	9.9	5.0	0.9	3.3	6.1	32.3	9.9	4.0	15.9
20	39075	Leawood city, Kansas	6.7	1.2	4.0	12.0	25.6	22.0	6.6	2.1	2.0
20	39350	Lenexa city, Kansas	10.5	4.2	2.8	9.0	19.4	21.8	6.7	2.1	3.0
20	39825	Liberal city, Kansas	11.9	1.6	4.2	2.1	1.3	13.5	9.3	7.1	5.2
20	44250	Manhattan city, Kansas	14.7	0.7	1.7	2.2	8.7	34.1	14.1	5.8	3.9
20	52575	Olathe city, Kansas	12.2	5.1	3.3	9.0	13.0	23.5	9.5	5.2	3.6
20	53775	Overland Park city, Kansas	10.9	2.5	5.2	11.5	19.3	22.0	6.9	4.4	3.1
20	56025	Pittsburg city, Kansas	11.2	4.2	0.3	0.8	5.3	40.6	8.4	2.3	4.5
20	57575	Prairie Village city, Kansas	7.9	0.0	3.7	17.1	21.7	22.8	5.4	7.8	1.9
20	62700	Salina city, Kansas	9.7	3.2	0.6	6.4	5.5	20.5	13.1	8.7	2.2
20	64500	Shawnee city, Kansas	9.6	4.5	3.2	9.8	11.6	23.3	8.0	3.8	5.6
20	71000	Topeka city, Kansas	11.4	5.9	1.3	8.6	8.2	25.2	9.9	5.5	7.4
20	79000	Wichita city, Kansas	13.5	3.4	2.1	4.8	9.0	21.8	9.6	4.5	2.3
21	00000	**KENTUCKY**	12.2	5.9	1.6	5.4	7.9	23.7	9.2	4.8	4.4
21	02368	Ashland city, Kentucky	14.8	4.0	2.7	2.4	8.0	33.7	12.3	1.9	4.6
21	08902	Bowling Green city, Kentucky	11.7	5.9	2.6	4.7	7.6	25.3	18.0	2.1	3.2
21	17848	Covington city, Kentucky	9.9	6.8	2.1	8.1	12.1	18.0	15.0	3.0	3.7
21	24274	Elizabethtown city, Kentucky	20.9	5.1	2.2	2.2	6.1	19.1	10.4	9.2	6.4
21	27982	Florence city, Kentucky	10.4	7.9	0.7	4.0	11.0	14.3	15.1	6.8	4.6
21	28900	Frankfort city, Kentucky	16.1	0.4	0.0	7.0	6.1	17.3	6.6	6.1	19.3
21	30700	Georgetown city, Kentucky	8.8	5.2	0.3	3.7	9.2	21.6	13.4	4.5	4.7
21	35866	Henderson city, Kentucky	12.9	4.2	2.2	3.7	4.5	22.1	12.8	4.6	3.9
21	37918	Hopkinsville city, Kentucky	11.8	2.8	1.1	1.8	8.8	27.5	8.3	6.5	4.8
21	39142	Independence city, Kentucky	10.8	16.8	0.9	8.1	11.3	20.7	6.4	0.6	3.2
21	40222	Jeffersontown city, Kentucky	16.4	3.0	1.0	8.1	10.3	21.0	8.5	6.1	4.7
21	46027	Lexington-Fayette urban county, Kentucky	12.6	2.3	2.0	4.4	12.0	28.4	11.3	5.5	3.7
21	48006	Louisville/Jefferson County metro government (balance), Kentucky	10.6	7.9	1.6	7.1	8.9	24.7	10.5	4.8	3.0
21	56136	Nicholasville city, Kentucky	23.2	5.8	1.1	0.5	9.0	30.4	7.8	1.0	4.4
21	58620	Owensboro city, Kentucky	13.9	2.0	1.3	7.7	7.2	24.5	11.3	7.3	4.4
21	58836	Paducah city, Kentucky	14.8	10.4	0.0	3.7	8.8	25.4	11.7	5.3	6.4
21	63912	Radcliff city, Kentucky	13.6	7.2	2.0	3.0	11.2	26.0	10.2	2.7	8.2
21	65226	Richmond city, Kentucky	18.3	2.9	0.4	2.0	6.2	26.7	14.6	6.5	6.7
22	00000	**LOUISIANA**	11.5	5.1	1.6	5.2	9.2	23.6	10.7	5.3	5.4
22	00975	Alexandria city, Louisiana	9.2	4.3	1.9	8.7	8.1	35.9	12.6	5.6	6.5
22	05000	Baton Rouge city, Louisiana	10.9	4.2	1.7	5.1	12.4	28.2	10.8	5.7	4.3
22	05210	Bayou Cane CDP, Louisiana	19.8	12.2	1.2	6.6	4.6	15.4	5.5	2.0	3.0
22	08920	Bossier City city, Louisiana	13.9	4.4	2.2	3.6	11.6	22.1	11.6	4.5	5.9
22	13960	Central city, Louisiana	8.0	1.6	0.4	8.2	15.8	18.1	8.5	6.5	9.3
22	14135	Chalmette CDP, Louisiana	13.5	3.1	2.3	3.6	10.6	22.4	10.6	9.1	4.0
22	32755	Hammond city, Louisiana	11.0	5.2	1.5	1.9	7.0	33.3	20.0	0.8	3.2
22	33245	Harvey CDP, Louisiana	14.4	8.5	0.0	9.1	5.4	14.6	11.7	3.9	7.0
22	36255	Houma city, Louisiana	11.3	6.4	0.6	5.1	5.1	26.4	7.3	2.8	4.3
22	39475	Kenner city, Louisiana	8.2	5.9	0.6	8.6	10.3	17.0	16.5	5.2	4.9
22	40735	Lafayette city, Louisiana	12.6	2.7	1.0	4.7	9.9	24.2	16.2	4.2	3.9
22	41155	Lake Charles city, Louisiana	11.2	2.8	0.8	4.8	7.4	28.1	20.1	5.0	4.3
22	42030	Laplace CDP, Louisiana	12.0	3.6	1.4	4.7	12.4	25.0	7.3	4.9	5.6
22	48785	Marrero CDP, Louisiana	9.4	3.7	2.5	2.5	8.7	18.7	21.2	4.4	10.1
22	50115	Metairie CDP, Louisiana	12.2	4.7	1.5	8.7	12.8	20.5	12.6	4.9	5.0
22	51410	Monroe city, Louisiana	12.4	5.0	4.7	6.9	13.5	28.6	15.0	4.1	2.7
22	54035	New Iberia city, Louisiana	9.9	3.5	0.5	5.5	9.0	20.3	14.0	9.8	4.2
22	55000	New Orleans city, Louisiana	9.8	5.1	1.9	4.8	12.9	25.1	17.6	5.3	5.4
22	62385	Prairieville CDP, Louisiana	15.5	5.2	2.8	7.2	8.3	27.5	2.5	3.6	5.5
22	66655	Ruston city, Louisiana	8.3	1.4	3.9	3.2	0.5	49.3	10.0	8.6	5.4
22	70000	Shreveport city, Louisiana	12.1	5.6	1.9	5.8	7.6	26.9	13.0	5.6	5.4
22	70805	Slidell city, Louisiana	17.4	6.7	3.7	5.4	10.9	16.6	13.3	1.8	8.2
22	73640	Sulphur city, Louisiana	11.8	3.7	0.3	5.8	9.8	22.4	11.5	6.0	1.9
22	75180	Terrytown CDP, Louisiana	6.5	7.1	0.7	10.3	14.4	12.7	14.3	3.6	10.8
23	00000	**MAINE**	13.1	3.8	1.9	6.3	8.3	28.0	8.7	4.6	3.9
23	02060	Auburn city, Maine	12.5	6.0	1.3	6.1	7.7	32.7	11.7	1.7	3.3

Table E. Cities—Labor Force, Employment, and Educational Data, 2015—*Continued*

FIPS state code	FIPS place code	State/city	Retail trade	Transportation and warehousing, and utilities	Information	Finance and insurance, and real estate and rental and leasing	Professional, scientific, and management, and administrative and waste management services	Educational services, and health care and social assistance	Arts, entertainment, and recreation, and accommodation and food services	Other services, except public administration	Public administration
23	02795	Bangor city, Maine	18.1	5.2	3.8	5.9	7.6	35.4	10.7	4.1	3.5
23	04860	Biddeford city, Maine	10.9	2.7	3.2	5.5	4.7	26.6	16.6	4.0	1.3
23	38740	Lewiston city, Maine	12.6	3.0	2.1	8.0	7.3	29.5	7.0	6.0	3.6
23	60545	Portland city, Maine	10.1	3.8	4.5	8.6	13.4	28.8	12.1	5.1	2.3
23	65725	Sanford city, Maine	15.9	2.1	2.3	3.2	6.7	21.4	11.6	4.2	4.7
23	71990	South Portland city, Maine	15.9	2.0	2.7	10.6	12.2	26.3	7.4	7.2	1.3
24	00000	**MARYLAND**	9.9	4.6	2.2	5.9	15.5	23.2	8.9	5.3	10.7
24	01600	Annapolis city, Maryland	11.2	3.2	3.2	3.2	13.7	22.7	18.4	6.4	7.4
24	01975	Arbutus CDP, Maryland	16.2	5.8	1.7	3.1	11.7	27.1	9.3	5.4	4.5
24	02275	Arnold CDP, Maryland	8.0	7.2	8.5	1.9	16.9	23.3	5.7	4.8	12.5
24	02825	Aspen Hill CDP, Maryland	10.6	4.9	2.1	3.9	17.3	24.3	9.6	5.1	8.7
24	04000	Baltimore city, Maryland	10.0	5.8	2.0	5.4	13.1	30.5	8.6	5.2	7.9
24	05825	Bel Air North CDP, Maryland	17.5	5.0	2.1	7.6	8.0	25.4	6.7	5.9	7.6
24	05950	Bel Air South CDP, Maryland	12.4	3.8	1.8	10.1	13.1	22.3	7.3	4.1	10.1
24	07125	Bethesda CDP, Maryland	4.1	0.5	4.3	9.7	28.4	21.4	7.1	6.8	13.1
24	08775	Bowie city, Maryland	5.5	6.1	2.2	5.0	16.6	24.4	6.8	6.3	21.0
24	12600	Camp Springs CDP, Maryland	14.0	8.4	1.3	6.2	13.5	17.7	7.2	5.2	18.3
24	13325	Carney CDP, Maryland	13.8	2.2	5.3	6.7	9.9	33.2	11.4	5.7	4.0
24	14125	Catonsville CDP, Maryland	8.8	1.0	2.3	7.8	16.2	29.8	8.6	4.5	6.9
24	16875	Chillum CDP, Maryland	8.7	6.0	1.7	1.3	14.5	23.3	15.0	6.7	2.5
24	17350	Clarksburg CDP, Maryland	4.7	2.3	2.2	10.7	28.7	22.3	6.9	6.2	7.8
24	17900	Clinton CDP, Maryland	9.2	7.9	1.0	5.5	16.6	18.0	8.0	4.3	19.7
24	18250	Cockeysville CDP, Maryland	11.8	3.5	2.6	9.4	14.0	24.8	7.8	7.4	4.8
24	18750	College Park city, Maryland	6.7	1.2	4.1	7.8	17.2	35.9	11.7	2.7	7.6
24	19125	Columbia CDP, Maryland	7.7	3.0	2.5	7.7	22.1	26.7	6.4	4.2	11.6
24	20875	Crofton CDP, Maryland	5.5	2.4	2.8	4.9	19.5	19.9	3.3	5.2	24.9
24	21325	Cumberland city, Maryland	9.8	4.9	4.9	5.2	9.6	24.7	14.8	3.5	6.1
24	23975	Dundalk CDP, Maryland	12.0	6.7	2.0	3.9	11.6	23.5	9.7	3.4	6.7
24	25150	Edgewood CDP, Maryland	19.9	7.0	0.7	1.8	8.3	26.2	4.2	6.7	7.2
24	25575	Eldersburg CDP, Maryland	6.0	3.1	4.8	7.5	15.0	23.9	9.0	5.0	12.0
24	26000	Ellicott City CDP, Maryland	6.2	2.9	3.0	5.6	21.7	26.1	6.6	4.5	12.5
24	26600	Essex CDP, Maryland	12.3	7.1	2.5	4.2	12.5	23.0	7.3	3.6	6.3
24	27250	Fairland CDP, Maryland	12.4	4.6	0.6	5.3	14.7	34.9	6.6	3.7	9.6
24	29525	Fort Washington CDP, Maryland	8.8	3.9	1.9	9.2	24.8	16.9	5.1	5.4	19.5
24	30325	Frederick city, Maryland	11.0	3.1	2.1	7.7	14.0	24.7	9.9	4.5	7.7
24	31175	Gaithersburg city, Maryland	7.9	2.8	1.3	5.7	25.9	19.0	11.2	5.3	8.0
24	32025	Germantown CDP, Maryland	10.5	3.7	2.6	6.5	20.8	19.9	11.0	5.6	7.9
24	32650	Glen Burnie CDP, Maryland	13.9	4.6	2.8	6.0	13.0	22.9	3.8	4.6	10.2
24	34775	Greenbelt city, Maryland	3.1	3.0	1.5	13.6	22.7	22.9	6.9	4.6	8.8
24	36075	Hagerstown city, Maryland	10.7	9.8	1.6	5.5	12.1	19.0	13.8	4.2	5.2
24	41475	Ilchester CDP, Maryland	5.6	3.0	3.5	5.5	21.5	22.1	11.7	2.2	13.9
24	45325	Landover CDP, Maryland	8.5	10.0	0.4	4.4	18.9	20.0	16.3	3.9	8.8
24	45525	Langley Park CDP, Maryland	7.1	1.5	0.0	8.3	12.4	8.1	10.8	7.9	0.3
24	45900	Laurel city, Maryland	12.5	3.9	3.3	5.6	17.9	24.5	9.8	5.2	10.3
24	47450	Lochearn CDP, Maryland	9.6	9.0	1.6	9.6	10.7	21.4	8.7	6.1	12.3
24	52300	Middle River CDP, Maryland	15.4	2.9	0.7	5.5	8.8	26.2	11.0	5.9	5.3
24	52562	Milford Mill CDP, Maryland	12.7	9.9	3.2	6.2	10.7	21.9	7.4	5.5	13.5
24	53325	Montgomery Village CDP, Maryland	6.1	3.8	1.3	6.4	21.3	18.0	8.2	9.3	9.7
24	56337	North Bethesda CDP, Maryland	4.3	0.8	2.4	8.1	26.2	16.7	16.1	4.1	14.2
24	56725	North Laurel CDP, Maryland	9.3	6.7	2.0	5.8	17.9	18.1	12.7	3.9	14.2
24	56875	North Potomac CDP, Maryland	7.9	1.0	2.1	5.4	33.8	20.1	6.5	7.4	9.4
24	58300	Odenton CDP, Maryland	8.6	5.1	1.1	5.4	15.3	12.5	10.6	2.7	24.9
24	58900	Olney CDP, Maryland	8.6	3.0	1.9	7.6	19.7	23.9	8.5	6.2	10.5
24	59425	Owings Mills CDP, Maryland	9.6	3.6	2.5	5.8	16.3	25.3	13.7	5.2	9.1
24	59500	Oxon Hill CDP, Maryland	8.4	5.4	1.6	4.9	13.8	20.6	13.2	4.0	13.7
24	60275	Parkville CDP, Maryland	15.2	6.9	0.8	4.6	9.2	32.3	12.9	3.0	5.7
24	60475	Pasadena CDP, Maryland	15.0	6.8	0.5	3.1	5.9	22.4	8.9	11.5	13.2
24	60975	Perry Hall CDP, Maryland	14.4	4.8	2.0	6.9	11.0	25.0	10.1	2.3	7.6
24	61400	Pikesville CDP, Maryland	7.8	1.7	2.4	11.2	10.0	38.5	5.5	3.4	6.8
24	63300	Potomac CDP, Maryland	7.8	1.0	3.6	9.0	26.1	21.3	2.9	6.7	14.6
24	64950	Randallstown CDP, Maryland	11.5	8.2	2.0	8.6	11.8	22.8	7.4	6.1	14.0
24	65600	Reisterstown CDP, Maryland	8.3	2.0	4.7	5.6	20.6	22.8	6.5	4.8	8.5
24	67675	Rockville city, Maryland	5.8	1.2	2.4	4.7	28.0	21.6	6.4	5.6	15.3
24	69925	Salisbury city, Maryland	14.5	4.2	0.3	3.5	6.4	25.1	12.5	5.2	3.3
24	71150	Severn CDP, Maryland	12.7	5.8	1.4	3.4	14.6	20.3	7.6	3.7	19.5
24	71200	Severna Park CDP, Maryland	7.7	1.7	0.9	6.7	19.7	27.3	3.5	2.4	12.3
24	72450	Silver Spring CDP, Maryland	5.8	3.2	1.6	5.4	20.8	22.7	9.3	9.6	11.3
24	73650	South Laurel CDP, Maryland	6.5	7.4	3.1	2.1	16.9	27.2	7.8	7.5	8.7
24	75725	Suitland CDP, Maryland	16.0	7.5	1.1	3.0	9.9	19.4	10.6	4.9	18.0
24	78425	Towson CDP, Maryland	10.4	2.8	3.2	9.9	16.0	29.6	10.1	6.3	4.2
24	81175	Waldorf CDP, Maryland	10.9	4.9	2.4	3.3	16.7	18.8	8.6	4.2	18.5
24	83775	Wheaton CDP, Maryland	11.3	2.6	3.7	3.8	20.3	13.6	13.7	6.7	8.4

Table E. Cities—Labor Force, Employment, and Educational Data, 2015—*Continued*

FIPS state code	FIPS place code	State/city	Retail trade	Transportation and warehousing, and utilities	Information	Finance and insurance, and real estate and rental and leasing	Professional, scientific, and management, and administrative and waste management services	Educational services, and health care and social assistance	Arts, entertainment, and recreation, and accommodation and food services	Other services, except public administration	Public administration
							Percent in each industry sector				
24	86475	Woodlawn CDP (Baltimore County), Maryland	12.6	5.8	2.4	5.9	10.5	25.7	9.4	5.6	13.2
25	00000	**MASSACHUSETTS**	10.6	3.7	2.4	7.4	13.5	28.1	9.1	4.4	3.6
25	00840	Agawam Town city, Massachusetts	13.8	4.3	2.3	5.4	9.2	33.9	7.5	3.1	2.8
25	01640	Arlington CDP, Massachusetts	5.3	1.6	6.9	7.9	19.3	30.3	7.5	4.9	3.5
25	02690	Attleboro city, Massachusetts	12.2	2.8	1.2	5.5	15.7	26.6	7.4	4.3	2.9
25	03690	Barnstable Town city, Massachusetts	13.4	2.4	3.1	4.9	10.8	20.5	11.2	9.0	2.2
25	05105	Belmont CDP, Massachusetts	6.5	1.2	2.9	6.9	21.6	35.2	6.2	3.1	2.7
25	05595	Beverly city, Massachusetts	12.4	2.2	2.4	7.8	11.1	27.3	13.6	5.9	1.9
25	07000	Boston city, Massachusetts	8.9	3.5	2.5	8.7	16.4	31.7	10.4	4.1	3.9
25	07740	Braintree Town city, Massachusetts	10.5	4.6	0.8	14.7	15.1	19.8	9.7	3.7	4.0
25	09000	Brockton city, Massachusetts	10.9	7.9	1.4	6.0	10.7	29.4	10.7	5.5	2.8
25	09210	Brookline CDP, Massachusetts	4.2	1.3	4.2	10.7	21.3	42.0	5.4	3.8	1.2
25	09875	Burlington CDP, Massachusetts	6.5	2.3	2.5	7.9	15.2	26.7	5.3	4.1	4.5
25	11000	Cambridge city, Massachusetts	4.2	1.7	3.0	5.5	22.8	42.0	5.7	2.9	2.9
25	13205	Chelsea city, Massachusetts	13.1	5.5	2.9	1.5	14.4	18.6	21.8	4.2	1.9
25	13660	Chicopee city, Massachusetts	17.0	7.3	3.6	5.0	4.5	29.0	7.8	2.0	3.7
25	16285	Danvers CDP, Massachusetts	13.7	6.2	1.5	10.3	10.0	22.2	4.7	5.2	3.4
25	16530	Dedham CDP, Massachusetts	12.6	6.6	4.6	7.7	6.9	32.1	6.5	6.2	3.1
25	21990	Everett city, Massachusetts	14.3	6.2	0.6	7.2	10.9	17.1	16.3	8.0	1.9
25	23000	Fall River city, Massachusetts	9.9	3.6	2.0	4.8	4.8	26.1	11.5	6.0	4.1
25	23875	Fitchburg city, Massachusetts	11.0	5.5	0.3	4.0	7.7	26.6	5.8	3.6	7.9
25	24960	Framingham CDP, Massachusetts	12.6	0.6	2.9	5.3	13.6	26.8	9.6	5.2	2.9
25	25172	Franklin Town city, Massachusetts	11.0	1.6	2.4	7.5	16.1	29.9	3.1	2.3	3.5
25	25485	Gardner city, Massachusetts	13.6	1.4	0.7	3.1	7.9	30.7	12.5	7.2	2.5
25	26150	Gloucester city, Massachusetts	10.9	2.7	1.9	7.2	8.5	26.9	13.3	2.8	2.7
25	29405	Haverhill city, Massachusetts	11.1	4.6	2.2	7.7	9.5	29.3	6.2	6.3	3.1
25	30840	Holyoke city, Massachusetts	13.8	5.7	1.5	4.3	12.1	26.8	6.9	3.8	4.0
25	34550	Lawrence city, Massachusetts	12.2	4.3	1.0	2.2	12.0	24.8	12.2	7.9	1.2
25	35075	Leominster city, Massachusetts	13.4	1.3	0.4	6.3	8.8	30.3	8.3	6.3	2.7
25	35250	Lexington CDP, Massachusetts	6.9	0.4	4.8	9.3	25.1	29.7	3.7	2.4	2.0
25	37000	Lowell city, Massachusetts	8.9	4.0	1.5	3.2	12.0	24.3	11.2	5.2	4.4
25	37490	Lynn city, Massachusetts	11.2	3.7	0.6	6.0	9.5	26.9	11.9	7.3	3.5
25	37875	Malden city, Massachusetts	9.4	4.7	2.1	6.7	16.2	32.0	10.9	4.1	2.6
25	38435	Marblehead CDP, Massachusetts	6.8	4.0	2.8	9.8	19.4	23.8	12.0	3.1	2.9
25	38715	Marlborough city, Massachusetts	11.8	4.1	2.1	6.6	11.7	23.7	8.2	6.4	1.6
25	39835	Medford city, Massachusetts	4.3	3.1	3.5	8.2	18.1	34.0	8.0	5.3	4.4
25	40115	Melrose city, Massachusetts	6.7	6.6	1.1	4.2	22.1	26.2	9.7	5.7	6.1
25	40710	Methuen Town city, Massachusetts	7.7	3.0	3.7	4.3	12.8	20.3	10.0	8.4	4.7
25	41200	Milford CDP, Massachusetts	10.9	4.3	1.7	9.9	18.4	22.1	6.7	4.9	3.3
25	41725	Milton CDP, Massachusetts	11.4	1.3	3.5	9.0	14.0	34.3	6.0	4.3	2.3
25	44140	Needham CDP, Massachusetts	2.1	0.5	2.4	13.0	20.3	38.2	4.8	5.6	1.6
25	45000	New Bedford city, Massachusetts	13.1	2.9	1.7	4.6	4.5	28.8	11.5	4.3	4.5
25	45560	Newton city, Massachusetts	5.2	2.1	4.8	10.7	19.1	35.0	5.0	5.1	3.7
25	46330	Northampton city, Massachusetts	12.9	0.7	3.1	3.6	10.8	49.5	8.6	3.7	2.4
25	50285	Norwood CDP, Massachusetts	17.3	2.2	0.8	4.9	18.1	29.5	5.3	2.6	4.5
25	52490	Peabody city, Massachusetts	15.8	3.7	1.2	5.6	14.9	24.5	10.2	4.4	4.1
25	53960	Pittsfield city, Massachusetts	14.0	3.2	2.1	3.9	9.6	24.1	14.4	7.5	4.2
25	55745	Quincy city, Massachusetts	11.3	4.8	2.8	9.6	13.3	24.0	15.2	2.9	3.8
25	55990	Randolph CDP, Massachusetts	10.0	6.5	1.4	14.6	8.2	30.9	10.6	2.5	1.7
25	56165	Reading CDP, Massachusetts	7.0	1.0	1.5	9.0	15.4	27.9	4.0	5.4	5.2
25	56585	Revere city, Massachusetts	8.4	11.2	0.4	5.2	11.0	22.6	14.0	6.2	4.6
25	59105	Salem city, Massachusetts	8.5	3.4	1.7	7.5	10.3	26.7	17.8	6.3	5.3
25	60050	Saugus CDP, Massachusetts	12.8	5.2	1.8	5.4	12.2	26.5	14.0	3.5	4.8
25	62465	Somerset CDP, Massachusetts	7.7	9.6	0.0	7.9	10.4	28.1	10.6	1.2	3.7
25	62535	Somerville city, Massachusetts	4.3	2.8	3.2	7.0	22.0	31.5	10.4	3.5	2.0
25	67000	Springfield city, Massachusetts	12.0	4.1	0.9	8.4	7.5	33.1	8.9	2.9	4.7
25	67700	Stoneham CDP, Massachusetts	11.1	7.0	1.5	8.2	11.7	26.3	8.2	4.1	5.9
25	69170	Taunton city, Massachusetts	18.5	2.7	2.3	4.8	7.3	25.3	8.3	3.5	3.8
25	72250	Wakefield CDP, Massachusetts	12.6	3.1	5.1	6.9	14.6	24.9	7.5	5.3	2.9
25	72600	Waltham city, Massachusetts	12.9	2.0	3.9	8.1	12.4	26.8	8.9	5.5	3.0
25	73440	Watertown Town city, Massachusetts	7.6	4.4	4.1	9.5	17.7	32.5	3.2	6.2	2.9
25	74210	Wellesley CDP, Massachusetts	8.4	0.4	2.5	21.7	21.1	26.1	6.2	2.3	1.4
25	76030	Westfield city, Massachusetts	11.0	4.9	4.2	8.1	7.4	26.7	10.9	3.9	4.8
25	77890	West Springfield Town city, Massachusetts	14.7	8.1	1.1	11.0	5.8	26.2	7.1	4.2	3.1
25	78972	Weymouth Town city, Massachusetts	12.5	6.2	2.9	7.6	12.0	30.5	4.3	4.0	3.7
25	80195	Wilmington CDP, Massachusetts	13.5	4.4	2.4	5.9	10.7	25.2	9.1	1.7	3.9
25	80545	Winchester CDP, Massachusetts	4.0	2.6	4.5	14.9	20.9	26.2	3.7	2.0	3.3
25	81035	Woburn city, Massachusetts	9.1	2.6	4.6	8.7	10.8	24.7	13.1	4.7	1.8
25	82000	Worcester city, Massachusetts	12.1	4.2	1.9	5.6	8.9	31.5	11.4	4.6	2.3

Table E. Cities—Labor Force, Employment, and Educational Data, 2015—*Continued*

FIPS state code	FIPS place code	State/city	Retail trade	Transportation and warehousing, and utilities	Information	Finance and insurance, and real estate and rental and leasing	Professional, scientific, and management, and administrative and waste management services	Educational services, and health care and social assistance	Arts, entertainment, and recreation, and accommodation and food services	Other services, except public administration	Public administration
26	00000	**MICHIGAN**	11.4	4.3	1.5	5.4	9.4	23.5	9.8	4.5	3.4
26	00440	Adrian city, Michigan	15.7	1.9	0.6	4.2	7.4	27.0	8.9	6.6	5.1
26	01340	Allendale CDP, Michigan	14.3	3.5	0.7	5.4	5.6	31.4	13.3	6.3	0.4
26	01380	Allen Park city, Michigan	12.1	6.1	0.8	4.9	12.9	21.7	10.7	5.6	3.8
26	03000	Ann Arbor city, Michigan	7.3	2.0	2.2	2.9	13.3	49.0	10.7	2.4	1.3
26	04105	Auburn Hills city, Michigan	12.5	2.4	0.4	4.3	10.5	18.0	10.6	6.0	2.0
26	05920	Battle Creek city, Michigan	10.5	3.9	1.1	4.5	10.6	19.4	6.9	4.2	5.9
26	06020	Bay City city, Michigan	21.5	3.1	0.6	6.9	8.3	23.1	8.8	6.0	1.5
26	08640	Birmingham city, Michigan	6.2	0.9	2.0	13.6	20.6	23.5	5.2	3.9	2.9
26	12060	Burton city, Michigan	16.3	4.4	0.9	7.9	10.4	21.5	8.7	5.0	2.5
26	21000	Dearborn city, Michigan	15.3	5.4	2.0	4.9	9.7	22.0	11.6	4.9	3.4
26	21020	Dearborn Heights city, Michigan	9.3	12.1	0.7	8.6	10.1	17.2	9.1	7.6	1.2
26	22000	Detroit city, Michigan	11.1	6.4	1.3	5.3	12.2	23.7	11.9	4.6	4.4
26	24120	East Lansing city, Michigan	8.4	1.9	0.5	5.2	5.1	47.8	20.0	3.0	2.5
26	24290	Eastpointe city, Michigan	7.7	4.5	0.3	3.1	7.5	29.2	9.6	3.4	4.6
26	27440	Farmington Hills city, Michigan	9.5	3.0	2.5	8.8	17.9	23.7	7.3	4.1	1.9
26	27880	Ferndale city, Michigan	6.8	2.3	2.0	6.1	22.3	17.3	18.6	6.6	3.1
26	29000	Flint city, Michigan	12.2	5.7	1.1	2.9	8.5	26.2	11.9	5.9	2.8
26	29580	Forest Hills CDP, Michigan	12.5	3.1	1.1	9.0	15.8	25.3	8.9	3.8	1.2
26	31420	Garden City city, Michigan	9.5	5.7	3.7	4.4	8.0	14.3	9.4	4.9	2.0
26	34000	Grand Rapids city, Michigan	13.1	3.8	1.7	4.2	10.1	23.9	11.2	4.1	1.8
26	36280	Hamtramck city, Michigan	17.2	3.8	2.5	1.3	6.6	9.0	12.0	6.7	1.1
26	37100	Haslett CDP, Michigan	6.0	1.5	4.3	7.1	14.1	32.5	7.5	3.9	8.6
26	38640	Holland city, Michigan	14.4	1.3	1.2	2.9	5.8	21.6	8.4	7.1	2.0
26	38780	Holt CDP, Michigan	12.2	5.7	1.8	8.9	8.4	30.3	5.0	5.0	11.2
26	40680	Inkster city, Michigan	11.9	11.5	0.0	2.5	12.3	13.6	14.3	5.2	3.5
26	41420	Jackson city, Michigan	11.9	4.2	0.7	5.3	6.6	23.7	15.1	3.1	4.0
26	42160	Kalamazoo city, Michigan	12.1	1.1	1.1	5.7	8.4	34.0	14.5	2.9	3.0
26	42820	Kentwood city, Michigan	9.7	6.0	2.9	7.3	12.8	18.1	7.5	4.7	2.9
26	46000	Lansing city, Michigan	13.5	4.7	1.7	7.3	9.4	27.7	10.4	5.9	5.0
26	47800	Lincoln Park city, Michigan	18.5	9.3	1.9	3.9	5.4	16.7	11.4	7.5	0.6
26	49000	Livonia city, Michigan	9.9	4.2	1.6	6.8	11.8	23.7	8.8	5.3	3.5
26	50560	Madison Heights city, Michigan	14.0	2.4	4.8	4.4	5.9	21.1	11.3	3.5	3.6
26	51900	Marquette city, Michigan	13.0	1.0	2.7	6.0	7.5	32.6	17.3	2.9	2.0
26	53780	Midland city, Michigan	12.7	1.7	0.2	5.7	6.6	18.9	13.4	4.0	2.5
26	55020	Monroe city, Michigan	9.5	6.6	0.4	2.8	6.3	22.7	14.2	6.3	1.8
26	56020	Mount Pleasant city, Michigan	8.8	3.5	0.6	3.4	6.0	34.2	25.3	4.2	2.3
26	56320	Muskegon city, Michigan	11.3	3.0	2.1	1.0	5.6	20.0	20.1	3.8	2.7
26	59140	Norton Shores city, Michigan	11.5	1.3	1.5	4.7	9.7	22.0	11.6	4.8	2.7
26	59440	Novi city, Michigan	9.9	2.0	2.3	5.9	12.2	17.0	9.2	3.9	1.8
26	59920	Oak Park city, Michigan	10.1	8.6	1.8	8.6	14.3	27.0	7.3	1.8	6.8
26	60340	Okemos CDP, Michigan	7.7	2.0	0.8	8.7	15.7	30.1	11.9	1.6	6.8
26	65440	Pontiac city, Michigan	11.0	7.1	0.9	4.6	12.7	20.4	18.5	2.6	3.2
26	65560	Portage city, Michigan	13.9	2.4	1.4	8.1	10.5	26.5	8.5	5.1	3.4
26	65820	Port Huron city, Michigan	14.9	6.6	0.0	2.0	5.4	18.7	15.6	3.4	1.4
26	69035	Rochester Hills city, Michigan	9.5	1.8	2.4	8.3	13.9	21.9	9.0	1.9	2.2
26	69420	Romulus city, Michigan	9.6	8.8	1.0	6.2	11.9	23.8	11.1	5.6	2.4
26	69800	Roseville city, Michigan	12.6	3.8	1.8	4.7	10.5	21.0	8.6	5.6	3.0
26	70040	Royal Oak city, Michigan	7.6	3.1	2.6	10.1	18.3	23.2	7.8	4.8	2.1
26	70520	Saginaw city, Michigan	14.4	4.1	1.5	2.3	6.5	25.9	15.8	5.8	2.3
26	70760	St. Clair Shores city, Michigan	11.8	3.6	1.0	6.2	13.9	19.7	9.8	4.1	3.6
26	74900	Southfield city, Michigan	7.3	5.1	3.5	7.3	10.4	33.3	7.3	4.7	3.3
26	74960	Southgate city, Michigan	9.5	5.8	0.0	4.6	9.6	22.7	7.7	5.8	2.3
26	76460	Sterling Heights city, Michigan	14.7	3.4	0.8	6.0	10.1	18.9	10.0	5.2	3.2
26	79000	Taylor city, Michigan	14.1	9.7	2.3	4.8	7.7	20.0	8.9	5.2	1.5
26	80700	Troy city, Michigan	6.6	1.9	1.8	5.1	18.2	30.1	4.5	4.1	2.1
26	82960	Walker city, Michigan	13.3	3.1	3.5	6.6	12.4	20.0	7.7	4.9	0.6
26	84000	Warren city, Michigan	11.0	5.9	1.3	4.7	10.2	19.7	7.0	4.3	2.7
26	84800	Waverly CDP, Michigan	9.9	3.0	2.9	9.6	5.7	24.9	10.2	5.6	8.9
26	86000	Westland city, Michigan	10.7	5.5	1.6	6.3	9.3	20.2	11.1	3.8	1.8
26	88900	Wyandotte city, Michigan	13.1	5.5	1.9	10.7	8.4	24.2	10.5	3.5	2.3
26	88940	Wyoming city, Michigan	15.9	3.7	0.8	4.5	7.5	15.5	6.7	4.7	0.7
26	89140	Ypsilanti city, Michigan	14.7	2.8	3.0	2.9	9.7	31.4	18.1	3.0	1.2
27	00000	**MINNESOTA**	11.0	4.6	1.7	7.3	9.8	25.0	8.4	4.5	3.1
27	01486	Andover city, Minnesota	9.2	5.6	1.4	8.4	6.8	25.7	8.6	3.3	3.6
27	01900	Apple Valley city, Minnesota	11.5	7.6	2.8	9.3	9.9	20.9	8.8	5.7	3.5
27	02908	Austin city, Minnesota	10.5	3.1	0.3	2.1	8.8	24.4	5.4	5.1	2.9
27	06382	Blaine city, Minnesota	12.9	5.5	1.6	6.8	11.4	25.8	6.6	6.7	2.2
27	06616	Bloomington city, Minnesota	14.2	5.6	2.0	11.9	11.6	19.0	8.5	5.6	2.5
27	07948	Brooklyn Center city, Minnesota	16.5	2.6	0.9	6.5	16.5	19.1	9.2	3.6	3.7
27	07966	Brooklyn Park city, Minnesota	10.5	4.8	0.5	11.4	8.5	28.2	5.0	4.8	2.7

Table E. Cities—Labor Force, Employment, and Educational Data, 2015—*Continued*

			Percent in each industry sector									
FIPS state code	FIPS place code	State/city	Retail trade	Transportation and warehousing, and utilities	Information	Finance and insurance, and real estate and rental and leasing	Professional, scientific, and management, and administrative and waste management services	Educational services, and health care and social assistance	Arts, entertainment, and recreation, and accommodation and food services	Other services, except public administration	Public administration
27	08794	Burnsville city, Minnesota	9.8	5.3	2.0	12.4	14.6	18.0	14.4	3.4	2.8
27	10846	Champlin city, Minnesota	16.1	3.7	0.3	8.9	11.7	24.5	3.3	3.7	2.4
27	10918	Chanhassen city, Minnesota	6.9	4.3	2.9	11.0	17.2	16.6	8.2	4.4	4.2
27	10972	Chaska city, Minnesota	9.2	3.8	2.1	8.9	17.7	17.3	13.7	2.9	1.1
27	13114	Coon Rapids city, Minnesota	11.1	4.8	1.4	9.2	9.1	23.6	8.2	4.3	2.7
27	13456	Cottage Grove city, Minnesota	12.6	4.6	1.2	8.4	6.7	23.5	6.5	3.2	6.8
27	14158	Crystal city, Minnesota	7.9	4.0	0.9	10.8	17.6	28.7	4.5	3.1	0.9
27	17000	Duluth city, Minnesota	14.9	3.8	1.1	6.4	7.5	34.9	14.9	3.7	2.5
27	17288	Eagan city, Minnesota	9.4	7.2	2.3	13.5	13.2	20.8	7.7	2.7	3.6
27	18116	Eden Prairie city, Minnesota	11.8	3.2	2.0	11.0	19.2	18.5	6.7	4.5	1.3
27	18188	Edina city, Minnesota	9.8	2.0	2.5	10.9	18.9	21.7	8.0	4.8	1.7
27	18674	Elk River city, Minnesota	7.3	4.1	0.0	5.2	13.1	24.6	8.3	5.0	3.2
27	20546	Faribault city, Minnesota	13.4	0.5	1.0	2.0	10.2	17.4	7.8	7.1	3.1
27	20618	Farmington city, Minnesota	16.7	5.7	5.1	9.2	6.0	21.3	4.5	2.0	2.6
27	22814	Fridley city, Minnesota	12.6	6.8	0.9	11.1	8.8	28.1	3.3	3.0	2.1
27	24308	Golden Valley city, Minnesota	11.2	2.8	2.5	14.2	16.3	21.0	7.7	3.3	3.0
27	27530	Hastings city, Minnesota	19.1	8.5	2.8	3.9	12.1	18.6	6.4	1.2	4.8
27	31076	Inver Grove Heights city, Minnesota	6.9	7.8	1.6	9.5	13.1	22.6	6.5	5.7	4.8
27	35180	Lakeville city, Minnesota	12.9	7.1	1.3	10.8	11.9	17.5	9.5	4.7	4.9
27	37322	Lino Lakes city, Minnesota	8.6	6.6	1.3	12.5	9.4	23.3	5.9	5.4	3.8
27	39878	Mankato city, Minnesota	14.9	2.6	2.3	3.4	8.0	32.1	12.4	4.5	1.5
27	40166	Maple Grove city, Minnesota	10.7	3.5	0.6	11.2	15.6	20.7	5.5	5.1	1.1
27	40382	Maplewood city, Minnesota	11.6	4.5	0.8	8.1	9.7	27.7	5.5	3.8	5.1
27	43000	Minneapolis city, Minnesota	10.4	3.5	2.4	7.3	15.0	26.4	13.2	4.8	2.6
27	43252	Minnetonka city, Minnesota	11.2	2.9	3.4	13.3	19.2	22.2	5.6	4.1	1.2
27	43864	Moorhead city, Minnesota	12.5	4.7	1.1	9.4	6.6	29.5	11.7	2.3	3.3
27	45430	New Brighton city, Minnesota	6.8	4.4	1.4	7.7	12.4	23.8	11.3	2.7	2.4
27	45628	New Hope city, Minnesota	13.4	2.1	0.9	10.9	14.6	20.2	10.6	2.1	2.3
27	46924	Northfield city, Minnesota	3.4	2.4	0.3	7.2	3.7	58.1	6.2	3.1	0.0
27	47680	Oakdale city, Minnesota	10.9	3.8	0.7	11.0	9.3	26.4	7.8	4.5	5.9
27	49300	Owatonna city, Minnesota	8.9	3.4	3.9	9.4	8.4	20.6	7.1	5.9	1.3
27	51730	Plymouth city, Minnesota	10.8	3.2	1.7	13.3	15.8	21.5	8.1	2.9	2.2
27	52594	Prior Lake city, Minnesota	12.7	7.4	1.1	10.6	8.8	14.4	16.4	6.1	1.0
27	53026	Ramsey city, Minnesota	7.9	4.8	2.7	11.6	9.0	21.1	6.7	2.7	4.9
27	54214	Richfield city, Minnesota	11.7	4.6	2.7	8.5	12.2	25.3	11.8	3.9	1.8
27	54880	Rochester city, Minnesota	10.8	2.4	2.3	3.1	7.2	47.1	7.1	4.0	1.9
27	55726	Rosemount city, Minnesota	11.0	7.7	2.8	8.8	9.9	22.5	8.7	6.7	6.0
27	55852	Roseville city, Minnesota	9.7	4.4	1.1	9.0	10.1	33.9	8.5	5.5	3.1
27	56896	St. Cloud city, Minnesota	16.2	5.1	1.9	4.1	7.7	30.2	11.2	4.5	2.2
27	57220	St. Louis Park city, Minnesota	10.7	1.3	1.9	13.4	18.5	27.6	5.2	3.2	3.0
27	58000	St. Paul city, Minnesota	9.9	3.3	2.1	7.1	11.6	28.1	10.8	4.9	3.9
27	58738	Savage city, Minnesota	8.1	5.1	2.0	11.1	13.6	22.1	5.9	4.9	2.0
27	59350	Shakopee city, Minnesota	11.8	6.3	2.1	9.9	8.1	16.9	12.0	4.2	1.1
27	59998	Shoreview city, Minnesota	11.1	2.6	1.9	10.0	15.6	26.3	7.2	2.9	4.0
27	61492	South St. Paul city, Minnesota	9.6	6.9	2.2	6.1	13.5	17.9	12.1	5.0	3.3
27	69970	White Bear Lake city, Minnesota	9.2	4.3	5.1	8.4	13.5	23.0	6.2	4.0	6.8
27	71032	Winona city, Minnesota	16.8	1.2	1.0	5.1	3.5	23.7	16.2	4.5	1.4
27	71428	Woodbury city, Minnesota	10.5	3.3	1.6	10.3	11.8	26.4	4.9	3.6	7.3
28	00000	**MISSISSIPPI**	11.9	5.8	1.2	4.7	6.7	24.2	9.5	4.5	5.3
28	06220	Biloxi city, Mississippi	13.2	1.3	0.8	4.4	3.4	21.3	22.6	5.0	6.1
28	08300	Brandon city, Mississippi	4.6	1.0	2.3	8.4	10.5	25.4	17.8	6.3	2.8
28	14420	Clinton city, Mississippi	9.1	1.7	4.3	3.8	9.1	34.5	14.3	4.8	3.4
28	15380	Columbus city, Mississippi	18.6	4.2	0.0	5.5	0.0	30.7	6.4	4.2	5.3
28	29180	Greenville city, Mississippi	13.7	7.7	1.7	1.1	6.2	34.2	10.8	4.0	7.0
28	29700	Gulfport city, Mississippi	12.7	7.9	0.9	4.9	9.3	18.6	19.0	3.8	7.2
28	31020	Hattiesburg city, Mississippi	22.5	2.5	1.1	1.3	9.4	25.5	13.1	3.7	6.0
28	33700	Horn Lake city, Mississippi	9.5	19.3	0.4	3.3	10.0	9.0	15.5	4.7	4.3
28	36000	Jackson city, Mississippi	10.2	6.1	1.8	3.7	11.1	29.0	11.5	4.7	9.0
28	44520	Madison city, Mississippi	10.4	3.7	2.8	12.4	10.6	25.3	7.9	2.4	2.7
28	46640	Meridian city, Mississippi	13.2	4.0	1.7	9.1	6.0	28.7	11.3	3.3	7.1
28	54040	Olive Branch city, Mississippi	12.6	12.4	1.6	9.0	6.0	20.9	10.7	3.5	3.0
28	54840	Oxford city, Mississippi	13.3	0.6	6.7	7.6	12.1	35.0	10.0	0.6	6.5
28	55360	Pascagoula city, Mississippi	16.3	3.7	3.0	4.7	7.2	20.6	8.0	7.1	1.2
28	55760	Pearl city, Mississippi	17.8	2.6	0.0	5.3	11.5	15.5	18.0	4.3	5.1
28	62520	Ridgeland city, Mississippi	9.4	2.3	4.7	14.6	4.7	25.6	8.9	3.2	7.9
28	69280	Southaven city, Mississippi	11.7	12.0	1.3	6.0	8.7	18.5	14.3	3.5	3.4
28	70240	Starkville city, Mississippi	5.8	4.4	0.0	2.3	6.2	46.2	12.6	3.4	5.5
28	74840	Tupelo city, Mississippi	16.0	3.4	1.3	6.5	6.0	20.5	15.7	3.2	3.7
28	76720	Vicksburg city, Mississippi	10.4	6.5	1.5	1.0	3.5	24.8	17.4	8.2	7.4
29	00000	**MISSOURI**	11.9	5.3	2.0	6.7	9.8	24.0	9.2	4.7	4.1
29	00280	Affton CDP, Missouri	10.3	4.1	0.9	7.9	10.5	26.5	18.3	1.7	5.0
29	01972	Arnold city, Missouri	17.1	5.3	3.7	10.0	8.1	12.5	12.0	10.8	1.5

Table E. Cities—Labor Force, Employment, and Educational Data, 2015—*Continued*

FIPS state code	FIPS place code	State/city	Retail trade	Transportation and warehousing, and utilities	Information	Finance and insurance, and real estate and rental and leasing	Professional, scientific, and management, and administrative and waste management services	Educational services, and health care and social assistance	Arts, entertainment, and recreation, and accommodation and food services	Other services, except public administration	Public administration
							Percent in each industry sector				
29	03160	Ballwin city, Missouri	13.6	2.2	1.9	15.0	15.6	23.6	5.7	6.8	3.3
29	04384	Belton city, Missouri	16.7	5.4	1.8	6.4	8.1	16.3	17.8	6.6	4.1
29	06652	Blue Springs city, Missouri	13.0	8.1	2.1	6.6	9.7	23.9	8.5	4.8	3.7
29	11242	Cape Girardeau city, Missouri	15.3	1.8	0.5	3.3	6.9	34.5	9.7	4.1	5.1
29	13600	Chesterfield city, Missouri	7.4	3.0	1.8	12.1	19.1	24.1	5.7	0.9	2.0
29	15670	Columbia city, Missouri	12.0	3.1	2.6	8.8	7.9	37.7	11.8	2.3	3.3
29	16030	Concord CDP, Missouri	10.5	3.1	1.0	7.6	14.6	24.4	13.8	6.8	2.2
29	23986	Ferguson city, Missouri	12.0	8.7	1.6	6.8	13.7	25.0	10.2	2.4	2.3
29	24778	Florissant city, Missouri	9.7	8.9	0.2	12.1	9.7	26.6	8.4	6.4	1.9
29	25264	Fort Leonard Wood CDP, Missouri	–	–	–	–	–	–	–	–	–
29	27190	Gladstone city, Missouri	15.6	5.4	4.3	7.6	14.2	21.1	6.2	2.9	3.2
29	28324	Grandview city, Missouri	14.6	4.8	4.4	5.4	9.8	23.2	7.2	3.3	4.1
29	31276	Hazelwood city, Missouri	10.3	8.2	1.0	5.5	7.1	19.0	16.7	2.4	2.1
29	35000	Independence city, Missouri	11.9	5.1	1.7	7.8	10.0	21.0	9.3	4.3	4.5
29	37000	Jefferson City city, Missouri	17.6	3.6	1.3	4.8	7.5	21.9	5.2	4.0	17.8
29	37592	Joplin city, Missouri	13.9	7.2	2.1	4.5	4.8	29.2	14.7	7.1	0.7
29	38000	Kansas City city, Missouri	11.4	6.2	2.4	6.9	13.9	21.6	10.8	4.5	4.7
29	39044	Kirkwood city, Missouri	8.7	5.1	2.2	12.2	15.6	26.6	6.2	2.6	1.1
29	41348	Lee's Summit city, Missouri	9.2	3.8	3.1	8.3	15.5	28.2	7.3	5.0	5.6
29	42032	Liberty city, Missouri	8.1	10.0	1.0	6.7	13.5	21.8	10.6	6.0	2.7
29	46586	Maryland Heights city, Missouri	10.0	3.5	1.8	8.6	17.6	22.4	9.8	4.5	0.7
29	47180	Mehlville CDP, Missouri	11.2	10.3	0.3	6.5	13.9	14.6	11.9	2.8	4.7
29	52616	Nixa city, Missouri	9.7	11.1	0.0	9.4	10.6	29.5	7.7	4.9	0.8
29	53876	Oakville CDP, Missouri	13.3	3.8	1.3	6.6	13.6	21.0	10.5	4.8	3.8
29	54074	O'Fallon city, Missouri	12.2	4.1	3.4	11.7	9.5	22.4	5.5	5.9	2.5
29	60752	Raymore city, Missouri	9.8	4.6	4.8	5.0	15.3	22.8	7.6	3.5	9.1
29	60788	Raytown city, Missouri	12.6	4.5	1.5	6.9	11.2	27.2	7.8	6.2	6.0
29	62912	Rolla city, Missouri	–	–	–	–	–	–	–	–	–
29	64082	St. Charles city, Missouri	10.3	4.8	3.6	8.3	9.0	24.0	11.9	4.6	2.6
29	64550	St. Joseph city, Missouri	9.5	5.1	2.0	5.5	9.7	23.5	11.8	3.0	3.6
29	65000	St. Louis city, Missouri	10.6	4.8	2.3	7.3	12.5	26.2	12.3	4.2	4.8
29	65126	St. Peters city, Missouri	12.5	4.4	2.7	9.8	10.7	22.5	12.6	3.3	3.1
29	66440	Sedalia city, Missouri	9.6	4.4	0.8	5.8	7.2	26.2	9.0	7.0	2.6
29	70000	Springfield city, Missouri	12.8	3.4	2.3	6.3	11.1	26.4	12.9	6.5	2.1
29	75220	University City city, Missouri	3.7	4.9	5.2	7.1	14.9	39.7	7.4	4.8	1.8
29	78154	Webster Groves city, Missouri	10.8	1.2	4.6	7.8	12.6	31.8	8.2	5.8	1.7
29	78442	Wentzville city, Missouri	10.2	4.2	2.5	10.3	9.3	17.7	15.0	7.7	4.4
29	79820	Wildwood city, Missouri	14.0	4.3	4.1	12.2	13.2	19.6	7.2	5.1	3.8
30	00000	**MONTANA**	11.4	4.6	1.9	5.4	8.0	24.2	10.4	5.1	6.4
30	06550	Billings city, Montana	11.4	4.3	3.5	7.6	10.6	24.4	10.6	4.6	4.4
30	08950	Bozeman city, Montana	18.3	2.9	0.7	3.8	7.3	29.8	12.5	3.8	4.0
30	11397	Butte-Silver Bow (balance), Montana	8.6	5.4	0.6	2.5	5.4	30.4	14.7	4.8	10.4
30	32800	Great Falls city, Montana	11.3	5.3	1.8	6.3	7.7	27.0	13.7	7.0	4.2
30	35600	Helena city, Montana	8.6	0.3	4.3	7.3	10.5	22.6	12.2	5.3	18.0
30	40075	Kalispell city, Montana	13.9	3.9	1.9	8.2	8.1	34.6	4.1	2.2	0.7
30	50200	Missoula city, Montana	13.6	4.1	2.9	5.6	11.0	28.7	13.4	5.6	3.9
31	00000	**NEBRASKA**	11.7	5.7	1.7	7.3	8.5	24.0	8.1	4.2	3.8
31	03950	Bellevue city, Nebraska	11.8	5.0	1.5	11.1	9.5	23.2	7.4	4.1	6.8
31	10110	Columbus city, Nebraska	8.4	6.9	1.8	3.8	4.9	17.7	5.0	5.5	2.1
31	17670	Fremont city, Nebraska	18.3	3.0	1.6	5.2	4.7	24.2	7.9	2.7	4.7
31	19595	Grand Island city, Nebraska	13.2	4.9	0.4	5.0	5.0	18.5	10.7	4.3	3.6
31	21415	Hastings city, Nebraska	11.6	1.9	0.0	5.7	7.3	25.9	10.2	2.4	3.0
31	25055	Kearney city, Nebraska	24.4	3.6	2.2	1.6	3.3	28.1	12.4	2.3	2.5
31	28000	Lincoln city, Nebraska	11.6	3.9	1.6	7.6	10.1	27.5	9.1	4.3	5.8
31	34615	Norfolk city, Nebraska	13.6	6.1	1.4	2.4	5.4	19.9	10.3	5.2	3.6
31	35000	North Platte city, Nebraska	21.0	14.2	0.9	8.0	3.6	27.8	10.4	1.4	1.6
31	37000	Omaha city, Nebraska	11.4	4.7	2.4	9.9	13.0	24.6	9.5	4.0	2.1
31	38295	Papillion city, Nebraska	9.9	5.6	3.0	10.7	14.7	23.2	10.3	1.8	3.2
32	00000	**NEVADA**	12.1	5.2	1.4	6.1	11.6	15.2	25.6	4.5	4.1
32	09700	Carson City, Nevada	11.6	3.3	2.1	3.7	5.3	15.3	19.9	3.8	13.4
32	22500	Elko city, Nevada	7.0	1.4	1.3	4.0	9.7	13.3	19.7	1.9	6.9
32	23770	Enterprise CDP, Nevada	12.5	5.9	1.4	6.5	10.0	12.3	34.0	3.9	3.7
32	31900	Henderson city, Nevada	10.6	4.6	1.7	8.4	12.3	18.5	22.3	4.1	4.0
32	40000	Las Vegas city, Nevada	11.9	4.2	1.7	6.2	13.0	15.6	26.3	5.2	4.1
32	51800	North Las Vegas city, Nevada	11.9	5.0	0.9	5.7	11.9	14.7	25.5	4.4	4.3
32	53800	Pahrump CDP, Nevada	17.0	8.0	1.9	7.6	12.7	14.8	14.2	6.5	5.5
32	54600	Paradise CDP, Nevada	13.1	6.1	1.1	5.4	9.4	13.1	34.4	3.9	2.8
32	60600	Reno city, Nevada	12.4	5.4	1.4	6.8	12.1	19.5	19.3	4.5	3.3
32	68400	Sparks city, Nevada	13.7	8.6	1.5	4.4	10.2	18.8	14.1	4.9	3.1
32	68585	Spring Valley CDP, Nevada	12.8	6.4	1.2	7.6	11.9	10.1	37.4	3.1	1.6
32	70900	Summerlin South CDP, Nevada	10.7	2.1	0.6	10.6	17.8	17.7	19.6	6.9	2.5
32	71400	Sunrise Manor CDP, Nevada	13.0	5.5	1.0	4.8	11.2	12.6	30.9	5.2	2.9

Table E. Cities—Labor Force, Employment, and Educational Data, 2015—*Continued*

FIPS state code	FIPS place code	State/city	Retail trade	Transportation and warehousing, and utilities	Information	Finance and insurance, and real estate and rental and leasing	Professional, scientific, and management, and administrative and waste management services	Educational services, and health care and social assistance	Arts, entertainment, and recreation, and accommodation and food services	Other services, except public administration	Public administration
32	71600	Sun Valley CDP, Nevada	14.0	3.6	0.6	2.4	18.7	7.5	20.5	12.7	0.4
32	83800	Whitney CDP, Nevada	17.5	5.1	1.0	7.3	11.3	11.3	29.4	3.2	0.9
32	84600	Winchester CDP, Nevada	11.0	2.1	1.1	3.3	16.7	8.4	39.3	5.2	0.8
33	00000	**NEW HAMPSHIRE**	12.3	4.0	2.1	6.3	10.9	25.1	8.4	4.1	3.7
33	14200	Concord city, New Hampshire	11.6	2.5	1.1	7.1	12.9	30.7	11.0	4.4	5.8
33	17860	Derry CDP, New Hampshire	21.6	11.1	2.0	6.0	9.7	16.9	6.0	3.0	2.7
33	18820	Dover city, New Hampshire	11.0	2.1	1.9	9.0	11.7	28.4	13.4	3.4	2.4
33	39300	Keene city, New Hampshire	10.0	5.9	0.4	3.1	6.2	35.4	14.8	3.4	2.2
33	45140	Manchester city, New Hampshire	14.0	3.1	1.8	7.3	13.7	24.8	9.1	5.3	3.0
33	50260	Nashua city, New Hampshire	11.4	3.4	2.7	7.4	13.9	19.8	9.5	4.8	1.7
33	62900	Portsmouth city, New Hampshire	11.1	1.4	1.5	12.9	14.8	22.9	10.6	3.8	2.9
33	65140	Rochester city, New Hampshire	16.3	6.9	1.2	6.3	8.1	19.7	11.9	3.5	4.7
34	00000	**NEW JERSEY**	11.3	5.8	2.8	8.5	13.3	23.6	8.6	4.6	3.9
34	02080	Atlantic City city, New Jersey	17.4	4.7	1.2	2.4	4.0	16.6	38.3	4.7	2.3
34	02350	Avenel CDP, New Jersey	23.8	18.8	1.6	5.8	12.5	19.5	1.3	6.1	1.1
34	03580	Bayonne city, New Jersey	9.4	9.2	1.5	8.6	10.1	30.5	6.7	3.5	5.1
34	05170	Bergenfield borough, New Jersey	11.5	4.5	3.6	5.4	8.0	39.5	7.2	4.3	2.7
34	07600	Bridgeton city, New Jersey	15.4	5.9	1.6	2.4	6.9	18.3	2.4	0.0	5.2
34	10000	Camden city, New Jersey	11.3	4.3	1.5	1.2	11.4	32.7	10.2	6.6	3.1
34	10750	Carteret borough, New Jersey	12.0	12.5	2.2	8.1	10.9	26.6	7.4	3.6	3.4
34	13570	Cliffside Park borough, New Jersey	13.5	7.0	1.1	11.4	11.8	14.3	12.4	9.6	3.9
34	13690	Clifton city, New Jersey	12.6	8.5	2.7	5.5	11.2	21.6	6.7	5.5	3.3
34	19390	East Orange city, New Jersey	14.0	8.1	2.7	3.8	8.6	31.8	7.4	6.3	5.5
34	21000	Elizabeth city, New Jersey	11.0	13.2	1.0	3.9	13.1	15.8	11.6	5.7	2.7
34	21300	Elmwood Park borough, New Jersey	15.6	8.6	1.7	5.6	13.4	18.4	6.7	4.5	1.7
34	21480	Englewood city, New Jersey	13.8	3.7	0.5	11.1	19.6	19.8	8.7	11.5	3.1
34	22470	Fair Lawn borough, New Jersey	14.0	6.0	1.6	9.5	14.5	25.3	6.9	6.6	3.5
34	24420	Fort Lee borough, New Jersey	12.5	4.6	4.1	12.1	13.4	21.0	4.7	7.5	1.4
34	25770	Garfield city, New Jersey	14.0	12.5	1.5	6.6	8.3	21.7	4.5	2.5	3.1
34	28680	Hackensack city, New Jersey	7.2	6.2	2.6	10.1	10.7	31.6	11.4	3.1	0.9
34	32250	Hoboken city, New Jersey	5.2	2.9	9.8	23.5	23.6	13.5	5.0	3.5	2.4
34	36000	Jersey City city, New Jersey	9.8	8.3	3.5	13.4	16.9	19.7	8.1	4.7	2.5
34	36510	Kearny town, New Jersey	9.3	10.2	2.2	3.4	10.0	25.3	6.5	4.4	2.2
34	38580	Lakewood CDP, New Jersey	14.5	1.0	1.1	2.3	8.0	41.4	6.5	5.6	1.1
34	40350	Linden city, New Jersey	15.8	9.0	0.3	4.0	9.5	27.6	5.8	3.5	6.7
34	41100	Lodi borough, New Jersey	15.9	5.8	3.3	8.3	14.2	23.4	8.0	3.3	2.6
34	41310	Long Branch city, New Jersey	10.5	3.5	1.5	7.9	11.3	23.3	12.1	5.0	3.3
34	46680	Millville city, New Jersey	19.5	6.3	0.0	3.6	6.1	28.4	9.8	4.1	4.6
34	51000	Newark city, New Jersey	11.0	11.2	1.6	4.6	10.6	24.8	10.4	5.4	4.2
34	51210	New Brunswick city, New Jersey	11.8	8.0	0.6	3.4	10.4	18.3	12.6	2.0	3.1
34	53280	North Plainfield borough, New Jersey	11.1	5.7	1.4	8.2	9.5	21.2	8.9	5.4	4.7
34	54690	Old Bridge CDP, New Jersey	17.4	7.2	0.2	12.3	10.0	21.0	6.6	4.0	2.3
34	55770	Palisades Park borough, New Jersey	10.8	6.2	3.9	12.0	12.3	10.9	14.5	12.6	1.0
34	55950	Paramus borough, New Jersey	13.2	3.2	3.8	10.5	13.9	20.6	7.2	1.6	2.4
34	56550	Passaic city, New Jersey	13.4	7.2	1.1	2.9	5.8	16.2	7.6	6.1	2.4
34	57000	Paterson city, New Jersey	12.2	10.4	1.8	4.5	9.8	21.8	6.4	5.7	2.1
34	58200	Perth Amboy city, New Jersey	14.6	13.2	0.8	3.9	12.0	18.8	7.3	5.2	2.4
34	59190	Plainfield city, New Jersey	11.6	3.7	2.2	3.9	17.1	18.6	10.3	5.4	4.2
34	59640	Pleasantville city, New Jersey	16.3	5.2	0.0	4.0	2.8	16.6	36.6	7.3	3.7
34	60900	Princeton, New Jersey	9.8	1.4	3.3	8.2	16.0	36.9	8.1	4.1	3.7
34	61530	Rahway city, New Jersey	8.5	13.8	2.5	8.5	9.9	21.2	3.6	1.9	5.9
34	63000	Ridgewood village, New Jersey	7.9	2.4	2.4	17.6	25.1	21.0	3.8	3.1	2.5
34	64620	Roselle borough, New Jersey	10.4	9.1	1.4	8.0	8.8	28.6	7.0	5.3	8.3
34	65790	Sayreville borough, New Jersey	10.1	7.3	2.2	12.7	13.1	20.0	8.3	5.8	3.9
34	68370	Somerset CDP, New Jersey	4.3	4.4	5.1	14.0	19.9	23.9	9.1	1.1	1.8
34	69390	South Plainfield borough, New Jersey	9.4	7.4	3.4	8.2	16.1	15.5	2.9	12.4	1.0
34	71430	Summit city, New Jersey	4.7	0.9	3.1	24.3	19.9	14.4	9.9	5.0	0.0
34	73110	Toms River CDP, New Jersey	16.2	7.6	1.3	6.8	9.4	25.7	7.9	5.2	5.4
34	74000	Trenton city, New Jersey	13.2	4.9	0.6	2.8	13.0	21.4	12.5	5.1	7.7
34	74630	Union City city, New Jersey	10.8	8.9	1.4	4.1	11.6	16.4	14.2	5.3	3.2
34	76070	Vineland city, New Jersey	6.9	4.7	0.7	4.7	9.2	30.1	6.4	2.4	5.7
34	79040	Westfield town, New Jersey	5.9	4.2	5.4	21.4	14.6	19.1	4.9	4.5	3.8
34	79610	West New York town, New Jersey	15.2	9.8	2.9	9.5	11.8	13.7	8.7	8.7	2.2
35	00000	**NEW MEXICO**	12.0	4.4	1.6	4.5	11.7	24.9	11.8	4.8	6.9
35	01780	Alamogordo city, New Mexico	19.9	4.6	0.8	7.6	3.6	26.3	9.8	4.9	12.2
35	02000	Albuquerque city, New Mexico	12.7	3.0	2.2	4.7	15.4	25.5	12.4	5.3	6.3
35	12150	Carlsbad city, New Mexico	11.7	8.5	0.3	1.1	6.5	24.4	7.4	5.4	3.3
35	16420	Clovis city, New Mexico	16.7	5.1	1.3	5.5	4.9	27.4	8.6	7.5	7.1
35	25800	Farmington city, New Mexico	9.3	7.0	1.0	3.0	8.2	21.4	11.3	7.8	4.2
35	28460	Gallup city, New Mexico	8.7	1.3	7.3	1.0	9.1	30.0	14.6	6.6	9.3

Table E. Cities—Labor Force, Employment, and Educational Data, 2015—*Continued*

FIPS state code	FIPS place code	State/city	Retail trade	Transportation and warehousing, and utilities	Information	Finance and insurance, and real estate and rental and leasing	Professional, scientific, and management, and administrative and waste management services	Educational services, and health care and social assistance	Arts, entertainment, and recreation, and accommodation and food services	Other services, except public administration	Public administration
							Percent in each industry sector				
35	32520	Hobbs city, New Mexico	9.1	9.3	1.4	3.8	4.4	23.4	9.6	4.1	4.1
35	39380	Las Cruces city, New Mexico	10.9	4.3	0.4	5.9	13.3	29.9	11.9	4.8	10.4
35	63460	Rio Rancho city, New Mexico	12.6	4.9	1.5	7.7	11.5	23.6	12.6	4.1	5.5
35	64930	Roswell city, New Mexico	11.6	8.0	0.4	7.1	5.7	29.7	8.4	4.7	6.2
35	70500	Santa Fe city, New Mexico	13.6	2.4	2.3	5.6	14.8	22.5	13.7	6.7	8.4
35	74520	South Valley CDP, New Mexico	10.8	2.3	0.5	7.3	5.5	19.9	16.2	5.3	6.8
36	00000	**NEW YORK**	10.6	5.4	3.0	7.9	11.7	27.4	9.8	5.0	4.4
36	01000	Albany city, New York	9.3	2.0	2.3	4.6	12.3	28.0	14.1	6.7	12.3
36	03078	Auburn city, New York	10.2	2.2	1.0	1.6	11.3	28.0	9.1	7.6	6.6
36	04143	Baldwin CDP, New York	12.3	9.0	2.6	4.9	9.7	27.9	9.8	4.6	7.7
36	04935	Bay Shore CDP, New York	10.1	5.1	2.4	7.2	6.1	25.2	11.9	5.3	3.9
36	06607	Binghamton city, New York	13.1	4.2	1.2	3.9	10.5	28.7	15.6	3.9	5.5
36	08026	Brentwood CDP, New York	12.3	4.8	2.2	5.3	14.1	19.7	9.4	3.6	2.3
36	08257	Brighton CDP, New York	9.2	3.2	2.6	4.6	14.6	36.7	4.9	5.5	3.0
36	11000	Buffalo city, New York	11.3	4.6	2.0	6.6	13.0	27.9	12.4	4.9	3.7
36	13376	Centereach CDP, New York	9.6	7.1	3.5	6.0	8.3	29.5	6.0	7.0	5.9
36	13552	Central Islip CDP, New York	13.0	5.2	1.5	5.0	13.4	18.2	8.9	5.0	7.4
36	15000	Cheektowaga CDP, New York	12.5	5.0	1.8	8.9	6.8	23.8	8.5	3.4	5.5
36	17530	Commack CDP, New York	9.2	7.1	2.2	8.3	14.0	28.5	6.7	4.0	5.1
36	18146	Copiague CDP, New York	18.3	9.0	2.5	4.7	9.3	14.3	14.4	4.7	2.4
36	18157	Coram CDP, New York	13.4	5.9	0.9	5.7	11.7	30.8	7.4	6.4	3.7
36	19972	Deer Park CDP, New York	10.5	6.8	5.8	10.1	5.4	26.8	7.1	3.7	4.1
36	20687	Dix Hills CDP, New York	12.5	7.5	4.7	7.7	17.4	25.7	3.3	3.6	3.5
36	22502	East Meadow CDP, New York	13.6	4.8	4.7	4.8	13.3	32.8	4.8	5.7	2.7
36	22612	East Northport CDP, New York	10.1	3.8	9.6	4.9	14.2	21.4	7.9	1.6	5.3
36	22733	East Patchogue CDP, New York	8.0	6.3	1.1	5.2	12.7	24.8	2.0	13.2	7.8
36	24229	Elmira city, New York	11.6	4.9	0.5	4.5	10.5	30.5	12.1	1.7	5.1
36	24273	Elmont CDP, New York	15.8	11.6	1.4	5.2	8.5	29.0	11.8	4.8	2.7
36	27309	Franklin Square CDP, New York	8.5	5.4	3.8	9.7	8.8	29.6	4.8	6.6	5.9
36	27485	Freeport village, New York	10.4	5.9	6.0	5.5	11.2	30.6	5.6	10.0	2.4
36	28178	Garden City village, New York	5.7	6.1	1.2	22.8	19.1	25.6	6.7	3.7	3.0
36	29113	Glen Cove city, New York	15.5	4.6	2.8	8.5	9.7	24.5	10.9	5.0	3.3
36	32402	Harrison village, New York	7.1	0.0	2.5	10.5	19.3	24.9	10.3	4.0	3.2
36	33139	Hempstead village, New York	17.7	8.1	1.1	3.7	7.3	23.1	12.6	7.8	2.8
36	34374	Hicksville CDP, New York	10.9	6.4	2.8	8.9	14.4	24.1	5.2	4.2	3.8
36	35056	Holbrook CDP, New York	14.3	5.7	2.5	4.2	14.0	27.7	6.6	1.7	7.5
36	35254	Holtsville CDP, New York	7.8	5.2	2.7	3.3	12.2	35.8	5.1	1.7	11.4
36	37044	Huntington Station CDP, New York	14.3	8.3	2.5	8.0	14.3	21.4	7.2	3.3	4.3
36	37737	Irondequoit CDP, New York	9.0	4.4	3.6	4.5	9.3	32.4	10.9	5.1	4.3
36	37869	Islip CDP, New York	9.3	9.1	3.4	6.8	11.7	21.2	5.1	8.0	3.1
36	38077	Ithaca city, New York	11.6	2.1	2.5	4.9	7.5	47.1	11.4	2.0	2.9
36	38264	Jamestown city, New York	13.1	1.9	1.1	4.1	6.4	28.4	10.9	4.2	2.8
36	39727	Kingston city, New York	8.4	5.2	0.7	11.0	9.0	32.2	9.2	7.1	6.7
36	39853	Kiryas Joel village, New York	15.1	2.1	0.0	9.1	11.3	35.9	0.6	3.9	2.0
36	40838	Lake Ronkonkoma CDP, New York	8.3	3.6	2.3	9.6	6.0	26.8	7.0	9.9	2.6
36	42081	Levittown CDP, New York	11.8	5.9	3.8	8.2	9.0	28.4	6.7	4.1	7.3
36	42554	Lindenhurst village, New York	12.4	5.5	2.9	7.5	7.0	20.6	9.3	6.6	7.9
36	43082	Lockport city, New York	17.4	4.1	2.3	6.8	12.3	19.4	5.0	4.3	2.0
36	43335	Long Beach city, New York	13.1	3.2	4.7	9.3	9.1	30.8	7.1	5.3	3.4
36	45986	Massapequa CDP, New York	7.3	12.5	4.7	11.3	9.3	29.7	4.5	1.9	5.0
36	46404	Medford CDP, New York	12.3	1.8	2.5	8.9	10.9	15.4	15.7	9.8	6.5
36	47042	Middletown city, New York	14.1	5.0	2.0	3.0	6.4	22.8	7.4	6.1	4.2
36	48010	Monsey CDP, New York	–	–	–	–	–	–	–	–	–
36	49121	Mount Vernon city, New York	11.0	5.9	2.7	3.9	13.4	35.0	7.2	7.7	3.4
36	49407	Nanuet CDP, New York	22.1	3.5	4.5	4.5	11.3	30.0	4.8	3.4	6.3
36	50034	Newburgh city, New York	11.3	8.9	2.1	2.1	11.9	20.4	8.5	10.3	2.7
36	50100	New City CDP, New York	10.2	3.5	2.3	9.5	12.4	33.8	7.8	2.7	6.0
36	50617	New Rochelle city, New York	11.0	3.2	3.6	10.2	13.7	30.3	8.3	4.5	3.6
36	51000	New York city, New York	9.4	6.3	3.8	9.3	13.4	26.6	11.3	5.5	3.6
36	51055	Niagara Falls city, New York	16.5	5.8	1.2	3.4	7.2	25.9	15.0	4.1	2.0
36	51396	North Amityville CDP, New York	9.0	10.3	0.9	9.9	8.7	28.5	10.3	2.5	2.5
36	53682	North Tonawanda city, New York	13.6	4.1	0.9	5.7	13.8	21.8	8.0	5.6	4.0
36	54441	Oceanside CDP, New York	7.1	4.1	3.2	10.1	13.9	31.4	8.3	6.1	3.5
36	55530	Ossining village, New York	14.0	5.9	1.9	4.6	11.5	20.8	5.7	12.7	3.4
36	56979	Peekskill city, New York	12.7	3.4	0.4	6.6	17.9	24.7	11.6	5.7	4.5
36	58442	Plainview CDP, New York	9.1	3.4	3.7	12.6	18.7	31.1	1.3	2.6	4.5
36	59223	Port Chester village, New York	14.6	1.2	1.4	5.4	15.4	14.2	17.8	9.0	1.9
36	59641	Poughkeepsie city, New York	10.3	6.2	0.9	3.5	9.1	31.5	14.9	7.4	3.1
36	63000	Rochester city, New York	12.5	4.6	2.1	2.7	10.0	33.7	10.8	6.3	3.5
36	63264	Rockville Centre village, New York	7.6	3.5	4.7	12.8	12.2	35.1	3.9	4.2	5.7
36	63418	Rome city, New York	19.7	1.2	1.2	3.1	11.5	23.9	8.4	4.4	9.6
36	63473	Ronkonkoma CDP, New York	10.4	7.9	3.0	6.2	10.6	23.3	8.9	4.0	6.9

Table E. Cities—Labor Force, Employment, and Educational Data, 2015—*Continued*

FIPS state code	FIPS place code	State/city	Retail trade	Transportation and warehousing, and utilities	Information	Finance and insurance, and real estate and rental and leasing	Professional, scientific, and management, and administrative and waste management services	Educational services, and health care and social assistance	Arts, entertainment, and recreation, and accommodation and food services	Other services, except public administration	Public administration
							Percent in each industry sector				
36	63924	Rotterdam CDP, New York	13.6	5.5	3.2	6.4	8.8	25.2	12.8	3.9	8.5
36	65255	Saratoga Springs city, New York	9.1	1.5	0.0	6.4	8.2	34.6	5.2	2.8	7.3
36	65508	Schenectady city, New York	12.0	6.7	4.0	7.5	8.3	26.1	10.0	2.3	8.8
36	67070	Shirley CDP, New York	9.3	8.0	2.0	5.2	12.4	31.7	6.9	2.7	4.6
36	67851	Smithtown CDP, New York	13.0	2.4	2.6	6.5	10.9	28.7	8.3	2.1	4.9
36	70420	Spring Valley village, New York	14.1	11.0	1.2	3.7	8.3	29.9	4.5	10.5	0.7
36	72554	Syosset CDP, New York	8.1	5.0	4.3	14.9	16.4	24.7	6.9	1.7	3.4
36	73000	Syracuse city, New York	12.3	5.3	2.3	4.0	10.1	34.5	13.3	3.9	4.1
36	74183	Tonawanda CDP, New York	13.4	3.9	0.6	11.0	7.1	30.2	10.8	4.7	2.6
36	75484	Troy city, New York	5.7	7.9	3.3	4.9	8.8	30.9	9.8	4.5	12.7
36	76089	Uniondale CDP, New York	12.8	6.1	3.2	3.4	6.7	32.6	6.4	4.3	4.2
36	76540	Utica city, New York	9.3	2.5	1.4	7.4	7.1	35.3	9.2	5.3	4.8
36	76705	Valley Stream village, New York	7.1	8.9	2.6	10.2	10.4	27.7	8.1	5.1	6.5
36	78146	Wantagh CDP, New York	10.6	7.1	0.0	9.7	11.4	27.1	9.1	1.5	9.5
36	78608	Watertown city, New York	17.3	2.6	2.2	3.1	4.5	31.9	12.5	7.3	10.0
36	79246	West Babylon CDP, New York	16.4	9.6	3.1	8.4	8.5	21.7	5.5	5.4	4.2
36	80225	West Hempstead CDP, New York	13.7	5.1	2.2	6.4	11.1	27.2	9.3	10.8	4.0
36	80302	West Islip CDP, New York	14.3	4.3	3.6	8.1	10.6	32.4	4.7	1.8	7.0
36	80907	West Seneca CDP, New York	9.8	6.8	2.1	9.3	8.9	28.2	5.8	4.5	5.7
36	81677	White Plains city, New York	8.5	3.1	2.6	11.7	17.8	25.0	10.8	6.4	2.8
36	84000	Yonkers city, New York	12.9	7.4	2.4	8.3	9.7	26.0	9.2	5.9	4.1
37	00000	**NORTH CAROLINA**	11.8	4.2	1.8	6.3	10.7	23.0	9.5	4.7	4.3
37	01520	Apex town, North Carolina	10.1	4.7	3.9	7.5	17.0	23.0	9.4	3.8	2.8
37	02080	Asheboro city, North Carolina	7.8	1.7	0.2	3.6	7.6	21.6	11.9	2.6	4.5
37	02140	Asheville city, North Carolina	13.6	2.5	0.9	5.5	14.0	26.1	18.5	4.5	3.3
37	09060	Burlington city, North Carolina	12.8	2.4	1.7	4.1	10.4	22.1	10.5	8.6	1.8
37	10620	Carrboro town, North Carolina	10.5	1.9	2.8	4.3	13.2	48.8	5.6	2.6	1.6
37	10740	Cary town, North Carolina	9.0	3.1	5.4	5.9	23.8	22.6	6.2	3.7	2.8
37	11800	Chapel Hill town, North Carolina	7.5	0.3	2.0	7.2	9.1	45.8	12.1	3.8	2.6
37	12000	Charlotte city, North Carolina	10.8	5.5	3.1	13.9	14.2	18.1	9.9	4.6	1.8
37	14100	Concord city, North Carolina	14.2	6.9	2.1	11.2	10.2	20.3	7.0	5.0	2.9
37	14700	Cornelius town, North Carolina	12.9	1.8	1.4	10.8	8.7	21.2	12.2	4.9	2.7
37	19000	Durham city, North Carolina	7.4	1.8	2.2	4.7	12.7	35.2	11.5	4.1	4.2
37	22920	Fayetteville city, North Carolina	13.9	3.0	2.0	3.4	10.3	28.1	12.2	6.3	8.1
37	25300	Fuquay-Varina town, North Carolina	16.3	1.1	7.9	8.7	16.2	13.3	8.0	3.3	7.1
37	25480	Garner town, North Carolina	9.7	6.4	4.6	5.4	14.2	18.0	11.9	3.5	8.4
37	25580	Gastonia city, North Carolina	15.5	4.6	1.8	6.4	6.3	18.9	12.8	3.6	2.3
37	26880	Goldsboro city, North Carolina	13.2	4.0	0.3	3.2	4.9	30.5	10.0	3.8	6.5
37	28000	Greensboro city, North Carolina	11.3	5.1	1.9	9.5	10.0	23.1	11.4	6.6	2.5
37	28080	Greenville city, North Carolina	13.0	2.7	1.5	4.6	5.4	30.3	18.0	5.7	5.2
37	30120	Havelock city, North Carolina	13.0	4.1	0.0	6.0	5.3	16.3	25.6	4.0	12.7
37	31060	Hickory city, North Carolina	13.4	2.3	1.8	4.9	7.4	19.3	9.0	3.6	1.3
37	31400	High Point city, North Carolina	10.7	4.7	1.4	5.2	11.8	21.8	10.6	4.9	2.9
37	32260	Holly Springs town, North Carolina	13.6	2.8	7.5	8.2	15.9	19.1	9.9	4.9	4.2
37	33120	Huntersville town, North Carolina	12.0	3.2	2.9	13.3	13.5	19.0	11.8	3.6	2.8
37	33560	Indian Trail town, North Carolina	14.1	4.9	2.6	11.1	14.2	19.9	7.2	2.6	3.1
37	34200	Jacksonville city, North Carolina	9.9	0.3	4.6	4.8	20.4	19.5	12.5	7.0	12.9
37	35200	Kannapolis city, North Carolina	12.5	3.5	1.4	5.6	8.2	22.4	11.4	4.4	4.4
37	35600	Kernersville town, North Carolina	17.9	3.9	2.0	4.5	9.6	21.7	8.3	1.3	3.6
37	35920	Kinston city, North Carolina	4.6	3.1	0.4	0.0	8.4	31.0	6.7	1.9	0.8
37	39700	Lumberton city, North Carolina	15.0	2.6	1.7	2.8	5.3	22.3	9.0	6.5	4.8
37	41960	Matthews town, North Carolina	16.2	3.5	1.4	12.0	11.8	22.0	7.3	7.6	1.4
37	43480	Mint Hill town, North Carolina	23.9	6.7	2.5	6.3	12.9	17.3	8.9	2.4	3.3
37	43920	Monroe city, North Carolina	8.7	3.7	1.7	2.1	12.5	23.1	10.6	3.8	1.6
37	44220	Mooresville town, North Carolina	16.3	3.5	1.2	4.0	9.7	21.9	12.2	6.2	1.3
37	44520	Morrisville town, North Carolina	10.3	1.9	2.8	12.3	26.8	13.9	9.2	3.0	5.5
37	46340	New Bern city, North Carolina	7.4	3.8	0.5	5.6	10.8	27.8	7.9	5.8	9.8
37	55000	Raleigh city, North Carolina	11.0	3.9	2.8	8.1	20.4	20.2	9.7	3.5	4.9
37	57500	Rocky Mount city, North Carolina	8.2	9.2	0.8	7.4	9.3	27.9	12.5	1.6	1.8
37	58860	Salisbury city, North Carolina	13.2	2.4	1.3	2.0	9.1	29.3	10.5	7.0	2.1
37	59280	Sanford city, North Carolina	12.0	3.0	1.6	1.6	8.3	19.8	7.0	8.6	4.4
37	61200	Shelby city, North Carolina	20.9	0.0	0.0	2.9	1.4	30.7	8.6	3.3	4.0
37	64740	Statesville city, North Carolina	13.9	5.7	0.5	8.0	11.0	24.6	7.8	6.8	0.9
37	67420	Thomasville city, North Carolina	14.5	7.4	2.2	2.1	5.5	18.7	4.2	4.6	1.9
37	70540	Wake Forest town, North Carolina	9.4	1.8	3.9	6.8	11.5	27.3	9.4	6.1	6.3
37	74440	Wilmington city, North Carolina	13.7	4.8	2.7	5.1	8.9	27.5	14.9	7.0	1.4
37	74540	Wilson city, North Carolina	7.9	3.6	0.0	6.1	7.3	24.3	7.9	8.6	3.3
37	75000	Winston-Salem city, North Carolina	10.4	3.5	1.6	6.1	11.5	28.8	10.1	5.6	2.8
38	00000	**NORTH DAKOTA**	11.6	5.8	1.2	5.1	6.9	23.9	8.2	4.7	4.4
38	07200	Bismarck city, North Dakota	12.0	6.5	1.2	5.6	8.7	26.3	8.4	3.8	6.5
38	19620	Dickinson city, North Dakota	9.9	7.7	3.2	2.9	1.9	18.1	10.1	4.6	2.5

Table E. Cities—Labor Force, Employment, and Educational Data, 2015—*Continued*

FIPS state code	FIPS place code	State/city	Retail trade	Transportation and warehousing, and utilities	Information	Finance and insurance, and real estate and rental and leasing	Professional, scientific, and management, and administrative and waste management services	Educational services, and health care and social assistance	Arts, entertainment, and recreation, and accommodation and food services	Other services, except public administration	Public administration
							Percent in each industry sector				
38	25700	Fargo city, North Dakota	11.5	4.0	0.9	7.7	11.3	24.5	11.5	5.0	2.4
38	32060	Grand Forks city, North Dakota	19.6	4.1	0.4	4.6	5.0	27.9	11.3	3.4	6.2
38	49900	Mandan city, North Dakota	10.4	7.9	1.8	2.9	5.7	31.5	4.5	5.2	8.4
38	53380	Minot city, North Dakota	16.3	8.5	1.1	4.2	8.2	21.0	11.3	7.8	4.4
38	84780	West Fargo city, North Dakota	9.5	4.4	0.7	7.1	8.9	23.5	7.5	4.4	1.1
38	86220	Williston city, North Dakota	6.9	9.4	0.7	7.5	8.4	20.2	4.6	5.6	1.8
39	00000	**OHIO**	11.7	5.1	1.6	6.5	9.3	23.8	9.4	4.5	3.8
39	01000	Akron city, Ohio	15.6	3.4	1.6	4.6	10.3	23.0	12.5	5.3	2.3
39	01420	Alliance city, Ohio	14.1	4.1	2.0	2.6	4.1	24.2	9.8	8.6	0.9
39	02568	Ashland city, Ohio	11.9	1.9	4.5	3.4	9.3	29.4	8.5	7.5	1.7
39	02736	Athens city, Ohio	6.8	1.8	2.7	4.7	0.3	50.4	21.9	2.7	2.2
39	03184	Austintown CDP, Ohio	13.0	3.6	1.4	5.3	8.5	22.8	9.4	6.7	5.8
39	03352	Avon city, Ohio	19.7	6.0	3.2	14.0	9.0	13.9	13.7	3.7	3.8
39	03464	Avon Lake city, Ohio	6.9	2.3	1.3	10.9	11.2	27.2	9.4	5.9	0.7
39	03828	Barberton city, Ohio	12.5	4.6	1.3	4.2	13.7	20.6	9.2	5.6	2.6
39	04720	Beavercreek city, Ohio	10.1	1.8	1.9	5.9	12.5	31.1	6.8	3.1	10.0
39	07454	Boardman CDP, Ohio	19.0	4.1	2.2	5.8	12.9	26.0	5.0	4.3	4.3
39	07972	Bowling Green city, Ohio	7.4	3.5	1.7	1.3	6.9	31.0	22.7	3.3	5.1
39	09680	Brunswick city, Ohio	14.8	5.2	1.4	8.9	8.4	24.5	8.1	5.0	5.6
39	12000	Canton city, Ohio	9.6	3.7	2.5	4.4	8.2	22.4	16.8	2.9	2.0
39	13190	Centerville city, Ohio	11.4	0.4	2.2	9.5	11.2	29.4	5.3	3.1	10.2
39	14184	Chillicothe city, Ohio	14.7	2.6	2.4	4.2	2.9	26.3	19.6	5.4	3.3
39	15000	Cincinnati city, Ohio	11.0	4.6	2.4	7.5	14.4	26.3	12.2	4.7	2.7
39	16000	Cleveland city, Ohio	12.3	5.1	1.7	5.8	8.3	24.4	13.7	3.6	4.8
39	16014	Cleveland Heights city, Ohio	6.4	2.3	1.2	6.9	12.4	38.5	12.2	4.3	1.7
39	18000	Columbus city, Ohio	12.9	6.7	2.3	10.3	12.3	23.4	11.2	3.9	3.8
39	19778	Cuyahoga Falls city, Ohio	13.2	4.3	1.7	6.4	10.5	25.7	5.7	3.9	3.7
39	21000	Dayton city, Ohio	10.4	3.9	2.1	3.8	10.1	28.7	14.1	2.7	4.3
39	21434	Delaware city, Ohio	12.1	2.5	3.5	8.9	12.7	24.0	8.4	1.8	5.8
39	22694	Dublin city, Ohio	10.9	3.0	2.9	21.4	14.3	18.0	6.5	2.0	3.9
39	25256	Elyria city, Ohio	10.4	4.2	1.6	2.8	8.5	23.7	7.3	3.7	5.4
39	25704	Euclid city, Ohio	10.2	3.9	1.8	7.8	11.0	30.0	9.9	3.9	5.2
39	25914	Fairborn city, Ohio	10.7	4.1	0.7	3.1	12.9	27.4	11.1	3.9	7.5
39	25970	Fairfield city, Ohio	13.4	3.1	3.1	8.7	12.3	19.1	9.6	4.4	1.6
39	27048	Findlay city, Ohio	11.2	5.2	1.1	4.6	6.6	22.3	8.6	6.2	2.2
39	29106	Gahanna city, Ohio	14.7	4.0	0.9	10.1	15.0	24.2	4.7	3.6	5.7
39	29428	Garfield Heights city, Ohio	12.9	6.4	0.7	6.1	5.5	29.9	8.3	5.7	0.8
39	31860	Green city, Ohio	11.6	5.1	0.9	4.5	10.2	23.7	13.8	1.9	3.8
39	32592	Grove City city, Ohio	12.4	4.9	0.5	11.4	12.7	27.4	8.3	2.5	5.6
39	33012	Hamilton city, Ohio	14.1	6.8	0.2	4.7	7.9	20.9	12.8	3.7	2.7
39	35476	Hilliard city, Ohio	14.2	3.2	3.9	12.1	13.4	28.2	6.4	3.2	3.1
39	36610	Huber Heights city, Ohio	10.1	5.6	1.6	4.7	12.2	22.5	9.9	4.2	5.3
39	36651	Hudson city, Ohio	4.9	3.7	2.1	9.4	16.6	24.4	7.5	4.8	1.3
39	39872	Kent city, Ohio	9.4	1.5	1.3	2.1	6.7	36.3	20.5	4.7	1.1
39	40040	Kettering city, Ohio	11.0	1.5	2.1	7.5	10.6	28.5	8.2	7.3	5.5
39	41664	Lakewood city, Ohio	9.5	2.4	2.3	7.4	11.7	26.3	12.9	3.8	4.1
39	41720	Lancaster city, Ohio	13.4	4.6	3.3	4.2	5.1	22.6	16.7	3.9	4.1
39	42364	Lebanon city, Ohio	18.0	4.2	0.8	6.2	7.1	15.8	9.4	6.3	5.1
39	43554	Lima city, Ohio	6.9	2.5	0.0	3.5	10.2	21.0	12.4	6.2	4.0
39	44856	Lorain city, Ohio	13.6	3.5	1.4	6.9	8.7	18.9	10.4	5.6	5.6
39	47138	Mansfield city, Ohio	8.8	6.3	0.9	3.9	5.4	25.7	16.7	4.4	5.5
39	47306	Maple Heights city, Ohio	12.4	5.4	4.2	5.4	7.6	33.9	11.2	3.7	4.9
39	47754	Marion city, Ohio	17.2	8.7	1.5	0.7	4.3	19.6	6.3	2.6	5.4
39	48160	Marysville city, Ohio	15.9	5.9	0.6	9.2	9.5	18.5	9.5	4.9	4.6
39	48188	Mason city, Ohio	10.7	1.9	4.5	5.5	11.1	27.0	9.4	4.4	4.3
39	48244	Massillon city, Ohio	18.8	6.0	2.1	4.0	6.8	16.5	11.1	6.3	1.8
39	48790	Medina city, Ohio	10.9	4.5	1.6	4.1	11.3	24.3	9.3	5.8	1.8
39	49056	Mentor city, Ohio	12.7	5.7	1.1	5.3	11.4	24.7	5.3	4.2	1.6
39	49434	Miamisburg city, Ohio	13.2	2.5	2.9	4.8	10.7	23.1	13.4	4.7	1.1
39	49840	Middletown city, Ohio	16.0	3.6	1.1	6.2	11.3	18.8	13.9	4.8	1.0
39	54040	Newark city, Ohio	17.1	2.6	1.2	7.1	10.2	18.5	9.8	4.5	5.8
39	56882	North Olmsted city, Ohio	13.3	4.1	2.0	6.7	13.2	18.5	9.0	6.2	3.8
39	56966	North Ridgeville city, Ohio	10.7	3.2	1.2	9.0	9.7	23.2	9.7	3.5	4.4
39	57008	North Royalton city, Ohio	11.1	5.0	1.2	15.1	6.8	22.8	10.8	5.3	3.9
39	58730	Oregon city, Ohio	9.5	8.8	0.0	3.2	6.2	25.1	14.2	4.2	5.6
39	59234	Oxford city, Ohio	7.2	2.6	2.5	2.8	3.5	44.8	16.9	2.7	6.7
39	61000	Parma city, Ohio	14.2	5.3	1.7	5.8	11.1	19.1	9.3	5.8	1.9
39	61028	Parma Heights city, Ohio	15.5	6.0	2.5	10.4	8.1	15.5	10.5	4.4	4.4
39	62148	Perrysburg city, Ohio	7.9	3.0	0.9	4.4	12.4	30.1	5.2	2.7	5.3
39	62848	Piqua city, Ohio	13.3	1.7	0.0	2.4	2.8	16.3	13.4	1.7	1.1
39	64304	Portsmouth city, Ohio	21.9	1.5	2.4	2.2	9.2	29.5	12.7	0.8	10.6
39	66390	Reynoldsburg city, Ohio	11.9	5.1	1.5	14.2	12.4	17.8	7.2	4.9	4.9
39	67468	Riverside city, Ohio	11.1	3.1	0.4	6.9	4.2	25.9	8.5	1.4	11.5

Table E. Cities—Labor Force, Employment, and Educational Data, 2015—*Continued*

FIPS state code	FIPS place code	State/city	Retail trade	Transportation and warehousing, and utilities	Information	Finance and insurance, and real estate and rental and leasing	Professional, scientific, and management, and administrative and waste management services	Educational services, and health care and social assistance	Arts, entertainment, and recreation, and accommodation and food services	Other services, except public administration	Public administration
							Percent in each industry sector				
39	68056	Rocky River city, Ohio	9.4	4.8	2.7	11.3	14.2	22.8	6.9	2.6	3.8
39	70380	Sandusky city, Ohio	13.2	2.3	0.9	1.5	7.0	22.1	22.5	3.4	2.4
39	71682	Shaker Heights city, Ohio	5.6	2.4	1.0	8.8	13.2	43.7	5.6	3.5	4.1
39	72424	Sidney city, Ohio	10.6	3.0	5.5	6.2	8.2	17.7	7.9	4.3	4.6
39	72928	Solon city, Ohio	6.2	1.9	1.0	10.0	15.3	26.8	9.5	4.9	2.8
39	73264	South Euclid city, Ohio	11.4	3.6	0.9	5.4	7.9	30.7	9.3	5.2	8.4
39	74118	Springfield city, Ohio	10.4	4.1	0.7	6.4	7.4	28.8	10.5	3.5	2.6
39	74944	Stow city, Ohio	8.5	4.2	4.1	6.5	11.5	29.3	8.2	5.9	4.2
39	75098	Strongsville city, Ohio	8.6	3.2	1.3	9.3	13.9	28.1	6.8	3.6	4.8
39	77000	Toledo city, Ohio	12.3	6.1	1.1	2.8	8.7	25.0	12.1	5.4	2.7
39	77504	Trotwood city, Ohio	13.2	2.5	0.3	6.6	7.6	31.6	13.7	2.5	3.9
39	77588	Troy city, Ohio	12.2	2.8	2.9	7.5	5.0	18.0	14.8	3.7	5.6
39	79002	Upper Arlington city, Ohio	9.9	2.6	1.1	13.1	17.4	29.5	4.7	2.9	5.3
39	80304	Wadsworth city, Ohio	12.0	7.4	0.6	6.7	7.4	29.8	8.8	4.2	2.8
39	80892	Warren city, Ohio	12.7	3.8	1.4	6.1	8.9	21.4	13.8	5.1	3.1
39	83342	Westerville city, Ohio	9.2	4.1	2.3	14.6	11.4	24.3	12.7	2.4	5.2
39	83622	Westlake city, Ohio	9.0	6.0	3.0	7.2	14.7	23.8	14.7	2.9	6.5
39	84812	White Oak CDP, Ohio	16.1	7.6	0.8	11.8	8.5	21.9	10.4	3.8	2.9
39	85484	Willoughby city, Ohio	10.0	3.6	1.0	7.0	4.6	24.4	9.0	1.7	5.2
39	86548	Wooster city, Ohio	7.1	3.2	0.6	2.9	6.8	36.7	11.1	3.1	1.1
39	86772	Xenia city, Ohio	15.4	3.4	0.0	8.2	8.0	26.6	6.1	7.7	8.2
39	88000	Youngstown city, Ohio	14.9	3.6	0.9	3.2	8.4	26.0	13.3	5.0	3.4
39	88084	Zanesville city, Ohio	16.5	4.0	1.5	4.0	2.3	33.2	15.9	2.8	0.4
40	00000	**OKLAHOMA**	11.8	5.2	1.7	5.6	8.5	22.3	9.5	5.2	5.8
40	02600	Ardmore city, Oklahoma	14.8	6.3	0.2	3.7	6.0	21.6	9.2	5.3	2.8
40	04450	Bartlesville city, Oklahoma	11.4	4.9	4.1	5.1	9.5	23.4	11.4	5.2	1.7
40	06400	Bixby city, Oklahoma	14.1	6.8	3.3	9.2	15.1	18.5	4.7	3.8	2.8
40	09050	Broken Arrow city, Oklahoma	11.6	5.5	2.1	7.7	11.4	20.4	8.6	5.8	3.5
40	19900	Del City city, Oklahoma	14.1	5.2	1.5	6.9	10.0	24.6	7.2	5.1	5.8
40	21900	Duncan city, Oklahoma	16.2	7.2	0.6	4.0	4.2	20.5	7.9	4.8	3.6
40	23200	Edmond city, Oklahoma	9.2	2.8	2.6	9.6	10.5	24.8	11.8	5.2	4.6
40	23950	Enid city, Oklahoma	14.6	7.2	1.6	3.5	6.4	19.1	6.8	5.9	5.7
40	37800	Jenks city, Oklahoma	8.7	4.6	2.7	8.8	14.1	27.9	8.8	3.8	4.5
40	41850	Lawton city, Oklahoma	13.3	3.3	2.6	8.4	10.0	21.1	9.5	8.3	9.6
40	48350	Midwest City city, Oklahoma	11.8	3.0	1.3	8.2	8.6	22.9	7.8	5.2	12.0
40	49200	Moore city, Oklahoma	11.5	4.7	2.3	6.7	9.2	25.4	10.9	3.1	8.8
40	50050	Muskogee city, Oklahoma	11.1	6.9	0.3	4.4	6.7	25.5	12.2	3.4	6.5
40	50100	Mustang city, Oklahoma	21.6	6.5	0.6	5.6	4.8	16.7	9.6	2.6	8.9
40	52500	Norman city, Oklahoma	11.5	3.3	1.5	5.3	8.9	31.8	12.5	4.9	5.2
40	55000	Oklahoma City city, Oklahoma	11.8	3.9	1.8	7.2	10.8	21.4	9.0	5.8	5.9
40	56650	Owasso city, Oklahoma	11.9	6.5	0.8	7.0	11.2	22.6	9.5	6.3	3.5
40	59850	Ponca City city, Oklahoma	18.1	4.7	0.7	3.2	5.5	20.7	14.5	5.1	2.4
40	65400	Sapulpa city, Oklahoma	14.5	4.0	0.5	2.8	11.3	18.1	12.6	3.7	5.2
40	66800	Shawnee city, Oklahoma	15.0	3.2	1.5	4.4	6.9	20.7	17.6	3.1	7.9
40	70300	Stillwater city, Oklahoma	12.9	1.1	3.1	2.6	4.6	38.1	12.0	6.0	5.2
40	75000	Tulsa city, Oklahoma	10.9	5.6	3.0	6.1	11.9	21.5	9.3	5.9	2.1
40	82950	Yukon city, Oklahoma	16.1	1.7	2.7	4.9	12.5	20.3	9.7	3.5	2.0
41	00000	**OREGON**	12.0	4.1	1.9	5.4	11.3	23.1	9.8	4.7	4.4
41	01000	Albany city, Oregon	15.2	1.6	1.1	2.5	8.6	30.3	5.9	4.2	5.9
41	01650	Aloha CDP, Oregon	13.3	4.0	4.3	4.9	11.0	20.1	9.8	2.9	4.0
41	03050	Ashland city, Oregon	13.1	1.5	1.7	6.3	15.0	24.2	13.9	4.1	4.8
41	05350	Beaverton city, Oregon	9.8	2.6	2.9	8.8	14.9	19.9	13.6	3.1	3.1
41	05800	Bend city, Oregon	9.4	1.4	4.0	5.4	16.6	23.7	10.9	8.5	1.4
41	05950	Bethany CDP, Oregon	9.9	0.4	2.1	7.4	11.4	23.4	4.3	0.7	9.2
41	15800	Corvallis city, Oregon	9.8	1.8	0.6	1.3	14.3	42.7	8.6	4.4	2.8
41	23850	Eugene city, Oregon	13.8	3.1	2.5	5.2	11.0	29.9	12.9	3.6	3.3
41	26200	Forest Grove city, Oregon	11.2	3.7	1.1	4.2	9.2	16.7	6.2	6.6	4.5
41	30550	Grants Pass city, Oregon	14.9	5.2	1.6	5.5	11.0	19.3	10.6	8.5	4.6
41	31250	Gresham city, Oregon	14.3	5.5	0.9	5.6	10.1	21.0	12.9	3.9	3.7
41	32850	Hayesville CDP, Oregon	10.1	2.0	1.7	6.5	13.8	22.9	3.0	0.0	3.0
41	34100	Hillsboro city, Oregon	8.5	2.3	2.5	4.7	13.9	18.6	4.9	4.7	5.2
41	38500	Keizer city, Oregon	15.3	0.8	0.0	9.0	9.0	24.9	4.3	5.8	7.2
41	39700	Klamath Falls city, Oregon	18.3	9.1	3.2	3.1	6.6	21.3	9.1	4.7	5.2
41	40550	Lake Oswego city, Oregon	9.5	2.6	2.1	10.6	14.6	24.4	10.4	4.1	2.9
41	45000	McMinnville city, Oregon	12.4	1.7	0.0	5.3	5.9	24.8	7.8	3.3	3.7
41	47000	Medford city, Oregon	13.1	4.1	1.7	4.1	8.7	25.6	11.5	5.9	5.3
41	48650	Milwaukie city, Oregon	11.6	4.0	1.4	3.9	6.8	33.6	6.8	6.3	1.1
41	52100	Newberg city, Oregon	10.1	4.4	3.1	4.3	6.5	20.9	17.9	1.5	2.9
41	55200	Oregon City city, Oregon	13.0	9.0	3.3	6.9	8.1	18.6	10.9	4.1	4.4
41	59000	Portland city, Oregon	10.0	4.1	2.5	6.1	14.9	26.7	11.6	4.9	3.1
41	61200	Redmond city, Oregon	8.6	3.6	4.2	2.9	13.8	23.6	12.0	7.2	1.3
41	63650	Roseburg city, Oregon	—	—	—	—	—	—	—	—	—

Table E. Cities—Labor Force, Employment, and Educational Data, 2015—*Continued*

FIPS state code	FIPS place code	State/city	Retail trade	Transportation and warehousing, and utilities	Information	Finance and insurance, and real estate and rental and leasing	Professional, scientific, and management, and administrative and waste management services	Educational services, and health care and social assistance	Arts, entertainment, and recreation, and accommodation and food services	Other services, except public administration	Public administration
							Percent in each industry sector				
41	64900	Salem city, Oregon	12.5	1.6	1.1	3.9	9.9	22.3	8.6	5.9	10.0
41	69600	Springfield city, Oregon	17.2	3.7	1.3	2.4	6.3	26.0	8.6	4.4	2.8
41	73650	Tigard city, Oregon	13.2	2.5	2.0	9.6	17.3	19.2	9.1	3.4	4.1
41	74950	Tualatin city, Oregon	15.0	4.9	1.4	8.5	15.6	17.9	8.1	2.5	2.6
41	80150	West Linn city, Oregon	6.1	2.7	0.9	9.7	17.1	24.8	11.5	4.4	1.0
41	82800	Wilsonville city, Oregon	11.0	8.1	2.1	3.4	23.1	15.0	12.3	2.4	1.6
41	83750	Woodburn city, Oregon	22.3	6.4	0.0	4.5	10.3	16.9	12.2	2.1	1.1
42	00000	**PENNSYLVANIA**	11.5	5.4	1.6	6.2	10.3	25.6	8.6	4.6	4.0
42	02000	Allentown city, Pennsylvania	11.1	8.1	0.7	4.2	13.2	23.9	11.1	3.3	1.4
42	02056	Allison Park CDP, Pennsylvania	12.0	5.4	0.6	10.1	12.8	31.1	8.2	7.2	1.5
42	02184	Altoona city, Pennsylvania	18.6	7.1	2.9	4.3	4.7	29.2	8.2	3.4	3.6
42	06064	Bethel Park municipality, Pennsylvania	14.2	4.1	2.3	9.0	15.8	22.0	11.5	3.1	3.0
42	06088	Bethlehem city, Pennsylvania	10.0	7.7	1.6	4.9	8.9	30.5	13.8	4.5	1.3
42	12536	Chambersburg borough, Pennsylvania	12.5	5.7	1.1	4.5	9.7	25.5	9.5	4.1	9.2
42	13208	Chester city, Pennsylvania	14.2	6.9	0.0	6.4	8.9	28.3	9.5	6.1	4.3
42	19920	Drexel Hill CDP, Pennsylvania	8.6	4.4	3.3	8.2	12.3	31.6	11.3	3.5	6.4
42	21648	Easton city, Pennsylvania	7.7	3.9	4.0	3.9	8.0	25.2	9.3	3.9	5.2
42	24000	Erie city, Pennsylvania	11.2	3.4	1.4	5.8	5.3	27.4	17.0	5.2	2.4
42	32800	Harrisburg city, Pennsylvania	11.2	4.7	1.5	8.9	11.8	19.1	12.4	4.6	11.0
42	33408	Hazleton city, Pennsylvania	23.7	9.5	1.0	2.3	10.8	16.8	9.1	1.9	3.2
42	38288	Johnstown city, Pennsylvania	18.1	3.4	0.7	8.2	5.6	22.1	17.4	8.7	5.5
42	41216	Lancaster city, Pennsylvania	12.7	4.2	1.1	4.0	9.8	20.4	14.2	4.0	2.7
42	42168	Lebanon city, Pennsylvania	8.4	9.5	0.0	3.3	6.6	23.9	13.4	2.7	7.4
42	42928	Levittown CDP, Pennsylvania	13.0	6.5	3.5	5.4	7.5	25.4	8.8	3.5	4.0
42	50528	Monroeville municipality, Pennsylvania	11.4	3.4	2.2	11.1	7.9	24.3	12.0	5.8	3.5
42	52432	Murrysville municipality, Pennsylvania	10.1	7.0	2.5	4.9	15.5	22.5	6.3	8.0	1.2
42	53368	New Castle city, Pennsylvania	16.8	10.1	1.1	2.6	4.0	26.4	8.6	4.4	5.0
42	54656	Norristown borough, Pennsylvania	9.8	4.7	2.2	6.7	14.7	30.5	10.0	1.3	2.3
42	60000	Philadelphia city, Pennsylvania	10.7	6.3	1.9	5.4	11.8	29.6	10.0	5.0	6.3
42	61000	Pittsburgh city, Pennsylvania	9.5	3.5	2.5	7.2	13.5	31.5	12.2	3.7	4.0
42	61536	Plum borough, Pennsylvania	17.8	0.9	2.8	8.7	12.6	23.6	7.3	4.8	2.1
42	62416	Pottstown borough, Pennsylvania	13.3	7.7	2.4	3.5	10.4	22.6	11.4	2.5	3.3
42	63624	Reading city, Pennsylvania	12.2	6.1	1.4	2.9	7.0	20.6	8.4	4.8	2.0
42	69000	Scranton city, Pennsylvania	10.9	5.4	2.3	5.7	8.4	28.9	9.0	6.5	2.8
42	73808	State College borough, Pennsylvania	7.6	1.7	0.7	1.3	9.2	44.7	20.2	3.0	1.0
42	79277	Upper St. Clair CDP, Pennsylvania	7.1	5.1	1.8	13.1	19.6	23.3	6.4	5.9	0.0
42	83512	West Mifflin borough, Pennsylvania	7.3	4.6	2.2	8.6	7.5	24.3	8.1	3.7	5.9
42	85152	Wilkes-Barre city, Pennsylvania	18.0	4.6	0.7	2.9	8.3	27.9	14.0	3.8	3.6
42	85312	Williamsport city, Pennsylvania	10.3	3.0	1.0	1.5	8.2	31.6	18.0	4.1	0.9
42	87048	York city, Pennsylvania	11.0	7.5	2.1	3.4	6.8	24.1	11.4	5.9	2.4
44	00000	**RHODE ISLAND**	11.7	3.7	1.6	6.5	9.3	27.4	11.1	4.4	4.1
44	19180	Cranston city, Rhode Island	12.0	2.4	3.8	8.3	8.0	25.8	10.6	3.7	5.8
44	22960	East Providence city, Rhode Island	12.5	7.0	0.4	6.7	6.1	28.3	10.9	6.1	3.5
44	49960	Newport city, Rhode Island	13.7	4.5	1.8	5.5	7.5	25.1	16.0	5.7	5.5
44	54640	Pawtucket city, Rhode Island	13.0	4.1	1.5	5.6	7.9	31.7	9.8	4.3	2.0
44	59000	Providence city, Rhode Island	11.8	3.2	2.0	5.1	9.5	30.3	10.2	4.8	1.8
44	74300	Warwick city, Rhode Island	10.9	5.3	1.2	6.4	8.9	26.6	12.2	4.1	4.9
44	76820	Westerly CDP, Rhode Island	8.9	1.9	1.7	2.9	6.3	25.7	16.7	4.8	2.6
44	80780	Woonsocket city, Rhode Island	19.9	6.9	2.4	4.0	9.0	21.7	12.7	2.5	2.5
45	00000	**SOUTH CAROLINA**	12.2	4.6	1.9	5.9	9.9	21.7	10.2	5.2	4.4
45	00550	Aiken city, South Carolina	13.0	5.1	0.5	1.9	16.5	27.9	10.7	7.4	2.9
45	01360	Anderson city, South Carolina	15.8	1.8	1.2	1.6	4.8	29.5	8.7	10.2	5.3
45	13330	Charleston city, South Carolina	8.1	4.2	2.8	5.9	17.5	24.8	15.2	4.6	3.0
45	16000	Columbia city, South Carolina	10.6	3.8	2.3	7.2	12.6	27.4	12.8	4.2	7.3
45	16405	Conway city, South Carolina	13.5	2.3	4.2	3.8	9.4	26.5	19.7	3.0	3.5
45	21985	Easley city, South Carolina	10.8	2.6	2.6	4.6	9.4	21.3	11.3	3.4	4.2
45	25810	Florence city, South Carolina	14.2	5.9	1.0	6.3	6.0	27.8	10.2	6.0	3.8
45	29815	Goose Creek city, South Carolina	11.1	3.1	2.1	4.9	11.9	17.5	10.3	5.6	8.9
45	30850	Greenville city, South Carolina	7.0	3.9	3.3	6.3	15.6	25.2	14.9	4.3	2.4
45	30895	Greenwood city, South Carolina	–	–	–	–	–	–	–	–	–
45	30985	Greer city, South Carolina	12.0	1.6	2.1	7.3	5.8	23.3	10.5	3.1	1.1
45	32065	Hanahan city, South Carolina	8.5	5.1	1.5	4.3	15.3	19.2	10.6	4.0	7.5
45	34045	Hilton Head Island town, South Carolina	13.4	3.5	3.9	7.5	12.5	20.2	16.9	5.0	1.9
45	41335	Lexington town, South Carolina	7.8	8.9	1.6	5.9	14.4	29.8	5.3	6.6	5.0
45	45115	Mauldin city, South Carolina	8.3	1.8	3.6	6.0	12.6	25.4	10.0	7.0	4.7
45	48535	Mount Pleasant town, South Carolina	8.5	5.4	1.5	14.5	16.5	24.4	13.8	3.0	3.5
45	49075	Myrtle Beach city, South Carolina	15.6	2.9	0.8	5.3	9.0	14.2	33.2	4.0	1.8
45	50695	North Augusta city, South Carolina	22.2	8.5	0.0	8.2	7.2	26.1	8.1	0.0	4.3
45	50875	North Charleston city, South Carolina	10.4	4.5	2.3	5.7	13.7	17.6	14.8	4.6	6.6
45	61405	Rock Hill city, South Carolina	15.0	5.0	1.9	8.7	11.2	19.1	11.5	5.2	3.1
45	62395	St. Andrews CDP, South Carolina	19.6	8.7	1.5	3.6	7.3	22.9	8.4	5.1	5.1
45	66580	Simpsonville city, South Carolina	16.1	2.5	5.2	2.9	10.2	21.9	8.0	6.6	6.2

Table E. Cities—Labor Force, Employment, and Educational Data, 2015—*Continued*

FIPS state code	FIPS place code	State/city	Retail trade	Transportation and warehousing, and utilities	Information	Finance and insurance, and real estate and rental and leasing	Professional, scientific, and management, and administrative and waste management services	Educational services, and health care and social assistance	Arts, entertainment, and recreation, and accommodation and food services	Other services, except public administration	Public administration
											Percent in each industry sector
45	67390	Socastee CDP, South Carolina	15.7	1.2	1.8	4.3	10.6	16.2	20.0	2.3	1.0
45	68290	Spartanburg city, South Carolina	11.3	3.0	2.8	2.2	5.6	20.8	11.1	7.4	1.4
45	70270	Summerville town, South Carolina	6.5	2.6	1.6	2.7	13.8	20.2	13.6	5.4	6.0
45	70405	Sumter city, South Carolina	8.9	2.5	2.9	6.6	6.1	22.2	10.4	2.7	8.8
45	71395	Taylors CDP, South Carolina	6.3	4.3	1.5	5.1	13.5	24.5	11.7	2.6	2.5
45	73870	Wade Hampton CDP, South Carolina	13.4	0.7	2.7	6.2	12.6	17.8	9.0	11.1	6.7
46	00000	**SOUTH DAKOTA**	10.5	4.6	1.5	7.0	6.5	24.3	9.5	4.4	4.4
46	00100	Aberdeen city, South Dakota	15.8	4.7	1.9	3.6	7.9	24.3	10.6	2.7	4.6
46	07580	Brookings city, South Dakota	10.6	4.1	1.7	3.1	4.3	30.3	12.2	5.3	1.7
46	52980	Rapid City city, South Dakota	12.1	4.0	1.0	8.3	10.2	25.5	13.5	5.9	4.1
46	59020	Sioux Falls city, South Dakota	10.8	3.8	1.9	10.7	7.9	25.9	8.5	3.9	2.2
46	69300	Watertown city, South Dakota	12.7	5.1	2.9	3.5	5.9	18.6	11.5	2.6	4.5
47	00000	**TENNESSEE**	12.3	6.5	1.8	5.7	9.9	22.4	9.5	5.1	4.0
47	03440	Bartlett city, Tennessee	14.1	8.4	1.3	4.4	10.4	18.4	9.0	5.2	6.9
47	08280	Brentwood city, Tennessee	9.0	2.1	2.6	15.0	15.2	28.4	5.7	4.9	1.9
47	08540	Bristol city, Tennessee	9.4	3.9	4.1	4.7	8.4	19.9	16.7	3.0	4.5
47	14000	Chattanooga city, Tennessee	13.3	6.9	1.8	7.1	11.9	21.4	11.7	4.7	1.9
47	15160	Clarksville city, Tennessee	14.1	5.2	1.7	4.1	11.2	22.3	9.3	3.6	8.1
47	15400	Cleveland city, Tennessee	9.8	4.9	1.8	7.7	7.3	20.4	16.2	7.3	2.9
47	16420	Collierville town, Tennessee	11.6	13.3	1.5	5.6	7.5	26.6	7.2	4.5	5.7
47	16540	Columbia city, Tennessee	15.6	5.4	2.3	5.3	10.8	26.3	5.9	4.1	2.2
47	16920	Cookeville city, Tennessee	13.4	4.6	1.1	3.1	10.1	29.1	17.1	4.3	2.4
47	22720	East Ridge city, Tennessee	6.2	7.9	3.1	8.2	6.6	15.4	9.8	7.6	2.8
47	25760	Farragut town, Tennessee	5.1	4.0	1.8	7.3	18.4	29.6	6.0	4.4	5.6
47	27740	Franklin city, Tennessee	8.9	3.0	3.8	10.2	15.2	23.3	10.1	5.8	5.0
47	28540	Gallatin city, Tennessee	10.3	5.8	3.8	2.7	8.3	28.5	8.1	3.4	2.6
47	28960	Germantown city, Tennessee	10.0	6.9	0.7	13.4	9.3	30.3	7.3	3.0	2.0
47	33280	Hendersonville city, Tennessee	14.3	4.6	1.9	7.3	11.7	21.0	9.6	7.6	3.7
47	37640	Jackson city, Tennessee	13.7	2.9	0.6	2.7	7.5	32.2	12.4	5.4	3.1
47	38320	Johnson City city, Tennessee	11.2	2.2	3.1	5.9	6.9	31.6	18.6	6.8	1.4
47	39560	Kingsport city, Tennessee	12.6	1.6	2.1	4.9	6.2	24.6	14.0	5.6	2.6
47	40000	Knoxville city, Tennessee	16.2	4.2	2.6	6.0	12.8	25.3	13.4	3.9	3.7
47	41200	La Vergne city, Tennessee	11.9	9.6	1.0	4.9	8.4	17.4	4.8	5.3	2.9
47	41520	Lebanon city, Tennessee	11.7	5.8	0.3	7.1	11.6	25.4	7.4	7.6	4.5
47	46380	Maryville city, Tennessee	14.2	4.1	2.3	6.0	12.2	23.2	10.9	8.9	3.2
47	48000	Memphis city, Tennessee	10.8	13.3	1.8	4.9	11.0	21.8	9.9	5.6	3.8
47	50280	Morristown city, Tennessee	6.4	3.4	2.0	3.5	7.3	24.4	10.8	1.5	0.5
47	50780	Mount Juliet city, Tennessee	12.2	5.1	3.2	10.3	15.5	18.9	9.2	5.8	6.3
47	51560	Murfreesboro city, Tennessee	12.4	6.2	3.3	7.2	8.5	24.3	13.5	4.3	2.1
47	52006	Nashville-Davidson metropolitan government (balance), Tennessee	10.9	5.0	2.6	7.8	12.6	23.7	12.6	5.1	4.0
47	55120	Oak Ridge city, Tennessee	16.1	2.6	1.6	5.6	24.7	19.1	9.5	5.4	3.0
47	67760	Shelbyville city, Tennessee	21.4	8.2	0.5	4.3	0.4	12.6	9.8	2.5	1.6
47	69420	Smyrna town, Tennessee	10.8	8.2	1.1	6.2	12.9	16.7	9.4	6.0	5.9
47	70580	Spring Hill city, Tennessee	13.8	1.2	6.0	9.7	12.0	12.5	17.5	9.5	2.4
48	00000	**TEXAS**	11.7	5.7	1.8	6.6	11.4	21.2	9.1	5.2	4.1
48	01000	Abilene city, Texas	12.7	5.7	0.9	5.7	6.2	30.1	12.1	6.0	5.8
48	01924	Allen city, Texas	13.6	2.0	4.5	10.5	14.8	21.6	6.6	3.8	3.4
48	02272	Alvin city, Texas	14.0	9.0	2.2	2.0	7.6	14.8	9.0	4.3	5.3
48	03000	Amarillo city, Texas	14.3	4.6	1.7	4.9	7.1	24.9	10.3	6.1	4.3
48	04000	Arlington city, Texas	12.4	6.8	2.4	7.8	11.2	20.6	9.7	5.9	3.3
48	04462	Atascocita CDP, Texas	11.1	10.7	1.3	6.4	3.4	27.8	8.0	3.4	4.8
48	05000	Austin city, Texas	9.6	2.9	3.2	7.6	18.1	19.5	11.6	5.2	5.4
48	05372	Balch Springs city, Texas	7.5	12.0	0.0	2.6	8.9	9.3	19.6	6.8	1.4
48	06128	Baytown city, Texas	10.6	7.6	0.6	1.7	11.0	16.8	10.4	5.0	2.7
48	07000	Beaumont city, Texas	12.2	4.0	0.7	3.6	9.3	25.5	13.0	4.6	5.4
48	07132	Bedford city, Texas	13.5	7.7	3.1	7.3	14.1	21.3	9.3	4.6	5.3
48	07492	Belton city, Texas	7.8	3.1	0.9	6.6	13.6	30.0	5.6	5.2	3.4
48	07552	Benbrook city, Texas	11.9	5.6	0.4	6.3	11.2	20.8	9.0	5.9	3.9
48	08236	Big Spring city, Texas	18.9	3.8	2.7	6.7	3.5	21.0	9.5	7.1	3.1
48	10768	Brownsville city, Texas	16.9	6.5	1.2	4.4	6.2	31.7	8.5	4.6	4.1
48	10897	Brushy Creek CDP, Texas	11.2	2.3	2.7	9.5	14.5	18.2	4.9	2.0	4.2
48	10912	Bryan city, Texas	15.3	2.9	1.0	4.0	8.7	24.1	13.2	4.4	3.7
48	11428	Burleson city, Texas	10.9	7.6	1.3	7.3	6.8	26.0	4.4	4.8	7.8
48	12580	Canyon Lake CDP, Texas	10.9	5.4	1.2	5.8	10.1	26.4	9.5	3.7	3.6
48	13024	Carrollton city, Texas	12.2	6.5	4.2	9.8	13.1	15.0	9.4	6.2	1.8
48	13492	Cedar Hill city, Texas	12.8	7.0	1.3	10.0	10.0	24.1	8.4	5.6	4.0
48	13552	Cedar Park city, Texas	11.0	1.2	2.8	10.9	21.4	25.0	3.8	2.0	4.7
48	14236	Channelview CDP, Texas	11.8	11.7	0.3	4.1	9.7	17.0	10.9	3.8	3.8
48	14920	Cibolo city, Texas	13.8	1.5	2.9	3.6	6.8	30.3	5.9	5.4	13.5
48	15364	Cleburne city, Texas	12.8	11.1	0.2	6.9	5.8	25.9	5.1	3.9	1.8
48	15628	Cloverleaf CDP, Texas	11.0	10.1	0.3	5.1	5.3	16.6	4.7	3.0	1.5
48	15976	College Station city, Texas	14.5	1.6	2.1	4.2	9.2	37.7	12.3	3.2	3.0

Table E. Cities—Labor Force, Employment, and Educational Data, 2015—Continued

									Percent in each industry sector		
FIPS state code	FIPS place code	State/city	Retail trade	Transportation and warehousing, and utilities	Information	Finance and insurance, and real estate and rental and leasing	Professional, scientific, and management, and administrative and waste management services	Educational services, and health care and social assistance	Arts, entertainment, and recreation, and accommodation and food services	Other services, except public administration	Public administration
48	15988	Colleyville city, Texas	8.8	3.3	1.7	11.7	19.6	14.9	3.7	7.2	6.7
48	16432	Conroe city, Texas	13.5	5.9	1.0	6.5	13.3	22.2	9.9	4.7	3.1
48	16468	Converse city, Texas	15.5	4.7	0.4	13.5	13.0	17.1	10.9	3.6	5.8
48	16612	Coppell city, Texas	6.1	5.0	5.1	13.5	18.3	19.7	5.6	4.3	2.4
48	16624	Copperas Cove city, Texas	12.6	4.2	1.7	7.3	11.9	28.8	7.3	3.6	12.5
48	16696	Corinth city, Texas	11.2	7.2	2.5	10.6	13.3	20.8	6.2	2.3	5.8
48	17000	Corpus Christi city, Texas	11.5	4.0	1.0	5.9	8.9	22.9	13.4	5.2	6.4
48	17060	Corsicana city, Texas	11.8	1.2	0.0	8.5	2.1	15.5	15.4	9.7	7.2
48	19000	Dallas city, Texas	10.1	5.5	2.3	8.8	15.0	17.6	11.2	5.8	1.7
48	19624	Deer Park city, Texas	11.9	9.4	0.7	4.5	6.5	27.0	6.5	5.1	2.8
48	19792	Del Rio city, Texas	10.9	7.9	0.3	4.0	5.7	20.8	14.8	3.8	14.6
48	19900	Denison city, Texas	12.6	3.7	1.1	7.1	6.1	26.5	10.5	8.7	3.4
48	19972	Denton city, Texas	12.5	4.1	1.8	5.0	8.8	29.1	13.1	5.0	3.2
48	20092	DeSoto city, Texas	9.2	9.7	2.3	10.5	9.9	19.1	8.0	5.0	7.7
48	21628	Duncanville city, Texas	14.1	10.4	1.6	7.4	8.8	17.0	8.1	9.1	3.7
48	21892	Eagle Pass city, Texas	10.8	9.7	0.9	5.2	5.4	27.7	12.4	2.8	7.3
48	22660	Edinburg city, Texas	12.1	4.9	1.1	1.5	11.2	37.5	9.2	5.0	6.3
48	24000	El Paso city, Texas	11.8	6.5	1.6	5.8	11.4	24.5	10.6	4.6	8.4
48	24768	Euless city, Texas	12.9	10.5	0.5	9.3	8.1	19.0	11.1	6.2	3.0
48	25452	Farmers Branch city, Texas	11.4	5.6	2.2	7.7	13.6	19.9	11.9	5.1	0.8
48	26232	Flower Mound town, Texas	9.1	7.1	2.5	12.8	16.0	17.0	8.1	4.4	4.6
48	26736	Fort Hood CDP, Texas	–	–	–	–	–	–	–	–	–
48	27000	Fort Worth city, Texas	10.7	7.9	2.2	5.9	10.5	20.8	9.6	4.4	3.7
48	27540	Fresno CDP, Texas	12.8	11.4	4.4	6.1	6.2	30.0	2.7	5.2	6.8
48	27648	Friendswood city, Texas	12.3	5.8	0.5	10.5	13.8	18.6	4.9	5.4	2.5
48	27684	Frisco city, Texas	11.7	2.4	4.3	13.5	20.1	19.1	6.2	3.2	1.8
48	28068	Galveston city, Texas	9.4	3.3	1.4	7.8	10.2	29.3	18.7	3.0	2.7
48	29000	Garland city, Texas	14.1	5.6	2.0	6.2	13.9	17.8	8.9	6.8	1.9
48	29336	Georgetown city, Texas	10.1	2.5	1.7	7.6	16.3	29.5	5.5	4.6	5.2
48	30464	Grand Prairie city, Texas	13.4	8.5	1.5	8.2	9.9	16.2	7.8	5.8	2.5
48	30644	Grapevine city, Texas	15.5	10.8	1.5	8.5	17.2	12.1	13.8	1.5	1.0
48	30920	Greenville city, Texas	14.2	1.8	2.0	3.8	10.7	18.9	7.3	7.9	4.3
48	31928	Haltom City city, Texas	15.8	6.3	0.7	1.6	14.6	15.0	9.5	9.0	1.2
48	32312	Harker Heights city, Texas	20.0	2.6	0.0	4.8	11.5	16.8	9.3	9.1	17.3
48	32372	Harlingen city, Texas	11.7	3.8	2.5	4.6	10.4	35.9	6.7	4.9	7.4
48	35000	Houston city, Texas	11.1	6.0	1.2	6.3	13.6	18.3	10.4	5.6	2.2
48	35528	Huntsville city, Texas	–	–	–	–	–	–	–	–	–
48	35576	Hurst city, Texas	17.0	8.3	2.4	9.4	10.8	19.6	7.4	7.3	3.6
48	35624	Hutto city, Texas	7.5	1.2	1.3	2.8	13.3	29.8	8.1	2.8	7.6
48	37000	Irving city, Texas	9.7	8.8	4.0	9.4	18.1	12.0	11.4	4.3	1.9
48	38632	Keller city, Texas	12.6	8.0	1.8	8.3	11.7	18.9	8.6	7.3	2.3
48	39040	Kerrville city, Texas	4.6	4.4	0.8	7.9	11.8	26.2	8.4	9.5	3.3
48	39148	Killeen city, Texas	12.8	3.2	1.2	4.6	11.4	19.5	12.3	3.9	15.4
48	39352	Kingsville city, Texas	7.0	2.8	0.0	4.7	2.5	21.8	10.7	5.9	1.8
48	39952	Kyle city, Texas	13.8	4.2	5.4	5.1	8.3	21.6	8.1	4.6	7.4
48	40588	Lake Jackson city, Texas	7.8	4.3	2.4	2.9	11.0	18.7	6.3	3.1	5.2
48	41212	Lancaster city, Texas	6.6	12.3	0.0	8.8	7.9	20.3	8.2	5.5	6.5
48	41440	La Porte city, Texas	7.9	9.4	0.3	3.5	14.3	17.3	3.3	6.0	4.5
48	41464	Laredo city, Texas	13.4	14.7	0.6	3.5	7.0	25.1	9.8	5.9	6.2
48	41980	League City city, Texas	8.9	4.2	2.1	8.0	12.1	25.2	7.5	3.5	6.6
48	42016	Leander city, Texas	8.8	4.8	4.3	8.8	13.5	26.1	6.9	2.0	4.8
48	42508	Lewisville city, Texas	14.0	5.8	2.1	7.6	14.0	15.4	13.1	7.0	2.3
48	43012	Little Elm city, Texas	8.5	9.9	4.4	13.7	10.9	23.0	7.7	6.4	2.4
48	43888	Longview city, Texas	18.7	3.0	0.4	4.4	9.4	22.7	9.4	6.7	1.9
48	45000	Lubbock city, Texas	13.6	3.9	2.1	5.9	7.7	29.7	11.0	5.8	3.1
48	45072	Lufkin city, Texas	7.9	4.4	0.5	2.9	11.4	28.6	7.8	5.7	5.5
48	45384	McAllen city, Texas	14.6	4.6	0.6	5.7	5.4	31.1	11.8	5.0	4.7
48	45744	McKinney city, Texas	10.9	2.8	2.7	12.2	13.4	21.1	9.4	4.5	2.7
48	46452	Mansfield city, Texas	9.7	5.1	1.6	12.6	11.3	23.8	6.1	5.2	5.5
48	46776	Marshall city, Texas	5.4	5.3	0.3	7.0	5.5	27.4	11.1	5.3	8.6
48	47892	Mesquite city, Texas	12.6	7.8	4.6	7.3	12.4	18.4	9.0	4.1	2.7
48	48072	Midland city, Texas	10.2	8.4	0.6	5.0	7.4	18.5	8.8	5.6	1.9
48	48096	Midlothian city, Texas	18.1	6.1	1.1	7.7	11.4	22.2	7.7	3.4	6.9
48	48768	Mission city, Texas	11.2	6.3	2.2	8.1	8.7	25.4	8.1	6.0	4.7
48	48772	Mission Bend CDP, Texas	11.5	5.1	1.5	8.4	6.1	23.2	15.4	5.6	2.6
48	48804	Missouri City city, Texas	13.1	6.2	1.7	8.1	14.1	24.2	5.1	5.5	3.3
48	50100	Murphy city, Texas									
48	50256	Nacogdoches city, Texas	4.0	4.2	3.1	3.3	9.6	44.4	5.5	3.7	3.4
48	50820	New Braunfels city, Texas	10.9	5.3	3.0	6.1	12.2	15.6	14.7	4.6	6.8
48	52356	North Richland Hills city, Texas	18.2	8.4	1.5	8.8	9.2	16.5	9.3	6.2	6.0
48	53388	Odessa city, Texas	12.1	5.3	1.2	4.8	5.8	17.0	10.9	6.7	2.5
48	55080	Paris city, Texas	25.1	4.3	0.0	2.8	5.7	21.5	5.4	2.8	3.7
48	56000	Pasadena city, Texas	11.7	7.7	0.8	4.4	9.2	15.4	9.9	5.5	2.5

Table E. Cities—Labor Force, Employment, and Educational Data, 2015—*Continued*

							Percent in each industry sector				
FIPS state code	FIPS place code	State/city	Retail trade	Transportation and warehousing, and utilities	Information	Finance and insurance, and real estate and rental and leasing	Professional, scientific, and management, and administrative and waste management services	Educational services, and health care and social assistance	Arts, entertainment, and recreation, and accommodation and food services	Other services, except public administration	Public administration
48	56348	Pearland city, Texas	8.5	6.9	2.3	6.3	11.3	35.0	3.5	3.8	5.0
48	57176	Pflugerville city, Texas	11.5	4.4	2.4	8.8	12.7	24.3	7.1	4.8	8.0
48	57200	Pharr city, Texas	16.5	5.9	0.0	2.2	5.9	26.8	10.9	7.2	2.8
48	57980	Plainview city, Texas	28.2	4.2	0.0	2.4	5.2	17.5	8.8	4.8	6.9
48	58016	Plano city, Texas	10.9	3.6	4.1	11.3	19.0	19.7	9.6	4.7	1.9
48	58820	Port Arthur city, Texas	13.4	4.8	1.6	3.7	5.4	17.3	7.7	5.1	4.1
48	61796	Richardson city, Texas	11.1	2.9	4.4	6.5	18.6	24.6	8.1	4.5	1.7
48	62828	Rockwall city, Texas	12.9	3.3	1.4	8.8	12.9	23.3	8.3	2.9	3.4
48	63284	Rosenberg city, Texas	16.9	1.2	0.4	1.5	7.5	22.8	8.3	5.1	3.1
48	63500	Round Rock city, Texas	11.2	4.6	3.6	6.4	16.7	18.5	8.6	4.7	4.8
48	63572	Rowlett city, Texas	12.2	3.2	3.4	11.4	11.3	26.4	5.5	4.6	3.1
48	64064	Sachse city, Texas	7.1	1.7	15.8	12.7	14.2	19.1	1.2	8.3	1.4
48	64112	Saginaw city, Texas	14.3	6.3	3.1	11.8	8.8	15.2	11.0	3.5	7.6
48	64472	San Angelo city, Texas	15.7	3.3	2.1	2.7	8.9	25.2	9.4	4.5	5.5
48	65000	San Antonio city, Texas	12.1	4.5	1.8	8.5	11.4	22.2	12.2	5.1	4.4
48	65036	San Benito city, Texas	11.0	3.3	1.3	5.7	3.3	29.4	10.0	8.8	4.5
48	65516	San Juan city, Texas	15.3	4.9	0.0	4.5	10.9	24.7	8.5	4.8	4.7
48	65600	San Marcos city, Texas	21.4	1.7	0.6	4.7	9.6	21.8	16.5	3.2	2.6
48	66128	Schertz city, Texas	12.2	6.2	3.1	7.0	8.6	20.1	9.6	6.6	13.6
48	66644	Seguin city, Texas	16.9	5.5	0.0	4.1	5.3	18.7	6.2	9.4	4.5
48	67496	Sherman city, Texas	7.8	2.3	1.4	2.8	5.2	31.3	10.7	6.7	4.7
48	68636	Socorro city, Texas	13.7	10.4	1.5	1.4	12.7	21.5	11.0	5.5	3.2
48	69032	Southlake city, Texas	14.3	3.5	2.3	23.5	17.6	15.9	5.4	2.5	0.7
48	69596	Spring CDP, Texas	11.5	9.6	2.6	8.1	9.4	17.9	6.9	7.8	4.8
48	70208	Stephenville city, Texas	13.8	3.6	0.7	1.6	8.1	22.3	11.1	4.7	4.8
48	70808	Sugar Land city, Texas	11.7	3.6	3.4	9.7	13.0	26.1	5.5	2.0	1.5
48	72176	Temple city, Texas	14.4	5.3	1.4	4.4	8.6	31.9	7.3	3.7	5.0
48	72368	Texarkana city, Texas	15.8	3.1	0.7	2.8	8.8	26.5	11.4	7.4	5.0
48	72392	Texas City city, Texas	12.4	5.1	0.4	3.9	9.1	24.2	13.2	6.5	5.8
48	72530	The Colony city, Texas	20.5	3.4	2.3	9.9	16.7	12.9	10.7	9.2	2.7
48	72656	The Woodlands CDP, Texas	6.5	6.5	0.4	7.1	14.3	15.4	6.6	5.2	3.6
48	73057	Timberwood Park CDP, Texas	16.3	5.3	3.7	15.7	8.5	25.1	6.6	4.6	8.5
48	74144	Tyler city, Texas	15.1	3.7	2.8	6.1	5.9	29.6	8.9	6.5	3.0
48	74492	University Park city, Texas	10.5	0.3	2.0	18.1	24.5	21.7	6.0	5.2	0.7
48	75428	Victoria city, Texas	18.0	4.6	1.2	3.0	5.2	27.9	8.7	4.1	5.5
48	76000	Waco city, Texas	13.7	3.5	1.1	6.8	8.3	24.5	10.8	5.5	5.7
48	76672	Watauga city, Texas	13.4	9.7	3.7	7.8	6.9	17.2	9.0	9.6	1.2
48	76816	Waxahachie city, Texas	15.4	4.0	1.6	9.7	8.7	23.2	7.1	4.2	1.8
48	76864	Weatherford city, Texas	18.7	6.8	0.0	9.5	5.0	21.3	5.6	4.1	2.9
48	77272	Weslaco city, Texas	17.4	2.9	1.6	5.3	8.8	32.7	4.1	10.6	5.8
48	77728	West Odessa CDP, Texas	10.8	7.9	1.3	7.9	2.3	17.2	3.5	12.2	2.9
48	79000	Wichita Falls city, Texas	15.8	4.2	2.5	2.3	7.7	25.3	13.9	4.9	5.9
48	80356	Wylie city, Texas	12.6	2.0	4.1	7.1	16.5	20.5	4.8	8.5	2.7
49	00000	**UTAH**	12.3	4.5	2.2	6.7	11.9	20.8	9.2	4.5	5.1
49	01310	American Fork city, Utah	13.1	1.7	1.5	3.9	20.4	24.4	5.5	2.5	4.8
49	07690	Bountiful city, Utah	10.6	4.5	2.0	8.4	13.6	22.5	8.2	4.8	6.5
49	11320	Cedar City city, Utah	4.8	3.6	2.8	7.7	9.7	31.2	13.4	1.8	3.7
49	13850	Clearfield city, Utah	15.4	9.8	1.4	3.2	9.1	12.9	10.8	4.9	9.9
49	14290	Clinton city, Utah	14.2	2.1	1.9	13.1	9.9	17.6	7.2	6.6	8.0
49	16270	Cottonwood Heights city, Utah	12.1	5.4	1.6	8.0	15.0	27.5	7.0	2.7	3.9
49	20120	Draper city, Utah	8.0	3.5	4.4	13.7	15.2	24.1	9.9	2.0	2.3
49	20810	Eagle Mountain city, Utah	18.5	3.1	3.5	5.0	17.7	14.2	3.7	1.4	5.7
49	24740	Farmington city, Utah	15.5	3.6	3.9	10.9	7.3	21.2	7.6	1.4	11.5
49	34970	Herriman city, Utah	8.5	9.2	4.3	7.9	5.2	14.8	11.3	1.7	7.0
49	36070	Holladay city, Utah	9.9	2.7	1.4	14.3	20.1	26.9	6.1	5.8	1.6
49	40360	Kaysville city, Utah	11.2	2.2	3.2	12.1	13.5	18.0	8.7	5.9	5.0
49	40470	Kearns CDP, Utah	11.8	8.0	3.2	5.2	10.5	11.2	7.3	5.9	2.3
49	43660	Layton city, Utah	13.9	5.2	1.2	5.7	11.7	17.7	9.5	3.5	8.7
49	44320	Lehi city, Utah	10.7	3.2	2.8	10.7	13.3	19.7	6.5	7.1	4.2
49	45860	Logan city, Utah	17.5	1.6	1.4	1.2	16.0	27.1	8.5	3.4	2.2
49	47290	Magna CDP, Utah	8.5	5.0	1.7	9.6	7.4	15.5	7.8	5.6	2.3
49	49710	Midvale city, Utah	12.4	6.4	2.5	8.5	18.0	17.8	8.8	4.7	2.6
49	50150	Millcreek CDP, Utah	11.7	3.2	1.7	8.2	17.6	27.2	8.0	3.3	3.0
49	53230	Murray city, Utah	10.0	4.1	1.7	9.7	12.9	20.1	10.0	3.9	3.1
49	55980	Ogden city, Utah	10.3	3.5	1.2	3.1	10.8	17.1	7.7	3.0	7.6
49	57300	Orem city, Utah	11.6	1.9	3.6	5.3	14.2	27.4	11.0	3.8	1.4
49	60930	Pleasant Grove city, Utah	13.0	5.5	2.2	3.6	11.5	26.2	8.8	6.3	4.9
49	62470	Provo city, Utah	12.2	1.8	2.9	3.7	13.0	31.2	9.8	7.3	3.1
49	64340	Riverton city, Utah	16.2	4.0	2.4	10.0	13.1	20.0	6.1	3.2	6.6
49	65110	Roy city, Utah	10.7	3.9	1.1	5.2	9.4	17.7	9.3	5.2	13.6
49	65330	St. George city, Utah	13.8	3.5	3.5	6.6	9.3	24.1	18.8	3.4	3.9
49	67000	Salt Lake City city, Utah	11.8	3.6	2.6	5.8	12.9	25.6	10.8	5.6	4.4

Table E. Cities—Labor Force, Employment, and Educational Data, 2015—*Continued*

FIPS state code	FIPS place code	State/city	Retail trade	Transportation and warehousing, and utilities	Information	Finance and insurance, and real estate and rental and leasing	Professional, scientific, and management, and administrative and waste management services	Educational services, and health care and social assistance	Arts, entertainment, and recreation, and accommodation and food services	Other services, except public administration	Public administration
							Percent in each industry sector				
49	67440	Sandy city, Utah	13.2	4.2	2.6	13.6	13.5	17.4	10.7	4.2	4.2
49	67825	Saratoga Springs city, Utah	12.1	1.9	6.8	10.1	13.5	23.3	2.9	3.5	1.9
49	70850	South Jordan city, Utah	10.7	5.1	0.7	11.8	15.2	19.9	5.9	2.4	6.0
49	71070	South Salt Lake city, Utah	18.7	9.4	0.4	10.2	9.4	12.8	10.3	4.6	4.2
49	71290	Spanish Fork city, Utah	13.6	2.0	1.9	4.7	9.3	24.9	8.3	3.0	2.5
49	72280	Springville city, Utah	8.2	4.0	5.2	4.4	10.4	23.6	9.5	3.8	2.3
49	74810	Syracuse city, Utah	11.9	3.2	2.1	3.0	12.6	25.9	8.0	2.4	9.0
49	75360	Taylorsville city, Utah	11.9	4.6	1.7	10.5	11.7	12.8	10.8	4.1	3.7
49	76680	Tooele city, Utah	17.0	3.4	0.4	4.6	10.9	10.2	5.8	7.5	13.8
49	81960	Washington city, Utah	23.7	4.8	1.5	7.5	5.1	14.0	11.0	3.4	3.9
49	82950	West Jordan city, Utah	14.0	5.6	2.4	8.4	10.8	15.9	9.9	3.8	4.7
49	83470	West Valley City city, Utah	12.7	6.4	1.7	6.9	11.8	12.8	11.1	6.1	2.3
50	00000	**VERMONT**	11.5	3.4	2.3	4.8	8.6	28.3	9.5	4.3	4.8
50	10675	Burlington city, Vermont	12.1	2.1	2.8	2.8	12.8	35.0	18.1	4.8	2.3
51	00000	**VIRGINIA**	10.8	4.2	2.0	6.4	14.7	21.9	9.1	5.5	8.7
51	01000	Alexandria city, Virginia	9.0	3.8	3.1	7.1	18.1	16.2	9.7	7.1	17.0
51	01912	Annandale CDP, Virginia	7.1	4.8	1.0	3.5	21.5	22.0	9.7	9.8	9.3
51	03000	Arlington CDP, Virginia	3.7	1.8	2.9	9.2	27.9	15.1	6.5	6.5	17.6
51	03320	Ashburn CDP, Virginia	8.6	4.6	7.5	9.8	25.7	12.7	8.2	4.7	10.0
51	04088	Bailey's Crossroads CDP, Virginia	5.6	4.4	4.0	4.1	20.7	12.8	20.1	5.6	10.9
51	07784	Blacksburg town, Virginia	–	–	–	–	–	–	–	–	–
51	08472	Bon Air CDP, Virginia	21.0	1.7	0.3	10.0	10.3	24.2	7.6	5.7	3.7
51	11464	Burke CDP, Virginia	7.7	1.7	2.6	3.6	23.0	22.6	6.4	4.6	18.6
51	13720	Cave Spring CDP, Virginia	6.2	5.5	0.0	9.6	17.4	26.7	12.5	5.3	5.5
51	14440	Centreville CDP, Virginia	10.6	4.1	2.6	5.7	23.3	20.2	10.0	6.5	8.4
51	14744	Chantilly CDP, Virginia	6.3	3.9	3.7	5.8	28.3	16.6	7.9	4.8	7.3
51	14968	Charlottesville city, Virginia	6.8	2.9	2.7	3.9	12.5	37.4	15.9	6.3	2.6
51	15176	Cherry Hill CDP, Virginia	11.6	3.5	0.5	8.3	19.4	24.7	6.4	4.4	15.5
51	16000	Chesapeake city, Virginia	10.1	4.9	2.3	6.8	11.3	25.5	7.1	5.7	9.4
51	16096	Chester CDP, Virginia	10.9	6.1	1.1	5.9	11.7	18.2	9.8	1.8	12.8
51	16608	Christiansburg town, Virginia	10.7	4.3	2.5	2.8	14.7	35.5	9.6	2.2	2.3
51	21088	Dale City CDP, Virginia	10.9	6.5	2.2	5.1	15.6	17.0	10.8	6.3	10.2
51	21344	Danville city, Virginia	11.3	3.7	1.3	7.0	9.3	31.7	12.4	2.5	3.0
51	26496	Fairfax city, Virginia	13.8	5.5	0.9	5.5	18.1	21.4	9.2	6.8	10.2
51	26875	Fair Oaks CDP, Virginia	8.7	1.2	2.7	11.5	19.4	22.8	11.2	6.9	9.6
51	29136	Fort Hunt CDP, Virginia	7.1	0.8	1.7	4.1	24.0	19.5	4.5	5.3	26.2
51	29744	Fredericksburg city, Virginia	10.0	1.9	1.7	10.6	14.3	17.8	10.7	10.5	13.4
51	35000	Hampton city, Virginia	11.4	3.7	0.6	7.2	10.8	23.7	7.4	5.5	8.7
51	35624	Harrisonburg city, Virginia	10.1	1.6	3.3	3.9	9.1	28.2	20.6	4.6	1.6
51	36648	Herndon town, Virginia	6.7	2.8	3.1	5.5	35.6	11.0	10.1	5.1	6.8
51	38424	Hopewell city, Virginia	10.7	5.7	1.7	11.0	7.7	14.6	12.4	6.1	6.1
51	39448	Idylwood CDP, Virginia	10.0	3.5	1.8	5.9	26.9	13.7	11.9	9.2	8.4
51	43432	Lake Ridge CDP, Virginia	12.1	1.8	1.1	5.1	20.3	20.6	7.1	5.4	16.7
51	44280	Laurel CDP, Virginia	12.3	5.5	0.9	12.2	6.6	24.9	8.1	6.1	8.3
51	44984	Leesburg town, Virginia	9.6	5.7	3.0	4.4	19.9	20.4	10.6	3.4	6.5
51	45784	Lincolnia CDP, Virginia	7.8	3.1	2.1	6.4	21.0	15.8	9.2	9.1	11.3
51	45957	Linton Hall CDP, Virginia	9.5	3.9	1.7	6.4	19.9	18.9	9.4	4.5	15.2
51	47064	Lorton CDP, Virginia	8.3	2.6	0.0	3.2	14.4	25.0	15.4	12.1	12.0
51	47672	Lynchburg city, Virginia	10.0	1.8	2.9	3.9	11.4	37.5	13.7	2.6	3.8
51	48376	McLean CDP, Virginia	3.2	1.4	3.4	6.9	30.3	19.0	5.8	8.4	14.2
51	48952	Manassas city, Virginia	11.6	7.4	0.8	1.7	15.9	17.2	8.3	5.1	7.3
51	49792	Marumsco CDP, Virginia	12.9	4.7	2.5	2.7	11.8	19.3	13.4	6.6	9.6
51	50856	Mechanicsville CDP, Virginia	12.4	6.2	2.8	7.8	10.8	25.4	6.0	4.9	7.5
51	52658	Montclair CDP, Virginia	8.0	1.3	2.5	6.4	22.1	19.1	8.2	3.2	22.4
51	56000	Newport News city, Virginia	13.6	3.6	1.7	4.6	10.3	21.0	8.8	4.2	9.2
51	57000	Norfolk city, Virginia	11.0	5.8	2.0	6.6	10.2	20.4	14.2	4.2	10.1
51	58472	Oakton CDP, Virginia	2.5	2.2	2.2	9.7	28.5	21.5	11.5	5.2	11.2
51	61832	Petersburg city, Virginia	16.9	9.5	0.8	2.8	7.7	23.1	13.9	8.0	3.5
51	64000	Portsmouth city, Virginia	12.3	5.6	1.3	3.8	8.9	26.0	7.7	4.8	9.7
51	66672	Reston CDP, Virginia	5.9	2.8	3.7	8.5	30.2	18.0	8.4	4.4	8.6
51	67000	Richmond city, Virginia	10.8	3.5	1.4	8.3	14.4	25.7	12.4	6.0	6.2
51	68000	Roanoke city, Virginia	11.7	5.0	1.6	7.8	5.8	24.5	13.4	5.4	5.1
51	68880	Rose Hill CDP (Fairfax County), Virginia	13.0	4.4	3.6	6.3	16.6	18.9	6.6	6.9	11.9
51	70000	Salem city, Virginia	10.7	3.6	1.3	13.9	8.1	28.5	7.2	1.0	4.2
51	72272	Short Pump CDP, Virginia	8.3	2.9	1.4	12.9	17.2	26.2	11.1	2.9	5.2
51	74100	South Riding CDP, Virginia	9.0	1.8	7.3	9.1	32.4	16.2	4.0	4.3	6.0
51	74592	Springfield CDP, Virginia	11.6	6.4	1.9	6.7	22.4	13.9	8.1	13.3	7.7
51	75216	Staunton city, Virginia	15.1	3.7	1.2	5.1	8.2	25.8	14.5	3.4	1.6
51	75376	Sterling CDP, Virginia	13.3	4.6	2.4	5.8	22.5	13.0	15.3	7.2	5.1
51	76432	Suffolk city, Virginia	12.3	3.7	1.2	4.1	11.1	23.4	7.0	6.1	10.1
51	79560	Tuckahoe CDP, Virginia	13.8	6.6	0.6	13.2	12.7	22.7	10.1	5.9	3.5

Table E. Cities—Labor Force, Employment, and Educational Data, 2015—*Continued*

			Percent in each industry sector								
FIPS state code	FIPS place code	State/city	Retail trade	Transportation and warehousing, and utilities	Information	Finance and insurance, and real estate and rental and leasing	Professional, scientific, and management, and administrative and waste management services	Educational services, and health care and social assistance	Arts, entertainment, and recreation, and accommodation and food services	Other services, except public administration	Public administration
51	79952	Tysons Corner CDP, Virginia	7.9	1.4	4.4	2.1	41.9	13.5	6.3	3.5	12.0
51	82000	Virginia Beach city, Virginia	11.5	3.3	2.2	7.0	11.6	22.5	11.6	4.6	9.5
51	83680	Waynesboro city, Virginia	22.1	4.1	2.2	2.3	11.1	24.0	7.6	4.3	4.6
51	84368	West Falls Church CDP, Virginia	6.4	0.8	2.8	5.6	21.1	12.0	13.3	12.2	8.8
51	84976	West Springfield CDP, Virginia	5.8	1.1	2.0	7.4	25.4	15.6	8.6	7.8	21.8
51	86720	Winchester city, Virginia	12.8	8.2	4.4	5.8	5.1	22.8	11.9	3.2	1.4
51	87410	Woodlawn CDP (Fairfax County), Virginia	10.8	7.0	0.8	1.1	15.3	13.6	20.9	6.9	7.2
53	00000	**WASHINGTON**	11.7	5.4	2.2	5.4	12.5	21.3	9.3	4.7	5.1
53	03180	Auburn city, Washington	12.4	6.9	1.1	5.6	9.5	18.6	8.5	3.3	4.9
53	03736	Bainbridge Island city, Washington	9.0	6.6	1.6	10.6	21.9	22.6	7.4	6.0	4.8
53	05210	Bellevue city, Washington	10.5	4.9	5.5	6.7	25.6	15.7	10.6	3.9	1.8
53	05280	Bellingham city, Washington	13.6	4.9	2.6	4.9	8.4	27.1	12.7	4.9	5.6
53	07380	Bothell city, Washington	11.7	2.6	2.3	7.3	17.1	18.7	9.9	4.4	4.4
53	07395	Bothell West CDP, Washington	8.3	6.3	3.1	9.9	15.3	17.0	7.8	5.1	0.5
53	07695	Bremerton city, Washington	7.2	3.7	2.2	4.8	11.0	17.0	17.3	6.6	9.8
53	08552	Bryn Mawr-Skyway CDP, Washington	6.1	4.3	3.7	12.3	13.8	14.6	6.7	5.6	5.2
53	08850	Burien city, Washington	9.9	7.8	0.3	7.0	11.5	17.4	11.3	5.0	2.3
53	09480	Camas city, Washington	6.9	3.1	2.0	6.9	14.9	18.1	13.7	4.4	2.6
53	14940	Cottage Lake CDP, Washington	9.8	4.6	6.6	10.1	19.4	23.1	2.7	2.6	2.4
53	17635	Des Moines city, Washington	8.6	5.0	3.5	6.2	12.1	18.8	11.6	6.0	4.1
53	19630	Eastmont CDP, Washington	10.6	3.9	0.7	6.8	7.3	15.4	7.2	7.4	3.1
53	20750	Edmonds city, Washington	10.4	5.2	3.2	7.2	15.1	24.8	8.2	5.5	1.3
53	22640	Everett city, Washington	11.7	5.3	4.8	5.4	12.8	15.5	9.1	3.7	4.0
53	23160	Fairwood CDP (King County), Washington	11.7	3.7	1.7	4.0	10.1	28.9	10.9	7.3	2.0
53	23515	Federal Way city, Washington	11.4	8.3	1.3	3.5	10.8	21.2	9.8	4.7	4.7
53	24188	Five Corners CDP, Washington	8.2	7.2	1.5	10.0	7.3	15.0	9.2	7.2	3.9
53	27785	Graham CDP, Washington	14.2	7.3	1.1	6.1	8.6	17.1	7.6	5.8	5.2
53	33805	Issaquah city, Washington	14.4	2.9	5.6	9.0	26.1	15.2	9.8	2.2	0.9
53	35170	Kenmore city, Washington	8.1	1.2	3.5	7.4	22.2	27.3	3.1	5.3	3.1
53	35275	Kennewick city, Washington	12.7	2.6	1.9	5.9	11.3	23.5	9.7	5.5	3.4
53	35415	Kent city, Washington	12.7	10.8	1.7	4.3	12.5	20.5	8.1	4.5	4.1
53	35940	Kirkland city, Washington	8.7	2.5	3.6	9.4	23.8	17.0	7.4	3.6	4.5
53	36745	Lacey city, Washington	11.1	4.1	1.4	2.5	13.4	21.1	8.1	3.2	19.1
53	37900	Lake Stevens city, Washington	11.6	4.3	1.2	6.1	10.2	19.7	8.0	5.0	6.5
53	38038	Lakewood city, Washington	10.7	5.8	1.0	5.3	9.2	26.3	12.9	5.0	6.2
53	40245	Longview city, Washington	18.2	2.7	1.7	4.3	6.8	24.7	6.4	3.7	4.4
53	40840	Lynnwood city, Washington	12.7	5.2	1.2	5.8	12.3	20.7	12.1	7.7	1.6
53	43150	Maple Valley city, Washington	13.0	3.4	2.7	4.7	17.6	22.6	2.5	1.6	4.4
53	43955	Marysville city, Washington	12.3	4.6	0.9	4.8	7.5	17.0	10.5	4.9	4.9
53	45005	Mercer Island city, Washington	9.0	0.4	3.7	15.8	21.8	29.7	6.6	2.4	2.2
53	45865	Mill Creek city, Washington	18.6	3.5	0.7	5.9	18.5	20.7	5.2	3.7	2.8
53	45870	Mill Creek East CDP, Washington	11.6	8.9	5.0	11.5	12.5	18.6	4.8	4.7	2.0
53	47245	Moses Lake city, Washington	5.1	0.0	0.9	7.5	7.4	20.6	17.1	4.3	3.2
53	47490	Mountlake Terrace city, Washington	12.2	0.8	1.2	10.2	11.6	27.5	13.8	6.2	2.3
53	47560	Mount Vernon city, Washington	7.8	3.2	0.5	1.6	9.5	19.0	13.7	4.4	3.3
53	47735	Mukilteo city, Washington	12.2	3.7	1.7	8.0	16.0	16.9	2.2	2.4	3.1
53	50360	Oak Harbor city, Washington	16.7	4.0	0.4	5.4	6.3	20.4	6.8	7.8	14.8
53	51300	Olympia city, Washington	9.8	2.1	2.8	4.7	8.6	18.1	12.6	6.8	23.0
53	51795	Orchards CDP, Washington	8.2	8.4	0.7	3.0	5.5	19.4	16.7	3.7	6.0
53	53335	Parkland CDP, Washington	15.5	4.4	1.5	5.1	10.2	23.6	9.8	3.3	5.7
53	53545	Pasco city, Washington	8.6	6.8	0.8	4.4	9.0	16.4	16.0	3.4	4.4
53	56625	Pullman city, Washington	12.3	0.6	0.8	1.1	6.2	47.9	12.3	4.4	2.4
53	56695	Puyallup city, Washington	15.2	5.8	0.8	7.1	6.8	21.0	9.7	5.3	5.8
53	57535	Redmond city, Washington	8.9	1.9	8.9	2.5	40.1	11.6	6.9	4.1	2.4
53	57745	Renton city, Washington	16.0	7.0	1.5	4.8	13.4	19.7	7.7	4.0	4.8
53	58235	Richland city, Washington	11.4	7.7	1.0	2.9	23.1	23.4	8.0	2.7	5.3
53	61000	Salmon Creek CDP, Washington	4.8	10.3	0.0	8.5	10.6	25.1	6.6	4.7	3.2
53	61115	Sammamish city, Washington	15.3	0.7	5.5	8.6	33.0	13.1	5.3	3.1	1.9
53	62288	SeaTac city, Washington	9.2	18.9	0.0	3.3	8.4	16.6	14.6	6.1	5.0
53	63000	Seattle city, Washington	12.0	3.2	3.8	6.4	20.3	23.3	11.5	4.6	3.0
53	63960	Shoreline city, Washington	12.1	5.8	4.9	4.8	13.6	26.4	9.6	4.9	0.9
53	64380	Silver Firs CDP, Washington	11.5	3.5	5.2	8.1	8.1	20.8	7.4	6.3	3.1
53	65922	South Hill CDP, Washington	15.4	9.2	2.7	4.1	8.9	22.1	5.1	3.1	5.7
53	66255	Spanaway CDP, Washington	16.3	9.5	3.9	6.1	5.2	20.9	8.1	5.1	4.2
53	67000	Spokane city, Washington	11.6	3.2	1.6	7.0	8.6	30.5	11.8	6.0	3.5
53	67167	Spokane Valley city, Washington	15.1	5.4	1.2	8.6	10.9	22.2	6.2	4.2	3.3
53	70000	Tacoma city, Washington	10.4	6.3	2.1	4.0	9.6	24.8	12.3	4.9	7.5
53	72625	Tukwila city, Washington	10.7	13.7	0.0	3.1	11.4	18.5	9.8	2.7	3.0
53	73307	Union Hill-Novelty Hill CDP, Washington	12.5	3.7	6.0	9.3	27.3	12.8	5.3	6.9	2.6
53	73465	University Place city, Washington	14.8	5.8	0.2	5.9	7.4	33.7	8.6	5.7	5.5

Table E. Cities—Labor Force, Employment, and Educational Data, 2015—*Continued*

FIPS state code	FIPS place code	State/city	Retail trade	Transportation and warehousing, and utilities	Information	Finance and insurance, and real estate and rental and leasing	Professional, scientific, and management, and administrative and waste management services	Educational services, and health care and social assistance	Arts, entertainment, and recreation, and accommodation and food services	Other services, except public administration	Public administration
							Percent in each industry sector				
53	74060	Vancouver city, Washington	13.3	5.2	2.6	7.6	11.6	19.6	9.3	5.3	3.1
53	75775	Walla Walla city, Washington	11.7	2.0	1.0	4.2	8.8	29.2	14.8	3.0	6.2
53	77105	Wenatchee city, Washington	18.6	5.2	1.4	7.1	8.1	19.4	12.3	3.8	3.9
53	80010	Yakima city, Washington	9.4	8.9	1.4	2.6	6.3	25.1	7.5	6.2	3.9
54	00000	**WEST VIRGINIA**	12.2	5.3	1.5	4.0	8.0	28.6	9.4	4.2	6.7
54	14600	Charleston city, West Virginia	9.9	2.0	1.6	5.1	12.4	32.2	12.0	2.3	13.0
54	39460	Huntington city, West Virginia	11.2	1.3	2.4	2.6	9.5	38.7	13.8	4.3	3.2
54	55756	Morgantown city, West Virginia	9.9	0.8	1.4	3.6	5.4	49.3	11.6	2.4	6.4
54	62140	Parkersburg city, West Virginia	17.8	2.9	1.8	4.7	12.7	24.6	10.0	2.8	4.7
54	86452	Wheeling city, West Virginia	14.3	3.9	0.9	4.6	6.4	33.3	10.0	3.4	4.7
55	00000	**WISCONSIN**	11.4	4.4	1.5	6.0	8.2	23.1	8.9	4.1	3.4
55	02375	Appleton city, Wisconsin	11.8	4.5	1.2	6.5	9.2	20.3	12.1	4.0	3.8
55	06500	Beloit city, Wisconsin	11.6	2.6	2.5	1.6	6.2	22.7	8.2	3.7	3.1
55	10025	Brookfield city, Wisconsin	8.7	2.6	2.4	15.1	12.5	26.1	6.0	5.0	1.6
55	11950	Caledonia village, Wisconsin	8.8	6.3	0.0	5.3	11.0	19.9	7.3	4.3	3.3
55	19775	De Pere city, Wisconsin	10.9	10.2	1.3	12.1	8.9	18.9	8.0	1.0	2.2
55	22300	Eau Claire city, Wisconsin	16.2	4.6	1.3	5.3	5.2	30.6	9.3	3.7	2.8
55	25950	Fitchburg city, Wisconsin	10.9	0.8	3.7	5.8	17.6	31.5	5.9	4.4	4.5
55	26275	Fond du Lac city, Wisconsin	14.9	5.2	2.3	7.2	5.0	22.8	9.8	4.7	2.2
55	27300	Franklin city, Wisconsin	5.5	6.1	0.4	10.6	14.6	32.5	6.7	2.6	3.2
55	31000	Green Bay city, Wisconsin	14.3	4.8	1.1	6.4	10.2	17.6	10.4	4.0	2.4
55	31175	Greenfield city, Wisconsin	11.1	5.0	0.7	8.1	10.2	20.7	8.5	6.2	2.9
55	37825	Janesville city, Wisconsin	16.1	3.9	2.0	4.6	5.2	23.1	9.1	3.4	2.6
55	39225	Kenosha city, Wisconsin	13.3	6.6	1.6	4.5	6.2	23.9	9.1	4.1	3.3
55	40775	La Crosse city, Wisconsin	14.9	3.3	2.1	5.4	4.6	30.8	15.6	5.1	2.6
55	48000	Madison city, Wisconsin	8.2	2.9	3.0	6.4	15.5	30.7	12.9	4.7	4.8
55	48500	Manitowoc city, Wisconsin	15.1	5.0	1.3	6.1	7.2	17.8	6.9	2.1	2.5
55	51000	Menomonee Falls village, Wisconsin	12.0	4.1	1.7	9.1	10.5	20.4	5.5	3.3	1.2
55	51150	Mequon city, Wisconsin	8.0	1.4	3.4	13.6	20.4	21.4	4.9	2.4	4.3
55	53000	Milwaukee city, Wisconsin	9.6	4.1	1.5	5.3	10.2	27.4	12.0	4.0	3.4
55	54875	Mount Pleasant village, Wisconsin	8.3	7.5	1.9	5.9	7.4	20.8	8.4	3.9	3.7
55	55275	Muskego city, Wisconsin	10.4	5.5	1.2	3.5	12.3	18.3	5.6	6.7	1.3
55	55750	Neenah city, Wisconsin	8.5	4.6	1.0	8.2	13.6	22.7	7.8	3.8	1.3
55	56375	New Berlin city, Wisconsin	7.8	3.1	2.4	7.7	9.7	31.0	6.7	5.3	2.7
55	58800	Oak Creek city, Wisconsin	10.9	8.5	0.4	6.7	10.0	20.4	7.1	3.5	5.7
55	60500	Oshkosh city, Wisconsin	15.5	3.6	1.1	4.1	6.8	22.5	11.3	4.5	3.8
55	63300	Pleasant Prairie village, Wisconsin	9.8	7.0	0.5	3.5	12.5	23.6	6.3	3.5	1.3
55	66000	Racine city, Wisconsin	11.6	4.8	1.4	3.4	9.8	24.9	10.0	3.8	2.4
55	72975	Sheboygan city, Wisconsin	10.0	3.8	0.4	5.6	6.7	13.3	10.0	4.5	2.7
55	75125	South Milwaukee city, Wisconsin	13.4	10.5	2.1	7.7	7.1	18.0	6.6	12.2	1.9
55	77200	Stevens Point city, Wisconsin	17.5	5.2	1.5	9.2	7.2	23.9	15.0	3.9	1.4
55	78600	Sun Prairie city, Wisconsin	11.0	2.9	1.8	14.6	11.7	17.5	11.5	3.0	8.2
55	78650	Superior city, Wisconsin	14.1	9.4	0.6	5.5	4.8	27.7	12.1	5.1	5.1
55	83975	Watertown city, Wisconsin	10.1	2.7	2.2	1.7	4.2	22.6	9.1	2.9	3.1
55	84250	Waukesha city, Wisconsin	12.5	2.9	1.3	6.5	12.5	22.0	11.0	4.1	1.9
55	84475	Wausau city, Wisconsin	14.1	4.7	0.3	12.4	8.0	24.1	9.4	1.9	2.6
55	84675	Wauwatosa city, Wisconsin	8.6	2.2	3.0	7.5	11.7	33.3	9.0	3.9	2.8
55	85300	West Allis city, Wisconsin	13.5	2.9	2.3	5.8	6.9	22.5	8.6	3.4	2.1
55	85350	West Bend city, Wisconsin	15.2	4.4	0.5	9.2	5.4	18.8	9.4	1.7	3.6
56	00000	**WYOMING**	11.9	5.7	1.4	3.8	6.4	22.2	11.3	4.7	6.4
56	13150	Casper city, Wyoming	15.3	4.0	1.5	3.9	8.6	20.0	11.7	6.7	5.8
56	13900	Cheyenne city, Wyoming	14.9	5.8	2.4	7.8	9.2	21.9	9.9	2.1	13.8
56	31855	Gillette city, Wyoming	11.3	6.0	1.1	1.4	4.7	19.7	12.3	5.9	2.0
56	45050	Laramie city, Wyoming	15.5	1.8	1.6	2.7	5.7	40.8	12.6	4.9	5.6
56	67235	Rock Springs city, Wyoming	8.8	8.8	4.1	2.2	4.5	23.1	6.6	2.1	2.3

Table E. Cities—Labor Force, Employment, and Educational Data, 2015

| | | | Educational attainment of persons age 25 years and older | | | | Median earnings in the past 12 months (in 2015 Inflation-adjusted dollars) | | | | |
| | | | | | | | | Men with earnings | | Women with earnings | |
FIPS state code	FIPS place code	State/city	Total population age 25 years and older	Less than high school graduate	High school graduate (includes equivalency)	Some college or Associate's degree	Bachelor's degree or higher	All persons age 16 and older with earnings in the past 12 months	All men with earnings	Men who worked full-time, year-round in the past 12 months	All women with earnings	Women who worked full-time, year-round in the past 12 months
00	00000	**UNITED STATES**	216,447,163	12.9	27.6	29.0	30.6	$31,394	$36,979	$49,938	$26,316	$39,940
01	00000	**ALABAMA**	3,282,252	15.1	31.0	29.7	24.2	$28,262	$34,804	$45,057	$22,998	$34,310
01	00820	Alabaster city, Alabama	22,090	10.8	21.4	35.1	32.7	$36,809	$47,818	$51,516	$24,315	$40,605
01	00988	Albertville city, Alabama	14,391	26.2	32.5	32.0	9.2	$23,636	$25,570	$27,789	$18,968	$30,084
01	01852	Anniston city, Alabama	12,959	18.7	27.4	32.1	21.9	$16,389	$20,794	$51,209	$13,627	$22,574
01	02956	Athens city, Alabama	18,134	17.9	27.0	30.1	24.9	$25,394	$31,630	$50,734	$16,751	$30,609
01	03076	Auburn city, Alabama	28,853	6.3	8.5	28.4	56.8	$17,900	$18,239	$52,193	$17,670	$36,708
01	05980	Bessemer city, Alabama	18,276	16.5	41.1	30.2	12.2	$23,845	$22,474	$35,972	$24,868	$31,140
01	07000	Birmingham city, Alabama	146,295	12.9	29.2	32.6	25.3	$23,167	$26,193	$40,276	$21,438	$31,349
01	19648	Daphne city, Alabama	17,278	5.1	19.2	28.2	47.4	$35,929	$48,064	$55,810	$28,758	$45,785
01	20104	Decatur city, Alabama	38,205	16.4	23.6	33.7	26.2	$26,288	$27,340	$40,967	$25,141	$31,990
01	21184	Dothan city, Alabama	46,150	12.3	28.9	34.1	24.8	$27,297	$35,207	$43,529	$21,998	$31,317
01	24184	Enterprise city, Alabama	18,200	9.3	22.6	39.1	29.0	$27,934	$35,096	$47,003	$24,321	$29,360
01	26896	Florence city, Alabama	25,215	17.2	24.9	29.1	28.8	$22,394	$24,946	$41,279	$16,624	$33,750
01	28696	Gadsden city, Alabama	24,063	24.0	32.5	28.3	15.2	$23,318	$27,026	$32,396	$19,744	$24,839
01	35800	Homewood city, Alabama	16,306	4.1	16.4	26.5	53.0	$33,561	$37,461	$54,325	$31,309	$50,435
01	35896	Hoover city, Alabama	57,598	3.8	14.1	28.0	54.1	$41,773	$54,289	$62,412	$35,442	$47,225
01	37000	Huntsville city, Alabama	131,333	8.6	21.4	27.7	42.3	$27,452	$32,351	$50,612	$22,479	$36,620
01	45784	Madison city, Alabama	32,087	4.0	12.7	24.1	59.2	$55,902	$90,840	$99,828	$36,824	$46,195
01	50000	Mobile city, Alabama	133,825	13.4	29.0	29.3	28.3	$26,277	$32,383	$39,915	$22,424	$31,095
01	51000	Montgomery city, Alabama	131,409	14.5	25.2	28.7	31.7	$26,460	$31,300	$40,833	$22,121	$32,535
01	51696	Mountain Brook city, Alabama						$61,882	$102,488	$111,603	$36,761	$61,787
01	55200	Northport city, Alabama	15,576	8.8	23.7	22.0	45.5	$40,120	$45,226	$55,309	$30,092	$41,104
01	57048	Opelika city, Alabama	17,787	6.3	32.7	33.4	27.5	$25,832	$26,512	$42,206	$24,995	$35,815
01	57576	Oxford city, Alabama	14,083	20.2	30.3	30.4	19.1	$26,499	$41,549	$45,560	$20,981	$34,476
01	58848	Pelham city, Alabama	14,299	5.1	16.4	36.0	42.6	$39,466	$50,674	$64,205	$32,355	$46,172
01	59472	Phenix City city, Alabama	24,303	14.2	24.1	44.9	16.8	$23,376	$32,784	$38,445	$17,618	$21,809
01	62328	Prattville city, Alabama	23,600	14.8	32.8	22.1	30.4	$28,300	$38,522	$40,934	$20,747	$31,551
01	62496	Prichard city, Alabama	12,883	18.3	38.3	35.4	8.0	$24,512	$30,780	$35,558	$18,953	$29,042
01	76944	Trussville city, Alabama	12,737	3.1	19.5	37.5	39.8	$55,402	$65,956	$75,856	$43,073	$56,271
01	77256	Tuscaloosa city, Alabama	54,778	13.2	26.3	22.7	37.8	$20,522	$23,753	$47,073	$15,632	$36,788
01	78552	Vestavia Hills city, Alabama	24,402	4.4	10.8	20.8	64.0	$50,525	$62,329	$71,771	$38,322	$50,323
02	00000	**ALASKA**	469,523	7.4	27.3	35.7	29.7	$35,552	$41,430	$55,752	$29,648	$43,455
02	03000	Anchorage municipality, Alaska	190,006	5.7	24.1	34.6	35.6	$37,838	$43,799	$55,883	$32,350	$47,188
02	05000	Badger CDP, Alaska	11,913	0.8	20.2	55.6	23.4	$31,908	$42,317	$60,221	$28,960	$31,473
02	24230	Fairbanks city, Alaska	17,211	8.1	19.6	38.1	34.2	$28,558	$34,537	$41,827	$25,067	$40,375
02	36400	Juneau city and borough, Alaska	22,782	5.6	20.9	34.2	39.4	$41,599	$43,731	$52,323	$40,418	$55,850
04	00000	**ARIZONA**	4,536,954	13.9	24.5	33.9	27.7	$30,110	$32,726	$44,421	$25,860	$37,084
04	02830	Apache Junction city, Arizona	29,262	15.2	26.1	39.9	18.7	$28,187	$35,115	$45,884	$22,928	$32,111
04	04720	Avondale city, Arizona	46,656	12.2	26.3	42.6	18.9	$31,266	$36,334	$40,362	$27,671	$32,402
04	07940	Buckeye city, Arizona	39,266	15.4	22.7	46.8	15.1	$32,001	$36,418	$42,496	$27,835	$34,858
04	08220	Bullhead City city, Arizona	29,733	16.3	42.6	30.9	10.1	$19,104	$24,343	$31,846	$16,941	$31,168
04	10530	Casa Grande city, Arizona	34,081	19.7	26.5	37.8	16.0	$26,471	$28,252	$37,282	$22,952	$37,635
04	10670	Casas Adobes CDP, Arizona	47,426	6.3	18.6	39.8	35.3	$31,719	$40,307	$48,718	$25,839	$37,361
04	11230	Catalina Foothills CDP, Arizona	38,839	1.4	11.2	20.9	66.5	$45,835	$54,410	$86,734	$33,001	$57,485
04	12000	Chandler city, Arizona	172,466	7.0	16.9	32.9	43.2	$40,581	$48,879	$61,756	$34,196	$42,361
04	20540	Drexel Heights CDP, Arizona	17,598	18.8	34.4	37.7	9.1	$30,144	$37,007	$40,405	$25,248	$29,900
04	22220	El Mirage city, Arizona	18,379	14.3	36.6	32.7	16.4	$31,408	$31,507	$36,562	$31,123	$36,123
04	23620	Flagstaff city, Arizona	33,612	5.6	16.2	33.5	44.7	$18,256	$20,614	$51,280	$16,963	$36,888
04	23760	Florence town, Arizona	25,118	27.4	25.1	33.3	14.3	$18,935	$13,443	$34,327	$22,911	$27,530
04	25030	Fortuna Foothills CDP, Arizona	23,109	14.6	32.6	37.5	15.3	$35,565	$36,669	$45,872	$28,252	$39,703
04	25300	Fountain Hills town, Arizona	20,048	7.3	14.2	34.4	44.1	$42,806	$70,000	$89,222	$31,465	$49,470
04	27400	Gilbert town, Arizona	150,007	4.2	18.4	36.8	40.5	$40,867	$51,417	$62,072	$31,960	$44,613
04	27820	Glendale city, Arizona	153,520	17.5	26.2	34.9	21.3	$27,397	$30,562	$38,474	$24,279	$35,040
04	28380	Goodyear city, Arizona	53,953	7.0	19.9	43.0	30.1	$36,427	$40,244	$49,826	$31,931	$42,584
04	29710	Green Valley CDP, Arizona	20,937	2.0	21.6	33.1	43.2	$23,542	$38,060	$54,049	$17,334	$32,309
04	37620	Kingman city, Arizona	21,235	11.3	33.6	39.1	16.0	$26,899	$25,688	$41,795	$27,655	$32,065
04	39370	Lake Havasu City city, Arizona	42,254	11.2	36.9	38.3	13.6	$26,523	$30,106	$37,563	$24,477	$29,626
04	44270	Marana town, Arizona	26,901	8.9	14.8	31.2	45.1	$36,552	$52,804	$65,293	$25,998	$36,920
04	44410	Maricopa city, Arizona	29,997	9.7	29.6	39.1	21.7	$33,954	$43,397	$50,551	$24,884	$41,637
04	46000	Mesa city, Arizona	314,920	12.9	25.1	36.9	25.2	$28,566	$31,231	$40,805	$24,591	$37,216
04	49640	Nogales city, Arizona	12,454	40.4	33.8	17.5	8.4	$21,333	$28,190	$38,739	$15,527	$20,889
04	51600	Oro Valley town, Arizona	34,105	3.4	17.9	31.5	47.2	$36,225	$54,969	$67,189	$24,863	$45,712
04	54050	Peoria city, Arizona	110,871	7.0	25.4	38.1	29.4	$35,331	$40,666	$51,696	$29,131	$40,630
04	55000	Phoenix city, Arizona	995,646	19.8	24.6	28.9	26.6	$30,084	$31,644	$40,455	$26,941	$36,543
04	57380	Prescott city, Arizona	32,129	5.7	16.5	39.8	38.1	$24,734	$28,142	$45,074	$21,140	$35,614
04	57450	Prescott Valley town, Arizona	29,707	15.9	28.4	35.3	20.4	$24,228	$30,322	$37,699	$18,056	$41,534
04	58150	Queen Creek town, Arizona	18,975	5.6	19.3	33.0	42.2	$51,406	$70,991	$86,753	$35,147	$54,856

Table E. Cities—Labor Force, Employment, and Educational Data, 2015—*Continued*

FIPS state code	FIPS place code	State/city	Total population age 25 years and older	Less than high school graduate	High school graduate (includes equivalency)	Some college or Associate's degree	Bachelor's degree or higher	All persons age 16 and older with earnings in the past 12 months	All men with earnings	Men who worked full-time, year-round in the past 12 months	All women with earnings	Women who worked full-time, year-round in the past 12 months
									Men with earnings		Women with earnings	
04	62140	Sahuarita town, Arizona	17,116	3.5	19.7	43.3	33.6	$37,807	$51,630	$55,350	$30,701	$37,143
04	63470	San Luis city, Arizona	16,467	67.3	8.5	15.8	8.3	$16,387	$21,426	$26,766	$13,151	$26,523
04	64210	San Tan Valley CDP, Arizona	47,702	10.3	28.2	46.4	15.1	$32,111	$40,335	$50,227	$27,658	$40,476
04	65000	Scottsdale city, Arizona	184,631	5.4	13.0	26.5	55.1	$46,688	$55,507	$66,691	$40,790	$52,500
04	66820	Sierra Vista city, Arizona	28,004	7.2	14.6	50.6	27.6	$34,105	$46,542	$53,615	$29,108	$34,978
04	70320	Sun City CDP, Arizona	41,973	8.1	38.5	32.6	20.8	$18,765	$19,462	$45,799	$18,697	$29,594
04	70355	Sun City West CDP, Arizona	24,450	6.1	26.4	36.0	31.5	$12,813	$13,321	$84,447	$9,943	$35,720
04	71510	Surprise city, Arizona	85,451	7.7	26.9	39.1	26.3	$35,645	$41,337	$48,404	$30,433	$37,923
04	73000	Tempe city, Arizona	102,347	7.7	16.0	32.4	43.8	$26,155	$30,036	$44,406	$23,008	$36,336
04	77000	Tucson city, Arizona	331,389	16.8	24.2	32.6	26.5	$21,785	$23,341	$36,718	$20,324	$31,553
04	85540	Yuma city, Arizona	58,611	22.3	24.5	35.2	18.0	$25,696	$29,288	$36,987	$21,174	$33,536
05	00000	**ARKANSAS**	1,987,819	14.6	34.1	29.5	21.8	$26,798	$31,104	$40,570	$22,642	$32,003
05	04840	Bella Vista city, Arkansas	21,574	2.7	25.8	34.4	37.1	$32,279	$39,996	$56,844	$30,193	$37,254
05	05290	Benton city, Arkansas	23,005	14.0	31.2	27.9	26.9	$26,778	$26,459	$37,132	$27,306	$40,945
05	05320	Bentonville city, Arkansas	27,684	8.9	22.9	22.3	45.9	$41,192	$61,607	$66,449	$31,986	$41,977
05	10300	Cabot city, Arkansas	16,626	11.9	24.7	38.3	25.1	$37,736	$42,602	$48,635	$30,640	$44,606
05	15190	Conway city, Arkansas	37,392	5.6	21.3	34.4	38.7	$24,022	$27,136	$40,850	$17,762	$39,198
05	23290	Fayetteville city, Arkansas	46,034	7.8	13.5	30.2	48.5	$25,390	$27,402	$42,136	$20,913	$38,314
05	24550	Fort Smith city, Arkansas	57,680	22.3	30.3	28.4	19.0	$23,705	$28,722	$32,804	$18,533	$28,196
05	33400	Hot Springs city, Arkansas	25,801	14.6	28.1	37.1	20.2	$17,811	$20,457	$27,600	$16,106	$36,569
05	34750	Jacksonville city, Arkansas	16,658	15.0	25.6	38.3	21.1	$28,442	$30,197	$36,389	$26,993	$38,050
05	35710	Jonesboro city, Arkansas	45,336	8.1	29.8	33.1	29.1	$24,224	$26,883	$38,287	$20,146	$32,078
05	41000	Little Rock city, Arkansas	133,452	9.2	21.6	29.4	39.7	$30,495	$31,971	$42,489	$28,072	$38,540
05	50450	North Little Rock city, Arkansas	41,627	16.8	29.5	29.0	24.6	$27,392	$26,655	$36,509	$29,015	$36,205
05	53390	Paragould city, Arkansas	17,966	15.7	46.0	25.4	12.9	$24,035	$31,061	$40,052	$16,966	$33,667
05	55310	Pine Bluff city, Arkansas	27,045	15.2	39.2	31.3	14.3	$23,174	$24,212	$38,222	$22,611	$31,846
05	60410	Rogers city, Arkansas	41,263	15.1	28.7	22.1	34.1	$32,104	$34,761	$40,471	$28,866	$32,330
05	61670	Russellville city, Arkansas	15,132	15.7	29.9	26.9	27.4	$14,093	$16,960	$37,370	$12,143	$27,301
05	63020	Searcy city, Arkansas	13,247	9.8	35.0	22.9	32.2	$14,667	$14,291	$38,490	$14,909	$26,156
05	63800	Sherwood city, Arkansas	20,826	8.0	28.6	34.2	29.2	$32,321	$40,025	$43,558	$30,404	$36,415
05	66080	Springdale city, Arkansas	48,055	24.5	31.2	21.9	22.4	$26,962	$27,755	$32,845	$24,489	$30,634
05	68810	Texarkana city, Arkansas	21,598	15.1	39.2	29.5	16.2	$22,999	$30,326	$37,165	$17,925	$30,678
05	71480	Van Buren city, Arkansas	15,019	12.9	34.4	29.5	23.2	$27,928	$36,007	$39,959	$21,535	$36,119
05	74540	West Memphis city, Arkansas	14,822	18.3	40.9	25.0	15.8	$24,170	$23,196	$35,214	$24,436	$35,446
06	00000	**CALIFORNIA**	26,085,263	17.8	20.8	29.1	32.3	$31,733	$36,556	$50,562	$27,038	$43,335
06	00296	Adelanto city, California	17,400	39.9	21.6	33.1	5.4	$21,585	$26,069	$35,568	$17,384	$23,162
06	00394	Agoura Hills city, California	14,654	7.8	18.6	21.9	51.7	$65,929	$100,010	$101,386	$35,304	$78,125
06	00562	Alameda city, California	58,780	7.1	12.3	26.1	54.5	$51,453	$54,597	$68,466	$50,294	$63,068
06	00884	Alhambra city, California	65,048	15.9	28.8	20.5	34.7	$31,091	$33,890	$41,658	$28,098	$36,233
06	00947	Aliso Viejo city, California	34,171	2.4	10.8	32.3	54.5	$52,365	$69,836	$83,436	$42,771	$60,953
06	01290	Altadena CDP, California	35,111	10.3	16.9	29.0	43.7	$35,215	$46,781	$71,335	$30,613	$52,810
06	01640	American Canyon city, California	13,988	12.7	17.4	43.8	26.1	$40,102	$44,613	$61,806	$28,019	$51,184
06	02000	Anaheim city, California	226,279	25.8	23.6	27.4	23.2	$27,614	$30,878	$37,962	$24,460	$38,901
06	02210	Antelope CDP, California	30,459	6.6	25.5	42.7	25.2	$41,172	$47,017	$51,974	$30,264	$45,252
06	02252	Antioch city, California	68,754	12.7	25.7	42.2	19.5	$33,540	$46,353	$58,615	$23,590	$42,062
06	02364	Apple Valley town, California	43,155	14.0	33.1	34.0	18.9	$26,423	$31,572	$50,505	$21,657	$40,242
06	02462	Arcadia city, California	42,102	8.2	15.4	23.5	52.9	$46,781	$51,024	$70,911	$44,053	$66,471
06	02553	Arden-Arcade CDP, California	71,326	9.7	21.5	34.9	33.8	$29,269	$31,339	$47,033	$26,460	$46,038
06	02924	Arvin city, California	11,952	71.3	17.6	8.9	2.3	$18,255	$18,964	$19,984	$14,632	$20,203
06	02980	Ashland CDP, California	16,317	22.9	19.3	38.5	19.3	$32,337	$37,949	$44,538	$26,787	$37,068
06	03064	Atascadero city, California	21,733	5.6	17.7	44.3	32.4	$40,959	$46,846	$60,935	$26,414	$49,080
06	03162	Atwater city, California	16,676	23.8	30.4	33.2	12.6	$22,064	$28,440	$38,956	$20,188	$26,215
06	03386	Azusa city, California	29,541	17.3	30.0	31.4	21.3	$25,525	$30,650	$39,907	$17,995	$36,205
06	03526	Bakersfield city, California	220,726	20.7	28.8	29.1	21.4	$30,859	$38,958	$48,557	$22,887	$35,658
06	03666	Baldwin Park city, California	50,201	34.3	31.1	20.6	13.9	$25,558	$27,278	$33,033	$23,293	$28,752
06	03820	Banning city, California	20,729	18.6	35.6	31.4	14.4	$25,557	$30,069	$42,144	$20,646	$27,157
06	04030	Barstow city, California	12,197	20.5	33.3	36.4	9.8	$19,753	$31,024	$51,302	$14,974	$25,556
06	04415	Bay Point CDP, California	16,505	34.7	27.2	28.4	9.7	$26,489	$31,952	$41,323	$18,194	$34,971
06	04758	Beaumont city, California	28,771	16.5	28.0	33.7	21.8	$33,772	$40,868	$49,773	$31,037	$42,231
06	04870	Bell city, California	21,075	52.6	23.8	16.1	7.5	$19,373	$23,430	$27,300	$15,438	$26,385
06	04982	Bellflower city, California	46,671	24.2	26.6	29.5	19.6	$32,062	$35,116	$41,150	$28,755	$40,207
06	04996	Bell Gardens city, California	24,095	53.2	25.6	15.1	6.1	$21,039	$24,088	$27,595	$18,348	$21,997
06	05108	Belmont city, California	19,772	5.4	9.3	24.6	60.7	$71,665	$95,589	$131,276	$50,278	$81,549
06	05290	Benicia city, California	20,790	3.0	17.1	31.7	48.2	$51,522	$60,342	$77,594	$43,821	$66,161
06	06000	Berkeley city, California	78,172	4.2	5.7	16.9	73.1	$32,156	$41,055	$78,462	$25,462	$55,808
06	06308	Beverly Hills city, California	24,569	4.5	10.3	18.5	66.8	$65,588	$82,408	$100,749	$50,878	$70,040
06	07064	Bloomington CDP, California	12,345	38.3	25.6	25.8	10.3	$26,796	$30,276	$34,606	$20,969	$31,159

Table E. Cities—Labor Force, Employment, and Educational Data, 2015—*Continued*

| | | | Educational attainment of persons age 25 years and older | | | | | Median earnings in the past 12 months (in 2015 Inflation-adjusted dollars) | | | | |
| | | | | | | | | | Men with earnings | | Women with earnings | |
FIPS state code	FIPS place code	State/city	Total population age 25 years and older	Less than high school graduate	High school graduate (includes equivalency)	Some college or Associate's degree	Bachelor's degree or higher	All persons age 16 and older with earnings in the past 12 months	All men with earnings	Men who worked full-time, year-round in the past 12 months	All women with earnings	Women who worked full-time, year-round in the past 12 months
06	08058	Brawley city, California	17,262	32.7	20.8	36.9	9.7	$20,219	$24,468	$48,657	$14,780	$30,529
06	08100	Brea city, California	27,883	7.6	12.6	31.7	48.2	$50,146	$60,572	$80,093	$41,727	$52,109
06	08142	Brentwood city, California	38,349	6.3	20.8	46.4	26.5	$45,248	$51,229	$76,838	$31,767	$50,535
06	08786	Buena Park city, California	55,156	18.8	20.2	30.1	30.8	$31,935	$33,930	$41,509	$30,946	$45,590
06	08954	Burbank city, California	74,116	8.7	18.4	34.4	38.4	$42,858	$46,895	$65,477	$40,750	$60,003
06	09066	Burlingame city, California	22,057	5.4	16.3	23.0	55.3	$51,151	$71,336	$96,027	$43,615	$60,803
06	09598	Calabasas city, California	15,175	4.3	14.1	23.3	58.3	$42,043	$70,002	$86,913	$37,594	$49,477
06	09710	Calexico city, California	23,217	37.1	16.6	28.6	17.6	$25,321	$31,822	$42,865	$17,988	$30,953
06	10046	Camarillo city, California	47,454	10.2	13.5	35.2	41.2	$40,667	$50,822	$63,531	$29,216	$49,214
06	10256	Cameron Park CDP, California	14,244	11.1	23.6	41.9	23.4	$42,253	$47,712	$66,790	$41,036	$65,724
06	10345	Campbell city, California	29,672	7.2	14.1	24.3	54.3	$60,229	$70,931	$81,700	$47,136	$61,667
06	11194	Carlsbad city, California	79,397	4.4	13.3	27.6	54.8	$48,754	$66,632	$80,492	$36,541	$72,062
06	11390	Carmichael CDP, California	44,791	8.2	21.8	38.0	31.9	$30,788	$37,327	$50,905	$28,454	$41,485
06	11530	Carson city, California	66,270	20.9	22.3	30.1	26.8	$33,544	$36,967	$48,572	$30,968	$48,450
06	11796	Castaic CDP, California	12,964	9.2	20.5	38.6	31.7	$41,875	$60,165	$77,614	$30,546	$51,742
06	11964	Castro Valley CDP, California	44,306	8.4	21.9	28.1	41.6	$50,100	$51,035	$65,097	$48,821	$56,610
06	12048	Cathedral City city, California	34,550	25.1	28.6	29.0	17.3	$22,706	$23,895	$27,751	$20,752	$34,000
06	12524	Ceres city, California	28,664	34.6	26.9	31.5	7.0	$25,331	$30,221	$38,149	$20,646	$27,203
06	12552	Cerritos city, California	36,264	6.9	11.7	28.5	52.9	$48,696	$55,451	$62,388	$40,128	$52,050
06	13014	Chico city, California	52,528	7.1	16.0	36.8	40.1	$22,059	$24,956	$44,321	$18,443	$41,939
06	13210	Chino city, California	59,901	24.9	24.1	34.0	17.0	$26,849	$35,020	$53,214	$23,482	$37,284
06	13214	Chino Hills city, California	55,055	7.5	14.9	34.5	43.1	$46,891	$52,110	$72,288	$41,191	$53,972
06	13392	Chula Vista city, California	169,025	17.7	18.8	33.7	29.8	$32,347	$38,517	$48,818	$27,639	$44,479
06	13588	Citrus Heights city, California	60,046	8.8	27.7	45.1	18.4	$31,198	$31,439	$41,500	$30,676	$42,326
06	13756	Claremont city, California	23,489	6.5	16.0	21.2	56.3	$31,804	$40,749	$71,980	$28,018	$58,244
06	14218	Clovis city, California	70,261	7.9	21.6	40.7	29.8	$33,585	$42,408	$60,062	$27,453	$45,467
06	14260	Coachella city, California	27,124	49.0	28.3	17.9	4.7	$20,655	$21,269	$23,403	$19,680	$25,098
06	14890	Colton city, California	34,505	22.0	31.5	33.8	12.7	$29,105	$31,638	$36,217	$25,342	$32,115
06	15044	Compton city, California	56,762	41.1	25.8	23.5	9.6	$22,487	$24,183	$27,558	$20,357	$31,949
06	16000	Concord city, California	92,753	13.3	19.6	33.6	33.5	$38,128	$41,207	$61,777	$32,920	$51,054
06	16224	Corcoran city, California	16,197	40.0	31.1	26.4	2.5	$14,549	$26,745	$37,808	$9,842	$21,162
06	16350	Corona city, California	109,374	14.2	25.5	32.8	27.6	$35,592	$45,272	$52,379	$25,612	$41,896
06	16378	Coronado city, California	16,624	4.6	12.1	18.4	64.9	$38,712	$34,719	$50,919	$39,274	$70,287
06	16532	Costa Mesa city, California	79,858	16.2	13.5	30.0	40.3	$40,177	$41,860	$54,574	$35,758	$46,563
06	16742	Covina city, California	30,970	15.7	21.4	36.0	26.8	$32,265	$40,832	$48,352	$26,764	$33,472
06	17498	Cudahy city, California	14,131	54.6	22.5	18.6	4.3	$19,229	$21,039	$25,092	$17,451	$20,502
06	17568	Culver City city, California	29,573	7.0	11.6	26.9	54.6	$46,499	$50,503	$56,340	$44,359	$60,971
06	17610	Cupertino city, California	40,262	2.9	4.6	15.2	77.2	$108,013	$142,160	$156,492	$63,587	$90,314
06	17750	Cypress city, California	34,762	7.6	23.8	30.9	37.8	$36,181	$47,356	$60,101	$30,524	$41,863
06	17918	Daly City city, California	79,292	13.3	18.4	32.8	35.6	$35,602	$37,990	$47,974	$32,025	$50,348
06	17946	Dana Point city, California	27,474	5.8	11.7	41.1	41.4	$40,388	$57,179	$81,830	$28,343	$53,462
06	17988	Danville town, California	28,076	2.1	7.3	19.6	71.0	$81,709	$110,511	$141,111	$50,995	$81,710
06	18100	Davis city, California	35,312	1.4	4.9	13.7	80.0	$21,980	$29,476	$69,757	$15,000	$61,897
06	18394	Delano city, California	31,278	42.4	29.2	20.5	7.8	$15,458	$16,110	$27,651	$14,016	$27,318
06	18996	Desert Hot Springs city, California	17,187	28.5	35.0	26.8	9.7	$18,186	$21,235	$31,574	$15,565	$26,885
06	19192	Diamond Bar city, California	39,692	5.8	13.1	23.9	57.2	$41,517	$51,319	$64,634	$31,888	$52,171
06	19318	Dinuba city, California	13,517	35.3	25.8	28.0	10.9	$21,708	$24,406	$31,293	$20,842	$31,605
06	19766	Downey city, California	76,268	24.2	21.5	34.1	20.2	$31,276	$35,051	$41,283	$27,684	$37,489
06	19990	Duarte city, California	16,064	14.4	25.1	34.5	26.0	$36,579	$44,220	$49,088	$30,583	$36,813
06	20018	Dublin city, California	40,202	6.9	13.2	18.9	61.0	$71,820	$81,002	$92,408	$60,536	$77,049
06	20802	East Los Angeles CDP, California	73,972	52.6	20.5	18.3	8.6	$24,028	$25,648	$28,953	$21,818	$27,995
06	20956	East Palo Alto city, California	17,429	34.6	23.1	23.2	19.0	$26,747	$27,632	$30,750	$24,407	$33,203
06	21230	Eastvale city, California	34,557	10.0	25.6	26.9	37.6	$37,315	$47,372	$58,455	$30,932	$51,535
06	21712	El Cajon city, California	66,029	18.0	28.8	34.1	19.2	$25,972	$27,844	$37,406	$23,278	$35,889
06	21782	El Centro city, California	25,009	34.5	18.2	27.9	19.4	$21,580	$25,132	$45,873	$15,632	$31,664
06	21796	El Cerrito city, California	19,839	6.8	11.0	21.4	60.9	$50,049	$55,518	$77,172	$41,993	$63,333
06	21880	El Dorado Hills CDP, California	30,461	2.6	12.4	27.4	57.7	$62,209	$75,390	$102,407	$47,979	$84,767
06	22020	Elk Grove city, California	105,494	9.3	18.3	36.1	36.3	$40,939	$42,285	$61,178	$38,412	$54,753
06	22230	El Monte city, California	78,371	43.0	26.6	17.1	13.2	$22,414	$24,760	$27,408	$21,285	$22,734
06	22300	El Paso de Robles (Paso Robles) city, California	19,802	15.5	22.0	42.1	20.3	$29,334	$40,278	$41,497	$23,270	$31,103
06	22678	Encinitas city, California	48,545	3.8	7.9	27.0	61.3	$49,843	$53,276	$80,166	$41,265	$66,817
06	22804	Escondido city, California	98,103	23.8	19.0	34.2	23.0	$24,537	$29,848	$40,539	$19,785	$35,494
06	23042	Eureka city, California	19,903	16.5	24.4	35.3	23.8	$22,202	$25,166	$31,093	$21,834	$23,781
06	23182	Fairfield city, California	72,458	13.3	23.6	36.6	26.5	$34,347	$40,004	$55,155	$28,094	$42,816
06	23294	Fair Oaks CDP, California	21,893	7.7	12.6	35.7	44.1	$39,567	$37,492	$73,719	$39,579	$61,282
06	23462	Fallbrook CDP, California	20,807	12.9	21.8	42.8	22.5	$30,349	$35,559	$42,321	$23,835	$36,089
06	24477	Florence-Graham CDP, California	38,673	58.3	21.3	13.4	7.0	$19,588	$21,883	$25,673	$17,268	$23,628
06	24498	Florin CDP, California	31,660	27.1	24.5	33.1	15.3	$21,662	$26,424	$36,694	$16,606	$35,965

Table E. Cities—Labor Force, Employment, and Educational Data, 2015—*Continued*

| | | | | | | | | Median earnings in the past 12 months (in 2015 Inflation-adjusted dollars) | | | | |
| | | | Educational attainment of persons age 25 years and older | | | | | | Men with earnings | | Women with earnings | |
FIPS state code	FIPS place code	State/city	Total population age 25 years and older	Less than high school graduate	High school graduate (includes equivalency)	Some college or Associate's degree	Bachelor's degree or higher	All persons age 16 and older with earnings in the past 12 months	All men with earnings	Men who worked full-time, year-round in the past 12 months	All women with earnings	Women who worked full-time, year-round in the past 12 months
06	24638	Folsom city, California	54,414	5.9	15.6	26.0	52.5	$60,779	$80,280	$93,557	$47,006	$66,230
06	24680	Fontana city, California	119,225	29.2	29.1	27.8	13.9	$26,820	$31,671	$41,427	$22,047	$35,634
06	24722	Foothill Farms CDP, California	22,007	12.2	37.4	33.2	17.2	$26,707	$28,063	$38,418	$24,055	$42,148
06	25338	Foster City city, California	23,647	3.2	6.5	19.0	71.3	$90,699	$106,546	$121,903	$71,667	$92,350
06	25380	Fountain Valley city, California	41,292	7.9	13.7	32.3	46.1	$41,573	$50,285	$65,723	$36,516	$51,921
06	26000	Fremont city, California	163,064	5.5	20.4	20.2	54.0	$60,994	$75,996	$90,529	$49,290	$62,312
06	26067	French Valley CDP, California	19,809	5.8	21.9	44.3	28.0	$60,110	$75,234	$86,972	$35,182	$60,283
06	27000	Fresno city, California	307,534	24.5	23.7	32.5	19.3	$22,878	$25,164	$38,395	$21,159	$38,498
06	28000	Fullerton city, California	91,548	16.5	16.3	26.9	40.3	$30,550	$35,868	$50,797	$22,562	$40,923
06	28112	Galt city, California	15,019	14.2	36.0	33.6	16.2	$36,522	$45,102	$51,833	$30,997	$51,975
06	28168	Gardena city, California	42,536	19.2	24.4	32.7	23.7	$30,016	$31,641	$37,175	$27,279	$43,313
06	29000	Garden Grove city, California	119,295	27.8	26.6	26.8	18.9	$25,723	$29,278	$36,058	$22,088	$36,589
06	29504	Gilroy city, California	32,806	23.9	19.5	34.7	21.9	$28,415	$39,711	$56,150	$19,085	$40,806
06	30000	Glendale city, California	153,031	13.9	20.3	26.4	39.4	$33,013	$38,091	$56,474	$30,492	$47,599
06	30014	Glendora city, California	35,144	8.3	16.0	37.7	38.0	$40,005	$50,354	$76,113	$34,595	$56,902
06	30378	Goleta city, California	21,456	3.2	19.6	27.2	49.9	$41,049	$56,413	$70,045	$31,387	$46,514
06	30693	Granite Bay CDP, California	15,162	2.9	12.4	30.9	53.9	$60,352	$77,137	$101,227	$41,188	$64,788
06	31596	Hacienda Heights CDP, California	42,007	14.1	23.1	28.9	33.9	$40,797	$50,222	$52,416	$33,606	$42,149
06	31960	Hanford city, California	34,980	20.6	22.2	34.8	22.3	$31,900	$36,377	$46,071	$26,220	$42,099
06	32548	Hawthorne city, California	57,414	25.7	27.6	30.1	16.6	$23,735	$25,102	$35,309	$22,666	$32,466
06	33000	Hayward city, California	106,912	17.3	30.3	26.9	25.5	$36,041	$40,893	$47,111	$30,665	$39,766
06	33182	Hemet city, California	52,243	20.9	30.5	38.5	10.0	$22,859	$30,714	$40,450	$19,493	$32,814
06	33308	Hercules city, California	18,584	5.0	12.6	34.0	48.4	$46,326	$47,312	$66,458	$45,692	$65,446
06	33434	Hesperia city, California	53,476	20.8	37.6	31.0	10.6	$25,542	$31,129	$42,952	$20,837	$31,283
06	33588	Highland city, California	33,999	22.9	24.2	33.4	19.4	$31,719	$40,448	$50,692	$25,492	$42,485
06	34120	Hollister city, California	23,523	26.4	24.0	34.7	14.9	$31,011	$40,880	$42,929	$22,238	$33,758
06	36000	Huntington Beach city, California	147,750	8.0	17.3	33.0	41.8	$41,379	$46,075	$61,514	$36,296	$57,926
06	36056	Huntington Park city, California	34,629	58.8	19.7	16.5	5.0	$20,464	$22,117	$25,938	$17,179	$22,209
06	36294	Imperial Beach city, California	16,537	18.0	22.5	40.0	19.4	$27,373	$35,499	$41,966	$20,577	$36,104
06	36448	Indio city, California	56,137	22.7	30.5	29.8	17.1	$26,400	$30,764	$40,020	$22,351	$35,431
06	36546	Inglewood city, California	73,306	26.7	20.6	34.8	17.9	$24,354	$24,276	$31,655	$24,484	$36,033
06	36770	Irvine city, California	167,677	3.4	8.3	19.3	69.1	$55,790	$71,147	$85,779	$41,003	$71,267
06	36868	Isla Vista CDP, California	2,449	19.9	16.5	5.6	58.0	$3,463	$3,528	$27,136	$3,413	$30,172
06	37692	Jurupa Valley city, California	61,778	31.2	28.0	28.1	12.7	$25,627	$27,950	$41,521	$20,872	$29,008
06	39003	La Cañada Flintridge city, California	14,379	1.5	5.5	16.0	77.0	$70,636	$100,256	$120,977	$45,968	$77,111
06	39114	Ladera Ranch CDP, California	16,402	7.6	9.0	24.3	59.2	$68,327	$104,390	$130,464	$43,934	$66,222
06	39122	Lafayette city, California	18,447	1.9	7.5	15.0	75.6	$72,987	$110,503	$147,256	$43,558	$100,040
06	39178	Laguna Beach city, California	16,823	1.3	7.6	22.1	68.9	$64,542	$91,076	$121,454	$39,951	$70,698
06	39220	Laguna Hills city, California	23,531	6.2	10.3	31.7	51.9	$32,245	$37,338	$70,438	$31,182	$61,313
06	39248	Laguna Niguel city, California	48,154	3.8	13.4	30.9	52.0	$40,367	$56,404	$86,773	$33,923	$50,770
06	39290	La Habra city, California	39,003	15.1	27.9	28.1	28.8	$31,095	$37,232	$45,552	$23,166	$40,687
06	39486	Lake Elsinore city, California	35,417	30.6	24.1	30.8	14.5	$30,257	$36,897	$45,897	$22,749	$47,848
06	39496	Lake Forest city, California	58,425	7.8	15.1	30.8	46.3	$48,454	$55,894	$76,745	$38,971	$59,973
06	39766	Lakeside CDP, California	15,557	8.2	33.1	42.1	16.6	$31,724	$38,093	$55,979	$28,119	$42,039
06	39892	Lakewood city, California	56,752	10.1	24.1	35.1	30.6	$41,458	$50,754	$60,792	$35,624	$51,732
06	40004	La Mesa city, California	43,287	9.6	20.4	37.2	32.8	$34,969	$43,259	$51,478	$28,376	$39,316
06	40032	La Mirada city, California	34,115	11.3	27.1	33.5	28.1	$36,535	$45,198	$60,135	$31,009	$46,220
06	40130	Lancaster city, California	99,135	15.0	29.6	40.1	15.2	$35,094	$42,024	$45,415	$30,531	$35,547
06	40326	La Presa CDP, California	27,420	18.6	25.6	40.6	15.3	$26,222	$29,539	$35,667	$21,890	$33,998
06	40340	La Puente city, California	25,771	41.7	27.0	22.9	8.3	$24,574	$30,336	$34,991	$21,365	$30,112
06	40354	La Quinta city, California	28,429	10.3	21.4	30.9	37.3	$32,729	$45,837	$72,074	$25,357	$50,302
06	40704	Lathrop city, California	13,130	27.1	25.3	30.7	16.9	$30,097	$30,567	$41,826	$29,349	$36,919
06	40830	La Verne city, California	22,795	12.6	13.7	38.2	35.6	$34,269	$46,683	$60,568	$30,421	$41,710
06	40886	Lawndale city, California	22,581	29.0	25.8	28.6	16.6	$24,308	$31,524	$40,370	$18,576	$34,180
06	41124	Lemon Grove city, California	18,449	17.0	24.2	39.0	19.8	$26,482	$31,284	$40,547	$19,809	$30,528
06	41152	Lemoore city, California	14,018	13.5	21.7	39.7	25.1	$31,787	$39,341	$43,936	$26,433	$35,383
06	41180	Lennox CDP, California	11,968	45.3	27.1	17.4	10.1	$21,799	$25,026	$28,268	$17,186	$26,081
06	41474	Lincoln city, California	33,343	13.2	18.4	37.5	30.9	$40,896	$50,933	$70,783	$31,524	$50,471
06	41992	Livermore city, California	59,740	6.8	16.2	34.7	42.3	$51,407	$66,332	$87,936	$41,857	$61,227
06	42202	Lodi city, California	41,738	15.1	29.1	38.7	17.1	$30,691	$33,413	$42,813	$25,750	$38,900
06	42370	Loma Linda city, California	17,011	10.6	19.6	24.5	45.3	$38,990	$48,010	$60,305	$34,016	$53,357
06	42468	Lomita city, California	13,793	12.7	24.6	35.0	27.7	$31,544	$49,651	$62,291	$18,431	$41,061
06	42524	Lompoc city, California	29,607	24.5	26.5	38.6	10.5	$25,640	$27,725	$31,968	$18,942	$31,498
06	43000	Long Beach city, California	316,064	21.1	19.2	30.2	29.5	$31,826	$34,528	$45,237	$30,166	$42,281
06	43280	Los Altos city, California	22,020	2.6	3.1	11.4	82.9	$107,011	$170,625	$190,103	$55,963	$120,179
06	44000	Los Angeles city, California	2,687,915	23.6	20.2	23.5	32.6	$27,662	$30,614	$40,261	$25,248	$40,060
06	44028	Los Banos city, California	20,660	34.3	19.3	31.8	14.5	$20,826	$27,839	$36,993	$14,406	$40,551
06	44112	Los Gatos town, California	22,802	4.5	8.9	21.2	65.3	$96,759	$120,522	$150,850	$70,987	$101,442

Table E. Cities—Labor Force, Employment, and Educational Data, 2015—*Continued*

| | | | Educational attainment of persons age 25 years and older | | | | Median earnings in the past 12 months (in 2015 Inflation-adjusted dollars) | | | | |
| | | | | | | | | Men with earnings | | Women with earnings | |
FIPS state code	FIPS place code	State/city	Total population age 25 years and older	Less than high school graduate	High school graduate (includes equivalency)	Some college or Associate's degree	Bachelor's degree or higher	All persons age 16 and older with earnings in the past 12 months	All men with earnings	Men who worked full-time, year-round in the past 12 months	All women with earnings	Women who worked full-time, year-round in the past 12 months
06	44574	Lynwood city, California	42,431	41.9	27.9	22.8	7.4	$21,893	$22,759	$30,124	$20,888	$28,798
06	45022	Madera city, California	34,591	42.3	22.5	25.7	9.5	$21,188	$21,436	$30,880	$20,612	$37,578
06	45400	Manhattan Beach city, California	24,579	2.0	6.0	20.5	71.6	$80,786	$101,459	$131,037	$61,540	$99,088
06	45484	Manteca city, California	47,820	17.0	33.8	35.2	14.0	$30,881	$36,013	$52,394	$26,254	$40,024
06	45778	Marina city, California	11,328	12.3	19.6	39.3	28.7	$31,268	$40,833	$57,442	$25,669	$40,129
06	46114	Martinez city, California	26,674	8.7	19.7	36.3	35.3	$40,678	$50,021	$69,726	$39,271	$56,487
06	46492	Maywood city, California	16,418	51.7	27.8	16.5	4.0	$20,668	$22,337	$26,038	$17,006	$21,202
06	46646	Mead Valley CDP, California	11,884	35.0	27.4	27.8	9.7	$21,428	$22,096	$49,514	$18,461	$26,766
06	46842	Menifee city, California	56,675	14.6	28.6	39.3	17.5	$35,267	$45,486	$52,360	$22,241	$43,472
06	46870	Menlo Park city, California	22,767	11.1	7.5	16.1	65.2	$50,928	$52,099	$130,568	$44,948	$91,570
06	46898	Merced city, California	46,493	25.4	24.6	30.4	19.5	$21,537	$24,505	$37,311	$17,440	$40,244
06	47486	Millbrae city, California	17,717	7.8	16.6	22.6	53.0	$61,631	$66,316	$90,676	$60,929	$71,993
06	47766	Milpitas city, California	53,705	11.1	16.2	25.6	47.1	$43,148	$51,872	$80,290	$36,434	$51,977
06	48256	Mission Viejo city, California	69,766	7.3	13.4	33.8	45.5	$47,075	$60,215	$84,891	$40,215	$56,612
06	48354	Modesto city, California	134,303	19.7	26.2	35.8	18.3	$30,407	$35,379	$47,984	$25,014	$41,625
06	48648	Monrovia city, California	26,158	9.7	19.8	37.3	33.2	$34,414	$36,838	$42,491	$28,587	$41,324
06	48788	Montclair city, California	24,525	31.8	28.6	23.7	16.0	$23,479	$26,198	$30,687	$20,766	$27,957
06	48816	Montebello city, California	42,966	24.9	30.8	24.8	19.5	$24,189	$24,801	$26,870	$22,349	$28,099
06	48872	Monterey city, California	21,243	13.1	9.7	28.3	48.9	$36,766	$41,685	$65,347	$24,795	$41,647
06	48914	Monterey Park city, California	46,237	20.3	23.5	24.6	31.6	$31,365	$33,281	$43,016	$28,961	$38,970
06	49138	Moorpark city, California	25,925	11.0	11.0	35.9	42.1	$36,944	$41,114	$66,620	$31,041	$65,025
06	49270	Moreno Valley city, California	120,971	26.0	28.9	30.1	15.0	$26,628	$31,074	$38,309	$21,838	$33,999
06	49278	Morgan Hill city, California	27,984	8.9	11.8	32.9	46.4	$44,316	$60,504	$86,688	$30,570	$71,772
06	49670	Mountain View city, California	55,960	5.9	12.7	15.5	65.9	$60,714	$85,276	$116,983	$51,555	$71,310
06	50076	Murrieta city, California	67,869	7.9	24.7	38.6	28.8	$32,268	$46,330	$66,903	$25,419	$41,211
06	50258	Napa city, California	54,331	17.9	18.1	34.0	30.1	$32,286	$37,425	$55,286	$29,366	$45,556
06	50398	National City city, California	40,011	25.1	31.3	32.0	11.5	$22,764	$24,012	$31,820	$20,971	$26,679
06	50916	Newark city, California	31,344	15.1	30.8	24.3	29.9	$42,460	$48,329	$52,445	$41,019	$50,905
06	51182	Newport Beach city, California	65,667	2.1	8.2	25.6	64.1	$64,288	$89,548	$103,453	$49,984	$66,634
06	51560	Norco city, California	19,003	13.6	33.2	38.1	15.1	$32,464	$36,769	$70,493	$27,106	$45,586
06	51924	North Highlands CDP, California	31,699	18.2	25.6	45.6	10.6	$21,848	$26,399	$37,280	$17,467	$31,468
06	52379	North Tustin CDP, California	17,069	3.3	9.7	26.5	60.5	$58,540	$81,843	$101,558	$40,650	$70,291
06	52526	Norwalk city, California	68,995	24.5	27.3	31.0	17.1	$28,845	$31,931	$36,900	$24,074	$31,624
06	52582	Novato city, California	40,740	6.6	13.9	29.4	50.1	$41,376	$47,472	$71,924	$32,164	$51,972
06	52694	Oakdale city, California	14,658	11.7	27.6	41.8	18.8	$29,332	$32,421	$43,935	$22,363	$35,446
06	53000	Oakland city, California	298,374	20.5	15.6	24.0	40.0	$31,846	$35,263	$50,138	$30,217	$50,136
06	53070	Oakley city, California	23,790	12.4	21.1	48.5	18.0	$45,823	$60,473	$66,518	$26,398	$47,096
06	53322	Oceanside city, California	122,453	13.0	21.5	37.1	28.4	$32,019	$38,391	$46,158	$29,842	$44,336
06	53448	Oildale CDP, California	19,182	16.6	32.4	38.1	12.9	$35,337	$41,020	$47,152	$23,684	$38,349
06	53896	Ontario city, California	102,597	27.9	27.6	28.9	15.6	$26,420	$29,362	$35,821	$23,995	$32,077
06	53980	Orange city, California	93,760	14.4	18.0	31.5	36.0	$36,750	$46,073	$57,142	$31,059	$48,019
06	54092	Orangevale CDP, California	25,805	5.3	26.5	36.1	32.1	$35,917	$49,639	$59,626	$27,586	$49,389
06	54120	Orcutt CDP, California	19,051	5.3	23.0	43.1	28.7	$34,175	$46,901	$65,980	$20,975	$43,844
06	54652	Oxnard city, California	124,686	34.3	21.3	27.7	16.7	$22,501	$25,125	$32,349	$20,592	$35,669
06	54806	Pacifica city, California	28,957	5.0	17.4	35.1	42.5	$47,523	$51,546	$64,202	$43,721	$62,197
06	55156	Palmdale city, California	95,674	23.5	27.7	35.4	13.3	$30,020	$35,806	$43,059	$23,501	$34,572
06	55184	Palm Desert city, California	40,815	8.9	21.3	34.4	35.4	$34,353	$33,389	$51,076	$34,588	$44,799
06	55254	Palm Springs city, California	38,204	10.9	19.1	35.3	34.7	$27,215	$26,189	$46,414	$30,537	$50,466
06	55282	Palo Alto city, California	46,870	3.6	3.2	13.4	79.9	$81,176	$112,145	$150,284	$57,243	$89,842
06	55520	Paradise town, California	19,294	8.7	20.1	50.8	20.4	$27,095	$26,595	$46,087	$28,280	$33,092
06	55618	Paramount city, California	33,956	37.1	24.4	26.6	11.9	$26,625	$30,035	$33,200	$22,881	$35,592
06	56000	Pasadena city, California	102,463	13.2	13.5	23.7	49.5	$40,974	$46,200	$65,399	$36,395	$51,334
06	56112	Patterson city, California	16,658	26.4	37.8	26.8	8.9	$40,117	$46,273	$47,355	$19,373	$36,776
06	56700	Perris city, California	39,425	37.3	27.9	27.9	6.9	$26,951	$30,749	$35,395	$17,797	$30,740
06	56784	Petaluma city, California	42,222	10.4	14.6	39.6	35.4	$34,455	$45,872	$63,895	$29,937	$50,420
06	56924	Pico Rivera city, California	43,373	32.3	30.7	27.1	9.9	$28,927	$29,333	$35,674	$27,373	$37,197
06	57456	Pittsburg city, California	44,654	20.8	23.8	35.3	20.0	$32,439	$34,587	$46,597	$30,771	$44,518
06	57526	Placentia city, California	34,405	15.7	16.5	35.6	32.2	$35,669	$40,345	$52,041	$30,600	$41,616
06	57764	Pleasant Hill city, California	24,305	3.6	8.0	31.4	57.0	$58,182	$61,876	$77,149	$46,791	$63,690
06	57792	Pleasanton city, California	53,012	5.6	11.0	21.4	61.9	$74,870	$101,144	$121,401	$47,529	$81,744
06	58072	Pomona city, California	94,234	31.4	22.8	26.1	19.7	$23,554	$28,935	$36,696	$20,129	$30,226
06	58240	Porterville city, California	30,663	31.2	28.0	29.7	11.1	$20,240	$20,832	$41,056	$19,043	$26,959
06	58296	Port Hueneme city, California	14,884	16.1	22.9	41.2	19.9	$32,746	$36,782	$41,944	$31,032	$33,721
06	58520	Poway city, California	34,355	10.6	18.3	29.2	41.9	$36,927	$51,385	$70,764	$28,914	$46,068
06	59346	Ramona CDP, California	16,118	10.5	40.1	29.3	20.1	$33,791	$49,949	$51,285	$29,675	$39,078
06	59444	Rancho Cordova city, California	47,979	9.8	23.8	39.3	27.0	$31,847	$38,735	$50,091	$26,345	$42,094
06	59451	Rancho Cucamonga city, California	110,449	7.3	21.6	39.6	31.4	$36,049	$42,666	$56,893	$30,233	$45,282
06	59514	Rancho Palos Verdes city, California	31,346	2.8	11.4	22.8	63.0	$51,398	$85,025	$110,076	$40,682	$56,288

Table E. Cities—Labor Force, Employment, and Educational Data, 2015—*Continued*

| | | | Educational attainment of persons age 25 years and older | | | | | Median earnings in the past 12 months (in 2015 Inflation-adjusted dollars) | | | | |
| | | | | | | | | | Men with earnings | | Women with earnings | |
FIPS state code	FIPS place code	State/city	Total population age 25 years and older	Less than high school graduate	High school graduate (includes equivalency)	Some college or Associate's degree	Bachelor's degree or higher	All persons age 16 and older with earnings in the past 12 months	All men with earnings	Men who worked full-time, year-round in the past 12 months	All women with earnings	Women who worked full-time, year-round in the past 12 months
06	59550	Rancho San Diego CDP, California	14,459	6.3	22.2	35.0	36.5	$30,861	$30,721	$54,955	$31,261	$50,678
06	59587	Rancho Santa Margarita city, California	32,286	6.0	9.9	28.2	55.9	$58,623	$75,458	$85,632	$41,045	$71,525
06	59920	Redding city, California	62,932	7.4	21.3	43.2	28.1	$26,809	$30,871	$40,094	$24,301	$37,239
06	59962	Redlands city, California	46,634	10.4	19.4	33.0	37.3	$36,311	$41,718	$54,027	$29,519	$42,463
06	60018	Redondo Beach city, California	52,565	3.3	10.2	26.1	60.4	$61,816	$75,647	$93,883	$45,677	$65,884
06	60102	Redwood City city, California	60,009	15.9	16.2	21.5	46.4	$51,300	$54,718	$79,411	$48,296	$63,969
06	60242	Reedley city, California	14,359	38.5	17.2	31.6	12.7	$19,688	$20,973	$34,586	$18,021	$32,804
06	60466	Rialto city, California	63,642	34.0	31.0	25.7	9.4	$23,894	$27,202	$36,712	$20,987	$31,940
06	60620	Richmond city, California	75,709	19.6	23.3	31.1	26.0	$31,341	$31,803	$43,570	$30,709	$42,400
06	60704	Ridgecrest city, California	18,408	7.9	29.6	38.6	24.0	$37,430	$46,895	$61,663	$23,958	$41,777
06	61068	Riverbank city, California	15,174	28.5	31.5	24.6	15.3	$30,614	$31,997	$41,115	$26,858	$37,321
06	62000	Riverside city, California	198,255	20.6	25.3	31.8	22.2	$27,064	$31,251	$41,046	$22,790	$36,842
06	62364	Rocklin city, California	40,473	3.4	17.5	35.3	43.7	$42,098	$52,482	$71,197	$33,010	$57,985
06	62546	Rohnert Park city, California	28,011	8.9	23.2	40.2	27.7	$27,343	$32,353	$50,616	$24,886	$47,473
06	62826	Rosamond CDP, California	13,102	16.2	21.1	44.1	18.6	$37,374	$41,614	$50,422	$28,029	$40,587
06	62896	Rosemead city, California	38,995	33.2	26.5	22.0	18.3	$26,551	$28,323	$34,302	$24,517	$32,047
06	62910	Rosemont CDP, California	14,817	8.9	24.6	40.5	26.0	$36,135	$41,500	$56,215	$35,418	$50,500
06	62938	Roseville city, California	88,068	7.5	17.6	37.7	37.2	$41,097	$51,366	$61,970	$32,316	$50,698
06	63218	Rowland Heights CDP, California	38,122	14.4	26.3	24.0	35.3	$26,843	$35,040	$41,468	$23,420	$32,181
06	64000	Sacramento city, California	323,209	16.6	21.9	31.2	30.3	$30,962	$32,370	$46,804	$28,751	$40,857
06	64224	Salinas city, California	92,015	43.5	19.3	24.0	13.1	$22,215	$25,098	$32,428	$20,312	$30,660
06	65000	San Bernardino city, California	121,274	31.4	28.3	28.0	12.2	$20,618	$22,985	$32,132	$16,742	$30,063
06	65028	San Bruno city, California	32,168	11.8	15.2	35.9	37.1	$50,040	$50,678	$61,954	$47,732	$60,697
06	65042	San Buenaventura (Ventura) city, California	77,005	14.0	19.9	34.7	31.4	$31,807	$37,927	$55,324	$29,194	$44,445
06	65070	San Carlos city, California	22,102	1.9	11.6	20.7	65.8	$71,730	$100,679	$125,353	$56,359	$90,336
06	65084	San Clemente city, California	47,216	5.5	11.1	31.3	52.1	$46,157	$55,405	$71,662	$36,579	$58,009
06	66000	San Diego city, California	945,996	12.9	15.8	27.0	44.3	$35,017	$40,613	$52,308	$29,411	$46,896
06	66070	San Dimas city, California	25,670	9.1	19.9	35.0	36.0	$41,489	$45,729	$60,236	$34,894	$58,103
06	66140	San Fernando city, California	15,703	38.2	29.6	21.5	10.7	$30,018	$32,019	$37,469	$23,399	$38,003
06	67000	San Francisco city, California	683,821	12.4	12.8	19.7	55.2	$51,884	$60,343	$80,764	$48,396	$66,965
06	67042	San Gabriel city, California	29,243	21.6	29.2	18.5	30.7	$25,868	$27,466	$35,368	$21,012	$30,568
06	67056	Sanger city, California	14,737	35.3	18.3	30.0	16.4	$22,380	$30,598	$46,850	$19,292	$29,340
06	67112	San Jacinto city, California	27,155	24.1	28.7	36.5	10.8	$25,508	$30,231	$40,673	$17,913	$39,817
06	68000	San Jose city, California	697,313	16.6	17.5	25.2	40.7	$40,728	$47,446	$62,905	$32,699	$52,259
06	68028	San Juan Capistrano city, California	23,732	12.2	26.3	27.4	34.1	$31,827	$35,542	$61,079	$22,350	$60,538
06	68084	San Leandro city, California	65,634	18.4	23.0	29.0	29.5	$31,826	$32,149	$40,843	$31,457	$43,637
06	68112	San Lorenzo CDP, California	17,141	18.5	19.9	28.6	33.0	$41,803	$40,229	$50,882	$46,474	$51,536
06	68154	San Luis Obispo city, California	25,383	7.1	13.0	29.7	50.1	$16,999	$22,310	$41,497	$11,800	$50,376
06	68196	San Marcos city, California	58,107	14.7	20.2	31.9	33.2	$30,669	$37,431	$52,060	$22,452	$41,547
06	68252	San Mateo city, California	74,215	12.0	12.9	23.6	51.5	$48,419	$57,098	$76,697	$41,449	$65,338
06	68294	San Pablo city, California	18,663	36.5	29.2	23.4	10.8	$21,890	$23,511	$30,287	$20,111	$27,066
06	68364	San Rafael city, California	40,926	17.7	12.3	18.9	51.0	$42,169	$45,425	$65,853	$40,287	$67,269
06	68378	San Ramon city, California	49,471	3.9	10.1	19.3	66.7	$75,085	$100,123	$116,893	$52,586	$75,040
06	69000	Santa Ana city, California	202,730	45.8	23.6	19.1	11.5	$22,287	$25,288	$27,518	$20,134	$26,173
06	69070	Santa Barbara city, California	63,973	15.2	13.0	23.4	48.4	$31,410	$34,810	$49,174	$27,500	$42,717
06	69084	Santa Clara city, California	88,652	8.6	14.3	21.9	55.3	$51,543	$60,382	$79,777	$42,836	$61,659
06	69088	Santa Clarita city, California	121,904	10.5	21.5	34.3	33.7	$40,424	$46,321	$67,572	$33,974	$51,542
06	69112	Santa Cruz city, California	34,849	7.3	11.8	31.3	49.6	$21,549	$21,960	$70,033	$21,025	$42,381
06	69196	Santa Maria city, California	58,821	43.0	18.7	25.9	12.3	$22,298	$24,893	$28,354	$20,467	$25,928
06	70000	Santa Monica city, California	72,955	3.7	10.7	20.2	65.3	$52,399	$63,621	$86,168	$47,244	$66,620
06	70042	Santa Paula city, California	17,769	39.8	20.3	28.3	11.5	$22,063	$25,548	$35,204	$20,550	$33,035
06	70098	Santa Rosa city, California	121,849	14.5	20.2	34.9	30.4	$30,753	$32,480	$47,114	$26,342	$41,376
06	70224	Santee city, California	39,960	4.8	28.6	39.1	27.5	$39,879	$41,678	$59,609	$35,640	$46,073
06	70280	Saratoga city, California	22,808	3.1	8.9	14.9	73.1	$101,035	$132,185	$151,431	$56,526	$101,667
06	70686	Seal Beach city, California	20,235	4.6	10.4	39.1	45.9	$41,966	$70,657	$81,655	$28,333	$52,408
06	70742	Seaside city, California	22,009	23.5	25.8	33.6	17.2	$22,936	$27,320	$41,113	$17,475	$31,353
06	70882	Selma city, California	12,606	33.3	28.8	26.0	11.9	$22,343	$22,478	$36,101	$21,791	$37,538
06	72016	Simi Valley city, California	84,935	10.1	21.7	32.5	35.7	$40,153	$46,259	$61,893	$35,834	$51,452
06	72520	Soledad city, California	17,299	36.3	26.5	30.1	7.0	$21,166	$22,347	$32,212	$19,073	$35,083
06	72996	South El Monte city, California	10,841	41.0	30.6	17.2	11.1	$23,306	$24,079	$30,244	$22,807	$25,927
06	73080	South Gate city, California	58,793	45.5	25.3	19.1	10.1	$24,204	$27,232	$31,981	$19,753	$30,072
06	73108	South Lake Tahoe city, California	10,927	11.6	26.5	38.3	23.7	$26,939	$26,639	$40,294	$30,425	$46,742
06	73220	South Pasadena city, California	18,100	7.5	13.9	22.3	56.3	$45,824	$55,868	$76,605	$42,853	$56,900
06	73262	South San Francisco city, California	47,636	22.1	21.1	28.4	28.3	$40,505	$40,207	$52,328	$40,910	$52,141
06	73290	South San Jose Hills CDP, California	13,834	40.8	27.6	22.1	9.4	$19,428	$20,652	$22,795	$16,326	$22,349
06	73430	South Whittier CDP, California	39,366	22.6	30.9	33.6	13.0	$30,091	$31,411	$35,630	$26,607	$35,890

Table E. Cities—Labor Force, Employment, and Educational Data, 2015—*Continued*

			Educational attainment of persons age 25 years and older				Median earnings in the past 12 months (in 2015 Inflation-adjusted dollars)	Men with earnings		Women with earnings	
FIPS state code	FIPS place code	State/city	Total population age 25 years and older	Less than high school graduate	High school graduate (includes equivalency)	Some college or Associate's degree	Bachelor's degree or higher	All persons age 16 and older with earnings in the past 12 months	All men with earnings	Men who worked full-time, year-round in the past 12 months	All women with earnings	Women who worked full-time, year-round in the past 12 months
06	73696	Spring Valley CDP (San Diego County), California	20,423	14.2	24.0	36.4	25.3	$34,837	$36,730	$46,695	$29,356	$41,102
06	73962	Stanton city, California	23,725	32.6	23.9	29.9	13.5	$27,036	$31,645	$41,689	$22,475	$32,026
06	75000	Stockton city, California	188,184	25.5	25.3	31.5	17.8	$26,087	$28,676	$40,089	$22,122	$36,096
06	75630	Suisun City city, California	19,081	12.5	22.8	46.3	18.4	$30,789	$36,526	$60,036	$25,439	$34,188
06	77000	Sunnyvale city, California	109,728	8.2	11.2	18.1	62.6	$70,620	$86,143	$101,052	$48,017	$76,911
06	78120	Temecula city, California	70,522	9.0	22.7	38.5	29.8	$35,189	$47,211	$57,336	$25,554	$40,746
06	78138	Temescal Valley CDP, California	16,009	8.0	22.8	44.0	25.1	$50,793	$74,430	$82,136	$27,466	$36,847
06	78148	Temple City city, California	24,797	13.4	17.3	26.3	43.0	$31,750	$34,470	$50,560	$25,881	$40,647
06	78582	Thousand Oaks city, California	90,117	6.7	14.9	29.4	49.0	$51,691	$66,310	$82,156	$40,196	$69,023
06	80000	Torrance city, California	103,150	5.3	17.0	30.9	46.8	$43,176	$51,694	$67,143	$35,048	$52,061
06	80238	Tracy city, California	54,187	15.4	21.6	35.0	28.0	$37,477	$41,148	$52,466	$31,223	$45,449
06	80644	Tulare city, California	35,523	26.9	25.5	32.2	15.4	$31,317	$34,881	$45,608	$29,240	$36,594
06	80812	Turlock city, California	46,822	16.8	27.0	29.6	26.7	$34,652	$41,247	$52,278	$26,963	$40,305
06	80854	Tustin city, California	52,026	13.5	17.3	27.8	41.4	$33,302	$38,017	$51,078	$28,764	$41,803
06	80994	Twentynine Palms city, California	12,525	5.9	26.6	49.5	18.1	$24,035	$23,908	$25,669	$24,743	$30,948
06	81204	Union City city, California	53,707	7.4	26.7	27.5	38.4	$48,040	$51,658	$60,892	$41,274	$55,074
06	81344	Upland city, California	53,226	11.9	21.1	37.5	29.5	$31,777	$35,414	$48,822	$29,967	$43,303
06	81554	Vacaville city, California	64,220	10.7	26.8	41.9	20.5	$36,670	$45,223	$61,243	$27,262	$46,189
06	81638	Valinda CDP, California	16,629	35.3	31.6	24.9	8.3	$25,763	$28,194	$40,460	$20,238	$32,428
06	81666	Vallejo city, California	85,197	13.5	25.0	37.3	24.3	$31,840	$36,281	$50,160	$27,971	$41,864
06	82590	Victorville city, California	72,581	21.9	26.9	35.1	16.2	$25,074	$28,547	$45,984	$21,853	$35,289
06	82852	Vineyard CDP, California	18,117	7.5	16.6	44.7	31.2	$39,858	$38,830	$55,090	$40,238	$46,218
06	82954	Visalia city, California	80,512	20.0	22.2	36.8	21.0	$30,170	$31,672	$45,676	$26,000	$40,601
06	82996	Vista city, California	59,863	21.7	24.3	31.3	22.8	$28,693	$32,051	$40,297	$22,466	$32,344
06	83332	Walnut city, California	22,921	5.1	17.1	23.7	54.1	$45,584	$61,246	$70,965	$32,862	$63,886
06	83346	Walnut Creek city, California	51,905	1.9	9.5	22.1	66.5	$60,343	$85,611	$102,175	$50,369	$62,272
06	83542	Wasco city, California	14,234	46.3	33.5	17.6	2.6	$17,044	$25,189	$37,764	$10,756	$20,959
06	83668	Watsonville city, California	30,729	46.4	27.1	19.9	6.6	$18,801	$21,852	$28,269	$15,592	$29,073
06	84144	West Carson CDP, California	17,205	13.4	18.8	28.1	39.7	$30,326	$26,696	$31,169	$35,264	$41,829
06	84200	West Covina city, California	76,147	15.1	26.7	31.6	26.6	$31,914	$36,518	$50,952	$29,630	$41,334
06	84410	West Hollywood city, California	32,417	1.7	9.7	18.7	69.9	$54,136	$60,078	$69,506	$52,748	$61,276
06	84550	Westminster city, California	67,691	21.9	20.8	33.2	24.1	$26,552	$31,033	$48,788	$21,298	$38,828
06	84592	Westmont CDP, California	21,367	30.4	28.3	34.3	7.0	$26,077	$26,541	$32,380	$25,308	$36,447
06	84774	West Puente Valley CDP, California	17,413	37.7	30.1	23.2	9.1	$28,890	$31,700	$35,532	$25,547	$31,699
06	84780	West Rancho Dominguez CDP, California	14,908	35.1	26.0	27.9	10.9	$30,050	$30,757	$36,590	$26,550	$36,367
06	84816	West Sacramento city, California	34,632	17.4	22.3	33.6	26.7	$32,230	$39,265	$49,985	$30,913	$41,375
06	84921	West Whittier-Los Nietos CDP, California	20,000	23.5	29.0	29.4	18.0	$35,013	$35,168	$36,852	$34,585	$39,526
06	85292	Whittier city, California	58,836	15.6	26.3	35.5	22.7	$36,339	$39,196	$46,207	$30,948	$43,693
06	85446	Wildomar city, California	22,942	12.0	29.9	41.4	16.7	$28,028	$34,903	$46,100	$22,640	$40,685
06	85922	Windsor town, California	19,230	14.6	19.9	36.4	29.1	$35,744	$47,083	$61,555	$24,907	$43,869
06	85992	Winter Gardens CDP, California	14,598	9.5	36.1	33.5	20.9	$34,245	$36,741	$40,519	$27,255	$36,243
06	86328	Woodland city, California	38,164	15.8	26.4	32.3	25.5	$30,526	$35,459	$49,542	$24,469	$37,072
06	86832	Yorba Linda city, California	47,781	5.4	13.2	28.5	52.9	$60,315	$81,179	$101,015	$38,604	$71,792
06	86972	Yuba City city, California	42,973	25.4	23.6	34.0	17.1	$25,674	$30,532	$44,870	$19,364	$34,991
06	87042	Yucaipa city, California	36,685	12.6	28.0	38.2	21.2	$37,057	$41,314	$51,128	$30,889	$50,275
06	87056	Yucca Valley town, California	15,463	8.2	32.6	46.1	13.2	$30,283	$56,216	$60,234	$17,788	$29,759
08	00000	**COLORADO**	3,671,853	8.8	21.7	30.2	39.2	$33,462	$40,186	$51,628	$28,642	$41,690
08	03455	Arvada city, Colorado	83,223	5.8	24.0	30.4	39.8	$41,000	$50,930	$59,137	$31,600	$46,724
08	04000	Aurora city, Colorado	231,628	12.5	25.7	32.9	29.0	$31,359	$32,990	$42,064	$29,675	$40,131
08	07850	Boulder city, Colorado	61,589	4.2	7.5	15.3	73.0	$23,087	$26,396	$66,621	$20,304	$49,611
08	08675	Brighton city, Colorado	24,016	18.8	27.4	30.5	23.4	$35,130	$41,524	$55,544	$27,063	$40,655
08	09280	Broomfield city, Colorado	44,959	3.0	14.9	25.9	56.1	$43,763	$50,596	$70,635	$40,156	$51,845
08	12415	Castle Rock town, Colorado	34,501	2.4	12.1	36.7	48.8	$43,762	$57,261	$68,563	$32,017	$50,444
08	12815	Centennial city, Colorado	77,042	2.6	12.7	29.1	55.6	$47,025	$59,868	$70,295	$38,101	$52,476
08	15165	Clifton CDP, Colorado	13,667	16.0	33.4	37.1	13.5	$26,007	$32,688	$39,848	$16,644	$29,689
08	16000	Colorado Springs city, Colorado	299,826	5.7	21.5	34.4	38.3	$30,740	$36,961	$50,732	$24,957	$37,687
08	16110	Columbine CDP, Colorado	18,267	0.6	18.2	35.5	45.7	$45,601	$60,992	$73,464	$31,783	$45,762
08	16495	Commerce City city, Colorado	31,123	20.0	33.7	29.1	17.2	$32,442	$39,158	$46,158	$26,294	$40,032
08	19150	Dakota Ridge CDP, Colorado	21,751	3.9	16.5	33.5	46.0	$36,979	$41,393	$61,657	$32,581	$45,825
08	20000	Denver city, Colorado	483,833	14.2	16.5	22.2	47.1	$37,346	$40,088	$49,598	$35,324	$46,483
08	24785	Englewood city, Colorado	25,315	11.0	26.7	26.3	36.0	$31,652	$34,963	$46,790	$29,234	$35,959
08	24950	Erie town, Colorado	13,073	6.3	6.1	25.8	61.8	$60,905	$81,433	$90,357	$36,430	$60,276
08	25280	Evans city, Colorado	14,026	18.2	34.9	36.7	10.2	$27,245	$30,245	$35,224	$23,062	$30,900
08	27425	Fort Collins city, Colorado	95,850	3.1	15.7	27.1	54.1	$26,868	$32,250	$52,836	$21,588	$42,162
08	27865	Fountain city, Colorado	16,579	3.0	27.8	54.4	14.7	$32,363	$44,005	$50,704	$23,137	$36,221
08	30835	Golden city, Colorado	12,580	6.5	14.6	21.3	57.6	$20,909	$17,097	$57,204	$30,066	$44,233
08	31660	Grand Junction city, Colorado	38,064	10.7	20.9	31.4	37.0	$20,722	$22,630	$50,756	$18,899	$37,045

Table E. Cities—Labor Force, Employment, and Educational Data, 2015—*Continued*

| | | | Educational attainment of persons age 25 years and older | | | | Median earnings in the past 12 months (in 2015 Inflation-adjusted dollars) | | | | |
| | | | | | | | | Men with earnings | | Women with earnings | |
FIPS state code	FIPS place code	State/city	Total population age 25 years and older	Less than high school graduate	High school graduate (includes equivalency)	Some college or Associate's degree	Bachelor's degree or higher	All persons age 16 and older with earnings in the past 12 months	All men with earnings	Men who worked full-time, year-round in the past 12 months	All women with earnings	Women who worked full-time, year-round in the past 12 months
08	32155	Greeley city, Colorado	58,189	16.9	25.7	32.7	24.7	$28,325	$35,493	$43,916	$20,137	$35,432
08	36410	Highlands Ranch CDP, Colorado	65,817	1.3	11.0	28.1	59.6	$55,376	$78,810	$91,756	$36,416	$56,729
08	40377	Ken Caryl CDP, Colorado	23,084	2.4	21.5	31.5	44.6	$42,237	$51,463	$61,012	$31,096	$45,277
08	41835	Lafayette city, Colorado	19,235	2.7	18.0	26.0	53.3	$32,936	$41,728	$52,495	$28,914	$58,038
08	43000	Lakewood city, Colorado	108,055	7.5	24.4	30.0	38.0	$35,021	$37,230	$43,197	$31,582	$45,309
08	45255	Littleton city, Colorado	34,237	3.9	16.2	33.4	46.5	$40,314	$46,124	$54,808	$32,343	$51,022
08	45970	Longmont city, Colorado	60,998	11.2	22.0	28.5	38.4	$30,452	$36,576	$50,958	$24,130	$41,062
08	46355	Louisville city, Colorado	12,833	1.9	9.8	15.9	72.3	$40,817	$55,899	$75,613	$31,918	$46,975
08	46465	Loveland city, Colorado	50,944	4.6	24.1	35.2	36.2	$33,601	$40,685	$51,971	$27,476	$40,403
08	54330	Northglenn city, Colorado	25,066	13.4	31.9	35.4	19.4	$31,127	$34,914	$42,406	$26,103	$37,472
08	57630	Parker town, Colorado	31,558	1.5	13.2	27.5	57.8	$56,066	$71,862	$80,482	$41,373	$60,361
08	62000	Pueblo city, Colorado	73,644	16.1	28.8	36.8	18.4	$22,306	$26,839	$37,206	$20,163	$30,501
08	62220	Pueblo West CDP, Colorado	18,429	4.3	29.2	38.6	28.0	$31,457	$45,017	$61,393	$26,262	$39,438
08	68847	Security-Widefield CDP, Colorado	23,929	6.1	31.2	42.9	19.8	$30,023	$36,356	$41,157	$22,979	$30,201
08	77290	Thornton city, Colorado	83,463	14.8	23.9	32.9	28.4	$37,018	$45,785	$52,194	$31,432	$39,899
08	83835	Westminster city, Colorado	80,204	8.7	23.5	30.6	37.2	$39,398	$43,716	$56,046	$35,429	$45,251
08	84440	Wheat Ridge city, Colorado	22,940	8.5	25.7	35.3	30.5	$36,239	$39,614	$48,793	$31,017	$41,318
08	85485	Windsor town, Colorado	16,831	2.6	22.4	30.7	44.3	$41,593	$53,859	$61,460	$32,087	$46,219
09	00000	**CONNECTICUT**	2,474,718	9.8	27.4	24.5	38.3	$40,009	$46,435	$61,666	$32,701	$50,802
09	08000	Bridgeport city, Connecticut	94,390	21.6	34.2	24.2	20.0	$26,063	$31,266	$45,346	$20,804	$35,775
09	08420	Bristol city, Connecticut	42,057	9.4	35.4	25.7	29.6	$41,458	$44,057	$60,436	$40,393	$48,856
09	18430	Danbury city, Connecticut	59,726	18.2	29.5	23.1	29.2	$31,352	$35,149	$45,425	$26,107	$40,112
09	18920	Darien CDP, Connecticut	12,635	1.4	8.2	12.5	77.8	$80,016	$137,147	$250,000	$31,312	$86,166
09	22700	East Hartford CDP, Connecticut	35,250	17.8	35.3	28.9	18.1	$36,982	$41,956	$51,701	$33,750	$45,152
09	22980	East Haven CDP, Connecticut	21,268	10.8	36.5	28.2	24.5	$41,478	$50,361	$58,633	$36,449	$45,918
09	37000	Hartford city, Connecticut	74,245	28.7	31.3	23.1	16.9	$22,847	$25,973	$36,681	$20,991	$32,565
09	44690	Manchester CDP, Connecticut	20,871	7.1	25.7	40.2	27.0	$35,265	$41,935	$48,346	$30,682	$39,128
09	46450	Meriden city, Connecticut	45,467	9.9	40.0	27.7	22.4	$38,794	$42,489	$47,400	$35,330	$43,721
09	47290	Middletown city, Connecticut	29,335	8.5	26.9	26.7	37.9	$40,906	$44,189	$60,800	$34,566	$55,596
09	47515	Milford city (balance), Connecticut	39,195	7.3	29.2	24.8	38.8	$46,451	$51,647	$61,383	$37,230	$60,109
09	49880	Naugatuck borough, Connecticut	21,674	10.4	33.7	27.7	28.2	$44,230	$53,523	$70,598	$31,534	$43,498
09	50370	New Britain city, Connecticut	46,257	17.4	38.9	23.3	20.4	$31,900	$35,832	$49,423	$30,166	$38,071
09	52000	New Haven city, Connecticut	79,312	15.4	29.7	19.8	35.1	$25,500	$26,365	$40,610	$24,154	$41,968
09	52210	Newington CDP, Connecticut	22,563	9.8	23.5	24.6	42.1	$41,902	$48,054	$59,654	$37,881	$46,723
09	52280	New London city, Connecticut	15,295	22.1	33.3	26.4	18.2	$18,739	$20,205	$40,969	$18,192	$38,611
09	54940	North Haven CDP, Connecticut	17,148	2.8	32.6	27.5	37.2	$44,159	$57,785	$70,447	$40,519	$45,345
09	55990	Norwalk city, Connecticut	63,581	12.2	27.8	19.9	40.1	$40,658	$45,276	$57,183	$36,068	$50,675
09	56200	Norwich city, Connecticut	27,768	13.5	40.8	30.8	15.0	$33,046	$38,863	$50,531	$23,768	$37,472
09	68100	Shelton city, Connecticut	29,502	8.0	29.6	19.5	42.9	$46,676	$51,686	$62,478	$42,098	$55,202
09	73000	Stamford city, Connecticut	89,256	9.1	20.5	23.1	47.3	$41,780	$50,909	$69,190	$37,691	$55,410
09	74260	Stratford CDP, Connecticut	38,408	7.0	34.8	24.1	34.2	$38,067	$47,829	$62,295	$33,868	$52,074
09	76500	Torrington city, Connecticut	25,651	14.9	33.1	30.9	21.1	$39,301	$45,784	$51,567	$30,482	$41,921
09	77270	Trumbull CDP, Connecticut	23,907	4.9	19.3	22.2	53.6	$60,681	$73,840	$86,413	$50,743	$80,228
09	80000	Waterbury city, Connecticut	71,584	22.4	39.5	25.0	13.1	$28,479	$31,304	$42,404	$26,410	$35,546
09	82660	West Hartford CDP, Connecticut	43,813	4.8	13.5	19.4	62.2	$51,197	$60,144	$79,274	$47,801	$66,156
09	82800	West Haven city, Connecticut	36,668	12.9	36.1	24.0	27.1	$31,153	$35,008	$43,772	$25,054	$42,033
09	83570	Westport CDP, Connecticut	18,578	2.4	9.6	14.2	73.8	$81,185	$152,393	$201,375	$52,288	$90,415
09	84970	Wethersfield CDP, Connecticut	20,173	6.1	24.9	24.8	44.2	$45,975	$50,902	$61,869	$39,640	$50,157
10	00000	**DELAWARE**	652,636	11.1	29.8	28.1	30.9	$35,139	$40,025	$51,037	$30,711	$45,192
10	21200	Dover city, Delaware	19,835	10.3	28.4	32.1	29.2	$21,587	$23,310	$41,648	$18,360	$42,347
10	50670	Newark city, Delaware	16,835	2.4	17.5	25.0	55.2	$12,979	$20,891	$55,302	$8,876	$46,250
10	77580	Wilmington city, Delaware	49,648	12.6	37.2	24.8	25.4	$30,200	$37,740	$46,431	$27,312	$35,525
11	00000	**DISTRICT OF COLUMBIA**	472,884	10.2	17.4	15.7	56.7	$49,891	$52,377	$72,230	$45,201	$62,191
11	50000	Washington city, District of Columbia	472,884	10.2	17.4	15.7	56.7	$49,891	$52,377	$72,230	$45,201	$62,191
12	00000	**FLORIDA**	14,394,281	12.4	29.2	30.0	28.4	$28,381	$31,441	$41,105	$25,382	$35,604
12	00410	Alafaya CDP, Florida	55,599	6.3	21.7	32.2	39.8	$35,236	$40,810	$47,218	$29,413	$34,767
12	00950	Altamonte Springs city, Florida	32,417	5.1	23.1	35.0	36.9	$34,324	$40,187	$45,787	$31,428	$36,622
12	01700	Apopka city, Florida	31,100	9.5	30.9	30.5	29.0	$33,164	$39,995	$50,814	$29,846	$36,865
12	02681	Aventura city, Florida	33,028	3.3	19.2	29.6	48.0	$39,249	$51,003	$69,561	$31,665	$45,052
12	04162	Bayonet Point CDP, Florida	21,686	15.8	37.6	32.0	14.6	$21,975	$25,787	$36,247	$20,467	$23,582
12	05462	Bellview CDP, Florida	15,976	7.7	27.1	43.0	22.2	$30,923	$32,523	$37,558	$27,863	$30,181
12	06875	Bloomingdale CDP, Florida	16,657	2.5	26.0	28.9	42.6	$41,234	$50,862	$55,459	$36,229	$40,227
12	07300	Boca Raton city, Florida	69,035	3.2	17.7	25.3	53.9	$36,468	$50,501	$76,522	$27,181	$46,127
12	07525	Bonita Springs city, Florida	42,635	11.1	27.1	29.9	31.9	$21,419	$19,257	$33,759	$27,514	$33,633
12	07875	Boynton Beach city, Florida	56,420	13.3	27.4	30.8	28.5	$29,195	$30,531	$42,205	$27,515	$43,844

Table E. Cities—Labor Force, Employment, and Educational Data, 2015—*Continued*

FIPS state code	FIPS place code	State/city	Educational attainment of persons age 25 years and older					Median earnings in the past 12 months (in 2015 Inflation-adjusted dollars)				
								All persons age 16 and older with earnings in the past 12 months	Men with earnings		Women with earnings	
			Total population age 25 years and older	Less than high school graduate	High school graduate (includes equivalency)	Some college or Associate's degree	Bachelor's degree or higher		All men with earnings	Men who worked full-time, year-round in the past 12 months	All women with earnings	Women who worked full-time, year-round in the past 12 months
12	07950	Bradenton city, Florida	37,915	17.1	32.2	30.3	20.3	$23,073	$25,878	$31,196	$21,728	$27,630
12	08150	Brandon CDP, Florida	78,180	7.8	24.1	35.9	32.3	$31,660	$35,013	$44,403	$30,636	$40,071
12	08300	Brent CDP, Florida	14,226	12.3	43.1	31.6	13.0	$17,772	$19,081	$36,101	$15,895	$31,720
12	09415	Buenaventura Lakes CDP, Florida	19,947	17.8	37.9	27.3	17.0	$20,903	$21,705	$22,561	$20,402	$21,166
12	10275	Cape Coral city, Florida	131,302	9.5	37.4	30.2	22.9	$29,832	$32,155	$37,360	$26,709	$35,843
12	10825	Carrollwood CDP, Florida	27,238	3.7	19.4	33.2	43.8	$32,759	$36,655	$41,001	$28,482	$39,038
12	11050	Casselberry city, Florida	19,403	5.4	25.2	43.4	26.0	$22,670	$24,102	$31,174	$21,355	$41,357
12	12425	Citrus Park CDP, Florida	18,486	7.1	23.4	35.3	34.2	$37,143	$41,661	$46,887	$31,555	$50,453
12	12875	Clearwater city, Florida	85,597	9.2	26.3	36.5	28.0	$30,421	$31,379	$41,540	$28,511	$37,492
12	12925	Clermont city, Florida	22,261	7.5	20.4	35.3	36.8	$31,032	$26,448	$38,279	$32,169	$41,308
12	13275	Coconut Creek city, Florida	41,213	5.2	34.6	28.9	31.3	$34,511	$40,062	$47,302	$31,544	$41,835
12	14125	Cooper City city, Florida	22,572	3.9	23.9	28.3	43.9	$39,569	$46,980	$65,708	$27,966	$45,037
12	14250	Coral Gables city, Florida	35,730	4.0	13.4	19.9	62.6	$48,298	$60,195	$76,782	$38,860	$57,859
12	14400	Coral Springs city, Florida	83,279	7.2	22.7	33.1	37.0	$32,045	$39,031	$50,021	$29,781	$41,661
12	14412	Coral Terrace CDP, Florida	19,939	17.5	33.0	19.1	30.5	$26,318	$27,411	$37,776	$21,680	$27,253
12	14895	Country Club CDP, Florida	31,888	16.4	32.1	30.1	21.5	$23,117	$28,545	$32,441	$21,049	$27,280
12	15475	Crestview city, Florida	13,320	5.9	27.6	44.3	22.2	$25,453	$32,430	$49,007	$20,388	$31,047
12	15968	Cutler Bay town, Florida	28,682	10.1	28.3	26.6	35.0	$38,750	$40,300	$45,408	$35,856	$43,972
12	16335	Dania Beach city, Florida	23,063	10.7	45.3	22.7	21.3	$26,468	$26,857	$37,150	$25,625	$36,119
12	16475	Davie town, Florida	72,585	9.0	26.8	27.7	36.5	$31,590	$33,854	$43,132	$30,970	$46,012
12	16525	Daytona Beach city, Florida	47,822	10.2	30.5	33.7	25.6	$22,107	$21,944	$30,974	$22,369	$36,738
12	16725	Deerfield Beach city, Florida	58,842	11.6	31.4	28.9	28.1	$27,370	$29,567	$37,658	$24,336	$32,499
12	16875	DeLand city, Florida	19,284	8.0	34.8	32.8	24.4	$26,388	$32,414	$40,998	$22,414	$35,184
12	17100	Delray Beach city, Florida	51,878	13.4	23.9	29.0	33.7	$27,689	$29,873	$46,475	$25,749	$36,080
12	17200	Deltona city, Florida	60,146	10.1	36.6	36.6	16.7	$26,390	$30,018	$35,427	$21,038	$31,114
12	17935	Doral city, Florida	32,952	6.2	15.8	20.4	57.7	$31,235	$45,414	$51,230	$25,521	$31,742
12	18575	Dunedin city, Florida	29,443	8.2	28.8	31.1	31.9	$35,371	$41,403	$54,696	$30,209	$36,705
12	19206	East Lake CDP, Florida	24,404	6.3	15.8	27.1	50.7	$41,991	$60,233	$71,271	$30,741	$45,986
12	19212	East Lake-Orient Park CDP, Florida	15,812	20.9	31.1	23.8	24.2	$25,005	$25,892	$30,414	$21,771	$28,707
12	19825	Edgewater city, Florida	16,965	9.4	41.0	35.9	13.7	$25,608	$29,449	$32,447	$21,741	$31,526
12	20108	Egypt Lake-Leto CDP, Florida	27,762	21.5	20.6	35.4	22.5	$22,424	$28,669	$31,685	$19,233	$25,447
12	20925	Ensley CDP, Florida	16,438	13.4	33.1	36.5	17.0	$22,912	$22,032	$35,710	$23,276	$28,296
12	21150	Estero village, Florida	24,615	5.0	22.2	24.2	48.6	$31,695	$38,033	$76,980	$21,881	$41,641
12	22275	Ferry Pass CDP, Florida	18,837	6.9	24.5	28.6	40.0	$24,760	$29,695	$40,833	$22,302	$36,019
12	22660	Fleming Island CDP, Florida	17,087	1.7	14.5	32.8	51.0	$35,417	$51,155	$72,794	$27,117	$42,344
12	23050	Florida Ridge CDP, Florida	14,733	18.6	31.0	27.3	23.1	$24,196	$25,918	$26,782	$20,112	$33,950
12	24000	Fort Lauderdale city, Florida	133,650	13.2	23.9	26.6	36.3	$29,962	$32,102	$47,474	$26,982	$39,111
12	24125	Fort Myers city, Florida	52,202	20.0	26.4	27.4	26.2	$25,098	$26,990	$38,775	$22,499	$30,670
12	24300	Fort Pierce city, Florida	27,624	24.5	36.1	26.4	13.1	$19,099	$19,315	$26,096	$18,974	$25,343
12	24475	Fort Walton Beach city, Florida	13,896	7.9	27.5	37.5	27.1	$27,888	$30,423	$35,283	$24,922	$31,568
12	24562	Fountainebleau CDP, Florida	44,269	15.9	30.1	22.9	31.1	$26,533	$29,111	$32,477	$25,388	$32,706
12	24581	Four Corners CDP, Florida	24,015	9.9	31.8	32.7	25.6	$27,108	$27,206	$32,072	$26,785	$29,183
12	24925	Fruit Cove CDP, Florida	23,108	2.1	18.9	28.4	50.6	$42,476	$65,157	$101,610	$35,700	$45,054
12	25175	Gainesville city, Florida	69,025	8.1	20.9	26.4	44.6	$18,606	$19,959	$40,521	$17,530	$35,148
12	26300	Golden Gate CDP, Florida	16,648	29.4	37.2	18.2	15.2	$20,896	$26,063	$31,571	$13,872	$20,927
12	26375	Golden Glades CDP, Florida	21,304	26.1	30.5	29.0	14.4	$23,768	$25,695	$31,791	$19,440	$32,190
12	27322	Greenacres city, Florida	28,581	22.2	23.7	30.1	24.0	$25,722	$27,260	$36,513	$21,746	$33,506
12	28400	Haines City city, Florida	16,271	24.4	36.3	24.6	14.7	$22,299	$25,497	$31,623	$20,796	$26,849
12	28452	Hallandale Beach city, Florida	29,689	14.7	27.9	25.9	31.6	$24,224	$28,442	$35,952	$19,396	$32,558
12	30000	Hialeah city, Florida	175,027	30.2	35.1	21.8	12.8	$21,348	$24,035	$30,176	$18,930	$24,202
12	30025	Hialeah Gardens city, Florida	19,114	26.7	34.9	21.6	16.8	$21,745	$31,891	$36,181	$18,150	$21,488
12	31075	Holiday CDP, Florida	15,186	15.1	43.9	29.3	11.7	$23,162	$25,176	$26,551	$21,680	$30,708
12	32000	Hollywood city, Florida	107,085	14.6	31.2	26.6	27.6	$26,038	$30,173	$38,132	$21,023	$35,702
12	32275	Homestead city, Florida	40,953	29.0	27.3	25.3	18.4	$25,320	$26,552	$29,737	$21,772	$33,385
12	32610	Horizon West CDP, Florida	15,657	3.1	14.5	22.3	60.1	$41,142	$48,216	$50,669	$37,552	$46,030
12	32967	Hunters Creek CDP, Florida	17,926	3.6	19.5	31.2	45.8	$34,855	$39,018	$39,946	$31,128	$50,230
12	33250	Immokalee CDP, Florida	16,876	57.9	24.4	13.8	3.9	$13,643	$13,091	$21,188	$14,510	$21,882
12	35000	Jacksonville city, Florida	583,153	11.6	28.3	32.5	27.7	$30,296	$32,123	$42,077	$26,631	$36,139
12	35050	Jacksonville Beach city, Florida	18,849	1.8	16.9	30.7	50.5	$47,525	$50,920	$52,197	$36,931	$50,635
12	35350	Jasmine Estates CDP, Florida	18,030	15.2	37.3	34.4	13.1	$22,454	$22,956	$30,467	$22,240	$27,377
12	35875	Jupiter town, Florida	46,908	6.8	20.3	31.8	41.1	$36,358	$44,964	$56,236	$31,199	$41,713
12	36062	Kendale Lakes CDP, Florida	43,690	14.2	31.5	31.5	22.8	$30,446	$31,156	$34,933	$28,593	$32,689
12	36100	Kendall CDP, Florida	56,951	9.1	17.4	27.5	46.0	$38,283	$41,903	$55,553	$34,789	$46,715
12	36121	Kendall West CDP, Florida	28,109	19.0	28.6	25.9	26.4	$27,162	$31,205	$37,113	$23,682	$29,424
12	36462	Keystone CDP, Florida	16,294	3.1	20.3	23.8	52.8	$51,349	$80,801	$93,010	$40,216	$51,904
12	36550	Key West city, Florida	19,949	8.2	19.4	33.6	38.8	$30,987	$31,418	$37,134	$29,363	$38,586
12	36950	Kissimmee city, Florida	47,550	13.1	33.4	36.1	17.4	$22,850	$25,817	$30,886	$21,524	$27,131
12	37648	Lake Butler CDP, Florida	13,248	4.7	6.3	22.1	66.9	$67,237	$85,296	$110,593	$47,487	$69,149

Table E. Cities—Labor Force, Employment, and Educational Data, 2015—*Continued*

| | | | | | | | | Median earnings in the past 12 months (in 2015 Inflation-adjusted dollars) | | | |
| | | | Educational attainment of persons age 25 years and older | | | | | | Men with earnings | | Women with earnings |
FIPS state code	FIPS place code	State/city	Total population age 25 years and older	Less than high school graduate	High school graduate (includes equivalency)	Some college or Associate's degree	Bachelor's degree or higher	All persons age 16 and older with earnings in the past 12 months	All men with earnings	Men who worked full-time, year-round in the past 12 months	All women with earnings	Women who worked full-time, year-round in the past 12 months
12	38250	Lakeland city, Florida	69,929	15.7	31.5	27.2	25.6	$27,185	$32,345	$40,472	$24,763	$34,548
12	38350	Lake Magdalene CDP, Florida	19,719	8.8	24.1	29.6	37.5	$31,535	$36,000	$41,823	$27,018	$39,356
12	38813	Lakeside CDP, Florida	21,297	9.5	38.2	33.2	19.1	$30,657	$39,113	$41,633	$20,624	$33,065
12	39075	Lake Worth city, Florida	26,259	23.2	27.6	27.0	22.1	$21,634	$21,548	$26,132	$21,732	$31,187
12	39200	Land O' Lakes CDP, Florida	25,175	5.4	21.3	33.8	39.5	$45,500	$48,808	$57,597	$41,286	$49,671
12	39425	Largo city, Florida	62,090	10.3	33.6	36.2	19.9	$27,458	$31,033	$36,841	$22,058	$34,452
12	39525	Lauderdale Lakes city, Florida	21,085	30.7	39.6	23.2	6.5	$17,373	$20,083	$37,121	$16,625	$23,566
12	39550	Lauderhill city, Florida	47,527	17.9	37.0	24.4	20.6	$24,498	$22,496	$31,750	$25,152	$30,719
12	39875	Leesburg city, Florida	15,193	13.3	39.3	34.8	12.6	$18,050	$22,473	$30,530	$13,484	$25,646
12	39925	Lehigh Acres CDP, Florida	75,565	20.2	37.4	28.1	14.3	$25,355	$30,373	$36,126	$20,486	$26,889
12	39950	Leisure City CDP, Florida	14,892	40.9	34.8	17.3	7.0	$17,199	$21,110	$31,934	$15,195	$21,310
12	41775	Lutz CDP, Florida	16,558	2.9	23.9	34.4	38.8	$31,112	$32,354	$41,035	$26,081	$41,573
12	41825	Lynn Haven city, Florida	13,217	2.7	17.9	38.6	40.8	$35,042	$39,203	$50,681	$30,747	$41,427
12	43125	Margate city, Florida	41,989	11.9	34.3	32.2	21.6	$27,185	$29,609	$40,392	$25,688	$31,635
12	43800	Meadow Woods CDP, Florida	22,037	16.2	24.9	29.2	29.7	$26,597	$21,903	$31,767	$30,110	$31,338
12	43975	Melbourne city, Florida	58,475	8.4	33.3	31.9	26.4	$30,020	$31,514	$42,042	$26,144	$31,752
12	44275	Merritt Island CDP, Florida	26,521	6.9	28.5	34.9	29.7	$26,818	$38,686	$47,743	$17,737	$37,868
12	45000	Miami city, Florida	331,782	25.6	29.5	19.2	25.7	$23,546	$25,992	$30,877	$20,783	$26,693
12	45025	Miami Beach city, Florida	73,773	10.6	18.5	22.8	48.1	$32,348	$40,016	$45,232	$27,114	$41,366
12	45060	Miami Gardens city, Florida	72,901	23.2	32.9	32.0	11.9	$24,176	$24,322	$35,004	$23,824	$31,235
12	45100	Miami Lakes town, Florida	22,081	8.5	16.1	36.6	38.7	$41,456	$50,485	$56,092	$32,096	$42,571
12	45975	Miramar city, Florida	90,893	9.0	21.9	34.8	34.3	$35,838	$37,645	$45,070	$31,884	$40,492
12	47625	Naples city, Florida	17,073	6.7	15.7	21.3	56.3	$32,993	$42,038	$50,917	$31,884	$50,256
12	48050	Navarre CDP, Florida	22,534	6.8	16.7	46.8	29.7	$35,584	$45,182	$56,882	$26,146	$36,166
12	48625	New Smyrna Beach city, Florida	19,701	6.8	25.0	36.6	31.7	$30,865	$41,908	$47,326	$23,611	$26,938
12	49260	Northdale CDP, Florida	16,549	4.7	25.2	37.2	32.9	$40,640	$47,143	$50,463	$32,276	$41,646
12	49350	North Fort Myers CDP, Florida	35,264	14.3	35.0	31.7	19.0	$26,579	$26,169	$32,107	$26,902	$35,464
12	49425	North Lauderdale city, Florida	28,179	16.1	39.9	25.6	18.5	$23,936	$26,205	$30,676	$20,728	$29,401
12	49450	North Miami city, Florida	41,065	23.5	29.2	25.4	22.0	$21,118	$22,078	$28,253	$20,182	$26,181
12	49475	North Miami Beach city, Florida	30,565	20.0	30.1	31.0	18.9	$23,789	$25,448	$32,429	$22,857	$26,744
12	49675	North Port city, Florida	42,141	8.1	38.1	29.2	24.6	$36,122	$38,794	$50,836	$35,113	$36,304
12	50575	Oakland Park city, Florida	34,479	18.9	33.0	24.8	23.3	$26,721	$29,081	$37,191	$21,231	$31,084
12	50630	Oakleaf Plantation CDP, Florida	15,311	14.7	24.9	29.0	31.5	$35,814	$41,883	$60,935	$25,560	$41,476
12	50638	Oak Ridge CDP, Florida	14,965	26.8	28.2	30.4	14.6	$21,432	$23,321	$26,295	$19,426	$25,882
12	50750	Ocala city, Florida	37,090	12.5	32.1	34.0	21.4	$26,800	$31,633	$38,507	$23,194	$31,102
12	51075	Ocoee city, Florida	27,491	10.7	26.1	38.2	25.0	$30,961	$32,221	$42,879	$27,465	$37,415
12	53000	Orlando city, Florida	189,403	9.9	24.1	30.5	35.5	$27,669	$31,147	$40,953	$25,647	$35,415
12	53150	Ormond Beach city, Florida	32,325	5.3	31.2	39.2	24.4	$27,957	$31,024	$37,183	$24,557	$35,491
12	53575	Oviedo city, Florida	24,910	4.9	18.0	37.4	39.8	$37,264	$42,120	$60,345	$34,808	$49,887
12	53725	Pace CDP, Florida	15,420	14.0	29.1	29.7	27.1	$27,459	$36,077	$56,473	$22,268	$32,366
12	54000	Palm Bay city, Florida	73,689	11.4	36.2	32.8	19.6	$26,311	$30,034	$36,546	$22,200	$29,510
12	54075	Palm Beach Gardens city, Florida	43,333	5.8	19.9	25.7	48.6	$42,329	$52,236	$61,226	$32,332	$45,239
12	54175	Palm City CDP, Florida	18,691	3.5	14.1	36.2	46.1	$36,128	$55,734	$61,061	$27,185	$47,059
12	54200	Palm Coast city, Florida	60,489	6.1	32.2	35.7	26.0	$25,501	$29,710	$36,780	$21,226	$30,338
12	54275	Palmetto Bay village, Florida	16,478	6.8	15.7	24.0	53.5	$42,525	$56,394	$80,698	$34,212	$40,264
12	54300	Palmetto Estates CDP, Florida	14,480	12.8	41.3	28.4	17.6	$22,195	$23,027	$26,532	$21,255	$25,814
12	54350	Palm Harbor CDP, Florida	45,526	3.4	24.7	36.6	35.4	$32,511	$33,775	$55,017	$31,599	$43,773
12	54387	Palm River-Clair Mel CDP, Florida	14,731	18.1	34.2	34.4	13.3	$28,870	$36,321	$45,876	$23,999	$28,093
12	54450	Palm Springs village, Florida	14,130	23.5	27.8	33.9	14.7	$23,169	$28,058	$30,884	$21,291	$26,843
12	54525	Palm Valley CDP, Florida	15,355	2.1	14.4	24.6	58.9	$44,529	$87,766	$108,705	$30,942	$51,957
12	54700	Panama City city, Florida	27,598	11.6	31.0	35.6	21.8	$22,260	$29,658	$41,034	$20,239	$31,580
12	55125	Parkland city, Florida	18,338	2.7	15.2	22.0	60.2	$66,528	$101,930	$120,531	$45,664	$66,077
12	55775	Pembroke Pines city, Florida	115,440	8.2	25.1	29.6	37.0	$36,347	$42,286	$52,308	$30,823	$42,128
12	55925	Pensacola city, Florida	33,908	6.6	24.6	36.4	32.5	$26,256	$27,489	$43,791	$25,348	$32,078
12	56825	Pine Hills CDP, Florida	42,673	21.1	30.2	31.2	17.5	$20,359	$21,625	$31,078	$19,734	$25,895
12	56975	Pinellas Park city, Florida	39,451	11.1	40.4	29.6	18.9	$30,205	$30,496	$35,383	$29,869	$34,268
12	57425	Plantation city, Florida	66,629	7.1	19.1	32.8	41.0	$36,011	$45,007	$51,359	$30,842	$43,283
12	57550	Plant City city, Florida	23,008	19.5	34.7	24.9	20.9	$27,315	$27,281	$35,007	$27,509	$32,430
12	57900	Poinciana CDP, Florida	46,394	13.1	39.0	30.9	16.9	$19,728	$19,460	$23,149	$20,432	$24,538
12	58050	Pompano Beach city, Florida	77,987	18.9	32.6	26.9	21.6	$26,164	$30,929	$39,879	$19,913	$31,380
12	58350	Port Charlotte CDP, Florida	47,010	11.7	42.1	28.5	17.8	$22,091	$25,595	$34,257	$20,191	$28,914
12	58575	Port Orange city, Florida	42,560	9.8	32.3	36.3	21.6	$26,995	$32,450	$45,183	$22,686	$33,698
12	58715	Port St. Lucie city, Florida	125,704	13.2	35.4	30.4	21.0	$29,502	$31,761	$38,923	$26,003	$31,674
12	58975	Princeton CDP, Florida	16,352	28.6	31.1	22.7	17.6	$29,567	$27,661	$34,586	$32,346	$35,550
12	60230	Richmond West CDP, Florida	21,104	15.3	32.3	28.2	24.3	$29,300	$30,293	$36,123	$26,850	$38,836
12	60950	Riverview CDP, Florida	54,923	7.6	24.0	38.0	30.4	$36,262	$40,752	$50,023	$34,353	$38,453
12	60975	Riviera Beach city, Florida	21,526	13.1	37.3	28.8	20.8	$23,367	$24,661	$31,629	$22,257	$31,507
12	61500	Rockledge city, Florida	20,661	7.6	24.7	31.9	35.8	$35,299	$42,044	$51,544	$22,845	$33,817

Table E. Cities—Labor Force, Employment, and Educational Data, 2015—*Continued*

FIPS state code	FIPS place code	State/city	Total population age 25 years and older	Less than high school graduate	High school graduate (includes equivalency)	Some college or Associate's degree	Bachelor's degree or higher	All persons age 16 and older with earnings in the past 12 months	All men with earnings	Men who worked full-time, year-round in the past 12 months	All women with earnings	Women who worked full-time, year-round in the past 12 months
					Educational attainment of persons age 25 years and older					Men with earnings		Women with earnings	
12	62100	Royal Palm Beach village, Florida	26,978	8.8	23.8	29.9	37.6	$35,766	$36,618	$46,864	$32,218	$42,651
12	62275	Ruskin CDP, Florida	16,346	16.7	28.8	38.8	15.7	$26,134	$26,060	$35,863	$26,145	$40,685
12	62625	St. Cloud city, Florida	28,921	11.4	34.7	35.6	18.4	$29,545	$31,092	$37,380	$26,846	$30,494
12	63000	St. Petersburg city, Florida	187,988	9.6	25.9	31.5	33.0	$30,911	$31,574	$42,381	$30,258	$40,525
12	63425	San Carlos Park CDP, Florida	11,838	12.7	20.9	41.1	25.3	$27,535	$32,214	$45,879	$23,219	$29,079
12	63650	Sanford city, Florida	37,845	10.6	30.2	41.6	17.7	$26,724	$32,113	$41,719	$22,195	$33,510
12	64175	Sarasota city, Florida	42,358	11.9	25.0	26.7	36.4	$28,613	$31,697	$40,229	$24,710	$31,062
12	64825	Sebastian city, Florida	18,685	8.0	41.2	31.1	19.6	$30,734	$32,189	$38,337	$23,382	$31,351
12	67258	South Bradenton CDP, Florida	21,019	17.2	41.7	27.3	13.8	$19,719	$24,284	$35,970	$16,588	$31,333
12	67575	South Miami Heights CDP, Florida	29,745	27.7	37.2	20.6	14.5	$22,243	$27,283	$31,375	$18,540	$26,218
12	68350	Spring Hill CDP, Florida	74,694	11.1	37.6	35.3	16.0	$27,352	$31,373	$39,738	$24,669	$35,446
12	69250	Sun City Center CDP, Florida	22,125	3.5	29.3	34.0	33.2	$25,228	$26,297	$50,117	$23,264	$51,779
12	69555	Sunny Isles Beach city, Florida	11,973	5.8	17.1	27.2	50.0	$30,791	$35,558	$41,669	$19,836	$36,011
12	69700	Sunrise city, Florida	65,375	12.9	27.2	35.4	24.5	$30,538	$31,806	$37,408	$28,663	$35,680
12	70345	Sweetwater city, Florida	13,471	32.5	33.7	13.5	20.3	$18,871	$23,388	$27,459	$16,878	$19,358
12	70600	Tallahassee city, Florida	99,740	7.1	16.9	30.4	45.6	$19,938	$20,538	$40,393	$18,934	$36,684
12	70675	Tamarac city, Florida	51,901	11.8	29.5	28.4	30.3	$28,823	$29,652	$40,485	$26,270	$36,535
12	70700	Tamiami CDP, Florida	48,429	22.3	33.1	22.0	22.7	$28,143	$29,090	$32,101	$26,943	$32,662
12	71000	Tampa city, Florida	247,802	13.1	26.9	24.5	35.5	$29,702	$32,266	$47,417	$26,480	$37,825
12	71150	Tarpon Springs city, Florida	19,485	12.4	31.2	35.3	21.1	$22,037	$22,141	$39,635	$21,945	$31,368
12	71400	Temple Terrace city, Florida	17,430	5.1	14.6	35.0	45.3	$32,051	$39,516	$51,374	$26,324	$35,666
12	71564	The Acreage CDP, Florida	24,354	12.7	34.1	34.2	19.0	$40,679	$45,299	$52,059	$32,344	$46,117
12	71567	The Crossings CDP, Florida	15,942	4.4	21.1	26.4	48.1	$36,374	$36,715	$46,041	$35,945	$48,993
12	71569	The Hammocks CDP, Florida	41,275	9.3	23.8	39.7	27.1	$30,151	$32,407	$36,950	$26,055	$31,923
12	71625	The Villages CDP, Florida	71,492	2.3	27.3	28.0	42.4	$29,877	$27,233	$80,494	$30,043	$49,143
12	71741	Three Lakes CDP, Florida	13,132	5.4	19.9	40.4	34.3	$35,029	$36,591	$46,279	$21,875	$40,239
12	71900	Titusville city, Florida	33,325	8.2	37.3	36.1	18.5	$25,885	$30,720	$46,343	$22,369	$29,575
12	72145	Town 'n' Country CDP, Florida	57,071	11.6	34.0	27.6	26.8	$31,361	$31,349	$40,516	$31,372	$40,279
12	73163	University CDP (Hillsborough County), Florida	26,430	22.7	25.0	24.7	27.6	$20,776	$21,442	$30,551	$19,105	$29,252
12	73172	University CDP (Orange County), Florida	11,854	15.1	33.9	22.3	28.6	$13,206	$16,135	$31,778	$11,641	$22,317
12	73287	University Park CDP, Florida	17,305	20.8	31.8	24.2	23.2	$25,406	$25,499	$27,274	$25,218	$31,767
12	73700	Valrico CDP, Florida	24,140	10.2	25.0	32.3	32.5	$44,394	$52,416	$61,163	$33,524	$37,934
12	73900	Venice city, Florida	20,379	3.9	28.0	28.4	39.8	$24,879	$21,937	$38,699	$25,721	$31,620
12	74200	Vero Beach South CDP, Florida	18,152	7.7	36.9	36.2	19.2	$22,306	$25,297	$37,585	$21,173	$27,939
12	75725	Wekiwa Springs CDP, Florida	16,552	1.7	10.3	35.3	52.7	$49,226	$62,298	$72,385	$31,969	$46,236
12	75812	Wellington village, Florida	42,226	4.0	19.2	28.4	48.4	$41,022	$50,436	$66,519	$33,041	$51,049
12	75875	Wesley Chapel CDP, Florida	35,039	7.4	20.1	38.0	34.5	$38,908	$41,461	$56,504	$33,304	$42,028
12	76062	Westchase CDP, Florida	16,600	5.5	16.6	21.8	56.1	$43,636	$57,268	$81,833	$35,964	$45,667
12	76075	Westchester CDP, Florida	22,915	23.5	29.0	23.7	23.7	$24,237	$22,372	$26,643	$25,731	$31,550
12	76487	West Little River CDP, Florida	21,374	28.7	45.0	18.6	7.7	$19,921	$17,512	$23,640	$21,356	$32,448
12	76500	West Melbourne city, Florida	16,362	5.5	33.0	33.8	27.7	$32,621	$33,716	$41,298	$32,526	$34,279
12	76582	Weston city, Florida	42,754	2.9	10.9	23.1	63.1	$42,389	$60,831	$83,000	$29,522	$48,817
12	76600	West Palm Beach city, Florida	76,754	14.2	26.1	26.1	33.6	$28,511	$30,312	$38,178	$26,840	$35,067
12	76675	West Pensacola CDP, Florida	14,733	12.4	37.6	36.7	13.3	$24,155	$27,668	$28,732	$19,691	$27,460
12	78250	Winter Garden city, Florida	25,049	8.7	28.9	26.3	36.0	$31,148	$33,240	$38,629	$28,812	$40,734
12	78275	Winter Haven city, Florida	27,298	15.5	41.3	29.1	14.1	$21,975	$26,158	$36,559	$20,916	$27,976
12	78300	Winter Park city, Florida	22,272	4.8	15.5	19.6	60.2	$44,700	$51,682	$70,664	$40,315	$46,396
12	78325	Winter Springs city, Florida	25,920	3.5	22.4	34.1	39.9	$35,720	$42,280	$60,445	$25,127	$44,613
12	78800	Wright CDP, Florida	18,284	9.4	30.9	35.5	24.1	$24,318	$33,592	$48,163	$21,731	$26,224
13	00000	**GEORGIA**	6,683,767	13.9	28.1	28.1	29.9	$30,284	$35,154	$45,396	$25,277	$36,650
13	00408	Acworth city, Georgia	13,201	6.2	25.6	35.4	32.8	$40,331	$30,778	$46,566	$42,134	$44,455
13	01052	Albany city, Georgia	43,839	17.9	32.8	30.3	19.0	$24,240	$27,800	$37,104	$22,952	$32,533
13	01696	Alpharetta city, Georgia	40,980	2.5	10.0	20.2	67.2	$47,477	$70,100	$100,933	$36,821	$48,994
13	03440	Athens-Clarke County unified government (balance), Georgia	65,121	15.1	18.6	21.5	44.8	$14,095	$20,659	$33,258	$11,145	$31,560
13	04000	Atlanta city, Georgia	320,178	10.4	19.3	22.1	48.3	$36,779	$41,222	$56,177	$32,349	$44,125
13	04204	Augusta-Richmond County consolidated government (balance), Georgia	128,275	17.1	29.3	32.5	21.1	$25,573	$30,220	$39,882	$21,807	$31,714
13	10944	Brookhaven city, Georgia	34,359	13.7	11.4	13.8	61.1	$41,732	$48,570	$61,417	$37,439	$55,280
13	12834	Candler-McAfee CDP, Georgia	15,629	15.9	33.9	25.6	24.6	$21,902	$24,485	$34,469	$21,416	$29,431
13	12988	Canton city, Georgia	16,044	17.6	18.5	29.4	34.5	$30,158	$39,951	$42,387	$22,370	$50,309
13	13492	Carrollton city, Georgia	12,784	20.0	20.4	25.6	34.0	$20,281	$23,309	$41,607	$15,595	$46,219
13	13688	Cartersville city, Georgia	13,854	21.8	38.2	23.0	16.9	$35,483	$45,943	$46,511	$27,666	$32,944
13	15172	Chamblee city, Georgia	19,364	29.3	17.7	13.3	39.8	$30,211	$30,028	$40,036	$30,458	$41,468
13	19000	Columbus city, Georgia	129,080	13.2	29.4	32.9	24.5	$25,204	$30,870	$42,392	$20,014	$31,348

Table E. Cities—Labor Force, Employment, and Educational Data, 2015—*Continued*

| | | | Educational attainment of persons age 25 years and older | | | | Median earnings in the past 12 months (in 2015 Inflation-adjusted dollars) | | | | |
| | | | | | | | | Men with earnings | | Women with earnings | |
FIPS state code	FIPS place code	State/city	Total population age 25 years and older	Less than high school graduate	High school graduate (includes equivalency)	Some college or Associate's degree	Bachelor's degree or higher	All persons age 16 and older with earnings in the past 12 months	All men with earnings	Men who worked full-time, year-round in the past 12 months	All women with earnings	Women who worked full-time, year-round in the past 12 months
13	21380	Dalton city, Georgia	20,457	41.6	16.7	26.7	15.0	$25,536	$27,169	$29,798	$23,099	$26,116
13	22052	Decatur city, Georgia	14,088	3.1	9.1	9.5	78.3	$60,330	$72,303	$86,654	$37,994	$81,043
13	23900	Douglasville city, Georgia	23,256	11.6	20.5	32.3	35.6	$35,499	$32,003	$46,900	$36,713	$42,199
13	24600	Duluth city, Georgia	19,238	8.6	17.9	27.2	46.2	$34,105	$37,248	$43,945	$32,540	$41,442
13	24768	Dunwoody city, Georgia	32,906	5.1	9.8	15.8	69.2	$56,371	$71,712	$82,484	$35,439	$52,325
13	25720	East Point city, Georgia	24,305	12.7	28.3	34.7	24.4	$28,232	$30,347	$38,189	$25,663	$36,390
13	28044	Evans CDP, Georgia	24,887	9.8	15.1	32.1	43.0	$46,898	$63,249	$70,886	$30,310	$47,604
13	31908	Gainesville city, Georgia	22,779	29.6	28.1	22.5	19.8	$25,849	$27,087	$35,785	$24,788	$30,702
13	35324	Griffin city, Georgia	12,567	22.7	32.8	27.2	17.3	$21,016	$32,168	$36,703	$16,438	$23,141
13	38964	Hinesville city, Georgia	20,870	9.0	30.9	42.1	18.0	$26,055	$30,122	$32,249	$22,958	$30,024
13	42425	Johns Creek city, Georgia	53,204	4.0	11.5	18.8	65.6	$51,153	$74,757	$101,711	$31,237	$60,709
13	43192	Kennesaw city, Georgia	22,317	12.8	21.6	33.7	31.9	$32,869	$33,046	$46,803	$32,771	$40,281
13	44340	LaGrange city, Georgia	19,320	20.4	33.1	29.9	16.5	$22,045	$26,743	$38,507	$20,859	$31,059
13	45488	Lawrenceville city, Georgia	20,423	12.0	29.9	31.9	26.2	$27,249	$29,418	$40,417	$25,608	$32,836
13	48288	Mableton CDP, Georgia	26,822	11.5	26.2	23.1	39.2	$29,529	$31,922	$41,097	$23,592	$38,555
13	48624	McDonough city, Georgia	15,577	14.4	32.2	29.7	23.7	$27,422	$30,894	$38,450	$24,603	$40,021
13	49008	Macon-Bibb County, Georgia	99,357	14.2	32.2	28.3	25.3	$26,430	$28,445	$39,690	$22,704	$34,726
13	49756	Marietta city, Georgia	38,323	13.7	20.4	27.3	38.6	$30,747	$35,258	$50,311	$26,203	$35,638
13	50036	Martinez CDP, Georgia	24,370	8.4	22.2	32.5	36.8	$33,708	$41,795	$47,162	$30,630	$34,132
13	51670	Milton city, Georgia	21,959	3.7	13.1	18.9	64.3	$48,135	$85,927	$121,112	$26,236	$60,743
13	55020	Newnan city, Georgia	22,140	10.2	32.4	30.6	26.8	$32,433	$47,708	$57,826	$25,000	$36,218
13	56168	North Druid Hills CDP, Georgia	15,836	5.0	16.1	18.5	60.4	$50,216	$61,398	$71,052	$45,350	$51,597
13	59724	Peachtree City city, Georgia	22,961	1.3	16.6	26.5	55.6	$50,885	$70,046	$90,623	$32,642	$56,747
13	59735	Peachtree Corners city, Georgia	27,048	7.3	12.2	22.8	57.6	$41,576	$47,590	$66,030	$36,595	$51,953
13	62104	Pooler city, Georgia	18,829	7.5	24.7	30.0	37.8	$31,336	$53,144	$64,754	$21,823	$33,049
13	63952	Redan CDP, Georgia	21,175	5.5	29.2	39.1	26.2	$27,915	$35,209	$39,016	$24,354	$33,471
13	66668	Rome city, Georgia	22,361	23.6	30.3	25.9	20.2	$25,116	$27,196	$31,572	$21,471	$29,502
13	67284	Roswell city, Georgia	63,428	6.6	14.7	22.6	56.2	$42,074	$47,457	$70,027	$36,926	$50,821
13	68516	Sandy Springs city, Georgia	72,940	5.6	12.9	19.4	62.1	$43,419	$51,173	$60,095	$38,596	$50,371
13	69000	Savannah city, Georgia	89,699	12.4	26.8	32.7	28.0	$20,870	$21,963	$31,350	$19,313	$27,716
13	71492	Smyrna city, Georgia	39,558	8.3	17.4	24.0	50.2	$37,438	$37,435	$51,154	$37,445	$50,147
13	73256	Statesboro city, Georgia	11,887	13.6	15.6	37.3	33.5	$10,897	$9,196	$30,569	$12,619	$22,008
13	73704	Stockbridge city, Georgia	17,771	13.3	20.0	30.8	35.9	$30,827	$35,402	$45,291	$30,275	$35,434
13	74180	Sugar Hill city, Georgia	13,293	6.1	22.3	26.4	45.2	$34,240	$36,719	$42,015	$32,173	$39,048
13	77652	Tucker CDP, Georgia	19,945	7.5	18.7	27.6	46.2	$40,831	$41,390	$50,494	$39,795	$58,018
13	78324	Union City city, Georgia	12,563	16.2	41.9	22.3	19.5	$19,262	$18,555	$25,653	$19,986	$40,652
13	78800	Valdosta city, Georgia	32,447	21.6	25.3	27.9	25.2	$17,999	$20,950	$32,077	$14,012	$23,106
13	80508	Warner Robins city, Georgia	45,278	9.4	25.0	46.2	19.4	$30,421	$36,100	$40,971	$23,620	$32,809
13	84176	Woodstock city, Georgia	18,597	3.7	13.2	34.6	48.4	$47,209	$50,705	$66,697	$40,639	$51,182
15	00000	**HAWAII**	985,914	9.1	27.1	32.4	31.4	$34,730	$38,276	$48,074	$30,911	$40,434
15	06290	East Honolulu CDP, Hawaii	35,372	3.3	17.6	26.0	53.1	$52,063	$66,750	$82,118	$41,099	$60,931
15	07470	Ewa Gentry CDP, Hawaii	14,587	6.1	21.4	41.5	31.1	$42,074	$60,055	$61,741	$36,124	$41,729
15	14650	Hilo CDP, Hawaii	29,934	5.3	28.2	29.2	37.3	$33,442	$36,292	$54,543	$32,040	$42,339
15	22700	Kahului CDP, Hawaii	20,288	16.6	37.5	27.8	18.1	$32,141	$33,576	$41,588	$31,573	$37,669
15	23150	Kailua CDP (Honolulu County), Hawaii	26,867	5.5	18.3	28.8	47.5	$40,280	$47,279	$70,685	$32,303	$47,625
15	28250	Kaneohe CDP, Hawaii	24,982	3.5	30.8	31.3	34.4	$41,647	$47,807	$55,878	$38,906	$46,544
15	30300	Kapolei CDP, Hawaii	13,365	7.2	31.9	34.5	26.4	$36,485	$45,168	$50,440	$26,227	$37,253
15	47600	Makakilo CDP, Hawaii	15,353	7.9	25.8	35.1	31.1	$35,318	$45,066	$58,605	$27,206	$37,075
15	51000	Mililani Mauka CDP, Hawaii	13,252	3.3	13.8	33.1	49.8	$50,520	$62,061	$76,595	$42,043	$50,796
15	51050	Mililani Town CDP, Hawaii	19,748	4.5	29.1	31.4	35.0	$40,049	$46,518	$54,717	$34,497	$44,142
15	62600	Pearl City CDP, Hawaii	30,577	6.9	26.1	38.1	29.0	$37,201	$40,707	$52,426	$36,401	$42,325
15	69050	Schofield Barracks CDP, Hawaii	8,308	2.3	22.4	56.3	19.1	$28,060	$30,105	$30,847	$16,786	$29,578
15	71550	Urban Honolulu CDP, Hawaii	262,999	13.1	23.7	27.8	35.4	$32,325	$36,889	$46,272	$30,589	$39,186
15	79700	Waipahu CDP, Hawaii	24,781	15.3	34.9	31.3	18.5	$27,932	$30,959	$37,074	$25,119	$31,235
16	00000	**IDAHO**	1,065,982	10.0	27.5	36.6	26.0	$25,680	$32,036	$43,264	$19,349	$31,808
16	08830	Boise City city, Idaho	142,993	5.4	20.5	34.4	39.7	$27,951	$32,352	$47,429	$23,081	$36,995
16	12250	Caldwell city, Idaho	29,601	22.3	33.4	30.5	13.9	$18,100	$23,982	$40,503	$15,046	$25,658
16	16750	Coeur d'Alene city, Idaho	34,550	7.9	23.0	45.3	23.8	$25,319	$26,682	$39,045	$23,009	$36,579
16	23410	Eagle city, Idaho	14,664	5.6	14.5	31.3	48.6	$36,926	$40,837	$62,115	$35,165	$50,384
16	39700	Idaho Falls city, Idaho	36,467	10.9	26.7	32.5	29.9	$20,887	$29,951	$48,866	$16,536	$30,159
16	46540	Lewiston city, Idaho	22,344	7.2	34.8	33.6	24.5	$31,309	$41,906	$50,156	$23,436	$34,634
16	52120	Meridian city, Idaho	60,530	5.9	22.8	36.1	35.2	$32,491	$42,972	$57,276	$21,375	$39,913
16	54550	Moscow city, Idaho	11,708	2.2	9.8	21.2	66.8	$11,920	$12,155	$38,269	$11,679	$36,312
16	56260	Nampa city, Idaho	54,230	12.9	34.3	34.6	18.2	$23,583	$28,167	$35,176	$18,279	$30,124
16	64090	Pocatello city, Idaho	33,154	8.0	26.9	36.6	28.6	$18,807	$24,147	$40,902	$14,221	$25,430
16	64810	Post Falls city, Idaho	20,688	13.4	30.9	40.9	14.8	$26,647	$34,508	$41,269	$21,161	$36,849
16	67420	Rexburg city, Idaho	9,608	4.4	20.6	40.5	34.5	$8,526	$11,743	$30,170	$6,041	$18,898

Table E. Cities—Labor Force, Employment, and Educational Data, 2015—*Continued*

| | | | Educational attainment of persons age 25 years and older | | | | | Median earnings in the past 12 months (in 2015 Inflation-adjusted dollars) | | | | |
| | | | | | | | | | Men with earnings | | Women with earnings | |
FIPS state code	FIPS place code	State/city	Total population age 25 years and older	Less than high school graduate	High school graduate (includes equivalency)	Some college or Associate's degree	Bachelor's degree or higher	All persons age 16 and older with earnings in the past 12 months	All men with earnings	Men who worked full-time, year-round in the past 12 months	All women with earnings	Women who worked full-time, year-round in the past 12 months
16	82810	Twin Falls city, Idaho	29,872	10.9	24.2	42.9	22.1	$20,663	$29,498	$41,027	$15,642	$27,320
17	00000	**ILLINOIS**	8,661,938	11.4	26.7	28.9	32.9	$32,904	$40,856	$52,161	$27,150	$41,327
17	00243	Addison village, Illinois	24,583	19.2	29.9	27.4	23.5	$28,548	$32,339	$48,594	$22,829	$41,438
17	00685	Algonquin village, Illinois	17,518	1.8	22.8	32.3	43.0	$37,513	$60,141	$85,055	$26,590	$51,246
17	01114	Alton city, Illinois	19,296	6.6	38.2	40.2	14.9	$28,314	$38,325	$50,256	$19,814	$35,173
17	02154	Arlington Heights village, Illinois	57,808	4.7	13.1	25.6	56.6	$50,848	$61,856	$75,128	$40,886	$60,470
17	03012	Aurora city, Illinois	122,593	23.9	20.7	25.6	29.8	$30,817	$36,895	$42,471	$25,669	$36,824
17	04013	Bartlett village, Illinois	27,865	6.6	20.7	30.5	42.2	$51,204	$62,033	$76,921	$32,406	$56,837
17	04078	Batavia city, Illinois	17,500	3.3	17.7	30.3	48.7	$41,367	$56,191	$72,000	$32,301	$54,403
17	04845	Belleville city, Illinois	27,998	7.4	26.4	40.3	25.8	$30,541	$34,101	$42,079	$26,208	$36,116
17	05092	Belvidere city, Illinois	16,652	24.6	29.9	33.0	12.5	$28,440	$35,873	$43,664	$21,315	$37,088
17	05573	Berwyn city, Illinois	34,893	22.8	29.9	25.8	21.5	$30,407	$33,417	$45,259	$27,288	$35,599
17	06587	Bloomingdale village, Illinois	16,996	8.5	22.4	37.3	31.8	$40,795	$42,736	$66,141	$34,506	$53,125
17	06613	Bloomington city, Illinois	52,286	4.8	24.8	19.4	50.9	$35,714	$44,117	$61,095	$29,591	$41,672
17	06704	Blue Island city, Illinois	15,007	21.1	33.8	39.8	5.3	$25,664	$23,785	$31,188	$26,265	$31,996
17	07133	Bolingbrook village, Illinois	45,224	11.6	21.4	31.5	35.4	$30,406	$37,049	$56,564	$23,130	$42,026
17	09447	Buffalo Grove village, Illinois	29,679	2.7	11.2	20.6	65.6	$60,846	$76,037	$90,068	$47,004	$63,658
17	09642	Burbank city, Illinois	18,624	20.6	40.7	27.9	10.8	$27,609	$36,867	$43,737	$18,478	$30,148
17	10487	Calumet City city, Illinois	25,375	15.9	32.9	34.5	16.7	$31,373	$40,060	$52,572	$28,232	$40,173
17	11163	Carbondale city, Illinois	12,886	7.4	13.0	31.7	47.9	$11,418	$11,644	$33,293	$10,970	$38,004
17	11332	Carol Stream village, Illinois	25,224	9.5	19.0	33.0	38.4	$35,040	$38,760	$50,971	$26,584	$43,663
17	11358	Carpentersville village, Illinois	22,052	28.3	20.4	30.6	20.7	$27,663	$32,434	$47,905	$22,459	$33,666
17	12385	Champaign city, Illinois	48,310	3.8	19.1	27.1	50.0	$23,883	$27,493	$50,236	$20,357	$41,676
17	12567	Charleston city, Illinois	9,585	5.8	27.2	27.4	39.6	$13,556	$20,810	$45,500	$11,978	$30,351
17	14000	Chicago city, Illinois	1,851,852	15.9	23.6	23.9	36.6	$32,326	$36,165	$50,396	$30,599	$45,150
17	14026	Chicago Heights city, Illinois	19,259	16.2	30.0	39.8	14.0	$25,579	$35,258	$41,693	$20,649	$31,615
17	14351	Cicero town, Illinois	46,527	37.5	32.2	22.0	8.3	$23,017	$27,062	$33,852	$20,238	$25,815
17	15599	Collinsville city, Illinois	17,362	9.8	28.8	30.5	30.9	$31,779	$39,290	$55,757	$30,113	$36,605
17	17458	Crest Hill city, Illinois	13,249	17.2	32.3	29.7	20.8	$21,939	$21,299	$46,649	$25,118	$36,940
17	17887	Crystal Lake city, Illinois	28,097	6.0	21.3	31.2	41.6	$43,478	$57,431	$66,332	$37,039	$46,129
17	18563	Danville city, Illinois	19,805	15.8	36.4	34.3	13.6	$24,934	$27,364	$35,791	$21,456	$32,979
17	18628	Darien city, Illinois	16,520	2.7	17.7	33.9	45.8	$58,299	$71,250	$84,870	$42,121	$61,543
17	18823	Decatur city, Illinois	49,723	12.6	34.0	32.7	20.7	$25,631	$31,107	$49,980	$22,487	$35,082
17	19161	DeKalb city, Illinois	21,772	9.9	20.7	29.9	39.5	$16,241	$19,852	$46,414	$13,718	$31,163
17	19642	Des Plaines city, Illinois	43,595	12.5	23.2	27.6	36.7	$37,042	$41,235	$51,389	$30,935	$45,388
17	20292	Dolton village, Illinois	15,357	12.0	25.4	40.8	21.8	$26,156	$31,472	$60,562	$22,953	$42,368
17	20591	Downers Grove village, Illinois	34,421	4.2	17.4	31.0	47.4	$46,014	$60,064	$77,023	$39,312	$51,755
17	22073	East Moline city, Illinois	16,407	17.6	34.1	24.8	23.5	$29,291	$41,415	$45,063	$17,157	$27,532
17	22164	East Peoria city, Illinois	16,056	7.6	28.4	39.1	25.0	$33,903	$37,416	$49,208	$28,198	$36,779
17	22255	East St. Louis city, Illinois	17,347	20.4	34.1	35.0	10.5	$13,026	$18,313	$36,706	$11,583	$25,921
17	22697	Edwardsville city, Illinois	13,931	2.1	16.2	24.6	57.2	$22,456	$16,596	$57,517	$24,541	$50,821
17	23074	Elgin city, Illinois	72,164	23.4	21.9	30.4	24.2	$30,259	$34,150	$45,378	$25,015	$36,150
17	23256	Elk Grove Village village, Illinois	25,956	6.6	22.8	37.4	33.3	$41,623	$48,794	$55,074	$35,337	$43,540
17	23620	Elmhurst city, Illinois	28,802	4.2	17.7	23.3	54.7	$57,903	$72,031	$90,753	$43,807	$69,363
17	23724	Elmwood Park village, Illinois	16,490	17.0	32.8	25.4	24.8	$34,155	$44,775	$52,298	$25,530	$37,999
17	24582	Evanston city, Illinois	49,260	5.2	14.4	14.5	65.8	$40,198	$46,457	$78,071	$31,832	$55,516
17	27884	Freeport city, Illinois	15,803	8.8	35.9	38.7	16.5	$22,318	$28,044	$40,782	$16,907	$24,986
17	28326	Galesburg city, Illinois	21,208	11.6	37.6	32.0	18.9	$19,911	$25,112	$36,859	$16,998	$31,178
17	28872	Geneva city, Illinois	15,703	2.4	19.8	20.7	57.1	$42,400	$79,290	$83,989	$31,707	$41,608
17	29730	Glendale Heights village, Illinois	22,953	25.2	22.3	27.7	24.8	$30,196	$32,229	$41,807	$26,190	$33,170
17	29756	Glen Ellyn village, Illinois	18,447	4.9	9.1	24.4	61.6	$46,342	$75,881	$102,413	$27,725	$56,773
17	29938	Glenview village, Illinois	32,783	3.7	12.7	17.5	66.1	$51,564	$80,855	$100,287	$39,797	$63,616
17	30926	Granite City city, Illinois	22,250	11.9	43.7	29.6	14.9	$31,128	$41,849	$52,761	$26,403	$31,747
17	31121	Grayslake village, Illinois	13,213	5.3	14.2	25.8	54.8	$36,841	$56,582	$65,982	$28,889	$54,602
17	32018	Gurnee village, Illinois	19,879	5.1	20.9	28.6	45.3	$37,078	$46,618	$69,257	$34,938	$60,751
17	32746	Hanover Park village, Illinois	24,901	20.1	26.0	25.2	28.6	$30,159	$37,371	$45,735	$22,355	$31,623
17	33383	Harvey city, Illinois	13,778	21.9	42.1	28.0	8.0	$21,174	$28,658	$40,110	$15,119	$21,599
17	34722	Highland Park city, Illinois	18,791	0.9	8.8	18.2	72.2	$62,392	$99,375	$130,878	$45,443	$66,062
17	35411	Hoffman Estates village, Illinois	36,531	10.5	17.6	25.1	46.8	$42,076	$51,955	$65,111	$33,405	$50,918
17	35835	Homer Glen village, Illinois	17,267	7.8	24.4	32.3	35.5	$49,526	$62,435	$81,245	$35,708	$50,144
17	36750	Huntley village, Illinois	17,141	1.9	28.9	36.0	33.2	$47,371	$61,239	$80,734	$41,115	$47,255
17	38570	Joliet city, Illinois	89,913	17.3	33.8	28.2	20.7	$28,878	$37,384	$52,029	$22,305	$35,232
17	38934	Kankakee city, Illinois	16,987	28.1	29.9	29.5	12.6	$21,401	$22,002	$37,588	$19,493	$37,787
17	41183	Lake in the Hills village, Illinois	18,058	4.9	25.7	35.4	34.0	$38,612	$44,642	$58,794	$31,656	$45,975
17	41742	Lake Zurich village, Illinois	13,456	10.1	13.7	19.0	57.2	$50,349	$56,946	$65,747	$37,500	$65,449
17	42028	Lansing village, Illinois	19,733	8.4	28.9	33.6	29.1	$38,509	$40,849	$52,284	$36,181	$45,385
17	43250	Libertyville village, Illinois	14,309	2.2	7.2	15.7	74.9	$42,340	$78,088	$100,568	$35,155	$57,604
17	43939	Lisle village, Illinois	15,011	4.7	13.3	21.2	60.8	$49,869	$50,423	$76,507	$48,772	$66,735

Table E. Cities—Labor Force, Employment, and Educational Data, 2015—*Continued*

| | | | Educational attainment of persons age 25 years and older | | | | | Median earnings in the past 12 months (in 2015 Inflation-adjusted dollars) | | | | |
| | | | | | | | | | Men with earnings | | Women with earnings | |
FIPS state code	FIPS place code	State/city	Total population age 25 years and older	Less than high school graduate	High school graduate (includes equivalency)	Some college or Associate's degree	Bachelor's degree or higher	All persons age 16 and older with earnings in the past 12 months	All men with earnings	Men who worked full-time, year-round in the past 12 months	All women with earnings	Women who worked full-time, year-round in the past 12 months
17	44225	Lockport city, Illinois	15,065	3.6	24.9	35.2	36.3	$48,445	$61,802	$71,695	$35,892	$41,783
17	44407	Lombard village, Illinois	30,764	7.1	17.5	29.3	46.0	$40,156	$46,792	$56,523	$35,554	$55,986
17	45031	Loves Park city, Illinois	15,133	9.7	30.6	35.9	23.7	$33,316	$34,615	$49,561	$32,063	$36,977
17	45694	McHenry city, Illinois	19,210	11.2	27.3	35.9	25.6	$39,869	$43,073	$58,466	$30,496	$40,654
17	45726	Machesney Park village, Illinois	15,885	13.6	42.8	29.6	14.0	$32,409	$41,082	$56,983	$26,193	$35,459
17	47774	Maywood village, Illinois	15,665	15.0	39.7	31.3	14.0	$25,368	$30,445	$36,048	$17,303	$36,411
17	48242	Melrose Park village, Illinois	16,970	30.6	29.9	26.4	13.1	$25,107	$30,028	$36,808	$19,988	$26,392
17	49867	Moline city, Illinois	28,601	15.4	22.1	36.7	25.7	$30,470	$37,272	$41,876	$20,312	$36,804
17	50647	Morton Grove village, Illinois	18,124	9.0	18.5	29.3	43.2	$41,831	$50,774	$55,685	$35,414	$55,869
17	51089	Mount Prospect village, Illinois	38,149	8.5	19.5	28.6	43.4	$38,013	$47,085	$56,144	$30,417	$51,490
17	51349	Mundelein village, Illinois	19,806	11.6	19.2	25.0	44.2	$41,621	$56,088	$62,303	$26,624	$44,111
17	51622	Naperville city, Illinois	95,630	2.4	10.6	21.4	65.5	$50,864	$79,253	$100,932	$32,110	$56,607
17	52584	New Lenox village, Illinois	17,270	3.6	29.2	32.2	34.9	$50,507	$65,716	$79,813	$34,838	$56,306
17	53000	Niles village, Illinois	23,241	17.7	28.4	24.4	29.5	$31,650	$31,461	$40,013	$32,241	$55,076
17	53234	Normal town, Illinois	24,824	2.7	25.2	26.1	46.0	$17,512	$20,340	$44,637	$16,871	$40,125
17	53481	Northbrook village, Illinois	24,919	3.6	9.4	20.1	66.9	$59,570	$91,767	$102,211	$29,405	$65,123
17	53559	North Chicago city, Illinois	14,320	20.9	27.7	31.3	20.1	$17,725	$17,968	$26,929	$17,253	$29,783
17	54638	Oak Forest city, Illinois	18,534	10.3	30.0	30.0	29.7	$38,205	$42,727	$51,991	$35,339	$45,630
17	54820	Oak Lawn village, Illinois	38,444	8.3	30.9	34.4	26.4	$35,622	$40,422	$49,170	$31,659	$42,076
17	54885	Oak Park village, Illinois	37,318	4.1	10.3	17.1	68.5	$53,953	$72,101	$80,856	$42,112	$61,222
17	55249	O'Fallon city, Illinois	18,503	2.8	17.4	35.7	44.1	$40,215	$52,493	$66,510	$26,874	$46,495
17	56640	Orland Park village, Illinois	42,369	6.5	24.9	26.6	42.1	$42,455	$60,271	$81,268	$36,615	$50,192
17	56887	Oswego village, Illinois	22,430	4.8	19.0	33.6	42.6	$46,116	$61,547	$88,744	$36,756	$42,041
17	57225	Palatine village, Illinois	48,725	13.0	17.9	24.5	44.7	$35,450	$41,481	$59,243	$30,728	$41,929
17	57732	Park Forest village, Illinois	15,671	5.4	19.8	49.9	24.9	$32,196	$40,040	$45,807	$31,099	$36,929
17	57875	Park Ridge city, Illinois	24,955	4.8	13.5	23.5	58.2	$55,000	$66,042	$86,222	$41,805	$65,368
17	58447	Pekin city, Illinois	24,825	10.8	38.6	32.4	18.1	$30,467	$40,156	$45,594	$25,484	$32,084
17	59000	Peoria city, Illinois	75,537	11.9	23.0	31.1	34.0	$31,659	$40,093	$54,511	$25,847	$40,344
17	60287	Plainfield village, Illinois	25,094	4.8	19.6	26.3	49.4	$47,199	$69,566	$73,664	$32,054	$43,982
17	62367	Quincy city, Illinois	28,187	7.1	40.4	30.7	21.8	$28,780	$33,952	$39,550	$21,751	$32,457
17	65000	Rockford city, Illinois	97,648	17.0	30.2	32.0	20.9	$23,567	$26,828	$42,443	$21,147	$33,787
17	65078	Rock Island city, Illinois	24,815	10.4	33.6	34.2	21.7	$27,058	$31,183	$46,860	$22,171	$36,270
17	65338	Rolling Meadows city, Illinois	15,348	13.2	18.5	30.3	38.0	$46,362	$49,128	$59,309	$42,264	$51,824
17	65442	Romeoville village, Illinois	26,483	14.6	29.7	28.2	27.5	$32,816	$49,464	$61,952	$20,485	$40,458
17	65806	Roselle village, Illinois	14,292	7.6	22.1	31.2	39.2	$35,506	$41,275	$59,552	$30,010	$50,153
17	66040	Round Lake Beach village, Illinois	16,833	27.2	30.9	27.6	14.3	$22,334	$30,106	$39,611	$18,305	$30,792
17	66703	St. Charles city, Illinois	20,301	4.6	12.0	36.9	46.4	$45,384	$61,577	$71,618	$30,956	$56,269
17	68003	Schaumburg village, Illinois	53,550	6.1	20.6	28.0	45.3	$41,866	$51,322	$61,781	$35,057	$50,926
17	70122	Skokie village, Illinois	47,205	9.9	20.9	24.8	44.4	$38,111	$41,283	$68,594	$35,552	$52,039
17	70720	South Elgin village, Illinois	15,906	16.6	28.7	24.3	30.3	$46,236	$58,494	$75,958	$30,852	$49,936
17	70850	South Holland village, Illinois	15,412	7.7	25.9	37.9	28.5	$36,714	$40,394	$50,352	$31,706	$51,644
17	72000	Springfield city, Illinois	80,461	9.8	25.2	28.8	36.2	$31,467	$39,802	$51,521	$25,324	$43,252
17	73157	Streamwood village, Illinois	28,568	16.5	23.4	30.1	29.9	$36,023	$37,471	$41,056	$35,285	$41,290
17	75484	Tinley Park village, Illinois	41,378	7.3	27.2	32.2	33.3	$42,064	$56,363	$62,374	$31,591	$50,829
17	77005	Urbana city, Illinois	21,464	2.6	15.2	20.0	62.2	$21,170	$22,646	$37,725	$18,900	$40,896
17	77694	Vernon Hills village, Illinois	16,434	2.1	9.6	21.4	66.8	$60,490	$75,997	$100,381	$47,663	$61,231
17	77993	Villa Park village, Illinois	15,184	6.7	22.3	33.7	37.4	$44,438	$51,056	$57,303	$31,102	$51,354
17	79293	Waukegan city, Illinois	53,716	26.2	32.6	22.8	18.4	$23,524	$26,790	$35,935	$20,737	$25,508
17	80060	West Chicago city, Illinois	18,018	30.6	22.0	22.6	24.8	$31,258	$36,290	$41,534	$20,845	$36,138
17	80645	Westmont village, Illinois	17,618	4.4	25.7	31.4	38.5	$40,691	$49,672	$62,485	$29,858	$51,002
17	81048	Wheaton city, Illinois	36,370	3.8	10.4	24.3	61.4	$41,955	$51,365	$73,550	$31,767	$52,325
17	81087	Wheeling village, Illinois	26,350	18.8	22.7	25.0	33.4	$33,106	$35,516	$40,919	$29,256	$40,511
17	82075	Wilmette village, Illinois	18,498	2.7	4.8	12.1	80.3	$66,351	$91,901	$112,118	$47,962	$74,517
17	83245	Woodridge village, Illinois	22,512	3.6	18.5	29.7	48.2	$42,214	$48,808	$60,706	$35,541	$50,582
17	83349	Woodstock city, Illinois	16,664	12.3	26.1	29.9	31.7	$32,782	$41,395	$51,022	$25,627	$44,521
17	84220	Zion city, Illinois	14,456	11.6	38.0	32.5	17.9	$28,237	$27,548	$34,384	$28,840	$41,791
18	00000	**INDIANA**	4,363,573	11.8	34.3	29.0	24.9	$30,229	$36,454	$47,092	$23,449	$35,753
18	01468	Anderson city, Indiana	37,099	13.3	39.2	30.7	16.8	$21,436	$25,511	$35,371	$16,928	$31,354
18	05860	Bloomington city, Indiana	37,794	7.0	13.8	24.1	55.1	$10,486	$13,767	$37,181	$7,416	$35,114
18	08416	Brownsburg town, Indiana	16,674	8.8	15.9	40.1	35.3	$30,496	$25,080	$41,512	$31,211	$42,030
18	10342	Carmel city, Indiana	57,737	2.7	9.7	17.8	69.8	$56,075	$79,994	$100,130	$37,347	$56,085
18	12934	Clarksville town, Indiana	14,805	17.3	39.1	27.5	16.1	$28,604	$33,591	$39,136	$19,312	$31,981
18	14734	Columbus city, Indiana	31,052	7.2	26.2	30.5	36.1	$32,185	$41,830	$50,203	$20,808	$35,532
18	16138	Crown Point city, Indiana	19,003	6.3	28.7	31.4	33.7	$41,392	$51,231	$61,082	$30,498	$51,981
18	19486	East Chicago city, Indiana	18,108	33.6	36.7	22.5	7.1	$21,640	$24,751	$31,932	$19,598	$33,377
18	20728	Elkhart city, Indiana	32,292	21.0	37.9	26.4	14.7	$25,740	$31,574	$40,099	$20,490	$26,988
18	22000	Evansville city, Indiana	81,290	12.8	38.0	29.1	20.1	$24,384	$29,736	$40,319	$21,270	$30,078

Table E. Cities—Labor Force, Employment, and Educational Data, 2015—*Continued*

| | | | | | | | | Median earnings in the past 12 months (in 2015 Inflation-adjusted dollars) | | | | |
| | | | Educational attainment of persons age 25 years and older | | | | | | Men with earnings | | Women with earnings | |
FIPS state code	FIPS place code	State/city	Total population age 25 years and older	Less than high school graduate	High school graduate (includes equivalency)	Some college or Associate's degree	Bachelor's degree or higher	All persons age 16 and older with earnings in the past 12 months	All men with earnings	Men who worked full-time, year-round in the past 12 months	All women with earnings	Women who worked full-time, year-round in the past 12 months
18	23278	Fishers town, Indiana	53,894	1.8	10.1	19.9	68.2	$57,263	$77,132	$86,130	$42,379	$55,615
18	25000	Fort Wayne city, Indiana	164,839	11.4	28.4	33.3	26.9	$28,782	$32,091	$41,518	$25,250	$32,382
18	25450	Franklin city, Indiana	17,354	10.2	34.8	25.6	29.4	$32,042	$39,784	$41,526	$23,190	$32,055
18	27000	Gary city, Indiana	49,873	12.1	37.2	38.1	12.6	$21,831	$26,479	$40,796	$19,769	$30,873
18	28386	Goshen city, Indiana	21,872	27.4	33.6	22.6	16.5	$23,496	$27,056	$31,699	$16,154	$26,221
18	28800	Granger CDP, Indiana	19,675	5.3	20.8	22.3	51.6	$44,515	$65,668	$92,602	$31,749	$44,684
18	29520	Greenfield city, Indiana	12,754	14.7	39.5	28.2	17.6	$37,637	$49,465	$52,473	$30,730	$40,072
18	29898	Greenwood city, Indiana	36,089	8.5	31.5	30.1	29.9	$38,409	$47,082	$54,334	$30,241	$42,081
18	31000	Hammond city, Indiana	50,967	18.0	39.8	28.2	14.0	$26,354	$31,034	$39,421	$21,199	$34,339
18	33466	Highland town, Indiana	18,204	7.8	36.7	29.7	25.8	$39,735	$45,682	$50,713	$31,894	$43,892
18	34114	Hobart city, Indiana	21,746	12.8	38.7	25.1	23.5	$35,217	$36,814	$60,456	$31,904	$41,843
18	36003	Indianapolis city (balance), Indiana	556,012	15.1	27.5	28.0	29.4	$27,798	$31,161	$41,111	$25,426	$35,861
18	38358	Jeffersonville city, Indiana	32,748	7.3	33.4	33.7	25.6	$35,346	$40,175	$45,182	$30,559	$41,231
18	40392	Kokomo city, Indiana	40,130	15.8	39.7	30.4	14.1	$29,055	$35,031	$47,418	$23,901	$31,355
18	40788	Lafayette city, Indiana	45,343	12.6	32.3	33.5	21.7	$24,785	$28,593	$36,735	$20,435	$27,833
18	42246	La Porte city, Indiana	14,568	16.8	40.7	29.0	13.6	$21,081	$29,128	$43,251	$17,065	$26,033
18	42426	Lawrence city, Indiana	31,764	19.2	24.4	24.3	32.2	$31,447	$34,648	$41,595	$30,493	$39,690
18	46908	Marion city, Indiana	18,498	16.1	49.9	24.4	9.6	$16,079	$25,173	$32,754	$12,983	$21,676
18	48528	Merrillville town, Indiana	23,726	8.9	26.2	39.3	25.6	$32,942	$48,228	$60,250	$22,495	$35,968
18	48798	Michigan City city, Indiana	21,604	15.2	37.0	29.4	18.4	$22,525	$29,121	$40,058	$16,493	$27,409
18	49932	Mishawaka city, Indiana	34,739	14.4	30.6	29.6	25.3	$26,052	$33,194	$41,161	$21,896	$31,140
18	51876	Muncie city, Indiana	36,779	11.3	36.0	31.2	21.5	$15,495	$18,841	$36,877	$12,795	$31,908
18	51912	Munster town, Indiana	14,896	8.7	21.1	24.0	46.1	$50,268	$56,186	$75,480	$36,655	$61,815
18	52326	New Albany city, Indiana	24,917	13.7	31.6	35.7	19.0	$30,354	$31,410	$46,400	$25,326	$33,508
18	54180	Noblesville city, Indiana	39,148	8.9	24.3	30.1	36.8	$35,552	$46,199	$52,138	$26,221	$40,101
18	60246	Plainfield town, Indiana	20,331	8.0	39.7	28.3	24.0	$34,372	$46,324	$51,068	$21,127	$35,760
18	61092	Portage city, Indiana	24,383	13.7	41.2	31.8	13.3	$29,608	$43,458	$52,246	$16,340	$30,081
18	64260	Richmond city, Indiana	23,411	24.3	34.2	25.8	15.7	$22,394	$22,522	$29,945	$22,159	$31,407
18	68220	Schererville town, Indiana	19,378	8.3	34.8	32.0	24.9	$29,924	$41,171	$65,282	$21,911	$40,278
18	71000	South Bend city, Indiana	63,271	17.2	32.1	28.0	22.8	$25,202	$28,686	$40,294	$23,119	$29,250
18	75428	Terre Haute city, Indiana	38,134	19.6	30.2	28.0	22.2	$16,685	$20,810	$34,459	$12,342	$35,162
18	78326	Valparaiso city, Indiana	21,738	5.0	24.8	29.3	40.9	$27,779	$37,332	$61,410	$18,148	$43,398
18	82700	Westfield city, Indiana	24,303	3.1	16.8	25.0	55.1	$42,031	$60,720	$69,626	$26,925	$50,541
18	82862	West Lafayette city, Indiana	13,218	9.1	6.3	12.8	71.8	$7,233	$8,793	$41,752	$5,732	$52,822
18	86372	Zionsville town, Indiana	17,305	1.5	10.9	16.9	70.7	$71,915	$82,021	$104,704	$52,496	$72,787
19	00000	**IOWA**	2,074,504	8.3	32.1	32.8	26.8	$30,916	$37,901	$47,298	$25,007	$36,264
19	01855	Ames city, Iowa	27,692	1.9	10.4	22.5	65.2	$12,247	$12,271	$50,861	$12,199	$41,117
19	02305	Ankeny city, Iowa	34,059	3.8	20.4	31.0	44.8	$37,027	$45,979	$57,258	$31,934	$42,104
19	06355	Bettendorf city, Iowa	24,357	2.9	20.8	29.1	47.2	$41,207	$56,133	$65,629	$31,778	$42,333
19	09550	Burlington city, Iowa	18,414	9.6	37.3	33.3	19.8	$27,161	$35,280	$45,054	$19,389	$37,780
19	11755	Cedar Falls city, Iowa	21,657	4.1	21.9	30.1	43.8	$25,467	$31,747	$50,571	$17,460	$41,063
19	12000	Cedar Rapids city, Iowa	86,501	6.4	29.6	35.0	29.0	$31,242	$37,373	$46,688	$25,142	$37,216
19	14430	Clinton city, Iowa	16,945	7.7	37.4	32.1	22.7	$27,407	$42,341	$56,049	$20,696	$28,007
19	16230	Coralville city, Iowa	12,117	7.2	24.7	22.9	45.1	$27,026	$28,368	$41,201	$26,569	$41,314
19	16860	Council Bluffs city, Iowa	41,997	15.9	34.0	31.7	18.4	$30,759	$36,586	$42,096	$24,239	$35,858
19	19000	Davenport city, Iowa	67,539	10.3	32.9	31.7	25.1	$29,479	$36,506	$44,996	$25,551	$31,756
19	21000	Des Moines city, Iowa	138,768	13.1	30.2	30.6	26.1	$29,596	$33,236	$42,451	$25,817	$34,665
19	22395	Dubuque city, Iowa	39,623	9.4	30.3	28.6	31.7	$26,013	$30,058	$45,624	$21,633	$35,666
19	28515	Fort Dodge city, Iowa	15,837	8.3	30.0	43.4	18.4	$21,270	$27,058	$45,966	$17,297	$26,509
19	38595	Iowa City city, Iowa	37,861	5.3	15.0	23.5	56.2	$17,295	$21,001	$42,850	$15,161	$45,185
19	39765	Johnston city, Iowa	14,945	5.8	17.2	24.2	52.7	$65,920	$71,086	$85,808	$55,865	$70,555
19	49485	Marion city, Iowa	26,036	2.2	25.9	37.0	34.9	$42,338	$55,407	$59,744	$35,081	$42,187
19	49755	Marshalltown city, Iowa	18,559	22.6	35.1	25.1	17.3	$26,059	$32,169	$41,007	$21,073	$34,337
19	50160	Mason City city, Iowa	17,809	5.4	29.8	48.1	16.8	$21,041	$31,840	$48,066	$12,195	$35,598
19	55110	Muscatine city, Iowa	16,493	11.1	34.4	33.9	20.6	$30,237	$35,825	$37,117	$22,014	$31,593
19	60465	Ottumwa city, Iowa	16,491	14.8	30.4	38.4	16.4	$30,264	$31,732	$39,625	$25,793	$34,369
19	73335	Sioux City city, Iowa	52,261	15.9	35.5	27.0	21.7	$27,948	$32,228	$41,889	$25,166	$31,816
19	79950	Urbandale city, Iowa	28,310	3.1	19.2	31.9	45.8	$38,578	$50,369	$60,927	$31,261	$40,973
19	82425	Waterloo city, Iowa	45,855	11.8	32.4	30.9	25.0	$27,397	$30,551	$42,103	$25,169	$31,778
19	83910	West Des Moines city, Iowa	46,033	5.3	12.9	28.1	53.7	$42,258	$52,068	$60,275	$36,014	$45,529
20	00000	**KANSAS**	1,888,479	9.7	26.5	32.0	31.7	$31,014	$37,240	$47,864	$24,650	$36,671
20	17800	Derby city, Kansas	15,988	3.2	19.6	34.7	42.5	$41,837	$50,090	$52,622	$31,273	$44,346
20	18250	Dodge City city, Kansas	15,406	25.6	29.4	27.4	17.6	$25,664	$29,934	$37,014	$22,002	$26,334
20	21275	Emporia city, Kansas	15,758	13.1	21.2	39.4	26.2	$20,775	$24,437	$33,382	$16,666	$31,173
20	25325	Garden City city, Kansas	16,312	30.4	19.7	30.6	19.4	$28,633	$32,954	$37,404	$20,008	$32,959
20	25425	Gardner city, Kansas	12,823	3.9	23.9	32.3	39.8	$37,934	$43,088	$47,214	$31,536	$43,454
20	31100	Hays city, Kansas	11,813	5.4	25.4	30.2	38.9	$19,856	$28,140	$50,959	$14,941	$36,250

Table E. Cities—Labor Force, Employment, and Educational Data, 2015—*Continued*

| | | | Educational attainment of persons age 25 years and older | | | | Median earnings in the past 12 months (in 2015 Inflation-adjusted dollars) | | | | |
| | | | | | | | | Men with earnings | | Women with earnings | |
FIPS state code	FIPS place code	State/city	Total population age 25 years and older	Less than high school graduate	High school graduate (includes equivalency)	Some college or Associate's degree	Bachelor's degree or higher	All persons age 16 and older with earnings in the past 12 months	All men with earnings	Men who worked full-time, year-round in the past 12 months	All women with earnings	Women who worked full-time, year-round in the past 12 months
20	33625	Hutchinson city, Kansas	27,801	12.6	29.7	37.7	20.0	$24,628	$27,347	$40,280	$22,372	$29,502
20	35750	Junction City city, Kansas	13,370	9.4	22.5	48.5	19.5	$31,935	$45,246	$47,083	$21,995	$31,914
20	36000	Kansas City city, Kansas	94,606	23.0	33.2	27.6	16.3	$26,067	$29,332	$36,665	$22,012	$31,422
20	38900	Lawrence city, Kansas	51,126	6.9	17.9	25.1	50.1	$20,854	$22,075	$50,141	$19,183	$37,190
20	39000	Leavenworth city, Kansas	22,106	10.9	25.2	32.2	31.7	$27,269	$32,240	$47,976	$22,169	$38,039
20	39075	Leawood city, Kansas	23,631	0.0	5.6	15.8	78.6	$70,685	$104,593	$136,689	$40,293	$75,066
20	39350	Lenexa city, Kansas	37,034	4.9	12.4	24.3	58.5	$45,405	$53,806	$61,794	$37,019	$47,917
20	39825	Liberal city, Kansas	12,015	39.9	25.0	25.2	9.9	$24,264	$24,701	$38,449	$23,184	$32,306
20	44250	Manhattan city, Kansas	27,045	5.1	15.6	33.2	46.1	$14,776	$20,672	$46,544	$11,039	$35,878
20	52575	Olathe city, Kansas	79,965	5.0	18.6	29.4	47.0	$37,190	$46,251	$61,727	$30,651	$41,113
20	53775	Overland Park city, Kansas	129,737	2.0	11.8	24.7	61.5	$45,107	$56,968	$75,011	$35,544	$48,226
20	56025	Pittsburg city, Kansas	10,654	13.0	21.5	30.9	34.6	$19,458	$24,211	$32,240	$15,636	$35,060
20	57575	Prairie Village city, Kansas	15,007	1.2	8.5	15.9	74.4	$48,915	$52,328	$73,570	$42,364	$54,252
20	62700	Salina city, Kansas	31,052	11.7	33.8	34.9	19.7	$25,831	$30,360	$32,916	$20,966	$28,293
20	64500	Shawnee city, Kansas	44,278	6.4	24.5	23.6	45.5	$40,069	$49,437	$61,122	$31,419	$51,475
20	71000	Topeka city, Kansas	84,431	11.1	28.2	31.5	29.3	$29,697	$30,996	$41,941	$28,368	$35,901
20	79000	Wichita city, Kansas	249,658	12.9	27.4	33.7	26.0	$29,749	$36,001	$45,471	$23,312	$34,817
21	00000	**KENTUCKY**	2,988,790	14.9	33.5	28.3	23.3	$27,807	$32,295	$43,037	$23,160	$35,294
21	02368	Ashland city, Kentucky	14,927	7.7	32.5	36.9	22.9	$26,132	$26,728	$61,088	$24,701	$37,542
21	08902	Bowling Green city, Kentucky	34,802	16.1	25.6	27.3	31.1	$19,610	$20,868	$32,584	$16,575	$29,365
21	17848	Covington city, Kentucky	27,854	16.7	35.7	28.1	19.6	$24,541	$27,388	$40,645	$21,016	$35,797
21	24274	Elizabethtown city, Kentucky	18,199	13.4	27.4	32.7	26.5	$22,684	$30,431	$42,094	$20,271	$36,875
21	27982	Florence city, Kentucky	20,836	7.7	27.4	39.7	25.2	$30,353	$31,715	$39,363	$25,570	$36,345
21	28900	Frankfort city, Kentucky	16,760	12.4	33.2	29.2	25.2	$29,865	$32,637	$38,588	$25,971	$36,938
21	30700	Georgetown city, Kentucky	21,023	10.7	31.1	29.4	28.8	$28,969	$35,754	$47,198	$22,799	$36,132
21	35866	Henderson city, Kentucky	20,167	15.6	34.4	32.9	17.1	$24,241	$30,612	$44,318	$21,320	$30,580
21	37918	Hopkinsville city, Kentucky	21,358	12.9	32.0	36.9	18.3	$21,306	$26,337	$38,325	$16,396	$19,971
21	39142	Independence city, Kentucky	17,704	11.3	32.3	31.2	25.2	$36,843	$45,018	$46,995	$30,058	$47,028
21	40222	Jeffersontown city, Kentucky	19,859	9.5	20.3	31.4	38.8	$35,190	$35,672	$45,140	$33,993	$41,724
21	46027	Lexington-Fayette urban county, Kentucky	203,167	10.0	20.4	28.1	41.6	$27,465	$31,307	$45,396	$23,595	$39,405
21	48006	Louisville/Jefferson County metro government (balance), Kentucky	417,075	10.5	29.5	29.9	30.1	$30,202	$33,767	$45,526	$25,855	$37,127
21	56136	Nicholasville city, Kentucky	18,227	14.8	33.1	26.8	25.4	$23,569	$27,797	$36,639	$19,909	$36,034
21	58620	Owensboro city, Kentucky	37,957	14.4	32.6	31.1	22.0	$26,466	$32,354	$44,638	$21,163	$30,069
21	58836	Paducah city, Kentucky	17,938	12.9	29.4	30.6	27.1	$30,373	$31,093	$36,928	$26,419	$35,901
21	63912	Radcliff city, Kentucky	14,752	12.8	26.8	38.2	22.2	$23,781	$26,648	$36,820	$17,351	$35,159
21	65226	Richmond city, Kentucky	18,121	14.2	26.8	26.5	32.5	$15,775	$26,225	$40,399	$10,189	$30,378
22	00000	**LOUISIANA**	3,095,255	15.4	34.1	27.3	23.2	$30,263	$37,630	$49,730	$23,460	$33,832
22	00975	Alexandria city, Louisiana	33,313	15.7	32.5	27.8	24.0	$23,576	$26,920	$37,042	$19,432	$31,738
22	05000	Baton Rouge city, Louisiana	136,406	10.8	27.6	28.8	32.9	$24,134	$30,062	$50,007	$20,262	$31,425
22	05210	Bayou Cane CDP, Louisiana	14,224	19.8	31.7	31.6	16.9	$35,585	$50,875	$48,545	$25,306	$31,824
22	08920	Bossier City city, Louisiana	43,795	13.4	27.1	39.0	20.5	$30,060	$33,400	$41,847	$25,673	$35,088
22	13960	Central city, Louisiana	19,785	5.8	41.9	22.6	29.8	$40,290	$53,244	$57,038	$30,214	$39,477
22	14135	Chalmette CDP, Louisiana	15,526	18.3	29.3	35.0	17.3	$26,105	$27,389	$36,459	$25,131	$41,177
22	32755	Hammond city, Louisiana	12,020	13.7	35.3	28.0	23.0	$16,087	$22,424	$39,659	$12,805	$26,658
22	33245	Harvey CDP, Louisiana	13,662	27.2	30.5	25.5	16.8	$28,252	$30,615	$31,591	$23,047	$30,118
22	36255	Houma city, Louisiana	23,828	12.6	44.3	25.1	18.0	$30,519	$36,114	$50,035	$22,092	$33,181
22	39475	Kenner city, Louisiana	44,843	16.7	32.1	28.3	22.9	$30,615	$32,491	$40,729	$26,610	$35,412
22	40735	Lafayette city, Louisiana	80,338	12.6	23.6	25.4	38.4	$25,620	$30,348	$50,019	$21,057	$33,194
22	41155	Lake Charles city, Louisiana	47,654	14.4	28.0	32.3	25.3	$22,454	$30,045	$41,049	$18,931	$26,888
22	42030	Laplace CDP, Louisiana	18,383	10.9	36.5	33.7	18.8	$34,329	$41,308	$47,844	$26,626	$35,370
22	48785	Marrero CDP, Louisiana	19,992	20.7	37.8	29.4	12.0	$30,800	$35,224	$38,750	$22,071	$30,832
22	50115	Metairie CDP, Louisiana	109,441	8.9	27.1	27.6	36.4	$32,095	$36,510	$46,202	$29,553	$37,995
22	51410	Monroe city, Louisiana	29,666	17.6	28.0	24.9	29.5	$20,784	$21,611	$30,624	$19,745	$29,165
22	54035	New Iberia city, Louisiana	19,867	23.1	43.1	18.5	15.3	$22,635	$25,264	$47,500	$20,156	$25,558
22	55000	New Orleans city, Louisiana	272,132	14.0	22.1	28.0	36.0	$29,366	$31,249	$42,066	$26,916	$38,611
22	62385	Prairieville CDP, Louisiana	21,963	7.4	27.0	28.3	37.3	$51,002	$65,425	$81,771	$35,701	$50,245
22	66655	Ruston city, Louisiana	9,992	12.9	14.4	30.6	42.1	$11,770	$22,756	$41,632	$9,485	$30,744
22	70000	Shreveport city, Louisiana	128,570	13.6	32.4	29.0	24.9	$24,481	$32,047	$42,100	$21,225	$31,912
22	70805	Slidell city, Louisiana	19,498	12.3	35.0	26.4	26.4	$30,982	$35,429	$46,643	$26,232	$32,299
22	73640	Sulphur city, Louisiana	15,851	15.4	34.3	31.0	19.3	$32,047	$52,697	$62,115	$19,849	$30,003
22	75180	Terrytown CDP, Louisiana	16,569	22.6	29.6	30.2	17.6	$25,660	$27,121	$34,275	$21,740	$36,223
23	00000	**MAINE**	961,240	8.3	32.7	28.9	30.1	$29,367	$34,492	$46,934	$25,045	$36,841
23	02060	Auburn city, Maine	15,570	13.4	29.5	32.5	24.6	$30,910	$41,256	$46,120	$22,684	$30,809
23	02795	Bangor city, Maine	23,194	6.6	29.8	36.4	27.2	$21,973	$23,822	$50,730	$20,876	$45,818
23	04860	Biddeford city, Maine	13,267	16.5	31.8	21.2	30.5	$23,151	$35,567	$55,503	$15,750	$31,580

Table E. Cities—Labor Force, Employment, and Educational Data, 2015—*Continued*

| | | | Educational attainment of persons age 25 years and older | | | | | Median earnings in the past 12 months (in 2015 Inflation-adjusted dollars) | | | | |
| | | | | | | | | | Men with earnings | | Women with earnings | |
FIPS state code	FIPS place code	State/city	Total population age 25 years and older	Less than high school graduate	High school graduate (includes equivalency)	Some college or Associate's degree	Bachelor's degree or higher	All persons age 16 and older with earnings in the past 12 months	All men with earnings	Men who worked full-time, year-round in the past 12 months	All women with earnings	Women who worked full-time, year-round in the past 12 months
23	38740	Lewiston city, Maine	24,897	17.3	34.6	28.4	19.7	$26,303	$29,492	$35,781	$24,107	$31,447
23	60545	Portland city, Maine	50,620	5.0	20.9	24.1	50.0	$31,839	$35,737	$47,671	$29,646	$40,308
23	65725	Sanford city, Maine	15,358	9.2	43.9	26.7	20.3	$27,304	$28,957	$41,944	$25,821	$30,510
23	71990	South Portland city, Maine	17,859	3.8	25.8	27.2	43.2	$31,105	$37,568	$60,097	$30,133	$45,469
24	00000	**MARYLAND**	4,102,486	10.4	25.1	25.7	38.8	$40,893	$46,509	$60,591	$35,647	$50,635
24	01600	Annapolis city, Maryland	29,275	12.5	24.6	20.8	42.1	$33,220	$37,913	$50,015	$32,126	$43,364
24	01975	Arbutus CDP, Maryland	15,947	9.8	30.2	29.5	30.5	$33,201	$36,598	$45,282	$24,907	$45,053
24	02275	Arnold CDP, Maryland	15,705	5.3	14.0	25.4	55.3	$51,964	$70,077	$86,711	$46,329	$58,088
24	02825	Aspen Hill CDP, Maryland	36,395	13.2	21.0	22.7	43.1	$34,528	$41,707	$56,554	$28,341	$50,354
24	04000	Baltimore city, Maryland	425,261	15.3	29.9	24.9	29.9	$32,248	$35,741	$46,556	$30,861	$41,796
24	05825	Bel Air North CDP, Maryland	21,895	5.7	27.6	29.3	37.4	$42,207	$59,731	$71,128	$27,482	$46,283
24	05950	Bel Air South CDP, Maryland	32,324	3.5	24.1	27.5	44.9	$46,081	$55,200	$70,054	$37,669	$51,442
24	07125	Bethesda CDP, Maryland	41,788	1.5	4.4	9.7	84.4	$72,323	$101,317	$136,792	$58,099	$82,042
24	08775	Bowie city, Maryland	41,745	4.7	17.3	26.9	51.1	$57,000	$60,468	$71,418	$55,750	$70,506
24	12600	Camp Springs CDP, Maryland	18,153	10.4	29.9	29.0	30.7	$39,180	$39,795	$43,343	$38,588	$60,876
24	13325	Carney CDP, Maryland	21,083	5.3	24.0	37.0	33.7	$31,687	$31,623	$46,990	$31,759	$40,717
24	14125	Catonsville CDP, Maryland	29,770	5.1	20.6	26.6	47.6	$45,984	$55,054	$65,231	$38,790	$55,072
24	16875	Chillum CDP, Maryland	27,523	35.0	23.9	21.9	19.2	$30,303	$31,202	$35,105	$23,750	$36,049
24	17350	Clarksburg CDP, Maryland	13,497	3.1	10.6	23.4	63.0	$62,184	$92,051	$103,008	$42,263	$70,608
24	17900	Clinton CDP, Maryland	27,716	5.4	32.5	39.7	22.4	$50,862	$53,333	$63,109	$48,634	$74,572
24	18250	Cockeysville CDP, Maryland	16,374	9.1	20.9	20.9	49.2	$37,433	$42,905	$60,731	$24,554	$46,346
24	18750	College Park city, Maryland	12,806	12.7	20.9	18.0	48.4	$7,427	$7,431	$71,623	$7,422	$45,721
24	19125	Columbia CDP, Maryland	70,254	4.3	11.7	21.2	62.8	$52,470	$61,612	$80,400	$47,054	$61,869
24	20875	Crofton CDP, Maryland	19,014	1.3	13.2	25.4	60.1	$70,042	$78,803	$90,474	$56,598	$76,082
24	21325	Cumberland city, Maryland	14,035	8.5	43.4	30.7	17.4	$19,630	$26,346	$33,898	$18,143	$30,075
24	23975	Dundalk CDP, Maryland	41,937	23.6	40.1	24.5	11.8	$31,032	$35,547	$45,543	$25,086	$42,462
24	25150	Edgewood CDP, Maryland	14,731	14.0	24.7	42.9	18.4	$35,299	$31,183	$41,074	$40,098	$50,720
24	25575	Eldersburg CDP, Maryland	21,679	7.4	20.7	27.4	44.5	$51,818	$62,778	$75,243	$41,200	$60,618
24	26000	Ellicott City CDP, Maryland	48,916	4.4	12.0	17.9	65.7	$66,354	$88,064	$101,020	$43,919	$70,779
24	26600	Essex CDP, Maryland	27,071	16.2	38.1	28.9	16.9	$35,045	$41,089	$51,240	$31,134	$36,367
24	27250	Fairland CDP, Maryland	18,722	6.8	18.1	28.7	46.4	$34,752	$40,133	$42,427	$26,874	$40,129
24	29525	Fort Washington CDP, Maryland	17,919	8.0	21.7	26.4	44.0	$47,371	$42,660	$61,873	$49,142	$62,721
24	30325	Frederick city, Maryland	46,485	9.8	25.1	28.0	37.2	$33,502	$35,633	$43,850	$30,601	$38,495
24	31175	Gaithersburg city, Maryland	45,405	13.3	14.1	20.2	52.4	$40,907	$45,199	$57,292	$37,094	$60,693
24	32025	Germantown CDP, Maryland	54,370	9.8	16.6	23.1	50.5	$50,886	$61,083	$66,844	$38,212	$54,803
24	32650	Glen Burnie CDP, Maryland	48,881	15.7	32.0	26.7	25.5	$40,529	$41,793	$51,504	$39,158	$45,207
24	34775	Greenbelt city, Maryland	15,470	8.2	14.7	24.3	52.8	$51,583	$50,912	$57,143	$52,808	$67,917
24	36075	Hagerstown city, Maryland	25,338	15.9	39.9	30.0	14.2	$26,401	$31,283	$40,160	$22,847	$30,364
24	41475	Ilchester CDP, Maryland	17,529	5.6	16.9	16.2	61.4	$57,277	$68,780	$81,627	$40,066	$60,604
24	45325	Landover CDP, Maryland	16,839	12.2	39.5	34.7	13.6	$31,234	$31,523	$49,368	$30,501	$45,037
24	45525	Langley Park CDP, Maryland	13,275	63.4	21.6	5.7	9.3	$26,382	$27,419	$30,200	$23,497	$26,607
24	45900	Laurel city, Maryland	16,500	8.5	18.9	23.5	49.0	$40,778	$41,237	$48,875	$39,345	$58,671
24	47450	Lochearn CDP, Maryland	18,430	11.5	25.0	36.7	26.9	$35,293	$39,106	$50,840	$30,660	$48,422
24	52300	Middle River CDP, Maryland	16,036	12.8	37.1	30.5	19.6	$29,870	$36,626	$46,490	$24,574	$50,360
24	52562	Milford Mill CDP, Maryland	20,217	6.1	34.1	24.6	35.1	$39,727	$39,934	$46,923	$38,707	$46,358
24	53325	Montgomery Village CDP, Maryland	19,467	14.8	17.8	22.5	45.0	$37,056	$42,345	$47,639	$32,053	$47,936
24	56337	North Bethesda CDP, Maryland	38,852	8.7	8.9	14.3	68.0	$50,988	$61,169	$80,803	$39,245	$60,329
24	56725	North Laurel CDP, Maryland	14,587	6.7	16.4	29.2	47.7	$48,515	$50,636	$55,335	$45,107	$70,079
24	56875	North Potomac CDP, Maryland	14,271	1.4	7.2	9.2	82.1	$71,165	$95,441	$113,797	$56,835	$87,366
24	58300	Odenton CDP, Maryland	27,615	6.4	17.9	29.6	46.2	$60,320	$62,680	$70,980	$50,550	$64,296
24	58900	Olney CDP, Maryland	24,616	5.5	10.3	25.0	59.1	$59,959	$66,235	$80,952	$51,197	$73,408
24	59425	Owings Mills CDP, Maryland	22,170	14.5	20.3	21.0	44.3	$37,364	$40,841	$52,083	$36,217	$56,677
24	59500	Oxon Hill CDP, Maryland	15,514	16.3	30.7	27.2	25.9	$37,023	$43,009	$60,780	$35,986	$56,073
24	60275	Parkville CDP, Maryland	22,471	10.6	30.2	31.4	27.8	$37,115	$39,726	$48,238	$35,284	$50,033
24	60475	Pasadena CDP, Maryland	17,919	5.0	32.8	31.8	30.4	$40,199	$49,583	$61,942	$35,169	$44,707
24	60975	Perry Hall CDP, Maryland	19,251	9.7	26.3	24.3	39.7	$50,277	$56,941	$67,042	$40,510	$53,326
24	61400	Pikesville CDP, Maryland	23,750	4.0	14.8	13.0	68.3	$49,376	$81,355	$88,455	$38,690	$51,388
24	63300	Potomac CDP, Maryland	31,748	2.4	5.2	10.6	81.8	$93,260	$135,079	$151,475	$50,169	$87,948
24	64950	Randallstown CDP, Maryland	27,092	5.2	27.0	35.8	32.1	$40,647	$37,131	$50,353	$41,308	$50,252
24	65600	Reisterstown CDP, Maryland	19,823	7.0	22.3	33.0	37.6	$41,755	$41,848	$51,395	$41,726	$46,587
24	67675	Rockville city, Maryland	46,438	7.2	10.2	16.6	66.0	$52,231	$62,416	$77,182	$47,381	$67,985
24	69925	Salisbury city, Maryland	18,798	12.9	31.7	29.6	25.8	$25,033	$29,225	$41,964	$21,239	$30,978
24	71150	Severn CDP, Maryland	35,600	8.5	22.8	29.4	39.3	$48,906	$60,890	$72,427	$37,375	$50,458
24	71200	Severna Park CDP, Maryland	26,352	2.5	12.3	23.8	61.4	$61,983	$91,783	$110,017	$38,404	$66,018
24	72450	Silver Spring CDP, Maryland	55,251	17.9	11.9	15.7	54.5	$36,840	$41,084	$58,224	$33,543	$51,222
24	73650	South Laurel CDP, Maryland	20,044	13.8	16.6	20.9	48.7	$41,714	$41,776	$51,058	$41,669	$51,055
24	75725	Suitland CDP, Maryland	15,403	13.5	44.7	28.2	13.5	$34,342	$32,336	$40,831	$36,007	$46,295
24	78425	Towson CDP, Maryland	34,388	4.0	15.0	21.2	59.8	$38,527	$50,090	$70,188	$33,940	$54,459

Table E. Cities—Labor Force, Employment, and Educational Data, 2015—*Continued*

| | | | Educational attainment of persons age 25 years and older | | | | Median earnings in the past 12 months (in 2015 Inflation-adjusted dollars) | | | | |
| | | | | | | | | Men with earnings | | Women with earnings | |
FIPS state code	FIPS place code	State/city	Total population age 25 years and older	Less than high school graduate	High school graduate (includes equivalency)	Some college or Associate's degree	Bachelor's degree or higher	All persons age 16 and older with earnings in the past 12 months	All men with earnings	Men who worked full-time, year-round in the past 12 months	All women with earnings	Women who worked full-time, year-round in the past 12 months
24	81175	Waldorf CDP, Maryland	48,089	3.5	32.5	35.8	28.2	$51,933	$57,188	$66,328	$47,324	$57,519
24	83775	Wheaton CDP, Maryland	32,643	21.7	21.5	19.1	37.6	$35,463	$40,764	$51,571	$30,447	$43,742
24	86475	Woodlawn CDP (Baltimore County), Maryland	27,236	10.0	26.5	26.5	37.0	$37,068	$40,873	$47,979	$31,983	$41,892
25	00000	**MASSACHUSETTS**	4,706,644	9.8	25.2	23.6	41.5	$38,648	$45,792	$61,761	$31,845	$51,343
25	00840	Agawam Town city, Massachusetts	21,753	6.1	32.1	36.2	25.5	$41,102	$42,373	$55,062	$31,886	$53,907
25	01640	Arlington CDP, Massachusetts	33,530	3.4	13.5	16.6	66.5	$52,336	$62,466	$90,284	$50,168	$69,312
25	02690	Attleboro city, Massachusetts	31,007	10.2	27.1	31.8	30.9	$40,506	$46,708	$56,361	$32,040	$51,029
25	03690	Barnstable Town city, Massachusetts	32,968	6.0	30.7	29.9	33.4	$31,516	$31,677	$50,700	$31,228	$39,770
25	05105	Belmont CDP, Massachusetts	17,729	3.2	8.2	11.9	76.7	$60,974	$66,377	$96,370	$52,226	$73,859
25	05595	Beverly city, Massachusetts	27,398	4.2	21.6	26.5	47.7	$31,279	$50,724	$66,563	$21,773	$47,857
25	07000	Boston city, Massachusetts	457,625	14.1	21.1	18.2	46.6	$36,059	$40,964	$57,997	$31,682	$51,432
25	07740	Braintree Town city, Massachusetts	26,253	7.1	28.6	25.9	38.4	$47,702	$51,383	$57,304	$40,317	$62,379
25	09000	Brockton city, Massachusetts	62,495	15.2	35.7	31.0	18.1	$27,167	$31,851	$41,958	$22,810	$36,502
25	09210	Brookline CDP, Massachusetts	39,368	4.2	5.2	8.8	81.7	$51,128	$66,366	$95,049	$48,322	$66,726
25	09875	Burlington CDP, Massachusetts	18,527	5.4	25.7	22.7	46.2	$47,167	$59,430	$74,310	$32,350	$62,317
25	11000	Cambridge city, Massachusetts	77,884	4.0	9.6	8.0	78.5	$42,219	$47,225	$67,076	$40,654	$62,180
25	13205	Chelsea city, Massachusetts	24,629	33.5	33.5	16.1	16.9	$25,449	$26,891	$40,013	$21,846	$34,890
25	13660	Chicopee city, Massachusetts	40,233	10.3	39.5	32.4	17.8	$32,272	$40,124	$50,003	$26,954	$40,484
25	16285	Danvers CDP, Massachusetts	21,651	5.3	25.2	34.2	35.4	$45,383	$55,562	$65,386	$36,008	$46,824
25	16530	Dedham CDP, Massachusetts	17,754	5.0	24.6	25.8	44.6	$41,056	$49,497	$72,449	$37,016	$51,628
25	21990	Everett city, Massachusetts	30,505	20.7	38.9	23.7	16.8	$26,933	$30,952	$37,344	$22,869	$36,386
25	23000	Fall River city, Massachusetts	63,848	26.1	35.6	24.8	13.5	$30,643	$36,183	$46,438	$26,502	$37,366
25	23875	Fitchburg city, Massachusetts	25,110	19.2	35.2	25.8	19.8	$32,239	$38,310	$50,200	$27,849	$48,331
25	24960	Framingham CDP, Massachusetts	50,165	12.1	23.9	17.4	46.6	$38,984	$40,938	$58,745	$31,209	$51,295
25	25172	Franklin Town city, Massachusetts	22,679	2.8	17.6	23.3	56.4	$66,360	$79,648	$94,641	$57,912	$70,468
25	25485	Gardner city, Massachusetts	14,453	14.3	37.1	28.3	20.3	$31,370	$35,696	$45,846	$30,007	$37,254
25	26150	Gloucester city, Massachusetts	22,383	10.9	26.9	24.5	37.7	$32,042	$39,003	$46,071	$26,548	$42,461
25	29405	Haverhill city, Massachusetts	43,993	8.8	28.8	31.6	30.7	$36,369	$45,757	$60,829	$31,889	$42,235
25	30840	Holyoke city, Massachusetts	27,016	20.1	32.6	27.0	20.3	$31,031	$36,550	$47,197	$27,798	$40,590
25	34550	Lawrence city, Massachusetts	48,622	31.7	36.2	22.4	9.7	$24,475	$26,813	$35,727	$19,338	$30,334
25	35075	Leominster city, Massachusetts	28,074	14.9	30.3	26.2	28.6	$31,760	$36,433	$52,457	$25,729	$38,158
25	35250	Lexington CDP, Massachusetts	23,445	3.0	6.2	8.4	82.4	$84,861	$102,226	$126,582	$63,160	$95,635
25	37000	Lowell city, Massachusetts	70,623	19.6	34.9	23.4	22.1	$30,322	$31,067	$41,995	$29,272	$40,777
25	37490	Lynn city, Massachusetts	59,970	21.2	31.6	27.8	19.5	$30,438	$31,354	$43,004	$27,212	$40,720
25	37875	Malden city, Massachusetts	44,466	13.2	26.5	24.0	36.3	$35,357	$41,659	$51,059	$27,433	$51,015
25	38435	Marblehead CDP, Massachusetts	15,381	1.7	10.1	20.3	67.9	$51,433	$71,947	$100,180	$39,538	$72,045
25	38715	Marlborough city, Massachusetts	26,458	6.8	28.3	25.6	39.2	$37,471	$47,627	$61,757	$30,023	$50,822
25	39835	Medford city, Massachusetts	41,169	8.7	25.4	20.6	45.2	$43,759	$50,766	$70,058	$41,217	$51,323
25	40115	Melrose city, Massachusetts	20,128	7.0	18.3	20.9	53.8	$43,991	$59,484	$73,471	$40,867	$57,484
25	40710	Methuen Town city, Massachusetts	34,236	11.3	30.5	28.6	29.6	$35,649	$43,280	$55,549	$28,834	$39,635
25	41200	Milford CDP, Massachusetts	17,288	8.5	30.5	26.8	34.2	$40,980	$49,043	$62,483	$30,484	$53,822
25	41725	Milton CDP, Massachusetts	18,102	4.0	16.5	21.0	58.5	$51,414	$58,508	$91,234	$51,144	$75,836
25	44140	Needham CDP, Massachusetts	20,317	1.9	12.1	12.2	73.9	$61,266	$82,051	$110,030	$42,232	$67,393
25	45000	New Bedford city, Massachusetts	64,468	27.0	33.5	22.1	17.3	$27,051	$31,234	$44,875	$23,622	$36,342
25	45560	Newton city, Massachusetts	59,400	2.6	10.6	10.2	76.6	$57,642	$68,919	$101,713	$41,900	$85,097
25	46330	Northampton city, Massachusetts	18,363	6.6	12.9	17.7	62.8	$26,593	$32,394	$61,594	$20,006	$56,233
25	50285	Norwood CDP, Massachusetts	21,139	2.7	23.8	26.6	46.8	$46,286	$52,060	$69,043	$41,074	$50,392
25	52490	Peabody city, Massachusetts	38,376	9.2	34.1	23.3	33.4	$41,332	$43,505	$61,334	$36,014	$50,033
25	53960	Pittsfield city, Massachusetts	31,678	12.4	32.0	30.6	24.9	$28,740	$35,472	$50,792	$23,283	$36,495
25	55745	Quincy city, Massachusetts	71,055	11.7	25.8	21.6	40.9	$39,079	$41,607	$60,749	$36,555	$55,756
25	55990	Randolph CDP, Massachusetts	23,335	12.1	32.4	30.1	25.4	$38,386	$38,358	$55,198	$38,425	$48,493
25	56165	Reading CDP, Massachusetts	16,930	3.3	16.2	20.9	59.5	$60,879	$87,048	$100,163	$44,447	$61,628
25	56585	Revere city, Massachusetts	40,680	17.8	41.5	22.4	18.3	$31,242	$31,812	$40,919	$30,193	$42,075
25	59105	Salem city, Massachusetts	28,492	8.2	26.9	25.5	39.5	$32,113	$46,490	$56,063	$20,687	$51,977
25	60050	Saugus CDP, Massachusetts	20,888	11.7	37.3	25.3	25.6	$37,585	$45,246	$60,637	$30,631	$46,028
25	62465	Somerset CDP, Massachusetts	13,733	9.6	28.9	34.3	27.3	$36,342	$46,911	$66,831	$31,662	$40,636
25	62535	Somerville city, Massachusetts	60,528	10.3	15.0	14.6	60.1	$43,800	$50,096	$61,382	$40,217	$51,442
25	67000	Springfield city, Massachusetts	92,173	22.9	32.7	27.0	17.5	$22,581	$24,554	$40,029	$21,157	$40,511
25	67700	Stoneham CDP, Massachusetts	16,123	5.8	25.9	26.7	41.6	$43,973	$42,715	$75,546	$45,202	$58,077
25	69170	Taunton city, Massachusetts	39,747	16.3	33.5	28.8	21.4	$36,624	$42,198	$50,305	$31,726	$46,160
25	72250	Wakefield CDP, Massachusetts	18,783	7.5	23.0	17.3	52.2	$46,985	$59,390	$70,153	$40,842	$52,178
25	72600	Waltham city, Massachusetts	44,519	6.7	22.4	20.6	50.3	$41,037	$45,634	$56,089	$32,217	$51,946
25	73440	Watertown Town city, Massachusetts	26,224	4.4	14.5	13.8	67.2	$56,582	$63,347	$75,134	$47,227	$65,459
25	74210	Wellesley CDP, Massachusetts	16,822	1.8	4.3	8.6	85.2	$52,157	$82,118	$120,488	$15,371	$110,330
25	76030	Westfield city, Massachusetts	27,291	7.1	27.6	28.8	36.5	$29,375	$33,936	$46,901	$24,509	$41,803
25	77890	West Springfield Town city, Massachusetts	20,559	9.6	30.9	31.4	28.1	$32,618	$41,310	$51,612	$27,938	$40,068
25	78972	Weymouth Town city, Massachusetts	42,705	6.7	29.3	28.5	35.5	$41,165	$48,217	$66,199	$37,070	$53,549

Table E. Cities—Labor Force, Employment, and Educational Data, 2015—*Continued*

| | | | | | | | | | Median earnings in the past 12 months (in 2015 Inflation-adjusted dollars) | | | |
| | | | Educational attainment of persons age 25 years and older | | | | | | | Men with earnings | | Women with earnings |
FIPS state code	FIPS place code	State/city	Total population age 25 years and older	Less than high school graduate	High school graduate (includes equivalency)	Some college or Associate's degree	Bachelor's degree or higher	All persons age 16 and older with earnings in the past 12 months	All men with earnings	Men who worked full-time, year-round in the past 12 months	All women with earnings	Women who worked full-time, year-round in the past 12 months
25	80195	Wilmington CDP, Massachusetts	15,703	5.6	30.1	29.9	34.4	$35,440	$41,030	$65,082	$30,767	$43,506
25	80545	Winchester CDP, Massachusetts	15,644	1.2	10.3	11.5	77.0	$86,255	$102,168	$111,825	$70,963	$87,162
25	81035	Woburn city, Massachusetts	29,008	4.2	30.1	24.9	40.8	$40,022	$42,459	$61,065	$31,073	$50,819
25	82000	Worcester city, Massachusetts	122,089	17.1	29.6	25.1	28.2	$30,275	$32,493	$45,608	$26,708	$40,151
26	00000	**MICHIGAN**	6,728,347	9.9	29.4	32.9	27.8	$29,704	$36,390	$50,479	$22,803	$37,486
26	00440	Adrian city, Michigan	11,435	17.0	30.0	34.8	18.3	$19,063	$22,004	$31,882	$14,803	$26,862
26	01340	Allendale CDP, Michigan	7,338	8.1	35.2	28.0	28.7	$9,660	$20,054	$31,295	$5,296	$31,775
26	01380	Allen Park city, Michigan	19,512	7.1	30.6	35.6	26.8	$36,792	$38,890	$51,589	$35,503	$45,821
26	03000	Ann Arbor city, Michigan	66,632	3.8	7.6	14.6	73.9	$22,539	$27,879	$52,975	$15,818	$50,556
26	04105	Auburn Hills city, Michigan	16,886	7.8	21.1	28.0	43.2	$27,236	$37,177	$56,878	$22,477	$41,891
26	05920	Battle Creek city, Michigan	34,236	9.8	36.7	32.3	21.3	$23,416	$27,604	$50,713	$20,992	$34,464
26	06020	Bay City city, Michigan	22,885	13.8	34.8	38.5	12.9	$24,221	$31,544	$40,540	$19,629	$29,681
26	08640	Birmingham city, Michigan	14,728	3.3	6.1	18.4	72.2	$73,793	$105,753	$121,588	$45,744	$95,422
26	12060	Burton city, Michigan	18,818	11.1	36.0	36.3	16.6	$24,280	$24,950	$45,393	$22,410	$37,260
26	21000	Dearborn city, Michigan	58,590	18.2	20.5	32.9	28.4	$26,644	$31,139	$48,233	$21,986	$41,393
26	21020	Dearborn Heights city, Michigan	35,344	12.8	34.0	32.7	20.5	$31,518	$32,792	$40,835	$24,723	$41,336
26	22000	Detroit city, Michigan	432,410	20.4	32.5	32.9	14.2	$20,158	$21,850	$32,445	$18,207	$29,716
26	24120	East Lansing city, Michigan	13,697	3.1	7.5	17.8	71.5	$5,778	$6,115	$51,697	$5,325	$39,085
26	24290	Eastpointe city, Michigan	20,526	10.2	32.6	41.9	15.3	$27,679	$32,752	$39,568	$23,132	$34,441
26	27440	Farmington Hills city, Michigan	58,136	5.2	14.9	27.7	52.2	$43,942	$62,256	$76,594	$30,663	$47,072
26	27880	Ferndale city, Michigan	15,433	4.5	18.6	41.3	35.5	$32,361	$47,354	$50,547	$28,182	$36,650
26	29000	Flint city, Michigan	63,607	15.6	36.5	36.1	11.8	$19,680	$20,156	$37,461	$18,704	$29,629
26	29580	Forest Hills CDP, Michigan	17,229	1.9	7.7	19.1	71.3	$52,551	$77,295	$92,047	$21,985	$65,459
26	31420	Garden City city, Michigan	18,257	11.1	36.7	41.0	11.2	$32,092	$38,152	$50,049	$21,489	$32,236
26	34000	Grand Rapids city, Michigan	126,174	14.6	22.4	29.4	33.6	$23,726	$27,165	$36,896	$20,826	$34,348
26	36280	Hamtramck city, Michigan	13,071	26.2	42.7	22.7	8.5	$18,183	$21,136	$30,269	$14,311	$21,407
26	37100	Haslett CDP, Michigan	13,722	5.3	14.1	23.6	57.0	$36,731	$40,275	$61,925	$32,321	$51,695
26	38640	Holland city, Michigan	19,420	12.8	25.2	30.8	31.2	$27,357	$31,560	$51,751	$24,255	$36,091
26	38780	Holt CDP, Michigan	17,935	3.0	21.3	37.5	38.2	$40,458	$46,117	$56,531	$34,368	$44,907
26	40680	Inkster city, Michigan	17,078	17.7	37.6	28.5	16.2	$22,010	$31,799	$40,114	$16,269	$27,336
26	41420	Jackson city, Michigan	19,489	17.9	37.4	27.7	17.0	$22,453	$24,484	$35,211	$19,116	$27,932
26	42160	Kalamazoo city, Michigan	40,114	7.8	21.1	35.1	36.0	$16,575	$18,400	$36,051	$15,235	$31,814
26	42820	Kentwood city, Michigan	34,068	11.0	25.6	29.7	33.7	$29,554	$36,835	$45,384	$25,058	$36,187
26	46000	Lansing city, Michigan	72,028	11.9	27.0	35.1	26.0	$23,149	$25,536	$35,003	$20,804	$33,579
26	47800	Lincoln Park city, Michigan	24,396	21.7	39.0	31.3	8.0	$24,664	$26,691	$37,255	$22,030	$36,906
26	49000	Livonia city, Michigan	70,300	6.2	24.9	34.6	34.3	$37,045	$48,207	$64,302	$28,348	$47,570
26	50560	Madison Heights city, Michigan	20,582	19.4	36.6	26.4	17.6	$27,487	$31,849	$37,760	$21,645	$30,049
26	51900	Marquette city, Michigan	12,928	4.5	24.7	29.6	41.2	$19,245	$24,554	$41,185	$15,349	$31,160
26	53780	Midland city, Michigan	29,918	3.8	25.6	27.3	43.3	$30,553	$39,493	$59,432	$21,779	$40,946
26	55020	Monroe city, Michigan	14,054	10.9	36.0	35.7	17.4	$28,941	$35,348	$47,120	$21,851	$31,433
26	56020	Mount Pleasant city, Michigan	10,743	6.6	27.6	19.5	46.3	$8,524	$8,488	$40,480	$8,599	$34,794
26	56320	Muskegon city, Michigan	25,831	16.6	35.2	33.8	14.5	$22,432	$26,516	$37,450	$21,887	$33,995
26	59140	Norton Shores city, Michigan	16,031	2.3	33.0	37.7	26.9	$27,166	$31,609	$44,454	$24,226	$31,841
26	59440	Novi city, Michigan	40,673	4.2	11.9	22.4	61.5	$57,986	$75,811	$89,423	$44,287	$58,169
26	59920	Oak Park city, Michigan	20,946	12.2	20.9	40.2	26.7	$22,272	$29,344	$41,250	$20,969	$37,832
26	60340	Okemos CDP, Michigan	14,079	0.3	6.3	18.7	74.7	$40,749	$50,962	$72,454	$26,221	$55,750
26	65440	Pontiac city, Michigan	36,602	18.7	31.7	36.8	12.8	$20,408	$22,378	$30,555	$18,224	$30,353
26	65560	Portage city, Michigan	32,891	2.9	23.5	30.2	43.4	$31,559	$40,553	$51,415	$25,785	$41,396
26	65820	Port Huron city, Michigan	18,566	12.8	38.1	36.3	12.8	$21,389	$26,318	$41,471	$15,635	$30,036
26	69035	Rochester Hills city, Michigan	50,360	3.2	14.6	27.8	54.5	$41,418	$57,360	$80,968	$26,928	$51,256
26	69420	Romulus city, Michigan	13,221	14.9	35.5	34.2	15.4	$24,409	$23,304	$36,647	$28,867	$37,335
26	69800	Roseville city, Michigan	33,960	12.8	37.7	37.7	11.8	$27,232	$35,877	$40,851	$20,502	$30,532
26	70040	Royal Oak city, Michigan	45,540	3.3	15.0	27.0	54.7	$45,933	$57,820	$66,541	$36,396	$49,410
26	70520	Saginaw city, Michigan	32,040	20.1	38.2	32.8	8.9	$19,360	$22,712	$35,229	$16,940	$28,199
26	70760	St. Clair Shores city, Michigan	44,927	6.9	30.0	39.2	23.9	$32,944	$39,807	$48,450	$26,198	$39,374
26	74900	Southfield city, Michigan	51,578	7.8	20.9	35.3	36.1	$32,701	$36,859	$47,275	$30,425	$41,481
26	74960	Southgate city, Michigan	21,050	12.9	33.4	34.5	19.2	$30,736	$40,419	$42,057	$23,562	$31,864
26	76460	Sterling Heights city, Michigan	92,843	14.1	28.2	32.3	25.4	$31,534	$39,063	$50,424	$25,981	$36,508
26	79000	Taylor city, Michigan	41,804	16.3	42.6	29.0	12.1	$28,943	$34,199	$46,550	$22,244	$31,710
26	80700	Troy city, Michigan	58,606	4.8	13.5	23.8	57.9	$51,399	$70,172	$96,795	$38,960	$53,962
26	82960	Walker city, Michigan	17,200	2.9	30.3	34.4	32.4	$31,010	$38,358	$49,084	$25,580	$31,376
26	84000	Warren city, Michigan	98,031	15.5	33.5	32.1	18.9	$28,528	$33,766	$42,046	$25,551	$32,491
26	84800	Waverly CDP, Michigan	17,304	5.7	20.0	38.8	35.5	$30,801	$36,810	$48,271	$25,683	$38,741
26	86000	Westland city, Michigan	58,278	10.5	33.8	36.0	19.7	$31,371	$35,576	$45,168	$29,013	$37,386
26	88900	Wyandotte city, Michigan	17,729	9.2	36.9	33.8	20.1	$35,452	$41,565	$51,922	$30,019	$41,939
26	88940	Wyoming city, Michigan	47,556	15.9	32.6	33.7	17.8	$26,117	$35,859	$43,738	$21,379	$29,384
26	89140	Ypsilanti city, Michigan	10,899	9.7	10.9	32.7	46.7	$12,975	$15,275	$31,884	$11,390	$22,620
27	00000	**MINNESOTA**	3,700,935	7.2	25.4	32.7	34.7	$35,147	$40,930	$51,979	$29,658	$42,137
27	01486	Andover city, Minnesota	19,857	4.6	20.7	40.6	34.1	$43,423	$53,572	$68,678	$35,385	$51,118

Table E. Cities—Labor Force, Employment, and Educational Data, 2015—*Continued*

FIPS state code	FIPS place code	State/city	Total population age 25 years and older	Less than high school graduate	High school graduate (includes equivalency)	Some college or Associate's degree	Bachelor's degree or higher	All persons age 16 and older with earnings in the past 12 months	All men with earnings	Men who worked full-time, year-round in the past 12 months	All women with earnings	Women who worked full-time, year-round in the past 12 months
			Educational attainment of persons age 25 years and older					Median earnings in the past 12 months (in 2015 Inflation-adjusted dollars)	Men with earnings		Women with earnings	
27	01900	Apple Valley city, Minnesota	34,964	3.8	21.8	27.0	47.3	$41,024	$46,063	$62,156	$36,404	$51,020
27	02908	Austin city, Minnesota	16,015	16.0	29.5	28.2	26.3	$30,783	$37,965	$44,697	$25,709	$31,854
27	06382	Blaine city, Minnesota	40,903	4.6	23.7	35.4	36.2	$41,213	$47,762	$61,226	$35,070	$46,979
27	06616	Bloomington city, Minnesota	62,814	6.7	20.2	31.2	42.0	$36,098	$41,229	$52,442	$31,501	$46,263
27	07948	Brooklyn Center city, Minnesota	18,944	18.5	30.1	33.3	18.0	$28,085	$31,394	$39,563	$24,693	$36,946
27	07966	Brooklyn Park city, Minnesota	50,669	10.1	24.6	37.6	27.6	$35,367	$40,531	$47,562	$30,973	$37,407
27	08794	Burnsville city, Minnesota	41,158	7.1	19.0	35.5	38.4	$36,466	$44,100	$51,477	$31,410	$40,200
27	10846	Champlin city, Minnesota	15,604	3.3	24.6	32.2	40.0	$42,186	$47,003	$59,095	$37,435	$46,143
27	10918	Chanhassen city, Minnesota	16,327	2.0	9.6	24.9	63.4	$56,282	$76,351	$92,927	$50,112	$75,097
27	10972	Chaska city, Minnesota	15,793	9.5	22.2	31.4	36.9	$36,637	$45,365	$61,954	$31,195	$42,846
27	13114	Coon Rapids city, Minnesota	44,057	5.2	28.3	39.2	27.2	$37,443	$42,668	$51,139	$35,585	$41,462
27	13456	Cottage Grove city, Minnesota	23,292	3.8	21.7	41.1	33.5	$41,528	$50,773	$55,377	$35,736	$50,998
27	14158	Crystal city, Minnesota	16,347	5.9	22.8	34.5	36.8	$40,827	$47,459	$52,149	$33,212	$41,243
27	17000	Duluth city, Minnesota	54,032	5.6	25.0	31.7	37.6	$23,332	$29,765	$46,626	$20,540	$37,574
27	17288	Eagan city, Minnesota	44,745	3.3	14.7	33.4	48.6	$40,735	$48,545	$65,546	$36,433	$50,487
27	18116	Eden Prairie city, Minnesota	44,366	3.0	9.5	25.2	62.3	$47,953	$57,041	$74,381	$37,070	$70,159
27	18188	Edina city, Minnesota	36,105	2.9	13.7	17.3	66.0	$46,073	$57,912	$83,155	$37,282	$71,923
27	18674	Elk River city, Minnesota	13,732	5.5	21.2	38.9	34.4	$37,124	$37,786	$54,181	$36,459	$48,611
27	20546	Faribault city, Minnesota	14,348	13.5	43.4	28.0	15.1	$24,273	$24,915	$40,190	$23,647	$35,585
27	20618	Farmington city, Minnesota	13,571	2.1	19.7	41.3	36.8	$45,535	$50,940	$60,886	$40,647	$47,451
27	22814	Fridley city, Minnesota	18,865	12.4	31.6	27.0	28.9	$36,736	$40,618	$46,950	$32,581	$41,220
27	24308	Golden Valley city, Minnesota	15,644	2.5	14.0	23.4	60.1	$50,425	$50,167	$61,608	$50,681	$67,300
27	27530	Hastings city, Minnesota	15,518	4.5	33.1	31.9	30.5	$38,177	$41,052	$48,521	$30,962	$47,012
27	31076	Inver Grove Heights city, Minnesota	23,234	7.3	24.2	37.0	31.4	$36,322	$42,203	$55,841	$28,654	$47,332
27	35180	Lakeville city, Minnesota	39,450	3.4	16.7	30.3	49.5	$47,409	$57,990	$71,078	$39,623	$51,941
27	37322	Lino Lakes city, Minnesota	13,477	4.0	19.9	36.1	39.9	$42,054	$48,417	$73,581	$40,984	$51,398
27	39878	Mankato city, Minnesota	20,743	5.6	20.5	34.7	39.3	$16,675	$20,945	$42,003	$13,777	$31,690
27	40166	Maple Grove city, Minnesota	46,885	2.0	16.0	30.5	51.5	$49,764	$64,587	$78,646	$38,823	$50,726
27	40382	Maplewood city, Minnesota	29,600	8.5	29.2	33.4	28.8	$35,053	$35,773	$47,325	$34,215	$45,682
27	43000	Minneapolis city, Minnesota	276,896	12.1	15.7	23.9	48.3	$31,675	$35,447	$50,117	$29,777	$46,535
27	43252	Minnetonka city, Minnesota	38,688	1.8	14.9	23.7	59.5	$50,711	$58,155	$74,364	$46,270	$62,459
27	43864	Moorhead city, Minnesota	24,288	6.8	22.8	33.0	37.4	$30,048	$40,534	$51,930	$21,017	$38,737
27	45430	New Brighton city, Minnesota	18,599	4.9	18.9	26.3	49.9	$40,179	$41,783	$52,317	$35,103	$51,255
27	45628	New Hope city, Minnesota	16,099	11.6	22.2	35.7	30.5	$34,346	$40,208	$51,388	$26,489	$45,192
27	46924	Northfield city, Minnesota	11,174	3.1	21.4	26.3	49.2	$11,079	$25,528	$47,353	$6,422	$40,107
27	47680	Oakdale city, Minnesota	18,789	6.6	25.4	36.6	31.4	$34,807	$35,705	$50,223	$34,368	$43,371
27	49300	Owatonna city, Minnesota	16,375	7.9	32.4	27.6	32.2	$40,763	$42,221	$47,231	$27,324	$47,991
27	51730	Plymouth city, Minnesota	52,710	1.7	14.2	27.9	56.2	$47,097	$51,703	$71,655	$45,044	$61,237
27	52594	Prior Lake city, Minnesota	16,678	2.4	17.7	37.1	42.8	$55,340	$60,409	$67,397	$42,201	$56,024
27	53026	Ramsey city, Minnesota	17,420	3.2	24.5	46.0	26.2	$45,519	$48,031	$60,260	$40,759	$51,109
27	54214	Richfield city, Minnesota	23,988	11.0	17.0	32.6	39.5	$35,454	$38,375	$50,211	$33,075	$43,384
27	54880	Rochester city, Minnesota	74,884	6.4	18.6	29.8	45.2	$35,977	$40,888	$53,444	$31,550	$48,123
27	55726	Rosemount city, Minnesota	14,963	3.2	12.7	38.1	46.0	$47,332	$57,174	$67,876	$38,651	$53,750
27	55852	Roseville city, Minnesota	24,567	8.3	16.5	27.6	47.6	$30,564	$35,121	$56,211	$24,323	$50,380
27	56896	St. Cloud city, Minnesota	40,281	9.8	24.7	36.3	29.2	$20,981	$22,366	$43,045	$20,279	$30,660
27	57220	St. Louis Park city, Minnesota	36,143	3.2	10.9	25.9	60.0	$44,469	$51,816	$62,032	$40,871	$47,029
27	58000	St. Paul city, Minnesota	190,130	13.4	20.9	25.9	39.8	$30,146	$31,335	$41,715	$26,607	$42,344
27	58738	Savage city, Minnesota	19,818	5.0	20.8	33.4	40.8	$42,774	$51,784	$62,220	$37,666	$47,199
27	59350	Shakopee city, Minnesota	24,339	7.3	26.8	36.0	29.8	$38,314	$47,926	$59,814	$31,465	$41,730
27	59998	Shoreview city, Minnesota	19,099	2.7	14.8	24.4	58.1	$46,649	$56,669	$71,216	$41,873	$60,150
27	61492	South St. Paul city, Minnesota	13,754	8.0	28.5	35.5	28.0	$35,326	$40,219	$52,060	$31,419	$41,465
27	69970	White Bear Lake city, Minnesota	17,226	3.1	25.9	36.4	34.6	$36,341	$44,362	$52,223	$30,776	$48,240
27	71032	Winona city, Minnesota	14,819	8.0	27.2	32.1	32.7	$20,019	$22,191	$40,363	$16,371	$30,388
27	71428	Woodbury city, Minnesota	45,020	2.7	15.4	21.4	60.5	$51,724	$71,067	$91,167	$38,851	$55,215
28	00000	**MISSISSIPPI**	1,952,337	16.5	31.0	31.6	20.8	$26,953	$31,700	$41,092	$22,381	$31,110
28	06220	Biloxi city, Mississippi	29,352	14.6	27.0	31.5	26.8	$22,453	$27,474	$35,215	$19,648	$24,978
28	08300	Brandon city, Mississippi	16,105	5.1	17.1	34.4	43.4	$40,330	$51,067	$66,929	$31,440	$40,533
28	14420	Clinton city, Mississippi	15,912	6.1	18.1	33.1	42.7	$31,203	$31,421	$45,050	$31,008	$42,496
28	15380	Columbus city, Mississippi	12,911	16.0	28.9	32.1	23.0	$19,867	$32,446	$41,784	$14,454	$21,458
28	29180	Greenville city, Mississippi	21,714	20.7	31.9	29.7	17.7	$24,895	$35,585	$39,943	$20,109	$26,425
28	29700	Gulfport city, Mississippi	46,661	14.7	30.1	34.7	20.5	$24,100	$28,085	$37,212	$22,630	$27,462
28	31020	Hattiesburg city, Mississippi	26,398	16.8	24.2	28.0	30.9	$16,800	$19,749	$29,190	$15,607	$25,833
28	33700	Horn Lake city, Mississippi	18,174	17.4	34.5	36.9	11.3	$30,381	$36,839	$41,266	$18,488	$31,159
28	36000	Jackson city, Mississippi	105,366	13.7	27.4	32.0	26.9	$23,573	$25,251	$35,780	$22,386	$30,494
28	44520	Madison city, Mississippi	17,835	1.2	9.2	33.3	56.4	$49,366	$60,732	$71,861	$40,330	$52,060
28	46640	Meridian city, Mississippi	25,991	14.7	26.1	42.7	16.6	$24,915	$27,744	$31,311	$22,267	$29,459
28	54040	Olive Branch city, Mississippi	22,532	8.4	30.5	34.2	26.9	$32,964	$40,839	$56,270	$30,871	$41,577
28	54840	Oxford city, Mississippi	9,024	4.3	1.8	28.0	65.9	$16,018	$18,992	$50,947	$11,722	$29,759
28	55360	Pascagoula city, Mississippi	16,171	14.7	30.1	35.9	19.2	$26,285	$40,415	$47,726	$18,060	$30,680

Table E. Cities—Labor Force, Employment, and Educational Data, 2015—*Continued*

| | | | | | | | | | Median earnings in the past 12 months (in 2015 Inflation-adjusted dollars) | | | |
| | | | Educational attainment of persons age 25 years and older | | | | | | | Men with earnings | | Women with earnings |
FIPS state code	FIPS place code	State/city	Total population age 25 years and older	Less than high school graduate	High school graduate (includes equivalency)	Some college or Associate's degree	Bachelor's degree or higher	All persons age 16 and older with earnings in the past 12 months	All men with earnings	Men who worked full-time, year-round in the past 12 months	All women with earnings	Women who worked full-time, year-round in the past 12 months
28	55760	Pearl city, Mississippi	17,322	14.4	33.6	34.5	17.4	$30,027	$33,139	$41,938	$24,753	$31,115
28	62520	Ridgeland city, Mississippi	17,114	6.6	15.7	22.7	55.0	$41,354	$43,310	$49,356	$40,133	$45,431
28	69280	Southaven city, Mississippi	32,730	10.6	31.4	33.9	24.2	$34,639	$36,938	$50,043	$32,338	$40,876
28	70240	Starkville city, Mississippi	13,161	10.3	21.4	20.6	47.7	$20,769	$21,714	$43,022	$20,239	$28,047
28	74840	Tupelo city, Mississippi	23,308	9.3	30.9	33.4	26.4	$26,058	$31,062	$44,285	$23,268	$26,608
28	76720	Vicksburg city, Mississippi	13,992	8.0	33.1	36.0	22.9	$23,145	$23,258	$28,773	$23,024	$26,433
29	00000	**MISSOURI**	4,097,212	11.1	31.0	30.1	27.8	$30,139	$35,628	$45,897	$24,872	$35,759
29	00280	Affton CDP, Missouri	14,402	7.6	21.3	35.6	35.5	$33,272	$41,207	$50,258	$26,070	$38,155
29	01972	Arnold city, Missouri	15,086	17.9	33.2	35.2	13.7	$27,876	$31,062	$50,506	$26,931	$36,616
29	03160	Ballwin city, Missouri	20,954	5.4	14.4	23.7	56.5	$47,042	$51,602	$69,610	$40,693	$50,571
29	04384	Belton city, Missouri	14,291	16.6	35.0	28.2	20.2	$28,049	$31,818	$40,367	$25,189	$31,066
29	06652	Blue Springs city, Missouri	35,525	7.7	25.1	33.9	33.3	$34,346	$45,291	$52,500	$25,850	$40,335
29	11242	Cape Girardeau city, Missouri	24,510	12.0	20.9	30.2	36.9	$25,035	$30,732	$42,461	$18,338	$36,048
29	13600	Chesterfield city, Missouri	35,450	1.6	11.1	18.1	69.1	$51,976	$72,279	$91,368	$40,243	$64,692
29	15670	Columbia city, Missouri	65,566	5.2	19.3	21.6	53.9	$24,998	$27,467	$41,265	$20,588	$37,886
29	16030	Concord CDP, Missouri	13,631	4.7	20.9	39.1	35.4	$35,139	$45,220	$50,709	$24,805	$39,413
29	23986	Ferguson city, Missouri	11,532	10.4	25.8	41.6	22.2	$30,208	$40,161	$41,679	$26,236	$34,808
29	24778	Florissant city, Missouri	35,051	11.9	26.4	39.5	22.2	$30,755	$35,240	$41,030	$26,751	$34,313
29	25264	Fort Leonard Wood CDP, Missouri	7,576	14.8	12.2	31.8	41.2	$17,026	$20,602	$30,142	$15,315	$25,010
29	27190	Gladstone city, Missouri	19,996	10.4	28.2	31.3	30.2	$30,902	$36,791	$46,399	$20,353	$46,176
29	28324	Grandview city, Missouri	15,607	11.3	33.8	36.3	18.7	$29,775	$28,598	$32,452	$30,786	$36,345
29	31276	Hazelwood city, Missouri	16,592	11.0	29.5	40.0	19.5	$30,516	$30,459	$37,211	$30,586	$33,588
29	35000	Independence city, Missouri	80,504	12.9	36.3	31.6	19.2	$30,770	$35,583	$41,185	$25,910	$33,852
29	37000	Jefferson City city, Missouri	31,145	7.4	26.2	31.5	34.9	$31,412	$41,618	$50,025	$26,957	$31,752
29	37592	Joplin city, Missouri	33,083	7.8	31.0	33.7	27.6	$22,476	$22,788	$36,435	$22,142	$33,196
29	38000	Kansas City city, Missouri	321,405	11.3	26.1	29.3	33.3	$31,678	$36,478	$44,253	$27,944	$38,844
29	39044	Kirkwood city, Missouri	20,765	4.0	12.1	22.2	61.6	$50,326	$62,259	$85,829	$42,080	$61,850
29	41348	Lee's Summit city, Missouri	61,016	3.6	16.8	33.0	46.6	$45,837	$51,708	$63,145	$38,344	$50,031
29	42032	Liberty city, Missouri	19,008	4.1	27.9	33.1	34.9	$35,670	$41,236	$52,305	$32,400	$43,250
29	46586	Maryland Heights city, Missouri	20,465	7.2	22.8	27.7	42.3	$33,146	$37,904	$51,435	$31,007	$34,834
29	47180	Mehlville CDP, Missouri	22,117	6.2	30.1	34.7	29.0	$32,192	$45,310	$48,451	$27,680	$33,517
29	52616	Nixa city, Missouri	15,618	7.1	32.5	37.4	23.0	$35,640	$36,867	$41,763	$29,837	$40,329
29	53876	Oakville CDP, Missouri	27,110	4.1	21.9	33.4	40.6	$38,700	$45,795	$60,048	$31,380	$41,563
29	54074	O'Fallon city, Missouri	55,080	6.2	24.4	32.5	36.9	$40,530	$48,666	$60,688	$31,730	$45,683
29	60752	Raymore city, Missouri	15,126	3.4	22.4	35.1	39.0	$45,378	$55,928	$64,487	$30,292	$49,342
29	60788	Raytown city, Missouri	19,619	5.0	37.6	32.0	25.5	$34,913	$40,860	$50,019	$31,631	$37,248
29	62912	Rolla city, Missouri	10,673	10.6	29.9	25.2	34.3	$19,034	$15,363	$30,785	$21,410	$38,720
29	64082	St. Charles city, Missouri	45,542	8.0	26.3	31.6	34.1	$31,088	$40,156	$53,141	$25,337	$41,697
29	64550	St. Joseph city, Missouri	51,080	10.4	36.4	32.4	20.8	$25,189	$30,741	$41,818	$19,765	$28,778
29	65000	St. Louis city, Missouri	219,675	14.2	23.9	27.2	34.7	$29,839	$32,644	$44,625	$26,330	$35,885
29	65126	St. Peters city, Missouri	39,896	4.8	27.4	33.2	34.5	$36,513	$42,055	$51,435	$31,079	$41,257
29	66440	Sedalia city, Missouri	14,265	16.7	31.1	36.7	15.5	$20,014	$22,254	$32,149	$16,565	$22,262
29	70000	Springfield city, Missouri	106,879	9.6	28.5	33.9	28.0	$21,489	$23,440	$35,126	$19,971	$30,303
29	75220	University City city, Missouri	24,111	3.5	18.2	21.3	57.0	$32,089	$32,293	$51,270	$31,930	$45,616
29	78154	Webster Groves city, Missouri	16,591	2.9	9.9	24.8	62.4	$46,196	$70,069	$81,687	$35,917	$54,848
29	78442	Wentzville city, Missouri	22,956	9.5	29.2	36.9	24.4	$35,001	$41,297	$51,158	$28,301	$35,782
29	79820	Wildwood city, Missouri	23,231	1.4	11.4	28.7	58.5	$50,755	$65,599	$95,248	$33,705	$62,161
30	00000	**MONTANA**	706,329	6.5	31.5	31.5	30.6	$27,317	$32,489	$46,123	$22,262	$33,443
30	06550	Billings city, Montana	75,152	6.6	29.6	29.9	33.9	$31,704	$40,620	$46,263	$25,028	$35,131
30	08950	Bozeman city, Montana	25,255	1.4	14.8	27.0	56.9	$19,543	$20,590	$36,513	$17,520	$33,109
30	11397	Butte-Silver Bow (balance), Montana	22,648	7.8	31.0	30.0	31.3	$25,961	$30,472	$46,307	$22,474	$35,505
30	32800	Great Falls city, Montana	39,415	8.8	34.2	30.7	26.3	$26,848	$30,467	$38,821	$25,251	$35,110
30	35600	Helena city, Montana	21,201	4.0	23.8	27.5	44.8	$29,402	$30,301	$46,721	$27,827	$40,882
30	40075	Kalispell city, Montana	16,601	5.8	37.9	31.3	25.0	$26,326	$31,214	$42,014	$22,296	$31,521
30	50200	Missoula city, Montana	46,211	2.0	23.2	28.3	46.5	$22,881	$24,670	$51,862	$18,733	$35,268
31	00000	**NEBRASKA**	1,232,583	9.0	26.9	33.9	30.2	$31,024	$36,817	$46,763	$25,264	$36,834
31	03950	Bellevue city, Nebraska	33,416	8.4	26.7	36.4	28.5	$31,479	$36,717	$46,612	$25,519	$35,207
31	10110	Columbus city, Nebraska	14,237	16.4	24.2	39.9	19.6	$31,890	$34,545	$39,459	$27,753	$35,261
31	17670	Fremont city, Nebraska	16,544	15.6	32.2	33.3	18.9	$26,540	$30,822	$40,703	$22,802	$31,138
31	19595	Grand Island city, Nebraska	31,519	18.6	32.3	30.6	18.6	$26,575	$30,643	$37,997	$24,677	$33,311
31	21415	Hastings city, Nebraska	16,484	13.6	28.8	32.2	25.3	$25,396	$27,167	$41,537	$20,809	$39,187
31	25055	Kearney city, Nebraska	19,146	3.1	26.5	32.5	38.0	$21,205	$26,055	$46,559	$15,547	$31,946
31	28000	Lincoln city, Nebraska	169,947	6.3	21.7	34.9	37.1	$27,547	$31,965	$45,645	$22,568	$36,718
31	34615	Norfolk city, Nebraska	15,763	11.9	31.7	35.8	20.6	$26,255	$30,813	$40,247	$21,786	$31,861
31	35000	North Platte city, Nebraska	16,995	7.7	24.5	43.0	24.8	$26,584	$28,344	$45,101	$21,841	$35,427
31	37000	Omaha city, Nebraska	289,085	11.1	23.2	31.0	34.8	$31,337	$35,221	$43,365	$26,868	$40,126
31	38295	Papillion city, Nebraska	12,947	4.1	22.6	36.9	36.4	$34,274	$46,194	$56,039	$26,048	$42,070
32	00000	**NEVADA**	1,968,167	14.4	27.9	34.1	23.6	$30,799	$33,560	$43,681	$26,848	$36,565
32	09700	Carson City, Nevada	38,334	15.0	25.6	37.7	21.7	$30,090	$34,444	$41,159	$25,115	$33,591

Table E. Cities—Labor Force, Employment, and Educational Data, 2015—*Continued*

| | | | Educational attainment of persons age 25 years and older | | | | Median earnings in the past 12 months (in 2015 Inflation-adjusted dollars) | | | | |
| | | | | | | | | | Men with earnings | | Women with earnings | |
FIPS state code	FIPS place code	State/city	Total population age 25 years and older	Less than high school graduate	High school graduate (includes equivalency)	Some college or Associate's degree	Bachelor's degree or higher	All persons age 16 and older with earnings in the past 12 months	All men with earnings	Men who worked full-time, year-round in the past 12 months	All women with earnings	Women who worked full-time, year-round in the past 12 months
32	22500	Elko city, Nevada	13,331	14.6	28.9	39.1	17.4	$36,463	$51,986	$65,741	$19,979	$35,640
32	23770	Enterprise CDP, Nevada	91,892	6.2	22.1	42.3	29.5	$38,354	$41,161	$50,110	$35,107	$41,886
32	31900	Henderson city, Nevada	207,985	6.7	26.5	35.4	31.3	$36,414	$41,194	$52,420	$32,018	$42,258
32	40000	Las Vegas city, Nevada	419,673	16.6	27.2	33.3	23.0	$30,722	$32,219	$41,863	$28,098	$36,608
32	51800	North Las Vegas city, Nevada	142,781	19.3	30.9	34.5	15.3	$27,060	$31,243	$38,210	$22,785	$31,788
32	53800	Pahrump CDP, Nevada	28,055	12.6	42.4	35.2	9.9	$26,450	$30,098	$51,858	$24,503	$31,310
32	54600	Paradise CDP, Nevada	164,666	17.3	30.7	30.5	21.5	$27,987	$30,325	$37,054	$25,594	$34,259
32	60600	Reno city, Nevada	162,711	13.3	21.4	34.0	31.3	$27,121	$30,562	$41,804	$25,125	$35,874
32	68400	Sparks city, Nevada	64,266	13.2	28.2	34.5	24.1	$32,309	$38,573	$44,576	$26,656	$35,953
32	68585	Spring Valley CDP, Nevada	136,664	11.6	29.2	34.5	24.7	$30,967	$33,289	$41,010	$27,193	$36,852
32	70900	Summerlin South CDP, Nevada	19,713	5.0	19.2	26.3	49.6	$53,261	$67,951	$71,363	$39,732	$61,120
32	71400	Sunrise Manor CDP, Nevada	118,118	26.9	34.8	27.6	10.7	$25,097	$26,680	$32,299	$22,572	$31,541
32	71600	Sun Valley CDP, Nevada	13,817	30.9	30.2	28.6	10.2	$25,779	$28,418	$30,333	$20,664	$31,308
32	83800	Whitney CDP, Nevada	28,884	15.0	30.1	39.8	15.1	$27,418	$30,669	$39,298	$25,957	$31,148
32	84600	Winchester CDP, Nevada	21,212	31.8	23.8	27.0	17.4	$21,040	$22,228	$40,912	$17,219	$27,379
33	00000	**NEW HAMPSHIRE**	937,214	6.9	28.5	28.9	35.7	$36,500	$42,344	$56,525	$30,621	$43,172
33	14200	Concord city, New Hampshire	30,521	6.8	22.8	35.7	34.7	$35,756	$39,992	$52,091	$31,242	$42,000
33	17860	Derry CDP, New Hampshire	15,180	3.5	42.2	31.4	22.8	$31,765	$36,101	$51,290	$30,610	$40,690
33	18820	Dover city, New Hampshire	21,005	4.6	19.3	26.8	49.4	$30,918	$39,787	$63,491	$26,739	$40,767
33	39300	Keene city, New Hampshire	14,792	7.4	27.9	21.5	43.1	$25,546	$35,096	$50,711	$14,089	$38,923
33	45140	Manchester city, New Hampshire	74,986	12.6	31.2	27.0	29.2	$31,993	$36,077	$46,680	$27,112	$40,297
33	50260	Nashua city, New Hampshire	61,892	8.8	24.7	31.5	35.0	$37,121	$44,308	$61,413	$33,008	$40,867
33	62900	Portsmouth city, New Hampshire	18,507	4.2	16.7	22.1	57.0	$49,139	$50,542	$56,496	$45,745	$52,231
33	65140	Rochester city, New Hampshire	21,249	15.3	29.0	32.3	23.5	$37,817	$38,533	$44,010	$29,710	$42,424
34	00000	**NEW JERSEY**	6,166,384	10.9	28.5	23.0	37.6	$39,245	$46,574	$61,462	$31,765	$50,373
34	02080	Atlantic City city, New Jersey	25,435	26.5	32.5	26.8	14.3	$21,620	$24,475	$31,246	$19,800	$29,242
34	02350	Avenel CDP, New Jersey	15,948	5.7	55.5	20.2	18.7	$40,976	$45,935	$46,543	$22,332	$36,980
34	03580	Bayonne city, New Jersey	46,525	13.1	33.4	20.6	32.9	$35,814	$39,677	$50,112	$32,325	$47,090
34	05170	Bergenfield borough, New Jersey	17,467	9.8	26.5	22.3	41.4	$46,711	$51,015	$57,429	$35,722	$51,293
34	07600	Bridgeton city, New Jersey	15,495	28.4	44.3	24.0	3.3	$15,910	$15,754	$27,372	$16,330	$21,975
34	10000	Camden city, New Jersey	42,761	32.5	33.5	24.5	9.5	$21,157	$21,956	$29,953	$20,615	$28,769
34	10750	Carteret borough, New Jersey	16,634	14.9	37.8	26.9	20.4	$36,080	$36,758	$52,230	$35,591	$60,310
34	13570	Cliffside Park borough, New Jersey	19,543	7.3	36.4	20.6	35.7	$42,419	$52,102	$61,280	$34,167	$47,240
34	13690	Clifton city, New Jersey	59,172	12.5	35.7	24.4	27.3	$35,884	$42,569	$52,539	$31,616	$37,220
34	19390	East Orange city, New Jersey	42,775	12.9	35.0	32.7	19.4	$26,472	$32,226	$45,722	$24,230	$35,232
34	21000	Elizabeth city, New Jersey	82,781	28.6	39.5	20.3	11.7	$25,104	$26,573	$32,929	$20,737	$27,688
34	21300	Elmwood Park borough, New Jersey	14,996	6.6	38.1	25.2	30.1	$40,950	$41,726	$51,348	$40,255	$55,835
34	21480	Englewood city, New Jersey	22,262	12.5	24.8	17.1	45.7	$35,288	$36,511	$47,105	$31,034	$40,508
34	22470	Fair Lawn borough, New Jersey	24,112	6.4	17.4	23.9	52.2	$50,731	$55,791	$72,223	$50,254	$61,412
34	24420	Fort Lee borough, New Jersey	28,202	6.7	17.6	15.2	60.6	$56,131	$60,546	$62,633	$50,776	$70,059
34	25770	Garfield city, New Jersey	21,775	11.0	42.0	27.7	19.3	$40,702	$41,552	$51,305	$37,695	$48,458
34	28680	Hackensack city, New Jersey	33,557	13.4	30.4	18.0	38.2	$39,149	$41,524	$49,339	$36,620	$50,262
34	32250	Hoboken city, New Jersey	42,013	5.2	8.7	6.1	80.0	$81,231	$100,428	$101,657	$70,459	$76,384
34	36000	Jersey City city, New Jersey	185,673	13.9	25.4	17.8	43.0	$39,001	$45,781	$58,644	$29,492	$50,687
34	36510	Kearny town, New Jersey	29,219	14.6	39.8	22.6	23.0	$30,488	$35,896	$44,778	$21,254	$42,267
34	38580	Lakewood CDP, New Jersey	19,092	18.2	33.8	25.6	22.4	$16,786	$21,689	$31,930	$15,453	$30,854
34	40350	Linden city, New Jersey	27,746	17.6	31.1	30.8	20.5	$31,771	$37,189	$50,324	$30,259	$33,306
34	41100	Lodi borough, New Jersey	17,392	17.1	29.8	28.0	25.2	$40,650	$42,125	$44,684	$29,128	$45,073
34	41310	Long Branch city, New Jersey	21,853	15.7	32.6	25.9	25.9	$28,579	$30,635	$41,964	$27,068	$40,221
34	46680	Millville city, New Jersey	18,227	11.9	47.8	22.1	18.2	$26,570	$33,819	$45,403	$25,608	$37,387
34	51000	Newark city, New Jersey	182,502	25.6	33.8	24.6	16.0	$23,120	$26,764	$33,041	$20,329	$31,382
34	51210	New Brunswick city, New Jersey	28,773	43.3	22.9	17.0	16.8	$24,382	$26,215	$34,262	$21,621	$31,354
34	53280	North Plainfield borough, New Jersey	15,998	10.3	34.6	30.9	24.2	$32,132	$33,777	$41,923	$31,750	$50,511
34	54690	Old Bridge CDP, New Jersey	17,317	11.4	21.7	27.3	39.5	$52,083	$61,828	$82,094	$31,944	$61,235
34	55770	Palisades Park borough, New Jersey	15,897	9.3	29.0	16.0	45.8	$35,735	$40,705	$50,680	$27,636	$36,942
34	55950	Paramus borough, New Jersey	20,373	7.3	29.4	20.1	43.1	$40,702	$40,397	$70,724	$41,135	$61,760
34	56550	Passaic city, New Jersey	41,683	36.0	35.5	14.9	13.7	$24,401	$26,371	$29,399	$18,708	$25,642
34	57000	Paterson city, New Jersey	92,361	30.0	41.5	19.4	9.1	$23,896	$26,441	$32,075	$21,319	$29,350
34	58200	Perth Amboy city, New Jersey	30,898	32.8	31.8	18.6	16.7	$30,855	$35,727	$41,459	$25,706	$31,271
34	59190	Plainfield city, New Jersey	32,179	29.1	31.6	23.7	15.6	$22,488	$22,400	$31,531	$22,925	$36,086
34	59640	Pleasantville city, New Jersey	13,710	23.9	40.2	22.1	13.9	$20,292	$19,616	$30,290	$20,747	$28,024
34	60900	Princeton, New Jersey	17,771	3.0	16.9	9.6	70.5	$31,967	$43,008	$101,501	$25,224	$100,508
34	61530	Rahway city, New Jersey	22,288	10.3	40.7	18.8	30.3	$35,432	$40,303	$51,582	$32,031	$47,520
34	63000	Ridgewood village, New Jersey	17,348	2.6	8.4	9.7	79.3	$72,957	$101,231	$111,354	$50,536	$71,834
34	64620	Roselle borough, New Jersey	16,448	13.7	35.1	34.6	16.5	$31,595	$35,049	$42,021	$27,460	$40,977
34	65790	Sayreville borough, New Jersey	29,745	10.6	32.5	24.0	32.9	$40,348	$50,524	$65,702	$33,257	$50,107
34	68370	Somerset CDP, New Jersey	17,588	3.2	18.3	27.6	50.9	$41,816	$42,358	$73,271	$40,266	$47,121
34	69390	South Plainfield borough, New Jersey	17,404	17.6	27.5	23.4	31.4	$41,805	$45,571	$55,833	$40,192	$56,278
34	71430	Summit city, New Jersey	13,415	3.3	11.4	11.2	74.0	$71,832	$113,089	$165,283	$45,250	$72,411
34	73110	Toms River CDP, New Jersey	60,549	6.8	37.1	23.1	32.9	$37,600	$46,944	$61,965	$31,654	$46,355

Table E. Cities—Labor Force, Employment, and Educational Data, 2015—*Continued*

| | | | | | | | | Median earnings in the past 12 months (in 2015 Inflation-adjusted dollars) | | | | |
| | | | Educational attainment of persons age 25 years and older | | | | | | Men with earnings | | Women with earnings | |
FIPS state code	FIPS place code	State/city	Total population age 25 years and older	Less than high school graduate	High school graduate (includes equivalency)	Some college or Associate's degree	Bachelor's degree or higher	All persons age 16 and older with earnings in the past 12 months	All men with earnings	Men who worked full-time, year-round in the past 12 months	All women with earnings	Women who worked full-time, year-round in the past 12 months
34	74000	Trenton city, New Jersey	55,073	26.9	36.8	24.6	11.8	$22,101	$22,334	$29,213	$21,817	$31,804
34	74630	Union City city, New Jersey	47,485	32.5	32.9	16.2	18.4	$22,708	$25,048	$27,347	$18,798	$27,990
34	76070	Vineland city, New Jersey	40,426	25.8	40.2	18.1	15.8	$27,116	$30,652	$37,991	$22,412	$36,657
34	79040	Westfield town, New Jersey	19,871	2.0	12.4	13.1	72.4	$89,516	$130,812	$151,907	$52,407	$81,159
34	79610	West New York town, New Jersey	39,083	24.5	26.9	19.9	28.7	$26,706	$32,176	$36,630	$20,047	$28,801
35	00000	**NEW MEXICO**	1,377,548	15.4	26.8	31.3	26.5	$26,244	$30,564	$41,440	$21,976	$35,070
35	01780	Alamogordo city, New Mexico	20,207	12.3	22.0	44.5	21.2	$20,978	$23,418	$40,598	$20,377	$28,958
35	02000	Albuquerque city, New Mexico	377,467	12.7	22.9	31.8	32.6	$28,260	$31,059	$41,903	$25,183	$36,643
35	12150	Carlsbad city, New Mexico	16,820	12.8	37.1	31.4	18.8	$28,122	$40,453	$56,625	$17,076	$35,643
35	16420	Clovis city, New Mexico	22,964	19.0	27.3	35.2	18.5	$20,415	$28,571	$40,089	$10,540	$27,336
35	25800	Farmington city, New Mexico	27,470	11.6	31.1	35.8	21.5	$30,188	$45,042	$54,905	$21,722	$32,248
35	28460	Gallup city, New Mexico	12,097	14.9	30.0	31.8	23.3	$21,754	$22,904	$46,966	$19,790	$42,770
35	32520	Hobbs city, New Mexico	22,610	25.8	32.2	22.1	19.9	$33,254	$42,335	$46,826	$20,294	$26,068
35	39380	Las Cruces city, New Mexico	62,574	15.8	22.8	33.0	28.4	$23,325	$25,664	$35,592	$20,427	$31,690
35	63460	Rio Rancho city, New Mexico	62,671	8.7	24.3	37.8	29.2	$31,425	$39,913	$51,223	$24,640	$40,735
35	64930	Roswell city, New Mexico	29,989	18.4	34.9	29.8	16.9	$25,185	$31,449	$40,861	$21,294	$31,467
35	70500	Santa Fe city, New Mexico	60,578	13.0	20.4	25.6	41.0	$31,034	$31,692	$37,043	$30,435	$42,440
35	74520	South Valley CDP, New Mexico	26,468	28.8	35.5	25.5	10.1	$21,998	$24,623	$26,785	$18,482	$28,984
36	00000	**NEW YORK**	13,641,473	14.0	26.5	24.4	35.0	$35,580	$40,570	$52,124	$30,878	$46,208
36	01000	Albany city, New York	62,539	12.0	26.7	25.2	36.1	$23,874	$25,449	$40,783	$22,144	$40,004
36	03078	Auburn city, New York	18,846	12.3	28.5	38.3	21.0	$30,669	$32,151	$51,742	$23,901	$36,253
36	04143	Baldwin CDP, New York	17,099	14.0	20.6	31.9	33.6	$42,336	$36,928	$65,395	$43,850	$52,604
36	04935	Bay Shore CDP, New York	19,983	22.1	26.5	24.1	27.3	$31,734	$30,419	$46,692	$36,059	$41,099
36	06607	Binghamton city, New York	28,536	13.3	33.0	31.1	22.6	$17,751	$18,078	$32,285	$17,616	$36,467
36	08026	Brentwood CDP, New York	40,877	33.0	33.1	21.2	12.7	$25,970	$30,626	$35,006	$21,613	$30,230
36	08257	Brighton CDP, New York	26,898	6.7	10.3	22.9	60.1	$45,101	$47,715	$55,344	$40,373	$52,000
36	11000	Buffalo city, New York	167,166	17.9	28.2	30.1	23.9	$25,401	$27,398	$40,589	$23,363	$36,655
36	13376	Centereach CDP, New York	23,586	6.7	31.7	34.3	27.3	$45,192	$61,259	$81,123	$36,199	$49,732
36	13552	Central Islip CDP, New York	20,000	26.2	38.1	24.0	11.7	$35,082	$39,410	$47,773	$30,283	$41,577
36	15000	Cheektowaga CDP, New York	54,565	9.6	36.2	33.5	20.7	$31,767	$35,950	$46,340	$30,351	$40,156
36	17530	Commack CDP, New York	26,340	3.2	25.3	22.0	49.6	$46,475	$61,996	$80,346	$31,280	$60,629
36	18146	Copiague CDP, New York	18,320	20.8	37.6	18.5	23.2	$30,592	$35,004	$41,518	$23,627	$36,615
36	18157	Coram CDP, New York	25,490	4.2	31.4	30.2	34.2	$42,776	$56,240	$67,478	$27,398	$48,887
36	19972	Deer Park CDP, New York	17,805	10.4	36.2	28.7	24.6	$35,444	$36,597	$49,282	$31,825	$42,453
36	20687	Dix Hills CDP, New York	17,795	2.4	19.5	19.0	59.2	$61,848	$76,570	$86,952	$50,921	$69,250
36	22502	East Meadow CDP, New York	27,484	10.2	28.9	23.5	37.3	$46,223	$51,645	$65,797	$40,754	$50,415
36	22612	East Northport CDP, New York	14,121	4.9	28.8	29.1	37.1	$36,464	$42,221	$71,997	$28,858	$42,183
36	22733	East Patchogue CDP, New York	16,099	10.2	32.7	26.2	30.9	$44,066	$55,961	$70,159	$33,367	$42,369
36	24229	Elmira city, New York	18,055	13.2	41.3	29.5	16.1	$20,988	$25,574	$40,868	$16,345	$30,806
36	24273	Elmont CDP, New York	23,599	11.3	33.5	29.6	25.6	$35,910	$41,167	$51,875	$30,426	$41,147
36	27309	Franklin Square CDP, New York	25,995	9.9	37.5	27.0	25.6	$39,379	$46,775	$61,550	$30,666	$47,418
36	27485	Freeport village, New York	28,783	16.7	32.2	21.3	29.9	$40,418	$46,551	$56,544	$32,708	$51,502
36	28178	Garden City village, New York	13,802	1.9	12.0	17.4	68.7	$66,847	$90,122	$128,929	$46,393	$90,518
36	29113	Glen Cove city, New York	18,572	13.5	31.9	15.4	39.2	$35,071	$45,257	$51,633	$27,400	$41,645
36	32402	Harrison village, New York	17,512	8.4	23.8	20.3	47.5	$37,346	$54,316	$101,399	$25,426	$47,325
36	33139	Hempstead village, New York	35,470	29.9	28.9	21.9	19.3	$25,587	$25,498	$31,078	$25,753	$40,806
36	34374	Hicksville CDP, New York	30,113	13.0	26.6	25.6	34.7	$41,837	$49,430	$67,359	$35,801	$50,926
36	35056	Holbrook CDP, New York	18,179	4.8	28.9	30.2	36.2	$48,119	$47,480	$70,408	$48,891	$60,371
36	35254	Holtsville CDP, New York	15,664	8.9	26.4	31.7	33.0	$47,144	$51,888	$71,604	$45,529	$52,299
36	37044	Huntington Station CDP, New York	22,727	19.9	23.9	19.1	37.1	$36,322	$40,402	$50,060	$31,397	$51,553
36	37737	Irondequoit CDP, New York	36,826	5.5	31.4	26.7	36.4	$36,782	$40,534	$48,721	$32,604	$43,736
36	37869	Islip CDP, New York	14,380	6.7	30.9	28.4	34.0	$38,448	$36,392	$52,100	$41,417	$57,045
36	38077	Ithaca city, New York	11,342	5.0	15.0	13.9	66.1	$10,160	$13,794	$54,135	$6,810	$44,608
36	38264	Jamestown city, New York	20,539	14.7	34.9	34.6	15.8	$22,485	$24,893	$36,205	$20,924	$30,381
36	39727	Kingston city, New York	16,835	16.5	30.5	24.9	28.1	$30,014	$30,947	$37,332	$25,745	$39,611
36	39853	Kiryas Joel village, New York	6,397	42.4	43.7	9.5	4.5	$22,202	$29,209	$44,052	$13,107	$19,950
36	40838	Lake Ronkonkoma CDP, New York	15,735	6.3	33.3	37.4	23.0	$48,336	$52,412	$61,760	$37,099	$50,220
36	42081	Levittown CDP, New York	37,714	6.8	30.2	30.8	32.2	$41,867	$47,358	$65,648	$37,362	$52,181
36	42554	Lindenhurst village, New York	18,361	11.9	34.1	29.7	24.4	$36,459	$48,490	$61,996	$27,438	$50,661
36	43082	Lockport city, New York	14,052	14.6	28.0	39.9	17.5	$27,979	$33,750	$40,018	$25,443	$40,325
36	43335	Long Beach city, New York	26,026	5.1	25.0	26.9	43.0	$44,892	$52,859	$72,439	$33,817	$66,107
36	45986	Massapequa CDP, New York	15,089	2.2	24.6	31.4	41.8	$55,566	$70,505	$76,425	$44,315	$57,384
36	46404	Medford CDP, New York	15,409	17.0	28.4	25.5	29.2	$31,648	$36,260	$51,567	$29,892	$48,588
36	47042	Middletown city, New York	18,084	12.6	36.5	29.5	21.4	$32,121	$35,318	$37,490	$31,128	$39,953
36	48010	Monsey CDP, New York	8,614	22.6	37.8	17.4	22.1	$21,973	$30,755	$35,968	$19,835	$38,536
36	49121	Mount Vernon city, New York	46,386	17.4	29.7	24.4	28.5	$35,704	$37,224	$45,897	$35,043	$44,204
36	49407	Nanuet CDP, New York	13,510	9.9	21.4	24.1	44.6	$46,790	$51,215	$62,482	$41,482	$74,191
36	50034	Newburgh city, New York	13,929	27.5	38.9	21.8	11.9	$25,963	$34,097	$36,714	$21,748	$29,245
36	50100	New City CDP, New York	25,004	5.4	12.4	20.4	61.9	$54,738	$65,975	$98,157	$49,375	$65,989

Table E. Cities—Labor Force, Employment, and Educational Data, 2015—*Continued*

| | | | Educational attainment of persons age 25 years and older | | | | Median earnings in the past 12 months (in 2015 Inflation-adjusted dollars) | | | | |
| | | | | | | | | Men with earnings | | Women with earnings | |
FIPS state code	FIPS place code	State/city	Total population age 25 years and older	Less than high school graduate	High school graduate (includes equivalency)	Some college or Associate's degree	Bachelor's degree or higher	All persons age 16 and older with earnings in the past 12 months	All men with earnings	Men who worked full-time, year-round in the past 12 months	All women with earnings	Women who worked full-time, year-round in the past 12 months
36	50617	New Rochelle city, New York	54,572	19.3	16.2	18.8	45.6	$42,372	$42,490	$62,085	$41,796	$60,654
36	51000	New York city, New York	5,948,515	19.1	23.9	20.2	36.8	$36,087	$40,087	$50,758	$32,121	$47,345
36	51055	Niagara Falls city, New York	32,209	15.8	40.7	25.4	18.1	$22,570	$23,487	$35,403	$21,431	$32,831
36	51396	North Amityville CDP, New York	14,300	27.2	35.5	17.4	19.9	$31,088	$31,768	$56,975	$30,579	$39,627
36	53682	North Tonawanda city, New York	22,515	10.4	30.5	38.1	21.0	$31,613	$31,700	$46,312	$31,430	$41,537
36	54441	Oceanside CDP, New York	22,452	8.2	24.7	22.3	44.9	$51,016	$53,750	$80,723	$48,734	$67,310
36	55530	Ossining village, New York	20,128	29.1	19.1	24.0	27.7	$26,437	$28,482	$35,882	$24,344	$42,090
36	56979	Peekskill city, New York	16,038	18.4	31.7	24.9	25.1	$30,538	$35,732	$50,663	$26,940	$36,039
36	58442	Plainview CDP, New York	19,297	3.3	19.1	13.7	63.9	$54,830	$77,033	$101,846	$36,818	$67,045
36	59223	Port Chester village, New York	20,164	28.0	29.5	18.2	24.4	$26,608	$30,144	$34,120	$23,038	$35,672
36	59641	Poughkeepsie city, New York	20,032	16.7	30.7	33.4	19.2	$27,128	$30,938	$40,081	$25,339	$36,846
36	63000	Rochester city, New York	129,744	21.4	27.9	29.1	21.6	$22,676	$26,316	$37,558	$20,450	$33,041
36	63264	Rockville Centre village, New York	16,620	7.1	16.5	18.6	57.8	$56,493	$75,675	$100,794	$46,239	$70,660
36	63418	Rome city, New York	22,905	13.6	35.9	31.2	19.4	$26,453	$31,343	$44,432	$19,309	$35,468
36	63473	Ronkonkoma CDP, New York	15,498	10.3	23.8	34.5	31.4	$37,186	$50,754	$60,886	$34,279	$51,413
36	63924	Rotterdam CDP, New York	13,060	11.0	36.4	31.2	21.3	$35,122	$36,136	$44,634	$31,665	$45,705
36	65255	Saratoga Springs city, New York	18,492	4.6	20.8	18.6	56.0	$48,057	$51,538	$64,265	$40,638	$55,534
36	65508	Schenectady city, New York	45,497	15.8	33.0	28.4	22.8	$25,692	$26,622	$42,352	$25,410	$38,949
36	67070	Shirley CDP, New York	17,660	14.9	39.2	24.1	21.9	$36,649	$40,761	$60,090	$35,252	$46,073
36	67851	Smithtown CDP, New York	19,263	5.6	21.9	29.7	42.7	$41,929	$61,261	$80,459	$31,997	$65,571
36	70420	Spring Valley village, New York	19,603	27.8	31.2	24.2	16.8	$25,805	$30,903	$45,069	$19,923	$38,832
36	72554	Syosset CDP, New York	12,973	7.0	13.2	18.3	61.5	$77,047	$100,313	$104,872	$51,463	$74,450
36	73000	Syracuse city, New York	86,596	18.0	28.3	24.7	29.0	$25,090	$27,728	$45,198	$20,971	$38,545
36	74183	Tonawanda CDP, New York	40,491	7.1	27.3	30.0	35.5	$36,093	$41,398	$47,090	$30,840	$38,700
36	75484	Troy city, New York	33,266	15.2	30.6	29.6	24.6	$26,702	$29,368	$43,684	$24,259	$33,586
36	76089	Uniondale CDP, New York	14,349	20.6	31.1	27.3	21.0	$34,171	$35,590	$42,472	$32,392	$40,826
36	76540	Utica city, New York	39,027	21.3	30.4	32.5	15.7	$22,068	$25,712	$36,403	$19,245	$31,072
36	76705	Valley Stream village, New York	25,294	14.1	25.9	27.8	32.3	$45,117	$45,281	$71,089	$44,107	$60,847
36	78146	Wantagh CDP, New York	14,116	2.7	24.1	22.7	50.5	$55,165	$57,099	$70,761	$47,073	$62,055
36	78608	Watertown city, New York	17,444	15.1	29.0	34.2	21.6	$21,485	$22,327	$32,312	$18,846	$27,799
36	79246	West Babylon CDP, New York	29,717	9.6	36.8	27.2	26.3	$37,087	$39,540	$62,096	$36,172	$42,322
36	80225	West Hempstead CDP, New York	14,532	11.2	29.9	24.1	34.8	$35,065	$42,874	$52,026	$33,377	$47,464
36	80302	West Islip CDP, New York	18,470	5.2	23.5	33.2	38.1	$47,856	$65,359	$82,263	$36,529	$54,618
36	80907	West Seneca CDP, New York	34,923	3.8	32.8	33.1	30.3	$36,247	$50,113	$55,583	$30,173	$37,065
36	81677	White Plains city, New York	41,238	16.1	14.8	17.4	51.8	$37,343	$41,825	$61,085	$34,621	$51,758
36	84000	Yonkers city, New York	137,787	16.4	26.6	25.4	31.5	$39,148	$41,873	$51,432	$34,702	$51,402
37	00000	**NORTH CAROLINA**	6,762,644	13.4	26.4	30.7	29.4	$29,355	$32,379	$42,039	$25,123	$36,113
37	01520	Apex town, North Carolina	28,900	5.5	11.8	19.4	63.3	$50,321	$66,154	$80,435	$33,073	$51,374
37	02080	Asheboro city, North Carolina	18,096	19.3	27.1	38.9	14.7	$27,125	$29,577	$35,340	$24,697	$29,978
37	02140	Asheville city, North Carolina	64,114	7.8	19.0	25.5	47.7	$25,873	$28,889	$38,249	$22,095	$36,332
37	09060	Burlington city, North Carolina	35,751	20.8	27.5	28.7	23.0	$23,173	$26,427	$32,374	$20,898	$30,086
37	10620	Carrboro town, North Carolina	11,895	5.8	5.4	16.1	72.7	$26,540	$27,405	$50,060	$25,374	$40,901
37	10740	Cary town, North Carolina	112,008	4.0	11.2	21.3	63.6	$50,647	$65,031	$81,294	$36,214	$54,124
37	11800	Chapel Hill town, North Carolina	31,831	4.9	10.9	11.9	72.4	$16,288	$24,299	$81,535	$11,355	$55,241
37	12000	Charlotte city, North Carolina	550,245	12.0	19.6	26.6	41.9	$32,366	$36,553	$46,536	$30,386	$41,008
37	14100	Concord city, North Carolina	56,802	10.4	24.5	32.7	32.4	$31,972	$39,129	$45,198	$27,137	$40,062
37	14700	Cornelius town, North Carolina	19,821	1.8	10.2	35.5	52.5	$52,457	$66,959	$88,507	$37,068	$56,363
37	19000	Durham city, North Carolina	171,181	13.9	16.7	22.4	47.0	$30,512	$31,147	$41,386	$29,247	$41,398
37	22920	Fayetteville city, North Carolina	123,801	8.4	24.2	40.5	26.8	$24,903	$28,507	$32,010	$20,739	$31,948
37	25300	Fuquay-Varina town, North Carolina	14,375	3.0	28.3	30.6	38.2	$30,438	$45,586	$56,703	$23,295	$45,872
37	25480	Garner town, North Carolina	18,414	8.2	22.1	33.3	36.4	$34,310	$35,062	$45,280	$32,303	$47,008
37	25580	Gastonia city, North Carolina	50,054	15.3	29.2	32.5	23.0	$28,323	$30,882	$37,253	$25,025	$32,567
37	26880	Goldsboro city, North Carolina	23,867	12.6	28.9	33.6	24.9	$22,958	$26,735	$36,197	$13,914	$29,355
37	28000	Greensboro city, North Carolina	189,322	9.8	22.5	32.4	35.2	$27,673	$31,889	$40,474	$23,569	$33,785
37	28080	Greenville city, North Carolina	46,946	9.7	22.3	31.2	36.8	$20,174	$24,555	$42,150	$17,494	$32,192
37	30120	Havelock city, North Carolina	8,056	6.7	17.0	57.0	19.3	$25,389	$26,988	$27,903	$17,160	$26,947
37	31060	Hickory city, North Carolina	28,457	14.4	23.3	28.3	33.9	$28,379	$32,084	$49,195	$25,500	$34,622
37	31400	High Point city, North Carolina	71,029	17.5	22.5	29.9	30.2	$26,189	$31,605	$41,045	$20,834	$34,290
37	32260	Holly Springs town, North Carolina	19,173	3.1	15.3	28.7	53.0	$51,150	$62,190	$81,569	$36,444	$50,990
37	33120	Huntersville town, North Carolina	32,835	3.6	12.2	26.6	57.5	$45,397	$53,721	$70,489	$36,263	$50,996
37	33560	Indian Trail town, North Carolina	22,223	3.8	24.9	38.2	33.0	$41,457	$48,297	$58,335	$32,950	$46,264
37	34200	Jacksonville city, North Carolina	31,703	6.4	30.3	42.9	20.4	$23,095	$25,217	$26,596	$18,128	$24,308
37	35200	Kannapolis city, North Carolina	29,008	16.8	28.2	33.5	21.4	$31,122	$35,820	$37,395	$25,869	$34,401
37	35600	Kernersville town, North Carolina	17,480	10.4	26.0	30.0	33.6	$31,513	$38,079	$42,403	$30,510	$35,782
37	35920	Kinston city, North Carolina	13,421	20.4	34.2	29.4	16.0	$21,058	$26,509	$40,163	$18,425	$27,190
37	39700	Lumberton city, North Carolina	14,291	20.1	39.0	26.3	14.7	$21,730	$25,780	$31,260	$20,310	$25,759
37	41960	Matthews town, North Carolina	21,427	6.1	16.9	23.3	53.8	$36,115	$51,017	$79,283	$23,257	$49,958
37	43480	Mint Hill town, North Carolina	16,746	6.0	23.1	31.1	39.8	$31,056	$32,468	$51,051	$30,418	$42,258

Table E. Cities—Labor Force, Employment, and Educational Data, 2015—*Continued*

| | | | Educational attainment of persons age 25 years and older | | | | | Median earnings in the past 12 months (in 2015 Inflation-adjusted dollars) | | | | |
| | | | | | | | | | Men with earnings | | Women with earnings | |
FIPS state code	FIPS place code	State/city	Total population age 25 years and older	Less than high school graduate	High school graduate (includes equivalency)	Some college or Associate's degree	Bachelor's degree or higher	All persons age 16 and older with earnings in the past 12 months	All men with earnings	Men who worked full-time, year-round in the past 12 months	All women with earnings	Women who worked full-time, year-round in the past 12 months
37	43920	Monroe city, North Carolina	22,705	21.5	26.8	35.0	16.7	$25,436	$27,583	$36,250	$25,094	$31,477
37	44220	Mooresville town, North Carolina	22,917	5.0	20.3	35.6	39.1	$33,810	$45,559	$52,475	$26,880	$37,101
37	44520	Morrisville town, North Carolina	18,780	4.2	10.0	14.2	71.5	$52,155	$60,295	$62,384	$39,396	$68,810
37	46340	New Bern city, North Carolina	22,060	10.6	26.3	37.1	26.0	$26,696	$28,702	$37,077	$26,403	$33,347
37	55000	Raleigh city, North Carolina	292,363	9.0	16.3	25.4	49.2	$32,635	$36,912	$46,038	$30,582	$40,685
37	57500	Rocky Mount city, North Carolina	34,690	15.2	27.1	36.1	21.6	$22,171	$29,896	$33,314	$19,392	$26,348
37	58860	Salisbury city, North Carolina	24,270	19.4	32.0	29.7	19.0	$24,212	$24,529	$34,065	$22,027	$30,668
37	59280	Sanford city, North Carolina	18,115	23.6	21.2	35.7	19.5	$28,049	$32,183	$42,757	$21,863	$30,621
37	61200	Shelby city, North Carolina	14,408	16.0	38.9	29.2	15.9	$28,109	$34,857	$43,580	$23,750	$41,480
37	64740	Statesville city, North Carolina	16,924	26.8	23.8	31.1	18.3	$25,502	$31,281	$41,689	$21,062	$27,009
37	67420	Thomasville city, North Carolina	19,460	19.5	35.6	26.3	18.6	$25,597	$30,562	$33,708	$22,979	$34,148
37	70540	Wake Forest town, North Carolina	24,166	5.4	16.9	24.5	53.2	$42,271	$59,290	$65,932	$30,895	$45,238
37	74440	Wilmington city, North Carolina	73,975	7.8	21.6	33.2	37.4	$22,421	$30,382	$45,266	$18,699	$34,844
37	74540	Wilson city, North Carolina	34,295	20.1	25.7	28.9	25.2	$27,957	$34,730	$39,544	$22,674	$35,496
37	75000	Winston-Salem city, North Carolina	153,249	12.6	24.8	27.2	35.5	$26,394	$30,364	$41,566	$22,496	$34,625
38	00000	**NORTH DAKOTA**	492,017	7.5	27.6	35.8	29.1	$34,336	$42,186	$52,031	$26,799	$37,016
38	07200	Bismarck city, North Dakota	49,141	8.0	22.3	34.6	35.1	$38,582	$45,346	$52,155	$31,591	$38,453
38	19620	Dickinson city, North Dakota	16,731	9.5	27.9	37.8	24.8	$41,272	$55,043	$68,201	$21,841	$39,866
38	25700	Fargo city, North Dakota	72,088	5.8	22.9	35.2	36.1	$27,732	$31,255	$47,459	$25,429	$36,071
38	32060	Grand Forks city, North Dakota	32,504	4.5	24.9	33.7	36.9	$25,269	$30,033	$47,451	$20,318	$36,232
38	49900	Mandan city, North Dakota	13,965	8.3	30.7	24.9	36.1	$40,086	$44,855	$51,211	$27,659	$37,304
38	53380	Minot city, North Dakota	29,816	6.1	29.0	34.2	30.7	$36,028	$42,413	$53,505	$28,016	$41,351
38	84780	West Fargo city, North Dakota	22,286	3.1	23.1	41.3	32.4	$37,273	$45,149	$52,068	$32,051	$35,328
38	86220	Williston city, North Dakota	14,883	7.4	26.1	36.9	29.6	$42,492	$56,617	$61,891	$31,479	$42,537
39	00000	**OHIO**	7,896,470	10.3	33.7	29.2	26.8	$30,635	$36,958	$50,051	$24,837	$37,365
39	01000	Akron city, Ohio	135,622	13.5	36.3	29.5	20.7	$25,348	$29,990	$40,219	$21,493	$30,558
39	01420	Alliance city, Ohio	14,945	15.6	45.6	24.9	14.0	$19,789	$25,155	$37,138	$15,730	$28,484
39	02568	Ashland city, Ohio	12,847	11.9	35.2	22.8	30.2	$20,442	$21,775	$38,845	$17,905	$31,381
39	02736	Athens city, Ohio	7,679	3.8	14.5	11.9	69.8	$5,659	$6,838	$52,113	$4,599	$40,216
39	03184	Austintown CDP, Ohio	20,942	7.7	41.1	33.8	17.4	$27,719	$35,348	$41,992	$21,898	$35,343
39	03352	Avon city, Ohio	13,060	4.9	19.1	33.8	42.1	$35,949	$57,328	$93,538	$25,755	$46,171
39	03464	Avon Lake city, Ohio	16,607	4.3	20.9	22.4	52.4	$43,778	$61,282	$72,287	$27,215	$60,485
39	03828	Barberton city, Ohio	17,654	15.6	46.3	24.7	13.4	$25,249	$35,386	$43,953	$20,198	$27,398
39	04720	Beavercreek city, Ohio	31,513	2.6	21.5	31.6	44.4	$41,426	$47,620	$60,575	$34,004	$51,261
39	07454	Boardman CDP, Ohio	25,545	4.5	30.9	30.7	33.8	$31,260	$35,189	$45,578	$27,756	$40,519
39	07972	Bowling Green city, Ohio	13,604	5.6	25.5	26.4	42.5	$7,896	$11,172	$52,415	$6,056	$40,164
39	09680	Brunswick city, Ohio	24,276	11.1	29.8	31.8	27.2	$38,577	$47,435	$60,203	$30,256	$40,976
39	12000	Canton city, Ohio	44,917	14.7	36.6	34.4	14.4	$23,266	$26,758	$35,443	$17,034	$32,696
39	13190	Centerville city, Ohio	16,934	2.6	13.4	23.4	60.5	$41,993	$50,820	$66,396	$39,085	$48,331
39	14184	Chillicothe city, Ohio	16,814	14.9	33.8	31.6	19.6	$22,230	$25,087	$34,107	$21,510	$35,867
39	15000	Cincinnati city, Ohio	195,344	11.0	25.9	28.8	34.3	$26,060	$27,834	$42,170	$24,423	$37,457
39	16000	Cleveland city, Ohio	257,937	21.3	32.3	30.2	16.2	$22,997	$25,571	$37,237	$21,238	$31,686
39	16014	Cleveland Heights city, Ohio	32,278	4.4	16.7	28.0	50.9	$32,981	$37,150	$50,447	$30,263	$46,484
39	18000	Columbus city, Ohio	560,012	10.9	26.2	28.1	34.8	$29,494	$31,148	$42,102	$26,935	$39,324
39	19778	Cuyahoga Falls city, Ohio	36,077	7.5	29.0	33.6	29.9	$33,194	$40,568	$50,380	$27,771	$41,555
39	21000	Dayton city, Ohio	87,575	16.9	30.2	34.9	18.1	$18,041	$19,666	$37,264	$17,280	$31,169
39	21434	Delaware city, Ohio	23,569	5.6	31.5	29.9	33.0	$33,911	$41,138	$51,118	$26,698	$40,262
39	22694	Dublin city, Ohio	29,268	1.3	8.0	13.8	76.9	$70,729	$90,727	$102,658	$46,362	$65,032
39	25256	Elyria city, Ohio	35,975	11.3	35.2	38.3	15.2	$25,937	$31,510	$41,222	$19,269	$33,912
39	25704	Euclid city, Ohio	32,413	11.4	32.4	36.2	20.1	$27,090	$30,213	$41,277	$25,500	$37,406
39	25914	Fairborn city, Ohio	20,529	13.8	27.8	30.6	27.8	$23,018	$31,819	$52,307	$16,913	$31,025
39	25970	Fairfield city, Ohio	30,602	14.1	33.5	26.1	26.3	$31,154	$36,282	$44,874	$28,956	$35,634
39	27048	Findlay city, Ohio	27,689	10.3	34.0	27.5	28.3	$25,742	$35,871	$50,142	$17,246	$38,628
39	29106	Gahanna city, Ohio	25,563	2.9	24.7	27.5	45.0	$48,256	$60,685	$67,301	$32,329	$52,409
39	29428	Garfield Heights city, Ohio	18,795	14.3	37.3	34.9	13.4	$28,934	$31,787	$39,142	$25,521	$36,933
39	31860	Green city, Ohio	18,979	5.4	31.7	25.6	37.3	$35,520	$47,723	$56,090	$22,034	$43,140
39	32592	Grove City city, Ohio	26,700	7.5	31.9	29.1	31.5	$40,719	$43,319	$49,970	$36,490	$44,539
39	33012	Hamilton city, Ohio	38,383	16.5	40.4	28.6	14.5	$29,390	$36,089	$45,894	$23,806	$35,027
39	35476	Hilliard city, Ohio	23,173	4.8	12.0	26.8	56.4	$45,218	$65,363	$71,146	$31,816	$51,912
39	36610	Huber Heights city, Ohio	26,055	8.3	31.3	40.5	19.9	$30,459	$35,223	$43,501	$24,978	$35,582
39	36651	Hudson city, Ohio	15,701	1.7	9.0	17.6	71.7	$51,224	$100,678	$120,447	$25,813	$62,404
39	39872	Kent city, Ohio	14,046	4.5	31.5	25.8	38.2	$11,487	$16,215	$47,098	$8,199	$42,012
39	40040	Kettering city, Ohio	38,407	6.1	23.2	35.4	35.3	$35,013	$41,294	$50,975	$28,866	$41,756
39	41664	Lakewood city, Ohio	36,575	7.7	23.3	26.2	42.9	$32,647	$31,923	$44,196	$34,090	$45,303
39	41720	Lancaster city, Ohio	26,569	10.3	40.4	31.6	17.6	$25,261	$30,368	$37,459	$21,909	$35,576
39	42364	Lebanon city, Ohio	13,941	8.7	26.9	42.3	22.1	$26,487	$36,482	$50,102	$20,915	$28,172
39	43554	Lima city, Ohio	24,131	10.7	44.3	30.2	14.8	$25,476	$30,393	$41,217	$21,597	$31,014
39	44856	Lorain city, Ohio	39,051	17.1	35.7	36.2	11.0	$20,731	$25,171	$37,004	$17,701	$26,297
39	47138	Mansfield city, Ohio	31,086	17.0	37.2	31.7	14.1	$22,609	$30,004	$41,440	$17,367	$30,547

Table E. Cities—Labor Force, Employment, and Educational Data, 2015—*Continued*

FIPS state code	FIPS place code	State/city	Total population age 25 years and older	Less than high school graduate	High school graduate (includes equivalency)	Some college or Associate's degree	Bachelor's degree or higher	All persons age 16 and older with earnings in the past 12 months	All men with earnings	Men who worked full-time, year-round in the past 12 months	All women with earnings	Women who worked full-time, year-round in the past 12 months
					Educational attainment of persons age 25 years and older				*All persons*	*Men with earnings*		*Women with earnings*	
39	47306	Maple Heights city, Ohio	15,997	13.5	39.7	30.5	16.3	$22,409	$22,431	$36,791	$22,396	$31,176
39	47754	Marion city, Ohio	26,266	19.9	44.5	28.1	7.6	$20,641	$24,173	$40,850	$18,237	$30,898
39	48160	Marysville city, Ohio	14,986	10.0	31.1	30.8	28.1	$35,862	$60,187	$62,156	$25,107	$36,761
39	48188	Mason city, Ohio	21,304	1.3	18.9	18.4	61.4	$51,449	$71,080	$100,678	$40,771	$76,888
39	48244	Massillon city, Ohio	21,531	13.1	42.8	29.6	14.4	$25,442	$29,520	$35,250	$21,495	$31,637
39	48790	Medina city, Ohio	16,747	5.1	26.5	27.9	40.5	$35,637	$38,776	$50,922	$29,837	$41,400
39	49056	Mentor city, Ohio	35,359	4.9	34.0	35.3	25.8	$41,393	$55,796	$60,439	$32,295	$40,990
39	49434	Miamisburg city, Ohio	15,677	7.0	37.0	34.8	21.3	$34,663	$46,205	$50,703	$22,231	$35,917
39	49840	Middletown city, Ohio	32,149	19.0	37.0	30.5	13.5	$26,177	$31,073	$40,592	$19,524	$31,695
39	54040	Newark city, Ohio	30,688	13.6	37.4	31.0	18.1	$23,934	$32,323	$48,446	$20,633	$26,897
39	56882	North Olmsted city, Ohio	23,437	7.4	33.9	34.4	24.2	$29,794	$36,197	$51,784	$26,049	$37,954
39	56966	North Ridgeville city, Ohio	23,842	7.7	30.3	31.0	31.0	$38,785	$46,789	$54,534	$36,008	$50,070
39	57008	North Royalton city, Ohio	22,039	6.7	29.2	27.9	36.2	$38,403	$50,172	$55,741	$31,615	$44,956
39	58730	Oregon city, Ohio	15,176	10.8	35.9	35.6	17.8	$31,318	$35,251	$42,009	$28,167	$39,114
39	59234	Oxford city, Ohio	6,529	7.0	15.4	14.6	63.0	$4,683	$10,213	$43,844	$3,485	$51,506
39	61000	Parma city, Ohio	57,484	8.8	40.2	30.9	20.0	$30,237	$38,545	$47,056	$24,908	$34,635
39	61028	Parma Heights city, Ohio	13,049	6.6	38.2	31.4	23.8	$30,325	$32,036	$37,087	$26,005	$36,872
39	62148	Perrysburg city, Ohio	15,803	4.8	18.9	22.9	53.4	$43,078	$58,496	$70,658	$37,684	$41,670
39	62848	Piqua city, Ohio	13,230	14.6	40.7	32.8	11.8	$25,829	$36,936	$41,082	$18,285	$29,167
39	64304	Portsmouth city, Ohio	12,191	21.3	31.4	34.7	12.7	$16,547	$41,698	$51,243	$11,488	$23,583
39	66390	Reynoldsburg city, Ohio	23,996	8.1	29.3	33.5	29.1	$27,804	$30,914	$50,492	$27,084	$37,137
39	67468	Riverside city, Ohio	16,453	10.4	30.3	33.4	25.9	$31,515	$39,700	$46,861	$24,077	$35,383
39	68056	Rocky River city, Ohio	14,573	5.0	15.5	24.8	54.7	$41,748	$50,283	$63,410	$40,131	$48,851
39	70380	Sandusky city, Ohio	16,279	14.1	42.7	30.3	12.9	$25,063	$27,077	$40,580	$19,873	$29,743
39	71682	Shaker Heights city, Ohio	17,991	3.4	9.7	25.3	61.7	$46,832	$70,643	$81,505	$34,602	$52,399
39	72424	Sidney city, Ohio	13,689	9.6	37.5	35.5	17.4	$27,480	$31,737	$41,019	$21,287	$34,209
39	72928	Solon city, Ohio	16,399	4.0	13.8	25.8	56.5	$43,756	$70,429	$87,234	$32,244	$65,140
39	73264	South Euclid city, Ohio	14,418	7.4	21.6	33.0	38.0	$32,921	$39,035	$45,983	$30,288	$45,181
39	74118	Springfield city, Ohio	39,927	19.1	38.3	30.0	12.6	$22,009	$26,654	$40,937	$20,372	$27,491
39	74944	Stow city, Ohio	25,094	3.3	24.0	26.5	46.2	$35,938	$43,995	$56,491	$30,186	$38,831
39	75098	Strongsville city, Ohio	32,999	4.4	24.9	26.6	44.1	$40,429	$46,759	$66,281	$32,221	$47,148
39	77000	Toledo city, Ohio	187,416	14.1	34.2	34.9	16.8	$25,087	$28,409	$40,558	$21,279	$32,056
39	77504	Trotwood city, Ohio	15,205	11.2	33.7	38.3	16.8	$20,023	$18,013	$29,926	$20,464	$25,278
39	77588	Troy city, Ohio	16,032	13.6	27.4	32.7	26.4	$26,726	$34,933	$53,043	$22,028	$27,305
39	79002	Upper Arlington city, Ohio	24,145	1.0	9.2	18.3	71.4	$57,270	$80,382	$93,908	$45,669	$69,564
39	80304	Wadsworth city, Ohio	15,778	2.7	33.5	26.9	36.9	$32,186	$42,701	$52,296	$25,919	$40,645
39	80892	Warren city, Ohio	26,577	13.1	45.7	28.4	12.8	$20,491	$23,444	$41,221	$16,907	$31,175
39	83342	Westerville city, Ohio	27,499	1.5	21.7	25.7	51.2	$42,171	$50,555	$62,460	$35,516	$55,151
39	83622	Westlake city, Ohio	23,375	3.8	16.3	28.2	51.7	$46,796	$60,228	$80,035	$34,214	$50,795
39	84812	White Oak CDP, Ohio	13,453	13.4	26.0	29.0	31.6	$26,265	$35,096	$45,738	$17,628	$43,141
39	85484	Willoughby city, Ohio	16,854	5.8	28.2	36.6	29.5	$42,996	$50,582	$52,373	$32,349	$48,251
39	86548	Wooster city, Ohio	17,447	9.9	32.7	22.7	34.6	$22,708	$36,046	$50,041	$15,902	$38,963
39	86772	Xenia city, Ohio	16,745	13.7	42.5	23.3	20.6	$24,816	$33,636	$46,882	$21,640	$36,165
39	88000	Youngstown city, Ohio	43,094	16.0	38.9	33.1	12.1	$18,011	$18,836	$30,935	$17,649	$25,171
39	88084	Zanesville city, Ohio	15,579	17.6	39.6	32.5	10.3	$21,638	$29,484	$42,428	$17,455	$27,053
40	00000	**OKLAHOMA**	2,557,863	12.7	31.6	31.1	24.6	$29,108	$35,488	$43,829	$22,889	$32,096
40	02600	Ardmore city, Oklahoma	16,184	15.3	36.3	32.0	16.4	$26,558	$40,088	$47,674	$21,180	$25,736
40	04450	Bartlesville city, Oklahoma	24,318	8.9	33.8	25.3	32.1	$29,010	$36,280	$47,964	$23,990	$33,931
40	06400	Bixby city, Oklahoma	16,875	4.3	17.9	37.1	40.7	$37,494	$48,318	$55,608	$28,236	$36,796
40	09050	Broken Arrow city, Oklahoma	68,861	6.4	23.8	40.0	29.7	$35,162	$45,439	$51,696	$26,701	$36,303
40	19900	Del City city, Oklahoma	14,905	15.3	33.7	35.8	15.2	$30,614	$36,112	$41,100	$26,940	$32,395
40	21900	Duncan city, Oklahoma	15,518	13.5	34.7	35.4	16.4	$22,548	$34,109	$51,131	$20,162	$24,703
40	23200	Edmond city, Oklahoma	55,466	4.6	17.7	25.2	52.5	$32,005	$42,130	$62,043	$26,124	$41,513
40	23950	Enid city, Oklahoma	34,121	15.8	32.5	27.0	24.7	$27,872	$37,381	$43,767	$20,424	$29,855
40	37800	Jenks city, Oklahoma	13,883	5.0	15.1	35.6	44.3	$45,824	$51,594	$60,246	$37,141	$46,468
40	41850	Lawton city, Oklahoma	58,933	11.3	32.3	36.7	19.7	$24,354	$29,438	$37,070	$20,647	$28,477
40	48350	Midwest City city, Oklahoma	36,314	14.7	32.6	34.8	17.9	$28,043	$31,224	$35,662	$25,713	$34,502
40	49200	Moore city, Oklahoma	38,804	8.8	27.5	35.2	28.5	$30,580	$35,670	$45,569	$26,890	$33,911
40	50050	Muskogee city, Oklahoma	23,688	18.6	33.9	28.8	18.7	$26,889	$32,915	$41,959	$20,483	$31,592
40	50100	Mustang city, Oklahoma	13,219	4.5	29.5	45.3	20.7	$33,324	$45,082	$52,022	$28,725	$35,090
40	52500	Norman city, Oklahoma	71,429	6.9	20.7	32.2	40.1	$25,745	$35,337	$43,516	$20,554	$31,678
40	55000	Oklahoma City city, Oklahoma	409,659	14.4	25.6	29.9	30.1	$30,383	$35,721	$44,728	$25,020	$35,551
40	56650	Owasso city, Oklahoma	22,211	5.6	26.6	32.5	35.3	$35,649	$48,122	$56,630	$25,539	$36,827
40	59850	Ponca City city, Oklahoma	17,078	14.0	35.3	31.4	19.3	$22,798	$30,630	$40,382	$18,375	$27,300
40	65400	Sapulpa city, Oklahoma	13,901	16.0	36.2	32.3	15.4	$25,612	$32,014	$35,751	$21,172	$26,683
40	66800	Shawnee city, Oklahoma	20,352	14.3	35.1	33.2	17.4	$20,675	$24,189	$35,438	$16,694	$30,591
40	70300	Stillwater city, Oklahoma	23,130	4.2	18.4	32.4	45.1	$17,076	$21,486	$27,363	$11,834	$25,723
40	75000	Tulsa city, Oklahoma	264,531	13.1	25.5	30.6	30.8	$28,048	$31,749	$40,911	$24,332	$33,350
40	82950	Yukon city, Oklahoma	17,595	4.4	33.0	37.8	24.8	$33,201	$36,739	$43,403	$28,940	$40,665

Table E. Cities—Labor Force, Employment, and Educational Data, 2015—*Continued*

| | | | | | | | | Median earnings in the past 12 months (in 2015 Inflation-adjusted dollars) | | | | |
| | | | Educational attainment of persons age 25 years and older | | | | | | Men with earnings | | Women with earnings | |
FIPS state code	FIPS place code	State/city	Total population age 25 years and older	Less than high school graduate	High school graduate (includes equivalency)	Some college or Associate's degree	Bachelor's degree or higher	All persons age 16 and older with earnings in the past 12 months	All men with earnings	Men who worked full-time, year-round in the past 12 months	All women with earnings	Women who worked full-time, year-round in the past 12 months
41	00000	**OREGON**	2,804,461	10.0	23.4	34.5	32.2	$28,933	$34,277	$48,001	$24,310	$38,774
41	01000	Albany city, Oregon	36,366	9.1	25.7	37.4	27.7	$28,969	$33,309	$49,170	$25,011	$35,873
41	01650	Aloha CDP, Oregon	35,138	10.5	24.6	35.7	29.1	$30,630	$36,582	$58,189	$26,104	$45,563
41	03050	Ashland city, Oregon	13,873	3.5	16.6	24.5	55.5	$21,983	$31,350	$49,905	$20,657	$35,123
41	05350	Beaverton city, Oregon	69,076	9.6	13.8	29.9	46.7	$34,820	$35,995	$53,644	$32,159	$44,651
41	05800	Bend city, Oregon	60,875	2.7	14.7	35.4	47.2	$29,661	$35,396	$49,800	$25,608	$40,794
41	05950	Bethany CDP, Oregon	13,301	2.2	9.3	18.2	70.3	$62,410	$100,230	$104,618	$51,753	$63,446
41	15800	Corvallis city, Oregon	30,248	5.8	13.3	20.4	60.5	$19,581	$22,439	$54,204	$16,480	$32,475
41	23850	Eugene city, Oregon	102,915	6.9	18.2	34.0	40.9	$20,992	$24,565	$42,312	$17,921	$35,611
41	26200	Forest Grove city, Oregon	14,111	24.2	22.3	35.9	17.5	$23,699	$32,002	$41,479	$17,572	$32,985
41	30550	Grants Pass city, Oregon	25,695	12.3	34.8	40.4	12.4	$22,801	$26,950	$37,192	$19,366	$25,338
41	31250	Gresham city, Oregon	74,664	16.5	26.8	35.5	21.2	$24,874	$27,774	$40,237	$21,763	$34,682
41	32850	Hayesville CDP, Oregon	12,868	28.0	27.5	27.9	16.6	$23,609	$25,986	$39,813	$20,830	$26,188
41	34100	Hillsboro city, Oregon	69,370	9.6	17.4	32.9	40.0	$40,267	$46,658	$59,669	$33,732	$47,715
41	38500	Keizer city, Oregon	24,386	11.7	24.9	39.5	23.8	$32,039	$45,036	$52,232	$26,658	$37,122
41	39700	Klamath Falls city, Oregon	14,297	11.5	29.6	42.4	16.5	$22,030	$26,735	$31,665	$20,809	$30,180
41	40550	Lake Oswego city, Oregon	27,961	2.4	7.3	23.2	67.2	$46,284	$60,924	$90,659	$32,795	$52,736
41	45000	McMinnville city, Oregon	21,887	14.1	30.9	35.8	19.2	$26,194	$31,046	$40,667	$19,988	$32,511
41	47000	Medford city, Oregon	54,873	14.1	28.9	36.1	20.9	$24,961	$26,668	$36,502	$23,213	$30,308
41	48650	Milwaukie city, Oregon	15,509	6.5	29.2	38.1	26.2	$30,828	$33,338	$45,421	$26,570	$47,518
41	52100	Newberg city, Oregon	13,257	12.3	16.5	40.8	30.3	$24,753	$32,996	$37,249	$18,311	$31,949
41	55200	Oregon City city, Oregon	25,120	7.5	28.7	37.2	26.6	$37,994	$42,029	$53,084	$30,655	$50,005
41	59000	Portland city, Oregon	462,743	8.7	15.0	27.7	48.6	$31,542	$35,570	$49,424	$29,216	$45,467
41	61200	Redmond city, Oregon	19,229	6.8	39.6	34.6	19.0	$26,740	$29,803	$37,453	$19,391	$35,670
41	63650	Roseburg city, Oregon	15,010	9.0	27.4	41.2	22.3	$31,862	$35,399	$47,606	$26,642	$35,475
41	64900	Salem city, Oregon	105,793	13.2	25.6	35.3	25.9	$24,904	$28,605	$39,669	$21,887	$33,497
41	69600	Springfield city, Oregon	39,837	14.2	31.9	36.4	17.5	$24,513	$28,225	$34,755	$21,812	$30,774
41	73650	Tigard city, Oregon	36,163	9.3	15.3	29.4	46.1	$36,692	$44,307	$59,897	$29,881	$46,340
41	74950	Tualatin city, Oregon	17,705	5.4	12.0	37.9	44.6	$37,401	$42,401	$66,879	$32,948	$43,564
41	80150	West Linn city, Oregon	17,034	3.9	12.1	23.9	60.1	$48,208	$62,085	$84,237	$28,934	$57,848
41	82800	Wilsonville city, Oregon	17,592	3.6	19.7	31.3	45.3	$41,416	$51,305	$60,179	$26,784	$39,262
41	83750	Woodburn city, Oregon	15,041	24.6	31.2	29.4	14.8	$22,105	$31,077	$42,847	$15,275	$32,197
42	00000	**PENNSYLVANIA**	8,895,727	10.3	35.7	24.3	29.7	$31,911	$39,778	$50,976	$26,505	$40,214
42	02000	Allentown city, Pennsylvania	75,847	22.4	35.5	27.0	15.1	$23,761	$27,467	$34,112	$19,667	$30,352
42	02056	Allison Park CDP, Pennsylvania	17,753	2.7	26.0	20.1	51.2	$38,776	$45,653	$78,395	$31,829	$41,317
42	02184	Altoona city, Pennsylvania	32,155	10.5	48.3	21.5	19.6	$30,372	$36,633	$46,334	$22,949	$36,243
42	06064	Bethel Park municipality, Pennsylvania	23,250	5.5	22.7	23.0	48.8	$40,833	$60,425	$66,902	$26,215	$46,250
42	06088	Bethlehem city, Pennsylvania	48,309	9.8	32.5	29.5	28.3	$25,225	$31,517	$43,968	$21,032	$35,688
42	12536	Chambersburg borough, Pennsylvania	14,002	21.4	32.1	19.4	27.1	$30,975	$33,754	$45,000	$28,167	$32,775
42	13208	Chester city, Pennsylvania	21,585	20.1	46.9	22.1	10.9	$16,320	$18,999	$32,142	$14,408	$26,994
42	19920	Drexel Hill CDP, Pennsylvania	18,740	3.3	28.0	28.1	40.6	$37,962	$45,469	$60,761	$31,923	$50,003
42	21648	Easton city, Pennsylvania	17,261	18.3	27.3	31.1	23.3	$26,058	$27,051	$36,015	$23,942	$32,068
42	24000	Erie city, Pennsylvania	64,341	12.6	41.7	25.1	20.5	$23,691	$29,705	$39,843	$20,506	$30,456
42	32800	Harrisburg city, Pennsylvania	30,480	21.6	32.4	25.6	20.4	$26,400	$26,981	$35,515	$25,896	$34,266
42	33408	Hazleton city, Pennsylvania	15,678	22.4	43.7	21.7	12.2	$25,804	$27,255	$30,822	$22,145	$32,106
42	38288	Johnstown city, Pennsylvania	12,615	10.9	51.3	25.4	12.4	$15,439	$15,536	$33,810	$15,342	$24,888
42	41216	Lancaster city, Pennsylvania	37,533	24.8	35.0	18.5	21.7	$22,603	$22,944	$34,158	$22,573	$30,764
42	42168	Lebanon city, Pennsylvania	15,813	25.2	47.6	16.3	11.0	$27,392	$30,103	$35,069	$24,716	$33,837
42	42928	Levittown CDP, Pennsylvania	32,996	9.0	43.1	28.8	19.1	$34,202	$41,163	$51,386	$30,740	$40,393
42	50528	Monroeville municipality, Pennsylvania	21,789	6.3	27.0	23.8	42.8	$38,353	$50,684	$60,104	$30,756	$41,967
42	52432	Murrysville municipality, Pennsylvania	14,173	2.9	19.5	29.3	48.3	$38,889	$42,277	$70,387	$31,258	$54,224
42	53368	New Castle city, Pennsylvania	17,644	14.4	49.0	22.8	13.9	$21,157	$25,098	$44,815	$19,751	$27,351
42	54656	Norristown borough, Pennsylvania	20,591	20.0	37.5	19.8	22.8	$26,582	$27,209	$40,513	$25,270	$37,412
42	60000	Philadelphia city, Pennsylvania	1,050,747	16.9	33.0	22.7	27.4	$30,188	$31,666	$43,880	$27,236	$40,848
42	61000	Pittsburgh city, Pennsylvania	204,143	8.0	27.8	22.9	41.3	$27,607	$31,148	$47,213	$25,110	$40,459
42	61536	Plum borough, Pennsylvania	21,585	6.3	26.3	28.9	38.5	$36,367	$40,534	$45,041	$28,718	$41,972
42	62416	Pottstown borough, Pennsylvania	16,854	16.7	42.5	25.8	15.0	$28,021	$38,179	$46,869	$20,333	$35,980
42	63624	Reading city, Pennsylvania	50,623	30.0	35.3	23.2	11.5	$17,231	$21,069	$30,514	$13,744	$26,301
42	69000	Scranton city, Pennsylvania	51,427	18.4	35.5	26.1	20.1	$23,350	$28,763	$39,601	$20,157	$30,371
42	73808	State College borough, Pennsylvania	12,355	3.6	9.9	18.2	68.2	$6,764	$8,496	$38,294	$5,203	$31,533
42	79277	Upper St. Clair CDP, Pennsylvania	13,288	1.2	12.3	21.6	64.9	$60,091	$81,529	$101,167	$34,803	$51,389
42	83512	West Mifflin borough, Pennsylvania	13,729	7.3	35.6	35.3	21.7	$32,132	$39,863	$45,945	$25,941	$32,417
42	85152	Wilkes-Barre city, Pennsylvania	24,998	15.2	41.0	27.8	16.0	$18,195	$19,589	$39,955	$15,620	$37,107
42	85312	Williamsport city, Pennsylvania	18,930	9.5	40.9	23.9	25.7	$23,119	$24,916	$36,667	$22,206	$32,267
42	87048	York city, Pennsylvania	26,260	21.7	37.6	26.6	14.1	$21,005	$25,164	$33,844	$16,645	$26,744
44	00000	**RHODE ISLAND**	730,083	12.3	28.0	27.0	32.7	$34,890	$40,264	$51,368	$30,200	$44,050
44	19180	Cranston city, Rhode Island	57,353	10.3	30.2	27.2	32.2	$40,009	$42,768	$51,052	$32,223	$50,657
44	22960	East Providence city, Rhode Island	33,835	18.0	36.1	22.4	23.5	$33,340	$37,284	$46,178	$31,257	$36,847

Table E. Cities—Labor Force, Employment, and Educational Data, 2015—*Continued*

| | | | Educational attainment of persons age 25 years and older | | | | Median earnings in the past 12 months (in 2015 Inflation-adjusted dollars) | | | | |
| | | | | | | | | Men with earnings | | Women with earnings | |
FIPS state code	FIPS place code	State/city	Total population age 25 years and older	Less than high school graduate	High school graduate (includes equivalency)	Some college or Associate's degree	Bachelor's degree or higher	All persons age 16 and older with earnings in the past 12 months	All men with earnings	Men who worked full-time, year-round in the past 12 months	All women with earnings	Women who worked full-time, year-round in the past 12 months
44	49960	Newport city, Rhode Island	17,937	6.5	16.7	26.4	50.4	$30,104	$35,769	$48,777	$25,281	$41,077
44	54640	Pawtucket city, Rhode Island	51,063	17.9	34.7	27.1	20.4	$30,107	$32,234	$41,056	$24,657	$40,751
44	59000	Providence city, Rhode Island	107,284	22.5	25.5	21.9	30.1	$23,991	$29,356	$40,079	$19,487	$40,073
44	74300	Warwick city, Rhode Island	60,902	7.6	27.3	30.9	34.2	$40,821	$43,834	$54,038	$36,486	$47,747
44	76820	Westerly CDP, Rhode Island	14,329	6.5	30.1	36.2	27.2	$30,554	$27,328	$41,156	$30,856	$43,703
44	80780	Woonsocket city, Rhode Island	29,109	16.8	36.7	28.4	18.1	$32,216	$36,712	$48,324	$30,242	$39,322
45	00000	**SOUTH CAROLINA**	3,319,832	13.7	29.4	30.1	26.8	$27,657	$31,974	$42,238	$23,796	$34,182
45	00550	Aiken city, South Carolina	23,181	11.1	21.1	23.3	44.4	$34,132	$61,005	$76,513	$21,797	$35,605
45	01360	Anderson city, South Carolina	18,019	19.2	26.1	33.1	21.6	$22,499	$24,667	$35,347	$20,813	$35,514
45	13330	Charleston city, South Carolina	95,643	5.3	19.7	24.8	50.2	$35,475	$38,714	$47,299	$30,786	$40,759
45	16000	Columbia city, South Carolina	74,381	12.0	19.9	27.4	40.7	$18,054	$19,962	$43,437	$16,796	$35,609
45	16405	Conway city, South Carolina	10,105	8.8	23.6	41.3	26.3	$14,843	$15,845	$37,066	$14,133	$27,436
45	21985	Easley city, South Carolina	14,398	12.5	37.4	29.2	20.9	$31,332	$31,861	$36,501	$30,899	$36,357
45	25810	Florence city, South Carolina	25,827	8.9	29.6	31.8	29.7	$26,038	$30,388	$37,483	$20,842	$35,836
45	29815	Goose Creek city, South Carolina	24,898	7.3	25.1	40.0	27.5	$30,076	$36,681	$42,198	$22,394	$35,892
45	30850	Greenville city, South Carolina	43,434	11.9	18.5	23.3	46.2	$30,937	$36,343	$50,330	$24,568	$36,533
45	30895	Greenwood city, South Carolina	14,397	20.0	28.7	26.7	24.6	$16,933	$16,492	$22,056	$19,460	$35,362
45	30985	Greer city, South Carolina	20,670	20.6	22.4	31.1	25.9	$31,237	$35,423	$45,117	$25,639	$41,995
45	32065	Hanahan city, South Carolina	14,970	10.7	23.4	33.4	32.5	$32,088	$32,359	$45,891	$31,703	$39,500
45	34045	Hilton Head Island town, South Carolina	32,121	6.1	17.7	23.3	52.8	$31,708	$35,833	$50,693	$29,028	$38,330
45	41335	Lexington town, South Carolina	14,622	6.1	19.2	32.5	42.2	$41,280	$47,185	$54,027	$39,277	$50,476
45	45115	Mauldin city, South Carolina	16,848	3.2	29.2	28.1	39.5	$36,061	$40,801	$50,753	$32,331	$36,908
45	48535	Mount Pleasant town, South Carolina	57,034	2.2	13.8	19.4	64.6	$48,453	$61,499	$75,922	$41,112	$50,496
45	49075	Myrtle Beach city, South Carolina	22,355	16.4	23.9	35.5	24.2	$21,284	$21,951	$31,546	$19,987	$32,236
45	50695	North Augusta city, South Carolina	15,237	8.4	27.7	31.2	32.7	$34,292	$37,026	$41,261	$31,158	$37,537
45	50875	North Charleston city, South Carolina	69,976	14.5	30.2	32.7	22.6	$26,748	$30,896	$39,031	$23,542	$30,463
45	61405	Rock Hill city, South Carolina	45,791	12.0	28.1	30.2	29.7	$26,357	$31,053	$36,923	$21,002	$34,918
45	62395	St. Andrews CDP, South Carolina	15,755	12.7	27.3	29.8	30.3	$24,422	$25,833	$37,208	$23,709	$31,556
45	66580	Simpsonville city, South Carolina	10,883	4.4	20.8	34.0	40.8	$38,510	$42,821	$62,079	$32,745	$36,913
45	67390	Socastee CDP, South Carolina	16,761	16.2	31.2	35.0	17.6	$22,733	$24,704	$39,612	$21,080	$30,777
45	68290	Spartanburg city, South Carolina	24,191	18.1	29.2	26.5	26.2	$22,822	$27,243	$36,017	$16,416	$30,005
45	70270	Summerville town, South Carolina	33,849	6.5	29.9	33.1	30.5	$40,455	$47,539	$60,428	$31,235	$40,498
45	70405	Sumter city, South Carolina	25,649	16.7	27.6	35.1	20.6	$25,075	$28,701	$34,366	$20,776	$30,809
45	71395	Taylors CDP, South Carolina	13,974	9.9	21.8	36.9	31.4	$30,559	$31,927	$46,036	$28,686	$32,306
45	73870	Wade Hampton CDP, South Carolina	16,848	14.3	22.2	30.0	33.4	$28,445	$30,750	$39,966	$24,434	$38,673
46	00000	**SOUTH DAKOTA**	563,108	8.9	31.2	32.4	27.5	$30,002	$35,574	$42,605	$25,063	$33,268
46	00100	Aberdeen city, South Dakota	18,518	9.4	33.4	29.6	27.6	$27,189	$35,688	$41,595	$19,958	$30,873
46	07580	Brookings city, South Dakota	10,514	6.3	23.8	27.6	42.4	$18,578	$20,677	$41,877	$14,626	$34,923
46	52980	Rapid City city, South Dakota	50,701	4.3	28.4	35.2	32.1	$27,186	$31,914	$42,291	$24,097	$31,827
46	59020	Sioux Falls city, South Dakota	113,568	9.8	24.6	32.1	33.5	$31,331	$35,818	$41,797	$27,359	$35,533
46	69300	Watertown city, South Dakota	15,548	8.4	35.7	33.5	22.4	$27,318	$36,399	$41,784	$21,621	$29,451
47	00000	**TENNESSEE**	4,473,487	13.9	33.1	27.2	25.7	$28,489	$32,734	$42,525	$23,982	$34,427
47	03440	Bartlett city, Tennessee	40,057	6.5	30.2	29.9	33.4	$40,983	$51,192	$61,046	$31,653	$42,453
47	08280	Brentwood city, Tennessee	26,442	0.9	7.6	15.1	76.4	$80,137	$102,197	$122,272	$41,925	$79,575
47	08540	Bristol city, Tennessee	18,962	12.6	28.3	33.3	25.9	$26,246	$31,205	$45,791	$22,737	$31,009
47	14000	Chattanooga city, Tennessee	117,791	17.1	29.0	27.9	26.0	$26,159	$30,826	$39,063	$21,593	$32,715
47	15160	Clarksville city, Tennessee	90,080	6.3	31.0	36.3	26.4	$28,977	$35,079	$40,835	$22,212	$30,775
47	15400	Cleveland city, Tennessee	27,666	19.7	25.3	33.4	21.5	$22,201	$26,908	$34,340	$14,026	$34,083
47	16420	Collierville town, Tennessee	30,495	3.3	14.1	26.7	55.9	$50,834	$55,753	$70,590	$42,355	$52,088
47	16540	Columbia city, Tennessee	24,816	11.9	40.6	31.5	16.0	$30,424	$40,533	$45,446	$22,816	$32,264
47	16920	Cookeville city, Tennessee	17,753	16.5	30.9	23.5	29.1	$21,962	$24,675	$31,109	$19,167	$27,999
47	22720	East Ridge city, Tennessee	15,861	17.1	25.7	37.5	19.7	$25,359	$25,765	$29,184	$24,684	$31,727
47	25760	Farragut town, Tennessee	15,325	1.8	15.2	20.7	62.3	$57,755	$99,673	$111,463	$26,701	$45,246
47	27740	Franklin city, Tennessee	47,461	5.3	13.6	23.4	57.7	$45,088	$61,157	$82,316	$33,195	$50,463
47	28540	Gallatin city, Tennessee	23,615	12.5	34.9	26.4	26.1	$32,379	$36,676	$40,667	$30,384	$37,101
47	28960	Germantown city, Tennessee	27,624	2.3	9.6	20.3	67.9	$49,853	$66,417	$81,305	$44,150	$55,074
47	33280	Hendersonville city, Tennessee	38,837	4.6	27.7	30.3	37.4	$31,771	$40,063	$51,473	$27,496	$39,091
47	37640	Jackson city, Tennessee	43,393	8.4	33.4	28.0	30.1	$26,046	$29,350	$42,120	$22,027	$31,792
47	38320	Johnson City city, Tennessee	42,860	9.0	24.4	26.3	40.3	$24,953	$31,164	$46,379	$20,014	$30,996
47	39560	Kingsport city, Tennessee	38,356	13.5	33.1	27.1	26.3	$24,506	$26,887	$41,615	$22,056	$30,146
47	40000	Knoxville city, Tennessee	118,114	11.1	29.1	30.6	29.2	$22,662	$25,062	$36,354	$21,598	$32,082
47	41200	La Vergne city, Tennessee	19,960	17.8	36.5	32.2	13.5	$30,537	$36,182	$40,168	$22,276	$30,000
47	41520	Lebanon city, Tennessee	20,296	14.9	35.8	23.1	26.2	$30,260	$32,269	$41,683	$26,419	$35,321
47	46380	Maryville city, Tennessee	18,349	9.7	27.0	30.1	33.3	$26,233	$26,617	$50,628	$25,608	$33,653
47	48000	Memphis city, Tennessee	422,148	16.0	30.7	28.4	24.9	$24,800	$26,739	$37,743	$22,438	$31,475
47	50280	Morristown city, Tennessee	19,987	24.0	41.6	23.0	11.4	$21,787	$24,283	$31,786	$21,224	$26,250
47	50780	Mount Juliet city, Tennessee	20,067	4.0	26.6	27.6	41.8	$37,126	$50,372	$66,033	$30,556	$42,044
47	51560	Murfreesboro city, Tennessee	75,570	8.0	24.6	28.0	39.5	$28,216	$35,693	$46,707	$24,910	$35,385

Table E. Cities—Labor Force, Employment, and Educational Data, 2015—*Continued*

FIPS state code	FIPS place code	State/city	Educational attainment of persons age 25 years and older					Median earnings in the past 12 months (in 2015 Inflation-adjusted dollars)				
									Men with earnings		Women with earnings	
			Total population age 25 years and older	Less than high school graduate	High school graduate (includes equivalency)	Some college or Associate's degree	Bachelor's degree or higher	All persons age 16 and older with earnings in the past 12 months	All men with earnings	Men who worked full-time, year-round in the past 12 months	All women with earnings	Women who worked full-time, year-round in the past 12 months
47	52006	Nashville-Davidson metropolitan government (balance), Tennessee	446,641	11.9	24.1	26.0	37.9	$30,895	$31,975	$41,205	$29,743	$38,849
47	55120	Oak Ridge city, Tennessee	21,252	9.0	28.9	24.4	37.7	$25,475	$27,189	$45,597	$17,068	$45,883
47	67760	Shelbyville city, Tennessee	13,691	28.8	41.9	22.4	6.9	$20,559	$25,690	$27,207	$8,539	$30,071
47	69420	Smyrna town, Tennessee	30,687	10.1	28.9	38.2	22.8	$32,097	$34,586	$41,208	$28,588	$36,558
47	70580	Spring Hill city, Tennessee	21,202	2.5	19.8	39.2	38.5	$41,215	$58,390	$66,161	$24,111	$27,104
48	00000	**TEXAS**	17,472,861	17.6	25.3	28.7	28.4	$31,038	$36,598	$46,791	$25,264	$36,934
48	01000	Abilene city, Texas	76,081	13.3	33.0	33.0	20.8	$24,526	$31,057	$35,903	$19,266	$28,443
48	01924	Allen city, Texas	62,303	5.1	14.6	28.4	51.8	$45,293	$51,651	$71,159	$40,576	$50,230
48	02272	Alvin city, Texas	15,424	21.9	27.4	38.4	12.3	$29,701	$32,310	$37,574	$15,852	$29,990
48	03000	Amarillo city, Texas	125,621	16.3	24.5	35.8	23.4	$29,077	$35,889	$45,892	$22,719	$33,556
48	04000	Arlington city, Texas	242,995	16.3	23.1	30.9	29.7	$29,523	$32,051	$42,168	$25,873	$35,633
48	04462	Atascocita CDP, Texas	48,220	7.7	20.2	35.9	36.2	$46,191	$51,118	$65,464	$37,409	$49,962
48	05000	Austin city, Texas	635,470	11.9	16.9	22.9	48.3	$35,193	$37,761	$48,263	$31,202	$42,089
48	05372	Balch Springs city, Texas	12,671	46.3	20.2	25.6	7.9	$23,727	$25,622	$31,276	$18,609	$29,592
48	06128	Baytown city, Texas	47,581	22.7	24.2	36.9	16.2	$31,159	$47,099	$56,468	$20,172	$33,265
48	07000	Beaumont city, Texas	72,582	14.5	30.5	31.5	23.5	$31,073	$39,835	$49,428	$24,702	$36,504
48	07132	Bedford city, Texas	34,405	3.5	23.0	38.6	34.9	$37,431	$43,068	$52,402	$31,426	$42,539
48	07492	Belton city, Texas	13,008	20.3	30.3	23.4	25.9	$21,490	$25,541	$31,845	$15,229	$28,760
48	07552	Benbrook city, Texas	17,205	5.4	27.4	34.6	32.7	$36,488	$39,565	$57,639	$32,908	$40,991
48	08236	Big Spring city, Texas	17,898	21.8	38.1	31.4	8.7	$26,484	$30,046	$40,316	$21,767	$31,376
48	10768	Brownsville city, Texas	104,842	36.0	22.6	25.3	16.1	$20,058	$23,235	$28,221	$16,918	$26,413
48	10897	Brushy Creek CDP, Texas	13,326	2.3	12.8	23.8	61.1	$52,056	$69,064	$80,253	$33,198	$56,730
48	10912	Bryan city, Texas	49,886	17.1	24.1	28.6	30.2	$25,222	$30,355	$39,749	$20,602	$31,014
48	11428	Burleson city, Texas	28,923	9.7	27.1	37.9	25.3	$41,202	$52,113	$59,047	$30,485	$40,117
48	12580	Canyon Lake CDP, Texas	17,871	9.7	27.3	37.9	25.1	$31,130	$41,558	$52,296	$21,190	$34,574
48	13024	Carrollton city, Texas	87,979	14.6	23.4	25.8	36.3	$38,067	$46,541	$55,516	$31,825	$41,325
48	13492	Cedar Hill city, Texas	30,260	8.5	26.1	37.8	27.6	$35,911	$34,602	$42,314	$36,385	$42,800
48	13552	Cedar Park city, Texas	40,140	5.5	15.3	33.4	45.8	$46,741	$61,325	$68,725	$40,215	$45,583
48	14236	Channelview CDP, Texas	26,368	33.3	34.2	25.6	6.9	$32,231	$40,866	$42,414	$25,422	$31,713
48	14920	Cibolo city, Texas	16,218	5.9	18.9	34.7	40.4	$42,108	$52,155	$61,250	$27,050	$36,471
48	15364	Cleburne city, Texas	18,433	16.2	33.6	26.1	24.1	$34,405	$38,111	$58,333	$24,000	$37,461
48	15628	Cloverleaf CDP, Texas	14,170	41.4	31.1	21.5	6.0	$27,321	$34,419	$35,924	$21,193	$30,311
48	15976	College Station city, Texas	46,725	8.3	12.2	25.0	54.5	$16,343	$18,603	$45,563	$13,907	$35,658
48	15988	Colleyville city, Texas	18,649	1.2	9.3	24.0	65.6	$61,939	$101,363	$125,453	$45,160	$71,270
48	16432	Conroe city, Texas	42,111	21.2	25.9	25.8	27.1	$28,162	$31,915	$44,759	$24,053	$37,122
48	16468	Converse city, Texas	11,692	8.4	20.4	46.2	25.1	$32,076	$40,102	$45,551	$29,167	$38,870
48	16612	Coppell city, Texas	27,173	1.9	8.9	21.0	68.2	$61,171	$85,952	$92,442	$43,391	$57,156
48	16624	Copperas Cove city, Texas	20,994	7.9	24.8	52.1	15.2	$32,321	$36,035	$37,143	$23,891	$35,282
48	16696	Corinth city, Texas	15,928	6.7	24.9	31.6	36.8	$38,145	$46,245	$58,750	$36,067	$42,420
48	17000	Corpus Christi city, Texas	210,127	18.9	28.8	31.4	20.9	$28,177	$35,737	$44,003	$22,037	$31,910
48	17060	Corsicana city, Texas	15,278	27.1	25.7	35.1	12.1	$26,048	$28,474	$33,966	$25,166	$30,498
48	19000	Dallas city, Texas	834,619	25.2	21.1	22.0	31.8	$30,170	$31,511	$37,112	$26,689	$37,084
48	19624	Deer Park city, Texas	19,719	12.5	25.6	40.7	21.2	$32,222	$41,632	$56,859	$27,314	$37,320
48	19792	Del Rio city, Texas	21,986	36.6	25.1	21.0	17.3	$24,378	$32,358	$46,544	$15,743	$28,995
48	19900	Denison city, Texas	16,579	15.5	29.7	31.9	22.9	$26,444	$29,482	$38,733	$25,754	$32,959
48	19972	Denton city, Texas	75,414	11.0	20.4	32.8	35.8	$21,874	$27,054	$40,443	$17,260	$33,420
48	20092	DeSoto city, Texas	36,268	13.8	18.4	34.9	32.8	$38,909	$40,127	$46,186	$38,317	$42,451
48	21628	Duncanville city, Texas	24,601	16.0	27.1	36.9	20.0	$27,859	$30,661	$37,953	$24,701	$31,037
48	21892	Eagle Pass city, Texas	16,883	31.9	23.9	35.0	9.2	$19,121	$26,760	$54,145	$16,250	$20,006
48	22660	Edinburg city, Texas	47,626	25.3	21.8	26.7	26.1	$24,358	$30,371	$40,629	$20,610	$37,948
48	24000	El Paso city, Texas	422,146	20.6	24.6	30.6	24.3	$26,103	$30,933	$38,498	$20,895	$31,458
48	24768	Euless city, Texas	35,597	10.9	19.8	32.3	37.1	$34,463	$37,091	$42,430	$30,208	$40,146
48	25452	Farmers Branch city, Texas	21,769	19.3	19.9	26.7	34.1	$32,452	$41,529	$50,496	$25,631	$40,750
48	26232	Flower Mound town, Texas	46,194	2.9	11.0	25.1	61.0	$55,605	$77,148	$90,749	$40,804	$57,258
48	26736	Fort Hood CDP, Texas	10,318	5.3	24.8	53.1	16.8	$22,877	$23,497	$24,266	$20,471	$22,627
48	27000	Fort Worth city, Texas	518,807	19.1	26.0	27.6	27.3	$31,583	$36,770	$47,284	$27,212	$38,175
48	27540	Fresno CDP, Texas	12,281	8.8	22.0	35.6	33.5	$36,979	$36,288	$41,002	$37,489	$40,404
48	27648	Friendswood city, Texas	26,456	4.7	17.9	32.5	45.0	$52,041	$72,714	$89,021	$45,174	$53,962
48	27684	Frisco city, Texas	95,043	3.3	10.3	26.1	60.3	$65,137	$86,858	$100,128	$42,369	$65,213
48	28068	Galveston city, Texas	34,009	17.7	25.4	30.2	26.6	$23,798	$30,218	$48,961	$20,684	$30,465
48	29000	Garland city, Texas	150,569	21.8	25.4	30.1	22.8	$26,810	$30,338	$37,808	$23,783	$32,779
48	29336	Georgetown city, Texas	48,502	6.0	20.9	34.1	39.0	$36,031	$46,114	$59,694	$29,683	$40,829
48	30464	Grand Prairie city, Texas	116,126	21.3	25.1	29.4	24.1	$30,465	$32,053	$40,327	$25,968	$39,801
48	30644	Grapevine city, Texas	33,758	5.8	16.0	34.1	44.1	$37,022	$45,106	$59,311	$31,228	$47,358
48	30920	Greenville city, Texas	15,204	19.5	30.7	29.3	20.5	$22,107	$30,434	$32,070	$14,565	$20,291
48	31928	Haltom City city, Texas	27,972	19.5	31.1	35.6	13.8	$25,234	$30,197	$32,493	$21,689	$27,822
48	32312	Harker Heights city, Texas	18,361	5.6	15.9	40.2	38.3	$30,330	$43,341	$61,915	$11,782	$37,022
48	32372	Harlingen city, Texas	37,970	26.7	25.1	32.3	15.8	$23,079	$27,498	$36,932	$18,249	$24,858

Table E. Cities—Labor Force, Employment, and Educational Data, 2015—*Continued*

FIPS state code	FIPS place code	State/city	Educational attainment of persons age 25 years and older — Total population age 25 years and older	Less than high school graduate	High school graduate (includes equivalency)	Some college or Associate's degree	Bachelor's degree or higher	Median earnings in the past 12 months (in 2015 Inflation-adjusted dollars) — All persons age 16 and older with earnings in the past 12 months	Men with earnings — All men with earnings	Men who worked full-time, year-round in the past 12 months	Women with earnings — All women with earnings	Women who worked full-time, year-round in the past 12 months
48	35000	Houston city, Texas	1,471,908	22.3	23.2	23.7	30.9	$28,936	$31,912	$40,785	$23,891	$36,556
48	35528	Huntsville city, Texas	23,772	12.7	37.8	23.2	26.3	$25,556	$25,888	$31,827	$23,833	$31,576
48	35576	Hurst city, Texas	26,580	11.2	28.7	31.6	28.4	$30,364	$34,183	$47,893	$25,980	$40,368
48	35624	Hutto city, Texas	11,727	11.7	26.9	39.2	22.2	$34,125	$40,543	$41,039	$26,889	$31,373
48	37000	Irving city, Texas	148,941	21.3	18.9	24.4	35.4	$31,149	$35,149	$40,957	$25,727	$36,364
48	38632	Keller city, Texas	29,810	3.8	12.0	26.0	58.3	$61,630	$81,404	$101,108	$36,520	$62,948
48	39040	Kerrville city, Texas	17,715	16.1	25.1	35.9	22.8	$23,641	$24,509	$33,709	$22,995	$36,088
48	39148	Killeen city, Texas	81,730	7.9	30.0	41.5	20.7	$27,404	$33,984	$40,391	$20,840	$31,400
48	39352	Kingsville city, Texas	11,735	23.0	28.9	19.7	28.3	$20,131	$23,085	$39,468	$16,054	$19,907
48	39952	Kyle city, Texas	21,916	10.4	22.3	36.7	30.6	$36,532	$42,011	$50,348	$27,223	$31,475
48	40588	Lake Jackson city, Texas	18,352	6.0	15.2	37.5	41.3	$50,171	$88,372	$100,391	$28,687	$36,955
48	41212	Lancaster city, Texas	22,364	13.5	29.1	41.9	15.5	$29,047	$31,458	$38,858	$27,301	$36,340
48	41440	La Porte city, Texas	24,515	8.8	33.9	39.3	18.0	$41,348	$60,459	$66,333	$31,577	$42,101
48	41464	Laredo city, Texas	141,051	32.5	27.7	22.0	17.8	$22,459	$28,173	$34,707	$18,130	$26,751
48	41980	League City city, Texas	65,946	3.5	15.8	33.3	47.3	$56,455	$71,033	$85,627	$45,979	$56,468
48	42016	Leander city, Texas	22,605	3.4	19.2	34.0	43.4	$41,892	$52,155	$57,373	$37,327	$40,953
48	42508	Lewisville city, Texas	67,117	12.8	21.8	32.4	33.0	$33,093	$36,703	$41,820	$30,722	$37,762
48	43012	Little Elm city, Texas	25,258	8.3	20.4	35.6	35.7	$39,077	$46,231	$51,635	$31,474	$40,293
48	43888	Longview city, Texas	53,183	18.0	29.2	32.4	20.4	$24,743	$32,152	$38,866	$18,702	$30,873
48	45000	Lubbock city, Texas	142,247	15.4	27.1	30.7	26.8	$22,544	$27,909	$41,008	$19,736	$31,020
48	45072	Lufkin city, Texas	23,941	19.7	27.1	33.8	19.3	$24,879	$26,636	$40,421	$21,242	$31,574
48	45384	McAllen city, Texas	84,494	26.0	20.8	25.2	27.9	$25,065	$27,058	$40,736	$21,890	$36,625
48	45744	McKinney city, Texas	103,183	7.7	17.8	27.3	47.2	$48,151	$57,922	$71,030	$40,725	$50,875
48	46452	Mansfield city, Texas	42,606	5.5	16.0	36.5	42.0	$48,050	$60,419	$71,451	$37,115	$51,073
48	46776	Marshall city, Texas	15,777	17.8	37.7	30.8	13.7	$25,210	$33,034	$38,934	$18,805	$26,005
48	47892	Mesquite city, Texas	90,157	20.9	30.9	30.9	17.3	$26,784	$30,165	$41,261	$25,235	$35,251
48	48072	Midland city, Texas	82,837	14.3	24.8	32.8	28.1	$42,450	$53,140	$60,850	$30,686	$46,860
48	48096	Midlothian city, Texas	14,356	6.7	24.7	43.9	24.8	$42,708	$45,908	$55,132	$42,271	$47,276
48	48768	Mission city, Texas	46,322	29.1	20.9	22.7	27.3	$26,517	$34,675	$45,294	$18,302	$30,236
48	48772	Mission Bend CDP, Texas	21,334	20.6	23.7	31.0	24.7	$26,861	$35,500	$40,884	$22,311	$30,733
48	48804	Missouri City city, Texas	48,865	6.2	16.7	29.6	47.4	$46,334	$50,726	$60,432	$41,830	$51,435
48	50100	Murphy city, Texas	16,274	9.4	8.9	19.8	61.8	$46,885	$65,090	$76,138	$27,119	$37,352
48	50256	Nacogdoches city, Texas	16,871	11.1	25.9	29.3	33.7	$18,128	$27,031	$43,601	$9,832	$35,103
48	50820	New Braunfels city, Texas	45,398	10.5	27.0	28.9	33.5	$31,018	$36,038	$46,766	$26,199	$40,640
48	52356	North Richland Hills city, Texas	48,065	8.4	23.5	40.8	27.3	$32,105	$40,197	$50,256	$26,588	$36,628
48	53388	Odessa city, Texas	71,357	19.9	28.4	32.1	19.5	$33,491	$44,442	$62,050	$24,286	$35,879
48	55080	Paris city, Texas	16,179	21.8	38.0	28.2	12.0	$22,026	$28,900	$42,422	$20,833	$24,293
48	56000	Pasadena city, Texas	93,706	29.8	30.1	26.2	13.8	$30,723	$36,941	$43,426	$21,739	$34,248
48	56348	Pearland city, Texas	73,433	3.4	18.4	29.6	48.6	$51,169	$60,991	$62,438	$45,365	$51,300
48	57176	Pflugerville city, Texas	35,708	9.9	21.1	33.3	35.7	$41,135	$43,750	$56,105	$40,025	$44,002
48	57200	Pharr city, Texas	40,465	40.6	22.9	26.9	9.5	$22,688	$26,481	$30,883	$17,533	$24,943
48	57980	Plainview city, Texas	12,416	21.3	29.4	30.0	19.3	$25,944	$24,553	$32,154	$26,497	$30,941
48	58016	Plano city, Texas	192,070	7.3	12.4	26.1	54.2	$45,769	$58,091	$71,355	$35,448	$50,452
48	58820	Port Arthur city, Texas	34,494	28.1	34.9	25.4	11.6	$26,002	$30,626	$32,411	$18,943	$27,049
48	61796	Richardson city, Texas	75,082	7.5	14.1	25.2	53.2	$41,292	$50,543	$61,386	$31,930	$51,978
48	62828	Rockwall city, Texas	28,698	8.2	15.6	36.2	40.0	$43,012	$50,364	$61,645	$35,800	$40,766
48	63284	Rosenberg city, Texas	21,130	28.4	35.0	23.4	13.2	$28,906	$33,930	$48,869	$20,816	$40,584
48	63500	Round Rock city, Texas	72,324	8.7	19.8	35.3	36.2	$36,056	$42,448	$50,501	$29,520	$37,111
48	63572	Rowlett city, Texas	38,266	6.7	23.9	35.6	33.8	$38,349	$40,914	$50,765	$36,980	$42,360
48	64064	Sachse city, Texas	14,149	12.3	19.9	34.1	33.8	$42,351	$51,631	$55,657	$29,381	$40,105
48	64112	Saginaw city, Texas	13,296	5.0	28.5	37.4	29.1	$41,382	$52,162	$60,934	$35,000	$38,820
48	64472	San Angelo city, Texas	63,027	17.1	28.8	30.7	23.4	$26,931	$31,420	$42,390	$21,801	$30,490
48	65000	San Antonio city, Texas	934,535	19.0	26.9	29.9	24.2	$27,074	$30,936	$39,235	$23,763	$32,486
48	65036	San Benito city, Texas	14,392	41.7	30.9	16.3	11.1	$18,718	$17,182	$25,665	$21,043	$31,061
48	65516	San Juan city, Texas	20,051	40.3	23.3	23.9	12.5	$22,493	$24,807	$31,021	$20,172	$25,865
48	65600	San Marcos city, Texas	29,145	15.0	26.2	28.0	30.8	$18,856	$23,375	$34,176	$12,322	$31,792
48	66128	Schertz city, Texas	24,829	8.1	24.3	33.3	34.3	$36,781	$52,104	$56,452	$23,327	$35,168
48	66644	Seguin city, Texas	17,929	17.4	34.3	30.2	18.0	$26,286	$37,145	$45,826	$20,620	$25,426
48	67496	Sherman city, Texas	25,982	16.5	33.7	32.1	17.6	$25,648	$28,517	$34,557	$19,381	$32,337
48	68636	Socorro city, Texas	18,456	46.2	26.3	21.7	5.8	$21,633	$26,372	$30,477	$14,252	$21,855
48	69032	Southlake city, Texas	18,054	1.1	5.6	23.6	69.8	$102,130	$152,252	$202,311	$52,493	$120,272
48	69596	Spring CDP, Texas	36,947	9.6	32.5	33.3	24.6	$37,078	$44,655	$51,399	$30,736	$34,390
48	70208	Stephenville city, Texas	9,126	7.7	31.1	31.4	29.8	$18,031	$17,874	$36,733	$18,132	$25,118
48	70808	Sugar Land city, Texas	61,033	5.5	12.1	22.5	59.9	$52,767	$72,021	$90,438	$41,964	$55,123
48	72176	Temple city, Texas	47,259	10.1	28.0	35.2	26.7	$25,731	$28,188	$34,119	$20,862	$30,478
48	72368	Texarkana city, Texas	22,820	15.6	30.8	36.4	17.2	$26,902	$30,949	$46,055	$26,039	$30,315
48	72392	Texas City city, Texas	32,111	16.2	34.9	34.6	14.3	$25,724	$30,335	$49,900	$17,385	$32,433
48	72530	The Colony city, Texas	29,186	4.8	25.1	36.0	34.1	$38,783	$49,303	$60,609	$31,365	$45,390
48	72656	The Woodlands CDP, Texas	76,072	2.6	9.4	24.6	63.4	$53,217	$90,366	$120,741	$35,179	$58,083
48	73057	Timberwood Park CDP, Texas	17,753	5.8	13.8	28.3	52.1	$51,835	$76,163	$82,331	$38,191	$60,077

Table E. Cities—Labor Force, Employment, and Educational Data, 2015—*Continued*

| | | | Educational attainment of persons age 25 years and older | | | | | Median earnings in the past 12 months (in 2015 Inflation-adjusted dollars) | | | | |
| | | | | | | | | | Men with earnings | | Women with earnings | |
FIPS state code	FIPS place code	State/city	Total population age 25 years and older	Less than high school graduate	High school graduate (includes equivalency)	Some college or Associate's degree	Bachelor's degree or higher	All persons age 16 and older with earnings in the past 12 months	All men with earnings	Men who worked full-time, year-round in the past 12 months	All women with earnings	Women who worked full-time, year-round in the past 12 months
48	74144	Tyler city, Texas	65,080	17.3	20.3	33.3	29.1	$26,447	$31,579	$41,420	$22,419	$30,663
48	74492	University Park city, Texas	13,136	0.6	2.2	7.8	89.4	$69,152	$100,160	$202,117	$40,756	$101,900
48	75428	Victoria city, Texas	44,099	17.2	30.1	29.0	23.7	$25,694	$31,516	$46,779	$22,055	$31,175
48	76000	Waco city, Texas	75,120	16.3	27.7	31.2	24.7	$21,773	$24,502	$36,943	$20,419	$30,654
48	76672	Watauga city, Texas	15,680	12.1	22.5	40.3	25.1	$31,275	$31,117	$41,889	$31,376	$34,918
48	76816	Waxahachie city, Texas	21,061	12.9	27.0	33.4	26.7	$30,877	$32,333	$41,644	$30,135	$42,614
48	76864	Weatherford city, Texas	18,962	14.6	28.3	34.4	22.7	$31,686	$45,258	$49,555	$20,665	$36,514
48	77272	Weslaco city, Texas	22,790	26.4	21.1	31.5	21.0	$22,168	$28,056	$32,371	$18,584	$24,967
48	77728	West Odessa CDP, Texas	15,201	36.2	32.3	28.0	3.6	$28,513	$48,115	$60,022	$16,640	$28,305
48	79000	Wichita Falls city, Texas	65,528	18.7	29.5	28.9	22.9	$22,327	$26,222	$36,460	$18,501	$33,282
48	80356	Wylie city, Texas	30,353	5.0	23.7	39.1	32.1	$41,950	$55,647	$61,308	$34,790	$41,185
49	00000	**UTAH**	1,741,949	8.5	24.2	35.5	31.8	$29,188	$36,791	$50,741	$21,143	$36,060
49	01310	American Fork city, Utah	15,506	7.4	16.0	40.0	36.6	$31,493	$38,875	$49,332	$22,573	$36,284
49	07690	Bountiful city, Utah	29,032	6.0	18.7	32.2	43.1	$31,222	$33,439	$52,445	$24,328	$41,196
49	11320	Cedar City city, Utah	15,020	5.7	26.6	28.6	39.2	$21,173	$28,965	$46,628	$10,499	$30,240
49	13850	Clearfield city, Utah	15,720	14.1	27.8	37.2	20.9	$23,561	$30,888	$32,683	$19,347	$24,416
49	14290	Clinton city, Utah	10,203	9.0	19.0	37.2	34.7	$28,654	$41,463	$50,766	$17,177	$41,139
49	16270	Cottonwood Heights city, Utah	23,471	2.5	19.6	33.5	44.4	$40,590	$50,513	$55,268	$30,625	$43,140
49	20120	Draper city, Utah	27,118	3.1	14.2	29.4	53.3	$40,156	$51,810	$79,858	$25,311	$55,007
49	20810	Eagle Mountain city, Utah	12,305	4.8	20.3	49.2	25.8	$40,091	$45,841	$51,018	$20,021	$36,308
49	24740	Farmington city, Utah	13,383	0.4	9.8	48.1	41.7	$40,932	$70,218	$80,793	$22,239	$41,001
49	34970	Herriman city, Utah	15,412	4.8	24.0	39.1	32.1	$41,371	$51,238	$61,240	$29,419	$41,647
49	36070	Holladay city, Utah	20,523	2.0	18.8	25.6	53.5	$37,283	$51,480	$70,183	$26,602	$36,697
49	40360	Kaysville city, Utah	15,605	1.5	20.0	33.3	45.1	$39,323	$56,520	$70,597	$20,233	$35,156
49	40470	Kearns CDP, Utah	23,535	28.1	35.4	26.0	10.5	$26,396	$29,764	$32,074	$22,083	$30,939
49	43660	Layton city, Utah	42,409	5.9	22.4	42.2	29.5	$30,319	$42,120	$55,094	$18,625	$34,118
49	44320	Lehi city, Utah	27,597	2.0	16.3	38.7	42.9	$36,934	$55,505	$66,569	$13,357	$40,388
49	45860	Logan city, Utah	23,650	12.2	20.7	34.8	32.4	$15,055	$17,964	$33,636	$11,097	$27,824
49	47290	Magna CDP, Utah	17,169	21.3	38.2	31.3	9.1	$29,295	$32,815	$41,192	$22,050	$28,705
49	49710	Midvale city, Utah	20,201	8.7	28.0	31.6	31.6	$31,726	$37,151	$43,540	$26,458	$32,069
49	50150	Millcreek CDP, Utah	41,584	8.3	17.3	27.0	47.4	$35,164	$47,866	$59,486	$27,276	$42,520
49	53230	Murray city, Utah	32,877	8.0	24.3	38.6	29.1	$30,729	$35,949	$46,777	$23,175	$37,565
49	55980	Ogden city, Utah	52,503	16.9	31.9	32.3	19.0	$24,409	$28,854	$32,170	$19,512	$29,137
49	57300	Orem city, Utah	49,415	11.6	14.3	38.7	35.4	$22,269	$30,387	$41,476	$15,451	$31,250
49	60930	Pleasant Grove city, Utah	20,071	6.3	18.9	40.3	34.6	$22,926	$36,282	$52,293	$16,628	$42,042
49	62470	Provo city, Utah	47,279	8.4	12.9	35.3	43.3	$12,394	$16,358	$38,388	$9,221	$26,716
49	64340	Riverton city, Utah	23,190	5.3	18.7	44.3	31.7	$43,475	$51,825	$66,216	$35,423	$51,519
49	65110	Roy city, Utah	21,594	6.8	36.8	35.9	20.5	$31,019	$39,043	$48,533	$23,774	$31,024
49	65330	St. George city, Utah	50,849	8.2	26.8	38.2	26.7	$24,723	$31,561	$44,525	$18,585	$31,946
49	67000	Salt Lake City city, Utah	128,718	9.5	20.2	25.8	44.4	$30,545	$35,150	$42,463	$25,609	$37,045
49	67440	Sandy city, Utah	58,531	5.2	21.8	34.0	38.9	$36,204	$46,868	$65,792	$24,625	$40,335
49	67825	Saratoga Springs city, Utah	10,619	2.4	15.7	30.9	51.1	$42,182	$70,580	$75,515	$27,451	$36,848
49	70850	South Jordan city, Utah	40,002	2.7	17.6	36.7	43.1	$39,800	$60,586	$75,298	$32,219	$46,056
49	71070	South Salt Lake city, Utah	16,328	13.7	30.7	36.6	18.9	$25,573	$26,662	$36,500	$20,412	$35,554
49	71290	Spanish Fork city, Utah	19,234	8.5	25.3	38.4	27.8	$26,064	$35,808	$51,310	$15,249	$31,502
49	72280	Springville city, Utah	16,004	7.0	18.9	36.2	37.9	$27,911	$35,942	$47,804	$17,483	$35,992
49	74810	Syracuse city, Utah	14,929	5.7	21.8	31.1	41.3	$38,262	$53,182	$61,798	$20,467	$38,182
49	75360	Taylorsville city, Utah	38,251	9.9	30.4	36.0	23.6	$30,023	$31,269	$41,005	$26,660	$36,432
49	76680	Tooele city, Utah	19,870	8.9	29.7	38.9	22.6	$36,716	$42,797	$50,210	$30,591	$37,987
49	81960	Washington city, Utah	14,272	8.7	20.2	41.2	29.9	$26,345	$50,157	$56,409	$18,280	$25,669
49	82950	West Jordan city, Utah	65,801	7.9	29.6	38.6	24.0	$30,823	$36,863	$50,080	$23,470	$35,830
49	83470	West Valley City city, Utah	81,210	21.3	34.4	30.6	13.7	$26,180	$29,392	$32,394	$23,895	$30,934
50	00000	**VERMONT**	438,654	8.3	29.0	25.8	36.9	$31,002	$35,502	$47,960	$26,541	$40,173
50	10675	Burlington city, Vermont	23,410	6.8	18.4	18.8	56.0	$18,292	$20,195	$41,093	$15,869	$35,104
51	00000	**VIRGINIA**	5,685,318	11.1	24.6	27.3	37.0	$35,296	$41,421	$54,392	$30,119	$42,342
51	01000	Alexandria city, Virginia	116,855	8.0	13.4	18.7	59.8	$51,253	$55,139	$74,440	$46,784	$62,377
51	01912	Annandale CDP, Virginia	34,150	14.5	19.1	20.7	45.8	$35,599	$38,814	$50,962	$32,180	$47,479
51	03000	Arlington CDP, Virginia	171,583	7.4	6.6	12.6	73.4	$66,217	$71,154	$86,926	$62,201	$75,111
51	03320	Ashburn CDP, Virginia	34,058	3.2	10.3	24.7	61.8	$56,084	$78,307	$96,214	$42,407	$66,087
51	04088	Bailey's Crossroads CDP, Virginia	17,841	17.7	20.8	14.1	47.4	$30,204	$37,759	$63,199	$26,132	$33,656
51	07784	Blacksburg town, Virginia	17,134	7.8	9.4	12.8	69.9	$10,103	$11,114	$50,374	$7,222	$39,045
51	08472	Bon Air CDP, Virginia	13,847	6.6	18.5	29.2	45.7	$36,042	$48,134	$59,417	$21,670	$40,216
51	11464	Burke CDP, Virginia	25,135	6.3	11.7	15.3	66.8	$58,183	$81,257	$112,167	$42,447	$72,172
51	13720	Cave Spring CDP, Virginia	19,225	5.6	14.9	25.1	54.3	$40,932	$51,092	$52,050	$27,347	$42,259
51	14440	Centreville CDP, Virginia	48,009	6.6	15.9	20.5	56.9	$46,518	$59,147	$69,167	$37,116	$52,413
51	14744	Chantilly CDP, Virginia	14,813	6.9	13.7	24.9	54.5	$51,337	$72,138	$80,523	$35,022	$59,727
51	14968	Charlottesville city, Virginia	29,789	7.0	19.4	24.0	49.6	$31,230	$32,423	$52,301	$28,332	$55,406
51	15176	Cherry Hill CDP, Virginia	14,219	9.7	20.2	31.0	39.1	$45,124	$46,484	$61,796	$40,183	$56,500

Table E. Cities—Labor Force, Employment, and Educational Data, 2015—*Continued*

FIPS state code	FIPS place code	State/city	Total population age 25 years and older	Less than high school graduate	High school graduate (includes equivalency)	Some college or Associate's degree	Bachelor's degree or higher	All persons age 16 and older with earnings in the past 12 months	All men with earnings	Men who worked full-time, year-round in the past 12 months	All women with earnings	Women who worked full-time, year-round in the past 12 months
									Men with earnings		Women with earnings	
51	16000	Chesapeake city, Virginia	157,207	8.3	23.5	36.4	31.8	$37,554	$44,374	$54,565	$31,037	$41,380
51	16096	Chester CDP, Virginia	16,392	12.1	29.5	37.6	20.8	$33,813	$41,797	$51,001	$23,984	$50,842
51	16608	Christiansburg town, Virginia	13,852	3.1	22.6	30.2	44.0	$34,164	$45,424	$60,437	$31,257	$37,879
51	21088	Dale City CDP, Virginia	45,100	19.3	24.9	31.0	24.7	$35,149	$38,849	$47,940	$30,185	$45,705
51	21344	Danville city, Virginia	29,184	22.3	29.9	29.6	18.2	$22,449	$26,042	$36,738	$20,696	$30,448
51	26496	Fairfax city, Virginia	16,923	4.1	15.6	23.8	56.5	$46,531	$57,587	$62,076	$34,576	$47,484
51	26875	Fair Oaks CDP, Virginia	21,046	2.6	13.2	19.2	65.0	$62,077	$76,904	$99,985	$47,134	$72,015
51	29136	Fort Hunt CDP, Virginia	12,671	1.5	6.1	13.8	78.6	$82,661	$106,991	$120,418	$65,982	$95,544
51	29744	Fredericksburg city, Virginia	16,589	8.5	28.1	33.1	30.2	$31,324	$36,382	$46,706	$25,293	$40,599
51	35000	Hampton city, Virginia	91,099	10.0	26.4	38.9	24.8	$30,195	$35,958	$46,967	$25,202	$35,585
51	35624	Harrisonburg city, Virginia	25,526	13.7	24.6	22.3	39.4	$16,292	$21,872	$40,403	$9,334	$34,643
51	36648	Herndon town, Virginia	15,770	12.8	23.9	15.8	47.5	$33,879	$46,072	$76,219	$25,143	$48,981
51	38424	Hopewell city, Virginia	14,328	18.5	33.9	31.9	15.7	$25,012	$26,134	$36,323	$24,563	$29,473
51	39448	Idylwood CDP, Virginia	13,271	16.3	12.3	13.3	58.1	$41,271	$45,948	$59,444	$37,092	$54,276
51	43432	Lake Ridge CDP, Virginia	26,955	8.2	14.8	33.1	43.9	$46,201	$51,536	$71,345	$41,761	$56,647
51	44280	Laurel CDP, Virginia	14,963	10.4	23.9	32.9	32.8	$27,465	$35,000	$39,876	$26,484	$32,173
51	44984	Leesburg town, Virginia	32,964	9.1	17.9	21.4	51.5	$45,183	$49,558	$64,443	$40,392	$53,147
51	45784	Lincolnia CDP, Virginia	17,677	14.2	21.3	21.4	43.1	$31,845	$40,993	$46,871	$25,723	$36,650
51	45957	Linton Hall CDP, Virginia	23,640	5.2	13.8	27.2	53.9	$61,237	$86,476	$91,045	$35,292	$57,076
51	47064	Lorton CDP, Virginia	11,633	12.6	9.0	30.3	48.1	$31,567	$58,820	$67,136	$25,442	$33,875
51	47672	Lynchburg city, Virginia	45,037	12.4	26.6	28.0	33.0	$17,078	$17,744	$42,276	$16,654	$31,824
51	48376	McLean CDP, Virginia	32,439	1.9	5.1	10.6	82.3	$99,085	$126,849	$150,667	$64,815	$96,667
51	48952	Manassas city, Virginia	25,757	23.4	26.8	24.0	25.8	$34,638	$40,116	$46,996	$31,147	$36,406
51	49792	Marumsco CDP, Virginia	24,465	25.4	25.4	22.1	27.1	$29,527	$30,598	$37,097	$26,013	$38,577
51	50856	Mechanicsville CDP, Virginia	26,263	8.0	26.7	30.6	34.6	$45,535	$51,248	$59,631	$38,882	$47,018
51	52658	Montclair CDP, Virginia	13,103	1.5	12.2	25.3	60.9	$56,748	$82,068	$93,990	$44,605	$60,596
51	56000	Newport News city, Virginia	115,693	9.3	27.5	38.6	24.6	$30,217	$34,752	$45,533	$25,986	$36,229
51	57000	Norfolk city, Virginia	150,965	12.7	28.5	32.1	26.6	$26,342	$29,504	$36,312	$23,272	$32,041
51	58472	Oakton CDP, Virginia	26,364	5.2	10.9	16.0	67.9	$60,839	$74,075	$90,269	$51,295	$71,402
51	61832	Petersburg city, Virginia	21,426	20.4	38.5	23.8	17.2	$20,540	$22,313	$30,465	$16,638	$24,747
51	64000	Portsmouth city, Virginia	62,610	14.9	27.6	34.0	23.6	$29,171	$35,631	$47,920	$26,606	$32,043
51	66672	Reston CDP, Virginia	43,533	4.9	13.8	16.6	64.7	$60,345	$76,468	$91,247	$45,162	$65,944
51	67000	Richmond city, Virginia	150,042	14.2	23.4	24.7	37.7	$26,035	$27,525	$41,487	$24,556	$38,081
51	68000	Roanoke city, Virginia	69,434	15.0	33.2	30.1	21.7	$25,786	$27,093	$37,973	$23,103	$33,539
51	68880	Rose Hill CDP (Fairfax County), Virginia	15,307	9.5	17.3	21.9	51.3	$45,170	$58,447	$71,829	$31,929	$51,607
51	70000	Salem city, Virginia	16,424	11.9	32.9	32.2	23.1	$30,845	$36,152	$42,804	$26,142	$35,648
51	72272	Short Pump CDP, Virginia	17,180	2.1	4.1	21.6	72.2	$54,020	$90,363	$100,043	$40,666	$51,075
51	74100	South Riding CDP, Virginia	18,500	2.9	12.7	18.2	66.2	$71,785	$99,158	$104,330	$51,644	$70,507
51	74592	Springfield CDP, Virginia	20,064	13.5	19.3	28.6	38.6	$35,740	$38,982	$54,679	$28,302	$49,733
51	75216	Staunton city, Virginia	18,162	12.0	32.6	25.4	30.1	$26,035	$31,421	$40,417	$23,019	$36,333
51	75376	Sterling CDP, Virginia	20,968	23.4	17.3	19.7	39.6	$30,472	$32,488	$46,473	$26,529	$35,375
51	76432	Suffolk city, Virginia	58,380	12.8	28.2	31.3	27.7	$32,347	$40,736	$52,596	$26,815	$36,678
51	79560	Tuckahoe CDP, Virginia	37,096	5.2	17.6	22.9	54.3	$31,108	$35,776	$50,800	$26,796	$42,266
51	79952	Tysons Corner CDP, Virginia	16,675	2.3	10.5	12.3	75.0	$71,245	$72,334	$90,236	$65,549	$91,963
51	82000	Virginia Beach city, Virginia	305,033	7.0	22.6	37.7	32.8	$35,133	$41,507	$49,193	$29,451	$39,612
51	83680	Waynesboro city, Virginia	13,626	18.8	39.3	24.9	17.0	$30,969	$36,356	$39,408	$22,487	$27,427
51	84368	West Falls Church CDP, Virginia	24,641	24.0	20.5	20.3	35.2	$32,409	$36,045	$41,777	$27,448	$51,210
51	84976	West Springfield CDP, Virginia	15,082	2.5	10.4	20.5	66.6	$56,923	$78,574	$90,306	$42,427	$72,320
51	86720	Winchester city, Virginia	17,055	18.7	20.0	26.1	35.2	$23,892	$33,619	$51,627	$17,049	$34,704
51	87410	Woodlawn CDP (Fairfax County), Virginia	14,940	20.5	29.8	32.4	17.3	$26,409	$28,476	$37,161	$22,236	$31,198
53	00000	**WASHINGTON**	4,889,314	9.2	23.1	33.6	34.2	$35,414	$41,859	$56,215	$28,451	$44,422
53	03180	Auburn city, Washington	50,842	11.5	31.3	32.2	25.1	$37,197	$45,522	$55,163	$31,835	$45,282
53	03176	Bainbridge Island city, Washington	17,306	2.6	7.8	19.8	69.9	$49,491	$70,429	$103,452	$34,914	$56,764
53	05210	Bellevue city, Washington	101,300	4.3	9.7	20.3	65.6	$56,121	$71,717	$91,839	$36,974	$72,170
53	05280	Bellingham city, Washington	51,443	4.9	19.9	34.1	41.1	$21,386	$23,706	$47,452	$20,154	$35,871
53	07380	Bothell city, Washington	30,682	7.7	17.4	30.9	44.0	$41,920	$49,880	$61,714	$30,607	$48,836
53	07395	Bothell West CDP, Washington	13,832	5.0	16.0	30.8	48.3	$50,392	$66,511	$79,990	$34,255	$52,208
53	07695	Bremerton city, Washington	25,494	5.8	21.4	48.6	24.2	$27,380	$30,432	$36,273	$22,659	$32,319
53	08552	Bryn Mawr-Skyway CDP, Washington	14,042	11.3	42.3	26.7	19.7	$29,578	$31,606	$50,327	$28,079	$35,678
53	08850	Burien city, Washington	33,243	19.5	27.5	30.2	22.7	$29,614	$35,020	$48,051	$25,365	$36,498
53	09480	Camas city, Washington	14,280	8.8	17.0	32.9	41.3	$42,413	$63,304	$80,761	$30,943	$49,287
53	14940	Cottage Lake CDP, Washington	14,542	1.5	11.6	25.2	61.7	$57,395	$101,623	$140,401	$38,430	$63,720
53	17635	Des Moines city, Washington	22,391	15.2	21.4	38.5	25.0	$30,840	$39,125	$50,955	$28,514	$50,772
53	19630	Eastmont CDP, Washington	14,694	7.8	21.7	32.4	38.1	$43,845	$52,082	$57,069	$36,891	$51,548
53	20750	Edmonds city, Washington	30,986	4.2	21.5	25.0	49.2	$41,096	$41,943	$56,107	$38,455	$61,639
53	22640	Everett city, Washington	74,884	12.1	27.6	38.1	22.1	$31,801	$36,453	$46,982	$25,473	$41,629

Table E. Cities—Labor Force, Employment, and Educational Data, 2015—*Continued*

								Median earnings in the past 12 months (in 2015 Inflation-adjusted dollars)				
			Educational attainment of persons age 25 years and older						Men with earnings		Women with earnings	
FIPS state code	FIPS place code	State/city	Total population age 25 years and older	Less than high school graduate	High school graduate (includes equivalency)	Some college or Associate's degree	Bachelor's degree or higher	All persons age 16 and older with earnings in the past 12 months	All men with earnings	Men who worked full-time, year-round in the past 12 months	All women with earnings	Women who worked full-time, year-round in the past 12 months
53	23160	Fairwood CDP (King County), Washington	15,757	5.3	18.9	35.4	40.3	$45,776	$57,303	$64,005	$39,797	$46,095
53	23515	Federal Way city, Washington	65,043	9.7	25.7	39.6	25.1	$35,254	$39,306	$49,410	$30,817	$44,801
53	24188	Five Corners CDP, Washington	13,541	9.6	32.8	41.5	16.2	$31,304	$35,802	$40,223	$24,983	$41,132
53	27785	Graham CDP, Washington	15,753	9.0	28.4	47.0	15.6	$41,038	$49,764	$56,370	$24,946	$38,869
53	33805	Issaquah city, Washington	24,148	3.4	8.2	23.2	65.2	$58,851	$77,194	$110,207	$41,285	$60,355
53	35170	Kenmore city, Washington	16,090	4.0	11.8	26.1	58.1	$52,092	$63,750	$76,172	$37,244	$61,630
53	35275	Kennewick city, Washington	48,072	12.4	23.2	42.0	22.4	$28,145	$36,825	$51,621	$23,494	$30,681
53	35415	Kent city, Washington	81,880	12.6	28.5	35.7	23.1	$31,733	$33,753	$50,287	$30,372	$38,695
53	35940	Kirkland city, Washington	66,021	5.1	11.7	25.0	58.3	$60,847	$75,366	$92,464	$51,203	$73,219
53	36745	Lacey city, Washington	29,917	6.8	17.4	42.8	33.0	$35,101	$41,452	$50,876	$26,183	$43,500
53	37900	Lake Stevens city, Washington	19,947	9.3	22.8	38.4	29.5	$42,077	$50,972	$60,485	$36,114	$46,068
53	38038	Lakewood city, Washington	40,143	10.9	29.3	40.6	19.2	$26,827	$28,755	$35,664	$24,612	$40,093
53	40245	Longview city, Washington	26,209	14.6	31.2	36.2	18.0	$26,076	$37,707	$42,504	$17,194	$31,612
53	40840	Lynnwood city, Washington	26,015	14.0	19.3	36.9	29.9	$31,969	$33,611	$46,413	$27,874	$46,172
53	43150	Maple Valley city, Washington	17,193	3.8	14.3	39.4	42.5	$56,705	$71,268	$78,040	$42,398	$54,206
53	43955	Marysville city, Washington	43,083	9.4	27.6	41.6	21.4	$36,851	$45,562	$57,187	$31,052	$41,126
53	45005	Mercer Island city, Washington	17,423	4.1	2.5	12.4	81.0	$80,307	$100,992	$130,426	$60,669	$87,431
53	45865	Mill Creek city, Washington	14,489	2.8	15.0	33.9	48.3	$43,891	$60,956	$81,822	$34,068	$47,309
53	45870	Mill Creek East CDP, Washington	12,847	3.0	16.4	32.7	47.9	$67,204	$86,244	$87,390	$42,198	$61,092
53	47245	Moses Lake city, Washington	11,253	14.0	29.7	33.3	23.1	$30,542	$35,984	$42,583	$25,403	$30,975
53	47490	Mountlake Terrace city, Washington	16,092	6.7	18.8	38.7	35.8	$36,987	$46,447	$51,375	$30,369	$46,022
53	47560	Mount Vernon city, Washington	21,928	14.2	24.8	35.6	25.4	$28,009	$35,767	$48,938	$19,022	$35,358
53	47735	Mukilteo city, Washington	15,676	1.8	15.7	23.0	59.5	$70,461	$81,869	$93,141	$42,037	$75,663
53	50360	Oak Harbor city, Washington	14,404	5.9	20.9	50.6	22.6	$26,470	$30,791	$36,560	$23,406	$42,246
53	51300	Olympia city, Washington	35,913	10.4	16.4	33.5	39.7	$36,159	$42,433	$56,005	$30,973	$51,281
53	51795	Orchards CDP, Washington	14,305	11.7	32.7	39.1	16.6	$32,453	$40,345	$51,161	$21,857	$41,063
53	53335	Parkland CDP, Washington	22,266	13.2	34.4	39.2	13.2	$25,442	$30,369	$46,154	$21,581	$32,340
53	53545	Pasco city, Washington	36,996	24.7	29.2	27.3	18.9	$29,814	$30,691	$40,077	$27,824	$37,380
53	56625	Pullman city, Washington	12,078	3.1	6.3	21.5	69.1	$11,083	$16,061	$27,474	$8,149	$31,292
53	56695	Puyallup city, Washington	28,510	8.9	28.9	36.2	26.0	$42,156	$45,555	$56,397	$36,335	$52,260
53	57535	Redmond city, Washington	42,472	3.5	8.2	17.2	71.1	$67,013	$92,410	$110,387	$42,449	$65,853
53	57745	Renton city, Washington	67,963	8.9	21.0	32.3	37.8	$40,020	$44,477	$57,279	$35,728	$52,911
53	58235	Richland city, Washington	37,185	4.8	20.4	28.0	46.7	$40,592	$57,223	$76,807	$27,438	$50,295
53	61000	Salmon Creek CDP, Washington	13,823	7.3	21.4	35.3	36.0	$32,315	$38,814	$77,472	$27,352	$40,794
53	61115	Sammamish city, Washington	34,436	2.3	5.3	18.9	73.5	$91,645	$122,348	$140,172	$49,398	$97,393
53	62288	SeaTac city, Washington	18,935	15.2	27.4	36.1	21.3	$25,833	$27,467	$37,049	$23,895	$38,303
53	63000	Seattle city, Washington	506,840	5.3	10.2	22.5	62.1	$46,454	$51,999	$70,616	$41,042	$56,934
53	63960	Shoreline city, Washington	41,399	8.4	17.2	31.1	43.3	$40,790	$50,802	$62,134	$32,726	$52,551
53	64380	Silver Firs CDP, Washington	13,072	3.4	16.1	30.9	49.5	$55,569	$72,616	$74,908	$36,463	$61,282
53	65922	South Hill CDP, Washington	34,756	5.8	31.7	40.7	21.8	$38,236	$50,800	$57,695	$28,193	$40,703
53	66255	Spanaway CDP, Washington	18,088	8.5	32.8	45.0	13.7	$36,690	$41,786	$45,812	$24,575	$40,297
53	67000	Spokane city, Washington	146,320	6.3	25.6	37.9	30.3	$26,938	$30,424	$44,244	$24,719	$35,906
53	67167	Spokane Valley city, Washington	64,806	8.2	29.8	40.1	21.8	$28,767	$33,861	$41,180	$22,671	$33,373
53	70000	Tacoma city, Washington	144,640	11.6	27.8	32.5	28.0	$32,139	$36,670	$48,643	$27,951	$40,691
53	72625	Tukwila city, Washington	12,803	14.8	29.6	33.5	22.1	$29,901	$36,469	$50,436	$29,461	$40,808
53	73307	Union Hill-Novelty Hill CDP, Washington	14,744	1.4	10.2	21.5	66.9	$67,000	$101,472	$116,115	$27,882	$60,552
53	73465	University Place city, Washington	20,891	3.5	17.1	43.8	35.6	$32,028	$42,178	$52,465	$21,870	$42,326
53	74060	Vancouver city, Washington	116,188	10.7	24.4	37.0	27.9	$34,891	$40,918	$48,347	$24,033	$40,531
53	75775	Walla Walla city, Washington	21,298	13.7	22.5	39.3	24.6	$23,892	$25,173	$35,493	$19,583	$40,024
53	77105	Wenatchee city, Washington	22,064	19.2	29.4	33.4	18.0	$31,247	$37,600	$41,913	$22,280	$35,369
53	80010	Yakima city, Washington	57,609	24.7	25.8	30.4	19.1	$25,394	$30,692	$36,030	$20,080	$30,094
54	00000	**WEST VIRGINIA**	1,300,347	14.0	40.7	25.7	19.6	$27,527	$33,822	$45,082	$22,951	$31,824
54	14600	Charleston city, West Virginia	34,563	5.7	27.5	26.1	40.7	$31,298	$37,461	$53,195	$26,495	$36,462
54	39460	Huntington city, West Virginia	29,872	11.2	25.9	34.1	28.9	$19,882	$23,226	$40,982	$16,455	$34,422
54	55756	Morgantown city, West Virginia	16,149	7.0	19.2	20.4	53.4	$17,642	$16,489	$52,860	$18,861	$34,773
54	62140	Parkersburg city, West Virginia	22,280	12.4	38.9	31.3	17.4	$20,935	$22,084	$35,866	$18,484	$25,429
54	86452	Wheeling city, West Virginia	19,497	8.9	31.1	28.2	31.8	$27,660	$33,618	$50,609	$22,081	$30,331
55	00000	**WISCONSIN**	3,918,997	8.6	31.2	31.8	28.4	$31,474	$37,774	$49,306	$26,173	$38,594
55	02375	Appleton city, Wisconsin	49,729	6.5	30.4	31.5	31.6	$30,603	$35,392	$46,054	$22,620	$37,757
55	06500	Beloit city, Wisconsin	22,376	19.1	35.8	28.2	16.9	$24,365	$25,922	$41,492	$23,624	$35,303
55	10025	Brookfield city, Wisconsin	27,343	4.2	17.4	22.1	56.3	$51,442	$60,789	$79,420	$38,500	$62,840
55	11950	Caledonia village, Wisconsin	17,592	4.3	32.8	34.6	28.3	$42,382	$51,932	$65,192	$31,615	$47,670
55	19775	De Pere city, Wisconsin	15,858	3.1	22.7	34.5	39.8	$36,362	$40,348	$47,815	$31,357	$42,598
55	22300	Eau Claire city, Wisconsin	40,782	7.4	20.5	38.7	33.4	$24,052	$26,927	$41,479	$21,396	$30,622
55	25950	Fitchburg city, Wisconsin	18,877	3.9	23.9	28.1	44.1	$29,597	$32,693	$45,324	$26,610	$35,333
55	26275	Fond du Lac city, Wisconsin	29,135	9.2	35.6	30.9	24.3	$28,901	$35,934	$47,008	$23,445	$32,639

Table E. Cities—Labor Force, Employment, and Educational Data, 2015—*Continued*

| | | | Educational attainment of persons age 25 years and older | | | | | Median earnings in the past 12 months (in 2015 Inflation-adjusted dollars) | | | | |
| | | | | | | | | | Men with earnings | | Women with earnings | |
FIPS state code	FIPS place code	State/city	Total population age 25 years and older	Less than high school graduate	High school graduate (includes equivalency)	Some college or Associate's degree	Bachelor's degree or higher	All persons age 16 and older with earnings in the past 12 months	All men with earnings	Men who worked full-time, year-round in the past 12 months	All women with earnings	Women who worked full-time, year-round in the past 12 months
55	27300	Franklin city, Wisconsin	27,645	7.3	20.2	30.6	41.9	$47,750	$58,333	$75,947	$37,400	$61,491
55	31000	Green Bay city, Wisconsin	66,537	12.0	31.7	31.6	24.7	$26,028	$30,374	$37,960	$20,826	$32,082
55	31175	Greenfield city, Wisconsin	26,308	9.3	29.1	33.9	27.6	$36,268	$39,928	$48,130	$33,798	$41,127
55	37825	Janesville city, Wisconsin	45,924	8.0	38.9	29.8	23.3	$30,950	$36,236	$46,717	$25,861	$39,212
55	39225	Kenosha city, Wisconsin	64,153	10.9	32.5	34.2	22.3	$26,045	$30,354	$41,535	$22,212	$35,757
55	40775	La Crosse city, Wisconsin	30,327	6.2	25.3	33.3	35.2	$18,568	$20,801	$36,842	$14,896	$32,129
55	48000	Madison city, Wisconsin	153,194	6.4	15.0	23.6	55.0	$27,918	$31,305	$52,398	$25,281	$40,428
55	48500	Manitowoc city, Wisconsin	23,387	14.2	30.6	34.4	20.8	$30,125	$36,031	$41,639	$23,591	$34,515
55	51000	Menomonee Falls village, Wisconsin	26,409	3.2	31.0	23.8	42.0	$42,086	$51,499	$60,655	$34,633	$46,681
55	51150	Mequon city, Wisconsin	15,720	1.5	14.4	21.1	63.0	$58,839	$77,004	$92,038	$36,735	$70,174
55	53000	Milwaukee city, Wisconsin	371,229	17.3	28.7	30.1	23.9	$25,762	$27,321	$40,514	$24,324	$36,146
55	54875	Mount Pleasant village, Wisconsin	18,354	5.7	29.9	32.5	31.8	$35,895	$50,719	$60,909	$27,692	$40,295
55	55275	Muskego city, Wisconsin	16,540	3.6	32.2	32.5	31.7	$40,657	$51,980	$69,340	$32,813	$47,198
55	55750	Neenah city, Wisconsin	17,181	5.1	29.1	31.6	34.2	$37,001	$42,928	$50,482	$31,584	$40,307
55	56375	New Berlin city, Wisconsin	29,530	3.2	20.6	33.4	42.8	$44,505	$61,245	$66,714	$35,149	$48,895
55	58800	Oak Creek city, Wisconsin	25,029	6.7	35.3	30.5	27.5	$39,659	$41,491	$54,722	$35,730	$51,087
55	60500	Oshkosh city, Wisconsin	41,234	10.2	35.1	32.0	22.7	$25,246	$30,965	$42,013	$20,709	$32,076
55	63300	Pleasant Prairie village, Wisconsin	15,318	7.4	25.6	36.7	30.3	$45,431	$51,296	$55,791	$27,947	$46,234
55	66000	Racine city, Wisconsin	49,240	18.7	27.6	35.9	17.7	$25,612	$28,508	$41,583	$23,575	$33,258
55	72975	Sheboygan city, Wisconsin	33,189	13.5	40.0	26.2	20.3	$31,225	$34,630	$45,419	$28,316	$34,299
55	75125	South Milwaukee city, Wisconsin	14,748	9.1	35.6	34.6	20.8	$30,707	$36,292	$48,684	$23,803	$38,658
55	77200	Stevens Point city, Wisconsin	14,095	7.7	25.6	28.7	38.1	$15,770	$17,956	$46,289	$13,943	$34,048
55	78600	Sun Prairie city, Wisconsin	22,566	2.9	21.8	34.9	40.3	$36,597	$39,644	$49,724	$30,793	$44,668
55	78650	Superior city, Wisconsin	18,531	5.8	36.9	38.8	18.5	$24,348	$28,576	$45,710	$20,009	$35,115
55	83975	Watertown city, Wisconsin	15,358	9.2	41.3	30.9	18.7	$27,807	$34,598	$42,069	$22,646	$27,246
55	84250	Waukesha city, Wisconsin	47,752	7.8	24.1	32.2	35.9	$33,299	$42,162	$52,164	$26,061	$42,052
55	84475	Wausau city, Wisconsin	28,099	11.1	28.8	32.6	27.5	$30,872	$33,835	$42,313	$27,706	$36,247
55	84675	Wauwatosa city, Wisconsin	33,305	3.0	15.5	24.2	57.4	$45,173	$51,715	$60,979	$40,642	$51,163
55	85300	West Allis city, Wisconsin	44,286	11.4	30.3	33.9	24.5	$35,500	$38,870	$44,218	$31,167	$39,886
55	85350	West Bend city, Wisconsin	21,953	7.9	33.8	31.4	26.9	$35,092	$46,117	$48,998	$23,438	$32,967
56	00000	**WYOMING**	388,747	7.8	28.8	37.2	26.2	$31,524	$42,376	$55,965	$22,526	$36,064
56	13150	Casper city, Wyoming	38,694	10.8	26.6	38.7	24.0	$31,289	$41,243	$51,553	$23,112	$33,444
56	13900	Cheyenne city, Wyoming	42,825	7.7	23.5	40.1	28.7	$35,369	$42,831	$51,597	$27,775	$36,836
56	31855	Gillette city, Wyoming	20,296	10.5	29.4	41.6	18.6	$36,582	$68,173	$76,786	$21,312	$31,724
56	45050	Laramie city, Wyoming	16,761	2.7	13.9	34.5	48.9	$17,353	$20,390	$43,997	$14,488	$31,292
56	67235	Rock Springs city, Wyoming	14,654	5.2	29.2	38.2	27.4	$33,892	$52,476	$66,647	$21,178	$38,891

PART F

CONGRESSIONAL DISTRICTS

PART F. CONGRESSIONAL DISTRICTS

- The average number of working age people in a congressional district (people age 16 years and older) in 2015 was 587,541. Oregon's third district was the largest apportioned congressional district with 670,728 people 16 years and older while the 2nd congressional district in Rhode Island was the smallest at 432,242.

- The congressional districts in the Midwest typically had the largest percentage of workers in manufacturing.

In the 2nd district in Indiana, 27.4 percent of workers were employed in manufacturing. Similarly, 26.6 percent of workers in the 4th district in Ohio were employed in manufacturing.

- In 2015, 192 congressional districts had a higher unemployment rate than the national average of 6.3 percent. District 13 in Michigan, which includes portions of Detroit, had the highest unemployment rate among all congressional districts at 14.6 percent.

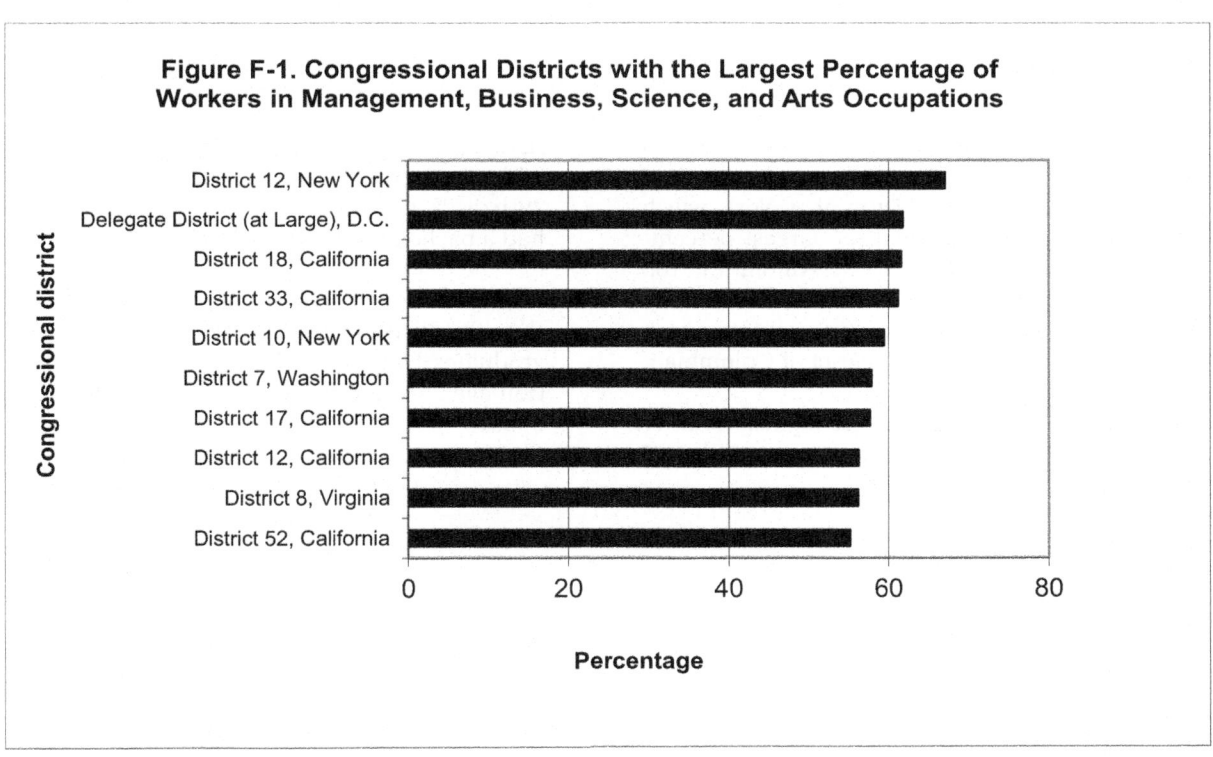

Figure F-1. Congressional Districts with the Largest Percentage of Workers in Management, Business, Science, and Arts Occupations

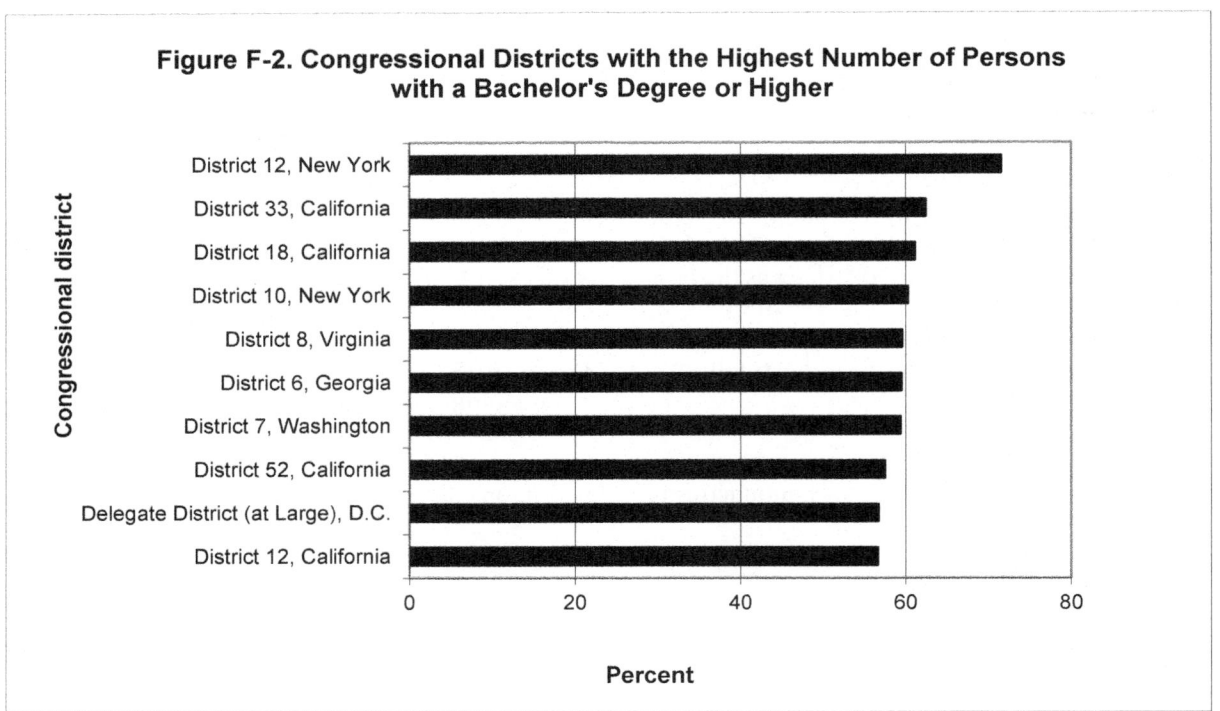

Figure F-2. Congressional Districts with the Highest Number of Persons with a Bachelor's Degree or Higher

- In the United States, 37.1 percent of the employed population worked in management, business, science, and arts occupations. The 12th district in New York, which includes parts of Manhattan, had the largest percentage of these workers at 67.0 percent. Among the top ten congressional districts for this occupation, five were located in California, two in New York, and one each in Washington, Virginia, and the District of Columbia.

- District 12 in New York also had the highest number of persons with a bachelor's degree or more with 71.5 percent followed by the 33rd district in California with 62.4 percent. Only 9.1 percent of people in the 29th district of Texas and the 21st district in California had a bachelor's degree or higher.

- Nearly half of the residents age 25 years and older in the 40th district in California were not high school graduates. Nationally, only 12.9 percent of the population age 25 and older were not high school graduates in 2015.

Table F. Congressional Districts—Labor Force, Employment, and Educational Data, 2015

State and District code	State/Congressional district (114th Congress)	Representative (115th Congress)	Total population age 16 and older	Percent in civilian labor force	Percent in armed forces	Civilian labor force participation by gender		Civilian labor force participation by age				Civilian unemployment rate
						Men	Women	Age 16 to 24	Age 25 to 54	Age 55 to 64	Age 65 and older	
0000	**UNITED STATES**		256,167,758	62.7	0.4	67.7	58.0	56.8	85.9	69.4	21.6	6.3
0100	**ALABAMA**		3,878,471	56.7	0.2	61.9	51.9	53.7	75.5	53.8	14.9	7.2
0101	District 1, Alabama	Bradley Byrne (R)	559,421	55.5	0.1	59.7	51.8	53.9	75.6	50.3	14.4	7.1
0102	District 2, Alabama	Martha Roby (R)	544,488	55.8	0.9	59.9	52.2	52.9	73.0	54.9	16.3	7.9
0103	District 3, Alabama	Mike Rogers (R)	565,432	56.2	0.4	61.6	51.2	53.9	75.3	52.4	14.4	7.1
0104	District 4, Alabama	Robert B. Aderholt (R)	545,336	52.8	0.0	60.4	45.7	53.8	72.0	50.9	11.7	6.0
0105	District 5, Alabama	Mo Brooks (R)	571,042	59.0	0.2	64.6	53.7	53.6	77.6	58.8	15.3	7.2
0106	District 6, Alabama	Gary J. Palmer (R)	554,231	62.8	0.1	70.1	56.2	59.5	80.7	61.2	18.5	5.1
0107	District 7, Alabama	Terri A. Sewell (D)	538,521	54.3	0.0	56.9	52.1	49.5	74.0	48.0	13.6	10.2
0200	**ALASKA**		571,393	67.4	3.1	70.3	64.2	61.1	79.2	69.4	23.5	7.9
0200	District (at Large), Alaska	Don Young (R)	571,393	67.4	3.1	70.3	64.2	61.1	79.2	69.4	23.5	7.9
0400	**ARIZONA**		5,393,214	58.5	0.3	63.2	53.9	57.7	77.7	59.2	14.0	6.9
0401	District 1, Arizona	Tom O'Halleran (D)	593,570	51.5	0.1	53.0	50.0	51.2	69.7	52.4	13.4	10.6
0402	District 2, Arizona	Martha McSally (R)	588,083	54.1	1.5	57.0	51.3	58.5	74.2	59.8	13.5	7.2
0403	District 3, Arizona	Raul M. Grijalva (D)	575,462	60.3	0.3	65.3	55.5	53.1	77.4	56.2	12.6	9.5
0404	District 4, Arizona	Paul A. Gosar (R)	613,778	45.7	0.5	48.4	42.9	58.0	70.5	48.4	9.6	7.9
0405	District 5, Arizona	Andy Biggs (R)	608,963	63.8	0.1	70.8	57.2	62.3	83.4	66.4	15.3	4.2
0406	District 6, Arizona	David Schweikert (R)	613,333	62.4	0.0	68.3	56.8	63.6	81.7	62.9	19.0	5.2
0407	District 7, Arizona	Ruben Gallego (D)	560,699	61.4	0.0	68.0	54.9	53.9	73.8	56.5	15.7	7.6
0408	District 8, Arizona	Trent Franks (R)	611,803	57.4	0.4	61.5	53.8	58.3	82.0	61.3	12.2	5.7
0409	District 9, Arizona	Kyrsten Sinema (D)	627,523	69.4	0.1	76.1	62.6	63.6	83.0	69.6	19.4	5.4
0500	**ARKANSAS**		2,352,507	57.4	0.2	62.4	52.7	56.3	75.8	55.9	15.7	5.8
0501	District 1, Arkansas	Eric A. "Rick" Crawford (R)	574,063	53.1	0.1	56.7	49.6	55.7	70.3	51.2	15.8	6.5
0502	District 2, Arkansas	J. French Hill (R)	600,965	60.5	0.7	66.3	55.1	56.9	78.9	58.0	16.2	5.4
0503	District 3, Arkansas	Steve Womack (R)	609,494	60.7	0.0	67.2	54.5	56.1	78.5	60.6	15.6	4.4
0504	District 4, Arkansas	Bruce Westerman (R)	567,985	54.8	0.0	58.8	51.1	56.4	74.6	54.1	15.3	7.4
0600	**CALIFORNIA**		31,068,647	62.6	0.4	68.7	56.8	52.2	79.9	63.8	17.5	7.3
0601	District 1, California	Doug LaMalfa (R)	582,891	52.4	0.1	54.6	50.2	54.6	72.2	56.1	14.0	7.9
0602	District 2, California	Jared Huffman (D)	593,887	60.6	0.2	64.2	57.0	57.8	77.2	67.3	23.7	6.0
0603	District 3, California	John Garamendi (D)	574,773	58.7	1.1	62.5	55.0	51.4	76.5	59.1	15.7	9.0
0604	District 4, California	Tom McClintock (R)	594,553	55.4	0.2	60.0	50.9	53.0	78.3	58.0	13.5	7.6
0605	District 5, California	Mike Thompson (D)	598,292	63.4	0.1	68.6	58.5	59.1	81.9	65.3	21.2	6.1
0606	District 6, California	Doris O. Matsui (D)	584,896	61.8	0.1	66.0	57.8	53.6	79.2	57.6	14.1	8.3
0607	District 7, California	Ami Bera (D)	586,885	62.7	0.0	66.9	58.9	54.6	81.6	62.1	15.2	8.3
0608	District 8, California	Paul Cook (R)	545,336	54.2	2.2	56.9	51.6	50.5	71.1	55.6	11.8	12.2
0609	District 9, California	Jerry McNerney (D)	565,706	59.6	0.1	66.1	53.4	52.2	76.8	58.2	15.4	10.0
0610	District 10, California	Jeff Denham (R)	563,852	60.6	0.1	67.7	53.7	54.8	76.5	61.8	12.7	10.9
0611	District 11, California	Mark Desaulnier (D)	602,294	64.2	0.0	71.2	57.7	57.0	81.2	69.2	20.1	6.8
0612	District 12, California	Nancy Pelosi (D)	661,618	70.9	0.0	75.1	66.5	59.6	87.4	67.1	18.7	4.8
0613	District 13, California	Barbara Lee (D)	627,623	67.0	0.2	71.2	63.1	54.8	83.6	66.1	21.4	6.3
0614	District 14, California	Jackie Speier (D)	623,193	68.0	0.0	73.7	62.5	58.1	86.0	71.5	19.2	5.6
0615	District 15, California	Eric Swalwell (D)	602,756	66.6	0.0	74.7	58.9	51.2	83.3	68.9	16.4	4.4
0616	District 16, California	Jim Costa (D)	536,942	57.2	0.0	64.9	49.6	50.3	70.9	53.1	16.6	11.6
0617	District 17, California	Ro Khanna (D)	614,866	66.4	0.0	75.1	57.4	52.6	82.4	67.1	14.6	5.1
0618	District 18, California	Anna G. Eshoo (D)	589,825	66.5	0.1	73.4	60.0	48.9	84.3	72.0	20.9	3.7
0619	District 19, California	Zoe Lofgren (D)	606,481	66.7	0.0	73.6	59.7	55.2	83.4	68.1	17.2	6.3
0620	District 20, California	Jimmy Panetta (D)	573,008	59.8	1.1	64.8	54.7	49.4	76.2	63.7	18.6	6.0
0621	District 21, California	David G. Valadao (R)	516,213	56.9	0.8	61.2	52.1	46.7	70.6	53.7	14.7	12.4
0622	District 22, California	Devin Nunes (R)	561,089	61.0	0.0	67.8	54.5	50.2	78.7	62.6	16.5	8.0
0623	District 23, California	Kevin McCarthy (R)	554,771	57.9	0.5	63.2	52.4	48.9	73.2	58.4	15.8	8.6
0624	District 24, California	Salud O. Carbajal (D)	601,537	61.4	0.7	65.9	56.9	53.0	81.8	66.5	21.3	5.7
0625	District 25, California	Stephen Knight (R)	556,597	61.9	0.1	69.7	54.1	48.5	77.5	64.8	17.9	7.4
0626	District 26, California	Julia Brownley (D)	570,675	64.1	0.6	70.4	58.2	56.5	81.5	69.7	18.7	7.1
0627	District 27, California	Judy Chu (D)	601,673	62.2	0.0	67.9	57.1	46.7	82.3	68.8	16.7	5.6
0628	District 28, California	Adam B. Schiff (D)	614,693	68.3	0.0	73.8	62.9	57.5	84.8	66.3	20.9	6.6
0629	District 29, California	Tony Cárdenas (D)	566,545	65.9	0.0	73.6	58.3	54.8	80.9	62.9	17.5	7.5
0630	District 30, California	Brad Sherman (D)	638,146	67.3	0.0	73.8	61.0	52.7	84.4	70.3	22.3	6.0
0631	District 31, California	Pete Aguilar (D)	563,594	61.4	0.1	67.6	55.5	51.6	76.9	59.9	15.3	8.2
0632	District 32, California	Grace F. Napolitano (D)	586,242	62.0	0.0	70.9	53.6	50.8	80.2	64.3	16.5	7.5
0633	District 33, California	Ted Lieu (D)	597,648	64.8	0.0	71.7	58.4	45.4	83.3	71.3	26.8	5.7
0634	District 34, California	Jimmy Gomez (D)	595,378	64.6	0.0	70.7	58.4	52.6	79.5	62.6	16.2	7.9
0635	District 35, California	Norma J. Torres (D)	563,108	63.1	0.0	69.1	57.1	54.7	76.3	56.4	15.5	9.0
0636	District 36, California	Raul Ruiz (D)	590,702	53.1	0.0	58.6	47.6	52.2	75.8	50.5	14.9	10.5
0637	District 37, California	Karen Bass (D)	598,895	65.6	0.0	71.7	59.8	50.8	82.1	66.8	19.8	7.8
0638	District 38, California	Linda T. Sánchez (D)	581,298	60.6	0.0	68.2	53.2	46.5	80.8	60.0	13.7	6.4
0639	District 39, California	Edward R. Royce (R)	591,301	63.3	0.0	70.3	56.8	49.7	82.1	67.9	17.4	6.6
0640	District 40, California	Lucille Roybal-Allard (D)	538,729	63.2	0.0	72.3	54.4	49.6	78.2	60.3	14.7	8.6
0641	District 41, California	Mark Takano (D)	571,729	63.0	0.1	71.6	54.6	54.3	78.1	62.8	14.1	9.7
0642	District 42, California	Ken Calvert (R)	590,959	61.9	0.3	70.2	54.1	50.7	78.0	63.6	14.4	9.1
0643	District 43, California	Maxine Waters (D)	580,207	63.9	0.0	70.5	57.9	51.2	80.4	64.9	15.9	7.7
0644	District 44, California	Nanette Diaz Barragan (D)	540,049	62.9	0.1	69.7	56.7	56.0	78.6	60.0	12.4	9.7
0645	District 45, California	Mimi Walters (R)	628,615	64.5	0.0	74.5	55.2	49.0	82.2	70.1	22.1	5.2
0646	District 46, California	J. Luis Correa (D)	562,872	67.1	0.0	75.1	58.9	56.0	81.9	64.5	14.1	5.9
0647	District 47, California	Alan S. Lowenthal (D)	578,854	63.0	0.1	68.4	57.8	47.1	80.8	64.0	17.4	5.6

Table F. Congressional Districts—Labor Force, Employment, and Educational Data, 2015—*Continued*

State and District code	State/Congressional district (114th Congress)	Representative (115th Congress)	Total population age 16 and older	Percent in civilian labor force	Percent in armed forces	Civilian labor force participation by gender		Civilian labor force participation by age				Civilian unemployment rate
						Men	Women	Age 16 to 24	Age 25 to 54	Age 55 to 64	Age 65 and older	
0648	District 48, California	Dana Rohrabacher (R)	600,834	64.7	0.1	71.4	58.3	54.6	83.6	67.9	20.3	5.0
0649	District 49, California	Darrell E. Issa (R)	589,241	62.1	4.4	66.6	57.6	46.9	81.3	69.7	19.8	5.4
0650	District 50, California	Duncan Hunter (R)	591,409	62.7	0.8	70.6	54.9	58.6	79.8	61.7	17.9	6.8
0651	District 51, California	Juan Vargas (D)	557,054	56.9	2.3	60.1	53.6	49.6	72.9	54.0	13.4	11.5
0652	District 52, California	Scott H. Peters (D)	625,396	64.5	2.7	68.1	61.0	48.8	81.6	67.4	21.1	5.1
0653	District 53, California	Susan A. Davis (D)	632,917	66.1	1.5	70.5	61.6	54.8	81.9	65.1	18.7	7.5
0800	**COLORADO**		4,333,738	67.3	0.7	72.4	62.2	62.1	83.6	67.6	19.6	5.2
0801	District 1, Colorado	Diana DeGette (D)	652,440	70.8	0.1	77.7	63.8	61.2	86.1	65.6	18.8	4.9
0802	District 2, Colorado	Jared Polis (D)	646,810	69.3	0.0	73.4	65.2	63.4	86.6	70.5	22.9	4.5
0803	District 3, Colorado	Scott R. Tipton (R)	591,307	62.3	0.1	67.0	57.5	61.8	82.1	61.3	19.2	7.1
0804	District 4, Colorado	Ken Buck (R)	605,023	67.4	0.1	73.6	61.2	62.7	82.7	70.1	20.4	4.7
0805	District 5, Colorado	Doug Lamborn (R)	609,507	60.4	4.4	62.5	58.2	56.9	74.6	64.8	16.6	6.4
0806	District 6, Colorado	Mike Coffman (R)	613,856	70.7	0.4	76.9	64.9	62.6	85.9	72.1	21.4	4.5
0807	District 7, Colorado	Ed Perlmutter (D)	614,795	69.6	0.0	75.2	64.1	66.3	86.2	69.6	17.9	4.7
0900	**CONNECTICUT**		2,922,877	66.4	0.3	70.7	62.5	59.4	84.1	73.9	21.1	6.9
0901	District 1, Connecticut	John B. Larson (D)	581,994	66.9	0.0	70.7	63.4	61.6	86.0	72.8	19.4	7.0
0902	District 2, Connecticut	Joe Courtney (D)	588,145	65.7	1.2	67.6	63.8	64.0	83.1	71.8	20.6	6.2
0903	District 3, Connecticut	Rosa L. DeLauro (D)	592,434	66.2	0.1	70.6	62.2	54.3	85.0	75.4	21.4	6.8
0904	District 4, Connecticut	James A. Himes (D)	583,906	67.5	0.0	74.6	61.1	57.8	83.6	76.1	23.6	7.7
0905	District 5, Connecticut	Elizabeth H. Esty (D)	576,398	65.9	0.0	70.1	61.9	59.5	83.0	73.8	21.0	7.0
1000	**DELAWARE**		765,250	62.1	0.4	65.9	58.7	57.9	82.1	65.4	17.0	5.8
1000	District (at Large), Delaware	Lisa Blunt Rochester (D)	765,250	62.1	0.4	65.9	58.7	57.9	82.1	65.4	17.0	5.8
1100	**DISTRICT OF COLUMBIA**		564,206	69.0	0.7	71.5	66.8	52.7	86.1	60.8	23.2	7.3
1198	Delegate District (at Large), District of Columbia	Eleanor Holmes Norton (D)	564,206	69.0	0.7	71.5	66.8	52.7	86.1	60.8	23.2	7.3
1200	**FLORIDA**		16,640,196	58.1	0.3	62.5	54.0	54.5	80.1	61.1	14.6	7.0
1201	District 1, Florida	Matt Gaetz (R)	609,465	57.6	3.5	60.2	55.0	57.1	75.9	58.9	13.1	7.3
1202	District 2, Florida	Neal P. Dunn (R)	592,675	56.9	0.6	57.2	56.7	60.8	71.7	53.6	16.8	8.3
1203	District 3, Florida	Ted S. Yoho (R)	588,928	53.4	0.3	54.5	52.4	47.5	74.1	56.1	12.5	8.2
1204	District 4, Florida	John H. Rutherford (R)	602,340	63.6	1.8	68.9	58.6	60.9	80.2	63.3	18.4	5.2
1205	District 5, Florida	Al Lawson (D)	576,815	64.0	0.3	66.4	62.0	60.5	79.9	59.7	17.3	10.4
1206	District 6, Florida	Ron DeSantis (R)	631,533	51.8	0.0	56.1	47.8	49.3	79.1	53.3	12.1	6.7
1207	District 7, Florida	Stephanie N. Murphy (D)	609,357	61.9	0.2	66.4	57.7	44.6	83.1	57.7	17.7	6.5
1208	District 8, Florida	Bill Posey (R)	613,472	52.8	0.3	57.1	48.8	52.8	78.8	59.0	12.5	6.8
1209	District 9, Florida	Darren Soto (D)	643,258	63.3	0.0	69.4	57.5	53.5	79.2	62.2	16.7	6.1
1210	District 10, Florida	Val Butler Demings (D)	635,271	60.6	0.0	64.7	56.8	61.0	81.7	60.3	13.5	5.7
1211	District 11, Florida	Daniel Webster (R)	636,324	40.4	0.0	42.3	38.6	48.1	70.3	49.8	8.4	9.3
1212	District 12, Florida	Gus M. Bilirakis (R)	612,924	56.3	0.2	60.8	52.4	58.0	79.5	61.3	13.3	6.3
1213	District 13, Florida	Charlie Crist (D)	612,954	58.5	0.1	62.3	55.1	61.8	83.0	64.5	15.5	5.3
1214	District 14, Florida	Kathy Castor (D)	614,190	64.2	0.5	67.9	60.7	54.0	81.9	59.2	16.2	8.3
1215	District 15, Florida	Dennis A. Ross (R)	583,296	60.8	0.2	66.7	55.1	52.5	80.7	62.7	15.1	6.6
1216	District 16, Florida	Vern Buchanan (R)	650,911	50.1	0.0	54.5	46.1	55.7	81.0	58.5	13.1	6.5
1217	District 17, Florida	Thomas J. Rooney (R)	620,408	48.2	0.3	52.4	44.2	52.7	75.6	54.6	10.9	7.4
1218	District 18, Florida	Brian J. Mast (R)	623,198	56.1	0.0	59.9	52.6	61.3	80.5	65.4	13.8	5.7
1219	District 19, Florida	Francis Rooney (R)	658,541	50.2	0.1	54.2	46.5	59.8	78.4	55.1	14.0	6.4
1220	District 20, Florida	Alcee L. Hastings (D)	612,520	64.4	0.0	67.9	61.2	60.6	82.8	62.2	17.2	11.7
1221	District 21, Florida	Lois Frankel (D)	617,860	60.6	0.0	67.0	55.1	54.7	85.7	70.5	16.9	6.6
1222	District 22, Florida	Theodore E. Deutch (D)	622,200	62.0	0.1	68.6	55.7	62.4	84.4	68.1	19.7	6.5
1223	District 23, Florida	Debbie Wasserman Schultz (D)	602,147	67.2	0.1	73.9	61.0	54.7	86.1	72.7	21.5	5.8
1224	District 24, Florida	Frederica S. Wilson (D)	597,323	61.9	0.0	66.6	57.7	50.2	78.9	63.5	15.8	9.4
1225	District 25, Florida	Mario Diaz-Balart (R)	618,351	60.3	0.0	65.3	55.7	50.5	81.7	63.2	14.2	5.6
1226	District 26, Florida	Carlos Curbelo (R)	635,956	61.9	0.2	68.5	55.6	45.1	80.9	64.3	16.9	5.4
1227	District 27, Florida	Ileana Ros-Lehtinen (R)	617,973	61.4	0.0	69.4	54.1	47.0	82.9	63.2	15.7	6.2
1300	**GEORGIA**		7,998,548	62.0	0.6	66.5	57.8	52.7	79.5	60.2	16.9	7.1
1301	District 1, Georgia	Earl L. "Buddy" Carter (R)	570,827	58.2	2.7	60.3	56.2	51.1	75.3	57.2	17.1	8.0
1302	District 2, Georgia	Sanford D. Bishop Jr. (D)	536,797	53.5	2.1	55.1	52.0	46.2	71.6	49.7	15.3	11.3
1303	District 3, Georgia	A. Drew Ferguson IV (R)	572,633	59.5	0.4	65.2	54.3	54.7	78.5	57.9	14.9	8.0
1304	District 4, Georgia	Henry C. "Hank" Johnson Jr. (D)	574,662	67.4	0.1	69.7	65.4	54.7	83.1	66.7	18.3	8.9
1305	District 5, Georgia	John Lewis (D)	605,539	66.5	0.1	68.5	64.6	56.0	83.9	57.2	15.3	8.2
1306	District 6, Georgia	Karen C. Handel (R)	559,887	71.6	0.1	79.2	64.2	56.9	86.2	72.6	26.1	5.2
1307	District 7, Georgia	Robert Woodall (R)	606,680	68.7	0.1	76.8	61.1	51.7	83.0	71.0	21.5	5.8
1308	District 8, Georgia	Austin Scott (R)	550,389	56.3	0.7	60.2	52.8	49.9	74.9	53.1	15.8	7.9
1309	District 9, Georgia	Doug Collins (R)	572,553	56.3	0.1	62.0	51.0	53.3	76.6	57.1	14.3	5.1
1310	District 10, Georgia	Jody B. Hice (R)	575,218	57.8	0.2	62.8	53.1	48.7	76.4	58.7	15.6	6.3
1311	District 11, Georgia	Barry Loudermilk (R)	588,335	68.2	0.0	75.1	61.9	58.7	84.0	70.3	18.7	4.9
1312	District 12, Georgia	Rick W. Allen (R)	560,517	54.1	1.9	55.8	52.5	44.9	70.6	54.3	14.9	7.4
1313	District 13, Georgia	David Scott (D)	573,693	67.0	0.0	72.0	62.8	54.9	83.9	60.5	17.8	8.2
1314	District 14, Georgia	Tom Graves (R)	550,818	61.0	0.0	66.5	55.9	59.0	79.5	55.4	15.3	5.4
1500	**HAWAII**		1,152,884	61.6	3.9	63.9	59.2	52.7	79.2	68.6	20.4	4.9
1501	District 1, Hawaii	Colleen Hanbusa (D)	581,946	62.8	4.0	65.8	59.8	53.2	79.9	72.1	21.4	4.0
1502	District 2, Hawaii	Tulsi Gabbard (D)	570,938	60.4	3.7	62.1	58.6	52.1	78.5	65.5	19.4	5.9

Table F. Congressional Districts—Labor Force, Employment, and Educational Data, 2015—*Continued*

State and District code	State/Congressional district (114th Congress)	Representative (115th Congress)	Total population age 16 and older	Percent in civilian labor force	Percent in armed forces	Civilian labor force participation by gender		Civilian labor force participation by age				Civilian unemployment rate
						Men	Women	Age 16 to 24	Age 25 to 54	Age 55 to 64	Age 65 and older	
1600	**IDAHO**		1,270,851	61.9	0.4	67.0	56.9	61.6	79.7	61.9	16.7	5.4
1601	District 1, Idaho	Raul Labrador (R)	660,483	59.7	0.3	63.9	55.5	59.9	79.1	58.1	15.8	5.9
1602	District 2, Idaho	Michael K. Simpson (R)	610,368	64.3	0.5	70.3	58.3	63.1	80.3	66.5	17.9	4.8
1700	**ILLINOIS**		10,240,058	65.0	0.2	70.3	60.1	59.3	83.0	66.4	17.4	6.9
1701	District 1, Illinois	Bobby L. Rush (D)	569,754	60.4	0.0	64.3	57.2	53.2	81.0	59.9	15.3	13.0
1702	District 2, Illinois	Robin L. Kelly (D)	558,222	60.8	0.0	64.6	57.5	56.9	80.5	58.1	14.4	14.5
1703	District 3, Illinois	Daniel Lipinski (D)	568,345	64.4	0.0	71.8	57.4	56.0	82.6	67.4	15.2	6.7
1704	District 4, Illinois	Luis V. Gutierrez (D)	543,741	68.1	0.1	76.8	59.4	58.0	82.6	60.3	16.4	7.1
1705	District 5, Illinois	Michael Quigley (D)	606,756	73.1	0.0	79.2	67.4	64.7	89.3	69.2	19.5	4.6
1706	District 6, Illinois	Peter J. Roskam (R)	577,451	68.7	0.0	76.7	61.2	59.1	85.9	74.2	23.4	4.4
1707	District 7, Illinois	Danny K. Davis (D)	591,766	63.3	0.1	64.7	62.0	50.6	80.2	59.7	17.7	10.4
1708	District 8, Illinois	Raja Krishnamoorthi (D)	561,502	71.7	0.1	78.4	65.0	67.5	86.1	74.2	22.4	5.4
1709	District 9, Illinois	Janice D. Schakowsky (D)	591,952	64.5	0.0	72.1	57.3	50.8	82.7	71.5	19.7	5.5
1710	District 10, Illinois	Bradley Scott Schneider (D)	555,990	66.5	1.8	72.5	60.7	56.5	83.0	74.0	22.2	5.6
1711	District 11, Illinois	Bill Foster (D)	557,091	70.1	0.1	76.5	64.1	65.3	84.7	71.9	19.0	5.3
1712	District 12, Illinois	Mike Bost (R)	562,340	59.2	0.6	61.9	56.7	58.5	78.7	58.3	12.3	8.1
1713	District 13, Illinois	Rodney Davis (R)	580,422	60.2	0.1	62.8	57.7	53.8	81.1	63.0	16.0	6.2
1714	District 14, Illinois	Randy Hultgren (R)	565,700	70.2	0.0	77.3	63.5	64.2	85.9	74.3	20.0	4.2
1715	District 15, Illinois	John Shimkus (R)	563,313	59.8	0.1	63.0	56.7	63.6	79.8	61.0	14.7	5.8
1716	District 16, Illinois	Adam Kinzinger (R)	561,395	63.6	0.0	68.1	59.3	66.2	82.5	67.0	16.6	7.1
1717	District 17, Illinois	Cheri Bustos (D)	553,486	61.5	0.1	64.4	58.7	66.8	81.7	62.5	14.9	7.9
1718	District 18, Illinois	Darin LaHood (R)	570,832	63.6	0.1	68.2	59.3	61.9	83.9	68.0	16.9	4.8
1800	**INDIANA**		5,215,392	63.5	0.1	68.7	58.6	61.7	81.7	64.7	16.1	5.8
1801	District 1, Indiana	Peter J. Visclosky (D)	568,766	60.5	0.0	65.9	55.5	56.8	78.8	62.5	14.7	8.1
1802	District 2, Indiana	Jackie Walorski (R)	564,541	61.5	0.0	67.5	55.7	59.4	78.7	65.9	17.2	5.3
1803	District 3, Indiana	Jim Banks (R)	565,685	65.2	0.1	72.1	58.8	66.7	83.1	68.1	15.3	4.7
1804	District 4, Indiana	Todd Rokita (R)	595,123	64.5	0.0	69.4	59.8	60.0	84.0	67.5	16.0	4.9
1805	District 5, Indiana	Susan W. Brooks (R)	593,657	68.9	0.1	74.5	63.8	66.0	86.2	68.9	19.8	4.3
1806	District 6, Indiana	Luke Messer (R)	580,063	61.3	0.0	66.7	56.1	63.2	81.2	63.0	13.8	5.4
1807	District 7, Indiana	André Carson (D)	573,398	66.0	0.0	68.8	63.5	66.5	80.3	60.7	15.7	9.1
1808	District 8, Indiana	Larry Bucshon (R)	579,256	60.8	0.0	66.0	55.7	60.2	80.2	61.8	16.3	5.1
1809	District 9, Indiana	Trey Hollingsworth (R)	594,903	62.7	0.2	67.5	58.2	57.9	82.6	63.1	16.3	5.4
1900	**IOWA**		2,475,140	67.4	0.1	71.9	63.1	68.3	87.0	70.9	18.6	4.2
1901	District 1, Iowa	Rod Blum (R)	614,592	67.5	0.0	72.0	63.1	69.9	87.8	70.8	18.3	3.5
1902	District 2, Iowa	David Loebsack (D)	620,046	66.1	0.0	70.3	61.9	66.8	85.1	68.5	19.4	4.7
1903	District 3, Iowa	David Young (R)	629,750	70.4	0.1	75.2	65.8	70.6	87.9	70.1	19.0	4.7
1904	District 4, Iowa	Steve King (R)	610,752	65.8	0.1	70.0	61.6	66.2	87.3	74.0	17.8	3.7
2000	**KANSAS**		2,270,108	65.5	0.9	70.1	61.0	62.9	82.5	70.0	20.2	4.7
2001	District 1, Kansas	Roger W. Marshall (R)	561,878	64.0	2.6	68.5	59.3	63.0	79.6	70.9	23.0	4.8
2002	District 2, Kansas	Lynn Jenkins (R)	568,514	62.6	0.4	66.1	59.2	62.5	81.2	66.7	17.5	5.1
2003	District 3, Kansas	Kevin Yoder (R)	581,808	70.7	0.1	76.6	65.1	65.5	86.2	73.8	22.4	4.2
2004	District 4, Kansas	Ron Estes (R)	557,908	64.5	0.5	69.0	60.1	60.7	82.1	68.8	18.1	4.5
2100	**KENTUCKY**		3,531,385	58.4	0.4	62.9	54.2	60.9	75.7	55.4	14.8	6.5
2101	District 1, Kentucky	James Comer (R)	577,699	53.8	1.4	57.8	50.1	56.4	72.5	53.2	13.7	6.3
2102	District 2, Kentucky	Brett Guthrie (R)	594,938	59.4	0.6	64.6	54.5	63.7	76.7	56.7	13.7	6.6
2103	District 3, Kentucky	John A. Yarmuth (D)	594,691	65.4	0.1	69.8	61.3	66.1	83.3	64.0	16.8	6.1
2104	District 4, Kentucky	Thomas Massie (R)	589,697	63.0	0.1	67.7	58.3	64.5	79.3	62.5	16.5	5.2
2105	District 5, Kentucky	Harold Rogers (R)	569,071	44.7	0.0	47.5	42.0	51.4	60.0	38.1	10.1	10.0
2106	District 6, Kentucky	Garland "Andy" Barr (R)	605,289	63.4	0.1	69.4	57.9	62.1	80.6	58.3	18.5	5.9
2200	**LOUISIANA**		3,676,681	59.7	0.4	64.0	55.6	54.3	76.8	58.3	17.4	7.1
2201	District 1, Louisiana	Steve Scalise (R)	641,278	63.0	0.2	69.7	56.9	54.7	81.1	63.3	20.9	5.8
2202	District 2, Louisiana	Cedric Richmond (D)	629,129	61.5	0.2	65.1	58.3	53.4	78.5	57.5	17.1	9.3
2203	District 3, Louisiana	Clay Higgins (R)	609,403	62.2	0.1	67.1	57.6	61.3	79.0	59.7	15.5	7.2
2204	District 4, Louisiana	Mike Johnson (R)	591,568	53.5	1.7	57.1	50.1	45.9	70.6	54.1	15.7	7.4
2205	District 5, Louisiana	Ralph Lee Abraham (R)	588,234	52.1	0.1	52.8	51.3	47.5	68.7	50.1	15.2	8.2
2206	District 6, Louisiana	Garret Graves (R)	617,069	65.0	0.1	71.7	58.8	61.4	81.4	64.2	19.9	5.0
2300	**MAINE**		1,103,834	62.1	0.2	65.6	58.8	66.6	80.9	65.3	19.3	5.4
2301	District 1, Maine	Chellie Pingree (D)	559,256	65.0	0.2	68.3	62.0	69.5	83.6	68.9	21.5	4.4
2302	District 2, Maine	Bruce Poliquin (R)	544,578	59.0	0.1	62.8	55.5	63.6	78.1	61.6	17.0	6.4
2400	**MARYLAND**		4,814,546	66.6	0.6	71.0	62.6	56.6	84.3	69.4	20.8	5.5
2401	District 1, Maryland	Andrew Harris (R)	590,605	63.7	0.1	68.4	59.2	59.3	83.5	68.8	21.1	5.2
2402	District 2, Maryland	C. A. Dutch Ruppersberger (D)	605,603	65.5	1.2	68.4	62.8	58.3	81.1	67.0	17.5	5.7
2403	District 3, Maryland	John P. Sarbanes (D)	612,625	68.2	1.5	73.4	63.4	55.0	86.9	70.1	21.6	5.4
2404	District 4, Maryland	Anthony G. Brown (D)	590,577	70.9	0.5	75.2	67.0	60.5	87.5	71.2	22.9	5.6
2405	District 5, Maryland	Steny H. Hoyer (D)	610,927	67.6	0.9	71.9	63.6	53.8	85.3	70.4	19.7	4.7
2406	District 6, Maryland	John K. Delaney (D)	601,131	65.9	0.4	70.4	61.6	56.1	83.1	70.0	19.5	4.5
2407	District 7, Maryland	Elijah E. Cummings (D)	591,071	61.0	0.1	64.2	58.1	52.0	79.0	61.3	17.9	8.4
2408	District 8, Maryland	Jamie Raskin (D)	612,001	70.1	0.4	76.0	64.7	58.7	87.5	76.1	25.5	4.6
2500	**MASSACHUSETTS**		5,578,648	67.0	0.1	71.2	63.2	61.8	84.6	71.6	21.1	5.8
2501	District 1, Massachusetts	Richard E. Neal (D)	601,971	63.2	0.0	66.8	60.0	64.5	81.3	68.8	16.7	6.9
2502	District 2, Massachusetts	James P. McGovern (D)	614,814	65.5	0.0	68.2	62.9	58.3	83.6	70.5	19.5	6.5
2503	District 3, Massachusetts	Niki Tsongas (D)	601,386	67.2	0.1	71.3	63.2	59.8	82.7	70.4	22.2	5.9
2504	District 4, Massachusetts	Joseph P. Kennedy III (D)	600,293	67.7	0.0	72.1	63.7	58.0	85.8	74.0	24.2	5.3

Table F. Congressional Districts—Labor Force, Employment, and Educational Data, 2015—*Continued*

State and District code	State/Congressional district (114th Congress)	Representative (115th Congress)	Total population age 16 and older	Percent in civilian labor force	Percent in armed forces	Civilian labor force participation by gender		Civilian labor force participation by age				Civilian unemployment rate
						Men	Women	Age 16 to 24	Age 25 to 54	Age 55 to 64	Age 65 and older	
2505	District 5, Massachusetts	Katherine Clark (D)	631,614	69.3	0.2	74.9	64.2	58.4	86.7	74.8	24.6	3.9
2506	District 6, Massachusetts	Seth Moulton (D)	621,191	67.3	0.1	72.2	62.9	64.1	85.4	74.5	22.2	5.1
2507	District 7, Massachusetts	Michael E. Capuano (D)	661,302	69.9	0.1	72.7	67.4	62.8	84.6	67.3	18.9	6.7
2508	District 8, Massachusetts	Stephen F. Lynch (D)	628,496	69.9	0.1	75.2	65.2	66.4	87.2	72.4	20.4	5.7
2509	District 9, Massachusetts	William R. Keating (D)	617,581	62.8	0.1	67.1	59.0	65.0	83.0	71.0	20.9	6.5
2600	**MICHIGAN**		7,982,332	60.9	0.1	65.5	56.5	62.6	80.7	58.8	14.0	7.2
2601	District 1, Michigan	Jack Bergman (R)	585,953	54.5	0.2	56.5	52.5	61.3	78.5	55.9	12.1	6.7
2602	District 2, Michigan	Bill Huizenga (R)	574,195	63.5	0.0	68.2	59.0	66.8	82.6	59.5	15.7	5.4
2603	District 3, Michigan	Justin Amash (R)	572,371	65.4	0.1	70.0	60.9	68.7	83.1	62.8	14.3	6.2
2604	District 4, Michigan	John L. Moolenar (R)	574,748	56.9	0.0	60.2	53.7	59.7	78.6	55.8	12.1	6.6
2605	District 5, Michigan	Daniel T. Kildee (D)	549,687	56.8	0.0	59.8	54.0	63.0	78.4	50.3	11.8	9.5
2606	District 6, Michigan	Fred Upton (R)	568,996	63.7	0.1	68.6	58.9	68.1	82.9	62.8	16.4	6.6
2607	District 7, Michigan	Tim Walberg (R)	564,545	59.0	0.1	62.9	55.1	60.9	78.5	59.2	13.2	5.4
2608	District 8, Michigan	Mike Bishop (R)	590,640	64.9	0.0	70.7	59.5	60.6	84.8	62.9	17.7	5.9
2609	District 9, Michigan	Sander M. Levin (D)	589,419	62.9	0.1	68.7	57.5	63.9	82.5	61.3	14.3	6.7
2610	District 10, Michigan	Paul Mitchell (R)	576,647	61.9	0.1	67.4	56.6	66.3	82.1	61.8	12.4	6.0
2611	District 11, Michigan	David A.Trott (R)	579,755	66.8	0.0	73.3	60.6	61.6	85.8	68.5	15.8	4.2
2612	District 12, Michigan	Debbie Dingell (D)	573,935	62.1	0.0	68.3	56.2	58.5	80.9	59.7	15.6	6.5
2613	District 13, Michigan	John Conyers Jr. (D)	532,565	55.1	0.0	58.7	52.1	58.0	72.3	47.4	10.2	14.6
2614	District 14, Michigan	Brenda L. Lawrence (D)	548,876	58.6	0.0	63.3	54.5	60.6	76.5	53.8	15.7	12.8
2700	**MINNESOTA**		4,349,038	69.9	0.0	73.8	66.1	71.1	87.8	72.7	18.1	4.2
2701	District 1, Minnesota	Timothy J. Walz (D)	533,183	69.3	0.0	72.9	65.7	74.1	88.1	75.7	18.6	3.9
2702	District 2, Minnesota	Jason Lewis (R)	539,488	73.6	0.1	78.1	69.3	73.9	90.2	74.5	18.5	3.7
2703	District 3, Minnesota	Erik Paulsen (R)	554,543	72.1	0.0	77.4	66.9	67.2	89.2	77.1	21.7	3.7
2704	District 4, Minnesota	Betty McCollum (D)	554,669	69.2	0.0	72.8	66.0	66.3	85.8	71.4	17.4	5.1
2705	District 5, Minnesota	Keith Ellison (D)	571,692	73.5	0.0	77.1	70.1	70.5	88.4	71.1	19.5	5.0
2706	District 6, Minnesota	Tom Emmer (R)	530,217	73.1	0.0	76.7	69.5	72.0	88.8	75.1	17.8	3.9
2707	District 7, Minnesota	Collin C. Peterson (D)	525,671	66.2	0.0	70.4	62.0	71.2	87.7	74.4	18.1	3.3
2708	District 8, Minnesota	Richard M. Nolan (D)	539,575	61.8	0.1	64.7	58.8	70.7	83.9	62.8	14.2	4.6
2800	**MISSISSIPPI**		2,345,713	56.5	0.5	60.4	52.8	49.8	75.7	54.0	15.0	8.9
2801	District 1, Mississippi	Trent Kelly (R)	597,597	58.4	0.2	63.7	53.6	52.5	78.4	55.3	15.9	7.7
2802	District 2, Mississippi	Bennie G. Thompson (D)	557,338	53.4	0.0	54.7	52.4	44.5	71.2	52.4	14.6	11.8
2803	District 3, Mississippi	Gregg Harper (R)	590,871	57.4	0.2	62.5	52.5	48.2	77.9	57.4	14.2	7.0
2804	District 4, Mississippi	Steven Palazzo (R)	599,907	56.5	1.4	60.5	52.7	53.6	75.1	50.8	15.2	9.4
2900	**MISSOURI**		4,851,761	62.7	0.4	66.8	58.8	61.9	81.7	63.0	16.4	5.3
2901	District 1, Missouri	William Lacy Clay (D)	591,475	66.3	0.1	69.8	63.3	62.6	84.0	62.9	16.0	8.7
2902	District 2, Missouri	Ann Wagner (R)	620,851	66.8	0.0	73.5	60.5	62.8	87.8	71.9	18.5	3.4
2903	District 3, Missouri	Blaine Luetkemeyer (R)	612,685	65.0	0.1	68.8	61.3	67.2	83.0	66.0	17.0	4.3
2904	District 4, Missouri	Vicky Hartzler (R)	611,401	57.9	2.9	61.1	54.8	52.3	77.6	59.5	15.2	5.7
2905	District 5, Missouri	Emanuel Cleaver (D)	601,724	64.8	0.1	69.1	60.9	65.2	82.8	62.1	16.7	5.0
2906	District 6, Missouri	Sam Graves (R)	602,537	64.1	0.1	68.3	60.0	63.8	82.6	64.5	17.9	4.7
2907	District 7, Missouri	Bill Long (R)	615,008	60.9	0.1	66.0	56.1	63.6	79.7	63.0	15.4	4.8
2908	District 8, Missouri	Jason T. Smith (R)	596,080	55.8	0.1	58.5	53.2	60.2	75.3	52.7	14.5	6.5
3000	**MONTANA**		829,911	61.8	0.4	65.5	58.1	59.2	81.9	64.8	18.8	4.5
3000	District (at Large), Montana	Greg Gianforte (R)	829,911	61.8	0.4	65.5	58.1	59.2	81.9	64.8	18.8	4.5
3100	**NEBRASKA**		1,476,487	69.1	0.4	73.8	64.4	68.1	85.7	74.6	22.3	3.2
3101	District 1, Nebraska	Jeff Fortenberry (R)	499,246	69.3	0.7	73.8	64.8	66.9	86.2	76.5	22.8	3.2
3102	District 2, Nebraska	Don Bacon (R)	498,985	70.9	0.4	75.1	66.9	69.3	84.7	71.8	20.7	3.5
3103	District 3, Nebraska	Adrian Smith (R)	478,256	66.9	0.0	72.5	61.4	68.4	86.6	75.5	22.9	2.9
3200	**NEVADA**		2,292,699	63.1	0.4	68.0	58.2	60.2	80.8	61.0	17.2	7.9
3201	District 1, Nevada	Dina Titus (D)	559,708	63.6	0.1	69.4	57.4	59.6	79.1	58.2	19.0	10.4
3202	District 2, Nevada	Mark E. Amodei (R)	565,290	63.2	0.3	67.8	58.6	65.4	81.4	62.5	18.5	6.5
3203	District 3, Nevada	Jacky Rosen (D)	610,807	65.8	0.1	70.9	60.9	59.8	84.4	63.6	18.6	6.4
3204	District 4, Nevada	Ruben J. Kihuen (D)	556,894	59.5	1.0	63.7	55.5	56.2	77.8	59.3	13.0	8.7
3300	**NEW HAMPSHIRE**		1,102,089	67.6	0.2	72.1	63.3	67.2	85.2	73.5	20.8	4.2
3301	District 1, New Hampshire	Carol Shea-Porter (D)	557,281	68.7	0.3	73.6	64.2	69.7	86.2	74.0	20.9	4.5
3302	District 2, New Hampshire	Ann M. Kuster (D)	544,808	66.4	0.1	70.5	62.4	64.3	84.2	73.1	20.7	3.9
3400	**NEW JERSEY**		7,193,921	65.1	0.1	70.8	59.8	52.4	83.4	70.8	20.3	6.6
3401	District 1, New Jersey	Donald Norcross (D)	591,094	66.2	0.1	71.0	61.9	58.1	84.7	67.8	19.0	7.8
3402	District 2, New Jersey	Frank A. LoBiondo (R)	585,342	61.3	0.3	65.2	57.6	59.3	79.7	67.8	18.2	8.2
3403	District 3, New Jersey	Thomas MacArthur (R)	603,223	62.8	0.9	67.0	59.0	60.9	82.0	71.6	18.8	7.3
3404	District 4, New Jersey	Christopher H. Smith (R)	580,530	62.6	0.1	69.2	56.5	54.4	84.1	69.2	19.2	5.0
3405	District 5, New Jersey	Josh Gottheimer (D)	599,299	67.1	0.0	73.7	60.9	53.0	85.4	76.3	25.3	4.7
3406	District 6, New Jersey	Frank Pallone Jr. (D)	606,212	63.9	0.0	70.2	57.8	40.2	82.7	68.9	20.4	5.9
3407	District 7, New Jersey	Leonard Lance (R)	595,866	68.2	0.0	75.0	61.8	54.8	85.8	76.4	22.5	5.1
3408	District 8, New Jersey	Albio Sires (D)	613,395	70.1	0.0	76.8	63.5	55.7	84.6	68.5	17.0	7.8
3409	District 9, New Jersey	Bill Pascrell, Jr. (D)	612,046	60.9	0.0	67.9	54.4	41.1	78.2	68.0	20.7	4.7
3410	District 10, New Jersey	Donald M. Payne, Jr. (D)	611,212	65.2	0.1	68.4	62.4	50.7	82.2	65.8	18.3	11.6
3411	District 11, New Jersey	Rodney P. Frelinghuysen (R)	593,542	67.7	0.0	73.5	62.4	53.9	87.1	76.3	24.1	4.4
3412	District 12, New Jersey	Bonnie Watson Coleman (D)	602,160	65.1	0.0	71.9	58.8	51.5	83.8	70.9	19.3	6.8

Table F. Congressional Districts—Labor Force, Employment, and Educational Data, 2015—Continued

State and District code	State/Congressional district (114th Congress)	Representative (115th Congress)	Total population age 16 and older	Percent in civilian labor force	Percent in armed forces	Civilian labor force participation by gender		Civilian labor force participation by age				Civilian unemployment rate
						Men	Women	Age 16 to 24	Age 25 to 54	Age 55 to 64	Age 65 and older	
3500	**NEW MEXICO**		1,642,487	57.9	0.6	62.4	53.5	56.2	75.1	60.7	16.5	7.4
3501	District 1, New Mexico	Michelle Lujan Grisham (D)	558,109	60.3	0.5	64.5	56.3	57.5	77.0	61.7	17.5	6.4
3502	District 2, New Mexico	Steve Pearce (R)	542,185	54.7	0.6	59.9	49.6	55.3	72.2	57.5	14.3	7.9
3503	District 3, New Mexico	Ben Ray Luján (D)	542,193	58.5	0.6	62.6	54.5	55.9	75.7	62.7	17.8	8.0
3600	**NEW YORK**		16,066,508	63.0	0.1	67.9	58.6	52.0	81.8	66.0	18.1	6.5
3601	District 1, New York	Lee M. Zeldin (R)	593,090	63.0	0.1	68.0	58.2	53.3	81.7	71.1	19.6	4.7
3602	District 2, New York	Peter T. King (R)	586,158	66.9	0.0	73.0	61.2	59.3	85.0	70.9	18.0	5.5
3603	District 3, New York	Thomas R. Souzzi (D)	587,027	61.8	0.1	69.7	54.6	46.1	83.1	72.4	21.1	4.4
3604	District 4, New York	Kathleen M. Rice (D)	579,368	66.3	0.1	72.3	60.8	49.4	85.8	73.4	24.9	4.8
3605	District 5, New York	Gregory W. Meeks (D)	625,786	65.4	0.0	69.7	61.5	52.3	82.7	68.6	17.5	9.2
3606	District 6, New York	Grace Meng (D)	612,837	62.2	0.0	69.8	55.5	45.2	82.4	63.6	15.4	6.0
3607	District 7, New York	Nydia M. Velázquez (D)	590,218	64.0	0.0	70.5	57.6	49.6	81.2	55.4	12.8	6.5
3608	District 8, New York	Hakeem S. Jeffries (D)	621,263	61.9	0.1	65.5	59.0	44.4	81.3	62.3	14.0	9.2
3609	District 9, New York	Yvette D. Clarke (D)	608,459	64.5	0.0	67.7	61.9	45.0	81.6	70.7	19.3	7.3
3610	District 10, New York	Jerrold Nadler (D)	601,127	67.5	0.0	74.0	61.6	40.8	85.1	71.2	26.1	5.3
3611	District 11, New York	Daniel M. Donovan Jr. (R)	583,528	58.9	0.1	65.4	53.0	41.4	78.2	63.4	15.1	6.0
3612	District 12, New York	Carolyn B. Maloney (D)	653,961	71.8	0.0	77.1	66.9	48.9	88.0	70.6	27.7	4.2
3613	District 13, New York	Adriano Espaillat (D)	641,648	64.7	0.0	69.7	60.4	56.4	80.9	56.0	13.0	10.6
3614	District 14, New York	Joseph Crowley (D)	587,905	63.9	0.0	72.2	55.8	48.6	80.8	65.7	14.9	6.6
3615	District 15, New York	José E. Serrano (D)	572,738	56.9	0.0	61.4	53.1	44.8	73.8	48.6	10.6	11.3
3616	District 16, New York	Eliot L. Engel (D)	596,776	63.9	0.0	68.9	59.6	52.3	82.6	70.7	21.6	7.5
3617	District 17, New York	Nita M. Lowey (D)	581,668	66.1	0.0	72.2	60.4	54.7	85.6	72.6	20.9	6.1
3618	District 18, New York	Sean Patrick Maloney (D)	571,395	62.4	0.8	67.6	57.4	52.8	79.6	66.4	21.5	5.9
3619	District 19, New York	John J. Faso (R)	587,620	59.0	0.0	62.1	55.8	51.7	78.9	64.4	19.8	6.1
3620	District 20, New York	Paul Tonko (D)	599,543	64.4	0.3	68.8	60.3	59.8	84.5	66.1	17.7	5.5
3621	District 21, New York	Elise M. Stefanik (R)	579,498	57.5	1.9	58.1	56.9	54.9	75.3	60.1	15.4	6.2
3622	District 22, New York	Claudia Tenney (R)	582,802	58.6	0.0	61.5	55.9	55.4	79.3	63.4	15.0	6.5
3623	District 23, New York	Tom Reed (R)	583,154	58.1	0.1	61.6	54.8	51.2	79.3	63.8	15.6	6.1
3624	District 24, New York	John Katko (R)	575,874	62.4	0.1	66.1	59.0	53.8	82.7	67.3	16.4	6.6
3625	District 25, New York	Louise McIntosh Slaughter (D)	587,420	64.6	0.0	68.8	60.8	65.2	83.7	65.7	16.4	6.7
3626	District 26, New York	Brian Higgins (D)	580,180	61.1	0.1	64.8	57.8	59.5	80.0	63.4	15.8	5.6
3627	District 27, New York	Chris Collins (R)	595,465	62.5	0.0	65.6	59.3	59.8	82.5	67.1	16.6	4.4
3700	**NORTH CAROLINA**		8,011,388	61.0	0.9	65.7	56.6	56.4	79.5	61.4	15.8	6.9
3701	District 1, North Carolina	G. K. Butterfield (D)	580,363	58.0	0.4	60.8	55.6	56.9	76.9	55.2	15.8	9.1
3702	District 2, North Carolina	George Holding (R)	612,538	59.9	3.7	64.4	55.8	50.7	75.4	65.1	15.9	7.0
3703	District 3, North Carolina	Walter B. Jones (R)	614,338	56.7	5.9	57.3	56.1	53.3	73.5	61.5	17.1	9.2
3704	District 4, North Carolina	David E. Price (D)	651,524	65.9	1.3	70.0	62.1	56.5	81.7	64.7	18.4	6.0
3705	District 5, North Carolina	Virginia Foxx (R)	616,097	59.6	0.1	65.5	54.1	53.3	80.5	62.7	15.2	7.0
3706	District 6, North Carolina	Mark Walker (R)	616,000	60.8	0.0	65.1	56.8	54.5	80.7	65.6	16.3	5.7
3707	District 7, North Carolina	David Rouzer (R)	629,749	57.8	0.2	61.7	54.1	53.8	79.0	55.7	16.4	6.3
3708	District 8, North Carolina	Richard Hudson (R)	591,045	58.8	0.1	63.5	54.3	56.8	77.6	58.5	13.7	7.6
3709	District 9, North Carolina	Robert Pittenger (R)	638,425	69.9	0.0	77.3	63.2	61.3	86.3	69.0	19.5	5.0
3710	District 10, North Carolina	Patrick T. McHenry (R)	609,300	58.0	0.1	64.5	52.1	60.2	77.3	58.0	14.0	7.6
3711	District 11, North Carolina	Mark Meadows (R)	616,255	54.1	0.1	58.8	49.7	58.5	76.0	55.8	13.6	5.6
3712	District 12, North Carolina	Alma S. Adams (D)	617,442	66.6	0.1	72.2	61.5	58.5	82.5	62.0	13.7	9.1
3713	District 13, North Carolina	Ted Budd(R)	618,312	66.0	0.2	72.8	59.7	61.2	83.2	65.8	17.9	5.1
3800	**NORTH DAKOTA**		603,014	68.9	1.1	73.1	64.5	67.1	87.0	71.8	19.6	2.6
3800	District (at Large), North Dakota	Kevin Cramer (R)	603,014	68.9	1.1	73.1	64.5	67.1	87.0	71.8	19.6	2.6
3900	**OHIO**		9,295,255	63.1	0.1	67.6	58.9	63.3	81.8	63.9	16.7	6.4
3901	District 1, Ohio	Steve Chabot (R)	573,635	65.4	0.1	68.7	62.2	58.5	82.5	67.5	19.7	6.9
3902	District 2, Ohio	Brad R. Wenstrup (R)	581,705	62.2	0.0	68.5	56.3	62.5	80.5	63.1	16.1	5.3
3903	District 3, Ohio	Joyce Beatty (D)	599,532	68.2	0.0	71.5	65.2	64.3	82.5	62.9	17.4	7.7
3904	District 4, Ohio	Jim Jordan (R)	570,627	61.8	0.0	66.3	57.6	64.5	79.8	65.8	15.1	6.0
3905	District 5, Ohio	Robert E. Latta (R)	576,356	65.3	0.1	70.9	60.0	66.1	85.2	69.3	17.7	4.7
3906	District 6, Ohio	Bill Johnson (R)	571,865	55.5	0.0	59.9	51.3	59.6	75.6	54.8	14.5	6.7
3907	District 7, Ohio	Bob Gibbs (R)	590,431	63.7	0.0	69.3	58.3	67.9	84.2	65.5	17.0	5.4
3908	District 8, Ohio	Warren Davidson (R)	575,201	63.2	0.0	68.1	58.7	63.1	82.0	64.5	17.0	5.7
3909	District 9, Ohio	Marcy Kaptur (D)	570,163	63.3	0.0	66.5	60.3	68.2	80.2	59.4	15.8	8.9
3910	District 10, Ohio	Michael R. Turner (R)	579,855	61.5	0.6	66.7	56.7	62.0	80.8	63.4	16.6	7.3
3911	District 11, Ohio	Marcia L. Fudge (D)	564,279	60.1	0.0	62.1	58.4	62.2	78.1	59.3	15.6	12.4
3912	District 12, Ohio	Patrick J. Tiberi (R)	604,116	66.9	0.1	71.5	62.4	61.0	85.0	65.3	19.7	4.8
3913	District 13, Ohio	Tim Ryan (D)	583,430	60.6	0.0	65.5	56.1	62.6	81.4	60.4	15.1	7.3
3914	District 14, Ohio	David P. Joyce (R)	580,736	64.3	0.0	69.7	59.2	63.3	84.8	70.0	19.3	4.5
3915	District 15, Ohio	Steve Stivers (R)	598,791	61.9	0.1	64.9	58.8	57.4	79.5	62.4	14.4	5.2
3916	District 16, Ohio	James B. Renacci (R)	574,533	65.1	0.0	70.4	60.2	70.3	86.7	69.3	17.1	4.2
4000	**OKLAHOMA**		3,053,371	60.7	0.6	66.2	55.5	58.7	78.0	59.9	18.3	5.5
4001	District 1, Oklahoma	Jim Bridenstine (R)	614,050	66.7	0.0	73.5	60.6	65.9	83.0	65.8	21.7	5.6
4002	District 2, Oklahoma	Markwayne Mullin (R)	593,012	52.9	0.0	56.5	49.4	55.4	72.0	51.6	13.7	6.6
4003	District 3, Oklahoma	Frank D. Lucas (R)	609,273	58.5	0.4	64.2	52.7	54.1	75.6	60.1	19.5	5.2
4004	District 4, Oklahoma	Tom Cole (R)	616,159	61.3	2.2	65.4	57.3	56.6	78.6	61.7	18.1	5.3
4005	District 5, Oklahoma	Steve Russell (R)	620,877	63.9	0.3	71.3	57.1	62.4	79.7	60.6	19.7	4.8

Table F. Congressional Districts—Labor Force, Employment, and Educational Data, 2015—*Continued*

State and District code	State/Congressional district (114th Congress)	Representative (115th Congress)	Total population age 16 and older	Percent in civilian labor force	Percent in armed forces	Civilian labor force participation by gender		Civilian labor force participation by age				Civilian unemployment rate
						Men	Women	Age 16 to 24	Age 25 to 54	Age 55 to 64	Age 65 and older	
4100	**OREGON**		3,268,296	61.8	0.1	66.2	57.5	60.6	81.7	60.9	15.1	6.8
4101	District 1, Oregon	Suzanne Bonamici (D)	655,053	65.7	0.1	72.8	58.9	62.0	82.7	63.7	16.5	5.8
4102	District 2, Oregon	Greg Walden (R)	642,611	57.3	0.0	60.4	54.2	62.6	78.5	57.5	15.4	7.6
4103	District 3, Oregon	Earl Blumenauer (D)	670,728	68.0	0.0	71.5	64.5	62.5	84.4	62.8	17.1	6.6
4104	District 4, Oregon	Peter A. DeFazio (D)	651,154	55.6	0.0	59.7	51.8	56.1	78.3	58.2	13.3	8.1
4105	District 5, Oregon	Kurt Schrader (D)	648,750	62.0	0.0	66.5	57.8	61.0	83.2	62.8	13.9	6.3
4200	**PENNSYLVANIA**		10,429,005	62.5	0.0	67.3	58.0	59.0	82.1	66.8	17.2	6.3
4201	District 1, Pennsylvania	Robert A. Brady (D)	567,009	64.1	0.0	68.5	60.2	53.7	78.4	61.6	18.1	10.3
4202	District 2, Pennsylvania	Dwight Evans (D)	601,435	57.2	0.0	58.7	56.0	46.9	76.0	55.8	17.2	10.3
4203	District 3, Pennsylvania	Mike Kelly (R)	572,766	59.1	0.0	64.6	53.8	61.3	79.3	61.5	14.7	5.9
4204	District 4, Pennsylvania	Scott Perry (R)	585,210	65.3	0.1	70.0	60.8	66.5	84.7	67.7	17.2	5.1
4205	District 5, Pennsylvania	Glenn Thompson (R)	585,374	56.7	0.0	58.9	54.5	51.9	77.4	63.3	13.8	6.1
4206	District 6, Pennsylvania	Ryan A. Costello (R)	583,291	67.6	0.0	73.7	61.7	61.9	86.3	74.3	19.4	4.5
4207	District 7, Pennsylvania	Patrick Meehan (R)	575,479	65.5	0.0	71.2	60.1	57.3	85.1	73.3	22.6	4.7
4208	District 8, Pennsylvania	Brian K. Fitzpatrick (R)	575,283	67.8	0.1	73.4	62.5	63.6	86.8	74.8	21.5	5.2
4209	District 9, Pennsylvania	Bill Shuster (R)	572,328	57.5	0.0	62.7	52.4	58.3	80.1	59.3	13.4	6.6
4210	District 10, Pennsylvania	Tom Marino (R)	580,169	59.0	0.0	63.6	54.5	62.3	78.5	64.6	14.6	5.2
4211	District 11, Pennsylvania	Lou Barletta (R)	578,571	61.1	0.1	65.2	57.2	59.5	82.1	64.9	15.9	5.3
4212	District 12, Pennsylvania	Keith J. Rothfus (R)	576,504	61.6	0.0	66.9	56.6	59.6	82.8	69.9	15.7	5.3
4213	District 13, Pennsylvania	Brendan F. Boyle (D)	575,053	65.4	0.0	70.5	60.8	59.6	83.4	68.1	19.5	7.7
4214	District 14, Pennsylvania	Michael F. Doyle (D)	593,272	62.5	0.0	66.9	58.5	57.5	83.6	64.9	16.9	6.7
4215	District 15, Pennsylvania	Charles W. Dent (R)	586,500	65.1	0.1	70.5	60.1	61.8	85.1	70.8	17.3	5.2
4216	District 16, Pennsylvania	Lloyd Smucker (R)	569,314	66.7	0.1	72.8	60.9	66.0	83.4	74.1	21.2	6.6
4217	District 17, Pennsylvania	Matt Cartwright (D)	566,547	59.6	0.0	63.9	55.4	56.7	80.5	63.4	14.8	7.6
4218	District 18, Pennsylvania	Tim Murphy (R)	584,900	63.5	0.1	69.7	57.8	64.0	84.5	68.3	17.0	5.0
4400	**RHODE ISLAND**		870,136	64.3	0.3	68.2	60.8	60.0	82.7	69.3	18.8	6.2
4401	District 1, Rhode Island	David Cicilline (D)	437,894	62.5	0.5	66.4	58.9	58.7	80.8	65.7	17.7	5.7
4402	District 2, Rhode Island	James R. Langevin (D)	432,242	66.2	0.0	69.9	62.7	61.5	84.7	72.5	20.0	6.7
4500	**SOUTH CAROLINA**		3,931,185	59.4	0.7	63.9	55.3	55.6	79.5	58.0	16.0	7.3
4501	District 1, South Carolina	Mark Sanford (R)	603,273	62.6	1.6	67.6	58.0	56.1	82.7	64.0	18.1	4.8
4502	District 2, South Carolina	Joe Wilson (R)	559,248	63.0	1.8	67.5	58.7	53.6	82.9	62.6	18.5	7.2
4503	District 3, South Carolina	Jeff Duncan (R)	552,340	56.3	0.0	61.0	51.9	53.8	77.2	56.0	14.4	7.0
4504	District 4, South Carolina	Trey Gowdy (R)	560,975	62.4	0.0	68.7	56.7	60.4	80.2	63.0	16.8	6.3
4505	District 5, South Carolina	Ralph Norman (R)	552,707	59.1	0.4	64.1	54.5	57.1	78.8	57.2	14.5	7.6
4506	District 6, South Carolina	James E. Clyburn (D)	535,404	56.5	0.9	57.7	55.4	51.8	74.8	52.4	16.6	10.2
4507	District 7, South Carolina	Tom Rice (R)	567,238	55.7	0.0	60.2	51.6	57.5	78.7	51.4	13.6	8.7
4600	**SOUTH DAKOTA**		671,301	67.8	0.4	72.4	63.2	67.9	85.5	73.0	21.7	4.0
4600	District (at Large), South Dakota	Kristi Noem (R)	671,301	67.8	0.4	72.4	63.2	67.9	85.5	73.0	21.7	4.0
4700	**TENNESSEE**		5,277,935	60.6	0.4	65.5	56.0	59.8	78.5	59.1	16.7	6.2
4701	District 1, Tennessee	David P. Roe (R)	587,927	55.4	0.0	59.3	51.6	61.8	74.4	53.9	15.4	6.3
4702	District 2, Tennessee	John J. Duncan Jr. (R)	596,919	61.2	0.0	67.2	55.7	63.3	81.0	60.1	16.3	5.5
4703	District 3, Tennessee	Chuck Fleischmann (R)	592,022	56.6	0.0	61.7	51.9	58.3	76.2	54.3	15.3	7.2
4704	District 4, Tennessee	Scott DesJarlais (R)	597,802	62.1	0.0	69.2	55.4	67.1	78.5	58.0	15.5	6.0
4705	District 5, Tennessee	Jim Cooper (D)	610,746	68.9	0.1	74.3	63.9	64.4	83.9	63.9	20.0	5.0
4706	District 6, Tennessee	Diane Black (R)	596,228	59.2	0.2	64.6	54.1	60.1	78.9	60.3	14.8	5.2
4707	District 7, Tennessee	Marsha Blackburn (R)	586,656	58.0	2.5	61.9	54.2	53.0	73.2	60.7	16.4	6.3
4708	District 8, Tennessee	David Kustoff (R)	563,683	59.4	0.2	63.8	55.2	52.0	78.7	60.3	19.5	4.9
4709	District 9, Tennessee	Steve Cohen (D)	545,952	64.6	0.2	67.7	61.9	56.5	80.7	61.4	19.0	9.9
4800	**TEXAS**		21,043,248	63.9	0.5	70.5	57.4	54.9	79.5	64.1	19.1	5.5
4801	District 1, Texas	Louie Gohmert (R)	557,077	57.3	0.0	62.6	52.4	55.4	75.5	56.7	17.4	6.6
4802	District 2, Texas	Ted Poe (R)	597,290	69.8	0.0	77.7	61.9	59.2	83.1	72.7	23.6	4.4
4803	District 3, Texas	Sam Johnson (R)	626,982	70.5	0.1	78.7	62.7	52.4	84.6	74.5	23.1	3.7
4804	District 4, Texas	John Ratcliffe (R)	567,393	58.4	0.1	65.5	51.7	55.8	77.5	59.4	16.3	6.4
4805	District 5, Texas	Jeb Hensarling (R)	573,762	60.7	0.1	65.5	55.7	60.0	75.8	60.1	16.1	5.8
4806	District 6, Texas	Joe Barton (R)	574,341	68.0	0.1	73.3	63.1	56.1	83.5	68.4	22.4	4.8
4807	District 7, Texas	John Abney Culberson (R)	593,360	70.1	0.0	80.1	60.2	51.9	83.6	70.9	28.8	4.7
4808	District 8, Texas	Kevin Brady (R)	621,970	59.3	0.1	65.7	52.8	49.7	74.4	60.9	20.0	5.2
4809	District 9, Texas	Al Green (D)	598,152	69.4	0.1	76.7	62.5	59.3	82.8	68.3	21.2	6.7
4810	District 10, Texas	Michael T. McCaul (R)	608,035	68.7	0.0	76.9	60.8	55.6	83.9	70.3	20.5	4.4
4811	District 11, Texas	K. Michael Conaway (R)	590,811	60.7	0.6	68.6	52.9	57.6	78.3	63.8	18.7	4.2
4812	District 12, Texas	Kay Granger (R)	610,486	66.2	0.2	73.1	59.9	60.3	82.9	63.3	19.8	6.3
4813	District 13, Texas	Mac Thornberry (R)	549,728	60.0	1.0	64.9	55.0	57.0	75.2	63.3	19.3	4.6
4814	District 14, Texas	Randy K. Weber Sr. (R)	583,014	60.1	0.2	64.9	55.1	56.3	74.6	60.2	19.0	6.9
4815	District 15, Texas	Vicente Gonzalez (D)	554,848	58.8	0.1	64.8	53.0	45.3	75.9	58.2	16.5	7.7
4816	District 16, Texas	Beto O'Rourke (D)	559,336	58.6	3.6	64.6	53.1	48.3	74.9	58.1	17.1	6.3
4817	District 17, Texas	Bill Flores (R)	596,263	62.8	0.0	68.1	57.7	51.5	80.8	66.0	18.7	4.5
4818	District 18, Texas	Sheila Jackson-Lee (D)	583,371	64.9	0.0	70.2	59.8	51.0	79.3	61.9	19.3	7.0
4819	District 19, Texas	Jodey C. Arrington (R)	561,660	60.0	0.8	64.5	55.4	53.9	76.3	64.9	19.6	4.5
4820	District 20, Texas	Joaquin Castro (D)	590,611	63.0	1.3	67.2	59.0	55.4	78.7	57.0	15.3	6.2
4821	District 21, Texas	Lamar Smith (R)	637,199	63.8	0.6	69.1	58.8	52.9	84.3	65.2	17.5	4.4
4822	District 22, Texas	Pete Olson (R)	650,309	67.5	0.1	75.6	59.9	50.6	82.8	68.1	21.8	3.7

Table F. Congressional Districts—Labor Force, Employment, and Educational Data, 2015—*Continued*

State and District code	State/Congressional district (114th Congress)	Representative (115th Congress)	Total population age 16 and older	Percent in civilian labor force	Percent in armed forces	Civilian labor force participation by gender		Civilian labor force participation by age				Civilian unemployment rate
						Men	Women	Age 16 to 24	Age 25 to 54	Age 55 to 64	Age 65 and older	
4823	District 23, Texas	Will Hurd (R)	561,310	58.1	0.8	64.3	51.8	49.8	74.7	58.2	17.6	7.1
4824	District 24, Texas	Kenny Marchant (R)	611,969	73.5	0.0	81.5	65.9	63.2	85.7	76.2	25.7	3.4
4825	District 25, Texas	Roger Williams (R)	598,184	60.8	2.0	66.9	55.1	49.3	76.8	65.5	17.5	4.5
4826	District 26, Texas	Michael C. Burgess (R)	618,247	72.5	0.0	79.0	66.4	62.9	86.0	71.8	21.6	4.5
4827	District 27, Texas	Blake Farenthold (R)	570,240	61.6	0.3	68.6	55.0	57.4	79.8	61.4	19.9	6.5
4828	District 28, Texas	Henry Cuellar (D)	524,033	60.0	0.3	67.9	52.7	52.0	76.4	60.4	14.9	8.3
4829	District 29, Texas	Gene Green (D)	542,632	65.0	0.1	76.5	53.2	57.2	77.1	62.1	16.8	5.9
4830	District 30, Texas	Eddie Bernice Johnson (D)	564,463	63.7	0.0	68.3	59.4	56.7	76.7	60.6	18.6	6.4
4831	District 31, Texas	John R. Carter (R)	612,224	64.8	3.1	69.9	59.8	56.3	80.3	63.9	16.4	5.9
4832	District 32, Texas	Pete Sessions (R)	587,203	70.4	0.0	78.2	63.0	60.5	84.5	75.7	25.6	4.2
4833	District 33, Texas	Marc A. Veasey (D)	529,857	65.2	0.0	76.3	53.9	58.1	77.8	61.2	15.8	6.2
4834	District 34, Texas	Filemon Vela (D)	532,523	53.6	0.1	59.4	48.0	47.1	71.3	53.9	13.2	8.3
4835	District 35, Texas	Lloyd Doggett (D)	631,201	66.0	0.2	72.0	59.8	60.4	79.9	56.7	16.6	5.4
4836	District 36, Texas	Brian Babin (R)	573,164	60.1	0.1	67.8	52.4	55.8	76.5	58.6	17.4	7.5
4900	**UTAH**		2,180,281	67.5	0.1	75.9	59.2	68.5	80.4	66.4	19.1	4.0
4901	District 1, Utah	Rob Bishop (R)	532,807	67.6	0.4	76.0	59.2	68.3	80.0	66.3	19.5	4.5
4902	District 2, Utah	Chris Stewart (R)	565,663	64.3	0.1	71.7	56.9	65.5	80.5	62.6	17.0	4.0
4903	District 3, Utah	Vacant	535,092	67.4	0.1	77.5	57.4	69.7	78.9	67.0	20.3	3.8
4904	District 4, Utah	Mia B. Love (R)	546,719	70.9	0.1	78.7	63.2	70.4	82.0	70.2	20.4	3.5
5000	**VERMONT**		521,616	65.3	0.0	68.4	62.4	61.4	84.6	72.8	21.2	3.8
5000	District (at Large), Vermont	Peter Welch (D)	521,616	65.3	0.0	68.4	62.4	61.4	84.6	72.8	21.2	3.8
5100	**VIRGINIA**		6,721,590	64.2	1.8	68.0	60.7	55.3	81.3	67.6	19.7	5.5
5101	District 1, Virginia	Robert J. Wittman (R)	604,439	63.1	2.5	67.6	58.7	51.4	81.3	67.1	18.5	4.7
5102	District 2, Virginia	Scott Taylor (R)	605,813	61.2	7.8	62.4	60.0	47.5	76.3	70.7	19.7	5.8
5103	District 3, Virginia	Robert C. "Bobby" Scott (D)	595,834	61.4	3.6	61.8	61.0	55.5	76.9	60.1	17.9	9.1
5104	District 4, Virginia	A. Donald McEachin (D)	601,201	61.3	2.0	62.7	60.0	58.3	76.8	63.1	17.2	6.1
5105	District 5, Virginia	Thomas A. Garrett, Jr. (R)	608,227	59.0	0.2	62.1	56.1	51.9	80.1	64.6	18.4	5.5
5106	District 6, Virginia	Bob Goodlatte (R)	612,092	59.4	0.1	64.2	54.9	53.0	79.9	65.8	17.1	5.3
5107	District 7, Virginia	Dave Brat (R)	619,913	68.3	0.1	72.8	64.3	61.0	86.1	74.3	20.7	5.0
5108	District 8, Virginia	Donald S. Beyer, Jr. (D)	650,364	75.2	1.9	79.8	70.7	65.5	86.9	74.5	28.2	4.6
5109	District 9, Virginia	Morgan Griffith (R)	597,965	53.3	0.1	57.3	49.4	51.5	73.4	54.8	14.2	6.4
5110	District 10, Virginia	Barbara Comstock (R)	614,092	71.1	0.5	77.5	64.9	56.4	86.0	74.8	25.2	3.5
5111	District 11, Virginia	Gerald E. Connolly (D)	611,650	72.1	0.9	78.3	66.3	60.6	85.9	75.2	25.4	5.0
5300	**WASHINGTON**		5,741,873	62.9	0.8	68.2	57.7	58.1	80.3	64.1	16.7	6.0
5301	District 1, Washington	Suzan K. DelBene (D)	567,070	65.8	0.1	71.9	59.6	57.8	81.2	69.1	18.8	4.3
5302	District 2, Washington	Rick Larsen (D)	589,583	63.2	1.4	68.7	57.8	61.4	80.3	66.4	16.9	6.0
5303	District 3, Washington	Jaime Herrera Beutler (R)	561,226	59.6	0.2	65.4	54.0	59.7	78.7	58.9	15.4	5.9
5304	District 4, Washington	Dan Newsome (R)	523,986	62.4	0.0	68.9	55.8	58.7	79.1	63.6	17.5	6.3
5305	District 5, Washington	Cathy McMorris Rodgers (R)	565,439	56.8	0.5	59.9	53.8	54.0	75.6	57.5	15.1	7.5
5306	District 6, Washington	Derek Kilmer (D)	567,030	54.5	2.5	58.4	50.6	55.8	74.9	55.7	13.9	7.3
5307	District 7, Washington	Pramila Jayapal (D)	640,075	71.7	0.1	75.8	67.6	64.0	87.8	70.4	20.2	4.8
5308	District 8, Washington	David G. Reichert (R)	573,269	65.6	0.1	72.7	58.8	54.9	82.7	67.5	17.3	5.2
5309	District 9, Washington	Adam Smith (D)	586,539	67.9	0.1	74.9	61.0	60.0	84.0	68.1	18.4	5.8
5310	District 10, Washington	Denny Heck (D)	567,656	60.4	2.8	63.9	57.0	55.3	75.4	64.8	14.9	7.5
5400	**WEST VIRGINIA**		1,508,224	52.8	0.1	57.6	48.2	52.7	72.7	51.6	12.8	7.3
5401	District 1, West Virginia	David McKinley (R)	510,335	54.4	0.0	59.4	49.5	52.5	74.9	54.2	12.9	6.4
5402	District 2, West Virginia	Alexander X. Mooney (R)	508,779	57.5	0.1	63.0	52.2	56.8	77.0	58.5	15.0	6.9
5403	District 3, West Virginia	Evan H. Jenkins (R)	489,110	46.3	0.0	50.1	42.8	48.8	65.8	41.9	10.4	8.9
5500	**WISCONSIN**		4,627,790	66.8	0.1	70.5	63.2	69.3	85.8	69.1	16.1	4.3
5501	District 1, Wisconsin	Paul Ryan (R)	571,244	66.7	0.1	69.9	63.6	67.3	85.6	70.0	15.6	4.8
5502	District 2, Wisconsin	Mark Pocan (D)	604,779	71.3	0.0	75.7	67.1	71.8	88.6	71.8	19.8	4.3
5503	District 3, Wisconsin	Ron Kind (D)	584,335	65.2	0.1	68.2	62.3	68.8	85.7	67.5	16.2	3.8
5504	District 4, Wisconsin	Gwen Moore (D)	554,459	65.6	0.0	66.8	64.5	62.1	81.2	61.1	16.5	7.6
5505	District 5, Wisconsin	F. James Sensenbrenner Jr. (R)	582,138	68.5	0.0	74.7	62.5	72.2	86.9	74.3	16.0	3.0
5506	District 6, Wisconsin	Glen Grothman(R)	576,908	65.4	0.0	69.2	61.7	69.8	84.8	69.9	15.5	3.8
5507	District 7, Wisconsin	Sean P. Duffy (R)	573,165	63.5	0.0	66.9	60.0	70.9	85.6	66.9	14.7	3.5
5508	District 8, Wisconsin	Mike Gallagher (R)	580,762	67.9	0.0	72.0	63.9	72.3	87.9	69.5	15.2	3.4
5600	**WYOMING**		460,730	67.4	0.5	72.3	62.4	65.7	84.5	68.8	21.0	4.8
5600	District (at Large), Wyoming	Liz Cheney (R)	460,730	67.4	0.5	72.3	62.4	65.7	84.5	68.8	21.0	4.8

Table F. Congressional Districts—Labor Force, Employment, and Educational Data, 2015

| | | Civilian employed population age 16 and older | | | | Class of worker for civilian employed population age 16 and older | | | | | | |
| | | | | | | Private for-profit wage and salary workers | | | Private not-for-profit wage and salary workers | Government workers | | |
State and District code	State/Congressional district (114th Congress)	Total	Men	Women	Percent women	Total private for-profit wage and salary workers	Employees of private companies	Self-employed in own incorporated business	Private not-for-profit wage and salary workers	Local government workers	State government workers	Federal government workers
0000	**UNITED STATES**	150,534,773	79,120,041	71,414,732	47.4	72.3	68.8	3.5	8.0	6.6	4.5	2.4
0100	**ALABAMA**	2,040,118	1,067,761	972,357	47.7	73.4	70.7	2.7	6.6	6.3	5.4	3.1
0101	District 1 , Alabama	288,779	148,095	140,684	48.7	76.4	73.2	3.2	6.7	6.5	3.7	1.8
0102	District 2, Alabama	280,010	141,961	138,049	49.3	70.2	67.7	2.4	6.2	7.0	7.0	4.3
0103	District 3, Alabama	295,040	156,830	138,210	46.8	74.6	72.4	2.1	5.0	6.1	5.7	3.3
0104	District 4, Alabama	270,799	149,505	121,294	44.8	74.5	71.5	3.1	5.6	6.9	5.2	1.4
0105	District 5, Alabama	312,777	167,346	145,431	46.5	72.3	70.4	1.8	6.6	5.4	4.3	6.3
0106	District 6, Alabama	330,254	174,954	155,300	47.0	74.4	70.7	3.6	8.0	6.0	4.5	2.5
0107	District 7, Alabama	262,459	129,070	133,389	50.8	71.6	68.8	2.8	7.9	6.4	8.0	1.9
0200	**ALASKA**	354,766	193,392	161,374	45.5	58.8	55.5	3.3	10.1	9.0	8.6	6.9
0200	District (at Large), Alaska	354,766	193,392	161,374	45.5	58.8	55.5	3.3	10.1	9.0	8.6	6.9
0400	ARIZONA	2,937,510	1,564,955	1,372,555	46.7	74.1	70.6	3.5	6.1	6.4	4.7	2.7
0401	District 1, Arizona	273,151	139,684	133,467	48.9	63.8	61.0	2.8	6.8	11.1	8.4	4.7
0402	District 2, Arizona	295,365	152,392	142,973	48.4	66.9	63.1	3.8	7.6	6.6	6.4	6.3
0403	District 3, Arizona	313,990	168,922	145,068	46.2	71.5	69.8	1.7	5.6	8.9	5.1	3.7
0404	District 4, Arizona	258,079	138,375	119,704	46.4	71.4	67.1	4.3	6.5	7.6	4.5	3.1
0405	District 5, Arizona	372,155	200,329	171,826	46.2	77.3	72.9	4.4	5.9	5.9	3.6	1.4
0406	District 6, Arizona	363,201	195,117	168,084	46.3	78.3	72.2	6.1	6.2	4.0	3.2	1.5
0407	District 7, Arizona	318,211	176,293	141,918	44.6	80.4	77.9	2.5	4.0	4.6	3.5	1.3
0408	District 8, Arizona	331,245	166,241	165,004	49.8	75.3	72.6	2.7	6.8	5.4	4.3	2.0
0409	District 9, Arizona	412,113	227,602	184,511	44.8	77.6	74.4	3.2	5.9	5.2	4.7	1.5
0500	**ARKANSAS**	1,271,063	670,323	600,740	47.3	70.6	67.8	2.8	7.2	5.5	8.0	2.1
0501	District 1, Arkansas	285,037	150,473	134,564	47.2	69.8	67.0	2.8	6.9	5.4	8.3	2.2
0502	District 2, Arkansas	343,958	181,045	162,913	47.4	67.3	64.0	3.3	9.0	5.5	9.4	3.1
0503	District 3, Arkansas	353,726	190,087	163,639	46.3	75.2	72.7	2.5	6.9	4.9	5.4	1.2
0504	District 4, Arkansas	288,342	148,718	139,624	48.4	69.7	67.0	2.7	5.9	6.2	9.3	2.0
0600	**CALIFORNIA**	18,045,450	9,771,350	8,274,100	45.9	71.8	68.5	3.3	6.5	7.5	4.0	1.8
0601	District 1, California	281,376	146,240	135,136	48.0	62.3	59.7	2.6	7.9	9.3	6.4	2.6
0602	District 2, California	338,233	176,511	161,722	47.8	60.2	56.1	4.2	9.4	9.2	5.1	1.3
0603	District 3, California	307,002	160,451	146,551	47.7	63.2	61.0	2.1	7.0	9.5	9.2	3.8
0604	District 4, California	304,238	160,622	143,616	47.2	65.1	61.4	3.7	8.1	9.0	6.0	1.8
0605	District 5, California	356,138	186,134	170,004	47.7	69.6	66.8	2.7	6.8	8.5	4.4	1.6
0606	District 6, California	331,490	170,445	161,045	48.6	67.0	65.6	1.4	6.4	7.1	11.8	1.5
0607	District 7, California	337,380	172,772	164,608	48.8	62.9	60.1	2.7	7.1	8.4	12.2	2.1
0608	District 8, California	259,449	133,885	125,564	48.4	66.8	64.8	2.0	6.1	10.5	3.6	4.6
0609	District 9, California	303,584	165,508	138,076	45.5	72.3	70.3	2.0	6.6	8.9	4.5	1.8
0610	District 10, California	304,073	170,097	133,976	44.1	73.8	71.4	2.4	5.9	9.1	3.5	1.5
0611	District 11, California	360,342	192,375	167,967	46.6	69.9	66.6	3.3	8.5	6.7	3.2	1.5
0612	District 12, California	446,732	241,657	205,075	45.9	72.6	69.8	2.8	8.9	5.2	3.4	1.5
0613	District 13, California	393,824	202,519	191,305	48.6	63.2	60.4	2.8	11.4	7.5	5.8	2.0
0614	District 14, California	399,823	211,871	187,952	47.0	73.2	70.2	3.0	7.5	7.4	2.9	1.7
0615	District 15, California	383,788	210,123	173,665	45.3	77.5	74.7	2.7	5.7	6.8	2.2	2.1
0616	District 16, California	271,480	155,394	116,086	42.8	72.9	71.8	1.1	5.2	9.6	4.2	1.6
0617	District 17, California	387,214	223,400	163,814	42.3	82.4	79.8	2.6	4.9	5.4	1.6	1.2
0618	District 18, California	377,605	202,072	175,533	46.5	72.6	68.7	4.0	9.1	6.7	2.2	1.1
0619	District 19, California	379,214	209,572	169,642	44.7	76.0	73.5	2.5	6.5	7.7	2.8	1.1
0620	District 20, California	322,351	177,518	144,833	44.9	69.8	66.8	3.0	6.8	7.5	4.9	1.9
0621	District 21, California	257,518	149,035	108,483	42.1	76.0	74.2	1.8	3.7	8.0	5.1	2.2
0622	District 22, California	314,786	169,179	145,607	46.3	67.6	64.9	2.7	6.8	10.3	7.2	1.8
0623	District 23, California	293,676	164,573	129,103	44.0	67.0	64.6	2.4	5.3	11.7	5.2	3.5
0624	District 24, California	348,483	188,459	160,024	45.9	65.8	62.0	3.8	8.2	7.6	7.3	1.3
0625	District 25, California	318,928	179,054	139,874	43.9	71.8	67.9	3.9	6.7	9.2	3.1	1.6
0626	District 26, California	340,023	182,310	157,713	46.4	74.1	70.0	4.1	4.4	8.1	2.8	2.5
0627	District 27, California	353,412	181,710	171,702	48.6	69.8	64.1	5.6	10.0	7.8	3.5	1.0
0628	District 28, California	392,029	210,193	181,836	46.4	69.9	64.1	5.8	7.9	5.8	2.3	0.7
0629	District 29, California	345,247	193,449	151,798	44.0	73.7	71.4	2.3	5.9	5.3	2.7	0.7
0630	District 30, California	403,627	216,664	186,963	46.3	73.9	66.8	7.0	5.9	4.6	2.9	0.9
0631	District 31, California	317,640	169,516	148,124	46.6	70.2	68.4	1.8	7.5	11.2	4.5	0.9
0632	District 32, California	336,134	186,768	149,366	44.4	76.3	73.7	2.6	5.4	8.3	2.1	1.3
0633	District 33, California	365,213	194,375	170,838	46.8	69.6	59.1	10.6	7.1	5.2	4.2	1.3
0634	District 34, California	354,331	197,212	157,119	44.3	72.4	70.2	2.2	6.1	6.5	1.6	0.7
0635	District 35, California	323,402	177,367	146,035	45.2	77.3	75.6	1.7	5.3	7.8	3.1	0.9
0636	District 36, California	280,700	154,574	126,126	44.9	71.6	68.3	3.3	6.0	8.1	3.8	1.1
0637	District 37, California	362,044	191,916	170,128	47.0	71.8	66.9	4.9	7.3	5.9	3.5	1.1
0638	District 38, California	329,917	181,760	148,157	44.9	74.9	72.7	2.2	6.2	8.8	3.0	1.1
0639	District 39, California	349,497	186,879	162,618	46.5	73.2	68.1	5.1	5.8	7.5	4.0	1.2
0640	District 40, California	311,326	179,436	131,890	42.4	81.0	79.1	1.9	3.0	6.4	1.3	0.9
0641	District 41, California	325,320	184,567	140,753	43.3	74.1	72.4	1.7	4.6	9.1	4.0	1.4
0642	District 42, California	332,676	184,164	148,512	44.6	73.2	68.7	4.4	4.5	8.4	3.5	2.4
0643	District 43, California	342,157	178,294	163,863	47.9	74.3	72.4	1.9	5.3	7.5	2.5	1.7
0644	District 44, California	307,105	165,117	141,988	46.2	78.7	76.8	1.8	4.5	7.0	2.6	1.3
0645	District 45, California	384,641	214,449	170,192	44.2	75.9	70.0	5.9	5.3	6.2	3.4	1.4

Table F. Congressional Districts—Labor Force, Employment, and Educational Data, 2015—*Continued*

State and District code	State/Congressional district (114th Congress)	Civilian employed population age 16 and older				Class of worker for civilian employed population age 16 and older						
						Private for-profit wage and salary workers			Private not-for-profit wage and salary workers	Government workers		
		Total	Men	Women	Percent women	Total private for-profit wage and salary workers	Employees of private companies	Self-employed in own incorporated business		Local government workers	State government workers	Federal government workers
0646	District 46, California	355,275	200,184	155,091	43.7	82.7	80.7	2.0	4.0	4.8	1.9	0.7
0647	District 47, California	344,068	182,989	161,079	46.8	73.9	71.1	2.8	5.1	7.6	3.8	1.9
0648	District 48, California	369,001	197,176	171,825	46.6	75.7	70.5	5.2	4.6	5.7	2.6	1.0
0649	District 49, California	346,352	189,886	156,466	45.2	72.1	67.2	4.9	5.9	5.8	2.4	3.0
0650	District 50, California	345,683	192,875	152,808	44.2	70.8	67.8	3.0	7.5	6.9	3.7	2.8
0651	District 51, California	280,238	148,157	132,081	47.1	71.9	70.4	1.5	4.5	8.0	4.6	3.7
0652	District 52, California	383,055	203,371	179,684	46.9	70.8	66.5	4.3	7.8	5.5	4.6	3.6
0653	District 53, California	386,610	206,526	180,084	46.6	66.8	63.8	3.0	8.2	6.8	5.0	5.7
0800	**COLORADO**	2,765,115	1,485,661	1,279,454	46.3	72.7	67.9	4.8	7.8	6.3	4.1	2.6
0801	District 1, Colorado	438,960	240,794	198,166	45.1	75.2	70.6	4.6	8.7	4.7	3.3	2.3
0802	District 2, Colorado	428,451	227,849	200,602	46.8	70.0	64.6	5.4	8.1	6.7	6.5	1.8
0803	District 3, Colorado	342,043	183,830	158,213	46.3	68.5	63.0	5.5	9.0	7.3	4.8	1.8
0804	District 4, Colorado	388,662	213,607	175,055	45.0	73.5	68.5	5.0	6.6	7.3	4.3	1.8
0805	District 5, Colorado	344,652	183,279	161,373	46.8	67.9	62.9	5.1	8.4	7.6	4.1	5.8
0806	District 6, Colorado	414,688	218,676	196,012	47.3	76.5	72.0	4.6	7.1	5.4	2.9	2.6
0807	District 7, Colorado	407,659	217,626	190,033	46.6	75.7	72.1	3.6	7.0	5.9	3.1	2.3
0900	**CONNECTICUT**	1,807,098	925,935	881,163	48.8	71.0	67.6	3.4	9.4	7.4	4.4	1.4
0901	District 1, Connecticut	361,863	180,707	181,156	50.1	71.8	68.6	3.2	9.6	7.0	5.9	1.1
0902	District 2, Connecticut	362,487	186,747	175,740	48.5	69.4	66.6	2.8	8.5	8.0	5.8	2.4
0903	District 3, Connecticut	365,678	184,301	181,377	49.6	68.7	66.0	2.7	12.7	7.1	4.0	1.6
0904	District 4, Connecticut	363,848	191,196	172,652	47.5	73.2	68.7	4.5	8.0	7.2	1.9	1.1
0905	District 5, Connecticut	353,222	182,984	170,238	48.2	71.8	67.9	3.9	8.3	7.9	4.4	0.7
1000	**DELAWARE** District (at Large),	447,516	225,225	222,291	49.7	73.4	69.7	3.7	8.2	3.2	8.8	2.1
1000	Delaware	447,516	225,225	222,291	49.7	73.4	69.7	3.7	8.2	3.2	8.8	2.1
1100	**DISTRICT OF COLUMBIA** Delegate District (at Large),	361,179	175,876	185,303	51.3	52.0	49.4	2.6	18.8	5.0	2.1	17.3
1198	District of Columbia	361,179	175,876	185,303	51.3	52.0	49.4	2.6	18.8	5.0	2.1	17.3
1200	**FLORIDA**	8,990,221	4,663,492	4,326,729	48.1	76.3	70.4	5.8	6.1	6.8	2.8	1.9
1201	District 1, Florida	325,496	171,921	153,575	47.2	68.9	65.2	3.7	8.0	6.9	2.8	6.0
1202	District 2, Florida	309,354	156,340	153,014	49.5	62.7	58.7	3.9	6.5	8.3	13.4	3.2
1203	District 3, Florida	289,051	146,327	142,724	49.4	68.2	64.0	4.2	7.5	7.4	8.5	3.4
1204	District 4, Florida	363,284	188,590	174,694	48.1	76.7	72.6	4.1	7.7	5.2	3.3	2.7
1205	District 5, Florida	330,930	159,340	171,590	51.9	77.4	74.8	2.5	6.4	6.3	3.1	2.0
1206	District 6, Florida	305,277	158,930	146,347	47.9	75.4	68.8	6.6	7.0	8.1	2.6	1.5
1207	District 7, Florida	353,000	182,818	170,182	48.2	77.1	71.2	5.9	8.2	5.6	2.8	1.2
1208	District 8, Florida	302,037	154,961	147,076	48.7	76.7	70.2	6.5	6.3	6.4	2.2	3.2
1209	District 9, Florida	382,399	204,277	178,122	46.6	78.6	74.8	3.8	6.3	6.8	2.1	1.7
1210	District 10, Florida	363,243	188,315	174,928	48.2	80.4	75.1	5.3	5.7	5.4	1.8	1.4
1211	District 11, Florida	233,160	116,582	116,578	50.0	75.4	69.9	5.6	4.5	8.7	2.7	1.3
1212	District 12, Florida	323,466	164,766	158,700	49.1	75.9	69.7	6.2	6.6	8.0	2.1	1.8
1213	District 13, Florida	339,968	171,754	168,214	49.5	77.0	70.8	6.3	6.3	6.2	1.9	2.1
1214	District 14, Florida	361,177	181,786	179,391	49.7	77.2	72.7	4.6	6.5	6.9	2.5	1.8
1215	District 15, Florida	330,920	176,065	154,855	46.8	75.4	70.9	4.5	7.6	7.6	3.1	1.9
1216	District 16, Florida	304,756	156,203	148,553	48.7	76.2	68.5	7.7	7.1	6.5	2.0	0.9
1217	District 17, Florida	277,255	147,384	129,871	46.8	76.6	70.7	5.9	6.2	6.8	2.6	1.6
1218	District 18, Florida	329,870	169,399	160,471	48.6	77.4	69.2	8.2	5.6	7.4	2.3	1.3
1219	District 19, Florida	309,473	161,360	148,113	47.9	77.0	68.5	8.5	6.4	6.2	1.6	1.3
1220	District 20, Florida	348,428	175,891	172,537	49.5	80.1	77.0	3.1	4.2	7.4	1.4	1.0
1221	District 21, Florida	349,825	180,259	169,566	48.5	78.1	69.9	8.2	3.9	7.3	2.1	1.3
1222	District 22, Florida	360,736	196,754	163,982	45.5	78.4	70.1	8.3	6.2	5.4	1.6	1.1
1223	District 23, Florida	381,506	203,369	178,137	46.7	78.3	68.6	9.6	5.0	6.6	1.6	1.3
1224	District 24, Florida	335,131	169,777	165,354	49.3	75.3	71.7	3.6	4.6	9.2	2.4	1.8
1225	District 25, Florida	352,089	185,491	166,598	47.3	80.3	74.1	6.2	4.0	5.1	1.1	1.2
1226	District 26, Florida	372,266	200,838	171,428	46.0	76.4	69.5	6.9	5.2	7.6	2.1	1.9
1227	District 27, Florida	356,124	193,995	162,129	45.5	78.1	70.8	7.3	5.3	5.5	1.7	1.4
1300	**GEORGIA**	4,605,633	2,379,783	2,225,850	48.3	73.6	69.7	3.9	6.1	6.9	4.8	3.0
1301	District 1, Georgia	305,821	156,268	149,553	48.9	72.3	68.9	3.4	6.2	6.4	5.6	4.9
1302	District 2, Georgia	254,595	126,605	127,990	50.3	67.6	65.4	2.3	6.6	7.8	7.7	4.7
1303	District 3, Georgia	313,658	165,646	148,012	47.2	73.2	69.5	3.8	6.2	7.6	5.3	2.8
1304	District 4, Georgia	352,712	169,021	183,691	52.1	72.4	69.0	3.4	6.8	8.2	4.7	3.4
1305	District 5, Georgia	369,333	179,380	189,953	51.4	71.4	67.3	4.0	9.0	7.1	5.3	2.6
1306	District 6, Georgia	380,302	210,126	170,176	44.7	79.9	74.2	5.7	5.7	3.9	2.4	1.5
1307	District 7, Georgia	392,794	214,870	177,924	45.3	79.3	74.4	4.9	5.3	5.0	1.8	2.0
1308	District 8, Georgia	285,665	148,027	137,638	48.2	66.5	63.5	3.0	6.3	8.1	6.7	7.2
1309	District 9, Georgia	305,772	163,035	142,737	46.7	73.4	69.3	4.1	4.9	8.4	4.0	1.4
1310	District 10, Georgia	311,276	163,072	148,204	47.6	70.8	66.4	4.4	5.9	7.7	8.2	1.7

Table F. Congressional Districts—Labor Force, Employment, and Educational Data, 2015—*Continued*

| | | Civilian employed population age 16 and older | | | | Class of worker for civilian employed population age 16 and older | | | | | | |
| | | | | | | Private for-profit wage and salary workers | | | | Government workers | | |
State and District code	State/Congressional district (114th Congress)	Total	Men	Women	Percent women	Total private for-profit wage and salary workers	Employees of private companies	Self-employed in own incorporated business	Private not-for-profit wage and salary workers	Local government workers	State government workers	Federal government workers
1311	District 11, Georgia	381,709	202,200	179,509	47.0	76.8	72.0	4.7	6.2	6.5	3.2	1.9
1312	District 12, Georgia	280,814	140,499	140,315	50.0	71.9	69.3	2.6	4.0	6.7	7.3	4.8
1313	District 13, Georgia	352,950	172,786	180,164	51.0	71.8	68.4	3.4	6.4	7.8	4.7	3.3
1314	District 14, Georgia	318,232	168,248	149,984	47.1	78.1	75.1	3.1	5.5	7.1	3.1	1.1
1500	**HAWAII**	675,214	354,372	320,842	47.5	65.1	61.6	3.5	7.7	3.6	9.2	7.1
1501	District 1, Hawaii	350,962	185,997	164,965	47.0	65.3	62.2	3.1	8.1	3.2	8.8	8.3
1502	District 2, Hawaii	324,252	168,375	155,877	48.1	64.9	61.1	3.9	7.2	4.0	9.7	5.8
1600	**IDAHO**	744,228	399,344	344,884	46.3	69.8	65.9	3.9	7.5	6.8	5.3	2.6
1601	District 1, Idaho	370,718	197,505	173,213	46.7	70.3	66.1	4.1	6.8	7.0	5.8	2.2
1602	District 2, Idaho	373,510	201,839	171,671	46.0	69.4	65.7	3.8	8.2	6.5	4.9	3.1
1700	**ILLINOIS**	6,196,524	3,246,265	2,950,259	47.6	74.9	71.4	3.5	8.7	6.5	3.6	1.6
1701	District 1, Illinois	299,695	143,294	156,401	52.2	70.5	67.6	2.9	10.5	9.0	3.6	2.6
1702	District 2, Illinois	290,095	140,910	149,185	51.4	72.2	70.0	2.2	9.6	8.5	4.1	2.3
1703	District 3, Illinois	341,262	185,258	156,004	45.7	76.9	72.6	4.3	6.7	8.7	2.5	1.4
1704	District 4, Illinois	343,803	193,795	150,008	43.6	79.3	77.3	2.0	8.8	4.8	1.7	0.6
1705	District 5, Illinois	423,185	223,987	199,198	47.1	75.6	71.5	4.1	9.9	6.4	1.9	1.1
1706	District 6, Illinois	379,280	205,456	173,824	45.8	78.6	73.2	5.4	8.0	5.7	2.2	1.1
1707	District 7, Illinois	335,417	159,096	176,321	52.6	72.6	69.4	3.2	11.7	6.2	3.3	1.8
1708	District 8, Illinois	380,785	209,298	171,487	45.0	82.6	78.8	3.7	5.5	5.5	1.7	1.2
1709	District 9, Illinois	360,866	196,938	163,928	45.4	70.1	65.0	5.0	13.6	6.6	2.0	1.1
1710	District 10, Illinois	349,179	188,952	160,227	45.9	80.4	75.5	4.9	6.0	5.4	1.8	1.8
1711	District 11, Illinois	369,956	196,068	173,888	47.0	81.4	78.0	3.4	6.0	5.9	2.1	1.4
1712	District 12, Illinois	306,069	153,806	152,263	49.7	70.6	68.0	2.6	7.9	5.9	7.0	3.2
1713	District 13, Illinois	327,853	164,537	163,316	49.8	66.8	63.7	3.0	10.3	6.3	10.7	1.4
1714	District 14, Illinois	380,665	204,661	176,004	46.2	77.9	73.0	4.8	7.3	7.0	2.4	1.2
1715	District 15, Illinois	317,256	165,746	151,510	47.8	72.1	69.6	2.6	7.7	5.9	5.7	2.1
1716	District 16, Illinois	331,962	175,204	156,758	47.2	72.7	69.8	2.9	8.5	7.4	4.7	1.2
1717	District 17, Illinois	313,461	159,917	153,544	49.0	74.4	72.3	2.1	9.3	5.7	3.5	2.1
1718	District 18, Illinois	345,735	179,342	166,393	48.1	69.7	66.6	3.1	10.7	5.9	6.3	1.6
1800	**INDIANA**	3,119,966	1,642,149	1,477,817	47.4	76.4	73.4	3.0	8.6	5.5	3.5	1.4
1801	District 1, Indiana	316,239	166,853	149,386	47.2	77.5	74.9	2.6	8.2	6.5	2.8	1.1
1802	District 2, Indiana	328,483	176,479	152,004	46.3	75.8	73.0	2.9	10.4	5.6	2.4	0.8
1803	District 3, Indiana	351,477	189,045	162,432	46.2	77.8	74.0	3.7	8.8	4.6	2.6	1.0
1804	District 4, Indiana	365,281	194,851	170,430	46.7	75.3	72.7	2.6	8.7	5.3	5.3	1.0
1805	District 5, Indiana	391,529	201,640	189,889	48.5	75.4	70.3	5.1	9.4	6.2	3.2	1.7
1806	District 6, Indiana	336,128	179,250	156,878	46.7	76.2	73.5	2.6	7.7	5.7	3.7	1.3
1807	District 7, Indiana	343,787	169,256	174,531	50.8	78.6	76.8	1.7	8.2	5.0	3.1	1.8
1808	District 8, Indiana	334,109	179,139	154,970	46.4	76.4	73.8	2.5	8.5	5.4	3.7	1.5
1809	District 9, Indiana	352,933	185,636	167,297	47.4	75.0	72.1	2.9	7.8	5.0	4.8	2.0
1900	**IOWA**	1,599,893	839,299	760,594	47.5	71.8	68.6	3.2	8.7	6.1	5.5	1.4
1901	District 1, Iowa	400,049	209,982	190,067	47.5	72.9	69.9	3.0	10.0	5.2	4.5	1.0
1902	District 2, Iowa	390,223	204,014	186,209	47.7	70.8	68.0	2.8	7.8	6.3	7.5	1.5
1903	District 3, Iowa	422,482	220,957	201,525	47.7	74.9	71.9	3.1	8.3	5.9	4.0	1.8
1904	District 4, Iowa	387,139	204,346	182,793	47.2	68.3	64.4	3.9	8.8	6.9	6.3	1.3
2000	**KANSAS**	1,417,069	749,555	667,514	47.1	70.9	67.3	3.6	8.1	7.2	5.6	2.1
2001	District 1, Kansas	341,960	186,500	155,460	45.5	66.9	62.9	4.1	7.6	8.3	6.7	2.0
2002	District 2, Kansas	337,507	173,569	163,938	48.6	65.9	62.7	3.3	8.9	8.2	8.7	2.7
2003	District 3, Kansas	394,038	208,143	185,895	47.2	75.0	71.1	3.9	8.4	5.7	3.5	2.1
2004	District 4, Kansas	343,564	181,343	162,221	47.2	75.0	71.9	3.1	7.5	6.9	3.7	1.5
2100	**KENTUCKY**	1,928,967	1,006,647	922,320	47.8	72.5	69.6	2.9	7.8	5.3	6.6	2.4
2101	District 1, Kentucky	291,481	152,342	139,139	47.7	71.3	68.0	3.3	6.6	5.8	7.0	2.6
2102	District 2, Kentucky	330,213	174,796	155,417	47.1	71.9	69.5	2.4	6.9	5.3	6.6	3.1
2103	District 3, Kentucky	364,911	183,754	181,157	49.6	75.0	72.3	2.8	9.8	4.3	4.5	1.8
2104	District 4, Kentucky	352,096	188,021	164,075	46.6	75.9	72.9	3.1	8.2	4.6	4.3	2.3
2105	District 5, Kentucky	228,857	117,402	111,455	48.7	67.5	65.1	2.4	8.1	6.3	10.0	2.4
2106	District 6, Kentucky	361,409	190,332	171,077	47.3	71.3	67.9	3.4	7.0	5.7	8.5	2.5
2200	**LOUISIANA**	2,037,812	1,049,048	988,764	48.5	73.1	69.4	3.8	6.2	7.2	5.6	2.3
2201	District 1, Louisiana	380,447	200,912	179,535	47.2	74.0	68.6	5.4	6.4	6.8	3.8	2.4
2202	District 2, Louisiana	351,121	175,264	175,857	50.1	73.8	71.0	2.8	6.9	6.6	4.5	2.7
2203	District 3, Louisiana	351,520	180,821	170,699	48.6	74.9	70.5	4.3	5.5	8.4	4.6	0.8
2204	District 4, Louisiana	292,917	151,778	141,139	48.2	70.9	68.0	2.9	6.3	6.5	5.6	5.0
2205	District 5, Louisiana	280,960	139,427	141,533	50.4	71.0	68.3	2.7	5.3	8.1	8.0	2.4
2206	District 6, Louisiana	380,847	200,846	180,001	47.3	73.3	69.4	3.9	6.3	6.8	7.8	1.0
2300	**MAINE**	648,414	327,487	320,927	49.5	65.5	61.5	4.0	12.6	6.5	4.2	2.2
2301	District 1, Maine	347,546	174,213	173,333	49.9	67.3	62.6	4.7	12.0	6.6	3.4	2.2
2302	District 2, Maine	300,868	153,274	147,594	49.1	63.3	60.2	3.2	13.2	6.5	5.1	2.2
2400	**MARYLAND**	3,031,466	1,541,470	1,489,996	49.2	64.1	60.6	3.5	9.7	7.5	4.1	9.8
2401	District 1, Maryland	356,356	184,892	171,464	48.1	68.3	63.8	4.5	7.9	8.5	5.0	4.6
2402	District 2, Maryland	373,656	183,819	189,837	50.8	67.0	64.3	2.6	10.0	7.4	4.1	6.9

Table F. Congressional Districts—Labor Force, Employment, and Educational Data, 2015—*Continued*

State and District code	State/Congressional district (114th Congress)	Total	Men	Women	Percent women	Total private for-profit wage and salary workers	Employees of private companies	Self-employed in own incorporated business	Private not-for-profit wage and salary workers	Local government workers	State government workers	Federal government workers
2403	District 3, Maryland	395,018	202,399	192,619	48.8	64.9	61.5	3.4	11.6	6.3	4.2	8.3
2404	District 4, Maryland	395,429	200,110	195,319	49.4	63.2	60.4	2.8	8.5	7.8	3.3	13.4
2405	District 5, Maryland	393,701	199,915	193,786	49.2	59.7	56.3	3.3	8.2	8.2	4.2	16.1
2406	District 6, Maryland	378,323	199,104	179,219	47.4	66.6	63.0	3.6	8.2	7.6	3.5	8.6
2407	District 7, Maryland	329,932	160,289	169,643	51.4	62.3	59.3	3.0	12.8	7.7	6.0	7.2
2408	District 8, Maryland	409,051	210,942	198,109	48.4	60.9	56.4	4.5	10.9	6.4	2.8	12.4
2500	**MASSACHUSETTS**	3,522,203	1,784,929	1,737,274	49.3	69.5	66.7	2.8	12.8	6.7	3.5	1.5
2501	District 1, Massachusetts	354,532	176,001	178,531	50.4	68.6	66.6	2.1	11.6	7.8	3.9	1.9
2502	District 2, Massachusetts	376,154	187,722	188,432	50.1	68.3	65.8	2.4	11.4	7.3	5.9	1.2
2503	District 3, Massachusetts	380,104	196,198	183,906	48.4	73.0	70.5	2.6	10.0	6.7	3.1	1.7
2504	District 4, Massachusetts	384,820	196,362	188,458	49.0	69.8	66.6	3.2	13.1	6.4	3.3	1.5
2505	District 5, Massachusetts	420,772	217,780	202,992	48.2	68.0	64.5	3.5	14.9	5.8	3.0	1.3
2506	District 6, Massachusetts	396,996	202,718	194,278	48.9	69.9	66.4	3.5	11.2	7.5	3.2	1.7
2507	District 7, Massachusetts	431,279	214,852	216,427	50.2	67.4	65.9	1.5	19.1	4.8	3.3	1.4
2508	District 8, Massachusetts	414,702	208,827	205,875	49.6	70.1	67.7	2.4	13.9	7.0	2.9	1.8
2509	District 9, Massachusetts	362,844	184,469	178,375	49.2	70.8	66.7	4.1	8.3	7.8	2.9	1.5
2600	**MICHIGAN**	4,512,641	2,356,179	2,156,462	47.8	75.3	72.0	3.3	9.5	5.0	4.0	1.4
2601	District 1, Michigan	297,829	155,215	142,614	47.9	69.0	65.1	3.9	10.2	6.4	5.6	1.6
2602	District 2, Michigan	344,887	179,910	164,977	47.8	77.2	74.5	2.7	10.0	4.7	2.6	0.9
2603	District 3, Michigan	351,028	187,587	163,441	46.6	74.2	70.7	3.5	11.9	4.6	3.3	1.1
2604	District 4, Michigan	305,545	159,603	145,942	47.8	72.5	69.5	3.0	8.7	5.7	5.6	1.2
2605	District 5, Michigan	282,380	140,561	141,819	50.2	77.7	75.3	2.4	8.9	5.0	3.1	0.9
2606	District 6, Michigan	338,465	178,197	160,268	47.4	74.4	71.6	2.9	10.1	5.0	3.5	1.1
2607	District 7, Michigan	315,090	166,370	148,720	47.2	72.5	69.4	3.1	9.8	5.6	5.1	1.4
2608	District 8, Michigan	360,853	190,354	170,499	47.2	72.5	69.1	3.4	9.3	5.2	7.0	1.0
2609	District 9, Michigan	345,827	178,539	167,288	48.4	79.0	75.7	3.3	8.7	3.9	2.5	1.9
2610	District 10, Michigan	335,471	179,145	156,326	46.6	78.2	73.9	4.3	7.0	5.4	2.8	2.0
2611	District 11, Michigan	370,875	199,155	171,720	46.3	79.0	74.0	5.0	8.7	4.4	2.2	1.2
2612	District 12, Michigan	333,135	177,052	156,083	46.9	72.6	69.7	2.8	10.6	5.1	6.4	1.6
2613	District 13, Michigan	250,907	123,715	127,192	50.7	81.4	79.5	1.9	7.2	3.2	2.7	1.7
2614	District 14, Michigan	280,349	140,776	139,573	49.8	74.9	70.8	4.1	11.0	5.0	3.3	1.4
2700	**MINNESOTA**	2,913,176	1,507,764	1,405,412	48.2	71.7	67.8	3.9	11.5	6.2	3.7	1.3
2701	District 1, Minnesota	354,861	184,507	170,354	48.0	67.4	64.2	3.2	15.5	6.4	3.2	0.9
2702	District 2, Minnesota	382,377	197,583	184,794	48.3	75.1	71.6	3.5	9.7	5.6	3.4	1.9
2703	District 3, Minnesota	384,757	201,215	183,542	47.7	77.0	71.7	5.4	9.6	5.0	2.2	1.2
2704	District 4, Minnesota	364,599	182,843	181,756	49.9	70.4	67.3	3.0	13.6	5.4	5.2	1.4
2705	District 5, Minnesota	399,431	203,538	195,893	49.0	71.1	67.8	3.3	13.1	5.8	4.3	0.9
2706	District 6, Minnesota	372,439	195,359	177,080	47.5	74.1	69.7	4.4	9.8	6.3	3.5	1.1
2707	District 7, Minnesota	336,560	177,332	159,228	47.3	68.5	64.2	4.3	9.6	7.9	3.9	1.5
2708	District 8, Minnesota	318,152	165,387	152,765	48.0	68.8	64.9	3.9	11.3	7.7	4.2	1.4
2800	**MISSISSIPPI**	1,206,679	622,777	583,902	48.4	70.9	67.7	3.2	5.9	5.6	9.2	3.2
2801	District 1, Mississippi	321,776	167,945	153,831	47.8	74.1	70.7	3.4	5.7	4.8	8.1	2.4
2802	District 2, Mississippi	262,679	126,084	136,595	52.0	68.0	65.4	2.6	5.4	7.2	11.3	3.5
2803	District 3, Mississippi	315,315	167,237	148,078	47.0	69.6	65.4	4.2	7.0	4.1	11.3	2.6
2804	District 4, Mississippi	306,909	161,511	145,398	47.4	71.5	68.8	2.7	5.4	6.4	6.6	4.3
2900	**MISSOURI**	2,880,309	1,484,020	1,396,289	48.5	71.6	68.6	3.0	10.6	5.6	4.3	2.2
2901	District 1, Missouri	357,843	171,251	186,592	52.1	71.0	68.7	2.3	15.0	5.6	1.8	2.5
2902	District 2, Missouri	400,400	211,960	188,440	47.1	75.2	70.8	4.4	12.3	4.5	1.7	1.5
2903	District 3, Missouri	381,462	198,481	182,981	48.0	73.8	71.2	2.6	8.4	5.3	5.6	1.4
2904	District 4, Missouri	334,027	174,672	159,355	47.7	67.0	64.1	2.9	8.6	6.2	6.8	3.9
2905	District 5, Missouri	370,442	188,775	181,667	49.0	74.0	71.1	3.0	10.1	5.5	3.0	3.2
2906	District 6, Missouri	368,098	191,742	176,356	47.9	71.0	68.0	3.1	8.9	6.4	4.6	2.5
2907	District 7, Missouri	356,771	187,245	169,526	47.5	70.4	67.6	2.8	11.7	5.6	4.0	1.6
2908	District 8, Missouri	311,266	159,894	151,372	48.6	69.5	66.4	3.0	9.6	5.6	7.4	1.4
3000	**MONTANA**	489,875	259,333	230,542	47.1	62.5	56.4	6.1	9.4	8.0	7.1	3.4
3000	District (at Large), Montana	489,875	259,333	230,542	47.1	62.5	56.4	6.1	9.4	8.0	7.1	3.4
3100	**NEBRASKA**	986,789	519,537	467,252	47.4	70.5	66.9	3.6	9.3	6.7	5.0	2.0
3101	District 1, Nebraska	334,987	177,352	157,635	47.1	68.7	65.6	3.1	9.2	7.0	7.0	2.5
3102	District 2, Nebraska	341,301	176,212	165,089	48.4	74.9	71.3	3.7	10.5	5.6	2.9	1.9
3103	District 3, Nebraska	310,501	165,973	144,528	46.5	67.7	63.7	4.0	8.1	7.4	5.2	1.6
3200	**NEVADA**	1,331,796	715,246	616,550	46.3	79.9	76.8	3.0	3.5	6.2	3.0	2.2
3201	District 1, Nevada	318,685	179,258	139,427	43.8	86.2	84.1	2.1	2.6	3.8	1.6	1.1
3202	District 2, Nevada	334,167	179,302	154,865	46.3	74.9	71.4	3.5	4.2	6.9	5.2	2.1
3203	District 3, Nevada	376,096	198,104	177,992	47.3	81.3	77.8	3.4	3.4	5.9	2.5	1.9
3204	District 4, Nevada	302,848	158,582	144,266	47.6	76.9	74.0	2.9	3.8	8.3	3.0	3.6
3300	**NEW HAMPSHIRE**	713,313	371,025	342,288	48.0	69.7	66.6	3.1	10.9	7.0	3.7	2.1
3301	District 1, New Hampshire	365,684	189,636	176,048	48.1	72.2	69.2	3.0	9.4	6.6	3.6	2.3
3302	District 2, New Hampshire	347,629	181,389	166,240	47.8	67.2	63.9	3.2	12.4	7.6	3.8	1.8

Table F. Congressional Districts—Labor Force, Employment, and Educational Data, 2015—*Continued*

State and District code	State/Congressional district (114th Congress)	Civilian employed population age 16 and older				Class of worker for civilian employed population age 16 and older						
						Private for-profit wage and salary workers			Private not-for-profit wage and salary workers	Government workers		
		Total	Men	Women	Percent women	Total private for-profit wage and salary workers	Employees of private companies	Self-employed in own incorporated business		Local government workers	State government workers	Federal government workers
3400	**NEW JERSEY**	4,374,536	2,298,798	2,075,738	47.5	75.2	71.3	3.9	6.6	6.9	4.6	1.6
3401	District 1, New Jersey	360,695	181,953	178,742	49.6	72.5	69.5	3.0	8.1	7.5	5.1	2.5
3402	District 2, New Jersey	329,659	170,422	159,237	48.3	72.0	68.7	3.3	6.4	8.6	5.5	1.9
3403	District 3, New Jersey	351,239	180,039	171,200	48.7	71.4	67.8	3.6	7.1	8.0	5.7	2.4
3404	District 4, New Jersey	345,305	183,436	161,869	46.9	73.5	68.7	4.7	7.7	7.9	4.9	1.5
3405	District 5, New Jersey	383,513	205,057	178,456	46.5	76.2	70.0	6.1	6.0	6.9	3.6	1.4
3406	District 6, New Jersey	364,521	196,580	167,941	46.1	77.3	72.9	4.4	6.4	5.7	4.5	1.5
3407	District 7, New Jersey	385,696	205,277	180,419	46.8	76.3	71.1	5.2	6.9	6.4	4.2	1.1
3408	District 8, New Jersey	396,661	219,453	177,208	44.7	80.6	78.5	2.1	4.8	5.9	2.8	0.9
3409	District 9, New Jersey	355,006	189,439	165,567	46.6	79.8	75.7	4.1	4.6	6.0	3.2	1.5
3410	District 10, New Jersey	352,289	174,591	177,698	50.4	73.0	71.0	2.1	6.5	6.7	6.9	2.4
3411	District 11, New Jersey	384,266	199,185	185,081	48.2	74.4	69.4	5.0	6.7	8.0	3.8	1.4
3412	District 12, New Jersey	365,686	193,366	172,320	47.1	74.0	71.1	2.9	8.2	6.0	6.0	1.1
3500	**NEW MEXICO**	879,807	463,219	416,588	47.3	64.6	61.2	3.4	7.4	8.5	7.8	5.2
3501	District 1, New Mexico	314,909	163,917	150,992	47.9	66.5	63.0	3.5	8.7	6.7	6.4	5.9
3502	District 2, New Mexico	272,966	147,497	125,469	46.0	64.7	61.3	3.4	5.3	9.7	9.6	4.4
3503	District 3, New Mexico	291,932	151,805	140,127	48.0	62.6	59.2	3.4	7.9	9.3	7.7	5.1
3600	**NEW YORK**	9,473,337	4,874,995	4,598,342	48.5	68.8	65.0	3.8	10.2	9.1	4.3	1.7
3601	District 1, New York	356,128	188,059	168,069	47.2	67.0	61.2	5.8	7.7	10.6	7.0	2.6
3602	District 2, New York	370,553	194,853	175,700	47.4	72.6	68.6	4.1	6.9	10.8	4.8	1.7
3603	District 3, New York	347,032	187,214	159,818	46.1	70.5	62.1	8.4	8.6	10.3	3.2	1.6
3604	District 4, New York	365,535	190,656	174,879	47.8	70.4	65.1	5.2	7.9	10.6	3.5	1.5
3605	District 5, New York	371,482	184,810	186,672	50.3	68.6	65.8	2.8	8.6	12.5	2.9	1.8
3606	District 6, New York	358,596	189,176	169,420	47.2	73.5	69.0	4.5	8.0	8.7	1.8	1.6
3607	District 7, New York	353,073	193,246	159,827	45.3	75.9	72.3	3.6	9.1	6.2	1.5	1.5
3608	District 8, New York	349,251	162,422	186,829	53.5	65.7	62.8	2.9	9.9	14.1	2.8	1.8
3609	District 9, New York	363,918	169,170	194,748	53.5	65.7	62.8	2.9	10.6	11.5	2.9	1.5
3610	District 10, New York	384,348	202,558	181,790	47.3	72.1	66.5	5.6	12.2	4.3	1.8	1.3
3611	District 11, New York	323,173	170,202	152,971	47.3	68.1	64.4	3.7	8.0	14.6	2.5	1.8
3612	District 12, New York	449,491	228,453	221,038	49.2	75.3	70.7	4.6	9.4	4.1	1.5	1.6
3613	District 13, New York	370,918	184,261	186,657	50.3	66.9	65.4	1.6	13.2	9.3	2.0	1.3
3614	District 14, New York	351,101	198,240	152,861	43.5	72.5	68.6	3.9	9.2	8.2	1.5	1.5
3615	District 15, New York	289,011	140,870	148,141	51.3	75.0	74.1	0.9	7.9	8.4	2.3	1.0
3616	District 16, New York	352,738	176,668	176,070	49.9	67.9	63.7	4.2	11.8	9.9	3.1	1.3
3617	District 17, New York	361,090	190,914	170,176	47.1	67.3	61.9	5.5	12.0	9.6	3.4	1.1
3618	District 18, New York	335,488	177,364	158,124	47.1	68.7	64.4	4.3	9.4	9.8	4.7	2.3
3619	District 19, New York	325,528	170,145	155,383	47.7	61.4	57.0	4.4	11.7	9.4	7.9	1.1
3620	District 20, New York	364,936	187,979	176,957	48.5	60.8	58.2	2.6	12.2	8.4	11.6	2.6
3621	District 21, New York	312,500	160,957	151,543	48.5	62.2	59.4	2.8	10.5	9.4	7.6	3.1
3622	District 22, New York	319,370	162,358	157,012	49.2	65.3	62.6	2.7	11.3	8.4	7.8	1.4
3623	District 23, New York	318,308	163,574	154,734	48.6	62.8	60.7	2.1	14.8	8.8	5.8	1.2
3624	District 24, New York	335,712	170,425	165,287	49.2	66.6	64.0	2.6	11.1	7.9	7.4	1.7
3625	District 25, New York	353,810	178,787	175,023	49.5	69.0	66.1	2.9	14.5	7.1	3.7	1.0
3626	District 26, New York	334,536	166,456	168,080	50.2	71.5	69.4	2.1	10.5	7.3	5.2	1.9
3627	District 27, New York	355,711	185,178	170,533	47.9	70.2	66.6	3.6	9.1	7.2	6.8	1.9
3700	**NORTH CAROLINA**	4,550,972	2,366,821	2,184,151	48.0	73.0	69.5	3.5	6.9	5.3	6.7	2.3
3701	District 1, North Carolina	306,077	149,304	156,773	51.2	70.7	68.9	1.8	7.4	5.3	9.1	2.4
3702	District 2, North Carolina	341,450	178,374	163,076	47.8	70.8	67.7	3.1	6.1	5.0	6.8	4.9
3703	District 3, North Carolina	316,554	161,873	154,681	48.9	68.8	65.3	3.5	5.1	5.9	7.1	7.1
3704	District 4, North Carolina	403,882	207,467	196,415	48.6	68.3	65.5	2.9	7.8	4.6	10.7	3.1
3705	District 5, North Carolina	341,477	181,763	159,714	46.8	72.0	68.2	3.8	8.5	5.7	5.5	1.7
3706	District 6, North Carolina	353,041	181,550	171,491	48.6	73.0	69.1	3.9	8.0	5.9	5.8	1.4
3707	District 7, North Carolina	341,093	175,472	165,621	48.6	72.2	68.0	4.3	5.2	6.6	7.8	1.7
3708	District 8, North Carolina	321,128	169,718	151,410	47.1	74.3	71.8	2.5	6.7	6.2	6.3	1.3
3709	District 9, North Carolina	424,009	223,115	200,894	47.4	79.7	74.5	5.2	7.2	4.0	3.4	0.7
3710	District 10, North Carolina	326,871	174,436	152,435	46.6	75.7	72.2	3.5	6.1	5.6	4.7	1.1
3711	District 11, North Carolina	314,754	164,544	150,210	47.7	70.0	66.3	3.7	7.0	5.6	7.2	2.0
3712	District 12, North Carolina	373,371	193,885	179,486	48.1	78.5	76.2	2.3	7.2	4.3	4.1	1.6
3713	District 13, North Carolina	387,265	205,320	181,945	47.0	72.6	68.4	4.1	6.3	5.4	8.3	1.8
3800	**NORTH DAKOTA**	404,589	220,613	183,976	45.5	66.6	63.4	3.3	10.4	6.9	5.1	2.8
3800	District (at Large), North Dakota	404,589	220,613	183,976	45.5	66.6	63.4	3.3	10.4	6.9	5.1	2.8
3900	**OHIO**	5,489,742	2,839,454	2,650,288	48.3	73.6	70.9	2.7	9.1	6.8	3.5	1.8
3901	District 1, Ohio	349,212	176,055	173,157	49.6	73.8	71.0	2.8	10.4	6.3	2.4	2.3
3902	District 2, Ohio	342,538	180,233	162,305	47.4	73.7	71.2	2.4	9.8	5.6	3.1	2.1
3903	District 3, Ohio	377,530	188,998	188,532	49.9	75.4	73.6	1.8	8.0	5.0	5.6	1.7
3904	District 4, Ohio	331,707	175,404	156,303	47.1	76.1	73.7	2.4	8.0	7.1	2.8	1.0
3905	District 5, Ohio	358,570	187,772	170,798	47.6	74.3	72.0	2.3	8.3	7.0	4.3	0.9
3906	District 6, Ohio	296,236	156,977	139,259	47.0	74.5	72.3	2.3	7.6	7.5	3.3	1.6
3907	District 7, Ohio	355,488	186,891	168,597	47.4	74.9	71.8	3.2	7.8	6.8	2.5	1.2

Table F. Congressional Districts—Labor Force, Employment, and Educational Data, 2015—*Continued*

State and District code	State/Congressional district (114th Congress)	Civilian employed population age 16 and older				Class of worker for civilian employed population age 16 and older						
						Private for-profit wage and salary workers			Private not-for-profit wage and salary workers	Government workers		
		Total	Men	Women	Percent women	Total private for-profit wage and salary workers	Employees of private companies	Self-employed in own incorporated business		Local government workers	State government workers	Federal government workers
3908	District 8, Ohio	343,113	179,086	164,027	47.8	75.9	73.3	2.7	8.0	6.6	2.8	1.4
3909	District 9, Ohio	328,828	166,311	162,517	49.4	73.7	71.6	2.1	9.8	7.8	2.4	1.8
3910	District 10, Ohio	330,534	172,955	157,579	47.7	69.8	67.2	2.6	10.1	7.1	2.2	5.4
3911	District 11, Ohio	297,073	139,857	157,216	52.9	68.9	66.4	2.5	14.4	7.9	2.4	2.9
3912	District 12, Ohio	384,798	201,297	183,501	47.7	71.2	68.1	3.0	9.1	6.8	5.7	1.6
3913	District 13, Ohio	327,699	168,242	159,457	48.7	77.4	74.9	2.5	7.7	5.6	3.4	1.1
3914	District 14, Ohio	356,586	186,265	170,321	47.8	74.4	70.2	4.3	9.6	7.4	2.0	1.3
3915	District 15, Ohio	351,267	184,655	166,612	47.4	70.1	67.4	2.6	9.2	7.0	7.3	1.4
3916	District 16, Ohio	358,563	188,456	170,107	47.4	72.9	69.4	3.6	9.2	7.2	2.5	1.7
4000	OKLAHOMA	1,753,445	937,290	816,155	46.5	70.9	67.3	3.6	6.7	5.5	6.9	3.8
4001	District 1, Oklahoma	386,901	204,755	182,146	47.1	76.0	72.7	3.3	7.7	4.3	4.2	1.9
4002	District 2, Oklahoma	293,006	153,345	139,661	47.7	67.1	63.9	3.2	6.1	7.2	9.0	3.8
4003	District 3, Oklahoma	337,784	187,408	150,376	44.5	69.3	65.7	3.6	6.0	6.3	8.0	3.7
4004	District 4, Oklahoma	358,028	190,264	167,764	46.9	68.4	64.6	3.8	5.9	5.5	8.2	6.5
4005	District 5, Oklahoma	377,726	201,518	176,208	46.6	72.5	68.2	4.3	7.5	4.5	5.7	3.6
4100	OREGON	1,881,255	987,483	893,772	47.5	69.3	65.3	4.0	9.5	6.2	5.3	2.1
4101	District 1, Oregon	405,530	219,474	186,056	45.9	74.5	70.9	3.6	8.9	4.9	3.6	1.6
4102	District 2, Oregon	340,080	178,255	161,825	47.6	67.4	62.7	4.6	7.4	6.7	5.1	3.0
4103	District 3, Oregon	425,585	220,285	205,300	48.2	67.7	63.9	3.8	12.1	6.2	4.1	2.1
4104	District 4, Oregon	333,045	172,123	160,922	48.3	65.0	61.5	3.5	10.1	7.3	7.4	2.7
4105	District 5, Oregon	377,015	197,346	179,669	47.7	71.0	66.5	4.5	8.5	6.2	6.9	1.4
4200	PENNSYLVANIA	6,109,670	3,168,719	2,940,951	48.1	72.9	70.2	2.7	11.7	5.1	3.2	2.0
4201	District 1, Pennsylvania	326,260	162,223	164,037	50.3	71.9	70.0	1.9	13.2	5.0	1.9	3.6
4202	District 2, Pennsylvania	308,561	142,686	165,875	53.8	64.0	61.6	2.5	18.0	7.1	3.0	3.0
4203	District 3, Pennsylvania	318,536	168,414	150,122	47.1	73.4	70.6	2.8	10.8	4.3	3.7	1.7
4204	District 4, Pennsylvania	362,468	187,837	174,631	48.2	73.8	71.3	2.4	9.4	4.5	4.6	2.8
4205	District 5, Pennsylvania	312,074	164,580	147,494	47.3	71.1	68.5	2.6	11.5	4.9	6.0	1.3
4206	District 6, Pennsylvania	376,302	200,243	176,059	46.8	78.6	75.4	3.2	8.6	4.9	2.1	1.1
4207	District 7, Pennsylvania	358,822	187,016	171,806	47.9	72.7	68.4	4.3	12.3	5.5	2.2	2.0
4208	District 8, Pennsylvania	369,562	192,290	177,272	48.0	78.3	74.2	4.1	9.0	4.4	1.9	1.4
4209	District 9, Pennsylvania	307,268	163,538	143,730	46.8	72.0	69.9	2.1	9.6	5.7	5.4	1.8
4210	District 10, Pennsylvania	324,478	173,684	150,794	46.5	71.1	68.3	2.8	10.6	5.1	4.9	1.8
4211	District 11, Pennsylvania	334,635	173,534	161,101	48.1	70.8	68.7	2.1	10.8	4.9	5.9	2.9
4212	District 12, Pennsylvania	336,244	177,184	159,060	47.3	73.0	69.8	3.1	13.4	4.2	2.7	1.6
4213	District 13, Pennsylvania	346,948	175,581	171,367	49.4	73.3	70.2	3.1	12.4	6.0	1.4	2.3
4214	District 14, Pennsylvania	346,222	176,858	169,364	48.9	69.1	67.3	1.8	17.5	5.1	2.0	1.9
4215	District 15, Pennsylvania	362,203	188,851	173,352	47.9	73.6	71.6	2.1	12.5	4.7	2.7	1.6
4216	District 16, Pennsylvania	354,352	187,861	166,491	47.0	74.0	71.7	2.3	10.5	4.9	3.1	1.2
4217	District 17, Pennsylvania	311,664	160,977	150,687	48.3	73.8	71.5	2.4	9.9	5.7	3.7	2.3
4218	District 18, Pennsylvania	353,071	185,362	167,709	47.5	75.4	72.2	3.2	11.5	4.8	2.1	1.2
4400	RHODE ISLAND	524,975	264,722	260,253	49.6	72.3	69.1	3.1	10.8	6.0	3.8	2.2
4401	District 1, Rhode Island	258,155	130,480	127,675	49.5	72.8	69.7	3.1	11.7	5.4	2.7	2.3
4402	District 2, Rhode Island	266,820	134,242	132,578	49.7	71.7	68.6	3.1	9.9	6.7	5.0	2.1
4500	SOUTH CAROLINA	2,165,702	1,115,610	1,050,092	48.5	73.6	70.6	3.0	6.2	5.4	7.1	2.2
4501	District 1, South Carolina	359,564	188,296	171,268	47.6	72.3	68.3	3.9	6.2	6.0	5.6	4.4
4502	District 2, South Carolina	326,896	169,015	157,881	48.3	70.5	67.0	3.5	5.8	5.2	10.5	2.8
4503	District 3, South Carolina	289,207	151,509	137,698	47.6	73.9	71.2	2.7	6.8	4.7	7.4	1.2
4504	District 4, South Carolina	328,178	172,695	155,483	47.4	76.2	73.1	3.2	8.4	4.5	4.4	0.9
4505	District 5, South Carolina	301,854	155,079	146,775	48.6	76.4	74.0	2.4	5.6	5.1	6.0	2.1
4506	District 6, South Carolina	271,557	131,182	140,375	51.7	71.3	69.2	2.1	5.0	6.3	9.9	2.3
4507	District 7, South Carolina	288,446	147,834	140,612	48.7	74.8	71.8	3.0	5.3	6.2	6.2	0.9
4600	SOUTH DAKOTA	436,852	231,215	205,637	47.1	65.8	61.6	4.2	11.4	6.8	4.5	2.9
4600	District (at Large), South Dakota	436,852	231,215	205,637	47.1	65.8	61.6	4.2	11.4	6.8	4.5	2.9
4700	TENNESSEE	2,998,814	1,562,444	1,436,370	47.9	72.1	70.1	2.1	7.6	7.0	4.1	2.4
4701	District 1, Tennessee	304,982	156,998	147,984	48.5	71.9	69.9	2.1	7.2	6.5	5.2	1.8
4702	District 2, Tennessee	345,344	181,330	164,014	47.5	72.1	69.7	2.4	8.2	6.6	4.5	2.6
4703	District 3, Tennessee	311,006	163,108	147,898	47.6	71.1	68.9	2.2	7.8	7.0	4.0	3.4
4704	District 4, Tennessee	348,816	189,173	159,643	45.8	74.0	72.6	1.4	5.6	6.9	4.4	2.2
4705	District 5, Tennessee	399,640	206,972	192,668	48.2	71.1	69.2	1.9	11.9	5.0	4.0	1.5
4706	District 6, Tennessee	334,390	178,173	156,217	46.7	72.0	69.8	2.2	6.0	8.0	3.6	1.5
4707	District 7, Tennessee	318,570	167,231	151,339	47.5	69.6	67.3	2.3	6.6	8.0	4.4	3.4
4708	District 8, Tennessee	318,226	164,969	153,257	48.2	72.2	69.7	2.5	6.9	8.4	4.2	2.3
4709	District 9, Tennessee	317,840	154,490	163,350	51.4	75.4	73.8	1.6	7.3	7.5	2.4	2.7
4800	TEXAS	12,693,901	6,906,093	5,787,808	45.6	75.0	72.2	2.7	5.5	6.3	4.5	2.1
4801	District 1, Texas	298,086	156,185	141,901	47.6	71.5	68.7	2.8	7.9	5.6	7.3	1.3
4802	District 2, Texas	398,374	220,314	178,060	44.7	78.1	75.0	3.1	6.0	5.3	3.0	1.5
4803	District 3, Texas	425,586	231,109	194,477	45.7	80.2	76.2	4.0	4.6	5.3	3.0	1.2
4804	District 4, Texas	310,435	169,901	140,534	45.3	73.1	70.3	2.8	4.7	6.9	5.2	2.4
4805	District 5, Texas	327,931	179,024	148,907	45.4	73.5	71.2	2.2	6.1	6.4	4.8	1.2

Table F. Congressional Districts—Labor Force, Employment, and Educational Data, 2015—*Continued*

| | | Civilian employed population age 16 and older | | | | Class of worker for civilian employed population age 16 and older | | | | | | |
| | | | | | | Private for-profit wage and salary workers | | | Private not-for-profit wage and salary workers | Government workers | | |
State and District code	State/Congressional district (114th Congress)	Total	Men	Women	Percent women	Total private for-profit wage and salary workers	Employees of private companies	Self-employed in own incorporated business	Private not-for-profit wage and salary workers	Local government workers	State government workers	Federal government workers
4806	District 6, Texas	371,688	190,286	181,402	48.8	76.9	73.6	3.2	5.2	7.0	3.4	2.2
4807	District 7, Texas	396,313	225,021	171,292	43.2	79.1	75.3	3.9	5.8	3.7	3.2	1.3
4808	District 8, Texas	349,821	197,421	152,400	43.6	74.6	71.6	3.0	5.1	5.7	5.5	1.1
4809	District 9, Texas	387,105	205,658	181,447	46.9	76.8	74.8	2.0	5.1	5.1	4.4	1.2
4810	District 10, Texas	399,263	220,144	179,119	44.9	74.7	71.3	3.4	6.0	6.1	5.5	1.2
4811	District 11, Texas	343,800	195,497	148,303	43.1	75.0	71.8	3.2	4.7	6.9	4.2	1.2
4812	District 12, Texas	378,604	200,690	177,914	47.0	74.8	72.0	2.8	7.9	7.1	2.5	2.1
4813	District 13, Texas	314,910	172,757	142,153	45.1	71.5	69.0	2.5	6.2	7.0	5.2	1.9
4814	District 14, Texas	325,917	177,945	147,972	45.4	75.8	74.1	1.8	4.9	6.4	5.9	1.7
4815	District 15, Texas	300,991	161,284	139,707	46.4	69.6	67.2	2.3	3.9	6.3	6.5	2.9
4816	District 16, Texas	307,397	164,830	142,567	46.4	67.1	65.4	1.6	5.1	9.5	5.3	6.4
4817	District 17, Texas	357,797	192,259	165,538	46.3	68.5	66.7	1.8	6.9	7.2	9.8	1.7
4818	District 18, Texas	352,050	186,281	165,769	47.1	78.7	76.9	1.8	4.5	5.4	3.2	1.1
4819	District 19, Texas	321,858	175,260	146,598	45.5	71.4	68.8	2.6	6.7	6.9	6.5	1.5
4820	District 20, Texas	349,049	179,247	169,802	48.6	75.3	74.2	1.1	6.1	5.4	4.3	4.4
4821	District 21, Texas	389,033	206,772	182,261	46.8	70.6	66.1	4.5	7.1	5.8	4.7	3.7
4822	District 22, Texas	422,996	230,075	192,921	45.6	76.9	73.5	3.5	6.4	6.6	3.8	1.1
4823	District 23, Texas	302,764	169,555	133,209	44.0	71.5	69.0	2.5	4.3	7.6	5.6	4.5
4824	District 24, Texas	434,492	235,008	199,484	45.9	81.6	78.6	3.0	4.8	4.1	1.8	1.4
4825	District 25, Texas	347,478	186,122	161,356	46.4	68.6	64.0	4.6	6.2	6.8	6.8	3.3
4826	District 26, Texas	428,261	228,440	199,821	46.7	76.8	73.9	2.9	5.4	6.9	3.9	1.4
4827	District 27, Texas	328,831	177,304	151,527	46.1	72.8	70.7	2.1	4.7	7.5	4.6	2.8
4828	District 28, Texas	288,375	157,231	131,144	45.5	71.5	68.7	2.8	4.5	7.1	5.5	4.0
4829	District 29, Texas	331,514	197,678	133,836	40.4	80.5	79.6	0.9	4.3	5.8	1.5	0.9
4830	District 30, Texas	336,394	171,403	164,991	49.0	78.1	76.5	1.6	5.1	6.4	2.9	2.2
4831	District 31, Texas	373,095	199,183	173,912	46.6	70.1	67.7	2.4	6.8	7.0	5.7	4.2
4832	District 32, Texas	396,159	214,128	182,031	45.9	78.8	74.2	4.6	6.3	5.1	2.4	1.4
4833	District 33, Texas	323,813	192,809	131,004	40.5	83.1	81.8	1.3	3.0	5.3	1.9	0.9
4834	District 34, Texas	261,555	140,571	120,984	46.3	70.8	67.7	3.1	3.8	9.5	5.4	2.1
4835	District 35, Texas	393,642	217,787	175,855	44.7	75.8	73.9	1.9	5.4	4.9	5.2	3.3
4836	District 36, Texas	318,524	180,914	137,610	43.2	75.5	73.3	2.2	4.6	7.7	5.3	1.6
4900	**UTAH**	1,414,337	793,605	620,732	43.9	73.4	69.2	4.2	7.6	5.6	5.5	3.1
4901	District 1, Utah	344,237	193,907	150,330	43.7	71.5	66.9	4.5	7.2	6.3	5.0	6.2
4902	District 2, Utah	349,028	193,311	155,717	44.6	71.9	67.9	4.0	7.2	5.7	7.0	2.7
4903	District 3, Utah	347,062	199,714	147,348	42.5	72.8	67.8	4.9	9.6	5.8	5.2	1.3
4904	District 4, Utah	374,010	206,673	167,337	44.7	77.0	73.6	3.4	6.6	4.7	5.0	2.1
5000	**VERMONT**	327,841	165,927	161,914	49.4	62.0	57.7	4.4	15.5	6.7	4.7	2.3
5000	District (at Large), Vermont	327,841	165,927	161,914	49.4	62.0	57.7	4.4	15.5	6.7	4.7	2.3
5100	**VIRGINIA**	4,081,600	2,106,890	1,974,710	48.4	67.2	63.9	3.3	7.9	7.5	4.1	8.2
5101	District 1, Virginia	363,121	189,988	173,133	47.7	63.8	60.1	3.8	6.7	8.6	3.7	12.9
5102	District 2, Virginia	349,128	176,995	172,133	49.3	68.1	65.0	3.1	6.9	8.1	3.3	9.5
5103	District 3, Virginia	332,455	160,026	172,429	51.9	67.9	66.0	2.0	7.7	7.9	5.3	7.0
5104	District 4, Virginia	346,106	172,765	173,341	50.1	68.8	65.8	2.9	6.2	8.8	4.4	7.5
5105	District 5, Virginia	339,381	173,862	165,519	48.8	66.3	62.7	3.7	9.1	7.7	8.0	2.2
5106	District 6, Virginia	344,319	180,338	163,981	47.6	71.2	68.0	3.3	9.2	7.5	5.0	2.1
5107	District 7, Virginia	402,412	203,815	198,597	49.4	71.1	67.2	3.9	7.4	8.2	4.6	3.3
5108	District 8, Virginia	466,344	244,242	222,102	47.6	59.9	57.2	2.7	10.8	4.7	1.7	17.4
5109	District 9, Virginia	298,321	157,440	140,881	47.2	69.4	66.9	2.5	6.1	8.1	8.3	2.2
5110	District 10, Virginia	421,067	225,691	195,376	46.4	70.4	65.6	4.8	6.9	6.9	1.7	8.4
5111	District 11, Virginia	418,946	221,728	197,218	47.1	64.6	61.0	3.6	8.8	6.6	1.8	13.1
5300	**WASHINGTON**	3,397,974	1,831,920	1,566,054	46.1	70.3	66.3	4.0	7.9	6.4	6.2	3.1
5301	District 1, Washington	357,023	195,919	161,104	45.1	75.5	70.6	4.9	6.1	6.4	4.6	1.5
5302	District 2, Washington	350,147	187,647	162,500	46.4	73.0	69.6	3.4	6.8	6.0	5.1	2.7
5303	District 3, Washington	314,789	171,117	143,672	45.6	72.3	67.9	4.4	7.2	6.8	5.3	2.4
5304	District 4, Washington	306,145	169,707	136,438	44.6	72.6	69.3	3.3	6.6	6.6	6.0	2.4
5305	District 5, Washington	297,034	155,429	141,605	47.7	65.7	61.1	4.5	9.6	6.3	8.8	2.6
5306	District 6, Washington	286,382	150,558	135,824	47.4	61.5	57.6	3.9	7.5	8.7	7.1	8.2
5307	District 7, Washington	437,018	233,763	203,255	46.5	68.2	63.7	4.5	11.2	5.4	7.0	1.5
5308	District 8, Washington	356,802	194,118	162,684	45.6	73.3	69.5	3.8	6.8	6.6	4.9	2.5
5309	District 9, Washington	375,293	207,065	168,228	44.8	74.2	70.8	3.4	8.9	5.1	3.9	2.1
5310	District 10, Washington	317,341	166,597	150,744	47.5	64.4	61.1	3.2	7.2	7.4	9.9	6.2
5400	**WEST VIRGINIA**	738,438	390,899	347,539	47.1	69.2	67.2	2.0	7.8	7.0	8.0	3.5
5401	District 1, West Virginia	259,834	139,695	120,139	46.2	70.8	68.8	2.0	8.0	5.7	8.4	3.0
5402	District 2, West Virginia	272,207	145,019	127,188	46.7	67.4	65.5	1.9	8.0	7.6	7.9	4.3
5403	District 3, West Virginia	206,397	106,185	100,212	48.6	69.5	67.5	2.0	7.4	7.8	7.6	3.1
5500	**WISCONSIN**	2,959,655	1,533,690	1,425,965	48.2	73.6	70.6	3.0	8.9	6.5	4.4	1.3
5501	District 1, Wisconsin	362,648	185,509	177,139	48.8	76.2	72.8	3.4	8.6	6.3	2.8	1.4
5502	District 2, Wisconsin	412,895	212,789	200,106	48.5	67.8	64.3	3.5	9.1	6.5	10.4	1.4
5503	District 3, Wisconsin	366,647	190,345	176,302	48.1	70.6	67.6	3.0	8.5	6.9	5.8	1.8
5504	District 4, Wisconsin	335,807	161,279	174,528	52.0	74.2	72.6	1.6	9.9	6.9	3.3	1.5

Table F. Congressional Districts—Labor Force, Employment, and Educational Data, 2015—*Continued*

State and District code	State/Congressional district (114th Congress)	Civilian employed population age 16 and older				Class of worker for civilian employed population age 16 and older						
						Private for-profit wage and salary workers				Government workers		
		Total	Men	Women	Percent women	Total private for-profit wage and salary workers	Employees of private companies	Self-employed in own incorporated business	Private not-for-profit wage and salary workers	Local government workers	State government workers	Federal government workers
5505	District 5, Wisconsin	386,753	205,748	181,005	46.8	77.0	74.1	2.9	10.2	5.6	2.2	1.0
5506	District 6, Wisconsin	363,318	192,055	171,263	47.1	76.0	72.4	3.6	8.1	5.9	3.4	1.1
5507	District 7, Wisconsin	350,818	185,687	165,131	47.1	71.4	68.0	3.4	9.0	7.3	3.3	1.4
5508	District 8, Wisconsin	380,769	200,278	180,491	47.4	76.1	73.4	2.7	7.7	6.5	3.2	0.8
5600	**WYOMING**	295,328	159,435	135,893	46.0	67.1	62.8	4.3	6.5	10.4	7.3	2.3
5600	District (at Large), Wyoming	295,328	159,435	135,893	46.0	67.1	62.8	4.3	6.5	10.4	7.3	2.3

Table F. Congressional Districts—Labor Force, Employment, and Educational Data, 2015

| State and District code | State/Congressional district (114th Congress) | Class of worker for civilian employed population age 16 and older | | Occupation for employed population age 16 and older | | | | | Industry for employed population age 16 and older | | |
		Self-employed in own not incorporated business	Unpaid family workers	Management, business, science, and arts occupations	Service occupations	Sales and office occupations:	Natural resources, construction, and maintenance occupations	Production, transportation, and material moving occupations:	Agriculture, forestry, fishing and hunting, and mining	Construction	Manufacturing
0000	**UNITED STATES**	5.9	0.2	37.1	18.0	23.6	9.0	12.3	1.9	6.4	10.3
0100	**ALABAMA**	4.9	0.2	33.9	16.3	23.7	9.7	16.4	1.7	6.3	14.3
0101	District 1 , Alabama	4.8	0.1	32.8	18.5	24.2	10.2	14.3	1.2	7.5	12.3
0102	District 2, Alabama	5.1	0.2	32.0	16.8	24.6	9.7	17.0	2.5	5.8	13.2
0103	District 3, Alabama	5.2	0.1	32.5	15.7	22.9	10.1	18.8	1.4	6.0	18.1
0104	District 4, Alabama	6.1	0.3	27.6	15.0	22.3	12.2	22.9	2.9	7.3	19.7
0105	District 5, Alabama	4.8	0.3	39.6	14.8	23.3	8.9	13.4	0.7	6.1	14.0
0106	District 6, Alabama	4.4	0.2	41.6	13.5	25.1	8.9	10.9	1.4	6.4	9.5
0107	District 7, Alabama	4.0	0.2	29.2	20.3	23.2	8.2	19.1	1.9	4.7	14.1
0200	**ALASKA**	6.3	0.3	36.4	17.7	22.6	12.1	11.1	5.3	7.2	3.2
0200	District (at Large), Alaska	6.3	0.3	36.4	17.7	22.6	12.1	11.1	5.3	7.2	3.2
0400	ARIZONA	5.8	0.2	34.6	19.8	26.2	9.1	10.2	1.5	6.6	7.1
0401	District 1, Arizona	4.7	0.5	32.1	23.2	23.4	10.3	11.0	3.9	6.2	7.2
0402	District 2, Arizona	6.1	0.2	38.4	20.9	24.8	7.9	7.9	1.3	6.6	5.4
0403	District 3, Arizona	5.1	0.1	24.7	22.6	26.6	12.8	13.3	3.6	7.8	5.7
0404	District 4, Arizona	6.8	0.1	29.4	23.0	25.2	10.3	12.1	2.7	6.1	6.2
0405	District 5, Arizona	5.7	0.2	40.9	16.2	27.3	7.1	8.5	0.6	5.8	10.0
0406	District 6, Arizona	6.5	0.3	44.1	16.9	26.3	5.9	6.9	0.4	4.6	5.9
0407	District 7, Arizona	6.2	0.1	20.6	23.7	25.4	14.5	15.7	0.7	10.9	8.9
0408	District 8, Arizona	6.0	0.1	35.7	16.8	30.0	8.3	9.2	0.6	6.7	6.0
0409	District 9, Arizona	5.1	0.2	40.1	18.1	26.0	6.8	9.1	0.6	5.3	7.6
0500	**ARKANSAS**	6.3	0.2	32.1	16.7	23.7	11.0	16.5	3.2	6.4	13.9
0501	District 1, Arkansas	7.0	0.3	27.9	18.4	22.3	12.2	19.2	4.8	6.2	15.8
0502	District 2, Arkansas	5.4	0.3	37.2	15.6	25.5	9.1	12.5	1.4	5.9	8.4
0503	District 3, Arkansas	6.2	0.2	33.9	15.1	24.8	10.1	16.2	2.5	6.0	15.9
0504	District 4, Arkansas	6.8	0.1	28.1	18.4	21.6	12.9	19.0	4.7	7.7	16.3
0600	**CALIFORNIA**	8.2	0.2	37.7	18.7	22.9	9.4	11.2	2.5	6.2	9.5
0601	District 1, California	11.3	0.3	32.7	23.1	24.1	10.5	9.6	4.6	6.7	6.1
0602	District 2, California	14.2	0.7	42.3	17.8	22.9	10.1	6.9	3.3	7.0	6.2
0603	District 3, California	7.0	0.3	33.4	20.0	21.7	12.8	12.1	5.9	7.0	7.2
0604	District 4, California	9.8	0.2	41.8	18.6	23.6	9.3	6.8	1.5	7.9	6.6
0605	District 5, California	9.0	0.1	34.2	21.1	22.1	11.3	11.2	3.3	7.8	9.2
0606	District 6, California	6.1	0.1	34.3	21.6	25.5	8.6	9.9	0.6	6.9	4.7
0607	District 7, California	7.0	0.3	42.3	17.1	25.2	6.2	9.2	0.8	5.6	6.7
0608	District 8, California	8.2	0.1	28.5	23.0	22.8	11.8	14.0	1.0	7.7	6.0
0609	District 9, California	5.8	0.1	28.4	18.0	24.0	14.2	15.5	4.6	8.9	8.0
0610	District 10, California	5.9	0.2	27.8	17.5	25.0	13.5	16.2	4.9	7.1	12.1
0611	District 11, California	10.1	0.1	43.8	17.4	22.2	8.4	8.2	1.0	7.6	6.2
0612	District 12, California	8.3	0.2	56.2	15.3	19.5	3.7	5.2	0.3	3.2	5.7
0613	District 13, California	9.9	0.2	48.6	17.3	19.2	5.9	9.0	0.5	5.1	6.1
0614	District 14, California	7.2	0.1	43.6	18.7	23.5	5.9	8.2	0.5	4.8	7.2
0615	District 15, California	5.5	0.2	47.2	14.5	20.9	7.6	9.7	0.5	5.6	11.8
0616	District 16, California	6.3	0.1	21.0	21.5	20.7	20.2	16.4	13.2	6.7	11.0
0617	District 17, California	4.4	0.0	57.6	12.9	17.2	4.8	7.5	0.1	3.0	20.6
0618	District 18, California	8.1	0.1	61.6	12.6	17.1	4.6	4.1	0.5	4.7	14.3
0619	District 19, California	5.8	0.1	39.0	21.0	19.7	9.4	10.9	0.9	7.5	16.4
0620	District 20, California	8.8	0.3	29.5	21.0	19.8	18.7	11.0	14.1	7.0	6.0
0621	District 21, California	5.0	0.1	16.8	19.1	17.4	32.5	14.2	29.4	4.7	6.2
0622	District 22, California	6.1	0.2	33.3	18.9	23.1	13.5	11.2	8.9	4.4	7.3
0623	District 23, California	6.8	0.4	32.9	17.7	21.6	14.8	13.0	9.7	6.6	5.6
0624	District 24, California	9.6	0.2	37.8	20.4	19.9	13.2	8.8	7.0	6.2	7.7
0625	District 25, California	7.5	0.1	39.1	17.3	24.6	9.3	9.7	0.8	6.8	9.9
0626	District 26, California	7.8	0.2	36.7	17.4	22.7	12.1	11.1	6.5	5.9	10.9
0627	District 27, California	7.8	0.2	45.9	16.4	23.8	5.4	8.5	0.3	4.9	8.0
0628	District 28, California	13.0	0.3	49.3	16.4	22.9	4.9	6.6	0.5	3.8	5.4
0629	District 29, California	11.5	0.2	26.1	24.5	22.9	12.3	14.2	0.7	9.0	9.4
0630	District 30, California	11.7	0.2	48.0	16.0	23.6	6.5	6.0	0.5	5.8	6.2
0631	District 31, California	5.6	0.1	29.7	20.1	25.1	8.6	16.6	0.5	6.5	8.5
0632	District 32, California	6.4	0.1	27.4	19.2	26.6	9.2	17.6	0.8	5.9	13.1
0633	District 33, California	12.5	0.1	61.2	9.7	22.8	1.9	4.4	0.4	2.8	8.0
0634	District 34, California	12.6	0.1	29.6	24.9	21.2	8.9	15.4	0.6	7.5	10.5
0635	District 35, California	5.4	0.1	22.1	19.3	25.5	11.1	22.1	0.7	7.9	12.9
0636	District 36, California	9.3	0.1	24.8	26.9	25.7	13.6	9.0	4.0	7.3	4.0
0637	District 37, California	10.2	0.1	41.5	20.3	21.8	6.3	10.1	0.5	5.2	6.0
0638	District 38, California	5.9	0.1	30.1	16.2	29.3	8.7	15.7	0.5	6.1	12.6
0639	District 39, California	8.1	0.2	43.5	14.9	26.1	6.6	8.9	0.5	5.2	12.7
0640	District 40, California	7.3	0.1	16.3	20.2	25.9	10.3	27.4	0.8	7.2	17.5
0641	District 41, California	6.6	0.2	23.8	20.0	23.5	13.7	19.0	1.1	10.8	9.2
0642	District 42, California	7.8	0.3	35.3	17.6	25.4	9.9	11.9	0.9	9.1	11.8
0643	District 43, California	8.7	0.1	30.1	22.2	25.7	7.2	14.8	0.4	5.1	9.6
0644	District 44, California	5.7	0.2	20.3	21.9	23.8	9.8	24.2	0.6	6.5	14.0

Table F. Congressional Districts—Labor Force, Employment, and Educational Data, 2015—*Continued*

State and District code	State/Congressional district (114th Congress)	Class of worker for civilian employed population age 16 and older		Occupation for employed population age 16 and older					Industry for employed population age 16 and older		
		Self-employed in own not incorporated business	Unpaid family workers	Management, business, science, and arts occupations	Service occupations	Sales and office occupations:	Natural resources, construction, and maintenance occupations	Production, transportation, and material moving occupations:	Agriculture, forestry, fishing and hunting, and mining	Construction	Manufacturing
0645	District 45, California	7.5	0.2	53.8	12.6	23.8	3.6	6.3	0.3	4.3	12.8
0646	District 46, California	5.9	0.1	22.5	24.4	22.8	11.8	18.5	0.8	8.7	14.5
0647	District 47, California	7.6	0.1	36.8	19.3	23.3	7.7	13.0	0.5	5.6	11.9
0648	District 48, California	10.1	0.2	46.1	15.6	24.9	5.3	8.2	0.9	4.8	12.2
0649	District 49, California	10.8	0.1	43.6	17.4	23.6	6.9	8.5	1.2	5.8	11.1
0650	District 50, California	7.9	0.3	32.9	22.3	24.2	10.9	9.7	1.6	8.7	8.6
0651	District 51, California	7.2	0.0	20.4	29.4	25.3	12.5	12.3	2.5	7.4	6.8
0652	District 52, California	7.6	0.1	55.1	15.3	21.2	3.9	4.4	0.3	3.3	10.6
0653	District 53, California	7.3	0.2	42.1	19.7	23.5	6.8	7.9	0.3	4.1	7.1
0800	**COLORADO**	6.3	0.2	41.2	16.8	23.7	9.4	8.9	2.6	7.9	6.9
0801	District 1, Colorado	5.7	0.1	45.7	16.4	21.3	8.5	8.0	1.3	8.3	5.5
0802	District 2, Colorado	6.9	0.1	48.3	16.5	21.4	6.9	6.9	2.0	6.4	8.6
0803	District 3, Colorado	8.3	0.3	34.2	19.4	23.3	12.8	10.4	5.2	9.8	4.8
0804	District 4, Colorado	6.3	0.2	39.8	15.9	23.2	10.8	10.3	5.8	7.9	8.6
0805	District 5, Colorado	5.8	0.3	38.6	18.7	25.3	9.4	8.0	1.0	7.0	5.6
0806	District 6, Colorado	5.2	0.2	42.1	15.0	26.1	7.9	8.9	1.7	7.0	6.2
0807	District 7, Colorado	5.9	0.2	37.1	16.8	25.7	10.1	10.3	1.6	9.2	8.6
0900	**CONNECTICUT**	6.2	0.2	42.4	17.0	23.6	7.6	9.4	0.4	6.0	10.4
0901	District 1, Connecticut	4.4	0.2	43.5	16.1	23.9	6.2	10.3	0.3	5.1	10.6
0902	District 2, Connecticut	5.7	0.3	40.4	18.9	22.7	8.6	9.4	1.0	6.0	12.1
0903	District 3, Connecticut	5.9	0.1	40.9	16.6	24.8	7.4	10.4	0.1	5.9	10.9
0904	District 4, Connecticut	8.3	0.3	47.1	16.8	23.0	7.2	5.9	0.2	6.1	6.5
0905	District 5, Connecticut	6.7	0.3	40.2	16.8	23.4	8.7	10.9	0.4	6.7	12.0
1000	**DELAWARE** District (at Large),	4.1	0.1	40.0	18.9	23.3	8.7	9.1	1.1	6.4	8.1
1000	Delaware	4.1	0.1	40.0	18.9	23.3	8.7	9.1	1.1	6.4	8.1
1100	**DISTRICT OF COLUMBIA** Delegate District (at Large),	4.7	0.1	61.8	15.7	17.0	2.1	3.4	0.1	2.6	1.4
1198	District of Columbia	4.7	0.1	61.8	15.7	17.0	2.1	3.4	0.1	2.6	1.4
1200	**FLORIDA**	6.0	0.2	34.5	20.1	27.0	9.2	9.3	1.1	7.1	5.1
1201	District 1, Florida	7.3	0.1	33.8	21.4	26.0	9.3	9.5	1.0	7.0	4.3
1202	District 2, Florida	5.7	0.2	35.9	22.1	26.1	8.1	7.8	1.5	5.5	3.6
1203	District 3, Florida	5.0	0.1	37.4	18.8	24.1	10.3	9.3	2.5	6.5	4.9
1204	District 4, Florida	4.3	0.1	39.5	15.6	27.7	7.4	9.7	0.4	5.1	7.3
1205	District 5, Florida	4.7	0.2	26.1	25.5	25.7	8.9	13.8	1.1	6.4	5.2
1206	District 6, Florida	5.2	0.1	36.8	20.0	25.8	9.2	8.2	1.0	6.8	7.2
1207	District 7, Florida	4.8	0.2	42.3	15.0	29.0	6.4	7.3	0.2	6.0	5.2
1208	District 8, Florida	5.0	0.2	36.2	20.2	26.0	8.4	9.1	1.1	7.0	8.5
1209	District 9, Florida	4.4	0.1	29.9	24.3	27.3	8.0	10.5	0.3	6.0	4.2
1210	District 10, Florida	5.1	0.2	38.7	19.5	26.8	7.0	7.9	0.7	6.5	4.9
1211	District 11, Florida	6.8	0.6	28.9	21.9	27.6	10.1	11.5	2.0	6.6	6.1
1212	District 12, Florida	5.3	0.3	39.2	16.4	28.2	8.1	8.2	0.5	7.1	5.1
1213	District 13, Florida	6.2	0.3	36.4	18.2	28.4	7.8	9.1	0.3	6.2	7.4
1214	District 14, Florida	5.0	0.1	35.7	20.0	26.3	8.8	9.2	0.7	7.3	4.5
1215	District 15, Florida	4.3	0.1	36.4	16.5	28.6	9.5	9.0	1.9	7.4	5.2
1216	District 16, Florida	7.2	0.2	34.7	20.0	26.6	9.5	9.2	0.5	8.0	6.9
1217	District 17, Florida	6.0	0.1	27.8	19.5	26.9	14.2	11.5	5.6	7.8	5.7
1218	District 18, Florida	5.8	0.2	34.1	21.8	27.0	9.8	7.3	1.1	8.6	4.2
1219	District 19, Florida	7.3	0.2	31.5	21.5	27.6	10.9	8.5	0.8	10.8	4.1
1220	District 20, Florida	5.8	0.1	23.7	26.3	27.5	11.0	11.6	1.4	7.6	4.2
1221	District 21, Florida	7.3	0.0	39.1	18.7	27.6	7.6	7.1	0.6	6.2	4.8
1222	District 22, Florida	7.2	0.2	39.5	19.6	24.4	9.4	6.9	0.5	8.2	3.9
1223	District 23, Florida	6.9	0.4	39.6	17.8	27.5	7.1	7.9	0.8	5.9	4.6
1224	District 24, Florida	6.7	0.1	28.6	25.7	26.7	8.2	10.8	0.4	6.0	3.7
1225	District 25, Florida	8.1	0.1	29.6	19.1	26.8	12.1	12.4	2.7	9.1	6.5
1226	District 26, Florida	6.7	0.1	32.5	18.8	30.8	10.4	7.5	1.9	7.2	3.7
1227	District 27, Florida	7.8	0.2	33.3	20.5	24.2	11.8	10.3	0.7	10.1	3.9
1300	**GEORGIA**	5.4	0.2	36.4	16.4	24.3	9.1	13.8	1.1	6.5	10.9
1301	District 1, Georgia	4.4	0.1	32.3	20.2	23.7	10.1	13.6	1.2	6.6	10.0
1302	District 2, Georgia	5.3	0.2	30.5	18.3	23.6	10.6	16.9	2.9	5.7	11.9
1303	District 3, Georgia	4.8	0.1	33.5	15.5	24.2	9.2	17.6	0.9	5.7	13.7
1304	District 4, Georgia	4.2	0.3	33.5	17.1	26.7	8.4	14.3	0.1	6.4	8.8
1305	District 5, Georgia	4.5	0.1	45.1	16.7	22.6	5.0	10.6	0.1	4.1	5.2
1306	District 6, Georgia	6.5	0.1	54.7	11.8	22.2	5.2	6.1	0.4	5.3	7.3
1307	District 7, Georgia	6.3	0.3	41.3	14.4	25.2	9.2	9.8	0.2	8.7	9.4
1308	District 8, Georgia	5.0	0.2	32.5	17.1	23.2	11.2	15.9	3.6	4.9	12.1
1309	District 9, Georgia	7.6	0.2	30.9	16.5	23.7	12.1	16.8	2.2	8.3	15.7
1310	District 10, Georgia	5.4	0.2	33.1	18.2	25.4	9.8	13.5	1.6	6.5	10.0
1311	District 11, Georgia	5.5	0.0	42.2	15.3	25.1	7.5	9.9	0.5	7.3	10.0
1312	District 12, Georgia	5.2	0.2	31.4	16.8	24.8	11.7	15.3	2.4	7.8	11.8

Table F. Congressional Districts—Labor Force, Employment, and Educational Data, 2015—*Continued*

State and District code	State/Congressional district (114th Congress)	Class of worker for civilian employed population age 16 and older — Self-employed in own not incorporated business	Unpaid family workers	Occupation for employed population age 16 and older — Management, business, science, and arts occupations	Service occupations	Sales and office occupations:	Natural resources, construction, and maintenance occupations	Production, transportation, and material moving occupations:	Industry for employed population age 16 and older — Agriculture, forestry, fishing and hunting, and mining	Construction	Manufacturing
1313	District 13, Georgia	6.0	0.1	31.8	18.1	24.7	10.1	15.1	0.5	7.3	7.2
1314	District 14, Georgia	4.9	0.1	27.1	15.2	24.8	10.5	22.5	0.9	6.6	23.0
1500	**HAWAII**	7.2	0.2	33.6	22.9	24.8	10.2	8.5	1.4	7.9	3.0
1501	District 1, Hawaii	6.1	0.2	34.9	22.5	25.3	8.5	8.8	0.4	6.6	3.5
1502	District 2, Hawaii	8.3	0.1	32.3	23.3	24.3	12.0	8.2	2.5	9.3	2.4
1600	**IDAHO**	7.8	0.2	33.7	19.1	23.0	11.4	12.9	5.2	6.6	9.5
1601	District 1, Idaho	7.8	0.2	33.2	18.8	24.4	10.9	12.7	4.1	7.1	10.1
1602	District 2, Idaho	7.7	0.2	34.1	19.4	21.6	11.9	13.1	6.3	6.1	8.9
1700	**ILLINOIS**	4.6	0.1	37.5	17.5	23.7	7.4	14.0	1.1	5.3	12.3
1701	District 1, Illinois	3.7	0.1	34.4	19.7	26.2	6.8	12.9	0.2	5.4	7.2
1702	District 2, Illinois	3.1	0.2	30.7	20.3	25.0	7.6	16.3	0.4	4.5	10.7
1703	District 3, Illinois	3.7	0.2	31.2	18.2	25.2	9.9	15.4	0.3	7.4	10.6
1704	District 4, Illinois	4.6	0.1	25.8	24.3	21.5	8.8	19.5	0.3	6.0	14.9
1705	District 5, Illinois	5.0	0.1	50.0	14.1	22.2	5.1	8.7	0.1	4.7	7.9
1706	District 6, Illinois	4.3	0.1	48.0	12.7	25.1	5.1	9.0	0.2	4.8	13.0
1707	District 7, Illinois	4.3	0.0	46.1	17.3	22.7	3.2	10.7	0.2	2.6	8.1
1708	District 8, Illinois	3.4	0.2	33.6	17.7	25.5	6.6	16.6	0.3	5.5	15.5
1709	District 9, Illinois	6.4	0.2	48.6	15.0	23.0	4.4	9.0	0.2	4.0	8.0
1710	District 10, Illinois	4.4	0.1	41.8	15.9	24.0	6.1	12.2	0.2	4.7	15.3
1711	District 11, Illinois	3.1	0.1	35.5	17.2	24.1	7.2	15.8	0.5	5.7	12.2
1712	District 12, Illinois	5.2	0.2	33.9	18.9	22.9	9.0	15.4	1.9	5.9	11.3
1713	District 13, Illinois	4.3	0.2	39.4	19.8	21.1	7.7	12.0	2.2	5.0	9.9
1714	District 14, Illinois	4.2	0.1	41.0	14.1	25.1	8.6	11.2	0.9	6.9	15.3
1715	District 15, Illinois	6.4	0.1	29.6	18.0	22.3	10.8	19.2	4.9	6.3	15.8
1716	District 16, Illinois	5.3	0.2	30.7	17.8	23.1	9.7	18.7	3.1	6.0	16.5
1717	District 17, Illinois	4.8	0.1	26.4	20.9	23.0	9.4	20.2	1.8	5.7	17.4
1718	District 18, Illinois	5.7	0.1	40.0	15.5	24.8	7.9	11.8	3.2	5.1	11.8
1800	**INDIANA**	4.4	0.2	32.9	16.5	22.8	9.0	18.8	1.5	5.9	19.0
1801	District 1, Indiana	3.7	0.1	31.1	17.5	23.3	9.8	18.4	0.4	6.5	17.1
1802	District 2, Indiana	4.6	0.3	30.1	15.1	21.6	8.6	24.6	1.7	5.0	27.4
1803	District 3, Indiana	5.0	0.2	30.3	15.6	21.4	8.9	23.7	2.0	5.8	25.9
1804	District 4, Indiana	4.2	0.2	33.2	16.1	21.2	9.8	19.7	2.0	5.8	20.0
1805	District 5, Indiana	4.0	0.1	45.0	13.9	25.3	6.0	9.8	0.9	5.0	12.0
1806	District 6, Indiana	5.1	0.3	29.9	17.2	21.9	10.0	20.9	1.9	6.1	22.6
1807	District 7, Indiana	3.1	0.2	29.1	19.1	26.0	8.4	17.5	0.3	6.0	10.9
1808	District 8, Indiana	4.3	0.2	29.7	17.7	21.2	11.0	20.3	2.9	7.0	19.4
1809	District 9, Indiana	5.3	0.1	35.2	17.1	22.8	9.1	15.8	1.2	6.3	17.1
1900	**IOWA**	6.2	0.2	34.4	16.8	22.2	9.5	17.0	3.8	6.3	15.7
1901	District 1, Iowa	6.0	0.3	33.6	16.9	21.9	9.2	18.3	3.7	5.8	18.4
1902	District 2, Iowa	5.8	0.2	33.2	17.9	21.1	9.2	18.6	2.9	6.4	18.0
1903	District 3, Iowa	5.0	0.1	37.6	15.8	24.2	9.2	13.3	2.3	6.9	10.5
1904	District 4, Iowa	8.2	0.3	33.1	16.7	21.5	10.5	18.2	6.4	6.1	16.4
2000	**KANSAS**	6.0	0.2	37.3	17.0	22.1	9.8	13.7	3.4	6.6	12.2
2001	District 1, Kansas	8.1	0.3	32.9	17.9	20.8	12.7	15.6	8.3	6.9	12.2
2002	District 2, Kansas	5.4	0.2	36.2	17.3	21.7	10.2	14.6	2.7	6.7	10.4
2003	District 3, Kansas	5.2	0.1	44.9	14.8	24.0	6.3	10.1	0.6	5.7	8.7
2004	District 4, Kansas	5.3	0.1	34.1	18.1	21.8	10.7	15.3	2.4	7.1	17.9
2100	**KENTUCKY**	5.2	0.1	33.2	16.7	23.8	9.2	17.1	2.5	5.8	14.3
2101	District 1, Kentucky	6.5	0.2	28.1	16.6	23.1	11.3	20.9	4.7	6.3	17.6
2102	District 2, Kentucky	5.9	0.2	28.4	16.7	23.1	10.3	21.5	2.2	6.9	17.7
2103	District 3, Kentucky	4.4	0.1	38.3	15.4	24.2	6.4	15.6	0.6	4.9	11.6
2104	District 4, Kentucky	4.5	0.1	36.7	15.4	24.3	8.4	15.2	1.7	5.3	13.8
2105	District 5, Kentucky	5.6	0.1	29.3	18.4	24.3	12.4	15.6	4.2	6.2	10.5
2106	District 6, Kentucky	4.9	0.1	35.8	18.3	23.5	8.2	14.1	2.9	5.6	14.1
2200	**LOUISIANA**	5.5	0.1	33.7	19.1	23.6	11.8	11.8	4.2	7.9	7.8
2201	District 1, Louisiana	6.5	0.1	36.5	16.8	26.2	11.1	9.4	2.9	8.7	6.1
2202	District 2, Louisiana	5.6	0.0	31.6	23.0	21.7	11.8	11.9	1.7	8.5	6.6
2203	District 3, Louisiana	5.7	0.1	31.7	19.7	23.0	12.6	13.0	8.7	6.7	8.9
2204	District 4, Louisiana	5.6	0.1	31.3	19.4	22.7	13.6	13.0	6.1	7.1	7.8
2205	District 5, Louisiana	5.1	0.1	30.3	21.2	24.1	12.0	12.4	4.3	7.5	6.6
2206	District 6, Louisiana	4.6	0.2	38.9	15.5	23.6	10.3	11.7	2.1	8.6	10.6
2300	**MAINE**	8.9	0.1	36.5	17.8	23.8	10.6	11.3	2.7	7.2	9.4
2301	District 1, Maine	8.3	0.1	39.6	17.3	24.1	9.5	9.6	2.0	6.8	9.4
2302	District 2, Maine	9.6	0.1	33.0	18.3	23.4	11.9	13.3	3.5	7.7	9.3
2400	**MARYLAND**	4.7	0.1	44.7	17.6	21.9	7.7	8.1	0.5	6.8	4.6
2401	District 1, Maryland	5.5	0.1	38.5	17.7	24.0	10.1	9.6	1.5	7.9	7.9
2402	District 2, Maryland	4.4	0.2	40.1	17.4	25.5	6.9	10.1	0.2	5.7	5.8

Table F. Congressional Districts—Labor Force, Employment, and Educational Data, 2015—*Continued*

State and District code	State/Congressional district (114th Congress)	Class of worker for civilian employed population age 16 and older		Occupation for employed population age 16 and older					Industry for employed population age 16 and older		
		Self-employed in own not incorporated business	Unpaid family workers	Management, business, science, and arts occupations	Service occupations	Sales and office occupations:	Natural resources, construction, and maintenance occupations	Production, transportation, and material moving occupations:	Agriculture, forestry, fishing and hunting, and mining	Construction	Manufacturing
2403	District 3, Maryland	4.5	0.1	50.4	15.4	21.2	6.1	6.9	0.1	5.5	4.7
2404	District 4, Maryland	3.6	0.1	38.4	21.2	22.0	9.6	8.8	0.2	8.4	2.2
2405	District 5, Maryland	3.6	0.2	43.9	18.4	21.4	9.1	7.2	0.5	8.2	2.8
2406	District 6, Maryland	5.4	0.1	46.0	17.0	21.1	7.9	8.0	0.7	7.1	5.5
2407	District 7, Maryland	3.9	0.1	45.4	17.4	23.2	4.6	9.4	0.2	4.3	4.7
2408	District 8, Maryland	6.4	0.1	53.7	16.2	17.7	7.1	5.3	0.5	6.5	3.6
2500	**MASSACHUSETTS**	5.9	0.1	44.9	17.8	21.9	6.8	8.7	0.4	5.4	9.0
2501	District 1, Massachusetts	6.1	0.1	35.1	20.9	24.5	7.5	12.0	0.8	4.7	11.1
2502	District 2, Massachusetts	5.6	0.3	42.6	17.5	22.9	6.7	10.3	0.6	4.8	11.0
2503	District 3, Massachusetts	5.4	0.1	43.0	18.5	20.4	7.3	10.8	0.3	5.6	14.1
2504	District 4, Massachusetts	5.8	0.1	52.0	12.3	22.1	6.5	7.1	0.2	5.2	9.1
2505	District 5, Massachusetts	7.1	0.0	54.0	15.5	19.1	5.8	5.6	0.2	5.1	7.7
2506	District 6, Massachusetts	6.4	0.0	45.9	17.0	22.4	6.7	8.0	0.2	6.0	9.7
2507	District 7, Massachusetts	4.0	0.1	45.7	21.5	20.2	4.8	7.8	0.1	3.9	5.3
2508	District 8, Massachusetts	4.2	0.1	47.8	16.6	22.2	6.1	7.3	0.3	5.1	6.1
2509	District 9, Massachusetts	8.7	0.1	35.4	20.3	23.7	10.3	10.3	1.0	8.6	7.9
2600	**MICHIGAN**	4.7	0.2	35.2	18.0	23.0	8.0	15.9	1.2	5.1	18.1
2601	District 1, Michigan	6.8	0.3	31.9	21.4	23.4	10.3	13.0	2.7	6.7	11.2
2602	District 2, Michigan	4.5	0.2	29.8	17.7	22.3	8.0	22.1	1.5	5.2	24.3
2603	District 3, Michigan	4.7	0.1	33.8	16.8	22.7	8.3	18.4	1.7	5.1	19.3
2604	District 4, Michigan	5.9	0.3	31.3	18.8	21.8	10.9	17.2	2.8	6.9	16.7
2605	District 5, Michigan	4.3	0.1	29.3	20.3	24.6	8.5	17.3	0.7	5.5	16.0
2606	District 6, Michigan	5.7	0.2	34.0	17.3	22.3	9.1	17.2	1.9	5.4	21.8
2607	District 7, Michigan	5.4	0.1	32.4	17.9	22.3	9.4	18.1	1.6	5.9	19.8
2608	District 8, Michigan	4.7	0.2	42.3	15.8	24.3	6.9	10.7	0.5	4.6	16.5
2609	District 9, Michigan	3.9	0.1	37.6	17.0	23.7	6.3	15.3	0.2	4.4	19.4
2610	District 10, Michigan	4.4	0.2	33.9	17.9	22.5	9.4	16.2	1.6	6.6	21.4
2611	District 11, Michigan	4.3	0.1	49.1	13.6	22.4	5.6	9.4	0.3	4.6	19.5
2612	District 12, Michigan	3.5	0.2	40.3	16.4	22.5	7.1	13.6	0.4	3.8	14.3
2613	District 13, Michigan	3.6	0.1	23.8	22.3	24.4	7.2	22.3	0.4	4.3	17.1
2614	District 14, Michigan	4.2	0.1	37.3	21.2	22.8	4.9	13.7	0.2	3.2	13.4
2700	**MINNESOTA**	5.4	0.2	40.2	16.3	22.3	8.2	13.0	2.2	6.1	13.4
2701	District 1, Minnesota	6.4	0.2	36.8	16.4	20.6	9.6	16.5	4.5	6.0	16.4
2702	District 2, Minnesota	4.2	0.1	40.5	15.4	23.5	8.0	12.7	1.3	6.1	12.9
2703	District 3, Minnesota	5.0	0.1	47.8	13.1	25.4	4.7	8.9	0.5	4.4	14.4
2704	District 4, Minnesota	4.0	0.1	45.2	17.1	21.7	4.9	11.1	0.3	4.1	12.6
2705	District 5, Minnesota	4.6	0.1	47.4	17.0	20.8	4.9	9.9	0.4	4.1	9.6
2706	District 6, Minnesota	4.9	0.2	36.3	15.7	23.4	10.6	14.1	1.4	8.6	15.0
2707	District 7, Minnesota	8.2	0.3	33.0	16.7	20.5	11.9	17.9	6.9	7.5	16.0
2708	District 8, Minnesota	6.3	0.2	31.8	19.6	22.5	12.0	14.2	3.0	8.8	10.6
2800	**MISSISSIPPI**	5.1	0.1	30.8	17.6	23.6	10.8	17.3	2.9	6.9	13.6
2801	District 1, Mississippi	4.8	0.1	29.3	15.0	24.6	9.2	22.0	1.9	5.9	18.1
2802	District 2, Mississippi	4.6	0.0	27.6	20.8	23.2	8.8	19.5	3.6	5.7	13.9
2803	District 3, Mississippi	5.1	0.3	35.5	16.6	22.5	11.1	14.3	3.7	6.9	11.6
2804	District 4, Mississippi	5.8	0.1	30.2	18.5	24.0	13.7	13.7	2.5	8.9	10.8
2900	**MISSOURI**	5.5	0.2	35.4	17.6	24.4	9.0	13.6	1.8	6.4	11.5
2901	District 1, Missouri	4.0	0.2	36.6	21.0	24.3	5.4	12.8	0.4	3.9	9.2
2902	District 2, Missouri	4.6	0.2	48.0	13.2	26.0	5.6	7.2	0.5	5.1	9.9
2903	District 3, Missouri	5.4	0.2	32.3	16.8	24.4	11.3	15.1	1.7	8.7	14.3
2904	District 4, Missouri	7.2	0.3	34.4	16.8	24.0	10.3	14.4	2.9	7.0	11.2
2905	District 5, Missouri	3.9	0.1	33.1	19.0	25.5	8.1	14.3	0.7	6.4	10.0
2906	District 6, Missouri	6.2	0.3	35.3	16.8	23.5	9.9	14.5	2.9	6.3	12.7
2907	District 7, Missouri	6.5	0.2	32.1	18.5	25.2	9.6	14.6	1.6	7.0	11.5
2908	District 8, Missouri	6.3	0.2	29.0	19.2	22.0	12.5	17.3	4.1	7.2	14.0
3000	**MONTANA**	9.1	0.5	38.1	18.7	21.3	13.7	8.2	7.0	9.3	4.1
3000	District (at Large), Montana	9.1	0.5	38.1	18.7	21.3	13.7	8.2	7.0	9.3	4.1
3100	**NEBRASKA**	6.3	0.2	36.6	16.6	23.5	10.1	13.3	4.5	6.9	10.5
3101	District 1, Nebraska	5.3	0.2	35.7	16.5	23.1	10.7	14.0	3.3	7.4	12.1
3102	District 2, Nebraska	4.1	0.1	41.6	16.3	25.0	7.2	9.9	1.0	6.6	7.9
3103	District 3, Nebraska	9.7	0.3	32.0	17.0	22.1	12.6	16.3	9.5	6.7	11.6
3200	**NEVADA**	5.1	0.1	27.4	27.4	26.2	8.8	10.2	1.6	6.2	4.5
3201	District 1, Nevada	4.6	0.1	17.2	36.4	24.7	9.8	11.9	0.3	7.3	3.5
3202	District 2, Nevada	6.6	0.2	30.2	21.3	26.3	10.4	11.8	4.5	6.4	7.2
3203	District 3, Nevada	5.0	0.1	33.2	26.4	27.1	5.7	7.7	0.3	4.3	4.1
3204	District 4, Nevada	4.3	0.1	27.7	26.1	26.7	9.9	9.5	1.4	7.1	3.1
3300	**NEW HAMPSHIRE**	6.5	0.1	40.1	15.9	23.7	8.5	11.7	0.8	6.6	12.7
3301	District 1, New Hampshire	5.8	0.1	40.1	15.7	24.3	8.3	11.6	0.6	6.2	12.4
3302	District 2, New Hampshire	7.1	0.2	40.1	16.1	23.2	8.7	11.9	1.1	7.1	13.1

Table F. Congressional Districts—Labor Force, Employment, and Educational Data, 2015—*Continued*

State and District code	State/Congressional district (114th Congress)	Class of worker for civilian employed population age 16 and older		Occupation for employed population age 16 and older					Industry for employed population age 16 and older		
		Self-employed in own not incorporated business	Unpaid family workers	Management, business, science, and arts occupations	Service occupations	Sales and office occupations:	Natural resources, construction, and maintenance occupations	Production, transportation, and material moving occupations:	Agriculture, forestry, fishing and hunting, and mining	Construction	Manufacturing
3400	**NEW JERSEY**	4.9	0.2	41.3	16.6	24.2	7.3	10.6	0.3	5.9	8.0
3401	District 1, New Jersey	4.1	0.2	39.5	17.1	25.6	7.1	10.7	0.2	5.4	7.2
3402	District 2, New Jersey	5.4	0.1	33.7	21.6	22.6	10.7	11.4	1.7	7.8	7.3
3403	District 3, New Jersey	4.9	0.4	39.3	16.8	26.0	7.7	10.1	0.4	6.5	6.1
3404	District 4, New Jersey	4.4	0.1	41.5	16.5	26.4	7.2	8.4	0.3	6.4	6.9
3405	District 5, New Jersey	5.7	0.2	46.8	12.6	25.3	7.2	8.0	0.4	6.1	7.3
3406	District 6, New Jersey	4.4	0.2	41.6	16.0	23.9	7.5	11.0	0.2	5.5	7.9
3407	District 7, New Jersey	5.1	0.1	50.0	12.7	24.3	6.0	7.0	0.6	5.1	10.3
3408	District 8, New Jersey	4.9	0.0	34.0	19.5	21.9	8.4	16.3	0.0	7.1	8.4
3409	District 9, New Jersey	4.7	0.2	35.6	16.4	24.1	8.0	15.9	0.0	6.1	10.8
3410	District 10, New Jersey	4.5	0.1	32.2	23.2	23.5	6.4	14.7	0.1	4.5	6.4
3411	District 11, New Jersey	5.5	0.2	52.4	12.9	24.2	5.0	5.6	0.1	4.6	8.1
3412	District 12, New Jersey	4.6	0.1	46.9	14.9	23.2	6.4	8.7	0.1	5.9	8.9
3500	**NEW MEXICO**	6.3	0.2	34.5	21.5	24.0	11.1	8.9	4.2	7.3	3.6
3501	District 1, New Mexico	5.7	0.1	39.0	20.8	23.5	9.5	7.2	1.2	7.4	3.7
3502	District 2, New Mexico	6.0	0.3	27.6	22.5	24.5	14.1	11.4	8.0	7.8	3.7
3503	District 3, New Mexico	7.3	0.1	36.1	21.2	24.0	10.1	8.5	4.0	6.6	3.4
3600	**NEW YORK**	5.9	0.1	39.9	20.2	23.3	7.3	9.4	0.6	5.6	6.1
3601	District 1, New York	5.0	0.1	40.0	17.7	24.5	9.8	8.1	0.6	8.3	5.8
3602	District 2, New York	3.0	0.1	34.7	18.2	26.9	9.9	10.3	0.2	6.9	7.7
3603	District 3, New York	5.6	0.2	50.5	13.0	24.3	6.0	6.3	0.2	6.0	5.3
3604	District 4, New York	5.9	0.2	42.4	17.1	25.4	6.8	8.3	0.2	5.6	4.1
3605	District 5, New York	5.5	0.1	27.6	27.0	24.5	9.4	11.5	0.1	7.3	3.5
3606	District 6, New York	6.2	0.2	38.8	21.7	23.6	6.8	9.2	0.2	6.2	4.1
3607	District 7, New York	5.8	0.1	38.5	23.6	21.5	7.2	9.3	0.1	6.1	4.6
3608	District 8, New York	5.6	0.1	38.0	24.6	22.4	5.5	9.4	0.2	3.8	2.6
3609	District 9, New York	7.7	0.1	41.4	25.6	20.0	5.5	7.6	0.0	4.4	2.2
3610	District 10, New York	8.3	0.1	59.4	12.3	20.4	3.4	4.4	0.2	3.4	3.3
3611	District 11, New York	5.1	0.0	40.4	18.5	23.7	9.0	8.4	0.1	7.6	3.0
3612	District 12, New York	8.0	0.1	67.0	9.5	18.7	2.1	2.7	0.0	1.6	3.0
3613	District 13, New York	7.2	0.1	34.8	29.0	21.6	5.3	9.3	0.0	4.2	3.1
3614	District 14, New York	7.2	0.1	29.4	27.5	22.0	8.4	12.7	0.3	7.1	4.9
3615	District 15, New York	5.2	0.2	19.6	38.3	23.0	7.5	11.6	0.1	5.2	2.9
3616	District 16, New York	5.8	0.2	41.6	21.5	23.3	6.5	7.0	0.2	5.6	3.4
3617	District 17, New York	6.4	0.1	46.7	18.1	22.4	6.8	6.0	0.1	6.0	4.9
3618	District 18, New York	5.0	0.1	39.2	18.7	25.4	7.0	9.6	0.5	6.2	7.4
3619	District 19, New York	8.1	0.4	36.5	18.9	22.8	10.7	11.0	2.1	8.0	7.3
3620	District 20, New York	4.3	0.1	42.8	17.7	25.2	6.3	7.9	0.3	5.0	6.9
3621	District 21, New York	7.0	0.2	31.4	20.9	23.7	10.4	13.6	2.3	7.0	9.3
3622	District 22, New York	5.6	0.1	34.3	19.1	24.5	8.8	13.2	1.5	5.5	11.2
3623	District 23, New York	6.3	0.3	35.2	20.3	21.3	9.0	14.2	2.8	5.6	13.7
3624	District 24, New York	5.1	0.1	38.5	17.5	24.8	8.3	10.9	1.4	5.9	9.5
3625	District 25, New York	4.5	0.1	41.0	17.6	24.5	6.3	10.6	0.3	4.6	10.5
3626	District 26, New York	3.6	0.1	36.5	19.7	26.6	5.7	11.6	0.1	4.1	9.6
3627	District 27, New York	4.9	0.0	37.1	16.9	23.7	10.1	12.1	1.7	7.0	13.0
3700	**NORTH CAROLINA**	5.7	0.2	36.6	17.1	23.0	9.8	13.5	1.2	7.2	12.5
3701	District 1, North Carolina	5.0	0.2	30.2	21.4	21.2	10.0	17.2	2.0	6.3	14.4
3702	District 2, North Carolina	6.2	0.1	39.4	15.5	22.0	9.4	13.6	1.3	6.6	13.1
3703	District 3, North Carolina	5.8	0.2	31.5	21.1	25.2	11.2	11.1	1.9	7.3	8.8
3704	District 4, North Carolina	5.3	0.1	42.6	17.7	22.7	8.1	8.9	0.6	6.3	6.9
3705	District 5, North Carolina	6.4	0.1	34.4	17.2	23.1	9.2	16.1	1.2	7.1	16.2
3706	District 6, North Carolina	5.8	0.2	38.4	15.8	23.4	10.1	12.3	1.0	7.1	13.5
3707	District 7, North Carolina	6.3	0.1	33.5	17.0	23.7	12.5	13.4	2.6	9.4	11.3
3708	District 8, North Carolina	5.1	0.1	30.3	17.4	21.3	12.7	18.3	1.5	9.5	16.1
3709	District 9, North Carolina	4.8	0.2	48.1	12.3	25.6	6.2	7.7	0.3	5.2	9.5
3710	District 10, North Carolina	6.7	0.2	31.2	17.9	22.1	9.3	19.5	0.7	5.9	19.5
3711	District 11, North Carolina	8.0	0.3	32.9	17.6	20.7	12.3	16.4	1.8	8.4	15.1
3712	District 12, North Carolina	4.1	0.1	30.8	20.5	23.1	10.2	15.4	0.4	8.6	10.0
3713	District 13, North Carolina	5.5	0.1	45.4	13.5	23.5	8.4	9.2	1.2	6.9	11.1
3800	**NORTH DAKOTA**	7.9	0.2	35.3	16.9	21.9	13.5	12.5	9.5	8.0	6.8
3800	District (at Large), North Dakota	7.9	0.2	35.3	16.9	21.9	13.5	12.5	9.5	8.0	6.8
3900	**OHIO**	5.1	0.1	35.7	17.3	23.3	7.5	16.1	1.1	5.0	15.5
3901	District 1, Ohio	4.7	0.1	41.6	16.9	24.1	5.8	11.7	0.4	4.9	12.2
3902	District 2, Ohio	5.7	0.1	38.6	16.3	23.8	7.6	13.7	1.0	5.1	14.7
3903	District 3, Ohio	4.4	0.1	33.2	19.2	26.5	6.2	14.8	0.2	4.4	7.2
3904	District 4, Ohio	4.8	0.2	28.0	16.2	20.5	8.5	26.7	1.7	5.0	26.6
3905	District 5, Ohio	5.1	0.1	33.8	15.4	20.3	8.8	21.7	1.8	5.4	23.1
3906	District 6, Ohio	5.3	0.2	27.8	18.6	23.5	11.4	18.7	3.3	6.1	14.4

Table F. Congressional Districts—Labor Force, Employment, and Educational Data, 2015—*Continued*

State and District code	State/Congressional district (114th Congress)	Class of worker for civilian employed population age 16 and older		Occupation for employed population age 16 and older					Industry for employed population age 16 and older		
		Self-employed in own not incorporated business	Unpaid family workers	Management, business, science, and arts occupations	Service occupations	Sales and office occupations:	Natural resources, construction, and maintenance occupations	Production, transportation, and material moving occupations:	Agriculture, forestry, fishing and hunting, and mining	Construction	Manufacturing
3907	District 7, Ohio	6.6	0.2	30.1	17.5	22.8	10.0	19.6	2.8	6.1	19.3
3908	District 8, Ohio	5.1	0.1	34.5	17.4	22.1	8.6	17.5	1.2	5.5	18.8
3909	District 9, Ohio	4.5	0.1	30.1	20.8	23.8	7.5	17.7	0.6	4.9	15.4
3910	District 10, Ohio	5.3	0.1	37.9	18.0	22.9	7.1	14.0	0.5	5.0	12.9
3911	District 11, Ohio	3.5	0.1	36.7	21.8	23.3	4.4	13.8	0.1	3.1	11.6
3912	District 12, Ohio	5.6	0.1	46.6	14.4	23.5	5.4	10.1	0.6	4.4	10.7
3913	District 13, Ohio	4.7	0.1	29.9	19.7	24.9	7.2	18.3	0.6	4.6	17.3
3914	District 14, Ohio	5.1	0.1	40.0	14.6	24.4	7.0	14.0	0.7	4.9	18.5
3915	District 15, Ohio	4.8	0.2	40.7	16.7	22.0	7.8	12.8	1.1	5.6	10.0
3916	District 16, Ohio	6.1	0.3	39.3	14.6	24.5	7.4	14.2	0.9	5.1	16.2
4000	**OKLAHOMA**	6.0	0.2	33.6	17.6	24.1	11.7	12.9	5.0	7.3	9.5
4001	District 1, Oklahoma	5.7	0.2	36.9	16.1	25.7	9.5	11.8	2.3	6.7	11.6
4002	District 2, Oklahoma	6.5	0.3	28.2	19.4	23.2	12.8	16.4	5.1	7.2	12.0
4003	District 3, Oklahoma	6.5	0.2	30.5	17.2	23.2	14.1	14.9	9.5	7.2	9.2
4004	District 4, Oklahoma	5.4	0.1	36.2	17.2	23.4	11.5	11.8	5.1	6.2	8.1
4005	District 5, Oklahoma	6.1	0.1	34.6	18.6	24.8	11.3	10.7	3.7	9.1	7.3
4100	**OREGON**	7.4	0.2	37.7	18.7	22.7	8.9	11.9	3.5	5.7	11.3
4101	District 1, Oregon	6.3	0.1	43.3	17.5	22.7	6.7	9.9	2.1	4.6	16.5
4102	District 2, Oregon	10.1	0.3	32.1	19.5	23.3	11.5	13.6	6.0	6.6	9.3
4103	District 3, Oregon	7.7	0.1	42.6	19.1	21.0	6.4	10.9	1.6	4.9	8.9
4104	District 4, Oregon	7.2	0.3	35.1	20.0	21.5	9.7	13.7	3.9	5.8	10.7
4105	District 5, Oregon	6.0	0.1	33.8	17.9	24.9	11.2	12.2	4.5	7.1	10.8
4200	**PENNSYLVANIA**	4.9	0.2	37.4	17.5	23.2	8.2	13.7	1.5	5.7	12.1
4201	District 1, Pennsylvania	4.3	0.1	35.2	23.3	22.5	6.0	12.9	0.4	4.4	7.3
4202	District 2, Pennsylvania	4.8	0.1	45.4	22.1	21.2	3.1	8.1	0.2	2.4	4.8
4203	District 3, Pennsylvania	5.9	0.2	32.3	19.4	22.3	9.0	17.0	1.9	5.7	16.3
4204	District 4, Pennsylvania	4.7	0.2	34.4	15.9	24.1	8.4	17.2	0.7	6.4	14.5
4205	District 5, Pennsylvania	5.0	0.3	33.9	17.6	20.3	10.4	17.8	3.0	5.7	16.6
4206	District 6, Pennsylvania	4.5	0.1	46.6	14.4	21.9	6.2	10.9	0.9	5.2	14.1
4207	District 7, Pennsylvania	5.2	0.1	47.2	13.8	23.2	7.9	7.9	1.7	6.5	9.7
4208	District 8, Pennsylvania	4.8	0.1	43.1	14.1	24.4	8.4	10.0	0.7	7.2	12.1
4209	District 9, Pennsylvania	5.3	0.2	29.5	18.1	23.4	11.2	17.8	3.5	6.9	13.3
4210	District 10, Pennsylvania	6.3	0.2	30.1	18.2	22.5	12.1	17.0	3.1	7.5	13.8
4211	District 11, Pennsylvania	4.7	0.1	32.6	18.1	24.6	8.0	16.6	1.4	5.2	12.2
4212	District 12, Pennsylvania	5.0	0.2	41.2	15.3	22.7	8.2	12.6	1.3	5.5	11.6
4213	District 13, Pennsylvania	4.5	0.1	38.5	18.8	23.5	7.3	11.9	0.1	5.3	10.1
4214	District 14, Pennsylvania	4.2	0.1	40.0	20.2	23.8	6.2	9.9	0.9	4.6	7.7
4215	District 15, Pennsylvania	4.8	0.1	35.2	17.7	24.0	7.0	16.1	0.8	5.1	13.7
4216	District 16, Pennsylvania	6.0	0.3	32.1	17.7	22.0	10.3	17.9	3.1	6.8	15.9
4217	District 17, Pennsylvania	4.3	0.2	31.8	17.5	25.3	8.5	16.9	1.1	5.0	13.9
4218	District 18, Pennsylvania	4.9	0.1	40.9	15.3	24.8	8.8	10.2	2.1	6.3	10.7
4400	**RHODE ISLAND**	4.8	0.1	38.2	18.9	24.4	7.2	11.3	0.4	5.2	11.4
4401	District 1, Rhode Island	5.1	0.1	38.7	18.6	24.3	6.7	11.6	0.6	5.1	10.3
4402	District 2, Rhode Island	4.6	0.1	37.7	19.1	24.6	7.6	11.0	0.3	5.3	12.5
4500	**SOUTH CAROLINA**	5.4	0.1	33.8	17.9	24.6	9.0	14.7	1.0	6.4	13.9
4501	District 1, South Carolina	5.4	0.1	40.0	17.4	24.2	8.6	9.8	0.5	6.2	8.2
4502	District 2, South Carolina	5.1	0.1	40.5	15.0	25.4	8.2	10.9	0.9	6.6	10.8
4503	District 3, South Carolina	5.8	0.2	30.2	17.3	23.4	10.0	19.1	1.3	6.0	22.9
4504	District 4, South Carolina	5.3	0.2	34.6	17.4	23.5	7.9	16.6	0.6	5.8	18.2
4505	District 5, South Carolina	4.6	0.1	30.9	15.5	26.0	9.1	18.5	0.9	6.3	16.5
4506	District 6, South Carolina	5.0	0.1	27.4	22.8	23.8	10.2	15.7	1.4	6.8	10.5
4507	District 7, South Carolina	6.5	0.1	30.4	20.8	26.1	9.2	13.4	1.7	7.4	11.3
4600	**SOUTH DAKOTA**	8.3	0.3	33.8	17.9	23.0	11.1	14.2	6.7	7.4	10.4
4600	District (at Large), South Dakota	8.3	0.3	33.8	17.9	23.0	11.1	14.2	6.7	7.4	10.4
4700	**TENNESSEE**	6.6	0.1	34.3	17.0	24.1	8.9	15.7	1.0	6.0	13.0
4701	District 1, Tennessee	7.1	0.2	30.5	20.4	23.2	10.1	15.7	1.2	6.9	15.8
4702	District 2, Tennessee	5.9	0.1	36.7	16.2	25.8	8.5	12.8	0.8	5.2	10.3
4703	District 3, Tennessee	6.7	0.1	32.8	17.7	24.2	8.3	17.1	0.8	5.4	15.7
4704	District 4, Tennessee	6.7	0.1	31.2	15.8	24.2	9.9	18.9	1.2	6.7	17.2
4705	District 5, Tennessee	6.3	0.1	39.2	16.5	23.9	8.4	12.0	0.2	5.9	8.1
4706	District 6, Tennessee	8.7	0.2	32.7	16.9	23.7	9.7	17.0	1.8	6.8	14.9
4707	District 7, Tennessee	7.9	0.2	37.9	15.4	23.6	8.6	14.5	1.3	6.3	14.2
4708	District 8, Tennessee	5.8	0.2	37.6	15.3	23.7	8.8	14.7	1.4	5.0	14.2
4709	District 9, Tennessee	4.5	0.1	28.9	19.4	24.5	8.1	19.1	0.1	5.4	8.1
4800	**TEXAS**	6.5	0.2	35.3	17.4	24.2	10.9	12.2	3.4	8.1	8.7
4801	District 1, Texas	6.2	0.2	30.4	18.5	23.2	12.7	15.1	5.8	7.0	9.9
4802	District 2, Texas	6.0	0.2	43.3	14.1	23.7	7.9	10.8	4.9	8.1	9.7
4803	District 3, Texas	5.6	0.1	53.3	12.6	23.8	4.5	5.8	0.8	4.6	9.2
4804	District 4, Texas	7.3	0.3	32.3	17.1	25.0	11.1	14.5	3.1	8.5	12.8

Table F. Congressional Districts—Labor Force, Employment, and Educational Data, 2015—*Continued*

State and District code	State/Congressional district (114th Congress)	Class of worker for civilian employed population age 16 and older — Self-employed in own not incorporated business	Unpaid family workers	Occupation for employed population age 16 and older — Management, business, science, and arts occupations	Service occupations	Sales and office occupations:	Natural resources, construction, and maintenance occupations	Production, transportation, and material moving occupations:	Industry for employed population age 16 and older — Agriculture, forestry, fishing and hunting, and mining	Construction	Manufacturing
4805	District 5, Texas	7.9	0.1	28.0	18.9	25.9	13.2	14.0	2.3	9.6	8.9
4806	District 6, Texas	5.3	0.0	36.6	12.9	28.3	8.3	13.9	1.2	5.8	10.3
4807	District 7, Texas	6.8	0.1	46.8	15.2	22.3	7.4	8.3	5.8	6.2	8.5
4808	District 8, Texas	7.9	0.1	39.9	14.9	23.5	10.8	10.9	6.5	7.8	9.4
4809	District 9, Texas	7.4	0.1	27.9	23.1	24.4	11.4	13.3	2.0	9.7	5.4
4810	District 10, Texas	6.2	0.2	41.4	15.4	23.5	9.4	10.2	3.8	8.1	9.8
4811	District 11, Texas	7.7	0.3	29.6	16.8	23.8	15.5	14.2	13.4	8.1	6.6
4812	District 12, Texas	5.5	0.1	37.1	15.1	26.1	9.3	12.4	2.9	6.0	11.3
4813	District 13, Texas	8.0	0.2	30.4	18.4	22.5	14.5	14.2	7.8	7.7	8.7
4814	District 14, Texas	5.2	0.1	36.6	17.1	21.6	11.8	12.9	1.8	10.9	12.5
4815	District 15, Texas	10.5	0.3	27.9	21.9	24.9	12.6	12.8	4.7	6.6	6.9
4816	District 16, Texas	6.4	0.1	30.4	20.2	28.3	8.4	12.6	1.1	4.5	6.5
4817	District 17, Texas	5.8	0.1	38.9	15.7	23.8	10.4	11.2	3.2	6.8	8.6
4818	District 18, Texas	6.9	0.1	28.2	19.5	23.3	12.3	16.6	2.8	10.3	9.3
4819	District 19, Texas	6.6	0.3	30.9	19.0	24.0	13.0	13.1	7.5	7.3	6.0
4820	District 20, Texas	4.5	0.0	32.7	20.5	25.7	11.1	10.1	1.2	8.1	6.1
4821	District 21, Texas	7.8	0.4	45.8	15.7	25.3	6.6	6.6	1.9	5.9	5.6
4822	District 22, Texas	5.2	0.0	49.8	11.8	23.0	6.7	8.8	5.4	5.7	10.2
4823	District 23, Texas	6.4	0.1	29.4	19.9	24.2	13.7	12.8	6.5	8.5	6.1
4824	District 24, Texas	6.1	0.2	44.4	13.9	25.4	6.9	9.5	1.1	5.3	7.9
4825	District 25, Texas	7.9	0.4	42.8	14.9	22.5	9.3	10.5	2.7	7.3	8.7
4826	District 26, Texas	5.6	0.1	44.7	14.3	26.0	6.4	8.5	1.1	5.2	8.0
4827	District 27, Texas	7.5	0.1	28.7	20.1	23.0	14.3	13.9	5.1	9.8	9.1
4828	District 28, Texas	7.2	0.1	27.4	21.9	25.3	12.8	12.6	4.3	8.5	3.7
4829	District 29, Texas	6.9	0.1	16.1	19.8	21.8	21.6	20.6	1.3	18.6	11.6
4830	District 30, Texas	5.1	0.2	28.7	17.9	25.3	11.6	16.4	0.6	10.2	8.6
4831	District 31, Texas	6.2	0.1	41.5	16.1	24.9	7.8	9.6	1.2	6.3	9.7
4832	District 32, Texas	5.9	0.2	43.5	15.1	25.0	7.7	8.6	1.2	6.8	8.2
4833	District 33, Texas	5.7	0.1	15.8	21.5	20.2	20.3	22.1	1.1	17.4	12.3
4834	District 34, Texas	8.2	0.2	26.2	25.6	23.8	12.9	11.5	6.0	7.5	5.3
4835	District 35, Texas	5.4	0.0	25.7	24.2	25.2	13.9	11.1	1.0	11.1	5.4
4836	District 36, Texas	5.1	0.1	31.0	15.8	22.0	15.4	15.8	3.8	11.2	14.8
4900	**UTAH**	4.6	0.2	36.7	15.4	26.1	8.6	13.2	2.0	6.8	11.3
4901	District 1, Utah	3.7	0.2	35.2	14.2	25.2	9.0	16.5	3.2	6.4	14.3
4902	District 2, Utah	5.4	0.1	35.1	16.6	25.9	9.0	13.3	2.2	6.4	10.9
4903	District 3, Utah	5.1	0.2	41.3	15.9	25.4	7.5	9.9	1.2	6.5	8.4
4904	District 4, Utah	4.2	0.3	35.4	14.9	27.8	9.0	13.0	1.4	7.6	11.7
5000	**VERMONT**	8.6	0.2	41.1	17.1	21.3	9.4	11.0	2.4	7.0	11.0
5000	District (at Large), Vermont	8.6	0.2	41.1	17.1	21.3	9.4	11.0	2.4	7.0	11.0
5100	**VIRGINIA**	5.0	0.1	43.0	16.8	22.1	8.5	9.6	1.0	6.5	7.2
5101	District 1, Virginia	4.0	0.1	43.3	16.7	22.6	9.4	8.1	0.6	7.8	6.1
5102	District 2, Virginia	4.2	0.1	38.9	17.6	24.3	10.3	8.9	1.0	6.9	8.5
5103	District 3, Virginia	3.9	0.3	31.1	21.4	25.5	8.4	13.6	0.3	5.2	8.8
5104	District 4, Virginia	4.4	0.1	36.7	16.8	24.2	10.7	11.7	1.1	7.4	9.7
5105	District 5, Virginia	6.5	0.2	36.9	17.8	22.3	10.2	12.7	1.9	7.5	9.2
5106	District 6, Virginia	4.9	0.1	33.8	18.7	23.3	10.8	13.4	1.7	7.2	11.2
5107	District 7, Virginia	5.1	0.2	44.5	14.2	25.4	7.9	8.1	1.0	6.5	5.6
5108	District 8, Virginia	5.4	0.1	56.1	16.2	16.7	6.5	4.5	0.2	6.4	2.3
5109	District 9, Virginia	5.6	0.2	33.9	16.4	22.8	9.8	17.1	3.2	5.1	15.1
5110	District 10, Virginia	5.5	0.2	53.1	13.8	19.9	6.3	6.9	0.8	6.1	4.8
5111	District 11, Virginia	4.9	0.2	53.3	16.8	19.3	5.5	5.2	0.2	5.2	2.4
5300	**WASHINGTON**	5.9	0.2	39.8	16.9	21.8	9.9	11.5	2.7	6.5	10.3
5301	District 1, Washington	5.6	0.2	47.4	12.6	21.5	8.7	9.8	1.7	6.9	13.3
5302	District 2, Washington	6.2	0.1	34.3	18.3	24.0	11.6	11.8	1.3	6.6	15.0
5303	District 3, Washington	5.8	0.2	32.4	17.4	24.1	11.5	14.6	1.7	8.7	11.6
5304	District 4, Washington	5.7	0.1	30.0	17.2	17.6	19.7	15.5	14.9	6.3	8.8
5305	District 5, Washington	6.8	0.2	36.6	19.0	24.3	8.3	11.8	2.8	5.5	8.9
5306	District 6, Washington	6.7	0.2	34.7	20.8	22.5	11.1	10.9	1.8	7.0	9.4
5307	District 7, Washington	6.5	0.2	57.8	14.1	17.9	4.4	5.7	0.3	4.2	6.6
5308	District 8, Washington	5.6	0.3	38.8	14.8	24.1	9.8	12.4	2.1	7.4	11.3
5309	District 9, Washington	5.5	0.2	42.8	18.1	19.9	6.9	12.3	0.5	5.7	10.3
5310	District 10, Washington	4.8	0.2	34.9	18.9	24.1	9.9	12.2	1.4	7.3	7.9
5400	**WEST VIRGINIA**	4.5	0.1	33.5	19.8	23.4	11.1	12.3	4.2	6.3	7.4
5401	District 1, West Virginia	4.2	0.0	33.3	19.3	24.0	11.4	11.9	4.3	6.4	7.8
5402	District 2, West Virginia	4.7	0.1	35.3	18.8	23.1	10.3	12.6	2.8	6.6	7.7
5403	District 3, West Virginia	4.5	0.1	31.2	21.7	22.9	11.7	12.4	5.8	5.8	6.6
5500	**WISCONSIN**	5.1	0.2	35.2	16.9	22.4	8.6	16.9	2.4	5.6	18.4
5501	District 1, Wisconsin	4.5	0.1	34.3	16.6	23.1	9.1	17.0	1.2	6.4	19.4
5502	District 2, Wisconsin	4.6	0.2	44.3	16.3	21.5	7.2	10.7	2.1	5.0	11.3
5503	District 3, Wisconsin	6.1	0.3	32.3	17.6	22.4	9.9	17.8	4.4	5.4	15.8

Table F. Congressional Districts—Labor Force, Employment, and Educational Data, 2015—*Continued*

State and District code	State/Congressional district (114th Congress)	Class of worker for civilian employed population age 16 and older		Occupation for employed population age 16 and older					Industry for employed population age 16 and older		
		Self-employed in own not incorporated business	Unpaid family workers	Management, business, science, and arts occupations	Service occupations	Sales and office occupations:	Natural resources, construction, and maintenance occupations	Production, transportation, and material moving occupations:	Agriculture, forestry, fishing and hunting, and mining	Construction	Manufacturing
5504	District 4, Wisconsin	4.0	0.1	34.2	22.0	21.8	6.2	15.9	0.5	4.2	14.6
5505	District 5, Wisconsin	4.0	0.1	40.1	15.0	23.7	7.0	14.2	1.1	5.1	20.3
5506	District 6, Wisconsin	5.2	0.3	31.9	16.8	21.6	8.4	21.3	2.8	5.2	24.9
5507	District 7, Wisconsin	7.3	0.3	31.0	16.3	21.9	11.2	19.6	4.6	6.7	19.2
5508	District 8, Wisconsin	5.5	0.2	32.3	15.2	23.1	10.2	19.2	2.3	7.1	22.5
5600	**WYOMING**	6.2	0.2	31.5	17.4	22.1	15.8	13.2	12.9	7.3	4.1
	District (at Large),										
5600	Wyoming	6.2	0.2	31.5	17.4	22.1	15.8	13.2	12.9	7.3	4.1

Table F. Congressional Districts—Labor Force, Employment, and Educational Data, 2015

State and District code	State/Congressional district (114th Congress)	Industry for employed population age 16 and older								
		Wholesale trade	Retail trade	Transportation and warehousing, and utilities	Information	Finance and insurance, and real estate and rental and leasing	Professional, scientific, and management, and administrative and waste management services	Educational services, and health care and social assistance	Arts, entertainment, and recreation, and accommodation and food services	Other services, except public administration
0000	**UNITED STATES**	2.7	11.5	5.1	2.1	6.5	11.3	22.9	9.8	4.9
0100	**ALABAMA**	2.5	11.8	5.3	1.7	5.5	9.6	22.5	8.4	5.2
0101	District 1 , Alabama	2.7	13.2	5.2	1.7	4.8	9.3	23.9	9.5	5.1
0102	District 2, Alabama	2.4	13.0	6.1	1.2	5.0	8.6	21.0	8.6	4.7
0103	District 3, Alabama	2.4	11.6	4.7	1.8	5.4	8.5	22.2	8.0	4.3
0104	District 4, Alabama	2.4	12.2	6.0	1.2	4.4	6.0	20.8	8.0	5.3
0105	District 5, Alabama	2.2	11.6	3.7	1.7	4.1	14.3	20.9	8.5	5.4
0106	District 6, Alabama	3.3	10.8	6.2	2.0	9.1	11.1	23.5	6.7	6.1
0107	District 7, Alabama	2.1	10.5	5.3	1.9	4.8	8.5	25.5	9.7	5.3
0200	**ALASKA**	2.0	11.0	7.6	1.9	3.6	8.6	23.4	9.7	4.7
0200	District (at Large), Alaska	2.0	11.0	7.6	1.9	3.6	8.6	23.4	9.7	4.7
0400	ARIZONA	2.3	12.5	5.0	1.9	8.2	12.2	21.7	11.2	4.7
0401	District 1, Arizona	1.3	11.9	4.7	1.5	4.6	7.7	25.0	13.0	3.9
0402	District 2, Arizona	1.5	12.7	3.3	1.5	5.2	13.5	25.5	11.3	4.8
0403	District 3, Arizona	2.6	13.4	6.2	1.3	5.4	10.4	20.4	11.9	4.2
0404	District 4, Arizona	2.0	14.2	5.5	1.5	5.5	9.3	21.8	12.9	5.8
0405	District 5, Arizona	2.5	12.5	5.3	2.0	10.4	12.5	21.0	8.7	4.9
0406	District 6, Arizona	2.6	10.9	4.0	2.6	12.8	15.4	20.8	12.0	4.7
0407	District 7, Arizona	3.1	12.4	5.4	1.6	6.7	12.6	17.0	11.6	5.5
0408	District 8, Arizona	2.7	13.9	6.1	1.9	10.5	11.0	23.1	8.2	4.6
0409	District 9, Arizona	2.4	11.6	4.7	2.5	10.1	14.9	21.3	12.1	4.2
0500	**ARKANSAS**	2.4	13.8	5.5	1.6	4.5	7.2	24.4	7.7	4.7
0501	District 1, Arkansas	2.8	12.6	5.9	1.5	3.7	5.0	24.7	7.7	4.5
0502	District 2, Arkansas	2.2	13.6	5.2	2.5	5.9	8.5	26.8	8.4	5.1
0503	District 3, Arkansas	2.8	16.2	5.7	1.3	4.8	8.7	22.2	6.9	4.6
0504	District 4, Arkansas	1.7	12.0	5.4	1.2	3.3	6.1	24.0	7.8	4.6
0600	**CALIFORNIA**	2.9	10.8	5.0	2.9	6.0	13.2	20.8	10.5	5.3
0601	District 1, California	1.6	12.4	3.7	2.0	4.8	9.0	24.8	11.9	5.1
0602	District 2, California	3.0	11.2	2.7	2.8	7.1	13.6	22.4	10.1	5.4
0603	District 3, California	1.9	12.0	5.7	1.3	4.5	10.0	23.6	9.4	3.9
0604	District 4, California	2.2	11.9	4.8	2.2	6.5	11.7	21.4	11.3	4.9
0605	District 5, California	3.4	11.2	5.1	1.7	5.9	10.4	21.5	11.5	4.7
0606	District 6, California	2.7	11.9	5.3	1.8	6.5	12.8	21.9	10.6	4.4
0607	District 7, California	2.6	10.5	5.7	1.8	7.7	11.9	22.7	8.0	4.4
0608	District 8, California	2.2	13.4	7.9	1.6	4.2	8.6	22.9	12.6	5.5
0609	District 9, California	3.0	12.0	8.0	1.6	5.3	9.5	21.9	7.6	4.9
0610	District 10, California	4.7	13.7	6.4	1.5	4.0	8.3	20.7	8.3	4.5
0611	District 11, California	2.5	10.5	5.1	2.5	9.0	16.7	20.4	9.1	5.8
0612	District 12, California	1.6	9.6	3.4	7.0	9.4	23.5	17.2	11.3	4.2
0613	District 13, California	2.5	8.6	5.1	3.8	5.4	17.8	24.2	10.8	6.0
0614	District 14, California	2.2	11.0	6.5	3.3	6.4	18.4	19.8	11.7	4.8
0615	District 15, California	2.8	9.3	6.2	3.4	7.2	18.6	19.1	7.3	4.7
0616	District 16, California	2.7	10.5	5.0	0.7	2.9	7.4	21.1	8.8	5.1
0617	District 17, California	2.2	8.0	2.9	5.1	4.7	24.0	16.3	7.2	3.6
0618	District 18, California	1.5	7.4	2.2	6.4	6.3	21.0	21.7	7.7	3.9
0619	District 19, California	2.0	10.3	3.6	2.8	4.1	15.2	18.5	10.4	4.9
0620	District 20, California	3.2	9.9	3.2	1.1	3.4	9.2	20.3	13.1	4.9
0621	District 21, California	2.9	9.7	4.3	0.6	1.9	6.1	16.7	7.1	4.3
0622	District 22, California	3.5	11.5	4.2	1.7	5.1	7.9	24.6	9.3	4.1
0623	District 23, California	2.7	10.9	5.1	1.2	4.5	8.6	23.3	8.6	5.1
0624	District 24, California	2.0	10.2	3.6	1.9	4.5	10.7	23.8	12.7	5.0
0625	District 25, California	2.4	12.0	4.4	4.0	7.5	10.7	21.8	9.3	5.4
0626	District 26, California	2.8	11.1	3.7	2.5	6.5	12.1	18.5	9.8	5.3
0627	District 27, California	3.3	8.9	4.7	3.2	8.4	13.7	24.7	10.8	5.7
0628	District 28, California	2.7	8.8	3.0	9.9	6.8	16.0	19.8	13.7	6.6
0629	District 29, California	2.6	11.4	5.1	4.2	5.0	12.9	18.8	11.4	7.2
0630	District 30, California	2.4	9.6	3.1	7.6	8.2	16.7	21.0	10.9	6.0
0631	District 31, California	3.3	12.8	8.5	1.4	4.9	9.8	24.7	8.5	5.1
0632	District 32, California	4.3	12.3	6.6	2.2	5.3	10.7	20.6	9.6	5.4
0633	District 33, California	3.3	8.4	3.9	7.0	10.2	17.8	21.5	10.4	4.1
0634	District 34, California	2.9	11.2	4.5	3.5	4.5	11.4	17.7	15.6	7.7
0635	District 35, California	4.0	13.1	10.1	1.1	4.4	9.0	17.8	9.5	5.8
0636	District 36, California	2.1	13.8	4.3	1.6	5.9	11.1	20.2	15.5	6.4
0637	District 37, California	1.6	9.6	5.0	6.5	5.9	16.7	21.6	11.8	7.1
0638	District 38, California	5.2	12.8	7.6	1.4	5.2	9.2	21.9	8.4	5.2
0639	District 39, California	5.2	10.6	4.0	2.3	8.5	11.6	22.5	9.3	4.2
0640	District 40, California	6.0	12.4	7.7	1.2	3.8	8.3	15.9	10.7	6.2
0641	District 41, California	2.9	13.8	7.8	1.3	4.0	9.0	21.5	8.9	5.5
0642	District 42, California	3.5	13.5	4.8	1.2	5.9	10.5	19.6	8.6	5.1
0643	District 43, California	2.5	11.1	9.0	3.2	5.5	13.1	19.7	11.6	6.0
0644	District 44, California	4.3	10.6	9.0	1.6	3.9	10.5	19.5	10.3	6.3
0645	District 45, California	3.6	9.0	3.4	2.4	10.7	16.0	20.3	9.1	4.9
0646	District 46, California	3.1	9.8	3.5	1.8	5.7	13.5	16.4	14.5	5.9

Table F. Congressional Districts—Labor Force, Employment, and Educational Data, 2015—Continued

State and District code	State/Congressional district (114th Congress)	Wholesale trade	Retail trade	Transportation and warehousing, and utilities	Information	Finance and insurance, and real estate and rental and leasing	Professional, scientific, and management, and administrative and waste management services	Educational services, and health care and social assistance	Arts, entertainment, and recreation, and accommodation and food services	Other services, except public administration
0647	District 47, California	3.4	9.9	6.0	1.7	6.0	12.1	21.7	11.8	5.7
0648	District 48, California	3.4	10.5	3.2	2.1	10.6	15.3	19.1	10.2	5.3
0649	District 49, California	4.2	11.2	2.9	2.7	6.3	15.3	19.3	11.2	5.2
0650	District 50, California	2.5	11.2	4.2	1.6	5.4	13.3	19.8	12.4	6.2
0651	District 51, California	2.4	12.5	5.3	1.2	3.6	10.9	20.4	14.1	6.8
0652	District 52, California	2.6	8.7	2.7	3.4	6.8	18.2	23.4	11.5	3.9
0653	District 53, California	2.3	9.9	4.6	2.2	6.2	14.7	23.3	12.6	6.0
0800	**COLORADO**	2.6	11.3	4.6	2.9	6.9	13.8	20.7	10.5	5.0
0801	District 1, Colorado	2.9	9.7	4.3	3.6	8.0	17.3	19.5	10.8	5.0
0802	District 2, Colorado	2.1	10.0	2.5	3.0	5.1	15.9	23.8	12.2	4.7
0803	District 3, Colorado	2.3	12.9	4.8	1.4	5.5	9.6	21.2	13.1	4.7
0804	District 4, Colorado	2.8	10.6	5.2	2.8	6.7	12.0	20.0	8.1	5.0
0805	District 5, Colorado	1.7	12.7	4.3	2.4	6.8	13.1	22.0	11.1	5.6
0806	District 6, Colorado	2.6	12.1	5.7	3.9	9.2	14.7	19.7	8.8	4.5
0807	District 7, Colorado	3.5	11.6	5.3	3.2	6.5	12.6	18.5	9.5	5.6
0900	**CONNECTICUT**	2.6	10.9	4.1	2.3	9.3	11.5	26.3	8.1	4.3
0901	District 1, Connecticut	2.6	10.0	4.5	2.5	11.2	10.6	27.0	6.7	4.0
0902	District 2, Connecticut	2.0	11.6	4.1	1.6	7.1	9.5	25.9	11.2	3.5
0903	District 3, Connecticut	2.6	10.5	4.1	2.4	6.9	10.6	29.9	7.4	5.0
0904	District 4, Connecticut	2.7	10.4	3.5	2.9	13.4	15.7	23.0	8.2	4.9
0905	District 5, Connecticut	2.8	12.1	4.1	2.1	7.8	11.2	25.6	6.9	4.3
1000	**DELAWARE** District (at Large),	1.6	12.3	4.0	1.5	9.8	10.1	25.0	10.1	4.5
1000	Delaware	1.6	12.3	4.0	1.5	9.8	10.1	25.0	10.1	4.5
1100	**DISTRICT OF COLUMBIA** Delegate District (at Large),	0.5	5.0	2.7	4.2	6.2	23.0	19.5	9.7	8.8
1198	District of Columbia	0.5	5.0	2.7	4.2	6.2	23.0	19.5	9.7	8.8
1200	**FLORIDA**	2.8	13.1	5.1	1.9	7.9	12.9	20.8	12.6	5.2
1201	District 1, Florida	1.9	14.3	4.7	1.3	7.8	12.2	18.6	12.9	6.4
1202	District 2, Florida	1.6	12.9	3.8	1.7	5.5	10.7	24.6	13.1	4.2
1203	District 3, Florida	2.3	11.9	4.7	1.7	6.3	11.1	28.4	8.7	5.1
1204	District 4, Florida	3.0	12.2	6.2	2.0	12.3	12.0	20.7	9.8	4.6
1205	District 5, Florida	2.4	13.6	6.3	1.9	6.1	11.2	20.1	16.2	5.3
1206	District 6, Florida	2.1	12.9	4.4	1.9	8.5	11.6	21.4	12.3	5.3
1207	District 7, Florida	2.9	12.0	4.3	2.5	10.7	14.9	22.9	11.6	3.8
1208	District 8, Florida	2.1	13.5	4.0	1.7	5.2	13.4	22.2	11.4	5.1
1209	District 9, Florida	2.3	13.9	6.1	1.7	5.1	13.1	18.5	20.8	4.3
1210	District 10, Florida	2.6	11.3	4.1	1.9	8.0	13.4	18.6	21.4	3.5
1211	District 11, Florida	2.5	15.2	5.4	1.4	7.0	10.0	22.6	11.7	4.8
1212	District 12, Florida	3.0	13.0	4.8	2.3	9.5	14.2	22.5	9.8	4.6
1213	District 13, Florida	2.4	14.0	3.4	2.1	9.7	14.6	19.9	11.2	5.5
1214	District 14, Florida	2.7	11.0	5.3	2.2	9.5	14.9	22.6	10.6	5.1
1215	District 15, Florida	3.4	14.1	4.1	2.0	9.6	12.0	21.9	9.4	4.2
1216	District 16, Florida	2.5	13.2	3.5	1.3	7.5	13.0	21.8	12.9	5.5
1217	District 17, Florida	2.8	14.9	5.9	1.4	7.1	10.6	20.2	9.4	5.0
1218	District 18, Florida	2.4	11.9	3.9	1.8	7.2	15.6	20.6	13.2	5.5
1219	District 19, Florida	2.1	15.4	3.6	1.9	8.5	12.7	18.7	13.8	4.8
1220	District 20, Florida	3.0	15.5	5.2	1.9	5.7	12.3	20.6	13.2	5.8
1221	District 21, Florida	3.3	14.3	4.1	2.3	8.6	14.5	21.2	10.7	5.7
1222	District 22, Florida	3.2	12.3	4.5	2.1	9.4	15.6	18.7	13.3	5.4
1223	District 23, Florida	4.0	12.4	5.6	2.5	9.4	14.4	19.3	11.9	5.8
1224	District 24, Florida	2.7	12.4	7.9	2.4	6.4	12.9	21.1	13.6	5.6
1225	District 25, Florida	4.6	12.5	7.9	2.0	6.2	12.2	16.7	10.0	6.9
1226	District 26, Florida	3.0	13.7	6.8	1.9	7.8	11.2	21.5	11.5	5.9
1227	District 27, Florida	4.0	10.2	7.2	2.0	7.2	13.1	19.5	12.1	6.9
1300	**GEORGIA**	2.9	12.0	6.0	2.6	6.0	11.8	20.9	9.2	5.1
1301	District 1, Georgia	1.8	13.5	6.8	1.2	4.6	8.6	21.9	11.8	5.6
1302	District 2, Georgia	2.4	11.4	4.4	1.2	6.8	7.2	25.0	8.3	5.4
1303	District 3, Georgia	3.4	10.5	8.6	2.6	5.0	9.8	21.2	8.5	5.1
1304	District 4, Georgia	2.4	12.4	8.1	3.1	5.6	11.7	22.2	8.9	4.7
1305	District 5, Georgia	2.6	10.1	7.5	3.7	6.3	16.6	23.1	11.1	4.8
1306	District 6, Georgia	3.2	9.5	3.8	4.7	10.7	21.7	16.6	9.4	5.0
1307	District 7, Georgia	3.8	12.4	3.6	3.5	8.2	16.0	15.8	9.8	5.7
1308	District 8, Georgia	2.3	12.8	5.1	1.2	3.9	8.2	22.9	8.2	5.0
1309	District 9, Georgia	3.8	13.1	4.5	1.6	4.9	7.7	20.3	8.3	5.5
1310	District 10, Georgia	3.2	13.9	6.0	1.9	4.3	9.4	23.5	9.8	5.7
1311	District 11, Georgia	2.6	12.2	4.7	3.7	7.5	15.2	19.0	8.6	4.9
1312	District 12, Georgia	2.1	13.0	6.0	1.3	4.1	7.9	25.3	8.2	4.1
1313	District 13, Georgia	3.4	11.6	9.8	2.6	5.5	11.0	20.6	9.7	5.0
1314	District 14, Georgia	3.2	11.6	5.6	1.5	4.1	7.9	19.3	7.3	5.3

Table F. Congressional Districts—Labor Force, Employment, and Educational Data, 2015—*Continued*

State and District code	State/Congressional district (114th Congress)	Wholesale trade	Retail trade	Transportation and warehousing, and utilities	Information	Finance and insurance, and real estate and rental and leasing	Professional, scientific, and management, and administrative and waste management services	Educational services, and health care and social assistance	Arts, entertainment, and recreation, and accommodation and food services	Other services, except public administration
					Industry for employed population age 16 and older					
1500	**HAWAII**	2.6	11.5	5.7	1.7	6.8	9.9	19.6	15.9	4.8
1501	District 1, Hawaii	2.9	11.6	6.1	1.7	6.8	10.0	20.3	15.5	5.0
1502	District 2, Hawaii	2.2	11.4	5.4	1.6	6.9	9.9	18.9	16.4	4.6
1600	**IDAHO**	2.8	11.9	4.9	1.8	5.0	9.9	23.4	9.5	4.8
1601	District 1, Idaho	2.9	12.1	4.8	1.6	5.7	9.3	23.4	8.8	5.1
1602	District 2, Idaho	2.7	11.7	5.0	1.9	4.3	10.6	23.3	10.2	4.4
1700	**ILLINOIS**	3.1	11.0	6.1	1.9	7.3	11.7	22.7	9.2	4.6
1701	District 1, Illinois	2.4	11.1	8.7	1.8	7.7	11.4	26.1	8.2	4.1
1702	District 2, Illinois	1.8	11.2	9.0	1.9	6.7	9.4	27.3	8.2	4.3
1703	District 3, Illinois	3.6	11.1	8.7	1.4	6.8	11.1	20.3	9.3	5.3
1704	District 4, Illinois	3.2	9.6	5.6	1.6	5.2	12.4	17.6	15.2	6.2
1705	District 5, Illinois	2.9	8.9	5.1	2.9	10.5	19.8	20.6	8.4	4.5
1706	District 6, Illinois	4.1	10.1	5.0	2.6	9.6	14.8	20.6	8.4	4.5
1707	District 7, Illinois	2.8	8.3	6.8	2.0	10.1	16.8	25.4	9.1	4.1
1708	District 8, Illinois	3.8	12.0	7.4	1.8	6.2	13.5	17.3	10.3	4.5
1709	District 9, Illinois	2.8	9.8	4.9	2.8	9.2	15.0	25.4	9.7	5.6
1710	District 10, Illinois	4.8	11.9	3.9	1.5	7.8	15.4	19.2	8.2	4.2
1711	District 11, Illinois	3.5	12.4	6.8	2.8	7.0	12.0	20.9	10.0	3.6
1712	District 12, Illinois	2.4	11.4	6.0	1.4	5.7	7.6	26.1	9.6	4.8
1713	District 13, Illinois	2.3	10.3	5.0	1.7	6.4	7.8	28.9	11.3	4.1
1714	District 14, Illinois	4.1	11.9	4.8	1.9	7.4	11.2	20.5	7.6	4.6
1715	District 15, Illinois	2.7	11.7	5.6	1.4	5.1	5.9	25.0	7.3	4.5
1716	District 16, Illinois	2.8	12.8	6.5	1.2	4.6	7.1	23.3	7.9	4.6
1717	District 17, Illinois	2.4	12.8	6.3	1.4	4.2	6.9	23.2	9.0	5.0
1718	District 18, Illinois	3.2	11.2	4.5	1.6	9.8	8.2	24.1	7.3	4.7
1800	**INDIANA**	2.7	11.5	5.1	1.6	5.3	8.3	22.2	9.0	4.5
1801	District 1, Indiana	2.1	12.5	6.4	1.1	4.5	9.2	23.5	9.0	4.4
1802	District 2, Indiana	2.2	10.8	3.9	1.7	4.0	6.4	22.1	7.1	4.6
1803	District 3, Indiana	2.5	11.1	3.9	1.6	6.0	6.4	20.0	7.7	5.1
1804	District 4, Indiana	2.6	10.9	5.6	1.5	4.4	7.3	24.0	8.3	4.5
1805	District 5, Indiana	3.3	10.9	3.7	2.5	8.2	12.6	23.9	8.5	4.9
1806	District 6, Indiana	2.6	11.4	4.4	1.0	4.2	7.0	22.0	9.5	3.7
1807	District 7, Indiana	3.4	13.8	8.0	1.7	5.8	10.7	19.6	11.1	5.0
1808	District 8, Indiana	3.1	10.7	4.8	1.6	4.6	7.2	21.3	9.4	4.1
1809	District 9, Indiana	2.3	11.8	5.0	1.9	5.7	7.1	23.4	10.1	4.4
1900	**IOWA**	2.7	11.7	4.6	1.7	7.3	7.1	24.3	7.7	4.0
1901	District 1, Iowa	2.6	12.5	4.7	2.0	5.8	7.1	23.7	7.1	4.0
1902	District 2, Iowa	2.1	11.4	4.2	1.5	5.3	6.5	26.8	8.1	3.9
1903	District 3, Iowa	2.8	11.4	4.9	1.9	12.8	9.3	22.3	7.4	4.0
1904	District 4, Iowa	3.4	11.3	4.7	1.5	4.9	5.4	24.4	8.1	4.3
2000	**KANSAS**	2.8	11.2	4.6	2.1	6.2	9.4	24.4	8.2	4.6
2001	District 1, Kansas	2.9	10.8	4.3	1.8	4.4	5.9	25.1	8.2	4.7
2002	District 2, Kansas	1.8	11.5	5.3	1.4	6.3	7.3	27.5	8.3	4.8
2003	District 3, Kansas	3.9	10.8	4.4	3.3	9.1	15.6	21.7	7.7	4.6
2004	District 4, Kansas	2.6	11.7	4.4	1.8	4.4	7.7	23.9	8.8	4.3
2100	**KENTUCKY**	2.4	12.2	5.9	1.6	5.4	7.9	23.7	9.2	4.8
2101	District 1, Kentucky	2.2	12.4	6.2	1.1	3.5	6.1	22.7	7.4	5.3
2102	District 2, Kentucky	2.3	11.7	6.1	2.0	5.4	6.5	21.4	8.8	4.9
2103	District 3, Kentucky	3.0	11.0	7.4	1.7	7.8	9.4	24.5	10.1	5.1
2104	District 4, Kentucky	3.0	11.9	6.7	1.8	6.9	9.4	21.5	9.8	3.8
2105	District 5, Kentucky	1.7	14.2	5.0	1.6	3.8	5.6	29.0	8.4	5.2
2106	District 6, Kentucky	1.7	12.8	3.7	1.3	3.9	9.0	24.6	10.0	4.6
2200	**LOUISIANA**	2.5	11.5	5.1	1.6	5.2	9.2	23.6	10.7	5.3
2201	District 1, Louisiana	3.1	11.1	5.5	1.6	6.9	11.2	21.5	11.4	5.1
2202	District 2, Louisiana	2.3	11.3	5.6	1.5	4.4	10.6	22.2	14.5	5.1
2203	District 3, Louisiana	2.4	12.2	4.2	1.1	4.1	7.9	23.1	11.5	5.3
2204	District 4, Louisiana	2.5	11.5	5.2	1.6	4.9	7.4	24.4	9.6	5.3
2205	District 5, Louisiana	1.7	12.2	5.3	2.2	4.6	6.4	27.5	9.2	5.7
2206	District 6, Louisiana	2.8	10.8	4.9	1.8	5.9	10.4	24.1	7.6	5.3
2300	**MAINE**	2.1	13.1	3.8	1.9	6.3	8.3	28.0	8.7	4.6
2301	District 1, Maine	2.3	12.6	3.1	2.2	7.5	9.6	26.8	9.4	4.6
2302	District 2, Maine	1.9	13.6	4.7	1.7	4.8	6.9	29.4	7.9	4.6
2400	**MARYLAND**	2.0	9.9	4.6	2.2	5.9	15.5	23.2	8.9	5.3
2401	District 1, Maryland	2.6	12.3	4.4	1.6	6.7	10.3	23.2	9.3	5.0
2402	District 2, Maryland	3.0	12.5	5.0	2.0	5.7	13.7	24.0	8.5	4.9
2403	District 3, Maryland	2.4	9.4	4.1	2.5	6.4	15.9	25.2	9.8	4.6
2404	District 4, Maryland	1.6	9.7	6.0	2.0	4.2	15.4	21.2	9.9	6.3

Table F. Congressional Districts—Labor Force, Employment, and Educational Data, 2015—*Continued*

State and District code	State/Congressional district (114th Congress)	Wholesale trade	Retail trade	Transportation and warehousing, and utilities	Information	Finance and insurance, and real estate and rental and leasing	Professional, scientific, and management, and administrative and waste management services	Educational services, and health care and social assistance	Arts, entertainment, and recreation, and accommodation and food services	Other services, except public administration
						Industry for employed population age 16 and older				
2405	District 5, Maryland	1.4	8.8	4.8	2.1	5.1	15.7	21.1	8.3	5.0
2406	District 6, Maryland	2.0	9.8	4.1	2.3	6.6	17.9	21.0	8.6	5.3
2407	District 7, Maryland	1.6	9.5	5.3	2.0	6.4	14.2	28.8	7.8	5.1
2408	District 8, Maryland	1.6	7.6	2.9	2.8	6.4	20.0	21.8	8.5	6.4
2500	**MASSACHUSETTS**	2.3	10.6	3.7	2.4	7.4	13.5	28.1	9.1	4.4
2501	District 1, Massachusetts	2.6	12.6	4.3	1.9	7.1	8.2	29.9	8.7	4.1
2502	District 2, Massachusetts	2.4	11.8	3.8	2.1	6.1	9.7	31.5	8.7	4.2
2503	District 3, Massachusetts	2.4	9.6	3.2	2.7	5.1	14.1	25.4	8.8	5.2
2504	District 4, Massachusetts	2.9	10.0	3.5	2.5	9.1	14.0	28.9	7.2	3.9
2505	District 5, Massachusetts	1.5	8.4	3.2	3.4	7.6	17.7	29.4	8.0	4.6
2506	District 6, Massachusetts	2.3	10.6	3.1	2.4	7.1	14.9	25.7	9.5	4.5
2507	District 7, Massachusetts	1.9	9.0	3.9	2.5	7.2	15.9	31.4	11.5	4.1
2508	District 8, Massachusetts	2.0	10.6	4.4	2.3	10.2	15.2	27.1	8.5	4.1
2509	District 9, Massachusetts	2.5	13.8	3.8	1.6	6.6	10.4	23.4	10.8	5.2
2600	**MICHIGAN**	2.5	11.4	4.3	1.5	5.4	9.4	23.5	9.8	4.5
2601	District 1, Michigan	2.0	13.2	4.4	1.6	4.8	6.1	25.1	13.3	4.4
2602	District 2, Michigan	3.4	11.7	3.5	1.4	4.5	7.8	20.3	8.8	4.9
2603	District 3, Michigan	3.3	11.3	3.9	1.3	5.4	9.0	22.3	9.2	5.1
2604	District 4, Michigan	2.0	11.5	4.3	1.0	4.5	7.0	24.5	9.8	4.3
2605	District 5, Michigan	2.4	14.3	4.6	1.4	4.5	7.9	24.8	9.7	5.1
2606	District 6, Michigan	2.2	10.9	3.9	1.0	5.1	7.7	23.2	9.9	4.1
2607	District 7, Michigan	2.1	10.9	4.8	1.1	4.4	7.5	23.8	8.6	4.8
2608	District 8, Michigan	2.9	10.5	3.2	1.7	6.8	11.3	24.8	9.5	3.8
2609	District 9, Michigan	2.6	11.0	3.7	1.5	6.5	12.1	21.5	9.5	4.5
2610	District 10, Michigan	2.3	11.2	4.1	1.4	5.4	7.3	21.3	8.9	4.7
2611	District 11, Michigan	2.9	10.2	3.0	1.9	6.6	13.0	22.4	8.9	4.1
2612	District 12, Michigan	2.1	11.7	5.7	1.8	4.6	9.9	29.3	9.8	4.1
2613	District 13, Michigan	2.7	11.3	6.5	1.2	5.8	11.0	21.3	11.0	4.6
2614	District 14, Michigan	1.7	10.6	5.1	2.2	6.7	13.2	24.6	10.6	4.6
2700	**MINNESOTA**	2.9	11.0	4.6	1.7	7.3	9.8	25.0	8.4	4.5
2701	District 1, Minnesota	2.6	11.2	3.7	1.6	3.9	6.3	29.6	6.9	4.6
2702	District 2, Minnesota	3.2	10.8	6.2	1.9	8.9	10.0	21.7	9.1	4.4
2703	District 3, Minnesota	3.6	11.2	3.9	1.7	11.3	14.2	21.3	7.1	4.4
2704	District 4, Minnesota	3.0	10.4	3.8	2.1	8.0	11.1	27.5	8.2	4.5
2705	District 5, Minnesota	2.5	10.6	3.5	2.3	8.5	14.7	25.9	11.1	4.4
2706	District 6, Minnesota	3.0	10.8	5.1	1.6	7.0	9.1	23.4	7.1	4.8
2707	District 7, Minnesota	3.5	11.1	4.9	1.2	4.7	5.2	24.3	7.3	4.0
2708	District 8, Minnesota	2.0	12.0	5.6	1.1	5.1	6.1	26.4	10.7	4.5
2800	**MISSISSIPPI**	2.7	11.9	5.8	1.2	4.7	6.7	24.2	9.5	4.5
2801	District 1, Mississippi	3.0	12.3	7.7	1.4	5.6	6.3	21.8	7.9	4.2
2802	District 2, Mississippi	2.8	10.9	5.8	1.0	3.3	5.7	26.7	9.3	4.1
2803	District 3, Mississippi	2.6	10.4	4.5	1.3	5.3	7.5	26.6	9.1	5.2
2804	District 4, Mississippi	2.1	14.0	5.3	1.1	4.4	7.3	22.1	11.9	4.6
2900	**MISSOURI**	2.7	11.9	5.3	2.0	6.7	9.8	24.0	9.2	4.7
2901	District 1, Missouri	2.2	11.1	6.0	2.1	7.2	12.3	26.7	10.8	4.7
2902	District 2, Missouri	3.6	11.8	3.8	2.3	10.4	13.6	23.0	8.5	4.8
2903	District 3, Missouri	2.6	12.0	5.0	1.9	6.7	7.9	20.4	9.0	4.7
2904	District 4, Missouri	2.0	13.0	4.9	2.0	5.9	7.6	25.0	8.8	4.5
2905	District 5, Missouri	2.7	11.8	5.9	2.1	6.8	11.8	23.2	9.5	4.5
2906	District 6, Missouri	3.1	10.6	6.1	2.3	6.0	9.7	23.0	8.2	4.4
2907	District 7, Missouri	2.4	12.4	6.1	1.7	5.2	8.8	24.2	11.0	5.2
2908	District 8, Missouri	2.4	12.2	5.0	1.3	4.3	5.5	27.5	7.4	4.6
3000	**MONTANA**	2.4	11.4	4.6	1.9	5.4	8.0	24.2	10.4	5.1
3000	District (at Large), Montana	2.4	11.4	4.6	1.9	5.4	8.0	24.2	10.4	5.1
3100	**NEBRASKA**	3.1	11.7	5.7	1.7	7.3	8.5	24.0	8.1	4.2
3101	District 1, Nebraska	2.7	11.6	5.1	1.6	6.6	8.1	24.0	7.9	4.4
3102	District 2, Nebraska	2.9	10.9	5.0	2.3	10.5	12.8	24.4	8.8	4.3
3103	District 3, Nebraska	3.6	12.9	7.0	1.2	4.5	4.3	23.6	7.7	3.9
3200	**NEVADA**	2.0	12.1	5.2	1.4	6.1	11.6	15.2	25.6	4.5
3201	District 1, Nevada	1.2	13.2	5.3	1.1	5.3	11.6	10.1	34.6	4.6
3202	District 2, Nevada	2.7	12.3	5.5	1.4	5.1	10.7	17.1	16.8	4.8
3203	District 3, Nevada	2.0	11.4	5.1	1.5	7.7	11.7	16.2	28.4	3.8
3204	District 4, Nevada	2.1	11.8	4.7	1.6	5.8	12.6	17.2	22.3	4.8
3300	**NEW HAMPSHIRE**	2.9	12.3	4.0	2.1	6.3	10.9	25.1	8.4	4.1
3301	District 1, New Hampshire	2.9	12.8	4.3	2.3	6.8	11.2	24.5	8.5	3.9
3302	District 2, New Hampshire	2.9	11.7	3.8	1.9	5.9	10.6	25.7	8.2	4.3
3400	**NEW JERSEY**	3.5	11.3	5.8	2.8	8.5	13.3	23.6	8.6	4.6
3401	District 1, New Jersey	3.0	11.2	5.6	1.9	7.6	12.2	27.7	9.1	4.5
3402	District 2, New Jersey	2.5	11.3	5.2	1.3	5.2	8.8	24.6	15.5	3.8

Table F. Congressional Districts—Labor Force, Employment, and Educational Data, 2015—*Continued*

State and District code	State/Congressional district (114th Congress)	Industry for employed population age 16 and older								
		Wholesale trade	Retail trade	Transportation and warehousing, and utilities	Information	Finance and insurance, and real estate and rental and leasing	Professional, scientific, and management, and administrative and waste management services	Educational services, and health care and social assistance	Arts, entertainment, and recreation, and accommodation and food services	Other services, except public administration
3403	District 3, New Jersey	3.4	13.4	5.7	2.0	7.5	11.8	25.2	8.0	3.9
3404	District 4, New Jersey	3.2	12.1	4.6	3.1	8.9	11.7	24.6	8.3	4.7
3405	District 5, New Jersey	4.6	11.9	4.4	3.2	9.4	13.9	24.6	7.5	4.1
3406	District 6, New Jersey	3.5	11.9	6.9	3.2	8.6	14.3	22.0	8.2	4.8
3407	District 7, New Jersey	3.6	10.4	3.8	3.5	11.3	15.3	21.7	7.3	4.2
3408	District 8, New Jersey	4.0	10.0	8.5	3.0	9.0	14.4	18.5	9.4	5.0
3409	District 9, New Jersey	4.0	12.6	7.3	2.8	7.7	11.5	20.6	7.4	6.0
3410	District 10, New Jersey	2.5	10.6	9.9	2.5	6.9	12.2	26.5	8.1	5.3
3411	District 11, New Jersey	3.6	10.1	3.4	3.5	10.0	16.3	24.9	7.6	4.2
3412	District 12, New Jersey	3.5	10.5	4.7	3.1	8.9	15.8	23.2	6.9	4.3
3500	**NEW MEXICO**	2.4	12.0	4.4	1.6	4.5	11.7	24.9	11.8	4.8
3501	District 1, New Mexico	2.3	12.2	3.0	1.9	5.0	14.8	24.6	12.5	5.5
3502	District 2, New Mexico	2.7	11.3	5.7	1.1	3.7	7.5	26.7	10.6	4.0
3503	District 3, New Mexico	2.3	12.3	4.6	1.8	4.7	12.2	23.7	12.2	4.8
3600	**NEW YORK**	2.5	10.6	5.4	3.0	7.9	11.7	27.4	9.8	5.0
3601	District 1, New York	2.9	11.3	5.1	2.7	6.1	11.5	27.7	7.8	5.2
3602	District 2, New York	3.1	11.6	6.8	2.9	7.7	10.8	26.0	7.7	3.7
3603	District 3, New York	3.5	9.2	5.3	3.5	11.7	14.1	26.9	6.8	3.9
3604	District 4, New York	3.4	10.7	6.0	3.3	8.9	11.6	29.7	7.0	5.2
3605	District 5, New York	2.0	10.0	10.7	2.3	6.7	9.0	29.1	8.5	4.9
3606	District 6, New York	3.3	10.3	6.4	2.3	8.5	12.4	23.9	10.6	8.0
3607	District 7, New York	2.5	10.5	5.0	4.5	7.1	15.1	20.6	15.5	5.8
3608	District 8, New York	1.5	9.4	8.5	3.3	6.3	12.4	32.3	8.9	5.7
3609	District 9, New York	1.7	8.7	6.5	5.0	7.0	12.6	33.7	8.0	6.1
3610	District 10, New York	2.6	6.7	3.5	6.0	16.6	19.0	22.2	10.1	4.1
3611	District 11, New York	2.0	10.3	6.8	2.3	9.9	11.3	28.5	8.1	4.3
3612	District 12, New York	2.6	7.2	2.2	7.8	17.9	23.3	18.7	9.6	3.5
3613	District 13, New York	2.4	9.4	5.5	2.8	6.6	10.3	30.2	17.3	5.6
3614	District 14, New York	2.1	10.8	8.6	2.3	6.4	10.1	21.9	15.7	6.4
3615	District 15, New York	2.0	12.6	7.9	1.3	5.9	8.6	30.2	14.6	6.5
3616	District 16, New York	2.1	9.9	5.0	3.0	9.7	11.9	31.3	8.0	5.6
3617	District 17, New York	2.8	10.1	3.5	2.7	8.5	14.2	28.7	8.8	5.8
3618	District 18, New York	3.0	12.1	5.5	3.1	7.0	10.1	26.1	8.7	4.4
3619	District 19, New York	2.6	11.6	4.9	1.9	5.2	8.4	29.0	9.3	4.5
3620	District 20, New York	2.1	10.5	4.0	2.3	7.4	10.3	26.8	8.8	4.8
3621	District 21, New York	1.7	14.4	3.9	1.6	3.9	7.0	27.5	10.3	4.0
3622	District 22, New York	2.4	12.9	4.4	1.3	4.6	7.6	29.5	9.6	4.6
3623	District 23, New York	1.7	11.9	3.8	1.4	3.1	6.6	31.0	9.4	4.4
3624	District 24, New York	2.9	11.5	5.2	2.1	5.5	9.4	29.1	9.1	4.2
3625	District 25, New York	2.4	11.6	3.8	2.7	5.0	11.9	30.6	8.5	5.1
3626	District 26, New York	2.9	11.7	4.5	1.6	7.9	10.5	27.8	11.0	4.4
3627	District 27, New York	2.6	11.3	4.4	1.4	6.0	8.6	25.8	8.9	4.5
3700	**NORTH CAROLINA**	2.6	11.8	4.2	1.8	6.3	10.7	23.0	9.5	4.7
3701	District 1, North Carolina	2.0	10.5	3.8	1.2	4.0	8.7	27.4	9.9	4.5
3702	District 2, North Carolina	2.2	11.0	4.4	2.3	4.5	12.8	22.3	8.4	5.1
3703	District 3, North Carolina	1.9	13.5	4.1	1.4	5.1	8.9	22.5	12.3	5.1
3704	District 4, North Carolina	2.0	10.9	3.4	2.0	5.7	14.9	27.9	10.9	3.7
3705	District 5, North Carolina	2.3	12.0	4.4	1.2	5.5	9.0	24.8	8.4	4.9
3706	District 6, North Carolina	3.2	12.3	4.1	1.1	6.0	9.5	25.6	8.0	5.0
3707	District 7, North Carolina	2.9	12.8	3.8	1.6	4.7	9.1	22.8	9.3	4.7
3708	District 8, North Carolina	2.8	11.7	5.5	1.2	5.2	6.8	22.2	8.6	4.9
3709	District 9, North Carolina	3.8	12.3	4.3	2.9	13.9	13.3	18.8	9.3	4.5
3710	District 10, North Carolina	2.8	13.4	4.6	1.3	4.4	8.5	20.3	10.2	4.7
3711	District 11, North Carolina	2.4	11.0	3.3	1.3	4.9	8.1	24.8	10.8	4.2
3712	District 12, North Carolina	2.5	10.9	6.1	2.3	8.8	12.3	20.1	10.4	5.4
3713	District 13, North Carolina	2.8	11.1	3.5	2.9	7.1	14.5	20.7	7.9	4.8
3800	**NORTH DAKOTA** District (at Large), North Dakota	4.0	11.6	5.8	1.2	5.1	6.9	23.9	8.2	4.7
3800		4.0	11.6	5.8	1.2	5.1	6.9	23.9	8.2	4.7
3900	**OHIO**	2.7	11.7	5.1	1.6	6.5	9.3	23.8	9.4	4.5
3901	District 1, Ohio	3.2	12.3	4.8	1.6	7.7	11.7	24.7	8.8	4.4
3902	District 2, Ohio	2.2	12.5	4.5	1.7	7.6	11.2	22.9	8.7	4.1
3903	District 3, Ohio	2.5	13.6	7.4	2.0	9.7	11.8	22.1	11.1	4.2
3904	District 4, Ohio	2.8	9.5	5.6	1.1	3.6	6.3	21.5	7.8	4.8
3905	District 5, Ohio	2.8	10.6	5.9	1.1	3.6	7.1	23.4	7.8	4.5
3906	District 6, Ohio	2.3	13.1	7.2	1.4	4.2	6.3	24.3	8.7	4.7
3907	District 7, Ohio	3.1	11.1	4.8	1.5	5.4	7.2	22.0	8.6	5.0
3908	District 8, Ohio	2.8	11.5	4.4	1.2	6.1	8.7	23.0	9.3	4.2
3909	District 9, Ohio	2.5	12.0	5.2	1.5	5.1	9.1	22.9	12.2	4.5
3910	District 10, Ohio	2.3	10.6	3.9	1.8	5.8	10.5	26.5	9.7	4.9

Table F. Congressional Districts—Labor Force, Employment, and Educational Data, 2015—*Continued*

State and District code	State/Congressional district (114th Congress)	Wholesale trade	Retail trade	Transportation and warehousing, and utilities	Information	Finance and insurance, and real estate and rental and leasing	Professional, scientific, and management, and administrative and waste management services	Educational services, and health care and social assistance	Arts, entertainment, and recreation, and accommodation and food services	Other services, except public administration
3911	District 11, Ohio	1.7	10.3	4.0	1.8	7.3	9.9	30.5	11.7	4.2
3912	District 12, Ohio	3.1	12.0	3.9	2.3	11.0	11.0	23.0	9.6	4.0
3913	District 13, Ohio	2.1	14.0	4.6	1.5	4.7	9.0	22.8	10.7	5.2
3914	District 14, Ohio	3.7	11.0	4.0	2.1	6.7	9.3	24.1	7.8	4.1
3915	District 15, Ohio	3.0	11.9	5.8	1.8	7.6	9.6	26.0	8.7	3.9
3916	District 16, Ohio	3.1	11.6	5.2	1.6	6.9	9.5	22.8	9.0	4.7
4000	**OKLAHOMA**	2.6	11.8	5.2	1.7	5.6	8.5	22.3	9.5	5.2
4001	District 1, Oklahoma	3.2	11.3	5.7	2.6	6.4	11.1	21.5	8.9	5.7
4002	District 2, Oklahoma	2.3	11.5	6.5	1.1	3.8	5.5	24.3	10.0	4.3
4003	District 3, Oklahoma	2.8	11.7	6.0	1.5	4.1	6.5	20.9	9.6	4.8
4004	District 4, Oklahoma	2.4	12.6	4.7	1.6	5.8	7.9	23.4	9.3	5.3
4005	District 5, Oklahoma	2.4	11.7	3.7	1.8	7.3	10.3	21.7	9.8	5.5
4100	**OREGON**	2.8	12.0	4.1	1.9	5.4	11.3	23.1	9.8	4.7
4101	District 1, Oregon	3.2	10.7	3.4	2.1	7.0	13.6	19.9	9.0	3.7
4102	District 2, Oregon	2.3	13.6	4.8	2.0	4.2	9.2	21.1	10.3	5.6
4103	District 3, Oregon	3.3	11.3	4.3	2.2	5.4	13.0	25.2	11.5	5.0
4104	District 4, Oregon	2.1	12.2	4.2	1.5	4.5	9.0	27.3	9.5	4.9
4105	District 5, Oregon	2.9	12.4	3.9	1.4	5.6	10.9	21.9	8.7	4.3
4200	**PENNSYLVANIA**	2.9	11.5	5.4	1.6	6.2	10.3	25.6	8.6	4.6
4201	District 1, Pennsylvania	2.2	10.8	6.9	2.0	6.2	11.7	27.9	10.2	5.0
4202	District 2, Pennsylvania	1.3	9.6	5.0	2.0	5.9	13.6	35.0	10.4	4.4
4203	District 3, Pennsylvania	2.3	12.1	5.2	1.3	5.3	7.2	25.6	9.0	4.8
4204	District 4, Pennsylvania	3.0	11.9	6.1	1.4	6.3	9.3	21.0	8.0	4.9
4205	District 5, Pennsylvania	1.6	11.3	4.7	1.0	3.8	6.6	27.5	9.2	5.0
4206	District 6, Pennsylvania	3.3	9.7	3.8	2.3	9.3	14.1	22.8	7.6	4.4
4207	District 7, Pennsylvania	3.0	9.7	4.0	2.2	8.5	13.4	25.8	7.4	4.5
4208	District 8, Pennsylvania	3.4	12.4	4.1	1.9	7.6	13.4	23.5	7.2	4.1
4209	District 9, Pennsylvania	2.6	12.6	7.3	1.4	4.4	6.1	24.5	8.5	4.3
4210	District 10, Pennsylvania	2.5	11.7	5.8	1.2	4.3	6.9	25.5	8.9	4.6
4211	District 11, Pennsylvania	2.9	12.5	7.0	1.3	5.4	8.0	25.2	8.0	4.0
4212	District 12, Pennsylvania	2.9	11.1	5.7	1.5	7.6	10.3	26.6	7.8	5.4
4213	District 13, Pennsylvania	3.3	11.5	4.9	2.0	7.0	12.0	25.9	8.1	5.1
4214	District 14, Pennsylvania	2.9	11.0	4.4	1.9	7.3	12.2	28.4	11.0	4.4
4215	District 15, Pennsylvania	2.9	12.4	6.4	1.6	5.6	10.0	24.8	9.5	4.4
4216	District 16, Pennsylvania	3.9	10.9	5.0	1.2	5.1	9.7	23.1	8.0	4.6
4217	District 17, Pennsylvania	3.5	12.6	6.3	1.7	4.4	8.4	26.0	8.4	4.5
4218	District 18, Pennsylvania	3.3	12.7	5.3	1.4	7.4	11.2	23.5	8.3	5.1
4400	**RHODE ISLAND**	3.1	11.7	3.7	1.6	6.5	9.3	27.4	11.1	4.4
4401	District 1, Rhode Island	3.1	12.3	4.1	1.6	6.2	9.5	29.1	10.7	4.1
4402	District 2, Rhode Island	3.1	11.2	3.3	1.5	6.7	9.1	25.7	11.5	4.7
4500	**SOUTH CAROLINA**	2.7	12.2	4.6	1.9	5.9	9.9	21.7	10.2	5.2
4501	District 1, South Carolina	2.4	11.0	4.1	2.3	7.0	14.3	21.2	12.7	4.9
4502	District 2, South Carolina	2.5	12.4	4.8	1.6	7.5	10.1	22.6	8.4	5.7
4503	District 3, South Carolina	2.0	11.4	4.2	1.6	4.2	7.8	22.9	7.1	5.6
4504	District 4, South Carolina	3.6	10.5	3.8	2.5	5.2	10.9	21.1	10.0	5.6
4505	District 5, South Carolina	3.3	12.6	5.8	2.0	6.8	9.0	19.0	8.4	5.2
4506	District 6, South Carolina	2.1	13.1	5.8	1.7	4.7	8.8	23.2	11.1	4.7
4507	District 7, South Carolina	2.7	14.5	4.2	1.4	5.2	7.4	22.5	13.9	4.5
4600	**SOUTH DAKOTA**	2.9	10.5	4.6	1.5	7.0	6.5	24.3	9.5	4.4
4600	District (at Large), South Dakota	2.9	10.5	4.6	1.5	7.0	6.5	24.3	9.5	4.4
4700	**TENNESSEE**	2.7	12.3	6.5	1.8	5.7	9.9	22.4	9.5	5.1
4701	District 1, Tennessee	1.9	12.8	3.9	1.5	4.3	7.3	23.9	12.6	5.0
4702	District 2, Tennessee	2.7	14.3	4.8	2.1	5.9	12.2	24.2	9.5	4.7
4703	District 3, Tennessee	2.6	12.6	6.8	1.4	6.1	10.5	20.6	8.6	5.3
4704	District 4, Tennessee	2.2	13.0	6.4	2.1	5.7	8.3	20.2	8.6	5.1
4705	District 5, Tennessee	2.2	11.2	4.9	2.5	7.5	12.5	23.8	12.1	5.0
4706	District 6, Tennessee	4.0	11.3	6.5	1.4	5.1	8.7	20.5	9.5	5.1
4707	District 7, Tennessee	2.3	11.8	4.6	2.1	6.2	10.1	23.6	7.9	4.8
4708	District 8, Tennessee	3.1	12.8	7.2	1.2	5.0	8.1	23.8	7.4	5.4
4709	District 9, Tennessee	3.5	11.4	13.5	1.9	5.0	10.8	21.2	9.4	5.6
4800	**TEXAS**	3.0	11.7	5.7	1.8	6.6	11.4	21.2	9.1	5.2
4801	District 1, Texas	2.2	12.6	4.7	1.5	4.5	7.8	27.4	7.7	5.5
4802	District 2, Texas	4.1	9.4	6.5	1.5	7.6	14.1	18.5	8.4	4.6
4803	District 3, Texas	2.9	11.7	2.9	3.7	11.4	16.8	20.2	8.6	4.7
4804	District 4, Texas	3.1	13.1	4.8	1.3	5.5	8.8	22.4	6.9	4.8
4805	District 5, Texas	2.2	12.4	5.9	2.7	5.9	10.9	19.0	9.9	6.0
4806	District 6, Texas	3.6	12.9	7.2	2.2	8.3	10.2	22.0	7.3	5.5
4807	District 7, Texas	4.6	9.5	4.7	1.4	8.0	17.0	18.5	8.9	5.0
4808	District 8, Texas	3.7	11.5	6.2	1.8	5.8	12.2	18.2	7.1	5.1
4809	District 9, Texas	2.2	13.5	6.6	1.1	6.2	11.1	22.8	10.1	6.7
4810	District 10, Texas	3.6	10.2	5.2	2.0	6.9	13.8	19.5	7.9	4.7

Table F. Congressional Districts—Labor Force, Employment, and Educational Data, 2015—*Continued*

		Industry for employed population age 16 and older								
State and District code	State/Congressional district (114th Congress)	Wholesale trade	Retail trade	Transportation and warehousing, and utilities	Information	Finance and insurance, and real estate and rental and leasing	Professional, scientific, and management, and administrative and waste management services	Educational services, and health care and social assistance	Arts, entertainment, and recreation, and accommodation and food services	Other services, except public administration
4811	District 11, Texas	3.0	11.5	5.8	1.3	4.6	7.4	20.6	8.2	6.1
4812	District 12, Texas	2.9	13.1	7.8	1.5	5.4	10.3	21.2	8.7	4.7
4813	District 13, Texas	3.4	12.2	5.2	1.5	4.3	6.3	22.4	10.2	5.8
4814	District 14, Texas	1.8	10.0	4.4	1.1	5.0	10.4	22.9	9.8	4.8
4815	District 15, Texas	3.3	14.1	5.4	0.8	4.0	8.1	27.2	8.9	5.4
4816	District 16, Texas	2.8	12.1	6.8	1.7	5.8	11.1	24.4	10.3	4.6
4817	District 17, Texas	2.6	11.8	4.6	1.7	6.1	10.3	25.2	9.1	4.7
4818	District 18, Texas	3.4	11.4	8.4	1.7	5.2	12.6	17.9	9.1	5.4
4819	District 19, Texas	2.5	12.6	5.5	1.6	5.4	6.0	26.5	9.6	5.4
4820	District 20, Texas	2.2	11.9	3.7	1.8	9.6	10.5	23.7	12.4	4.3
4821	District 21, Texas	2.7	11.2	3.9	2.7	8.0	15.2	21.2	10.9	5.0
4822	District 22, Texas	3.5	11.3	5.0	1.4	6.8	12.9	24.4	6.3	3.8
4823	District 23, Texas	2.4	11.2	7.1	1.3	7.1	8.4	21.6	9.0	4.2
4824	District 24, Texas	3.8	10.9	7.7	3.3	10.9	15.6	16.5	9.8	5.1
4825	District 25, Texas	2.7	10.8	4.2	2.2	6.4	13.8	22.0	8.3	4.4
4826	District 26, Texas	4.0	12.2	6.2	2.9	9.0	13.2	19.5	9.6	5.6
4827	District 27, Texas	2.5	12.4	5.1	1.1	4.9	7.7	21.8	10.3	4.7
4828	District 28, Texas	3.3	12.3	8.8	1.1	5.1	7.5	24.8	8.7	5.6
4829	District 29, Texas	3.2	11.8	8.4	0.9	3.6	9.1	14.5	9.2	5.8
4830	District 30, Texas	2.6	11.2	8.1	1.4	7.7	12.0	19.5	9.4	5.3
4831	District 31, Texas	2.7	11.3	3.8	2.2	6.9	14.6	22.9	8.0	4.1
4832	District 32, Texas	2.8	11.5	4.1	3.5	9.8	16.1	19.8	8.9	5.6
4833	District 33, Texas	3.5	10.0	6.4	1.0	4.6	10.4	13.4	12.0	6.0
4834	District 34, Texas	2.5	13.3	5.1	1.3	4.1	7.0	29.0	7.8	5.8
4835	District 35, Texas	2.9	12.8	4.7	2.2	5.3	11.4	18.6	13.7	5.9
4836	District 36, Texas	3.0	10.3	6.5	0.6	4.2	8.4	20.2	7.4	5.2
4900	**UTAH**	2.8	12.3	4.5	2.2	6.7	11.9	20.8	9.2	4.5
4901	District 1, Utah	2.5	11.8	4.4	1.5	5.3	10.8	19.6	8.1	4.3
4902	District 2, Utah	2.3	12.6	4.9	2.0	6.1	11.0	21.3	10.2	5.0
4903	District 3, Utah	3.3	12.3	3.3	2.8	6.8	12.9	24.8	9.7	4.6
4904	District 4, Utah	3.1	12.6	5.1	2.3	8.5	12.7	17.8	8.9	4.0
5000	**VERMONT**	2.2	11.5	3.4	2.3	4.8	8.6	28.3	9.5	4.3
5000	District (at Large), Vermont	2.2	11.5	3.4	2.3	4.8	8.6	28.3	9.5	4.3
5100	**VIRGINIA**	2.0	10.8	4.2	2.0	6.4	14.7	21.9	9.1	5.5
5101	District 1, Virginia	1.7	11.4	4.0	1.5	5.7	14.2	19.9	8.6	4.9
5102	District 2, Virginia	2.4	11.3	3.3	2.0	6.6	11.1	22.0	11.1	4.6
5103	District 3, Virginia	1.6	12.9	5.5	1.6	5.9	10.5	23.6	11.1	5.2
5104	District 4, Virginia	2.7	11.4	5.2	1.6	6.5	9.7	22.8	8.1	5.4
5105	District 5, Virginia	2.1	11.2	4.4	1.4	4.6	9.9	28.0	8.6	5.9
5106	District 6, Virginia	2.6	12.3	4.6	1.6	5.6	8.9	25.3	10.3	4.7
5107	District 7, Virginia	3.1	12.1	4.6	1.9	10.5	12.3	23.1	8.4	5.1
5108	District 8, Virginia	0.9	7.0	2.8	2.6	7.0	22.5	15.9	9.8	7.3
5109	District 9, Virginia	1.9	13.1	4.3	1.3	4.4	8.4	27.0	7.0	5.0
5110	District 10, Virginia	1.6	9.3	4.4	3.6	6.3	23.6	18.2	8.2	5.1
5111	District 11, Virginia	1.3	9.0	3.3	2.5	6.4	23.4	19.3	9.1	6.2
5300	**WASHINGTON**	2.9	11.7	5.4	2.2	5.4	12.5	21.3	9.3	4.7
5301	District 1, Washington	2.8	10.8	4.5	3.1	6.0	16.7	18.3	7.1	4.3
5302	District 2, Washington	2.8	12.8	4.9	2.1	5.3	10.3	19.9	9.6	5.1
5303	District 3, Washington	3.0	11.7	7.2	1.9	5.8	9.3	20.3	8.8	4.9
5304	District 4, Washington	3.5	9.5	6.5	0.9	3.4	9.0	20.0	8.5	4.2
5305	District 5, Washington	2.9	12.4	4.5	1.5	6.1	8.6	28.0	8.8	5.4
5306	District 6, Washington	2.1	10.9	4.8	1.3	4.7	9.6	22.3	12.0	5.0
5307	District 7, Washington	2.4	11.9	3.4	3.7	6.4	19.5	23.9	10.6	4.4
5308	District 8, Washington	4.0	12.6	6.5	2.3	5.4	13.2	19.2	7.6	4.1
5309	District 9, Washington	2.7	11.6	7.2	2.6	5.8	15.3	19.3	10.4	4.9
5310	District 10, Washington	2.4	12.6	5.3	1.6	4.8	8.8	22.9	9.4	5.1
5400	**WEST VIRGINIA**	2.2	12.2	5.3	1.5	4.0	8.0	28.6	9.4	4.2
5401	District 1, West Virginia	2.0	13.2	4.9	1.3	3.8	8.0	29.3	8.5	4.3
5402	District 2, West Virginia	2.4	11.2	5.5	1.8	4.8	8.5	26.6	9.9	3.8
5403	District 3, West Virginia	2.3	12.4	5.4	1.3	3.0	7.3	30.5	9.9	4.4
5500	**WISCONSIN**	2.6	11.4	4.4	1.5	6.0	8.2	23.1	8.9	4.1
5501	District 1, Wisconsin	3.1	11.2	5.1	1.4	5.4	8.6	23.0	8.2	4.4
5502	District 2, Wisconsin	2.3	11.0	3.1	2.4	6.7	11.6	26.1	9.5	4.4
5503	District 3, Wisconsin	2.1	13.3	5.0	1.3	5.5	5.9	25.1	8.4	4.2
5504	District 4, Wisconsin	2.3	9.6	4.2	1.7	5.9	10.3	27.1	11.9	4.3
5505	District 5, Wisconsin	3.6	11.7	3.4	1.6	7.2	8.9	23.1	8.1	3.6
5506	District 6, Wisconsin	2.2	11.3	4.1	1.2	5.5	7.4	19.9	8.0	4.0
5507	District 7, Wisconsin	2.6	11.2	5.4	1.2	5.8	5.3	21.9	8.4	4.0
5508	District 8, Wisconsin	2.5	11.5	5.0	1.4	6.1	7.3	18.9	8.6	3.7
5600	**WYOMING**	1.8	11.9	5.7	1.4	3.8	6.4	22.2	11.3	4.7
5600	District (at Large), Wyoming	1.8	11.9	5.7	1.4	3.8	6.4	22.2	11.3	4.7

Table F. Congressional Districts—Labor Force, Employment, and Educational Data, 2015

State and District code	State/Congressional district (114th Congress)	Industry for employed population age 16 and older Public administration	Educational attainment for the population age 25 and older Total population age 25 and older	Less than high school graduate	High school graduate (includes equivalency)	Some college or Associate's degree	Bachelor's degree or higher
0000	**UNITED STATES**	4.6	216,447,163	12.9	27.6	29.0	30.6
0100	**ALABAMA**	5.2	3,282,252	15.1	31.0	29.7	24.2
0101	District 1 , Alabama	3.5	479,549	13.9	33.6	28.6	23.9
0102	District 2, Alabama	7.9	461,931	16.5	31.8	30.4	21.4
0103	District 3, Alabama	5.6	467,978	16.7	30.5	32.0	20.8
0104	District 4, Alabama	3.7	471,090	19.7	35.0	29.2	16.1
0105	District 5, Alabama	6.6	485,955	12.6	27.4	28.6	31.3
0106	District 6, Alabama	3.8	478,893	10.3	25.4	29.0	35.3
0107	District 7, Alabama	5.5	436,856	16.6	33.8	30.1	19.5
0200	**ALASKA**	11.7	469,523	7.4	27.3	35.7	29.7
0200	District (at Large), Alaska	11.7	469,523	7.4	27.3	35.7	29.7
0400	ARIZONA	5.1	4,536,954	13.9	24.5	33.9	27.7
0401	District 1, Arizona	9.0	493,095	13.8	27.4	35.6	23.2
0402	District 2, Arizona	7.5	495,911	9.6	21.7	35.7	33.0
0403	District 3, Arizona	7.2	453,105	24.7	26.8	32.9	15.6
0404	District 4, Arizona	6.4	544,011	13.3	30.4	37.7	18.6
0405	District 5, Arizona	3.9	522,755	7.3	21.9	35.7	35.1
0406	District 6, Arizona	3.2	540,304	9.4	18.8	29.8	42.0
0407	District 7, Arizona	3.4	446,437	31.9	29.1	25.1	13.8
0408	District 8, Arizona	4.8	532,137	7.8	25.7	38.7	27.7
0409	District 9, Arizona	2.6	509,199	11.3	19.3	32.5	36.9
0500	**ARKANSAS**	4.6	1,987,819	14.6	34.1	29.5	21.8
0501	District 1, Arkansas	4.9	494,186	16.0	38.7	29.9	15.4
0502	District 2, Arkansas	6.1	506,004	11.8	29.5	29.7	29.0
0503	District 3, Arkansas	2.3	503,405	14.8	30.2	28.5	26.5
0504	District 4, Arkansas	5.3	484,224	15.9	38.5	29.7	15.9
0600	**CALIFORNIA**	4.3	26,085,263	17.8	20.8	29.1	32.3
0601	District 1, California	7.3	495,933	10.1	24.9	40.8	24.2
0602	District 2, California	5.2	516,850	10.4	17.8	31.0	40.7
0603	District 3, California	7.7	464,014	15.7	24.3	35.1	24.9
0604	District 4, California	7.0	520,023	7.4	22.3	38.2	32.0
0605	District 5, California	4.3	514,708	13.4	21.0	35.3	30.3
0606	District 6, California	9.9	489,731	16.6	23.4	33.3	26.6
0607	District 7, California	11.6	504,838	9.2	20.6	36.7	33.4
0608	District 8, California	6.3	447,551	17.4	28.6	36.6	17.4
0609	District 9, California	4.8	468,237	19.7	25.5	35.7	19.1
0610	District 10, California	3.8	466,747	21.1	28.2	32.8	17.9
0611	District 11, California	3.5	520,392	12.1	17.1	27.8	43.0
0612	District 12, California	3.5	602,854	12.2	12.2	19.0	56.6
0613	District 13, California	4.0	535,374	15.3	14.1	23.2	47.5
0614	District 14, California	3.6	540,833	12.5	15.9	26.7	44.9
0615	District 15, California	3.6	526,877	10.2	20.4	25.9	43.6
0616	District 16, California	4.9	428,028	33.6	25.5	28.7	12.1
0617	District 17, California	2.2	536,869	8.8	15.5	20.6	55.1
0618	District 18, California	2.4	514,417	7.0	11.5	20.4	61.1
0619	District 19, California	3.4	510,787	19.5	18.5	27.8	34.2
0620	District 20, California	4.5	463,276	26.8	19.0	28.1	26.1
0621	District 21, California	6.0	410,597	41.4	26.4	23.1	9.1
0622	District 22, California	7.5	458,410	19.0	22.1	35.3	23.5
0623	District 23, California	8.0	459,154	17.3	28.5	33.7	20.5
0624	District 24, California	4.5	469,164	15.7	18.9	31.7	33.6
0625	District 25, California	5.0	461,718	14.5	24.3	34.2	27.0
0626	District 26, California	4.5	479,338	18.3	17.8	31.6	32.4
0627	District 27, California	3.5	527,871	14.3	19.5	24.4	41.8
0628	District 28, California	3.0	547,502	12.1	17.4	25.5	45.1
0629	District 29, California	2.3	470,101	31.3	25.7	23.3	19.7
0630	District 30, California	2.0	550,306	11.2	18.4	27.7	42.7
0631	District 31, California	5.5	454,614	19.8	25.2	32.8	22.2
0632	District 32, California	3.2	487,997	25.8	25.9	28.1	20.2
0633	District 33, California	2.3	512,904	4.1	10.5	23.0	62.4
0634	District 34, California	2.3	498,181	35.1	20.8	20.0	24.1
0635	District 35, California	3.8	452,019	30.4	27.3	27.4	14.9
0636	District 36, California	4.0	507,182	21.0	27.6	31.9	19.6
0637	District 37, California	2.7	496,763	19.8	17.7	24.9	37.7
0638	District 38, California	3.9	481,583	20.4	27.2	30.1	22.3
0639	District 39, California	3.6	499,620	11.8	18.4	28.7	41.1
0640	District 40, California	2.4	429,000	47.4	22.8	20.3	9.5
0641	District 41, California	4.2	445,505	25.6	27.2	30.3	17.0
0642	District 42, California	5.5	495,903	14.1	26.3	35.5	24.1
0643	District 43, California	3.1	482,622	22.4	24.1	29.4	24.0
0644	District 44, California	2.9	435,217	36.1	25.3	25.2	13.4
0645	District 45, California	3.3	528,854	6.5	12.0	26.7	54.7
0646	District 46, California	1.9	459,120	35.2	24.0	24.0	16.8
0647	District 47, California	3.7	489,826	19.5	20.1	30.1	30.2
0648	District 48, California	2.4	527,472	10.4	14.6	30.6	44.3

Table F. Congressional Districts—Labor Force, Employment, and Educational Data, 2015—*Continued*

State and District code	State/Congressional district (114th Congress)	Industry for employed population age 16 and older	Educational attainment for the population age 25 and older				
				Educational attainment			
		Public administration	Total population age 25 and older	Less than high school graduate	High school graduate (includes equivalency)	Some college or Associate's degree	Bachelor's degree or higher
0649	District 49, California	3.6	489,800	9.1	16.5	30.9	43.5
0650	District 50, California	4.4	500,937	13.5	23.7	35.0	27.7
0651	District 51, California	6.1	447,940	32.0	24.9	29.4	13.6
0652	District 52, California	4.6	526,385	5.3	12.1	25.0	57.5
0653	District 53, California	6.6	533,319	11.7	17.8	33.8	36.7
0800	**COLORADO**	4.4	3,671,853	8.8	21.7	30.2	39.2
0801	District 1, Colorado	3.7	571,021	12.8	17.1	23.4	46.7
0802	District 2, Colorado	3.6	523,544	3.6	16.0	25.8	54.6
0803	District 3, Colorado	4.9	507,664	10.3	26.8	32.7	30.2
0804	District 4, Colorado	4.5	516,688	9.3	23.6	33.1	34.0
0805	District 5, Colorado	6.7	502,867	5.8	23.6	35.8	34.8
0806	District 6, Colorado	3.9	523,869	7.8	19.6	31.4	41.1
0807	District 7, Colorado	4.1	526,200	11.7	25.8	30.3	32.1
0900	**CONNECTICUT**	3.8	2,474,718	9.8	27.4	24.5	38.3
0901	District 1, Connecticut	4.8	499,296	11.0	26.8	25.5	36.7
0902	District 2, Connecticut	4.4	489,467	8.1	29.3	27.7	34.9
0903	District 3, Connecticut	3.7	493,649	9.5	30.0	24.6	35.9
0904	District 4, Connecticut	2.4	493,239	9.6	22.0	19.9	48.6
0905	District 5, Connecticut	3.9	499,067	10.8	29.0	24.6	35.6
1000	**DELAWARE** District (at Large),	5.3	652,636	11.1	29.8	28.1	30.9
1000	Delaware	5.3	652,636	11.1	29.8	28.1	30.9
1100	**DISTRICT OF COLUMBIA** Delegate District (at Large),	16.3	472,884	10.2	17.4	15.7	56.7
1198	District of Columbia	16.3	472,884	10.2	17.4	15.7	56.7
1200	**FLORIDA**	4.2	14,394,281	12.4	29.2	30.0	28.4
1201	District 1, Florida	7.5	515,293	9.6	27.0	36.6	26.8
1202	District 2, Florida	11.2	474,363	12.7	29.7	31.0	26.6
1203	District 3, Florida	5.9	479,355	11.7	31.6	30.9	25.8
1204	District 4, Florida	4.4	518,845	8.5	27.2	31.9	32.5
1205	District 5, Florida	4.2	478,412	17.6	32.6	32.4	17.4
1206	District 6, Florida	4.6	555,352	8.4	30.1	32.4	29.2
1207	District 7, Florida	2.9	504,460	6.7	24.7	34.0	34.6
1208	District 8, Florida	4.8	541,067	8.7	30.8	32.7	27.8
1209	District 9, Florida	3.7	545,785	12.5	30.0	32.8	24.7
1210	District 10, Florida	3.1	554,778	10.3	28.1	31.3	30.3
1211	District 11, Florida	4.8	574,658	11.0	37.2	31.0	20.8
1212	District 12, Florida	3.6	539,577	9.4	28.8	33.1	28.8
1213	District 13, Florida	3.2	553,765	9.0	29.8	32.5	28.7
1214	District 14, Florida	3.6	524,186	14.2	28.0	29.0	28.8
1215	District 15, Florida	4.7	486,338	11.8	29.1	30.0	29.2
1216	District 16, Florida	3.4	585,328	9.3	30.8	28.6	31.3
1217	District 17, Florida	3.7	547,866	15.4	36.8	28.6	19.2
1218	District 18, Florida	4.2	555,117	11.0	28.1	30.4	30.6
1219	District 19, Florida	2.8	591,350	11.8	28.3	28.9	31.0
1220	District 20, Florida	3.5	520,708	20.3	33.4	26.8	19.6
1221	District 21, Florida	3.6	539,257	8.0	24.0	30.2	37.9
1222	District 22, Florida	3.1	558,762	10.4	22.0	28.8	38.9
1223	District 23, Florida	3.3	529,016	9.4	24.8	26.5	39.4
1224	District 24, Florida	5.0	506,401	21.2	28.3	28.0	22.5
1225	District 25, Florida	2.9	533,759	20.0	29.6	23.8	26.6
1226	District 26, Florida	4.0	542,699	16.5	28.7	27.9	26.9
1227	District 27, Florida	3.1	537,784	20.6	28.8	20.7	29.9
1300	**GEORGIA**	5.0	6,683,767	13.9	28.1	28.1	29.9
1301	District 1, Georgia	6.2	476,109	12.7	30.2	32.8	24.3
1302	District 2, Georgia	7.5	443,195	18.3	34.6	29.3	17.9
1303	District 3, Georgia	5.0	476,480	12.9	31.8	29.5	25.8
1304	District 4, Georgia	5.7	484,765	13.2	25.4	30.9	30.5
1305	District 5, Georgia	4.8	497,961	12.4	22.3	24.7	40.6
1306	District 6, Georgia	2.4	489,462	6.8	13.3	20.4	59.5
1307	District 7, Georgia	2.9	506,380	11.0	21.9	27.1	40.0
1308	District 8, Georgia	9.8	458,206	16.4	34.3	29.3	19.9
1309	District 9, Georgia	4.1	490,387	17.3	31.8	28.0	23.0
1310	District 10, Georgia	4.2	461,294	14.8	33.3	26.9	25.0
1311	District 11, Georgia	3.7	494,130	10.2	21.4	27.2	41.2
1312	District 12, Georgia	5.9	458,969	17.3	32.6	29.3	20.8
1313	District 13, Georgia	5.8	484,095	11.9	29.4	29.5	29.3
1314	District 14, Georgia	3.8	462,334	20.1	33.9	29.0	17.0
1500	**HAWAII**	9.0	985,914	9.1	27.1	32.4	31.4
1501	District 1, Hawaii	9.5	500,290	10.0	24.7	31.0	34.3
1502	District 2, Hawaii	8.5	485,624	8.2	29.7	33.8	28.3

Table F. Congressional Districts—Labor Force, Employment, and Educational Data, 2015—*Continued*

State and District code	State/Congressional district (114th Congress)	Industry for employed population age 16 and older	Educational attainment for the population age 25 and older				
					Educational attainment		
		Public administration	Total population age 25 and older	Less than high school graduate	High school graduate (includes equivalency)	Some college or Associate's degree	Bachelor's degree or higher
1600	**IDAHO**	4.8	1,065,982	10.0	27.5	36.6	26.0
1601	District 1, Idaho	4.9	561,323	9.5	29.0	36.9	24.7
1602	District 2, Idaho	4.6	504,659	10.6	25.8	36.2	27.4
1700	**ILLINOIS**	3.6	8,661,938	11.4	26.7	28.9	32.9
1701	District 1, Illinois	5.7	474,502	11.4	28.0	33.7	26.9
1702	District 2, Illinois	4.6	467,901	11.9	30.5	35.6	22.0
1703	District 3, Illinois	4.0	477,892	14.1	31.7	28.1	26.2
1704	District 4, Illinois	2.1	449,460	27.8	26.9	21.9	23.4
1705	District 5, Illinois	3.7	534,242	8.9	18.5	20.6	52.0
1706	District 6, Illinois	2.3	494,448	5.6	17.8	27.2	49.5
1707	District 7, Illinois	3.4	494,655	14.1	23.1	22.2	40.6
1708	District 8, Illinois	2.2	483,648	15.4	22.7	28.7	33.3
1709	District 9, Illinois	2.7	519,474	9.4	17.5	21.7	51.4
1710	District 10, Illinois	3.0	466,785	10.7	20.4	24.6	44.3
1711	District 11, Illinois	2.7	465,805	13.9	24.3	28.4	33.4
1712	District 12, Illinois	5.8	480,245	10.1	31.7	35.7	22.5
1713	District 13, Illinois	5.0	456,470	8.1	31.3	29.9	30.8
1714	District 14, Illinois	3.0	479,087	5.9	23.8	30.3	40.0
1715	District 15, Illinois	3.8	480,561	11.0	35.2	34.8	19.0
1716	District 16, Illinois	3.6	476,590	10.3	34.7	33.3	21.7
1717	District 17, Illinois	3.9	471,766	12.6	35.2	33.9	18.4
1718	District 18, Illinois	5.4	488,407	6.7	30.2	31.1	32.0
1800	**INDIANA**	3.3	4,363,573	11.8	34.3	29.0	24.9
1801	District 1, Indiana	3.3	481,961	11.2	35.2	30.9	22.7
1802	District 2, Indiana	3.1	474,076	15.1	36.1	27.9	21.0
1803	District 3, Indiana	1.9	477,226	12.5	35.2	29.9	22.4
1804	District 4, Indiana	3.1	478,326	9.6	34.5	30.1	25.8
1805	District 5, Indiana	3.5	513,410	7.2	23.8	25.0	44.0
1806	District 6, Indiana	3.5	483,850	11.3	40.0	29.0	19.8
1807	District 7, Indiana	3.8	478,686	17.8	31.1	29.0	22.2
1808	District 8, Indiana	3.9	487,974	11.9	38.3	30.1	19.7
1809	District 9, Indiana	3.6	488,064	9.8	35.2	29.2	25.8
1900	**IOWA**	3.0	2,074,504	8.3	32.1	32.8	26.8
1901	District 1, Iowa	2.3	514,893	7.7	33.8	32.9	25.6
1902	District 2, Iowa	2.9	518,268	8.0	33.3	32.4	26.2
1903	District 3, Iowa	3.5	540,177	8.7	28.4	31.6	31.3
1904	District 4, Iowa	3.3	501,166	8.6	32.9	34.5	24.0
2000	**KANSAS**	4.3	1,888,479	9.7	26.5	32.0	31.7
2001	District 1, Kansas	4.5	455,292	12.2	28.5	35.7	23.7
2002	District 2, Kansas	5.9	464,263	9.0	30.4	32.9	27.7
2003	District 3, Kansas	3.9	497,709	7.5	19.6	25.9	47.0
2004	District 4, Kansas	3.0	471,215	10.5	28.2	34.0	27.3
2100	**KENTUCKY**	4.4	2,988,790	14.9	33.5	28.3	23.3
2101	District 1, Kentucky	4.6	489,347	15.6	39.2	28.3	16.9
2102	District 2, Kentucky	4.1	497,544	14.6	35.7	29.9	19.8
2103	District 3, Kentucky	3.0	510,434	9.9	27.6	29.8	32.7
2104	District 4, Kentucky	4.4	505,877	11.7	32.6	29.2	26.5
2105	District 5, Kentucky	4.8	488,672	24.3	37.9	24.5	13.2
2106	District 6, Kentucky	5.9	496,916	13.3	28.5	28.1	30.1
2200	**LOUISIANA**	5.4	3,095,255	15.4	34.1	27.3	23.2
2201	District 1, Louisiana	4.9	550,479	12.6	30.2	27.9	29.4
2202	District 2, Louisiana	5.7	529,491	18.1	31.7	27.4	22.8
2203	District 3, Louisiana	4.1	513,651	16.9	36.1	26.8	20.2
2204	District 4, Louisiana	6.6	498,110	15.3	36.4	29.0	19.3
2205	District 5, Louisiana	6.7	495,408	18.9	38.9	24.6	17.6
2206	District 6, Louisiana	5.0	508,116	10.9	32.1	27.8	29.3
2300	**MAINE**	3.9	961,240	8.3	32.7	28.9	30.1
2301	District 1, Maine	3.7	486,234	6.2	29.1	27.3	37.3
2302	District 2, Maine	4.1	475,006	10.4	36.4	30.5	22.8
2400	**MARYLAND**	10.7	4,102,486	10.4	25.1	25.7	38.8
2401	District 1, Maryland	7.2	501,228	9.5	32.4	27.1	31.0
2402	District 2, Maryland	9.1	513,452	11.6	28.8	28.6	31.1
2403	District 3, Maryland	9.3	530,221	9.1	20.8	22.8	47.3
2404	District 4, Maryland	12.9	507,543	13.1	25.5	28.4	33.0
2405	District 5, Maryland	16.2	507,157	8.6	26.9	29.7	34.9
2406	District 6, Maryland	9.1	512,252	10.5	24.3	24.2	41.0
2407	District 7, Maryland	10.1	501,913	11.3	25.8	25.8	37.0
2408	District 8, Maryland	11.4	528,720	9.4	16.8	19.8	53.9
2500	**MASSACHUSETTS**	3.6	4,706,644	9.8	25.2	23.6	41.5
2501	District 1, Massachusetts	3.9	504,253	12.0	30.8	28.1	29.1
2502	District 2, Massachusetts	3.3	501,918	9.8	27.6	25.9	36.7
2503	District 3, Massachusetts	3.5	509,119	11.4	27.8	23.4	37.4

Table F. Congressional Districts—Labor Force, Employment, and Educational Data, 2015—*Continued*

State and District code	State/Congressional district (114th Congress)	Industry for employed population age 16 and older	Educational attainment for the population age 25 and older				
					Educational attainment		
		Public administration	Total population age 25 and older	Less than high school graduate	High school graduate (includes equivalency)	Some college or Associate's degree	Bachelor's degree or higher
2504	District 4, Massachusetts	3.3	510,199	7.2	20.2	22.7	49.9
2505	District 5, Massachusetts	3.2	545,205	6.8	19.5	17.8	55.9
2506	District 6, Massachusetts	4.0	531,908	7.5	25.4	24.6	42.4
2507	District 7, Massachusetts	3.1	521,958	15.9	23.1	18.8	42.2
2508	District 8, Massachusetts	4.0	548,664	7.4	23.6	23.7	45.3
2509	District 9, Massachusetts	4.7	533,420	10.1	29.0	27.8	33.1
2600	**MICHIGAN**	3.4	6,728,347	9.9	29.4	32.9	27.8
2601	District 1, Michigan	4.5	506,404	8.1	33.5	33.6	24.9
2602	District 2, Michigan	2.7	476,339	10.3	31.8	32.9	25.1
2603	District 3, Michigan	3.2	485,093	9.4	28.7	31.8	30.2
2604	District 4, Michigan	4.6	475,992	9.8	35.8	33.7	20.7
2605	District 5, Michigan	3.2	470,032	10.7	33.6	36.2	19.5
2606	District 6, Michigan	2.8	471,771	9.0	29.6	33.4	28.1
2607	District 7, Michigan	4.6	483,768	8.8	33.5	34.3	23.4
2608	District 8, Michigan	3.9	476,341	5.9	22.1	33.0	39.0
2609	District 9, Michigan	3.1	515,299	10.7	27.6	32.9	28.8
2610	District 10, Michigan	3.8	496,858	9.2	32.7	35.2	22.8
2611	District 11, Michigan	2.5	504,151	5.4	19.0	29.7	46.0
2612	District 12, Michigan	2.6	460,334	10.6	25.5	29.6	34.3
2613	District 13, Michigan	2.9	442,439	18.2	33.6	32.9	15.3
2614	District 14, Michigan	3.8	463,526	13.0	25.3	31.9	29.7
2700	**MINNESOTA**	3.1	3,700,935	7.2	25.4	32.7	34.7
2701	District 1, Minnesota	2.6	442,943	7.8	30.4	33.5	28.2
2702	District 2, Minnesota	3.5	460,273	5.1	23.1	33.9	37.8
2703	District 3, Minnesota	2.1	485,420	4.4	18.3	29.3	48.0
2704	District 4, Minnesota	4.2	468,338	8.3	21.0	27.4	43.2
2705	District 5, Minnesota	2.5	483,057	10.6	18.0	26.2	45.1
2706	District 6, Minnesota	3.2	446,483	5.7	27.0	38.0	29.3
2707	District 7, Minnesota	3.4	449,056	8.6	33.2	36.5	21.6
2708	District 8, Minnesota	4.0	465,365	7.3	33.4	37.0	22.3
2800	**MISSISSIPPI**	5.3	1,952,337	16.5	31.0	31.6	20.8
2801	District 1, Mississippi	4.1	495,307	17.3	31.5	31.4	19.9
2802	District 2, Mississippi	7.2	462,722	19.6	32.2	30.5	17.7
2803	District 3, Mississippi	5.3	492,001	14.0	29.3	31.4	25.2
2804	District 4, Mississippi	5.0	502,307	15.4	31.2	33.1	20.4
2900	**MISSOURI**	4.1	4,097,212	11.1	31.0	30.1	27.8
2901	District 1, Missouri	3.4	495,661	12.1	26.3	31.1	30.5
2902	District 2, Missouri	2.7	543,234	5.2	19.7	27.9	47.2
2903	District 3, Missouri	5.2	521,754	10.0	34.5	31.0	24.5
2904	District 4, Missouri	5.1	494,084	11.7	33.9	29.2	25.2
2905	District 5, Missouri	4.5	515,163	11.8	31.0	30.0	27.2
2906	District 6, Missouri	4.5	509,205	9.3	33.9	29.4	27.3
2907	District 7, Missouri	2.9	508,664	11.1	32.9	32.0	24.0
2908	District 8, Missouri	4.6	509,447	17.8	36.5	30.2	15.6
3000	**MONTANA**	6.4	706,329	6.5	31.5	31.5	30.6
3000	District (at Large), Montana	6.4	706,329	6.5	31.5	31.5	30.6
3100	**NEBRASKA**	3.8	1,232,583	9.0	26.9	33.9	30.2
3101	District 1, Nebraska	5.1	404,616	8.3	27.1	34.8	29.9
3102	District 2, Nebraska	2.6	423,227	8.6	21.3	31.6	38.5
3103	District 3, Nebraska	3.6	404,740	10.1	32.7	35.4	21.9
3200	**NEVADA**	4.1	1,968,167	14.4	27.9	34.1	23.6
3201	District 1, Nevada	2.0	470,959	24.3	31.2	29.1	15.4
3202	District 2, Nevada	5.4	486,045	13.2	25.5	35.3	26.0
3203	District 3, Nevada	3.5	536,051	7.0	25.1	36.0	31.8
3204	District 4, Nevada	5.5	475,112	14.2	30.2	35.8	19.8
3300	**NEW HAMPSHIRE**	3.7	937,214	6.9	28.5	28.9	35.7
3301	District 1, New Hampshire	3.6	469,588	6.7	28.2	28.8	36.3
3302	District 2, New Hampshire	3.7	467,626	7.1	28.8	29.1	35.1
3400	**NEW JERSEY**	3.9	6,166,384	10.9	28.5	23.0	37.6
3401	District 1, New Jersey	4.5	504,414	10.2	31.6	27.3	30.9
3402	District 2, New Jersey	5.0	507,330	13.9	35.5	25.3	25.3
3403	District 3, New Jersey	6.1	523,107	7.1	31.9	28.7	32.3
3404	District 4, New Jersey	5.1	500,032	7.5	27.7	26.1	38.7
3405	District 5, New Jersey	2.8	516,520	7.2	24.5	22.2	46.1
3406	District 6, New Jersey	3.0	505,844	12.2	27.5	21.8	38.5
3407	District 7, New Jersey	2.9	513,896	5.5	21.5	20.8	52.2
3408	District 8, New Jersey	2.7	532,047	20.9	28.8	18.4	31.9
3409	District 9, New Jersey	3.3	520,543	15.1	32.4	20.4	32.1
3410	District 10, New Jersey	4.5	511,464	15.1	32.5	24.6	27.8
3411	District 11, New Jersey	3.4	515,458	5.6	22.7	19.8	52.0
3412	District 12, New Jersey	4.3	515,729	10.6	25.6	20.5	43.3

Table F. Congressional Districts—Labor Force, Employment, and Educational Data, 2015—*Continued*

State and District code	State/Congressional district (114th Congress)	Industry for employed population age 16 and older	Educational attainment for the population age 25 and older				
		Public administration	Total population age 25 and older	Educational attainment			
				Less than high school graduate	High school graduate (includes equivalency)	Some college or Associate's degree	Bachelor's degree or higher
3500	**NEW MEXICO**	6.9	1,377,548	15.4	26.8	31.3	26.5
3501	District 1, New Mexico	6.1	473,069	13.1	24.3	31.0	31.6
3502	District 2, New Mexico	7.2	446,377	19.0	29.6	31.3	20.1
3503	District 3, New Mexico	7.5	458,102	14.2	26.7	31.7	27.4
3600	**NEW YORK**	4.4	13,641,473	14.0	26.5	24.4	35.0
3601	District 1, New York	5.0	502,649	8.1	28.3	29.3	34.3
3602	District 2, New York	4.8	495,809	12.0	30.8	27.2	30.0
3603	District 3, New York	3.7	511,558	6.8	20.6	20.7	51.8
3604	District 4, New York	4.3	494,810	10.9	25.3	23.1	40.7
3605	District 5, New York	5.7	526,389	19.7	29.0	27.0	24.3
3606	District 6, New York	3.7	545,184	16.2	26.2	21.5	36.2
3607	District 7, New York	2.7	498,903	27.9	24.1	15.0	33.0
3608	District 8, New York	5.1	524,517	17.0	28.2	23.8	30.9
3609	District 9, New York	4.0	521,947	14.8	26.2	21.6	37.3
3610	District 10, New York	2.3	525,330	12.9	14.1	12.8	60.3
3611	District 11, New York	5.8	507,344	13.1	29.0	23.5	34.4
3612	District 12, New York	2.5	582,868	6.6	9.7	12.2	71.5
3613	District 13, New York	2.5	546,327	26.7	21.1	20.7	31.5
3614	District 14, New York	3.3	505,561	24.5	29.7	20.2	25.6
3615	District 15, New York	2.2	457,955	36.1	27.4	22.6	13.9
3616	District 16, New York	4.2	507,601	15.1	23.6	22.6	38.7
3617	District 17, New York	4.1	494,628	13.0	21.0	21.7	44.4
3618	District 18, New York	5.9	475,291	8.9	28.0	28.6	34.6
3619	District 19, New York	5.3	498,390	10.4	32.6	28.8	28.3
3620	District 20, New York	10.7	495,914	8.2	26.4	29.0	36.4
3621	District 21, New York	7.1	488,156	10.9	35.9	30.6	22.6
3622	District 22, New York	5.0	483,323	10.5	34.4	31.7	23.4
3623	District 23, New York	4.7	474,666	9.9	35.0	28.8	26.3
3624	District 24, New York	4.2	482,165	9.9	28.9	30.7	30.5
3625	District 25, New York	3.1	493,505	10.5	24.8	28.5	36.3
3626	District 26, New York	3.8	486,488	11.4	29.2	29.7	29.8
3627	District 27, New York	4.8	514,195	7.8	31.0	32.0	29.3
3700	**NORTH CAROLINA**	4.3	6,762,644	13.4	26.4	30.7	29.4
3701	District 1, North Carolina	5.4	484,762	19.9	30.4	29.0	20.7
3702	District 2, North Carolina	5.8	523,837	12.7	24.9	31.4	31.0
3703	District 3, North Carolina	7.3	480,004	10.1	29.4	35.9	24.5
3704	District 4, North Carolina	4.8	520,777	10.9	19.7	27.6	41.8
3705	District 5, North Carolina	3.1	517,695	14.5	28.5	30.2	26.8
3706	District 6, North Carolina	3.3	528,226	12.5	26.1	31.5	29.9
3707	District 7, North Carolina	4.9	546,823	14.7	27.9	33.3	24.1
3708	District 8, North Carolina	4.2	499,933	17.0	32.5	32.5	18.0
3709	District 9, North Carolina	2.0	556,382	6.2	16.9	27.4	49.5
3710	District 10, North Carolina	3.6	525,157	15.6	30.7	30.5	23.2
3711	District 11, North Carolina	4.0	537,158	14.8	29.5	32.3	23.4
3712	District 12, North Carolina	2.3	504,059	17.8	26.9	29.8	25.6
3713	District 13, North Carolina	5.6	537,831	9.0	21.4	28.2	41.3
3800	**NORTH DAKOTA**	4.4	492,017	7.5	27.6	35.8	29.1
3800	District (at Large), North Dakota	4.4	492,017	7.5	27.6	35.8	29.1
3900	**OHIO**	3.8	7,896,470	10.3	33.7	29.2	26.8
3901	District 1, Ohio	3.3	481,311	8.7	28.7	28.4	34.2
3902	District 2, Ohio	3.7	505,017	10.3	30.6	28.6	30.5
3903	District 3, Ohio	3.9	490,586	12.6	30.8	29.4	27.2
3904	District 4, Ohio	3.7	486,641	10.2	42.1	30.7	17.0
3905	District 5, Ohio	2.9	482,834	7.5	36.5	30.8	25.2
3906	District 6, Ohio	3.9	497,265	12.3	42.6	29.4	15.8
3907	District 7, Ohio	3.1	504,813	12.5	40.0	28.0	19.5
3908	District 8, Ohio	3.3	481,065	11.4	36.4	28.4	23.7
3909	District 9, Ohio	4.1	481,013	13.6	34.1	30.7	21.6
3910	District 10, Ohio	5.8	488,949	9.3	28.9	32.8	29.1
3911	District 11, Ohio	3.8	474,170	14.2	29.1	30.8	26.0
3912	District 12, Ohio	4.5	515,979	6.9	25.8	27.3	40.0
3913	District 13, Ohio	3.1	493,433	10.4	39.2	29.0	21.4
3914	District 14, Ohio	3.1	504,201	8.1	30.8	27.6	33.5
3915	District 15, Ohio	4.9	509,905	9.9	32.5	26.8	30.8
3916	District 16, Ohio	3.3	499,288	7.2	32.1	28.4	32.3
4000	**OKLAHOMA**	5.8	2,557,863	12.7	31.6	31.1	24.6
4001	District 1, Oklahoma	3.1	520,610	10.4	27.5	32.7	29.4
4002	District 2, Oklahoma	6.5	504,073	15.7	36.6	30.4	17.3
4003	District 3, Oklahoma	6.4	503,592	12.8	35.5	29.7	22.1
4004	District 4, Oklahoma	7.6	503,777	10.4	31.9	33.6	24.1
4005	District 5, Oklahoma	5.7	525,811	14.2	27.0	28.9	29.9
4100	**OREGON**	4.4	2,804,461	10.0	23.4	34.5	32.2
4101	District 1, Oregon	4.1	565,397	8.8	18.9	31.9	40.4

Table F. Congressional Districts—Labor Force, Employment, and Educational Data, 2015—*Continued*

State and District code	State/Congressional district (114th Congress)	Industry for employed population age 16 and older — Public administration	Educational attainment for the population age 25 and older — Total population age 25 and older	Less than high school graduate	High school graduate (includes equivalency)	Some college or Associate's degree	Bachelor's degree or higher
4102	District 2, Oregon	5.0	559,115	10.5	28.6	36.9	24.0
4103	District 3, Oregon	3.3	585,668	10.2	18.8	31.1	39.9
4104	District 4, Oregon	4.4	543,272	9.9	25.9	38.3	25.9
4105	District 5, Oregon	5.6	551,009	10.3	25.0	34.7	29.9
4200	**PENNSYLVANIA**	4.0	8,895,727	10.3	35.7	24.3	29.7
4201	District 1, Pennsylvania	5.0	482,239	17.1	35.5	21.4	26.0
4202	District 2, Pennsylvania	5.4	486,451	13.7	28.3	22.3	35.6
4203	District 3, Pennsylvania	3.4	490,156	9.5	41.2	24.2	25.1
4204	District 4, Pennsylvania	6.5	500,843	10.6	38.1	25.8	25.5
4205	District 5, Pennsylvania	3.9	477,235	9.2	43.3	23.7	23.8
4206	District 6, Pennsylvania	2.4	500,249	7.1	28.5	22.0	42.5
4207	District 7, Pennsylvania	3.5	495,068	7.3	28.6	21.7	42.4
4208	District 8, Pennsylvania	2.5	499,792	6.7	29.0	25.2	39.1
4209	District 9, Pennsylvania	4.7	490,204	11.3	47.5	22.8	18.4
4210	District 10, Pennsylvania	4.3	497,136	12.1	41.9	24.7	21.3
4211	District 11, Pennsylvania	6.9	496,623	10.4	40.9	25.8	22.8
4212	District 12, Pennsylvania	2.7	510,233	6.8	35.6	25.1	32.4
4213	District 13, Pennsylvania	4.7	495,853	12.0	29.7	24.0	34.3
4214	District 14, Pennsylvania	3.4	499,640	8.1	32.4	26.5	32.9
4215	District 15, Pennsylvania	3.0	495,187	11.2	34.3	25.9	28.6
4216	District 16, Pennsylvania	2.9	477,593	15.7	35.5	23.3	25.6
4217	District 17, Pennsylvania	4.3	487,685	11.4	40.2	26.7	21.7
4218	District 18, Pennsylvania	2.6	513,540	6.0	32.4	26.2	35.4
4400	**RHODE ISLAND**	4.1	730,083	12.3	28.0	27.0	32.7
4401	District 1, Rhode Island	3.3	366,315	13.8	28.1	25.4	32.7
4402	District 2, Rhode Island	4.9	363,768	10.9	27.8	28.6	32.7
4500	**SOUTH CAROLINA**	4.4	3,319,832	13.7	29.4	30.1	26.8
4501	District 1, South Carolina	5.2	521,530	6.9	23.5	30.0	39.6
4502	District 2, South Carolina	6.3	467,919	10.6	26.0	29.9	33.5
4503	District 3, South Carolina	3.1	462,263	16.5	32.0	31.7	19.8
4504	District 4, South Carolina	2.3	474,056	15.2	25.7	29.0	30.2
4505	District 5, South Carolina	4.1	469,048	15.4	31.2	30.3	23.1
4506	District 6, South Carolina	6.1	430,757	17.0	34.4	29.4	19.2
4507	District 7, South Carolina	3.3	494,259	15.1	34.1	30.2	20.6
4600	**SOUTH DAKOTA**	4.4	563,108	8.9	31.2	32.4	27.5
4600	District (at Large), South Dakota	4.4	563,108	8.9	31.2	32.4	27.5
4700	**TENNESSEE**	4.0	4,473,487	13.9	33.1	27.2	25.7
4701	District 1, Tennessee	3.1	506,890	16.8	37.5	26.5	19.2
4702	District 2, Tennessee	3.4	499,491	11.4	30.7	28.1	29.9
4703	District 3, Tennessee	3.6	510,806	16.4	34.8	26.3	22.5
4704	District 4, Tennessee	3.4	498,068	15.0	35.1	28.3	21.6
4705	District 5, Tennessee	4.0	518,774	12.3	25.5	25.8	36.4
4706	District 6, Tennessee	4.4	510,395	14.1	37.4	27.0	21.6
4707	District 7, Tennessee	4.9	498,864	11.6	32.7	27.3	28.4
4708	District 8, Tennessee	5.2	478,259	12.4	32.8	26.3	28.5
4709	District 9, Tennessee	3.9	451,940	15.5	31.6	29.7	23.2
4800	**TEXAS**	4.1	17,472,861	17.6	25.3	28.7	28.4
4801	District 1, Texas	3.4	465,543	17.8	29.9	32.1	20.3
4802	District 2, Texas	2.5	504,616	11.9	20.1	27.9	40.1
4803	District 3, Texas	2.4	533,973	6.7	14.2	26.5	52.6
4804	District 4, Texas	4.8	484,509	14.2	34.1	32.2	19.5
4805	District 5, Texas	4.2	482,638	20.3	30.1	29.7	20.0
4806	District 6, Texas	3.5	475,887	12.7	24.2	33.3	29.8
4807	District 7, Texas	1.8	514,487	11.0	16.9	23.5	48.6
4808	District 8, Texas	4.6	523,413	14.5	27.0	28.9	29.6
4809	District 9, Texas	2.5	491,055	22.2	25.1	27.6	25.1
4810	District 10, Texas	4.4	525,353	13.1	21.6	27.0	38.3
4811	District 11, Texas	3.4	490,418	17.9	29.7	31.3	21.0
4812	District 12, Texas	4.4	516,263	11.7	26.3	31.8	30.1
4813	District 13, Texas	4.6	458,283	17.3	30.2	31.9	20.5
4814	District 14, Texas	4.6	491,179	15.1	28.5	32.2	24.2
4815	District 15, Texas	4.7	444,120	31.6	24.4	25.3	18.7
4816	District 16, Texas	8.3	453,216	20.2	25.0	30.5	24.3
4817	District 17, Texas	5.4	459,621	13.6	25.1	30.7	30.7
4818	District 18, Texas	2.6	481,194	24.9	27.5	26.6	21.0
4819	District 19, Texas	4.1	441,504	17.8	30.8	30.9	20.5
4820	District 20, Texas	4.5	474,681	19.2	26.4	31.1	23.3
4821	District 21, Texas	5.9	538,423	7.6	18.4	29.4	44.6
4822	District 22, Texas	3.1	548,608	9.3	19.5	26.4	44.7
4823	District 23, Texas	6.7	457,673	24.3	27.5	27.1	21.1
4824	District 24, Texas	2.1	526,707	9.7	18.1	27.5	44.7
4825	District 25, Texas	6.3	502,767	9.9	23.0	30.0	37.0
4826	District 26, Texas	3.5	519,165	7.5	19.3	31.6	41.6

Table F. Congressional Districts—Labor Force, Employment, and Educational Data, 2015—*Continued*

State and District code	State/Congressional district (114th Congress)	Industry for employed population age 16 and older	Educational attainment for the population age 25 and older				
		Public administration	Total population age 25 and older	Less than high school graduate	High school graduate (includes equivalency)	Some college or Associate's degree	Bachelor's degree or higher
4827	District 27, Texas	5.3	473,689	19.1	30.8	30.8	19.3
4828	District 28, Texas	6.1	420,453	29.4	27.4	24.8	18.4
4829	District 29, Texas	1.9	436,377	39.0	30.0	22.0	9.1
4830	District 30, Texas	3.4	468,291	24.4	27.3	28.2	20.0
4831	District 31, Texas	6.4	512,957	7.9	23.0	33.9	35.2
4832	District 32, Texas	1.8	499,103	13.1	17.5	26.4	43.0
4833	District 33, Texas	1.9	429,223	42.4	28.1	19.1	10.4
4834	District 34, Texas	5.3	431,596	33.2	27.9	24.3	14.6
4835	District 35, Texas	5.0	516,371	22.9	30.9	27.3	18.9
4836	District 36, Texas	4.4	479,505	16.1	33.1	32.6	18.2
4900	**UTAH**	5.1	1,741,949	8.5	24.2	35.5	31.8
4901	District 1, Utah	7.9	426,430	8.0	27.5	35.7	28.7
4902	District 2, Utah	5.0	462,808	9.4	25.1	34.3	31.2
4903	District 3, Utah	3.4	398,739	6.6	17.6	36.3	39.6
4904	District 4, Utah	4.1	453,972	9.6	26.1	35.7	28.6
5000	**VERMONT**	4.8	438,654	8.3	29.0	25.8	36.9
5000	District (at Large), Vermont	4.8	438,654	8.3	29.0	25.8	36.9
5100	**VIRGINIA**	8.7	5,685,318	11.1	24.6	27.3	37.0
5101	District 1, Virginia	13.5	513,324	9.0	25.4	30.6	35.0
5102	District 2, Virginia	9.4	499,579	8.6	24.8	35.7	30.9
5103	District 3, Virginia	7.8	479,552	14.1	29.2	32.0	24.6
5104	District 4, Virginia	8.4	511,534	11.2	28.5	32.9	27.3
5105	District 5, Virginia	5.3	519,344	14.1	30.3	29.2	26.5
5106	District 6, Virginia	3.9	499,557	13.4	32.9	27.5	26.2
5107	District 7, Virginia	5.8	536,674	8.6	24.0	26.2	41.1
5108	District 8, Virginia	15.2	574,680	10.0	12.9	17.5	59.6
5109	District 9, Virginia	4.2	501,375	17.1	32.9	29.3	20.7
5110	District 10, Virginia	8.0	530,347	7.7	16.8	20.8	54.7
5111	District 11, Virginia	11.4	519,352	8.7	15.5	21.1	54.7
5300	**WASHINGTON**	5.1	4,889,314	9.2	23.1	33.6	34.2
5301	District 1, Washington	4.3	495,359	6.3	19.9	30.7	43.1
5302	District 2, Washington	4.2	494,937	8.0	23.8	37.2	31.0
5303	District 3, Washington	5.1	485,065	10.1	26.7	39.0	24.3
5304	District 4, Washington	4.4	436,578	20.9	27.4	31.2	20.6
5305	District 5, Washington	4.7	465,649	7.7	25.9	38.2	28.2
5306	District 6, Washington	9.1	486,012	7.5	25.9	37.8	28.8
5307	District 7, Washington	2.7	550,966	5.2	11.7	23.7	59.4
5308	District 8, Washington	4.4	488,540	9.4	24.7	32.6	33.3
5309	District 9, Washington	3.6	506,328	9.6	20.1	29.1	41.3
5310	District 10, Washington	10.3	479,880	8.7	26.9	38.1	26.3
5400	**WEST VIRGINIA**	6.7	1,300,347	14.0	40.7	25.7	19.6
5401	District 1, West Virginia	6.1	429,890	11.3	39.6	26.6	22.5
5402	District 2, West Virginia	8.3	444,566	12.9	40.5	25.1	21.5
5403	District 3, West Virginia	5.4	425,891	17.8	42.1	25.5	14.5
5500	**WISCONSIN**	3.4	3,918,997	8.6	31.2	31.8	28.4
5501	District 1, Wisconsin	2.6	493,792	8.9	31.2	33.1	26.9
5502	District 2, Wisconsin	4.6	494,775	6.5	24.1	29.4	40.0
5503	District 3, Wisconsin	3.6	473,714	7.8	33.8	33.9	24.5
5504	District 4, Wisconsin	3.4	454,897	15.3	27.4	30.2	27.2
5505	District 5, Wisconsin	2.3	502,598	5.9	26.9	31.4	35.9
5506	District 6, Wisconsin	3.5	493,649	8.7	35.3	31.5	24.6
5507	District 7, Wisconsin	3.8	505,765	8.5	35.8	33.4	22.3
5508	District 8, Wisconsin	3.1	499,807	7.5	35.2	31.7	25.7
5600	**WYOMING**	6.4	388,747	7.8	28.8	37.2	26.2
5600	District (at Large), Wyoming	6.4	388,747	7.8	28.8	37.2	26.2

APPENDIXES

APPENDIX A. GEOGRAPHIC CONCEPTS AND CODES

GEOGRAPHIC AREAS COVERED

Education and the American Workforce presents American Community Survey (ACS) data for the United States, all states, all metropolitan areas, all counties, and cities with populations of 20,000 or more. ACS population sizes are based on the most recent population estimates from the Census Bureau's Population Estimates Program. Also included are some national tables from the Bureau of Labor Statistics.

STATES AND COUNTIES

Data are presented for each of the 50 states, the District of Columbia, and the United States as a whole. The states are arranged alphabetically and counties are arranged alphabetically within each state. Data are presented for 3,142 counties and county equivalents.

County equivalents

In Louisiana, the primary divisions of the state are known as parishes rather than counties. In Alaska, the county equivalents are the organized boroughs, together with the census areas that were developed for general statistical purposes by the state of Alaska and the U.S. Census Bureau. Four states—Maryland, Missouri, Nevada, and Virginia—have one or more incorporated places that are legally independent of any county and thus constitute primary divisions of their states. Within each state, independent cities are listed alphabetically following the list of counties. The District of Columbia is not divided into counties or county equivalents—data for the entire district are presented as a county equivalent. New York City contains five counties: Bronx, Kings, New York, Queens, and Richmond.

METROPOLITAN AREAS

Data are included for 381 metropolitan statistical areas and 31 metropolitan divisions, which are located within the 11 largest metropolitan statistical areas. The metropolitan statistical areas are listed alphabetically, and the metropolitan divisions are listed alphabetically under the metropolitan statistical area of which they are components.

The U.S. Office of Management and Budget (OMB) defines metropolitan and micropolitan statistical areas according to published standards. The major purpose of defining these areas is to enable all U.S. government agencies to use the same geographic definitions in tabulating and publishing data. The general concept of a metropolitan or micropolitan statistical area is that of a core area containing a substantial population nucleus, together with adjacent communities that have a high degree of economic and social integration with the core.

New delineations of these Core Based Statistical Areas (CBSAs) based on the 2010 census were released in February 2013. Standard definitions of metropolitan areas were first issued in 1949 by the Bureau of the Budget (the predecessor of OMB), under the designation "standard metropolitan area" (SMA). The term was changed to "standard metropolitan statistical area" (SMSA) in 1959, and to "metropolitan statistical area" (MSA) in 1983. The term "metropolitan area" (MA) was adopted in 1990 and referred collectively to metropolitan statistical areas (MSAs), consolidated metropolitan statistical areas (CMSAs), and primary metropolitan statistical areas (PMSAs). The term "core based statistical area" (CBSA) became effective in 2000 and refers collectively to metropolitan and micropolitan statistical areas.

The 2010 standards provide that each CBSA must contain at least one urban area of 10,000 or more population. Each metropolitan statistical area must have at least one urbanized area of 50,000 or more inhabitants. Each micropolitan statistical area must have at least one urban cluster of at least 10,000 but less than 50,000 people.

Under the standards, a metro area contains a core urban area of 50,000 or more population, and a micro area contains an urban core of at least 10,000 (but less than 50,000) population. Each metro or micro area consists of one or more counties and includes the counties containing the core urban area, as well as any adjacent counties that have a high degree of social and economic integration (as measured by commuting to work) with the urban core.

If specified criteria are met, a metropolitan statistical area containing a single core with a population of 2.5 million or more may be subdivided to form smaller groupings of counties referred to as "metropolitan divisions."

As of February 28, 2013, there were 381 metropolitan statistical areas. The largest city in each metropolitan or micropolitan statistical area is designated a "principal city." Additional cities qualify if specified requirements are met concerning population size and employment. The title of each metropolitan statistical area consists of the names of up to three of its principal cities and the name of each state into which the metropolitan or micropolitan statistical area extends. Titles of metropolitan divisions also typically are based on principal city names, but in certain cases consist of county names. The principal city need not be an incorporated place if it meets the requirements of population size and employment. Usually such a principal city is a census designated place (CDP).

In view of the importance of cities and towns in New England, the 2010 standards also provide for a set of geographic areas that are defined using cities and towns in the six New England states. These New England city and town areas (NECTAs) are not included in this volume.

CITIES

This book presents data for 2,215 cities with estimated populations of 20,000 or more. Corresponding data for states are also provided. The states are arranged alphabetically and the cities are ordered alphabetically within each state.

As used in this volume, the term *city* refers to *places* as defined by the Census Bureau. These include places that have been incorporated as cities, boroughs, towns, or villages under the laws of their respective states, as well as Census designated places (CDPs). CDPs are delineated by the Census Bureau, in cooperation with states and localities, as statistical counterparts of incorporated places for purposes of the decennial census and the ACS. CDPs comprise densely settled concentrations of population that are identifiable by name but are not legally incorporated places.

Included with the incorporated cities are the principal portions of seven consolidated cities. A consolidated city is an incorporated place that has combined its government functions with a county or subcounty entity but contains one or more other semi-independent incorporated places that continue to function as local governments within the consolidated government. Consolidated cities are not included in this book, but the "consolidated city (balance)" portions are treated as incorporated places in the ACS data. Consolidated city (balance) portions included in this volume are Milford, Connecticut; Athens-Clarke County, Georgia Augusta-Richmond County, Georgia; Indianapolis, Indiana; Louisville-Jefferson County, Kentucky; Butte-Silver Bow, Montana; and Nashville-Davidson, Tennessee.

Towns in the New England states and New York are treated as minor civil divisions (MCDs) and are not included in this book.

CONGRESSIONAL DISTRICTS

The congressional districts shown in this volume are the districts used for the election of the 114th Congress, which convened in January 2015. These are the districts that were established following the 2010 Census and are based on population data from that census. Data are shown for the 435 regular districts plus the District of Columbia, which has a non-voting delegate, but no representative. Corresponding data for each state also are included. States are listed alphabetically and districts numerically within each state. The Representatives shown were elected for the 115th Congress which convened in January 2017. Boundary changes between the 114th and 115th congresses occurred in Florida, Minnesota, North Carolina, and Virginia

GEOGRAPHIC CODES

The tables in this book provide a geographic code or codes for each area.

For counties, a five-digit state and county code is given for each state and county. The first two digits indicate the state; the remaining three represent the county. Within each state, the counties are listed in order, beginning with 001, with even numbers usually omitted. Independent cities follow the counties and begin with the number 510. In the state-level tables, a two-digit state code is provided. The state code is a sequential numbering, with some gaps, of the states and the District of Columbia in alphabetical order from Alabama (01) to Wyoming (56).

These codes have been established by the U.S. government as Federal Information Processing Standards and are often referred to as *FIPS codes*. They are used by U.S. government agencies and many other organizations for data presentation. The codes are provided in this volume for use in matching the data given here with other data sources in which counties are identified by FIPS code.

The metropolitan area tables provide metro area codes for each metropolitan area, as well as metropolitan division codes where appropriate.

For cities, a seven-digit state and place code is included. The first two digits identify the state and are the same as the FIPS codes described above. The remaining five digits are the place FIPS codes established by the U.S. government.

INDEPENDENT CITIES

The following independent cities are not included in any county; their data are presented separately in this volume.

Maryland
Baltimore (separate from Baltimore County).

Missouri
St. Louis (separate from St. Louis County).

Nevada
Carson City.

Virginia

Alexandria
Charlottesville
Chesapeake
Danville
Fairfax
Fredericksburg
Hampton
Harrisonburg
Hopewell
Lynchburg
Manassas
Newport News
Norfolk
Petersburg
Portsmouth
Richmond
Roanoke
Salem
Staunton
Suffolk
Virginia Beach
Waynesboro
Winchester

Data in this book are from the Bureau of Labor Statistics (BLS) and the Census Bureau. Part A presents national data from the BLS Occupational Employment Statistics Program, and a table that was compiled by BLS from the American Community Survey (ACS), the Census Bureau's ongoing survey of detailed social and economic characteristics.

Most of the data in the book—all of the data in Parts B through E—are from the ACS. Annual ACS data are released for all geographic entities with populations of 65,000 or more, and are used for Part B (states), Part D (metropolitan areas), and Part F (congressional districts.) For areas with populations between 20,000 and 65,000, 1-year Supplemental Estimates are released with less precise categories than the regular 1-year estimates. These 1-year Supplemental Estimates are used for Part E (cities). For areas with populations below 20,000, only 5-year estimates are available. In order to include data for all counties, these 5-year estimates are used in Part C (counties). Covering the years 2011 through 2015, these 5-year county data can mask changes over time.

PART A. NATIONAL DATA

It is always critical to remember that all estimates are subject to sampling error. On the Census Bureau's website, every ACS number is accompanied by its margin of error. In the interests of space and simplicity, this book does not include the margins of error, but all users are encouraged to consult the Census Bureau's website and to understand some basics: small differences are very likely to represent no difference at all; do not draw conclusions from small numbers; use these numbers as a starting point to explore the wealth of information from the ACS.

Table A-1. Number of Employees, Wages and Salaries, and Job Requirements for Detailed Occupations in the United States

The number of employees, median hourly wage, and median annual salary are from the Occupational Employment Statistics Program. https://www.bls.gov/oes/tables.htm.

The typical education needed, years of experience and on-the-job training come from the Education and Training data of the Employment Projections program. https://www.bls.gov/emp/

Table A-2. Educational Attainment for Workers 25 Years and Older by Detailed Occupation, 2014–2015

The educational attainment table was developed by the Employment Projections Program of the BLS from the Public Use Microdata Samples of the 2014 and 2015 American Community Survey. Many of the occupations represent combinations of similar occupations to conform to the ACS occupation coding scheme. https://www.bls.gov/emp/ep_table_111.htm

Table A-3. Fastest Growing Occupations, 2014 and Projected 2024

Table A-4. Fastest Declining Occupations, 2014 and Projected 2024

The projections are from the Employment Projections Program of the BLS.
https://www.bls.gov/emp/ep_table_103.htm
https://www.bls.gov/emp/ep_table_105.htm

PART B. STATE DATA
PART C. COUNTY DATA
PART D. METROPOLITAN AREA DATA
PART E. CITY DATA
PART F. CONGRESSIONAL DISTRICT DATA

This section of source notes is generally derived from: https://www2.census.gov/programs-surveys/acs/tech_docs/subject_definitions/2015_ACSSubjectDefinitions.pdf

The data were assembled from the ACS detailed tables on American FactFinder. https://factfinder.census.gov/faces/nav/jsf/pages/index.xhtml

The following notes reference the numbers of those detailed tables on American FactFinder. Also included in each table title is the table's universe, which is the total number of units (e.g., individuals, households, businesses, in the population of interest). Many of the data items can also be found in ACS profiles, subject tables, geographic comparison tables, and other formats available on the ACS website.

In this section, table numbers beginning with B or C are from the 2015 1-year ACS estimates used in Part B (states), Part D (metropolitan areas) and Part F (congressional districts), and also from the 2011–2015 5-year ACS estimates used in Part C (counties). Table numbers beginning with K are from the 2015 1-year supplemental ACS estimates used in Part E (cities).

Topics are listed in alphabetical order.

CLASS OF WORKER

Sources:

B24080. Sex by Class of Worker for the Civilian Employed Population 16 Years and Over;
K202402. Class of Worker for the Civilian Employed Population 16 Years and Over.

For employed people, the data on **class of worker** refer to the person's job during the previous week. For those who worked two or more jobs, the data refer to the job where the person worked the greatest number of hours. For unemployed people, the data refer to their last job. The information on **class of worker** refers to the same job as a respondent's industry and occupation and categorizes people according to the type of ownership of the employing organization. The class of worker categories are defined as follows:

Private wage and salary workers includes people who worked for wages, salary, commission, tips, pay-in-kind, or piece rates for a private for-profit employer or a private not-for-profit, tax-exempt or charitable organization. Self-employed people whose business was incorporated are included with private wage and salary workers because they are paid employees of their own companies.

Government workers includes people who were employees of any local, state, or federal governmental unit, regardless of the activity of the particular agency. Employees of foreign governments, the United Nations, or other formal international organizations controlled by governments were classified as "federal government workers." The class of worker government categories includes all government workers, though government workers may work in different industries. For example, people who work in a public elementary or secondary school are coded as local government class of workers.

Self-employed includes people who worked for profit or fees in their own unincorporated business, profession, or trade, or who operated a farm.

Unpaid family workers includes people who worked 15 hours or more a week without pay in a business or on a farm operated by a relative.

EARNINGS

Sources:

B20004. Median Earnings in the Past 12 Months (In 2015 Inflation-Adjusted Dollars) by Sex by Educational Attainment for the Population 25 Years and Over;
B24012. Sex by Occupation and Median Earnings in the Past 12 Months (in 2015 Inflation-Adjusted Dollars) for the Civilian Employed Population 16 Years and Over;
B24032. Sex by Industry and Median Earnings in the Past 12 Months (in 2015 Inflation-Adjusted Dollars) for the Civilian Employed Population 16 Years and Over;
K202002. Median Earnings in the Past 12 Months (in 2015 Inflation-Adjusted Dollars) by Sex by Work Experience in the Past 12 Months for the Population 16 Years and Over with Earnings in the Past 12 Months.

Earnings are defined as the sum of wage or salary income and net income from self-employment. "Earnings" represent the amount of income received regularly for people 16 years old and over before deductions for personal income taxes, Social Security, bond purchases, union dues, Medicare deductions, etc. An individual with earnings is one who has either wage/salary income or self-employment income, or both. Respondents who "break even" in self-employment income and therefore have zero self-employment earnings also are considered "individuals with earnings."

The median divides the earnings distribution into two equal parts: one-half of the cases falling below the median and one-half above the median. Median earnings is restricted to individuals 16 years old and over with earnings and is computed on the basis of a standard distribution.

Wage or salary income includes total money earnings received for work performed as an employee during the past 12 months. It includes wages, salary, armed forces pay, commissions, tips, piece-rate payments, and cash bonuses earned before deductions were made for taxes, bonds, pensions, union dues, etc.

Self-employment income includes both farm and non-farm self-employment income.

Farm self-employment income includes net money income (gross receipts minus operating expenses) from the operation of a farm by a person on his or her own account, as an owner, renter, or sharecropper. Gross receipts include the value of all products sold, government farm programs, money received from the rental of farm equipment to others, and incidental receipts from the sale of wood, sand, gravel, etc. Operating expenses include cost of feed, fertilizer, seed, and other farming supplies, cash wages paid to farmhands, depreciation charges, cash rent, interest on farm mortgages, farm building repairs, farm taxes (not state and federal personal income taxes), etc. The value of fuel, food, or other farm products used for family living is not included as part of net income.

Non-farm self-employment income includes net money income (gross receipts minus expenses) from one's own business, professional enterprise, or partnership. Gross receipts include the value of all goods sold and services rendered. Expenses include costs of goods purchased, rent, heat, light, power, depreciation charges, wages and salaries paid, business taxes (not personal income taxes), etc.

EDUCATIONAL ATTAINMENT

Sources:

C15002. Sex by Educational Attainment for the Population 25 Years and Over;
C15002H. Sex by Educational Attainment for the Population 25 Years and Over (White Alone, Not Hispanic or Latino);
C15002B. Sex by Educational Attainment for the Population 25 Years and Over (Black or African American Alone);
C15002I. Sex by Educational Attainment for the Population 25 Years and Over (Hispanic or Latino);
C15002D. Sex by Educational Attainment for the Population 25 Years and Over (Asian Alone);
C16010. Educational Attainment and Employment Status by Language Spoken At Home for the Population 25 Years and Over;
K201501. Educational Attainment for the Population 25 Years and Over.

Data on **educational attainment** were derived from a question that asked respondents for the highest level of school completed or the highest degree received. Persons currently enrolled in school are instructed to report the level of the previous grade attended or the highest degree received. Persons who had passed a high school equivalency examination were considered high school graduates. Schooling received in foreign schools was to be reported as the equivalent grade or years in the regular American school system.

Specifically excluded are vocational and technical training, such as barber school training; business, trade, technical, and vocational schools; or other training for a specific trade.

No high school diploma includes all persons who have not received a high school diploma.

High school graduate includes persons whose highest degree was a high school diploma or its equivalent, including those who passed a high school equivalency examination.

Some college or associate's degree includes people who attended college but did not receive a degree or received an associate's degree. The category "associate's degree" includes people whose highest degree is an associate's degree, which generally requires two years of college level work and is either in an occupational program that prepares them for a specific occupation, or an academic program primarily in the arts and sciences.

Bachelor's degree includes persons who have received bachelor's degrees.

Graduate or professional degree includes persons who have received master's degrees, professional school degrees (such as law school or medical school degrees), or doctoral degrees.

EMPLOYMENT STATUS

Sources:

C23001. Sex by Age by Employment status for the Population 16 Years and Over;
C23002H. Sex by Age by Employment Status for the Population 16 Years and Over (White Alone, Not Hispanic or Latino);
C23002B. Sex by Age by Employment Status for the Population 16 Years and Over (Black or African American Alone);
C23002I. Sex by Age by Employment Status for the Population 16 Years and Over (Hispanic or Latino);
C23002D. Sex by Age by Employment Status for the Population 16 Years and Over (Asian Alone);
C16010. Educational Attainment and Employment Status by Language Spoken at Home for the Population 25 Years and Over;
K201301. Employment Status for the Population 16 Years and Over.

The **civilian labor force** consists of all persons 16 years old and over who are either employed or unemployed, not including those in the armed forces.

The **labor force participation** rate represents the proportion of the population that is in the civilian labor force.

The percent in the **Armed Forces** represents people on active duty in the United States Armed Forces as a percentage of the total population.

Total employment includes all civilians 16 years old and over who were either (1) "at work"—those who did any work at all during the reference week as paid employees, worked in either their own business or profession, worked on their own farm, or worked 15 hours or more as unpaid workers in a family farm or business; or were (2) "with a job, but not at work"—those who had a job but were not at work that week due to illness, weather, industrial dispute, vacation, or other personal reasons.

Unemployment includes all persons who did not work during the survey week, made specific efforts to find a job during the previous four weeks, and were available for work during the survey week (except for temporary illness). Persons waiting to be called back to a job from which they had been laid off and those waiting to report to a new job within the next 30 days are included in unemployment figures.

The **unemployment rate** represents the number of unemployed people as a percentage of the civilian labor force.

Full-Time, Year-Round Workers are people 16 years old and over who usually worked 35 hours or more per week for 50 to 52 weeks in the past 12 months. The data pertain to the number of weeks during the past 12 months in which a person did any work for pay or profit (including paid vacation and paid sick leave) or worked without pay on a family farm or in a family business. Weeks of active service in the Armed Forces are also included. The question on usual hours worked per week was asked of people 16 years old and over who indicated that they worked during the past 12 months.

FIELD OF DEGREE

Sources:

B15010. Detailed Field of Bachelor's Degree for First Major for the Population 25 Years and Over with a Bachelor's Degree or Higher Attainment;
C15010. Field of Bachelor's Degree for First Major for the Population 25 Years and Over with a Bachelor's Degree or Higher Attainment;
C15010H. Field of Bachelor's Degree for First Major for the White Alone, Not Hispanic or Latino Population 25 Years and Over with a Bachelor's Degree or Higher Attainment;
C15010B. Field of Bachelor's Degree for First Major for the Black or African American Alone Population 25 Years and Over with a Bachelor's Degree or Higher Attainment;
C15010I. Field of Bachelor's Degree for First Major for the Hispanic or Latino Population 25 Years and Over with a Bachelor's Degree or Higher Attainment;
C15010D. Field of Bachelor's Degree for First Major for the Asian Alone Population 25 Years and Over with a Bachelor's Degree or Higher Attainment.

Data on field of bachelor's degree were derived from answers to a question that was asked only of persons with a bachelor's degree or higher. Eligible respondents were asked to list the specific major(s) of any bachelor's degree received. This question does not ask for the field of any other type of degree earned (such as master's or doctorate). An automated computer system coded write-in responses into 192 areas. Clerical coding categorized any write-in responses that could not be autocoded by the computer. Respondents listing multiple fields were assigned a code for each field, with a maximum of 10 fields per respondent.

The full list of the field of degree codes and how they are grouped can be found in the *2015 Code Lists* document at: https://www.census.gov/programs-surveys/acs/technical-documentation/code-lists.2015.html

HEALTH INSURANCE

Source:

B27019. Health Insurance Coverage Status and Type by Age by Educational Attainment for the Civilian noninstitutionalized population 25 years and over

Respondents were instructed to report their current health insurance coverage and to mark "yes" or "no" for each of the eight types listed:

a. Insurance through a current or former employer or union (of this person or another family member)

b. Insurance purchased directly from an insurance company (by this person or another family member)

c. Medicare, for people 65 and older, or people with certain disabilities

d. Medicaid, Medical Assistance, or any kind of government-assistance plan for those with low incomes or a disability

e. TRICARE or other military health care

f. VA (including those who have ever used or enrolled for VA health care)

g. Indian Health Service

h. Any other type of health insurance or health coverage plan (Respondents who answered "yes" were asked to provide their other type of coverage type in a write-in field.)

Health insurance coverage in the ACS and other Census Bureau surveys define coverage to include plans and programs that provide comprehensive health coverage. Plans that provide insurance for specific conditions or situations such as cancer and long-term care policies are not considered coverage. Likewise, other types of insurance like dental, vision, life, and disability insurance are not considered health insurance coverage.

In defining types of coverage, write-in responses were reclassified into one of the first seven types of coverage or determined not to be a coverage type. Write-in responses that referenced the coverage of a family member were edited to assign coverage based on responses from other family members. As a result, only the first seven types of health coverage are included in the categories in this table.

An eligibility edit was applied to give Medicaid, Medicare, and TRICARE coverage to individuals based on program eligibility rules. TRICARE or other military health care was given to active-duty military personnel and their spouses and children. Medicaid or other means-tested public coverage was given to foster children, certain individuals receiving Supplementary Security Income or Public Assistance, and the spouses and children of certain Medicaid beneficiaries. Medicare coverage was given to people 65 and older who received Social Security or Medicaid benefits.

People were considered insured if they reported at least one "yes". People who had no reported health coverage, or those whose only health coverage was Indian Health Service, were considered uninsured. For reporting purposes, the Census Bureau broadly classifies health insurance coverage as private health insurance or public coverage. Private health insurance is a plan provided through an employer or union, a plan purchased by an individual from a private company, or TRICARE or other military health care. Respondents reporting a "yes" to the types listed in parts a, b, or e were considered to have private health insurance. Public health coverage includes the federal programs Medicare, Medicaid, and VA Health Care (provided through the Department of Veterans Affairs); the Children's Health Insurance Program (CHIP); and individual state health plans. Respondents reporting a "yes" to the types listed in c, d, or f were considered to have public coverage. The types of health insurance are not mutually exclusive; people may be covered by more than one at the same time.

HOME-OWNERSHIP

Source:

B25013 Tenure by Educational Attainment of Householder for Occupied Housing Units

A **housing unit** is a house, apartment, mobile home or trailer, group of rooms, or single room occupied or, if vacant, intended for occupancy as separate living quarters. Separate living quarters are those in which the occupants do not live and eat with any other person in the structure and which have direct access from the outside of the building or through a common hall.

The occupants of a housing unit may be a single family, one person living alone, two or more families living together, or any other group of related or unrelated persons who share living arrangements.

Occupied housing units are classified as either owner occupied or renter occupied. A housing unit is classified as occupied if it is the usual place of residence of the person or group of persons living in it at the time of enumeration, or if the occupants are only temporarily absent from the residence for two months or less, that is, away on vacation or a business trip. If all the people staying in the unit at the time of the interview are staying there for two months or less, the unit is considered to be temporarily occupied and classified as "vacant."

A housing unit is **owner occupied** if the owner or co-owner lives in the unit even if it is mortgaged or not fully paid for. The owner or co-owner must live in the unit and usually is Person 1 on the questionnaire. The unit is "Owned by you or someone in this household with a mortgage or loan" if it is being purchased with a mortgage or some other debt arrangement such as a deed of trust, trust deed, contract to purchase, land contract, or purchase agreement. The unit also is considered owned with a mortgage if it is built on leased land and there is a mortgage on the unit. Mobile homes occupied by owners with installment loan balances also are included in this category.

INDUSTRY

Sources:

C24030. Sex by Industry for the Civilian Employed Population 16 Years and Over;
K202403. Industry for the Civilian Employed Population 16 Years and Over.

For employed people, the data on **industry** refer to the person's job during the previous week. For those who worked two or more jobs, the data refer to the job where the person worked the greatest number of hours. For unemployed people, the data refer to their last job.

Written responses to the industry questions are coded using the industry classification system developed for Census 2000 and modified in 2002, 2007, and again in 2012. This system consists of 269 categories for employed people, including military, classified into 20 sectors. The modified 2012 census industry classification was developed from the 2012 North American Industry Classification System (NAICS) published by the Executive Office of the President, Office of Management and Budget. The NAICS was developed to increase comparability in industry definitions between the United States, Mexico, and Canada. It provides industry classifications that group establishments into industries based on the activities in which they are primarily engaged. The NAICS was created for establishment designations and provides detail about the smallest operating establishment, while the American Community Survey data are collected from households and differ in detail and nature from those obtained from establishment surveys. Because of disclosure issues, ACS data cannot be released in great detail, and the industry classification system, while defined in NAICS terms, cannot reflect the full detail for all categories.

The tables in this book use ACS grouped categories and do not include the full 269 industries.

The industry category, "Public administration," is limited to regular government functions such as legislative, judicial, administrative, and regulatory activities. Other government organizations such as public schools, public hospitals, liquor stores, and bus lines are classified by industry according to the activity in which they are engaged.

The list of the 269 ACS industry codes and how they relate to the NAICS codes can be found in the *2015 Code Lists* document at: https://www.census.gov/programs-surveys/acs/technical-documentation/code-lists.2015.html

INTERNET ACCESS

Source:

B28006. Educational Attainment by Presence of a Computer and Types of Internet Subscription in Household for Household population 25 years and over

The computer use question asked if anyone in the household owned or used a computer and included three response categories for a desktop/laptop, a handheld computer, or some other type of computer. The Category **Household has dial-up or broadband Internet subscription** includes housing units where someone pays to access the Internet through a service such as a data plan for a mobile phone, a cable modem, DSL or other type of service. This will normally refer to a service that someone is billed for directly for Internet alone or sometimes as part of a bundle. Not included in this category are those respondents who may live in a city or town that provides free Internet services for their residents, or

attend a university that provides Internet services. These persons may be able to access the Internet without a subscription, but are not included in this category.

LANGUAGES SPOKEN

Source:

C16010. Educational Attainment and Employment Status by Language Spoken at Home for the Population 25 Years and Over

Language Spoken at Home. The American Community Survey questionnaire instructed respondents to mark "Yes" if they sometimes or always spoke a language other than English at home, and "No" if a language was spoken only at school—or if speaking was limited to a few expressions or slang. Respondents printed the name of the non-English language they spoke at home. If the person spoke more than one non-English language, they reported the language spoken most often. If the language spoken most frequently could not be determined, the respondent reported the language learned first.

The questions referred to languages spoken at home in an effort to measure the current use of languages other than English. This category excluded respondents who spoke a language other than English exclusively outside of the home.

Most respondents who reported speaking a language other than English also spoke English. The questions did not permit a determination of the primary language of persons who spoke both English and another language.

Household Language. In households where one or more people spoke a language other than English, the household language assigned to all household members was the non-English language spoken by the first person with a non-English language. This assignment scheme ranked household members in the following order: householder, spouse, parent, sibling, child, grandchild, other relative, stepchild, unmarried partner, housemate or roommate, and other nonrelatives. Therefore, a person who spoke only English may have had a non-English household language assigned during tabulations by household language.

OCCUPATION

B24010. Sex by Occupation for the Civilian Employed Population 16 Years and Over
K202401. Occupation for the Civilian Employed Population 16 Years and Over

For employed people, the data on **occupation** refer to the person's job during the previous week. For those who worked two or more jobs, the data refer to the job where the person worked the greatest number of hours. For unemployed people, the data refer to their last job.

Written responses to the occupation questions are coded using the occupational classification system developed for the 2000 census and modified in 2010. This system consists of 539 specific occupational categories, including military, for employed people, arranged into 23 occupational groups, and further combined into five major groups. This classification was developed based on the *Standard Occupational Classification (SOC) Manual: 2010*, published by the Executive Office of the President, Office of Management and Budget. The 539 categories used in the ACS have been collapsed from the 840 categories in the SOC.

The list of the 539 ACS occupation codes and how they relate to the SOC codes can be found in the *2015 Code Lists* document at:
https://www.census.gov/programs-surveys/acs/technical-documentation/code-lists.2015.html

Descriptions of all 840 occupations in the SOC can be found at:
https://www.bls.gov/soc/major_groups.htm

RACE AND HISPANIC ORIGIN

Several of the tables in this book include information by race and Hispanic origin for four groups with the largest populations.

The concept of race, as used by the Census Bureau, reflects self-identification by people according to the race or races with which they most closely identify. These categories are socio-political constructs and should not be interpreted as being scientific or anthropological in nature. Furthermore, the race categories include both racial and national-origin groups. The racial classifications used by the Census Bureau adhere to the October 30, 1997, *Federal Register Notice* entitled, "Revisions to the Standards for the Classification of Federal Data on Race and Ethnicity," issued by the Office of Management and Budget (OMB). These standards govern the categories used to collect and present federal data on race and ethnicity. The OMB requires five minimum categories (White, Black or African American, American Indian or Alaska Native, Asian, and Native Hawaiian or Other Pacific Islander) for race. The race categories are described below with a sixth category, "Some other race," added with OMB approval. In addition to the five race groups, the OMB also states that respondents should be offered the option of selecting one or more races, resulting in "alone or in combination" estimates which are not available for the tables used in this book.

The **White** population includes persons having origins in any of the original peoples of Europe, the Middle East, or North Africa. It includes people who indicate their race as "White" or report entries such as Irish, German, Italian, Lebanese, Near Easterner, Arab, or Polish.

The **Black** population includes persons having origins in any of the Black racial groups of Africa. It includes people who indicate their race as "Black, African American, or Negro," or provide written entries such as African American, Afro-American, Kenyan, Nigerian, or Haitian.

The **Asian** population includes persons having origins in any of the original peoples of the Far East, Southeast Asia, or the Indian subcontinent including, for example, Cambodia, China, India, Japan, Korea, Malaysia, Pakistan, the Philippine Islands, Thailand, and Vietnam. It includes Asian Indian, Chinese, Filipino, Korean, Japanese, Vietnamese, and Other Asian.

The race groups not included in this book are **American Indian or Alaska Native, Native Hawaiian or Other Pacific Islander, Some Other Race, and Two or More Races.**

The question on the **Hispanic or Latino** population was asked of all people. The terms "Spanish," "Hispanic," and "Latino" are used interchangeably. Some respondents identify with all three terms, while others may identify with only one of these three specific terms. Hispanics or Latinos who identify with the terms "Spanish," "Hispanic," or "Latino" are those who classify themselves in one of the specific Hispanic or Latino categories listed on the questionnaire — "Mexican," "Puerto Rican," or "Cuban" — as well as those who indicate that they are "other Spanish/Hispanic/Latino." People who do not identify with one of the specific origins listed on the questionnaire but indicate that they are "other Spanish/Hispanic/Latino" are those whose origins are from Spain, the Spanish-speaking countries of Central or South America, the Dominican Republic, or people identifying themselves generally as Spanish, Spanish-American, Hispanic, Hispano, Latino, and so on.

Hispanic or Latino persons can be of any race. This book uses ACS tables that include all Black and Asian persons, both Hispanic and non-Hispanic, but there are tables that include White persons who are not of Hispanic origin. Most Hispanic or Latino persons identify themselves as White or Some other race.

CPSIA information can be obtained
at www.ICGtesting.com
Printed in the USA
BVOW09*0514081217

501947BV00003B/3/P